Oxford Dictionary of National Biography

Volume 35

Oxford Dictionary of National Biography

IN ASSOCIATION WITH
The British Academy

From the earliest times to the year 2000

Edited by
H. C. G. Matthew
and
Brian Harrison

Volume 35
Macan–Macpherson

OXFORD
UNIVERSITY PRESS

OXFORD
UNIVERSITY PRESS

Great Clarendon Street, Oxford OX2 6DP

Oxford University Press is a department of the University of Oxford.
It furthers the University's objective of excellence in research, scholarship,
and education by publishing worldwide in

Oxford New York

Auckland Bangkok Buenos Aires Cape Town
Chennai Dar es Salaam Delhi Hong Kong Istanbul Karachi
Kolkata Kuala Lumpur Madrid Melbourne Mexico City Mumbai Nairobi
São Paulo Shanghai Taipei Tokyo Toronto

Oxford is a registered trade mark of Oxford University Press
in the UK and in certain other countries

Published in the United States
by Oxford University Press Inc., New York

© Oxford University Press 2004

Illustrations © individual copyright holders as listed in
'Picture credits', and reproduced with permission

Database right Oxford University Press (maker)

First published 2004

British Library Cataloguing in Publication Data
Data available

Library of Congress Cataloging in Publication Data
Data available: for details see volume 1, p. iv

ISBN 0-19-861385-7 (this volume)
ISBN 0-19-861411-X (set of sixty volumes)

Text captured by Alliance Phototypesetters, Pondicherry
Illustrations reproduced and archived by
Alliance Graphics Ltd, UK
Typeset in OUP Swift by Interactive Sciences Limited, Gloucester
Printed in Great Britain on acid-free paper by
Butler and Tanner Ltd,
Frome, Somerset

LIST OF ABBREVIATIONS

1 General abbreviations

AB	bachelor of arts
ABC	Australian Broadcasting Corporation
ABC TV	ABC Television
act.	active
A$	Australian dollar
AD	*anno domini*
AFC	Air Force Cross
AIDS	acquired immune deficiency syndrome
AK	Alaska
AL	Alabama
A level	advanced level [examination]
ALS	associate of the Linnean Society
AM	master of arts
AMICE	associate member of the Institution of Civil Engineers
ANZAC	Australian and New Zealand Army Corps
appx *pl.* appxs	appendix(es)
AR	Arkansas
ARA	associate of the Royal Academy
ARCA	associate of the Royal College of Art
ARCM	associate of the Royal College of Music
ARCO	associate of the Royal College of Organists
ARIBA	associate of the Royal Institute of British Architects
ARP	air-raid precautions
ARRC	associate of the Royal Red Cross
ARSA	associate of the Royal Scottish Academy
art.	article / item
ASC	Army Service Corps
Asch	Austrian Schilling
ASDIC	Antisubmarine Detection Investigation Committee
ATS	Auxiliary Territorial Service
ATV	Associated Television
Aug	August
AZ	Arizona
b.	born
BA	bachelor of arts
BA (Admin.)	bachelor of arts (administration)
BAFTA	British Academy of Film and Television Arts
BAO	bachelor of arts in obstetrics
bap.	baptized
BBC	British Broadcasting Corporation / Company
BC	before Christ
BCE	before the common (*or* Christian) era
BCE	bachelor of civil engineering
BCG	bacillus of Calmette and Guérin [inoculation against tuberculosis]
BCh	bachelor of surgery
BChir	bachelor of surgery
BCL	bachelor of civil law
BCnL	bachelor of canon law
BCom	bachelor of commerce
BD	bachelor of divinity
BEd	bachelor of education
BEng	bachelor of engineering
bk *pl.* bks	book(s)
BL	bachelor of law / letters / literature
BLitt	bachelor of letters
BM	bachelor of medicine
BMus	bachelor of music
BP	before present
BP	British Petroleum
Bros.	Brothers
BS	(1) bachelor of science; (2) bachelor of surgery; (3) British standard
BSc	bachelor of science
BSc (Econ.)	bachelor of science (economics)
BSc (Eng.)	bachelor of science (engineering)
bt	baronet
BTh	bachelor of theology
bur.	buried
C.	command [identifier for published parliamentary papers]
c.	*circa*
c.	*capitulum pl. capitula*: chapter(s)
CA	California
Cantab.	Cantabrigiensis
cap.	*capitulum pl. capitula*: chapter(s)
CB	companion of the Bath
CBE	commander of the Order of the British Empire
CBS	Columbia Broadcasting System
cc	cubic centimetres
C$	Canadian dollar
CD	compact disc
Cd	command [identifier for published parliamentary papers]
CE	Common (*or* Christian) Era
cent.	century
cf.	compare
CH	Companion of Honour
chap.	chapter
ChB	bachelor of surgery
CI	Imperial Order of the Crown of India
CIA	Central Intelligence Agency
CID	Criminal Investigation Department
CIE	companion of the Order of the Indian Empire
Cie	Compagnie
CLit	companion of literature
CM	master of surgery
cm	centimetre(s)

Cmd	command [identifier for published parliamentary papers]		edn	edition
CMG	companion of the Order of St Michael and St George		EEC	European Economic Community
			EFTA	European Free Trade Association
Cmnd	command [identifier for published parliamentary papers]		EICS	East India Company Service
			EMI	Electrical and Musical Industries (Ltd)
CO	Colorado		Eng.	English
Co.	company		enl.	enlarged
co.	county		ENSA	Entertainments National Service Association
col. *pl.* cols.	column(s)		ep. *pl.* epp.	*epistola(e)*
Corp.	corporation		ESP	extra-sensory perception
CSE	certificate of secondary education		esp.	especially
CSI	companion of the Order of the Star of India		esq.	esquire
CT	Connecticut		est.	estimate / estimated
CVO	commander of the Royal Victorian Order		EU	European Union
cwt	hundredweight		ex	sold by (*lit.* out of)
$	(American) dollar		excl.	excludes / excluding
d.	(1) penny (pence); (2) died		exh.	exhibited
DBE	dame commander of the Order of the British Empire		exh. cat.	exhibition catalogue
			f. *pl.* ff.	following [pages]
DCH	diploma in child health		FA	Football Association
DCh	doctor of surgery		FACP	fellow of the American College of Physicians
DCL	doctor of civil law		facs.	facsimile
DCnL	doctor of canon law		FANY	First Aid Nursing Yeomanry
DCVO	dame commander of the Royal Victorian Order		FBA	fellow of the British Academy
DD	doctor of divinity		FBI	Federation of British Industries
DE	Delaware		FCS	fellow of the Chemical Society
Dec	December		Feb	February
dem.	demolished		FEng	fellow of the Fellowship of Engineering
DEng	doctor of engineering		FFCM	fellow of the Faculty of Community Medicine
des.	destroyed		FGS	fellow of the Geological Society
DFC	Distinguished Flying Cross		fig.	figure
DipEd	diploma in education		FIMechE	fellow of the Institution of Mechanical Engineers
DipPsych	diploma in psychiatry			
diss.	dissertation		FL	Florida
DL	deputy lieutenant		*fl.*	*floruit*
DLitt	doctor of letters		FLS	fellow of the Linnean Society
DLittCelt	doctor of Celtic letters		FM	frequency modulation
DM	(1) Deutschmark; (2) doctor of medicine; (3) doctor of musical arts		fol. *pl.* fols.	folio(s)
			Fr	French francs
DMus	doctor of music		Fr.	French
DNA	dioxyribonucleic acid		FRAeS	fellow of the Royal Aeronautical Society
doc.	document		FRAI	fellow of the Royal Anthropological Institute
DOL	doctor of oriental learning		FRAM	fellow of the Royal Academy of Music
DPH	diploma in public health		FRAS	(1) fellow of the Royal Asiatic Society; (2) fellow of the Royal Astronomical Society
DPhil	doctor of philosophy			
DPM	diploma in psychological medicine		FRCM	fellow of the Royal College of Music
DSC	Distinguished Service Cross		FRCO	fellow of the Royal College of Organists
DSc	doctor of science		FRCOG	fellow of the Royal College of Obstetricians and Gynaecologists
DSc (Econ.)	doctor of science (economics)			
DSc (Eng.)	doctor of science (engineering)		FRCP(C)	fellow of the Royal College of Physicians of Canada
DSM	Distinguished Service Medal			
DSO	companion of the Distinguished Service Order		FRCP (Edin.)	fellow of the Royal College of Physicians of Edinburgh
DSocSc	doctor of social science			
DTech	doctor of technology		FRCP (Lond.)	fellow of the Royal College of Physicians of London
DTh	doctor of theology			
DTM	diploma in tropical medicine		FRCPath	fellow of the Royal College of Pathologists
DTMH	diploma in tropical medicine and hygiene		FRCPsych	fellow of the Royal College of Psychiatrists
DU	doctor of the university		FRCS	fellow of the Royal College of Surgeons
DUniv	doctor of the university		FRGS	fellow of the Royal Geographical Society
dwt	pennyweight		FRIBA	fellow of the Royal Institute of British Architects
EC	European Community		FRICS	fellow of the Royal Institute of Chartered Surveyors
ed. *pl.* eds.	edited / edited by / editor(s)			
Edin.	Edinburgh		FRS	fellow of the Royal Society
			FRSA	fellow of the Royal Society of Arts

FRSCM	fellow of the Royal School of Church Music
FRSE	fellow of the Royal Society of Edinburgh
FRSL	fellow of the Royal Society of Literature
FSA	fellow of the Society of Antiquaries
ft	foot *pl.* feet
FTCL	fellow of Trinity College of Music, London
ft-lb per min.	foot-pounds per minute [unit of horsepower]
FZS	fellow of the Zoological Society
GA	Georgia
GBE	knight or dame grand cross of the Order of the British Empire
GCB	knight grand cross of the Order of the Bath
GCE	general certificate of education
GCH	knight grand cross of the Royal Guelphic Order
GCHQ	government communications headquarters
GCIE	knight grand commander of the Order of the Indian Empire
GCMG	knight or dame grand cross of the Order of St Michael and St George
GCSE	general certificate of secondary education
GCSI	knight grand commander of the Order of the Star of India
GCStJ	bailiff or dame grand cross of the order of St John of Jerusalem
GCVO	knight or dame grand cross of the Royal Victorian Order
GEC	General Electric Company
Ger.	German
GI	government (*or* general) issue
GMT	Greenwich mean time
GP	general practitioner
GPU	[Soviet special police unit]
GSO	general staff officer
Heb.	Hebrew
HEICS	Honourable East India Company Service
HI	Hawaii
HIV	human immunodeficiency virus
HK$	Hong Kong dollar
HM	his / her majesty('s)
HMAS	his / her majesty's Australian ship
HMNZS	his / her majesty's New Zealand ship
HMS	his / her majesty's ship
HMSO	His / Her Majesty's Stationery Office
HMV	His Master's Voice
Hon.	Honourable
hp	horsepower
hr	hour(s)
HRH	his / her royal highness
HTV	Harlech Television
IA	Iowa
ibid.	*ibidem*: in the same place
ICI	Imperial Chemical Industries (Ltd)
ID	Idaho
IL	Illinois
illus.	illustration
illustr.	illustrated
IN	Indiana
in.	inch(es)
Inc.	Incorporated
incl.	includes / including
IOU	I owe you
IQ	intelligence quotient
Ir£	Irish pound
IRA	Irish Republican Army

ISO	companion of the Imperial Service Order
It.	Italian
ITA	Independent Television Authority
ITV	Independent Television
Jan	January
JP	justice of the peace
jun.	junior
KB	knight of the Order of the Bath
KBE	knight commander of the Order of the British Empire
KC	king's counsel
kcal	kilocalorie
KCB	knight commander of the Order of the Bath
KCH	knight commander of the Royal Guelphic Order
KCIE	knight commander of the Order of the Indian Empire
KCMG	knight commander of the Order of St Michael and St George
KCSI	knight commander of the Order of the Star of India
KCVO	knight commander of the Royal Victorian Order
keV	kilo-electron-volt
KG	knight of the Order of the Garter
KGB	[Soviet committee of state security]
KH	knight of the Royal Guelphic Order
KLM	Koninklijke Luchtvaart Maatschappij (Royal Dutch Air Lines)
km	kilometre(s)
KP	knight of the Order of St Patrick
KS	Kansas
KT	knight of the Order of the Thistle
kt	knight
KY	Kentucky
£	pound(s) sterling
£E	Egyptian pound
L	lira *pl.* lire
l. *pl.* ll.	line(s)
LA	Lousiana
LAA	light anti-aircraft
LAH	licentiate of the Apothecaries' Hall, Dublin
Lat.	Latin
lb	pound(s), unit of weight
LDS	licence in dental surgery
lit.	literally
LittB	bachelor of letters
LittD	doctor of letters
LKQCPI	licentiate of the King and Queen's College of Physicians, Ireland
LLA	lady literate in arts
LLB	bachelor of laws
LLD	doctor of laws
LLM	master of laws
LM	licentiate in midwifery
LP	long-playing record
LRAM	licentiate of the Royal Academy of Music
LRCP	licentiate of the Royal College of Physicians
LRCPS (Glasgow)	licentiate of the Royal College of Physicians and Surgeons of Glasgow
LRCS	licentiate of the Royal College of Surgeons
LSA	licentiate of the Society of Apothecaries
LSD	lysergic acid diethylamide
LVO	lieutenant of the Royal Victorian Order
M. *pl.* MM.	Monsieur *pl.* Messieurs
m	metre(s)

m. *pl.* mm.	membrane(s)		ND	North Dakota
MA	(1) Massachusetts; (2) master of arts		n.d.	no date
MAI	master of engineering		NE	Nebraska
MB	bachelor of medicine		*nem. con.*	*nemine contradicente*: unanimously
MBA	master of business administration		new ser.	new series
MBE	member of the Order of the British Empire		NH	New Hampshire
MC	Military Cross		NHS	National Health Service
MCC	Marylebone Cricket Club		NJ	New Jersey
MCh	master of surgery		NKVD	[Soviet people's commissariat for internal affairs]
MChir	master of surgery		NM	New Mexico
MCom	master of commerce		nm	nanometre(s)
MD	(1) doctor of medicine; (2) Maryland		no. *pl.* nos.	number(s)
MDMA	methylenedioxymethamphetamine		Nov	November
ME	Maine		n.p.	no place [of publication]
MEd	master of education		NS	new style
MEng	master of engineering		NV	Nevada
MEP	member of the European parliament		NY	New York
MG	Morris Garages		NZBS	New Zealand Broadcasting Service
MGM	Metro-Goldwyn-Mayer		OBE	officer of the Order of the British Empire
Mgr	Monsignor		obit.	obituary
MI	(1) Michigan; (2) military intelligence		Oct	October
MI1c	[secret intelligence department]		OCTU	officer cadets training unit
MI5	[military intelligence department]		OECD	Organization for Economic Co-operation and Development
MI6	[secret intelligence department]		OEEC	Organization for European Economic Co-operation
MI9	[secret escape service]		OFM	order of Friars Minor [Franciscans]
MICE	member of the Institution of Civil Engineers		OFMCap	Ordine Frati Minori Cappucini: member of the Capuchin order
MIEE	member of the Institution of Electrical Engineers		OH	Ohio
min.	minute(s)		OK	Oklahoma
Mk	mark		O level	ordinary level [examination]
ML	(1) licentiate of medicine; (2) master of laws		OM	Order of Merit
MLitt	master of letters		OP	order of Preachers [Dominicans]
Mlle	Mademoiselle		op. *pl.* opp.	opus *pl.* opera
mm	millimetre(s)		OPEC	Organization of Petroleum Exporting Countries
Mme	Madame		OR	Oregon
MN	Minnesota		orig.	original
MO	Missouri		OS	old style
MOH	medical officer of health		OSB	Order of St Benedict
MP	member of parliament		OTC	Officers' Training Corps
m.p.h.	miles per hour		OWS	Old Watercolour Society
MPhil	master of philosophy		Oxon.	Oxoniensis
MRCP	member of the Royal College of Physicians		p. *pl.* pp.	page(s)
MRCS	member of the Royal College of Surgeons		PA	Pennsylvania
MRCVS	member of the Royal College of Veterinary Surgeons		p.a.	per annum
MRIA	member of the Royal Irish Academy		para.	paragraph
MS	(1) master of science; (2) Mississippi		PAYE	pay as you earn
MS *pl.* MSS	manuscript(s)		pbk *pl.* pbks	paperback(s)
MSc	master of science		*per.*	[during the] period
MSc (Econ.)	master of science (economics)		PhD	doctor of philosophy
MT	Montana		pl.	(1) plate(s); (2) plural
MusB	bachelor of music		priv. coll.	private collection
MusBac	bachelor of music		pt *pl.* pts	part(s)
MusD	doctor of music		pubd	published
MV	motor vessel		PVC	polyvinyl chloride
MVO	member of the Royal Victorian Order		q. *pl.* qq.	(1) question(s); (2) quire(s)
n. *pl.* nn.	note(s)		QC	queen's counsel
NAAFI	Navy, Army, and Air Force Institutes		R	rand
NASA	National Aeronautics and Space Administration		R.	Rex / Regina
NATO	North Atlantic Treaty Organization		*r*	recto
NBC	National Broadcasting Corporation		*r.*	reigned / ruled
NC	North Carolina		RA	Royal Academy / Royal Academician
NCO	non-commissioned officer			

RAC	Royal Automobile Club		Skr	Swedish krona
RAF	Royal Air Force		Span.	Spanish
RAFVR	Royal Air Force Volunteer Reserve		SPCK	Society for Promoting Christian Knowledge
RAM	[member of the] Royal Academy of Music		SS	(1) Santissimi; (2) Schutzstaffel; (3) steam ship
RAMC	Royal Army Medical Corps		STB	bachelor of theology
RCA	Royal College of Art		STD	doctor of theology
RCNC	Royal Corps of Naval Constructors		STM	master of theology
RCOG	Royal College of Obstetricians and Gynaecologists		STP	doctor of theology
RDI	royal designer for industry		*supp.*	supposedly
RE	Royal Engineers		suppl. *pl.* suppls.	supplement(s)
repr. *pl.* reprs.	reprint(s) / reprinted		s.v.	*sub verbo / sub voce*: under the word / heading
repro.	reproduced		SY	steam yacht
rev.	revised / revised by / reviser / revision		TA	Territorial Army
Revd	Reverend		TASS	[Soviet news agency]
RHA	Royal Hibernian Academy		TB	tuberculosis (*lit.* tubercle bacillus)
RI	(1) Rhode Island; (2) Royal Institute of Painters in Water-Colours		TD	(1) *teachtaí dála* (member of the Dáil); (2) territorial decoration
RIBA	Royal Institute of British Architects		TN	Tennessee
RIN	Royal Indian Navy		TNT	trinitrotoluene
RM	Reichsmark		trans.	translated / translated by / translation / translator
RMS	Royal Mail steamer		TT	tourist trophy
RN	Royal Navy		TUC	Trades Union Congress
RNA	ribonucleic acid		TX	Texas
RNAS	Royal Naval Air Service		U-boat	*Unterseeboot*: submarine
RNR	Royal Naval Reserve		Ufa	Universum-Film AG
RNVR	Royal Naval Volunteer Reserve		UMIST	University of Manchester Institute of Science and Technology
RO	Record Office		UN	United Nations
r.p.m.	revolutions per minute		UNESCO	United Nations Educational, Scientific, and Cultural Organization
RRS	royal research ship			
Rs	rupees		UNICEF	United Nations International Children's Emergency Fund
RSA	(1) Royal Scottish Academician; (2) Royal Society of Arts		unpubd	unpublished
RSPCA	Royal Society for the Prevention of Cruelty to Animals		USS	United States ship
			UT	Utah
Rt Hon.	Right Honourable		*v*	verso
Rt Revd	Right Reverend		v.	versus
RUC	Royal Ulster Constabulary		VA	Virginia
Russ.	Russian		VAD	Voluntary Aid Detachment
RWS	Royal Watercolour Society		VC	Victoria Cross
S4C	Sianel Pedwar Cymru		VE-day	victory in Europe day
s.	shilling(s)		Ven.	Venerable
s.a.	*sub anno*: under the year		VJ-day	victory over Japan day
SABC	South African Broadcasting Corporation		vol. *pl.* vols.	volume(s)
SAS	Special Air Service		VT	Vermont
SC	South Carolina		WA	Washington [state]
ScD	doctor of science		WAAC	Women's Auxiliary Army Corps
S$	Singapore dollar		WAAF	Women's Auxiliary Air Force
SD	South Dakota		WEA	Workers' Educational Association
sec.	second(s)		WHO	World Health Organization
sel.	selected		WI	Wisconsin
sen.	senior		WRAF	Women's Royal Air Force
Sept	September		WRNS	Women's Royal Naval Service
ser.	series		WV	West Virginia
SHAPE	supreme headquarters allied powers, Europe		WVS	Women's Voluntary Service
SIDRO	Société Internationale d'Énergie Hydro-Électrique		WY	Wyoming
			¥	yen
sig. *pl.* sigs.	signature(s)		YMCA	Young Men's Christian Association
sing.	singular		YWCA	Young Women's Christian Association
SIS	Secret Intelligence Service			
SJ	Society of Jesus			

2 Institution abbreviations

All Souls Oxf.	All Souls College, Oxford		Garr. Club	Garrick Club, London
AM Oxf.	Ashmolean Museum, Oxford		Girton Cam.	Girton College, Cambridge
Balliol Oxf.	Balliol College, Oxford		GL	Guildhall Library, London
BBC WAC	BBC Written Archives Centre, Reading		Glos. RO	Gloucestershire Record Office, Gloucester
Beds. & Luton ARS	Bedfordshire and Luton Archives and Record Service, Bedford		Gon. & Caius Cam.	Gonville and Caius College, Cambridge
Berks. RO	Berkshire Record Office, Reading		Gov. Art Coll.	Government Art Collection
BFI	British Film Institute, London		GS Lond.	Geological Society of London
BFI NFTVA	British Film Institute, London, National Film and Television Archive		Hants. RO	Hampshire Record Office, Winchester
BGS	British Geological Survey, Keyworth, Nottingham		Harris Man. Oxf.	Harris Manchester College, Oxford
Birm. CA	Birmingham Central Library, Birmingham City Archives		Harvard TC	Harvard Theatre Collection, Harvard University, Cambridge, Massachusetts, Nathan Marsh Pusey Library
Birm. CL	Birmingham Central Library		Harvard U.	Harvard University, Cambridge, Massachusetts
BL	British Library, London		Harvard U., Houghton L.	Harvard University, Cambridge, Massachusetts, Houghton Library
BL NSA	British Library, London, National Sound Archive		Herefs. RO	Herefordshire Record Office, Hereford
BL OIOC	British Library, London, Oriental and India Office Collections		Herts. ALS	Hertfordshire Archives and Local Studies, Hertford
BLPES	London School of Economics and Political Science, British Library of Political and Economic Science		Hist. Soc. Penn.	Historical Society of Pennsylvania, Philadelphia
BM	British Museum, London		HLRO	House of Lords Record Office, London
Bodl. Oxf.	Bodleian Library, Oxford		Hult. Arch.	Hulton Archive, London and New York
Bodl. RH	Bodleian Library of Commonwealth and African Studies at Rhodes House, Oxford		Hunt. L.	Huntington Library, San Marino, California
Borth. Inst.	Borthwick Institute of Historical Research, University of York		ICL	Imperial College, London
Boston PL	Boston Public Library, Massachusetts		Inst. CE	Institution of Civil Engineers, London
Bristol RO	Bristol Record Office		Inst. EE	Institution of Electrical Engineers, London
Bucks. RLSS	Buckinghamshire Records and Local Studies Service, Aylesbury		IWM	Imperial War Museum, London
CAC Cam.	Churchill College, Cambridge, Churchill Archives Centre		IWM FVA	Imperial War Museum, London, Film and Video Archive
Cambs. AS	Cambridgeshire Archive Service		IWM SA	Imperial War Museum, London, Sound Archive
CCC Cam.	Corpus Christi College, Cambridge		JRL	John Rylands University Library of Manchester
CCC Oxf.	Corpus Christi College, Oxford		King's AC Cam.	King's College Archives Centre, Cambridge
Ches. & Chester ALSS	Cheshire and Chester Archives and Local Studies Service		King's Cam.	King's College, Cambridge
Christ Church Oxf.	Christ Church, Oxford		King's Lond.	King's College, London
Christies	Christies, London		King's Lond., Liddell Hart C.	King's College, London, Liddell Hart Centre for Military Archives
City Westm. AC	City of Westminster Archives Centre, London		Lancs. RO	Lancashire Record Office, Preston
CKS	Centre for Kentish Studies, Maidstone		L. Cong.	Library of Congress, Washington, DC
CLRO	Corporation of London Records Office		Leics. RO	Leicestershire, Leicester, and Rutland Record Office, Leicester
Coll. Arms	College of Arms, London		Lincs. Arch.	Lincolnshire Archives, Lincoln
Col. U.	Columbia University, New York		Linn. Soc.	Linnean Society of London
Cornwall RO	Cornwall Record Office, Truro		LMA	London Metropolitan Archives
Courtauld Inst.	Courtauld Institute of Art, London		LPL	Lambeth Palace, London
CUL	Cambridge University Library		Lpool RO	Liverpool Record Office and Local Studies Service
Cumbria AS	Cumbria Archive Service		LUL	London University Library
Derbys. RO	Derbyshire Record Office, Matlock		Magd. Cam.	Magdalene College, Cambridge
Devon RO	Devon Record Office, Exeter		Magd. Oxf.	Magdalen College, Oxford
Dorset RO	Dorset Record Office, Dorchester		Man. City Gall.	Manchester City Galleries
Duke U.	Duke University, Durham, North Carolina		Man. CL	Manchester Central Library
Duke U., Perkins L.	Duke University, Durham, North Carolina, William R. Perkins Library		Mass. Hist. Soc.	Massachusetts Historical Society, Boston
Durham Cath. CL	Durham Cathedral, chapter library		Merton Oxf.	Merton College, Oxford
Durham RO	Durham Record Office		MHS Oxf.	Museum of the History of Science, Oxford
DWL	Dr Williams's Library, London		Mitchell L., Glas.	Mitchell Library, Glasgow
Essex RO	Essex Record Office		Mitchell L., NSW	State Library of New South Wales, Sydney, Mitchell Library
E. Sussex RO	East Sussex Record Office, Lewes		Morgan L.	Pierpont Morgan Library, New York
Eton	Eton College, Berkshire		NA Canada	National Archives of Canada, Ottawa
FM Cam.	Fitzwilliam Museum, Cambridge		NA Ire.	National Archives of Ireland, Dublin
Folger	Folger Shakespeare Library, Washington, DC		NAM	National Army Museum, London
			NA Scot.	National Archives of Scotland, Edinburgh
			News Int. RO	News International Record Office, London
			NG Ire.	National Gallery of Ireland, Dublin

NG Scot.	National Gallery of Scotland, Edinburgh
NHM	Natural History Museum, London
NL Aus.	National Library of Australia, Canberra
NL Ire.	National Library of Ireland, Dublin
NL NZ	National Library of New Zealand, Wellington
NL NZ, Turnbull L.	National Library of New Zealand, Wellington, Alexander Turnbull Library
NL Scot.	National Library of Scotland, Edinburgh
NL Wales	National Library of Wales, Aberystwyth
NMG Wales	National Museum and Gallery of Wales, Cardiff
NMM	National Maritime Museum, London
Norfolk RO	Norfolk Record Office, Norwich
Northants. RO	Northamptonshire Record Office, Northampton
Northumbd RO	Northumberland Record Office
Notts. Arch.	Nottinghamshire Archives, Nottingham
NPG	National Portrait Gallery, London
NRA	National Archives, London, Historical Manuscripts Commission, National Register of Archives
Nuffield Oxf.	Nuffield College, Oxford
N. Yorks. CRO	North Yorkshire County Record Office, Northallerton
NYPL	New York Public Library
Oxf. UA	Oxford University Archives
Oxf. U. Mus. NH	Oxford University Museum of Natural History
Oxon. RO	Oxfordshire Record Office, Oxford
Pembroke Cam.	Pembroke College, Cambridge
PRO	National Archives, London, Public Record Office
PRO NIre.	Public Record Office for Northern Ireland, Belfast
Pusey Oxf.	Pusey House, Oxford
RA	Royal Academy of Arts, London
Ransom HRC	Harry Ransom Humanities Research Center, University of Texas, Austin
RAS	Royal Astronomical Society, London
RBG Kew	Royal Botanic Gardens, Kew, London
RCP Lond.	Royal College of Physicians of London
RCS Eng.	Royal College of Surgeons of England, London
RGS	Royal Geographical Society, London
RIBA	Royal Institute of British Architects, London
RIBA BAL	Royal Institute of British Architects, London, British Architectural Library
Royal Arch.	Royal Archives, Windsor Castle, Berkshire [by gracious permission of her majesty the queen]
Royal Irish Acad.	Royal Irish Academy, Dublin
Royal Scot. Acad.	Royal Scottish Academy, Edinburgh
RS	Royal Society, London
RSA	Royal Society of Arts, London
RS Friends, Lond.	Religious Society of Friends, London
St Ant. Oxf.	St Antony's College, Oxford
St John Cam.	St John's College, Cambridge
S. Antiquaries, Lond.	Society of Antiquaries of London
Sci. Mus.	Science Museum, London
Scot. NPG	Scottish National Portrait Gallery, Edinburgh
Scott Polar RI	University of Cambridge, Scott Polar Research Institute
Sheff. Arch.	Sheffield Archives
Shrops. RRC	Shropshire Records and Research Centre, Shrewsbury
SOAS	School of Oriental and African Studies, London
Som. ARS	Somerset Archive and Record Service, Taunton
Staffs. RO	Staffordshire Record Office, Stafford

Suffolk RO	Suffolk Record Office
Surrey HC	Surrey History Centre, Woking
TCD	Trinity College, Dublin
Trinity Cam.	Trinity College, Cambridge
U. Aberdeen	University of Aberdeen
U. Birm.	University of Birmingham
U. Birm. L.	University of Birmingham Library
U. Cal.	University of California
U. Cam.	University of Cambridge
UCL	University College, London
U. Durham	University of Durham
U. Durham L.	University of Durham Library
U. Edin.	University of Edinburgh
U. Edin., New Coll.	University of Edinburgh, New College
U. Edin., New Coll. L.	University of Edinburgh, New College Library
U. Edin. L.	University of Edinburgh Library
U. Glas.	University of Glasgow
U. Glas. L.	University of Glasgow Library
U. Hull	University of Hull
U. Hull, Brynmor Jones L.	University of Hull, Brynmor Jones Library
U. Leeds	University of Leeds
U. Leeds, Brotherton L.	University of Leeds, Brotherton Library
U. Lond.	University of London
U. Lpool	University of Liverpool
U. Lpool L.	University of Liverpool Library
U. Mich.	University of Michigan, Ann Arbor
U. Mich., Clements L.	University of Michigan, Ann Arbor, William L. Clements Library
U. Newcastle	University of Newcastle upon Tyne
U. Newcastle, Robinson L.	University of Newcastle upon Tyne, Robinson Library
U. Nott.	University of Nottingham
U. Nott. L.	University of Nottingham Library
U. Oxf.	University of Oxford
U. Reading	University of Reading
U. Reading L.	University of Reading Library
U. St Andr.	University of St Andrews
U. St Andr. L.	University of St Andrews Library
U. Southampton	University of Southampton
U. Southampton L.	University of Southampton Library
U. Sussex	University of Sussex, Brighton
U. Texas	University of Texas, Austin
U. Wales	University of Wales
U. Warwick Mod. RC	University of Warwick, Coventry, Modern Records Centre
V&A	Victoria and Albert Museum, London
V&A NAL	Victoria and Albert Museum, London, National Art Library
Warks. CRO	Warwickshire County Record Office, Warwick
Wellcome L.	Wellcome Library for the History and Understanding of Medicine, London
Westm. DA	Westminster Diocesan Archives, London
Wilts. & Swindon RO	Wiltshire and Swindon Record Office, Trowbridge
Worcs. RO	Worcestershire Record Office, Worcester
W. Sussex RO	West Sussex Record Office, Chichester
W. Yorks. AS	West Yorkshire Archive Service
Yale U.	Yale University, New Haven, Connecticut
Yale U., Beinecke L.	Yale University, New Haven, Connecticut, Beinecke Rare Book and Manuscript Library
Yale U. CBA	Yale University, New Haven, Connecticut, Yale Center for British Art

3 Bibliographic abbreviations

Adams, *Drama* W. D. Adams, *A dictionary of the drama*, 1: *A–G* (1904); 2: *H–Z* (1956) [vol. 2 microfilm only]

AFM J O'Donovan, ed. and trans., *Annala rioghachta Eireann / Annals of the kingdom of Ireland by the four masters*, 7 vols. (1848–51); 2nd edn (1856); 3rd edn (1990)

Allibone, *Dict.* S. A. Allibone, *A critical dictionary of English literature and British and American authors*, 3 vols. (1859–71); suppl. by J. F. Kirk, 2 vols. (1891)

ANB J. A. Garraty and M. C. Carnes, eds., *American national biography*, 24 vols. (1999)

Anderson, *Scot. nat.* W. Anderson, *The Scottish nation, or, The surnames, families, literature, honours, and biographical history of the people of Scotland*, 3 vols. (1859–63)

Ann. mon. H. R. Luard, ed., *Annales monastici*, 5 vols., Rolls Series, 36 (1864–9)

Ann. Ulster S. Mac Airt and G. Mac Niocaill, eds., *Annals of Ulster (to AD 1131)* (1983)

APC *Acts of the privy council of England*, new ser., 46 vols. (1890–1964)

APS *The acts of the parliaments of Scotland*, 12 vols. in 13 (1814–75)

Arber, *Regs. Stationers* F. Arber, ed., *A transcript of the registers of the Company of Stationers of London, 1554–1640 AD*, 5 vols. (1875–94)

ArchR *Architectural Review*

ASC D. Whitelock, D. C. Douglas, and S. I. Tucker, ed. and trans., *The Anglo-Saxon Chronicle: a revised translation* (1961)

AS chart. P. H. Sawyer, *Anglo-Saxon charters: an annotated list and bibliography*, Royal Historical Society Guides and Handbooks (1968)

AusDB D. Pike and others, eds., *Australian dictionary of biography*, 16 vols. (1966–2002)

Baker, *Serjeants* J. H. Baker, *The order of serjeants at law*, SeldS, suppl. ser., 5 (1984)

Bale, *Cat.* J. Bale, *Scriptorum illustrium Maioris Brytannie, quam nunc Angliam et Scotiam vocant: catalogus*, 2 vols. in 1 (Basel, 1557–9); facs. edn (1971)

Bale, *Index* J. Bale, *Index Britanniae scriptorum*, ed. R. L. Poole and M. Bateson (1902); facs. edn (1990)

BBCS *Bulletin of the Board of Celtic Studies*

BDMBR J. O. Baylen and N. J. Gossman, eds., *Biographical dictionary of modern British radicals*, 3 vols. in 4 (1979–88)

Bede, *Hist. eccl.* *Bede's Ecclesiastical history of the English people*, ed. and trans. B. Colgrave and R. A. B. Mynors, OMT (1969); repr. (1991)

Bénézit, *Dict.* E. Bénézit, *Dictionnaire critique et documentaire des peintres, sculpteurs, dessinateurs et graveurs*, 3 vols. (Paris, 1911–23); new edn, 8 vols. (1948–66), repr. (1966); 3rd edn, rev. and enl., 10 vols. (1976); 4th edn, 14 vols. (1999)

BIHR *Bulletin of the Institute of Historical Research*

Birch, *Seals* W. de Birch, *Catalogue of seals in the department of manuscripts in the British Museum*, 6 vols. (1887–1900)

Bishop Burnet's History *Bishop Burnet's History of his own time*, ed. M. J. Routh, 2nd edn, 6 vols. (1833)

Blackwood *Blackwood's [Edinburgh] Magazine*, 328 vols. (1817–1980)

Blain, Clements & Grundy, *Feminist comp.* V. Blain, P. Clements, and I. Grundy, eds., *The feminist companion to literature in English* (1990)

BL cat. *The British Library general catalogue of printed books* [in 360 vols. with suppls., also CD-ROM and online]

BMJ *British Medical Journal*

Boase & Courtney, *Bibl. Corn.* G. C. Boase and W. P. Courtney, *Bibliotheca Cornubiensis: a catalogue of the writings ... of Cornishmen*, 3 vols. (1874–82)

Boase, *Mod. Eng. biog.* F. Boase, *Modern English biography: containing many thousand concise memoirs of persons who have died since the year 1850*, 6 vols. (privately printed, Truro, 1892–1921); repr. (1965)

Boswell, *Life* *Boswell's Life of Johnson: together with Journal of a tour to the Hebrides and Johnson's Diary of a journey into north Wales*, ed. G. B. Hill, enl. edn, rev. L. F. Powell, 6 vols. (1934–50); 2nd edn (1964); repr. (1971)

Brown & Stratton, *Brit. mus.* J. D. Brown and S. S. Stratton, *British musical biography* (1897)

Bryan, *Painters* M. Bryan, *A biographical and critical dictionary of painters and engravers*, 2 vols. (1816); new edn, ed. G. Stanley (1849); new edn, ed. R. E. Graves and W. Armstrong, 2 vols. (1886–9); [4th edn], ed. G. C. Williamson, 5 vols. (1903–5) [various reprs.]

Burke, *Gen. GB* J. Burke, *A genealogical and heraldic history of the commoners of Great Britain and Ireland*, 4 vols. (1833–8); new edn as *A genealogical and heraldic dictionary of the landed gentry of Great Britain and Ireland*, 3 vols. [1843–9] [many later edns]

Burke, *Gen. Ire.* J. B. Burke, *A genealogical and heraldic history of the landed gentry of Ireland* (1899); 2nd edn (1904); 3rd edn (1912); 4th edn (1958); 5th edn as *Burke's Irish family records* (1976)

Burke, *Peerage* J. Burke, *A general [later edns A genealogical] and heraldic dictionary of the peerage and baronetage of the United Kingdom* [later edns *the British empire*] (1829–)

Burney, *Hist. mus.* C. Burney, *A general history of music, from the earliest ages to the present period*, 4 vols. (1776–89)

Burtchaell & Sadleir, *Alum. Dubl.* G. D. Burtchaell and T. U. Sadleir, *Alumni Dublinenses: a register of the students, graduates, and provosts of Trinity College* (1924); [2nd edn], with suppl., in 2 pts (1935)

Calamy rev. A. G. Matthews, *Calamy revised* (1934); repr. (1988)

CCI *Calendar of confirmations and inventories granted and given up in the several commissariots of Scotland* (1876–)

CClR *Calendar of the close rolls preserved in the Public Record Office*, 47 vols. (1892–1963)

CDS J. Bain, ed., *Calendar of documents relating to Scotland*, 4 vols., PRO (1881–8); suppl. vol. 5, ed. G. G. Simpson and J. D. Galbraith [1986]

CEPR letters W. H. Bliss, C. Johnson, and J. Twemlow, eds., *Calendar of entries in the papal registers relating to Great Britain and Ireland: papal letters* (1893–)

CGPLA *Calendars of the grants of probate and letters of administration* [in 4 ser.: England & Wales, Northern Ireland, Ireland, and Éire]

Chambers, *Scots.* R. Chambers, ed., *A biographical dictionary of eminent Scotsmen*, 4 vols. (1832–5)

Chancery records chancery records pubd by the PRO

Chancery records (RC) chancery records pubd by the Record Commissions

CIPM	*Calendar of inquisitions post mortem*, [20 vols.], PRO (1904–); also *Henry VII*, 3 vols. (1898–1955)
Clarendon, *Hist. rebellion*	E. Hyde, earl of Clarendon, *The history of the rebellion and civil wars in England*, 6 vols. (1888); repr. (1958) and (1992)
Cobbett, *Parl. hist.*	W. Cobbett and J. Wright, eds., *Cobbett's Parliamentary history of England*, 36 vols. (1806–1820)
Colvin, *Archs.*	H. Colvin, *A biographical dictionary of British architects, 1600–1840*, 3rd edn (1995)
Cooper, *Ath. Cantab.*	C. H. Cooper and T. Cooper, *Athenae Cantabrigienses*, 3 vols. (1858–1913); repr. (1967)
CPR	*Calendar of the patent rolls preserved in the Public Record Office* (1891–)
Crockford	*Crockford's Clerical Directory*
CS	Camden Society
CSP	*Calendar of state papers* [in 11 ser.: domestic, Scotland, Scottish series, Ireland, colonial, Commonwealth, foreign, Spain [at Simancas], Rome, Milan, and Venice]
CYS	Canterbury and York Society
DAB	*Dictionary of American biography*, 21 vols. (1928–36), repr. in 11 vols. (1964); 10 suppls. (1944–96)
DBB	D. J. Jeremy, ed., *Dictionary of business biography*, 5 vols. (1984–6)
DCB	G. W. Brown and others, *Dictionary of Canadian biography*, [14 vols.] (1966–)
Debrett's Peerage	*Debrett's Peerage* (1803–) [sometimes *Debrett's Illustrated peerage*]
Desmond, *Botanists*	R. Desmond, *Dictionary of British and Irish botanists and horticulturists* (1977); rev. edn (1994)
Dir. Brit. archs.	A. Felstead, J. Franklin, and L. Pinfield, eds., *Directory of British architects, 1834–1900* (1993); 2nd edn, ed. A. Brodie and others, 2 vols. (2001)
DLB	J. M. Bellamy and J. Saville, eds., *Dictionary of labour biography*, [10 vols.] (1972–)
DLitB	Dictionary of Literary Biography
DNB	*Dictionary of national biography*, 63 vols. (1885–1900), suppl., 3 vols. (1901); repr. in 22 vols. (1908–9); 10 further suppls. (1912–96); *Missing persons* (1993)
DNZB	W. H. Oliver and C. Orange, eds., *The dictionary of New Zealand biography*, 5 vols. (1990–2000)
DSAB	W. J. de Kock and others, eds., *Dictionary of South African biography*, 5 vols. (1968–87)
DSB	C. C. Gillispie and F. L. Holmes, eds., *Dictionary of scientific biography*, 16 vols. (1970–80); repr. in 8 vols. (1981); 2 vol. suppl. (1990)
DSBB	A. Slaven and S. Checkland, eds., *Dictionary of Scottish business biography, 1860–1960*, 2 vols. (1986–90)
DSCHT	N. M. de S. Cameron and others, eds., *Dictionary of Scottish church history and theology* (1993)
Dugdale, *Monasticon*	W. Dugdale, *Monasticon Anglicanum*, 3 vols. (1655–72); 2nd edn, 3 vols. (1661–82); new edn, ed. J. Caley, J. Ellis, and B. Bandinel, 6 vols. in 8 pts (1817–30); repr. (1846) and (1970)
DWB	J. E. Lloyd and others, eds., *Dictionary of Welsh biography down to 1940* (1959) [Eng. trans. of *Y bywgraffiadur Cymreig hyd 1940*, 2nd edn (1954)]
EdinR	*Edinburgh Review, or, Critical Journal*
EETS	Early English Text Society
Emden, *Cam.*	A. B. Emden, *A biographical register of the University of Cambridge to 1500* (1963)
Emden, *Oxf.*	A. B. Emden, *A biographical register of the University of Oxford to AD 1500*, 3 vols. (1957–9); also *A biographical register of the University of Oxford, AD 1501 to 1540* (1974)
EngHR	*English Historical Review*
Engraved Brit. ports.	F. M. O'Donoghue and H. M. Hake, *Catalogue of engraved British portraits preserved in the department of prints and drawings in the British Museum*, 6 vols. (1908–25)
ER	The English Reports, 178 vols. (1900–32)
ESTC	*English short title catalogue, 1475–1800* [CD-ROM and online]
Evelyn, *Diary*	*The diary of John Evelyn*, ed. E. S. De Beer, 6 vols. (1955); repr. (2000)
Farington, *Diary*	*The diary of Joseph Farington*, ed. K. Garlick and others, 17 vols. (1978–98)
Fasti Angl. (Hardy)	J. Le Neve, *Fasti ecclesiae Anglicanae*, ed. T. D. Hardy, 3 vols. (1854)
Fasti Angl., 1066–1300	[J. Le Neve], *Fasti ecclesiae Anglicanae, 1066–1300*, ed. D. E. Greenway and J. S. Barrow, [8 vols.] (1968–)
Fasti Angl., 1300–1541	[J. Le Neve], *Fasti ecclesiae Anglicanae, 1300–1541*, 12 vols. (1962–7)
Fasti Angl., 1541–1857	[J. Le Neve], *Fasti ecclesiae Anglicanae, 1541–1857*, ed. J. M. Horn, D. M. Smith, and D. S. Bailey, [9 vols.] (1969–)
Fasti Scot.	H. Scott, *Fasti ecclesiae Scoticanae*, 3 vols. in 6 (1871); new edn, [11 vols.] (1915–)
FO List	*Foreign Office List*
Fortescue, *Brit. army*	J. W. Fortescue, *A history of the British army*, 13 vols. (1899–1930)
Foss, *Judges*	E. Foss, *The judges of England*, 9 vols. (1848–64); repr. (1966)
Foster, *Alum. Oxon.*	J. Foster, ed., *Alumni Oxonienses: the members of the University of Oxford, 1715–1886*, 4 vols. (1887–8); later edn (1891); also *Alumni Oxonienses … 1500–1714*, 4 vols. (1891–2); 8 vol. repr. (1968) and (2000)
Fuller, *Worthies*	T. Fuller, *The history of the worthies of England*, 4 pts (1662); new edn, 2 vols., ed. J. Nichols (1811); new edn, 3 vols., ed. P. A. Nuttall (1840); repr. (1965)
GEC, *Baronetage*	G. E. Cokayne, *Complete baronetage*, 6 vols. (1900–09); repr. (1983) [microprint]
GEC, *Peerage*	G. E. C. [G. E. Cokayne], *The complete peerage of England, Scotland, Ireland, Great Britain, and the United Kingdom*, 8 vols. (1887–98); new edn, ed. V. Gibbs and others, 14 vols. in 15 (1910–98); microprint repr. (1982) and (1987)
Genest, *Eng. stage*	J. Genest, *Some account of the English stage from the Restoration in 1660 to 1830*, 10 vols. (1832); repr. [New York, 1965]
Gillow, *Lit. biog. hist.*	J. Gillow, *A literary and biographical history or bibliographical dictionary of the English Catholics, from the breach with Rome, in 1534, to the present time*, 5 vols. [1885–1902]; repr. (1961); repr. with preface by C. Gillow (1999)
Gir. Camb. opera	*Giraldi Cambrensis opera*, ed. J. S. Brewer, J. F. Dimock, and G. F. Warner, 8 vols., Rolls Series, 21 (1861–91)
GJ	*Geographical Journal*

Gladstone, *Diaries*	*The Gladstone diaries: with cabinet minutes and prime-ministerial correspondence*, ed. M. R. D. Foot and H. C. G. Matthew, 14 vols. (1968–94)
GM	*Gentleman's Magazine*
Graves, *Artists*	A. Graves, ed., *A dictionary of artists who have exhibited works in the principal London exhibitions of oil paintings from 1760 to 1880* (1884); new edn (1895); 3rd edn (1901); facs. edn (1969); repr. [1970], (1973), and (1984)
Graves, *Brit. Inst.*	A. Graves, *The British Institution, 1806–1867: a complete dictionary of contributors and their work from the foundation of the institution* (1875); facs. edn (1908); repr. (1969)
Graves, *RA exhibitors*	A. Graves, *The Royal Academy of Arts: a complete dictionary of contributors and their work from its foundation in 1769 to 1904*, 8 vols. (1905–6); repr. in 4 vols. (1970) and (1972)
Graves, *Soc. Artists*	A. Graves, *The Society of Artists of Great Britain, 1760–1791, the Free Society of Artists, 1761–1783: a complete dictionary* (1907); facs. edn (1969)
Greaves & Zaller, *BDBR*	R. L. Greaves and R. Zaller, eds., *Biographical dictionary of British radicals in the seventeenth century*, 3 vols. (1982–4)
Grove, *Dict. mus.*	G. Grove, ed., *A dictionary of music and musicians*, 5 vols. (1878–90); 2nd edn, ed. J. A. Fuller Maitland (1904–10); 3rd edn, ed. H. C. Colles (1927); 4th edn with suppl. (1940); 5th edn, ed. E. Blom, 9 vols. (1954); suppl. (1961) [see also *New Grove*]
Hall, *Dramatic ports.*	L. A. Hall, *Catalogue of dramatic portraits in the theatre collection of the Harvard College library*, 4 vols. (1930–34)
Hansard	*Hansard's parliamentary debates*, ser. 1–5 (1803–)
Highfill, Burnim & Langhans, *BDA*	P. H. Highfill, K. A. Burnim, and E. A. Langhans, *A biographical dictionary of actors, actresses, musicians, dancers, managers, and other stage personnel in London, 1660–1800*, 16 vols. (1973–93)
Hist. U. Oxf.	T. H. Aston, ed., *The history of the University of Oxford*, 8 vols. (1984–2000) [1: *The early Oxford schools*, ed. J. I. Catto (1984); 2: *Late medieval Oxford*, ed. J. I. Catto and R. Evans (1992); 3: *The collegiate university*, ed. J. McConica (1986); 4: *Seventeenth-century Oxford*, ed. N. Tyacke (1997); 5: *The eighteenth century*, ed. L. S. Sutherland and L. G. Mitchell (1986); 6–7: *Nineteenth-century Oxford*, ed. M. G. Brock and M. C. Curthoys (1997–2000); 8: *The twentieth century*, ed. B. Harrison (2000)]
HJ	*Historical Journal*
HMC	Historical Manuscripts Commission
Holdsworth, *Eng. law*	W. S. Holdsworth, *A history of English law*, ed. A. L. Goodhart and H. L. Hanbury, 17 vols. (1903–72)
HoP, *Commons*	*The history of parliament: the House of Commons* [*1386–1421*, ed. J. S. Roskell, L. Clark, and C. Rawcliffe, 4 vols. (1992); *1509–1558*, ed. S. T. Bindoff, 3 vols. (1982); *1558–1603*, ed. P. W. Hasler, 3 vols. (1981); *1660–1690*, ed. B. D. Henning, 3 vols. (1983); *1690–1715*, ed. D. W. Hayton, E. Cruickshanks, and S. Handley, 5 vols. (2002); *1715–1754*, ed. R. Sedgwick, 2 vols. (1970); *1754–1790*, ed. L. Namier and J. Brooke, 3 vols. (1964), repr. (1985); *1790–1820*, ed. R. G. Thorne, 5 vols. (1986); in draft (used with permission): *1422–1504*, *1604–1629*, *1640–1660*, and *1820–1832*]
IGI	*International Genealogical Index*, Church of Jesus Christ of the Latterday Saints
ILN	*Illustrated London News*
IMC	Irish Manuscripts Commission
Irving, *Scots.*	J. Irving, ed., *The book of Scotsmen eminent for achievements in arms and arts, church and state, law, legislation and literature, commerce, science, travel and philanthropy* (1881)
JCS	*Journal of the Chemical Society*
JHC	*Journals of the House of Commons*
JHL	*Journals of the House of Lords*
John of Worcester, *Chron.*	*The chronicle of John of Worcester*, ed. R. R. Darlington and P. McGurk, trans. J. Bray and P. McGurk, 3 vols., OMT (1995–) [vol. 1 forthcoming]
Keeler, *Long Parliament*	M. F. Keeler, *The Long Parliament, 1640–1641: a biographical study of its members* (1954)
Kelly, *Handbk*	*The upper ten thousand: an alphabetical list of all members of noble families*, 3 vols. (1875–7); continued as *Kelly's handbook of the upper ten thousand for 1878* [1879], 2 vols. (1878–9); continued as *Kelly's handbook to the titled, landed and official classes*, 94 vols. (1880–1973)
LondG	*London Gazette*
LP Henry VIII	J. S. Brewer, J. Gairdner, and R. H. Brodie, eds., *Letters and papers, foreign and domestic, of the reign of Henry VIII*, 23 vols. in 38 (1862–1932); repr. (1965)
Mallalieu, *Watercolour artists*	H. L. Mallalieu, *The dictionary of British watercolour artists up to 1820*, 3 vols. (1976–90); vol. 1, 2nd edn (1986)
Memoirs FRS	*Biographical Memoirs of Fellows of the Royal Society*
MGH	*Monumenta Germaniae Historica*
MT	*Musical Times*
Munk, *Roll*	W. Munk, *The roll of the Royal College of Physicians of London*, 2 vols. (1861); 2nd edn, 3 vols. (1878)
N&Q	*Notes and Queries*
New Grove	S. Sadie, ed., *The new Grove dictionary of music and musicians*, 20 vols. (1980); 2nd edn, 29 vols. (2001) [also online edn; see also Grove, *Dict. mus.*]
Nichols, *Illustrations*	J. Nichols and J. B. Nichols, *Illustrations of the literary history of the eighteenth century*, 8 vols. (1817–58)
Nichols, *Lit. anecdotes*	J. Nichols, *Literary anecdotes of the eighteenth century*, 9 vols. (1812–16); facs. edn (1966)
Obits. FRS	*Obituary Notices of Fellows of the Royal Society*
O'Byrne, *Naval biog. dict.*	W. R. O'Byrne, *A naval biographical dictionary* (1849); repr. (1990); [2nd edn], 2 vols. (1861)
OHS	Oxford Historical Society
Old Westminsters	*The record of Old Westminsters*, 1–2, ed. G. F. R. Barker and A. H. Stenning (1928); suppl. 1, ed. J. B. Whitmore and G. R. Y. Radcliffe [1938]; 3, ed. J. B. Whitmore, G. R. Y. Radcliffe, and D. C. Simpson (1963); suppl. 2, ed. F. E. Pagan (1978); 4, ed. F. E. Pagan and H. E. Pagan (1992)
OMT	Oxford Medieval Texts
Ordericus Vitalis, *Eccl. hist.*	*The ecclesiastical history of Orderic Vitalis*, ed. and trans. M. Chibnall, 6 vols., OMT (1969–80); repr. (1990)
Paris, *Chron.*	*Matthaei Parisiensis, monachi sancti Albani, chronica majora*, ed. H. R. Luard, Rolls Series, 7 vols. (1872–83)
Parl. papers	*Parliamentary papers* (1801–)
PBA	*Proceedings of the British Academy*

Pepys, *Diary*	*The diary of Samuel Pepys*, ed. R. Latham and W. Matthews, 11 vols. (1970–83); repr. (1995) and (2000)
Pevsner	N. Pevsner and others, Buildings of England series
PICE	*Proceedings of the Institution of Civil Engineers*
Pipe rolls	*The great roll of the pipe for . . .*, PRSoc. (1884–)
PRO	Public Record Office
PRS	*Proceedings of the Royal Society of London*
PRSoc.	Pipe Roll Society
PTRS	*Philosophical Transactions of the Royal Society*
QR	*Quarterly Review*
RC	Record Commissions
Redgrave, *Artists*	S. Redgrave, *A dictionary of artists of the English school* (1874); rev. edn (1878); repr. (1970)
Reg. Oxf.	C. W. Boase and A. Clark, eds., *Register of the University of Oxford*, 5 vols., OHS, 1, 10–12, 14 (1885–9)
Reg. PCS	J. H. Burton and others, eds., *The register of the privy council of Scotland*, 1st ser., 14 vols. (1877–98); 2nd ser., 8 vols. (1899–1908); 3rd ser., [16 vols.] (1908–70)
Reg. RAN	H. W. C. Davis and others, eds., *Regesta regum Anglo-Normannorum, 1066–1154*, 4 vols. (1913–69)
RIBA Journal	*Journal of the Royal Institute of British Architects* [later *RIBA Journal*]
RotP	J. Strachey, ed., *Rotuli parliamentorum ut et petitiones, et placita in parliamento*, 6 vols. (1767–77)
RotS	D. Macpherson, J. Caley, and W. Illingworth, eds., *Rotuli Scotiae in Turri Londinensi et in domo capitulari Westmonasteriensi asservati*, 2 vols., RC, 14 (1814–19)
RS	Record(s) Society
Rymer, *Foedera*	T. Rymer and R. Sanderson, eds., *Foedera, conventiones, literae et cuiuscunque generis acta publica inter reges Angliae et alios quosvis imperatores, reges, pontifices, principes, vel communitates*, 20 vols. (1704–35); 2nd edn, 20 vols. (1726–35); 3rd edn, 10 vols. (1739–45), facs. edn (1967); new edn, ed. A. Clarke, J. Caley, and F. Holbrooke, 4 vols., RC, 50 (1816–30)
Sainty, *Judges*	J. Sainty, ed., *The judges of England, 1272–1990*, SeldS, suppl. ser., 10 (1993)
Sainty, *King's counsel*	J. Sainty, ed., *A list of English law officers and king's counsel*, SeldS, suppl. ser., 7 (1987)
SCH	Studies in Church History
Scots peerage	J. B. Paul, ed. *The Scots peerage, founded on Wood's edition of Sir Robert Douglas's Peerage of Scotland, containing an historical and genealogical account of the nobility of that kingdom*, 9 vols. (1904–14)
SeldS	Selden Society
SHR	*Scottish Historical Review*
State trials	T. B. Howell and T. J. Howell, eds., *Cobbett's Complete collection of state trials*, 34 vols. (1809–28)
STC, 1475–1640	A. W. Pollard, G. R. Redgrave, and others, eds., *A short-title catalogue of . . . English books . . . 1475–1640* (1926); 2nd edn, ed. W. A. Jackson, F. S. Ferguson, and K. F. Pantzer, 3 vols. (1976–91) [see also Wing, *STC*]
STS	Scottish Text Society
SurtS	Surtees Society

Symeon of Durham, *Opera*	*Symeonis monachi opera omnia*, ed. T. Arnold, 2 vols., Rolls Series, 75 (1882–5); repr. (1965)
Tanner, *Bibl. Brit.-Hib.*	T. Tanner, *Bibliotheca Britannico-Hibernica*, ed. D. Wilkins (1748); repr. (1963)
Thieme & Becker, *Allgemeines Lexikon*	U. Thieme, F. Becker, and H. Vollmer, eds., *Allgemeines Lexikon der bildenden Künstler von der Antike bis zur Gegenwart*, 37 vols. (Leipzig, 1907–50); repr. (1961–5), (1983), and (1992)
Thurloe, *State papers*	*A collection of the state papers of John Thurloe*, ed. T. Birch, 7 vols. (1742)
TLS	*Times Literary Supplement*
Tout, *Admin. hist.*	T. F. Tout, *Chapters in the administrative history of mediaeval England: the wardrobe, the chamber, and the small seals*, 6 vols. (1920–33); repr. (1967)
TRHS	*Transactions of the Royal Historical Society*
VCH	H. A. Doubleday and others, eds., *The Victoria history of the counties of England*, [88 vols.] (1900–)
Venn, *Alum. Cant.*	J. Venn and J. A. Venn, *Alumni Cantabrigienses: a biographical list of all known students, graduates, and holders of office at the University of Cambridge, from the earliest times to 1900*, 10 vols. (1922–54); repr. in 2 vols. (1974–8)
Vertue, *Note books*	[G. Vertue], *Note books*, ed. K. Esdaile, earl of Ilchester, and H. M. Hake, 6 vols., Walpole Society, 18, 20, 22, 24, 26, 30 (1930–55)
VF	*Vanity Fair*
Walford, *County families*	E. Walford, *The county families of the United Kingdom, or, Royal manual of the titled and untitled aristocracy of Great Britain and Ireland* (1860)
Walker rev.	A. G. Matthews, *Walker revised: being a revision of John Walker's Sufferings of the clergy during the grand rebellion, 1642–60* (1948); repr. (1988)
Walpole, *Corr.*	*The Yale edition of Horace Walpole's correspondence*, ed. W. S. Lewis, 48 vols. (1937–83)
Ward, *Men of the reign*	T. H. Ward, ed., *Men of the reign: a biographical dictionary of eminent persons of British and colonial birth who have died during the reign of Queen Victoria* (1885); repr. (Graz, 1968)
Waterhouse, *18c painters*	E. Waterhouse, *The dictionary of 18th century painters in oils and crayons* (1981); repr. as *British 18th century painters in oils and crayons* (1991), vol. 2 of *Dictionary of British art*
Watt, *Bibl. Brit.*	R. Watt, *Bibliotheca Britannica, or, A general index to British and foreign literature*, 4 vols. (1824) [many reprs.]
Wellesley index	W. E. Houghton, ed., *The Wellesley index to Victorian periodicals, 1824–1900*, 5 vols. (1966–89); new edn (1999) [CD-ROM]
Wing, *STC*	D. Wing, ed., *Short-title catalogue of . . . English books . . . 1641–1700*, 3 vols. (1945–51); 2nd edn (1972–88); rev. and enl. edn, ed. J. J. Morrison, C. W. Nelson, and M. Seccombe, 4 vols. (1994–8) [see also *STC, 1475–1640*]
Wisden	*John Wisden's Cricketer's Almanack*
Wood, *Ath. Oxon.*	A. Wood, *Athenae Oxonienses . . . to which are added the Fasti*, 2 vols. (1691–2); 2nd edn (1721); new edn, 4 vols., ed. P. Bliss (1813–20); repr. (1967) and (1969)
Wood, *Vic. painters*	C. Wood, *Dictionary of Victorian painters* (1971); 2nd edn (1978); 3rd edn as *Victorian painters*, 2 vols. (1995), vol. 4 of *Dictionary of British art*
WW	*Who's who* (1849–)
WWBMP	M. Stenton and S. Lees, eds., *Who's who of British members of parliament*, 4 vols. (1976–81)
WWW	*Who was who* (1929–)

Macan, Sir Arthur Vernon (1843–1908), gynaecologist and obstetrician, born at 9 Mountjoy Square, Dublin, on 30 January 1843, was the eldest of three sons in a family of five children of John Macan, of a co. Sligo family, a leading QC on the Connaught circuit, and first commissioner in bankruptcy in the high court in Ireland, and his wife, Maria Perrin, daughter of a Liverpool merchant of Huguenot extraction. Of his brothers, Jameson John Macan (*d.* 1910) for several years assisted in editing the *British Gynaecological Journal*; and Reginald Walter Macan became master of University College, Oxford, in 1906.

Arthur Macan was educated at St Columba's College (1858–9), co. Dublin, entered Trinity College, Dublin, in 1859, and graduated BA in December 1864. He studied medicine in the school of physic, Trinity College, and at the House of Industry Hospital. He proceeded MB and MCh in 1868, and took the degree of MAO in 1877. Having joined a class in London with a view to entering the Army Medical Service, he changed his mind, and early in 1869 he went to Berlin. The next three years were spent in intermittent study abroad, working under B. von Langenbeck, F. Hebra, C. Rokitansky, and others. Of robust physique, Macan was fond of outdoor sports and varied his work by prolonged walking tours, in one of which he walked from Berlin to Milan and then to Vienna. In 1870 he served as volunteer with the Prussian army, and was at Versailles when the royal palace was used as a German military hospital. Returning to Dublin in 1872, he was appointed assistant physician at the Rotunda Lying-in Hospital, and after three years' tenure of this post was elected gynaecologist to the City of Dublin Hospital.

Macan married, on 30 January 1877, Mary Agnes, daughter of John Bradshaw Wanklyn, of Cheam, Surrey. There were three sons and four daughters of the marriage. In 1877 he was elected fellow of the King and Queen's College of Physicians in Ireland, and in 1878 was appointed lecturer in midwifery in the Carmichael school of medicine. His chief opportunity came in 1882, when he succeeded Lombe Atthill as master of the Rotunda Hospital, a post which was the prize of the obstetric profession in the United Kingdom.

Macan, who throughout life was a radical and a reformer, found, on his return from abroad, obstetric practice in the United Kingdom far behind that on the continent. He set out to introduce the newer methods, in face of the opposition of the profession. He and other progressives were dubbed the 'German band', and treated with scant courtesy at medical meetings. Although not the discoverer of the newer methods in obstetrics and gynaecology, Macan was a reformer and introduced many new techniques to Ireland. He reintroduced the clinical method of abdominal palpation as a means of diagnosis in labour and also the use of the obstetric chair. He reported the first successful case of caesarean section from Ireland in 1889. The use of silver nitrate preparations as prophylaxis against gonococcal eye infections in the newborn was begun during his term as master of the Rotunda.

Macan developed the clinical area of gynaecology. He reported vaginal hysterectomy and also a series of successful ovarian removals by abdominal operation. Also interested in the field of hospital administration, Macan modified and upgraded hospital policies and facilities. A major problem of the period was the terrible mortality from infection after childbirth. Macan became master of the Rotunda Hospital at a time when there was serious debate whether the very existence of maternity hospitals was justified, as sepsis was much more common following delivery in the hospital setting. As one of the earliest to apply the Listerian principles of antisepsis to midwifery, Macan developed the reforms which had been instituted by his predecessor, Lombe Atthill. During the last eighteen months of Macan's term of office at the Rotunda there was no death from septic causes. Just before the usual term of seven years at the Rotunda Hospital expired, Macan was elected king's professor of midwifery in the school of physic, Trinity College, a post which carried with it the duties of obstetric physician and gynaecologist to Sir Patrick Dun's Hospital.

Macan's wife died in 1886 of puerperal sepsis, the disease which few had done more to combat than Macan. He married for a second time on 5 February 1889. His bride, an American, Mary Catherine Lynch, claimed to be a widow, but her husband, Oliver Lynch, appeared on the scene and took an action against Macan. The newly-weds separated but Macan granted his second 'wife' a handsome annual gratuity.

From 1902 to 1904 Macan was president of the Royal College of Physicians of Ireland, and in 1903 he was knighted. He was also president of the British Gynaecological Society (1890), of the section of obstetrics of the Royal Academy of Medicine in Ireland (1886–7; 1899–1901), and of the obstetric section of the British Medical Association in 1887. He was honorary president of the obstetric section of the International Congress of Medicine in Berlin in 1890, and of the Congress of Gynaecology and Obstetrics in Geneva in 1896, and in Amsterdam in 1899. It was by Macan's force of character that he influenced the development of obstetrics in the United Kingdom. Although he wrote no book, he published no fewer than seventy reports and communications in the *Dublin Journal of Medical Science* between 1872 and 1908. Many others appeared elsewhere.

Macan died on 26 September 1908 of heart failure at his residence, 53 Merrion Square, Dublin. He was buried on 29 September in Mount Jerome cemetery, Dublin.

R. J. ROWLETTE, *rev.* MICHAEL J. O'DOWD

Sources *Journal of Obstetrics and Gynaecology*, 14 (1908), 344–50 · 'In memoriam', *Dublin Journal of Medical Science*, 126 (1908) · T. D. O'D. Browne, *The Rotunda Hospital, 1745–1945* (1947) · T. P. C. Kirkpatrick, *History of the medical teaching in Trinity College, Dublin, and of the School of Physic in Ireland* (1912) · C. A. Cameron, *History of the Royal College of Surgeons in Ireland*, 2nd edn (1916) · J. D. H. Widdess, *A history of the Royal College of Physicians of Ireland, 1654–1963* (1963) · A. Browne, ed., *Masters, midwives, and ladies in waiting: the Rotunda Hospital, 1745–1995* (1995) · J. B. Lyons, *Brief lives of Irish doctors* (1978) · *BMJ* (3 Oct 1908), 1049

Archives Royal College of Physicians of Ireland, Dublin, Kirkpatrick MSS
Likenesses D'Arcy, photograph, repro. in *Dublin Journal of Medical Science*, 412 · S. Purser, oils, priv. coll. · photograph, Royal College of Physicans, Dublin; repro. in *Journal of Obstetrics and Gynaecology*, 345
Wealth at death £14,150 2s. 9d.—in England: Irish probate sealed in England, 2 Feb 1909, *CGPLA Eng. & Wales*

Mac an Bhaird family (*per. c.*1400–*c.*1695), Gaelic poets, was an Irish family (clann an Bhaird, 'the children of the bard') famous for poetry and learning. The name suggests an early link with learning, through descent from a bard, the earliest kind of poet attested among the Celtic peoples, who was in medieval Ireland regarded as inferior to the learned *file*. The surname is first attested in the annals in 1173, when Máel Ísu Macc in Baird died bishop of Clonfert, a see in co. Galway.

What has been regarded as the senior learned line, and possibly the kin of Máel Ísu of 1173, first appears in the annals in 1408 with the death of Mac an Bhaird of Cúl an Urtainn, *ollamh* of Uí Mhaine in co. Galway, of which the family of Ó Ceallaigh (O Kelly) were the leaders. The term *ollamh* is usually translated as 'chief poet', but he also had enormous power as the chief's political counsellor. The first name of this *ollamh* is not known, and none of his work, nor that of any of the co. Galway family, is known to have survived. Families of Mac an Bhaird (in various Anglicizations, including Ward) are still on record in the Ó Ceallaigh country in the seventeenth century, but by then the learned tradition of the family had moved on. Possibly members of this same branch of the poetic family did continue to produce verse (of some kind) for several centuries, while leaving no written evidence of it; they might conceivably include a group of 'McEwards', 'rymers' in Ballymote, co. Sligo, who were 'pardoned' by Queen Elizabeth in 1603.

A second branch of the family was clearly in evidence by 1488, when the annals record the death of 'Mac an Bhaird Oirghiall', the head of the branch belonging to Oirghialla (Oriel), an Ulster territory approximating to co. Monaghan; he was Nuadha, son of Seán Cam, and his grandfather Cú Uladh probably lived about 1400. This is usually taken to be an offshoot of the Mac an Bhaird family of Uí Mhaine, but there is a hint in Roderic O'Flaherty's *Ogygia* (1685) that in fact the Mac an Bhaird family of Oriel was just as ancient as that of Uí Mhaine. None of the Oriel family, however, is identified as a poet before the mid-sixteenth century. After that there are several extant poems composed by a poet (or poets) called Aodh mac Diarmada (Mhic an Bhaird) to patrons in that area, notably Ó Raghallaigh leaders in co. Cavan in 1596–8, and a Maguire (Fermanagh) aristocrat in 1566.

The third branch of the family, the most important and (as far as is known) the most productive, was based in Tír Conaill (co. Donegal), and it is usually assumed to have derived from one of the two branches already mentioned. This may be correct, but the beginnings of the Donegal family have been placed about the year 1400, very much the same time that the other two families are first heard of. In 1510 the annals record the death of Eoghan Ruadh

Mac an Bhaird, *ollamh* to Ó Domhnaill (O Donnell) of Tír Conaill, and it is as poets to the O Donnell family that Clann an Bhaird are best known thereafter. This Eoghan Ruadh may have been the son of Gofraidh mac Eoghain, who died in 1478 and is the first Mac an Bhaird Tíre Conaill (head of the Donegal family) on record; the earliest surviving Mac an Bhaird poem is one composed on the death of an O Donnell chief in 1420 by **Eoghan Mac an Bhaird** (*fl.* 1420), Gofraidh's father. It may be to this Eoghan that a seventeenth-century poet of the family refers when he claims to belong to 'Sliocht Eoghain mhóir Mhic an Bhaird' (descendants of the great Eoghan Mac an Bhaird) (Mhág Craith, 1.120). Poets of the Donegal family are fairly well documented, both in the annals and in their poetic works, for the next two centuries. Another *ollamh*, Aodh, was killed in 1522.

Conchobhar Ruadh died in 1541 as *ollamh* to O Donnell, and he was apparently author of an extant poem of 1505 on the death of the O Donnell chief. His brother Cormac (*d.* 1534) was also a poet. Conchobhar's son Cú Uladh and grandson Maol Muire (*d.* 1597) were both learned poets, as were Cormac's sons Flann and Uilliam Óg (*d.* 1576). Uilliam Óg was *ollamh* to O Donnell, and had two sons who were poets, **Eoghan Ruadh Mac an Bhaird** (*b. c.*1570, *d.* after 1625) and a second Uilliam Óg, who was still composing in 1641. He seems also to have had a third son, Fearghal, whose son Somhairle flourished as a poet about 1649. An unbroken poetic line can thus be identified from Cormac in the early sixteenth century to his great-grandson, Somhairle, about 1649.

Eoghan Ruadh may have been regarded as *ollamh* to O Donnell about the turn of the seventeenth century, and his life and verse are both closely tied to the varying political fortunes of the O Donnell family. He accompanied his chief in the historic 'flight of the earls' in 1607, when Gaelic rule in Ulster was effectively ended. He was living in Flanders when O Donnell died in 1608, and he later went on to Rome; but his poems continue to show his central concern with the misfortunes and hopes of the O Donnells and Ireland. A volume of his work was edited in 1930 (O Raghallaigh). Walsh's verdict on it is that it is 'very indifferent' (Walsh, 204); none the less Eoghan Ruadh was one of the two most prolific and important poets of the Donegal family. In 1612 Eoghan Ruadh received a pension from Philip III of Spain, and he seems to have died in Rome some time after 1625.

Quite possibly a son of Eoghan Ruadh (though there is no overwhelming evidence to that effect) was Aodh Buidhe Mac an Bhaird, Father Hugh *Ward (1592–1635), who was born in co. Donegal, became a Franciscan, and went to the Irish College at Louvain in 1622 as professor of philosophy.

The other most important Mac an Bhaird poet is **Fearghal Óg Mac an Bhaird** (*d.* 1618x30), who lived about the same time as Eoghan Ruadh but belonged to a different kin within the Donegal family. His father, who died in 1550, is named in the annals as Fearghal, 'mac domhnaill ruaidh saoí fhirdhana, 7 oide sccol' (which has been translated as 'a learned poet, a master of schools'), and both

Fearghal's sons were poets. One, Eoghan Ruadh, was hanged in 1572. Fearghal Óg may have been born in the 1540s and in 1581 he was in Scotland, where he may even have had King James VI among his patrons, and where he reports his distress, clearly amounting to 'culture-shock' (Ó Macháin, 56), at the effects of the Reformation there. He may also have been something of a rebel among Irish poets, for he seems to be the subject of a poem (O. Bergin, *Irish Bardic Poetry*, 1970, 118) by another professional chiding him for composing poetry while out riding his horse: true *filidheacht* should be composed indoors, in the dark, and involve serious brainstorming. Fearghal also once threw a goblet of wine in the face of Mág Uidhir (the Maguire chief), and apologized poetically for it. Later in life he lived for a while on the continent, and there are a few unhappy poems from there. He is known to have visited Louvain after 1618 and then to have returned to Ireland, where he died before 1630, but beyond these facts little is known of his life.

Fearghal Óg left more of his work than any other Mac an Bhaird poet, about sixty poems, his patrons being aristocrats in all parts of the northern half of Ireland, but of course principally the O Donnell leadership; however, primacy as O Donnell poet about 1600 seems to have gone to Eoghan Ruadh (mac Uilliam Óig). One critic thought that Fearghal Óg 'was a voluminous composer of simple, if not very distinguished verse' (E. Knott, *An Introduction to Irish Syllabic Poetry of the Period 1200–1600*, 1928, 82). Bergin's opinion is more enthusiastic: 'many of Fearghal Óg's poems have a natural grace and charm beyond the miracles of technique admired and imitated in the schools' (O. Bergin, *Irish Bardic Poetry*, 1970, 118). It has been suggested that a specimen of Fearghal Óg's handwriting is extant in the National Library of Scotland's manuscript Adv. 72.1.1, which he may have owned at one point.

It is becoming clear that these conservative professional poets, like their masters, were quite willing to collaborate fully, when necessary, with the new English world being imposed by King James. The leading Donegal poets Eoghan Ruadh and Fearghal Óg have been classed among the great 'innovators' of the 1600 period because of the willingness evidenced in their poetry to face up to the grim reality of life under the new masters (Caball, 4, 12). In 1603 Eoghan Ruadh was a member of an official 'inquisition' in Donegal, looking into the extent of the O Donnell lands. In 1922 Eleanor Knott wrote as follows of the introduction of new political themes to professional verse:

> Towards the end of the 16th century we find Eóghan Ruadh Mhac an Bhaird attempting to express a more intellectual outlook in verses which reflect a faint gleam of the humanizing influence which was beginning—too late—to rise over the schools.   (Knott, *Bardic Poems*, 2.xxxiv)

Despite the central importance of the Donegal family, the Oriel branch of Clann an Bhaird is also worthy of note. In the sixteenth century Laoiseach Mac an Bhaird, probably a member of the Oriel family and still living in co. Monaghan in 1601, scolds a neighbour (in technically perfect *deibhidhe* metre, of course) for following 'English ways' of dress and hairstyle (O. Bergin, *Irish Bardic Poetry*, 1970, 49);

but he is perhaps also the author of two 'courtly' love poems that have survived. Gofraidh mac Briain Mhic an Bhaird, of the Oriel family, is an important figure in early seventeenth-century verse, with fifteen professional poems extant, to O Donnell leaders and other Ulster and Connaught figures, as well as religious verse. Gofraidh Óg Mac an Bhaird (whose father Gofraidh was also a poet, perhaps the same Gofraidh mac Briain) left a poem lamenting an O Donnell chief who died in 1655. Later there is a Pádraig Óg Mac an Bhaird (whose *floruit* date has been given as c.1690, but whose family links are unknown) and his son, another Fearghal Óg, producing poetry.

A Louvain Franciscan priest who called himself in Latin Cornelius Wardaeus—doubtless for **Conchobhar Mac an Bhaird** (d. 1641)—can be firmly linked to the poetic family. Probably a member of the Donegal family, he volunteered in 1624, with other Franciscans (and with the authority of Aodh Mac an Bhaird among others), to take part in a mission to the highlands of Scotland, where Catholics had had few, if any, Gaelic-speaking priests since the Reformation (in 1560). He came to Muckairn, Argyll, and the published English summary of his Latin report to Rome reads:

> Campbell of Calder was laird; Calder was a man of great importance, but a heretic; it was very difficult to gain access to him; knowing, however, that Calder held poets in high regard, Ward, having composed a poem in praise of Calder, disguised himself as an Irish poet; then, accompanied by a singer, carrying a harp, he presented himself before Calder [*mox cum uno cytharoeda, et cantore (ut moris erat) ingredior*], and was graciously received; Ward continued in the guise of a poet for three days, and then disclosed to Calder who he actually was; ... later, ... the latter became a catholic. (Giblin, 53–4)

Whatever may be meant by the word 'disguised', Mac an Bhaird clearly knew what was involved in being a professional *file*. He was imprisoned at the Gatehouse in London between 1630 and 1632, and remained on the Scottish mission until it ended in 1637. He then returned to Ireland, where he died in 1641.

The practice of composing syllabic praise poems for patrons did not end with English conquest, but hung on, in places, even into the 1690s. A good example is **Diarmaid mac Laoisigh Mhic an Bhaird** (*fl.* 1675–1695), who left nine poems, six of them in praise of Mac Mathghamhna (MacMahon) leaders in co. Monaghan. A modern scholar calls him 'one of the last fully-trained classical poets practising his art in this country' (Hughes, 1987, 67). Little is known about his life, but he can safely be regarded as a late representative of the Oriel family, although some sources say that he belonged to co. Down.

Diarmaid also took part in the last, almost laughably late, poetic *iomarbhágh* or 'contention', of which the four extant component poems are in the Book of Clanranald (in the National Museum of Scotland), probably written in the 1680s. The contention is about the heraldic right to the symbol of the Red Hand, which Diarmaid claims for the Mac Aonghusa family of co. Down; Eoghan Ó Donnghaile disputes this and claims it for the Ó Néill family, and the Scottish poet Niall Mac Muireadhaigh (c.1637–1726) writes a reply to each of the Irish poets, claiming the Red Hand for Clann Dòmhnaill (the MacDonalds). This *iomarbhágh* echoes the much larger poetic contention in which, early in the seventeenth century, numerous Irish poets squabbled learnedly about the relative merits of the north and south of Ireland, just as the English conquest was in the process of destroying their old Gaelic world forever, following the battle of Kinsale. If that earlier *iomarbhágh* exemplified the unreal ivory tower world of the learned poets, the Red Hand contention shows that nothing much had changed in the run-up to the battle of the Boyne.

COLM Ó BAOILL

Sources P. Ó Macháin, 'Poems by Fearghal Óg Mac an Bhaird', 2 vols., PhD diss., U. Edin., 1988 · P. Walsh, *Irish men of learning*, ed. C. O Lochlainn (1947) · T. O Raghallaigh, *Duanta Eoghain Ruaidh Mhic an Bhaird* (1930) · C. McGrath, 'Eoghan Ruadh mac Uilliam Óig Mhic an Bhaird', *Measgra i gcuimhne Mhichíl Uí Chléirigh*, ed. S. O'Brien (1944), 108–16 · C. Mhág Craith, *Dán na mBráthar Mionúr*, 2 vols. (1967–80) · C. A. Empey and K. Simms, 'The ordinances of the White Earl and the problem of coign in the later middle ages', *Proceedings of the Royal Irish Academy*, 75C (1975), 161–87 · C. Giblin, *Irish Franciscan mission to Scotland, 1619–1646* (1964) · T. Ó Concheanainn, 'A feature of the poetry of Fearghal Óg Mac an Bhaird', *Éigse*, 15 (1974), 235–51 · A. J. Hughes, 'Fuar leam Longphort mo Charad', *Celtica*, 19 (1987), 61–74 · A. J. Hughes, 'The seventeenth-century Ulster/Scottish contention of the Red Hand: background and significance', *Gaelic and Scots in harmony*, ed. D. S. Thomson (1990), 78–94 · J. O'Donovan, *The tribes and customs of Hy-Many* (1843) · L. Mac Cionnaith, *Dioghluim Dána* (1938) · L. MacKenna, *Aithdioghluim Dána*, 2 vols. (1939–40) · A. Cameron, *Reliquiae Celticae*, 2 (1894) · D. Greene, *Duanaire Mhéig Uidhir* (1972) · M. O Riordan, *The Gaelic mind and the collapse of the Gaelic world* (1990) · M. Caball, *Poets and politics: continuity and reaction in Irish poetry, 1558–1625* (1998) · E. Knott, *The bardic poems of Tadhg Dall Ó Huiginn (1550–1591)*, 2 vols. (1922–6) · K. Nicholls, *Gaelic and Gaelicised Ireland in the middle ages* (1972)

Mac an Bhaird, Conchobhar (*d.* 1641). *See under* Mac an Bhaird family (*per. c.*1400–*c.*1695).

Mac an Bhaird, Eoghan (*fl.* 1420). *See under* Mac an Bhaird family (*per. c.*1400–*c.*1695).

Mac an Bhaird, Eoghan Ruadh (*b. c.*1570, *d.* after 1625). *See under* Mac an Bhaird family (*per. c.*1400–*c.*1695).

Mac an Bhaird, Fearghal Óg (*d.* 1618x30). *See under* Mac an Bhaird family (*per. c.*1400–*c.*1695).

Mac an t-Saoir, Donnchadh Bàn. *See* Macintyre, Duncan Bàn (1723?–1812).

Macanward, Hugh Boy. *See* Ward, Hugh (1592–1635).

Macara, Sir Charles Wright, first baronet (1845–1929), cotton spinner, was born at Strathmiglo, Fife, on 11 January 1845, the only child of the Revd William Macara, minister of the Free Church of Scotland, and his wife, Charlotte Grace, daughter of Thomas Cowpar, of Memus, Kirriemuir, Forfarshire, and niece of Sir Archibald Galloway, sometime chairman of the East India Company. Macara's father was a Scottish divine of the old school, whose life, writes Macara in his *Recollections*, 'was a standing exhortation to me to find out what was good and hold on to it'. He refers also to the influence of his mother, an equally vivid personality.

Educated in his native village and at a school in Edinburgh, Macara began work in 1862, at the age of seventeen, with a Scottish merchant in Manchester. In 1875 he married Marion (1848–1938), daughter of William Young of Bournemouth, granddaughter of one of the founders of the firm of Henry Bannerman & Sons, cotton spinners and merchants of Manchester, and cousin to Sir Henry Campbell-Bannerman. In 1880 Macara was made managing partner in this firm. In 1884 he fought a strike, with ruthless success, and in 1899 took a leading part in establishing the Manchester Cotton Employers' Parliamentary Association; but he also claimed to have been 'one of the forces which have extended and solidified the operatives' unions' (Macara, 16). His belief was that all workers and all employers should join their respective unions and organizations and that between employers and employees, so organized, there need be no ill feeling. In the famous twenty weeks' strike in the cotton-spinning industry in 1892 and 1893, which was ended by the signing of the Brooklands agreement (March 1893), Macara had to fight both the workers on the question of wages, which had originated the strike, and his fellow employers on the wider issue of full recognition of the workers' right to have a say in industry. The Brooklands agreement provided rules for the settlement of future disputes by conciliatory methods and, in Macara's view, inaugurated a new era 'not in the cotton industry alone, but in all industry' (ibid., 24). Macara's reputation is based on his role in bringing the 1892–3 dispute to an end. Contemporaries looked upon him as the architect of the agreement, together with James Mawdsley, the leader of the operatives. Macara and his biographer, Haslam Mills, encouraged this view, though later research questioned this. He became prominent in the dispute in the final weeks, but the Brooklands agreement had originally been drafted by the Oldham solicitor and later member of parliament for the town, Robert Ascroft. Probably the truth will never be known, but it was Macara's partnership with Mawdsley that contemporaries perceived as the reason for industrial peace in the cotton-spinning industry and Macara used that view of himself to great effect, emerging as the spokesman for the industry as a whole.

In 1894 Macara was elected president of the Federation of Master Cotton Spinners' Associations and he held this position until 1914. During all that time there occurred only one strike concerning wages (in 1908) which affected the whole industry; whereas before his presidency the industry was known as the cockpit of industrial strife. Macara took a leading part in all public movements connected with the cotton trade, including the inauguration in 1894 of the Manchester Cotton Association, which had for its object the direct importation of raw cotton to Manchester by the ship canal, and of the British Cotton Growing Association. In 1902 he headed a delegation, representing both employers and workers, to the China Shipping Conference, where he secured a reduction in freights; this was calculated to have saved the Lancashire trade about £100,000 a year. Spurred on by the cotton crisis of 1903–4, Macara founded in 1904 the International Federation of

Master Cotton Spinners' and Manufacturers' Associations, of which he was chairman from 1904 to 1915, and which he regarded as one of the most important movements in the history of international co-operation. He also did much to assist the establishment of the International Institute of Agriculture.

By the Edwardian era, Macara was the most influential figure in the Lancashire cotton industry, but he was also a figure of controversy. Although not involved in party politics, he vigorously opposed tariff reform and was responsible for the Cotton Employers' Parliamentary Association, the organization which he had helped to found in 1899, and the cotton unions issuing a joint statement in 1903 condemning tariff reform. This statement was to arouse controversy in both the 1906 and 1910 general elections, when his support of free trade was resented by Conservatives in Lancashire. This may help to explain why the Liberal government looked favourably on his proposal of 1911 for ending industrial conflict, and adopted his proposal for an industrial council consisting of leading employers and trade unionists, including Macara. It was not very effective, though its chairman, Sir George Askwith, emerged as the government's main industrial arbitrator and conciliator.

Macara resigned as president of the Federation of Master Cotton Spinners' Associations during the war, but he continued to comment on the fortunes of the industry as well as on more general economic and social issues. He was particularly critical of the response of the federation to the inter-war crisis of the cotton industry, its solution to the loss of export markets being to seek wage reductions. Macara became president of the provisional emergency cotton committee, which advocated a return to the wartime Cotton Control Board, with fixed prices and elimination of excess capacity. Their proposals were later adopted by the government in the 1930s. Macara ended his career as the chief critic of the very organization he had helped to build.

Macara published numerous articles on labour questions, the organization of trade, philanthropic movements, and lifeboat work, the last reflecting the involvement of himself and his wife as residents of St Anne's-on-Sea, Lancashire, from 1884, in the Lifeboat Saturday movement, following the disaster at St Anne's in 1886, in which the local lifeboat was sunk with the loss of all crew.

Macara was created a baronet in 1911, and received many foreign decorations. He died at his home, Friar's Croft, Hale, Cheshire, on 2 January 1929, leaving one son, William Cowper Macara, who succeeded to the baronetcy, and four daughters. His wife also survived him. He was buried in the town cemetery, St Anne's-on-Sea, on 5 January.

Sir Charles Macara was the last great spokesman produced by the Lancashire cotton industry. No one was to enjoy such wide support after 1914 or again speak with such authority on the industry's problems. Macara set out to create a stable and peaceful industrial environment. He believed that industrial progress could only come from social harmony between capital and labour. Perhaps he

was fortunate in emerging as a leading figure in the industry as the great depression of 1873–96 came to a close. Similarly his period of influence was over before cotton faced the intractable problems of the inter-war years.

Macara could not, however, have been so successful without a similar figure representing the operatives' side. It was Macara's good fortune to be associated with James Mawdsley, the general secretary of the Amalgamated Association of Operative Cotton Spinners. Mawdsley and Macara were both determined in 1893 to put the relationship between capital and labour in cotton spinning on a new footing in order to try to avoid future disputes. The personal relationship these two men established is illustrated by Macara's often-quoted remark that if the people of Lancashire had known James Mawdsley as well as he had, they would put up a statue to him, and by the fact that, even after Mawdsley's death in 1902, the spinners' union presented Macara with an illuminated address on the announcement of his baronetcy.

H. WITHERS, *rev.* ALAN FOWLER

Sources W. Haslam Mills, *Sir Charles W. Macara, Bart: a study of modern Lancashire* (1917) · C. W. Macara, *Recollections* (1921) · A. J. McIvor, 'Macara, Sir Charles Wright', *DBB* · *Manchester Guardian* (3 Jan 1929) · *Textile Mercury* (5 Jan 1929) · *Cotton Factory Times* (4 Jan 1929) · A. Bullen, 'The making of Brooklands', *The barefoot aristocrats: a history of the Amalgamated Association of Operative Cotton Spinners*, ed. A. Fowler and T. Wyke (1987), 93–114 · P. F. Clarke, *Lancashire and the new liberalism* (1971) · A. McIvor, *Organised capital: employers' associations and industrial relations in northern England, 1880–1939* (1996) · R. F. Dyson, 'The development of collective bargaining in the cotton spinning industry', PhD diss., U. Leeds, 1971 · *The crisis in the cotton industry: report of the proceedings of the Provisional Emergency Cotton Committee*, Provisional Emergency Cotton Committee, 3 vols. in 4 (1923–5) · *CGPLA Eng. & Wales* (1929) · *Cotton Factory Times* (11 Jan 1929)
Archives Greater Manchester County RO, Federation of Master Cotton Spinners' Association annual reports · JRL, Manchester and District Employers' Association minutes
Likenesses A. P. F. Ritchie, cartoon, NPG; repro. in *VF* (13 March 1912) · photographs, repro. in Macara, *Recollections* · photographs, repro. in Haslam Mills, *Sir Charles W. Macara, Bart*
Wealth at death £15,842 18s. 9d.: resworn probate, 18 March 1929, *CGPLA Eng. & Wales*

Macardell, James (1727/8–1765), mezzotint engraver, was born in Cow Lane, Dublin, in 1727 or 1728, possibly the son of Patrick Macardell. He learnt engraving in John Brooks's workshop, probably from Brooks's assistant Andrew Miller. His earliest work appears to be a head of Archbishop Boulter in an engraving altered from one by Brooks of Bishop Robert Howard. Brooks moved to London early in 1746, accompanied by his ablest assistants, where Macardell almost immediately sought to establish himself as an independent artist. He very soon supplanted the ageing John Faber as the engraver employed by the two leading portrait painters Thomas Hudson and Allan Ramsay, eventually scraping twenty-one mezzotints after Hudson and fourteen after Ramsay. He was also employed by the circle of George Knapton, Arthur Pond, and Rhoda Astley, and by various printsellers, for whom he produced designs as well as engravings. It was probably through Pond that Macardell was introduced to David Garrick. He

James Macardell (1727/8–1765), by Richard Earlom, pubd 1771 (after self-portrait, 1765)

engraved portraits of the actor and his leading lady Peg Woffington in 1748 for Pond, but before 1754 he had scraped three more portraits of Garrick, keeping the plates. In his early years in London Macardell was much drawn to the theatre, producing portraits of *Mr Woodward in the Character of the Fine Gentleman in Lethe* (c.1750), *Mr Quin in the Character of Sir John Falstaff* (c.1750), *Mr Blakes in the Character of M. le Médecin* (c.1750), *Mr Lowe and Mrs Chambers in the Characters of Captain Macheath and Polly* (1752), Beard (c.1752), and Hannah Pritchard (c.1750). Three of these reproduced his own drawings. All this substantiates the claim made in 1825 that Macardell 'was a jolly companion at the artists' clubs, and well known in the Green Room. Quin and he were sworn brothers' (Elmes, 1.14). The finest of these early portraits was *Mr Garrick in Hamlet* (1754), after a painting by Benjamin Wilson, showing the expression of terror on seeing the ghost of Old Hamlet, for which Garrick was famous.

By 1754 Macardell had established himself at the Golden Head on the corner of Henrietta Street and Southampton Street, Covent Garden, a few doors away from Garrick's home in Southampton Street. Now he was able to publish and sell his own work, secure in his reputation as the best mezzotint engraver in London. 1754 was also the year in which Joshua Reynolds published *Lady Charlotte Fitzwilliam*, the first print after one of his paintings, selecting Macardell to engrave it. It was the beginning of a fruitful association, driven by Reynolds's appreciation of Macardell's ability to promote him: 'by this man I shall be immortalized', he once said (Strickland, 45). Macardell scraped thirty-eight of Reynolds's portraits with accuracy

and sensitivity, often in the large full-length format employed for one of his finest portraits, that of Frances Ann Greville and her brother as Psyche and Cupid, exhibited in 1762. Reynolds painted Macardell's portrait in the late 1750s.

During the 1750s Macardell engraved several paintings by Rembrandt, and more particularly by Rubens and Van Dyck, demonstrating his virtuosity through his tonal interpretation of the luxuriant flesh and fabric of the Flemish school. He began to engrave the series of portraits by Peter Lely known as the 'Windsor Beauties', but completed only three. Macardell's success was a magnet for other talented Irishmen. Both Edward Fisher and James Watson seem to have spent time working with Macardell on their arrival in London from Dublin, Watson probably as a pupil. Macardell joined the Society for the Encouragement of Arts, Manufactures and Commerce in 1760, and exhibited from the first exhibition. In recognition of his eminence he was made an original director of the Society of Artists upon its incorporation in 1765. Although he avoided the perils of drink to which several of the Irish engravers succumbed, he died at the age of thirty-seven on 1 June 1765. Macardell loved to take the country air of Hampstead and his friends arranged for his burial at St John's, Hampstead, where a memorial stone in the churchyard rightly declared him to be 'the most eminent in his art in his time'. He was unmarried, his estate being administered by his brother Philip Macardell of Dublin.

TIMOTHY CLAYTON and ANITA MCCONNELL

Sources W. G. Strickland, *A dictionary of Irish artists*, 2 (1913); repr. with introduction by T. J. Snoddy (1989), 42–55 · C. Smith, 'James Macardell', *Dublin University Review*, 2 (1886), 331–41 · J. T. Gilbert, *A history of the city of Dublin*, 3 vols. (1854–9), 2.17; 3.275, 345, 347 [repr. 1972] · D. Alexander, 'The Dublin group: Irish mezzotint engravers in London, 1750–75', *Quarterly Bulletin of the Irish Georgian Society*, 16 (1973), 73–92 · F. Cullen, 'McArdell, James', *The dictionary of art*, ed. J. Turner (1996), 19.867 · private information (2004) [Society of Genealogists] · *GM*, 1st ser., 35 (1765), 299 · *GM*, 1st ser., 56 (1786), 420 · T. Clayton, *The English print, 1688–1802* (1997) · J. C. Smith, *British mezzotinto portraits*, 4 vols. in 5 (1878–84) · G. Goodwin, *British mezzotinters: James MacArdell* (1903) · J. Elmes, *The arts and artists*, 3 vols. (1825) · administration, PRO, PROB 6/141, fol. 250v

Likenesses J. Reynolds, oils, 1756–60 · R. Earlom, mezzotint, pubd 1771 (after self-portrait, 1765), BM, NG Ire. [*see illus.*]

Macarius [Macarius Scotus] (*supp. d.* in or before **1153**), supposed abbot of St James's, Würzburg, was an Irish monk about whom little certain is known. As in several other south German episcopal towns, there was a group of Irish monks in Würzburg by the 1130s; by about 1140 this embryonic foundation had become the monastery of St James, dedicated by Bishop Embricho following his pilgrimage to Santiago in 1138. Later traditions, beginning with the *Vita Mariani Scoti* (composed between 1180 and 1185) claimed that Macarius had come from Ireland (in the tradition preserved at Regensburg he had come via that city) to be St James's first abbot, a man distinguished for his asceticism—ordered by Bishop Embricho to drink wine at a feast, he prayed to God, who turned the wine into water—and monastic rigour. However, Embricho's 'foundation charter' for Macarius of 1140 is a forgery of the 1220s, and the first documented abbot is Christian (recorded between 1153 and 1177). If Macarius preceded Christian in office he was therefore dead by 1153; the Regensburg necrology records his death date as 6 January, while his feast day is kept on 23 January in Würzburg.

Macarius's reputation took off in the sixteenth century. Johann Tritheim, abbot of St James's from 1506 to 1516, had his tomb opened and wrote a life of Macarius, now lost, and a largely legendary account of the early history of St James's. From the late sixteenth century Macarius was given a new prominence by exiled Scottish Catholics, who were attempting to reclaim the eleventh- and twelfth-century Irish Benedictine monastic foundations for themselves, on the grounds that they had originally been founded by Scotsmen (a misreading of the *Scoti* of the Latin sources). His relics were translated in 1615, and he was gradually provided by such authors as Wilhelm Eysengrein and Thomas Dempster with a legendary history as a writer, associate and correspondent of Pope Eugenius III, and worker of miracles. Allegedly, it was Macarius's relics which saved the sight of the Old Pretender when still a small child. A local cult survived into the twentieth century, though the relics were lost or destroyed in bombing in 1945. His tombstone, dating from about 1615, is preserved in the Marienkapelle at Würzburg.   TIMOTHY REUTER

Sources J. Trithemius, 'Compendium breve fundationis monasterii S. Jacobi ordinis S. Benedicti', *Geschicht-Schreiber von dem Bischoffthum Wirtzburg*, ed. J. P. Ludewig (Frankfurt, 1713), 993–1003 · D. O'Riain-Raedel, 'Das Nekrolog der irischen Schottenklöster: Edition der Handschrift Vat. lat. 10100 mit einer Untersuchung der hagiographischen und liturgischen Handschriften der Schottenklöster', *Beiträge zur Geschichte des Bistums Regensburg*, 26 (1992), 7–119 · P. A. Breatnach, *Die Regensburger Schottenlegende: Libellus de fundacione ecclesie consecrati Petri* (1977) · P. Johanek, *Die Frühzeit der Siegelurkunde im Bistum Würzburg* (1969) · M. Wieland, 'Das Schottenkloster zu St. Jakob in Würzburg', *Archiv des historischen Vereins von Unterfranken und Aschaffenburg*, 16 (1863), 1–183 · K. Arnold, *Johannes Trithemius, 1462–1516* (1971) · M. Dilworth, *The Scots in Franconia* (1974) · H. Flachenecker, *Schottenklöster: irische Benediktine konvente im hochmittelalterlichen Deutschland* (1995) · A. Wendehorst, *Das Bistum Würzburg*, 1 (1962) · 'Vita Mariani Scoti', *Acta sanctorum: Februarius*, 2 (Antwerp, 1658), 361–72 · W. Eysengrein, *Catalogus testium* (1565)
Likenesses stone statue, 17th cent. (after earlier statue), church of St James, Würzburg, Germany · tombstone, *c*.1615, Marienkapelle, Würzburg, Germany

MacArthur family (*per.* 1715–1839), pipers, were hereditary pipers to the MacDonalds of Sleat in the Isle of Skye. The first authenticated mention of them is in an early seventeenth-century satirical poem, *Seanchas na pìob o thùs* ('The Story of the Pipes of Old'), ascribed to the famous bard Niall Mór MacMhuirich, though some would ascribe it to his son Niall Òg. The pipers referred to were Iain and Dòmhnall MacArtuir, and the poet's dislike of the pipes reflects their increasing dominance over the *clarsach* (Celtic harp), which was the traditional bardic instrument. The next record is of **Angus MacArthur** (*fl.* 1715), who held the property of Hunglator in Trotternish, Isle of Skye, at the time of the 1715 forfeitures, his son **Charles MacArthur** (*fl.* 1733) later sharing the same property, 'but the deponent being the Laird's piper for his pains he is allowed to retain three fourths of the haill rent' ('Judicial rental of the lands of Slate and Troterness', 1733, NA Scot., GD 221/14/1(I)). Charles accompanied Sir Alexander MacDonald during the latter's student days in St Andrews, and he was paid a salary of £66 13*s*. 4*d*. in addition to his tenure at Peingown in Kilmuir, where the hillock Cnoc Phàil is remembered as the place where they liked to perform. Charles's tombstone in Kilmuir, Isle of Skye, reads: 'Here lie the remains of Charles MacKarter whose fame as an honest man and remarkable piper will survive this generation, for his manners were easy and regular as the music and melody of his fingers.'

The MacArthurs were not the only pipers to Lord MacDonald, there being mentions also of a John and a Ewan McIntyre, pipers, during the same period. Nor were the MacArthurs confined to the MacDonalds. A **Niel MacArthur** (*d.* 1762), piper to the 77th regiment (Montgomery's Highlanders), died during an expedition to Havana in 1762 (NA Scot., C.C.8), and a **Charles MacArthur** (*fl.* 1781–1839) was a piper to the earls of Eglinton (the Montgomeries) between 1781 and 1839, the Montgomeries having married into the MacDonalds of Sleat.

In 1769 and 1771 the names of John and Donald MacArthur feature in the MacDonald household accounts; but in 1782 a Charles MacArthur received 'two pecks of meal as maintenance till he had an opportunity of going out of the country', the hereditary piper going the same way as had gone the hereditary *clarsair*. Charles's son Alexander sent a petition and letter dated 22 December 1800 to Lord MacDonald requesting his appointment 'as Piper on the Estate to the Family' (NA Scot., GD 221/53/35/1 and GD 221/53/35/2), but the petition was not granted. Thomas Pennant records that he took 'a repast at the house of Sir Alexander Mac-donald's piper, who, according to ancient custom, by virtue of his office, holds his lands free … the owner was quite master of his instrument, and treated us with several tunes' (Pennant, 301). Pennant goes on to state that the 'Mac-Karters' were the piping family in question and that they, and the MacCrimmons, had run piping colleges in the past. In 1775 a MacArthur piper 'exhilarated' Boswell and Johnson at dinner at the MacDonald seat in Armadale, Isle of Skye. Forty years later Alexander Campbell, music tutor to Sir Walter Scott, heard an Archibald MacArthur, piper to Sir Reginald MacDonald of Staffa, play 'The Flowers of the Forest', 'with pathos' in Fingal's cave on Staffa on 3 August 1815 (Edinburgh University Library, MS 235).

The MacArthurs are best remembered as performers and tradition-bearers; however, at least six piobaireachd are reliably attributed to them, including 'Murray of Abercairnie's Salute', 'Sir James MacDonald's Lament', and 'Lady MacDonald's Lament' (see Buisman, Wright, and Cannon, xxii–xxxi).   JOHN PURSER

Sources F. Buisman, A. Wright, and R. Cannon, eds., *The MacArthur–MacGregor manuscript of piobaireachd (1820)* (2001) · K. Sanger,

'The MacArthurs', *Piping Times*, 35/8 (1982–3) • K. Sanger, 'Neil Mac-Arthur', *Piping Times*, 38/9 (1985–6) • T. Pennant, *A voyage to the Hebrides* (1762)
Archives NL Scot., MacArthur–MacGregor manuscript, MS 1679

MacArthur, Angus (*fl.* 1715). *See under* MacArthur family (*per.* 1715–1839).

MacArthur, Charles (*fl.* 1733). *See under* MacArthur family (*per.* 1715–1839).

MacArthur, Charles (*fl.* 1781–1839). *See under* MacArthur family (*per.* 1715–1839).

McArthur, Charles (1844–1910), politician and writer on marine insurance, born at Kingsdown, Bristol, in May 1844, was the son of Charles McArthur of Port Glasgow and his wife, Harriet. Educated at Bristol grammar school, McArthur entered the Liverpool office of North, Ewing & Co., underwriters and marine insurance brokers, in 1860. He made his mark in his profession by the publication in 1871 of *The Policy of Marine Insurance Popularly Explained, with a Chapter on Occasional Clauses* (2nd edn, 1875). In 1874 he went into business on his own account as an average adjuster and established the firm of Court and McArthur of Exchange Buildings, Liverpool, and Cornhill, London. In 1885 he published *The Contract of Marine Insurance* (rev. 2nd edn, 1890). McArthur became chairman of the Association of Average Adjusters of Great Britain, and was made chairman of the commercial law committee of the Liverpool chamber of commerce in 1887, vice-president of the chamber in 1888, and president from 1892 to 1896. In 1892 he read an important paper on the reform of bills of lading at the international conference at Genoa on the codification and reform of the law of nations. In 1895 he advised the government on the Marine Insurance Bill and the Companies Amendment Act. His services were acknowledged by the presentation to him at Liverpool on 8 September 1896 of a service of plate.

McArthur entered parliament in November 1897 as Liberal Unionist member for the Exchange division of Liverpool, after a close contest with Russell Rea. He was re-elected by an increased majority in 1900, but lost the seat in 1906, when he stood as a Conservative free-trader. He was returned for another division of Liverpool (Kirkdale) in September 1907, was re-elected in January 1910, and retained the seat until his death. In the House of Commons he was an active champion of shipping and commercial interests. Though a convinced free-trader, he advocated subsidies to British shipping companies to enable them to meet foreign state-aided competition, and the creation of one bounty to balance another. He also urged the improvement of the status of the merchant service by the establishment of training ships on the coasts and a pension scheme for sailors, and the transference of the cost of lighthouses and beacons to the Board of Trade. He was on the select committee of 1904–5 which reported in favour of the application of British statutory regulations to foreign ships in British ports.

As a strong evangelical, McArthur played in parliament a persistent, if not very effective, part in church questions. His views were set out in *The Evidences of Natural Religion and the Truths Established Thereby* (1880). In May 1899 he moved unsuccessfully the second reading of a bill 'to secure a prompt and inexpensive means' for settling ritualistic disputes. He resisted the appointment of the royal commission on ecclesiastical discipline in 1904, but in 1908 he introduced the Ecclesiastical Disorders Bill, in which he claimed to give effect to the commission's report. To the bill for amending the royal accession declaration (carried in 1909) he offered a stout resistance.

McArthur married Jessie, daughter of John Makin of Liverpool; they had no children. He died rather suddenly on 3 July 1910 at his home, 25 Army and Navy Mansions, London, survived by his wife. He was buried at Wallasey cemetery, Liverpool.

G. Le G. Norgate, *rev.* H. C. G. Matthew

Sources *The Times* (4 July 1910) • *The Times* (7 July 1910) • *Liverpool Daily Post and Liverpool Mercury* (4 July 1910) • *WW* • *Dod's Parliamentary Companion* (1910) • *CGPLA Eng. & Wales* (1910)
Likenesses portrait, repro. in *Liverpool Daily Post*
Wealth at death £1397 15s. 8d.: probate, 16 Aug 1910, *CGPLA Eng. & Wales*

McArthur, David Charteris (1808–1887), banker, was born on 20 September 1808 in Gloucester, one of four children of Captain Donald McArthur, soldier, and his wife, Elizabeth, *née* Wemyss. Of Scottish descent, McArthur was educated in Scotland, and was engaged by the North British and Mercantile Insurance Company in Edinburgh in 1826, where he received a mercantile training. In 1835 he took a post as a teller in the Sydney office of the newly established Bank of Australasia. Within three years McArthur was promoted to the managership of the new branch in Melbourne, a city to be made fabulously wealthy by wool and gold. McArthur was to play a significant role in the affairs of the first British overseas bank to enter Australia, rising to occupy its highest managerial post. He was also to play a leading role in the cultural and commercial life of the city of Melbourne.

McArthur belonged to the first generation of expatriate British bankers whose isolation from their London boards thrust responsibility upon them. His career was propelled forward by two forces. McArthur's Australian superiors quickly recognized his talents and promoted him to higher office in 1843 in the face of some opposition from London. He was second in command from 1848 until finally assuming the mantle of superintendent in 1868. Secondly, the gold discoveries of the 1850s transformed the position of the Melbourne office to such an extent that the headquarters was transferred there from Sydney in 1860.

McArthur's stature in the bank grew dramatically from the 1850s. He became a financial adviser to the newly independent colony of Victoria, and was largely instrumental in arranging its first issue of bonds in 1854. This issue became the model followed by all Australian colonies for the next forty years. As other banks became parties to government capital issues, an informal association of bankers, which became the Associated Banks of Victoria, acted as a forum and as a mouthpiece for the industry. McArthur was a central figure in this body for many years.

Within his own bank he was responsible for a number of important initiatives, including the opening of branches in New Zealand from the 1860s, the creation of a staff pension fund, and a strengthening of the local administrative structure in the early 1860s. He was exceptional in being the first man who, having spent an entire career in Australia, then became chief executive.

Despite these considerable earlier achievements, relations between the ageing McArthur and the court of directors were unhappy through most of his term as superintendent and he was dismissed in 1876. It has been suggested that McArthur was too old to handle this most demanding job, and that he was too lenient in his dealings with his managers. Certainly he disagreed with the directors on a number of issues and occasionally expressed his views intemperately. But to suggest that he failed seems unduly harsh, as during his nine years as superintendent the Bank of Australasia performed as well as its competitors: it was the fourth largest British overseas bank in 1860 and by 1890 had gained second place.

After his retirement McArthur decided to remain in Melbourne, where he enjoyed an enviable reputation as the grand old man of Australian banking and as a civic worthy. A kindly and gregarious man, a *bon vivant* and sportsman, McArthur enjoyed a wide circle of friends and acquaintances. He married Caroline Wright, and lived from 1840 until his death at 'Charterisville', Heidelberg, many miles to the east of Melbourne. They had no children. He served suburb and city through his involvement with road boards, the public library, the botanical gardens, the mechanics institute and Melbourne Athenaeum, the Austin Hospital for Incurables, and the Old Colonists Association, and as president of the Melbourne Cricket Club. McArthur's business interests continued to expand as he became a local director of the Bank of Australasia, and the North British and Mercantile Insurance Company; he was also a director of the Trustees Executors and Agency Company Ltd. He served God as well as Mammon by playing an important role in the administration of the diocese of Melbourne, and by being deeply involved in the affairs of St James in the city, and of the Anglican church St John's in the suburb of Heidelberg. McArthur died at his home after suffering a heart attack on 15 November 1887 in his eightieth year. He was survived by his widow.   D. T. MERRETT

Sources S. J. Butler, *Australia and New Zealand Bank: the Bank of Australasia and the Union Bank of Australia Limited, 1828–1951* (1961) · G. Blainey, 'McArthur, David Charteris', *AusDB*, vol. 5 · *Australasian Insurance and Banking Record* (16 Dec 1887), 765 · *Bankers' Institute of Australasia* (Nov 1887), 212–14 · bank records, Bank of Australasia · G. Jones, *British multinational banking, 1830–1990: a history* (1993)
Archives ANZ Banking Group, 90 Bourke Street, Melbourne, Victoria, Australia, archive, corresp. with London
Likenesses E. a'Beckett, oils, 1884, ANZ Art Collection, Melbourne, Australia
Wealth at death £30,215: Blainey, 'McArthur, David Charteris'

Macarthur, Sir Edward (1789–1872), army officer, was born on 16 March 1789 at the White Hart inn, Bath, the first of the nine children of Captain John *Macarthur (1766–1834) and his wife, Elizabeth *Macarthur (1766–

Sir Edward Macarthur (1789–1872), by Richard Daintree and Antoine Fauchery, c.1858

1850) [*see under* Macarthur, John], the daughter of Richard Veale, a landowner, of Lodgeworthy, Devon. He was the brother of James *Macarthur, William *Macarthur [*see under* Macarthur, James], and John *Macarthur [*see under* Macarthur, John]. The family emigrated to New South Wales on the Second Fleet in 1790, and John and Elizabeth became noted sheep-farming pioneers in the new colony. Edward spent his childhood at the family's Elizabeth Farm in Parramatta, Sydney, before being sent in 1799 to England for his education. He attended Dr James Lindsay's school, Grove Hall, Bow, London, and returned to Australia in 1806.

Finding some of the jobs around the family estate 'distasteful' (King, 'Sir Edward Macarthur', 315), Macarthur decided to pursue his interest in a military career, and in 1808 he returned to England; in December of that year he joined the 60th regiment and he saw service at Corunna and Sicily before receiving promotion to the rank of lieutenant in the 39th regiment. He fought in a number of campaigns of the Napoleonic wars and in the Anglo-American War of 1812–14, and served with occupation forces in France and Ireland in the following years. In 1821 he purchased a captain's commission in the 19th regiment, and in 1824 he returned to Australia on leave. He sought appointment to an official position in the colony, but was unsuccessful. He achieved the rank of major in 1826.

In 1830 Macarthur was appointed to the post of secretary to the lord chamberlain, in which role he continued until 1837, after which he became assistant adjutant-general in Ireland. He achieved promotion to lieutenant-colonel, and in 1851 was made deputy adjutant-general in the Australian military command, based in Sydney.

In 1854 Macarthur was promoted colonel and the command headquarters moved to Melbourne. The following year he succeeded to the post of commander-in-chief of the forces. On the death of the governor of Victoria in December that year Macarthur, as senior military officer in the colony, assumed the post of acting governor until a successor was appointed twelve months later. Macarthur saw it as a central part of his role to maintain stability in the colony, and the popularity of the crown, by exhibiting 'cheerfulness, hospitality and truthfulness toward all with whom ... I can have relations' (King, 'Sir Edward Macarthur', 324). In this he was very successful. One resident warmly praised him as 'an industrious, kind-hearted, Christian gentleman' (Hill).

Macarthur resumed his role as commander of the military forces, a post he held until his retirement in 1860. He then returned to England, and on 18 November 1862 he married Sarah (d. 1889), the third daughter of Lieutenant-Colonel W. Smith Neill, of Ayrshire. They had no children. In that year Macarthur was also made a KCB, and in 1866 he was promoted lieutenant-general. He died at his London home—27 Princes Gardens, Kensington—on 4 January 1872 and was buried at Brompton cemetery.

MARC BRODIE

Sources H. King, 'Lieutenant-General Sir Edward Macarthur: expatriate Australian?', *Journal of the Royal Australian Historical Society*, 74 (1989), 315–28 · J. M. Ward, *James Macarthur, colonial conservative, 1798–1867* (1981) · A. J. Hill, 'Macarthur, Sir Edward', *AusDB*, vol. 5 · L. Bickel, *Australia's first lady: the story of Elizabeth Macarthur* (1991) · *DNB* · *IGI* · H. King, *Elizabeth Macarthur and her world* (1980) · H. King, *Colonial expatriates: Edward and John Macarthur junior* (1989) · *CGPLA Eng. & Wales* (1872)

Archives BL, campaign journal, Add. MS 44022 · Mitchell L., NSW, corresp. and papers | Lpool RO, letters to fourteenth earl of Derby · NA Scot., corresp. with G. W. Hope · U. Durham L., letters to third Earl Grey

Likenesses R. Daintree and A. Fauchery, photograph, *c.*1858, State Library of Victoria, Melbourne, La Trobe picture collection [*see illus.*] · W. Strutt, oils?, Parliament House, Melbourne · W. Strutt, pencil and watercolour drawing, Mitchell L., NSW · bust, St John's Church, Parramatta, New South Wales

Wealth at death under £35,000: administration with will, 12 June 1872, *CGPLA Eng. & Wales* · £4000: Australian probate, *AusDB*

Macarthur, Elizabeth (1766–1850). *See under* Macarthur, John (1766–1834).

McArthur, Ellen Annette (1862–1927), historian, was born on 19 June 1862 at Duffield, near Belper, Derbyshire, one of at least four daughters of the Revd Charles Chapman McArthur (d. 1892) and his wife, whose name was probably Annette Cohen. Her father was employed by the Church Missionary Society and was at the time of her birth a missionary at Jaffna, Ceylon; he returned to England in 1867, and later became rector of Burlingham, Norfolk. She was educated at home, at the Diakonissen Anstalt in Hilden, Germany, and at St Andrews School for Girls (St Leonard's School, St Andrews), Fife; her teacher there, Louisa Lumsden, became a lifelong friend. She served as a junior mistress at the school before winning a scholarship to enter Girton College, Cambridge. In 1885

she gained first-class honours in the relatively new historical tripos, although at that date she was not permitted to graduate from the university. The following year she began teaching at Girton, holding various posts, including vice-mistress in 1895–6. From 1896 to 1907 she was the principal historian at Girton.

Ellen McArthur was the first woman examiner for the Oxford and Cambridge schools examinations board, and in 1894 the first woman lecturer employed by the Cambridge local lectures syndicate. She had many supporters in Cambridge and in the profession generally. She did graduate work with Dr (later Archdeacon) William Cunningham, and they collaborated on *Outlines of English Industrial History* (1895). When Cunningham stopped lecturing on economic history in Cambridge in 1902, Ellen McArthur began lecturing for Girton and Newnham students on the subject. In response to a request from tutors of several men's colleges, she also allowed their students to be admitted to her lectures. She was elected a fellow of the Royal Historical Society in 1906 (sponsored by Hubert Hall and H. E. Malden).

Between 1894 and 1900 Ellen McArthur wrote three articles on fifteenth- and sixteenth-century wage assessments for the *English Historical Review* and several entries for the *Dictionary of Political Economy* (3 vols.), edited by R. H. I. Palgrave. Her contributions covered a broad range, including the history of the exchequer to the mid-nineteenth century, Sir Anthony Fitzherbert, the peasants' revolt, and the Russia and South Sea companies, among others. She also reviewed for the *Cambridge Review*, *International Journal of Ethics*, *Economic Journal*, and *Vierteljahrschrift für Sozial und Wirtschaftsgeschichte*.

When Trinity College, Dublin, offered degrees to the women of Cambridge and Oxford, Ellen McArthur was the first recipient of the DLitt in 1905, on the basis of her published work. Probably her best known article is her last: 'Women petitioners and the Long Parliament', in the *English Historical Review* of 1909. She was dedicated to preparing her students not only to pass examinations, but also to go on to advanced work in history. She taught a generation of influential historians: E. M. Leonard, Lilian Knowles, Dorothy George, Alice Radice, Annie Abram, O. Jocelyn Dunlop, M. G. Jones, and Eileen Power.

From 1896 to 1903 Ellen McArthur personally ran a hostel for women postgraduate students at 3 Green Street, Cambridge. Between 1907 and 1910 she represented the Certificated Students (the organization of graduates, an important advocate for establishing research posts) on the Girton College council. From 1896 she was on the council of the Cambridge Training College for Teachers. She was elected an honorary member of Newnham College in 1902. While continuing to lecture in Cambridge, she agreed in 1907 to head the history department at Westfield College, London, standing in during the illness of her former student, Caroline Skeel. She was immediately elected a member of the faculty of arts, a member of the historical board, and a recognized teacher in the University of London. She continued at Westfield, spending one night each week in London, until Caroline Skeel returned to work in 1911.

Ellen McArthur worked for the Cambridge Association for Women's Suffrage, and in the historic march to the Albert Hall in the summer of 1908 carried the banner at the head of the university women. She served on the local committee from at least 1909, and was elected to the executive committee of the National Union of Women's Suffrage Societies in 1910. Unfortunately, the 'reserved nature' that her colleagues remembered is only too evident in the weekly minutes of the Cambridge committee and the fortnightly minutes of the executive committee.

Early in 1912 Ellen McArthur suffered a serious illness whose exact nature is nowhere recorded; it seems likely that overwork played a part. She made an unexpected recovery, but remained a semi-invalid until her death. She continued her work with the Cambridge Training College for Teachers (now Hughes Hall), only giving up the office of registrar in 1920, remaining chairman in 1921–2 and then vice-chairman until her death. She remained a fellow of the Royal Historical Society until 1920, and from 1916 until her death served as a vice-president of the Historical Association. She died of ovarian cancer at her home, 10 Huntingdon Road, Cambridge, on 4 September 1927. She was cremated, and her ashes scattered in the Garden of Rest, Golders Green, Middlesex. It was her 'sincerity and real kindliness', her 'unfailing grasp of business procedure', and her 'unusually brilliant gifts as an organiser and as a teacher' that her friends and colleagues remembered. Her 'striking personality' is glimpsed in two photographs of her that survive in the Girton College archives. Nothing else of hers remains in the archives of any institution with which she was connected.

Ellen McArthur left a £150 fund in memory of her sister, Henrietta McArthur, founder of the United Girls' Schools Mission, to assist 'women workers in need of a change or holiday after illness which they cannot afford'. The bulk of her £8617 estate she left to Cambridge University, to establish a prize for economic history, open to men and women students alike. That prize—and the studentship and lecture series which the Ellen McArthur Fund also established in the early 1970s—has since been awarded to a large number of men and a very few women. (Precise numbers are unavailable because the records of the fund are patchy and unsorted.) Many of the prize-winning essays (until 1973) were published in a special series by Cambridge University Press, which bears the benefactor's name. Having dedicated her life to the professional advancement of women, the preponderance of men among the beneficiaries of Ellen McArthur's largesse is partly explained by the time at which she died: in 1923, women were granted titular degrees and allowed to attend lectures as a right instead of a privilege; and just the year before she died, university teaching posts, prizes, scholarships, and studentships were opened to women. In her enthusiasm, and with unaccustomed inattention to detail, she did not specify the management of her fund. It has been administered ever since by the professor of economic history and two faculty representatives, all of whom have always been men. Ellen McArthur surely did not imagine that women would not become full university members until more than sixty years after her own student days, nor that, in a system of patronage, they might not be treated equally even then.

AMY LOUISE ERICKSON

Sources K. T. Butler and H. I. McMorran, eds., *Girton College register, 1869–1946* (1948), 635 · *Girton Review*, Michaelmas term (1927) · *The Times* (6 Sept 1927) · *Woman's Leader* (9 Sept 1927) · *Cambridge Review* (14 Oct 1927) · R. McWilliams-Tullberg, *Women at Cambridge* (1975) · J. Sondheimer, *Castle Adamant in Hampstead: a history of Westfield College, 1882–1982* (1983), 61 · records of Royal Historical Society, London · records of Historical Association, London · Newnham College Records, Newnham College, Cambridge · Hughes Hall Records, Hughes Hall, Cambridge · minutes, Cambridge Association for Women's Suffrage, Cambs. AS · minutes of the National Association for Women's Suffrage, Women's Library, London · records of Ellen McArthur Fund, U. Cam., faculty of history · Crockford · will, Principal Registry of the Family Division, London · *CGPLA Eng. & Wales* (1927) · b. cert. · d. cert.
Likenesses two photographs, 1905–1912?, Girton Cam.
Wealth at death £8617 8s. 0d.: probate, 9 Nov 1927, *CGPLA Eng. & Wales*

McArthur, Gerald Elwyn (1916–1996), police officer, was born on 28 May 1916 at 22 Clarence Place, Newport, Monmouthshire, the son of Gerald West McArthur, insurance superintendent, and his wife, Eleanor, *née* Lewis. He was educated at Newport grammar school. His driving ambition to succeed in whatever field he entered made leaving depression-era south Wales an inevitability. In 1935 he joined the Metropolitan Police. It was at that time unusual for a grammar school boy to deem the police a suitable career, but McArthur thrived in the capital, and rapidly established himself as a rising star of the Criminal Investigation Department (CID). In 1941 he was promoted detective constable and posted to the commissioner's office. On 10 August in the same year he married Marion Rose (1917/18–2001), daughter of Stanley Ivor George, a chartered shipbroker, of Newport. They had two daughters.

During the latter stages of the Second World War McArthur served as a pilot with Coastal Command, reaching the rank of flight lieutenant. After demobilization in 1946 he returned to the Metropolitan Police, and after a further year in the commissioner's office he was transferred to the company fraud squad. Promotions to detective sergeant, detective inspector, and detective chief inspector followed rapidly, and McArthur acquired a reputation as a dedicated and astute detective. In 1963 he was promoted to detective superintendent in charge of the Met's murder squad.

However, it was robbery rather than homicide that established McArthur's reputation, for within days of his appointment a coalition of two south London criminal firms stole over £2.5 million from the Glasgow to London night train. The train had been halted by men wearing army uniforms at Bridego Bridge, Buckinghamshire, the driver received head injuries, and the robbery team retreated to their hideout at nearby Leatherslade Farm. The plans for the 'great train robbery' had been circulating among London's professional criminal fraternity for years, and despite the stories of the robbery being master-minded by a 'mister big' or an ex-Nazi commando leader, the combination of the two loose-knit gangs was enough to pull off a crime that became known as 'the crime of the century'.

Brigadier Cheyney, the chief constable of Buckingham-shire, contacted the Metropolitan Police for assistance, and McArthur was seconded to the subsequent investiga-tion. From his base in Aylesbury he proved especially adept at handling the media interest in what the robber Bruce Reynolds was later to describe as the 'first televised crime'. McArthur kept media interest alive by calling regular press conferences, and it is quite likely that his announcement that the robbers were still within a 30 mile radius of the crime hastened their departure from Leath-erslade Farm some 27 miles away, contributing to a break-down in the robbers' hallmark discipline and profession-alism. Many other detectives later took credit for their role in the successful convictions (along with the exces-sive sentences) of the robbers, and a number of books and biographies feature these officers in nothing less than heroic detail. Gerald McArthur, however, studiously avoided publicity throughout his glittering career, and this hard-nosed professionalism stood him in good stead during his next period of intense combat with London's villainy.

In 1964 McArthur was promoted to chief superintend-ent in charge of the Hertfordshire CID, and the following year the skill he had displayed during the train robbery investigation as a mediator between competing police for-ces was acknowledged in his appointment as the co-ordinator of no. 5 regional crime squad. He was simul-taneously appointed assistant chief constable of Hertford-shire. Soon after his appointment he was approached by a man called Taggart with accusations concerning the activ-ities of Charlie and Eddie Richardson and their associates, who included underworld icon 'Mad' Frankie Fraser. The Richardsons were without doubt the most astute British criminals of their generation, and were ahead of their time in many ways, especially in their ability to penetrate the legitimate economy. The subsequent investigation was unique at the time, as McArthur and his team investi-gated accusations of torture that were little short of fan-tastic, and to this day are fervently contested. However, the frauds that lay at the heart of the Richardsons' oper-ations, although ingenious, were less contentious. What became known as the 'torture trial' resulted in the Rich-ardsons being 'weighed off' with twenty-five years each. Looking back at the details of the case it is hard not to have some sympathy with Charlie Richardson, who later incredulously stated that despite the 'torture trial' hype, 'I was actually charged with a bit of fraud and five counts of grievous bodily harm. Nobody was dead, maimed or even scarred … I had slapped five hooligans around and had defrauded large companies' (The Independent, 17 Sept 1996). Successful cases against lorry hijackers, which involved sealing off the exits of the M1, and against car park fraud-sters at London airport followed. In 1966 McArthur

received the queen's police medal, and in 1968 he was appointed MBE.

McArthur was an old-fashioned, cigarette-smoking British detective, seldom seen in public without his trilby hat. He shunned publicity and viewed the world in simple black and white terms. Dedicated to his job, he once inter-rupted the morning school run with the successful pur-suit of a villain, an episode that left his elder daughter with a novel excuse for her lateness at school. McArthur retired from the police in 1969, and became security adviser to the Tobacco Advisory Council until 1975. During his long retirement he was an active member of the Air-crew Association and an enthusiastic bowls player. He died of bronchial cancer at his home, 80 Bury Hill, Hemel Hempstead, Hertfordshire, on 20 July 1996. He was sur-vived by his wife and their two daughters.

RICHARD HOBBS

Sources *The Times* (23 July 1996) · *Daily Telegraph* (23 July 1996) · *The Independent* (17 Sept 1996) · P. P. Read, *The train robbers* (1978) · B. Reynolds, *The autobiography of a thief* (2000) · private information [Gillian Langdon, daughter] · b. cert. · m. cert. · d. cert.
Likenesses photograph, *c.*1963, repro. in *The Times* · photograph, 1963, repro. in *Daily Telegraph* · photograph, repro. in *The Inde-pendent*
Wealth at death under £180,000: probate, 13 Nov 1997, *CGPLA Eng. & Wales*

Macarthur, Hannibal Hawkins (1788–1861). *See under* Macarthur, John (1766–1834).

Macarthur, James (1798–1867), politician, was born on 15 December 1798 at his parents' home, Elizabeth Farm, near Parramatta, New South Wales, the fifth of the seven sur-viving children of John *Macarthur (1766–1834) and his wife, Elizabeth *Macarthur, *née* Veale (1766–1850) [see under Macarthur, John]. His parents had arrived in the col-ony in 1790, his father being then an officer in the New South Wales Corps. James and his younger brother, Wil-liam [see below], his life-long companion, were taught at home until 1809, when they went with their father to Eng-land. Their education was completed at Dr James Lind-say's school, Grove Hall, Bow, London. Another brother was Edward *Macarthur.

In 1815–16 James and William travelled with their father through France and Switzerland, and in 1817 all three returned to Australia. Thereafter the brothers lived at the family estate, Camden Park, 40 miles south-west of Syd-ney. A new house was completed there in 1834, and they formed a substantial tenant-farming community, with a village well positioned on the Sydney–Melbourne road. They were energetic and popular landlords, and Camden became the foundation for their wider authority.

During his second visit to England (1828–31), James Mac-arthur offered to the Colonial Office a paper on crown land policy in New South Wales, a sketchy but significant argument for more ambitious management. His optimis-tic understanding of the colonial penal system led him always to believe in the ramifying duties of government. At the same time he hoped to refine and strengthen local opinion. In 1831, following his return, he brought

James Macarthur (1798–1867), by Thomas Woolner, 1854

together various parties with the hope of influencing imperial land policy, and in 1833 he tried to do the same for constitutional reform. In 1836 he went again to England, where he consulted frequently with the Colonial Office, and where he published his *New South Wales: its Present State and Future Prospects* (1837). In London, on 14 June 1838, he married Emily Stone (1806–1880), the daughter of a City banker. Macarthur called himself a liberal conservative, and the liberal aspects of his thinking were due partly to his wife. They had one daughter, Elizabeth, born in 1840 (later Mrs Macarthur-Onslow).

From June 1840 Macarthur was a member of the original legislature of New South Wales, a nominated body. He failed to be chosen for the first partly elected legislative council (1843), but his membership of the two subsequent councils (1849–55) allowed him to achieve numerous ambitions for the colony. Convict transportation had ended in 1840, and he had a central part in several projects for political, social, and economic reform, designed to establish a self-governing community free of the stigma of convictism. He was one of the founders of the University of Sydney (1850) and of the non-sectarian (or national) system of elementary education.

Macarthur's main contribution to Australian public life arose from his inspired interest in political and administrative process. He had a powerful understanding of the idea of public morality, and of the role which a visionary conscience might play in government. His achievements are therefore to be found as much in the minutiae of debate and legislation as in major items of reform.

In 1851–3 council devised a new bicameral constitution (for enactment by the British parliament), with Macarthur once again playing a leading role. He sat in the lower house of the first two colonial parliaments (1856–9) and he was a member, without portfolio, of the short-lived first cabinet under responsible government (April–August 1856). In 1859 he was offered a knighthood, but his complex attitude to honours for Australians led him to decline it.

With his wife and daughter Macarthur was in Europe from 1860 to 1864, and on his return he was given a seat in the nominated upper house (October 1866). However, he died on 21 April 1867, at Camden Park, of heart failure.

After a service on 28 April at St John's Church, Camden, he was buried in the family graveyard at Camden Park.

The younger brother of James Macarthur, **Sir William Macarthur** (1800–1882), pastoralist and scientist, was born at Elizabeth Farm, near Parramatta, on 15 December 1800. The main concerns of his life were centred on Camden Park, where his experimental vineyard, orchard, and gardens were a source of plants for others throughout Australia. He made a remarkable collection of indigenous trees and was among the first in Australia to attempt photography. He was an elected member of the legislative council (1849–55) and he sat in the upper house of the colonial parliament (1864–82). He was a commissioner for the colony at the Universal Exhibition in Paris in 1855, and was afterwards awarded a knighthood and the Légion d'honneur. He died, unmarried, at Camden Park on 29 October 1882 of embolism of the cerebral artery and, after a service at St John's Church, Camden, was buried in the family graveyard in Camden Park on 31 October 1882.

ALAN ATKINSON

Sources A. Atkinson, 'The political life of James Macarthur', PhD diss., Australian National University, 1976 · A. Atkinson, 'James Macarthur as author', *Royal Australian Historical Society Journal and Proceedings*, 67 (1981), 264–71 · A. Atkinson, 'Time, place and paternalism', *Australian Historical Studies*, 23 (1988–9), 1–18 · A. Atkinson, *Camden: farm and village life in early New South Wales* (1988) · A. Atkinson, 'James Macarthur', *Australian political thinkers*, ed. G. Melleuish and G. Stokes (1996) · J. M. Ward, *James Macarthur: colonial conservative, 1798–1867* (1981) · R. Teale, 'Macarthur, Sir William', *AusDB*, vol. 5 · *Sydney Morning Herald* (31 Oct 1882) [Sir William Macarthur] · parish register (baptism), April 1802, Parramatta, St John · family gravestone, Camden Park, New South Wales · d. cert. · d. cert. [Sir William Macarthur]

Archives Mitchell L., NSW

Likenesses miniature, c.1820, Camden Park, New South Wales, Australia · miniature, c.1820 (Sir William Macarthur), Camden Park, New South Wales, Australia · miniature, on ivory, c.1820, Mitchell L., NSW · Scanlan, oils, 1838, Camden Park, New South Wales, Australia · T. Woolner, bronze medallion, 1854, Mitchell L., NSW · T. Woolner, bronze medallion, 1854, priv. coll. [*see illus.*] · A. Capalti, oils, 1862, Camden Park, New South Wales, Australia · A. Capalti, oils, 1862 (Sir William Macarthur), Camden Park, New South Wales, Australia · A. Capalti, oils, 1863, University of Sydney, Australia · C. Summers, marble bust, 1870, Legislative Council, Sydney, Australia · C. Summers?, marble bust, 1870, Camden Park, New South Wales, Australia · W. Macarthur, photographs, Camden Park, New South Wales, Australia · W. Macarthur, photographs (Sir William Macarthur), Camden Park, New South Wales, Australia · oils (Sir William Macarthur), Australian Club, Sydney, Australia · silhouette, Camden Park, New South Wales, Australia

Wealth at death £5000: probate, *AusDB* · £38,000—Sir William Macarthur: probate, *AusDB*

McArthur, John (1755–1840), seaman and author, details of whose upbringing and parents are unknown, entered the navy in 1778 as assistant clerk on the *Eagle* on the North American station. On her return McArthur was moved into the cutter *Rattlesnake*, and on 22 March 1779 was promoted purser for his gallantry in boarding a French privateer in an engagement off Le Havre on 14 March. In November the *Rattlesnake* assisted the *Tartar* in capturing the Spanish frigate *Santa Margarita*, and McArthur was promoted purser of the prize when she was commissioned in the British navy. During the American War of Independence he was often stationed to observe signals, and was confronted with the many defects of the current system. In order to address them he prepared a revised signal book which Admiral Robert Digby issued on 5 October 1782, and which was used experimentally by a small cruiser squadron for three months (MOD, NM/76 and NMM, KE 1/S/9).

McArthur followed these lines of study during the peace, while still purser of the *Santa Margarita*, and in 1790, according to his own statement, laid a new code of signals before the Admiralty. In his publication of 1782 he had sought to clarify the existing system by which individual flags flown in particular places in the rigging indicated an intention to execute particular tactical movements described in the book of fighting instructions. By contrast this new code employed a system developed by the Chevalier du Pavillon for the French navy, by which a two-flag hoist of flags, flown where they could best be seen, directed the recipient to look in the appropriate line and column of a chart which in turn referred to the fighting instructions. This procedure was a definite improvement on the older system, but it was unnecessarily complicated, and its capacity was more limited than that ultimately adopted by the navy, which used hoists of three numeric flags in conjunction with a numbered signal book. McArthur's system was somewhat incoherent as it had four different code charts with overlapping applications, but the provision he made for changing the meaning of signals for security purposes, while technically unsatisfactory, was ahead of his time.

McArthur's signals caught the attention of Lord Hood, then first sea lord, who, in the Russian armament of 1791, made McArthur his secretary. Hood was eager to try McArthur's signals; but the Admiralty preferred to retain Lord Howe's. McArthur was employed to simplify his system in line with Howe's, but only succeeded in adding to its complexity. However, after approval by Howe, it was tested and used in the experimental cruise of 1792. In 1807 McArthur wrote that 'from that period it has been universally adopted in the service, and is, it is believed, continued with little or no variation in form or substance at the present day'. But in this McArthur was certainly wrong, for Sir Home Popham's code had been generally adopted some years before. As early as 1799 McArthur claimed (in 'Thoughts on several plans combining a system of universal signals', *Naval Chronicle*, 1.509, 2.70) to be the real author of the code known by the name of Lord Howe; it appears probable, however, that his contribution was reserved to seeing it through the press.

McArthur was again Hood's secretary when the admiral went out as commander-in-chief in the Mediterranean in 1793. He was also appointed purser of the flagship *Victory*. McArthur's duties at this time were onerous and important. In addition to the ordinary work of secretary, the occupation of Toulon and the intimate association of the Spanish and Italian forces required him to undertake a correspondence in three languages, without, he says, any assistance. He had also acted as Hood's interpreter, and as his representative in the disbursements of public money,

both to the British forces and to those of the allies. For some time there was no British commissary-general, a role he also fulfilled. In addition, he was prize agent for the fleet; and though his duties as purser of the *Victory* were performed by a deputy, the responsibility, pecuniary and otherwise, rested on him. When Hood, after returning to England, was ordered to strike his flag, McArthur went back to the Mediterranean solely as the *Victory's* purser. As soon as the ship joined the fleet Rear-Admiral Man hoisted his flag on her, and in the action of 14 July 1795 McArthur volunteered to observe the signals. He was afterwards secretary to Sir Hyde Parker (1739–1807), and returned to England with him early in 1796.

In 1803 Lord Nelson offered to take McArthur as his secretary to the Mediterranean. McArthur, however, declined, 'as Lord Hood's accounts with the treasury were then pending before the auditors'. This was the official reason, but he was probably more directly influenced by his literary engagements. As a young man McArthur had published *The army and navy gentleman's companion, or, A new and complete treatise on the theory and practice of fencing* (1781). In 1792, while secretary to Lord Hood, he brought out *A Treatise of the Principles and Practice of Naval Courts-Martial* which, in the second edition, appeared as *Principles and Practice of Naval and Military Courts-Martial* (1805); in this form it ran through many editions, and was long the standard work on the subject. McArthur may also have been one of the 'Literary and professional men' who assisted with the *Naval Chronicle* under its first editor, James Stanier Clarke. He certainly collaborated with Clarke in the preparation of a *Life of Lord Nelson* which set a new standard in the use of primary sources. This was published in 1809 and was extensively used by later editors of the *Naval Chronicle* in the preparation of biographical memorials.

In 1801 McArthur published an octavo volume of *Financial and Political Facts of the Eighteenth Century* which, with a change of 'century' into 'and present centuries', ran through several editions; he followed this in 1806 with *A translation from the Italian of the Abbé Cesarotti's historical and critical dissertation respecting the controversy on the authenticity of Ossian's poems*, in which he described himself as a member of the committee of the Highland Society of London employed to superintend the publication of Ossian in Gaelic. On 22 July 1806 McArthur received the degree of LLD from the University of Edinburgh. He was at this time living in York Place, Portman Square, London, but afterwards he settled down at Hayfield in Hampshire, where he died on 29 July 1840. He left a widow and, apparently, one daughter, Mrs Conway.

J. K. LAUGHTON, *rev.* NICHOLAS TRACY

Sources 'The memorial of John McArthur, 9 Nov. 1807', PRO, ADM 1/4883 · B. Tunstall, *Naval warfare in the age of sail: the evolution of fighting tactics, 1650–1815*, ed. N. Tracy (1990) · N. Tracy, ed., *The Naval Chronicle: the contemporary record of the Royal Navy at war*, 5 vols. (1998–9) · *GM*, 2nd ser., 14 (1840), 436 · R. Beatson, *Naval and military memoirs of Great Britain*, 2nd edn, 4 (1804), 556

Archives PRO, ADM 1/4883 | BL, corresp., mainly with Lord Nelson, Add. MSS 34902–34992

Likenesses G. Romney, oils, 1795, Scot. NPG

Macarthur, John (1766–1834), merchant and wool-grower, was probably born on 18 August 1766 and was baptized on 3 September 1767 at Stoke Damerel, near Plymouth, Devon, one of three known children of the expatriate Scot Alexander Macarthur (1720?–1790), mercer and draper, and his wife, Katherine (d. 1777). Another son believed him self-educated, 'having been cast upon the world at 14 years old' ('Memorandum of William Macarthur', [n.d.], Macarthur MSS, A2897, 263), though in December 1782 John Macarthur became an ensign in a minor defence body (Fish's corps). The corps was disbanded in April 1783 and he remained on half-pay until April 1788, when he exchanged into the 68th (Durham) regiment of foot. At Bridgerule, Devon, on 6 October 1788 he married Elizabeth Veale, the step-daughter of a local farmer. Macarthur joined the New South Wales Corps in June 1789, and the following June he arrived at Botany Bay with Elizabeth and their son, Edward *Macarthur.

Like other officers, Lieutenant Macarthur readily engaged in trafficking, and while regimental paymaster from 1792 he ordered military slops from his brother at Plymouth. He was one of the first to cultivate land (Elizabeth Farm) at Parramatta, where he was inspector of public works from 1793. In 1795 he was promoted captain. A leading landholder by 1800—when he contemplated a return to England—he estimated his worth at £4000. This enviable progress had been punctuated by jarring feuds, carried on particularly, but not exclusively, with every governor since Arthur Phillip. Governor Hunter complained of Macarthur's 'restless, ambitious and litigious disposition' (Hunter to the duke of Portland, 25 July 1798, HRA, 1st ser., 2, 1914, 160) and, following a duel with his commanding officer in 1801, the 'Perturbator' was ordered to England for court martial by Governor King, who trenchantly condemned his 'art, cunning, impudence and … baselisk eyes' (Governor King to Under-Secretary King, 8 Nov 1801, HRA, 1st ser., 3, 1915, 322). During the voyage Macarthur befriended the son of the royal physician Sir Walter Farquhar, who generously supported Macarthur's interest after he reached London. When it was eventually decided that his offence required to be tried in New South Wales, Macarthur prudently resigned his commission, in 1804.

In the search for exportable colonial resources, specimens of wool from Spanish merino sheep brought to Sydney in 1797 had been sent to Sir Joseph Banks for appraisal. Macarthur owned several of these sheep and had taken similar samples to London. The favourable reaction of some English cloth manufacturers, concerned about wartime supplies, stimulated Macarthur into presenting a 'scheme' for the production of fine wool in New South Wales. His memorandum reached the committee for trade and plantations and was considered by Lord Camden. In 1805 Macarthur returned to Sydney with merinos from the royal flock and authority to select 5000 acres (which he named Camden Park) to aid his development of fine wool. He also returned with partnership interests in trade and in the Pacific fisheries.

Very shortly Macarthur ran foul of Governor Bligh and,

John Macarthur (1766–1834), by unknown engraver

in particular, his efforts to control the colony's notorious rum trade. Macarthur's importation of spirit stills and his flouting of certain obligations as a shipowner brought him to trial in January 1808. When Bligh refused Macarthur bail, Major George Johnston of the New South Wales Corps ordered his release and deposed the governor. Macarthur then arbitrarily administered the colony as 'colonial secretary' until July. He sailed for England in March 1809, and attended Johnston's court martial in 1811. Despite a 'deep-rooted prejudice' against him at the Colonial Office (John Macarthur to Elizabeth Macarthur, 8 Dec 1814, Macarthur MSS, A2898, 277), Macarthur, as a civilian, escaped trial for treason, but was advised that he would be liable to arrest in New South Wales as the 'leading Promoter and Instigator' of the rebellion (Castlereagh to Macquarie, 14 May 1809, HRA, 1st ser., 7.81).

Stranded and hoping to do something in the mercantile way, Macarthur found the times 'frightfully hazardous'. Rising wool prices revived him, and his wife and nephew were instructed to transform the wool from his flocks into a commercial commodity. Although he occupied himself in investigating wool processing and marketing, he fretted over a cramped exile (shared with his younger sons, James and William), in which 'Our only beverage is water and our most sumptuous fare a mutton chop and a potato' (John Macarthur to Elizabeth Macarthur, 26 July 1814, Macarthur MSS, A2898, 212). As a result of the persistent diplomacy of his son John, he was allowed to return to New South Wales in 1817 on condition that he avoid public affairs. He was thus conveniently reinstated in time delicately to court and impress Commissioner Bigge, whose crucial recommendation for the future direction of the colony ultimately coincided with Macarthur's: it endorsed a wool-based pastoralism of large estates, serviced by convict labourers, that would create a resource for British industry while reducing government penal expenditure.

Privately, Macarthur was aware that his own promotion of fine wool 'still creeps on almost unheeded' (John Macarthur to Davidson, 3 Sept 1818, Macarthur MSS, A2897, 22B). However, some of his wool brought high prices in London in 1821, and he acquired medals from the Society of Arts in 1822 and 1824 for its quantity and quality. In 1824 the richly subscribed and chartered Australian Agricultural Company was launched—a cherished objective shepherded to completion by his son John in London. But in New South Wales, Macarthur remained deeply unpopular and was often baited in the local press. His nomination in December 1825 to the legislative council brought serious public protest. Yet he continued to fuel controversy, agitating against the chief justice, Francis Forbes, and showing hostility towards Governor Darling. In 1828 he seized local control of the Australian Agricultural Company and caused its shares to collapse. His mental instability accelerated and he was declared insane in 1832. He died on 11 April 1834, survived by his wife, three sons (his son John had died in 1731), and three daughters, and was buried at his Camden Park estate. Complex, tortured, and ruthless, Macarthur achieved his essential ambition to be a landed esquire. His insistence on the potential of a colonial wool staple—a vision neither unique nor original—was secondary to that ambition but a testimony to his abilities and to his skill as a publicist.

His wife, **Elizabeth Macarthur** (1766–1850), was born on 14 August 1766 at Bridgerule, Devon, the daughter of Richard Veale (d. 1772), farmer, and his wife, Grace, who remarried in 1778. The first cultivated woman to reach Sydney, Elizabeth was 'abundantly content' (Elizabeth Macarthur to Bridget Kingdon, 7 March 1791, Macarthur MSS, A2906, 19) in her new life, charmed by its advantages and unfamiliar natural environment. Though fashionably romantic, she proved adaptable and sensible, nurturing seven surviving children (including James *Macarthur) in an ordered domestic world and providing a 'moral entrenchment' against the 'plagues' of convictism. In the 1804 convict uprising she made a nocturnal flight to Sydney with her children, accepting this responsibility as calmly and uncomplainingly as all others heaped on her during Macarthur's absences. She diligently carried out her husband's instructions from England concerning their affairs, eventually deriving pleasure from some of the routines of pastoral management. Essentially gregarious and a natural arbitrator for her husband's 'peculiar and sudden' disturbances (Elizabeth Macarthur to Edward Macarthur, 4 March 1827, Macarthur MSS, A2906, 2), she was respected for her patient good nature and fortitude. She died on 9 February 1850, at Sydney, and was buried a week later at Camden Park.

John Macarthur (1794–1831), their second son, was born on 10 May 1794, at Elizabeth Farm, Parramatta. In 1801 his father took him to Britain, where he was educated at a private academy in London, and then at Glasgow University and Caius College, Cambridge (BA, 1817; MA, 1823). He was called to the English bar in 1818, and he gave evidence before the parliamentary select committee on gaols in 1819. His father's favourite, he was groomed to be the family's personal agent, to supervise wool sales, and to cultivate officials and strategic social contacts. The architect of the Australian Agricultural Company, he guided its charter and was a director from 1824 to 1830. In 1827 he was appointed a commissioner in bankruptcy. Having played a vital role in the foundation and progress of the family's interests, he died in London, unmarried, in a fit of apoplexy, on 19 April 1831, and was buried at St Martin's Church, London.

Hannibal Hawkins Macarthur (1788–1861), entrepreneur and politician, was born on 16 January 1788 at Plymouth, Devon, son of James Macarthur, draper, and his wife, Catherine, *née* Hawkins. Hannibal accompanied his uncle John to Sydney in 1805, becoming his general factotum, and between 1812 and 1817 he managed Macarthur's flocks, wool processing, and export. In 1812 he married Anna Maria King, daughter of the ex-governor. A director of the Australian Agricultural Company, Hannibal Macarthur was chairman of the Bank of Australia and a member (1830–48) of the legislative council. His trading and extensive pastoral interests collapsed in the depression of the 1840s, and he was declared insolvent in 1848. In 1853 he returned to England, where he died on 26 October 1861, at Upper Norwood, Surrey.　　MARGARET STEVEN

Sources Mitchell L., NSW, Macarthur MSS and Index • M. H. Ellis, *John Macarthur* (1955) • H. King, *Elizabeth Macarthur and her world* (1980) • H. King, *Colonial expatriates: Edward and John Macarthur junior* (1989) • S. M. Onslow, *Early records of the Macarthurs of Camden* (1912) • A. T. Atkinson, 'John Macarthur before Australia knew him', *Journal of Australian Studies*, no. 4 (June 1979) • J. M. Ward, *James Macarthur, colonial conservative, 1798–1867* (1981) • *AusDB*, vol. 2 • J. C. Garran and L. White, *Merinos, myths and Macarthurs: Australian graziers and their sheep, 1788–1985* (1985) • parish register, St Andrew's Church, Stoke Damerel, 3 Sept 1767, Devon RO [birth] • parish register, Bridgerule, 6 Oct 1788, Devon RO [marriage] • G. Aplin, S. G. Foster, and M. McKernan, eds., *Australians, a historical dictionary* (1987) • *CGPLA Eng. & Wales* (1861) [Hannibal Hawkins Macarthur] • d. cert. [Hannibal Hawkins Macarthur] • *Sydney Herald* (17 April 1834) • parish register, St Bridget's, Bridgerule, 1 Oct 1766, Devon RO [baptism, Elizabeth Macarthur]
Archives Mitchell L., NSW, MSS | Derbys. RO, letters to Sir R. J. Wilmot-Horton
Likenesses engraving, National Archives of Australia [*see illus.*] • oils, Dixson Gallery, Sydney, Australia • oils (Elizabeth Macarthur), Dixson Gallery, Sydney, Australia • watercolour, priv. coll. • watercolour, priv. coll. • watercolour (John Macarthur junior), Mitchell L., NSW
Wealth at death 60,000 acres; also stock and town allotments • £200—Hannibal Hawkins Macarthur: will, 1861

Macarthur, John (1794–1831). *See under* Macarthur, John (1766–1834).

MacArthur, John Stewart (1856–1920), metallurgical chemist, was born on 9 December 1856 at 12 Norfolk Street, Hutchesontown, Glasgow, one of six sons and a

John Stewart MacArthur (1856–1920), by G. Comrie Smith

daughter (two other sons died in infancy) of Robert McArthur (spelled thus on the birth certificate; *b.* 1819), tailor, of Glasgow, and his wife, Elizabeth Stewart. He left school at fourteen and became an apprentice with the Tharsis Sulphur and Copper Company—part of the great Glasgow international chemical empire generated by the Tennant family. In the evenings he studied metallurgy and mathematics until the age of twenty-two. With two physicians, William Forrest and Robert Wardrop Forrest, he formed a private research syndicate, seeking improved methods of recovering gold from complex ores.

In 1886 another Tennant subsidiary in Glasgow, the Cassel Gold Extracting Company, collapsed following a scandal involving H. R. Cassel, its American founder, and MacArthur was called upon to restructure the company. This he did successfully, first moving its works from Gray's Inn Road, London, to Glasgow. He based the restructuring on his own researches rather than Cassel's discredited process. MacArthur married, on 19 October 1888, Agnes Ann (1858–1948), daughter of William Marshall, woollen merchant, of Glasgow. They had one son, John Stewart MacArthur, who became a cleric.

Between 1886 and 1888 MacArthur and the Forrests registered patents in Britain covering a new process of gold and silver recovery, based on dissolving crushed ore in potassium cyanide solution and subsequent filtration through metallic zinc. The process was assigned to the Cassel Company, international patents obtained, and MacArthur began to train young chemists and dispatch them with plant to virtually every gold-producing country.

The world's gold-mining industry was stagnating, refining only about 45 per cent of metal from complex ores: the new process enabled 98 per cent extraction, and was hailed as the saviour of the industry. However, in 1896 the South African mining bureaucracy took MacArthur through the courts to prove an esoteric weakness in the patent, which allowed them to avoid royalty payments to the man who had rejuvenated their industry. A century later, however, MacArthur was still given credit in South Africa for his contribution to that country's economy. He continued to introduce his process throughout the world, travelling abroad extensively. He also took an interest in cyanide production and in refining processes for copper and antimony.

In 1911 MacArthur concentrated on radium refining on an industrial scale, initially in Runcorn in Cheshire, and from 1915, until his death, in Balloch on Loch Lomond. This pioneering, dangerous, and chemically intensive work was as significant as that on gold, most work on radium being at that time confined to the laboratory.

MacArthur was concerned to apply science for the benefit of industry and humanity, but was unwilling to endure the politics of international business. He was the first gold medal winner (1902) of the Institution of Mining and Metallurgy, his obituary in *Nature* noting: 'It is given to few men to discover a process which has had such a far-reaching effect in almost every branch of civilised life'. Cyanide is still in wide use in gold and silver extraction, but some recent cases of incompetent management of the technology have resulted in large-scale contamination of the environment. MacArthur died on 16 March 1920 in Pollokshields, Glasgow, and was buried three days later in Cathcart cemetery. He was survived by his wife.

D. I. HARVIE, *rev.*

Sources D. I. Harvie, 'John Stewart MacArthur, 1856–1920', *Scottish Industrial Heritage Society Newsletter* (Dec 1988), 3–5 · D. I. Harvie, 'John Stewart MacArthur: pioneer gold and radium refiner', *Endeavour*, new ser., 13 (1989), 179–84 · *Nature*, 105 (1920), 112 · *CCI* (1920) · election certificate, RS
Archives Balliol Oxf.
Likenesses G. Comrie Smith, photograph, Balliol Oxf. [*see illus.*] · photographs, Balliol Oxf.
Wealth at death £34,154 6s. 2d.: confirmation, 21 Sept 1920, *CCI*

Macarthur [*married name* Anderson], **Mary Reid** (1880–1921), women's labour organizer, was born at Glasgow on 13 August 1880, the eldest daughter of John Duncan Macarthur, proprietor of a drapery business, and his wife, Anne Elizabeth Martin. She was one of six children, of whom only three survived. Educated at Glasgow Girls' High School, she also studied in Germany before working as a bookkeeper for her father. She initially endorsed her family's Conservative politics and was a member of the Primrose League, but was unexpectedly impressed by a meeting she attended in 1901 to discuss the establishment of a branch of the Shop Assistants' Union in Ayr and

Mary Reid Macarthur (1880–1921), by unknown photographer

became an advocate of trade unionism. Within months she was chairing the new Ayr branch.

Mary Macarthur rapidly graduated to presidency of the Scottish national district council of the union and by 1903 was the first woman on its national executive. She moved to London and became honorary secretary of the Women's Trade Union League (WTUL). She encouraged trade unions with women members to affiliate and dramatically increased membership. Her colleagues and friends included Sir Charles and Lady Emilia Dilke and Margaret Bondfield. She travelled to the International Congress of Women in Berlin in 1904. For a time she was the only woman delegate to the London Trades Council. Mary Macarthur is perhaps best known for founding the National Federation of Women Workers (NFWW) in 1906. She began as president, but then exchanged offices with Gertrude *Tuckwell (1861–1951) to become general secretary. By the end of its first year the NFWW boasted seventeen branches in Scotland and England and about two thousand members. Mary Macarthur was especially concerned about the relationship between low wages and women's lack of organization. In 1907 she began (and edited) the monthly paper the *Woman Worker*, which was soon transformed into a weekly with a circulation of about 20,000.

A tireless campaigner on behalf of sweated workers, Mary Macarthur sat on the executive of the Anti-Sweating League, gave evidence to the select committee on homework (1908), and advocated a legal minimum wage. She regarded the establishment of trade boards as a legislative revolution, and helped to set up the lace-mending and finishing board in Nottingham and sat on the chain-making board; she then helped to organize the Cradley Heath women chainmakers when they struck to secure implementation of their rightful new rates. In the summer of 1911 she organized an estimated 2000 women involved in twenty concurrent strikes in Bermondsey and elsewhere. The character of Miss Doremus in Kathleen Woodward's story *Jipping Street* (1928), set in the Bermondsey area, is allegedly based on Mary Macarthur. As an adult suffragist,

and honorary secretary to the People's Suffrage Federation, she saw her primary commitment as providing protection for working-class women rather than concentrating on the voting rights of women.

Mary Macarthur was a member of the national council of the Independent Labour Party (ILP) from 1909 to 1912. On 21 September 1911 she married William Crawford *Anderson (1877–1919), a self-educated, working-class journalist, who chaired the executive committee of the ILP. Their first child died at birth in 1913 but two years later a daughter, Anne Elizabeth (Nancy), was born. From 1914 to 1918 William Anderson was MP for Attercliffe, Sheffield. Once she was enfranchised, Mary Macarthur stood for parliament. She was defeated as Labour candidate for Stourbridge, Worcestershire, in 1918; some attributed this to the fact that although she had campaigned as Mary Macarthur the returning officer had insisted on describing her on the polling card as Mrs W. C. Anderson. By 1919 she was on the executive of the Labour Party and the following year became one of the pioneer women magistrates. During the First World War she had been the WTUL representative on the War Emergency Workers' National Committee and sat on many committees in addition to her work for the NFWW. Through her position as secretary to the queen's Work for Women Fund she struck up a working friendship with Queen Mary.

William Anderson died suddenly and prematurely in February 1919. In the following year Mary Macarthur made several trips to America, one as a British representative to the International Labour Organization. Although she was instrumental in negotiating the transfer of the NFWW into a mixed general union, the General and Municipal Workers' Union, she did not live to see this. She developed cancer in 1920 and after two unsuccessful operations died at home, 42 Woodstock Road, Golders Green, Middlesex, on new year's day 1921, being cremated at Golders Green crematorium three days later. She was only forty at her death. The Mary Macarthur Educational Trust and Mary Macarthur Homes for Working Women were established in her memory.

Mary Macarthur's contemporaries were well aware of her vitality, motivation, and ability to act as a catalyst for change. Gertrude Tuckwell, who first met her in 1903, commented that 'with Mary, something great was always going to happen, and she created an atmosphere in which it did' (*Labour Woman*). Nevertheless, both Gertrude Tuckwell and Mary Macarthur faced severe difficulties in organizing working-class women, who still encountered enormous obstacles to being accepted as an integral part of the workforce. As members of trade unions they allayed the suspicions of some male workers, but convincing most men and women of the importance of women's trade unionism was never an easy task, particularly for a woman from a middle-class background. At the same time some feminists were concerned about Mary Macarthur's sense of priorities, which was manifested, for example, in her commitment to adult suffrage. Yet her ability to work effectively with people of all classes facilitated her huge task and this, combined with her personal energy and commitment, helped to ensure the importance of the National Federation of Women Workers in peace and especially in war. As Beatrice Webb noted, Mary Macarthur was 'the axle round which the machinery moved' (ibid.).   ANGELA V. JOHN

Sources M. A. Hamilton, *Mary Macarthur: a biographical sketch* (1925) · M. Cole, *Women of today* (1922) · D. Thom, 'The bundle of sticks: women, trade unionists and collective organization before 1918', *Unequal opportunities: women's employment in England, 1800–1918*, ed. A. V. John (1986), 260–89 · *DLB* · B. Drake, *Women in trade unions* (1920) · O. Banks, *The biographical dictionary of British feminists*, 1 (1985) · S. Lewenhak, *Women and trade unions: an outline history of women in the British trade union movement* (1977) · K. Woodward, *Jipping Street* (1961); repr. (1983) · *Labour Woman* (Feb 1921), 22–6 [tributes, editorial, and portrait] · *DNB* · m. cert. · d. cert.
Archives BLPES, corresp. with the independent labour party · London Metropolitan University, TUC collections, corresp. and newspaper cuttings · London Metropolitan University, TUC collections, Gertrude Tuckwell papers | People's History Museum, Manchester, War Emergency Workers' National Archive
Likenesses group photograph, *c.*1908, U. Hull, Varley collection · Mendoza, photograph, repro. in *Labour Woman*, 25 · four photographs, TUC · photograph, GMB · photograph, People's History Museum, Manchester [*see illus.*]
Wealth at death £7264 0s. 2d.: probate, 7 March 1921, *CGPLA Eng. & Wales*

MacArthur, Niel (d. 1762). *See under* MacArthur family (*per.* 1715–1839).

Macarthur, Sir William (1800–1882). *See under* Macarthur, James (1798–1867).

McArthur, Sir William (1809–1887), woollen merchant and politician, was born at Malin, Donegal, Ireland, on 6 July 1809, the fifth child and second son of John McArthur (d. 1840) and Sarah, *née* Finlay (d. 1861). His father was a poor Scots-Irish farmer who had converted to Methodism in the 1790s and turned to itinerant preaching in the 'linen triangle' of Ulster. William attended schools in Stranorlar and Newtownstewart, but at the age of twelve he was sent away from home to be apprenticed to a Methodist woollen draper in Enniskillen. Subsequently he worked as a clerk for a Methodist tobacco and spirit merchant in Lurgan, and briefly as a travelling agent for a Dublin woollen draper, before he and a partner of about his own age set up a woollens export business in Londonderry in 1831. The firm prospered and acquired new suppliers in the north of England, and when his partner, John Cather, emigrated to Canada in 1835 McArthur assumed control.

A modest if solid provincial enterprise was transformed into a major commercial house in consequence of a visit made to New South Wales in 1841 by one of McArthur's younger brothers. By the late 1840s Alexander McArthur (1814–1909) had established branches of the firm in Sydney, Melbourne, Adelaide, and Auckland, to deal in McArthur textiles and Australasian exports. When the 'gold rush' happened in 1851 McArthur Brothers was well placed to profit enormously from both the great demand for durable woollens and from the high profits to be made in gold exporting. Australian success led the firm to open a London office in 1854. Three years later William McArthur himself moved to London and subsequently became a City

figure of great wealth and some influence. By the mid-1860s the two brothers (Alexander moved to London in 1863) had extended their activity into banking and insurance, and they sat on the boards of a number of other firms dealing in colonial and foreign investments.

McArthur had deferred matrimony until his business was soundly established, and in 1843 he married Marianne (1819?–1889), the only child of Archibald McElwaine, an Ulster businessman and a Methodist. They had no children and from the 1850s Marianne was a semi-invalid; for reasons of health she often lived apart from her husband.

McArthur was elected to the Londonderry town council in 1841 as a Conservative, though his politics were more Methodist Connexional than tory partisan. When he moved toward the Liberals in the 1850s, he was driven in large measure by the protestant issues of sectarian education and anti-Catholicism. It was not until 1865, however, that he became interested in a parliamentary seat. By this time he was well established in the City of London, had become a prominent benefactor of Methodist educational and charitable institutions, and lived in a south London suburb, Brixton Hill, among a community of wealthy nonconformist professionals and businessmen like himself. Following an invitation from the Methodists of the West Riding borough of Pontefract, McArthur contested the seat as a moderate Liberal but was narrowly defeated. He subsequently took a larger role in City affairs, served a term as sheriff for London and Middlesex in 1867, hired a political agent, and stood successfully in 1868 for the south London (Surrey) borough of Lambeth. He held this constituency, which included his own residence in Brixton Hill, until 1885, though with increasing challenge from the radical wing of metropolitan Liberalism.

Although many of McArthur's philanthropic and evangelical interests cut across partisan lines in the House of Commons, he was, like the other Methodist MPs, a generally loyal Gladstonian, and embraced most of the domestic reforms of the first and second Gladstone governments. As one of the most prominent (and wealthy) Methodist laymen of the time, he was not merely a spokesman for Connexion in parliament but played a considerable role in shaping the Methodist political agenda. For McArthur, the most compelling item on this agenda was the furtherance of Methodist missionary enterprise, especially in the south Pacific. Here he was strongly influenced by his brother Alexander and his Australian Methodist friends and relatives.

McArthur's persistent campaign in parliament and at Whitehall in the early 1870s for the annexation of the Fiji Islands, where there was a well-developed Methodist missionary presence, was vigorously resisted by Gladstone, but it ultimately triumphed when Disraeli's government accepted the sovereignty of the islands in 1874. Earlier McArthur had helped to promote, as did many nonconformist Liberals, causes which were often critical of colonial administration (the British and Foreign Anti-Slave Society, the Aborigines Protection Society, the Anglo-Oriental Society for Suppression of the Opium Trade, and

J. S. Mill's Jamaica Committee to prosecute Governor Eyre). The Fiji success, however, and the alliances he made in achieving it, encouraged in McArthur an enthusiasm for the empire (in 1884 he was ardent in his support for W. E. Forster's Imperial Federation League), and helped to widen the rift between McArthur and Liberal radicalism in his later years.

McArthur was elected alderman for the Coleman Street ward of the City in 1872, and he served on committees concerned with sewerage, the police, gas and water, and various charities, and lent his name and resources to a number of civic and philanthropic organizations. He was a founding member of the London chamber of commerce in 1881, and he supported the campaigns of the Metropolitan Free Bridges Association and the Public Museums and Free Libraries Association. In his mind civic reform was inextricably tied to moral reform, a conviction reflected in his support for the Central Association for Stopping the Sale of Intoxicating Liquors on Sundays and the National Association for Repeal of the Contagious Diseases Acts. Primacy of place was, however, always reserved for explicitly Methodist demands on his time and money: the Wesleyan Methodist Missionary Society, the Methodist Chapel Building Fund, and the Methodist college at Belfast. From 1872 until his death he was a lay representative to both the English and Irish Wesleyan conferences.

McArthur's turn as lord mayor of London came in 1880, and the pious tone he set at Mansion House—no wine, card playing, or dancing, and prayer meetings for the Evangelical Alliance—drew sarcastic comment from some quarters about his parvenu religiosity and lack of sophistication. After the end of his year in office Gladstone created him KCMG (an award commonly associated with colonial service), rather than bestow the baronetcy which many former lord mayors received, an apparent slight which McArthur and his friends resented.

McArthur had relished the robes of office, which he wore to chapel services in Brixton, and the dignity of his position, feeling that they honoured, through him, both provincial nonconformity and self-made men of commerce. He added a considerable amount of aldermanic flesh to his large frame, and a growing sense of his importance in the City and in the Wesleyan community led him to take a large, elegant house at 79 Holland Park, appropriate to the style of the merchant prince he considered himself to be. However, his removal to west London, the grandness of his style, his foreign travel, his increasing absence from the House of Commons, and his lack of interest in the 'low' radicalism of the left of the Liberal Party made McArthur vulnerable in Lambeth. Although he endorsed land reform and extension of the franchise, there were limits to his ability to accommodate the radical programme, and his failure in 1883 to vote for the Affirmation Bill which would have allowed the atheist Charles Bradlaugh to take his seat in the Commons resulted in a deputation from his constituents demanding that he resign his seat. McArthur—heavy, elderly, and never a very confident orator—saw a parliamentary seat as a reward rather than a battleground, and, rather than struggle against a coming generation in a large, demanding metropolitan constituency, he chose not to contest Lambeth in the general election of 1885. Nonconformists in the newly created east Kent district of Newington West invited him to stand, but here too there was a radical challenge which split the Liberal vote and gave the seat to a tory—with McArthur trailing a distant third.

The humiliation of his loss embittered McArthur in his last years. Like his protégé Hugh Price Hughes he abandoned Gladstone over home rule, and he turned to the satisfying and complicated business of arranging and rearranging the many charitable legacies in his will. McArthur remained in robust health until his sudden death from heart failure on 16 November 1887, *en route* on the London Underground to a City board meeting. Survived by his wife and also by his brother Alexander, McArthur was buried at Norwood cemetery. He left a considerable fortune, amounting almost to £0.5 million, more than £150,000 of which was left to Methodist charities.

Rising from an obscure apprenticeship to dignity, honour, and a mercantile fortune, McArthur's life fitted the pattern described by Samuel Smiles. He attributed his success to simple virtues, inscribing his stationery with the motto *Fide et opera*. The recognized spokesman for the Wesleyan Methodist laity, an avid promoter of missionary imperialism, and a minor pillar of nonconformist support for Gladstonian Liberalism, McArthur remained a confirmed back-bencher, alternately useful and embarrassing to the Liberal leadership. He was a great man to many of his Methodist contemporaries, but in London, in the larger world, regard for his money was inevitably tempered by condescension. McArthur's girth and broad, coarse features belied his character, which was not particularly expansive or gregarious. His strict evangelical and sectarian approach to all aspects of his public and commercial life—the very means by which he struggled out of a narrow Ulster poverty—also worked to prevent him from developing larger sympathies with either the world of high politics or that of his working-class constituents, and so limited the influence which his wealth might have commanded. H. L. MALCHOW

Sources T. McCullagh, *Sir William McArthur* (1891) · H. L. Malchow, *Gentlemen capitalists: the social and political world of the Victorian businessman* (1991) · Boase, *Mod. Eng. biog.*

Archives Bodl. RH · JRL, Methodist Archives and Research Centre | Bodl. Oxf., corresp. with Lord Kimberley · SOAS, Wesleyan Methodist Missionary Society MSS

Likenesses Spy [L. Ward], cartoon, NPG; repro. in *VF* (8 Oct 1881) · photograph, GL · woodcut, NPG

Wealth at death £481,443—incl. estate in the colonies: Boase, *Mod. Eng. biog.* · £120,937 2s. 5d.: probate, 23 Dec 1887, *CGPLA Eng. & Wales* · no value given: probate, 1888, resworn

MacArthur, Sir William Porter (1884–1964), army medical officer, was born at Belmont, co. Down, on 11 March 1884, the second child and only son of John Porter MacArthur, partner in a firm of tea importers in Belfast, and his wife, Margaret Rainey, daughter of William Baird MD of Donemara and grandniece of Andrew Baird FRS. His father's forebears had emigrated from Argyll in the latter

Sir William Porter MacArthur (1884–1964), by Bassano, 1937

part of the eighteenth century. MacArthur received his medical education in Queen's University, Belfast, and graduated MB BCh (Royal University of Ireland) in 1908. He received the diploma in public health at Oxford in 1910, the degree of MD at Belfast in 1911, and the diploma in tropical medicine and health at Cambridge in 1920. He was elected FRCP (Ireland) in 1913 and FRCP (London) in 1937.

In 1909 MacArthur joined the Royal Army Medical Corps as a lieutenant and while serving in Mauritius from 1911 to 1914 acquired a keen interest in tropical medicine which remained with him throughout his life. He treated cases of typhoid fever with a polyvalent vaccine which he himself prepared and claimed considerable success. For the excellence of this work he was officially congratulated by the director-general. In 1915 he was posted to the British expeditionary force in France where he served until he was wounded and invalided home in 1916, and appointed to the DSO.

In 1919 MacArthur became commanding officer and chief instructor at the Army School of Hygiene at Blackpool, which he had been instrumental in helping to found. In 1922 he was transferred to the Royal Army Medical College in London as professor of tropical medicine, an appointment which he held until 1929 and again in 1932–4. Before taking up his duties he studied 'medical' entomology at the London School of Tropical Medicine and acquired a comprehensive collection of those arthropods which are disease vectors. This collection became the basis of a unique and valuable course of entomology

which he introduced into the training curriculum at the college. He was greatly esteemed as teacher and lecturer and his enthusiasm and initiative did much to raise the standard of instruction.

In subsequent appointments, as consulting physician to the army (1929–34) and as director of studies and commandant of the Royal Army Medical College (1935–8), MacArthur maintained his interest in teaching. His bent was towards clinical and preventive medicine rather than research, but he made one important original discovery. He found that so-called idiopathic epilepsy (believed to result from constitutional or inborn causes) could in certain cases be caused by invasion of the brain by the larval or cysticercus stage of the pork tapeworm, *Taenia solium*, a common parasite of pigs in the East, with which man can become infected. Sixty-three cases of men invalided out of the army with idiopathic epilepsy were traced and in all of them cysticercus infection was found. After vigorous representations by MacArthur their condition was accepted as attributable to service and retrospective disability pensions were granted.

After an earlier period in the War Office as deputy director-general of the Army Medical Services (1934–5), MacArthur was made director-general in 1938, with the rank of lieutenant-general. It was a somewhat unhappy appointment: his experience of the administrative aspects of the medical services was limited and he chafed at the restrictions imposed by red tape. Sensing the imminence of war in 1938, for instance, he side-tracked a ruling by a cabinet subcommittee and laid in a much needed store of equipment for medical field units due to be mobilized when war was declared. This earned him a severe rebuke from the financial authorities but found its justification a year later. Although well able to cope with peacetime problems, he found himself somewhat at sea in the hurly-burly of war when quick decisions had to be given on matters of which he had inadequate past experience. His difficulties were not lessened by the fact that on certain subjects, notably the functions of psychiatrists in the army, he did not see eye to eye with the adjutant-general. He was distressed by a press campaign which adversely, and in his opinion unjustly, criticized the medical services. This, however, he was well able to counter: he addressed members of parliament and representatives of the press with such success that the campaign came to an abrupt end. However, an injury to his right arm gave him severe pain for a long time and made sleep difficult, and this, combined with the cumulative worries and frustrations of his appointment, undermined his health and led to his resignation in 1941, a year before the normal termination of his period of office. He had been appointed CB in 1938 and KCB in 1939, and was honorary physician to the king from 1930 to 1941.

In his later years MacArthur found a congenial outlet for his energy as lecturer in tropical medicine and additional member of the faculty of medicine at Oxford, as consultant in tropical diseases at the Royal Masonic Hospital, and as editor of the *Transactions* of the Royal Society of Tropical

Medicine and Hygiene. He was colonel commandant of the Royal Army Medical Corps from 1946 to 1951.

Although dedicated to his professional career, MacArthur had other absorbing interests. Pride in his highland ancestry and love for all things Gaelic played a great part in his life. He had been one of the founders of the Gaelic Society in Queen's University and to perfect his knowledge of the Gaelic language, which he came to speak fluently, he spent long holidays in the far west of Donegal. Later in life he frequently visited Argyll where he found the Gaelic dialect very similar to that of Donegal, and so he was able to converse freely with the country people and to hear their folklore. He was fascinated by the mysterious Appin murder, on which he wrote a short book (1960), and of which a fictitious account is woven into R. L. Stevenson's *Kidnapped*.

MacArthur was also well versed in Old English and had a working acquaintance with Latin. This repertoire enabled him to read and interpret original documents and records and so to pursue his lifelong hobby, the study of medical history. He was particularly interested in the history of plague, typhus, and leprosy.

MacArthur's researches were the basis of papers published in various journals and of numerous lectures. He was a lecturer of outstanding ability, capable of holding his audience enthralled, speaking from memory, using no notes, and interlarding his remarks with long word-perfect quotations. Medals awarded in appreciation of his historical researches included the Arnott (1929), Chadwick (1935), Robert Campbell (1951), and the Scott-Heron (1957).

MacArthur was of medium height and build. His Celtic ancestry revealed itself in his robust bearing and forthright manner. He possessed vast stores of energy, and tenaciously pursued to its conclusion any task which he undertook: 'A dour exterior and a formidable manner, as so often happens, concealed a spirit of great sensibility and kindness' (*BMJ*, 388).

In 1914 MacArthur married Marie Eugénie Thérèse, third daughter of Louis Ferdinande Antelme MD of Mauritius; they had two sons, the elder of whom became a director of the Rank Organization and the younger, Ian (*b.* 1925), was Conservative member of parliament for Perth and East Perthshire from 1959 to 1974. MacArthur died in London on 30 July 1964. JOHN BOYD, *rev.*

Sources personal knowledge (1981) · *BMJ* (8 Aug 1964), 388–9 · *The Lancet* (8 Aug 1964), 321 · *WWW* · *WW*
Archives Royal Army Medical College, Millbank, London
Likenesses Bassano, photograph, 1937, NPG [*see illus.*] · Lewis, oils, Royal Army Medical Corps, Camberley, Surrey
Wealth at death £36,096: probate, 14 Dec 1964, *CGPLA Eng. & Wales*

Macartney, (William John) Allan (1941–1998), political scientist and politician, was born on 17 February 1941 at the Scottish mission house, Christiansborg, Accra, Gold Coast, the second of three children of the Revd William Macleod Macartney (1912–1999), minister of religion of the Church of Scotland and church missionary, and his wife, Jessie (Jay) Helen Inch Low (1912–1995). His mother

was an English teacher before her marriage. He was brought up in Africa until the age of four. He was successively educated at Coldingham School, Bridge of Weir public school, Greenock Academy, West End School, Elgin, and, between 1952 and 1957, Elgin Academy. He attended the universities of Tübingen and Marburg in Germany (1957–8) and then the University of Edinburgh (1958–62), where he graduated with an honours MA in political economy. While at Edinburgh he became president of Edinburgh University Nationalist Club and was co-founder of the Federation of Student Nationalists, of which he became founding president.

On 2 September 1963 Macartney married (Jane Dorothy) Anne Forsyth (*b.* 1941), a geographer and later university administrator, whom he had met as a student in Edinburgh. After their marriage they worked together as voluntary teachers in Nigeria. On their return, Macartney undertook postgraduate studies for a BLitt in politics at the University of Glasgow (1964–6) before becoming a lecturer in the University of Botswana, Lesotho, and Swaziland (1966–74), where he learned to speak Sesotho and seTswana (added to some Igbo, learned earlier in Nigeria). He was one of the few Scots able to sing a 'click' song. On the basis of his African experiences he later wrote a thesis entitled 'Local government and the politics of development in Botswana', for which he obtained a PhD from the University of Edinburgh in 1978.

In 1975 Macartney took up a post as staff tutor in social sciences with the Open University. Based in Edinburgh, he travelled extensively throughout Scotland. He loved his time with the Open University and was heard to comment that it was the greatest achievement of the 1960s Labour administration under Harold Wilson. He took a very practical view of his subject and became a specialist in the mechanisms of voting systems. He was a genial and witty man. One fellow staff tutor recalled his 'brilliantly subversive sense of humour' (private information). He also served with the Unit for the Study of Government in Scotland and was a fellow in the politics department of Edinburgh University. His publications included *Readings in Boleswa Government* (1971), *The Referendum Experience* (1981), *Islands of Europe* (1984), *Self-Determination in the Commonwealth* (1987), *Towards 1992* (1989), and *Asking the People* (1992).

Macartney never wavered from his support for Scotland's national sovereignty. He happened to be on leave from Africa when he stood as a Westminster parliamentary candidate for the Scottish National Party (SNP) in West Renfrewshire in the general election of 1970. He stood again in Berwick and East Lothian (1979), Tweeddale, Ettrick, and Lauderdale (1983), Clackmannan and East Stirlingshire (1987), and Kincardine and Deeside (1991 and 1992). Nothing diminished his appetite for helping the SNP even in seats where the prospects of success were minimal. Then he made the breakthrough. Having been narrowly defeated as the SNP candidate for North East Scotland in the European parliament election in 1989, he surged home in 1994 with a huge majority of 31,227.

Macartney immediately made his mark in Europe. He

had contacts with political movements in Flanders, Brittany, Catalonia, the Basque country, Friesland, the Faeroe and Åland islands, and other parts of Europe submerged in the imperial state-building of the nineteenth century. He had a command of languages such as Dutch, French, and German in addition to his African repertory, although his proficiency in Gaelic left him at times wishing for improvement. Nevertheless, he was an able communicator, and his open-minded and tolerant approach to others combined with his internationalism caused his work to be respected. He was appointed vice-president of the fisheries committee and a member of the joint assembly of the agreement between the African, Caribbean, and Pacific states and the European Union.

In 1996 Macartney convened a working party of experts, mainly from outside the SNP, to produce a seminal report on how to achieve the transition to independence. He was responsible in 1998 for introducing changes to the SNP constitution to give a democratic say to party members in the selection of party list candidates for the Scottish and European parliaments. In 1997 he was elected rector of Aberdeen University, and he took great pride in working for his student electors and promoting the university. Among other responsibilities, he was chairman of the Scottish Flag Trust (1991–8) and an active member of the St Andrew Society. He was a convinced Christian, an elder of the Church of Scotland (1976), and a member of the church's influential church and nation committee (1989–96).

Macartney died suddenly of heart failure at his home, 57 Forest Avenue, Aberdeen, on 25 August 1998, and was buried at Sunnyside cemetery, Alloa, Clackmannanshire, on 31 August. He was survived by his wife, Anne, his daughter Jean, his sons, John and Andrew, and four grandchildren. Aberdeen University established a scholarship in his memory. He was an unassuming man who would have been surprised by the many tributes of respect and affection from across the political divide that followed his death. His experience and calmness were greatly missed by his colleagues in the Scottish national movement. His contribution to the SNP at a time of great change was substantial. He never lived to see the recall of the Scottish parliament, but he knew from the successful outcome of the devolution referendum in 1997 that it was on its way.

GORDON WILSON

Sources *The Scotsman* (26 Aug 1998) · *The Guardian* (26 Aug 1998) · *Daily Telegraph* (26 Aug 1998) · *The Times* (27 Aug 1998) · *The Independent* (27 Aug 1998) · *The Herald* (26 Aug 1998), 1, 7 · *Who's who in Scotland* (1998) · *WWW* · personal knowledge (2004) · private information (2004) [Mrs J. D. Anne Macartney] · b. cert. · m. cert. · d. cert.
Archives priv. coll., MSS
Likenesses photograph, 1991, repro. in *Daily Telegraph* · double portrait, photograph, 1994 (with Alex Salmond), repro. in *The Independent* · photograph, repro. in *The Scotsman* · photograph, repro. in *Daily Telegraph* · photograph, repro. in *The Times*
Wealth at death £95,819.38: confirmation, 18 Dec 1998, *CCI*

Macartney, Carlile Aylmer (1895–1978), historian of central Europe, was born on 24 January 1895 at Newlands, Crockham Hill, Westerham, Kent, the youngest of five children of Carlile Henry Hayes Macartney (1842–1924),

barrister, landscape artist, and horologist, and his wife, Louisa, *née* Gardiner. The family, whose most renowned member was George, Earl Macartney, was of Scottish origin but long resident in Ulster. Aylmer's infancy and much of his boyhood were spent at Foxhold, a small house at Crockham near Newbury, Berkshire. In 1909 he went to Winchester College as a Pitt exhibitioner and scholar. He was elected to a scholarship at Trinity College, Cambridge; but, as he matriculated in October 1914, his classical studies were cut short by the war, in which he fought in France and was wounded in the leg. His only brother, Maxwell, fifteen years his senior, was already widely respected as a reporter for *The Times*, specializing in central Europe and the Balkans. Aylmer began to share many of his interests, travelling to Vienna, where he was acting vice-consul from 1922 to 1925. While there he married Nedella (c.1902–1990), daughter of Colonel Dimitri Mamarchev, of the Bulgarian army.

In his first book, *The Social Revolution in Austria* (1926), Macartney drew on his experiences of the new, post-Habsburg republic, emphasizing the disparities between living conditions in the huge capital city and the rural or mountainous provinces around it. But his attention soon shifted to Hungary, the inter-war 'kingdom without a king', whose problems, historical and contemporary, were to fascinate him throughout his academic life. He became fluent in Magyar, visited every region in the country, and established personal contacts with scholars and with some leading Calvinist landowning families. In 1930 he published a study entitled *The Magyars in the Ninth Century*, subsequently analysing the earliest Hungarian chronicles in a series of critical articles published in Budapest over several years. This scholarly achievement he made available for Western students in *The Medieval Hungarian Historians* (1953). Meanwhile he worked in the international department of the League of Nations Union from 1928 to 1936 and was recognized by the Royal Institute of International Affairs (Chatham House) as the leading authority on the problems of the Danube basin, and the relationship between 'national states and national minorities', a title he chose for a judicious study published in 1934. This problem was also at the heart of his *Hungary and her Successors* (1938), a survey of the political and economic consequences of the treaty of Trianon of 1920, by which two-thirds of pre-war 'historic Hungary' was ceded to neighbouring states.

In 1936 Macartney was elected a research fellow of All Souls College, Oxford. When war came in 1939 he was attached to the research department of the Foreign Office. Hungary remained neutral until June 1941, and early in 1940 Macartney travelled to Budapest for talks with the prime minister, Count Pal Teleki, and others who hoped to curb the mounting Nazi influence in their country. Subsequently Macartney began broadcasting regularly in Magyar for the BBC's World Service. Although firmly anti-German in content, the broadcasts showed a tolerant understanding of the existing order in Hungary which, by 1942, angered more radical colleagues. The Foreign Office backed Macartney, realizing that his combination of restrained comment and gently ironic reproach offered his listeners an impartiality lacking in their own media and German propaganda. 'Macartney acquired a reputation in Hungary which survived the vicissitudes of the war', the official history of British broadcasting observes (A. Briggs, *History of Broadcasting in the United Kingdom*, 3.428).

Until 1949, when the republic adopted a Soviet-style constitution, Macartney maintained links with scholars under the new regime as a foreign member of the Hungarian Academy. He interviewed detainees in occupied Germany (including the former regent, Horthy) and survivors of the war years in Budapest, from whom he received several unpublished memoirs and other documents. This varied material, supplemented by information from émigrés, encouraged him to write a two-volume history of Hungary between 1929 and 1945, which he entitled *October Fifteenth* to recall that confused Sunday in 1944 when Horthy vainly sought a separate peace with the allies. The critical assessment of his sources took Macartney almost nine years but in 1956 *October Fifteenth* was at last published by the University of Edinburgh, where from 1951 to 1957 he held the chair of international relations.

In November 1956 Macartney was on the Austrian frontier during the flight of refugees after the failure of the uprising in Budapest against Soviet occupation. He continued to help Hungarian exiles in London, but in his academic work he abandoned recent history to study the Habsburg lands as a whole, from Leopold II's accession to the end of dynastic rule, and concentrating on domestic affairs. His *The Habsburg Empire, 1790–1918* (1968) was an undertaking affectionately contemplated for forty years; it grew into a book of half a million words, not easy reading, but a quarry of detailed scholarship into which no dedicated student of the region could fail to hack. Other works, smaller in compass, included: *Independent Eastern Europe: a History* (1962), in collaboration with A. W. Palmer; a single-volume history of Hungary (1962); and a brief life of Maria Theresa (1969).

Macartney was elected a fellow of the British Academy in 1965, the year he retired from All Souls. In *Who's Who* he listed 'travel' as his recreation: he was able to visit the USA and was welcomed once more in Hungary and Bulgaria. He retained the thin, ascetic figure of a good walker. Perhaps his greatest pleasure in later years came from cultivating the irises at Hornbeams, his home on Boars Hill, south of Oxford. There, in early June each summer, with flag flowers in full colour, the Macartneys would welcome friends to a garden party. On 18 June 1978, a few days after the last of these celebrations, Aylmer Macartney collapsed and died at Hornbeams. A funeral service in the chapel of All Souls College, Oxford, on 23 June was followed by private cremation at Oxford crematorium.

ALAN PALMER

Sources *The Times* (20 June 1978) · personal knowledge (2004) · Bodl. Oxf., Macartney MSS · b. cert.
Archives Bodl. Oxf., papers concerning studies of Eastern Europe
Likenesses photograph, Bodl. Oxf., Macartney MSS

Wealth at death £81,499: probate, 7 Aug 1978, *CGPLA Eng. & Wales*

Macartney, George (*c.*1660–1730), army officer, was born in Belfast about 1660, the elder son of George Macartney, a recent settler from Scotland, and his wife, Martha Davies. One of the vanguard of a new, steady flow of Scots into Ulster, his father set up as a merchant and prospered. His mother came from the family of a prominent lawyer and politician, Sir John Davies (*d.* 1626), who had been attorney-general for Ireland. Macartney's younger brother Isaac belonged to the more civilized, urban element in an Ireland still regarded as semi-barbarous; he and his sons became influential in the expanding commercial life of Belfast, which by 1700 'had replaced Limerick as the fourth port of Ireland' (Foster, 127).

Macartney was educated at home, and then in France. He may have been sent there to qualify for foreign commerce, like Francis Osbaldistone in Scott's *Rob Roy*. Like Francis, he broke away from any such prudent course. With or without paternal approval, he joined the Scots guards, and from then on was an army man to the backbone. Much of his career was to be linked with his ancestral Scotland. His military and Scottish bent showed even in his marriage, to the widow of a General Douglas. There were offspring, but this branch of the family, unlike Isaac's, died out before making its mark.

Macartney rose as a soldier, climbing the ladder from 'volunteer' to lieutenant-colonel, with the Nine Years' War (1688–97) in his ears. Only a brief interval of peace divided this from the last of Louis XIV's challenges to Europe, the War of the Spanish Succession (1702–13). Macartney's service in the field belonged to the years 1706 to 1710, when he was in his forties, and when promotion could be swift for a man of courage and enterprise. In April 1703—the year before Marlborough's first grand victory, at Blenheim—he was appointed to the colonelcy of a new infantry regiment, to be raised in Scotland, and to be in a sense his own corps in an army still run largely by private enterprise. It was soon seeing action in Flanders, that 'cockpit of Europe', and before the end of 1705 Macartney was a brigadier. Not much later he and his men were sent to take part in the fighting in Spain. In April 1707 at the battle of Almanza, in the south-east, near Albacete, he was at the head of a brigade. His commander was Ruvigny, a Huguenot exile now earl of Galway, of whose 15,000 men only one-third were British. Ruvigny was outnumbered, and after severe losses had to effect a withdrawal. Macartney's regiment was cut to pieces, and he was captured.

Before long Macartney was free again, by an exchange; Marlborough knew his value and took a personal interest in getting him back. He was soon displaying a side of his nature—and of his Ireland—by some drunken misbehaviour to an old woman. She proved to be a clergyman's widow and took her complaint to the bishop of London, who carried it to Queen Anne; the latter summarily dismissed the culprit from the army. He had to sell his regiment, which after its wear and tear may not have been worth much; then, going back to his early beginnings, he rejoined the army as a gentleman volunteer.

Circumstances favoured Macartney. In 1709 Marlborough was trying to penetrate northern France. His bloodiest encounter took place at Malplaquet, just inside the frontier, in September. Very large forces were engaged on each side; Marlborough could claim victory, but with far more severe losses than those of his opponent Villars, who had occupied a better position. It was the kind of situation where Macartney could be at his best, and the following year saw him promoted major-general, directing the siege of Douai. But Marlborough and his war policy were losing favour, and in August 1710 the whig ministry was replaced by a tory government headed by Harley and St John. In December, Marlborough was deprived of all his posts and charged with peculation, and Swift could crow, in his letters to Stella, over the dismissal of Macartney and other like-minded officers.

A duel was to be the cause of Macartney's next discomfiture, though the quarrel was not his own. His fellow tory-hater Charles, fourth Baron Mohun, had for years been at loggerheads with James, fourth duke of Hamilton, a Scottish ally of the tories and high in favour with the queen. With everyone anxiously awaiting Anne's death, politicians' nerves were under acute strain.

In November 1712 the bitterness between Mohun and Hamilton erupted in a challenge, and the former enlisted Macartney as his second. There is no sign of any close friendship between the two men, and the link must have been chiefly political. The affray, in Hyde Park on 15 November 1712, ended with both principals mortally wounded. Their seconds seem to have made only a show of using their swords; but at a privy council enquiry the duke's second, another Hamilton, declared on oath that Macartney had given the death blow to the helpless duke. Macartney hid for a few days, and escaped to the Netherlands with a price on his head. He was in exile for four years and thus missed the Jacobite rising of autumn 1715, following Anne's death; however, its failure enabled him to return and submit to the law.

In June 1716 Macartney was tried for murder and virtually acquitted; Hamilton had more or less withdrawn his accusation, and been retired from the army. Macartney was clearly the kind of man that a new dynasty, still insecure, stood in need of as a prop. He was immediately reinstated in the army with the rank of colonel and soon raised to lieutenant-general. There were no more wars in store for him, but in 1718 he was made governor of the strategic border town of Berwick, and in 1722 he became a comptroller of army accounts; later he was commanding general in Ireland and governor of Portsmouth. Macartney died in 1730. He was a man of no great note on his own account, but he belonged to a band of fighting-men who built an army that in some degree altered the course of European history. V. G. KIERNAN

Sources DNB · R. S. Forsythe, A noble rake: the life of Charles, fourth Lord Mohun (1928) · H. T. Dickinson, 'The Mohun–Hamilton duel: personal feud or whig plot?', Durham University Journal, 57 (1964–5), 159–65 · V. L. Stater, Duke Hamilton is dead! A story of aristocratic life and death in Stuart Britain (1999) · J. Kelly, That damn'd thing called honour: duelling in Ireland, 1570–1860 (1995) · L. H. Addington, The patterns of war through the eighteenth century (1990) · The Spectator (1711–12) · The Spectator (1714) · F. M. A. de Voltaire, Voltaire's The age of Louis XIV, trans. M. P. Pollack [1926], chaps. 18–23 · W. Coxe, Memoirs of the duke of Marlborough, with his original correspondence, rev. J. Wade, 3rd edn, 3 vols. (1847–8); repr. (1905–8) · C. Maxwell, Country and town in Ireland under the Georges (1940) · R. F. Foster, Modern Ireland, 1600–1972 (1988) · T. C. Smout, A history of the Scottish people, 1560–1832 (1969)

Macartney, George, Earl Macartney (1737–1806), diplomatist and colonial governor, was born in co. Antrim or Dublin on 3 May 1737, the only son of the three children of George Macartney (d. 1779), a landowner, of Lisanoure, co. Antrim, and his wife, Elizabeth (d. 1755), the youngest daughter of the Revd John Winder, prebend of Kilroot and rector of Carmony, Antrim. His paternal grandfather, another George Macartney, had represented Belfast in the Irish parliament. After attending Dr Thompson's school in Leixlip from 1745, he studied at Trinity College, Dublin, from 1750 to 1754, whence he proceeded MA in 1759. The Revd William Dennis, a friend of Edmund Burke, was also his tutor until 1757, when he entered Lincoln's Inn; he migrated to the Middle Temple the following year. Macartney inherited £150 from his grandfather in 1757 and property from his uncle in 1759. On the grand tour he lingered in Italy in 1760 and wintered in Geneva, where he met Stephen Fox, Lord Holland's heir, with whom he returned to London. He frequented Holland House, his host trusting him to curb Stephen's gambling. From December 1761 he was Stephen's minder in Geneva, and while there he met and became friends with Rousseau and Voltaire. In 1763 he and Stephen were met in Paris by the Hollands, and together they toured France and the Netherlands; Macartney later went on to Germany with Stephen's younger brother Charles James Fox. On their return Lord Holland made him an interest-free loan (unrepaid) and tried unsuccessfully to get him into parliament for Midhurst; however, he did secure him an envoyship-extraordinary to Russia. Macartney was appointed on 4 October 1764, was knighted on 19 October, had his portrait painted by Reynolds, and reached St Petersburg on 27 December.

Envoy in Russia Commended in London for his good looks, social accomplishments, and ready mind, Macartney was expected to impress the Empress Catherine, but he omitted to produce his credentials on meeting her. He then fell ill, thereby delaying negotiation of a fresh commercial treaty and consideration of any Anglo-Russian alliance proposals. A commercial treaty he signed without authority in August 1765 maintained Britain's preferential status in Russia and permitted merchants to settle anywhere, but it failed to unlock the transit trade with Persia. Macartney received a rebuke from London, and after renegotiation the treaty was concluded in 1766. By then Lord Chatham, who was premier, craved a Russian alliance, which involved the substitution of Hans Stanley for Macartney (whose diplomacy had faltered over the Turkish question). Stanley never went, but Macartney left St Petersburg on 3 April 1767 and returned via Copenhagen in August. He was decorated with the White Eagle of Poland and published privately an *Account of the Russian Empire* (1767). On 20 November 1767 he was named ambassador to Russia, but he withdrew, having damaged his prospects by seducing two Russian court ladies. Soon afterwards, on 1 February 1768, he married Lady Jane Stuart (1742–1828), the daughter of the former prime minister John *Stuart, third earl of Bute (1713–1792), and his wife, Mary Wortley Montagu, Baroness Mount Stuart of Wortley; his mother-in-law vetoed any move to Russia. A mission to Turin was talked of as an alternative posting, as was the secretaryship at war. As Macartney needed to be in parliament, Lord Holland offered him the resources to contest Stockbridge, but he still feared the expense. A bid to win a peerage failed, but Bute secured his return for Cockermouth on Sir James Lowther's interest in 1768. There he was soon pressurized by Lowther to vacate, and he reluctantly accepted the chief secretaryship to Lord Townshend, the Irish viceroy, on 1 January 1769; he gave up Cockermouth in March.

Chief secretary in Ireland Macartney owed his appointment to Bute, whose oldest political friend was Townshend. His initial misgivings about his new position grew when Townshend added to his administrative duties the management of the Irish Commons; he had already been voted member for Armagh in absentia in 1768. He was sworn of the Irish privy council on 30 March 1769 and visited Dublin to meet the Dublin Castle undertakers or parliamentary managers, but soon returned to represent Townshend in London. In September, lacking cabinet consent to viceregal reforms, he returned to Dublin. His wish to become ambassador to Spain was frustrated, but Townshend promised recompense. In October he opened proceedings in the Irish Commons, promoting a money

bill, which had been rejected in 1768, to augment the military. He was heckled and the bill failed again, so parliament was prorogued. An Irish peerage, as Lord Balmaine, for which Townshend applied in vain, would have released him from his duties. In 1770 he lobbied London for Townshend's scheme to sidestep parliament by raising indirect revenues, but he still hankered after the diplomatic posting to Spain, whereby he hoped to settle the Falklands dispute and to augment his salary of £3000 per annum. When the Irish Commons convened in 1771, Townshend, who despaired of Macartney's management, requested a pension of £2000 for him, but the king disliked creating a precedent. Foregoing an alternative appointment as muster-master-general, he was finally assured his pension and also obtained a second knighthood, this time of the Bath (29 May 1772). Although this honour allowed him to castellate and improve his property at Lisanoure, he stayed on unwillingly, suffering caricature in the Irish patriot publication *Baratariana*, until November 1772. He urged in vain that his replacement be spared the vexing duties of parliamentary management. Despite his unhappy experience of Irish politics, his *Account of Ireland in 1773* showed his firm grasp of Irish economics and his commitment to imperial government. He continued to sit for Armagh, nominally, until 1776.

Disqualified from membership at Westminster by his pension, Macartney was allowed to substitute the governorship of Toome Castle, which he subsequently sold to pay debts contracted during his time in Russia. Bute secured his return for Ayr burghs in 1774. One speech availed him: he opposed the London merchants' petition against the trade embargo on the American colonies in January 1775. In November he was appointed governor of

George Macartney, Earl Macartney (1737–1806), by Lemuel Francis Abbott, *c.*1786–8 [left, with his secretary, Sir George Leonard Staunton, first baronet]

Grenada, Tobago, and the Grenadines. He vacated his seat in January, and he and Lady Jane reached St George on 3 May 1776. On 19 July he became Baron Macartney in the Irish peerage. Enjoying an income of £6000 a year, he admired the islands' beauty and racial variety but found the principal residents riven by bigotry, and he dissolved the Tobago assembly. While investigating economic problems, he feared French retaliation during the American war and projected a militia. This came too late, as the French invaded Grenada in 1779 and transported him a prisoner to Limoges that July. His wife escaped, but his property was looted. Macartney returned to London in November through an exchange of prisoners of war, and early the following year Lord North sent him on a confidential mission to Dublin; however, his advocacy of Anglo-Irish union fell on deaf ears.

Governor of Madras Macartney next canvassed for the governorship of Madras, then worth £15,000 per annum. Regarded as an interloper in Indian politics, he emphasized his commercial acumen and local impartiality. Backed by Lord Sandwich at the Admiralty, he won over the East India Company directors and court and succeeded in being the first non-company servant to be appointed. He vacated his parliamentary seat of Berealston, for which he had just been elected, on the Northumberland interest and sailed for India on 21 February 1781. He was accompanied by his secretary in Grenada, George Staunton, but not his wife, who suffered increasingly from deafness. His first mission was to seize the Dutch settlements, in order to counter the Franco-Dutch alliance in support of American independence. Negapatam was duly taken on 12 November 1781 and Trincomali in January 1782, despite his quarrel with the commander-in-chief in India, General Sir Eyre Coote, who had defeated Haidar Ali of Mysore, invader of the Carnatic, at the battle of Porto Novo in July 1781. Warren Hastings, governor-general in Calcutta, halted Macartney's initiatives by making Coote military supremo in Madras. To counter the French and Haidar, Macartney needed to finance the East India Company's military forces, and did so by taking over the revenue collection of the debt-ridden nawab of the Carnatic. This policy created a rift with Hastings, who upheld the nawab's objection to Macartney's appointment of revenue collectors, but Hastings gave way, subject to the nawab's approval, on 2 December 1781. Macartney had set up a committee of assigned revenue, headed by Paul Benfield, to whom he owed £6000 for his passage to India, but, alerted to Benfield's graft, he replaced him. When Benfield subsequently intrigued against him, he repaid his personal debt in 1782 and urged the company to boycott him. Meanwhile, the French naval threat having materialized, Macartney commandeered the nawab's revenue. This action was then approved by Hastings, but by May 1783 he had turned against Macartney, who refused to rehabilitate the nawab. In October, having prevented Macartney from negotiating with Haidar, Hastings tried unsuccessfully to suspend him in council. Even when the French made peace in 1783 Hastings continued to veto any

negotiation and yielded only when Haidar's heir, Tipu Sultan, made overtures. Tipu renounced all claim to the Carnatic by treaty on 11 March 1784. The nawab's omission from this treaty rankled in Calcutta, but Macartney stuck to his guns, risking suspension from office. The company directors, backed by the newly established government, the Board of Control for India, annulled his revenue takeover on 15 October 1784. Macartney sent his secretary, Staunton, to London to plead his cause, which led to Edmund Burke's exposure in a speech to the Commons on 28 February 1785 of the corruption enmeshing the nawab's affairs. By this point Hastings had resigned as governor-general, and Macartney was chosen as his successor on 17 February 1785. Unaware of his new appointment, Macartney resigned the governorship of Madras on 7 June 1785, *en route* for Calcutta, where the council, headed by Benfield's crony Sir John Macpherson, rebuffed him. He left India to argue his case in London on 13 August, and reached London in December. Addressing the company on 13 January 1786, he stated his terms and argued that both the military under the commander-in-chief, and the council in Calcutta, should be made subordinate to the governor-general; he also recommended Macpherson's dismissal. He met Pitt and Henry Dundas on 20 January, and their failure to mention a British peerage, while accepting his manifesto, probably clinched matters; he declined the governor-generalship, which was awarded instead to Lord Cornwallis. The company rewarded Macartney for his service with plate worth £1600 and a pension of £1500, commending him for rejecting the customary bribes in India.

Macartney had made several enemies in India and had fought a duel with Anthony Sadleir in September 1784, in which he had been wounded. His dispute with Coote's successor as commander-in-chief in India, Major-General James Stuart, whom he had dismissed in favour of Sir John Burgoyne, was played out in a duel in Hyde Park on 8 June 1786. This time Macartney was seriously wounded, and only the king's intervention in the quarrel prevented another duel between the two men. Disillusioned with India, Macartney withdrew from the political limelight. With his savings of over £30,000 he purchased a house in Curzon Street, Mayfair, and an estate in Surrey at Parkhurst. He also renovated his house at Lisanoure. He took his seat in the Irish Lords on 12 March 1788. Macartney served as *custos rotulorum* of Antrim, as a trustee of linen manufacture, and as a colonel in the yeomanry in Ulster. He became president of the Literary Club and was elected FRS in 1792 and FSA in 1795.

Viscount Macartney in Peking Macartney's next posting was dictated to some extent by his old masters, the East India Company. The company, together with the government, was anxious to ameliorate conditions for trade with China and sent Macartney on an embassy to Peking (Beijing). He was sworn of the privy council on 2 May 1792, awarded a salary of £10,000 and an allowance of £5000, and created Viscount Macartney on 28 June 1792. His party, which numbered ninety-four, including Staunton and a galaxy of experts, embarked in the *Lion* on 26 September 1792. Samples of the best British manufactures, with mechanical toys to entertain the octogenarian emperor Qianlong, were shipped. After enjoying the customary spectacles enjoined by Chinese hospitality, Macartney was presented to Qianlong at Jehol on 14 September 1792. The event, in which Macartney alone was able to avoid making the ceremonial *kowtow* to the emperor, was caricatured by Gillray. Thereafter he barely glimpsed the emperor. The premier Heshan refused to negotiate a treaty of trade and friendship, and Macartney was handed his dismissal on 3 October, a week after reaching Peking. His journals, which display ample appreciation of China, were later published in Barrow's life of Macartney (1807); Staunton published an acclaimed account of their mission in 1797. Macartney concluded that China could easily be bombarded, but accepted that the potential for commercial expansion by British traders was thwarted by the Chinese refusal to allow a resident minister in Peking. He returned home via Canton (Guangzhou), where he held talks about improving conditions for the British merchants, but he made no progress on reforming the unsatisfactory system then in operation.

Following his return, Macartney was raised to an earldom in the Irish peerage on 1 March 1794, but he was still ambitious for a British barony. He accordingly undertook another mission, on 10 July 1795, this time to Verona, to the exiled French king, Louis XVIII. Lord Grenville, as foreign secretary, wished to moderate French royalist aspirations. Louis accepted a personal grant of £10,000, but he had already dictated a defiant restoration manifesto and objected to leaving Verona; he wanted British recognition to promote rebellion in France against the revolutionary regime. By February 1796 Macartney had given up; he proceeded to Naples and was received at court. In April he returned to London, where the offer of the post of governor of the Cape awaited him, together with a British barony (granted on 8 June). He took his seat in the Lords on 27 September.

Governor of the Cape Macartney was enticed to accept the governorship of the Cape with a salary of £10,000 a year, an annual allowance and pension of £2000, and permission to leave peremptorily if his health failed; gout had long plagued him. He was appointed on 30 December 1796 and reached Cape Town on 4 May. In Lady Macartney's absence Lady Anne, the wife of his official secretary, Andrew Barnard, acted as first lady. His brief was to conciliate the Dutch, which he affably attempted, by concession and reform; military intimidation was seldom necessary, and he prevented clashes between the Boers and tribal pastoralists by halting the latter across the Great Fish River. The burghers were made to swear allegiance to George III. John Barrow, one of two private secretaries with him in China, mapped the colony for Macartney, who was confined to his Cape Town residence. He checked a naval mutiny at Simonstown, discouraged the slave trade, on which he had given evidence to the Lords in 1792, and abolished judicial torture. Surveying its

resources, he concluded that retention of the Cape was advantageous merely to safeguard India and suggested that the East India Company should manage the colony. He left for England on 21 November 1798, eschewing half pay until he was replaced, after making a declaration of administrative integrity. It was his last office: he declined Addington's offer of the chair of the Board of Control in 1801.

Latterly Macartney seldom attended parliament and instead consolidated his Antrim estate; he established a market town at Dervock. He was a trustee of the British Museum from 1801. After selling his Parkhurst estate in 1799, he rented Corney House in Chiswick. He died at Curzon Street on 31 March 1806 and was buried privately at Chiswick, as he wished, on 9 April. Childless, he left his widow handsomely provided for, and he bequeathed his realty to his niece Mrs Elizabeth Hume, whose heir was to assume the surname Macartney. She erected a cenotaph to his memory in Lisanoure church. His well-stocked library was sold in 1854 together with a first batch of his papers, which, after subsequent sales, have travelled even farther than he.   ROLAND THORNE

Sources *Macartney of Lisanoure, 1737–1806*, ed. P. Roebuck (1983) · H. H. Robbins, *Our first ambassador to China* (1908) · J. Barrow, *Some account of the public life and a collection from the unpublished writings of the earl of Macartney*, 2 vols. (1807) · *The private correspondence of Lord Macartney, governor of Madras*, ed. C. Collin Davies, CS, 3rd ser., 77 (1950) · *Macartney in Ireland, 1768–72: calendar of the chief secretaryship papers of Sir George Macartney*, ed. T. Bartlett (1979) · M. Roberts, *Macartney in Russia* (1974) · L. S. Sutherland, 'Lord Macartney's appointment as governor of Madras, 1780: the treasury in East India Company elections', *EngHR*, 90 (1975), 523–35 · J. Cranmer-Byng, *An embassy to China, being the journal kept by Lord Macartney during his embassy* (1962) · J. Cranmer-Byng, 'Lord Macartney's embassy to Peking in 1793 from original Chinese documents', *Journal of Oriental Studies*, 4/1–2 (1957–8) · J. L. Cranmer-Byng and T. H. Levere, 'A case study in cultural collision: scientific apparatus in the Macartney embassy to China, 1793', *Annals of Science*, 38 (1981), 503–25 · M. M. Drummond, 'Macartney, Sir George', HoP, *Commons, 1754–90* · *GM*, 1st ser., 76 (1806), 387, 475, 556 · *DNB* · J. Almon and others, eds., *The debates and proceedings of the British House of Commons*, 72 vols. (1766–94), vol. 1, pp. 109, 422 [From 1774–94 called The parliamentary register...] · *The letters of Lady Anne Barnard to Henry Dundas*, ed. A. Lewin Robinson (1973) · W. Fryer, 'The mirage of restoration: Louis XVIII and Lord Macartney, 1795–6', *Bulletin of the John Rylands University Library*, 62 (1979–80), 87–114, 388–422

Archives BL, accounts of Russia and Ireland, King's MSS 106–107, 189–190 · BL, corresp. and papers, Add. MSS 6826, 12438, 19814–19825, 22415–22464, 36811, 37846, 37876, 38717–38718, 39856–39858, 51389, 58834, 62665 · BL, Grenada papers, Egerton MS 2135, fols. 54–72 · BL, Hardwicke papers, letters, Add. MSS 37535–37536 · BL, Holland House papers, letters, Add. MSS 51388–51389 · BL OIOC, MSS Eur. C 22, C 229, E 87–89, E 273, E 291, F 190 · BL OIOC, home misc. series, corresp. and papers relating to India · Bodl. Oxf., corresp. and papers · Bodl. Oxf., corresp. and letters relating to India, MSS Eng. hist. b. 173–185, c. 66–118, 399, d. 142–143 · Bodl. Oxf., private letter-book, MSS Eng. hist. c. 399; Eng. lett. b. 23, d. 373–374; Eng. misc. b. 162, c. 625, d. 938–939, e. 879, f. 533–535 · Bodl. RH, corresp. and papers relating to West Indies and Cape Colony, MS W. Ind. 5.9, MS Afr. t. 2–4 · Boston PL, letters and papers · Boston University, corresp. relating to West Indies · Brenthurst Library, Johannesburg, corresp. and papers relating to Cape Colony · Cornell University, Ithaca, corresp. and papers relating to China · Coutts Bank archives, London, bank accounts · CUL, corresp. and memoranda · Deccan College, Poona, Postgraduate & Research Institute, corresp. and papers relating to Madras · Duke U., Perkins L., corresp., mainly relating to Madras · HF Oppenheimer, Johannesburg, letters and account of the Cape · Hunt. L., commonplace book · Kimberley Public Library, corresp. relating to Cape Colony · L. Cong., corresp. and papers relating to West Indies · L. Cong., Phillipps collection, letter-books · National Archives of India, New Delhi, papers relating to India · NL Ire., sketch of the revenue of Ireland, MS 11967 · NYPL, papers relating to West Indies · PRO NIre., corresp. and papers, D 426, 557, 572, 1062, 1184, 2225, 2731, T 2408, 2480–2483, 3169, 3428; TD 4779, 177, 221, 227, 395, 405, 407; Indian papers, D 2225 · Tōyō Bunko Oriental Library, Tokyo, journal of embassy to China · Tamil Nadu Government Oriental Manuscript Library, Madras, corresp. relating to India · U. Mich., Clements L., papers relating to West Indies · UCL, school of Slavonic and east European studies, draft of account of Russia · University of Minnesota, Minneapolis, Ames Library of South Asia, corresp. relating to Madras · University of Natal, Durban, Killie Campbell Africana Library, corresp. and papers relating to Cape Colony · University of Pennsylvania, Philadelphia, Van Pelt Library, corresp. relating to East India Co. · University of Witwatersrand Library, Johannesburg, corresp. and papers mainly relating to Cape Colony · Wellcome L., journal of voyage to China [copy] · Wellcome L., papers relating to Madras · Yale U., Beinecke L., corresp. and papers relating to Russia and China · Yale U., Beinecke L., journal of embassy to China [copy] | BL, corresp. with Francis Drake, Add. MS 46825 · BL, corresp. with Lord George Germain, Add. MSS 38717–38718 · BL, corresp. with Warren Hastings, Add. MSS 29146–29205 · BL, corresp. with Lord Holland, Add. MS 51388 · BL, corresp. with Lord Wellesley, Add. MSS 37278, 37283 · Bodl. Oxf., corresp. with Eyles Irwin · Derbys. RO, letters to Sir Robert Wilmot · Hants. RO, corresp. with William Wickham · NA Ire., corresp. with Lord Townshend, u 733 · NA Scot., corresp. with Lord Melville · NMM, corresp. with Lord Sandwich · NMM, letters to Sir William Hamilton · NRA, priv. coll., corresp. with Lord Stormont · PRO, official corresp., SP, CO, FO, T classes · Sheff. Arch., corresp. with Edmund Burke, X.151–2 (1978) · Suffolk RO, Bury St Edmunds, corresp. with duke of Grafton · Washington State University, Pullman, papers relating to China

Likenesses R. Hunter, oils, 1758?, repro. in Robbins, *Our first ambassador to China* · J. Reynolds, oils, exh. 1764, Petworth House, Sussex · line engraving, pubd 1781 (after unknown artist), BM, NPG · oils, c.1786, repro. in Burtchaell & Sadleir, *Alum. Dubl.*, 1st edn · L. F. Abbott, double portrait, oils, c.1786–1788 (with Sir George Staunton), NPG [*see illus.*] · H. Hudson, mezzotint, pubd 1790 (after M. Brown), BM · J. Gillray, caricature, etching, pubd 1792 (*The reception of the diplomatique and his suit at the court of Peking*), NPG · C. Townley, mezzotint, pubd 1793 (after S. de Koster), BM, NG Ire. · L. Schiavonetti, stipple, pubd 1807 (after pastel by H. Edridge, exh. RA 1801), NG Ire. · G. Bartolozzi, drawing, 1817 (after H. Edridge), BM · S. Reynolds, engraving, 1820 (after portrait by J. Reynolds) · G. S. Bartolozzi, chalk drawing (after H. Edridge), BM · J. Hall, line engraving (after T. Hickey), BM, NPG; repro. in A. Anderson, *A narrative of the British embassy to China*, 2 (1796) · K. A. Hickel, group portrait, oils (*The House of Commons, 1793*), NPG · O. Humphrey, oils, repro. in H. D. Love, *Vestiges of old Madras, 1640–1800*, 4 vols. (1913) · G. Lundberg, pastel drawing, Ulster Museum, Belfast · J. Singleton, stipple (after O. Humphrey), BM, NPG; repro. in *European Magazine* (1796) · caricature, BM; repro. in *Baratariana: a select collection of fugitive political pieces*, 2nd edn (1773) · oils, Scone Palace, Tayside Region, Scotland · sketch, BL, Add. MS 33931 fol. 2

Wealth at death under £40,000: PRO, death duty registers, IR 26/110; *Macartney of Lisanoure*, ed. Roebuck

Macartney, Sir George (1867–1945), diplomatist, was born at Nanking (Nanjing), China, on 19 January 1867, the eldest child of Sir (Samuel) Halliday *Macartney (1833–1906), a Scottish officer in Chinese service, and his first wife (d. 1878), a near relative of a rebel Taiping prince killed in 1863. George grew up in Nanking, but moved to Britain with his father in 1876. He was educated at Dulwich College and in France at the Collège de Bernay, Eure, and Caen University, where he obtained his *bachelier ès lettres* in 1886. In 1888, disappointed in his hopes of a consular post in China, he accepted a lowly job as Chinese interpreter with the Burma commission. He was a dapper, trim man, not obviously Chinese in appearance; nevertheless, his Foreign Office aspirations were probably thwarted by his mixed-race parentage, especially as it was coupled with an almost excessive modesty and shyness.

At the close of 1888 Macartney accompanied the British expedition to expel the Tibetans from Sikkim. In 1890 he was assigned as interpreter to Francis Younghusband on his mission to Chinese Turkestan (Sinkiang or Xinjiang) to block an unclaimed corridor of land between Afghan and Chinese territory which was menaced by the Russians. Younghusband thought highly of Macartney's linguistic skills and tact, and in July 1891 when he pulled out of Kashgar, the administrative capital of western Sinkiang he left Macartney behind him as Britain's sole representative in central Asia. Over the next twenty-eight years, in the absence of clear instructions from India, Macartney carved out his own goals: the protection of British subjects in Sinkiang, the collection of information about Russian activities in the region; the maintenance of friendly relations with the Chinese authorities and, through them, the containment of Russian influence. He was surprisingly successful in these goals (and especially so in freeing British-born subjects from slavery and protecting Indian merchants)—a remarkable achievement for one who for almost twenty years had no official status. With only two turbanned escorts and an Indian clerk in his consular retinue, he managed to maintain in Chinese eyes a rough diplomatic equivalence with his ambitious and well-armed Russian rival, M. Petrovsky. His father's position as secretary to the Chinese legation in London was no doubt of some assistance.

On 17 September 1898, while on leave, Macartney married a family friend, Catherina Theodora, second daughter of James Borland of Castle Douglas, Kirkcudbrightshire. She had never travelled before but revealed an exemplary ability to 'make do', hosting numerous Russian and Chinese diplomatic guests as well as any passing travellers from home. Travellers such as Ralph Cobbold and the archaeologist Sir Aurel Stein repeatedly expressed their amazement to the India and Foreign offices at the unsupported state in which Macartney attempted to represent British interests in Kashgar. These recommendations bore fruit in 1890 when Macartney was made CIE and again in 1913 when he was promoted to KCIE, an elevation which coincided with the completion of a grand new consulate-general on the site of his old native house, Chini Bagh. The building had gone ahead after he had finally been recognized by the Russians and Chinese as consul-general in 1910.

On his retirement in August 1918 Macartney left Kashgar amid warm farewells. He travelled first to Tashkent, where a British mission was endeavouring to establish friendly relations with the Bolsheviks. The Russians held Macartney in high esteem but the mission nevertheless failed, whereupon Macartney, despairing of reaching England through the warring fronts of 1918, turned round and undertook the long journey back to India. Ironically, after twenty-eight years without military assistance, the first formal bodyguard arrived to protect the Kashgar consulate-general just as he was leaving it.

On his arrival in Britain, Macartney recorded his experiences in 'Bolshevism as I saw it at Tashkent in 1918' (*Journal of the Royal Central Asian Society*, 7, 1920, 42–55). Much earlier he had published a monograph on Chinese imperialism, *Eastern Turkistan: the Chinese as Rulers over an Alien Race* (1909), but otherwise he remained silent about his career. His wife was less reticent and in 1931 published an amusing account of her Kashgar years, *An English Lady in Chinese Turkestan*. In retirement Macartney settled at Jersey. He lived just long enough to see the Channel Islands freed from German occupation, dying at his home, 4 Overseas Dicq Road, St Saviour, Jersey, after a long illness on 19 May 1945. His wife and their three children, Eric, Sylvia, and Robin, survived him. KATHERINE PRIOR

Sources C. P. Skrine and P. Nightingale, *Macartney at Kashgar* (1973) · Lady Macartney, *An English lady in Chinese Turkestan* (1931) · *DNB* · *The Times* (25 May 1945), 7 · T. L. Ormiston, *Dulwich College register, 1619 to 1926* (1926)
Archives BL OIOC, Bailey corresp., MS Eur. F 157 · Bodl. Oxf., Stein MSS · Mitchell L., NSW, G. E. Morrison corresp.
Likenesses photograph, 1913, repro. in Skrine and Nightingale, *Macartney at Kashgar*, facing p. 132
Wealth at death £11,535 12s. 9d.—in England: administration with will, 13 Aug 1946, *CGPLA Eng. & Wales*

Macartney, Sir (Samuel) Halliday (1833–1906), official in Chinese government service, born near Castle Douglas on 24 May 1833, was the youngest son of Robert Macartney of Dundrennan House, Kirkcudbrightshire, and Elizabeth, daughter of Ebenezer Halliday of Slagnaw. Educated at the Castle Douglas Academy, at the age of fifteen Halliday went as a clerk into a merchant's office in Liverpool, and in 1852 entered Edinburgh University to study medicine. In 1855, while still a medical student, he joined the medical staff of the Anglo-Turkish contingent in the Crimean War, and was with them at the occupation of Kerch. He graduated MD at Edinburgh in 1858, and, after joining the army medical department, was in September of that year promoted to the 99th regiment as third assistant surgeon. He accompanied his regiment to Calcutta, where it remained until, early in 1860, it was ordered to China. He served in the Chinese war of that year, taking part in the advance on Peking (Beijing). Thus began his long connection with China.

From December 1860 Macartney was stationed for fifteen months in Canton (Guangzhou), and at the end of February 1862 he went with two companies to Shanghai, which was then threatened by the Taipings. He served under General Charles William Dunbar Staveley but,

Sir (Samuel) Halliday Macartney (1833–1906), by unknown photographer

seeking a wider career than that of an army doctor, in October 1862 he resigned in order to join the service of China. Faced with increasing pressure from Western powers and, internally, the Taiping uprising, the Chinese authorities had begun to cast off their traditional suspicion of foreigners. In 1860 an American adventurer, Frederick T. Ward, was engaged by the Chinese business community in Shanghai to set up a 'foreign legion' to divert the Taiping insurgents from their city, which in 1862 received from the emperor the name Ever Victorious Army. In November 1862 Macartney became military secretary to Ward's successor, Henry A. Burgevine, and was spoken of as a possible successor on Burgevine's dismissal. Macartney, however, desired permanently to enter the Chinese government service in the capacity of interpreter and adviser, for which he had qualified himself by learning the language.

Macartney became closely attached to Li Hongzhang, later one of China's great statesmen, who appointed him, with the grade of colonel in the Chinese service, to command a separate contingent of Chinese troops which co-operated with Gordon. In the late summer of 1863 he took Fengching (Fengqing) and Seedong. At this time also he turned to account his knowledge of chemistry acquired at Edinburgh by instructing the Chinese in the manufacture of gunpowder, percussion caps, and other munitions. With Li Hongzhang's support he began an arsenal at Sungkiang (Songjiang), which was developed at Soochow (Suzhou) after it was recaptured from the Taipings; finally, after the end of the uprising the arsenal was permanently established in 1865 at Nanking (Nanjing). Chinese reliance on the technical expertise of Westerners—it has been described as 'a blind faith in the ability of foreigners, regardless of their training and experience' (Hsü, 283)—was in this case misplaced: it was discovered in 1874 that the guns cast at Nanking were useless for the defence of Formosa (Taiwan), being capable of firing only dummies for salutes.

Macartney's diplomatic tact and knowledge of Chinese language and character were brought into play when he was called upon to act as intermediary between Gordon and the Chinese generals, especially Li Hongzhang, with whom Gordon was incensed for the massacre of the Taiping leaders at Soochow after the surrender of that city. Macartney's intervention aroused Gordon's resentment, and he denounced Macartney in a letter which was published in a blue book in 1864, but subsequently friendship between the two men was renewed. In 1864 Macartney married at Soochow a Chinese lady, occasionally described as a member of a princely family, with whom he had a daughter and three sons; the eldest son was Sir George *Macartney (1867–1945). Mrs Macartney died in 1878.

Macartney was in charge of the arsenal at Nanking for ten years (1865–75), during which he paid a short visit to Europe in 1873–4. In 1875 his appointment was terminated, owing to disagreement with the Chinese authorities, but the Margary incident of the same year led to the sending of a Chinese mission to London and the permanent appointment of a Chinese representative at the court of St James in 1877. Macartney was appointed secretary to the embassy, and went back to England. He never returned to China, but remained in Europe, helping to organize the diplomatic relations of the Chinese government, visiting Paris and St Petersburg; for nearly thirty years, from 1877 to 1906, he held the position first of secretary and then of counsellor and English secretary to the Chinese legation in London. In that capacity he advised the Chinese government in all negotiations and entirely identified himself with Chinese interests. He was made a mandarin of the second degree, with the distinction of the peacock's feather, and was given the second-grade order of the Double Dragon of China, and the first class of the Chinese order of the Precious Star. He was made a CMG in 1881 and KCMG in 1885. On 12 August 1884 he married Jeanne (d. 1904), daughter of Jean Leon du Sautoy of Fontainbleu, with whom he had a further three sons and a daughter. He retired at the beginning of 1906. He died at his home at Kenbank, Dalry, Kirkcudbrightshire, on 8 June in that year, and was buried in the family burying-ground at Dundrennan. C. P. LUCAS, rev. K. D. REYNOLDS

Sources D. C. Boulger, The life of Sir Halliday Macartney (1908) · The Times (9 June 1906) · London and China Telegraph (11 June 1906) · I. C. Y. Hsü, The rise of modern China, 5th edn (1995) · A. J. Sargent, Anglo-Chinese commerce and diplomacy (1907) · Burke, Peerage · WWW

Likenesses photograph, repro. in Boulger, Life of … Macartney [see illus.]

Wealth at death £13,993 15s.: probate, 25 July 1906, CGPLA Eng. & Wales

Macartney, James (1770–1843), anatomist, was born on 8 March 1770 at Armagh, the youngest of the six surviving children of James Macartney (d. 1790), gentleman farmer of Ballyrea, co. Armagh, and Mary (d. 1788), the eldest of the five children of John Maxwell, a Presbyterian minister in Armagh, and former moderator of the Presbyterian synod, and Rose Carson of Strabane. Macartney was educated privately and at the classical school, Armagh, but had an inability to remember lessons, retain information derived from books, or to master Euclid and maths (Thornton, 164). He was a radical Presbyterian and may have inherited his unitarian beliefs from his mother. Macartney's father, though nominally a Presbyterian, associated himself with no particular church and rarely attended service.

Macartney served as a clerk to his cousins' linen business in Newry but on the death of his father in 1790 he returned home to farm the family property with his brothers until he moved to Dublin to study surgery. In March 1794 he was apprenticed to William Hartigan, professor of anatomy in the Royal College of Surgeons in Ireland, and on 10 August 1795 he married Mary Ekenhead of Newry. He also studied chemistry at Trinity College. In 1796, with Hartigan's consent, Macartney moved to London to continue his professional education and during the next three years attended several of the London hospital schools, as well as the Great Windmill Street school. In 1798, the final year of his apprenticeship, Macartney was appointed demonstrator in anatomy to Abernethy at St Bartholomew's Hospital at a salary of £50 per year. He dissected so much during the summer of 1799 that his health became weakened, so that he was unable to walk without the aid of a stick. On 6 February 1800 Macartney became a member of the Royal College of Surgeons of London and immediately afterwards was appointed lecturer in comparative anatomy at St Bartholomew's medical school, commencing his first course of lectures in March 1800. He continued to lecture there until his resignation in 1811. Macartney had illustrated his lectures with anatomical specimens made partly at his own expense. The hospital then claimed these as their own property, forcing Macartney to pay for a duplicate set. It was this, plus further disputes, which caused Macartney to resign his post. Macartney combined his lecturing duties rather improbably with the position of surgeon to the Radnor militia, to which he was appointed early in 1803. Macartney also supervised William Ross's Lectures on Comparative Anatomy (1802), a translation of Georges Cuvier's Leçons d'anatomie comparée. In March 1811 Macartney was elected a fellow of the Royal Society and in August of that year he returned to Ireland with his regiment.

On the termination of his military duties in 1812 Macartney determined to remain in Ireland and to seek the chair of anatomy and surgery in Trinity College—given that its holder, his old master, Hartigan, was seriously ill. Hartigan died in December 1812 and on 21 June of the following year Macartney was appointed in his place. He had obtained the degree of MD from the University of St Andrews a month earlier. On 3 July 1813 he was given an honorary MD degree by Trinity College.

As professor of anatomy Macartney was obliged to deliver a course of twelve public lectures, open to all students of the university, as well as a course of systematic lectures on five days of the week, and to superintend the work of the dissecting room. The professorship carried with it the office of clinical physician to Sir Patrick Dun's Hospital and Macartney had to deliver clinical lectures in the hospital to the students of the medical school. The theme of his introductory lecture, delivered to 'an overflowing house' (Crosse, 59), on 1 November 1813 was the importance of anatomy in medical study. It appears that Macartney also took part in body snatching and in February 1814 was arrested by soldiers but subsequently released (Crosse, 64). In Macartney's first year fifty-three students entered for the systematic course and twenty-one for dissections. In the following year he and Arthur Jacob established the National Eye Dispensary in North Cumberland Street. He obtained leave from the board of the university for Jacob to lecture in the medical school on the anatomy and diseases of the eye, and for John Pentland, afterwards master of the Rotunda Hospital, to lecture on midwifery, a subject that was not at the time taught in Trinity College. The number of students increased rapidly, reaching 303 in 1820. It would be incorrect to attribute the entire expansion in medical student numbers to Macartney—the numbers in arts were also rising at the time—but his reputation, his acknowledged ability in general science, physiology, surgery, and comparative anatomy attracted many Irish students who would otherwise have gone to Edinburgh, and even a few from England and Scotland. William Stokes later referred to the Trinity medical school of 1820 as 'a grammar school of anatomy and book medicine and little more' but, according to R. B. McDowell and D. A. Webb, it was this very programme as taught by Macartney that drew in the students who were later to benefit from the clinical teaching of Stokes and his equally renowned colleague, Robert James Graves (McDowell and Webb, 89). On 16 August 1824 he was elected to an honorary fellowship of the King and Queen's College of Physicians in Ireland and on 25 October 1824 he was admitted a licentiate. On 21 August 1833 an honorary MD from the University of Cambridge was conferred on him.

Macartney resigned his chair on 11 July 1837 after a protracted and bitter dispute with his faculty colleagues and the board of the university over the time of his lectures. Alexander Macalister claimed in his memoir that 'by their own act, and by a continuous course of petty annoyances and persecutions, the University of Dublin lost the services of the greatest teacher, the best anatomist, the most philosophic surgeon that Ireland has ever produced'. This was typical Macalister hagiography. Macartney's resignation owed more to his own disputatious and truculent nature than to intransigence on the university's part. He was an able and progressive teacher, conscientious and hard-working, and committed to the cause of educational and medical reform. He was, in the eyes of his contemporaries, the finest anatomist and physiologist that Ireland had produced. But he was also egotistical, quarrelsome, hot-tempered, outspoken, difficult, obdurate, and unpopular with his medical and academic colleagues. His obituarist in the *Dublin Medical Press* (8 March 1843, 160)—possibly his old associate, Arthur Jacob, who was one of the joint owners and editors—in a balanced appraisal, wrote:

> Dr Macartney had, like every other man, his faults and his failings, which, unlike the majority of men, he neither concealed nor varnished; but, on the other hand, he had his perfections and his merits. He nurtured in his breast a spirit of independence rarely to be met with, and a conscientious respect and regard for truth and honour not often found among persons making greater professions.

However, in his diary Macartney claimed that he had been wrongly seen as:

> supposed unrelenting to solicitation—devoid of compassion, more tenacious of my own opinion than desirous to find the truth—penurious & even miserly, harsh & tyrannical to those in my power … I have also been considered by some people as unsteady in carrying my purposes into effect & of being indolent & changeable & I have been told that I have no predilection for the fair sex, nor love for children by Le Deville the phrenologist. If I was to name any person whom I have ever known as possessing the opposite qualities in the greatest degree that person would be myself. (Thornton, 164–5)

In politics Macartney was an active member of The Society of United Irishmen and while in Newry 'formed a similar organization at Armagh' (Thornton, 167).

In 1836 Macartney sold the museum of anatomical and pathological preparations that he had collected in Dublin to Cambridge University for an annual payment of £100 for ten years. He died at his residence, 31 Upper Merrion Street, Dublin, on 6 March 1843, probably from apoplexy. He was buried at Mount Jerome cemetery three days later. LAURENCE M. GEARY

Sources A. Macalister, *James Macartney* (1900) · Royal College of Physicians of Ireland, Kildare Street, Dublin 2, Kirkpatrick Archive · R. B. McDowell and D. A. Webb, *Trinity College, Dublin, 1592–1952: an academic history* (1982) · T. P. C. Kirkpatrick, *History of the medical teaching in Trinity College, Dublin, and of the School of Physic in Ireland* (1912) · *The Lancet*, 8 (1825), 85–9, 248–52, 308 · *Dublin Medical Press* (8 March 1843), 160; (29 March 1843), 287 · J. L. Thornton, 'A diary of James Macartney (1770–1843): with notes on his writings', *Medical History*, 12 (1968), 164–73 · V. M. Crosse, *A surgeon in the early nineteenth century: the life and times of John Greene Crosse* (1968) · records, Mount Jerome cemetery, Harold's Cross, Dublin

Archives priv. coll., diary [transcript in medical library of St Bartholomew's Hospital, London]

Likenesses plaster bust, 1832 (after R. J. H. Troy), U. Cam. · W. F. Fry, engraving (after Kiernan), Royal College of Physicians of Ireland, Dublin; repro. in Macalister, *James Macartney*

MacAskill, Henry (*fl.* 1948). *See under* Knoydart, Seven Men of (*act.* 1948).

Macassey, Sir Lynden Livingston (1876–1963), industrial lawyer, was born on 14 June 1876 in Carrickfergus, Larne, co. Antrim, the eldest son of Luke Livingston Macassey, a civil engineer of Belfast and later a barrister and parliamentary draftsman in London, and his wife, Agnes White.

His younger brother Ernest Livingston Macassey (*d.* 1947) became a Church of England clergyman, whose pastoral work was principally in deprived London parishes. He was educated at Upper Sullivan School, Holywood, co. Down; Bedford School; Trinity College, Dublin; and the University of London. He was trained as an engineer, at one stage serving an apprenticeship on the Clyde where he was later to figure so prominently in labour disputes. Like his father he turned to law, being called to the bar in 1899 by the Middle Temple. He received a BA and LLB from Dublin in 1900 (proceeding to MA and LLD in 1905). On 15 April 1903 he married Jeanne, only child of Robert McFarland of Melbourne and Barooga, New South Wales; they had two sons and one daughter. From 1901 to 1909 he lectured on economics and law at the London School of Economics, and from 1903 to 1906 he was secretary to the royal commission on London traffic, for which he visited the major cities of the United States. He meanwhile practised at the bar and became KC in 1912.

During the First World War, Macassey's combination of the professions of engineer and lawyer led to his appointment as a Board of Trade arbitrator in shipbuilding and engineering disputes from 1914 to 1916. He was particularly involved in the industrial unrest among munitions workers on the Clyde. He was a member of a government commission on Clyde munitions workers' grievances and in that capacity produced, with Lord Balfour of Burleigh, a report in 1915. Many of its recommendations were incorporated into the 1916 Munitions of War (Amendment) Act, in particular those designed to prevent employers' abuse of leaving certificates (which had been introduced to prevent skilled men leaving work of national importance but were used by some employers to discipline their workforce).

Macassey soon became a more controversial figure on the Clyde. A principal source of unrest in the munitions industry was the government's need, given the shortage of labour, to 'dilute' the workforce through the introduction of women or relatively unskilled men into jobs previously reserved for craftsmen who had served their apprenticeships. In January 1916 he was sent to the Clyde as the head of a body of dilution commissioners to implement this policy. From his regular contacts with ordinary workmen, he was convinced that most unrest was the consequence of small grievances which were allowed to fester. He therefore targeted the key factories and negotiated agreements with both sides of industry, securing the appointment of joint committees of employers and shop stewards to oversee their implementation and record any agreed divergences. He made himself available 'at all times of day and night'. In March 1916, however, the dilution commissioners led an attack on the Clyde Workers' Committee, which they believed was leading the continued resistance to dilution, and they secured the deportation from Glasgow of one of its leaders, David Kirkwood, and four colleagues. This action, because of its implications for civil liberties and workers' control, became a *cause célèbre* for labour historians during the industrial militancy of the 1970s. From his own reports to the Ministry of Munitions, it is clear that Macassey had recommended deportation as early as December 1915 and during March 1916 was subject to major mood swings and paranoia about the presence of German spies in Glasgow (McLean, 70, 83–4). Unlike the other participants, he never recanted these views (*Parl. papers*, 1914–16, 29, Cd 8136).

Following the Clyde Workers' Committee deportations dilution was accepted on the Clyde, and Macassey set about enforcing dilution in Barrow in Furness. In 1917 he was appointed KBE and became director of shipyard labour for the Admiralty until 1918. From 1917 to 1919 he served on the war cabinet committees on labour and on women in industry. He then became one of the labour assessors for the British government on the Permanent Court of International Justice at The Hague. In 1920 he represented the employers in the court of inquiry at which Ernest Bevin earned himself the title of 'the dockers' KC' by his advocacy of the workers' case. It is generally agreed that the employers' choice of lawyer, and his heavy reliance on bald statistical evidence to combat Bevin's more emotional arguments, were mistakes (Clegg, 257).

In 1922 Macassey wrote *Labour Policy: False and True* and thereafter occupied many honorific positions in public life, being at times a bencher (1922) and treasurer (1935) of the Middle Temple, and an honorary fellow and chairman of the governors of Queen Mary College, London, master of the Drapers' Company, and president of the Institute of Arbitrators. He also had a long association with the Scottish Amicable Life Assurance Society Ltd, and was its president until 1962. He died at his London home, 37 Alexandra Court, Queen's Gate, on 23 February 1963.

RODNEY LOWE

Sources DNB · *The Times* (25 Feb 1963) · *WWW* · *Thom's Irish who's who* (1923) · Walford, *County families* (1919) · J. Harris, *William Beveridge*, 2nd edn (1997) · I. McLean, *The legend of red Clydeside* (1983) · J. Hinton, 'The Clyde Workers Committee and the dilution struggle', *Essays in labour history*, ed. A. Briggs and J. Saville (1971) · H. A. Clegg, A. Fox, and A. F. Thompson, *A history of British trade unions since 1889*, 2 (1985) · *CGPLA Eng. & Wales* (1963)
Archives PRO, ministry of munitions MSS, MUN 5/73
Wealth at death £5425 16s.: probate, 23 May 1963, *CGPLA Eng. & Wales*

Mc Ateer, Edward [Eddie] (1914–1986), politician, was born on 25 January 1914 at Coatbridge, near Glasgow, the second son of Hugh Mc Ateer (1879–1963) and his wife, Bridget Doherty (1879–1961), who were both migratory farm labourers from the north of Ireland. When Eddie was two his family returned to Derry, where his father obtained work as a docker. As a youth, Eddie Mc Ateer was charged, along with his three brothers, with IRA offences, but was acquitted. A brilliant student at the nearby Brow of the Hill Christian Brothers' School, he secured high marks in the Northern Ireland civil service examination of 1930, and was employed in the income tax department.

After studying accountancy at night, Mc Ateer abandoned the civil service and went to work for the Derry firm of accountants McCambridges, before starting his own practice (which survived his death). On 28 February 1941 he married Rose Ellen McGee (1916–1988), the daughter of a local publican. Active in the local nationalist organization, Mc Ateer was elected to the Stormont parliament for the Mid-Derry constituency in June 1945. He was instrumental, in November of that year, in setting up the Anti-Partition League (APL), which strove for a rejuvenated campaign against the division of Ireland, and involved all 'nationally minded' groups and representatives, acting in liaison with southern Irish political parties and overseas interests, including sympathizers among the new British Labour government. Mc Ateer was elected vice-chairman of the APL.

The hopes of the APL soon proved to be illusory: most well-disposed British labourites were more concerned with the discriminatory practices of the Belfast government than with the partitionist settlement, and opinion in the twenty-six counties of the south remained apathetic. In May 1948 Mc Ateer, speaking in Galway, accused southern Irish public opinion of being 'more concerned with the price of beef and eggs' (Staunton, 'The northern nationalist political tradition', 238) than with the plight of co-religionists across the border. Later that year, in an appeal to northern nationalist self-reliance, he called for a civil disobedience in a pamphlet entitled *Irish Action*. Within months, however, southern support unexpectedly materialized when the twenty-six counties declared themselves to be a republic and left the Commonwealth. When Britain reaffirmed the integrity of the Union, a decision later formalized in the Ireland Act, and Lord Brookeborough, the prime minister of Northern Ireland, called a snap general election for February 1949, the southern parties in a burst of national feeling convened an anti-partition conference, which floated a fund raised by chapel gate collections in the republic to finance APL candidates, without having first consulted the APL. In a bitterly fought sectarian contest, the nationalist vote increased to more than 100,000, with nine of its seventeen candidates being returned, including Mc Ateer. But the Unionist vote was almost two and a half times that figure, and their stock was at its height with both the British and American establishments, who remembered with some bitterness Éire's wartime neutrality. It was an unpropitious time to promote the cause of Irish nationalism.

After the defeat of Congressman Fogarty's anti-partition resolution in the US congress in 1950, it was downhill all the way for the league. By 1953, in the face both of increasing southern disengagement and northern nationalist demoralization, Mc Ateer was reportedly contemplating a breakup of the organization, which was by then fragmenting into three groups: one in Omagh, co. Tyrone, centred on the *Ulster Herald* newspaper chain; a south Armagh faction linked to militant republicanism; and Mc Ateer's own Derry City stronghold, which he now represented in the Belfast parliament (he transferred to the Foyle constituency in 1953 to oppose the sitting member, Patrick Maxwell, whose nationalism he regarded as increasingly ineffectual). Mc Ateer, who understood better than most the inevitability of a republican resurgence (his brother Hugh had been IRA chief of staff in the 1940s

and continued to act as a link man between that movement and the Dublin government) counselled a more proactive approach by that government to halt their advance. When in late 1954 the southern parliament (the Dáil) decisively rejected a proposal that northern nationalists be given a symbolic voice in its chambers, he condemned its 'Kathleen Mavourneen policy on partition' (Staunton, 'The northern nationalist political tradition', 286), and in 1956 displayed a strict neutrality as the Omagh Group unsuccessfully attempted to reverse the Sinn Féin electoral advance in the previous year's Westminster election. When the IRA campaign commenced in late 1956 Mc Ateer informed the Dublin government's department of external affairs that Unionist politicians had recognized to a colleague that the violence had its roots in the 'secondary aspects of partition' (ibid., 317–20), that is, in discrimination and gerrymandering, and he therefore proposed that a new, intergovernmental initiative should focus on these matters.

This approach and the internal discussion it generated may be seen justifiably as the beginning of Dublin's new course on Northern Ireland, later to become synonymous with the premiership of Sean Lemass. But Mc Ateer was no advocate of conciliation within the northern province. In 1958 he was instrumental in having a decision that the Nationalist Party become the official opposition at Stormont reversed, although he was defeated at the same meeting in a contest for the leadership of the party by the proposer of the motion, the ageing Joe Stewart. The same year he rejected as treachery the demands for Catholic co-operation with the state which were advanced at the social studies conference in Garron Tower, co. Antrim.

In 1964, on Stewart's death, Mc Ateer became leader of the Nationalist Party, and introduced a thirty-nine point plan for a new, streamlined organization with more vibrant policies. The following year he led the party into the role of official opposition, on the advice of Cardinal Conway. Increasingly, his belief in the Lemass line, that membership of the European Economic Community would lead to a 'lowering of the border', gave way to a fear of abandonment by Dublin. Active in the lobbying of representatives on the issue of discrimination, he lent support to the campaign for social justice and later to the Northern Ireland Civil Rights Association, and though he counselled moderation, he marched in the 5 October 1968 demonstration in Derry city, where he was among those savagely batoned by the Royal Ulster Constabulary.

Electorally, Mc Ateer's position had been under challenge since the late 1950s, with Labour candidates securing up to, and more than, one third of the vote. In February 1969 John Hume, a young Credit Union manager associated with the civil rights movement, succeeded in ousting him from his parliamentary seat. In an attempt to stage a comeback in the assembly elections of 1973 Mc Ateer approached the republican movement with a request that they encourage their abstentionist supporters to back him against Hume's Social Democratic and Labour Party (SDLP), but was turned down. In 1977 he supported his son Fergus in the formation of the Irish

Independence Party (IIP), as a more nationalist alternative to the SDLP but unconnected with the violence of the IRA, and joined the party's Derry city branch. He warmly welcomed a suggestion by the republic's taoiseach, Jack Lynch, that amnesties for paramilitaries would be considered by his government in the event of a ceasefire. When the IIP vanished from the scene after Sinn Féin's electoral interventions of the 1980s, he retired. Eddie Mc Ateer died of a stroke in Derry city on 25 March 1986, and was buried in the city cemetery on 27 March in a funeral attended by a large gathering, which included representatives of both Sinn Féin and the SDLP. His wife survived him.

A grey-haired and avuncular man of imposing physical presence and ready wit, the father of ten children (six boys and four girls), Mc Ateer was in many respects ahead of the prejudices within his own community. In the clericalist 1950s he was, for instance, only one of two nationalist representatives who were not members of the Catholic church-linked, semi-secret organization, the Knights of Columbanus. It was ultimately his tragedy that he was too old to capture the popular imagination when the grievances of northern Catholics, which he had articulated throughout his adult life, finally gained the attention of a hitherto indifferent world.   ENDA STAUNTON

Sources E. Staunton, 'The northern nationalist political tradition', PhD diss., Queen's University, Belfast, 1993 · E. Staunton, 'A matter of votes', *Fortnight* (Feb 1997) · E. Staunton, *The nationalists of Northern Ireland* (2001) · private information (2004)
Archives NA Ire., Department of Taoiseach 'S' files and Department of Foreign Affairs files · NRA, priv. coll. · PRO NIre., corresp. | PRO NIre., Cahir Healy MSS | FILM RTE Archive Library, Dublin, news footage | SOUND RTE Archive Library, Dublin
Likenesses photographs, repro. in *Derry Journal*

Macaulay, Aulay (1758–1819), Church of England clergyman and writer, was born at Lismore, Argyll, on 20 October 1758, the eldest son of John *Macaulay (1720–1789) [*see under* Macaulay, Zachary], Church of Scotland minister, and his second wife, Margaret Campbell (d. 1790). Zachary *Macaulay was his brother and Thomas Babington Macaulay was his nephew. He was educated at home and then at Glasgow University, whence he graduated MA in 1778. While in residence he contributed to *Ruddiman's Magazine* under the pseudonym Academicus. After acting for three years as tutor to the sons of Joseph Foster Barham at Bedford he took holy orders in the Church of England and obtained a curacy at Claybrooke, Leicestershire, in 1781. He remained there until 1789, when he was appointed rector of Frolesworth, in the same county, but he resigned that living in 1790. In 1785 he had been admitted at Sidney Sussex College, Cambridge, to study divinity but, although he completed the course, he decided against the expense of graduation.

In 1793 Macaulay went on a tour in Holland and Belgium, writing an account of his travels for the *Gentleman's Magazine* (1793–4). In 1794, as travelling tutor to one of the sons of Sir Walter Farquhar, he visited the court of the duke of Brunswick and gave English lessons to his daughter, afterwards Queen Caroline, in the course of which he

gained the regard of her mother, the duchess. In 1796, after his return, Macaulay was presented by his brother-in-law Thomas Babington MP to the living of Rothley in Leicestershire. He married Ann Heyrick (*bap.* 1774), daughter of John Heyrick, town clerk of Leicester, and his wife, Mary, at St Margaret's, Leicester, on 19 September 1797. In 1815 he made another tour on the continent, again publishing accounts in the *Gentleman's Magazine* (1815–17).

Macaulay spent over thirty years working on a life of Melancthon but this massive project was never published. He also considered editing an abridged version of Alexander Pope's works. His own published works include *Essays* (1780), *The History and Antiquities of Claybrooke*, which was published separately as well as in John Nichols's *Queries Proposed to the Nobility, Gentry, and Clergy, of Leicestershire* (1787?), and sermons recommending the Anglican liturgy and Sunday schools. He died of apoplexy on 24 February 1819 and was survived by his wife and eight sons. He should not be confused with Aulay Macaulay (1673–1758), father of Kenneth Macaulay.

Macaulay's second son, **Colin Campbell Macaulay** (*bap.* 1800, *d.* 1853), solicitor and historian, was baptized at Rothley on 7 January 1800. Having been educated at Rugby School he travelled in Portugal, and in 1831 he became partner in a firm of solicitors at Leicester. He was president of the Leicester Literary and Philosophical Society in 1847 and 1848, and contributed historical papers on Cardinal Wolsey (1849), the duke of Marlborough (1850), and Queen Elizabeth (1851). On 30 April 1850 he married Mary Kendall Wood, eldest daughter of Richard Warner Wood; they had a son and a daughter. He died on 20 October 1853 at Knighton Lodge, Leicester, and was buried at Rothley.

G. LE G. NORGATE, *rev.* EMMA MAJOR

Sources *GM*, 1st ser., 89/1 (1819), 276–7 · Venn, *Alum. Cant.* · ESTC · G. O. Trevelyan, *The life and letters of Lord Macaulay*, 2 vols. (1876) · Nichols, *Lit. anecdotes*, 9.82–6 · IGI
Archives Trinity Cam., letters to John Nichols Babington

Macaulay [*née* Young], **Carola** (*b.* 1682), milliner and shopkeeper, was born on 19 February 1682 at Kippen, Stirlingshire, one of three children of the Revd Robert Young, minister at Kippen, and Margaret MacFarlane. She is a good example of an eighteenth-century woman from a professional family background who, even after her marriage, continued in business. She had no inherited right to trade but was allowed to do so on payment of an annual due to the Edinburgh Merchant Company. Before her marriage she set up in partnership as a milliner and shopkeeper with Helen Gilchrist under the name of Carola Young & Co. Her business with the merchants John Bell and Robert Blackwood, the latter an agent for many well-known merchants and traders in the burgh, shows her as part of the Edinburgh trading community. Significantly, Blackwood was a witness to the baptism of her first child.

In 1710 Carola Young married Archibald Macaulay (*d.* 1761), later lord provost of Edinburgh and an elder of West Kirk, Edinburgh. When Macaulay, also from outside Edinburgh, asked to enter the Edinburgh Merchant Company in 1710 it was noted in the minutes that 'he is now married to Carola Young', implying that he made use of her right to trade, she already being a member of the company (Merchant Company of Edinburgh minute books). The Macaulays had three children: Carola (*b.* 29 Nov 1712), George (*b.* 28 Sept 1716), and Anne (*b.* 26 April 1723). Many of Carola's bills survive in family papers, signed either Carola Young or Carola Macaulay. In 1748, when Carola sued a debtor, a witness, Margaret Christie, described herself in court as 'shopkeeper to Mrs Macaulay', stating that she knew Mrs Macaulay had 'sold and furnished the goods' and that she herself had assisted in making them up and had seen them delivered (Edinburgh commissary court processes, 1748). The date of Carola's death is unknown. Archibald Macaulay died on 7 January 1761; Carola's name does not appear on his large tombstone in Greyfriars kirkyard, Edinburgh.

ELIZABETH C. SANDERSON

Sources Edinburgh City Archives, Merchant Company of Edinburgh, minute books, 1681–1724 · ledger of John Bell, Edinburgh merchant, NA Scot., GD 241/434 · letter book of Robert Blackwood, Edinburgh merchant, NA Scot., GD 1/564/12 · parish register extract from Kippen, Stirlingshire, NA Scot., Cunningham-Graham MSS, GD 22/1/146 · Edinburgh commissary court register of testaments, NA Scot., 7 Jan 1761 · Edinburgh commissary court processes, 1748, NA Scot. · *Fasti Scot.*, new edn
Archives NA Scot., ledger of John Bell, Edinburgh merchant · NA Scot., ledger of Robert Blackwood, Edinburgh merchant

Macaulay [*née* Sawbridge; *other married name* Graham], **Catharine** (1731–1791), historian and political polemicist, was born on 2 April 1731 at Olantigh in the parish of Wye, Kent, second daughter of John Sawbridge (1699–1762), landowner, and Elizabeth Wanley (*d.* 1733), daughter of London banker George Wanley of Tottenham, Middlesex. As well as her elder sister, Mary, she had two brothers, Wanley and John *Sawbridge, who made a name for himself in radical politics.

Family and education The family's origins were among Warwickshire yeomanry, and when some of the family moved south in the early seventeenth century one branch gravitated towards Kent. Catharine's great-grandfather Isaac Sawbridge was in business in London and her grandfather Jacob, banker and stockbroker, was born in Canterbury. The Sawbridge family had already acquired some notoriety long before Catharine Macaulay was born, when Jacob Sawbridge became involved in the South Sea Bubble. Believing that an extension of credit was essential to the prosperity of the country, and resenting the monopoly position enjoyed by the Bank of England and its close relation to government, Jacob and his partners, 'the three capital sharpers of Britain', as Defoe called them, set out to exploit the South Sea scheme. When the crash came Sawbridge was deeply implicated. Despite the expropriation of a large part of his assets, he nevertheless managed to emerge a rich man. When half a century later Catharine Macaulay sought to vindicate her grandfather's memory, she argued that many from both houses of parliament were involved but managed to escape all punishment, and that Sawbridge was merely the unfortunate scapegoat.

Catharine Macaulay (1731–1791), by Robert Edge Pine, *c.*1775

Family fortunes, however, did not suffer long as Catharine's father was fortunate in marrying an heiress, and on her death in childbirth in 1733 he inherited her fortune, which he used to improve the family estate at Olantigh. Devastated by his wife's death, Sawbridge tended to cut himself off from society, and played little part in his daughters' education. In consequence Catharine had much time to herself. She and her sister were privately educated, and were left in the care of an antiquated and ignorant governess. Some have suggested her education was the result of daily foraging in her father's well-stocked library. Others insist her education was 'by no means distinguished from that of other young ladies of the same rank' (*European Magazine and London Review*, 4, 1783, 330). What is certain is that Catharine was a prolific reader, particularly in her twenties. She read Greek and Roman history, probably in translation, and later claimed that this had been the source of her republicanism and the inspiration to her turning historian. Her upbringing without parental direction was undoubtedly lonely and may well have made for a 'wayward, headstrong, young woman' but it gave her a rare independence and intellectual self-sufficiency (Peach, 117n.). Elizabeth Carter, meeting her in 1757 at a Canterbury assembly, was impressed by this 'fine, fashionable, well-dressed lady whose train was longer than anybody's train' and who 'took her mightily by way of conversation' (*Series of Letters*, 2.260–61).

Marriage, the *History*, and politics On 18 June 1760 Catharine married Dr George Macaulay (1715/16–1766), a Scottish physician, a few months after the death of his first wife, Leonora Maria Bathurst. He had left Edinburgh for London in 1752 and became physician and treasurer of the British Lying-in Hospital at Brownlow Street. Little is known of him, but Richard Baron was a close friend and he and Thomas Hollis were regular visitors at the Macaulays' house. Baron described George Macaulay as 'a most worthy and benevolent man' (*Diary of Sylas Neville*, 20). From all accounts the marriage was a happy one. Baron was fascinated and more than a little frightened by Catharine Macaulay. He described her as 'quite a phenomenon—a woman without passions', and thought her face 'as abstract as the print of Mr Locke' (Hollis, diary, entries for 6 and 13 Dec 1766). In 1766 George Macaulay died, aged fifty, leaving his widow with their only child, Catherine Sophia.

It was in the brief period of her first marriage that Catharine Macaulay embarked on her eight-volume *History of England*. For a woman to have conceived of such a project in the eighteenth century was extraordinary. That her husband actively encouraged her was equally remarkable. When her first volume was published in 1763 it was greeted with acclaim. Overnight she became 'the celebrated Mrs Macaulay'. But behind the praise she received there was condescension and the belief that the writing of history was not for women. On her first volume, for instance, the *Monthly Review* concentrated not on the nature of the history but on the fact that she was a woman. She was referred to as 'the fair Macaulay', 'our fair Historian'. After mild praise the *Review* expressed the wish that 'the same degree of genius and application had been exerted *in more suitable pursuits*', for the writing of history was not recommended 'to the practice of our lovely countrywomen' (*Monthly Review*, 29, 1763, 373).

The whigs welcomed the first volumes as a timely answer to what was seen as David Hume's tory interpretation of events. As the *History* proceeded, however, it became increasingly clear that Macaulay was no mere whig. It was when she reached her fourth volume in 1768, that dealt with the trial and execution of Charles I, that the gulf between her views and those of the whigs was revealed. It was in this volume that she talked for the first time of 'the rise of the republicans' who 'looked forward to the reformation of the principles, as well as the executive, of the government' (C. Macaulay, *History of England*, 4.160). The Commonwealth she saw as 'the brightest age that ever adorned the page of history' (ibid., 5.382). For her the events of the seventeenth century remained vividly alive, and they were in the process of being re-enacted in the present. Such views caused the Rockingham whigs to virtually abandon her, and such freely expressed republican ideas were an increasing embarrassment, as was her warmly expressed sympathy with the American colonists.

Catharine Macaulay further expounded her political views in two polemical pamphlets, *Loose remarks on certain positions to be found in Mr Hobbes's 'Philosophical rudiments of government and society'* (1767) and *Observations on a pamphlet entitled 'Thoughts on the cause of the present discontents'* (1770). Her *Observations* threw into relief her differences with the Rockingham whigs and emphasized her own startlingly radical politics. Burke and Macaulay differed fundamentally in their views of the causes of the political corruption which both believed threatened liberty. Burke believed in the perfection of the constitution established by the revolution settlement of 1688–9 and thought that the causes of the 'present discontents' lay in the recent resurgence of the power of the crown from which only strong and principled government of the Rockingham whigs could save the country. Macaulay thought that the revolution settlement itself had been the work of those who called themselves whigs but were in reality the 'enemies of public liberty' (Macaulay, *Observations*, 6–7, 10–11) and had diverted the revolution from its original radical course. Her proposed cures involved reactivating their radical programme by introducing shorter parliaments, a system of rotation of office, a place bill, and a more extended and equal power of election. For Americans the pamphlets had the effect of undermining their earlier conviction that the British constitution was the very best form of government and helped them to abandon constitutional monarchy as a model for a free government.

In this period Catharine Macaulay moved in at least two social circles in London. The first had originally been formed around John Wilkes and the Society of the Supporters of the Bill of Rights. Her brother John Sawbridge played a central role in the campaign organized by London radicals on Wilkes's behalf and for a time Catharine Macaulay frequently entertained John Wilkes and his daughter Polly. The second circle was a group of dissenters who tended to share her republican views, namely Thomas and Timothy Hollis, Richard Baron, and Sylas Neville. The growing hostility of the Rockingham whigs, combined with the criticisms levelled at the *History*, may have contributed to her decision to leave London for Bath in 1774 to improve her health that had been badly affected by the effort of completing volume 5 of the *History*.

Macaulay's claim to scholarship Catharine Macaulay's *History* has been attacked as a 'masterly example of how not to write history' and it has been claimed that she was no scholar (Peardon, 60). But research into the contents of her library, revealed by her *Catalogue of Tracts* of 1790, and careful examination of the sources she used in her *History* reveal a meticulous scholar. The *Catalogue of Tracts* (her purpose in publishing the catalogue remains obscure) consisted of 200 pages listing nearly 5000 tracts and sermons, mostly from the seventeenth century. Its range of tracts from the period 1640–50 is remarkable—even by present standards. She made good use of manuscripts in her *History* (seven are referred to in volume 1 alone). If it had not been for her public expressing impatience with the footnotes in her early volumes we might have had even more evidence of the sources she used and the care she took over them. The *Monthly Review* in assessing her first volume described it as 'collecting and digesting the political fragments which have escaped the researches of so many learned and ingenious men' (*Monthly Review*, 29, 1763, 373). It also suggests her originality in using sources others had passed over. She made extensive use of the *Parliamentary History*, and made constant reference to standard works such as Rushworth, Clarendon, Burnet, Ludlow, the state papers of John Thurloe, *Commons Journals*, Carte, and Whitelocke. She frequently cited Clarendon and Hume with whom she fundamentally disagreed, and her work reveals a familiarity with other historians, her friend William Harris, Rapin-Thoyras, James Ralph, and William Guthrie. It is no longer possible to dismiss her *History* as 'the clumsy old volumes'—as Lucy Donnelly described it. Remarkably, given the frequency with which her first four volumes appeared, no further volumes of the *History* were published during the following four years. She may well have found it difficult to resume without the facilities she enjoyed in London. Instead she produced in 1778 one volume of *The history of England from the revolution to the present time in a series of letters to a friend* [the Revd Thomas Wilson].

On arriving in Bath, Catharine Macaulay had taken a house in St James's Parade. She had been a widow for eight years and her daughter was still a child. She must have missed the social life of London and the involvement in London politics. Without the British Museum it was more difficult to work on her *History*. It was in these circumstances that the offer of a former acquaintance, an elderly member of the Society of the Supporters of the Bill of Rights, the Revd Thomas Wilson (1703–1784), a friend of both Wilkes and her brother, to share his house in Bath was irresistible. She was promised the free run of his library. She and her daughter were soon settled into Alfred House. Wilson at the time was seventy-three, a widower, and a lonely man much in need of company. He was reputed to give generously to charity but he was well able to afford it. His generosity extended to Catharine Macaulay. Shortly after her arrival in Alfred House, David Hume wrote to Hugh Blair:

> There is one Dr. Wilson, a man zealous for Liberty, who has made her a free and full Present of a house of £2,000 Value, has adopted her Daughter by all the Rites of Roman Jurisprudence, and intends to leave her all his Fortune, which is considerable. (*Letters of David Hume*, 2.321)

A cultured man, Wilson had an extensive library and was something of a book collector. He was a fervent Wilkite and remained loyal to Wilkes until his death.

Catharine Macaulay's decision to move into Alfred House proved a serious mistake. Wilson, increasingly senile, was clearly besotted with her. To celebrate her forty-sixth birthday, he seated her on a throne, so that she could attend to six odes of little poetic merit, written in her honour, and numerous adulatory addresses. The occasion did little to enhance her reputation. For all Wilson's devotion, her residence at Alfred House was not a happy one, and her health suffered.

In 1777 for reasons of health Macaulay decided to make a visit to Nice. Constant illness meant she got no further than Paris. There she began to recover her strength and eventually to entertain a very select group—the chevalier de Rigemont, the abbé de Colbert, the duc de Harcourt, the ducs de La Rochefoucauld-Liancourt, and the count of Sarsfield, as well as Madame Bocage and Madame Geoffrin. She was clearly gratified by her reception and the attentions of the great. Turgot, on asking her whether she wished to see Versailles, was told: 'I have no desire to see the residence of tyrants' (*Mémoires de Brissot*, 2.237). No doubt for reasons of security she was very careful in her relations with Benjamin Franklin, the American envoy, and did not entertain him. Throughout her visit she was constantly made aware of the excitement generated by the American revolution.

The second marriage and completion of the *History* On 19 December 1778, less than two years after moving in to Alfred House, Catharine Macaulay announced her marriage, to William Graham, a mate to a ship's surgeon, aged twenty-one. The scandal that followed was due less to her marrying beneath her and the discrepancy between the ages of bride and bridegroom than to the rumours of an earlier sexual liaison with Dr Graham, her new husband's brother. A celebrated quack doctor, he had recently moved to Bath and begun to treat Catharine Macaulay, who recommended him to her friends. Her second marriage and the ensuing scandal fatally damaged her reputation. From being the focus of public interest she passed into relative obscurity. Of the last thirteen years of her life very little is known.

Despite predictions that her second marriage would end Catharine Macaulay's career as historian, the *History* continued—two more volumes appeared in 1781 and the eighth and final volume in 1783. It was also predicted that the marriage would not last. It did, and to all appearances proved a happy one. In 1784 with her second husband she left for a visit to America of nearly a year. Already she and her *History* were well known in America. Among ideas that had influenced the course of the American War of Independence her *History* played a significant role. Through it she had become acquainted with Benjamin Franklin, Josiah Quincy, Benjamin Rush, Richard Henry Lee, John Adams, Ezra Styles, and Jonathan Mayhew, many of whom had come to Britain, where the Club of Honest Whigs welcomed them. Catharine Macaulay had frequently entertained them. On reaching America her first visit was to Mercy Otis Warren, wife of James Warren and sister of James Otis. With Mercy she had much in common. Indeed, it may have been Catharine Macaulay's influence that persuaded Mercy to become a historian. She went briefly to New York and met Richard Henry Lee who at this time was president of the continental congress. She spent ten days with the Washingtons at Mount Vernon. She continued to correspond with her many friends in America after she had returned to Britain.

Final works and death Ill health had dogged Catharine Macaulay's visit to America and on her return she went straight to the south of France in an effort to find a cure. When four years later news of the French Revolution reached England she was jubilant. The American revolution, she was convinced, had been its inspiration. In 1790 she published *Letters on Education*. It covered a wide range of ideas. She was in favour of co-education and called on parents to reject 'the absurd notion, that the education of females should be of an opposite kind to that of males' (C. Macaulay, *Letters on Education*, 1790, 47). She expressed enlightened views on the upbringing of children. Children, she wrote, should be fed on fruit, eggs, and vegetables, and only very occasionally should be given meat. Sugar was bad for the teeth. They should be encouraged to wash regularly. It was a mistake to use baby talk in addressing them. She also argued passionately against capital punishment, and declared that if there had to be executions they should not be public events. She also argued in favour of reform of penal law and the abolition of slavery, decrying the deplorable 'treatment given by some of our countrymen to their African slaves' (ibid.).

On the position of women, Macaulay argued that if it was better than it had been under slavery, 'we ... have no great reason to boast of our privileges, or of the candour and indulgence of the men towards us' (Macaulay, *Letters on Education*, 210). She criticized women for their passive acceptance of the claimed natural superiority of men. Women's weaknesses were the result of 'situation and education only'. The education of women was an essential ingredient to a happy marriage. She was under no illusion about the operation of the sexual double standard in eighteenth-century society. The reason for the very different attitudes adopted towards any 'deviations from chastity in the two sexes', was, she thought, the result of men treating women as their property and women being denied any rights over 'their own persons' (p. 220). But while Catharine Macaulay was clearly sympathetic to the condition of her sex, it was not a priority in her thought. Neither in her *History* nor in her political polemic do women occupy a place and she was not really concerned with the state of women's political representation. Until women were better educated, she thought, there was no hope of achieving political equality.

In 1790 Catharine Macaulay also published an impassioned response to Burke's *Reflections on the Revolution in France* (1790). This gave rise to a brief correspondence between her and Mary Wollstonecraft, in which both praised the other's work. Her answer to Burke raised once again their very different interpretations of the revolution of 1688 and what, if anything, it had achieved.

Recurring ill health forced Catharine Macaulay out of London to Binfield in Berkshire, where she died on 22 June 1791 'after a long and very painful illness' (*GM*). She was a remarkable woman. No other woman before her had written history of the kind that she wrote. Though not strictly a feminist she always behaved as though equality between the sexes already existed. She refused to go out of the room with the ladies after dining in mixed company. When she visited the British Museum while writing her earlier volumes, she asked to see the letters exchanged between James I and the duke of Buckingham. The librarian, 'observing that many of them were wholly unfit for the inspection of any one of her sex', asked that he might be allowed to select a few. 'Phoo', said she, 'a historian is of no sex', and then deliberately read through them all (Taylor, 1.209).   BRIDGET HILL

Sources *The diary of Sylas Neville, 1767–1788*, ed. B. Cozens-Hardy (1950) · *Mémoires de Brissot*, ed. M. F. de Montrol, 4 vols. (1830) · *Memoirs of Thomas Hollis*, ed. F. Blackburne, 2 vols. (1780) · T. Hollis, diary, Harvard U., Houghton L. · Walpole, *Corr.* · *GM*, 1st ser., 61 (1791), 589 · B. Hill, *The republican virago: the life and times of Catharine Macaulay* (1992) · B. Hill and C. Hill, 'Catharine Macaulay's *History* and her "Catalogue of tracts"', *Seventeenth Century*, 8 (1993), 269–85 · L. M. Donnelly, 'The celebrated Mrs Macaulay', *William and Mary Quarterly*, 6 (1949), 173–207 · *The letters of Mrs Elizabeth Montagu*, ed. M. Montagu, 4 vols. (1809–13) · *A series of letters between Mrs. Elizabeth Carter and Miss Catherine Talbot ... to which are added, letters from Mrs. Elizabeth Carter to Mrs. Vesey*, ed. M. Pennington, 2 vols. (1808) · J. Taylor, *Records of my life*, 2 vols. (1832) · T. P. Peardon, *The transition in historical writing* (1933) · *The letters of David Hume*, ed. J. Y. T. Greig, 2 vols. (1932) · R. E. Peach, *Historical houses in Bath* (1883) · 'Account of the life and writings of Mrs Catherine Macauley Graham', *European Magazine and London Review*, 4 (1783), 330–34 · E. Hasted, *The history and topographical survey of the county of Kent*, 2nd edn, 12 vols. (1797–1801); facs. edn (1972) · M. Hays, *Female biography, or, Memoirs of celebrated and illustrious women, of all ages and countries*, 6 vols. (1803), vol. 5
Archives BL, MS of history of England 1628–60, Add. MSS 28192–28195 · New York Historical Society | New York Historical Society, letters to Thomas Wilson
Likenesses J. Spilsbury, mezzotint, pubd 1764 (after C. Read), BM, NPG · J. Basire, line engraving, 1767 (after G. B. Cipriani), BM; repro. in C. Macaulay, *History of England* (1767), vol. 3 · R. E. Pine, oils, *c*.1775, NPG [*see illus.*] · J. F. Moore, marble statue, 1778, Reference Library, Warrington · R. Samuel, group portrait, oils, exh. 1779 (*The nine living muses of Great Britain*), NPG · M. le Jeune, stipple (after unknown artist), NPG · line engraving, BM, NPG · oils, NPG

Macaulay, Colin Campbell (*bap.* 1800, *d.* 1853). *See under* Macaulay, Aulay (1758–1819).

Macaulay, James (1817–1902), author, born in Edinburgh on 22 May 1817, was the eldest son of Alexander Macaulay (1783–1868), MD and FRCS Edinburgh, who in his later years moved from Edinburgh to practise in London, and was author of a *Dictionary of Medicine Designed for Popular Use* (1828). James was educated at the Edinburgh Academy, where A. C. Tait, the future archbishop of Canterbury, was among his fellow students. He then proceeded to Edinburgh University, where after taking the arts course he studied medicine. With his fellow student and lifelong friend, Edward Forbes (1815–1854), he went to Paris in 1837–8, and witnessed François Majendie's experiments on animals. According to Macaulay, both left the room 'disgusted less by the cruelty of the professor than by the heartlessness of the spectators'. Subsequently, Macaulay became a staunch anti-vivisectionist. After graduating both MA and MD at Edinburgh in 1838, he published *An Essay on Cruelty to Animals* (1839), which he followed many years later with *A Plea for Mercy to Animals* (1875) and *Vivisection: is it Scientifically Useful or Morally Justifiable?* (1881), both questions being answered in the negative.

On leaving university, Macaulay travelled as a tutor in Italy and Spain, and spent some months in Madeira, contributing 'Notes on the physical geography, geology and climate' of the island to the *Edinburgh New Philosophical Journal* for October 1840. He produced the letterpress for *Madeira, Illustrated by A. Picken* and edited *The Stranger*, both published in the same year. On settling in London, he joined the staff on the *Literary Gazette* in 1850, and married on 24 February 1860 Fanny Stokes, daughter of the Revd

George Stokes of Hope, Hanley. From 1858 to 1885 he was the editor of two weekly periodicals, the *Leisure Hour* (founded in 1852) and *Sunday at Home* (founded in 1854); he shared the editorship with William Stevens from 1885 to 1894. Both papers had moral and religious aims, and long enjoyed a wide circulation among young readers. Contributors to Macaulay's *Leisure Hour*, who were usually anonymous, included Archbishop Richard Whately, the naturalist F. T. Buckland, Canon George Rawlinson, and Arminius Vambéry. In July 1862 Macaulay was elected FRCS Edinburgh, but he preferred to pursue his literary career. He was the general editor of the Religious Tract Society's periodicals for many years, and the *Boy's Own Paper* and *Girl's Own Paper* were founded in 1879 and edited under his direction.

In 1871 Macaulay toured the United States of America and wrote a series of articles in the *Leisure Hour* called 'First impressions of America', which were collected as *Across the Ferry* (1871). A visit to Ireland the following year produced *Ireland in 1872: a Tour of Observation* (1873), in which Macaulay advocated restricted home rule. Most of Macaulay's independent publications were narratives of adventure for children, including *All True: Records of Peril and Adventure by Sea* (1879), *Gray Hawk: Life and Adventures among the Red Indians* (1883), and *Stirring Stories of Peace and War by Land and Sea* (1885). He also published *Victoria, R. I.: her Life and Reign* (1887) and edited the *Speeches and Addresses of the Prince of Wales* (1889). He died at 4 Wynnstay Gardens, Kensington, London, on 18 June 1902.

G. Le G. Norgate, rev. Nilanjana Banerji

Sources *British Weekly* (25 June 1902) · Allibone, *Dict.* · *The Times* (19 Feb 1868) · *WWW* · *Men and women of the time* (1899) · *Seed time and harvest*, 15th edn (1899) · m. cert.
Wealth at death £3382 3s. 4d.: probate, 22 Aug 1902, *CGPLA Eng. & Wales*

Macaulay, Sir James Buchanan (1793–1859), lawyer in Canada, was born on 3 December 1793 at Newark (Niagara-on-the-Lake), Upper Canada, the second son of James Macaulay, an army surgeon, and his wife, Elizabeth Tuck Hayter. The family was moderately wealthy and well connected, and in 1805 James joined the sons of the Upper Canadian élite in the Revd John Strachan's school in Cornwall. In 1809 he was commissioned ensign with the 98th regiment of foot and in 1812 joined the Glengarry light infantry fencibles. He saw action against American forces at Sackets Harbor, Ogdensburg, Lundy's Lane, and Fort Erie. After the end of the war he began to study law (1816); in 1822 he was called to the bar and in 1825 he became a bencher of the Law Society.

He was industrious and successful at the bar, and his high social standing was consolidated when, on 1 December 1821, he married Rachel Crookshank (1799/1800–1883), the daughter of John Gamble, an army surgeon and colleague of Macaulay's father. They had four daughters and one son and lived quietly in Toronto. Macaulay was a devout Anglican, active in church affairs, and a member of a small coterie of conservatives described derisively as the 'Family Compact'.

In 1825 Macaulay was appointed by Sir Peregrine Maitland to the executive council, but he withdrew in 1829 after becoming a judge in the court of king's bench. He was concerned principally with matters of civil litigation and was in general fair, if conservative, in his judgments. He tended towards clemency and was concerned about prison conditions. He was a colonel in the militia and during the rebellion of 1837 in Upper Canada he helped organize the defence of the colony. In 1839 he was asked to report on the Indian department, but he showed little understanding of native concerns, suggesting that the plight of the 'degenerate races', as he called them, be relieved by Christian charity. He was asked, between 1839 and 1849, to undertake a fuller investigation of the Indian department and of the executive council, earning the approval of the governor-general, Lord Sydenham. In 1840 he began the first revision of Upper Canadian statute law, and he served on the commission of 1842 and 1843 inquiring into the court of chancery. In 1843 he was appointed to the court of appeal and in 1849 he became chief justice in the court of common pleas, which post he held until age and increasing deafness forced him to retire in 1856. In that year he was appointed QC and began the revision of the statute law of Upper and Lower Canada, a responsibility which he carried out meticulously. Despite poor health he was appointed to the bench of the court of error and appeal in 1857. In 1858 he was made CB and in 1859 he was knighted. He died on 26 November 1859 after suffering a heart attack at Osgoode Hall, Toronto, leaving his widow the family home at Wykeham Lodge in the city and an estate worth (Canadian) $40,000. A moderate conservative of good judgement, Macaulay helped shape policy on a wide range of questions.

G. C. Boase, rev. Elizabeth Baigent

Sources *DCB*, vol. 6 · D. B. Read, *The lives of the judges of Upper Canada and Ontario* (1888) · W. R. Riddell, *The legal profession in Upper Canada in its early periods* (1916)
Archives Public Archives of Ontario, Toronto
Likenesses portrait, *c*.1854, Law Society of Upper Canada, Osgoode Hall, Toronto, Canada
Wealth at death C$40,000: *DCB*

Macaulay, John (1720–1789). *See under* Macaulay, Zachary (1768–1838).

Macaulay, Kenneth (1723/4–1779), Church of Scotland minister and local historian, was the third son of Aulay Macaulay (*d*. 1758), minister of Harris, and Margaret Morrison (*d*. 1771), daughter of Kenneth Morrison, minister of Stornoway, Isle of Lewis. He was educated at King's College, Aberdeen, where he graduated MA on 1 April 1742. On 15 November 1749 he was appointed missionary to Lochaber, but declined the post. On 20 November 1751 he was ordained as assistant and successor to his father, on whose death in 1758 he became sole pastor. On 4 August of the same year he married Penelope Macleod (*d*. 1799); the eldest of their five children, Neil, later became a missionary minister in Harris. Macaulay was presented by Archibald, third duke of Argyll, to the parish of Ardnamurchan, Argyll, and was admitted there on 15 July 1761. On 17

November 1772 he was translated to Cawdor in the presbytery of Nairn.

In 1758 Macaulay visited St Kilda on behalf of the Society in Scotland for the Propagation of Christian Knowledge (SSPCK), and in 1764 he published in London as his own composition *The history of St Kilda, containing a description of this remarkable island, the manners and customs of its inhabitants, the religious and pagan antiquities there found; with many other interesting particulars.* James Boswell showed the book to Samuel Johnson before their visit to the Hebrides in 1773, and Johnson pronounced it 'very well written, except for some foppery about liberty and slavery' (Boswell, *Life*, 2.150). The two travellers visited Macaulay on their journey to the Hebrides and from conversation with him came to the conclusion that he could not have written the book. 'There is', Johnson said, 'a combination in it of which Macaulay is not capable' (ibid., 5.119). Johnson may have been influenced in his opinion by a discussion he had on the English clergy with Macaulay, who was by no means respectful towards episcopal claims. Johnson pronounced him a 'bigot to laxness' (ibid., 5.120). Boswell was told that the book had been written by John Macpherson of Skye from materials supplied by Macaulay, but it is now generally accepted that the bulk of the book is Macaulay's own work, with some contributions from Macpherson. Macaulay died at the age of fifty-five on 2 March 1779 and was survived by his wife, who died on 7 May 1799.

T. F. HENDERSON, rev. RODERICK MACLEOD

Sources *Fasti Scot.*, new edn, 4.107, 6.439, 7.189 · Boswell, *Life*, vols. 2, 5 · M. Harman, *An isle called Hirte: history and culture of the St Kildans to 1930* (1997), 91–2
Archives NL Scot., corresp.

Macaulay, Dame (Emilie) Rose (1881–1958), author, was born at Rugby on 1 August 1881, the second of the seven children of George Campbell Macaulay (*b.* 1854), assistant master at Rugby School, and his wife, Grace Mary Conybeare (*b.* 1855), daughter of the Revd William John *Conybeare. Among her Macaulay antecedents was the historian T. B. Macaulay, a first cousin of her paternal grandfather. For eight years of her childhood her family lived at the seaside town of Varazze, near Genoa—a time of great happiness for her—and she received her early education mostly from her parents. As a child, she was a tomboy who believed she would grow to be a man, a gender ambiguity which pervades her later fiction. After the Macaulays returned to England in 1894, she attended the Oxford high school. In 1900, with financial assistance from her uncle and godfather, Reginald Macaulay, she went to Somerville College, Oxford, where she read modern history and acquired a lasting interest in the seventeenth century. She was awarded an *aegrotat* in 1903. University life stimulated Macaulay's independence and she lost the intense shyness from which she had suffered since her return from Italy.

On leaving Somerville, Macaulay moved with her family to Aberystwyth in Wales, but in 1905 her father was appointed lecturer in English at Cambridge, where she lived until 1913. Her early poems were published in the *Westminster Gazette*, and her first novel, *Abbots Verney*,

Dame (Emilie) Rose Macaulay (1881–1958), by Howard Instead, 1920s

appeared in 1906. By 1914 she had written six more novels. Her early fiction was sombre, concerned with a woman's life at home and its problems; it incorporated themes of loss and isolation from society, yet was combined with a witty, aphoristic style. She did not reach public notice as a novelist until *The Lee Shore* was awarded first prize in a Hodder and Stoughton novel competition in 1913. Its success, together with the £1000 prize-money and, once more, the generosity of her uncle, enabled her to leave home and buy her own flat in London.

Once settled in her flat in Marylebone, she began to move in literary circles. In 1914 she published *The Making of a Bigot*, a comic novel, and two years later, *The Two Blind Countries*, a collection of poems. Her poetry never had the success of her fiction, and by 1919 she had given up writing verse altogether. During the First World War she worked as a nurse and a land girl until 1916, when she became a civil servant in the War Office, with responsibilities for exemptions from service and conscientious objectors. At the War Office she met Gerald *O'Donovan (1871–1942) in February 1918, a novelist ten years her senior, with whom she formed a close friendship. O'Donovan was already married and had children, and Macaulay's religious convictions and moral scruples made her reluctant to begin a relationship with him but, nevertheless, two years into their friendship, they became lovers, and she ceased taking communion in the Anglican church. O'Donovan never left his family, but Macaulay's relationship with him lasted until his death.

After the war Macaulay worked as a publisher's reader for Constable, and it was in the twenties, the middle period of her fiction, that her talent as a novelist flowered.

Her gentle irony, effervescent wit, fastidious turn of phrase, and lightness of touch in exposing the absurdities of the day won for her a large, varied, and enthusiastic public. *Potterism* (1920) was her first best-seller, followed by *Dangerous Ages* (1921), which was awarded the Femina Vie Heureuse prize. In 1921 she rather self-consciously entered the Bloomsbury circle, forming a—sometimes strained—friendship with Virginia Woolf. Her popularity continued with *Told by an Idiot* (1923), a family history outlining shifts in social, religious, and political thought over the previous forty years. It drew comparisons with Woolf's *Orlando*. *Orphan Island* (1924), *Crewe Train* (1926), and *Keeping Up Appearances* (1928), all written in a vein of detached amusement at the follies of the human race, also sold well. At this time she was also writing many lively articles for the daily press, as well as books of essays with a more learned flavour: *A Casual Commentary* (1925) was followed by *Catchwords and Claptrap* (1926), which reflected the pleasure she derived from the English language and her insistence on verbal precision.

In 1930 Macaulay published a biography of Milton, described as 'refreshing and informed', and during the thirties she became increasingly absorbed in the seventeenth century, her specialist area of study from her time at Somerville College. The result of her prolonged meditation on the period was *They Were Defeated* (1932), her only historical novel, centring upon the poet Robert Herrick, and her own favourite among her books. In it she considers the position of the woman writer through her heroine Julian, a promising poet defeated by social pressures. She deliberately restricted the characters' vocabulary to the words known to have existed at that period, yet her dialogue remained fluent and credible. This novel, and her brief, scholarly study *Some Religious Elements in English Literature* (1931), initiated a new stage in her writing, one having a decidedly more academic emphasis. Her anthology of verse, *The Minor Pleasures of Life*, was published in 1934, as was her novel *Going Abroad*. In 1935 she began writing a weekly column, 'Marginal comments', for *The Spectator* and also published her best volume of essays, *Personal Pleasures*. A book of literary criticism, *The Writings of E. M. Forster*, was published in 1938. In 1932 Q. D. Leavis had described Macaulay's books as upper-middlebrow best-sellers, 'to be found on the shelves of dons, the superior type of schoolmaster (the other type has Kipling, Ian Hay and P. G. Wodehouse), and in the average well-to-do home' (Leavis, 37). By the end of the thirties, however, her work had gained greater prestige.

During the Second World War, Macaulay wrote little. For nearly three years she served as a voluntary part-time ambulance driver in London and her life was disrupted by the loss of all her belongings when her flat was bombed. In 1941 O'Donovan was diagnosed as suffering from terminal cancer and given six months to live. Macaulay's distress at watching him die was heightened by the necessary secrecy of their relationship, which meant she was unable to express anything more than a friend's concern for his welfare. In her grief after his death in 1942, she became ill and depressed and was supported by her friend Rosamond Lehmann. She wrote nothing until 1946, when *They Went to Portugal* and *Fabled Shore* three years later established her as a writer on travel and travel history, a field she continued to explore in *Pleasure of Ruins* (1953). Throughout her life she delighted in foreign countries and was especially fond of the Mediterranean region.

After the war Macaulay discovered that her name had been on the German list of writers to be exterminated after the Nazi invasion of Britain. Although in earlier life she had called herself a 'High Church Agnostic', she began to correspond with a distant cousin, the Revd J. H. C. Johnson, and in 1950 re-entered the Church of England after a long estrangement. Two volumes of her letters to Johnson were published after her death as *Letters to a Friend* (1961) and *Last Letters to a Friend* (1962). She resumed writing fiction with *The World my Wilderness* (1950), which showed that new depths of pity had transmuted her satirical approach. A revivified understanding of the human heart was even more evident in her final brilliant novel, *The Towers of Trebizond* (1956), which was awarded the James Tait Black memorial prize. Partly inspired by her trip to Turkey in 1954, it was a picaresque compendium of her interests. The narrator, Laurie, unhappily estranged from the church owing to an adulterous relationship, describes her aunt Dot's eccentric attempts to liberate Muslim women in Turkey into high Anglicanism. John Betjeman described it as 'the best book she has written and that is saying a lot', and it was a literary sensation, a best-seller in both Britain and the United States. *The Towers of Trebizond* brought Macaulay celebrity status: to her great amusement, she was invited to dine at Buckingham Palace with Queen Elizabeth, the duke of Edinburgh, and Princess Margaret, on its account.

During Macaulay's last years she wrote prolifically for periodicals such as the *Times Literary Supplement*, *The Spectator*, the *New Statesman*, *The Observer*, and *The Listener*. In 1951 Cambridge University conferred an honorary LittD upon her and in 1958 she was made a DBE by Harold Macmillan. She died suddenly of a heart attack at her home, 20 Hinde House, Hinde Street, London, on 30 October 1958. *Letters to a Sister*, a selection of letters to her sister Jean, accompanied by a fragment of *Venice Besieged*, the novel she was working on when she died, was published posthumously in 1964.   CONSTANCE BABINGTON SMITH, *rev.*
KATHERINE MULLIN

Sources *The Times* (31 Oct 1958) · P. Schlueter and J. Schlueter, eds., *An encyclopedia of British women writers* (1988) · J. Emery, *Rose Macaulay: a writer's life* (1991) · W. Ruddick, 'Macaulay, (Emilie) Rose', *Reference guide to English literature*, ed. D. L. Kirkpatrick, 2nd edn, 2 (1991), 893–4 · C. B. Smith, *Rose Macaulay* (1972) · A. R. Bensen, *Rose Macaulay* (1969) · Q. D. Leavis, *Fiction and the reading public* (1932) · *CGPLA Eng. & Wales* (1959)

Archives Ransom HRC, MSS and letters · Trinity Cam., corresp. and papers · Yale U., Beinecke L. | BL, corresp. with Society of Authors, Add. MS 56742 · Bodl. Oxf., corresp. with Gilbert Murray · King's AC Cam., letters to J. M. Keynes · U. Warwick Mod. RC, corresp. with Sir Victor Gollancz

Likenesses H. Instead, photograph, 1920–29, NPG [*see illus.*] · C. Beaton, photograph, NPG · Mann, photographs, repro. in Emery, *Rose Macaulay*

Wealth at death £89,547 15s. 7d.: probate, 12 Jan 1959, *CGPLA Eng. & Wales*

Macaulay, Thomas Babington, Baron Macaulay (1800–1859), historian, essayist, and poet, was born on 25 October 1800, the son of Zachary *Macaulay (1768–1838) and Selina Mills (d. 1831). Zachary Macaulay was the son of John Macaulay, minister of Cardross in Dunbartonshire. After apprenticeship to a merchant in Glasgow, Zachary became an overseer on a West Indian plantation, where he formed a deep hatred for the institution of slavery. In 1793 he was made the first governor of the settlement which the first abolitionists had founded as a refuge for escaped slaves in Sierra Leone. Zachary's sister Jean had married Thomas Babington of Rothley Temple, Leicestershire, and Babington inspired his brother-in-law with many of his evangelical beliefs. Selina Mills was the daughter of a Quaker family who had been a pupil and later an assistant of Hannah More, the evangelical writer who had founded a school in Bristol. The two met when Zachary returned from Africa in 1796 to recover his health, but were not married until he had returned from a second visit to the colony in 1799. In his absence Selina had frequently stayed at Rothley Temple. On his return, he became secretary to the Sierra Leone Company and took a house in Lambeth. But Thomas was born in Rothley Temple and the house was a second home to him, as it was to all the Macaulay children. When raised to the peerage he became Baron Macaulay of Rothley.

Childhood and education From both parents Thomas derived strong religious views. In 1802 Zachary Macaulay moved his family from Birchin Lane, Cornhill, to a home in the High Street, Clapham. It was here that most of the Macaulay children were brought up, among Wilberforces, Thorntons, Grants, and other evangelical families devoted to the cause of slavery abolition. All the settings of his childhood, from Rothley, the house of the Misses More in Barley Wood, near Clifton, and in Clapham reinforced the evangelical influences upon Macaulay. He was a highly precocious and sensitive child. He was reading by the age of three, and even as a small boy he astonished adults with his odd learning and recondite vocabulary. He very early showed the two salient features of his published work, a love of rhetoric and a highly retentive memory. The Bible in King James's version was the earliest and probably the greatest influence. When as a little child he found a maid had thrown away the oyster shells with which he had marked out a plot in the garden, he came into his mother's drawing-room and declared, 'Cursed be Sally: for it is written, Cursed is he that removeth his neighbour's landmark.' This childish outburst illustrates the pattern of Macaulay's more mature controversies. His reading was so insatiable, his head so filled with eloquent phrases that his response was often quite unsuited to the occasion. Interior conviction was always more important to him than its social effects. Even when he had shed the evangelical outlook, the language of the Bible shaped his style. He was shocked when supposedly educated people

Thomas Babington Macaulay, Baron Macaulay (1800–1859), by Maull & Polyblank, 1856

displayed an ignorance of scripture. In times of sorrow or loss his language became more biblical and sonorous. When he wanted to learn a new language he bought a Bible in it to save the trouble of using a dictionary. Later influences were Milton (he could say *Paradise Lost* by heart), Shakespeare, and Scott. The *Lay of the Last Minstrel* and *Marmion* inspired him to write a poem called 'The Battle of Cheviot'. He wrote hymns and commemorative verse, and even a religious tract to convert the native inhabitants of Malabar.

His parents, aware that he showed 'marks of uncommon genius', strove to keep him humble, a plan applied more consistently by Zachary, who criticized him freely, than by Selina, who adored him and tried to soften the effects of her husband's severity. But his education as Zachary's heir and successor could not but mark him out as special. His siblings received less attention and seem to have accepted the fact. The two girls nearest him in age, Selina (b. 1802) and Jane (b. 1804), were largely taught at home. The third daughter, Frances (b. 1808), was too young to be a playmate of her brilliant brother, but too old to be an admirer. She never married, and she became the maid of all work who nursed her father in his last years. Henry (b. 1806) was apprenticed to a Liverpool merchant. Charles (b. 1813) was apprenticed to a surgeon. Only Thomas and John (b. 1805) went to university. John, after a short attempt in commerce, graduated from Queens' College, Cambridge, and became a clergyman.

Thomas alone had a gentleman's education. In 1812 he

was sent to a school run by an evangelical clergyman, Matthew Preston, at Little Shelford, near Cambridge. Here he was thoroughly drilled in the Latin and Greek classics and evangelical Christianity. In 1818 he entered Trinity College, Cambridge. There he distinguished himself in classical scholarship and literary feats. He attended the lectures of a Trinity fellow, J. H. Monk, who became the biographer of Richard Bentley, a former master of Trinity and a figure whom Macaulay greatly admired. But he found the mathematics which loomed so large in a Cambridge education much less congenial. He won a Trinity scholarship in April 1820, the Craven scholarship in March 1821, and in June that year the chancellor's medal for English verse. But in January 1822 he withdrew from the mathematics examination which was required for honours and had to be content with a plain BA. The reverse upset him less than it did his family. Besides his formal studies he had laid the foundations of an extraordinary knowledge of the classics of European literature, in Italian and French. His classical scholarship encouraged a scepticism about the foundation documents of Christianity which generated an impatience and contempt for the simplicities of the evangelical creed. He also encountered, in men like Charles Austin and the Romilly brothers, the philosophy of the utilitarians Bentham and James Mill.

Utilitarianism for a short time gave an uncompromising edge to Macaulay's ethics, and helped form the public man with his carapace of aggressive self-confidence which concealed a deeply emotional nature. This first appears in his childhood letters to his mother, but in the middle 1820s he began to develop an affection for his sisters Hannah (1810–1873) and Margaret (b. 1812) which involved the deepest emotional relationship of his life. His letters to them read like love letters, and when Margaret married Edward Cropper he described his feelings like a spurned lover. After her death, which was a terrible blow to him, he depended on Hannah and her family. All through his public career the famous man, who held distinguished political office and was 'lionized' in society, needed the reassurance of an admiring family circle in which he could take refuge and return to the unselfconscious playfulness of childhood. He could be abrasive in company and critical of cant, especially of the religious sort. But his abiding affection for his family prevented any overt revolt against his religious inheritance; if he felt any scepticism for the central doctrines of Christianity he was discreet in the family circle, and in his published writings his real opinions were buried in an admiration for the grandeur of Christian civilization.

Début as a reviewer After his degree Macaulay took up, without much more enthusiasm than he felt for mathematics, the study of the law. He was admitted a student of Lincoln's Inn on 25 January 1822. He could still however hope to gain a fellowship of Trinity and, after a disappointment in 1823, was elected to one on 1 October 1824. His most productive years at Cambridge followed. While ostensibly studying for the bar, he was still living there, debating regularly in the Cambridge Union, and writing his first articles for reviews. In June 1824 he began, with a few Cambridge contemporaries, writing for *Knight's Quarterly Magazine*, to his father's distress. In January 1825 he made his début in the *Edinburgh Review* with an article on West Indian slavery. The following August the *Edinburgh* published his 'Milton' essay, which made him famous.

Macaulay's formal education was completed before financial disaster struck his family. When Sierra Leone became a crown colony in 1808 Zachary's secretaryship ended and he set up as a merchant in partnership with his nephew Thomas Gisborne Babington. At first the business prospered. The Macaulay family moved in 1818 from Clapham to a larger house in Cadogan Place. But Zachary's part in the campaign for the abolition of slavery took more and more of his time, and in 1823 he handed over effective control of the business to his nephew. The family moved again, to 50 Great Ormond Street. In the following three years Babington rashly overextended the firm's commitments and in 1826 it became clear that it was insolvent. The partnership was dissolved in December 1828 and Zachary resumed control, but thereafter he and his family became dependent on the charity of others. Tragedy struck, in the death of the ailing sister Jane in 1830, a blow which hastened her mother's death the following year. They were not destitute, but they had to retrench and Thomas had for the first time in his life to consider a profession.

Political opinions Macaulay was not very successful at the law. Although called to the bar in February 1826 he never made a profit at his profession. The law could lead to a political career, but Macaulay was more interested in literature than politics. His nephew and biographer, G. O. Trevelyan, claimed that he became 'a staunch and vehement Whig' (Trevelyan, *Life*, 1.120). This seems unlikely, first because the leaders of the Clapham Sect had a tradition of being above party; and second because Macaulay made his political début when the prospects of the whig party in parliament were poor. For the 'saints' of Clapham Sect, political influence was less important than doing God's work, and Thomas Macaulay retained something of this otherworldly attitude. If he did not retain his father's religious fervour he always had a conviction that the actions of politicians were ephemeral and that the works of great writers were more enduring. He certainly shared the impatience of his Cambridge contemporaries at the stuffiness and traditionalism of their elders, but his political opinions, as they appear in his early articles, are not so much whig as a mixture of Burkean toryism with its high regard for tradition and the historic constitution, and utilitarianism, with its critique of aristocratic government, the established church, and the law. The two themes are reconciled in the developing conviction that political abuses could be peacefully reformed and violent revolution avoided if the movement for popular education were to include teaching ordinary people the main events of their nation's past and encouraging them to value its achievements as their own.

The conviction that this was the key to peaceful reform and that Macaulay could provide the historical work which would be both accurate and vivid had formed by

1828. In that year he was approached to write a history of England for the Society for the Diffusion of Useful Knowledge, and he wrote his essay 'History' and a long review of Hallam's *Constitutional History of England* in the *Edinburgh Review*. 'History' argues the romantic case that narratives which deal only with rulers, battles, and treaties miss the 'noiseless revolutions' which alter the lives of the majority; that the materials for these more profound changes in the structure of ordinary lives have been appropriated by the novelist, and that the historian must recover them. The review of Hallam applies this theme to a historian Macaulay admired but considered too dry and too traditional. These two essays were followed in 1829 by the famous assault on James Mill's *Essay on Government* in which Macaulay repudiated the utilitarian view that a science of politics could be derived deductively from certain principles of human nature. The three articles attacking Mill and his followers are in Macaulay's most powerful polemical style, and they are a notable contribution to the quarrel between the *Edinburgh Review* and its radical rival the *Westminster Review*, the organ of Benthamite utilitarianism; but they also elaborate Macaulay's conception of an inductive social science and his repudiation of the a priori method of the utilitarians and political economists. They provide an important clue to the method he used in the *History of England* twenty years later, and they suggest that by 1829 Macaulay had, at least sketchily, conceived the ingredients of that popular success.

Parliamentary and official career Zachary Macaulay's business failure put these plans in abeyance, and made some steady alternative source of income essential. Despite his liberal, not to say radical, views, Thomas's political career began in a very traditional way. In December 1828 Lord Lyndhurst, the lord chancellor in Goderich's short-lived ministry and in the Wellington ministry which followed, appointed him to a commissionership in bankruptcy, which he held until the duke's fall. It was not renewed when Henry Brougham succeeded Lyndhurst as lord chancellor. Macaulay's relations with Brougham were already marred by mutual jealousy over their capacity to influence the *Edinburgh Review*, Brougham claiming it as an organ of the party he led, Macaulay reluctant to contribute to any periodical reputedly controlled by Brougham. When in February 1830 Lord Lansdowne offered Macaulay a seat in parliament for his borough of Calne, Brougham was very annoyed that it was not offered to his friend Denman. When Brougham told Napier, the *Edinburgh's* editor, to countermand an article by Macaulay on the French revolution of July 1830, Macaulay resigned from the *Review*. The quarrel was made up, at least outwardly, when Brougham offered a church living to John Macaulay, and a charity commissionership to Zachary, but Thomas remained unforgiving. He called Brougham 'a kind of Semi-Solomon. He *half knows* everything from the cedar to the hyssop', and he refused to enter his house when invited (*Letters*, 1.314).

Macaulay was elected for Calne on 15 February 1830 and took his seat three days later. He made his maiden speech on 5 April 1830 in support of a motion for the repeal of Jewish disabilities, but he made his name as an orator with the introduction of the whig government's Reform Bill in March 1831. He made five major speeches in support of the reform of parliament. They were carefully prepared, replete with literary and historical learning, and they held the House of Commons entranced with the richness of their language and the vehemence of the speaker. They were not however debating speeches. The whig diarist Greville called them 'harangues and never replies' (C. C. F. Greville, *Memoirs*, ed. Strachey and Fulford, 1938, 2.203). Macaulay was not skilled at impromptu replies to interruptions: 'Answer me', he said on one occasion, 'but do not interrupt me' (Macaulay, *Speeches*, ed. Young, 1935, 31). He was also hampered and embarrassed by the fact that he himself sat for the sort of close borough (nominally a close corporation but with only twenty-four electors) the Reform Bill was supposed to abolish. For the first time too, he had to endure public correction. When one of his historical assertions was demolished by J. W. Croker in the debate of 20 September 1831, he did not answer in the house but took his revenge in a review of Croker's edition of Boswell's *Life of Johnson* in the *Edinburgh Review*. Soon after the Reform Act was law, he sought a change of seat, and in the first elections for the reformed parliament he stood for Leeds. The election was marked by his polemic in the *Edinburgh* against his tory opponent Sadler, whom he ridiculed for his anti-Malthusian views. He was returned on 14 December, second on the poll after John Marshall the flax-spinner. Marshall had 2012 votes, Macaulay 1984, and Sadler 1596. Macaulay held the seat for a little more than a year.

Promotion when it came was probably due more to his Clapham connections than to his loyalty to the ministry. In June 1832 he had been appointed to the Board of Control, whose president was Charles Grant, 'the only saint in the ministry' of Grey, and son of Zachary Macaulay's Clapham friend. In December 1832, just before the Leeds election, he was made the board's secretary and thereby a spokesman in the House of Commons for Indian affairs. Grant was an amiable but indecisive chief, and Macaulay claimed on one occasion that he ran the board himself. His loyalty to his father's friends was in one case stronger than his loyalty to the ministry. When the government proposal for the abolition of slavery included a scheme for the freed slaves' wages to be used to help compensate the owners, the Clapham party objected and Macaulay agreed with them. He twice offered to resign his post but the offer was declined; in this way, as he said, he saved both his honour and his place. But in any case, the family's money difficulties combined with his own disillusionment with the ministers to convince him that he must leave office. In 1833 the government's Charter Act, presented to parliament by Grant, created a new supreme council for India, with a fourth post for a 'law member'. It was offered (probably not without some lobbying on his part) to Macaulay. The post in India would, he thought, enable him to be away from England while political parties regrouped and new questions arose. While in India, he could save money (he calculated on saving half his salary of £10,000) and 'return with a competence honestly earned' which would give his family security and himself independence (*Letters*, 2.301).

Indian exile In early March 1834 Macaulay resigned his seat for Leeds, and on the 15th he sailed for India. He had persuaded his sister Hannah to go with him, and he also took a large library of books, as if for a prolonged exile. The voyage took nearly three months. They arrived in Madras early in June, and Macaulay immediately joined Lord William Bentinck, the governor-general, at Ootacamund, while his sister went on to Calcutta to stay with the bishop. Macaulay joined her at the end of September. Within a few weeks he suffered two blows. The first was Hannah's engagement to Charles Edward *Trevelyan, a rising star of the Bengal civil service. Macaulay approved of Trevelyan as a vigorous, reforming official of strong character, but noticed his manners were brusque and his reading limited. The loss of Hannah was a severe shock. She and Trevelyan were married in December and while they were away on their honeymoon the news arrived of Margaret Cropper's death from scarlet fever. Macaulay's distress was so extreme that the Trevelyans returned early to be with him. He recovered, and it was some comfort to him that the three decided to keep house together, but the loss of Margaret marked him deeply. It strengthened his preference for books over people. 'Literature has saved my life and my reason,' he wrote, adding, 'Even now I dare not, in the intervals of business, remain alone without a book in my hand' (*Letters*, 3.158). The books he read and reread were his beloved classical editions. In his stay in India he read most of the extant authors of ancient Greece and Rome. He took no interest in Indian literature or antiquities save as a mark of the superiority of things European. He avoided Calcutta society and incurred a lot of unpopularity for doing so. He lost something of his exuberant enjoyment of controversy, and as between politics and writing, he felt the balance of his interests tipping towards the latter. He recurred to the idea of 'some great historical work' (ibid.) instead of a return to politics. Above all, he became more conservative, more distrustful of change, and more respectful of the efforts of the rulers and administrators as against the radicals and theorists. His schoolboy love of the heroic now settled into a preference for the soldier and the pioneering adventurers whose courage had created British rule in India.

Macaulay left his mark on British administration, less in actual change than in memorable arguments on disputed issues. These have been taken as more typical of British attitudes to India than the work of more hardened but more obscure men. His most famous contribution, in which he joined Trevelyan, was to the controversy between orientalists and Anglicizers over the allocation of a sum of money to native students in higher education, one party favouring instruction in Sanskrit and Arabic, the other pressing for all instruction in English. Macaulay's *Minute on Indian Education* (2 February 1835) argued vigorously for the latter, on the grounds previously advanced by James Mill, that instruction in English would convey the findings of a more advanced culture and so the money would be more usefully spent. The *Minute* has become famous as a landmark in the dispute, but it owes its fame mainly to the fact that G. O. Trevelyan printed it in an appendix to his book *The Competition Wallah* (1864).

In March 1836 Macaulay defended the so-called Black Act which ended the privilege enjoyed by European settlers to appeal from the Suddur courts of the company to the supreme court, and put them instead on a par with the native inhabitants in the company's jurisdiction. In September 1836 he defended the decision of Bentinck's government to end censorship of the press, writing a minute which persuaded Lord Auckland, Bentinck's successor, to leave the decision unaltered. But the largest undertaking of Macaulay's Indian years was the penal code, the work of a commission in which he was joined by John Macleod and Charles Hay Cameron. As their health gave way, Macaulay completed the code more or less single-handed in May 1837. He pronounced it superior to Napoleon's and to Livingston's for Louisiana. He then gave notice of his intention to return home early in 1838. He had been abroad not five years but four. He sailed with the Trevelyans, and they arrived early in June, three weeks after Zachary Macaulay's death.

Italian tour Macaulay found the political scene much changed. While in India he had expected the English radical party to grow stronger. The general election of 1837 had reduced the whig government's majority but also wiped out the radical party in parliament. London was in a ferment of sentimental loyalty for the young Queen Victoria. At first Macaulay savoured his independence. When Greville met him, he said he was still a radical. In October 1838 he set out for Rome, partly to visit the scenes of the events which he described in what would become his *Lays of Ancient Rome*, partly in imitation of Gibbon meditating *The Decline and Fall*. Being alone, he kept a journal which has some of the vividness of his letters to his sisters, and in which he meditated upon the history of the city, its past greatness and present dependence. He saw the squalor of papal administration which he thought 'Brahminical' (*Letters*, 3.268), but also the grandeur of papal power which captivated him. He made frequent visits to St Peter's and called it a 'glorious place'. After Christmas he travelled to Naples and saw Pompeii under snow.

Politics pursued him. On his journey out, while he was in Florence, he received a letter offering him the post of judge advocate. He refused it. 'The offer did not strike me as even tempting.' A man in office, but out of the cabinet, he reflected, was 'a mere slave' (Trevelyan, *Life*, 1909, 357). He wrote to Lord Melbourne saying he would support the government in parliament but hold no subordinate office. But in Naples he talked to Frederick Lamb, the premier's brother, and was relieved to hear the government had weathered the crisis in Canada and the scandal of Durham's mission. He returned by sea to Marseilles and coach through France, arriving in London in February 1839. He began work on the *History of England* the following month.

Cabinet minister In May he was invited to stand as parliamentary candidate for Edinburgh in place of James Abercromby, who had been raised to the peerage. He was elected on 4 June, making the famous declaration of whig allegiance, 'I entered public life a Whig; and a Whig I am determined to remain.' He had actually gone to India to avoid whig collapse. Now he declared, 'While one shred of the old banner is flying, by that banner will I at last be found' (*Speeches*, 182). He took his seat in parliament after the 'bedchamber' crisis: had he done so before, he might have had to vote against the ministry in the Jamaica debate which precipitated it. But he soon found independence impossible. In a weak ministry with a slender majority his talents were likely to be in greater demand, and on 17 September he was offered the cabinet post of secretary at war. He began his official duties with an unfortunate gaffe, when he addressed a letter to his constituents from Windsor Castle, and was much mocked for his arrogance. His two years in the cabinet were relatively uneventful, if only because the ministry was too weak to propose any major legislative measures. Macaulay spoke in its defence on a no-confidence motion on 29 January 1840, but failed to hold his own against a hostile opposition. He presented his department's estimates in March with more authority, having worked long at the details. His speech on the debate on war with China on 7 April was more successful. He began to like the official routine and confessed, 'I became too mere a bookworm in India, and on my voyage home' (*Letters*, 3.321–2). But the government was sadly irresolute over the major issue of the corn laws, and to this debate Macaulay contributed nothing, being a convinced supporter of free trade but disliking the leaders of the Anti-Corn Law League. He was relieved when in early June 1841 the government was defeated in the debate on the corn laws and he was able to return to his *History*.

He seems at first to have thought he could write it in his intervals of leisure. At the general election of July 1841 he had retained his seat in parliament and continued to speak, occasionally but very effectively. In February 1841 he had done more than any other speaker to destroy Sergeant Talfourd's Copyright Bill, which proposed extending copyright to sixty years from the death of an author. The following year Lord Mahon brought in another bill, reducing the term to twenty-five years. Macaulay proposed an amendment, giving forty-two years from the date of publication, on the grounds that the best work was generally published late in a writer's life and was most unfairly penalized if the copyright dated only from his death. Macaulay's speech involved very much the same display of vast reading in the annals of literature, great and trivial, which he used to such effect in his critical reviews. It is a sign of the respect in which he was held that the motion was carried. On 3 May 1842 he showed his deep distrust for popular radicalism when he opposed the reception of the Chartist petition. His reasons were again utilitarian: he thought the non-electors had shown that they did not know their own best interests. He also spoke on Irish affairs in July 1843 and February 1844 and again on

14 April 1845 in the debate on the Maynooth grant, when his speech closed with a famous criticism of Peel's career.

These efforts made it quite natural that he should be considered as a minister in any future Liberal ministry. When, on Peel's resignation early in December 1845, Lord John Russell tried to form a ministry, Macaulay was to have been paymaster-general, though he did not expect to be in office long. 'If I give to my history the time which I used to pass in transacting business when I was Secretary at War, I shall get on nearly as fast as when I was in opposition.' In the event the ministry foundered on Lord Grey's refusal to work with Lord Palmerston. It was Macaulay's indiscreet letter to his constituents, containing the sentence 'All our plans were frustrated by Lord Grey,' which made the matter public (*Letters*, 4.280–81). It was not until Peel's resignation the following June that Russell formed a ministry and Macaulay became paymaster-general. By then, however, his liberal views on economic policy were not sufficient to satisfy his Edinburgh constituents, and a motley collection of critics, from free church presbyterians who disliked his preference for the kirk, to members of the kirk who disliked his sympathy for the Catholics in Ireland, and many others who questioned if he was a Christian at all, gathered against him. At the general election in July 1847 he was third in the poll. He was personally very hurt and indignant, but to a friend he merely said he felt 'manumitted, after the old fashion, by a slap in the face' (ibid., 342). He resigned his office in April the following year.

Return to literature In 1839 Macaulay's happiness was threatened by the prospect that the Trevelyans would be returning to India. He may have been instrumental in the appointment which staved this off, when Trevelyan was offered and accepted the post of assistant secretary to the Treasury. For some months in 1840 he and the Trevelyans lived together in a house in Great George Street. The Trevelyans decided to move to Clapham, however, and in September 1841 Macaulay himself moved to the Albany where much of the *History of England* was written. He called it 'a very pleasant student's cell' but his life there, in central London, was not devoted exclusively to study. He was close to the clubs and the British Museum. He entertained friends to breakfast. While in office he gave formal dinners. He travelled a good deal, not always in search of materials for the *History*, and wherever he went in London he walked at least some of the way, often reading a book. He regularly walked to Clapham to see the Trevelyans. The *History* was not even his sole literary activity. He was able to establish a reputation outside reviewing with the *Lays of Ancient Rome*, published in 1842. These were based on a hypothesis of the historian Niebuhr, himself reviving the theory of a Dutch scholar of the seventeenth century, Perizonius, that the early books of Livy's *History* had been based on stories taken from oral poetry, since lost, and rendered into prose. Macaulay's aim was to put the stories back into ballad form for English readers. They were begun in India, and at first shown in manuscript form to friends. The poetry (for which Macaulay was always modest) was accompanied, and buttressed, by prose introductions, each offering a historical explanation of individual poems, in which Macaulay displayed considerable scholarship. He was sharply aware from precedents such as Talfourd's *Ion* and Bulwer-Lytton's *Last Days of Pompeii* of the dangers of historical anachronism. He thought the *Lays* might be unpopular, but asserted that 'no man who is not a good scholar can attack it without exposing himself' (*Letters*, 4.68). In fact the book was a great popular success. A first edition of 750 was sold out by December when a second of 500 was printed.

By then he was obliged by the threat of a pirated edition in America to consider the reprinting of his review articles. At first he was against this, because he thought papers intended for a natural life of six weeks would look superficial in a more permanent format. Longman, however, disagreed and the three volumes appeared in April 1843. They contain all that Macaulay thought the least impermanent of his articles, and proved more popular than the collections of reviewers who in their own time had been equally famous. In 1849 he noted that while Francis Jeffrey's collected articles had reached a second edition and Sydney Smith's a fourth, his own *Critical and Historical Essays* were reprinting for the seventh time. This may have been because he had left out his juvenilia in *Knight's Quarterly Magazine* and his early political articles in the *Edinburgh Review*. He included his 'Milton' but not his 'Dryden' (1828), which is biographically as interesting. He also omitted his attacks on James Mill and the utilitarians from a feeling of gratitude to Mill who had subsequently supported his appointment in India. He did not reprint the attacks on his old Leeds antagonist Sadler. Three polemics which he did reprint, probably with a certain vindictive relish, were his articles on Southey's *Colloquies* (1830), Robert Montgomery's *Poems* (1830), and Croker's edition of Boswell's *Life of Johnson* (1831).

Composition of the *History of England* Macaulay did not reprint the 1828 essay, 'History'. It may have seemed to him too crude. Some writers have taken it as a prospectus for the *History of England*. But in the following twenty years his literary ambitions changed, as did his political views. Unfortunately we cannot follow them in detail: he had kept a journal of his visit to Italy in 1838–9, but abandoned it when he became a minister, resuming it again in 1848 when he was out of politics. So his plans for the *History* from 1839 onwards must be inferred from his other writings and references in his letters. On his return from India he was given custody of the papers which Sir James Mackintosh had gathered for his unfinished *History of the Revolution of 1688* and these included many transcriptions of official correspondence which Macaulay later called 'the rudest ore of history'. Already he had an intimate knowledge of English literature after 1660, and Mackintosh's work may have focused his attention on the political events of the reigns of James II and William III. But his stay in Rome gave Macaulay's reflections an international

dimension. It was there that he decided to begin the *History* at 1685. The revolution could be set in the context of the struggle between Catholicism and protestantism, with William III's accession finally tipping the balance of influence in Europe in favour of the latter. Here was a revolution of vital importance for the modern world, not only for English readers. The small stage of seventeenth-century England became the scene of a titanic struggle. The idea broached in the 1828 essay that the important changes in history are 'noiseless revolutions' was retained, but played down. Macaulay's sympathy for the life of the common people, never very strong, had been further weakened by the Chartist experience. He still held the utilitarian view that societies could progress only if people were freed from the controls of superstition, but he wanted enlightened leadership, not democracy, and he loathed disorder. He did not subscribe to any of the contemporary schemes (utilitarian, socialist, or positivist) for explaining or accelerating social progress. He merely wanted the energies of the individual freed for his own and therefore society's betterment. He assumed that the ignorant would agree with the better informed in such an arrangement. Yet he also wanted his *History* to be popular, and he kept to his old aim of reclaiming for history the materials which had been assumed by the novelist. He did this not by extensive research in statistics of wages, poor relief, or demographic records, but by drawing on his encyclopaedic knowledge of the popular literature of the time—chapbooks, ballads, popular songs, theatre, and what he called 'the lighter literature of the age'.

Macaulay has been criticized for using novels and plays as if their characters were based on real people. On the contrary, he thought he could write a history which was as accessible and readable as a novel, yet which told a story that was true, and would on that account, 'supersede the last fashionable novel on the tables of young ladies' (*Letters*, 4.15). It was accordingly written in a much more simple, modest, and undogmatic style than that used in his reviews. They were designed to be read once; the *History* to be read again and again. Macaulay's long-standing conviction that literature outlasts politics and has greater influence in shaping opinion than the decisions of governments, enabled him to be, much more than is supposed, above party. Of course he did not conceal his opinion that England had in two hundred years become better governed and more humane, or hesitate to praise those he thought had contributed to make it so, and to condemn their opponents. It is clear that he favoured the forces of progress. But within that limitation he distributed praise and blame impartially on whig or tory. In any society there were, he said, supporters of change and innovation and supporters of tradition and order: but 'the best specimens of each class are to be found not far from the common frontier'. In times of crisis they co-operate; in 1660 their co-operation restored the monarchy, and in 1688 again it restored 'constitutional liberty'. In 1848, the year of revolution, this was a doctrine to please Englishmen of both parties. In the *History of England* Macaulay told his readers why they had escaped the fate of European governments:

'It is because we had a preserving revolution in the seventeenth century that we have not had a destroying revolution in the nineteenth.' The message of the *History of England* was not democratic, but its appeal was popular.

The first two volumes, which took the story to the proclamation of William and Mary in February 1689, were published on 2 December 1848. Macaulay was very aware of their faults. 'As compared with excellence the work is a failure. But as compared with other similar books I cannot think it so' (Trevelyan, *Life*, 2.243). When the first sales passed expectations he thought there would be a reaction. But the sales continued to be spectacular. Twelve days from publication 3000 copies had been sold. By 10 January 1849 a second edition of 3000 had gone, and of a third edition of 5000, 1250 had been already ordered. Macaulay was praised in every social gathering he attended. Reviews were flattering. He was particularly touched in May 1849 by a letter from a group of working men in Dukinfield, near Manchester, thanking him for the pleasure of having the book read aloud to them every Wednesday evening for the past few months.

Critics of the *History* The two volumes had their critics. Macaulay expected strong censure from the religious sects, 'Papists, churchmen, puritans and Quakers'. The Quakers were the first. A deputation of five came to him by appointment on 5 February 1849 to protest at his treatment of William Penn. Macaulay seems to have borne them down with a volley of evidence. 'Never was there such a rout,' he wrote, 'They had absolutely nothing to say' (G. O. Trevelyan, *Life and Letters of Lord Macaulay*, 1909 edn, 521). Perhaps they were given no time to say it: one of the delegation later recalled that Macaulay was 'extremely rude, treating the Friends with contempt' (*Letters*, 5.6n). He had expected criticism from churchmen, and especially Tractarians, for his description in the third chapter of the clergy in 1685. He had a courteous but bruising exchange with the high-church bishop of Exeter, Henry Phillpotts. Another pamphlet by a Cambridge cleric, Churchill Babington, Macaulay dismissed as 'a silly book'. In April 1849 appeared a long-awaited critique in the *Quarterly Review* from his old antagonist, J. W. Croker. Croker had had the assistance of various contributors, and Macaulay thought the length and tediousness of the review had done him a service. In fact it makes a number of shrewd criticisms which deserve more space, and exposes many practical errors which Macaulay silently corrected for subsequent editions. Its main weakness was that Croker had no quarrel with Macaulay's political interpretation of the revolution, and spent all his ingenuity in exposing small errors of fact and taste, paying little attention to the overall design. Much more damaging was the criticism of John Paget a decade later. Paget examined closely particular episodes and people in Macaulay's *History* and his essays were published in *Blackwood's Magazine*. Macaulay never replied to them.

Volumes 3 and 4 of the *History* Amid all the critical acclaim, Macaulay began work on the next volume of the *History of England*. He worked with more concentration than before.

There were distractions. For six years from 1849 he took the Trevelyans on an Easter tour to some cathedral city to see fine buildings and savour historical associations. In November 1848 he had been elected lord rector of the University of Glasgow, and the following March he was inaugurated and made a learned and uplifting address. But when in July he was offered the regius chair in history at Cambridge he refused it. 'It would be strange if, having sacrificed for liberty a seat in the cabinet and 2,500£ a year, I should now sacrifice my liberty for a chair at Cambridge at 400£ a year' (Trevelyan, *Life*, 2.261). He travelled, but his journeys, even the Easter tours, were to gather inspiration and colour for the *History*. In mid-August he took a three-week tour in Ireland. He crossed to Dublin at night and sat on deck in his greatcoat. 'As I could not read', he recorded in his journal, 'I used an excellent substitute for reading. I went through Paradise Lost in my head. I could repeat half of it, and the best half. I really never enjoyed it so much' (ibid., 263). After working for a few days in Dublin he took the train to Drogheda and traced the course of William III's battle. From Dublin he went to Limerick and on to Killarney, thence to Kilkenny, Cork, and back to Dublin. At the end of August he went to Londonderry and acquired the close knowledge of its layout which makes his account of the siege of the city in chapter 12 so vivid. He returned on 4 September and immediately set out with his friend Ellis to France, a short trip which included some work in Parisian archives. They returned on 17 September. The Irish chapter was written in the autumn of 1849 when the memory of Ireland was still fresh. But the next chapter, on Scotland, was begun, and largely written in draft, before his Scottish tour in June and July 1850. These tours were essential for the graphic descriptions of the *History* but they took their toll. In the winter of 1850 he suffered much from what he thought were rheumatic pains and congestion of the chest. By spring he had recovered and in June and July he went with his sister Hannah, now Lady Trevelyan, and her daughter, Margaret, on a tour of Scotland. On his return, while on holiday at Ventnor, Isle of Wight, that September, he wrote his account of the battle of Killiecrankie. His journal however has frequent complaints of difficult respiration, sleeping badly, and, what worried him most, flagging inspiration. But he did his Easter tours in 1851 and early 1852. In June 1852 he was asked to stand again for Edinburgh and took the request as a sign of contrition for the electors' mistake of five years before, and his acceptance as a demonstration that a large city electorate 'should not expect slavish obedience from men of spirit and ability'. He refused from a mixture of pride and ill health to canvass or even to travel to Edinburgh. He went to Clifton for a change of air and on his return suffered a heart attack. He managed to address his constituents only in November. His recovery was slow. He later said of this crisis, 'I became twenty years older in a week, and shall never be young again' (*Letters*, 5.318).

Macaulay soon found parliamentary life a strain. He spoke on 1 June 1853 against a bill for excluding the master of the rolls from the House of Commons. The measure was defeated, but he was exhausted by the effort. He supported the same month a measure for competitive examinations for appointees to the East India Company, but could not complete the speech, though he chaired the committee appointed to draw up rules for the examination which published its report in December 1854. His last speech in the Commons was on 19 July 1853. Then he went to Tunbridge Wells where he began preparing an edition of his speeches to combat the pirated edition by Henry Vizetelly. The volume was published the following year and is really his farewell to politics. He had by this time become convinced that he was too ill to continue an MP, and had ceased to attend late sessions. He was confined to his rooms throughout the winter and 1855 was the first year since 1849 in which he made no Easter tour. Instead he finished the fourth volume of the *History*. The two volumes, 3 and 4, appeared in December 1855. Only in January 1856 did he retire from parliament.

Last years Macaulay had expected a cooler reception for the two volumes, but they sold as well as the first two. In ten weeks 26,500 copies were sold, and in March 1856 Longman's paid him the famous cheque for £20,000. But he no longer had any hopes of meeting his original aim, to take the narrative into the Hanoverian era. He had reached 1697 with chapter 22, the last of volume 4. After volume 4 his literary aims rapidly contracted. He moved out of the Albany when he bought Holly Lodge, Campden Hill, Kensington, where he moved in May 1856. He seized eagerly what diversions he could still manage. He resumed the Easter tours in 1856, but they were shorter. He went with his friend T. F. Ellis on an Italian tour in August. He did not take up volume 5 of the *History* until November 1856, and then 'with little expectation of living to publish anything more'. He thought, privately, that he would have done his duty if he completed a history of the reign of William III. He still enjoyed the reading and writing for the work, but its composition was not a race against time. He was able to fit in five biographical essays, on Atterbury, Bunyan, Goldsmith, Johnson, and William Pitt for the *Encyclopaedia Britannica*, edited by his friend and former constituent Adam Black. He also accepted in August 1857 a peerage offered by Palmerston, taking his seat in the Lords (where he never spoke) in December. In October that year he was elected high steward of the borough of Cambridge, and the installation was deferred until the warm weather, in May 1858. He arranged a French tour with Ellis in the autumn, but in his hibernation which was now a necessity he received the blow he had been spared in 1839. Sir Charles Trevelyan was appointed governor of Madras, and his wife would have to follow him to India. He left England on 18 February, and in May, Macaulay knew that Hannah and the children would follow. He took them on a two-week tour of Scotland in late July and August. In October Hannah told him, by letter, that she would leave for India in February. He tried to find comfort in his books and writing, but was oppressed with the certainty that he would never see her again. In mid-December he had a heart attack, and he died in his study at Holly Lodge on 28 December 1859. He was buried in Westminster Abbey on 9 January 1860, in Poets' Corner, at the feet of the statue of Addison.

Macaulay was a short, stout, physically awkward man who, in common with other men of genius, was indifferent to his appearance and to adverse comments on it. He was much more sensitive to his literary reputation, which he came to realize was likely to suffer from a career in politics. He was not a natural politician. He was a fine orator in a parliament which still admired elaborate, polished, and learned speeches on great occasions, but he was too proud to use the common methods of acquiring and keeping political influence and too fastidious for intrigue. He hid his distaste for the political process behind a touchy independence. He had most impact on issues like Indian administration and the laws of copyright, where neutral votes could be swayed by specialist knowledge. His polemical writing was more often driven by private moral feeling than by political opinion. He was quite capable of discharging ministerial duties efficiently and thoroughly, but they bored him. So did debates when the issues did not seem to compete for historic significance with the men and events he was reading about. For all his political experience he preferred the world of literature and especially of drama and epic poetry to that of everyday reality, and was never happier than in his study engaging in a dialogue with his favourite authors. 'With the dead there is no rivalry. In the dead there is no change. Plato is never sullen. Cervantes is never petulant. Demosthenes never comes unseasonably. Dante never stays too long' (Macaulay, *Critical and Historical Essays*, 2.282). The great exception to this preference for books over people was his family, at least those members of it who had not forfeited his esteem by financial irregularity or religious enthusiasm. He never outgrew the need to escape from the strains of public life into an intimate circle in which he could behave unselfconsciously and receive sincere love and admiration. In one way this domestic anchorage restricted the movement and range of his sympathy. Though he shed his religious fundamentalism he remained very rigid in his ethical standards, especially towards sexual infidelity. In another way however his love of family life served him well. It was the foundation for the extraordinary clarity of his writing. He loved to read his writings aloud in the family circle, in his boyhood to his mother and sisters, in later years until his last illness to Hannah Trevelyan and her children. He had an actor's feeling for his audience. He loved the company of children and the experience of introducing them, through word games and quizzes and nonsense verses, to the rich heritage of their language and its subtle nuances. If he had lived to read Matthew Arnold's condescending remark that his writings were 'pre-eminently fitted to give pleasure to all who are *beginning* to feel enjoyment in the things of the mind' (quoted in G. S. Fraser, 'Macaulay's style as an essayist', *Review of English Literature*, 1/4, Oct 1960, 16) he would have taken it as a compliment. It is the foundation of his enduring popularity. WILLIAM THOMAS

Sources G. O. Trevelyan, *The life and letters of Lord Macaulay*, 2 vols. (1876) · *The letters of Thomas Babington Macaulay*, ed. T. Pinney, 6 vols.

(1974–81) • J. L. Clive, *Thomas Babington Macaulay: the shaping of the historian* (1973) • W. Thomas, *The quarrel of Macaulay and Croker: politics and history in the age of reform* (2000) • M. J. Trevelyan, *Life and letters of Zachary Macaulay* (1900) • [M. Macaulay], *Recollections of a sister of T. B. Macaulay* (1864) • G. O. Trevelyan, *Marginal notes by Lord Macaulay* (1907) • A. N. L. Munby, *Macaulay's library* (1966) • H. R. Trevor-Roper, *The Romantic movement and the study of history* (1969) • J. W. Burrow, *A liberal descent: Victorian historians and the English past* (1981) • J. Hamburger, *Macaulay and the whig tradition* (1976) • *The works of Lord Macaulay*, ed. Lady Macaulay, 8 vols. (1866)

Archives BL, letters, Add. MS 63092 • CKS, corresp. and papers • Col. U., Rare Book and Manuscript Library, papers • CUL, corresp. • Edinburgh Central Reference Library, letters on Edinburgh elections • Hunt. L., letters • LUL, corresp. • NL Scot., letters • NL Scot., MSS of biographical articles for Encyclopaedia Britannica • Trinity Cam., corresp., journals, commonplace book, and literary papers • University of Chicago Library, papers • University of Virginia, Charlottesville, papers | BL, letters to Lord Broughton, Add. MSS 47227–47229 • BL, letters to Lord and Lady Holland, Add. MSS 51838, 51843, 51850–51855 • BL, letters to Leigh Hunt, Add. MSS 38109–38110, 38524 • BL, letters to Zachary Macaulay, M/566 [copies] • BL, Napier MSS, Add. MS 34613 • BL, letters to Macvey Napier, Add. MSS 34614–34626 • BL, letters to Royal Literary Fund, loan 96 • Bodl. Oxf., letters to Mary Somerville • Bodl. Oxf., letters to Wilberforce family • Borth. Inst., letters to Lord Halifax • Borth. Inst., letters to Sir Charles Wood • Harvard U., letters to Zachary Macaulay • Herts. ALS, letters to Lord Lytton • Hunt. L., letters to Zachary Macaulay • Hunt. L., Zachary Macaulay MSS • NL Scot., letters to Adam Black • NL Scot., letters to John Burton • NL Scot., corresp. with Robert Cadell • NL Scot., letters to Dundas family and papers relating to his funeral • NL Wales, letters to Sir George Cornwall Lewis • Notts. Arch., letters to Lord Belper • NRA, priv. coll., letters to John Swinton • PRO, corresp. with Lord John Russell, PRO 30/22 • Trinity Cam., letters to Thomas Babington and others • Trinity Cam., letters to Lord Houghton • Trinity Cam., letters to William Whewell • U. Nott. L., corresp. with Lord Bentinck • U. Nott. L., letters to J. E. Denison • U. Reading, archives of Thomas Longman • U. Reading L., letters to Longman's • Yale U., Beinecke L., letters to Thomas Flower Ellis and Marion Ellis

Likenesses L. Haghe, lithograph, c.1832 (after J. N. Rhodes), BM • Inchbold, lithograph, pubd 1832 (after I. Atkinson), Trinity Cam. • S. W. Reynolds, group portrait, oils, 1832 (*The Reform Bill receiving the king's assent*), Palace of Westminster, London • S. W. Reynolds senior, mezzotint, pubd 1833 (after S. W. Reynolds junior), BM, NPG • F. Bromley, group portrait, etching, pubd 1835 (*The Reform banquet, 1832*; after B. R. Haydon), NPG • H. Inman, oils, 1844–5, Pennsylvania Academy of Fine Arts, Philadelphia • P. Park, plaster bust, 1846, Wallington, Northumberland • C. Marochetti, bronze medallion, 1848, National Liberal Club, London • C. Marochetti, two bronze medallions, 1848, NPG, Scot. NPG • J. W. Gordon, oils, 1850, U. Glas.; related portrait Scot. NPG • W. Holl, stipple, c.1850 (after G. Richmond), BM • F. Grant, oils, 1853, NPG • E. M. Ward, oils, 1853, NPG • Maull & Polyblank, photograph, 1856, NPG [*see illus.*] • G. Scharf, group portrait, pen-and-ink, 1860 (*The funeral of Lord Macaulay*), NPG • T. J. Barker, group portrait, mixed engraving, pubd 1864 (*The intellect and valour of Great Britain*; after C. G. Lewis), NPG • G. Burnard, marble bust, 1866, Westminster Abbey, London • T. Woolner, marble statue, 1868, Trinity Cam. • J. Archer, oils, 1880 (after photograph by Claudet, c.1856), Reform Club, London • J. Brown, stipple (after E. U. Eddis), BM, NPG; repro. in *Bentley's Miscellany* (1852) • J. Doyle, two caricature drawings, BM • W. Greatbach, line engraving (after E. U. Eddis), NPG; repro. in T. B. Macaulay, *Critical and historical essays*, 2 vols. (1857) • G. Hayter, group portrait, oils (*The House of Commons, 1833*), NPG • Maull & Co., carte-de-visite, NPG • J. Partridge, group portrait (*The fine arts commissioners, 1846*), NPG; oil study, 1849–53, NPG • photogravure (after Claudet), NPG • prints (after photographs by Claudet, and Maull & Polyblank), NPG

Wealth at death under £70,000: resworn probate, Aug 1860, *CGPLA Eng. & Wales*

Macaulay, Zachary (1768–1838), slavery abolitionist, was born on 2 May 1768 in Inveraray, the third son of the twelve children of **John Macaulay** (1720–1789), Church of Scotland minister, and his second wife, Margaret(*d.* 1790), daughter of Colin Campbell of Inveresragan. John Macaulay was the eldest son of Angus Macaulay, and was minister successively of South Uist (1746), Lismore (1756), Inveraray (1765), and Cardross (1775). He dined with Samuel Johnson and suffered his anger during Boswell and Johnson's journey to Scotland in October 1773. Aside from Zachary, the other children from his second marriage included Aulay *Macaulay and Colin (1760–1836), who served in the Indian army and at Seringapatam, was imprisoned along with Sir David Baird by Haidar Ali, and served as MP for Saltash from 1828 to 1830. Promoted to the rank of major-general in August 1830 and subsequently lieutenant-general, Colin Macaulay died at Clifton on 20 February 1836. John Macaulay died on 30 March 1789.

Given only a rudimentary education, Zachary Macaulay taught himself Latin and Greek and read the English classics voraciously. At fourteen he went to work in a merchant's office in Glasgow. Here, according to an autobiographical fragment which he wrote in 1797, he fell in with a group of university students who undermined his faith and indulged his passion for conversation and debate. Urged on by his colleagues at the counting-house, he also started to drink excessively.

At the end of 1784 Macaulay obviously suffered some kind of personal embarrassment, although the precise details are unclear. To escape the 'labyrinth' in which he found himself he determined to go abroad. Not yet seventeen, he took up a position as an under-manager or book-keeper on a sugar plantation in Jamaica. Initially repulsed by the sights he saw around him, not least the violence of the slave system, he soon adapted to his new surroundings and by his own account became 'callous and indifferent'. Nevertheless, he kept up his languages (Horace, he said, was his constant companion), moderated his drinking, and, as he had in Glasgow, proved himself to be a more than capable worker. In fact, he became a 'prodigy' among bookkeepers. Despite his protestations, he also took an interest in the welfare of the slaves.

Macaulay returned to Britain in 1789, lured by the offer of a position from an uncle in London. Soon after his arrival he went to stay with his sister Jean, who in 1787 had married Thomas Babington, a country gentleman who owned Rothley Temple in Leicestershire. The visit was to change his life. Babington was a young man of strong evangelical views, and under his influence Macaulay's better nature began to assert itself. At some point during his time at Rothley Temple he underwent a conversion experience and, as a result, he became an intimate of Babington and his circle, which included Henry Thornton and William Wilberforce.

Through his association with Babington, Macaulay was invited to visit Sierra Leone, the west African colony

Zachary Macaulay (1768–1838), by F. Slater

founded in 1787 to provide a home for emancipated slaves. Setting sail at the end of 1790 he did not see his friends again until the spring of 1792. No sooner had he returned to Britain than he was sent out again to Sierra Leone, this time as one of the council members. In March 1794 he became governor. A tireless and painstaking administrator, Macaulay steered the colony through a difficult period in its short history. Undeterred by a hostile environment and disputes among the settlers, he opened trade negotiations with the Fula kingdom and in September 1794 successfully resisted an invasion by French revolutionary forces. When he handed over the governorship in 1799 the capital, Freetown, was a bustling settlement of some 1200 inhabitants and the centre of a considerable trade with the interior.

On 26 August 1799 Macaulay married Selina Mills (d. 1831), the daughter of Thomas Mills, a Bristol bookseller. The couple, who had been introduced by their mutual friend Hannah More, eventually settled in Clapham, Surrey, where they raised their nine children, five daughters and four sons born between 1800 and 1814. To support himself Macaulay became secretary to the Sierra Leone Company, a position he held until 1808, when the colony was transferred to the British crown. It was not long, however, before he became absorbed in philanthropic endeavours, chief among them being the campaign to abolish the slave trade. Macaulay, of course, had direct personal experience of the trade, both in the West Indies and on the west coast of Africa, and it was this experience that he brought to bear on the early nineteenth-century abolitionist movement.

In 1804 Macaulay was elected a member of the Society for the Abolition of the Slave Trade, which had only recently been revived by William Wilberforce. He quickly emerged as a leading figure in the parliamentary campaign which in 1807 resulted in victory for Wilberforce and his supporters. Throughout these proceedings Macaulay worked in the background, collecting information, drafting reports, and assisting his friends in the House of Commons. A brilliant statistician blessed with a prodigious memory, Macaulay had a rare gift for being able to master and abridge the most intractable sources. He was also scrupulously fair and accurate. When information was required Wilberforce would say, 'Look it out in Macaulay' (Booth, 65).

After 1807 Macaulay played a major part in trying to ensure that the new legislation was enforced and that other European countries followed Britain's example. He became honorary secretary of the African Institution, which replaced the Society for the Abolition of the Slave Trade, and, following his resignation in 1812, continued to serve on the committee. In 1814, during the temporary peace in Europe, he travelled to Paris to present the British case for abolition of the slave trade by the continental powers. Macaulay was also in regular contact with the duke of Wellington and Lord Castlereagh at the Congress of Vienna (1815), and with them fought unsuccessfully to block French efforts to revive the slave trade in those parts of Africa where it had already been suppressed. It was later said that Macaulay was the only one of the 'saints' whom Wellington liked.

By the early 1820s Macaulay was contemplating a more direct attack on West Indian planters, namely the gradual abolition of slavery itself. In 1823 he helped to organize the Anti-Slavery Society and became editor of its monthly publication, the *Anti-Slavery Reporter*. Through the pages of the *Reporter* and pamphlets such as *East and West India Sugar* (1823) and *Negro Slavery* (1824), both of which were published anonymously, Macaulay sought to reveal the true enormities of the slave system and to counter claims that conditions in the West Indies had actually improved. In doing so, he provided Thomas Foxwell Buxton and his colleagues with the evidence on which they could take their stand in the Commons. For the most part Macaulay preferred to work behind the scenes. Even so, he was frequently the target of scurrilous attacks by pro-slavery interests, notably in the periodical *John Bull*, all of which he resisted with patience and great courage.

Macaulay and his colleagues focused their attention on working through parliament. As time went on, however, the ideas and methods of the Anti-Slavery Society came under increasing pressure from young men like George Stephen who favoured taking the campaign out into the country. The result was the agency committee, organized in 1831. Like many conservatives within the movement, Macaulay looked askance at the populist appeal of the committee, its revivalist tone, and its support for the immediate abolition of slavery. Nevertheless, he assisted the new organization and gave it his tacit support.

Macaulay was also involved in a number of other philanthropic endeavours. He helped to start the *Christian Observer*, the official organ of the Clapham Sect, and served as its editor from 1802 to 1816. He was a fellow of the Royal Society and an active member of the British and Foreign Bible Society, the Church Missionary Society, and the Society for the Suppression of Vice. He also found time to promote Sunday and infant schools. Macaulay took a keen interest in educational movements; he supported Andrew Bell's claim to be the originator of the monitorial system, for instance, and was one of the principal founders of the University of London.

These various activities, and the many demands on his time, undoubtedly had an adverse effect on Macaulay's business interests. Soon after he stepped down as secretary of the Sierra Leone Company he started a business of his own, trading with Africa and the East Indies. He also acted as an agent for captains and shipowners seeking compensation, usually in the form of prize money, for their part in the suppression of the slave trade. By 1818 Macaulay was reputed to be worth £100,000. But then disaster struck. In 1823 he handed over control of his trading company to his nephew, Thomas Babington, who proved unequal to the task. It soon became apparent that what had once been a thriving business was on the verge of bankruptcy. In 1828 the family was forced to move from Cadogan Place into smaller premises in Great Ormond Street. Macaulay's financial circumstances steadily worsened, so much so that in 1834 he was exiled to Paris. With the help of his son Henry all of his debts were liquidated but the business was wound up and Macaulay spent the last years of his life in lodgings in Clarges Street, London.

Macaulay had been born with a defect in one eye and as a boy suffered a serious accident to his right arm which required extensive surgery. He was repeatedly ill in Jamaica and his health broke down again in Sierra Leone, probably from overwork. In later life his financial embarrassments also took their toll. Macaulay died at Clarges Street on 13 May 1838 and was buried in Mecklenburgh Square, London. At a meeting held on 30 July 1838, with Sir Thomas Foxwell Buxton in the chair, it was agreed to erect a memorial to Macaulay in Westminster Abbey. The bust, which was designed and executed by Henry Weekes, incorporates a figure of a kneeling slave together with the motto 'Am I not a Man and a Brother?'

An intense, tenacious, and imperturbable man, Macaulay holds an important place in the history of British anti-slavery. His was not a particularly glamorous role. But through calm and reasoned argument Macaulay laid the foundations for the campaign that would lead in 1834 to the abolition of slavery throughout Britain's colonial possessions. Nothing escaped his notice. He was the perfect foil to firebrands like Sir James Stephen and did as much as anyone to give the anti-slavery movement intellectual respectability. Macaulay was a demanding husband and parent, whose stern moralism inevitably caused friction, not least with his eldest son, Thomas Babington *Macaulay. Nevertheless, the family remained close-knit.

J. R. OLDFIELD

Sources J. L. Clive, *Thomas Babington Macaulay: the shaping of the historian* (1973) · C. Booth, *Zachary Macaulay* (1934) · M. J. Holland, *Life and letters of Zachary Macaulay* (1900) · H. Temperley, *British anti-slavery, 1833–1870* (1972) · J. R. Oldfield, *Popular politics and British anti-slavery* (1995) · D. B. Davis, *The problem of slavery in western culture* (1966) · D. Eltis, *Economic growth and the ending of the transatlantic slave trade* (1987) · R. Fogel, *Without consent and contract: the rise and fall of American slavery* (1989)
Archives Hunt. L., corresp. and papers · Trinity Cam. | BL, Broughton MSS · BL, Thomas Clarkson MSS · BL, Hamilton and Greville MSS · BL, Liverpool MSS · Bodl. Oxf., corresp. with William Wilberforce · Bodl. RH, corresp. relating to Anti-Slavery Society · Bodl. RH, corresp. with Thomas Buxton · Derbys. RO, letters to Sir R. J. Wilmot-Horton · Hunt. L., Thomas Clarkson MSS · LUL, corresp. with Charles and Mary Booth · NL Scot., letters to Lord Stuart de Rothesay · PRO NIre., corresp. with Lord Castlereagh, D3030 · Surrey HC, corresp. with Henry Goulburn · Trinity Cam., letters to Thomas Babington · Trinity Cam., letters to Thomas Babington Macaulay · U. Durham L., letters to second Earl Grey · U. Edin., New Coll. L., letters to Thomas Chalmers · U. Hull, Brynmor Jones L., letters to Thomas Perronet Thompson
Likenesses H. Weekes, bust, 1842, Westminster Abbey, London · F. Slater, drawing [*see illus.*] · print, NPG
Wealth at death nearly went bankrupt in 1828; probably had very little money at time of death; became increasingly dependent on his sons: Booth, *Macaulay*

McAuley [McGauley], **Catherine Elizabeth** [*name in religion* Mary Catherine] (**1778?–1841**), Roman Catholic nun, was born at Stormanstown House, Dublin, probably on 29 September 1778, though her birth year is sometimes given as 1781. She was one of three children, two girls and a boy, born to James McGauley or McAuley (*c.*1723–1783) and his wife, Elinor, *née* Conway (*c.*1753–1798). Her parents belonged to the prosperous Dublin professional middle class by virtue of her father's work as an architect and builder and her mother's family involvement in the medical trades. They were both Roman Catholics, though her father seems to have been by far the more committed. At his death the three young children and their mother were left well provided for and remained in Dublin. Little is known of McAuley's education other than that it was undertaken at home and in the social and intellectual milieu of fashionable medical families. Much has been made of the children's indifference to their Catholicism after their father's death and their subsequent sojourns in protestant as well as Catholic households, but they made their first holy communion and were confirmed. Shortly after her mother's death in 1798 McAuley joined her brother and sister in the household of the protestant apothecary Armstrong, leaving there in 1803 for the home of another apothecary and physician, William Callaghan and his Quaker wife Catherine.

The Callaghans, who had no children, treated McAuley as their adopted daughter and for the next twenty years her life centred on them, her own extended family, and the charitable activities which she undertook among the poor in the locality of the Callaghans' estate at Coolock House in north-east Dublin. She continued to practise her faith, attending St Mary's, Liffey Street, and she became well known to a number of priests who were leading figures within Irish Catholicism, including Dean Andrew Lubé, Dr Daniel Murray, and Father Michael Blake. During this period she became involved in the contemporary debates about how best to combat poverty and was particularly concerned about the precariousness of life for young working-class women. Ideas for a lay organization appealed to her but she took no definite steps. This phase of her life ended with the deaths of Catherine Callaghan in 1819 and William in 1822, at which point she became sole heir to their considerable estate. From 1822 until her death she made use of this legacy and her independent status to put into practice some of her earlier ideas.

McAuley's focus was the establishment of a permanent institute for educational, religious, and social services for women and children. To this end she leased a property in Baggot Street in south-east Dublin in June 1824 and commissioned a new building. Known as the House of Mercy, the institute opened in September 1827 as a school for the education of poor girls and a residence for homeless women and girls; McAuley also adopted nine children, seven of whom were either orphaned or motherless members of her own family. She soon invited other women to work with her, particularly those 'who prefer a conventual life, and are prevented embracing it from the nature of property or connections' (Sullivan, 11). By 1830 there were twelve in the community and they had added visiting the sick poor to their activities. A devotional life was practised from the outset and a chapel was dedicated in the house in 1829, but McAuley's original intention was for a lay and not a religious community. In 1830, however, she and her companions experienced a change of heart and took steps to found a new religious congregation for women, beginning in September of that year with a period of formation with the Presentation Sisters in Dublin. The first members of the new congregation, the Sisters of Mercy, made their vows on 12 December 1831 and McAuley was appointed superior by Archbishop Murray. In addition to the usual vows of poverty, chastity, and obedience, the Sisters of Mercy took a fourth vow: to devote themselves for life to the service of the poor, sick, and ignorant. The first chapters of the constitutions and rule were submitted to Rome in December 1833, leading to initial approval of the congregation in March 1835. Branch houses of the Sisters of Mercy were opened in McAuley's lifetime in other parts of Ireland and in England (1839), while plans were agreed for a mission to Newfoundland.

McAuley was one of the pioneers of the active religious life in the English-speaking world, creating a highly adaptable and stable organization which spread rapidly throughout the English-speaking world and then beyond, to Newfoundland (1842), the United States (1843), Australia (1845), Scotland (1849), New Zealand (1849), and South America (1856). McAuley died on 11 November 1841 at the House of Mercy, Baggot Street, Dublin, from pulmonary tuberculosis and an internal abscess, and was buried in the convent cemetery at Baggot Street. She was declared venerable in 1990.   SUSAN O'BRIEN

Sources M. I. Neumann, *The letters of Catherine McAuley* (1969) · M. B. Degnan, *Mercy unto thousands: the life of Mother Mary Catherine McAuley* (1958) · M. C. Sullivan, *Catherine McAuley and the tradition of mercy* (1995) · M. A. Bolster, *Documentary study for the canonization process of…Catherine McAuley…poritio super virtutibus*, 2 vols (1985) · E. Bolster, *Catherine McAuley: venerable for mercy* (1990) · *Mantle of mercy* (c.1963) · R. B. Savage, *Catherine McAuley: the first sister of mercy* (1950)

Archives Carysfort Park Catholic Archives, corresp., prayers, and other MSS, 1985, pp. 44–45 · Sisters of Mercy, Baggot Street, Dublin · Sisters of Mercy, Thornhill, Derry · Sisters of Mercy, Limerick · Sisters of Mercy, Bermondsey, London

Likenesses M. Henderson, bronze sculpture, Institute of Mercy, Dublin

Macauley, Elizabeth Wright (1785?–1837), actress and socialist, was born in York, probably in 1785. Her father, a poor man, died when she was only two, leaving his family destitute. According to her sketchy autobiographical memoirs, Macauley's first career was as an actress. She began by performing in barns in Kent, but by 1805 she had moved to London, where for the next twenty years she went from one low-paid and badly reviewed theatrical production to another. Eventually a long period of unemployment forced her to depart the stage, leaving in a flurry of tracts denouncing the selfishness of her more illustrious male colleagues and the philistinism of the metropolitan theatre owners. Nothing daunted, she immediately began to turn her performing talents in other directions. The late 1820s found her preaching from the pulpit of a little 'Jacobinical' chapel in Grub Street, and from there she moved to the platforms of Owenite co-operation, becoming, in her own words, a 'good Co-operative woman'.

Owenism in the early 1830s was a vigorous working-class movement, promoting economic self-help through co-operative manufacture and trading, and encouraging the establishment of communities of mutual association. Its ethos was utopian–socialist and democratic, and the equality of the sexes was an important theme in its propaganda. All this appears to have been well suited to Macauley's insubordinate temperament, and by 1832 she was deeply involved in London Owenite activities. She served as manager of the largest labour exchange (an Owenite institution where workers exchanged goods and services on the basis of the number of labour hours invested in them), and became a well-known lecturer, delivering lectures on subjects as varied as financial reform, child development, the evils of Christian orthodoxy, and women's right to full social equality. 'Women have too long been considered as playthings, or as slaves', she told a London audience in July 1832, 'but I hope the time is at hand, when we shall hold a more honourable rank in the scale of creation' ('Address on responsibility', *The Crisis*, 7 July 1832, 66). She also offered acting lessons to her fellow socialists, including to a group of French Saint-Simonians visiting London in the early 1830s.

All these activities were undoubtedly motivated as much by economic necessity as by Owenite socialist conviction. Employment opportunities for single women such as Macauley were few and far between, and the small sums paid by the Owenites to their publicists would have been very welcome. Writing for publication was a more typical resource for such women—and Macauley also turned her hand to this, penning small volumes of essays on edifying topics, 'poetic effusions', and other such ladylike potboilers, while at the same time also producing a steady stream of pamphlets denouncing her enemies in the theatre, attacking the magistracy, and defending various patrons against scurrilous detractors—the traditional stuff of Grub Street hacks. But 'literary pursuits are the most arduous of any … and subject to the most mortifications—particularly for females', as she complained (E. W. Macauley, *Effusions of Fancy*, 1812, ix), and by 1835 she was to be found publishing her memoirs (funded by subscription) from a cell in the Marshalsea debtors' prison. She died in York, while on a lecture tour, on 22 February 1837.

BARBARA TAYLOR

Sources B. Taylor, *Eve and the new Jerusalem: socialism and feminism in the nineteenth century* (1983) · E. W. Macauley, *Autobiographical memoirs* (1835) · *GM*, 2nd ser., 8 (1837), 96 · E. W. Macauley, 'Miss Macauley's address on responsibility', *The Crisis* (7 July 1832), 66
Wealth at death see Macauley, *Autobiographical memoirs*

M'Avoy, Margaret (1800–1820), impostor, was born at Liverpool of respectable parentage on 28 June 1800. Of sickly constitution, she appeared to become totally blind in June 1816. Her case attracted considerable contemporary attention from the readiness with which she was alleged to distinguish, by touch, colours of cloth, silk, and stained glass. She could also accurately describe the height, dress, bearing, and other characteristics of her visitors, and even decipher letters in a printed book or manuscript with her fingers' ends, so as to be able to read with tolerable fluency. Sir Joseph Banks, the naturalist, asked William Roscoe of Liverpool to investigate; Roscoe concluded that M'Avoy could see, and that her demonstrations were an elaborate fraud. She died at Liverpool on 18 August 1820.

GORDON GOODWIN, *rev.* H. C. G. MATTHEW

Sources G. Smeeton, *Biographia curiosa, or, Memoirs of remarkable characters in the reign of George the Third* (1822) · *European Magazine and London Review*, 78 (1820), 183 · *The Quiz* (Jan 1818) · H. Roscoe, *The life of William Roscoe*, 2 vols. (1833)
Likenesses portrait, repro. in Smeeton, *Biographia curiosa*

Macbain, Alexander (1855–1907), philologist, was born at Balguish Farmhouse, Glenfeshie, Badenoch, Inverness-shire, on 22 July 1855, the illegitimate son of John Macbain, farmservant, and Margaret Mackintosh, maidservant. A fluent Gaelic speaker who grew up in poverty as a cowherd, he learned English when at Insh General Assembly school, Badenoch, between 1863 and 1870, under its teacher Alexander Mackenzie. Himself in sole charge of Dunmullie School at the age of fifteen, he developed an insatiable thirst for education. Between two spells at Baldow school, Badenoch, he worked for the Ordnance Survey in Scotland and Wales (1871–4). He went as a bursar to Old Aberdeen grammar school (1874) and King's College, Aberdeen (1876), graduating MA with honours in philosophy.

In 1880, Raining's school, Inverness, founded in 1727, was expanded to provide secondary education for the whole highland area. Macbain became its rector in July of that year, and presided with distinction over the last and finest period in its history. In 1894–5 it was incorporated into the High Public School, where Macbain remained until his death. In 1901 Aberdeen University made him an LLD, and in 1905 he received a civil-list pension of £90.

Macbain contributed much to the proceedings of the

Gaelic Society of Inverness and the Inverness Field Club, and many of his papers grew into substantial works. His first book, *Celtic Mythology and Religion*, was published in 1885 and reprinted in 1917. *Personal Names and Surnames of Inverness* appeared in 1895. His most important work, *An Etymological Dictionary of the Gaelic Language*, was first published in 1896: its philological judgements have stood the test of time. The first edition was sold out within a year; the second, in preparation at his death, was published in Stirling in 1911, and reprinted in 1982.

On the death in 1888 of the Revd Dr Alexander Cameron of Brodick (a native of Badenoch and Scotland's senior Celtic scholar), Macbain and his close friend the Revd John Kennedy, another Badenoch man, set about preparing Cameron's voluminous transcripts of manuscript texts for publication. These appeared as *Reliquiae Celticae* (1892–4), a treasure-house of primary materials whose usefulness to scholars has proved enduring. Equally, Macbain's 1902 edition of W. F. Skene's *Highlanders* launched a prolonged period of reassessment for the work of that influential but over-confident historian. Macbain's excursus and notes display the forensic intelligence which, in contrast with Skene's, obliges us to rank Macbain among twentieth- rather than nineteenth-century scholars.

Macbain also edited *The Book of Deer* and Alexander Mackenzie's *History of the Mathesons*, jointly edited Evan MacEachen's *Gaelic Dictionary*, and wrote on the Picts in *Chambers's Encyclopaedia*. He wrote much for newspapers and magazines, and was sole editor of the *Celtic Magazine* from 1886 to 1888, joint editor of the *Highland Monthly* from 1889 to 1902, and author of the review section of the *Transactions of the Gaelic Society of Inverness* (1880–1903). His *Gaelic Reader* went through three editions, and his *How to Learn Gaelic* (co-authored with John Whyte) through four.

From about 1888 to 1907, Macbain appears to have been the lynchpin of a group who met frequently in Inverness and Edinburgh and who may be described collectively as the Gaelic intelligentsia. As the sole representative of the generation born between 1839 and 1859, he provided a bridge between the older members (Alexander Nicolson, Alexander Carmichael, Donald Mackinnon) and the younger (Father Allan McDonald, William Watson, and ex-pupils of his own such as George Henderson and Kenneth MacLeod). If Carmichael was the group's heart, Macbain was its head. His intellectual stimulus was such that both Henderson and Watson went on to fill the kind of academic posts in Celtic studies which were his by right had he survived.

Macbain was a full-blooded man who worked hard, enjoyed life to the full, and never married. He died of a cerebral haemorrhage at the Station Hotel, Stirling, on 4 April 1907, and was buried in Rothiemurchus churchyard, Badenoch.

RONALD BLACK

Sources W. J. Watson, *Celtic Review*, 3 (1906–7), 381–6 · T. M. Murchison, 'Raining's School, Inverness: a seed-bed of talent', *Transactions of the Gaelic Society of Inverness*, 52 (1980–82), 405–59 · W. J. Watson, introduction, in A. Macbain, *Celtic mythology and religion* (1917), v–xviii · J. A. Smith, 'An educational miscellany', *Transactions of the Gaelic Society of Inverness*, 53 (1982–4), 248–309 · A. Macbain, journal,

vol. 1, 1855–71, U. Edin. L., Carmichael–Watson collection, MS 50A · d. cert. · *DNB*
Archives U. Edin. L., journal, notebooks and corresp.
Likenesses group photograph (with students), repro. in Macbain, *Celtic mythology and religion* · photograph, repro. in *Celtic Review*, 381
Wealth at death £434 10s. 5d.: probate, 4 July 1907, *CGPLA Eng. & Wales*

MacBain, Sir James (1828–1892), businessman and politician in Australia, born on 19 April 1828 at Kinrives, Ross-shire, was the youngest son of Smith MacBain, a farmer, and his wife, Christina Taylor. While he was still an infant his family moved to Scotsburn, and thence to Invergordon. His education was much interrupted by poor health, after his fall from a horse. In 1845 he was apprenticed for five years to Andrew Smith, a draper and warehouseman, of Inverness, and became his bookkeeper and cashier. In 1852 he was employed as a traveller for John Milligan & Co., of Bradford. He married in May 1853 Jessie, the daughter of William Smith of Forres, the brother of his Inverness employer, and the couple immediately emigrated to Melbourne. For four years MacBain held a clerkship in the Bank of New South Wales. In 1857 he paid a visit to Britain, and on his return to Melbourne the following year became managing partner for a branch of the firm of Gibbs, Ronald & Co., mercantile and squatting (pastoral land) agents. In 1863 he became partner in the London house, as well as the colonial branches, and when, two years later, the business was bought by the Australian Mortgage (Mercantile) Land and Finance Company, he became chairman and managing director, a post he retained for over twenty-five years. He was also director of two leading and several other banks and many insurance offices, and engaged extensively and successfully in speculation in agricultural land.

In 1864 MacBain was elected to the legislative assembly of Victoria as member for the Wimmera district, a scattered constituency, which he represented for sixteen years. He was a prominent advocate of the abolition of state aid to religion, but opposed both the 1872 Education Act and the Land Tax Act as injudicious and imperfect. He supported free trade and the end of squatting after fair compensation to the squatter.

In 1880 MacBain was elected to represent the central (on redistribution of districts in 1882 the South Yarra) province in the legislative council. From August 1881 to March 1883 he was minister without portfolio representing Sir Bryan O'Loghlen's government in the council (he had declined previous offers on account of his business commitments). A solid tory, on 27 November 1884 he became president of the legislative council, and, having fulfilled his duties creditably, was created knight bachelor in 1886 and KCMG in 1889.

MacBain visited England in 1874–5, and again in 1883, when he acted as chairman of the Victorian commissioners at the Amsterdam Exhibition. In 1888 he was president of the executive commission of the Melbourne Centennial Exhibition.

MacBain was a leading member of the Presbyterian church and took an active and generous part in church affairs. He was a trustee of the Scotch College in Melbourne, the Presbyterian Ladies' College, the Melbourne Working Men's College, the Victorian National Gallery, and other institutions, and was president of the Royal Caledonian Society and, for many years, of the board for the protection of Aborigines. After having suffered for some time from the effects of hepatitis, he died, on 4 November 1892, at his home, Scotsburn, Toorak, a Melbourne suburb. He was survived by his widow and their adopted son, MacBain's nephew. He was buried at Booroonda cemetery, Melbourne, on 7 November.

C. A. HARRIS, rev. ELIZABETH BAIGENT

Sources *AusDB* · *The Argus* [Melbourne] (5 Nov 1892) · J. D. Bailey, *A hundred years of pastoral banking: a history of the Australian Mercantile Land and Finance Company* (1966)
Wealth at death £2753: administration with will, 7 June 1893, *CGPLA Eng. & Wales* · £48,000 in Australia: probate, *AusDB*

McBane, Donald (1664–c.1730), army officer and writer on swordsmanship, was the son of a farmer and publican near Inverness. Little is known of his background and life other than what appears in his colourful memoir *The Expert Swordsman's Companion* (1728). Aged twenty-three, McBane enlisted in the army and over the next quarter of a century he claimed to have taken part in sixteen battles and fifty-two sieges. His 'first Adventure with the sword' came following a disagreement with a senior officer to whom he had been assigned and whom McBane accused of drawing his pay (McBane, 84). In a bid to settle the dispute McBane took lessons in swordsmanship from a sergeant accomplished in the short sword. Two weeks later he confronted his adversary and, though soundly beaten, showed the stubbornness and pugnacity that were to stand him in good stead throughout his life. McBane returned to his teacher, received advice on how to fight with a broad sword, and again demanded his rightful pay. On this occasion he was able to avoid the officer's cut at leg and, having thrust his opponent through the body and then the leg, claimed victory.

After service at the siege of Namur (1695), McBane returned to Inverness-shire but, finding his widowed mother too impoverished to support him, he soon after re-enlisted in the army, where he took additional fencing lessons and set himself up as a master. In order to prove his ability McBane was required to fight on twenty-four occasions before other masters of defence. After adding a gaming tent and a brothel to his business, he now lived comfortably and in 1701 married, though details of his wife are unknown. Two years later he was in the field as a swordsman with sixteen mistresses and in 1704 marched with the duke of Marlborough to the Danube, where he supervised sixty women and sixteen 'professors of the sword'. On one occasion he and his men took fourteen women from the Dutch quarters and were confronted the following day by twenty-four Dutch swordsmen who arrived to retrieve them. In the ensuing fight eleven Dutchmen and seven of his men were killed. By the battle of Malplaquet (1709) he and his wife had at least two children, who accompanied the couple in battle. McBane's laconic description of how his three-year-old son was shot in the arm at Malplaquet before being tended to by an army surgeon and collected by his mother is typical of his memoir's blend of terse statement and visceral detail.

In 1712 McBane returned to England, where he kept an ale house and took up stage-fighting in London, where he fought for thirty-seven prizes at the Bear Garden. However, following the Jacobite rising of 1715 he re-enlisted and was charged with guarding the Hanoverian standard at the battle of Preston. Subsequently he appears to have lived at Fort William. He made his last appearance as a fighter at Edinburgh in 1726, in his early sixties, when he fought a young man, 'gave him seven wounds and broke his arm with the fauchion'. He thereafter retired determined to 'repent for my former wickedness' (McBane, 152). Two years later his *Expert Swordsman's Companion* was published in Glasgow, with a detailed account of his life and advice to the practical swordsman. One of the last fighting masters, McBane's treatise was intended to alert readers to the trickery of 'Ruffins' rather than gentlemen, and in this sense differed markedly from guides of contemporaries such as Sir William Hope, who wrote specifically for the gentleman fencer. If never as popular as works such as Hope's *New Method of Fencing*, McBane's practical style—keeping a guard with the point threatening the opponent's hand, wrist, and arm—none the less anticipated the mid-nineteenth-century development of épée fencing. McBane died about 1730.   MALCOLM FARE

Sources D. McBane, *The expert swordsman's companion* (1728) · J. D. Aylward, *The English master of arms* (1956)

Macbean, Alexander (*d.* 1784), writer and amanuensis, of whose origins nothing is known, was employed as an amanuensis by the encyclopaedist Ephraim Chambers. After this he became one of the six amanuenses employed by Samuel Johnson on his *Dictionary*. About 1758 Johnson obtained for him the post of librarian to Archibald Campbell, third duke of Argyll. When, on the duke's death in 1761, Macbean was left 'without a shilling', he became mainly dependent upon charity. Johnson, who praised his learning and faculty for languages, but described his 'ignorance of life' as complete, subsequently advised him to write a geographical dictionary, and wrote a preface for his *Dictionary of Ancient Geography* when it appeared in 1773. The book was well conceived, but Johnson confessed to Madame D'Arblay it destroyed his hopes of Macbean's doing anything properly 'when he found he had given as much labour to Capua as to Rome' (Fanny D'Arblay, *Diary*). Two years later, when Macbean was starving, as his former colleague, Peyton, had already done, Johnson gave him 4 guineas and collected more (Piozzi, 1.218), and in 1780, through his influence with Lord Thurlow, obtained him admission as a poor brother to the Charterhouse. There he died on 26 June 1784, removing, Johnson lamented, 'a screen between him and death' (cf. *Works of the Rev. Jonathan Swift*, 11.246). Johnson said of him: 'He was very pious; he was very innocent; he did no ill, and of doing good a continual tenour of distress allowed him few opportunities.'

Besides the *Dictionary of Ancient Geography* Macbean published, in 1743, *A synopsis or short analytical view of chemistry, translated from the high Dutch of Dr Godfrey Rothen*, and in 1779 he compiled *A Dictionary of the Bible*. He also compiled numerous indexes, including that to Johnson's edition of the *English Poets* (Nichols, *Lit. anecdotes*, 5.30).

THOMAS SECCOMBE, *rev.* MICHAEL BEVAN

Sources *Letters to and from … Samuel Johnson*, ed. H. L. Piozzi, 2 vols. (1788) · *Boswell's Life of Johnson*, ed. G. B. Hill, 1 (1887), 187; 2 (1887), 379; 3 (1887), 440 · *Memoirs, journal and correspondence of Thomas Moore*, ed. J. Russell, 1 (1853), 94 · *The works of the Rev. Jonathan Swift*, ed. T. Sheridan, new edn, 11 (1803), 246 · Nichols, *Lit. anecdotes*, 5.30

McBean, Angus Rowland (1904–1990), photographer, was born on 8 June 1904 in Newbridge, Monmouthshire, the elder child and only son of Clement Philip James McBean, surveyor, and his wife, Irene Sarah, *née* Thomas. He was educated at Monmouth grammar school from 1915 to 1921 and, briefly, at Newport Technical College. His childhood was spent far away from the metropolitan sophistication which he later encountered in the 1930s and 1940s as Britain's most prominent and inventive theatre photographer. But photography had become significant to him long before he emerged as a professional. The teenage purchase of a simple Kodak camera gave him his first glimpse of the possibilities of the medium. Amateur dramatics, organized by an aunt, introduced McBean to the magical world of theatre—he designed posters and costumes, and began to experiment with the mask-making which intrigued him for the rest of his life.

McBean was a bank clerk from 1921 to 1924. After the death of his father in 1924, McBean's mother moved her family to London, and Angus worked for the department store Libertys (1926–33), as an antiques salesman. Like many of his generation, he was attracted by the Germanic cult of health and beauty and joined the Kibbu Kift movement, where he met Helena Wood, whom he married in 1923. They were separated in 1924 and there were no children.

By the end of the 1920s McBean was obsessed by theatre. He met the Motleys (Percy and Sophia Harris and Elizabeth Montgomery [*see* Motley]), three young stage designers who encouraged his interest in prop-making and helped him to secure his first design commission—work for the 1933 production of *Richard of Bordeaux*.

McBean continued to photograph, and in 1934 (after his first photographic exhibition, at the Pirates' Den teashop in London) he became assistant to the Bond Street portraitist Hugh Cecil. Though he disliked Cecil's soft-focus romanticism, he was an adept studio worker, and soon began to develop the aesthetic and technical skills which distinguished his later career. In 1935 McBean opened his own studio in London. He photographed Ivor Novello in *The Happy Hypocrite* in 1936. His stage photographs were boldly lit and dramatic, and soon he was photographing at the Old Vic, documenting now classic productions: Laurence Olivier in *Hamlet*, Edith Evans in *The Country Wife*, and Diana Wynyard in *Pygmalion*. McBean's photographs were now appearing in all the London glossy magazines.

Angus Rowland McBean (1904–1990), by Roger George Clark, 1979 [in the garden of Flemings Hall, Suffolk]

But it was the mounting in London of the 1936 exhibition of surrealist art which inspired McBean to begin radical experiments with photographic portraiture. By 1937 he had begun to use the styles and devices of surrealism to create fantastical portraits of theatrical stars—Vivien Leigh, enveloped in a plaster of Paris gown and posed among cotton-wool clouds, Flora Robson erupting from a desolate landscape, the impresario H. G. (Binkie) Beaumont as a giant puppet-master, and Patricia Hilliard emerging from a sea shell. He photographed himself too, in striped pyjamas with an umbrella, in a neo-classical aquarium, as King Neptune, and as a Roman bust, and sent the photographs out as Christmas cards to an ever-widening circle of friends and associates. With his flowing beard and his deep theatrical voice, he became a well-known and much admired character in the London of the 1930s. Immediately after the end of the Second World War (during the course of which he spent some time in prison as a conscientious objector), he opened a bigger studio in Covent Garden, and during the 1940s and 1950s he was inundated with commissions from London's major theatre companies.

In the early 1960s McBean photographed the Beatles for the cover of their first album. But as the decade wore on, and fashions in both theatre and photography began to alter, McBean's style, so rooted in the aesthetics of the 1950s, became unpopular. McBean had made those he portrayed into elegant stars. On the new realist stage, however, actors simply wanted to look like ordinary people.

Angus McBean's appearance was flamboyant. His thick beard marked him out immediately as one who wished to be considered an artist rather than a craftsman, and his colourful and often handmade clothes indicated an enduring interest in design and costume. When McBean retired in 1970 and moved to Flemings Hall near the village of Eye in Suffolk, he became almost immediately obscure. He sold his glass plate negatives to Harvard University and in Suffolk moved back into the design work which had so fascinated him in his early years. Flemings Hall, where he lived with his companion (and long-time assistant) David Ball, became a fitting arena for McBean's fantastical imagination. When his photographs were shown in 1976, as a retrospective exhibition at Impressions Gallery, York (and two years later at the National Theatre), the significance of his work within the history of British photography was finally recognized. Acknowledged too was his place as an elder statesman of the burgeoning and culturally progressive international gay community. During the 1980s there were major exhibitions of his work, television documentaries, and numerous photographic commissions. No longer a half-forgotten name from the unfashionable past, Angus McBean, much to his delight, was once more in demand. He died on 8 June 1990 at Ipswich Heath Road Hospital, Ipswich. The Harvard Theatre Museum has a collection of his photographs and plates. VAL WILLIAMS, *rev.*

Sources C. Naylor, ed., *Contemporary photographers*, 2nd edn (1988) · A. Woodhouse, *Angus McBean* (1982) · typescript of an unpublished autobiography, c.1972, priv. coll. · *CGPLA Eng. & Wales* (1990) · personal knowledge (1996) · private information (1996) [D. Ball]

Archives Harvard TC, collection of his photographs and plates

Likenesses K. Hutton, photograph, 1940, Hult. Arch. · A. R. McBean, self-portrait, photograph, c.1940, NPG · A. R. McBean, self-portrait, photograph, 1953, NPG · R. G. Clark, photograph, 1979, NPG [*see illus.*]

Wealth at death £115,155: probate, 16 Aug 1990, *CGPLA Eng. & Wales*

Macbean, Forbes (1725–1800), army officer, was born at Inverness on 1 July 1725, the son of Alexander Macbean (c.1684–1762) and his wife, Marjory (d. 1766). His father was minister of the High Church in Inverness and so militant a Presbyterian as to earn the nickname John Knox of the North; he was also fiercely anti-Jacobite and in the circumstances it is hardly surprising that Forbes and two of his foster brothers, Robert and William, sons of the Revd Archibald Bannatyne, minister of Dores, Inverness-shire, should follow military careers. Forbes Macbean entered the Royal Military Academy, Woolwich, as a cadet-matross on 3 August 1743 and passed out as a lieutenant-fireworker, Royal Artillery, on 4 April 1745. He was immediately posted to Flanders and had charge of two guns at the battle of Fontenoy. Having been ordered home in 1745, in consequence of the Jacobite rising, he joined the army of William Augustus, duke of Cumberland, at Lichfield and served at the siege of Carlisle in December. He did not accompany the duke to Scotland but the fact of his being a serving officer subsequently enabled his father to intercede with Cumberland on behalf of some deserters condemned to death after Culloden. In the meantime Forbes returned to Flanders, where he commanded a pair of light battalion guns attached to the 19th foot at the battle of Rocoux, and again at Laffeldt in the following year.

In November 1753 one of Macbean's foster brothers, Robert Bannatyne, joined the East India Company's Madras army, and some months later Macbean too volunteered to go to India with one of three Royal Artillery companies ordered there under Major John Chalmers. His application was unsuccessful, which was probably just as well, for only four of the twenty-two officers in the three companies ever returned home and Robert Bannatyne was killed at the storming of Conjeeveram in 1759. Nevertheless as a result of the departure of these companies Macbean was promoted lieutenant on 1 March 1755 and further promoted captain-lieutenant on 1 April. Next, offered a posting to Ireland, he instead purchased the adjutancy at Woolwich, a post that he held until promoted captain on 1 January 1759. In April of that year he was ordered to Germany, where he commanded a brigade of heavy artillery, most notably at Minden on 1 August 1759, after which he received an autograph letter from the allied commander, Duke Ferdinand of Brunswick, who wrote: 'I have reason to be infinitely satisfied with your behaviour, activity and zeal' (*Fasti Scot.*, 6.457), together with a rather more practical gratuity of 500 crowns. He again distinguished himself at Warburg, on 30 July 1760, and at Fritzlar, on 12 February 1761, before returning home on sick leave.

In 1762 Macbean went to Portugal with Count Wilhelm von Lippe, who had formerly been the allied artillery commander under Brunswick and had been commissioned to modernize the rather dilapidated Portuguese army. At Lippe's request Macbean was commissioned a colonel in the Portuguese artillery in 1763 and made inspector-general of Portuguese artillery two years later. Having relinquished this appointment in 1769 Macbean then commanded a company of Royal Artillery in Canada until 1773, before returning home, having been made a brevet major on 23 July 1772. A brevet lieutenant-colonelcy followed on 29 August 1777, and in March 1778 he was appointed commander, Royal Artillery, in Canada, in succession to Major-General Thomas Phillips. In anticipation of an invasion in 1780 he was assigned a field command at Sorel but the Americans failed to oblige and he saw no further action. Thereafter however he was successively promoted colonel (brevet) on 20 November 1782 and colonel, Royal Artillery, on 1 December, major-general on 12 October 1793, and lieutenant-general on 1 January 1798; on 25 September 1793 he was appointed colonel-commandant of the invalid battalion Royal Artillery. It is not known when or where he married his wife, Ann (1729/30–1818), but two sons followed him into the army. The elder, Frederick, was colonel of the 6th foot and had six sons of his own, all soldiers. Two died young; two, Frederick and Forbes, became colonels; and two, William and Archibald, became generals. Forbes Macbean, regarded as a scientific

soldier, was made fellow of the Royal Society in 1786. He died at his home, at Woolwich Common, on 11 November 1800; his wife, who survived him by many years, died at Greenwich in 1818, aged eighty-eight.   STUART REID

Sources M. E. S. Laws, 'War services of officers of the royal artillery, 1716–1763', MS, Royal Artillery Institution, Woolwich • *Army List* • *Fasti Scot.*, new edn, vol. 6 • C. Dalton, *The Waterloo roll call*, 2nd edn (1904); repr. (1971) • *Gunner at large: the diary of James Wood, R.A., 1746–1765*, ed. R. Whitworth (1988) • *GM*, 1st ser., 70 (1800), 1117 • parish register, Inverness [baptism], 1/7/1725

Archives Royal Artillery Institution, Woolwich, London, papers | BL, corresp. with Sir Frederick Haldimand, Add. MSS 21796–21798, 21816 • BL, corresp. with Lord Loudoun, Add. MSS 44069–44082, *passim*

Macbeth [Mac Bethad mac Findláich] (d. **1057**), king of Scots, was the son of Findlaech mac Ruaidrí (d. 1020), king of Moray, and (probably) *nepos* (nephew or grandson) of *Malcolm II (d. 1034). Macbeth became king of Moray in 1032 when his cousin Gille Comgáin mac Maíl Brigte was burnt with fifty of his followers, possibly at Macbeth's instigation. Gille Comgáin and his brother Mael Coluim (d. 1029) had killed Macbeth's father, Findlaech, in 1020. Macbeth married Gille Comgáin's widow, Gruoch, the daughter of Boite mac Cinaeda, who was probably a son of Kenneth II (d. 995). As king of Moray, Macbeth had to contend with the growing power of Earl Thorfinn of Orkney. The Norse *Orkneyinga Saga* (a source of dubious reliability) relates how Karl Hundason (probably to be identified with Macbeth) campaigned unsuccessfully to assert his control over Caithness and Sutherland. Macbeth had better fortune against *Duncan I, king of Scots, whose campaign against Moray in 1040 culminated in Duncan's death in battle against Macbeth, probably at Pitgaveny near Elgin on 14 August. What had been Duncan's opportunity in the crisis of succession in 1034 now became Macbeth's, and Macbeth became king of Scots.

Whatever dynastic claim Macbeth may have had, it is notable that both his father, Findlaech, and his cousin Mael Coluim were described as 'king of Scotland' in their obits, even though their power base seems to have been Moray. Perhaps Macbeth's accession was simply the culmination of Moray's increasing dominance over the more prestigious kingship of 'Scotland'. Macbeth also had land and influence beyond Moray (perhaps through his wife, Gruoch, who belonged to the once dominant lineage of descendants of Kenneth I), and is recorded as a benefactor of the Céli Dé of Loch Leven, to whom he and his wife granted estates in Fothriff (west Fife). Macbeth's kingship did not go uncontested, however. In 1045 he defeated and killed Duncan I's father, Crinán, abbot of Dunkeld. But by 1050 Macbeth's position was sufficiently stable to allow him to make a pilgrimage to Rome—the only reigning king of Scotland to do so—where he 'scattered money like seed to the poor' (Anderson, *Early Sources*, 1.588). He was alive to developments in the wider world, and in 1052 took two Norman knights into his service—the first Scottish king to take such recruits. In 1054 he faced a strong challenge from Duncan I's now adult son, Malcolm Canmore [see Malcolm III], who was backed by a powerful Northumbrian army. A bloody battle took place on 27 July, probably at Dunsinane (in what is now Perthshire), after which Macbeth was forced to give Malcolm some lands and position. This set up Malcolm to challenge Macbeth, and he killed him on 15 August 1057 at Lumphanan in Mar. The chief beneficiary, however, was Macbeth's stepson, Lulach [see below], who became king. His father, Gille Comgáin, had been killed by Macbeth. It may be that when Macbeth was finally overcome it was by the combined might of the sons of the kings he had killed in the advancement of his own career. A late (and debatable) source alleges that he was buried on Iona.

The Macbeth of Shakespeare's play was largely drawn from Ralph Holinshed's *Chronicles*, published in 1577. Holinshed followed the history of Hector Boece, who copied and enlarged the narrative in Andrew Wyntoun's metrical chronicle, written in the early fifteenth century. Wyntoun described Macbeth as 'thane of Cromarty' and 'thane of Moray'. Whether or not Macbeth was 'thane of Cromarty' cannot now be ascertained, but he was certainly not a mere 'thane' of Moray. Boece, without any apparent authority, altered these titles to the 'thane of Glamis' and 'thane of Cawdor' and Shakespeare followed this baseless attribution.

Lulach [Lulach mac Gille Comgáin] (*d.* 1058), king of Scots, was the son of Gille Comgáin mac Maíl Brigte (*d.* 1032), king of Moray from 1029, and Gruoch, who was the daughter of Boite mac Cinaeda and who subsequently married Macbeth. King-lists of the twelfth and thirteenth centuries describe him as *fatuus* ('stupid') or *infelix* ('unlucky'). He became king on Macbeth's death on 15 August 1057. It is usually argued that, despite defeat against Malcolm Canmore, son of Duncan I, Macbeth's followers were still able to seize the kingship for Lulach ahead of Malcolm. Lulach was soon defeated and killed 'by treachery' by Malcolm on 17 March 1058, at Essie, near Rhynie, in Strathbogie (in what is now Aberdeenshire). An alternative scenario, however, is that Lulach and Malcolm had been allies against Macbeth, who may have been responsible for the deaths of both their fathers. A late (and debatable) source says Lulach was buried on Iona. He had a son, Mael Snechta (*d.* 1085), king of Moray until dispossessed by Malcolm Canmore in 1078, and an unnamed daughter, whose son Angus (Óengus) was king of Moray until his death at the battle of Stracathro in 1130.

DAUVIT BROUN

Sources A. O. Anderson, ed. and trans., *Early sources of Scottish history, AD 500 to 1286*, 1 (1922), 551, 571, 580–604 · A. O. Anderson, ed., *Scottish annals from English chroniclers, AD 500 to 1286* (1908), 84–6 · A. A. M. Duncan, *Scotland: the making of the kingdom* (1975), vol. 1 of *The Edinburgh history of Scotland*, ed. G. Donaldson (1965–75), 90–100 · M. O. Anderson, *Kings and kingship in early Scotland*, rev. edn (1980), 265–89 · B. E. Crawford, *Scandinavian Scotland* (1987), 71–4 · H. Pálsson and P. Edwards, eds. and trans., *The Orkneyinga saga: the history of the earls of Orkney* (1978)

Macbeth, Ann (1875–1948). *See under* Glasgow Girls (*act.* 1880–1920).

Macbeth, George Mann (1932–1992), writer and radio broadcaster, was born at Hill Road, Shotts, Lanarkshire,

George Mann MacBeth (1932–1992), by Christopher Barker

Scotland, on 19 January 1932, the only child of George MacBeth (*d.* 1941), a coalminer, and Amelia Morton Mary Mann (*d.* 1951). His parents moved to Billingham, Cleveland, before settling in Sheffield where his father was killed in an air raid in October 1941 while serving in the Home Guard. His mother died of cancer ten years later. Educated at King Edward VII School, Sheffield, MacBeth was a clever child and received a scholarship to New College, Oxford, where he read classics and philosophy, gaining a first-class degree in 1955. At Oxford he ran the poetry society, founded and co-edited *Trio*, and published *A Form of Words*, his first collection of poetry, in 1954 with the Fantasy Press. On 3 August 1955 he married a fellow student, Elizabeth Browell Robson, later the distinguished geneticist.

On leaving Oxford he joined the BBC as a producer in the Overseas Talks department and for the next twenty-two years worked as a BBC radio producer on programmes such as *Poets' Voice*, *New Comment*, and *Poetry Now*. As the producer and editor of these programmes, MacBeth exercised a very considerable literary influence. A zealot in the cause of modern literature, and poetry in particular, he was in touch with a wide congregation of poets from staid traditionalists to avant-garde concrete poets and visualists. His exceedingly eclectic tastes and superb editorial judgement resulted in his programmes not only broadcasting the best and latest work of the established poets but also a considerable body of poetry from unknown, up-and-coming writers. Furthermore, all programme contributors read their own work, a new departure for the BBC which had previously relied predominantly upon actors. Through his radio programmes MacBeth was instrumental in developing—even in some instances kick-starting—the careers of many poets who went on to become major writers, such as Adrian Henri, Peter Porter, and Alan Brownjohn. In the recording studio, he was sensitive and professional to every poet whom he produced, treating everyone as equal: he was never above gently instructing even the most famous in order to get their best performance. Indeed, it was due to MacBeth's tutelage that the standard of spoken poetry rose so sharply. He also introduced British poetry audiences to foreign writers, of whom they would otherwise have been ignorant: this led to his bringing fresh influences to British verse. MacBeth was utterly unpartisan. He abhorred literary cliques and prophesied, accurately, that they would eventually stem the nation's poetic tide that was running hard during the 1960s and 1970s.

From the 1950s MacBeth was a central figure of The Group, a loose company of poets including Edward Lucie-Smith, Philip Hobsbaum, Alan Brownjohn, and Ted Hughes, whose aim was to modernize verse, to bring it away from the tight confines of the past. This group metamorphosed into the Poets' Workshop, of which MacBeth was a leading figure, religiously attending meetings to offer incisive and always impartial criticism on the work of the other seventy or so members. In his own right MacBeth was a remarkably adroit and skilful poet. With his second and third collections, *The Broken Places* (1963) and *The Doomsday Book* (1965), his reputation was assured and he published twenty-one verse collections. His talent, once described by an antagonistic critic as being 'magnificently wasted', ranged from sound poetry ('The Lax Cheer') to tightly structured traditional forms ('My Father's Patents'). He was a master with any poetic form, any genre. His personal verse ('The Land-Mine', 'The Drawer') was remarkable for its intensity of emotion while his comic poems, such as 'The Flame of Love, by Laura Stargleam (a Mills & Boon Poem)' and 'Pavan for an Unborn Infanta', a poem lamenting the inability of two London Zoo pandas successfully to mate, were not only hilarious but often trenchant. As a performer of his own poetry MacBeth was a consummate literary entertainer. He could judge an audience the minute he walked into a room and his poetry readings drew large followings. MacBeth's popularity as a poetry performer, however, rankled with some who did not share his generous non-partisan stance and were jealous of his position. Consequently his work was frequently attacked by establishment critics who not only took against him but found his work hard to pigeonhole. Despite occasional critical opprobrium, his poetry earned him the prestigious Geoffrey Faber memorial award in 1964 for *The Broken Places*, and the Cholmondeley award in 1977. MacBeth also wrote for children and was an outstanding anthologist. His three anthologies for Penguin, the *Penguin Book of Sick Verse* (1963), *Animal Verse* (1965), and *Victorian Verse* (1969), were remarkable for their range while his *Poetry 1900–1975* (1979), an enlightened educational anthology, was widely used in schools. His anthology *The Book of Cats* (1976)—MacBeth was an enthusiast for cats—remained in print for over twenty-five years. He also taught creative writing to American undergraduates (both in London and the USA) and travelled internationally on reading tours.

In 1975 MacBeth's marriage was dissolved. In that same year, a watershed in MacBeth's life, he quit the BBC to make his living by his pen and published his first novel, *The Transformation*. His prose was never as popular as his poetry. Each novel—he wrote nine in all—was utterly unlike the last: several were erotic to the point of the pornographic, and all seemed somehow self-indulgent. Only one, *Anna's Book* (1983), received critical acclaim. On 4 March 1982 MacBeth married the writer Lisa St Aubin de Terán (b. 1953), with whom he was overjoyed to have a son. Later that decade she left him and the marriage was dissolved in 1989. This was devastating, as he was to show in his poetry, collected in a powerfully emotive volume entitled *Anatomy of a Divorce* (1988) and in a novel, *Another Love Story* (1991). On 28 September 1989 he married Penelope Ronchetti-Church and settled in Ireland. He was again made happy by the birth of a daughter. By this time, however, MacBeth had contracted motor neurone disease, from which he died at Moyne Park, Tuam, co. Galway, Ireland, on 16 February 1992. His last collection, published posthumously, was *The Patient* (1992), in which he dealt touchingly and courageously—even humorously—with his condition. The book cemented his position as one of Britain's most important post-war poets.

MacBeth was tall and always extremely thin, moustachioed, bespectacled and eccentric, especially in his dress; he once shocked the then staid BBC hierarchy by coming to work wearing a cream leather suit. Unconceited, generous, and always good-humoured, he never played the part of the poet. He was too busy living a life that included owning a run-down Ferrari (to which he wrote a funeral ode), collecting samurai swords, and buying Edwardian furniture for the vast, semi-derelict houses he revelled in owning. He was once asked, if he had not been a poet, what would he have liked to have been? He replied, without hesitation, 'A general'.   MARTIN BOOTH

Sources personal knowledge (2004) · *WWW* · G. MacBeth, *A child of the war* (1987) · b. cert. · d. cert. · m. certs.
Archives State University of New York, Buffalo, papers · TCD, papers from his time in Éire, photographs, childhood diaries, memorabilia · U. Cal., Los Angeles, William Andrews Clark Memorial Library, papers | NL Scot., corresp. with Duncan Glen · U. Reading L., poems and letters to I. Fletcher | SOUND BBC Archives
Likenesses C. Barker, photograph, priv. coll. [*see illus.*]
Wealth at death £202,510: probate, 16 Oct 1992, *CGPLA Éire*

Macbeth, Norman (1821–1888), portrait painter, was born on 7 November 1821 at Port Glasgow, Renfrewshire, the son of James McBeath, an excise officer, and Janet Lees, his wife. As a boy he moved to Glasgow and served a seven years' apprenticeship as an engraver. He then moved to London, where he studied at the Royal Academy Schools, and made copies in the National Gallery. Afterwards he travelled to Paris, where he studied in the Louvre. In 1845 he established himself as a portrait painter in Greenock, moving to Glasgow in 1848, but was practising in Greenock again by 1856. He was a regular exhibitor at the Royal Scottish Academy from 1845. In 1861 he went to Edinburgh, where he gained much employment as a hardworking portrait painter of both public and private commissions. Macbeth was elected an associate of the Royal Scottish Academy in 1870, and an academician in 1880.

Macbeth's works, which include *Sir John Steel RSA, Sculptor* (1878; Royal Scottish Academy, diploma collection), *Alexander Whitelaw MP* (1880; Glasgow Museums and Art Galleries), and *William Forrest HRSA* (1886; Royal Scottish Academy), are conventional and competent but lack any distinction in either their treatment or ability to capture character. He also painted some genre subjects and landscapes, particularly of Arran early in his career, and of Switzerland in 1883, and of Berkshire in the last years of his life. On 21 April 1846 Macbeth married Mary Walker and among their children were the painters James Macbeth, Robert Walker *Macbeth, and Henry Macbeth-Raeburn. He moved to London in 1886 and died there, at his home, 10 Belsize Avenue, Hampstead, on 27 February 1888. He was buried in Glasgow on 2 March.

JOANNA SODEN

Sources *Annual Report of the Council of the Royal Scottish Academy of Painting, Sculpture, and Architecture*, 61 (1888), 13–14 • C. B. de Laperriere, ed., *The Royal Scottish Academy exhibitors, 1826–1990*, 4 vols. (1991), vol. 3, pp. 90–94 • Graves, *RA exhibitors*, 5.125–6 • J. L. Caw, *Scottish painting past and present, 1620–1908* (1908), 178 • P. J. M. McEwan, *Dictionary of Scottish art and architecture* (1994), 344 • Wood, *Vic. painters*, 2nd edn • *DNB* • m. cert. • b. cert. • correspondence, Royal Scot. Acad.
Archives Royal Scot. Acad., corresp.
Likenesses photograph, Royal Scot. Acad.
Wealth at death £1511 0s. 4d.: confirmation, 27 June 1888, CCI

Macbeth, Robert Walker (1848–1910), painter and etcher, was born on 30 September 1848 in Glasgow, the son of Norman *Macbeth (1821–1888), a well-known portrait painter, and his wife, Mary, *née* Walker. His younger brother, Henry Macbeth-Raeburn (1860–1947), also became an artist. In 1861 the family moved to Edinburgh, where Macbeth went to school. This was followed by a period of study in Friedrichsdorf in Germany. On his return Macbeth entered the Royal Scottish Academy School. He had his first work accepted for the Royal Scottish Academy's annual exhibition in 1867, when he showed a portrait of his father. He exhibited for the first time in London at the Dudley Gallery in 1869 and moved to London the following year, joining the staff of the newly founded newspaper *The Graphic*, where his friends John Gregory and Hubert von Herkomer also worked. From 1871 to 1872 he also attended the Royal Academy Schools.

At the start of his career Macbeth worked mostly in watercolour, and in 1871 he was appointed an associate member of the Royal Watercolour Society (he became a full member in 1901). As a watercolour painter, together with J. W. North, Fred Walker, and George Pinwell, Macbeth is classed as one of the idyllic school, painting idealized scenes of English country life. In oils he also often chose to depict romanticized pastoral scenes. Such work was strongly influenced by the art of George Heming Mason and Walker, and fits more easily into the English rather than the Scottish school. However the painterly quality of Macbeth's work and his rich use of colour links him to Robert Scott Lauder and his pupils, many of whom Macbeth would have known.

In 1873 Macbeth exhibited for the first time at the Royal Academy, and he continued to do so every year until 1904. He also exhibited at the Grosvenor Gallery. His work was well received, both by the critics and by the art-buying public, and he became well known for his pastoral scenes, one of which, *The Cast Shoe* (1890; Tate collection), was purchased under the terms of the Chantrey bequest for £630. Macbeth's subject matter was, however, quite varied and included lively seascapes, as in *Fishing Boats off Yarmouth*, scenes of modern domestic life, such as *Our First Tiff* (1878) (both Walker Art Gallery, Liverpool), and also period pieces in the manner of W. Q. Orchardson and John Pettie, such as *Stroller's Reverie* (1904; Aberdeen Art Gallery and Museums). He painted historical subjects, such as *Study for 'The Opening of the Royal Exchange by Queen Victoria'* (1844; corporation of London), and even a few mythological subjects, such as *Diana Hunting* (1896; Dundee Museum and Art Galleries). Macbeth was elected an associate of the Royal Academy in 1883 and Royal Academician in 1903. On 9 August 1887 he married Lydia Esther, the eldest daughter of General John Bates of the Bombay native cavalry. They had one daughter (later Mrs Reginald Owen).

Macbeth retained studios in London but from the mid-1870s to the late 1880s spent prolonged periods in the Lincolnshire fenlands. Several paintings inspired by these sojourns were exhibited, including *A Lincolnshire Gang* (1876), *Potato Harvest in the Fens* (1877), *A Fen Flood* (1883), and *Sheep-Shearing in the Fens* (1889; Aberdeen Art Gallery and Museums). J. L. Caw notes how Macbeth's subsequent move to Somerset brought about a clear change in his art—the gentler landscape of Somerset leading to a 'softer charm' in Macbeth's pastoral scenes.

It was as an etcher that Macbeth was most widely known. From 1880 onwards he etched a series of large plates after paintings by Velásquez and Titian in the Prado, Madrid. He also etched *Le chant d'amour* by Edward Burne-Jones, many works by Mason and Walker, and less well-known contemporary works, such as *The Top of the Hill*, after a painting by W. Dendy Sadler. He was an original member of the Society of Painter–Etchers (from 1880) and was appointed an honorary member of the same society in 1909. He illustrated F. G. Jackson's *A Thousand Days in the Arctic* (1899) and contributed to *Once a Week* (1870), the *Sunday Magazine* (1871), and the *English Illustrated Magazine* (1883–5).

During his later years Macbeth lived chiefly at Washford, near Dunster, and hunted with the Exmoor staghounds. He died at his home near London, Brentbrook, Wentworth Road, Golders Green, on 1 November 1910 and was buried in Golders Green.　JENNIFER MELVILLE

Sources J. L. Caw, Scottish painting past and present, 1620–1908 (1908), 277–80 • P. J. M. McEwan, Dictionary of Scottish art and architecture (1994) • J. Halsby, Scottish watercolours, 1740–1940 (1986) • W. D. McKay and F. Rinder, The Royal Scottish Academy, 1826–1916 (1917); repr. (1975) • Graves, RA exhibitors • J. Melville, 'Aberdeen Artists Society exhibitors', priv. coll. [typescript] • J. Turner, ed., The dictionary of art, 34 vols. (1996) • S. Penketh, ed., Concise illustrated catalogue of British painting in the Walker Art Gallery and at Sudley (1995) • W. Hardie, Dundee City Art Gallery: the permanent collection of paintings, drawings and sculpture (1973) • W. Hardie, Scottish painting, 1837–1939 (1976) • b. cert. • m. cert. • d. cert. • CGPLA Eng. & Wales (1911)
Likenesses N. Macbeth, oils, 1866, Aberdeen Art Gallery • R. W. Macbeth, self-portrait, oils, 1883, Aberdeen Art Gallery • G. Manton, group portrait, watercolour, 1891 (Conversazione at the Royal Academy), NPG • R. W. Macbeth, self-portrait, pencil and wash on paper, c.1894, Aberdeen Art Gallery • R. W. Macbeth, etching, BM • R. W. Robinson, photograph, NPG • wood-engraving, NPG; repro. in ILN (12 May 1883)
Wealth at death £169 10s. 10d.: probate, 7 Feb 1911, CGPLA Eng. & Wales

McBey, James (1883–1959), etcher and painter, was born on 23 December 1883 at Newmill, Foveran, near Newburgh, 12 miles north of Aberdeen, the son of James McBey, a farmer, and Annie Gillespie, a blacksmith's daughter. His father abandoned them shortly after his birth, and McBey was brought up by his mother and her parents. Always closest to his grandparents, McBey had a difficult relationship with his mother, who never showed him affection and made him call her Annie rather than mother. To his shock she killed herself in 1906, and he himself discovered her body.

McBey was educated at the local school in Newburgh, and left at the age of fifteen to become a clerk in the Aberdeen branch of the North of Scotland Bank. His interest in etching was first aroused by an article in the Boy's Own Paper, but in 1902, in Aberdeen Public Library, he found a copy of Maxime Lalanne's Traité de la gravure à l'eau-forte, translated by S. R. Koehler, and from this he learned the detailed practicalities of etching. It greatly inspired him, and in 1902 he produced his first etching, a view of Point Law in Aberdeen, the plate drawn before the subject. McBey first printed it using a mangle, but later made his own press from a propeller shaft found in a scrapyard. A series of plates of Aberdeen scenes followed, drawn surreptitiously to avoid the anticipated mockery of his fellow bank clerks. McBey was transferred to the Edinburgh branch of the bank in 1904, and a series of views of the city followed. This move also enabled him to see the Whistler exhibition there that year, by which he was greatly influenced. He was encouraged by the acceptance of his etching Old Torry for the Royal Scottish Academy 1905 annual exhibition, and its resulting praise.

Although his banking career had progressed well, in 1910 McBey took the drastic step of resigning. He immediately travelled to Amsterdam, determined to see the scenes which Rembrandt had etched with so much mastery. That summer he produced twenty-one plates, as well as numerous small oils. After a brief period in Aberdeen, in 1911 he settled in London to pursue his career as an artist. In July he visited Spain, and in November had his first exhibition at the Goupil Gallery in London. Malcolm Salaman, the accepted etching critic of the day, immediately saw the value of the young artist's work, as did Martin Hardie, who was himself also an etcher as well as a curator at the Victoria and Albert Museum. The result of their praise was that all available prints were sold, and the future publication of McBey's works was taken up by Gutekunst in London and Davidson in Glasgow. McBey now had enough money to set out once again on his travels. He visited the Netherlands again and then Morocco, but between 1911 and 1914 he also produced etchings of Cornwall, Kent, and the Thames in London. It was the last of these which gave him the subjects for two of his most successful early plates, The Lion Brewery (1914) and The Pool (1914). Both of these display his debt to Whistler, whom McBey recognized as his second master after Rembrandt, and whose book The Gentle Art of Making Enemies (1890) had been a rich source of inspiration for him when he first became interested in art.

After several rejections, in 1916 McBey was commissioned as a second lieutenant, and while attached to the army printing and stationery office in Boulogne and Rouen made drawings of the battlefields. However, the following year he was appointed official war artist to the Egyptian expeditionary force, and he remained in the Near East until 1919. He painted General Allenby, the Emir Feisal, and T. E. Lawrence (1918, Imperial War Museum, London), and made hundreds of watercolours and drawings of key moments of the campaign as well as scenes of daily life. Much of this work, including his famous Dawn: Camel Patrol Setting out, is in the Imperial War Museum. Issued as three sets of etchings between 1919 and 1921, McBey's war subjects were greeted with great acclaim. In 1924 and 1925 he went to Venice, where he strove to emulate Whistler's later, looser manner. The etchings from these trips were also greeted with critical praise and sold well. By this time McBey was one of the best-known and most successful etchers of his generation, and he was fortunate in finding himself at the height of his powers during the 'etching boom' of the 1920s. His prints were signed either 'McBey' or 'James McBey' in the plate; if additionally signed by hand, this was usually in the fuller form. In 1925 Hardie published a catalogue raisonné of his etchings and prints and in 1929 Salaman, who in 1924 had included him in the Studio series of Modern Masters of Etching, published a well-illustrated account of his life and work. Some of McBey's plates sold at very high prices, at the time the highest ever realized by the work of a living etcher. His paintings and drawings were equally sought after.

An energetic man, McBey was strong in physique and character and possessed of a good sense of humour, which came through in witty stories he related about himself and his life. He kept meticulous diaries, and had a strong sense of purpose and destiny. In addition to his self-portrait in the Imperial War Museum, a pencil portrait sketch by Hardie (National Portrait Gallery, London) and a watercolour also by him of McBey sketching (Aberdeen Art Gallery) record details of his appearance and character. On 13 March 1931 he married the artist and illustrator Marguerite Huntsberry, the daughter of Adolf and Hortense Loeb of Philadelphia; in 1939 they moved to New York and in 1942 he himself became an American citizen. From 1946 the couple lived in Tangier; in the spring of 1950 McBey revisited Newburgh and Aberdeen, where the university had awarded him an honorary LLD in 1934, for the last time. He died at his home, El Foolk, in Tangier on 1 December 1959. He was buried in a large park he owned overlooking the Strait of Gibraltar.

There are examples of McBey's work in the British Museum, Victoria and Albert Museum, National Maritime Museum, and all the principal print rooms of Great Britain and America. His archive is held by Aberdeen Art Gallery, which also has a James McBey Room and Art Library, where there is a comprehensive collection of his working drawings, watercolours, trial proofs, and etchings given by the American collector H. H. Kynett. In America a similar collection is at Boston Public Library given by Albert Wiggin, and another in the National Gallery of Art in Washington, given by Lessing Rosenwald. The Cummer Art Gallery in Jacksonville, Florida, also holds a large collection of McBey's work.

JAMES LAVER, *rev.* ROBERT UPSTONE

Sources N. Barker, *The early life of James McBey: an autobiography, 1883–1911* (1977) · *James McBey, 1883–1959* (1983) [exhibition catalogue, Aberdeen Art Gallery] · M. Hardie, *Etchings and dry points from 1902 to 1924 by James McBey* (1925) · C. Carter, ed., *Etchings and dry points from 1924 by James McBey* (1962) · M. Salaman, *The etchings of James McBey* (1929) · J. Melville, *James McBey's Morocco* (1991) · M. C. Salaman, ed., *James McBey* (1924), vol. 2 of *Modern masters of etching* (1924–32)
Archives Aberdeen Art Gallery · IWM | Boston PL, Wiggin Gift collection · National Gallery of Art, Washington, DC, Lessing Rosenwald Gift collection · NL Scot., papers incl. corresp. with James Grieg · U. Glas., Archives and Business Record Centre, letters to Lord Rowallan · U. Glas. L., letters mainly to Renee Goode
Likenesses J. McBey, self-portrait, chalk and watercolour drawing, 1918, IWM · M. Hardie, pencil drawing, 1919, NPG · B. Schotz, bronze bust, 1924, Aberdeen Art Gallery and Museums; copy, Cummer Gallery of Art, Jacksonville, Florida · G. L. Brockhurst, engraving, 1931, AM Oxf. · G. L. Brockhurst, oils, *c.*1931, Boston PL · J. McBey, self-portrait, oils, 1952, priv. coll. · M. Hardie, watercolour, Aberdeen Art Gallery and Museums · J. McBey, self-portrait, ink and watercolour drawing, Aberdeen Art Gallery and Museums

Mac Brádaigh, Fiachra (*c.*1690–*c.*1760), poet and scribe, may have been born in the townland of Drumgallon in the parish of Drung, co. Cavan, where he later lived. He taught in a 'hedge school' in Stradone in the nearby parish of Laragh, and was dubbed 'a witty schoolmaster' and 'a tolerably good poet' (O'Reilly, ccx). Some half-dozen of his poems are extant, three of them in his own hand. The titles, or opening lines, of three others are known but they appear not to have survived. Mac Brádaigh's most celebrated compositions are his 'Aisling' ('Vision poem'), his

'Faoistin' ('Confession'), and his 'Seachrán' (a humorous account of his wanderings, including a journey to Dublin). The first and last of these appeared in print within a generation of his death, in a Dublin magazine, *Anthologia Hibernica* (October and December 1793). 'The rollicking drollery of his verses' has been remarked on, as has the fact that 'he puts the stamp of his locality and of his own individuality on his compositions' (Ó Mórdha, 6).

Mac Brádaigh's scribal work survives in a manuscript in the British Library (MS Egerton 135) and, indirectly, in a manuscript in the Royal Irish Academy, Dublin. The former contains three of his own poems and some genealogical material addressed to three friends who may well have been former pupils from his school in Stradone. Two of them were working as clerks in the Dublin Linen Hall and the third may also have been resident in the capital. The material in Mac Brádaigh's hand, dated September 1755, appears to have been intended as a rough draft; in a note he asks Muiris Ó Gormáin, the celebrated south Ulster scribe, then based in Dublin, to rewrite it 'with good ink and plaine writing' (Ó Mórdha, 13). The Royal Irish Academy manuscript is a careful early nineteenth-century copy, penned in co. Cork, of an interesting collection of early modern Irish prose tales and some short pieces of poetry which Mac Brádaigh compiled in Drumgallon early in 1722. The original, produced for a local gentleman and landholder named Ros Mac Cába, or Ross Mac Cabe, of Lappan, also in the parish of Drung, appears to be lost.

The precise date and place of Mac Brádaigh's death are uncertain. One tradition suggests that he died in his native place, while a conflicting one indicates, enigmatically, that he was buried in Dunsandle, presumably the place of that name in co. Galway. The suggestion, sometimes made, that Fiachra was a brother to the rather notorious Pilib Mac Brádaigh (alias Pilib an Ministéir or Parson Brady) is without foundation.

NOLLAIG Ó MURAÍLE

Sources DNB · S. P. Ó Mórdha, 'Fiachra Mac Brádaigh, poet and scribe of central Cavan', *Heart of Breifne*, 1/3 (1890), 4–23 · E. O'Reilly, *A chronological account of … four hundred Irish writers … down to … 1750, with a descriptive catalogue of … their works* (1820)

Mac Brádaigh, Pilip. See Macbrady, Philip (*fl.* 1711).

Mac Brádaigh, Risteard. See Brady, Richard (*d.* 1607).

Macbrady, Fiachra. See Mac Brádaigh, Fiachra (*c.*1690–*c.*1760).

Macbrady, Philip [Pilip Mac Brádaigh] (*fl.* **1711**), Irish scholar, was born in co. Cavan. He was brought up a protestant and became vicar of the parish of Inishmagrath, in the diocese of Kilmore—hence the by-name Pilip Ministeir by which he was also known. He translated into Irish a sermon preached by John Tillotson, archbishop of Canterbury, before William III and Mary II at Hampton Court in April 1689, on St Luke 10. 42, and this was included in a book of sermons compiled by Charles Lynegar and John Richardson, printed in Irish type, but with a title-page in

Roman letters, by Elinor Everingham, entitled *Seanmora ar na priom Phonicibh na Chreideamh* (1711).

Macbrady was a friend of the blind harpist Turlough Carolan and wrote an Irish poem addressed to him, besides other verses and epigrams. Nothing is known of his family life, other than a verse written on seeing his daughter weep at the report of the death of a youth. He suspected it was her lover, and asked why she wept. 'Some snuff I was taking', was her reply, but her father saw the true cause, recited this Irish verse, found the report of the youth's death to be mistaken, sent for him, and consented to the marriage. He is now known mainly for the humorous Irish compositions in which he features, some having passed into the oral tradition of his native Cavan.

NORMAN MOORE, *rev.* ANITA MCCONNELL

Sources B. Ó'Cuív, 'Irish language and literature, 1691–1845', *A new history of Ireland*, ed. T. W. Moody and others, 4: *Eighteenth-century Ireland, 1691–1800* (1986), 374–419

MacBrayne, David (*bap.* 1817, *d.* 1907), shipowner, was baptized on 25 December 1817 in the Barony parish of Glasgow, the son of David MacBrayne, registrar of births in the Barony parish, and Elizabeth Stevenson Burns, daughter of the Revd Dr John Burns of the Barony Church. After initial training as a typefounder, he joined a shipping firm to train as a clerk. This was probably in the office of his uncles, George and James Burns, who in 1830 had established the City of Glasgow Steam Packet Company, trading between Glasgow, Liverpool, Belfast, and Londonderry. The Burns's partners in this were two Liverpool Scots, David and Charles MacIver; it was George Burns and David MacIver who joined with Samuel Cunard as founding partners of what became the Cunard Line.

In developing their Scottish business G. and J. Burns acquired the Castle Line in 1845, a west highland service. However, in 1848 they sold it to a partnership of their shipping clerk, David Hutcheson, his brother Alexander, and their young nephew David MacBrayne. The new company was operated as David and Alexander Hutcheson & Co., with MacBrayne as a junior partner. This company was early into the competition to open up access to the western highlands and islands, where the advent of the steamer offered the prospect of developing regular services for freight and passengers. Another potential market, in the tourist trade, was simultaneously emerging. Queen Victoria had travelled by track boat through the Crinan Canal in 1847, then onward by steamer via Loch Linnhe to Fort William, and through the Caledonian Canal to Inverness. The 'royal route' through the wild splendour of the Western Isles and highlands had been pioneered, and David MacBrayne and his partners were quick to develop it, initially with second-hand tonnage. New purpose-built vessels quickly followed, the first being the *Iona* in 1855. This introduced Hutchesons' 'crack' steamers offering a new style of service combining speed, regularity, comfort, and economy, all under the watchful eye of David MacBrayne, who was responsible for the supervision of the ships and their accommodation. This formula brought them success during thirty years of partnership from 1848 to 1878, during which time the Hutchesons and MacBrayne developed a fleet of fifteen steamers, competing vigorously with the railway ones. The Hutchesons retired between 1876 and 1878 leaving MacBrayne as sole proprietor of his renamed David MacBrayne & Co.

This was the prelude to ten years of vigorous expansion, even though MacBrayne was in his sixties. Ten new vessels were added to make MacBrayne's the pre-eminent service to the islands and highlands. He also skilfully captured a large part of the seasonal tourist trade by developing a variety of daily tours, and longer excursions for which he wrote and published a full-coloured guide in 1878. By the end of the 1880s he operated 28 ships employing 750 men afloat and 700 onshore. This earned the company the famous tag:

> The earth it is the Lord's and all that it contains,
> Except the Western Isles and they are all MacBraynes.

Loyalty was a strong feature of the company, most of his men having twenty-five years' or more service with him. His red-funnelled vessels developed a high reputation under his careful and detailed administration.

David MacBrayne was totally absorbed by his shipping business, and did not marry until 1860. His wife, Robina Eckford Robertson, was the daughter of an Edinburgh banker, Lawrence Robertson. They had two sons and a daughter. The sons, David Hope MacBrayne and Lawrence MacBrayne, joined their widowed father as partners in 1902, when he was already in ill health. David MacBrayne finally withdrew from active business in 1905, the partnership converting to a limited company with the elder son, David, as chairman and managing director. Even then David MacBrayne kept in constant touch with the affairs of the business, which had been his life for nearly sixty years. He had had little time for, or interest in, other commitments, though he served dutifully on the Clyde Navigation Trust in the 1860s, and as a JP for Glasgow. He died at his home, 11 Park Circus Place, Glasgow, on 26 January 1907. At his death, his name was synonymous with shipping services to the highlands and the western and northern isles. His sons actively developed the business bearing his name, which was subsequently absorbed into a larger conglomerate.

ANTHONY SLAVEN

Sources A. Slaven, 'Macbrayne, David', *DSBB* · *The Bailie* (7 Aug 1878), 1–2 · *The Bailie* (27 June 1888), 1–2 · *Glasgow of today* (1888) · *Glasgow and its environs* (1891) · *The Engineer* (1 Feb 1907) · *Glasgow Herald* (28 Jan 1907) · *The Scotsman* (28 Jan 1907) · G. E. Todd, *Who's who in Glasgow in 1909* (1909) · inventory of estate, NA Scot., SC 36/48/07 · trust disposition and settlement, NA Scot., SC 36/51/144 · d. cert. · IGI

Likenesses caricature, engraving, repro. in *The Bailie*, 12/303 (7 Aug 1878) · engraving, repro. in *The Bailie*, 32/819 (27 June 1888) · photograph, repro. in *Glasgow Biographic Notices*, 16, 145

Wealth at death £28,397 4s. 8d.: confirmation, 22 Aug 1907, CCI · £329 15s. 6d.: additional estate, 30 June 1908, CCI

Mac Briain, Donnchad [Donough O'Brien] (*d.* 1064), king of Munster, was the son of *Brian Bóruma (*d.* 1014) and of Gormlaith (*d.* 1030), the sister of Máel Mórda Ua Fáeláin, king of Leinster, and former wife of Olaf (Amlaíb), king of the Dublin vikings. The battle of Clontarf in 1014 greatly weakened Brian's descendants, the Uí Briain of Dál Cais in north Munster. This was a time of intense competition among the provincial Irish kings and Mac Briain had great difficulty in retaining power over Munster. He had little prospect of continuing his father's attempts to extend control over much of Ireland and faced internal opposition. His half-brother Tadc was an equal claimant to the kingship and several Munster dynasties began to assert themselves at this time. In 1023 Donnchad had Tadc assassinated and at this point he began to show his power. In 1025 he marched north into Connacht, plundered the capital Cruachu, and returned with hostages. The following year he began to extend his influence to the east, taking hostages from Meath, Brega, Norse Dublin, and Leinster, and returned with the king of Osraige to Kincora, an Uí Briain stronghold. A significant recognition of his authority is recorded in this year when Abbot Amalgaid of Armagh and his 'venerable clerics' (annals of Inisfallen, s.a. 1026) spent Easter at Kincora.

Events in east Munster and Leinster cut short Donnchad Mac Briain's advance. Toward the end of the decade the kingdom of Osraige reached the zenith of its power under Donnchad Mac Gilla Pádraig. The ruling Leinster dynasty of Uí Dúnlainge lost out to the rising Uí Chennselaig led by the dynamic Diarmait mac Máel na mBó, whose wife was Derbforgaill (d. 1080), Donnchad Mac Briain's daughter. Both Mac Gilla Pádraig and Diarmait—frequently acting together—resisted the ambitions of the king of Munster. From this point, Mac Briain's influence was contained to the north-west by the powerful Áed Ua Conchobair, king of Connacht, and balanced by Diarmait mac Máel na mBó in Leinster to the south-east. However, it was the emergence of Toirdelbach *Ua Briain, the son of his assassinated brother, that brought about the powerful combination of these two forces and Mac Briain's downfall.

In 1051 Áed Ua Conchobair invaded Munster and Donnchad Mac Briain's son Domnall Bán died in the encounter. Although Áed and Diarmait mac Máel na mBó were Donnchad's natural enemies, it is likely that their concerted attacks on Munster about 1054 were the result of Toirdelbach Ua Briain's intrigues. In that year Áed, with the support of Toirdelbach, attacked north Munster while Diarmait and the men of Osraige attacked from the east. In 1058 Toirdelbach, with the backing of Diarmait, again marched against his uncle. Donnchad had no choice but to flee before their advance, preferring to burn the city of Limerick rather than see it fall into their hands. When he did engage his enemies shortly after, at the battle of Slíab Crot, he suffered defeat. These events probably forced on Donnchad the realization of how destructive a joint assault could be. To outmanoeuvre Toirdelbach and escape such combined attacks in the future, Donnchad submitted to King Áed of Connacht in 1060. The tactic was unsuccessful, for in 1061 Áed destroyed Donnchad's fort of Kincora and burned the Dál Cais ecclesiastical centre of Killaloe. Diarmait of Leinster and Toirdelbach marched into Munster and secured the submission of the nobles of the plain of Munster. Donnchad's son, Murchad in Scéith Girr ('Murchad of the Short Shield'), resisted Toirdelbach without success. When Diarmait departed, Toirdelbach

was confronted by an army put in the field by Donnchad and his son. Again, Toirdelbach emerged victorious and was soon supported by the return of Diarmait. Mac Briain acknowledged defeat and left on pilgrimage for Rome, where he died in 1064. He is buried in the church of Santo Stefano Rotondo on the Caelian Hill, where a later plaque records him as king of Cashel and Thomond.

Although Donnchad Mac Briain's career has been seen as disappointing when compared to that of his father, Brian Bóruma, he did manage to secure his position as king of Munster and retained the kingship for four decades. In the early, dynamic, period of his career he attempted to continue his father's campaign to control Leinster and the east, a campaign that was realized in the reigns of his nephew Toirdelbach Ua Briain and great-nephew Muirchertach *Ua Briain. An entry inserted in the annals of Inisfallen recording Mac Briain's marriage in 1032 to a daughter of Ragnall testifies to his interest in establishing dynastic links with the Norse. The genealogies in the Book of Lecan record that Donnchad had twelve sons, and elsewhere Gormlaith, daughter of Ua Donnocáin, king of Ára, is named as Murchad's mother. Donnchad's activity in proclaiming ecclesiastical ordinances and his convening of a Munster synod show a ruler intent on extending royal prerogatives and also point the way to the reforming practices of his Uí Briain successors, who made Munster the centre of church reform. The annals of Inisfallen record how Donnchad enacted a law in 1040 which attempted to enforce strict sabbatarianism. The annals of the four masters refer to a Munster synod held in 1050 at Killaloe under Donnchad's presidency 'where they enacted a law and a restraint upon every injustice, from small to great. God gave peace and favourable weather in consequence of this law' (AFM, s.a. 1050). Despite the exaggeration that can be expected from such sources, Donnchad Mac Briain's career was indeed largely peaceful. At a time when a ruler's success was measured by his ability to wage war, perhaps a different criterion should be applied to Donnchad and due recognition be given to his achievement in maintaining both peace and his grip on power.   DAMIAN BRACKEN

Sources AFM · S. Mac Airt, ed. and trans., *The annals of Inisfallen* (1951) · *Ann. Ulster* · D. Murphy, ed., *The annals of Clonmacnoise*, trans. C. Mageoghagan (1896); facs. edn (1993) · *The Book of Lecan*, ed. K. Mulchrone (1937) · W. M. Hennessy, ed. and trans., *Chronicum Scotorum: a chronicle of Irish affairs*, Rolls Series, 46 (1866) · W. M. Hennessy, ed. and trans., *The annals of Loch Cé: a chronicle of Irish affairs from AD 1014 to AD 1590*, 2 vols., Rolls Series, 54 (1871) · W. Stokes, ed., 'The annals of Tigernach [8 pts]', *Revue Celtique*, 16 (1895), 374–419; 17 (1896), 6–33, 119–263, 337–420; 18 (1897), 9–59, 150–97, 267–303, 374–91; pubd sep. (1993) · M. A. O'Brien, ed., *Corpus genealogiarum Hiberniae* (Dublin, 1962) · M. C. Dobbs, ed. and trans., 'The Banshenchus [3 pts]', *Revue Celtique*, 47 (1930), 283–339; 48 (1931), 163–234; 49 (1932), 437–89 · J. Ryan, 'The O'Briens in Munster after Clontarf', *North Munster Antiquarian Journal*, 2 (1940–41), 141–52; 3 (1942–3), 1–152 · 'The Dalcassians', *North Munster Antiquarian Journal*, 3 (1942–3), 189–202 · F. J. Byrne, *Irish kings and high-kings* (1973) · J. Hogan, 'The Ua Briain kingship in Telach Óc', *Féilsgribhinn Eóin Mhic Néill*, ed. J. Ryan [E. Ua Riain] (1940) · D. Ó Corráin, *Ireland before the Normans* (1972) · D. Ó Corráin, 'The career of Diarmait mac Máel no mBó, king of Leinster', *Journal of Old Wexford Society*, 3 (1970–71), 27–35 · D. Ó Cróinín, *Early medieval Ireland, 400–1200* (1995) ·

K. Hughes, *The church in early Irish society* (1966) • M. T. Flanagan, *Irish society, Anglo-Norman settlers, Angevin kingship: interactions in Ireland in the late twelfth century* (1989)

Macbride, David (1726–1778), chemist and physician, was born on 26 April 1726 at Ballymoney, co. Antrim, Ireland, one of three children of Robert *McBride (1686/7–1759) [*see under* McBride, John] and his wife, the daughter of Mr Boyd of Killabeg, co. Down. His father was a Scottish minister, and John *Macbride (d. 1800) was his brother. He was educated at the village school, and after serving an apprenticeship to a local surgeon he entered the Royal Navy, where he was a mate aboard a hospital ship and then a surgeon during the war of Austrian succession (1741–8). The seafaring life enabled him to observe scurvy—the scourge of the eighteenth-century British navy—and this shaped his lifelong search for an effective antiscorbutic.

After the peace of 1748 Macbride studied anatomy with Monro Secundus in Edinburgh and with William Hunter in London, where he also studied midwifery with William Smellie. He returned to Ballymoney in 1749 and moved to Dublin in 1751. He soon won the affections of Dorcas Evory, but her father made her marry George Cumming, a Dublin merchant, and Macbride went on to marry Margaret Armstrong on 20 November 1753 at St Audoen's Church, Dublin. In due course, however, the widowed Macbride married his widowed 'first love' in the same church on 5 June 1762. He had no children by either marriage.

Macbride set up practice as a surgeon and accoucheur in 1752, but bashfulness limited his practice for several years. His real abilities were known only to his family and close friends, who appreciated him not only for his pleasant nature and agreeable manner but also for his general knowledge of painting, music, and polite literature. Attracted to the Enlightenment world of polite and useful learning, he joined and read papers before the Medico-Philosophical Society, formed in 1756 in Dublin; he became its secretary in 1762. His medical practice expanded considerably in 1764, when the publication of his *Experimental Essays* brought him into notice and when the University of Glasgow made him MD. With this qualification in hand, Macbride started a course of medical lectures in his home in the winter of 1766–7. He published them in 1772 as *A Methodical Introduction to the Theory and Practice of Physic*, which was translated into Latin in 1774 and reissued in an enlarged edition in Dublin in 1776. Macbride's interest in useful knowledge was also evident in December 1767, when he made a new discovery in the art of tanning, substituting lime-water for water in part of the process. For this discovery he was, in 1768, made an honorary member of the Dublin Royal Society, which also awarded him a silver medal. In 1769 the Society of Arts of London gave him a gold medal, and his 'Account of the improved method of tanning leather' was published in the *Philosophical Transactions* of 1778.

Macbride is remembered mainly for his work on scurvy in his *Experimental Essays*. The object and method of his researches were characteristic of Enlightenment medicine, which looked to science to curb the diseases of modern institutional populations, in gaols, in hospital ships, and in military camps. The most important of these diseases were fevers. In the early 1750s John Pringle emphasized the putrid nature of gaol fever, dysentery, and scurvy, and tested various substances for their antiseptic or restorative qualities. Interpreting these results within a theoretical framework shaped by the work of Stephen Hales and Joseph Black in pneumatic (gas) chemistry, Macbride related putrefaction to the loss of fixed air (carbon dioxide) and the efficacy of antiseptics or antiscorbutics in the prevention of, or restoration from, this loss. As a cheap and readily available source of fixed air, Macbride recommended to the Admiralty in 1767 the use of fresh wort, or infusion of malt, in the treatment of scurvy. While his brother, Admiral John Macbride, reported some success with the remedy on a voyage in 1765–7, the results obtained on Cook's expeditions were confused and ambiguous; in the early 1790s the Admiralty finally decided in favour of James Lind's recommendation of lemon juice. Macbride's experimental results also sparked Joseph Priestley's interest in the medicinal possibilities of the new gases he was discovering, and this research led to the work of Thomas Beddoes and the Pneumatic Institute.

The attention focused on Macbride in the wake of his *Experimental Essays* also had its adverse effects. The resulting demand for his medical services induced in his gentle and uncertain nature a state of chronic tension and insomnia. This enfeebling condition led to a fever, brought on by a cold, from which he died, in his house in Cavendish Row, Dublin, on 28 December 1778; he was buried in St Audoen's Church. Although a minor figure in eighteenth-century science and medicine, Macbride was nevertheless remembered by many—not least the anxious women he aided through the perils of eighteenth-century birthing; for them he was 'the hope of weeping eyes' (*Dublin Quarterly Journal of Medical Science*, 289).

JOHN G. McEVOY

Sources 'Memoir of Dr Macbride', *Dublin Quarterly Journal of Medical Science*, 3 (1847), 281–90 • K. J. Carpenter, *The history of scurvy and vitamin C* (1986) • E. L. Scott, 'The "Macbridean doctrine" of air: an eighteenth-century explanation of some biochemical processes including photosynthesis', *Ambix*, 17 (1970), 43–57 • C. Lawrence, 'Priestley in Tahiti: the medical interests of a dissenting chemist', *Science, medicine and dissent: Joseph Priestley (1733–1804)*, ed. R. G. W. Anderson and C. Lawrence (1987), 1–10 • DNB
Likenesses J. T. Smith, stipple and line engraving, pubd 1797 (after Reynolds of Dublin), BM, NPG • W. H. Lizars, stipple, pubd 1847 (after Reynolds of Dublin), NG Ire.; repro. in *Dublin Quarterly Journal of Medical Science* • Reynolds of Dublin, portrait

MacBride, Ernest William (1866–1940), biologist, was born on 12 December 1866 in Belfast, the first of the five children of Samuel MacBride, linen manufacturer, and his wife, Mary, daughter of a Presbyterian minister. He was educated at the Royal Belfast Academical Insitution and Queen's College in Belfast, and then studied zoology at University College, London, where he obtained a BSc in 1889. He moved to St John's College, Cambridge, where he was elected fellow in 1893 after having obtained a first-class BA in zoology in 1891.

After a brief period of study at the Stazione Zoologica in Naples, MacBride returned to Cambridge as university demonstrator in animal morphology. Then in 1897 he was appointed professor of zoology at McGill University, Montreal. There he supervised the building of new laboratories and taught a zoology course, primarily to medical students. While in Canada, in 1902 he married Constance Harvey, daughter of H. Chrysler KC, an Ottawa barrister; they had two sons. In 1909 MacBride was appointed assistant to Adam Sedgwick, professor of zoology at Imperial College, London. He remained at Imperial until his retirement in 1934, succeeding Sedgwick in 1914 and developing a successful postgraduate research school.

MacBride built his scientific reputation on his studies of the embryology of invertebrates, especially the echinoderms (including starfish and sea-urchins). He published a series of papers and also the *Textbook of Embryology* (1914). When he trained in London and Cambridge, the minute study of embryological development was still seen as a vital source of information on evolutionary relationships. MacBride remained loyal to this belief, even when the vast majority of biologists turned away to other interests. Indeed, he was one of the last British scientists to defend in detail the theory that the development of the embryo recapitulates the evolutionary history of its species. Nevertheless, it was through the application of this theory that he made his most enduring contribution: his recognition that echinoderms (which are now characterized by radial symmetry) have evolved by degeneration from a bilaterally symmetrical form. He showed that the cushion star, *Asterina*, passes through a larval stage in which it is attached to the sea-bed. This he interpreted as the relic of an evolutionary stage in which the ancestors of the echinoderms gave up their free-swimming habits and began to degenerate into radial symmetry. He was one of the first to recognize that the ancestors of the echinoderms must have been closely related to the earliest chordates, from which the vertebrates have descended.

MacBride continued to defend the recapitulation theory long after most biologists rejected it in favour of new approaches to the study of development and heredity. He condemned the new science of genetics as based on the study of artificially induced characters. MacBride favoured the Lamarckian theory of the inheritance of acquired characteristics: he believed that changes in bodily structure produced by new habits would gradually become incorporated into the species' inheritance. In effect, he maintained, heredity represents a memory of the species' past evolutionary modifications. In the 1920s he played a prominent role in defending the Lamarckian biologist Paul Kammerer against attacks by the geneticists. As a fluent German-speaker, MacBride provided on-the-spot translations for Kammerer when the latter visited London in April 1923.

MacBride's Lamarckism has deflected historians' attention from his extreme position on social issues. Through the 1920s he played a prominent role in the Eugenics Society, eventually becoming vice-president. He strongly endorsed claims that persons of 'inferior' character should be prevented from reproducing, as a means of purifying the population. He argued for the compulsory sterilization of the least fit members of the British population, whom he identified as those of Irish descent. According to MacBride (who was of Ulster protestant stock), the Irish race had evolved in a less challenging environment than that which had produced the hardy Anglo-Saxons. His views on compulsory sterilization were not endorsed by the membership of the Eugenics Society, and in 1931 he resigned as vice-president. He defended the fascist side in the Spanish Civil War, and in 1937 he expressed support for German military policy.

Less controversially, MacBride served on the council and also as chairman of the Marine Biological Association. In 1913 he was appointed to a committee of the Board of Agriculture and Fisheries, formed to draw up a programme of investigation into Britain's fisheries. In 1919 he joined the advisory committee on fisheries research set up by the Development Commissioners, and was appointed chairman of the committee in 1933.

After his retirement MacBride moved to Alton in Hampshire, where he died at his home, Westbank, on 17 November 1940 and was buried on 25 November at St Lawrence's Church there. His wife survived him. He was remembered with affection by many of his students, who preferred to concentrate on his enthusiasm as a teacher rather than on his outdated theoretical opinions and controversial political stance.

PETER J. BOWLER

Sources W. T. Calman, *Obits. FRS*, 3 (1939–41), 747–59 · P. J. Bowler, 'E. W. MacBride's Lamarckian eugenics', *Annals of Science*, 41 (1984), 245–60 · A. Koestler, *The case of the midwife toad* (1971) · G. R. Searle, 'Eugenics and politics in Britain in the 1930s', *Annals of Science*, 36 (1979), 159–69 · *Nature*, 146 (1940), 831–2 · *The Times* (23 Nov 1940) **Archives** U. Cam., department of zoology, lecture notes | CAC Cam., corresp. with A. V. Hill · Rice University, Houston, Texas, Woodson Research Center, corresp. with Sir Julian Huxley **Likenesses** F. A. de Biden Footner, drawing, 1934, repro. in Calman, *Obits. FRS* **Wealth at death** £5271 15s. 10d.: administration with will, 18 April 1941, *CGPLA Eng. & Wales*

McBride, John (*c*.1650–1718), minister of the Presbyterian General Synod of Ulster and religious controversialist, may have been the son of John McBryd, merchant, admitted a freeman of Belfast in 1644. He clearly came from Scottish stock but was almost certainly born in the north of Ireland, since on entering Glasgow University in 1666 he styled himself 'Hibernus'. Having graduated in 1673 McBride was ordained in 1679 as minister of Clare, co. Armagh. In or before 1687 he had married Margaret (*d*. in or after 1718?), daughter of William Fairlie of Tullyreavy, co. Tyrone. They had three sons and a daughter, to whom McBride was a loving if heavy-handed and even irascible parent. He left in 1688 to take charge of the parish of Borgue in Kirkcudbrightshire, and attended the national assembly of the Church of Scotland in 1692. A popular preacher, rigorously orthodox, and with a sharp if heavily sardonic wit, he was called to Ayr in 1691, but the presbytery refused to translate him. By June 1694 he was back at Clare, and attending the General Synod of Ulster, and later that year succeeded Patrick Adair at Belfast. Through his friendship with the third earl of Donegal he was able to obtain a site for a new church in Rosemary Lane (subsequently Rosemary Street), to which the congregation removed in 1695.

McBride's intellectual capacity and force of character propelled him to the forefront of the Presbyterian community in Ireland. As early as 1695 he was involved in canvassing the Irish parliament in a vain attempt to secure a toleration act, and afterwards threw himself into the paper war over the issue ignited by the Dublin dissenting minister Joseph Boyse's *Case of the Dissenting Protestants of Ireland*. Boyse had been answered by three Anglican clergymen, bishops Pullein of Dromore and Dopping of Meath, and a future archbishop, Edward Synge, and McBride's *Animadversions on the Answer to the Case*, published in 1697, took issue with each of Boyse's detractors: the pamphlet was undeniably effective, if remorselessly ponderous. The same year he was elected moderator of the general synod. At the beginning of the next synod, in June 1698, he preached as outgoing moderator; the sermon, a strong defence of Presbyterian church organization and of synodical authority in particular, was deemed sufficiently important to be printed. The style, 'minister of Belfast', accorded him on the title-page, and a passage in which he appeared to claim that synods were legal even without the consent of the secular power, enraged Bishop Edward Walkington of Down and Connor, who alerted the Dublin government. As good whigs the lords justices were unwilling to prosecute, and instead McBride was summoned to a special hearing, presided over by the lord chancellor, John Methuen, assisted by the chief justices, and in the presence of six bishops. He successfully defended himself, pointing out that the composition of the title-page was not his responsibility, and that the offending passage of text had been qualified by a saving phrase. The lord chancellor was thus able to dismiss him with nothing more than an admonition to behave 'rectably' for the future towards the established church.

McBride's stature among Ulster's Presbyterians was such that in 1700 the new patent for the *regium donum* (the royal grant towards the maintenance of ministers) was lodged with him for safe keeping. He plunged into print again in 1702 with a *Vindication of Marriage, as Solemnized by Presbyterians in the North of Ireland*, a point by point refutation of the case made by the established church, in pamphlets and lawsuits, against the legality of marriages performed by Presbyterian ministers. He had thus made himself a prime target for Anglican revenge when the passage of the English statute of 1703 imposing an abjuration oath in England and Ireland exposed him to prosecution. Together with two other ministers McBride refused the oath rather than (as he saw it) commit himself to uphold episcopacy, and swear to something he could not know, the Pretender's illegitimacy. As he explained to his old friend Sir Hans Sloane, 'my scrupling the oaths is not from

the least disaffection to her Majesty's person or government' but was a simple obedience to conscience, that 'incommunicable jewel, the loss whereof nothing can repair or requite' (BL, Sloane MS 4043, fol. 68). Fearing arrest he spent the winter of 1703–4 in Scotland, where the abjuration did not apply, but was back in Belfast to attend the synod in June 1704. However, local tory magistrates eventually secured a warrant, and in 1705 he was obliged to take refuge again in Scotland. There is a story (the supposed evidence for which is still visible) that the mayor of Belfast, who came to arrest him, was so enraged at finding the bird flown that he drew his sword and stabbed the portrait of McBride which hung in the manse.

McBride remained in Glasgow until 1708, supplying the Blackfriars kirk but declining a chair in divinity at the university. He was chosen moderator of Glasgow presbytery in 1708. In the meantime the General Synod of Ulster had appointed James Kirkpatrick to assist him in Belfast, and then, following a petition from some of the elders, which McBride had at first endorsed, divided the congregation into two. There were factional, and perhaps, doctrinal tensions between the two churches (Kirkpatrick and his friends being associated with advanced theological and philosophical ideas), and a group of McBride's supporters disputed the practical arrangements which the synod had made for the division. Thinking himself safe under a whig viceroy, McBride returned to Ireland to help settle matters. He was duly discharged by magistrates at Carrickfergus in respect of the earlier warrant, but within two years his situation had once more deteriorated. There were quarrels with those other Presbyterian ministers who were prepared to take the oaths, and in summer 1710 some high-flying JPs, anticipating political changes in Ireland in the wake of the impeachment of the high-church clergyman, Henry Sacheverell, in England, took out new warrants against the nonjurors. McBride returned to Glasgow while appeals were made to the English ministry. He was sufficiently encouraged to reappear in Ireland, but withdrew for a third time in 1712 following a presentment against him by the co. Antrim grand jury.

In McBride's absence the general synod advised ministers to take the abjuration, but only 'if they have clearness to it' (*Records of the General Synod*, 1.283) and at the same time renewed an earlier appointment to McBride to write 'an history of this church' (ibid., 1.284), with Kirkpatrick to help him. What he produced was a polemical defence of the Presbyterians' political record against tory charges of disloyalty. The particular object of McBride's indignation was his neighbour in Belfast, the Church of Ireland parson William Tisdall, whose *Sample of Trew-Blue Presbyterian Loyalty* (1709) provided the occasion for his own reply, *A Sample of Jet-Black Pr—Tic Calumny*, published anonymously in Glasgow in 1713. Although concerned with contemporary political developments (and from time to time defending himself, in the third person), he offered a typically learned and laborious disquisition, essentially historical in structure and argument and lacking the verve and incisiveness of his Anglican antagonist.

Despite being subject to an outstanding warrant McBride returned to Ireland for good in June 1713. Orders were given for his arrest but the sub-sheriff ignored them. After the Hanoverian succession McBride remained true to his principles and would not take the oaths to George I, but the authorities now left him alone. Although increasingly infirm and racked with gout he joined his fellow nonjuror Alexander McCracken in 1716–17 in opposing moves to accept a legal toleration on any other basis than subscription to the Westminster confession, a prelude to the great controversy over subscription which would divide the general synod in 1720–26. He died on 21 July 1718, 'aetatis suae 68', and was buried in Belfast on 23 July. His wife almost certainly outlived him. Their younger children were each left a guinea in his will, since, as he said, he had already during his lifetime adequately provided for them.

Robert McBride (1686/7–1759), eldest son of John, was also educated at Glasgow. He was always intended for the ministry, and while still a probationer preached on the king's birthday in 1716 to the Belfast company of independent volunteers, a sermon which was subsequently printed. In September that year he was admitted as minister of Ballymoney, co. Antrim, where he stayed for the rest of his life and was remembered as the model of a conscientious and efficient pastor. A strong supporter of orthodox theology, and of the principle of subscription, he frequently clashed with the New Light faction in the general synod, and especially with his father's successor, Samuel Haliday. At one point he was sent over to Scotland to obtain the opinion of the general assembly, and on his return found himself accused of misrepresenting the views of the non-subscribers. In or before 1726 he married the daughter of a Mr Boyd of Killabeg, co. Down. They had a daughter and two sons, David *MacBride and John *MacBride, both of whom joined the Royal Navy. In 1726 he contributed a pamphlet to the controversy, the *Overtures Transmitted by the General Synod, 1725, in a Fair Light*. In 1728 he was elected moderator. He died on 2 September 1759 in his seventy-third year, and was buried in Ballymoney churchyard. A memorial tablet inside the parish church described him as 'truly pious, always cheerful, moderate in his principles … universally beloved and lived in friendship with the good men of all persuasions' (Witherow, 211), perhaps in unconscious irony, in view of his father's long record of conflict with the established church.

D. W. HAYTON

Sources T. Witherow, *Historical and literary memorials of presbyterianism in Ireland, 1623–1731* (1879), 109–25, 209–16 · *DNB* · J. S. Reid and W. D. Killen, *History of the Presbyterian church in Ireland*, 3 vols. (1834–53) · *Records of the General Synod of Ulster, from 1691 to 1820*, 3 vols. (1890–98), vols. 1–2 · *The correspondence of the Rev. Robert Wodrow*, ed. T. M'Crie, 3 vols., Wodrow Society, [3] (1842–3), vol. 1 · BL, Sloane MSS, 4038–4039, 4043, 4056–4057 · A. G. Brown, 'Irish Presbyterian theology in the early eighteenth century', PhD diss., Queen's University, Belfast, 1977 · *Fasti Scot.*, 1/2.701 · R. M. Young, ed., *The town book of the corporation of Belfast, 1613–1816* (1892), 251, 315 · J. Agnew, ed., *Funeral register of the First Presbyterian Church of Belfast, 1712–31* (1995), 12, 20, 43 · J. S. Porter, 'History of the First Presbyterian Congregation, Belfast', *Bible Christian*, 1/4 (1836), 112–15 · J. B. Armour and others, *A short history of the Presbyterian church of Ballymoney* (1898) · G. Benn, *A history of the town of Belfast*, 2 vols. (1877), 2.405 · C. Innes, ed., *Munimenta alme Universitatis Glasguensis / Records of the University of Glasgow from its foundation till 1727*, 4 vols., Maitland Club, 72 (1854), vol. 3

Archives BL, letters to Sir Hans Sloane, Sloane MSS 4038–4039, 4043, 4056–4057 · NL Scot., Wodrow MSS · U. Glas. L., Stirling MSS

Likenesses oils, Presbyterian church, Rosemary Street, Belfast; repro. in J. Agnew, *Belfast merchant families in the seventeenth century* (1996), 69

Wealth at death 'seems to have possessed a considerable amount of property': Benn, *A History*, vol. 2, p. 405n.

Macbride, John (c.1735–1800), naval officer and politician, was one of three children of Robert *McBride (1686/7–1759) [*see under* McBride, John (c.1650–1718)], a Presbyterian minister of Ballymoney, co. Antrim, and his wife, *née* Boyd, of Killabeg, co. Down. David *Macbride, chemist and physician, was his elder brother. John entered the Royal Navy about 1754, having served for some years in the merchant marine. His early days were spent as a midshipman, master's mate, or able seaman in the *Garland* in the West Indies. He was promoted lieutenant on 27 October 1758.

Macbride came to public attention in August 1761 while in command of the cutter *Grace*. He secured permission to lead some small boats into the roadstead at Dunkirk and captured a French privateer anchored there. In April 1762 he was promoted to command the fireship *Grampus*, and shortly afterwards he took over several other vessels, all in home waters. In 1766 he took the frigate *Jason* to the Falkland Islands, about which he published *A Journal of the Winds and Weather … at Falkland Islands from 1 Feb 1766 to 19 Jan 1767* (1770?). He then commanded several more vessels in home waters, on one occasion, in May 1772, escorting the queen of Denmark to the Scheldt. On 14 July 1774 he married Ursula, daughter of William Folkes of Hillington Hall, Norfolk. The couple had one son, John David *Macbride, who later became principal of Magdalen Hall, Oxford. In 1776 he was appointed to command the line of battle ship *Bienfaisant* (64 guns) and in her he was engaged in the tactically indecisive action off Ushant on 27 July 1778. Macbride did not play a significant part in the fighting; however, his evidence in favour of Viscount Keppel was instrumental in securing the commander-in-chief's acquittal when court martialled for misconduct in February 1779. Macbride was less supportive of Sir Hugh Palliser when he resigned from the Admiralty and was in turn court martialled.

In December 1779 Macbride sailed in the *Bienfaisant* with Sir George Rodney to relieve Gibraltar and *en route*, on 8 January 1780, he captured a Spanish 54-gun vessel. Macbride's ship took an important part in the battle of Cape St Vincent eight days later. The Spanish ship *San Domingo* blew up while engaged with the *Bienfaisant*, and then the *Phoenix*, flagship of Admiral Don Juan de Langara, surrendered to her. Because of a smallpox outbreak on the British vessel, Macbride agreed to let Langara and his officers remain on the *Phoenix*, but they were to act as if they were prisoners on the British ship. Both vessels eventually arrived safely in Gibraltar harbour.

Macbride was sent back to Britain with Rodney's dispatches and in March 1780 resumed command of *Bienfaisant*. His next notable action occurred shortly afterwards when, in the company of three other vessels, he went in search of a French privateer with which he eventually made contact off the Old Head of Kinsale on 13 August. Macbride's vessel opened fire first on the French ship, the *Comte d'Artois* (64 guns; over 600 men). After just over an hour, with the arrival of one of Macbride's supporting vessels, the French surrendered. Of the British squadron only *Bienfaisant* had suffered any serious casualties. In January 1781 he was appointed to command the former enemy frigate *Artois* (40 guns), and in her he took part in the battle of the Dogger Bank (5 August). In the aftermath of the battle he briefly took command of the line of battle ship *Princess Amelia*, whose captain had been killed in the action. He then returned to the *Artois* and on 3 December was engaged in another sharp fight with privateers, which resulted in his capturing two Dutch vessels in the North Sea. In April 1782, while cruising in the English Channel, Macbride was able to observe a French fleet heading for the West Indies, and reported their position to the main fleet, which intercepted and captured about half of them. In June he was stationed in Ireland, where he was employed to impress men for service with the fleet.

With the return of peace Macbride's career took a new turn. In 1784 he was elected MP for Plymouth, a seat he held until 1790 despite being appointed to command the Plymouth guardship *Cumberland* in 1788. As an MP Macbride spoke on naval affairs on several occasions. He was one of the naval members of the duke of Richmond's commission which investigated the state of the Portsmouth and Plymouth defences (1785–6) and he spoke out and voted against the proposals in the House of Commons.

Macbride went back to active service with the outbreak of war against France in February 1793. Promoted rear-admiral on 1 February, he became commander-in-chief of a frigate squadron patrolling the downs. He was then placed in command of a squadron off Brest and in December 1793 he led a small fleet to Brittany and Normandy, attempting to create a diversion on behalf of French royalists. On 4 July 1795 he was promoted vice-admiral and by early 1796 he was back in the North Sea, watching the Dutch fleet in the Texel. In February 1799 he was appointed admiral of the blue. His last appointments do not seem to have been especially successful, though for much of his career he was a popular and well-respected officer. He died following a stroke on 17 February 1800 at the Spring Garden Coffee House in London. His wife survived him.

MICHAEL PARTRIDGE

Sources *DNB* · *Naval Chronicle*, 19 (1808), 265–72 · J. Charnock, ed., *Biographia navalis*, 6 (1798), 555–63 · J. Ralfe, *The naval biography of Great Britain*, 4 vols. (1828) · J. Ralfe, *The naval biography of Great Britain*, 1 (1828), 401–6 · *GM*, 1st ser., 70 (1800), 285 · commission book, 'John Macbride', 27 Oct 1750, PRO, ADM 6/18, fol. 553 · R. Beatson, *Naval and military memoirs of Great Britain*, 2nd edn, 6 vols. (1804) · *GM*, 4th ser., 5 (1868), 393–4 · M. M. Drummond, 'Macbride, John', HoP, *Commons, 1754–90*, 3.79–80

Archives Hertford College, Oxford, commonplace and order book | NMM, letters to Lord Sandwich
Likenesses H. R. Cook, stipple, pubd 1808 (after Smart, 1760), NPG · J. Fittler, line engraving (after J. Northcote), BM, NPG · J. Northcote, oils, NMM

MacBride, John (1868–1916), Irish revolutionary and officer in the Irish brigade of the Boer army, was born on 7 May 1868 in The Quay, Westport, co. Mayo, Ireland, the youngest of five sons of Patrick MacBride, a shopkeeper and importer, and his wife, Honoria Gill. His father's family originated from the north of Ireland. MacBride was educated at the Christian Brothers' school, Westport, and at St Malachy's College, Belfast. For a while MacBride was employed in a draper's shop in Castlerea, co. Roscommon, during which time he involved himself in advanced Irish nationalist politics, being a member of both the Irish Republican Brotherhood (IRB—the Fenian movement) and of the politico-sporting Gaelic Athletic Association. MacBride moved to Dublin and worked as a clerk in Moore's wholesale chemist business in Yarnhall Street. By now he had come to the notice of the anti-insurgency G division of the Dublin Metropolitan Police, especially after he joined the extreme splinter group of the IRB, the Irish National Alliance. As a senior member MacBride attended the 1895 Irish republican convention in Chicago.

In 1896 MacBride, like several other prominent Irish republicans, emigrated to Transvaal (South African Republic), where he worked on Block B of the Langlaagte gold mine outside Johannesburg. Eighty years later reports emerged of a son being born at about this time to MacBride and a woman of mixed race. Within months of his arrival MacBride hijacked the politically moderate Irish club in the town and soon the Irish National Foresters, which included Arthur Griffith in its ranks, was a fervently active pro-Irish republican and pro-Kruger government organization. The centenary of the Irish insurrection of 1798 was prominently celebrated by the Irish in Johannesburg, more so than in Dublin, clearly demarcating the Irish as the 'odd man out' in Uitlander society. It was no surprise, therefore, that as Transvaal and Britain drew towards war in 1899 MacBride and his associates prepared to raise an Irish commando unit to fight alongside the Boer forces. Grandly termed the Irish brigade, it comprised about 300 men and was led at MacBride's suggestion by a former American cavalry lieutenant, John Blake, who took the title of colonel. MacBride was number two, with the title of major. He was also made a Transvaal citizen and a justice of the peace.

Frequently MacBride was in charge of the Irish commando and when Blake left to join another commando he was in full command (7 June to 23 September 1900); in Ireland, where pro-Boer fever swept through nationalist Ireland, the commando was invariably called MacBride's brigade. This small, wiry redheaded man (known as Foxy Jack) was popular with most of his men. As a unit his commando did sterling work outside Ladysmith guarding one of the great Long Tom creusot siege guns. MacBride and his men also fought well at the battles of Talana Hill, Lady-smith, Colenso, and Tugela Heights, and fought in the rear of the Boer army as it retreated across the Orange Free State and later eastern Transvaal. In his absence from Ireland, in May 1900, the advanced wing of Irish nationalism put MacBride's name forward against a home-rule candidate in a by-election in South Mayo. Despite his reputation he was defeated on a low poll. Another setback was the establishment by an Irish-Australian, Arthur Lynch, of a second, and rival, Irish commando unit in South Africa.

When MacBride's unit reached Komatipoort on the frontier with Portuguese Mozambique with the British cavalry less than a day behind them, most of what remained of the commando, including MacBride, crossed the border into neutral territory. Eventually MacBride made his way to Paris, where he was welcomed by a small Irish nationalist expatriate group dominated by (Edith) Maud *Gonne (1866–1953). She accompanied him for part of a not very successful lecture tour in the United States. Returning to Paris, MacBride worked as a journalist's runner. On 21 February 1903, against the advice of his friends, he married the beautiful Maud Gonne, then very much the muse of the poet W. B. Yeats. Arguably, he was dragooned into it by her: she later said that she thought she was marrying Ireland. A son, Seán *MacBride, was born in 1904, but the difference in temperament, wealth, education, and social status was more than the marriage could bear and by 1906, amid bitter recriminations which still resound in scholarly debate, a French court had granted a separation.

A newly elected Liberal government in Britain meant that MacBride could now return to Ireland unmolested by the authorities. He was a war hero among the nationalist population, but his heavy drinking and the publicity surrounding the collapse of his marriage had tarnished his image. A close friend of the republican Fred Allan, with whom he lived for a while, MacBride renewed his involvement with the IRB and for a period served on its supreme council. He was also a vice-president of Griffith's Cumann na nGaedheal and later a member of Sinn Féin. The truth, however, was that MacBride was politically marginalized even among the advanced nationalists. He made occasional political speeches and in 1906–7 he published a series of thirteen articles in the *Freeman's Journal* on his wartime experiences. Eventually he got a mundane job as water bailiff in the port of Dublin.

MacBride was excluded from the planning of the 1916 Easter rising. Coming into central Dublin to attend a wedding he stumbled on Thomas MacDonagh and his military unit on their way to occupy Jacobs' factory. MacDonagh immediately made MacBride his number two, and by all accounts MacBride fought well and hard during the following week. When the surrender took place he made no effort to escape or disguise his identity. He was court martialled, condemned, and shot in Kilmainham gaol on 5 May 1916, then interred there the same day. Overnight MacBride's reputation was restored from Yeats's 'drunken, vainglorious lout' of the poem 'Easter 1916' to national martyr. DONAL P. MCCRACKEN

Sources A. J. Jordan, *Major John MacBride, 1865–1916* (Westport, CT, 1991) · A. J. Jordan, *The Yeats–Gonne–MacBride triangle* (Dublin, 2001) · D. P. McCracken, *MacBride's brigade: Irish commandos in the Anglo-Boer War* (Dublin, 1999) · b. cert.
Archives NL Ire., Allan papers
Likenesses portrait, National Archives of South Africa, Pretoria · portrait, Kilmainham gaol, Dublin · portrait, repro. in M. Davitt, *The Boer fight for freedom* (1902)

MacBride, John Alexander Patterson (1819–1890), sculptor, was born in February 1819 at Campbeltown, Argyll, the son of Archibald MacBride. 'His mother was a McKenzie, and his grandmother a McKinnon' (*The Graphic*). He was trained as a sculptor at Liverpool in the studio of William Spence and also studied drawing at the Liverpool Art School with fellow students Richard Ansdell and Samuel Huggins. At the same time he studied anatomy at the Liverpool medical school under the eminent surgeons James Long and Alfred Higginson. In 1841, on the completion of his time with Spence, MacBride moved to London where he continued his studies at the British Museum. In 1844 his life-size group *Margaret of Anjou and her Son* was highly commended in the first sculpture contest at Westminster Hall. This work received mixed reviews. The *Literary Gazette* considered Margaret 'a virago' and her son 'a poor attenuated, impudent lad' (Gunnis, 247) but the work so impressed one of the judges, Samuel Joseph, that he took MacBride into his studio without charging his usual fee of 500 guineas. In Joseph's studio MacBride was a 'premier pupil'; he was appointed studio manager and became Joseph's chief assistant. After Joseph's bankruptcy MacBride returned to Liverpool and by 1848 was an associate of the Liverpool Academy. He became a full member in 1850. MacBride was an enthusiastic supporter of the Pre-Raphaelites and as secretary of the Liverpool Academy in 1851 and 1852 was instrumental in these years in awarding the annual prize of 50 guineas to Holman Hunt and John Everett Millais.

After establishing himself in Liverpool MacBride continued to exhibit at the Royal Academy between 1848 and 1853 but his principal source of patronage was the area in which he spent most of his working life, the city of Liverpool and its environs. MacBride was most commonly sought to execute the standard form of nineteenth-century sculpted memorial, the marble classicizing bust. Notable examples are *Sir William Brown* (Bart) for St George's Hall; the *Revd Dr T. S. Raffles* (exh. Liverpool Academy, 1865) for the Great George Street Chapel, Liverpool; his friend the author *Philip James Bailey* (Scottish National Portrait Gallery, Edinburgh); *John Laird* (1863) for Birkenhead Hospital; *Lieutenant-Colonel Peter Thomson* (mayor of Liverpool) (Walker Art Gallery, Liverpool); and *General Lord Viscount Combermere* (1853). MacBride carved the statue of Sir Hugh Myddelton for the Royal Exchange, London; statues of *The Four Seasons* for Garswood Hall, Lancashire, for Sir John Gerrard; and a statue of the Wesleyan minister Dr Adam Clarke for Portrush, co. Antrim. For St Mary's Church, Birkenhead, he carved the tablet in memory of Dr Stevenson (1854). This was noted by Timothy Stevens to be 'an outstanding example' of the nineteenth-century practice of illustrating the occupation of the departed on a monument, and 'represents Stevenson, the first medical man to settle in Birkenhead, holding a watch and feeling the pulse of a patient' (Stevens, 48). The monument is now in the Oratory, St James's cemetery, Liverpool. For reproduction by Messrs Minton of Stoke-on-Trent he modelled statuettes of Lord Clyde, Lord Havelock, Prince Albert, H. M. Stanley (his last work), and a reduced-size version of his *Margaret of Anjou* group. Models of his *Lady Godiva* were awarded by the Liverpool Art Union as one of their prizes in 1850. He lobbied for the commission for a statue to commemorate the duke of Wellington to surmount the Liverpool Column, but this went instead to the sculptor George Lawson, whose brother Andrew designed the column (1862–3).

MacBride was also sought after as an art critic and lecturer: he delivered courses on sculpture at the British Museum, at the Crystal Palace, and for the corporations of Liverpool, Bradford, and Greenock, among others. About 1883 he moved to London and then, in deteriorating health, to Southend-on-Sea, where he died on 4 April 1890. ALBERT NICHOLSON, *rev.* ROBIN L. WOODWARD

Sources R. Gunnis, *Dictionary of British sculptors, 1660–1851* (1953); new edn (1968) · *The Graphic* (3 May 1890), 508 · T. Stevens, 'Sculptors working in Liverpool in the early nineteenth century', *Patronage and practice: sculpture on Merseyside*, ed. P. Curtis (1989), 42–9 · B. Read, 'From basilica to Walhalla', *Patronage and practice: sculpture on Merseyside*, ed. P. Curtis (1989), 32–41
Archives Walker Art Gallery, Liverpool, JCS file, MSS letters; corresp.
Likenesses engraving (after photograph), repro. in *The Graphic*

Macbride, John David (1778–1868), college head, was born on 28 June 1778 at Plympton St Maurice, Devon, the only son of John *Macbride (*c.*1735–1800), naval captain (later MP for Plymouth, 1784–90, and admiral, 1799), and his wife, Ursula, eldest daughter of William Folkes, of Hillington Hall, Norfolk. The physician David *Macbride was his uncle. After being educated at Cheam School, Surrey, he matriculated at Exeter College, Oxford, on 28 March 1795, graduating BA in 1799. On 9 July 1800 he became a fellow of Exeter, vacating the fellowship on his marriage (19 July 1805) to Mary (1770/71–1862), second daughter of Sir Joseph Radcliffe, bt, and widow of Joseph Starkie, of Redvales. The couple had one child, a daughter.

Macbride then took up legal studies, becoming both BCL and DCL in November 1811; he served as assessor of the chancellor's court of Oxford University from 1812 to 1840. He also interested himself in oriental literature, and in 1813 was appointed lord almoner's reader in Arabic (from 1862, professor). In 1813 he also became a fellow of the Society of Antiquaries, and was appointed principal of Magdalen Hall, succeeding Henry Ford in both this and the readership. He retained these Oxford appointments until his death. He held several other university offices, being a perpetual delegate of privileges from 1813, a perpetual delegate of the university press from 1814, a commissioner of sewers (1823–45), and of the market (1825–66).

Macbride was made principal of Magdalen Hall to supervise its projected transfer to the site of the former Hertford College, which it acquired in 1816; this move, made more urgent when the hall's original buildings adjoining Magdalen College were damaged by fire in 1820, was completed in 1822. The hall prospered under him, and especially under his energetic vice-principal from 1832 to 1848, William Jacobson, afterwards bishop of Chester; shortly after Macbride's death it achieved college status as the present Hertford College (1874). In 1863 the jubilee of his headship was marked by the foundation of the Macbride scholarship; he was also commemorated by the annual Macbride university sermon, which he endowed in 1848.

Macbride published three volumes of his theology lectures, and a few other articles and speeches, but his principal work was *The Mohammedan Religion Explained* (1857), a polemic with no pretension to original research, despite its impressive number of Arabic quotations. He was not a man of deep learning, but a profoundly religious layman of the 'old' evangelical school, politically a moderate Conservative, and in character kind, sincere, and humorous. Well off himself, he was known for his generosity to the poor. He died at Oxford on 24 January 1868 and was buried on 30 January in Holywell cemetery; he was mourned as one of the last links with the Oxford of the previous century. R. S. SIMPSON

Sources *The Times* (25 Jan 1868), 9f; repr. in *Manchester Guardian* (29 Jan 1868), 131 · *GM*, 4th ser., 5 (1868), 393–4 · C. W. Boase, *Registrum Collegii Exoniensis*, 2 vols. (1879–94), 118, 215 · Boase, *Mod. Eng. biog.* · private information (1893) · J. Foster, *Oxford men and their colleges* (1893), 588, 594 · Foster, *Alum. Oxon.* · *Oxford University Calendar* (1813–68) · J. W. Burgon, *Lives of twelve good men*, [new edn], 2 (1889), 297 · C. Hibbert, ed., *The encyclopaedia of Oxford* (1988), 182, 480 · *DNB* · *The Times* (31 Jan 1868), 76
Likenesses W. Salter, oils, Hertford College, Oxford
Wealth at death under £20,000: probate, 11 Feb 1868, *CGPLA Eng. & Wales*

McBride, Robert (1686/7–1759). *See under* McBride, John (*c.*1650–1718).

MacBride, Seán (1904–1988), Irish nationalist and politician, was born on 26 January 1904 at Les Mouettes, Coleville, in Normandy. His father, Major John *MacBride (1868–1916), was a member of the Irish Republican Brotherhood from co. Mayo, who organized and led the Irish brigade in the Second South African War and was later executed for his part in the Easter rising of 1916 in Dublin. His mother, (Edith) Maud Gonne MacBride (1866–1953) [*see* Gonne, (Edith) Maud] was the daughter of English parents, who spent part of her childhood in Ireland and became an activist in the cause of Irish nationalism in the 1880s.

A half-brother, George, who died in infancy and a half-sister, Iseult Gonne [*see* Stuart, Iseult Lucille Germaine], were the children of Maud Gonne and the French nationalist politician Lucien Millevoye. Maud Gonne and John MacBride separated shortly after Seán's birth. Seán was baptized Seaghan (the old Irish form of the name) MacBride in Dublin on 1 May 1904 but spent his early years in France and spoke with a strong French accent throughout

Seán MacBride (1904–1988), by unknown photographer, 1948

his life. He was educated at St Louis de Gonzague in Paris and Mount St Benedict in co. Wexford. In 1919 during the War of Independence he joined Na Fianna Éireann, the junior branch of the Irish Republican Army, when aged fifteen. A year later, falsifying his age, he became a full member of the IRA, coming to the attention of Michael Collins, whom he accompanied to London during the treaty negotiations in 1921. In the split that followed the signing of the treaty MacBride took the anti-treaty side and participated in the occupation of the Four Courts by the IRA. In June 1922 the Four Courts was shelled and its occupants imprisoned. MacBride escaped from custody eighteen months later and spent the next few years as a leading member of the IRA, an activity which he managed to combine with journalism and legal studies at University College, Dublin, and later the King's Inns, Dublin.

On 26 January 1925 MacBride married Catalina (Kid) Bulfin (1901–1976), who had been active in Cumann na mBan. The couple moved to Paris and then to London, where he worked as a journalist before returning to Ireland over a year later. They had a daughter, Anna (b. 1927), and a son, Tiernan (b. 1934).

MacBride held various posts in the IRA, including chief of staff in 1936, but left the movement, probably in 1937. He was called to the Irish bar in 1937 and made his name defending republican prisoners, most prominently in the Burke case, in which he successfully challenged in the Supreme Court the constitutional validity of internment without trial under the Offences Against the State Act (1939). The act had been introduced to curb an IRA bombing campaign in Britain, which posed a potential threat to

Irish neutrality. The case led to the second amendment of the constitution in 1941.

Convinced that physical-force republicanism had no future, MacBride founded a new party, Clann na Poblachta, on 6 July 1946, and was returned under its banner in a by-election of 1947 to the Dáil Éireann. Eight months later he became minister for external affairs in the first inter-party government. These post-war years saw Ireland redefining its relationship with Britain and Europe and MacBride played an important role in this process. The decision to repeal the External Relations Act, by which Ireland formally ceased its membership of the British Commonwealth, is widely attributed to Mac-Bride's influence. A lifelong opponent of the partition of Ireland, he raised the issue both at the Council of Europe and with European and American governments and initiated an anti-partition campaign which supported nationalist candidates in Northern Ireland elections. MacBride successfully opposed Ireland's entry to NATO, on the basis that the country should not enter a military alliance until the partition issue had been solved. As a constitutional lawyer he took a prominent part in the creation of the Council of Europe, established in May 1949. He was responsible for Ireland's long-term recovery programme under which the country qualified for Marshall Aid loans and he was appointed negotiator with the American government for the sixteen-country group of Marshall Aid recipients. He served as vice-president of the Organization for European Economic Co-operation and in 1949–50 was president of the committee of ministers of the council. He helped to draft the European convention on human rights.

The inter-party government fell in May 1951, following a crisis over the mother and child scheme introduced by MacBride's party colleague Dr Noël Browne, the minister for health. In the face of opposition from doctors and the Catholic hierarchy to the introduction of the scheme, MacBride had demanded Browne's resignation, thereby alienating many of Clann na Poblachta's supporters. He was re-elected in 1951 and 1954, supporting but not participating in the second inter-party government of 1954, until he successfully tabled a motion of no confidence in January 1957, but his party's popularity declined and it was eventually wound up in 1965. In the meantime MacBride returned to his legal practice and defended a number of important constitutional cases. In 1956, when the British government deported the Greek-Cypriot leader and future president of Cyprus, Archbishop Makarios, to the Seychelles, MacBride fought his case at the European Court of Human Rights and secured his release. In the Lawless case in 1957 he challenged the Fianna Fáil government's reintroduction of internment, taking the case through the Supreme Court to the European Commission of Human Rights.

In 1961 MacBride helped to establish Amnesty International to campaign on behalf of prisoners of conscience throughout the world, and he acted as chairman of its international executive from 1961 to 1974. In 1963 he was appointed secretary-general to the International Commission of Jurists, based in Geneva; in 1969 he became executive chairman of the International Peace Bureau in Geneva and in 1974 its president. At the same time he chaired another Geneva-based body, the special committee of international non-governmental organizations on human rights, and in 1983 he became president of its committee on disarmament. In 1973 he was vice-chairman of the congress of world peace forces in Moscow and from that year he served as vice-president of the World Federation of United Nations Associations. At the height of the cold war he campaigned for complete general disarmament, particularly in nuclear weapons.

In 1973 MacBride was appointed by the general assembly of the United Nations as its commissioner for Namibia, with the rank of assistant secretary-general to the UN. The following year he was awarded the Nobel peace prize; the text of his speech was published as *The Imperatives of Survival* (1975). In 1977 he received the international prize for peace from the government of the Soviet Union, while the following year he was presented with the American medal of justice and received an honorary doctorate of law from Trinity College, Dublin. In 1979 he presided over the international commission of inquiry into racist and apartheid regimes in South Africa. In 1980, as President of UNESCO's international commission for the study of communications problems he was responsible for its report, *Many Voices, One World*, which criticized Western news agencies' treatment of 'third world' issues. In 1982 he chaired an international commission to examine violations of international law by Israel during its invasion of the Lebanon. In the following year his name was mooted as a candidate for the Irish presidency but the idea gained insufficient support.

Much of MacBride's career in the 1960s and 1970s was spent abroad, but he maintained an interest in Irish affairs. Socially conservative, if politically radical, he supported a referendum in 1983 to write the prohibition against abortion into the Irish constitution and opposed the introduction of divorce in Ireland. While disagreeing with the tactics of the Provisional IRA, he was sharply critical of repressive measures taken against IRA prisoners in Northern Ireland. He lent his name to a set of nine principles proposed by the Irish National Caucus in 1983, in an attempt to make contracts from the USA to Northern Ireland firms conditional on the introduction of employment equality measures. On 4 October of the same year he made a submission to the New Ireland Forum, established to review political thinking on the Northern Ireland question. An activist and speaker as much as a writer, MacBride produced at least twenty-five publications, several of which are either reports or published speeches. Some of those not previously referred to are *Civil Liberty* (1947); *Report of the Commission of Enquiry into the Irish Penal System* (1980); *Israel in Lebanon: report of the international commission to enquire into reported violations of international law by Israel during its invasion of the Lebanon* (1983); and *A Message to the Irish People* (1985).

Seán MacBride died at his home, Roebuck House, Clonskeagh, in Dublin, on 15 January 1988, eleven days before his eighty-fourth birthday. On 16 January he was buried beside his wife and mother in the republican plot at Glasnevin cemetery.   CARLA KING

Sources A. J. Jordan, *Seán MacBride: a biography* (Dublin, 1993) · *Irish Times* (16 Jan 1988) · N. Cardozo, *Maud Gonne: lucky eyes and a high heart* (1979) · M. Ward, *Maud Gonne: Ireland's Joan of Arc* (1990) · A. J. Jordan, *Major John MacBride* (Westport, 1991) · B. Whelan, *Ireland and the Marshall Plan* (Dublin, 2000) · J. Bowyer Bell, *The secret army: a history of the IRA, 1916–1970* (1970) · T. P. Coogan, *The IRA* (1970) · J. Horgan, *Noël Browne: passionate outsider* (Dublin, 2000) · N. Browne, *Against the tide* (Dublin, 1986) · J. Whyte, *Church and state in modern Ireland* (Dublin, 1980) · H. Boylan, *A dictionary of Irish biography*, 3rd edn (1998)
Archives priv. coll., papers | FILM BFI NFTVA, current affairs footage · BFI NFTVA, news footage · Radio Telifís Éireann, interview footage · Radio Telifís Éireann, *Seán MacBride remembers*, 28 Feb and 7 March 1989 · Radio Telifís Éireann, *States of Mind* · Radio Telifís Éireann, *The late late show*, 21 Jan 1984 · Radio Telifís Éireann, *Wednesday Report*, 8 April 1970 | SOUND BL NSA, performance recording · Radio Telefís Éireann, diary of 1949
Likenesses photograph, 1948, Hult. Arch. [*see illus.*] · B. Doyle, photographs, repro. in Jordan, *Seán MacBride* · photographs, *Irish Times* archive · photographs, Hult. Arch.
Wealth at death £300,552: probate, 1989, *CGPLA Éire*

MacBrody, Anthony. See Bruodin, Anthony (d. 1680).

Mac Bruaideadha family (*per.* 1558–1636), historians and Gaelic poets, became prominent in the later sixteenth and early seventeenth centuries. They ran a school in co. Clare attended by bardic students from Munster and Ulster. Three main branches of the family are recorded, though their relationship is unclear. Flann and Bernard, sons of Conchobhar son of Maoilín Mór, resided about 1637 in the parish of Moynoe on an ancestral holding in the termon, or 'sanctuary lands', of St Caimín, patron saint of Iniscaltra. Flann and his father before him claimed headship of the family. They were keepers of the so-called psalter of St Caimín, and are described as professional men of learning, or *aos ealadhna* (Esposito, 79; McGrath, 60–61).

Another branch, with the patronymic Mac Dáire, were court poets to the earls of Thomond, as perhaps one of their ancestors had been. An ode to the Ó Briain chief, Mathghamhain (d. 1369), elsewhere attributed to Maolmhuire *bacach* Mág Raith, is sometimes ascribed to an otherwise unknown Seaán Buidhe Mac Bruaideadha (Royal Irish Academy, MSS 3, 7, 1387). The first datable poem of **Domhnall mac Dáire Mhic Bhruaideadha** (*fl.* 1558–1570), *Lá dá rabha ós ráith Luimnigh*, celebrated the installation of Conchobhar Ó Briain as third earl of Thomond in 1558. In *Ceolchar sin, a chruit mo ríogh*, he laments the same earl's brief flight to France in 1570. He addressed a poem, *Cia as sine cairt ar chrích Néill*, to the leader of the Desmond revolt, James fitz Maurice FitzGerald (d. 1579), and another to the earl of Clanricarde's son John, on his first assuming arms in the late 1560s, *A mhic, gur mheala t'arma*. A number of religious poems are also doubtfully ascribed to this author. Domhnall was the son of Dáire Mac Bruaideadha and Finola Gray; Tadhg mac Dáire Mhic Bhruaideadha is stated to have been brother to this Domhnall (McGrath, 57).

Maoilín Óg Mac Bruaideadha (*d.* 1602) belonged to a branch of the family who were mainly historians or *seanchaidhe*, though he himself composed bardic verse to the professional standard known as *dán díreach*. His now lost book of annals, covering the late sixteenth century, was drawn on by the four masters and a Westmeath scribe in the early seventeenth century. Presumably this was the original source for the obituary in 1563 of Diarmaid Mac Bruaideadha, *ollamh* of Uí Bhracáin and Uí Fhearmaic (territories of Mac Gormáin and Ó Deagha). Diarmaid's brother and successor was Maoilín Óg's father, Maoilín the elder, who had risen to be *ollamh* in history to Ó Briain before his death in 1582, at which a third brother, Giolla Brighde, became *ollamh*. The title had passed to Maoilín Óg ('M. the younger') by 1599.

In that year the insurgent army of Aodh Ruadh Ó Domhnaill plundered co. Clare. Maoilín Óg entered their camp and secured the return of his cattle by reciting a praise poem to Aodh Ruadh, of which only one verse survives (Walsh, 1.210). Another, though undated, expression of anti-government feeling comes in the poem *Bráthair don bhás an doidhbhreas* where he complains that an Ó Briain chief, probably Sir Toirdhealbhach of Ennistimon (*Catalogue of Irish Manuscripts*, 1.394), has dismissed him, and he appears to mock his patron's protestantism, desertion of old Gaelic customs, and indifference to relatives and poets. Yet before the poet's death on 31 December 1602 he had served the protestant cause by joining other Irish scholars at the new Trinity College near Dublin to prepare the text of an Irish translation of the New Testament for publication (McGrath, 61n.). Naturally the four masters' notice of his death lists his long historical poems on the genealogies of Ó Briain, Mag Cochláin, Mág Gormáin, and others as his greatest achievements, combining literary merit and erudition. They awarded him the title *file*, or 'learned poet', seldom used by annalists about any scholar later than the twelfth century.

The four masters' own annalistic compilation is prefaced by a letter of recommendation from Maoilín Óg's son, **Conchobhar Mac Bruaideadha** [Mac Bruadan] (*fl.* 1631–1636), then head of his family and successor to Tadhg mac Dáire as conductor of a school of history and literature at Lettermoylan, co. Clare, which had been attended by, among others, the German planter Matthew de Renzy. Antonius Bruodinus (*d.* 1680) [see Bruodin, Anthony], Scotist theologian and controversialist, guardian of the Irish Franciscan college in Prague, and a great-nephew of Domhnall and Tadhg mac Dáire, was the latest and arguably best-known scholar of this family.

KATHARINE SIMMS

Sources C. McGrath, 'Materials for a history of clann Bhruaideadha', *Éigse*, 4 (1943–4), 48–66 • AFM • M. Esposito, 'On the so-called psalter of St Caimín', *Proceedings of the Royal Irish Academy*, 32C (1913–16), 78–86 • S. O'Grady, R. Flower, and M. Dillon, eds., *Catalogue of Irish manuscripts in the British Library (formerly British Museum)*, 2 vols. (1926–53); repr. (1992) • L. Ó Cléirigh, *The life of Aodh Ruadh Ó Domhnaill*, ed. P. Walsh and C. Ó Lochlainn, 1, ITS, 42 (1948) • J. Frost, *The history and topography of the county of Clare* (1893) • O. Bergin, ed., *Irish bardic poetry*, rev. D. Greene and F. Kelly (1970), 52–60 • T. F. O'Rahilly, ed., *Measgra Dánta: miscellaneous Irish poems* (1927), 41–4, 79–81 • *The Irish fiants of the Tudor sovereigns*, 4 vols. (1994) • T. F. O'Rahilly, 'Irish poets, historians and judges in English historical documents, 1538–1615', *Proceedings of the Royal Irish Academy*, 36C (1921–4), 86–120 • P. Walsh, *Gleanings from Irish manuscripts*, 2nd edn (1933) • B. MacCuarta, 'Conchubhar Mac Bruaideadha and Sir Matthew de Renzy (1577–1634)', *Éigse*, 27 (1993), 122–6

Mac Bruaideadha, Conchobhar (*fl.* 1631–1636). *See under* Mac Bruaideadha family (*per.* 1558–1636).

Mac Bruaideadha, Maoilín Óg (*d.* 1602). *See under* Mac Bruaideadha family (*per.* 1558–1636).

Mac Bruaidín [Mac Bruaideadha], **Tadhg mac Dáire** (*b. c.*1570, *d.* in or after 1625), Gaelic poet and genealogist, was from Knockanalban (Knockanalbanie or Cnoc an Albanaigh), barony of Ibrickan, in the parish of Kilmurry, co. Clare, one of a large family of sons and daughters of Dáire Mac Bruaideadha and Finola Gray of Knockanalban. Mentioned in the fiants of Elizabeth as resident at Knockanalban in 1586 and 1602 (*Fiants*, nos. 4860, 6615), Tadhg also appears as a witness (Teige Mac Brody) of a conveyancing agreement dated 1594 (Hardiman, 83). Information concerning him is supplied by his descendant Anthony Bruodinus OFM in a work published in Prague in 1669, and in a work published two years later under a pseudonym in which he responded to his detractor Thomas Carew. Of his brothers, Domhnall mac Dáire is also known as a poet and the compositions of both are sometimes confounded in the sources.

According to Bruodinus, Tadhg knew Greek, Latin, and English, and became tutor to Donnchadh Ó Briain, the future earl of Thomond. The latter is said to have been fostered for the first seven years of his life in the house of Tadhg's sister Finola, and to have been attended by Tadhg during his education at the English court, where he went for two years at the age of twenty-one. The same is known to have been residing in the court of Elizabeth in 1577. Following Donnchadh Ó Briain's succession as fourth earl of Thomond in 1580 Tadhg is said to have served as *aulae prefectus* in his household (Bruodinus, *Propugnaculum*, 851) and to have acted as district sheriff. (Tadhg is not mentioned among the list of high sheriffs of co. Clare, however; see McGrath, 62). Tadhg married Anna Mohuny with whom he had six children, and his estate passed to his son Jacobus on his death. According to O'Flanagan (1808), Tadhg was assigned Dunogan Castle (barony of Ibrickan) by the earl of Thomond, but this cannot be verified (McGrath, 62). Irish sources refer to him commonly as Tadhg mac Dáire, while his full name sometimes appears as Tadhg mac Dáire M(h)ic Bhruaideadha (Mhic Bhruaidín) from which it is concluded that he did not become head of the surname (that is, 'Mac Bruaideadha') in his lifetime.

In all approximately thirty compositions attributed to Tadhg have survived. Among these are a number which can be dated approximately to the early 1580s. Ten members of the O'Briens of Thomond and the Burkes of Clanricarde are remembered in the elegy 'Anois díolam an deachmhaidh', apparently written about 1580 (O'Grady, 390). The poet recalls other former Connaught patrons in

'A mhacaoimh shénas mo sheirc' (O Lochlainn), including a 'Mhaol Mórdha'. He can be identified as M. Mac Suibhne of Sligo (d. 1581) for whom Tadhg composed jointly with Tadhg Dall Ó hUiginn a *crosántacht* 'Tugam aghaidh ar Mhaol Mórdha'. A further composition by him in that genre, 'Rannam le chéile a chlann Uilliam' (Mac Cionnaith, no. 111), was composed for two of the Burkes of Clanricarde some time before 1582 (Bruodinus, *Anatomicum Examen*, 116). The poem 'Teallach flaithis fine Caoimh' which gives the martial roll of the ancestors of Art (son of Art) Ó Caoimh was written before about 1583 (Walsh, 7).

Several compositions are addressed by Tadhg to Donnchadh Ó Briain, among the earliest of which is the widely disseminated 'Mór atá ar theagasc flatha', a poem of advice which was composed possibly to mark the earl's succession in 1580 (O'Flanagan). Much copied also is the short didactic poem to the same patron 'Mo cheithre rann duit a Dhonnchaidh', but less so the short composition 'Aoidhe ó Cais na chrích féin' which deals with the earl's martial exploits. Tadhg's elegy written on the occasion of the death of the earl in 1624, 'Easgar Gaoidheal éag aoinfhir' (Ó Cuív), is transmitted in only one independent copy. The genealogical poem 'Mithid dul d'fhagháil m'fhiach' addresses another of the O'Briens, namely Donnchadh, son of Brian of Carraig Ó gConaill. The short composition 'Ní tráth dod dhol a Dhiarmaid' is a touching prayer for the recovery from illness of Diarmaid Ó Briain, fifth baron of Inchiquin (d. 1624). In contrast, 'Tairgidh mo sheachna a shíol mBriain' represents a sharply worded warning to certain of the O'Briens not to interfere with his property, lest they be made to feel the power of his satire. Similar in theme and tone is 'Fóiridh mo leisge a Leath Chuinn', a threatening satire against a member of the Burkes who joined in stealing cattle from the poet during a foray into his district led by Red Hugh O'Donnell in 1599 (Mac Cionnaith, no. 95). Apart from the poems for Art Ó Caoimh and Donnchadh Ó Briain (Carraig Ó gConaill), further evidence of Tadhg's activity as a professional genealogist is in a tract on Clann Uí Dhuibhdhabhoireann ascribed to him to which is appended a poem on the same subject '[Ní crann] aontoraidh an uaisle' (incomplete) (Macnamara).

Tadhg is chiefly known, however, as the initiator and chief protagonist of the poetic contention known as 'Iomarbhágh na bhfileadh' dealing with the rival historical claims to supremacy in Ireland of the descendants of the mythical Éibhear representing the northern half of Ireland, and those of Éireamhón representing the southern half. In all he contributed nine poems of varying length to the controversy, beginning with 'Olc do thagrais a Thorna', a criticism of claims in favour of the northern half by the ancient author Torna Éigeas. In a letter from Dublin dated June 1617 he issued an invitation to other protagonists to meet at Gort, co. Galway, in order to submit the dispute to arbitration by judges to be nominated by both sides. The letter with his own signature survives (Breatnach, 97–9).

A number of religious compositions are also ascribed to Tadhg's authorship including an address to the cross of Christ ('A chroch Dé déana mo leigheas') and a nativity poem ('Déanadh go subhach síol Ádhaimh') (Mac Cionnaith, nos. 2, 17).

A tradition recorded by nineteenth-century co. Clare sources tells that Tadhg was murdered in 1652 by a Cromwellian soldier who was granted his Dunogan lands, but no verification is available and the date given conflicts with the evidence of Bruodinus who understood his relation to have died about 1621 (McGrath, 62). The only contemporary evidence that Tadhg lived beyond that date is found in a list of names drawn up by Don Philip O'Sullivan Beare about the year 1625 in which 'Thaddaeus MacBruodinus' is mentioned among a list of contemporary Irish lawyers and doctors and poets on the continent at the time of writing (Gwynn, 11). It may be therefore that Tadhg left Ireland following the death of Thomond in 1624.   PÁDRAIG A. BREATNACH

Sources *Fiants of Elizabeth* (1879–86) [11th to 18th reports of the deputy keeper of the public records in Ireland] · J. Hardiman, 'Ancient Irish deeds and writings', *Royal Irish Acad. Trans.*, 15/Antiq. 3–95 (1826) · C. McGrath, 'Materials for a history of clann Bhruaideadha', *Éigse*, 4 (1943–4), 48–66 · A. Bruodinus, *Propugnaculum Catholicae veritatis* (Prague, 1669) · A. Bruodinus, *Anatomicum examen authore Cornelio O Mollony* (Prague, 1671) · DNB [Donough O'Brien] · S. H. O'Grady, ed., *Catalogue of Irish manuscripts in the British Museum*, 1 (1926) · 'Advice to a prince', *Transactions of the Gaelic Society of Dublin*, ed. T. O'Flanagan (1808) · C. O Lochlainn, 'A poem by Tadhg mac Dáire Mhic Bhruaideadha', *Éigse*, 1 (1939–40), 2–6 · P. Walsh, *Catalogue of Irish manuscripts in Maynooth College Library* (1943) · B. Ó Cuív, 'An elegy on Donnchadh Ó Briain, fourth earl of Thomond', *Celtica*, 16 (1984), 87–106 · L. Mac Cionnaith, *Dioghluim dána* (1938) · G. U. Macnamara, 'The O'Davorens of Cahermacnaughtern, Burren, co. Clare', *Journal of the North Munster Archaeological Society*, 2 (1912), 63–93, 149–64 · P. A. Breatnach, 'Litir ó Thadhg Mac Bruaideadha', *Éigse*, 28 (1994–5), 97–99 · A. Gwynn, 'An unpublished work of Philip O'Sullivan Bear', *Analecta Hibernica*, 6 (1934), 1–11

Archives Royal Irish Acad., MSS · St Patrick's College, Maynooth MSS

MacBryde, Robert (1913–1966). *See under* Colquhoun, Robert (1914–1962).

McBurney, Charles Brian Montagu (1914–1979), prehistoric archaeologist, was born on 18 June 1914 at Stockbridge, Massachusetts, USA, the only son of Henry McBurney (1875–1956), engineer and farmer, and his wife Dorothy Lilian Rundall (d. 1958), daughter of Colonel Montagu Rundall and his wife, Margaret Willoughby Weston. His father was American and his mother English. Charles was the younger of two children, having an elder sister. His early life was divided between the family farm in Massachusetts and western Europe, where his parents, nervous of the fact that he suffered from colitis, arranged private education by a succession of tutors, mainly in Switzerland. He settled permanently in England in 1930, not however becoming a British citizen until 1950.

In 1933 McBurney entered King's College, Cambridge, as an undergraduate, recommended by one of his former tutors: he initially read modern languages, but transferred in his third year to archaeology and anthropology. This proved a defining moment, for he encountered Miles Burkitt and subsequently Dorothy Garrod as teachers of palaeolithic archaeology at a time of many exciting discoveries in that discipline: he never relinquished his sense of debt to these two scholars for his own subsequent achievements. After his finals, King's awarded him a graduate studentship in 1937, and a research fellowship in 1940, which he held until 1953. The Second World War profoundly affected McBurney's graduate career, though not entirely adversely, as it turned out. He joined the Royal Air Force Volunteer Reserve (USA), training first in air photographic interpretation, on which several distinguished Cambridge archaeologists worked in the 1940s, before a Royal Air Force posting to north Africa. Here he evidently kept his eyes on the ground as well as the skies, discovering several important palaeolithic sites, and planning to return in more peaceful times.

In 1948 McBurney completed his doctoral thesis, entitled 'The prelude to the upper palaeolithic in western Europe: a comparative study of the earlier industries from cave deposits'—a first embodiment of the major interests that would dominate his subsequent research and writing, including stone artefacts, the peculiar art and special rewards of excavating caves, and the relationship between Neanderthals and modern humans. By then, he was energetically following up his north African wartime reconnaissance, initially with the geologist Richard Hey: their joint book *Prehistory and Pleistocene Geology in Cyrenaican Libya* was published in 1955, and McBurney's admirable Pelican book *The Stone Age of Northern Africa* followed in 1960. His greatest Libyan site was the vast Haua Fteah Cave, where excavations in 1951, 1952, and 1955 yielded a deep stratified sequence from the end of the local lower palaeolithic through middle palaeolithic, early and late upper palaeolithic to the neolithic. Painstaking study of the extremely prolific finds by McBurney and many generations of Cambridge students culminated in his important monograph *The Haua Fteah (Cyrenaica) and the Stone Age of the South-East Mediterranean* (1967).

From the outset, McBurney recognized the close link at various stages of the palaeolithic between north Africa and the Near East: he was particularly interested, like his mentor Dorothy Garrod, in the origins and spread of the first blade-using industries of the upper palaeolithic. In the 1960s and early 1970s he led several expeditions to find new cave sites and conduct trial excavations in what seemed a key area, Iran and Afghanistan. Surprisingly, no early upper palaeolithic material was found, though some important middle palaeolithic and epi-palaeolithic sites were examined, the latter including the cave of Ali Tappeh I at the south end of the Caspian Sea.

Concurrently, McBurney actively pursued his interests in the European middle and upper palaeolithic, following up new ideas and rapidly assimilating new discoveries or methodological advances. A visiting fellowship at the Soviet Academy of Sciences in 1975 greatly enhanced his overview of the west European sites, as expounded in his Albert Reckitt lecture that year to the British Academy—he had been elected FBA in 1966. In Britain he excavated at upper palaeolithic cave sites in Somerset, south Wales, and Derbyshire (1958–60), and at the important middle palaeolithic site of La Cotte de St Brelade, Jersey, from 1961 to 1978, the results from the latter site being published in 1986 in a volume edited by his colleagues Paul Callow and Jean Cornford.

McBurney's excavations enabled generations of Cambridge students to participate in important current research: since he taught worldwide palaeolithic archaeology, he viewed each site in the broadest context. The inspiration and stimulation he transmitted to his brightest students, in the field, lecture room, and laboratory, were extraordinary and many subsequently had distinguished careers in archaeology. The abundant time and trouble he devoted to them was often reflected in their own care of undergraduate and research students. Most could also imitate affectionately his distinctive high-pitched voice and mannerisms, but none ever attained his sublime level of absent-mindedness, simultaneously lovable and lethal.

In 1962 McBurney became a fellow of Corpus Christi College, Cambridge, to which he gave devoted service. He received his Cambridge ScD in 1968, and a personal chair in quaternary prehistory in 1977. His many other achievements and honours are recorded by Desmond Clark and Patrick Wilkinson in their sensitive appreciation written for the memorial volume *Stone Age Prehistory* (1986), edited by G. N. Bailey and P. Callow. He married his second cousin, Anne Frances Edmonstone Charles (*d.* 2002), on 21 March 1953; they had three children. The marriage was idyllically happy, with the family home a welcoming place, where domestic and academic endeavours seemed to merge inextricably. McBurney was only sixty-five, and had suffered from diabetes for some years, when cancer was diagnosed in 1979. He died on 14 December 1979 at his home, 5 Grange Road, Cambridge: his ashes were interred five days later in the garden of remembrance next to Corpus Christi College.   DEREK A. ROE

Sources J. D. Clark and L. P. Wilkinson, 'Charles Brian Montagu McBurney (1914–1979): an appreciation', *Stone Age prehistory: studies in memory of Charles McBurney*, ed. G. N. Bailey and P. Callow (1986), 7–25 [incl. bibliography] · personal knowledge (2004) · private information (2004) [Anne McBurney, Gerard McBurney]
Archives U. Cam., Museum of Archaeology and Anthropology, personal MSS
Likenesses photograph, department of archaeology, Downing Street, Cambridge, McDonald Institute for Archaeological Research · photograph, repro. in Bailey and Callow, eds., *Stone Age prehistory*, frontispiece
Wealth at death £89,553: probate, 28 March 1980, *CGPLA Eng. & Wales*

Mac Cába, Cathaoir (*fl.* 1728–1739), poet and harper, was born at Cloghballybeg in the parish of Mullagh, co. Cavan. Throughout his life he was the intimate friend of the celebrated harper Turlogh O'Carolan (Toirdhealbhach Ó Cearbhalláin; 1670–1738), who addressed two poems to him, one of them on hearing a report of his death—the report, which was false, originated as a practical joke played on O'Carolan by his friend. Mac Cába addressed several poems and some miscellaneous verses to O'Carolan. Many of these were humorous (such as his contribution to a 'scolding match' between the two) but one of them was a lament on the great harper's death which has been adjudged to evince 'a competence in versification and a depth of feeling to which [O'Carolan] could hardly attain' (O'Sullivan, 1.68). Mac Cába had dealings in 1727–8 with the noted scholar Charles O'Conor (1710–1791) and spent some periods at the latter's home at Belanagare, co. Roscommon, where they exchanged harp tunes. Mac Cába was friendly with the O'Donnell family of Larkfield, near Manorhamilton, co. Leitrim, and he composed a lament in 1736 for a relation of that family's, Colonel Manus O'Donnell of Newport, co. Mayo. In addition to a small number of other extant poems, there is record of at least two other works by Mac Cába that seem not to have survived. While it has been suggested that Mac Cába may have died as early as 1739, one authority declares that he outlived O'Carolan by many years and that, 'having obtained a licence to teach, as a "Popish school-master", he earned a scanty subsistence in his old age and finally died in want' (Hardiman, 1.lxii). He was said to have been buried in the churchyard of Mullagh, near the well of St Ultan.   NOLLAIG Ó MURAÍLE

Sources *DNB* · D. O'Sullivan, *Carolan: the life, times and music of an Irish harper*, 1 (1958), 67–81 · J. Hardiman, ed., *Irish minstrelsy, or, Bardic remains of Ireland*, 2 vols. (1831)
Archives NL Ire. · Royal Irish Acad., poems

Maccabe, Cathaoir. *See* Mac Cába, Cathaoir (*fl.* 1728–1739).

McCabe, Edward (1816–1885), cardinal and Roman Catholic archbishop of Dublin, born at Dublin on 14 February 1816, was the son of poor parents. He was educated at Father Michael Doyle's school at Arran Quay, Dublin. In 1833 he entered St Patrick's College, Maynooth, where he was ordained on 24 June 1839. He was for some time curate at Clontarf, co. Dublin, and then transferred to the pro-cathedral parish of Dublin. Daniel Murray and his successor to the archbishopric, Paul Cullen, recognized his organizing talent; he was appointed a canon in 1855 and he refused a nomination to the bishopric of Grahamstown, Cape Colony, in the same year. In 1856 Cullen appointed him parish priest of St Nicholas Without, and he was promoted to the post of vicar-general of the archdiocese. His health gave way under the strain of work, and in 1865 he was removed to the parish of Kingstown (Dún Laoghaire). There he built a new church at Monkstown and opened a local hospital. In 1872 he drew up the address given by the Catholics of the archdiocese of Dublin in answer to the remarks of William Nicholas Keogh, the judge in the celebrated Galway election case. As Cardinal Cullen was becoming infirm, McCabe was on 25 July 1877 consecrated bishop of Gadara *in partibus infidelium*, and appointed as his auxiliary. After Cullen's death in 1878, McCabe became archbishop of Dublin on 23 March 1879. He at once issued a circular calling attention to the position of Irish Roman Catholics with regard to university education (*The Times*, 1 April 1879). He was installed as archbishop on 4 May 1879, and on 12 March 1882 was created a cardinal.

In his politics McCabe was opposed to the campaign for home rule and land reform led by Charles Stewart Parnell

Edward McCabe (1816–1885), by Fratelli D'Alessandri

and Michael Davitt. Though aware of the plight of tenant farmers and appalled by wholesale evictions, he had sympathy for the economic difficulties facing landlords. He regularly condemned agrarian outrages and in October 1881 issued a pastoral letter denouncing in fierce terms the Land League's 'no rent' manifesto. McCabe zealously sought to keep priests from engaging in political agitation. All of this left him isolated among his fellow prelates and increasingly alienated from the generality of Irish nationalist opinion. So great was his unpopularity that his return from Rome in 1882 with the red hat passed almost unnoticed in his native city, and on one occasion his life was threatened. He was a member of the senate of the Royal University of Ireland, and served in 1880 on the Mansion House committee in Dublin for the relief of famine throughout Ireland. Sandwiched between the reigns of Cullen and Walsh, two giant figures in ecclesiastical and political spheres in nineteenth-century Ireland, McCabe's period as archbishop might be dismissed as a mere interlude were it not for the eventful times in which he lived. None the less, he enjoyed the confidence of the papacy at a time when Anglo-Vatican relations were undergoing a temporary thaw. He was also the last archbishop of Dublin to be made a cardinal. Plagued by ill health during the latter part of his administration, McCabe died at his home in Eblana Avenue, Kingstown, on 11 February 1885 and was the first archbishop of Dublin to be buried at Glasnevin.

W. A. J. ARCHBOLD, *rev.* DAVID C. SHEEHY

Sources B. J. Canning, *Bishops of Ireland, 1870–1987* (1987) • E. Larkin, *The Roman Catholic church and the creation of the modern Irish state, 1878–1886* (1975) • C. J. Woods, 'The politics of Cardinal McCabe, archbishop of Dublin, 1879–85', *Dublin Historical Record*, 26/3 (1972–3), 101–10 • *Freeman's Journal* [Dublin] (11 Feb 1885) • *The Times* (12 Feb 1885) • *The Times* (18 Feb 1885)
Archives Dublin Roman Catholic archdiocese, archives, corresp. and papers
Likenesses Fratelli D'Alessandri, photograph, NPG [*see illus.*] • T. Farrell, recumbent figure on tomb, Glasnevin cemetery • Judd & Co., lithograph, NPG; repro. in *Whitehall Review* (22 Nov 1879) • wood-engraving, NPG; repro. in *ILN* (22 April 1882)
Wealth at death approx. £750

McCabe, Joseph Martin [*pseud.* Arnold Wright; *name in religion* Antony] (**1867–1955**), freethinker, was born at 14 Chestergate, Macclesfield, Cheshire, on 12 November (not 11 November, as he said) 1867, the second son of William Thomas McCabe, a weaver and draper of Irish descent, and his wife, Harriet Kirk, a milliner of Scottish and English descent—poor but respectable Roman Catholics.

When McCabe was a child the family moved to Gorton, Manchester, where he was educated at a Catholic elementary school until he was thirteen. He worked as an office boy for three years, but then trained as a Franciscan friar in Manchester, Killarney, and Forest Gate, London, taking the religious name of Brother Antony. In 1890 he was ordained priest and appointed a professor of philosophy, and he did parochial work in England and academic work in England and Belgium. In 1895 he became rector of St Bernardine's College, Buckingham, but in 1896 his growing doubts led him to abandon his post, his order, his church, and his religion.

For the rest of his life McCabe worked as a freelance writer and speaker, and he became the most industrious and influential campaigner in the freethought movement throughout the English-speaking world. He announced his position in an essay, *From Rome to Rationalism, or, Why I Left the Church* (1896), expanded as a book, *Twelve Years in a Monastery* (1897), and also in a pseudonymous novel, *In the Shade of the Cloister* (1907). He spent a few years as a lecturer and journalist for the Union of Ethical Societies and then as secretary of the Leicester Secular Society, where he met his future wife. On 17 August 1899 he married Beatrice Alice Ann Lee, a hosiery worker and the daughter of William Lee, also a hosiery worker, at the Leicester register office.

McCabe spoke at the South Place Ethical Society from 1896 to 1954 (longer than anyone else), and served as an appointed lecturer from 1905 to 1923. He was one of the founders of the Rationalist Press Association in 1899, served as a director until 1902, and became an honorary associate in 1908. His translation of Ernst Haeckel's book *The Riddle of the Universe* in 1900 and his lectures on evolution from 1903 were the first public successes of the RPA, and he remained its busiest writer and speaker until a long-lasting breach in 1926. During this period he wrote several books on religion and science, history, and biography, the most important being the authorized *Life and Letters of George Jacob Holyoake* (1908) and *A Biographical Dictionary of Modern Rationalists* (1920).

McCabe attended international freethought congresses in Europe from 1904 to 1924, made several lecture tours of Australasia from 1910 to 1923 and of North America from 1914 to 1930, as well as travelling widely in Europe and America, and was a member of the committee of honour for the international freethought congress in London in 1938. From 1926 he collaborated with the leading American freethought publisher, Emanuel Haldeman-Julius (1889–1951), writing a series of substantial partworks which appeared as periodicals or Little Blue Books and sold millions of copies around the world. From 1934 he also wrote again for the Rationalist Press Association, and he continued to lecture to ethical and secular societies until the 1950s. His last major works were *Eighty Years a Rebel* (1947), a candid autobiography for Haldeman-Julius, and *A Rationalist Encyclopaedia* (1948), an idiosyncratic reference book for the Rationalist Press Association.

McCabe claimed to have written more than anyone else alive, and he produced thousands of articles, hundreds of books and booklets, and dozens of translations and pamphlets, under his own name and several pseudonyms; he also gave thousands of lectures and took part in hundreds of debates all over the world. He never claimed to be a scholar, describing himself rather as 'a peddler in culture' (McCabe, *Eighty Years a Rebel*, 5), yet he not only mastered several languages, natural and social sciences, theology, philosophy, economics, and above all ancient, medieval, and modern history, but he also displayed an unrivalled ability to explain complex issues in simple terms, both in writing and in speaking.

McCabe called himself first an agnostic and rationalist and later an atheist, materialist, republican, and socialist. Although he never joined any political organization, he became an uncritical fellow traveller with the communist regime in the Soviet Union and later an early advocate of nuclear disarmament. He was always a devastating controversialist, and often a difficult colleague. He himself attributed his irascible and pugnacious temperament to lifelong dyspepsia, and he had a grim face and voice to match. He had little respect for most of the leaders of the organizations he worked for, and he had little sympathy with moderate freethinkers; in the last year of his life he joined the more militant National Secular Society.

Although McCabe ended his long life in virtual isolation and relative poverty, he was widely recognized as the most formidable British opponent of religion in general and of Roman Catholicism in particular, as well as of other forms of superstition, during the first half of the twentieth century. He was always mainly concerned with the negative work of challenging false beliefs and evil behaviour in religion and politics, but he was also committed to the positive work of advancing better ideas in their place. He had a naïve faith in freedom and reason and science, and a naïve trust that their combination—which was beginning to be called 'humanism' (a term he avoided)—would lead to a new era of peace and prosperity, the cause to which he devoted unremitting labour for more than half a century.

The McCabes had two sons and two daughters; they separated in 1925, and he lived alone with a housekeeper for the rest of his life. He died of pneumania following prostate cancer at his home, 22 St George's Road, Golders Green, Middlesex, on 10 January 1955, and was cremated four days later at Golders Green crematorium after a secular ceremony. During his lifetime Isaac Goldberg described him as 'an unpriestly priest of an unchurchly church' (Goldberg, 14); after his death the obituary in *The Times* called him 'an old-fashioned Rationalist', and the obituary in the Ethical Union *News and Notes* (March 1955) stated that 'McCabe's name was revered by the rank and file of the movement more than anybody else's'.

NICOLAS WALTER

Sources J. McCabe, *Twelve years in a monastery* (1897) · J. McCabe, *Eighty years a rebel* (1947) · *The Freethinker* (21 Jan 1955) · *The Freethinker* (28 Jan 1955) · *The Freethinker* (4 Feb 1955) · *Monthly Record* (March 1955) · *Monthly Record* (May 1955) · *Literary Guide and News & Notes* (March 1955) · *The Times* (26 Jan 1955) · M. Haldeman-Julius, *Talks with Joseph McCabe, and other confidential sketches* (1931) · I. Goldberg, *Joseph McCabe: fighter for freethought* (1936) · E. Haldeman-Julius, *My second 25 years* (1949) · J. R. Burr, 'Joseph McCabe', *The encyclopedia of unbelief*, ed. G. Stein (1985) · B. Cooke, 'Joseph McCabe: an intellectual biography' · N. Walter, 'Joseph McCabe, 1867–1955'
Archives BL, corresp. with Marie Stopes, Add. MS 58543
Likenesses photographs, repro. in McCabe, *Eighty years a rebel*
Wealth at death £4817 6s. 10d.: probate, 21 April 1955, CGPLA Eng. & Wales

MacCabe, William Bernard (1801–1891), journalist and historian, was born in Dublin on 23 November 1801, of Roman Catholic parents. In 1823 he joined the Dublin *Morning Register* as a reporter; for the next decade he worked for the Dublin press, reporting many of Daniel O'Connell's early speeches and editing several papers. About 1833 he moved to London, where he worked as a parliamentary reporter on the *Morning Chronicle* and (from 1835) also served on the staff of the *Morning Herald*. During the parliamentary recesses he spent much time abroad, acting as a foreign correspondent; he also wrote critical reviews for both papers. In 1847 he was appointed consul in London for the Oriental Republic of Uruguay; he resigned this post and all other London appointments about 1851, when he moved back to Ireland to become editor (until 1857) of the *Weekly Telegraph*, a Roman Catholic newspaper under the influence of Cardinal Wiseman. Subsequently he seems to have lived for some time in Brittany.

In 1847–54 MacCabe published, in three enormous volumes, *A Catholic History of England*, a work consisting of extracts from monastic chroniclers, dovetailed to form a continuous narrative. MacCabe aimed not only to introduce his readership to neglected works of early English literature, but also to allow them to form their own historical opinions from primary sources. His footnotes reveal him to be extremely erudite, but almost criminally naïve in his neglect of such rudimentary critical approaches as were then practised: he fails to contextualize his sources fully, and analysis of their content and credibility is limited to simplistic comparisons with other sources for the same events. However, the second volume of the *Catholic History* was reviewed enthusiastically in September 1849 in the *Dublin Review* (to which MacCabe himself was a contributor): praising it as 'a solid and instructive … an orderly and agreeable narrative' (*Dublin Review*, 130), the critic emphasized its value in correcting the anti-Catholic perspectives of such historians as Sharon Turner and Samuel Laing. MacCabe had originally intended to continue his history up to at least the English Reformation, but no further volumes of the *Catholic History* were published.

MacCabe also wrote several turgid historical novels, set in early medieval Europe and later translated into several continental languages: these included *Bertha* (3 vols., 1851) and *Adelaide, Queen of Italy* (1856). In 1861 he published the more interesting *Agnes Arnold* (1861), a novel set in the time of the 1798 Irish rising. MacCabe translated several works into English, including J. J. I. von Dollinger's *Christentum und Kirche* (1860), which appeared as *The Church and Churches* in 1862. He contributed to *Once a Week* and *Notes and Queries*, and also published articles in the Catholic *Dublin Review* on subjects ranging from Spanish novelists to the 1848 revolutions. MacCabe died on 8 December 1891 at his home, 2 Eglinton Terrace, Donnybrook, co. Dublin.

ROSEMARY MITCHELL

Sources Boase, *Mod. Eng. biog.* · *Men of the time* (1875) · D. J. O'Donoghue, *The poets of Ireland: a biographical and bibliographical dictionary* (1912) · *DNB* · review of *A Catholic history of England*, *Dublin Review*, 27 (1849), 128–46 · *Wellesley index* · D. Griffiths, ed., *The encyclopedia of the British press, 1422–1992* (1992) · J. Sutherland, *The Longman companion to Victorian fiction* (1988) · CGPLA Ire. (1892)
Wealth at death £5656 16s. 4d.: probate, 21 Jan 1892, CGPLA Ire.

McCabe, William Putnam (c.1776–1821), Irish nationalist and cotton manufacturer, was born in Belfast, the third of four children of Thomas McCabe (c.1739–1820), watchmaker, cotton manufacturer, and United Irishman, and his first wife, Jean Woolsey (d. June 1790), daughter of John Woolsey, merchant of Portadown. His middle name, Putnam, derived from a distant relative who served under George Washington. He was educated in Belfast, specializing in mechanics and drawing, before working in his father's mill. Being somewhat unruly as a young man, he was sent to train in Glasgow and Manchester in the hope that this would have a maturing effect. After returning to Belfast he joined the Society of United Irishmen and was employed as an emissary by the Belfast committee, being sent to Connaught in late 1796. McCabe travelled around Ireland, organizing civilian societies into military units.

An excellent mimic, McCabe adopted various Irish and Scottish dialects to conceal his identity from the authorities. He took great care to avoid arrest, but his reputation was such that a price of £500 was placed on his head. A description was circulated thus: 'height five foot four inches: well made: walks smart: full face: black or dark eyes: dark hair: whiskers: good complexion: not corpulent but pretty lusty: a great deal of vivacity: wears pantaloons and boots' (McCabe, 17). McCabe's escapes from capture are legendary. Arrested in Dublin in May 1798, he persuaded his Dumbarton fencible guards that he was an innocent Scot, wrongly apprehended while out for a stroll. So convinced were they by his accent that he was released. On another occasion McCabe evaded capture by fooling his pursuers into thinking that he had escaped through his open bedroom window when, in fact, he had hidden under the mattress. The troops scoured Belfast's streets in search of the elusive William Putnam McCabe!

McCabe was aide-de-camp to the rebel commander-in-chief Lord Edward Fitzgerald. His role in the rising is, however, unclear. Some accounts place him at Naas and Kildare before he joined the belated French invasion force under Humbert, which landed in the west in August 1798. The insurrection crushed, McCabe returned to Dublin, thence to Wales and Scotland. He travelled regularly between Dublin, London, Hamburg, and Paris, continuing his intrigue on behalf of the United Irishmen by, for example, conspiring with the United Britons and Colonel Edward Despard in 1802. In 1801 he married Elizabeth McNeil, née Lockhart (d. 1806), widow of a Captain McNeil and sister of Sir Alexander McDonald Lockhart of Lee, Scotland. They had one daughter, Elizabeth (b. c.1802).

McCabe then went to France and established a cotton business near Rouen, where he received a gift of 4000 francs from Napoleon, who visited the factory. There McCabe is said to have helped train Irish émigrés for Robert Emmet's 1803 uprising. Upon selling his mill at Rouen, he loaned money to the United Irishman Arthur O'Connor, whose failure to repay the debt led to protracted court battles, in both France and Ireland. McCabe returned to Ireland regularly between 1810 and 1814 to pursue his claims, but was arrested in 1814, only to be freed by order of the chief secretary, Robert Peel, on condition that he leave Ireland. On returning again in 1817 he was arrested and sent to Kilmainham gaol, Dublin, where he languished for eighteen months. At the end of 1818 he returned to France, but was detained again in Glasgow the following year.

Towards the end of his life McCabe was infirm with rheumatism. He died in Paris on 6 January 1821 and was buried at the Vaugirard cemetery in Paris. His daughter, Elizabeth, married Andrew Nesbitt of co. Meath two weeks after McCabe's death. Nesbitt promptly spent the several thousand pounds left by McCabe to his daughter, and when he died in 1839 Elizabeth and her children were left destitute. KENNETH L. DAWSON

Sources J. McCabe, 'A United Irish family: the McCabes of Belfast', *Familia* (1997), 1–24 · R. R. Madden, *Antrim and Down in '98* (1888) · W. A. Maguire, ed., *Up in arms: the 1798 rebellion in Ireland: a bicentenary exhibition* (1998) · R. Wells, *Insurrection: the British experience, 1795–1803* (1983) · J. Smyth, *The men of no property* (1992) · DNB · M. Elliott, *Partners in revolution: the United Irishmen and France* (1982) · NA Ire., Rebellion MSS, 620 collection
Archives BL, letters and papers, Add. MSS 40204–40235
Wealth at death several thousand pounds

MacCaghwell, Hugh [Hugo Cavellus, Aodh Mac Aingil] (1571?–1626), Roman Catholic archbishop of Armagh and theologian, was born at Sall, co. Down. The names of his parents are unknown, but he was a member of a bardic family originally seated at Clogher in co. Tyrone, the name of his clan being generally Latinized as Cavellus. On reaching adulthood he went to the Isle of Man to study the classics and dialectics. By 1599 he was recalled to Ulster by Hugh O'Neill, earl of Tyrone, who appointed him tutor to his sons, Henry and Hugh. In 1600 Tyrone sent him and Henry to Spain, where they settled at Salamanca. There MacCaghwell attended a philosophy course at the university and joined the Franciscans in 1604. He may later have taught briefly theology at Salamanca. About 1606 he went to the Spanish Netherlands, having being appointed chief chaplain of the Irish regiment in Flanders in December 1605. There he became one of the leading figures in the local Irish émigré community, part of the so-called northern clique. This highly influential group adopted a strongly anti-English line and effectively controlled the flow of patronage from the Spanish crown to the Irish exiles. MacCaghwell played a key role in securing the foundation of a college for Irish Franciscans at Louvain in 1607, becoming professor of theology and guardian of the college in the same year. Over the next seven years he successfully devoted himself to establishing the college on a firm financial basis, going on many fund-raising tours outside the Netherlands.

In 1613 MacCaghwell was approached by English agents who wanted to open negotiations with Tyrone, who had fled Ulster in 1607, for the earl's peaceful return to Ireland. Nothing came of this as the Spanish preferred to keep Tyrone and the English estranged. Generally, MacCaghwell stayed out of political matters, preferring to concentrate on his administrative duties and theological studies. In 1618 he published under his Irish name Aodh Mac Aingil *Scáthán shacramuinte na haithridhe* or 'A mirror of the sacrament of penance', a devotional work written in Irish. Although this acknowledged James I as the rightful ruler of Ireland, it also identified Ireland as a Catholic nation and demonstrates a very modern sense of national consciousness. Moreover, the work is a prominent example of how the literary language of contemporary Irish poets was used to produce a readable prose text. As a theologian MacCaghwell was held in high regard and specialized in the works of John Duns Scotus, whose doctrines he strongly defended. He published a number of theological tracts under his Latinized name Hugo Cavellus in the 1620s, including editions of a number of Scotus's works, which brought him a high reputation throughout Europe.

In 1620 MacCaghwell represented his province at the chapter-general of the Franciscans held in Spain. He was subsequently made definitor-general of the Franciscan order and spent most of 1622 in Paris, reforming the Parisian Franciscan convent. He was summoned in 1623 to Rome, where he read theology at the convent of Ara Coeli and was highly regarded by Pope Urban VIII. Partly through MacCaghwell's influence an Irish college was established at St Isidore's in Rome. When an election to the generalship of the Franciscan order was held in 1624 he was second in the poll. Subsequently, when the archbishopric of Armagh fell vacant with the death of Peter Lombard in 1625, John O'Neill, earl of Tyrone, Albert

O'Donnell, earl of Tyrconnell, and Luke Wadding all strongly urged MacCaghwell's promotion to that see. He was consecrated on 7 June 1626 and immediately prepared to journey to Ireland. However, he fell ill suddenly and died of a fever at St Isidore's on 22 September 1626. A highly ascetic lifestyle combined with a delicate constitution contributed heavily to his death. He was buried in the church of St Isidore, where Tyrone had a monument placed over his grave. There is a fresco of him by Emmanuele di Como in the theological hall at St Isidore's College.   TERRY CLAVIN

Sources C. P. Meehan, *Rise and fall of the Franciscans* (1872), 156–9 · L. Renehan, *Collections on Irish church history* (1861), vol. 1, pp. 20–24 · G. Henry, *The Irish military community in Spanish Flanders* (1992), 103 · *Report on Franciscan manuscripts preserved at the convent, Merchants' Quay, Dublin*, HMC, 65 (1906), 1, 74, 84 · M. K. Walsh, *An exile of Ireland* (1996), 111–13 · B. Jennings, *Wild geese in Spanish Flanders* (1964), 82, 121, 128, 130, 166–7, 173 · T. W. Moody and others, eds., *A new history of Ireland*, 3: *Early modern Ireland, 1534–1691* (1976); repr. with corrections (1991) · *DNB*
Likenesses E. di Como, fresco, 1672, St Isidore's College, Rome

MacCaig [McCaig], **Norman Alexander** (1910–1996), poet, was born at 53 East London Street, Edinburgh, on 14 November 1910, the only son and the fourth child of Robert McCaig (1880–1950?), a chemist, and his wife, Joan, *née* MacLeod (1879–1959). His father was a lowland Scot from Dumfriesshire and his mother came from Scalpay on the island of Harris in the Outer Hebrides. A few months before his fifth birthday he was sent to school in the primary department of the Royal High School, Edinburgh, moving from there, in 1922, to the upper school. In 1928 he proceeded to Edinburgh University to read classics and graduated in 1932 with an honours degree. After university he attended Moray House College in Edinburgh to train as a teacher.

It was a difficult time to become a teacher and McCaig, unable to find a full-time job teaching classics, took on a series of part-time posts. For a few years he taught Latin, including a period at Portobello High School, where the art teacher, George Findlay McKenzie, painted the portrait which now hangs in the school of Scottish studies at Edinburgh University. After a series of temporary posts he accepted a permanent post in Craiglockhart primary school, and all his teaching thereafter, until 1970, was in primary schools. He was at Craiglockhart in 1939 when war broke out.

On 6 April 1940 McCaig married Isabel Robina Munro (1910–1990), a teacher, whom he had met at university, and they settled in a house in Broughton Street, Edinburgh. They had two children, Joan, born in 1942, and Ewen, born in 1944. McCaig lived in Edinburgh throughout his life but, 'a threequarter Gael' (MacCaig, 81), he spent most of his summers in a cottage in Achmelvich on the coast of Sutherland.

McCaig had been writing poems of what he called 'an elaborate and increasing awfulness' (MacCaig, 86) since his senior years at the Royal High School and during the 1930s and early 1940s he became involved with the short-lived New Apocalypse movement, which published his first poems in 1939, in the anthology *The New Apocalypse*.

These were followed by two books, *Far Cry* (1943) and *The Inward Eye* (1946), which collected his various periodical publications and added to them; they were all a reflection of his association with the New Apocalypse movement and were publications that he later desperately wished to disown. Many years later he declared that these two books illustrated not a revelation but an obscurement, and he totally repudiated them. Always a joker, he frequently used to tell the story that a friend to whom he had lent the second of these two volumes returned it to him with the words 'When are you publishing the answers?' (MacCaig, 85); so, he explained, he set about looking for the answers and they were not in the New Apocalypse Movement. Certainly, the poems from both books were completely expunged from his *Selected Poems* (1971) and from the later *Collected Poems* (1985).

During the Second World War McCaig was a conscientious objector, though not on religious grounds for, as he asserted in an interview, 'I was born an atheist' (Murray, 88). Yet he was a pacifist and objected to war for humanistic reasons, insisting that nothing could persuade him to 'drop bombs on Hamburg' (Murray, 96). When he was called up in 1941 he refused to serve in the armed forces. At the tribunal, however, he agreed to do non-military work and was drafted into the non-combatant corps. Later, when asked to service tanks, he refused and was court-martialled; as a result he was sent briefly to Winchester prison and then to Wormwood Scrubs, where he spent the official prescribed three months before being released and directed to 'war work' as a gardener.

After the war McCaig returned to teaching, which he loved. He was a marvellous teacher, full of wit, and a fountain of great stories. Despite Hugh MacDiarmid's well-known assertion that conscientious objection ruined McCaig's life, Norman enjoyed his years as a primary school teacher. They perhaps gave him the freedom to think and write, which intellectually more demanding and time-consuming grammar school teaching would have been likely to impede. The Scottish Renaissance movement which MacDiarmid nurtured in the 1920s aimed to revive the use of the Scots language in contemporary literature and at the same time to dissociate it from the sentimentality of the 'kailyard' school. Despite his admiration for MacDiarmid, Norman was not persuaded that he should write in a language not his own, and his own language, he often asserted, was English. Furthermore, he was out of sympathy with his friend's political interests, describing himself as 'a-political'. He nevertheless went to New York with MacDiarmid in 1967 and counted him as one of his closest friends.

Some time between 1946 and 1955 McCaig adopted the spelling MacCaig, which he used for his publications, keeping the original for family matters. When asked about the change, he generally replied that it was because people kept mis-spelling it. His real poetic début came in 1955 with the publication of *Riding Lights*. The poems in this book show an awareness of nature in all its variety, of the cycle of the months and the seasons, and, in almost every poem, the poet himself is present in some way. The poems move between Edinburgh, MacCaig's physical home, and the highlands and islands of his spiritual home; they embrace landscape and history as well as the carefully carved cameos of familiar nature. The imagery is colourful and striking, as in 'End of a Cold Night':

> The pond has closed its frozen eyelid,
> The grass clump clenched its frozen claws.

Most of the poems in this volume are in formal rhyming four-line stanzas, with the occasional incursion of six-, eight-, or twelve-line stanzas. Sometimes there are no rhymes; sometimes assonance is used.

The structural formality of *Riding Lights* is maintained, though with increasing variety, through the next three volumes, *The Sinai Sort* (1957), *A Common Grace* (1960), and *A Round of Applause* (1962). By the mid-sixties, however, in *Measures* (1965), there is a noticeable emphasis on different forms and by the time *Surroundings* was published in 1966 MacCaig seemed to have accomplished a painless shift to the use of free verse. In discussing his gradual move to his own particular brand of free verse, he commented, 'How many free verse poems are ruined by the lack of a thorough-going rhythm to articulate the whole and by line-endings which are purely arbitrary and serve no functional purpose whatever' (MacCaig, 83). This remark encapsulates the significance for him of rhythm in all his poetry, formal or free.

In 1967 MacCaig was appointed creative writing fellow at Edinburgh University and on his return to teaching in 1969 he became headmaster of Inch primary school, Liberton, south Edinburgh. The following year, however, he left schoolteaching for good when he was appointed, first as lecturer, and then as reader in poetry at Stirling University, where he remained until he retired in 1978. During this time and for the next ten years he continued to write poetry; another eight volumes were published at fairly regular intervals, the last one, *Voice-over*, in 1988, making sixteen in all.

MacCaig was essentially a writer of short poems and throughout his career he continued with his descriptions of landscapes and places, as well as choosing as his subjects the living world around him—animals, birds, flowers, and people—treating them with understanding and compassion. He was well known for his acerbic wit, though he frequently described himself as 'a big softy at heart'; both these qualities are apparent in the poem 'Responsibility':

> They left the horse standing for two days
> with a shattered leg
> till the vet signed a paper.
> Then they dug a hole beside it
> and put a bullet in its skull. ...
> This could have been worse only
> if they had had to wait
> till the horse signed a paper.
> Some day they'll dig a hole
> near enough to the vet's bed, for him to know it's there.

Here, the pronounced rhythmic patterning and the paralleling of the death of the horse with that of the vet is typical of MacCaig's free verse of this period.

MacCaig was always a cheerful, sociable man and during the 1940s and 1950s he frequented the various bars in Rose Street, Edinburgh, where he could be found talking with fellow Scottish poets—Hugh MacDiarmid, Sorley Maclean, Sidney Goodsir Smith, Tom Scott, George Mackay Brown, and others. He was later to become acquainted with Iain Crichton Smith and, later still, struck up a warm friendship with Seamus Heaney. Though he is best-known as a poet, MacCaig also delighted in music, both classical and traditional Scottish; he had a good singing voice and played the violin more than competently. He frequently claimed that he preferred music to poetry and that Bach, in particular, was a source of great solace to him.

As MacCaig grew older and the deaths of friends such as MacDiarmid and Angus MacLeod occurred, his poems began to reflect ideas of old age and death. In his summers away from Edinburgh in the wild countryside of Sutherland, MacLeod was his dearest friend and MacCaig found his loss hard to bear. The sequence of 'Poems for Angus' in *The Equal Skies* (1980) comprises some of his most beautiful and moving work. They voice the simplicity of his memories of MacLeod, represented in 'In Memoriam' as 'a top branch ... on the biggest tree in my garden', which, though broken off, remains held up by the 'living branches'; his feeling of loss is intensified in 'Angus's Dog':

> in that blank no-time, no-place where
> you can't even greet your master.

During the 1970s and 1980s MacCaig was much in demand to read his poetry to audiences of students, schoolchildren, and others. He was a popular reader, presenting his poems with a laconic wit and a wealth of funny stories to accompany them. One of his most potent weapons was the pregnant pause; his audience could hardly bear to wait until he came out with his punchline. He was a tall, loose-framed man, very imposing as he stood on a rostrum or sat on a classroom desk; his craggy features, the sometimes rather wistful set of his mouth, and, as he grew older, his silver flyaway hair gave him an endearing air of authority and his audiences, particularly the children, loved him. Asked about his methods of composition, he would tell them with appropriate dramatic gestures that his poems came straight out of his head onto the page and, miming screwing up a piece of paper and throwing it into a waste-paper basket, that he never laboured over his poems; if they were unsatisfactory he destroyed them. A glance through his *Collected Poems*, however, will show that he certainly hoarded some of them for many years; of the hundred or so new poems in that book, twenty-seven date from the 1950s.

MacCaig's well-known public trademark was the cigarette held in his left hand as he explained or disputed a point. He repeatedly claimed that it took him two 'fags' to write a poem. When he tried to give up smoking, he found that his muse disappeared. He was ordered for medical reasons to stop smoking, but despite many efforts it proved impossible.

In the last fifteen years or so of his life MacCaig received considerable public recognition, with honorary doctorates from Stirling, Edinburgh, St Andrews, and Dundee. In 1979 he was made an OBE and in 1986 received the queen's medal for poetry. Though he wrote neither in Gaelic nor in Scots, MacCaig was one of the most influential of the Scottish poets writing in the second half of the twentieth century. Writing in English, he nevertheless celebrated the Scottish landscape, Scottish characters, Scottish music, Scottish culture. He will remain a major Scottish poet.

Norman MacCaig never really recovered from his wife's death in 1990. Three years later he had a slight stroke and was no longer able to write. Early in 1996 he had another stroke and was taken to Astley Ainslie Hospital, Edinburgh, where he died on 23 January. He was cremated on 29 January at Warriston crematorium, Edinburgh.

Even though MacCaig always declared that he threw away all the poems he did not intend to publish, his son, Ewen McCaig, discovered after his death a mass of unpublished material, now part of the Norman MacCaig archive, Edinburgh University.   HILDA D. SPEAR

Sources U. Edin. L., special collections division, university archives • M. McNeill, *Norman MacCaig: a study of his life and work* (1996) • N. MacCaig, 'My way of it', *As I remember*, ed. M. Lindsay (1979) • J. Hendry and R. Ross, eds., *Norman MacCaig: critical essays* (1990) • I. Murray, ed., *Scottish writers talking* (1996) • personal knowledge (2004)
Archives NL Scot., letters and poems • U. Edin., archive, MS 3198–MS 3210 • U. Edin., corresp. and literary papers • U. Edin., papers | NL Scot., corresp. with Duncan Glen • U. Edin., letters to Trudy Wallace
Likenesses G. F. McKenzie, oil on canvas, 1936–7, U. Edin., school of Scottish studies • A. Moffat, oil on panel, 1968, Scot. NPG • A. Moffat, group portrait, oils, 1980 (*Poets' Pub*), NPG • M. Knowles, oils, 1988, BBC Gallery, Edinburgh • L. Westwater, plaster bust, U. Edin. L.

Mac Cairteáin, Uilliam [William MacCartan] (**1667/8–1724**), poet and scribe, was born in Munster; a manuscript in his own hand records that he was aged thirty-four on 30 March 1702 (Royal Irish Academy, MS 23 H 18, p. 137). The names of his parents are not known. His wife's name was Cáit, and she was evidently related to another Cork poet and scribe, Eoghan *Ó Caoimh (1656–1726). In his youth Uilliam Mac Cairteáin served in the cavalry of the army of James II in Ireland and was a participant in the ambush of Williamite soldiers at Béal Átha Salainn (Six Mile Water) close to his home in co. Cork in April 1691. After the war he lived as a farmer just north of Cork city on a farm straddling the parishes of Carraig na bhFear and Teampall Geal (Whitechurch). The locality was renowned for its poetic and scribal tradition. Approximately thirty of his poetic compositions survive including works in praise of local Catholic gentry and laments on exiled gentry and clergy. He also composed humorous poems. Little information survives concerning his family, but a fellow poet's composition on the occasion of the marriage of his son in 1725 reveals that he had a son named Dónall who was himself a poet and inherited his books. Traditional sources suggest he also had sons named Tadhg and Séan and daughters whose names are not recorded.

A small number of manuscripts in Irish transcribed by Mac Cairteáin survives, containing stories from the Fiannaíocht (Ossianic) tradition, selected poetry, principally by fellow Munster poets Dáibhí Ó Bruadair and Eoghan Ó Caoimh, and devotional texts. Mac Cairteáin's scholarly contacts included John Sleyne, Catholic bishop of Cork from 1693 to 1703, from whom he borrowed manuscripts and for whom he wrote poetry. He may also have been employed by Sleyne to copy manuscripts. He was part of the same scholarly circle as the Revd Conor Mac Cairteáin (1658–1737) who may have been his parish priest. Mac Cairteáin was closely associated with the poet and scribe Eoghan Ó Caoimh and was godfather to Eoghan's son Art, who died in France in 1709 while studying for the priesthood. Their association was not without its tensions. Mac Cairteáin wrote poetry in praise of Dónall Ó Colmáin's prose satire *Parliament na mBan*. In his own locality Mac Cairteáin enjoyed the patronage of the McCarthy family. He may also have enjoyed the patronage of the prominent Cork Jacobite Sir James Cotter (*d.* 1705), and he was an admirer of both Sir James and his son. One of his poems revealed that Sir James had been responsible for the death of the regicide John Lisle in 1664.

After the death of Diarmaid Mac Seáin Buí Mhic Carthaigh in 1705 Mac Cairteáin became head of the local court of poetry which had been based at Gleann na Rátha, Blarney, co. Cork, and later at Teampall Geal. This assembly sought to maintain standards of poetic composition. The poetry of a younger poet from the same locality, Seán Ó Murchú na Ráithíneach (1700–1762), indicates that he was indebted to the encouragement he received from Mac Cairteáin who also lent him books. On Mac Cairteáin's death in November 1724 he was succeeded as chief poet by Liam ruadh Mac Coitir (*c.*1690–1738) who was in turn succeeded by Seán na Ráithíneach. Mac Cairteáin was buried in the parish of Teampall Geal, co. Cork, and was long remembered in the locality for his wit and humour.   BERNADETTE CUNNINGHAM

Sources B. Ó Conchúir, *Scríobhaithe Chorcaí, 1700–1850* (1982), 17–19 • A. Heusaff, *Fílí agus cléir san ochtú h-aois déag* (1992) • *Faiche na bhFílí: Carraig na bhFear, Cuimhneacháin-Souvenir* (1962) • Royal Irish Acad., MS 23 H 18 • M. Ní Urdail, *The scribe in eighteenth- and nineteenth-century Ireland: motivations and milieu* (2000)
Archives NL Ire., MSS G113–G114 • Royal Irish Acad., MS 23 H 18

Mac Caírthinn mac Cainnig (*d.* **506**). *See under* Ulster, saints of (*act. c.*400–c.650).

McCall, Annie (**1859–1949**), physician and promoter of antenatal and maternity care, was born on 23 September 1859 at Dudley Bank Cottage, Whalley Range, Moss Side, Manchester, the third child of five born to William McCall (1810/11–1863), an insurance agent, and his wife, Mary (1831–1921), daughter of Andrew Meiklejohn, an indigo planter. Her father died of tuberculosis when she was four and in 1871 her mother took the children to Germany to extend their education and so that they could learn a second language. Mrs McCall was widely read, 'a walking gazetteer' (Barrass, 24), and a strong influence, encouraging her daughter's wish to qualify as a doctor, which was difficult for women at that time. On the advice of Elizabeth

Annie McCall (1859–1949), by Deneulain

Garrett Anderson, a friend of her mother's, McCall studied at the London School of Medicine for Women from 1880 to 1884, specializing in midwifery, and afterwards at Bern, where she gained her degree as doctor of medicine in 1885, one of the first fifty women to do so. She studied obstetrics in Vienna before returning to England and taking an appointment in 1885 as medical officer at the Conference Hall, 143 Clapham Road, London, a mission hall and surgery run by Mrs Susannah Meredith. She was there for fifteen months and then continued the work of the outpatients' clinic for poor women and children from January 1887 at her own home, 131 Clapham Road.

McCall had always intended to open a maternity hospital, and to prepare for this had established a committee of supportive women and opened an antenatal clinic in 1886, which, McCall said:

> set out to deal with the absolute needs of expectant mothers. It is my belief that it was also the first thing of its kind in the country. Here we dealt with such things as the occupation of the mother, food preparation, the question of rest, leisure and exercise. Eventually it embodied a kind of post-natal work too, which we called the *Mother's Welcome*.
> (Barrass, 43)

Other outpatient establishments for women and children were at 2 Stockwell Road, 377 Wandsworth Road, and 2 Fentiman Road.

The Clapham Maternity Hospital (renamed the Annie McCall Maternity Hospital in 1936) was opened in 1889 at 74 Jeffreys Road, Stockwell, moving to 41–3 Jeffreys Road in 1892 and rebuilt on that site in 1913. In 1931 there were fifty beds and fees were 3 guineas a week. It closed in 1970

and the adjacent road has been named Annie McCall Close. It was financed originally by private subscriptions and legacies; in 1898 income included McCall's temperance lecture fees, donations from Elizabeth Blackwell and Louisa Garrett Anderson, and the sale of caps made by Mrs McCall. Small mortgages were taken out and grants received from the King Edward's Hospital Fund for London. Priority was given to admitting single women, unusual at this time, when being an unmarried mother was considered a disgrace and could result in the mother being cast out of the family home and the baby being born in the workhouse. McCall believed in the importance of antenatal care, natural childbirth, and conservative midwifery. 'Masterful inactivity' was her watchword and she also emphasized diet, recommending that no meat or eggs be eaten in the last months of pregnancy. Internal examinations were avoided if possible and forceps were used in only 3 per cent of births. Great emphasis was given to training and high standards; the resulting maternal mortality rates were low—1.6 per 1000—from 1889 to 1942. The skills of midwifery and obstetrics were being developed in Clapham at a time when their importance was not recognized elsewhere, before midwives had to be registered. McCall had been shocked at the low standard of care she had experienced during her early training in London hospitals. She and Marion Ritchie did 'much for obstetrics especially during a period when this branch of practice was looked upon as beneath the notice of the physician and surgeon' (*The Lancet*).

McCall had also established the Clapham School of Midwifery, which opened in 1887, with three students based at her home. It was run in conjunction with the hospital and set its own examinations, marked by external women doctors. The school trained midwives, monthly nurses, and doctors in midwifery. There was also a class in operative midwifery for medical students and missionaries going abroad. The examination was in three parts; written, *viva voce*, and practical on the wards. Only women, staff, and students, were admitted to both the school and hospital. Many women came from Christian missions abroad. The first Nigerian arrived in 1912; 'It is character, not colour, that counts', said McCall (Barrass, 75). She was a member of the Central Midwives' Board from its establishment in 1902 until 1931 and an examiner, as well as being vice chairman of the London county council committee for the Midwives' Act. She was also interested in tuberculosis, running a clinic at the hospital and a sanatorium at her other home in Rudgwick, Sussex.

McCall was confirmed into the Lutheran church while in Germany and believed in the power of prayer. She was fierce in her opposition to alcohol, and a vocal member of the temperance movement, bequeathing her house at 165 Clapham Road to the United Temperance Council. She was an autocrat, who expected her orders to be carried out in every detail, but was 'tender to the unmarried mother, even… a second time' (Barrass, 6). She worked until 1941 and one mother remembered her in the 1930s peering down to stitch up, as her eyesight deteriorated. She was described as an ardent suffragette and refused to write her degree dissertation about vivisection, requesting another subject instead. McCall was severe in appearance. One student wrote describing her clothes: black costumes, white blouses, black tie, woollen stockings, and boots. 'She seemed to us to have shed frills forever. I will say no more in that line' (Barrass, 117). For relaxation she enjoyed travel and her garden at her later home, 165 Clapham Road, with its mulberry tree. Members of her family lived near by at 56 Jeffreys Road; close friends included her cousin Marion Ritchie, who was an able hospital administrator and who until her death in 1931 softened McCall's forceful character, and Constance Watney, matron for a time, whom McCall described as 'my friend and close companion and business advisor' (Barrass, 107).

McCall died on 9 September 1949 at her last home, Kings, in Rudgwick and was buried in the Holy Trinity churchyard at Rudgwick on 13 September. She left an estate valued at over £92,000, most of which was willed to the London School of Medicine for Women to set up an Annie McCall scholarship in midwifery; she cared passionately that all women should have the best possible maternity care.   BERYL M. BARROW

Sources P. Barrass, *Fifty years in midwifery: the story of Annie McCall M.D.* (1950) · B. M. Barrow, 'Annie McCall', *Lambeth archives women's pack* (1990–97) [*Women's pack* consists of individually dated sections, 'Annie McCall' is from 1994] · *Annual Report* [Clapham Maternity Hospital] (1899–1939) · *The Lancet* (24 Sept 1949) · *South London Press* (16 Sept 1949) · *West Sussex County Times* (16 Sept 1949) · LMA, King Edward's Hospital Fund for London archives, 1911–66 · LMA, National United Temperance Council records · 'Safety first for our mothers', *Clapham Observer* (15 May 1936) · *London Directory* · Lambeth voters' registers, Lambeth Archives, London · *Medical Directory* (1910) · *Hospital Yearbook* (1931) · private information (2004) · Royal Free Hospital, Hampstead, London, London Free Hospital archives · *CGPLA Eng. & Wales* (1949) · b. cert. · d. cert. · m. cert. [parents]
Archives Lambeth Archives, London · LMA
Likenesses photograph, *c*.1945, repro. in Barrass, *Fifty years in midwifery*, frontispiece · Deneulain, photograph, Wellcome L. [*see illus.*]
Wealth at death £92,821 7s. 7d.: probate, 10 Dec 1949, *CGPLA Eng. & Wales*

Maccall, William (1812–1888), writer and public lecturer, was born in Largs, Ayrshire, on 25 February 1812, the eldest child of six sons and six daughters of John Maccall (*b*. 1793), a builder, and his wife, Elizabeth Murdoch (*b*. 1792). He later told the biographer Francis Espinasse (1823–1912) that he enlisted in the dragoons but was soon bought off. Then, intended for the ministry in the evangelical United Secession church, to which his parents belonged, he matriculated in the University of Glasgow in 1827. By the time he left the university in 1833 doubt had set in, and he was attracted by the preaching of the Revd George Harris (1794–1859), the Unitarian minister at Glasgow, who secured his appointment as minister at Greenock in 1833–4.

Maccall then entered a theological seminary in Geneva, where he learned German and became an ardent disciple of Rousseau. On returning to England he supplied pulpits in London, and in 1837 became minister at Moor Lane Chapel, Bolton, where Harris had been the first and only truly successful pastor. By 1840 the declining congregation was unable to pay a stipend, and Maccall resigned. After a brief involvement with the anti-corn law and Chartist agitations, he failed in candidacies at Bristol and Brixton. A visit to James Forrest (*d*. 1858), minister at Devonport, whom he had known at Glasgow and who had succeeded him at Greenock, led to his appointment at Crediton, in Devon, in 1841. After three months he moved to Coseley but, disliking it, returned to Crediton, where he preached until 1846, supplementing his stipend of £100 by teaching languages.

While at Bolton, Maccall had courted Mary (1819–1837), fifth child and fourth daughter of John Haselden (1785?–1835), a cotton manufacturer who belonged to Moor Lane. Five months after her death, at the age of eighteen, he proposed to her older sister Alice (1813–1878); they were married on 3 March 1842, helped by a small legacy from her uncle. Any expectations from the Haselden inheritance collapsed with the failure of the family firm following a disastrous mill fire in November 1842. Their only child, Elizabeth, was born the next year.

In 1839, in a sermon published as *The Clergy and the Nation*, Maccall told the Unitarian congregation at Todmorden that they must demand that their ministers preach and act in politics or choose those who would. He later insisted that he did not preach politics at Crediton, making only appropriate references to the game laws and the corn laws; but one member of the congregation organized a campaign against his 'indecent political declamation'. While the congregation supported their minister, his stipend was reduced to £40 by what he alleged was the trustees' financial mismanagement. He resigned in midsummer 1846 and moved to London, supplying pulpits— 'of the least *tight-laced* Unitarian species' Carlyle called them (T. Carlyle to O. Blewitt, 6 March 1853, Archives of the Royal Literary Fund)—and trying to maintain himself and his family by writing and lecturing.

The most curious surviving instance of Maccall's potboiling is a collection of materials for the history of amber, translated mostly from German and published in *Cope's Tobacco Plant*, the house organ of a Liverpool tobacco manufacturer. More seriously, in 1854 he translated Spinoza's *Tractatus politicus*, a French textbook in biology in 1877, and *Christian Legends*, from the collection by Karl Eduard von Bulow (1803–1853), in 1884. He had mixed success in writing for periodicals, quarrels or changes in editorship cutting short his contributions to *The Spectator*, *The Critic*, *Fraser's Magazine*, and the *Gentleman's Magazine*. Many of his reviews and essays were subsequently republished in books.

A tall, erect man, with a wonderful conversational gift, Maccall profoundly impressed John Sterling (1806–1844), who met him on a stagecoach in 1842 and whose letter written at the time led in 1848 to a meeting with Thomas Carlyle, who went out of his way to help with connections. When Maccall suffered a serious illness and mental collapse, Carlyle gave impressive support for an application in 1853 to the Royal Literary Fund that resulted in a grant of £40. Carlyle continued to think well of Maccall, though he described him as 'harsh-edged, as a rusty *lipped* [broken-edged] razor' and suspected that his difficulties with his congregations had been largely of his own making (T. Carlyle to M. Carlyle, 13 Feb 1856; *New Letters of Thomas Carlyle*, 2.144–5). Certainly his aggressiveness and savagery alienated editors and some well-disposed friends, and the continued sympathy of both John Stuart Mill and George Eliot did not prevent his harshly criticizing their work in publications such as *The Newest Materialism* (1873). Espinasse remarked that, while Maccall could be indulgent with foreign writers, he 'seemed to regard as a criminal offence the mere writing of an English book' (Espinasse, 251).

Predictably, these qualities were better adapted to the lecture platform, although even there Maccall's self-absorption could alienate audiences. He had given up the Unitarian connection by the 1850s, distressed, like his friend Forrest, by what he came to see as Unitarian frigidity, shallowness, and narrowness (Maccall, *Via crucis*, 21), but he remained a Christian of a cloudy and expansive sort, suggested in the medieval ideals set out in the preface to his 1884 translation of *Christian Legends*.

Most of Maccall's subsequent work must, however, be seen as flowing from *The Elements of Individualism*, thirty-five lectures given to his Crediton congregation in 1845–6 and published in book form by John Chapman in 1847. This elaborate credo, rambling and self-indulgent, is a call to the fullest individual development, to reveal God existing in every man and woman, and a passionate plea for toleration. John Stuart Mill saw the work as a major predecessor of his *On Liberty* (1859), one of the books Maccall reviewed so stringently. He also revealed a Carlylean prophetic streak, hailing the hero both as individual—notably in his 1857 panegyric on Charles James Napier (1782–1853)—and as archetype in *The Agents of Civilization* (1840; repr. 1893), shallow, inspirational ruminations on the hero, poet, priest, artist, prophet, philosopher, apostle, and martyr. In *National Missions* (1855) each of the great national cultures is matched to a single characteristic: Egypt and religion, Greece and beauty, Palestine and faith, Italy and art, France and manners, England and science, and so on.

In 1878 Alice Maccall died after long suffering from a blood disorder. *Via crucis* (1880) is a husband's passionate lament and a harrowing revelation of his own life of failure and misery. He died on 19 November 1888 at his home, Fountain Villa, Woolwich Road, Bexleyheath, Kent.

R. K. WEBB

Sources W. Maccall, *The elements of individualism* (1847) · W. Maccall, *Via crucis: record of a divine life and picture of a divine death* (1880) · F. Espinasse, *Literary recollections and sketches* (1893) · BL, Archives of the Royal Literary Fund, case no. 1314, reel 49 [s.v. Maccall] · *New letters of Thomas Carlyle*, ed. A. Carlyle (1904) · *Christian Pioneer*, 14 (1840), 423–32, 455–60 · *Christian Life* (24 Nov 1888) · *The George Eliot letters*, ed. G. S. Haight, 2 (1954), 13–14; 6 (1956), 278–9 · *The later letters of John Stuart Mill, 1849–1873*, ed. F. E. Mineka and D. N. Lindley, 4 vols. (1972), vols. 14–17 of *The collected works of John Stuart Mill*, ed. J. M. Robson and others (1963–91), vol. 1, p. 38 · J. S. Mill, *On liberty* (1859), preface · parish register (birth), 25 Feb 1812, Largs, Ayrshire · *CGPLA Eng. & Wales* (1889)

Likenesses mezzotint, BM

Wealth at death £696 11s.: probate, 23 Jan 1889, *CGPLA Eng. & Wales*

MacCallum, Andrew (1821–1902), landscape painter, was born at Nottingham and baptized at St Mary's Church on 15 December 1822. His father, also Andrew MacCallum, was of highland descent and an employee of the hosiery manufactory William Gibson & Sons. It was into this trade that MacCallum was later apprenticed. His pleasure, however, came from sketching in Sherwood Forest. Though his family had little time for his talents, he was encouraged by the newspaper editor Thomas Bailey, who allowed the young man to study his own art collection. MacCallum also attended drawing classes run at the Nottingham Mechanics' Institution in the late 1830s by the Derby painter Moses Webster.

On his twenty-first birthday the penniless MacCallum set up on his own in Nottingham, maintaining himself by teaching elementary drawing to students at the city's People's College and selling the occasional painting. He is thought to have sold his first picture to the Nottingham town clerk Mr Enfield. When he was twenty-two he became a student of the newly opened Nottingham School of Design. In 1846 he exhibited his first work, a landscape, at the Birmingham Society of Artists' Exhibition, and this was followed the next year by another landscape at the Liverpool Academy. In 1849 his picture of Flint Castle appeared at the British Institution in London. About the same time he enrolled at the Government School of Design at Somerset House, London, and found lodgings not far away, at York Chambers, Adelphi. There his teachers included Richard Redgrave and J. R. Herbert. In 1850 MacCallum exhibited his first painting at the Royal Academy, entitled *The Old Grey Stone; Study from Nature—Ambleside*. Later in the same year he moved to Manchester, where he worked as assistant master at the Manchester School of Art, then under the directorship of John Astbury Hammersley, MacCallum's teacher at Nottingham. In 1852 he moved to the School of Practical Art at Stourbridge, living at the Old Parsonage, New Street. The school's headmaster was Henry Alexander Bowler, and it is possible to see his Pre-Raphaelite influence on MacCallum's work. That same year he married, on 30 December, Susan (d. 1875/6), the daughter of John Tetlow, an oil merchant from Altrincham, Cheshire. In 1854 MacCallum was awarded a scholarship by the government's Department of Science and Art to travel throughout Italy for the purposes of copying examples of mural decorations for use in the government art schools. He recorded his impressions in a manuscript, 'Report of a sojourn in Italy from the year 1854 to 1857', now in the National Art Library at the Victoria and Albert Museum. Although he was greatly impressed by Italian art of earlier centuries, the manuscript reveals his belief that the contemporary artists of modern Italy were far inferior to their British counterparts. The many illustrations of door knockers, altar cloths, and stained glass also show that MacCallum was equally interested in applied and fine art.

After returning to England in 1857, MacCallum was commissioned to decorate the interior of the first lecture theatre at the South Kensington Museum (now the Victoria and Albert Museum). A little later he decorated the western exterior of the museum's Sheepshanks Gallery with portraits of famous artists. In 1858 MacCallum leased a studio in Kensington which had previously belonged to the artist Thomas Webster.

MacCallum spent much of the 1860s travelling in Europe. Towards the end of 1861 he was at Fontainebleau, in 1864 he saw Switzerland and the Rhine, in 1866 he was in Italy, and in the winter of 1866–7 he was in Paris. But his travels did not prevent him from contributing works to exhibitions in Britain. In 1865 he sent four paintings to the Nottingham School of Art and in 1866 he exhibited six watercolours and twenty-nine oils at the Dudley Gallery. These included the large paintings *Charlemagne Oak, Forest of Fontainebleau* and *A Glade in Sherwood Forest*, which helped to establish MacCallum's reputation as a painter of trees. The exhibition received mixed reviews. The *Art Journal* found MacCallum's works 'so full of suggestion as to fill the mind with the most vivid imagery' (*Art Journal*, 28, 1866, 218), while the *Illustrated London News* considered his style 'somewhat artificial and mechanical' (*ILN*, 23 June 1866). The meticulous realism that characterized MacCallum's style received renewed criticism in 1871, when P. G. Hamerton praised his technical and observational skill but found him lacking in spiritual imagination: 'Not one of his pictures ever affects us when we stand before it, or haunts us when we have left it … this is the special weakness of our scientifically accurate art' (Hamerton, 61). Nevertheless, MacCallum's pictures were popular with the public. He was awarded a silver medal by the Society of Arts and exhibited a total of fifty-three paintings at the Royal Academy, as well as a few at both the British Institution and the Society of British Artists. He sent works to the international exhibitions of 1870–71 and showed fourteen works at the Midland Counties' Exhibition of Fine and Industrial Art at the Nottingham Exchange in 1872. Favourite subjects included Windsor Forest, Sherwood Forest, and Burnham Beeches in Buckinghamshire.

In 1870 MacCallum made the first of several visits to Egypt. In 1875 he was invited by a patron, Lady Ely, to paint for Queen Victoria at Balmoral. Although Lady Ely warned the queen that his prices were steep, he was commissioned to paint three views near Balmoral. Soon afterwards MacCallum travelled to the south of France with his dying wife, a cultured woman who accompanied her husband on his travels and introduced him to several important patrons. After her death MacCallum returned to Balmoral, and Queen Victoria was said to be very kind to him in his bereavement. She later granted him the upper storey of a tower in Windsor Great Park to use as a studio, and they corresponded occasionally. In 1876 MacCallum

sent his *Sultry Eve* to the Centennial Exhibition at Philadelphia. Perhaps responding to the criticism that his style was overly realistic, in the late 1870s he sent to the Royal Academy two imaginary scenes, *The Eve of Liberty* and the *Dream of Ancient Egypt*. On reviewing the latter in 1878, *The Times* recommended that MacCallum confine himself to nature painting.

MacCallum died from bronchitis on 22 January 1902 at 5 The Studios, Holland Park Road, Kensington. He had lived in the neighbourhood since 1858. He was survived by two sons from his second marriage, to a Miss Salway of Ludlow, one who served in the Second South African War and the other an electrical engineer. It is understood that he raised the boys alone after separating from his wife. A number of his works are in public collections, including the Tate collection, the Victoria and Albert Museum, Nottingham Castle Museum and Art Gallery, Manchester City Galleries, and the Guildhall Art Library, London.

B. S. LONG, *rev.* MARY GUYATT

Sources H. Williams, 'The lives and work of Nottingham artists from 1750–1914, with special consideration of their association with the lace industry and society at large', PhD diss., U. Nott., 1981 · D. Millar, *The Victorian watercolours and drawings in the collection of her majesty the queen*, 2 vols. (1995), 594 · file of correspondence, Nottingham Castle Museum and Art Gallery · J. Dafforne, 'The works of Andrew MacCallum', *Art Journal*, 39 (1877), 321–4 · P. G. Hamerton, *English painters of the present day* (1871), 60–61 · *ILN* (23 June 1866) · 'The works of A. MacCallum', *Art Journal*, 28 (1866), 218 · *The Times* (4 May 1878), 12 · J. Physick, *The Victoria and Albert Museum: the history of its building* (1982), 29, 37 · Graves, *RA exhibitors* · C. E. Clement and L. Hutton, *Artists of the nineteenth century*, 2 vols. (1879), 80 · *Fifty years of public work of Sir Henry Cole*, ed. A. S. Cole and H. Cole, 2 vols. (1884), 329–33 · J. Beavington Atkinson, 'Exhibitions of the year', *Fine Arts Quarterly Review*, 1 (1866), 1.373 · m. cert. · d. cert.

Archives Castle Museum, Nottingham, corresp. with Castle Museum · V&A, report MS

Likenesses J. H. Sylvester, portrait, 1888 · carte-de-visite, NPG

Wealth at death £230: administration with will, 11 Aug 1902, CGPLA Eng. & Wales

McCallum [*married name* Richardson], **Janet Hutchison** [Jenny] (1881–1946), trade unionist and suffragette, was born on 21 July 1881 at Hospital Hill, Dunfermline, the eldest of the thirteen children of John McCallum (1857–c.1905), stonemason, and his wife, Janet (1860–1933). Jenny McCallum's early childhood was spent in the town of Inverkeithing, where her father worked on the construction of the Forth Bridge; but she probably received her elementary schooling at St Leonard's School in Dunfermline when her father returned to seek work in the local quarries. There were at least three linen-weaving factories within a few hundred yards of her home at 89 Woodmill Street and it was inevitable that she would start her working life in one of these.

As a young woman Jenny McCallum showed some interest in local trade union activities but when, in 1907, the Women's Social and Political Union expanded its organization in Scotland she threw her energies into the struggle for women's suffrage. In west Fife the year's activities centred on a 'great demonstration', planned for the autumn, which was to be attended by Christabel Pankhurst and other national leaders. Jenny McCallum organized and presided over a series of successful open-air meetings, often sharing the platform with the highly charismatic figure of Anna Munro, later to be the Scottish organizer of the Women's Freedom League. In October she was delegated to attend a conference on sweated labour in Glasgow. As a factory worker she understood as well as any the wider basis of women's oppression. This, as well as the example of Anna Munro, certainly influenced her decision to join the newly created Women's Freedom League.

In the summer of 1908 Jenny McCallum was active in the attempt to force women's suffrage into the forefront of by-elections in Liberal strongholds in the east of Scotland. After these campaigns she was fully committed to the women's cause and, leaving her job as a winder in Bothwell Street linen works, she travelled to London to take part in demonstrations aimed at Westminster politicians. On 27 October 1908 she was in a group of Women's Freedom League members who, climbing onto a mounted statue in Old Palace Yard, attempted to hold a public meeting. She was arrested along with thirteen other activists. The following morning, after refusing to pay a fine of £5, all fourteen were sentenced to one month's imprisonment. After serving her sentence in Holloway prison she travelled north and spent a period at the league's new Scottish headquarters in Glasgow. There she took the decision to return to her home in Dunfermline, where, although her mother and sister had been supportive of her political activities, her contribution as a wage-earner had been important. Effectively blacklisted by employers, however, it was over a year before she secured a job in a local mill. Resuming her trade union activities, she eventually became full-time organizer and secretary of the Textile Workers' Union.

On 17 December 1915, at the age of thirty-four, Jenny McCallum married Harry Richardson (b. 1879), an engine fitter at the newly constructed dockyard at Rosyth. They had three children. In the summer of 1919, as a mother with a young family, she joined the leadership of a group of striking Scottish National Housing Company tenants in Rosyth. Placing women at the centre of the struggle she drew on her trade union and suffragette experience and organized a series of mass meetings, marches, and pickets. The Rosyth rent strike, although ultimately abortive, attracted national attention and generated sympathetic action by miners and Admiralty workers in other parts of the country. When court proceedings were taken against a group of Rosyth tenants she enlisted the aid of Sylvia Pankhurst to speak on their behalf.

In the mid-1920s the dockyard workforce was rapidly scaled down and the Richardsons were obliged to seek a living by emigrating to South Africa. Ironically, Jenny McCallum had been able to use her hard-won vote on only a handful of occasions. She died, several years after her husband, on 24 March 1946 at 16 Maltzan Street, Pretoria.

CHRIS NEALE

Sources L. Leneman, *A guid cause: the women's suffrage movement in Scotland* (1991) · *The Times* (29 Oct 1908) · *The Times* (30 Oct 1908) · 'Suffragists at Westminster', *Dunfermline Journal* (31 Oct 1908) · *Dunfermline Journal* (June–Dec 1919) · 'Dunfermline suffragette', *Dunfermline Journal* (2 March 1968) · private information (2004) · b. cert. · m. cert.

Likenesses photograph, 1908, repro. in *Dunfermline Journal* (2 March 1968)

McCallum, Ronald Buchanan (1898–1973), historian and college head, was born on 28 August 1898 at Paisley, Renfrewshire, the last of four sons of Andrew Fisher McCallum, master dyer, of Paisley, and his wife, Catherine Buchanan, *née* Gibson. He was educated at Paisley grammar school and Trinity College, Glenalmond. He did two years' service in the labour corps of the British expeditionary force in France (1917–19) and then read modern history at Worcester College, Oxford, obtaining first class honours in 1922. After a year at Princeton and another as a history lecturer at Glasgow University, in 1925 McCallum was elected to a fellowship and tutorship in history at Pembroke College, Oxford; among his colleagues there were R. G. Collingwood and J. R. R. Tolkien. After holding several college offices McCallum was elected master of Pembroke in 1955, becoming the first non-clerical head of the college since Queen Anne's annexation of the mastership to a canonry of Gloucester Cathedral.

McCallum was quintessentially an Oxford don whose centre of life was the college and university. He tutored several generations of undergraduates in British and foreign history and political institutions, and conducted an important university seminar on British parliamentary procedure; some of its participants became prominent political leaders in Britain and the United States. He was senior proctor (1942–3) and pro-vice-chancellor (1961) of the university and university member of the city council (1958–67), and played a part in the creation of Nuffield College. He was senior treasurer of the union and edited and contributed regularly to the *Oxford Magazine*. His vignettes of Oxford, published there under a pseudonym, give an amusing picture of university life.

The twelve years of McCallum's mastership saw a marked transformation of Pembroke. The number of tutorial fellows increased and began to include natural scientists. The quality of undergraduates and their academic performance improved. A new quadrangle was created in 1962 by converting and incorporating a row of historic houses between Pembroke Street and Beef Lane. McCallum was an ideal master for this expansionary period in the history of the college. He combined traditional beliefs in the virtues of Oxford education with the recognition of a need to bring the college into the era established by the Butler Education Act of 1944. His sense of fairness and toleration of views with which he disagreed were valuable qualities in a governing body that became increasingly large and diverse.

Steeped in the tradition of Scottish Presbyterianism and Liberalism at home, McCallum was a lifelong Liberal himself and a prominent member of the Unservile State Group. His political background nurtured his academic interests. His first published work was a life of Asquith

Ronald Buchanan McCallum (1898–1973), by Walter Stoneman, 1955

(1936) and one of the last was *The Liberal Party from Earl Grey to Asquith* (1963). He contributed a chapter on Liberalism to *Law and Opinion in England in the Twentieth Century* (1959, ed. Morris Ginsberg) and published, with an introduction, the political writings of John Stuart Mill (1946) in Blackwell's series of political texts, which he edited jointly with C. H. Wilson. In his most controversial work, *Public Opinion and the Last Peace* (1944), which analysed British attitudes to the treaty of Versailles, McCallum sought to correct what he considered to be serious distortions in the accounts of J. M. Keynes and other writers. With *The British General Election of 1945* (1947), written with Alison Readman, McCallum inaugurated the well-known series of Nuffield election surveys. Although the work gave currency to 'psephology' (a word McCallum coined as a name for the academic study of elections) it eschewed any sociological approach; like the rest of his books it was a fine example of traditional historical scholarship. McCallum's special gift as a historian was for the analysis of political opinions. He was also a very gifted letter writer and conducted with friends, colleagues, and former pupils (such as Senator J. W. Fulbright) an extensive correspondence, which is remarkable for its attractive style and graphic quality. He loved serious conversation and had an unusually good memory. His portly figure dominated any gathering he attended.

In 1967 McCallum resigned the mastership, shortly before retirement, in order to become principal of St Catharine's, Cumberland Lodge, Windsor Great Park, a position which he held until 1971. He was an honorary fellow of Pembroke (1968) and Worcester (1961) colleges and honorary LLD of Dundee University (1967), the latter in recognition of his advice on the new university's constitution and development.

McCallum was married twice: first, in 1932, to Ischar Gertrude (*d.* 1944), of Wallasey, Cheshire, daughter of Frederick Bradley, schoolmaster; and second, in 1950, to Evelyn Margaret, daughter of Sir Douglas *Veale, registrar of Oxford University. There were two daughters of the first marriage, and two sons and a daughter of the second. McCallum died on 18 May 1973 at his home, the Old Vicarage, Letcombe Regis, Berkshire, and was cremated at Headington crematorium, Oxford.

Z. A. PELCZYNSKI, *rev.*

Sources *The Times* (21 May 1973) · *Pembroke College Record* (1974) · J. W. Fulbright, The first R. B. McCallum memorial lecture, 24 Oct 1975 · personal knowledge (1986) · private information (1986)
Archives Pembroke College, Oxford, corresp. | JRL, letters to the *Manchester Guardian*
Likenesses W. Stoneman, photograph, 1955, NPG [*see illus.*] · J. Gunn, oils, Pembroke College, Oxford · J. Ward, portrait, Pembroke College, Oxford
Wealth at death £28,936: probate, 2 Aug 1973, *CGPLA Eng. & Wales*

McCalmont, Frederick Haynes (1846–1880), statistician and barrister, born at home on 13 October 1846, was the first son of the Revd Thomas McCalmont of Highfield, near Southampton, and formerly of Belfast, and his second wife, Emily Georgina, daughter of Frederick Hill of the 1st Life Guards. He was a relative of Hugh McCalmont Cairns, first Earl Cairns and lord chancellor. He was educated at Eton College (1859–62) and at Oriel College, Oxford, where he graduated BA in 1869, proceeding MA in 1872. He was called to the bar from the Inner Temple in April 1872 and began to practise on the western circuit later that year. He lived at Southampton, where he was a member of the endowed school board and, from 1877, an alderman. He was a prominent freemason, being master of the Shirley and Southampton lodges, and was a 'staunch Conservative in politics' (*Southampton Times*, 6 Nov 1880). He was tory candidate for Southampton, but withdrew his candidacy in 1878 on the death of his brother, Alfred Leighton McCalmont (*b.* 1851), mayor of Southampton.

McCalmont is a name known to all students of British parliamentary elections. In such elections, the returning officer returned the name of the winning candidate only, not the names of other candidates or the numbers of votes cast, or any information about the parties of the candidates. There was therefore no official record of such details, although much information was given in local and national newspapers. **James Acland** (1799–1876) had begun compiling electoral statistics, published as *The Imperial Poll Book of All Elections from 1832 to 1864* (1865; 2nd edn, 1869). Acland was a radical, who had been a clerk, an actor, sub-editor of the journal the *British Traveller*, and editor of

The Portfolio, or, Memoirs and Correspondence of an Editor (1831–3), after which he worked in Paris and then, from 1838 to 1846, as a lecturer for the Anti-Corn Law League. His experience as an election agent from 1846 onwards led naturally to his book.

McCalmont took Acland's work much further, in content and accuracy. He decided to compile information not merely on the dates, names of candidates, parties, and votes of all parliamentary elections since 1832, but also to display it conveniently together with details of the size and ratable value of constituencies, and the numbers of electors. His *Parliamentary Poll Book of All Elections* was first published in 1879. The book was successively revised, initially by W. H. Rowe, until the general election of January 1910. An eighth edition, with material covering the period from February 1910 to the general election of 1918, was edited by J. Vincent and M. Stenton in 1971. For many years McCalmont's single-volume work was the most convenient and accurate record of nineteenth-century elections; *British Parliamentary Election Results*, compiled and edited by F. W. S. Craig (4 pts, 1969–89), largely superseded McCalmont as the standard work.

McCalmont, who was unmarried, was a diabetic and suffered from insomnia and heart disease. Following tory success in the local elections in Southampton in 1880, he was reported to have been 'somewhat unduly elated'. On 3 November 1880 he bought a bottle of syrup of chloral hydrate and died in bed in Radley's Hotel, Southampton, his body being found on the morning of 4 November. The coroner's jury found that he died from natural causes as a result of his heart condition. He was buried in Southampton cemetery.   H. C. G. MATTHEW

Sources *Southampton Times* (6 Nov 1880) · *Southern Reformer* (24 July 1880) · Foster, *Alum. Oxon.* · d. cert. · Boase, *Mod. Eng. biog.* [James Acland]
Likenesses Adams & Stilliard, photograph, repro. in *Southern Reformer*

McCalmont, Harry Leslie Blundell (1861–1902), racehorse owner, was born on 30 May 1861 at Hampton Court, Middlesex, the only son (in a family of three children) of Hugh Barklie Blundell McCalmont (1836–1888), barrister of Lincoln's Inn, and his wife, Edith Florence, daughter of Martin Blackmore of Bonchurch, Isle of Wight. At Eton College he excelled at rowing and football, passing his military exams before joining the 6th regiment of foot in 1881. From 1885 to 1889 he was a lieutenant in the more fashionable Scots Guards. He married on 9 December 1885 Amy Hyacinth (d. 1889), daughter of Major-General John Miller.

McCalmont's great-uncle Hugh McCalmont, of Abbeylands, co. Antrim, a member of the City of London firm McCalmont Brothers & Co., died unmarried on 20 October 1887 leaving his fortune to McCalmont. It was held in trust for seven years but in 1894 McCalmont received capital and interest totalling some £4 million. From 1887 he set out to enjoy his greatly altered circumstances: he purchased the Cheveley estate at Newmarket and built a grand neo-Palladian mansion, bought the first of his three

yachts, *Giralda*, and soon joined the Royal Yacht Squadron.

His wealth allowed McCalmont to indulge his taste for racing and betting. He purchased Sefton Lodge and its stables in Newmarket from the duke of Montrose for £12,000 and soon became one of the most successful owners and popular racing figures of the period. He had steeplechasers trained by Captain D. L. Beattie in Wicklow, and asked Captain Machell, who owned the Newmarket Bedford Cottage stable, to act as his stable manager on the flat. Machell began by buying the well-proven four-year-old Timothy, who carried McCalmont's light blue and scarlet-quartered colours (the Eton football strip) to win the gold cup and Alexandra plate at Ascot in 1888. McCalmont also purchased from Machell a reportedly useless thoroughbred mare, Deadlock, to breed from. Put to Isonomy, in 1890 she produced Isinglass, the best horse McCalmont ever owned. Isinglass was only beaten once in twelve races and won £57,455 in prize money, a total that remained an English record until 1952. In 1893 Isinglass won a rare turf triple crown of the Two Thousand Guineas, the Derby, and the St Leger; in 1894 his successes included the Princess of Wales stakes and the Jockey Club stakes; and in 1895 he won the Ascot Cup. However, from 1895 until 1902 McCalmont was less successful. Machell was too ill to give racing his full attention so in 1898 McCalmont bought Bedford Cottage and installed as trainer Charles Beattie, son of his former trainer.

McCalmont stocked Cheveley Park lavishly with game, and his guests experienced generous hospitality and good shoots. He successfully bred sheep and pigs, and set up a small thoroughbred breeding stud. Isinglass, who went to stud in 1894, was of limited success as a stallion but became the sire of two later classic winners. McCalmont also set up a steeplechase course on his estate. He was elected as a member of the Jockey Club in 1893.

McCalmont was elected as Conservative MP for East Cambridgeshire on 29 July 1895: his narrow majority may have been helped by his famous tour of the constituency on polling day to rally support, in which he covered some 87 miles in under twelve hours. Following the death of his first wife he married, on 5 July 1897, Winifred (d. 1943), widow of William Atmar Fanning and daughter of General Sir Henry Percival De Bathe, fourth baronet. After the outbreak of the Second South African War he served in South Africa as colonel of the 6th battalion of the Royal Warwickshires, and was on active service at the time of his re-election to his Cambridgeshire seat in October 1900. He was made CB in 1900 for his South African services.

In 1901 McCalmont returned to England, determined to restore his racing prestige. His home-bred horse Rising Glass won £12,000 in what was a very successful 1902 racing season. Earlier in that year (16 January 1902) he moved in the House of Commons the address in reply to the king's speech. On 8 December 1902 he died of heart failure at his London house, 11 St James's Square; he was buried in the churchyard at Cheveley. He left no children, and the bulk of his £2 million estate passed to his second cousin Dermot McCalmont.   M. J. HUGGINS

Sources *The Times* (9 Dec 1902) · *The Sportsman* (9 Dec 1902) · *Sporting Times* (9 Dec 1902) · *Ruff's Guide to the Turf* (1887–1903) · *Baily's Magazine*, 63 (1895), 297–9 · *Badminton Magazine* (Feb 1903) · H. Dixon, *From Gladiateur to Persimmon* (1901) · R. Mortimer, R. Onslow, and P. Willett, *Biographical encyclopedia of British flat racing* (1978), 361 · R. Onslow, *The heath and the turf: a history of Newmarket* (1971); rev. edn pubd as *Headquarters: a history of Newmarket and its racing* (1983), 172–8 · G. Plumptre, *The fast set: the world of Edwardian racing* (1985), 109–11 · A. T. C. Pratt, ed., *People of the period: being a collection of the biographies of upwards of six thousand living celebrities*, 2 vols. (1897) · Burke, *Gen. Ire.* (1958)

Likenesses Spy [L. Ward], caricature, NPG; repro. in *VF* (5 Dec 1889) · Spy [L. Ward], caricature, NPG; repro. in *VF* (9 Jan 1896) · photograph, repro. in Plumptre, *The fast set*, 108 · photograph, repro. in R. Onslow, *Headquarters: a history of Newmarket and its racing* (1983), 173

Wealth at death £2,000,000: probate, 3 Jan 1903, *CGPLA Eng. & Wales*

MacCalzean, Euphame (*d.* 1591). *See under* North Berwick witches (*act.* 1590–1592).

McCance, Sir Andrew (1889–1983), steelmaster and metallurgist, was born at 12 Adder Steps, Cadder, Dunbartonshire, on 30 March 1889, the third of four children and younger son of John McCance, a cloth factor, and his wife, Janet Ferguson McGaw. His father subsequently worked for the Graham Joint Stock Shipping Company of Glasgow, engaged in trade with the East. McCance was brought up in Crieff, where he attended Morrison's Academy before moving to Allan Glen's School in Glasgow. He graduated in metallurgy at the Royal School of Mines in 1910.

After graduation McCance was given the run of the melting shop of William Beardmore & Co., unpaid until a vacancy was found for him six months later as an assistant chemist. After making a contribution to the prevention of cracking in armour plate ingots, he was made assistant armour manager. In the armour shop he conducted far-reaching experiments into the annealing process. Experimental work carried out at the Royal Technical College and at the University of Glasgow supplemented his investigations at Beardmores. These investigations, which were always rooted in technical problems encountered in the workplace, resulted in a number of papers—perhaps the most important of which was his 'Contribution to the theory of hardening' (*Journal of the Iron and Steel Institute*, 89, 1914, 199–244)—and were recognized by the award of a DSc by London University in 1916. There followed further pioneering studies on non-metallic inclusions in steel.

Believing that there was no future in armour steel McCance left Beardmores in 1919 in order to establish himself as a manufacturer of alloy and special steels. He went into partnership with T. M. Service, the armour manager at Beardmores who had first seen his potential, and the two metallurgists asked John Craig (1874–1957) whether David Colville & Sons would lease the derelict Inshaw works to them for conversion into a steel foundry and take an interest in the proposed company. The approach was welcomed by Colvilles. A new company, Clyde Alloy, was created with a capital of £60,000 in ordinary £1 shares. Colvilles took up 48,000 of the shares, of

Sir Andrew McCance (1889–1983), by Walter Bird, 1966

which 8000 were to be held for sale to McCance and Service when they were in a position to purchase them.

For the next ten years the creation of Clyde Alloy dominated McCance's life. It was a very difficult period—the 'black decade' of the British steel industry—made even more so for McCance by his partner's recall to Beardmores in 1921. McCance did everything from supplying the management, providing the technical expertise, and marketing the product, to keeping the accounts. For long periods he never left the works, sleeping on the premises and cooking breakfast on the office fire. But slowly he built up connections with the beleaguered shipbuilders and with the more buoyant motorcar manufacturers, Ford, Austin, Swift, and Vulcan lorries. Meanwhile, he continued his scientific investigations and his published papers constituted a major contribution to the knowledge and understanding of the physical chemistry of steel-making.

As chairman of Clyde Alloy, John Craig was so impressed with McCance's ability and energy that when Colvilles Ltd was formed in 1930 by a merger of David Colville & Sons and the iron and steel interests of Sir James Lithgow, McCance was made general manager of the Colville Group and offered a place on the board. Thus began a partnership which was to shape the future development of the Scottish steel industry. As Craig and Lithgow painfully gained control of over 80 per cent of Scotland's steel making capacity, McCance undertook its rationalization. Later critics of the nature and pace of the technical integration of the Colville Group have failed to appreciate the social, financial, and demand constraints that inhibited more radical policies: the ideal of a vast integrated tidewater plant was subordinated to the piecemeal modernization of Colvilles' existing works. This ideal was originally proposed in the Brassert report on the manufacture of iron and steel of 1929. Glengarnock and Dalzell were remodelled and the blast furnaces at Clyde Iron modified to permit the production of pig iron at a cost below the current market price of English and Indian pig. This remarkable achievement was followed by the integration of Clyde Iron with Clydebridge by the construction of a bridge across the Clyde, over which molten iron from the former was conveyed to the open-hearth furnaces of the latter, thereby making possible large-scale hot-metal working in Scotland for the very first time.

McCance's position within Colvilles became increasingly powerful during the war when overcoming the problems arising from hard-driving plant with a chronic shortage of spares and time for proper maintenance, the use of low-grade Northampton ores, and the increasing complexity of producing and handling ferro-alloys for aircraft production demanded the exercise of the full range of his technical abilities. Awarded the Bessemer gold metal by the Iron and Steel Institute in 1940 and elected a fellow of the Royal Society in 1943, McCance was perhaps at the height of his scientific prowess during the war years. Certainly, Colvilles became heavily dependent upon his practical virtuosity. This was formally recognized in 1944, when McCance was appointed deputy chairman and joint managing director of the group. He was knighted in 1947.

The problems did not cease with the ending of hostilities. Already in 1943-4 McCance had devised the company's post-war plan. Relatively modest in its objectives, its formulation was shaped by the company's social responsibilities, McCance's projection of long-term future trends in demand (totally at odds with the predictions of the Iron and Steel Board), and the difficulties envisaged in the acquisition of adequate supplies of coking coal of metallurgical quality. In essence, McCance wished to complete the interrupted programmes of rationalization embarked upon in 1936.

Colvilles' plans were not well received by the Iron and Steel Federation, whose adviser, Dr T. P. Colclough, one of the authors of the Brassert report, argued for the development of an entirely new works located on a tidewater site at Inchinnan or Erskine Ferry. In the event, the alliance of Sir John Craig's diplomatic skills and McCance's technical knowledge resulted in the reluctant acceptance of Colvilles' development scheme by the federation and the second Iron and Steel Board in 1954. Approval was given for the modernization of the group's existing plant and the creation of a new integrated iron and steel works on a greenfield site at Motherwell, the Ravenscraig works.

As the first stage of the Ravenscraig project neared completion, the group's future development seemed clearly charted. It was then that the strip mill question intervened. Urged by industrialists, trade unionists, the news media, and above all by the government to undertake the building of a strip mill, McCance, since 1956 the chairman

of the company, demurred. There was, he argued, neither the necessary coking coal available nor, more importantly, an adequate local demand for steel strip to make such a mill commercially viable. Eventually, after intense political pressure, Colvilles were persuaded to put down a strip mill at Ravenscraig. Commissioned in 1962, it was, as McCance had predicted, a financial disaster: the cost of its construction brought the Colville Group to the brink of bankruptcy. Only nationalization in 1967 saved the firm from liquidation.

Meanwhile, in 1965, McCance had retired. In thirty years he had welded together a steelmaking complex from the untidy collection of works so patiently assembled by Sir John Craig, only to have its delicate internal balance destroyed by succumbing to political pressure, the object of which was not economic efficiency but the pursuance of misguided regional employment policy. McCance ruled his empire autocratically. His boardroom colleagues were always conscious that although they might advise him, *he* made the decisions. McCance came to meetings, seeking guidance perhaps, but always ready to present his plan, which was invariably carefully thought out, scientifically precise, and fully documented. It was said that the first task facing his successor, T. R. Craig (Sir John's elder son), was to teach the board how to direct. It was a role most of them had forgotten.

A shy, reserved, immaculately dressed, and immensely dignified man, McCance found relaxation in music and the composition of a stream of scientific papers. In 1936 he married Joya Harriett Gladys, daughter of Thomas B. Burford, a licensee. They had two daughters, and his wife's death in 1969 was a grievous blow to him. He served on numerous committees established by bodies within the iron and steel industry. He was president of the West of Scotland Iron and Steel Institute in 1933-4, of the Iron and Steel Institute in 1948-50, and of the British Iron and Steel Federation in 1957-8. He was chairman of the Mechanical Research Board, Department of Scientific and Industrial Research, from 1952 to 1958. Intensely interested in educational matters, it was during his chairmanship of the Royal Technical College at Glasgow that it became the Royal College of Science and Technology and in 1961 received confirmation that it would be granted independent degree-awarding status as the University of Strathclyde. McCance was among the first recipients of an honorary doctorate of the new institution. His fruitful connections with the University of Strathclyde is commemorated in the names of the McCance and Colville buildings, the latter housing the metallurgy department.

McCance, active in scientific enquiry until nearly the end of his long life, died at the age of ninety-four, on 11 June 1983 at Davidson Hospital, Girvan, Ayrshire. He was survived by his two daughters. He was cremated at Masonhill crematorium, Ayr, on 15 June.   PETER L. PAYNE

Sources NA Scot., British Steel records, GD 464 · P. L. Payne, *Colvilles and the Scottish steel industry* (1979) · N. J. Patch and L. Barnard, *Memoirs FRS*, 30 (1984), 389–405 · *Colvilles Magazine* (May–June 1947) · *Colvilles Magazine* (spring 1957) · D. Burn, *The steel industry, 1939–1959: a study in competition and planning* (1961) · D. W. Heal, *The* *steel industry in post-war Britain* (1974) · K. Warren, 'Locational problems of the Scottish iron and steel industry', *Scottish Geographical Magazine*, 81 (1965) · K. Warren, 'Coastal steelworks: a case for argument', *Three Banks Review*, 83 (1969) · J. Vaizey, *The history of British Steel* (1974) · *DNB* · *The Scotsman* (14 June 1983) · personal knowledge (2004)

Archives U. Glas., Archives and Business Records Centre, corresp. and papers · University of Strathclyde, Glasgow, corresp., papers, and photographs | NA Scot., British Steel records, records relating to the Colville group, GD 464
Likenesses J. Gunn, oils, 1943, University of Strathclyde, Glasgow, Collins Art Gallery, GLAEX A329 · W. Bird, photograph, 1966, NPG [*see illus.*] · photograph, repro. in 'A technical survey of the Colville Group', *Colvilles Magazine* (1957?), 4 · photographs, repro. in *Colvilles Magazine*

McCance, Robert Alexander (1898–1993), physician and research physiologist, was born on 8 December 1898, at Woodbourne, near Dunmurry, south-west of Belfast, the third son of John Stouppe Finlay McCance (1865–1926), barrister and linen merchant, and Mary Letitia, *née* Bristow (1865–1948). (Through a mistake on his father's part, his birth certificate wrongly recorded his birth date as 9 December.) He had a younger sister, Elizabeth. At the age of eight he began his formal education at Mourne Grange, a preparatory school near Kilkeel, co. Down, and when he was thirteen he entered St Bees School, Cumberland, where his brothers Finlay and Harry had preceded him. In 1947 he was appointed a governor of the school, and he held this office for thirty-five years.

On leaving school in 1916 McCance applied for a commission in the Royal Naval Air Service. He was called up in 1917 and trained to fly single-seater aircraft (Camels), but later flew two-seater aircraft from a wooden platform mounted over the midship gun turrets of the battle cruiser *Indomitable*. He was demobilized in 1919 and, deciding to make agriculture his career, was advised to obtain the diploma in agriculture at the University of Cambridge. After six months working on a farm in northern Ireland he entered Sidney Sussex College, Cambridge, in 1919. On his tutor's advice he took the natural sciences part one course first, and obtained first-class honours in 1921. He gave up the idea of agriculture as a profession, and took the part two physiology course under Sir Joseph Barcroft, achieving second-class honours in 1922. In the same year he married Mary Lindsay (Mollie) MacGregor (1898–1965), daughter of Dr Duncan Otto MacGregor, physician, of Glasgow, and a student at Girton; they had one son and one daughter. McCance spent the next three years in the department of biochemistry under Sir Frederick Gowland Hopkins, which led to a PhD in 1926. By this time McCance had decided to study medicine, and his next move was to King's College Hospital, London. He obtained his MB in 1927 and MD in 1929, and was made MRCP in 1930 and FRCP in 1935. He was interested in diabetes, and spent a year assisting R. D. Lawrence in the new diabetic clinic. Although insulin had recently become available it was still important for diabetics to regulate the amount of carbohydrate in their diet. Because published values for the carbohydrate content of foods were unsatisfactory he analysed more than a hundred plant foods for available

carbohydrate, and published the values with Lawrence as a Medical Research Council Special Report in 1929.

A new biochemical laboratory was set up at King's College Hospital in the early 1930s, and McCance was appointed as its head. Although he was responsible for the biochemical requirements of the hospital, he was able to spend time on research, and in the mid-1930s made his seminal studies of the effects of salt deficiency on the human body. The analysis of foods continued, and plant, meat, fish, and other common foods were analysed for ten constituents. The results were published by McCance and his colleague Elsie M. Widdowson in 1940, as a Medical Research Council Special Report entitled *The Chemical Composition of Foods*.

In 1938 McCance accepted an invitation from J. A. Ryle, regius professor of physic in Cambridge, to return there as reader in medicine. He was allocated laboratories in the pathology department and beds in Addenbrooke's Hospital for patients with rare diseases. The laboratories were soon occupied by research and junior staff, and visiting scientists from the UK and overseas.

Food analysis continued, and second and third editions of the tables, containing the composition of more foods, were published in 1946 and 1960. The Ministry of Food then took over the responsibility for updating the tables, which at the time of writing are in their fifth edition. They are the standard publication on the composition of foods in the UK, and are used worldwide.

McCance (Mac or Prof to his colleagues) was not a lone worker, and always had one or more collaborators; he was interested in the physiology of the whole body, and the subjects of his research ranged widely. During the early part of the Second World War he was engaged with Andrew Huxley, James Robinson, Widdowson, and others in a study of rationing, which involved living on a diet extremely low in fat for three months before cycling the 200 miles from Cambridge to the Lake District, and walking 36 miles up hill and down dale in one day, in deep snow and with heavy rucksacks. The study concluded that such rationing was unlikely to lead to any loss of physical fitness; it was also the origin of the proposal to add calcium to flour used for bread-making to offset the effects of rationing of dairy products. Later in the war McCance chaired a joint Medical Research Council and Royal Navy committee on survival at sea which for the first time demonstrated conclusively that it was better to drink nothing at all than to drink seawater. Among other things, the committee's work led also to the development of new pills for seasickness, and a new design for covered inflatable life-rafts, which subsequently saved many shipwrecked seamen from death through exposure. In 1945 the University of Cambridge, jointly with the Medical Research Council, created a personal chair for McCance and, as a tribute to the French scientist Claude Bernard, he chose the title professor of experimental medicine, the first of such titles in the UK.

In the years before his retirement, one of McCance's major interests was the physiology of the newborn infant. He found that at birth the kidneys are immature and an excess of certain nutrients in manufactured milk formulae may do harm. This work inspired others to study the physiology of infancy, which became a subject in its own right. The Neonatal Society was founded, with McCance as first president, and it now holds an annual McCance lecture. On his retirement in 1966 the Medical Research Council asked him to go to Uganda as temporary head of their Infantile Malnutrition Research Unit in Kampala. He spent two years there, and greatly enjoyed the experience.

In 1968 he returned to Cambridge, where he spent the rest of his life. He was fond of walking, but his favourite mode of travel was cycling, which gave him 'uninterrupted time to think'. His bicycle was fitted with a cyclometer, and between 1939 and 1969 he cycled 200,000 miles, equivalent to eight times round the world. In the late 1970s he was knocked off his bicycle, fracturing a femur, which led to a shortening of his right leg. However, he continued to walk several miles a day until he had another fall about ten years later, which resulted in a fractured pelvis. He then became more and more disabled, and had to move to sheltered accommodation. His many friends, including past colleagues and students, visited him when they could, often seeking his advice. All had valued the years they spent working with him. He published more than 300 papers in scientific journals, six Medical Research Council Special Reports, and, with E. M. Widdowson, a book entitled *Breads, White and Brown; Their Place in Thought and Social History* (1956).

He died of a chest infection at the home where he lived, Shelford Lodge, 144 Cambridge Road, Great Shelford, Cambridgeshire, on 5 March 1993, and was cremated on 11 March at Cambridge crematorium; his ashes were taken to Sidney Sussex College garden. A memorial service was held in the college chapel on 16 April. His wife had died in 1965, but he was survived by a son and daughter, seven grandchildren and twelve great-grandchildren.

ELSIE WIDDOWSON

Sources 'Links with the Past: the McCances of Suffolk and Knock Na Goney', 1984, PRO NIre. · R. A. McCance, 'Reminiscences', Sidney Sussex College, Cambridge · M. Ashwell, *McCance and Widdowson: a scientific partnership of 60 years* (1993) · personal knowledge (2004) · private information (2004) [D. Ogilvy] · WWW · E. M. Widdowson, *Memoirs FRS*, 41 (1995), 261–80
Archives Wellcome L., notebooks relating to nutrition, GC/97
Likenesses photograph, 1966, repro. in *Memoirs FRS*, 262 · W. E. Narraway, pencil, 1978, Sidney Sussex College, Cambridge; repro. in *The Independent* (17 March 1993) · M. Bulman, bronze head, 1995, RS
Wealth at death £598,367: probate, 28 June 1993, *CGPLA Eng. & Wales*

McCance, William (1894–1970), artist and writer on art, was born on 6 August 1894 at 69 Westburn Rows, Newton, parish of Cambuslang, near Glasgow, the seventh child and youngest son of the eight children of James McCance (d. 1911), a coalminer who originally came from Ulster, and Elizabeth MacBride, from an Ayrshire weaving family. He was educated at Hamilton Academy and then attended the Glasgow School of Art (1911–15), where he studied under Fra Newbery; he won the Haldane travelling scholarship in his last year. Following a year's teacher training at Kennedy Street School, he was imprisoned in 1917 for refusing to go on parade when serving with the Scottish Rifles. He was subsequently incarcerated in Wormwood Scrubs, Knutsford, Dartmoor, and Warwick prisons before being discharged from the army in 1920, though he married, on 6 July 1918, a former student at the Glasgow School of Art, Agnes Miller *Parker (1895–1980), the daughter of William McCall Parker, an analytical chemist. She became one of the most distinguished woodengravers of her generation.

In 1919 or 1920 McCance moved to London, and he immediately adopted the style he retained for the rest of his life; derived in part from foreign artists such as Fernand Léger, Francis Picabia, and Albert Gleizes, it also owed much to the English vorticists of the pre-war era. (The vorticist William Roberts rented a room in the McCances' apartment at this period.) McCance began to make sculptures, such as his blocky, faceted *Cat* (1921–2, priv. coll.), and became art critic of *The Spectator* (1923–6). His friends included the sculptor Eric Kennington, and in 1925 his work was the subject of an article in the *Scottish Educational Journal* by Hugh MacDiarmid (writing under the name C. M. Grieve), with whom his friendship lasted forty years. In 1928 he first exhibited his work in London, in a group show with Agnes Miller Parker, Blair Hughes-Stanton, and Gertrude Hermes, at the St George's Gallery. The Scottish National Gallery of Modern Art in Edinburgh houses a number of his works from this period, such as his *Study for a Colossal Steel Head* (1926).

Appointed controller of the Gregynog Press in 1930, McCance moved to Newtown, Montgomeryshire. Despite his lack of previous experience of publishing fine books, he was responsible for some magnificent productions, and himself designed a number of very successful initial letters, such as those for *The Fables of Esope* which was illustrated with woodcuts by Agnes Miller Parker. Some abstract experiments, such as *Speed Doodle* (1930), were executed with lettering pens as a result of his new interest in calligraphy and letter-forms. A passionate Scottish nationalist, he contributed an article entitled 'Idea in art' to the *Modern Scot* (2, 1930), and cartoons in favour of social credit to the *Free Man*, such as *Scots! Unite!* which appeared on 4 February 1933.

After three successful years at the Gregynog Press McCance and his wife moved to Albrighton, near Wolverhampton, Staffordshire, to live in a windmill where he made terracotta portraits, masks, reclining figures, and cats, as well as paintings, monotypes, and linocuts. In 1936 they moved again, to Hambleden, near Henley-on-Thames, Oxfordshire, where McCance became friendly with John Piper. He continued to write art criticism, and powerful articles by him on Jacob Epstein in the *News Chronicle* (1937) and *Picture Post* (1939) so pleased the sculptor that he reprinted them in his autobiography *Let there be Sculpture* (1942). McCance also worked on an 85,000-word treatise on art, which he finished in 1941 but which remains unpublished. In 1943 he took over from Robert

Gibbings as lecturer in typography and book production at the University of Reading; his first, belated, one-man exhibition was at the Reading Art Gallery in 1960. He and Agnes Miller Parker separated in 1955, and on his retirement in 1963 he returned to Scotland, settling in Girvan, Ayrshire, following his marriage on 6 April to Dr Margaret Eva Chislett (b. 1926/7), a microbiologist who had also lectured at Reading; she was the daughter of Stuckey Wesley Chislett, a retired farmer. McCance's *Self-Portrait* (oils, 1916, Scottish National Portrait Gallery, Edinburgh) depicts a strong, angular face, and later photographs show him bearded, with thick, wiry, upstanding hair on his vigorous head. He died at Girvan on 19 November 1970.   ALAN WINDSOR

Sources P. Elliott, *William McCance, 1894–1970* (1990) · *William McCance, 1894–1970* (1975) [exhibition catalogue, Central Museum and Art Gallery, Dundee] · C. M. Grieve [H. MacDiarmid], 'William and Agnes McCance', *Scottish Educational Journal* (20 Nov 1925) · b. cert. · m. certs. · R. Garton, ed., *British printmakers, 1855–1955* (1992) · B. Hughes-Stanton, *William M'Cance, Gertrude Hennes, Agnes Miller-Parker* (1928) [exhibition catalogue, St George's Gallery, London, Feb–March 1928]
Likenesses W. McCance, self-portrait, oils, 1916, Scot. NPG

McCardie, Sir Henry Alfred (1869–1933), judge, was born on 19 July 1869 at 57 Wellington Road, Edgbaston, Birmingham, one of several sons and fifth of the seven children of Joseph William McCardie, merchant, of Edgbaston, an Irishman, and his English wife, Jane Elizabeth Hunt. His father dying when McCardie was still a child, he owed much to his mother's determination. McCardie was educated at King Edward VI Grammar School, Birmingham. Lively and intelligent but preferring sport and skylarking to study, he was jolted by the challenge of a sceptical schoolmaster into adopting what became the industrious habits of a lifetime. He left school at sixteen, needing to earn a living but uncertain of his future. Some years spent in an auctioneer's office he looked back on as valuable exposure to commercial practice. After several false starts, he decided on the bar. He was admitted to the Middle Temple in 1891 and was called to the bar on 18 April 1894.

After joining the chambers of James Parfitt, in Birmingham, McCardie soon made a name on the midland and Oxford circuits for his exceptional grasp of legal principle—the fruit of intense study—and for clear, logical, and attractive argument. He also proved an enterprising, confident, and persuasive advocate in appeals. 'If you have a bad case,' he would say, 'you have nothing to lose and much to gain' (Pollock, 14). A decade of outstanding success in Birmingham emboldened him to try his luck in London. He joined forces with a fellow barrister, and took chambers in the Temple in 1904.

McCardie's optimism was amply justified. Solicitors vied for his services, and were equally satisfied whether he was briefed to appear alone or led by the senior counsel of the day. McCardie's success lay in immense application and thoroughness of preparation, concealed by a relaxed, informal style of advocacy. He put to good use an inability to sleep for more than six hours a night: his chambers became known as 'the lighthouse' from his lucubrations into the small hours. He handled a heavy and varied caseload with unruffled temper despite the pressures on him: his diary for one day records twenty-one cases in twenty-one different courts. His knowledge of case law, aided by a photographic memory, was encyclopaedic. He was also steeped in the intricacies of interlocutory pleadings before 'masters'. He impressed judge and jury by his businesslike presentation of cases and his skill in clarifying the issues—'he could summarize an intricate argument in a sentence' (Pollock, 19). In cross-examination he never sought to browbeat; rather he triumphed by a quiet, friendly approach, a modest, winning charm, and an easy good humour, free of any self-assertion, his wig cheerfully askew.

McCardie was popular and respected at the bar. A question of professional etiquette arose when his leader, Marshall Hall, indignant at a judge's hostility, walked out of court in the middle of a case, and McCardie followed him. The consensus was that, as the most experienced junior in the Temple, McCardie must be right. He represented the main banks and railway companies and many titled litigants and theatrical stars. In his last ten years at the bar his was by far the largest junior practice in the Temple. His annual earnings averaged over £20,000, an enormous sum for the time. He declined to enter politics, despite the promise from Joseph Chamberlain of a safe seat—being unwilling, as he said, to submit to any 'party creed' (Pollock, 23).

In 1910 McCardie submitted his name to Lord Chancellor Loreburn for consideration for silk; but Loreburn's well-known conscientiousness led to a long delay in reaching a decision, and this delay damaged McCardie's practice. McCardie withdrew his application, letting his reason be known, and refused to reapply even when Loreburn offered to grant it. McCardie was thus still a junior barrister when, on 12 October 1916, on the promotion of Sir Thomas Scrutton to the Court of Appeal, Lord Chancellor Buckmaster appointed McCardie a judge of the King's Bench Division at the recommendation of the prime minister, H. H. Asquith. He was knighted on 23 October.

Comprehensive judgments As a judge McCardie at once displayed two characteristics, neither hitherto suspected, which place him in a class of his own. His reserved judgments were as comprehensive and as carefully crafted as though written for a legal monograph. He made a point of reviewing all available authorities, however many there might be, in order to extract from the totality of precedents their common principle and to reduce that principle to a limpid and authoritative statement of the law. His ability to trace a line of reasoning in clear and simple language lent his dicta the stamp of applied common sense. 'What McCardie says seems so obvious—after he has said it,' said one admirer (Pollock, 188). In *Cohen v. Sellar* (1926), ruling on a point not previously determined, he held that a man who breaks off his engagement is not entitled to the return of the ring. McCardie reached this conclusion after an exhaustive review of precedents, Roman and continental, as well as English.

Such lengthy excursuses seemed otiose to the senior judges. Lord Justice MacKinnon deplored what he called McCardie's 'prolix disquisitions'. To cite 'every case ever decided upon any topic', he complained, 'is not the method of the great judge' (MacKinnon, 238). But McCardie was convinced (as he said in *Gayler and Pope* v. *Davies*) of 'the importance of principle and of the need for a greater co-ordination of case law'; and student, scholar, and practitioner may still find profit and example in his learned, compendious, and methodical judgments. *MacLenan* v. *Segar* (1917) remains a classic authority on a hotelier's liability for the safety of his premises, *Said* v. *Butt* (1920) on a theatre's right to 'sell or refuse to sell tickets at its own option'. *Pratt* v. *The British Medical Association* (1918) is a pioneering judgment in the civil law of conspiracy. *Heddon* v. *Evans* (1919) confirms that decisions of military tribunals are justiciable by the civil courts. McCardie's ruling in *Hartley* v. *Hymans* (1920), relieving a party when appropriate from the letter of his contract, set the future Lord Denning on the fruitful path of 'promissory estoppel' (Denning, 201). In the leading case of *Phillips* v. *Britannia Hygienic Laundry Co.* (1923) McCardie held that breach of a statutory order does not of itself necessarily furnish a cause of action to a plaintiff injured thereby. In *Gayler and Pope* v. *Davies* (1924), reviewing the law on straying animals, he ruled that if a horse is left untended in a public street and bolts, its owner is prima facie liable in negligence. In *Fisher* v. *Oldham Corporation* (1930), where his researches extended to the *English Historical Review*, he ruled that police officers are officers of the crown, not agents of the corporation, and that an action for false imprisonment would not lie against the latter.

A controversial judge McCardie's second characteristic as a judge caused surprise and even consternation. Having been known for 'his infallible tact as an advocate' (*The Times*, 12 Oct 1916), he showed himself on the bench to be a rebel and a crusader, a critic and opponent of much in the system he was appointed to administer. He denied that anyone was ever reformed by prison or borstal. He thought the current divorce laws a disgrace and said so in open court. The duties of the king's proctor were 'repulsive' (Pollock, 47), suits for restitution of conjugal rights— 'a hollow mockery' (ibid., 68). The divorce laws themselves were shaped by 'the dead hand of the old canon law' (ibid.); and they and such actions as suits for breach of promise of marriage would, he rightly predicted, be looked on with incredulity thirty years hence. Holding passionately that the law should move with the times and reflect the standards of educated opinion, McCardie did not hesitate to speak out. 'Iconoclasm', he wrote, 'is the basis of moral and social progress' (Carr, 290). So far as the law allowed, he strove to act on his belief, informed by wide reading and reflection, that while judicial decision making was necessarily grounded in case law, considerations of social problems should also influence it. No judge held the common law in greater veneration and few were more deeply versed in it: one lord chancellor described him as 'the greatest master of case-law of our

time' (*DNB*); but for McCardie himself the elasticity, expansiveness, and vitality of the common law were as essential as its certainty. 'The law', he said, 'must be stable, yet it cannot stand still' (Pollock, 48). Impatient of judicial 'paralysis'—'my task', he insisted, 'is not merely that of an automaton' (ibid.)—he supported his judgments with observations on the realities of modern life, especially the position of women, and with arguments in favour of birth control, lowering the age of consent, and the legalization of abortion.

McCardie's bold expression of controversial views irritated and dismayed his fellow judges. They 'shuddered to read' in the popular press of 'Mr Justice McCardie's latest' or the opinions of 'the Bachelor Judge' (*Solicitors' Journal*, 291) on women's fashions, including their lingerie. His conviction of the dynamic role of law in society aroused equal disquiet. 'I have no respect', he declared with typical robustness, 'for a rule of law whose sole claim to esteem is based on its antiquity and its remoteness from everyday life' (Pollock, 51). While such forthright assertions cheered the hearts of a younger generation of lawyers— McCardie identified easily with the young, and bridged, it was said, the generation gap between pre-1914 and interwar England—his repeated breaches of judicial convention sowed resentment. In *Place* v. *Searle* (1932) a husband sought damages from his wife's enticer. McCardie, finding against him, denounced actions for enticement, from the viewpoint of 'the lawyer who possesses sociological vision', as an absurd and degrading anachronism. 'The fact is', he concluded, 'that many of the old decisions require adjustment, if not abolition, in view of the conditions of modern life.' The Court of Appeal ordered a retrial on the evidence. In a mordant and personalized judgment, Lord Justice Scrutton, questioning McCardie's credentials as a bachelor to comment on marital relations and women's underwear, added tartly that the less 'sociological knowledge' entered into legal decisions, the better. Stung to the quick, McCardie delivered what he called a 'public rebuke to Lord Justice Scrutton' (Pollock, 214), stating that he would no longer pass on his case notes to any court of appeal of which Scrutton was a member. This was an extraordinary act of defiance. On the intervention of the master of the rolls, McCardie agreed to comply with the normal procedure.

McCardie also exposed himself to political controversy. *O'Dwyer* v. *Nair* (1924) was a libel suit, centring on the 1919 'massacre' at Amritsar in India, where General Dyer ordered his troops to fire on a crowd of 20,000 unarmed rioters, killing 400. In his book the defendant accused Dyer's superior, the lieutenant-governor of Punjab and plaintiff in the action, of responsibility for an 'atrocity'. Summing up, McCardie gave it as his considered opinion that Dyer's order was justified in the circumstances and that his subsequent dismissal from the army was wrong. McCardie had every right to express his views, coupled as they were with a warning that the jury was under no obligation to agree with them. The socialist intellectual Harold Laski, who was a juryman in the case, dissented from

McCardie's view, but none the less commended his 'magnificent impartiality' (*Holmes–Laski Letters*, 613). But McCardie caused grave offence in Liberal and Labour circles generally as well as in India, where 'Amritsar' was a synonym for colonial oppression. In the House of Commons, the Labour MP George Lansbury urged McCardie's removal from the bench and McCardie's comments were censured by the prime minister, Ramsay MacDonald. Ironically, McCardie's name had been among those submitted to MacDonald as a possible lord chancellor in the first Labour government (Lewis, 18–19). During the financial crisis of 1931, when MacDonald's National Government reduced the judges' salaries by 20 per cent, McCardie protested to Lord Chancellor Sankey at this breach of contract. While his immediate concern was a drop in his net income to one-tenth of what it was during his heyday at the bar, it was subsumed in the collective remonstrance by the High Court judges that the measure was unconstitutional under the settlement of 1689.

Among criminal cases heard by McCardie, two involved crimes of passion: the trials of Lieutenant Malcolm (1917) for killing his wife's seducer, and of Roland Hurn (1929) for the murder of his wife. The cases of *R. v. Jacoby* and *R. v. True* (1922) caused a public outcry. Jacoby, an eighteen-year-old pantry-boy, was executed despite the jury's strong recommendation for mercy, fully endorsed by McCardie; while the well-connected Ronald True, convicted with McCardie's clear approval, was reprieved by the home secretary on the grounds of insanity. Public outrage at the reprieve was such that Lord Chancellor Birkenhead appointed a committee under Lord Atkin to reconsider the McNaghten rules on criminal insanity.

Unfulfilled law reformer Popular as a barrister, McCardie had to steel himself against the criticism he received as a judge. He was so often its target, he said, that he had 'forgotten what it feels like not to be attacked' (Pollock, 34). Most of the laws whose obsolescence he exposed have long since been swept away. But the unreflecting and sometimes ill-natured acrimony provoked at the time by his outspoken pronouncements saddened and hurt him. Sensitive to what he prized as 'the brotherhood of the Bar' (ibid., 44), he was wounded by the hostility of Lord Justice Scrutton, Mr Justice Avory, and the lord chief justice, Lord Hewart. Even so temperate a lawyer as Lord Buckmaster came to regret that he had ever raised McCardie to the bench (MacKinnon, 238).

McCardie loved the law. Even as a judge he still thought of himself as a law student (Pollock, 239). In particular he loved the common law. He found it 'aflame with interest and adventure' (ibid., 240), 'one of the most stupendous products of the human mind' (ibid., 244), and the proper vehicle of progress. He was courteous and kindly on the bench, tending, as he said, to side 'with those who are weak and those who are poor' (ibid., 52). He preferred a bind-over or probation order to a custodial sentence, and in any event 'the helping hand afterwards' (ibid., 157). While he believed in both corporal and capital punishment, he loathed having to pass a death sentence; and his voice was instrumental in the repeal of the death penalty

for infanticide under the Infanticide Act (1922). The public warmed to his patent goodwill, and he received an astonishing number of letters asking for advice. He often helped, anonymously but from his own pocket, families of those he had sentenced. In his large humanity and accessibility, his wide sympathies, and his obvious desire to do justice and to make the law serve the changing needs of society, McCardie saw himself in the creative tradition of Mansfield and Bowen. He was a Denning before his time, though denied promotion to an appellate court from where, like them, he might have reshaped the law.

Like Denning, Harry McCardie was an inspiration to the young: youthful in his enthusiasm and smiling good humour, his frank, open face, his spontaneity, optimism, and generosity of spirit. 'Bitterness', as he said, 'is a very small thing and it does not carry a man far in life' (Pollock, 166). Despite his comments on women's fashions, he was remarkably careless of his own. Despite a copious wardrobe, he wore the same set of clothes, worn and creased because he put them away in a drawer, never on hangers. He would gad about, down at heel, indifferent to torn hatband, frayed trousers, or leaking boots. Arrayed in his judge's robes, he had an odd habit of jerking up his ermine cuffs at moments of strain.

A bencher of the Middle Temple since 1916, McCardie, on becoming reader for 1927, revived the ancient custom, in abeyance since 1680, of delivering an address. He used the occasion to respond obliquely to his critics by insisting on a judge's right to speak out. 'The judges seek no popularity,' he declared. 'They will not yield to the passing winds of popular excitement' (Pollock, 138). Though he never attended university, he was highly cultivated and widely read in history and literature, as his judgments show. He was an active member of the Horatian Society, a connoisseur of old china, and an avid collector of watercolours, which crowded every room, including the bathroom, of his small flat in Queen Anne's Mansions, St James's Park, Westminster. McCardie had a powerful, stocky physique, was fond of boxing, shooting, and fishing, a keen golfer, and at the age of sixty still a formidable tennis player. He was a member of the Reform Club and the Athenaeum.

Early in 1933, while on circuit, McCardie suffered in succession three debilitating bouts of influenza which left him deeply depressed and unable to sleep. On 26 April 1933, alone in his flat, he shot himself. The coroner returned a verdict of suicide while the balance of his mind was disturbed. Suicide was certainly on his mind during the last year of his life (Rentoul, 130–31). One of the last cases tried before him was a libel action brought by Mrs Meurig Morris, a self-styled medium, whose attempts to turn the court into a séance sorely tried his patience. It was said that during the trial McCardie received an anonymous letter, purportedly from the spirit world, which foretold his own fate. Be that as it may, the circumstances of his death were sad enough. McCardie had incurred massive gambling debts. It also appears that he was being blackmailed. McCardie was a great lawyer, whose progress as a judge was barred by his fearless independence and outspokenness. His judicial reformism was not adequately appreciated by his contemporaries or allowed full scope. A. LENTIN

Sources G. Pollock, *Mr Justice McCardie: a biography* (1934) · *DNB* · *The Times* (27 April 1933) · *The Times* (29 April 1933) · *The Times* (17 June 1933) · *The Times* (12 Oct 1916) · *Law reports* · F. MacKinnon, 'An unfortunate preference', *Law Quarterly Review*, 61 (1945), 237–8 · *Solicitors' Journal*, 77 (1933), 291 · H. Montgomery Hyde, *Norman Birkett: the life of Lord Birkett of Ulverston* (1964) · H. A. McCardie, *The law, the advocate and the judge* (1927) · *Judicial wisdom of Mr Justice McCardie*, ed. A. Crew (1932) · R. C. Carr, ed., *Red rays: essays of hate from Oxford* (1933) · J. B. Williamson, ed., *The Middle Temple bench book*, 2nd edn, 1 (1937) · E. Bowen-Rowlands, *In court and out of court: some personal recollections* (1925) · G. Lewis, *Lord Atkin* (1983) · G. Lang, *Mr Justice Avory* (1935) · J. D. Crawford, *Reflections and recollections* (1936) · R. Jackson, *The Chief: the biography of Gordon Hewart, lord chief justice of England, 1922–40* (1959) · A. T. Denning, *The discipline of law* (1979) · *Holmes–Laski letters: the correspondence of Mr Justice Holmes and Harold J. Laski*, ed. M. De Wolfe Howe (1953) · G. Rentoul, *Sometimes I think: random reflections and recollections* (1946) · *WWW*, 1929–40 · D. G. Browne, *Sir Travers Humphrey: a biography* (1960) · G. Goodwin, *The Middle Temple: the society and fellowship* (1954) · b. cert.
Archives Bodl. Oxf., corresp. with Lord Hanworth
Likenesses Elliott & Fry, photograph, repro. in Pollock, *Mr Justice McCardie* · L. N. A., photograph, repro. in Pollock, *Mr Justice McCardie* · M. Milwood, bronze head, Middle Temple, London · Press Portrait Bureau, photograph, repro. in Pollock, *Mr Justice McCardie* · W. Thomas, photograph, repro. in Pollock, *Mr Justice McCardie* · photographs, repro. in Pollock, *Mr Justice McCardie*
Wealth at death £7323 2s. 3d.: resworn administration, 17 June 1933, CGPLA Eng. & Wales

McCarrison, Sir Robert (1878–1960), army medical officer and nutritional physiologist, was born in Portadown, co. Armagh, on 15 March 1878, the second son of Robert McCarrison, a flax buyer, and his wife, Agnes McCullagh. He received his medical education at Queen's College, Belfast, and the Richmond Hospital, Dublin, and qualified with first-class honours in 1900.

Like many of his compatriots who possessed high ability but had limited financial resources he joined the Indian Medical Service (IMS), and sailed for the East on his twenty-third birthday. He spent the earliest formative years of his service in Chitral, as regimental medical officer (1902–4), and Gilgit, as agency surgeon (1904–11). Both these valleys were in the mountainous north-west of British India where, in McCarrison's words, 'nature makes large-scale experiments on man'. While in Gilgit, in 1906, he married Helen Stella (d. 1968), third daughter of John Leech Johnston of the Indian Civil Service. Their only child, a daughter, was stillborn in 1910.

During his first season in Chitral, McCarrison found his garrison suffering from an apparently novel and undescribed 'three-day fever'. By careful observation and investigation he correctly identified the sandfly (*phlebotomus*) as the vector. This experience whetted his appetite for research, and other features of the health of the mountain people of the north-west became the main themes of his research career. The first of these was thyroid disease. Goitre and cretinism were endemic in mountain populations, but not uniformly distributed. In Gilgit, McCarrison was able to demonstrate, by an experiment

on himself and several volunteers, that suspensible impurities from certain surface water sources were goitrogenic, enhancing the iodine deficiency common to the whole area and explaining the variation in goitre incidence between Gilgit's villages. This work may have helped him to secure his position at the Pasteur Institute at Kasauli in 1912. An Indian Research Fund Association (IRFA) grant supported his work there, which was initially on goitre in animal models. He received widespread recognition from the outset, with the award of the kaisar-i-Hind gold medal for public service in 1911, the Prix Amussat of the Académie de Médecin of Paris in 1914, and election to fellowship of the Royal College of Physicians in the same year. He had delivered the Milroy lectures to the college in 1913.

McCarrison's second and best-remembered area of research was work on the patterns of disease associated with various human diets and the balance of nutrients found in them. In public lectures he attributed his interest to his encounters with the people of the Hunza valley, who displayed great vitality and little ill health, and whose diet appeared to mark them out from their mountain neighbours. McCarrison's laboratory work on deficiency disease was started in 1913, following the publication of Frederick Gowland Hopkins's 1912 paper on accessory food factors, later called vitamins. The method McCarrison evolved was a blend of clinical and laboratory models of research. Populations of animals were fed various actual human diets, or modified foodstuffs. He made clinical observations of these animals' health while alive, and subsequently conducted detailed post-mortem examinations.

McCarrison's research career suffered many interruptions. The first of these was the outbreak in 1914 of the First World War, during which he was on active service with the Indian army, largely in Egypt. In March 1918 he returned to India as lieutenant-colonel and was assigned an empty room in the Pasteur Institute at Coonoor, southern India. The project was officially styled 'The beri-beri inquiry'; his only equipment was a microscope and a microtome, and his staff was a clerk borrowed from the post office, and his wife's cook. He was soon joined by assistant surgeon Mula Singh, who was to remain his assistant, and at times his only colleague, until 1935. When illness took McCarrison back to England in 1920 he paid for Mula Singh to accompany him to Charles Sherrington's Oxford laboratory for training in histological techniques. The following year McCarrison made a lecture tour of the USA, which included talks at the Mayo Foundation and Johns Hopkins University. During this period he also published *Studies in Deficiency Disease* (1921). Widespread recognition for his thyroid and nutritional research did not protect him from the retrenchment measures of the 1922 Inchcape commission. In 1923 he was appointed CIE, but also had his IRFA grant withdrawn, forcing him to stop laboratory work until 1925.

McCarrison made much of these interruptions in the evidence he gave to the royal commission on agriculture in India when it visited Coonoor in 1926. The commission was broadly concerned with the problems of agriculture in India, a concern sharpened by recurrent famines and endemic disease on the subcontinent. McCarrison was able to speak directly of the links between various regional diets, agricultural practices, and ill health, using his own experimental data. He argued that crop, animal, and human nutrition were part of the same process and should be studied together. One commission member, the raja of Parlakimedi, was so impressed that he immediately donated a lakh of rupees. Lord Linlithgow's interest as viceroy effectively ended McCarrison's funding problems. His modest laboratory grew to become the Nutrition Research Laboratories. He was the director, with the rank of major-general, until his retirement in 1935. McCarrison was made honorary physician to the king (1928–35) and was knighted in 1933.

After retirement from the IMS in 1935 McCarrison returned to England, to live in Oxford. In 1936 he gave the Royal Society of Arts Cantor lectures, published as *Nutrition and National Health* (1944). In 1938 he and Sir Albert Howard, whose agricultural research work was also carried out in India, lectured together at a meeting in Crewe that led eventually to the setting up of the Soil Association. Between 1939 and 1945 he chaired the local medical war committee and was regional adviser in medicine to the Emergency Medical Service from 1944. After the war he served as director of postgraduate medical education in Oxford until 1955. A Festschrift containing his most important papers was produced for his seventy-fifth birthday, and was later published as *The Work of Sir Robert McCarrison* (1953).

McCarrison died in Oxford, aged eighty-two, on 18 May 1960. He was survived by his wife. The McCarrison Society was set up shortly after his death to promote the study of the relationship between nutrition and health.

A. D. Gardiner, McCarrison's obituarist in the *British Medical Journal*, said of him: 'he knew more about nutrition and less about income tax than anyone I know of' (*BMJ*, 1818). He was a man of great charm, tenacity, and scientific ability, with skills not only in experimentation, but also in communicating his findings, teaching, and enthusing others. Of his many achievements perhaps the greatest was to build from nothing an institution which trained generations of Indian nutritionists and which, in its new home in Hyderabad, has continued to thrive. His distinctive style of experimentation related patterns of disease to whole diets eaten by real populations, demonstrating the broad role of 'faulty' nutrition in causing disease. McCarrison developed an understanding of diet and disease that was complex in detail, but which he distilled into elegant and practical concepts and guidance, accessible to clinicians, scientists, and lay people. For those concerned, as he himself was, to promote nutrition as central to health and disease, McCarrison was perceived as an early bearer of an important message. As for his subsequent influence, or lack of it, he once commented, 'It is my business to do the work, it is the business of others to see it is continued' (BL OIOC, royal commission, 100).

H. M. SINCLAIR, *rev.* ANDREW A. G. MORRICE

Sources *The work of Sir Robert McCarrison*, ed. H. M. Sinclair (1953) [Festschrift containing most of McCarrison's important papers, extracts from his lectures, and a complete bibliography] · A. D. Gardiner, 'Sir Robert McCarrison', *BMJ* (11 June 1960), 1818–19 · *BMJ* (28 May 1960), 1663–4 · *BMJ* (4 June 1960), 1743–4 · R. McCarrison and H. M. Sinclair, *Nutrition and Health* (1953) [The Cantor lectures, with a postscript by Sinclair] · *Royal commission on agriculture in India: evidence*, 1 (1927) · R. McCarrison, 'Adventures in research', *Transactions of the Medical Society of London*, 60 (1936) · private information (1996) · L. Picton, *Thoughts on feeding* (1943) · M. Harrison, *Public health in British India: Anglo-Indian preventive medicine, 1859–1914* (1994) · *CGPLA Eng. & Wales* (1960)
Archives Wellcome L.
Likenesses Lady Kennet, bust, priv. coll. · photograph, repro. in Sinclair, ed., *Work of Sir Robert McCarrison*, frontispiece
Wealth at death £5582 12s. 7d.: probate, 19 July 1960, *CGPLA Eng. & Wales*

MacCartan, William. *See* Mac Cairteáin, Uilliam (1667/8–1724).

Mac Cárthaigh Riabhach, Finian. *See* MacCarthy Reagh, Florence (1562–c.1640).

MacCarthy. For this title name *see* MacCarthy Reagh, Justin, Count MacCarthy in the French nobility (1744–1811).

M'Carthy [*formerly* Guéroult], **Sir Charles** (1764–1824), colonial governor and army officer, came from the Irish sept of the name. He was the second son of Jean Gabriel Guéroult and Charlotte Michelle, granddaughter of Michael MacCarthy, who went to France with James II. An uncle, Charles Thaddeus François MacCarthy, knight of St Louis, and an officer of the guards of Louis XV, persuaded M'Carthy to adopt his mother's maiden name. M'Carthy's elder brother (1765–1793), a captain in the Irish brigade in the French service, died unmarried; a sister married Charles François, Comte Fontaine de Morvé, and died childless.

After the revolution the Irish brigade, formerly in the service of France, was reorganized in British pay and M'Carthy was appointed on 1 October 1794 ensign in the regiment of James Henry, Count Conway—afterwards called the 5th regiment of the Irish brigade—with which he served in the West Indies. He was made a lieutenant on 31 December 1795 and captain on 1 October 1796. In 1800 he was appointed captain 52nd foot and, on 14 April 1804, major in the New Brunswick fencibles (afterwards the Old 104th foot), a fine body of backwoodsmen which he commanded for several years. On 30 May 1811 he was promoted to lieutenant-colonel in the Royal African Corps, and the year after was made governor of Senegal and Gorée. When these settlements were returned to France under the treaty of 1814 M'Carthy was transferred to Sierra Leone as governor, and when Cape Coast Castle was taken out of the hands of the Royal African Company, he was sent to govern there as well. On 22 November 1820 he was knighted (KCMG), and on 19 July 1821 attained the rank of colonel.

In December 1823, M'Carthy received news that the Asante, incensed at the protection given to the Fante, were moving down in force against Cape Coast. After arranging the defence of the settlement by African auxiliaries, on 10 January 1824 M'Carthy set out with a small advance force, consisting of a company of the Royal Africans, and some colonial militia and volunteers. Exhausted with marching in the heavy rains, and having expended its ammunition, on 21 January 1824 the little band was routed by an overwhelming force of Asante. M'Carthy was mortally wounded, and his head taken by the Asante as a war trophy. M'Carthy had tried to advance Christianity and Western customs, particularly in the villages set up for recaptives.

H. M. CHICHESTER, rev. LYNN MILNE

Sources LondG · Army List · H. I. Rickett, Narrative of the Ashantee War (1831) · D. D. Daly, 'Brigadier-General Sir Charles MacCarthy Kt. 1764–1824', Journal of the Society for Army Historical Research, 10 (1930), 143–9 · J. E. Flint, ed., The Cambridge history of Africa from c.1790 to c.1870 (1976), vol. 5 of The Cambridge history of Africa, ed. J. D. Fage and R. Oliver (1975–86)
Archives NAM, papers | LPL, Carewe MSS · NAM, letters to James Chisholm

MacCarthy, Cormac Oge Laidhir, lord of Muskerry (d. **1536**), chieftain, was the son of Cormac MacCarthy, lord of Muskerry (d. 1495), and Mary, daughter of Edmund Fitzmaurice, baron of Lixnaw. In 1498 Cormac Oge killed his uncle Eóghan MacCarthy, lord of Muskerry, who three years earlier had killed his father and taken over the lordship. In this he was aided by his brother-in-law Thomas fitz Thomas Fitzgerald, subsequently eleventh earl of Desmond, the two proving firm allies and important actors in Munster's political history in the early sixteenth century. In 1501 Cormac Oge became lord of Muskerry. He continued to be involved in events outside his lordship and participated in the expedition led by the lord deputy, Gerald Fitzgerald, eighth earl of Kildare, against Teige O'Brien of Thomond in 1510. In 1516 he joined with his brother-in-law Thomas in support of James fitz Maurice Fitzgerald, subsequently tenth earl of Desmond, then in conflict with John fitz Thomas Fitzgerald, subsequently twelfth de facto earl of Desmond. In 1520, however, they sided against James, who had succeeded as tenth earl earlier that year, and inflicted a very heavy defeat on him at the battle of Mourne, co. Cork. Cormac and Thomas again attacked James in December 1527 when they joined Piers Butler, earl of Ormond, in besieging him at Dungarvan.

Thomas fitz Thomas succeeded as eleventh earl of Desmond in 1529, and when he died five years later Cormac supported Thomas's grandson and heir James fitz Maurice *Fitzgerald, twelfth de jure earl, who was married to Cormac's daughter Mary. He provided James with military support and wrote to Henry VIII on his behalf in 1535, but James was opposed by the majority of the Desmond Geraldines and was in England by the following year. Cormac met Lord Lieutenant Thomas Howard, earl of Surrey, at Waterford in 1520 and appeared willing to hold his lands of the crown, but nothing came of the meeting.

Cormac Oge married Katherine, daughter of John, Lord Barry, with whom he apparently had at least five sons: Tadhg, who succeeded as lord of Muskerry (d. 1565), Diarmuid, Eóghan, Ceallachán, and Cormac; there were also at least three daughters: Julia (Shely, Cicely), Ellen (Joan), and Mary. He died in 1536 and was buried at Kilcrea, co. Cork.

ANTHONY M. McCORMACK

Sources PRO, State papers Ireland, Henry VIII, SP 60 · State papers published under … Henry VIII, 11 vols. (1830–52), vols. 2–3 · AFM · H. Webb Gillman, 'Sir Cormac McTeige MacCarthy and the sept lands of Muskerry, co. Cork, with a historical pedigree', Journal of the Cork Historical and Archaeological Society, 1 (1892), 193–200 · T. W. Moody and others, eds., A new history of Ireland, 9: Maps, genealogies, lists (1984), 156 · DNB

McCarthy, D'Alton (1836–1898), lawyer and politician in Canada, was born on 10 October 1836 at Oakley Park, Blackrock, Ireland, the son of D'Alton McCarthy and Charlesina Hope Manners. His father was a lawyer who decided in 1847 to emigrate to Upper Canada (later Ontario). After attending schools in Ireland, McCarthy finished his education at the grammar school in Barrie, Upper Canada. His father resumed legal practice in Barrie in 1855 after a disappointing attempt at farming. McCarthy joined the firm in 1858, and was called to the bar the following year, elected a bencher of the Law Society of Upper Canada in 1871, made a queen's counsel in 1872, and appointed solicitor for Simcoe county in 1873.

McCarthy's early adulthood was devoted as much to family formation and establishment of a country estate as to the practice of the law. His first marriage, in Barrie on 23 October 1867, was to Emma Catherine Lally, who died in 1870 having borne a son and a daughter. On 15 July 1873, McCarthy married his late wife's sister, Agnes Elizabeth Lally, the widow of Richard Barrett Bernard, who was related to the prime minister, Sir John A. Macdonald. They had no children. McCarthy developed country property on which he oversaw the growing of crops, and the raising of cattle, horses, and pigs. He became a prominent member of the rural society in his area, and aspired to the status of country gentleman.

Although McCarthy retained both his farming and legal ties to the Barrie district, his legal practice soon took him to Toronto and his political skills drew him to Ottawa. In 1876 he established a branch of his law firm in Toronto; in 1877 he founded the powerful firm of McCarthy, Hoskin, Plumb, and Creelman; and in 1879 he moved his residence to Toronto. After several unsuccessful attempts to win a seat in the commons between 1872 and 1876, he was elected for Simcoe North in the general election of 1878, beginning a turbulent political career that was to last until his death.

McCarthy's political career was marked successively by his Conservative partisanship, support for Macdonald's policies of national consolidation and development, growing disenchantment with Quebec and the official recognition of the French language, a desire to reform the protective tariff in the interests of the farming community, a break with the Conservative Party in 1893, and an influential role as leader of a third party from 1894 until his agreement to enter the cabinet of the Liberal prime minister Sir Wilfrid Laurier in 1898. His strenuous partisanship on behalf of the Conservatives focused in the early 1880s on fighting court challenges after elections

D'Alton McCarthy (1836–1898), by William James Topley, 1890

and then on championing Macdonald's desire to create a highly centralized federation in which the national government would dominate the provinces. In support of the latter cause, McCarthy was the federal government's leading barrister in a series of cases pitting the assertive province of Ontario against the federal government, cases which often brought McCarthy to argue the federal side unsuccessfully before the judicial committee of the privy council.

McCarthy's close identification with the campaign for centralization and his leadership of the Canadian branch of the Imperial Federation League from 1885 to 1891 earned him the distrust of French-speaking Conservative politicians. For his part, by the mid-1880s McCarthy had come to regard Quebec as the primary obstacle to a variety of projects that he considered essential to Canada's successful development. By 1889 he was criticizing Quebec's demands for respect for its language and Roman Catholic religion as a source of division in the country. Adopting the linguistic notions of E. A. Freeman and Max Muller, in 1890 McCarthy denounced linguistic duality as a barrier to national unity and called for steps to recognize only English on an official level outside Quebec. Although McCarthy, an Anglican, was not anti-Catholic, his views on language earned him the enmity of Quebec opinion leaders and alienated many of his Conservative colleagues who, like Macdonald, regarded support in the Francophone province as essential to the party's success.

When the rupture between McCarthy and the Conservative leadership came in 1893, it was over commercial rather than linguistic policies. Since at least the general election of 1891, McCarthy had worried that Ontario farmers were deserting the Conservatives in large numbers for the opposition Liberal policy of freer trade with the United States. After Macdonald's death in 1891 McCarthy found fewer personal ties held him to the party. When his increasingly vocal advocacy of tariff reform led the party's official newspaper to attack him, he left the Conservatives in 1893.

The remainder of McCarthy's political career was devoted to two causes: promoting tariff reform nationally, and opposing attempts to restore denominational schools, which he regarded as a means of perpetuating French, in Manitoba. His tariff views allowed him to work co-operatively with a new agrarian movement, the Patrons of Industry; and his opposition to denominational schools in Manitoba drew him closer to the provincial Liberal party there. McCarthy was a key adviser to the Manitoba Liberals during their contest with the federal cabinets that sought until the election of 1896 to resolve the differences over Manitoba schools in order to placate Quebec. He helped directly to frustrate attempts to settle the schools question in a manner satisfactory to Catholics, and indirectly to generate support for Liberals and their policy of freer trade.

McCarthy found the policies of Laurier's government generally pleasing after 1896. Its first budget introduced an imperial tariff preference, which appealed both to McCarthy's support for imperial co-operation and his advocacy of tariff reform. He also found Laurier's compromise settlement of the Manitoba schools question acceptable because it did not restore a distinct system of Catholic schools that could be used to perpetuate French language and identity. He had agreed to enter Laurier's cabinet, most likely in the justice portfolio, shortly before a carriage accident on 8 May 1898 led to his death three days later, at his home in Beverley Street, Toronto. He died widely respected, though not universally liked. His erect bearing and piercing glance overshadowed a warm personality.   J. R. MILLER

Sources L. L. Kulisek, 'McCarthy, D'Alton', *DCB*, vol. 12 · L. L. Kulisek, 'D'Alton McCarthy and the true nationalization of Canada', PhD diss., Wayne State University, Detroit, 1973 · J. R. Miller, *Equal rights: the Jesuits' Estates Act controversy* (1979) · J. R. Miller, '"As a politician he is a great enigma": the social and political ideas of D'Alton McCarthy', *Canadian Historical Review*, 58 (1977), 399–422 · J. R. Miller, 'D'Alton McCarthy, equal rights, and the origins of the Manitoba schools question', *Canadian Historical Review*, 54 (1973), 369–92 · P. B. Waite, *Canada, 1874–1896: arduous destiny* (1971) · J. R. Miller, 'D'Alton McCarthy, Jr: a protestant Irishman abroad', *Boswell's children: the art of the biographer*, ed. R. B. Fleming (1992), 191–203 · C. Cole, 'McCarthy, Osler, Hoskin, and Creelman, 1882–1902: establishing a reputation, building a practice', *Beyond the law: lawyers and business in Canada, 1830–1930*, ed. C. Wilton (1990), 149–66 · 'Amicus', 'The late D'Alton McCarthy, Q.C., M.P.: an appreciation', *Canadian Magazine*, 21 (1903), 31

Archives NA Canada · University of Western Ontario, Ontario, D. B. Weldon Library | NA Canada, Gowan MSS · NA Canada, Laurier MSS · NA Canada, Macdonald MSS · NA Canada, Sifton MSS · NA Canada, Thompson MSS

Likenesses W. J. Topley, photograph, 1890, NA Canada [*see illus.*] · photograph, NA Canada, PA-24698

McCarthy, Daniel (1883–1957), sports administrator and politician, was born at 50 Upper Dorset Street, Dublin, on 22 January 1883, the son of John McCarthy, a coach finisher, and his wife, Bridget, *née* Rabbit. A product of the reawakening of Irish culture in the late nineteenth century who pursued his beliefs into the political arena, he was active in the Gaelic Athletic Association (GAA), founded in 1884. As a movement committed to the revitalization of Irish culture, the GAA drew the attention of the radical Irish Republican Brotherhood and later of Sinn Féin. McCarthy quickly became involved in the politics of the nationalist cause. In 1913 he stood, and was elected, as a member of the Dublin corporation for Sinn Féin. In the same year he enthusiastically embraced the Irish Volunteers, led by John Redmond and formed as a counterweight to the Ulster Volunteer Force to protect home rule for Ireland. McCarthy was quick to link the physical force ideals of the volunteer movement to the masculinity and physicality of the GAA.

With the onset of the First World War, McCarthy refused to enlist in the British army, and stayed in Ireland. As a radical nationalist he took an active role in the Easter rising of 1916, and was interned by the British because of his role. In the fighting of 1916 he suffered serious injury that would affect his health for the remainder of his life. On his release from prison he became an activist, working for Sinn Féin in Dublin. By the time of the 1918 election McCarthy had been appointed chief elections organizer for Sinn Féin. In addition to organizing the successful campaign that would give the party the largest number of seats in Ireland, McCarthy was also elected to the first Dáil Éireann as a member for one of the Dublin constituencies. In the 1916–18 period he had formed a close relationship with W. T. Cosgrave. In the wake of the Anglo-Irish treaty of 1921, and the ascent to power of Cosgrave's pro-treaty Cumann na nGaedheal, McCarthy became Cosgrave's parliamentary secretary. From 1921 until 1923 he also served as the chief whip for the Cumann na nGaedheal Party in the Dáil.

In 1923 McCarthy left active politics to give more time to his role within the GAA. He had been elected to the presidency of the GAA following the resignation of James Nowlan in 1921, and he held the post until 1924. His period of office was important to the GAA. Although he was a protreaty politician, he had to steer the GAA through the period of post-treaty fall-out and disagreement, and then attempt to preserve unity during the years of civil war in Ireland. That the GAA emerged into the mid-1920s as a unified organization that had not, unlike so many other bodies within the new Irish Free State, divided along the lines of the treaty, is a testament to McCarthy's skill. At the end of his period as president he returned to his original occupation as a sales representative, and worked with the Irish Hospitals Trust promoting their various sweepstakes. He died, unmarried, at his home, 1 Malahide Road, Clontarf, Dublin, on 2 March 1957, and was buried on 5 March.

MIKE CRONIN

Sources M. de Búrca, *The G. A. A.: a history of the Gaelic Athletic Association* (1980) · W. F. Mandle, *The Gaelic Athletic Association and Irish nationalist politics, 1884–1924* (1987) · *A century of service, 1884–1984*, Gaelic Athletic Association (1984) · *Gaelic Weekly* (9 March 1957) · *Irish Times* (3 March 1957) · b. cert.

MacCarthy, Denis Florence (1817–1882), Young Irelander and poet, was born at 24 Lower Sackville Street, Dublin, on 26 May 1817, the son of John (1786/7–1857) and Sarah MacCarthy (1787/8–1845). A strong Catholic, he wanted to become a priest and went to Maynooth, but after two years of study, he changed to law at Trinity College, Dublin; he was called to the bar in 1846. However, his main interest was literature, and he also developed a keen interest in foreign languages, especially Spanish. His first poem, 'My Wishes', was published in the *Dublin Satirist* on 12 April 1834, and for the next two years he contributed both prose and verse to this magazine.

MacCarthy supported Daniel O'Connell's Loyal National Repeal Association, but his political interests were always subordinate to his literary tastes. Nevertheless, he employed his literary talents to encourage a cultural revival in Ireland, believing that it would lead to a repeal of the Union between Great Britain and Ireland. On 14 October 1843 his first contribution appeared in *The Nation*, to which he afterwards regularly contributed political verse and poetry under the pseudonyms of Desmond, Vig, Trifolium, Antonio, and S.E.Y., or above his initials. Some of his poems were published in the new edition of *The Spirit of the Nation* (1844). In 1845 he was a founder member of the '82 Club, a half-military organization, formed by upper-class members of the Repeal Association and Young Ireland.

In 1846 he edited *The Poets and Dramatists of Ireland* and *The Book of Irish Ballads* for Young Ireland's Library of Ireland, with introductory essays on the history and religion of the Irish, and on ballad poetry. In 1847 he was a member of the original council of the Irish Confederation, but 'was seldom seen at a committee' (Duffy, *Four Years*, 441). The following year he ceased to be a member of the council. Duffy maintains that MacCarthy was part of the Young Ireland movement because of his close friendship with *The Nation* writers, rather than because of passionate political convictions. He describes him as having a good sense of humour, and being charming in society, but reluctant to make public speeches (Duffy, *Young Ireland*, 133ff.). This reluctance to attract public attention might perhaps explain his absence in purely political activities, rather than being due to a lack of strong convictions. He certainly was no radical, and was not involved in the revolutionary activities of the Confederation in 1848. However, he resumed writing for the new *Nation* in 1849, albeit contributing to it less frequently than before.

During the time of his involvement in Young Ireland, he married Elizabeth Donnelly (1820/21–1874). The couple had nine children, six of whom predeceased him. His eldest son, John, published a collection of his father's poems in 1882. His daughter, Sister Mary Stanislaus MacCarthy OSD, was also a poet, publishing predominantly religious poetry.

Most of MacCarthy's original work and his translations from Spanish, German, French, Italian, Greek, and Latin poetry were published in periodicals. In 1850 the first collection of his poetry, *Ballads, Poems, and Lyrics Original and Translated*, appeared. In 1853 MacCarthy published *Dramas of Calderon*, his first translations of the works of the Spanish dramatist Calderon. All in all, MacCarthy translated fifteen of Calderon's plays. On the other hand, some of MacCarthy's early poems were translated into French by Le Chevalier de Chatelain and published in 1863–4.

In 1853–4, MacCarthy was appointed to a professorship in English literature at the Catholic University, Dublin, but being of a restless nature, he resigned after a few months, because he did not like the sedentary nature of the post. In 1857 he published *'The Bell-Founder' and other Poems* and *'Underglimpses' and other Poems*. In 1864 the ill health of some members of his family forced MacCarthy to leave Ireland for long periods of time. He travelled extensively on the continent, before finally settling in London in 1871, where he was granted a civil-list pension of £100 a year. In 1872 he published *Shelley's Early Life*, and from 1873 onwards he regularly wrote religious poetry and prose for the *Irish Monthly*. At the request of the committees in charge of the celebrations, MacCarthy wrote the centenary odes in honour of Daniel O'Connell (1875) and Thomas Moore (1879). He was also elected a member of the Real Academia of Spain. In 1881 it presented him with a commemorative medal of Calderon's bicentenary, in recognition of MacCarthy's work in Spanish literature. MacCarthy spent the last few months of his life in Ireland, and died at his home, 4 Herbert Terrace, Blackrock, co. Dublin, on 7 April 1882. He was buried on 11 April in the family vault in Glasnevin cemetery, Dublin. A committee was set up in Dublin to honour his memory.

BRIGITTE ANTON

Sources J. MacCarthy, introduction, in D. F. MacCarthy, *Poems* (1882) · [M. Russell], 'Sister Mary Stanislaus MacCarthy', *Irish Monthly*, 25 (1897), 495–6 · [M. Russell], 'Denis Florence MacCarthy's daughter', *Irish Monthly*, 25 (1897), 560–74, 617–23 · [M. Russell], 'Denis Florence MacCarthy', *Irish Monthly*, 10 (1882), 388–90; 445–8 · [M. Russell], 'The poems of Denis Florence MacCarthy', *Irish Monthly*, 10 (1882), 649 [review] · T. F. O'Sullivan, *The Young Irelanders*, 2nd edn (1945) · A. Leventhal, 'Denis Florence MacCarthy: national scholar–poet', *Thomas Davis and Young Ireland, 1845–1945*, ed. M. J. MacManus (1945), 105–8 · C. G. Duffy, *Young Ireland: a fragment of Irish history, 1840–1845*, rev. edn, 2 vols. (1896) · C. G. Duffy, *Four years of Irish history, 1845–1849: a sequel to 'Young Ireland'* (1883) · *The Nation* (22 March 1845) · *The Nation* (July–Oct 1846) · *The Nation* (Oct 1846–Dec 1847) · *The Nation*, 6 (1848) · *The Nation* (15 April 1882) · *The Nation* (22 April 1882) · *Freeman's Journal* [Dublin] (18 March 1845) · *Freeman's Journal* [Dublin] (9 April 1857) · *Freeman's Journal* [Dublin] (10 April 1882) · *Irish Times* (25 Aug 1874) · *Irish Times* (10–12 April 1882) · C. G. Duffy, *My life in two hemispheres*, 2 (1898); facs. edn (Shannon, 1969) · J. S. Crone, *A concise dictionary of Irish biography* (1928) · DNB · *The Athenaeum* (15 April 1882), 477 · *Thom's directory* (1848) · *Thom's directory* (1883) · R. J. Hayes, ed., *Manuscript sources for the history of Irish civilisation*, 3 (1965) · R. J. Hayes, ed., *Manuscript sources for the history of Irish civilisation: first supplement, 1965–1975*, 1 (1979) · P. J. Hamell, *Maynooth: students and ordinations index, 1795–1895* (1982) · *Dublin University Calendar* (1835–7) · *Dublin University Calendar* (1839) · *Dublin University Calendar* (1842)
Archives NL Ire. · TCD, notebooks · TCD, commonplace book | Mitchell L., Glas., Glasgow City Archives, letters to Sir Stirling Maxwell · NL Ire., letters to Mary 'Eva' Kelly · TCD, letters to Sir William Rowan Hamilton · TCD, Archdeacon O'Hagan MSS
Likenesses bust, City Hall, Dublin · drawing, repro. in O'Sullivan, *Young Irelanders*, 315 · oils, NG Ire. · photograph, repro. in C. G. Duffy, *Young Ireland*, 135
Wealth at death £1922 (in England): Irish probate sealed in England, 13 June 1882, *CGPLA Eng. & Wales*

MacCarthy, Sir (Charles Otto) Desmond (1877–1952), literary reviewer and drama critic, was born at Plymouth, Devon, on 20 May 1877, the only child of Charles Desmond MacCarthy (1832/3–1895), bank agent, and Louise Jeanne Wilhelmine de la Chevallerie (1854–1938). His ancestors were English, Irish, and German. He spent his childhood in Leeds, and went on to attend Eton College (1888–94), where he was educated, he said, by the boys, and then Trinity College, Cambridge, where his education was continued by his friends and himself. Elected to the Apostles, he came to know G. M. Trevelyan and R. C. Trevelyan, Roger Fry, Bertrand Russell, E. M. Forster, and especially G. E. Moore, whose closest friend he became. Through friendship with younger Apostles and other members of Trinity, such as Lytton Strachey, Leonard Woolf, and Clive Bell, he became involved with the Bloomsbury group. MacCarthy read history and graduated aegrotat in 1897, started to study philosophy with Moore for a further degree, and after a term at Leipzig University prepared to be a novelist by reading extensively. He was acquainted with Samuel Butler, George Meredith, Leslie Stephen, and Henry James, all of whom influenced his development. On the death of his father in 1895 (his possessive mother survived until 1938) MacCarthy inherited about £150 a year and remained impecunious for most of his career. He began, therefore, in 1903 to write not fiction but reviews. By 1906 he had become the drama critic for the Liberal *Speaker*, and recognized the importance of the Vedrenne-Barker productions at the Court Theatre, particularly those of George Bernard Shaw's plays. MacCarthy's reviews, collected in his first book, *The Court Theatre* (1907), were, Shaw told him, closer to the mark than those of other critics. MacCarthy applied Moore's ideas in *Principia ethica* to the plays, and his criticism is still among the best that has been written of Shaw.

On 29 August 1906 MacCarthy married Mary Warre-Cornish [see below] and began to edit the *New Quarterly*, which a Cambridge friend financed for him; it lasted for three years and published significant work by Butler, Russell, Moore, and Fry. In 1910 MacCarthy became the secretary for Fry's celebrated first post-impressionist exhibition, and the introduction that he wrote for the catalogue became his most widely quoted work. He reviewed intermittently for various periodicals until 1913, when at Shaw's suggestion he was invited by Beatrice and Sidney Webb to become the drama critic for the *New Statesman*. (A lifelong Liberal, MacCarthy wrote most of his work for socialist and then Conservative papers.) During the First World War he served with the Red Cross and then joined naval intelligence. He became literary editor of the *New Statesman* under Clifford Sharp in 1920, and wrote a weekly column signed with the fitting pseudonym Affable

Hawk. MacCarthy later described how rude Sharp could be about his exasperating elusiveness: Sharp 'would glare and I would despair—but not reform' (MacCarthy, *Experience*, xv). As an editor he helped train many reviewers, including his successors Raymond Mortimer and Cyril Connolly. In 1927 MacCarthy began speaking on books for the BBC and over the next twenty-five years he broadcast hundreds of popular talks. The next year he succeeded Edmund Gosse as the principal reviewer for the *Sunday Times*. With a readership that reached 500,000, the paper made him the most influential literary journalist of the time. Also in 1928 he started *Life and Letters*, a general literary monthly underwritten by another patron. MacCarthy's involvement lasted until 1934, and in the course of his editorship he published work by Butler, Russell, Max Beerbohm, Hilaire Belloc, Thomas Hardy, Aldous Huxley, Virginia Woolf, Clive Bell, and many others.

MacCarthy had a wide literary and social acquaintance, and his charm as a sympathetic conversationalist (rather than a talker, for he was not a monologist) was legendary. But his development continued to be a disappointment to himself and his friends. Leonard Woolf thought the influence of Moore's high standards might have been to blame, and MacCarthy conceded that high standards and indolence had blighted his career. Only by procrastinating, he once explained, could he avoid spending 'a preposterous amount of time titivating' (Cecil and Cecil, 286). After abandoning attempts to write a novel before the war, MacCarthy planned to make a study of John Donne. In the 1920s Byron became his subject, and he gave the unpublished Clark lectures on him in 1929; in the 1930s it was to be a biography of Tolstoy. But the only books MacCarthy produced were collections of journalism. The second, called *Remnants*, was published in 1918. A selection of his biographical sketches appeared as *Portraits*: volume 1 came out in 1931, but no second volume followed. Subsequent collections of reviews appeared as *Criticism* (1932), *Experience* (1935), *Drama* (1940), and *Shaw* (1951). Three posthumous selections reusing some material from earlier books were *Memories*, *Humanities* (both 1953), and *Theatre* (1954). MacCarthy was knighted in 1951 and died in a nursing home in Cambridge of asthma, emphysema, and pneumonia, on 7 June 1952, shortly after receiving an honorary DLitt. He was buried in St Giles's churchyard, Cambridge.

MacCarthy accurately described himself as 'an acute and balanced critic who sometimes writes uncommonly well' (Cecil and Cecil, 292); yet as a weekly reviewer he was forced to serve up unripe thoughts and 'translate at once every feeling into intellectual discourse' (MacCarthy, *Portraits*, viii). He was distressed by 'an involved limpness' in some of his writing (MacCarthy, *Experience*, xi), and his good friend Virginia Woolf, who, like others, was entranced by his charm, complained of the 'damnable tepidity' of his review of *The Waves* (*Diary of Virginia Woolf*, 4.56). Something of MacCarthy's charm as well as tepidity is captured in the character of Bernard in that novel. MacCarthy was a traditional, eclectic, somewhat sceptical,

rather unoriginal, but very widely read critic. His viewpoint was formed before the First World War and he regarded modernist writing with misgiving. (He confessed to being a backward and reluctant admirer of Woolf.) MacCarthy himself best described his critical theory in the preface to *Criticism*, where he argued that 'aesthetic taste is only further discrimination upon preferences determined by other causes'. Part of the critic's job was to discuss ideas current both now and in the author's time, he continued, and therefore the reader's psychology was as much the critic's concern as the book being read. Perhaps MacCarthy's deepest literary conviction was that 'a work of art whatever its theme must somehow, somewhere, suggest the desirability of life' (*Drama*, 152).

Mary Josepha [Molly] **MacCarthy** [*née* Warre-Cornish], Lady MacCarthy (1882–1953), writer, was born in August 1882, the daughter of Francis Warre Warre-*Cornish (1839–1916), vice-provost of Eton, and Blanche Ritchie (1848–1922), novelist, whose eccentric sayings were collected as *Cornishiana*. Her marriage to Desmond MacCarthy on 29 August 1906 produced two sons, Michael and Dermod, and a daughter, Rachel (Lady David Cecil). An original, amusing, if diffident and distracted, personality, Molly MacCarthy has been credited with coining the term 'Bloomsbury' as applied to her friends; in 1920 she founded Bloomsbury's Memoir Club to encourage Desmond's writing. Her novel *A Pier and a Band* (1918) amusingly represents characters resembling herself and her husband. An engaging memoir, *A Nineteenth-Century Childhood*, appeared in 1924. She suffered from her husband's feckless gregariousness. Deafness cruelly increased her isolation from his social life, but she continued to write, publishing biographical studies in *Fighting Fitzgerald and other Papers* (1930) and *Handicaps: Six Studies* (1936), and then a volume of miscellaneous sketches, entitled *Festival, etc.* (1936). A sequel to her childhood memoir was never completed. Molly MacCarthy died of heart failure on 28 December 1953 at Garrick's Villa, Hampton, Twickenham, Middlesex.   S. P. ROSENBAUM

Sources D. MacCarthy, *Portraits* (1931) · D. MacCarthy, *Criticism* (1932) · D. MacCarthy, *Experience* (1935) · D. MacCarthy, *Drama* (1940) · D. MacCarthy, *Shaw* (1951) · D. MacCarthy, *Humanities* (1953) · D. MacCarthy, *Memories* (1953) · D. MacCarthy, *Theatre* (1954) · H. Cecil and M. Cecil, *Clever hearts: Desmond and Molly MacCarthy: a biography* (1990) · L. Woolf, *Sowing: an autobiography of the years 1880–1904* (1960) · L. Woolf, *Beginning again: an autobiography of the years 1911–1918* (1964) · *The diary of Virginia Woolf*, ed. A. O. Bell and A. McNeillie, 5 vols. (1977–84) · S. P. Rosenbaum, ed., *The Bloomsbury group: a collection of memoirs and commentary*, rev. edn (1995) · S. P. Rosenbaum, *Victorian Bloomsbury* (1987) · S. P. Rosenbaum, *Edwardian Bloomsbury* (1994) · S. P. Rosenbaum, *Georgian Bloomsbury* [forthcoming] · D. Cecil, introduction, *Desmond MacCarthy: the man and his writings* (1984) · R. Mortimer and C. Connolly, 'Forewords', in D. MacCarthy, *Memories* (1953) · C. Connolly, 'A portrait', in D. MacCarthy, *Memories* (1953) · Q. Bell, 'The MacCarthys', *Elders and betters* (1995), 129–39 · F. Partridge, *A pacifist's war* (1978) · F. Partridge, *Memories* (1981) · F. Partridge, *Everything to Lose* (1985) · M. Beerbohm and others, 'Tributes to Desmond MacCarthy', *The Listener* (26 June 1952), 1031–2 · *DNB* · d. cert. [Mary Josepha MacCarthy]

Archives Indiana University, Bloomington, Lilly Library, corresp., literary papers, and writings · NRA, corresp. and literary papers • Ransom HRC | Bodl. Oxf., corresp. with Sibyl Colefax • Bodl. Oxf., letters to Jack W. Lambert • CUL, letters to G. E. Moore • Herts. ALS, letters to Lady Desborough • King's AC Cam., letters to Oscar Browning • King's AC Cam., letters to J. M. Keynes • King's Cam., Charleston MSS • LUL, letters to T. S. Moore • McMaster University, Hamilton, Ontario, letters to Bertrand Russell • Som. ARS, corresp. with Mary Herbert • U. Sussex, letters to Virginia Woolf | SOUND BBC WAC • BL NSA, 'Desmond MacCarthy', 16 June 1952, 29E BBC18145/07 • BL NSA, oral history interview • BL NSA, performance recordings

Likenesses D. Grant, pencil drawing, 1938, NPG • R. Guthrie, pencil drawing, 1938, NPG • H. Lamb, oils, 1940, NMG Wales • Q. Bell, clay bust, 1940–1949?, Charleston, Sussex • D. Grant, two oils, 1942–4, NPG • V. Bell, oil sketch, 1943, repro. in Rosenbaum, ed., *The Bloomsbury Group*, cover • D. Glass, photograph, repro. in MacCarthy, *Humanities*, jacket • photograph (with Mary MacCarthy in early marriage), repro. in Cecil and Cecil, *Clever hearts*, 96

Wealth at death £9958 0s. 5d.: probate, 30 July 1952, CGPLA Eng. & Wales

MacCarthy, Donough, first earl of Clancarty (1594–1665), politician and army officer, was the second son of the staunchly Catholic Charles MacCarthy, first Viscount Muskerry (d. 1640), and Margaret, daughter of Donough *O'Brien, fourth earl of Thomond. With the death of his elder brother, Cormac, Donough became heir to vast estates in Munster. Blarney Castle, just north of Cork city and 'a place of great strength' was the family's principal residence. Thanks to his father's prudent management (and unlike so many of his Irish neighbours) the family finances were healthy and the estates unencumbered. Donough's mother died in or before 1599 when his father married as his second wife Ellen (d. in or after 1610), widow of Donell MacCarthy Reagh, and daughter of David Roche, seventh Viscount Fermoy. Created a baronet about 1638, Donough MacCarthy had married by 1641 Eleanor (or Ellen; 1612–1682), the eldest daughter of Thomas Butler, Viscount Thurles, and sister of James, later duke of Ormond. MacCarthy thus enjoyed a formidable range of kinship links—they included the Butlers of Ormond and Cahir and the houses of Thomond, Fermoy, Buttevant, Courcy of Kinsale, and Kerry—and, according to one contemporary, 'These advantages of birth and fortune strengthened him with a numerous kindred, and a multitude of dependants' (*Irish Confederation*, ed. Gilbert, 1.68).

In the parliaments of 1634 and 1640 MacCarthy sat as MP for co. Cork and served as a member of the committee which presented grievances to Charles I in 1640. In the same year he succeeded his father as second Viscount Muskerry. News of the outbreak of the Irish rising of October 1641 reached him after a dinner party attended by the earl of Cork, lords Broghill and Barrymore, 'and some other men of quality of the Irish nation, with whom they lived in an easy and familiar way' (Budgell, 38). According to a later account 'My lord Muskerry, who was a facetious man, and an excellent companion, employ'd all the wit he was master of to turn the whole story into ridicule' (Budgell, 39). The insurrection proved to be no laughing matter. It quickly spread from Ulster throughout the country and during the early months of the war Muskerry attempted to protect local protestant refugees against the onslaughts of his Catholic tenants and to provide safe convoys for them. However in March 1642 he threw in his lot with the insurgents on the grounds that the rebellion was the only means of preserving Catholicism, the king's prerogative, and the 'antient privileges of the poore kingdome of Ireland established and allowed by the Common Law of England' (BL, Add. MS 25277, fol. 58).

Muskerry, working closely with Colonel Garret Barry, a veteran from Spanish service in Flanders, now led the Catholic war effort in Munster. He raised troops and from his base at Rochfordstown near Cork led forays against the protestant forces mobilized by the earl of Cork and his kinsmen. The local commander, Murrough O'Brien, Lord Inchiquin, retaliated and early in April 1642 captured Rochfordstown, taking 'very good booty and provision, and amongst the rest, choice armor of the Lord of Muskeries' (*A Letter of the Earle of Corke, to the State at Dublin*, 1642, 3). On 16 May, Muskerry and Lord Roche captured and then pillaged Castle Lyons (though Barrymore was allowed to escape unharmed). He went on to lay siege to Limerick Castle but on 25 August suffered a major defeat at the hands of Inchiquin at Liscarrol. At a national level he sat as a member of the third, fourth, fifth, and eighth supreme councils and served as a commissioner of trust (1649) and president of the confederate high court of admiralty. In 1644 he headed the delegation sent to Oxford to treat with the king and, as a member of the peace faction within the confederation, negotiated with the royalists throughout the 1640s. While Muskerry was in Dublin with Ormond, his wife and son, Charles, welcomed the papal nuncio Rinuccini to their castle at Macroom shortly after his arrival in Ireland in October 1645. Lady Muskerry's civility delighted the nuncio, and his secretary described her as 'a lady of noble bearing, accomplished and exceeding tactful, well and wisely able to take her place and sustain her authority as lady of the house' (Massari, 1916, 220).

Ultimately Muskerry's support for Ormond and the conclusion of a peace with the king led him to cross swords with Rinuccini and his faction. But after a short period of imprisonment (late 1646) he briefly took command of the Munster army, relinquishing it to his ally Viscount Taaffe in July 1647. Early in 1648 the eighth confederate general assembly appointed him as one of their agents to secure approval from the royalist court in exile for their decision to invite the prince of Wales either to come in person to Ireland or to nominate a Catholic lord deputy. Muskerry arrived in Paris in February and immediately joined forces with Ormond and Henrietta Maria in planning a royalist revival in Ireland as part of a wider strategy to secure the three kingdoms for the Stuarts. On his return to Ireland he supported the royalist cause with enthusiasm and, as the Cromwellian conquest gathered momentum, he led the anti-parliamentarian forces in Munster. Despite suffering a number of defeats, especially one against Lord Broghill (July 1651), he fought on before finally surrendering at Ross Castle (27 June 1652) and fleeing to the continent.

Despite being exempted from pardon of life and estate by the Act for the Settling of Ireland (August 1652), Muskerry returned to Ireland late in 1653. In December the

Cromwellian authorities tried him for being an accessory to murder during the early months of the rising. After being acquitted he thanked the court: 'It is one of the greatest providences that ever I met with … I can live without my estate, but not without my credit' (Hickson, 2.204). He was retried in February 1654 for his part in royalist conspiracies, but thanks to the influence that Lady Ormond enjoyed with the Cromwellian authorities was again acquitted. He returned to the continent where he served as a confidant of Ormond and Charles II who in 1658 elevated him to the earldom of Clancarty.

By Charles II's 'gracious declaration' (30 November 1660) Clancarty recovered his extensive Munster patrimony and throughout the 1660s Ormond protected the estates from litigious tenants and avaricious adventurers. His restoration in large part stemmed from the close personal relationship that he enjoyed with Ormond, his loyalty to the Stuarts, and to the fact that Charles II needed to secure the continued support of reliable powerbrokers in remote areas. In June 1661 he took his seat in the Irish House of Lords, where he also held Inchiquin's proxy, and sat on various *ad hoc* committees, including the committee of privileges and grievances; he attended regularly until April 1663 when he moved to London. He died at Ormond's residence at Moor Park in August 1665. Ormond later reassured his wife that 'he wanted nothing … for disposing of himself to die as a Christian of the persuasion he was'. The duke had ensured that a priest was present since he believed that 'it is the part of a good Christian to help another die like one in his own way, nor yet believing that the merciful God hath so limited his Salvation as passionate and interested men have done' (Bodl. Oxf., MS Carte 128, fol. 386).

Contemporaries clearly regarded Clancarty as a man of integrity and honour. Richard Bellings later noted 'his excellent parts and judgement', qualities which were 'in the great scarcity and fatall barrenesse of abilityes among the then sett of noblemen' (*Irish Confederation*, ed. Gilbert, 1.68). Despite the turmoil of the civil wars, Clancarty appears to have died a wealthy man. His will, made shortly before his demise, left his Blarney estate, worth £2000 per annum, to his wife together with all of the family plate and household goods. From various bonds and mortgages he held, he bequeathed his sons, Justin *MacCarthy, later Viscount Mountcashel, and Callaghan, annuities of £500 and he provided for his daughters (£3000 each to Helen, who had married William Bourke, seventh earl of Clanricarde, and Margaret, who married Luke, earl of Fingall) and for other family members, servants, and friends. He made no specific provision for pious uses but asked his wife to provide £100 for the clergy and 'my soul'. Since his eldest son, Charles, who had married Margaret, only daughter of Ulick, marquess of Clanricarde in 1660, had perished in March 1665 aboard the *Royal Charles* in a battle against the Dutch, the remainder of his estate passed to his heir and grandson, Charles James MacCarthy.

JANE OHLMEYER

Sources *History of the Irish confederation and the war in Ireland … by Richard Bellings*, ed. J. T. Gilbert, 7 vols. (1882–91) · J. T. Gilbert, ed., *A contemporary history of affairs in Ireland from 1641 to 1652*, 3 vols. (1879–80) · J. A. Murphy, *Justin MacCarthy, Lord Mountcashel, commander of the first Irish brigade in France* (1959) · B. McGrath, 'A biographical dictionary of the membership of the Irish House of Commons, 1640–41', 2 vols., PhD diss., TCD, 1997 · T. FitzPatrick, 'Waterford during the civil war', *Journal of the Waterford and South-East of Ireland Archaeological Society*, 15 (1912), 6–23, 71–96, 138–53 · G. Radcliffe, *The earl of Strafforde's letters and dispatches, with an essay towards his life*, ed. W. Knowler, 2 vols. (1739) · T. Carte, *An history of the life of James, duke of Ormonde*, 3 vols. (1735–6); new edn, pubd as *The life of James, duke of Ormond*, 6 vols. (1851) · E. O'Keeffe, 'The family and marriage strategies of James Butler, first duke of Ormonde, 1658–1688', PhD diss., U. Cam., 2000 · *CSP Ire.*, 1633–47 · E. Budgell, *Memoirs of the lives and characters of the illustrious family of the Boyles: particularly of the late eminently learned Charles, earl of Orrery* (1737) · D. Massari, 'My Irish campaign', *The Catholic Bulletin*, 6 (1916); 7 (1917); 8 (1918); 9 (1919); 10 (1920) · *A collection of the state letters of … Roger Boyle, first earl of Orrery*, ed. T. Morrice (1742); later edn 2 vols. (1743) · Count de Grammont [A. Hamilton], *Memoirs of the life of count de Grammont*, trans. A. Boyer (1714) · M. A. Hickson, *Ireland in the seventeenth century*, 2 vols. (1884) · political and miscellaneous papers, BL, Add. MS 25277, fol. 58 · Bodl. Oxf., MS Carte 128, fol. 386 · will, NA Ire., RC 5/19/part3a/ pp. 269, 271 · *DNB* · J. Lodge, *The peerage of Ireland*, rev. M. Archdall, rev. edn, 7 vols. (1789) · GEC, *Peerage* · J. Fenlon, 'French influence in late seventeenth century portraits', *GPA Irish artists review yearbook* (1989–90), 158–65

Archives BL, political and other papers, Add. MS 25277, fol. 58 | Bodl. Oxf., Carte papers · PRO, state papers, Ireland · Sheff. Arch., Strafford papers · TCD, 1641 depositions

Wealth at death recovered considerable estates after Restoration; seemingly reasonable income: will, NA Ire., RC 5/19/part3a/ pp. 269, 271

Maccarthy, Donough, styled fourth earl of Clancarty

(1668–1734), Jacobite army officer, was born in Blarney, co. Cork, the only son of Callaghan Maccarthy, third earl of Clancarty (d. 1676), and Elizabeth, daughter of George Fitzgerald, sixteenth earl of Kildare. Maccarthy was the grandson of Donough *MacCarthy, second Viscount Muskerry, a general of the Irish forces in Munster supporting Charles I during the revolution. In exile the viscount was created earl of Clancarty, and he returned to Ireland after the restoration of Charles II. During this period the Clancartys, staunch Catholics and loyal to the Stuart kings, were one of the noblest and richest families in Ireland, with estates in Cork and co. Kerry. On his father's death on 21 November 1676 Maccarthy became the fourth earl of Clancarty. The family's wealth and power ensured that the young earl would be drawn into the Catholic-protestant struggles for control over the Irish kingdom. His mother, Elizabeth, a protestant, was appointed Clancarty's guardian by her late husband. To fend off Catholic influences and ensure a proper protestant education for her son, she placed him under the care of John Fell, bishop of Oxford and dean of Christ Church.

It was while Donough was at Oxford that he drew the attention of Charles II and became the subject of one of the greatest scandals of the day. Charles, concerned that there were too many 'old Cromwellians' in the Irish army, intended to root out the protestant veterans of the interregnum and replace them with loyal Catholic royalists. In 1684 Charles began to reorganize the army under Richard Talbot, the first earl of Tyrconnell, and purge Irish officers, replacing them with loyal Catholics. The first commission he granted was to Colonel Justin *MacCarthy, Clancarty's uncle. Justin, a veteran of the armies of Louis XIV of France, had strong ties to the Stuart cause and Catholic factions at court. Married to Arabella, daughter of Thomas Wentworth, earl of Strafford, MacCarthy was also an adviser to James, duke of York. It was MacCarthy who proposed to enlist the young earl of Clancarty in the Catholic cause. The king sent a letter, countersigned by the earl of Sunderland, to John Fell commanding that the young earl should 'keep his Christmas at London with his uncle'. Fell suspected subterfuge but, unable to contact the earl's mother and unwilling to dismiss the king's wishes, sent the boy to Sunderland's London house. On his arrival in London, Clancarty (aged fifteen or sixteen years old) was quickly married to Sunderland's second daughter, Lady Elizabeth Spencer (d. 1704), who by various accounts was between eleven and thirteen years old, at Westminster Abbey on 31 December 1684. The marriage caused a great scandal. Intended to bind one of Ireland's most powerful families more closely to the Stuart cause, it was seen by many as a crude attempt by the king to advance his Irish policies. The Sunderlands enlisted the aid of the diarist John Evelyn to break the news to the earl's distraught mother. Gilbert Burnet, bishop of Salisbury, wrote an account of the incident in his *History of my Own Time*. Attempting to cover up Sunderland's role in Charles's 'sinister' policies, Burnet later deleted references to his friend in a subsequent draft that was eventually published.

Clancarty was immediately recalled to Ireland, before consummating his marriage and without his new bride. In defiance of his mother, he converted to Catholicism within a year. On the accession of James II, Clancarty received command of a troop of horse, giving the Stuarts another loyal Catholic officer in the Irish army. The appointment prompted a letter of complaint from the earl of Clarendon that the commission deprived a Captain Brook 'of his troop of horse in Lord Ardglasse's regiment though he gave sixteen hundred pounds for it not two years ago'. Serving with his uncle Justin MacCarthy under the command of Tyrconnell, Clancarty's service amounted to little more than licensed banditry. He had a reputation as a brutal, even sadistic, commander. Clancarty allegedly had a man hung up by his hair and ordered that another, a butcher in Mallow, be tossed in a blanket. According to J. P. Kenyon, Clancarty also took a second wife and fathered a son. In May 1689, though under age, he was granted a royal dispensation that allowed him to sit in the Irish House of Lords.

At the outbreak of the revolution of 1688 Clancarty, a loyal supporter of James II, greeted the deposed king when James invaded Ireland in 1689. Clancarty was appointed lord of the bedchamber and later colonel of the 4th regiment of foot, later called Clancarty's regiment. Fighting beside his uncle, who was now a general titled by James II as Viscount Mountcashel, Clancarty participated throughout the ill-fated Irish campaign. Mountcashel was wounded and captured during the campaign. He later broke parole and entered the army of Louis XIV. Clancarty

surrendered to Marlborough at the siege of Cork in October 1690 and was sent to the Tower of London. The earl's estate (yielding a rent of about £10,000 a year) was seized, though the dowager countess and her daughters were provided a pension. He was attainted and his title forfeited on 11 May 1691. The bulk of the forfeited estates went to William Bentinck, Lord Woodstock.

On 27 October 1694 Clancarty escaped from the tower by leaving a 'periwig block' dressed up in his bed to fool the watch. The guards allegedly found a note pinned to the blanket with the inscription 'this block must answer for me'. He joined James II's court at St Germain as commander of the second troop of Horse Guards, disbanded in 1697 after the peace of Ryswick. By this time, Clancarty was thoroughly estranged from the earl of Sunderland, who considered him little more than a dissolute brigand. Sunderland refused to support a petition for the return of Clancarty's confiscated estates and blocked the earl's efforts to reunite with his wife, Sunderland's daughter. Nevertheless Clancarty, who had not seen Lady Clancarty in over a decade, returned to England in secret. On an evening in late December he sent for her. Elizabeth, now in her twenties, a slim woman with dark good looks, expressive eyes, and a high forehead, was still loyal to Clancarty and agreed to meet him at his mother's house. Clancarty tried to convince her to consummate their marriage, but she refused. The earl persisted, following her that night to Norfolk House at St James Square, London, where she went to bed with him. Lady Clancarty's maid revealed the earl's presence to a porter, who ran to Sunderland's house. Sunderland went to Whitehall and, finding the secretary of state, Sir James Vernon, working late, had a warrant sworn out for Clancarty's arrest. Accompanied by armed soldiers, Sunderland dragged Clancarty from Elizabeth's bed and deposited him in London's Newgate prison. Elizabeth took refuge with the family of Jael Boscawen, where she mounted a campaign to secure her husband's release. For the second time controversy over the Clancarty marriage became the talk of London. In defiance of her parents, Elizabeth enlisted the aid of a long list of members of court to plead her husband's case before William III. William remarked that 'he never was so teased about anything so much as petitions and requests in behalf of that little spark Lord Clancarty' (Kenyon, 303). Clancarty was pardoned on condition of leaving the kingdom. In addition, he received a small pension of £300 a year and Lady Clancarty received a grant of £2000 a year 'out of the first fruits of office'.

The earl and countess of Clancarty went to Hamburg and then took up residence on an island in the Elbe River, near Altona. They had a daughter, Charlotte, and two sons, Robert *Maccarthy and Justin, before Lady Clancarty's death in 1704. Clancarty himself died on 19 September 1734 at Praals-Hoff. His daughter, Charlotte, married John West, the seventh Lord Delawarr. Justin served as an officer in the Neapolitan army. The eldest son, Robert, became Viscount Muskerry and titular earl of Clancarty. He entered the British navy and served as governor of Newfoundland from 1733 to 1735. After returning to Britain and failing in efforts to recover the family estate he went back to sea, rising to command the *Adventure*. He left the navy in 1741 to support Charles Edward Stuart and the Jacobite cause. He was granted a pension of £1000 a year by Louis XV of France and retired to Boulogne. The last Clancarty to champion the Stuart claim to the throne, he died on 19 September 1769.

The scandals of the Clancarty marriage were retold in Lord Macaulay's *History of England*. The story was later adopted by Tom Taylor as an 'original drama' and first produced at the Royal Olympic Theatre in London on 9 March 1874. Clancarty's life and marriage remain of enduring interest not only as what Macaulay called a 'romantic history', but as a tale reflective of the web of political, religious, and military conflicts that strained the Irish aristocracy during the Stuart age.   JAMES JAY CARAFANO

Sources DNB · *Burnet's History of my own time*, ed. O. Airy, new edn, 2 (1900) · *A supplement to Burnet's History of my own time*, ed. H. C. Foxcroft (1902) · *The life and letters of Sir George Savile … first marquis of Halifax*, ed. H. C. Foxcroft, 2 (1898) · T. B. Macaulay, *The history of England from the accession of James II*, 5 vols. (1858–61) · E. M. Thompson, ed., *Correspondence of the family of Hatton*, 2 vols., CS, new ser., 22–3 (1878) · *The correspondence of Henry Hyde, earl of Clarendon, and of his brother Laurence Hyde, earl of Rochester*, ed. S. W. Singer, 2 vols. (1828) · *Diary of the times of Charles the Second by the Honourable Henry Sidney (afterwards earl of Romney)*, ed. R. W. Blencowe, 2 vols. (1843) · J. Childs, *The army of Charles II* (1976) · J. G. Simms, *The Williamite confiscation in Ireland, 1690–1703* (1956); repr. (1976) · J. P. Kenyon, *Robert Spencer, earl of Sunderland, 1641–1702* (1958) · Evelyn, *Diary*

McCarthy, James Joseph (1817–1882), architect, was born in Dublin on 6 January 1817, the son of Charles McCarthy (*fl. c.*1800–1831), who came of a Kerry family. He was educated from 1831 at the Christian Brothers' O'Connell School in Dublin. He was trained in the Royal Dublin Society Schools (1834–7) and the office of William Farrell. He seems to have spent the years 1843–6 in England, absorbing the latest developments in church architecture then being vigorously pursued by Augustus Welby Pugin and the Cambridge Camden Society. By 1846 he was back in Dublin, and a church to his design, which he claimed as the first uncompromisingly true church of the old type erected in the archdiocese of Dublin, was begun at Glendalough, co. Wicklow. A parish church at Kilskyre, co. Meath (begun 1847), and a chapel for All Hallows Missionary College, Dublin (1848), soon followed.

James McCarthy was a talented architect. He took to heart Puginian principles of truth to materials, honesty of construction, and fitness of purpose, and he followed Pugin in believing that medieval styles were the only ones possible for a Christian country, particularly in Ireland, where they would be a revival of the venerable architecture of our Catholic forefathers. He could build a simple country church, giving a strong sense of solidity and permanence, but he was also good at grand buildings in Decorated Gothic that fitted the increasingly triumphalist mood of the Catholic church.

McCarthy's success is attributable not just to his talent as an architect, but to his remarkable gift for publicizing that talent. By the late 1840s notices of his work were appearing in the Irish Catholic press, and, from the 1850s, in *The Builder* and the *Building News*. He wrote on architecture in *Duffy's Irish Catholic Magazine*. His biggest coup, however, was his involvement with the Irish Ecclesiological Society, founded in 1849, which gave him access to a network of senior clergy. The only publication of the society, *Suggestions on the Arrangement and Characteristics of Parish Churches* (1851), was written by McCarthy. He sent a copy to Pugin, who told him that he was a man raised up to do great things in Ireland, and offered him the supervision of his Irish work. This came to nothing as Pugin died in 1852, though McCarthy succeeded Pugin as architect at Killarney and Enniscorthy cathedrals, and at Maynooth College, where he designed the infirmary (1862) and chapel (1875).

It was McCarthy's good fortune to be a Catholic architect at a time when increased prosperity after the famine, and tightening-up of church organization following the Synod of Thurles in 1850, gave rise to a boom in church building. His practice was almost exclusively religious. He attracted the attention of Archbishop Paul Cullen, and got several commissions that were virtually in Cullen's gift—the completion of Armagh Cathedral in 1851, and the design of the new Catholic university buildings in Dublin in 1862. By the time of his death McCarthy had eighty or so major commissions to his credit, including two more cathedrals, Monaghan (1861) and Thurles (1865). He had become a member of the architectural establishment, and penetrated institutions not readily accessible to Catholics of humble origin: the Royal Irish Academy (1853) and the Royal Hibernian Academy (1861).

Although J. J. McCarthy's public life is fairly well documented, little is known about his private life. From 1851 he lived at various addresses in Rathmines. He and his wife, Agnes (1819–1885), had four children: twins Charles and Emily (*b.* 9 Dec 1858), Frances, and Agnes, who became a nun. Their son, Charles J. McCarthy (1858–1947), was city architect of Dublin from 1893 to 1920. J. J. McCarthy died, after a long illness, at his house, Charleston House, Leinster Road, Rathmines, on 6 February 1882 and was buried in Glasnevin cemetery, Dublin. Sometimes known as 'the Irish Pugin', McCarthy's importance lies in the large number of churches he designed, and in the fact that he established ecclesiologically correct Gothic as the style for Catholic church building in Ireland.

JEANNE SHEEHY

Sources J. Sheehy, *J. J. McCarthy and the Gothic revival in Ireland* (1977) · R. O'Donnell, 'Roman Catholic church architecture in Great Britain and Ireland, 1829–1878', PhD diss., U. Cam., 1983 · D. S. Richardson, *Gothic revival architecture in Ireland* (1983) · J. Sheehy, 'Irish church building', *The Victorian church: architecture and society*, ed. C. Brooks and A. Saint (1995), 133–50 · 'A famous architect of the Gothic revival in Ireland', *Irish Builder*, Jubilee issue (1909), 68 · *Irish Builder* (1 March 1882), 309 · *The Builder*, 42 (1882), 309 · gravestone, Glasnevin cemetery, Dublin · register, O'Connell School, Dublin

Likenesses Hardman & Co., double portrait, window, *c.*1860 (with his wife, Agnes), parish church, Celbridge, co. Kildare, Ireland

Wealth at death £7069 11*s.* 7*d.*: probate, 28 April 1882, *CGPLA Ire.*

MacCarthy, John George (1829–1892), land commissioner and author, born at Cork in June 1829, was the son of John

MacCarthy, merchant, of Cork, and his wife, Jane, daughter of George O'Driscoll, distiller, of Cork. He was educated at St Vincent's, a local private school. In 1851 MacCarthy made a continental tour and wrote his first book entitled *Letters on the Land Tenures of Europe*. He was admitted a solicitor in 1853, and continued to practise in Cork until 1881. In 1859 he married Maria Josephine, daughter of John Hanrahan of Mount Prospect, Cork, and they had a family of at least three sons.

MacCarthy was an early supporter of Isaac Butt's home rule efforts and had written, in 1871, *A Plea for Home Government of Ireland*. From 1874 to 1880 he represented Mallow in parliament as a home-ruler. While in parliament he devoted his attention to the Irish land question, and his mastery of the subject led to his appointment as an assistant commissioner under the Land Act of 1881. On the passing of the Land Purchase Act in 1885, MacCarthy was appointed one of the two commissioners selected to carry out that measure. He was a firm believer in the efficacy of peasant proprietorship, and administered the different Land Purchase Acts with justice and fairness.

MacCarthy was connected with many philanthropic institutions, notably the Cork Young Men's Society, of which he was for a long period president, and in recognition of services to the Roman Catholic church he was made a knight of the order of St Gregory by Pope Leo XIII. In addition to several legal pamphlets he was the author of historical works and a further book on the Irish land question. MacCarthy died at the Eastern Hotel, Drummond Street, London, on 7 September 1892, and was buried in Glasnevin cemetery, Dublin, on the 10th.

[ANON.], *rev.* DAVID HUDDLESTON

Sources *Irish Law Times and Solicitors' Journal* (10 March 1888), 116 · *WWBMP* · *Irish Law Times and Solicitors' Journal* (8 Oct 1881), 520–21 · *Irish Monthly*, 20 (1892), 548–9 · D. Thornley, *Isaac Butt and home rule* (1966) · *Freeman's Journal* [Dublin] (8 Sept 1892), 4 · *Thom's directory* (1892), 374 · *Irish Law Times and Solicitors' Journal* (10 Sept 1892), 484 · *Irish Law Times and Solicitors' Journal* (17 Sept 1892), 506 · *Irish Law Times and Solicitors' Journal* (13 Oct 1892), 542–3
Wealth at death £4907 5*s.* 1*d.*: probate, 17 Oct 1892, *CGPLA Ire.*

MacCarthy, Justin, first Viscount Mountcashel (*c.*1643–1694), army officer, was the third and youngest son of Donough *MacCarthy, first earl of Clancarty (1594–1665), and Eleanor Butler (1612–1682), sister of James Butler, the first duke of Ormond. He was brought up in exile in France, where his eldest brother commanded a regiment. About 1663 he married Lady Arabella (*b. c.*1628), a daughter of Thomas *Wentworth, first earl of Strafford, a lady some fifteen years his senior. They had no children. MacCarthy's military career began in French service, probably in the Irish regiment raised in 1671 by his cousin Sir George Hamilton. In 1676 MacCarthy was appointed lieutenant-colonel of the duke of Monmouth's regiment, then in French pay, and served against the Dutch. He returned to England in 1678, where it was Charles II's intention to employ him in Ireland. He was given the colonelcy of a regiment of foot in succession to Sir Thomas Dongan, but the accidental discovery of MacCarthy in the houses of parliament in the wake of the uncovering of the Popish Plot caused an uproar when it was revealed that he, an Irish Catholic, held the king's commission. The secretary of state Sir Joseph Williamson was sent to the Tower for countersigning this and other commissions, and MacCarthy fled to Ireland and applied to join the Danish army.

Both MacCarthy's brothers were dead by 1676, and his nephew Donough *Maccarthy (1668–1734) succeeded as the fourth earl of Clancarty. In 1684, when Clancarty was sixteen, his protestant mother entrusted his education to Dr John Fell (of the celebrated epigram), bishop of Oxford. While in London, 'to pervert his nephew, as well as make his own court, [McCarthy] got the king to write to the bishop to let the young lord come up and see the diversions of the town at Christmas' (Burnet, 2.448), where he was instrumental in arranging his marriage to the fourteen-year-old daughter of the secretary of state Robert Spencer, second earl of Sunderland, and his conversion to Roman Catholicism. In January 1685 MacCarthy was again given the colonelcy of an Irish regiment despite objections that he was a Catholic. Following the accession of James II, he was in 1686 made a privy counsellor and promoted to major-general, the second most senior post in the Irish army. Although he was at first recommended for the post by Clarendon, the lord lieutenant, the two men fell out over the deductions that were made from subsistence pay which had become widespread in the Irish army and which Clarendon saw as an abuse. Clarendon was abruptly recalled in early 1687 and MacCarthy kept his post throughout Tyrconnell's purge of protestants in the army.

In February 1689, just before King James arrived in Ireland, the protestants of Bandon declared themselves for William III. MacCarthy marched his regiment into the town while the population were at their Sunday services and installed eight of his men as a garrison to keep the peace. On the next day ('bloody Monday') these Irish troops were either killed or chased out, the town gates were shut, and a flag proclaiming 'no surrender' was raised. MacCarthy returned to the town, forced his way in, rounded up the culprits, and took them back to Cork, where they petitioned King James for mercy. This provided James with an opportunity of showing his goodwill to his protestant subjects: 'You may now see you have a gracious king' (*Full and True Account*, 2).

In May 1689, following James's abortive mission to Londonderry, MacCarthy was made master-general of the ordnance in place of Viscount Mountjoy, who was then in the Bastille. In the Dublin parliament of that month MacCarthy sat as a member for co. Cork. On 22 May he brought up to the House of Lords the bill for repealing the Act of Settlement. On the following day he was created Baron Castleinch and Viscount Mountcashel and he took his seat in the upper house on 24 May.

In the summer of 1689, while the best part of King James's Irish army was besieging Londonderry, MacCarthy was ordered to lead a force of some 4000 men to attack the second stronghold of Williamite resistance, Enniskillen. He was instructed to join forces with Patrick Sarsfield, who was south of the Erne, and James Fitzjames, duke of

Berwick, who was at Trillick, and mount a combined attack on Enniskillen. Once an English fleet had been spotted on Lough Swilly, Berwick was recalled to Londonderry and, without contacting Sarsfield, MacCarthy marched on alone. His orders were first to attack Crom Castle, on Upper Lough Erne, which he did unsuccessfully on 30 July 1689. Alerted to his presence, William Wolseley led a force from Enniskillen 15 miles away. On 31 July MacCarthy detached Anthony Hamilton with his dragoons to attack a body of Enniskillen horsemen. Hamilton was defeated and his men chased away. MacCarthy met Wolseley at Newtownbutler, where the Enniskilliners charged through a bog and scattered his army. Once the battle had been decided, MacCarthy led a few horsemen in a desperate charge on those troops who had captured his artillery. He was shot from his horse and taken prisoner to Enniskillen. He told his captors that 'he came with a design to lose his life, and was sorry that he had missed his aim, being unwilling to outlive the disgrace of that day' (Harris, 225). MacCarthy's wounds were treated and once he had given his parole he was allowed to walk in the town. Following a rumour that the Irish intended to free him, he was confined in a cell. Considering himself no longer bound by parole, he escaped by bribing his guard, Sergeant Acheson, who was later executed. 'The General [Schomberg] was much concerned when he heard of *Mackarty's* Escape, and said he took him to be a Man of Honour, but he would not expect that in an Irish Man any more' (Story, 51).

When MacCarthy arrived back in Dublin at the end of December, he was greeted with bonfires and a procession to Dublin Castle, where he was received by King James. He was chosen to command a force of 5000 Irish recruits, who were to serve in France in exchange for a like number of veteran troops to be sent by Louis XIV to support James's army. MacCarthy was delighted. He had written to the French minister of war that this command was 'the thing I most desire in the world ... If they should send another that would cause me the greatest grief and I would only think of retiring for the rest of my days' (Murphy, 28). The French ambassador, D'Avaux, commented at the time that MacCarthy's short sight would prevent him from ever becoming a great general. John Michelburne more graphically recalled 'my colonel, old Justin Maccartie, looks damn'd squinting upon me with his blind eyes' (Michelburne, 5).

Throughout the spring, with some difficulty, the troops for the 'Mountcashel brigade' were recruited and MacCarthy set sail from Cork on 18 April 1690. On his arrival in Brest he was acquitted by a French tribunal of any wrongdoing in breaking his parole in Enniskillen. He was received by Louis XIV at Versailles, had money lavished upon him, and was promoted to the rank of lieutenant-general. In the late summer of 1690 Mountcashel's brigade marched across France to join Marshal Catinat in Italy. In September they were in action in Savoy, where the Irish troops were said to have 'performed miracles' (*Journal ... Dangeau*, 3.225), although MacCarthy was shot and dangerously wounded in the chest. He wintered at King James's court in exile at St Germain, where he was

involved in the palace plots to discredit Tyrconnell. He campaigned for an audience for the delegation sent to France by Sarsfield and circulated his correspondence from Ireland. By the summer of 1691 he had sufficiently recovered to be sent to Catalonia to serve under Marshal Noailles. In 1692 he joined the army on the Rhine and remained there until the spring of 1694. His old wounds rendered him unfit for command, and he travelled to Barèges in the French Pyrenees to take the curative waters. He died there on 1 July 1694, and was buried there. His wife survived him. By a will dated 8 May 1693 he adopted his distant cousin Florence Callaghan MacCarthy of Carrignavar, co. Cork, as his son and sought to bequeath his title to him. PIERS WAUCHOPE

Sources *A full and true account of the landing and reception of the late King James at Kinsale* (1689) · *Journal of the Proceedings of the Parliament in Ireland* (1689) · W. MacCarmick, *A farther impartial account of the actions of the Inniskilling men* (1691) · G. Story, *An impartial history of the wars of Ireland* (1693) · J. Michelburne, *Ireland preserv'd, or, The siege of London-Derry*, 2 pts (privately printed, London, 1705) · W. Harris, *The history of the life and reign of William-Henry* (1749) · *The correspondence of Henry Hyde, earl of Clarendon, and of his brother Laurence Hyde, earl of Rochester*, ed. S. W. Singer, 2 vols. (1828) · *Journal du marquis de Dangeau*, ed. E. Soulié and others, 19 vols. (Paris, 1854–60) · G. Bennet, *History of Bandon* (1869) · J. C. O'Callaghan, *History of the Irish brigades in the service of France* (1886) · J. C., 'Justin MacCarthy, Lord Mountcashel', *Journal of the Cork Historical and Archaeological Society*, 2nd ser., 13 (1907) · J. A. Murphy, *Justin MacCarthy, Lord Mountcashel* (1959) · S. Mulloy, ed., *Franco-Irish correspondence, December 1688 – February 1692*, 3 vols., IMC (1983–4) · *Bishop Burnet's History* · GEC, *Peerage*

Likenesses P. Lely, oils, *c.*1665, repro. in 'Justin MacCarthy, Lord Mountcashel', p. 164

Wealth at death suffered attainder and confiscation of property following Williamite victory in Ireland: Murphy, *Justin MacCarthy*

McCarthy, Justin (1830–1912), politician and writer, was born at Dunmanway, near Cork, on 22 November 1830. He was the second child and elder son of Michael Francis McCarthy, clerk to the Cork city magistrates, and Ellen FitzGerald. Brought up, as he said, in 'genteel poverty' with a view to the bar, at about seventeen he completed his education and, finding his family dependent on him, secured employment on the *Cork Examiner*. While in Cork he joined the temperance institute and helped to found the Cork Historical Society. He initially visited England in 1852 and served as secretary to the parliamentary commission on fairs and markets before taking up employment with the *Northern Daily Times* (subsequently *Northern Daily News*) in Liverpool in the following year. In 1855 he married Charlotte (d. 1879), daughter of W. G. Allman of Bandon, co. Cork. They had two children: a son, Justin Huntley, a novelist and politician from 1884 to 1892, and a daughter, Charlotte. After moving to London in 1860, he was on the staff of the radical *Morning Star*, first as a member of the reporters' gallery of the House of Commons, then as foreign editor and finally, from 1864, as editor, until his resignation in 1868.

McCarthy authored or co-authored more than fifty novels; the first, *Paul Massie*, was published anonymously in 1866 and was quickly followed by a second, *Waterdale*,

Justin McCarthy (1830–1912), by Walery, pubd 1890

published under his own name in 1867. On leaving the *Morning Star* he travelled in September 1868 to the United States, where he toured widely, visiting thirty-five of the then thirty-seven states. He returned in mid-1871 to London, where he subsequently wrote for several periodicals including the *Fortnightly Review*, *Contemporary Review*, and *Nineteenth Century*. Soon after his return he also became a leader writer on the Liberal *Daily News*, where he was employed for the next twenty-three years.

During the 1860s and 1870s McCarthy established a reputation as a novelist. His *Dear Lady Disdain* (1875) was a popular success and then his non-fictional *A History of our Own Times* (1878) sold immensely well and was reprinted numerous times. He also took an interest in Irish affairs, becoming a member of the Westminster Home Rule Association when it was formed in 1877. The financial rewards from his *History* enabled him to seek parliamentary honours. On 4 April 1879 he was returned unopposed as a home-ruler at the by-election for co. Longford because, as he later recalled in *Story of an Irishman* (1904), 'I was not likely to go into extremes on the one side or the other' (*Story of an Irishman*, 203) in the dispute between Isaac Butt and Charles Stewart Parnell over parliamentary 'obstruction'. McCarthy's pleasant demeanour and refusal to 'go to extremes' characterized his political dealings. He supported Parnell's triumphant bid for the chairmanship of the Home Rule Party on 17 May 1880 and became vice-chairman himself in December 1880, a position which he held until December 1890. Though he became a member

of the Land League in August 1881, McCarthy played only a small role in the land agitation, and never wholly separated himself from his many Liberal friends. He also was an original shareholder in *United Ireland*, which commenced publication on 13 August 1881. In the 1880s he continued with his newspaper work and wrote novels, beginning in the mid-1880s a partnership with Mrs Campbell Praed, whom he met initially in 1884.

Although regularly in attendance in the House of Commons, McCarthy played a minor part in the political disputes of the 1880s and was not identified with any significant cause, although he held fast to his liberal opinions on most questions, becoming quite well known to Gladstone. At the general election of 1885 he contested both North Longford and Londonderry City, narrowly losing the latter. At the general election of 1886, however, he captured Londonderry City and sat for this constituency until being defeated there at the general election of 1892. Polling for North Longford was a week later and he captured this seat, which he retained until retiring from parliament in 1900. Undoubtedly his greatest political trial came as a consequence of the Parnell divorce case. Gladstone, intentionally or otherwise, gave conflicting messages to McCarthy and John Morley. Speaking to the former Gladstone conveyed the impression that, although he disapproved of Parnell, he would continue to fight for home rule, whether or not the Irish Parliamentary Party re-elected Parnell as chairman. In a subsequent letter to Morley, however, Gladstone threatened to resign if Parnell were to be re-elected. It was the publication of this letter that led to the split in the Irish party. On 6 December McCarthy led the withdrawal of the majority of nationalist MPs, who thereafter, under his chairmanship, were generally known as 'anti-Parnellites'. Despite the bitterness of the split, his affable nature did not desert him and he remained on cordial terms with the fallen leader. It was at this time that Parnell referred to him famously, as 'a nice old gentleman for a quiet tea party' (*United Ireland*, 27 Dec 1890), a phrase that stuck. McCarthy retained the largely thankless task of being chairman of the majority section of nationalists until February 1896, when he surrendered the post.

McCarthy's finances were devastated by the liabilities resulting from the failure of the Irish Exhibition held at Olympia, London, from June to November 1888. As a consequence of the strain, he became seriously ill in 1897 and thereafter suffered nearly complete blindness. He nevertheless continued to write by dictation, his last substantial work, *Irish Recollections*, being published in 1911. To ease his financial plight, the Conservative prime minister, Arthur Balfour, nominated him in 1902 for a civil-list pension of £300 a year for his services to literature, and his daughter, Charlotte, looked after him. A lifelong Roman Catholic, McCarthy died in London on 24 April 1912 and was buried at Hampstead cemetery.

S. L. GWYNN, *rev.* ALAN O'DAY

Sources *Freeman's Journal* [Dublin] (25–6 April 1912) · *The Times* (26 April 1912) · H. Boylan, *A dictionary of Irish biography*, 2nd edn

(1988) • *WWBMP*, vol. 2 • *Dod's Parliamentary Companion* • D. Thornley, *Isaac Butt and home rule* (1964) • F. S. L. Lyons, *The Irish parliamentary party, 1890–1910* (1951) • C. C. O'Brien, *Parnell and his party, 1880–90* (1957) • F. S. L. Lyons, *John Dillon: a biography* (1968) • F. S. L. Lyons, *The fall of Parnell, 1890–91* (1961) • F. Callanan, *The Parnell split* (1992) • A. Plunkett, 'Justin McCarthy: an eminent Victorian', PhD diss., University of Virginia, 1992 • J. McCarthy, *Reminiscences*, 2 vols. (1899)

Archives NL Ire., diaries | BL, corresp. with W. E. Gladstone, Add. MSS 44384–44520, *passim* • NL Ire., letters to F. X. O'Brien • Richmond Local Studies Library, London, letters to Richard Sladen • TCD, corresp. with John Dillon • U. Birm. L., corresp. with Joseph Chamberlain • U. Leeds, Brotherton L., letters mainly to Bram Stoker • University of Missouri at Kansas City Library, corresp. with Chatto and Windus

Likenesses London Stereoscopic Co., carte photograph, *c.*1881, NPG • Walery, photograph, pubd 1890, NPG [*see illus.*] • H. White, oils, *c.*1907, NG Ire. • Barraud, photograph, NPG; repro. in *Men and women of the day*, 4 (1891) • W. & D. Downey, woodburytype photograph, NPG; repro. in Cassell, *Cabinet portrait gallery* (1893), vol. 4 • H. Furniss, pen-and-ink cartoons, NPG • S. P. Hall, pencil drawing, NG Ire. • S. P. Hall, pencil drawings, NPG • F. Pegram, pencil drawing, V&A • C. P. Renouard, charcoal drawing, NG Ire. • Spy [L. Ward], chromolithograph caricature, NPG; repro. in *VF* (23 May 1885) • photograph, repro. in *Daily News* (26 April 1910) [1912?]

McCarthy, Lila Emma [Lillah; *married names* Lila Emma Barker; Lila Emma Keeble, Lady Keeble] (**1875–1960**), actress and theatre manager, was born in Cheltenham on 22 September 1875, the seventh of the eight children of Jonadab McCarthy FRAS, a furniture broker with wide intellectual interests, and his wife, Emma Price. After disastrous early attempts at school, Lila Emma, as she was called, was educated at home from the age of eight by her father, her greatest early influence; the lessons included declaiming Milton, Bunyan, Shakespeare, and Blake. When Frank Benson brought his company to Cheltenham to play Shakespeare, Jonadab arranged for his daughter to recite from *King John* for the young actor–manager; Benson declared that she had talent, and in 1893 the family moved to London so that she could study elocution with Hermann Vezin and voice production with Emil Behnke. She took the stage name Lillah in May 1895 when as an amateur she played Lady Macbeth for the Shakespeare Society at St George's Hall. G. B. Shaw complimented her appearance and talent in fateful words in the *Saturday Review*: 'she can hold an audience whilst she is doing everything wrongly … some years of hard work would make her a valuable recruit to the London stage' (Shaw, 1.139–40).

McCarthy took his advice literally, touring in Shakespeare for Ben Greet and gaining the part of Berenice in *The Sign of the Cross* in London in 1896 with Wilson Barrett. This pitiful Christians-and-lions melodrama, written by Barrett himself, became her drama school, as she then joined Barrett's company to play the virginal female lead Mercia for eight years in England, Australia, New Zealand, and South Africa, undertaking a number of other roles, including Desdemona and Ophelia. She returned to London in 1905 as an accomplished actress—tall, statuesque, dark haired, and exceedingly beautiful—and she wrote to Shaw that her ten years of tutorial exile were completed. At that moment Shaw was in difficulty over casting the

Lila Emma McCarthy (1875–1960), by Bassano

part of Ann Whitefield for the initial production of his *Man and Superman*, which Harley Granville *Barker (1877–1946) was to mount in 1905 as part of his famous seasons at the Court Theatre. Shaw wrote:

> I was in despair of finding what I wanted, when one day there walked into my rooms at Adelphi Terrace a gorgeously goodlooking young lady in a green dress and huge picture hat … with the figure and gait of a Diana … And with that young lady I achieved performances of my plays which will probably never be surpassed. (McCarthy, 5)

As it turned out Lillah would get many more Shavian roles, almost all of them parts for passionate, dominating women, including four or five written specifically for her. Barker, as well as running the company at the Court, played the rich revolutionary John Tanner in *Man and Superman*. On 24 April 1906 he and Lillah were wed, just like their characters in the play.

At the Court in 1905–6 she also played Nora in a revival of *John Bull's Other Island*, Gloria in *You Never Can Tell*, and she originated Jennifer Dubedat in *The Doctor's Dilemma*, all written by Shaw. Elsewhere she used her sense of aristocratic comedy in J. M. Barrie's *What Every Woman Knows* (1908), her experience in melodrama in John Masefield's countrified *The Tragedy of Nan* (1908), and demonstrated her range with the working-class character Madge Thomas in John Galsworthy's *Strife* (1909), the last two directed by her husband, as was her performance in Masefield's adaptation of *The Witch* by H. Wiers-Jensen (1911).

Lillah's marriage was the most important fact of her life, though unfortunately it was not so for Barker. None the less their personal and professional lives were thoroughly intertwined for a crucial decade. In 1911, after the failure of a number of projects designed to create an art theatre in London, Barker was in a great depression and he considered moving to Germany. Lillah took action: she went into theatrical management herself by leasing the Little Theatre in Adelphi, offering her husband the opportunity to direct again. Here she played Hilde in Ibsen's *The Master Builder* and she settled in as Margaret Knox in Shaw's *Fanny's First Play*, which ran for 623 performances.

That play and McCarthy's management transferred to the Kingsway Theatre in 1912, where she took another lead, in Euripides' *Iphigenia in Tauris* in Gilbert Murray's translation; she also played Jocasta in Max Reinhardt's monumental staging of Sophocles' *Oedipus the King* at Covent Garden. In September the McCarthy-Barker partnership began a series of Shakespeare plays at the Savoy that revolutionized British production of the national dramatist. Now at the peak of her career Lillah was seen to full advantage as a powerful Hermione in *The Winter's Tale*, as a boyish Viola in *Twelfth Night*, and as a long-tressed Helena in *A Midsummer Night's Dream*. In 1913 they engaged the St James's Theatre for three months in another repertory experiment; here she played in Shaw's *Androcles and the Lion*, the Christians-and-lions play of the new drama, and revived some of her earlier roles. She was no match for Barker's intelligence, but she grew in strength as an actress as he grew as a coach; she flourished under his direction and found fulfilment as his ally.

McCarthy also had considerable charm off-stage, and a number of illustrious men sought her for social engagements. She graced the dinner table of the Asquiths frequently and managed to turn erotic interest in her into material interest for her art: Lord Howard de Walden financed her management in 1911 and Lord Lucas, who admitted he had been in love with her since he saw her Mercia in Oxford, generously backed the Shakespeare series at the Savoy. In her autobiography she speaks warmly of her few meetings with Lucas and it is reasonable to conclude that his feeling for her was reciprocated. Yet McCarthy's commitment to Barker did not waver. In 1915 they took their recent repertory to New York and performed Greek plays, with Lillah in the lead, at sports stadia on the American east coast. But all changed when Barker, having found an American soul mate in Helen Huntington, informed Lillah the next year that he was not returning to her. She strongly resisted but eventually took Shaw's advice and bowed to the inevitable; the divorce was granted in 1917, a devastating blow to her. Typically Shaw tried to help by writing her a new play, *Annajanska, the Bolshevik Empress*, a short 'bravura piece' Shaw called it, which capitalized on Lillah's own bravura characteristics. She had other brief engagements in London after the war, but her career was effectively over. On 27 March 1920 Lillah McCarthy married the botanist Professor Sir Frederick William *Keeble (1870–1952) and they enjoyed a happy and peaceful life at Boars Hill, near Oxford. She gave occasional recitals of poetry and dramatic scenes throughout

the country and remained friends with a number of theatrical colleagues, including Masefield and Shaw. She was living in London when she died at her home, flat 6, Cranley Mansions, 160 Gloucester Road, on 15 April 1960, aged eighty-four. She had no children.

Lillah McCarthy's part in raising the general quality of theatre in the Edwardian era was noteworthy. She became the chief interpreter of Shaw's women during the period, and she was central to Barker's reforming project, but without Barker to guide her she tended to return to the older style of declamation that she had learned from her father. Like many beautiful women of the time, she relied on men for a sense of direction. Her autobiography, *Myself and my Friends* (1933), is a flat and gushy book, most notable for the absence of Barker's name—angered by her intention to relate the story of their breakup, he had insisted that all references to him be removed.

DENNIS KENNEDY

Sources *The Times* (16 April 1960), 8 · L. McCarthy, *Myself and my friends* (1933) · *Who was who in the theatre, 1912–1976*, 4 vols. (1978) · G. B. Shaw, *Our theatre in the nineties*, 1 (1931) · C. B. Purdom, *Harley Granville Barker* (1955) · D. Kennedy, *Granville Barker and the dream of theatre* (1985) · E. Salmon, *Granville Barker: a secret life* (1983) · DNB · WWW, 1951–60 · m. certs.
Archives BL, corresp., Add. MS 47897 · Harvard U., Houghton L., papers · Ransom HRC, letters and notebooks · Theatre Museum, London, scrapbooks | BL, corresp. with Marie Stopes, Add. MS 58539
Likenesses W. & D. Downey, photograph, c.1906, NPG · C. Shannon, oils, 1907, Cheltenham Art Gallery and Museum · Daily Mirror Studios, photograph, 1913, NPG · C. Shannon, oils, c.1917–1918, Cheltenham Art Gallery and Museum · A. McEvoy, print, chromolithograph, 1919, V&A · A. McEvoy, oils, c.1920, NPG · Bassano, photograph, NPG [*see illus.*] · photographs, Theatre Museum, London · photographs, Ransom HRC · photographs, repro. in McCarthy, *Myself and my friends*
Wealth at death £46,338 4s. 3d.: probate, 18 July 1960, CGPLA Eng. & Wales

MacCarthy, Mary Josepha, Lady MacCarthy (1882–1953). *See under* MacCarthy, Sir (Charles Otto) Desmond (1877–1952).

McCarthy, Dame (Emma) Maud (1858–1949), army matron-in-chief, was born on 22 September 1858 at Sydney, New South Wales, Australia, the eldest daughter of William Frederick McCarthy, solicitor, and his wife, Emma Mary à Beckett. She was educated privately, and after spending three years in England decided to enter the London Hospital to train as a nurse (1891–3), thereby following a strong philanthropic tendency towards medicine and nursing that had been evinced in her family for generations; one of her ancestors was William Harvey.

On the outbreak of war in South Africa, McCarthy, then a ward sister, was one of the six nurses selected from the London Hospital by Queen Alexandra (then princess of Wales) to go to South Africa as her own special nursing sisters. McCarthy served with distinction throughout the war, and received the queen's and king's medals, the Royal Red Cross (to which in 1918 she was awarded a bar), and a special decoration from Queen Alexandra on her return to England in 1902. She became closely concerned

Dame (Emma) Maud McCarthy (1858–1949), by Frank O. Salisbury, 1917

with the formation of Queen Alexandra's Imperial Military Nursing Service (later Queen Alexandra's Royal Army Nursing Corps) in which she served as a matron until 1910, when she became principal matron at the War Office.

On the outbreak of war in 1914 McCarthy went to France in the first ship to leave England with members of the British expeditionary force. In 1915 she was installed at Abbeville as matron-in-chief of the British armies in France, in charge of the whole area from the channel to the Mediterranean, wherever British, imperial, and American nurses were working. In August 1914 the numbers in her charge were 516; by the time of the armistice there were 5440 nurses on the lines of communication and a further 954 in casualty clearing stations. They came from Canada, Australia, New Zealand, South Africa, Portugal, and the United States as well as from the United Kingdom; not all were trained nurses, for some 1729 were from voluntary aid detachments. To keep this vast body working harmoniously and efficiently called for administrative talent of the highest order. In 1917 and 1918 there were casualties from air raids and in the latter year the influenza epidemic also took its toll. The constant shortage of trained nurses, the continual movements of position, and the personal requirements of individuals all raised problems that McCarthy solved with tact and skill. It is believed that she was the only head of a department in the British expeditionary force who remained in her original post throughout the war—a great tribute to her strength of body, mind, and spirit. She was appointed GBE in 1918 and awarded the Florence Nightingale medal and several foreign decorations. When in August 1919 she sailed for

England from Boulogne, to where she had transferred her headquarters the previous year, representatives of the French government and medical service were among those who assembled to do her honour.

In 1920 McCarthy was appointed matron-in-chief of the Territorial Army Nursing Service, and although she retired five years later the advancement of nursing remained her great interest until she died. She had the highest ideals in her profession and an unselfish, modest character. Her devotion to duty and self-sacrifice were an inspiration to all who worked with her. To her own family she was a tower of strength and in every circumstance they turned to her for advice and comfort. She died, unmarried, at the age of ninety, at 6 St Luke's Street, London, on 1 April 1949.   H. S. GILLESPIE, *rev.*

Sources W. G. MacPherson, *Medical services: general history*, History of the Great War, 2 (1922) · *The Times* (8 April 1949), 7e · *The Times* (16 April 1949), 6e · private information (1959) · I. Hay, *One hundred years of army nursing: the story of the British army nursing services from the time of Florence Nightingale to the present day* (1953) · WWW · WW (1946) · WW (1947)
Archives Queen Alexandra's Royal Army Nursing Corps Museum, Aldershot, MSS
Likenesses F. O. Salisbury, portrait, 1917, NPG [*see illus.*] · A. O. Spare, pastel drawing, IWM
Wealth at death £3249 18s. 5d.: probate, 6 July 1949, CGPLA Eng. & Wales

MacCarthy, Nicholas Tuite [*known as* the Abbé de Lévignac] (**1769–1833**), Jesuit, was the son of Justin *MacCarthy Reagh (1744–1811), of Springhouse, co. Tipperary, and his wife, Mary Winifred (*b.* 1747), daughter of Nicholas Tuite, an Irish plantation owner on the West Indian island of Ste Croix, then a Danish possession. Born in Dublin on 19 May 1769, at four years of age he was taken to Toulouse, where his father was naturalized (1776) and ennobled by Louis XVI as Count MacCarthy. At the age of seven he was sent to the Collège du Plessis in Paris, and at fourteen received the tonsure at St Magloire seminary, being styled, from a property near Bordeaux purchased by his father, the Abbé de Lévignac. His relative Arthur Dillon, archbishop of Narbonne, would have given him a benefice *in commendam*, but MacCarthy would not accept a sinecure. The French Revolution interrupted his studies at the Sorbonne, and he returned to Toulouse, where he took advantage of his father's magnificent library and helped to educate his younger brothers, one of whom, Viscount Robert MacCarthy, was later deputy for the Drôme (1815–20).

Because of ill health MacCarthy delayed his ordination to the priesthood until 1814, after which date he soon won fame as a preacher. In 1817 he was offered the bishopric of Montauban but declined preferment, having determined to join the Society of Jesus. This he did in 1820, after which he continued to be in demand as a preacher at court, in the principal French towns, and at Geneva. The revolution of 1830 led him to retire to Savoy, but he was summoned to Rome on a preaching mission which undermined his health. He died on 3 May 1833 in the bishop's palace at

Annecy, France, and was buried in the cathedral. His posthumously published sermons were translated into Spanish, Italian, English, and German. They are characterized by moral rigorism and fervent denunciation of rationalism and revolution.

J. G. ALGER, *rev.* G. MARTIN MURPHY

Sources Collombet, 'MacCarthy, l'Abbé Nicolas Tuite de', *Biographie universelle, ancienne et moderne*, ed. L. G. Michaud and E. E. Desplaces, new edn (Paris, 1843–65), vol. 25 · Abbé Deplace, Memoir, *Sermons du R. P. MacCarthy*, 4 vols. (1834–6), preface · A. de Backer and others, *Bibliothèque de la Compagnie de Jésus*, new edn, 5, ed. C. Sommervogel (Brussels, 1894), 238–41 · H. de Gensac, 'MacCarthy, Nicholas Tuite de', *Dictionnaire de spiritualité ascétique et mystique: doctrine et histoire*, ed. M. Viller and others (1937–95) · 'MacCarthy', *Annuaire de la pairie* (1845), 230–33 · S. E. Green-Pedersen, 'Tuite, Nicholas', *Dansk biografisk leksikon*, ed. C. F. Bricka and others, 3rd edn, ed. S. Cedergreen Bech (Copenhagen, 1979–84)

Maccarthy, Robert, styled fifth earl of Clancarty (*d.* 1769), Jacobite sympathizer and Royal Naval officer, was the eldest son of the scandalous union between Donough *Maccarthy, styled fourth earl of Clancarty (1668–1734), and Elizabeth (*d.* 1704), the second daughter of Robert Spencer, second earl of Sunderland, who was aged between eleven and thirteen years at their marriage on 31 December 1684. Lord Clancarty left his wife without consummating the marriage and returned to Ireland, where he participated in James II's unsuccessful invasion attempt of 1689. A decade after his marriage Clancarty returned from exile against the wishes of Sunderland and was rearrested by government troops. Clancarty was finally pardoned by William III (though his estates and title were forfeited to William, earl of Portland), and he and his wife went to Hamburg, where they lived on a government pension.

After his mother's death in 1704 Robert Maccarthy (styled Viscount Muskerry) returned to England and, with his sister Charlotte, was befriended by Sarah, duchess of Marlborough, a former associate of the countess of Clancarty. While the duchess did not approve of a Stuart restoration, she kept many in her circle who, like Robert, maintained a Jacobite connection. A profligate youth who combined hard drinking with a rough temper, Muskerry lost the sight of an eye during a drunken brawl at a tavern. His sister once remarked that 'his judgement is not his brightest side' (Harris, 326). On 14 December 1722 he married his first wife, Joanna (1693–1759), daughter of Henry Player of Alverstone, Hampshire.

Through his association with the duchess, Muskerry received a commission in the British navy, and at the time of his father's death in September 1734 he commanded a ship off Newfoundland. Muskerry now assumed his father's title as fifth earl of Clancarty, but failed to have it recognized in Britain. At this date the British government also cancelled his father's pension, but in lieu the duchess of Marlborough granted Clancarty an annuity of £400 and provided him with an apartment in the courtyard of Marlborough House. From 1733 to 1735 Muskerry served as governor of Newfoundland. On his return to England he attempted to recover the family estates, which had made

his ancestors some of the wealthiest and largest landholders in Ireland. The suit provoked severe disruption within the Irish aristocracy. John Boyle, fifth earl of Orrery wrote to Jonathan Swift that 'Lord Clancarty's Thunderbolt will destroy half of our most wealthy Neighbours' (*Correspondence of Jonathan Swift*, 5.360). Clancarty continued to draw heavily on support from the duchess of Marlborough, who allegedly paid the legal bills for his suit. In addition the French minister, Cardinal Fleury, pleaded Clancarty's case with Sir Robert Walpole. Despite their backing, the claim proved unsuccessful. Having failed in his efforts, Clancarty returned to sea, rising to command the *Adventure* at the outbreak of the War of Jenkins's Ear (1739) before leaving the navy in 1741. At the death of Sarah, duchess of Marlborough (18 October 1744), he received a gift of £1000 and a further £1000 a year, as well as a manor in Buckinghamshire.

However, Clancarty left England to join the ranks of adventurers who travelled to Paris to support Charles Edward Stuart, the Young Pretender, and the Jacobite forces planning to invade Scotland. Clancarty did not accompany the prince, and after the uprising's collapse he was to be found, often drunk and dishevelled, unsuccessfully scheming for the Jacobite cause in France. Excluded from the 1747 Act of Indemnity, Clancarty never returned to England. After the death of his first wife in January 1759, he married Elizabeth Farnelly (*d.* 1790). Granted a pension of £1000 a year by Louis XV, Clancarty had by now retired to Boulogne. There he gained a reputation as a pleasant storyteller and generous host who 'generally finished the evening in an oblivion of all former cares' (*Works of Jonathan Swift*, 18.412). A heavy drinker his whole life, apparently he finally drank himself to death on 19 September 1769. He was survived by two sons, who took commissions in the French army. Clancarty's life was chronicled in the July and August editions of *Walker's Hibernian Magazine* (1796)—a portrait of a minor, ineffective, but certainly colourful champion of the ill-fated Stuart cause.

JAMES JAY CARAFANO

Sources DNB · F. Harris, *A passion for government: the life of Sarah, duchess of Marlborough* (1991) · H. Douglas, *Jacobite spy wars: moles, rogues, treachery* (1999) · *The correspondence of Jonathan Swift*, ed. H. Williams, 5 vols. (1963–5) · A. Coville, *Duchess Sarah* (1904) · *Walker's Hibernian Magazine* (July–Aug 1796) · *The works of Jonathan Swift*, ed. W. Scott, 2nd edn, 19 vols. (1824) · GEC, *Peerage*

MacCarthy Reagh, Florence [Finian Mac Cárthaigh Riabhach] (1562–*c.*1640), chieftain and writer on Ireland, was probably born at Kilbrittan Castle, the eldest son of Sir Donough MacCarthy Reagh (*d.* 1576), the second of the MacCarthy chiefs, the others being the MacCarthy of Muskerry and the MacCarthy More, the greatest. His mother was a daughter of James FitzMaurice of Desmond and the aunt of the last earl of Desmond. His father, who was lord of Carberry in west Cork, and a loyal subject of the crown, taught his son the arts of Gaelic politics and dissimulation, in which he would so excel. MacCarthy began his career by exacting tribute from and laying other impositions upon his father's dependants, which attracted the attention of the local authorities. Upon Sir

Donough's death, the chieftainship passed to his younger brother, Sir Owen (Eoghan) MacCarthy. Finian was made a ward of the president of Munster, Sir William Drury, and was left with twenty-seven ploughlands worth £1500 a year by his father. He became of age about 1578, when he entered the royal army with 300 of his own men and gained a reputation as a good fighting man on the side of the crown in the Desmond rebellion in Munster.

After the suppression of the rebellion in 1583, MacCarthy went to London, where Elizabeth I received him and awarded him £1000 for his services and gave him an annual pension of £100. He spent some considerable time at the court over the next five years, took up the fashions of the typical English courtier, learned to speak good English, and Anglicized his forename to Florence. He returned to Ireland and was present in 1585 at the opening of the Irish parliament in Dublin held by Sir John Perrott. Throughout his life he played a double game both as an English gentleman and as a Gaelic lord, and was in consequence increasingly distrusted by both sides. He remained a Catholic after he became of age, but refused to sue for livery of his estates, which would have necessitated his taking the oath of supremacy. He developed a liking for Spanish culture and learned to speak Spanish, having several relatives at the Spanish court at Madrid. He was described in one dispatch as being 'more Spanish than English' (CSP Ire., 1596–7, 232). It subsequently transpired that he had had connections with Sir William Stanley, who in 1586 had betrayed the English garrison at Deventer to the Spanish.

Florence stood second in succession to the title of MacCarthy Reagh behind his uncle Sir Owen and his cousin Donal-na-pipi. He stood opposed to Donal's claims to the clan title, in virtue of a patent given the latter by his father some years before. In 1583–4 the clan MacCarthy Reagh made Donal swear that he would not divert the succession from Florence, on payment of a bond of £10,000. Florence also had aspirations of becoming the MacCarthy More, and to that end in 1588 he eloped with and married the sole heir, Ellen (also known as Eileen), daughter of Donal McCarthy, first earl of Clancare, the current MacCarthy More. It had already been arranged that she should marry Nicholas, son of Sir Valentine Browne, an undertaker (planter) in co. Kerry of English birth, who held lands by mortgage from the earl. The prospect of one man with well-known Spanish sympathies holding the titles of both MacCarthy Reagh and MacCarthy More caused consternation among the authorities. Florence and his wife were taken prisoner. He was put in Cork gaol for six months and on 10 February 1589 sent to the Tower of London. Clancare promised to persuade his daughter to divorce Florence, who, to forestall this, had her removed from imprisonment in Cork on 18 February. He was questioned by the privy council on 23 March in relation to his Spanish connections, which he denied. He remained in the Tower until his marriage to Ellen was finally accepted by the authorities and she was permitted to come out of hiding and visit her husband in London. He was released from the Tower on 19 January 1591 on condition that he remain in London. The earl of Ormond later stood surety for Florence, and he was permitted to return to Ireland in November 1593.

In his absence Florence's properties in Munster had fallen prey to the depredations of local magnates and settlers, and he incurred huge legal expenses in prosecuting suits against Lord Barry, whom he blamed for being the author of his misfortunes. The earl of Clancare died in 1596 and Florence's claims to his lands were regarded sympathetically by the authorities, who considered him a useful pawn in a situation of growing unrest among the northern Gaelic chieftains. In 1598 Clancare's illegitimate son, Donal, had proclaimed himself the MacCarthy More and offered his support to Hugh O'Neill, earl of Tyrone, in his rebellion against the crown. But Florence's brother-in-law, the O'Sullivan More, refused to inaugurate Donal as MacCarthy More, and thereby negated his claim to it. On 16 March 1598 the English privy council ruled that Florence and not Valentine Browne should inherit Clancare's lands.

Florence finally returned to Munster in 1599, to claim the title of MacCarthy More. He hired 500 Connaught mercenaries or bonaghs, sealed off the entrances to his country, defeated Donal, and was inaugurated on 1 January 1600 as the MacCarthy More. In February the earl of Tyrone marched into Munster and called all the lords of the province to a parley. Florence's useful Spanish connections swayed Tyrone into accepting him as an ally. Tyrone therefore banished Donal and reinstalled Florence as the MacCarthy More and gave him 600 mercenaries. Florence promptly wrote to the English authorities informing them of his loyalty to the queen. In April the Munster commissioners under Captain Flower sent a force of 1000 to despoil the MacCarthy country. Florence laid an ambush for them as they were returning between Kinsale and Cork on 21 April. The ensuing battle, in which the Irish forces were eventually defeated after forcing an initial retreat by the English, was the one and only time that Florence actually encountered royal troops in the field. Upon Sir George Carew's arrival in Ireland as treasurer at war and subsequently lord justice and president of Munster, he invited a nervous Florence to a meeting on 29 October on a promise of safe conduct, at which he assured Carew of his neutrality and promised to send his eldest son to Cork as a pledge if the queen would grant him the Desmond estates and confirm his title of MacCarthy More. It is likely that Florence spent the next several months making arrangements with the Spanish for a landing in Munster, while at the same time protesting his loyalty to both the English authorities and the Irish rebels, especially Tyrone. It is most likely that his behaviour was inspired by the fear of being sent back to the Tower.

After the capture in late May 1601 of the súgán ('straw') or pretender earl of Desmond, James FitzThomas, who had been appointed by Tyrone, Carew felt himself to be in a position to take matters finally into his control. He arrested Florence, even though he still remained under the protection of the great seal, and was sent under a spurious pretext to the Tower; here and at the Marshalsea, with two periods of liberty within England, he spent the rest of his long life. He was never tried with any offence and continued to try to regain his escheated lands. But he was apparently treated with some leniency and given special privileges, including access to his books, which enabled him to compose 'A treatise on the antiquity and history of Ireland', a history of Ireland from mythical times to the Norman conquest, a work of some scholarship. He died in London about 1640. His schemings and dealings with both English and Irish left him with an unedifying reputation among his contemporaries as a vain, ambitious, and foolish man, who tried to please both sides and pleased neither. The eldest of his four sons, Tadhg, died as a boy in the Tower, so he was succeeded as the MacCarthy More by his second son, Donal, who married Sarah, the daughter of Randal MacDonnell, earl of Antrim. Their relationship had long since become estranged: she had held Castle Lough in Desmond with her own supporters against him and was to receive a government pension for informing on her husband to Carew.   AIDAN BREEN

Sources CSP dom., 1598–1601, 82, 402, 438 • APC, 1587–8, 326–7 • J. S. Brewer and W. Bullen, eds., Calendar of the Carew manuscripts, 6 vols., PRO (1867–73), vol. 3, p. 482; vol. 4, pp. 28–30, 139, 328–30 • Calendar of the manuscripts of the most hon. the marquis of Salisbury, 24 vols., HMC, 9 (1883–1976), vol. 3, pp. 450–53; vol. 4, pp. 486–7; vol. 5, pp. 431–2, 444; vol. 7, pp. 236, 290–91 • Fourth report, HMC, 3 (1874), 109–10 • D. MacCarthy, The life and letters of Florence MacCarthy Reagh (1867) • P. O'Sullivan Beare, Ireland under Elizabeth: chapters towards a history of Ireland in the reign of Elizabeth, ed. and trans. M. J. Byrne (1903), 114, 133 • S. O'Grady, Pacata Hibernia, or, A history of the wars in Ireland during the reign of Queen Elizabeth, especially within the province of Munster under the government of Sir Geo. Carew (1896), vol. 1 • C. Falls, Elizabeth's Irish wars (1950), 257–9, 282–3, 288–9 • M. MacCarthy-Morrogh, The Munster plantation (1986), 81–5
Archives BL, Add. MS 4793 • Bodl. Oxf., MSS Laud misc. 611, 614 • TCD, MS 786, D.3.16
Likenesses portrait, c.1776; formerly in the possession of a descendant of Donal-na-Piér

MacCarthy Reagh, Justin, Count MacCarthy in the French nobility (1744–1811), book collector, was born on 18 August 1744 at Springhouse, co. Tipperary, the son of Denis MacCarthy Reagh (1718–1761), landowner, of Springhouse and his wife, Christine French of Rahasane, co. Galway. His father took refuge in France from the penal laws against Catholics in Ireland, and at his death at Argenson in 1761 Justin sold his Irish estates and settled permanently at Toulouse. In September 1776 he acquired French nationality and the title of count, and in February 1777 he was admitted to the French court on the strength of his pedigree. The MacCarthy Reagh branch of the sept claimed descent from the ancient princes of Carbery. In 1765 he had married Mary Winifred (b. 1747), the daughter of the wealthy Irish West India merchant Nicholas Tuite, owner of sugar plantations in Montserrat and St Croix and honorary chamberlain of the king of Denmark (to which St Croix belonged). Tuite is said to have settled £10,000 on his daughter, but according to MacCarthy Reagh's will (Diary of John Baker, 62) did not honour the pledge.

MacCarthy Reagh was a lifelong book collector, with a predilection for books printed on vellum and for Mainz printings. He gave an account of the history of his collection in a letter of 15 November 1800 to J.-B.-B. van Praet, keeper of printed books at the Bibliothèque Nationale (Hobson, 517–19). He was a major beneficiary of the Gaignat and Girardot de Préfond sales. In 1771 he took the English bookbinders Richard Wier and his wife to Toulouse to carry out a programme of de luxe morocco binding.

Though he attended the general assembly of the nobility of the diocese of Toulouse in January 1789, MacCarthy Reagh took little part in public life, preferring to devote himself to his family—described by a Paris bookseller to William Beckford as 'une des plus polies et des plus aimables qu'on puisse rencontrer' (Hobson, 517)—and to his collection. His library escaped depredation at the Revolution, when he sought temporary asylum in England. Some of its contents were sold in London by Leigh and Sotheby in May 1789.

MacCarthy Reagh died at Toulouse on 31 December 1811. A two-volume catalogue of his collection, including 601 books printed on vellum, all in superb condition, was published by the De Bure brothers at Paris in 1815. The most notable items included a Complutensian polyglot Bible of 1514 (one of only three sets to be printed on vellum, which MacCarthy Reagh had bought at the Pinelli sale for what was then the record sum of £483), a Gutenberg Bible, two Mainz psalters of 1457 and 1459, and a Sarum missal of 1500 printed by Richard Pynson. The MacCarthy family had hoped to sell the collection as a whole, but rejected an immediate offer of £20,000 from the sixth duke of Devonshire, and an auction sale held by the De Bure brothers in January 1817 realized only £16,000, reflecting the depressed state of the market. The 1457 psalter (the earliest dated printed book) was acquired by van Praet for Louis XVIII, and the polyglot Bible went to George Hibbert for £650, while other items passed into the King's Library (now part of the British Library) and to English collectors such as Francis Douce, Thomas Grenville, and Lord Spencer. Unsold books were advertised by De Bure in further fixed-price catalogues of 1817 and 1822.

MacCarthy Reagh was survived by his six sons and three daughters. Nicholas Tuite *MacCarthy (1769–1833), known as the Abbé de Lévignac, became a notable preacher, while his younger brother Count Robert MacCarthy (1770–1827) was aide-de-camp to the prince de Condé and later a deputy in the French assembly.

G. MARTIN MURPHY

Sources S. T. MacCarthy, The MacCarthys of Munster (1922), 153–7 • Lainé, Archives généalogiques et historiques de France, 5 (1836) • A. Hobson, 'A letter from Count MacCarthy Reagh to J. B. B. van Praet', Festschrift Otto Schäfer (1987), 515–22 • [J. Roche], Critical and miscellaneous essays by a nonagenarian, 1 (1850), 232 • Catalogue des livres rares et précieux de la bibliothèque du feu le comte de MacCarthy Reagh, 2 vols. (Paris, 1815) • The diary of John Baker, ed. P. C. Yorke (1931), 62 • R. B. Sheridan, Sugar and slavery (1974), 444–5 • A. N. L. Munby, Connoisseurs and medieval miniatures, 1750–1850 (1972) • M. Callanan, 'Irish wills', Irish Genealogist, 1 (1938), 123–4 • T. F. Dibdin, The bibliographical decameron, 3 (1817), 162–80 • G. De Bure, Catalogue des livres rares et précieux du cabinet de M. L. C. D. M. par Guillaume De Bure (Paris, 1779) • A catalogue of a very elegant and curious cabinet of books lately imported from France, the property of a gentleman lately resident in that *kingdom* (1789) [sale catalogue, Leigh and Sotheby, 18 May 1789] · *Biographie toulousaine*, 2 (1823), 1–3

Archives Bibliothèque Nationale, Paris, Fonds français MSS 1014, 3230, 4642 (no. 636, p. 117)

Maccartney, George. *See* Maccartney, George (*c*.1660–1730).

McCartney [*née* Eastman; *other married name* See], **Linda Louise**, Lady McCartney (1941–1998), photographer and promoter of vegetarianism, was born on 24 September 1941 in Scarsdale, New York, USA, the second child and eldest daughter in the family of one son and three daughters of Lee Eastman, formerly Leopold Vail Epstein (*b.* 1910), lawyer, and his wife, Louise Sara (1911–1962), daughter of Max Dryfoos Lindner of Cleveland, Ohio. Both her parents were Jewish. Despite the widespread belief to the contrary, the family was not related to the Eastmans of Eastman Kodak. She was educated at Scarsdale high school, spending the summers in the family house at Cape Cod, where her parents entertained artists including Willem de Kooning, and musicians such as the bandleader Tommy Dorsey. After briefly attending the University of Arizona she studied photography at a local arts centre, and married John Melvyn (Mel) See (*d.* 2000), a geologist, on 18 June 1962. There was one daughter, Heather, from this marriage. After her divorce in 1965, she moved back to New York and took a job as an editorial assistant with *Town and Country* magazine.

Linda Eastman's career as a photographer of rock and roll groups was launched in 1966, after she photographed the Rolling Stones at a press reception on a boat in New York harbour. At Fillmore East Auditorium, the New York rock venue, she photographed all the most famous bands and singers of the 1960s, including The Who, The Animals, Jim Morrison and The Doors, Frank Zappa and the Mothers of Invention, and the Grateful Dead, and particularly admired Jimi Hendrix. Her photographs were much sought after, and appeared in magazines such as *Life* and *Mademoiselle*. A selection of these photographs, *Sixties: Portrait of an Era*, was published in 1992.

Linda Eastman met Paul McCartney (*b.* 1942), songwriter and member of The Beatles rock group, in 1967, and they were married on 12 March 1969: he adopted Heather and they had three further children, Mary, Stella, and James. The Beatles were breaking up at the time of their marriage, and the media and the fans accused her and John Lennon's wife, Yoko Ono, of being responsible for this. She helped Paul McCartney to start writing songs again, and the first song in his solo album *McCartney* (1970) was 'The Lovely Linda'. She helped him to form a new band, Wings, in 1971, and although she had no musical training he persuaded her to join the band as keyboard player and singer, contributing to albums including *Ram* (1971), *Band on the Run* (1973), and *Venus and Mars* (1975). The Wings' recording of 'Mull of Kintyre' became the then highest-selling single ever. The band toured regularly, including a thirteen-month world tour in 1975–6 which ended at Wembley Stadium. In 1977 she wrote and recorded her first solo song, 'Seaside Woman', and this served as the soundtrack for the animated film made by Oscar Brill

which won the Golden Palm for Best Short at the Cannes Film Festival in 1980. Wings was disbanded in 1980. Paul McCartney, who continued to enjoy a successful solo career, was knighted in 1997.

Linda McCartney became a vegetarian in the early 1970s, and wrote *Home Cooking* (1989) to encourage people who wanted to cook without using meat. After this success—over 400,000 copies were sold—she continued to publish cookery books, including *Linda McCartney's Home Cooking* (1994) and *Linda's Kitchen* (1995). *Linda McCartney on Tour* (1998) was published posthumously. She promoted the idea of cooking vegetarian food disguised as meat, advocating the use of textured vegetable protein, and went on to launch her own line of frozen vegetarian meals, Linda McCartney's Meatless Entrées, in 1991, with dishes including Beefless Burgers and Ploughman's Pie, extending her range to include Chili Non-Carne and Bavarian Goulash. In 1995 she opened a factory in Fakenham, Norfolk, with 500 employees, but although highly successful in Britain, Linda McCartney's Home Style Cooking did not succeed in the United States, where it was launched in 1994, partly because the meals were high in calories, and contained a large proportion of fat. She became a prominent animal rights campaigner, working with People for the Ethical Treatment of Animals.

Linda McCartney's photographs became known to a wider public in the 1980s, with several exhibitions, including one at the Royal Photographic Society in Bath in 1987, and her *Sun Prints* were shown at the Victoria and Albert Museum in 1988. She was diagnosed as suffering from breast cancer in 1995 and died on 17 April 1998 at the McCartneys' ranch near Tucson, Arizona. Four of her photographs, including 'The Beatles and Yoko Ono' (1969), are in the permanent collections of the National Portrait Gallery in London and the Smithsonian Institution in Washington, DC. ANNE PIMLOTT BAKER

Sources D. Fields, *Linda McCartney* (2000) · L. McCartney, *Sixties: portrait of an era* (1992) · *Daily Telegraph* (20 April 1998) · *The Guardian* (20 April 1998) · *The Independent* (21 April 1998) · *The Times* (21 April 1998) · m. cert.

Likenesses photograph, 1972, repro. in *The Independent* · photograph, 1975, repro. in *Daily Telegraph* · photograph, repro. in *The Guardian* · photograph, repro. in *The Times* · photographs, repro. in Fields, *Linda McCartney* · photographs, Hult. Arch.

Wealth at death £3,888,256—gross: probate, 2001, *CGPLA Eng. & Wales* · £3,884,731—net: probate, 2001, *CGPLA Eng. & Wales*

Maccarwell, David. *See* Mac Cearbhaill, David (*d.* 1289).

McCaul, Alexander (1799–1863), Hebrew scholar and missionary to the Jews, was born of protestant parents in Dublin on 16 May 1799. He was educated at a private school, entered Trinity College, Dublin, on 3 October 1814, graduated BA in 1819, and proceeded MA in 1831; he was created DD in 1837. He was for some time tutor to the earl of Rosse, but becoming interested in the Jews he was sent in 1821 to Poland as a missionary by the London Society for Promoting Christianity among the Jews. He studied Hebrew and German at Warsaw, and at the close of 1822 went to St Petersburg, where he was received by the tsar, who took some interest in his work. After returning to England he was ordained and served the curacy of Huntley, near Gloucester, where he became friendly with Samuel Roffey Maitland.

In 1823 McCaul married and returned to Poland, where he lived at Warsaw as head of the mission to the Jews and as English chaplain until 1830. He was supported by the Grand Duke Constantine, but had disputes with the Lutheran congregations, and withdrew to Berlin, where he was befriended by Sir Henry Rose, the English ambassador, and by Crown Prince Friedrich Wilhelm of Prussia, who had known him at Warsaw. To improve his health he visited Ireland, and returned for a short time to Poland in 1832. He finally decided to settle in London, and took up residence in Palestine Place, Cambridge Road; there he actively supported the London Society and helped to found the Jews' Operatives Converts Institution. In 1837 he began the publication of *Old Paths*, a weekly pamphlet on Jewish ritual, which continued for sixty weeks. In 1840 he was appointed principal of the Jewish college founded by the London Society; and in the summer of 1841, through Friedrich Wilhelm IV of Prussia, he was offered the bishopric of Jerusalem, though he declined it because he thought it would be better held by one who had earlier been of the Jewish faith. In the same year McCaul succeeded Michael Solomon Alexander as professor of Hebrew and rabbinical literature at King's College, London; in 1846 he was also elected to a chair of divinity and later he was also professor of ecclesiastical history. He held these three chairs until 1863.

In addition to these offices McCaul in 1843 was appointed rector of St James's, Duke's Place, London; in 1845 he became prebendary of St Paul's, and in 1847 he declined Archbishop Howley's offer of any one of the four new colonial bishoprics. In 1850 he became rector of St Magnus, St Margaret, and St Michael, Fish Street Hill. When the sittings of convocation were revived in 1852, McCaul was elected proctor for the London clergy, and he represented them until his death. At first strongly opposed to the revival of the ancient powers of convocation, he modified his views and worked dogmatically with the highchurchmen, opposing the relaxation of the subscription to the articles, and seconding Archdeacon Denison's motion for the appointment of a committee (of which he was afterwards a member) for the assessment of Bishop Colenso's works on the Old Testament.

McCaul published many single sermons and pamphlets, and several books, the chief being *A Hebrew Primer* (1844), *Warburtonian lectures* (2 sers., 1846–52), *Rationalism, and the Divine Interpretation of Scripture* (1850), a critique of *Essays and Reviews*, entitled *Some Notes on the First Chapter of Genesis* (1861), and *An Examination of Bishop Colenso's Difficulties with Regard to the Pentateuch* (2 vols., 1863–4). McCaul died at his rectory, 39 King William Street, London, on 13 November 1863, and was buried at Ilford, Essex. He left several sons, his wife having apparently predeceased him. His friends donated a stained-glass window in his memory in King's College chapel.

W. A. J. ARCHBOLD, rev. H. C. G. MATTHEW

Sources *Guardian* (18 Nov 1863) • Crockford (1860) • F. J. C. Hearnshaw, *The centenary history of King's College, London, 1828–1928* (1929) • W. T. Gidney, *The history of the London Society for Promoting Christianity amongst the Jews, 1809–1908* (1908) • *CGPLA Eng. & Wales* (1864) • d. cert.
Likenesses W. T. Davey, mezzotint (after E. J. Fisher), BM
Wealth at death under £1500: probate, 11 Jan 1864, *CGPLA Eng. & Wales*

McCausland, Dominick (1806–1873), judge and religious writer, was born at his father's residence, Roe Park, co. Londonderry, on 20 August 1806, the third of four sons of Marcus Langford McCausland and his wife, a daughter of John Kennedy of Cultra, co. Down, and aunt of Sir Arthur Edward Kennedy. His father died when McCausland was still an infant and he was taught at the Revd Dr Moore's school, Parkhill, Gloucestershire, and for two years at the Royal School, Dungannon. In 1822 he went to Trinity College, Dublin, where he graduated BA in 1827, winning the gold medal for science in his year. He proceeded LLD and LLB in 1859. Ill health contributed to his missing a fellowship, and he went on a tour of the continent for two years.

After his tour McCausland returned to Ireland to study law and was called to the Irish bar in 1835. He selected the north-western circuit, and became QC in 1860. In the second administration of Lord Derby (1858–9), McCausland was appointed crown prosecutor, and immediately afterwards was elected 'father', or president, of the circuit bar. Notwithstanding the demands of a busy practice he found time to write several religious works, including *On the Latter Days of the Jewish Church and Nation, as Revealed in the Apocalypse* (1841), and *The Times of the Gentiles as Revealed in the Apocalypse* (1852). These works were later republished in a combined second edition as *The Latter Days of Jerusalem and Rome as Revealed in the Apocalypse*. Other works were *Sermons in Stones* (1856), which went into thirteen editions, *Adam and the Adamite* (1864), and *The Builders of Babel* (1871). McCausland died at his home, 12 Fitzgibbon Street, Dublin, on 28 June 1873, and was buried at St George's, Dublin, on 1 July. His wife, Emily, and at least three of their sons, survived him.

B. B. WOODWARD, rev. DAVID HUDDLESTON

Sources W. D. Ferguson, *Memoir of Dominick McCausland* (1873) • *Irish Law Times and Solicitors' Journal*, 7 (1873), 354 • Burtchaell & Sadleir, *Alum. Dubl.* • [J. H. Todd], ed., *A catalogue of graduates who have proceeded to degrees in the University of Dublin, from the earliest recorded commencements to … December 16, 1868* (1869), 384 • *The Athenaeum* (5 July 1873), 17 • *CGPLA Ire.* (1873)
Wealth at death under £2000 in Ireland: administration, 23 July 1873, *CGPLA Ire.* • under £600 in England: administration with will, 23 July 1873, *CGPLA Ire.*

Mac Cearbhaill, David (d. 1289), archbishop of Cashel, held the archbishopric from 1253 until his death in 1289. Before his episcopal appointment he held the deanery of Cashel, but apart from this virtually nothing is known of his early career. His family background was predominantly Irish and his election was opposed by Henry III on the grounds of his affinity with the king's enemies. Pope Innocent IV confirmed his election in August 1254 and royal assent was eventually obtained in February 1255.

The new archbishop did fealty to the king in person and was consecrated in Cashel in the summer of 1255.

One of Mac Cearbhaill's earliest actions as archbishop was to hold a provincial council at which various disputes with his suffragan bishops and clergy were settled. Nevertheless, in the following years Archbishop David was involved in serious quarrels with both the suffragan bishop of Lismore and the dean of Cashel. His reputation as a contentious prelate is given further substantiation by the events of 1266, when he confirmed, and in one case consecrated, suffragan bishops before royal assent had been obtained. In 1267 he was summoned into the king's presence and pardoned for these offences.

The archbishop had strong sympathies with the Cistercian tradition. In 1255 he had petitioned the general chapter for permission to have the services of two Cistercian monks to help him in his administration. In 1269, fourteen years after his consecration, he himself took the habit of a Cistercian monk. This marked a turning point in his career and he became very involved in the affairs of that order. In 1272, having removed a Benedictine community, he founded Hore Abbey in Cashel, bringing monks from Mellifont. In 1274 he attended the chapter general at Cîteaux and was granted his petition that all the daughter houses removed from Mellifont's jurisdiction by Abbot Lexington in 1228 were to be restored.

In this same year the archbishop was present at the Council of Lyons; and he made a vow to go on pilgrimage to the Holy Land which he does not appear to have fulfilled. He was in England in January 1275 and then returned to Ireland to oversee the reorganization of the Cistercian houses. He provoked the hostility of many of the English in Ireland who complained of his anti-English sentiments and actions. It was alleged that his abbey in Cashel was full of rogues who killed English people and that the archbishop had made an Irish boy of twenty-two years bishop of Cork, to humiliate the English. His personal relations with the king, however, appear to have been cordial and despite being branded anti-English he was one of the prime movers in the unsuccessful attempts in the period 1277–81 to extend English law to the Irish. With his suffragan bishops of Emly and Killaloe, he spent the best part of four years in England negotiating with royal officials. Together with five other bishops of the Cashel province they pledged all their temporalities to guarantee payment of the proposed fine of 10,000 marks. When the negotiations broke down, Mac Cearbhaill returned to Cashel. Little is known of the last six years of his life. He died in Cashel on 1 August 1289 and may have been buried in Hore Abbey.

Although the evidence points to Mac Cearbhaill having been a quarrelsome prelate, he also emerges as able and courageous. He placed himself firmly within native Irish ecclesiastical tradition, while at the same time attempting to establish a working relationship with the crown. The contradictory evidence of his career is, in the words of J. Watt, 'an expression of the conflict facing every Irish prelate who ministered in the *terre Engleis*' (Watt, 160).

MARGARET MURPHY

Sources A. Gwynn, 'Edward I and the proposed purchase of English law for the Irish, *c.*1276–80', *TRHS*, 5th ser., 10 (1960), 111–27 · J. A. Watt, *The church and the two nations in medieval Ireland* (1970) · J. Otway-Ruthven, 'The request of the Irish for English law, 1277–80', *Irish Historical Studies*, 6 (1948–9), 261–70 · G. Hand, *The church in the English lordship, 1216–1307* (1968), vol. 2/3 of *A history of Irish Catholicism* · S. Phillips, 'David MacCarwell and the proposal to purchase English law, *c.*1273–*c.*1280', *Peritia*, 10 (1996), 253–73

McCheyne, Robert Murray (1813–1843), Church of Scotland minister, was born on 21 May 1813 at 14 Dublin Street, Edinburgh, the youngest of the five children of Adam McCheyne (*d.* 1854), lawyer and writer to the signet, and his wife, Lockhart Murray Dickson (*d.* 1854), youngest daughter of David Dickson, proprietor of Nether Locharwood, in Dumfries. While Robert was recovering from scarlet fever at the age of four, his father taught him to read and write the Greek alphabet. The following year he was sent to George Knight's school. Two years later the family moved to 56 Queen Street, Edinburgh, and sixteen years later to 20 Hill Street. From October 1821 McCheyne attended Infirmary Street high school, Edinburgh. He matriculated at Edinburgh University in 1827. In 1831 he entered the Divinity Hall. At university he won prizes in all his classes. He had a particular love for natural scenery, and many of his letters are illustrated by sketches that testify to his skill in drawing.

On 8 July 1831 McCheyne's brother David died at the age of twenty-six—of the effects of a cold caught while hill walking. The two brothers had been close, and David often shared his evangelical Christian faith with Robert. David's death strongly contributed to Robert's conversion, which occurred soon afterwards. In 1835 he went before Edinburgh presbytery for his licence to preach. He later wrote that, 'For a good hour … all heckled me, like so many terriers on a rat' (Smellie, 45). However, because the Edinburgh presbytery was so busy, McCheyne undertook further examinations, and was instead licensed by the presbytery of Annan on 1 July 1835, and became, as he expressed it, 'a preacher of the Gospel, an honour to which I cannot name an equal' (ibid., 46). In November he became assistant to John Bonar in the parishes of Larbert and Dunipace, near Stirling.

McCheyne's fame as a preacher spread quickly and, along with Andrew Bonar and Alexander Somerville, he was considered by the new church of St Peter in Dundee. It was McCheyne who was called and he was ordained there on 24 November 1836. From the start of his ministry the church was full, with some 1100 people attending, many having to stand. People were not drawn by his oratory or voice, but by the power, simplicity, freeness, and sufficiency of the gospel he preached. As one of his contemporaries, a Mr Hamilton of Regent Square, London, commented, 'few ministers preach with the fervour, the Christ-exalting simplicity, and the prayerful expectancy of Robert McCheyne' (Bonar, 172). In his first year of ministry he received three further calls offering far more than the £200 yearly stipend he was receiving, but he rejected each one. He became actively involved in the cause of church extension, and in 1837 became secretary to the Forfarshire Association.

Robert Murray McCheyne (1813–1843), by John Le Conte (after Hope J. Stewart, after self-portrait, c.1834)

In late 1838, being thoroughly exhausted, McCheyne was forced to leave Dundee and return to his family's Edinburgh home. A little later he joined the Church of Scotland's mission of inquiry to Israel, its remit being to inquire into the number, condition, and character of the Jews. The mission left England on 29 March 1839, and returned on 6 November. The details of its visit were recorded and subsequently published in the *Narrative of a Mission of Enquiry to the Jews from the Church of Scotland, in 1839* (1842). McCheyne had been worried about leaving his congregation during his visit to Israel, but he was relieved when William C. Burns successfully took his place.

In November 1842 McCheyne was a member of the convocation and would have led his church into the Free Church had he lived to see the Disruption. In early 1843 he took part in a number of evangelistic missions, one of which crossed the border into Northumberland. In February 1843 he journeyed to the north-east of Scotland, to the districts of Deer and Ellon, where he preached and spoke twenty-seven times in twenty-four different places.

McCheyne never married, but he was twice engaged. His first fiancée was a Miss Maxwell, the daughter of a Dundee physician; possibly her parents prevented the marriage. He was later engaged to Jessie Thain of Heath Park near Blairgowrie.

In 1843 typhus was prevalent in Dundee, but McCheyne visited freely among the sick. Being weak himself, he soon caught the infection and quickly became gravely ill. On Saturday 25 March, in his own bedroom with Dr James Gibson beside him, McCheyne died while raising his hands as if to pronounce the benediction. All Dundee was

moved by the news of his death. His parents agreed to the wish of St Peter's that McCheyne be buried in St Peter's graveyard, rather than in the family's own burial-ground in Edinburgh. He was buried on Thursday 30 March, with perhaps 7000 people attending the funeral.

McCheyne was esteemed by his contemporaries for the remarkable results of his short period of ministry, the hymns he wrote (including 'Jehovah Tsidkenu' and 'The Barren Fig-Tree'), and his published diary and sermons, collected in A. A. Bonar's *Memoir and Remains* (1844; 2nd edn, 1892). Some indication of the success of, and interest in, McCheyne's life and ministry may be seen in the fact that this work had, by 1910, sold more than 500,000 copies. MICHAEL D. MCMULLEN

Sources A. A. Bonar, *Memoir and remains of the Rev. Robert Murray M'Cheyne*, new edn (1892) · A. Smellie, *Robert Murray McCheyne* (1913) · J. C. Smith, *Robert Murray McCheyne* (1910) · *Fasti Scot.* · J. L. Watson, *Life of Robert Murray McCheyne* (1882)
Archives U. Edin., New Coll. L., corresp. and papers
Likenesses J. Le Conte, stipple (after H. J. Stewart, after self-portrait, c.1834), NPG [*see illus.*]

McClean, Frank (1837–1904), astronomer and educational benefactor, was born at Glasgow on 13 November 1837, the only son of the six children of John Robinson McClean MP FRS FRAS (1813–1873), a civil engineer of repute, and his wife, Anna, *née* Newsam. He entered Westminster School in 1850, then proceeded in 1853 to the University of Glasgow, where he was influenced by William Thomson (Lord Kelvin) and won several prizes, and in 1855 to Trinity College, Cambridge, where he gained a scholarship and from where he graduated twenty-seventh wrangler in 1859. After articled training as an engineer in 1862 he became a partner in his father's company. On 24 May 1865 he married Ellen, the daughter of John Greg, a gentleman of Escowbeck, Lancaster; they had two daughters and three sons. In 1870 McClean came into money and retired from business; he maintained a residence in London, at South Kensington, and a country house in Kent. Relishing craftsmanship, he collected methodically to illustrate evolution in early arts, and mastered French and Italian in order to perfect his collection.

In 1875 McClean built an observatory at Ferncliffe, near Tunbridge Wells, and studied stellar spectra and solar prominences. In 1884 he built Rusthall House nearby, with a laboratory and heliostat. From 1887, in *Monthly Notices of the Royal Astronomical Society*, his papers and photographic atlases presented large-scale solar spectra, and laboratory spectra including a range of rare metals, to facilitate line identification.

In 1895 McClean installed a twin $^{12}/_{10}$ inch Grubb photovisual refractor and became a pioneer of objective prism spectrography, in which a prism is placed in front of the object glass. He avoided the small-scale multi-spectra per plate method of the Harvard observatory, and his prism yielded one wide-dispersion spectrum per plate of each star brighter than magnitude 3.5. Those he could enlarge, analyse, and discuss. An artist at heart, McClean could not bear another's hand on his work; he executed every detail himself, and in 1896 he completed his survey of 160 northern stars (published in *Philosophical Transactions of the Royal Society*, 191, 1898), and in 1897 used the same prism at the Cape observatory to photograph the 116 southern stars. Shortly after H. C. Vogel, he identified stars with neutral helium absorption lines, deduced they were early in the stellar sequence, and was the first to show the coincidence of 'helium stars' lying in regions of gaseous nebulae. Not least, in 1897, by recognizing oxygen absorption in Beta Crucis, he first detected direct evidence of oxygen beyond our planet. McClean thus contributed to disputed schemes of stellar evolution by temperature classification, which were plagued by determining which stars were actually hottest. Spectroscopists before 1914 lacked the advances in nuclear theory that could make interpretation significant. Since McClean's data came after Harvard's Draper memorial catalogue, which extended to much fainter stars, it was of relatively minor importance, but his high-detail spectra compelled reclassification of some stars, and the quality and completeness of the research justified the award to McClean in 1899 of the Royal Astronomical Society's gold medal.

McClean enabled Britain to pursue astrophysical work in the southern hemisphere by offering the Cape observatory in 1894 the 24/18 inch photovisual Victoria telescope, building, dome, and equipment; it finally became operational in 1901. He displayed a pernickety trait, driving the maker Howard Grubb to distraction by constantly challenging Grubb's designs or imposing design detail.

McClean permanently distinguished himself as a benefactor of astronomical education. When British research appeared disadvantaged by the German PhD system, thirty years before those degrees became available at Cambridge, and when funding for pure research was very scarce, he ensured that the best aspirants could be drawn into astronomical work. In 1890 he gave £12,500 to establish at Cambridge three Isaac Newton studentships in astronomy and physical optics, each worth £200 per annum (£250 after 1930) for up to three years. Professor H. H. Turner rightly emphasized that the only comparable 'directive force' in astronomy were the professorships founded at Oxford in 1619 by Savile and at Cambridge in 1704 by Plume and in 1749 by Lowndes; these funded individual careers by appointment. McClean's genius was to provide sufficient to start careers by merit, through competitive examination; by 1939 there were fifty-six beneficiaries. In 1903 McClean also augmented two existing stipends to found the Stokes and Cayley mathematical lectureships at Cambridge.

Having been elected a fellow of the Royal Astronomical Society in 1877, McClean served on its council from 1891 until his death, but would not accept office, nor serve the council of the Royal Society, after his election as FRS in 1895. Instead, and typically encouraging others to advance in their own way, he was a founder member of the British Astronomical Association, and served on its council from 1900 to 1902. He was an honorary LLD of the University of Glasgow (1894).

H. H. Turner reported 'with unfeigned sorrow'

McClean's death from pneumonia at Brussels on 8 November 1904. He was buried in Kensal Green cemetery, London. Bequests from his will included £5000 each to the department of physical science at the new University of Birmingham, and another to improve the instrumental equipment of the Newall observatory. McClean thus gave vital impetus to the development of solar physics at Cambridge: H. F. Newall erected a new solar telescope and spectrograph. The results obtained significantly influenced the government's 1913 relocation of the solar physics observatory from South Kensington to Cambridge, which complemented the Isaac Newton studentships in consolidating Cambridge's growing domination of British astrophysics. McClean's collections, which were left to the Fitzwilliam Museum, Cambridge, included illuminated manuscripts and early printed books, and were the most notable bequest since its foundation.

H. P. HOLLIS, rev. ROGER HUTCHINS

Sources H. H. T. [H. H. Turner], *Monthly Notices of the Royal Astronomical Society*, 65 (1904–5), 338–42 · H. F. N. [H. F. Newall], *PRS*, 78A (1907), xix–xxiii · J. B. Hearnshaw, *The analysis of starlight: one hundred and fifty years of astronomical spectroscopy*, new edn (1990), 9, 94, 99–100, 134 · I. S. Glass, *Victorian telescope makers: the lives and letters of Thomas and Howard Grubb* (1997), 155–6, 158–66, 168–9, 171, 173–5, 177–9 · H. F. Newall, 'Frank McClean', *The Observatory*, 27 (1904), 448–9 · R. S. Ball, address, *Monthly Notices of the Royal Astronomical Society*, 59 (1898–9), 315–24 · A. J. Meadows, *Science and controversy: a biography of Sir Norman Lockyer* (1972), 299–301 · W. W. Bryant, *A history of astronomy* (1907), 335 · [H. H. Turner], *The Observatory*, 27 (1904), 457 · *Journal of the British Astronomical Association*, 15 (1904–5), 47 · *The historical register of the University of Cambridge, supplement, 1921–30* (1932), 34–5, 279 · *The historical register of the University of Cambridge, supplement, 1931–40* (1942), 54 · H. H. Turner, *Modern astronomy* (1901), 243–4

Archives RAS, letters to Royal Astronomical Society · RAS, Royal Astronomical Society papers, 55-2 · South African Astronomical Observatory, Cape Town, archive, corresp. relating to Victoria telescope

Likenesses photograph, South African Astronomical Observatory, Cape Town, archive; repro. in Glass, *Victorian telescope makers*, 157

Wealth at death £306,953 19s. 8d.: resworn probate, 26 Nov 1904, *CGPLA Eng. & Wales*

Macclesfield. For this title name *see* Gerard, Charles, first earl of Macclesfield (c.1618–1694); Gerard, Charles, second earl of Macclesfield (c.1659–1701); Brett, Anne [Anne Gerard, countess of Macclesfield] (1667/8–1753); Parker, Thomas, first earl of Macclesfield (1667–1732); Parker, George, second earl of Macclesfield (c.1697–1764); Parker, George, fourth earl of Macclesfield (1755–1842).

Macclesfield [Maxfield], **Thomas** (1585–1616), Roman Catholic priest and martyr, was probably born at Chesterton Hall in Staffordshire, the seventh of the eleven children of William Macclesfield (c.1553–1610), gentleman, of Chesterton and Maer, Staffordshire, and his wife, Ursula (c.1557–c.1607), daughter of Francis Roos of Laxton, Nottinghamshire, and Chapel Chorlton parish, Swineshead, Staffordshire. An elder son, Simon, also became a priest. The family's two main residences were Chesterton Hall,

Chesterton, in the parish of Wolstanton, and Maer Hall, Maer, the family seat. The estate at Maer Hall consisted of land comprising some 3000 acres. Thomas Macclesfield's father, William, 'was Catholike, a man of worthy pietie … and who under the reign of two princes was much renowned for his patient sufferance of a long imprisonment, confiscation of all his goods' (*Miscellanea*, 33). In July 1587 he was condemned to death with Erasmus Wolseley of Wolseley Hall and other gentlemen at Stafford assizes for aiding a recusant priest, Robert Sutton. They were also caught attending mass in gaol. The judge reprieved them. William Macclesfield was convicted at least nine times for recusancy, and is said to have spent nineteen years in prison in total.

Thomas Macclesfield 'was nurst and brought into the world, both parents being in prison' (*Miscellanea*, 33). He attended a Staffordshire grammar school. On 16 March 1603 he entered the English College, Douai, with his elder brother Simon. They adopted the alias Field. Thomas also used the alias John Cleaton, probably emanating from the Clayton family of Maer. However, he was sent home for health reasons in 1610. In 1612 he was readmitted to the English College, Douai, and ordained at Arras on 29 March 1614. He was sent to England on 17 July 1615. On arrival he took lodgings in the Strand and went to visit Father Harries, a friend, at the Gatehouse prison in Westminster where he celebrated his first mass in England. He carried out missionary work for three months and was then arrested. He confessed to being a priest and was put in the Gatehouse prison. On 14 June 1616 'a barr of the windowe being broken, he attempted to escape, but alas, whilst he was descending … by a rope … a fellow caught him' (ibid., 33). On recapture he was put in a tiny cell in such a position that he could not stand upright, lie down, or turn over. On 17 June he was moved to Newgate prison. As a result of converting two of his fellow prisoners to his religion, he was put with other recusants.

At the Old Bailey, Macclesfield was indicted under the statute of 27 Elizabeth for having been ordained overseas and acting as a priest in England. At the trial he was convicted of high treason and condemned to death, 'yet had his pardon offer'd, if he would submit to the oath of allegiance, which he … refused' (Dodd, 2.378). In prison he was visited by many persons of distinction and by his mother, his brother Peter, and his sisters. His letters to some of them and to Matthew Kellison were preserved and later given to St Edmund's College, Ware. Despite the intercession of the Spanish ambassador, the count of Gondomar, with James I, he was executed at Tyburn on 1 July 1616. On the night before his execution people decorated the gallows with flowers. When, at his execution, he tried to explain that seminary priests were not traitors, he was silenced and the cart was drawn from under him. He was then hanged, drawn, and quartered. After his death his bones were taken to Spain, where they were venerated as those of a martyr in the family chapel of the count of Gondomar in Galicia. The relics are currently at Downside Abbey, Somerset. His portrait hangs in St Alban's College,

Valladolid. Thomas Macclesfield was one of the 136 martyrs beatified by the pope in 1929. He was beatified as Thomas Maxfield. ANTONY CHARLES RYAN

Sources *Miscellanea III*, Catholic RS, 3 (1906), 30–58 · G. Anstruther, *The seminary priests*, 2 (1975), 214–16 · A. Dunn, 'The pedigree and history of the Macclesfield family', 1994, William Salt Library, Stafford · Gillow, *Lit. biog. hist.* · A. F. Allison and D. M. Rogers, eds., *The contemporary printed literature of the English Counter-Reformation between 1558 and 1640*, 2 (1994), 46, 113 · H. Bowler, *Recusants in the exchequer pipe rolls, 1581–1592*, ed. T. J. McCann, Catholic RS, 71 (1986), 115–19 · C. Dodd [H. Tootell], *The church history of England, from the year 1500, to the year 1688*, 2 (1739), 378–9 · Foster, *Alum. Oxon.*, 1500–1714 · *Calendar of the manuscripts of the most hon. the marquis of Salisbury*, 24 vols., HMC, 9 (1883–1976), vol. 1, p. 576; vol. 4, p. 272 · G. Holt, *St Omers and Bruges colleges, 1593–1773: a biographical dictionary*, Catholic RS, 69 (1979) · T. F. Knox and others, eds., *The first and second diaries of the English College, Douay* (1878) · M. E. Williams, *St Alban's College, Valladolid: four centuries of English Catholic presence in Spain* (1986)
Archives Biblioteca Nacional, Madrid, full account of subject in Latin, dated 4 July 1616, MS 18420
Likenesses portrait, St Alban's College, Valladolid, Spain; repro. in *Miscellanea*, 30

Macclesfield [Mykelfeld], **William of** (d. 1303), Dominican friar and theologian, was presumably born at Macclesfield, near Chester, and probably entered the order at the Chester convent. He studied theology in Paris, where he preached sermons in 1293–4, but he then studied theology at Oxford, under Thomas Sutton, and incepted there as master in 1298. On 11 October 1300 he was licensed to hear confessions in the diocese of Lincoln. On 14 October 1300 Edward I granted him and a confrère safe conduct to go to Rome on Dominican business, and in February 1302 he was among the arbitrators in the dispute between the Dominicans and the chapter of Exeter Cathedral. He was elected diffinitor of the English province by the Dominican provincial chapter held at Bristol in 1302 and in that capacity attended the general chapter at Besançon on 26 May 1303. It was on his return journey from here that he died at Canterbury, presumably some time in the summer, but this news had not reached Rome by 18 December, when Pope Benedict XI made William titular cardinal of Santa Sabina.

Various lost treatises have been attributed to William of Macclesfield on slender evidence, but a number of works survive which there are good grounds to believe are his. Besides sermons (in Kremsmünster, Stadtsbibliothek, MS 83), the questions on the prologue to the *Sentences* (in Bruges, Bibliothèque Communale MS 491; cf. fragments in Bologna, Biblioteca Archiginnasio MS A. 913 for identification) and perhaps those on book 1 are his. Since this commentary defends Aquinas's teaching against the attacks of Henri de Gand and Giles of Rome, it has been suggested that it is the work which, according to the fourteenth-century catalogue of Stams, William wrote 'against the sayings of Henry in which he attacked Thomas' (*Laurentii Pignon*, 60). Two *quaestiones* on angels in the Bruges manuscript (also defending Aquinas) may also, on the evidence of early catalogues, be William's. In Worcester Cathedral Library, MS Q. 99 and Troyes, Bibliothèque Municipale MS 501, are found records of some of William's *quaestiones disputatae*, most of them on the Trinity, including the one that was discussed when he incepted as master.

According to the Stams catalogue William of Macclesfield also wrote *Contra corruptorem Thome*—that is, one of the *Correctoria corruptorii* directed by the Dominicans against the Franciscan William de la Mare's *Correctorium*, his critique of Aquinas's supposedly heretical positions. William's strong advocacy of Aquinas elsewhere makes this testimony very plausible. Pallmon Glorieux, the editor of the *Correctorium 'Sciendum'*, claimed it for William, but this work has now been shown to be by Robert Orford. William may, however, have written the *Correctorium 'Quaestione'* (ed. J. P. Muller, 1954). Although this *Correctorium* must have been written in the early 1280s, almost a decade before the first records of William's activity, it is possible that William of Macclesfield had already studied, taught, and written in England before he went to Paris about 1290.   JOHN MARENBON

Sources D. A. Callus, review of J.-P. Muller, ed., *Le Correctorium corruptorii 'Quaestione'*, *Bulletin Thomiste*, 9 (1954–6), 643–55, esp. 653–5 · A. G. Little and F. Pelster, *Oxford theology and theologians*, OHS, 96 (1934), 270–75 · F. Pelster, 'Theologisch und philosophisch bedeutsam Quästionen des W. von Macclesfield O.P., H von Harclay und anonymer Autoren der englischen Hochscholastik in Cod. 501 Troyes', *Scholastik*, 28 (1953), 222–40 · V. Doucet, 'Commentaires sur les *Sentences*: supplément au répertoire de M. Frédéric Stegmueller', *Archivum Franciscanum Historicum*, 47 (1954), 88–170, esp. 113 · *Laurentii Pignon catalogi et chronica*, ed. G. Meersseman (Rome, 1936), 56–77 · J. Koch, 'Kritische Studien zum Leben Meister Eckharts', *Archivum Fratrum Praedicatorum*, 29 (1959), 5–51, esp. 12–13 · T. Kaeppeli, *Scriptores ordinis praedicatorum medii aevi*, 2 (Rome, 1975), 116–18 · Emden, *Oxf.*, 2.1200–01 · F. J. Roensch, *Early Thomistic school* (1964), 51–7 · *Hist. U. Oxf.* 1: *Early Oxf. schools*, 502–3 · C. H. Lohr, 'Medieval Latin Aristotle commentaries', *Traditio*, 24 (1968), 149–295, esp. 202 · [Robert of Orford], *Le Correctorium corruptorii 'Sciendum'*, ed. P. Glorieux (Paris, 1956) · J. P. Muller, ed., *Le 'Correctorium Corruptorii "Quaestione"'* (1954)
Archives Biblioteca Archiginnasio, Bologna, MS A. 913 · Bibliothèque Communale, Bruges, MS 491 · Bibliothèque Municipale, Troyes, MS 501 · Stadtsbibliothek, Kremsmünster, MS 83 · Worcester Cathedral, MS Q. 99

Mac Cliabhair, Eusebh D. *See* Cleaver, Euseby Digby (1826–1894).

McClintock, Sir (Francis) Leopold (1819–1907), naval officer and Arctic explorer, born at Dundalk, co. Louth, on 8 July 1819, was the eldest son of Henry McClintock, formerly of the 3rd dragoon guards, customs collector of Dundalk, and his wife, Elizabeth Melesina, daughter of the Ven. George Fleury, archdeacon of Waterford. He entered the navy in 1831 and passed his examination in October 1838; but promotion then was slow and uncertain, and McClintock remained a mate nearly seven years. He was promoted lieutenant on 29 July 1845, when serving in the steamer *Gorgon* on the South American station, and a few days later was moved into the sloop *Frolic* (16 guns), on which he served two years in the Pacific. On 7 February 1848 he was appointed to the *Enterprise* (Captain Sir James Clark Ross) for a voyage to the Arctic, and in February 1850 was chosen first lieutenant of the *Assistance*, sailing on a

Sir (Francis) Leopold McClintock (1819–1907), by Stephen Pearce, 1859

similar voyage of discovery. In these expeditions he established his reputation as an Arctic traveller, especially by an unprecedented sledge journey of 760 miles in eighty days in the winter and spring of 1851, when the *Assistance* was frozen up at Griffith Island. On his return home he received his promotion to commander, dated 11 October 1851.

In February 1852 a larger Arctic expedition of five ships was fitted out under the command of Captain Sir Edward Belcher. Two of the ships had auxiliary steam power, and McClintock was given the command of one, the *Intrepid*, which was officially described as tender to the *Resolute* (Captain Kellett), under whose immediate orders he was. The *Intrepid* wintered on the south side of Melville Island, from where many sledge expeditions were sent out. McClintock himself made a journey of 1210 geographical miles in 105 days, during which time he examined and charted the west coast of Prince Patrick Island and Ireland's Eye; Cape Leopold McClintock was named after him. He also made improvements in Arctic sledge travelling. In summer 1854 Belcher decided to abandon the *Intrepid* and three other ships, and the party returned home in the *North Star* and two relief ships.

On 22 October 1854, one day after McClintock received his promotion to captain, the Arctic explorer John Rae arrived back in England with the first certain intelligence of the fate of Sir John Franklin's expedition. The Admiralty was satisfied of the truth of the news and took no action to confirm it, but Lady Franklin determined on a search expedition. For this purpose she bought the yacht

Fox and had her fitted out, principally at her own cost, giving the command to McClintock, who, like the other officers of the expedition, offered his services gratuitously. In 1859 McClintock published an account of this service in *The voyage of the Fox in the Arctic seas: a narrative of the fate of Sir John Franklin and his companions*, a work which went through many editions. The expedition returned to England in 1859, bringing with it the written memorandum of Franklin's death, the abandonment of the ships, and the fate of the whole party. In recognition of his success McClintock was allowed by the Admiralty to count his command of the *Fox* as sea-time, and in 1860 he was knighted.

From February 1861 to December 1862 McClintock commanded the frigate *Doris* in the Mediterranean, and in November 1863 he commissioned the *Aurora* for service with the channel squadron. In her he cruised in the North Sea during the Prussian-Danish War of 1864, and on 9 May of that year, by his presence at Heligoland, prevented the development of what might have been a serious problem in international law. From 1865 he was for three years commodore-in-charge at Jamaica, and on 1 October 1871 he reached flag rank. From April 1872 to May 1877 he served as admiral-superintendent of Portsmouth Dockyard, and on 5 August 1877 was promoted vice-admiral. In November 1879 he was appointed commander-in-chief on the North America and West Indies station, where, with his flag in the *Northampton*, he remained for the customary three years. This was his last active service. In February 1884 he was elected an elder brother of Trinity House, and on 7 July reached admiral, one day before the age for retirement. He was created a KCB in 1891, and was made honorary LLD at Cambridge and Dublin and honorary DCL at Oxford.

McClintock stood for Drogheda at the general election of 1868 but withdrew in consequence of dangerous rioting. In 1870 he married Annette Elizabeth, second daughter of Robert Foster Dunlop of Monasterboice, co. Louth. One son, John William Leopold, also entered the navy. McClintock died in London on 17 November 1907 and was buried at Kensington Hanwell cemetery at Hanwell, Middlesex.   L. G. C. LAUGHTON, *rev.* ROGER MORRISS

Sources C. Markham, *Life of Admiral Sir Leopold McClintock* (1909) · *The Times* (18 Nov 1907) · *The Times* (23 Nov 1907) · *GJ*, 31 (1908) · F. L. McClintock, *The voyage of the Fox in the Arctic seas: a narrative of the fate of Sir John Franklin and his companions* (1859) · O'Byrne, *Naval biog. dict.* · L. H. Neatly, *The search for Franklin* (1970) · E. S. Dodge, *The polar Rosses* (1973) · *WWW* · Kelly, *Handbk*
Archives NA Canada, Arctic journals and papers [copies] · NMM, corresp., journals, log books, and papers · Scott Polar RI, corresp. and meteorological registers | RGS, Franklin search journal [copied material]
Likenesses S. Pearce, oils, 1856, NPG; second version, 1856, NPG · S. Pearce, oils, 1859, NPG [*see illus.*] · J. R. Kirk, marble bust, exh. 1862, Royal Dublin Society · F. Yates, portrait, 1901; in possession of Lady McClintock, 1912 · Lock & Whitfield, woodburytype photograph, NPG; repro. in T. Cooper, *Men of mark: a gallery of contemporary portraits* (1878) · W. H. Mote, stipple, NPG · D. J. Pound, stipple and line engraving, NPG; repro. in D. J. Pound, *Drawing room portrait gallery of eminent personages* (1859–60) · carte-de-visite, NPG · chromolithograph, NPG · photograph, NPG · portrait (after photograph), repro. in Markham, *Life of Admiral Sir Leopold McClintock* · wood-engraving (*The Arctic searching squadron*; after photograph by Beard), NPG; repro. in *ILN* (1 May 1852) · wood-engraving (after photograph by Beard), NPG; repro. in *ILN* (8 Oct 1859)

McCloughry, Edgar James Kingston- (1896–1972), air force officer and author, was born Edgar James McCloughry on 10 September 1896 at Hindmarsh, South Australia, the second son of James Kingston McCloughry, a draper from Larne in Ireland, and his Australian wife, Charlotte Rebecca (*née* Ashton). His elder brother, Air Vice-Marshal Wilfred Ashton McClaughry CB DSO DFC (1894–1943), who changed the spelling of his surname, flew operationally in both world wars.

McCloughry briefly attended Adelaide University and later became a fellow of the South Australian School of Mines and Industries. He was commissioned into the Australian engineers in May 1915, advancing to lieutenant later that year. He went with the Australian Imperial Force in December 1915 to Egypt, then to France, before transferring to the Australian Flying Corps on 24 May 1917. Flying with 23 squadron, he was grounded by an accident, but on 15 April 1918 in France he joined 4 squadron, which was commanded by his brother Wilfred as temporary captain and flight commander. In four months from June he accounted for four balloons and seventeen aircraft. 'A bold and fearless officer, who has performed many gallant deeds of daring' (*London Gazette*, 3 Dec 1918), wounded in action on 31 July, he gained a DFC and bar on 21 September, and was awarded the DSO on 3 December for single-handedly attacking a train and ten enemy machines on 24 September despite being seriously wounded.

On 8 January 1919 McCloughry entered Trinity College, Cambridge; he gained a BA in mechanical sciences in 1920 and after the statutory period an MA. Having settled in England and now known as Kingston-McCloughry, on 5 December 1922 he joined the Royal Air Force as a temporary flight lieutenant, and thirteen days later he was posted for instruction to the School of Naval Co-Operation at Lee-on-Solent, Hampshire. He remained there after qualifying as a marine observer on 15 September 1923. On 16 January 1924, giving his profession as 'of independent means' (m. cert.), in a Congregational chapel near Hanover Square, London, Kingston-McCloughry married Freda Elizabeth (*b.* 1901), second daughter of Sir Alfred Lewis, a banker, of Conebury, Lower Kingswood, Reigate, Surrey. They had two daughters; the marriage ended in divorce.

Confirmed as flight lieutenant on 1 July 1925 and posted to the directorate of scientific research at the Air Ministry on 23 September 1925, Kingston-McCloughry became a student at the RAF Staff College, Andover, on 19 September 1927. Meanwhile, in 1924 he had won first place in the Gordon-Shephard memorial prize essay competition and third (1925) and first (1927) prizes in the R. M. Groves memorial essay competition. While based at Andover he travelled to the United States and produced a report on the United States air services in December 1928. On 12 February 1929 Kingston-McCloughry was posted to the staff of RAF India at Simla, joining 20 (army co-operation) squadron at Peshawar on 24 March 1932. After returning to England, he attended the army Staff College, Camberley, as a student from 21 January 1934, there advanced to squadron leader on 1 October 1934, and graduated at the end of 1935. He went to 4 (army co-operation) squadron at South Farnborough on 16 January 1936 and to the RAF College at Cranwell as an instructor on 4 March 1937; at the latter he became wing commander and assistant commandant on 1 January 1938.

Kingston-McCloughry moved to the directorate of organization at the Air Ministry on 16 January 1939, was promoted group captain on 1 December 1940 and posted to South Africa. Back in England, he commanded 44 group from 1942 to 1943, advancing to temporary air commodore on 1 June 1943. In December 1943 he was appointed chief operational planner for the allied expeditionary air force involved in Operation Overlord. He chaired its bombing committee, which examined Professor Solly Zuckerman's plan to attack the transportation infrastructure in France and the moral implications of collateral damage to civilian personnel and property. Apart from needing to fend off objections from Sir Arthur Harris and the United States air force general Carl Spaatz to diversion of heavy bombers from raids on Germany, Kingston-McCloughry encountered fears from Churchill and the Foreign Office that local French casualties would provide manna for the German propaganda machine. He and Zuckerman conducted an official inquiry into the bombing of Caen on 7 July 1944 following claims that the enemy's fighting capacity had not been significantly affected. They concluded that delay in launching the ground attack undermined the effectiveness of the aerial onslaught.

Kingston-McCloughry became acting air vice-marshal on 1 April 1946 (substantive from 1 July 1947), and sat on committees examining the frontiers of India (1944) and reorganization of its armed forces (1945). He became successively senior air staff officer, RAF India, in April 1946; air officer commanding 18 group and senior air officer, Scotland, in January 1947; senior air staff officer, Fighter Command, 1948–50; air officer commanding, 38 group, in 1950; and chief air defence officer at the Ministry of Defence, 1951–3. He left the RAF on 6 May 1953 to become director of an engineering firm before 'retiring to his Scottish sheep farm' (The Times, 16 Nov 1972).

Kingston-McCloughry was an associate fellow of the Royal Aeronautical Society and a member of the Royal Institute for International Affairs, the Institute of Strategic Studies, and the Oxford and Cambridge Club. He wrote a wide range of books and articles, principally on military aviation, including Winged Warfare (1937), about imperial policing; War in Three Dimensions (1949), on aerial warfare and imperial defence; The Direction of War (1955), on allied decision making during the Second World War; Global Strategy (1957), on Britain and world defence; Defence: Policy and Strategy (1960), calling for a unified British defence policy; and The Spectrum of Strategy (1963), which he dedicated to John F. Kennedy, about the strategic implications of the American nuclear deterrent. Reviewing The Strategic Air Offensive Against Germany, the four-

volume official history, in 1962 Kingston-McCloughry castigated pre-war politicians and staff officers for not facing up 'to the realities of war in which air forces were to take part … The planners in each Service, and often in each separate Command, all too frequently amplified and distorted … basic intelligence to suit their own wishes and requirements'. It was necessary to create an overarching Ministry of Defence: 'The Second World War illustrated the ineptness of three separate Service views of strategy and the waste and inefficiency which could result from the lack of proper co-ordination and co-operation' (Kingston-McCloughry).

Kingston-McCloughry produced, too, a vast number of papers, pamphlets, and reports, not all of them published. He wrote two short works about India between 1929 and 1933, covering his life as a junior officer and the RAF's role in containing disturbances. He was appointed CBE in 1943, and CB in 1950. In later life he lived at Fordel Croft, Glenfarg, Perthshire, and he died at the Royal Infirmary, Edinburgh, on 13 November 1972, 'a trenchant mind and a kind comrade' (The Times, 16 Nov 1972). In his will, he bequeathed his body for medical education. If that proved impossible, there should be a cremation 'privately without the presence of relatives or friends' (Dundee Courier and Advertiser). His papers were left to the Imperial War Museum in London.

From his essays as a junior officer onwards, Kingston-McCloughry self-confidently expounded his views on professional issues. Specifically, the Australian academic Sebastian Ritchie has revealed that at the Air Ministry in 1940 he composed several memoranda criticizing RAF preparations for war, inaccurate aircraft figures submitted to the cabinet, and, in particular, the fitness of chief of the air staff (Air Chief Marshal Sir Cyril Newall) for his post, which found their way into the hands of politicians and newspaper editors. Kingston-McCloughry later defended himself on the grounds of overriding national interest, but advancement rarely visits those who openly criticize senior officers and unofficially consort with politicians. He may therefore have been right to reflect that his failure to be promoted beyond air vice-marshal stemmed from his actions in 1940. He was surely wrong, though, to claim credit for engineering Newall's removal, which owed more to intervention from two former chiefs of the air staff, Sir John Salmond and Lord Trenchard. Kingston-McCloughry wrote widely about warfare in the nuclear age, but so did a vast number of other international figures. His precise influence on policy making in this field, therefore, remains debatable.

JOHN SWEETMAN

Sources Army List · Air Force List · C. Shores and others, Above the trenches: a complete record of the fighter aces and units of the British empire air forces, 1915–1920 (1990) · T. Henshaw, The sky their battlefield: air fighting and the complete list of allied air casualties from enemy action in the first war (1995) · J. Terraine, The right of the line: the Royal Air Force in the European war, 1939–1945 (1985) · E. Kingston-McCloughry, 'The strategic air offensive', Journal of the Royal United Service Institution, 107 (1962), 61–4 · The Times (14 Nov 1972) · The Times (16 Nov 1972) · Dundee Courier and Advertiser (2 Feb 1973) · WWW, 1971–80 · AusDB, vol. 10 · m. cert. · d. cert. · S. Ritchie, 'A political intrigue against the chief of the air staff: the downfall of Air Chief Marshall Sir Cyril Newall', *War and Society*, 16/1 (May 1998), 83–104

Archives IWM, diaries, corresp., and papers | King's Lond., Liddell Hart C., corresp. with Sir B. H. Liddell Hart | FILM IWM FVA, actuality footage

Wealth at death £91,086: *Dundee Courier and Advertiser* · £54,119.89: confirmation, Scotland, 1973

McCluer, John (1759?–1795), hydrographer, joined the Bombay marine as a volunteer about 1777. He was promoted second lieutenant on 18 February 1780 and first lieutenant on 8 January 1784. His hydrographic career probably began in March 1785 when, in the *Scorpion*, he surveyed Muscat and Matruh harbours at the entrance to the Gulf of Oman, a project which he followed by conducting a survey from Muscat to Bushehr. He continued to work in the Persian Gulf in 1786–7, thus enabling Alexander Dalrymple to publish from his surveys a chart extending from the entrance to the Persian Gulf to Basrah. Later in 1787 he made the first comprehensive survey of Bombay harbour, after which he was employed for two years in the *Experiment*, his task being to conduct a detailed survey of the west coast of India; he was assisted by John Proctor in a pattamar, a locally lateen-rigged sailing vessel.

Early in 1790, assisted by Lieutenant John Wedgbrough, McCluer carried out a number of surveys in Laccadive, thus completing a comprehensive survey of the west coast of India from Diu Head to Cape Cormorin. At some stage he also surveyed Mocha Road at the southern end of the Red Sea. On 23 August 1790, when by his own submission he was thirty-one years old, he was sent to the Palau Islands in the *Panther*, with the *Endeavour* (Lieutenant William Drummond) as consort, to inform the king of the death in London of his son, Prince Lee Boo. McCluer first called at several ports to embark seeds, plants, and cattle and to rate his chronometers. His course then took him through Sallawatty Strait between Sallawatty and the western end of the island of New Guinea. He reached the Palau Islands on 21 January 1791, where he broke the news to the king of his son's death. McCluer then proceeded to Macao for supplies, leaving John Proctor in the *Endeavour* (Drummond having died) to commence a survey of the Palau Islands.

McCluer returned to the islands and then sailed for New Guinea with the *Endeavour* to carry out a survey of the western end of the island in accordance with his instructions, during which voyage the *Panther* became the first English vessel for seventy years to call at Amboyna for supplies. Continuing his survey, he discovered an extensive inlet at the south-western end of New Guinea, which was subsequently named McCluer inlet (Teluk Berau). He then followed the south coast of New Guinea to the east as far as Cape Valsche (Ug Salah) before turning south and running a line of soundings, during December 1791 and January 1792, off the north coast of Australia, which he sighted at intervals. His soundings were later incorporated by Matthew Flinders into his small-scale chart of Australia. After calling at Timor, McCluer made for Bencoolen on the west coast of Sumatra to report his discoveries to the East India Company, one of which was that nutmeg grew near

the coast of New Guinea. He returned to the Palau Islands via the island of Sulu, where he embarked grain, seeds, and cattle. On his arrival in the islands on 20 January 1793 McCluer sent Proctor in the *Endeavour* to Macao to inform the court of directors of the East India Company that he intended to remain in the Palau Islands to establish an English settlement. On 2 February he handed over the command of the *Panther* to Wedgbrough, who returned in her to Bombay.

After fifteen months McCluer, who was promoted captain on 27 June 1793, decided to return to the service of the East India Company. Leaving the islands in the *Panther*'s launch, which had been left behind for him, McCluer made a remarkable nineteen-day voyage to Macao. Here he bought the barque *Venus* with the intention of returning in her to Bombay after first calling at the Palau Islands to embark his native wives and family. However, before he could sail Captain John Hayes, a fellow officer in the Bombay marine, arrived in Macao from Batavia with the news that a settlement he had established in Dorey harbour in Geelvink Bay on the north coast of New Guinea was urgently in need of provisions. McCluer was persuaded to undertake its relief. He sailed from Macao on 24 July 1794 and, after calling at the Palau Islands to embark his family, he continued to New Guinea. Having relieved the settlement, McCluer sailed for Bencoolen, calling at Amboyna and Timor *en route*. From here six of his women were taken to Bombay in a Bombay frigate, while he continued to Calcutta. He sailed from the latter port in August 1795 and was never heard of again, the *Venus* having probably foundered in a storm in the Bay of Bengal. In his will, dated 12 February 1793, he made provision for 'a female named Elizabeth Tennel' and 'a child named Margaret by a Malabar mother'.

McCluer was a talented artist and drew many coastal views as aids to navigation during his career. His surveys and views were published by Dalrymple as hydrographer to the East India Company in some forty charts, plans, and sheets of coastal views. His charts of the west coast of India survived as Admiralty charts until the mid-nineteenth century. Dalrymple also published three memoirs giving details of McCluer's surveys in the Persian Gulf and of the west coast of India, while James Horsburgh published McCluer's directions for Mocha and made considerable use of his sailing directions for the west coast of India and the Laccadive Islands in his *India Directory*. ANDREW C. F. DAVID

Sources C. R. Low, *History of the Indian navy, 1613–1863*, 2 vols. (1877) · J. P. Hockin, 'A supplement to the account of the Pelew Islands', in G. Keate, *An account of the Pelew Islands*, 5th edn (1803) · A. Delano, *A narrative of voyages and travels in the northern and southern hemispheres: comprising three voyages round the world; together with a voyage of survey and discovery* (1817) · C. R. Markham, *A memoir on the Indian surveys*, 2nd edn (1878) · I. Lee, *Commodore Sir John Hayes: his voyage and life* (1912) · J. McCluer, 'Journal of a voyage from Bombay to the Pelew Islands, in the E. India Company's ship *Panther*, by Capt John McCluer, 23 Aug 1790–28 Dec 1792 (20 Jan 1793)', BL, Add. MS 19301 · H. T. Fry, *Alexander Dalrymple … and the expansion of British trade* (1970) · H. T. Fry, 'Alexander Dalrymple and New Guinea', *Journal of Pacific History*, 4 (1969), 83–104 · A. Dalrymple, *An … account of the navigation between India and the Gulph of Persia* (1786) ·

A. Dalrymple, *Description of the coast of India (Malabar)* (1789) • A. Dalrymple, *Continuation of the description of the coast of Malabar* (1791) • J. Horsburgh, *India directory, or, Directions for sailing to and from the East Indies*, 2 vols., 3rd edn (1826) • A. Dunlop, *A memorabilia of the McClures* (1972) • will, 12 Feb 1793, BL OIOC, L/AG/34/29/342
Archives BL, 'Journal of a voyage from Bombay to the Pelew Islands, in the E. India Company's ship *Panther* by Capt John McCluer 23 Aug 1790–28 Dec 1792', Add. MS 19301 • BL, manuscript chart of the island of Geby (Gebe), Add. MS 33765, fol. 42 • Hydrographic Office, Taunton, manuscript charts of his Persian Gulf and Palau Islands surveys | NL Scot., Melville MSS
Wealth at death provision for Elizabeth Tennel and child by Malabar mother; had sent £500 home to mother: will, BL OIOC, L/AG/34/29/342

McClung [*née* Mooney], **Nellie Letitia** (1873–1951), suffragist and writer, was born at Chatsworth, Grey county, Ontario, Canada, on 20 October 1873, the youngest of seven children and the third daughter of John Mooney (*c*.1813–1893), an Irish immigrant farmer and his Scottish-born wife, Letitia McCurdy. Her father's Methodism competed with her mother's sterner Presbyterianism to produce a lively household. When hard work failed to make the farm profitable, the family sought free homesteads in the new province of Manitoba in 1880. As the first volume of McClung's autobiography, *The Clearing in the West* (1937), makes clear, the Mooneys were part of a frontier of European imperialism, matter-of-factly displacing indigenous and mixed-race peoples. Self-confident farmers, they set the stage for the western challenge to Canadian politics dominated by Ontario and Quebec.

A much loved child, Nellie Mooney grew up determined to challenge limits on women and westerners, going so far, in siding with her sister Hannah, as to defend métis grievances during the 1885 north-west rebellion. A keen Methodist, she became a youthful critic of male privilege and abuse, particularly alcohol-fuelled violence against women and children. Nellie Mooney was late in starting school but by 1890 she had earned a second-class teaching certificate, attended the Winnipeg Normal School, and started teaching, first at a one-room rural Manitoba schoolhouse. In 1894 she gained her first-class certificate. She immersed herself in local affairs as a teacher, active Methodist, and member of the Woman's Christian Temperance Union, the leading women's organization of the day and, in its critique of male violence and early endorsement of women's enfranchisement, among the most radical. She soon experimented with capturing her observations in non-fiction and short stories. In (Robert) Wesley McClung, the pharmacist son of an active member of the Woman's Christian Temperance Union and a Methodist minister, she also found a lifelong soulmate. When they wed in 1896, like other married women she had to abandon teaching.

As a wife and mother to four children born between 1897 and 1911, Nellie McClung juggled domestic responsibilities with writing and reform commitments. She and her busy household relied on immigrant domestics, whose contributions were gratefully acknowledged in the second volume of her autobiography, *The Stream Runs Fast* (1945). She drew on her own family life to conclude that

Nellie Letitia McClung (1873–1951), by C. Jessop

women had special responsibility and capacity for nurture and care. Men should be encouraged to develop such qualities but McClung counted on the exercise, in private and public life, of supposedly universal maternal sensibilities to provide a more balanced and better world.

Living in the small town of Manitou until 1911, Nellie McClung was active in the influential Christian social gospel movement with its efforts to uplift the nation's material and spiritual life and the suffrage crusade with its questioning of male authority in everything from homestead rights to employment. Friends included James Shaver Woodsworth of Winnipeg's All People's Mission and the *Winnipeg Free Press* columnists Cora Hind and Lillian Beynon Thomas. Like many other women writers she added to family resources by selling short stories and reviews for children and adults. These provided the genesis for her first Canadian best-seller, *Sowing Seeds in Danny* (1908), which saw her touring western towns. This inspirational story, the first in an eventual trilogy (*The Second Chance*, 1910, and *Purple Springs*, 1921), focuses on a youthful prairie heroine, Pearlie Watson, who reforms the hard-hearted of her community and in the process rescues unfortunate victims. By 1910 McClung was speaking before Ontario audiences and sharing a Toronto platform with Ethel Snowden, a noted British suffragist. While she was increasingly linked to a wider world, her early stories, and many later as well, drew inspiration from the virtues of farm and small town Canada. She nevertheless remained keenly aware of the dangers of rural isolation and poverty.

In 1911 Nellie McClung moved to Winnipeg, Manitoba's booming capital, where her husband took employment with an insurance company. Welcomed by friends and readers, she quickly moved to the forefront of the province's suffrage and temperance movements, entertaining the visiting English suffragette Emmeline Pankhurst in her home in 1911. Allied with like-minded women and men, she founded Manitoba's Political Equality League. A quick wit, that produced devastating comic caricatures of the powerful, won her a national and continent-wide reputation. After the 1912 publication of the short story collection, *The Black Creek Stopping-House*, she turned for almost a decade from fiction to concentrate more directly on reform causes. The provincial Conservative government of Sir Rodmund Roblin, with its resistance to prohibition and suffrage, was an easy target. When the premier remained unmoved by a 1913 suffrage delegation, as by the plight of women and girls working in Winnipeg's sweatshops, McClung lampooned him in a triumphant women's parliament in the city's largest theatre. A move to Alberta in 1914 meant that McClung did not get the cabinet post, that had been predicted, upon Roblin's defeat a year later. She did, however, immediately become active in Alberta's feminist and temperance politics and barnstormed both Canada and the United States as one of the most popular of suffrage speakers. By the time that Manitoba, Alberta, and Saskatchewan brought in the provincial franchise in 1916, followed by British Columbia and Ontario in 1917, and Ottawa introduced the federal franchise, partially in 1917 and somewhat more completely in 1919, McClung was the best-known national campaigner.

Like many liberal-minded Canadians, McClung was deeply ambivalent about the First World War. Only when she concluded that Germany was morally bankrupt and that Canadians could use the war to re-energize democracy, self-sacrifice, and co-operation, did she support conscription. Her speeches and essays published as *In Times Like These* (1915) constitute a classic document of the first feminist movement. A trenchant mixture of the ironic, the comedic, and the serious, this volume engages feminism in a brilliant dissection of the ideas of leading antifeminists such as the McGill University humorist Stephen Leacock and Britain's Sir Almroth Wright. *The Next-of-Kin* (1917), written after the enlistment of her eldest son, expresses her faith that war's dreadful costs would usher in the land of the fair deal. McClung's hopes for an all-out war effort explain her support for the union government of Sir Robert Borden but, objecting to its distinction between British and foreign-born citizens, she opposed the Wartime Elections Act of 1917. In early 1918 she participated in Ottawa's women's war conference and celebrated federal prohibition as a war measure that March.

Dry Canada did not long survive but Nellie McClung remained optimistic about women voters. Elected to the Alberta legislature as a prohibitionist Liberal in 1921–6 for the city of Edmonton, she joined an erstwhile suffrage ally, Irene Parlby, minister without portfolio in the United Farmers of Alberta government, in championing a minimum wage for women, mothers' pensions, and equality in divorce and citizenship. A move to Calgary contributed to McClung's defeat in 1926 and she never again held public office. She did, however, join with Henrietta Muir Edwards, Irene Parlby, Emily Murphy, and Louise McKinney as the 'Famous Five' in successfully petitioning the judicial committee of the privy council to recognize women as 'persons' for the purpose of appointment to the Canadian senate. Her activism went well beyond such politics. A dedicated Methodist and, after 1925, United church member, she joined the Canadian delegation to the ecumenical Methodist conference in London in 1921 and insisted on women's right to ordination, a dream unrealized until 1936.

McClung also kept writing. Fiction and non-fiction for newspapers and magazines joined two volumes of autobiography and other books: *When Christmas Crossed 'the Peace'* (1923), *The Beauty of Martha* (1923), *Painted Fires* (1925), *All We Like Sheep and other Stories* (1926), *Be Good to Yourself* (1931), *Flowers for the Living* (1931), *Leaves from Lantern Lane* (1936), and *More Leaves from Lantern Lane* (1937). While slighted by modernist interpreters of the Canadian literary canon, McClung's works are increasingly recognized for their anti-romanticism and domestic realism.

In 1932 McClung and her husband made their last move, to Victoria, British Columbia. Gardening, friendships, and travel kept her busy but she kept up her social commentary in newspaper columns and on public platforms. In 1936 she accepted an appointment to the board of governors of the new Canadian Broadcasting System and in 1938 she joined the Canadian delegation to the League of Nations. While critical of many radical unionists and communists, she also despised xenophobia and championed the poor, Dukhobors and Japanese in Canada, and Jews in Europe. A supporter of the Oxford Group and Moral Re-Armament in the 1930s, she fought failing health in the 1940s and concentrated on completing her autobiography and periodical writing. She never relinquished her enthusiasm for women's rights, supporting day-care, contraception, and equal wages until her death in Victoria, British Columbia, on 1 September 1951. She was buried on 5 September in Victoria. Her husband survived her.

VERONICA STRONG-BOAG

Sources M. Hallett and M. Davis, *Firing the heather: the life and times of Nellie McClung* (1994) • R. R. Warne, *Literature as pulpit: the Christian social activism of Nellie L. McClung* (1993) • N. L. McClung, *In times like these*, ed. V. Strong-Boag (1992) • *Stories subversive: through the field with the gloves off. Short fiction by Nellie L. McClung*, ed. M. I. Davies (1996)
Archives Provincial Archives of British Columbia, Victoria
Likenesses C. Jessop, photograph, NA Canada [*see illus.*] • photographs, British Columbia Archives and Records Service, Victoria, British Columbia, Canada

McClure, Sir John David (1860–1922), schoolmaster, was born at Wigan, Lancashire, on 9 February 1860, the eldest son of John McClure (d. 1904) of Wigan, a Congregational businessman whose ancestors came originally from Skye. His mother was Elizabeth (d. 1871), daughter of James

Hyslop, who came from Kirkcudbrightshire and who lived for a time at Wigan. He was educated at Holly Mount College, near Bury (1874–6), and at Owens College, Manchester (1876–7), graduating with a London University BA degree in 1878. He took up schoolteaching in order to finance his further studies, becoming an assistant master at Holly Mount (1877–8) and at Hinckley grammar school, Leicestershire (1878–82). During this period music became, as it remained, one of the dominant influences in his life. In 1882 he won a sizarship at Trinity College, Cambridge, where he read for the mathematical tripos and gave much time to the work of the Nonconformist Union, to lay preaching in neighbouring free churches, and to music; he took his degree with a second class in 1885, but, remaining a further year at Trinity (as Walker prizeman), graduated LLB in 1886 (LLD, 1897), and entered the Inner Temple, where he was called to the bar in 1890. His marriage on 15 July 1889 to Mary, the daughter of James Johnstone, a Scottish businessman living at Holcombe, Lancashire, with whom he had one son and two daughters, made a settled career necessary. The free church ministry, the law, music, or education were all open to him as professions: he chose the last, and after five years (1885–91) of extramural lecturing for the Cambridge University extension syndicate he was appointed headmaster of Mill Hill School in 1891. He also held, from 1889 to 1894, the chair of astronomy at Queen's College, London.

McClure remained at Mill Hill until the end of his life, and saw it grow from a comparatively unknown nonconformist school of sixty boys into a successful public school, with over 300 names on its books. His impressive personality, his remarkable memory for names and faces, his sense of humour, and his unfailing fund of stories, of which he was a born raconteur, made him a popular and effective figure not only in the school but in wide circles outside. He moved in many such circles, as an educationist, a musician, and one of the leading free churchmen of his time.

McClure, who regretted that there were very few free churchmen among the headmasters of secondary schools in England, took a prominent part in educational bodies, though he avoided becoming publicly involved in the nonconformists' campaign against the 1902 Education Act. In 1900 he was elected a member of the senate of London University and in 1902 a member of the council of Mansfield College, Oxford; he was joint honorary secretary of the Incorporated Association of Headmasters from 1904 to 1912, president in 1914–15, and treasurer from 1920 to 1922. He strongly believed in a unified teaching profession, and tried to bridge the divisions between secondary and elementary teachers. Partly through his contacts with Robert Morant, the Teachers' Registration Council, with a single register of teachers, was brought into being in 1912. For his services to education he was knighted in 1913.

McClure became a MusB of London University in 1903, a DMus in 1909, was elected to the corporation of Trinity College of Music in 1906, and became its chairman in 1920. The Congregational Union elected him chairman in 1919,

and he was largely responsible for compiling its new hymnal between 1909 and 1916. He received the freedom of the borough of Wigan in 1920. During the First World War he served on many local committees and did valuable work in the interests of teachers on the Professional Classes War Relief Council, of which he was a founder. In 1921 he was invited to stand as a university representative in the House of Commons, but his health was beginning to fail. He died at Mill Hill, after a week's illness, on 18 February 1922, and was survived by his wife.

McClure's chief work was the making of Mill Hill School. But he made, also, important contributions to the educational, musical, and religious life of his time, all marked by a broad-mindedness and a devotion to truth which were characteristic. His open-minded attitude towards the Church of England sometimes distanced him from the stricter free church circles, but made him an effective advocate of the cause of reunion between the churches. After the war, which he had regarded as necessary to resist German militarism, though he loathed jingoism and the arms trade, he became a strong supporter of the League of Nations. Sociable and ready to take up causes, he was much in demand for committee work. His power of marshalling facts and of presenting a balanced and reasoned case made him a telling advocate, and some of his most effective public work was done as a mediator in difficult situations. He wrote no books, but contributed an article, 'Preparation for practical life', to *Cambridge Essays on Education* (1917), edited by A. C. Benson; as he said in a speech addressed to the old boys of Mill Hill School: 'If I have written no books ... my writings are happily more lasting, and they are round about me.'

M. L. JACKS, *rev.* M. C. CURTHOYS

Sources [K. M. J. Ousey], *McClure of Mill Hill: a memoir* (1927) · private information (1937) · Venn, *Alum. Cant.* · Walford, *County families* (1919)

Likenesses F. Yates, oils, 1912 · Alfieri Picture Service, photograph, 1920, repro. in Ousey, *McClure of Mill Hill* · Estelle, photograph, 1920, repro. in Ousey, *McClure of Mill Hill* · J. Russell & Sons, photograph, repro. in Ousey, *McClure of Mill Hill*, frontispiece

Wealth at death £9016 13s. 9d.: probate, 24 March 1922, *CGPLA Eng. & Wales*

McClure, Sir Robert John Le Mesurier (1807–1873), naval officer, son of Robert McClure (*d.* 1806), captain in the 89th regiment, and his wife, Jane, daughter of Archdeacon Elgee, rector of Wexford, Ireland, was born at Wexford on 28 January 1807, five months after his father's death. Captain John Le Mesurier of Alderney, Channel Islands, an old comrade of his father, was his godfather and guardian. McClure was educated at Eton College and the Royal Military College, Sandhurst, and entered the navy in 1824. He passed his examination in 1830, and in 1836–7 was mate of the *Terror* in her Arctic voyage under Captain George Back. On the return of the *Terror* in September 1837 McClure was promoted lieutenant. In 1838–9 he served on board the *Niagara* (20 guns), the flagship of Commodore Sandom, on the Great Lakes in Canada during the uprising; and from 1839 to 1842 he was in the *Pilot* (16 guns) in the West Indies. From 1842 to 1846 he commanded the *Romney*, receiving

Sir Robert John Le Mesurier McClure (1807–1873), by Stephen Pearce, 1855

ship at Havana. In December 1846 he was appointed to the coastguard, which he left in 1848 to go as first lieutenant of the *Investigator* with Captain Bird in the Arctic expedition of Sir James Clark Ross. On Ross's return in autumn 1849 it was at once decided to send the same two ships to renew the search for Sir John Franklin by way of the Bering Strait. Captain Richard Collinson was appointed to the *Enterprise* as senior officer of the expedition, and McClure, who had shown energy and resourcefulness, was promoted on 4 November 1849 to the command of the *Investigator*.

The ships sailed from Plymouth on 20 January 1850. As they passed into the Pacific on 16 April they were separated in a gale and did not meet again. When McClure arrived off Honolulu on 1 July, he found that the *Enterprise* had gone on ahead of him, having been fearful of losing the short remains of the summer. The *Investigator* sailed for the north on 4 July and joined the *Plover* in Kotzebue Sound, Alaska, on 29 July. The *Enterprise* had then got into a streak of contrary winds and was a fortnight behind. McClure had faint hope of meeting her at the next rendezvous, off Cape Lisburne; and on departing from Kotzebue Sound he left a letter for the Admiralty explaining the course he proposed to follow in the event of not meeting the *Enterprise*.

The *Investigator* fell in with the *Herald* some 30 miles past Cape Lisburne, but though Captain Kellett did not think that the *Enterprise* had passed, and suggested that the *Investigator* had better wait, he would not order her to do so. McClure therefore went on alone, until his progress was

stopped by the firm ice of Melville Sound. He was compelled to turn southward, and by 10 October had completed the arrangements for wintering in Prince of Wales Strait. He journeyed along the coast of Banks Island and arrived at its north-eastern extremity on 26 October, where he climbed a hill some 600 feet high and looked across the ice to Melville Island and to 'Parry's farthest'— the furthest point reached by Sir William Edward Parry in 1820. No land lay between. The north-west passage was discovered. It was not until several years later that it was known that Franklin and his companions had discovered another passage more than four years before.

In summer 1851 McClure, finding it impossible to advance into Melville Sound, retraced his steps, hoping to be able to cross Banks Strait to 'Parry's farthest'. However, the strait was then as impassable as it has always been found, and on 23 September the *Investigator* was forced into a bay on the northern shore of Banks Island, which, with a sense of immediate relief, McClure named the Bay of Mercy. The ship remained there.

In April 1852 McClure, with a sledge party, succeeded in crossing the strait and actually arriving at Winter Harbour on Melville Island. He found a notice of Lieutenant Francis Leopold McClintock's having been there the previous June, but no stores nor news of probable relief. The summer of 1852 passed and the *Investigator* was still blocked up in the Bay of Mercy. Provisions were running short, the men were falling ill, and McClure had made his arrangements for abandoning the ship in April 1853, when on the 6th Lieutenant Bedford Pim of the *Resolute* reached them from Melville Island. McClure's first idea was to get what relief was possible from the *Resolute*, and remain, in the hopes of getting the *Investigator* free in the course of the summer. He crossed over to Melville Island to consult with Kellett, but after a medical survey of the *Investigator*'s crew it was resolved that further stay was inadvisable and that the ship must be abandoned. The men were therefore conveyed across the ice to the *Resolute*. The season, however, proved very unfavourable. The *Resolute* was unable to get to the eastward, and the *Investigator*'s men thus passed a fourth winter in the ice. In April 1854 they were transferred to the *North Star* and finally arrived in England on 28 September. The news of their safety and of their great discovery had been brought home by Lieutenant Cresswell in the *Phoenix* (Captain Inglefield) in the previous October.

McClure was, as a matter of form, court-martialled for the loss of his ship, and honourably acquitted. He was knighted on 21 November 1855 and promoted captain (commission dated back to 18 December 1850). In the session of 1855 parliament awarded a grant of £10,000 to the officers and crew of the *Investigator*.

In 1856 McClure was appointed to the *Esk* for service on the Pacific station. In the following year he brought her to China to reinforce the squadron there, and in December commanded a battalion of the naval brigade at the capture of Canton (Guangzhou). He was afterwards for some time senior officer in the Strait of Malacca, was made a CB on 20 May 1859, and returned to England in 1861. He had no further service, but was promoted rear-admiral on 20

March 1867, and vice-admiral, on the retired list, on 29 May 1873. In 1869 he married Constance Ada, daughter of Richard H. Tudor of Birkenhead, Cheshire.

McClure, according to the navigator and writer Sherard Osborn, who knew him well, was cool and bold in all perils, a severe disciplinarian, yet modest, and would in war have been a great leader. McClure died at his home, 25 Duke Street, St James's, London, on 17 October 1873 and was buried on the 25th in Kensal Green cemetery. His wife survived him. J. K. LAUGHTON, *rev.* ROGER MORRISS

Sources 'Our portrait gallery, no. LXXII', *Dublin University Magazine*, 43 (1854), 334–58 • O'Byrne, *Naval biog. dict.* • *Journal of the Royal Geographical Society*, 44 (1874), cxxxix • *The Times* (21 Oct 1873) • *The Times* (22 Oct 1873) • *The Times* (27 Oct 1873) • R. J. le M. McClure, *The discovery of a north-west passage by HMS Investigator*, ed. S. Osborn, 4th edn (1865) • A. Armstrong, *A personal narrative of the discovery of the north-west passage: ... five years' continuous service in the Arctic regions ... in search of the expedition under Sir John Franklin* (1857) • S. Cresswell, *Eight sketches of the voyage of HMS Investigator* (1854) • Boase, *Mod. Eng. biog.* • C. Holland, *Arctic exploration and development, c. 500 BC to 1915: an encyclopedia* (1994) • T. H. Levere, *Science and the Canadian Arctic: a century of exploration, 1818–1918* (1993) • M. Graf, *Arctic journeys: a history of exploration for the north-west passage* (1992) • *CGPLA Eng. & Wales* (1873)
Archives NMM, corresp. and papers | PRO, letters to Sir John Ross, BJ2
Likenesses lithograph, pubd 1854, NPG • S. Pearce, oils, 1855, NPG [*see illus.*] • engraving, repro. in *The Graphic*, 8 (1873), 412
Wealth at death under £9000: administration, 29 Nov 1873, *CGPLA Eng. & Wales*

McCluskie, Samuel Joseph (1932–1995), trade unionist, was born into a Roman Catholic family at 97 St Andrew Street, Leith, on 11 August 1932, son of James McCluskie, riveter and later barman, and his wife, Agnes McHenry. Sent to the local St Mary's primary school and to Holy Cross Academy, Edinburgh, he left without academic qualifications. 'I played truant because I hated school', he explained. 'We received corporal punishment for truancy so I decided the only way to avoid punishment was not to go back to school at all' (*The Independent*, 18 Sept 1995). He began an apprenticeship with George Gibson of Leith, and worked in trawler engine rooms before doing his national service with the army (the navy found him 'too fat') and going to Korea. On demobilization, he spent a year 'mucking about in Japan' (*Daily Telegraph*, 18 Sept 1995)—a formative experience which bred a passionate belief in workers' co-operation, and co-operation with well-intentioned employers. He returned home to nine months' unemployment, before joining the Union Castle Line in 1955 as a ship's steward, soon becoming ship's chef instead. His travels were a political education: South African apartheid, Latin American right-wing dictatorships, and eastern bloc left-wing ones all earned his suspicion and dislike. On 29 September 1961 he married Alice Lowrie Fletcher, *née* Potter (*b.* 1925/6), a widowed bonded warehouse worker. They had a daughter and two sons, one of whom died young.

McCluskie was first spotted by the National Union of Seamen (NUS) in 1960 when he was involved in an unofficial strike. He was persuaded to become a branch delegate in 1963 after complaining about an increase in union dues, and in 1964 he became a land-based full-time official, living in Bo'ness, West Lothian, and representing Grangemouth and the east coast of Scotland. He spent some years as a branch secretary in ports around the country, from Plymouth, to Liverpool (where he consolidated his position during the strike of 1966), to Hull (where he spotted the young John Prescott), before arriving at Maritime House, Clapham, the union's headquarters, as a national organizer in 1969. Supported by Catholic moderates and soft left Tribunites, he made an early bid for the general secretaryship of the union in 1974, but was beaten by the hard left candidate, Jim Slater. He became assistant general secretary in 1976.

Baulked of the job he wanted, McCluskie threw himself into Labour Party politics, and won a seat on the party's national executive committee in the same year, which he kept until his death, also serving as treasurer (1984–92). He was party chairman in 1983 at the nadir of the Labour Party's fortunes, and chaired the party conference in Brighton that year. Bullying, cajoling, charming the delegates by turn, with all the skills accumulated during interminable rough trade-union meetings, McCluskie played an important part in bringing the party back from the edge of oblivion. He was an authentic working-class leader, whose style was breezy, blunt, and unmalicious, although he could be blazingly angry, whereupon his language became both picturesque and unprintable.

In 1986 McCluskie achieved his old ambition, and was elected general secretary of the NUS. 'Sam the Man' was a skilled fixer and classic operator in 'smoke-filled rooms'; he was viewed by employers and arbitrators as a moderate, a man with whom business could be done, despite his public stance of unbending socialism and contempt for shipowners. Behind the scenes he sought to avoid confrontation with P. & O. in 1988, but when the strike began, he took a high-profile role. The protracted and increasingly bitter strike began after 2000 members of the NUS in Belfast and Dover rejected new contracts and were served with dismissal notices. The British merchant shipping industry was in trouble, and the P. & O. chairman, Sir Jeffrey Stirling (a friend of the prime minister, Margaret Thatcher), took advantage of the anti-union legislation of recent years to force a confrontation with the NUS. When McCluskie announced a ballot of his members for a national strike in support of the sacked men, a High Court judge ruled that the union's assets could be seized. McCluskie insisted on holding the ballot, a strike was called, and in May 1988 the union was fined heavily. The union's assets were sequestered, and it was evicted from Maritime House: McCluskie then conducted the strike from the Prince of Wales pub (which he called 'our annexe') opposite Maritime House. In July the threat of a second, heavier fine forced the NUS to withdraw support from its members' main picket at Dover, and the strike collapsed. Within two years, the financial state of the NUS and dwindling membership led the union into a merger with the National Union of Railwaymen. McCluskie served as executive officer of the amalgamated Rail, Maritime and Transport Union for a year (1990–91) before he retired quietly, having suffered poor health for some time. He died from cancer in St Columba's Hospice, Edinburgh, on 15 September 1995, survived by his wife.

TAM DALYELL

Sources personal knowledge (2004) · *The Independent* (18 Sept 1995) · *Daily Telegraph* (18 Sept 1995) · *The Times* (18 Sept 1995) · *The Guardian* (18 Sept 1995) · *The Scotsman* (18 Sept 1995) · b. cert. · m. cert. · d. cert. · *CCI* (1995)
Likenesses photograph, repro. in *The Independent*
Wealth at death £49,250.33: confirmation, 27 Dec 1995, *CCI*

McCoan, James Carlile (1829–1904), politician and journalist, born at Dunlow, co. Tyrone, on 14 July 1829, was the only son of Clement McCoan of Charlemont, Armagh, and his wife, Sarah, daughter of James Carlile of Culresoch, Moy. After education at Dungannon School and at Homerton College, London, he matriculated at University College, London, in 1848. He entered the Middle Temple in November 1851, but did not seek to practise the law in England. Instead, he turned to journalism, and acted as war correspondent for the *Daily News* during the Crimean War. At the end of the conflict he travelled in Georgia and Circassia, and afterwards settled at Constantinople. On 2 June 1857 he married Augusta Janet, youngest daughter of William Jenkyns of Elgin, with whom he had a son and a daughter.

McCoan practised in the supreme consular court in Constantinople until 1864, and founded and edited the first English-language newspaper in Turkey, the *Levant Herald*. The paper was for a time subsidized by the British government, until in 1870 McCoan disposed of it—apparently under pressure from the Turkish authorities—and returned to England. He proceeded to publish several works on Egypt, which he had visited during his Levantine sojourn: *Consular Jurisdiction in Turkey and Egypt* (1873), *Egypt as it is* (1877), and *Egypt under Ismail* (1889). He also contributed to *Fraser's Magazine* articles on Turkey, which he published as *Our New Protectorate: Turkey in Asia, its Geography, Races, Resources, and Government* (2 vols., 1879).

In April 1880 McCoan stood for parliament for Drogheda as a home-ruler, but was unsuccessful. The following month he was elected for county Wicklow as a Parnellite. In January 1881 he took part in the home-rulers' filibustering over the introduction of an Irish coercion act—Henry Lucy observed that if the length and 'unrelieved dulness' of his speech were typical of his outpourings, it was small wonder that the Turks, a proverbially patient people, had 'politely, but firmly' invited the editor of the *Levant Herald* 'to go away' (Lucy, 117)—and he was one of those suspended by the speaker. Subsequently, however, he voted against the Parnellites on the second reading of the Land Bill, and was censured by his party, from which he eventually resigned in 1883. He thereafter gave independent support to the government, and stood unsuccessfully as a Gladstonian Liberal at Lancaster in 1885, at Southampton in 1886, and at Macclesfield in 1892.

McCoan died at his residence, 42 Campden Hill Square, Kensington, on 13 January 1904 and was buried at Kensal Green. His wife survived him by only five days.

G. LE G. NORGATE, *rev.* K. D. REYNOLDS

Sources *The Times* (15 Jan 1904) · *Daily News* (16 Jan 1904) · H. W. Lucy, *A diary of two parliaments*, 2 (1886) · R. F. Foster, *Charles Stewart Parnell: the man and his family* (1976) · private information (1912)
Wealth at death £16,216 17s.: probate, 2 March 1904, *CGPLA Eng. & Wales*

Maccoby, Chaim Zundel (1858–1916), Zionist and preacher, was born near the town of Kobrin, Poland, the son of 'Simche'. Little is known of his parents, except that they were poor, devoutly Orthodox Jews. Maccoby had a thoroughly religious education, studying Talmudic subjects first in Kobrin and later in Brisk and Prusznin, where he delved into secular subjects; and he became a rabbi. At the age of sixteen Maccoby married Hannah Blumah Belber (*d.* 1921), whose parents lived in Prusznin. There were four sons and four daughters of the marriage.

As a rabbinical authority Maccoby was not in the first rank. But his powers as an orator were widely recognized, and he found himself in demand as a preacher of extraordinary charisma. In 1874 he accepted a call to become the *maggid* (or preacher) of the town of Kamenitsk, and though his sojourn there was little more than two years he became known thereafter as the Kamenitsker *Maggid*.

Maccoby had many followers, but he made many enemies, both among anti-Zionist Orthodox rabbis and within the Russian government of Poland. Though not a supporter of political Zionism, which sought to re-establish a Jewish nation state in the Holy Land (an ambition which he regarded as heretical), he was none the less an early adherent of the Chovevi Zion ('Lovers of Zion') movement, which merely supported Jewish settlement in Palestine. In 1883 he became the first full-time preacher for Chovevi Zion, and spent the next six years travelling widely in Russia, Poland, and Lithuania to gather support for the cause. This peripatetic activity became highly controversial, the more so as he had no compunction about censuring fellow rabbis for having failed to do anything to alleviate the condition of Jews living under tsarist rule. The Russian authorities eventually forbade his lecturing activities, and in January 1890 he fled with his family to England, where he had previously agreed to serve as rabbi of a small congregation in London's East End.

Maccoby's arrival in London coincided with a number of developments central to the future direction of London Jewry. The practicality of Jewish settlement in Palestine was a matter of wide discussion, and Maccoby played a part in the formation of an English branch of Chovevi Zion in London in April 1890. Militant socialism was spreading among the Jewish poor of the East End. Maccoby preached the virtues of Chovevi Zion, but also spoke out against the vices of socialism and atheism. His ability to draw crowds to his lectures was evident. In 1892 Samuel Montagu, the Liberal MP for Whitechapel and founder (1887) of the Federation of Synagogues in east London, suggested that he finance Maccoby's appointment as official *maggid* of the federation. Maccoby accepted the post in February 1894 and retained it until his death.

Maccoby's task, for which Montagu had appointed him, was to counter the propaganda of socialists and atheists.

In 1895 Theodor Herzl, the founder of political Zionism, made the first of several visits to England, where his ideas found enthusiastic audiences among the Yiddish-speaking refugees. Herzlian Zionists established the English Zionist Federation; in December 1902 the English branch of Chovevi Zion was wound up. Maccoby regarded Herzl as a false messiah, and his movement as a threat to the preservation of Orthodox Jewish values. But in his bitter opposition to Herzl we may detect more than a vague hint of wounded pride. He spoke out ever more vehemently against Herzl, the self-confessed atheist, and his followers, refusing to preach at one federation synagogue because it dared to host a branch of the Zionist Federation. Maccoby's relationship with Montagu and the Federation of Synagogues deteriorated, and he seems to have withdrawn from social gatherings, offering his strict vegetarianism as a pretext. In 1910 his health began to break down. He died of kidney disease at his home, 4 St Agnes Terrace, South Hackney, London, on 4 April 1916, and was buried at the Edmonton cemetery of the Federation of Synagogues. A collection of Maccoby's sermons was published in 1929 under the title *Chayim* ('Life').

GEOFFREY ALDERMAN

Sources J. Jung, *Champions of orthodoxy* (1974) · G. Alderman, *The Federation of Synagogues, 1887–1987* (1987) · d. cert.
Archives Federation of Synagogues, minute books and papers
Likenesses photograph, repro. in Jung, *Champions of orthodoxy* · photograph, repro. in Alderman, *Federation of Synagogues*

MacCodrum, Iain [John] (1693?–1779), Scottish Gaelic poet, was born at Aird an Runnair in North Uist, the son of Farquhar MacCodrum (*d. c.*1740), a crofter. MacCodrum lived in various locations in North Uist throughout his life. Apart from a youthful satirical piece, there are no dated poems ascribed to him until the late 1740s. Two of his poems appeared, without acknowledgement, in Alasdair Mac Mhaighstir Alasdair's collection of 1751. He had apparently been visited by his famous contemporary, who came again about 1755, when the two poets recited scurrilous songs at a local gathering attended by the Revd Donald MacQueen, and remembered in local tradition.

In 1760 James Macpherson, on one of his tours collecting Ossianic balladry, visited MacCodrum, who had a large fund of traditional verse and story, but Macpherson's companion took umbrage at MacCodrum's humorous slighting of his brand of Gaelic, and they left without milking this rich source of lore. In 1763 Sir James MacDonald of Sleat, baronet, met MacCodrum in Uist, and appointed him as his family bard, giving him a rent-free holding of land, and annual quantities of meal and cheese, and a small annual payment. MacDonald listened regularly to MacCodrum's recitations of Ossianic verse, and tried to improve his own knowledge of Gaelic. No doubt this sequence of events was triggered by the public prominence of James Macpherson's work at that time.

After his appointment MacCodrum composed a series of songs in praise of Sir James MacDonald and other chiefs and lairds, and an elegy for Sir James in 1766. Sir James's successor continued to pay the bard's emoluments, and MacCodrum travelled to neighbouring islands, and to

Skye, meeting the descendants of the famous Mac-Mhuirich poets in South Uist, and Captain Allan MacDonald, husband of the famous Flora, in Skye. MacCodrum died in 1779 and was buried in North Uist. He had been married three times, and was survived by his third wife, Mary Robertson, and by a daughter.

MacCodrum's poetry was widely known in his home island, and his twentieth-century editor, William Matheson, reported that in the early 1930s there was a man in North Uist who knew seventeen of his poems, from traditional sources. Matheson's edition, published in 1938, is compiled from oral tradition and from a long list of books and manuscripts dating from 1751 to 1933, including Alasdair Mac Mhaighstir Alasdair's 1751 collection, the McLagan Manuscripts, the Eigg collection of 1776, John Mackenzie's *Beauties of Gaelic Poetry* of 1841, and the collection of work by Uist bards (1894).

MacCodrum's songs in praise of the chiefs and lairds tend to be extended, and fairly conventional, using many of the stereotypes common in such verse, and referring to a succession of clans and their military prowess, but showing a good knowledge of Gaelic legend and history. He uses a variety of metrical forms, three-line, seven-line, and eight-line stanzas, and some more extended ones. In a poem composed during the Seven Years' War (1756–63) he comments quite knowledgeably on the participants in that struggle, but then concentrates on a local altercation.

The songs concerning local events and personalities are the most successful part of MacCodrum's output, combining wit, observation, and satire, and making what can probably be regarded as an early and major contribution to the corpus of so-called 'village verse' which was to retain its popularity into the late twentieth century. He has songs about old age, a dispute between the Friend and the Enemy of Whisky, satires on individuals, a satire on Uist tailors, a light-hearted complaint about his wife, a song about a bout of fever, and so on.

MacCodrum's verse has been authoritatively edited by William Matheson, in the edition published by the Scottish Gaelic Texts Society in 1938, and Matheson draws on tradition and manuscripts to establish the main pattern of his life. Donald Archie MacDonald, a fellow North Uist man, added his own perspective to MacCodrum's work in an article in *Gairm*, 129 (1985).

DERICK S. THOMSON

Sources *The songs of John MacCodrum*, ed. W. Matheson, Scottish Gaelic Texts Society (1938) · D. S. Thomson, *An introduction to Gaelic poetry*, 2nd edn (1990) · *Gairm*, 129 (1985)

MacColl, Dugald Sutherland (1859–1948), painter and museum administrator, was born at 276 St Vincent Street, Glasgow, on 10 March 1859, the eldest child and only son of the Revd Dugald MacColl (1826–1882), a Free Church of Scotland minister, and his wife, Janet Scott Mathieson (*d.* 1895), daughter of a banker. His schooling began at Glasgow Academy in 1869, and from 1873, when his father became minister of the Kensington Presbyterian Church, London, he spent three years at University College School,

Hampstead. In 1876 he entered University College, London: he graduated MA and won the Gerstenberg prize for political economy in 1881, and was made a fellow of his college in 1882. In 1881 he proceeded to Lincoln College, Oxford, where he was a scholar. He won the Newdigate prize for poetry in 1882 and was placed in the second class of the honours list in *literae humaniores* in 1884. The years from 1887 to 1889 were occupied with travel in Italy and Greece, with a visit to Constantinople and a glance at Germany, Holland, and Belgium.

MacColl travelled mainly to familiarize himself with great works of art, and, once back in England, he took art lessons from Frederick Brown at the Westminster School of Art. Between 1890 and 1896 he was art critic to *The Spectator*, then, after a short interval, until 1906 on the *Saturday Review*. In his writings he praised the French impressionists and their English followers, and criticized the conservatism of the Royal Academy. Supported by a small private income left to him by his mother, he was able to pursue a very active career as a painter, critic, editor, and lecturer. In December 1893 the new Goupil Gallery opened with an exhibition of his watercolours; and he was a regular exhibitor at the New English Art Club from 1892, becoming a member in 1896. In 1902 he published *Nineteenth Century Art*, a large and authoritative work which was one of the earliest books to appreciate the importance of the French impressionists; in 1900, at the Glasgow Exhibition, he had organized the first British exhibition devoted to the painters of this school.

MacColl edited the *Architectural Review* from 1901 to 1905 as representative of the committee for literary direction. During 1903, in the *Saturday Review*, he engaged in the first of the controversies which were to punctuate his career. Examining the will of the sculptor Sir Francis Chantrey, who had bequeathed the reversionary interest of most of his property to the Royal Academy, to fund the purchase for the nation of outstanding works of art, he declared that the administrators were departing from its terms, implying that they had long been buying mediocre works. His *Administration of the Chantrey Bequest* appeared in book form in 1904, and soon afterwards a government committee initiated reforms. MacColl also urged the government to spend more on art, and it was largely through his efforts that the National Art Collections Fund was founded in 1903. He fought hard for new artists he admired, among them P. Wilson Steer, William Rothenstein, and Muirhead Bone.

In 1906 MacColl was appointed keeper of the Tate Gallery, where he carried out an energetic and progressive programme which included showing many Turners unearthed from store for the first time, and the opening of an Alfred Stevens room. In 1911, under the threat of tuberculosis, he resigned and went to Fiesole, just outside Florence, to recuperate. His fears proved groundless and in the same year he became curator of the Wallace Collection, where he remained until 1924. Here again he acted with characteristic vigour, rehanging and recataloguing the whole collection and carrying out useful researches. He served as a trustee of the Tate Gallery from 1917 to 1927,

and as a member of the Royal Fine Arts Commission from 1925 to 1929.

In 1919 MacColl published the collection of his poems *Bull and other War Verses*. He started writing again for the *Saturday Review* in 1921, but when Gerald Barry, the editor, parted company with his proprietor and founded the *Week-End Review* in 1930, MacColl went over with the rest of the staff. During the late 1920s he was engaged in the most violent of all his artistic campaigns—and the only one to be unsuccessful. John Rennie's Waterloo Bridge had begun to collapse, and for several years MacColl advocated its repair and preservation against Herbert Morrison and the London county council, who advocated—at length successfully—its demolition and replacement.

MacColl entered an energetic old age, continuing to paint, write, and participate in controversies. His *Confessions of a Keeper*, a collection of his criticism, appeared in 1931; in 1940 he collected the *Poems* written over a period of sixty years; in 1945, at the age of eighty-six, he won the James Tait Black memorial prize with his *Life, Work and Setting of Philip Wilson Steer*, one of the most notable artistic biographies of the period. Lecturer, connoisseur, critic, poet, curator, and a watercolourist of sensitive technique and with a fine feeling for colour, he was versatile, volcanically energetic, generous-minded, and utterly honest and self-confident. Loyal to his friends and his causes, he had a keen business sense which perhaps owed something to the banking line to which his mother's family belonged. His marriage in 1897 to Andrée Adèle Désirée Jeanne (d. 1945), daughter of Dr Emile Zabé, of Neuilly, Seine, was a most successful one. Elegant, witty, skilled in all the social graces, Andrée MacColl was a noted beauty, whose portrait by Steer (National Gallery of Scotland, Edinburgh) was one of that artist's more successful figure pieces. The couple had two sons, Andre Dugald, born in 1898, and René *MacColl, born in 1905.

MacColl received the honorary degrees of LLD from Glasgow (1907) and DLitt from Oxford (1925). He was a council member (1925) of the British School at Rome, and a founder member of the Contemporary Art Society, as well as an honorary associate of the Royal Institute of British Architects and an honorary member of the English and Scottish royal societies of painters in water colours. MacColl died at his home, 1 Hampstead Way, Hampstead Garden Suburb, on 21 December 1948. His remains were cremated at Golders Green crematorium on 28 December.   H. B. GRIMSDITCH, *rev.* ROBERT UPSTONE

Sources M. Borland, *D. S. MacColl: painter, poet, and art critic* (1995) · *The Times* (22 Dec 1948) · RIBA *Journal*, 56 (1948–9), 142–3 · D. S. MacColl, 'A batch of memories', *Week-End Review* (20 Dec 1930) · private information (1959) · Tate collection, Tate Gallery catalogue file · *CGPLA Eng. & Wales* (1949)

Archives U. Glas. L., corresp. | BL, corresp. with Sir Sydney Cockerell, Add. MS 52733 · Bodl. Oxf., corresp. with Lewis Harcourt · Girton Cam., corresp. with Eugenie Strong · Harvard U., Houghton L., letters to Sir William Rothenstein · JRL, letters to Samuel Alexander · LUL, corresp. with W. P. Ker · NL Scot., corresp. with A. E. Borthwick · NL Scot., letters to Ronald Gray · Tate collection, corresp. with Lord Clark · TCD, corresp. with Thomas Bodkin

Likenesses A. Legros, silverpoint, 1897, NPG · G. C. Beresford, photograph, 1906, NPG · D. G. MacLaren, oils, c.1906, Tate collection · M. Beerbohm, caricature drawing, 1907 (*A quiet morning at the Tate Gallery*), Tate collection · W. Orpen, group portrait, oils, 1909 (*Homage to Manet*), Man. City Gall. · P. Evans, pen sketch, 1922, Athenaeum, London · J. Kerr-Lawson, pencil, 1933, Wallace Collection, London · F. Dodd, chalk drawing, 1939, NPG · D. Gordine, bronze bust, priv. coll. · D. G. MacLaren, pencil drawing, Scot. NPG · D. G. MacLaren, watercolour caricature (Some members of the New English Art Club), NPG · W. Orpen, group portrait, oils (*The selecting jury of the New English Art Club, 1909*), NPG · W. Orpen, pencil, pen and ink, watercolour and wash, NPG · J. Russell & Sons, photograph, NPG · P. W. Steer, watercolour sketch, Athenaeum, London · H. Tonks, caricatures, repro. in J. Hone, *Life of Henry Tonks* (1939) · H. Tonks, double portrait, watercolour over pencil caricature (as Don Quixote, with William Rothenstein as Sancho Panza), BM · P. Wilson Steer, drawing, priv. coll.

Wealth at death £18,191 1s. 1d.: probate, 22 April 1949, *CGPLA Eng. & Wales*

MacColl, Ewan [*formerly* James Miller] (1915–1989), songwriter, folk-singer, and playwright, was born James Miller on 25 January 1915 in Salford, Lancashire, the youngest and only surviving child in the family of three sons and one daughter (one of each sex was stillborn and one son died at the age of four) of William Miller, ironmoulder, of Salford, and his wife, Betsy Hendry, charwoman. He was educated at Grecian Street School, Salford. He left school at the age of fourteen after an elementary education and was immediately unemployed. He joined the Young Communist League (he was not to leave the Communist Party until the early 1960s) and then found work as a motor mechanic, factory worker, and street singer. He first began writing for factory newspapers, composing satirical songs and political poems, while also taking a keen interest in amateur dramatics, in 1931 forming a political street theatre group, the Red Megaphones, which performed sketches on the streets of Salford and Manchester. Both his parents were fine traditional singers, and he had begun to sing and write songs while a teenager. One of his first and finest protest songs, 'The Manchester Rambler', dealt with the 'mass trespass' campaigns of the 1930s, in which hikers fought pitched battles with gamekeepers when they invaded privately owned grouse moors.

It was two decades before he devoted his energies to music. He spent most of the 1930s involved in experimental theatre projects after joining forces with his future wife, Joan Littlewood, with whom he formed a 'workers' experimental theatre', the Theatre of Action, at Manchester in 1933. Miller wrote and co-produced a series of political satires and dance dramas, and was arrested and charged with disturbing the peace after the police stopped performances of his 'living newspaper', 'Last Edition'. In the Second World War he was called up, joined the army, and was arrested for desertion, although he claimed there had been a case of mistaken identity. He was discharged on medical grounds. He continued with his drama projects after the war, and he and Littlewood formed Theatre Workshop, for which he became art director and resident dramatist. He changed his name to Ewan MacColl in 1945. Between 1945 and 1952 he wrote eleven plays, including *Uranium 235* (1952), a drama with music, and *Landscape with*

Ewan MacColl (1915–1989), by Brian Shuel, 1962 [with Peggy Seeger]

Chimneys (1951), which included one of his best-known songs, 'Dirty Old Town', written in a matter of hours on the opening night to cover a scene change.

MacColl severed his professional links with Littlewood in 1952 and gradually withdrew from the Theatre Workshop. From 1952 onwards he worked to establish a folksong revival in Britain. He saw folk music not as some quaint historical curiosity but as a political force, an expression of working-class culture, and he wanted to develop a style in which 'songs of struggle would be immediately acceptable to a lot of young people'. With help from American folklorist Alan Lomax and A. L. (Bert) Lloyd, he mixed politics, British and American folk music, and jazz in a radio series, *Ballads and Blues* (1953). He founded the Ballads and Blues Club, later renamed the Singers' Club, in London, and by the mid-1950s was considered one of the leading folk-singers in the country.

Initially, MacColl had encouraged the fashion for American folk and blues (he and Lomax had even started a skiffle group, which included another American singer and songwriter, Peggy Seeger, who was to become his third wife), but by the late 1950s he became concerned that British traditional music was being swamped by American styles. He therefore introduced his controversial 'policy rule'—singers had to perform songs from their own tradition, depending on whether they were British or American.

In 1957, when he claimed there were 1500 folk clubs around Britain, MacColl returned to experimental multimedia work, this time with a distinctively British flavour. The *Radio Ballads*, broadcast on the BBC Home Service from 1958 to 1964, dealt with the everyday lives of British workers, from railwaymen to boxers or fishermen, and used a montage of interviews and new songs written by MacColl. He wrote many of his best songs for this widely praised series, including 'Shoals of Herring' and 'Freeborn Man'.

A fiery, authoritative, opinionated figure, MacColl never deviated from his staunch left-wing views. From 1965 to 1971 he trained young singers in folk-singing and theatre technique in his Critics Group, which performed an annual review of the year's news, the 'Festival of Fools'. He collected folk-songs, and co-wrote two books with

Peggy Seeger (*Travellers' Songs from England and Scotland*, 1977, which was praised for its scholarship, and *Till Doomsday in the Afternoon, the Folklore of a Family of Scots Travellers*, 1986). With her he founded Blackthorne Records, which specialized in their own recordings. In the 1980s, by which time his jet-black hair and red beard had turned white, he wrote songs to support the miners' strike and the anti-apartheid movement. Considering his enormous and varied output, it was ironic that his only financial success came from his song 'The first time ever I saw your face', a no. 1 hit in America for Roberta Flack in 1972. It won the Ivor Novello award in 1973. MacColl was awarded an honorary degree by Exeter University in 1986.

In 1935 MacColl married Joan Littlewood, who did not know the identity of her father, but was brought up by a stepfather, Jimmy Morritt, asphalter. They were divorced in 1948 and in 1949 he married Jean, daughter of William Newlove, a wartime director of regional supplies and part-time artist. They had a son, Hamish, and a daughter, Kirsty Anna *MacColl, a very successful singer–songwriter. They were divorced in 1974 and he married his third wife, the singer Peggy Seeger, with whom he had lived since the 1950s, in 1977. She was the daughter of Charles Seeger, musicologist, and sister of the singer Pete Seeger. MacColl died on 22 October 1989 in the Brompton Hospital, London, after complications following heart surgery, and his autobiography *Journeyman* was published the following year.   ROBIN DENSELOW, rev.

Sources interview with Ewan MacColl, priv. coll. · E. MacColl, *Journeyman* (1990) · J. Littlewood, *Joan's book* (1994) · *The Independent* (30 Oct 1989) · private information (1996) · *CGPLA Eng. & Wales* (1990)
Archives Ruskin College, Oxford, papers relating to his life and work | NL Scot., letters to Hamish Henderson
Likenesses B. Shuel, photograph, 1962, Redferns Music Picture Library [see illus.]
Wealth at death £80,500: probate, 12 Oct 1990, *CGPLA Eng. & Wales*

MacColl, John (1860–1943), player and composer of highland bagpipe music, was born at Kentallen in Appin, Argyll, on 6 January 1860, youngest of the four sons and three daughters of Dugald MacColl, tailor and traditional musician, and his wife, Elizabeth McInnes. On 21 June 1894 he married Helen Carruthers (b. 1863/4), a housemaid at Dunach House, Argyll, daughter of John Carruthers, manager of the Kilberry estate in Knapdale. They had two sons and two daughters.

After early teaching from his father, MacColl entered his first competition at the Bonawe highland games in 1877. He was so impressed by the playing of the music publisher and bagpipe maker Donald MacPhee (1841–1880) that he took a job at Bonawe quarry to save enough money to study with him in Glasgow. When MacPhee died in December 1880 MacColl returned to the family home, now in Oban, working and studying with Pipe-Major Ronald MacKenzie (d. March 1911, a Skye man and former pipe-major in the Black Watch; prize pipe, Inverness 1873, gold medal, Inverness 1875) on the nearby estate of Dunach. His employer, Neil M. MacDonald, came from a leading

highland musical family and was grandson of the piobaireachd editor Niel MacLeod of Gesto. MacColl went on to a glitteringly successful competitive career, winning all the top awards: the gold medal at the Argyllshire Gathering in 1881, and a silver cup for previous winners in 1883; the prize pipe at the Northern Meeting in Inverness in the same year; the special centenary gold medal at Inverness in 1888; and the clasp in 1900. In 1902 he took the first prize for piping at the Paris Exhibition. Like many piping contemporaries, he was a member of the volunteer force, serving as pipe-major of the 3rd battalion, Black Watch, and later with the Scottish Horse. He worked part-time training pipers in the territorial battalions during the winter months and as an instructor for the Piobaireachd Society.

MacColl's career shows the transformation of opportunity for leading pipers with the growth of the mass entertainment industry in the second half of the nineteenth century, which brought the music-hall, the seaside holiday, and, in Scotland, the highland games. The games hosted a competition circuit for professional pipers, and those at the top could earn a comfortable living, going the rounds of Dunoon, Braemar, Oban, Inverness, and a host of smaller events. MacColl was a talented dancer and athlete as well as a piper. His son recalled him:

> finishing a dance, throwing off his kilt (having running shorts underneath), competing in the hundred yards race and then putting his kilt and things on ready for the next dance … He was away from home practically all summer travelling round the Games … he could earn £40 in an afternoon from piping, dancing and athletics. (MacNeill)

Pipe-Major Willie Ross described a foursome reel including John MacColl and his fellow piper D. C. Mather as the best he had ever seen. MacColl was also an expert yachtsman and golfer, a shinty internationalist, a fiddle player, and Gaelic singer.

Along with a friend, the piper and dancer William McLennan (1860–1892), MacColl worked to advance the interests of professional players. Pipe-Major Robert Meldrum described an incident at the Northern Meeting in 1885:

> William McLennan met me and … explained that they had protested against the smallness of the prizes and they were not going to play … Eventually Angus Macrae and [John MacDougall] Gillies played, although they had protested, but MacColl and McLennan did not. They got into some trouble for booing those who had played … I was second. The judges praised my playing but for my reed. Someone had removed my own reed and substituted another. (Meldrum)

His technical gift made MacColl a formidable competitor, and he was widely considered the best march player of his generation. Some thought that he lacked expression in piobaireachd, but John MacDonald of Inverness described his playing 'I got a kiss of the king's hand' at Birnam as 'one of the most harmonious performances I have listened to'.

Along with William Laurie and G. S. McLennan, John MacColl was one of the leading pipe music composers of the later nineteenth and early twentieth centuries. His piobaireachd compositions included 'Donald MacPhee's

Lament' and 'N. M. MacDonald's Lament', but he was best known for his superbly inventive and tuneful marches, including 'John MacFadyen of Melfort', 'Jeannie Carruthers', and 'Mrs John MacColl'. These set new standards in technical demand and significantly extended the expressive possibilities of the form.

In 1908 MacColl became manager of R. G. Lawrie's bagpipe firm in Glasgow, from which he retired about 1936. In 1923 he gave the first known piping broadcast, playing the tune 'Johnnie Cope'. John MacColl died, aged eighty-three, on 8 June 1943 at his home, 34 Claddens Quadrant, Glasgow. At his funeral John MacDonald of the Glasgow police played 'The Lament for the Children'.

WILLIAM DONALDSON

Sources W. Donaldson, *The highland pipe and Scottish society, 1750–1950* (2000) • S. MacNeill, 'The life and times of John MacColl', *Piping Times*, 50/5–8 (1998) • 'A famous piper, John MacColl', *Oban Times* (17 Aug 1935) • 'A veteran piper', *Oban Times* (12 Dec 1942) • J. Campbell, 'The Argyllshire Gathering—the early years', *Piping Times*, 42/11 (1990), 40–45 • J. Campbell, 'Patrons of piping, part 3: the MacDonalds of Dunach', *Piping Times*, 51/9 (1999), 46–7 • J. Campbell, *Highland bagpipe makers* (2001) • R. Meldrum, 'Reminiscences', *Oban Times* (29 June 1940–4 Jan 1941) • J. MacDonald, 'The piping reminiscences of John MacDonald M.B.E.', *Oban Times* (21 March 1942) • D. Ross, 'Some of the old pipers I have met', *Piping Times*, 26/4 (1974), 9–17 • 'Death of a noted piper. A native of Skye. Pipe-Major Ronald Mackenzie', *Oban Times* (18 March 1911) • A. Fairrie, *The Northern Meeting, 1788–1988* (1988) • b. cert. • m. cert. • d. cert. **Archives** College of Piping, 16–24 Otago Street, Glasgow, MSS **Likenesses** photograph, repro. in *Piping Times*, 50/5 (1998), 19 • photograph, repro. in *Piping Times*, 53/3 (2000), 9

MacColl, Kirsty Anna (1959–2000), singer and songwriter, was born on 10 October 1959 at Mayday Hospital, Thornton Heath, Surrey, the daughter of Ewan *MacColl (1915–1989), singer, songwriter, and folk-song revivalist, and his wife, Jean Mary, née Newlove (b. 1923), dancer and choreographer. Her parents separated shortly after her birth, and she was brought up by her mother, in Selsdon, near Croydon. About the age of six she developed severe asthma, which proved highly distressing and disrupted her education. She spent prolonged periods in bed, where she read, wrote, painted, and enjoyed a lively education from her mother. She was a highly musical and conspicuously intelligent child, who at the age of nine wrote a contribution to Edward Blishen's *The School that I'd Like*. She declined a scholarship to Millfield because of her debilitating asthma, but was a high-performing pupil at Monks Hill comprehensive school in Selsdon. While a pupil there, her imagination was captivated by Neil Young's album *Harvest* (1972) and by the Beach Boys' vocal arrangements.

When she left school in 1977 MacColl resisted pressure to study science at university and instead attended Croydon Art School for six months and night courses at Goldsmiths' College (1977–8). Soon, under the name of Mandy Doubt, she was backing singer in a punkish band called the Drug Addix. Stiff Records arranged for her to record her début solo single, 'They don't know' (1979), which gained much radio airplay. Its sales were mediocre because of a distribution strike at Stiff, but it was later a big chart hit for Tracey Ullman. Despite achieving her first

top twenty hit with 'There's a guy works down the chip shop (swears he's Elvis)' (1981), MacColl had difficulty in establishing herself, partly because of her fear of live performances. Once, at a gig in Ireland, she rushed through her material so quickly that she exhausted her repertory and had to sing her songs over again. Her first album, *Desperate Character* (1981), sold disappointingly, but her version of Billy Bragg's song 'New England' (1985) reached Britain's top ten.

On 18 August 1984 MacColl married Stephen Alan Lillywhite (b. 1955), invariably known as Steve, son of Geoffrey Alan Lillywhite, an accountant, and himself a record producer of considerable energy and success. She was a cheerful, attentive, but not anxiously over-protective mother to their two sons, who appear on her songs 'Innocence' (1989) and 'Happy' (1989). Lillywhite and other producers used her talents—including perfect pitch and the ability to record harmony vocals on the first take—as a backing singer on records. She featured on discs by The Smiths, Talking Heads, Simple Minds, and Happy Mondays. Her collaboration with Shane MacGowan and the Pogues on their whisky-sodden 'Fairytale of New York' (1987) was her biggest hit. In 1988 she made a guest appearance on the French and Saunders comedy television series (singing 'Trains and boats and planes' with the band Raw Sex), and regularly sang during the third series of 1989. She also appeared in several memorable promotional music videos, including 'Fairytale of New York' and 'Miss Otis regrets' (1990) with the Pogues, and a video from *French and Saunders* of her own song 'Don't come the cowboy with me, sonny Jim!' (1989).

Not only did Kirsty MacColl have a superb voice; she was a versatile, droll lyricist (likened by Bono of the Irish rock band U2 to Noël Coward) and a harmonically inventive and evocative songwriter. Her tender and amusing solo album *Kite* (1989) was anti-bimbo and anti-yuppie. It included a track, 'Free world', that mocked Thatcherism, while other numbers were scathing about the way that the pop music industry packaged women performers. MacColl's next album, *Electric Landlady* (1991), shot into the top twenty on its release and included such songs as 'Walking down Madison', about New York's homeless inhabitants. The sequel album, *Titanic Days* (1994), is more pensive, and reflected the breakdown of her marriage; although praised by critics, it had modest sales. Her biggest-selling album was a compilation of her hits, *Galore* (1995). The album *What do Pretty Girls do?* (1998), with its title taken from a song of 1989, was another compilation. Although MacColl's work never had a mass following, it was never unfashionable. Initially she was malleable with recording companies, but she became increasingly assertive about making records on her own terms. Forced to shift from one company to another, she became alienated from the industry. Her aim, always, was to sell enough records to be able to make another record and continue working. Occasionally she suffered writer's block, but usually she was a pragmatic and efficient worker.

Kirsty MacColl once said that she liked 'to make jangly, luscious, melodic pop music but with lyrics that are a bit more biting and down to earth than the average stuff' (O'Brien, 55). Her approach was always eclectic—managing to combine country and western, rock, and electronic dance music—but from 1991 she became enthused by the music of Brazil and Cuba. She learned Portuguese and Spanish, regularly revisited Cuba, and supported the Cuban Solidarity Movement's opposition to US economic sanctions against the island. Her final album, *Tropical Brainstorm* (2000), was witty, beautifully crafted, and showed the influence of Cuban and Latin American music. A series of radio programmes, entitled *Kirsty MacColl's Cuba*, was recorded just before she died. The Music Fund for Cuba, which provided instruments for children, was established in her memory, and the library at Havana School of Music was renamed in her honour in 2002.

Kirsty MacColl was distinctive in both appearance and character. She had dark, mischievous looks with richly coloured red hair. Her outlook was feisty, earthy, and irreverent. She had a raunchy laugh, was gregarious, and gave very good parties. She worked hard at determining what was important to her, but was unable to hide what she found unimportant or pretentious in other people: she described herself as 'mouthy' (O'Brien, 55). Her uncompromising intelligence was sometimes an obstacle to success: so too was her impatience with 'dopey cows in frilly dresses singing, "Oh baby, I can't live without you"' (James, 402). Her marriage broke up in 1994 and was dissolved in 1997. In 1999 she met the saxophonist James Knight (*b.* 1974) and they began living together the following year. On 18 December 2000 she was accidentally killed by a recklessly steered pleasure boat when swimming at Cozumel, Mexico. She was cremated at Mortlake crematorium, London, on 5 January 2001. A memorial service was held at St Martin-in-the-Fields on 20 January, and in August 2001 a commemorative bench was placed in London's Soho Square, which had provided the title for one of her songs.   RICHARD DAVENPORT-HINES

Sources private information (2004) [Jean MacColl, James Knight] · K. O'Brien, *Hymn to her* (1995), 47–59 · A. James, 'The queen of rock and droll', *Marie Claire* (Oct 2001), 400–02 · B. Bragg, 'Kirsty MacColl', *Folk Roots*, 213 (March 2001), 14 · *The Independent* (20 Dec 2000) · *The Guardian* (20 Dec 2000) · *The Times* (20 Dec 2000) · *Daily Telegraph* (20 Dec 2000) · www.kirstymaccoll.com [incl. complete discography] · *Croydon Advertiser* (20 Dec 2000) · *New Musical Express* (20 Jan 2001) · E. Blishen, *The school that I'd like* (1969) · b. cert. · m. cert.

Archives priv. coll., personal family papers | SOUND *Kirsty MacColl's Cuba*, BBC Radio 2 (2001)

Likenesses photograph, 1991, repro. in *Daily Telegraph* · photograph, 1994, repro. in *The Times* · C. Dickins, photograph, 1995, repro. in O'Brien, *Hymn to her*, 45 · T. Craig, photograph, 1999, repro. in *The Independent* · G. Smith, photograph, *c.*2000, repro. in *The Guardian*

MacColl, Malcolm (1831–1907), Church of England clergyman and religious controversialist, was born on 27 March 1831 at Glenfinnan, Inverness-shire, the third son of the four sons and two daughters of John MacColl of Glenfinnan and his wife, Martha, daughter of Malcolm Macrae of Kintail. His father, a tenant farmer, died when Callum (as he was known in the family) was young, and he was reared

by his mother, who spoke only Gaelic. Callum was baptized an Episcopalian, but his mother was a strict sabbatarian. She moved the family to Kintail, where the children learned English, and then to Ballachulish. A wealthy local lady became Callum's patron, having him educated at a seminary for teachers at Dalkeith. Having qualified there he taught in Callander, Stonehaven, and Perth. At Callander he acted as a lay reader at a mission chapel and was encouraged to enter Trinity College, Glenalmond, as a divinity student, where he won a scholarship for his Gaelic abilities. He early showed the argumentativeness which became his best-known characteristic and by 1853 was in print in *The Guardian* and elsewhere. He was ordained deacon in 1856 and priest in the Scottish Episcopal church in 1857. Caught in the controversies then engulfing that church, he wrote for help to W. E. Gladstone (as one of the founders of Glenalmond and then quite prominent in Episcopalian church politics), thus inaugurating a relationship that lasted to the end of Gladstone's long life. Several further posts in Scotland followed, before MacColl accepted the non-stipendiary principalship of a teaching institution in Soho, London. In 1861 he became curate of St Barnabas, Pimlico, a high-church centre, and in 1862 transferred to St Paul's, Knightsbridge. In 1863 he visited Russia as domestic chaplain to the British ambassador, Lord Napier, and established important contacts with Russian Orthodox churchmen and -women. The anomalous position of MacColl's orders was regularized by a Lambeth MA in 1864, and his close links with the Episcopal church were in effect severed. MacColl was thus launched on the London social scene, for his incumbencies in London were all in high-profile society churches, and on the national scene as a liberal high-church controversialist, for the letters and pamphlets he wrote as Scrutator soon gained general attention. 'He was a hot-blooded Highlander, with a bulldog tenacity; very loyal and affectionate to friends, but a merciless opponent', commented a colleague (Russell, 21).

MacColl became something of an in-house journalist for Gladstone, involving himself in the Oxford University election of 1865 (when Gladstone lost) with a pamphlet by Scrutator, *Mr. Gladstone and Oxford*, and in a series of other causes. He wrote for *The Times*, but complained at Delane's rewriting of his articles. Having been curate at St Paul's, Knightsbridge, again in 1864–7, a chaplain in southern Italy in 1867–9, and curate of Addington, Buckinghamshire, in 1869, he was rewarded by Gladstone's appointment of him in April 1871 to St George's, Botolph Lane, London, a mistake by both appointer and recipient, for MacColl was not by nature a good parish priest. His biographer records that 'his disposition was not pastoral. He shrank from that personal dealing with individual souls which is the most vital portion of the pastor's work' (Russell, 33). MacColl soon realized that he was wrongly placed and contemplated joining the Central African Mission; nothing came of this, and he drew his stipend from St George's even after it closed in 1891.

MacColl was a prominent opponent of the Public Worship Act of 1874 and its various successors, though he did not see himself as a ritualist (the group against which the acts were aimed). His *Lawlessness, Sacerdotalism, and Ritualism* (1875) was a clever attack on the judicial committee of the privy council. He attended the second conference on Anglican–Old Catholic–Orthodox reunion held by J. J. I. von Döllinger in Bonn in August 1875, and his contacts with Orthodox Christians equipped him to play a prominent part in the campaign against Turkish atrocities on Christians in the Balkans which began in 1876. In July 1876 he and H. P. Liddon travelled through Serbia and his messages to Gladstone encouraged the retired prime minister to action. MacColl had little of the caution which lay in the small print of Gladstone's statements on the Eastern question; he had 'a greater horror of Disraeli than you [Gladstone] appear to have' (letter of 5 Nov 1879; Russell, 63). MacColl was the most prominent of the liberal high-churchmen who took part in the campaign. He was also to the fore in attacking Conservative policy over Afghanistan in 1878–80, being the chief author of *Causes of the Afghan War* (1879).

Despite his strong identification with the Liberals, MacColl attempted to act as broker between Gladstone and Salisbury on two important occasions. In 1884, when the Lords were rejecting the Reform Bill, MacColl tried to persuade Salisbury of Gladstone's political moderation and, more seriously, in November 1885 he encouraged Salisbury in the view that Gladstone would trade a parliament in Dublin for a tory-led solution to the question of Irish home rule. Both these experienced political hands treated MacColl's interventions with more apparent gravity than they perhaps really felt. MacColl was useful to Gladstone in the late 1880s as a reporter of opinion and developments among the Liberal Unionists, with whom MacColl retained good relations despite his own home-rule views, described in *Reasons for Home Rule* (1886; much reprinted).

In July 1884 Gladstone made MacColl canon of Ripon, where he was initially unhappy, finding the parochial work excessive and offering resignation (declined) in July 1885. In the 1890s MacColl was again prominent as a campaigner, for the rights of the Armenians against their Russian and Turkish persecutors. His links with Salisbury, at that time foreign secretary as well as prime minister, were a useful but not very effective entrée for the campaigners. When, with Gladstone's death in 1898, the high-church element of Liberalism was much diminished, MacColl reduced his contacts with the party for which he had worked so energetically for so long and, increasingly attracted by Salisbury's high-churchmanship, transferred his allegiance to the tories, formally making the break with the Liberals over the education question in 1902–3.

MacColl was not merely a person of political interests. His pamphlet on the Oberammergau passion play (1870; often enlarged and reprinted) did much to popularize it in Britain. *Christianity in Relation to Science and Morals* (1889), on the Nicene creed, was a substantial work, as was *The Reformation Settlement Examined in the Light of History and Law* (1899), with a preface by Sir William Harcourt.

In the late 1890s MacColl's health declined: he had heart trouble and was seriously ill following a holiday in Greece. In 1904 he married Consuelo Albinia, youngest daughter of Major-General W. H. Crompton-Stansfield of Esholt Hall, Yorkshire; they had no children. In March 1906 he was given the cross of the order of the Redeemer by the king of Greece for his services to that country. MacColl died at his house, 4 Beaufort Gardens, London, on 5 April 1907 and was buried on 10 April at Kirkby Overblow, near Ripon. An altar was erected to his memory in St Wilfrid's Chapel, Ripon Cathedral.

MacColl was often seen as sycophantic and interfering. To an extent he was both. But he established for himself an unusual niche in British public life, for he brought no wealth, patronage, or office to support his involvement, and yet he was for forty years not only an indefatigable publicist but an elegant and very well-informed correspondent with two demanding prime ministers.

H. C. G. MATTHEW

Sources DNB · G. W. E. Russell, *Malcolm MacColl* (1914) · Crockford (1870–1907) · *Clergy List* (1860–1907) · *The Times* (6 April 1907) · *The Guardian* (10 April 1907) · Gladstone, *Diaries* · *Correspondence on church and religion of William Ewart Gladstone*, ed. D. C. Lathbury, 2 vols. (1910) · A. B. Cooke and J. Vincent, *The governing passion: cabinet government and party politics in Britain, 1885–86* (1974) · R. T. Shannon, *Gladstone and the Bulgarian agitation, 1876* (1963) · A. Jones, *The politics of reform, 1884* (1972)
Archives BL, corresp. with W. E. Gladstone, Add. MSS 44242–44245 · BL, letters to Sir Edward Hamilton, Add. MS 48618 · Bodl. Oxf., letters to Sir William Harcourt · Hatfield House, Hertfordshire, Salisbury MSS · LPL, corresp. with A. C. Tait · NL Scot., corresp. with Lord Rosebery
Wealth at death £15,775 6s. 7d.: probate, 18 June 1907, *CGPLA Eng. & Wales*

MacColl, Norman (1843–1904), journal editor and Spanish scholar, was born on 31 August 1843 at 28 Ann Street, Corstorphine, Edinburgh, the only child of Alexander Stewart MacColl and his wife, Eliza Fulford of Crediton. His grandfather, Donald MacColl, was an Episcopalian clergyman who later became factor to the duke of Gordon at Lochaber. Having been educated at home by his father, a classical scholar who kept a private school at Edinburgh, MacColl entered Christ's College, Cambridge, in 1862, but migrated the following year to Downing College and was awarded a scholarship there in 1865. He graduated BA in 1866 with a first class in the moral sciences tripos, and in 1868 won the Hare prize with an essay, 'Greek sceptics, from Pyrrho to Sextus', which was published in 1869. He was elected to a fellowship at Downing the same year. An early supporter of the campaign to admit women to degrees, in 1869 he was one of the first tutors at the establishment at Hitchin which was the forerunner of Girton College. He became a student of Lincoln's Inn on 21 January 1872 and was called to the bar on 17 November 1875. He never practised law, but retained his chambers until his death.

At Cambridge, MacColl made the acquaintance of Sir Charles Dilke (1843–1911), who, soon after becoming proprietor of *The Athenaeum*, appointed him to the editorship of that paper, a post which he held for almost thirty years, from 1871 to 1900. Under his judicious guidance *The Athenaeum* regained its prestige, and in the 1870s and 1880s became the most influential literary weekly in the country, respected for its fair-minded, authoritative criticism and high standards of scholarship. Its regular contributors included D. G. Rossetti, Theodore Watts-Dunton (the chief poetry reviewer), Edmund Gosse, Andrew Lang, W. E. Henley, Richard Garnett, and Henry Sidgwick. Though remaining independent of party, MacColl shared Dilke's liberal outlook, and *The Athenaeum* came to embody the intellectual ethos of the late Victorian era, encompassing science and philosophy as well as literature. As an editor he was open-minded and self-effacing; though he had the laconic incisiveness expected of a Scots classicist he wrote little himself, preferring to devote his time to cultivating his reviewers and hewing their style.

MacColl was a friend of Leslie Stephen and regularly took part in the latter's Sunday 'tramps'. When in 1882 Stephen undertook the editorship of what was to become the *Dictionary of National Biography*, MacColl offered him the freedom of his pages to publicize the venture and attract contributors. The first manifesto of the dictionary appeared in *The Athenaeum* of 23 December 1882, and over a period of fourteen years (1883–97) lists of the names proposed for inclusion in successive volumes were published at six-monthly intervals; readers were invited to comment on the lists and applications were called for from suitable contributors. MacColl himself wrote entries on Thomas Campbell and on the elder Dilkes, among others.

A frequent traveller on the continent, MacColl made one tour of Spain, and from 1874 dedicated himself to the serious study of Spanish literature. In 1888 he published an edition for the general reader of select plays of Calderón, of whom he was an ardent but not uncritical admirer, and in 1902 he contributed a two-volume translation of the *Exemplary Novels* to a collection of the translated works of Cervantes edited by his friend James Fitzmaurice-Kelly (1857–1923). By his will, he endowed the Cambridge lectureship in Spanish and Portuguese which bears his name, and bequeathed his Spanish books to the university library.

Reserved and taciturn by nature, MacColl shunned publicity and mixed little in society, but was notable for many acts of unobtrusive private generosity, especially to the young. He never married, and died suddenly of heart failure at his home, 4 Campden Hill Square, Notting Hill, on 15 December 1904. He was buried at Charlton cemetery, Blackheath, London, in the grave of his parents.

G. MARTIN MURPHY

Sources *The Athenaeum* (24 Dec 1904), 874–5 · L. A. Marchand, *The Athenaeum: a mirror of Victorian culture* (1941) · G. Fenwick, 'The *Athenaeum* and the *Dictionary of National Biography*, 1885–1901', *Victorian Periodicals Review*, 23 (1990), 180–88 · Venn, *Alum. Cant.* · G. Fenwick, *The contributors' index to the Dictionary of National Biography, 1885–1901* (1989) · DNB
Archives Bodl. Oxf., corresp. with Sir Henry Burdett · King's AC Cam., letters to O. Browning · NL Scot., letters to Blackwoods · NL Wales, letters to Johnes family · U. Edin. L., corresp. with James Halliwell-Phillips

Likenesses C. Wilkinson, oils, *c.*1900, Downing College, Cambridge · H. Furniss, group portrait, sketch, repro. in *Punch* (28 March 1885)
Wealth at death £24,949 16s. 8d.: probate, 23 Jan 1905, *CGPLA Eng. & Wales*

MacColl, René (1905–1971), journalist and author, was born on 12 January 1905 in London, the younger son of Dugald Sutherland *MacColl (1859–1948), a Scot, keeper of the Tate Gallery from 1906 to 1911, and later of the Wallace Collection, and his French wife, Andrée Adèle Désirée Jeanne (d. 1945), daughter of Dr Émile Zabé of Neuilly, Seine. He was educated at University College School, London, and went up to Lincoln College, Oxford, in 1923 to read modern history, but left two years later without a degree. He found a job working for the Antwerp branch of a British firm which dealt in secondhand jute sacks, but had to leave after sixteen months when it was closed down in December 1926. At a loss for what to do next, he was introduced to Van-Lear Black (1875–1930), an American millionaire, president of the Fidelity Trust Company and publisher of the *Baltimore Sun*, who was taking an extended holiday in London, and he was engaged as his personal assistant. Van-Lear Black developed a passion for flying, leased a single-engined Fokker plane and two pilots from the Dutch airline KLM, and, accompanied by MacColl, flew over 200,000 miles in Europe, Africa, and the Dutch East Indies between January and September 1927. When Black returned to the United States in September 1927, he offered MacColl a job on the *Baltimore Sun*, and he began work as a district reporter, covering the Baltimore waterfront. While in America MacColl married Helen (d. 1945), daughter of Walter Edwards of Boyertown, Pennsylvania, in 1928: they had one son and one daughter.

MacColl returned to England and joined the *Daily Telegraph* in 1929, covering events at home and abroad. He reported on several royal occasions, including the silver jubilee of George V in 1935, the coronation of George VI in 1937, and the state visit of George VI and Queen Elizabeth to France in 1938. His foreign assignments included India in 1932 to cover the riots in Bombay, the wedding of King Zog of Albania in 1938, and the Spanish Civil War, where he was one of those who entered Madrid when it fell to Franco in April 1939. With war imminent, he sent his wife and children to her parents in Pennsylvania, and was commissioned in the Royal Air Force Volunteer Reserve. In October 1939 he was posted to Rheims, headquarters of the advanced air striking force of Bomber Command, where he served as a liaison officer between the RAF and the war correspondents until the fall of France in May 1940. He was seconded from the Royal Air Force Volunteer Reserve in November 1940 and sent to New York to become the first head of the press and radio division of the British Information Services in the United States, and remained there until February 1946, when he joined the *Daily Express*. His first wife died in 1945, and in 1946 he married (Margaret) Hermione, daughter of Lieutenant-Colonel Kenneth Bruce DSO.

As Washington correspondent of the *Daily Express* from

1946 to 1948, MacColl reported the first of the trials of Alger Hiss, accused of passing state department documents to a Soviet spy, before the House Un-American Activities Committee, and he covered the 1948 presidential election. From 1949 to 1950 he was Paris correspondent, before returning to the United States from 1951 to 1952. He was in Washington when President Truman relieved General Douglas MacArthur of his command of the United Nations troops in Korea in 1951, and covered the 1952 presidential election. From 1953 to 1958, although based in London, he spent at least six months of each year on foreign assignments: he accompanied Clement Attlee's mission to China in 1954, and was the first British reporter to visit the USSR for several years when he spent three months there in 1954. MacColl was the chief foreign correspondent of the *Daily Express* from 1959 to 1969, flying over 1 million miles during these years. Of all the world leaders and heads of state he interviewed, he was the most impressed by President Tito of Yugoslavia.

A highly respected journalist, MacColl also published several books, the best-known of which was *Roger Casement: a New Judgement* (1956). He also wrote two autobiographies, *A Flying Start* (1939) and *Deadline and Dateline* (1956); a novel, *No Idea!* (1952); an account of his visit to Russia, *Just back from Russia: 77 Days Inside the Soviet Union* (1954); and a travel book, *The Land of Genghis Khan: a Journey in Outer Mongolia* (1963). René MacColl died on 20 May 1971 in Crowborough Hospital, Sussex. ANNE PIMLOTT BAKER

Sources R. MacColl, *Deadline and dateline* (1956) · R. MacColl, *A flying start* (1939) · *The Times* (21 May 1971) · *Lincoln College Record*, 1970–71, 28–9 · *WWW* · *Who was who in America* · *CGPLA Eng. & Wales* (1971)
Archives IWM, corresp. and papers | Bodl. RH, corresp. with Sir R. R. Welensky · U. Glas., letters to D. S. MacColl | SOUND BL NSA, documentary recording
Likenesses photograph, 1945, repro. in MacColl, *Deadline and dateline* · photograph, repro. in *The Times*
Wealth at death £29,335: probate, 27 July 1971, *CGPLA Eng. & Wales*

McColl, Robert Smyth (1876–1959), footballer and retailer, was born on 13 April 1876 at 49 Holmhead Street, Glasgow, the son of Donald McColl, a bookkeeper, and his wife, Jemima Smyth. He showed an aptitude for association football at an early age and started playing with a local junior side, Benmore, before moving in January 1894 to play for Queen's Park, at that time the senior side in Scotland. During the first eight years of his career he played no league football because until 1900 Queen's Park would have nothing to do with payment for play and stayed out of the Scottish League, which had been founded in 1890 and had introduced professionalism in 1893. McColl's reputation as the Prince of Centre Forwards was made in the famous match of 1900 between England and Scotland, the 'Rosebery international', when the Scottish players forsook their customary dark blue colours to play in the primrose and pink racing colours of the former prime minister, the earl of Rosebery. McColl scored three of the goals in Scotland's 4–1 victory. Two years later he captained the Scottish side in what became known as the 'Ibrox disaster' match (5 April 1902), when

wooden terracing collapsed and killed twenty-six spectators.

McColl was at the centre of controversy when, on 28 October 1901, he resigned from Queen's Park to join Newcastle United, where he became a professional player. He returned to Scotland, however, in September 1904 to play for Queen's Park's great rivals in Glasgow, Rangers, and in 1907 he took the unprecedented step of applying to revert to amateur status as a member of Queen's Park. It had been an inviolable rule of the Queen's Park club that any dalliance with professional football entailed permanent removal from the membership roll. McColl's involvement with professional football had been neither fleeting nor insignificant yet, to the consternation of many, he was readmitted to membership by the casting vote of the president in August 1907. He won the last of his international caps against Ireland in 1908, and retired from club football in 1910.

McColl's return to Queen's Park may have been prompted by the realization that it was a businessman's club, and could assist a commercial career. Former players' ambitions did not normally extend beyond running a corner-shop or public house, but in 1910 McColl began to build up a chain of confectioner's shops. At first this was confined to Glasgow, but later the business expanded to include retail news agencies throughout the north of England. 'Toffee Bob', as McColl was later known, died in Glasgow on 25 November 1959, his death curiously unnoticed by newspapers of record. ROBERT A. CRAMPSEY

Sources R. A. Crampsey, *The Scottish Football League: the first 100 years* (1990) · R. Robinson, *The history of Queen's Park FC, 1867–1917* (1920) · P. Joannou, *The history of Newcastle United* (1980)
Likenesses photograph, repro. in A. Gibson and W. Pickford, *Association football and the men who made it*, 4 vols. (1906), vol. 3. facing p. 192

MacColla, Alasdair [Sir Alexander MacDonald] (*d.* 1647), clan leader, was the third son of Col MacGillespie (*d.* 1647)—also known as Coll Ciotach or Colkitto, names that many sources wrongly assign to his son—and (probably) Mary MacDonald, who had been repudiated by her former husband, Ranald MacDonald of Benbecula. Alasdair's father was a claimant to chieftancy of the clan Ian Mor, the southern branch of the now fragmented MacDonald clan that had once dominated the lordship of the isles. Since the lordship had been abolished at the end of the fifteenth century other clans (above all the Campbells) had taken advantage of the weakness and internal feuds of the MacDonalds to build up their own power. Kintyre and Jura passed to the Campbells in 1607, and Islay too was handed over to them after a bitter succession feud among the MacDonalds led them into a confused rebellion. Coll Ciotach played a prominent part in these internal struggles that sought to save the clan's lands but instead hastened their loss, and emerged in possession of the island of Colonsay. Alasdair MacColla's youth was spent in this surviving fragment of the old MacDonald empire, doubtless with visits to his close kinsmen in Ireland, the MacDonnells of Antrim. In 1638 the earl of Antrim sought to exploit the conflict between Charles I and the Scottish covenanters by offering the king military help in Scotland in return for former MacDonald lands in Scotland. This provoked the earl of Argyll, as chief of the Campbells, into imprisoning Coll Ciotach and two of Alasdair's brothers, and driving the remnants of the family into exile.

Alasdair MacColla and his brother Ranald escaped to Antrim, and from there they led a small-scale and brief raid on Islay in November 1640. When the Irish uprising began in October 1641 Alasdair served as a captain in a regiment raised in Antrim to resist the rebels, but the tensions in a regiment which mixed Roman Catholic officers and men, like Alasdair, with protestants in fighting a war in which the two sides were largely defined by religious allegiance were intolerable. In January 1642 Alasdair and his co-religionists attacked their protestant colleagues and led local Catholics in joining the uprising. He commanded a force which won a notable victory at the battle of the Laney on 11 February, but soon eastern Ulster was occupied by an army from Scotland, the MacDonnell lands in Antrim being garrisoned by a Campbell regiment under Argyll's command. At Glenmaquin, co. Donegal, Alasdair persuaded the Irish commander, Sir Phelim O'Neill, to attack a protestant force on 16 June, and in the defeat that followed he was severely injured.

Alasdair's priorities lay, as always, in protecting his family and clan, and he now reconsidered his position. Alliance with the Irish had seemed a way of fighting the Campbells and regaining clan lands in Scotland and freedom for his father and brothers, but now the Irish cause was faltering. Alasdair and Ranald therefore negotiated a secret agreement with the earl of Leven (general of the Scottish army in Ireland) whereby they would desert the Irish and in return his relatives would be freed and family property restored. The brothers duly deserted, but their agreement with the Scots army soon broke down and they returned to the rebel cause, by one account because Alasdair was 'so generous as he would in no termes take service against the Irishes, with whom he had once syded' (Gordon, 64).

In 1643 Alasdair became involved in Antrim's plans to bring help from Ireland to Charles I against his English and Scottish enemies, and in November 1643 he led a raid on Islay and Colonsay. He was soon driven back to Ireland, but there Antrim gave him command, with the rank of major-general, of a mixed Irish and highland Scots expeditionary force which was intended to land in the west highlands and join Scottish royalists in war against the covenanting regime. He landed his troops (about sixteen hundred strong, far fewer than had been planned) in Morvern and Ardnamurchan in July 1644, but quickly found that he lacked credibility. His orders from the king were to join the marquess of Huntly, but the latter's attempt at a rising against the covenanters had been defeated months before, and even royalist-inclined chiefs were reluctant to rise in arms under a man whose previous landings had been failures, and whose arrival was seen as much or more as an Irish invasion than as a royalist rising.

Alasdair marched his men through the highlands in search of support, unaware that at the same time the royalist marquess of Montrose was making his way to the highlands hoping to find men to lead in a rising. When the two men learned of each other's movements is not clear, but they met in Atholl. The meeting was momentous. Montrose's leadership provided Alasdair's force with Scottish royalist noble leadership, providing a degree of respectability and credibility, while Alasdair provided Montrose with a body of veterans already in arms around which to build an army. It was to form the nucleus of the royalist army in the campaigns that followed. From September 1644 to August 1645 six successive victories were achieved, Alasdair himself playing a major part in all but one of them. However, difference in ambitions between the two men caused frequent tension. Montrose was fighting for the king, hoping to subdue Scotland then intervene in England to bring victory to Charles in the English civil war, whereas Alasdair and his men had specifically Irish and highland agendas. To Alasdair, the war was fought on behalf of family and to regain clan lands in Scotland. After the victories at Tippermuir (1 September 1644) and Aberdeen (13 September) Alasdair went back to the highlands on expeditions valuable to Montrose in that men were recruited to strengthen his army, but which he probably had no alternative to sanctioning, as such opportunities to wage war on the Campbells were the price of Alasdair's continuing support. At the end of 1644 Montrose at first planned to quarter for the winter in the lowlands, but Alasdair and his men persuaded him instead to undertake a campaign in the west. This culminated in the routing of the Campbells at Inverlochy (2 February 1645).

Alasdair played a central role in turning near defeat into victory at Auldearn (9 May), but was absent from Alford (2 July), being again in the west fighting and recruiting. He returned in time to fight in the last victory of the campaign, at Kilsyth (15 August), but the divergence between his and Montrose's objectives then contributed to disaster. Montrose, determined to break into England, moved south to the border, while Alasdair, though knighted by Montrose, insisted on taking most of his men back to Argyllshire to prevent any resurgence of Campbell power. The fact that he left 700 of his Irish troops with Montrose may indicate an element of compromise, and is perhaps a sign that Alasdair intended, as in the past, to rejoin Montrose after his foray. But Montrose's army was destroyed at Philiphaugh (13 September) and he was forced to flee back to the highlands to try to rebuild an army. Alasdair failed to rejoin him, choosing instead to continue his war in Argyllshire. When in mid-1646 Charles I (then a prisoner of the Scottish army in England) ordered royalist forces in Scotland to disband, Montrose duly went into exile, but Alasdair remained in arms. He had co-operated with the royalist cause, but now put clan ambitions first, refusing to surrender the lands in Argyllshire that he had overrun. In 1647 lowland covenanting forces combined with the Campbells in a campaign against him and his resistance disintegrated. Driven into Kintyre, he and some of his men escaped first to Islay and then to Ireland, while the remnants of his army were massacred.

Alasdair hoped to receive Irish aid for a prompt return to Scotland, but there was no hope of Irish confederates, now fighting for survival, engaging in another Scottish venture. Instead Alasdair was appointed lieutenant-general of Lord Taaffe's Munster army and governor of Clonmel. On 13 November 1647 Taaffe's army faced Lord Inchiquin's at Knocknanuss, co. Cork. Alasdair led the right wing in a successful charge and plundered the enemy baggage train, but the collapse of the rest of the confederate army then exposed him and his men to cavalry charges, and they were slaughtered or dispersed. Alasdair was evidently captured, but shot immediately after the battle by a junior officer, perhaps in a dispute over who should have credit for taking so important a prisoner.

Most accounts of the 1644–5 royalist campaign in Scotland present Alasdair's role as a limited one: he was brave and a good leader in battle, but blundering and untrustworthy. He thus becomes a useful scapegoat for Montrose's occasional mistakes and final failure. Certainly his strategic vision was limited, and his focus on clan was frustrating to Montrose. But without Alasdair he would not have had an army, and there is strong evidence that the tactic that was to bring highland armies repeated success in the century that followed (up to the battle of Falkirk in 1746)—the highland charge—was developed by Alasdair from older Gaelic tactics. His men would drop their muskets after firing one volley, and charge their enemies with their swords, thus catching them off guard, as they were still struggling to reload their muskets, without (until the end of the seventeenth century) bayonets to defend themselves. It was such fast and wild highland charges, timed to bring tactical advantage, that won most of Montrose's battles.

In Gaelic sources Alasdair shares fully with Montrose in credit for the 'year of victories'. In the words of Neil MacMhuirich the Gaels were 'the men who did all the service' (MacBain and Kennedy, 2.203), and Alasdair was their leader. The many tales that circulated for generations in Ireland and the highlands about his great size and strength, and the myths of supernatural signs that accompanied his birth and his deeds, are reflections of the status he achieved among his own people. Poets, male and female, sang his praises. Of his personal life all that is known is that, probably during the 1644–5 campaign, he married a daughter of Hector MacAllister of Loup.

DAVID STEVENSON

Sources D. Stevenson, *Alasdair MacColla and the highland problem in the seventeenth century* (1980); repr. as *Highland warrior: Alasdair MacColla and the civil wars* (1994) · D. Stevenson, 'The way of the warrior: Alasdair MacColla', *King or covenant?* (1996), 133–49 · P. Gordon, *A short abridgement of Britane's distemper*, ed. J. Dunn, Spalding Club, 10 (1844) · 'The book of Clanranald', *Reliquiae Celticae*, ed. A. MacBain and J. Kennedy, 2 vols. (1892–4), 2

Mac Colla, Fionn. *See* MacDonald, Thomas Joseph Douglas (1906–1975).

McColvin, Lionel Roy (1896–1976), librarian, was born on 30 November 1896 at Heaton, Newcastle upon Tyne. He was the second son and third child of John Andrew McColvin, a portrait painter, and his wife, Isabel (*née* Stewart); there were two more children, of whom one, Eric Raymond (*b.* 1904), was afterwards librarian at the polytechnic, Regent Street. In 1901 the family moved to London and finally settled at 38 Lebanon Road, East Croydon. McColvin attended Portland Road primary school, and, at the age of eleven, won a scholarship to Croydon Council Boys' Secondary School, later part of Selhurst grammar school. In 1911 he became a junior assistant in the central library in Katharine Street, following his elder brother, Norman. McColvin enlisted in the 24th Middlesex regiment in 1915, transferred to the 2nd Border regiment, and fought in the third battle of Ypres in October 1917. He returned to Croydon public libraries in 1919 and was later appointed reference librarian. He attended the school of librarianship at University College, London, and passed the Library Association examinations in 1920–21; his diploma thesis, *Music in Public Libraries*, completed and approved in 1923, was published in 1924. Appointed chief assistant at Wigan Public Library on 1 April 1921, he there met and on 18 April 1922 married Mary Carter, the only daughter of William and Esther Carter.

McColvin became chief librarian at Ipswich in the summer of 1924 and the new central library opened in September 1924. He took an active part in planning the interior, and made much of it open-access for the first time. Helped by William Paul, a local corn merchant, he secured enough money to restock the shelves; he promoted musical activities, created a children's library, encouraged extension work and the drama, and actively publicized the library service. A keen amateur musician, he organized celebrity concerts in Ipswich and through them met many famous musical figures. He contributed to *The Sackbut*, the *Musical Times*, and other musical papers. Between 1920 and 1929 McColvin contributed to *Library World* under the pseudonym Aristonymous, and, under another pseudonym, John Molvin, wrote plays, two of which were published, and most of which were produced by the Ipswich library players. This culminated in his Ipswich pageant play *To Kill the Queen*, produced between 17 and 20 June 1931.

In 1931 McColvin was appointed chief librarian at Hampstead and curator of the Keats House Museum. His principal achievement was the new Belsize Library, but he also rejuvenated the lending library stock and introduced chamber music concerts. In 1936 he undertook a survey of public libraries in the United States, part of an international project undertaken by the Library Association, and the results, edited by McColvin, appeared in 1938. While at Hampstead he published a number of influential books: *Library Stock and Assistance to Readers* (1936); *Libraries and the Public* (1937); and *Music Libraries* (2 vols., 1937–8). On 1 April 1938 he became city librarian at Westminster and remained there until his retirement on 30 November 1961. In 1940 he was put in charge of the civil defence report centre for Westminster, but still found opportunity, granted six months' paid leave of absence, to undertake extended tours around the country for an inquiry into the public library service, published as *The Public Library System of Great Britain* (1942): the McColvin report. But its recommendations were not then accepted.

McColvin served on the Library Association's council from 1925; he was also a member of the wartime emergency committee, honorary secretary (1934–51), editor of the *Library Association Record* (1941–5), president (1952), and honorary fellow (1961). He was made CBE in 1951. McColvin worked for UNESCO and was a member of its British co-operating committee; he also worked for the British Council and travelled extensively on its behalf, and was a member of the International Federation of Library Associations (IFLA) as vice-president and chairman of the public libraries section, and of the Society of Municipal and County Chief Librarians, which he was instrumental in establishing. In Westminster, in the post-war period, he opened a new branch library in Charing Cross Road and founded the central music library. He was a member of the Roberts committee, whose report (1959) led to the 1964 Public Libraries and Museums Act. He was forced to retire in 1961, affected by defective memory caused by two strokes, and died on 16 January 1976 at Southgate. He was cremated at Golders Green.

McColvin (Mac) was personally unassuming and not especially gregarious. A pipe-smoker and beer-drinker, he was always accessible to colleagues, no matter how junior, and was willing to listen, quick-witted, a fluent speaker, and an excellent committee man; he wrote and published prolifically. He was agnostic, although his wife was a Roman Catholic. His eldest son, (Kenneth) Roy, later became librarian of Lambeth. McColvin was the most influential British public librarian of the twentieth century. He was best-known for his promotion of cultural extension activities in libraries, and his insistence on the key role of public libraries in community life.

B. C. BLOOMFIELD

Sources R. F. Vollans, ed., *Libraries for the people* (1968) · *Library Review*, 32 (1983), 114–44 · K. C. Harrison, 'McColvin, IFLA and international librarianship', *IFLA Journal*, 3 (1976), 133–6 · *World encyclopedia of librarianship*, 3rd edn (1993) · T. Landau, ed., *Who's who in librarianship* (1954) · *WWW*, 1981–90 · *The Times* (24 Jan 1976), 14f · private information (2004) · *CGPLA Eng. & Wales* (1977)
Likenesses photograph, 1968, Library Association, London
Wealth at death £2643: probate, 16 Nov 1977, *CGPLA Eng. & Wales*

McComb, William (1793–1873), poet, son of Thomas McComb, a draper, was born at Coleraine, co. Londonderry, on 17 August 1793. His mother's surname was Foster. After receiving an elementary education in his native town, he was apprenticed to Thomas O'Neill, a Belfast wholesale draper, but after a short time left him, and, after training with the Kildare Place Society, Dublin, became a teacher of Brown Street daily school in Belfast.

In 1816 McComb married Sarah Johnson of Hillsborough, Belfast, and a year later published *The Dirge of O'Neill and other Poems* in Belfast. The collection commemorated Arthur O'Neill, a blind harpist considered the last of the Irish itinerant bards, who had died in co. Armagh the previous year. One of the poems, 'O Erin my country!

although thy harp slumbers' became particularly popular. McComb followed this moderate success with *The School of the Sabbath* in 1822, a long poem 'adapted to inspire pity for the ignorant poor, and augmented energy for the promotion of Sunday Schools' (McComb, 402).

In 1827 McComb's wife, Sarah, died, and he abandoned teaching to start business as a bookseller in High Street, Belfast. In 1830 he married Eliza Barkley, the widow of Captain Robert Walkinshaw Campbell of Belfast, and the couple had several children. In 1840 he established *McComb's Presbyterian Almanac*, which became a highly popular annual in the north of Ireland. He took a deep interest in many of the charitable institutions of Belfast, and was one of the founders and the first treasurer of the Ulster Institution for the Education of the Deaf and Dumb and the Blind.

The Voice of a Year, or, Recollections of 1848, McComb's third collection of poems, appeared in 1849. 'Its theme is Revolution' remarked the *Belfast News-Letter*, 'and its moral the guilt and misery of attempting to change the institutions of a nation by the prowess of the popular sword, instead of the power of popular opinion' (McComb, 420).

In 1864 McComb retired from business, and later that year published a collected edition of his poetry, *Poetical Works*, to much acclaim from the protestant and unionist press. The *Belfast Protestant Journal* claimed 'Mr McComb's reputation as a poet is not local, but national', and compared him to Thomas Moore (McComb, 404). McComb's 'national' appeal was, however, limited by his virulent anti-Catholicism, demonstrable in lines from *The Voice of a Year* such as:

> Princes and Potentates from thrones were hurled
> Wherever haughty Rome her blood-red flag unfurled
> (stanza 41)

and 'Antichrist, arrayed in papal power' (stanza 42). On 13 September 1873 McComb died at home, in Colin View Terrace, Belfast. He was interred in Hillsborough churchyard.

THOMAS HAMILTON, rev. KATHERINE MULLIN

Sources W. McComb, *Poetical works* (1864) · K. Newmann, 'Arthur O'Neill', *Dictionary of Ulster biography* (1993), 207 · *McComb's Presbyterian Almanac* (1874)
Likenesses portrait, repro. in McComb, *Poetical works*, frontispiece
Wealth at death under £450: probate, 1 Dec 1873, *CGPLA Ire.*

McCombie, William (*bap.* 1805, *d.* 1880), cattle breeder, was born at Home Farm, Tillyfour, Aberdeenshire, and baptized on 3 August 1805, the younger son of Charles McCombie, a farmer and cattle dealer, who was descended from an old highland family, and his wife, Anne, *née* Black. He was educated at the parish school and Marischal College, Aberdeen.

McCombie worked with his father until he leased the Tillyfour farm from him in 1829, and in 1832 he founded a polled Angus herd. Realizing that there was no future in driving lean cattle from the north of Scotland to be fattened in the south, he turned to the breeding of black polled cattle, carrying on the work of Hugh Watson of Keiller (1789–1865), the first to improve Aberdeen Angus cattle. McCombie became famous as an exhibitor of prize stock, and was the first Scottish exhibitor of fat cattle at Birmingham. He won more than five hundred prizes, including Prince Albert's cup for the best animal in the French or foreign classes at Poissy in 1862, and a similar prize at the Paris Exhibition in 1878. After his champion ox, Black Prince, won the blue riband at Smithfield in 1866, Queen Victoria asked him to bring it to Windsor, and following this the queen visited Tillyfour in 1867 to inspect McCombie's herd. McCombie also wrote *Cattle and Cattle Breeders* (1867), which ran to four editions. He was one of the largest farmers in Aberdeenshire, with 1200 acres of arable land, and he was one of the earliest presidents of the Scottish chamber of agriculture.

From 1868 until 1876 McCombie was MP for West Aberdeenshire, the first tenant farmer to be an MP in Scotland. He resigned in 1876 because of failing health. The McCombie prize for black polled cattle, an annual prize, was set up in Aberdeen in his honour. McCombie spent the rest of his life at Tillyfour, which he had bought in 1875, on the death of his eldest brother. He died unmarried at Home Farm on 1 February 1880.

J. R. MacDonald, *rev.* Anne Pimlott Baker

Sources R. Trow-Smith, *A history of British livestock husbandry, 1700–1900*, 2 vols. (1957–9) · *The Times* (3 Feb 1880) · W. McCombie, *Cattle and cattle breeders*, ed. J. Macdonald, 4th edn (1886) · Irving, *Scots.* · Boase, *Mod. Eng. biog.* · Ward, *Men of the reign* · IGI

McCombie, William (1809–1870), farmer and journalist, was born on 7 May 1809 at Alford, Aberdeenshire, the son of William McCombie, farmer, and his wife, Marjory Wishart. McCombie received little formal education and was largely self-educated under the influence of his mother. *The Spectator* regarded him as the greatest example of the autodidact in Scotland after his fellow journalist Hugh Miller (*The Spectator*, 14 May 1870). His early life was spent on his father's farm with his spare time devoted to the composition of essays on religious and philosophical subjects. These essays were collected in 1835 under the title of *Hours of Thought* (1835), which reached a third, expanded edition by 1856; a second early work, *Moral Agency and Man as a Moral Agent* (1842), was an attack on Calvinist theology. In early 1840 McCombie married Anne, daughter of Joseph Robertson of Aberdeen. In this period McCombie was also active in the Mutual Improvement Movement which operated in the north-east of Scotland, becoming honorary president of the Aberdeenshire and Banffshire Mutual Instruction Union. The activities of this organization extended beyond adult education and provided a link between the Free Church of Scotland, the Liberal Party, and the conservative peasantry. It is in connection with a lecture for a Mutual Improvement Society in 1850 that a description is provided of McCombie as 'a tall slightly stooping man, in the prime of life … with a fine intellectual face, a keen searching, yet pleasant and slightly humorous glance and expression' (Smith, 67).

From 1849 McCombie was on the staff of the *Aberdeen Gazette*, and soon became the editor, changing the title of the paper to the *Aberdeen Free Press* in 1853. The paper was a supporter of the Liberal cause and of the Free Church which was powerful in Aberdeen, although McCombie himself was a Baptist. Under McCombie's editorship it supported some quite advanced causes such as universal suffrage. In journalistic terms McCombie's regime saw an improved standard of editorship but this may have had more to do with his assistant and successor, William Alexander, than with McCombie, who devoted more time to farming than to day-to-day editorial duties. McCombie was a keen Liberal in politics and wholly behind the Liberal cause, being particularly active in the cause of tenant farmers who became increasingly restive throughout Scotland in the 1860s, especially on the issue of the Game Laws. His cousin, William McCombie of Tillyfour (*bap.* 1805, *d.* 1880), the famous cattle breeder, was Liberal MP for West Aberdeenshire from 1868 to 1876 and president of the Scottish chamber of agriculture. The *Aberdeen Free Press* also reported at great length on the American Civil War, which was an important influence on Scottish Liberalism in the mid-nineteenth century. McCombie positioned himself firmly behind the North on the grounds of the evil of slavery, which he felt had been forced on the South by Britain in the eighteenth century.

McCombie's final publication in 1869 was a pamphlet entitled *The Irish land question practically considered: a letter to the Rt Hon William E. Gladstone, M.P.* (with whom he had corresponded during the 1860s). In order to prepare himself for constructive comment on the Irish land issue McCombie toured Ireland in the autumn of 1868. In the pamphlet he argued that Irish nationalism was 'exotic' (p. 13) and was only sustained by the continuing injustices of the land system and the church. If these two issues were dealt with then, in McCombie's view, it would 'speedily die' (ibid.). He was critical of both tenants and landowners, the former for their lack of initiative and exertion and the latter for their selfishness and 'utter disregard for the public interest' (ibid., 33). Nevertheless, he felt that 'were the resources and capabilities of the soil properly developed it might maintain in comfort as large a population as that before the famine' (ibid., 10). This pamphlet was perhaps McCombie's most accessible and most practical piece of work; his other writings were, like much of his journalism, rather abstract and even metaphysical.

McCombie was an active lay preacher in the John Street Baptist Church in Aberdeen and his *Sermons and Lectures* (1871) were prepared for posthumous publication by his daughter. He also published two volumes commemorating the work of George Murray, a shoemaker and journalist (*Literary Remains of George Murray*, 1860) and Alexander Bethune, a farmer poet (*Memoirs of Alexander Bethune*, 1845). His other principal publication was a collection of essays on the subject of education: *On Education in its Constituents, Objects and Issues* (1857).

McCombie remained a practical farmer throughout his career, first on his father's farm at Cairnballoch, and then, from the late 1860s, at Milton of Kemnay, also in Aberdeenshire. *The Spectator* recorded in 1870 that 'he rapidly made his fine farm a model for both the completeness of its arrangements and the quality of its stock' (14 May

1870). Indeed, McCombie's reputation as an agriculturist did much to improve the profile of the *Aberdeen Free Press* which until his editorship had been in the shadow of the *Aberdeen Journal*.

In early 1870 McCombie was laid low with a severe attack of bronchitis and chronic dyspepsia, ailments from which he had suffered for most of his life, and which resulted in his death on 6 May 1870 at 9 Broadford Place, Aberdeen. He was survived by his widow and their four sons and two daughters.

McCombie could be characterized merely as a provincial newspaper editor and obscure essayist, but within the confines of the north-east of Scotland, however, he was much more than this. The very clear regional identity of this part of the country, allied to his political activities, especially concerning the fate of tenant farmers, assured him a wider prominence. He was also well known as a practical farmer. Much of his literary output, with the possible exception of his *Hours of Thought* and his pamphlet, *The Irish Land Question*, was rather obscure; on his death *The Spectator* commented 'the world has never given a welcome to his books … his written dissertations were not distinctive or complete enough to be singled out for special remembrance' (14 May 1870). His contemporary prominence stemmed from his editorship of the *Aberdeen Free Press* which was sustained and developed by his successor, William Alexander, who turned the paper into a daily in 1872. McCombie's life, however, fits a nineteenth-century Scottish stereotype which emphasized his self-education, his piety, and his contribution to his locality.

EWEN A. CAMERON

Sources *Aberdeen Free Press* (13 May 1870) · *The Spectator* (14 May 1870) · *The Scotsman* (9 May 1870) · R. H. Smith, *An Aberdeenshire village propaganda forty years ago* (1889) · I. R. Carter, *Farm life in the north-east, 1840–1914: the poor man's country* (1979) · I. R. Carter, 'The mutual improvement movement in north east Scotland in the 19th century', *Aberdeen University Review*, 46 (1975–6), 383–92 · W. Donaldson, *Popular literature in Victorian Scotland* (1986) · R. M. W. Cowan, *The newspaper in Scotland: a study of its first expansion, 1815–1860* (1946) · F. M. Szasz, 'Scotland, Abraham Lincoln and the American Civil War', *Northern Scotland*, 16 (1996), 127–40 · Gladstone, *Diaries*
Wealth at death £2929 11s. 8d.: confirmation, 14 Dec 1870, NA Scot., SC 1/36/67/847–52

Mac Conmara, Donnchadh Ruadh (1714/15–1810), Irish-language poet, is of uncertain origins. There are no written sources for his birth and the two accounts which purport to be based on reliable oral tradition show some discrepancies. O'Grady writing in 1853 states that he was 'guided by information carefully collected from such of the posterity of our poet as are still living, as well as from others in that part of the county of Waterford where he spent the greater part of his life' and goes on to say that Mac Conmara was born in Cratloe (An Chreatlach in Irish) in co. Clare 'in, or shortly after the year 1709' (Hayes, 3). Of Seaghan Pléimeann, or John Fleming, it is said that he had access to a similar type of informant: 'he was acquainted not only with some of Donogh's pupils, but also with one of his grandsons, and had many of his facts from living witnesses' (Ó Flannghaile, viii). Writing in 1881–2, Fleming states that Mac Conmara was born 'early in the last century' (ibid., 1), and he cites, in agreement with O'Grady, Cratloe as place of birth. Fortunately, a contemporary newspaper, the *Freeman's Journal* (5 November 1810), recorded Mac Conmara's death at the age of ninety-five and, while the caveat as to the reliability of such oral sources as were available to the newspaper must remain, it is not unreasonable to posit 1714 or 1715 as Mac Conmara's date of birth.

O'Grady and Fleming are in agreement that, having been educated first at home, Mac Conmara was sent to Rome in order to study for the priesthood. This would indicate either that his parents, of whom nothing is known, lived in relatively comfortable circumstances, or that his education was sponsored from the outset by some well-off relation or patron. He spent some five years in Rome and was then expelled from whatever college he had been attending for some misdemeanour of which nothing is known. These formative years equipped him for life with a thorough knowledge of Latin, which he demonstrated in the elegy he wrote for fellow poet Tadhg Gaelach Ó Súilleabháin in 1795. Donnchadh Ruadh was doubtlessly fluent in Irish from childhood, he acquired English in the course of his education, and it is not unreasonable to assume a knowledge on his part of some other continental languages gained during the course of his travels. Ó Foghludha rejects the opinion of O'Grady and Fleming that Mac Conmara studied in Rome, arguing that the Latinity the poet undoubtedly possessed would have been accessible to him in Ireland (Ó Foghludha, *Donnchadh Ruadh*, iii; Ó Foghludha, *Donnchadh Ruadh MacComara*, 10). While the reason put forward by Ó Foghludha for his opinion is valid, the unanimous opinion of the earlier commentators is bolstered by a well-established and widespread practice, which lasted up to the end of the eighteenth century, of young Irishmen going abroad to study for the priesthood. In the absence of documentary evidence to the contrary, the traditions of the poet's time spent in Rome must be allowed to stand. Ó Foghludha's attitude to this question may well have been influenced by an understandable desire, when he produced his two editions, to disseminate a certain orthodox and, therefore, simplified view of Gaelic Ireland in the eighteenth century.

About 1740 Mac Conmara arrived from the continent and settled in the Decies country in Waterford. The strong scholastic and literary traditions of that district would have been attractive to Mac Conmara, though it cannot be ruled out that his decision to settle there had to do with his determination not to return to his native parts following his fall from grace in Rome. He taught school in various districts of Waterford, first in the parish of Seskinane in either the townland of Ballynaguilkee or of Knockboy under the auspices of fellow poet Uilliam Ó Móráin. O'Grady and Fleming claim that at about this time he married Máire Ní Ógáin, but Ó Foghludha's dissenting opinion (Ó Foghludha, *Donnchadh Ruadh MacComara*, 13–14) on this matter does not lack cogency. Unhappy with the life of a peripatetic schoolmaster, it seems that Mac Conmara set out for Newfoundland some time after 1745. The voyage across the Atlantic features in his most ambitious poem, entitled *Eachtra Ghiolla an Amaráin*, 'The Voyage of the Luckless Fellow'. While it is not possible to state how long he spent in Newfoundland, it is clear that he had returned to Waterford by 1758 when he compiled the Maynooth manuscript M 85 (4 A 11) in which are found autograph copies of three of his poems, including the 'Voyage'. In 1764 Mac Conmara, having appealed to and having won the favour of James Ducket, of White's Town, became clerk of the protestant church in Kilmacthomas. He converted to the tenets of that church in order to get the clerkship and composed what must have been to his Catholic fellows a challenging poem that sets down boldly the reasons for his tergiversation. However, as in the case of his relationship with the Catholic church, his reluctance to toe the line had him in disagreement with the authorities in the new denomination, and he returned to Catholicism. In Mac Conmara's latter years he composed a formal poem of repentance, but does not refer at all to his denominational oscillations. It seems that he had married some years prior to 1764, for in his appeal to Ducket in that year, in the form of a poem, he alludes to his inability to provide for his *naíonáin* or 'infant children' (ibid., 14). From approximately 1800 he spent some years teaching the Power family in the parish of Kill in co. Waterford, but eventually retired to the home of his son Donnchadh Óg, a weaver by trade, in Newtown near Kilmacthomas, where he died on 6 October 1810; he was buried in Newtown.

Mac Conmara will be best remembered for 'The Voyage of the Luckless Fellow' which can be classed as belonging to a category of narrative poetry. In these 291 lines a long sea journey is recounted, including a battle at sea, and an interval in the other world where characters from classical and Irish myth and history are encountered. It is worth noting, however, that his song in praise of Ireland, *Bánchnoic Éireann Óighe*, which he based on an existing song, was probably composed while in Newfoundland, and is one of the best-known songs in the Irish language folk repertoire today. Despite, or, perhaps, because of the fact that he crossed swords with the Catholic church early in life, he had a lasting interest in the affairs of the clergy, which is reflected in what survives of his verse. In the most comprehensive and most acute analysis to date of Jacobite literature in Ireland (Ó Buachalla, 646–7) a hitherto unpublished satire by Donnchadh Ruadh is singled out for its biting invective in attacking the Catholic clergy of Ireland for seeking a *rapprochement* with the Hanoverian kings and government. The concentrated and sustained criticism of the political tendencies of the church as found in these ninety-six lines of verse compensates for a certain flaccidity and lack of focus in Mac Conmara's other poems. This piece also foreshadows his willingness to break, if only temporarily, with the Catholic–Jacobite nexus in order to give priority to earning his bread as a protestant clerk through the offices of a protestant but Irish-speaking landowner.   L. P. Ó MURCHÚ

Sources S. Hayes, ed., *Adventures of Donnchadh Ruadh Mac Conmara, a slave of adversity, written by himself. Now for the first time edited, from an original Irish manuscript* (1853) • [D. R. Mac Conmara], *Eachtra Ghiolla an Amaráin, or, The adventures of a luckless fellow, and other poems by Red Donough Macnamara*, ed. T. Ó Flannghaile (1897) [incl. biography by J. Fleming] • *Donnchadh Ruadh cct.: díoghluim ina bhfuil suim de sna duanógaibh is fearr dár cheap Donnchadh Ruadh mac Conmara, 1715–1810*, ed. R. Ó Foghludha (1908) • *Donnchadh Ruadh MacComara, 1715–1810*, ed. R. Ó Foghludha (1933) • B. Ó Buachalla, *Aisling Ghéar: Na Stíobhartaigh Agus An tAos Léinn, 1603–1788* (1996) • P. Ó Fiannachta and P. Walsh, *Lámhscríbhinní Gaeilge Choláiste Phádraig Má Nuad*, [8 pts] (1943–73) • T. O'Rahilly and others, *Catalogue of Irish manuscripts in the Royal Irish Academy*, 30 vols. (Dublin, 1926–70), vol. 20 • *Freeman's Journal* [Dublin] (5 Nov 1810)

Archives Royal Irish Acad., Irish manuscript collection, MS 24 L 27 • St Patrick's College, Maynooth, Murphy papers, MS M 85 (4 A 11)

Mac Con Midhe, Giolla Brighde [Gilbride MacNamee] (*d.* 1272?), poet, was a member of a family which for more than three centuries acted as hereditary poets of the Cenéal Eóghain, the Ó Néill family, and related septs. He sprang from one of these septs, the Cenéal Moáin, settled around Ardstraw in Tyrone, although he tells that his mother was a member of the Cenéal Conaill. The *Ceart Uí Néill*, a traditional listing of Ó Néill's tributes, places the land of Mac Con Midhe, known as 'the Reciter's land', at Lough Uí Mhaoldubháin, which has been identified as the modern Lough Katherine at Baronscourt. Giolla Brighde Mac Con Midhe has at times been confused with an earlier poet, Giolla Brighde Albanach (surname unknown) who addressed a number of poems to Cathal Croibhdhearg Ó Conchobhair, king of Connacht (*d.* 1224), but this is now rejected as mere scribal error, based on the identity of forenames.

Of the twenty-one poems clearly attributable to Giolla Brighde Mac Con Midhe, the earliest dateable ones are addressed to Domhnall Mór Ó Domhnaill, king of Tír Conaill (*d.* 1241), containing allusions appropriate to the period of political weakness in Tír Eoghain in the years after 1230. He also eulogized Domhnall Mór's four sons, Maoilsheachlainn, Gofraid, Aodh, and Domhnall Óg, three of whom succeeded their father in the kingship of Tír Conaill. His most famous composition, however, was an elegy of some eighty-one verses lamenting the death of Brian Ó Néill and his vassal chiefs at the battle of Down in 1260. In this composition he makes clear that he held the position of *ollamh*, or court poet, to Ó Néill, who awarded him twenty cows as the price of a poem, and a stipend of twenty cows on May day, besides presents of gold and clothing. Presumably after Ó Néill's death, Mac Con Midhe entered a similar relationship with Domhnall Óg Ó Domhnaill, who ruled Tír Conaill from 1258 to 1281, and he records receiving twenty cows with their calves from this king each May day. Single compositions of his to other contemporary chiefs survive, and some formal religious poems, but most touching is his poem of supplication to God for a surviving son, all his previous children having died 'while they drank their first milk', a situation particularly distressing for a poet, since Irish custom demanded a more stringent monogamy from this profession than from ordinary laymen. As with many of his other poems, this supplication ends by invoking the saint 'Bridget, after whom I was baptized'.

A fifteenth-century poet from the same family, Briain Ruadh Mac Con Midhe, recalled a tradition that Giolla Brighde died while his patron, Domhnall Óg Ó Domhnaill, was on a plundering expedition to the Erne. Ó Domhnaill is said to have raided Cenéal Moáin on his way back, but, learning that he had met no resistance because the inhabitants were in the act of burying their celebrated poet, he returned the prey. If true, this would place Giolla Brighde Mac Con Midhe's death certainly before 1281, when Domhnall Óg himself died, and possibly in the year 1272, when the king is recorded as going on an expedition to Lough Erne and Lough Oughter. KATHARINE SIMMS

Sources N. J. A. Williams, *The poems of Giolla Brighde Mac Con Midhe* (1980) • G. Murphy, 'A vision concerning Rolf MacMahon—Giolla Brighde Mac Con Midhe, cc.', *Éigse*, 4 (1943), 79–108 • B. Ó Cuív, 'A poem for Cathal Croibhdhearg Ó Conchubhair', *Éigse*, 13 (1969–70), 195–202

McConnell, Primrose (1856–1931), farmer and writer, was born on 11 April 1856 at Lessnessock, Ochiltree, Ayrshire, the son of Archibald McConnell (1821–1898) and his wife, Agnes Milroy (1830–1897). At this time his father held the tenancy of Lessnessock Farm, Ochiltree, but in 1862 he took the tenancy of Castle Mains Farm, New Cumnock, a few miles to the east, and there McConnell spent his boyhood. He was sent to Ayr Academy, and from there he took up an engineering apprenticeship in Glasgow, which he did not complete. Instead he went to the University of Edinburgh to read agriculture, and in 1878 he obtained the diploma of the Highland and Agricultural Society. In 1889, when the university instituted the degree in agriculture, he returned to take the examinations and was the second student to be awarded the BSc.

By the 1880s the reduction in land and sea transport costs, resulting from the expansion of the American railway network and the introduction of steamships on the north Atlantic, had had the effect of reducing cereal prices in those European countries which adopted free trade practices. The then prevalent farming systems on the Essex clays were ill-equipped to cope with falling prices. McConnell was one of the first of many who had been brought up on small Scottish dairy farms to see the potential other use of such land, relatively close to large urban markets. In 1883 he took the tenancy of Ongar Park Hall farm near Epping, converted it to milk production, and farmed there, initially in partnership with his father, until 1905. As soon as he was established in farming, McConnell married on 10 January 1884 Katherine Anderson (1857–1930), daughter of the Free Church minister at New Cumnock, whom he had known since childhood. They had a daughter and two sons. In 1905, following a dispute over farming methods with his landlord, he gave up his tenancy and bought the 500 acre North Wycke Farm at Southminster, near the coast between the Crouch and Blackwater estuaries. There he remained for the rest of his life, dairy farming—he built up a much visited herd of 100 cows, an enormous number in that period—and writing.

Farming, and writing about farming, formed the core of McConnell's life. As a profit maximizing adopter of science based farming techniques, he was a pioneer of twentieth-century farming methods. In addition to making careful evaluations of new devices, such as milking machines, he also developed his own: principal among these was the hay sweep, which he claimed to have introduced from the United States of America and adapted to English conditions. He also lectured, at various times, at the universities of Glasgow and Oxford. But he was most widely known as a writer. He began with journalism, writing to the farming papers at the age of eighteen. Indeed, he later claimed that some articles he had written for the Scottish agricultural press in 1883 formed one of the motivating forces in the influx of Scottish farmers to Essex. His first and best-known book, *The Agricultural Notebook*, was published in 1883, the year he took on his first farm. It went through eleven editions and sold 45,000 copies in his lifetime, and it remained in print in its nineteenth edition in 1996 as an agricultural textbook written by a team of authors. McConnell also wrote *Elements of Agriculture* (1896), *The Complete Farmer* (1908, 2nd edn 1910), a more detailed agricultural textbook, and many other contributions to textbooks and journals. *The Elements of Agricultural Geology* (1902) brought together his professional concerns with agriculture and his serious amateur interest in geology (he became a fellow of the Geological Society in 1900), in an account of the relationship between the underlying rocks and associated farming systems.

From 1905 McConnell edited his own journal, *Farm Life*. Some of the pieces he wrote for this were later reprinted as *The Diary of a Working Farmer* (1906), his only non-technical book. It contains some of his most engaging writing and the only surviving published photographs in which he can be definitely identified; they show him at about the age of fifty, a full-bearded man of middling height and build, with a piercing gaze. His personality, too, appears through the pages of the diary: he was a teetotaller and dissenting churchman with immense energy, fond of the physical work of the farm, surrounded, in his later years at least, by piles of manuscripts and proofs, but always able to find time to play with his grandchildren; he was irascible and tolerant in turn, insatiably curious, and unwilling to take himself too seriously.

McConnell died on 7 July 1931, at North Wycke, and was buried four days later in the nonconformist burial-ground at Southminster. PAUL BRASSLEY

Sources P. Brassley, 'A pioneer in everything: Primrose McConnell, 1856–1931', *Journal of the Royal Agricultural Society of England*, 156 (1995), 172–8 • *Burnham-on-Crouch and Dengie Hundred Advertiser* (11 July 1931) • *University of Edinburgh Journal*, 4 (1930–31), 297–8 • P. McConnell, *The diary of a working farmer* (1906) • private information (2004) • *CGPLA Eng. & Wales* (1931) • d. cert.
Likenesses group portrait, photograph (aged about fifty; with his sons), repro. in McConnell, *Diary of a working farmer*, facing p. 272 • photograph (aged about fifty), repro. in McConnell, *Diary of a working farmer*, frontispiece
Wealth at death £7942 12s. 4d.: administration with will, 8 Oct 1931, *CGPLA Eng. & Wales*

McConnell, William (1831–1867), cartoonist and illustrator, was born in Warwick Street, London, on 29 September 1831, the son of an Irish tailor, and had a sister, Annie (who survived him). After seeing some of his early sketches

Mark Lemon, the first editor of *Punch*, sent him to study wood-engraving with Joseph Swain. His first contribution to *Punch* (aged eighteen) seems to have been an illuminated capital (vol. 18, January–June 1850). Thereafter he produced some sixty illustrations for the magazine, notably two whole-page political cartoons: 'Louis Napoleon Viewing the Body of Liberty', published on 4 December 1851, and 'The Rivals, or, A Military Position', published on 28 February 1852. In July 1852 he left after a dispute over money and 'the contumelious and shabby treatment meted out to him by Mark Lemon' (Spielmann, 460). He also contributed to the *Illustrated London News* (1851–60) and the short-lived *Diogenes* (1853–4, including the strip cartoon 'How Mr Poppleton Enjoyed a Masquerade').

In 1855 McConnell began drawing for the *Illustrated London Magazine*. He served as the first staff comic artist and political cartoonist on the *Illustrated Times* (1855–61) and later on *The Train* (launched on 1 January 1856). In 1857 he illustrated a series of articles by George Augustus Sala for the *Leisure Hour*, and the following year he began contributing to another short-lived magazine, *Town Talk* (1858–9); for the latter he supplied both full-page cartoons and a strip-cartoon series, 'The Adventures of Mr Wilderspin on his Journey through Life', by Andrew Halliday, which was later published as a book (1861). In the same year he illustrated Sala's 'Twice round the clock'—an account of life in London during a 24-hour period—which was published in instalments from the first issue of the *Welcome Guest* (1 May 1858) and later (1859) became a very successful book. Another *Welcome Guest* serial which he illustrated for Sala was 'Make your game, or, The adventures of the stout gentleman, the thin gentleman and the man with the iron chest', later also published as a book (1860). In 1863 he contributed to the short-lived *Comic News* (1863–4), in particular the strip 'The Adventures of Mr Swellington Fipps', and in 1864 he began drawing for *London Society* and the *Churchman's Family Magazine* and then the *Sunday Magazine* (1865).

Among the books for which McConnell provided illustrations were G. Godwin's *London Shadows* (1854, though the title-page credits only John Brown); Oliver Oldfellow's *Our School* (1857); G. F. Pardon's *The Months* (1858); A. W. Cole's *Lorimer Littlegood Esq.* (1858); *Tom Thumb's Alphabet* (c.1860); R. J. Shields's *The Knights of the Red Cross* (1861); W. Smith's *Advertise: How? When?* (1863); *The Beautiful Picture Book* (1865); and the posthumous *My Pet's Picture Book* (1868), *The Turtle Dove's Nest* (1886), and *Nursery Rhymes* (1890). In April 1867 he sketched fifteen double portraits which, if inverted, showed animals (*As Brave as … a Lion*, *As Greedy as … a Pig*, and so on). However, illness prevented him engraving them himself, and they were later published posthumously as *Upside Down, or, Turnover Traits* (1868), with verses by Thomas Hood the younger.

In appearance McConnell was 'a handsome little fellow, bright, alert, and full of originality. He was always exceptionally well dressed' (Spielmann, 460), and was clean-shaven with dark hair and a short dark moustache. He signed himself M'Connell, McConnell, M^cC, WM^c, Mc, or one of two combinations of W and M which also include an A, suggesting another forename. An accomplished cartoonist and pioneer comic-strip artist, and 'one of the most successful book illustrators of our time' (*Art Journal*, 172), he was 'a good and improving draughtsman, especially of horses; and he revelled in beggars, "swells" and backgrounds' (Spielmann, 461). McConnell died of consumption at his home, 17 Tavistock Street, London, on 14 May 1867 aged thirty-five.   MARK BRYANT

Sources DNB · Boase, *Mod. Eng. biog.* · M. H. Spielmann, *The history of 'Punch'* (1895) · M. Bryant and S. Heneage, eds., *Dictionary of British cartoonists and caricaturists, 1730–1980* (1994) · S. Houfe, *The dictionary of British book illustrators and caricaturists, 1800–1914* (1978) · D. Kunzle, *The history of the comic strip: the 19th century* (1990) · G. Everitt, *English caricaturists and graphic humourists of the nineteenth century* (1886) · *Art Journal*, 29 (1867), 135, 172 · *The life and adventures of George Augustus Sala*, 2 vols. (1895) · P. Collins, 'Introduction', in G. A. Sala, *Twice round the clock* (1859) [repr. 1971] · Bryan, *Painters* (1886–9) · [G. Dalziel and E. Dalziel], *The brothers Dalziel: a record of fifty years' work … 1840–1890* (1901) · A. McConnell, 'Preface', in W. McConnell and T. Hood, *Upside down* (1868)
Archives GL | Courtauld Inst., Witt Library
Likenesses H. Watkins, albumen print, 1855–9, NPG · Southwell Brothers, photograph, repro. in Spielmann, *History of Punch*

Maccormac, Henry (1800–1886), physician, was born at Carnan, co. Armagh, the fifth of the eight children of John Maccormac (d. 1811), a linen merchant, and his wife, Anne (d. 1846), daughter of Joseph Hall, a distiller from co. Armagh. He studied medicine in Dublin and then in Paris, where he studied at the L'Hôtel Dieu under the famous surgeon Guillaume, Baron Dupuytren, before graduating MD at Edinburgh in 1824 with a thesis entitled 'De clabo secalino'. In the same year he became a licentiate of the Royal College of Surgeons of Edinburgh.

Following the completion of his studies Maccormac visited Africa, travelling by land from the Cape of Good Hope to Sierra Leone where his brother John was a magistrate. During this journey he nearly died of yellow fever. He subsequently made two voyages to the United States and Canada. He was appointed physician in 1828 to the Belfast Fever Hospital, where in 1832 he successfully limited the spread of an outbreak of cholera in the city. In recognition of this work he received a public testimonial from the citizens of Belfast. In 1833 he married Mary Newsam (or Newsham; 1811–1871); they raised a family of two sons and three daughters.

In 1835 a faculty of medicine was established in the Belfast Academical Institution and Maccormac was appointed to the chair of theory and practice of medicine, a post he held until 1848. During this time he was also, from 1840 to 1845, dean of the faculty of medicine. In 1849 Maccormac unsuccessfully applied for the chair of medicine in the new Queen's College. In the same year he was appointed physician to the Belfast Lunatic Asylum, a position which he held until his death. He brought about a marked change in the quality of the life of the patients, introducing an active healthy regimen to the asylum and improving the patients' diet. In 1849 cholera again struck Belfast, but owing to Maccormac's methods there were no deaths in the asylum.

Maccormac's medical writings cover a broad range of

subjects but he devoted particular attention to the cause and cure of tuberculosis. In the mid-nineteenth century a wide variety of theories were advanced to explain the cause of the disease. Without a common belief in the contagious nature of tuberculosis, causes such as physical predisposition, hereditary inheritance, poverty, and alcoholism were suggested. Maccormac believed that the disease was caused by re-breathed air and advocated the benefits of fresh air as a cure. He was in good company as this view was shared by Florence Nightingale. However, the stubborn way in which Maccormac put forward his ideas, refusing to see reason in any of those who opposed him, did not endear him to his peers. He demanded that his patients follow his advice and open the windows of their homes to ensure good health. On one occasion he had to appear in court for breaking the window panes of the house of a patient who had refused to heed his advice.

In 1861 Maccormac gave a paper to the Royal Medical and Surgical Society in London on 'the true nature and absolute preventibility of tubercular consumption' in which he presented his belief that foul and impure air was the only possible source of tuberculosis. This paper was so badly received by the society that its members refused to pass a vote of thanks to him and calls were made for all future papers to be reviewed by a committee before being read to the society. Undaunted by this slight, Maccormac immediately replied robustly to his critics in the pages of the *Dublin Medical Press*. The event was not forgotten by Maccormac, and twenty years later he published another letter to the society on the subject asking them to reconsider their earlier actions. The attitude of the members of the Royal Medical and Surgical Society was not shared by all of Maccormac's contemporaries. His ideas on the open-air treatment of tuberculosis were embraced in Europe. Indeed a street was named after him in Copenhagen in recognition of his contribution to the treatment of the disease.

About 1866 Maccormac retired from his practice, though he continued to attend the asylum, and devoted himself to his literary and scientific studies. He wrote on a wide variety of subjects including medicine, insanity, religion, philology, and classical antiquity. He also concerned himself with the well-being of animals, writing a work advocating a way of killing animals for food that was more humane than the practices of the time. Although a deeply religious man, he did not adhere to any particular faith. One of his daughters, Mary, remained unmarried and looked after her father after the death of his wife in 1871. One of his sons was the distinguished surgeon Sir William *MacCormac. Henry Maccormac died on 26 May 1886 at Fisherwick Place, Belfast.   KARL MAGEE

Sources I. Fraser, 'Father and son—a tale of two cities', *Ulster Medical Journal*, 37 (winter 1968), 1–39 · Dr Burden, 'Biographical sketch of the late Dr. Henry Maccormac', *Dublin Journal of Medical Science*, 86 (Aug 1888), 161–4 · 'A pioneer of open-air treatment, Henry Maccormac (1800–1886)', *BMJ* (2 May 1942) · *DNB* · 'Rude and unseemly attack on Dr. Maccormac of Belfast by the Medico-Chirurgical Society of London', *Dublin Medical Press* (8 May 1861) · H. Maccormac, 'Correspondence to the members of the London Medico-Chirurgical Society', *Dublin Medical Press* (8 May 1861) · Royal College of Physicians of Ireland, Dublin, Kirkpatrick archive · F. B. Smith, *The retreat of tuberculosis* (1988), chap. 2

Archives U. Edin., MD thesis | Royal College of Physicians of Ireland, Dublin, Kirkpatrick archive

Likenesses bust, Ulster Medical Society Museum · portrait, Ulster Medical Society Museum

Wealth at death £986—effects in England: probate, 23 June 1886, *CGPLA Eng. & Wales*

MacCormac, Sir William, baronet (1836–1901), surgeon, was born at Belfast on 17 January 1836, the elder son of Henry *Maccormac (1800–1886), a physician of Belfast, and his wife, Mary (1811–1871), daughter of William Newsham. The younger son, John, became a director of the Northern Linen Company at Belfast.

After education at the Royal Belfast Academical Institution, MacCormac studied at Dublin and Paris. In October 1851 he entered Queen's College, Belfast, as a student of engineering, and gained engineering scholarships there in his first and second years. He then transferred to the arts course, graduating BA in the old Queen's University in 1855 and proceeding MA in 1858. He won the senior scholarship in natural philosophy in 1856, and next year was admitted MD, subsequently receiving the honorary degrees of MCh in 1879 and of DSc in 1882, with the gold medal of the university. The honorary degrees of MD and MCh were bestowed upon him in later life by the University of Dublin in June 1900.

After graduation MacCormac studied surgery in Berlin, where he made lasting friendships with von Langenbeck, Billroth, and von Esmarch. Becoming MRCS England in 1857, he was elected in 1864 FRCS Ireland. MacCormac practised as a surgeon in Belfast from 1864 to 1870, becoming successively surgeon, lecturer on clinical surgery, and consulting surgeon to the Royal Hospital.

At the outbreak of the Franco-Prussian War in 1870 MacCormac volunteered for service. Appointed to hospital duties at Metz, he was treated on his arrival as a spy and returned to Paris. Here he joined the Anglo-American association for the care of the wounded, and eventually became second in command to Dr Marion Sims. MacCormac performed many hundreds of operations in difficult conditions and gained a considerable reputation as an operative surgeon. His experiences in France were written up and published in 1871 as *Notes and Recollections of an Ambulance Surgeon*.

Returning to London at the end of the Franco-Prussian War, MacCormac was elected in 1871 as fellow of the Royal College of Surgeons of England on the strength of his reputation and Irish fellowship. In the same year he became, after a severe struggle, assistant surgeon at St Thomas's Hospital, which had just moved to the Albert Embankment. He was made full surgeon in 1873 on the resignation of Frederick le Gros Clark and he was for twenty years lecturer on surgery in the medical school. He was elected consulting surgeon to the hospital and emeritus lecturer on clinical surgery in the medical school on retiring from active work in 1893.

Meanwhile MacCormac saw more war service. In 1876, as chief surgeon to the National Aid Society for the Sick

Sir William MacCormac, baronet (1836–1901), by Prince Pierre
Troubetzkoy, 1891

and Wounded during the Turco-Serbian campaign, he was
present at the battle of Alexinatz. His war service was still
further extended, and his great practical knowledge was
utilized in the Boer campaign of 1899–1900, when he was
appointed 'government consulting surgeon to the field
force'. In this capacity he visited all the hospitals in Natal
and Cape Colony, and went to the front on four occasions.
In 1901 he became KCB for his work in South Africa, and an
honorary serjeant-surgeon to King Edward.

MacCormac became a leading figure at St Thomas's and
was very active in professional circles in London. He was a
pivotal figure in the spread of Listerian antiseptic surgery.
His address on the topic at the metropolitan branch of the
British Medical Association in 1879 provoked an extended
debate and led to MacCormac's editing the first British
book on the subject. MacCormac was honorary secretary
general to the International Medical Congress held in London in 1881 and edited its *Transactions*. He was knighted in
the same year. MacCormac's organizational abilities and
strong links with continental medicine allowed him to
bring together the leading clinicians and medical scientists of the day, arranging among others the first meeting
between Louis Pasteur and Robert Koch. MacCormac's
main surgical interests were in fractures and abdominal
operations. He was a master of surgical technique and
always willing to try innovations. In 1885 he began to publish a planned series entitled Surgical Operations; however, only the first two parts were completed.

MacCormac was also surgeon to the French, the Italian,
Queen Charlotte's, and the British lying-in hospitals. He

was an examiner in surgery at the University of London
and for her majesty's naval, army, and Indian medical services. In 1897 he was created a baronet and was appointed
surgeon-in-ordinary to the prince of Wales, afterwards
King Edward VII; on 27 September 1898 he was made
KCVO in recognition of professional services rendered to
the prince when he injured his knee.

At the Royal College of Surgeons of England, MacCormac was elected a member of the council in 1883, and in
1887 of the court of examiners. He delivered the Bradshaw
lecture in 1893, taking as the subject 'Sir Astley Cooper
and his surgical work', and he was Hunterian orator in
1899. He was elected president in 1896, and enjoyed the
honour of re-election on four subsequent occasions, during the last of which he presided over the centenary meeting held on 26 July 1900.

MacCormac was 6 feet 2 inches tall, and well built in proportion. He enjoyed fishing and golf. His industry, mastery of detail, rapidity of work, and Irish bonhomie made
him a first-rate organizer. 'He was soft-voiced, singularly
courteous in manner, and apparently—but only apparently—inattentive to what was being said to him' (Plarr, 748).
At home in the medical circles of Europe, he broke down
the insularity which militated against the progress of English surgery, and he learned and taught what was done at
home and abroad. He abducted, and married on 30
November 1861, Katharine Maria, sixth daughter of John
Charters of Belfast, but left no children. He died at Bath on
4 December 1901, and was buried at Kensal Green on 9
December. He was survived by his wife.

D'A. POWER, *rev.* MICHAEL WORBOYS

Sources *The Lancet* (7 Dec 1901), 1618–22 · *BMJ* (14 Feb 1902), 1771–
5 · *Belfast News-Letter* (5 Dec 1901) · *Northern Whig* (5 Dec 1901) · *St
Thomas's Hospital Reports*, new ser., 30 (1903), 322–7 · private infor-
mation (1912) · personal knowledge (1912) · Burke, *Peerage* ·
WWW · V. G. Plarr, *Plarr's Lives of the fellows of the Royal College of Sur-
geons of England*, rev. D'A. Power, 2 vols. (1930)
Archives RCS Eng., papers
Likenesses G. Jerrard, photograph, 1881, Wellcome L. · P. Trou-
betzkoy, oils, 1891, RCS Eng. [*see illus.*] · photoprint, 1891, Well-
come L. · Spy [L. Ward], chromolithograph caricature, 1896, NPG,
Wellcome L.; repro. in *VF* (1 Oct 1896) · H. H. Brown, oils, 1897,
Queen's University, Belfast, N. Ireland · Beynon & Company, litho-
graph (*Buildings and famous alumni of St Thomas's Hospital*), Wellcome
L. · A. Drury, marble bust, St Thomas's Hospital, London; replica,
RCS Eng. · W. & D. Downey, woodburytype photograph, NPG;
repro. in W. Downey and D. Downey, *The cabinet portrait gallery*, 5
(1894) · oils, St Thomas's Hospital, London
Wealth at death £23,133 13s. 8d.: resworn probate, June 1902,
CGPLA Eng. & Wales

McCormack, John Francis (1884–1945), singer, was born
on 14 June 1884 in the Bawn, Mardyke Street, Athlone, co.
Westmeath, Ireland, the second son and fifth of the eleven
children (five of whom died in infancy or childhood) of
Andrew McCormack, a foreman at the Athlone Woollen
Mills, and his wife, Hannah Watson. Both parents were
from Galashiels, Scotland, where his father had worked in
the tweed mill, although his paternal grandfather was
from Sligo, in the west of Ireland. His father had a fine

John Francis McCormack (1884–1945), by Sir William Orpen, 1923

voice and sang in the church choir, but although McCormack sang from an early age he had no formal singing lessons. He was educated by the Marist Brothers before winning a scholarship to the Diocesan College of the Immaculate Conception, Summerhill, Sligo, in 1896. Leaving school in 1902 he narrowly failed to win a scholarship to the Dublin College of Science, and was working as a clerk while preparing for the civil service entrance examination when he was encouraged by his friends to audition for the Palestrina Choir at the pro-cathedral in Dublin. He sang in this choir for two years under the direction of Vincent O'Brien, and won the gold medal in the solo tenor class at the Feis Ceoil, the National Irish Festival in Dublin, in 1903. This led to an invitation to America to take part in the musical entertainment in the Irish village at the St Louis World Fair in 1904. On his return he raised funds to study singing with Vincenzo Sabatini in Milan from 1905 to 1906. On 2 July 1906 he married Lily, daughter of Patrick Foley, a Dublin innkeeper. A soprano, she had been another gold medal winner at the 1903 Feis Ceoil. They had one son and one daughter, and in 1918 adopted another son, the sixteen-month-old child of Lily's brother.

McCormack made his opera début on 13 January 1906 at Savona, near Genoa, using the name Giovanni Foli, as Fritz in Pietro Mascagni's *L'Amico Fritz*, but after failing to get any engagements in Milan he returned home early in 1907 and moved to London, where he began to build a reputation as a ballad singer in concerts and at private parties. After a successful appearance in one of Arthur Boosey's Queen's Hall Ballad Concerts in 1907 he was taken up by Sir John Murray Scott, a wealthy patron of the arts, who arranged an audition at Covent Garden. McCormack made his Covent Garden début on 15 October 1907 as Turiddu in Mascagni's *Cavalleria rusticana*, the youngest tenor to sing a major role at the Royal Opera House. This was followed by Don Ottavio in Mozart's *Don Giovanni*. He was then engaged for the 1908 season, and sang in the gala performance to celebrate the state visit of the French president, Emile Loubet. He was re-engaged as a *primo tenore* for the grand season each summer until 1914, performing sixteen roles, including Alfredo in Giuseppe Verdi's *La traviata* with Luisa Tetrazzini, and Rodolfo—his favourite role—in Giacomo Puccini's *La Bohème* with Nellie Melba.

McCormack's European reputation grew as he was invited to sing at the Salzburg Festival by Felix Weingartner, and to perform in Verdi's *Rigoletto* at the Teatro San Carlo in Naples in 1909, and in 1909, thanks to Tetrazzini, he was invited to New York by Oscar Hammerstein. He made his New York début at the Manhattan Opera House with Tetrazzini in *La traviata*, and after the Metropolitan Opera bought the Manhattan Opera Company in 1910, changing its name to the Chicago–Philadelphia Opera Company, McCormack remained for the 1910–11 season, making his first appearance at the Metropolitan Opera on 29 November 1910 with Nellie Melba in one of the company's weekly performances there.

McCormack's concert career began to take off in America in 1912, and in 1914 he made New York his home, eventually taking American citizenship. But he became unpopular in England because of his outspoken Irish nationalism, and he did not sing there from 1914 until 1924. He gave up opera soon after the war. He had always been a poor actor, and his voice was lighter than that of the leading Italian operatic tenors. Although Enrico Caruso regarded McCormack (known as the Irish Caruso) as the finest tenor of his time, he had never been universally admired as an opera singer. But as a recitalist he was unsurpassed, and he had an enormous popular following, especially in America. He toured throughout the world in the 1920s and 1930s, his concerts always starting with serious songs by Handel or Mozart, and German lieder, usually by Brahms or Hugo Wolf, before moving on to the Irish ballads and sentimental popular songs. Although often accused of pandering to his audience's craving for sentimental songs he claimed never to have sung music he did not want to sing. His most famous songs were 'I hear you calling me', which he recorded eight times, and 'Mother Machree'. He always sang with his head raised, his eyes shut, and his legs wide apart, with a closed book clasped to his chest. His voice declined rapidly after 1932, and he retired from the concert platform in 1938, when he sold his house in Hollywood and settled in Ireland. He made one film, *Song o' my Heart*, in 1929, and in 1936 made a brief appearance in *Wings of the Morning*, the first British film to be shot in Technicolor. He came out of retirement at the beginning of the Second World War to make a concert tour with Gerald Moore on behalf of the Red Cross, and appeared in the first series of the *Irish Half Hour* in 1941 to 1942 on the BBC. But he was unable to sing after 1942, when he developed emphysema.

What was most striking about McCormack's voice was the beauty and sweetness of his tone, and the clarity of his enunciation. He became famous partly through his gramophone recordings, starting in 1904 when he made eight recordings on wax cylinders for the Edison Bell Company. Most of his recordings were of the lighter side of his repertoire, but one of the most famous was 'Il mio tesoro', from *Don Giovanni*.

A devout Catholic, McCormack was honoured many times by the pope for his services to Catholic charities, and he was especially proud of his hereditary title of papal count, awarded by Pope Pius XI in 1928. When the Eucharistic Congress was held in Dublin in 1932, and the pontifical high mass was celebrated by the papal legate in Phoenix Park, McCormack, wearing his uniform as count of the papal court, sang César Franck's *Panis angelicus* before a congregation of one million. He became a privy chamberlain of cape and sword to the pope in 1933.

Although slim as a young man McCormack developed a vast appetite, and became very fat. He lived extravagantly and had expensive hobbies, with an art collection that included Corot's *Nymphs Bathing*, Franz Hals's *Man*, and a Rodin sculpture, and he was addicted to horse-racing, although he never realized his ambition to own a Derby winner. James Joyce used him as a model for Shaun the Post in *Finnegans Wake* (1939). McCormack died of pneumonia on 16 September 1945 at his home, Glena, Booterstown, overlooking Dublin Bay, and was buried at Dean's Grange cemetery, Dublin.   ANNE PIMLOTT BAKER

Sources N. Douglas, *More legendary voices* (1994), 133–52 · L. McCormack, *I hear you calling me* (1950) · G. T. Ledbetter, *The great Irish tenor* (1977) · R. Foxall, *John McCormack* (1963) · L. A. G. Strong, *John McCormack* (1949) · G. O'Brien, *John McCormack and Athlone* (1992) · G. Moore, *Am I too loud?* (1962), 122–8 · J. Scarry, 'Finnegan's wake III, i: a portrait of John McCormack', *Irish University Review*, 3 (1973), 155–62 · *New Grove*, 2nd edn · *The Times* (18 Sept 1945) · *WWW* · *DAB* · private information (2004)
Likenesses photograph, 1918, repro. in Douglas, *More legendary voices* · W. Orpen, portrait, 1923, priv. coll. [*see illus.*] · photographs, *c.*1923–1930, Hult. Arch. · J. Lavery, group portrait, 1924; formerly at Municipal Gallery of Modern Art, Dublin, 1930 · group portrait, photograph, 1924, Hult. Arch. · photographs, 1939, Hult. Arch. · Tunbridge, photograph, 1941, Hult. Arch. · D. Wilding, photograph, repro. in Moore, *Am I too loud?*, p. 197 · photograph, repro. in Strong, *John McCormack*, p. 132
Wealth at death £14,300 in USA; £503 in England: Foxall, *John McCormack*

McCormick, Charles (*c.*1755–1807), historian and biographer, was born in Ireland, the son of Charles McCormick of Rathkeal, near Limerick. He was educated at the Middle Temple, London, and on 18 July 1783 matriculated at St Mary Hall, Oxford, graduating BCL on 18 June 1794. Thereafter he abandoned law for literature. His principal published works are *The History of England, from the Death of George the Second to the Peace of 1783* (n.d.), *The Secret History of the Court and Reign of Charles the Second* (1792), and *Memoirs of … Edmund Burke* (1797), a supposedly 'disgraceful piece of party virulence' (Lowndes, 1434). In 1805 he published

Light Reading at Leisure Hours, and followed this with a continuation of Rapin's *History of England*. His death from dropsy, in London on 29 July 1807, meant his proposed history of Ireland remained unfinished.

McCormick's writing brought him little financial reward. On his death his wife, of whom no further details are known, was left in such poverty that a public appeal was set up for her support.

THOMPSON COOPER, *rev.* PHILIP CARTER

Sources *GM*, 1st ser., 77 (1807), 889, 973–4 · Foster, *Alum. Oxon.* · W. T. Lowndes, *The bibliographer's manual of English literature*, ed. H. G. Bohn, [new edn], 6 vols. (1864)

MacCormick, John MacDonald (1904–1961), Scottish nationalist, was born on 20 November 1904 at 12 Leslie Street, Glasgow, the son of Donald MacCormick, a sea captain, and his wife, Marion, *née* Macdonald. He was educated at Woodside School, Glasgow, and studied law at the University of Glasgow (1923–8). He became involved in Scottish politics while at university, and joined the university Labour Club and the Independent Labour Party (ILP). In September 1927 he left the party and formed the Glasgow University Scottish Nationalist Association, which was designed to promote Scottish culture and nationalism and self-government. The association was sufficiently neutral to act as the honest broker between the various nationalist organizations which would form the National Party of Scotland in April 1928. MacCormick was a talented speaker and organizer, and was promoted to national secretary of the NPS. The failure of the NPS to make an electoral breakthrough led him to question current tactics and he concluded that the party's fundamentalist wing was frightening away potential support because of its support for republicanism and separatism. In consequence, MacCormick initiated a campaign to redefine the policy of the NPS, to make it more moderate and to tone down demands for independence. He first stood for parliament in 1929, when he was defeated at Glasgow Camlachie in the general election, with five per cent of the votes.

In 1932 MacCormick began to make overtures to the right-wing Scottish Party, believing that, as the Scottish Party included a number of members of the Scottish 'establishment', their conversion to the cause of home rule would enhance the credibility of the nationalists. In order to secure an accommodation, MacCormick purged the NPS of radical elements, and moved the policy of the NPS towards that of the Scottish Party. His endeavours paid dividends, and in 1934 the two organizations merged to form the Scottish National Party (SNP). MacCormick himself was not a dogmatic politician, and described himself as a radical, by which he meant a form of centrist Liberal. His response to the failure of the SNP to make an electoral impact in the mid-1930s was to search for alternative strategies. He considered the basic problem to be that, although many people in Scotland favoured home rule, they were not, on the whole, willing to put the issue above conventional party loyalties. The solution, MacCormick argued, was to make the other parties take home rule seriously, and to demonstrate widespread support for the cause. In 1939 he launched the idea of a Scottish national convention, which would bring together all sections of Scottish society and all shades of Scottish political opinion in favour of home rule. He had made contact with both the Labour and Liberal parties, and although the first meeting, scheduled for September 1939, was cancelled because of the outbreak of war, MacCormick pushed negotiations throughout the war. On 10 September 1938 he married Margaret Isobel Miller (b. 1908/9), with whom he had two sons and two daughters. Their younger son (Donald) Neil MacCormick (b. 1941) became regius professor of public law at Edinburgh University and a vigorous SNP candidate at elections.

As a leading figure in the SNP, 'King John' MacCormick came under increasing attack from the rank and file members for his failure to maintain party structure and organization. He considered that his preferred strategy of co-operation with other organizations meant that there was little need for the SNP to function as a mainstream political party. He endeavoured to present an acceptable face of Scottish nationalism, and did much to reverse the party's official anti-conscription policy following the outbreak of the Second World War.

MacCormick's opportunist streak came into full play in the decision to contest wartime by-elections, which he viewed as an opportunity to exert pressure on the Labour Party, which was fearful of nationalist interventions. This policy collapsed after the nationalists failed to make any impact at the Cathcart by-election in 1942. The SNP was now a discredited force, and Thomas Johnston, the secretary of state for Scotland, did not feel the need to include the nationalists in his various committees of inquiry into Scottish post-war reconstruction. MacCormick's policy suffered a further defeat at the SNP's annual conference in 1942, when the party endorsed Douglas Young, the anti-conscriptionist, as chairman. MacCormick believed this would discredit the nationalist movement, and it also signalled an end to his policy of co-operation with other organizations. As a result, he and his followers left the SNP to set up the Scottish convention, which succeeded in 1947 in setting up an assembly along the lines planned in 1939. The assembly endorsed home rule, and, in following years, drew up the Scottish covenant, which had over 2 million signatories (a number of which were shown to be bogus). MacCormick's attempts to demonstrate real political support for home rule failed when, in 1948, he stood as an independent candidate at the Paisley by-election with what he erroneously believed to be Liberal and Conservative support, and lost. His failure discredited claims as to the popularity of home rule, and further served to reinforce notions that the Scottish convention was an anti-Labour organization. MacCormick's failure left the SNP with a monopoly of the cause of home rule.

MacCormick continued to encourage Scottish nationalism, albeit in an increasingly non-party political fashion. He was elected lord rector of Glasgow University in 1950, in which year he became involved with the theft by some students of the stone of Scone from Westminster Abbey. He also mounted a legal challenge to the right of the new queen to be designated Elizabeth II in Scotland, on grounds that there had been no previous Scottish Queen Elizabeth. The Scottish convention faded out, and in June 1951 MacCormick founded the Scottish Covenant Association to press for the establishment of a Scottish parliament within the framework of the United Kingdom, but it did not attract much support. He was awarded an honorary LLD degree by Glasgow University in 1951, and in 1955 published *The Flag in the Wind*, an account of the nationalist movement and his part in it. He made the last of his six unsuccessful bids to become a member of parliament in 1959, standing as a Liberal, and died on 13 October 1961 in Glasgow. His wife survived him.   RICHARD J. FINLAY

Sources R. J. Finlay, *Independent and free: Scottish politics and the origins of the Scottish national party, 1918–1945* (1994) · J. M. MacCormick, *The flag in the wind* (1955) · NL Scot., Muirhead MSS · *WW* · *Glasgow Herald* (14 Oct 1961) · *The Times* (14 Oct 1961) · C. Harvie, *Scotland and nationalism* (1977) · *The Scotsman* (17 Oct 1961) · b. cert. · m. cert. **Archives** NL Scot., Donaldson MSS · NL Scot., McIntyre MSS · NL Scot., Muirhead MSS **Likenesses** photographs

Maccormick, Joseph (1733–1799), Church of Scotland minister, was born at St Andrews on 22 January 1733, the son of John Maccormick, a minister in that town. He graduated MA at St Andrews University in 1750 and was granted a bursary in theology from the university exchequer in the same year. After serving as tutor in the Hepburn family at Clarkington, he entered in 1756 upon trials before the presbytery of Dalkeith. Maccormick was early affiliated with the moderate literati settled in the general vicinity of Edinburgh, including William Robertson, Alexander Carlyle, and John Home. His attendance at performances of Home's *Douglas* in 1756 was opposed by the presbytery of Dalkeith, which consequently transferred his trials to the presbytery of Edinburgh. He was there licensed on 30 March 1757 and ordained minister of Kilmany, Fife, on 17 April 1758. He was presented by Robert Hepburn of Baads to the living of Temple on 21 November 1760, and while there, in 1766, had the degree of DD conferred upon him by St Andrews University. He married, on 7 May 1770, Mary (d. 1822), daughter of Joseph Simson, a Bristol merchant; they had one son and three daughters.

Through the favour of Janet, countess of Hyndford, Maccormick was transferred in 1771 to Prestonpans, where he edited his only major work, *State-papers and letters, addressed to William Carstares … to which is prefixed the life of Mr. Carstares* (1774). The documents included in this collection had come into the hands of Charles Mackie, professor of civil history at Edinburgh University, as trustee to Carstares's widow. He in turn entrusted them to Maccormick, who was Carstares's great-nephew, along with some materials for a life. Prefixed to the letters are memoirs of the correspondents taken from the manuscript of 'The characters of the court of Great Britain', in the earl of Hyndford's library. William Robertson, Maccormick's long time friend and ally, was active in helping him secure a publisher.

In May 1782 Maccormick was elected moderator of the

general assembly, and in the following July, thanks again to the support of Robertson, he was presented by George III to the charge of St Leonards in his native presbytery in conjunction with the principalship of the United College of St Andrews. He was appointed one of the deans of the Chapel Royal on 19 July 1788, and he was a non-resident fellow of the Royal Society of Edinburgh.

Alexander Carlyle's judgement of him is well known, 'rather a Merry Andrew, than a Wit' (*Autobiography*, ed. Burton, 134), as is Walter Scott's complaint that as a boy he 'yawnd under the inflictions of a Doctor M'Cormick, a name in which dullness seems to have been hereditary' (*Journal*, 602). But these comments obscure his genuine accomplishments as a steadfast supporter of the moderate party. A member of the general assembly on seven occasions, he was one of the speakers backing Robertson's effort to repeal the Catholic penal laws in 1778. The documents comprising the *State-Papers* have been relied upon by later historians and biographers. Maccormick's life of Carstares, with its portrayal of Carstares's public role as leader of the Church of Scotland and of his private character as embodying tolerance, charity, and moderation, was a significant contribution to moderate ideology. Maccormick died at Edinburgh on 17 June 1799.

THOMAS SECCOMBE, *rev.* JEFFREY R. SMITTEN

Sources *State papers and letters addressed to William Carstares*, ed. J. M'Cormick (1774) · *The principal acts of the general assembly of the Church of Scotland* (1782) · *Fasti Scot.*, new edn · *Autobiography of the Rev. Dr. Alexander Carlyle … containing memorials of the men and events of his time*, ed. J. H. Burton (1860); repr. as *Anecdotes and characters of the times*, ed. J. Kinsley (1973) · R. B. Sher, *Church and university in the Scottish Enlightenment: the moderate literati of Edinburgh* (1985) · *The journal of Sir Walter Scott*, ed. W. E. K. Anderson (1972) · NL Scot., MSS 582, fols. 48–9; 583, fols. 334, 390–91 · Duke U., Perkins L. · Bayerische Staatsbibliothek · U. Edin. L., MS La.II 241, Dc.4. 41, fols. 63–71 · BL, MS Eg. 2182, fols. 39–40 · *The Drennan–McTier letters*, ed. J. Agnew, 1 (1998) · *Scots Magazine*, 50 (1788), 363 · *Scots Magazine*, 61 (1799), 424 · M. F. Conolly, *Biographical dictionary of eminent men of Fife* (1866) · W. Anderson, *The Scottish biographical dictionary* (1845) · L. Sharp, 'Charles Mackie, the first professor of history at Edinburgh University', *SHR*, 41 (1962), 23–45
Archives NL Scot., corresp. | U. Edin. L., letters to Alexander Carlyle

McCormick, (William) Patrick Glyn (1877–1940), Church of England clergyman, was born at Hull, Yorkshire, on 14 June 1877, the fourth child and third son of the eight children of Joseph McCormick (1834–1914), vicar of Holy Trinity Church, Hull, afterwards canon of York Minster, rector of St James's Church, Piccadilly, and an honorary chaplain to the king, and his wife, Frances (*d.* 1913), daughter of Lieutenant-Colonel Gregory Haines, of the East India Company's service, and granddaughter of Hugh, first Viscount Gough. McCormick was educated at Llandaff Cathedral school, Exeter School, and St John's College, Cambridge (BA, 1899; MA, 1907).

McCormick was ordained deacon in 1900 and priest in 1901. In 1902 he went to South Africa as an army chaplain, intending to make this his career, but soon after became a missionary on the Rand, in 1903 moving to Jumpers Deep mine, Cleveland, where he lived with the men in their quarters. This was a tough mining area and McCormick's presence was ridiculed by the workers, but he gathered some respect by his sporting prowess at rugby football and cricket. He became the first vicar of St Patrick's, Cleveland, raising the money for building the church and vicarage. In 1910 he was appointed rector of St John's Church, Belgravia, Johannesburg. On 1 December 1910 McCormick married (Ada) Miriam, daughter of George Herbert Shelton, of the stock exchange, a kinsman of William Morris. They had a son and three daughters.

McCormick again joined the army as a chaplain in 1914, seeing active service in France. From 1915 to 1917 he was senior chaplain to the guards division; from 1917 to 1918 deputy assistant chaplain-general to the 14th corps, becoming in 1918 to 1919 assistant chaplain-general at Boulogne. In 1917 he was made DSO, and he was four times mentioned in dispatches. On his return to England in 1919 he was appointed vicar of Croydon; from 1923 to 1927 he was an honorary canon of Canterbury Cathedral; and from 1928 until his death he was an honorary chaplain to the king.

In Croydon, McCormick sought to demonstrate his belief in greater social equality, of which he said 'many of us believe that the old system under which we have lived for so long is not the right system' (Northcott, 57). In 1927 he was appointed vicar of St Martin-in-the-Fields, and here he began to combine his concern for the poor with a talent for popular appeal. He made a call for a million shillings to assist church work, and sat on the steps of his church for ten hours to collect contributions. He made regular religious broadcasts for the BBC, of which it was said his unique 'sincerity and humility' gave these a popularity as never before (Northcott, 70). He became the first parson to be televised, on Christmas day 1937.

The '"down and outs" and the welfare of the sick and the poor was ever in his thoughts', it was said of McCormick. Through the great popularity of his broadcasts, sermons, and writings, and his personality, he managed to promote these views, in their religious context, to a wide and attentive audience. He died at the vicarage, St Martin-in-the-Fields, on 16 October 1940 and was cremated at Golders Green on 18 October. McCormick was survived by his wife. A memorial plaque of him was erected in the crypt of St Martin-in-the-Fields.

C. J. E. HOLLINS, *rev.* MARC BRODIE

Sources R. J. Northcott, *Pat McCormick* (1941) · *The Times* (17 Oct 1940) · *The Times* (19 Oct 1940) · *WWW* · Venn, *Alum. Cant.* · *CGPLA Eng. & Wales* (1941)
Likenesses H. Coster, negatives, NPG · photographs, repro. in Northcott, *Pat McCormick*, frontispiece
Wealth at death £6561 7s. od.: probate, 7 Feb 1941, *CGPLA Eng. & Wales*

McCormick, Robert (1800–1890), naval surgeon, explorer, and naturalist, born at Runham, near Great Yarmouth, Norfolk, on 22 July 1800, was the only son of Robert McCormick (*d.* 1817), surgeon in the navy, son of Robert McCormick of Ballyreagh, co. Tyrone, where the family had been settled for several generations. He spent his childhood near Great Yarmouth, and was educated by his mother and sisters. Despite his father's death in the wreck of the *Defense* in December 1817, he decided to become a naval surgeon. He studied medicine in 1821, under Sir Astley Cooper, at Guy's and St Thomas's hospitals in London; on 6 December 1822 became a member of the Royal College of Surgeons; and in 1823 entered the navy as an assistant surgeon. He was sent out to the West Indies, where he remained for two years, seeing most of the islands and the coast of the Spanish main. In the summer of 1825 he was invalided home with yellow fever, and, after a year in a cutter in the North Sea, volunteered for Arctic service with William Edward Parry, with whom he sailed in the *Hecla*, in the expedition to the north of Spitsbergen in the summer of 1827. He took no part in the sledging expeditions, but contributed by keeping the crew healthy and by studying the natural history of Spitsbergen. On his return he was promoted surgeon on 27 November 1827.

Two years later McCormick was again sent out to the West Indies, very much against his will, and within three months he was invalided home. His next appointment was to a surveying brig on the coast of Brazil. That, too, he found uncomfortable, and got superseded after a few months. In 1828 he was appointed to a sloop employed for some time in the blockade of the coast of Holland. Early the next year she was sent out to the West Indies, and McCormick, with a rooted dislike to the station, and especially in a small craft, was invalided home for a third time. He was now on half pay for upwards of four years, and in the intervals of study made many excursions on foot through England and Wales, travelling some 3440 miles, and pursuing his favourite studies of geology and natural history. In 1839 he was appointed, as much in the capacity of naturalist as surgeon, to the *Terror*, then going on a voyage to the Antarctic, under the command of Captain James Clark Ross. He worked on all branches of science, although his zoological findings were published only considerably later, by John Gray and Sir John Richardson on orders from the Admiralty, after the task had remained undone for some time after the expedition; McCormick apparently lacked the necessary ability.

When the expedition returned to England, in the autumn of 1843, McCormick was disappointed of promotion. In September 1845 he was appointed surgeon to the *William and Mary* yacht at Woolwich. He understood that this appointment was for life, or until promotion, and was very angry at being, after two years, moved to the *Fisgard*, the flagship attached to Woolwich Dockyard, from which he was superseded in December 1848. His next idea was to conduct a party in search of Sir John Franklin, and he laid before the Board of Admiralty a proposal to undertake such a search in small boats and sledges in Wellington Channel, the Boothia peninsula, and King William Island. Although his suggestions were soundly based, as McClintock was later to prove, the Admiralty dismissed his plan as dangerous. However, in 1852, while surgeon of the *North Star*, he was able to carry it out to some extent. In the

Forlorn Hope he explored the Wellington Channel, covering 240 statute miles, mapping the east side of the channel, but finding no trace of Franklin. He afterwards published *Narrative of a Boat Expedition up the Wellington Channel in the Year 1852* (1854).

McCormick returned to England in the *Phoenix* in October 1853 and was awarded the Arctic medal in 1857. He had never ceased to urge on the Admiralty his claims for promotion, contending that his service with the Antarctic expedition was exceptional and ought to be exceptionally rewarded. The Admiralty at last promoted him, on 20 May 1859, to be deputy inspector of hospitals. He had, however, no employment, and in July 1865 he was put on the retired list, the Admiralty refusing him the honorary rank of inspector of hospitals. His friends, as well as himself, thought that he was badly used. He was a man of considerable ability, although lacking the single-mindedness of his successful scientific colleagues such as Hooker and Lyell; but in his relations with the Admiralty he was sadly wanting in tact. He disagreed with each of the medical directors-general of his time and in his avoidance of Caribbean duty was almost insubordinate. He died, unmarried, on 28 October 1890 at his home, Hecla Villa, 22 Ridgway Place, Wimbledon. The accounts of his several voyages and expeditions, together with a very detailed autobiography, were published as *Voyages of Discovery in the Arctic and Antarctic Seas and Round the World* (2 vols., 1884), but came too late to arouse much interest. As Robert Johnson has remarked, 'he thought it the harbinger of a distinguished future, but, in the event, the *Forlorn Hope* was his first, last and only command' (*DCB*). None the less, he is remembered in several place names in the Arctic and Antarctic.   J. K. LAUGHTON, *rev.* ELIZABETH BAIGENT

Sources DCB, vol. 11 · H. Berkeley, 'Naval biography: deputy inspector-general Robert McCormick, RN, FRGS', *Illustrated Naval and Military Magazine*, new ser., 1 (1889), 607–11 · J. J. Keevil, 'Robert McCormick, RN, the stormy petrel of naval medicine', *Royal Naval Medical Journal*, 29 (1943), 36–42 · *CGPLA Eng. & Wales* (1890) · d. cert.
Archives BL, sketches, Add. MS 33930 · Wellcome L., diaries, lecture notes, and papers, MSS 3356–3382 | BL, letters to John Barrow, Add. MSS 35307, 35309 · BL, letters to James Robert Brown, Add. MSS 42712–42713
Likenesses S. Pearce, oils, 1853, NPG · portraits, repro. in R. McClintock, *Voyages of discovery in the Arctic and Antarctic seas and round the world*, 2 vols. (1884)
Wealth at death £3139 4s.: resworn probate, Dec 1891, *CGPLA Eng. & Wales* (1890)

McCormick, Sir William Symington (1859–1930), English scholar and educational administrator, was born at Dunbar Terrace, Dumfries, Scotland, on 29 April 1859, the elder son of William McCormick, an ironmonger and maker of agricultural implements in that town, and his wife, Agnes Ann, daughter of the Revd William *Symington, professor of divinity in the Reformed Presbyterian Church of Scotland (the Cameronians), and niece of Andrew Symington. He was educated at Dumfries high school and at Glasgow University, graduating in 1880. For a short time he lectured in mathematics at Glasgow as assistant to Professor Hugh Blackburn; afterwards he went to the universities of Göttingen and Marburg in order to study literature. On his return to Glasgow, McCormick became in 1884 assistant to John Nichol, professor of English literature, and after the transference of Queen Margaret College for women to the university in 1893 he was put in charge of the department of English language and literature. For a time he was also in partnership with a Mr Wilson in a publishing business.

In 1890 McCormick was appointed to the chair of English literature at University College, Dundee, to which was added later a lecturership in English at the University of St Andrews, where he transferred his home. In 1897 he married Mabel Emily (d. in or after 1930), younger daughter of Sir Frederick Lucas Cook, second baronet, head of the firm of Cook, Son & Co., warehousemen, St Paul's Churchyard, London, and had one son and two daughters. He was an admirable lecturer, and he was continuously engaged in literary work and in university administration throughout this period of his life. He published a volume of *Three Lectures on Literature* (1889), edited *Troilus and Cressida* for the Globe edition of Chaucer's works (1901), and formulated his theory of English rhythms, based on the continuity of the Old English four-beat line, which, unfortunately, was never published.

In 1900 McCormick prepared a report for the General Medical Council on preliminary examinations for medical students, which established his reputation as an academic administrator. In the following year Andrew Carnegie invited him to become the first secretary of the trust for the universities of Scotland which he had endowed with a fund of £2 million. This changed the whole course of McCormick's life, for thenceforth he was to become primarily an administrator, although he never lost his interest in literature, especially in Chaucer. In his last years he prepared for the Clarendon Press, on the basis of photostat copies presented to him by the University of Chicago, a critical description of the known MSS (fifty-seven complete and twenty-eight fragmentary) of the *Canterbury Tales*, which shows the nature and order of the contents of each manuscript, with the divisions marked and headings supplied by the scribe, together with all additions, omissions, transpositions, and other structural variants from the text adopted as standard. McCormick was led to undertake this work (published in 1933 as *The MSS of Chaucer's Canterbury Tales, a Critical Description*) in preparation for a full critical edition of the *Tales*, by a study of the *Pardoner's Tale* which he had made in 1900, which was printed but not published. Through his contacts with Abram Flexner, the American academic administrator, he helped to secure funding for the Chicago edition of the text of the *Canterbury Tales* (8 vols., 1940), which was dedicated to McCormick's memory.

On his appointment as secretary of the Carnegie Trust, McCormick moved to Edinburgh, where he lived until he went to London in 1920. The new work revealed his administrative ability, and when the Liberal government came into power in 1906, R. B. Haldane, one of the Carnegie trustees, secured McCormick's appointment as a member of the advisory committee set up 'to advise the Treasury as to the distribution of grants in aid of colleges furnishing education of a university standard'. From 1906 onwards McCormick was closely involved with every important step taken by the government to aid university education. In 1907 he served on the departmental committee of the University of Wales and the Welsh colleges. From 1909 to 1913 he was a member of the royal commission on university education in London. In 1911 the Treasury advisory committee was transferred to the Board of Education, and McCormick became its chairman. In 1919 this became the Treasury University Grants Committee (UGC) and McCormick became its first chairman, holding the post until his death. He secured for these bodies the confidence of academics, many of whom were wary of state funding and control. At the UGC he applied the system of quinquennial planning successively developed by the Carnegie Trust.

In 1915 McCormick also became chairman of the Advisory Council for Scientific and Industrial Research, at first attached to the Board of Education, but transferred in 1916 to a new Department of Scientific and Industrial Research under the lord president. The First World War had exposed Britain's scientific shortcomings in the face of German competition, and the study made of the universities by McCormick and his committee had convinced the government that systematic encouragement of scientific research was urgently needed in the national no less than in the industrial interest. Although McCormick's appointment was initially criticized by some scientists, he was trusted by the universities. Industrial firms, however, proved less inclined to treat scientific research as a matter of urgency, but the fund of £1 million granted by the government, on McCormick's initiative, to the new department towards the maintenance of co-operative research associations to be established and run by the industries themselves, helped to overcome apathy. When McCormick died fifteen years later, the department controlled an annual expenditure of over £700,000 on a series of large national research stations and in support of research conducted in the universities and by industry. The Royal Society in 1928 admitted McCormick to be a fellow as a person who, in the opinion of the council, 'had rendered conspicuous service to the cause of science'.

McCormick was an original trustee of the Carnegie United Kingdom Trust, formed in 1913, and chairman of its music committee, which published Tudor and Elizabethan church music and the work of modern British composers, assisted the musical competition festivals, and helped to save the Old Vic Theatre. As a member of its library committee, he was active in the development of the rural libraries, the formation of the Central Library for Students (later the National Central Library in Malet Place, London), and the school of librarianship at University College, London. He also became chairman of the British National Opera Company and a member of the committee of management of the Old Vic. He was knighted in 1911 and created a GBE in 1929. He died at sea on 23 March 1930.   H. F. HEATH, *rev.* M. C. CURTHOYS

Sources R. T. and H. T. T., *PRS*, 130A (1930–31), xv–xxiii • personal knowledge (1937) • private information (1937) • R. D. Anderson, *Education and opportunity in Victorian Scotland: schools and universities* (1983) • D. S. L. Cardwell, *The organisation of science in England*, rev. edn (1972) • *CGPLA Eng. & Wales* (1930)
Likenesses W. Orpen, oils, 1920, Tate collection
Wealth at death £20,780 10s. 1d.: probate, 19 May 1930, *CGPLA Eng. & Wales*

McCosh, James (1811–1894), philosopher and college head, was born at the family home, Carskeoch, Patna, Ayrshire, on 1 April 1811, the fifth of seven children of Andrew McCosh, farmer, and his wife, Jean, daughter of James Carson, farmer. McCosh grew up at Carskeoch, in an area with a long history of defiant protestantism. He received religious inspiration from both parents and regularly walked with them the several miles to the Straiton parish church. Andrew McCosh died when James was nine, and, an older brother having died at the age of three, James was the only male family member left to work the farm.

McCosh attended the local parish school and in 1824 entered Glasgow University. In 1829 he began his studies for the ministry at Edinburgh University. He became closely attached to Thomas Chalmers, in the chair of divinity, and also acquainted with David Welsh, professor of church history. The philosopher Sir William Hamilton also taught at Edinburgh and McCosh became absorbed in his writings. He received his master of arts degree from Edinburgh in 1834 and was licensed by the presbytery of Ayr (26 March 1834) as a member of the Church of Scotland.

In October 1835 McCosh began his ministry at the abbey church of Arbroath on the eastern coast of Scotland. Here he attended to a heavily working-class parish. Shortly, he began a collaboration with Thomas *Guthrie of nearby Brechin. Guthrie had joined other evangelicals in the fight against patronage in the national church. In January 1839 McCosh became minister of the cathedral church of Brechin. He now made the movement for complete separation of church and state his main cause. At St Andrew's Church in Edinburgh, on 18 May 1843, McCosh joined Chalmers, Welsh, and Guthrie in seceding from the general assembly meeting and reconvening to form the Free Church of Scotland. He was from 1844 to 1851 minister of the East Free Church, Brechin. On 29 September 1845 McCosh married Isabella Guthrie (d. 1909), daughter of Alexander Guthrie, older brother of Thomas and a noted physician. They had five children: Mary Jane (b. 1846), Andrew (1848–1849), Alexander Guthrie (b. 1850), Margaret Sarah (b. 1852), and Andrew James (b. 1858).

McCosh's interest in philosophy led to the publication in 1850 of his first book, *The Method of the Divine Government, Physical and Moral*. The book was read and admired by the earl of Clarendon, lord lieutenant of Ireland, and helped secure McCosh's appointment (14 November 1851) as professor of logic and metaphysics at the newly established Queen's College, Belfast. In philosophy McCosh sought a viable middle ground between what he considered an overzealous intuitionism that cannot validate a real world, and a strenuous materialism that honours no spiritual reality. He confronted these problems within the tradition of Scottish philosophy. He praised Thomas Reid and Dugald Stewart for defending the truths of consciousness but faulted them for not successfully connecting them with a world of experience. He believed that Thomas Brown had left philosophy in a similarly dubious state by restricting it to the immediately knowable, the laws of the mind itself. He praised Hamilton, however, for insisting that we do not know attributes without knowing substance. In *The Intuitions of the Mind, Inductively Investigated* (1860) McCosh sought to demonstrate that all intuitions are of something and that they must connect to experience. His 'intuitional realism' thus stayed within the general thematic emphasis of the Scottish school but his more emphatic empiricism gave McCosh his distinct place in it. On the other hand, McCosh believed that Hamilton's negative idea of the absolute had damaging implications for religious belief. McCosh paid his highest respects to Scottish philosophy in *The Scottish Philosophy, Biographical, Expository, Critical, from Hutcheson to Hamilton* (1875). It remains a useful intellectual history.

In 1868 McCosh accepted an invitation to become president of the College of New Jersey (Princeton) in the United States; he delivered his inaugural speech on 27 October that year. He had become well known in certain quarters of America, particularly in the protestant religious press, where his books were widely reviewed and often praised for making a useful alliance with Christianity. At Princeton he announced his intention to open the college to new areas of learning. He modernized the curriculum and expanded the faculty. McCosh held two public debates with Charles William Eliot, president of Harvard and major defender of the elective system. Free choice, McCosh said, would enable students to bypass not just the ancient classics but the modern sciences, now a necessary component of the higher learning.

McCosh proved to be a successful academic politician at Princeton. He made new connections with wealthy Presbyterians who welcomed his effort to transform Princeton from a provincial college to a national university. On several occasions he called on such individuals to provide money to support new academic programmes or buildings. He worked with Princeton alumni to establish new chapters around the United States as he sought to broaden the geographical base of the student body. McCosh also won the support and affection of a group of students, whom he called 'me bright young men', and who shared his vision of a renewed Princeton. Woodrow Wilson—in the class of 1879 and editor of the student newspaper *The Princetonian*—championed McCosh's causes.

Although he maintained a strict moral regime at Princeton and made religion prominent at the college, McCosh's liberal views on evolution brought him enemies. His writings on science had begun at Queen's and there his work with James Dickie had led to a co-authored book, *Typical Forms and Special Ends in Creation* (1855). Their discussions of 'collocation' and 'homologies' outlined a dynamic teleological process at work in nature and prepared McCosh's receptivity to all theories of evolution, including Darwin's. But some individuals in Princeton's board of trustees denounced McCosh for his accommodationist stance. By 1880 he felt frustrated with the reactionary temper of the trustees and prevailed in his quest to have an alumni trustee position created. Furthermore, in a significant reversal, McCosh, determined to see the success of his changes at Princeton, began appointing to faculty positions some of his best former students, several of whom became noted scholars.

To friend and foe alike McCosh was a commanding figure at the college. His tall and imposing physique had become stooped in his older years, but students flatteringly attributed that posture to his scholarly habits. He sported lengthy sideburns and spoke with a rough Scottish brogue that gave piquancy to his speech. A proud man, he boasted unabashedly of his accomplishments at Princeton, where the students gave him the nickname Old Jimmie. Always referring to 'me college', he would escort visitors to Princeton around the campus, pointing at new buildings and saying 'that's mine; I built that'. Students who might at first have found him intimidating soon learned to see through his 'big bow-wow', as one of them called it. Many later remembered his personal kindness toward them. McCosh resigned the presidency in June 1888, but continued teaching. He died at his college home, in Princeton, New Jersey, on 16 November 1894 and was buried in the president's plot at the college on 20 November.   J. DAVID HOEVELER

Sources J. D. Hoeveler, jr, *James McCosh and the Scottish intellectual tradition: from Glasgow to Princeton* (1981) [incl. bibliography of McCosh's writings] · J. McCosh, 'Incidents of my life in three countries', Princeton University Archives, New Jersey · *The life of James McCosh: a record chiefly autobiographical*, ed. W. M. Sloane (1896) [based mainly on McCosh's 'Incidents'] · McCosh correspondence, Princeton University Library, rare books and special collections department · Princeton University Archives, New Jersey, college and faculty minutes · minute book, 1829–42, Abbey Church, Arbroath, Angus, Scotland · 'Records of the kirk session of Brechin: beginning with the year 1831, at the Brechin Cathedral', Brechin, Scotland · minutes of the West Free Church kirk session, NA Scot. · priv. coll. · *Fasti Scot.* · Boase, *Mod. Eng. biog.* · *Memorial book of the sesquicentennial celebration of … Princeton University* (1898) · W. Libby, 'The funeral exercises', *Princeton College Bulletin*, 7 (1895), 11–19

Archives UCL, G. C. Robertson MSS

Likenesses portrait, *c.*1870, BM · A. Saint-Gaudens, bronze relief, Princeton University, New Jersey, Marquand Chapel · portrait, repro. in Sloane, ed., *Life of James McCosh* · portrait, repro. in J. A. Wylie, *Disruption worthies* (1881), vol. 3, pp. 343–8 · portrait, repro. in J. M. MacBain, *Eminent Arbroathians* (1897) · portrait, repro. in J. M. MacBain, *America's celebrities* (1895) · portrait, repro. in *The Princeton College Bulletin* (Feb 1895)

MacCourt, James. *See* Mac Cuarta, Séamas Dall (*c.*1645–1733).

McCoy, Sir Frederick (1821/2–1899), palaeontologist, was born in Dublin, the second of three children of Simon Henry McCoy (1794/5–1875), medical practitioner, and his wife, Bridget (1798/9–1876). Although he initially studied for the medical profession, McCoy's consuming interest was in the natural sciences and this became his life's

work. There were few periods throughout his career when he did not have some curatorial role in a natural history museum. During his late teens and early twenties he was employed to identify, arrange, and catalogue the fossil collections of the Geological Society of Dublin, the Royal Dublin Society, and Richard Griffith's geological survey of Ireland. In 1842 or 1843 he married Anna Maria (1819/20–1886), daughter of Thomas Harrison, attorney, and his wife, Eliza. They had five children, only two of whom reached adulthood: Emily Mary (1842–1891) and Frederick Henry (1843–1887).

In 1845 McCoy joined the geological survey of Ireland as an assistant field geologist. He resigned late in 1846 and was then invited by Adam Sedgwick, professor of geology in Cambridge University, to classify and catalogue the geological museum's fossil collection. This occupied him full-time until 1849 when he was appointed to the foundation chair of geology and mineralogy in Queen's College, Belfast, and made curator of its museum. During this period he returned to Cambridge each summer to complete his work for Sedgwick, who described him in a letter to Roderick Murchison, dated 6 October 1851, as 'an excellent naturalist, an incomparable and most philosophical palaeontologist, and one of the steadiest and quickest workmen that ever undertook the arrangement of a Museum' (Clark and Hughes, footnote to p. 194).

McCoy was appointed foundation professor of natural science in the University of Melbourne in 1854 and director of the Museum of Natural and Applied Sciences in 1857, either of which would have been a full-time job for a man of lesser drive and capacity. Contemporaries described him as: 'strongly built and ruddy of countenance'; 'though somewhat peppery when thwarted, he was really warm-hearted and friendly' (Scott, 34). When, in 1856, the Victorian government moved to disband the small public museum it had set up in 1854, McCoy persuaded it, against strong opposition from the Philosophical Institute, to re-establish the museum in the grounds of the university. A separate building was provided in 1862 and the public museum remained there under McCoy's stewardship until his death. He was also state palaeontologist, served on a number of royal commissions, and was an active member of many learned societies.

McCoy saw museums as 'the most ready and effectual means of communicating the knowledge and practical experience of the experienced few to the many' (*The Argus*, 29 May 1857). Typically, he put this vision into practice by providing scale models of gold-mining tools, plant, and equipment for the enlightenment of 'new-chum' miners making their way through Melbourne to the goldfields.

Government funding for the museum was always niggardly and the governing trustees hostile. McCoy, almost single-handedly, built up the collection over four decades, mainly by trading Australia's unique flora and fauna with museums around the world. At his death, the museum contained over 500,000 specimens and was internationally recognized. McCoy was one of Australia's principal scientists of his time.

As an academic McCoy was less successful and arguably

his major achievement at the university was the establishment of a systematic botanic garden that was a key resource for the study of botany and medicine. McCoy lectured in chemistry, mineralogy, botany, anatomy, physiology of animals, zoology, and geology. For the first decade his lectures were well attended, but as the years went by and McCoy aged and sickened, his popularity with the students waned and they complained of irrelevance, an excess of theory, and insufficient practice in his subjects.

McCoy's professional achievements were recognized and honoured widely. He was fellow of the Geological Society of London (1852), winner of its Murchison medal (1879), honorary member of the Cambridge Philosophical Society (1853), fellow of the Royal Society (1880), CMG (1886), DSc (Cantab.) *honoris causa*—the first recipient (1886)—and KCMG (1891); he also received a number of awards and decorations from other European countries. He wrote seminal works on the palaeontology of Ireland and of Great Britain, and the palaeontology and zoology of Victoria, Australia, and he was a prolific contributor to learned journals.

Born a Roman Catholic, McCoy joined the Church of England some time between 1846 and 1854. He died of renal failure on 13 May 1899 at his home, Maritima, 45 South Road, Brighton, Melbourne, and was buried on 15 May in the Anglican section of Brighton cemetery, Melbourne. Inconclusive evidence suggests that he made a deathbed recantation.   MALCOLM CARKEEK

Sources Mitchell L., NSW, McCoy correspondence, CY reel 499 · Museum of Victoria, Melbourne, archives · University of Melbourne archives · CUL, department of manuscripts and university archives, Sedgwick MSS · GS Lond. · Geological Survey of Ireland, Dublin, archives · G. L. Herries Davies, *Sheets of many colours: the mapping of Ireland's rocks, 1750–1890* (1983) · T. W. Moody and J. C. Beckett, *Queen's, Belfast, 1845–1949: the history of a university*, 2 vols. (1959) · E. Scott, *A history of the University of Melbourne* (1936) · J. W. Clark and T. M. Hughes, *The life and letters of the Reverend Adam Sedgwick*, 2 vols. (1890) · R. T. M. Pescott, *Collections of a century: the history of the first one hundred years of the National Museum of Victoria* (1954) · N. H. Olver and G. Blainey, *The University of Melbourne: a centenary portrait* (1956) · R. W. Home, ed., *Australian science in the making* (1988) · A. Moyal, *A bright and savage land* (1986) · d. cert. [Simon Henry McCoy]

Archives Geological Survey of Ireland, Dublin, corresp. and MSS · GS Lond., corresp. and MSS · Mitchell L., NSW, corresp. and MSS, CY reel 499 · Museum of Victoria, Melbourne, corresp. and MSS · University of Melbourne, corresp. and MSS | CUL, department of manuscripts and university archives, Sedgwick MSS, corresp. and MSS

Likenesses oils, Museum of Victoria, Melbourne

Wealth at death £6873: undated newspaper cutting

McCracken, Henry Joy (1767–1798), businessman and Irish nationalist, was born at 39 High Street, Belfast, on 31 August 1767, the fifth child of Captain John McCracken (1721–1803), shipowner and textile manufacturer, and his wife, Ann Joy (1730–1814). Both the Joy and McCracken families were Presbyterian, industrious, and prominent; his mother was a great-granddaughter of George Martin, sovereign (mayor) of Belfast in 1645, and the daughter of Francis Joy, a public notary of Huguenot descent, and founder of one of Ireland's first newspapers, the *Belfast News-Letter*. In 1777 the families joined economic forces to create one of Belfast's first mechanical cotton-spinning mills, Joy, McCabe, and McCracken. McCracken displayed an early talent for mechanics and, following his education at a local school run by David Mason, was apprenticed to the family business: by 1789, he was managing the mill. A humane and popular employer, he followed in the philanthropic family tradition by creating a lending library for the poor, and in 1788 created, with his sister Mary Ann *McCracken (1770–1866), social reformer, Belfast's first non-denominational Sunday school.

A crusader by temperament, McCracken was influenced by his family's advanced political ideas. In 1788 Belfast had been at the forefront of the volunteer movement. His father and four of his relatives were founding members of the 1st Belfast volunteer company, and an uncle, Henry Joy, had been a delegate to the Dungannon convention of February 1782, which had demanded greater legislative freedom for Ireland. His family, like many other Ulster Presbyterians, had sympathized with the rebellious American colonies, and McCracken later embraced the more revolutionary ideals of the French Revolution and the ideas of Tom Paine's *The Rights of Man*. After the Society of United Irishmen was formed in 1791, the McCracken family welcomed to Belfast the Dublin lawyer Theobald Wolfe Tone. Tone joined the society, was elected an honorary member of the 1st Belfast volunteer company, and began a chapter of the society in Dublin. Although not a founding member, McCracken formally joined the United Irishmen in March 1795, at a time when it was being reorganized into a secret revolutionary society dedicated to the military overthrow of British rule, with French aid, and the creation of an Irish republic.

Before Tone left Belfast for exile in Philadelphia, he, McCracken, and other Belfast radicals climbed Cave Hill in Belfast and swore an oath to undermine British rule and create a republic. While McCracken remained lukewarm to the notion of the necessity of obtaining French military aid, he played a crucial role in forging an alliance between the Catholic Defenders and the largely Presbyterian United Irishmen of Ulster. Before the French invasion fleet floundered outside Bantry Bay the authorities struck against the United Irishmen in the north: in October 1796 McCracken was arrested and imprisoned in Kilmainham gaol, Dublin. Although he initially refused to accept bail, his increasing ill health led him to accept bail and release in November 1797. Having returned to a province suffering under the full weight of the suspension of habeas corpus and the repressive measures carried out by the military under the provisions of the Insurrection Act of 1796, McCracken threw himself into the planning of a United Irishmen rebellion. Expecting another French invasion in the spring of 1798, the Ulster directory of the Society of United Irishmen dispatched McCracken to Dublin to help co-ordinate an effective rising.

On his return to Belfast, McCracken informed the Ulster leaders that an attack on Dublin, together with the simultaneous stopping of all mail-coaches to hamper government intelligence on 27 May, would signal a general uprising under the leadership of Lord Edward Fitzgerald. The betrayal of the Leinster directory to the authorities and the subsequent arrest of Fitzgerald led to the easy suppression of the Dublin revolt; yet, when a more serious and successful rebellion broke out in co. Wexford, on 26–7 May, McCracken urged Robert Simms, the adjutant-general of Antrim, to mobilize forces. Dismayed at Simms's refusal, McCracken, by then deputy chief of the Antrim Defenders, pressed the issue and replaced Simms on 3 June, thereby becoming in effect the United Irish commander-in-chief in Ulster. The plans for an Ulster rising had already been betrayed to General George Nugent, but, having issued a stirring proclamation on 6 June, McCracken, with approximately 1500 men, attacked the county town of Antrim on 7 June.

In a short, sharp action, McCracken's forces initially captured the town in a battle which took the life of John, Lord O'Neill. They were eventually forced to retreat by the arrival of forces dispatched by Nugent, and a similar rising in co. Down was also defeated by Nugent at the battle of Ballynahinch on 12–13 June. Following his defeat McCracken took refuge in the mountains outside Ballymena, hoping to secure passage to the United States. He was recognized by three Carrickfergus yeomen, and was arrested, brought to Belfast, and, following a court martial, hanged, to the great dismay of the townspeople, on 17 July 1798, outside the market house. As a final act of humanity, General Nugent allowed McCracken's body to be quickly cut down and entrusted to the care of his sister; he was buried the following day in St George's churchyard, Belfast.

Although McCracken never married, an illegitimate daughter was brought to Mary Ann McCracken two weeks following his execution. It is usually assumed that Mary Bodel was the mother, and the child, Maria, was brought up in the McCracken household, the constant companion of Mary Ann. In later life Maria married another Belfast radical, William McCleery. In 1998 the Republic of Ireland issued five commemorative stamps remembering the 1798 rising: one bore the portrait of the Ulster Presbyterian Henry Joy McCracken. RORY T. CORNISH

Sources A. T. Q. Stewart, *The summer soldiers: the 1798 rebellion in Antrim and Down* (1995) · R. R. Madden, *The United Irishmen: their lives and times*, 2nd edn, 4 vols. (1857–60) · E. Fitzhenry, *Henry Joy McCracken* (1936) · T. Pakenham, *The year of liberty: the great Irish rebellion of 1798* (1978) · M. McNeill, *The life and times of Mary Ann McCracken, 1770–1866: a Belfast panorama* (1960); repr. (1988) · N. J. Curtin, *The United Irishmen: popular politics in Ulster and Dublin, 1791–1798* (1994)
Archives PRO NIre., family corresp., T. 1210 | Linen Hall Library, Belfast, Joy MSS, TD2777 · TCD, letters to Madden
Likenesses T. H. Lynch, lithograph, pubd 1843 (after J. Comerford), NG Ire.; repro. in Madden, *United Irishmen* · S. C. Harrison (after miniature), Belfast Muncipal Museum and Art Gallery

McCracken, Mary Ann (1770–1866), social reformer, was born on 8 July 1770 at 39 High Street, Belfast, the sixth of the seven children of Captain John McCracken (1721–1803), a master mariner with entrepreneurial interests, and his wife, Ann Joy (1730–1814). Mary Ann was the sister of the United Irishman Henry Joy *McCracken. The Joys were a family of Huguenot descent who contributed

Mary Ann McCracken (1770–1866), by unknown photographer

much to the development of Belfast as a modern industrial city, including the founding of its first newspaper, the *Belfast News-Letter*, in 1737, and the nurture of its early textile industry. Mary Ann was especially close to her elder brother Henry, and came to share much of his political idealism. They received part of their education in the school founded by David Manson, whose methods of teaching children 'by way of amusement' and reward rather than punishment (D. Manson, *Belfast News-Letter*, 17 Oct 1755) were then regarded as outlandish, and they grew up as lively and public-spirited young people who alarmed their elders by reading and admiring the works of William Godwin, Mary Wollstonecraft, and later Tom Paine.

At that time the Ulster Presbyterians, who were excluded from the charmed circle of the protestant ascendancy, shared many grievances with Irish Catholics, and were regarded with suspicion by the government, largely because of their sympathy with the revolutionaries in America and France. When Henry became a member of the Society of United Irishmen, Mary Ann gave him her full support and did not waver from it when it became clear that he was deeply involved in plotting revolution. He was arrested in October 1796 and imprisoned in Dublin but released in December 1797. When rebellion burst out in Ireland on 23 May 1798 the north remained quiet, to the amazement of the authorities. The truth was that the chosen leader in co. Antrim had refused to act without a French invasion, but two weeks later Henry Joy McCracken took his place and raised the standard of revolt. The rebels were routed at Antrim town on 7 June 1798 and McCracken became a fugitive. Although Belfast was under stringent military curfew Mary Ann set out to seek news of her brother, ascending Cave Hill and combing the bleak moorland until she found him, with the few followers who remained loyal to him. On her return to Belfast she at once began to arrange his escape to America. The plan went forward, but McCracken had the bad luck to be recognized by an acquaintance when he reached the coast. He was arrested, tried by court martial, and executed in Belfast on 17 July 1798. With immense courage Mary Ann sat by her brother during his trial and walked hand in hand with him to the gallows. She later confessed, 'I did not weep till then' (Madden, 2.494).

Mary Ann McCracken devoted the rest of her long life to caring for the poor and disadvantaged and campaigning for the rights of women and children. Much of her time was dedicated to work for the Belfast Charitable Institution, which her uncles Robert and Henry Joy had helped to create in 1771. Apart from the needs of the poor of Belfast, other causes claimed her enthusiasm: campaigns to improve conditions in prisons, to foster education, and to abolish the use of climbing boys in chimney sweeping, and cruelty to animals. For years she abstained from eating sugar, though she had a sweet tooth, to support antislavery. Like most of her co-religionists, she eventually made her peace with the British government, declaring on Queen Victoria's accession that all their grievances had been righted (McCleery, 192). She died on 26 July 1866 in Belfast, at the age of ninety-six, having lived long enough to be the subject of a clear and striking photograph, now in the Ulster Museum in Belfast. Her grave in the new burying-ground at Clifton Street remained unmarked until 1909, when the exhumed remains of her brother were placed in it and a stone erected which recorded that she 'wept by her brother's scaffold'.

A. T. Q. STEWART

Sources McCracken MSS, TCD, Madden MSS · McCracken MSS, PRO NIre., Madden MSS, T 1210 · Linen Hall, Belfast, Joy MSS · PRO NIre., Drennan MSS · PRO NIre., Drennan–Bruce MSS · A. McCleery, 'Life of Mary Ann McCracken', *Historical notices of old Belfast and its vicinity*, ed. R. M. Young (1896) · M. McNeill, *The life and times of Mary Ann McCracken, 1770–1866: a Belfast panorama* (1960) · E. C. Fitzhenry, *Henry Joy McCracken* (1936) · A. T. Q. Stewart, *The summer soldiers: the 1798 rebellion in Antrim and Down* (1995) · R. R. Madden, *The United Irishmen: their lives and times*, 2nd ser., 2 (1843) · A. C. W. Merrick and R. S. J. Clarke, *Old Belfast families and the new burying ground* (1991)
Archives PRO NIre., Madden MSS · TCD, Madden MSS
Likenesses W. Thompson, oils, repro. in R. M. Young, ed., *Historical notices of old Belfast* (1896) · photograph, Ulster Museum, Belfast [*see illus.*]
Wealth at death under £100: probate, 1 Sept 1866, *CGPLA Ire.*

Mac Craith, Seaán mac Ruaidhrí (*fl.* mid-14th cent.), historian, was a member of the Mac Craith family of hereditary bardic poets, which appears in the sixteenth-century *Fiants* of Queen Elizabeth I as settled near Pallas Green in east co. Limerick and Clogheen in south co. Tipperary. The death of 'the son of Mac Raith, the *file*' (or learned poet), is recorded in the annals of Inisfallen as early as 1097. The annals of the four masters, under the year 1098, add that he was 'arch-poet of Munster'. The next representative of the line to appear in the annals was Ruaidhrí Mac Craith

(d. 1343), described by the four masters as *ollamh le dán* or 'master-poet' to the southern half of Ireland. This Ruaidhrí is depicted in the elaborate historical narrative *Caithréim Thoirdhealbhaigh* ('The triumphs of Toirdhealbhach'), which celebrates Toirdelbach Ó Briain (d. 1306), as lamenting the slain warriors after the battle of Corcomrua Abbey, which took place in 1317 between rival factions within the Ó Briain dynasty. The *Caithréim* (which survives in copies at the Royal Irish Academy and Trinity College, Dublin) takes as its main themes the power struggle within the Uí Briain from the mid-thirteenth century, promoting the cause of the Clann Toirdelbaig over that of the Clann Briain Ruaid, and the relationship of the Uí Briain with the Anglo-Norman Clares, whom it vilifies. According to the heading in a copy of *Caithréim Thoirdhealbhaigh* which was written in 1721 by the co. Clare scribe Aindrias Mac Cruitín, the tract was composed by Seaán mac Ruaidhrí Mac Craith in 1459. However, literary and historical critics since T. J. Westropp in 1904 have agreed that on internal evidence the tract was composed in the mid-fourteenth century, most probably for the chief Diarmait Ó Briain (d. 1364), the 1459 date being either a misreading by Mac Cruitín, or applying to an intermediary copy of the original text. A mid-fourteenth-century date for the tract's composition increases the likelihood that the author, Seaán, was a son of the poet Ruaidhrí who is twice mentioned in the tract itself.

Other Mac Craith poets who flourished in the fourteenth century were Murchadh gan Crios ('the Beltless'), who addressed a poem to Sir William Bermingham (d. 1332?), Maolmhuire Bacach ('the Lame'), who eulogized the chiefs Muircheartach Ó Briain (d. 1343) and Aodh Reamhar Ó Néill (d. 1364), and Eoghan an t-Órthóir ('the Gilder') who composed an ode to Art Mac Murchadha Caomhánach (d. 1417), paramount chief of Leinster. The family continued to supply professional court poets to the aristocracy of Munster and Leinster up to the early seventeenth century, one of the later members, Eoghan, son of Donnchadh Maol ('the Bald') Mac Craith, also being the author of a number of religious poems.

KATHARINE SIMMS

Sources S. Mac Ruaidhrí Mac Craith, *Caithréim Thoirdhealbhaigh / The triumphs of Turlough*, ed. S. H. O'Grady, 2 vols., ITS, 26–7 (1929); repr. (1988) · A. Nic Ghiollamhaith, 'Dynastic warfare and historical writing in north Munster, 1276–1350', *Cambridge Medieval Celtic Studies*, 2 (1981), 73–89 · T. F. O'Rahilly, 'Irish poets, historians and judges in English historical documents, 1538–1615', *Proceedings of the Royal Irish Academy*, 36C (1921–4), 86–120 · AFM · L. F. McNamara, 'An examination of the medieval Irish text *Caithréim Thoirdhealbhaigh*', *North Munster Antiquarian Journal*, 8 (1958–61), 182–92 · T. J. Westropp, 'On the external evidences bearing on the historic character of the "Wars of Turlough" by John son of Rory MacGrath', *Transactions of the Royal Irish Academy*, 32C (1902–4), 133–98 · A. M. Freeman, ed. and trans., *Annála Connacht / The annals of Connacht* (1944); repr. (1970) · S. Mac Airt, ed. and trans., *The annals of Inisfallen* (1951) · A. Nic Ghiollamhaith, 'Kings and vassals in later medieval Ireland', *Colony and frontier in medieval Ireland: essays presented to J. F. Lydon*, ed. T. Barry and others (1995), 201–16

McCrea, Jane (1752?–1777), murder victim and folk heroine in America, was born near Bedminster or Lamington, Somerset county, in the colony of New Jersey, the younger of the two daughters among the seven children of James McCrea (*d.* 1769), a Presbyterian minister, and his wife, Mary Graham (*d.* 1753), both Scots-Irish immigrants to America in the 1730s. The family name is variously spelled M'Crea, MacCrea, M'Kray, McCrae, and M'Crae, but always McCrea in Jane's case. Her friends called her Jenny. She was tall for a woman and had unusually long hair.

In 1770 the recently orphaned young woman moved into the home of her eldest brother, John, a Princeton-educated lawyer practising in Argyle, Washington county, New York. The two apparently got along well at first but increasingly disagreed about politics. Jane remained loyal to the crown during the American War of Independence, while John was colonel of a New York militia regiment under General Philip Schuyler, and their brother Stephen served another New York regiment as surgeon. She fell in love with David Jones, a loyalist from the upper Hudson River valley who enlisted in the British army under Lieutenant-General Sir John Burgoyne in 1776 and was commissioned lieutenant in 1777. They planned to be married during Burgoyne's Saratoga campaign. McCrea's loyalist friend Sarah Fraser Campbell McNeil, a cousin of Burgoyne's brigadier Simon Fraser, arranged a rendezvous for her with Jones.

On the morning of 27 July 1777 McCrea travelled from her home in Argyle to McNeil's home near Fort Edward. The two women were captured by Indians, stripped naked, and dragged towards the British camp. McNeil survived, but McCrea was killed and scalped. The facts of her death have become irretrievably lost in legend, romance, propaganda, and conflicting accounts. Some say the Indians were Ottawas, others say Mohawks, but all agree that they were Burgoyne's allies. Some maintain that McCrea died from tomahawk blows, others from gunshots. Some assert that American pickets accidentally killed her with musket fire as they tried to rescue her. Even the colour of her hair is disputed. Most agree that David Jones saw her scalp when the Indians brought it into the British camp and recognized it from the length of its tresses.

Burgoyne himself believed that McCrea was killed by Wyandot Panther, a particularly unruly member of the Ottawa tribe. He first intended to hang Panther, but when he was advised that, if he did so, the Ottawas would revolt and harass the British lines all the way back to Canada, he reconsidered. Finally he did nothing. The Ottawas deserted anyway. Jones, disgusted by Burgoyne's decision, deserted the British army and took refuge in Canada, where he died many years later, unmarried and despondent. He is supposed to have kept McCrea's scalp as a relic and had it buried with him.

American propagandists made the most of the McCrea incident. They argued that, if Burgoyne could not protect even his own civilian supporters from the barbarity of his Indian allies, how much less safe were the wives and children of rebel soldiers. In private correspondence with Burgoyne, the American general Horatio Gates strongly protested against the various atrocities that Burgoyne's Indians committed and accused Burgoyne of buying the scalps of white settlers, including McCrea's. Burgoyne indignantly denied such collusion, but his reputation as Gentleman Johnny suffered irreparable harm, especially when Gates made his accusations public. McCrea immediately became a martyr to the revolutionary cause. Her death rallied the Americans against Burgoyne, checked desertions, prompted enlistments, and was an important morale factor in the American victory at Saratoga in October 1777. In the following decades she became a popular subject for novelists, artists, historians, and poets, such as Joel Barlow and Philip Freneau. The irony that their heroine was a tory apparently did not matter to them or else it remained subordinate to the sincerity of her emotions and the brutality of her death.

McCrea was first buried beside Three Mile Creek, about 3 miles south of Fort Edward, then removed to the old Fort Edward burial-ground. In the nineteenth century her remains were reinterred beside those of her niece, Sarah Hanna Payne, in Union cemetery, Hudson Falls, New York.   ERIC V. D. LUFT

Sources J. Namias, 'McCrea, Jane', *ANB* • J. A. Holden, 'Influence of the death of Jane McCrea on the Burgoyne campaign', *Proceedings of the New York State Historical Association*, 12 (1913), 249–310 • J. Namias, *White captives: gender and ethnicity on the American frontier* (1993) • D. Wilson, *The life of Jane McCrea, with an account of Burgoyne's expedition in 1777* (1853) • R. Furneaux, *Saratoga: the decisive battle* (1971) • G. Tomkinson, 'Jane McCrea: a martyr of the revolutionary war', *Dalhousie Review*, 49 (1969–70), 399–403
Archives Fort Edward Historical Association, Fort Edward, New York • Old Fort House Museum, Fort Edward, New York
Likenesses J. Vanderlyn, oils, 1804, Wadsworth Atheneum, Hartford, Connecticut
Wealth at death probably negligible

McCrea, Sir William Hunter [Bill] (1904–1999), astrophysicist, was born on 13 December 1904 in Dublin, the elder son and eldest child of Robert Hunter McCrea (1877–1956), a schoolmaster, and his wife, Margaret, *née* Hutton (1879–1962). His parents, of Irish stock, were strict nonconformists, but by the age of eighteen he had become a confirmed Anglican, a faith he retained all his life. By 1907 the family had moved to Chesterfield, Derbyshire, where he attended first the central (elementary) school and then the grammar school, from which he won an entrance scholarship in mathematics to Trinity College, Cambridge. He read for the mathematics tripos, becoming a wrangler in 1926.

As an undergraduate McCrea specialized in those branches of mathematical physics which were stimulating exciting research at Cambridge, and after graduating he began research as one of the many pupils of R. H. Fowler (to whom he paid warm tribute on his centenary in 1989). Although he worked initially on basic problems in quantum physics and relativity, and also on related problems in pure mathematics, his interest gradually focused on the application of theoretical physics to the astronomical universe, ranging from the constitution of stellar atmospheres, through the formation of planets and stars, to cosmology, the study of the universe as a whole. Recognition came early with a Cambridge University Rayleigh prize, a Trinity College Rouse Ball senior studentship, a

Sheepshanks exhibition, and an Isaac Newton studentship.

Academic career After spending the year 1928–9 as visitor at Göttingen University in Germany, McCrea began his rapid rise up the regular academic ladder as lecturer in the Edinburgh department of mathematics, headed by Edmund Whittaker. While at Edinburgh he met Marian Nicol Core (1911–1995), second daughter of Thomas Webster, a mining engineer, of Burdiehouse, Edinburgh. They were married on 28 July 1933. They had two daughters, Isabella and Sheila, and a son, Roderick.

In 1932 McCrea became reader in mathematics at Imperial College, London. In 1936 he moved to Queen's University, Belfast, as professor of mathematics. In 1943 he was given leave from Belfast while doing operational research in the Admiralty in the team led by Patrick Blackett. After VE-day in 1945, with the rank of captain in the Royal Naval Volunteer Reserve, he had the task of interviewing German naval officers in Schleswig-Holstein. He did not return to Belfast, having in 1944 been appointed professor at Royal Holloway College, London, and taken up the appointment at the end of the war.

McCrea remained at Holloway until 1966, when he took up his last appointment as research professor of theoretical astronomy (supported by the Science Research Council) at the recently established University of Sussex. Shortly after the war, he had urged the setting up of a national institute of theoretical astronomy. The subsequent rather tortuous negotiations led to the establishment of the Institute of Theoretical Astronomy in Cambridge (later united with the Cambridge observatories to form the Institute of Astronomy), and the smaller Sussex Astronomy Centre, with McCrea as the first research professor and Roger Tayler as the first professor supported by the University Grants Committee. With the enthusiastic support of the astronomer royal, Sir Richard Woolley, and the other senior staff at the Royal Greenwich Observatory, McCrea and Tayler jointly put Sussex on to the world astronomy map.

Contributions to astrophysics and relativity McCrea was a versatile astrophysicist. Many of his papers profoundly affected the way in which subsequent workers formulated problems. One of his earliest papers proposed turbulent pressure as the means of support of the solar chromosphere—the layer between the surface and the hot corona, observable through the emission of spectral lines by calcium and other elements. His paper 'Model stellar atmospheres', published in 1931, followed on from the basic mathematical treatments of Karl Schwarzschild, Arthur Eddington, and E. Arthur Milne. For a gas of given chemical composition McCrea pioneered the now standard procedure that constructs the degree of ionization and so also the coefficient of opacity by the direct application of quantum mechanics and statistical mechanics. From his careful studies he came to the cautious but prescient conclusion that 'hydrogen is of importance in some stars in some parts of their spectra' (W. H. McCrea, 'Model

stellar atmospheres', *Monthly Notices of the Royal Astronomical Society*, 91, 1931, 836–57). The later discovery by Rupert Wildt of the strong contribution to the opacity in cool stars of the negative hydrogen ion effectively removed the objections, noted by Milne, to hydrogen being in fact the dominant element, as had been urged earlier by Cecilia Payne-Gaposchkin, and which McCrea himself had surmised from his study of the chromosphere. This conclusion—of great cosmological significance—was supported by the parallel studies of Bengt Strömgren and others, extending Eddington's theory of stellar structure.

McCrea had a lifelong interest in the physics and dynamics of stellar and planetary formation. Just before his birth, James Jeans had introduced the picture of the breakup of a uniform gaseous medium through 'gravitational instability'. A rigorous discussion of this fragmentation into bodies with the 'Jeans mass' requires a self-consistent treatment of the initially unperturbed medium. Parallel to Rolf Ebert and William Bonnor, McCrea gave an approximate but elegant treatment of the equilibrium of an isothermal gas cloud, as a balance between internal pressure, self-gravitation, and external pressure. Under steadily increasing external pressure, the cloud density goes up until the Jeans mass becomes less than the cloud mass, and gravitational collapse begins. As emphasized by Fred Hoyle, for the collapse to persist and lead to possible breakup into masses of stellar order, the heat of compression must be largely radiated away. Together with Derek McNally, McCrea pioneered the study of the formation of molecules in dusty interstellar clouds, especially the hydrogen molecule, which is a powerful cooling agent.

The comparatively few but very bright O and B stars have lifetimes much less than the galactic age. McCrea explored the possibility that they are born as stars of moderate mass but subsequently grow by gravitational accretion of gas from the interstellar medium, as discussed by Hoyle, Ray Lyttleton, and Hermann Bondi. He argued that this would occur occasionally when an already slowly moving star enters a gas cloud and is reduced almost to rest through dynamical drag. However, he was well aware that studies in cosmogony which ignored angular momentum could be suggestive but not definitive. One of his later papers attempted to give a unified picture of the formation of the sun and the surrounding planets through the spontaneous evolution of a rotating disc with a highly supersonic turbulence. He argued that the very process by which the turbulence decays, by the mutual collision and adherence of 'floccules', moving randomly and with supersonic speeds, acts broadly like a gross macro-viscosity, yielding a slowly rotating, condensed core containing most of the mass, surrounded by a Keplerian disc containing very little mass but most of the angular momentum. Altogether his contributions to cosmogony warranted a permanent place in the literature, though, like many of his generation, he was slow to appreciate the importance of electromagnetic processes in astronomy.

McCrea made many contributions to both special and

general relativity theory. In a famous controversy with Herbert Dingle, he vigorously rebutted misunderstandings of the so-called 'twin paradox' that kept reappearing in the literature. Together with Arthur Milne he showed that the various cosmological models emerging from Einstein's theory had simply-understood Newtonian analogues. In a profound paper entitled 'Observable relations in cosmology' (*Zeitschrift für Astrophysik*, 9, 1935, 290–314), the first in a series, he spelt out the different possible definitions of distance in cosmology, showing how counts of galaxies and their observed change of brightness with distance can in principle be used to constrain the parameters in standard homogeneous, isotropic models of the expanding universe. Later he argued that the cosmical constant Λ that appeared in Einstein's modified version of general relativity, leading to the 'cosmical repulsion', can be regarded as determining the zero point of density and stress. Einstein subsequently regretted his introduction of the Λ-term, calling it 'the biggest blunder of my life' (G. Gamow, *My World Line*, 1970, 64). However, most other workers in relativistic cosmology were happy to retain it, and in fact it is currently cited as a likely explanation of the observationally inferred acceleration of the cosmical expansion.

A decade or so later, when evolutionary cosmology appeared to face observational difficulties, McCrea showed a commendable flexibility of mind in taking seriously the alternative steady-state theory proposed in 1948 by Thomas Gold, Hermann Bondi, and Fred Hoyle. The experience gained from his thorough studies of the mathematical structure of general relativity enabled him to show how, with a suitable modification of the equation of state, the steady-state model could be treated within the framework of general relativity. (Later work on inflationary 'big bang' cosmology was likewise concerned with the appropriate equation of state.) However, he later accepted that the steady-state theory, at least in its original form, could no longer hold up against the accumulating evidence from optical and radio observations. In his later years he appeared in private conversation to backtrack from the theme of his earlier work, expressing a growing scepticism about the feasibility of the whole cosmological enterprise.

Publications and honours In addition to his many papers and reviews, McCrea wrote the texts *Relativity Physics* (1935) and *Analytical Geometry of Three Dimensions* (1942), the less technical *Physics of the Sun and Stars* (1950), a history of *The Royal Greenwich Observatory* (1975), and, together with Tayler, the second volume of the *History of the Royal Astronomical Society* (1987). Over his long life, he knew personally many of the great figures in twentieth-century physics and astronomy. His personal recollections of Jeans and Eddington, his essay review on the origin of wave mechanics written for Erwin Schrödinger's centenary, and his article 'Cambridge physics, 1925–1929: diamond jubilee of golden years', published in the *Interdisciplinary Science Reviews* for 1986, were all lasting contributions to the history of science.

McCrea was elected a fellow of the Royal Society of Edinburgh in 1931 and of the Royal Society of London in 1952. He received many invitations from all over the world. He was a bye-fellow at Caius College, Cambridge, and visiting professor or lecturer at Berkeley, the Case Institute at Cleveland, the University of British Columbia at Vancouver, Louvain, Cairo, Istanbul, and Otago, among others. Like Tayler's, his services to astronomy went far beyond his technical contributions. He was successively council member, secretary, president, foreign correspondent, and treasurer of the Royal Astronomical Society, and for some years he was editor of *Observatory* and of the society's *Monthly Notices*. He received the society's gold medal in 1976. He also served on the councils of the Royal Society, of the London Mathematical Society, and of the Royal Institute of Philosophy, and gave public service as a school governor. He was knighted in 1985.

McCrea was a kindly, rather shy man with hidden reserves of strength, and remained intellectually active well into his nineties. His personal integrity was patent; his public services, especially to the Royal Astronomical Society, were so much appreciated because everyone instinctively trusted him. His somewhat formal manner was rather misleading: he was a gregarious figure, especially committed to the Royal Astronomical Society and the Royal Society dining clubs. His death, in Lewes, Sussex, on 25 April 1999, was mourned worldwide by colleagues and friends, and not least by former undergraduate and graduate students, who recalled with gratitude his help and warm encouragement. He was buried at Lewes, survived by his three children, his wife having predeceased him.

LEON MESTEL

Sources W. H. McCrea, 'Clustering of astronomers', *Annual Review of Astronomy and Astrophysics*, 25 (1987), 1–22 · W. H. McCrea, 'Cambridge physics, 1925–29', *Interdisciplinary Science Reviews*, 11 (1986), 269–84 · *Daily Telegraph* (28 April 1999) · *The Times* (30 April 1999) · *The Independent* (30 April 1999) · *The Guardian* (3 May 1999) · *The Scotsman* (21 May 1999) · J. D. Barrow and D. McNally, 'Sir William Hunter McCrea, 1904–1999', *Astronomy and Geophysics*, 40/6 (Dec 1999), 35–6 · *WWW* · personal knowledge (2004) · private information (2004) [Isabella Stevens]
Archives CAC Cam., MSS · Royal Holloway College, Egham, Surrey, papers
Likenesses photograph (as president of the Royal Astronomical Society), Burlington House, Piccadilly, London · photograph, repro. in McCrea, 'Clustering of astronomers' · photograph, RS · photograph (with Subrahmanyan Chandrasekhar), repro. in Barrow and McNally, 'Sir William Hunter McCrea', 36
Wealth at death £302,643—gross; £299,665—net: probate, 16 July 1999, CGPLA Eng. & Wales

M'Creery, John (1768–1832), printer, was born at Burndennet near Strabane in co. Tyrone; his father was probably James M'Creery (*c*.1745–1811), a printer in Strabane. John M'Creery came to Liverpool, where he was apprenticed to George Wood (1754–1815), printer of Princes Street. M'Creery set up as a printer in Houghton Street, Liverpool, his earliest imprints being dated 1792, when he printed Thomas Hall's *Achmet to Selim, or, The Dying Negro*, a slim quarto. M'Creery became acquainted with William Roscoe, who played a leading part in many Liverpool institutions, and who became M'Creery's principal patron, entrusting to him the printing of his *Life of Lorenzo de' Medici* (2 vols., 1796). M'Creery produced much ephemeral work for those Liverpool institutions with which Roscoe was associated. While these are no better than the jobbing work of his time, he aspired to fine printing, as he clearly indicates in the preface to the first part of his *The Press: a Poem* (1803), which was set in the transitional typeface cut by William Martin for the Boydell Shakespeare, printed by William Bulmer; it was illustrated with wood-engravings by Henry Hole, a former apprentice of Thomas Bewick. In this preface, expatiating on the 'art' of printing, M'Creery also makes clear his belief that his 'remote' situation in Liverpool prevented his achieving fine printing. However, a study of his output suggests that his later work did not improve upon the substantial books that he produced for Roscoe while in Liverpool.

Nevertheless, in 1805, with William Martin's advice, M'Creery moved to London, establishing himself in Black Horse Court, Fleet Street, and registering his press under the Seditious Societies Act on 28 December of that year. He became free of the Stationers' Company by redemption on 4 February 1806, and was immediately cloathed in the livery; he was active on the committee of master printers, which was at that time negotiating wages with the journeymen compositors and pressmen. He still relied to a considerable extent on his former Liverpool patrons, especially Roscoe, for work, though initially he gained some support in London, printing *Bibliomania* (2 vols., 1811) for the demanding author T. F. Dibdin. In spite of Dibdin's praise M'Creery's business declined, and by 1817 he had only a single compositor at work. He published a second part of *The Press* in 1827. He appears to have been a poor man of business, and had retired by June 1828. Soon afterwards he returned to Liverpool. In the autumn of 1831 M'Creery visited Paris with his wife and daughters, and on 18 April 1832 he died there of cholera. His body was brought back to England, and he was buried in London at Kensal Green cemetery.   PETER ISAAC

Sources J. R. Barker, 'John McCreery: a radical printer, 1768–1832', *The Library*, 5th ser., 16 (1961), 81–103 · T. F. Dibdin, *The bibliographical decameron*, 2 (1817), 407–11 · J. R. Barker, 'Cadell and Davies and the Liverpool booksellers', *The Library*, 5th ser., 14 (1959), 274–80 · *GM*, 1st ser., 102/1 (1832), 649 · *GM*, 1st ser., 81/2 (1811), 197 · G. Chandler, *William Roscoe of Liverpool* (1953), 88 · C. H. Timperley, *Encyclopaedia of literary and typographical anecdote*, 2nd edn (1842), 920–21 · *IGI*
Archives Lpool RO, corresp. with William Roscoe · NL Scot., corresp. with Cadell and Davies
Likenesses sketch, repro. in *Liverpool Worthies*, 2 (1910), 16

McCreery, Sir Richard Loudon (1898–1967), army officer, was born at Kibworth Harcourt, Leicestershire, on 1 February 1898, the eldest son of Walter Adolph McCreery, of Bilton Park, Rugby, and his wife, Emilia, *née* McAdam. He was educated at Eton College (1911–15) and the Royal Military College, Sandhurst. He was commissioned in the 12th royal lancers in 1915, with whom he served in France from 1915 to 1917 (lieutenant 1917) and from August to November 1918, winning the MC (1918) for a fine reconnoitring action with his troop which enabled the 50th division to advance quickly and effectively. After the war, despite a leg wound which doctors claimed would prevent his riding, McCreery quickly established himself as a leading horseman, winning the grand military gold cup at Sandown Park twice (once on a favourite mare, Annie Darling), as well as many other steeplechases; winning also sword, lance, revolver, and dummy thrusting competitions at Olympia, hunting regularly, and playing polo for his regiment, eventually leading it to victory in the interregimental competition in 1936. On 18 April 1928 he married Lettice (*b.* 30 Oct 1902), second daughter of Lord Percy St Maur (second son of Algernon, fourteenth duke of Somerset); they had four sons and a daughter.

McCreery was an exceptionally promising soldier. After promotion to captain in 1923 and major in 1927 he entered Staff College in 1928 (graduated 1929) and was brigade-major, 2nd cavalry brigade from 1930 to 1933. From 1935 to 1938 (when he was promoted colonel) he commanded the 12th lancers—an armoured car regiment, one of the first cavalry regiments to be mechanized. He made them train hard. Only the best would do, so that in 1940 they acquitted themselves well against the German Panzer troops. By then Dick McCreery was commanding 2nd armoured brigade. At the outbreak of war in 1939 he had been principal staff officer (GSO1) to Harold Alexander, then commanding 1st division at Aldershot, and they served together in France during the 'phoney war' period from September 1939 to May 1940.

During the last phase of the battle for France, so gallantly and skilfully did McCreery conduct his brigade's withdrawal that he was awarded the DSO (1940). He was promoted major-general, and commanded an armoured division in England for two years, before going to the Mediterranean theatre in 1942, at first as adviser on armoured fighting vehicles at general headquarters Cairo. On Alexander's arrival there, McCreery returned to his old master as chief of staff (Middle East), and had decisive influence during the Alamein battle. Long afterwards McCreery broke his silence in an article (1959) in his regimental journal, criticizing Montgomery's conduct of this battle, and alleging his tactics had been unnecessarily costly in infantry and his pursuit overcautious, so failing to cut off Rommel. He also criticized Montgomery's intolerance and inflated ideas. Alexander described McCreery himself as that rare creature, a brilliant staff officer and an inspiring commander. He served in Tunisia in 1943 and in Italy from 1943 to 1945.

In 1943 McCreery became lieutenant-general and took command, under Lieutenant-General Mark Clark, USA, of the Eighth Army's 10th corps (two infantry and one armoured division); and in the Salerno landings (September 1943) and ensuing critical battles his calm courage, personal example, and dynamic influence did much to carry the day. During the fighting in 1943 and 1944 he was regularly at the front line so that his thrusting subordinate generals would often find McCreery further forward than they were. He was appointed CB and KCB in 1943. In September 1944 he assumed command of the Eighth Army, and after the Gothic line (German defences in the

Apennines) battles, closed up to the Senio River in preparation for the great spring offensive of 1945. This was a brilliant success, and after a battle lasting twenty-three days the enemy forces surrendered unconditionally on 2 May 1945.

After the war McCreery commanded the British forces of occupation in Austria, and was the British representative on the allied commission for Austria in 1945–6. He had considerable success in negotiating with Marshal Koniev and apparently earned the respect of the Russians. He was appointed KBE in 1945, and promoted full general in 1946. When Sir Archibald Nye became governor of Madras in 1946 Alanbrooke wanted McCreery to succeed him as VCIGS, but Montgomery disagreed and a compromise was found in Sir Frank Simpson. McCreery commanded the British Army of the Rhine in 1946–8, during the difficult period of its run-down and retraining, and finally he was the British army representative on the United Nations military staff committee in 1948–9. He was appointed GCB and retired in 1949. From 1947 to 1956 he was colonel-commandant of the Royal Armoured Corps.

McCreery was deeply religious, and very much a family man. After his retirement he devoted much time to his regiment: he was colonel of the 12th lancers in 1951–60, and of the amalgamated 9th/12th lancers in 1960–61. He was also colonel of the 14th/20th hussars, and the 3rd/4th County of London yeomanry. He gave much time to racing and was steward at Wincanton and Sandown; also to boys' clubs; and he took pride in his horses, his home at Stowell Hill, Templecombe, Somerset, his farm, his garden, and his flowers. He was a man for whom nothing was too much trouble: family, friends, and regiment, soldiers and servants received his consideration and kindness.

McCreery was tall and thin, quiet in manner, and restrained in speech; he was a man of fierce loyalties and without humbug. A legendary horseman, he became the doyen of the British cavalry. He died at 232 Cranmer Court, Chelsea, on 18 October 1967.

JOHN STRAWSON, *rev.* ROGER T. STEARN

Sources *The Times* (19 Oct 1967) · personal knowledge (1980) · private information (1980) · *WWW* · Burke, *Peerage* (1959) · *The Eton register*, 8 (privately printed, Eton, 1932) · J. Gooch, ed., *Decisive campaigns of the Second World War* (1990) · B. Bond, *British military policy between the two world wars* (1980) · *CGPLA Eng. & Wales* (1968)
Archives FILM IWM FVA, 'Front line Y.M.C.A.', Army Film Unit, 21 Oct 1943, A 571/1/2 · IWM FVA, actuality footage · IWM FVA, news footage | SOUND IWM SA, 'American commander of allied campaign in Italy, 1943–1945', Thames TV, 1972 · IWM SA, oral history interview
Likenesses W. Stoneman, photograph, 1946, NPG
Wealth at death £60,199: probate, 14 May 1968, *CGPLA Eng. & Wales*

Mac Creiche mac Pessláin (*fl.* late 6th cent.). *See under* Munster, saints of (*act. c.*450–*c.*700).

McCrie, Thomas (1772–1835), Original Secession minister and ecclesiastical historian, was born at Duns, Berwickshire, in 1772 and baptized on 22 November, the eldest son of Thomas McCrie, manufacturer and merchant in Duns, and his first wife, Mary, daughter of John Hood, a farmer near Duns. His parents belonged to that branch of the

seceders from the Church of Scotland in 1733 known as the Anti-Burghers, who had split from the original seceders by 1747 over the burgess oath, which was held to imply an acknowledgement of the Church of Scotland. Reared in that seceding tradition and encouraged by his maternal grandfather, Thomas received a classical education at Duns parish school, and before he had reached the age of fifteen served as an elementary teacher in two country schools near by. In 1788 he became an usher or assistant teacher first at the parish school at Kelso, Roxburghshire, and then in East Linton, Haddingtonshire, before entering Edinburgh University in December of that year. His arts course included classes in Latin, Greek, Hebrew, mathematics, logic, and moral philosophy, to whose professor, Dugald Stewart, among all his college teachers, he was most indebted. As was not unusual, he did not graduate; and in May 1791 he was appointed teacher at a private Anti-Burgher school in Brechin, Forfarshire. During the harvest months from September 1791 he attended the Divinity Hall at Whitburn, Linlithgowshire, where he studied for the ministry of his denomination under the Revd Archibald Bruce, professor of theology in the Anti-Burghers' General Associate Synod—an office to which McCrie succeeded in 1816. In May 1794 he left his teaching post at Brechin and spent the summer at the home of his maternal uncle near Dunbar, Haddingtonshire, before returning to Edinburgh University in the winter to complete his arts course by attending the natural philosophy class. Licensed on 9 September 1795 by the associate presbytery of Kelso, he declined to express a view on the magistrate's power in religious matters, for the subject was then pending before the General Associate Synod, and was admitted minister of the second associate congregation in Potterrow, Edinburgh, on 26 May 1796. On 24 December that year he married Janet (*IGI* gives Jessie) Dickson (*d.* 1821), daughter of William Dickson, a farmer in Swinton parish, Berwickshire. They had four sons and one daughter: Thomas *McCrie (1797–1875), professor of church history and systematic theology in the English Presbyterian College, London; William, a merchant in Edinburgh; Jessie, who married Archibald Meikle of Flemington; John, who died aged twenty-eight on 4 October 1837; and George, minister of Clova, Aberdeenshire.

From 1793 the Anti-Burghers, to McCrie's dismay, developed scruples on the civil magistrate's role within the church, which led them to revise their adherence to the teaching of the Westminster confession of faith on the magistrate's duty to promote true religion. Their 'new testimony', adopted by the General Associate Synod in May 1804, led McCrie with five other ministers, including his mentor Archibald Bruce, vigorously to protest at the synod's action. McCrie remained attached to the standards and constitution of the Church of Scotland 'as settled in her reforming periods', upheld the principle of an established church, and condemned the complete separation of church and state. On 28 August 1806 he and three other 'Old Light' ministers formed themselves into the Constitutional Associate Presbytery. Deposed from his ministry by the synod on 2 September 1806 and ejected from his Potterrow meeting-house after a lawsuit in March 1809, McCrie assembled his people for worship in a chapel at the foot of Carrubber's Close, Edinburgh, until in 1813 a new church was built in West Richmond Street, where he preached for the rest of his life. By 1827 the 'constitutionalists' were joined by former brethren who, dissatisfied with the union of the Burgher and Anti-Burgher synods in 1820, had split to form the Associate Synod of Protesters, and who merged with McCrie's Constitutional Presbytery on 18 May as the Associate Synod of Original Seceders, a designation intended to denote that they stood precisely on the same ground as that occupied by the original seceders; later they adopted the name Original Secession church.

In these disputes McCrie's stand was reinforced by his study of Scottish church history since the Reformation, and he proved a formidable scholar in defending Presbyterian traditions. His earlier writings on church history included a study of the Hussites and essays on the covenanting minister Alexander Henderson; Patrick Hamilton, first Scottish martyr in the Reformation; Francis Lambert of Avignon, the French reformer of Hesse; André Rivet, French protestant and professor at Leiden; and John Murray, a Scottish Presbyterian opponent of James VI. His first major work, a scholarly and sympathetic biography of John Knox, published in 1811, sought to counter the prevailing 'enlightened' view of Knox in the histories of David Hume and William Robertson as a fierce and gloomy bigot, the foe to polite learning and innocent enjoyment, who stirred up vulgar enthusiasm to effect a revolution against Rome and France in defiance of the crown. The evangelical revival helps account for the widespread popularity of McCrie's *Knox* and for a renewed interest in the principles of the Scottish Reformation. On 3 February 1813 Edinburgh University conferred on him the degree of doctor of divinity. His next study, appropriately, was a biography of Andrew Melville (1545–1622), the champion of presbytery and adversary of James VI's bishops, in which McCrie made extensive use of manuscript material to elucidate the principles of early presbyterianism. That work, first published in 1819, did not gain the popularity of his study of Knox, though it involved 'a hundred times more labour', yet its scholarship remains unsurpassed nearly two centuries later. On the 'second reformation' of the covenanting period, McCrie took to task Sir Walter Scott's view in *Old Mortality* that the covenanters, far from defending political freedoms, were no more than religious enthusiasts determined to impose an ecclesiastical tyranny. For McCrie, the Reformation principles of Scotland combined political and religious liberty, and the covenanters had played a crucial role in the struggle for national and individual rights. His literary output extended to histories of the Reformation in Italy (1827), translated into French, German, and Dutch (and placed on the papal *Index expurgatorius*) and in Spain (1829), and, at the end of his life, an uncompleted study of Calvin.

After the death of his first wife on 1 June 1821, McCrie

sailed for the Netherlands in May 1822, visiting The Hague, Leiden, Haarlem, Amsterdam, and Utrecht, and preached at the Scots Kirk in Rotterdam. At home he served as a founding member of the Gaelic School Society, opposed whig plans for Irish education in 1832, petitioned the House of Commons against Roman Catholic emancipation in 1829, and gave evidence in 1834 to a House of Commons committee on church patronage, which he considered to be at variance with Presbyterian principles. On 4 October 1827 he married Mary Chalmers, the fourth daughter of Robert Chalmers, minister of Haddington. McCrie died in Edinburgh on 3 August 1835 and was buried on 12 August in Greyfriars churchyard; a deputation from the general assembly of the Church of Scotland attended his funeral.   JAMES KIRK

Sources T. McCrie, *Life of Thomas McCrie, by his son Thomas McCrie* (1840) · *Miscellaneous writings of Thomas McCrie*, ed. T. McCrie (1841) · J. M'Kerrow, *History of the Secession church*, rev. edn (1848)
Archives U. Edin. L., extracts relating to church and historical matters | NL Scot., letters to John Lee · U. Edin. L., letters to David Laing
Likenesses J. W. Gordon, oils, Scot. NPG

McCrie, Thomas (1797–1875), ecclesiastical historian and Free Church of Scotland minister, was born in Edinburgh on 7 November 1797, the eldest in a family of four sons and a daughter of Thomas *McCrie (1772–1835), Secession church minister, and his wife, Janet Dickson (*d.* 1821). He was educated at the high school and university in Edinburgh before entering the theological hall of the Original Secession church. Licensed on 15 August 1820, McCrie was ordained minister of a congregation at Crieff, Perthshire, in 1821, but it was so poorly supported that he demitted the charge in July 1826. He was inducted to a church at Clola, Aberdeenshire, on 16 April 1829. On 28 December 1830 he married Walteria Chalmers (*d.* 1875), the daughter of a Secession minister and sister of his father's second wife. There were no children. McCrie succeeded his father in Davie Street Church, Edinburgh, on 9 June 1836 and in the same year succeeded Dr George Paxton as the theological professor of the Original Secession church. McCrie received the degrees of DD from Marischal College, Aberdeen, in 1848 and LLD from Glasgow University in 1850.

McCrie was moderator of his church's synod when it united with the Free Church of Scotland in 1852 and moderator of the Free Church general assembly in 1856. In October of that year he demitted his charge in order to serve as professor of church history and exegesis to the English Presbyterian synod. He remained in London until, his sight affected by cataract, he retired to Gullane, East Lothian, in 1866.

A good preacher, McCrie is chiefly remembered for his publications, which included his father's collected works in four volumes, a biography of his father, several titles for the Wodrow Society, and *Sketches of Scottish Church History*, which passed through several editions. For several years McCrie was editor of the *British and Foreign Evangelical Review* and he was also a contributor to *The Witness* under

Hugh Miller. He enjoyed a close friendship with James Aitken Wylie (1808–1890), whose background, interests, and conservative outlook were similar to his own.

He died on 9 May 1875 at his home, 39 Minto Street, Edinburgh, and was buried beside his father in Greyfriars churchyard on 14 May. His wife predeceased him by a matter of weeks.

W. A. J. ARCHBOLD, *rev.* LIONEL ALEXANDER RITCHIE

Sources *The Scotsman* (11 May 1875) · *Free Church of Scotland Monthly Record* (1 July 1875) · D. Scott, *Annals and statistics of the Original Secession church* (1886), 295, 544–6 · J. A. Wylie, *Disruption worthies: a memorial of 1843*, ed. J. B. Gillies, new edn (1881), 349–56 · R. Small, *History of the congregations of the United Presbyterian church from 1733 to 1900*, 1 (1904), 515–16; 2 (1904), 624 · private information (1893) [C. G. McCrie]
Archives U. Edin. L., corresp. with David Laing
Likenesses portrait (aged fifty-nine), repro. in Gillies, ed., *Disruption worthies*, facing p. 349
Wealth at death £1354 17s. 9d.: confirmation, Scotland, 29 June 1875, NA Scot., SC 70/1/175, 1131–8

MacCrimmon family (*per.* 1600–1746), pipers, were hereditary pipers to the MacLeods of Dunvegan, Isle of Skye, holding tenancies at Boreraig, Galtrigill, and Borrodale. The origins of the MacCrimmons are obscure. Genealogies of the family have been produced, based mostly on James Logan's unreliable introduction to Angus Mackay's *A Collection of Ancient Piobaireachd* (1838). They rely more on tradition, inference, and even invention, than on accurate records. However, through the tangle of romance attached to the name, there is no doubt that the MacCrimmons were masters and renowned teachers of *ceòl mòr*—the classical music of the highland bagpipes, also known as piobaireachd (pibroch).

In May 1651 a 'John M'gyurmen' was declared by his fellow pipers to be 'the Prince of Pipers' (NL Scot., 3658, Wardlaw MS p. 379). Charles II called him forward and permitted him to kiss his hand, upon which the piper composed the piobaireachd *Thug mi pòg do làimh an righ*. Opinion has it that 'M'gyurmen' (a name otherwise unknown) is a rendering of the name MacCrimmon though, as piper to the 'Earle of Sutherland', the player in question would not have been employed by the MacLeods.

Further evidence of the family's employment and status can be found in the records of the MacLeod estates, but they do not appear on the rent rolls as they probably held their lands rent-free, as did Roderick Morison. That they were formally recognized as teachers is reflected in an entry for 1698 referring to the 'Prentisep of McIntyre ye pyper with McCrooman'. Their musical prowess is mentioned in the Gaelic poems of Mary MacLeod—notably *Crònan an taibh* (composed shortly after 1666), which refers to Pàdraig Mòr and his 'pìob nuallanach mhòr' or 'great shrill-voiced pipe' (*Gaelic Songs of Mary MacLeod*, ed. J. Carmichael Watson, 1934, 44–5). Thomas Pennant refers to the MacCrimmons as hereditary pipers to the MacLeods of Skye, holding land rent-free and receiving pupils at their piping college; and when Boswell and Johnson visited the MacLeod stronghold of Dunvegan in 1773, Johnson recorded, 'There has been in Sky, beyond all time of memory, a college of pipers, under the direction of Macrimmon, which is not quite extinct.'

The main members of the family were **Donald Mòr MacCrimmon** (*fl.* 1600–1614), **Patrick Mòr MacCrimmon** (*fl.* 1640–1670), **Patrick Óg MacCrimmon** (*fl.* 1650), **Malcolm MacCrimmon** (*fl.* 1743), **Domhnall Bàn MacCrimmon** (*d.* 1746), and **Donald Ruadh MacCrimmon** (*fl.* 1731); and to them are attributed a number of piobaireachd, often on legendary rather than historical grounds, their skills having been originally acquired from the fairies—a common motif in Gaelic mythology. However, there is historical as well as stylistic support for some of the attributions. Donald Mòr is credited with the composition of 'MacLeod's Salute', a tune which shares a characteristic fingering feature with others attributed to him. A remission granted under the great seal on 13 January 1614 refers to a piper called Donald MacCruimien, and it is assumed that this is the same man. Patrick Mòr is said to have composed 'The Lament for the Children', one of the most famous and extended of piobaireachd. Others attributed to him also tend to be extended, though 'Cumha Dhomhnaill an Lagain' is an exception. It was said that this lament for Donald of Laggan was played nightly in Dunvegan as Donald's daughter, wife to the MacLeod, could not sleep without hearing it.

Patrick Óg is particularly remembered for the lament for Iain Garve of Raasay and the beautiful and gentle lament for Mary MacLeod, who was unofficial bard as well as nurse to the MacLeods and who died in 1707.

Patrick Óg's son Malcolm is said to have composed a lament for his half-brother Domhnall Bàn, known both as a song, 'Cha till mi tuille', and in piobaireachd form as 'MacCrimmon's lament'. It was believed to have been composed after MacCrimmon foresaw his own death following the rout of Moy (1746), and there is some evidence to support the story (see Blankenhorn, 1978).

The MacCrimmons were far from being the only major family of hereditary pipers. The MacArthurs and MacKays too ran piping schools. However, the MacCrimmons were undoubtedly leading figures in the development of piobaireachd, though the publication of a thorough scholarly study of the family and its music is still awaited.

JOHN PURSER

Sources R. D. Cannon, *The highland bagpipe and its music* (1988) · D. Thomson, ed., *The companion to Gaelic Scotland* (1983) · K. Sanger and A. Kinnaird, *Tree of strings* (1992) · V. S. Blackenhorn, 'Traditional and bogus elements in "MacCrimmon's lament"', *Scottish Studies*, 22 (1978), 45–67 · T. Pennant, *A voyage to the Hebrides* (1762) · S. Johnson, *A journey to the Western Islands of Scotland* (1775)

MacCrimmon, Domhnall Bàn (*d.* 1746). *See under* MacCrimmon family (*per.* 1600–1746).

MacCrimmon, Donald Mòr (*fl.* 1600–1614). *See under* MacCrimmon family (*per.* 1600–1746).

MacCrimmon, Donald Ruadh (*fl.* 1731). *See under* MacCrimmon family (*per.* 1600–1746).

MacCrimmon, Malcolm (*fl.* 1743). *See under* MacCrimmon family (*per.* 1600–1746).

MacCrimmon, Patrick Mòr (*fl.* 1640–1670). *See under* Mac-Crimmon family (*per.* 1600–1746).

MacCrimmon, Patrick Óg (*fl.* 1650). *See under* MacCrimmon family (*per.* 1600–1746).

McCrindle, John Ronald (1894–1977), lawyer and airline executive, was born on 29 November 1894 at The Grange, Middlesbrough, the only child of James Ronald McCrindle MB CM, physician and surgeon, and his wife, Elizabeth Pullan Kealabow, both of Scots descent. He was brought up in Kingston, Jamaica, where his father was in practice. Following early education at Jamaica College, he went on to Glasgow University to study medicine. In August 1914—not yet qualified—he was gazetted a second lieutenant in the territorial brigade of the Gordon Highlanders, and seconded to the Royal Flying Corps in November 1914. For the next four years, as a pilot in France, Mesopotamia, Egypt, and Palestine, he was three times mentioned in dispatches, awarded a Military Cross in 1917, and ended the war as a major in the Royal Air Force.

In December 1918 McCrindle was posted to command 1 (communications) flight, RAF, formed on 13 December to operate regular, daily, air services between London and Paris for the peace conference at Versailles. Appointed OBE in November 1919 and fluent in French, he was posted for special duties with the British delegation on the council of ambassadors in Paris. On 26 December 1921 he married in New York, Odette, the daughter of Joseph Fuller Feder. Early the following year he retired from the RAF, and joined the Harvard business school, from where he graduated in 1924. Called to the bar at Lincoln's Inn in 1927, McCrindle practised at the chancery bar until 1934. He kept his links with aviation through the London Aeroplane Club at Stag Lane, where he owned and flew a DH Cirrus Moth. He returned to work in aviation in 1932 as legal adviser to the small, independent Hillman bus company at Romford, Essex, from where in April 1933 he and Edward Hillman initiated a London (Maylands) to Paris (Le Bourget) air service with the first DH Dragon aircraft, at fares of £3 10s. single and £5 10s. return. When Edward Hillman died, aged only forty-five, on 31 December 1934, McCrindle became managing director of Hillman's Airways and, supported by his second wife (the writer Susan Ertz, whom he had married on 6 August 1932, following his divorce from Odette), he negotiated the absorption by Hillman's Airways of three other small airlines, Spartan, United, and British Continental, forming a new company known as British Airways, to compete with Imperial Airways on the London to Paris and Brussels air routes, and on to Cologne, Hanover, Stockholm, and the Western Isles in 1936.

In April 1937 the enterprising British Airways began fast (one hour twenty minutes) services between London and Paris, flying new American Lockheed Electra monoplanes, in competition with the two and a quarter hours of Imperial Airways. Following the 1938 Cadman inquiry into the operation of British air transport, the airline was granted increased services into Europe, and the pioneering of scheduled British air services to South America.

Operating the advanced American Lockheed aircraft, British Airways was chosen in September 1938 to fly the prime minister to and from the Munich meetings with Hitler. In April 1940 it merged with Imperial Airways to form the state-owned British Overseas Airways Corporation (BOAC), with Sir John Reith as chairman, and McCrindle as deputy director-general. Already, in 1945, he had been in the lead in forming the post-war International Air Transport Association in which, with BOAC, for the next twelve years he was an active and respected representative in London, Montreal, Chicago, and Bermuda.

McCrindle retired in 1969, but continued to enjoy contacts with his wide circle of friends throughout the world of air transport. He and his wife entertained with flair and enjoyment at their country house, Lossenham Manor, near Hawkhurst in Kent, where McCrindle was described by a leading American diplomat as, 'A British gentleman of the first order'. In addition to his Military Cross and OBE, McCrindle became a CMG in 1948, and received numerous honours from abroad. He suffered a stroke and died at his home on 12 March 1977.

PETER G. MASEFIELD

Sources personal knowledge (2004) · private information (2004) · *Who's Who in British Aviation* (1936–70) · P. G. Masefield, 'McCrindle, John Ronald', *DBB* · *The Aeroplane*, 49 (1935) · *The Aeroplane*, 50 (1936) · J. Stroud, *The annals of British commonwealth air transport* (1962) · R. D. S. Higham, 'British Airways Ltd, 1935–40', *Journal of Transport History*, 4 (1959–60), 113–23 · H. J. Dyds and L. D. H. Aldcraft, *British Transport* (1969), ch. 13 · P. S. Bagwell, *The transport revolution* (1974), ch. 9, sect. 9 · *WW* (1977) · *WWW*, 1971–80 · *CGPLA Eng. & Wales* (1977)
Archives International Air Transport Association, Montreal · International Air Transport Association, Geneva · Royal Air Force Museum, Hendon
Wealth at death £50,147—gross: probate, 21 June 1977, *CGPLA Eng. & Wales*

McCrone, Guy Fulton (1898–1977), novelist, was born on 13 September 1898 at 93 Westbourne Road, Birkenhead, the elder son of Robert McCrone, margarine manufacturer from Ayrshire, and his wife, Jane, daughter of Hugh Osborne, cheese merchant. The family moved to Glasgow where McCrone was educated at Glasgow Academy. He graduated in economics at Pembroke College, Cambridge, before studying singing in Vienna under Jean de Reske. He married Sylvia Louise Shanks (*b.* 1899/1900) on 30 April 1931.

McCrone took an active part in Glasgow musical life, being a member of the local grand opera and chamber music societies. He sang Aeneas in a Glasgow production of Berlioz's *Les Troyens* in 1935, the first British performance of the complete opera. With his cousin the playwright Osborne Henry Mavor (James Bridie) he was involved in founding Glasgow Citizens' Theatre in 1943, being at different periods business manager and managing director. McCrone had no experience in theatre management but, a colleague later wrote, 'Bridie had decided that Mr McCrone would somehow rise to the occasion … [He] settled nobly to his pioneer task … when he might have been writing [a best-selling novel] like his *Wax Fruit*' (Bannister, 208–9).

McCrone's first novel, *The Striped Umbrellas*, was published in 1937. He began to write *Antimacassar City*, which later became part 1 of *Wax Fruit*, before the outbreak of the Second World War and finished it during the spare moments of his wartime job as an air-raid warden. Published in 1940, it was always planned as the first part of a trilogy about a middle-class family of provision merchants in Victorian Glasgow, but the second and third parts, *The Philistines* and *The Puritans*, were not published separately at that time. All three appeared in one volume as *Wax Fruit: the Story of the Moorhouse Family* (1947), the novel for which McCrone remains best known. Because of paper rationing the original print run was fairly small, but the novel was chosen as a book of the month in America and became a best-seller. It was later translated into French and German. By the time of McCrone's death it had sold 1 million copies.

Wax Fruit was especially popular with Glasgow readers and there was a persistent belief that it was possible to identify the real-life originals of the characters. McCrone explicitly denied this in dedicating *Wax Fruit* to 'Glasgow readers': 'No. You must forgive me. But I did not have the impertinence to draw for you portraits of your grandparents and their friends'. The novel and its sequels *Aunt Bel* (1949) and *The Hayburn Family* (1952), which together cover the period 1870–1901, are, however, the product of considerable research into Glasgow social history. McCrone wrote: 'It is fleeting detail that matters to the novelist and gives him his background. In the newspapers, it is not the great things that are remembered to this day. It is such things as the advertisement columns' (McCrone). Guy McCrone retired to the Lake District with his wife in 1965 and died of heart disease at his home, Brackenmere, Birthwaite Road, Windermere, on 30 May 1977. He was survived by his wife.   MOIRA BURGESS

Sources G. McCrone, *Scottish Field* (March 1952), 36 · *Glasgow Herald* (1 June 1977) · W. Bannister, *James Bridie and his theatre* (1955) · private information (2004) [Sylvia McCrone, widow, and Ronald Mavor, relative] · A. Downie, 'Guy's TV diet of *Wax fruit*', *Glasgow Herald* (3 Jan 1975) · *DSBB*, vol. 1
Likenesses photograph, repro. in McCrone, *Scottish Field* · photograph, repro. in J. Vinson, ed., *Contemporary novelists*, 2nd edn (1976) · photograph, repro. in *Glasgow Herald* (1 June 1977)

Mac Cruitín, Aindrias. *See* MacCurtin, Andrew (*c.*1670–1738).

Mac Cruitín, Aodh Buí. *See* MacCurtin, Hugh (1680?–1755).

Mac Cuarta, Séamas Dall [James MacCourt or Maccuairt] (*c.*1645–1733), Irish-language poet, may have been born in the area known as Créamhainn (the tribal territory of Creamhthainn or Uí Chreamhthainn in early medieval times), on the borders of co. Louth and co. Monaghan, although some authorities have argued for a birthplace in the vicinity of Dundalk, others for one in co. Meath, and still others—with perhaps greater probability—in the district of Omeath, co. Louth, with which he is most closely identified. He spent most of his life in and around Omeath

but also had close links with the vicinity of the Boyne, particularly with the townland of Kellystown in the parish of Monknewtown, barony of Upper Slane. He lost his sight as a boy, in unexplained circumstances, and—like many of his contemporaries who shared his affliction—spent most of his life as a wandering minstrel.

Mac Cuarta's poetry reflects a familiarity with Irish literature and history, the classics (Greek and Latin), and the Bible. His surviving work—the earliest of which appears to date from about 1690—runs to more than fifty poems and is to be found in approximately 130 manuscripts. One of the manuscripts dates from as early as 1724–5 and no fewer than fifteen of his poems occur in manuscripts that were penned either during his lifetime or immediately after his death.

Much of Mac Cuarta's work echoes the political events of his time, such as the catastrophic battle of Aughrim (1691)—which inspired 'Tuireamh Shomhairle Mhic Dhomhnaill' (a lament for a Catholic leader who fell in that battle)—and the subsequent subjugation of his people by the English, who are condemned both as foreigners and heretics. (Strangely enough, Mac Cuarta does not mention the battle of the Boyne.) He bitterly laments the loss of the traditional local chieftains, the O'Neills of the Fews, in south Armagh, where their great castle at Glasdrummond now lay broken and deserted. He is especially bitter about those Irishmen whom he deems to have betrayed their compatriots and accordingly praises local men of non-noble lineage—whom others consider upstarts—who are willing to challenge the English, however futile their efforts, and he never loses hope that eventually the Englishry will be destroyed and the exiled leaders will return.

Mac Cuarta's great love of nature (despite his blindness) is most poignantly reflected in his poem to the cuckoo—'Fáilte don éan' ('Welcome to the bird')—said to date from 1707. His work includes a body of religious poetry that is characterized by strong Marian devotion and a fiercely anti-protestant tone. Other poems on ecclesiastical matters include one welcoming the appointment of James O'Shiel OFM as bishop of Down and Connor in 1717 and a lament for a priest named Pilib Ó Raghallaigh. His poems of 'exile' (which relate to his being some twenty or thirty miles removed from some of his favourite haunts), 'Beannacht Bóinne' and 'Dúiche Chréamhainn', are noteworthy, as are his elegies, particularly that on his close friend Niall Óg Mac Murchaidh who died in 1714. He also mourned the death of his two brothers Ruairí and Brian, in 1717. He composed numerous poems in praise of chieftains—Toirealach Ó Néill, Brian Mac Naois, Brian Mac Eoghain, Mac Airt Uí Néill, the baron of Slane, and others—as well as several in praise of women; these latter works are rather pedestrian and lacking in passion.

One of Mac Cuarta's most justly celebrated works is his well-crafted, delicious little satire 'Tithe Chorr an Chait' on the niggardly inhabitants of the village of Corrakit. A more bitter one is his attack, 'Scanradh an Daill', on the miscreant who had callously stolen 18 guineas from the blind poet. Mac Cuarta was a noted practitioner of the verse form known as 'trí rainn agus amhrán' (consisting of three quatrains in traditional—albeit rather loose—syllabic metre and a stanza in song metre). He was also famed for his sociability and his great friendship with his fellow poets and musicians, most notably Niall Óg Mac Mhurchaidh, Pádraig Mac Giolla Fhiondáin (1665–1733), and Toirdhealbhach Ó Cearbhalláin (Turlogh O'Carolan; 1670–1738)—they praised, mocked, and mourned one another, as appropriate. For example, Mac Cuarta lamented Niall Óg and Mac Giolla Fhiondáin lamented Mac Cuarta. From the latter lament comes the knowledge that Mac Cuarta died in February 1733, but there is no indication of where he was buried. Two editions of his writings (neither complete) have appeared, the first in 1925 and the second in 1971.   NOLLAIG Ó MURAÍLE

Sources DNB · S. Ó Gallchóir, *Séamus Dall Mac Cuarta: Dánta* (1971) · S. S. Ó Gallchóir, 'Fiíocht an Daill Mhic Cuarta', *An tUltach* (Sept–Nov 1972), 3–6, 23; 3–4, 11; 3–4, 15 · L. Ua Muireadhaigh, *Amhráin Sheumais Mhic Chuarta*, An Cheud Chuid (1925)

McCudden, James Thomas Byford (1895–1918), airman, was born at the Female Hospital, Brompton, Gillingham, Kent, on 28 March 1895, the third child and second son of William Henry McCudden (1864–1920), a sergeant-major and later a warrant officer in the Royal Engineers, of Carlow, Ireland, and his wife, Amelie Emma Byford (d. 1955), of Chatham, Kent. He was educated first at a small private school and then at the Royal Engineers' School, Brompton barracks, Gillingham, and the garrison school at Sheerness. At fourteen McCudden left school, becoming a Post Office messenger boy until, in the following year (1910) he was eligible to enlist in the Royal Engineers as a bugler. At eighteen he applied for a transfer to the Royal Flying Corps, following his elder brother, William, who had in August 1913 qualified as an NCO pilot, and after initial training was posted as mechanic to 3 squadron at Netheravon, Wiltshire. There he occasionally flew as a passenger and was given several strictly unofficial flying lessons by his brother.

Promoted first-class air mechanic on 1 April 1914, McCudden went to France with 3 squadron at the outbreak of war, and was promoted corporal in November 1914 and sergeant in April 1915. In January 1916 his efficiency and devotion to duty were recognized by the award of the French Croix de Guerre. In June 1915 he undertook his first official sortie as an observer, but he did not fly regularly until November. An earlier application for pilot training had been frozen since skilled engine mechanics were in short supply, but on 31 January 1916 he was posted for instruction and he qualified for his pilot's brevet at Gosport, Hampshire, on 16 April. After a period as an instructor he joined 20 squadron in France on 4 July, flying FE 2d two-seaters on offensive patrols and photographic work, but in August he was transferred to 29 squadron, equipped with single-seat DH2 scouts. He brought down his first enemy machine on 6 September and his overall good work as a scout pilot was acknowledged in the award, on 1 October, of the Military Medal. He was in action continually during the autumn and early winter, a period of heavy squadron losses.

James Thomas Byford McCudden (1895–1918), by Sir William Orpen

After being commissioned on 1 January 1917, McCudden was shot down (unhurt) for the only time in his career on the 23rd of that month, but on the 26th he scored his second victory, and by the time he returned to England on 23 February he had five to his credit. In recognition of his achievements he was awarded the Military Cross, gazetted on 12 March. Posted to Joyce Green, near Dartford, Kent, he served as an instructor there and at Dover, and took part in the defence of London against German daylight raids in June and July. Following his promotion to captain on 1 June 1917 he was posted on 11 July for a brief refresher course in France with 66 squadron, and shortly after his return to England he was posted to 56 squadron as a flight commander, returning to France on 14 August 1917.

The pre-eminent scout squadron in the Royal Flying Corps at this time, 56 squadron was equipped with the superlative SE 5a, superior to any type then in German service, and McCudden rapidly increased his score of victories, which reached twenty-three by the end of November 1917. December brought a further fourteen, his highest monthly total, to which were added another twenty before he was posted back to England on 5 March. His forty-seventh victory, on 2 February, made him the top-scoring British pilot, and his total had reached fifty-seven when he left France. During this period he received a bar to his Military Cross (gazetted 2 October 1917), and the Distinguished Service Order (15 December 1917) and bar (3 January 1918).

On 29 March 1918 McCudden was awarded the Victoria Cross in recognition of his service on aerial patrols between August 1917 and March 1918. The citation in the

London Gazette (2 April 1918) referred to his conspicuous bravery, exceptional perseverance, and high devotion to duty. It was stated that as a patrol leader he not only exercised the utmost skill in attacking and destroying the enemy, but also minimized casualties by protecting newer members of his flight.

McCudden instructed for three months at the 1 school of aerial fighting at Ayr and Turnberry in Scotland, but he agitated for a posting to France and was appointed to command 60 squadron, with the rank of major, from 9 July. That day he flew to France in a new SE 5a, and landed at Auxi-le-Château, 5 miles from the squadron's base at Boffles, to ask for directions, taking off again immediately. Within ninety seconds McCudden had crashed into a wood adjoining the aerodrome. He was taken to hospital unconscious, with a fractured skull, died that evening, and was buried the following day, 10 July 1918, in the small British war cemetery at Wavans, near Auxi-le-Château.

Given McCudden's reputation for prudence and cool judgement, it was inevitable that the circumstances surrounding his death would excite rumour and controversy. The facts are clear. After take-off he made a near-vertical turn, after which the aircraft rolled at low altitude, lost height, and crashed into the wood. Two reasons for what happened seem possible, based on eyewitness accounts. One simply posits pilot error, with McCudden misjudging a roll at low altitude. The other argues engine failure, perhaps, as has been suggested, because the wrong type of carburettor was fitted (Cooksley, 148). Here too, pilot error might have been involved, since McCudden would have broken a cardinal rule in attempting to turn back to the aerodrome when his engine cut out.

McCudden's remarkable success as a fighter pilot derived from a combination of qualities. He was both a gifted pilot and a skilled mechanic, devoting many hours to ensuring that his aircraft had achieved optimal performance. He also became a fine shot. But the key to his success was without doubt a matter of personality. Of almost legendary coolness in judgement, he also possessed extraordinary patience, which was particularly valuable in respect of his forte: shooting down two-seat reconnaissance aircraft, forty-five of which were included in his total of fifty-seven victories. This was not easy; the German reconnaissance aircraft of the last two years of the war were fast, with a fine altitude performance, and hence hard to reach and bring down. McCudden studied their habits, the psychology of their pilots, and the weaknesses of each aircraft type, and, working alone, stalked such machines sometimes for up to forty-five minutes before placing himself where a kill could be assured. On other occasions, however, McCudden achieved success with remarkable speed. He twice brought down four opponents in a day. On 13 January 1918 he shot down three two-seaters in twenty minutes, and on 30 January he shot down two single-seat fighters within a minute.

As a solitary fighter McCudden was unsurpassed, but his reputation as a flight commander has been contested, some claiming that he was selfish and others that he kept too tight a rein on his flight. In fact the records show that his tactics allowed the experienced members of his flight to fight as they chose, but restricted the less skilled so that they might survive to become valuable members of the team. The few losses in his flight while he was with 56 squadron attests to the success of his tactics and his emphasis on teamwork and discipline.

McCudden was a cheerful, modest man and good company, but felt by many to be something of an enigma. He eschewed publicity and particularly disliked that which followed the award of his Victoria Cross. He wrote to a friend:

> I see the papers are making a fuss again about the ordinary things one does. Why, that's our work. Why fuss about it? I'm so tired of this limelight business. If only one could be left alone a bit more, and not so much of the hero about it. (Cole, 173–4)

Of natural good manners, he adjusted well to the translation from other ranks to officer, although he confided to a friend that 'I always wish I had had the advantage of a public school. After I joined the Officers' Mess I often felt ill at ease when chaps were talking about things I didn't understand' (Cole, 203). That he could hold his own in such company, however, is well illustrated by the book he completed just before his death, *Five Years in the Royal Flying Corps*. It is a remarkable achievement by a man of little formal education: lucidly and economically written, highly accurate, and entirely without self-glorification. As one of the few personal accounts of the early Royal Flying Corps it is of the highest value and deservedly admired.

McCudden was not only the top-scoring British fighter pilot in the First World War, but also one of the first to think deeply about fighter combat tactics. Not charismatic, like 'Mick' Mannock, in his cool efficiency, as Cole has suggested, he more closely resembles than any other British ace his German counterpart, Manfred von Richthofen. Respecting his opponents, and striving always to hone his own skills, he was the consummate professional.   DAVID GUNBY

Sources J. T. B. McCudden, *Five years in the royal flying corps* (1918) [republished as *Flying fury* (1930) and *Flying fury: five years in the royal flying corps* (1987)] · C. Cole, *McCudden V. C.* (1967) · C. Shores and others, *Above the trenches: a complete record of the fighter aces and units of the British empire air forces, 1915–1920* (1990), 268–70 · P. G. Cooksley, *VCs of the First World War: the air VCs* (1996), 136–50 · C. Bowyer, *For valour: the air VCs* (1978), 121–31 · register, Commonwealth War Graves Commission, Maidenhead

Archives IWM, letters relating to service with RFC · Royal Air Force Museum, Hendon, papers |SOUND IWM SA, oral history interview

Likenesses group photograph, *c*.1917, Hult. Arch. · E. Newling, oils, 1919, IWM · W. Orpen, oils, IWM [*see illus.*] · photographs, repro. in Cole, *McCudden V. C.* · photographs, IWM

Wealth at death £266 14*s.* 3*d.*: administration, 24 Nov 1919, *CGPLA Eng. & Wales*

Mac Cuilinn mac Cathmoga (*d.* 496). *See under* Meath, saints of (*act. c*.400–*c*.900).

MacCullagh [McCullagh], **James** (1809–1847), mathematician, was born in Landahussy, in the parish of Upper Badoney, Tyrone, Ireland, the eldest of twelve children of

James MacCullagh (1777–1857), farmer, and his wife, Margaret (1784–1839), *née* Ballentine(?). While MacCullagh was still young his father left his mountain farm and the family moved to Strabane, where MacCullagh's mathematical talent first became apparent. He attended the schools of the historian the Revd John Graham and of the classicist the Revd Thomas Rollestone at Lifford in co. Donegal. On 1 November 1824 he was admitted to Trinity College, Dublin, as a pensioner and on 1 June 1825 he was a successful candidate for a sizarship. On 24 June 1826 he took up residence in the college, where he lived until his death. He was elected a foundation scholar on 11 June 1827 and graduated a bachelor of arts on 2 March 1829.

MacCullagh benefited greatly from the renaissance in mathematical education at the college initiated by Bartholomew Lloyd, and his rapid promotion owed much to the patronage of Lloyd. In June 1829 he was an unsuccessful candidate in the highly competitive fellowship examination. Following the failure of a second attempt in 1831 he sent the provost, Lloyd, a letter containing several theorems relating to a geometrical theory of rotation and to the theory of attraction. The publication in 1834 of Louis Poinsot's theory of rotary motion meant that MacCullagh's work had been superseded but his letter was published in 1844 in the *Proceedings of the Royal Irish Academy*. He competed successfully for a fellowship in 1832 and was elected a junior fellow on 18 June 1832. Shortly afterwards he was made junior assistant to the Erasmus Smith professor of mathematics and assistant to the lecturer in Greek.

In the course of the eighteen years of his career MacCullagh wrote some thirty-nine papers, presented for the most part to the Royal Irish Academy and published in its *Proceedings* or *Transactions*. Most of his papers were republished posthumously, together with his lectures on the rotation of a solid body and on the attraction of ellipsoids, in *The Collected Works of James MacCullagh* (1880). His first two papers dealt with geometrical theorems on the rectification of conic sections, and with double refraction in a crystallized medium, in which context he provided a description of Fresnel's wave surface. Evidence of his profound understanding of double refraction in crystals is evident in his first major paper 'Geometrical propositions applied to the wave theory of light' (1833). In the following years he set about trying to improve the derivation by Fresnel of the laws governing the reflection of light and to extend them to crystalline surfaces. For an ether having the same density everywhere, he assumed (unlike Fresnel) that the vibrations were parallel to the plane of polarization and (like Fresnel) that the incident transverse waves give rise only to transverse reflected and refracted waves. His theory of crystalline reflection and refraction (1835–7) was identical with a theory of Franz Ernst Neumann announced in 1835 and published in 1837. In papers of 1836 MacCullagh treated the optical behaviour of quartz and the reflection of light from metals.

MacCullagh's most important paper on light, 'An essay towards a dynamical theory of crystalline reflexion and refraction', in which he set forth equations which describe a light-bearing ether having the properties necessary to justify the assumptions he had made in earlier work on crystalline reflection, was read on 9 December 1839 (final version published 1843). In it he followed the method adopted by George Green in an 1838 investigation of the propagation of waves in a real elastic medium. Early in 1840 he was able to reconcile his theory of optical activity in quartz with his dynamical theory, and in May 1841 he gave an account of how his theory could be extended to include total reflection. In 1843 he published the results of experiments carried out in 1837 on metallic reflection with the assistance of Thomas Grubb. However, he remained sceptical as to the truth of the wave theory of light. At the British Association meeting at Manchester in 1842, where a vigorous discussion of the wave theory took place, he adopted an agnostic stance, and suggested that the theory was still lacking in physical principles.

Although MacCullagh had provided a mathematical framework for the description of a wide range of optical phenomena, his work was received with scepticism. However, his dynamical theory found supporters, particularly among Anglo-Irish scientists, decades after his death. In 1880 George Francis FitzGerald provided an interpretation of his theory of reflection and refraction so as to bring it into harmony with Maxwell's electromagnetic theory. George Gabriel Stokes was particularly critical of MacCullagh's work but Joseph Larmor and Lord Rayleigh considered this judgement too harsh.

Despite his preoccupation with the physical problem of the propagation of light, MacCullagh's primary talent was as a geometer. His success in developing his ether theory was due in part to his geometrical skills. He had been interested in surfaces, especially the ellipsoid and second-order surfaces, since 1829 when he first investigated the Fresnel wave surface. The ellipsoid was also relevant to his early investigations of the rotation of a solid body. The first part of his major mathematical work, 'On surfaces of the second order' (1843), dealt with the generalization of the focus-directrix property of conic sections; the second considered various properties of second-order surfaces. Inversive geometry and the use of reciprocal surfaces had been used to good advantage both in his elucidation of the Fresnel wave surface and in his treatment of the rotation of a solid body. This idea was extended in his 1843 paper to what is referred to as the modular generation of surfaces such as the ellipsoid. As with all his mathematical writing this paper is characterized by its elegance and simplicity of style.

In 1835 the chair of mathematics at Trinity College, Dublin, became vacant, and MacCullagh was appointed. He was a lay fellow of the college, and in the following year he was freed, at his own request, from the requirement to take holy orders. In the summer of 1838 the degrees LLB and LLD were conferred on him. He had previously been elected (in February 1833) a member of the Royal Irish Academy, and was now elected to the academy's council and was awarded its Cunningham medal for his paper on the laws of crystalline reflection and refraction, the presentation being made by William Rowan Hamilton on 25

June 1838. On this occasion Hamilton referred to Neumann's paper but gave priority to MacCullagh. This claim was disputed by Neumann in a letter of 8 October read at the meeting of 30 November. MacCullagh insisted on his priority in publication and the independence of his work.

MacCullagh made an important contribution to the development of the school of mathematics at Trinity College, Dublin, and helped establish a geometrical bias there. He delivered a special course of lectures to the fellowship candidates and from 1837 to 1843 was an examiner at the annual fellowship examinations. He was an inspiring lecturer and of his graduate students, after 1835, twenty became fellows and a number were to make original contributions in mathematics. He was instrumental in the establishment of the school of engineering in 1841 and subsequently shared responsibility for teaching mechanics and physics to engineering students. On 4 December 1843 he was appointed Erasmus Smith professor of natural and experimental philosophy, in succession to Humphrey Lloyd, and he was allowed to substitute a course of physics lectures in place of those he had previously provided for fellowship candidates.

MacCullagh's other scholarly interests included Egyptian chronology and Irish culture. He devoted much effort to building up the Royal Irish Academy's Museum of Antiquities (now part of the National Museum of Ireland) donating from his own funds for the purchase of Irish antiquities. He was awarded the Copley medal of the Royal Society in 1842, and was elected a fellow in the following year. He attended the annual meetings of the British Association for the Advancement of Science in Dublin (1835), Bristol (1836), Manchester (1842), and Cork (1843), and he travelled to the continent on at least three occasions (1840, 1842, 1846). Together with Charles Babbage he attended a scientific meeting at Turin in September 1840. He was elected to the Athenaeum in February 1842.

The last months of MacCullagh's life were marked by an involvement in politics. In the general election of 1847 he decided to compete for one of the two Dublin University seats at Westminster, in opposition to the sitting members who were Oxford graduates. He was a liberal but without party affiliation or political experience, and in a constituency that was strongly tory he was inevitably an outsider: he received 374 out of 2224 votes cast, finishing last of four candidates. The Young Irelanders applauded his patriotism after his death, an obituary notice in *The Nation* (30 October 1847) describing him as a 'warm and ardent nationalist'. It is likely, however, that he was a nationalist only in the sense that he believed Irishmen should show self-respect and promote their own national institutions. He made no pronouncements on constitutional issues.

MacCullagh's powerful drive for achievement was frustrated by a series of disappointments in science and politics. His personality was characterized by excessive sensitivity, introspection, and a lack of stability. An impetuous temperament combined with suspicion or fear of plagiarism caused him to make extravagant claims on occasions. He died on the evening of Sunday 24 October 1847, being found in his college apartment with his throat cut. An inquest the next day returned a verdict of suicide. No trace of his collection of manuscript papers was found after his death. A funeral service was held in the college on 30 October and he was buried in the family vault in the graveyard of St Patrick's parish church of Upper Badoney, co. Tyrone. He is commemorated by a brass plaque in the church and by a marble tablet on the family grave erected by his sister Isabella (1823–1894). Three sisters and a younger brother were dependent on him at the time of his death and an appeal to the prime minister, with the support of important academics and politicians, helped procure a civil-list pension for his sisters.   JAMES G. O'HARA

Sources *The collected works of James MacCullagh*, ed. J. H. Jellett and S. Haughton (1880) · B. K. P. Scaife, 'James MacCullagh, 1809–47', *Proceedings of the Royal Irish Academy*, 90C (1990), 67–106 [incl. an annotated list of publications] · T. D. Spearman, 'James MacCullagh', *Science in Ireland, 1800–1930: tradition and reform*, ed. J. R. Nudds and others (1988), 41–59 · *Proceedings of the Royal Irish Academy*, 4 (1847–50), 103–16 · *Abstracts of the Papers Communicated to the Royal Society of London*, 5 (1843–50), 712–18 · T. D. Spearman, 'Mathematics and theoretical physics', *The Royal Irish Academy: a bicentennial history, 1785–1985*, ed. T. Ó. Raifeartaigh (1985), 210–39 · T. L. Hankins, *Sir William Rowan Hamilton* (1980) · R. P. Graves, *Life of Sir William Rowan Hamilton*, 3 vols. (1882–9) · A. J. McConnell, 'The Dublin mathematical school in the first half of the nineteenth century', *Proceedings of the Royal Irish Academy*, 50A (1944–5), 75–88 · J. G. O'Hara, 'The prediction and discovery of conical refraction by William Rowan Hamilton and Humphrey Lloyd, 1832–1833', *Proceedings of the Royal Irish Academy*, 82A (1982), 231–57 · *The Nation* (30 Oct 1847)

Archives AM Oxf., Griffiths Institute, Davidson MSS · BL, corresp. with Charles Babbage · TCD, corresp. with W. R. Hamilton

Likenesses C. Moore, marble bust, exh. RA 1849, TCD · F. W. Burton, four pencil sketches, NG Ire.

McCulloch, Derek Ivor Breashur [*performing name* Uncle Mac] (**1897–1967**), broadcaster, was born on 18 November 1897 at 6 Sussex Place, Plymouth, Devon, the youngest child of (William) Lionel Breashur McCulloch and his wife, Bertha Russell. As he lived within sight of Plymouth Sound, his childhood ambitions lay with the Royal Navy, but a change in family circumstances following the death of his father caused him to leave his local preparatory school in 1906 for Croydon high school. In early 1915 he enlisted as a private soldier in the public schools battalion of the 16th Middlesex regiment, in which his elder brothers were serving.

McCulloch landed in France on his eighteenth birthday, and was present at the battle of the Somme in July 1916 where he suffered near-fatal wounds: stranded in no man's land 20 yards from the German front line, he was fired on by an enemy stretcher party and lost his right eye. He lay in a shell hole for three days and nights, suffering numerous further injuries from shrapnel, before crawling back to his own lines. His war wounds, and the misfortune of a motor accident in 1938 which cost him his left leg, necessitated over fifty operations throughout his life, and he was never to be free of pain. None the less, after the

Derek Ivor Breashur McCulloch [Uncle Mac] (1897–1967), by Kurt Hutton, 1946

war he travelled in Europe and South America. He was working for the Central Argentine Railway when his health deteriorated, and he returned to Europe where a bullet was extracted from his lung. In January 1926 McCulloch successfully applied to the British Broadcasting Company for the post of announcer.

McCulloch's earliest years with the BBC were not entirely happy. Continuing medical problems and some dissatisfaction with his microphone style meant that he was taken away from front-line announcing and given miscellaneous work. This included sport (he was assistant commentator on the BBC's first running commentary on an association football match in 1927) and compèring variety programmes. More significantly, McCulloch was first heard in *Children's Hour* as Uncle Mac. A breakdown in health while working for the Belfast station in 1929 threatened a premature end to his BBC career, but a permanent job was found for him in *Children's Hour*. By 1931 he was second-in-command, and on 13 June that year he married Eileen Hilda Barry (*b.* 1907/8), a BBC secretary, with whom he was to have two daughters. His wife was the daughter of a glove buyer, James Barry. In 1933 he was appointed *Children's Hour* organizer.

Children's Hour had been part of the BBC's output since 1922, and had evolved from its original dependence on spontaneous banter, fairy stories, and whimsy. McCulloch's philosophy was simple, and rigidly adhered to:

> Our established policy is that nothing but the best is good enough for children … our wish is to stimulate their imagination, direct their reading, encourage their various interests, widen their outlook, and inculcate the Christian principles of love of God and their neighbour. (*BBC Quarterly*, Jan 1948, 229)

This policy was applied throughout what McCulloch saw as 'a microcosm of broadcasting'—drama, music, talks, variety, religion, and charitable appeals. His zeal brought his department, hitherto an unlikely adjunct to features and drama, autonomy in 1938. Aside from his administrative work, he employed his gifts of humour and personality on air, both presenting programmes and appearing in them. The playwright Dennis Potter recalled 'a kind of stiff gentleness wholly suited to a favourite uncle' (*Daily Herald*, 14 Feb 1964). The perennial *Children's Hour* favourite

was S. G. Hulme Beaman's series of *Toy Town* playlets. McCulloch played the central role of Larry the Lamb, and his baa-ing vibrato was heard from the 1920s to the 1960s.

By 1939 *Children's Hour* was a national institution with a juvenile audience of some four million. With the war came the evacuation of large numbers of this audience, and for them *Children's Hour* acquired the added significance of a link with their home lives, emphasized by McCulloch's poignant sign-off 'Goodnight, children … everywhere'. It was a source of pride to him that, in October 1940, Princess Elizabeth made her radio début in a *Children's Hour* broadcast to the empire. By 1950 McCulloch was tired, and, wishing to devote more time to writing, he resigned from the BBC to become children's editor of the *News Chronicle*. He continued to broadcast, however, as chairman of *Nature Parliament* (a series he had started in 1946), and was a compère of the record programme *Children's Favourites* until 1965.

In 1964 the BBC—citing figures which showed that the audience for children's radio had dwindled to 24,000—discontinued the daily programme. McCulloch was predictably saddened: 'I am surprised. I would have thought a lot of children still listened to Toy Town' (*Daily Herald*, 17 Jan 1964). He did not long outlive the institution with which he was so closely identified. On 1 June 1967 he died at St Francis Hospital, Haywards Heath. He was cremated at Longview, Snowdenham Links Road, Bramley, Surrey.

JEFF WALDEN

Sources files, BBC WAC, L 1/278 [1926–67]; RCONT 1 [1939–62]; RCONT 12 [1963–8] · *The Times* (3 June 1967) · *Desert island discs*, transcript, 23 June 1958, BBC WAC · 'Derek McCulloch tells his own story', *Weldon's Ladies' Journal* (July 1950) · D. McCulloch, 'A pilgrim on the Somme', *Daily Telegraph* (17 July 1933) · D. McCulloch, 'The children's hour is for children', *Radio Times* (26 Feb 1937), 5 · 'Uncle Mac married', *Birmingham Gazette* (15 June 1931) · *Daily Herald* (14 Feb 1964) · *Daily Herald* (17 Jan 1964) · 'Radio's "Uncle Mac" dies at 69', *Daily Telegraph* (3 June 1967) · D. McCulloch, 'Entertaining the young listener', *BBC Quarterly*, 2/4 (Jan 1948), 229 · b. cert. · m. cert. · d. cert. · WWW

Archives BBC WAC, internal/external corresp., scripts, articles | SOUND BL NSA

Likenesses K. Hutton, photograph, 1946, Hult. Arch. [*see illus.*]

Wealth at death £17,550: probate, 12 Dec 1967, CGPLA Eng. & Wales

McCulloch, George (1848–1907), mine owner and art collector, was born on 22 April 1848 in Glasgow, the son of James McCulloch, a contractor, and was educated at Anderson's University. He travelled in Mexico and South America to study farming before, in the 1870s, deciding to seek his fortune in Australia. Here his uncle, James McCulloch, appointed him manager of a large sheep station, Mount Gipps, near Broken Hill, giving him an eighth share in the business. It was at Broken Hill that Charles Rasp discovered large deposits of silver in 1883: McCulloch thus became a member of the syndicate owning the mine, and went to London to raise more capital in 1885. He later rose to be manager and chairman of the Broken Hill Proprietary Co. Ltd, and thanks to this, and other investments in west Australian goldfields, became enormously rich, a multi-millionaire by Victorian standards.

There is an enduring legend that McCulloch won the

Broken Hill mine in a game of penny nap with another miner. The truth is more prosaic: McCulloch already owned a share in the syndicate, and he acquired a further fourteenth share in a game of euchre (an American card game resembling whist) with an English prospector. He is described as 'large in build … [a man who] delighted in feats of strength and practical jokes' (*AusDB*). McCulloch was portrayed by contemporaries as a self-made man, but his background was respectable, middle class, and educated.

In 1893 McCulloch returned to Britain, and on 11 May he married Mary Agnes Mayger, the widowed daughter of a miner, William Smith. He promptly set about acquiring the trappings of wealth and social position, buying a large house at 186 Queen's Gate, London, to which he added several large galleries, and thereafter devoting himself to forming a major collection of modern art. His adviser was David Croal Thomson, who was an art dealer, connoisseur, and critic: he was editor of the prestigious *Art Journal*, and a director of the Goupil Gallery, and later Agnews, but at the time such a combination of roles was not considered to represent a conflict of interests.

In little over ten years McCulloch spent more than £200,000, buying over 300 pictures. His taste was conventional, and he preferred narrative pictures and landscapes, both English and French. He was, however, a friend of J. S. Sargent, and acquired pictures by him and by Whistler and Orpen. He also admired the works of Scottish artists, such as William Quiller Orchardson, John Pettie, David Murray, and John Lavery. McCulloch's collection was certainly one of the most remarkable late Victorian accumulations, and among its stars were major works by Millais, Leighton, G. F. Watts, Burne-Jones, J. W. Waterhouse, and George Clausen. These included *Sir Isumbras at the Ford* by Millais (Lady Lever Art Gallery, Port Sunlight), *The Garden of the Hesperides* and *The Daphnephoria* by Leighton (also both Lady Lever Art Gallery), *Fata Morgana* by Watts, *Saint Cecilia* and *Ophelia* by Waterhouse, and *Love among the Ruins* (Wightwick Manor) and *The Wedding of Psyche* (Museum of Modern Art, Brussels) by Burne-Jones. McCulloch also bought one of the sets of Holy Grail tapestries designed by Burne-Jones for Morris & Co.

McCulloch died on 12 December 1907 at 186 Queen's Gate, leaving an estate of £436,000. In 1909 his collection was shown at the Royal Academy winter exhibition, arousing considerable controversy: the academy was accused of commercialism in exhibiting a private collection which was about to be sold. Eventually McCulloch's collection was dispersed in 1913 at a series of sales at Christies, from 23 to 30 May. The 326 lots made a total of £136,859, showing a poor return on McCulloch's investment. A major buyer at the sale was William Lever, first Lord Leverhulme, later the founder of the Lady Lever Art Gallery. McCulloch's widow married the Scottish artist James Coutts Michie.   CHRISTOPHER WOOD

Sources D. S. Macleod, *Art and the Victorian middle class: money and the making of cultural identity* (1996) · *AusDB*, 5.139–40 · S. Houfe, 'David Croal Thomson, Whistler's "aide de camp"', *Apollo*, 119

(1984), 112–19 · *The McCulloch collection of modern art* (1909) [exhibition catalogue, RA, winter exhibition, 1909] · *The Times* (5–30 Jan 1909) · A. C. R. Carter, *Let me tell you* (1940), 80 · G. Agnew, *Agnew's, 1817–1967* (1967), 44 · *Lord Leverhulme* (1980), 30–31 [exhibition catalogue, Royal Academy] · R. Treble, ed., *Great Victorian pictures: their paths to fame* (1978), 95 [exhibition catalogue, Leeds, Leicester, Bristol, and London, 28 Jan – Sept 1978] · *CGPLA Eng. & Wales* (1908)

Likenesses double portrait, photograph (with Mary McCulloch), repro. in *McCulloch collection of modern art*

Wealth at death £436,679 6s. 7d.: resworn probate, 6 Jan 1908, *CGPLA Eng. & Wales*

McCulloch [Macculloch], **Horatio** (1805–1867), landscape painter, was born in Glasgow in November 1805, the son of Alexander McCulloch (*d. c.*1827), cotton merchant, and his wife, Margaret Watson. He studied art under John Knox, the landscape, portrait, and panorama painter in Glasgow, and was a friend of the artists Daniel Macnee and William Leighton Leitch. McCulloch and Macnee left Glasgow to work at Cumnock in Ayrshire, then moved to Edinburgh where they were employed by William Home Lizars, the engraver.

McCulloch's earliest documented work, *Portrait of a Boy*, was shown by a Glasgow printseller in 1819. In 1828 the Glasgow Dilettanti Society's first exhibition had four works by McCulloch, including two studies; his tendency to show sketches aroused some criticism. From 1829 he exhibited with the Scottish Academy in Edinburgh and was elected an associate in 1834. Although he occasionally contributed to exhibitions in Manchester, Liverpool, Dublin, Belfast, and London, his work was not that well known in England. His early paintings reflect the style of Alexander Nasmyth and John Knox in their classical composition and meticulous technique but, following his move to Edinburgh, he came under the influence of the Revd John Thomson of Duddingston, then Scotland's most admired landscape artist, in his Romantic vision of the country and exuberant brushwork, and Hugh William 'Grecian' Williams. McCulloch's painting became more spontaneous and fluid and he can be regarded as a pioneer of a freer style of watercolour painting. Although contemporary critics emphasized the 'natural' quality of his works, Alexander Fraser, his fellow artist, friend, and biographer, wrote that he 'did not want to know too much of anything; for him objects of sight were to be studied only as they were objects of taste—food for imagination, or as they appealed to his sense of beauty or grandeur' (Fraser, 37).

McCulloch was an outstanding and influential painter of the Scottish landscape whose work appeared in a variety of settings. Robert Napier, the renowned marine engineer, had him decorate panels for steamships; his views were used to illustrate the *Steam Boat Companion* (1831), published by James Lumsden, a major patron; they also appeared in *The Scottish Annual* (1836), William Beattie's *Scotland Illustrated* (1838), and *Scotland Delineated* (1847–54). His work was acquired by the art unions in Glasgow and Edinburgh as well as by private collectors. McCulloch was particularly drawn to the western highlands and islands, Stirlingshire, Lanarkshire, and Renfrewshire. The Isle of Skye also provided great inspiration and it was there that he married Marcella McLellan on 6 September 1847.

In the 1850s and 1860s McCulloch's style changed; this is most obvious in his outdoor studies, which reveal a greater interest in detail and composition. Some of his best-known and most popular pictures date from this period, including *My Heart's in the Highlands* (1860, Glasgow Art Gallery and Museum), commissioned by the Royal Association for the Promotion of the Fine Arts in Scotland and engraved by William Forrest for its *Illustrated Songs of Robert Burns* (1861). *Glencoe* (1864, Glasgow Art Gallery and Museum), regarded as one of the most pictorially successful of the later works, is the most reproduced of all his images of Scotland. He and Landseer, more than any other mid-nineteenth-century artist, contributed to the popular Victorian image of the highlands, revealing nature in all its elements.

Alexander Fraser wrote that, as a young man, McCulloch was popular for his 'good-heartedness, and merry, harem-scarem disposition' (Fraser, 19). One portrait by Daniel Macnee (1842, Glasgow Art Gallery and Museum) captures a fresh-faced artist gazing eagerly; it contrasts with the more rugged appearance photographed by Thomas Annan in the 1860s and included in Fraser's monograph. McCulloch died at his home, St Colm Villa, Trinity, Leith, near Edinburgh, on 24 June 1867 and was buried in Warriston cemetery in Edinburgh on 28 June. His works are in the collections of the Glasgow Art Gallery and Museum; the National Gallery of Scotland, Edinburgh; Perth Museum and Art Gallery; McManus Galleries, Dundee; and other public collections.

GEORGE FAIRFULL SMITH

Sources S. Smith, *Horatio McCulloch, 1805–1867* (1988) • A. Fraser, *Scottish landscape: the works of Horatio Macculloch RSA* (1872) • Chambers, *Scots.*, rev. T. Thomson (1875), vol. 5 • J. L. Caw, *Scottish painting past and present, 1620–1908* (1908) • D. Irwin and F. Irwin, *Scottish painters at home and abroad, 1700–1900* (1975) • C. B. de Laperriere, ed., *The Royal Scottish Academy exhibitors, 1826–1990*, 4 vols. (1991), vol. 3 • *Glasgow Herald* (13 Sept 1847) • *Glasgow Herald* (26 June 1867) • J. Halsby, *Scottish watercolours, 1740–1940* (1986) • R. Brydall, *Art in Scotland, its origin and progress* (1889) • d. cert. • NA Scot., SC 70/1/138/173–178 • R. Billcliffe, ed., *The Royal Glasgow Institute of the Fine Arts, 1861–1989: a dictionary of exhibitors at the annual exhibitions*, 4 vols. (1990–92), vol. 3 • J. Hedderwick, *Backward glances, or, Some personal recollections* (1891) • *DNB*

Archives NL Scot. • Royal Scot. Acad. | University of Strathclyde, Glasgow, Glasgow Dilettanti Society Archive

Likenesses D. Macnee, chalk drawing, 1828, Scot. NPG • D. Macnee, oils, 1842, Glasgow Art Gallery and Museum • R. Adamson and D. O. Hill, calotype, c.1845, Scot. NPG • J. Smyth, line engraving, 1847 (after D. Macnee), BM, NPG; repro. in *Art Union Journal* (1847) • P. Park, marble bust, exh. 1849, Royal Scot. Acad. • D. Brown, photograph, 1855–6, Glasgow School of Art • D. Macnee, oils, 1858, NG Scot. • T. Annan, photograph, c.1860, repro. in Fraser, *Scottish landscape* • T. F. Heaphy, double portrait, ink drawing (with W. B. Johnstone), Scot. NPG • T. F. Heaphy, ink • D. Macnee, oils, Scot. NPG • J. G. Tunny, carte-de-visite, NPG

Wealth at death £3584 11s. 0d.: confirmation, 4 March 1868, NA Scot., SC 70/1/138/173–178

McCulloch, Sir James (1819–1893), politician and entrepreneur in Australia, the son of George McCulloch, a carter, and his wife, Jean Thomson, was born on 19 March 1819 at Glasgow. After a rudimentary education he entered the office of the merchants J. and A. Dennistoun. On 1 August 1841 he married Susan, the daughter of the Revd James Renwick of Muirton, Forfar. In 1853 Dennistouns sent him to open a branch in Melbourne, where his energy, connections, and lively personality quickly made him a leader in the business community, public charities, and institutions. In 1854 he was nominated to the legislative council of Victoria, and in October 1856 he was elected to the first legislative assembly under responsible government.

Described as a mercantile liberal, in the next seven years McCulloch was in and out of the legislative assembly, twice held office amid constant ministerial changes, twice visited Britain, was twice president of the chamber of commerce, formed a new company, McCulloch, Sellar & Co., in succession to Dennistouns, was elected a member of the Melbourne Club, and began to acquire pastoral interests. In 1863, dissatisfied with Charles Duffy's radical and disastrous land selection act which had enabled pastoralists, acting largely through dummies, rather than agricultural selectors, to buy crown lands, he helped to defeat the existing administration and, allied with some of his former radical opponents, became premier and chief secretary in the first stable ministry that Victoria had had.

McCulloch immediately took a strong stand against British proposals to increase convict transportation to Western Australia, and then, after the legislative council, elected on a restricted franchise which strongly favoured squatters and conservatives, twice rejected government land legislation, he went to the country in November 1864 on a programme which included a new land bill, council reform, and moderate tariff increases. He won handsomely and the council was virtually compelled to accept another land bill, which, despite continued dummying, achieved partial success. Partly in revenge, the council opposed the tariff in the name of free trade. McCulloch then 'tacked' the customs duties to the appropriation bill, which the council consequently rejected. Uproar ensued; public payments were maintained by the government's borrowing money from the London Chartered Bank, of which McCulloch was the local director (other banks refusing to lend), to which it confessed judgment when sued under the Crown Remedies and Liabilities Act. Compromise failing and his majority dwindling, McCulloch appealed to the country, and in February 1866 was returned with a crushing and more radical majority. The council then passed the tariff, but its power remained intact.

The dispute was renewed in May 1866 when the imperial government recalled the governor, Sir Charles Darling, for partisanship with the ministry and McCulloch proposed to vote Lady Darling £20,000 in compensation. Colonial government regulations prevented this, until Sir Charles resigned from government service; McCulloch then, in July 1867, put the grant on the estimates, and refused to put it up separately. The council rejected the appropriation bill, and deadlock returned. Fresh elections in February 1868 sent the government back stronger than before, and when London instructed the governor that the grant must be reintroduced separately, McCulloch resigned. His huge majority made a conservative ministry impotent, but eight weeks later, in July, news of Darling's re-entry into the colonial service made the grant unacceptable and unnecessary. McCulloch resumed office, now becoming treasurer as well as premier and chief secretary. Radical disappointment at the inconclusive end of the crises and the concessions to pastoralists which accompanied easier terms for selection in a new land act the following year, together with corruption scandals, weakened his government. It fell on a minor issue in September 1869. McCulloch was knighted in 1870 and became premier and chief secretary again in April of that year. He succeeded in abolishing state aid to religion and won the 1871 elections promising to establish state secular education, but he was defeated in June when his proposals for modest tariff increases dissatisfied the more ardent protectionists in his party, and proposals for a property tax alienated many uncommitted members.

After resigning his seat in March 1872, McCulloch acted as agent-general for Victoria in London during early 1873; the following year his KB was converted to KCMG. He then returned to Australia and re-entered the assembly at the 1874 elections. Although his old party was in power, he first helped to defeat it on taxation, then rejoined it to overthrow the radical Berry ministry, and he became premier and treasurer in October. Berry launched systematic parliamentary obstruction; McCulloch defeated this by introducing the closure, but his attempts to establish a balanced system of direct taxation failed. In May 1877 Berry, campaigning for a land tax on great estates, won a devastating electoral victory. A year later McCulloch resigned from parliament.

McCulloch then devoted himself to business, holding several directorships and helping establish the frozen meat trade. Having been a trustee of the public library, museums, and national gallery of Victoria since 1870, he could now work for it more strenuously, and he played a considerable part in selecting pictures for it. He retired to England in 1886, and died on 30 January 1893 at his residence, Garbrand Hall, Ewell, Surrey, leaving an estate valued at more than £22,000. He was survived by his second wife, Margaret Boak, the daughter of his associate William Inglis of Walflat, Dumbarton, whom he had married on 17 October 1867, but he had had no children from either of his marriages. McCulloch was an honest, energetic, determined, and very effective politician. At times he was ready to compromise, on other occasions he seemed opportunistic and unscrupulous, but he was a consistent liberal who carried out several important reforms.   G. R. BARTLETT

Sources C. G. Duffy, *My life in two hemispheres*, 2 (1898); facs. edn (Shannon, 1969) · G. Serle, *The golden age: a history of the colony of Victoria, 1851–1861* (1963) · G. M. Dow, *George Higinbotham: church and state* (1964) · F. K. Crowley, 'Aspects of the constitutional conflicts ... Victorian legislature, 1864–1868', MA diss., University of Melbourne, 1947 · G. R. Bartlett, 'Political organisation and society in Victoria, 1864–1883', PhD diss., Australian National University,

1964 · R. A. Johnson, 'Groups in the Victorian legislative assembly, 1861–1870', PhD diss., Latrobe University, 1975 · R. Wright, *A people's counsel: a history of the parliament of Victoria, 1856–1990* (1992) · G. R. Bartlett, 'McCulloch, Sir James', *AusDB*, vol. 5 · *The Argus* [Melbourne] (20 Aug 1859) · *The Argus* [Melbourne] (4 Feb 1893) · parish register (births and baptisms), 19 Mar 1819, Glasgow · parish register (banns and marriages), 1 Aug 1841, Montrose, Forfar, Scotland · *CGPLA Eng. & Wales* (1893) · D. McCaughey, N. Perkins, and A. Trumble, *Victoria's colonial governors, 1839–1900* (1993) · *DNB* · d. cert. · *Weekly Times* [Melbourne] (4 Feb 1893) · *Illustrated Australian News* [Melbourne] (1 March 1893) · *The Leader* [Melbourne] (27 June 1863)
Likenesses photograph, repro. in Wright, *A people's counsel*
Wealth at death £22,390 10s. 9d.: probate, 17 April 1893, *CGPLA Eng. & Wales*

MacCulloch, John (1773–1835), surgeon and geologist, was born on 6 October 1773 at his grandparents' home on Guernsey. He was the third of eight children born to James MacCulloch (1746–1832), wine merchant of Roscoff, and his wife, Elizabeth de Lisle, daughter of Thomas de Lisle, a Guernsey jurat. John early showed his solitary and precocious nature, so his father sent him to schools in Cornwall between 1778 and 1790. In M'Gilvray's Grammar School, Lostwithiel, MacCulloch served as head pupil, and there he was inspired to become a doctor. He studied medicine at Edinburgh University from 1790 to 1794. He also read chemistry under Joseph Black and natural history under John Walker. In 1793, he graduated MD, presenting a dissertation, *De igne electreo*, reviewing uses of electricity to cure intermittent fevers. However, postgraduate studies were curtailed by his parents' internment during the French Revolution.

On 15 August 1795 MacCulloch became surgeon's mate in the Royal Artillery, rising to senior assistant surgeon by 1803, then being drafted to the ordnance chemical department, becoming ordnance chemist in 1806 and retiring from the army with a small military pension. In September 1808 he became a licentiate of the Royal College of Physicians and settled at Blackheath, where he practised privately until 1811 when ordnance duties necessitated prolonged absences for geological surveys. Always an opportunist, in 1820 he became physician to Prince Leopold, later king of the Belgians. MacCulloch's principal contribution to medicine was his compilation and analysis of data on fevers. He attributed recurrent fevers to bad air which he made the theme of his book, *Malaria* (1827). His description of symptoms and analysis of causes showed an appreciation of the role of the environment in propagating malarial disease. He published *An Essay on the Remittent Diseases* in 1828 and argued that there were causal links between malaria and other intermittent fevers but ignored some contrary evidence.

As ordnance chemist MacCulloch prepared chemicals, analysed materials, and gave lectures on chemistry, first to students of the Royal Military Academy at Woolwich, then to East India Company military cadets at Addiscombe. He lectured at Woolwich (1803–21) and at Addiscombe (1814–35). During the Napoleonic wars he was responsible for analysing purity of sulphur and nitrate shipments for the gunpowder mills and he checked the efficacy of gunpowder delivered from them. When the

John MacCulloch (1773–1835), by Benjamin Rawlinson Faulkner

powdermill wheels of Belgian limestone wore out in 1809, MacCulloch was assigned the task of locating British replacement limestone; thus began his paid geological fieldwork.

MacCulloch's growing interest in geology evinced itself in diaries of tours in the Lake District in 1805 and the west country in 1807, during which he visited mines and commented upon rocks, but his zeal was best expressed when he joined the Geological Society of London in 1808 and promptly read a paper on Channel Island geology. Between 1809 and 1813 he conducted geological surveys in Wessex, Wales, and Scotland, searching for silica-free limestone for millwheels. He located appropriate rocks in Skye and Sutherland but the quarries were difficult to work so no wheels were delivered.

Each summer from 1814 to 1821 MacCulloch acted as geologist to the ordnance trigonometrical survey. His tasks were to examine the geology of rocks around the survey stations to determine whether they were dense enough to distort the position of the vertical plumb line and so introduce errors in the survey, and also to find a detached mountain of simple geological structure where the deflection produced by a known mass could be measured exactly. In eight seasons he examined the geology of hundreds of Scottish peaks, completed a geological map of west Scotland, and recommended Ben Stack and Ailsa Craig for the deflection experiment.

Thorough descriptions of MacCulloch's discoveries concerning Scottish rocks were published in the *Transactions of the Geological Society of London* where his closely reasoned and well illustrated papers epitomized the Baconian skills

advocated by the society. He served as Geological Society president in 1816–18, but his wide scientific expertise was best attested by his election as fellow of the Royal Society in 1820. Unexpectedly, survey work took its toll; after he suffered enlargement of the spleen in 1821, he was unfit for duty until 1822, and remained unhealthy thereafter.

In 1824 ordnance establishments were being cut; the chemical department was abolished, with MacCulloch retiring on pension, and the geological survey was transferred to the Treasury. Until 1832 MacCulloch spent each summer surveying central and southern Scotland to complete his map. Costs exceeded £1000 per year but although the Scottish geological fraternity challenged the expenditure in parliament during 1830–31, the survey was completed. MacCulloch suffered a stroke in 1831, but he rallied to draft the final reports and map which were demanded by the Treasury when prompted by Robert Jameson, who roused the Highland Society to seek publication.

Latterly MacCulloch was alienated from geological peers who had hailed his success in 1819 on publishing *A Description of the Western Islands of Scotland* and again in 1821 when he released *A Geological Classification of Rocks*, which served ten years as textbook for his geology lectures in the East India College. Those books embodied the results of careful field observation and demonstrated understanding of crystalline rock origins, and the power of erosion. From 1821 onwards writing was an auxiliary source of income and occupation and MacCulloch wrote dozens of scientific papers, book reviews, and articles for the *Edinburgh Encyclopaedia*. His most controversial book, *The Highlands and Western Islands of Scotland* (1824), stated that lazy highlanders should be cleared from the land, and met virulent opposition. MacCulloch's scientific reputation was marred by his last geology book, *The System of Geology*, published in 1831. He wrote it before 1824 but found no funds to publish until 1830 when his ideas, largely based on studies of crystalline rocks, had become unfashionable. Fossils had become the favoured analytical tool in geology, but MacCulloch belittled their value.

MacCulloch was a handsome, charming man in his prime, about 1820 when Faulkner painted him, but as his health deteriorated his face became puffy and his manner acerbic. Nevertheless, he married Louisa Margaretta White of Croydon on 6 July 1835 at St Martin-in-the-Fields, London. On honeymoon in Cornwall he suffered severe injuries in a carriage accident near Penzance and died after the amputation of a leg on 20 August 1835. He was buried at Gulval church near Penzance.

The 4 mile to an inch Scottish geological map by MacCulloch appeared in 1836 and was criticized for topographical and geological inaccuracy, but it was not superseded for many years. His widow published his *Proofs and Illustrations of the Attributes of God* in 1837. In it he argued that geological evidence revealed the work of God in creation, an idea well received by the Church of England, but tested by Charles Darwin against his embryonic theory of evolution.

MacCulloch bequeathed money which supported his widow for twenty-three years and he left publications on medicine and geology which acted as the solid observational basis for later theoretical development. A contemporary, Charles Lyell, praised MacCulloch as an observer and commented on the powerful and lasting value of his written work. A twentieth-century biography considered that MacCulloch's work 'greatly advanced general knowledge of the varied rock formations of Scotland, especially that of the igneous rocks' (Eyles, 593–5). Finally, MacCulloch exemplified early scientific professionalization in Britain, first challenging government bureaucracy to meet administrative and financial burdens involved in geological research.   DAVID A. CUMMING

Sources D. A. Cumming, 'John MacCulloch: pioneer of Precambrian geology', PhD diss., U. Glas., 1982 [2 vols.] • L. J. Bruce-Chwatt, 'John MacCulloch, 1773–1835: the precursor of the discipline of malariology', *Medical History*, 21 (1977), 156–65 • *Annual Biography and Obituary*, 20 (1836), 24–34 • J. MacCulloch, *A description of the western islands of Scotland*, 3 vols. (1819) • J. MacCulloch, *A geological classification of rocks, with descriptive synopses of the species and varieties, comprising the elements of practical geology* (1821) • C. Lyell, 'Address to the Geological Society delivered at the anniversary on the 19th February 1836', *Proceedings of the Geological Society of London*, 2 (1833–8), 357–90 • V. Eyles, 'MacCulloch, John', *DSB*
Likenesses portrait, 1826–9 • marble bust, 1830–39, GS Lond. • C. E. Wagstaff, mezzotint, pubd 1837, BM • B. R. Faulkner, oils, RS [*see illus.*]
Wealth at death substantial; incl. £600 p.a. from pensions and fees at Addiscombe: will, 1853

McCulloch, John Ramsay

McCulloch, John Ramsay (1789–1864), political economist, was born on 1 March 1789, in Whithorn, Wigtownshire, the eldest of two sons of William McCulloch and of Sarah, daughter of the Revd James Laing DD, minister of the parish of Glasserton. The family owned the freehold of a small estate, Auchengool, in the stewartry of Kirkcudbright, and when John Ramsay was five years old, William McCulloch died, a year before his own father, upon which Sarah's father took charge of their home and property and assumed guardianship of the two boys. Sarah herself escaped from her father's domination by marrying a cousin, Dr David Dempster, but it was not until sixteen-year-old John Ramsay formally inherited Auchengool, together with his father's house and small farm in Whithorn, that he and his brother went to live with their mother and stepfather. Although Dr Laing pursued until 1809 his litigious endeavours to dispute John Ramsay's inheritance, the latter (according to H. G. Reid, his biographer, son-in-law, and personal assistant) was to recall his maternal grandfather gratefully, in later years, as a good classical scholar with a taste for modern as well as ancient literature, whose well-stocked library nourished his youthful passion for books.

Early interest in political economy In October 1807, after moving with the Dempsters to Edinburgh, McCulloch entered the university there, where he studied various subjects (including mathematics, agriculture, and metaphysics); there is no evidence, however, that he attended Dugald Stewart's lectures in political economy. He left without graduating, returned in August 1811 to his house in Whithorn, and on 12 November of that year married Isabella Stewart. He then took employment in Edinburgh

John Ramsay McCulloch (1789–1864), by Sir Daniel Macnee, exh. RA 1840

as a lawyer's clerk and it was there that he became interested in political economy. In 1815 he wrote his first *Essay on the Question of Reducing the Interest of the National Debt*, which he boldly sent to David Ricardo for comment. The 27-year-old was rewarded for his temerity in addressing the leading British political economist of the day by receiving a generously full critical comment on his *Essay*. A few months later he sent Ricardo a much enlarged and duly revised edition of the pamphlet—which did not altogether accept the master's critique. By the time Ricardo's classic *Principles of Political Economy* was published McCulloch had joined the staff of *The Scotsman*, a new liberal newspaper for which he reviewed the book in May 1817. More significant, however, in establishing his early reputation as a well-informed economic journalist, in close touch with recent thinking on political economy, was the substantial review article on Ricardo's *Principles* that was McCulloch's first contribution to the influential *Edinburgh Review* (June 1818). He remained that journal's principal economic writer for almost twenty years and was regarded by himself, and his contemporaries—including Ricardo—as the latter's principal popularizer.

Relations with David Ricardo By the end of 1818 McCulloch had published more than fifty articles on current politico-economic themes—mainly in *The Scotsman* (of which he was editor from 1817 to 1821) or the *Edinburgh Review*—and had written two of the twenty major articles he was to contribute to the 6th, 7th, and 8th editions of the *Encyclopaedia Britannica* and its supplements. He was then sending Ricardo first drafts or proofs of his articles and getting back both constructive advice and warm encouragement. Moreover, after Ricardo took his seat as an MP, early in 1819, McCulloch had no hesitation either in using him to extract from other MPs or officials factual data and perspectives relevant to his current journalistic projects, or in urging him to speak in Commons debates on issues of special concern to politically minded Scots. Over the next four to five years the congenial, often lengthy, argumentative letters passing between these two seekers after truth in the new science of political economy created a professional relationship valued by each of them. They first met in May 1823, when McCulloch visited London to spend six weeks in lively discussion with Ricardo and his circle and participated in a meeting of the Political Economy Club. This was after he had already delivered the third of his annual course of lectures to Edinburgh students—to an audience that reached sixty in early 1823. A cordial letter from Ricardo, which arrived after McCulloch's return home, anticipated his next London visit, the following year, to give a similar course which ought to prove instructive to 'some of the grown gentlemen in the House of Commons' (*Works and Correspondence*, 9.301). However, Ricardo died two months later. So, although McCulloch did return to London (in April 1824) to lecture to an audience that included government ministers and MPs, it was James Mill and his friends who had raised the funds to endow a Ricardo memorial lectureship on political economy for ten years and ensured that McCulloch would be the first incumbent.

Professor in London The Ricardo Memorial Lectures were so successful that in the first year McCulloch was persuaded to repeat them in Liverpool in the autumn of 1824. In 1825 and 1826 his London audiences (at times including such eminent dignitaries as the chancellor of the exchequer, the president of the Board of Trade, and the lord mayor) were so large that he gave twenty-six lectures, twice weekly, at a City as well as a West End location—supplementing them with private classes in his own rooms for the more earnest of his regular listeners. He also gave occasional one-off lectures, one of which—a discourse delivered at the opening of the City of London Literary and Scientific Institution—was said to have attracted nearly 800 auditors. In spite of his fame as a teacher of political economy in London, McCulloch's friends failed in their campaign to establish an Edinburgh chair in the subject, for which they saw him as the best-qualified candidate. The reason was that, during his years as an outspoken editor of *The Scotsman*, he had made a bitter enemy of (among others) John Wilson, Dugald Stewart's successor in the chair of moral philosophy, who though totally without interest in, or knowledge of, political economy, could (and did) claim it as being within his own professorial brief. McCulloch had not yet affronted influential Londoners, however, when he was offered, and in 1828 accepted, the chair of political economy in the newly founded University of London. It proved a disappointing episode in his career. After buying an expensive house in fashionable Fitzroy Square, he quarrelled continuously with the university council (mainly about money matters,

but also on educational issues) and was confronted by dwindling student audiences. Money was, of course, a pressing consideration for a middle-aged man who took his family responsibilities seriously. Isabella bore him twelve children, of whom four boys (including William *McCulloch) and six girls survived, and McCulloch was anxious to add to the small return generated by his Scottish properties a basic salary of the kind attached to public office. He vacated the London University chair in 1837, and eventually, in 1838, he was appointed comptroller of the Stationery Office at a salary of £600 per annum, which rose gradually to £1200 in 1854. There he gained a deserved reputation among government ministers for his vigorous efforts to cut the costs of paper and printing in government offices—tempered by a humane consideration for those members of his staff who faced personal financial crises. According to the obituary published in the 1864 *Annual Register*, McCulloch's economy drive achieved annual savings that 'far exceeded the cost of the department he presided over' (*Annual Register*, 196).

The first professional economist Meanwhile McCulloch continued to justify Ricardo's assessment of him as a 'zealous advocate for the correct principles of political economy' (*Works and Correspondence*, 9.155). He was arguably the first professional economist. He published a steady stream of seriously researched and lucidly expounded articles, pamphlets, and books. From 1820 (when he first offered private classes in political economy to Edinburgh students) to 1837, when he left his London chair, he was also a conscientious lecturer in the subject. As early as 1822 his reputation was such that he was invited to write the first substantive article on political economy to appear in the *Encyclopaedia Britannica*. As usual, he submitted it for Ricardo's approval and was duly encouraged by the latter's response: 'Besides a valuable historical sketch, you have given so clear an exposition of all the important principles of the science that you have left nothing for me to wish for' (ibid., 9.275). This was the article that McCulloch expanded into his popular textbook, *Principles of Political Economy, with a Sketch of the Rise and Progress of the Science* (1825), which went through five editions. Apart from a best-selling annotated edition of Adam Smith's *Wealth of Nations* (1828) and a (less successful) edition of David Ricardo's works (1845), he also produced the first systematic account of the theory and policy of public finance: *Treatise on the Principles and Practical Influence of Taxation and the Funding System* (1845).

McCulloch reached an even wider audience, however, and added substantially to his annual income with his three statistical reference books, of which the most financially rewarding was his *Dictionary, Practical, Theoretical, and Historical of Commerce and Commercial Navigation* (1832), a virtually single-handed work which he revised, expanded, and updated nine times. These 'dictionaries' were not simply compilations of statistical and other facts; for McCulloch was a pioneer in critical assessment and analytical treatment of economic information he gathered from a variety of public and private sources. None of his contemporaries, for example, was better informed or more outspoken on the deficiencies of the broad range of official statistics then available. The many journalists, public officials, MPs, and government ministers who used his figures to buttress their arguments and policy recommendations had no excuse for ignoring the fragility of the basic data. At the same time, this most prolific author was an avid reader. Few, if any, writers on economic matters had read so widely and so exhaustively on the science and substance of their subject—as effectively illustrated by his 400-page bibliography *Literature of Political Economy* (1845). Nor did he confine his reading to economic questions. A keen bibliophile, McCulloch built up a valuable library of over 10,000 books which, after his death, his friend Lord Overstone bought for £5000.

Reputation and death Although McCulloch's association with Ricardo and his circle helped to enhance his early reputation as an expert in the new science of political economy, it seems to have obscured, until recently, his distinctive qualities as an applied economist for later historians of economic thought. The fact is that McCulloch was never converted to the Ricardian abstract style of theorizing—even during the three years before Ricardo's death, when their eager exchange of views and information was at its peak. McCulloch's own interest in political economy stemmed always from his immediate concern with questions of practical policy. He judged economic theories in terms of their usefulness when applied to urgent current problems. As he continued to address a widening range of contemporary economic problems and to amass the relevant statistics and other data, and as he continually revised and updated his *Principles* in the light of experience, his divergence from the orthodox Ricardian model became increasingly obvious. In his own time he was probably more famous, more widely read by those engaged in making or debating economic policy, and more often singled out for attack by critics of the 'dismal science' than any other economist. Although Sir Robert Peel, for example, had crucially failed in 1825 to support the claim for a separate chair of political economy in Edinburgh, he was frankly impressed in the 1830s by McCulloch's views on public finance, and in 1846 he was to acknowledge his services to the science of political economy by getting him an annual state pension of £200. McCulloch was by then internationally famous. His *Principles* was a familiar text for American undergraduates and was translated into French, German, Portuguese, Spanish, and Italian. In 1843 he was elected a foreign associate of the Institut de France. Evidently this early example of a professional economist was a public personality in his own time. The obituary in *The Scotsman*, for example, referred to his 'great sagacity and manly commonsense' as well as to 'an independence of judgment that occasionally revelled in arbitrary assertion and cherished prejudice', and went on to notice 'something almost Johnsonian in his intellectual aspect and style' (*The Scotsman*, 13 Nov 1864).

On the other hand, given McCulloch's eclectic use of economic theory, and his dauntingly large output of articles, pamphlets, and books, realistically (if often repetitiously) focused on a variety of specific nineteenth-century problems, subsequent commentators have found it hard to put his contribution into perspective and have tended to underrate him—at least until Professor O'Brien's comprehensive account and evaluation of his work as a whole was published in 1970. It is now apparent that for most of the half-century preceding his death this hard-working, largely self-educated Scot did more than any other economist of his day to introduce the new science of political economy to an interested public. In particular, for example, although McCulloch neither invented nor developed the classical wage-fund theory, he used it to such effect that, according to Joseph Schumpeter, 'he established himself as the leading exponent of the wage-fund doctrine' (J. A. Schumpeter, *History of Economic Analysis*, 1955, 669). He continued to keep in touch with new thinking on economic affairs, not only by reading voraciously, but also by exchanging ideas and arguments with other economists—for example at the London Political Economy Club, where he participated regularly from 1839 to 1852 and made many good friends. His distinctive technique was to marry to current economic data theories developed by such leaders in classical political economy as Smith, Hume, or Ricardo and to furnish the analysis with insights arising out of his own interpretation of recent economic events, or borrowed from friends (such as the banker Lord Overstone) who were themselves active agents in crucial decision-making processes.

McCulloch was still working on an 11th edition of his *Commercial Dictionary*, and still in charge of HM Stationery Office in Prince Street, Westminster, when he died there (of the chronic bronchitis that had afflicted him for most of his life) on 11 November 1864. He was buried a week later in Brompton cemetery, where Isabella—to whom he had been happily married for fifty-three years—was laid beside him three years later.

PHYLLIS DEANE

Sources D. P. O'Brien, *J. R. McCulloch: a study in classic economics* (1970) · H. G. Reid, 'Biographical notice', in J. R. McCulloch, *Dictionary of commerce and commercial navigation*, ed. H. G. Reid (1871) · *The works and correspondence of David Ricardo*, ed. P. Sraffa and M. H. Dobb, 11 vols. (1951–73), vols. 7–9 · *Annual Register* (1864) · *The Scotsman* (13 Nov 1864) · *Wellesley index*

Archives UCL, corresp. | BL, letters to William Huskisson, Add. MS 38746 · BL, letters to Macvey Napier, Add. MSS 34612–34630 · BL, letters to Sir Robert Peel, Add. MSS 40512–40603 · Bodl. Oxf., letters to Benjamin Disraeli · CUL, letters to David Ricardo · Derbys. RO, letters to Sir R. J. Wilmot-Horton · LUL, letters to Lord Overstone · Mitchell L., Glas., Strathclyde Regional Archives, corresp. with John Strang · NRA, letters to William Ritchie · UCL, letters to the Society for the Diffusion of Useful Knowledge · UCL, letters relating to UCL

Likenesses D. Macnee, oils, exh. RA 1840, NPG [*see illus.*] · W. Bewick, chalk drawing, Scot. NPG · lithograph, BM, NPG · wood-engraving (after photograph by J. C. C. Watkins), NPG; repro. in *ILN* (1864)

Wealth at death under £16,000: resworn probate, July 1868, *CGPLA Eng. & Wales*

McCulloch, William (1691–1771), Church of Scotland minister, was born at Whithorn, Wigtownshire, the son of a parish schoolmaster from Anwoth. He received his early education under his father, and was then sent to the universities of Edinburgh and Glasgow; he graduated with an MA from Glasgow on 26 April 1712. A man of uncommon abilities, he excelled in languages (showing exceptional skill in Hebrew) and mathematics in particular, and taught classes for a time in astronomy and geography at Glasgow University. His real interest, however, was the ministry, and he was licensed to preach by the presbytery of Wigtown on 28 August 1722. While waiting for a call to a parish ministry, he lived with a Mr Hamilton of Aitkenhead in Cathcart, and supported himself by serving the family as a tutor and a chaplain. During the same period he volunteered to serve as a minister in the Carolinas in the American colonies, but applied too late to be accepted. He was eventually ordained to the parish of Cambuslang in Lanarkshire on 29 April 1731, where he ministered until his death on 18 December 1771. He married Janet Dinwoodie, daughter of a Glasgow merchant, on 29 April 1736; she survived him by eight years, dying on 13 October 1779. They had one child, Robert, born on 21 July 1740, who became minister of Dairsie and whose daughter, Janet, became a close friend of Thomas Chalmers, Church of Scotland minister and social reformer.

McCulloch was, according to one contemporary, 'a learned, unostentatious scholar, a slow, cautious and prudent parish minister' (Stanley, 137). His son noted that he 'was not a very ready speaker; though eminent in learning and piety, he was not eloquent … very different from that of popular orators' (ibid., 15–16). But his preaching was marked by a deep sincerity and courage; despite his lack of eloquence, a great religious awakening known as the 'Cambuslang Revival' occurred under his preaching in 1742. During the revival he preached five to six times a week, receiving assistance from neighbouring ministers and from the English evangelist George Whitefield who, at the height of the awakening, is estimated to have preached to a gathering of upwards of 30,000–40,000.

McCulloch took particular care to record the spiritual experiences of many of his parishioners, and as a result has left one of the best-documented conversion accounts on record of the rank and file, constituting, in effect, Scotland's first oral history project. The two bound manuscript volumes, which record the spiritual awakenings of 110 individuals, were preserved and later deposited at New College, Edinburgh, by McCulloch's granddaughter, Janet Coutts. In addition McCulloch edited and published the first religious periodical in Scotland, the *Glasgow Weekly History Relating to the Late Progress of the Gospel at Home and Abroad* (1742). He also encouraged the growth of prayer societies and helped to foster renewed interest in foreign missions. His works include *An Account of some Remarkable Events at Cambuslang* (1742) and *Sermons on Several Subjects*, published posthumously by his son in 1793.

C. W. Mitchell

Sources DNB · *Fasti Scot.*, new edn, 3.237–8 · A. Fawcett, *The Cambuslang revival: the Scottish evangelical revival of the eighteenth century* (1971) · R. MacCulloch, 'A sketch of the life and character of the author', in W. MacCulloch, *Sermons on several subjects* (1793) · T. C. Smout, 'Born again at Cambuslang: new evidence on popular religion and literacy in eighteenth-century Scotland', *Past and Present*, 97 (1982), 114–27 · A. P. Stanley, *Lectures on the history of the Church of Scotland* (1872) · C. W. Mitchell, 'Jonathan Edwards's Scottish connection and the eighteenth-century Scottish revival, 1735–1750', PhD diss., U. St Andr., 1997
Archives U. Edin., New Coll. L., MS study of participants in Cambuslang revival

McCulloch, William (1816–1885), army and political officer in India, the eldest son of John Ramsay *McCulloch (1789–1864), political economist, and his wife, Isabella, *née* Stewart (d. 1867), was born on 28 February 1816 in the parish of St Cuthbert's, Edinburgh. He attended the Edinburgh high school and joined Addiscombe College as a cadet, on the nomination of James Rivett Carnac, on 15 February 1833. He was commissioned ensign on 12 December 1834, and arrived at Fort William on 21 July 1835. He was appointed successively to the 56th native infantry at Dinapore (8 August), 30th native infantry at Benares (12 August), and 13th native infantry at Bareilly (24 September), and he commanded the detachment at Deolia employed on cordon duty. After becoming lieutenant on 18 February 1839, he was appointed interpreter and quartermaster to his corps in July 1839, and assistant to the political agent at Manipur in April 1840. Although he temporarily acted as superintendent of Cachar from 2 February to 7 November 1842, he continued to hold his office at Manipur until the middle of 1845, when he was promoted to the post of political agent there. He obtained the rank of captain on 30 June 1848 and of major on 4 September 1857, and retired from the army with the rank of lieutenant-colonel on 31 December 1861. In 1863 his place at Manipur was taken by assistant surgeon Dillon, but Dillon's failure led to McCulloch resuming office late in 1864. He finally retired in 1867. He was author of an *Account of the Valley of Munnipore and the Hill Tribes* (1859). McCulloch died at Shillong, Assam, on 4 April 1885.

J. M. Rigg, *rev.* Roger T. Stearn

Sources Boase, *Mod. Eng. biog.* · H. M. Vibart, *Addiscombe: its heroes and men of note* (1894) · CGPLA Eng. & Wales (1885)
Wealth at death £916 15s. 5d.: probate, 1 Sept 1885, CGPLA Eng. & Wales

Mac Cumhaigh [Mac Cooey], **Art** (c.1738–1773), Irish-language poet, was probably born in the parish of Creggan (perhaps in the townland of Mounthill), co. Armagh; he also had links with nearby Kilcurly, co. Louth. His poetry displays a knowledge of the classics, but he spent his short life as a labourer, gardener, and herdsman, most of it in the employment of various priests and of a protestant minister, the Revd Hugh Hill.

One of the best-known episodes in Mac Cumhaigh's life was his dispute with the parish priest of Creggan, the Revd Terence Quinn, whom he attacked—as did his fellow poet Peadar Ó Doirnín—for being overbearing, partial towards the well-to-do, and imposing heavy financial exactions on his parishioners. He also satirized the priest's sister and housekeeper in a celebrated poem as

'Máre Chaoch' ('Blind—or squint-eyed—Mary'). But, contrary to local tradition, the poem was not the sole—nor perhaps even the primary—cause of the poet's rift with the parish priest. That was more likely to have resulted from his abducting and marrying a second cousin Máire Ní Luain (Mary Lamb), in the protestant church, about 1770, an action that incurred his double excommunication. Ostracized by his neighbours, Mac Cumhaigh fled to Howth, co. Dublin, where he worked as a gardener. During his sojourn there, he composed his celebrated 'aisling' ('Ag cuan Bhinn Éadain ar bhruach na hÉireann') in which he bemoaned his exile from his beloved Creggan. Within a year the excommunication was lifted and the poet returned to Creggan by permission, not of Father Quinn, but of the vicar-general of the archdiocese of Armagh. He then composed 'Cúilfhionn Ní Choinne' in reparation to the offended housekeeper; the work has been described by Tomás Ó Fiaich as 'a fulsome tribute which is metrically perfect and patently insincere' (Ó Fiaich, *Mac Cooey*, 14). He spent the remaining few years of his life working as a herd on a local farm.

In all, some two dozen of Mac Cumhaigh's compositions survive. His poems in praise of the local Gaelic lords, the O'Neills of the Fews—now in Spanish exile following the Williamite victory in the 'War of the Two Kings'—include two on the ruined O'Neill stronghold of Glasdrummond Castle and an elegy of 262 lines on the death of Art Óg Ó Néill, heir of the O'Neills of Creggan, who died in 1769 aged twenty-six (and for whom the poet had earlier composed a praise poem). A second elegy composed in that same year was a lament for his fellow poet Peadar Ó Doirnín. Following his return from 'exile' in Howth Mac Cumhaigh composed two savage satires entitled 'Bodaigh na hEorna' ('The Churls of the Barley') on the O'Callaghans of Cullaville, a well-to-do local Catholic family whose reputed snobbery, materialism, and philistine disregard for literature and music incurred the poet's wrath. Several of his poems relate to ecclesiastical matters, including a dialogue between the Catholic church at Faughart and the protestant church at Forkill, a succinct explanation of protestant doctrine addressed to a priest friend, and praise poems for two priests, the Franciscan Seán Ó hAnluain and Dominick Bellew, future bishop of Killala. There are poems in praise of a local tory or raparee, of a young woman, of a doctor who had healed an ulcer on the poet's leg, and on a member of the Catholic gentry. As well as some satirical or humorous pieces, there are a couple of vision poems known as *aislingí*, one of which, 'Úrchill an Chreagáin', has been described as 'one of the most interesting and sweetest aisling-poems in the Irish language' (Ó Fiaich, *Art Mac Cumhaigh*, 170, original statement in Irish). It is noteworthy that these *aislingí* by Mac Cumhaigh lack the strong Jacobite sentiments of their Munster counterparts.

Art Mac Cumhaigh was known locally as 'Art na gCeolta' (Art of the songs). Indeed most of his compositions were meant to be sung and the airs of many of the more popular items have been recorded.

Mac Cumhaigh's untimely death, which occurred a short distance north of Crossmaglen probably on 5 January 1773, was almost certainly brought about by overindulgence in alcohol. He was buried in Creggan churchyard in an unmarked grave. The bicentennial of his death was marked by the unveiling of a fine monument at the spot where he is traditionally said to be buried. A collection of his poetry first appeared in print in 1916 and the bicentennial of his death saw the publication of a comprehensive edition of his work, including a detailed analysis of Mac Cumhaigh's life and times and the historical context of his poetry, and an appraisal of his surviving work, by Tomás Ó Fiaich. NOLLAIG Ó MURAÍLE

Sources *Art Mac Cumhaigh: dánta*, ed. T. Ó Fiaich (Baile Átha Cliath, 1973) · T. Ó Fiaich, *Art Mac Cooey and his times* (1973) · *Amhráin Airt Mhic Chubhthaigh agus Amhráin Eile | Art Mac Cooey's and other poems*, ed. E. Ó Muirgheasa (Dundalk, 1916); 2nd edn, 2 vols. (1926)

MacCunn, Hamish [James] (1868–1916), composer and conductor, was born James MacCunn at 15 Forsyth Street, Greenock, Renfrewshire, on 22 March 1868, the second son of a prosperous shipowner, James MacCunn of Thornhill, Greenock, and his wife, Barbara Neill. He benefited from cultured surroundings much fostered by his mother, who had studied with the composer and pianist Sir William Sterndale Bennett. As a child of eight he was taken to concerts at the Crystal Palace in London, and in 1883 he was awarded a composition scholarship to the Royal College of Music in London, one of the first from the newly founded institution. He left the college without a degree because he lacked respect for the qualification and was dissatisfied with the attitude of his superiors, a feeling pungently put in a letter to his composition teacher Hubert Parry.

Early fruit of MacCunn's composition studies included the cantata *The Moss Rose*, performed at the Royal College of Music in 1884, and the overture *Cior Mhor*, which was given by August Manns in a Saturday concert at the Crystal Palace on 27 October 1885, a performance procured through the good offices of George Grove. MacCunn's reputation as one of the most remarkable talents of his generation was assured by a string of choral and orchestral works composed in short order, mostly in 1888, and all based on Scottish subjects, chief among them the work by which he became best-known after his death, the overture *The Land of the Mountain and the Flood*, given at the Crystal Palace on 5 November 1887 and published two years later. Two notable orchestral 'ballades' followed, *The Ship o' the Fiend* (1888) and *The Dowie Dens o'Yarrow* (1888), both of which were published. The virtues of appealing melody and clear dramatic expression mark the contemporary choral works, *Lord Uillin's Daughter*, *Bonny Kilmeny*, and *The Lay of the Last Minstrel* (all 1888) and *The Cameronian's Dream* (1889).

In 1888 MacCunn married Alison Quiller, the daughter of the distinguished Scottish painter John *Pettie (1839–1893). The latter painted the couple, before their marriage, in a picture entitled *Two Strings to her Bow*. From 1888 to 1894 MacCunn was professor of harmony at the Royal Academy of Music. His composing career was much advanced by a commission for an opera from the Carl Rosa

Hamish MacCunn (1868–1916), by J. B. B. (after John Pettie, 1886)

company. The result, *Jeanie Deans*, after Sir Walter Scott's *The Heart of Midlothian*, was the first Scottish opera based on the Waverley novels; premièred in Edinburgh in 1894, it was a major success, and the work remains one of the most distinguished British operas of the late nineteenth century. His second opera, *Diarmid*, was given with somewhat less success at Covent Garden in 1897. MacCunn continued his association with the Carl Rosa company by conducting two seasons from 1898, which included the premières in English of Wagner's *Tristan* and *Siegfried*. He continued as a conductor in a number of companies, notably at the Savoy from after Sir Arthur Sullivan's death in 1900 to 1905, at Covent Garden, deputizing for Thomas Beecham (1910), and at the Shaftesbury Theatre (1915); he also passed on the benefits of his experience as a composer, teaching composition at the Guildhall School of Music from 1912. Struck down by illness in 1916, MacCunn died in London on 2 August 1916 and was survived by his wife and his only son.

MacCunn's music, solidly founded in early Romantic technique, was flavoured by a range of influences including Mendelssohn, Dvořák, and Wagner. His melodic accent, shaded by pentatonic intervals and often supported by warm, plagal harmonies, was one of the most distinctive from these islands in the late nineteenth century; he also had an unrivalled ear for effective orchestration. He had a marked predilection for programmes and text-inspired composition, with the vast majority of his works reflecting an interest in Scottish subject matter. His most effective music, including *Lord Ullin's Daughter*, *The Lay of the Last Minstrel*, and *Jeanie Deans*, was composed during the late 1880s and the first half of the 1890s. While later works, such as *The Masque of War and Peace* (1900), are less strongly characterized, perhaps reflecting his greater involvement with conducting, they nevertheless display MacCunn's customary sophisticated craft.

JAN SMACZNY

Sources *MT*, 57 (1916), 410 · *DNB* · 'MacCunn, Hamish (James)', *New Grove*, 2nd edn · N. Temperley, ed., *Music in Britain: the Romantic age, 1800–1914* (1981) · J. C. Dibble, *C. Hubert H. Parry: his life and music* (1992) · M. Musgrave, *The musical life of the Crystal Palace* (1995) · 'MacCunn, Hamish (James)', Grove, *Dict. mus.* (1954) · *CGPLA Eng. & Wales* (1916) · b. cert.
Archives U. Glas., autograph scores and related papers
Likenesses J. Pettie, double portrait, 1887 (with Alison Pettie; *Two strings to her bow*), Glasgow Art Gallery and Museum · J. B. B., engraving (after J. Pettie, 1886), NPG [*see illus.*]
Wealth at death £140: probate, 22 Dec 1916, *CGPLA Eng. & Wales*

MacCurtin, Andrew [Aindrias Mac Cruitín] (*c*.1670–1738), poet and scribe, was born in the townland of Moyglass, about 5 miles south of Milltown Malbay, in the parish of Kilmurry, co. Clare. His father, Roland Mac Cruitín, is reputed to have been a prosperous farmer but nothing else is known about his immediate family. MacCurtin's work displays a familiarity with older forms of the Irish language and with the syllabic metres employed by the professional bardic poets of earlier centuries—suggesting that his education included elements of the curriculum of the bardic schools which had disappeared in the early seventeenth century. This is consistent both with the cultural conservatism of Clare, a region which was partially sheltered from the rapid social change that affected most of Ireland in the seventeenth century, and also with the MacCurtins' status as members of the hereditary learned caste of medieval Ireland.

The MacCurtins had acted as hereditary antiquaries to the O'Briens, lords of Thomond, since the fourteenth century, a role which had evolved into that of scribes and notaries by the early seventeenth century. Andrew MacCurtin maintained the scholarly tradition of his ancestors by establishing a school in his native parish, where he appears to have resided throughout his life. The extant manuscripts in his hand contain copies of several long texts, including devotional works such as Geoffrey Keating's *Trí Bior-Ghaoithe an Bháis* and *Eochair Sgiath an Aifrinn*; linguistic works such as Mícheál Ó Cléirigh's *Foclóir nó Sanasán Nua* and Hugh MacCurtin's *Elements of the Irish Language Grammatically Explained in English*; and historical works such as *Caithréim Thoirdhealbhaigh* and Geoffrey Keating's *Foras Feasa ar Éirinn*. The fact that at least five copies of the last work survive in MacCurtin's hand leaves little doubt that he supplemented his income from teaching by copying manuscripts. MacCurtin wrote a modernized version of *Beatha Sheanáin*, the life of St Senán, and a holograph copy (St Patrick's College, Maynooth, MS C41) dating from 1721 was the exemplar used by several later scribes.

More than forty of MacCurtin's poems are extant. Several are written in the older syllabic metres and extol the virtues or lament the deaths of members of the co. Clare gentry, particularly the O'Briens of Leamaneh and Ennistimon, the MacDonnells of Kilkee, and the O'Loghlens of Burren. A *duanaire* or compendium of encomiastic verse

(Royal Irish Academy, MS E iv 3) that MacCurtin wrote for one of the O'Loghlens in 1727, contains poems by himself and other authors, and is one of the last such volumes to have been compiled.

While Andrew MacCurtin's *œuvre* is not as politicized as that of his relative, fellow poet, and contemporary Hugh MacCurtin, a composition which begins '*Ar mbeith sealad domhsa in aicis mhór cois taoide*' and appears to date from 1718–19 is an early example of a Jacobite *aisling* or vision poem, a genre which became popular with Munster poets from the middle of the eighteenth century onwards. Another of his political poems, the work beginning '*Go cúig roimh luis dá dtugadh grásaibh Dé*', has been dated to 1735 and is noteworthy for its prediction that an invasion of Britain would take place in 1745. But MacCurtin's best-known poem is probably a more personal composition beginning '*Beannú doimhin duit, a Dhoinn na Duimhche*' in which the aged poet appealed to Donn, the fairy king of a range of sandhills in west Clare, for hospitality at a time when no patronage was forthcoming from members of the gentry.

The date of MacCurtin's death is given as 1738 in a manuscript (TCD, MS H.6.11, 23) written in 1754, and this seems more likely than the alternative date of 1749 which is mentioned in later sources. He was buried in Kilfarboy churchyard, near Milltown Malbay, and was lamented by Hugh MacCurtin in a poem beginning '*Ní buan brón go bás ollaimh*'.   VINCENT MORLEY

Sources St Patrick's College, Maynooth, MS SF 2, 159–163 · TCD, MS H.6.11, 23 · L. Ó Luaighnigh, *Dánta Aindréis Mhic Cruitín* (1935) [incomplete edn of his poems] · V. Morley, *An crann os coill: Aodh Buí Mac Cruitín, c. 1680–1755* (1995) [critical biography of Hugh Mac-Curtin]

Archives BL, Add. MS 27910 · NL Ire., MS G.599 · Royal Irish Acad., MS E iv 3, MS 23 I 29, MS 23 O 10, MS 3 C 18, MS 23 G 9, MS 23 I 15, MS 23 M 52, MS 23 E 10 and MS 23 M 47 · St Patrick's College, Maynooth, MS C 37, MS C 41, MS C 58 and MS R 66 · TCD, MS H.1.18

MacCurtin, Hugh [Aodh Buí Mac Cruitín] (**1680?–1755**), poet and antiquary, was born near Liscannor in the parish of Kilmacrehy, co. Clare. Nothing is known of his immediate family except that his father was named Conchobhar Óg Mac Cruitín. The MacCurtins were one of the hereditary learned families of medieval Irish society and acted as antiquaries to the O'Briens, lords of Thomond, from the fourteenth century, a role which had evolved into that of scribes and notaries by the seventeenth century. MacCurtin was educated locally, at least partly in the school run by Andrew MacCurtin, a relative and fellow poet.

Some fifty poems by Hugh MacCurtin are extant. His corpus includes encomiastic verse addressed to patrons and written in the obsolescent syllabic metres employed by the professional bards of earlier centuries; Jacobite verse written in the stressed metres of popular song and intended for a mass audience; and a small number of works dealing with more personal themes. MacCurtin worked as a scribe and teacher, and there is evidence to suggest that the prominent patriot Charles Lucas may have been one of his pupils. His early compositions include laments for Daniel O'Brien, fourth Viscount Clare, and Charles O'Brien, fifth Viscount Clare, two brothers who were successive colonels of the *régiment de Clare*, an Irish regiment in the French service. A poem which denounced those who took an oath abjuring the Pretender (James Francis Edward Stuart) probably dates from 1709. MacCurtin married and had at least two daughters, but the poem beginning '*Is trua do chás a shuaircbhean bhreá*' suggests that the marriage was not a success. Addressed to an unnamed woman, it expresses the poet's sorrow that he must leave her and return to 'three women' in co. Clare, presumably his wife and two daughters.

By 1713 MacCurtin had moved to Dublin where he found employment copying and translating Irish manuscripts. His patrons there included William Hawkins, Ulster king of arms; the Revd Anthony Raymond, an aspiring histor-ian and friend of Jonathan Swift; and Aaron Crossly, author of *The Peerage of Ireland* (1724). While in Dublin, MacCurtin associated with the literary circle grouped around the poet and schoolmaster Tadhg Ó Neachtain, and published his first book, *A Brief Discourse in Vindication of the Antiquity of Ireland* (1717), which is little more than an abridged translation of Geoffrey Keating's *Foras Feasa ar Éirinn*. MacCurtin was imprisoned about this time and, in 1749, Charles Lucas alleged that the detention was a conse-quence of the trenchant criticism of Sir Richard Cox's *Hibernia Anglicana* contained in MacCurtin's *Discourse*. This seems unlikely since Cox, a leading tory, was out of favour with government after 1715, and the large number of prominent Jacobites whose names appeared on MacCur-tin's list of subscribers may have been a more relevant factor.

MacCurtin had returned to co. Clare by 1721, but in 1724 he composed a lament on the death of Edmund Byrne, Roman Catholic archbishop of Dublin, at the request of Tadhg Ó Neachtain. What is arguably his best known poem, '*Ar aonach má théid sin ar uair de ló*', a satire on the social pretensions of ignorant but newly prosperous peas-ants, also seems to date from the 1720s. MacCurtin left Ire-land about 1727 and travelled to the Irish Franciscan col-lege at Louvain where his second book, *The Elements of the Irish Language Grammatically Explained in English*, was pub-lished in 1728. This is a work of considerable scholarship, but it is clear that MacCurtin drew heavily from an unpub-lished manuscript grammar by Francis Walsh.

MacCurtin crossed into France later in 1728 and enlisted in the *régiment de Clare*, a unit which contained many sol-diers from his native county. A work composed during his period of military service, '*Is grinn an tsollamhain chím fén Nollaig seo*', anticipates a French invasion of Britain and the execution of George II. After his discharge in 1729 he pro-ceeded to Paris where he assisted Conchobhar Ó Beag-laoich with the preparation of *The English Irish Dictionary*, the first dictionary of its kind, which was published in 1731. It is likely that MacCurtin's assistance in the prepar-ation of the dictionary was largely clerical, but he contrib-uted an initial dedicatory poem. He appears to have remained in France until 1739 when he returned to co. Clare.

MacCurtin spent his final years as a schoolteacher in his native parish of Kilmacrehy and appears to have written little after 1745. He died in 1755 and is variously reported to have been interred in Kilmacrehy churchyard, and in Kilvoydane churchyard, near Corrofin, co. Clare. The latter may be the more likely resting place as his daughters were living nearby in 1761.   VINCENT MORLEY

Sources V. Morley, *An crann os coill: Aodh Buí Mac Cruitín, c. 1680–1755* (1995) [a critical biography] · S. S. Ó Mainnín, 'Filíocht Aodha Bhuí Mhic Cruitín', MA diss., University College Galway, 1961 [edn of his poetry] · V. Morley, 'Hugh MacCurtin: an Irish poet in the French army', *Eighteenth-Century Ireland*, 8 (1993), 49–58
Archives NL Ire., MS 96 and MS 560 · NL Ire., MS G.693 · Royal Irish Acad., MS C iv 1, MS 23 L 25 and MS 24 G 11 · St Patrick's College, Maynooth, MS C 57, MS C 67, MS M 86 and MS M 107

McDaniel, Stephen (*fl.* 1741–1755), thief-taker, was born in Ireland. Little is known of his personal life: by trade he was a sword cutler, but he was also an officer at Marshalsea prison and at one time kept a public house in Scroop's Court, Holborn, London.

McDaniel was a violent and dangerous man, who habitually went armed, sometimes with a sword, sometimes with a pistol, and sometimes with a horsewhip that doubled as a cosh. He also carried a concealed knife. His first known appearance as a prosecution witness was in 1741, when he saved his own neck by turning king's evidence against his accomplices. After that date he appeared regularly as a prosecution witness at the Old Bailey, and his activities have also been traced at assize trials in Kent, Surrey, and Essex. He did not act alone; he had a number of accomplices, and it is clear that thief-taking was simply the most visible part of his gangland activities.

McDaniel and his accomplices manipulated the criminal justice system for personal gain. In an attempt to encourage prosecutors, parliament had provided a system of rewards to those who secured conviction in cases of serious crimes such as highway robbery and burglary. The standard reward (£40) was in itself a substantial sum, equivalent to perhaps eighteen months' wages for an artisan in mid-eighteenth-century London, but at times of particular anxiety about high crime rates, further rewards might be offered either by central government or by local organizations (and sometimes by both). The McDaniel gang became expert in securing convictions irrespective of the merits of individual cases, so that they could share the proceeds of these rewards.

In August 1754 it seemed pure bad luck that two young highway robbers (Peter Kelly and John Ellis) had been caught at all. It was still more unfortunate that the goods they had stolen were readily traced, and that the accomplice who had suggested the crime in the first place was now prepared to save himself by testifying against them. The involvement of Stephen McDaniel and his fellow thief-taker John Berry as arresting officers seemed almost peripheral—but it was not. Every event that led Kelly and Ellis to trial had been carefully planned. The accomplice (Thomas Blee) was himself part of the McDaniel gang. So was the victim (James Salmon). So was the man to whom they sold the stolen goods (James Eagan). Moreover, the stolen goods actually belonged to McDaniel and had been carefully chosen for ease of identification and recovery. Even the site of the robbery had been predetermined in order to add a local reward to the statutory one.

Immediately after the conviction of Kelly and Ellis, Joseph Cox, high constable of Blackheath, arrested McDaniel and his 'hellish crew' on a charge of conspiracy. Whether Cox was motivated by altruism or was himself involved with some of McDaniel's gangland rivals is unclear. Certainly the arrests brought nothing but embarrassment to the legal establishment, who feared that the scandal might undermine the criminal justice system. McDaniel, Berry, Salmon, and Eagan were tried and convicted for the murder of Joshua Kidden, a young man whom they had sent to the gallows nearly a year earlier on perjured evidence. However, judgement was respited, probably because of establishment fears that a conviction might deter prosecutors in other cases. Later commentators have assumed that the attorney-general's refusal to argue the case rested on the premise that 'murder by perjury' is not an offence at common law, though it would appear that at the time Mansfield and other judges strongly supported the validity of the indictment. The four men were thus fortunate to escape the gallows. They were sentenced to seven years' imprisonment and to be pilloried twice on the lesser charge of conspiracy. Officials protected McDaniel and Berry when they were pilloried in 1755. They were either less willing or less able to protect Eagan and Salmon—both of whom died from the injuries they received at the hands of the outraged London crowd.

McDaniel's subsequent fate is unknown.

                                                        RUTH PALEY

Sources J. Cox, *A faithful narrative of the most wicked and inhuman transactions of that bloody minded gang … * (1756) · R. Paley, 'Thief-takers in London in the age of the McDaniel gang, c.1745–1754', *Policing and prosecution in Britain, 1750–1850*, ed. D. Hay and F. Snyder (1989), 301–42 · *The proceedings on the king's commission of the peace* [Old Bailey sessions papers] · home circuit assize records, PRO · J. C. Hogan, 'Murder by perjury', *Fordham Law Review* (30 Dec 1961)

MacDermot, Hugh Hyacinth O'Rorke [*called* the MacDermot] (1834–1904), lawyer, was born on 1 July 1834 at Coolavin, co. Sligo. He was the eldest of the twelve children of Charles Joseph MacDermot (*d.* 1873) titular 'prince of Coolavin' and his wife, Arabella O'Rorke, the last lineal descendant of the Breffny family. Educated at home by his father until 1852, at eighteen he entered the Royal College of St Patrick, Maynooth, as a candidate for the priesthood. He remained at Maynooth until 1856, when he abandoned the ecclesiastical career, and obtaining a burse on the nomination of the bishops, entered in November the Catholic University in St Stephen's Green, Dublin, of which Newman was rector. There during 1857 and 1858 he gained various distinctions in classics and English.

On leaving the university in 1859 MacDermot read law in Dublin and London, and won a studentship of £50 a year given by the Council of Legal Education in London. Admitted a student of the King's Inns, Dublin, in Michaelmas term 1857, he was called in Michaelmas term 1862, and was summoned to the inner bar in February 1877. He was elected a bencher on 11 January 1884.

MacDermot went the Connaught circuit, on which he became the chief junior. He later acquired leading Dublin business. Although no great orator, he was a first-rate lawyer, and understood the management of witnesses and juries. At the celebrated Galway election petition in 1872 before Judge Keogh, MacDermot held the junior brief for Colonel Nolan, the sitting member. He was a senior counsel in the action for libel brought against Lord Clanricarde by Frank Joyce, his former agent, in 1883; and appeared for A. M. Sullivan in the prosecution for sedition in 1880, and for Wilfrid Scawen Blunt in an attempt to quash on *certiorari* Blunt's conviction by a crimes court in 1887. After taking silk MacDermot held a leading brief in nearly every important case from the west of Ireland, especially in those of a political complexion, almost invariably taking the 'popular' side.

On the death of his father on 5 December 1873 MacDermot became the MacDermot and titular prince of Coolavin. A strong Liberal in politics, he was made in May 1885 solicitor-general for Ireland in Gladstone's second administration. He retired with the ministry in the following July, but held the office again from February to August 1886 in Gladstone's third administration. When Gladstone became prime minister for the fourth time in 1892, MacDermot was made attorney-general and was sworn of the Irish privy council. He remained attorney-general until 1895. MacDermot never sat in the House of Commons; he failed in his only attempt to obtain a seat in 1892, when he contested West Derbyshire against Victor Cavendish, later ninth duke of Devonshire. He said laughingly that the voters mistook him for the Great Macdermott, the music-hall singer Gilbert Hastings Macdermott.

MacDermot married twice: first, on 1 December 1861, Mary (*d.* 1871), daughter of Edward Howley, deputy lieutenant, of Belleek Castle, with whom he had three sons; and second, in 1872, Henrietta Maria, daughter of Henry Blake JP, with whom he had five sons. He died on 6 February 1904 at his home, 10 Fitzwilliam Place, Dublin, and was buried in the Catholic church, Monasteraden, co. Sligo.

DAVID FITZGERALD, *rev.* PETER GRAY

Sources A. T. C. Pratt, ed., *People of the period: being a collection of the biographies of upwards of six thousand living celebrities*, 2 vols. (1897) · *Annual Register* (1904) · *Irish Times* (8 Feb 1904) · *Freeman's Journal* [Dublin] (8 Feb 1904) · Burke, *Gen. GB*
Likenesses wood-engraving, NPG; repro. in *ILN* (3 Dec 1887)
Wealth at death £11,153 8s.—effects in England: Irish probate sealed in London, 9 June 1904, *CGPLA Ire.* · £34,311 13s.: probate, 30 March 1904, *CGPLA Ire.*

Macdermott, Gilbert Hastings (1845?–1901), music-hall entertainer, about whose background nothing is known, was originally surnamed Farrell. In 1869, after a period in the Royal Navy, he began his stage career as a 'utility' actor in Dover under the name Gilbert Hastings. He moved to London probably in 1870, where he adopted the name G. H. Macdermott, and immediately had considerable success as a melodramatic actor. In 1874–6 he accompanied the *opéra bouffe* artiste Julia Matthews to America as stage-

Gilbert Hastings Macdermott (1845?–1901), by unknown photographer

manager and actor. He also enjoyed some success as a playwright with melodramas, including *The Headsman's Axe* (1870), *Driven from Home* (1871), and *Brought to Book* (1876).

Although Macdermott maintained a strong interest in the theatre—he wrote the successful comedy *Racing* for the Grand, Islington, as late as 1887—his ultimate reputation was made on the music-hall stage. His début came at the London Pavilion in 1873, when he sang Henry Pettitt's 'If ever there was a damned scamp', adopting the performance style of the *lions comiques*, comic singers who both celebrated and burlesqued the habits of the leisured upper-class male and his imitators. The song which made him literally a household name was the composition by George William *Hunt, published as 'Macdermott's Warsong' but invariably termed 'The Jingo Song'. Probably first performed on 2 May 1877, it dealt with the threat posed to Britain's Mediterranean interests by Russia's declaration of war against Turkey. Its chorus, beginning 'We don't want to fight, but by jingo if we do', was adopted as the anthem of Conservative Party factions pressing for naval action against Russia. Macdermott was accused by Liberal politicians of being in the tories' pay and, while there is no evidence that this was the case, he certainly appreciated the commercial possibilities, particularly in West End halls, stemming from broad support of their policies and criticism of their opponents. Later successes, for example, included a second war song, 'Waiting for the Signal' (1878), and 'True Blue for Ever' (1879) and 'The Flower our Hero Loved' (1881), both celebrations of the life of Benjamin Disraeli.

While 'the Great Macdermott', as he was increasingly billed, continued to use political material throughout the remainder of his career, his repertory incorporated much else besides. With the aid of Hunt and his other major songwriters, he became a master of the not always subtle *double entendre* in songs such as 'Turn off the Gas at the Meter', concerning a miserly Scot and his young house-maid, the chorus to which ended 'Every night he would go, to the regions below, to turn off the gas at the meter'. His unsurprising lack of popularity with critics of music-hall morality was more than matched by his massive pop-ularity with audiences. In the mid-1880s he was earning £60 per week for London engagements and an average of £1200 to £1500 per annum. He went bankrupt in 1885 after losing money in a theatre building project, the situation compounded, as *The Era* reported, because 'the balance of his earnings over and above his living expenses had been lost on horse racing'. His career began to wane, and he eventually left the music-hall stage in 1894. He wrote a number of successful music-hall sketches at about this time, notably the patriotic 'Our Lads in Red' (1894), many of which featured his second wife, Annie Milburn. He then moved into management: he bought the Hoxton Theatre of Varieties and the Foresters' Music Hall and, in 1899, became the managing director of the South London Palace. He also worked as a music-hall agent in the 1890s.

Macdermott died of cancer at his home, 240 Clapham Road, London, on 8 May 1901 and was buried at West Nor-wood at a service well attended by members of the music-hall profession, testimony to his important role in the industry's history. While allowing for the licence that often decorates obituaries, *The Era* was probably not claiming too much when it stated that, at his height, he 'attained to a position never reached by any previous per-former on the variety boards'. Although he was not par-ticularly innovative in terms of style or content, his suc-cess in the late 1870s and early 1880s, above all with 'The Jingo Song', helped considerably to raise the profile of the music-hall in the public consciousness.

DAVE RUSSELL

Sources *The Era* (6 May 1877) · *The Era* (8 Aug 1885) · *The Era* (11 May 1901) · *The Era* (18 May 1901) · G. H. Macdermott and D. Braham, *Macdermott's comic song album* [1891–2]
Likenesses photograph, repro. in *The Era* (11 May 1901) · photo-graph, V&A [*see illus.*] · twenty-five prints, Harvard TC

MacDermott, John Clarke, Baron MacDermott (1896–1979), lord chief justice of Northern Ireland, was born in Belfast on 12 April 1896, the third surviving son and sixth of seven children of Revd John MacDermott DD, minister of Belmont and moderator of the Presbyterian Church in Ireland, and his wife, Lydia Allen, daughter of Robert Wil-son, solicitor, of Strabane. Educated at Campbell College, Belfast, and awarded a scholarship at Queen's University (1914), before reading law there he served in the machine

gun battalion (51st Highland division) in France, and won the MC (1918). In 1921 he graduated LLB (with a first class and the Dunbar Barton prize). He was Victoria prizeman and exhibitioner at King's Inns, Dublin, and, with first-class honours in his bar final, was called to the bar in both Dublin and Belfast.

Endowed with ability, learning, and industry, MacDermott's progress was sure. His sense of relevance, his courteous but firm approach, pleasant and clear voice, and his impressive appearance, constituted a formidable armoury. His height was 6 feet 4 inches, his face hand-some and strong and his turn-out impeccable (but without a hint of pride or affectation). In 1926 he married Louise Palmer, daughter of the Revd John Corry Johnston DD, another moderator of the general assembly; they had two sons (one a High Court judge in Northern Ireland from 1973 and the other a Presbyterian minister) and two daughters. He lectured in jurisprudence at Queen's Uni-versity 1931–5 while conducting a busy practice. On taking silk in 1936, he was immediately as busy as ever.

In 1938 MacDermott entered the parliament of North-ern Ireland as a Unionist member for Queen's University but joined the army as a major RA in 1939. After Dunkirk he was released at government request to be minister of public security (in which post he showed resolution and also an organizing genius typical of the man but unusual in his profession) and was sworn of the privy council of Northern Ireland in 1941. Appointed attorney-general in 1941 and a High Court judge in 1944, his judicial quality was soon apparent. In 1947 he became a privy councillor, a life peer, and the first lord of appeal appointed from Northern Ireland. Frequently in the minority, many of his dissenting speeches exemplify the quality of his legal thinking.

With his roots still in Belfast, MacDermott was happy to accept appointment as lord chief justice of Northern Ire-land (1951–71) when a vacancy arose on the death of Sir James Andrews. He still sat occasionally in London, and on retirement often sat as an additional judge, devoting him-self largely to wardship, an interest fostered by his love of family and curiosity about human nature. As a judge, he was inspired by a deep sense of right and wrong based on Christian standards. Knowing every branch of the law, he was its master, not just its servant. His eye for the merits and his sense of justice, while not causing him to spurn the law (which he loved and respected), helped him to reach the goal by way of the law and not in spite of it.

Although he inspired affection, MacDermott was often severe. To those who did not know him, and to some who did, he was not only formidable but frightening, an impression not lessened by his dominating presence. Some felt that, appointing himself the agent of retribu-tion, he adopted as his text the words 'Whom the Lord loveth he correcteth.' A more accurate summation of his philosophy would be 'Train up a child the way he should go, and when he is old, he will not depart from it.' Slack-ness he could not tolerate. Not to do your best was a fault; not to do your best and be paid for it was a crime. But, while censorious of minor failings, he was generous, compassionate, and understanding when the trouble was real. Strong in his views, he could be magnanimous in argument. The enjoyment of conversation which he experienced and imparted was obvious and infectious. Fond of travel, he would render a fascinating account of his latest expedition, which showed his ability to assimilate facts and ideas. He was a practical expert, as befitted an old machine-gunner, knew about cameras and car engines, and was a first-class woodworker.

MacDermott's courage was shown when, aged over eighty, he offered in 1977 to redeliver at the Ulster College a lecture interrupted by a bomb meant for him which had severely wounded him. In 1957 he chose as his subject for the Hamlyn lectures 'Protection from power' and therein merged two favourite themes: the importance of the rule of law and the rights and personality of the individual. He maintained with enthusiasm the connection with Gray's Inn, which had elected him an honorary bencher in 1947; he was also an honorary bencher of King's Inns and an honorary LLD of Queen's University (1951), Edinburgh (1958), and Cambridge (1968). He was chairman of the committee on road and rail transport in Northern Ireland (1939), the National Arbitration Tribunal (1944–6), the commission on the Isle of Man constitution (1958), and the Northern Ireland branches of the Multiple Sclerosis Society and the Cancer Research Centre. He was Northern Ireland president of the Boys' Brigade, a governor of Campbell College (1934–59), and pro-chancellor of Queen's University (1951–69).

MacDermott died at home in Belfast on 13 July 1979.

LOWRY, *rev.*

Sources J. C. MacDermott, *An enriching life* (privately published, 1980) · personal knowledge (1986) · private information (1986) · *WWW* · *Daily Telegraph* (17 July 1979)
Likenesses photograph, Judges' Assembly Room, Belfast · portrait, Bar Library, Belfast

MacDermott, Martin (1823–1905), poet and architect, was born of Roman Catholic parents at 8 Ormond Quay, Dublin, on 8 April 1823. His father, John MacDermott (1785–1842), was a merchant; his mother, Amelie Therese Boshell, was of French descent. He was educated as a Catholic in Dublin and Boulogne, but became a protestant in early life.

MacDermott was articled to Patrick Byrne RHA, a well-known Dublin architect, but his studies were interrupted by participation in the Young Ireland movement. He often contributed poems to *The Nation* and the *Irish Felon* under the pseudonym of M.M^cD from 1840 onwards. When in 1848 the Young Irelanders tried to gain the support of the French government in their struggle for Irish independence, MacDermott represented *The Nation* in the delegation sent to Paris to interview Lamartine, then foreign minister in the new republican government. Lamartine made the delegation a glowing speech of welcome but published so disappointingly colourless a report of the interview in the official *Moniteur* as to convince them of the impossibility of practical help.

MacDermott remained in Paris as the representative of *The Nation*, but soon after its suppression in 1848 went to Birkenhead, where he completed his training in a local architect's office. In 1850, he entered the London office of Charles Liddell, and was employed chiefly on the stations of the Metropolitan Railway extension. In 1860 MacDermott married Martha Melladew of Liverpool, and they went on to have nine children. Shortly after marriage, he obtained the post of chief architect to the Egyptian government, and spent some years in Alexandria from 1866 onwards. Twelve years later he retired and settled in London.

MacDermott's subsequent years were devoted to literary work. In 1860 he translated a work by Viollet-le-Duc as *Essay on the Military Architecture of the Middle Ages*, which was revised and reissued as *Military Architecture* in 1879, and ran to a third edition in 1907. A close friend of Sir Charles Gavan Duffy, from 1892 to 1895 MacDermott helped him with the New Irish Library scheme, a series of books designed to continue the successful National Library inaugurated in 1843. For the series, MacDermott edited an anthology of Irish poetry called *The New Spirit of the Nation* (1894). His collection was reissued as *Songs and Ballads of Young Ireland* in 1896, and published in the Masterpiece Library series in 1899. In 1897 MacDermott edited and prefaced Thomas Moore's *The Memoirs of Lord Edward Fitzgerald*, which became a classic nationalist account of the Irish rising of 1798.

MacDermott died at his residence at Cotham, Bristol, on 25 April 1905. He was survived by three sons and three daughters. Two of MacDermott's poems, 'The Coulin' and 'Exiles Far Away', achieved great popularity. He was represented in Stopford Brooke's and T. W. Rolleston's bestselling *Treasury of Irish Poetry in the English Tongue* (1905) by 'Girl of the Red Mouth'.

D. J. O'DONOGHUE, *rev.* KATHERINE MULLIN

Sources D. J. O'Donoghue, *The poets of Ireland: a biographical dictionary with bibliographical particulars*, 1 vol. in 3 pts (1892–3) · S. A. Brooke and T. W. Rolleston, *A treasury of Irish poetry in the English tongue* (New York, 1923) · C. G. Duffy, *Young Ireland*, 2 vols. (1880–83) · *Freeman's Journal* [Dublin] (27 April 1905) · private information (1912)

MacDhomhnaill, Somhairle Buidhe. *See* MacDonnell, Sorley Boy (*b.* in or before 1508, *d.* 1590).

MacDhomnuill, Raonuill [Ranald MacDonald; called Raonuill Dubh] (*b.* 1728, *d.* after 1807), folklorist, was the son of Alexander *MacDonald (Alasdair Mac Mhaighstir Alasdair) (*c.*1695–*c.*1770), the Gaelic poet, and his wife, Jean MacDonald of the Dalness family. He took his father's place as SPCK schoolmaster in Ardnamurchan in 1744, and his youngest sister was born while the family was on the run, after the battle of Culloden, in 1746 or early 1747.

MacDhomnuill was the compiler of the first printed collection of Scottish Gaelic songs, which he titled *Comhchruinneachadh orannaigh Gaidhealach le Raonuill MacDomhnuill ann 'n eilean Eigg, vol. 1* (1776), now usually referred to as the Eigg Collection. His English introduction makes it clear that his book was the first produced in response to the revival of interest in the Ossianic legends and in Gaelic verse, aroused by the publication of James MacPherson's *Temora* in 1763. MacDhomnuill dedicated his book to the advocate James Grant (*c.*1743–1835) of Coriemony, who later wrote *Thoughts on the Origin and Descent of the Gael* (1814) and discussed the Ossianic question. MacDhomnuill's second volume was never completed; according to his introduction to the first, it was to have contained 'poems of much older date than these of the first', and might well have included genuine Ossianic ballads, such as were later collected and printed by J. F. Campbell of Islay.

In 1776 MacDhomnuill was living on the island of Eigg as tacksman or tenant of the farm of Laig, the lease of which he had obtained from Old Clanranald before 1766. In the introduction to his book he refers to having 'been at much labour and expense, during the course of two years, in collecting the poems now offered to the public'. It is clear from the variations in orthography that he must have collected them from a variety of sources. Colm Ó Baoill has shown that five of them were probably copied from the collection of Dr Hector MacLean of Grulin, on the island of Mull, which was taken to Nova Scotia in 1819 by John MacLean, the Tiree bard, and is now in the public archives of Halifax, Nova Scotia. The interest of Raonuill MacDhomnuill and his father in MacLean's poetry was probably based on their personal acquaintance with the Revd John MacLean, minister of Kilninian (the part of Mull nearest to Ardnamurchan) from 1702 to 1752; Alasdair Mac Mhaighstir Alasdair's poem in praise of the Gaelic language was clearly influenced by the Revd John MacLean's poem addressed to Edward Lhuyd, printed in the latter's *Archaeologia Britannica* (1707).

The Eigg Collection contains 106 Gaelic poems totalling 9681 lines of Gaelic verse, plus a few translations. Among the most important poems are seven composed by, and three later attributed to, Raonuill's father; of these, seven were not included in the 1751 edition of Alasdair Mac Mhaighstir Alasdair's poetry. The most important of the ten is the 566-line poem on the voyage of Clanranald's galley from Loch Eynort in South Uist to Carrickfergus in Ulster, of which there is also a manuscript version in the library of the Royal Irish Academy.

The Swiss geologist Necker de Saussure visited the island of Eigg in 1807 and met Raonuill MacDhomnuill while sitting out a storm that had delayed his crossing to Rum. Saussure wrote that nothing was more singular than this good old man's way of life; he had the tone, the manners of an already long-past epoch, and of a generation which would soon disappear. He recorded that MacDhomnuill had planted the only trees growing on the island of Eigg, and described how he sang Gaelic songs, some of which imitated bagpipe music. MacDhomnuill also showed Saussure a Gaelic manuscript which had belonged to his grandfather. Editions of the Eigg Collection appeared in 1782 and 1809, the latter edited by Peter Turner, who published his own collection of Gaelic poetry in 1813; Turner was a well-known collector of Gaelic manuscripts, and may have acquired those belonging to

MacDhomnuill. Raonuill MacDhomnuill's name is not among the list of Turner's subscribers, which suggests that he had died before Turner's book was projected.

J. L. CAMPBELL

Sources R. MacDhomnuill, ed., *Comh-chruinneachadh orannaigh Gaidhealach* (1776) · L. A. Necker de Saussure, *Voyage en Écosse et aux îles Hébrides*, 2 (Geneva, 1821), pt 2, 471–5 [10 Sep 1807] · J. L. Campbell, 'The early printed sources of Scottish Gaelic poetry. 1. The Eigg Collection', *An Gaidheal*, 28, 162–4 · C. Ó Baoill, 'Raghnall Dubh and Hector MacLean', *Scottish Gaelic Studies*, 12/2 (1976), 209–19 · Society in Scotland for Promoting Christian Knowledge minutes, Edinburgh RO, Edinburgh

MacDiarmada, Seán [John MacDermott] (1883–1916), Irish revolutionary, was born in Kiltyclogher, co. Leitrim, probably on 26 January 1884 (his birth was officially registered as 29 March, but his baptism is recorded as having taken place on 29 January), the son of Daniel MacDermott (*d.* 1913), a farmer, and his wife, Mary McMorrow. He was educated at Corradoona national school and, having twice failed to get into teacher training college, spent some time working in Scotland before returning to Ireland, where he learned bookkeeping and Irish at night school in Tullynamoyle, co. Cavan.

In 1905 MacDiarmada moved to Belfast, where he worked as a tram conductor and barman and became active in politics, joining the Ancient Order of Hibernians and the Gaelic League. He helped to organize the Dungannon clubs, the precursors to Sinn Féin; for the latter he was party organizer in its (unsuccessful) campaign in the 1908 North Leitrim by-election. About this time he was drawn to the revived Irish Republican Brotherhood (IRB). It is possible that he was sworn into the organization while still living at home, as his father was a member. He became a full-time organizer for the IRB in Dublin and enjoyed a strong friendship with Tom Clarke, alongside whom he was a prime mover in the power struggle for the leadership of the supreme council of the organization that took place in 1910–11. This battle was also over control of the IRB's journal, *Irish Freedom*, of which MacDiarmada became manager. This role, together with his secretaryship of the IRB and—of most significance—his membership, with Clarke, of its all-important three-man executive, put him in a powerful position. He and Clarke were responsible for creating the IRB military council, which planned the 1916 rising—plans that were unknown even to the brotherhood's supreme council.

In 1911 MacDiarmada organized demonstrations against loyalist displays during the king's visit. The following year he was left partially disabled by an illness often identified as polio, but which may have been tuberculosis of the right hip. His incapacity—he walked with a stick thereafter—was said to have sharpened his sense of purpose. He was instrumental in bringing the Gaelic League under the control of advanced nationalists in 1915, and his commitment to revolution received another boost when he was handed a four-month prison sentence with hard labour for his campaign against the recruitment of soldiers in Ireland for the British army in the First World War.

MacDiarmada's highest profile in Irish nationalism was achieved as an organizer of and participant in the Easter rising of 1916; he was one of the seven signatories of the proclamation of the provisional government of the Irish republic. The nationalism which he had always believed in and promoted was that of active revolution and the 'blood sacrifice' approach of Padraic Pearse; in a speech to members of the IRB in co. Kerry in 1914 MacDiarmada declared that 'Irish patriotic spirit will die forever unless a blood sacrifice is made in the next few years' (Boyce, 308), with the clear inference that some would have to offer themselves as martyrs. At the Dublin post office in 1916, injuries to others left the direction of the fight in his hands, and the final dispatch from the garrison has been attributed to him. After surrender he was singled out for particular ill treatment by certain guards, and was fatalistic: 'There will be executions; I suppose I will be shot; but the executions will create a reaction in this country that will wipe out the slavish pro-English spirit' (Travers, 37). He was duly executed by firing squad at Kilmainham gaol on 12 May, thus gaining martyrdom status; he was unmarried. His grave is in Arbour Hill cemetery, Dublin.

MacDiarmada was a popular figure, and an able recruiting sergeant for both the IRB and for the Irish Volunteers. He has been described as a man of charm, enthusiasm, and good looks, 'of average height, with strong, dark hair [and] well marked eyebrows over dark blue eyes' (Travers, 4). Latterly he wore a beard, but he reputedly borrowed a razor to shave with from a British soldier during his final incarceration, telling him, 'I have to make a nice corpse, you know' (Maclochlainn, 167). Appropriately for a former transport worker, the bus depot at Store Street, Dublin, was named after him in recognition of his role in 1916, though a full reappraisal of his significance had to wait until the 1960s when, in a series of radio lectures, F. X. Martin identified him as the 'mainspring' of the rising (Travers, 39). While the importance of his role in turning the IRB into a revolutionary unit was no longer in doubt by the early twenty-first century, he still awaited a full biographical study.   SALLY WARWICK-HALLER

Sources transcript of a radio broadcast, c.1940, by Thomas MacDonagh, NL Ire., MS 33,694/E · K. B. Nowlan, 'Tom Clarke, MacDermott, and the IRB', *Leaders and men of the Easter rising*, ed. F. X. Martin (1967) · M. Foy and B. Barton, *The Easter rising* (1999) · www.rootsweb.com/~fianna/history/east1916.html, 26 April 2001 · L. Óbroin, *Revolutionary underground and the story of the IRB, 1858–1924* (1976) · D. G. Boyce, *Nationalism in Ireland* (1982) · *Irish Freedom* (Nov 1910–Dec 1914) · T. W. Moody and others, eds., *A new history of Ireland, 6: Ireland under the Union, 1870–1921* (1996) · D. Lynch, *The IRB and the 1916 rising*, ed. F. O'Donoghue (1957) · P. F. Maclochlainn, *Last words* (1971) · C. J. Travers, 'Sean MacDiarmada', *Breifne*, 3/9 (1966), 1–40
Likenesses S. O'Sullivan, portrait, c.1930–1934, National Museum of Ireland, Dublin · A. Power, bronze bust, NG Ire. · photograph, repro. in *Oidreacht, 1916–1966* [a commemorative booklet] · photographs, Kilmainham gaol, Dublin · photographs, postcards, Kilmainham gaol, Dublin · portrait (shortly after death), Kilmainham gaol, Dublin

Macdiarmid, Sir Allan Campbell (1880–1945), steel manufacturer, was born at Glasgow on 18 August 1880, the youngest son of Allan Macdiarmid, a partner in a Glasgow merchants (James Anderson & Co.), and his wife, Elizabeth, *née* Tulloch. Educated at Kelvinside Academy in Glasgow, and then at Uppingham School, Macdiarmid declined to follow his two elder brothers to Cambridge and instead trained as an accountant with a local firm, McClelland, Ker & Co.

In 1909 Macdiarmid began his career in the steel industry, becoming company secretary to Stewart and Lloyds, a firm he was to be associated with throughout his career. It had been formed in 1903 as an Anglo-Scottish merger of two steel-tube producing interests: Stewart and Menzies on Clydeside and Lloyd and Lloyd of Birmingham. Profitable and relatively efficient, the combine produced about half the UK's output of steel-tube products and exported nearly one-half of its finished tubes and fittings. Controlled by family interests (the Stewarts in Scotland and the English Lloyd and Howard families) and commercially tough and competitive, the company, under its chairman, John G. Stewart, offered Macdiarmid both an opportunity and a training. He soon made his mark as a board-room adviser, making contributions to both accounting systems and some policy decisions.

In 1918 Macdiarmid joined the board of Stewart and Lloyds and immediately set up an important policy unit—the general purposes advisory committee. This organization helped the drive towards centralization and modernization in the 1920s. Macdiarmid's influence was felt in some pioneering improvements in information systems, which sought to give better control of capital requirements and cash flows. By the mid-1920s, Macdiarmid had become J. G. Stewart's most logical successor. When the latter died in 1925 he became briefly deputy chairman; then in June 1926 he was appointed chairman.

Macdiarmid now entered the most dynamic phase of his career as he pursued Stewart and Lloyds' long-term policy objectives. These included international competitiveness and a leading position in the domestic steel-tube business, based on the cheapest production of steel tubes in the country. These objectives had been traditional ones at Stewart and Lloyds, but Macdiarmid refined them for the more difficult era of the inter-war years.

> To these tasks he brought formidable supplies of guile, nerve and persistence. He became a pastmaster particularly at stonewalling and playing hard to get, exuding mystery or noncommittal helpfulness, taking a long view and plotting forward sequential moves well in advance. (*DSBB*)

Macdiarmid brokered important agreements to supply oil companies, absorbed rival tube makers, negotiated for both domestic and international cartels, and sought best-practice tube technology from the USA and Germany.

Stewart and Lloyds was relatively well-placed in the early 1920s. The older dynastic family elements within the firm, which had crippled many other steel firms, had given way at Stewart and Lloyds to professional managers, such as Macdiarmid. The firm's restrained financial policies meant that it had also avoided the kind of heavy debts that other firms had incurred in the brief post-war boom. However, Macdiarmid recognized that the firm's relative prosperity was threatened by its fragmented lay-out, which prevented the use of the newest tube technologies. Macdiarmid's answer was to build a major new integrated iron and tube works at Corby, Northamptonshire. This aimed to produce the cheapest bulk steel in Europe. For this undertaking a canny negotiator like Macdiarmid was able to utilize government support, which came in the form of advice, financial help (through the Bankers' Industrial Development Company (BID Co.), and protectionism. This enabled Stewart and Lloyds to build its works cheaply and to consolidate its hold on the steel-tube business, despite the opposition of some powerful voices within the industry, such as the United Steel Companies. There were some negative aspects. Corby was an ecological blot on the landscape and labour relations at the company were uninspired. Macdiarmid's critics found him rapacious, and his hard-nosed attitude to BID Co. and other firms, such as Colvilles, did not win him admirers everywhere. The company stood aloof from some important developments: it refused to affiliate, for example, to the new British Iron and Steel Federation (BISF), and was also choosy about following voluntary price controls set by the import duties advisory committee of the BISF. However, the Corby initiative was fortuitously well timed—it was built quickly and economically and came on stream at the end of 1934 as steel demand began to recover—and Stewart and Lloyds became one of the few British steel firms to break decisively and successfully from its Victorian past.

Within the firm Macdiarmid was an autocrat who by the early 1930s dominated the board-room. Like many of the old Victorian owner–managers, he acted as both chairman and managing director. Like them, he needed help, which came, notably, from leading managers such as Guy McClay and Francis McClure (his double brother-in-law), J. H. Lloyd (marketing), and R. Menzies Wilson (works management). One of Macdiarmid's sons, Niall, was also to become chairman and managing director of Stewart and Lloyds. However, the elder Macdiarmid was the dominating presence at the company, maintaining his position by the force of his personality and his successful policies. He evidently cared little for great wealth or social status. A shy man who disliked formal occasions and had no particular interest in religion, he had few commitments outside his family (which consisted of his wife, Grace Buchanan, née McClure, whom he had married in 1910, and two daughters and three sons). In business he found rewards in the pursuit of trade as a great intellectual game, in which his success could not be doubted. By the late 1930s Stewart and Lloyds was returning record profits. The approach of war had obviously helped: however, it was 'in many ways a copy book case of successful competitive strategy' (*DSBB*).

In the Second World War, Stewart and Lloyds became a major shell producer. Such was the level of demand, even activity in Scotland began to revive. Macdiarmid threw himself into the armaments drive with his usual energy, developing closer ties with Whitehall and giving some thought to the reconstruction of the industry after the war. He became president of the BISF in 1944, healing his former rift with that body. He was knighted in 1945. However, just as it looked as though he was about to emerge as an industrial statesman for the post-war steel industry, his career was ended by his death in London on 14 August 1945. He was survived by his wife.

GEOFFREY TWEEDALE

Sources J. S. Boswell, 'Macdiarmid, Sir Allan Campbell', *DSBB* · J. S. Boswell, *Business policies in the making: three steel companies compared* (1983) · S. Tolliday, *Business, banking and politics: the case of British steel, 1918–1939* (1987) · D. L. Burn, *The economic history of steelmaking, 1867–1939* (1940) · J. C. Carr and W. Taplin, *History of the British steel industry* (1962) · *CGPLA Eng. & Wales* (1946)
Archives British Steel East Midlands Regional Records Centre, Irthlingborough, Stewart & Lloyd records
Wealth at death £111,217 12s. 4d.: probate, 15 Jan 1946, *CGPLA Eng. & Wales*

MacDiarmid, Hugh. *See* Grieve, Christopher Murray (1892–1978).

Macdiarmid, John (1779–1808), journalist and author, was born at Weem, Perthshire, where his father, James Macdiarmid (1743–1828), was parish minister. His mother was Catherine, only child of John Buik, minister of Tannadice, Forfarshire. A brother, James, was an officer in the army. After receiving elementary education at home, he studied at Edinburgh and St Andrews Universities, and for a short time was a private tutor. In 1801 he settled in London, where he wrote for various periodicals, and edited the *St James's Chronicle*. When war with France broke out in 1802 he especially studied the subject of national defence, and in 1805 published, in two volumes, *An Enquiry into the System of National Defence in Great Britain*, deprecating the substitution of volunteers for a strong standing army. In 1806 appeared his *Enquiry into the Principles of Civil and Military Subordination*, soon after which he suffered a paralytic stroke. In spite of it, with the help of a friend, he was able to publish in 1807 his best-known work, *Lives of British Statesmen*, reprinted in 1820 and 1838, comprising the biographies of Sir Thomas More, Lord Burleigh, Lord Stafford, and Lord Clarendon. A second stroke and paralysis, however, proved fatal, and Macdiarmid died in poverty in London on 7 April 1808.

T. W. BAYNE, rev. NILANJANA BANERJI

Sources Allibone, *Dict.* · I. D'Israeli, *Miscellanies of literature*, new edn (1840) · Chambers, *Scots.* (1835)

M'Diarmid, John (1790–1852), newspaper editor, born at Glasgow, was the son of Hugh M'Diarmid, minister of the Gaelic church in Glasgow. After some education, mainly in Edinburgh, he became, at an early age, owing to his father's death, a clerk in an Edinburgh counting-house, whence he passed into the head office of the Commercial Bank, Edinburgh, remaining there until 1817. He devoted his leisure to study, attending several classes in the university, and for two years spent his evenings as amanuensis to Professor John Playfair, who gave him access to his classes and his library. He was a distinguished member of a college debating society, and of the Edinburgh Forum, a club that helped to train many good speakers, and he wrote some clever verses. He formed friendships with Sir Walter

Scott and his circle. In 1819 he married Anne, *née* McKnight (*d.* 1850), of Dumfries.

On 25 January 1817 M'Diarmid joined Charles Maclaren and William Ritchie in preparing the first number of *The Scotsman* newspaper, and in the same month he moved to Dumfries to become editor of the *Dumfries and Galloway Courier*, which he edited until his death. M'Diarmid became an authority on Dumfriesshire, especially its agriculture, and wrote many attractive descriptions of his journeys about the county. In 1820 he declined the editorship of the *Caledonian Mercury* in Edinburgh, receiving at the same time an interest in the property of the *Courier*, of which he became owner in 1837. His paper followed the liberal political line common in lowland Scotland at that time. His son, William Ritchie M'Diarmid, became a partner in the paper in 1843.

When, in September 1832, Dumfries suffered heavily from cholera, M'Diarmid's appeal for a relief fund brought in £2900, which he skilfully distributed. He was the trusted adviser of Robert Burns's widow, Jean, until her death in 1834, when he was her executor. M'Diarmid published editions, with memoirs, of William Cowper (1817) and Oliver Goldsmith (1823). In 1820 the first volume of his *Scrap Book*, consisting of selections and original contributions, appeared. A second series speedily followed, and both were frequently reprinted. In 1825 he started the *Dumfries Magazine*, which ran for three years. In 1830 he reprinted *Sketches from Nature* from the *Courier*, and in 1832 he contributed to an *Illustrated Picture of Dumfries*, an account of the town and district. He also wrote a description of Moffat and a life of William Nicholson (1782–1849), the Galloway poet.

M'Diarmid died of erysipelas at Dumfries on 18 November 1852, and was buried next to his wife in Dumfries cemetery.   T. W. BAYNE, *rev.* H. C. G. MATTHEW

Sources *Dumfries and Galloway Courier* (30 Nov 1852) · *Dumfries and Galloway Courier* (7 Dec 1852) · Irving, *Scots.* · Chambers, *Scots.* (1868–70) · W. Anderson, *The Scottish nation*, 3 vols. (1866–77) · *Memoir of John McDiarmid* (1853)

MacDonagh, Terence (*d.* 1713), army officer, lawyer, and politician, was born in Creevagh, Kilmactranny, co. Sligo, the second son of Terence (Turlough) MacDonagh (*fl.* 1640–1656), administrator, of Creevagh, and his wife, Mary, daughter of Tadhg Ó hUigínn (Higgins) of co. Sligo. This branch of the MacDonaghs had retained their lands, or part of them, for much of the seventeenth century. Nothing is known of Terence's early years, but during the 1650s he appears to have served overseas as a lieutenant, in Charles II's interest, and returned to Ireland on the restoration of the monarchy in 1660. He received grants of land in the barony of Gallen, co. Mayo, under the restoration settlement, and was sufficiently wealthy in later years to purchase the interest of the Cromwellian grantee of his father's lands at Creevagh. About 1670 he married Mary O'Rorke (*d. c.*1740), who came from a prominent Gaelic Irish family. They had no children.

Having been admitted to the Middle Temple in 1683 as Terence Donno of Creevagh (at a time when he must have been over forty), MacDonagh seems to have practised law with some success, and was one of several Catholic barristers who became king's counsel after the accession of James II. In the Williamite war (1689–91) he was once again in arms, serving as a captain in Colonel Henry Dillon's regiment of infantry. Given command of a garrison at Ballymote Castle, co. Sligo, he was to earn respect for his determination and loyalty, if not for his military abilities. He provided poor intelligence for Jacobite forces under Patrick Sarsfield, which led to an ill-prepared attempt to take Ballyshannon. MacDonagh himself was in command of an infantry party providing cover for field guns firing into the town. After the Jacobites were routed by Enniskilleners under Thomas Lloyd, MacDonagh was taken prisoner, which was a considerable blow to Jacobite morale in co. Sligo. He was released in an exchange of prisoners forced on Gustavus Hamilton, governor of Enniskillen, by Patrick Sarsfield's detention of all co. Sligo's protestants. After his release he seems to have travelled to Dublin to sit in James II's Irish parliament as member for Sligo borough, of which he was already a burgess under the new charter granted by Tyrconnel in 1687. Like the majority of MPs he supported enthusiastically legislation for the restoration of former Catholic proprietors, despite James II's anxieties about its propaganda value to his erstwhile subjects in England. A later anecdote has MacDonagh standing in the Commons lobby and declaring in Tyrconnel's hearing, with his hand on the hilt of his sword, that its unsheathing 'would be in defence of the rights and privileges of an Irish parliament' (MacDonagh, 'Counsellor Terence MacDonagh [pt 1]', 310).

Promoted to lieutenant-colonel, MacDonagh continued to serve in north-west Ireland, being present for a time at the siege of Londonderry, and holding Ballymote Castle until 1690. He was stationed in Sligo when it capitulated to Williamite forces in September 1691. The Jacobite garrison was permitted to join the Irish army at Limerick, and was subsequently covered by both the civil and military articles of the treaty of Limerick (October 1691).

His army days over, MacDonagh returned to co. Sligo and his legal practice. Using his legal skills to maximum benefit he petitioned for permission to practise on the basis of both the articles of Limerick and a provision in the Westminster act appointing new oaths for Ireland. Later he was among a number of claimants seeking adjudication under the articles of Limerick. By whatever means, he retained his lands in co. Mayo and co. Sligo, residing mainly at Creevagh and apparently also in Dublin. Occasionally he was the object of official suspicion. There were reports of his involvement in subversion in 1698 and again in 1708, when he was arrested during a Jacobite scare. In 1712 Edward Tyrrel, the priest-catcher, declared in the court of queen's bench that the Roman Catholic bishop of Killala, Tadhg O'Rorke, MacDonagh's brother-in-law, lived in his house, and a similar claim, that the titular bishop resided in 'counties Mayo and Sligo at counsellor MacDonagh's' (MacDonagh, 'Counsellor Terence Mac-Donagh [pt 1]', 316), was made by the Church of Ireland archbishop of Tuam. But MacDonagh was never charged with any infringement of the Bishops' Banishment Act, and seems to have lived relatively undisturbed until his death.

There is a folkloric quality to the tales of the legal prowess of MacDonagh the Great Counsellor. His other sobriquet, Blind MacDonagh, or in Irish, Turlogh Caech, is usually interpreted as indicating his blindness in one eye, but it may have arisen from a civil claim in which he successfully represented a young defendant sued by another youth, with whom he had been fishing, for having hooked out his eye when saving him from drowning in a swollen river. Less flatteringly MacDonagh was the subject of an eleven-verse street ballad, 'The Young Squire, or, The Counsellor Outwitted', in which he was mocked for having inadvertently advised his manservant on avoiding the legal penalties of elopement, only to find that the woman in question was his niece, Dolly MacDonagh.

MacDonagh's main claim to fame as a lawyer rests on his role in the successful restoration of lands (about 700 acres) to his brother-in-law Donogh O'Conor, father of Charles O'Conor of Belanagare. Sometimes represented as a legal triumph over a rapacious protestant landowner, John French of Frenchpark, it seems in fact to have been a collusive settlement, arranged by MacDonagh, within the letter if not the spirit of the law. The debt to MacDonagh was not forgotten in subsequent O'Conor historiography.

In his day MacDonagh had a reputation for generosity to the surviving Gaelic poets, Catholic clergy, and not least the impoverished scholar Roderick O'Flaherty. MacDonagh himself wrote poetry in Irish, including a satire on his brother Eoin and other neighbouring landowners who had conformed to the established church. When he died in May 1713 at least two poets wrote verse grieving at the loss. A lament for Terence MacDonagh is attributed to Torlach Carolan. His wife, who survived him by many years, was sole beneficiary of his will, which was unspecific about the extent of 'my real and personal estates' (O'Rorke, 2.232). He was buried in Ballindoon Abbey. A memorial slab commissioned by his wife in 1737 was moved from Belanagare in 1819 by members of the MacDonagh family and placed over his tomb.

JAMES MCGUIRE

Sources J. C. MacDonagh, 'Counsellor Terence MacDonagh [pt 1]', *Studies: an Irish Quarterly Review*, 36 (1947), 307–18 · T. O'Rorke, *The history of Sligo: town and county*, 2 vols. (1892) · D. O'Sullivan, *Carolan: the life, times and music of an Irish harper*, 2 vols. (1958) · H. A. C. Sturgess, ed., *Register of admissions to the Honourable Society of the Middle Temple, from the fifteenth century to the year 1944*, 3 vols. (1949) · C. O'Conor, 'Charles O'Conor of Belanagare: an Irish scholar's education', *Studies: an Irish Quarterly Review*, 23 (1934), 124–43 · P. Wauchope, *Patrick Sarsfield and the Williamite war* (Blackrock, co. Dublin, 1992) · R. Doherty, *The Williamite war in Ireland, 1688–1691* (Dublin, 1998) · C. C. Trench, *Grace's card: Irish Catholic landlords, 1690–1800* (Cork, 1997) · J. C. MacDonagh, 'Counsellor Terence MacDonagh [pt 2]', *Studies: an Irish Quarterly Review*, 37 (1948), 65–74

MacDonagh, Thomas Stanislaus (1878–1916), poet and critic, was born on 1 February 1878 in Cloughjordan, co. Tipperary, one of the eight children of Joseph MacDonagh (1834–1894), a schoolteacher, and his wife, Mary, née Parker (d. 1908), also a teacher. His parents were both Roman Catholics; his mother, formerly a protestant, had converted before her marriage. MacDonagh inherited his good humour from his father, his literary leanings from his mother, and from an early age displayed a lively imagination, delighting in jokes, riddles, and ghost stories. He also developed an interest in poetry and put together small books of rhymes.

At fourteen MacDonagh was sent to Rockwell College, near Cashel, co. Tipperary, founded by the Holy Ghost Fathers, a French religious order. A junior scholasticate attached to the college prepared priests for missionary work. Academically, the school had a good record and MacDonagh was a conscientious though not outstanding student. In 1894, the year of his father's death, he decided to enter religious life. As a novice he wore the clerical garb of the order and taught English, French, and Latin to junior pupils, but in 1901 he abandoned his studies for the priesthood and left Rockwell.

MacDonagh's next teaching post was at St Kieran's College, Kilkenny. There he joined the Gaelic League, receiving his 'baptism in Nationalism' (Parks and Parks, 8) and in 1902 he visited the Aran Islands to improve his command of spoken Gaelic. MacDonagh's first book of poetry, *Through the Ivory Gate*, had been published at his own expense in 1902. It was dedicated to W. B. Yeats to whom he had sent the manuscript, requesting advice. Yeats advised against publication because he felt that MacDonagh had not found himself as a poet. A second book, *April and May*, followed in 1903. Religion, nationalism, beauty, and nature were the dominant themes in these early efforts and were to recur in his later work. In 1903 he began teaching at St Colman's College, Fermoy, co. Cork. A sacred cantata, *The Exodus*, for which he wrote the lyrics, won the prize at the 1904 Dublin Feis Ceoil, and in 1908 he published another book of poetry, *The Golden Toy*.

In 1908 MacDonagh joined Patrick Pearse as assistant head teacher at the newly established St Enda's school for boys in Dublin, where all aspects of Gaelic culture were enthusiastically promoted and Irish plays and pageants were regularly performed. MacDonagh was himself a playwright but he made little lasting impact. *When the Dawn is Come*, performed at The Abbey in 1908, depicts an Irish rising against English rule and centres on the antagonism between two of the leaders. One reviewer described it as the 'first Sinn Féin drama' and hailed it as the best Abbey production for two years (Parks and Parks, 102–3). Pupils of St Enda's returned from a performance 'yearning for rifles' (ibid., 104). All told, however, the play was not deemed to be a success.

By this time, in addition to his several volumes of poetry, MacDonagh had published articles in such journals as *The Nation* (London), *The Leader*, and *T. P.'s Weekly*. He was well known in Dublin literary and theatrical circles, with friends and acquaintances including Padraic Colum, James Stephens, George Russell (A. E.), Arthur Griffith, and James Connolly. His closest friends were Pearse and Joseph Plunkett. In appearance, MacDonagh was of stocky build with brown hair, grey eyes, a prominent nose, and a friendly expression. On formal occasions he wore a kilt. He was active on many fronts. In 1909 he was a founder member of the Association of Secondary Teachers of Ireland. He was also a member of both the Irish Women's Franchise League and the National Literary Society, but he had become disillusioned with the Gaelic League.

In 1910 MacDonagh was awarded a BA, having studied part-time at University College, Dublin, and spent time in Paris studying French literature and philosophy. *Songs of Myself* (1910), the title reflecting Walt Whitman's influence, included two of MacDonagh's best poems, 'John-John' and 'Envoi'. A year later he received an MA for his thesis 'Thomas Campion and the art of poetry' and with Colum, Stephens, and David Houston founded the monthly *Irish Review*. Later in the year he was appointed lecturer in English at University College, Dublin.

In 1910 MacDonagh's love affair with Mary Maguire (later to marry Colum) ended. A relationship with Muriel Gifford led to marriage on 3 January 1912. Muriel Gifford was one of twelve children of a mixed marriage and had been brought up as a protestant. MacDonagh considered that he and his wife were of the same religion, neither Catholic nor protestant, and they attended neither church nor chapel (Parks and Parks, 28). Her parents did not approve of the marriage, but the couple set up house at 32 Baggot Street near St Stephen's Green, later moving to 29 Oakley Road in Ranelagh, a southside suburb. A son, Donagh, was born in November 1912 and a daughter, Barbara, in 1915.

MacDonagh's second play, *Metempsychosis*, was staged in the Theatre of Ireland in 1912. A satire on theosophy and reincarnation, it had as one of the central characters Lord Winton Winton de Winton, a caricature of Yeats. Reviews were poor. In the meantime the *Irish Review* was plagued by money troubles and in 1913 Plunkett assumed the financial burden and replaced Colum as editor.

During the momentous industrial dispute that shook Dublin in 1913 MacDonagh was a member of the Dublin Industrial Peace Committee. Giving evidence to an inquiry into disturbances during the dispute, he told of a street riot where he heard the 'continual rapping of [police] batons on people's heads' (Kee, 2.199).

Lyrical Poems (1913) is MacDonagh's most accomplished work and combined a selection of old and new poems, most notably 'The night hunt'. His 'Yellow bittern', a translation of 'An Bunán Buí' by the eighteenth-century poet Cathal Buí Mac Giolla Ghunna, showed real poetic advance. However, MacDonagh never fully matured as a poet. He tended to rush into print and his work suffered from insufficient revision. Much of his poetry was obscure and baffling, especially his mystical poems.

MacDonagh's MA thesis was published as *Thomas Campion and the Art of English Poetry* in 1913. A treatise on English metrics and rhyme, it asserted that there were two main types of English verse: song verse and speech verse; a third type, chant, lay somewhere between the two. The assumption that Campion was of Irish extraction was strongly disputed.

Through their involvement in amateur drama productions, MacDonagh and Plunkett became convinced of the need for a new professional theatre to stage Irish and continental drama. It was left to MacDonagh to get the project off the ground. Financed in large measure by Edward Martyn and managed by MacDonagh's brother John, the Irish Theatre finally opened in November 1914, but MacDonagh had little time for literary endeavour in the last two years of his life. Late in 1913 he joined the Irish Volunteers on their foundation and became a member of the central provisional committee. He wrote the 'Marching song of the Irish Volunteers' and, as commander of one of the four companies of the Dublin brigade, was active in overseeing the training of recruits. He also addressed recruiting rallies around the country and was involved in the Howth gun-running in 1914.

When the volunteers split over attitudes to the war, the Redmondite majority became known as the National Volunteers. The minority Irish Volunteers appointed a new headquarters staff with MacDonagh as director of training. He was confident that Irish freedom would be secured by 'zealous martyrs', through peace, he hoped, but by war if necessary (Parks and Parks, 52).

In 1915, the year that he was sworn into the Irish Republican Brotherhood (IRB), MacDonagh was a member of the committee that took charge of the funeral arrangements of the exiled Fenian Jeremiah O'Donovan Rossa, who had died in the United States. The IRB seized the opportunity to stage a militant nationalist pageant. The National Volunteers and the Irish Citizen Army took part. But it was the Irish Volunteers who fired the volley over the grave and Pearse who gave the oration. In a Rossa funeral souvenir, MacDonagh wrote of the volunteer's ideal 'that leads him now to battle, to sacrifice and to victory' (Parks and Parks, 55).

Pagans, based on the poem 'John-John', was presented at the Irish Theatre in 1915. A literary drama, it explored the conflict between the conventional and bohemian philosophies of life. It was not without merit but was ill served by an inferior production.

MacDonagh took to turning up for classes at University College, Dublin, in uniform, complete with officer's sword. One of his students, Austin Clarke, remembered him placing a revolver on the desk during a lecture (Norstedt, 121). There were complaints and MacDonagh reverted to wearing civilian attire at work.

By spring 1916 the IRB's plans for revolt were well advanced. Irish volunteer activities were stepped up. There were frequent marches through the streets of Dublin and, when plans were announced for Easter Sunday manoeuvres, MacDonagh instructed all volunteers to turn up with full equipment. 'Boys' he told the men directly under his command, 'some of us may never come back' (Kee, 2.270). On hearing of Roger Casement's arrest in Kerry, the volunteers' chief-of-staff Eoin MacNeill issued eleventh-hour instructions rescinding the orders for Easter Sunday. Confusion ensued and a military council that included MacDonagh met on Sunday and determined that the rising would proceed the following day. MacDonagh was one of the seven signatories of the proclamation of the provisional government read by Pearse outside the

General Post Office at noon on Easter Monday. The rising, largely confined to Dublin, enjoyed little popular support. It quickly became clear that it would fail. MacDonagh, in command of the garrison at Jacob's biscuit factory which was near Dublin Castle, was initially reluctant to obey Pearse's order to surrender. Only when he was convinced that resistance was futile did he comply.

Courts martial were held without delay and on Tuesday 2 May, MacDonagh was tried and found guilty. A priest heard his confession in his cell at Kilmainham gaol and he also received communion. His only other visitor was his sister Mary, Sister Francesca of the Sisters of Charity. In a farewell letter to his wife MacDonagh wrote, 'I am ready to die, and I thank God that I die in so holy a cause. My Country will reward my dust richly' (Parks and Parks, 70). At 3.30 am on Wednesday 3 May he was executed by firing squad. His body was buried in an unmarked grave in Arbour Hill barracks the same day. His sister-in-law Grace Gifford married Joseph Plunkett hours before he too was executed.

MacDonagh's *Literature in Ireland: Studies Irish and Anglo-Irish* was published posthumously in 1916 and advanced an inclusive theory of the Irish literary tradition. MacDonagh rejected Arnold's 'Celtic note' in favour of the term, the 'Irish mode'. At its best, he contended, Irish literature in English had its own unique qualities that drew on race and nationality and which echoed the patterns and rhythms of Gaelic speech and song. The Anglo-Irish literature that mattered was the work of first-generation English speakers of rural origin. MacDonagh borrowed freely from the ideas of others but the strength of his literary criticism derived from his synthesis of these ideas and his passionate advocacy of them. *Literature in Ireland* broke new ground and continues to be of relevance.

The poet Francis Ledwidge, a member of the British army who died at Ypres in 1917, wrote an elegy 'He shall not hear the bittern cry' for MacDonagh. A. E., who did not support the rising, also paid tribute in 'Salutation', while Yeats, in 'Easter, 1916', wrote of MacDonagh's unfulfilled promise.

MacDonagh's widow, Muriel, was received into the Roman Catholic church at Easter 1917. She drowned in July of that year while swimming in the sea at Skerries, north of Dublin. The children were embroiled in a custody dispute between the MacDonagh and Gifford families that marred their childhood years. Thomas MacDonagh's son and a granddaughter continued the family literary tradition.   PATRICK GILLAN

Sources J. A. Norstedt, *Thomas MacDonagh: a critical biography* (1980) · E. W. Parks and A. W. Parks, *Thomas MacDonagh: the man, the patriot, the writer* (1967) · D. MacDonagh, 'Plunkett and MacDonagh', in F. X. Martin, *Leaders and men of the Easter rising, Dublin, 1916* (1967), 165–76 · R. Kee, *The green flag*, 3 vols.; *The bold Fenian men*, 2 (1976) · J. J. Lee, *Ireland 1912–1985: politics and society* (1989)
Archives NL Ire., corresp. and literary papers, MS 10843–10858 | NL Ire., Nuala MacDonagh papers · priv. coll., letters to Dominick Hackett
Likenesses O. Kelly, bronze bust, University College, Dublin, staff common room · O. Kelly, bronze bust, NG Ire. · S. O'Sullivan, pencil drawing, NG Ire.

Wealth at death £120; two children insured for £100 each to be paid at the age of twenty-one: letter, dated 2 May 1916, from MacDonagh to wife, cited Parks and Parks, *Thomas MacDonagh*, pp. 70–72

Mac Dónaill, Seán Clárach (1691–1754), Irish poet and scribe, was born near Charleville (Ráth Luirc), in northern co. Cork. The epithet 'Clárach' was apparently descriptive of his large forehead, and not a toponym linking him with co. Clare. In his youth he lived in the parish of Baile an Teampaill, co. Cork, moving to a farm and mill at Killtoohig (Cill Tuathaigh), south of Charleville, after his marriage. He may subsequently have lived in Charleville itself. Traditional sources record that his wife, Agnes White, was a protestant, and that the marriage was not a success. No information about his family has been traced.

Mac Dónaill himself records that he was educated alongside Richard Walsh, who later served as Catholic bishop of Cork from 1748 to 1763 and was a patron of Gaelic scholars and poets. It has been speculated that both were educated at the school established in Charleville by Roger Boyle, earl of Orrery. Mac Dónaill was certainly well educated and knew English, Latin, and Greek as well as his native Irish language. He was both a poet and a scribe. The few extant manuscripts in his hand contain historical material, including a 1720 transcript of Geoffrey Keating's *Foras feasa ar Éirinn*. According to Sylvester O'Halloran, his former student, Mac Dónaill was writing a history of Ireland in the Irish language towards the end of his life but illness prevented him from completing it. The bulk of his manuscripts were reputedly destroyed by the sheriff's men.

Mac Dónaill became chief of the court of poetry at Ráth Luirc and maintained contact with similar assemblies at Carraig na bhFear, co. Cork, and at Lios na Rígh in Bruree in the neighbouring county of Limerick. These assemblies were social gatherings as well as cultural and perhaps political occasions. Mac Dónaill's poetic associates included Seán Ó Tuama, Aindréas Mac Craith, Nioclás Ó Dónaill OFM, Liam Inglis, Liam Rua Mac Coitir, and Liam dall Ó hIfearnáin. Over sixty of his Irish poetic compositions survive, and he features in more than a dozen poems by his contemporaries, including songs lamenting his death written by Seán na Ráithíneach, Seán Ó Tuama, and Éamonn de bhFál. Mac Dónaill wrote political poetry in Irish in support of the Jacobite cause. Many of these poems were set to popular tunes and provided commentary, sometimes allegorical, on contemporary political developments. His vision poems continually expressed confidence in the Jacobite cause, even after the defeat at Culloden in 1746. He also used poetry to support the attempt by young Robert, earl of Clancarty, to regain the MacCarthy family's estates in 1735. He engaged in poetic controversy with Eoghan Ó Caoimh, a Cork poet many years senior to him, and later with another Munster poet, Tadhg Gaelach Ó Súilleabháin. He composed poems in praise of and laments on the deaths of prominent local clergy and fellow poets and wrote informed songs about the war in Europe in the 1740s. To the tunes of well-known Jacobite airs he rejoiced in the triumphs of Philip V, king of Spain. A satire written after the death of James Dawson drew the wrath of the Dawson family and forced Mac Dónaill to leave his home temporarily about 1737–8. Some sources suggest that he spent time overseas, but a poem composed by Seán Ó Tuama and the evidence of manuscript annotations indicate that he may simply have pretended to have left his home. Two 'exile' poems were composed in co. Tipperary and co. Clare respectively. His reputed role as a recruiting officer for the Jacobites would explain the need for him to be secretive about his movements.

After his death at Charleville on 7 January 1754 Mac Dónaill was buried at Holy Cross cemetery, Ballysallagh, close to Charleville, where the Latin inscription on his tombstone recorded that he had been 'a poet of no common genius'. BERNADETTE CUNNINGHAM

Sources R. Ó Foghladha, *Seán Clárach* (1932) · B. Ó Conchúir, *Scríobhaithe Chorcaí, 1700–1850* (1982), 17–19 · A. Heusaff, *Filí agus cléir san ochtú h-aois déag* (1992) · P. Ua Duinnín, *Amhráin Sheagháin Chláraigh Mhic Dhomhnaill* (1902) · B. Ó Buachalla, *Aisling ghéar: na Stiobhartaigh agus an t-aos léinn, 1603–1688* (1996) · P. Ó Héalaí, 'Seán Clárach Mac Dónaill', *Léachtaí Cholm Cille*, 4 (1975), 88–110 · É. Ó Ciardha, *Ireland and the Jacobite cause, 1685–1766: a fatal attachment* (2002)
Archives Royal Irish Acad., Irish MSS

MacDonald. For this title name *see* Macdonell, Alastair, of Glengarry, Jacobite first Baron MacDonald (*d.* 1724).

MacDonald family [MacDhomnaill, MacDonald de Ile] (*per. c.*1300–*c.*1500), magnates, ruled a semi-independent lordship or kingdom in the west coast and islands of Scotland, with the title *rí Innse Gall* ('king of the Hebrides') or *dominus insularum* ('lord of the Isles'). The titles appear to have been interchangeable, depending on which language was used. As late as 1549 a writer could refer to the 'lord of the Isles ore as the heighland men calls him king of the Isles' (*Monro's Description*, 92).

The MacDonalds and the lordship of the Isles Descended from Somerled, king of the Isles and lord of Argyll (*d.* 1164), the MacDonalds ruled over the varied and scattered series of communities stretching at the height of their power from the Butt of Lewis to the Mull of Kintyre, and linked by an intricate web of sea lanes through which their galleys could move widely in peace and in war. Their mainland territories were held from the king of Scots, and the islands (until they were ceded to Scotland under the treaty of Perth in 1266) from the king of Norway. The family separated into three great divisions—the MacDonalds based in Islay, the MacDougalls of Lorn, and the MacRuairis, whose lands of Garmoran by the fourteenth century, at least, extended from Moidart to Barra and the Uists. Overlordship passed by turns among the three kindreds, but the MacDougalls, by taking the Balliol side in the wars of independence owing to a Comyn relationship, lost in both land and influence, while the others supported Robert I and prospered.

Angus MacDonald [Angus Óg MacDonald] (*d.* 1314x18),

king of the Hebrides, was of Islay kindred. With his supporters he helped to win victory over the English at Bannockburn and was rewarded with lands in Lochaber, Ardnamurchan, Morvern, Duror, and Glencoe. He married an Irish chief's daughter, Aine Ni Cathan, and (as well as a daughter, Mary, who married William *Ross, fifth earl of Ross [*see under* Ross family]) had a son, **John MacDonald** (*d. c.*1387), who succeeded his father as king of the Hebrides, and was the first of four members of the family known to have adopted the designation *dominus insularum*, which he used in a letter to Edward III of England in 1336. His lands, with the custody of the royal castles of Cairnburgh Mor and Beg in the Treshnish Isles off Mull and Dunchonnuil in the Garvellochs, were confirmed to him by David II in 1343, and he consolidated the power of clan Donald over the other descendants of Somerled. This process was assisted by his two marriages, for which he obtained papal dispensations in 1337 and 1350 respectively. His first wife was Amie, sister of Ruairi of Garmoran, on whose death in 1346 she inherited all his lands, which were then joined with John's territories in Kintyre, Islay, and Mull, while the clan Ruairi was absorbed into clan Donald. In 1354 the possessions of John and his kinsman John (MacDougall) of Lorn were divided under an agreement that emphasized the latter's subordinate position. With Amie MacRuair, John had three sons, including Ranald (or Reginald) from whom the MacDonalds of Clanranald and Glengarry are descended.

John MacDonald's second wife was Margaret, daughter of Robert Stewart (who became king as *Robert II in 1371), and, while the MacRuairi lands went to Amie's son, it was **Donald MacDonald** (*d.* 1420x25), the eldest son of his father's marriage to Margaret Stewart, who succeeded as second lord of the Isles 'with the consent of his brethren and the nobles of the Isles' according to one family annalist, 'but contrary to the opinion of the men of the Isles' (Cameron, 161). As well as their own kindred, the lordship now comprised great clans like the Macleans and MacLeods, and lesser ones such as the MacKinnons and MacQuarries, and both groups had a share in the administration as well as in the territory of the Isles. Three of Donald's charters apparently composed in feudal form to his brother-in-law Lachlan Maclean of Duart (1390) and one to his nephew Hector Maclean (1409) are known through later crown confirmations; but the most singular survival in the original manuscript is the only specimen of a charter of the lord of the Isles (here signing McDomhnaill with no other designation) in the Gaelic language and traditional phrasing, granting lands in Islay to Brian Vicar Mackay in 1408. Donald's marriage to Mary, a daughter of Euphemia, countess of Ross in her own right, and her husband, Sir Walter Leslie, led to a claim to the Ross earldom in which Donald was opposed by the powerful Albany family, leading to the memorable but indecisive battle of Harlaw (1411) near Aberdeen.

Earls of Ross Although the earldom remained in the hands of the crown after the elimination of the Albany Stewarts in 1425, Donald's son and successor **Alexander MacDonald**, twelfth earl of Ross (*d.* 1449), styled himself 'lord of the isles and master [heirs] of the earldom of Ross' (Munro and Munro, 34) in a charter dated at Finlaggan (where he had a 'mansion' on an island in the loch) in 1427, while his mother was still living. The third lord of the Isles, Alexander, was one of the highland chiefs arrested when James I came to Inverness in 1428, but though taken to Perth he managed to escape, gathered his forces, and faced a royal army in Lochaber where he gave himself up without a battle, and after a humiliating submission at Edinburgh, 'clad only in short and drawers' (Bower, 8.488–90), in August 1429, was imprisoned in Tantallon Castle. In Alexander's absence his cousins Donald Balloch and Alasdair Carrach carried on the rebellion, and after their defeat of the king's army at Inverlochy in 1431, terms were agreed and Alexander was released. He kept within the law thereafter and co-operated with the crown, and shortly before the death of James I was issuing charters as fully established twelfth earl of Ross. He administered the lordship and earldom as a single unit, with one council including leading men of his own kin and other clans from both areas; and for a time he was justiciar north of the Forth. But his loyalty was less than wholehearted, if it was he who entered into an offensive and defensive league with the earls of Douglas and Crawford in 1445–6, with serious consequences that followed in the next generation. However, no evidence exists as to exactly which earls of Douglas, Ross, and Crawford were involved, nor of the contents of the bond, which may never have been written down. The only exact date assigned to the bond, 7 March 1445, comes from an unreliable seventeenth-century source, while 1450–51 has also been suggested, when Douglas was already threatened by James II, and Alexander's son was out of favour because of his Livingston connections.

Alexander MacDonald had a wife, Elizabeth (apparently a Haliburton of Dirleton, and not a Seton as has been supposed), but his sons Celestine of Lochalsh and Hugh of Sleat, whose descendants were to claim succession to the lordship, were not the children of any recorded marriage. His daughter, Florence, was the mother of Farquhar *Mackintosh [see under Mackintosh family (per. c.1491–1606)]. A Ross chronicle says that Alexander died at Dingwall on 9 May 1449, and was buried at the chanonry of Ross (Fortrose). His successor, as fourth lord of the Isles and thirteenth earl of Ross, was his lawful son **John MacDonald** (c.1434–1503), possibly still a minor. John's early marriage to Elizabeth, daughter of James Livingston of Callendar (d. 1467), chamberlain of Scotland, apparently took place with James II's encouragement shortly before her father's imprisonment in 1450, from which he escaped and took refuge with his son-in-law. The exact chronology of events is unclear, but it seems that John's revolt, during which he took the royal castles of Inverness, Urquhart, and Ruthven, strengthening the two former and demolishing the latter, took place on Livingston's behalf in the spring of 1451, when the king was already threatening the Douglases. This revolt was probably one of the causes, rather than the result, of the killing of the earl of Douglas on 22 February 1452, for which the bond between Douglas and MacDonald was the immediate excuse. There was no northern rising after the slaying, though raids in the Clyde region by John's cousin Donald Balloch may have taken place at this time at the request of the new earl of Douglas. James Livingston recovered his lands and office before the middle of 1454, as the king tried to build up support against the Douglases. The castles of Inverness and Urquhart were granted to Livingston for three years, and then to the lord of the Isles for life.

The end of the lordship The minority of James III saw unrest in Lorn and renewed pressure from the exiled earl of Douglas, who was used by the Yorkists in England when on the look-out for allies in the Wars of the Roses. Douglas promoted a treaty with John of the Isles (Donald Balloch and his son John being also associated) and Edward IV of England in 1461–2, by which the two Scots as vassals of King Edward agreed to divide Scotland between them. Three years later, after John had ravaged Inverness, a fifteen-year truce between the Scots and English left him free to make his peace with James III's government. When the truce with England was converted to a peace in 1474, the terms of the treaty of Westminster–Ardtornish (as it has been called) came to light, and John was forfeited, but on his renouncing the earldom of Ross, the lordships of Kintyre and Knapdale, and the sheriffships of Inverness and Nairn, he was pardoned, reinstated in 1476 in his other lands, and created a lord of parliament as lord of the Isles. Thereafter his hold on the lordship was uneasy. His only son, **Angus MacDonald** [Angus Óg MacDonald] (d. c.1490), rebelled against his father, and was supported by leaders of clan Donald, but after a sea battle at Bloody Bay off Mull they were reconciled. John still failed to control his people, and was finally forfeited in 1493, after a further rebellion led by his nephew Alexander MacDonald of Lochalsh. The former lord of the Isles died as a pensioner of the royal court while the king was at Dundee in 1503, survived by his wife and a daughter, Elizabeth.

Angus MacDonald, who had been recognized as his heir in 1476 and was using the style 'master of the Isles' in 1485, died before his father, allegedly murdered by an Irish harper at Inverness in 1490. Having married a daughter of the first earl of Argyll, Angus left a son, Donald Dubh *MacDonald, who spent many years in prison, but during brief spells of freedom attempted to rally support for a revival of the island lordship until his death in Ireland in 1545. His efforts were doomed to failure, and with the ending of this hope there expired any prospect of a permanent and independent centre of Gaelic power and culture surviving on the 'Celtic fringe' of the Scottish realm.

The lords of the Isles were unlike the other magnates of late medieval Scotland. The feudal elements introduced by the MacDonalds had some features that could combine easily with the Gaelic concept of a kin-based society, but embodied others that were hostile to it. A major difference lay in succession practices, with primogeniture replacing the former pattern by which the headship of the kindred alternated among the leaders of the three divisions of the descendants of Somerled. The lords of the Isles adopted the feudal practice, but after 1493 there was a revival of the old system, leading to much confusion and bloodshed. On the other hand, landholding was readily translatable into feudal terms, with galleys being required in place of knight service. The church and the law were supported, and the lords had a council to advise them, making it plausible to say in retrospect that 'in their time there was great peace and wealth in the Isles through the ministration of justice' (*Monro's Description*, 57). Compared with the period of anarchy that followed the forfeiture, this was a time when the arts could flourish; the sculptured stones and crosses scattered widely around the west highlands and islands, and the bardic verse composed in the same period, notably by a number of generations of the MacMhuirich family and others whose work appears in the Book of the Dean of Lismore, alike survive as a reminder of what was looked back upon as a golden age. R. W. MUNRO and JEAN MUNRO

Sources J. Munro and R. W. Munro, eds., *Acts of the lords of the Isles, 1336–1493*, Scottish History Society, 4th ser., 22 (1986) · K. A. Steer and J. W. M. Bannerman, *Late medieval sculpture in the west highlands* (1977) · J. W. M. Bannerman, 'The lordship of the Isles', *Scottish society in the fifteenth century*, ed. J. M. Brown (1977), 209–40 · D. S. Thomson, ed., *The companion to Gaelic Scotland* (1983) · T. Dickson and J. B. Paul, eds., *Compota thesaurariorum regum Scotorum / Accounts of the lord high treasurer of Scotland*, 1–11 (1877–1916) · A. Cameron, ed., 'Book of Clanranald', *Reliquiae Celticae* (1892–4) · J. R. N. Macphail, ed., 'History of the Macdonalds', *Highland Papers*, 1, Scottish History Society, 2nd ser., 5 (1914) · W. M. Hennessy and B. MacCarthy, eds., *Annals of Ulster, otherwise, annals of Senat*, 4 vols. (1887–1901) · A. Grant, 'Scotland's "Celtic fringe"', *The late middle ages: the British Isles, 1100–1500*, ed. R. R. Davies (1988), 118–41 · T. Maclauchlan and W. F. Skene, eds., *The dean of Lismore's book* (1862) · *Scots peerage*, vol. 5 · *Monro's description of the western islands of Scotland*, ed. R. W. Munro (1961) · W. Bower, *Scotichronicon*, ed. D. E. R. Watt and others, new edn, 9 vols. (1987–98), vol. 8

MacDonald family (*per. c.*1475–1616), clan chiefs, of Sleat, traced their descent from **Hugh MacDonald** (*d.* 1495/1498), a natural son of Alexander *MacDonald, third lord of the Isles (*d.* 1449) [*see under* MacDonald family (*per. c.*1300–*c.*1500)], who in 1469 had a charter from his elder brother John of lands in Skye and Uist, and had these lands confirmed by James IV in 1495 after the fall of the lordship. Hugh was followed by his son John, who apparently lost his right to much of his territory (including Sleat itself with the castle of Dunscaith) to the family of MacDonald of Clanranald, although his successors seem to have recovered possession. On his death in 1505 he was followed by the first of a series of Donald MacDonalds, distinguished from each other by a Gaelic by-name. This was his half-brother Donald Gallach (*d.* 1506), 'the Stranger'—his mother came from Caithness—whose time as head of the family was short but notable for his marriage with Agnes, daughter of John (Cathanach) MacDonald of Dunyvaig and former wife of Torquil MacLeod of Lewis. This connection was to be close and important through several generations, though confusion of records makes it difficult to plot the several Lewis marriages exactly. Donald was murdered by his half-brother Archibald MacDonald (Gilleasbuig Dubh) who took control of the family and brought up his nephew **Donald Gruamach MacDonald** (*d.* 1534?), an able and energetic man who undertook the rehabilitation of the family; his by-name means 'the

Grim'. After the death of his cousin Donald Gallda ('the Foreigner'—he was brought up at court) MacDonald in 1519 he was regarded as the nearest claimant in the attempts made to restore the lordship of the Isles while the true heir, Donald Dubh MacDonald, was a royal prisoner.

In the 1520s Donald Gruamach made alliances with a number of mainland families including Campbell of Cawdor in 1521, Mackintosh in 1524, and Munro of Foulis and Rose of Kilravock in 1527. But in 1528 he started a long-running feud with MacLeod of Dunvegan when he invaded Trotternish in northern Skye which, while claimed by the Sleat family, had been granted in 1498 to both the MacLeods of Dunvegan and the MacLeods of Lewis. On his death, probably in 1534, he was succeeded by his son Donald Gorm ('Sombre') (*d.* 1539). His reign as chief was short but notable for his brief attempt to regain the lordship of the Isles. Supported by MacLeod of Lewis and others he first invaded Trotternish and then attacked Mackenzie lands and besieged their castle of Eilean Donan, where Donald was killed by an arrow. His son **Donald Gormson MacDonald** (*d.* 1575) succeeded as a minor and the clan was led by his uncle Archibald the Clerk. Donald Gormson was considered too young to press his claim effectively after the death of Donald Dubh in 1545, but he spent some time at the English court to escape the Scottish government, who still considered him a threat. On his return he inherited feuds with a number of his neighbours, including the Mackenzies after his father's attack in 1539, the MacLeods of Dunvegan in the ongoing struggle for Trotternish, and in 1560 he joined the MacDonalds of Dunyvaig in their feud with the MacLeans. He became involved in the family turmoils of the MacLeods of Dunvegan concerning the disputed succession of the heir Mary in the course of which the fifth earl of Argyll tried to arrange a compromise over Trotternish.

Donald Gormson was followed in 1575 by his son **Donald Gorm Mor MacDonald** (*d.* 1616), likewise a minor, who was in the temporary care of his great-uncle James MacDonald of Castle Camus. In his time the feuds with the Mackenzies and MacLeans appear to have become less intense, and he obtained a feu charter of Trotternish in 1596 and soon after transferred his home from Dunscaith in Sleat to Duntulm in the north of Trotternish. In spite of Donald's repudiation of his first wife, a daughter of Norman MacLeod of Dunvegan, which led to several years of warfare, an agreement was reached between the two families in 1601 though not finalized until 1618. The MacLeods of Lewis were at this time involved in a succession struggle in which Donald Gorm Mor was marginally concerned through his mother, and this so weakened them that they finally lost their lands in Lewis to the Mackenzies in 1610. The Scottish government made strenuous efforts to impose law and order on the western highlands and islands, and Donald was among the chiefs who in 1609 accepted the regulations known as the statutes of Iona. Donald Gorm Mor ('the Great') died without issue in 1616 to be succeeded by his nephew Donald called Gorm Og ('the Young') (*d.* 1643). For more than a century after the forfeiture of the lordship of the Isles the MacDonalds of Sleat held a prominent position as heirs to the imprisoned Donald Dubh, and were consequently the object of suspicion to the central government, and also aroused jealousy and mistrust in some of their neighbours for their very active part in many of the resulting battles and feuds.

R. W. MUNRO and JEAN MUNRO

Sources D. Gregory, *The history of the western highlands and the isles of Scotland* (1836) · D. J. MacDonald, *Clan Donald* (1978) · J. Munro and R. W. Munro, eds., *Acts of the lords of the Isles, 1336–1493*, Scottish History Society, 4th ser., 22 (1986)
Archives Clan Donald Centre, Armadale, Isle of Skye · U. Hull, Brynmor Jones L., title deeds, estate and household papers

Macdonald sisters (*act.* 1837–1925), four daughters of a Methodist minister, George Browne Macdonald (1805–1868), and his wife, Hannah, *née* Jones (1809–1875), went on to have notable lives through either marriage or parenthood. George Macdonald was an easy-going and energetic man and a kind father, although often absent. Hannah was the stricter parent, at times overwhelmed and depressed by the task of raising her large family on a minister's income. Her children remembered her as an excellent nurse and a family prohibition against idleness was relaxed only when one of the children was ill, which may have contributed to a family tendency to hypochondria. Both parents were well educated—the children were allowed great freedom to use their father's library and were well taught by their mother. The family was musical and the children made a great deal of their own entertainment. Owing to the Methodist church's custom of relocating its ministers every three years the household was what the Macdonalds referred to as a 'moving tent'. This constant moving undoubtedly contributed to Hannah Macdonald's melancholy but also ensured an unusual degree of closeness among her two sons and six daughters (three children died in infancy and one daughter, Carrie, in her teens). Despite the drawbacks of this peripatetic life, the Macdonalds, especially the sisters, grew up to be spirited, witty, and a little wild.

The eldest surviving daughter, **Alice Kipling** [née Macdonald] (1837–1910), mother of (Joseph) Rudyard *Kipling, was born in Sheffield on 4 April 1837. The story that she once baked a mouse in pastry and dared a friend to eat it may be a family myth but she was certainly bold enough to try it and tough enough to find it amusing. By her teens she was engaged to an Oxford friend of her brother's who was studying for the ministry.

In 1853 the family moved to London. They found London life exceedingly stimulating and the girls spent a lot of time with the Pre-Raphaelite artists, among them Edward Burne-Jones, whom they knew from childhood. Alice was writing poetry and attributed her failure to get into print to gender discrimination. She was not ready to settle down as a clergyman's wife and her engagement quietly died. She later made quite a hobby of getting engaged, most notably to the poet William Allingham, and her father had to speak to her about her flirting. In 1863 she

met John Lockwood Kipling (1837–1911), an artist working for the Department of Science and Arts in South Kensington. They married in 1865 and immediately embarked for India, where Kipling had gained a post in an art school in Bombay. His calm good nature complemented her quick, sharp wit—her brother observed how her words tumbled over each other in her haste to get them out. It is fortunate that she was happy in her marriage because she hated India. She turned her social talents to gaining professional advancement for her husband and to social advantage for them both.

The birth of Alice's first child, Rudyard, late in 1865 was so difficult that the Kiplings decided any future children must be born in England. In 1868 she took Rudyard to England, where he stayed with her parents while she gave birth to her daughter Alice, known in the family as Trix. Something went wrong on this trip: perhaps Rudyard, the spoiled darling of an Indian ayah, was too much for the Macdonalds (George Macdonald was ill and died shortly after their visit), perhaps the sisters, now well married to husbands more prosperous than hers, annoyed Alice; whatever it was, the visit was a disappointment and may have led her to make the greatest mistake of her life. When her third child, John, died weeks after his birth in 1870, the Kiplings decided that the time had come for Rudyard and Trix to return to England. Possibly because Alice was at odds with her family, the children were sent not to their family but to strangers in Southsea, where they boarded for over ten years. The experience may not have been as traumatic as Rudyard later depicted it, but he suffered a breakdown as a result of it and Trix suffered mental illness for a large part of her life. The family coolness existed largely in Alice's mind and the family kept an eye on the two children; Georgiana and Edward Burne-Jones rescued Rudyard when he was in danger of going blind and alerted his mother to his condition.

While the children were suffering in England, their parents were unhappy in India, missing their children but believing in the rightness of their actions. Alice's attempts to advance her husband's career bore fruit in 1875 when he was made principal of a new art school in Lahore. Both wrote in their free time and their social life prospered. They were introduced to the viceroy when John designed and Alice helped to make a series of banners for the Delhi durbar and thereafter they moved in the highest circles of Anglo-Indian society. This effort was not mere social climbing but was rather the means to financial security for themselves and their family. It financed a long trip home, as Alice realized that all was not well with her children. It set in place a network of connections that Alice could use to promote her son's career upon his return.

By 1883 both children were back in India. The Kiplings rejoiced in being again what they called the family square. Indeed, their efforts at family unity seem a little fevered, as if to make up for all the years of separation. Nevertheless, they claimed to be ecstatically happy together. All four of them wrote and Alice proved Rudyard's fiercest critic. Alice's connections obtained Rudyard his first newspaper job. When Trix shocked Anglo-Indian society by attracting his son, the viceroy appealed to Alice Kipling to send her daughter away in order to prevent a misalliance. The viceroy blinked first and his son returned to England. The Kiplings were not universally liked in their last years in India, but they were respected, and Alice had her share in that.

The Kiplings left India for good in 1893 and settled in Tisbury, in Wiltshire. The divisions between Alice and her sisters were largely healed and she spent a great deal of time with them. Neither of her children's marriages brought her the kind of satisfaction she might have hoped for— Rudyard's wife was as formidable a personality as Alice herself, and equally determined to control his affairs, while Trix's marriage was always shaky and Alice believed that it was responsible for Trix's mental breakdowns. In her later years Alice looked after Trix herself and sometimes seemed as disturbed as her daughter. Only Rudyard Kipling's success gave cause for satisfaction. Alice died at Tisbury on 23 November 1910; John outlived her by only two months.

Alice Kipling like many women of her time lived in the career of her husband and son. She probably had the greater impact on the former, although it is for the latter that she is remembered.

The fifth Macdonald child and second surviving daughter, **Georgiana Burne-Jones** [née Georgiana Macdonald], Lady Burne-Jones (1840–1920), wife and biographer of Sir Edward Coley Burne-*Jones, first baronet, was born in Birmingham on 21 July 1840. Like her elder sister, she was educated largely at home. When she was twelve the family first met Edward Burne-Jones, a schoolfriend of their elder brother. When the family moved to London, Georgie enrolled at the Government School of Design in Kensington. Although she appears to have had some talent, she saw her training as an adjunct to her main role as helper to Burne-Jones, to whom she was officially engaged at the age of fifteen. Their parents allowed the sisters a great deal of freedom to associate with Burne-Jones and his friends, all of whom repaid this trust with impeccable behaviour. Georgie was the quiet, steadfast sister, tiny in stature, with large, striking eyes whose gaze often seemed to be judging weaker mortals. Her patience was to be a singular asset to her married life.

They were married in 1860. Burne-Jones fell ill, as was his habit in any stressful situation, and Georgie spent her honeymoon nursing him. A family biographer records an otherwise composed Georgie breaking a necklace in their hotel room and scrabbling on the floor to collect the lost beads (Baldwin, 135). She found that Burne-Jones was less inclined to encourage artistic endeavour in a wife than in a fiancée and this together with her awe at the abilities of her husband and his friends prevented her from developing her own talent. The birth of her first child, Philip, in 1861 separated her further from the artists' world, and her husband's inability to handle money led her to take command of the family's financial affairs. Yet the early years of marriage were happy. She always felt that happiness

was a debit in an account that must be paid off by suffering in the future, and so it seemed to be when she fell seriously ill with scarlet fever in 1864, giving birth to her second son prematurely. She recovered but the baby died. Edward, predictably, was prostrated and in the way they dealt separately with their sorrow, something in the marriage was lost. It was said that Georgie always looked a little pale and faded afterwards, and she wrote years later that she felt the presence of the 'little shadowy babe' she had lost for the rest of her life (Flanders, 273). After the birth of their daughter in 1866 Edward embarked on a very public affair. They repaired their marriage but it was never quite the same.

At this point Georgie embarked on a life less dependent on her husband. She had a series of influential friendships—with William Morris (with whom she shared an interest in socialism and the experience of a disloyal spouse), with Rosalind Howard, who tried to interest her in women's suffrage, and with George Eliot, who encouraged her to educate herself. Georgie did educate herself, adopted Morris's politics, and bought a house. The house at Rottingdean, near Brighton, was always more hers than Edward's and she spent more time there as the years passed. When the Local Government Act of 1894 empowered villages to elect parish councils, she ran as an independent and became the only woman member of the Rottingdean council, serving until 1901.

Edward Burne-Jones died suddenly in 1898. He had asked Georgie to write his biography and she took great pride in doing so, producing a book that is still respected today, although she avoided excessive frankness about some of the personal details. She was close to her nephew Rudyard Kipling and his family, who had settled nearby. She opposed the Second South African War and was once rescued from an angry crowd by the pro-war Kipling when she hung out a banner proclaiming her beliefs. The villagers considered her eccentric but admired her fearlessness, while she gained an iconic status within the family. She left the parish council in 1901 and died at 55 Holland Road, Kensington, London on 2 February 1920.

Georgiana Burne-Jones was perhaps the most complex of the Macdonald sisters. Although starting married life as they did, determined to live her life through her family, the deficiencies of her husband and the opportunities offered within their social circle enabled and encouraged her to find interests of her own. She was the strong one of the family, who sorted out everyone else's crises, but she made a good job of her own life too, a life that all too easily disappeared in the shadow of her family.

The Macdonalds' third surviving daughter, **Agnes Poynter** [née Macdonald], Lady Poynter (1843–1906), wife of Sir Edward John *Poynter, first baronet, was born in Leeds on 25 September 1843. She was an excellent pianist and had a more placid and sunny nature than her sisters; the latter shared a fondness for what the family called 'the joy of grief' (Taylor, 21). She was thought the best-looking of the sisters—John Lockwood called her 'tyrannously pretty'—and attracted suitors from her early teens (ibid., 52). Although she enjoyed the company of the Pre-Raphaelite artists whom she met at Burne-Jones's studio, she gravitated to more mainstream fashionable society, preferring the modish crinoline to the plain aesthetic dress favoured by Georgie. This preference for the fashionable may explain why she married the dour and temperamental Edward Poynter.

Satirized in George Du Maurier's novel *Trilby* as Lorrimer, 'the industrious apprentice', Poynter achieved enormous financial and social success as an academic painter, specializing in epic canvases with classical themes, and as an administrator, becoming president of the Royal Academy. Poynter and Agnes were married in 1866 and embarked on a glittering social career that took its toll on their marriage and their health. Their son Ambrose was born in 1867 and Agnes was often unwell, suffering from headaches, possibly neuralgia or, as unkind observers guessed, from a difficult marriage. Edward Poynter worked for seven days a week and collapsed when a painting was finished; his working pattern suggests manic depression. He obviously loved Agnes, grieving almost excessively when she died, but he was quite unable to show emotion, and she was probably unique in feeling any sympathy for him.

This bleak outlook, beneath the façade of social and professional success, was lightened somewhat when Agnes became pregnant unexpectedly in her late thirties. Her embarrassment about what was then considered very late motherhood was increased when she went into labour at a dinner party and was obliged to give birth in her hosts' house. The birth of her second son, Hugh, caused great mirth in her family and seems to have lightened the gloom that had settled over her household. Poynter does not appear to have been a cruel man—his nephews Stanley Baldwin and Rudyard Kipling got on well with him—but everyone agreed that any lightness and charm within that household emanated from Agnes.

In later life the Poynters travelled in Europe but Agnes's health declined rapidly after 1900. In 1903 she underwent an operation, probably for cancer. She kept going, possibly to reassure her husband, even travelling to Turkey in 1905 to attend Hugh's wedding. She died in London on 12 June 1906.

Agnes Poynter enjoyed the greatest marital and worldly success of all the sisters, judged by the standards of their time, but her life was in its way the least satisfactory. Her family blamed her husband for the sad life of this most loved sister, but he may not have been entirely at fault. Agnes illustrates how a certain lack of resourcefulness might overtake a pretty and vivacious woman when the dissatisfactions of mature life began to overtake the promise of youth and other consolations had to be found to take their place. At the same time, she was plainly indispensable to her husband, supplying the social grace and charm that he so conspicuously lacked.

The fourth surviving daughter, **Louisa Baldwin** [*née* Macdonald] (1845–1925), mother of Stanley *Baldwin, was born in Wakefield on 25 August 1845. She was quiet and somewhat lacking in self-confidence, perhaps overshadowed by the stronger personalities of her older sisters. In her teens she modelled for Burne-Jones and his friends, became proficient at making woodcuts, wrote fiction, and studied at the Wolverhampton School of Art. She had the reputation of being somewhat aloof, possibly because of her poor vision, which made it difficult for her to recognize people she did not know well. By the time she came of age the family was deeply involved in the art world, through the marriages of the two older sisters, but Louisa accepted the proposal of the earnest Worcestershire ironmaster Alfred *Baldwin and married him in a double wedding with her sister Agnes in 1866. He converted her to high-church Anglicanism without difficulty, but she seems to have had some trouble adjusting to life in rural Worcestershire, where they settled to be near the business. She may have been lonely with a husband often preoccupied with the demands of a successful business and two sisters living in London. This may have contributed to the illness that overtook her after the birth of Stanley Baldwin in 1867. She appears to have had one and perhaps two miscarriages after his birth, and she may simply have settled on ill health as a way of ensuring that she had no more pregnancies. The causes and nature of her illness are mysterious, but it was extremely debilitating; she spent most of her time lying down, often in a darkened room, and if she went out at all it was in a bath chair. She tried a dazzling variety of cures and treatments, the most startling of all being the champagne cure, which caused her to fall down. Her three-year-old son emulated her by putting cushions on a chair and announcing 'Stanley poorly back' (Flanders, 128). The 1870s were spent travelling in pursuit of health—biographers have based their diagnosis of hypochondria on Louisa's sudden return to energy and mobility when abroad or visiting her sisters (ibid., 149).

Despite her poor health, Louisa's life does not seem to have been unhappy. Released from the duties of housekeeping, she read widely, studied languages, and wrote novels, poetry, and collections of stories. Her nephew Rudyard Kipling was a gentle critic. She was not a very good writer, but writing passed the time and gave her the creative outlet she craved. Nor did illness ruin her marriage—Louisa and Alfred shared a strong religious faith that enabled them to view her illness as a trial sent to strengthen them. It was, however, what her brother-in-law John Kipling called a 'caded' life, sheltered to the extent that Louisa could not grow, either as a person or as a writer (Taylor, 102).

In 1883 Louisa suddenly began to get well. The reason for her recovery is as mysterious as the cause of her illness. She took over a number of good works in Wilden, the Worcestershire village where they lived, including teaching in the Sunday school and running groups for the wives of her husband's workers. In 1892 Alfred was elected to parliament and they spent more time in London. Her recovery did not last long, and she gradually returned to a state of permanent invalidity, especially after Alfred's death in 1908. She lived to see her son become prime minister and commissioned Morris & Co. to design stained-glass windows for Wilden church as memorials to her family, after drawings by Burne-Jones. She died at Wilden on 16 May 1925 and was buried in Wilden churchyard.

Louisa Macdonald Baldwin is in many ways the hardest of the sisters to capture. If more were known about her health, it might be proved either that she was a hypochondriac or that she genuinely suffered from a painful undiagnosed illness. Whether through her own lack of will or through circumstances outside her control, Louisa remains a frustrating case of a life that never quite took shape.

The Macdonald sisters illustrated almost the whole range of roles open to women of their class in Victorian England. Alice exemplified the ambitious wife and mother; Georgie began as the self-sacrificing wife and ended as a parish councillor, a political force in her own right; Agnes was the model wife for a successful man, offering the social polish he lacked; and the life of Louisa, also a loyal wife, reflected the frustrations and limitations inherent in such a life. As a group they were strong-willed and somewhat intolerant—their standards were high, and they made no effort to adapt to those who could not meet them. On the other hand they were intelligent and artistic, bringing out the talents of their spouses and descendants. Georgie's great-grandson Colin MacInnes said of them that they were 'the sort of family that one would perhaps rather read about than belong to' (Flanders, 329).

ELIZABETH J. MORSE

Sources J. Flanders, *A circle of sisters: Alice Kipling, Georgiana Burne-Jones, Agnes Poynter and Louisa Baldwin* (2001) · I. Taylor, *Victorian sisters* (1987) · A. W. Baldwin, *The Macdonald sisters* (1960) · E. Macdonald, *Annals of the Macdonald family* (1928) · F. W. Macdonald, *As a tale that is told* (1919) · F. MacCarthy, *William Morris: a life for our time* (1994) · A. Wilson, *The strange ride of Rudyard Kipling* (1977) · C. Carrington, *Rudyard Kipling: his life and work* (1955) · P. Fitzgerald, *Edward Burne-Jones: a biography* (1975) · A. Thirkell, *Three houses* (1986) · P. Williamson, *Stanley Baldwin: conservative leadership and national values* (1999) · W. C. Monkhouse, *Sir Edward J. Poynter, president of the Royal Academy: his life and work* (1897) · *CGPLA Eng. & Wales* (1920) [Georgiana Burne-Jones] · *CGPLA Eng. & Wales* (1925) [Louisa Baldwin]
Archives FM Cam., Burne-Jones papers [Georgiana Burne-Jones] · U. Sussex, John Lockwood Kipling papers [Alice Kipling]
Likenesses E. Burne-Jones, group portrait, 1858 (*Kings' daughters*), repro. in Flanders, *A circle of sisters* · E. Burne-Jones, group portrait, 1864 (*Green summer*), repro. in Flanders, *A circle of sisters*
Wealth at death £12,683 13s. 4d.—Georgiana Burne-Jones: probate, 1920 · £5,399 11s. 8d.—Louisa Baldwin: probate, 1925

Macdonald, Agnes Syme (1882–1966), suffragette and campaigner for women's citizenship, was born on 8 September 1882 at 23 Dublin Street, Edinburgh, the fifth child and only daughter of the six children of Alexander Macdonald and his wife, Euphemia Henderson. Alexander Macdonald, from Kiltarlity, Inverness, was a wine and spirit merchant in Edinburgh; Euphemia, who was born in Kinross, took over the business in 1893.

Agnes 'was one of the many daughters of the house who stayed at home' and she later said that was why she joined the Women's Social and Political Union (WSPU). 'Possibly it's because I was a so-called "lady of leisure" … At that time there were too many women running around with no training to do anything' (*Evening Dispatch*, 12 Dec 1962). In the autumn of 1911 the truce in suffragette militancy ended when the government announced that no further time would be given to the Conciliation Bill, which would have introduced a measure of women's suffrage. The most dramatic protests so far took place in early March 1912, with window-smashing raids on the West End and Whitehall. A number of Scottish women travelled to London to take part. Using 'a hammer, which we wore round the neck on a rope and a bit of string' (ibid.), Agnes broke a police office window. She was charged with malicious damage on 5 March 1912 and, in common with others who had attacked government property, was given two months' hard labour. That period in Holloway was formative. 'We learned a lot about social conditions, particularly from the women who cleaned out our cells. It was a tremendous experience, and later it helped me after I trained to become a secretary, and took up social work' (ibid.). That social work was primarily women's movement organization and campaigning on social and equality issues.

Agnes was secretary of the Edinburgh branch of the WSPU for a short time in 1913, but became alienated by what she saw as extreme militant activity. In 1918, with other women from both militant and constitutional suffrage campaigns, she set up the Edinburgh Women Citizens' Association (WCA); she was its first and longest-serving secretary. Women's citizens' associations were formed throughout Britain at this time to organize and educate women voters into a political force and to promote women's representation. The Edinburgh association was inaugurated in Edinburgh city chambers on 9 May 1918 when 'The Lord Provost presided, and the hall was filled to overflowing with women, who showed keen interest and great enthusiasm in the new movement' (minutes, Edinburgh WCA, 1918–19). In 1919 fifteen Scottish women's citizens' associations formed the Scottish Council of Women Citizens' Associations; they remained independent of the London-based National Women Citizens' Association.

Agnes remembered the inter-war Edinburgh WCA as busy and effective. 'There was such efficiency and drive! Deputations to Government Departments and town councils! Meetings all over the country, constant efforts to get things done. And we did get things done' (*The Scotsman*, 31 March 1962). Organized citizenship was seen as the next stage for the women's movement; as well as continuing to campaign for the franchise on equal terms to men, they believed women's status as citizens would lead to feminist and social reforms. Their programme was ambitious, encompassing efforts to get more women elected to central and local government (the latter successfully) and campaigning for equal pay and promotion for women teachers and council employees, against marriage bans in employment, for pre-school nursery and play facilities, and on mental illness and handicap, public health, and social housing. With other women's organizations in 1920 they launched a campaign on 'child outrage' (child sexual abuse), and from 1925 began to lobby for a national maternity service.

In July 1939 Agnes retired as secretary of the Edinburgh WCA; at that time she was caring for her younger, disabled brother, Roddy, with whom she shared a house in Strathfillan Road, Edinburgh. She had joined the Society of Friends and her organizational skills found outlet in Quaker relief work for European refugees and as a member of the management committee of Barns School in the Scottish borders. Set up in 1940 for delinquent city boys, it was run on progressive principles and was highly controversial. Agnes is well remembered by Edinburgh Friends for her strong, left-leaning beliefs and sense of injustice, her efficiency, energy, and enthusiasm, and sharp wit. Quakers who were children then remember her as 'the pan drop lady' who brought peppermints to meeting for them. She was also active on the Edinburgh Old People's Welfare Council.

Agnes Macdonald died, unmarried, on 21 October 1966, aged eighty-four, after a period in a nursing home, at St Raphael's Home, Blackford Avenue, Edinburgh.

SUE INNES

Sources b. cert. · d. cert. · *Evening Dispatch* (12 Dec 1962) · minutes, Edinburgh Women Citizens' Association, 1918–19, NA Scot. · *The Scotsman* (28 Oct 1966) · private information (2004) [Society of Friends] · *The Scotsman* (31 March 1962)
Likenesses photograph, repro. in *Evening Dispatch*
Wealth at death £4749 5s.: confirmation, 11 Nov 1966, *CCI*

MacDonald, Alexander, twelfth earl of Ross (d. 1449). See under MacDonald family (per. c.1300–c.1500).

MacDonald, Alexander, of Dunyvaig and the Glens (d. 1536×9), clan chief, was the eldest son of John Cannoch or Cattenach MacDonald (d. 1499) of Dunyvaig and the Glens, and his wife, Cecilia Savage. His father, who was hanged with his father, Sir John *MacDonald of Dunyvaig and the Glens, and two of his brothers by James IV's orders in 1499, had been the heir to the chieftainship of the clan Iain Mhòir, also known as the clan Donald south, the senior and most powerful of the cadet lines of the clan Donald. The clan had important holdings on both sides of the North Channel, in Kintyre and Islay in western Scotland, and the Glens of Antrim in Ulster. Alexander took refuge in the latter after his father's death, while his inheritance in Islay was granted to Sir John MacIan of Ardnamurchan, who had captured John Cannoch and his sons in 1494. Alexander MacDonald is said to have defeated an expedition by MacIan into Ulster, but he remained there and established a formidable reputation as a leader of the Scottish mercenaries who flocked to Ireland from the Hebrides in the sixteenth century. He settled his feud with John MacIan and married the latter's daughter Caitirfhiona (or Katherine), with whom he had nine sons (including James *MacDonald of Dunyvaig and the Glens, and Sorley Boy *MacDonnell) and two daughters.

Following the battle of Flodden in 1513 Alexander MacDonald's forfeiture was remitted. His marriage had brought him into the orbit of the earls of Argyll, the crown's principal agents in filling the power vacuum left by the disappearance of the lordship of the Isles. On 7 March 1516 'Alexander Johne Caynachis sone' was described as one of the 'familiaris and servandis to Coline erle of Ergile' (*Registrum secreti sigilli*, no. 2722). But his reconciliation with MacIan did not last long. By March 1517 Alexander was supporting the bid by Donald Gallda MacDonald of Lochalsh to gain the lordship of the Isles, and later that year they came upon MacIan at Craiganairgid in Morvern and defeated and killed him. Donald died without an heir in 1519, and Alexander became the leading MacDonald in the Isles.

By now the central government was aware of the need to win Alexander MacDonald over. On 13 March 1517 the council recorded its awareness that the clan Iain Mhòir was in revolt 'because thai have na heritage' (Hannay, 80), and proposed that if Alexander agreed to submit and give hostages for good behaviour he should be given a renewed remission and a grant of lands. Following the death of Donald Gallda he made his peace and recovered his inheritance in Kintyre and Islay, on condition that his followers 'keep guid reule and mak na extorsioun on the Kingis liegis, gevand plegis sufficient' (Macdonald and Macdonald, 2.516). Alexander also had to settle with the Campbells, and in 1520 he entered into a bond of gossipry and manrent with Sir John Campbell of Cawdor, a younger brother of the third earl of Argyll, whereby Campbell leased to MacDonald lands in Islay and Jura and the island of Colonsay. Although relations between the two men soon became strained, there is evidence that the king's government accepted MacDonald as de facto lord of the Isles at this time.

The re-establishment of the clan Iain Mhòir threatened the position of Lachlan Cattanach Maclean, the pre-eminent islander since 1493, and Alexander MacDonald gained most from Lachlan's murder in 1523, but even more important to Alexander were his relations with the Campbells and with the king. In 1528 he went into rebellion once more. In that year James V assumed power, and Argyll was made his lieutenant in the west, where the king had ordered the annulment of recent infeftments of crown lands. The beneficiaries of these had included Alexander MacDonald, and their revocation must have been a principal cause of his revolt, reinforced by his suspicion of Argyll's ambitions. An expedition against the Isles in 1529 was cut short by the earl's death. Summoned before the king MacDonald did not appear, but as preparations were made for a royal expedition he came to James at Stirling in June 1531 and submitted, on terms which included handing over his son James as a hostage. He was rewarded with £100 and a purple velvet gown. Soon afterwards the fourth earl of Argyll accused him of 'divers and sindry greit faltis' (Cameron, 234), but MacDonald appeared before the council in November to answer them, and when Argyll did not attend presented his own complaints against the earl, who was subsequently dismissed as chamberlain of Kintyre.

In 1532, in a westward extension of that year's Anglo-Scottish hostilities, MacDonald led 7000 men to Ulster, and spent most of the rest of his life there. In 1533 he and Hector Maclean of Duart attacked the Isle of Man and captured an English ship, the *Mary Willoughby*, which they handed over to King James. The king sent bows and arrows to MacDonald, who, however, was also active on his own behalf, to the extent that on 30 August 1535 he was outlawed for a piratical attack on a Glasgow merchant's ships off the Mull of Kintyre. No further action followed, perhaps because MacDonald died in 1536, as stated in the annals of Ulster, or because MacDonald was reconciled with the crown; he may have been the Alexander mentioned in a letter from Archbishop John Allen of Dublin as active in the service of James V in 1538. He was dead by 1539, when his son James was described as 'of Dunyvaig'.

NICHOLAS MACLEAN-BRISTOL

Sources K. Nicholls, 'Notes on the genealogy of clann Eoin Mhoir', *West Highland Notes & Queries*, ser. 2, 8 (Nov 1991) · G. Hill, *An historical account of the MacDonnells of Antrim* (1873) · W. M. Hennessy and B. MacCarthy, eds., *Annals of Ulster, otherwise, annals of Senat*, 4 vols. (1887–1901), vol. 3 · M. Livingstone, D. Hay Fleming, and others, eds., *Registrum secreti sigilli regum Scotorum / The register of the privy seal of Scotland*, 1 (1908) · A. J. N. Macdonald and A. Macdonald, *The clan Donald*, 3 vols. (1896–1904) · J. Cameron, *James V: the personal rule, 1528–1542*, ed. N. Macdougall (1998) · R. K. Hannay, ed., *Acts of the lords of council in public affairs, 1501–1554* (1932) · J. M. Hill, *Fire and sword: Sorley Boy MacDonnell and the rise of Clan Ian Mor, 1538–1590* (1993)

MacDonald, Sir Alexander. *See* MacColla, Alasdair (*d.* 1647).

Macdonald, Alexander, of Glencoe [Alasdair Maciain; *called* Alasdair Ruaidh] (*d.* **1692**), clan chief and victim of massacre, was probably born in Glencoe between the early 1620s and early 1630s, the son of Alexander Macdonald (Alasdair Maciain; *d.* in or after 1657), who by 1627 was chief (reputedly eleventh chief) of a branch of the clan Donald inhabiting Glencoe in Lorn, Argyllshire. Tradition asserts that he was educated in Paris, one of several indications that the clan were Roman Catholics, although it has also been suggested that they were episcopalians. Since the mid-sixteenth century Glencoe had been owned by the Campbells, earls of Argyll, whose policy was to prevent the Macdonalds from gaining legally secure rights to their lands. During the civil wars the latter were among the clans which rose unsuccessfully under the marquess of Montrose against the Campbells, but they avoided vengeance afterwards. The later tradition of a constant Macdonald–Campbell feud is groundless. Between local and national crises, they linked themselves by bonds of manrent (clientage), friendship, business, and marriage. Similarly, the glen was not the inaccessible robbers' nest of myth. Like other clans in the area the Glencoe Macdonalds were notorious for cattle raiding and robbery, but Argyll was still able to use its rents for security in deeds and peacefully lease out its woods. The scale of violence decreased until, in the later seventeenth century, except in time of wars, cattle raiding was perpetrated by small groups of displaced caterans (marauders) and chiefs could profit (perhaps not always honestly) from supplying the watches against them.

Alexander Macdonald (sometimes called Alasdair Ruaidh on account of his red hair, but most usually known as Maciain) succeeded his father as putative twelfth chief some time after January 1657, when the two men signed a bond of friendship with Sir John Campbell of Glenorchy and his eldest son, John Campbell (1635–1716). Intended to guard against repetition of heavy gentry casualties such as the Campbells had sustained in the 1640s, the bond agreed that there would be mutual warning of impending danger. By the early 1660s Maciain had married: clan tradition that his wife was the daughter of Archibald Gillespie (*d.* 1683), chief of the Macdonalds of Keppoch, seems implausible owing to the youth of the latter's sons when he died, and no plausible alternative has been advanced. At any rate, Maciain and his wife had two sons, John (Iain) and Alexander (Alasdair) Og, who were serving soldiers in 1685 and married by 1692.

In 1665 Maciain, who of the two hundred or so families in the clan could send about one hundred men to war, dispatched a contingent to support Ewen Cameron of Lochiel in his confrontation over lands with Lauchlan Mackintosh of Torcastle; this dispute was settled peaceably. East highland cattle raiding by some of the inhabitants of Glencoe rendered Argyll, as owner, and John Campbell, as temporary lessee, liable to pay the resulting penalties and in 1673 Argyll sold on the glen to Sir James Campbell of Lawers. That year Maciain, still an established local figure, was able to visit the Inveraray justice eyre even after substituting the wrong defendant in one trial. However, soon after, and probably not for the only time, he murdered two of his own clansmen, according to tradition because they had informed on a cattle raid. However bad the affair, he could have disposed of opponents with a veneer of legality had he possessed the judicial rights enjoyed by many other chiefs. Since he lacked them, it was probably for this crime that Argyll imprisoned him at Inveraray, but he escaped, and in April 1674 the privy council reported that he had committed several murders and robberies since. The affair was soon lost in the greater disruption caused by Argyll's campaign to dispossess the Maclean chiefs of their estate and the Maclean–Macdonald resistance, but Edinburgh lawyers dwelt on the worst highland atrocities to justify extending their cumbersome and costly system there in all matters. One of them, Sir John Dalrymple, remembered the story: he still referred to 'the murderer McIain' in 1692 (NL Scot., MS 7014, fol. 8).

The Maclean–Macdonald coalition's struggle of 1674–80 against Argyll ended in defeat, but in the meantime it had enabled an adroit chief like Maciain and his clan to profit considerably through offering protection to some of the Campbells. The clan's raiding against other Campbells increased so enormously that Argyll determined to buy back the glen from Lawers, evict the clan (who, he believed, neglected farming for robbery), and plant it with honest tenants; but he lacked the money. Meanwhile, on the other side, many Glencoe men served for pay in John Campbell's highland company, and some fought for him against the Caithness Sinclairs in 1680. If a letter printed in 1817 is genuine, a large contingent also accompanied the highland host in plundering the richer lowland west: they were not John Campbell's men, but he dared not leave them behind near his undefended estates.

In 1680 Maciain was one of two men who acted as executors to Angus (Aeneas), Lord Macdonell and Aros, an officially recognized position of trust. A formidable figure, well over 6 feet high, he was still strong and active in old age, with his beard curled in horns. A contemporary's description, 'much loved by his neighbours ... a person of great integrity, honour, good-nature and courage' (MacKnight, 321), is corroborated by the bards' praise for him as a wise chief and counsellor, although the context was the edge of legality. A peaceful period was broken in 1685 by Argyll's rebellion, during which Maciain and both his sons served on the government side. Like many others from the general down, they plundered widely and fairly indiscriminately. Glencoe was sold in 1687 to the Tutor of Appin, chief of the Stewarts, Glencoe's western neighbours. He wanted their fighting men as vassals, to make the Stewarts a powerful clan. This gave greater practical security of tenure. Maciain in 1688 sent sixty men who, with other clan contingents, joined Macdonald of Keppoch in opposing his oppressive landlord, Mackintosh, in the last private clan battle, Mulroy.

When the Jacobite rising of John Graham, Viscount Dundee, broke out in 1689, Maciain joined it, serving with the Stewarts. During Dundee's abortive Strathspey campaign, he plundered Williamite enemies, but he tried to restrain a Maclean contingent which had begun plundering friendly inhabitants—until a second-sighted man warned him of the dragoons about to attack the Macleans, and he retired. The Appin and Glencoe men were not at Killiecrankie, since a force under the tenth earl of Argyll was advancing towards their country. It fled at the news, and Maciain and his men joined the highland army, commanded after Dundee's death by Major-General Cannon, for an uninspired campaign and the defeat at Dunkeld. He was one of the chiefs who on 24 August, before they dispersed, signed a bond promising to reassemble.

In October Glencoe men were in one party sent out by Cannon to destroy the castle at Achallader of John Campbell, by this time earl of Breadalbane, in order to prevent the government from establishing a garrison, and in another which ravaged Glenlyon, thus preventing the laird, Robert Campbell, from redeeming his estates from the marquess of Atholl. Victorian writers deduced that this made Breadalbane and Glenlyon specially vindictive against the Macdonalds of Glencoe. In reality, Breadalbane knew they had acted under orders; in November, he privately praised Maciain's forbearance towards Campbells on a spectacular raid down Loch Lomond. Glenlyon blamed Atholl.

In February 1690 Maciain was among the chiefs who signed a letter to King James promising to fight on following the arrival of a new Jacobite commander, Major-General Thomas Buchan. His second son, Alasdair Og, became a captain in Buchan's new regiment, and took part in the spring campaign which ended disastrously at Cromdale. That autumn, the enemy closed in. A force

under Argyll captured the Stewarts' castle, and would next have overrun Glencoe had a crisis not diverted it to Mull. Most ordinary Glencoe clansmen submitted to Colonel John Hill, the honest governor of the new Fort William; by May 1691 Maciain was considering it.

The next month, as part of a government initiative to end the war, Breadalbane offered the chiefs, gathered at Achallader, money to buy out troublesome feudal superiorities over them, in return for taking the oaths to King William before the sheriffs in the shire towns by a deadline finally extended to 1 January 1692. The Glencoe men had previously helped Breadalbane frighten away an intruding presbyterian minister, but when Maciain attended at Achallader, the earl quarrelled with him and threatened him over stolen cattle; Maciain later said that he feared a mischief from nobody so much. Yet Breadalbane obtained for him the promise of £150 to buy the superiority of Glencoe and pardon for the murder. The earl's selfish but constructive plans, for a huge highland militia with himself as general (and including a Glencoe contingent camouflaged under the Tutor's name), depended on a total and genuine pacification.

However, Breadalbane's political enemies subsequently tempted the major chiefs into posturing about fighting on with insincere promises of larger rewards: Alasdair Macdonell of Glengarry was the most extreme, and Maciain probably followed him blindly, distracted by talk of the Catholic chiefs going abroad rather than taking the oaths. He failed to check the procedure, though the second-sighted man's prophecy that he would be killed in his own house frightened him. In the event, more because of fear of a government campaign of repression than because of King James's belated authorization, just before the deadline, the chiefs rushed to submit. On 31 December 1691 Maciain appeared at Fort William, wrongly supposing that Hill was entitled to administer the oath. Hill sent him off to Inveraray with a recommendation. Immediately afterwards, Glengarry offered terms for surrender, which, verbal mention but not the document made clear, were intended to protect Maciain also. Maciain hurried southwards through the snow. He encountered Argyll's regiment marching to Fort William, and Captain Thomas Drummond briefly detained him. Only on 6 January 1692, after desperate pleading, did he take the oath before sheriff-depute Sir Colin Campbell of Ardkinglass. Returning, he found that Argyll's regiment had stayed one night in Glencoe without harming it.

However, news of Maciain's belated submission did not reach secretary of state Sir John Dalrymple. A false report that he had submitted on time was corrected by Argyll, but not superseded by the truth. When Dalrymple realized that Glengarry, having a castle, might defeat a midwinter attack, and that his surrender should therefore be accepted, he selected as an alternative scapegoat Maciain, whom he saw as a murderer, at the head of people who were cattle thieves and papists. Therefore, instructions to Hill (duplicated to Major-General Sir Thomas Livingstone) on the surrender terms, drafted by Dalrymple and signed by William on 16 January, included the observation that 'it will be a proper vindication of public justice to extirpate that sect [sept] of thieves' (Gordon, 65). Dalrymple's covering letters, demanding that for 'a just example of vengeance' they should 'be rooted out in earnest' (ibid., 66), made clear his personal enthusiasm.

Hill, himself politically vulnerable, knew that the Glencoe men had submitted and had rights to protection, but dared not oppose Dalrymple openly. Livingstone, in the same position, also hated the Glencoe men and despised Hill. On 23 January 1692 he sent an order for the attack to Hill's scheming lieutenant-colonel, James Hamilton. Hill, while passively hoping for a countermand, let Hamilton and Major Robert Duncanson, commanding Argyll's regiment, plan the attack. They introduced the outrageous idea that troops quartered on the inhabitants should slaughter their hosts. On 1 February 1692 two companies under Captain Campbell of Glenlyon, who did not know the plan, and Captain Drummond, who probably did, entered Glencoe, reassured the Macdonalds, and were quartered among the settlements—technically a penalty for unpaid taxes, but they were treated, and behaved, as guests. Maciain had a dozen in his house. He sent away the unmarried girls and, fearing a disarmament, hid the clan's weapons elsewhere; otherwise, the mutual duties highland hospitality traditionally imposed seemed sufficient protection.

On 12 February Hamilton arranged a rendezvous in Glencoe at 7 a.m. the next day with Duncanson, quartered nearby. Duncanson wrote secretly that evening to Glenlyon, ordering him at 5 a.m. 'to fall upon the Rebells, the McDonalds of Glenco, and putt all to the sword under seventy. you are to have a speciall care that the old Fox and his sones doe upon no account escape your hands ...' (NL Scot., MS Adv. 23.6.24). Threatened with dismissal and ruin, Glenlyon decided to obey and dissembled, accepting Maciain's invitation to dinner the next day. A blizzard arose.

Between 4 a.m. and 5 a.m. on 13 February Lieutenant John Lindsay, Ensign Lundie, and soldiers from Glenlyon's company arrived at Maciain's house, in Polveig. As he rose from his bed to greet them, they shot him in the back, killing him, pulled the body outside by the heels and left it lying naked. His wife tried to dress and escape, but the soldiers stripped her naked and pulled her rings off her fingers with their teeth. Her sons found her, but, like other Glencoe women, she died of exposure and ill treatment that day or the next. Several of the clan gentry were also murdered; perhaps thirty-eight men and half a dozen women and children in all. Maciain's sons and their families, warned by suspicious servants, escaped. Duncanson's two-hour anticipation of Hamilton's arrival, other changes in his order, and the raging blizzard allowed the inhabitants to escape through the unguarded passes out of the glen, though an unknown number, especially women and children, died of exposure. The troops burnt the houses and departed with all the clan's livestock and moveable property. When they dared return, the survivors buried Maciain in Eilean Munde, their burial isle in the glen's sea loch.

The news hastened the submissions of other chiefs. Breadalbane, almost alone, was shocked enough to declare his innocence, but this merely increased suspicions of his guilt. Hill, recovering his courage, began applying for permission to resettle the survivors in Glencoe, but even when Dalrymple heard the full truth, he suggested sending them to Ireland, the plantations, or anywhere else in Scotland. Hill applied elsewhere, and in August 1692 received permission to allow them back.

Although totally impoverished, the clan, under Maciain's son John Macdonald (d. after 1710) as chief, remained quiet. In 1695, he and other survivors testified before the parliamentary inquiry into the massacre, but their appeal for compensation had almost no result. Some prosperity probably returned about 1706. In 1711, ownership of the glen was transferred to the Stewart chief, Appin. Argyll was still the latter's superior, but Stewart ownership created a protective buffer. Indeed, the Argyll family by then were treating their rebel vassals more mildly than the state did Jacobite landowners. Alexander Macdonald, John's son and successor, who joined the 1715 rising but submitted early, fairly soon regained practical control of the glen; and it was not long lost to the family even after he also joined Prince Charles Edward in 1745. A member of the prince's council, he was afterwards imprisoned until 1749. PAUL HOPKINS

Sources P. A. Hopkins, *Glencoe and the end of the highland war*, rev. edn (1998) · NA Scot., Breadalbane papers, GD 112 · J. Gordon, ed., *Papers illustrative of the political condition of the highlands of Scotland, 1689–1696* (1845) · J. Prebble, *Glencoe: the story of the massacre* (1966) · A. Macdonald and A. Macdonald, *The clan Donald*, 3 vols. (1896–1904) · D. J. Macdonald, *Slaughter under trust* (1965) · A. I. Macinnes, *Clanship, commerce and the house of Stuart, 1603–1788* (1996) · Blair Castle, Perthshire, Atholl manuscripts · NA Scot., duke of Hamilton papers, GD406, bundle 633 · NL Scot., Tweeddale MSS 7010–7020 · U. Glas. L., MS 1577 · *Reg. PCS*, 3rd ser. · J. A. Maclean, 'The sources, particularly the Celtic sources, for the history of the highlands in the seventeenth century', PhD diss., U. Aberdeen, 1939 · 'A copie of a letter from the host about Glasgow, 1 Feb 1678', *Blackwood*, 1 (1817), 68–9 · A. Kincaid, ed., *An account of the depredations committed upon the clan Campbell and their followers during the years 1685 and 1686* (1816) · *Memoirs of Sir Ewen Cameron of Locheill*, ed. J. Macknight, Abbotsford Club, 24 (1842) · J. Aubrey, 'Miscellanies', *Three prose works*, ed. J. Buchanan-Brown (1972) · NL Scot., Adv. MS 23.6.24 · Scottish Catholic Archive, Edinburgh, Blair's letters · J. Philp, *The grameid*, ed. A. D. Murdoch (1888) · J. Prebble, 'Religion and the massacre of Glencoe', *SHR*, 46 (1967), 185–8

Wealth at death cattle and other livestock; household goods

MacDonald, Alexander [*pseud.* Alasdair Mac Mhaighstir Alasdair] (*c.*1695–*c.*1770), Scottish Gaelic poet, was born at Dalilea on the north bank of Loch Shiel; he was the second son of the Revd Alexander MacDonald (Maighstir Alasdair; *c.*1655–1724), the episcopalian clergyman in the wide parish of Ardnamurchan, and of his wife, who was a MacLachlan from Morven. His eldest brother was Angus, and he had several sisters. His father came from South Uist; his paternal grandfather, Ranald, was a son of Allan MacDonald, chief of Clanranald, and his grandmother belonged to the family of the MacDonalds of Islay. Flora MacDonald of the Jacobite rising of 1745 was the poet's first cousin. The Revd Alexander MacDonald had graduated MA from the

University of Glasgow in 1674, going on to study divinity thereafter. He seems to have been settled at Dalilea not later than 1687, and probably earlier. His son Alasdair is said to have attended Glasgow University also; his father may have intended him for the ministry and the chief of Clanranald apparently wished him to follow the law. He may have served Clanranald for some time in a quasi-legal capacity, but by 1729 or a little earlier he was employed as teacher and catechist (posts funded by the general assembly of the Church of Scotland and by the Scottish Society for the Propagation of Christian Knowledge), and he held various posts in locations from Islandfinnan to south Morven, until 1745. Shortly before the outbreak of the 'Forty-Five he seems to have officially converted to Roman Catholicism, a conversion that may have been as much political as religious. Alasdair married Jane Mac-Donald of Dalness; their son, Ranald [see MacDhomnuill, Raonuill], was a folklorist. Ranald was old enough to hold the school fort for his father when Alasdair was preparing for the rising in 1744-5. There were several daughters of this marriage also, the youngest born about 1746-7.

Alasdair played a prominent part in the 'Forty-Five; he held a captain's commission, made the acquaintance of Prince Charlie soon after his landing, and acted as the prince's Gaelic tutor. A journal of the 'Forty-Five campaign was compiled by Alasdair and some prominent Mac-Donald relatives and friends, and this was published in *The Lockhart Papers*, while various interviews with Bishop Forbes (between December 1747 and April 1751) later appeared in *The Lyon in Mourning*. Alasdair seems to have been involved in the entire campaign, from the welcome at Glenfinnan—via the battles of Prestonpans and Falkirk, the entries to Edinburgh and Glasgow, the march to Derby, and the skirmish at Clifton near Penrith—to the battle of Culloden. Some references in *The Lockhart Papers* and early poems referring to the battle of Sheriffmuir suggest that he may have taken part in the Jacobite rising of 1715 also, but this cannot be verified. His surviving poetry includes many songs and poems connected with the 'Forty-Five and with the political events of 1745-8. Some of these describe battles, or praise the highland clans, or propose toasts to the Stewarts, or vilify Cumberland and the anti-highland measures taken by the government after the rising. One or two also assess the situation, and its historical background, in a calm, judicious way.

Approximately 6000 lines survive of verse ascribed to Alasdair. It is likely that this represents only part of his total output. This verse has a wide range, as is indicated by a brief listing of topics: the origins of the Gaelic language, an address to the muses, an elegy for a pet dove, poems describing summer and winter and other poems of natural description, the idyllic 'Praise of Morag' and the scurrilous 'Dispraise of Morag', a bridal song, a fierce satire of an anti-Jacobite poetess, a satire of a priest and his parish, a satire of dissolute octogenarians in Ardnamurchan, a lengthy mixture of fun and satire directed at a catalogue of Campbells (named 'The Ark'), and a long poem of over 560 lines on Clanranald's galley ('Birlinn Chlann Ragh-naill'). This poetry shows Alasdair's acquaintance with the earlier traditions of Gaelic verse and saga, with classical literature to some extent, and probably with the work of earlier Scots poets such as Gavin Douglas, and with the contemporary eighteenth-century poet James Thomson, author of *The Seasons*. These influences surface in various poems, but never dominate them. The poet is his own master, in terms of construction, development of theme, and felicity of language. He deploys a huge vocabulary, and continually shows inventive genius. His two seasonal poems owe something to an ancient Gaelic tradition of nature description and also to Thomson's *Seasons*, but they also carry the clear stamp of Alasdair's own genius; a succession of eighteenth-century Gaelic poets followed him in this particular seasonal poetry track. His 'Praise of Morag' has a delicate erotic felicity and his galley poem a detailed dramatic development, while his satires explore the language of depravity with brilliance. There is some earlier evidence of his involvement with Gaelic vocabulary, for he edited a Gaelic–English vocabulary for the Scottish Society for the Propagation of Christian Knowledge in the mid-1730s. This was published in 1741 and is partly based on an existing vocabulary of English and on Edward Lhuyd's *Archaeologia Britannica* (1707). A manuscript in the special collections department of Glasgow University Library includes copies, apparently in the poet's hand, of Irish grammars, one from an English–Irish dictionary published in Paris in 1732. The poet's *Vocabulary* was the first secular Gaelic book to be printed and the collection of his own poetry published in 1751 was the first printed collection of secular Gaelic verse.

Relatively little is known of Alasdair's later years after his last meeting with Bishop Forbes in 1751. It is known that he lived for a short period on the Isle of Canna, where he apparently composed at least part of the galley poem. Later he lived in Moidart, Knoydart, Morar, and Arisaig, apparently dying about 1770 in isolation from his family, but reciting with his final breaths some newly composed lines to two youngsters who were watching over him on his deathbed. He was buried at Arisaig. It is not known when his wife died. His son, Ranald, by 1770 was living on the Isle of Eigg, and in 1776 he published an anthology of Gaelic verse, apparently using his father's papers and including a few items of his father's verse. There has been a succession of editions of Alasdair's poetry, most of them rather uncritical. The most complete works, with an English translation, appeared in 1924; a critical edition of the 'Birlinn' in 1933 (A. MacLeod, *Sàr Orain, Three Gaelic Poems*, 1933); an important collection of his political poems in 1933 (*Highland Songs of the 'Forty-Five*, ed. J. L. Campbell, 1933; repr., 1984); and an edition of *Selected Poems*, using a wide range of sources, in 1996 (*Alasdair Mac Mhaighstir Alasdair, Selected Poems*, ed. D. S. Thomson).

DERICK S. THOMSON

Sources R. Black, *Mac Mhaighstir Alasdair: the Ardnamurchan years* (1986) · *Eigg collection*, ed. R. MacDonald (1776) · R. Forbes, *The lyon in mourning, or, A collection of speeches, letters, journals … relative to … Prince Charles Edward Stuart*, ed. H. Paton, 3 vols., Scottish History Society, 20–22 (1895–6); repr. (1975) · G. Lockhart, *The Lockhart papers: containing memoirs and commentaries upon the affairs of Scotland from 1702 to 1715*, 2 vols. (1817) · A. Mac-Dhonuill, *Ais-eiridh na Sean*

Chanoin Albannaich (1751) · *The poems of Alexander MacDonald* (1924) · C. MacDonald, *Moidart, or, Among the Clanranalds* (1889); repr. (1989) · D. Thomson, 'Alasdair mac Mhaighstir Alasdair's political poetry', *Transactions of the Gaelic Society of Inverness*, 56 (1988–90), 185–213 · D. S. Thomson, *An introduction to Gaelic poetry*, 2nd edn (1990)

Archives NL Scot., Adv. MS 72.2.15 · Royal Irish Acad., R.I.A. MS E ii 1 (746) · U. Glas., MS gen 9 | U. Glas., McLagan MSS

MacDonald, Alexander (1736–1791), vicar apostolic of the highland district, the son of Ranald MacDonald, laird of Bornish, was born at Bornish on the island of South Uist. He entered the Scots College, Rome, on 20 January 1754, was ordained there on 10 August 1764, and returned to Scotland in April 1765. He was sent to the island of Barra, where he remained a missionary until 1780. On the death of Bishop John MacDonald (1727–1779) he was elected vicar apostolic by the priests of the highland district. He was nominated titular bishop of Polemonium on 30 September 1779, and was consecrated by Bishop Hay at Scalan on 12 March 1780. In 1783 he refounded the highland seminary at Samalaman, where he died on 9 September 1791, and was probably buried on St Finnan's Isle on Loch Moidart.   THOMPSON COOPER, *rev.* CLOTILDE PRUNIER

Sources J. Darragh, *The Catholic hierarchy of Scotland: a biographical list, 1653–1985* (1986) · Scottish mission vote slips, Scottish Catholic Archives, Edinburgh, 4/20/2 · C. Johnson, *Developments in the Roman Catholic church in Scotland, 1789–1829* (1983) · J. F. S. Gordon, *Ecclesiastical chronicle for Scotland, 1–2: Scotichronicon* (1875)

Archives Scottish Catholic Archives, Edinburgh, Blairs letters

MacDonald, Alexander (1755–1837), Roman Catholic priest and Scottish Gaelic scholar, was born in the west highlands of Scotland. Aged eleven he was received into the Roman Catholic seminary of Bourblach, in North Morar, by Bishop Hugh Macdonald. Alexander Macdonald was later sent to the Scots College in Rome, where, aged twenty-three, he was ordained priest by dispensation. In 1782 he returned to Scotland and, being a good student of Gaelic, he was placed at Balloch, near Drummond Castle, Perthshire, to attend the highlanders resident in that mission. Ten years later he was appointed missionary of the Gaelic chapel in Blackfriars' Wynd, Edinburgh. Afterwards he returned to Balloch, and eventually he built a chapel at Crieff, Perthshire, where he passed the remainder of his life, except for a short interval in 1827–8, when he took charge of the congregation at Leith.

A talented classical as well as Gaelic scholar, Macdonald was employed to give the Latin significations of the words for two letters of the alphabet in the *Dictionarium Scoto-Celticum: a Dictionary of the Gaelic language*, published under the direction of the Highland Society of Scotland in 1828. He himself published *Phingateis, sive, Hibernia liberata, epicum Ossianis poema, e Celtico sermone conversum, tribus praemissis disputationibus, et subsequentibus notis* (1820), dedicated to Augustus Frederick, duke of Sussex. Macdonald died at Crieff on 13 July 1837.

THOMPSON COOPER, *rev.* PHILIP CARTER

Sources *Dictionarium Scoto-Celticum: a dictionary of the Gaelic language*, 2 vols. (1828), preface · C. Johnson, *Developments in the Roman Catholic church in Scotland, 1789–1829* (1983) · D. S. Thomson, ed., *The companion to Gaelic Scotland*, new edn (1994)

Macdonald, Alexander (1791?–1850), antiquary, was employed at an early age as a clerk in the General Register House, Edinburgh, where he assisted Thomas Thomson in the preparation of *Acts of the Scottish Parliament* and other works. In 1824 he was elected a fellow of the Society of Antiquaries of Scotland, and in 1836 he was joint curator of the society's museum. For some years he had acted as curatorial assistant to James Skene, and had played an important part in the transfer of the society's collections to its new rooms in the Royal Institution building at the Mound. In 1836 he was appointed principal keeper of the register of deeds and probate writs or protests at Register House.

Macdonald is said to have supplied a considerable amount of the material for Sir Walter Scott's notes to the Waverley novels. Certainly it was his custom to provide scholars and men of letters with historical material extracted from the records in his care. In 1829, for instance, he transcribed for Scott lengthy extracts from the Orderly Book of the duke of Cumberland's army in Scotland in 1745–6; and Scott indeed incorporated portions of this in *Tales of a Grandfather*. (Macdonald's manuscript is in the National Library of Scotland.) Earlier, in 1825, Scott had stated that nothing could be more civil than the way Macdonald was superintending the work of gathering source material on King James VI and I. An invitation from Scott to Abbotsford in 1829 was clearly a great event in Macdonald's life. That year he had found an amanuensis for Scott. Many scholars acknowledged their debt to him. As Robert Chambers put it in 1826, by his assistance to him and to others Macdonald helped to advance the 'invaluable cause of antiquarian literature' (NL Scot., MS 3134, 219).

It was, however, as editor of the publications of the Maitland Club that Macdonald rendered most service to historical research. The volumes edited by him were: *The Register of Ministers, Exhorters, and Readers of the Church of Scotland* (1830); *Maitland Club Miscellany* (vols. 1 and 2, 1834); Adam Blackwood's *History of Mary, Queen of Scots* (1834); and *Report on the State of Certain Parishes in Scotland* (1835). He also edited *Letters to King James the Sixth* (1835), *Papers Relative to the Royal Guard of Scottish Archers in France* (1835), and *Letters to the Argyll Family* (1839). For the Bannatyne Club he edited *Registrum honoris de Morton*, published posthumously in 1853. Macdonald died at Edinburgh on 23 December 1850, aged about fifty-nine. His library at 5 Regent Terrace, rich in works on Scottish history and related matters, was sold by Tait and Nisbet on 7 May 1851.

T. F. HENDERSON, *rev.* IAIN GORDON BROWN

Sources D. Laing, 'Anniversary address on the state of the Society of Antiquaries of Scotland, from 1831 to 1860', *Archaeologia Scotica*, 5/1 (1890), 24 [address delivered on Monday, 9 Dec. 1861] · *Edinburgh Evening Courant* (26 Dec. 1850), 2 · *GM*, 2nd ser., 35 (1851), 317 · A. S. Bell, ed., *The Scottish antiquarian tradition* (1981), 67, 74 · NL Scot., MS 31134

Archives NL Scot., corresp. and historical notes and collections

MacDonald, Alexander (1794–1860), granite manufacturer, was born at Foss on the banks of the Tummel in Perthshire, the son of William MacDonald, farmer, and his wife, Isabella Stewart. Little is known about his early life, but after completing an elementary education, he worked as a farm labourer before serving an apprenticeship as a stonemason. In 1820 at the age of twenty-six he moved to Aberdeen where he opened up a stone-cutting yard in the Denburn district. Two years later he moved to larger premises in West North Street before finally settling in his yard in Constitution Street.

A man reputedly diligent in business, MacDonald initially worked principally in marble and in freestone, and it was not until 1829 that he turned his attention to cutting and polishing granite, the native rock of Aberdeenshire. Although granite had been quarried and worked in and around Aberdeen since the middle of the eighteenth century, few attempts had been made to polish the stone because of the time and expense involved. MacDonald was aware of the existence of examples of ancient Egyptian polished granite in the British Museum and went to examine these on a visit to London. On his return to Aberdeen he began experimenting in polishing the Aberdeenshire granites. His early implements and methods were crude, but he did succeed in polishing the stone, and it was from this that the Aberdeen granite manufacturing industry grew.

Polishing by hand using sea sand, emery sand, and oxide of iron proved painfully slow and MacDonald had to content himself by making small tombstones of simple design, mantelpieces, and bust pedestals. Such limitations provoked him to try to speed up the process through the application of steam power. Using a steam engine borrowed from John Stewart's nearby Aberdeen Combworks, MacDonald eventually succeeded in achieving a firm, high-quality, even polish on granite. The local market proved receptive to his product and in 1832 he sent a machine-polished headstone to Kensal Green cemetery in London, where it aroused considerable interest in the London monumental masonry trade. Orders came quickly and a healthy export trade ensued. What MacDonald's early processes and machinery were like is not known, but he is credited with inventing the three main polishing machines: the lathe, the pendulum, and the carriage or waggon. These dominated the industry until the latter decades of the nineteenth century, and were occasionally used beyond 1914.

MacDonald also made a major contribution to the working of granite by adopting the patent axe or bush hammer, as it was more commonly called, to cut and carve stone. Originating in the United States, the bush hammer was brought to Aberdeen by a local textile magnate, James Hadden, who had obtained one on a visit to New York. By a circuitous route via various building masons, a bush hammer came into MacDonald's possession. Until then he, like other monumental masons in Aberdeen, had been content to cut and carve granite using the five-pointed chisels that were introduced to the city manufacturers by itinerant freestone masons in 1818. MacDonald found the bush hammer was ideal for cutting granite, and after his own success it became the standard cutting tool in the industry until 1945.

It was the introduction of the bush hammer that enabled MacDonald to make his final contribution to granite manufacturing: cutting and carving statues, elaborate monuments, and sarcophagi. It was with bush hammers that the magnificent statue of the fifth duke of Gordon and Prince Albert's sarcophagus were cut in MacDonald's yard. Indeed, in consequence of these developments, Aberdeen granite masters in general quickly established themselves in the field of high-quality stone carving in granite, and gained a worldwide reputation.

At the time of his death in 1860, MacDonald employed over a hundred men at the Constitution Street works, and his yard was considered the best equipped in Aberdeen. He was married to Jessie Paterson (d. 1873), and owing to his dominant position in the industry succeeded in amassing a considerable fortune. This enabled him to purchase the estate of Johnston in the Garioch for £26,000 and also the small property of Shannaburn near Maryculter. Despite his achievements he was an extremely shy and retiring man and played no part in Aberdeen's public life. A Baptist by religion, he was generous to the Scottish Baptist church with which he had been associated throughout his years in Aberdeen. He died from a severe attack of bronchitis at his home, 7 Bon Accord Square, Aberdeen, on 23 March 1860 and was interred at Nellfield cemetery, where his wife was also laid to rest thirteen years later.

THOMAS DONNELLY

Sources T. Donnelly, 'The development of the Aberdeen granite industry, 1750–1939', PhD diss., U. Aberdeen, 1975 · W. Black, *The rise and progress of the Aberdeen granite industry* (1948) · *Aberdeen Journal* (28 March 1860)

Macdonald [*formerly* McDonald], **Alexander** (1821–1881), trade unionist and politician, was born on 27 June 1821 at Dalmacoulter Farm, New Monkland, Lanarkshire, the eldest of seven children of Daniel McDonald and his wife, Ann, *née* Watt. His father was a former seaman in the Royal Navy, who was employed as an agricultural labourer at the time of Alexander's birth, and subsequently worked as a coal and ironstone miner. The spelling of the family name was traditionally McDonald; Alexander adopted the Macdonald form in the 1870s. The family moved around the Lanarkshire coalfield before settling at Wattston near Airdrie in 1840. Although Macdonald was a regular church attender in his early years and a pupil at the parish school, his religious faith seems to have faded in later life, and it would appear that he had no particular religious affiliation by the time of his death. Macdonald never married but he always maintained close and cordial relations with his extended family.

After a brief spell at New Monkland parish school, from the age of nine in 1830 until 1846 Macdonald worked as a coal and ironstone miner. Although a hard-working and successful miner, working on occasion as an oversman, the lowest rung of the mining managerial ladder of the time, he also seems to have been active in attempts to organize the miners into trade unions, and suffered some victimization from employers as a consequence. He took one of the few routes out of the pit by extending his

Alexander Macdonald (1821–1881), by unknown engraver, pubd 1874

meagre education using his earnings to finance evening-class studies in Greek and Latin. This eventually allowed him to attend Glasgow University full-time between 1846 and 1849. Attending university in the winter, he worked as a miner in the summer months to fund his education. Macdonald did not take a degree, but his certificates of attendance allowed him to follow a career as a teacher. Life at university left its mark, and in later years when he had sufficient wealth he was able to bequeath £1000 to Glasgow University to provide two annual bursaries for young miners keen to pursue full-time studies at that institution.

From 1850 to 1855 Macdonald made a living as a teacher and private tutor in Airdrie. His ability to engage easily with social groups outside the labouring classes was to become a key factor in his success as an advocate of organized labour, but it also brought accusations of social snobbery, and even betrayal, by some contemporaries and later commentators. Macdonald's involvement in colliery enterprises, which grew out of contacts he acquired at university and as a private tutor, always added to the suspicion that his commitment to organized labour was compromised by his status as an owner of capital. It was, however, the small fortune he accumulated from speculative investment in the mining industry which allowed him the time and security to engage in labour activism. An effective and engaging public speaker, he could be rather censorious about the perceived weaknesses of the working men he led, but he was also hostile to middle- or upper-class paternalism.

Macdonald was among the first trade union leaders to achieve national standing, but he saw himself as an agent and advocate of labour working within, rather than challenging, the economic order. His rise to national prominence began in October 1855 when he created a unified Scottish coal and ironstone miners' union. While this union was little more than a co-ordinating body, with Macdonald as its sole paid official, it did try to convert the older traditions of Scottish mining unionism, which sought restriction of output and control over the entry of workers into mining, into a more formal regulatory relationship with the employers. It also established Macdonald's belief in lobbying parliament as a means of redressing the grievances of working men, especially in relation to long-standing abuses such as the truck system or raising the minimum working age. It was an outlook reinforced by a dispute which engulfed the coal industry in Scotland in 1856. Against Macdonald's advice, the Scottish miners came out on strike in the spring of 1856 seeking to reverse wage cuts imposed by the owners. By the early summer the strike and the newly formed union had collapsed.

Macdonald's belief in negotiation and lobbying was to bring him into frequent conflict with union activists who sought a more confrontational strategy. It was a conflict of perspective and outlook which was to be exposed most starkly with the establishment of the Miners' National Association in 1863. This was the culmination of earlier attempts by Macdonald to create a union linking all the British coalfields. In 1858 an informal co-ordinating body headed by Macdonald had been established; this he used as a platform to lobby parliament and government ministers. It paid off in the enactment in 1860 of the Mines Act, which included the vital provision for the election by miners of a checkweighman at each pit to ensure fair payment of wages. The creation of this post was to give a great fillip to union organization in the coalfields. Despite Macdonald's success, there was often a feeling that the interests of the mine workers were being sacrificed by leaders who were too close to the owners in terms of mentality and lifestyle. In 1864 this debate over strategy resulted in a short-lived schism in the miners' ranks. Led by the radical journalist John Towers, and the former Chartist lawyer W. P. Roberts, critics of Macdonald withdrew from the National Association and established the Practical Miners' Association which tried to pursue a more aggressive industrial policy. This breakaway organization collapsed within two years, but there remained an undercurrent of suspicion and hostility to the leadership of Macdonald. His well-known friendship with the wealthy Scottish tory coal owner Lord Elcho did little to allay such misgivings. Yet despite this opposition, he does seem to have retained the confidence of ordinary members of his association, and was the recipient of a number of collections and donations subscribed by them.

Macdonald was elected to the first parliamentary committee of the Trades Union Congress in 1871, and he served as chairman of the committee in 1872 and 1873. He lobbied the Liberal government over changes relating to trade union activities in the Criminal Law Amendment Act of 1871, and the Mines Regulation Act of 1872. In addition Macdonald accepted a place on the royal commission on trade unions which reported in 1875. However, he issued a dissenting statement, arguing for more extensive reforms of labour laws than the majority report had advocated.

From 1869 Thomas Halliday and his Amalgamated Association of Miners, which recruited mainly in Lancashire and south Wales, provided another challenge to Macdonald's parliament focused strategy. However, relations between Macdonald and Halliday were never acrimonious and this threat to Macdonald's national supremacy also faded in the later 1870s. His enthusiasm for the parliamentary road to improved conditions culminated in Macdonald's election as MP for Stafford in 1874. As the endorsed candidate of the Labour Representation League, Macdonald is recognized, alongside Thomas Burt, the MP for Morpeth returned at the same election, as one of the first two overtly labour, albeit Liberal/labour, members of parliament. While he took the Liberal whip Macdonald always adopted a fairly independent stance, and made 'labour' questions and resolution of the Irish problem the focus of his parliamentary work. Towards the end of his life young activists in the Scottish coalfields, such as James Keir Hardie, again questioned Macdonald's collaborative strategy. Re-elected as MP for Stafford in 1880, he served briefly as a government back-bencher until his death in 1881.

Towards the end of his life Macdonald purchased a small estate at Wellhall near Hamilton, where he died on 31 October 1881. He was buried in the churchyard at New Monkland on 6 November. While some of his critics, both contemporary and recent, have seen his leadership as flawed, he is rightly regarded as one of the founding fathers of mining trade unionism and labour politics.

RICHARD LEWIS

Sources G. M. Wilson, *Alexander McDonald: leader of the miners* (1982) · R. C. Challinor, *Alexander Macdonald and the miners* (1968) · A. B. Campbell, *The Lanarkshire miners: a social history of their trade unions, 1775–1974* (1979) · F. Reid, 'Alexander Macdonald and the crisis of the independent collier, 1872–1874', *Independent collier*, ed. R. Harrison (1978) · R. C. Challinor and B. Ripley, *The Miners' Association: a trade union in the age of the chartists* (1968) · R. Challinor, *A radical lawyer in Victorian England: W. P. Roberts and the struggle for workers' rights* (1990) · R. P. Arnot, *A history of Scottish miners from the earliest times* [1955] · J. E. Williams, *The Derbyshire miners: a study in industrial and social history* (1962) · A. J. Taylor, 'The Miners' Association of Great Britain and Ireland, 1842–48: a problem of integration', *Economica*, new ser., 22 (1955), 45–60 · A. J. Youngson Brown, 'Trade union policy in the Scottish coalfields, 1855–1885', *Economic History Review*, 2nd ser., 6 (1953–4), 35–50 · 'Macdonald, Alexander', *DLB*, vol. 1

Archives NA Scot., Wemyss MSS, corresp. with Lord Elcho
Likenesses engraving, pubd 1874, NPG [*see illus.*] · portrait, repro. in Wilson, *Alexander McDonald*
Wealth at death £3487 3s. 3d.: probate, 19 May 1882, CCI

McDonald, Allan (1859–1905), Roman Catholic priest and folklorist, son of John McDonald and his wife, Margaret, *née* MacPherson, was born at Kilmallie, on the borders of Argyll and Inverness-shire, on 25 October 1859. He was educated at Blairs College, Kincardineshire, and at the Colegio Real de los Escoceses, at Valladolid, Spain. He was ordained by Archbishop Eyre at St Andrews Cathedral in the summer of 1882. He was then appointed to the Oban mission under Bishop Angus MacDonald, and in 1884

became parish priest of Dalibrog with Eriskay in South Uist, an almost wholly Gaelic-speaking community, where he perfected his knowledge of the Gaelic language and of its South Uist dialect in which most of his writing was done.

Probably encouraged by the Revd Alexander Campbell, a priest born in South Uist about 1819, McDonald began in 1887 to note down local traditions, songs, proverbs, and customs, often giving the actual Gaelic words of his respondents. By December 1892, well before the folklorist movement showed an interest in the Hebrides, he had filled two large notebooks. By 1900 he had amassed a substantial collection, which included examples of second sight, Gaelic hymns, and his poetry. He published a collection of Gaelic hymns for children in 1889 and a larger collection in 1893. His reputation spread beyond the Hebrides and in 1895, soon after his health had broken down and his duties had been confined to the island of Eriskay, he was visited by Ada Goodrich Freer in connection with the Society for Psychical Research's inquiry into second sight. The inquiry came to little, but Freer returned with abundant literary and folklore material, which she soon began to publish. She did this with McDonald's perhaps naïve permission and she acknowledged his help, but she gave the impression that McDonald was little more than her assistant and that some of his material had in fact been collected by her. The extent of her reliance on McDonald later became apparent. McDonald was visited by several folklorists including, in the summer of 1905, Marjory Kennedy-Fraser, whom he also generously helped.

McDonald was active in South Uist affairs and was briefly a member of Inverness-shire county council. He built a new church on Eriskay in 1903, financed by the sale of his manuscripts to Walter Blackie, the publisher. He was dean of the Isles, and died of pneumonia on 8 October 1905 on Eriskay, where he was buried.

After McDonald's death his notebooks and papers were dispersed, and by the 1920s were thought completely lost. However, from 1947 this contributor, with the help of friends, was able to trace many of them and they are now chiefly in the Carmichael MSS in Edinburgh University Library and in the Henderson MSS in Glasgow University Library. McDonald's role in the timely collection of a fast-vanishing Hebridean folklore cannot be too strongly emphasized.

J. L. CAMPBELL

Sources J. L. Campbell, *Fr Allan McDonald of Eriskay*, 2nd edn (1956) · J. L. Campbell, 'The late Fr Allan McDonald, Miss Goodrich Freer and Hebridean folklore', *Scottish Studies*, 2 (1958), 175–88 · 'An Sithean Ruadh', *Celtic Review*, 3 (1906–7), 77–83 · *Catholic Directory for Scotland* (1906) · J. L. Campbell and F. Collinson, *Hebridean folksongs* (1969) · A. Murray, *Father Allan's island* (1920) · F. Rea, *A school in South Uist*, ed. J. L. Campbell (1964)

Archives priv. coll. | U. Edin., Carmichael MSS · U. Glas., Henderson MSS
Wealth at death £350 5s. 8d.: probate, 5 April 1906, CCI

Macdonald, Andrew [*pseud.* Matthew Bramble] (1757–1790), poet and playwright, was born at Edinburgh on 27 February 1757, the son of George Donald, a gardener, and his wife, Janet Elliot. He was educated at the grammar school in Leith and at Edinburgh University, under the sponsorship of Bishop Forbes of Ross and Caithness, who shared his father's Stuart sympathies. He received deacon's orders in the Scottish Episcopal church in 1775, when he lengthened his surname to Macdonald. After acting as a private tutor for a year to Oliphant of Gask's children, in Gask, Perthshire, he was appointed in 1777 to a charge in Glasgow. In 1782 he published *Velina, a Poetical Fragment*, and the following year, *The Independent*, a novel. Although apparently a good preacher, his income was diminishing with his congregation, and marrying the maidservant at his lodgings injured his prospects further. His tragedy *Vimonda* had been performed in Edinburgh to much acclaim, and he resigned his charge to move there as a writer. After living beyond his means for a while, he left Edinburgh to seek his fortune in London, where he made many friends and his prospects brightened. *Vimonda* was produced at the Haymarket on 5 September 1787, to an encouraging reception, and was printed in 1788. Macdonald's other dramatic efforts, however, were failures. As Matthew Bramble, he amused London for some time with poetical burlesques, cleverly modelled on John Wolcot (Peter Pindar), which brought him popularity but little remuneration. Macdonald's health quickly deteriorated and he died of consumption in Kentish Town, London, on 22 August 1790, leaving his widow and infant daughter destitute. A posthumous volume of sermons (1790) secured some further popularity, and Macdonald's *Miscellaneous Works*, including all his known writings, appeared in 1791. T. W. BAYNE, *rev.* SARAH COUPER

Sources [J. Robertson], *Lives of Scottish poets*, 3 (1822), 3 · Chambers, *Scots.* (1835) · D. E. Baker, *Biographia dramatica, or, A companion to the playhouse*, rev. I. Reed, new edn, rev. S. Jones, 3 vols. in 4 (1812) · *GM*, 1st ser., 60 (1790), 770 · Genest, *Eng. stage*, vol. 6 · [I. D'Israeli], *Calamities of authors*, 1 (1812) · *IGI* · L. Baillie and P. Sieveking, eds., *British biographical archive* (1984) [microfiche] · *N&Q*, 2nd ser., 9 (1860), 321–2

MacDonald, Angus (d. 1314×18). *See under* MacDonald family (*per. c.*1300–*c.*1500).

MacDonald, Angus (d. *c.*1490). *See under* MacDonald family (*per. c.*1300–*c.*1500).

MacDonald, Angus, of Dunyvaig and the Glens (c.1548–1613), chief of clan Iain Mhòr or clan Donald south, was born probably in Dunyvaig Castle, in Islay, the family seat. He was the second of six legitimate sons of James *Mac-Donald, sixth chief (*c.*1515–1565), and his wife, Lady Agnes *Campbell (d. in or after 1590), daughter of the third earl of Argyll, who was allegedly abducted into this, her second marriage, in 1545. After her husband's death Lady Agnes was married for a third time, in 1569, to Turlough Luineach O'Neill of Tír Eoghain, or Tyrone, a political union which greatly facilitated the lucrative hire of her son's mercenaries by the native Irish. Angus succeeded to the chiefship, as eighth chief, after the death of his elder brother, Archibald MacDonald, in 1568. He is likely to have received a traditional Gaelic education, befitting the son of a chief, from members of hereditary learned families who taught literacy in common classical Gaelic,

bardic verse, seanchus or history, harping and bagpiping, and the exercise of military prowess, such as sword fighting and use of the cudgel. He was born into the Catholic faith, though it was illegal to practise it in Scotland throughout his chiefship. With his wife, Fynvola MacLean of Duart, he had at least two legitimate sons, James and Angus Og MacDonald, and a daughter, Margaret; he also had two natural sons, Gillespie or Archibald MacDonald of Gigha and Ranald Og MacAllester. In 1597, according to the state papers for Ireland, he also accepted the eldest son of Hugh O'Neill, second earl of Tyrone, under the Gaelic system of fosterage.

The clan Donald south, a fragment of the old lordship of the Isles, was one of the most powerful on the western seaboard of Scotland in the late sixteenth century, with extensive lands in Kintyre, Islay, and Jura, and the Glens of Antrim. Angus MacDonald was not an impressive figure. Sir Arthur Chichester said of him in 1602 that he was 'a perpetual drunkard ... [and] his men of base and treacherous disposition, inclined to dissolute and licentious living' (*CSP Ire.*, 1601–3, 335). But he had the additional misfortune to be chief when a lethal combination of external forces and internal dissension had begun to prey upon the stability of the clan. The main external threat came from his mother's family, the house of Argyll. The Campbells, who had long coveted the clan's territory in Kintyre, were often employed by the lowland government in the 1580s and 1590s, as it became increasingly determined to bring the clans under control. In addition, the English government was constantly trying to limit the involvement of Angus's mercenaries in Ireland, and in this it increasingly had the support of James VI, looking ahead to the day when, as king of England and Ireland, he inherited all the problems associated with Anglo-Irish condominium. There was also almost continuous conflict between the clan and Angus's wife's family, the MacLeans of Duart, over the title to the Rhinns of Islay, a dispute which eventually gave the government an additional excuse for intervention.

The MacDonald–MacLean feud, begun under James MacDonald, continued under his son, and reached a peak of violence in May 1586, when the massacre of MacLean prisoners by Angus's men led to the enactment of the statute known as 'murder under trust'. Eventually, in 1590, Angus was summoned with Lachlan MacLean and Donald Gorm MacDonald of Sleat under a safe conduct to Edinburgh, to discuss the governance of their territories. They were imprisoned instead, to be released a year later on surety of 10,000 merks each, and equal amounts in annual rent. Angus's heir, James [*see below*], was imprisoned in Edinburgh Castle as surety for his father, and remained there almost continually over the next five years, with only brief periods of liberation to try and persuade his father to agree to terms. Angus was also compelled to find surety for his clansmen's good behaviour in Ireland. By 1594, however, both he and Lachlan MacLean had been placed under sentence of forfeiture for refusal to submit to the king. MacLean submitted in June 1596 and agreed to augment his rents, but Angus held out. In the same month, according to intelligence from Knockfergus, Angus sought the help of O'Neill, earl of Tyrone, whereupon the exasperated king gave MacLean a lease of the Rhinns of Islay, and commissioned Sir William Stewart of Houston to lead an expedition against the clan Donald south, with orders to take its main castles. Angus still refused to submit, but his affairs were made still more complicated by a dispute with his kinsmen in northern Ireland. The two branches of clan Donald south had co-operated under the leadership of Sorley Boy (Somhairle Buidhe) *MacDonnell, but after the latter's death in 1590 his son James MacSorley quarrelled with Angus, principally over the Glens of Antrim, held by Angus of the English crown and administered by his son Angus Og. In 1596 James took forcible possession of the glens, and in the following year submitted a claim to Kintyre and Islay as well, declaring that Angus was illegitimate; the allegation was a useful weapon against Angus for James VI. With Argyll controlling the movement of fighting men between Scotland and Ireland, Angus could hope for no support from O'Neill.

Beset on every side, and with no effective allies, in November 1596 Angus MacDonald submitted to King James. The settlement imposed by the king was potentially ruinous, since it required Angus to withdraw from Kintyre and Gigha. His agent in these negotiations was his son **Sir James MacDonald of Knockrinsay** (c.1570–1626), and Angus's inability to control the divisions within his own clan was most poignantly manifested in the utter breakdown of relations which followed between himself and his heir. James MacDonald was now in his midtwenties. Knighted between 1594 and 1596, he married Margaret, sister of Campbell of Cawdor, about 1597, but had no children. He spent several years in custody as a result of the government's hostage diplomacy, thereby losing all faith in his father. The terms he obtained in 1596 would have required him yet again to stay at court. Sir James understood, where his father did not, that prolonged passive resistance could no longer force an issue with the government. He felt that the clan should make a tactical withdrawal from Kintyre so that it could at least retain Islay. Angus disagreed. Having abandoned hope of persuading his father to submit to the crown, and bitter at the years of imprisonment in his stead, Sir James set fire to his father's house of Askomull, in Campbeltown in Kintyre, in February 1598, in the full knowledge that his parents were inside. But though he was badly burnt, Angus survived to be imprisoned by Sir James, who now assumed leadership of the clan.

The MacLeans took the opportunity of this internecine strife to drive the MacDonalds out of Islay, and make good their lease from the crown. Battle ensued on 5 August 1598 at Loch Gruinart, where MacLean was killed. Sir James went to Edinburgh, offering to carry out the promises which his father had made in 1597 to evacuate Kintyre, to surrender Dunyvaig Castle, and to pay crown rents, and offered to pay his father a pension of 1000 merks per annum, for which he wished to be confirmed in the title to Islay. But thanks to the intervention of John Campbell of

Cawdor and the seventh earl of Argyll, Sir James was not granted the feu. When Angus escaped from imprisonment in 1600, father and son vied for the leadership. Angus succeeded in capturing his son in 1603, and handed him over to Argyll, who nevertheless worked against Angus in the privy council to gain a feu of the crown lands in Kintyre and Jura, which had been forfeited by him.

By 1605 Angus had effectively lost control of Kintyre and Jura, which were formally granted to Argyll in 1607. He held on to Colonsay and Islay, however, and like other chiefs consequently remained subject to pressure from the crown. A show of force in 1608, during which Dunyvaig Castle was occupied, was followed in 1609 by a commission led by Bishop Andrew Knox, which held a justiciary court to which the island chiefs were summoned, including Angus. The statutes of Iona which Knox then promulgated continued the process of reducing chiefly power; Angus MacDonald, brought to submission by the previous year's expedition, also agreed to pay £3000 arrears of rent. By this time he was probably worn down by his efforts to preserve his heritage. The last significant transaction of his life was effectively an acknowledgement of failure. By a deed of 1 January 1612 he surrendered his patrimony in Islay to Sir John Campbell of Cawdor, in exchange for other lands and a payment of 6000 merks, thereby continuing the absorption of MacDonald territory by the Campbells. By the time Angus died, probably in Rothesay, between January and 17 March 1613, the clan Donald south had effectively disappeared as a territorial clan.

Meanwhile Sir James MacDonald had been put on trial in May 1609 for 'treasonable' breaking of ward and also for imprisoning and trying to kill his father. The court was presided over by Argyll himself, and inevitably Sir James was convicted, but though he was condemned to death he was not executed, but was placed in custody once more. Then, following Angus's death, his illegitimate son Ranald Og seized Dunyvaig Castle in spring 1614, triggering off a rising in Islay. Although Sir James made an offer from prison to recapture the castle, and to pay 8000 merks for the crown lands of Islay, a feu charter was instead issued to Cawdor. In May 1615 Sir James escaped from Edinburgh Castle, and with the support of MacDonald of Sleat and MacDonald of Clanranald drove Cawdor's men from Islay. In a letter to the secretary of state he insisted that 'if his Majestie be not willing that I sall be his heignes tennent in Ila, for Goddis cause let his Majestie hauld it in his awin hand; for that is certane, I will die befoir I sie a Campbell posses it' (Pitcairn, 21). But when Argyll arrived as royal lieutenant to repress the rising, assisted by English ships, Sir James was obliged to escape to Galway, and then to Spain. Although he was pardoned in 1620, he was never permitted to return to Scotland, but lived in London until his death there in 1626.   F. A. MACDONALD

Sources J. R. N. MacPhail, ed., *Highland papers*, 3: 1662–1667; Scottish History Society, 2nd ser., 20 (1920), Denmylne MSS · R. Pitcairn, ed., *Ancient criminal trials in Scotland*, 3, Bannatyne Club, 42 (1833) · C. Fraser-Mackintosh, *The last MacDonalds of Isla* (1895) ·

D. Stevenson, *Alasdair MacColla and the highland problem in the seventeenth century* (1980) • 'Observations of Mr Dioness Campbell Deane of Limerick on the west isles of Scotland', *Miscellany of the Maitland Club*, ed. J. Robertson, 4, pt 1 (1847), 41–57; Maitland Club, 67 • A. MacDonald and A. MacDonald, *The clan Donald*, 3 vols. (1896–1904) • *CSP Ire.*, 1509–73; 1592–6; 1601–3 • *CSP Scot.*, 1596–7 • G. A. Hayes-McCoy, *Scots mercenary forces in Ireland* (1937) • D. Gregory, *The history of the western highlands and isles of Scotland, 1493 to 1625*, 2nd edn (1881) • G. Hill, *An historical account of the MacDonnells of Antrim* (1873) • E. J. Cowan, 'Clanship, kinship and the Campbell acquisition of Islay', *SHR*, 58 (1979), 132–57 • N. Maclean-Bristol, *Murder under trust* (1999) • J. Goodare, 'The statutes of Iona in context', *SHR*, 77 (1998), 31–57 • A. I. Macinnes, *Clanship, commerce and the house of Stuart, 1603–1788* (1996) • J. Goodare, *State and society in early modern Scotland* (1999) • J. M. Hill, 'The rift within clan Ian Mor: the Antrim and Dunyveg MacDonnells, 1590–1603', *Sixteenth Century Journal*, 24 (1993), 865–79 • *Collectanea de rebus Albanicis*, Iona Club, 1 (1847)

Macdonald, Angus (1836–1886), obstetrician, was born in Aberdeen on 18 April 1836, the son of James Macdonald (*d.* 1846), road contractor, and Margaret Bannerman. He had little schooling until after the death of his father, when his mother, a woman of character and intellect, moved with her young family to Grange in Banffshire; he then attended Grange parish school, being taught by an inspiring schoolmaster, Arthur Gerrard. Macdonald received only a total of two years of formal education, having to work as an agricultural labourer while studying; however, Gerrard gave him a thorough grounding in Latin, which enabled him to sit the bursary competition for King's College, Aberdeen, and to win an award at the comparatively late age of nineteen. Macdonald matriculated in arts in 1855 and followed the four-year course, tutoring during term-time and labouring at home in the summer and autumn. He graduated MA in 1859 and left Aberdeen to read theology at the Divinity Hall of the United Presbyterian church in Edinburgh.

After one session of theology Macdonald found he was more interested in medicine, and in 1860 he entered the medical faculty of Edinburgh University, without abandoning his deeply held religious beliefs. His teachers included James Syme, John Goodsir, Robert Christison, J. Y. Simpson, and J. H. Bennett. Macdonald still had to augment his small funds with private tutoring in general and medical subjects, and he established a reputation as a teacher. He also found time for running and walking, which he enjoyed. In his midwifery finals he was examined on accidental haemorrhage and abortion. He graduated MD in 1864. Once qualified, he began in practice in Edinburgh, and lectured in the extramural school and at the Royal Infirmary on materia medica, midwifery, and the diseases of women. He published a revision of Scoresby-Jackson's materia medica with a supplement containing the new preparations introduced into the British pharmacopoeia of 1867. Another book, *The Bearings of Chronic Heart Disease on Pregnancy*, was published in 1878.

In 1866 Macdonald married Annie Finlayson (1839–1917), daughter of an Edinburgh Presbyterian minister, Thomas Finlayson, and Janet Carrick Chrystal. The couple lived at 41 Northumberland Street, Edinburgh, where Macdonald practised with increasing success as he concentrated more on obstetrics. He was admitted a fellow of the Royal College of Surgeons of Edinburgh in 1865, and of the Royal College of Physicians of Edinburgh in 1869. As physician to the Royal Maternity Hospital he kept up assiduously with new developments in his subject. Operations for the removal of ovarian cysts and fibroid tumours of the uterus as well as extra-uterine pregnancy now became the mainstay of his practice, and some of his work showed a talent for bold innovation. His contributions to the *Edinburgh Medical Journal* showed his development as a surgeon and his application to detail in the meticulous operations of which he became master. In 1882 the strain of overwork combined with a cold led to an attack of pleuropneumonia which forced him to stop work and to travel to the French riviera for warmth and rest.

Macdonald's career had been unusually prosperous. He had moved both his home and his consulting rooms to the fashionable Charlotte Square (while retaining the plain, approachable manner of the northern Scottish doctor), and he was now the father of seven children: Thomas Finlayson, Jessie Chrystal, Angus, Robert John, Margaret Bremner, George Andrew, and Ranald, the last born in 1881. On his return from France in 1882 Macdonald cut his workload, but the pulmonary trouble flared up again early in 1886. He died in Edinburgh on 10 February 1886, and was buried nearby in the Grange cemetery. His widow died in Edinburgh in 1917. Their eldest son, Thomas, became a doctor, but died in 1896 at the age of twenty-seven.

Macdonald's singular achievement was the remarkable advance he made in his chosen field in spite of early poverty and a late start in life. His writing, particularly in his papers for the Edinburgh Obstetrical Society, was noted for its clarity. He enhanced the reputation of the Edinburgh medical school, and greatly influenced the next generation of obstetricians. JO CURRIE

Sources *Edinburgh Medical Journal*, 31 (1885–6), 990–98 • student schedule, U. Edin. L., special collections division, university archives • census returns for Northumberland Street, Edinburgh, 1871 • census returns for Charlotte Square, Edinburgh, 1881 • m. cert.
Likenesses photograph, repro. in J. D. Comrie, *History of Scottish medicine* (1927); new edn (1932)
Wealth at death £11,888 7s. 6d.: confirmation, 28 April 1886, *CCI*

Macdonald, Angus (1938–1999), piper, was born at 429 Parliamentary Road, Glasgow, on 20 October 1938, the son of Alexander Macdonald and his wife, Helen Chalmers Donald. His father was originally from Glenuig and had served with the Cameron Highlanders before joining the Glasgow police and becoming a member of the famous Glasgow police pipe band, which won the world pipe band championship six times between 1936 and 1951. Angus Macdonald therefore was born into a piping environment, with many relatives and family friends among the top pipers of the time. Macdonald's mother died when he was only nine years old, leaving his father to bring up the boy and his younger sister, Ella. This was difficult for a serving policeman, so Ella went to stay with an aunt and Angus went as a boarder to the Queen Victoria School, Dunblane. Here he had piping tuition from Pipe Major George Sanderson and soon became boy pipe major of the school.

In December 1953 Macdonald enlisted in the Scots Guards as a boy soldier, beginning a thirty-year career. In the guards he received tuition from pipe majors K. G. and J. S. Roe, piobaireachd tuition from Pipe Major Alexander Macdonald, the queen's piper, and further tuition from Captain John A. MacLellan at the Army School of Piping. Macdonald served in France, Germany, Borneo, Malaya, Sharjah, and Northern Ireland. In 1965 he was promoted to pipe major and appointed household piper to the queen. In 1974 he was put in charge of the piping school at the guards' depot, where he remained for four years before serving with the 1st battalion and the regiment's recruiting team. He was then appointed senior instructor at the Army School of Piping and personal piper to the general officer commanding Scotland and governor of Edinburgh Castle. He was appointed MBE and retired from the army in 1983.

In the field of solo competing piping Macdonald's achievements were formidable. He won the gold medal at the Argyllshire Gathering in 1963, the clasp at the Northern Meeting in 1982, the Bratach Gorm in London in 1975, the piobaireachd and light music prizes at the Falkirk Tryst in 1981, the former winners' march, strathspey, and reel prizes in London six times, and the former winners' silver star at the Northern Meeting three times. He also won the Grants championship twice, and took numerous other prizes on the highland games circuit.

From 1974 Macdonald competed with the grade 1 British Caledonian Airways Pipe Band, then from 1990 to 1993 was a member of the Glencorse Pipe Band. From 1994 to 1999 he was a member of Callander and District Pipe Band, where he put a lot of time and effort into tutoring juvenile band members. A competition established in his memory, with the Angus Macdonald memorial trophy as prize, became an annual event at the Callander highland games.

After leaving the army Macdonald took employment with the bagpipe makers Grainger and Campbell in 1984, then in 1988 became an instructor at the College of Piping in Glasgow. He went to Oman to instruct the sultan's pipers for a time but returned to the College of Piping in 1990 and remained there until 1996, when he was asked to become senior instructor at the new piping centre. During his time at the College of Piping, Macdonald taught students from all over the world, and travelled widely to teach at summer schools abroad. He is remembered with affection in many places where he taught, and competitions have been held in his memory in the United States. He made two solo recordings of bagpipe music, *Ceol beag from the Castle* in the early 1980s and *The World's Greatest Pipers*, volume 1, in 1985. In 1995 he published two collections of music, including many of his own compositions, several of which have become popular with pipers and pipe bands. Macdonald's marriage to Anne Ivy Thomas ended in separation. They had a daughter, Fiona. Macdonald died of cancer in the Fairmile Marie Curie Centre, Edinburgh, on 25 June 1999. A funeral service was held at St Mungo's Chapel, Linn crematorium, Glasgow, on 3 July.

ROBERT WALLACE

Sources *The Scotsman* (30 June 1999) · *The Times* (9 July 1999) · *The Guardian* (12 July 1999) · *The Independent* (30 Sept 1999) · College of Piping records, College of Piping, Glasgow · b. cert. · d. cert. **Archives** College of Piping, Glasgow, records **Likenesses** photograph, repro. in *The Scotsman* · photograph, repro. in *The Guardian*

MacDonald, Angus Óg. See MacDonald, Angus (*d.* 1314x18), *under* MacDonald family (*per. c.*1300–*c.*1500); *see* MacDonald, Angus (*d. c.*1490), *under* MacDonald family (*per. c.*1300–*c.*1500).

Macdonald, Archibald [*name in religion* Benedict] (1739–1814), Benedictine monk and author, was born at Lochaber, Inverness, Scotland, the son of the Jacobite Ranald Macdonald (*d.* 1745) and his wife, Mary Cameron. He was educated at St Gregory's, Douai, and joined the Benedictine community there in September 1756. He was the first Benedictine monk to serve the mission of St Mary's, Liverpool, in 1783, and from here he founded the Benedictine mission of St Peter's, Seel Street, Liverpool, five years later.

Despite a busy (and at times controversial) pastoral life Macdonald published some literary works which had an extensive local circulation in their day and which represented a significant contribution to English Catholic devotional writing in the late eighteenth century. These included a number of small booklets designed to enhance the liturgy, which were popular with Benedictine missioners in the latter part of the century, and like contemporary Cisalpine authors he favoured a vernacular Catholic liturgy. Macdonald believed in the importance of congregational participation in Sunday afternoon devotions, arguing in the preface to one of his booklets (*The Layman's Afternoon Devotion*, 1778) that it was 'equally pleasing to God and more edifying to the people when able to join their pastor with one voice as St. Chrysostom observes' (Gillow, *Lit. biog. hist.*, 4.370). Macdonald's Jacobite sympathies caused a fellow monk to advise against his appointment as chaplain to the Towneley family at Standish in Lancashire, observing that he had 'too much of the North-Britton' (Bulmer to Nayler).

Macdonald is notable for his defence of the authenticity of James Macpherson's edition of the poems of Ossian against the attacks of Dr Johnson and Malcolm Laing. Macdonald himself translated some of Ossian's lesser poems in 1805, and in 1808 published *Fingal: an Epic Poem Rendered into Verse*. He also published *A Companion to the Altar, or, Prayers for Morning and Afternoon Service, on Sundays and Holydays* (1792), *Moral Essays, Chiefly Collected from Different Authors* (2 vols., 1796), and *Select Discourses on the Gospels for All the Sundays and Holydays throughout the Year* (1801). Macdonald was a controversial figure who continually quarrelled with any monks who were appointed to assist him. Paradoxically, given that he was a prolific writer, he was accused by his superiors of being a poor communicator.

Despite this he was honoured by his brethren with the offices of definitor of the regimen in 1806 and cathedral prior of Rochester in 1810. He died at St Peter's, Seel Street, Liverpool, on 29 July 1814. ALBAN HOOD

Sources T. B. Snow, *Obit book of the English Benedictines from 1600 to 1912*, rev. H. N. Birt (privately printed, Edinburgh, 1913), 130 · Gillow, *Lit. biog. hist.* · G. Scott, *Gothic rage undone: English monks in the age of Enlightenment* (1992), 92, 103–5, 141 · *GM*, 1st ser., 84/2 (1814), 298 · J. C. H. Aveling, *The handle and the axe* (1976), 332 · M. Bulmer to P. Nayler, 21 April 1770, Nancy Archives, Meurthe-et-Moselle, Meurthe H77
Archives Ampleforth Abbey, Yorkshire, Allanson MSS · Downside Abbey, near Bath, account book of Dom Benedict Steare · Downside Abbey, near Bath, profession book of St Gregory's
Likenesses oils, Ampleforth Abbey, York

Macdonald, Sir Archibald, first baronet (1747–1826), judge and politician, was born on 13 July 1747 at Armidale Castle on the Isle of Skye, the third and posthumous son of Sir Alexander Macdonald, seventh baronet (1711–1746), and his second wife, Margaret (*d.* 1799), daughter of Alexander *Montgomerie, ninth earl of Eglinton. He must have begun his education in Scotland because in later life he referred to Thomas Erskine as 'my old school-fellow' (*State trials*, 21.62) but in the aftermath of Culloden the government was anxious to limit Jacobite influence over the Macdonald boys and recommended that they be sent to England. Macdonald became a king's scholar at Westminster School in 1760 and was elected to a studentship at Christ Church, Oxford, in 1764, where he graduated BA in 1768 and MA in 1772. In this pattern of élite education he may have followed the example of another scion of the Scottish aristocracy, William Murray, first earl of Mansfield; like Mansfield he was entered at Lincoln's Inn, in 1765, and called to the bar, on 24 November 1770.

Macdonald's connections provided early employment for him as junior counsel in some appeals to the House of Lords but the first important case that he argued in his own right was *Campbell* v. *Hall*, or the *Case of the Island of Grenada*, tried before Lord Chief Justice Mansfield in May 1775. The case was very important because it was designed to test the issue of the crown's right to impose a duty on the inhabitants of a colony by prerogative; it came on just as the American War of Independence was breaking out and the second continental congress was meeting at Philadelphia. Citing *Calvin's case* and several civil law authorities Macdonald contended that no such tax could be imposed by prerogative after the cessation of hostilities, for in a settled colony the power of legislation was confined to king and parliament, as demonstrated by the Declaratory Act of 1766. Mansfield commented that he had raised 'one of the greatest constitutional questions that, perhaps, ever came before this Court' (*State trials*, 20.306).

Although such praise must have assisted his progress the turning point of Macdonald's career came in 1777. In February of that year he was elected to the House of Commons for the borough of Hindon, in Wiltshire, probably by dint of large-scale bribery among its inhabitants; on 26

Sir Archibald Macdonald, first baronet (1747–1826), by Sir Francis Legatt Chantrey, 1818

December he married Lady Louisa (*d.* 1827), daughter of Granville Leveson-Gower, second Earl Gower, lord president of the council and leader of the Bedford whigs. With such political advantages Macdonald could hardly fail to be promoted and it was no coincidence that he was granted a patent of precedence at the bar less than a month later, in January 1778. Later the same year he was one of several counsel retained on behalf of the governors and officers of Greenwich Hospital on their application to the court of king's bench for an information alleging libel against Captain Thomas Baillie, who had accused them of corrupt administration. On this occasion he failed to satisfy Mansfield, who discharged the rule for an information on the grounds that the writing in question had not been published, in the full sense of the word, and that Baillie had already been punished by the governors.

In parliament Macdonald dutifully followed the line of his father-in-law, even to the extent of public inconsistency and occasional apostasy. With Gower he supported the North administration's prosecution of the American war but he launched an artificially savage attack on North after Gower resigned in November 1779 and then abjectly apologized upon his father-in-law's signal of continued support for the North ministry. At the general election of 1780 he was returned for Gower's borough of Newcastle under Lyme and given a government place as second judge of the Carmarthen circuit in Wales. Becoming more confident in debate he assisted the administration's resistance to economical reform in 1781, despite having previously supported John Dunning's motion against the influence of the crown; and on the occasion of the younger William Pitt's motion for reforming parliamentary representation, debated on 7 May 1782, he declared 'that as the present form of the constitution had stood from Charles the 2nd's time, without any material alteration, he could see no reason for any amendment to it at present' (Cobbett, *Parl. hist.*, 22.1429). Like Gower he opposed the Fox–North administration from the start. In the debate of March 1783 on the Foxite motion pressing the king to install the new coalition he said that 'It did not deserve the respectable name of coalition; it was a perversion of words to call it so' (ibid., 23.674). Fox thereupon reminded the house of the sequel to his previous assault on North, but Macdonald had signalled his loyalty to the king's friends by declaring that 'He thought the democracy more to be feared than the regal power' (ibid., 675), and in November he argued strenuously against Fox's India Bill as 'a trap … for the liberties of the nation' (ibid., 1298), thereby hitching his fortunes firmly to Pitt's rising star. He had his reward after Gower returned to government in Pitt's ministry, when he became solicitor-general at the dissolution of parliament in March 1784 and attorney-general four years later. He continued to represent Newcastle under Lyme until his elevation to the judicial bench, and as a principal law officer he spoke regularly on legal affairs. Most notably, in 1785 he introduced a bill promoting a new scheme for securing the peace in the City of London, Westminster, and Southwark, principally by establishing district police establishments under a metropolitan commission and increasing the frequency of the Old Bailey sessions. Though the bill was defeated by the vested interests of local authorities and traditional fears of centralized authority it anticipated later reforms and, in aiming 'to render detection certain, and punishment with a moderate degree of severity, unavoidable' (ibid., 25.889), Macdonald articulated advanced ideas. He also rendered valuable support to Pitt at the time of the regency crisis in 1788–9, arguing strongly for the power of parliament to determine the powers of a regent against the Foxite claims for automatic reversion to the prince of Wales.

In his other capacity as a leader at the bar Macdonald proved to be competent rather than outstanding. Unusually for a law officer he maintained only a moderate private practice, principally in chancery and in the equity side of the exchequer. On being made attorney-general in June 1788 (when he was knighted) he became responsible for state prosecutions but his tenure pre-dated the main crisis of government reaction to the French Revolution, and in the trials that he prosecuted he was distinguished mainly by his easy confidence and good humour. In December 1789 he prosecuted the bookseller John Stockdale for publishing a pamphlet critical of the impeachment proceedings against Warren Hastings. Although it was an *ex officio* information the prosecution was not inspired by the government; it had been promoted by an address to the king originally moved by Charles Fox, on the basis that the publication was a libel against the House of Commons, and Macdonald's speech was correspondingly restrained. He opened by saying that 'The solemnity of the situation in which I am placed on this occasion, obliges me to address the intellect both of the court and the jury, and neither their passions or their prejudices' (*State trials*, 22.249). In the event his speech was completely overshadowed by Erskine's oration for the liberty of the press, which secured an acquittal, and later in his career he complained that 'He had more than once prosecuted, in obedience to the commands of the House, when he knew a conviction could not be expected' (Cobbett, *Parl. hist.*, 30.132). A year later he led for the crown in *R.* v. *John Frith*, who was indicted for high treason after throwing a stone at the king's coach. On this occasion he had little to do, since the defendant was found unfit to plead on grounds of insanity, although Lord Chief Justice Kenyon praised his characteristic moderation and indulgence to the prisoner (*State trials*, 22.310). But he was much less forbearing when prosecuting Thomas Paine for a criminal libel in December 1792. The case against Paine had the full support of the government, who were alarmed by the wide circulation of the second part of his *Rights of Man*, and Macdonald clearly identified his personal convictions with the prosecution. In loyal and patriotic tones he spoke up forcefully against Paine's 'gross, contemptible, and abominable falsehood' on the constitution (ibid., 385–6) and became righteously indignant over the author's sarcasm at the capacity of the king and his sons for government. The jury's hostile reaction to Erskine's exculpation of Paine for the defence showed that he had caught the public mood, and they gave a verdict for the prosecution without withdrawing from court.

Macdonald was appointed lord chief baron of exchequer on 12 February 1793, following Sir James Eyre's promotion to the court of common pleas. Cases in the exchequer were generally of limited significance and the promotion therefore constituted retirement from the front line of public affairs. But he was commissioned to take part in some important state trials, including the prosecution of Thomas Hardy for treason in late 1794, although Eyre presided and Macdonald said little. Macdonald presided himself at the trial of Colonel Joseph Wall for murder at the Old Bailey in January 1802. The case was one of considerable public interest because the alleged offence had taken place in 1782, when Wall was governor of the garrison of Goree off the coast of Africa, and it concerned the death of a sergeant after a punishment of 800 lashes, administered with a rope's end. In his defence Wall claimed that he had been confronted with a mutiny and had convened a summary court martial but the evidence was quite contradictory, and after reviewing it all very impartially Macdonald left the issue to the jury, who brought in a guilty verdict. He retired from the bench with a baronetcy in 1813, when his eyesight failed, but he maintained his interest in the reform of criminal law, appearing personally before a House of Commons select committee in 1819. On that occasion he argued again for the principle of certainty rather than severity in punishment, and advocated the restriction of capital punishment in favour of imprisonment with hard labour.

Although he was a conservative in politics and one of a generation who were alarmed by the implications of the French Revolution, Macdonald never became a reactionary, unlike his contemporaries John Scott, first earl of Eldon, and Edward Law. Indeed an unwillingness to participate in repressive measures may account for his sidelining in 1793, just when the Pitt government began to move decisively against popular radicalism. Near the end of his career he said that when he drew penal statutes as solicitor- and attorney-general 'I was always an exceedingly strong advocate for the milder course' ('Select committee on criminal laws', 48); and as a judge in criminal trials that 'I would always desire to give the prisoner the benefit of every thing that I could discover in his favour … I always felt it my duty to be counsel for him' (ibid., 50). Macdonald died at his home in Duke Street, Westminster, on 18 May 1826, and was buried in Kensington parish church. He was survived by his wife, who died eight months later, and by three children, James (1784–1832), who succeeded to the baronetcy, Louisa (1781–1862), and Caroline Diana (1790–1867). DAVID LEMMINGS

Sources J. A. Cannon, 'Macdonald, Archibald', HoP, Commons, 1754–90 · R. G. Thorne, 'Macdonald, Sir Archibald', HoP, Commons, 1790–1820 · E. Foss, Biographia juridica: a biographical dictionary of the judges of England … 1066–1870 (1870) · Cobbett, Parl. hist., vol. 19, 4 Dec 1778; vol. 20, 6 Dec 1779; vol. 21, 10 April 1780; vol. 22, 7 May 1782; vol. 23, 24 March 1783; vol. 25, 23 June 1785; vol. 30, 17 Dec 1792 · State trials, 20.287–306; 21.61–5; 22.247–93, 307–18, 357–472; 28.51–178 · GM, 1st ser., 96/1 (1826), 561–3 · 'Select committee on criminal laws', Parl. papers (1819), 8.46–52, 54–5, no. 585 · D. Lemmings, Professors of the law (2000), 119, 181, 339, 352 · W. R. Williams, The history of the great sessions in Wales, 1542–1830 (privately printed, Brecon, 1899), 184–5 · DNB · Sainty, King's counsel · Sainty, Judges · Burke, Peerage (1999)
Archives Edinburgh Central Reference Library, estate account book · Keele University Library, 'outline of legal history of the press in England' | BL, corresp. with earl of Liverpool, Add. MSS 38214–38234, 38307–38309, 38471, passim
Likenesses J. Gillray, caricature, etching, pubd 1787, NPG · G. Romney, oils, 1793–5, Christ Church Oxf. · F. L. Chantrey, marble bust, 1818, V&A [see illus.] · oils, Harvard U., law school
Wealth at death freehold house in Duke Street, Westminster; property at East Sheen, Surrey; also investments in Mersey canal navigation and public funds

MacDonald, Archibald (fl. 1948). See under Knoydart, Seven Men of (act. 1948).

MacDonald, Sir Claude Maxwell (1852–1915), diplomatist, the son of Major-General James Dawson (Hamish) MacDonald and his wife, Mary Ellen, née Dougan, was born on 12 June 1852. Educated at Uppingham School and Sandhurst, he entered the 74th highlanders in 1872. MacDonald had a varied early career as soldier and administrator. He served in the Egyptian campaign of 1882 and was promoted to major. He was military attaché to Lord Dufferin during the latter's tenure in Egypt, with particular responsibility for the courts martial of Egyptians, in

which he took a tough line. He was also attaché to Sir Evelyn Baring when he succeeded Dufferin in 1884. MacDonald served in the Suakin expedition of 1884–5 and was wounded at Tamai. In 1887 he became consul-general at Zanzibar. In 1889 he began a period of service in west Africa, during which he was sent on a mission to Berlin to delimit the frontier between the Oil Rivers Protectorate and the Cameroons. In 1891 he became the first commissioner and consul-general in the protectorate, where he proved a capable administrator. He became KCMG in 1892, and on 17 December in the same year married Ethel (d. 1941), daughter of Major W. Cairns Armstrong and widow of P. Craigie Robertson. They had two daughters.

MacDonald's claim to significance rests on his career as a diplomatist in China and Japan. In 1896, to the surprise of many, and the adverse comment of some, he became minister to China, a post he owed to the good opinion held of him by Baring and by Lord Salisbury, prime minister and foreign secretary. He was described in The Times as 'an elongated man of forty-five, with a long nose, reproachful eyes, and long, lovingly waxed moustaches' (Wilgus, 80). His appointment came as the hitherto unchallenged predominance of Britain among trading powers in China was coming under threat. The weakness of China, revealed by defeat at the hands of Japan in 1895, encouraged rivals to advance their interests. China was becoming an economic battleground where British enterprise had to meet keen competitors backed by their governments. This situation, developing as popular imperialism was at its height in Britain, called for defence of the British position and a strong man in Peking (Beijing) to conduct it. MacDonald proved an excellent choice. As the battle of concessions intensified in 1898 he was energetic and forceful in extracting from the hapless Chinese compensation for concessions granted to rivals. He obtained a lease of Weihaiwei to counter the Russian presence at Port Arthur and several railway contracts for British syndicates. In July 1898 Salisbury was made despondent by railway concessions gained by competitors, but by 1899 the China scene was much more satisfying to British opinion. China undertook not to alienate the Yangtze (Yangzi) region and pledged the appointment of a British subject at the head of Chinese maritime customs, so long as British trade was predominant. In south China counter-measures against the spread of French influence secured the opening of the West River to commerce, while the extension of Hong Kong was obtained in 1898 by the leasing of territory on the adjacent mainland. He was, moreover, 'an unabashed Russophobe', and was almost as suspicious of France (Wilgus, 83–4).

MacDonald had done well. If he had shown occasional rashness and inadequate grasp of the reasons for Salisbury's cautious policy towards rival powers in China, he had raised morale among the British community. His stock rose higher in public esteem during the siege of the Peking legations by the Boxer insurgents from 20 June to 14 August 1900, when he commanded the defenders. Following this he was appointed KCB (military), complementing the KCB (civil) conferred on him in 1898.

In October 1900 MacDonald was posted to Tokyo as minister, and from 1905 as the first British ambassador to Japan. He was to remain in Tokyo until 1912, a lengthy period in one post. There, as in Peking, the personalities and hospitality of the MacDonalds made them well liked by the staff and community, though MacDonald had been criticized for neglecting the consular service during his time in Peking. In Tokyo he soon established and maintained cordial relations with official and non-official Japanese society.

Two episodes of note marked MacDonald's period in Tokyo. In May 1901, as Britain was edging towards alliance with Japan, he was called to London at short notice for consultation. There he had meetings with Salisbury, Lansdowne (the foreign secretary), the king, and the Japanese minister Hayashi Tadasu, which offer some justification for his claim to have played a significant role in the making of the first Anglo-Japanese alliance. Little is on record of what passed in his conversations with British ministers, but it seems that as well as supplying the British with insights into opinion in Tokyo and presenting his own favourable views on alliance, MacDonald was able to indicate to the Japanese minister the trend of thinking in the Foreign Office before the matter was officially broached. MacDonald played no special part in the recasting of the alliance in 1905, and during years of cordiality in Anglo-Japanese relations he was not involved in critical issues. The British decision in 1911 to renew and extend to 1921 the alliance, concluded in 1905 for a ten-year period, was taken with little consultation with the Tokyo embassy. However, no doubt to the surprise of the Foreign Office, where he was regarded as Japanophile, MacDonald made clear his view that for the present no extension should be contemplated. Uncertainty as to renewal, he maintained, would be a restraint upon an assertive, forward policy by Japan in the immediate future. His argument, reflecting wariness among the British community in the Far East as to Japan's aims, came too late to influence the decision for renewal already taken in London for reasons of global policy. MacDonald went to London in 1911 for the coronation but did not take part in negotiation of the new treaty. He retired in 1912. Salisbury had held him in high esteem, though in the foreign service his abilities were not highly regarded. He was, as he said himself, 'a soldier outsider'.

MacDonald was sworn of the privy council in 1906 and in the same year was appointed GCVO. He died at 40 Chester Square, London, on 10 September 1915. Lady MacDonald lived on until 20 March 1941. She was active in charitable work, particularly for overseas nursing, and was created DBE in 1935. She has been described as 'a model Ambassadress' during her time in Tokyo (Nish, 'Sir Claude and Lady Ethel MacDonald', 143).   E. W. EDWARDS

Sources M. H. Wilgus, *Sir Claude MacDonald, the open door, and British informal empire in China 1895–1900* (1987) · L. K. Young, *British policy in China, 1895–1902* (1970) · E. W. Edwards, *British diplomacy and finance in China, 1895–1914* (1987) · I. H. Nish, *The Anglo-Japanese alliance* (1966) · I. H. Nish, *Alliance in decline* (1972) · P. Lowe, *Great Britain and Japan, 1911–1915* (1969) · *DNB* · *The Times* (15 Sept 1915) · C. Pearl, *Morrison of Peking*, new edn (1971) · I. Nish, 'Sir Claude and Lady Ethel MacDonald', *Britain and Japan: biographical portraits*, ed. I. Nish, 1 (1994), 133–45 · G. P. Gooch and H. Temperley, eds., *British documents on the origins of the war, 1898–1914*, 8 (1932); 11 (1926) · O. Ikime, 'Sir Claude MacDonald and the Niger coast protectorate – a reassessment', *Odù*, 3 (1970), 22–44 · WWW

Archives Bodl. Oxf., letters to Sir Horace Rumbold · CUL, letters to Lord Hardinge · PRO, Lansdowne, Satour, Jordan MSS

Likenesses Spy [L. Ward], chromolithograph caricature, NPG; repro. in *VF* (10 Oct 1901)

Wealth at death £20,435 15s. 6d.: probate, 23 Nov 1915, *CGPLA Eng. & Wales*

MacDonald, Donald (*d.* 1420×25). *See under* MacDonald family (*per. c.*1300–*c.*1500).

MacDonald, Donald (1766/7–1840), bagpipe maker and music publisher, was born at Glenhinisdale, Skye. He was a piper in the 2nd battalion Caithness fencible regiment from 1795 to about 1802, and pipe major in the Argyllshire militia from about 1811 to 1817. By 1806 he was a bagpipe maker in Edinburgh, and from 1823 pipe maker to the Highland Society, taking over that role from the previous best-known maker, Hugh Robertson. Although he also manufactured and taught the Irish and Northumbrian pipes, it is his work with the large highland bagpipe and its classical repertoire of piobaireachd ('pibroch') that is still remembered.

There is no early record of how MacDonald himself was taught to play the pipes, but he wrote in 1828 that he had fifty years' experience, which implies that he was a boy about ten years old when he began playing, and would still have been living in Skye. An acquaintance, A. MacGregor, who knew him in the 1820s wrote in 1878 that he had 'acquired a correct knowledge of piobaireachd from the last of the MacArthurs'—the famous hereditary pipers to the MacDonalds of the Isles. He entered the annual pibroch competitions in Edinburgh at various times from 1801, winning first prize in 1817.

MacDonald's great invention was a system of writing highland bagpipe music in staff notation which is both clear and complete, with all the grace notes, most of which are not ornaments but essential elements in playing technique. As early as 1806 he responded to a call from the Highland Society to produce manuscripts of pipe music, and eventually he published the first serviceable collections of pibroch (*c.*1820), and of the smaller bagpipe music, comprising marches, reels, and other music (1828). Thus he founded the two traditions of bagpipe music writing which have flourished ever since. A second volume of his pibroch collection is extant in manuscript. He died at 529 Castlehill, Edinburgh, on 11 October 1840, and was buried four days later at Canongate churchyard, Edinburgh.

In his notations of pibroch MacDonald recorded styles of playing which were evidently current in his day, but were later eclipsed by that of Angus MacKay (1813–1859), who edited a further collection in 1838. In the late twentieth century, however, there has been a revival of interest in earlier ways of playing. Part of this revival consists of piping competitions, held in Skye, at which Donald Mac-Donald's versions of tunes are prescribed. At the time of writing a complete edition of his pibrochs is being prepared, to be published by the Piobaireachd Society.

RODERICK D. CANNON

Sources K. Sanger, 'Donald MacDonald', *Piping Times*, 49/1 (1996–7), 24–31 • I. I. MacInnes, 'The highland bagpipe: the impact of the Highland societies of London and Scotland, 1781–1844', MLitt diss., U. Edin., 1988 • F. Buisman, 'The earliest editions of Donald Mac-Donald's Collection of the ancient martial music of Caledonia, called piobaireachd', *Piping Times*, 50/1 (1997), 51–5; 50/2 (1997), 32–4 • A. MacGregor, 'John MacDonald—adherent of Prince Charles', *Celtic Magazine*, 3 (1878), 462–6 • C. S. Thomason, *Ceol mor notation: a new and abbreviated system of musical notation for the piobaireachd* (1893); repr. (1975) • R. H. MacLeod, 'The Highland Society of London and the publication of piobaireachd', *Piping Times*, 34/9 (1981–2), 25–31; 34/11 (1981–2), 28–32 • R. D. Cannon, *A bibliography of bagpipe music* (1980) • R. D. Cannon, *The highland bagpipe and its music* (1988) • *The Post Office Edinburgh directory* [annuals] • parish register (burials), 15 Oct 1840, Canongate church, Edinburgh • K. Sanger, 'Uillean pipes from Donald MacDonald', *Common Stock: the Journal of the Lowland and Border Pipers' Society*, 9/2 (1994), 19–20 • K. Sanger and R. D. Cannon, 'Donald MacDonald, the man and his music', *Proceedings of the Piobaireachd Society Conference* (March 2000), 1–32 • private information (2004) [K. Sanger]

MacDonald, Donald Dubh (d. 1545), rebel, was the son of Angus (Angus Óg) *MacDonald [see under MacDonald family (per. c.1300–c.1500)] and a daughter (perhaps named Mary) of Colin Campbell, first earl of Argyll. Angus died about 1490, and so did not live to see the event which above all else shaped the life of his son, namely the forfeiture of the lordship of the Isles in 1493 by Donald's grandfather, John MacDonald, and the consequent eclipse of his family. Archibald Campbell, who became second earl in 1493, must have consented to his sister's imprisonment in Innis Chonnell Castle on Loch Awe and young Donald claimed to have been born in captivity. He escaped in 1501, and found shelter first with Torquil MacLeod of Lewis and then with Maclean of Duart, and was welcomed as the rightful heir to the lordship of the Isles. Lochaber was invaded and Badenoch plundered, while as part of the king's response a Scottish fleet was gathered in 1504, with Andrew Wood and Robert Barton taking part. One account says that Donald took refuge in the castle of Cairnburgh in the Treshnish Isles off Mull; recaptured in 1506, he was brought to the lowlands and lodged in Edinburgh Castle. After being held in ward for nearly forty years 'until his hair got grey', reports show that he was free by May 1543. That was the year when Matthew Stewart, earl of Lennox, returned to Scotland from abroad, and it was not long before Donald, with Lennox as intermediary, was in touch with Henry VIII and other enemies of the Scottish crown.

In June 1545 Donald Dubh MacDonald (the epithet means 'black') was being blamed by the privy council for the harrying and slaying of the young queen's subjects both in the islands and on the mainland, assisted by the king of England, and he was threatened with dire penalties if he and his supporters did not cease from such treasonable and rebellious conduct. Donald acted with the advice and consent of his barons, who formed a revived council of the Isles on the model of that which had met during the heyday of the lordship; this included, besides the leading men of his own clan, the Maclean chief and cadets, MacLeods, MacNeills, Mackinnon, and MacQuarrie. Meeting near Islay in July and at Knockfergus in northern Ireland in the following month, this body, along with Donald himself, took oaths of allegiance to King Henry and agreed to operate under Lennox's command. They were to assist in the invasion and conquest of Scotland, where Donald would hold the lordship lands (once they had been reclaimed) of King Henry, from whom he was to have an annual pension of 2000 crowns for his services.

Two commissioners were appointed to put these proposals to the king; calling himself earl of Ross and lord of the Isles of Scotland, Donald Dubh MacDonald wrote a personal letter of humble submission in Latin to King Henry; after communing with Lennox (now married to Henry's niece) and his council, Henry received the two island commissioners in September, and an agreement was drawn up taking into account the articles submitted through them. This was readily accepted, and as an assurance of good faith Henry's advisers were given examples of the persecution suffered by those in what were called 'the wyld Ilis of Scotland' which had made them always the enemies of the Scottish realm. Donald has been credited with aiming to revive a form of Celtic kingship for himself under the English flag; observers say that he had 180 galleys and 4000 men with him when he sailed across the narrow seas to Ireland, and another 4000 at home to keep Huntly and Argyll busy when they were active in the North and South Isles on behalf of the Scottish government. At Knockfergus, Donald was joined by Lennox, but after some delay a full-scale invasion of Scotland from the west was postponed. What proved to be the last substantial attempt to re-establish the lordship of the Isles ended late in 1545 with Donald's death of a fever at Drogheda, without any direct heir to succeed him, but leaving a 'base son' whom he bequeathed to the English king's service.

R. W. MUNRO and JEAN MUNRO

Sources A. MacDonald and A. MacDonald, *The clan Donald*, 1 (1896) • H. MacDonald, 'History of the MacDonalds', *Highland papers*, ed. J. R. N. Macphail, 1, Scottish History Society, 2nd ser., 5 (1914), 1–102 • A. Cameron, 'The book of Clanranald', *Reliquiae celticae*, ed. A. Macbain and J. Kennedy (1894) • *Facsimile of the national manuscripts of Scotland* (1871), no. 29 • D. Gregory, *The history of the western highlands and the isles of Scotland* (1836) • *LP Henry VIII*, vol. 20 • *APS* • J. Munro and R. W. Munro, eds., *Acts of the lords of the Isles, 1336–1493*, Scottish History Society, 4th ser., 22 (1986)

MacDonald, Donald Gorm Mor (d. 1616). See under MacDonald family (per. c.1475–1616).

MacDonald, Donald Gormson (d. 1575). See under MacDonald family (per. c.1475–1616).

MacDonald, Donald Gruamach (d. 1534?). See under MacDonald family (per. c.1475–1616).

Macdonald, Duncan George Forbes (1827/8–1884), agricultural engineer and writer, was the youngest son of John *Macdonald (1779–1849) and his second wife, Janet, eldest daughter of Kenneth Mackenzie, of Millbank. Initially he devoted himself to the study and practice of agriculture on his father's extensive glebe, before starting business on his own account in 1848, as an agricultural engineer in London and Dingwall, Ross-shire. He also worked as a civil engineer, in addition to acquiring practical knowledge of farming.

Macdonald was a prolific writer, producing publications on a multitude of different aspects relating to British agriculture and on his visits to the colonies. His first work, *What the Farmers may Do with the Land*, appeared in 1852; the subtitle, *Practical Hints for their and its Improvement*, effectively summarized the content of the text. Later Macdonald went to British Columbia, where he became a member of the government's survey staff and one of the commissioners responsible for adjusting the boundary line of British North America. This led, following his return to Britain, to the publication of *British Columbia and Vancouver Island*. The text provided a detailed analysis of the physical characteristics and climate of the area, in addition to assessing the manners and customs of the native people. Rather controversially, in this work he opposed immigration to the area on the grounds that the land was not as rich and fertile as his contemporaries believed. His views were also reiterated in subsequent lectures on the topic.

After the deposition of Napoleon III Macdonald wrote a pamphlet entitled *Napoleon III, the Empress Eugénie, and the Prince Imperial*. The rest of his life was devoted to agricultural and similar interests. He became drainage engineer of improvements under the control of the enclosure commissioners for England and Wales, and engineer-in-chief to the inspector-general of highland destitution. Macdonald was a fellow of the Geological Society and of the Royal Geographical Society; he also became a justice of the peace, and was made LLD. He died on 6 January 1884 at 23 West Hill Road, Brighton.

[ANON.], rev. JOHN MARTIN

Sources Boase, *Mod. Eng. biog.* • *The Times* (9 Jan 1884) • D. G. F. Macdonald, *What the farmers may do with the land, or, Practical hints for their and its improvement* (1852) • d. cert.
Likenesses V. Brookes, engraving, repro. in D. Macdonald, *Hints on farming and estate management*, 3rd edn (1865)

MacDonald, Ethel Camilia (1909–1960), anti-parliamentary socialist, was born on 24 February 1909 in Bellshill, Lanarkshire, one of nine children. She went to Motherwell high school, and became a member of the Independent Labour Party Guild of Youth. At sixteen she left home for good. She worked at various low-paid jobs but in Glasgow in 1933 became unemployed. After the labour exchange sent her for a non-existent waitressing job in Dumfries, she sought Guy Aldred's advice. The anarchist–communist propagandist invited her to be his secretary and assist with an advice bureau he was opening at 145 Queen Street, Glasgow. She began attending Aldred's meetings, joining the Anti-Parliamentary Communist Federation (APCF). When, shortly after, Aldred left the APCF to set up the United Socialist Movement (USM), she became its secretary. To be closer to the centre of political activity, she moved from lodgings on Cathcart Road to

Ethel Camilia MacDonald (1909–1960), by unknown photographer, 1938 [speaking at Hyde Park]

a top-floor flat at 24 Gibson Street, her home for the rest of her life.

In October 1936 Ethel MacDonald went to Spain at the request of the CNT–FAI (the anarchist federations) to work for their international information service, making nightly broadcasts on Radio Barcelona. She had an enormous influence on her worldwide audience, not only because of her uncompromising anarchist views (at odds with orthodox republican socialism and communism) but also, as one American editor noted, because she had 'the most wonderful radio speaking voice' (*Evening Citizen*, 2 Dec 1960).

With Jenny Patrick, Ethel MacDonald experienced the momentous May days in Barcelona in 1937. As the communist-led forces attacked the anarchist headquarters, Ethel MacDonald was loading rifles for the defenders. Aided by a conniving censor she sent an account of this 'Stalinist counter-revolution' back to Aldred in Glasgow. Recognizing its importance, he rushed the *Barcelona Bulletin* into print.

Persecution of the anarchists (and of the independent Marxist POUM) intensified. Many of Ethel MacDonald's comrades were imprisoned but she worked fearlessly on, even assisting escapes. She was imprisoned twice herself: first on the technicality of failure to renew her residence permit, then, more ominously, for 'visiting, harbouring, and associating with counter-revolutionary aliens'. Nevertheless, in prison she persisted in engineering escapes, becoming known as the Spanish Scarlet Pimpernel. In Glasgow an Ethel MacDonald defence committee was organized and campaigned vigorously; with eventual consular intervention she was released in September 1937. Her arrival at Glasgow's Queen Street Station on 7 November was greeted by a cheering crowd. At meetings in Glasgow, Edinburgh, and Aberdeen, and in newspaper articles, she revealed the developing tragedy in Spain and the plight of thousands of imprisoned comrades. Communism, she declared, was destroying 'the struggle and all the efforts of the Spanish people. Stalinism, which had betrayed so many hopes of the workers in the past, had to be arrested in Spain'. Her collection of revolutionary papers and posters (later deposited in the Mitchell Library) was exhibited in Glasgow on May day and at the USM's hall on Stirling Road in 1937.

In 1938 the International Working Men's Association (AIT) invited Ethel to Paris to assist their propaganda work. After her return to Glasgow, she helped set up the Strickland Press at 104–6 George Street in the summer of 1939. For twenty years she played her part with Guy Aldred, Jenny Patrick, and John Caldwell in printing and circulating socialist and anarchist literature, notably *The Word*, organ of the USM. With Jenny Patrick she stood firm against trade union denial of women's right to do typographical work.

In May 1959 Ethel MacDonald was taken ill. Multiple sclerosis spread rapidly and without remission, leaving her completely paralysed. Her strong, forthright personality, impatient of the irresolute, made her long illness all the more terrible for her to bear and for her friends to witness. She died in Knightswood Hospital, Glasgow, on 1 December 1960, bequeathing her body to medical science.

A small, dark-haired woman, at equal ease with a spanner, a sewing machine, or a paintbrush, she was a person of wide ability, sterling courage, and unswerving principle. JOHN T. CALDWELL and BOB JONES

Sources personal knowledge (2004) · J. T. Caldwell, *Come dungeons dark: the life and times of Guy Aldred* (1988) · *News From Spain* [Glasgow], 1/1 (1 May 1937) · *Barcelona Bulletin* [Glasgow] (12 May 1937) · *Bellshill Speaker* [Glasgow] (12 March–16 April 1936) · *The Word* [Glasgow] (1938–61), vols. 1–22 · *The Word*, 22/3 (Jan 1961) · *The Word*, 22/10 (Aug 1961), 86–8 · *The Word*, 22/8 (June 1961), 68 · *Regeneracion* [Glasgow] (29 July–7 Oct 1936), nos. 1–19 · *Regeneracion* [Glasgow], new ser., 1/1–4 (21 Feb–14 March 1937) · *Forward* [Glasgow] (1937) · *Forward* [Glasgow] (1938) · *Advance* [Glasgow] (Sept 1936–7 Aug 1937), vol. 1, nos. 1–6 · *Workers' Free Press* [Glasgow] (Sept–NovxDec 1937), nos. 1–3/4 · *Sunday Mail* [Glasgow] (12 Dec 1937) · *Sunday Mail* [Glasgow] (19 Dec 1937) · *Sunday Mail* [Glasgow] (26 Dec 1937) · *The Leader* [London] (19 Feb 1938) · E. MacDonald, *Monarchy Spain and the class struggle* (1938) [2pp. leaflet] · *Evening Citizen* [Glasgow] (2 Dec 1960)
Archives Mitchell L., Glas., papers and posters collected by her in Spain | Mitchell L., Glas., letters to Guy Aldred from Spain and Paris, and personal corresp.
Likenesses photograph, 1938, Northern Herald Books, Brighouse, Yorkshire [*see illus.*] · G. P. Miller, drawing, 1959, priv. coll. · photographs, Mitchell L., Glas., G. Aldred collection · photographs, priv. coll. · photographs, repro. in *News From Spain* (May 1937), 3, 4 · photographs, repro. in *The Word*, 22/3 (Jan 1961), 17–19 · photographs, repro. in *The Word*, 22/8 (June 1961), 68
Wealth at death Nil; personal knowledge

MacDonald, Finola (*d.* in or after **1610**). *See under* Campbell, Lady Agnes (*d.* in or after 1590).

MacDonald, Flora (1722–1790), Jacobite heroine, was born at Milton on the island of South Uist, Outer Hebrides, the third and last child of Ranald MacDonald (*d.* 1723), tacksman or leaseholder of Milton and Balivanich on South Uist, and his second wife, Marion (*d.* before 1771), daughter of the Revd Angus MacDonald and his wife, Flora. Flora is an Anglicization of the Gaelic name Fionnghal, and sometimes she signed herself Flory. The day and month of her birth are unknown, and her birthplace has been demolished, but a cairn marks its site just off the main north–south road on the island. Flora was not a poor peasant girl as legend often presents her, but came of a good family, and was raised and continued to practise as a Presbyterian. Her father was a cousin of the chief of the MacDonalds of Clanranald, and was related to the powerful Argyll Campbells. Her mother could claim connection to the MacDonalds of Sleat, the lords of the Isles. Flora had two older brothers: Angus, who eventually inherited the Milton tack, and Ranald, who died in an accident as a young man.

Their father died in 1723, and Marion remarried in 1728. Her second husband, Hugh MacDonald of Sartle in Skye, who could claim connection to two chiefs, MacDonald of Sleat and MacLeod of Raasay, was a great swordsman and had led an adventurous life as a young man. He was known as Uisdean Cam, or One-Eyed Hugh, because he had lost an eye either in a childhood accident or while serving with the French army.

Flora grew into a cultured young woman, who sang well, played the spinet, and danced. There is no evidence, however, to support a claim of early biographers that she went to school in Edinburgh, or that the Clanranald or Sleat chiefs' wives helped with her education.

By 1745, when Prince *Charles Edward arrived in Scotland, Flora's brother had taken over the tack of Milton, and Flora had moved to Armadale in Skye with her mother and her stepfather. Skye remained untouched by the 1745 campaign because the chief of Sleat refused to join the prince, but raised an independent militia regiment among his clansmen in support of the government. One-Eyed Hugh became one of its captains. After Charles Edward's defeat at Culloden in April 1746, his flight took him to the friendly Clanranald island of South Uist, where Flora happened to be visiting her brother. On learning of the prince's presence in the Outer Hebrides, government forces began a systematic search of the islands, which came close to capturing him. Unknown to Flora, a plan was devised to spirit Charles off the outer isles and back to Skye disguised as her Irish maid, Betty Burke, and the first she learned of the scheme was when the prince was brought to her secretly on the night of 20 June at a hut on a shieling or summer pasture on Sheaval Hill, where she

Flora MacDonald (1722–1790), by Allan Ramsay, 1749

had been sent to tend her brother's cattle. He was accompanied by one of Flora's kinsmen, Neil MacEachain, and by Captain Felix O'Neil, who each gave differing accounts of the meeting, but from Flora's account it would appear to have been the prince himself who asked her to help him. She agreed reluctantly.

Who planned the escape has never been explained, but her stepfather must be the chief suspect. He commanded the militia at the ford between South Uist and Benbecula at the time, and ordered the release of Flora and MacEachain when they were captured at the crossing. The journey was arranged with suspicious ease, and it was Hugh who supplied the pass to permit Flora to make the journey to Skye, accompanied by 'one Bettie Burke, an Irish girl, who, she tells me, is a good spinster' (Forbes, 2.32, 46). Lady Clanranald helped to make the Betty Burke dress, and the prince and Flora set sail from Benbecula to Skye on the night of 28–9 June in a small boat crewed mainly by militiamen. Many tales were told afterwards about the escape, but Flora's favourite was the one in which she said she forbade Charles to carry his pistols under the petticoat of his dress, telling him that, if searched, they would give him away. 'If we shall happen to meet with any that will go so narrowly to work in searching as what you mean, they will certainly discover me at any rate', the prince replied (ibid., 1.111).

Charles Edward landed at Trotternish in Skye, close to Monkstadt, home of MacDonald of Sleat, who was away at Fort Augustus at the time. Flora brought the prince to Sleat's house where the chief's wife, Lady Margaret MacDonald, gave him a meal and sent him south to the Sleat factor's house at Kingsburgh. Unfortunately the boatmen

were sent back to Uist, where they were arrested and confessed. Flora and the factor were arrested, but the prince fled first to Raasay and then to the mainland, where he remained in hiding until he was picked up by two French ships on 19 September.

Flora was taken aboard the *Furnace* and questioned by Major-General John Campbell of Mamore, whom she faced with great courage and apparent openness, but her answers concealed as much as they revealed. Like many other prisoners she was sent to London, but Campbell ordered that she should be treated well during the voyage aboard the *Bridgewater*. Unsubstantiated tradition claims she was held in the Tower of London for a few days, but for most of her imprisonment she was at the house of a messenger-at-arms, along with other important prisoners, until her release some days after the general amnesty was declared in July 1747. She remained a further few days with the Jacobite sympathizer Lady Primrose, who raised a subscription of £1500 for her, then left for Edinburgh, where she arrived on 2 August. Flora did not travel back to the Hebrides immediately, apparently unable to face returning to the islands, but spent the winter of 1746–7 in Edinburgh, taking lessons to improve her handwriting. The Revd Robert Forbes, who at this time was collecting first-hand accounts of those involved in the rising of 1745 (subsequently published in 1895–6 as *The Lyon in Mourning*), tried hard to persuade her to tell her story, but she did so reluctantly through an intermediary, John Burton. She returned to Skye in July 1747 but was back in London before the end of the year, apparently to arrange her finances.

On 6 November 1750 Flora married her kinsman Allan MacDonald (1722–1792) of Kingsburgh, a good-looking, amiable young man with advanced farming ideas but with a poor business sense, and they farmed at Flodigarry until Allan succeeded his father as Sleat factor. They had seven children, Charles (1751–1795), Anne (1754–1834), Alexander (1755–1781), Ranald (1756–1782), James (1757–1807), John *MacDonald (1759–1831), and Frances (b. 1766). The Flodigarry years swallowed up Flora's fortune, and Allan quarrelled with his chief, leaving them in sore financial straits. It was during this period that Samuel Johnson and James Boswell visited Kingsburgh, and Boswell described Flora, now fifty-one, as 'a little woman of genteel appearance, and uncommonly mild and well-bred'. Allan was 'completely the figure of a gallant Highlander'. Flora was taken with Johnson, and confided more of her story to him than she ever did to others: she even joked with him and told him that while she was on the mainland she had heard that Mr Boswell was on his way to Skye, 'a young English buck with him' (*Boswell's Journal*, 159). Johnson was accorded the honour of sleeping in the bed Prince Charlie had slept in the night he stayed at Kingsburgh in 1746.

In 1774 Allan and Flora emigrated to North Carolina, where members of their family were already living, and settled at Cheek's Creek in Anson (now Montgomery) County. However, before their seed was properly through the ground in the spring of 1775 the American War of Independence broke out, and neither Flora nor Allan doubted that their duty lay with George III. Flora encouraged highlanders to join the Royal Highland Emigrants 84th regiment, in which her husband, son, and son-in-law all served. The highland army was defeated by the patriots at Moore's Creek Bridge on 27 February 1776, and Allan was taken prisoner. Flora wrote that he 'and about 30 other gentlemen were draged [sic] from gaol to gaol for 700 miles, till lodged in Philadelphia gaol, remaining in their hands for 18 months before exchanged' (F. Macdonald to Sir John MacPherson, 21 Oct 1789, NL Scot.). Flora and her husband have been accused of involving themselves 'needlessly and recklessly' in the war (Maclean, 35), but Flora herself wrote,

> When the American Rebellion brock [sic] out, and [Continental] Congress, forcing her husband to joyne them, being a leading man among the highlanders, and seeing he would be obliged to joyne either party, he went in disguise to Fort Johnston on to mouth of the river Capefear, and there settled the plan of riseing the Highlanders in arms, with Governor Martin. (F. Macdonald to Sir John MacPherson, 21 Oct 1789, NL Scot.)

She suffered great hardship, and was brought before a patriot committee of safety during Allan's imprisonment, but was eventually allowed to travel to New York in April 1778 to be reunited with him. After he rejoined his regiment in Nova Scotia, Flora travelled to Fort Edward, near Windsor, to be with him, but she still had not recovered from her Carolina ordeal, and felt ill, lonely, and homesick. At the end of 1779 she returned to Britain. Her second son, Alexander (Sandy), who had been a prisoner with his father, was lost at sea in 1781, and only a year later her third son, Ranald, was drowned when his ship, the *Ville de Paris*, foundered off Newfoundland. Her health broken, Flora settled in Skye, where Allan joined her in 1785; he would have settled in Nova Scotia, but received only £440 plus £276 for loss of income in compensation for his war service and North Carolina losses—too little to begin a new life in Nova Scotia.

They ended their days at Penduin, near Kingsburgh, Skye, comfortably off, thanks to their son John, who made his fortune in the East. Almost the only clue Flora gave to her reason for agreeing to assist Prince Charlie's escape lies in the answer to George II's son, Prince Frederick, whom she met in London. When he asked why she had helped his father's enemies, she replied that she would have done the same for him had she found him in distress. Flora died at Penduin on 4 March 1790, and her husband, Allan, two years later, on 20 September 1792. Both were buried on Skye, at Kilmuir, 16 miles north of Kingsburgh.

The journey over the sea to Skye became a legend from the day it was made, and even as a prisoner in London in 1746 Flora was treated as a heroine. But oral tradition in the Hebrides largely ignored her, and even Lady Nairne failed to use such obvious material for a pro-Jacobite song. In 1870 the heroine's granddaughter, Flora Frances Wylde, produced a highly coloured *Autobiography* so full of obvious inaccuracies that it could not have been written by the heroine, and the Revd Alexander MacGregor's *Life*, written ten years later and said to have been based on information from Flora's daughter, Anne, had no more basis in truth.

Flora's memory was better served by James Hogg, Robert Louis Stevenson, and many others, who were moved to write poems in her honour. However, it is Harold Boulton's 'Skye Boat Song' that has best caught the spirit of her adventure, although it makes no more than a passing reference to Flora. By the time that song was written in the 1880s the world had come under the spell of the Flora MacDonald legend, which was carried round the world by emigrant Scots. Nowhere was it more enthusiastically accepted than in North Carolina and Nova Scotia. In North Carolina, the most Scottish of all the states of the USA, schools and colleges have been named after her, and her memory is greatly respected in spite of her support for the British at the revolution. A great upsurge of Scottish interest followed in that state during the second half of the twentieth century, and highland games began to be held annually at Grandfather Mountain in 1956. All through Flora's story legend has insinuated itself into truth, but the words of Samuel Johnson when he visited her in 1773 sum up both the woman and her legend: 'A name that will be mentioned in history, and if courage and fidelity be virtues, mentioned with honour' (Johnson, 67).

HUGH DOUGLAS

Sources H. Douglas, *Flora MacDonald: the most loyal rebel* (1993) · R. Forbes, *The lyon in mourning, or, A collection of speeches, letters, journals … relative to … Prince Charles Edward Stuart*, ed. H. Paton, 3 vols., Scottish History Society, 20–22 (1895–6) · F. MacDonald to J. Mac-Pherson, 21 Oct 1789, NL Scot., MS 2618 · A. R. MacDonald, *The truth about Flora MacDonald* (1938) · *Boswell's journal of a tour to the Hebrides with Samuel Johnson*, ed. F. A. Pottle and C. H. Bennett (1936) · S. Johnson, *A journey to the western islands of Scotland*, ed. M. Lascelles, vol. 9 of *The Yale edition of the works of Samuel Johnson* · R. H. MacLeod, *Flora MacDonald: the Jacobite heroine in Scotland and North America* (1995) · R. O. de Mond, *Loyalists in North Carolina during the revolution* (1979) · D. Meyer, *The highland Scots of North Carolina, 1732–76* (1961) · R. E. Wicker, *Miscellaneous ancient records of Moore County* (1971) · A. MacGregor, *The life of Flora MacDonald* (1882) · F. F. Wylde, *The autobiography of Flora MacDonald* (1870) · J. P. Maclean, *Flora Macdonald in America* (1909)
Archives NL Scot., letter to Sir John MacPherson
Likenesses R. Wilson, oils, 1747, Scot. NPG · mezzotint, pubd 1747 (after I. Markluin), BM · J. Macardell, engraving, pubd 1749 (after A. Ramsay), NPG · A. Ramsay, oils, 1749, AM Oxf. [*see illus.*] · W. Robertson, oils, 1750, Kelvingrove Museum and Art Gallery, Glasgow · J. Faber, mezzotint (after T. Hudson), BM, NPG · J. Highmore, oils, North Carolina Museum of Art, Raleigh · A. Ramsay, chalk drawing, Scot. NPG · R. Wilson, oils, NPG · oils (after A. Ramsay), Scot. NPG
Wealth at death lived on annuity from son

Macdonald, Frances Eliza (1873–1921). *See under* Mackintosh, Margaret Macdonald (1864–1933).

MacDonald, George (1824–1905), poet and novelist, was born on 10 December 1824 at Duke Street, Huntly, Aberdeenshire, the second of the four surviving sons of George MacDonald (1792–1858) and his first wife, Helen (1800–1832), daughter of Captain Alexander MacKay of Duardbeg, Sutherland, and sister of the Gaelic scholar McIntosh MacKay; his maternal grandmother was Helen Falconer, daughter of the Revd Alexander Falconer.

George MacDonald (1824–1905), by William Jeffrey, c.1852–60

Ancestry, early years, and education Both MacDonald's parents were Scottish, and he was fiercely proud of his ancestry. His Jacobite great-grandfather William, the official piper and resident of Portsoy, lost his sight at Culloden. William escaped with his father from Glencoe and migrated to Portsoy, Banffshire, where he began a business quarrying and polishing marble. From Portsoy the family eventually moved to Huntly, where Charles Edward (1746–1819), the author's grandfather, became proprietor of a linen and bleaching firm and later built a thread factory and introduced banking facilities. His energetic grandfather was a good businessman and had a reputation for being tolerant and devout, with a jovial and good-natured personality.

In 1778 Charles Edward married Isabella Robertson (1756–1848) of Huntly, a religious and determined woman, who taught herself to read; she gave birth to ten children and adopted four orphans. The grandmother in *Robert Falconer* is an accurate biographical portrait of her. The three sons—Charles, George (the author's father), and James—became partners in their father's linen and bleaching business. George MacDonald sen. built a house on Bogie (Duke Street), where two of his sons, Charles Francis (1823–1905) and George (the author), were born. His paternal grandmother lived in the house next door, at the corner of Church Street, with a communicating door linking the two houses.

In 1826 George MacDonald the elder and his brother James moved with their families to a stone cottage which they built at Pirriesmill; it was called Bleachfield Cottage and later was known as The Farm. Here three of George MacDonald's brothers, James MacKay (1826–1834), Alexander (1827–1853), and John Hill (1830–1858), were born. George MacDonald often recalled with nostalgia the bucolic scenes of his boyhood at The Farm: the changing seasons—how the stormy winter wind 'howled in the chimney, against the windows & down at the kitchen door' (*Expression of Character*, 56). He later described in his autobiographical novel *Ranald Bannerman's Boyhood* (1871) the attic room which he occupied as a young boy. He began his formal education at an Adventure school, supported mainly by dissenters or missioners. In 1832 his mother died and seven years later, in 1839, his father married Margaret McColl (1804–1904), the daughter of Alexander Stewart of Edinburgh. She was a devoted stepmother and also gave birth to three daughters: Isobel (1841–1855), Louise (b. 1843), and Jane or Jeanie (b. 1846).

In preparation for sitting the bursary at King's College, Old Aberdeen, George MacDonald spent three months at the Aulton (Old Town) grammar school, Aberdeen, where he studied mainly Latin, and won twelfth place in the competition, winning the Fullarton Bursary of £14 per annum, enough to cover expenses for the five months' session. He attended King's College for four sessions: 1840–45, missing 1842–3, presumably for lack of funds. Because of his frail health he was unable to work at The Farm and spent the summer months 'in a certain castle or mansion in the far North', the locality of which is uncertain, 'in cataloguing a neglected library' (*MacDonald and his Wife*, 72–3), possibly the library of Thurso Castle, owned at the time by Sir George Sinclair. At King's College he studied Latin, Greek, maths, chemistry, natural history, and moral philosophy. He became interested in the relation of poetry and science, and won the third prize in chemistry, was fourth in natural philosophy, and in moral philosophy was seventeenth. As a student he was 'studious, quiet, sensitive, imaginative, frank, open, speaking freely what he thought' (ibid., 76). In a lengthy narrative poem 'A Hidden Life' (*Poems*, 1857) he gave a graphic description of his rural and university life.

'Already a poet who saw symbolic meanings in what others found commonplace, MacDonald was regarded by the students as something of a visionary' (*DNB*). He attended Blackfriars Street Church, Aberdeen, where the Calvinistic doctrines of everlasting punishment and election that he had heard as a child continued to disturb him. In 1845 he took the MA and published in February 1846 in the *Scottish Congregational Magazine* his first poem, 'David', consisting of 114 lines in blank verse.

Uncertain about his vocational career and in need of a livelihood, MacDonald became a tutor and moved to London, where through his beautiful cousin Helen MacKay, who was married to Alexander Powell, he met James Powell's third daughter, Louisa (1822–1902). She was plain, but he admired her sense of humour, honesty, and frankness, and a romance ensued. Still unsure about his career, he gave up tutoring and entered Highbury Theological College, Middlesex, in 1848, to train as a Congregational minister. Finding his studies at Highbury College uncongenial, he took itinerant preaching engagements and did not finish his course, but was ordained in his first and only pastorate, the Trinity Congregational Chapel at Arundel, Sussex, in 1850. On 8 March 1851 he and Louisa Powell were married. Because MacDonald refused to subscribe to any sectarian position, 'neither of Arminian nor Calvinist' (*Expression of Character*, 34), some members of his congregation were offended and unable to grasp his poetic sermons, influenced by his translation *Twelve of the Spiritual Songs of Novalis* (privately published for friends in 1851). The reduction of his small stipend led to his resignation in May 1853.

First writings, 1855–1868: poetry and novels In need of financial support for his growing family and still determined to continue preaching, MacDonald moved to Manchester, where his brother Charles lived. There he became friends with Alexander John Scott, principal of Owens College, who greatly influenced him intellectually, and with Henry Septimus Sutton, a religious poet. Unable to find another pastorate, he took a room in Renshaw Street and began preaching on Sundays to some friends. He also contributed regularly to the *Christian Spectator*, and completed in 1855 his first book, *Within and Without*, a dramatic poem dedicated to his wife, the first draft of which had been written at Arundel in the winter of 1850. Its overly complicated plot entails reversal of fate and tragic circumstances, in which Count Jullian, who has become a monk, escapes from a monastery, rescues Lilia, a lady he has loved in the past, from a wicked noble, stabs the villain, and elopes with her; thereby MacDonald hoped to communicate to his wife that marital love is only an outgrowth of devotion to God. Filled with religious symbolism, the poem demonstrates MacDonald's lyrical talent as well as his failings as a dramatist. It won, however, the appreciation of Tennyson and the intense admiration of Lady Byron, who became at once one of MacDonald's closest friends and supporters. *Poems* (1857) strengthened MacDonald's reputation, and in 1858 he published *Hymns and Sacred Songs*. Also in 1858 his first major book appeared, *Phantastes: a Faerie Romance for Men and Women*, a prose romance of Spenserian allegory and fairy tales, which takes rank with La Motte-Fouqué's *Undine* and other classics of its kind. It contains some of MacDonald's most fascinating and impressive lyrics.

Throughout MacDonald's literary career he experimented with various forms of poetry and prose. For the next ten years, from 1862 to 1872, he concentrated on building his reputation as a novelist and lecturer. Hoping he might gain a wider audience, he turned to drama, writing a play ('If I had a Father'), which he subsequently turned into a novel ('Seekers and Finders'), but this was never published. Encouraged by George Murray Smith, the publisher of *Phantastes*, to write novels, he wrote 'prose fiction of two kinds, one of which dealt with the mystical and psychic and the other described humble life in Scotland' (*DNB*). *David Elginbrod* (1863), dedicated to the

memory of Lady Byron, *Adela Cathcart* (1864), and *The Portent: a Story of the Inner Vision of the Highlanders, Commonly Called the Second Sight* (1864) were early works in the first category, which effectively challenged nineteenth-century materialism and contributed to the interest in psychic experiences. *Alec Forbes* (1865) and *Robert Falconer* (1868) are autobiographical novels that 'rank among the classics of Scottish literature in their powerful delineation of Scottish character, their sense of the nobility of country work, and their appreciation of ideal beauty' (ibid.). In succeeding novels, chiefly in Scottish settings, MacDonald pursued the same aim in *Malcolm* (1875) and its sequel, *The Marquis of Lossie* (1877). In the English novel *Paul Faber, Surgeon* (1879), in which philosophic reflection predominates, he explores the conflict of the scientific mind and spiritual belief. In *Sir Gibbie* (1879) MacDonald returns to his autobiographical sources in a fictionalization of scenes from his student days in Aberdeen. In this novel a motherless mute street urchin loyally attends to his kind but drunken father, once a man of wealth but now a poor cobbler. After his father's death he flees to the countryside, where he is taken by a cotter and her husband; eventually he recovers his lost fortune, marries, and lives happily ever after. Similarly in *Castle Warlock: a Homely Romance* (1882) MacDonald pursues successfully his favourite theme of the love of father and son and family pride. Of the English novels, *Wilfrid Cumbermede* (1872), a *Bildungsroman* set in the early nineteenth century, and *Thomas Wingfold, Curate* (1876), are the most notable.

Juvenile fiction and fantasy In 1867 MacDonald published his first collection of fairy tales, *Dealings with the Faeries*, which includes two of his classic shorter tales: 'The Light Princess', about a little girl who must learn self-sacrifice in order to regain her physical gravity, and 'The Golden Key', in which he tried to depict the spiritual process of birth, maturation, and the future state—the lifelong activity of becoming a child, as he defined 'childlikeness'. From the scenes of his own boyhood—the bleaching fields around The Farm, the ruined castle nearby, the intriguing idle looms standing silent in the deserted thread-spinning factory, and, most impressive to him, the transporting power of the wind—MacDonald constructed the symbolic landscapes of his fairy tales.

Although MacDonald acquired a remarkable reputation during his lifetime as a poet and novelist, he is more highly regarded today as a writer of children's fiction and fantasy, and for his religious writings. He is known best for his ability—defined by C. S. Lewis—as a mythopoeic writer, that is, one who creates a fantasy hovering between the allegorical and the mythopoeic. He has been credited in this regard with establishing in the nineteenth century a tradition of symbolic fantasy fiction that has many modern admirers and imitators, including writers and artists like C. S. Lewis and Maurice Sendak. MacDonald's individualistic expression of his belief in immortality and in the presence of an inherent goodness in the universe ('Yet I know that good is coming to me— that is always coming, though few have at all times the simplicity and the courage to believe it'; *Phantastes*, 323) continues to attract religious readers to his sermons, which are frequently quoted and have been anthologized and reprinted.

MacDonald's special talent was to create literary parables which borrowed heavily from fairy tale, myth, and biblical tradition. Having published the first of a series of *Unspoken Sermons* (1867), he initiated his career as a writer for children by accepting the co-editorship of *Good Words for the Young*, in which he serialized, in 1868–9, his classic of childhood fantasy, *At the Back of the North Wind* (1871). This was followed by *Ranald Bannerman's Boyhood* (1871) and *The Princess and the Goblin* (1872). In 1875 he published *The Wise Woman*, and the sequel to the Princess books, *The Princess and Curdie*, appeared in 1882.

As a writer for children, MacDonald converted the popular nineteenth-century Dickensian pattern of the rags to riches orphaned child into parabolic fantasies, which in their moral and philosophical complexity surpass both the traditional fairy tale and the stories of his contemporaries. The child in his stories not only experiences fantasy adventures of co-inhabiting two worlds, as Diamond does in *At the Back of the North Wind*, or going up castle stairs to the timeless tower room, inhabited by the great-great-grandmother Wise Woman, as Princess Irene does in *The Princess and the Goblin*, but he or she must learn also several important lessons about the meaning of life and death, generally stated in unanswerable questions. Diamond's conversations with North Wind and Princess Irene's encounters with her great-great-grandmother are filled with paradoxical situations and statements, which suggest that the stories hold meaning for readers of all ages.

In *At the Back of the North Wind*, enhanced greatly by Arthur Hughes's illustrations, MacDonald contrasts the real world of the child Diamond, who sleeps in a loft over a stable, with his dream adventures with Mistress North Wind, who takes him on her flights over London and beyond. He tells her that he wants to go to the country at her back; she answers him that this is very difficult to do but she finally consents. The curious country to which he is taken is a dreamland of fictional parables representing daily life, events, and circumstances, ending with death itself. Similarly in *The Wise Woman, or, The Lost Princess: a Double Story*, Princess Rosamond and the shepherd's daughter Agnes have educational confrontations with the invincible Wise Woman (Mistress North Wind in disguise), who teaches them the true meaning of life's virtues—lessons which are learned also by 'The day boy and the night girl' in *The History of Photogen and Nycteris: a Day and Night Märchen* (1879), the last of his collected fairy tales, reprinted in 1882.

All of MacDonald's stories for children are—as G. K. Chesterton suggests—disguises of some sort: 'The fairy-tale was the inside of the ordinary story and not the outside.' Because 'George MacDonald did really believe that people were princesses or goblins and good fairies', he 'dressed them up as ordinary men and women' (*MacDonald and his Wife*, 11). It is perhaps for this reason that the children in his stories do not doubt the existence of the fairy tale inhabitants in them. His classics for children—the

Princess books and *The Wise Woman*—challenge readers to ask themselves questions about the nature of goodness, the limitless power of the unseen, and belief in a hereafter.

Despite his writing and preaching without intermission, MacDonald's income was still small. He took over the full editorship of *Good Words for the Young* (1872–3) and for a short time held an evening lectureship at King's College, London. In 1872 he went on a lecturing tour in America, where he found enthusiastic audiences. There he met John Greenleaf Whittier, Henry Wadsworth Longfellow, Oliver Wendell Holmes, C. D. Warner, Richard Watson Gilder, Ralph Waldo Emerson, Phillips Brooks, and later discussed co-operation on a novel with Samuel Clemens (Mark Twain), who visited the MacDonalds on their return from America to London at The Retreat, Hammersmith, later occupied by William Morris, and known then as Kelmscott House. MacDonald continued lecturing and wrote another, less well-known, romance for children, *Gutta Percha Willie: the Working Genius* (1873), about Willie MacMichael, who becomes a talented blacksmith, shoemaker, carpenter, and mechanic. Eventually he grows up and becomes a doctor and provides healing waters for the patients from a medicinal spring in an ancient priory, which he and his father restored.

The last period, 1880–1898 By 1880 MacDonald had achieved an international reputation as a poet, novelist, lecturer, and preacher. Two of his most famous friends were Robert Browning and John Ruskin, the latter of whom was a visitor at MacDonald's London home, and who ranked MacDonald's poem *Diary of an Old Soul* (1880) with Longfellow's *Hiawatha* and Keble's hymns. His wide range of friends included the Carlyles, William Morris, Edward Burne-Jones, Lord Tennyson, Octavia Hill, Dean Stanley, Matthew Arnold, the eighth duke of Argyll, John Stuart Blackie, Lord Houghton, Lord and Lady Mount-Temple, Arthur Hughes (whose nephew became engaged to MacDonald's daughter Mary Josephine), and Charles Dodgson (Lewis Carroll). In 1868 he was awarded the honorary degree of LLD by Aberdeen University and was granted a civil-list pension of £100 in 1877.

At fifty-seven MacDonald wrote in an attempt to summarize the meaning of his life to a close friend, Professor George Rolleston:

> All my life, I might say, I have been trying to find that one Being, and to know him consciously present; hope grows and grows with the years that lead me nearer to the end of my earthly life; and in my best moods it seems ever that the only thing worth desiring is that his will be done. (*Expression of Character*, 331)

In 1880 he privately published *A Book of Strife*, in the form of the Diary of an Old Soul, which contains some of his most moving devotional poetry. In 1893 he published the two volumes of his *Collected Poetry*. His last major work, *Lilith*, appeared in 1895, the companion to his romance *Phantastes*. This is a classic work of fantasy fiction, in which MacDonald explores the difficult subject of converting evil into good, and struggles with his own belief in immortality as, in the final years of his life, he was forced to face the death of some of his own children. Having had to endure poor health for most of his life, MacDonald spent the greater part of each year with his family from 1881 to 1901 at Casa Coraggio, Bordighera, Italy. The house was built by himself largely out of contributions from friends. At Bordighera as in London, where his charitable activity was unceasing, he proved a friend to all the neighbouring poor. In spite of his failing health he published his last novel, *Salted with Fire*, in 1897, in which he returns to recollections of his early life and only pastorate, and expresses his lifelong interest in the nature of goodness, repentance, and the symbolic meaning of marital love as an expression of love for God.

After the death of his beloved wife in 1902, MacDonald's own health deteriorated significantly—and shortly afterwards he suffered a stroke. This left him partially paralysed, and he returned to England to live in a house built for him by his eldest son at Haslemere. He died after a long illness at Sagamore, Ashtead, the home of his youngest daughter, Lady Troup, on 18 September 1905. Of a family of six sons and five daughters, five sons and two daughters survived their father. His ashes after cremation at Woking were buried in the English cemetery at Bordighera, and a memorial to him exists in the MacDonald family churchyard at Drumblade, near Huntly.

GLENN EDWARD SADLER

Sources Greville MacDonald, *George MacDonald and his wife* (1924) · R. MacDonald, 'George MacDonald: a personal note', *From a northern window* (1911), 21–79; repr. (Eureka, CA, 1989) · J. M. Bulloch, *A centennial bibliography of George MacDonald* (1925) · M. Hutton, 'The George MacDonald collection', *Yale University Library Gazette*, 51/2 (Oct 1976) · G. E. Sadler, 'The cosmic vision: a study of the poetry of George MacDonald', PhD diss., U. Aberdeen, 1966 · *An expression of character: the letters of George MacDonald*, ed. G. E. Sadler (1994) · W. Raeper, *George MacDonald* (1987) · D. S. Robb, *George MacDonald* (1987) · C. E. Troup, 'Notes on the boyhood of George MacDonald', *Deeside Field Club* (1925) · W. D. Geddes, 'George MacDonald as a poet', *Blackwood*, 149 (1891), 361–70 · private information (2004) [Charles Francis MacDonald; Maurice MacDonald, grandson; Christopher MacDonald, great-great grandson; Naomi Lewis; Mrs Freda Lawson] · M. Gray, 'A brief sketch of the life of George MacDonald', *The Bookman*, 29 (1905) · R. J. Troup, 'Huntly and George MacDonald', *Transactions of the Buchan Club*, 18/1 (1964) [repr.] · *The Times* (21 Sept 1905) · R. Hein, *George MacDonald: Victorian mythmaker* (1993) · E. Saintsbury, *George MacDonald: a short life* (1987) · W. Raeper, 'Diamond and Kilmeny: MacDonald, Hogg and the Scottish folk tradition, 7', *Anglo-American Literary Review*, 2 (1994), 63–72 · R. B. Shaberman, *George MacDonald: a bibliographical study* (1990) · *DNB* · bap. reg. Scot. · *CGPLA Eng. & Wales* (1906)
Archives Harvard U., Houghton L., corresp., literary MSS and papers · Hunt. L., letters · Huntly Branch Library, Huntly, Aberdeenshire, literary MSS, collected material · Man. CL, Manchester Archives and Local Studies, manuscripts · North Aberdeenshire Museums, MacDonald/Troup Collection, corresp., MSS, and letters · U. Aberdeen, corresp. and literary MSS · Yale U., Beinecke L., corresp. | Balliol Oxf., MSS · BL, MSS and letters · Bodl. Oxf., MSS and letters · DWL, letters to Henry Allon · FM Cam., MSS · King's Lond., corresp. and poems · Mitchell L., Glas., MSS · NL Scot., letters to Lord Mount-Temple and Lady Mount-Temple and poems · NYPL, letters · Shakespeare Centre, Stratford upon Avon, MSS · U. Cal., Los Angeles, letters · U. Nott. L., Hallward Library, letters to Henry Septimus Sutton · Wheaton College, Illinois, Marion E. Wade Center

Likenesses W. Jeffrey, *c*.1852–1860, NPG [*see illus.*] · G. Reid, oils, 1868, NPG · G. Reid, oils, 1868, Marischal College, Aberdeen · G. A. Lawson, copper bust, 1873?, Royal Scot. Acad.; [on loan to Scot. NPG] · C. Harrison, oils, 1897, Scot. NPG · G. Cook, stipple (after photograph by Elliott & Fry), NPG · attrib. C. L. Dodgson, photograph, NPG · Elliott & Fry, cabinet photograph, NPG · Elliott & Fry, carte-de-visite, NPG · A. Munro, bronze medallion, Scot. NPG · Dr Wallich, carte-de-visite, NPG · H. J. Whitlock, carte-de-visite, NPG · chromolithograph, BM
Wealth at death £1148 7*s*. 4*d*.: resworn probate, 3 Feb 1906, *CGPLA Eng. & Wales*

Macdonald, Sir George (1862–1940), classical scholar and civil servant, was born at Elgin on 30 January 1862, the third son of James Macdonald, a master at Elgin Academy and an antiquary, and his wife, Margaret Raff. He was educated at Ayr Academy, of which his father was then rector, and at Edinburgh University, where he graduated with first-class honours in classics in 1882. After periods of study in Germany and France, he entered Balliol College, Oxford, in 1884, and obtained a first class in classical moderations (1885) and in *literae humaniores* (1887). From 1887 to 1892 he was a member of the staff of the Kelvinside Academy, Glasgow, where his father was now rector, and was subsequently (1892–1904) a senior assistant in Greek at Glasgow University. He married in 1897 Margaret Tannahill, daughter of George Younger, a Glasgow merchant; they had a son and a daughter who predeceased her father.

In 1904 Macdonald left academic life on appointment as senior examiner at the Scottish education department. He was soon placed in charge of the department's Edinburgh office, at a time (1908 onwards) when a growing part of its administration was being transferred from London. His career culminated in appointment as secretary of the Scottish education department (1922–8). In educational circles Macdonald is best remembered for establishing the Leaving Certificate Examination and for introducing the first superannuation scheme for teachers in Scotland. With colleagues he was stiff and formal, even autocratic, though at the same time his natural kindness and integrity were visible to all. He was appointed CB in 1916 and KCB in 1927 for his services to the Scottish education department.

Besides being a distinguished administrator, Macdonald was also a skilled numismatist and an eminent authority on Romano-British history and antiquities. The Hunterian collection of coins in Glasgow University had long claimed his attention; between 1899 and 1906 he produced his catalogue of *Greek Coins in the Hunterian Museum*, a work which placed him in the front rank of numismatists and which was 'crowned' by the Académie des Inscriptions et Belles-Lettres and which brought him the award of the prix Allier de Hauteroche (1907). In 1905 he was made honorary curator of the Hunter Coin Cabinet, a post he retained until his death. He delivered in Edinburgh the Rhind lectures in archaeology which were published as *Coin Types: their Origin and Development* (1905). Several important surveys by him of newly found Roman coins appeared in the *Proceedings of the Society of Antiquaries*

SIR GEORGE MACDONALD K.C.B

Sir George Macdonald (1862–1940), by Maurice Greiffenhagen, 1929

of Scotland. In 1935 he was president of the Royal Numismatic Society, which had awarded him its medal in 1913.

With an interest inherited from his father in the Antonine wall between the Forth and the Clyde, Macdonald devoted much of his leisure to establishing its line and to excavating its forts. A course of Dalrymple lectures delivered in Glasgow in 1910 on this subject subsequently formed the main strand of his *Roman Wall in Scotland* (1911), of which a revised and enlarged edition appeared in 1934, incorporating the results of much excavation and fieldwork over the previous two decades by himself and others. A close friendship with F. J. Haverfield led to the publication in 1924, after Haverfield's death, of his Ford lectures in their joint names under the title of *The Roman Occupation of Britain.* Macdonald's authoritative work on Romano-British history was fully recognized abroad, especially in Germany.

Macdonald's interests came together in appointments to the royal commission on national museums and galleries (1927–30) and the subsequent standing commission (1931); he was also a member of the Royal Fine Art Commission for Scotland on its institution in 1927. From 1918 onwards he was one of the two reporters for the Carnegie Trust for the universities of Scotland under the research scheme. He was also a member of the University Grants Committee from 1933 onwards. Many academic honours were conferred upon him. He received honorary degrees from the universities of Edinburgh, Glasgow, Oxford, and Cambridge. He was elected a fellow of the British Academy in 1913, and an honorary fellow of the Royal Society of Edinburgh in 1933 and of Balliol College, Oxford, in 1936; he was also an honorary member of the Royal

Scottish Academy and a trustee of the National Library of Scotland. He was president of the Society for the Promotion of Roman Studies (1921–6) and of the Classical Associations of England and Wales (1931) and of Scotland (1936). A volume of the *Journal of Roman Studies* (22, 1932) was issued in his honour, with a bibliography of his writings. At the time of his death he was president of the Society of Antiquaries of Scotland, chairman of the Royal Commission on the Ancient and Historical Monuments of Scotland, and vice-chairman of the Ancient Monuments Board for Scotland. He died of a heart attack in Edinburgh on 9 August 1940, and was buried at Dean cemetery, on the 13th.   A. O. CURLE, *rev.* L. J. F. KEPPIE

Sources A. O. Curle, 'Sir George Macdonald, 1862–1940', *PBA*, 27 (1941), 433–51 · I. A. Richmond, 'Sir George Macdonald', *Archaeologia Aeliana*, 4th ser., 19 (1941), 177–87 · A. Graham, 'In piam veterum memoriam', *The Scottish antiquarian tradition*, ed. A. S. Bell (1981), 212–26 · 'A bibliography of Sir George Macdonald's published writings', *Journal of Roman Studies*, 22 (1932), 3–8 · J. G. C. Anderson, 'Sir George Macdonald: a bibliographical supplement', *Journal of Roman Studies*, 30 (1940), 129–30 · *Scottish biographies* (1938) · *The Times* (12 Aug 1940) · *Glasgow Herald* (10 Aug 1940) · *Glasgow Herald* (14 Aug 1940) · *CCI* (1940)

Archives U. Edin. L., corresp. and papers | Bodl. Oxf., letters to O. G. S. Crawford

Likenesses W. Stoneman, photograph, 1917, NPG · M. Greiffenhagen, oils, 1929, priv. coll. [*see illus.*] · W. and E. Drummond Young, photograph, repro. in 'A bibliography of Sir George Macdonald's published writings', frontispiece

Wealth at death £15,659 11s. 4d.: confirmation, 16 Oct 1940, *CCI*

Macdonald, George (1903–1967), malariologist, was born at 7 Summerfield, Ecclesall, Bierlow, Sheffield, on 22 June 1903, the son of John Smyth Macdonald (1867–1941), professor of physiology at Sheffield University and later at Liverpool, and his wife, Katherine Mary Stewart of Stornoway, Isle of Lewis. He was educated at the King Edward VII School in Sheffield, and, after the family moved to Liverpool in 1914, at the Liverpool Institute and the University of Liverpool, where he graduated MB ChB in 1924; in the same year he took the diploma of tropical medicine at the Liverpool School of Tropical Medicine.

In 1925 Macdonald was appointed research assistant at the Sir Alfred Jones Research Laboratory at Freetown, Sierra Leone, the Liverpool school's field station. He was there for four years, during which he carried out important research into the epidemiology of malaria in children, noticing that parasitaemia in African children was mathematically related to the number of infective bites in the population. He then went to India and, after two years as a malaria research officer with the Malaria Survey of India, was appointed medical officer for the Mariani Medical Association in Assam in 1932. It was also in 1932 that he obtained the degree of MD from Liverpool and the diploma in public health from London. On 27 July that year he married Mary (*b.* 1906/7), daughter of Sir Roger Gaskell Hetherington (1876–1952), chief engineering inspector at the Ministry of Health; they had one son and two daughters.

In 1937 Sir Malcolm Watson offered Macdonald the post of assistant director at the Ross Institute for Tropical

Hygiene. As a result, Macdonald spent eighteen months in Ceylon as malariologist to the Ross Institute's malaria control scheme for tea and rubber estates. Soon after his return to Britain in 1939 war broke out and he joined the Royal Army Medical Corps, where he soon was promoted to the rank of brigadier. In 1940 the War Office appointed him to form and command successively nos. 1, 2, and 3 malaria field laboratories in the Middle East and central Mediterranean, and it was claimed that the low incidence of malaria among the British troops was the result of his influence. In 1943 he was mentioned in dispatches. He returned to the Ross Institute as director in 1945.

Macdonald was next appointed to the chair of tropical hygiene in the University of London, in 1946. He became MRCP in 1948 and was appointed a member of the expert panel on malaria of the World Health Organization (WHO). In 1952 he led the WHO mission to Korea and in 1954 he was awarded the Darling foundation medal and prize by the World Health Assembly for his work on the epidemiology of malaria. Macdonald had been appointed CMG in 1953 and he was elected FRCP two years later. His classic work, *The Epidemiology and Control of Malaria*, was published in 1957. However, though he worked extensively in the field of malaria control, Macdonald's methods were not compatible with that of some of the other malariologists at the London School of Hygiene and Tropical Medicine. His epidemiological approach was based on mathematical work to establish biological models which could be understood by non-mathematicians. Professor P. C. C. Garnham, professor of protozoology at the school, differed from Macdonald, concentrating on the parasitology of malaria. This led to an unfortunate diversification of effort within the school and a considerable amount of ill feeling, as both men could be scathing in their comments.

In 1964 Macdonald transferred his attention to schistosomiasis, applying his mathematical analysis to its epidemiology, so that work according to his models run on a computer showed a striking similarity to that done in the field. Macdonald was elected president of the Royal Society of Tropical Medicine and Hygiene in 1965, a position that he held until shortly before his death. He was diagnosed with lung cancer in late 1966 and died in University College Hospital, London, on 10 December 1967. Until a few weeks before his death he was working on the application of mathematical models to the epidemiology of insect-borne diseases. His funeral at St Michael's Church, Highgate, London, on 12 December, was followed by cremation.

George Macdonald's work on the epidemiology of malaria expanded the initial work of Sir Ronald Ross and provided a basis from which subsequent developments have stemmed. Despite his acerbic tongue and intolerance of sub-standard work, he was helpful and kind to those who turned to him for assistance. The *Times* obituary of 15 December stated, 'he was not apt to display himself as a great man. But he had the qualities of greatness, and his friends miss him' (*The Times*).　　　MARY E. GIBSON

Sources Munk, *Roll* · *The Times* (15 Dec 1967) · L. J. Bruce-Chwatt, 'Professor George Macdonald', in G. Macdonald, *Dynamics of tropical disease*, ed. L. J. Bruce-Chwatt and V. J. Glanville (1973), 3–4 · P. C. C. Garnham, *Transactions of the Royal Society of Tropical Medicine and Hygiene*, 62 (1968), 160 · L. J. Bruce-Chwatt, *BMJ* (23 Dec 1967), 749 · *The Lancet* (23 Dec 1967), 1370–71 · private information (2004) · L. Wilkinson, 'Conceptual conflict: malaria control and internecine warfare within a London postgraduate school', *Parassitologia*, 40 (1998), 239–44 · b. cert. · m. cert. · d. cert. · *WWW*, 1941–50 [John Smyth Macdonald] · *WWW*, 1951–60 [Hetherington, Roger Gaskell] · *The Times* (12 Dec 1967)

Archives Wellcome L., papers

Likenesses photograph, *c*.1965, repro. in Graham, *Transactions of the Royal Society of Tropical Medicine and Hygiene* · photographs, London School of Hygiene and Tropical Medicine

Wealth at death £27,101: probate, 5 March 1968, *CGPLA Eng. & Wales*

Macdonald, Georgiana. *See* Jones, Georgiana Burne- (1840–1920), *under* Macdonald sisters (*act*. 1837–1925).

Macdonald, Sir Hector Archibald (1853–1903), army officer and popular hero, youngest of five sons of William Macdonald, a crofter and mason, and his wife, Ann, daughter of John Boyd of Killiechoilum and of Cradlehall, was born at Rootfield, Urquhart, Ross-shire, on 4 March 1853. Gaelic-speaking outside school, he attended the local Mulbuie School, left aged twelve, and worked as a hotel stable boy in Dingwall, then from 1868 as a draper's apprentice there and later in Inverness, where he also joined the Inverness rifle volunteers, attached to the Cameron Highlanders. On 11 June 1870, mis-stating his age and despite his parents' and friends' disapproval, he enlisted in the 92nd Gordon Highlanders. He served in India and rapidly won promotion: corporal (1872), sergeant (1873), colour sergeant (1874).

Macdonald first saw active service in the Second Anglo-Afghan War. On 27 September 1879 he showed bravery and skill in driving the Mangals from the Hazardarakt Pass near Karatiga, enabling Roberts to continue his march to Kushi. He again distinguished himself 'in a very daring manner' (Roberts, 406) at Charasia on 6 October, and was mentioned in dispatches. He served in the Maidan expedition, in the operations round Kabul in December 1879, including the defence of the Sherpur cantonments, the attack upon Takht-i-Shah, the engagement of Childukhtan, and the second action at Charasia. He was on Roberts's march from Kabul to Kandahar in August 1880, and at the reconnaissance of 31 August and at the battle of 1 September, distinguishing himself at the capture of Ayub Khan's camp at Baba Wali. His dash and prowess in battle, which won him the nickname Fighting Mac, led Roberts to promote him at Kabul second lieutenant in the Gordon Highlanders; his commission was ratified on 7 January 1880, when his sword was presented by his brother officers. Such commissioning from the ranks was then exceptional. Returning from India, Macdonald and two companies of the 92nd were landed in Natal to join Sir George Colley in the First South African War. At Majuba Macdonald showed 'conspicuous gallantry'. He was taken prisoner, but so impressed General Joubert that on release

Sir Hector Archibald Macdonald (1853–1903), by Elliott & Fry, 1890s

his sword was returned to him. He was mentioned in dispatches, and became full lieutenant on 1 July 1881.

In 1881 under Hugh Childers's reorganization the 92nd became the 2nd battalion, the Gordon Highlanders, with which Macdonald served in Edinburgh. In January 1884 he married Christina McDonald Duncan (d. 11 March 1911), aged sixteen, daughter of Alexander MacLouchan Duncan, schoolmaster, of Leith. They married secretly at her parents' home, 2 Kew Terrace, Murrayfield, Edinburgh, by exchange of consents without witnesses (a form then legal in Scotland) and the marriage was kept secret. On 17 July 1894, on his wife's application, it was registered at the court of sessions. She lived in England and they had one child, Hector Duncan (1887–1951), who was educated at Dulwich College, trained as an engineer, lived at North Shields, and reportedly was 'warped, a bitter man, latterly a recluse' (Royle, 147). Macdonald provided for but seldom saw his wife and son; apparently in nineteen years of marriage he saw his wife on only four brief occasions.

In 1884 Macdonald went to Egypt with the 1st battalion for the Gordon relief expedition, and served as garrison adjutant at Asyut from January to June 1885. Lacking the private income usually necessary to a British infantry officer, from 1885 he served with the Egyptian army under the sirdars Sir Francis Grenfell and then Kitchener. Macdonald had an important part in training the Egyptian army, and commanded the 11th Sudanese battalion,

which he modelled on the highlanders. He was promoted captain in January 1888. He and his Sudanese fought successfully against the Mahdists at Toski (3 August 1889) and the capture of Tokar (19 February 1891). He was awarded the Mejidiye (3rd class), the DSO (25 February 1890), and the Osmanieh (3rd class). He was promoted major on 7 July 1891 (nominally attached to the Royal Fusiliers, he remained in Egypt). In 1896, when Kitchener began the reconquest of the Sudan, Macdonald commanded an Egyptian infantry brigade in the Dongola offensive. Successful at Firket on 7 June and Hafir on 19 September, he was promoted brevet lieutenant-colonel on 18 November 1896. He served also on Kitchener's 1897–8 offensive, commanding an Egyptian brigade at the capture of Abu Hamed (7 August 1897), and at the Atbara (8 April 1898). He was made CB (22 June 1897). He was friendly to journalists, and his reputation was boosted by the war correspondents Bennet Burleigh and G. W. Steevens. Steevens described Old Mac as 'one of the soundest soldiers in the Egyptian or British armies' with 'a rare gift for the handling of troops' (Steevens, 57). His skill and coolness at the battle of Omdurman (2 September 1898) in meeting an unexpected Mahdist flank attack by the difficult manoeuvre, under fire, of wheeling his largely Sudanese 1st Egyptian brigade through a half circle, half battalion by half battalion, turned perilous potential disaster to victory. Omdurman was the zenith of his career. Much praised, Fighting Mac returned to Britain a popular hero, and was fêted, lionized, and honoured in London and in Scotland. He was made aide-de-camp to the queen and brevet colonel (16 November), thanked by both houses of parliament, and awarded an LLD by Glasgow University, with the organ playing 'Soldiers of the Queen'. He received admiring letters from youngsters throughout the empire, to which he always replied.

From 24 October 1899 until 3 January 1900 Macdonald was a brigadier-general in India, commanding the Sirhind district in the Punjab with headquarters at Ambala; he became major-general on relinquishing the command. After the death of Major-General Andrew Wauchope at Magersfontein (10 December 1899) Macdonald succeeded him in command of the Highland brigade, and at once went to South Africa. There he maintained his reputation. He prepared the way for Roberts's march to relieve Kimberley by seizing Koodoosberg (5–8 February 1900) and distracting the Boers from the main advance. He was at the operations resulting in Cronje's surrender at Paardeberg (16–27 February 1900). In Kitchener's bungled, unsuccessful attack on the Boer laager on 18 February Macdonald was, while leading the Highland brigade, slightly wounded in his left foot. During the reduction of the Orange Free State he was with the 9th division under Sir Henry Colvile. On the march from Lindley to Heilbron he took part in several actions (27–31 May 1900), and was on the operations that led to Prinsloo's surrender at Brandwater. During the guerrilla war he directed forces in the south-east Orange River Colony, being from the beginning of 1901 stationed at Aliwal North, where he was rumoured to have had a homosexual relationship with a

Boer prisoner. In April 1901 Kitchener had Macdonald sent home; his alleged sacking was questioned in the House of Commons. On 14 May he was knighted (KCB). Before and after the Second South African War he publicly advocated conscription. He was commander of the Belgaum district, southern India, in 1901. In May 1902 he was transferred to the command of the troops in Ceylon, a better-paid and more senior appointment.

Macdonald was about 5 feet 9 inches tall, stocky, broad-shouldered, with a 'strong, square face' (Cromb, 75), pene-trating dark eyes, and dark hair and moustache. Steevens described him as 'so sturdily built that you might imagine him to be armour-plated under his clothes' (Steevens, 58). Conan Doyle described him as 'a bony, craggy Scotsman, with a square fighting head and a bulldog jaw' (Doyle, 308).

In Ceylon Macdonald did not ingratiate himself with official and planter society, and offended by his treatment of the Ceylon militia, a planter-officered volunteer unit—like 'a sergeant with a band of recruits' (Royle, 123). He preferred the company of Burghers (Eurasians). He allegedly indulged in homosexual activity with local schoolboys, some of it allegedly witnessed in a railway carriage, and it was rumoured he had seduced the governor's son. In February 1903 the governor, Sir Joseph West Ridgeway, sent Macdonald on leave to Britain, cabling the Colonial Office, 'his immediate departure is essential to save grave public scandal' (Royle, 126). Macdonald saw Roberts, the commander-in-chief, who told him he could not stay in the army unless he cleared his name by court martial in Ceylon. He left for Ceylon (20 March) by the Marseilles route. In Paris on the morning of 25 March 1903, after seeing a *New York Times* report of a 'grave charge' against him, he shot and killed himself in room 105 of the Hotel Regina, rue du Rivoli. According to his brother William, 'It was the act of a proud and sensitive man' (Macleod, *Victims of fate*, v). According to Thomas Pakenham, 'He died like a gentleman: to save the army, and his wife, from scandal' (Pakenham, 574). His body was returned to Scotland. His Scottish admirers wanted a public funeral in Ross-shire, but at his widow's insistence he was privately, quickly buried in Dean cemetery, Edinburgh, in the early morning of Monday 30 March.

The sudden, unexpected allegations against, and death of, their hero shocked the public. There was massive public grief in Scotland: 'in death as in life he was their hero still' (Cromb, 92). On the first Sunday after his burial some 30,000 people visited his grave; so many flowers were brought that the cemetery superintendent refused to allow any more. Rumours spread: that Macdonald had been 'done away with' (Montgomery, 149), that he had been the victim of English jealousy and class prejudice, and of a plot involving Kitchener or Ridgeway or both, and that he was not dead but still in France. Later it was rumoured he was serving with the Russians against the Japanese, and during the First World War that he was a French officer, and that he was the German general Von Mackensen. Macdonald was commemorated by a tower at Dingwall, paid for by subscriptions from Scotland and the

Scottish diaspora. Macdonald's rise from private soldier to general officer was unprecedented in the Victorian army. A brave soldier and a competent commander, his NCO's obsession with drill and discipline served him well at Omdurman. At the time of the mass-circulation press and popular imperialism, military enthusiasm and 'highlandism', he was 'Scotia's darling', adored by the public. His life and tragedy have continued to fascinate and—despite biographies, articles, and pamphlets—there are questions still unanswered on his last years and death.   ROGER T. STEARN

Sources DNB · D. L. Cromb, *Hector Macdonald: the story of his life* (1903) · T. Royle, *Death before dishonour: the true story of Fighting Mac* (1982) · J. Montgomery, *Toll for the brave: the tragedy of Major-General Sir Hector Macdonald, KCB, DSO, ADC* (1963) · K. I. E. Macleod, *A victim of fate: a curious sequel, with reference to the death by suicide of Major-General Sir Hector Archibald Macdonald, KCB, DSO, ADC, LLD, the true hero of Omdurman, 1898* (1978) · K. I. E. Macleod, *The Ranker: the story of Sir Hector Macdonald's death* (privately printed, Cortland, NY, 1976) · *Hart's Army List* (1891) · T. Pakenham, *The Boer War* (1979) · G. W. Steevens, *With Kitchener to Khartum* (1898) · R. Hyam, *Empire and sexuality: the British experience* (1991) · Lord Roberts [F. S. Roberts], *Forty-one years in India*, 31st edn (1900) · B. Robson, *The road to Kabul: the Second Afghan War, 1878–1881* (1986) · F. M. Richardson, *Mars without Venus: a study of some homosexual generals* (1981) · M. Barthorp, *War on the Nile: Britain, Egypt and the Sudan, 1882–1898* (1984) · A. C. Doyle, *The great Boer War: a two years' record, 1899–1901*, 15th edn (1901) · P. Mansfield, *The British in Egypt* (1971)
Archives NAM, corresp. and papers; papers · Scottish United Services Museum, Edinburgh, corresp. and MSS
Likenesses Elliott & Fry, photograph, 1890–99, NPG [*see illus.*] · Spy [L. Ward], chromolithograph caricature (*A general group*), NPG; repro. in *VF* (29 Nov 1900) · photograph, repro. in Cromb, *Hector Macdonald* · photograph, repro. in Royle, *Death before dishonour* · photograph, repro. in Montgomery, *Toll for the brave*
Wealth at death £4402 11s. 6d.: confirmation, 4 July 1903, CCI

Macdonald, Hector Munro (1865–1935), mathematician and physicist, was born on 19 January 1865 in Edinburgh, the elder son of Donald Macdonald, originally of Kiltearn, Ross-shire, and his wife, Annie, daughter of Hector Munro of Kiltearn. His earliest education was in Edinburgh, but after the removal of his parents to Fearn in Easter Ross he went to school there, and later to the Royal Academy, Tain, and Old Aberdeen grammar school. He graduated at the University of Aberdeen in 1886 with first-class honours in mathematics and was awarded a Fullerton scholarship. Proceeding to Clare College, Cambridge, as a foundation scholar, he graduated as fourth wrangler in 1889, was elected to a fellowship at Clare in 1890, which he held until 1908, and in 1891 was awarded the second Smith's prize.

In the last years of the nineteenth century Macdonald published many papers on pure mathematics, on the relations between convergent series and asymptotic expansions, the zeros and the addition theorem of Bessel functions, various Bessel integrals, spherical harmonics, and Fourier series. However, his permanent reputation as a discoverer rests chiefly on his research in mathematical physics, which originated in the announcement by Cambridge University in 1899 of the Adams prize subject for 1901—'The improvement of existing knowledge in respect of … the modes and periods of free electric vibrations in systems of charged bodies, and the radiation from them … the theory of wireless telegraphy': Macdonald's essay won the prize. The great advance he made was the solution of the problem of diffraction at the edge of a perfectly conducting (that is, totally reflecting) prism; his method could be extended to any transparent or metallic prism of which the optical constants are known. Macdonald's essay was published under the title *Electric Waves* in 1902.

About this time, Guglielmo (afterwards Marchese) Marconi succeeded in sending wireless signals across the Atlantic, and the problem of explaining the transmission mechanism attracted the attention of mathematicians. The question may be put thus: the electric waves generated by the sending apparatus differ from waves of light only in having a longer wavelength, which is, nevertheless, small compared with the radius of the earth; the curved surface of the earth may, therefore, be expected to form a sort of shadow, effectively screening the receiving apparatus at a distance; how, then, does it happen that in practice the waves penetrate into the region of the shadow? To Macdonald belongs the credit of having been the first to formulate the problem as one of diffraction, and of having, in a series of papers published between 1903 and 1914, solved it.

Macdonald's later papers (eight of which were produced when he was in his sixties) and his book *Electro-Magnetism* (1934) continued the main study of his life, the radiation, transmission, and reflection of electric waves. He never seemed to be affected by the tremendous upheaval caused by the discoveries of the twentieth century—relativity and quantum mechanics.

In 1904 Macdonald left Cambridge to take up the chair of mathematics in his old university of Aberdeen, where his ability as an administrator soon made him the most influential member of the senatus. In 1907 he was elected as one of the representatives of the senatus on the university court, of which he remained a member (except when absent on government service during the war) for the rest of his life, attending his last meeting only a week before his death. Having been brought up on a farm, and with the further experience of estate management gained as acting senior bursar of Clare, he naturally took up specially the oversight of the university lands and buildings; his conception of a *cité universitaire* for the neighbourhood of King's College has left a permanent impress on that area.

The value of Macdonald's scientific work was recognized by his election in 1901 to the fellowship of the Royal Society, of which he was awarded a royal medal in 1916. He was president of the London Mathematical Society in 1916–18, was elected into an honorary fellowship at Clare in 1914, and received the honorary degree of LLD from Glasgow University in 1934. He never married. He died at his home, 52 College Bounds, Aberdeen, after a short illness, on 16 May 1935.

E. T. WHITTAKER, rev. ISOBEL FALCONER

Sources E. T. Whittaker, *Obits. FRS*, 1 (1932–5), 551–8 · *The Times* (17 May 1935) · personal knowledge (1949) · *CGPLA Eng. & Wales* (1935)

Likenesses W. Stoneman, photograph, 1931, NPG · R. G. Eves, oils, 1933, Scot. NPG · R. G. Eves, oils, 1933, U. Aberdeen · photograph, repro. in Whittaker, *Obits. FRS*, facing p. 551 · two photographs, RS

Wealth at death £30,887 10s.: confirmation, 29 July 1935, *CCI* · £554 19s. 5d.: eik further grant, 25 Nov 1935, *CCI*

MacDonald, Hugh (d. 1495/1498). *See under* MacDonald family (*per. c.*1475–1616).

Macdonald, Hugh (1699–1773), vicar apostolic of the highland district, son of Alexander Macdonald (*fl.* 1698–1726) of Morar and his second wife, Mary Macdonald of Kinlochmoidart, was born at Morar on 2 February 1699. In 1714 he entered the highland seminary at Loch Morar, then in 1716 went to Scalan seminary, where he was ordained priest on 18 September 1725. He served at Morar until 1730. On 12 February 1731 he was nominated titular bishop of Diana and vicar apostolic of the newly formed highland district. Having lived at the Scots College, Paris, from July 1730 to September 1731 preparing for his future duties, he received episcopal ordination at Edinburgh on 18 October 1731. His headquarters remained at Morar.

At this time the Jansenist controversy divided the highland clergy deeply but eventually it died away. After Prince Charles Edward arrived in Scotland in July 1745 Bishop Macdonald, having failed to persuade him to return to France, blessed the prince's standard raised at Glenfinnan on 19 August 1745. Macdonald remained hidden in Morar after the defeat at Culloden, until in September 1746 he sailed for France, where he was given a pension for life by the French crown. Although he returned to Scotland in August 1749, he remained mostly outside his district. In July 1755 he was arrested at Edinburgh, and sentenced to perpetual banishment in March 1756, but the sentence was not enforced and he lived quietly in the north of Scotland, mainly in upper Banffshire, outside the highland district, then at Aberchalder, a few miles west of Fort Augustus. In 1758 he visited Paris.

In 1761 Macdonald ordained his nephew, John *Macdonald (1727–1779), as his coadjutor bishop and successor. He died at Aberchalder on 12 March 1773, one of only two men who had played a leading part at Glenfinnan to die peacefully in Scotland, and was buried in Kilfinnan cemetery on Loch Lochy side. Macdonald priests of a certain social rank, including several bishops, were to form a sort of caste and have great influence in the Roman Catholic church in the highlands for the next two centuries.

THOMPSON COOPER, rev. MARK DILWORTH

Sources J. Darragh, *The Catholic hierarchy of Scotland: a biographical list, 1653–1985* (1986) · F. Forbes and W. J. Anderson, 'Clergy lists of the highland district, 1732–1828', *Innes Review*, 17 (1966), 129–84 · R. Forbes, *The lyon in mourning, or, A collection of speeches, letters, journals … relative to … Prince Charles Edward Stuart*, ed. H. Paton, 3, Scottish History Society, 22 (1896) · J. F. McMillan, 'Jansenists and anti-Jansenists in eighteenth-century Scotland', *Innes Review*, 39 (1988), 12–45 · A. Macdonald and A. Macdonald, *The clan Donald*, 3 (1904) · W. M. Brady, *The episcopal succession in England, Scotland, and Ireland, AD 1400 to 1875*, 3 vols. (1876–7) · B. M. Halloran, *The Scots College, Paris, 1603–1792* (1997)

Macdonald, Hugh (1817–1860), journalist, born in Bridgeton, Glasgow, on 4 April 1817, was apprenticed, after a scanty education at a night school, to a block-printer. He subsequently kept a provision shop in Bridgeton, and ultimately returned to his trade in Paisley. He began to write verse in the *Glasgow Citizen*, to which he also contributed a series of letters defending Robert Burns from an attack by George Gilfillan. In 1849 he gave up his trade and joined the staff of the *Glasgow Citizen*, contributing to it, and to the *Glasgow Times*, the series of descriptive papers subsequently collected under the titles of *Rambles Round Glasgow* (1856), and *Days at the Coast* (1874). In 1855 he joined the *Glasgow Sentinel*, soon afterwards became editor of the *Glasgow Times*, and in 1858 literary editor of the *Morning Journal*, a post that he held until his death on 16 March 1860. In 1883 a rustic stone fount, with a medallion bust of Macdonald, was erected to his memory on the site of 'the bonnie wee well', which is the subject of one of his songs. All his literary work shows an intense love for nature, but his prose is better than his verse. His poetical works were published, with a memoir, in 1863.

J. C. HADDEN, rev. H. C. G. MATTHEW

Sources H. Macdonald, *Poems and songs ... with a memoir of the author* (1863) · C. Rogers, *Leaves from my autobiography*, Grampian Club (1876) · R. Brown, *Paisley poets: with brief memoirs of them and selections from their poetry*, 2 vols. (1889–90) · NA Scot., SC 36/48/46/407–8
Likenesses medallion bust, *c*.1883 · A. S. Mackay, oils, Art Gallery and Museum, Glasgow
Wealth at death £160 15*s*. 8*d*.: confirmation, 1 Sept 1860, NA Scot., SC 36/48/46/407–8

Macdonald, Ian Wilson (1907–1989), accountant and banker, was born on 28 May 1907 at Cumnock, Ayrshire, the son of Alexander Buchanan Macdonald, minister of religion, and Mary Bowman Wilson, doctor of medicine. His only brother died in infancy. His very early childhood was spent in Ayrshire, but the family soon moved to Perthshire, where his mother was medical officer for Perthshire schools during the First World War. Macdonald's school education was begun at Perth Academy and completed at Edinburgh Academy. To complete the triangle he went to Glasgow University. Thereafter he served his apprenticeship as a chartered accountant with the Glasgow firm of Kerr, Macleod, and Macfarlan, and qualified in 1930. Three years later his firm assumed him as a partner; and it was then that he married Helen, daughter of James Nicholson, a Glasgow rubber and paint manufacturer. They had three children.

Macdonald's busy career in professional practice brought him into contact with a wide range of businesses and business people. Yet he also kept his academic contacts, and in 1938 he was appointed to the part-time chair in accountancy at Glasgow University. He held this post until 1950. In 1945 he became joint auditor of the Commercial Bank of Scotland, and two years later he joined the bank's board as non-executive director. A failure in planned succession led him to be offered the general manager's job in 1953. The appointment of a chartered accountant to the top job in a bank was somewhat controversial.

Macdonald was 'an energetic man of progressive views', who 'thrived on change' (*The Times*, 16 Jan 1989). He devised a three-point strategy for the future of the bank, which included growth by diversification of the business, amalgamation, and the development of a merchant bank. In 1954 Macdonald became the first British banker to acquire a hire-purchase company. He had not thought it necessary to consult the Bank of England, who were somewhat lukewarm to the idea of banks diversifying in this way. However, four years later, in under three months, all the English and Scottish clearing banks purchased stakes in finance houses dealing in hire purchase. Another progressive idea, which came to fruition in Edinburgh only in 1964, was for a ladies' branch.

It took a little longer for Macdonald to achieve his second objective, amalgamation, but in 1959 the Commercial Bank of Scotland acquired the National Bank of Scotland in a share exchange deal with its owner, Lloyds Bank, who retained 36 per cent in the new National Commercial Bank of Scotland. The sizeable hire-purchase interests of the National Commercial and Lloyds were combined and traded for many years as Lloyds and Scottish. Macdonald became chairman not only of the National Commercial Bank, but also of Lloyds and Scottish. The youngest bank chairman in Britain, his progression from general manager to chairman was 'unique in the field of British banking' (*The Times*, 16 Jan 1989). Macdonald also became a director of Lloyds Bank. By the late 1960s the growth of industry and commerce dictated the logic of further mergers among the banks, and Macdonald worked hard to secure a merger with one of Scotland's oldest, but smaller banks, the Royal Bank of Scotland. The Royal Bank name was used for the operating arm of the merged bank, and Macdonald served as chairman from the date of the merger in 1969 until 1972. The holding company from 1969 to 1979 was the National Commercial Bank of Scotland Group Ltd, and Macdonald was deputy chairman from 1969 until 1978.

Macdonald was less successful in his third aim of building a merchant bank. In 1964 National Commercial and Schroeders Ltd was set up, with Macdonald as chairman, but its growth was modest and Macdonald himself considered this venture something of a black mark on his career. Despite an exceptionally busy life with the Commercial Bank, Macdonald was able to serve on other boards including that of United Biscuits. His public service included membership of a number of government committees, including the committees of investigation and courts of inquiry into port transport (1945), shipbuilding (1947), fishing (1957–60), and ports and harbours (1961–2). He was also on the General Claims Tribunal (1943–58), the South of Scotland Electricity Board (1956–61), and the Civil Aviation Authority (1972–5). Macdonald retired from the boards of public companies at the age of seventy, and pursued his retirement interests as chairman of the Scottish Hospitals Endowment Research Trust, and as a member of the review body on doctors' and dentists' remuneration.

Described in the *Times* obituary as 'modest and unpretentious', Macdonald had 'a dour style, alleviated by dry humour' (*The Times*, 16 Jan 1989). As a son of the manse he retained his membership of the Church of Scotland, and was for many years an elder in the kirk session of St Giles's Cathedral, Edinburgh, where he also served as church treasurer. His recreational interests included shooting, fishing, and golf; he was a member of the Honourable Company of Edinburgh Golfers at Muirfield, and the Caledonian Club (London).

Macdonald played a leading role in the transformation of Scottish banking. Although his wide-ranging policies often made him seem an *enfant terrible*, they had a lasting influence at a time when post-war financial controls were yielding to competitive and rationalized banking. Macdonald died at Edington Cottage Hospital, North Berwick, on 8 January 1989. He was survived by his wife.

CHARLES W. MUNN

Sources S. G. Checkland, *Scottish banking: a history, 1695–1973* (1975) · M. Gaskin, *The Scottish banks: a modern survey* (1965) · b. cert. · d. cert. · *The Times* (16 Jan 1989) · private information (2004) **Likenesses** group portrait, photograph, 1971, Hult. Arch. · portrait, Royal Bank of Scotland, 42 St Andrew Square, Edinburgh **Wealth at death** £173,408.43: confirmation, 2 March 1989, *CCI*

MacDonald, James, of Dunyvaig and the Glens (*d.* 1565), clan chief, was the eldest son of Alexander *MacDonald of Dunyvaig and the Glens (*d.* 1536×9) and his wife, Caitirfhiona (Katherine) MacIan of Ardnamurchan. In 1531 his father handed him over as a hostage to James V, who entrusted him to the keeping of William Henderson, a canon of Holyrood. James returned home following his father's death. In 1540 he met the king during the royal expedition to the Isles and gave his brother Coll as a hostage. When Donald Dubh MacDonald escaped from prison in 1543 and claimed the lordship of the Isles, allying himself with England and the earl of Lennox, James MacDonald was almost alone among the chiefs of the Isles in remaining loyal to the Scottish crown (though his brother Angus joined Donald, presumably to safeguard James's interests). In 1544 Lennox ravaged Kintyre, and in the following year Hector Maclean of Duart used his influence with the fourth earl of Argyll to compel James to surrender the Rinns of Islay to him.

Not for the last time MacDonald showed himself to be both acquisitive and politically adroit. In 1545 he was rewarded for his loyalty by the crown with the grant in heritage of lands in north Kintyre which he had formerly leased; together they constituted the barony of Bar. He also settled his father's dispute with Argyll and married the earl's sister Agnes *Campbell. Then when Donald Dubh died late in 1545 MacDonald at once changed his political stance. His father had held a position akin to that of lord of the Isles, and he himself now aspired to the lordship. To that end he wrote to Henry VIII in January 1546, styling himself 'aperand aeyr of the Yllis' and offering to assist Lennox (Macdonald and Macdonald, 1.388). But when he found he could get little support from the islesmen he soon returned to his Scottish allegiance,

while Maclean was induced to return the Rinns of Islay. On 12 October 1550 he purchased Ardnamurchan from Argyll.

MacDonald now turned his attention increasingly to Ireland, where his clansmen were steadily infiltrating Antrim. Some of his cousins who had allied with the English had occupied the Glens of Antrim, but in 1550 these were driven out, and in 1551 MacDonald defeated a retaliatory attack on Rathlin Island. His activities alarmed the English government, and in 1556 he was himself driven from Ulster by the lord deputy, Lord Fitzwalter, from 1557 third earl of Sussex. He returned the next year, and although he defeated Sussex he also tried to make peace, but without success, and in autumn 1558 the English ravaged Arran and Kintyre. The casualties included MacDonald's principal residence, Saddell Castle, granted to him by the earl of Arran two years earlier. Meanwhile Reformation politics had begun to impinge on western Scotland, as Mary of Guise tried to build up James MacDonald, who was a Catholic, as a counterweight to the protestant fifth earl of Argyll. But her efforts failed, as James joined the lords of congregation with 700 foot soldiers.

In September 1562 Queen Mary gave MacDonald a tack of lands in Islay and Kintyre, but during that year he quarrelled with Hector Mor Maclean of Duart, ostensibly over 'the slaying of a man' (*CSP Scot.*, 1545–69, 593), in reality as part of a continuing contest for pre-eminence in the former lordship of the Isles. Argyll tried unsuccessfully to settle their quarrel, which had once more embraced the Rinns of Islay. In July 1563 the two men came before Mary at Glasgow and were instructed to produce their documents. The case was heard on 24 April 1564 and was decided in MacDonald's favour. Meanwhile MacDonald had bought substantial estates in South Uist.

In 1558, when England faced a hostile Franco-Scottish alliance, Sir Henry Sidney expressed fears that James MacDonald would invade Ulster, with native support from as far away as the Dublin pale. In 1563 an English agent even claimed that it was Scottish policy to make James MacDonald 'Lord of all the Isles of Scotland' (*CSP Ire.*, 1509–73, 228). This is unlikely—before 1560 the Scottish government had supported James's activities in Ireland, but now England and Scotland were at peace. In any case MacDonald's last expedition across the North Channel was an essentially private affair. In 1565 he raised a large army of mercenaries to attack Shane O'Neill, an ally of the Macleans who was endeavouring to subjugate the MacDonalds in Ulster. Moreover O'Neill had married James's daughter but sent her home as unsuitable. But MacDonald was outmanoeuvred by O'Neill and heavily defeated in Glenshesk near Ballycastle on 2 May. Both he and his youngest brother, Somhairle Buidhe (Sorley Boy *MacDonnell) were captured, and James died of his wounds at Castle Corcke, no later than 25 August. There were rumours that O'Neill had hastened the process. MacDonald's widow, with whom he had had three sons and two daughters, subsequently married Turlough Luineach

O'Neill, Shane's cousin. Her first husband was remembered in Irish tradition as 'a paragon of hospitality and prowess, a festive man of many troops and a bountiful and munificent man' (*AFM*, 5.1605).

NICHOLAS MACLEAN-BRISTOL

Sources *AFM*, 2nd edn, vol. 5 · K. Nicholls, 'Notes on the genealogy of clan Eoin Mhoir', *West Highland Notes & Queries*, ser. 2, 8 (Nov 1991) · D. Gregory, *History of the western highlands* (1881) · H. Paton, *The clan Campbell*, 8 (1922) · J. M. Thomson and others, eds., *Registrum magni sigilli regum Scotorum / The register of the great seal of Scotland*, 11 vols. (1882–1914), vol. 4 · PRO, State Papers Ireland, XIII, 38 · A. J. N. Macdonald and A. Macdonald, *The clan Donald*, 3 vols. (1896–1904) · N. Maclean-Bristol, *Warriors and priests: the history of the clan Maclean, 1300–1570* (1995) · D. J. Macdonald, *Clan Donald* (1978) · T. W. Moody and others, eds., *A new history of Ireland*, 3: *Early modern Ireland, 1534–1691* (1976) · J. B. Paul, ed., *Compota thesaurariorum regum Scotorum / Accounts of the lord high treasurer of Scotland*, 6 (1905) · *CSP Ire.*, 1509–73 · *CSP Scot.*, 1545–69 · G. A. Hayes-McCoy, *Scots mercenary forces in Ireland* (1937), 342

MacDonald, Sir **James, of Knockrinsay** (*c.*1570–1626). *See under* MacDonald, Angus, of Dunyvaig and the Glens (*c.*1548–1613).

Macdonald, Sir **James Ronald Leslie** (1862–1927), army officer, was born on 8 February 1862, the eldest son of surgeon-major James Macdonald. He was educated at Aberdeen grammar school (1873?–1877) and the University of Aberdeen where he was an arts student (1877–80), but took no degree. He proceeded to the Royal Military Academy, Woolwich, where he quickly made his mark, and passed out in 1882 well ahead of the rest of his year, having gained many prizes, the Pollock medal, and the sword of merit. He was gazetted lieutenant in the Royal Engineers, and took the two-year course at Chatham School of Military Engineering (1882–4).

Macdonald sailed for India in 1884, and after a short period of attachment to the Bengal Sappers and Miners, was posted for duty to the military works department. From 1885 to 1887 he was employed on survey work for the construction of the Harnai Railway in Baluchistan. His first experience of active service was with the Hazara expedition of 1888; he was mentioned in dispatches. Having been promoted captain in 1890, Macdonald carried out the survey for the Kabul River Railway, and in 1891 was employed in the Zhob Valley Railway survey. When due to return home on leave he was offered, and accepted, the appointment of chief engineer on the preliminary survey for the projected railway between Mombasa and Lake Victoria—the Uganda Railway. He had just completed this long and arduous survey when he was ordered to return to Uganda, where civil war had again broken out, to report on the causes of the religious wars and on the conduct of the British East Africa Company officials. Macdonald's report criticized Captain F. D. Lugard, and influenced Sir Gerald Portal, the imperial commissioner, to recommend the establishment of a British protectorate over Uganda. Following Portal's departure in May 1893, Macdonald was made acting commissioner of Uganda, a post he held until the arrival of Colonel Henry Colvile in November. Macdonald was engaged for two years in quelling the Muslim rebellion, and in expeditions against the Wavuma and,

while acting as chief of staff to Colville, against the slave raider Kabarega. For his services he was made a brevet major and received the brilliant star of Zanzibar, second class. Macdonald was himself criticized following the publication of Lugard's *The Rise of our East African Empire* in 1893, and his own account, *Soldiering and Surveying in British East Africa, 1891–1894*, was not published until 1897.

On 16 October 1894 Macdonald married Alice Margaret (*b.* 1864/5), youngest daughter of General George Pringle, Indian Staff Corps, at Cheltenham; they had no children. When he resumed duty in the military works department, India, Macdonald was attached to the headquarters staff at Simla. In 1896 he returned to Chatham for the Royal Engineers 'refresher course'. In 1897 he was selected to lead an expedition to find the source of the Juba River, which formed the northern boundary of the new British East Africa Protectorate. The secret purpose was to explore the region between Lake Rudolf and the Nile at a time which coincided with Kitchener's reconquest of the Sudan, and to effect a union at Fashoda. However, a mutiny by Sudanese troops and the revolt of Buganda Muslims engaged Macdonald for many months in operations over a very wide stretch of country. Following a battle at Lubwa's Hill on 19 October 1897, three British hostages were murdered by the mutineers. Macdonald's younger brother, Lieutenant Norman Macdonald, was killed in another battle on 11 December. Macdonald conducted successful operations near Lake Choga in January 1898, and after several other engagements finally assured the safety of Uganda. He was able to complete his explorations between June 1898 and March 1899, and was rewarded with a CB in 1900 and made a brevet lieutenant-colonel. Macdonald was refused permission by the Foreign Office to publish his account, *Uganda in Revolt*, because it was feared he would reveal the real purpose of the expedition. An edited account was later published by Lieutenant H. H. Austin, *With Macdonald in Uganda* (1903).

Shortly after the beginning of the Second South African War in October 1899 Macdonald was put in charge of the balloon factory at Aldershot, but on the outbreak of the Boxer uprising in 1900 he went out to China as director of balloons. This post, however, provided insufficient scope for one of his ability and experience, and he was given the post of director of railways for the China expeditionary force. He was mentioned in dispatches, received the China medal, and was promoted brevet colonel. Macdonald returned to India, and was employed in military works at Quetta until 1903. The government of India decided to send a political mission to Tibet in order to counter Russian intrigues and to stabilize relations with Tibet by means of a treaty. Lord Curzon, the viceroy of India, appointed Sir Francis Younghusband to lead the mission, while Lord Kitchener, commander-in-chief in India, selected Macdonald to command the military escort. A degree of friction arose between the two men which reflected that between their respective superiors, and endangered the mission. The party entered Tibet on 12 December 1903, their advance broken by several engagements with the Tibetans, especially in the neighbourhood of Gyantse. Although the fort there surrendered without resistance on 12 April, the capture of Gyantse was not finally consolidated until 7 July, when the monastery was secured. The last stage began on 13 July and the mission arrived at Lhasa on 3 August 1904, where a treaty was duly concluded. For his services Macdonald was made KCIE, the king having intervened to prevent his appointment as KCB.

In 1905 Macdonald was promoted colonel and given command of the presidency brigade at Calcutta. Two years later he took command of the Lucknow infantry brigade. In 1908 he was promoted major-general, and in 1909 appointed general officer commanding, Mauritius. He held this post until 1912, when under medical advice he resigned and returned to England. He was compelled, through ill health, to retire in the following year, and although he offered his services immediately on the outbreak of the First World War in 1914, his health precluded active service. In December 1914 he was appointed military member of the Aberdeen district emergency committee, and he served on that body with untiring zeal until the end of the war. In July 1915 he was appointed deputy lieutenant of the county of Aberdeen. In 1924 he was appointed colonel commandant of his own corps, the Royal Engineers. He died at his home, 70 Wellington Road, Bournemouth, on 27 June 1927.

C. V. Owen, rev. A. J. L. Blond

Sources J. R. L. Macdonald, *Soldiering and surveying in British East Africa, 1891–1894* (1897) • H. H. Austin, *With Macdonald in Uganda* (1903) • A. T. Matson, 'Introduction', in H. H. Austin, *With Macdonald in Uganda* (1973) • F. D. Lugard, *The rise of our East African empire*, 2 vols. (1893) • M. Perham, *Lugard*, 1: *The years of adventure, 1858–1898* (1956) • *The Times* (29 June 1927) • Aberdeen City Archives • U. Aberdeen, MS UI, p. 135 • Parliamentary debates, official report, 4th series (1898), Lords, 3 March 1898, 433–440; commons, 504–577 • P. Fleming, *Bayonets to Lhasa: the first full account of the British invasion of Tibet in 1904* (1961) • m. cert. • d. cert. • *CGPLA Eng. & Wales* (1927)
Archives Aberdeen City Archives • Bodl. RH, Uganda railway survey notebook • U. Aberdeen | Bodl. RH, letters to Ernest Gedge • PRO, Foreign Office MSS; Africa, Macdonald reports, C.8718, C.8941, C.9027 (1898); C.9123, C.9232, C.9503 (1899) • Royal Engineers, Brompton Barracks, Chatham, Kent, professional papers of the corps
Likenesses photograph, repro. in Austin, *With Macdonald in Uganda*
Wealth at death £5634 10s. 9d.: probate, 31 Aug 1927, *CGPLA Eng. & Wales*

MacDonald, John (d. c.1387). See under MacDonald family (per. c.1300–c.1500).

MacDonald, John, thirteenth earl of Ross (c.1434–1503). See under MacDonald family (per. c.1300–c.1500).

MacDonald, Sir John, of Dunyvaig and the Glens (d. 1499), clan chief, was the son of Donald MacDonald (d. 1476/1481) and his wife, Siobhan O'Donnell, and the great-grandson of John MacDonald, first lord of the Isles (d. c.1387), and his second wife, Margaret Stewart. His epithet refers to Dunyvaig on Islay and the Glens of Antrim in Ulster. His grandfather Iain Mor, who married the heiress of Bisset of the Glens, was founder of the southern branch of clan Donald based on Kintyre. John was associated with

his father in the treaty of Westminster–Ardtornish with Edward IV of England (1462) and appears as *rí Innse Gall* ('king of the Isles') in Irish annals in 1499, having been called heir to John, fourth and last lord of the Isles, during his son Angus's rebellion in 1484. After the forfeiture of the lordship in 1493 MacDonald of Dunyvaig and Alexander MacDonald of Lochalsh submitted to James IV and were knighted. The chronology of events at this point is not clear. According to the usually accurate annals of Ulster, Alexander was slain on Oronsay on 14 October 1494 by John Cattanach, Sir John's son, but a seventeenth-century source states that John MacIan of Ardnamurchan was the killer and was rewarded. (While the charter he received in June 1494 was a confirmation of lands already held by him, it was specifically granted in return for his obedience and good service.)

King James came to the west in July 1494 to take control of the castles of Tarbert and Dunaverty in Kintyre, and it was probably this that caused Sir John MacDonald to revolt. He captured Dunaverty and is said to have hanged the governor within sight of the king's fleet. MacDonald and his sons were summoned for treason; they fled to Islay and were taken by MacIan at Finlaggan at an unknown date. In July 1499 they were hanged at Edinburgh. The executions may have been intended to instil a fear of royal justice in the men of the Isles, and also to ensure that the MacDonalds of Dunyvaig did not become a focus for future opposition to the crown and its agents. MacDonald married a sister of Colin Campbell, first earl of Argyll; his grandson Alexander *MacDonald succeeded as MacDonald of Dunyvaig and the Glens, carried on the family in Ulster, and was an ancestor of the earls of Antrim.

R. W. Munro and Jean Munro

Sources J. Munro and R. W. Munro, eds., *Acts of the lords of the Isles, 1336–1493*, Scottish History Society, 4th ser., 22 (1986) • K. A. Steer and J. W. M. Bannerman, *Late medieval sculpture in the west highlands* (1977) • K. Nicholls, 'Notes on the genealogy of clann Eoin Mhoir', *Notes and Queries of the Society of West Highland and Island Historical Research*, 2/8 (1991) • W. M. Hennessy and B. MacCarthy, eds., *Annals of Ulster, otherwise, annals of Senat*, 4 vols. (1887–1901) • N. Macdougall, *James IV* (1989) • N. D. Campbell, tenth duke of Argyll, Argyll transcripts, Inveraray Castle, Argyll

MacDonald, John [known as Iain Lom] (c.1624–c.1710), Scottish Gaelic poet, the son of Donald MacDonald (d. 1646?), was apparently descended from Iain Alainn, who succeeded to the chiefship of the MacDonalds of Keppoch c.1497–8. He has a high reputation as a political and clan poet, commenting on the affairs of the Keppoch MacDonalds and on the turbulent political events of a long period from the mid-1640s to the union of the parliaments in 1707. Tradition reports that he went to the Scots College at Valladolid in Spain to prepare for the priesthood, but left after disagreement. The range of his interests and references would seem to support the idea that he had some extended educational opportunities. At various points he is found using English and Scottish words and phrases in the body of his verse.

Among Iain Lom's earliest poems there is one on the battle of Inverlochy, during the Montrose wars, when the

MacDonalds inflicted a humiliating defeat on the Campbells in 1645. Lom gloats over the Campbells' craven retreat, as he sees it. He is said to have given valuable advice, from his knowledge of the terrain, to Alasdair MacColla in the run-up to the battle. It was probably in the following year (1646) that he composed a lament for the young Keppoch chief who was killed in a skirmish at Sròn a' Chlachain near Killin in Perthshire. The poet's father was also killed in this skirmish, but protocol required the main emphasis to be on the chief's death. There are three other laments composed by Iain Lom in this decade: for Alasdair MacColla in 1647, for the marquess of Huntly in 1649, and for the marquess of Montrose in 1650.

Gaelic poets continued throughout the seventeenth century to have official or semi-official status within clans, whether they were trained poets using the classical Gaelic language or vernacular poets who had looser attachments to patrons, and in this context much of Iain Lom's poetry is connected with the public activities of his clan, their allies, and their enemies. A series of poems deals with the murder of the young chief of Keppoch and his brother in 1663, and the successful campaign to avenge these murders. There are poems in praise of allies, such as Maclean of Duart and the MacDonalds of Sleat and of Glengarry, and some elegies for chiefs of these septs or clans. As part of this continuing commentary there are poems about specific battles, for example that of Tom a' Phubaill (c.1680) and Killiecrankie (1689), and a poem on the massacre of Glencoe (1692).

The latest poem ascribed to Iain Lom is one on the union of the parliaments in 1707. Some doubt has been cast on this ascription, but it shows the sharp, witty, satirical style in which Iain Lom excelled. The poet clearly accepted that bribery had played a part in this transaction, as appears from his reference to Lord Dupplin:

Lord Dupplin, without delay
the vent to your throat opened,
a turbulence rose in your heart
when you heard the gold coming;
you swallowed the hiccoughs of avarice,
your lungs inflated and swelled,
control over your gullet was relaxed,
and the traces of your arse were unloosed.

This is not simply a case of an old man's outspokenness, for we see him in 1649 reproaching the future Charles II for his 'sorry slumber' and listlessness. In 1660 he was to celebrate this king's coronation, and it is said that he enjoyed a royal pension for a short time. He died about 1710, and is thought to have been buried in the graveyard of Cill Choiril at Brae Lochaber.

Iain Lom's surviving verse, running to about 3000 lines, provides a valuable commentary on political events and arguments. Characteristically, he employs vivid and figurative language across a wide tonal range from gentle adulation to fierce invective. His uncompromising, usually satiric, vision of these events also reveals a sharp, intellectual mind. DERICK S. THOMSON

Sources A. M. Mackenzie, *Orain Iain Luim*, Scottish Gaelic Texts Society (1964) • D. S. Thomson, *An introduction to Gaelic poetry*, 2nd edn (1990) • T. Royle, *The mainstream companion to Scottish literature* (1993)
Archives U. Glas., McLagan MSS

Macdonald, John (1727–1779), vicar apostolic of the highland district, was born at Ardnamurchan, Argyll, the son of Donald Macdonald of Ardnamurchan and Catherine Macdonald of Morar, and nephew on his mother's side to Bishop Hugh *Macdonald. After attending the highland seminary at Guidal he entered the Scots College, Rome, in 1743, was ordained there in 1752 and returned to Scotland in April 1753. He officiated as missionary on the island of South Uist until 1761. A man of 'learning, and exceeding good nature and temper' (Blairs letters, 3/146/2), he was nominated titular bishop of Tiberiopolis and coadjutor to his uncle in February 1761, and was consecrated at Preshome on 27 September of the same year. On Bishop Hugh Macdonald's death in 1773 he succeeded him as vicar apostolic of the highland district of Scotland. He died on 9 May 1779 at Knoydart, Inverness-shire, and was buried there.

THOMPSON COOPER, *rev.* CLOTILDE PRUNIER

Sources J. Darragh, *The Catholic hierarchy of Scotland: a biographical list, 1653–1985* (1986) • J. F. S. Gordon, *Ecclesiastical chronicle for Scotland*, 1–2: *Scotichronicon* (1875) • Blairs letters, Scottish Catholic Archives, 3/146/2 • F. Forbes and W. J. Anderson, 'Clergy lists of the highland district, 1732–1828', *Innes Review*, 17 (1966), 129–84
Archives Scottish Catholic Archives, Edinburgh

Macdonald, John (b. 1741), domestic servant and memoirist, was born in the parish of Urquhart, Inverness-shire, the son of a gentleman cattle dealer whose wife, from a Mackay family, died two years after Macdonald's birth. Macdonald's father fought with the Jacobite highlanders and was killed at the battle of Culloden in 1746. The orphaned John and his two small brothers, led by their fourteen-year-old sister, Kitty, and her 'heroic disposition' (Macdonald, 5), then walked 150 miles to Edinburgh within two months. There they found various positions in service, and Macdonald at the age of nine became the 'littlest postilion in Scotland or any other country' (ibid., 18). He was also taught to read by his employers. After Edinburgh he took up employment with various Jacobite families in Scotland. In the early 1760s he travelled around Ireland with a new master, and finished up in London in 1763.

In London Macdonald joined the household of John Crauford of Errol, 'just come from Paris, one of the gayest young gentlemen and the greatest gambler that ever belonged to Scotland' (Macdonald, 82). With Crauford, Macdonald travelled around the continent, although he advised his master that the British Isles offered a richer source of amusement and instruction. Crauford was an acquaintance of Laurence Sterne, and is thought to have told him the story which Sterne transformed into the final chapter of *A Sentimental Journey*, 'The case of delicacy'. Back in London in 1768 Macdonald was sent by Crauford to enquire after the bedridden Sterne's health, and in fact witnessed the novelist's death.

In 1769 Macdonald sailed to India with his new master, Alexander Dow, the close friend of James Macpherson and author of several accounts of Indian history. They seem to have spent several years in India and Macdonald's observations on Indian manners and customs are frank and tolerant. Following his return to Europe Macdonald, whose talents at dressing hair made him extremely desirable, continued to travel around Europe as valet to a variety of gentlemen, including Macpherson and James Coutts the banker. In London again, in 1778 Macdonald courted ridicule by sporting a new French accessory in the streets: nevertheless, the umbrella soon became 'a great trade in London' (Macdonald, 236).

Macdonald himself returned to Toledo in Spain in the summer of 1778 to discover that a night of passion he had enjoyed with a certain Malilia the previous year had produced a son, John England. Thereafter he and Malilia married and settled in Toledo, and he found a job at the Hôtel de Naples (Macdonald, 249) and wrote his memoirs, which were published in 1790 as *Travels, in Various Parts of Europe, Asia, and Africa*. They not only provide all the biographical evidence available on Macdonald's own colourful life, but paint a vivid picture of the European beau monde, and indeed the Indian subcontinent, from the unusual perspective of a servant. His observations offer a wry commentary on aristocratic travelling habits. His own amorous exploits with servant girls (which may account for his frequent changes of employer) feature prominently in the *Travels*, to the disapproval of contemporary reviewers, one of whom expressed anxiety that the publication would only 'increase the assurance of footmen' (*Analytical Review*, 8.63). Macdonald's date and place of death are unknown.

KATHERINE TURNER

Sources J. Macdonald, *Travels, in various parts of Europe, Asia, and Africa, during a series of thirty years and upwards* (1790) · A. H. Cash, *Laurence Sterne: the later years* (1986) · *Analytical Review*, 8 (Sept 1790), 59–63

Macdonald, John (1759–1831), military engineer and cartographer, was born in Flodigarry, Isle of Skye, on 30 October 1759, the fifth and youngest son of Allan Macdonald of Kingsburgh, a captain in the 84th Royal Highland Emigrants, and Flora *Macdonald (1722–1790), the Jacobite heroine. He attended the grammar school at Portree and then the Royal High School, Edinburgh. In 1780 he was granted a cadetship in the army of the East India Company and joined the Bombay infantry. Because of his interest in fortification he transferred to the Bombay Engineers on 6 April 1782 but, unhappy with the conditions of service, he travelled to Calcutta and, through the influence of a relative, was commissioned in the Bengal Engineers instead in September 1782 and resigned his Bombay commission. As an ensign his first appointment was as assistant engineer at Bencoolen, west Sumatra.

In 1784 Macdonald was employed to survey the west coast of Sumatra from Batang Kapas to Padang. His survey work was of such significance that he was noted by the government as a 'young officer of great merit and highly deserving of encouragement' (*Memoir*, 8) and given a brevet captaincy. The same year, at Fort Marlborough, he married Nancy Scott Bogle, *née* Salmon (1760/61–1786), the young widow of Lawrence Bogle, a Bengal civil servant, and the daughter of George Salmon. On account of the

high standard of his work, the East India Company ordered Macdonald to Pulo Penang (Penang Island) in 1786 to carry out a survey, but on arrival he found that Captain Alexander Kyd (1754–1826) of the Bengal Engineers had already commenced the survey. He proceeded to Calcutta and, given revised orders, returned as military and civil engineer to Bencoolen, where he was given command of the artillery with permission to develop and test an experimental fuse he had designed, the results of which were sent to Calcutta on 4 October 1786. During the next twelve months the unhealthy climate at Bencoolen claimed his family: his wife died on 28 October 1786, shortly after giving birth to their second daughter, Nancy, who died fifteen days later; their two-year-old elder daughter died on 27 June 1787. Macdonald, however, continued to serve at Bencoolen, and was promoted lieutenant on 16 December 1794 (retaining his honorary rank of captain), and was on the Fort Marlborough establishment during an unsuccessful attack by the French that year. During his final years in Sumatra he produced a *Plan of Fort Marlbro and its Environs*, later published by Alexander Dalrymple (27 August 1797), and wrote a paper, *Natural Productions of Sumatra—Camphor, Coral and Copper*, which was published in Calcutta in 1795.

Macdonald returned to Scotland in 1796 on sick leave. During his voyage home in a small American vessel he remained for several months on St Helena and consolidated his earlier work on variations of the magnetic needle. The results were later published in the *Philosophical Magazine*, submitted to the Royal Society, and earned him election as a fellow of the society in 1800. Many of his maps and charts were later deposited in the British Museum.

Macdonald was promoted captain on 8 January 1798 and, with the East India Company's permission, became a captain in the Royal Edinburgh volunteer artillery, a corps of pikemen formed from gentlemen of Edinburgh. During this service he wrote a treatise on the practice and theory of artillery. On 4 March 1799 he was commissioned as a major into Lord Macdonald's western fencibles, and served until June 1800. He took half pay on 30 July 1800, but was then promoted lieutenant-colonel in the Royal Clan alpine fencible artillery, and served with that unit in Ireland until its disbandment in 1801.

Following the peace of Amiens Macdonald travelled to France; he later published translations of several French military works. On 24 October 1799 he had married Frances Maria Chambers (1774/5–1860), the eldest daughter of Sir Robert *Chambers (1737–1803) and Frances Wilton; they had seven sons and two daughters. Macdonald's last military appointment was in 1804, when Pitt, as lord warden of the Cinque Ports, raised the Cinque Port Volunteers and granted him a commission as major. He held the post until the reduction of the unit in 1806.

Macdonald's family latterly moved to Exeter, where, in addition to his charitable works, he used his military experience to write *A treatise explanatory of a new system of naval, military and political telegraphic communication* (1817), which included his 'military anthropo telegraph for field service'. He died at his home at Summerlands Place, Exeter, on 16 August 1831 and was buried in the south transept of Exeter Cathedral, where his grave is marked with a brass plaque. He was an exemplary military officer and engineer who received little acknowledgement during his lifetime for his years of dedicated service.

ALAN HARFIELD

Sources J. MacInnes, *The brave sons of Skye* (1899) · V. C. P. Hodson, *List of officers of the Bengal army, 1758–1834*, 4 vols. (1927–47) · C. E. Buckland, *Dictionary of Indian biography* (1906) · *Memoir of Lieut.-Col. John Macdonald* (1831) · A. Harfield, *Bencoolen: a history of the Honourable East India Company's garrison on the west coast of Sumatra, 1685–1825* (1995) · *List of officers of the several regiments and corps of fencible cavalry and infantry officers of the militia* (1800) · The Hodson index of officers who served in the East India Company and Indian armies, NAM · K. K. Datta and others, eds., *Fort William–India House correspondence*, 21 (1969) · Sumatra factory records, BL OIOC, MS G/35/150, letters dated 2 Sept 1782, 24 Feb 1783, 19 June 1783; minute dated 22 July 1783 · Sumatra factory records, BL OIOC, MS G/35/156, letter dated 19 Oct 1785; report, fols. 67, 89–117A · *GM*, 1st ser., 102/2 (1832), 85–7 · *DNB*
Archives BL, maps and plans of the west coast of Sumatra · Devon RO, letter-book relating to Sumatra, London and Exeter · NL Scot., practical tracts of artillery | BL, letters to earl of Liverpool, Add. MSS 38249–38295, 38410, 38574 *passim*
Likenesses portrait (after miniature), repro. in MacInnes, *Brave sons of Skye*

Macdonald, John (1779–1849), Free Church of Scotland minister, was born at Reay, Caithness, on 12 November 1779, second son of James Macdonald or MacAdie (1735–1830) and his second wife, a daughter of John Mackay. His father, originally a weaver, was the local catechist. John was educated at the parish school and soon showed remarkable mathematical ability, being employed by the local farmers to help with their accounts. He went on to King's College, Aberdeen, graduating MA in 1801. He was licensed by the presbytery of Caithness in July 1805. In September, and at the request of Sir John Sinclair, he went on an expedition to research Ossianic traditions in the north-west highlands. He returned to serve as missionary at Achreny and Halladale for six months. In September 1806 he was ordained missionary minister at Berriedale. It was in that year that he married Georgina Ross of Gledfield, with whom he had three children before her death in August 1814.

In January 1807 Macdonald became minister of the Gaelic chapel, Edinburgh, which was supported by the Society in Scotland for the Propagation of Christian Knowledge (SSPCK), and it was here that he established his reputation as a preacher. In September 1813 he was presented to the parish of Urquhart, Ross and Cromarty, by Duncan George Forbes of Culloden, in succession to Charles Calder. Using this as a base, he conducted an itinerant ministry in Caithness and Ross which, because of its implied criticism of them, was greatly resented by neighbouring ministers. This practice was condemned by the general assembly of 1818. It was on 11 May of this year that he married again, his second wife being Janet, eldest daughter of Kenneth Mackenzie of Millbank, with whom he had a further seven children, including Duncan George Forbes *Macdonald.

Macdonald's missionary impulses, which earned him the sobriquet 'Apostle of the North', were channelled to less controversial effect when he took an interest in the spiritual welfare of the remote island community of St Kilda. At the request of the SSPCK he visited the islands between 1822 and 1824, eventually raising sufficient money to keep a minister there, whom he introduced to the islanders in 1830. He also visited London in 1823, at the request of the London Missionary Society, where he met Samuel Wilberforce. In 1827 he was invited to visit Ireland by Robert Daly, rector of Powerscourt and later bishop of Cashel. He was able to adapt his Gaelic sufficiently for an Irish audience. In 1842 he was honoured with the degree of DD from the University of New York.

Macdonald's influence and position were confirmed at the Disruption of 1843, where he was credited with much of the Free Church's success in the highlands. In David Octavius Hill's representational painting of that event he is a central figure, shown standing behind Patrick Macfarlan, waiting to sign the deed of demission. In 1845 he acted as Gaelic moderator when the Free Church general assembly met for a second time that year in Inverness. His publications included the diary of his visits to St Kilda (1830), sermons, and Gaelic verses (1848). He died at Urquhart on 16 April 1849 and was buried there beside his revered predecessor, Charles Calder, on 24 April.

W. A. J. ARCHBOLD, *rev.* LIONEL ALEXANDER RITCHIE

Sources *Fasti Scot.* · W. Ewing, ed., *Annals of the Free Church of Scotland, 1843–1900*, 1 (1914), 222 · J. Kennedy, *The apostle of the north* (1866) · R. Macgregor, *Life of John Macdonald, DD* (1881) · J. A. Wylie, *Disruption worthies: a memorial of 1843*, ed. J. B. Gillies, new edn (1881) · *DSCHT* · *Free Church Magazine* (1849), 142–5 · D. Becton, *Some noted ministers of the northern highlands* (1929), 157–70
Archives NA Scot., journals of visits to St Kilda · U. Edin., New Coll. L., sermon notes
Likenesses J. Kay, etching, 1813, NPG · J. Sinclair, mezzotint, pubd 1850, NPG · W. T. Fry, stipple, BM; repro. in *Evangelical magazine* (1823) · D. O. Hill, oils, Free Church College, Edinburgh · lithograph, repro. in Wylie, *Disruption worthies*, facing p. 357

Macdonald, Sir John (d. 1850), army officer, was distantly connected with Flora Macdonald, the Jacobite heroine. His military service began as an ensign in the 89th foot (15 April 1795), advancing in that regiment to lieutenant (2 February 1796) and captain (22 October 1802). He served with the 89th in Ireland during the 1798 rising, taking part in several encounters, including those at Ross and Vinegar Hill. After brief periods in garrison on Minorca and at Messina, the regiment took part in the siege of Valletta and capture of Malta (1799–1800). Macdonald also fought with it in Egypt in 1801, during the opposed landing on the 8th, skirmish on the 13th, and battle of Alexandria on 21 March, after which he received the military general service medal with campaign bar. On 28 February 1805 he became a half-pay major and shortly afterwards served as brigade major to Lieutenant-General Lord Cathcart in England before securing a majority in the 43rd foot (20 February 1806). He accompanied Cathcart as his military secretary when he commanded the King's German Legion in Swedish Pomerania during 1806–7, earning Cathcart's special praise. Macdonald acted in the same capacity with

Cathcart during the expedition to Denmark and bombardment of Copenhagen in 1807. He became a half-pay lieutenant-colonel in the 1st garrison battalion on 17 March 1808, and the following year acted as deputy adjutant-general for Lieutenant-General the Hon. Sir John Hope's reserve, tasked to clear the enemy from south Beveland during the disastrous Walcheren expedition. On 24 February 1810 Macdonald was appointed deputy adjutant-general under Lieutenant-General Thomas Graham in southern Spain, first at Cadiz and then during the battle of Barossa (5 March 1811), where his 'unwearied exertions' were mentioned in dispatches (Forbes, 277). Towards the close of the action, Macdonald decisively ordered the 67th foot to clear enemy artillery from a prominent ridge dominating the British position.

In March 1812 Macdonald became military secretary to Hope, commander-in-chief in Ireland, and from 25 September 1813 acted as his assistant adjutant-general in the Peninsula, taking part in the battle of the Nive (10 November 1813) and blockade of Bayonne early in 1814. When Hope was wounded and taken prisoner during an enemy sortie on 14 April 1814, Macdonald obtained permission to enter the French city to look after him. For his services in the Peninsula, Macdonald received a gold medal with one clasp for Barossa and the Nive.

Macdonald became a brevet colonel and CB (4 June 1814), and from 14 August 1818 served for almost twelve years as assistant adjutant-general at the Horse Guards in London under three successive commanders-in-chief of the army, the dukes of York and Wellington and Lord Hill. Hill remained in office until 1842, when Wellington returned as commander-in-chief. Meanwhile, Macdonald had been promoted to adjutant-general (27 July 1830), and would retain that post until his death, representing continuous service at the Horse Guards of over thirty-one years, advancing to major-general (27 May 1835) and lieutenant-general (28 June 1838). He was appointed KCB (13 September 1831) and GCB (24 September 1847). As adjutant-general, Macdonald was directly responsible to the commander-in-chief for military discipline in the cavalry and infantry (the ordnance forces then being a separate command under the master-general of the ordnance), and, after consulting the judge-advocate-general, advised him on courts martial. The adjutant-general arranged the passage of troops going overseas, dealt with problems of inter-regimental transfers, and supervised the establishment of regimental schools. He exercised responsibility for army clothing, taking note of the recommendations of the board of general officers appointed to oversee it, and ensured the supply of small arms to all regiments. His responsibilities in these matters extended to reserve forces (militia, yeomanry, and enrolled pensioners), and all military commanders in the United Kingdom and abroad (whether in garrison or on campaign) submitted regular reports to him. Scotland had a deputy adjutant-general in Edinburgh; Ireland, foreign stations, and overseas expeditions had their own adjutant-general. However, all these officers were answerable to the Horse Guards, as were assistant adjutants-general in military districts at home,

who were appointed on the adjutant-general's recommendation. Questioned by Lord Ebrington's select committee on army and navy appointments in 1833, Macdonald explained that such a vast amount of work had been acquired since expansion of colonial possessions post-1815, that 'the great variety of details' prevented him from giving a comprehensive summary of departmental responsibilities (Sweetman, 81). By 1836 the establishment at the Horse Guards comprised four officers with subordinate military and civilian staff; ten years later its cost amounted to almost £13,000 per year. One enduring legacy of Macdonald's time as adjutant-general was outlined by the commander-in-chief's general order of 1 January 1836: 'An account of the services of every regiment in the British army shall be published under the superintendence of the adjutant-general' (Cannon, preface).

Macdonald proved an able and effective adjutant-general: 'His official demeanour was courteous and kind, and his sincerity and candour were seldom found to border on abruptness or roughness, and never on rudeness or insult' (Naval and Military Gazette, 30 March 1850). Macdonald was also a clear writer of minutes and orders. He had been appointed colonel of the 67th foot (25 August 1828), then of the 42nd foot (15 March 1844). He died at his residence in Bruton Street, London, on 28 March 1850, and was buried in Kensal Green cemetery.

JOHN SWEETMAN

Sources Army List · R. G. A. Levinge, *Historical records of the forty-third regiment, Monmouthshire light infantry* (1868) · R. Brinckman, *Historical record of the 89th Princess Victoria's regiment* (1888) · M. Cunliffe, *The royal Irish fusiliers, 1793–1950* (1952) · A. Forbes, *The black watch: the record of an historic regiment* (1896) · C. T. Atkinson, *Regimental history: the royal Hampshire regiment, 1: To 1914* (1950) · S. G. P. Ward, *Wellington's headquarters: a study of the administrative problems in the Peninsula, 1809–14* (1957) · Fortescue, *Brit. army*, vol. 7 · J. Sweetman, *War and administration* (1984) · J. L. R. Samson, ed., *Officers of the black watch, 1725 to 1986* (1987) · R. Cannon, ed., *Historical record of the first, or king's regiment of dragoon guards* (1837) · *Naval and Military Gazette* (30 March 1850)

Archives priv. coll. | BL, corresp. with Lord Holland, Add. MSS 51542 · BL, letters to second Earl Spencer · Bodl. Oxf., letters to Sir William Napier · NL Scot., corresp. with Sir George Brown · NL Scot., letters to Lord Lynedoch · NRA, priv. coll., corresp. as aide-de–camp to Lord Cathcart · NRA, priv. coll., letters to Sir John Hope · priv. coll., Cathcart MSS · U. Southampton L., letters to first duke of Wellington · W. Sussex RO, letters to duke of Richmond · Woburn Abbey, Bedfordshire, letters to Lord George William Russell

Likenesses portrait, c.1893, repro. in Samson, ed., *Officers of the black watch* · portrait, repro. in E. Linklater and A. Linklater, *The black watch: the history of the Royal Highland Regiment* (1977), 92 · stipple, NPG

MacDonald, John (1818–1889), Roman Catholic bishop of Aberdeen, was born in Ballicladich, Strath Glass, Inverness-shire, on 2 July 1818, the son of William MacDonald and his wife, Hannah Fraser, both Catholics. He was educated locally, and later by the Benedictines at the Scottish seminary, St James's, Regensburg, in Bavaria (1830–37). He entered the Scots College, Rome, in June 1837. In ill health and accompanied by Bishop James Kyle, vicar apostolic of the northern district, he returned to Scotland as subdeacon in June 1840. In the following year, after attending Blairs College, he was ordained at Preshome by Bishop Kyle. He then served in the following missions: as assistant at Tombae, Banffshire (December 1841 – February 1842); alone at Glenmoriston, Inverness-shire, with Dornie Kintail, Ross-shire, as well for about a year (February 1842 – May 1844); Braemar, Aberdeenshire (May 1844–May 1845); as assistant at Inverness (May 1845 – May 1846) and later as sole priest (1846–8); Fassnakyle, Upper Strathglass, (1848–56); and Eskadale, Lower Strathglass (1856–68). At Eskadale he was chaplain to Simon Fraser, thirteenth Lord Lovat.

MacDonald was chosen as coadjutor by Kyle, and accepted in Rome, with the title of bishop of Nicopolis, on 11 December 1868. The appointment of a Scot, amid the bitter Irish-Scottish Catholic internecine feuding, was a relief to Kyle and the other Scottish bishops. Unfortunately Kyle died the previous day and so MacDonald immediately became vicar apostolic. As he was only the second bishop consecrated in Aberdeen since the Reformation, his installation aroused considerable public interest: the ceremony took place at St Mary's Aberdeen, and the Irish-born bishop John Lynch of the western district was not invited.

In 1869–70 MacDonald attended the First Vatican Council in Rome. On the restoration of the Scottish hierarchy in 1878 he was translated to the diocese of Aberdeen. During his episcopacy, Rome restored Wick and Caithness as well as Orkney and Shetland, some 262 miles distant, to his diocese (in 1860 they had been taken from Scottish episcopal jurisdiction and placed under the Arctic mission). Kincardine and part of Inverness-shire were also added to the former north district vicariate territory to make his new diocese. After an initial residence in Eskadale, he settled in Aberdeen in February 1869, making St Mary's Aberdeen his cathedral from 1886.

Reputedly the tallest man at the Vatican Council, MacDonald was a handsome and imposing figure, but possessed a shy, retiring, and diffident character. He was very conscientious in his religious duties but played very little part in public affairs. In 1868 his appointment represented a return to quiet competence; less assertive than Kyle, he was also unlike the enthusiastic and zealous Archbishop Gillis of Edinburgh or the tempestuous Bishop Lynch of Glasgow.

MacDonald presided over a vast area, with only about 11,000 faithful, the vast majority of them poor, with hardly half a dozen considerable families of substance. During his episcopate, however, solid progress was made: the number of churches, chapels, and stations more than doubled to 88; the number of clergy grew from 35 to 53 priests; religious orders of women in the diocese increased more than threefold; and the number of convents more than quadrupled. He also encouraged Lord Lovat's foundation of the Benedictine abbey at Fort Augustus, and orphanages, homes for the elderly, and education received his attention. All this was accomplished without debts, or political or sectarian disturbance: his was a safe pair of hands. From 1875 MacDonald suffered increasingly

from ill health; he deteriorated rapidly in late 1888 and died on 4 February 1889 at 20 Queen's Road, Aberdeen. He was buried in St Mary's Cathedral, Aberdeen.

BERNARD ASPINWALL

Sources Scottish Catholic archives, Drummond Place, Edinburgh · Scots College archives, Rome · archives of Propaganda Fide, Rome · *Catholic Directory for Scotland* (1890), 190–94; (1892), 62 [also issues 1870–89] · W. M. Brady, *Annals of the Catholic hierarchy in England and Scotland* (1877) · J. Darragh, *The Catholic hierarchy of Scotland: a biographical list, 1653–1985* (1986) · *The Tablet* (9 Feb 1889), 221 · *The Tablet* (16 Feb 1889), 262 · C. Johnson, *Scottish secular clergy, 1879–1989* (1991) · C. Johnson, 'Scottish secular clergy: the northern and eastern districts', *Innes Review*, 40 (1989), 24–68 · *DNB* · d. cert.
Archives Archivio Vaticano, Vatican City, archives of Propaganda Fide · Scots College, Rome, archives · Scottish Catholic Archives, Edinburgh
Likenesses black and white silhouette, Blairs College, Aberdeen · portrait, bishop's house, Aberdeen
Wealth at death £6626 18s. 5d.: confirmation, 31 July 1889, CCI

MacDonald, John (1865–1953), player and teacher of the highland bagpipe, was born on 26 July 1865 in Glentruim, in the parish of Laggan, Inverness-shire, the oldest son of the three sons and three daughters of Alexander MacDonald (1834/5–1883), piper, and his wife, Jane Lamont (1840/41–1931). He attended the local parish school of Insh and made his early living as a gamekeeper and piper before becoming a commercial traveller. He was pipe major of the 1st volunteer battalion of the Queen's Own Cameron Highlanders (which became the 4th Camerons) from 1890 to 1914. He was twice married, first to Christina Todd (d. 1925) and second to Helen Gibb (1875/6–1932), and twice widowed.

MacDonald received his first instruction in piping from his father, who had been a pupil of Donald Cameron, but his most important teacher was Malcolm MacPherson, the celebrated Calum Pìobaire (1833–1898), of Catlodge, Badenoch, who 'would … take away all books and pipe music, then sing in his own canntaireachd the ground and different variations of the particular piobaireachd he wished me to learn' (MacDonald, 5). Later he studied with Colin and Sandy Cameron, and Angus MacDonald of Morar. His traditional teaching in piobaireachd was thus linked, through the MacPhersons and Camerons, with the MacKays of Raasay, the Bruces of Glenelg and the later MacCrimmons, a glittering pedigree which he summed up wryly as 'the Apostolic Succession'.

MacDonald's first major prize was the gold medal for piobaireachd at Inverness in 1890, followed by the clasp for former gold medallists—the highest award in competitive piping—in 1903. He was also a formidable competitor in light music, and quickly became a much sought-after teacher. His classes in Inverness and South Uist were supported by the Piobaireachd Society, formed by a group of gentlemen enthusiasts in 1903, under whose auspices he established the first army course for pipers in October 1910 at Inverness. He was about to move to Edinburgh as first instructor of what eventually became the Army School of Bagpipe Music when the First World War broke out. Invalided out of the 4th Camerons, he returned to commercial travelling as the representative in the north and west highlands for Youngers, the drinks firm, declining the post of instructor to the army class in 1919. He remained highly active in piping as a teacher and competitor, being given annual leave by Youngers to pursue these activities, and stayed with the firm until his retirement.

John MacDonald's superb expressive gift and brilliant execution made him a legend in his own lifetime and, although he placed little value on competition as an end in itself, he remained at the top for almost fifty years, winning eight clasps, five of them after the age of sixty, the last in 1934 at his final public appearance. He made the first commercial recordings of piobaireachd with Columbia in 1927, playing the grounds and opening variations of 'Lament for the Children', 'MacCrimmon's Sweetheart', 'The Little Spree', and 'Lament for Patrick Og'. Efforts by two of his most prominent amateur pupils, John Peter Grant of Rothiemurchus and General Frank Richardson, to have further recordings made failed to secure funding.

Short and latterly stout, John MacDonald was a private man, quiet and unassuming, noted for his general kindliness and charm, and for the uncompromising ferocity of his teaching. He taught, as he had been taught, by canntaireachd, and his leading professional pupils, Robert Urquhart Brown and Robert Bell Nicol, devoted themselves to passing on his instruction until the latter's death in 1978. MacDonald was honorary piper to the Gaelic Society of Inverness, was appointed MBE for services to piping in 1935, and became honorary piper to George V.

After a slight stroke in 1935 ended his competitive career, MacDonald remained in high demand as a teacher. As the Piobaireachd Society's paid instructor, he had been expected to teach, and lend his authority to, the published texts it issued as a fixed standard for use in competition. While he offered little public criticism of the society's publications, his judgement that their printed texts misrepresented piobaireachd was well remembered by his pupils. His disappointment that in his long-standing role as private adviser to the society he had been unable to prevent this is reflected in his rejection of *The Kilberry Book of Ceol Mor*, brought out in 1948 by the society's editor, Archibald Campbell, as 'the beginning of the end of our traditional piobaireachd playing' (Eagle, 229). MacDonald's career and subsequent reputation is central to the debate about the interpretation and transmission of piobaireachd which continued throughout the twentieth century.

John MacDonald died of heart disease at the age of eighty-seven at his home, 3 Perceval Road, Inverness, on 6 June 1953, and was buried on 8 June at Cluny Hill cemetery, Forres.   WILLIAM DONALDSON

Sources J. MacDonald, 'The piping reminiscences of John MacDonald M.B.E.', *Oban Times* (4 April 1942) • W. Donaldson, *The highland pipe and Scottish society, 1750–1950* (2000) • *Oban Times* (1902–53) • NL Scot., Piobaireachd Society MS Acc. 9103 • F. Richardson, 'Interpretation', *Piobaireachd and its interpretation*, ed. S. MacNeill and F. Richardson (1987), 64–122 • D. MacLeod, 'Some memories of John MacDonald', *Piping Times*, 14/6 (1961–2), 6–7; 14/8 (1961–2), 14–15 • A. Macpherson, *A highlander looks back* (1970) • B. Mackenzie, *Piping traditions of the north of Scotland* (1998) • G. Moss, 'Ceol Mor playing: old and new styles', *Piping Times*, 8/11 (1955–6), 18–19 • G. Moss, 'Piobaireachd playing', *Piping Times*, 9/8 (1956–7), 6–7 • D. J. S. Murray, 'The maverick: George Moss, 1903–1990', *The Voice* (spring 1997), 31–5 • D. J. S. Murray, 'More on "The way it was"', *The Voice* (spring 1998), 35–8 • R. Eagle, *Seton Gordon: the life and times of a highland gentleman* (1991) • W. Stewart, J. P. Grant, and A. Campbell, *Piobaireachd Society Collection* [title varies], 1st ser., 1–5; 2nd ser., 1–10 (1905–63) • b. cert. • d. cert. • d. cert. [Helen Macdonald] • CCI (1953)

Archives NL Scot., Piobaireachd Society MSS, corresp. and photographs, Acc. 9103

Likenesses photograph, *c*.1928, repro. in *The Voice* [Newark, Delaware] (summer 1996), p. 21 • photographs, repro. in Mackenzie, *Piping traditions of the north of Scotland*, 7, 9, 10, 40 • photographs, NL Scot., Piobaireachd Society papers

Wealth at death £1964 13s. 6d.: confirmation, 27 July 1953, CCI

Macdonald, Sir John Alexander (1815–1891), prime minister of Canada, was born in Glasgow on 11 January 1815, one of the five children (and the only male to reach adulthood) of Hugh Macdonald (*d*. 1841), a merchant, and his wife, Helen Shaw.

Childhood and family life Although the origins of both his parents were in the Scottish highlands and Macdonald always spoke with a slight Scottish accent, he spent little of his youth in his native land. When he was five his parents emigrated to Kingston, near the eastern edge of Upper Canada. His father, who had left Scotland because his business ventures had failed, eventually acquired a small milling business in Prince Edward county, but never achieved much financial success and for a few years before his death in 1841 was employed as a bank clerk. Macdonald attended local grammar schools, where he acquired the habit of reading widely, particularly British fiction and constitutional history, but his formal education came to an end when at the age of fifteen he was articled to George Mackenzie, a Kingston lawyer. Macdonald had a quick mind and a natural aptitude for the law, and when he was only seventeen he was placed in charge of a branch office in the nearby town of Napanee. In August 1835 he opened his own office in Kingston and on 6 February 1836 was called to the bar.

Macdonald came of age in exciting times. In December 1837 he served in the militia during the Upper Canadian uprising and took part in the attack on the rebels' headquarters in Montgomery's Tavern in York (later Toronto). Yet in 1838, when Upper Canada was threatened by raids from across the American border, he courageously, though unsuccessfully, acted as the defence counsel for the rebels involved in one of the raids.

During the 1840s Macdonald concentrated on building up his Kingston law firm, became a specialist in commercial law, and purchased real estate and mortgages in many parts of the province, sometimes acting as the agent for British speculators. He invested in banks and road and shipping companies, acquired directorships in a number of Canadian and at least two British companies, and in 1864 became president of the British-backed St Lawrence Warehouse, Dock, and Wharfage Company in Quebec. None the less, money—or rather the lack of it—was a recurring problem for the young Macdonald. He lived well, but he had no inherited wealth and his income was

Sir John Alexander Macdonald (1815–1891), by unknown photographer

unstable. In 1842, apparently using substantial winnings from gambling, he went on a six months' holiday to Britain, during which he had a whirlwind courtship with a Scottish cousin, Isabella, the daughter of Alexander Clark of Dalnavert, Inverness-shire. They were married on 1 September 1843 and were a happy couple, but after 1845 Isabella became an invalid. Despite her illness she gave birth in August 1847, but John Alexander jun. died after thirteen months. In March 1850 Isabella gave birth to a second son. Hugh John survived, but Isabella was racked with pain, mitigated only by massive doses of opium, until her death in 1857. Hugh followed his father into law, becoming his partner, and into politics, serving as member of the Canadian House of Commons for Winnipeg in 1891, briefly as minister of the interior in 1896, and as premier of Manitoba for a year in 1900, but Macdonald spent little time with his son and their later relationship was frequently troubled. During the late 1850s, as Macdonald focused on his political career, he resided in the capital of the united province of Canada, which alternated between Toronto and Quebec City until permanently transferred in 1865 to Ottawa. Like many of his contemporaries, Macdonald was a heavy drinker. His wife's prolonged illness added to his financial difficulties and he seems frequently to have sought solace in the bottle. After her death his social life revolved increasingly around drinking bouts with his political cronies.

Politics in the united province Macdonald's first political office was as secretary of a district school board in 1834. He was active in a host of religious and ethnic organizations in Kingston, including the Orange lodge, the masons and the Celtic and St Andrew's societies, and he served as an alderman from 1843 to 1846. In 1841 Upper and Lower Canada were amalgamated into the united province of Canada and in October 1844 Macdonald was elected to the assembly from Kingston, which would return him to parliament in ten elections between 1844 and 1874. In 1844 he campaigned as a Conservative and a supporter of

Governor-General Sir Charles Metcalfe, and in the legislature he opposed the introduction of responsible government, the abolition of primogeniture, and an extended franchise, and he defended state support for the established church and for denominational schools. But he also showed a willingness to compromise, and he gravitated into the camp of the moderate Conservatives, led by William Henry Draper. In 1846 he was made a queen's counsel and in May 1847 Draper brought him into the cabinet as receiver-general. Macdonald held the post for seven months and then served for three months as commissioner of crown lands until the Reformers came to power in March 1848.

The most controversial measure introduced by the Reform administration was the Rebellion Losses Bill, which became a test of responsible government. When Governor-General Lord Elgin signed the bill, his carriage was stoned and the parliament buildings in Montreal were burnt by Conservatives disgruntled by the bill and by the imperial parliament's decision to abolish the preferential tariff on Canadian timber and wheat. A number of Conservatives even signed a manifesto advocating annexation to the United States. Macdonald dissociated himself from the extremists by participating in the British North America League, which was committed to the imperial connection. Macdonald also sought to persuade the Conservatives to abandon some of their more unpopular policies, including their opposition to responsible government, and he applauded the decision of the Conservative leader, Sir Allan Napier MacNab, to enter into a new political alliance in 1854 with the French-Canadian Reformers, who formed the largest single bloc in the assembly. The English-Canadian Reformers saw responsible government not as an end in itself but as a step towards creating a more liberal society, a goal not shared by the increasingly conservative French-Canadian leadership. The new coalition, out of which emerged the Liberal Conservative Party, had a clear majority in the assembly, and in September 1854 Macdonald took office as attorney-general for Upper Canada, a position he held until 1862 and again from 1864 to 1867. In 1861–2 and 1865–7 he also served as minister of militia affairs.

As attorney-general Macdonald was responsible for steering through the legislature much of the government's contentious legislation, such as the bill abolishing the clergy reserves and the 1855 act which entrenched Catholic separate schools in Upper Canada. He also presided over the expansion of the provincial penitentiary system and was largely responsible for the creation of separate provincial institutions for juvenile offenders and the criminally insane. Macdonald's influence was not entirely positive, since he believed that prisons should be more concerned with punishment than rehabilitation. In fact, he was a competent but hardly an innovative or outstanding administrator. His real forte was in the nitty-gritty of politics. He was a master in the art of distributing patronage, a formidable public speaker both in the assembly and on the hustings, and a likeable and popular politician.

Although the united province had been created as a legislative union, Upper Canada and Lower Canada retained
their separate identities, and cabinets were effectively
headed by two premiers, one drawn from each section. In
1856 Macdonald helped to push MacNab into retirement
and assumed the leadership of the Conservatives in Upper
Canada. He became joint premier of the united province
of Canada with Étienne-Paschal Taché, who was himself
replaced in 1857 by George-Étienne Cartier. From 1857
until 1862, except for two days in 1858, Macdonald and
Cartier remained joint premiers of the united province,
and Macdonald again served as joint premier with Taché
briefly in 1864. Even the temporary loss of power in 1858
was an accident. Because the politicians were unable to
agree on where to locate the capital, Cartier and Macdonald decided to refer the question to Queen Victoria, who
chose Ottawa. When the decision was announced the government was forced to resign. Two days later Macdonald
and Cartier were back in power when the Reformers
proved unable to sustain the support of a majority in the
assembly.

By the late 1850s the united province was increasingly
divided along sectional and sectarian lines. The predominantly protestant and British Upper Canada was growing
faster than the predominantly Catholic and French-
Canadian Lower Canada. The Liberal–Conservative alliance was based on an acceptance of equal representation
of both Canadas within the united province and a protection of minority protestant rights in Lower Canada and
minority Catholic rights in Upper Canada. But the evangelical protestants of Upper Canada, led by George Brown,
were angry that they were prevented from abolishing
state-supported Catholic separate schools by the votes of
French-Canadian Catholics in Lower Canada. To end the
supposed domination of the union by the French-
Canadian minority, the Reformers of Upper Canada
demanded that the principle of equal representation be
replaced by representation on the basis of population.
Partly to head off this threat, the Liberal–Conservatives
proposed the creation of a federal union of British North
America when they came back into power in 1858, but neither the Colonial Office nor the maritime colonies showed
any great enthusiasm for the measure. Nor did Macdonald. The Conservatives were the minority party in Upper
Canada, and federation—particularly a decentralized federation—might permanently deprive them of power.
Macdonald preferred the existing legislative union of the
Canadas and opposed the introduction of representation
by population.

Confederation Only when the demand for constitutional
reform had become irresistible did Macdonald throw his
weight behind confederation. His conversion was motivated by a careful evaluation of political realities, but he
was also influenced by the American Civil War. As Anglo-
American relations deteriorated, in May 1862 as minister
of militia Macdonald introduced a bill increasing the size
and costs of the militia. The bill was defeated and the Conservatives resigned, but the new government headed by
John Sandfield Macdonald held power only precariously

after the election of 1863. On 30 March 1864 the Conservatives returned to power, but on 14 June they too were
defeated. A way out of this political crisis was suggested by
a parliamentary committee chaired by George Brown,
which recommended that the united province be
replaced by a federal union, either of British North America or, if that proved impossible, of the two Canadas. Macdonald, a member of the committee, refused to sign the
report, but on 30 June 1864 he reluctantly agreed to join in
a coalition with Cartier and Brown. As Macdonald made
clear to his Conservative followers, he joined the coalition
not out of enthusiasm for constitutional change, but
because he believed that he had no choice. Macdonald still
preferred the status quo, but if change was inevitable he
preferred confederation to the other options available.
Like his contemporaries he was also frightened by the
implications of the victory of the North in the American
Civil War. As attorney-general in the coalition he established a small secret-service unit to gather information in
the United States, and after August 1865, as minister of
militia, he was responsible for making preparations to
defend Canada against the Fenian raids in 1866.

Partly because of his political skill and partly because of
his superior legal knowledge, Macdonald played a central
role in the constitutional negotiations at the Charlottetown and Quebec conferences in 1864, and he chaired the
meetings at the London conference in 1866–7. Thomas
D'Arcy McGee claimed that Macdonald was the author of
fifty of the seventy-two Quebec Resolutions which formed
the basis of the British North America Act of 1867 which
created the dominion of Canada. This undoubtedly exag-
gerates Macdonald's personal influence, for he could
impose his will upon neither his colleagues in the coalition nor the maritime delegates, and the British North
America Act did not entirely embody his ideals. Macdonald would have preferred a legislative union similar to the
union of England and Scotland, but he recognized that
legislative union was unacceptable to the French Canadians and to many Canadians of British origin. He therefore sought to create a highly centralized federal union in
which the provinces would be little more than municipal
bodies. The division of powers between the federal government and the provinces reflected these intentions, as
did the authority given to the federal government to
appoint provincial lieutenant-governors and to disallow
provincial legislation.

Whether these were desirable achievements is controversial. Macdonald was not trying to create a highly centralized modern state which could manage the economy
and provide a wide variety of social services; he was a
nineteenth-century Conservative, who believed in a very
limited role for government. His commitment to central-
ism was derived from his intense Conservatism. Macdonald feared the movement towards democracy, and sought
to contain it by creating large electoral units and a second
chamber composed of members appointed by the federal
government for life. Intensely anti-American, he was convinced that the American Civil War was a product of weaknesses in the American constitution which gave too much

authority to the states and to the people, and he believed British parliamentary institutions were superior because they included barriers against uncontrolled democracy. Ironically the constitution which Macdonald played such a major part in designing never functioned as it was supposed to. As minister of justice from 1867 until 1873, Macdonald sought to impose his will on the provinces, frequently resorting to the use of the power of disallowance. He was minister of the interior (1878–83), superintendent of Indian affairs (1878–87), and minister of railways and canals (1889–91), but he still kept a watchful eye on the provinces. His *bête noir* was Oliver Mowat, the premier of Ontario and his own former law student. Mowat challenged and eventually constrained Macdonald's partisan use of the power of disallowance, effectively turning it into a rarely used emergency power. Mowat also persuaded the judicial committee of the privy council to hand down a series of important decisions favouring provincial rights. Contrary to Macdonald's fears, decentralization did not lead to the collapse of the federal union.

First dominion prime minister, 1867–1874 Macdonald was more clearly successful in his political ambitions. He quickly established himself as the dominant partner in the 'Great Coalition', particularly after the resignation of George Brown in 1865, and he impressed the imperial authorities by his loyalty and constitutional knowledge. In 1865 he was awarded an honorary DCL by the University of Oxford, and on 1 July 1867 was appointed the first prime minister of Canada. He was created KCB, to the chagrin of colleagues given lesser honours. Macdonald was responsible for constructing the first federal cabinet and for turning the Liberal Conservative Party into the first national party and leading it to success in the first federal election in 1867.

In 1867 Macdonald's party swept to victory in the newly created provinces of Ontario and Quebec, but did less well in New Brunswick, and disastrously in Nova Scotia, where seventeen of the eighteen members elected were committed to repeal of the union. Macdonald sought to appease the leaders of the repeal movement, especially Joseph Howe, by offering better terms, and in 1869 Howe, having been rebuffed in London, agreed to the terms, and entered the cabinet. In 1869 the Macdonald government also made one of the largest land purchases in history when it bought out the Hudson's Bay Company's vast territorial claims in western Canada. The negotiations in London proceeded smoothly, but the government did little to prepare those already living in the west for the transition to Canadian rule. In particular the government ignored the existence of a substantial community of métis, the offspring of marriages between European fur traders and native women, settled along the Red River. The métis reacted by establishing a provisional government headed by Louis Riel, turned back the Canadian-appointed lieutenant-governor, took control of the Hudson's Bay Company fort, and arrested all those who supported the Canadian take-over, including a number of surveyors sent out by Ottawa. They even executed one of the surveyors, an Ontario Orangeman named Thomas Scott, for refusing

to accept the authority of the provisional government. The métis wanted their land titles confirmed, and demanded that Manitoba should be given immediate provincial status with guarantees for the equality of the French and English languages and for Catholic separate schools. Although Macdonald felt the grant of provincial status was premature, he agreed to the métis' demands, which were embodied in the Manitoba Act of 1870. At the same time, faced with an angry outcry from Ontario against the execution of Scott, Macdonald dispatched a military force to Manitoba and refused to extend a full pardon to Louis Riel, who was forced into exile. The integration of the west into Canada enabled the federal government to open negotiations with British Columbia, which became Canada's sixth province in 1871, in return for the promise of a railway to the rest of Canada within a decade. In 1873 Macdonald also completed negotiations which culminated in Prince Edward Island's entry into Canada. Only Newfoundland proved unresponsive to Canada's siren call.

In 1871 Macdonald served as one of the five British commissioners sent to Washington to settle various Anglo-American disputes which had arisen out of the American Civil War. Eventually the negotiations resulted in the treaty of Washington, a treaty Macdonald signed with great reluctance, since it gave the Americans access to Canada's Atlantic fisheries and to the St Lawrence River. Macdonald had opposed these concessions unless Canada received adequate compensation, preferably in the form of a renewal of the reciprocity treaty which the Americans had abrogated in 1866, but he could not prevail, and in the end was forced to accept the treaty in the interests of Anglo-American harmony. This decision proved a considerable handicap in the election of 1872, when he was accused of betraying Canada's national interests. Although the Conservatives did win a majority, it began to disappear following the election, when it was revealed that Macdonald and several of his colleagues had accepted enormous campaign contributions from Sir Hugh Allan, the head of the syndicate to be given the contract for building the Canadian Pacific Railway to British Columbia. Although Macdonald denied that he had benefited personally from the contributions and that the railway contract had been awarded to Allan for his generosity, he could not convince his own followers, and he was forced to resign on 5 November 1873 because of defections. In the election of 1874 his party suffered a disastrous defeat because of the Canadian Pacific Railway scandal.

The opposition years Macdonald was partly the author of his own misfortune. In 1864 his legal partner had died and he had found himself deeply in debt. Overworked and worried, he had begun to drink even more heavily. In 1866 the Canadian delegates were forced to delay their departure to London until Macdonald recovered from a binge, and in London he was almost killed when (presumably drunk) he fell asleep in his hotel room with the candle burning. The trip was not entirely a personal disaster. While walking in Bond Street he ran into Susan Agnes Bernard (*d.* 1920), the sister of his private secretary. Born in

Jamaica, the daughter of T. A. Bernard, an official in Jamaica, but brought up in Upper Canada, Agnes had moved to England in 1865. The two were married in Hanover Square on 16 February 1867. Two years later they had their only child, Margaret Mary Theodora. Mary was an invalid throughout her life and Macdonald was deeply attached to her. Agnes provided her husband with a secure and supportive home. Under her influence Macdonald, who was never a very devout Christian, abandoned the Presbyterian church and became a member of the Church of England.

In 1870 Macdonald fell seriously ill when passing a gallstone and almost died. During his illness it became apparent that he was virtually bankrupt, and his friends raised a fund, which eased his financial problems by providing him with $4000 per annum. None the less, he again began to drink heavily, so heavily that he had only a hazy memory of what he had really promised the railway contractor Allan. After his defeat in 1874 he went into an intense depression. He was forced to return to the practice of law. He had moved his legal firm to Toronto in 1871 and he moved his residence there in 1874. Increasingly he left the management of party affairs in the hands of Charles Tupper, who had not been tainted by the Pacific scandal. It was widely rumoured that Macdonald's retirement was imminent, but the rumours were premature. Macdonald's defeat coincided with hard times and, as the popularity of the Liberals waned, he gradually regained his confidence, brought his drinking under control, and re-established his authority as leader.

In 1876 Macdonald committed the Conservatives to a policy of raising tariffs to protect Canadian industries, mainly from competition from the United States, which had consistently declined all offers to renegotiate reciprocity. In 1878 the Conservatives swept back into power, promising a 'national policy' of tariff protection. Ironically Macdonald was defeated in Kingston, but he was elected in two western seats and chose to sit for Victoria, British Columbia (even though he had never been there). In 1882 he became the member for Carleton, Ontario, but in 1887 and 1891 returned to representing Kingston.

The old chieftain In 1879 the Conservatives raised the Canadian tariff to new levels. There was a substantial growth in Canadian manufacturing after 1879, but during the 1880s the economy grew slowly, Canada held few of the immigrants it attracted and saw many of the native-born leave for the United States, and there was a growing demand for reciprocity with the United States. Equally controversial was the other national policy to which the Macdonald administration was committed—the completion of a transcontinental railway. At first the government continued the policy of building the line themselves, but in 1880 Macdonald helped to negotiate a contract with the Canadian Pacific Railway Company (CPR), headed by George Stephen. The contract was a generous one, too generous in the minds of the opposition. Even so, the CPR returned in 1884 and 1885 to ask for large government loans to finish the project.

Macdonald was sympathetic to the CPR's requests, but he might not have been able to convince even his own followers to agree to the second loan had there not been another rebellion in the north-west. Once again the chief cause of the rebellion was the discontent of the métis, particularly the French-speaking métis who had settled along the South Saskatchewan River. In 1885 they invited Louis Riel to return from the United States and lead their protest movement. Although the federal government promised to examine the métis' grievances, Macdonald believed that the métis had been adequately compensated for their land claims after the first rebellion, and when the protest turned into a serious armed insurrection he responded not with efforts at conciliation but by sending west a substantial force of Canadian militia to suppress the rebellion. Since the force went west on the CPR, Macdonald was able to persuade the Canadian parliament to grant the additional loan requested by the company. In 1886 Macdonald made his first trip west, travelling to British Columbia on the recently completed line.

During 1885 the federal government also faced a series of scattered acts of native violence. In the case of the métis rebellion Macdonald's responsibility for the bloodshed was at least indirect, since he had handed over the ministry of the interior in 1883 to his old and increasingly inactive friend Sir David Macpherson. But Macdonald remained superintendent-general of Indian affairs. Although poorly advised by his subordinates, Macdonald ignored abundant evidence that the native peoples were facing starvation because of the disappearance of the buffalo. Macdonald's humanitarianism was always limited and he was completely unmoved by their appeals for assistance. He reacted with severity to the disorganized acts of violence that resulted from the native peoples' frustration, and all of those suspected of complicity received severe punishments. Macdonald was less vindictive towards the métis, but he did believe that Riel should be tried for treason. Riel's trial created enormous rancour between English Canada, which believed his actions merited the death penalty, and French Canada, which believed that there were sufficient mitigating circumstances, particularly Riel's mental instability, to merit a lesser sentence. Macdonald was at the centre of this controversy. His own lack of sympathy for Riel was clear, and he refused to yield to what he saw as political pressure from Quebec. Riel went to the gallows in 1885, but Macdonald was not forgiven by Quebec. He lost ground there in 1887 and after 1891 the Liberals dominated the province.

Macdonald and the empire Quebec's alienation was probably inevitable. During the 1880s and 1890s imperial enthusiasm grew stronger in Canada. Macdonald believed imperial federation was impracticable and undesirable, but he was genuinely committed to preserving the imperial connection. He had grown up in a community composed of United Empire loyalists and British immigrants, and he sought to transfer as many British institutions as possible to his adopted homeland. Many of Macdonald's contemporaries retired to Britain (as did his wife, who, after his death, was raised to the peerage of the United

Kingdom as Baroness Macdonald of Earnscliffe). Macdonald might also have returned to Britain, for he visited it whenever he could. He admired British politicians, particularly Benjamin Disraeli, to whom he bore a striking physical resemblance, and he eagerly sought imperial honours. In 1872 he was appointed to the British privy council and in 1884 was awarded a GCB. On the other hand he saw little to admire in the United States, which he rarely visited. In 1890 he even ordered that all official documents use British rather than American spellings. Confederation in 1867 he viewed not as the creation of a new nation but as a consolidation of several smaller colonies into a larger one. He would have called it the kingdom of Canada if he had not been overruled by the imperial authorities, who feared antagonizing the United States, but he assured Queen Victoria that Canada would remain under the British crown forever. Macdonald did not support Canadian participation in imperial wars in Africa and Asia, but he was not opposed to imperial expansion. In fact, he argued that in building the CPR and in opening up the vast territories in the west to British settlers, Canada was making an important contribution to the empire, and he showed little sympathy for those, like the métis and the native peoples, who stood in the way of expansion across the continent.

Macdonald's alliance with the French Canadians in the 1850s was born out of political necessity and was undoubtedly made easier by Cartier's own Anglophilia. After Cartier's death in 1873 none of Macdonald's French-Canadian colleagues possessed anything like Cartier's influence. Macdonald never learned to speak French. Although he was prepared to give French equal status in the federal parliament and courts and in Quebec, he only reluctantly consented to a bilingual Manitoba and he did nothing to assist the Acadian minority in New Brunswick in its struggles. During the discussions over allowing Quebec to acquire the territory in the north previously under Hudson's Bay Company jurisdiction, he expressed reservations about creating a barrier between the maritime provinces and Ontario. He refused to condone the activities of Dalton McCarthy's Equal Rights Association, and in 1890, when Manitoba stripped the Catholic minority of its state-funded separate schools, he promised to restore minority rights. But Macdonald was not enthusiastic about extending those rights where they had not existed before confederation, and he believed that Canada must be essentially a British nation and English the dominant language.

Macdonald's last hurrah, death, and burial By 1891 Macdonald's administration had lost much of its vitality and his health was rapidly deteriorating, but he was handed victory in the election of 1891 when the Liberals under Sir Wilfrid Laurier campaigned for unrestricted reciprocity with the United States. Appealing to Canadians to stand by 'the Old Man, the Old Flag, and the Old Policy', Macdonald used the loyalty cry to win a narrow victory at the polls. It was his last. Shortly after the election, on 6 June 1891, he died in Ottawa of heart failure. His body was transported in state by the CPR to Kingston, where he was buried beside his parents and first wife in Cataraqui cemetery. Seventeen months later a white marble bust was erected to his memory in the crypt of St Paul's Cathedral, London, inscribed with the slogan he had used during the 1891 election: 'A British Subject I was born, a British Subject I will die'.

Macdonald in perspective During his lifetime Macdonald aroused intense emotions. To his enemies (and they were many) 'Old Tomorrow' was a procrastinator without principles who gained and held office by the unscrupulous use of power and patronage. This was not entirely an unfair portrait. Macdonald grew up in a political environment where there was no clear conception of conflict of interest. He used his political influence to promote legislation to advance his own financial interests and those of his friends. He had no objection to using liquor and money to help voters arrive at the right decision, and, while he preferred not to appoint incompetents to the civil service, he was not above doing so out of political necessity. In fact, there was very little that he was not prepared to do out of political necessity, as he showed during the Pacific scandal and in 1885 when he ruthlessly gerrymandered the electoral districts in Ontario. Many of the reforms for which he might claim paternity, such as removing the common-law restrictions on labour unions in 1872, were based purely on partisan considerations and not on lofty principles.

Macdonald's friends did not deny his weaknesses, but they defended him as a statesman who always kept in sight the greater good and who played a major part in the creation of Canada. Sir Joseph Pope, for many years Macdonald's private secretary, published the first important biographical defence of Macdonald as well as a selection from his voluminous private papers. The historian who did most to establish Macdonald's reputation was Donald Creighton, in an evocative two-volume biography in the 1950s, which portrayed Macdonald as a hero for the times, the man who defined the Canadian national identity by resisting the growth of provincial power and the imperial ambitions of the United States. While Creighton was perhaps the most influential historian in Canada in the 1950s and 1960s, his views were refined by a number of his students and admirers, including Donald Swainson and Peter B. Waite, both of whom published more popular biographies of Macdonald. Keith Johnson, who demonstrated the extent of Macdonald's personal ambition, did not deny his essential greatness, and he was co-author with Peter Waite of the sympathetic entry in the *Dictionary of Canadian Biography* (1990). Even Macdonald's weaknesses—his heavy drinking and his cynical approach to politics—have come to be seen as positive virtues, signs of his basic humanity and willingness to compromise. Since he was the first prime minister of Canada and held the post for nearly two decades, it was probably inevitable that he became increasingly popular after his death. Yet his influence, while great, is easily exaggerated and was not entirely praiseworthy. Indeed, given his intense Conservatism, his cultural chauvinism, and his lifelong commitment to the promotion of British imperialism, he is in many ways a strange candidate to have become enshrined as the national hero of a country which has rejected so many of the ideals in which he believed.

PHILLIP BUCKNER

Sources D. G. Creighton, *John A. Macdonald*, 2 vols. (Toronto, 1952–5) · J. K. Johnson and P. B. Waite, 'Macdonald, Sir John Alexander', *DCB*, vol. 12 · P. B. Waite, *Macdonald: his life and world* (1975) · J. Pope, *Memoirs of the Right Honourable Sir John Alexander Macdonald*, 2 vols. (1894) · J. Pope, *The day of Sir John Macdonald* (1915) · D. Swainson, *Sir John A. Macdonald: the man and the politician*, 2nd edn (1989) · J. K. Johnson, 'John A. Macdonald', *The pre-confederation premiers: Ontario government leaders, 1841–1867*, ed. J. M. S. Careless (1980), 197–245 · J. K. Johnson, 'John A. Macdonald, the young non-politician', *Historical Papers* [Canadian Historical Association] (1971) · J. K. Johnson, 'John A. Macdonald and the Kingston business community', *To preserve and defend: essays on Kingston in the nineteenth century*, ed. G. Tulchinsky (1976), 141–55 · *Affectionately yours: the letters of Sir John A. Macdonald and his family*, ed. J. K. Johnson (1969) · M. Bliss, *Right honourable men: the descent of Canadian politics from Macdonald to Mulroney* (1994) · L. Reynolds, *Agnes: the biography of Lady Macdonald* (1990) · R. Cartwright, *Reminiscences* (1912) · P. B. Waite, *The life and times of confederation, 1864–1867* (1962) · P. B. Waite, *Canada, 1874–1896: arduous destiny* (1971) · G. T. Stewart, *The origins of Canadian politics: a comparative approach* (1986) · G. T. Stewart, 'John A. Macdonald's greatest triumph', *Canadian Historical Review*, 63 (1982), 3–33 · J. M. S. Careless, *Brown of The Globe*, 2 vols. (1959–63) · J. M. S. Careless, *The union of the Canadas: the growth of Canadian institutions, 1841–1857* (1967) · W. L. Morton, *The critical years: the union of British North America, 1857–1873* (1964) · D. N. Sprague, *Canada and the Metis, 1869–1885* (1988) · B. Forster, *A conjunction of interests: business, politics, and tariffs, 1825–1879* (1986)
Archives NA Canada | BL, corresp. with Lord Ripon, Add. MSS 43623–43624 · Bodl. Oxf., corresp. with Lord Kimberley · CCC Cam., corresp. with sixteenth earl of Derby · Glos. RO, corresp. with Sir Michael Hicks Beach · NA Canada, letters to the ninth duke of Argyll · NA Canada, Tupper MSS · NRA, priv. coll., letters to the ninth duke of Argyll · NRA, priv. coll., letters to Lord Monck · PRO NIre., corresp. with Lord Dufferin
Likenesses Notman, photograph, *c.*1868, National Archives of Canada, C30440 · three photographs, *c.*1872–1889, National Archives of Canada, C10144, C5329, C5327 · portrait, *c.*1877, National Archives of Canada, C2090 · G. E. Wade, white marble bust, 1892, St Paul's Cathedral, London · Bassano, two photographs, NPG · C. B. Birch, plaster statuette, NPG · A. D. Patterson, oils, National Archives of Canada · W. M. Reynolds-Stephens, bronze bust, D. E, Ottawa · G. E. Wade, bronze statue, Montreal, Canada · chromo-lithograph, NPG · photograph, NPG [*see illus.*] · photogravure, NPG · portraits, National Archives of Canada
Wealth at death approx. C$80,000 and a house: Johnson and Waite, 'Macdonald, Sir John Alexander'

MacDonald, John Alexander (1897–1996), Free Church of Scotland minister, was born on 5 July 1897 in the Gaelic-speaking island of Boreray, Outer Hebrides, Inverness-shire, the eldest of eight children of Alexander MacDonald (1864–1912), crofter, and his wife, Margaret (1870–1958), daughter of Donald MacLean and his wife, Kirsty McIntyre.

Lying between North Uist and St Kilda, Boreray is now uninhabited but in the late nineteenth century there was a population of 118 people, supported mainly by crofting and fishing. There was a primary school (where MacDonald learned English) and two libraries on the island. For secondary education pupils had to go to North Uist or Skye, and John MacDonald went to Bayhead School in North Uist.

The year 1912 brought radical changes to the MacDonald family. Alexander MacDonald died, his death perhaps hastened by the absence of medical care on the island. Left with the care of seven children, one of whom died soon after her father, Mrs MacDonald had no difficulty in accepting an invitation from a brother-in-law, Donald MacDonald, to come under his care in British Columbia, Canada. The journey to Canada was not uneventful in that young John MacDonald caught pneumonia on board ship, and his condition necessitated the ship's diversion to Halifax, Nova Scotia, so that he could be hospitalized. On recovery he joined the family in Vancouver.

Some years later MacDonald felt called to the Christian ministry and studied arts at Queen's University in Kingston, Ontario. From there he went to Scotland to study in the Free Church of Scotland college in Edinburgh in preparation for the ministry of that church. His studies in Edinburgh covered the years 1924–7. He was ordained on 21 September 1927. That year he married Elizabeth MacKay from Tain in Ross-shire, and they both set out as missionaries to South Africa, their base to be Keiskamma-hoek in the eastern Cape Province, where conditions at that time were somewhat primitive. Once more John MacDonald faced bereavement, partly because of the absence of quick medical help: his wife died in 1928, aged twenty-two. MacDonald brought his wife's body back to Tain for burial. The experience was so devastating that he did not return to South Africa, but after a few months was inducted as minister of the Free Church at Helmsdale in Sutherland.

MacDonald's ministry there was brief, as in 1932 he transferred to Kiltearn in the east of Ross-shire; and to the Christian needs of this parish—pastoral, evangelistic, and social—he devoted himself for the next thirty-two years. Throughout those years he proved to be exemplary in every department of the Christian ministry, amply realizing the ideal portrait described so long ago by Geoffrey Chaucer:

Cristes lore and his apostles twelve
He taughte, and first he followed it himselfe.
(*The English Parnassus*, 1940 edn, 11)

On 18 April 1933 MacDonald married May Fraser Urquhart (1901–1991), a medical doctor from Dundee with family roots in Ross-shire. The marriage produced three sons. The manse of Kiltearn became widely known for its generous hospitality, which proved an effective element in the pastoral and evangelical thrust of John MacDonald's ministry. He was an interesting preacher, and his strong resonant voice ensured that he was easily heard by everyone. To young colleagues in neighbouring towns and parishes MacDonald was an unfailing source of help and encouragement. A member of the Ross and Cromarty education committee, in 1952 he was elected moderator of the general assembly of the Free Church of Scotland.

In 1964 MacDonald retired from the pastorate of Kiltearn and went to live in nearby Muir of Ord. His house was called Torwood, a name by which he was always known locally. His retirement endured as long as his ministry in Kiltearn, but it was in no sense a relinquishment of work, for he continued preaching until he was in his nineties. In 1991 MacDonald's wife died. On 19 October 1996 he himself died at Torwood, just months short of his century. He was buried on 23 October beside his wife in the Kiltearn cemetery.　　　　　　　　CLEMENT GRAHAM

Sources personal knowledge (2004) · private information (2004) [family] · G. N. M. Collins, *Annals of the Free Church of Scotland, 1900–1986* [n.d., 1987?] · *The Scotsman* (25 Oct 1996)
Wealth at death £160,232.77: confirmation, 30 Oct 1996, NA Scot., SC/CO 957/102

McDonald, John Blake (1829–1901), historical genre and landscape painter, son of James McDonald, a wood merchant, and his wife, Mary Black, was born at Boat of Bridge, Boharm, Moray, on 31 May 1829. He was educated there, but in 1852 enrolled at the Trustees' Academy in Edinburgh. He studied there under Robert Scott Lauder, and from 1859 to 1862 continued his studies at the life school of the Royal Scottish Academy, where in 1862 he won first prize for figure painting. McDonald's work retained the chiaroscuro of Scott Lauder, but, despite a strength and vigour of handling, his paintings can feel heavy-handed and his colours dull. They were effective, however, and popular in his day, especially when they dealt with turbulent episodes of Jacobite history. McDonald was a regular exhibitor at the Royal Scottish Academy from 1857 until 1901. In 1862 he was elected an associate of the Royal Scottish Academy; he became an academician in 1877.

McDonald's early works were domestic genre paintings, landscapes, and some portraits, but he was soon attracted to the Scottish highlands and their history. Probably his best-known work was *Lochaber No More; Prince Charlie Leaving Scotland* (1863; Dundee Museums and Art Galleries), which attracted the attention of Queen Victoria when she visited the Edinburgh International Exhibition of 1886. Another strong image is his diploma work of 1877, *Glencoe, 1692* (Royal Scottish Academy, Edinburgh), which presents a woman finding the corpse of one of her McDonald clansmen after the infamous massacre. Although dour in colouring and theatrical in presentation, the painting effectively presents the full horror of that episode. In 1874 McDonald visited Venice and other European cities. From this time onwards he increasingly turned to landscape painting, both in oils and in watercolours, and after 1878 he virtually abandoned figure work. McDonald was married twice. The identity of his first wife is unknown; his second wife, whom he married on 5 April 1894, was Margaret Hogg, probably his housekeeper. McDonald died at his home, 4 St Peter's Place, Viewforth, Edinburgh, on 20 December 1901, and was survived by his second wife and children from his first marriage. He was buried on 23 December in the Warriston cemetery, Edinburgh.

　　　　　　　　JOANNA SODEN

Sources *Annual Report of the Council of the Royal Scottish Academy of Painting, Sculpture, and Architecture*, 75 (1902), 9–10 · *The Scotsman* (21 Dec 1901) · C. B. de Laperriere, ed., *The Royal Scottish Academy exhibitors, 1826–1990*, 4 vols. (1991), vol. 3, pp. 112–15 · Graves, *RA exhibitors*, 5.134 · P. J. M. McEwan, *Dictionary of Scottish art and architecture* (1994), 351 · b. cert. · m. cert. · d. cert. · Royal Scot. Acad., archives

Archives Royal Scot. Acad., archives, letter collection · Royal Scot. Acad., archives, minute books
Likenesses J. B. Abercromby, wash drawing, 1898, Scot. NPG · photograph, Royal Scot. Acad.

Macdonald, Sir John Denis (1826–1908), naval medical officer and biologist, born at Cork on 26 October 1826, was the youngest son of James Macdonald, an artist, and his wife, Catherine, daughter of Denis McCarthy of Kilcoleman, co. Cork. His father was the representative of the Castleton branch of the Macdonald family and claimant of the Annandale peerage through his great-grandfather, the Hon. John Johnston of Stapleton. Macdonald was privately educated, and after attending the Cork school of medicine went to King's College medical school in London to finish his course. Having qualified, he entered the navy as assistant surgeon in 1849 and was appointed to the Royal Naval Hospital, Plymouth. In 1852 he was appointed to the *Herald* and continued in her on surveying service in the south Pacific until 1859.

In 1859 Macdonald was elected FRS for his microscopic studies with the aid of the sounding lead, dredge, and towing-net, and was promoted to surgeon. In 1862 he was awarded the Makdougall–Brisbane medal by the Royal Society of Edinburgh for his deep-sea investigations. In 1864 he was appointed to Haslar Royal Naval Hospital, Hampshire, and in June 1870 as staff surgeon to the *Lord Warden*, flagship in the Mediterranean. He was awarded the Gilbert Blane medal in 1871. In March 1872 he was appointed to the flagship at Portsmouth for service as professor of naval hygiene at Netley, a post he continued to hold after his promotion to deputy inspector-general in February 1875. In July 1880 he was promoted inspector-general, and in that rank was in charge of the Royal Naval Hospital at Plymouth from 1883 to 1886. He retired on 24 May 1886 and was made KCB in 1902. His chief publications are *The Analogy of Sound and Colour* (1869), *Outlines of Naval Hygiene* (1881), and *Guide to the Microscopical Examination of Drinking Water* (1883).

Macdonald was twice married: first, in 1863 to Sarah Phoebe (d. 1875), daughter of Ely Walker of Stainland, Yorkshire, with whom he had two sons and two daughters; second, to Erina, daughter of William Archer, prebendary of Limerick; she died childless in 1893. Macdonald died at his home, 42 Granada Road, Southsea, Hampshire, on 7 February 1908.

　　　　　　L. G. C. LAUGHTON, rev. ROGER MORRISS

Sources *The Times* (11 Feb 1908) · private information (1912) · W. L. Clowes, *The Royal Navy: a history from the earliest times to the present*, 7 vols. (1897–1903), vol. 7 · *WWW* · *CGPLA Eng. & Wales* (1908)
Wealth at death £1042 15s.: administration, 22 Feb 1908, *CGPLA Eng. & Wales*

Macdonald, Sir John Hay Athole, Lord Kingsburgh (1836–1919), judge, was born at 29 Great King Street, Edinburgh on 27 December 1836, the second son of Matthew Norman Macdonald (subsequently Macdonald-Hume), writer to the signet, and his second wife, Grace, daughter of Sir John Hay, fifth baronet, of Smithfield and Haystoun, Peeblesshire. He was educated at Edinburgh Academy and the universities of Basel and Edinburgh, and was called to condensed exposition of Scots criminal law. His book soon became established, as did he at the criminal bar. However, *Macdonald*, the book, is probably better known now to the Scottish legal profession than Macdonald, the man.

Macdonald's tenure of the office of lord advocate was appropriately marked by the passing of the Criminal Procedure (Scotland) Act of 1887, which effected a great simplification of proceedings in criminal cases. Macdonald was thoroughly familiar with the subject and he helped to pilot the bill through parliament. As lord justice-clerk he conducted many criminal trials with conspicuous ability.

Few men were better known in Scotland in his day than Macdonald. The remarkable reputation which he enjoyed was founded chiefly on his wide range of interests outside the law. A stalwart Conservative in politics, he fought a number of elections unsuccessfully, but ultimately he sat in the House of Commons as Conservative member for the universities of Edinburgh and St Andrews, from 1885 to 1888. In the Commons he favoured an extension of scientific education and called for enhanced standards of qualification for medical practitioners.

Throughout his life Macdonald was an ardent army volunteer. He served for fifty years and in that time worked his way through the officer ranks. When he was required to retire by reason of age in 1901 he held the rank of brigadier-general, commanding a volunteer infantry brigade. He also served, holding various ranks, in the king's bodyguard for Scotland. He was a founder of the Scottish Rifle Association and he captained a British rifle-shooting team at a competition in Philadelphia in 1876. His remarkable knowledge of technical military subjects is shown in his numerous books and pamphlets on training and tactics, which enjoyed a high reputation among professional soldiers and led to many improvements in drill. In 1869 he recommended to Gladstone the introduction of postcards to the British postal system, believing that this would facilitate military communication. The suggestion was widely supported and received effect in 1870.

Macdonald was always interested in practical matters: when a student at the University of Edinburgh he attended concurrently the Watt Institution to learn carpentry. He was also attracted by scientific pursuits and took a special interest in practical applications of science. He was, for example, a member of the Society of Telegraphic Engineers and Electricians. Several inventions stand to his credit and brought him various international awards. He was a fellow of the Royal Society and of the Royal Society of Edinburgh, and president of the Royal Scottish Society of Arts. In the development of motor transport he was an enthusiastic pioneer, and he was president of the Scottish Automobile Association. All forms of athletics appealed to him; he was president of the Scottish Amateur Athletic Association, captain of the Royal and Ancient Golf Club of St Andrews, and arbiter in international football disputes. He was, as president of the Cockburn Association, a jealous guardian of the beauties of the city of Edinburgh. He was also instrumental,

Sir John Hay Athole Macdonald, Lord Kingsburgh (1836–1919), by George Fiddes Watt, 1911

the Scottish bar in 1859. In 1864 he married Adelaide Jeannette (*d.* 1870), daughter of Major John Doran of Ely House, co. Wexford.

Macdonald became successively sheriff of Ross, Cromarty, and Sutherland (1874–76), solicitor-general for Scotland (1876–80), queen's counsel (1880), sheriff of Perthshire (1880–85), dean of the Faculty of Advocates (1882–5), and lord advocate (1885–6 and 1886–8). In 1888 he was promoted to the bench as lord justice-clerk in succession to the first Baron Moncreiff, and assumed the judicial title of Lord Kingsburgh, derived from the part of Skye with which his highland ancestors, who included the Jacobite Flora Macdonald, had been associated. He is seldom referred to by that title. In this capacity he presided for twenty-seven years over the second division of the Court of Session. He retired in 1915.

As a counsel Macdonald found his most congenial sphere in jury trials, and on the bench he was at his best on questions of fact. An obituary in the *Scots Law Times* noted that he could handle a jury in a way which was excelled by none of his colleagues. His judgments were characterized by directness and robust common sense. From the outset he specialized in criminal law. In his early years at the bar he produced his *Practical Treatise on the Criminal Law of Scotland* (1867). He produced two later editions in 1877 and 1894; fourth and fifth editions were published in 1929 and 1948. Later criticism of the book was sharp but, at the time that Macdonald wrote his book, other works in the field were dated and there was practically no instruction given in criminal law at the universities, which treated it as peripheral. Macdonald sought only to produce a practical and when lord advocate, in securing Dover House, in White-hall, London, for the Scottish Office.

Macdonald was well liked by his contemporaries. However, he seems to have dissipated his attention on too many subjects. He dealt admirably as a judge with matters of fact but it was said that on matters of law (other than criminal law) he was superficial and perfunctory. He was at his most thorough on any subject that interested him. He was in his element at public gatherings of a social character, and the genial pages about his volunteer experiences, and his random autobiography, in *Fifty Years of it* (1909) and in *Life Jottings of an Old Edinburgh Citizen* (1915), faithfully reflect his temperament and outlook. One contemporary noted, however, that there were few men about whose personal affairs or personal movements so little was known. *Our Trip to Blunderland*, first published by Macdonald in 1877 under the pseudonym of Jean Jambon, displays his sense of fun and his sympathy with children.

Macdonald was made a privy councillor in 1885, KCB in 1900, and GCB in 1916. Throughout his life he was a devoted member of the Catholic Apostolic church. He died in Edinburgh on 9 May 1919 and was survived by his two sons. MACMILLAN, *rev.* ROBERT SHIELS

Lawrence Macdonald (1799–1878), by John Hutchison, 1860

Sources J. H. A. Macdonald, *Life jottings of an old Edinburgh citizen* (1915) · J. H. A. Macdonald, *Fifty years of it* (1909) · *Scots Law Times: News* (17 May 1919) · *WWW, 1916–28* · *WWBMP*, vol. 2 · D. M. Walker, *The Scottish jurists* (1985) · D. M. Walker, *The Oxford companion to law* (1980) · J. H. A. Macdonald, *Practical treatise on the criminal law of Scotland* (1867) · C. N. Johnstone, 'Lord Justice Clerk Macdonald and his Edinburgh', *Juridical Review*, 35 (1923), 107 · L. Farmer, *Criminal law, tradition and legal order* (1997) · *The Scotsman* (10 May 1919), 8 · *CCI* (1919)
Archives NL Scot., letters to Blackwoods
Likenesses Spy [L. Ward], chromolithograph caricature, *c.*1888, repro. in *VF* (23 June 1888) · G. F. Watt, oils, 1911, Faculty of Advocates, Parliament Hall, Edinburgh [*see illus.*] · W. Stoneman, photograph, 1917, NPG
Wealth at death £22,076 9*s.* 6*d.*: confirmation, 13 Oct 1919, *CCI*

MacDonald, Joseph (1739–1763). *See under* MacDonald, Patrick (1729–1824).

Macdonald, Lawrence (1799–1878), sculptor, was born on 15 February 1799 at Bonnyview, Findo Gask, Perthshire, a younger son of Alexander Macdonald, a village violinist who was blind (or partially sighted), and his wife, Margaret Morison, a nurse. He was apprenticed to a Perth mason, Thomas Gibson, and in 1822 moved to Edinburgh where he worked as an ornamental carver. He entered the Trustees' Academy there on 26 February 1822; seven months later he left for Rome in the company of his patrons, the Oliphants of Gask.

Macdonald set up as a sculptor of portrait busts in Rome, and in 1822–3 he was one of the founder members of the British Academy of Arts in the city. Macdonald, together with John Gibson and Richard James Wyatt, the leading British sculptors working in the neo-classical style in the nineteenth century, were to form the nucleus of the 'Anglo-Roman' school active in the mid-Victorian period.

In 1826 Macdonald returned to Edinburgh. He exhibited at the (Royal) Scottish Academy in its early years and at the Royal Academy. His work was enthusiastically promoted by Scottish patrons and the press. In 1829 he held a special exhibition at the Royal Institution in Edinburgh of his colossal plaster group, *Ajax and Patroclus*, which was engraved on the front page of *The Scotsman* (31 October 1829). A second private exhibition followed in 1830, when the *Edinburgh Literary Journal* described him as 'our Canova'. In the early 1820s he was made an associate of the Royal Institution for the Encouragement of the Fine Arts in Scotland (RIEFAS). In 1829 he became academician of the Royal Scottish Academy but resigned in 1858 and was elected an honorary member.

In 1832 Macdonald returned to Rome and settled there permanently. He moved into the sculptor Bertel Thorvaldsen's former studio in the piazza Barberini in 1844, by which time he had established himself as the leading bust portraitist for British visitors to Rome. According to the *Art Journal*, his studio was filled with 'the peerage done into marble, a plaster galaxy of rank and fashion' (Florentia, 351), and his sitters included the earls of Yarborough, the politician Sidney Herbert, the Liverpool merchant John Gladstone, the author Walter Scott, and the actress Fanny Kemble. He was assisted in the studio by John Macdonald, his older brother, and, from the 1860s, by Alexander Macdonald (*b.* 1847), his son.

Macdonald continued to make ideal statues. Examples included *Eurydice* for the sixth Viscount Powerscourt (1837; National Gallery of Ireland, Dublin) and *Hyacinthus* (1852; Royal Collection) for Prince Albert. Perhaps his finest work is the reclining figure of the countess of Winchilsea (1850; Victoria and Albert Museum, London), formerly in Eastwell church, Kent.

Macdonald's work was assured, carefully executed, and adherent to neo-classical principles of idealized form and high finish. His portrait busts were conventional and decorative rather than strongly individualized, combining the imagery of antique Roman portraiture with contemporary dress and hair-styling. He was described by Peter Robert Drummond as 'somewhat impassioned and self-asserting' in his youth, but later became 'an enthusiastic artist and genial companion' (Drummond, 112). In 1853 he wore a 'long brown beard, of orthodox Italian cut … His fingers were bedizened with gems, the gifts of his admirers; and his air was that of a man who moved amongst the upper ten thousand' (ibid., 126). Lawrence Macdonald died in Rome on 4 March 1878 and was buried in the protestant cemetery there; his son Alexander carved the marble medallion portrait on his tombstone. A marble bust of Macdonald, also by Alexander, is in the collection of the Accademia Nazionale di San Luca, Rome, and another (exh. RSA 1861) by John Hutchison is in the Royal Scottish Academy, Edinburgh.

MARTIN GREENWOOD

Sources H. Smailes, 'Thomas Campbell and Laurence Macdonald: the Roman solution to the Scottish sculptor's dilemma', *Virtue and vision: sculpture and Scotland, 1540–1990*, ed. F. Pearson (1991), 65–72 · P. R. Drummond, 'Lawrence Macdonald', *Perthshire in bygone days* (1879), 109–26 · R. Gunnis, *Dictionary of British sculptors, 1660–1851*, new edn (1964), 248–9 · R. L. Woodward, '19th century Scottish sculpture', PhD diss., U. Edin., 1977, 126–30 · Graves, *RA exhibitors* · W. D. McKay and F. Rinder, *The Royal Scottish Academy, 1826–1916* (1917), 234 · *DNB* · B. Read, *Victorian sculpture* (1982) · M. Greenwood, 'Macdonald, Lawrence', *The dictionary of art*, ed. J. Turner (1996) · H. Le Grice, *Walks through the studii of the sculptors at Rome … * (1841), 77–82 · Florentia, 'A walk through the studios of Rome', *Art Journal*, 16 (1854), 350–55 · *Art Journal*, 40 (1878), 136 · private information (2004)

Archives NL Scot., corresp. with George Combe

Likenesses J. Hutchison, marble bust, 1860, Royal Scot. Acad. [*see illus.*] · A. Macdonald, marble bust, *c.*1870–1878, Accademia Nazionale di San Luca, Rome · A. Macdonald, marble medallion on tombstone, 1878, protestant cemetery, Rome

Macdonald, Malcolm [Callum] (1912–1999), publisher, was born on 4 May 1912 at 10 Breaclete on the island of Bernera, Isle of Lewis, in the Outer Hebrides, the sixth of the eleven children (there were six brothers and five sisters) of Murdo Macdonald (1873–1951), crofter, and Mary Ann Maclean (1879–1968) of Breanish, Uig. Both parents were Gaelic speakers and Macdonald did not learn English until he went to primary school. Because the Scottish education system at the time made no provision for teaching Gaelic, Macdonald was taught to read and write the language at home by his father, who insisted that all his children should read daily verses from the family Bible. Macdonald's secondary education was at the Nicolson Institute in Stornoway on the Isle of Lewis. After leaving in 1931 he entered the University of Edinburgh but despite winning the class medal in economic history he did not take his degree, preferring to move to London to establish an agency for marketing lobsters for the fishermen of Bernera. Before leaving Edinburgh he married Williamina Seaforth Ross (1916–1986) of Scarp, Harris, on 21 June 1934. There were six children of the marriage.

At the outbreak of the Second World War Macdonald immediately enlisted in the Royal Air Force. Having served two tours of flying operations with Coastal Command he was commissioned as a signals officer and was posted to Gibraltar. In 1944 with the rank of squadron leader he was appointed head of 10 radio school in technical training command before taking over the command of air operating training at no. 4 radio school. A peacetime regular commission was offered to him but he was determined to return to civilian life and he was released from the service in 1947.

Macdonald and his wife then settled in Edinburgh where they opened a small stationery and bookselling business in the suburb of Marchmont. Anxious to expand, he bought a hand-printing machine and taught himself the rudiments of typesetting; a more sophisticated Heidelberg machine replaced it and in 1951 his literary interests encouraged him to set himself up as a publisher. His close friendship with the poet Sydney Goodsir Smith, whom he had met in 1944, was also a spur and through him he was introduced to other Scots poets of the same generation including Hugh MacDiarmid, Robert Garioch, Norman MacCaig, and Sorley MacLean.

With their encouragement Macdonald came to be the publisher of a literary magazine. In 1952 Alan Riddell, an Australian-born poet studying in Edinburgh, had produced a broadsheet called *Lines*, the first issue being in honour of Hugh MacDiarmid's sixtieth birthday. When it ran into financial difficulties the following year, Macdonald was persuaded by his growing number of literary friends to take it over. An editorial board was formed with MacDiarmid as chairman; it was decided to rename the magazine *Lines Review* and to publish it on a quarterly basis. Riddell remained as editor for only two further issues but returned to edit the magazine between 1962 and 1967. Other editors included the poets J. K. Annand and Robin Fulton.

As publisher Macdonald preferred to remain in the background but his influence helped to shape *Lines Review*. He insisted that while the magazine was published in Scotland it should have an international outlook and, above all, that literary quality should be its yardstick. A pattern began to emerge of publishing British and European writers but the magazine also promoted the work of Scottish poets. In the 1960s there was a shortage of publishing outlets for them, especially if the poetry was written in Scots or Gaelic, and Macdonald was anxious to encourage a younger generation, including the poets Alan Bold and Iain Crichton Smith.

That the magazine thrived owed everything to the hard work put into it by Macdonald and his family, all of whom were involved in the enterprise. Although Macdonald rejected the constraints of conformist religious belief and never practised any form of public worship, he did acknowledge that the impetus for succeeding came from the Presbyterian work ethic inculcated in his childhood. The business soon expanded and in 1968 it moved to larger premises at Loanhead outside Edinburgh. Macdonald received no public support for his efforts until he started receiving modest grants from the Scottish Arts Council in 1966. In addition to *Lines Review* he also published collections of poetry and literary prose works, most notably Goodsir Smith's novel *Carotid Cornucopius* (1964), which was compared favourably with the work of James Joyce.

Although reserved, but invariably polite, Macdonald

was at his happiest in the company of close literary friends and revelled in the society of Edinburgh's Rose Street pubs in the 1950s and 1960s. He was generous and affable, and his conversation ranged over military history, classical literature and politics but, being impatient of bores and pedants, he always wore his learning lightly. Throughout his career he insisted on high standards of dress and public behaviour and in later life his white hair and aesthetic looks gave him a patrician air which suited his role as a literary publisher.

In 1982 Macdonald retired to live in Innerleithen, near Peebles in the Scottish borders, but he remained as a director with responsibility for overseeing the company's literary output. He was appointed MBE in 1992. Three years after the death of his wife in 1986 he married the poet Tessa Ransford (b. 1938) on 7 December 1989. She was also the last editor of *Lines Review* and with Macdonald took the decision to publish the final issue of the magazine in spring 1998. By then Macdonald was ill with lung disease; he died of a pulmonary embolism at Hay Lodge Hospital, Peebles, on 24 February 1999 and was cremated at Morton Hall crematorium, Edinburgh. His ashes were buried at Dean cemetery, Edinburgh on 2 March.

TREVOR ROYLE

Sources J. MacInnes, *Callum Macdonald: Scottish literary publisher* (1983) · *The Scotsman* (25 Feb 1999) · *The Independent* (4 March 1999) · *The Herald* (27 Feb 1999) · d. cert. · private information (2004) [family]
Archives NL Scot., papers; personal and business coresp. and papers
Likenesses V. Crowe, oils, 1996, Scot. NPG · A. Catlin, photograph, NL Scot.
Wealth at death £240,335.45: confirmation, 8 July 1999, *CCI*

MacDonald, Malcolm John (1901–1981), politician and diplomatist, was born on 17 August 1901 at Lossiemouth, Scotland, the second of the three sons (among six children) of (James) Ramsay *MacDonald (1866–1937), journalist, politician, and later prime minister, and his wife, Margaret Ethel Gladstone *MacDonald (1870–1911), daughter of John Hall *Gladstone FRS, a distinguished scientist, and an active social and religious worker.

Early life and education Throughout their marriage Ramsay and Margaret MacDonald worked closely together on political and social issues, and from his earliest years Malcolm got to know early socialist pioneers such as Keir Hardie from among the stream of visitors who came to their crowded flat in Lincoln's Inn Fields which doubled as an office-cum-workplace as well as a family home. Margaret died in September 1911 at forty-one, just eighteen months after the birth of her third and youngest son, David, who also soon died. Thereafter Malcolm, his elder brother, Alister, and his three sisters were drawn even closer to their widowed father. Malcolm's career in particular was crucially affected by that of his father right up to the latter's retirement as prime minister in June 1935.

Malcolm MacDonald was at Bedales School, near Petersfield in Hampshire, for eight years from 1912 to 1920, the same school that Alister attended. Both brothers later testified to the tolerance and friendships they enjoyed

Malcolm John MacDonald (1901–1981), by Leo Whelan, exh. Royal Society of Portrait Painters 1937

there, despite the public reviling and criticism their father suffered during the First World War for his conspicuous role as a Labour leader and conscientious objector to military service. At that time Bedales was best-known for being the only co-educational boarding-school for teenagers in England. Malcolm, especially in his final two or three years, was much influenced by the remarkable founding headmaster of Bedales, John Haden Badley. By his last year he had achieved what he later termed, somewhat laconically in his unpublished autobiography, 'a certain eminence' (MacDonald papers). He captained the soccer team and was vice-captain of the cricket eleven; he was a school record-breaking swimmer and athlete, captain of the fire brigade, and head prefect. He was a leading actor and producer in school plays. He seemed to shine at everything except scholarship, where his performances were adequate but undistinguished, though he did win a minor history exhibition to Queen's College, Oxford.

MacDonald's four years at Oxford from 1920 to 1924 set him on course for a career in politics, and for his lifetime interest in travel and in international affairs. After a slow and rather quiet start in his first two years, he gradually became a relatively frequent and increasingly skilful debater at the Oxford Union, and in 1924 he was runner-up in the contest for presidency of the union to Gerald Gardiner, forty years later lord chancellor in Harold Wilson's Labour government. In that year his father became Britain's first Labour prime minister and he was able to invite some of his Oxford friends to visit the prime minister's country residence at Chequers. He was president for one term during his last year of the prestigious Ralegh Club, was active with several of his Canadian friends in Oxford at the 'Oh Canada! Club', and was a founder member of the Queen's-based informal Paragon Club. He obtained a second-class degree in modern history in 1923. He stayed on for a further postgraduate year, reading for a diploma in economics (in substance mostly economic history) and politics, and gained a distinction in 1924 which later encouraged him to comment rather wryly about economic expertise.

From August 1924 until June 1925 MacDonald enjoyed, as one of a three-man debating team from Oxford, an extensive—and busily social—tour of the United States, Canada, Hawaii, Fiji, New Zealand, and Australia. Then he visited Hawaii and Kyoto in 1927 and 1929 respectively as secretary to the British delegation to conferences of the Institute of Pacific Relations. Although unsure whether he wished to pursue a lifetime career in politics he served as a member of the London county council from 1927 to 1930; and in 1929, at his third attempt (having been defeated in 1923 and 1924), MacDonald was elected to the House of Commons as Labour member for the Bassetlaw division of Nottinghamshire.

Politician and high commissioner In August 1931 the formation of the National Government split the Labour Party and MacDonald followed his father as one of a small group of National Labour MPs. He was immediately appointed parliamentary under-secretary in the dominion office and in this capacity moved the third reading of the Statute of Westminster. Between 1935 and 1940 he was a cabinet minister holding one or both of the offices of secretary of state for dominion affairs and secretary of state for the colonies. In Whitehall and Westminster circles in the 1930s, Malcolm MacDonald had to prove to himself and to others that he owed successive ministerial offices to merit rather than merely to his father, although he was unashamedly a close confidant and supporter of his father, especially in Ramsay's last years.

MacDonald played as well as worked hard. Throughout the 1930s his long active days (of 12–14 hours) were mostly devoted to Whitehall. Yet he often spent the evening and small hours consorting with an extensive company of actor and actress friends in or around London's theatreland. These included Ivor Novello, Noël Coward, Laurence Olivier, Beatrice Lilley, and, above all, Dorothy Dickson. Ministerially he was intimately involved in the controversies in these years over Éire, Palestine, the West Indies, and the promotion of colonial development and welfare policy, becoming the first active ministerial advocate of Commonwealth as a desirable outcome of empire. As dominions secretary from 1935 to 1939 he negotiated the end of the British–Irish trade war and settled the annuity and 'treaty ports' disputes in 1938. He was well nigh unique among British ministers in gaining the trust and perhaps the friendship of Eamon de Valera, partly because of a shared interest in ornithology. During 1940–41, with Winston Churchill's reluctant concurrence, he visited de Valera in Dublin three times to discuss Ireland's role in the war, albeit not productively.

Although MacDonald lost his parliamentary seat at the general election of 1935, he was re-elected to the House of Commons at a by-election in 1936 for Ross and Cromarty; and he remained its MP, even through his war years in Canada, until 1945. In Churchill's government of 1940 he was minister of health, a post which involved him in such matters as food rationing, hospitals, and air-raid shelters during the blitz; this last responsibility involved him in inspecting London's war damage, occasionally in the company of the king and queen.

In 1941 MacDonald was appointed Britain's high commissioner to Canada, and his youngest sister, Sheila [see below], accompanied him as his hostess. During his five years there he played a significant and characteristically unpublicized role in smoothing relations between the prickly bachelor Canadian prime minister, W. L. Mackenzie King, through a time when Canada's contribution to the war effort and to post-war planning was of the utmost importance. The fact that King virtually regarded MacDonald as an adopted son was a considerable asset to Britain. MacDonald was present at the Quebec conferences between Churchill and Roosevelt, nominally attended by King too. It was indicative of the regard and confidence King reposed in him that when the activities of the Soviet spy Igor Gouzenko were being investigated by Canadian intelligence, MacDonald was told of this earlier and was given details that King did not reveal to all his cabinet colleagues.

King and many of his cabinet colleagues attended Malcolm MacDonald's wedding in Ottawa in December 1946. This was to a young Canadian war widow, Audrey Marjorie Rowley, daughter of a civil servant, Kenyon Fellowes. They met on a ski slope north of Ottawa, not long before his high commissionership came to an end. His wife had a son and a daughter from her first marriage. The couple also had a daughter, Fiona, born in 1949. Because of her father's itinerant life, and because her mother lived in Ottawa much of the time to look after her aged mother, Fiona wrote rather wistfully in the late 1990s: 'I thought of him more as a statesman than a father' (private information).

South-east Asia and India On his return from Ottawa, having ceased to be an MP in 1945, MacDonald was appointed governor-general of the Malay States and Singapore in 1946, refusing Attlee's offer of office in his government or some other prestigious post. Thus began what turned out to be more than eight years of being based in south-east Asia. During that time MacDonald worked hard for intercommunal co-operation, for civil government, and for an eventual federalizing of Britain's Malayan possessions. In late 1946 British Borneo had been added to his responsibilities. In 1948 his direct responsibilities over the myriad territories later joined together in Malaya were superseded by the more general and undoubtedly ambiguous role of being in charge of overseeing and helping to co-ordinate Britain's relationships with the former Indo-China, as UK commissioner-general for south-east Asia. This was no easy task, with the Foreign Office, the Colonial Office, and the War Office being just three of the most prominent Whitehall interests actively involved in Malaya throughout the counter-insurgency war, euphemistically known in official British parlance as 'the Emergency' (1948–60). MacDonald's commission was, however, reconfirmed several times by Conservative as well as Labour governments. In a remarkable tribute to his interest and high standing among Borneo peoples, he was adopted as a 'son' of the Iban paramount chief Temonggong Koh.

MacDonald was Britain's high commissioner to India from 1955 to 1960, years that saw a considerable increase in both Soviet and American interest, as rivals, in the subcontinent and some consequent diminution of British interest in military and economic matters. The years 1954 to 1958 also marked a high point in official Sino-Indian cordialities before border disputes and other matters led to a swift decline and then war in 1962. During MacDonald's five years in New Delhi the British diplomatic presence in India was extensive, with large offices in Bombay, Madras, and Calcutta as well as the main mission in the capital city. MacDonald toured extensively around India (occasionally meeting elderly Indians who purported to remember the visit of his parents much earlier in the century), entertained an extensive retinue of visitors, and extended his ornithological interests by writing (with the help of his Singapore-Chinese friend Christina Lohe) a book entitled *Birds in my Indian Garden* (published in 1961), in addition to lengthy dispatches ruminating on aspects of Indian life.

First and foremost, however, the second half of MacDonald's high commissionership was notable for his efforts, largely successful, to repair official Indo-British relations after the Suez misadventure in late 1956. This fence-mending was helped by Nehru's knowledge that MacDonald had criticized Eden's Suez Canal policy from the start. Once the canal zone had been invaded MacDonald drafted a letter resigning his high commissionership; but the swift passage of events and Eden's illness and resignation as prime minister made this unnecessary.

It was a mark of Malcolm MacDonald's unique standing and experience that he was soon called out of his subsequent semi-retirement in England to be co-chairman and leader of the British delegation at the international conference on Laos held in Geneva in 1961–2. Here his tact, patience, and diplomatic skills were fully stretched: he played an important role involving China constructively with the enterprise, a process aided by his friendship with China's foreign minister, the sagacious Zhou Enlai.

Africa In 1963 at the urging of Duncan Sandys, the colonial secretary, MacDonald agreed to become Britain's last governor and commander-in-chief in Kenya in the period leading to independence, a process he came to believe should be hastened, especially as the project for an East African Federation foundered and was abandoned by Britain. He was governor-general for the two critical years of transition (1963–4). Then, as a clear testimony to the trust and standing he enjoyed with Jomo Kenyatta, MacDonald returned as Britain's second high commissioner (1964–5) to independent Kenya, succeeding Sir Geoffrey de Freitas,

who was disappointed and disillusioned by the failure of the East African Federation scheme. MacDonald's friendship with Kenyatta, Tom Mboya, and a few other key Kenyans undoubtedly smoothed what could otherwise have been very strained UK–Kenyan relations.

For three more years, from 1967 to 1969, MacDonald served as a roving ambassador in Africa for Harold Wilson's Labour government. His many contacts and his open and friendly sympathy for post-colonial leaders, peoples, and societies helped to diminish suspicion and opposition to British policies in Africa—especially stemming from Rhodesia and Ian Smith's illegal regime, and Nigeria's civil war. However, despite being a loyal servant of the crown he was privately somewhat uncertain of the bona fides of the Wilson administration, and found his position trying and uncomfortable. As he wrote in a letter to his wife on 22 August 1967: 'It is quite a job trying to cope with the affairs of a dozen different countries in different parts of eventful Africa' (MacDonald papers).

Character and achievements Early in his adult life Malcolm MacDonald became an enthusiast for the Commonwealth, and throughout his life he helped to sharpen the contrast between empire and Commonwealth in practical terms and without gratuitously disavowing Britain's imperial past. In this he used to say that he was helped by being Scottish not English—though indubitably he was always British, as well as a self-styled citizen of the world. No linguist—at best he knew a little French—his character and broad interests and sympathies nevertheless brought him friends in many countries. His hobbies (especially bird-watching and collecting books, porcelain, and pictures) intermingled, sometimes creatively, with his official life.

MacDonald had been sworn of the privy council in 1935 but he was markedly reluctant to accept 'social' honours and discouraged several overtures regarding a knighthood or a peerage. The notable exception came in 1969 when he accepted the Order of Merit. He received, however, many academic and some civic honours, and was made freeman of the city of Singapore in 1955 and of the burgh of Lossiemouth in 1969. His continuing devotion to young people and to education was shown in many ways: as a Rhodes trustee from 1948 to 1957, chancellor of the University of Malaya from 1949 to 1961, visitor for the University College of Kenya, a senior research fellow at the University of Sussex (1971–3), and chancellor of the University of Durham.

MacDonald was small, wiry, and remarkably friendly, with something of a reputation as a ladies' man. He wore spectacles from youth to middle age and then, following an accidental breakage during the Second World War, he found that he was able to do without them. In later life he ate one main meal a day, though his diary sometimes registered two or three 'tea-times' in a single afternoon, usually at the Royal Commonwealth Society. In fact he always ate sparingly, turning his plate over at public mealtimes to indicate that he was forgoing a particular course. He required no more than a few hours' sleep each night. His painstaking application often kept him working late into the night, but he was usually up at dawn to renew his passionate interest in ornithology, which led him to produce books on the birds of Ottawa, Delhi, and Kenya. His other published writings were either reminiscences and pen portraits of people he had known or travelogues; they included *People and Places* (1969) and *Titans and Others* (1972).

In early manhood there was a certain bespectacled gawky toothiness about MacDonald's appearance, and in the Whitehall of the 1930s his dress generally conformed with the formal wear of senior civil servants and ministers. From middle age he matured into a more distinguished-looking silver-haired statesman, albeit one who generally dressed casually in old age, dispensing with a necktie and the more formal clothes of earlier life. For years he listed his recreations in *Who's Who* as 'ornithology, collecting, skiing'; the first two undoubtedly occupied much more of his time than the third—his collection of Chinese porcelain is now at Durham University. MacDonald died at his home, Raspit Hill, Ivy Hatch, near Sevenoaks in Kent, on 11 January 1981. He had gone outside late on a frosty night to ensure that his greenhouses were properly closed, and suffered a heart attack.

A nondenominational service of thanksgiving for Malcolm MacDonald's life and work was held in Westminster Abbey on 3 March 1981. In the commemorative address Sir Shridath Ramphal, the Commonwealth secretary-general, summed up his richly varied life by saying that he was a quintessential Commonwealth man. He stressed how MacDonald had brought to his extensive representational work the highest diplomatic qualities: he was 'the supreme interlocutor'.

MacDonald's youngest sister, **Sheila Ramsay Lochhead** [*née* MacDonald] (1910–1994), prison visitor, was born on 7 December 1910 in London. Her mother died less than a year after her birth, and she was for a time looked after by family friends. She grew up immersed in Labour Party politics. She attended North London Collegiate School, where she became head girl, and Somerville College, Oxford, where she won a hockey blue and narrowly missed a first in philosophy, politics, and economics. She hoped to enter politics and in the 1931 election, her father wrote, 'made a fine beginning on the political platform' (Marquand, 780), but her father's decision to form the National Government effectively ended her political career. When her eldest sister, Ishbel, married she became her father's political hostess, while also working as a classifying officer at Wormwood Scrubs prison. She accompanied her father on several visits overseas, and was with him in November 1937 on the voyage to South America on which he died. She then lived with her brother Malcolm in London—where during the war she helped establish a primary school for unevacuated children—and in Canada. In 1948 she married Andrew Van Slyke Lochhead (*b.* 1911), a lecturer in social administration; they had three children. They lived in Swansea, where he worked at the University College. She continued prison visiting and from 1962 was also a magistrate. She advocated penal reform and was active in the National Association of Prison Visitors, of which she was national chairwoman for three years. In Swansea she established a hostel for former prisoners and a shelter for homeless persons. In 1993 she published *Outside in*, a history of prison visiting. In 1993 a major stroke paralysed her down one side. She died on 22 July 1994 at her home, 43 Langland Road, Swansea, and was survived by her husband and their three children.

PETER LYON

Sources MacDonald papers, U. Durham L. [incl. unpubd autobiography, 'Constant surprise' in typescript] · C. Sanger, *Malcolm MacDonald: bringing an end to empire* (1995) · R. F. Holland, *Britain and the commonwealth alliance, 1918–39* (1981) · K. Kyle, *The politics of independence of Kenya* (1999) · Provost's entrance book, 1920–1922, Queen's College, Oxford · J. M. Brown and W. R. Louis, eds., *The Oxford history of the British empire*, 4: *The twentieth century* (1999) · M. MacDonald, *Titans and others* (1972) · M. MacDonald, *People and places* (1969) · J. Garner, *Commonwealth office, 1925–1968* (1978) · *WWW* · *CGPLA Eng. & Wales* (1981) · private information (2004) · *The Times* (12 Jan 1981) · D. Marquand, *Ramsay MacDonald* (1977) · *The Times* (26 July 1994) · *CGPLA Eng. & Wales* (1994)
Archives Bodl. RH, corresp. relating to African affairs · U. Durham L., corresp. and papers; additional papers | BL, letters to Albert Mansbridge, Add. MS 65253 · Bodl. Oxf., letters to Sir Alfred Zimmern · Bodl. RH, corresp. with Sir Harry Batterbee; corresp. with Sir Henry Brooke-Popham; corresp. with Sir Granville Orde Browne; corresp. with Arthur Creech Jones; corresp. with Lord Lugard; corresp. with J. H. Oldham; corresp. with Margery Perham and related papers; corresp. rel. to African affairs · HLRO, letters to Lord Samuel · Mitchell L., Glas., corresp. with J. L. Kinloch · NA Scot., corresp. with Lord Lothian · Rice University, Houston, Texas, Woodson Research Center, corresp. with Sir Julian Huxley · Ruskin College, Oxford, letters to James Middleton · State Library of Victoria, Melbourne, corresp. with John Jones · U. Durham, additional papers
Likenesses L. Whelan, oils, exh. Royal Society of Portrait Painters 1937, NPG [*see illus.*]
Wealth at death £400,704: probate, 2 April 1981, *CGPLA Eng. & Wales* · £416,091—Sheila Lochhead: probate, 25 Oct 1994, *CGPLA Eng. & Wales*

Macdonald, Margaret. *See* Mackintosh, Margaret Macdonald (1864–1933).

MacDonald, Margaret Ethel Gladstone (1870–1911), socialist and feminist, was born on 20 July 1870 at 17 Pembridge Square, London, the only daughter of John Hall *Gladstone (1827–1902), professor of chemistry at the Royal Institution, and his second wife, Margaret Thompson King (*d.* 1870), daughter of a Presbyterian minister and niece of Lord Kelvin. Margaret's mother died soon after her birth and she was brought up with half-sisters from her father's previous marriage in a religious and socially aware household. John Gladstone was a committed Liberal who served on the London school board for twenty-one years and was a founder member of the Young Men's Christian Association. Margaret Gladstone was educated at the Doreck College for Girls in Bayswater and the women's department of King's College and studied political economy under Millicent Fawcett. She was attracted to evangelicalism and taught a weekly class for servant girls at the Nassau Senior Training Home when she was seventeen. In 1889 she took Sunday school classes for boys and worked in boys' clubs. By the age of twenty-three she had become manager for several board schools, secretary

Margaret Ethel Gladstone MacDonald (1870–1911), by Elliott & Fry, 1906

of the Hoxton and Haggerston Nursing Association, and a visitor for the Charity Organization Society in Hoxton.

This was a common pattern of activities for young women who wished to lead purposeful lives. In Margaret Gladstone's case, however, contact with working-class poverty led to more radical political ideas. Initially influenced by the Christian socialists Charles Kingsley and F. D. Maurice, she was drawn further towards socialist politics in the 1890s by the speeches of the trade union leader Ben Tillett and by reading *Fabian Essays* (1893). Her work for the Charity Organization Society and the influence of an old schoolfriend, Lily Montagu, the organizer of the West London Jewish Girls' Clubs, brought her into contact with the Women's Industrial Council (WIC), a body which investigated women's working conditions and promoted policies to improve them. Inspired by Amelia Jane (Amie) Hicks and Mrs Hogg, both active members of the WIC, she acknowledged by 1895 that she was now a socialist. It was in the same year that she met her future husband, (James) Ramsay *MacDonald (1866–1937), who, after her death, was to become the first Labour prime minister. Margaret Gladstone joined the Independent Labour Party in April 1896 and was married in November of the same year. The MacDonalds set up home at 3 Lincoln's Inn Fields which became a centre for labour activists at home and from abroad. They had three daughters and three sons, including Malcolm John *MacDonald, and David, who died in 1910.

Margaret MacDonald had a private income of £460 a year and is most often remembered for the financial and emotional support and security that she gave to her husband. However, the importance of her own contribution to the labour movement has come to be recognized. She was one of a small group of middle-class women who concentrated on improving the lives of female industrial workers. The Women's Industrial Council, which she joined in 1894, provided a focus for her activities. She was secretary of the council's legal and statistical committee, and a member of its investigations and education committees. On behalf of the WIC she carried out investigations into home working in London, the results of which were published in 1897, and gave evidence to the 1906 select committee on home work. She helped to produce a series of studies on women workers, one of which, *Women in the Printing Trades* (1904), was edited by her husband. In the early 1900s Margaret MacDonald drew attention to the needs of unemployed women. Through her efforts the central unemployment board of London appointed a special women's work committee which established municipal workrooms for clothing workers. She helped to organize a march of unemployed women in Whitehall in 1905 and in 1907 initiated a national conference on the unemployment of women dependent on their own earnings. In the same year she gave evidence to the royal commission on the poor laws and provided a memorandum on women's unemployment. Industrial education for women and girls was another interest of Margaret MacDonald. She was partly responsible for the decision of the London county council to establish the first trade school for girls at the Borough Polytechnic in 1904 and organized national conferences on the industrial training of women and girls in 1907 and 1908.

Alongside her work for the WIC Margaret MacDonald also took an active part in the National Union of Women Workers. As chairman of the industrial committee and secretary of the legislation committee she was involved in a wide range of issues including housing, the registration of midwives and nurses, the early closing of shops, and the appointment of women probation officers. She gave many lectures on these subjects, and between 1899 and 1909 wrote most of the industrial section of the *Englishwoman's Year Book*. One of her last campaigns was to attempt to gain better terms for women under the National Insurance Act of 1911 by urging Lloyd George to include non-working wives and married home workers. In the last few years of her life Margaret MacDonald was president of a new organization, the Women's Labour League, which was established in 1906 to encourage women to become involved in Labour politics and to seek improvements in the work and family lives of working-class women. Margaret MacDonald supported women's enfranchisement from an adult suffrage position, but was never willing to give the issue priority. Despite her long-standing interest in working conditions, and her own attempts to combine motherhood and public activities, she believed that women's most important role was in the home and she was consistent in her opposition to married women's paid employment.

With so many causes to pursue and several young children to bring up it is little wonder that Margaret MacDonald's life at Lincoln's Inn Fields was chaotic. Margaret Bondfield, the trade union leader and socialist, recalled that she would beg Margaret MacDonald: 'Come back to my rooms, then I can be sure of getting your attention! What with babies, telephones and callers, etc. … it is impossible at your home' (Collette, 44). Margaret MacDonald was eulogized by her husband in a sentimental memoir published in 1912, but other contemporaries remembered her as a strong-minded campaigner who could be tenacious in her opinions. Her opposition to the Trade Board Bill, which would have set a minimum wage for home workers, led to a fundamental disagreement between herself and Clementina Black, president of the WIC, which split the council. Margaret MacDonald's involvement in the relationship between George Belt, a married organizer for the Independent Labour Party, and Dora Montefiore, a wealthy socialist and suffragist, in which she was sued for libel, showed a moralistic side to her character which was also revealed in her crusade to abolish the employment of women as barmaids.

Margaret MacDonald died unexpectedly, aged forty-one, on 8 September 1911 at her home, 3 Lincoln's Inn Fields, from blood poisoning due to an internal ulcer. Overwork and stress were thought to have contributed to her early death. After months of controversy, she had been obliged to sever her connections with the Women's Industrial Council, and this caused her acute distress. Services were conducted on 12 September at her home and at Golders Green crematorium, where she was cremated. Two services were also held for her at Leicester (where her husband had his parliamentary seat) and her ashes were buried at Spynie churchyard near Lossiemouth. Three memorials were created: a baby clinic was set up in her memory at North Kensington and a new ward was named after her at Leicester Children's Hospital by the Women's Labour League; a bronze statue, designed by her husband, was unveiled in Lincoln's Inn Fields, on 19 December 1914.   JUNE HANNAM

Sources J. Saville and J. Schmiechen, 'MacDonald, Margaret Ethel Gladstone', *DLB*, vol. 6 · C. Collette, *For labour and for women: the Women's Labour League, 1906–1918* (1989) · E. Mappen, *Helping women at work: the Women's Industrial Council, 1889–1914* (1985) · J. R. MacDonald, *Margaret Ethel MacDonald* (1912) · D. Marquand, *Ramsay MacDonald* (1977) · *The Times* (9 Sept 1911) · *The Times* (12 Sept 1911) · *The Times* (18 Sept 1911) · *Women's Industrial News* (Oct 1911) · Women's Labour League, obituary notices, 1912
Archives BLPES, corresp. and papers · PRO, personal and family corresp. and papers, PRO30/69 | BLPES, corresp. with the independent labour party · Swarthmore College, Swarthmore, Pennsylvania, Friends Historical Library, letters to Jane Addams
Likenesses Elliott & Fry, photogravure, 1906, repro. in MacDonald, *Margaret Ethel MacDonald* [*see illus.*] · R. Macdonald, bronze statue, unveiled 1914, Lincoln's Inn Fields, London · photographs, repro. in MacDonald, *Margaret Ethel MacDonald*
Wealth at death £271 11s. 2d.: probate, 22 Jan 1912, *CGPLA Eng. & Wales*

MacDonald, Sir Murdoch (1866–1957), engineer, was born on 6 May 1866 in Inverness, the seventh of the nine children of Roderick MacDonald, of Faillie, Strathnairn, carter, and his wife, Margaret Mackay, of Croy. He was educated at Dr Bell's Institution, later known as Farraline Park School, Inverness. On leaving school he served as an articled clerk in the Highland Railway and then was apprenticed to the chief engineer. In 1891–4 he was resident engineer to the Black Isle Railway and he then worked in the engineering office, engaged on design and superintendence of extensions of the railway.

In 1898 MacDonald resigned from the Highland Railway, and the following year married Margaret (d. 1956), daughter of Alexander Munro, postmaster of Lochalsh, Wester Ross; they had two sons. On leaving the Highland Railway he had immediately begun a period of service in Egypt where British engineers were converting its basin irrigation systems to a perennial irrigation system to enable cultivation of cash crops, notably cotton, after the British invasion in 1882. He was appointed assistant engineer on the Aswan Dam in 1898 and after its completion in 1902 was retained in the Egyptian service as resident engineer for the regulation of the dam and the construction of protecting aprons downstream. He supervised the heightening of the Aswan Dam in 1908, as a result of which the temples of Philae were drowned, and the building of the Esna barrage (finished 1912). He also designed and rebuilt a regulator on the delta barrage following its collapse. For this work he was appointed CMG (1910), and in 1912 he became under-secretary, and later adviser, to the Egyptian ministry of public works. He then became responsible for developments in irrigation in Egypt, in particular for the drainage and reclamation of waste land in the north of the delta. Schemes to extend cultivation by means of the Sennar Dam on the Blue Nile, and the Jebel Aulia Dam on the White Nile, which MacDonald helped project, were delayed by the First World War and not effected until 1925 and 1937 respectively, by which time he had retired. MacDonald, who was made KCMG in 1914, served as a colonel in the Royal Engineers to advise on engineering matters connected with the defence of the Suez Canal and water supply for the advance across the Sinai Desert. He was appointed CB in 1917.

About this time MacDonald was attacked by Sir William Willcocks, designer of the Aswan Dam, with charges of incompetence and falsification of information. The charges were scrutinized by two commissions and finally by the British supreme court in Egypt, each of which declared the charges to be without foundation. In 1920 MacDonald published *Nile Control* (2 vols.) and in 1921 retired from Egyptian government service, although he continued to act as consultant for irrigation and power schemes in the region. During his service he received six decorations, the highest being the grand cordon of the Nile, and on his retirement he was granted a substantial pension in recognition of his work in Egypt.

In 1921 MacDonald founded the London firm of MacDonald and MacCorquodale, consulting engineers, afterwards Sir Murdoch MacDonald & Partners, of which his elder son became the senior partner after his death. While MacDonald was working the firm carried out further work on Nile dams and barrages, which, however, were superseded by the Aswan High Dam scheme. The firm was also employed on irrigation, drainage, hydroelectric power, and harbour projects in Europe, the Middle East, and Pakistan.

From 1922 to 1950 MacDonald was Liberal MP for Inverness and was a very conscientious constituency member. The welfare of the highlands was his major concern as an MP, and he was involved in persuading the secretary of state for Scotland to issue an order protecting the Loch Ness monster. He was made a freeman of Inverness in 1930. MacDonald was slightly above average height, with a well-developed head and impressive manner. He played football and billiards well and was a good shot. In 1898 he was vice-president of the North of Scotland Football Association.

MacDonald was president of the Institution of Civil Engineers (1932, and twice received the Telford gold medal); of the Junior Institution of Engineers (1927–8); and of the Smeatonian Society of Civil Engineers (1952). He was a member of the Society of Engineers (gold medallist), of the Royal Institution, and of the Royal Astronomical Society, and a consulting engineer to the North of Scotland hydroelectric board. MacDonald died at Greystones, Seafield Street, Nairn, on 24 April 1957.

H. E. HURST, rev. ELIZABETH BAIGENT

Sources *The Times* (25 April 1957) · *The Engineer* (3 May 1957) · W. Willcocks, *The Nile projects* (1919) · W. Willcocks and J. Ireland, *Egyptian irrigation*, 2 vols. (1913) · D. R. Headrick, *The tentacles of progress: technology transfer in the age of imperialism, 1850–1940* (1988) · *Inverness Courier* (26 April 1957) · private information (1971) · personal knowledge (1971) · *WW* · d. cert. · *CGPLA Eng. & Wales* (1957) **Archives** Highland Council Archive, corresp. relating to his private practice · U. Durham L., archives and special collections, papers | U. Durham L., corresp. with Sir Reginald Wingate **Likenesses** W. Stoneman, photograph, 1932, NPG · G. Barron, bronze head, c.1933, Inverness Town Hall, Inverness · J. Gunn, oils, Inst. CE **Wealth at death** £39,302 13s. 10d.: confirmation, 25 Oct 1957, CCI

MacDonald, Patrick (1729–1824), music collector and publisher, was born on 22 April 1729 in Durness manse, Durness, Sutherland, the eldest of four sons and seven daughters of the Revd Murdoch (Murdo) MacDonald (b. 1696) and his wife, Agnes Coupar (Cooper). Although a Presbyterian minister, Murdoch was also a musician and Gaelic scholar who provided translations of Alexander Pope and probably transcribed the poems of his neighbour, the Gaelic poet Rob Donn MacKay, whose elegy described Murdoch as

> Ged bu bheartach do chràbhadh,
> Bha do mheas air gach talànn,
> 'S tu a thuigeadh na dàinte,
> 'S am fear a dheanadh na rainn.
> (Although rich in piety
> You showed appreciation for every talent,
> And well did you understand the songs
> And the one who composed the verses.)
> (*MacDonald's Compleat Theory*)

Murdoch, 'a most melodious and powerful singer' (*Fasti Scot.*), 'taught his children the principles of music, besides encouraging them in that art' (Glen). Patrick and his brother **Joseph MacDonald** (1739–1763), born on 26 February 1739, both played the violin; Patrick was regarded as an excellent amateur; Joseph also sang, and played the flute, oboe, and bagpipes. They and their sister Florence (Flora) all probably composed melodies for some of Rob Donn MacKay's verses.

Patrick spent some time from 1737 with his grandfather in Pittenweem, Fife, then returned home, later attending the University of Aberdeen and becoming licensed as a preacher in 1756 before he became a missionary at Strontian, Ross-shire. Patrick, who was 'tall of stature, with a commanding figure, light blue eyes, … remarkable ability … and a striking figure in his district' ('MacDonald of Kilmore'), began his lifelong ministry at Kilmore, south of Oban, Argyll, in 1757, the same year he married Barbara MacDonald, a Roman Catholic, 'who attended neither public nor family worship with her husband' (*Fasti Scot.*, 60). They had nine sons and four daughters.

Patrick wrote his parish's account for Sinclair's *Statistical Account of Scotland* (1791–9) and published the important *Collection of Highland Vocal Airs* (1784), which contained music he had collected in Argyll, Perthshire, and, probably with Joseph (who visited Patrick there), in Ross-shire, while the Sutherland section, 'North Highland Airs', was Joseph's own; music from the Hebrides came from correspondents. The successful collection, which went into five editions, contains the first printed versions of various Scottish and Gaelic melodies, as well as music thought to be originally for bagpipe and clarsach (the highland harp), which influenced many later figures, including Robert Burns, who wrote some of his poems to its melodies.

In contrast, Joseph, who at fourteen already spoke English, Gaelic, and French, and knew Latin, was sent to study in Haddington, then moved to Edinburgh, where he 'had an opportunity of being frequently in company with Signor Pasquali [Nicolò Pasquali, a violinist], and the other masters of that period, and thereby of extending his musical knowledge, and improving his taste', as his father wrote in 1753 (*MacDonald's Compleat Theory*). He also enjoyed painting, and included a picture of a young piper, perhaps a self-portrait, with his manuscript. Although Murdoch had hoped Joseph would become a professional musician, he joined the East India Company, leaving Scotland for Calcutta in 1760. He gave the music he had collected in Sutherland to his sister Florence, but took with him his own collection of bagpipe music, which he planned to publish. The manuscripts were lost after his death, aged twenty-four, from a malignant fever, in May 1763, until Sir John MacGregor Murray, a member of the highland societies of London and Scotland, rediscovered one part in India in 1784.

The manuscript returned to Patrick, who, to his great credit, was finally able to publish Joseph's *A Compleat Theory of the Scots Highland Bagpipe* in 1803. As far as is known, Joseph was 'the first piper to ever write on the subject or to attempt to record in notation the music [now known] as piobaireachd [pibroch]' (*MacDonald's Compleat Theory*). Patrick was also farsighted in the presentation of the music, having grace-note stems up and melody stems down, which later became standard pipe notation. The significance of Joseph's work was recognized only in 1948 when Archibald Campbell published a piobaireachd collection, the *Kilberry Book of Ceol Mor*. Campbell quoted extensively from *A Compleat Theory*, now acknowledged as the earliest primary source, describing it as the 'first reliable written evidence about the Highland bagpipe and Highland bagpipe music, the work of the first practical piper to endeavour to put his knowledge into writing' (ibid.).

Although Patrick's wealth at his death, on 25 September 1824, may have been substantial, since he had, according to Murdoch, 'one of the best livings in that country, as minister of Kilmore in Lorne', Joseph left, according to Cannon, 'three books of Highland music in Manuscript', '4 vols. of Correlli's Works', '3 Books of Highland Musick in manuscript partly blank', and '1 small box with a parcel of Old Bagpipes'. As Grimble perceived them, 'Patrick and Joseph were reared in a cultural tradition unstifled by political or religious prejudice, just as Rob Donn had been, and their contribution to it was complementary to that of the bard'; their lasting legacies are the invaluable cultural resources which their keen interest and research have provided.   MARY ANNE ALBURGER

Sources M. A. Alburger, *Scottish fiddlers and their music* (1983); repr. (1996) · *Joseph MacDonald's Compleat theory of the Scots highland bagpipe (c. 1760)*, ed. R. D. Cannon, new edn (1994) · R. D. Cannon, *The highland bagpipe and its music*, new edn (1995) · F. Collinson, *The traditional and national music of Scotland* (1966) · J. Glen, *The Glen collection of Scottish dance music*, 1 (1891) · I. Grannda, *Orain le Rob Donn* (1899) · I. Grimble, *The world of Rob Donn* (1979) · K. N. MacDonald, 'Rev. Patrick MacDonald of Kilmore', *Celtic Monthly*, 6 (1897) · B. MacKenzie, *Piping traditions of the north of Scotland* (1998) · *Fasti Scot.* · OPR

Likenesses K. Macleay, portrait, *c*.1896, priv. coll. · silhouette, Scot. NPG

Wealth at death had 'one of the best livings in the country as minister of Kilmore in Lorne': Grimble, *Rob Donn* · 'three books of Highland music in manuscript'; Joseph MacDonald: inventory, Cannon, *Highland bagpipe*, 2 · '4 vols. of Correlli's Works'; '3 Books of Highland Musick in manuscript partly blank', sold to James Ashburner; '1 small box with a parcel of Old Bagpipes', sold to 'Captn. Campbell'; Joseph MacDonald: BL OIOC, India office records, mayor's court inventories, range proceedings, 194/63, dated 8 Aug 1763; Cannon, *Highland bagpipe*, 110

Macdonald, Sir Peter George (1898–1983), biscuit entrepreneur, was born on 20 February 1898 at Darnaway, near Forres, Morayshire, the son of William Macdonald, head gamekeeper to the earl of Moray, and his wife, Annie Cameron. He was educated at Forres Academy, but left early and joined a sequence of Scottish regiments during the First World War. These included the Black Watch and the Lovat Scouts, a corps of highlanders skilled in hunting and stalking.

After demobilization Macdonald trained with the earl's Edinburgh solicitors to become a land agent. However, with an ex-serviceman's grant he studied law at Edinburgh University and moved into wider legal spheres in the firm of W. and J. Burness, with which he was associated (latterly as a consultant) until his death. In 1927 he

became a writer to the signet, and two years later he married Rachel Irene (*d.* 1990), daughter of the Revd Robert Forgan DD of Edinburgh. They had one son and two daughters.

Through his friendship in the 1930s with Sir Alexander Grant, also from Morayshire, Macdonald was made legal adviser to the biscuit manufacturers McVitie and Price. After Grant's death in 1937 he worked closely with his son and successor as chairman, Sir Robert McVitie Grant. During the Second World War Macdonald served as regional deferment officer for the Board of Trade's Edinburgh office; he was also on the staff of the regional commissioner for Scotland. When Sir Robert Grant died in 1947, Macdonald was elected chairman and managing director of McVitie and Price.

In 1948 McVitie and Price and the Glasgow-based Macfarlane Lang & Co. Ltd amalgamated as United Biscuits Ltd; their joint pre-merger profits were £450,000. As the first group chairman Macdonald set his stamp on the new enterprise through a combination of personality (he could be ruthless) and brainpower. He possessed great financial acumen, and backed the bold policy of concentrating McVitie and Price's output on a few leading brands of biscuit, most notably Digestive and Rich Tea. Group profits exceeded £2 million in 1957. However, United Biscuits remained no more than a holding company, with the respective units producing and marketing independently of each other.

Between 1962 and 1966 three further biscuit companies, William Crawford & Sons Ltd, William Macdonald & Sons Ltd, and Meredith and Drew Ltd, joined the group. The resulting organizational upheavals, and the pressures of intensified outside competition, led Macdonald in 1964 to hire the management consultants McKinsey & Co. They recommended the complete integration of all activities, and in 1965 Hector Laing (later Baron Laing of Dunphail), a grandson of Sir Alexander Grant, became group managing director, charged with carrying out this restructuring. In consequence, four out of the five Scottish factories had to be closed and administration was concentrated in London. By 1967, when Macdonald retired, United Biscuits was the largest biscuit company in Britain, with a turnover of £67 million and pre-tax profits of over £5 million. The national market leader in biscuits, it had also diversified into snack foods, packaged cakes, and bakery products.

A committed delegator, Macdonald undertook a range of outside activities. He became a director of several major insurance companies and chairman of various textile firms. He sat on the council of the Institute of Directors and was founder of the institute's Scottish branch. A Conservative, he was knighted in 1963 for political and public services. He supported many charities, but without publicity.

With large features and an impressive physical presence, Macdonald had a lawyer's concern for 'small print' but also the entrepreneur's urge to think big. He frequently used his recreations of fishing, shooting, and golf to foster business contacts. He served as JP for the city of

Edinburgh and in 1966 as deputy lieutenant for Edinburgh. An active but undoctrinaire member of the Church of Scotland, he was an elder in Greyfriars Church, Edinburgh, and by his own efforts raised from industry no less than £250,000 to finance an extension scheme for the Church of Scotland. He maintained his Scottish roots to the last, dying at his home, 18 Hermitage Drive, Edinburgh, on 21 July 1983. T. A. B. CORLEY

Sources S. Hamilton, 'Macdonald, Sir Peter', *DSBB* · J. S. Adam, *A fell fine baker: the story of United Biscuits* (1974) · P. Pugh, *A clear and simple vision* (1991) · D. F. Channon, *The strategy and structure of British enterprise* (1973) · *The Times* (26 July 1983) · *WWW* · Burke, *Peerage*
Likenesses photograph, repro. in Adam, *A fell fine baker*
Wealth at death £396,407.15: confirmation, 13 Oct 1983, *CCI* · £64,391.20—estate held abroad: confirmation, 13 Oct 1983, *CCI*

MacDonald, (James) Ramsay (1866–1937), prime minister, was born on 12 October 1866 in a 'but-and-ben' cottage in Lossiemouth, a small fishing port on the coast of Moray in north-east Scotland. He was the illegitimate son of Anne Ramsay, a Lossiemouth farm servant, and John MacDonald, a highlander from the Black Isle of Ross, who worked as a ploughman on the same farm. For most of his life he was known as James Ramsay MacDonald, but his birth certificate described him as 'James MacDonald Ramsay, child of Anne Ramsay'.

Early influences and first steps MacDonald was an only child, brought up by two devoted women—his mother and his grandmother Isabella (Bella) Ramsay. Perhaps because of this he was always more at ease with women than with men. It is not an accident that he was the first prime minister to give cabinet office to a woman (Margaret Bondfield) or that his faithful private secretary Rose Rosenberg played a significant role in his political activities. Some of his less happy traits may also have stemmed from the circumstances of his birth. The insecurities of a fatherless boy never quite disappeared. He came, he once wrote, 'of a people who were as ready to use their dirks as their tongues' (Marquand, 50); and throughout his life he was quick to take offence and apt to dwell on wounds which he would have been wiser to forget. The legacies of place and culture, on the other hand, were much more fortunate. MacDonald spent most of his adult life in London, but Lossiemouth was in his blood. He returned there whenever he could and, for form's sake, attended the free kirk on Sundays; his ashes, like those of his wife, were buried in nearby Spynie churchyard. The dogged determination and appetite for hard work that helped to take him to the summit of politics were part of his inheritance. So were the brooding Celtic emotions which helped to make him one of the most inspiring platform speakers of his generation.

MacDonald owed a special debt to the parish school at Drainie, and to the dominie, James McDonald. At fifteen, after a few months working on a nearby farm, MacDonald was appointed as the dominie's pupil teacher. His appointment saved him from the fields and gave his talents room to flower. During his time as pupil teacher he read widely in English literature, founded the Lossiemouth field club, whose members went on scientific

(James) Ramsay MacDonald (1866–1937), by Olive Edis, 1926

expeditions in the neighbourhood and read scientific papers to each other, and spoke regularly at the mutual improvement society. He owed a different kind of debt to the stubborn radicalism of the fishermen and farm workers among whom he grew up. He subscribed to the *Christian Socialist* and read Henry George's *Progress and Poverty*. Among his papers are the drafts of painstaking, argumentative youthful speeches condemning superstition, attacking landlords, and calling for land nationalization (MacDonald papers, PRO).

MacDonald's pupil teachership ended in April 1885. He left Lossiemouth to help set up a boys' club at a Bristol church. The venture failed, and by the end of the year he was back in Lossiemouth, but he soon left home again, this time for London. He arrived to find that the post he expected to take had been filled. For some weeks he tramped the streets in search of work, living on oatmeal sent from home, an occasional beefsteak pudding, and hot water in place of coffee or tea. He found a job addressing envelopes at 10s. a week, but it lasted for only four weeks. In May 1886, after another spell of unemployment, he was taken on as an invoice clerk in the City at 12s. 6d. a week, rising to 15s. On that, he claimed later, he lived 'like a fighting cock' (Elton, 54). He also began to cut his political teeth. In Bristol he had joined the Social Democratic Federation (SDF), founded in 1884 by the wealthy Marxist convert H. M. Hyndman. In the uproar that followed the discovery that the Conservatives had helped to finance at least two SDF candidates in the general election of 1885, MacDonald sided indignantly with Hyndman's critics. In

London he joined the breakaway Socialist Union, and contributed to its journal, *Socialist*. He was present in Trafalgar Square on the notorious 'bloody Sunday' of 13 November 1887, when a free-speech demonstration was broken up by soldiers and mounted police. But in his early London days politics were a secondary interest. He spent his lunch hours reading in the Guildhall Library, went to evening classes in science at the Birkbeck Institute, and worked for a scholarship in science at the South Kensington Museum. A mysterious breakdown prevented him from sitting his examination and shattered his hopes of a scientific career. Only then did political ambitions displace scientific ones.

Political apprenticeship and marriage MacDonald's first step on the political ladder came early in 1888, with his appointment as private secretary to a radical home-ruler and tea merchant, Thomas Lough. The salary was £75 a year, rising to £100—affluence after 15s. a week. He organized Lough's campaign as Liberal candidate for West Islington, and began to write for the radical press. He was an avid joiner, still unsure of his future path. He became a star of the 'St Pancras parliament', where would-be local politicians taught themselves parliamentary procedure, served briefly as secretary of the London committee of the Scottish Home Rule Association, and joined the recently founded Fabian Society. Like many social reformers of his generation, anxious to reconcile a Christian inheritance with the scientific advances of the time, he also joined the growing ethical movement, which hoped to base a secular, but morally uplifting ethics on a conception of man 'as a rational being, fighting out his spiritual battles within himself' (*Ethical World*, 18 June, 2 July 1898). More idiosyncratically, he played a leading part in an obscure socialist sect called the Fellowship of the New Life, which held that 'a reform of the ideals of individuals' was a prerequisite for a socialist society (*Seedtime*, April 1892). For a while he was the secretary of a co-operative (if flea-ridden) New Life household in Bloomsbury, whose members included Edith Lees, who later married Havelock Ellis, and the former Fabian essayist and future Labour minister Sydney Olivier.

In 1892 MacDonald left Lough to throw himself into labour and socialist politics, relying on the meagre earnings of his pen to make ends meet. It was an exhilarating but confusing period in labour history. The burgeoning labour movement faced a profound and divisive strategic question, which in one form or another was to haunt MacDonald for more than twenty years. How should it relate to the Liberal Party, the dominant anti-Conservative force in Britain, whose values most socialists and Labour people shared even when they castigated its timidity? Like the Fabians and the 'lib–labs' of the so-called Labour Electoral Association, MacDonald's initial answer was to try to work within the Liberal Party in the hope that it could be persuaded to pay more heed to labour interests. In 1892 the Labour Electoral Association in Dover selected him as its prospective parliamentary candidate. In 1894 the Southampton association tried unsuccessfully to win him the nomination as the second of two Liberal candidates in that two-member constituency. But his approaches to his putative Liberal allies were more menacing than supplicatory. Labour and the Liberals should come together in a 'great progressive party', he told his Dover adoption meeting. Pending that, Labour would adopt 'no shibboleth which will tie us to the old parties' (*Dover Express*, 7 Oct 1892, in Marquand, 34–5). The obvious implication was that if the Liberals spurned Labour's advances, Labour would fight on its own. When the Southampton Liberals turned him down, he duly announced that he would stand as an Independent Labour candidate anyway. Soon afterwards, the Liberals of the Attercliffe division of Sheffield followed Southampton's example and refused to adopt a trade unionist run by the local Labour Electoral Association. MacDonald promptly joined Keir Hardie's recently founded Independent Labour Party (ILP), which proclaimed a rugged independence from both the old parties.

MacDonald was bottom of the poll when the general election came in 1895, but his Southampton campaign changed his life. It brought him into contact with Margaret Gladstone (d. 1911) [see MacDonald, Margaret Ethel Gladstone], a vivacious and unconventional charity organization visitor from Bayswater, whose experience of social work in the East End had converted her to socialism. The Gladstones were a solid professional family; Margaret's father, John Hall *Gladstone, was professor of chemistry at the Royal Institution. She and MacDonald met in the summer of 1895 and married in November 1896. They had six children, one of whom died of diphtheria in early childhood. Their second child, John Malcolm *MacDonald (1901–1981), followed his father into politics and later held a series of high commissionerships in Africa and Asia. Margaret had a private income of about £460 a year— enough for them to live in a roomy, chaotic flat at 3 Lincoln's Inn Fields, where they gave regular 'at homes' for British and foreign radicals and socialists, and to indulge a mutual passion for foreign travel. Notable examples are a visit to the United States in 1897, to South Africa immediately after the Second South African War, to Canada, Australia, and New Zealand in 1906, and to India in 1910.

Building a party MacDonald's decision to throw in his lot with the ILP was a milestone too. The ILP catered for both sides of his character: for the practical organizer of Lough's committee rooms and for the utopian idealist of the Fellowship of the New Life. In doing so, it gave him a political home as well as a political base. Not that MacDonald was an orthodox ILP-er. He remained an active Fabian until 1900, when he resigned from the society in disgust because it refused to condemn the Second South African War. He had no patience with the sectarianism that frequently marked ILP attitudes to cross-party co-operation. He was an instinctive coalition builder, anxious to build bridges to potential allies in different camps; on a deeper level, his brand of gradualist socialism was an outgrowth of the radical Liberalism he had absorbed in his youth, not an alternative to it. He never abandoned the dream of a 'great progressive party', that would include 'advanced and sturdy Radicals' (MacDonald to Hardie, 12 July 1899 PRO, MacDonald papers). In that spirit he played a leading part in the Rainbow Circle, a discussion group of progressive intellectuals whose debates foreshadowed the new Liberalism of the following decade; other members included J. A. Hobson, the pioneer of underconsumptionist economics, and Herbert Samuel, the future Liberal leader. But after Southampton he shared the fundamental ILP premise that Labour would have to be prepared to fight the Liberals to win a fair share of seats, as well as its view that the official Liberal Party was moribund. In 1896 he was runner-up in the elections to the ILP's ruling body, the national administrative council (NAC); by the end of the decade he was unmistakably one of the party's leading figures, along with Hardie, Philip Snowden, and Bruce Glasier.

MacDonald was ideally placed to exploit the shift in trade-union attitudes which paved the way for the creation of the Labour Party early in the twentieth century. He could reassure trade unionists who feared that socialism might be rammed down their throats as well as socialists who feared for their ideological purity. It is not certain what role he played in the manoeuvres that led to the foundation conference of the Labour Representation Committee (LRC) in February 1900. His role in the sequel was pre-eminent. The LRC conference unanimously elected him as secretary of the new body. He was the only person in the entire LRC whose responsibility was to the whole rather than to any of the constituent parts. He had no salary, little formal power, and few resources. But on the strategic questions that determined its fate, his was the decisive voice.

The crucial question was how to deal with the Liberals. It was given extra edge by the 'khaki election' of September 1900. Only two LRC candidates out of fifteen were successful. In the two-member constituency of Leicester, MacDonald had two Liberal candidates to contend with, and came bottom of the poll. The obvious moral was that the LRC could not make an electoral breakthrough without a deal with the Liberals, and a few months after the election MacDonald put out feelers to Jesse Herbert, private secretary to the Liberal chief whip, Herbert Gladstone. Before long, the Taff Vale judgment of 1901, which made the unions liable for damages caused by their members in pursuance of a trade dispute, provoked a flood of new trade-union affiliations to the LRC and made it possible for MacDonald to negotiate with the Liberals from a position of strength. He played his hand with great skill, mixing blandishments with threats; and in September 1903 he and Gladstone reached an imprecise but far-reaching secret understanding, ensuring that about thirty LRC candidates faced no Liberal opponent (Bealey and Pelling, 157; Marquand, 78–80). In many ways it was the most portentous achievement of his life.

Evolutionary socialism: theory and practice Party management and electoral strategy went hand in hand with polemical journalism and socialist theory. From 1901 to 1905 MacDonald contributed a weekly column to the Liberal *Echo* and wrote substantial articles for the *New Liberal Review*. He published two important pamphlets: a savage attack on British policy during and after the Second South African War (*What I Saw in South Africa*, 1902) and a collectivist critique of the tariff reform movement, arguing that it was a diversion from the task of industrial modernization (*The Zollverein and British Industry*, 1903). Above all, he produced an elaborate statement of the case for an evolutionary socialism, distinct from both the class-war Marxism of the SDF and the social liberalism of his radical friends, designed to give the new labour alliance a theoretical rationale (*Socialism and Society*, 1905). He started from the organic conception of society then current in progressive circles. Society was an organism, to be understood in terms of Darwinian biology; it was evolving inexorably towards socialism. Marx was wrong in thinking that socialism would come through revolution; in social evolution, as in biological, higher forms of life slowly emerged out of lower forms. Individualistic theorists were wrong too: they were like 'cell philosophers' trying to prove 'that the body existed for them and that the modifying and moving force in the organism was the individual cell'. Biology also held the key to socialist politics. Parties had finite lives; the Liberal Party's was moving to a close. No gulf of principle prevented socialists from working with Liberals. 'Socialism, the stage which follows Liberalism, retains everything of value in Liberalism by virtue of being the hereditary heir of Liberalism.' But the proper place for socialists was a Labour Party, inevitably socialist in spirit, even if not in declared policy.

The MacDonald–Gladstone pact passed its first big test with flying colours. In the general election of 1906 twenty-nine LRC candidates were elected, only three against official Liberal opposition. In Leicester, MacDonald won comfortably, with Liberal support. The LRC members, together with a miners' MP who joined them after the election, elected Keir Hardie as their chairman, MacDonald as secretary, and Arthur Henderson as chief whip. The annual conference of the LRC then changed its name to 'Labour Party'. The evolutionary theory sketched out in *Socialism and Society*, however, had a more bumpy ride. Central to MacDonald's whole argument was the proposition that the Liberal Party was dying. Now it had been restored to health; indeed, the new Labour Party owed its parliamentary presence to a Liberal triumph. Not only did the mostly untried Labour MPs have to contend with one of the biggest government majorities of modern times; they had to do so in circumstances that called into question their reason for existence.

MacDonald stuck to his evolutionary guns. The government was not afraid of 'socialist speeches', he insisted, but it could be influenced by 'successful criticism in details' (*Labour Leader*, 10 May 1907). Like the Benthamites in the nineteenth century, socialists could shape the 'common sense' of the age by offering practical solutions to immediate problems (*Socialism and Government*, 1909, 2.86). He practised what he preached, overcoming his early qualms about speaking in the chamber, and turning himself into a powerful debater. Balfour thought him a 'born parliamentarian' (*DNB*); J. R. Clynes remembered him as a 'bitter and dour fighter' in debates on unemployment (J. R. Clynes, *Memoirs, 1869–1924*, 1937, 124).

Unfortunately, the stolid trade unionists on the Labour benches were ill suited to the role MacDonald had sketched out for them. Though Snowden rivalled him in forensic ability, the party's performance was, in general, lacklustre. Morale gradually sagged, even in the parliamentary party; outside parliament the euphoria of 1906 gave way to a mood of disillusioned acrimony. It was concentrated in the ILP, which saw itself as the socialist leaven in the Labour lump, and which became increasingly restive with the constraints imposed by the trade-union alliance and the pact with the Liberals. MacDonald, the ILP chairman from 1906 to 1909, had to devote most of his political energies to a long, dragging struggle to quell a rank-and-file rebellion against the electoral and political strategies he had done so much to shape, symbolized by the magnetic, ill-starred figure of Victor Grayson. The battle evoked one of the most powerful platform speeches of his life—a passionate affirmation at the ILP conference in 1909 of his commitment to parliamentary methods—and ended in defeat for the rebels. But it led him to resign from the NAC and left an ominous residue of bad blood.

Leader and widower In parliament and the wider Labour Party MacDonald's star continued to rise. The 'people's budget' of 1909, the struggle over the veto power of the House of Lords, and the two general elections of 1910 brought Labour and the Liberals closer together, and strengthened the case for a politics of non-sectarian progressivism. They also gave MacDonald a tailor-made opportunity to shine, and added to his following, particularly on the trade-union right of the party. In February 1911 he was unanimously elected as chairman of the parliamentary party, on the understanding that the term of office would no longer be restricted to two years and that he would relinquish the party secretaryship in favour of Arthur Henderson.

MacDonald's chairmanship was soon blighted by personal tragedy. On 8 September 1911 Margaret MacDonald died of blood poisoning. Part of MacDonald died with her. For some weeks he was in shock. The day after her cremation at Golders Green, Bruce Glasier remembered later, MacDonald told him, 'I have sorrowed so much and wept so much that I have no more sorrow or tears left' (Thompson, 173). To his ten-year-old son Malcolm

> my father's grief was absolutely horrifying to see. Her illness and death had a terrible effect on him of grief; he was distracted; he was in tears a lot of the time when he spoke to us, and, as I say, it was almost frightening to a youngster like myself. (Marquand, 134)

Little by little MacDonald gathered up the threads of his life. Financially, his circumstances were unchanged. The income from Margaret's trust fund—now about £800 a year—was paid to him. A housekeeper was engaged to look after the children; the household at Lincoln's Inn Fields went on. He wrote a memoir of Margaret which was privately printed, and a fuller biography which was published in the ordinary way. Both were among the most

revealing things he ever wrote, but they produced no catharsis: the wound never healed. As time went on he made warm friendships with a number of women—Lady Margaret Sackville, Molly (Mary Agnes) Hamilton, Cecily Gordon-Cumming, Marthe Bibesco, Lady Londonderry—who gave him some of the emotional support he needed. But at the centre of his life there was an aching loneliness.

Grief-stricken though he was, MacDonald was soon back in harness. It was a more onerous one than he could have foreseen at the time of his election. The turn to the left on which the government had embarked in the budget of 1909 continued; in doing so, it deepened the fissures in the labour movement. MacDonald and the bulk of the parliamentary party drew ever nearer to the Liberals, becoming for all practical purposes part of a tacit progressive coalition embracing most of anti-Conservative Britain. In the ILP, and among a younger more militant generation of trade unionists, the compromises of coalition politics seemed pusillanimous or even treacherous. The National Insurance Act (1911) was the most striking case in point, and confronted MacDonald with the first big test of his leadership. It was the most radical measure of the period and one of the most radical in modern British history. MacDonald hailed it as an advance of the sort that happened 'about once every century' (*Hansard 5C*, 26, 1911, 718–36). He and most of his parliamentary colleagues voted for it, and in detailed negotiations with ministers obtained significant concessions for the trade unions. But their gains won them no credit from the socialist left. The scheme was based on the contributory principle, anathema to the normally moderate Fabian Society as well as to the ILP. But MacDonald strongly supported it, on ideological grounds as well as on grounds of political expediency. The result was a deep party split, pitting socialists against trade unionists and parliamentarians, which soon extended well beyond the contributory principle to the even more sensitive questions of purpose, unity, and discipline.

The years 1912 and 1913 saw more splits: over strikes in the railways, docks, and coalfields; over the party's attitude to suffragette militancy; and, more embarrassingly, over the Labour national executive's refusal to put MacDonald's seat at risk by contesting a by-election in Leicester in violation of the MacDonald–Gladstone pact. By the early months of 1914 MacDonald and the majority of the parliamentary party were closer, on most issues, to the Liberal government than to the ILP. Meanwhile, the logic of progressivism increasingly pointed towards an open coalition between the Liberal and Labour parties in place of the existing tacit one. In March 1914 Lloyd George and the Liberal chief whip offered MacDonald and Henderson a wide-ranging deal, involving an early election on Irish home rule, an agreed election programme, a substantial increase in the number of Labour candidates to whom the Liberals would give a clear run, and Labour representation in the cabinet (Marquand, 159–60). Nothing came of it. But there is not much doubt that MacDonald was attracted, or that the offer was a striking vindication of the evolutionary socialism he had preached for more than a decade.

Peace campaigner and public enemy It was the last such vindication for some time. The outbreak of the First World War in August 1914 fractured the tacit progressive coalition beyond repair, set in motion the most far-reaching political realignment of the century, transformed the balance of power in the Labour Party, and swept MacDonald from the moorings he had occupied since his pact with Herbert Gladstone. On a deeper, emotional level he went through a time of trouble more testing than any he had faced in his political life before. Having been a quintessential insider, at any rate in Labour politics, he became an outsider, in lonely rebellion against the leadership in which he had been a pivotal figure since the party's birth. Paradoxically, however, his rebellion helped to equip the party with a distinctive programme which paved the way for its transformation from a trade-union pressure group into the main anti-Conservative force in the state.

In 1914 most of the Labour Party rallied to the flag; so did most Liberals. Most of the ILP opposed the war, as did a small number of radical intellectuals, some of whom were Liberal MPs. MacDonald's position was characteristically complex, but he stuck to it for four years of obloquy and misrepresentation. He did not want Germany to win. He was not a pacifist. He accepted that war might in certain circumstances be justified; he even had a certain respect for the military virtues. Yet no pacifist could have loathed violence and the hatreds bred by violence more than he did. In the particular case of the First World War he believed that Britain and Germany were equally to blame, that the British government was lying when it claimed to have gone to war for Belgium, and that the bellicose emotions it had let loose would lead to a punitive peace and sow the seeds of future wars. The true cause of the war, he thought, lay in the 'policy of the balance of power through alliance' (*Labour Leader*, 5 Aug 1914). If that policy continued after the war, the result would be 'new alarms, new hatreds and oppositions, new menaces and alliances; the beginning of a dark epoch, dangerous, not merely to democracy but to civilisation itself' (ibid., 29 Aug 1914). The only hope was to change opinion. That could be done only by exposing the true nature of the diplomacy which had made war inevitable in the first place, and by mobilizing support for a democratic alternative. That in turn implied that the British people had to be convinced that they were following dishonest leaders in a bad cause—a hard lesson for a nation engulfed by the first total war in history.

MacDonald's breach with the pro-war majority of his own party opened on 5 August 1914, when the Parliamentary Labour Party voted for war credits, thereby making nonsense of the anti-government line, which he had put forward on its behalf only two days before. He promptly resigned from the chairmanship, and in collaboration with a group of anti-war radicals, including Arthur Ponsonby, Charles Trevelyan, E. D. Morel, and Norman Angell, helped to set up the Union of Democratic Control (UDC) to campaign for parliamentary control over foreign policy,

negotiations with the democratic forces on the continent, and peace terms which would not humiliate the losers. By the end of the year he had become the leading figure in a bitterly unpopular but passionately committed cross-party campaign for a negotiated peace, centred on the UDC and the ILP.

In the labour movement memories of his wartime stand eventually became a priceless political asset, winning MacDonald the support of a war-radicalized left which saw him, for a while, as a mixture of hero and martyr and forgot his pre-war flirtations with the Liberal government. At the time he paid a heavy price. As the casualty lists lengthened, the anti-war movement became ever more isolated and MacDonald, its most prominent embodiment and symbol, became the target of a savage campaign of press vilification. Sometimes his meetings were broken up; occasionally he was stoned. More often the press reported disturbances when none had taken place, so as to deter proprietors from letting their halls to him. Two episodes in particular cut deep. The first came in September 1915, when Horatio Bottomley's journal *John Bull*, which had been running an anti-MacDonald campaign for months, published a facsimile reproduction of his birth certificate in an article headed 'James MacDonald Ramsay. Leicester MP's name and origin—can he sit in Parliament?' According to his diary, the article gave MacDonald 'hours of the most terrible mental pain' (Marquand, 191). The second episode hurt even more. It came a year later, when the Lossiemouth golf club voted by seventy-three to twenty-four to expel him from membership, on the ground that he had endangered the character and interests of the club. He never played on the Lossiemouth links again.

The British Kerensky In public MacDonald preserved a stoic front, but the scars were not difficult to detect. Political isolation accentuated the suspiciousness, defensiveness, and self-righteousness which were among the most unfortunate legacies of his fatherless childhood. He became ever more sceptical of human nature in the mass, ever more aware of the fickleness of public moods. ('In youth one believes in democracy', he noted in a diary entry shortly after the war ended; 'later on, one has to *accept* it,' (PRO, MacDonald papers, diary, 20 March 1919).) He also became more convinced both of his own rectitude and of his opponents' lack of moral fibre. In particular, he became steadily more contemptuous of the pro-war trade-union MPs who, as he saw it, had allowed themselves to become 'pliable putty' in the government's hands (Marquand, 195). When Arthur Henderson, his successor as chairman of the parliamentary party, joined the coalition cabinet which Asquith formed in May 1915, the breach between the pro- and anti-war factions widened further. When Henderson took office in the much more bellicose Lloyd George coalition of December 1916, an act which provoked MacDonald to make his first public attack on the majority's good faith, an outright split seemed to be on the cards.

Yet within a few months the UDC's struggle began to bear fruit. The February revolution in Russia and the emergence of a regime committed to a peace without annexations or indemnities gave a much needed psychological fillip to the British anti-war left and brought MacDonald in from the political cold. 'A spring-tide of joy had broken out all over Europe', he told the ILP conference in April 1917 (*ILP Conference Report*, 1917). If his diary is to be believed, he detected a revolutionary spirit even in sober Leicester (Marquand, 208). In June 1917 he was a keynote speaker at the so-called Leeds convention of anti-war socialists, which called for councils of workers' and soldiers' delegates on the Russian model—an act which led Lloyd George to opine in retrospect that he might have become the Kerensky of a British revolution (*War Memoirs of David Lloyd George*, 1938, 2.1124).

Leeds was a detour. The real significance of the February revolution for British politics lay elsewhere. It was no longer possible to dismiss MacDonald and the UDC as disloyal eccentrics: in Petrograd their heresies were orthodoxies. Shortly after the Leeds convention the government granted him a passport to visit Petrograd and confer with the Russian leaders; though the visit was aborted in the end, the responsibility lay with the violently pro-war seamen's union, not with the government. Little by little, a change of heart took place on the pro-war right of the Labour Party, exemplified most dramatically by Arthur Henderson's resignation from the war cabinet in August 1917. Thereafter MacDonald and Henderson worked together—warily, even suspiciously, but nevertheless successfully—for a statement of British war aims on UDC lines. Relations between the pro-war trade-union wing of the Labour Party and the anti-war ILP remained uneasy—not least because the new constitution which the party adopted in February 1918 gave the unions even more power within it than they had enjoyed before. On the central issue of the peace terms, however, the two factions gradually came together. When a more or less united Labour Party went in to the general election of 1918 with an essentially UDC foreign policy, MacDonald and Henderson could both claim the credit. But MacDonald was the true victor.

In the short run the victory availed him little. The Lloyd George coalition won a crushing majority in the election. Though Labour emerged as the largest opposition party, most of its leading figures lost their seats. In Leicester West MacDonald received only a paltry 6437 votes against the coalitionist candidate's 20,510. At fifty-two he was out of parliament, his career apparently in ruins. The parliamentary party was dominated by his opponents. With Lenin in power in Petrograd, and a victors' peace soon to be promulgated in Paris, the values for which he had stood since his earliest days in politics seemed to be in universal retreat.

Recovery As so often, opinion was more volatile than it looked. The hot blood of total war soon cooled. Lloyd George's popularity faded. The Versailles settlement lost its glitter. Cracks appeared in the coalition's imposing façade. The political realignment which had begun in August 1914, and of which Lloyd George's election victory was a delusive epiphenomenon, proceeded apace. By 1922

MacDonald was in parliament again, and leader of the opposition to boot. It was one of the most remarkable political recoveries in twentieth-century British history. It was made possible by a seismic shift of political allegiances, reflecting the split in the Liberal Party, the growth in trade-union membership, and the upsurge of class-consciousness which the war had brought in its train. But it would not have occurred without MacDonald's determination, flair, and personal magnetism.

Three interwoven themes dominated MacDonald's political life in these years. He played a leading part in a long, complex, and ultimately successful struggle to construct a post-war successor to the social-democratic second international of pre-war days. He consolidated his hold on the ILP, contriving with masterly ambiguity to combine the roles of darling of the left and hammer of the communist international which the Bolsheviks set up in March 1919. Slowly but surely he fought his way back into the inner councils of the Labour Party and re-established himself as its natural leader. In each of these arenas he adopted broadly the same line, expressed most powerfully in one of the most effective polemics he ever wrote: a 30,000 word defence of parliamentary socialism against the communists' call for a dictatorship of the proletariat (J. R. MacDonald, *Parliament and Revolution*, 1919). Lenin, MacDonald insisted, offered 'a tyranny to end all tyrannies', as dangerous a notion as the militarists' war to end all wars. The communist short cut to socialism was a blind alley. If the society concerned was ripe for socialism, socialists could win power through the ballot box; if it was not, they could not ripen it by force. In essence, this was his old evolutionary argument in a new guise. Yet the flavour and tone were subtly different. 'Before the war', he confessed in a booklet of 1918, 'I felt that what was called "the spirit of the rebel" was, to a great extent, a stagey pose. It is now required to save us' (MacDonald, *Socialism after the War*, 17). His campaign against communism was conducted in that spirit. He fought on two fronts, not one—against the former pro-war socialists to his right as well as against the communists on his left—and his attacks on the tyrannous intolerance of the third international were coupled with bitter criticisms of the feebleness and pusillanimity of the second. In a diary entry of July 1920 he noted that he had spent the preceding year 'calling on the ILP to be strong & upon the Labour Party … to forget the purple bondage & the flesh pots of Egypt which were its reward for the sorry part it played in the war' (MacDonald papers, PRO). That was the leitmotif of his politics on the long road back to Westminster. It epitomized the mood of a labour movement seething with discontent, yet wedded to democratic norms.

MacDonald suffered one bad setback before his recovery was complete. In January 1921 ill health forced the veteran Labour MP Will Crooks to resign his seat in Woolwich East. The national executive invited MacDonald to stand at the by-election, and after some initial hesitations he duly did so. After a bitter campaign—trams passing through Woolwich were covered with placards asking 'A Traitor for Parliament?'—he was narrowly defeated. He had already been selected as prospective candidate for the south Wales seat of Aberafan, however, and his exalted oratory and air of brooding mystery were ideally suited to a political culture still saturated with the influence of the chapel. In 1918 Aberafan, like most of Wales, had been a Lloyd George fief, but when the general election came in November 1922 MacDonald was elected with a majority of 3207.

Eight days after the general election the new parliamentary party met to elect its officers for the coming session. In normal circumstances the incumbent chairman, J. R. Clynes, a Manchester Labour MP since 1906 and minister of food control in the closing stages of the wartime coalition, could legitimately have expected to be re-elected. But the circumstances were far from normal. The Labour Party had increased its representation by more than eighty seats. Most of the leading figures of the pre-war years were back, together with an impressive array of newcomers. One hundred of the 142 Labour members belonged to the ILP, where attacks on the parliamentary leadership's alleged feebleness were almost *de rigueur*. Before the parliamentary party met, the ILP group agreed to nominate MacDonald for the chairmanship. He was elected with sixty-one votes to Clynes's fifty-six. The ILP paper the *New Leader* commented enthusiastically that MacDonald would 'infallibly become the symbol and personification of the party' (*New Leader*, 24 Nov 1922).

Prime minister MacDonald's overarching aim as leader of the opposition was to complete the realignment which had begun during the war: to elbow the Liberals aside and make Labour the permanent alternative to the Conservatives in a new two-party system. Three corollaries followed. He had to position his turbulent and inexperienced party as the natural custodian of the liberal tradition of ordered progress through the ballot box. He had to show that it was now a potential party of government, capable of exercising power, not in an already egalitarian society, contemptuous of class distinctions, but in the class-divided, hierarchical, and deferential Britain of the 1920s. And he had to do all this without stifling the *élan* and sense of mission which had accompanied its mushroom growth since pre-war days.

MacDonald's first big test came sooner than he could have expected. In November 1923 the new Conservative prime minister, Stanley Baldwin, suddenly called a general election. The Conservatives lost their majority, but with 259 seats they were still easily the largest party in the House of Commons. Labour, with 191 seats, was comfortably ahead of the barely reunited Liberals with 159. The prospect of a Labour government provoked extravagant expressions of horror in the more excitable sections of the political class, and a revealing mixture of incredulity and apprehension in much of the labour movement, but when Asquith, the Liberal leader, made it clear that he would not keep the Conservatives in office or join a coalition to keep Labour out, horror and apprehension both subsided. In the new year Baldwin presented a king's speech to the new parliament and lost the vote on the address. On 22 January 1924 he left office and MacDonald

kissed hands as prime minister. The king complained about the singing of the 'Red Flag' and the 'Marseillaise' at a Labour victory demonstration at the Albert Hall a few days before. MacDonald told him that if he had tried to stop it there would have been a riot, and that it had required all his influence to prevent his followers from singing the 'Red Flag' in the House of Commons itself when Baldwin fell.

Labour's musical tastes had little bearing on the government's conception of its task. The cabinet was one of the least experienced of modern times (though it was more so than Blair's in 1997). After some hesitation MacDonald decided to be his own foreign secretary. The Treasury went to Snowden, and the Home Office to Henderson. Thus, of the three great offices of state, only one was held by a former minister. Inexperienced though it was, however, the government bent over backwards to demonstrate its respectability. On the left, some thought it should ride for a fall, introduce socialist legislation which the opposition parties would be bound to vote down, and call a general election on ground of its own choosing. To MacDonald such ideas were anathema. As he saw it, he and his colleagues were in office not to defy or even to subvert the established order, but to infiltrate it—to show that they could carry on the king's government with as much authority and competence as the old parties had displayed, and in so doing to consolidate their lead over the Liberal Party. To do that they had to persuade a sceptical country that a Labour government was now part of the normal scheme of things, and they had to behave accordingly. There is no evidence that any minister quarrelled with this assertive moderation. The alternative of riding for a fall had no friends on Labour's front bench. MacDonald's decision to give high office to two non-Labour dignitaries—the former Liberal minister Viscount Haldane, who became lord chancellor, and the lifelong Conservative Lord Chelmsford, who became first lord of the Admiralty—provoked no discernible opposition. The cabinet was united in deciding to invoke emergency powers to quash a threatened transport strike in London. Curiously, MacDonald's most contentious concession to respectability was his willingness to appear at Buckingham Palace arrayed in the traditional splendour of court dress. But the mutterings which could be heard in the more Cromwellian sections of the Labour Party were not echoed in the cabinet.

One reason was that respectability paid dividends. Public opinion polls had not then been invented, but the evidence of by-elections and press comment suggests that the government's stock rose fairly steadily during its first six months. There were some bad parliamentary hiccups at the beginning, largely owing to lack of co-ordination in the cabinet, but after MacDonald instituted a regular weekly meeting of an inner group of senior ministers matters improved. Snowden's tax-cutting budget, proudly described by its author as 'the greatest step ever taken towards the Radical idea of the free breakfast table', was popular as well as adroit. So were the housing policies followed by the Clydeside health minister John Wheatley.

Despite frequent ministerial meetings the government discovered no domestic solution to the endemic unemployment problem, but it was not alone in that. It shared the prevailing view that economic recovery at home depended on a revival of British exports, and believed that the key to such a recovery lay in a return to normality in international relations, above all in the relationship between France and Germany, a goal which could hardly be reached overnight. It failed to reach an understanding with the Liberals, on whose support its tenure of office depended, partly because MacDonald could not help resenting the patronizing tone which Asquith habitually adopted towards him and his ministers, but chiefly because the Liberal and Labour parties were inevitably in competition for the role of principal anti-Conservative party. As a result, the government could never count on getting its business through and had to live, in parliamentary terms, from hand to mouth. But when the house rose for the summer recess in July 1924 few doubted that MacDonald and his party had both added to their stature.

Foreign secretary The credit was due to MacDonald the foreign secretary's assiduous pursuit of normality abroad even more than to MacDonald the prime minister's conduct of affairs at home. When Labour entered office an ugly international crisis, springing from the reparations burden imposed on Germany at Versailles, had just entered a new phase. In January 1923 French and Belgian troops occupied the Ruhr in response to a German default on deliveries of coal and timber. The occupation dealt a savage blow to the fragile Weimar republic and provoked a German campaign of passive resistance as well as a catastrophic fall in the value of the mark. Eventually the reparations commission set up two expert committees to find a way of reconciling Germany's formidable obligations under the peace settlement with its diminished resources. The first, chaired by the American General Dawes, started work a week before the change of government in Britain. MacDonald had consistently denounced the 'madness' of the Versailles settlement (*Labour Leader*, 22 May 1919) and the diplomatic approach it reflected. Now the onus was on him to show that his alternative was more effective as well as more uplifting: that a foreign secretary operating in the spirit of the UDC could succeed where Balfour and Curzon had failed.

It was not an easy task. Behind the reparations crisis lay profound conflicts of interest and perception which could not be wished out of existence. MacDonald had to devote seven months to a bravura display of personal diplomacy before the French were persuaded to leave the Ruhr on terms which Germany and Britain could accept. Though the appearance of the Dawes report in April was a big step forward, it was not until the final stage of a major, and frequently stormy, international conference in London from 16 July to 16 August that a settlement was reached. In a genial closing speech MacDonald told his fellow negotiators that the agreement they had reached 'may be regarded as the first Peace Treaty, because we have signed it with a feeling that we have turned our backs on the terrible years of war and war mentality' (*Proceedings of the London Reparations Conference*, 2.7–8). The boast was hard-won. At the time, it also seemed well founded.

After London, however, the government's fortunes turned down. At the beginning of September MacDonald made a triumphant appearance at the League of Nations assembly at Geneva. In another bout of intensive diplomacy he and the French prime minister, Edouard Herriot, hammered out a joint resolution that paved the way for the so-called Geneva protocol—a comprehensive plan for a system of collective security, linking compulsory international arbitration, disarmament, and sanctions, which might have sucked the poison out of Franco-German relations and tied Britain in to a new concert of Europe. But it was a false dawn. The protocol was never implemented; and well before it was agreed the opposition parties were joining forces to turn Labour out. A miscellany of leading Liberals, including both Asquith and Lloyd George, joined the Conservatives in furious denunciation of the government's hard-won and recently concluded commercial and general treaties with the Soviet Union. Meanwhile MacDonald's prestige and morale had both been dented by the discovery that the biscuit manufacturer Alexander Grant—who had been awarded a baronetcy in the honours list—had previously given him the use of a chauffeur-driven Daimler and the interest on £30,000 worth of McVitie and Price preference shares. Adding to the government's woes, the political world was awash with rumours that the attorney-general, Sir Patrick Hastings, had been improperly subject to instructions from the cabinet when he had decided, in mid-August, to withdraw his earlier decision to prosecute John Campbell, a decorated war veteran and temporary editor of the Communist paper the *Weekly Worker*, for incitement to mutiny.

The rumours were false: Hastings had consulted the cabinet, as he had every right to do, but the decision to withdraw the prosecution was his own. Unfortunately, the cabinet minutes did not make this clear; and the relevant minute leaked out. On that less than awesome rock the government fell. In answer to a private notice question when the house resumed after the summer recess, MacDonald said untruthfully and provocatively that he had not been consulted either about the institution or about the withdrawal of the proceedings against Campbell. Understandably, the opposition parties, whose leaders realized that he had misled the house, insisted on a debate. The Conservatives put down a motion censuring the government for its handling of the affair. More insidiously, Asquith put down an amendment calling for a select committee to investigate. The Conservatives voted against their own motion and for the Liberal amendment, which was duly carried by a majority of 168. The king then granted MacDonald a dissolution, and one of the most savagely fought general elections of the century began.

Red letter and direct action The Conservative Party and press did their best to make sure that the campaign was dominated by the twin themes of the Campbell case and the Russian treaties, and that both merged into the simpler theme of the red peril. When the *Daily Mail* published the now notorious 'Zinoviev letter'—almost certainly a White Russian forgery, purporting to have been sent to the British Communist Party by Grigory Zinovyev, the president of the Comintern, and instructing the British Communist Party to set up cells in the army and navy and to intensify the struggle for ratification of the Russian treaties—it looked as if they had succeeded. For the embattled and hard-pressed Labour Party the Foreign Office's reaction was even more embarrassing than the letter itself. After only perfunctory checks on the letter's authenticity, it prematurely released the text of a draft protest to the Russian chargé d'affaires in London, thus giving the impression that the letter was genuine, despite MacDonald's well-merited suspicion that it was not. MacDonald had seen the draft protest, and had substantially rewritten it in the intervals between Aberafan electioneering, but he had carefully refrained from initialling it; when it was published he was 'dumbfounded' and appeared both evasive and incoherent (PRO, MacDonald papers, diary, 31 Oct 1924; *'A Most Extraordinary and Mysterious Business': the Zinoviev Letter of 1924*, foreign and commonwealth office, 1999; Marquand, 381–7). He was not alone. Labour's campaign was thrown into confusion as unbriefed Labour candidates improvised hasty and uncoordinated responses. Yet the political impact of the affair can easily be exaggerated. The Conservatives won a crushing majority, but Labour also gained votes, despite losing forty seats. The real victims were the Liberals, who lost 119 seats and saw their share of the vote plummet from 29.6 per cent to 17.6 per cent. The realignment which MacDonald had tried so hard to push forward was not quite complete, but the goal of a new two-party system was clearly in sight.

MacDonald's achievement was soon under threat. As so often after losing office, Labour shifted to the left. The ILP fell increasingly under the influence of the flamboyant and intransigent Clydeside group of MPs, who thought socialism would come through stepping up the class war and radicalizing the masses. Clifford Allen, the party chairman, was an ally of MacDonald's, but in November 1925 he resigned from the chairmanship, giving the Clydesiders effective control of the NAC. Still more ominous from MacDonald's point of view was a parallel movement among the trade unions. The early post-war years had seen a rising tide of union militancy. It had subsided when the post-war boom broke in 1921, but even before the 1924 election there had been signs that the pendulum of union opinion was swinging back towards militancy, and after the election it swung much harder. The threat of wage cuts in the coalmines, which dominated the industrial scene in the summer of 1925, gave it a further push. So did the events of 'red Friday', 31 July 1925, when the government surrendered to the unions' threat to embargo the movement of coal, and announced a six months' subsidy to the mining industry, together with a royal commission to inquire into it. Despite misgivings among some trade union leaders, the tide continued to

flow towards direct action until it reached its high-water mark in the general strike of 1926.

MacDonald watched these developments with horrified dismay. Direct action was the negation of the parliamentary socialism he had preached since his twenties. Apart from his philosophical objections to it, he believed that in a conflict between the state and organized labour, the state would be sure to win. But, like Neil Kinnock during the miners' strike in 1984–5, he could not risk a head-on attack on the unions. From the sidelines he gave occasional coded warnings of the dangers they were courting, but during the run-up to the strike he was little more than a spectator; and he was careful to make no public criticism of the miners, despite his growing contempt for their general secretary, the wayward firebrand A. J. Cook. At the Memorial Hall meeting of trade union executives which decided to issue strike notices MacDonald made what Walter Citrine, the TUC general secretary, later described as a 'glorious speech' (W. Citrine, *Men and Work*, 1964, 163). Once the strike began, McDonald's main objectives were to keep the party together and to maintain its morale. He pleaded for negotiations, defended the miners, and kept his criticisms of the unions to himself.

Labour and the nation MacDonald's circumspection paid dividends. The failure of the strike, the crushing defeat which the government and the coal owners proceeded to inflict on the miners, and the passage of the Trade Disputes Act (1927), which made sympathetic strikes illegal, transformed the climate of working-class opinion. The union pendulum swung back to parliamentary politics. MacDonald still had to walk warily. For him, the moral of the general strike was plain. As he put it soon after the strike, it was now clear that industrial action could be used for political purposes only 'with arms in our hands' (*Forward*, 22 May 1926). But he did not want to rub salt into the wounds of potentially friendly union leaders or to exacerbate the inevitable demoralization of the rank and file; though a wounding note of 'I told you so' occasionally crept into his public comments, he was generally content to let the facts speak for themselves. His reward was a *rapprochement* between the industrial and political wings of the movement which gave him a seemingly unassailable hold on the Labour Party at large.

MacDonald's ascendancy over it sprang from deeper sources as well. Towards the end of the 1924 parliament the German Social Democrat Egon Wertheimer thought MacDonald had become 'a legendary being—the personification of all that thousands of downtrodden men and women hope and dream and desire. Like Lenin ... he is the focus for the mute hopes of a whole class' (Wertheimer, 176–7). No doubt one reason was that his ideological imprecision, with its fluctuating mixture of immediate pragmatism and distant hope, mirrored his party's. His commanding presence, handsome features, and uplifting oratory also deserved part of the credit. In his early thirties the *Labour Leader* had judged MacDonald to be one of the two best-looking men in the ILP (*Labour Leader*, 21 April 1900). A quarter of a century later the dashing, matinée-idol good looks of his early manhood had given way to a statesmanlike, yet still romantic, *gravitas*, accentuated by greying hair and deeply etched lines on an expressive face. A similar combination of *gravitas* and romanticism marked the stirring yet elusive platform style which led the Glasgow ILP-er P. J. Dolan to call MacDonald the 'Gladstone of Labour' (K. Middlemas, *The Clydesiders*, 1965, 79) and Molly Hamilton to see him as one of those great speakers 'who can seize and play on the nerves of their hearers' without engaging in exaggerated histrionics (Hamilton, 123). MacDonald's expansive gestures and exalted language were already a little old-fashioned; and it is worthy of note that he was slower than Baldwin to exploit the new media of radio and film (Williamson, *Baldwin*, 78–86). But Labour was in many ways an old-fashioned party. In the inner circle of Labour MPs criticisms of MacDonald's aloofness and brusqueness were rife, but he dominated the party's annual conference as no leader, with the possible exception of Neil Kinnock in the 1980s, has dominated it since.

As so often, however, the ILP was an odd man out. On the eve of the general strike its annual conference had adopted a famous resolution calling for 'socialism in our time'. Ironically, it was based on the report of a party commission chaired by MacDonald's old friend J. A. Hobson, advocating a minimum wage to mop up unemployment (the so-called 'living wage'). MacDonald welcomed the 'living wage' report, but 'socialism in our time' was a different matter. The terminology was a deliberate challenge to the gradualism he had preached for a quarter of a century; the content threatened his entire strategy as party leader. On a deeper level he believed that its proponents were betraying the true vocation of the ILP. Socialism would come, he insisted again and again, only when society had been persuaded to 'think socialistically' (*Forward*, 16 April 1927). The true task of the ILP was to preach 'economic justice made kinetic by reason of human idealism', not to immerse itself in the everyday 'patching and puttying', which should be left to the Labour Party (ibid., 25 July 1927, 11 Aug 1928). But his attempts to halt the ILP's leftward turn got nowhere. When the general election came in 1929 his old base was unmistakably hostile territory.

Compounding the challenge from the left was a more threatening challenge from the centre. In 1926 Lloyd George succeeded Asquith as leader of the reunited but virtually comatose Liberal Party, into which he managed to breathe new life. The most spectacular result was the celebrated Liberal 'yellow book' of 1928 setting out an ambitious programme of state-led economic development. Early in 1929 this was followed by the equally celebrated campaign document *We can Conquer Unemployment*. MacDonald's claim that Labour was now the true repository of the liberal tradition was called into question, while the realignment which had seemed on the verge of completion in 1924 began to look problematic.

MacDonald's response to the Lloyd George challenge resonated powerfully with the constituency for which they were both in competition. He devoted the lion's share of his parliamentary and electioneering energies to disarmament and foreign policy, the issues about which

he cared most and on which his reputation stood high and Lloyd George's low. He largely determined the content and approach of Labour's election programme *Labour and the Nation*, a blend of moralism and scientism, well calculated to appeal to progressive middle opinion. Unlike the government, however, he shrewdly refrained from attacking the Liberal programme head-on. Instead he dismissed it as an electioneering stunt. Lloyd George, he insisted, was 'an old performer at familiar tricks'. His promise to conquer unemployment was on a par with his promise in 1918 to build homes for heroes; the 'yellow book' was a modern equivalent of 'Joanna Southcott's box' (Marquand, 463–4, 486–7). Electorally, at least, his judgement was vindicated. When the election came in May 1929 Labour emerged with 288 seats—a net gain of 137—making it the largest party in the Commons. The Conservatives were down to 260. With 57 seats the Liberals were still a poor third. MacDonald, who had left Aberafan for the much safer seat of Seaham Harbour, was returned with a majority of more than 28,000. This time Baldwin resigned before meeting parliament. On 5 June 1929 MacDonald became prime minister for the second time.

Hopes dimmed As in 1924, MacDonald hated cabinet-making. Particularly hateful was Henderson's refusal to take charge of unemployment policy and his insistence on taking the Foreign Office instead. As a result, cabinet responsibility for unemployment went to J. H. Thomas, MacDonald's original choice as foreign secretary. In spite of his defeat at Henderson's hands, however, MacDonald's mood was noticeably more confident than in 1924. Trade seemed to be reviving; neither of the opposition parties had any reason to force an early election; Labour could reasonably hope for a honeymoon of some months in which to prepare for another election at a time of its own choosing, preferably with some demonstrable successes to its credit. In the closing years of the old parliament MacDonald had warned repeatedly of the dangers of a naval race between Britain and the United States, and he had fought the election largely on the ticket of peace and disarmament. It must have seemed to him that the best way to achieve dramatic short-term success was to concentrate his energies on naval disarmament, and it is not surprising that this became the central theme of the opening months of his second term.

It embroiled MacDonald in long and complex negotiations, first with the United States alone and then with the French, Italians, and Japanese as well. At the end of September he paid a much acclaimed visit to the United States, the first such visit by a prime minister in office, which paved the way for an Anglo-American agreement effectively conceding the American demand for parity. This was followed by a difficult five-power conference in London, at which the French and Italians proved immune to all MacDonald's displays of charm and moral earnestness. The conference ended in April 1930 with a limited five-power treaty, covering all the conference participants, within which was contained a more far-reaching three-power agreement between the British, Americans, and Japanese. As MacDonald was the first to recognize, the achievement was only partial, but he could legitimately boast that his government had done more for disarmament than any of its predecessors.

The political benefits were disappointing. By April 1930 the worst depression of the century was well under way; and the intricacies of naval disarmament paled into insignificance beside the rising tide of unemployment. The political repercussions were as alarming as the figures themselves. Early in February a cabinet committee had been set up to examine the so-called Mosley memorandum—a sparkling if breathless paper by Sir Oswald Mosley, chancellor of the duchy of Lancaster and supposedly an aide to J. H. Thomas, calling for a loan-financed programme of public works on the familiar lines set out in the Liberals' election manifesto, coupled with a drastic overhaul of the machinery of government. Psychologically and intellectually MacDonald was ill prepared for the storm which was now about to break. The evolutionary socialism he had preached since his twenties was based on the premise that capitalism was, in its own terms, a success. It was not easy for him to come to terms with the notion that it was in crisis. On a different level, he was instinctively suspicious of grandiose schemes of the sort that appealed to Mosley and Lloyd George. Yet he did not object in principle to the economic thinking underpinning the memorandum, and he was no friend to the orthodoxies against which Mosley was in revolt. The quasi-Keynesian economics espoused by Mosley were not far removed from the under-consumptionist teaching of his old friend and mentor J. A. Hobson; and it was no accident that his economic adviser was Hubert Henderson, a protégé of Keynes and part author of the Liberals' unemployment policies. Moreover, he liked Mosley, admired his energy, and wanted to keep him in his government. He seems to have hoped that committee investigation would produce a compromise acceptable to all concerned.

If so, he had reckoned without the Treasury. The cabinet committee was chaired by Snowden, once again chancellor of the exchequer; its report was an uncompromising expression of Treasury thinking. Mosley's administrative proposals, it declared, 'cut at the root' of cabinet government. His proposals for loan-financed public works would disrupt the capital market, undermine local democracy, and have little or no effect on the unemployment figures. MacDonald still sought compromise, but to no avail. On 20 May Mosley resigned to carry the fight first to the parliamentary party and then to the party conference. A week later the Conservatives more than doubled their majority in a by-election in Central Nottingham. The government survived a censure motion in the House of Commons by twenty-nine votes, but there was no doubt that it had been severely damaged.

Marking time Its troubles were only beginning. Unemployment continued to mount. By December 1930 2,725,000 people were out of work; by June 1931 the figure had risen to 2,735,000, against the seasonal trend. Three broad approaches were on offer. Snowden and the Treasury clung to Gladstonian orthodoxy: balanced budgets, free trade, and the gold standard. Mosley, Lloyd George,

and part of the Liberal Party were for loan-financed public works, centred on an ambitious programme of road building. The Conservative Party and a widening swathe of business opinion, eventually supported by Keynes and Hubert Henderson, were for protection.

MacDonald was appalled by the bleak negations of his chancellor. Under pressure from the Liberals he was even prepared to flirt for a while with the public works alternative. But the flirtation was short-lived. The Treasury was joined in its opposition by the Ministry of Transport, which argued powerfully and passionately that it was impossible to build roads on the necessary scale in time to make a significant difference to the unemployment total. The combination of Treasury mandarins and Ministry of Transport engineers was too strong to beat; and at the end of September 1930 the cabinet explicitly decided that nothing more could be done through public works. Protection fared no better. MacDonald favoured it himself, but the only senior minister who agreed with him was J. H. Thomas, by now a broken reed. Snowden and Henderson were both passionately opposed. So was Willy Graham, the president of the Board of Trade and, as such, the departmental minister most closely involved. The Liberals stuck to their free-trade tradition; most Labour MPs would probably have been reluctant to break with theirs. Not surprisingly MacDonald shrank from a fight on the issue; and in the absence of a lead from the top the protectionist alternative languished in limbo. With public works and protection both ruled out, only Treasury orthodoxy was left. But although Snowden accepted the Treasury doctrine, and would have liked nothing better than to apply it in practice, the balance of forces in the Labour Party made it impossible for him to make the cut in the soaring total of unemployment insurance expenditure which it logically entailed.

Thus, all roads were blocked. The government was too orthodox for new approaches, but not orthodox enough to make the old ones work. It talked deflation, but failed to control a swelling deficit. In autumn 1930 exasperation with the prevailing *immobilisme* fuelled a good deal of speculation about the need for a national government to overcome the crisis. On the whole, however, it emanated from the fringes of politics rather than from the summit; the Conservative leadership, by now on course to win a party majority in the next election, had no interest in an arrangement which would, at best, postpone a single-party Conservative government, and at worst prevent it altogether (Williamson, *National Crisis*, 133–62). MacDonald blew hot and cold, but on the whole his response was hostile. Though he appears to have mentioned the possibility to Baldwin, he beat a hasty retreat when Baldwin produced the flimsy objection that protection ruled it out. The policy log-jam remained, but talk of a national government to break it died down. Meanwhile, MacDonald, like other beleaguered heads of government, before and since, found some respite from domestic crisis in overseas affairs. From November 1930 to January 1931 he presided with his usual panache over a contentious, but in the end surprisingly successful, round-table conference designed to pave the way for eventual Indian self-government. When Baldwin went out of his way to support him, in defiance of the die-hards in his own party, he could legitimately congratulate himself on a striking vindication of the consensus politics he had practised for most of his life.

Despite the steady rise in unemployment, the omens for domestic politics seemed to be improving too. In September 1930 the cabinet had decided that it would try to make a deal with the Liberals over electoral reform, and then recommend it to the party executive. Earlier in the year MacDonald had vigorously opposed such a deal on the grounds that it would give the Liberals a 'permanent corner on our political stage' (PRO, MacDonald papers, diary, 3 Feb 1930) and his opposition had carried the day. But as the economic skies darkened he changed his mind. In December 1930 the cabinet agreed to include the alternative vote in an electoral reform bill as the price for sustained Liberal support. Thereafter, co-operation between the two left-of-centre parties gradually became closer. The Liberals abstained on the government's bill to amend the Trade Disputes Act (1927), ensuring it a second reading; the government accepted a Liberal motion calling, in effect, for a watered-down version of their familiar policy of loan-financed national development; joint committees on which Liberal spokesmen sat alongside Labour ministers were set up to look at telephone development, rural housing, and town planning. By spring 1931 MacDonald, Lloyd George, and their leading colleagues were holding weekly talks. Though the evidence is fragmentary, it seems clear that by July MacDonald was seriously exploring the possibility of an early Liberal–Labour coalition, with himself as prime minister and Lloyd George in a major cabinet post (Marquand, 583–603; Williamson, *National Crisis*, 229–52).

Crisis MacDonald's explorations came too late. Following the collapse of the great Austrian bank the Kreditanstalt in May 1931, a spiralling international financial crisis rapidly undermined confidence in sterling. At the end of July the May committee, set up under Liberal pressure to inquire into possible cuts in government spending, forecast a budget deficit of £120 million and recommended sweeping economies, including a cut of nearly £67 million in unemployment spending. Pressure on sterling redoubled. By 7 August the Bank of England was warning that the reserves were almost exhausted. It was clear that the parity could be held only if confidence were restored, and that the only way to restore confidence was to make heavy cuts in government spending. Keynes thought the parity was past saving and urged the suspension of gold convertibility as the first step towards the creation of a new currency union. But his was a lone voice. The Treasury, the bank, and even Keynes's protégé Hubert Henderson all thought it essential to defend the parity, and all drew the inescapable conclusion that expenditure would have to be cut on May report lines.

There is no direct evidence of MacDonald's reactions when the crisis broke, but there is not much doubt about his priorities. Though he had often been exasperated with Snowden's negativism, he was at one with his chancellor on the need for drastic expenditure cuts. As far back as December 1930 he had gone out of his way to promise Snowden his backing 'in any proposal you make to reduce expenditure'; and it is clear from his diary that he had no patience with the majority cabinet view that spending on unemployment was sacrosanct (Marquand, 587–8). Not only was he a cutter by instinct; he also believed that, if the cabinet flinched from making the cuts that were needed to save the pound, Labour's claim to be a party of government would be destroyed.

At first it looked as if MacDonald would have his way. When the May report appeared, the cabinet set up an economy committee, consisting of MacDonald, Snowden, Arthur Henderson, Thomas, and Graham. It recommended tax increases of £89 million and spending cuts of £78.5 million, £43.5 million of which was to come from spending on unemployment insurance. This was less than the Treasury had asked for, but Snowden seems to have been content with the package. When it reached the cabinet, however, it was picked apart. The cut in unemployment spending was whittled down to around £20 million, and the global expenditure cut to £56 million. These figures were far too small to satisfy the Bank of England or, *a fortiori*, foreign sterling holders. They were also too small to satisfy the government's Liberal allies, without whom no package would get through the House of Commons. It soon became clear, however, that they were too big for the TUC. In the evening of 20 August a deputation from the general council told the economy committee that it would not 'acquiesce in new burdens on the unemployed' and rejected spending cuts altogether. For MacDonald, as he put it in a disgusted diary entry, 'it was practically a declaration of war' (PRO, MacDonald papers, diary, 20 Aug 1931).

It was a war which MacDonald was determined to fight. For thirty years he had believed that the sectional interests of the trade unions came second to the Labour Party's view of the national interest: that citizenship came before class. He had fought trade-union domination in the name of political principle during the war. As he saw it, he now had to fight the same battle all over again. 'If we yield now to the TUC', he noted belligerently the day after the meeting with the general council deputation, 'we shall never be able to call our bodies or souls or intelligences our own' (PRO, MacDonald papers, diary, 22 Aug 1931, referring to 21 August). As during the war, however, Henderson reacted in precisely the opposite way. Before the TUC's *démarche* he had grudgingly accepted the economy committee's package, including the cuts in unemployment spending. Now he swung into opposition.

The story of the next three days was, above all, the story of a battle to the death between MacDonald and Henderson for the soul of the 1929 government. MacDonald fought with all his old diplomatic skill, backed by a kind of dour passion. In a series of complex negotiations he persuaded the Bank of England and the opposition parties to accept an economy package of £76 million, including a 10 per cent cut in unemployment benefit. Against all the odds, he then won a cabinet majority for it of eleven to nine. But Henderson and an unknown number of his fellow dissidents made it clear that they would resign rather than accept the majority view. It was clear that the government could not carry on. In the evening of Sunday 23 August, at the end of one of the most poignant cabinet meetings of the century, MacDonald was authorized to inform the king that all members of the cabinet had placed their resignations in the prime minister's hands.

National saviour At that stage MacDonald assumed that he would leave office along with his colleagues, that he would then resign from the Labour leadership and announce his support for cuts in unemployment benefit, and that Baldwin would form a Conservative government, presumably with Liberal support. Already, however, he had come under pressure—first from Neville Chamberlain and Herbert Samuel, and then from the king—to stay on as prime minister at the head of a national government. Their case was hard to refute. A potentially ruinous confidence crisis was well under way. A national government, headed by MacDonald, would stand a much better chance of halting it than would a Conservative government or even a Conservative–Liberal coalition. It is clear from his diary and from contemporaneous notes made by his son Malcolm and his daughters Sheila and Ishbel that MacDonald was profoundly reluctant to accept that logic (Marquand, 627–37). In the end, however, his resistance crumbled. At a Buckingham Palace meeting with the king, Baldwin, and Samuel in the morning of 24 August he agreed to form a temporary national government to restore British credit. That done, there would be a general election fought on normal party lines.

These expectations were soon belied. The cabinet was genuinely non-party. There were four Labour ministers: MacDonald himself, Snowden, Thomas, and Sankey, the lord chancellor. The Conservatives also had four places, and the Liberals two. Only a tiny number of Labour MPs followed MacDonald (partly, perhaps, because he made virtually no attempt to win Labour support), but the government's policies were as consensual as possible. Its economy programme, presented to parliament on 11 September, involved a total cut of £70 million, less than the total which had been accepted by a majority of the outgoing cabinet. Thirteen million pounds came from the 10 per cent cut in unemployment benefit which the Labour dissidents had rejected; with only trivial variations, the rest of the package was the old £56 million programme which the entire Labour cabinet had endorsed. None of this, however, cut any ice with the Labour Party, now free from the restraints of government. MacDonald and Snowden were heckled fiercely in the house, while Labour's front-bench spokesmen came close to denying that they had accepted even the £56 million programme. That was bad enough for foreign confidence, and worse followed. On 15 September units of the Atlantic fleet at Invergordon refused to muster, in protest against the government's pay cuts. After a brief recovery when the National Government was formed, sterling had started to weaken again. Now the drain accelerated. On 20 September the cabinet bowed to the inevitable and decided to leave the gold standard after all.

Devaluation transformed the political landscape. Demands for an early election had already come from sections of the Conservative Party. Now they intensified. At first MacDonald dragged his feet, but when the Labour Party executive voted to expel all members and associates of the National Government his resistance evaporated. Parliament was dissolved on 7 October, and after a three-week campaign the government swept back into power with a majority of nearly 500. The Labour vote fell by 1.5 million; with fifty-two seats (only forty-six won by officially endorsed Labour candidates) it had fewer MPs than in 1918. MacDonald's personal fate mirrored his government's. He had insisted on fighting his existing Seaham Harbour seat. Against what most observers had considered to be the odds at the start of the campaign, he was returned with a majority of nearly 6000.

Few victories can have had a more bitter taste. MacDonald had been the prime mover in crushing the party to which he had devoted his political life. He, more than anyone else, had embodied the national appeal which had given the Conservatives an overwhelming majority over all parties. For his pains he had become their prisoner. He was surprisingly successful in fending off Conservative place-seekers. Four of the twenty members of the new cabinet belonged to the minuscule National Labour group. There were five Liberals and only eleven Conservatives. But Conservative restraint over place was not matched by restraint over policy. They had campaigned on their historic ticket of protection; they had won a decisive majority for it; they also believed that it held the key to economic recovery. They were understandably determined to use their victory to carry it through—if not under a national government, then under a purely Conservative one—and no one could doubt that they would sooner or later do so.

The implications for MacDonald were both painful and paradoxical. He was no longer a free-trader, if he ever had been. On the merits of the case he sided with the Conservatives. But he knew that his government's shaky claim to non-party status, and, by the same token, his own claim to embody a national consensus, rested on the continued adhesion of the free-trade Liberals, led by Herbert Samuel. For the best part of a year he did his best to square the circle, arguing that the real issues lay elsewhere, that the fiscal question was one of practicality not ideology, and that in any event it mattered less than the government's survival. At first he seemed to be succeeding. In January 1932 the free-trade ministers agreed to a remarkable compromise whereby they were allowed to speak and vote against government legislation imposing a tariff, while still holding office. In the end, however, he had to admit defeat. At the Ottawa conference in the summer of 1932 the British delegation, led by Baldwin, agreed to a far-reaching scheme of imperial preference. This was more than the free-traders could stomach. Samuel and his followers resigned, accompanied by Snowden. MacDonald was left behind at the head of a virtually Conservative government, albeit with an increasingly implausible national label.

Labour scapegoat From then on MacDonald's prime ministership was a long diminuendo. His health had already begun to deteriorate. In 1932 he had two operations for glaucoma, one on each eye. They were both successful, but each had to be followed by weeks out of circulation. Altogether he was out of action for two months in the first half of the year. He was increasingly plagued by insomnia and depression, and, worse still, by the consciousness of failing powers. His memory began to fail, and he found it increasingly difficult to concentrate. Increasingly he dreaded his appearances at the dispatch box and did his best to avoid the public platform: with good reason, since his speeches were often virtually incomprehensible. By June 1934 his eyes were once again giving trouble. His doctors diagnosed a 'retrograde movement' and persuaded him to take three months' holiday. While he was away his morale improved, but once he was back in harness his mental and physical decline accelerated again. To judge by his photographs, MacDonald at sixty-five, though obviously worn and tired, still had the erect bearing and more than a trace of the personal magnetism of his earlier years. At seventy he looked an exhausted old man, years older than his real age, peering uncertainly into the camera as though not quite sure what was happening (Marquand, 693–700).

Physical and mental decline went hand in hand with emotional strain. MacDonald may have been blackmailed by a mysterious Viennese woman, known as Frau Foster and variously described as a 'cocotte' and a 'vamp', with whom he had had an affair in the 1920s and to whom he had written compromising letters (Roskill, 3.162; Marquand, 700–01). In the Labour Party he was the obvious scapegoat for the failures of the 1929 government and the disasters of 1931. Most of his old followers vilified him as a vain and treacherous social climber seduced out of his allegiance by the flattery of the governing class, a charge reinforced by the publication of Philip Snowden's acidulous autobiography alleging that, after the formation of the National Government, MacDonald had told him that 'tomorrow, every duchess in London will be wanting to kiss me' (Snowden, 2.957). Almost certainly, the remark was meant ironically, but Snowden was in no mood to appreciate irony and nor were his Labour readers. Some Labour people also believed that MacDonald had deliberately plotted to form the National Government, and had taken advantage of, or perhaps even engineered, the financial crisis in order to do so: that, in Sidney Webb's acid phrase, he had been the 'author, producer and principal actor' in a drama whose *dénouement* he had foreseen long in advance (S. Webb, 'What happened in 1931: a record', *Political Quarterly*, Jan–March 1932). Only a tiny handful of old Labour friends remained on speaking terms with him. The reporter, Sidney Campion, recalled later that in the House of Commons Labour MPs behaved towards MacDonald like hounds 'straining at the leash to kill' (Marquand, 680).

No cold-blooded and duplicitous traitor would have reacted as MacDonald did. Outwardly, he maintained a belligerent front. In letter after letter he denounced the new Labour leaders as cowardly time-servers who had abandoned the socialism of old days. It is clear from his diary, however, that their attacks drew blood: 'The desolation of loneliness is terrible', he noted in a particularly poignant entry late in 1932. 'Was I wise? Perhaps not, but it seemed as though anything else was impossible' (PRO, MacDonald papers, notebook, 27 Dec 1932). For some years he corresponded with a spiritualist medium, Grace Cooke, who sent him messages from his dead wife, but it is doubtful whether the correspondence did much to mitigate his desolation. For a while friendship with the flamboyant Conservative hostess Lady Londonderry was a more potent solace. MacDonald and she had got to know each other in the 1920s, and had discovered a mutual interest in highland folklore, but although he scandalized some of his followers by going to her parties at Londonderry House, the relationship did not become an important part of his life until the early 1930s. For some years after 1931, however, he was deeply attached to her. Yet even then, their friendship was only a palliative for his sense of isolation, not a cure.

Downward path In spite of failing powers and deteriorating health, it would be wrong to picture MacDonald as a mere figurehead with no influence on events after 1931. He rarely intervened in domestic affairs, and when he did so the record suggests that his interventions were mostly ineffectual. Yet the mere fact that he was still prime minister, and that the Conservatives would have been damaged politically if he had broken openly with them, gave him a kind of negative influence, at least until his three months' absence in 1934. On foreign policy, moreover, he played a leading role, both in shaping and in executing government policy, for most of the 1931 parliament. Anthony Eden, a junior minister at the Foreign Office from 1931 until his elevation to the foreign secretaryship in 1935, wrote later in his memoirs that when MacDonald spoke on foreign affairs in cabinet, he was conscious 'of the touch of the master' (Eden, 23). In 1932 MacDonald led the British delegation at two major international conferences: the long-awaited, but ultimately ill-starred disarmament conference which opened at Geneva in February, and the apparently successful Lausanne conference on reparations in June and July. He spent more time at the Geneva disarmament conference in the early months of 1933, and presided over the long-drawn-out but abortive world economic conference in London in the summer of that year. He also presided over the disarmament committee of the cabinet, which gradually extended its scope until it became a kind of inner cabinet for foreign and defence policy. As late as April 1935 he led the British delegation to the ill-fated Stresa conference, at which the British, French, and Italians fruitlessly discussed how best to respond to Hitler's violations of the peace settlement.

These, however, were milestones on a downward path. Conference diplomacy, of the sort that MacDonald had excelled at in the 1920s, was too tender a plant for the harsher climate of the 1930s. By 1932 the Weimar republic was tottering; in January 1933 Hitler came to power. The liberal, neo-Gladstonian assumptions which had underpinned MacDonald's foreign policy since UDC days were in ruins. There is no way of telling how far his slow, grudging, and painful realization that it was time to look for alternative assumptions contributed to his physical and mental decline, but it must have been an additional source of stress. What is clear is that the deterioration in his health accelerated. In a diary entry before leaving for Canada in June 1934 he noted apprehensively that he was 'more troubled by my overworked brain than my overworked eyes' (PRO, MacDonald papers, diary, 19 June 1934); no sooner had he returned to London in October than his headaches and insomnia returned, while his eyesight started to deteriorate again. There were complaints of his 'rambling incoherence' in cabinet; and by early 1935 it was clear both to his doctor, Sir Thomas Horder, and to the cabinet secretary, Maurice Hankey, that he could not carry on as prime minister for much longer (Marquand, 761–3).

The rest of the story is soon told. MacDonald struggled on as prime minister until summer 1935, but with diminishing influence on events. On 7 June, shortly after the jubilee of George V, he and Baldwin swapped offices: Baldwin became prime minister and MacDonald lord president of the council. In October Baldwin called a general election; after a bitter campaign, in which he was frequently denied a hearing, MacDonald lost Seaham Harbour to his old protégé Emmanuel Shinwell, with only 17,882 votes to Shinwell's 38,380. He stayed on as lord president, however, and in February 1936 he was elected for the Scottish universities in a convenient by-election. He held office for another seventeen months—a forlorn and almost forgotten figure, with no patronage and no following, who looked increasingly like a ghost from a vanished era. The end of his ministerial life came on 28 May 1937, a couple of weeks after the coronation of George VI, when Baldwin and he left office together. Baldwin, Neville Chamberlain (Baldwin's successor), and the king each offered him a peerage, but on each occasion he declined. He spent most of the summer pottering about in Lossiemouth, and on 5 November he and his daughter Sheila set sail in the liner *Reina del Pacifico*, for a visit to South America. On 9 November 1937 MacDonald died of heart failure, following a game of deck quoits. His body was returned to Britain on the naval cruiser, HMS *Apollo*. After a public funeral in Westminster Abbey and a private service in Golders Green, his ashes were taken by train to Lossiemouth and buried on 27 November in the grave at Spynie churchyard overlooking the Moray Firth where Margaret's had been buried twenty-six years before.

Shifting perspectives When MacDonald died his reputation was in tatters. The Conservatives had never taken him to their hearts, and for most of them he had become a pathetic, if not ludicrous, encumbrance. In the labour movement he was seen as, at best, a vain and weak-willed tool of the governing class, and at worst as a scheming traitor who had deliberately plotted to do down his party

and his cause. Death sometimes brings rehabilitation; in MacDonald's case it brought more disdain. In 1938 his former parliamentary private secretary, L. MacNeill Weir, published a savagely critical biography of him (*The Tragedy of Ramsay MacDonald*). A year later Lord Elton, Malcolm's former tutor and a National Labour peer, published the first of what was to have been a two-volume biography (*Ramsay MacDonald*), but although this gave a favourable and perceptive account of MacDonald's career up to 1919, it did not redress the balance. MacDonald appeared, thinly disguised, as the opportunistic anti-hero of Howard Spring's novel, *Fame is the Spur* (1940), while the memoirs and biographies of other Labour politicians were almost all hostile to him, albeit in varying degrees. By the early 1950s the part he had played in creating and cementing the Labour alliance in the first place, and then in establishing the Labour Party as the main anti-Conservative party in the state, had been forgotten. On the left he was remembered only for his alleged perfidy in 1931. On the right he was barely remembered at all.

Though he remained a bogey for some Labour left-wingers until well into the 1970s, the next twenty-five years brought a change of perspective. Labour historians discovered that MacDonald had contributed more to the formation and growth of the early Labour Party than a later generation had realized (Frank Bealey and Henry Pelling, *Labour and Politics, 1900–1906*). Reginald Bassett, a former Labour supporter who had followed MacDonald in 1931, published a meticulous, blow-by-blow account of the 1931 crisis, demolishing the plot theory which had become the received wisdom of the left (*1931: Political Crisis*). At a lunch in the House of Commons in October 1966, commemorating the centenary of MacDonald's birth, Harold Wilson, the first leader of the Labour Party too young to have played an active part in politics when the National Government was formed, paid him a warm and compassionate tribute. Eleven years later the present writer published the first biography of MacDonald to be based on his voluminous private papers. It was self-consciously revisionist in aim and perspective. It stressed his ideological consistency, his political skill, and his pivotal role in the growth of the Labour Party and the politics of inter-war Britain. He was depicted as 'a decent and likeable man who, for most of his term of office, led his party with conspicuous skill'. The true moral of his career was not that he had betrayed his convictions, but that he had been too slow to jettison cherished assumptions in the face of changing realities (Marquand, 795).

There was an irony in that judgement which was not apparent when it was made. The revisionism of the 1970s was soon to need revising. Implicit in the judgement that MacDonald should have been quicker to jettison the assumptions he had cherished in the past was the equally time-bound assumption that it would have been better to take Keynes's advice in 1931 than that of the Bank of England: that in following the nostrums of pre-Keynesian orthodoxy MacDonald was in thrall, albeit understandably, to a dogma which the Keynesian revolution was soon to supersede. But although it was still possible to view the events of 1931 through an essentially Keynesian prism in the mid-1970s, it soon ceased to be possible. In the harsher world of the 1980s and 1990s it was no longer obvious that Keynes was right in 1931 and the bankers wrong. Pre-Keynesian orthodoxy had come in from the cold. Politicians and publics had learned anew that confidence crises feed on themselves; that currencies can collapse; that the public credit can be exhausted; that a plummeting currency can be even more painful than deflationary expenditure cuts; and that governments which try to defy the foreign exchange markets are apt to get their—and their countries'—fingers burnt. Against that background MacDonald's response to the 1931 crisis increasingly seemed not just honourable and consistent, but right.

The 1980s and 1990s taught more complex lessons as well. The 1981 split in the Labour Party, the formation of the Social Democratic Party and later of the Liberal Democrats, the accompanying upsurge in third-party voting, Neil Kinnock's revisionist policies as Labour leader, the emergence of Tony Blair's 'new labour' party, and the ideological overlap between the anti-Conservative forces all invited comparison with the fluid and sometimes schismatic politics of MacDonald's day. The stable party loyalties and ideological commitments of the post-war period were as much a thing of the past as the Keynesian economics of the same period. In this climate MacDonald's willingness to defy the dictates of party loyalty seemed less a proof of perfidy than a portent of things to come. On a deeper level, labour and social democratic parties everywhere had learned—often painfully—that the constraints of global capitalism had become much tighter than they had been in the post-war period, and that the scope for ameliorative reformism had narrowed correspondingly. These discoveries threw new light, not just on MacDonald's actions in the supreme crisis of his career, but on the cautious and non-sectarian progressivism he had preached since his twenties. Here too he was no longer an honourable, but misguided prisoner of outworn orthodoxy: he was the unacknowledged precursor of the Blairs, the Schröders, and the Clintons of the 1990s and 2000s.   DAVID MARQUAND

Sources D. Marquand, *Ramsay MacDonald* (1977); repr. (1997) · MacDonald papers, PRO · Lord Elton [G. Elton], *The life of James Ramsay MacDonald* (1939) · J. R. MacDonald, *Margaret Ethel Macdonald* (1912) · J. R. MacDonald, *Socialism and society* (1905) · *DNB* · M. A. Hamilton, *Remembering my good friends* (1944) · P. Snowden, *Autobiography* (1934) · R. Bassett, *1931: political crisis* (1986) · F. Bealey and H. Pelling, *Labour and politics, 1900–1906* (1958) · E. Wertheimer, *Portrait of the Labour Party* (1929) · J. R. MacDonald, *What I saw in South Africa* (1902) · J. R. MacDonald, *The Zollverein and British industry* (1903) · J. R. MacDonald, *Parliament and revolution* (1919) · P. Williamson, *Baldwin* (1999) · P. Williamson, *National crisis and national government: British politics, the economy and empire, 1926–1932* (1992) · S. W. Roskill, *Hankey, man of secrets*, 3 vols. (1970–74), vols. 2–3 · A. Eden, *The Eden memoirs* (1962) · G. Cooke, *Plumed serpent: a story of reincarnation and the ancient wisdom* (1942) · L. MacNeill Weir, *The tragedy of Ramsay MacDonald* (1938) · L. Thompson, *The enthusiasts* (1971) · *CGPLA Eng. & Wales* (1938)

Archives BL, corresp. rel. to Codex Sinaiticus, Add. MSS 68923–9 · BLPES, misc. corresp. and papers · BLPES, corresp. and papers rel. to the ILP · Durham RO, letters · JRL, corresp. and papers · Labour History Archive and Study Centre, Manchester, corresp.

and papers · NL Scot., albums of letters of condolence on his wife's death, misc. letters and papers · NL Scot., originals of political articles by him · NL Scot., misc. corresp. and tribute to T. Hardy · NL Scot., misc. corresp. mainly with P. Geddes · PRO, corresp. and papers, 30/69 · PRO, Cabinet corresp. and papers, CAB 127/282–95 | Birm. CA, corresp. with C. J. Simmons · BL, corresp. with Lord Cecil, Add. MS 51081 · BL, corresp. with Lord D'Abernon, Add. MSS 48926–48931 · BL, corresp. with A. Mansbridge, Add. MS 65253 · BLPES, letters to W. John · BLPES, letters to T. Nodin · BLPES, letters to H. Bryan · BLPES, corresp. with the Fabian Society · BLPES, corresp. with E. D. Morel · Bodl. Oxf., corresp. with H. A. Gwynne · Bodl. Oxf., corresp. with G. Murray · Bodl. Oxf., corresp. with Lord Ponsonby · Bodl. Oxf., corresp. with H. Rumbold · Bodl. Oxf., corresp. with Lord Sankey · Bodl. Oxf., corresp. with Lord Simon · Bodl. Oxf., corresp. with A. Zimmern · Bodl. Oxf., letters to E. Marvin · Bodl. RH, corresp. with F. E. Colenso · CAC Cam., official corresp. with E. Phipps · CAC Cam., letters to R. G. Vansittart · CKS, corresp. with J. H. Thomas · CUL, Templewood Papers, corresp. with S. Hoare · CUL, letters to H. Young · Cumbria AS, Carlisle, letters to Lord Howard of Penrith · Harvard U., Houghton L., letters to W. Rothenstein · HLRO, letters to D. Lloyd George · HLRO, corresp. with H. Samuel, memoranda · HLRO, corresp. with Lord Beaverbrook · HLRO, corresp. with J. St Loe Strachey · JRL, corresp. with C. P. Scott, FO 800 · Leics. RO, letters to the Leeson family · Lpool RO, corresp. with earl of Derby · NA Scot., corresp. with Lord Lothian · NL Scot., letters to S. Gordon · NL Scot., letters to Sir A. Grant · NL Scot., corresp. with Lord Haldane · NL Scot., letters to J. K. Annand · NL Scot., letters to H. P. Macmillan · NL Wales, corresp. with Lloyd George · Norfolk RO, corresp. with H. W. Massingham · PRO, corresp. · PRO NIre., letters to Lord Londonderry · PRO NIre., corresp. with Lady Londonderry · Queen's University of Belfast Library, letters to O. Kyllmann · Ruskin College Library, Oxford, corresp. mainly with J. M. Middleton · U. Aberdeen L., letters to J. Leatham · U. Birm. L., special collections department, corresp. with W. H. Dawson · U. Glas. L., Archives and Business Records Centre, corresp. with first Viscount Weir · U. Lpool, department of special collections and archives, corresp. with J. B. Glasier · U. Newcastle, Robinson L., corresp. with W. Runciman · U. Newcastle, Robinson L., corresp. with C. P. Trevelyan · UCL, letters to K. Pearson

Likenesses W. Small, two pencil drawings, 1889, Scot. NPG · B. Stone, photograph, 1907, NPG · S. J. Solomon, oils, *c.*1912, NPG · G. C. Beresford, photograph, *c.*1920, NPG · W. C. Dongworth, miniature, *c.*1920–1930, NPG · O. Edis, photographs, *c.*1920–1930?, NPG [*see illus.*] · W. Rothenstein, sanguine drawing, 1923, Man. City Gall. · W. Stoneman, photograph, 1923, NPG · B. Partridge, pen and ink caricatures, 1923–31, NPG; repro. in *Punch* · M. Beerbohm, caricature drawing, 1924, Man. City Gall. · D. Low, pencil caricature, *c.*1926, NPG · A. McEvoy, oils, *c.*1926, Scot. NPG · print, 1926 (after D. Low), NPG · E. J. Walters, oils, 1929, NMG Wales · P. Angus, oils, 1930–39, NPG · J. Lavery, oils, 1931, NPG · Central Press Photos Ltd, double portrait, photograph, *c.*1932–1934 (with Lord Londonderry), NPG · J. Epstein, bronze bust, 1934, NPG · A. Wysard, pencil and gouache, 1936, NPG · M. Beerbohm, pencil, ink, and watercolour caricature, Columbus Gallery of Fine Arts, Ohio; chalk study, NPG · T. Cottrell, cigarette card, NPG · J. Epstein, bronze bust, Scot. NPG · J. Lavery, group portrait, oils (*House of Commons, 1924*), Art Gallery and Museum, Glasgow · L. M. Mayer, miniature, NPG · A. P. F. Ritchie, cigarette card, NPG · J. J. Tissot, lithograph, NPG; repro. in *VF* (1 April 1876) · cigarette card (after unknown artist), NPG

Wealth at death see confirmation, 19 March 1938, *CGPLA Eng. & Wales*

MacDonald, Ranald. *See* MacDhomnuill, Raonuill (*b.* 1728, *d.* after 1807).

MacDonald, Ranald (1756–1832), vicar apostolic of the highland and western districts, was born at Edinburgh, the son of Ranald MacDonald (*fl. c.*1714–*c.*1756) of Fersit and Margaret MacDonald of Cranachan. He received his education in the Scots College at Douai, and after ordination returned to Scotland in 1780. He was first stationed in Glen Gairn, Aberdeenshire; after two years he was transferred to Lochaber. In 1785 he was sent to Glen Garry, and in 1805 to South Uist, where he remained until 1820.

MacDonald succeeded Dr Aeneas Chisholm as vicar apostolic of the highland district, his brief to the vicariate, and see of Arindela *in partibus infidelium* being dated 24 August 1819. In 1827 he became the first vicar apostolic of the newly created western district of Scotland. He was blind in later life, and died at Fort William on 20 September 1832. Initially buried at Fort William, his body was later moved to the Cille Choreil cemetery, Lochaber, Inverness-shire.

THOMPSON COOPER, *rev.* ALEXANDER DU TOIT

Sources J. Darragh, *The Catholic hierarchy of Scotland: a biographical list, 1653–1985* (1986) · J. F. S. Gordon, *Ecclesiastical chronicle for Scotland*, 4 vols. (1867) · 'The vicar-apostolic of Scotland', *London and Dublin Orthodox Journal*, 4 (Jan–June 1837), 120–22 · *Edinburgh Catholic Magazine*, 1 (1832–3), 192 · W. J. Anderson, 'The autobiographical notes of Bishop John Geddes', *Innes Review*, 18 (1967), 36–57 · F. Forbes and W. J. Anderson, 'Clergy lists of the highland district, 1732–1828', *Innes Review*, 17 (1966), 129–84 · C. Eubel and others, eds., *Hierarchia Catholica medii et recentioris aevi*, 8 vols. (Münster and Passau, 1913–78); repr. (Münster, 1960–82) · A. MacDonald and A. MacDonald, *The clan Donald*, 3 vols. (1896–1904) · W. M. Brady, *The episcopal succession in England, Scotland, and Ireland, AD 1400 to 1875*, 3 vols. (1876–7)
Archives Scottish Catholic Archives, Edinburgh, corresp.

Macdonald, (John) Sandfield (1812–1872), lawyer and politician in Canada, was born on 12 December 1812 at St Raphael West, in Glengarry county, Upper Canada, the eldest of the five children of Alexander Sandfield Macdonald, of the clan Ranald, and his wife, Nancy Macdonald (*d.* 1820/21), a distant cousin of her husband. His father had emigrated to Canada as a child in 1786. Sandfield, as he was generally known, took a slow route to a law career. He rarely attended school, and twice ran away from home, before becoming a store clerk in Lancaster and then in Cornwall. At the age of twenty he entered the Eastern District grammar school in Cornwall, from which he graduated with top honours. He articled for law under Archibald McLean and William H. Draper, and was called to the bar in June 1840. Later that year, in New York, he married Marie Christine Waggaman (*b.* 1824?), the daughter of George Augustus Waggaman and his wife, Camille Armault. Two sons and four daughters survived childhood.

Macdonald maintained a law office, specializing in commercial law, from 1840 to 1872. He sat as a member of parliament in the province of Canada from 1841 to 1867 and then in both the Ontario legislature and the dominion House of Commons between 1867 and 1871, a record of continuity unmatched in its day. He represented Glengarry until 1857 and Cornwall thereafter. From 1849 to 1851 he was solicitor-general in the cabinet of Robert Baldwin and Louis-Hippolyte LaFontaine. When he did not succeed Baldwin as attorney-general he settled for being speaker (1852–4); in his finest political moment he

defended the rights of legislators against a governor-general who dissolved parliament prematurely. He was appointed attorney-general (Canada West) in the famed two-day short ministry headed by George Brown and A. A. Dorion.

Macdonald was premier and attorney-general (Canada West) in ministries he formed with L. V. Sicotte in 1862–3 and with A. A. Dorion in 1863–4. During his second ministry, representation by population was an open question. Macdonald would accept ridings of equal electoral size within each section but not across the province; that is, all ridings in Canada West (Ontario) would be equal, but all would be larger than the ridings in Lower Canada (Quebec). This guarded against the majoritarian impulse implicit in representation by population, but it meant accepting a diminished role for the eastern district.

Macdonald believed he never wavered in twenty-five years as a Reformer. He steadily believed that government should help the unfortunate, that education should be extended and universal, and that governments should be frugal and economical, avoid compromises with powerful interests and interest groups, and keep promises. However, the setting shifted more than he acknowledged. He had voted against responsible government, separate schools, and confederation, all of which he came to accept and promote. But he consistently opposed innovations that undermined fundamental agreements within the constitution. He identified with minorities, and with those with least access to power.

Macdonald became the first premier of Ontario on 11 July 1867. He worked closely with Sir John A. Macdonald, who shared his belief in the need for a spirit of coalition; indeed, their 'patent combination' of Conservatives and some Reformers had won the election of 1867. Macdonald established the civil service and essentially developed Ontario policies with respect to education, land, and forestry, as well as other areas of provincial jurisdiction. With his near-namesake, he helped to clarify the limits of authority; for example, since provinces could not legislate on criminal matters, but paid the expenses, the federal government allowed revenue from fines to go to the provinces. The experience of the old province of Canada, and Macdonald's efforts for administrative and legislative reform, informed his initiatives and responses. He always favoured honest, efficient government, and the government of Ontario operated with large financial surpluses. Despite failing health he did well in the election of 1871, when some voters may have voted on federal issues, such as better rights for Nova Scotia and the events surrounding Louis Riel in Manitoba. But he lost power in the legislature, partly because the Liberals tightened their hold on independent Reformers but mostly because the Liberals used loopholes in Macdonald's election law.

Macdonald died at Cornwall, Ontario, on 1 June 1872 and was buried on 4 June at St Andrew's, Ontario. Although he was cautious about constitutional change, he was venturesome in his efforts to preserve fundamental understandings. The only politician to sit in all eight parliaments of the united province of Canada (1841–67), he understood that the legislative union survived by nourishing federal forms. No other politician of his generation was committed to the idea of the double majority as a principle that no government should pass general legislation without a majority from each of the two sections united in 1841, and no legislation of local interest should pass without the support of a majority of the legislators from the relevant section. Practically, for most politicians, since all governments were effectively coalitions, it was enough to have a broad-based majority support. Contemporaries rated him highly as an administrator, but felt he was damaged by a gruff exterior and a slowness to forgive such politicians as George Brown and Francis Hincks.

ELWOOD JONES

Sources B. W. Hodgins, 'Macdonald, John Sandfield', *DCB*, vol. 10 · B. W. Hodgins, 'John Sandfield Macdonald', *The pre-confederation premiers: Ontario government leaders, 1841–1867*, ed. J. M. S. Careless (1980), 246–314 · B. W. Hodgins and E. H. Jones, 'A letter on the reform party, 1860: Sandfield Macdonald and the *London Free Press*', *Ontario History*, 57 (1965), 39–45 · E. H. Jones, 'The great reform convention of 1859', PhD diss., Queen's University, 1971 · J. G. Harkness, *Stormont, Dundas and Glengarry: a history, 1784–1945* ([Oshawa, ON], 1946); repr. (1972) · *Proceedings at the unveiling of the statue of John Sandfield Macdonald, first prime minister of Canada in the Queen's Park, Toronto, November 16th, 1909* (1909) · W. J. Rattray, *The Scot in British North America*, 2 (1880) · J. M. S. Careless, *Brown of The Globe*, 2 vols. (1959–63) · P. Baskerville, 'Imperial agendas and "disloyal" collaborators: decolonization and the John Sandfield ministries, 1862–1864', *Old Ontario: essays in honour of J. M. S. Careless*, ed. D. Keane and C. Read (1990), 234–56 · S. J. R. Noel, *Patrons, clients, brokers: Ontario society and politics, 1791–1896* (1990) · J. D. Livermore, 'The Ontario election of 1871: a case study of the transfer of political power', *Ontario History*, 71 (1979), 39–52 · G. Martin, *Britain and the origins of Canadian confederation, 1837–67* (1995)
Archives NA Canada, MSS, MG24, B30 | NA Canada, George Brown MSS, MG24, B40 · NA Canada, John A. Macdonald MSS, MG26, A · NA Canada, MS census, 1871 · University of Western Ontario, Ontario, Josiah Blackburn MSS
Likenesses T. Hamel, group portrait, oils, *c*.1850, House of Commons, Ottawa, Canada · S. B. Waugh, oils, *c*.1850, NA Canada · *Canadian Illustrated News*, photograph, 1870, NA Canada · photograph, 1925, NA Canada, C. P. Meredith collection, PA26869 · Ewing, photograph, NA Canada · Notman & Fraser, photograph, NA Canada · W. J. Topley, photograph, NA Canada · caricature, National Library of Canada, Ottawa · photograph, NA Canada, C. B. Smeaton collection, C52349 · photograph, National Library of Canada, Ottawa; repro. in *Canadian Illustrated News* (18 Dec 1869) · photograph, National Library of Canada, Ottawa; repro. in *Canadian Illustrated News* (11 Nov 1871) · photograph, National Library of Canada, Ottawa
Wealth at death over $200,000: Harkness, *Stormont, Dundas and Glengarry*

MacDonald, Thomas Joseph Douglas [*pseud.* Fionn Mac Colla] (**1906–1975**), novelist, was born on 4 March 1906 at 9 White's Place, Montrose, the younger of the two children of Donald MacDonald, shoemaker, and his wife, Jessie Anderson Douglas. The family were Plymouth Brethren, and in accordance with their beliefs MacDonald was not baptized as an infant; he was later to react strongly against the Calvinist theological background which dominated his childhood experience. His father was a Gaelic speaker from Inverness, and in adult life MacDonald came to espouse passionately the cause of the Gaelic language; his mother was a native of north-east Scotland.

MacDonald's early years were spent in Montrose with his parents and elder sister, Elizabeth; he was educated at Montrose Academy (*c*.1917–1923) and Aberdeen Teacher Training College (1923–5), coming out first in Scotland in his final examination. In his youth he became friendly with the great Scottish poet C. M. Grieve (Hugh MacDiarmid), a near neighbour in Links Avenue, Montrose, whose Scottish nationalist convictions he shared, and who was to offer great encouragement to the literary aspirations of the precociously talented young man.

At the early age of nineteen MacDonald took up his first appointment as headmaster of Laide public school in the district of Gairloch in Ross-shire. Here he was deeply affected by the legacy of the highland clearances and by what he saw as the life-denying assaults of highland Calvinism on the Gaelic language and culture. His anger was later to find a devastating satirical outlet in his first novel, *The Albannach* (1932), the story of the frustrations (eventually in part overcome) of a young contemporary highlander. For this novel he adopted the pseudonym Fionn Mac Colla, which was retained for the remainder of his writing career.

In 1926 MacDonald left Scotland to teach for three years at the United Free Church of Scotland's college at Safed in Palestine. One of the subjects he taught was history, and while teaching it he was by his own account powerfully struck by 'two marks of historical Catholicism—its conception of man's Unity and its faculty of self-renewal' (Mac Colla, *Too Long in this Condition*, 77). On his return from Palestine he made contacts in the predominantly Roman Catholic parts of the Outer Hebrides, and it was a priest at Iochdar in South Uist who introduced him to the works of Jacques Maritain and to Thomist philosophy, an influence which (together with his passion for the classics of Russian literature) was to prove decisive in the formation of both his peculiar cast of mind and his means of expression.

In 1929 MacDonald returned to Scotland to devote himself to the Scottish movement (the National Party of Scotland had been formed the previous year), and to writing. For a year he studied Gaelic at Glasgow University, but was forced to give up through lack of funds. In 1930 he moved to Edinburgh to work on the journal the *Free Man*, and later was for a time employed as a literary adviser by the New University Society; but the 1930s were years of sporadic employment and great economic hardship. Hugh MacDiarmid arranged for the publication of *The Albannach* by the firm of John Heritage, of which he was a director, and praised the novel in print both uncompromisingly and acutely. During the years 1934–8 MacDonald was working on his second book, *And the Cock Crew*, perhaps his masterpiece, a classic novel of the highland clearances notable for its grandeur of language and conception and its acute psychological and socio-historical insights. Hopes of early publication were dashed by the outbreak of the Second World War, and the novel did not appear until 1945. Regarded by Hugh MacDiarmid as by far the most radical products of the Scottish Renaissance movement in the field of fiction, these two novels failed however to reach a wide public and remained the only two of Mac-Donald's works of fiction to be published in their entirety during his lifetime.

MacDonald was received into the Roman Catholic church at Dundee on 31 December 1935, and shortly there-after, on 24 January 1936, he married Mary Doyle (1911–1999) at St Peter's and St Paul's Roman Catholic Church, Dundee. They were to raise a family of ten children (three sons and seven daughters). Determined to bring up his family in a Catholic and Gaelic-speaking environment, MacDonald moved in January 1941 to the Western Isles as headmaster of Torlum School on Benbecula, transferring to a similar post on the island of Barra in 1946. In all he spent nearly twenty years in the Gaidhealtachd, years which he was later to describe as 'a never-ending horror of totally schizoid activity' (Mac Colla, 'Mein bumpf'), for he felt that the exigencies of his position had forced him against his will to participate in the de-Gaelicization of his pupils and to strangle his own creative and speculative talent.

Nevertheless, MacDonald continued to write. His major effort during these years was a historical novel which attempted to penetrate to the root causes of the Reforma-tion within the human soul, and to address once again the profound interrelatedness of the three developments with which he was preoccupied all his writing life: the loss of Scottish nationhood, the decline of the Gaelic lan-guage, and the ascendancy in Scotland of Reformation protestantism. Uncompromising in theme and approach, and making few concessions to the ordinary reader (much of the dialogue reflects sixteenth-century Scots usage), *Move up, John* failed to find a publisher, and a pattern of rejection and frustration was established which was to dog MacDonald for the rest of his career. Fragments were issued separately as *Scottish Noël* (1958) and *Ane Tryall of Heretiks* (1962); the complete novel was published post-humously only in 1994. Another novel from these years, a little more optimistic in outlook, depicts with acerbic psychological observation what happens in a west high-land parish when the minister starts having mystical experiences; it was published as *The Ministers* in 1979, four years after the author's death. In the 1950s he wrote one more novel, 'Facing the Muzhik' (still unpublished; National Library of Scotland, deposit 265), which, using the framework of an adventure story in the manner of John Buchan, addresses questions about the political and social development of Russia in terms of its religious his-tory; but it too failed to find an outlet.

In 1960 MacDonald left the Western Isles to settle in Edinburgh, where he taught until his retirement in 1967, living first at 40A Morningside Park and latterly, when most of his children had left home, at 51 Warrender Park Road. By this time he had abandoned any real hope of the publication of his later fiction. He did, however, publish a brilliant exposition of his philosophical ideas in *At the Sign of the Clenched Fist* (1967), and made a final attempt to propagate his religious and political convictions in the form of a lively, idiosyncratic, and opinionated autobio-graphical work, *Too Long in this Condition*, which appeared in 1975 about a month after his death.

As a personality, Tom MacDonald was complex and arresting. With a tall and distinguished physical presence and impressive facial features, he had latterly much of the look of an Old Testament prophet; and the prophet, too, was an essential ingredient of his temperament. Ebullient and witty when in good form, and a brilliant talker and anecdotalist, he could also be moody, depressed, touchy, and difficult to deal with. In his later years he was undoubtedly an embittered and frustrated man, and not without reason. As well as the three novels which remained unpublished at the time of his death, he left manuscripts of an account of the Russian prison system under the tsars, entitled 'The tsars' white hell' and dating from the early 1950s, and an untitled continuation of his autobiography. He was stung equally by the lack of any general recognition of his achievements as a writer (though his work was often highly praised by perceptive commentators), and by what he saw as his failure to com-municate to a wide public the urgency of the ideas which he so vehemently advocated. He continued committed to the end, however, taking, for instance, an active part in the upsurge of Scottish nationalist politics of the late 1960s and early 1970s.

MacDonald died of heart failure in Edinburgh Royal Infirmary on 20 July 1975. He was cremated at Mortonhall crematorium, and his ashes were buried at Mount Vernon cemetery, Edinburgh, on 24 July 1975. His wife survived him. After his death MacDonald's reputation grew stead-ily if unspectacularly, and with the publication of two of his later novels it became possible to attempt a more accurate assessment of his work as a whole. It is undoubt-edly true that the achievement of his full potential as a novelist was frustrated by the conflict between what he distinguished as the 'creative' and 'speculative' sides of his talent: his great novelistic gifts never quite overcame his penchant for abstract philosophical analysis, so that, especially in his later fiction, the ideas were imperfectly integrated into the overall structure of the novels. Yet he was a born writer with a strong and subtle intellect, whose powers of precise and telling expression exactly matched his capacity for physical and psychological observation. In spite of structural imperfections his works have a linguis-tic power and a largeness of conception which succeed in imparting an acute and original vision of the forces which have shaped Scottish reality, both historical and contemporary.   JOHN HERDMAN

Sources F. Mac Colla, *Too long in this condition* (1975) · F. Mac Colla, 'Mein bumpf', *Essays on Fionn Mac Colla*, ed. D. Morrison (1973), 11–30 · autobiographical work, NL Scot., deposit 265, item 19 · private information (2004) · personal knowledge (2004) · W. R. Aitken, 'Fionn Mac Colla's books — a check list', *Essays on Fionn Mac Colla*, ed. D. Morrison (1973), 79–80

Archives NL Scot., corresp. and literary papers, deposits 239, 265 | SOUND NL Scot., cassette tapes, deposit 265, items 42–45

Likenesses photograph, 1930–39, repro. in F. Mac Colla, *The min-isters* (1979) · H. B. Cruickshank, photographs, May 1936, priv. coll. · photograph, 1960–64, repro. in F. Mac Colla, *At the sign of the*

clenched fist (1967) · G. G. Wright, photographs, 1970–71, priv. coll. · photograph, 1970–74, repro. in D. Morrison, ed., *Essays on Fionn Mac Colla* (1973), frontispiece

Wealth at death   £8594.18: confirmation, 12 Dec 1975, *CCI*

MacDonald, Walter (1854–1920), Roman Catholic priest and theologian, was born of tenant farmer stock and baptized at Emil, Piltown, co. Kilkenny. Educated at St Kieran's College, Kilkenny, he studied for the priesthood at St Patrick's College, Maynooth, between 1870 and 1876. Ordained in that year for the diocese of Ossory, co. Kilkenny, he taught at St Kieran's before returning to Maynooth as professor of theology in 1881. He was made prefect of the Dunboyne Establishment in Maynooth, a centre for doctoral and advanced studies, in 1888.

A bishopric usually followed for professors of theology at Maynooth. MacDonald received no such preferment in his lifetime. He was a person of fiercely independent views. As an academic and theologian he was seldom out of difficulties with his superiors. MacDonald held strong political views and did not hide his allegiances even when they placed him on the opposite side to the majority of the hierarchy. He remained a controversial figure throughout his lifetime. But he was not a controversialist. Well liked as a teacher, he was held in high respect by younger priests, who also remembered him with deep affection. His episcopal and college superiors did not share that same warmth of feeling towards a cleric and an academic who never ceased to take on the authorities in defence of an academic principle. According to a contemporary, 'he fought his corner fairly and was always an amiable opponent'.

MacDonald had a strong rival in his fellow professor and future bishop of Cork Daniel Cohalan. Patrick Corish has described the latter as 'a guardian of orthodoxy, a man of the manuals' (Corish, 252). In 1894 Cohalan held that the doctrine of grace in a number of propositions drafted by MacDonald for a public disputation was clearly opposed to the faith. The college authorities took Cohalan's side and MacDonald tried to appeal to Rome. In 1898 MacDonald published *Motion: its Origin and Conservation*, which sought to examine in a scientific context the theology of grace. The Holy See condemned the book in a decree on 15 December 1899 which was not to be made public. MacDonald, willing to abjure, sought clarification of what exactly was unorthodox in his book. He was not fully enlightened. In 1903 he published *The Principles of Moral Science*, for which he received an imprimatur from the archbishop of Dublin, but he was never subsequently free from controversy. He and Cohalan were in further dispute over the thesis of one of his doctoral students in 1913.

MacDonald was a radical social thinker. He strongly disapproved of the papal condemnation of the Plan of Campaign during the Irish land wars in the 1880s, when tenants withheld rent and boycotted their landlords. He continued to support Charles Stewart Parnell after the divorce case in 1890 and the split in the Irish parliamentary party. MacDonald was an admirer of the radical trade union leader James Larkin and a supporter of his Irish Transport and General Workers' Union during the 1913 lockout. He was also a strong advocate of radical educational reform and a defender of the right of Catholics to attend Trinity College, Dublin. When the episcopal trustees of Maynooth dismissed Michael O'Hickey (of Carrick-on-Suir, co. Tipperary) from his professorship in 1908 over his views on compulsory Irish, MacDonald helped him frame his appeal to Rome, which was lost in 1910.

MacDonald continued to work in Maynooth until his death on 2 May 1920. In 1906 he founded the *Irish Theological Quarterly*. He wrote two works, *Some Ethical questions of Peace and War* (1919) and *Some Ethical Aspects of the Social question* (1920), which were published in London with an imprimatur from the archdiocese of Westminster. His autobiography, *Reminiscences of a Maynooth Professor*, edited by Denis Gwynn, was published posthumously in 1925. Of his days as a student in Maynooth he wrote:

> The independence of the life at Maynooth had a charm for me. I knew no fear, whether of professor or dean; and if called on, would have spoken truth, however unpleasant, to the College of Cardinals; for I had no notion that an honest, well-meaning man could be injured by any one, and especially by an ecclesiastic. I was very innocent; but I loved my Alma Mater, and was proud of her.   (MacDonald, 67)

Even in death he tormented his tormentors.

DERMOT KEOGH

Sources W. MacDonald, *Reminiscences of a Maynooth professor* (1925) · *WWW* · P. J. Corish, *Maynooth College, 1795–1995* (1995)
Archives St Patrick's College, Maynooth, MSS
Likenesses portrait, repro. in MacDonald, *Reminiscences*

Macdonald, William Bell (1807–1862), linguist, was born in Glasgow on 24 December 1807, the eldest son of Donald Macdonald, merchant, and his wife, Mary, daughter of William Bell of Rammerscales, near Lockerbie, Dumfriesshire. He was educated at the University of Glasgow, where he graduated BA in 1827. After studying medicine he served as surgeon in Sir Pulteney Malcolm's flagship in the Mediterranean from 1828 to 1831, and was afterwards a commissioner of supply. On 17 March 1839 he married Helen, third daughter of Thomas Johnstone of Underwood.

Macdonald was a great linguist, making a special study of Coptic, and he could translate an old Scottish song into German, Latin, Greek, or Hebrew. Macdonald published *Lusus philologici. ex museo Gul. B. Macdonald* (1851), *Ten Scottish Songs Rendered into German* (1854), and *Sketch of a Coptic Grammar Adapted for Self-Tuition* (1856). To the Ray Society in 1846 he communicated reports on zoology and botany translated from the German.

On the death of an uncle named Bell, Macdonald succeeded to the estate of Rammerscales, where he collected a large and valuable library. He was noted for 'his love of learning and his genial hospitality' (*Dumfries Herald*). For some years he represented the burgh of Lochmaben in the general assembly of the Church of Scotland. Macdonald died at 114 West Campbell Street, Glasgow, on 5 December 1862, and was buried in Dalton churchyard.

G. C. BOASE, rev. JOHN D. HAIGH

Sources *GM*, 3rd ser., 14 (1863), 390 · R. Inglis, *The dramatic writers of Scotland* (1868) · *Dumfries and Galloway Standard and Advertiser* (17

Dec 1862), 64 · BL cat. · Allibone, *Dict.* · Boase, *Mod. Eng. biog.* · bap. reg. Scot. · m. reg. Scot. · d. cert.
Archives NRA, priv. coll., corresp. and papers | Museum of Scotland, Edinburgh, letters to Sir William Jardine · NL Scot., letters to J. S. Blackie

Macdonald, William Russell (1787–1854), writer, was in early life editor and part proprietor of *Bell's Life in London*, the *Sunday Herald*, the *British Drama*, and the *Literary Humourist*, besides contributing largely to other periodicals. 'An entire change of opinion and sentiment', says his obituarist Thomas Butler, 'subsequently induced him to seek other channels for the exercise of his varied literary talents.' He wrote *Christianity, Protestantism, and Popery, Compared and Contrasted* (1829), published anonymously, and several poems, including *A Paraphrase of Dodsley's 'Economy of Human Life'* (1817) and *Fudges in Ireland* among other more ephemeral poems. But the most useful of Macdonald's productions were his numerous books for the young, to which he devoted the latter period of his life until he lost his sight. Among them were *The Book of Quadrupeds* (1838), *First and Second Lessons for the Nursery*, *Simple Tales for the Young*, and *The Child's Cheerful Companion*. Macdonald died on 30 December 1854 in Great James Street, Bedford Row, London, leaving a widow and two sons.

GORDON GOODWIN, rev. VICTORIA MILLAR

Sources GM, 2nd ser., 43 (1855), 211

Macdonell, Alastair, of Glengarry, Jacobite first Baron MacDonald (d. 1724), Jacobite army officer, was the eldest son of Ranald Macdonell of Scotus or Scothouse (d. 1694), chief of clan Macdonnell of Glengarry, and Flora MacLeod, daughter of Alexander MacLeod of MacLeod. On the death in 1680 of his cousin Aenas Macdonell of Glengarry, Lord Macdonell and Aros, Ranald Macdonell succeeded to the estate of Glengarry and the chieftainship of the Macdonnell clan. Like his father an episcopalian and a loyal supporter of the Stuarts, Alastair Macdonell raised 300–400 men during Viscount Dundee's rising in 1689 and joined Ewen Cameron of Lochiel in Lochaber. Macdonell and Lochiel were considered the leading highland supporters of the rebellion.

In June 1689 Macdonell refused the Williamite General Hugh Mackay's request to join the government side. At Killiecrankie on 27 July he was the first Jacobite leader to urge Dundee to attack Mackay's army, and carried the Stuart royal banner on the right of the first line amid a troop of thirty horsemen. The clan regiment served in the centre of the line. In battle the Glengarry Macdonnells lost more than sixteen men, including Donald, Alastair's son from his second marriage, to Lady Mary Mackenzie (d. 1726), daughter of Kenneth, third earl of Seaforth. With Mary, Macdonell had four more sons; his first marriage to Anne Fraser, daughter of Hugh, seventh Lord Lovat, also produced one daughter, Anne, who married Robert Mackenzie of Applecross.

On 24 August 1689 Macdonell signed the Jacobite bond of association at Blair Castle in which he promised to levy 200 men. On 3 January of the following year he was declared a rebel by the privy council, and by parliament on 14 June.

Despite the Jacobite defeats at Dunkeld and Cromdale, Macdonell and his father opposed other Jacobite chiefs who now sought to make accommodations with the Williamite government. The intransigence of the Glengarry Macdonnells was inspired as much by their hatred of the Campbells, including the marquess of Breadalbane, as by their loyalty to James VII. On 15 May 1691 Colonel Hill, governor of Fort William, reported that Macdonell's residence, Invergarry Castle, was being fortified with an earthwork and palisade. This show of defiance, coupled with the remoteness of Invergarry, led Sir John Dalrymple to exclude the Glengarry Macdonnells from his expedition against some of the more notorious Jacobite clans. In fact, the Macdonnells' decision to surrender on terms before 31 December 1691 eliminated any pretext to include the clan as part of the expedition, with the result that Dalrymple's forces were concentrated on the Macdonalds of Glencoe. Following the Glencoe massacre of February 1692 Macdonell was active in gathering evidence against government forces for the Scottish parliament's commission to investigate Dalrymple's actions.

The death of Ranald of Glengarry in 1694 gave Alastair Macdonell a free hand in running the Glengarry clan. However, his authority was in part circumscribed by the presence of a government garrison at Invergarry after 1692. None the less Glengarry was able to increase his income by cattle droving, which enabled him to purchase Knoydart about 1700. By 1703 Lord Tarbet reported that the 'popishly inclined' Glengarry Macdonnells could muster several hundred men (Brown, 131). On 3 August 1704 Glengarry petitioned the Scottish parliament for the removal of the garrison and for reparations. Though his petition failed, he now dropped his fanatical support of the Jacobite cause. Of all the Macdonald chiefs he alone, having allied himself with Atholl, refused to sign the engagement of 7 May 1707 in favour of the chevalier de St George (James VIII).

In the wake of the Hanoverian succession Glengarry followed a course similar to that of the earl of Mar. Thus, having sent a letter to the earl promising allegiance to George I, he was one of Mar's first adherents when he raised the Jacobite standard at Braemar on 27 August 1715. In September he led 500 men to reclaim Invergarry Castle from a seventeen-strong garrison. At the battle of Sheriffmuir on 13 November his clansmen held a position to the right of the flank and, following the death of Allan MacDonald of Moidart, chief of Clanranald, Glengarry rallied his wavering clansmen with a call for revenge. Inspired by Glengarry, the Clanranald regiment quickly routed the left wing of the duke of Argyll's army.

After Sheriffmuir Glengarry returned to Invergarry. However, he was soon a target for the newly zealous whig Simon Fraser, claimant to the chiefship of the Lovat Frasers and the title Lord Lovat. On 9 April 1716 Glengarry submitted at Inverness to the Hanoverian General Cadogan after negotiations with Robert Munro of Foulis the younger. Even so, the clan's refusal to surrender their weapons led government forces to burn down Invergarry on 24 August. As a reward for his loyalty, Glengarry was made Baron MacDonald by the Pretender on 28 September 1716 with descent limited to his heirs male. Among the Jacobite leadership, worried about retaining support after the failure of the 1715 rising, Glengarry became an exemplar of loyalty.

Two years later the duke of Argyll purchased MacDonald's debts, but came to an accommodation with him instead of claiming his lands. The Jacobite rising of 1719 placed him under suspicion, especially after he refused to appear when summoned for questioning. MacDonald claimed that he feared wrongful arrest and was preoccupied by concern for his dying wife (who lived for several more years). His allegiance to the Stuarts continued, despite his failure to join the rising of 1719. In the following year he was named by the Old Pretender as one of his trustees for managing affairs in Scotland. Lord MacDonald died at Invergarry on 28 October 1724, 'a man of profound judgment and great courage … brave, loyall and wonderfully sagacious and long-sighted' (*Memoirs*, ed. Drummond, 255, 261).

MacDonald was succeeded in the chiefship and the Jacobite peerage by his son John (*d.* 1754), who married a daughter of Colin Mackenzie of Hilton. Like his father he supported the Jacobite cause and offered to raise his clan during the rising of 1745, though he refused to go out himself. Arrested in 1746 during the pacification of the highlands, he was imprisoned at Edinburgh until he successfully petitioned against illegal imprisonment in October 1749. He died on 1 September 1754 and was survived by his eldest son, Alasdair Ruadh MacDonnell, also known as Pickle the Spy.   EDWARD M. FURGOL

Sources DNB · H. Mackay, *Memoirs of the war carried on in Scotland and Ireland*, ed. J. M. Hog and others, Bannatyne Club, 45 (1833) · *Memoirs of Sir Ewen Cameron of Lockeill*, ed. J. Drummond (1842) · *Calendar of the Stuart papers belonging to his majesty the king, preserved at Windsor Castle*, 7 vols., HMC, 56 (1902–23) · *The Jacobite attempt of 1719: letters of James Butler, second duke of Ormonde, relating to Cardinal Alberoni's project for the invasion of Great Britain on behalf of the Stuarts, and to the landing of a Spanish expedition in Scotland*, ed. W. K. Dickson, Scottish History Society, 19 (1895) · *Letters relating to Scotland in the reign of Queen Anne by James Ogilvy, first earl of Seafield and others*, ed. P. Hume Brown, Scottish History Society, 2nd ser., 11 (1915) · A. MacDonald and A. MacDonald, *The Clan Donald*, 3 vols. (1896–1904) · N. H. MacDonald, *The Clan Ranald of Knoydart and Glengarry*, 2nd edn (1995) · A. I. MacInnes, *Clanship, commerce and the house of Stuart, 1603–1788* (1996) · K. Tomasson and F. Buist, *Battles of the '45* (1962)
Archives Inveraray Castle, Argyll, Argyll papers

Macdonell, Alexander (1762–1840), vicar apostolic for Upper Canada and Roman Catholic bishop of Kingston, was born on 17 July 1762 in Scotland, somewhere between Inverness and Fort William. His father, Angus Macdonell, was a Roman Catholic; his mother, a member of the Cameron family, was a protestant, but after her husband's death she fulfilled his wish to have their son educated for the Roman Catholic priesthood. Macdonell studied at the Scots College in Paris from about 1775 to 1777 and at the newly organized Scots College in Valladolid, Spain, from 1778 to 1787. At Valladolid on 16 February 1787 he was ordained to the priesthood.

From 1787 to 1791 Macdonell served as a highland missionary priest among the Gaelic-speaking Roman Catholics of Badenoch. Troubled by the economic distress of the highlands, he helped large numbers of Roman Catholic highlanders to settle in Glasgow as mill workers. Subsequently, when the mill economy slumped, he sought new employment for them by helping to form a regiment of Roman Catholic highlanders, called the Glengarry fencibles. Macdonell was appointed the chaplain of the regiment, contrary to the anti-Catholic laws in effect at that time. The Glengarry fencibles served uneventfully in Guernsey from 1795 to 1798; in Ireland, where they were located from 1798 to 1802, they took an active part in the suppression of the rebellion of 1798. When the regiment was disbanded after the peace of Amiens Macdonell's thoughts turned to schemes to help resettle the men as emigrants in Canada.

Macdonell arrived in Canada late in 1804. After receiving the approval of his new superior, the French Canadian bishop of Quebec, he settled at St Raphaels in Glengarry county, Upper Canada. In Glengarry and Stormont counties (thus named in 1792) in this part of Upper Canada numbers of Roman Catholic highlanders, many of them Macdonells and some of them relatives of the chaplain, had settled as United Empire loyalists in the 1780s and afterwards as emigrants directly from Scotland: Macdonell was therefore among his 'own people'. According to legend and many printed sources, several hundreds of highlanders from the disbanded Glengarry fencible regiment accompanied him to Canada to settle in Glengarry county, but it seems likely, on the basis of the documentary evidence, that in fact only a limited number came to Upper Canada and very few to Glengarry county.

At the time of Macdonell's arrival there was only one Roman Catholic bishop, that of Quebec, in the British colonies of North America, and only two priests in Upper Canada. He energetically toured the province, conducting services and encouraging the founding of parishes and the building of churches. Until 1832, he said, he seldom travelled less than 2000 miles a year. At St Raphaels, which remained his home until about 1832, he built a massive stone church which was opened for services in 1826 (destroyed by fire in 1970). As a step towards establishing a diocese of Upper Canada, Macdonell was made vicar apostolic for Upper Canada in 1819 and bishop of Rhesaena *in partibus infidelium* in 1820. In 1826 he became bishop of Upper Canada with the title of bishop of Kingston or Regiopolis.

Since his early days Macdonell had enjoyed courting the well born and powerful, among them the distant but distinguished connections of his own relatively obscure family. In Upper Canada he was a friend of the governors and the ruling élite; in 1830 he was named to the legislative council of the province, and he had important friends in the North West Company of fur traders. The bishop's firm toryism, which made him a pillar of the state in all emergencies, was coupled with the belief, often emphasized in his correspondence with men of power, that it was in the public interest to maintain and increase government financial support (begun just after his arrival in Upper Canada) for the growing Roman Catholic church. In the area of Scottish settlement in eastern Upper Canada he was a friend and patron of the humble, both Roman Catholic and protestant, and was always ready to lend a helping hand in case of problems with the complicated land-granting procedures. His relations with protestants, both lay and clergy, were marked by a friendliness and tolerance underlined in the memory of later generations by the long period of sectarian strife which set in soon after his death. As a highly visible public figure, loved especially by the highland Scots, who remembered him as the Big Bishop or Easbuig Mor, he merged into folklore in his lifetime, and innumerable legends and anecdotes about him survive. Macdonell was a most eloquent and emotional letter writer whose florid romanticism of literary style captured the character of the man himself. The town of Alexandria, Ontario, which grew up around a grist mill he founded about 1817, is named after him. He died at Dumfries on 14 January 1840, on one of his return journeys to Britain. The body was buried in Edinburgh, but in 1861 was removed and reinterred on 26 July in St Mary's Cathedral, Kingston, Canada.   ROYCE MACGILLIVRAY

Sources K. M. Toomey, *Alexander Macdonell: the Scottish years, 1762–1804* (1985) · J. E. Rea, 'McDonell, Alexander', *DCB*, vol. 7 · R. MacGillivray and E. Ross, *A history of Glengarry* (1979) · W. J. Macdonell, *Reminiscences of … Alexander Macdonell* (1888) · J. A. Macdonell, *A sketch of the life of … Alexander Macdonell* (1890) · [A. Macdonell], 'A page from the history of the Glengarry highlanders', *Canadian Literary Magazine* (April 1833), 3–11 · [A. Macdonell and others], *A short account of the emigration from the highlands of Scotland, to North America* (1839) · H. J. Somers, *The life and times of … Alexander Macdonell* (1931) · M. McLean, *The people of Glengarry: highlanders in transition* (1991) · L. J. Flynn, *Built on a rock: the story of the Roman Catholic church in Kingston* (1976) · R. Choquette, *L'Église catholique dans l'Ontario français du dix-neuvième siècle* (1984) · F. A. Walker, *Catholic education and politics in Upper Canada* (1956)

Archives archdiocesan archives, Kingston · archdiocesan archives, Toronto · Scottish Catholic Archives, Edinburgh | NAM, corresp. with Lieutenant-Colonel James Chisholm

Likenesses C. Turner, mezzotint, pubd 1825 (after M. A. Shee), BM · M. A. Shee, oils, NA Canada · oils, repro. in Macdonell, *Reminiscences* · wax medallion, repro. in J. Douglas Stewart and I. E. Wilson, eds., *Heritage Kingston* (1973) [exhibition catalogue, Agnes Etherington Art Centre, Kingston, Ont., 3 June–28 Oct 1973]

Macdonell, Alexander Ranaldson, of Glengarry (1773–1828)

Macdonell, Alexander Ranaldson, of Glengarry (1773–1828), chief of clan Macdonell or Macdonnell of Glengarry and soldier, was born on 15 September 1773 at Invergarry, Inverness-shire, the first of nine children of Duncan Macdonell (c.1744–1788), chief of clan Macdonell of Glengarry, and Marjory Grant (1744–1792), of Dalvey. General Sir James *Macdonell GCB (d. 1857) was his brother. In July 1788 he succeeded as chief of clan Macdonell, one of the great branches of clan Donald, inheriting estates stretching from Glengarry in the Great Glen to Knoydart on the Atlantic coast. Traditionally his clan was Roman Catholic but the chiefly house had become protestant, allowing Macdonell to matriculate at University College, Oxford, in October 1790.

In February 1793, following the outbreak of war with

Alexander Ranaldson Macdonell of Glengarry (1773–1828), by Sir Henry Raeburn, 1812

France, Macdonell received a captain's commission to recruit a company for the Strathspey fencibles, raised by his kinsman Sir James Grant. In August 1794, while still only twenty, he received a colonel's commission to raise the first fencible regiment of Glengarry Highlanders. Recruits were drawn principally from the Glengarry estates, threats of eviction being used where persuasion failed. His earlier attempt to raise an avowedly Catholic regiment failed because of official concern about whether such a unit would be publicly acceptable. Macdonell served with his regiment on garrison duty in Guernsey until August 1796, when he resigned command. His ambition for a career in the regular army was frustrated by opposition from the commander-in-chief, the duke of York—possibly inspired by adverse reports from Macdonell's service with the Grant fencibles and by concerns about his character.

When the Glengarry fencibles were disbanded in 1802 Macdonell's failure to honour his earlier pledge to find land for the men resulted in a mass emigration to Canada led by Father Alexander Macdonell, the regimental chaplain, later first bishop of Upper Canada. In 1803 Macdonell raised the 4th Inverness volunteer battalion, later to become the 2nd Inverness-shire local militia. He continued in command until the local militia units were stood down in 1814.

Macdonell, whose Gaelic nickname Alasdair Fiadhaich (wild, or fierce, Alasdair) persuasively suggests his nature, was a man of violent disposition. In May 1798, following a quarrel at a ball, he fought a duel near Fort George, Inverness-shire, with Lieutenant Norman MacLeod of the 42nd foot. MacLeod died of his wounds and Macdonell stood trial for murder at the high court in Edinburgh in August 1798. He was acquitted, the jury's justification being his attempt to be reconciled to MacLeod before the exchange of shots. In 1807 he was found guilty of assaulting a tenant and ordered to pay £2000 damages, the court also questioning his fitness to continue as a justice of the peace and deputy lord lieutenant of Inverness-shire.

Macdonell travelled on the continent in 1799–1800 and suffered a mental breakdown in Vienna, resulting in his temporary confinement in the Narrenturm, the city's asylum. Following his return home, on 20 January 1802 he married Rebecca (1779–1841), the second daughter of Sir William Forbes of Pitsligo, an Edinburgh banker. They had thirteen children; six of their seven sons died in infancy. The family homes were at Invergarry House, near Fort Augustus; Inverie, in Knoydart; and Garry Cottage, Perth.

Macdonell of Glengarry—Mac Mhic Alasdair to give him his Gaelic patronymic—was a passionate advocate of a fast-vanishing traditional highland way of life, travelling with his 'tail'—the traditional highland chief's band of retainers. He maintained a family bard, and in 1815 founded the Society of True Highlanders, a coterie of like-minded highland grandees. His apparently genuine attachment to Gaeldom and tradition did not however preclude his clearing much of his land for the introduction of large-scale sheep farming—a policy inimical to preserving the traditional way of life for his tenants, whose numbers fell sharply during his period of control. Walter Scott, who knew him well and probably modelled the figure of Fergus MacIvor in *Waverley* on him, described him as 'a kind of Quixote in our age … He seems to have lived a century too late' (*The Journal of Sir Walter Scott*, ed. D. Douglas, 2 vols., 1891, 1.120).

Macdonell pursued a bitter dispute over the title of chief of Clanranald with Ranald George MacDonald of Clanranald—a controversy centring on the alleged illegitimacy of a sixteenth-century Clanranald. Macdonell vainly applied to the Court of Session to have Clanranald's arms declared invalid, and frequently signed himself Macdonell of Glengarry and Clanranald, asserting his house's claim to the headship of clan Donald.

Although aggressive estate management had increased his rents, an extravagant lifestyle faced Macdonell with serious financial problems. On 17 January 1828 he was travelling to Edinburgh on the steamship *Stirling Castle*, to take legal advice about his finances, when it ran aground in Loch Linnhe. Macdonell, anxious for the safety of his two daughters, who had been taken ashore, jumped overboard, struck his head on a rock, and died later that day at Inverscaddle. He was buried in the family mausoleum at Kilfinnan, Inverness-shire, on 1 February.

The trustees for his son, Æneas Ranaldson, a nineteen-year-old Edinburgh University student, found debts amounting to £80,000. Invergarry House was let; Garry Cottage in Perth was sold. In 1836 the Glengarry estate was sold, and later the adjacent Glen Quoich estate also was sold. Such was the complexity of Macdonell's finances that it was not until 1847 that an inventory of his personal estate was completed.   BRIAN D. OSBORNE

Sources B. D. Osborne, *The last of the chiefs* (2001) · N. H. MacDonald, *The Clan Ranald of Knoydart and Glengarry* (1995) · L. C. R. Macdonell, 'Glengarry and his family: some reminiscences of a Highland Chief', *Blackwood*, 153 (1893), 323–39 · L. C. R. Macdonell, 'A highland chief and his family: some reminiscences', *Blackwood*, 157 (1895), 520–36 · A. MacDonald and A. MacDonald, *Clan Donald* (1896–1904) · *DNB* · *IGI* · University College, Oxford, archives · m. reg. Scot.
Likenesses A. Kauffman, oils, 1800, Scot. NPG · H. Raeburn, oils, 1812, NG Scot. [*see illus.*]
Wealth at death debts of £80,000 · £18,650: inventory, 1847, Inverness Sheriff Court

Macdonell, Archibald Gordon (1895–1941), writer and journalist, was born on 3 November 1895 in Poona, India, the younger son in a family of two sons and one daughter of William Robert Macdonell LLD, East India merchant and chairman of the Bombay chamber of commerce, later a distinguished figure in Scotland, and his wife, Alice Elizabeth, daughter of John Forbes White, classical scholar and patron of the arts. He was brought up in Scotland and educated at Horris Hill preparatory school and Winchester College, where he was a scholar and which he left after the summer term of 1914. He served as a lieutenant in the Royal Field Artillery of the 51st Highland division in 1916–18; it was an experience which heavily influenced his subsequent life. After the war he worked with the Friends' Emergency and War Victims Relief Committee, a Quaker mission, on reconstruction in eastern Poland (1921), and on famine in Russia (1922). Between 1922 and 1927 he was on the headquarters staff of the League of Nations Union. In the general elections of 1923 and 1924 he stood unsuccessfully as Liberal candidate for Lincoln. On 31 August 1926 he married Mona Sabine Mann (*b.* 1895/6), daughter of the artist Harrington Mann; they had one daughter.

Macdonell began his career as an author in 1927 by writing detective stories, sometimes under the pseudonyms Neil Gordon or John Cameron. By 1933 he had produced nine of these, including *The Seven Stabs* (1927), *The Professor's Poison* (1928), and *The Factory on the Cliff* (1928). He was secretary of the Sherlock Holmes Society of London and attended a dinner of the American Baker Street Irregulars in New York, recounting his experiences in *A Visit to America* (1935). At the same time he contributed to the *London Mercury*, founded in 1919 by John Collings Squire. A pugnacious as well as perceptive drama critic, Macdonell at one point occupied twelve pages of the *London Mercury* with a criticism of the art of Noël Coward. His comment on *Private Lives* offers a sample of his style: 'Mr Coward's plot is the contrast between brilliant cosmopolitanism and stodgy Anglo-Saxondom, his standby is Infidelity and his device of stage-craft is the Bicker.'

Squire did not admire Macdonell's early fiction and advised him to write more from observation. There followed in 1933 *England their England*, a collection of satirical essays on English social and sporting life including an attack on fox-hunting and a description of a village cricket match against a team of authors, most of them recognizable characters in Squire's own team, the Invalids. Winning instant acclaim, it also became required reading in schools at the time.

In 1934 Macdonell capitalized on this success with another satire, *How Like an Angel* (1934), which parodied the 'bright young things' and the British legal system. The military history *Napoleon and his Marshals* (1934) signalled a new direction; although Macdonell thought it poorly rewarded financially, the book was admired by military experts, and it illustrated the range of his abilities. Between 1933 and 1941 Macdonell produced eleven more books, including a return to fiction with *Lords and Masters* (1936), *Autobiography of a Cad* (1938), and the best of his thrillers, *The Crew of the Anaconda* (1940). He also wrote a play, *What next, baby?* (1939), and a volume of short stories, *The Spanish Pistol* (1939). *Lords and Masters* and *The Crew of the Anaconda* explored the question of rearmament and fear of a holocaust; Macdonell at this period was particularly anxious to depict the way in which he perceived woman's role to have changed—from nurturer to exterminator. Macdonell's marriage to Mona Sabine was dissolved in 1937, and on 22 June 1940 he married Rose Paul-Schiff, a Viennese, whose family was connected with the banking firm of Warburg Schiff and had come to England just before the *Anschluss*.

A talented and active broadcaster since the 1930s, Macdonell contributed to the BBC's short-wave service to the empire and the United States in the summer of 1940. Part of this task, for which he was admirably suited, was to dwell on the absurdities of enemy broadcasts monitored by the BBC.

A tall, athletic man with a close-cropped moustache, he was remembered as a complex individual, 'delightful … but quarrelsome and choleric' by Alec Waugh, who called him the Purple Scot, and by J. B. Morton as a man of conviction, with a quick wit and enthusiasm and, surprising in a military man, 'a sense of compassion for every kind of unhappiness' (Vickers). His health had not been strong, however, from the time of his service in the First World War (although he was a keen sportsman). Macdonell died suddenly of heart failure in his bath at his Oxford home, 14A Broad Street, on 16 January 1941. His wife survived him. DEEDES, *rev.* CLARE L. TAYLOR

Sources H. Vickers, 'Introduction', in A. G. Macdonell, *England their England* (1986) · S. J. Kunitz and H. Haycraft, eds., *Twentieth century authors: a biographical dictionary of modern literature* (1942) · *WWW* · R. Fry, *A Quaker adventure: the story of nine years' relief and reconstruction* (1926) · personal knowledge (1993) · m. certs. · d. cert.
Archives BL, corresp. with Macmillans, Add. MS 54963 · King's Lond., Liddell Hart C., corresp. with B. H. Liddell Hart · Ransom HRC, MSS and corresp.

Wealth at death £7891 6s. 0d.: probate, 25 April 1941, *CGPLA Eng. & Wales*

Macdonell, Arthur Anthony (1854–1930), Sanskritist, was born on 11 May 1854 at Muzaffarpur in Tirhut, north Bihar, India, the elder son of Colonel Alexander Anthony Macdonell (1822–1870), of the 40th Bengal native infantry, and his wife, Margaret Jane Lachlan (b. 1831), of Rum, Scotland. He was descended from Alasdair Ruadh MacDonnell of Glengarry (c.1725–1761), who spied for the British government on Prince Charles and the Jacobites. Sent to England with his mother in 1861, he was then placed in a school in Dresden (Neustadt, 1866–9), where a boyish adventure resulted in a permanent weakness of his lower limbs, which caused him to concentrate on intellectual interests. In 1875, after four years at the Göttingen Gymnasium, he matriculated in the university of that city and under Professor Theodor Benfey began the study of Sanskrit and comparative philology. At Oxford, as an exhibitioner (1876) of Corpus Christi College, he obtained a second class in honour moderations in 1878 and a third class in *literae humaniores* in 1880. He also won the Taylorian scholarship in German (1876), the Davis Chinese scholarship (1877), and the Boden Sanskrit scholarship (1878), besides rowing in his college eight and taking an active share in the life of the college.

Macdonell worked with Professor Friedrich Max Müller and was appointed Taylorian lecturer in German in 1880 and lecturer in Sanskrit to Indian Civil Service probationers in Balliol College in 1884. He then revisited Germany for the purpose of reading with the distinguished Sanskrit scholar Professor Rudolf von Roth, and graduated PhD at Leipzig University. In 1888 he was appointed deputy to Sir Monier Monier-Williams, the Boden professor of Sanskrit at Oxford and keeper of the Indian Institute. In 1890 he married Marie Louise, youngest daughter of William Lowson JP DL, of Balthayock, Perthshire. She survived him with their two daughters. Their only son was killed in the First World War in 1915.

On Monier-Williams's death in 1899 Macdonell was appointed his successor in both offices and also in a professorial fellowship at Balliol College. Retiring in 1926, he received the title of emeritus professor, and in 1928 he was elected an honorary fellow of Balliol. His connection with Corpus Christi College had been restored in 1921 by his election to an honorary fellowship there. As keeper of the Indian Institute, Macdonell interested himself in the development of the library and the museum (the growth of which was arrested in 1911). He also administered the Max Müller Memorial Fund, which he had raised in 1900, with the object of providing for subventions, acquisitions, and publications.

Outside Oxford, Macdonell was active in various ways. Elected in 1906 a fellow of the British Academy, he represented it from 1911 to 1913 on a committee of the International Union of Academies which was concerned with promoting a critical edition of the Sanskrit epic, the *Mahābhārata*. Macdonell was a signatory to an appeal for funds, addressed to the princes and nobles of India, and subsequently, by means of an independent appeal in conjunction with a colleague, elicited contributions amounting to about £1500. He served on the council of the Royal Asiatic Society of Great Britain and Ireland and was its vice-president from 1921 to 1924. Between 1881 and 1912 he usually participated in the quasi-triennial international congresses of orientalists. At his last attendance he secured assent for an Oxford congress, which, frustrated in 1915 by the First World War, was realized in 1928, when he was no longer able to take an active part in it. Of two visits which he made to India, the first (1907–8) led to the acquisition by the Bodleian Library of a large collection of Sanskrit manuscripts and produced some hundreds of mainly archaeological photographs, subsequently presented to the Indian Institute. During this visit he developed views regarding Indian temple architecture and iconic sculpture, which he expounded in lectures (1909) before the British Academy and the Royal Society of Arts. The second visit (1922–3) was for the purpose of delivering in the Calcutta University a course of Stephanos Nirmalendu Ghosh lectures on comparative religion (published in 1925). In 1904 Macdonell represented the Sanskrit language and literature at a congress of arts and sciences held at St Louis, Missouri, and in 1912 he visited Canada. His war service (1915–20) was performed in the intelligence department of the Admiralty, for which he compiled three historical memoirs.

Macdonell received various honorary distinctions and degrees, and in 1913 he was chosen by the Bombay branch of the Royal Asiatic Society to receive its Campbell memorial medal, in which connection he propounded, at a gathering in the rooms of the society in London, the idea of an institute of research in India on the lines of the British School at Athens.

As a Sanskrit scholar Macdonell worked chiefly on Vedic. His major publications in that area were: *Vedic Mythology* (1897), *Vedic Grammar* (1910), *Vedic Index of Names and Subjects* (in collaboration with A. B. Keith, 2 vols., 1912), and editions of two Vedic texts, *Sarvānukramanī* (1886), and *Bṛhaddevatā* (2 vols., 1904). Plans for an English translation of the complete ṚgVeda were never realized; but his enthusiasm for teaching led Macdonell to produce *A Sanskrit Grammar for Beginners* (1886, an abridgement of Max Müller's work), *A History of Sanskrit Literature* (1900), *A Sanskrit Grammar for Students* (1901), *A Vedic Grammar for Students* (1916), *A Vedic Reader for Students* (1917), *A Practical Sanskrit Dictionary* (1924), and, aimed at a wider audience, *India's Past: a Study of the Literatures, Languages, Religions, and Antiquities* (1927).

As a young man, Macdonell was distinguished by an abounding vitality, which made his various activities a proverb in Corpus Christi College. He was fond of boating and camping: he published *Camping Voyages on German Rivers* (1890) and *Camping out* (1892). His humour and fondness for jocular anecdote enlivened both his conversation and the earnestness of his teaching. A stroke, following his second Indian journey, resulted in his retirement from his professorship in 1926 and seriously curtailed his powers of work. He suffered a second stroke during the summer of 1930 and died at his home, 13 Belbroughton Road, Oxford, on 28 December of that year. He was buried at Holywell cemetery, Oxford.

At the end of the twentieth century, Macdonell was remembered above all for his work on the Vedic language. Generations of students in Indology and Indo-European comparative linguistics have been introduced to the Ṛg̣Veda by Macdonell's *Vedic Reader* and *Vedic Grammar for Students*. The method of description adopted by Macdonell in his more detailed *Vedic Grammar*, which gives lists of attested forms rather than paradigms, has also ensured this book's lasting usefulness as a work of reference.

F. W. Thomas, *rev.* Elizabeth Tucker

Sources *The Times* (29 Dec 1930), 12 · L. R. Farnell, *The Times* (2 Jan 1931), 12 · *Oxford Mail* (29 Dec 1930), 5 · L. R. Farnell, *Oxford Magazine* (29 Jan 1931), 367–8 · F. W. Thomas, 'Arthur Anthony Macdonell, 1854–1930', *PBA*, 17 (1931), 415–36
Archives Bodl. Oxf., corresp. with Sir Aurel Stein · U. Edin. L., A. B. Keith MSS
Likenesses W. Stoneman, photograph, 1918, NPG
Wealth at death £367 10s. 1d.: probate, 3 Feb 1931, *CGPLA Eng. & Wales*

MacDonell, Sir Hugh Guion (1832–1904), diplomatist, was the second son of Hugh MacDonell, who as British consul-general at Algiers rendered important services. With his second wife, daughter of Admiral Ulrich, the Danish consul-general, the elder MacDonell went through a period of great personal suffering and danger during Lord Exmouth's mission and the bombardment of the town in 1816. Owing to subsequent protests of the dey against his continuance in the office of consul-general, he was pensioned off, and retired to Florence, where Hugh Guion was born on 5 March 1832, being one of a family of two sons and six daughters. The elder brother, General Sir Alexander F. MacDonell, died in 1891. MacDonell's eldest sister, married to the marqués de Las Marismas, was *dame du palais* to the Empress Eugénie and died in 1908.

MacDonell was educated for the army at the Royal Military College, Sandhurst. He joined the rifle brigade in 1849, and served for three years in British Kaffraria. He retired from the army on 11 March 1853, and entered the diplomatic service in the following year, becoming attaché at Florence. He was promoted to be paid attaché at Constantinople in December 1858, and served there until 1866, when he was transferred to Copenhagen. In 1869 he was appointed secretary of legation at Buenos Aires, was transferred to Madrid in 1872, and after three years of service there was promoted to be secretary of embassy at Berlin (1875–8) and subsequently at Rome (1878–82). After serving as chargé d'affaires at Munich from 1882 to 1885, he held in succession the appointments of British envoy at Rio de Janeiro (1885–8), Copenhagen (1888–93), and Lisbon (1893–1902). The outbreak of war between Great Britain and the two South African republics in October 1899 raised some very difficult and delicate questions between Britain and Portugal, whose port at Delagoa Bay was directly connected with the Transvaal by rail and was the principal, if not the only, channel for supplies and external communications when access through the British colonies had been closed. MacDonell's management of the discussions on these subjects was tactful and conciliatory, and contributed in no small degree to the maintenance of cordial relations.

MacDonell's services were recognized by the distinction of CMG in 1889; CB in 1890; KCMG in 1892; and GCMG in 1899. On his retirement in 1902 he was sworn of the privy council. In July 1870, while at Buenos Aires, MacDonell married Anne, daughter of Edward Lumb of Wallington Lodge, Surrey, with whom he had four sons and one daughter. He died at his home, 53 Cornwall Gardens, London, on 25 January 1904, his wife surviving him.

T. H. SANDERSON, rev. H. C. G. MATTHEW

Sources The Times (26 Jan 1904) · FO List (1905) · R. L. Playfair, The scourge of Christendom: annals of British relations with Algiers prior to the French conquest (1884)
Archives BL, corresp. and papers, Add. MS 64076 | BL, letters to Sir Austen Layard, Add. MSS 39003–39007, 39037 · Bodl. Oxf., corresp. with Lord Kimberley · Hatfield House, Hertfordshire, Salisbury MSS · PRO, letters to Lord Ampthill, FO918
Wealth at death £1364 17s. 10d.: probate, 19 Feb 1904, CGPLA Eng. & Wales

Macdonell [Macdonnell], **Sir James** (d. 1857), army officer, third son of Duncan Macdonell (d. 1788), chief of clan Macdonnell of Glengarry, and his wife, Marjorie Grant, and brother of Colonel Alexander Ranaldson *Macdonell of Glengarry, was born at Glengarry House, Inverness-shire. He entered the army as ensign in an independent company in 1793. He became lieutenant in the 78th Ross-shire Buffs on its formation in 1794, captain-lieutenant in the 101st (Colonel Fullarton's) the same year, and captain in the 17th light dragoons on 1 December 1795, in which regiment he commanded a troop for nine years. In 1804 a new second battalion was formed for the 78th Ross-shire Buffs at Fort George, near Inverness, of which Macdonell was appointed one of the majors. He was with the battalion under Sir John Moore at Hythe, and served with it in Naples and Sicily, including the campaign in Calabria in 1806 and the battle of Maida, and in the unsuccessful expedition to Egypt in 1807, where he distinguished himself by surprising a Turkish battery near Alexandria. He became lieutenant-colonel in the 78th on 7 September 1809, and was briefly appointed to the Portuguese army staff. On 21 February 1811 he was made lieutenant-colonel of 2nd garrison battalion, and on 8 August of the same year he exchanged, as captain and lieutenant-colonel, into the 2nd foot (Coldstream) Guards. He served with the 1st battalion Coldstream Guards in the Peninsula from May 1812 to the end of January 1814, including the battles of Salamanca, Vitoria, Nivelle, and Nive, and commanded the 2nd battalion in the Netherlands from May to September 1814. He was made CB on 4 June 1815.

The night before the battle of Waterloo Macdonell was sent with some companies of his regiment and the 3rd (Scots) guards to occupy the château of Hougoumont, the garden and orchard of which were defended by other companies under Alexander George Fraser, Lord Saltoun.

Macdonell received the duke of Wellington's high praise for the determination with which he held that post—the key of the duke's position—during sustained attacks by the French in the early part of the battle. On one occasion, when the French were forcing their way into the courtyard, Macdonell, who was wounded, and a small party of officers and soldiers closed the gates on them by sheer physical strength. For these services he was made KCB (20 April 1838) and received the Waterloo medal.

Macdonell served in the Coldstream Guards, of which he became regimental lieutenant-colonel and colonel in 1825, until he was promoted to major-general in 1830. He commanded the Armagh district from 1831 to 1838. He commanded the brigade of guards sent out to Canada when Lord Durham was appointed governor-in-chief there during the troubles of 1838. Macdonell succeeded to the command of the troops in Canada, which he held until promoted to lieutenant-general's rank in 1841. He became a full general in 1854, and was made GCB in 1855. He was a KCH (1837), had Austrian and Russian decorations, and was colonel in succession of the 79th (Cameron Highlanders) and 71st (Highland) light infantry. Macdonell died at 15 Wilton Place, London, on 15 May 1857.

H. M. CHICHESTER, rev. JAMES FALKNER

Sources Army List · Naval and Military Gazette (31 March 1838) · Hart's Army List · J. F. G. Ross-of-Bladensburg, A history of the Coldstream guards (1896) · A. Mackenzie, History of the Macdonalds (1881) · C. Dalton, The Waterloo roll call, 2nd edn (1904) · Boase, Mod. Eng. biog.
Likenesses W. Salter, group portrait, oils (Waterloo banquet at Apsley House), Wellington Museum, Apsley House, London · W. Salter, oil study (for Waterloo banquet at Apsley House), NPG · attrib. F. R. Say, oils, Scot. NPG · miniature, NPG

Macdonell, James (1841–1879), journalist, was born on 21 April 1841 at Dyce, Aberdeenshire, and baptized there on 2 May, the eldest son of James Macdonell (1810–1858) of the Glengarry Macdonells and Rachel Allardyce. His father was a Roman Catholic and his mother a protestant. An exceptionally bright scholar in local parish schools in Dufftown and Rhynie, the death of his father in 1858 forced Macdonell from Bell's school, Inverness, into a clerkship at Messrs Piries' paper mills. He also doubled as an excise officer, his father's former occupation. Already a precocious book reviewer, in 1858 Macdonell was introduced to the mysteries of newspapers at the Aberdeen Free Press, an advanced organ of political Liberalism. Here, as a leader writer in embryo, he formulated the main studies of his life: ecclesiastical controversies and church dialectics. He became a lifelong passionate Francophile, admiring French literature, history, and character.

Noted as an intensely earnest young man, easily carried away by his subject but blessed by a brilliant literary style, in 1862 Macdonell moved to the notoriously sectarian Edinburgh Daily Review. After less than a year he saw himself as 'pitchforked … at a ridiculously early age' (Nicoll, 97) into the editorship of the Northern Daily Express in Newcastle at £150 per annum. Circulation rose rapidly, but a buy-out by William Saunders in 1865 hastened his departure to Fleet Street. Macdonell had reacted fiercely to the decision to use syndicated news (including leaders, his own province), which had resulted in the paper's politics coming from London daily by train, in a box. In a letter to William McCombie dated 1 May 1865, the youthful editor objected to the London establishment owned by Saunders where

> a staff of journalists prepare the news of the day, and write leaders on the principal current topics. The matter thus obtained is put in type; then stereotyped … and then the blocks are sent by afternoon train to Plymouth, Hull, and other places in which the firm have papers of their own. … Not one single leading article will be written in this office. … For Mr Saunders thinks … that it is not the duty of a journalist to write strongly, or to commit his paper to the advocacy of any opinion or any principle.   (Nicoll, 108–9)

Aged twenty-four, Macdonell reluctantly declined a senior post on *The Scotsman* and thus sacrificed certain Scottish prominence in favour of an assistant editorship on the *Daily Telegraph*. Thanks to his friend Hugh Gilzean Reid (1836–1911), the northern newspaper magnate, he secured the position of 'confidential helper' to Edward Levy (1833–1916), a son of the principal proprietor. His first article in a national daily appeared on 8 July 1865, inevitably on a Scottish topic. Well-versed in philosophy and church history, Macdonell brought a real highland charge to the *Telegraph* from 1865 to 1875. Numbered by Matthew Arnold among the 'magnificent roaring of the young lions' of that paper (Nicoll, 199), his cogently argued leaders best met the needs of the day, perceived as perfectly formed literary gems in essay form. In addition to visits to war-threatened Paris in 1870 and 1871, he was at this time writing six leaders a week for his editor, another for the *Leeds Mercury*, and one for the *Levant Herald*.

Eager to find the widest possible recognition Macdonell, after a trial period beginning 26 March 1875 as a leader writer on *The Times*, parted from the *Daily Telegraph* on 4 July of that year, moving immediately to Printing House Square. Within five days he brought his graceful literary style, scholarship, keen analysis, and cultural breadth to topics as diverse as Burma, Spain, Russia, Canada, and ironclad warships. Now the consummate journalist enjoying a European audience, occasionally Macdonell's pronounced radicalism proved intrusive. His powerful material on current affairs, moral theories, and religious trends in *The Spectator*, *Fraser's Magazine*, and the *North British Review* between 1865 and 1873 had no place in 'The Thunderer'. But, unlike his previous employers whose edict against journalistic freedom was absolute, the editorial diaries kept by J. T. Delane reveal how leading articles were assigned to the writers best inclined to debate and liberal expression. Not always, however, was he in harmony with the paper's direction. Most notably, Gladstone's handling of the eastern question found sympathetic support from Macdonell, ardent to commit *The Times* to a pro-Russian line. An irate Delane had to curtail a much needed holiday with the prince of Wales at Dunrobin Castle in October 1876 to telegraph that his chief foreign affairs writer should be 'shunted to safer topics' (Nicoll, 294).

Macdonell married Anna Jemima, daughter of Daniel

Harrison, on 22 August 1871 in Beckenham, Kent; they had three sons, including Sir Philip James *Macdonell. Her sister, Agnes, in 1873 married his younger brother, Sir John *Macdonell (1845–1921), a barrister and useful contributor concurrently to *The Times* on legal and philosophical subjects. Macdonell died suddenly at his home, 78 Gower Street, London, on 2 March 1879, widely revered by his contemporaries in the media and politics. Even when ill, in the year running up to his death he wrote often for days without a break on French politics, and his posthumous volume of collected essays, *France since the First Empire* (1879), edited by his politically aware and articulate wife, admirably summarizes his power of expression and high culture. He was buried on 6 March in Beckenham, Kent.

GORDON PHILLIPS

Sources W. R. Nicoll, *James Macdonell, journalist* (1890) • [S. Morison and others], *The history of The Times*, 2 (1939) • D. Griffiths, ed., *The encyclopedia of the British press, 1422–1992* (1992) • News Int. RO, *The Times* archive • *Wellesley index* • m. cert. • bap. reg. Scot.
Likenesses H. Manesse, etching, repro. in Nicoll, *James Macdonell*
Wealth at death under £1500: probate, 7 April 1879, CGPLA Eng. & Wales

Macdonell, Sir John (1845–1921), jurist, born on 11 August 1845 at Brechin, Forfarshire, was the second son of James Macdonell (1810–1858), of the Glengarry Macdonells, and his wife, Rachel Allardyce of Dyce, Aberdeenshire; he was the younger brother of the journalist James *Macdonell. In 1852 his father, an excise officer, moved to Rhynie, Aberdeenshire, and here John Macdonell received his early education under the classical scholar, Revd George Stewart. This was followed by a year at Aberdeen grammar school. Macdonell entered Aberdeen University in 1861, and graduated with honours in classics in 1865. Although most of his boyhood was spent in a remote village, there was no lack of intellectual stimulus at home, and perhaps he owed something of his later outlook on life to the fact that his father was a fervent though tolerant Roman Catholic, while his mother and many of his father's friends were protestants.

After a brief time as a classical tutor at Leamington, Macdonell obtained an appointment on the staff of *The Scotsman*, then edited by Alexander Russel. A series of articles contributed to that journal formed the basis of his first book, *A Survey of Political Economy* (1871). Meanwhile, he had entered the Middle Temple in 1870. He was called to the bar in 1873, and in the same year married Agnes, third daughter of Daniel Harrison, of Beckenham, Kent, and niece of the writer Mary Howitt. Agnes Macdonell (who died in 1925) was herself a gifted writer and a constant helper of her husband in all his work. They had two daughters, who survived them.

During the early years of his professional career Macdonell wrote *The Land Question, with Particular Reference to England and Scotland* (1873) and *The Law of Master and Servant* (1883). In 1890 he brought out an edition of J. W. Smith's *Compendium of Mercantile Law*. He was at the time in good practice as counsel to the Board of Trade and to the London chamber of commerce, and in 1884 was appointed revising barrister for Middlesex. In these years he also began a connection with *The Times* which lasted forty years, writing reviews and leading articles. In 1889 he was made a master of the Supreme Court, and in 1912 he became senior master and king's remembrancer, retaining both these offices until the year before his death. In 1901 he was appointed Quain professor of comparative law at University College, London, and he held the chair until 1920. In 1908 he became the first dean of the faculty of law in the University of London. He was made CB in 1898, knighted in 1903, and promoted KCB in 1914.

Macdonell was known as a steady and persistent law reformer. He edited the *Reports of State Trials, New Series*, volumes 1–3 (1888–91), and in 1894 was appointed by the lord chancellor, Lord Herschell, to a committee to inquire into the civil judicial statistics. The committee recommended that when the statistics were published attempts should be made to analyse the figures, draw conclusions from them, and point out important changes. Macdonell was appointed editor of the *Civil Judicial Statistics for England and Wales*, which he compiled for the Home Office until 1919. Macdonell's statistics lived up to the aims of the committee: comprehensive statistics were complemented by extensive commentary and interpretation, informed by a good knowledge of comparative continental materials. He also assisted in the production of the *Criminal Judicial Statistics*, writing introductions to them in 1899, 1902, and 1905. He was a member of Lord Gorell's committee (1909) which inquired into the relations between the High Court and the county courts, and he gave evidence and prepared statistical returns for the royal commission on divorce and matrimonial causes (1909–12). He also gave evidence before the joint select committee of the houses of parliament on the King's Bench Division of the High Court (1909), and he gave evidence and prepared statistical materials for the royal commission on delay in the King's Bench Division (1912–13). He served on the royal commission on shipping combinations (1906–7) and signed the minority report, and he was one of the two sub-commissioners sent to take evidence in South Africa.

In November 1918 Macdonell was asked by the attorney-general, Sir Gordon Hewart, to chair a committee of experts to advise the cabinet on breaches of international law committed by German forces during the First World War, and to examine what proceedings should be taken against those responsible, particularly the Kaiser. With the war cabinet in favour of trials for those suspected of war crimes, Macdonell continued to work on the committee, collecting and sifting evidence. The legal questions involved were often difficult, and the scrutinizing of questions of fact took up an enormous amount of labour, which overtaxed his strength. In accordance with the treaty of Versailles, a list of a hundred names was drawn up by the British government at the start of 1920; however, with the Kaiser remaining in the Netherlands and with the Germans opposing trial by an international court, the proposal to hold a major series of trials for wartime outrages came to nothing, and in the end only a handful of defendants were tried by the German imperial court in Leipzig in March 1921.

Macdonell was an active member of numerous learned bodies, being a founder member of the Grotius Society, a member of the Society of Comparative Legislation (whose *Journal* he edited from 1897 until his death), and an associate (from 1900) and subsequently a member (from 1912) of the Institut de Droit International. He acted as president of the Society of Public Teachers of Law in 1912–13 and as president of the Grotius Society from 1919 to 1921, and was also at other times vice-president of the Royal Statistical Society and vice-president of the Medico-Legal Society. In 1913 he was elected a fellow of the British Academy.

Macdonell was a frequent contributor to numerous periodicals, notably the *Fortnightly Review*, the *Nineteenth Century*, and the *Contemporary Review*. He also lectured regularly, and at University College he aimed his lectures (for which he charged no fee) at a wider audience than an exclusively legal one. Through his Quain lectures he influenced legal thinkers of many nationalities, among whom were jurists from China and Japan. He had a strong belief in the rational principles of law, and looked to the development of these principles in an international context as a way to counteract what he saw as an increasing drift to fragmentation and anarchy. Macdonell died at his home, 31 Kensington Park Gardens, London, on 17 March 1921.

MICHAEL LOBBAN

Sources *The Times* (19 March 1921) · *DNB* · *British Yearbook of International Law*, 2 · O. R. McGregor, *Social history and law reform* (1981), 28–31 · C. W. Brooks, *Lawyers, litigation, and English society since 1450* (1998), 108–13
Archives BLPES, letters to James Bonar
Likenesses J. Russell & Sons, photograph, NPG
Wealth at death £34,220 2s. 8d.: administration with will, 13 May 1921, *CGPLA Eng. & Wales*

Macdonell, Sir Philip James (1873–1940), judge, was born in London on 10 January 1873, the eldest son of the journalist James *Macdonell (1841–1879) and his wife, Anna Jemima (Annie), daughter of Daniel Harrison, of Beckenham, Kent, and niece of the writer Mary Howitt. He was nephew of the jurist Sir John Macdonell. After being educated at Clifton College under J. M. Wilson he went up to Brasenose College, Oxford, as a Hulme exhibitioner at the age of seventeen. He was president of the union in 1895, after obtaining a first class in modern history in 1894. He took his BA degree in 1897, in which year he represented Oxford against Cambridge as a fencer.

In 1900 Macdonell was called to the bar by Gray's Inn (of which he was Bacon scholar), but the same year he went out to South Africa and was war correspondent of *The Times* until 1902. This proved to be a turning point in his life and thenceforth he served the British empire in three continents. Beginning his legal career in Transvaal and continuing it in Northern Rhodesia, he was secretary to the Transvaal native commission in 1903 and assistant crown prosecutor (Witwatersrand court) from 1907 to 1908. In the last-named year he was appointed public prosecutor and legal adviser to the Chartered Company in north-west Rhodesia, and from 1911 to 1918 filled the same posts in Northern Rhodesia. In 1910 Macdonell married

Aline, youngest daughter of William Drew, chartered accountant, of Glasgow; they had no children.

During a visit to England in 1911 Macdonell took his BCL degree. From 1918 to 1927 he was a judge of the Northern Rhodesia high court. Even after he had left Africa Macdonell retained to the end of his life a love of that country and an intense interest in its peoples and problems. He became chief justice of Trinidad and Tobago and president of the West Indian court of appeal in 1927, and from 1930 to 1936, when he retired, he was chief justice of Ceylon.

Macdonell was knighted in 1925, and in 1939 was sworn of the privy council and became a member of the judicial committee. In 1938, two years after his retirement, he was sent on a commission to report and advise (to the Colonial Office) on a complicated problem of inter-tribal jurisdiction in the Balovale district, Northern Rhodesia. He wrote characteristically of this work:

> I cannot tell you what a pleasure the work is—to get back into the old atmosphere; to be received on an equality by men who are absolutely *au fait* with native matters; the constant dialogues of experts day after day; and the having to try and master a most delicate and intricate problem—truly I am a lucky man to have been given this duty. (private information)

Macdonell always keenly enjoyed his work; his memory was remarkable and his mind moved extraordinarily fast. 'I never knew a man who got through work faster' (private information), said a fellow judge. A natural impatience and vehemence—perhaps inherited from highland ancestors—were tempered by quick kindness and generosity. He had many and lasting friendships. He was a good classical scholar and was wont to take Homer's *Odyssey* with him on his constant voyages. In 1940 he was elected an honorary fellow of Brasenose College. The later years of his life were spent in Scotland—for which he had a romantic attachment—at Gatehouse of Fleet, Kirkcudbrightshire. Early in the Second World War he undertook to preside over the tribunal dealing with military exemptions sitting in Manchester. Worn out by overwork he fell ill there and died at a nursing home in Southport on 15 December 1940.   AMICE LEE, *rev.*

Sources personal knowledge (1949) · *WWW* · *Brazen Nose*, 7 (1939–44) · private information (1949) · *CGPLA Eng. & Wales* (1941)

Macdonlevy, Cormac. *See* Mac Duinnshléibhe, Cormac (*fl.* c.1459).

MacDonnell, Alasdair Ruadh, of Glengarry [*alias* Pickle the Spy] (*c.*1725–1761), spy and chief of clan Macdonnell of Glengarry, was the eldest son of John MacDonnell (*d.* 1754), chief of Glengarry, and his wife, the daughter of Colin Mackenzie of Hilton. Known as young Glengarry until he succeeded his father as clan chief, Alasdair was brought up in the Roman Catholic church. He was sent to France while still a boy, and became a captain in Lord John Drummond's Scots Royals regiment in 1743, when the French were planning to invade England under pretext of restoring the Stuarts. There he met Charles Edward Stuart, who had arrived from Rome unannounced to join the expedition, and was with him in Paris among the scheming pro-Charles and pro-Pretender factions after the invasion collapsed. He visited Scotland early in 1745, but returned to France to warn that clan chiefs would support a rising only if backed by French money and arms. By the time he reached France Prince Charles had sailed for Scotland.

That autumn, young Glengarry sailed with the Scots Royals to reinforce the successful Jacobite army, but the *Espérance*, aboard which he was travelling, was captured off Deal and he was imprisoned in the Tower of London. On his release in 1747 he returned to Paris in dire poverty and in debt to the French government. Prince Charles and the Pretender both refused him financial help, and when he asked to be recommended to succeed Lochiel as colonel of the Scots-French Albany regiment, he was passed over. All the Pretender offered him was a duplicate of his grandfather's warrant as a Jacobite peer—with an assurance that the document was genuine.

By the end of 1749 young Glengarry was living in London in dire poverty, secretly trying to obtain permission to settle in Britain. Yet only months later he was in funds, having helped himself to the Loch Arkaig treasure, gold sent from France too late to be of use to the prince in 1746. Glengarry was accused of forging James's signature to obtain this money, and became caught up in the clan quarrels surrounding it, which took him to Rome to present his version of events to the Pretender.

The historian Andrew Lang exposed the extent of the young Glengarry's treachery, which culminated in betrayal of the Elibank plot to kidnap the Hanoverian royal family in 1752 and the subsequent execution of Archibald Cameron. The British government had Cameron executed on an old warrant instead of bringing him to trial in order to avoid exposing their agent, who now went by the alias Pickle the Spy, from Tobias Smollett's novel *Peregrine Pickle*. Pickle continued to spy until 1754, when his paymaster, Henry Pelham, died, and he succeeded to the Glengarry chiefship on his father's death in September of the same year. He never married, and on his death in Glengarry in 1761 was succeeded by his nephew, Donald, son of his brother, Aeneas.

Why or when Pickle began his espionage career is not known, but it is probable that he was driven to it by poverty during his imprisonment in the Tower of London. Continuing lack of funds, clan feuds, and disillusionment with the Stuarts kept him loyal to his spymasters. His brother had been killed accidentally by a Cameron clansman at Falkirk, and he and his father had suffered imprisonment during the rising, yet afterwards neither Prince Charles nor the Pretender would provide financial support or career preferment. Although suspected, Pickle was never exposed during his lifetime; a fact that may owe something to his alignment with the prince's party and Charles Edward's stubborn refusal to accept criticism of members of his faction. Andrew Lang revealed his identity 150 years later with the help of one blindingly simple clue—in his correspondence and reports Glengarry always wrote 'how' when he meant 'who' (Lang, *Pickle the Spy*, 147, 162).

HUGH DOUGLAS

Sources DNB · A. Lang, *Pickle the Spy* (1897) · A. Lang, *Companions of Pickle* (1898) · M. F. Hamilton, ed., 'The Loch Arkaig treasure', *Miscellany … VII*, Scottish History Society, 3rd ser., 35 (1941), 133–68 · F. J. McLynn, *France and the Jacobite rising of 1745* (1981) · J. S. Gibson, *Ships of the Forty-Five* (1967) · H. Douglas, *Jacobite spy wars: spies, moles and treachery* (1999) · A. Mackenzie, *History of the Macdonalds* (1881) · W. B. Blaikie, ed., *Itinerary of Prince Charles Edward Stuart*, Scottish History Society, 23 (1897) · J. Browne, *History of the highlands*, 4 vols. (1832–3)
Archives BL, letters and informations, Add. MSS 32730–33050 · U. Nott., narrative of and information from, while working as a government agent
Likenesses oils, Museum of the Isles, Armadale, Skye, Clan Donald Lands Trust · two photogravures, NL Scot., Blaikie Collection

MacDonnell, Alexander, third earl of Antrim (1615–1699), army officer and politician, was the younger son of Randal *MacDonnell, Viscount Dunluce and first earl of Antrim (*d*. 1636), and Alice O'Neill (*d*. *c*.1664), and heir to his elder brother, Randal *MacDonnell, first marquess of Antrim (1609–1683). Reared at Dunluce Castle in co. Antrim and fluent in both Irish and English, he apparently received no formal education though he spent three years (1636–9) touring France, Germany, and Italy. On his father's death in 1636 he inherited the barony and castle of Glenarm which, in return for 'a certain sum of money yearly for his maintenance', he handed over to his elder brother (*Fifth Report*, HMC, 6).

With the outbreak of the Irish rising in 1641 MacDonnell, who initially took no part in the insurrection, hurried first to Edinburgh and later to London in search of further instructions about how best to proceed. The following year he threw in his lot with the Irish confederates and raised a regiment for the Catholic cause (hence he became known as Colonel Alexander). In 1644 he helped to recruit troops for his brother's expeditionary force to Scotland and in 1645, again acting on his brother's behalf, promised to send 1200 men to Flanders in return for arms and munitions. However, as the 1640s progressed he became increasingly embroiled in confederate politics and, after 1644, was regularly returned to the general assembly and sat as the representative for Ulster on its executive body, the supreme council. He was considered a moderate and served as a member of the committee of treaty, whose job it was to broker a lasting peace with the king. Though he initially supported the papal nuncio Rinuccini's censure of the first Ormond peace (1646), he later threw in his lot (unlike his brother) with the peace party and in 1649 became a commissioner of trust mediating between Ormond and the disbanded confederates. After 1651 he served in the army of Ulster under the bishop of Clogher until Sir Theophilus Jones captured him.

MacDonnell spent the early 1650s imprisoned in the Tower of London before returning to Ireland. Despite the fact that his co. Antrim estates had been confiscated and he had been granted—in lieu of them—7000 acres in co. Galway, he appears to have spent the remainder of the 1650s at Glenarm struggling to pay off his brother's debts

(for which he stood jointly liable). In 1665 the Act of Settlement and Explanation finally restored him to his lands (35,345 statute acres) in the barony of Glenarm and the same year he married Elizabeth Annesley (*d*. 1669), daughter of the staunchly protestant statesman Arthur, first earl of Anglesey (the marriage portion of £3000 was used to help pay off some of his brother's debts). The union proved disastrous. According to one account Elizabeth 'was most arrogantly rude with her husband, and he, of a pleasant humour, would onely and usually return in his Irish language, "how can it be otherwise with a man that has maryed the daughter of the devil"' (Hill, 361). Elizabeth died in 1669 and later, aged sixty-five, MacDonnell married Helena (*d*. 1710), daughter of Sir John Burke of Derrymaclaughney and a granddaughter of the sixth earl of Clanricarde, with whom he had a daughter, Mary, and a son and heir, Randal (later fourth earl of Antrim).

On the death of his elder brother in 1683 MacDonnell became third earl of Antrim, inheriting an estate that Richard Dobbs described as 'impaired, mangled, and engaged in debts, mortgages, grants and otherwise' (Hill, 377). During the brief reign of James II he enjoyed prominence as a privy councillor and lord lieutenant of co. Antrim and during the 'Wars of the Three Kings' he sided with the Catholic monarch. Late in 1688 the king ordered him to garrison his troops in Londonderry, but the sight of Antrim's redshanks (many of them over 6 feet tall) so terrified the inhabitants of the city that thirteen young apprentices shut the gates. In fact this 'vast swarm of Highland and Irish Roman Catholics' was commanded by MacDonnell's illegitimate son Daniel (who, after Limerick, served in France) and not the aged MacDonnell who did, however, take his seat in the 1689 parliament (R. Simpson, *The Annals of Derry*, 1847, facs. edn, 1987). In 1689 he was outlawed in England but his confiscated estates were finally restored to him in 1697 under the terms of the second article of Limerick. For much of the 1690s he acted as the London agent for the remaining Catholic Irish landowners. MacDonnell died on 11 June 1699 near the capital and was buried at Holywell, Flintshire, Wales. Though he lived most of his life under the shadow of his brother, he was an interesting and important figure in his own right and serves as an excellent example of a seventeenth-century Irish Catholic who survived the vicissitudes of two major civil wars with his lands intact.

JANE OHLMEYER

Sources G. Hill, *An historical account of the MacDonnells of Antrim* (1873); repr. (1978) · J. H. Ohlmeyer, *Civil war and Restoration in the three Stuart kingdoms: the career of Randal MacDonnell, marquis of Antrim, 1609–1683* (1993) · T. Carte, *An history of the life of James, duke of Ormonde*, 3 vols. (1735–6), pubd as *The life of James, duke of Ormond*, 6 vols. (1851) · B. O'Ferrall and D. O'Connell, *Commentarius Rinuccinianus de sedis apostolicae legatione ad foederatos Hiberniae Catholicos per annos 1645–1649*, ed. J. Kavanagh, 6 vols., IMC (1932–49) · *History of the Irish confederation and the war in Ireland … by Richard Bellings*, ed. J. T. Gilbert, 7 vols. (1882–91) · M. Ó Siochrú, *Confederate Ireland, 1642–1649: a constitutional and political analysis* (1999) · H. McDonnell, 'Jacobitism and the third and fourth earls of Antrim', *The Glynns*, 13 (1985), 50–54 · H. McDonnell, *The wild geese of the Antrim MacDonnells* (Dublin, 1996) · M. Hickson, ed., *Ireland in the seventeenth century, or, The Irish massacres of 1641–2*, 2 vols. (1884) · CSP

Ire., 1633–47; 1666–70 • *CSP dom.*, 1651–4 • R. C. Simington, *The transplantation to Connacht*, 1654–58, IMC (1970) • W. A. Maguire, ed., *Kings in conflict: the revolutionary war in Ireland and its aftermath, 1689–1750* (1990) • NL Ire., Plunkett MS 345 • Bodl. Oxf., MSS Carte • *Fifth report*, HMC, 4 (1876)

Archives PRO NIre., Antrim estate papers

Likenesses portrait, priv. coll.

McDonnell, Sir Alexander, baronet (1794–1875), civil servant, eldest son of James McDonnell MD and his wife, Elizabeth, daughter of J. Clarke, was born at Belfast. He gained a king's scholarship at Westminster School in 1809, and was elected in 1813 to Christ Church, Oxford, where he held a studentship until 1826. He graduated BA in 1816 and MA in 1820, and won four university prizes—those for Latin and English verse and for the Latin and English essays—an accumulation of honours only once before achieved. He was called to the bar at Lincoln's Inn on 23 November 1824, went the midland circuit, attended the Leicester and Northampton sessions, and served as a commissioner of inquiry into public charities. He married in 1826 Barbara (d. 1865), eldest daughter of Hugh Montgomery of Benvarden, co. Antrim, and widow of Richard Staples. They had no children.

McDonnell was of an exceedingly sensitive temperament, and broke down in pleading a case before a committee of the House of Lords. Mortified beyond expression, he renounced the bar, returned to Ireland, and accepted the position of chief clerk in the chief secretary's office under Thomas Drummond (1797–1840). In 1839 he was appointed resident commissioner of the Board of Education, and quickly assumed an influential role. While himself an ardent protestant, he persistently sought to provide for his countrymen the religious instruction of their choice. He was made a privy councillor of Ireland in 1846, resigned his commissionership in December 1871, and was created a baronet on 20 January 1872. Study of the classics and history formed the chief solace of his retirement. He died at 32 Upper Fitzwilliam Street, Dublin, on 21 January 1875, and was buried at Kilsharvan, near Drogheda. A statue of him by Farrell stands in Marlborough Street School, Dublin.

G. C. BOASE, rev. DAVID HUDDLESTON

Sources A. J. Webb, *A compendium of Irish biography* (1878) • *The Spectator* (20 Feb 1875), 240–41 • Burke, *Gen. Ire.* (1976), 757 • *ILN* (30 Jan 1875), 115 • J. Welch, *The list of the queen's scholars of St Peter's College, Westminster*, ed. [C. B. Phillimore], new edn (1852) [476] • K. Newmann, *Dictionary of Ulster biography* (1993), 155 • D. H. Akenson, *The Irish education experiment: the national system of education in the nineteenth century* (1970) • *The Times* (25 Jan 1875), 7 • CGPLA Ire. (1875)

Likenesses Farrell, statue, *c*.1875, Marlborough Street School, Dublin

Wealth at death under £40,000: probate, 27 Feb 1875, CGPLA Ire.

Macdonnell, Alexander (1798–1835), chess player, born in Belfast, the son of Alexander Macdonnell (d. 21 April 1843), a Belfast physician, was intended for a career in commerce, and carried on an extensive business at Demerara between 1820 and 1830. He became a vigorous propagandist for the slave-owning sugar planters in the West Indies, publishing an account of the condition of slaves in Demerara (1824), a defence of the corn laws, navigation laws, and commercial protection generally (1826), and a justification of the West Indian legislatures' handling of the slavery question (1826). Soon after 1830 he was appointed secretary to the West India Committee of Merchants, his duties being to watch the parliamentary progress of bills connected with the West Indies, notably the emancipation of slaves.

Macdonnell was trained as a chess player by William Lewis, but, once he had got over the odds of 'pawn and move', Lewis refused to meet him on equal terms, and from the foundation of the Westminster chess club in 1831 Macdonnell was tacitly admitted to be the best English player.

In June 1834 Louis Charles Mahé de Labourdonnais, secretary of the Paris chess club, and a pupil of the old French champion Alexandre des Chapelles, visited Britain and challenged Macdonnell's supremacy. Then commenced at the Westminster club in Bedford Street a match that was 'a landmark in the history of the game ... analysed by leading masters to an extent not previously known' (Hooper and Whyld, 56). Labourdonnais spoke no English and Macdonnell no French, and the only word that passed between them was 'check'. The struggle began with three drawn games of great length, thanks to Macdonnell's frequent agonized pondering of a single move over an hour and a half. Slowly, however, the Frenchman obtained the advantage, and of some eighty-five games he won about forty-four, thirteen games being drawn (accounts of the details vary slightly). Commentators have generally criticized Macdonnell's openings, which in fact were so habitually dangerous that he generally lost when playing white. He gained, however, a period of advantage by adopting the Evans gambit, of whose inventor, Captain William Evans, he had been an early victim in 1829. The fiftieth game of the series 'may be called the greatest game ever won by a British player' (Matthews, 19). The duel was at length interrupted by Labourdonnais's recall to Paris. Before the antagonists could again meet, Macdonnell—who was suffering from Bright's disease—died, at the boarding-house in Tavistock Square where he had long lived, on 14 September 1835. He was buried in Kensal Green cemetery, where five years later his great opponent was also interred. Macdonnell was unmarried. The first great British player, he had scaled the heights after only a few years' serious acquaintance with chess, lending credence to George Walker's belief that a little more experience would have made him a match for Labourdonnais in what was effectively a world championship contest. The time, however, was not afforded him.

THOMAS SECCOMBE, rev. JULIAN LOCK

Sources *Chess-players' Chronicle*, 1–4 (1841–3) • G. Walker, 'The games of Labourdonnais and MacDonnell', *Chess-players' Magazine*, 2 (1864), 161–6 • G. Walker, *Chess studies: comprising one thousand games*, ed. E. Freeborough (1893), chaps. 1, 3 • 'Glimpses of the genius of Caissa: MacDonnell and Labourdonnais', *Chess-players' Magazine*, 2 (1864), 72–5, 104–9, 138–43, 176–81, 203–5, 235–42 • D. Hooper and K. Whyld, *The Oxford companion to chess*, 2nd edn (1992), 239–40 • K. Matthews, *British chess* (1948) • G. Walker, 'The battles of MacDonnell and De La Bourdonnais', *Chess and chess players* (1850), 364–84 · H. Staunton, *The chess-player's handbook* (1847); facs. edn (1985) · private information (1893) · *GM*, 2nd ser., 4 (1835), 442 · H. E. Bird, *Modern chess* (1887)

Macdonnell, Angus [Aeneas], **Lord Macdonnell and Aros** (*d.* **1680**), chief of clan Macdonnell of Glengarry, was the son of Alasdair (or Alexander) Macdonnell of Glengarry and Jean, daughter of Allen Cameron of Lochiel, chief of clan Cameron. He was brought up a Roman Catholic, although it is unclear if he remained so after the late 1640s. By 23 November 1641 his father had died, and Angus was the heir apparent of his grandfather Donald Macdonnell, chief of the Glengarry Macdonnells, and, since the latter was nearly 100 years old, effectively in charge of the clan. That day Sir Donald MacDonald of Sleat, Skye, acted as cautioner to the sum of 10,000 merks that Macdonnell would appear in Edinburgh before the privy council within eight days, in connection with the murder on 15 August that year in Inverness of two followers of William Mackintosh of Torcastle by a group of Glengarry Macdonnells. The murderers had been put to the horn on 20 September, but failed to appear. Macdonnell refused to provide caution for the offenders and the council committed him to Edinburgh Castle. On 1 March 1642, after thirteen weeks in prison, he relented. Sir John Mackenzie of Tarbat acted as his cautioner for compliance to the sum of £10,000 Scots. Between 29 October 1642 and 24 January 1643 Macdonnell and Torcastle sought to resolve the issue of compensation for the Mackintoshes; the former's supporters in the arbitration included Tarbat, Thomas Fraser of Strechine, and William Fraser of Culbokie. Some idea of the armament of the Glengarry clan comes from a letter, which refers to Macdonnell's retinue 'neir the parts of Innernes with blowin pipes, bowes, gunnes and other offensive weapons' (*Reg. PCS*, 2nd ser., 1.575–6). The final judgment demanded that he pay 2300 merks to the victims' widows and orphans.

In December 1644 Macdonnell's grandfather sided with the royalist army of James Graham, marquess of Montrose, and Macdonnell, as effective military leader of the clan, took the field. His regiment fought in the centre of the royalist line at Montrose's victory at Inverlochy on 2 February 1645. That day his grandfather died and Angus became chief of the clan. In April he and his men served at the storming of Dundee and during the harrowing retreat from the burgh; on 9 May they helped the marquess win the desperate battle of Auldearn; on 2 July Glengarry commanded the centre of Montrose's army at the victory at Alford; and on 15 August he led 500 Macdonnells in the rout of covenanters at Kilsyth. In the next few months he allied with Alasdair MacColla MacDonald in attacking the covenanter Campbells in Argyll. On 8 September 1646 the synod of Argyll excommunicated him for being an unrepentant royalist, but by the end of that year he had ceased military operations and earned a pardon from the covenanter regime. In June 1647 he reluctantly led some clansmen to Ireland when Alasdair retreated at the approach of David Leslie's covenanter army, and joined the papal-Gaelic faction of the confederates at Charlemont,

Armagh. Cardinal Rinuccini divided the force and sent Glengarry to serve with General Thomas Preston's Leinster army in an attempt to take Dublin. On 8 August at Dungan Hill the chief led a regiment to bloody defeat. Few of his men survived the battle, but Glengarry escaped and continued to serve with a contingent of Scots and Irish in the papalist faction. In October 1648 royalist confederates captured him and others in the battle of Wexford, but Randal Macdonnell, marquess of Antrim, successfully pleaded for his release. Glengarry now went into a double exile, travelling to the court of the prince of Wales on the continent. The covenanter regime forfeited him for his royalist and anti-Campbell actions in 1649.

Glengarry returned to Scotland with Charles II at Garmouth on 24 June 1650, and during the next decade played a large role in highland affairs. During the English rule of Scotland he stoutly opposed the conquerors. In mid-August 1652 he raised 4000 men, and, as acting general of the Scottish royalists, sent a messenger to Charles II. In September to October he headed a coalition of Macdonnells, Macleans, Macleods, Lovat Frasers, and other clans and requested the dispatch of arms and John Middleton as the official commander. On 22 January 1653 English intelligence reported that Glengarry had between 1500 and 2000 men, but that he had failed to hold a royalist conference. In mid-February his army disbanded. Following meetings of royalists in the highlands, Glengarry joined William Cunningham, earl of Glencairn's 1200-man army. By December, despite royalist successes, Glengarry and his allies had retreated into Badenoch. In early April 1654 Glencairn had over 5000 men, but rifts weakened the royalist rising. Glencairn wounded the professional soldier Sir George Monro (serving in his army) in a duel after the latter called the highlanders, chiefly the Glengarry Macdonnells, thieves and robbers. Glengarry himself became involved in a bitter dispute with John Murray, earl of Atholl, that nearly led to a duel when the latter's tenants paid taxes to the English. An earlier difference (spring 1653) with Archibald Campbell, Lord Lorne, over Glencairn's position as leader, nearly caused a duel in September. In October to December, with a warrant from Glencairn, Glengarry sought to arrest Lorne. This dispute eventually quieted down. Meanwhile Lochiel had become disenchanted with Glengarry for failing to make a royalist rendezvous, but instead meeting with the English Colonel William Brayne.

On 31 October 1653 Glengarry received a royal commission as major-general in Scotland. During the year Charles wrote that he had 'a very good opinion of his affection and ability to serve' (Firth, *Scotland and the Commonwealth*, 310–11), but denied promising him the earldom of Ross. However, on 6 February 1654 the king issued a warrant to John Campbell, earl of Loudoun and chancellor, making Glengarry 'Lord MackDonald and Earle of' (Firth, *Scotland and the Protectorate*, 31). On 30 May Glengarry was noted as the 'only person for dyvers months that adhered to my Lord Glencarne' (ibid., 111). In August he was reputedly leading 1550 men. But by October–November the Macdonnells had become reluctant to follow their chief, probably owing to the English laying waste to the clan lands. In December Glengarry failed in an attempt to rouse the Camerons to loyalty to the royalist cause. The following May he agreed to treat with the English. On 8 June he surrendered in hopes of securing an indemnity for his acts of 1644–55. However, the English forfeited him, and gave his lands to Archibald Campbell, marquess of Argyll, who in turn granted them to Lochiel. In autumn 1656 General George Monck had the chief arrested owing to fears of a royalist rising. On 5 October 1658 Glengarry went to Inverlochy to hear Richard Cromwell proclaimed as lord protector. Between 12 August and 7 September 1659 he signed the engagement for peaceable behaviour with Monck. Nevertheless, some of his clansmen were in arms in November and had started robbing people, which caused the English to give Lochiel a commission against them.

The Restoration brought a positive uplift to Glengarry's fortunes. Although he failed in his attempt to secure the earldom of Ross, which would have given him precedence over all the other Macdonald chieftains, on 20 December 1660 he received a charter of nobility as Lord Macdonnell and Aros and in practice the Scottish government occasionally called him the leader of all MacDonalds. His military career for the Stuarts had burdened him with debts of £148,000 Scots by 1661, but on 23 February that year the Scottish privy council granted him an annuity of £300, which increased to £500 on 7 February 1676. With his status enhanced and a degree of financial security achieved, Macdonnell became an *habitué* of the court in London, a house near Inverness, and the parliament in Edinburgh. He attended the last in 1661, 1662, 1663, 1667, 1669, and 1670. On 15 April 1661 the estates overturned the forfeiture imposed on him in 1649. In 1662 it assigned him recompense for his losses as a royalist from the marquess of Argyll's forfeited estates. Parliament also recognized his local prominence by making him a commissioner of supply for Inverness-shire in 1667 and 1678.

However, the Restoration period was not without problems for the new peer. Macdonnell maintained a consistent hostility to certain parties—chiefly the Campbells led by Archibald, ninth earl of Argyll—until his death. In 1665 he joined the Macleans, the MacIans of Glencoe, the Camerons, and the MacDonalds of Keppoch in holding Mull against the earl. His feud with the burgh of Inverness in 1666 led the privy council to demand that both parties post caution of 20,000 merks for peaceful behaviour. In 1667 he found himself pursued by the council due to a charge from the earl of Seaforth. The earl claimed that Macdonnell had stopped a messenger from delivering a summons on 30 October 1667, and that twenty-four Macdonnells armed with swords, pistols, muskets, and dirks had threatened and robbed the messenger. In mid-February 1669 Macdonnell appeared at the council in Edinburgh and signed a bond for peaceable behaviour of his highlanders. Two weeks later, on 4 March, the council found Seaforth's charge unproven, and ordered the earl to pay Macdonnell £600 Scots. In November 1670 Macdonnell was at feud with Cameron of Lochiel, and the council ordered both to keep the peace. His earlier

troubles with the Mackintoshes continued; for on 18 July 1672 the council ordered Macdonnell to find caution of 5000 merks due to some of his clansmen troubling the laird of Mackintosh Torcastle. Unsurprisingly, Macdonnell's dispute with the Campbells endured. In 1674 he had joined with other MacDonalds, the MacQuarries, Camerons, and Macleans in opposing the earl of Argyll's quest to gain Mull. Nevertheless, on 18 September 1677 he managed to gain a commission for maintaining peace in the highlands at an annual stipend of £200. The commission continued until mid-November 1678, but thereafter he refused to obey the council. His disobedience in the midst of fears of a highland dimension of the Popish Plot, which led to a council order for disarming Catholic clansmen, was definitely ill-timed. A herald's attempt to cite him to the council or be charged a rebel led to an attack on the official that Christmas at Invergarry by a group of Macdonnell men dressed as women. His fortunes plunged further on 12 April 1679 when the council gave Argyll a commission to pursue the now outlawed Lord Macdonnell. On 27 May the council declared him to be in rebellion, and on 14 August he suffered his third forfeiture. In 1679 Argyll finally managed to overrun Mull and the other Maclean lands, despite Macdonnell's opposition. The change in government (with the fall of Argyll's patron Lauderdale in August to October and the arrival of James, duke of York, as regent in December) rescinded the declarations against Macdonnell. Still, on 15 March 1680 he was publicly rebuked for threatening the lord treasurer in Edinburgh.

Macdonnell had married in 1646 Margaret, eldest daughter of Sir Donald MacDonald of Sleat. They had a daughter who married Montgomery of Coilsfield, Ayrshire. Macdonnell died in Edinburgh on 6 December 1680, and was buried in Holyrood Abbey. Lacking a direct male heir, the peerage lapsed, and the chiefship fell to his nephew Ranald Macdonnell of Scotus. The judgements on Macdonnell's lengthy career were harsh, even from fellow royalists. Lochiel concluded, 'Glengarry … had he behaved himself with the same integrity to his neightbours [*sic*] as he did to his Prince, he had dyed with a very unblemished character' (Cameron, 259–60). The leading seventeenth-century Gaelic poet Ian Lom MacDonald also condemned him:

> You seem to me to be along time in England, being ruined by
> gaming. I would prefer you in a coat and plaid than in a cloak
> which fastens; and that you would walk in a sprightly
> manner in trews made of tartan cloth and visit for a spell in
> grassy Glenquoich [the glen in the midst of the clan lands].
> (Macinnes, 128)

EDWARD M. FURGOL

Sources *Reg. PCS*, 1st ser., vols. 6–14 · *Reg. PCS*, 2nd ser. · *Reg. PCS*, 3rd ser. · *APS* · C. H. Firth, ed., *Scotland and the Commonwealth: letters and papers relating to the military government of Scotland, from August 1651 to December 1653*, Scottish History Society, 18 (1895) · C. H. Firth, ed., *Scotland and the protectorate: letters and papers relating to the military government of Scotland from January 1654 to June 1659*, Scottish History Society, 31 (1899) · *Memoirs of Sir Ewen Cameron of Locheill*, ed. J. Macknight, Abbotsford Club, 24 (1842) · D. Stevenson, *Alasdair MacColla and the highland problem in the seventeenth century* (1980) ·

F. D. Dow, *Cromwellian Scotland, 1651–1660* (1979) • E. J. Cowan, *Montrose for covenant and king* (1977) • GEC, *Peerage* • A. I. Macinnes, *Clanship, commerce, and the house of Stuart, 1603–1788* (1996) • D. C. MacTavish, ed., *Minutes of the synod of Argyll*, 2 vols., Scottish History Society, 3rd ser., 37–8 (1943–4) • A. F. Mitchell and J. Christie, eds., *The records of the commissions of the general assemblies of the Church of Scotland*, 3 vols., Scottish History Society, 11, 25, 58 (1892–1909)

MacDonnell, Antony Patrick, Baron MacDonnell (1844–1925), colonial and British civil servant, was born on 7 March 1844 at Palmfield House, Carracastle, in the district of Srah (or Shragh), near Swinford in co. Mayo, Ireland. He was the eldest son of Mark Garvey MacDonnell (1807–1889), a Catholic gentleman who owned a small estate (*c.*863 acres valued at £121), whose galloglass forebears (professional soldiers or mercenaries who emigrated to Ulster from the Scottish highlands in the thirteenth and fourteenth centuries) had moved to Mayo in the seventeenth century. His mother, Bedelia, was the daughter of Michael O'Hara of Springtown, co. Roscommon. After attending Summerhill, a Catholic boarding-school in Athlone, the precocious son proceeded (aged fifteen) to Queen's College, Galway, where he had a brilliant career, excelling in debate and taking an honours degree in modern languages. Having scored high on the Indian Civil Service entrance exam, he embarked for India in 1865.

India, 1865–1901 Beginning his Indian career in Bengal, MacDonnell soon proved his ability as an administrator, showing not only a clear and decisive mind but mastery of the smallest details. In 1866–7 he saw the suffering caused by crop failures in Orissa, and when famine struck Bihar and Bengal during 1873–4 he was ready to implement relief measures that saved countless lives. Inspired, no doubt, by his own country's ordeal in 1845–9, MacDonnell became an expert on famines and wrote the long and meticulous *Report on the food-grain supply and statistical review of the relief operations in the distressed districts of Behar and Bengal* (1876), which served as a model for dealing with the causes and effects of crop failures in India. Twenty years later he supervised famine relief operations in the Allahabad and Banda districts of the North-Western Provinces. And in 1901 he presided over the famine commission, which produced a report that served as the standard guide for many years. While working in Bengal in 1883 he urged his superiors to create a department of agriculture that would gather data relating to climate, crop conditions, and food prices. His concern for the rights of tenants found expression in the Bengal Tenancy Act of 1885, which protected ryots or tenant farmers from rack-rents and arbitrary eviction. And while serving as lieutenant-governor of the North-Western Provinces and Oudh he helped to pass a similar measure there in 1901. Just as in Ireland, some of the wealthy landowners (known as talukdars and zemindars) resented these measures as threats to their privileged position. A conservative liberal in matters of imperial rule, MacDonnell advocated the appointment of élite Indians to village and district councils so that they could have a voice in spending money raised by local taxes. At the same time he wanted to broaden the powers of provincial legislative councils.

In November 1878, during a period on leave, MacDonnell married Henrietta (*d.* 1934), the younger daughter of Ewen MacDonell, a highland laird, of Insch, Lochaber. They had only one surviving child, Anne, who did not marry. MacDonnell's sharp mind, devotion to duty, and masterful personality enabled him to rise steadily up the ladder of preferment in the Indian Civil Service. In the 1880s he served successively as accountant general, home secretary, and revenue secretary to the Bengal government, and then as acting chief commissioner of Burma (1889–90), chief commissioner of the central provinces (1890–91), acting lieutenant-governor of Bengal (1893), member of the viceroy's council (1893–5), and finally lieutenant-governor of the North-Western Provinces and chief commissioner of Oudh (1895–1901). In 1898 he had to decline the lieutenant-governorship of Bengal owing to fatigue and the frail health of his devoted wife.

During his thirty-five years in India, MacDonnell thus played a leading role in governing four great provinces. Something of a taskmaster who demanded much of himself and his subordinates, he instilled fear in the hearts of slackers or incompetents. But he also won the respect of such viceroys as Dufferin, Lansdowne, Elgin, and Curzon. In addition to attaining high office he became a knight commander in the Order of the Star of India in 1893 and was promoted to grand commander in 1898. Known as 'the Bengal Tiger', he had the kind of prickly personality that prompted one Indian Civil Service colleague to observe: 'If Antony and another are cast away in an open boat and only one of them can live, it will not be Antony who is eaten' (P. Mason, *The Guardians*, vol. 2 of *The Men who Ruled India*, 1963, 188). Although even Curzon found him somewhat cold and lacking in 'generosity' of character, he too recognized MacDonnell's astute qualities. Writing from India to a colleague in London, he declared: 'It is such a God-send in this pigmy-ridden country to find a man who at least has mental stature' (D. Gilmour, *Curzon*, 1994, 157).

Ireland In 1901 Lady MacDonnell's heart condition and MacDonnell's own health problems finally moved him to resign office and leave India. Shortly after arriving in London he turned down the offer of a seat in parliament as an independent Irish nationalist (his brother Dr Mark Anthony MacDonnell was the home rule MP for Queen's county from 1892 to 1906). Lord Lansdowne, who, while viceroy of India, had come to admire him, asked him to accept the arduous post of permanent under-secretary of Ireland. Uneasy about serving a Conservative Unionist administration, MacDonnell sought the advice of some close friends and ex-Indian officials. In Dublin he told the Irish chief secretary, George Wyndham, that he was a Roman Catholic and an Irishman with 'nationalist leanings', although not a home-ruler. Keen to do some good for his country, he made it clear that he could not function as a glorified policeman in charge of law and order and insisted on having some say in shaping policy. Both Wyndham and Lansdowne accepted these conditions, which went well beyond civil service protocols. At the same time MacDonnell received a seat on the Council of India so that he would have an escape route should he run into trouble in Ireland.

MacDonnell arrived in Ireland at a crucial time, when moderation seemed to prevail within both the landlord and the nationalist camps despite the outbreak of an agrarian agitation aimed at breaking up the ranches of cattle graziers in the west. Sharing Wyndham's enthusiasm for constructive reforms, he supported the Land Conference of December 1902, which brought together the representatives of moderate landlordism and tenant right, who wanted to see a bold measure that would enable tenants to buy their farms from the landlords at a fair price. This consensus resulted in the drafting and passing of the famous Wyndham Act of 1903, which facilitated the sale of holdings on estates to the occupying tenants by means of state loans to be repaid through purchase annuities paid in yearly instalments over some sixty-eight years. (One of the earliest vendors under the new measure, MacDonnell sold his Shragh estate in June 1904 for £3206.)

Hoping to sustain the goodwill engendered by the Land Conference and land purchase, Wyndham and MacDonnell worked together in the autumn of 1903 on a scheme to streamline the maze-like bureaucracy of Dublin Castle, which contained some forty-five departments and boards, some of which overlapped. During the summer of 1904 MacDonnell became involved in the so-called devolution scheme by collaborating with a dozen or so 'liberal' landlords, led by the fourth earl of Dunraven, who wanted to transfer control over Irish fiscal and administrative matters from Westminster to Dublin in a manner consistent with the Act of Union. Reconstituting themselves as the Irish Reform Association, these moderate (southern) unionist landowners published a short manifesto on 31 August 1904 outlining their ideas about reform. Pressed for clarification, Dunraven asked MacDonnell to draw up a more precise plan for a political and financial council in Dublin that would deal with 'purely Irish affairs'. Convinced that he had the support of Wyndham and Lord Dudley, the Irish viceroy, MacDonnell drafted the second devolution manifesto on Dublin Castle notepaper and sent it off to Dunraven, who had it published on 26 September. It did not take long for rumours to reach the leaders of Ulster Unionism that the under-secretary, whose loyalty to the union they doubted, had aided and abetted the Irish Reform Association. Sensing betrayal, they launched attacks on the Dublin Castle regime. Wyndham's prompt repudiation of the devolution scheme in a letter to *The Times* failed to appease such militant Unionists as William Moore, MP for Antrim North, who was Wyndham's parliamentary secretary. Although the cabinet formally censured MacDonnell in December for having exceeded his authority, the fury of Ulster Unionists against both Wyndham and MacDonnell intensified in February 1905. Reluctantly, Balfour sacrificed his old friend Wyndham, who resigned early in March. Walter Long, a staunch tory unionist, replaced him as chief secretary. But northern loyalists were still bent on

ousting or punishing MacDonnell. Unable to defend himself in parliament, the under-secretary appealed for help from several aristocratic friends who had served in India, insisting that he had kept both Wyndham and Dudley fully informed about his work on behalf of devolution and that he had construed their silence as approval.

Although the evidence is sketchy, the cabinet may well have refrained from yielding to Ulster Unionist demands that MacDonnell be sacked not just because they feared more embarrassing disclosures about the terms of his appointment but also because a few ministers knew that he enjoyed the king's confidence. Apparently, MacDonnell had a standing invitation to Buckingham Palace whenever he was in London. During his state visit to Ireland in July 1903, Edward VII had dissuaded him from accepting the governorship of Bombay on the grounds that Ireland needed him more than India. (On that occasion the king awarded him a GCVO.) The whole story of the Wyndham–Dudley–MacDonnell imbroglio will never be known because the participants did their best to conceal all they knew about the Dunraven plan. Shortly before his death MacDonnell shut himself in his study and burnt many important letters pertaining to the devolution affair. The gaps in his papers for this period strongly suggest a wish to conceal any signs of royal support for his efforts to Indianize the Irish government by means of semi-elective councils designed to make it more efficient and responsive to Irish needs. MacDonnell's ability to survive the fierce attacks on his integrity that lasted well into the autumn of 1906 indicates the presence of some very powerful friends. At the same time he refused to become the scapegoat of what he called 'the Orange Faction'.

The devolution fiasco embarrassed Balfour's ministry at a time when the tariff reform dispute and other problems were tearing the Unionist Party apart. After Balfour surrendered office in December 1905, James Bryce became Irish chief secretary in the Liberal regime and relied heavily on MacDonnell's expertise. In 1906 they drafted a more ambitious devolution scheme, called the Irish Councils Bill, which called for the creation of an executive council and a grand committee of Irish MPs, who would deal with purely Irish legislation. Militant home-rulers promptly denounced this measure as a feeble attempt to buy their support. Dreading a split within his party, John Redmond repudiated the bill, which died unmourned in June 1907. After Augustine Birrell succeeded Bryce as chief secretary in January 1907, MacDonnell continued to press the Treasury for funds to finance land purchase while urging a university bill for Catholics. But serious personality and policy clashes with Birrell drove him to resign his post in July 1908, when the Asquith ministry honoured him with a barony.

In the House of Lords, MacDonnell spoke out on both Indian and Irish matters, taking a special interest in constitutional reform. In 1912 he chaired the royal commission on the civil service and gave advice on ways to improve recruitment for the Indian Civil Service. During and after the debates on the third Home Rule Bill he recommended proportional representation as the best way to ensure the rights of the protestant minority and avoid the evil of partition. In 1917 he served on the Irish Convention, which the government created to buy time after the Easter rising. Devoted to the cause of conciliation, he took part in the peace conference held in Dublin in 1920.

MacDonnell died in London on 9 June 1925, and was buried on 12 June in Putney Vale cemetery. The barony became extinct upon his death. Lacking private wealth, he had often worried about money matters. (At his death the value of his personal estate barely exceeded £10,000.) Short of stature and long on resolution, with eyes that glowed intensely beneath bushy eyebrows, MacDonnell was one of those rare Catholic Irishmen who saw no contradiction in being an Irish patriot and a loyal servant of the British empire.   L. PERRY CURTIS JUN.

Sources Bodl. Oxf., MacDonnell MSS · BL, Balfour MSS · Bodl. Oxf., Bryce MSS · A. Gailey, *Ireland and the death of kindness* (1987) · A. Jackson, *The Ulster unionist party* (1989) · F. S. L. Lyons, 'The Irish unionist party and the devolution crisis of 1904–5', *Irish Historical Studies*, 6 (1948–9), 1–22 · T. R. Metcalf, *Land, landlords, and the British raj: northern India in the nineteenth century* (1979) · J. W. Mackail and G. Wyndham, *The life and letters of George Wyndham*, 2 vols. (1925) · Earl of Dunraven, *Past times and pastimes*, 2 vols. (1922) · Lord Newton [T. W. Legh], *Lord Lansdowne: a biography* (1929) · W. O'Brien, *An olive branch in Ireland* (1910) · private information (1966)

Archives Bodl. Oxf., corresp. and papers relating to India and Ireland | BL, OIOC, letters to Sir Harcourt Butler, MSS Eur. F 116 · BL, corresp. with Lord Ripon, Add. MS 43542 · Bodl. Oxf., Bryce MSS · Plunkett Foundation, Long Hanborough, Oxfordshire, corresp. with Sir Horace Plunkett · TCD, corresp. with W. J. M. Starkie · Wilts. & Swindon RO, corresp. with Sir Walter Long and others · Bowood, Wiltshire, Lansdowne MSS

Likenesses W. Orpen, oils, c.1904, Hugh Lane Gallery of Modern Art, Dublin · G. Frampton, statue, 1907, Lucknow, Oudh, India · H. H. Brown, oils, exh. RA 1916 · W. Stoneman, photograph, 1920, NPG · Spy [L. Ward], cartoon, NPG; repro. in *VF* (3 Aug 1905) · W. H. Warburton, photograph, NPG · J. B. Yeats, oils, Hugh Lane Gallery of Modern Art, Dublin

Wealth at death £10,757 gross value of estate at death; £10,012 net personalty: *The Times* (27 Aug 1925)

Macdonnell, John. *See* Mac Dónaill, Seán Clárach (1691–1754).

MacDonnell [née Manners; *other married name* Villiers], **Katherine**, duchess of Buckingham and marchioness of Antrim (1603?–1649), noblewoman, was the only daughter of Francis *Manners, sixth earl of Rutland (1578–1632), the leading noble of the midlands and a prominent courtier, and his wife, Frances Knyvet (*d.* 1605), the daughter and heir of a rich Wiltshire gentleman. Her mother died shortly after she was born and her father then remarried and had two sons, who both died young. Thus Katherine was sole heir both to her mother's fortune and to extensive, unentailed portions of the Manners estates in Northamptonshire and Yorkshire, together with estates in Buckinghamshire and Leicestershire and the barony of Ros. Her wealth and good looks made her particularly attractive to James VI and I's young favourite

Katherine MacDonnell, duchess of Buckingham and marchioness of Antrim (1603?–1649), by Sir Anthony Van Dyck, 1620–21 [*Sir George Villiers and Lady Katherine Manners as Adonis and Venus*]

George *Villiers, marquess (and later first duke) of Buckingham (1592–1628), and the young couple fell passionately in love. On 16 May 1620, at the tender age of seventeen, Katherine married Buckingham (having first renounced her Catholicism) and over the course of the next nine years they had five children, of whom three survived infancy: George *Villiers, later second duke of Buckingham (1628–1687), Lord Francis Villiers (1629–1648), and Lady Mary *Villiers (1622–1685). Katherine and her children quickly became great favourites of the king. Following Buckingham's assassination in 1628 she inherited, together with her sons, an enormous fortune, which included Buckingham's London mansions—Wallingford House, Walsingham House, and York House—together with nineteen more modest properties on the Strand and a mansion in Chelsea; in addition she received an annual income of roughly £4550 from the Irish customs and a state pension of £6000. She reverted to Catholicism and remained a devout Catholic for the rest of her life; she later noted that she 'would pour out my life in defence of [Catholicism] … nothing can frighten me from my faith' (O'Ferrall and O'Connell, 2.757). An intimate of the papal agent George Con (who addressed her as 'fond Kate'), she was instrumental in converting 'women of quality' (including Endymion Porter's wife and Lady Newport) to Catholicism.

Next to Henrietta Maria the duchess of Buckingham, as one of Charles I's favourites, was probably the most important and influential woman at the Caroline court and, together with her daughter Mary, her sister-in-law Susan Feilding, Lady Denbigh, and the Catholic countess of Roxburghe, she held a position of honour in the queen's household. Thanks to her Villiers connections she was related to the earls of Desmond, Arundel, Suffolk, Northampton, Nithsdale, Pembroke, and Hamilton (who replaced her husband as the royal favourite). Loyalty to the late duke's memory also brought the support of numerous old Buckingham clients, including Endymion Porter, Sir Robert Pye, Sir Edward Conway, and Secretary Windebank. The second marriage of Katherine's daughter Lady Mary to James Stewart [see Stuart, James], fourth duke of Lennox (and, after 1641, of Richmond), in the summer of 1637, secured the patronage of Charles's closest blood relative and one of his most intimate friends. However, Katherine's most important and influential patron was William Laud, archbishop of Canterbury.

With Buckingham's death Katherine had become the most eligible widow at court, and in April 1635 she married Randal *MacDonnell, Lord Dunluce (1609–1683), heir to the first earl of Antrim. The duchess was forced to pay a high price for marrying a Catholic from Ireland several years her junior. Every measure was taken to ensure that Dunluce, who was obviously regarded by many at court as something of a gold digger, should have no jurisdiction over her children's inheritance. In addition her contemporaries snubbed her. According to Laud her friends were all 'ill-satisfied with her marriage' (Works, 7.137), which had lost her much ground 'with the king himself as well as all others of quality' (ibid., 135). However, within a relatively short period of time the court, led by the king, became reconciled to the match and the duchess was restored to her former position of favour. She continued to use her former title.

During the early years of their marriage (during which time Katherine miscarried at least twice) the couple lived at York House, but in an effort to cut down on expenditure they moved to Ireland in 1638 and made Dunluce Castle their primary residence. The outbreak of the Irish rising in October 1641 disrupted their peaceful existence and the duchess immediately left Ireland and joined Charles I's court in York. During the 1640s she divided her time between the royalist court in England, Ireland, and Flanders and she repeatedly importuned the king and other leading figures, such as the dukes of Hamilton and Ormond, on her husband's behalf, and in 1645 helped to secure him his marquessate. From October 1647 she remained in Ireland, administering her husband's privateering business and involving herself in confederate politics, including Antrim's abortive rising against Ormond in October 1648. In August 1649 she received permission to join her son and the exiled royal court in France but lack of funds forced her to remain in Waterford. Her health took a dramatic turn for the worse in late October. Shortly afterwards, in November 1649, she died, perhaps from the plague that was raging through Ireland, and was buried outside the walls of Waterford. A monument was erected in Westminster Abbey. Her extensive English estates and properties all passed to her son George, second duke of Buckingham.

Of Katherine's personality little is known though Clarendon described her as a woman of 'very great wit and spirit' (Clarendon, Hist. rebellion, 3.509). An examination of her household accounts between 1629 and 1634, which she carefully annotated in her rather childish hand, suggests that she was pampered and extravagant yet fastidious, resilient and an extremely shrewd businesswoman. Extant letters confirm this and illustrate her loyalty and devotion to—and her passion for—her husbands. In Antrim's case she was his closest confidante and adviser, acting as his deputy, secretary, and watchdog.

JANE OHLMEYER

Sources G. Hill, An historical account of the MacDonnells of Antrim (1873); repr. (1978) · J. H. Ohlmeyer, Civil war and Restoration in the three Stuart kingdoms: the career of Randal MacDonnell, marquis of Antrim, 1609–1683 (1993) · G. Radcliffe, The earl of Strafforde's letters and dispatches, with an essay towards his life, ed. W. Knowler, 2 vols. (1739) · The works of the most reverend father in God, William Laud, ed. J. Bliss and W. Scott, 7 vols. (1847–60) · R. Lockyer, Buckingham: the life and political career of George Villiers, first duke of Buckingham, 1592–1628 (1981) · M. A. E. Green, ed., Calendar of the proceedings of the committee for compounding … 1643–1660, 5 vols., PRO (1889–92) · T. Carte, An history of the life of James, duke of Ormond, 3 vols. (1735–6); new edn, pubd as The life of James, duke of Ormond, 6 vols. (1851) · B. O'Ferrall and D. O'Connell, Commentarius Rinuccinianus de sedis apostolicae legatione ad foederatos Hiberniae Catholicos per annos 1645–1649, ed. J. Kavanagh, 6 vols., IMC (1932–49) · History of the Irish confederation and the war in Ireland … by Richard Bellings, ed. J. T. Gilbert, 7 vols. (1882–91) · CSP Ire., 1633–60 · CSP dom., 1635–9 · J. Finet, Ceremonies of Charles I: the note books of John Finet, 1628–1641, ed. A. J. Loomie (1987) · GEC, Peerage · Clarendon, Hist. rebellion
Archives Bodl. Oxf., accounts of the household of the duchess of Buckingham, MS misc. eng · V&A NAL, papers relating to the sale to her daughters of a quantity of plate and jewels in 1637 | BL, Harley MS 6987 · Bodl. Oxf., Carte MSS · PRO, state papers
Likenesses A. Van Dyck, group portrait, 1620–21 (Sir George Villiers and Lady Katherine Manners as Adonis and Venus), priv. coll. [see illus.] · Reubens, oils, c.1629, Dulwich College Picture Gallery · H. Le Sueur, effigy, in or before 1634, Westminster Abbey, London · G. Honthoust, group portrait, oils (duchess and duke of Buckingham and family), Hampton Court · C. Janssen, group portrait, oils (duchess and duke of Buckingham and family), Buckingham Palace

MacDonnell, Randal, first earl of Antrim (d. 1636), chieftain and landowner, was the fourth of the five sons of Sorley Boy *MacDonnell (b. in or before 1508, d. 1590), Scots-Irish chieftain, and his wife, Mary (d. 1582), daughter of Con O'Neill, first earl of Tyrone. He was apparently called Arranagh owing to the fact that as a child he was fostered by the Stewart family of the Scottish island of Arran. In 1597 he helped his elder brother Sir James MacDonnell fortify Dunluce and defeat an English expedition commanded by Sir John Chichester, governor of Carrickfergus. In April 1601, on Sir James's death, MacDonnell became chieftain of the Glens and Route in preference to Sir James's teenage son. In December he joined Hugh *O'Neill, second earl of Tyrone, on his march south with 400 men. Only thirty survived their defeat at Kinsale. In August 1602 he submitted to Lord Deputy Mountjoy, undertaking to serve against Tyrone with 500 foot and forty horse at his own expense, and was knighted.

On 23 May 1603 MacDonnell was granted his territories as a personal estate by Mountjoy. Initially James I favoured the claim of the clan chieftain, MacDonald of Dunyvaig, but in 1604 MacDonnell's grant was confirmed and Rathlin included. Subsequently the Dublin administration reduced the grants to the Ulster chieftains, excluding church lands and significant strongholds. In 1606 Dunluce, Olderfleet Castle at Larne, three-quarters of the fishing rights on the Bann, and church lands, including the priory of Coleraine, were removed from MacDonnell, leaving him 333,907 acres stretching from Larne to Coleraine. Dunluce was returned to him in 1615.

About 1604 MacDonnell married Alice (b. 1582/3, d. in or after 1663), Tyrone's daughter with his second wife, Siobhán (or Joanna). He was acquitted of complicity in the 'flight of the earls' in 1607, and is notable for avoiding the embroilments which caused the flight or arrest of most Ulster chieftains by 1610, leaving almost six counties available for the plantation. This collapse of Gaelic society left MacDonnell as the greatest landowner in Ulster. He dealt astutely with the settlers, selling 2000 acres around Coleraine to the Irish Society and supplying them with building lime free of charge. In consequence he became an alderman, received a townhouse as a 'retreat for his life', and avoided further territorial encroachments.

In 1614 Alexander and Sorley, the elder sons of Sir James MacDonnell, plotted with certain dispossessed Ulster families to overthrow the new order. The conspiracy failed, and Sorley fled into exile. MacDonnell broke discontent by generosity: he brought up Sorley's son in his household, and granted Alexander 15,000 acres. Long leases for large tracts of land were made to MacDonnell kinsmen, other highland families which had come to Antrim in the sixteenth century, and important local septs. Simultaneously he gave much land to incoming lowland Scots. Rabbit warrens, deer parks, salt pans, quarries, manor courts, and markets were established, and the horse collar and heavy plough, previously unknown in Gaelic Ulster, were introduced. There was also extensive building, initiated both by himself and by leading tenants. Fortified dwellings in a distinctly Scottish style, mills, roads, townships, bridges, and imposing residences at Dunluce and Glenarm were erected. His foster family, the Stewarts, became tenants and land agents, as did his Scottish cousins the MacNaughtens. Their understanding of developing Scottish society must have aided this transition from traditional Gaelic society into a modern monetary economy.

MacDonnell inherited lands on Kintyre from his brother, lost them in 1607, attempted to acquire Islay about 1613, and again in 1627, and to buy Kintyre in 1635. This probably reflects an ambition to revive the clan Donald south under his leadership. In important respects he remained strongly part of native culture: his sons were brought up in the 'highland manner', wearing neither hats nor shoes, and speaking Irish; he gave estates to two bards who composed poetry and legally useful documents

for him; and he was a staunch, if discreet, Catholic, erecting on his lands three churches for the Church of Ireland but only a chapel for the Franciscans. However, he also built chapels at the Catholic shrines of Brideswell, co. Roscommon, and Lough Derg, co. Donegal, to which he made pilgrimages, and validated the presence of priests on his lands by declaring them his chaplains. He supported a Franciscan mission to the western isles, and gave £300 to their Louvain college when his illegitimate son Daniel became its guardian.

Two other illegitimate sons also joined the Franciscans at Louvain, while a fourth, Maurice, followed MacDonnell's nephew Sorley into the O'Neill regiment in Spanish Flanders. Links were thus maintained with the exiled Irish, and MacDonnell's two legitimate sons, Randal *MacDonnell, the future marquess of Antrim, and his younger brother Alexander, toured the continent extensively before spending many years at the Stuart court, while an illegitimate daughter, Alice, married Sir Phelim O'Neill's brother, both men becoming prominent rebels in the 1640s. MacDonnell, however, always avoided confrontation with the authorities, and was anxious that his legitimate sons should be integrated members of Stuart society, encouraging them to find wealthy English or Scottish wives.

MacDonnell was created Viscount Dunluce on 28 May 1618 and earl of Antrim on 12 December 1620. He died at Dunluce on 10 December 1636 and was buried at Bonamargey Abbey, Ballycastle. His will divided the estate between his legitimate sons. Randal inherited the baronies of Dunluce and Kilconway, and Alexander that of Glenarm. His five legitimate daughters were left £2800 each. Three married into important Old English Catholic families of the pale: Anne married Christopher Nugent, Viscount Devlin, then William Fleming, nineteenth Baron Slane; Mary married Lucas, Viscount Dillon, then Oliver Plunket, sixth Baron Louth; Catherine married Edward Plunket of Castlecor, co. Meath. By contrast Sarah, the third daughter, married Neale Oge O'Neill of Killileagh, then Sir Charles O'Connor Sligo, then Donald MacCarthy More. The youngest, Rose, married in 1642 Colonel George Gordon, brother to the earl of Sutherland, who had come to Antrim that year with the invading covenanting army. He helped her brother Randal escape from imprisonment at Carrickfergus in 1643.

MacDonnell's career was highly unusual. Unlike Tyrone and many others, he successfully made the transition from chieftain to modernizing landowner. At his death, astonishingly, he left no significant debts. James I expressed his administration's general satisfaction when he remarked that MacDonnell's 'civil and orderly life' allowed the 'reformation and civilising of those rude parts' of Ulster (James I to Chichester, 6 May 1613, BL, Add. MS 4794, fol. 233).   HECTOR MCDONNELL

Sources G. Hill, *An historical account of the MacDonnells of Antrim* (1873) · J. H. Ohlmeyer, *Civil war and Restoration in the three Stuart kingdoms: the career of Randal MacDonnell, marquis of Antrim, 1609–1683* (1993) · H. McDonnell, *The wild geese of the Antrim MacDonnells* (Dublin, 1996) · *CSP Ire., 1590–1636* · C. Giblin, *Irish Franciscan mission* to Scotland, 1619–1646 (Dublin, 1956) · C. Fraser-Mackintosh, *The last MacDonalds of Isla* (1895) · G. A. Hayes-McCoy, *Scots mercenary forces in Ireland* (Dublin, 1973) · D. Stevenson, *Alasdair MacColla and the highland problem in the 17th century* (1980) · H. McDonnell, 'Agnews and OGnimhs', *The Glynns*, 15, 34–50 · GEC, *Peerage*

Archives PRO NIre., MSS | Bodl. Oxf., MSS Carte · NA Scot., Breadalbane muniments · PRO, state papers, Ireland · PRO, state papers, Scotland

Wealth at death co. Antrim estate of 333,907 acres: Hill, *Historical account of the MacDonnells* · divided lands between two legitimate sons; left no significant debts

MacDonnell, Randal, marquess of Antrim (1609–1683), politician, was the eldest legitimate son of Randal *MacDonnell, first earl of Antrim (d. 1636), and Alice (b. 1582/3, d. in or after 1663), daughter of Hugh *O'Neill, second earl of Tyrone (c.1550–1616), magnate and rebel, and his second wife, Siobhán (or Joanna). He had one younger brother, Alexander *MacDonnell (1615–1699), four illegitimate brothers (James, Alistair, Daniel, and Maurice), and six sisters (Anne, Mary, Sarah, Catherine, Rose, and Ellis).

Background and early career Reared at Dunluce Castle in co. Antrim and fluent in both Irish and English, MacDonnell was 'bred the highland way' wearing 'neither hat, cap, nor shoe, nor stocking' until he was seven or eight years old (Hill, 252). In 1625 he left Ireland to spend eighteen months in France to complete his education and to master the language. In the spring of 1627 as Viscount Dunluce—described as 'a tall, clean-limbed, handsome man with red hair' (Clarendon, *Hist. rebellion*, 3.509)—he returned from France and was presented at the English court, where he sought a suitable spouse. In 1628 he jilted Lady Lucy Abercorn (to whom he had been affianced in 1613) in favour of one of the sisters of James Stuart, fourth duke of Lennox. Nothing came of this match and so he turned to Honora Burke, a half-sister of the earl of Essex and the daughter of Frances Walsingham and the fourth earl of Clanricarde and St Albans, the most powerful Old English grandee in Connaught. After much wrangling the countess of St Albans dismissed the match as 'most inconvenient and dangerous' (BL, Add. MS 46188, fols. 124, 126). Undaunted he married, in April 1635, Katherine Villiers (*née* Manners), duchess of Buckingham (1603?–1649) [see MacDonnell, Katherine], the most eligible widow at court, and through her secured the patronage of—among others—Archbishop William Laud and the king himself.

On his father's death in 1636 MacDonnell became second earl of Antrim and inherited the baronies of Dunluce, Cary, and Kilconway, co. Antrim, together with Dunluce Castle, and took control over his brother's estates in the barony of Glenarm. His empire covered nearly 340,000 acres, making him the largest landowner in Ulster and one of the greatest in Ireland. Determined to improve his estates he travelled to Ireland in 1637 and later boasted:

> I have compounded my affairs here with my tenants wherein I was not so inward to my [own] profit as to the general good and settlement by binding them to plant [trees] and husband their holdings so near as may be to the manner of England. (Sheffield Archives, Strafford MS 17, fol. 151)

Contemporary valuations suggest that he received an

Randal MacDonnell, marquess of Antrim (1609–1683), by unknown artist

approximate annual rental from his Irish lands of between £6000 and £8300.

Ultimately Antrim's power rested not on his estates but on the influence he exercised over a heterogeneous pool of people both in Ulster and along the western seaboard of Scotland. To begin with he commanded the loyalty and support of many of his co. Antrim tenants (especially the native Irish and highland Scottish ones) and the various branches of the Irish MacDonnells. He enjoyed extensive contacts in Scotland: the MacDonnells of Antrim, the MacDonalds of Dunyvaig and the Glens, of Clanranald, of Glengarry, of Keppoch, and of Sleat all shared a common heritage and outlook and were united by an overriding ambition to rid the Western Isles of their arch-rivals, the clan Campbell. The earl was also closely allied to the great Catholic Scottish house of Gordon and, as an opponent of Campbell hegemony, was supported by the Ogilvies, the Hamiltons, and the lesser clans of MacLeod of Lewis, MacNeils of Gigha, MacAllasters of Loup, and MacFies of Colonsay. These ties of blood and animosity were supplemented by bonds of marriage. Thanks to the carefully calculated marriages of his siblings the earl was allied with leading Old English families in the pale (the Westmeaths, Slanes, Dillons, and Louths), and native Irish ones in Munster (MacCarthy More) and in Connaught (the O'Connors). Their strongest connections were in Ulster, where they had intermarried with most of the leading Gaelic families (the O'Neills, O'Haras, O'Cahans, MacQuillans, and O'Donnells) and even with English protestant settlers such as Sir Moses Hill. Given these links and the English patronage networks he had access to through his wife, Antrim enjoyed the rare privilege of truly being a man of the 'three kingdoms'.

After spending three years living at court 'in great expense and some lustre' (Clarendon, *Hist. rebellion*, 3.509), excessive debts forced the couple to move to Ireland in September 1638. Surviving figures suggest that Antrim's debts probably hovered between £40,000 and £42,000 during the late 1630s, and by the end of 1638 there was hardly a leading merchant or tradesman in London and Dublin to whom he did not owe money. Hence he mortgaged many of his own—and his wife's—properties, including the barony of Cary, the lordship of Ballycastle, Rathlin Island, and his English mansion in Hampshire, and other assets in order to raise money. Ironically, however, being in debt also had a positive side, and in Antrim's case his indebtedness—particularly to leading landowners in Ulster and to members of the London business community—helped to ensure his political survival. At the Restoration his creditors formed a powerful pressure group which lobbied for the earl's restoration principally to ensure that the money he owed them from the late 1630s might at last be repaid. In the long term, therefore, his debts bought him political and tenurial security, while in the middle term (1640s and 1650s) his indebtedness was relative since the majority of his class was similarly embarrassed. However, his debts had their dangers in the short term (the late 1630s) because they put him in severely straitened circumstances. Frequently he could neither meet his current expenses nor raise the capital he so desperately needed to support the king during the first bishops' war.

War and politics, 1638–1648 In May 1638 the marquess of Hamilton—who was eager to foster an anti-Campbell alliance—recommended Antrim to the king and suggested using the MacDonnells on both sides of the north channel as bulwarks against the covenanters in western Scotland. Hamilton suggested that an army levied and paid for by Antrim, and supplemented where possible by Lord Deputy Wentworth, should be the first line of royalist offence in the west of Scotland. In return Charles promised the earl that 'whatsoever land he can conquer from them [the Campbells], he, having pretense of right, he shall have the same' (*Strafforde's Letters*, 2.319). By spring 1639 Antrim had levied an army of 5000 foot and 200 horse. These men were drawn from the leading Irish families in Ulster: the O'Neills, O'Haras, O'Lurgans, Magennisses, MacGuires, MacMahons, MacDonnells, MacHenrys; or, as the lord deputy charmingly phrased it, 'as many Oe's and Macs's as would startle a whole council board' and 'in a great part the sons of habituated traitors' (*Strafforde's Letters*, 2.300). Ultimately the expedition was frustrated by Charles I's inconsistent attitude towards it and by Wentworth's hostility to it. Yet the abortive expedition was not without significance. On the one hand, it destabilized affairs in Scotland by alienating support for the king and forcing Argyll and his followers into the covenanting camp. On the other, the king's willingness to conspire with an Irish papist against his protestant subjects (albeit Scottish ones) did little to dispel the rumours of popish plots which were circulating around London.

Antrim played no part in the second bishops' war and from the summer of 1640 until the outbreak of the Irish rising he appears to have lived principally in Dublin, where Sir Adam Loftus, a senior government official, leased the couple his house. From here Antrim continued to plot with the king. According to his own account (made in May 1650), some time early in May 1641 Charles I sent Antrim and Ormond a messenger with instructions that Wentworth's new army should be increased to 20,000, 'armed out of the store of Dublin, and employed against the parliament' (Hill, 448–51). This Antrim plot came to nothing and it was the O'More–Maguire plot which gave rise to the insurrection of October 1641. With the outbreak of rebellion Antrim remained in Dublin and agreed to act as an intermediary with the 'discontented gentlemen' (as he termed the insurgents). In order to negotiate more effectively he moved to the earl of Castlehaven's house at Maddenstown in co. Kildare, where he harboured 'a great number of English protestants that had been robbed by the rebels' and then helped them find their way to safety (TCD, MS 813, fols. 285–285v). It was there that he learned that his followers in co. Antrim had joined the rising and that a Scottish army, under the command of Robert Monro, had occupied his patrimony. The need to recover his estates became his priority for the next twenty years, and he was prepared to do almost anything in order to secure their return.

In an attempt to do so by forging a deal with the Scottish commander in Ulster, Antrim travelled to Dunluce, where he was captured in May 1642. Six months later he escaped when a friend procured a passport for an invalid to leave Carrickfergus Castle, and Antrim, disguised as an invalid, fled to a waiting ship bound for Carlisle; from there he journeyed to York, where he joined his wife some time in November. He spent most of his time at York plotting an invasion of Scotland with the queen, the details of which were made public in May 1643 when he was captured by a Scottish colonel off the coast of co. Down. Following another dramatic escape from Carrickfergus he hurried to Waterford, where the third general assembly of the confederate Catholics had just convened. Almost at once he secured the support of the general assembly for an invasion of Scotland. The confederates promised to raise and transport 2000–3000 men to the Western Isles to join forces with troops levied by the Scottish royalists under the command of the marquess of Montrose. The following June some 1600 fully armed soldiers under the command of Alasdair MacColla left Ireland to form the backbone of Montrose's very successful army.

Delighted, the king rewarded Antrim with a marquessate in February 1645. However, the need to reinforce his brigade in Scotland now preoccupied him. Unable to secure additional aid from the confederates he turned to the Spaniards. In May 1645 he signed a contract with Manuel de Moura y Cortereal, marqués de Castel Rodrigo, governor-general of the Spanish Netherlands, promising to recruit, from among his Irish and Scottish dependants, '2,000 men, of which he is to be the colonel' (B. Jennings, ed., *Wild Geese in Spanish Flanders*, 1964, 368). In return Castel Rodrigo gave him two Dunkirk frigates which he collected late in 1645. Rather than sail directly to Scotland, as originally planned, in November 1645 Antrim led his armada instead to Falmouth in Cornwall, where he rescued the prince of Wales and provided supplies, subsequently stored in Pendennis Castle, for the beleaguered royalist garrisons in Cornwall. Early in 1646 he returned to Ireland and set his frigates up as privateers. Within a short period he had acquired at least four other vessels which provided him with a lucrative, if erratic, source of income and enabled him to ship supplies and reinforcements to Scotland.

In May 1646 Antrim arrived in the Western Isles with between 600 and 800 men. Even before he had disembarked his troops, the political situation in all three Stuart kingdoms was transformed when Charles I handed himself over to the Scots near Newark in Nottinghamshire on 5 May 1646. Almost immediately the king sent orders that all men in arms in Scotland in his name should disband their forces. Fired both by his desire to keep the traditional clan Donald heartland under his command and by the hope that his continued presence there would free his lands in co. Antrim from the Scottish army of occupation, Antrim refused. Then during the late summer and autumn of 1646 Antrim mooted 'a design to raise … 30,000 men … to reduce Scotland this winter … and from hence to march into England'. Their quarrel, royalists at the exiled court in France later reported to the king, 'is to be, to free your majesty from imprisonment' (Scrope and Monkhouse, 2.271). Antrim's military endeavours in Scotland were thus no longer merely an embarrassment, but rather a serious threat to any chance of securing a British peace. Only after Charles I personally intervened did the marquess order his army to disband, his compliance purchased by an express verbal undertaking that as soon as Argyll's estates in Kintyre could be forfeited he would receive all those lands that he claimed belonged to the MacDonnells.

Antrim returned to Ireland in January 1647 and played a key role in the seventh confederate general assembly by leading the opposition to any peace with Ormond. In March the general assembly elected him president of the new supreme council and he became responsible for the day-to-day administration of the confederate armies, for the smooth running of the confederate provincial assemblies, and for the distribution of confederate material and financial resources. His eagerness to serve as a member of the supreme council and his enthusiastic adherence to the papal nuncio, Rinuccini, marked a new phase in his political career and illustrated his willingness to be formally associated with the Irish Catholic—as opposed to the royalist—cause. Despite his ties to the increasingly unpopular nuncio, Antrim was nominated by the eighth general assembly as part of a confederate delegation to treat with the royalist court in exile. He arrived at St Germain in March 1648 but was outwitted by Ormond during the subsequent negotiations. Furious and increasingly marginalized, Antrim resorted to armed rebellion in an

effort to undermine Ormond (who returned to Ireland in September 1648 at the head of a pan-archipelagic royalist coalition). The plan ran awry from the start and the insurrection was quashed, forcing Antrim to flee late in 1648 to the safety of Owen Roe O'Neill's camp in Ulster.

Later life and assessment With the death of his wife in November 1649 Antrim's prospects looked increasingly bleak, yet in another remarkable volte-face he clandestinely threw in his lot with the Cromwellians. Though the details are obscure, he appears to have been in fairly close contact with the parliamentarian commander, Michael Jones, since he returned from France in the autumn of 1648 and quickly made contact with Henry Ireton, Cromwell's son-in-law, when he arrived in Ireland late in the summer of 1649. He demonstrated his willingness to serve the Cromwellians by securing the surrender of New Ross (19 October 1649), by persuading his former followers to surrender Carlow peacefully (July 1650), and by disrupting the Scottish royalists' war effort during the third civil war. The administration in Dublin, though it refused to restore his estates, rewarded him financially for his loyalty to the regime. In addition to an annual pension of £500 (later increased to £800), he received occasional additional contributions towards everyday expenses and the Cromwellians also paid off a number of his creditors. In 1653 Antrim married a protestant heiress, Rose O'Neill (1631–1695), daughter of Sir Henry O'Neill and Martha Stafford. Rose *MacDonnell and her husband remained in east Ulster throughout the 1650s.

With the restoration of Charles II, Antrim was immediately imprisoned in the Tower of London, where he languished until May 1661. However, thanks to an extraordinary combination of factors—especially the tenacity of his creditors, and the support and generosity of his family, the queen mother, and members of her court, combined with the fact that his enemies were disorganized, disunited, and unprepared—he finally regained his estates. In July 1663 Charles II declared the marquess 'innocent of any malice or rebellious purpose towards the crown' and ordered Ormond to assist him to recover his estates by making known the king's wishes to the commissioners of the court of claims (Hill, 467–8). Adventurers and soldiers—led by Sir John Clotworthy, later Lord Massareene—who had acquired farms on the Antrim estate during the 1650s immediately protested and the publication of a pamphlet entitled *Murder Will Out* (August 1663) drew public attention to their grievances. But the marquess's tenacity was eventually rewarded and clause 173 of the Act of Explanation (December 1665) granted him a full pardon and restored him to his property in co. Antrim.

With this, Antrim's dramatic political career came to an end and he distanced himself from international and even national affairs—dividing his time between Dunluce, his summer residence at Ballymagarry, and his wife's estate near Randalstown. He passed his time hunting, gaming, arranging suitable matches for his family and friends, interfering in county politics, socializing with other local grandees, and settling his debts. Just before he died he mortgaged his entire estate for thirty-one years so that his financial obligations to roughly 220 individuals—some incurred nearly fifty years before—could be honoured. On 3 February 1683 he died 'at his dwelling near Dunluce'. Since he had not produced an heir the marquessate died out and his younger brother Alexander succeeded him as the third earl. Antrim's body lay in state until 14 March 1683 when he was finally buried, after an elaborate funeral, alongside many of his ancestors in the family vault at the Franciscan friary of Bonamargy, near Ballycastle.

Antrim's extraordinary career as a Caroline loyalist, Catholic confederate, Cromwellian collaborator, and Restoration pragmatist caused him to be vilified by his contemporaries and by later historians. There was undoubtedly an unsavoury, greedy, myopic side to Antrim's character and he was willing to twist ruthlessly every opportunity to his own advantage. However, there was also a very positive (and overlooked) dimension to his personality. He remained loyal to his family and kinsmen, devoted to Catholicism, and was charming, determined, dynamic, enterprising, and resourceful. These qualities, combined with the fact that he was an important political power broker in a remote and unstable corner of the three kingdoms, ensured that he survived the upheavals of the mid-seventeenth century with his inheritance, religion, political influence, and head intact.   JANE OHLMEYER

Sources J. H. Ohlmeyer, *Civil war and Restoration in the three Stuart kingdoms: the career of Randal MacDonnell, marquis of Antrim, 1609–1683*, pbk edn (2001) [repr. 2001] · G. Hill, *An historical account of the MacDonnells of Antrim* (1873); repr. (1978) · G. Radcliffe, *The earl of Strafforde's letters and dispatches, with an essay towards his life*, ed. W. Knowler, 2 vols. (1739) · *The works of the most reverend father in God, William Laud*, ed. J. Bliss and W. Scott, 7 vols. (1847–60) · Clarendon, *Hist. rebellion* · T. Carte, *An history of the life of James, duke of Ormonde*, 3 vols. (1735–6); new edn, pubd as *The life of James, duke of Ormond*, 6 vols. (1851) · B. O'Ferrall and D. O'Connell, *Commentarius Rinuccinianus de sedis apostolicae legatione ad foederatos Hiberniae Catholicos per annos 1645–1649*, ed. J. Kavanagh, 6 vols., IMC (1932–49) · *History of the Irish confederation and the war in Ireland … by Richard Bellings*, ed. J. T. Gilbert, 7 vols. (1882–91) · J. T. Gilbert, ed., *A contemporary history of affairs in Ireland from 1641 to 1652*, 3 vols. (1879–80) · *CSP Ire., 1608–70* · *CSP dom., 1635–61* · R. C. Simington, *The transplantation to Connacht, 1654–58*, IMC (1970) · R. Scrope and T. Monkhouse, eds., *State papers collected by Edward, earl of Clarendon*, 3 vols. (1767–86) · GEC, *Peerage* · Strafford papers, Sheff. Arch., Wentworth Woodhouse muniments · Bodl. Oxf., MSS Carte · SP, PRO · depositions, 1641, TCD · NL Ire., Plunkett MS 345 · estado Inglaterra, Simancas, Spain
Archives PRO NIre., estate MSS
Likenesses M. Wright, portrait, priv. coll. · portrait, priv. coll. [*see illus.*]
Wealth at death after death estate 'much altered, impaired, mangled, and engaged in debts, mortgages, grants and otherwise': Hill, *Historical account of the MacDonnells*

McDonnell, Randal John Somerled, eighth earl of Antrim (1911–1977), chairman of the National Trust, was born in Kensington, London, on 22 May 1911, the second of four children and elder son of Randall Mark Kerr McDonnell (1878–1932), then Viscount Dunluce and, from 1918, seventh earl of Antrim, and his wife, Margaret Isabel, daughter of John Gilbert Talbot, privy councillor and MP for Oxford University. He was educated at Eton College

(1924–9) and at Christ Church, Oxford, where he studied modern history. He left without a degree.

In 1932, the year he succeeded his father in the earldom, McDonnell was appointed honorary attaché in Tehran but resigned the following year to take up a post as clerk in the House of Lords. He resigned his clerkship in 1934 to pursue his plans for developing his Glenarm estate in co. Antrim, particularly its farming which was his lifelong interest. He started many local enterprises to create employment—hotels, coalmines, and fisheries. In the same year he became an Antrim JP and deputy lieutenant. In 1934 he married Angela Christina (d. 1984), daughter of Sir Mark *Sykes, sixth baronet (1879–1919), traveller, soldier, and politician. They had three sons, the second of whom died at a day old, and a daughter.

When war broke out in 1939 Antrim joined the Royal Naval Volunteer Reserve and commanded a motor torpedo boat until swept by Lord Louis Mountbatten into a series of staff appointments. On taking command of the Ulster division in 1954 (a post he held until 1957) he was promoted captain.

In 1948 Antrim was appointed chairman of the National Trust's committee for Northern Ireland. In 1965 he became chairman of the National Trust, on whose evolution and development he was to make a greater impact than any previous chairman. His mettle was soon tested. In 1967 a group of members requisitioned an extraordinary general meeting. It was long and disorderly, and a number of accusations were made. The trust had until then enjoyed an immaculate reputation. Now, though the meeting, and a later poll of all members, decisively rejected the critics, the trust received bad publicity. Antrim's great contribution at this crucial stage was to see that only by making changes in the trust's constitution and organization could its reputation be restored. To recommend what should be done an advisory committee was set up, consisting of three members of the trust's council, with Sir Henry Benson, an eminent chartered accountant, as chairman. Benson recommended greater control over the trust's policy by its members, greater access to its historic houses, and big changes in organization. Not all these ideas were palatable to Antrim's more traditional colleagues. All had to be steered through them, the council, the annual general meeting, and, since the trust's constitution was embodied in a private act of parliament, through parliament.

Antrim put all his energy (and charm) into this task of persuasion and the longer work of implementing the changes. He knew that the great increase in the number of properties accepted—many more were in prospect—made it essential for regional committees to take over much of the management from head office committees. He set regionalization in progress, simultaneously improving head office liaison and introducing effective control of the ever-increasing budget. He made the staff changes needed, some of them painful.

In 1977 Antrim's health was failing and he announced his wish to retire. By then regionalization was virtually completed and the new constitution was working. Rapport with members had been greatly improved, especially by setting up seventy-four new local centres; only eleven had existed in 1965. Fifty further historic houses had been accepted and 50,000 acres added to the 400,000 in hand. Enterprise Neptune, the appeal he had promoted to save the coastline, had extended the protected coast from 187 to 380 miles. A membership drive, at one time thought indecent, had brought numbers up from 150,000 to 600,000. New sources of revenue, including shops at historic houses, enabled an annual expenditure of £11 million to be financed. The reputation of the trust was as high as ever.

Antrim would never have claimed that the restoration and modernization of the National Trust was his doing. However, those who worked with him knew that, without his leadership and drive, these objectives would not have been secured. The trust was his paramount interest and he led others to give it the same devotion, masking his fervour behind great natural charm and an irrepressible sense of humour.

He worked not only for buildings and landscape. In 1959 he became chairman of the new Ulster Television station, where many potential explosions were defused by his wisdom, wit, and good humour. From 1966 he was chairman of the St Peter's group of hospitals in London. No figurehead, he visited constantly and was known by all the staff. He promoted actively the group's urological and nephrological research. In 1972–4 he was a member of the Sports Council.

Antrim was appointed KBE in 1970. In 1972 he became honorary FRIBA and received a DLitt from the New University of Ulster. Antrim died at his Chelsea home on 26 September 1977 and was succeeded in the earldom by his elder son, Alexander Randal Mark, Viscount Dunluce (b. 1935), who became keeper of conservation at the Tate Gallery.　　　　　JOHN WINNIFRITH, rev.

Sources *The Times* (27 July 1977) · personal knowledge (1986) · *WWW* · Burke, *Peerage* (1980) · G. Murphy, *Founders of the National Trust* (1967)
Archives PRO NIre., corresp. relating to National Trust

Macdonnell, Sir Richard Graves (1814–1881), colonial governor, was born in Dublin on 3 September 1814, the eldest son of Dr Richard MacDonnell (d. 1867), later provost of Trinity College, Dublin, and his wife, Jane, daughter of Richard Graves, dean of Ardagh. He was educated at Trinity College, Dublin, from which he graduated BA in 1835, LLB in 1845, and LLD in 1862. He was called to the Irish bar in 1838, and to the English bar, at Lincoln's Inn, in 1841. He married in 1847 Blanche Ann, daughter of Francis Skurray of Brunswick Square, Brighton.

On 20 July 1843 Macdonnell was appointed chief justice, and on 1 October 1847 governor, of the Gambia. Here he explored the interior from the Gambia to the Senegal rivers and quelled tribes hostile to European river traders. In 1852 he was nominated governor of St Lucia, but proceeded instead on 10 January 1853 to St Vincent as lieutenant-governor. In June 1855 he became governor of

South Australia, where he encouraged further exploration and settlement, and became embroiled in controversy over the readiness of that colony for responsible government. He took a strong line on the effective authority of the governor, which he took with him to his next appointment, in Nova Scotia, in May 1864, after two years of inactivity. Sent to foster the idea of union between the maritime communities, Macdonnell was profoundly critical of proposals for a wider Canadian confederation, and was embarrassed when the British Colonial Office took up that scheme. He departed for Hong Kong in October 1865, where he exercised his final governorship; he retired in 1872. In Hong Kong, as elsewhere, Macdonnell's abrasive personality made him deeply unpopular: Rutherford Alcock apparently described him as 'coarse, bumptious, and exceptionally uncouth and uncourteous' (Coates).

Macdonnell had become CB in 1852, was knighted in 1856, and was created KCMG in 1871. He died at Hyères, France, on 5 February 1881, and was buried in Kensal Green cemetery on 14 February. He was survived by his wife.　　　　　G. C. BOASE, rev. LYNN MILNE

Sources *The Times* (8 Feb 1881) · P. Burroughs, 'MacDonnell, Sir Richard Graves', *DCB*, vol. 11 · C. C. Manhood, 'MacDonnell, Sir Richard Graves', *AusDB*, vol. 5 · *ILN* (5 March 1881), 220, 222 · P. D. Coates, *The China consuls: British consular officers, 1843–1943* (1988) · Walford, *County families*
Archives NRA, priv. coll., letters to Lord Monck · State Library of South Australia, Adelaide, Mortlock Library of South Australiana, South Australian Archives, Finniss MSS · U. Durham L., corresp. with Lord Grey
Likenesses wood-engraving, NPG; repro. in *ILN*, 220
Wealth at death under £18,000: probate, 10 March 1881, *CGPLA Eng. & Wales*

McDonnell, Robert (1828–1889), surgeon, born in Dublin on 15 March 1828, was the second son of John McDonnell (1796–1892), surgeon, and his wife, Charity, *née* Dobbs. He was a grandson of Dr James McDonnell, of Belfast, and a descendant of Ian Vohr of Isla and Kintyre, whose great-grandson was Alaster MacColl Macdonald. After a private education McDonnell entered Trinity College, Dublin, in 1844. In the following year he was apprenticed to Richard Carmichael, on whose death in 1849 he was transferred to Robert Moore Peile. McDonnell graduated BA and MB in 1850, obtained the licence of the Royal College of Surgeons in Ireland on 22 February 1851, and was admitted a fellow on 24 August 1853. He afterwards visited Edinburgh, Paris, and Vienna. In 1855, during the Crimean War, he was attached to the British hospital at Smyrna, and he volunteered as civil surgeon to serve in the general hospital in the camp before Sevastopol. For his services he received the British medal and clasp and the Turkish medal.

In 1856 McDonnell became demonstrator of anatomy in the Carmichael school of medicine; he later lectured there on anatomy and physiology. In 1857 he became MD at the University of Dublin, and in 1864 he was admitted to the degree of MD at the Queen's University of Ireland. He was appointed surgeon to Jervis Street Hospital in 1863, and three years later he was elected surgeon to Dr Steevens' Hospital and professor of descriptive anatomy in its medical school. In 1865 he married Mary McAuley (d. 1869). He later married Susan McCausland (d. 1891); they had at least one son.

In 1857 McDonnell was appointed medical superintendent of Mountjoy prison. In carrying out his official duties he came into collision with the prison's board over questions of the food supply and general treatment of the prisoners under his charge. He held that the medical officer should exercise an unfettered discretion in such matters. As the board decided otherwise, he resigned in 1867. Some demur was made to granting him a pension, but in the interests of his profession he fought out the battle, eventually obtaining the pension. The money thus acquired he contributed annually to the Medical Benevolent Fund. 'One must embrace the profession with ardour, and pay it no divided allegiance', McDonnell told his students (Buckley, 66).

On new year's day 1847 John McDonnell was the first Irish surgeon to use ether; and according to J. D. Widdess the first recorded transfusion of blood to a human in Ireland was performed in Jervis Street Hospital on 20 April 1865 by Robert McDonnell, using his own blood (Widdess, 13). The patient, a victim of tetanus, died, but in February 1870 McDonnell transfused blood to a 24-year-old woman exsanguinated by post-partum haemorrhage. She survived. The donor on that occasion was the lady's husband; fortunately their bloods were compatible, for blood groups were then unknown. McDonnell wrote no books but was MRIA and FRS; his remarkably varied contributions to surgical and scientific literature were so numerous that they fill a column of the Royal Society's *Catalogue of Scientific Papers*. He edited a volume of the works of Abraham Colles for the New Sydenham Society in 1881.

McDonnell died suddenly from heart disease at his home, 89 Merrion Square, Dublin, at 1 a.m. on 6 May 1889, and was buried at Kilsharvan, the family cemetery, near Drogheda, co. Louth.   D'A. POWER, rev. J. B. LYONS

Sources C. A. Cameron, *History of the Royal College of Surgeons in Ireland*, 2nd edn (1916) · J. D. H. Widdess, 'Robert M'Donnell: a pioneer of blood transfusion; with a survey of transfusion in Ireland, 1832–1922', *The Irish Journal of Medical Science*, 313 (Jan 1952), 11–20 · C. McD. Buckley, 'Robert McDonnell (1828–1889)', *Journal of the Irish Colleges of Physicians and Surgeons*, 3 (1973), 66–9 · *The Lancet* (11 May 1889) · *BMJ* (11 May 1889), 1092 · CGPLA Eng. & Wales (1889)
Likenesses S. Purser, portrait, 1891, Royal College of Surgeons of Ireland · A. B. Joy, marble bust, 1892, Royal College of Surgeons of Ireland
Wealth at death £2172 10s. 0d.—in England: probate, 1889, CGPLA Eng. & Wales

MacDonnell [née O'Neill], **Rose, marchioness of Antrim** (1631–1695), noblewoman, was the daughter of Sir Henry O'Neill (d. 1638), from one of the pro-English cadet branches of the O'Neills of Clandeboye, and Martha Stafford (d. 1678), daughter of the English administrator and governor of Ulster Sir Francis Stafford. On her father's side she was related to local native Irish families, including Sir Arthur Magenis, later Viscount Iveagh, and the MacDonnells of Antrim. Rose had three brothers and one sister but since her siblings were declared insane she inherited, on her father's death in 1638, his estates of

Edenduffcarrick (also known as Shane's Castle) in the barony of Toome, co. Antrim. Though the details are obscure Rose spent some time at the Caroline court, and in 1642 she accompanied the eleven-year-old Princess Mary to Holland after her marriage to William II of Orange. As a protestant Rose appears to have spent most of the civil wars of the 1640s on her estates in co. Antrim, which were spoiled by the Scottish soldiers garrisoned on them. Despite this the property allegedly brought in an annual rental of £1600, even during the 1650s.

In 1653 Rose married, as his second wife, the Catholic statesman Randal *MacDonnell, marquess of Antrim (1609–1683), whose vast patrimony had been confiscated. Despite this Antrim enjoyed favour with the Cromwellians and in 1655–6 Rose was allotted 26,664 Irish acres of good quality land 'with convenient accommodation' in Connaught. There is no evidence to suggest that she ever left Ulster and she appears to have lived at her husband's seat at Dunluce. After the Restoration she lobbied vigorously for the return of her husband's estates and mortgaged chunks of her own property in an attempt to help him pay off his vast debts. Between 1665, when Antrim was restored to his patrimony, and his death on 3 February 1683, the couple divided their time between their various properties in east Ulster and involved themselves primarily in local affairs. In January 1690 one society gossip reported that a Monsieur Schomberg had married Rose. Presumably Rose met Frederick Herman *Schomberg, duke of Schomberg (1615–1690), commander and chief of the Williamite forces in Ireland, during the late summer of 1689, when his troops were garrisoned in east Ulster. An extant order from Schomberg, dated August 1689, required 'all officers, soldiers and all others … not to molest Lady Antrim or any of her tenants … either in their persons or estates' (Glenarm Castle MSS). Their alleged union proved short-lived since Schomberg perished at the battle of the Boyne six months later. No doubt Rose also used her earlier contacts with the house of Orange to ensure that her relatives, including her brother-in-law Alexander *MacDonnell, third earl of Antrim, suffered as little as possible as a result of the Williamite confiscations after 1689. Rose died, childless, on 27 April 1695 and her estate passed to John O'Neill, her first cousin, who had intermarried with a cadet branch of the MacDonnells. She was buried in the church of St Nicholas, Carrickfergus, beside her parents and her grandfather.

JANE OHLMEYER

Sources G. Hill, *An historical account of the MacDonnells of Antrim* (1873); repr. (1978) · H. McDonnell, 'A noble pretension', *The Glynns*, 8 (1980), 20–33 · J. H. Ohlmeyer, *Civil war and Restoration in the three Stuart kingdoms: the career of Randal MacDonnell, marquis of Antrim, 1609–1683* (1993) · *CSP Ire.*, 1647–70 · R. C. Simington, *The transplantation to Connacht, 1654–58*, IMC (1970) · W. A. Maguire, ed., *Kings in conflict: the revolutionary war in Ireland and its aftermath, 1689–1750* (1990) · GEC, *Peerage*
Archives Bodl. Oxf., Carte MSS · Hunt. L., Hastings MSS · PRO NIre., Antrim estate MSS
Likenesses portrait, priv. coll. · portrait, priv. coll.

McDonnell, Sir Schomberg Kerr (1861–1915), civil servant, was born at Glenarm Castle, co. Antrim, Ireland, on

22 March 1861, the fifth son of Mark McDonnell, fifth earl of Antrim (1814–1869), of the second creation, and his wife, Jane Emma Hannah (d. 1892), daughter of Major Turner Macan. He was known as Pom throughout his life. Educated at Eton College and at University College, Oxford, where he did not take a degree, he afterwards gained experience as private secretary to the fourth earl of Carnarvon and to the sixth duke of Buccleuch. This experience, and his own ability, left him well suited to fill the position of principal private secretary to the prime minister, the third marquess of Salisbury, in 1888. It was the start of a long and important relationship which lasted until Salisbury's death in 1903.

McDonnell was devoted to Lord Salisbury and referred to him as the 'chief'. He provided an invaluable channel of communication with the Conservative Party and was one of an inner circle, along with the chief whip, Aretas Akers-Douglas, and the chief party agent, Richard Middleton, who were in continual liaison. In 1892, when Lord Salisbury left office, he retained the services of McDonnell as his political private secretary, and he played a prominent part in party organization, especially in the work of the Conservative central office. Three years later, when the Conservatives returned to power, McDonnell again took up the duties of principal private secretary. In 1902 the announcement that he was leaving to succeed Viscount Esher as secretary to the office of works foreshadowed the imminent retirement of Lord Salisbury.

On his appointment to the office of works McDonnell was created KCB and during his period in office he was responsible for the funeral of Edward VII, the coronation of George V, and the investiture of the prince of Wales at Caernarfon Castle. An impressive looking man with piercing blue eyes, finely chiselled features, and upturned moustache, he became an important personality in court life. He retired in 1912 due to ill health, although it also seems likely that his career may have been cut short by his appearance in the divorce courts as a co-respondent in the case of an American, Mrs Harrison. On 26 February 1913 he married Ethel Henry (d. 1916), formerly wife of Captain Harrison, and daughter of Major Alexander H. Davis of La Floridiana, Naples. They had no children.

McDonnell appears to have possessed an impetuous and patriotic streak, characterized by his enlistment in the City of London Imperial Volunteers and active service in South Africa in 1900. After the outbreak of the First World War, he acted as a chief intelligence officer in London. However, he gave up this position and, aged fifty-four, joined the 5th Cameron Highlanders. Within three weeks he was mortally wounded on the western front in Flanders; he died on 23 November 1915 at Abeele, and was interred in the Lijsseuthoek military cemetery at Poperinge.   DAVID HUDDLESTON

Sources E. McDonnell, *Life of Schomberg McDonnell* (privately printed) [copy in PRO NIre., D/4091/A/11/8/1] · *DNB* · *The Times* (27 Nov 1915), 11 · Burke, *Peerage* · P. Marsh, *The discipline of popular government: Lord Salisbury's domestic statecraft, 1881–1902* (1978) · J. F. A. Mason, 'Lord Salisbury: a librarian's view', *Salisbury: the man and his policies*, ed. Lord Blake and H. Cecil (1987), 10–29 · R. Shannon, *The age of Salisbury, 1881–1902: unionism and empire* (1996) · J. Balfour, *Reminiscences of the McDonnells: the uncles* (privately printed) [copy in PRO NIre., D/4091/E/2/1] · S. Lee, *King Edward VII*, 1 (1925) · G. Cecil, *Life of Robert, marquis of Salisbury*, 4 vols. (1921–32) · K. Rose, *King George V* (1983) · *Dod's Peerage* (1904) · *WW* · Commonwealth War Graves Commission, www.cwgc.org [debt of honour register]
Archives PRO NIre., D/4091 | BL, Curzon MSS, 10C · Bodl. Oxf., L. Harcourt MSS · CKS, Akers-Douglas MSS
Likenesses B. Scott & Son, photograph, 1880, PRO NIre. · Maull & Fox, photograph, c.1897, PRO NIre. · Elliott & Fry, photograph, c.1900, PRO NIre. · W. & D. Downey, photograph, 1909, PRO NIre.
Wealth at death £51,003 0s. 3d.: resworn probate, 16 May 1916, CGPLA Eng. & Wales

MacDonnell, Sorley Boy [Somhairle Buidhe MacDhomhnaill] (*b.* in or before **1508**, *d.* **1590**), chieftain, was traditionally said to have been born and to have died at Dunanynie near Ballycastle Bay, co. Antrim, Ireland, the sixth and youngest son of Alastair or Alexander *MacDonald of Dunyvaig and the Glens (d. 1536x9), chieftain, of clan Iain Mhòir or clan Donald south in Scotland, and his wife, Katherine or Caitirfhiona, daughter of John MacIan, lord of Ardnamurchan. He was called Boy (Gaelic, Buidhe) because of his fair hair. During Sorley's youth his father, a cousin of John MacDonald, fourth lord of the Isles, built up a power base for his family in both Scotland and Ulster, receiving land grants on Islay, Colonsay, and Kintyre from Colin Campbell, third earl of Argyll, and his brother in 1519 (confirmed by James V in 1531).

Early career, 1538–1567 After Alexander MacDonald's death his eldest son, James *MacDonald of Dunyvaig and the Glens, the new chieftain, made his third brother, Colla (d. 1558), captain of his Antrim possessions. Sorley was Colla's active partner, and about 1550 was imprisoned in Dublin Castle for the constant encroachments of the Antrim Scots in the 'Route' of Antrim and the Glens; he remained there for over a year until he was exchanged, in September 1551, for men captured by James and Colla during the abortive raid of the lord deputy, Sir James Croft, on Rathlin Island during the summer. Sorley then attacked Carrickfergus and captured Walter Floddy, the castle constable, before releasing him on payment of a ransom.

During the 1550s Colla and Sorley extended the family territory westwards, seizing from the MacQuillans the coastal strip of the lordship of the Route from Ballycastle to Coleraine and capturing the greatest stronghold north of Carrickfergus, Dunluce Castle. A Southern Clandonald foothold was also established in Lecale, co. Down. On Colla's death in 1558 James offered the captaincy to his brothers in order of seniority, and as the others declined, the position fell to the youngest, Sorley. In 1560 Sorley made overtures to the English authorities, and in January 1561 he and James made an agreement with Elizabeth I's government. The MacDonnells—the name by which the MacDonalds of the Glens became known to Irish history written in English—undertook to deploy their forces against any 'rebels' between Carrickfergus and Lough Foyle in return for a grant of their lands for twenty-one years. This agreement was largely directed against Shane *O'Neill (c.1530–1567), who was regarded by the government as a greater threat, though positions soon changed.

In March 1563 the English attacked the MacDonnells holding Lecale, and two of Sorley's cousins were killed. Shane then signed a treaty with the English in September, and announced his intention of expelling the MacDonnells from Antrim.

In spring 1565 Shane attacked the Glens, burnt Red Bay Castle, and marched northwards, to defeat the MacDonnells at Glenshesk near Ballycastle, co. Antrim, on 2 May. Sorley and James were captured. Another brother, Eneas, was killed, and James died of his wounds, though it was rumoured that Shane hastened his end. However, by 1567 Shane was in such difficulties that he applied through his prisoner, Sorley, for reinforcements from the Scottish MacDonalds. On 2 June, after first sailing to Carrickfergus to parley with the English authorities there, they met Shane at Cushendun, co. Antrim, lured him out of sight of his own men, and murdered him. Sorley was freed at the same time.

Chieftain, 1567–1588 Sorley next went to Scotland, gathered a force of 600–700 fighting men, and landed at Ballycastle Bay in November 1567. Rory Oge MacQuillan, who had recovered his family's territory after Glenshesk, opposed their landing. According to tradition they fought three successive battles, the first at Bonamargy Friary, close to the shore, and the others in Glenshesk, as a result of which Sorley expelled the MacQuillans from the Ballycastle area, and Rory Oge's three sons were killed. However, before the year's end, and to the English government's alarm, peace was established between the three warring families of O'Neill, MacDonnell, and MacQuillan. In 1569 Turlough Luineach O'Neill, the new O'Neill, married Lady Agnes *Campbell (d. in or after 1590), James MacDonald's widow, on Rathlin Island. Sorley had already married Shane's sister Mary (d. 1582), daughter of Conn Bacach O'Neill, first earl of Tyrone, and his second wife, Sorcha, earlier in the 1560s, and MacQuillan married Turlough Luineach's daughter.

In 1571 Sir Thomas Smith proposed to colonize northern Ulster and expel the Scots. Sorley brought over reinforcements, and in February 1572 he attacked Carrickfergus, where he was wounded. He then petitioned Elizabeth, asking for legal recognition of his possessions. Smith's efforts achieved little, and on 14 April 1573 Sorley was offered a patent of denization in return for active support against any opponents of the crown in Ulster. But the situation altered as the government encouraged English plantation as a better means of bringing order to Ulster than negotiation with the Scots and Irish. Walter Devereux, first earl of Essex, received a grant of Clandeboye, the Glens, the Route, and Rathlin Island, and landed at Carrickfergus in August bringing 400 colonists with him. He joined forces with Smith and negotiated (unsuccessfully) with Sir Brian mac Phelim O'Neill of Clandeboye. Sorley offered his submission again, and 1574 was spent in complex negotiations, until in November mac Phelim O'Neill and MacQuillan were seized by Essex during a parley and killed. Sorley, however, remained, as the outstanding conveyor of 'redshanks' (mercenaries from western Scotland)

to the Ulster chieftains, and Elizabeth insisted that all the MacDonnells must be expelled.

On 27 July 1575 Essex made peace with Turlough Luineach, who submitted. He had won a battle against Sorley near Toome earlier in the month, and launched a naval attack commanded by John Norris against Rathlin Island from Carrickfergus. Sorley had 'put most of his plate, most of his children and the children of his gentlemen with their wives' on the island for their safety (PRO, SP 63/52/70). Norris brought 300 foot and eighty horse on three frigates, and the people on the island fled into a castle held by fifty of Sorley's men. The castle surrendered after a two-day siege, and Norris slaughtered the 500–600 people on the island and garrisoned the castle. This catastrophe did little to damage the MacDonnells' fighting strength. In November Sorley attacked Carrickfergus, took the townsmen's cattle, and killed 100 soldiers. On 28 September Sir Henry Sidney, the lord deputy, reported Sorley's country to be 'full of corn and cattle' and Sorley himself 'very haughty and proud by reason of the late victories he hath had' (Collins, 1.77). However, he agreed to end hostilities, and again asked for legal recognition of his position. Sidney returned Rathlin Island to him and proposed that the Glens should be held by Sorley rather than by Angus *MacDonald of Dunyvaig and the Glens, the clan chieftain, son of Sorley's brother James and Lady Agnes Campbell.

It was a constant anxiety for the English government that Sorley would bring in large numbers of Scots to extend his areas of control, or that Lady Agnes Campbell would strengthen Turlough Luineach's position by importing redshanks either through her nephew, Colin Campbell, sixth earl of Argyll, or else through Sorley. A certain number of redshanks did come across every year, and in 1582 Sorley brought 2000 men for an O'Neill–O'Donnell expedition to support a rising in Connaught. At this point the English administration decided to eject the MacDonnells completely. The consequent expedition of 1583 consisted of a mixed force of Clandeboye O'Neills, MacQuillans (anxious to retake their territory in the Route), and English soldiers. O'Neill of Clandeboye and seventy English musketeers attacked the men in the Glens led by Sorley's nephew, Angus of Dunyvaig, forcing them to flee to Scotland. They then regrouped, marched northwards through the Route, and tried to cross over a pass near Orra Mountain into the northern Glens so as to join forces with some discontented clansmen. However, Sorley had been forewarned and had prepared a trap. The invaders were tricked into charging into boggy ground, where O'Neill and MacQuillan were slain with many of their men, as well as the seventy English soldiers and their two captains. Sorley himself had been too old to fight, and watched the battle from a distance.

In 1584 the new lord deputy, Sir John Perrot, tried to reverse this defeat. In August and September he moved through Antrim with another mixed force of English companies and O'Neill and MacQuillan fighting men. Sorley quickly moved west of the Bann river, and Perrot took Dunluce after a brief siege. The most notable booty he found there was 'Holy Columkill's Cross, a god of great veneration with Surley Boy and all Ulster' (PRO, SP 63/111/94). Perrot then garrisoned both Dunluce and Dunanynie. Sorley meanwhile sailed to Scotland for reinforcements. He returned briefly in November, and at the beginning of January 1585 brought 2000 redshanks to Cushendun. This rescued Angus of Dunyvaig and his brother Donnell Gorm, whose territory was being threatened by English detachments under Sir William Stanley and Sir Henry Bagenal. Bagenal retreated to protect Carrickfergus, and on 5 January the MacDonnells attacked Stanley and his men, who had stationed themselves inside Bonamargy Friary. Donnell Gorm torched the building, and Sorley sailed south to Red Bay to prevent Bagenal returning from Carrickfergus. Stanley staunchly retained his position at Bonamargy, and on 5 February Sorley again offered to submit, promising a son as a pledge if his strongholds were returned and legal recognition granted. However, by March the MacDonnells' situation had deteriorated. Angus of Dunyvaig took most of his men back to Scotland, while another English expedition forced Sorley to retreat to Toome, where he found the Bann crossing blocked by Turlough Luineach's troops. On 22 March Perrot reported that the MacDonnells were a broken force; Sorley and Donnell Gorm had sailed for Scotland, he had established an English garrison on Rathlin Island, and only Sorley's son Alexander and 120 redshanks remained. Elizabeth told Perrot to halt all military operations in Ulster, and in April Angus of Dunyvaig submitted to James VI in Edinburgh, promising to prevent 'undesirable Scots' from going to Ireland (PRO, SP 63/109/37).

Nevertheless, by August Sorley was back with more men. They re-established control over the Glens, recaptured Dunluce in early November, and in February 1586 it was reported that Angus of Dunyvaig was going to bring over another 2000 redshanks. Sorley's eldest son, Alexander MacDonnell, described as his right arm by Perrot, was killed in a skirmish with an English detachment in March, but the attempt to eject the MacDonnells had clearly failed. Sorley had tried to negotiate throughout the winter of 1585-6, and in April he again asked for terms from Perrot, who was ordered by Elizabeth to make 'some reasonable composition' with Angus of Dunyvaig and Sorley (PRO, SP 63/122/no. 94). Angus of Dunyvaig submitted, through his mother, to the Dublin authorities in May, and received a grant of the Glens, and in June Sorley came in himself. He entered the cathedral on 18 June, 'threw his sword before your Majesty's picture, kissed the same and swore his allegiance' (PRO, SP 63/139/7). Sorley received a patent of denization, a grant of the territories between Ballycastle and Coleraine, and constableship of Dunluce Castle. The Route was divided between himself and MacQuillan. Eneas or Angus MacDonnell (d. after 1607), Sorley's fifth son, remained at Dublin as a pledge of his obedience.

Final years, 1588–1590 For some months Angus of Dunyvaig continued to act aggressively. He attacked MacQuillan in Antrim and Sir John O'Dogherty in Donegal, and sent 600 men under two of his sons to support the Burkes'

uprising in western Ireland. This ended after his two sons and many of their men were killed at Ardnaree in co. Mayo on 22 September 1586. Sorley, meanwhile, had some dealings in autumn 1586 with Hugh O'Neill, second earl of Tyrone, who had previously fostered his son Eneas. Sorley warned him that the MacLeans intended to land in Lough Foyle to assist his rivals, the sons of Shane, and he also supplied the earl with troops commanded by his son James MacDonnell (d. 1601).

In October 1588 a spy in Turlough Luineach O'Neill's company reported that an Armada ship had sunk near Dunluce, and that three survivors had come with Sorley to Strabane in Tyrone, 'where they certified of the late shipwreck' (CSP Ire., 1588–92, 64). Sorley went there in order to 'get O'Neill's daughter to wife', despite being over eighty, and having 'incisions made in his forehead for the recovery of his sight, which he hath almost lost' ('Perrot papers'). Mary, his first wife, had died in 1582 and he married an O'Neill in October 1588. In July 1589 Sorley commissioned a Scot to 'weigh the ordnance' of the Armada wreck, which was also supposed to have 'a great store of Gold and silver' (G. Hill, 190). Sorley died in January 1590, and according to tradition was buried at Bonamargy Friary. He had five sons with his first wife, two of whom predeceased him: Donnell, fighting Turlough Luineach in 1577, and Alexander in 1586. Sir James MacDonnell succeeded Sorley, and died suddenly at Dunluce on 13 April 1601, after which his brother, Sir Randal *MacDonnell (d. 1636), became head of the family. The fifth son, Eneas, died soon after 1607. There was an illegitimate son, Ludar, who took part in a conspiracy against Randal in 1615. Sorley and his first wife also reportedly had five daughters.

Despite the best efforts of the government over forty years, it proved impossible to eject the Antrim Scots from Ulster by force. Sorley was central to the continued entrenchment of his family in Ireland.

HECTOR MCDONNELL

Sources state papers, Ireland, Henry VIII–Elizabeth, PRO, SP 60; SP 61; SP 62; SP 63 · state papers, Scotland, Elizabeth, PRO, SP 52 · PRO NIre., MST350: II · CSP Ire., 1509–92 · CSP Scot., 1547–1603 · C. MacNeill, ed., 'The Perrot papers', Analecta Hibernica, 12 (1943), 3–65 · AFM · G. Hill, An historical account of the MacDonnells of Antrim (1873) · A. MacDonald and A. MacDonald, The clan Donald, 3 vols. (1896–1904) · H. Sydney and others, Letters and memorials of state, ed. A. Collins, 2 vols. (1746) · J. M. Hill, Fire and sword: Sorley Boy MacDonnell (1993)
Archives PRO, state papers, Ireland, Henry VIII–Elizabeth · PRO, state papers, Scotland · PRO NIre., Antrim MSS
Wealth at death territory covered c.100,000–150,000 acres; held on grants from crown for limited periods

Macdonnell and Aros. For this title name see Macdonnell, Angus, Lord Macdonnell and Aros (d. 1680).

Macdonogh, Sir George Mark Watson (1865–1942), army officer, was born on 4 March 1865, the son of George Valentine Macdonogh, deputy inspector of the Royal Naval Hospital, Greenwich. Macdonogh was commissioned lieutenant in the Royal Engineers on 5 July 1884. Of considerable intellectual ability and with a penetrating analytical mind, the diffident and taciturn Macdonogh, who was to spend most of his military career in staff appointments without seeing active service, was promoted captain on 22 October 1892. He and his fellow engineer, James Edmonds, passed the entrance examinations for the Staff College, Camberley, in 1896 so far ahead of other candidates that the publication of results was delayed and the usual order varied to try and conceal the degree of their intellectual superiority. Neither found the course stimulating and, while Edmonds used the opportunity to write a history of the American Civil War, Macdonogh qualified as a barrister at Lincoln's Inn in 1897. An excellent linguist, Macdonogh married a Finnish woman, Aline Borgström of Helsingfors (Helsinki), on 8 November 1898, and became fluent in a number of Scandinavian languages; their only son died in 1915.

After graduation from Camberley, Macdonogh's first staff appointment was as deputy assistant adjutant-general in Dublin from November 1898 to November 1899, and this was followed by that of secretary to the School of Military Engineering at Chatham from December 1899 to August 1903, in the course of which Macdonogh received his majority on 1 April 1901. He was then deputy assistant quartermaster-general for the Thames district; but he found his real vocation when appointed general staff officer, grade 3 (GSO3), in the War Office on 27 October 1906; he advanced to GSO2 in January 1908 and to GSO1 in December 1912, and was promoted lieutenant-colonel on 22 January 1909 and colonel on 30 October 1912. Macdonogh was responsible with Edmonds, whom he succeeded in charge of MO5 in the military operations directorate, for the drafting of measures to control aliens in the event of war. However, Macdonogh enjoyed an uneasy relationship with the director of military operations, Henry Wilson, who distrusted Macdonogh for his conversion from Methodism to Roman Catholicism. It was a distrust heightened by Macdonogh's being one of the few officers in the War Office prepared to contemplate coercing Ulster into accepting Irish home rule during the Curragh incident in March 1914.

On the outbreak of war in August 1914 Macdonogh was posted as GSO1 for intelligence to the general headquarters (GHQ) of the expeditionary force, and on 7 November 1914 he became brigadier-general, general staff. Macdonogh served GHQ well, especially during the first battle of Ypres and again when providing timely warning of a forthcoming gas attack on the Second Army in December 1915. He was summoned back to the War Office on 3 January 1916 as director of military intelligence with the rank of major-general. In this capacity he pushed for operations which would contribute to the weakening of German domestic morale, presenting a paper to this effect to the war cabinet in October 1917. He had created the propaganda department, MI7(b), as soon as he reached the War Office and from the summer of 1917 onwards carefully orchestrated what became a model subversion campaign. Macdonogh's agents and painstaking methodology provided him with an extremely accurate picture of the state of the German army so that by May 1917 he had compiled an entire order of battle for their forces in the west with the exception of a single *Landwehr* unit. He was also able to predict the date, time, and location of the German spring offensive in March 1918. However, Macdonogh was distrusted by Sir Douglas Haig and by Haig's chief of intelligence, John Charteris, not only because of his Catholicism but also because he did not share their over-optimistic assessments of the imminent collapse of the German army. Thus Haig recorded in his diary on 15 October 1917 that Macdonogh 'is a Roman Catholic and is (perhaps unconsciously) influenced by information which reaches him from tainted [that is, Catholic] sources' (Haig MSS). In turn, Macdonogh had considerable doubts about Haig's strategy, and engaged in a particularly acrimonious correspondence with Charteris, whom Macdonogh regarded as 'a dangerous fool' (Kirke MSS).

Macdonogh was appointed adjutant-general with the rank of temporary lieutenant-general on 11 September 1918, substantive rank as lieutenant-general coming on 1 January 1919. He was briefly considered as a possible liaison officer to the White Russian army of Admiral Kolchak, but remained adjutant-general until 10 September 1922, and retired from the army on 11 September 1925. For his wartime services Macdonogh was created CB in 1915 and KCMG in 1917, the appointment as KCB following in 1920 and the GBE on his retirement.

Macdonogh then entered business, held a variety of directorships in banking and manufacturing, and became president of the Federation of British Industries in 1933–4. He was also active in a number of institutions such as the London Zoological Society and the Royal Institute of International Affairs, while his interest in the plight of his wife's country brought him the presidency of the Anglo-Finnish Society, the vice-presidency of the Finland Fund, and membership of the Finnish Aid Bureau in 1940. He was also a commissioner for the Imperial War Graves Commission, a member of the royal commission on local government from 1923 to 1929, and, between 1939 and 1941, a member of the central committee for the regulation of prices. Macdonogh died in the Memorial Hospital, Teddington, London, on 10 July 1942.

IAN F. W. BECKETT

Sources M. Occleshaw, *Armour against fate: British military intelligence in the First World War* (1989) · *The military correspondence of Sir Henry Wilson, 1918–1922*, ed. K. Jeffrey (1985) · D. French, 'Failures of intelligence', *Strategy and intelligence*, ed. M. Dockrill and D. French (1996), 67–95 · J. Marshall-Cornwall, *Wars and rumours of wars* (1984) · T. Travers, *The killing ground* (1987) · I. F. W. Beckett, ed., *The army and the Curragh incident, 1914* (1986) · J. Gooch, *The plans of war: the general staff and British military strategy, c.1900–1916* (1974) · *The military correspondence of Field-Marshal Sir William Robertson, chief of the imperial general staff, December 1915 – February 1918*, ed. D. R. Woodward (1989) · J. Ferris, *The British army and signals intelligence during the First World War* (1992) · D. French, 'Sir John French's secret service on the western front', *Journal of Strategic Studies*, 7/4 (1984), 423–40 · *Army List* · *WWW* · Burke, *Peerage* · *CGPLA Eng. & Wales* (1942) · NL Scot., Haig MSS · IWM, Kirke papers
Archives PRO, papers, WO 106/1510-17 | CAC Cam., corresp. with Sir E. L. Spears · CUL, corresp. with Lord Hardinge · CUL, corresp. with Sir Samuel Hoare · IWM, Kirke MSS · King's Lond., Liddell Hart C., Charteris MSS · King's Lond., Liddell Hart C., letters to Sir J. E. Edmonds · NL Scot., Haig MSS · PRO, corresp. with John Charteris, WO 158/897

Wealth at death £53,784 1s. 10d.: probate, 19 Oct 1942, *CGPLA Eng. & Wales*

McDouall [Macdowall], **Andrew**, Lord Bankton (1685–1760), judge, was probably born at Logan, Wigtownshire, the younger son of Robert Macdowall of Logan, and Sarah, daughter of Sir John Shaw (or Schaw) of Greenock. He was probably the Andrew McDouall who matriculated at Edinburgh University in 1698, but further details of his education are unknown. He was admitted advocate on 24 February 1708 and practised as a civil lawyer. His career was helped by his kinsman Patrick MacDowell of Crichen, writer to the signet; important clients, whom he continued to advise into the 1730s, were the Murrays of Broughton and Cally, also relatives from Wigtownshire, one of whom, John Murray, was secretary to Prince Charles Edward during the Jacobite rising of 1745.

According to F. J. Grant in *The Faculty of Advocates in Scotland* (1944), McDouall was first married to Marion, daughter of David Dunmuir, advocate, but Grant's source for the statement is unknown. On 11 April 1717 he married Anne, daughter of Alexander Lesslie of Glaswell, who died within ten years of their marriage. His second wife was Marion, daughter of James Stewart of Alantoun, whom he married in Edinburgh on 30 July 1727. She had died by 1738. By the 1720s his practice was large and distinguished, and by the 1730s he was living at the good address of James Court, Edinburgh, and was the principal guardian ('tutor sine qua non') of his under-age nephew, the laird of Logan. He was said to be a whig in politics. In 1737 he was appointed a counsel for the government in the Porteous riot trials. His main business was in the court of session, but on occasions he practised also in other civil courts in Edinburgh. A contemporary assessment was: 'a gentleman of the most generous and lovely character' (*Duncan Forbes of Culloden*, 57–8). His written pleadings are learned and to the point. Though the style is vigorous and maintains the older form of being in the first person, they do not support the view of John Ramsay of Ochtertyre—hardly a contemporary, writing over fifty years later for effect—that he was disorganized and eccentric.

McDouall extended his territorial connections to Peeblesshire; by 1738 he had acquired the estate of Kingseat (including Slipperfield) near West Linton from the Russells, a decayed family of Jacobite sympathies, and on 23 July that year, in Edinburgh, he married Isobel Geddes (*d.* 1741), daughter of James Geddes of Rachan, Peeblesshire, and sister of James *Geddes (1710–1749), writer on classical literature. Though his wife died in 1741, McDouall continued an active proprietor, being involved in a question about the church fabric and leases and acting for at least one tenant in litigation (not a unique instance where he acted for less prosperous clients with whom he was connected), and he remained associated with the Geddes family.

The death of Crichen by 1741 'utterly insolvent' (*Creditors of M'Dowal v. M'Dowal*) may be the background to McDouall's acquiring the further property of Carrouchtrie in Wigtownshire. This insolvency and the decade of resulting litigation may have affected his prospects generally, but his practice flourished and on 17 April 1743, at Edinburgh, he married Helen Grant (*d.* 1771), sister of William *Grant, later Lord Prestongrange, and daughter of Sir Francis *Grant, first baronet, Lord Cullen. After 1745 he added to his properties Bankton, formerly Over Olivestob, at Prestonpans (renamed by the earlier proprietors, the Hamiltons, after a small property they had owned elsewhere) from the estate of Colonel James Gardiner, who had been killed on the government side in the battle of Prestonpans beside his garden. He supported the reforms of laws affecting major landholdings that followed the Jacobite rising of 1745, but in his *Essay upon Feudal Holdings*, published anonymously in London in 1748, warned against radical reform of the feudal system.

Between 1751 and 1753 McDouall brought out his famous work, *An Institute of the Laws of Scotland*, probably the product of very many years. Still cited 250 years later, it was an up-to-date, large, comprehensive work, reflecting the development of the law in his time, including, where relevant, discussion of the law in continental Europe together with a unique comparative treatment of English law, which he had cited as counsel as early as 1737 in the Porteous riots case. The *Institute* perhaps influenced his being appointed a judge of the court of session, as Lord Bankton, on 5 July 1755 at the age of seventy. He had been on 20 December 1754 appointed vice-dean of the Faculty of Advocates, deputizing for Robert Dundas, the culmination of his involvement with the affairs of the faculty, but resigned on being raised to the bench. His judicial appointment was made on the nomination of Philip Yorke, first earl of Hardwicke, lord chancellor, dedicatee of the second volume of the *Institute*, whose son, Charles Yorke, was in a case Bankton left on joining the bench. A contemporary considered him one of the four 'principal lawyers' (*Diary of George Ridpath*, 189) on the bench. A later assessment by Henry Mackenzie mentions 'ultra impartiality' (Mackenzie, fol. 94v). Ramsay of Ochtertyre's suggestions of eccentricity and tension with Robert Craigie of Glendoick, lord president of the court of session, seem exaggerated and again doubtful. Shortly before their appointments, he had acted along with Craigie as counsel.

McDouall died at Bankton House, Prestonpans, Haddingtonshire, in his seventy-fifth year, on 22 October 1760, having had no children, and is thought to have been buried in Greyfriars churchyard, Edinburgh. He was survived by his wife Helen, who died on 24 November 1771. He left his estates entailed. The entail was challenged unsuccessfully by the countess of Dalhousie.   JOHN BLACKIE

Sources W. M. Gordon, 'Bankton's life', *An institution of the laws of Scotland*, ed. W. M. Gordon, vol. 3; Stair Society, 43 (1995), vii–xxiv · *Diary of George Ridpath, minister of Stichel, 1755–1761*, ed. J. B. Paul (1922) · NA Scot., Broughton and Cally muniments, GD 10/1421 · P. MacDowell of Crichen, letters, NA Scot., GD 124/15/879 · Professor Hannay's papers, NA Scot., GD 214/711/2; GD 214/716 · memorial for William McLauchlane, 17 March 1737, NA Scot., Nha. Misc. 13 · *Duncan Forbes of Culloden* (1748), 57–61 · W. Chambers, *A history of Peeblesshire* (1864) · S. Shaw, *An accurate alphabetical index of the register of entails in Scotland* (1784) · 'Proceedings between Sir

J. Schaw and Lord Cathcart', MS, NA Scot., AWBNS 4 82 6 (1–14) • H. Mackenzie, 'Anecdotes', MS, NA Scot., MS 6377
Archives BL, corresp. with Lord Hardwicke and Charles Yorke, Add. MSS 35447–35448, 35633–35635, *passim* • NA Scot., Broughton and Cally muniments • NA Scot., Professor Hannay's papers • NA Scot., Cathcart of Genoch muniments

M'Douall [McDouall], **Peter Murray** (*c*.1814–1854), Chartist and medical practitioner, was born in Newton Stewart, Wigtownshire, the son of Andrew M'Douall. He served an apprenticeship with a surgeon in his home town, studied at Glasgow and Edinburgh, and in summer 1835 was admitted to the Royal College of Surgeons in Edinburgh. He subsequently moved to Lancashire, where he first managed a Burnley practice and then built up his own extensive and prosperous practice in the small cotton town of Ramsbottom. There he developed an intense interest in the medical effects of the factory system (he gave a British Association paper on the subject) and became involved in the ten-hour agitation. After his own arrest in December 1838, Joseph Rayner Stephens recommended M'Douall should take his place in the forthcoming Chartist convention as delegate for Ashton under Lyne, the militant Chartist centre with which M'Douall was to be closely associated for the rest of his life.

In the first convention (1839) M'Douall was a foremost advocate of physical force and, later, of the 'sacred month'. He was arrested in July 1839 while attempting to calm the crowd in the Birmingham Bull Ring, and the following month was sentenced at Chester assizes to twelve months' imprisonment for sedition and attending an illegal meeting at Hyde in April. According to Gammage, he was 'of an ardent fiery temperament, and though naturally possessing strong reflective powers, was impulsive to the last degree, and by no means deficient in the quality of courage'. 'In stature M'Douall was rather short … in personal appearance he was decidedly handsome … his hair which was light, approaching to sandy … was parted in the centre, and hung in long graceful curls behind his ears, and his whole appearance was highly interesting' (Gammage, 66–7). For Adams he was a 'picturesque figure … whose long cloak and general style helped to give him the appearance of a hero of melodrama' (Adams, 1.211–12).

On his release in August 1840 M'Douall was fêted as he toured the north of England and Scotland; that year, or the following, while in Glasgow, he married Mary Ann, the daughter of a warder at Chester Castle, where he had served his sentence. An advocate of the organization of Chartism in occupational groups, M'Douall played a prominent role in the recently formed National Charter Association, and headed the poll for the executive in both 1841 and 1842; he also published his own *Chartist and Republican Journal* in 1841. He stood for parliament at Northampton in June 1841 as a Chartist, but came bottom of the poll. After representing Ashton in the convention of April 1842, he was (with Thomas Cooper) the principal supporter of the general strike movement in August and it was he who drafted the executive's very forceful address to the people. The government offered a £100 reward for

his apprehension, but he escaped to France, where, sustained by Chartist collections, he lived for the next two years. He was able to return to Britain without prosecution during 1844 and resumed the life of a Chartist agitator, publishing *The Charter: What It Means! The Chartists: What They Want!* (1845) and unsuccessfully contesting the parliamentary seat of Carlisle in June 1848. In 1848 he was a member of the national assembly and, once more elected to the executive, was at the heart of the first insurrectionary conspiracy of the summer. During the two years' hard labour at Kirkdale gaol to which he was sentenced in August for his part in a meeting at Ashton, great hardship was suffered by his wife and children, the eldest of whom, a ten-year-old girl, actually died; and after release in 1850 his efforts to publish *McDouall's Manchester Journal* and to establish a medical practice in Ashton both failed. The *Northern Star* had observed in 1848:

> When he came among you he had good property in Scotland, a profession and a practice, which realized him several hundred pounds annually, besides a large sum of accumulated money in the bank. All of which has been spent long ago in the advocacy of the rights of the people. (Challinor, 80–81)

In the summer of 1853 M'Douall emigrated to Australia but he died shortly after arrival in 'about May, 1854' (*Newcastle Weekly Chronicle*, 8 March 1884). One apparently fallacious story of several which circulated was that he had drowned in a shipwreck. After his death M'Douall's family returned to an uncertain future in England. As Harney was to recall, 'no man in the Chartist movement was better known than Dr McDouall'. He was one of the half-dozen outstanding leaders of Chartism.

DAVID GOODWAY

Sources P. Pickering and S. Roberts, 'Pills, pamphlets and politics: the career of Peter Murray McDouall (1814–54)', *Manchester Region History Review*, 11 (1997), 34–43 • H. Weisser, 'M'Douall, Peter Murray', *BDMBR*, vol. 2 • R. Challinor, 'Peter Murray McDouall and "physical force chartism"', *International Socialism*, 12 (spring 1981), 53–84 • P. M. M'Douall, *The charter: what it means! The chartists: what they want!* (1845) • 'Portraits of delegates, no. 6', *The Charter* (7 April 1839) • R. G. Gammage, *History of the Chartist movement, 1837–1854*, new edn (1894) • 'Vicissitudes of a chartist leader's family', *Daily News* (5 Aug 1856) • Q., letter, *Newcastle Weekly Chronicle* (8 March 1884) • W. E. Adams, *Memoirs of a social atom*, 2 vols. (1903) • W. H. Maehl, ed., *Robert Gammage: reminiscences of a chartist* (1983) • G. J. Harney, 'Acknowledgements', *Newcastle Weekly Chronicle* (27 Feb 1897) • 'Dr. P. M. M'Douall', *Star of Freedom* (17 July 1852)
Likenesses engraving, repro. in Gammage, *History of the chartist movement*, facing p. 157 • woodcut, repro. in 'Portraits of delegates, no. 6'

M'Dougal [MacDougall], **Sir John** (1790–1865), naval officer, born in Edinburgh, was the second son of Patrick M'Dougal or MacDougall of Dunolly Castle, Argyll, lineal representative of the MacDougalls of Lorne, and his wife, Louisa, youngest daughter of John Campbell of Achallader, Argyll. His elder brother, Alexander, captain in the 5th regiment of foot, was killed in 1812 at the storming of Ciudad Rodrigo. John M'Dougal entered the navy in December 1802 on the sloop *Cruiser*, actively employed on the north coast of France through 1803. In 1804 he was in the frigate *Doris* with his cousin, Patrick Campbell. When the *Doris* was burnt in January 1805, he was appointed to the *Hero*, in which he was present in the action off Cape Finisterre on 22 July 1805. He was afterwards again with Campbell in the *Chiffonne*; and in the *Unité* from June 1806 to November 1809 he was repeatedly engaged in boat actions in the Adriatic. On 25 November 1809 he was promoted by Lord Collingwood lieutenant of the *Ville de Paris* (confirmed by the Admiralty on 3 January 1810).

In May 1811 M'Dougal was again appointed to the *Unité* (Captain Chamberlayne), still in the Adriatic. The service was very severe, and he was again frequently in boat actions. In November 1811 he was in command of a prize to take her to Malta, when he met three French warships. He returned to inform the senior officer, Captain Murray Maxwell, and two of the French ships were captured. Towards the end of 1812 he was invalided from the *Unité*. In 1814 he was in the *Leander* on the coast of North America; and in 1816 was a lieutenant of the *Superb* (Captain Ekins) at the bombardment of Algiers on 27 August, when he was twice wounded. In 1819 he was flag lieutenant to Rear-Admiral Donald Campbell in the West Indies, and he was officially thanked by Frederick VI, king of Denmark, for saving the crew of a Danish ship wrecked in a hurricane at St Thomas. He was promoted commander on 9 February 1820. On 28 August 1826 he married Elizabeth Sophia, only daughter of Commander Charles Sheldon Timins RN, of Oriel Lodge, Cheltenham, Gloucestershire. Their six sons and three daughters included Patrick Charles Campbell, who died a naval commander in 1861, and Somerled, who became a captain on the retired list.

From 1833 to 1835 M'Dougal commanded the *Nimrod* (20 guns) on the coast of Portugal, and on 16 August 1836 was promoted captain. In February 1845 he commissioned the paddle-frigate *Vulture* for the East India station, and in April 1847, then senior officer at Hong Kong, escorted the governor, Sir John Davis, with a strong force of troops up the river to Canton (Guangzhou), capturing the Bogue (Humen) forts on the way, spiking upwards of 500 guns and destroying the ammunition. Apparently the Chinese were taken unawares, and the forts were not fully garrisoned. He returned to England in 1848, and was appointed Admiralty superintendent of packets at Southampton in 1855. He had no further service, and was promoted rear-admiral on 12 May 1857. He was made a KCB on 10 November 1862, attained vice-admiral on 3 November 1863, and died at Dunolly Castle on 12 April 1865.

J. K. LAUGHTON, rev. ANDREW LAMBERT

Sources D. Syrett and R. L. DiNardo, *The commissioned sea officers of the Royal Navy, 1660–1815*, rev. edn, Occasional Publications of the Navy RS, 1 (1994) · G. S. Graham, *The China station: war and diplomacy, 1830–1860* (1978) · *GM*, 3rd ser., 18 (1865) · *The Times* (17 April 1865) · O'Byrne, *Naval biog. dict.*
Wealth at death £1942 14s. 3d.: confirmation, 8 Sept 1865, NA Scot., SC51/32/14, 53–7

MacDougal, Maurice [Mauritz Duwall] (**1603–1655**), army officer in the Swedish service, was born in Sweden, one of nine sons of the Scot Albert MacDougal (1541–1641) of Mackerston and Ursula Von Stralendorf (d. 1651), one of

his three wives from Mecklenburg. Little is known of MacDougal's life before he entered Swedish military service with his brothers, although his social success was typical of the ease with which Scotsmen and their sons became integrated into Swedish society at the time. He was known as Mauritz Duwall in Sweden.

MacDougal first served as an ensign in 1624 in Gustaf Horn's Norrland regiment, and his military career advanced rapidly from then on. He had become a lieutenant in his brother James MacDougal's regiment by 1626, a captain two years later, a lieutenant-colonel by 1633, and a full colonel the following year. In 1638 he was in charge of conscription in the Västerbotten region of Finland. That year he was also ennobled and introduced into the Swedish house of nobility on the merits of his father's long service to the Swedish crown. His brother Axel had been ennobled in 1626. MacDougal's claims to noble origins were supported by a fellow Scottish officer, James Forbes, and the Swedish chancellor's son, Johan Oxenstierna, who reported upon their return from a diplomatic mission to Scotland in 1634 that the MacDougals were a well-known noble family.

MacDougal became involved in disputes between the dowager queen Kristina, Gustav II Adolf's mother, and the Swedish government in 1640. He felt a strong loyalty towards Kristina as his father had served her before him. Not only had the queen sought financial aid from MacDougal, which was considered an illegal action, but he had also prevented another Swedish noblewoman, Kristina Bielke, from moving into the dowager queen's property in Örby. In 1641 MacDougal appeared before the Riksråd (the Swedish state council) to answer several charges of unlawful and disgraceful behaviour. He defended himself well, was reinstated to his former position, and by 1644 was being considered by the Riksråd for the position of colonel of the mountain troops. He consolidated his position in Sweden by buying land from his brother Colonel and Commandant Tobias MacDougal in 1652—land which had originally been procured with Gustav II Adolf's permission in 1629. This meant that he held land in Hallkved, Broby, and Sund in Funbo parish, and Kåttslinge in Vendels parish. Little is known of MacDougal's later activities or of his marriage. He died in 1655.

A. N. L. GROSJEAN

Sources G. Elgenstierna, *Den introducerade svenska adelns ättartavlor med tillägg och rättelser*, 9 vols. (1925–36), vol. 2 · *Svenska sändebuds till utländska hof och deras sändebud till Sverige*, 1841, Riksarkivet, Stockholm · *Katalog öfver sköldebref*, Riddarhusarkivet (Swedish nobility archives), Stockholm, Sweden · military muster rolls, Krigsarkivet, Stockholm, 1624/4, 5; 1625/4–6; 1626/5, 7, 9; 1628/10, 12, 13; 1629/22–24; 1630/18, 36; 1633/24; 1637/12 · N. A. Kullberg, S. Bergh, and P. Sondén, eds., *Svenska riksrådets protokoll*, 18 vols. (Stockholm, 1878–1959), *passim* · S. Bergh and B. Taube, eds., *Sveriges ridderskaps och adels riksdags-protokoll*, 17 vols. (1871) · B. Hildebrand, 'Duwall', *Svenskt biografiskt lexikon*, ed. B. Boëthius, 11 (1945) · J. Kleberg, *Krigskollegii historia biografiska anteckningar, 1630–1865* (1930)

MacDougall, Alexander, lord of Argyll (d. 1310), magnate, succeeded his father, Ewen *MacDougall (d. in or after 1268), as head of his kindred. Himself the son of a king—for Ewen had been king in the Hebrides under the crown of Norway—he served two kings of Scots, Alexander III (r. 1249–86) and John (John de Balliol, r. 1292–6), and two kings of England, Edward I (r. 1272–1307) and Edward II (r. 1307–27), and bitterly opposed a third king of Scots, Robert I (r. 1306–1329). For a time he seemed set to recreate the hegemony of his ancestor Somerled (d. 1164), king of the Hebrides and regulus of Argyll and Kintyre; but he died in old age, in exile, in English service.

In 1275 MacDougall was one of the leaders of a Scottish expedition sent to subdue the Isle of Man. In 1284 he was among the Scottish magnates who took the oath acknowledging Margaret, the Maid of Norway, as heir-presumptive to the crown. Subsequently Alexander supported John de Balliol in the competition for the throne of Scotland and acted as one of his auditors. MacDougall's wife was a Comyn of Badenoch, and this, together with the fact that his dynastic rivals, the MacDonalds, supported the Bruce claimant, helps to explain his support for Balliol, who as king conferred important administrative powers on MacDougall as part of a policy of extending royal authority in western Scotland. But private quarrels continued, and in 1299 Alexander MacDougall killed Alexander MacDonald, chief of his kindred, who may have been his son-in-law—'the person who was best for hospitality and excellence that was in Ireland and Scotland', according to the Ulster annals (Hennessy and MacCarthy, 2.393). Some years previously the MacDougalls had accounted for Cailin Mor Campbell, head of another prominent west highland family.

After the deposition of John, king of Scots, in 1296, MacDougall at first opposed Edward I. Later, however, he and his son, John *MacDougall of Argyll, became committed supporters of the English king, and in 1305 Alexander was appointed to Edward I's council for Scotland. The slaughter of John Comyn of Badenoch in 1306 intensified the MacDougalls' opposition to Robert Bruce, who was inaugurated king of Scots in that year. In 1307 and 1308 King Robert broke Comyn and MacDougall power. After the fall of his mainland castle of Dunstaffnage in 1308, Alexander MacDougall (although not his son John) came briefly into the king's peace, and attended his parliament at St Andrews in 1309. Shortly afterwards, however, he fled to England, where both Alexander and John attended a council held by Edward II at Westminster in June 1310. Alexander MacDougall died at the end of 1310, perhaps in Ireland, where he and John had been directed in English service.

From Alexander MacDougall and his son John descend the later chiefs of clan MacDougall to the present day, some accounts to the contrary notwithstanding. A daughter, Christian, married Maolmuire Lamont, and another married Lachlan MacRuari. W. D. H. SELLAR

Sources W. D. H. Sellar, 'Hebridean sea-kings: the successors of Somerled, 1164–1316', Alba: Celtic Scotland in the middle ages, ed. E. J. Cowan and R. A. McDonald (2000), 187–218 • R. A. MacDonald, The kingdom of the isles: Scotland's western seaboard, c.1100–c.1336 (1997) • C. M. MacDonald, History of Argyll (1950), 112–39 • G. W. S. Barrow, Robert Bruce and the community of the realm of Scotland, 3rd edn (1988) • R. Nicholson, Scotland: the later middle ages (1974), vol. 2 of The Edinburgh history of Scotland, ed. G. Donaldson (1965–75), 79–80 • W. D. H. Sellar, 'MacDougall pedigrees in MS 1467', Notes and Queries of the Society of West Highland and Island Historical Research, 29 (Aug 1986), 3–18 • W. M. Hennessy and B. MacCarthy, eds., Annals of Ulster, otherwise, annals of Senat, 4 vols. (1887–1901) • CDS, vol. 3, no. 191 • G. Barrow, 'The battle between John MacDougall of Lorn and Robert Bruce in 1308 or 1309', West Highland Notes and Queries, 2nd ser., 19 (March 1999), 3–11 • A. A. M. Duncan, 'The battles of Ben Cruachan', West Highland Notes and Queries, 2nd ser., 20 (Aug 1999), 3–20

McDougall, Alexander (1732–1786), army officer and revolutionary politician in America, was born in July or August 1732 in Kildalton, Islay, Scotland, the son of Ronald McDougall, a farmer and dairyman, and his wife, Elizabeth. His Presbyterian parents were part of the highland Scottish and northern Irish migration to the American 'back country' of the mid-eighteenth century, prepared to brave a war-ridden frontier rather than continuing to endure conditions in their homeland. Ronald McDougall found, however, that the projected settlement at Fort Edward in northern New York which he planned to join had failed. So he opened a dairy in New York city.

With such a beginning, his son Alexander had no prospect of formal education. He went to sea in his youth and commanded a privateer during the Seven Years' War. His war profits enabled him to establish himself as a merchant, working in the intercolonial trade rather than doing business across the Atlantic. His rise above his father's situation was significant. But his fellow colonials addressed him as 'Captain', to recognize his maritime career, rather than with the more honorific 'Mr'. He married his distant cousin Nancy McDougall (d. 1763) in 1751 and Hannah Bostwick in 1769.

McDougall emerged into fame in 1769 after he published his broadside, To the Betrayed Inhabitants of the City and Colony of New-York, with the pseudonym A Son of Liberty. The reference was both to the description of rebellious Americans in parliament by Isaac Barre and to the informal association of radicals that was orchestrating popular resistance. McDougall's highly partisan subject was his objection to the provincial assembly's compliance with parliament's insistence that the American colonies provide for the material welfare of the British forces stationed within them. British troops and sailors had become very unpopular, and McDougall struck a sore nerve. When the assembly discovered his authorship it ordered his imprisonment. His refusal to co-operate led to his becoming the American equivalent of John Wilkes, the MP and subsequent lord mayor of London who was persecuted for his political stance at about the same time. So close was the parallel that supporters of McDougall fêted him with forty-five instances of every category that crossed their minds. The reference was to no. 45 of Wilkes's paper the North Briton, the contents of which had led to its author's imprisonment. McDougall himself was threatened with the 'long, hard penalty' of being crushed to death with stones when he refused to co-operate with the assembly's investigation of his case.

An active radical within the patriot movement, McDougall took a leading part in generating resistance both to Britain and to the colonial government. His political base was New York city's artisan community. He was involved in their purchase of a headquarters, which they named Liberty Hall. He was very active in the unfolding crisis that followed the Boston Tea Party (December 1773), serving on successive revolutionary committees and in two provincial congresses. McDougall presided when New York's adult male population gathered in 'the Fields' to elect a revolutionary committee in June 1774.

For McDougall the revolution meant an unexpected opportunity. When he wrote his incendiary broadside in 1769 he had been well enough off to have the free time required to watch the assembly at work, but he never could have hoped to be in the centre of public affairs himself. Now, however, he emerged to institutional prominence. When war broke out in April 1775 he shifted his energy from street and committee politics to military organization. He rose from colonel in the New York militia (1775) to major-general in the Continental army (1777), spending his active-duty career in the New York theatre. He assumed command at West Point following the discovery of Benedict Arnold's plot to surrender it to the British. He survived a court martial in 1782 that tried him for insubordination to his superior, General William Heath.

By the end of the revolutionary war McDougall's politics had shifted from the positions he had taken as a pre-independence popular leader. As a major-general in the Continental army, he had come to share the undoubted grievances of his brother officers, including both lack of pay and lack of recognition. He took part in the abortive movement that might have led to a coup by the officer corps in 1783, and he presented the officers' case to congress. He served two terms in congress itself, and he was also a state senator from 1783 until his death.

Undoubtedly McDougall had been one of the American revolution's genuine radicals, both politically in terms of militancy about the problem between the colonies and Britain, and socially in terms of colonial society. His advance from outsider who had the time to observe events to insider who shaped events in both political and military terms is a measure of the difference between the colonial order and what followed. But his post-war life speaks to that radicalism's partial dissipation. His daughter Elizabeth married the New York city merchant John Laurence, a close associate of Alexander Hamilton in the socially and politically conservative movement that would lead to the United States constitution. McDougall himself joined in Hamilton's project to establish the Bank of New York, as a bulwark of what they both considered sound financial policies, and he became the bank's first president. When he died of fever in New York city on 9 June 1786 he had come a very long distance from his humble birth and youth, his ill education, his time at sea, and his imprisonment. Like many others, including such one-time county-level notables as George Washington and John Adams, he had found in the American revolution his own chance to rise in the world, and he had taken it.

EDWARD COUNTRYMAN

Sources R. J. Champagne, *Alexander McDougall and the American revolution in New York* (1975) • P. Maier, *From resistance to revolution: colonial radicals and the development of American opposition to Britain, 1765–1776* (1972) • E. Countryman, 'McDougall, Alexander', *ANB*
Archives New York Historical Society
Likenesses J. Ramage, miniature on ivory, New York Historical Society

Macdougall, Allan [*called* Ailean Dall] (1750?–1829), poet, was born in Glencoe, Argyll. As a boy he was apprenticed to a tailor, who, according to the local custom, travelled between farms wherever his services were called for, and on his working peregrinations Macdougall was able to acquire a deep knowledge of Gaelic song and story. His blindness, according to tradition, was the result of an attack upon him by a fellow apprentice who took umbrage at Macdougall's habitually sarcastic tongue; he was thereafter known as Ailean Dall ('Blind Allan'). Following his incapacitation, Macdougall turned particularly to music and became a competent fiddle player, earning a scanty living entertaining at country celebrations. About 1790 Macdougall moved with his family to Inverlochy, near Fort William, where a man named Stewart who owned a large farm granted him the use of a small property on his land. In this neighbourhood Macdougall's reputation as a poet and entertainer grew and, with the assistance of Ewan Maclachlan, a fellow poet and tradition-bearer, he collected together poems and poem versions of his own (along with some work of Maclachlan's), material which was published in Edinburgh as *Orain Ghaidhealacha* (1798). After the good reception of this volume, Colonel Alasdair Ronaldson MacDonell of Glengarry employed Macdougall as his family bard. In 1828 Macdougall travelled the counties of Argyll, Ross-shire, and Inverness-shire seeking (and obtaining 1000) subscriptions for a new, enlarged edition of *Orain Ghaidhealacha*, but he died the following year while his project was in press. He was buried at Kilfinan, Argyll.

Macdougall specialized in poetic pieces of a panegyric and ribald nature, as well as in song. One of his most notorious and resonant poetic gambits was his attack on lowland shepherds whose brand of farming signalled, for Macdougall, the depopulation of the highlands.

GERARD CARRUTHERS

Sources J. Mackenzie, ed., *Sar-obair nam bard Gaelach, or, The beauties of Gaelic poetry* (1841) • D. S. Thomson, ed., *The companion to Gaelic Scotland* (1983)

MacDougall, Archibald (1927–1999). *See under* Knoydart, Seven Men of (*act.* 1948).

Macdougall [MacDougall], **Sir Duncan** (1787–1862), army officer, son of Patrick MacDougall of Soroba, near Oban, Argyll, and his wife, Mary, daughter of Duncan M'Vicar, was born at Soroba. Educated at Edinburgh, he entered the army as ensign in 1804, and served in the 53rd and 85th regiments on the Cape Colony frontier, at the Cape, and in the Peninsular War. He took part in the third siege and in the capture by storm of Badajoz on 6 April 1812, and in the capture on 27 June of the forts of Salamanca. In the battle of Salamanca on 22 July he gallantly saved the colours of his regiment and was severely wounded. He was present at the siege of Burgos in September and October 1812 and the subsequent retreat, at the siege and capture on 31 August 1813 of San Sebastian, at the passage of the Bidassoa in October, at the battles of Nivelle (10 November) and Nive (9–13 December), and at the investment of Bayonne.

Macdougall took part in the Anglo-American War in 1814; he was present at the battle of Bladensburg on 24 August, the capture of Washington, and the attack on Baltimore on 12 September, when he was aide-de-camp to Major-General Robert Ross, who was killed. He also served in the operations against New Orleans in December 1814 and January 1815, was aide-de-camp to Lieutenant-General Sir Edward Pakenham, who was killed at the assault on 7 January, and took part in the siege of Fort Bowyer in Florida. Following service in France, Ireland, and Nova Scotia, Macdougall assumed command of the 79th highlanders in 1832, and quelled civil disturbances in Montreal. In 1835 he relinquished the command of his regiment and retired from the active list in order to join the British Auxiliary Legion of Spain as quartermaster-general and second in command under Sir De Lacy Evans. For his services in Spain he received from Queen Isabella II the order of knighthood of St Ferdinand.

On 18 July 1838 he was knighted at St James's Palace. He was twice married: first, in 1817, to Anne, daughter of Colonel Smelt, governor of the Isle of Man, with whom he had a son, Patrick Leonard *MacDougall, and, second, in 1844, to Hannah, widow of Colonel Nicholson of Springfield House, Liverpool. In later years Macdougall raised the Lancashire artillery militia and became a prominent figure in the volunteer movement. He presided at the great meeting at St Martin's Hall, London, at which the movement was inaugurated. His publications included the pamphlet *Hints to Volunteers on Various Subjects* (1860) and *The History of the Volunteer Movement* (1861). He died on 10 December 1862 at his home, 112 Eaton Square, London, and was buried in St Paul's Cathedral, London, where a monument with a bust by Adams was erected to his memory. R. H. VETCH, rev. JAMES FALKNER

Sources *Army List* · *Hart's Army List* · *Historical records of the Queen's Own Cameron Highlanders*, 7 vols. (1909–62), vol. 1 · *Colburn's United Service Magazine*, 3 (1849), 147 · Boase, *Mod. Eng. biog.* · *Dod's Peerage* (1858)

Archives NA Scot., report on Hottentot weapons | NA Scot., corresp. with Lord Panmure · U. Southampton L., letters and memorandum to Palmerston

Likenesses G. G. Adams, bust on monument, 1862, St Paul's Cathedral, London

Wealth at death under £3000: probate, 15 April 1863, *CGPLA Eng. & Wales*

MacDougall, Ewen, lord of Argyll (*d.* in or after 1268), king in the Hebrides, was the son of Duncan of Argyll, king in the Hebrides, and grandson of Dugald, also king in the Hebrides. Dugald, who is the eponym of the clan Mac-Dougall, was the son of Somerled (*d.* 1164), king of the Hebrides and *regulus* of Argyll and Kintyre.

In 1248 MacDougall and his kinsman Dugald mac Ruairi sailed to Bergen seeking the title of king in the Hebrides (or Sudreys) from King Hákon of Norway (*r.* 1217–63), who claimed overlordship. Hákon recognized Ewen as king and, on the death of Harald Óláfsson, king of Man and the Hebrides, in 1249, sent Ewen to the isles with a general commission to act on his behalf. However, Alexander II, king of Scots, MacDougall's overlord in Argyll, who sought to incorporate Man and the Hebrides into his own kingdom, led an army to Argyll, and demanded that Ewen renounce his allegiance to Hákon and surrender his castles. No man can serve two masters, said Alexander. On the contrary, said Ewen, it was quite possible so long as the masters were not enemies. Ewen refused to give up his Norwegian allegiance. Alexander pressed on against him but caught fever, and on 8 July 1249 died on the island of Kerrera, by Oban, in the heart of Ewen's territories. 'While wishing to disinherit an innocent man', wrote Matthew Paris, 'he unexpectedly breathed out with that ambition the breath of life' (Paris, *Chron.*, 5.89).

In 1250 MacDougall was in the Isle of Man, where he gave offence to the Manxmen by adopting the style *rex insularum*, and was driven out. In 1253 he and Dugald were again in Bergen, from where they sailed with King Hákon against Denmark. In 1255, through the mediation of Henry III of England, Ewen was restored to Argyll.

In 1263 MacDougall again found himself in confrontation with a major ruler. Hákon of Norway sailed in person to the Hebrides to assert his rights against the Scots. He required his sub-kings in the Hebrides, including Ewen, to join the expedition. Ewen refused and was dispossessed. The Norwegian expedition met with disaster, however, King Hákon dying in the Orkneys on his return to Norway after the battle of Largs. By the treaty of Perth between Scotland and Norway in 1266 Man and the Hebrides were ceded to Scotland, and MacDougall was restored to his island possessions. His last recorded appearance is in 1268.

Descended from many generations of Hebridean seakings, Ewen MacDougall seems to have been equally at home in the Gaelic and Scandinavian worlds. His many castles included Dunstaffnage in mainland Argyll, the impressive hall house of Aros on Mull, and the island stronghold of Cairnburgh between Mull and Tiree. He defied two powerful kings in the space of twenty years yet retained all his lands. It has been argued that Ewen left only daughters. However, there seems little doubt that he was the father of Alexander *MacDougall of Argyll, with other sons, and the lineal ancestor of the later chiefs of MacDougall. Ewen's daughter Mary married in succession Magnus Óláfsson, king of Man and the Hebrides (*d.* 1265), Malise, earl of Strathearn (*d.* 1271), Hugh, lord of Abernethy (*d.* 1291/2), and Warin Fitzwarin (*d.* 1299)—a wide selection which gives some indication of the status and far-ranging connections of Ewen MacDougall and his family.

Ewen's name occurs in contemporary sources in a variety of disguises, the Gaelic Eoghan (Ewen) being readily confused with Eoin (for John). Thus he appears in the Manx chronicle as Johannes Dugaldi, and in Norwegian sources as Jon Duncansson. Matthew Paris calls him Oenus of Argyll. His Gaelic style may well have been

Eogan MacSomairle. In his sole surviving charter he names himself Eugenius. During the thirteenth century the descendants of Somerled split into three distinct segments: the MacDougalls, the MacDonalds, and the MacRuaris. Later generations looked back to Ewen as a chief of the MacDougalls.   W. D. H. Sellar

Sources A. A. M. Duncan and A. L. Brown, 'Argyll and the Isles in the earlier middle ages', *Proceedings of the Society of Antiquaries of Scotland*, 90 (1956–7), 192–220 • E. J. Cowan, 'Norwegian sunset – Scottish dawn: Haakon IV and Alexander III', in N. H. Reid, *Scotland in the reign of Alexander III, 1249–1286* (1990), 103–31 • C. M. MacDonald, *History of Argyll* (1950), 103–11 • G. W. S. Barrow, *Kingship and unity: Scotland, 1000–1306* (1981), 105–21 • A. A. M. Duncan, *Scotland: the making of the kingdom* (1975), vol. 1 of *The Edinburgh history of Scotland*, ed. G. Donaldson (1965–75), 549–51, 578–82 • W. D. H. Sellar, 'Hebridean sea-kings: the successors of Somerled, 1164–1316', *Alba: Celtic Scotland in the middle ages*, ed. E. J. Cowan and R. A. McDonald (2000), 187–218

McDougall, Francis Thomas (1817–1886), bishop of Labuan and Sarawak, was born at Sydenham, Kent, on 30 June 1817, the second child and only son of Captain William Adair McDougall, of the 88th Connaught Rangers, and his wife, Catherine, *née* Gell. General Patrick McDougall of the East India Company was his grandfather. From his military forebears came his courage and quick resource; he was always at his best in emergency. From an Armenian grandmother he inherited his dark complexion and black hair. He passed a happy, carefree boyhood in Corfu, Cephalonia, and Malta, growing up 'ever at heart a sailor' (Bunyon, 4), according to his biographer and brother-in-law C. J. Bunyon. At Valletta in Malta he resolved to take up surgery as he watched glass splinters being removed from his own foot.

At sixteen McDougall returned to England to study medicine at King's College, London, where he won a gold medal. He became FRCS in 1854. At Oxford he graduated from Magdalen Hall, where he was remembered as a boisterous character who kept a dog in his rooms. He once dived into the river at Iffley, trying to rescue a sculler who had gone over the weir. 'Tuned to fiddle strings' he 'pulled bow' (Bunyon, 10, 13) in the Oxford crew which beat Cambridge in the boat race in 1842. The teachings of J. H. Newman and E. B. Pusey turned him into a lifelong high-churchman, and he decided to seek holy orders. First, however, he went to south Wales and managed an ironworks. At Pembrey, Carmarthenshire, on 11 July 1843, he married Harriette Bunyon (1818–1886) [see McDougall, Harriette]. He was ordained at Norwich in 1845.

After two curacies McDougall was persuaded by his wife to offer to go to Borneo as a pioneer missionary. Sir James Brooke, the English raja of Sarawak, was trying to introduce into his troubled realm the ideals of peace, justice, and thrift. Although not an orthodox believer himself, inclining towards deism rather than Anglicanism, the raja hoped that a Christian mission would help to turn the local Dyak headhunters into amiable citizens. At the inaugural meeting of the Borneo Church Mission in London in 1847 McDougall characteristically made clear to the raja and his supporters that the church about to be founded must be episcopal. Otherwise, he said, there

would be no unity of purpose or strength to produce fruit. The missionaries left England in a sailing ship in December and arrived in Kuching, Sarawak, on 29 June 1848.

Notwithstanding an uncomfortable start McDougall within two years was living in a good house, and his church, St Thomas's, was consecrated on 22 January 1851 by Daniel Wilson, bishop of Calcutta; McDougall had designed both buildings and laboured to construct them. He was uncommonly versatile. A home school was started and a dispensary opened for Chinese immigrants. There was much missionary encouragement. The Malays seemed deaf to the gospel but many Dyaks and Chinese were eager to hear it. Alongside his missionary labours McDougall performed amputations, treated cataracts, and did much gynaecological work. Social relations within the small English community were cordial. Nevertheless those first years were 'a stormy seedtime' and marked by domestic grief as five of the McDougalls' sons died in infancy.

In England, between 1852 and 1854, McDougall worked hard to secure the financial stability of the mission, which was transferred from the Borneo Mission Society to the Society for the Propagation of the Gospel in 1853; to arrange for his own consecration (which eventually took place in Calcutta in 1855) as first bishop of Labuan; and to promote the good name of Raja James Brooke, now being called into question in parliament. A commission of inquiry, exculpating the raja but bitterly resented by him, met in Singapore in the autumn of 1854. The McDougalls reached Kuching again in May 1855.

The insurrection of 1857 by the goldwashers from Bau was the most acute crisis of Raja Brooke's rule. Every government house in Kuching was destroyed by fire. Some English men and children were murdered. Only the mission and its occupants were spared, though both house and church were ransacked. The raja escaped by swimming across the river and staying hidden. The bishop found himself having to treat insurgents and tend the wounded. He succeeded in saving his own party by crossing the river and, having given away his gun 'as not helpful in swimming' (McDougall to Bunyon, 17 April 1857, Brooke MSS, Bodl. RH), joined his wife and two children at Lingga. Eventually Charles Johnson, the raja's younger nephew, recovered Kuching with Dyak forces. There was great slaughter of Chinese people both innocent and guilty. The episode was disastrous for the mission and for the raja's peaceful policies. The stress of this experience, following so soon after the inquiry and his illness from smallpox, made James Brooke's behaviour increasingly erratic, and his relations with the bishop became ever more difficult. The bishop may not have been altogether blameless, since his saying that 'The Rajah may quit his country; I must get back to my Diocese' (L. V. Helms, *Pioneering in the Far East*, 1882, 164) was doubtless reported.

In June 1859 the bishop sailed his own schooner to Labuan and back—more than 400 miles each way. At this time two government officers were murdered in a Malay plot. Anxiety was great in Kuching but there was no outbreak of trouble. On 15 May 1862 the bishop accompanied

John Brooke Brooke, the raja's heir, up the coast in a small gunboat. They encountered a fleet of six well-armed pirate boats from Celebes. In two fierce actions the pirates were destroyed and 165 of their wretched victims saved. The bishop, Brooke wrote, 'was very industrious with his Terry-repeater rifle' (J. Brooke Brooke to Lady Grant, 28 May 1862, Brooke MSS, Bodl. RH, 6420). At the Raja Mudah's request the bishop wrote a long letter to *The Times*, calling for British action to police the south China seas. The consequence was a prolonged campaign of criticism in England at the bishop's participation in the battle, though Archbishop Longley pronounced in his favour. The action, he said, was not of Bishop McDougall's seeking and he seemed justified in defending himself and his companions. McDougall also worked hard in treating the sick and wounded, whether friends or foes, and was described at the Colonial Office as 'a rollicking mixture of Bishop, Surgeon and Sea-Captain with a good deal of shrewdness and observation' (F. Rogers, minutes, 10 May 1869, Foreign Office).

In February 1863 James Brooke dismissed his elder nephew and acknowledged heir with ignomiy, in favour of his younger nephew Charles, forbidding Brooke Brooke's return to Sarawak on penalty of death. The McDougalls' sympathy was wholly with Brooke Brooke; but duty required them to pursue the church's work regardless of their reservations about the succession. In 1864, 1865, and 1866 the bishop held diocesan synods; he also rewrote *A Malay Prayer Book*, first published by the SPCK in 1857, and wrote *A Catechism for the Use of Missions of the Church in Borneo* (1868).

McDougall attended the Lambeth Conference of 1867 and then resigned his see on the grounds of ill health. He ministered briefly as vicar of Godmanchester, Huntingdonshire, and afterwards as canon residentiary, first at Ely and then at Winchester; finally he was archdeacon of the Isle of Wight, from 1874. McDougall became a friend and assistant to Bishop E. H. Browne. He died at Winchester on 16 November 1886, six months after his wife, and was buried at Shorwell, Isle of Wight.

R. H. W. REECE and A. J. M. SAINT

Sources C. J. Bunyon, *Memoirs of Francis Thomas McDougall* (1889) · M. Saint, *A flourish for the bishop and Brooke's friend Grant: two studies in Sarawak history, 1848–1868* (1985) · G. Saunders, *Brookes and bishops, 1848–1941: the Anglican mission and the Brooke raj in Sarawak* (1992) · H. McDougall, *Sketches of our life at Sarawak* (1882); repr. with an introduction by R. H. W. Reece and A. J. M. Saint (1992) · H. McDougall, *Letters from Sarawak: addressed to a child* [1854] · m. cert.
Archives Bodl. RH, letters · Bodl. RH, incl. family corresp. | Bodl. Oxf., Wilberforce MSS, letters to Samuel Wilberforce
Wealth at death £4685 19s. 8d.: probate, 21 March 1887, *CGPLA Eng. & Wales*

McDougall [*née* Smith], **Grace Alexandra** (1887–1963), commanding officer of the FANY, was born at 67 Dee Street, Dee Village, Aberdeen, on 3 June 1887, the fifth child of Charles Smith, master grocer and wine merchant, and his wife, Isobel Copland (d. 1919). She was educated at Albyn's School for Girls, Aberdeen, with her three sisters, Agnes, Isobel, and Carolyn. Her two brothers, Charles and

William, were killed in action in the First World War. Having left school she spent a year at Aberdeen University, studying physical training, riding, and fencing, and then went to a convent in Brussels for two years to learn French. She was an excellent horsewoman, a superb fencer, and won the Empire cup for rifle shooting at Bisley in 1911. She disliked her second name, Alexandra, and as a teenager adopted the surname Ashley-Smith, influenced apparently by her second home, Ashley Lodge, in Great Western Road, Aberdeen.

In 1910 Ashley-Smith read an advertisement appealing for new members of the First Aid Nursing Yeomanry (FANY), which had been founded by Sergeant-Major Edward Charles Baker in 1907 as a corps of nurses on horseback 'tending Britain's soldiers on the field' (Terry, 25). When Ashley-Smith joined in January 1910 the corps entered a new phase:

> She was an energetic, forceful personality with a flair, which never deserted her, for seeing where there were openings for the FANYs to operate … It was fortunate for the movement that a woman of Ashley-Smith's calibre should have been attracted. (Ward, 34)

This forcefulness, best demonstrated by her admission in a notable mixed metaphor, 'Red tape never cut any ice with me' (Popham, 26), often caused resentment; 'Such a difficult lady to deal with,' a harassed FANY secretary remarked of her (ibid., 45). With Lilian Franklin, who had joined in 1909, she knocked the organization back into shape and was responsible for 'almost the second founding of the Corps' (ibid., 8). She later wrote:

> I had taken jumps without reins or stirrups, and gone over with my face to the horse's tail. I could jump on to a horse when it was cantering, and it was solely because of the title Yeomanry I had sought out the Corps. (Ward, 34)

In the next two years a power struggle occurred within the corps. This ended on 6 January 1912, when the final break with the Bakers (Katie Baker had joined her father in running the corps in February 1909) took place. The corps was now under new management, with Lilian Franklin as second-lieutenant and Ashley-Smith as sergeant-major. It was the latter, described as a genius at arranging things (Popham, 12), who became the chief organizer of events. Her photograph in uniform, which appeared in an advertisement for Sandow's corsets in *Women and War: Official Gazette of the First Aid Nursing Yeomanry Corps and Cadet Yeomanry*, of which she was 'editress', reveals her as a good-looking young woman, with curly brown hair, wide-set eyes, and a firm mouth with a hint of humour at the corners. 'My mother was never one to let a chance go by of raising funds for her beloved FANY corps', her son Desmond explained.

By the end of the FANY summer camp in 1914 Ashley-Smith was convinced that the corps was ready to perform a useful service if war broke out. She left the affairs of the corps in the hands of Lilian Franklin, and on 25 July sailed on the *Edinburgh Castle* for South Africa to visit her sister Carolyn. When war was declared on 4 August 1914 Ashley-Smith promptly sent a wireless message to Cape Town to book her passage home. She was ashore for only four hours. Coincidentally her path must have crossed that of the man she would later marry, Ronald McDougall (1877–1947), who was on his way from South Africa to Britain to enlist. They met in France and Ashley-Smith became the first war bride to marry in khaki. The marriage took place in All Saints' Church, Boyne Hill, Maidenhead, on 22 January 1915.

In September 1914 Ashley-Smith persuaded a grudging War Office official to grant her a military pass to cross the channel and join a British field hospital in Antwerp. She began her war service by driving a Belgian ambulance and picking up wounded from the trenches, often under fire. The city fell to the Germans on 10 October and Ghent fell a few days later. Scorning repatriation with the last party of British after the withdrawal of the allied armies, she stayed behind at the Hôtel Flandria to nurse and—surrounded by German soldiers—subsequently to bury a wounded British officer, Lieutenant Richard Foote. Though she was a prisoner of the Germans she managed to smuggle letters back home to her mother, and in one dated 14 October 1914 she rather recklessly wrote:

> German aeroplanes go about all day … I am going to try and blow up their aerodrome with dynamite. It is quite near here. It wouldn't be such a chance as getting their big guns but I fear that is hopeless. I suppose if this falls into their hands I shall be shot!

Instead, with the aid of Belgian friends and a friendly Dutch consul, she managed to escape to the Netherlands.

Back in London Ashley-Smith persuaded a fellow Aberdonian garage proprietor to donate a brand new motor ambulance to the FANY corps. 'I recognised his accent at once and told him I came from Aberdeen, too, so of course he couldn't refuse', she explained (*The Bulletin*). She crossed the channel once more, in command of five other members of the corps, accompanied by three trained nurses, two men dressers, and her brother Bill, who drove the ambulance. The FANYs reached Calais on 27 October and found the docks to be the living reality of war. The first battle of Ypres was reaching a crisis point 50 miles to the east and casualties were heavy. More than 8000 wounded were evacuated through Calais during the first five days that the FANY were there. Rows of wounded, sick, and dying men lay waiting patiently for places on the few hospital ships. It was icy cold, there were not enough blankets, and there was nothing to eat and no one to care for them. The FANY were posted to a dilapidated convent school, known as Lamarck, in the rue de la Rivière, opposite the cathedral. It had been taken over by the Belgians and turned into a makeshift hospital. The beds were straw-filled palliasses laid out on the floor, and the 100 patients, many of them suffering from typhoid, were ranged cheek by jowl. The FANY stayed at Lamarck for two years, improvising where necessary and willing to perform the toughest and most revolting tasks. By 1918 the FANY had units with all the allied armies, but the Belgians and Lamarck will always find special places in the annals of the corps.

In 1917 the FANY heard that the British War Office and the British Red Cross Society (BRCS) proposed to abolish all FANY units except the Calais British convoy. McDougall, as she was then, was running the Calais Belgian convoy and was determined to maintain the independence of the corps. She went to see a friendly Belgian officer and that afternoon the FANYs were paraded at the Belgian *État majeur*, and in the presence of the base commandant and Colonel Dieu-Donné, his chief of staff, they were weighed, measured, photographed, finger-printed, and sworn in as *soldats* of the corps de transport de Calais (Belge). The next day the BRCS party stormed into the FANY mess 'in a belligerent mood, to find themselves confronted by the Belgian base commandant and his staff officers'. They were informed that the FANY were *soldats de l'armée Belge* and therefore no concern of the BRCS. 'It was checkmate to any future designs to prevent the use of FANY by allied armies' (Ward, 56).

Illustrative of McDougall's scant heed of conformity are two 75mm shell cases that survive as family heirlooms. After her younger brother, William, was killed in action on 22 January 1916, nine months after the death of his elder brother, Charles, McDougall persuaded Belgian gunners to allow her to fire two shells against the Germans, one for each of her two brothers. The Belgian gunners engraved the shell cases '*Tiré sur les Boches par Madame McDougall, Septembre 5, 1916*'.

McDougall ended the war with decorations from the French and the Belgians: the ordre de la Couronne, the ordre de Leopold II (Belge), the Mons medal, the 1914–18 service medal, the Victory medal, the Croix de Guerre (silver star), the médaille d'honneur (French), the médaille des épidémies, the médaille secours des blessés militaires, and the médaille de la reine Elisabeth (Belge); she was also one of the few women to earn the rosette to the Mons star. After the war she and her husband went to Southern Rhodesia (later Zimbabwe) to farm. Though he loved the solitude, she felt isolated and lonely. After three years of drought the farm bankrupted them and in the late 1920s Ronald took a job with Rhodesia Railways as a surveyor. They had three children, Charles (1920–1970), Rona (1924–1989), and Desmond (b. 1926). Grace McDougall published two books, one anonymous and entitled *Nursing Adventures: a F.A.N.Y. in France* (1917), and a novel, *The Golden Bowl* (1926). She died at Filsham House, St Leonards, Sussex, on 19 January 1963.   ROY TERRY

Sources T. Ward, *F.A.N.Y. invicta* (1955) · H. Popham, *F.A.N.Y.: the story of the Women's Transport Service, 1907–1984* (1984) · G. Ashley-Smith, diary, 1909–19, IWM · R. Terry, *Women in khaki* (1988) · *Nursing adventures: a F.A.N.Y. in France* (1917) · private information (2004) · *The Bulletin* (10 Nov 1988) [c/o F.A.N.Y. archives, Duke of York's Barracks, London] · m. cert. · d. cert. · *CGPLA Eng. & Wales* (1963)

Archives IWM, Ashley-Smith diary

Likenesses photographs, priv. coll.

Wealth at death £980 0s. 2d.: administration, 21 Nov 1963, *CGPLA Eng. & Wales*

McDougall [*née* Bunyon], **Harriette** (1818–1886), missionary, was born at 6 The Crescent, New Bridge Street, Blackfriars, London, on 30 August 1818, the second daughter of Robert John Bunyon, the London secretary of the Norwich Union Fire and Life Insurance Company, and his wife,

Frances (*née* Bignold). The Bunyon family had evangelical missionary interests: Edward Bickersteth of Watton, Hertfordshire, was Harriette's uncle, and her older sister, Frances, married John Colenso, afterwards bishop of Natal. Frederick Denison Maurice was a family friend and a lifelong influence on her spirituality.

Educated privately, Harriette was gifted in painting and music. She was fair-haired, slight, and vivacious, 'the flower of the flock', her sister wrote (Frances Colenso to Sophia Colenso, 1881, McDougall MS, Bodl. RH). On 11 July 1843 she married Francis Thomas *McDougall (1817–1886) at Pembrey, Carmarthenshire. A professional soldier's son, he had qualified in surgery at King's College, London, and was ordained in 1845.

Harriette McDougall encouraged her husband to offer for pioneer missionary work in Borneo at the invitation of the first white raja of Sarawak, Sir James Brooke, under the auspices of the Borneo Church Mission. With an infant son and his nursemaid, the McDougalls arrived at Kuching on 29 June 1848 after a six months' voyage. Nothing had been prepared for them but within two years they had built a large wooden church and a spacious house. They also started an orphan school and a medical dispensary. Harriette conducted the choir and played for services; she was also responsible for a large household frequently swelled by visitors.

The McDougalls worked in Sarawak for twenty years, with three periods of English leave. They lost five sons in five years. Despite this grief, political hazards, unreliable assistants, and malicious criticism from both the raja and his secretary, Spenser St John, they planted the Anglican church firmly within the Chinese and Dyak communities. Parishes with schools were established at Quop, Lingga, Banting, Lundu, and Bintulu. At first Harriette had the company of Elizabeth Richardson, her children's nursemaid; she was later a friend of her husband's cousin Elizabeth Woolley, who married Walter Chambers, afterwards second bishop of Labuan and Sarawak.

Harriette McDougall was a prolific correspondent; 130 of her letters survived, along with fragments of her journal. She also published two books: *Letters from Sarawak: Addressed to a Child* (1854) consists of letters written to her eldest child, Charley, and *Sketches of our Life at Sarawak* (1882) was written long after her return to England. She made watercolour paintings of local scenes and wrote a national anthem for Sarawak adapted from what she described as 'a German nonsense catch'.

These writings communicate serenity, especially at times of grief and physical danger, and also bear witness to a strong religious faith. In February 1857 Harriette experienced the privations of flight and homelessness with two young children when Chinese goldwashers rebelled against the raja's authority and occupied Kuching. She was often ill and anxious about her husband's health and had to manage the affairs of the mission single-handed when he visited Labuan and the outstation mission posts. Especially grievous to her was the mental deterioration of the raja after he had been stricken by smallpox in 1854, and his increasing mistrust of his

nephew and heir, John Brooke Brooke: the raja disinherited him in February 1863, confiscating his property and threatening to have him cut down should he ever return to Sarawak. Harriette's letters of this period offer a moving testament to her compassion. She also played an important part by mediating between the raja and her husband, after their relationship deteriorated upon McDougall's consecration as bishop of Labuan in 1855, and when the bishop's forthright manner antagonized his missionary colleagues. The mission could never have succeeded without her quiet wisdom.

After their return to England the McDougalls recovered in health. They worked first at Godmanchester, Huntingdonshire, and then at Ely and at Winchester, where he was canon residentiary. One of Harriette's tasks in later life was to act as temporary foster mother to the infant Charles Vyner Brooke, afterwards third raja. She died at the vicarage, Shorwell, Isle of Wight, on 7 May 1886, six months before her husband. Her body was buried at Shorwell churchyard, and the inscription on her memorial in Winchester Cathedral records simply that 'She first taught Christ to the women of Borneo.'

R. H. W. REECE and A. J. M. SAINT

Sources C. J. Bunyon, *Memoirs of Francis Thomas McDougall* (1889) · M. Bramston, *An early Victorian heroine* (1910) · M. Saint, *A flourish for the bishop and Brooke's friend Grant: two studies in Sarawak history, 1848–1868* (1985) · H. McDougall, *Sketches of our life at Sarawak* (1882); repr. with an introduction by R. H. W. Reece and A. J. M. Saint (1992) · H. McDougall, *Letters from Sarawak: addressed to a child* [1854] · G. Saunders, 'Harriette McDougall', *Adventurous women in south-east Asia*, ed. J. Gullick (1995) · *CGPLA Eng. & Wales* (1886) · m. cert. · d. cert.
Archives Bodl. RH | Bodl. RH, Basil Brooke and Turner MSS
Likenesses photographs, priv. coll. · photographs, Bodl. RH
Wealth at death £1121 8s.: probate, 14 July 1886, *CGPLA Eng. & Wales*

MacDougall, John, lord of Argyll (d. 1316), magnate, was the son of Alexander *MacDougall, lord of Argyll (d. 1310), with whose career his own is largely intertwined, the grandson of Ewen MacDougall, lord of Argyll and king in the Hebrides, and a descendant of Somerled (d. 1164), king of the Hebrides and *regulus* of Argyll and Kintyre. John's mother, it would appear, was a member of the powerful Comyn family, probably a daughter of John Comyn, lord of Badenoch (d. 1277). Although later historians have almost invariably styled him John of Lorne and he is better known to generations of Scots as such, contemporary accounts style him John of Argyll (*de Ergadia*). There seems to be no contemporary authority for the byname Bacach ('the Lame'), now often attached to him. This may have arisen through confusion with a cousin and namesake.

MacDougall first appears on record in 1291 when he swore fealty to Edward I. He followed his father, Alexander, in supporting the Balliol party, with whom the Comyns were closely connected. By tradition it was John who was responsible for the death of Cailin Mor, chief of the Campbells, in a skirmish at the String of Lorne about 1296. Like Alexander, John became a committed supporter of Edward I, who expressed his trust in him in a letter written in 1304. In 1305 Alexander was named a member of the advisory council of John of Brittany (d. 1334), Edward I's lieutenant in Scotland. John MacDougall's cousin, the former guardian John Comyn of Badenoch, was slain by Robert Bruce in the church of the Greyfriars in Dumfries in 1306. Later that year MacDougall defeated Robert, now king of Scots, and dispersed his followers at Dalrigh in Argyll, all but bringing to a premature end both his career as king and his life. According to Barbour, MacDougall compared Robert's near miraculous escape to that of Goll MacMorna from Finn MacCumhail. It was on this occasion that a dying MacDougall is said to have wrested from the fugitive king the brooch of Lorne.

In 1307 Edward II appointed MacDougall sheriff of Argyll and Inchegall (the Hebrides). In 1308, however, John wrote to Edward explaining that his position was becoming increasingly desperate and seeking assistance against the advancing forces of Robert I. No help was forthcoming, and later that year Robert defeated MacDougall by Ben Cruachan ('the battle of the Pass of Brander') and took the MacDougall headquarters of Dunstaffnage. John fled to England to be joined there later by his now elderly father, who had temporarily entered King Robert's peace. (Barbour's statement that John was captured by Robert and sent to Dumbarton and then to Lochleven, where he died in captivity, is without foundation.) Both John and Alexander attended Edward II's council at Westminster in 1310. In 1311 and 1314 John (named as Monsire Jehan Dargail) was appointed admiral and captain of an English fleet, and in 1315 he recovered the Isle of Man for England. He was granted a pension by Edward II in 1316 and died in September that year at Ospring in Kent on pilgrimage to Canterbury, having appointed as his executor another displaced Scot, Dungal MacDowall of Galloway.

The name of MacDougall's wife is not known. His sons Ewen and Alan were members of the household of Edward II of England, the former when Edward was still prince of Wales. Gaelic genealogical tradition gives John two further sons, Somhairle and Alexander Og. He had at least two daughters: Mary, who married John Stirling of Rathoran, and an unnamed daughter married to Patrick Graham. MacDougall's reputation has suffered on account of his opposition to Robert I, yet it is impossible not to discern in the accounts of Barbour in the fourteenth century and Blind Hary in the fifteenth, relayed again in Sir Walter Scott's *Tales of a Grandfather* (1828–30), more than a little grudging respect.

John's son Ewen appears to have returned briefly to Scotland in the 1330s in the following of Edward Balliol, but it was John's grandson and namesake, by his son Alan, who re-established the MacDougalls in Argyll, though the circumstances remain obscure. This **John MacDougall**, lord of Lorne (d. in or after 1371), is on record in 1338. Known traditionally as John Gallda ('the Foreigner') and usually styled John of Lorne, he styled himself lord of Argyll in an agreement concerning lands in dispute that he entered into with his remote cousin John MacDonald, chief of his name and lord of the Isles. He married Jonet Isaac, daughter of Thomas Isaac and Matilda Bruce, daughter of Robert I and full sister of David II. MacDougall

renewed the family's foothold in Argyll in a modest way, but it never regained the power and status which it had enjoyed before the wars of independence. John seems to have died in or after 1371, leaving two daughters, Isabel and Jonet, married respectively to Sir John Stewart of Innermeath and his brother Sir Robert Stewart of Durrisdeer. The lordship of Lorne passed to John and Isabel and their descendants. MacDougall also appears to have left a son, Alan, perhaps from an uncanonical union. The later chiefs of MacDougall descend from this Alan, rather than from a brother of Alexander of Argyll, named Duncan, as is usually claimed.   W. D. H. SELLAR

Sources W. D. H. Sellar, 'Hebridean sea-kings: the successors of Somerled, 1164–1316', *Alba: Celtic Scotland in the middle ages*, ed. E. J. Cowan and R. A. McDonald (2000), 187–218 · G. W. S. Barrow, *Robert Bruce and the community of the realm of Scotland*, 3rd edn (1988) · R. Nicholson, *Scotland: the later middle ages* (1974), vol. 2 of *The Edinburgh history of Scotland*, ed. G. Donaldson (1965–75), 74, 79–80, 94, 155–6, 178 · R. A. McDonald, *The kingdom of the isles: Scotland's western seaboard, c.1100–c.1336* (1997) · C. M. MacDonald, *History of Argyll* (1950), 117–73 · W. D. H. Sellar, 'MacDougall pedigrees in MS 1467', *Notes and Queries of the Society of West Highland and Island Historical Research*, 29 (Aug 1986), 3–18 · T. Stapleton, 'A brief summary of the wardrobe accounts of the tenth, eleventh and fourteenth years of King Edward the Second', *Archaeologia*, 26 (1836), 318–45 · G. Barrow, 'The battle between John MacDougall of Lorn and Robert Bruce in 1308 or 1309', *West Highland Notes and Queries*, 2nd ser., 19 (1999), 3–11 · A. A. M. Duncan, 'The battles of Ben Cruachan', *West Highland Notes and Queries*, 2nd ser., 20 (1999), 3–20 · J. Barbour, *The Bruce*, ed. A. A. M. Duncan (1997) · *Johannis de Fordun Chronica gentis Scotorum / John of Fordun's Chronicle of the Scottish nation*, ed. W. F. Skene, trans. F. J. H. Skene, 2 (1872), 360 · 'Lorn', GEC, *Peerage* · *Hary's Wallace*, ed. M. P. McDiarmid, 2 vols., STS, 4th ser., 4–5 (1968–9) · J. R. N. Macphail, ed., *Highland papers*, 1, Scottish History Society, 2nd ser., 5 (1914)

MacDougall, John, lord of Lorne (d. in or after **1371**). *See under* MacDougall, John, lord of Argyll (d. **1316**).

Macdougall, Sir John. *See* M'Dougal, Sir John (1790–1865).

McDougall [née Long], **Kate Florence** [Kay] (1910–1999), psychiatric social worker, was born on 6 November 1910 at 55 Pantel Road, Camberwell, London, the eldest of the three children of Richard Sylvester Long, brass finisher, and his wife, Kate Adelaide, née Griffin. Both her parents were Londoners, living for many years in Camberwell, where her father ran his own business. He held firm ethical and human values based on socialist principles. Her mother's sisters were wardrobe mistresses at Drury Lane theatres: the young Kate thus developed a lifelong love of the theatre and clothes. At school and in extracurricular activities she demonstrated her creative and leadership skills, writing plays for the local Church of England youth club and for the Brownies, where she later became tawny owl, ensuring parts for all, including children with learning disabilities.

Kay, as she was known throughout her professional life, left school at sixteen and took a job as a clerk with a city wine merchant. Determined to extend her knowledge, she went to evening classes run by Morley College and the Workers' Educational Association, before going full-time to Hillcroft College, Surbiton, in 1931. She often recalled the excellence of her teachers in those years: C. E. M. Joad for philosophy; Barbara Wootton for economics and psychology; Fanny Street, head of Hillcroft; and Elsie Whetnall, philosophy and logic tutor. After Hillcroft she went to work at a girls' approved school in Surrey and later became assistant matron at the first school for maladjusted girls in Northampton. Her first link with the London School of Economics (LSE) was made in 1934. After winning an Ernest Cassell scholarship she took the social science course, intending to become an industrial welfare officer. When she discovered that this would entail becoming a manager she opted to stay at the LSE for a second year to take the mental health course, helped by the award of a Commonwealth of America scholarship.

In 1936 Kay qualified as a psychiatric social worker. At a time when the primary preoccupation of most psychiatric social workers was with the small but growing child-guidance movement and its concern with the treatment and prevention of delinquency, she was the first psychiatric social worker to be appointed to Warlingham Park Hospital, Croydon, then designated a lunatic asylum. It is perhaps difficult to realize how revolutionary it was then for the occupants and outpatients of mental hospitals to be identified as individuals with a social history and family connections, not just examples of some unfortunate category of humanity with strange inexplicable behaviours. Social definitions of lunacy were only just becoming of interest to medicine. Initially the only social worker, with four psychiatrists and 1000 patients, Kay helped to promote new approaches to treatment for adults. By 1945 she had also been instrumental in the establishment of the Croydon child guidance clinic as part of the local authority hospital service. On 12 October 1939 she married Robert Percy McDougall (1916–1987), a printer, son of Robert John McDougall, commercial clerk. Her husband served with the Royal Artillery throughout the Second World War. Theirs proved to be a long and happy marriage. They had no children of their own, but were regarded with great filial affection by at least two overseas students for whom they acted as guardians.

At the end of the war Kay McDougall was appointed to the staff of the mental health course at the LSE, to which she brought experience and enthusiasm for work both with adults with mental illness and with children. This balance, together with her experience as a lecturer at the Maudsley Institute of Psychiatry working with a range of doctors and nurses, stood her in good stead when in 1947 she was appointed head of the mental health course. She strengthened and expanded the course, which became a leader in social work education in this country and also made an impact on the LSE itself. She was constant in her efforts to help improve the physical conditions and quality of life of sick and deprived people from all spheres of the community, and brought a breadth of approach to the study of human behaviour which was an essential counterbalance to those who saw its future as almost exclusively based on psychoanalytic theory.

Social work education in the 1950s was dominated by strenuous arguments about specialist and generic training. By 1954 the LSE was running three social work qualifying courses: the mental health course, the child care course, and the applied social studies course (funded by the Carnegie Foundation). A period of painful organizational conflict developed. A review of the position recommended that there should be a single social work course. Kay McDougall was identified as the person best able to lead the reorganization and to get the best from staff, which she did successfully, though not without scars which remained for many years. The mental health course eventually became an advanced course in social work.

Kay McDougall was a believer in lifelong learning. During these years she contributed many papers to social work and other professional conferences and journals. With Una Cormack she wrote two chapters for the first major British text for social workers, *Social Casework in Great Britain* (1950), edited by Cherry Morris. In 1954, conscious of the lack of British material on social work practice, she founded and published *Case Conference*, a monthly magazine which she was to edit for the next sixteen years. She encouraged professionals from the various branches of social work to write, and to examine and exchange ideas on the nature of their work. The quality of the material published made a major contribution to the development of social work and continued to do so until the magazine ceased publication in 1970, when the British Association of Social Workers and its journal, *Social Work Today*, were established. Professor Richard Titmuss, who wrote the first article in the first number, reflected in the last issue that '*Case Conference* has contributed throughout this period to sustaining and promoting a spirit of enquiry and a broad forward-looking approach to social change and the future of social work' (*Case Conference*, 16/12, April 1970). Kay was greatly supported in this enterprise by the encouragement and enthusiasm of her husband and a friend, Mrs R. V. Andrews, who acted as secretary and circulation manager.

In 1965, on returning from a sabbatical in Ghana evaluating the social administration unit at the university, Kay McDougall was invited to succeed David Jones, principal of the National Institute of Social Work, as chair of the Standing Conference of Organisations of Social Workers. An ardent believer in the value of professional association, she was an early member of the British Federation of Social Workers and later of the Association of Psychiatric Social Workers, and therefore willingly took on the delicate task of helping to weld together several disparate bodies to form a unified professional body. The British Association of Social Workers was established in June 1970, and Kay was delighted to become member number 1.

Kay McDougall's contribution to social work did not end with her retirement from the LSE in 1971. It had been marked with her appointment as OBE in 1967, and in the same year she was awarded a personal readership at the LSE to acknowledge her contribution to the school. In 1972, after a world tour with her husband during which she renewed contact with many former students, she became a consultant to the short course programme at the National Institute of Social Work. She was a humble and practical colleague, sharing her knowledge and experimenting with new teaching methods to meet the needs of directors of social services as they took on changing roles in local authority departments in the post-Seebohm era. She also served on numerous committees. She was the first non-doctor to chair the central health service committee of the National Association of Mental Health (MIND), and from 1981 to 1997 she was a trustee of the Social Workers Educational Trust.

One of the last of her generation of liberalizing and humanitarian influences on the care and treatment of people with mental illness, Kay McDougall was also a pioneer of renown in the development of social work education. A woman of considerable intellect, modesty, and outstanding integrity, she had a strong sense of social justice and set high standards. Seen as formidable by some students, she was always kind and fair. Her commitment to social work was rooted in her personal values. In 1970 she took the view that as social workers:

> we cannot make our professional life a nine to five persona
> … the need for other interests and for not taking client
> problems home with us are important, but a profession is a
> way of life and not a job of work. We are judged in the end by
> how we are seen to behave towards clients and towards each
> other.   (Baraclough, 4)

Her joy in her many diverse friendships and in the achievements of her students was very evident, while the warmth and generosity of the hospitality which she and her husband dispensed from their home by the River Mimram in Welwyn was renowned, as was their zest for living.

Kay McDougall died of cancer at the Queen Elizabeth II Hospital, Welwyn Garden City, Hertfordshire, on 29 June 1999, and was cremated at Garston crematorium on 22 July 1999. A memorial meeting was held at the LSE on 5 August 1999.   JOAN BARACLOUGH

Sources *Case Conference*, 16/12 (April 1970) · *The Guardian* (29 July 1999) · *LSE Magazine*, 42 (Nov 1971) · J. Baraclough, *Professional Social Work* (Aug 1999), 4 · personal knowledge (2004) · private information (2004) · b. cert. · m. cert.
Archives British Association of Social Workers, Birmingham, *Case Conference* archives · University of Warwick, British Association of Social Workers predecessor archives | FILM BFI NFTVA, '100 years of health related social work', K. Richards (producer) [produced for BASW]
Likenesses photograph, 1970, repro. in Baraclough, *Professional Social Work*, 4 · photograph, repro. in *The Guardian* · photograph, repro. in *LSE Magazine*
Wealth at death £264,544: probate, 7 Oct 1999, *CGPLA Eng. & Wales*

MacDougall, Sir Patrick Leonard (1819–1894), army officer and military writer, born at Boulogne, France, on 10 August 1819, was the son of Sir Duncan *Macdougall (1787–1862), army officer, and his first wife, Anne, daughter of Colonel Cornelius Smelt, governor of the Isle of Man. Educated at the private Scottish Naval and Military Academy, Edinburgh, and the Royal Military College, Sandhurst, he was commissioned second lieutenant in

Sir Patrick Leonard MacDougall (1819–1894), by unknown photographer, *c.*1860

the Ceylon rifle regiment on 13 February 1836, exchanging in July into the 79th Cameron Highlanders and on 26 July 1839 into the 36th foot. His promotions were: lieutenant (by purchase), 11 May 1839; captain (by purchase), 7 June 1844; major (by purchase), 9 February 1849; brevet lieutenant-colonel, 17 July 1855; brevet colonel, 17 July 1858; major-general, 6 March 1868; lieutenant-general, 1 October 1877; colonel of the 2nd battalion, West India regiment, 21 December 1881; general, 1 October 1883; and colonel of the Leinster regiment, 26 August 1891.

In 1840 MacDougall entered the senior department of the Royal Military College, Sandhurst; he left in 1842 with the highest class certificate and special commendation. Transferred on 25 June 1844 to the Royal Canadian rifle regiment, he joined it at Toronto and for the next ten years served as a regimental officer there and at Kingston. On 3 March 1854 he was appointed superintendent of studies at Sandhurst, but the following year was sent to the Crimea, where he acted as assistant quartermaster-general on the staff of Brigadier-General D. A. Cameron in the expedition to Kerch in May 1855, and attended Lord Raglan in the trenches at the unsuccessful assaults on the Redan on 18 June. He received a brevet lieutenant-colonelcy. He resumed his Sandhurst appointment, which he held until February 1858. He was one of the 'new army school' of officers who, influenced by the Crimean War failures, wanted army reform.

In 1856 MacDougall's book *The Theory of War: Illustrated by Numerous Examples from Military History* was published. This advanced no original theories, but was largely a digest from the classic European military writers, and also advocated more scientific education of officers. An immediate success, it became a standard textbook, was translated into French and German, and gave MacDougall a leading place among British military writers. His 1857 pamphlet, *The Senior Department of the Royal Military College*, asserted the lack of proper instruction for staff officers, and probably led to his appointment to the new Staff College at Camberley. He was its first commandant, from February 1858 to September 1861. He published in 1858 a treatise for students of military history, *The Campaigns of Hannibal Arranged and Critically Considered*.

At the Staff College he was an industrious writer and lecturer. His subjects included 'Napoleon's campaign in Italy in 1796', 'The military character of the great duke of Marlborough', and 'General Sir Charles James Napier as conqueror and governor of Sind'. He wrote *The Times* obituary of Napier.

In December 1861, during the *Trent* crisis, MacDougall advised the War Office on the defence of Canada, asserting the crucial importance of control of the Great Lakes and proposing an offensive into Maine. He also recommended linking Canadian militia units to British regular units in Canada. He visited Canada and the United States in 1862, and published in the same year *Forts versus Ships* and *Defence of the Canadian Lakes and its Influence on the General Defence of Canada*, both written while crossing the Atlantic. In 1864 his life of his father-in-law, the historian of the Peninsular War, Sir William Francis Patrick Napier, was published in two volumes—though (for reasons now unclear) under the name of H. A. Bruce (later Lord Aberdare), husband of another of Napier's daughters. MacDougall studied and was much influenced by the American Civil War. His *Modern Warfare as Influenced by Modern Artillery* (1864) was the first work by a British officer to incorporate lessons from the civil war, and argued that firepower would give an immense advantage to the defence, that there would be more trenches, and that the cavalry's role would decrease. Early in 1865 he contributed articles on Sir William Napier to both the *Edinburgh* and *Quarterly* reviews.

In May 1865 MacDougall was appointed adjutant-general of Canadian militia. In part responding to inadequacies revealed by its 1866 anti-Fenian mobilizations, he successfully reorganized it, grouping the independent companies into localized battalions, and grouping the battalions with regular battalions into brigades. Lord Monck, the governor-general, praised his achievement in creating an inexpensive, unoppressive, and efficient military system. MacDougall sometimes lectured on military subjects. In 1865 he published an anonymous pamphlet arguing that Canada could be defended. After he left Canada he continued to be concerned about its defence, and he tried to prevent the Gladstone government from withdrawing all British troops.

In April 1869 MacDougall returned to England. Convinced of the necessity of army reform, then a controversial issue, he published his pamphlet *The Army and its Reserves* (1869), warning against rigidly copying the Prussian system, and proposing for regulars relatively short service followed by reserve service, as well as—drawing on his Canadian experience—a revived militia as a reserve to reinforce the regulars, and organizationally linked to them. From October 1871 to March 1873 he was deputy inspector-general of the auxiliary forces at the War Office. He was chairman of Cardwell's crucial 1871 'localization committee', which included Wolseley, who also had Canadian experience. Its report, substantially adopted from 1872, proposed a system, influenced by both Prussian and Canadian models, of the fusion of the regular, reserve, and auxiliary forces to form one army, and of linked battalions, in order to have always one at home and one abroad, with depots for enlisting and training recruits. In 1873 MacDougall published *Modern Infantry Tactics*, arguing against the tendency to accept Prussian teaching, particularly on the offensive, reasserting lessons from the American Civil War, and asserting that modern firepower favoured the defence.

In 1873 Cardwell established the new intelligence branch at the War Office, based on the existing topographical and statistical department but with more than double the staff. MacDougall, by then 'one of the most respected and influential major generals' (Fergusson, 53), was its first head (deputy adjutant-general for intelligence and later deputy quartermaster-general) from April 1873 to May 1878. An excellent choice, he made an important contribution to British military intelligence, attempting to ensure quality through the appointment only of Staff College graduates to permanent posts, and expanding the branch's role to include involvement in defence planning. It rose from relative obscurity to increased prestige and real importance in the War Office, and by the time he left it was firmly established. He was made KCMG in May 1877.

In 1878 MacDougall was appointed to the command in North America, when relations with Russia were strained after the Russo-Turkish War. He undertook to have 10,000 trained Canadian volunteers available for service, wherever required, a few weeks after the offer of their service was accepted, instituting a precedent which was later followed not only by Canada but by most of the self-governing colonies to the great advantage of the empire.

MacDougall returned to England in May 1883, and retired from the active list in July 1885. He was twice married: first, in 1844, to Louisa Augusta (*d.* 1856), third daughter of Sir William Francis Patrick Napier; and, secondly, in 1860, to Marianne Adelaide, who survived him, daughter of Philip John Miles of Leigh Court, Somerset. There were no children in either marriage.

MacDougall published many articles in the reviews and magazines, and also *Emigration: its Advantages to Great Britain and her Colonies, Together with a Detailed Plan for the Promotion of the Proposed Railway between Halifax and Quebec* (1848) and *Short Service Enlistment and the Organisation of our Infantry* (1883). He died at his residence, Melbury Lodge, Kingston Hill, Surrey, on 28 November 1894, and was buried at Putney cemetery, the sergeants of the Kingston depot carrying his body to the grave.

R. H. VETCH, *rev.* ROGER T. STEARN

Sources war office records, PRO · *The Times* (30 Nov 1894) · J. Luvaas, *The education of an army: British military thought, 1815–1940*, new edn (1965) · B. Bond, *The Victorian army and the Staff College, 1854–1914* (1972) · T. G. Fergusson, *British military intelligence, 1870–1914* (1984) · E. M. Spiers, *The late Victorian army, 1868–1902* (1992) · R. Biddulph, *Lord Cardwell at the war office: a history of his administration, 1868–1874* (1904) · Boase, *Mod. Eng. biog.* · *Hart's Army List* (1891)
Archives Bodl. Oxf., corresp. with Sir William Napier · NL Scot., corresp. with Blackwoods
Likenesses photograph, *c*.1860, Jermit Services Command and Staff College, Bracknell, Berkshire [*see illus.*] · Notman, miniature, priv. coll.
Wealth at death £2757 7s. 4d.: probate, 31 Jan 1895, *CGPLA Eng. & Wales*

McDougall, William (1871–1938), psychologist, was born at Mills Hill, Tonge, Chadderton, Lancashire, on 22 June 1871. He was the second son of Isaac Shimwell McDougall, a chemical manufacturer, and his wife, Rebekah Smalley. After attending a private school, and following a spell at a *Realgymnasium* in Weimar, Germany, with his elder brother, McDougall entered Manchester University at fifteen; he graduated with first-class honours in general science in 1889 and obtained a scholarship to St John's College, Cambridge. McDougall's career continued auspiciously with a first in the Cambridge natural sciences tripos (part one 1892; part two 1894). Considering a medical career, he did laboratory work under C. S. Sherrington at St Thomas's Hospital, London (1894), qualifying MB, BChir, and MA (Cantab.) in 1897. His research earned him a fellowship of St John's in 1897, but reading William James's *Principles of Psychology* persuaded him that medicine would be insufficiently satisfying.

In 1898 McDougall won the Grainger prize at Cambridge and joined A. C. Haddon's Cambridge anthropological expedition to the Torres Strait (New Guinea) with W. H. R. Rivers and C. S. Myers, on which the first experimental psychological field studies of 'primitive' people were undertaken, McDougall tackling cutaneous sensation and weight judgement. A visit to Borneo during his return journey eventually yielded *The Pagan Tribes of Borneo* (1912), written with C. Hose. On 23 May 1900 McDougall married Annie Amelia Hickmore (*b.* 1878/9), daughter of Henry Hickmore, a government contractor; they had three sons and two daughters. With James Ward's encouragement McDougall spent a period researching perception and attention under G. E. Müller, the eminent Göttingen-based German psychologist. In 1901 McDougall was a co-founder of the British Psychological Society and, as reader in experimental psychology at University College, London (under James Sully), from 1901 to 1907, he continued his research into perception, particularly opposing the perceptual theory of Ewald Hering. In 1904 he became Wilde reader in mental philosophy, Oxford, holding this jointly with the University College readership, a part-time post until 1907. The Wilde readership explicitly prohibited experimental research, but McDougall ignored this condition and, with the collusion of some sympathetic colleagues, proceeded to help establish a presence for psychology at Oxford, despite claiming that while he was 'neither fish, flesh, nor fowl. I was neither a scientist or philosopher *pur sang*' (*Obits. FRS*, 41). His first book,

the brief *Physiological Psychology*, appeared in 1905. While becoming internationally the most prominent and prolific of early twentieth-century British psychologists, McDougall's career arguably peaked during these years with the extraordinarily successful *Introduction to Social Psychology* (1908), which went through twenty-three editions by 1936. The title was somewhat misleading in that it was centrally concerned with expounding a Darwinian evolutionary instinct theory of human motivation as the theoretical basis for a social psychology proper (presented in the less successful *Group Mind*, 1920). McDougall's concept of social psychology had almost no influence on the way that the discipline subsequently developed, especially in the USA. *Psychology: the Study of Behaviour* (1912) followed, consolidating his growing reputation. The outbreak of war in 1914 curtailed McDougall's psychoanalysis by Carl Jung. Like many professional contemporaries he spent the First World War treating shell-shock victims, and served as a major in the Royal Army Medical Corps from 1915 to 1919. Offered the prestigious and unrefusable William James chair of psychology at Harvard, he emigrated to the USA in 1920, remaining until 1927, when he accepted the psychology chair at Duke University, North Carolina. Increasing deafness made life difficult for him in the following years and most of his summers were spent in England at his house in Wendover, Buckinghamshire.

McDougall then increasingly devoted his energies to producing popular works on contemporary issues, often rather polemical and written from a eugenic perspective. The first, *Is America Safe for Democracy?* (1921, published in Britain as *National Welfare and National Decay*), immediately identified him with the immigration control and 'race differences' camp. This strong Galtonian eugenic position regarding social problems alienated increasing numbers of American psychologists from the mid-1920s as race-differences doctrines came under attack and 'race prejudice' emerged as a topic in American social psychology. McDougall, however, doggedly stuck by his 1898 findings of differences in skin sensitivity and weight discrimination ability, despite the (by then generally recognized) methodological flaws and interpretational ambiguities of this research. His own research interests now veered towards psychic phenomena and Lamarckian inheritance, thereby exacerbating his marginalization within the discipline. An inveterate controversialist, McDougall figured prominently in the heated debates (characteristic of this period) between various psychological schools. Behaviourism was a frequent target but he also challenged psychoanalysis and Gestalt psychology while sometimes claiming priority for anticipating their more positively valuable ideas. His more substantial general textbooks, *An Outline of Psychology* (1923) and *An Outline of Abnormal Psychology* (1926), remained popular none the less and he retained a high public profile to the end (publishing over forty full-length works).

While instinct-centred, McDougall's theoretical and philosophical position, which he termed 'hormic', was marked by a commitment to mind–body dualism (lengthily expounded in *Body and Mind: a History and Defence of Animism*, 1911) and the need to maintain a teleological approach to understanding human nature. This in itself set him fundamentally at odds with the main inter-war developments in American psychology. In retrospect, the range of perspectives he sought to integrate, from psychoanalysis to psychometrics, remains impressive. His views on the role of instincts partially anticipated those more successfully proposed later by the ethologists, while the purposiveness on which he always insisted received a demystified rehabilitation in post-1950 cognitivist theory.

Handsome and athletic in his youth, McDougall claimed to represent 'that blend of the Mediterranean and Nordic races which has produced the English people' (*Obits. FRS*, 39). He clearly possessed a degree of charisma. To this, however, were added a combative temperament and a generally élitist ideological outlook, which ill served his interests in the USA. McDougall himself acknowledged his 'intellectual arrogance and an invariable tendency to rebel against dominance and support scientifically unpopular doctrines' (*Obits. FRS*, 41). The loss of two of his six children undoubtedly cast a shadow over his later, professionally embattled, years. Almost unrivalled in his time as a popularizer of psychology, posterity's verdict on McDougall's work has not been generous, many considering his pre-1914 physiological work to be his best. Emigration, it is now plain, badly injured his career, his arrival at Harvard coinciding with the widespread, almost evangelical, rejection by young American psychologists of precisely the kind of psychology that McDougall represented. His academic honours included election as FRS and fellowship of Corpus Christi College, Oxford (both 1912), honorary DSc from Manchester University (1919), and honorary fellowship of St John's College, Cambridge (1938). McDougall died at Durham, North Carolina, on 28 November 1938.   GRAHAM RICHARDS

Sources C. Murchison, ed., *History of psychology in autobiography*, 1 (1930), 191–223 · F. A. Pattie, *American Journal of Psychology*, 52 (1939), 303–7 · A. L. Robinson, *William McDougall: a bibliography together with a brief outline of his life* (1943) · b. cert. · m. cert. · M. Greenwood and M. Smith, *Obits. FRS*, 3 (1939–41), 39–53 · *CGPLA Eng. & Wales* (1939)
Archives Duke U. | JRL, letters to Samuel Alexander
Likenesses W. Stoneman, photograph, 1917, NPG · group photograph (with his children), repro. in W. McDougall, *National welfare and national decay* (1921) · photograph, repro. in Murchison, ed., *History of psychology* · photograph, repro. in R. B. Cattell and others, *Human affairs* (1937) · photograph, repro. in Greenwood and Smith, *Obits. FRS*
Wealth at death £8309 1s. 3d.: administration with will, 6 April 1939, *CGPLA Eng. & Wales*

Macdowall, Andrew. *See* McDouall, Andrew, Lord Bankton (1685–1760).

McDowall, Roderick Andrew Anthony Jude [Roddy] (1928–1998), actor, was born on 17 September 1928 at 204 Herne Hill Road, Herne Hill, London, the younger child and only son of Thomas Andrew McDowall (1896–1978), a Scottish-born officer in the merchant marine, and his Irish wife, Winsfriede L. (Wynn) Corcoran (1899–1965). He

Roderick Andrew Anthony Jude McDowall (1928–1998), by unknown photographer, c.1955

was educated at St Joseph Roman Catholic College, Beulah Hill, and the Hanover Academy of Dramatic Art, both in London. His talent was soon spotted, and after winning several acting prizes he made his film début in *Scruffy* (1938). Sixteen films followed in three years. These included *I See Ice* with George Formby and *Murder in the Family* (both 1938); and *Poison Pen*, *Just William*, in which he played Ginger, and *Convict 99*, with Will Hay (all 1939). In most, though, he had only bit parts.

Evacuated in 1940 to New York with his sister (and accompanied by his mother), McDowall was soon in Hollywood, where he was cast by Twentieth Century Fox in Fritz Lang's *Man Hunt* (1941) before playing the pivotal role of Huw in John Ford's Oscar-winning *How Green was my Valley* (1941). His impact immediately placed him at the forefront of child actors; his innocent face and precise diction were in demand. He played children with responsibility thrust early upon them, as in *Confirm or Deny* (1941) and *The Pied Piper* (1942); other examples were his appearances as younger versions of Tyrone Power in *Son of Fury* (1942), of Gregory Peck in *The Keys of the Kingdom* and of Peter Lawford in MGM's *The White Cliffs of Dover* (both 1943). But it was three animal films for which he would be remembered in this period: *My Friend Flicka* (1943), the sequel *Thunderhead, Son of Flicka* (1945), and, particularly, MGM's *Lassie Come Home* (1943). The last teamed him with Elizabeth Taylor, who remained a lifelong friend. Twentieth Century Fox however, did not renew his contract, and his films for a number of years, including several for the 'poverty row' studio Monogram and Orson Welles's *Macbeth*

(1948) in which he played Malcolm, were mostly nondescript.

McDowall had renewed his education at the Twentieth Century Fox schoolroom for child actors in 1940, and graduated from University high school in Santa Monica in 1947. In 1949 he became an American citizen. In 1952, with producers continuing to treat him as a juvenile, he decided to change direction. 'I didn't know what acting meant. I had no tools … I had to learn my craft' (Parish, 85). He moved to New York, centre of the burgeoning television industry, and embraced the medium with great enthusiasm, appearing in a vast number of television shows over the next forty-five years. He had made his stage début (in *Young Woodley*) in 1946 and played in Welles's stage version of *Macbeth* in 1947. Now he studied acting with Mira Rostova and David Craig and made his Broadway début in Shaw's *Misalliance* (1953). 1955 was perhaps a turning point, with notable successes in Shaw's *The Doctor's Dilemma* off Broadway, in *The Tempest* (as Ariel) and *Julius Caesar* (as Octavius) in the Shakespeare festival at Stratford, Connecticut, and in the Ira Levin comedy *No Time for Sergeants*. In 1957 he played his favourite stage role, the homosexual killer Artie Strauss, in *Compulsion* (based on the Leopold–Loeb case). 1960 was a busy year: he won a 'supporting actor' Tony award for his role in O'Casey's *The Fighting Cock*, and a 'supporting actor' Emmy for his television performance in *Not without Honor*; he won the part of Mordred in the Lerner and Loewe stage musical *Camelot*, alongside Richard Burton; and he returned to the screen in *The Subterraneans* and *Midnight Lace*.

McDowall and Burton both left *Camelot* after a year to film *Cleopatra* (1963) in Rome with Elizabeth Taylor. McDowall received some of the film's few favourable reviews. He appeared in two more epics, *The Longest Day* (1962) and *The Greatest Story Ever Told* (1965). He was a high-school student (although now aged thirty-eight) in *Lord Love a Duck* (1966) and featured in the final film of his close friend Montgomery Clift, *The Defector* (1966). He appeared in *Planet of the Apes* (1968) as a chimpanzee, a part he loved despite being unrecognizable in heavy make-up. (He made three sequels and was in the subsequent television series.) In that year he also directed *Tam Lin*, starring Ava Gardner, but it was poorly received when finally released in 1971. From the 1960s to the 1990s he made almost 120 films, many of them television movies and 'mini-series', and continued as a seemingly ubiquitous guest star in television shows. Although he did not always choose too wisely, among his better later films were several for Disney, *The Poseidon Adventure* and *The Life and Times of Judge Roy Bean* (both 1972), and two excellent horror films, *The Legend of Hell House* (1973) and *Fright Night* (1985). His last stage role was in New York as Scrooge in *A Christmas Carol* (1997).

Having pursued photography since childhood, McDowall developed a second career as a celebrity photographer. His work appeared in many major magazines, and he published five compilation volumes, the first being *Double Exposure* (1966). He also built up a vast collection of movies and movie memorabilia. He was at one stage board member of the Academy of Motion Picture Arts and Sciences and worked actively for the Motion Picture and TV Fund. In 1991 the latter honoured him with its silver medallion for his humanitarian efforts. In December 1998 the former named its photograph archive of several million negatives and stills after him.

McDowall often said that his main interest in life was 'collecting friends'. He was a fine raconteur, especially about Hollywood, but never a malicious gossip. As a result he maintained a huge circle of friends and was held in great affection by the industry. He died of lung cancer at his California home, 3110 Brookdale Road, Studio City, on 3 October 1998. His body was cremated and the ashes scattered at sea. He never married.   ROBERT SHARP

Sources *The Scotsman* (5 Oct 1998) · *Daily Telegraph* (5 Oct 1998) · *The Independent* (5 Oct 1998) · *The Guardian* (5 Oct 1998) · *The Times* (5 Oct 1998) · www.smithway.org, 9 Feb 2001 · www.uk.imdb.com, 9 Feb 2001 · www.ameritech.net, 9 Feb 2001 · J. R. Parish, *Great child stars* (1976)
Likenesses photograph, *c*.1955, Hult. Arch. [*see illus.*] · double portrait, photograph, 1996 (with Elizabeth Taylor), repro. in *The Scotsman* · photograph, repro. in *Daily Telegraph* · photograph, repro. in *The Times*

McDowall, William (1815–1888), newspaper editor and antiquary, born at Maxwelltown, Kirkcudbrightshire, on 21 July 1815, was the son of James McDowall (*d.* 1826), a traveller for a cabinet-making firm, and his wife, Mary, née Todd (*d.* 1849). He was educated in Dumfries and learned bookbinding there; he then enlarged his experience in Glasgow and London. At the Disruption in 1843 he became a Free Churchman, and was appointed to the editorial staff of the *Scottish Herald*, an Edinburgh Free Church paper, and was afterwards for a short time reporter on the *Banner of Ulster*. In 1846 he became editor of the *Dumfries and Galloway Standard*, and, after a short interval about 1853–4 during which he edited a Sunderland paper, he continued editing it until his death, raising it to an influential position. A public-spirited citizen, he was connected with all the leading institutions of his burgh; in his *History of Dumfries* (1867, enlarged in 1873), he wrote a work that remains the point of departure for its subject. He married, first, Anne Dawson, who died on 3 May 1867, and second, on 20 November 1877, Susan Annie Scott Donaldsan, third daughter of David Scott, a deceased solicitor. He died at Dumfries on 28 October 1888, his second wife surviving him.

McDowall displays grace of fancy and expression in *The Man of the Woods, and other Poems* (1844; 2nd edn, 1882). Two chapters of his *History of Dumfries*, on Robert Burns, were also published as *Burns in Dumfriesshire* (1870). In 1876 he published *Memorials of St Michael's*, a compilation of antiquarian and biographical value. *The Mind in the Face* (1882; 3rd edn, 1888) was on physiognomy. McDowall's substantial volume *Chronicles of Lincluden, as an Abbey and as a College* was published in 1886, and his last work was a study of ballad writers, *Among the Old Scottish Minstrels* (1888).

T. W. BAYNE, *rev.* H. C. G. MATTHEW

Sources *Dumfries and Galloway Standard and Advertiser* (31 Oct 1888) · *Dumfries and Galloway Standard and Advertiser* (8 May 1867) ·

Dumfries and Galloway Standard and Advertiser (21 Nov 1877) · M. M. Harper, ed., *The bards of Galloway* (1889) · Ewart Library, Dumfries, MS Gk 22 (718) · *CCI* (1889)

Wealth at death £203 3s. 6d.: confirmation, 28 Jan 1889, *CCI*

McDowell, Benjamin (1739–1824), minister of the Presbyterian General Synod of Ulster, fifth son of Ephraim McDowell, an Irish emigrant, from Connor, co. Antrim, was born at Elizabethtown, New Jersey, on 25 December 1739. He was educated at the College of New Jersey and Glasgow University. Although his parents had belonged to the Reformed Presbyterian church, he joined the established Church of Scotland, and was licensed by the Glasgow presbytery on 3 July 1766. While visiting his relatives at Connor, he received a call to the congregation of Ballykelly, co. Londonderry, and was there ordained by the Route presbytery on 3 September 1766. He succeeded John Nelson, who had been compelled to resign on the ground of heterodoxy. At a time when New Light sentiments were prominent in the General Synod of Ulster, McDowell proved an able defendant of Presbyterian orthodoxy, publishing a series of pamphlets in response to attacks on the Westminster confession of faith—a dress rehearsal for what would become an increasingly divisive issue in Irish Presbyterianism.

In 1778 McDowell accepted a call to Capel Street, Dublin, which had just, after rebuilding, assumed the name St Mary's Abbey, and in the following years the synod made use of both his conviction and talent. From 1786 he took a leading part in negotiations between the Presbyterians and the government on a range of issues, including the 'regium donum'. In these negotiations he acted with William Campbell, a prominent leader of the New Light party, who left a good-humoured account of their theological relations in his manuscript 'Sketches' (1803). McDowell was elected moderator in 1786 and two years later was appointed by the synod, together with Robert Rodgers, minister of Corboy, co. Longford, to visit and inspect the Presbyterian churches in the 'frontier' towns of the west and south-west of Ireland. He was awarded the degree of DD by Edinburgh University on 22 January 1789, and in 1791 he travelled to France, though not because of any sympathy with the revolution.

In Dublin, meanwhile, McDowell exerted considerable influence as a pioneer of the late eighteenth-century religious revival, supporting the interdenominational General Evangelical Society, and influencing the early life of the Revd Benjamin Williams Mathias, to whom he was appointed guardian, and who was later the founder of the Hibernian Bible Society. Under his guidance, St Mary's increased its originally small membership to over 2000, and was widely considered to be the centre of evangelical Presbyterianism in Dublin.

McDowell died on 13 September 1824 in Dublin, leaving a family, and was succeeded by James Carlile, who had been appointed as his assistant in 1813. A marble tablet to McDowell's memory was placed in his meeting-house, and was removed in 1864 to the new building in Rutland Square.   ALEXANDER GORDON, *rev.* MYRTLE HILL

Sources T. Witherow, *Historical and literary memorials of presbyterianism in Ireland, 1731–1800* (1880), 145–60 · J. S. Reid and W. D. Killen, *History of the Presbyterian church in Ireland*, new edn, 3 (1867) · *A history of congregations in the Presbyterian Church in Ireland, 1610–1982*, Presbyterian Church in Ireland (1982) · W. B. Kirkpatrick, *Memorial services in connexion with the removal of the congregation of St Mary's Abbey, Dublin* (1865)

MacDowell [Maydland, Madwell, Maydwell], **John** (*b. c.*1500, *d.* in or after 1566), Dominican friar and evangelical reformer, was born in Galloway, entered the Dominicans at an unknown date, and was created bachelor of theology by 1524, when the general chapter of his order recorded this fact; it is probable that he studied at Cologne like his fellow friar, John Macalpine, whose degree was recorded at the same time. In 1530 MacDowell was incorporated as a sub-prior of Glasgow in Glasgow University. By 1533–4 he was prior of Wigtown, but had probably left the country by May of that year, bound it seems for France. A certain 'Dr Maydland' was alleged to have preached treason against Henry VIII and Anne Boleyn in the London Blackfriars in 1534; this was clearly MacDowell, though he was only a theology bachelor. He went on to the port of Rye, where he stayed with a Scottish priest-physician, Peter Cochrane, and borrowed from the vicar a book by Johann Eck attacking Henry VIII. Under the skilful management of one of Thomas Cromwell's agents, however, he won the patronage of Cromwell and rapidly altered his views. Presented to a chantry of the London Carthusians, on whom he was urged as a preacher once a week by the agent, he was refused, but he did inspect their library.

MacDowell is next heard of as chaplain to the reformed bishop of Salisbury, Nicholas Shaxton, and in 1537 he was commissioned to preach the Lenten sermon. The civic authorities disliked his preaching, and he responded in a sermon at St Edmund's, Salisbury. Cromwell tried to make peace between the parties. On 1 March 1536 MacDowell had been licensed by Cranmer to hold any non-resident benefice, provided he cast aside his Dominican habit. He became a naturalized Englishman in July 1537 (when the vicar of Croydon complained that he damned all singing and organ playing) and in October was made rector of Hawkchurch, Dorset. In 1549 he was in London and preached at St Mary Staining, and also at the burial service for the merchant Christopher Machyn. Arrangements are found in a Sussex will for him to preach in Pett parish church with another reformed preacher, Mr Thomas Rose. MacDowell also preached against King Edward's first prayer book of 1549, which roused the London aldermen against him, so that he soon went briefly into exile. Along with the wives of John Rogers and others, his foreign wife and children were granted English nationality after a petition dated March 1552; in the previous month, as a bachelor of divinity, MacDowell was given licence to preach. However, the accession of Mary Tudor as queen forced him into exile again, and he is mentioned in two lists of exiles from 1557, which record him as Madwell and Maydwell respectively. In 1566 Knox said he was a burgermeister in the 'Steads', presumably Friesland or north Germany. Nothing further is recorded of Mac-Dowell, and it is not known when he died.

JOHN DURKAN

Sources J. Durkan, 'Some local heretics', *Transactions of the Dumfriesshire and Galloway Natural History and Antiquarian Society*, 3rd ser., 36 (1959), 67–77 · J. Durkan, 'Scottish evangelicals in the patronage of Thomas Cromwell', *Records of the Scottish Church History Society*, 21 (1981–3), 127–56 · J. Durkan, 'Heresy in Scotland: the second phase', *Records of the Scottish Church History Society*, 24 (1990–92), 342–3 · J. L. Chester, *John Rogers* (1861), 441 · S. Brigden, *London and the Reformation* (1989) · D. S. Chambers, ed., *Faculty office registers, 1534–1549* (1966), 46 · R. G. Rice and W. H. Godfrey, eds., *Transcripts of Sussex wills*, 2, Sussex RS, 42 (1937), 290–91 · R. E. G. Kirk and E. F. Kirk, eds., *Returns of aliens dwelling in the city and suburbs of London, from the reign of Henry VIII to that of James I*, Huguenot Society of London, 10/1 (1900), 172 · J. Strype, *Ecclesiastical memorials*, 2/2 (1822), 276 · W. Page, ed., *Letters of denization and acts of naturalization for aliens in England, 1509–1603*, Huguenot Society of London, 8 (1893), 160 · *John Knox's History of the Reformation in Scotland*, ed. W. C. Dickinson, 1 (1949), 23 · B. M. Reichert, ed., *Acta capitulorum generalium ordinis praedicatorum*, 4 (Rome, 1898), 206 · C. Innes, ed., *Munimenta alme Universitatis Glasguensis / Records of the University of Glasgow from its foundation till 1727*, 2, Maitland Club, 72 (1854), 156 · G. Burnett and others, eds., *The exchequer rolls of Scotland*, 21 (1901), 336 · E. M. Thompson, *The Carthusian order in England* (1930), 420–24 · *LP Henry VIII*, vols. 9–10, 12–13

MacDowell, Patrick (1799–1870), sculptor, was born in Belfast on 12 August 1799, the son of a tradesman. While he was still an infant his father died and he was sent in 1807 to a school run by an engraver named Gordon, who encouraged him in his drawing. In 1811 he moved with his mother to Hampshire, where he attended a school run by a clergyman. He moved to London in 1813 and was apprenticed to a coach-builder until 1817, when the latter became bankrupt. He lodged at 23 Charles Street, Middlesex Hospital, in the house of the sculptor Peter Francis Chenu, where he began to draw from antique casts and to practise modelling. One of his earliest works was a small figure after Donatello which impressed Chenu, who purchased it. After his mother's death he moved to Seymour Street, Euston Square.

MacDowell resolved on the career of a sculptor. In 1822 he first exhibited at the Royal Academy and continued to exhibit there throughout his life. He submitted a design for a posthumous memorial to Major Cartwright (exh. RA, 1826) but failed to get the commission. In June 1830 he became a student of the Royal Academy Schools on the recommendation of the painter John Constable and stayed two years. He began to establish his reputation by doing portrait busts (which remained his staple output). However, he also modelled poetic subjects, early examples of which were a group based on Thomas Moore's popular poem *The Loves of the Angels* (exh. RA, 1827), bought by George Davidson of Belfast, and *Cephalus and Procris* (1834), bought by E. S. Cooper, MP for Sligo, of Markree Castle, co. Sligo.

MacDowell's first important patron was Sir James Emmerson Tennant, MP for Belfast. Tennant was instrumental in the commission for a self-portrait bust (Belfast City Hall) and a memorial relief, *The Parting Glance*, commemorating William Tennant (d. 1832), for Rosemary Street Presbyterian Church, Belfast. As a fellow Belfast man Tennant did everything he could to assist the sculptor, and through Tennant MacDowell was introduced to his most important patron, T. W. Beaumont, MP for Northumberland, who lived at Hyde Park Terrace, Piccadilly. He commissioned busts of his family, and ideal subjects such as *Love Triumphant* (1831), *Early Sorrow* (1847, Ulster Museum, Belfast), *Girl Reading* (1838, National Gallery of Ireland, Dublin), and *Girl Going to Bathe* (1841). These works established his public profile, leading to his election as an ARA in 1841, when Beaumont paid for him to study in Rome for eight months. In 1846 he became a full member of the Royal Academy and submitted a *Nymph* as his diploma work.

During the 1840s and 1850s MacDowell was at the height of his career. The Belfast connection led to a commission for a marble of Frederick Richard Chichester, earl of Belfast (d. 1853) (Belfast Castle chapel), which is his best piece and one of the finest examples of Victorian sculpture. It depicts the death of the young earl, who is attended by his mother, Harriet Anne, marchioness of Donegal. He also executed sculptures of Admiral Edward Pellew, Lord Exmouth (exh. RA, 1840; Royal Naval Hospital, Greenwich), William Pitt (exh. RA, 1857; St Stephen's Hall, Westminster Palace, London), Viscount Fitzgibbon, who died at Balaklava (bronze, formerly Sarsfield Bridge, Limerick; des.), Sir Michael O'Loughlen and William Lord Plunkett (both formerly in the Four Courts, Dublin; des.), J. M. W. Turner (1851, St Paul's Cathedral, London), and the earl of Eglinton (formerly St Stephen's Green, Dublin; des.).

MacDowell created a substantial body of ideal sculpture, the early works for Beaumont having established him in this genre. He went on to make *Eve* (exh. RA, 1849; Victoria and Albert Museum, London), and *Leah* (Egyptian Hall, Mansion House, London). The largest and best-known of his ideal works was his allegorical group of *Europe* (with emblematic figures of England, France, Italy, and Germany)—one of the four corner groups at the base of the Albert Memorial, Kensington Gardens, London—which was completed after his death. Besides the Royal Academy, he also exhibited at the British Institution, the Society of British Artists, and the Royal Hibernian Academy in Dublin. Owing to failing health he resigned from the Royal Academy in 1870 and died at his home in Wood Lane, Highgate, Middlesex, on 9 December, leaving a son, Redmond, who was also a sculptor. He was buried in Highgate cemetery. MacDowell's work belongs to the neoclassical style of Victorian sculpture, though in some instances he tempered this with a greater depth of feeling and realism which gives his work its appeal and shows him at his best. *The Athenaeum* passed its verdict in his obituary that he was 'a careful sculptor [and] his designs were generally graceful, occasionally charming, but some of them were rather trite'.

JOHN TURPIN

Sources W. G. Strickland, *A dictionary of Irish artists*, 2 (1913), 59–63 · 'The triumph of love: the autobiography of P. MacDowell', *Art Journal*, 12 (1850), 8–9 · *Art Journal*, 33 (1871), 41 · H. Potterton, 'Patrick MacDowell, 1799–1870', *Hibernia*, 35 (1971) · R. Gunnis, *Dictionary of British sculptors, 1660–1851* (1953), 249–50 · H. Potterton, *Irish* *church monuments, 1570–1880* (1975), 58 · *The Athenaeum* (24 Dec 1870), 846–7 · *CGPLA Eng. & Wales* (1871) · S. C. Hutchison, 'The Royal Academy Schools, 1768–1830', *Walpole Society*, 38 (1960–62), 123–91 · J. Turpin, 'MacDowell, Patrick', *The dictionary of art*, ed. J. Turner (1996)

Likenesses etching, pubd 1851 (after C. Grey), NG Ire.; repro. in *Dublin University Magazine*, 38 (1851) · Maull and Polyblank, photograph, carte, NPG · wood-engraving (after photograph), BM; repro. in *ILN* (1870) · woodcut, BM, NPG; repro. in *Art Journal* (1850), 8

Wealth at death under £300: probate, 21 Jan 1871, *CGPLA Eng. & Wales*

Macdowell, William (*b.* 1590, *d.* in or before 1666), diplomatist, was born in October 1590 in Makerstoun, Roxburghshire, the son of Thomas Macdowell, a minor landowner locally, and his wife, Johanna Kerr. He was educated at Musselburgh School and between 1605 and 1609 at St Andrews University. He was philosophy master at St Leonard's College even before taking his degree, and in 1614 he accepted the professorship of philosophy at Groningen University. In 1617 he married his first wife, Bernardina Van Frittema. He was president of the council of war in Groningen and Friesland from 1627 and provost-marshal of the Scottish regiment in Groningen, and he visited London as the province's envoy in 1629, 1633, and 1635 and impressed Charles I sufficiently to be considered for a Scottish privy councillorship until war intervened.

Macdowell's reputation among the Scottish Presbyterian community in the Low Countries brought him to prominence in the course of Charles II's negotiations with the Scots, and on 4 June 1650 he succeeded Sir William Boswell as the king's agent at The Hague, resigning his local offices. In spite of financial losses and overwork, he represented Charles once he returned to Scotland but complained to the secretary of state, Robert Kerr, earl of Ancram, 'I am rowing against wind, streams, and tide' (*Correspondence of Sir Robert Kerr*, 2.340–42). By this time he was styling himself knight but there is no record that he was knighted by Charles I or Charles II. His forensic abilities came into their own when the United Provinces prepared to receive Commonwealth ambassadors Walter Strickland and Oliver St John early in 1651. Macdowell presented a list of royalist objections to the states general, arguing against the precedent of recognizing dispossessors of rightful owners and citing the Old Testament case of Naboth's vineyard; he made representations on behalf of godly ministers and thousands of subjects oppressed by the regicides and reminded the states of the Commonwealth's arrogance and demands for colonial compensation. The ambassadors were harassed by local royalists, and their talks were delayed and unfruitful.

The envoys' departure in July was Macdowell's finest moment, and his published *Answer* to their arguments was smuggled into England as royalist propaganda, eliciting confiscation and an official reply. But he regarded his own sophistry rather than England's harsh terms on commerce and a federal alliance as responsible, and sought to conduct policy independently of Charles's advisers in Paris. Protesting at his unauthorized memorandum

requesting the states general to open Dutch ports to deserting English shipping, Hyde expostulated at his arrogance and foolishness and called him 'the veryest coxcomb I have heard of' (Macray, 2.189). Charles duly ordered Macdowell to act only on Secretary Nicholas's orders and, having distrusted the Presbyterians since events in Scotland in 1650, ignored Macdowell's optimistic encouragement to seek their aid. Sidelined and complaining of Charles's neglect, Macdowell was still important enough for Cromwell to persuade the states general to banish him at Whitsun 1653 as talks resumed. He appears to have returned to Amsterdam by late 1654. Meanwhile his second wife, Elizabeth Alberada Van Botnia, *née* Van Zandt, had died in 1652.

At the Restoration Charles offered to reinstate Macdowell in his post as resident; preferring to seek a Scottish judgeship instead, Macdowell was unsuccessful. He visited London to request payment of £2820 13*s*. 4*d*. for official services between 1650 and 1653 and £691 3*s*. 4*d*. for extraordinary disbursements, and was awarded £300 for money lent to the king. He died, probably in Amsterdam or Groningen, before July 1666, when Charles was petitioned for unpaid debts which had been promised in Macdowell's will. He was thus not the Dr Macdowell appointed by the council in 1665 to collect Dutch intelligence and arrested in 1666: this man appears to have been one Andrew Macdowell. A learned and loyal royal adviser but over-confident and of limited realism, William Macdowell's role had been frustrated by his own shortcomings and by royal antipathy to his co-religionists.

TIMOTHY VENNING

Sources *CSP dom.*, 1637; 1651–60; 1660–61; 1664–7 · W. A. Shaw, ed., *Calendar of treasury books*, 1, PRO (1904) · *Calendar of the Clarendon state papers preserved in the Bodleian Library*, 2: 1649–1654, ed. W. D. Macray (1869) · *Effigies et vitae professorum Academiae Groningae & Omlandiae* (Groningen, 1654) · *Correspondence of Sir Robert Kerr, first earl of Ancram, and his son William, third earl of Lothian*, ed. D. Laing, 2 vols., Roxburghe Club, 100 (1875) · BL, Add. MS 15858 · J. Ferguson, ed., *Papers illustrating the history of the Scots brigade in the service of the United Netherlands, 1572–1782*, 1, Scottish History Society, 32 (1899) · M. Wood, ed., *Extracts from the records of the burgh of Edinburgh, 1642–1655*, [9] (1938)

Likenesses line engraving, BM · portrait, repro. in *Effigies et vitae professorum academiae Groningae*

Wealth at death large debts still owed to him by Charles II for services to royalist cause; other legatee(s) had to apply to king for their own debts from Macdowell to be paid out of money owed by king: *CSP dom.* 1665–6, 532

Macduff (*fl.* 1057–1058). *See under* Dubh (*d.* 966).

Macduff family, earls of Fife (*per. c.*1095–1371), magnates, were the premier mormaers or (as they came to be known) earls in medieval Scotland. Closely associated with the Canmore dynasty, they were important in promoting acceptance of Anglo-Norman feudal practices in Scotland in the twelfth and thirteenth centuries.

The Macduffs and the first earls, *c.*1095–*c.*1136 The earls of Fife before Duncan (I) (*d.* 1154) are poorly documented and remain shadowy figures. Æthelred, the third or fourth son of Malcolm III and Margaret (both *d.* 1093), has been described as the first earl on record. In a later memorandum of his grant of lands in Fife to the Culdees of Loch Leven he is styled 'a man of venerable memory, abbot of Dunkeld and moreover earl of Fife' (Lawrie, no. 14). However, this is the only evidence to name Æthelred as earl of Fife, and there are many problems with accepting it at face value, or, indeed, with regarding Æthelred as having had any connection with the earldom of Fife. If Fife is not here an error for another name (unlikely in this context) the scribe may have attributed the title to him when he was in fact only the temporary recipient of the revenues of Fife, before the accession or restoration of **Constantine** [Constantine Macduff], earl of Fife (*d.* in or after 1128), who is more usually considered to have been the first earl. The date of Constantine's promotion is uncertain. He witnessed a charter of Edgar in 1095, but only by means of the attestation 'Signum filii Magdufe Constantini' (Lawrie, no. 15)—he is not styled earl; but he is earl in the confirmation of Æthelred's gift by Alexander and David, datable to before 1107. He last appears as a witness in a charter of *c.*1128, along with his successor Gille Micheil Macduff, who can plausibly be described as earl-in-waiting.

Even if Æthelred is excluded from their number, it nevertheless remains likely that the first earls were closely connected to the royal house. This is suggested by the fact that two of the first earls, Constantine and Gille Micheil, are called 'Macduff'—a Scoticized form of two Gaelic words, *mac* and *Dubh*, meaning 'son of Dubh'. In Scotland the only person of note to bear the name Dubh was *Dubh, king of Scots from 962 to 966, making it virtually certain that the Macduffs were descended from him. The surname Macduff for his descendants may have come into use as early as 1128. According to the later chroniclers John Fordun (*d.* 1384) and Andrew Wyntoun (*d. c.*1422) the prominence of the Macduffs stemmed from their support for Malcolm III against Macbeth. Wyntoun records *Macduff of Fife [*see under* Dubh] as requesting from Malcolm the privilege for himself and his successors of enthroning the kings of Scots, while Fordun makes Malcolm promise that Macduff will be the first in the kingdom. However, the historicity of these accounts remains highly contentious, and it seems more likely that the Macduffs represent a dynastic segment descended from King Dubh, who abandoned their claims to the kingship within the old kin-based system of succession in return for a privileged position which made them foremost among the Scottish nobles. The hypothesis that the earls of Fife were related to the ruling house is strengthened by the use of shared names such as Duncan, Malcolm, and especially the rare Constantine.

Constantine, called 'filii Magdufe' in King Edgar's charter of 1095, is the first earl to be firmly recorded as such and also the first to bear what became the established name of the lineage. Most of what is known of him derives from the record of a complaint made by the Culdees of Loch Leven against Robert the Burgundian in 1128. Constantine appears in the document as 'earl of Fife, great *judex* in Scotia' ('comes de Fyf, magnus judex in Scotia') and is also referred to as 'a man of the greatest discretion'

('*viri discretissimi*'; Lawrie, no. 80). Constantine and two other *judices*, Mael-Domhnaich, son of Macbethad, and Dubgall, son of Mocche, acted as judges, and judgment was pronounced in favour of the Culdees. It is possible that *justitia*, justice, may have been confused with *judex* in this account, and that Dubgall was *judex* of Fife while Constantine held the new office of justice in Scotia. It has also been suggested that Constantine must have attended a native law school to allow him to participate in the proceedings, and it is possible that he presided over the court of the *judex* in his capacity as justice. Whatever the case may have been, Constantine certainly presents an early example of the transition between old and new in Scottish society. Moreover, the reference in this document to the multitude of men, mostly from Fife, and the provincial army or armies, is a reminder of the ancient responsibility of the mormaer for leading the common host of his province.

Constantine's successor was Gille Micheil, who appears to have held the earldom only from about 1128 to about 1136. His identity remains something of a mystery, as does his relationship to his predecessor, but in a confirmation of King David to Dunfermline Priory of *c.*1128 he appears as 'Gillemichel mac duf'. Gille Micheil was clearly one of the most important men in the kingdom. In the 1128 charter to Dunfermline he was the first of the non-comital witnesses, and in another charter of David I to Dunfermline, *c.*1130, he was the first comital witness, appearing before even the important newcomer, Hugh de Morville (*d.* 1162). He was dead by 1136, when his successor appears on the record.

Duncan (I) and the development of primogeniture, c.1136–1154
Duncan (I) Macduff, third earl of Fife (*d.* 1154), had succeeded Gille Micheil by 1136, but their relationship remains uncertain despite frequent claims that he was the son of his predecessor. With Duncan (I) the seniority of the earls of Fife among the Scottish nobility becomes readily apparent. He was a regular witness in the charters of David I, and, like his predecessors, appears in a prominent position in witness lists. With Earl Duncan the significance of the earls of Fife in promoting the acceptance of new feudal ideals flowing north from England is evident, for about 1136 the earldom of Fife was transformed into a fief held of the king in return for fixed service. Although the exact terms of the grant are not known, there can be little question that Fife was now held in return for knight service. An episode near the end of the life of Earl Duncan (I) is also illustrative of the premier position of these earls. Following the death in 1152 of Earl Henry, King David's son and designated successor, the king made provision to ensure the peaceful succession of Henry's eldest son, Malcolm, in which the earl of Fife played a crucial role. The twelve-year-old Malcolm was entrusted to the care of Earl Duncan, who was given a large army and ordered to take the boy throughout Scotia and proclaim him heir to the kingdom. This demonstrates not only the seniority of the earls of Fife, but also the fact that their allegiance to the Canmore dynasty was unquestioned. It has even been suggested that this duty of escorting the young prince shows

that Duncan was meant to act as an unofficial guardian until Malcolm came of age.

One major controversy surrounding the first earls is their relationship to one another. It has been noted that earls Constantine and Gille Micheil 'Macduff' both appear as witnesses to David I's charter to Dunfermline Priory about 1128, and that the latter is assumed to have been Constantine's son. But Gille Micheil is unlikely to have been styled Macduff in a Latin witness list if he were Constantine's son, and he is probably best regarded as tanist, or designated heir, to Constantine, perhaps a brother, nephew, or cousin. This same old-fashioned system of appointed succession makes it more likely that Duncan (I), Gille Micheil's successor as earl, was a son of Constantine rather than a son of Gille Micheil himself. But following the transformation of Fife into a fief in the time of Earl Duncan (I), primogeniture became the governing principle behind the succession. Thus, even though Gille Micheil did have a son named Aedh (Hugh), who might otherwise have been tanist to Duncan (I), on the latter's death it was his (presumed) son Duncan (II) who succeeded as earl, while Aedh became the ancestor of the lords of Abernethy.

Royal service and territorial expansion, 1154–c.1228 Earl Duncan (I)'s obit was recorded by the chronicle of Holyrood under the year 1154, and he was succeeded by **Duncan (II) Macduff**, fourth earl of Fife (d. 1204), who seems to have been a minor at the time—his first appearance as a witness did not occur until 1159, five years after his succession to the earldom, and he did not take Fife's accustomed position at the head of the comital witnesses to royal charters until as late as 1163. Duncan (II)'s tenure of the earldom was one of the longest on record, and the close connections between the earls of Fife and the royal house are readily apparent throughout his lifetime. Like his immediate predecessor, Duncan (II) was a regular witness to royal acts, and was in close attendance on the king. His seniority among the native earls is demonstrated by the fact that he had the privilege of speaking first in King William's council of 1173 when the decision was taken (against his advice) to go to war with Henry II of England; Duncan led a contingent of troops into Northumbria in the ensuing conflict. Following King William's capture at Alnwick in the summer of 1174 and his submission to Henry at York in 1175, the earl of Fife was one of several hostages given to secure the settlement. Between c.1172 and 1199 he was justice in Scotia, responsible under the crown for the administration of justice north of Forth and hearing pleas civil and criminal. He may also have sat in the exchequer, probably established in Scotland in the 1180s or 1190s.

In the thirteenth century the earldom of Fife passed regularly from father to son. Duncan (II)'s successor was his son Malcolm (I) who had been a frequent witness to royal charters from c.1177. One of the prominent themes in the history of the earldom from the middle of the twelfth century is highlighted in the time of Malcolm (I), namely, the extension of the bounds of the earldom through royal grants and marriage alliances. Not only was Malcolm confirmed in lands in the west of Lothian that had been granted to his father and grandfather in return for knight service, but he also received further extensive grants from King William, including the area around Culross. The bounds of the earldom were extended further when Malcolm married Matilda, the daughter of Earl Gilbert of Strathearn, probably some time between 1194 and 1198. With this marriage came extensive lands held of the earl of Strathearn, but, more importantly, the marriage represents an alliance between a family that had continually demonstrated its allegiance to the house of Canmore and one whose loyalty had recently wavered, for Gilbert's father, Ferteth, had been involved in an attempt to capture King Malcolm at Perth in 1160. It was through such marriages that the social and political structures of feudalism were further spread throughout the Scottish kingdom, with the earls of Fife, as the senior members of the Scottish élite, once more prominent in their promotion.

The thirteenth-century earls, c.1228–1289 Malcolm (I) died about 1228, and was buried in the Cistercian monastery at Culross which he had founded in 1217. He left no children, and on his death the earldom passed to his nephew, Malcolm (II), the son of Duncan, a younger son of Earl Duncan (II). As might be expected, the name of Malcolm (II) figures prominently in the list of those nobles who guaranteed the treaty of York between Alexander II and Henry III in 1237, while in 1260 he was one of the Scottish nobles to whom the English king pledged the safe return of the queen of Scotland and her child. On the other hand, neither Malcolm nor his immediate successors, Colban and Duncan, made many appearances as witnesses to royal charters, and Malcolm himself seems to have played a curiously negligible role in the events surrounding the turbulent minority of the young Alexander III in the mid-1250s. He had been present at the inauguration of the young king (no doubt in his capacity as inaugural official), and was one of those named to the new regency council in 1255, but when this council was ousted in a counter-coup in 1257–8, Malcolm simply dropped out of sight, neither punished nor favoured by the king, until his reappearance in 1260. Perhaps this should be attributed to the Comyn ascendancy at this period, but, whatever the case, little more is known of his activities before his death in 1266.

The next two earls of Fife succeeded as minors and enjoyed only brief tenure of the office. Malcolm (II) was succeeded by his teenaged son, Colban, who died c.1270. Young though he was, Colban must have married, for on his death he left behind an eight-year-old son, **Duncan (III) Macduff**, eighth earl of Fife (c.1262–1289). In the latter's minority the wardship of the earldom was held by Alexander, the son of Alexander III, and Duncan received authority over the earldom only when the king's son died in 1284. Two years later, in an assembly at Scone in April 1286, Earl Duncan was among the six guardians chosen to carry on the government of Scotland following the death of Alexander III on 19 March. In the light of Duncan's youth and inexperience, the assembly was probably paying homage to the senior position of his earldom, but the earl may also have been a supporter of Robert (V) de Brus

(d. 1295) in his claim to the throne. He is known to have been in England in 1286–7, and also to have married Joan, the daughter of Gilbert de Clare, earl of Gloucester (d. 1295). Earl Duncan was inexplicably murdered at Pitpollok near Brechin in early September 1289 by Sir Patrick Abernethy (a descendant of Aedh mac Duff) and Sir Walter Percy, and was buried at Coupar Angus Abbey. One chronicler attributes the murder to his cruelty and greed, but a more reasonable explanation is that his death was a result of the growing unrest in Scotland as tensions between the Brus and Balliol factions began to boil over into open conflict.

The wars of independence, 1290–1315 Duncan (IV) Macduff, ninth earl of Fife (1289/90–1353), was a posthumous child, born in late 1289 or early 1290 after the death of his father, and his minority was spent in England. This made it impossible for him to undertake the traditional role of the earls of Fife at the inauguration of John de Balliol as king of Scots on St Andrew's day 1292, which was therefore delegated by Edward I to Sir John de St John (d. 1302). In 1306–7 Edward I and Edward II arranged his marriage to the nine-year-old Mary de Monthermer, daughter of the earl of Gloucester, for which a papal dispensation was granted in 1307.

During the years of Duncan (IV)'s wardship in England, two other members of the house of Fife assumed prominence. The first was Macduff, a younger son of Earl Malcolm (II), who claimed to have been dispossessed of certain lands given to him by his father, and to have been denied justice by King John. In spite of the famous appeals which he made to Edward I on this issue in 1293, Macduff remained a patriot, for in 1297 he and his two sons joined William Wallace, and he fought and died at the head of the men of Fife at the battle of Falkirk in 1298. No less prominent in this period was Isabella *Buchan (née Macduff), countess of Buchan, the sister of Duncan (III), who in the absence of the earl of Fife placed Robert Bruce on some substitute for the stone of enthronement at Scone on 25 March 1306, and was subsequently incarcerated by the English in a cage at Berwick Castle, from which she was not released until 1310.

Following the judgment of forfeiture at the Cambuskenneth parliament of 6 November 1314, Earl Duncan freed himself from English tutelage, and, leaving behind his wife (who did not join him in Scotland until January 1320), came into King Robert's peace. The earliest evidence that he was restored to his lands comes from an inquest of October 1316, but his seal was attached to a document of April 1315, which may indicate that he had been received into the king's peace by that date. Part of the reason for Duncan's restoration may have lain with King Robert's need to make a declaration on the succession, and the central part played by the earl of Fife in the inauguration of the king would make his adherence to the cause of the crown more important than that of any other noble. The details of the restoration were worked out by 23 August 1315, when an indenture was made between the king and Earl Duncan at Crichton. By its terms the earl resigned his earldom to the king and received it back, with

an entail which eventually brought it to Robert Stewart, duke of Albany (d. 1420). Thus, at the age of about twenty-five, the earl of Fife was restored to his lands, due in large measure to the seniority of the earldom and the role of the house of Fife in the inauguration of the Scottish monarchs.

The last years of the independent earldom, 1315–1371 Earl Duncan (IV) maintained his allegiance to Robert I during that king's lifetime. He was the first of the Scottish nobles named in the letter of the Scottish barons to Pope John XXII (the so-called 'declaration of Arbroath') in 1320, and he was present in Edinburgh in 1328 for the conclusion of peace between the two realms. Duncan fought with the Scots at Dupplin in August 1332 against 'the disinherited' of Edward Balliol, and Fordun records that 360 men-at-arms were killed fighting under his banner. But he was subsequently captured, and, in return for his liberty, joined Balliol. Thus, when Balliol was inaugurated as king in September, it was the earl of Fife, along with William Sinclair, bishop of Dunkeld (d. 1337—formerly one of King Robert's most ardent supporters), who performed the ceremony. With the return of King David II from France in 1341, Duncan again changed sides, and was captured with that monarch and many other Scottish magnates at the battle of Nevilles Cross on 17 October 1346. He was subsequently tried for treason by Edward III and sentenced to a traitor's death, but he obtained mercy and was allowed to return to Scotland to raise money for his ransom, set at 1000 marks, in 1350. He died in 1353, and his daughter Isabella succeeded as countess of Fife. There were no children of any of her four marriages, and in 1371, some eighteen years before her death, she resigned the earldom to Robert Stewart; it passed to the crown after the forfeiture of the Albany Stewarts in 1425.

The earls of Fife were the wealthiest of the Scottish magnates. In 1294–5 the lands of the earldom, then in wardship, were assessed at £432 per year, with the majority of this income derived from rents. Although this placed them on a par only with a modest English baron, their income was fully three times that of Neill, earl of Carrick, who died in 1256. Befitting their status as the premier nobles in the kingdom, the earls of Fife were generous benefactors of the church. Earl Malcolm (I) founded a Cistercian monastery at Culross, while Earl Duncan (I) had endowed a Cistercian nunnery at North Berwick between about 1136 and 1150. Duncan (I) was probably also responsible for the foundation of two hospitals, at Ardross and North Berwick, on the north and south ends of the ferry across the Forth. The patronage of reformed religious orders by these native lords represents yet another way in which they were instrumental in striking a balance between old and new in Scottish society.

ANDREW MCDONALD

Sources J. Bannerman, 'Macduff of Fife', *Medieval Scotland: crown, lordship and community*, ed. A. Grant and K. J. Stringer (1993) · A. A. M. Duncan, *Scotland: the making of the kingdom* (1975), vol. 1 of *The Edinburgh history of Scotland*, ed. G. Donaldson (1965–75) · R. Nicholson, *Scotland: the later middle ages* (1974), vol. 2 of *The Edinburgh history of Scotland*, ed. G. Donaldson (1965–75) · *Scots peerage,* vol. 4 · G. W. S. Barrow, 'The earls of Fife in the 12th century', *Proceedings of the Society of Antiquaries of Scotland*, 87 (1952–3), 51–62 · G. W. S. Barrow, *Robert Bruce and the community of the realm of Scotland*, 3rd edn (1988) · J. Bannerman, 'The king's poet and the inauguration of Alexander III', *SHR*, 68 (1989), 120–49 · G. W. S. Barrow, *The kingdom of the Scots* (1973) · G. W. S. Barrow, *The Anglo-Norman era in Scottish history* (1980) · A. C. Lawrie, ed., *Early Scottish charters prior to AD 1153* (1905) · A. O. Anderson, ed. and trans., *Early sources of Scottish history, AD 500 to 1286*, 2 (1922) · A. O. Anderson, ed., *Scottish annals from English chroniclers, AD 500 to 1286* (1908) · *Johannis de Fordun Chronica gentis Scotorum*, ed. W. F. Skene (1871) · A. Wyntoun, *Orygynale cronykle of Scotland*, ed. D. Laing (1872) · W. Bower, *Scotichronicon*, ed. D. E. R. Watt and others, new edn, 9 vols. (1987–98), vols. 5 and 6 · *Jordan Fantosme's chronicle*, ed. and trans. R. C. Johnston (1981) · *CDS* · A. A. M. Duncan, ed., *The acts of Robert I, king of Scots 1306–29* (1988) · G. W. S. Barrow, ed., *The acts of Malcolm IV, king of Scots 1153–65* (1960) · G. W. S. Barrow, ed., *The acts of William I, king of Scots 1165–1214* (1971) · J. Stevenson, ed., *Documents illustrative of the history of Scotland*, 2 vols. (1870)

Likenesses seal, 1249? (inauguration scene on Scone Abbey showing earl of Fife) · seals (seals of Malcolm I, Duncan III show them as knights on horse)

Macduff, Duncan (I), third earl of Fife (*d.* 1154). *See under* Macduff family, earls of Fife (*per. c.*1095–1371).

Macduff, Duncan (II), fourth earl of Fife (*d.* 1204). *See under* Macduff family, earls of Fife (*per. c.*1095–1371).

Macduff, Duncan (III), eighth earl of Fife (*c.*1262–1289). *See under* Macduff family, earls of Fife (*per. c.*1095–1371).

Macduff, Duncan (IV), ninth earl of Fife (1289/90–1353). *See under* Macduff family, earls of Fife (*per. c.*1095–1371).

Mac Duinnshléibhe [MacDonlevy], **Cormac** (*fl. c.*1459), physician and translator of medical texts, was descended from a royal family of twelfth-century Ulster (modern counties Down and Antrim), who were overthrown by the Anglo-Norman invaders. A branch of the family migrated to Tír Conaill (modern co. Donegal) where they became hereditary physicians to the Ó Domhnaill. Mac Duinnshléibhe calls himself *basiller a fisigeacht* ('bachelor of medicine'; BL, Arundel MS 333, fol. 113v25), a qualification recorded in a number of the scribal colophons that name him as translator, one of which (NL Ire., MS G 12, p. 30b13–19) also credits him with a degree in arts. The identity of the university from which he graduated is not specified.

Nine translations from Latin into Irish are attributed to Mac Duinnshléibhe, all of them undated. British Library, Arundel MS 333, fols. 112–13, is a holograph copy of his translation of a section of the *Diete particulares* of Isaac Judaeus (*d.* 959), written for Deinis Ó Eachthigheirn, member of a Munster family, and belongs, apparently, to the second half of the fifteenth century. His translation of Gualterus Agilon's (*fl. c.*1250) *De dosibus medicinarum* (published as S. Sheahan, *An Irish Version of Gaulterus 'De dosibus'*, 1938), made for Diarmaid (mac Domhnaill) Ó Leighin, member of an important medical family in Munster, was completed by 29 March 1459, the date of the anonymous scribe's colophon to the copy of the work found in British Library, Harley MS 546, fols. 1r–11r.

Three of Mac Duinnshléibhe's works comprise translations of treatises by the distinguished physician and professor of medicine in the University of Montpellier, Bernard de Gordon (*c.*1258–*c.*1318). His rendering of Gordon's *De pronosticis* (1295) (Dublin, Royal Irish Academy, MS 439 (3 C 19), fols. 241–88) had been completed by *c.*1468, the date of writing of the digest of that work found in National Library of Ireland, MS G 11, pp. 425–38. His major work, a translation of Gordon's monumental *Lilium medicine* (1303–5; Dublin, Royal Irish Academy, MS 443 (24 P 14), pp. 1–327), which achieved great popularity among the medical fraternity of the Gaelic-speaking world, was completed by 1482, the date of writing of the copy of the work contained in British Library, Egerton MS 89, fols. 13ra1–192vb13. The earliest extant copy of his rendering of Gordon's short treatise, *De decem ingeniis curandorum morborum* (1299) (National Library of Ireland, MS G 12, pp. 23a1–30b19), is evidently of early sixteenth-century date.

Four further works comprise: a translation of the first tractate of the French surgeon Gui de Chauliac's *Chirurgia* (1363; NL Ire., MS G 453, fols. 110–27; TCD, MS 1436, pp. 17a–35a), a brief extract from which occurs in British Library, Arundel MS 333, fol. 37va17–21 in a scribal hand dated 18 March 1514 (fol. 35v20–29); a rendering of Bertrandus's *Lucidarius, vel, Almagest*, a unique copy of which is found in Oxford, Corpus Christi College, MS 129, fols. 56v14–57v2 (cf. Bodl. Oxf., MS Digby 79, fols. 176r1–177r16), written in 1527; a translation of a section of the *Rosa Anglica* (*c.*1314) of John Gaddesden, the earliest extant copy of which (NL Ire., MS G 12, pp. 14–22) is evidently of early sixteenth-century date; and, finally, a translation of an opusculum of St Thomas Aquinas, *De operationibus occultis naturae*, a unique copy of which is found in the sixteenth-century manuscript, National Library of Scotland, MS Adv. 72.1.12, fol.10ra1–10vb36.   AOIBHEANN NIC DHONNCHADHA

Sources S. Sheahan, *An Irish version of Gaulterus 'De dosibus'* (1938) · H. C. Gillies, *Regimen sanitatis: the rule of health* (1911) · F. Shaw, 'Medieval medico-philosophical treatises in the Irish language', *Féilsgríbhinn Eóin MhicNéill*, ed. J. Ryan (1940), 149, § 9 · L. Thorndike and P. Kibre, *A catalogue of incipits of mediaeval scientific writings in Latin*, rev. edn (1963)
Archives BL, Arundel MS 333, fols. 112–13 · BL, Egerton MS 89, fols. 13ra1–192vb13 · BL, Harley MS 546, fols. 1r–11r · Bodl. Oxf., MS Digby 79, fols. 176r1–177r16 · CCC Oxf., MS 129, fols. 56v14–57v2 · NL Ire., MSS G 11, pp. 425–38; G 12, pp. 14–22, 23a17–30b19; G 453, fols. 110–27 · NL Scot., MS Adv. 72.1.12, fol. 10ra1–10vb36 · Royal Irish Acad., MSS 439 (3 C 19), fols. 241–88; 443 (24 P 14), pp. 1–327 · TCD, MS 1436, pp. 17a–35a

Mace, Daniel (*bap.* 1692?, *d.* 1756), Presbyterian minister and biblical scholar, was possibly the son of Daniel Mace of Compton Abdale, Gloucestershire, baptized on 25 July 1692, but little is known with certainty about his early years. His first ministerial appointment may have been at Beckington, Somerset. However, it is well documented that in 1727 Mace succeeded Joseph Standen as minister at the Presbyterian meeting-house in Toomer's Court, Newbury, Berkshire, and remained in that office until 1753. He appears to have been a popular preacher who was held in high regard by the members of his congregation. William Whiston, who heard Mace preach twice at Whitsun 1748, described him as a 'worthy' minister (Whiston, 429). Judging from the long list of subscribers' names, who included David Hartley and the Hebraist John Taylor, affixed to his volume of *Sermons* he was well known and respected by the nonconformist community in the west of England as well as by some of the clergy of the established church. In his religious sentiments Mace was opposed to orthodox Calvinism but it is not clear what precisely were his views on the doctrine of the Trinity. There are indications of antitrinitarianism in the text of his *New Testament in Greek and English* while the author of the brief account of his life in the *Christian Reformer* believed 'his opinions most nearly approached Arianism' (*Christian Reformer*, 1832, 315).

Although Mace cannot be regarded as a prolific writer his two published works aroused considerable attention, especially the anonymously published *The New Testament in Greek and English* (2 vols., 1729) that was attributed initially to William Mace, lecturer in civil law at Gresham College. His edition is remarkable for the colloquial tone of the English translation, the eccentric typography, and the pugnacious tone of the notes justifying his departure from the traditional text—the *textus receptus*. According to Metzger, 'In a high proportion of these alterations Mace anticipated the opinions of much later scholars', but his innovatory edition 'was either vehemently attacked or quietly ignored' (Metzger, 110–11). His other published work was a collection of *Sermons* (1751) written on diverse religious and ethical themes, including 'Submission to the will of God', 'Of communion with God and Christ', and 'The grace of God manifested in the gospel'.

On 7 May 1728 at Newbury, Mace married Hannah Carter, daughter of Richard Carter of Newbury and niece of Elizabeth Snow. They had eight children between 1729 and 1744 but only three survived childhood: Benjamin (*b.* 1734) who married Hannah Sealey on 9 October 1769; Mary (*b.* 1739) who died unmarried in 1763; and Sarah (*b.* 1741) who married Thomas Mallum on 7 August 1767. By 1750 Mace's health was clearly in decline. In 1753 he was obliged to resign his ministerial post and on 12 October of that year he drew up his last will and testament, which appointed his wife as his sole beneficiary. He died at Newbury on 10 September 1756 and was buried in the meetinghouse in Toomer's Court, close to the pulpit where he had preached for twenty-six years. His wife died shortly afterwards on 18 February 1757.

ALEXANDER GORDON, rev. M. J. MERCER

Sources DWL, Mace and Mallum family MSS, 38.91 and 38.92 · *Christian Reformer, or, New Evangelical Miscellany*, 18 (1832), 314–16 · C. Surman, index, DWL · G. E. Evans, *Vestiges of protestant dissent* (1897), 181 · W. Whiston, *Memoirs of the life and writings of Mr William Whiston: containing memoirs of several of his friends also* (1749) · B. M. Metzger, *The text of the New Testament: its transmission, corruption, and restoration*, 3rd edn (1992) · E. Reuss, *Bibliotheca Novi Testamenti Graeci* (1872), 175ff. · H. McLachlan, 'An almost forgotten pioneer in New Testament criticism', *Hibbert Journal*, 37 (1938–9), 617–25 · IGI

Archives DWL, family MSS

Mace, James [Jem] **(1831–1910)**, pugilist, was born on 8 April 1831 at Beeston-next-Mileham, Norfolk, the son of William Mace (*d.* 1860), blacksmith, and his wife, Ann (*née* Rudd). As a boy he showed an aptitude for fisticuffs and

James [Jem] **Mace (1831–1910)**, by Reginald Haines, *c.*1904

violin playing and, although sent to a cabinet-maker to learn the trade, soon embarked on a vagabond life during which he put these talents to good use. While exhibiting his milling and musical abilities at fairs and race-meetings, he attracted the attention of celebrated middleweight Nat Langham, whose boxing booth he was invited to join.

Mace had, according to his autobiography, many local encounters before his 'official connection with the ring' began on 2 October 1855, when he defeated a Norwich man named Slack at Mildenhall, Suffolk, in nineteen minutes. His introduction to the London ring came with an eighteen-round victory over Bill Thorpe on 17 February 1857. However, respect for him plummeted following two occasions when he forfeited to Mike Madden. On 20 October 1857 Mace refused to fight under the referee appointed, and in May of the next year he fled at the sight of his would-be antagonist (*Bell's Life*, 16 May 1858). Further humiliation ensued in the September when he was knocked out of time, under dubious circumstances, by Bob Brettle within three minutes.

Described as 'one of the most chicken-hearted men that ever pulled a shirt off' (*Bell's Life*, 30 Jan 1859), Mace started to repair his reputation with an eleven-round success over Ned (Posh) Price. Bob Travers was next defeated on 22 February 1860, after police had intervened the previous day. His redemption was completed with a win over Brettle, on 19 and 20 September, which resulted in Mace becoming middleweight champion. An eight-round victory on 18

June 1861 over Sam Hurst, when at a huge physical disadvantage, then gained him the championship of England. On 28 January 1862 he quelled the challenge of Tom King in sixty-eight minutes, only to lose the championship to him by an unlucky blow in the following November.

With King's brief retirement Mace immediately reclaimed the title, although the committee of the Pugilistic Benevolent Association insisted the champion's belt had to be fought for. His subsequent nineteen-round conquest of Joe Goss did not meet the criterion since the combatants were confined to weight. A proposed match with Joe Coburn, in Ireland in October 1864, ended in a farce and, after inevitable recriminations, the stakes were drawn. In September 1865 a forthcoming fight for the championship between Mace and the by then recognized holder Joe Wormald ended in the latter forfeiting. A further contest with Goss for the championship occurred on 24 May 1866 and, after seventy-four minutes of harmless posturing, the men consented to a draw. The disgust felt at this pitiful display prompted *Bell's Life* to state that Mace's decisive win over Goss less than three months later could not be for the title. A championship match with Ned Baldwin (O'Baldwin) on 15 October 1867 came to nothing as Mace was arrested on the eve of battle and bound over to keep the peace.

Mace had long combined boxing with other diverse enterprises. Having been the landlord of The Swan, Swan Lane, Norwich, he took over the running of the Old King John, Holywell Lane, Shoreditch, on 13 December 1860. He also toured with various circuses: Howes and Cushing's and Pablo Fanque's during 1861, Ginnett's in 1862, and his own in 1862 and 1863. In his capacity as boxing instructor at the famous Myrtle Street gymnasium in Liverpool, he was present at the formal opening of this establishment on 6 November 1865. The next year he became proprietor of the Strawberry Hotel and Grounds, West Derby Road, Liverpool, which he advertised would provide such recreational facilities as a 'bowling-green, race-grounds, croquet-grounds, quoit, skittle court, &c.' (*Sporting Life*, 4 April 1866).

In 1869, finding the prize ring virtually dead in Britain, Mace went to America. On 10 May 1870 he beat Tom Allen in ten rounds, for the American championship, at Oakland Plantation, near New Orleans. He then met Coburn, for the championship of the world, on 11 May of the following year near Port Dover, Canada, when for over one hour they participated in 'a "mill" without a blow struck' (*Weekly Leader*, Toronto, 19 May 1871). Coburn failed to appear for a renewed match in Kansas City and they finally fought a 3 hr 38 min. draw on 30 November, 40 miles from New Orleans, in what was to be Mace's last bare-knuckle fight. After arrests and a wrangle over a referee had prevented a meeting with Baldwin in August 1872, Mace left for Britain on 19 September. He does not seem to have fought again competitively until, after having returned to America, he twice beat Bill Davis, on 16 December 1876 and 26 January 1877.

On 3 March 1877 Mace arrived in Australia. There he toured successfully, exhibiting with the renowned Harry Sallars, Tom Curran, Larry Foley, and John Christie, and opened a hotel in Melbourne. He also spent some time in New Zealand, where he discovered protégé Herbert Slade, who was with him when he again returned to America on Christmas day 1882. Deemed too old to fight American champion John L. Sullivan in 1883, Mace nevertheless met Sullivan's great rival Charlie Mitchell at Glasgow seven years later and was defeated in a £1000 four-round match.

Although at one time a wealthy man, Mace, described as an 'instructor of boxing', was declared bankrupt at Brighton in 1894 (*The Times*, 18 April 1894). Back in America in 1896 he sparred with Mike Donovan in their joint benefit on 14 December. This led to a drawn contest between the two for a so-called 'veteran championship of the world' in Birmingham on 3 September 1897. At the turn of the century he was landlord of the Black Lion, Coleshill Street, Birmingham. His globe-trotting days not being over, at the end of 1903 he visited South Africa, where he impressed in sparring demonstrations with Jack Valentine. During his last years he was closely associated with showman William Le Neve and his wife, Norah Sullivan, with whom he fulfilled many engagements.

On 21 July 1851 Mace married schoolmaster's daughter Mary Ann Barton, with whom he had several children. In 1864 he instigated divorce proceedings on the grounds of her adultery. The petition was dismissed, however, owing to the fact that he himself had a mistress, Selina Hart, who had borne him a child. On 18 February 1864 he entered into a bigamous marriage with Hannah Boorn, with whom he also had offspring. Mace appears to have married again later in life and fathered yet more children, his partner, Alice Caroline Stokes, dying in 1908. Mace died of senile decay at 6 Princess Street, Jarrow, on 30 November 1910 and was buried in Anfield cemetery, Liverpool, on 6 December; the ceremony was conducted by his son Alfred. No headstone was erected at the time but, largely due to the efforts of the Merseyside Former Boxers' Association, this was rectified in 2002. A memorial cross to Mace, which stands next to his father's grave in the churchyard at Beeston-next-Mileham, was unveiled in 1976. He is further commemorated in Norfolk by a plaque sited in Swan Lane, Norwich.

Mace was, at his best, a most gifted fighter, with a deadly left, swift on his feet and equally quick with his head. He preached the gospel of straight hitting and always practised what he preached. At his death his earlier indiscretions had long been forgotten. Often considered the father of the modern scientific school of pugilism, it has been said that he taught the Australians how to box and they passed the art on to the Americans. Nevertheless he still maintained the old bare-knuckle sport to be superior.

TONY GEE

Sources fight reports, etc., *Bell's Life in London*, *Sporting Life*, *The Times*, *New York Times*, *Weekly Leader* [Toronto], *Chicago Tribune*, *San Francisco Chronicle*, *Evening News* [Sydney], *South Australian Register*, *Daily Telegraph* [Melbourne], *The Sportsman*, *Cape Times*, *Evening Citizen* [Glasgow], *Otago Witness*, *New York Tribune*, *Daily Picayune* [New Orleans], *Montreal Herald and Daily Commercial Gazette*, *Pittsburgh Gazette* • *Sporting Life* (1 Dec 1910) • *Sporting Chronicle* [Manchester] (1

Dec 1910) • *The Times* (1 Dec 1910) • *Manchester Guardian* (1 Dec 1910) • *Sydney Herald* (2 Dec 1910) • *The Sun* [Sydney] (1 Dec 1910) • *Northern Weekly Leader* (3 Dec 1910) • *Eastern Daily Press* (1 Dec 1910) • *San Francisco Chronicle* (1 Dec 1910) • *The Leader* [Melbourne] (3 Dec 1910) • *The Australasian* (3 Dec 1910) • *The Argus* [Melbourne] (2 Dec 1910) • *The Age* [Melbourne] (2 Dec 1910) • *The Bulletin* [Sydney, NSW] (8 Dec 1910) • *Newcastle Daily Chronicle* (1 Dec 1910) • J. Mace, *Fifty years a fighter: the life story of Jem Mace* (1908) • H. D. Miles, *Pugilistica*, 3 (1880), 444–88 • *The life and fights of Jem Mace, England's veteran hero*, Health and Strength (1909) • 'The last survivor of the prize ring', *Manchester Guardian* (2 April 1910) • bankruptcy adjudication, *The Times* (18 April 1894) • petition for divorce report, *The Times* (2 July 1864) • petition for divorce report, *Morning Advertiser* (1 July 1864) • petition for divorce report, *Morning Post* (1 July 1864) • W. E. Harding, 'Jem Mace', *The champions of the American prize ring* (New York, 1881); repr. (1993), 30–32 • A. Alexander, *A wayfarer's log* (1919), 6–7, 10, 179–80 • F. Henning, *Fights for the championship: the men and their times*, 2 (1899), 440–50, 453–61, 474–501 • L. Fitz-Barnard, *Fighting sports* (1921); repr. (1983), 261–4 • M. T. Isenberg, *John L. Sullivan and his times* (1988), 135–8 • d. cert. • parish register, Beeston-next-Mileham, 1813–48, Norfolk RO, PD 377/6 [baptisms] • private information (2004) [Chris Shaw, descendant of Mace's uncle] • m. cert. [Mary Ann Barton] • m. cert. [Hannah Boorn]

Likenesses R. Haines, photograph, *c.*1904, NPG [*see illus.*] • black and white tint, Ploughshare Inn, Beeston, Norfolk • black and white tint, repro. in *Licensed Victuallers' Gazette and Hotel Courier* (14 April 1899) • engraving, repro. in Miles, *Pugilistica*

Mace, Thomas (1612/13–1706?), musician and writer on music, was born in either York or Cambridge; in the title-page of his *Riddles, Mervels and Rarities, or, A New Way of Health from an Old Man's Experience* (1698) he describes himself as 'being now in the Eighty Six Year of his Age'. Although precise details of his parentage are unknown, there were branches of the Mace family in York and Cambridge. Thomas Mace may have been a chorister in one or other city. He certainly was an accomplished singer, being appointed clerk (that is, a singing man) at Trinity College, Cambridge, on 10 August 1635, and continuing to reside there for much of the rest of his life, dividing his time between his duties in Trinity College chapel and those as a teacher and performer. During part of the civil war he evidently fled Cambridge for York (possibly on account of his known royalist sympathies), and was in York in 1644 when the city was besieged by the parliamentary party. Following his return to Cambridge, he seems only infrequently to have left it, even enduring the plague years of 1665–6, whereas others departed for safer territory. He may have been the Thomas Mace who on 25 April 1656 married Mary Blackley at St Benedict's Church, Cambridge. Mace's youngest son John learned to play the lute almost solely by reading the manuscript of his father's *Musick's Monument*.

Mace visited London in 1676 to arrange for the publication of the book for which he is most famous, *Musick's monument, or, A remembrancer of the best practical musick, both divine, and civil, that has ever been known, to have been in the world* (1676). This is a volume of remarkable interest divided into three parts dealing, respectively, with psalm singing in parish churches ('also shewing, How *Cathedral Musick*, may be much *Improved* and *Refined*'); playing the lute (an instrument on which Mace was evidently highly skilled); and 'The *Generous Viol*, In its *Rightest Use* … and *Musick in General*'. *Musick's Monument* was written between

Thomas Mace (1612/13–1706?), by William Faithorne the elder, pubd 1676 (after Henry Cooke)

1671 and 1676 and shows Mace to have been of a conservative frame of mind in musical matters, defensive of traditions and chiefly of English music as it stood in the early seventeenth century (preferring, for instance, viols to violins—'Squaling-Scoulding Fiddles'), and deeply suspicious of newly imported French idioms that accompanied the restoration of Charles II. His conservatism is apparent too in the dozen or so fantasias, lessons, and suites for lute and theorbo appended to *Musick's Monument*. Paradoxically, he was one of the few writers on music in seventeenth-century England to grasp the importance of the affective element in music, advising his students to consider carefully, in learning to play a piece on the lute, not only the technicalities of its composition, but also its 'humour', that is, its emotional content. Towards the end of the book, he turns attention towards suitable acoustics for musical performances, implying an awareness of the growing importance of public concerts.

In 1675 Mace published 'for a Public Good' a non-musical work, *Profit, conveniency and pleasure to the whole nation. Being a short rational discourse, lately presented to his majesty concerning the highways of England: their badness, the causes thereof, the reasons of the causes.* In this he announced the imminent publication of *Musick's Monument*, which was subsequently published on subscription by Thomas Ratcliffe and Nathaniel Thompson at 12*s.* a copy.

Mace's only other known foray outside Cambridge was a

trip in 1690 (at the age of seventy-seven) to sell some of his musical books and instruments, which advancing deafness had rendered of little use to him in his declining years. In an attempt to combat his affliction he had invented a 'Dyphone: or Double Lute, The Lute of Fifty Strings', which is described in *Musick's Monument*. The records of Trinity College, Cambridge, show that on 17 April 1706 a singing man's place in the chapel had been 'voided' by 'Mr Mace', possibly referring to Thomas's death; there are no further references to him after this date.   JOHN IRVING

Sources H. Watson, 'Thomas Mace: the man, the book, and the instruments', *Proceedings of the Musical Association*, 35 (1908–9), 87–107 • R. M. Thackery, 'Thomas Mace', *MT*, 92 (1951), 306–7 • E. D. Mackerness, 'Thomas Mace: additions to a biography', *Monthly Musical Record*, 83 (1953), 43–9 • E. D. Mackerness, 'Thomas Mace and the fact of reasonableness', *Monthly Musical Record*, 85 (1955), 211–17, 235–40 • T. Mace, *Musick's monument, or, A remembrancer of the best practical musick* (1676); facs. edn with commentary by J. Jacquot and R. Souris (Paris, 1958) • T. Mace, *Riddles, mervels and rarities, or, A new way of health, from an old man's experience* (1698) • IGI

Likenesses W. Faithorne the elder, line engraving (after H. Cooke), BM, NPG; repro. in Mace, *Musick's monument* [*see illus.*]

MacEachainn, Eoghan [Evan Maceachen] (1769–1849), Roman Catholic priest and Gaelic scholar, was born at Arisaig, Inverness-shire, and educated in a school at Ruthven, near Huntly, Aberdeenshire. He was sent in 1788 to the Scots College at Valladolid, where he was ordained priest in 1798. On his return to the mission he was stationed at Arisaig. In 1801 he was removed to Badenoch, and thence was sent, about 1806, in the capacity of professor, to the seminary of Lismore. In 1814 he was appointed to the mission of Aigas in Strathglass, from which he was transferred in 1818 to Braemar. In consequence of failing health he retired in 1838 to Ballogie, and in 1847 he removed to Tombae, Banffshire, where he died on 9 September 1849.

MacEachainn was an important Gaelic scholar, translating various religious works, and leaving several in manuscript including the New Testament. His Gaelic–English dictionary, first published in 1842, was expanded and revised after his death and remained in print in its fifth edition until about 1940.

THOMPSON COOPER, rev. H. C. G. MATTHEW

Sources *Catholic Directory for Scotland* (1850) • J. A. Stothert, *The Catholic mission in Scotland*

Maceachen, Evan. *See* MacEachainn, Eoghan (1769–1849).

MacEachern, Angus Bernard (1759–1835), missionary and bishop of Charlottetown, was born on 8 February 1759 at Kinlochmoidart, Inverness-shire, the youngest of eight children born to Hugh MacEachern, or Hugh Ban, and Mary MacDonald. According to family tradition Hugh MacEachern was for many years the laird of Kinloch's gardener, and so was 'in fairly easy circumstances' (Macmillan, 56). In 1772, with social and economic conditions deteriorating in the highlands, Hugh MacEachern and his family joined the settlement expedition of John MacDonald, eighth laird of Glenaladale, to the new colony of St John's Island (after 1799, Prince Edward Island) in British North America. Angus was left behind to study for the

Roman Catholic priesthood. Given the penal laws in force against Roman Catholicism, this had to be done discreetly. MacEachern appears to have attended the secret highland Catholic college at Buorblach during the early 1770s before proceeding to the Royal Scots College at Valladolid, Spain, in 1777. He was ordained there on 20 August 1787.

After returning to Scotland, MacEachern spent three years as a missionary in the Inner Hebrides, but the tide of emigration was flowing strongly out of the region. With the reluctant consent of his superiors, he sailed for St John's Island in company with some 300 highland Catholic settlers. When MacEachern arrived in the colony in August 1790, its scattered population of Acadian, Irish, and Scots Catholics had been five years without a resident priest. Establishing himself at St Andrew's, in the heart of the Scots Catholic settlement, he was immediately placed in spiritual charge of the island. From 1791 until 1793, and again from 1798 to 1802, his jurisdiction was enlarged to include the Gaelic-speaking Scottish settlements of Cape Breton and Nova Scotia's gulf shore. MacEachern's early experience set the pattern for the rest of his career. He would spend most of the next forty-five years journeying endlessly back and forth across his jurisdiction, a pioneer missionary in a primitive environment tending a far-flung and impoverished flock.

In administrative terms, Catholics in the Maritime colonies (New Brunswick, Nova Scotia, Prince Edward Island, and Cape Breton Island until its integration into Nova Scotia in 1820) were members of the sprawling diocese of Quebec, which encompassed most of British North America. Its French Canadian bishops had few human or financial resources to spare to outlying areas, and as English-speaking Irish and Gaelic-speaking highland settlers streamed into the Maritimes, the area's overworked missionaries became increasingly alienated from the Quebec hierarchy. After 1812 MacEachern involved himself in a series of schemes to convince Rome to grant the region ecclesiastical independence from Quebec. At the same time, acutely aware of the precarious position then occupied by Roman Catholics in Britain, he took care not to antagonize government officials and to avoid stirring up religious animosities.

MacEachern's lobbying efforts bore fruit when, on 12 January 1819, he was created titular bishop of Rosen, responsible for Prince Edward Island, New Brunswick, and the Magdalen Islands. But the appointment fell far short of ecclesiastical independence; MacEachern was, in effect, merely a vicar-general with no real power. Dubious of the region's poverty, Rome still hesitated to grant it diocesan status. MacEachern gradually lost patience. Writing to Archbishop Bernard-Claude Panet of Quebec in June 1829 he railed at 'responsibility without authority, time lost to my flock, expenses without remuneration, a decision without effect' (Archives of the Archdiocese of Quebec, 210 CN, I, 115). Finally, on 11 August 1829, the diocese of Charlottetown, comprising Prince Edward Island, New Brunswick, and the Magdalen Islands, was officially established. MacEachern, now seventy years old, was named its first bishop.

Part of MacEachern's impetus for seeking diocesan status had been, paradoxically, one of the reasons it had been so long withheld: the lack of clergy in the region. In 1831, two years after winning diocesan status, he realized a long cherished dream when St Andrew's College was opened in his episcopal residence to educate prospective seminarians and lay leaders for Maritime Catholic society. Established in partnership with Bishop William Fraser, vicar apostolic of Nova Scotia, the tiny school was the first Roman Catholic college in what is now Maritime Canada.

The founding of his college notwithstanding, MacEachern's life's work had been largely accomplished by the time he was appointed bishop of Charlottetown. Aside from the Herculean nature of his missionary work, his chief legacy had been the establishment of the diocese itself. Distracted by quarrels with his Irish laity in New Brunswick and slowed by age, he carried on until the spring of 1835, when, during his Easter visit to the missions of King's county, Prince Edward Island, he suffered a massive stroke. He died at his home in Canavoy, Prince Edward Island on 22 April and was buried three days later at nearby St Andrew's, beneath the sacristy of the little church he had built there.

Angus MacEachern was one of the leading figures in the Maritime colonies during the early British colonial period. In an era when Roman Catholics were more tolerated than accepted, his long and difficult labours earned him the respect of both government officials and protestant colonists. Personal qualities, charm, wit, tact, and a disarming lack of pretension, made him genuinely popular as well. Already, by the time of his death, MacEachern had achieved heroic stature among his fellow Roman Catholics, particularly the highland Scots. Within a generation, his exploits had passed into folklore.

G. EDWARD MACDONALD

Sources Archives of the Archdiocese of Quebec, Quebec City, Quebec, 210 CN, I [microfilm copy at the Charlottetown Public Library, Charlottetown] · correspondence of A. B. MacEachern and W. Fraser to P. MacPherson and A. MacDonald, Archives of the Scots College, Rome (Pontifical), Vicars Apostolic · [A. E. Burke], 'Notes on Bishop MacEachern', Archives of the diocese of Charlottetown, Prince Edward Island · [A. E. Burke], 'The Right Reverend Æneas B. MacEachern', Archives of the diocese of Charlottetown, Prince Edward Island · J. C. Macmillan, *The early history of the Catholic church in Prince Edward Island* (1905) · F. W. P. Bolger, 'The first bishop', in M. F. Hennessey, *The Catholic church in Prince Edward Island, 1720–1979*, 22–57 · will, Supreme Court of Prince Edward Island, Estates Division, liber 3, fol. 71 · *Royal Gazette* [Charlottetown, PEI] (28 April 1835) · A. A. Johnston, *The early history of the Catholic church in eastern Nova Scotia*, 1 (1960) · G. E. MacDonald, 'The good shepherd: Angus Bernard MacEachern, first bishop of Charlottetown', *The Island Magazine*, 16 (autumn–winter 1984), 3–8 · E. J. Mullally, 'The life and times of the Right Reverend Angus Bernard MacEachern, the first bishop of the diocese of Charlottetown', *Report* [Canadian Catholic Historical Association], 13 (1945–6), 71–106 · T. Murphy, 'The emergence of Maritime Catholicism, 1781–1830', *Acadiensis*, 13/2 (1983–4), 29–49

Archives Archives of the Archdiocese of Quebec, Quebec City, Quebec, lettres d'évêques de missionaires et des laïcas addressés aux évêques de Québec, 210 CN, I, vol. 1, 2 [microfilm copy at Charlottetown Public Library, Charlottetown] · Scots College, Rome, archives, vicars apostolic corresp. of A. B. MacEachern and William Fraser to Paul MacPherson and Angus MacDonald (pontifical)

Likenesses R. Harris, oils, 1890–1899?, St Dunstan's Basilica, Charlottetown, Prince Edward Island · H. Purdy, stained glass window, St Dunstan's Basilica, Charlottetown, Prince Edward Island · charcoal sketch, St Mary's Convent, Charlottetown, Prince Edward Island · oils, chancery office, Dun Glaston, Charlottetown, Prince Edward Island

Wealth at death see will, Supreme Court of Prince Edward Island, Estates Division, liber 3, fol. 71

McEgan, Owen [Eoghan O'hAogain] (*d.* 1603), Roman Catholic bishop-designate of Ross and rebel, was born in Ireland but nothing is known about his family. He was probably educated in a seminary in Spain. By 1595 he was a priest and had graduated BA and MA. On 1 November 1595 he was granted the spiritual livings to Mourne Abbey and on 30 May 1597 was appointed vicar apostolic of Ross, both in co. Cork. By then, he was also a DTh. In February 1600 he and Dermot McGrath, Catholic bishop of Cork and Cloyne, met Hugh O'Neill, second earl of Tyrone, at Kilnamanach, co. Tipperary. McEgan accompanied Tyrone on his progress through Munster and encouraged other Irish chieftains to support the earl's rebellion. Florence McCarthy Reagh then 'wrote another letter to Donnaught McCartie [Donough MacCarthy] and his brother (being rebels) persuading to rebellion, in which letter there joined with him Owen McKegan usurping the name of bishop of Rosse'. That summer McEgan travelled to Rome to appeal for aid on Tyrone's behalf and to petition 'for an excommunication to all that did not rebel, which excommunication was divulged after' (Brewer and Bullen, 1589–1600, 314–15). One of his requests was that a papal nuncio be appointed to Ireland. After much procrastination Clement VIII appointed Luigi Mansoni, an Italian Jesuit, on 17 May 1601. This was a disappointment; Tyrone had pressed for a Spanish nuncio. Perhaps as a consolation, at some point in 1601 the pope granted McEgan the spiritual livings in co. Kerry at Ballybeg Priory and Morr Abbey and made him dean of Cork. In December Clement granted McEgan's petition to become vicar apostolic of Ardfert, co. Kerry.

In autumn 1601 McEgan accompanied Mansoni to Spain, and they arrived at the court, which was then in Valladolid, on 21 December. By then, a Spanish expeditionary force had landed at Kinsale, co. Cork, but a few weeks later news arrived of the rebel forces' annihilation by the English outside the town. However, about 5000 rebels continued to hold out in counties Cork and Kerry and appealed to Spain for aid. In March 1602 Philip III chose McEgan to deliver them a supply of money and arms, assuring him that another Spanish force would be sent as soon as possible. McEgan also travelled armed with papal authority to dispose of all the spiritual livings in Munster.

After some delays, McEgan landed at Kenmare Bay, co. Kerry, on 5 June 1602. On 18 June the key stronghold of Dunboy, co. Waterford, fell to the English. Demoralized, the rebels were on the point of surrendering or fleeing, but news of McEgan's arrival, and more pertinently the

20,000 ducats he brought, stiffened their resolve. Through Spanish money, slightly disingenuous assurances of the arrival of another Spanish expedition, and his own personal resolve and determination, McEgan probably prolonged resistance in Munster by another six months. Donough and Finin MacCarthy and Sir Cormac MacDermot of Muskerry were among those who accepted money from McEgan in return for continuing in rebellion. McEgan prosecuted the war with intense vigour, literally fighting for the Counter-Reformation and confessing and absolving prisoners immediately before their execution. However, all the major strongholds in Munster were in English hands and the rebels struggled to carry out guerrilla warfare in a famine-stricken province. As hopes of further help from Spain faded, one by one the leading rebels either submitted or withdrew from Munster.

By the start of 1603, only 400 rebels still held out at Carberry, co. Cork. McEgan, still vainly expecting relief from Spain, was among them. On 4 January about 400 soldiers under William Taaffe engaged them and a fierce battle ensued, ending only on 5 January when McEgan was killed. Sir Thomas Carew, lord president of Munster, memorably describes McEgan as dying with a sword in one hand and rosary beads in the other, while attempting to force the soldiers back. Indeed, Carew was somewhat obsessed with McEgan, describing him as cruel and inhumane, and generally exaggerating his importance. This probably reflects Carew's desire to portray the Irish rebellion as part of an international Catholic conspiracy against English protestantism. However, McEgan had some effect. The antiquary, Sir Thomas Stafford, noted that the last vestiges of rebellion in Carberry collapsed: 'a principall means of this suddaine and universalle reduction was the death of the traitorly priest, Owen MacEggan, which doubtlesse was more beneficialle to the state than to have gotten the head of the most capitall rebell in Munster' (Stafford, *Pacata Hibernia*, 367). McEgan was buried in the convent of Timoleague, co. Cork, and a cross was placed over his tomb. TERRY CLAVIN

Sources J. S. Brewer and W. Bullen, eds., *Calendar of the Carew manuscripts … at Lambeth, 1515–1624*, 6 vols. (1867–73), 1589–1600, 314–15; 1601–3, 61, 251, 267, 354, 406–7 · *CSP Ire.*, 1601–3, 425, 517–18, 537–9 · F. M. Jones, 'Canonical faculties on the Irish mission', *Irish Theological Quarterly*, 20 (1953), 152–71 · P. Ó Maidín, 'Collation of Eogham Ó hAogáin', *Cork Historical Association Journal*, 73 (1988), 52–9 · M. O'Reilly, *Lives of the Irish martyrs* (1880) · P. O'Sullivan Beare, *Ireland under Elizabeth: chapters towards a history of Ireland in the reign of Elizabeth*, ed. and trans. M. J. Byrne (1903); repr. (Port Washington, NY, 1970) · M. V. Ronan, *The Irish martyrs of the penal laws* (1935) · T. Stafford, *Pacata Hibernia: Ireland appeased and reduced, or a historie of the late wars of Ireland* (1633); repr. 2 vols. (1896), 2.185, 207, 211, 219, 229, 287–9, 344–51

McElligott, James John (1893–1974), civil servant in Ireland, was born on 26 July 1893 in Tralee, co. Kerry, a son of Edmund John McElligott, a local shopkeeper, and his wife, Catherine Slattery, also of co. Kerry. After attending Father Buckley's school, Tralee, he went to University College, Dublin, where he graduated with an honours BA degree in classics in 1913. Having competed successfully for a post as first-division clerk in the civil service, he was assigned to the Local Government Board in Dublin. He was also in the Irish Volunteers and, returning from the races in Fairyhouse on Easter Monday, 1916, he reported to the General Post Office (GPO) and took part in the rising. As the GPO became untenable, he led a small party of rebels in a sortie across O'Connell Street which involved kicking their way under fire through large plate-glass windows. These revolutionary activities cost him his job and led to his imprisonment in various English gaols. He ended up in Stafford, in a neighbouring cell to Michael Collins.

On returning to Dublin in 1917 McElligott completed a postgraduate degree in economics and took up financial journalism, becoming in 1921 managing editor of *The Statist*, a London financial weekly. He accepted in 1923 an invitation to rejoin the Irish civil service as assistant secretary in the department of finance and he succeeded his friend Joseph Brennan as secretary in 1927. In that year, on 23 February, he married Ann Gertrude (1893–1971), daughter of Denis Fay, a cattle salesman of Edenderry. They had a daughter.

McElligott shared with Brennan a reputation for tenacious pursuit of economy and efficiency in the administration of the public finances—a policy described by critics as remorseless pressure for retrenchment but one which did much to gain for the new state a reputation for soundness and stability. Their years of co-operation were marked by singular achievements, none more astounding than the oversubscription, in the immediate aftermath of a civil war, of the first national loan for £10 million, a sum equivalent in 1998 to £350 million. It now seems incredible that annual public expenditure had been lowered by the end of the 1920s to £25 million and that the aggregate of wartime budget deficits was a mere £16 million.

McElligott was a small, wiry man, remarkably tolerant of the cold, and sharing only coffee and a bun with Brennan as a working lunch. A younger colleague pictures him 'sitting in a cold narrow room, wearing a black linen coat, a model of the austerity he preached'. In time, however, that colleague discovered, behind the mask of severity, 'a warm, even emotional man, who could be reasoned with' (Whitaker, 162). He was in the end persuaded that some state expenditure, even of borrowed moneys, could be justified to promote competitive export industries and raise living standards. In his early years he had, unlike Brennan, been prepared to back the pioneering Electricity Supply Board scheme to harness the Shannon. In general, however, his sympathies lay with Adam Smith rather than with Keynes, whom he once described as belonging to the 'escapist school' (Lee, 566). His education in and love of the classics were reflected in the clarity and grace of his writing.

McElligott was in the forefront of all the major public inquiries and economic and financial developments of his time, and represented Ireland at many international conferences, notably the Ottawa conference of 1932. He was honoured with a doctorate of laws by the National University of Ireland in 1946 and became the first president of the Economic Research Institute in 1961.

McElligott died at his home, Oak Lodge, South Hill

Avenue, Blackrock, co. Dublin on 24 January 1974, within hours of his attending a board meeting of the Central Bank, of which he had been governor from 1953 to 1960 and the first to activate its rediscounting function. He had been continuously on the board of the bank and its predecessor, the Currency Commission, for forty-seven years, and had devotedly served his country for more than sixty. He was buried at Dean's Grange cemetery, co. Dublin, on 26 January.   T. K. WHITAKER

Sources R. Fanning, *The Irish department of finance, 1922–58* (1978) · J. J. Lee, *Ireland 1912–1985, politics and society* (1989) · M. Moynihan, *Currency and central banking in Ireland, 1922–60* (1975) · L. Ó Broin, *No man's man: a biographical memoir of Joseph Brennan* (1982) · T. K. Whitaker, *Interests* (1983) · m. cert. · private information (2004)
Archives NA Ire., department of finance files

McElwain, Timothy John (1937–1990), cancer physician, was born on 22 April 1937 in Wellington, New Zealand, the only child of Allan R. McElwain, freelance foreign correspondent, and his wife, Marjorie (Miranda) Simpson, a commercial artist specializing in fashion. Because of the peripatetic nature of his father's employment, McElwain was educated in both Australia and England. He attended St Peter's College, Adelaide, from 1947 to 1949, and then Sloane School in London (1949–51). Back in Australia, he went to Haileybury College, Melbourne, from 1951 to 1957. He returned to London in 1957 to go to the London Polytechnic to study physics, chemistry, zoology, and botany for a first MB exemption. He duly achieved this, with passes in all subjects. He also became president of the students' union, chairman of the debating society, and president of the faculty club. He was keen on water sports and rowing. He was admitted to St Bartholomew's Hospital medical college in October 1960, being about five years older than the average student. His maturity is reflected in the fact that he had no difficulty with examinations, passing MB, BS finals with honours in 1965, when he obtained a distinction in applied pharmacology and therapeutics. He was awarded the Hayward prize in recognition of his contribution to student activities.

McElwain did his house physician appointments at Bart's, where he worked for Gordon Hamilton Fairley, a pioneer of the drug treatment of cancer. His interest and ability in therapeutics ensured Hamilton Fairley's support, and he obtained one of the first Leukaemia Research Fund fellowships (1968–70), to work on childhood leukaemia at the Hospital for Sick Children, Great Ormond Street. He passed his MRCP in 1968, and, after registrar appointments at Bart's (1967–8), and posts as lecturer (1970–71) and senior lecturer (1972–3) at the Royal Marsden Hospital, London, he was appointed in 1973 consultant physician at the Royal Marsden. He became head of the section of medicine in 1980, and was subsequently appointed Cancer Research Campaign professor of medical oncology in the University of London in 1983. He had been elected at an early age to the fellowship of the Royal College of Physicians, London, in 1977.

McElwain brought to the Royal Marsden Hospital an appreciation of the importance of the discipline of internal medicine, not only in the proper use of drugs to combat cancer, but also in the expert general medical care necessary to the exploration of the drugs' potential. He pushed intensive therapy, using high doses of anti-cancer drugs, to the limit, and his resultant success in the care of myeloma, a highly malignant form of cancer, serves as a confirmation of the value of his work. This could not have been achieved without prolonged, intensive effort, and courage in facing the inevitable institutional resistance and resentments.

As professor of medical oncology McElwain was in great demand from organizations abroad and at home. He was always generous with his time, holding such posts as consultant in medical oncology at the Tata Memorial Cancer Centre in Bombay, India, external assessor to the Chinese University of Hong Kong, and referee for research grant applications to the Medical Research Council of New Zealand. In Great Britain he was chairman or member of several important committees in such institutions as the Royal College of Physicians, London, the Medical Research Council, and the Wolfson Foundation. However, the position that gave him most pleasure was his presidency of the Association of Cancer Physicians. He was a member of the editorial boards of many specialist journals. He was a popular member of societies, and of national and international committees, where his knowledge, combined with good common sense and a pithy expression of his views, could often rescue a meeting that was faltering.

McElwain was a large man, with a bald head, who loved food, wine, and music, and had a remarkable knowledge of contemporary literature. He had a library of over 2000 records of classical music. With his wit and his expansive personality, he was a charming and thoughtful host, and an invitation to his home was not to be missed. In 1970 he married Sheila Glennis, daughter of Richard Howarth, accountant, after a whirlwind courtship while he was a junior doctor at the Hospital for Sick Children, Great Ormond Street. She brought love and security to his life and, while carving out a distinguished medical career for herself, was able to give him an elegant and happy home. There were no children. McElwain died at his home, 94 Clapham Common North Side, London, on 26 November 1990.   J. S. MALPAS, *rev.*

Sources *BMJ* (5 Jan 1991), 46 · *The Lancet* (8 Dec 1990) · *British Journal of Cancer*, 63 (1991) · CGPLA Eng. & Wales (1991)
Wealth at death £61,067: administration, 25 Feb 1991

MacEntee, Seán Francis (1889–1984), Irish nationalist and politician, was born in College Square North, Belfast, on 1 January 1889, the eldest son of James MacEntee, a prosperous Catholic publican, merchant, and sometime town councillor. He was educated at St Malachy's College and the Belfast College of Technology before entering an apprenticeship in electrical engineering with the city engineer. An early interest in politics led him to join James Connolly's Irish Socialist Republican Party about 1910. In January 1914 MacEntee took employment as assistant to the town engineer of Dundalk, co. Louth, where he joined Sinn Féin and the Irish Volunteers. He contributed several poetical works to periodicals before 1916, earning himself a reputation as something of an intellectual. A selection later appeared as *The Poems of John Francis MacEntee* (1918). During the Easter rising in April 1916 he took part in operations locally and then made his way to the General Post Office in Dublin. His version of these events is recounted in *Easter Fires* (1943) and *Episode at Easter* (1966). He was arrested, court-martialled, and condemned to death, though the sentence was commuted to life imprisonment. He was sent to Dartmoor, Lewes, and Portland prisons; during this time he first met Eamon de Valera.

After his release from confinement under the general amnesty of June 1917, MacEntee played an active part in Sinn Féin and the Irish Republican Army, serving on the executives of both. In December 1918 he was elected MP for Monaghan South but like other members of Sinn Féin declined to take his seat, instead sitting in Dáil Éireann when it was formed in January 1919. In May 1921 he was returned unopposed for co. Monaghan in the second Dáil. Although a supporter of de Valera, MacEntee was never overawed by him. He sought to preserve the principle of Dáil authority, criticizing de Valera's mission to the United States because it lacked the authorization of the assembly and objecting to the appointment of Erskine Childers as head of propaganda because he was not a member of it. Also, as an adumbration of his later concern for social welfare, he forced the Dáil government to drop plans to end the £8000 subsidy for school meals in the slums of Dublin. He was a voluble supporter of the economic boycott of the north in response to the ousting of Catholics from employment in Belfast, arguing that 'they could not reduce Belfast by force of arms, but they could bring her to reason by economic force' (Mitchell, 171). In 1935 he again gave attention to the expulsion from employment of Catholics in Belfast. On 19 May 1921 he married Margaret Browne (*d.* 1976), of Grange Mockler, Carrick on Suir, co. Tipperary, daughter of Maurice Browne, a teacher; they had two sons and a daughter (Máire MacEntee, who married the author and politician Conor Cruise O'Brien and became a considerable scholar and poet in her own right).

MacEntee, the sole Belfast-born member of the second Dáil, opposed the Anglo-Irish treaty signed in December 1921. In the Dáil debates on the treaty in January 1922 he was one of the few who based his opposition to it on the division of the island. During the Irish civil war (1922–3) he was imprisoned by the Irish Free State. Subsequently he concentrated mainly on his profession, being a partner in a firm of electrical engineers and a prominent member of the Institute of Engineers. Indeed, he owed his release from prison in 1923 to this expertise; the then mayor of Waterford declined to pay contractors for their work on the electrification of the city until MacEntee was freed to inspect it. MacEntee unsuccessfully contested Dáil elections in 1923 and 1924. He was a founder of Fianna Fáil in 1926 and secured a seat for co. Dublin in the Dáil at both general elections in 1927. He was elected again in 1932, and with de Valera's party's succession to the office MacEntee himself began on 9 March a long spell as minister of finance (1932–9). On taking office he calmed worries about

the intentions of the new government by announcing that key officials would continue in post, and by pursuing orthodox fiscal policies. He introduced eight budgets, in which he raised old-age pensions, brought in widows' pensions and unemployment insurance, promoted children's allowances, and launched a housing programme. This was a difficult period for the Irish economy, and MacEntee was a key figure in resolving the Anglo-Irish trade war in 1938. He negotiated the electricity link with Northern Ireland and, in an echo of his earlier profession, took a keen interest in rural electrification during his time as a minister.

MacEntee possessed an insatiable thirst for information and was renowned as a diminutive figure with a huge appetite for parliamentary warfare and for public speaking, in spite of a slight stammer. He was noted also for being 'woefully long-winded' and prolix on paper. In 1939 he moved to the portfolio of industry and commerce (1939–41) and then to local government and public health (1941–6) before transferring to local government (1946–8). After a period in opposition, he returned to finance (1951–4), and when Fianna Fáil was again returned to power in 1957 he was minister for social welfare (1957–61), minister for health (1959–65), and *tánaiste* (deputy prime minister) (1959–65), before retiring from office and then from politics altogether in 1969. In this later phase of ministerial life, the social concerns of his early years returned to the fore, especially in the Health Act (1957), which left him at odds with the medical profession.

MacEntee spent a lengthy and happy retirement with his family in suburban Dublin. He was an honorary LLD of the National University of Ireland and a knight of the grand cross, Pian order. He died at his home, 30 Trimleston Avenue, Booterstown, co. Dublin on 9 January 1984, his wife having predeceased him in 1976, and after a funeral in the church of Our Lady Queen of Peace, Merrion Road, was interred in Glasnevin cemetery, Dublin.

ALAN O'DAY

Sources *Irish Times* (10 Jan 1984); (12 Jan 1984) · *The Times* (12 Jan 1984); (18 Jan 1984) · R. Fanning, *The Irish department of finance, 1922–58* (1978) · A. Mitchell, *Revolutionary government in Ireland* (1995) · C. C. O'Brien, *Memoirs: my life and themes* (1998) · L. Ó Broin, *Just like yesterday: an autobiography* (1986) · D. Fitzpatrick, *The two Irelands, 1912–1939* (1998) · E. O'Halpin, *Defending Ireland: the Irish state and its enemies since 1922* (1999) · F. Pakenham [Lord Longford], *Peace by ordeal* (1935) · D. Macardle, *The Irish republic* (1937) · S. MacEntee, *Easter fires: pages from personal records of 1916* (1943) · S. MacEntee, *Episode at Easter* (1966) · m. cert. · d. cert. · *CGPLA Ire.* (1984)
Archives University College, Dublin, corresp., O'Malley · University College, Dublin, corresp., de Valera | FILM BFI NFTVA, advertising footage | SOUND BL NSA, documentary recording
Likenesses H. Boylan, portrait, repro. in *Dictionary of Irish biography* (1998)
Wealth at death £153,748: probate, 1984, *CGPLA Éire*

Mac Eochada, Niall. See Niall mac Eochada (*d.* 1063).

MacEoin, Seán Joseph [John Joseph McKeown] (1893–1973), Irish republican, was born John Joseph McKeon at Bunlahy, Granard, co. Longford, on 30 September 1893, eldest child of Andrew MacEoin or McKeon, a blacksmith, and Catherine, *née* Treacy, of Ballinglough, co. Longford.

He was educated in the Kilshrule national school and by correspondence course. On leaving school at fifteen he was apprenticed as blacksmith in his father's forge; later he also took up farming.

One of the most famous fighters in the Anglo-Irish War and later one of the country's most colourful political figures, MacEoin was known widely as 'the blacksmith of Ballinalee' because of his feat of leading a major ambush on British troops (Black and Tans) at Ballinalee, co. Longford, on 5 November 1920. He had been engaged in politics from an early age. At Bunlahy he attended Gaelic League classes and at sixteen became a member of the North Longford United Irish League, and subsequently joined the Irish Volunteers. MacEoin's experience in the Irish Republican Brotherhood (IRB) shaped his subsequent thinking, notably that the IRB, citizen army, and volunteers should, combined, form the army of the new republic. He was a company commander in the Irish Volunteers in 1919, becoming battalion commander of the first battalion, Longford Volunteers and commandant in the IRA with the rank of general. He gained fame by leading the Longford flying column in 1920 and 1921. As he was supporting his widowed mother, he had been reluctant to take a major role in the struggle; it was Michael Collins, who bested him at wrestling, who overcame his reservations. Like Collins, MacEoin was a man of action and a natural military leader but he was not equally adept at the minutiae of organization and paperwork. To overcome his administrative lapses Collins assigned Erskine Childers to MacEoin in an attempt to bring greater order to the command but the arrangement ended abruptly after a month. In spite of his essentially military orientation MacEoin saw the Irish Republican Army's function as that of carrying out the policy of the Dáil government. Apart from his escapade at Ballinalee, he had other notable encounters with British forces: on several occasions he was captured but escaped. On 7 January 1921 he led an ambush in which District Inspector McGrath of the royal Irish constabulary and two auxiliaries were killed. On 21 March 1921 he was wounded and captured in Mullingar. He was moved to the King George V Hospital in Dublin and then incarcerated in Mountjoy prison. While held there, charged with the murder of McGrath, he was elected a member of the southern Ireland parliament for Longford-Westmeath at the general election on 24 May, following which the Sinn Féin members constituted themselves into the second Dáil Éireann. Collins, well aware of the fate that probably awaited his friend, organized an abortive rescue attempt before MacEoin could be tried. On 14 June a court martial meted out the expected death sentence. During the truce the British government released all political prisoners with the exception of MacEoin, but Collins was insistent that he be released. The British received an ultimatum from Eamon De Valera, backed by the Dáil cabinet, making this a condition for the negotiations and he was duly freed on 8 August. At Collins's direction he nominated De Valera in the Dáil as president of the Irish republic on 26 August.

MacEoin supported Collins over the treaty, seconding Arthur Griffith's motion for its acceptance on 19 December 1921 in the Dáil. His concurrence with the treaty was partly from personal loyalty to Collins and also from an assessment that the republican forces were in no position to renew the armed struggle. In December he took command of the midland division of the IRA and received possession of the Longford barracks from the British forces in January 1922. While in charge MacEoin oversaw raids into northern Ireland in February 1922 but when the civil war began he supported Collins and the pro-treaty side. MacEoin participated in the negotiations with the anti-treaty rebels who seized the Four Courts in Dublin. In June 1922 (in the presence of Collins and Griffith) he married Alice C. Cooney, eldest daughter of John Cooney, Gurteen House, Killashee, co. Longford. He had to interrupt his honeymoon to help dispatch the anti-treaty forces operating nearby. On 31 July he informed Collins that 'in Midland Divisions all posts and positions of military value are in our hands' (Hopkinson, 152). MacEoin had been re-elected to the Dáil at the general election on 16 June 1922 but at Collins's request he resigned his seat in August 1922 in order to become general officer in command of the western command. Because of his immense prestige MacEoin's support for the free state was held to be crucial, although the western command was regarded as somewhat inefficient. Subsequently he was general officer in charge Curragh command, quartermaster-general, and then from February to June 1929 chief of staff. He was involved in the National Defence Association formed in 1929, but left it when the government decreed that serving officers could not be members.

MacEoin resigned from the army in 1929 in a clash with Desmond FitzGerald over dress, deportment, and the deference due to the military, and entered the Dáil again at a by-election on 7 June for Sligo-Leitrim. At the general election on 16 February 1932 he was elected for Longford-Westmeath and represented the same constituency in its various guises until 1965. MacEoin joined the Army Comrades Association (the Blueshirts) in summer 1932 and the new Fine Gael party on its formation the following year. Although an opponent of Fianna Fáil and Eamon De Valera, he sometimes supported the policies of the new government and his politics might be described as eclectic. In April 1932 he spoke in favour of the bill for removal of the oaths of allegiance to the crown. He drew attention in 1938 to the impoverished state of some surviving MPs from the pre-1918 Irish party, calling upon old Sinn Féin members of the Dáil to apologize to them: 'we blackguarded them up and down the country because we were not aware of the facts' (Manning, 142). He upheld Irish neutrality in the Second World War, a policy at odds with some members of Fine Gael. In the presidential election of 1945 he stood for the presidency, losing, on the second count after the third contestant Patrick McCartan's votes were redistributed, to Seán T. O'Kelly, the Fianna Fáil candidate, by 453,425 to 565,165.

During the first inter-party government formed in 1948 MacEoin was minister for justice (February 1948 – March 1951), transferring to defence (March–June 1951), and in the second inter-party government he was again minister for defence (1954–7). Among his cabinet colleagues MacEoin's ministerial career was not without controversy. In his memoir Noel Browne claimed to have objected to MacEoin's cavalier use of patronage for the benefit of friends, constituents, and supporters (Browne, 126); he irritated several younger colleagues by his obsequious deference to the Catholic church hierarchy on social issues. James Dillon recalled that when an adoption bill came before the cabinet in 1951 MacEoin consulted the archbishop of Dublin and announced to his colleagues, '"he won't have it" and that was the end of the matter as far as he [MacEoin] was concerned' (Manning, 242). He lined up with the bishops against the 'mother and child' health scheme in 1951, a proposal to provide a non-compulsory health care system for all mothers and children up to the age of sixteen, which would not be means tested, and in 1955 succeeded in having the Fine Gael Ard-Fheis (annual party conference) drop a motion in favour of legalizing the opening of public houses on Sundays: 'I, for one, am not prepared to get a stroke of a crosier for any publican' (Maye, 93). In 1959 he stood for the presidency a second time as the 'man of the people' (O'Farrell, *Seán Mac-Eoin*, 103), being defeated in a straight contest with Eamon De Valera by 538,003 to 417,536 votes. MacEoin was dismayed by De Valera's candidacy, believing that there had been an understanding when O'Kelly was elected that he would succeed him unopposed. In 1965 he lost his seat in the Dáil in a disputed election which ended his career in politics.

MacEoin travelled widely, and was twice received in private papal audiences (popes Pius XI and Pius XII). He was a member of the knights of St Columbanus and for a decade from 1958 chairman of the *Catholic Standard*. While in Argentina in 1957 he was awarded the navy order of merit of the grand cross of Argentina. MacEoin was prominent in the creation of the garden of remembrance opened in Dublin in 1966, which commemorates all who died in the struggle for Irish independence. In April 1972 MacEoin was admitted to St Bricin's Military Hospital, Dublin, where he died on 7 July 1973 after a long illness. Three days later, following a state funeral in Ballinalee church, he was interred in St Emer's cemetery, Longford. His wife survived him.   ALAN O'DAY

Sources *Irish Times* (9 July 1973) · *Irish Independent* (9 July 1973) · *Irish Independent* (11 July 1973) · M. Hopkinson, *Green against green: the Irish civil war* (Dublin, 1988) · M. Manning, *James Dillon* (Dublin, 1998) · N. Browne, *Against the tide* (Dublin, 1986) · B. Maye, *Fine Gael, 1923–1987* (Dublin, 1993) · M. Farry, *The aftermath of revolution: Sligo, 1921–23* (Dublin, 2000) · M. Forester, *Michael Collins the lost leader* (1971) · P. O'Farrell, *Who's who in the Irish War of Independence* (Dublin, 1997) · M. Gallagher, *Political parties in the Republic of Ireland* (1985) · J. Duggan, *The Irish army* (Dublin, 1991) · P. O'Farrell, *The Seán MacEoin story* (1981) · b. cert. · d. cert.
Archives University College, Dublin, papers | priv. coll., James Dillon MSS
Likenesses Walshe, group portrait, photograph, 1922 (*Commander McKeown*), Hult. Arch. · Walshe, photograph, 1922 (with Michael Collins), Hult. Arch. · portrait, repro. in *Irish Independent* (9 July 1973)

Maceroni, Francis [*known as* Count Maceroni] (1788–1846), soldier and mechanical inventor, was born in the suburbs of Manchester. His father, Peter Augustus Maceroni, with two brothers, had served in a French regiment in America during the War of Independence, and after a roving life settled down at Manchester as an Italian agent for British goods. He married in 1786 the daughter of Benjamin Wildsmith of Sheffield, who was a Roman Catholic; they moved to London in 1792, having lost their fortune on the outbreak of war between France and Italy. Francis attended three Catholic schools: at the first, at Bridzor in Wiltshire, the pupils were underfed and neglected; he was removed to a school at Carshalton, Surrey, where the teachers were Dominican friars, refugees from Douai; and he then went on to the college at Old Hall Green, near Puckeridge, Hertfordshire, presided over by Dr William Poynter, later Roman Catholic bishop of London. In his memoirs, he paid 'humble tribute to the moral excellence of the community', and to his teachers, also Douai friars, from whom he acquired elementary scientific training. In 1803 he was sent by his father to Rome, where one of his uncles was the papal postmaster-general, ostensibly to learn banking and book keeping. He appears to have idled away the next ten years at Naples and Rome, in company with other young Englishmen. He claimed to have introduced archery and cricket into Italy, and started a swimming-bath for ladies, where he acted as instructor. He dabbled a little in scientific experiments, and in 1813 applied himself to the study of anatomy and medicine.

Maceroni recommended himself to Joachim Murat, king of Naples, who on 1 January 1814 made him one of his aides-de-camp, with the rank of colonel of cavalry, and sent him on missions to London, where he was when Murat's forces were defeated by the Austrians at Tolentino in May 1815. Meanwhile 'Count' Maceroni, as he styled himself, had proceeded to Paris to further his master's interests. He claimed to have been made at this time a chevalier of the Légion d'honneur in the name of the emperor. When the allied armies were advancing on Paris after Waterloo, he was employed as an agent of the 'commission of government' to endeavour to obtain an armistice, so as to delay the re-entry of the Bourbons; in this he was unsuccessful. In his memoirs he gives minute details of his interviews with the duke of Wellington, whose published papers, however, contain no mention of the subject. Maceroni was afterwards sent as the representative of the allied powers to offer Murat an asylum in the Austrian dominions. Murat refused to allow Maceroni to accompany him on his last, fatal expedition. Maceroni states that a number of Corsican patriots at this time asked him to place himself at their head, shake off the French yoke, and offer the island to Great Britain. He returned to France, and was subsequently thrown into a French prison for alleged illegal interference on Murat's behalf. He was released, without compensation, and in January 1816 returned to England, which was his home for the rest of his life. In 1817 he published his *Interesting Facts Relating to the Fall and Death of Joachim Murat, King of Naples*, which went through several editions. He also wrote a pamphlet in French and English containing Santini's representations of Napoleon's ill usage at St Helena.

Maceroni was associated with Gregor MacGregor, afterwards cacique of Poyais, in raising troops and acquiring supplies in England and Europe to aid General Bolívar in the struggle for Colombian independence. He eventually fell out with MacGregor, whom he described as a coward and a mountebank, when the Scot squandered his men and munitions in disastrous attacks on Portobello and Rio de la Hache. In 1821 he married: his wife's identity is unknown. He then went to Spain with General Pepè, and meddled in Spanish and Neapolitan politics, always on the popular, and, as events turned out, the losing side. On his return to England he was in communication with the Spanish ambassador in respect of a project of ship communication between the Atlantic and Pacific oceans. He promoted a company, styled the Atlantic and Pacific Junction and South American Mining and Trading Company, with a capital of a million pounds sterling in £100 shares. The company collapsed in the commercial panic of 1825.

About this time Maceroni designed 'the best paddlewheel in the world', some improved rockets, a design for an armoured ship, and other military and naval inventions which were never patented. He also wrote *Hints to Paviours* (1827), in which he advocated asphalt paving. In 1829 he went to Constantinople on receipt of £1000 to assist the Turks against the Russians, and returned two years later 'poorer than he went'. At the time of the first Reform Bill he published a physical-force pamphlet, entitled *Defensive Instructions for the People, Containing New and Improved Combination of Arms, Called Foot Lancers* (1832). The combination was a fowling piece and a 10 foot lance for street fighting. Maceroni says that he had great difficulty in finding a printer for the pamphlet, which he published without any return when he and his children were in great poverty.

Maceroni next turned his attention to an improved model of 'steam-coach' for common roads, the most important of his inventions. An engineering treatise of the day speaks of it as 'a fine specimen of indomitable perseverance' (Gordon). In this undertaking Maceroni was associated with a Mr Squire, the owner of a factory on Paddington Green, by whom the invention was patented and worked out. Accounts of the successful performances of the steam-coach in the neighbourhood of London and Brussels appeared in a number of newspapers in 1833 and 1834. But the railways ruined the project, the partners fell out, and Maceroni was for some time a prisoner for debt. At the time of writing his memoirs in 1838 he and his children were in most distressed circumstances. He died at 1 Mortimer Terrace, Latimer Road, Shepherd's Bush, Middlesex, on 25 July 1846.

H. M. CHICHESTER, *rev.* K. D. REYNOLDS

Sources F. Maceroni, *Memoirs and adventures of Colonel Maceroni, late aide-de-camp to Joachim Murat, king of Naples*, 2 vols. (1838) · N&Q, 11 (1855), 35–6 · N&Q, 2nd ser., 4 (1857), 74 · A. Gordon, *An historical and practical treatise upon elemental locomotion* (1832) · *Morning Chronicle* (7 Oct 1833) · *Morning Chronicle* (16 Oct 1833) · *The Times* (10 Oct 1834) · *The Scotsman* (9 March 1834) · d. cert.

Archives UCL, letters to G. B. Greenough

Likenesses C. Picart, stipple, pubd 1822 (after A. Wivell), BM

MacEvilly, John (1816–1902), Roman Catholic bishop of Galway and archbishop of Tuam, was born on 24 April 1816 at Bunowen, Louisburgh, co. Mayo, one of eight children of William McEvilly (1786–1872), a tenant farmer, and Sarah, *née* Boland (1786–1886). MacEvilly received his early education at St Jarlath's College, Tuam, co. Galway, before entering St Patrick's College, Maynooth, to prepare for the priesthood in 1833. He was ordained priest for the diocese of Tuam in June 1840 and he spent a further two years in study before being appointed professor of sacred scripture at St Jarlath's College by the archbishop of Tuam, John MacHale.

MacEvilly became a prominent figure in the diocese and he appeared on public platforms in support of national movements, such as Daniel O'Connell's Repeal Association and the Tenant League. On 22 March 1857 he was consecrated bishop of the neighbouring diocese of Galway, having been recommended for the post by the reforming archbishop of Dublin, Paul Cullen, the most influential Catholic ecclesiastic of his time. The two became close friends and, until Cullen's death in 1878, MacEvilly consistently looked to his mentor for advice on all issues, local and national. This close relationship with the archbishop of Dublin meant inevitably that MacEvilly incurred the displeasure of his former archbishop, John MacHale, who opposed all of Cullen's attempts to establish a centralized Irish Catholic church with a unified, disciplined clergy. MacHale was outraged when MacEvilly was appointed coadjutor archbishop of Tuam with right of succession in 1878. Although MacHale steadfastly refused to recognize the appointment, he was to be succeeded as archbishop by his enemy on his death in November 1881.

As bishop of Galway, MacEvilly's determination to implement Cullenite reforms in the diocese immediately brought him into conflict with Peter Daly, an ageing parish priest of immense wealth and influence in Galway city. When MacEvilly prohibited Daly from sitting on a public board, it marked the beginning of a protracted and complicated struggle which saw Daly, with the support of Archbishop MacHale, openly challenging the authority of his bishop and appealing his case to Rome. Predictably, Rome upheld the authority of the bishop and Daly was ordered to submit. Daly continued to employ the tactics of evasion and prevarication before eventually agreeing to comply with his bishop's demands.

'There is no other question which so intimately affects the faith of today as the question of education' (Norman, 190), declared John MacEvilly and from the outset, he made the provision of a Catholic system of education a top priority. Unlike MacHale in Tuam, he encouraged the establishment of state primary schools, since he was confident that they would, *de facto*, be controlled by the Catholic hierarchy. However, he discouraged parents, under threat of excommunication, from sending their children to the 'model' schools, which were managed directly by the state, setting up secondary schools, run by Catholic religious orders, in opposition to them.

Although MacEvilly had been publicly active in political affairs as a young priest, when he became bishop he took his lead from his friend Cullen and fought shy of public involvement in election contests. He was not averse, however, to working behind the scenes and to bringing his considerable influence to bear on events at election times. His intervention in the 1868 election contest, when the clergy of Galway demanded pre-election pledges of allegiance to Gladstone's Liberal Party from all candidates, led directly to the withdrawal of the sitting MP George Morris.

Throughout his career MacEvilly was opposed to all political movements involving popular agitation. Like Cullen he was an implacable opponent of Fenianism and later, he refused to lend his support to land reform movements. Privately, he was opposed to the Land League and prohibited the clergy of Galway, and later Tuam, from involving themselves publicly in the league's affairs and from lending their support to any form of agitation. He was a late and reluctant convert to the home rule movement but he remained deeply suspicious of Parnell, who he felt was not fitted to lead a Catholic people. Not surprisingly when Parnell lost the leadership of the Irish party, MacEvilly and the priests of Tuam were vociferous in their condemnation of the fallen leader and actively supported anti-Parnellite candidates in the subsequent elections. In his later years, however, MacEvilly did adopt a more nationalist attitude and gave his support to emerging popular movements such as the Gaelic League.

MacEvilly was a stern, austere man and a hard taskmaster. He was conscious of his position of influence and he was not slow to use it in promoting friends and punishing opponents. He was a strong man physically and he lived a full, active life into old age. In his later years he suffered from rheumatism and sciatica and he died at Tuam on 26 November 1902. He was buried in the grounds of Tuam Cathedral on 30 November. LIAM BANE

Sources L. Bane, The bishop in politics (1993) · L. Bane, 'John Mac-Hale and John MacEvilly: conflict in the nineteenth century Catholic hierarchy', Archivium Hibernicum, 39 (1984), 45–51 · L. Ó Báin, 'An tArdeaspag Mac Héil agus an Cairdinéal Ó Cuilinn (Archbishop MacHale and Cardinal Cullen)', Leon an Iarthair: aistí ar Sheán Mac Héil, árdeaspag Thuama, 1834–1881, ed. A. Ní Cheannain (1983), 67–71 · L. Bane, 'Bishop John MacEvilly and the Catholic church in late nineteenth century Galway', Galway history and society: interdisciplinary essays on the history of an Irish county, ed. G. Moran and R. Gillespie (1996), 421–44 · J. Healy, Maynooth College: its centenary history (1895) · E. A. D'Alton, History of the archdiocese of Tuam, 2 vols. (1928) · E. R. Norman, The Catholic church and Ireland in the age of rebellion, 1859–1873 (1965) · L. Bane, 'John MacEvilly (1816–1902)', MA diss., University College, Galway, 1979 · B. O'Reilly, John MacHale, archbishop of Tuam, his life, times, and correspondence, 2 vols. (1890) · P. J. Corish, Maynooth College, 1795–1995 (1995)
Archives Galway diocesan archives | Dublin Roman Catholic archdiocese, archives, Paul Cullen, Edward McCabe, William Walsh papers · Elphin diocesan archives, Laurence Gillooly papers
Likenesses oils, Maynooth College, co. Kildare

Wealth at death £2682 9s. 5d.: probate, 18 March 1903, CGPLA Ire.

McEvoy, (Arthur) Ambrose (1878–1927), painter, was born in Crudwell, Wiltshire, on 12 August 1878, the elder son of Captain Charles Ambrose McEvoy (d. in or after 1893) and his wife, Jane Mary. The younger son, Charles, gained some distinction as a playwright. Their father was an Irish-American mercenary who, after serving in the Confederate army in the American Civil War, became an authority on submarine warfare, including inventing an antisubmarine hydrophone in 1893; after his American service he settled in England. Captain McEvoy was a friend of James Abbott McNeill Whistler (one of whose brothers had served with him in the Confederate army), and Whistler joined with him in encouraging Ambrose McEvoy's ambition to become a painter. At the age of fifteen McEvoy entered the Slade School of Fine Art in London, where he studied under Frederick Brown, and he frequently worked in the National Gallery copying Titian, Rembrandt, Velázquez, Hogarth, and Gainsborough. His close friends at the Slade included Augustus John, with whom he later shared a studio for a short time at 76 Charlotte Street, London. In 1898 he embarked on a stormy affair with John's sister, the painter Gwen *John (1876–1939). Their paintings of this period bear a close similarity, though probably more by virtue of shared interests than of any direct influence on McEvoy's part. In 1900 Gwen John was devastated when McEvoy suddenly announced his engagement to Mary Augusta Spencer Edwards [see below], a fellow Slade student and daughter of Lieutenant-Colonel Henry Hutchins Spencer Edwards of Abbotsleigh, Freshford, Somerset. They were married at Freshford on 16 January 1902. In 1906 they moved to 107 Grosvenor Road on the Embankment, London, where they lived for the rest of their lives. They had a son, Michael, and a daughter, Anna.

McEvoy had been exhibiting his quietist and eclectic small paintings of figures in interiors, such as The Letter (c.1905, Walsall Art Gallery, Staffordshire) and The Earring (1911, Tate collection), at the New English Art Club from 1900. In 1909 he went to Dieppe with Walter Sickert and in the following years his painting began to show signs of the broader, looser treatment which was characteristic of his later work. Following the success of the portrait of his wife, Madame (Musée National d'Art Moderne, Paris), exhibited at the National Portrait Society in 1915, he suddenly found himself in huge demand as a painter of fashionable women, including Consuelo, duchess of Marlborough, and Lady Diana Cooper (both 1916, priv. coll.), and the actress Lillah McCarthy (1919, National Portrait Gallery, London).

His delicate and fluttering brushwork, his experiments in colour, tone, and surface quality, and his device of using mixed daylight and artificial lighting thrown up from below, all give strong individuality to every portrait, even if, like Silver and Grey (Mrs Charles McEvoy 1915; Manchester City Galleries), they are camouflaged by Whistlerian titles. He painted landscapes throughout his career, and watercolours which he would draw and paint solidly, then put under running water, and then scrub and scrape, adding accents in chalk or ink and floating on colours which fused into delicate opalescent harmonies.

In 1916 McEvoy was attached to the Royal Naval division, spent three months on the western front, and later was with the fleet in the North Sea, eventually producing a series of portraits of naval officers now in the Imperial War Museum in London. That he could render masculine qualities successfully is shown also in his striking portraits of Augustine Birrell (1918, National Gallery of Canada, Ottawa) and of his principal patron, Claude Johnson, chairman of Rolls-Royce, who was also responsible for commissioning the strangely reticent portrait of the aviator Sir John Alcock (1919, National Portrait Gallery, London). In 1920 McEvoy was invited to New York to undertake commissions for American patrons and was given a prestigious exhibition at the Duveen Galleries.

At the height of his career McEvoy was painting up to twenty-five oil portraits a year. He was elected an associate of the Royal Academy in 1924, a member of the Royal Society of Portrait Painters in 1924, and an associate of the Royal Society of Painters in Water Colours in 1926. Overwork and over-indulgence soon took its toll and he died of pneumonia at the Empire Nursing Home, Vincent Square, Westminster, London, on 4 January 1927. He was survived by his wife. He was cremated at Golders Green crematorium, Middlesex, on 7 January and his ashes were interred in the wall of All Saints' Church in Grosvenor Road. Of very distinctive appearance, McEvoy was described by his friend William Rothenstein as looking 'like a Pre-Raphaelite, with his strikingly large eyes in a long, angular face; and he spoke in an odd, cracked voice' (W. Rothenstein, *Men and Memories*, 1, 1931, 333–4). As an artist he was often compared in his lifetime with Gainsborough, though a tendency to flashiness in his post-war work did much to destroy his posthumous reputation. His unique contribution to early twentieth-century British painting remains still largely unacknowledged.

Ambrose McEvoy's wife, **Mary Augusta McEvoy** [née Spencer Edwards] (1870–1941), painter, was born in Freshford, Somerset, on 22 October 1870. After leaving the Slade School of Fine Art, London, she exhibited at the New English Art Club between 1900 and 1906 and then virtually abandoned painting until after her husband's death in 1927. She exhibited flower pieces and portraits at the Royal Academy from 1928 until 1937 and died at Abbotsleigh Cottage, Freshford, Somerset, on 4 November 1941. The Tate collection has her *Interior: Girl Reading* (1901) and there are later works in the City Art Gallery, Southampton, and the Hugh Lane Municipal Gallery of Modern Art, Dublin.   MARTIN HARDIE, *rev.* ROBIN GIBSON

Sources *Ambrose McEvoy* (1968) [exhibition catalogue, Ulster Museum, Belfast, 8–28 May 1968] · *Ambrose McEvoy, 1878-1927: paintings and drawings* (1974) [exhibition catalogue, Morley Gallery, London, 21 Feb – 13 April 1974] · M. Chamot, D. Farr, and M. Butlin, *The modern British paintings, drawings and sculpture*, 2 vols. (1964–5) [catalogue, Tate Gallery, London] · *WWW* · *Who's who in art* (1934) · S. Chitty, *Gwen John* (1981) · *The Times* (5–8 Jan 1927) · Wigs, ed., *The work of Ambrose McEvoy* (1923) · C. Johnson, ed., *The works of Ambrose McEvoy from 1900 to May 1919* (privately printed, 1919) · R. M. Y. Gleadowe, *Ambrose McEvoy* (1924) · *CGPLA Eng. & Wales* (1927) · m. cert. · d. cert. [Mary Spencer McEvoy] · private information (1937)

Archives NRA, priv. coll., diaries · Tate collection, corresp. and business papers, diaries, notebooks

Likenesses A. John, chalk drawing, c.1894–1898, NPG · A. John, chalk drawing, c.1900, NPG · A. John, drawing, c.1900, Art Institute of Chicago, Chicago · A. A. McEvoy, self-portrait, pencil-and-pen-and-ink drawing, 1900, Tate collection · A. John, oils, c.1900–1903, Durban Art Gallery, South Africa · A. A. McEvoy, self-portrait, pencil drawing, c.1912, NPG · F. D. Wood, bronze head, 1915, NPG, RA · A. A. McEvoy, self-portrait, oils, 1919, priv. coll. · A. A. McEvoy, self-portrait, oils, 1927, priv. coll. · A. John, oils, Durban Art Gallery, South Africa · W. Orpen, group portrait, oils (*The selecting jury of the New English Art Club, 1909*), NPG · A. Rutherston, pencil drawing, AM Oxf.

Wealth at death £9742 3s. 9d.: resworn probate, 6 April 1927, *CGPLA Eng. & Wales* · £3987 9s. 10d.—Mary Augusta McEvoy: probate, 1942, *CGPLA Eng. & Wales*

McEvoy, Harry (1902–1984), industrialist and food manufacturer, was born on 16 August 1902 in Bradford, the younger of twin sons (there were no other children) of Thomas McEvoy, weaver (later a grocer), and his wife, Polly Taylor, daughter of a Norwegian sea captain. He was educated at Bradford grammar school, and as a young man worked in his father's grocery business in Yorkshire. In 1926 he married Hilda (d. 1979), daughter of Enoch Wood, a Bradford mill owner. They had two daughters.

In his late twenties McEvoy studied at Columbia University, USA, where in 1930 he obtained a degree with distinction in American business methods and administration. In the following year he joined the export division of the American Kellogg Company, manufacturers of cereal foods, and after a year spent learning the business in Canada and the USA, returned to England and worked as assistant to the manager of the new Kellogg Company of Great Britain. In 1934 he was appointed managing director of the company. During the next four years he did much to persuade the British public, normally conservative in their eating habits, to accept packaged cereal foods as a healthy constituent of the British breakfast—not an easy task, as these products were at the outset treated with some suspicion. By 1936 some 400,000 packets of Kellogg's cereals were being sold each week, and it was decided that, in preference to importing them from America, a factory should be opened in Britain.

In 1938 McEvoy chose Stretford, Manchester, as the site for what would become the largest food-processing factory outside the USA. During the Second World War he worked with Frederick James Marquis, earl of Woolton, at the Ministry of Food, and was responsible for setting up the committee which dealt with cereal breakfast foods to ensure that the civilian population was adequately fed, in spite of the destruction of British shipping by German U-boats. The Stretford works continued in production despite near misses from bombing and fires. Output doubled; vast quantities of breakfast foods went to the armed forces, and civilian supplies had to be rationed. When it became impossible to import maize and rice from America and Canada, wheat flakes and bran cereal had to be manufactured from home-grown wheat.

When the war ended McEvoy planned and supervised the extension of the factory in Manchester, overcoming serious difficulties in procuring cement and steel. In 1938 there had been a workforce of 250; by 1968 it had risen to 1700, and the turnover of products being sold in supermarkets and grocery shops throughout Britain had increased eightfold.

McEvoy saw that the breakfast cereals industry needed some centralized organization to deal with problems of common interest, and in particular to provide a forum for consultation and discussion with the government when post-war legislation was under consideration. Together with the directors of other firms dealing in breakfast foods, he was a founder member of the Association of Cereal Food Manufacturers, and was its chairman from its inception in 1955 until his retirement in 1967. In pursuing its interests he played an important part in negotiations between the association and the Board of Trade which led to the inclusion of special provisions covering cereal foods in the Weights and Measures Act of 1963.

During his thirty-three years as managing director of the Kellogg Company of Great Britain McEvoy was the driving force in the extension of the cereal foods industry to western Europe, Scandinavia, and South Africa. According to The Times, 10 November 1984, 'more than any man he influenced the present trend towards a natural cereal-based diet'. A man of dynamic energy, his sense of humour and consideration for others earned him widespread respect and affection. In 1968 the McEvoys retired to Sydney, Australia. Hilda died in Australia in 1979, and in 1983 Harry McEvoy returned to Britain and settled in Douglas, Isle of Man. He died at his home there on 3 November 1984.　　　H. F. OXBURY, rev. CHRISTINE CLARK

Sources *The Times* (10 Nov 1984) · private information (1990) · *The history of the Kellogg Company* (1986)

McEvoy, Mary Augusta (1870–1941). *See under* McEvoy, (Arthur) Ambrose (1878–1927).

McEvoy, Sir Theodore Neuman (1904–1991), air force officer, was born on 21 November 1904 at 3 Claremont Road, Cricklewood, Middlesex, the second son and youngest of three children of the Revd Cuthbert McEvoy (1870–1944), Congregational minister, and his wife, Margaret Kate (1871–1961), daughter of John Birt Ulph and his wife, Laura Louise Daniell. Advances in aviation during the First World War attracted the teenage McEvoy to flying. Also, his much loved elder brother was an air 'ace' on the Italian front, transferring later to the newly formed Royal Air Force. The new service's cadet college at Cranwell opened in 1920, but the fees were prohibitive amounting to half McEvoy's father's stipend. After leaving Haberdashers' Aske's School in May 1922, McEvoy started overhauling aero engines at the Aircraft Disposal Co. near Croydon, hoping that the work would lead to flying lessons. However, his qualities were recognized at the firm and he was encouraged to try again for the RAF. His failure of a cadet test was challenged and the War Office found he had in fact passed with high marks. Benevolent relatives then offered to pay for a crammer course and, if necessary,

Cranwell's fees. From the Kensington Coaching College, McEvoy gained first place into Cranwell (or Sandhurst had he wished), winning a full scholarship.

Aircraft between the wars were by present-day standards much affected by weather and regular engine failure. However, they could be landed in any suitable field, which was fortunate for McEvoy, who survived nine forced landings, two while he was still training. Graduating with the sword of honour, he served his apprenticeship in front-line fighter squadrons on his way to becoming an exceptional fighter pilot and taking part in the Hendon air pageant with 41 squadron. At this time McEvoy began to suffer pain from a progressive and crippling disease of the spine which eventually fused, giving him a pronounced stoop. That he was able to continue piloting until his retirement despite this permanent affliction reflected his determination and the flexibility of medical and air staffs who recognized his value to the service.

A two-year engineering course developed McEvoy's analytical and logical skills and allowed time for sport; he became the RAF sabre champion. Next came a two-year posting to Iraq in charge of the aircraft servicing depot, where he tested aircraft and was involved in technical development and parachute trials. He also flew with 55 bomber squadron carrying out air control of the fractious tribes in the area. On the ship returning from UK leave he met Marian Jane Benson (b. 1913), daughter of William Alfred Coxon, a medical practitioner working in Egypt. They married on 17 September 1935.

The period of mounting tension as the Second World War approached saw McEvoy at the peak of his piloting skills in two élite squadrons—1 and 43—at Tangmere. In 1937 he widened his experience at the RAF Staff College. His two children, Jill (b. 1938) and Robin (b. 1940), saw less of their father than they would have liked as the intensity of the war increased. His considerable flying experience led to his transfer to the Air Ministry in operational and intelligence posts, from which he emerged in 1941 as a group captain to command the fighter station at Northolt with its Polish squadrons. True to form, he flew with the squadrons when shortage of pilots justified, and on a 'sweep' over France was wounded by cannon fire, managing to nurse his damaged Hurricane back to the English coast. Appointed OBE, he was also recognized by the Poles for his moral and practical support for their pilots by his appointment as a commander of the order of Polonia Restituta.

Inevitably McEvoy's staff appointments reflected his background of fighter operations. As senior air staff officer of 11 fighter group, and of 84 group in the Tactical Air Force, formed to support the invasion of Europe, he had ample scope for his administrative skills, particularly in the entirely new organization of mixed-role squadrons in the tactical groups. Planning and supervising the achievement of air superiority over the bridgehead, and the subsequent move of squadrons to the temporary landing grounds on the continental toehold, McEvoy moved with the victorious armies until virtually the end of the war. By now an air commodore, he was mentioned in dispatches for his part in the success of the Tactical Air Force and advanced to CBE in the victory honours. From now on increasingly senior staff appointments were inevitable, although he made every effort to keep in flying practice, which maintained the confidence and respect of those he commanded. After the course in 1948 at the Imperial Defence College came command of 61 group involving the reserve units of the RAF, particularly the squadrons of the Royal Auxiliary Air Force, whose Spitfires he was well qualified to fly.

Promoted to air vice marshal in 1950 as assistant chief of the air staff (training), McEvoy convinced the service of the need to adopt all-jet-engined flying training, in spite of the cost and the high ability required of the cadets. In the post-war era this helped the RAF to maintain professional excellence as the majority of experienced pilots were demobilized; this was recognized by his appointment as CB. Following two years as an instructor at the Imperial Defence College came a return to Europe as chief of staff of allied air forces, central Europe. This involved air planning for the event of a Soviet attack on the central front and ensuring that NATO squadrons based there were at the highest level of efficiency. Promoted to air marshal and knighted (KCB) in 1956, he epitomized the concept of deterrence—'being ready, able and willing to fight so as not to have to do so'. The last three years until McEvoy retired in 1962 were spent as air secretary and as an air aide-de-camp to the queen. The former involved identifying and grooming 'high flyers' in the service (its future leaders) as well as filling the day-to-day senior appointments, where his understanding of people made him an ideal choice for this task.

Retirement in Buckinghamshire gave McEvoy the opportunity to continue flying—this time in gliders. He attained a considerable facility at this sport and became vice-president of the British Gliding Association. The precision he had learnt as an engineer and his co-ordination of hand and eye produced a skilled calligrapher, glass engraver, and golfer. His anti-communist stance through the organization Common Cause enabled him to expose the myths of this political system, and he lived to see the ultimate collapse of the USSR. He died at his home, Hurstwood, West Drive, Aldwick Bay Estate, Bognor Regis, on 28 September 1991; his wife survived him. After cremation at Chichester crematorium his ashes were interred in Tangmere churchyard.   FREDERICK SOWREY

Sources RAF officers record of service, RAF Personnel and Training Command, Gloucester · personal knowledge (2004) · private information (2004) [Robin McEvoy, son] · *WWW*, 1991–5 · *The Times* (3 Oct 1991) · d. cert.
Likenesses group portrait, *c.*1960, Royal Air Force, Cranwell · portrait, repro. in *The Times*; copies, priv. coll.
Wealth at death £105,823: probate, 23 Jan 1992, *CGPLA Eng. & Wales*

MacEwan, (Alfred) Sydney Marley (1908–1991), singer and Roman Catholic priest, was born on 19 October 1908 at 130 Keppockhill Road, Glasgow, the younger of the two sons of John Smith MacEwan, commercial traveller, and

his wife, Jane (*née* Marley). His father left the family when Sydney was very young, and when he was five, although the family lived in Springburn, he was given permission to attend St Saviour's School, Govan, where his Irish mother taught. Aged twelve (his brother having put his name forward), he won the sum of 5*s.* singing in a talent competition in Dunoon. In 1920 he entered St Aloysius's (Jesuit) College in Garnethill, where he was unhappy, partly because Latin was not taught. He attended evening classes for violin and singing, as well as Latin, before making a happy move to Hillhead High, a protestant school where he and his brother were the only two Catholic pupils. His 'intense affection' for the church led him to study for the priesthood, and in 1925 he entered the Jesuit noviciate at Manresa House, Roehampton, London, where conversation was in Latin except at recreation. After finding himself unsuited to his calling, he left after six months and was admitted to Glasgow University in October 1926. At about this time he sang for the first time as a tenor and was taught by Mr Reid at The Athenaeum, the city of Glasgow's school of music. He was afterwards to describe Reid as 'the finest teacher in all my experience' (MacEwan, 90). He graduated MA and spent one year in teacher training at Jordanhill College, with music as his special subject. Aged twenty-two he entered the Royal Academy of Music in London, where he was taught by Sir Henry Wood, John Barbirolli, and Harry Plunkett-Greene. An unknown benefactor (widely thought to have been Compton McKenzie) paid his fees.

In 1932 MacEwan signed a recording contract with Parlophone which lasted more than thirty years. Compton McKenzie, whom he had met in Glasgow, arranged for the celebrated tenor John McCormack to hear him; McCormack later asked MacEwan to sing for him in Dublin just before he died, and bequeathed him the black notebook in which he recorded the words of his songs, and his prayer book. On 17 March 1936 MacEwan sailed on the *Tamaroa* with Duncan Morison (1902/3–1998), his accompanist, for a tour of New Zealand sponsored by the New Zealand Broadcasting Corporation; this was so successful it was extended to Australia. Tours followed to Canada and the USA, with a repertory of mainly Scottish and Irish folk songs, including 'Bonnie earl of Moray', 'Believe me if all those endearing young charms', and 'Ho-ro my nut-brown maiden'. Following a hurricane on a ship from Honolulu to Canada, MacEwan made a decision to become a priest. This decision was kept secret while the remainder of his concert obligations were discharged. In 1938 MacEwan entered the Scots College, Rome, which he later described as 'a gay, jolly eventful place' (MacEwan, 192). His three-year course was cut to two, and he was able to travel home each summer.

When the Second World War broke out, MacEwan was in South Uist and was not able to return to Rome, attending instead a seminary at Bearsden, Glasgow. He was ordained on 24 June 1944 in St Andrew's Cathedral, Glasgow, and the following day, before a packed attendance, celebrated his first mass in St Aloysius's, Garnethill, remembered by many for years afterwards. An ailing John

McCormack sent a telegram to mark the occasion. MacEwan's appointment as curate at St Andrew's prompted radio news all over the world, and an hour of Sydney MacEwan records was played on Australian radio. In carrying out his duties as a priest he was surprised to find 40 per cent of parishioners not practising their faith, and described himself as 'daily face to face with abject poverty' (MacEwan, 209). Processions of fans had to be turned away, and he received visitors only on parish business. In 1948 he flew to Melbourne to represent the bishops at the centenary of the Melbourne archdiocese, where he met both Cardinal Spellman and Eamon de Valera, celebrated many masses, and gave a series of concerts (extended from a planned three to fifteen). On his return he asked to be released from the cathedral and be sent to Lochgilphead on Loch Fyne, Argyll, where he remained for the next seventeen years, commuting regularly to London to sing for the BBC and to attend recording sessions. During a tour of Australia (accompanied by his mother) he suffered from nervous exhaustion and was admitted to hospital in Perth. He continued to America and as a result donated a cheque for 'thousands of pounds' to the church. In 1954, 1955, and 1956, he toured America where he attended many society dinner parties and on one occasion met the young John F. Kennedy.

MacEwan was anxious to promote 'real' folk music, rather than synthetic 'popular' tunes, and always refused to sing 'When Irish eyes are smiling', although often requested to do so, especially in the United States. His versions of 'She moved through the fair' and 'The lark in the clear air' were particularly well received. He recorded a mass in Rome (at 3 a.m. because of street noise) but the result was never issued in the UK. He was unhappy with an edition of *This is your Life* which he described as a 'trivial little cameo' (MacEwan, 306). His mother died at the age of eighty-nine but, as the death occurred in Holy Week, she was denied the requiem mass he had promised her.

Earlier in his life MacEwan had suffered from Ménière's disease, and when this worsened he spent several months in the kinder climate of Malaga. After recovering somewhat, he returned to become the parish priest in Kingussie in Speyside. He died of renal failure and acute pancreatitis in the Southern General Hospital, Glasgow, on 25 September 1991. In his introduction to MacEwan's autobiography, *On the High C's (a Light-Hearted Journey)*, published in 1973, Compton Mackenzie wrote 'At this time [the 1950s], he was the greatest living interpreter of Celtic music', and indeed his reception at the docks on his various tours to America was more akin to that usually accorded to film or pop stars.   KATHERINE MANVILLE

Sources S. MacEwan, *On the high C's (a light-hearted journey)* (1973) · b. cert. · *The Times* (2 Nov 1991) · *The Scotsman* (27 Sept 1991) · *Glasgow Herald* (27 Sept 1991) · d. cert.
Archives SOUND BL NSA, performance recordings
Wealth at death £47,543.22: confirmation, 1991, Scotland

McEwan, William (1827–1913), brewer and politician, was born at Alloa, Scotland, on 16 July 1827, the third of five children (two daughters and three sons) of John McEwan, a local shipowner, and his wife, Anne Jeffrey, whose father

William McEwan (1827–1913), by Walter William Ouless, exh. RA 1901

was a farmer at Throsk on the other side of the River Forth. Alloa had a thriving harbour and industries, including malting, brewing, distilling, glass making, and textiles. McEwan's father was a partner in a small shipping enterprise from 1814, and when he died in 1832, he left shares in four vessels. The executors maintained an interest in one vessel, named the *Fame*, to provide an income for the family. A new *Fame*, a schooner of 85 tons, was built in 1835. Later, in 1852, the partnership acquired two other vessels, but the business remained modest and did not offer any employment opportunity to McEwan.

After attending Alloa Academy, McEwan went to work at the offices of the Alloa Coal Company in 1843. Seeking to improve himself, he moved two years later to Glasgow, where he joined a firm of merchants, Patersons, as a clerk, at a salary of £30 per annum. He found this post uncongenial and spent his spare time improving his education by attending lectures at the university, and visiting the theatre. After two and a half years, McEwan was offered a job in offices in Huddersfield, but on arriving there found he was not to be engaged as a cashier in the commercial department, but as a clerk in a spinning mill at Honley, which in his diary he described as a 'village without society' (Topen, 35). Nevertheless, his salary was enhanced, first to £70 and then to £100.

McEwan's eldest sister, Janet (*b.* 1823), married James Younger, of the Alloa brewing family, in 1850; other family connections also proved useful. In 1851 McEwan began five years' technical and management training with his uncle, John Jeffrey, who since 1835 had been proprietor of the Heriot brewery, Edinburgh. By 1856 his brewing apprenticeship was completed, and, using family and borrowed capital, he established his own business at the Fountain brewery, near the eastern terminus of the Union Canal and adjacent to the Caledonian Railway.

With the rapid expansion of the brewing industry after the late 1850s working in his favour, McEwan was remarkably successful. Within four years his turnover was reported to be in the region of £40,000 per annum. Taking advantage of cheaper and more efficient transport, he penetrated markets in Glasgow and the west of Scotland, and this proved so successful that the area soon accounted for more than half McEwan's trade. The firm also sold widely in central and northern Scotland, established a foothold on Tyneside, and during the 1860s built up a profitable trade further afield in the British colonies—hence the origin of one of its most famous products, McEwan's Export ale. These initiatives proved so successful that the business soon rivalled longer-established Scottish competitors.

In 1874, McEwan's nephew, William Younger, began an apprenticeship with his uncle, and after its completion played an increasingly important role in the firm. When, in 1886, McEwan entered parliament, Younger became manager. His effectiveness evidently matched that of his uncle, for the average annual profit between 1885 and 1889 was £92,000 and, when registered in 1889, William McEwan & Co. was reported to be worth £408,000. The company, with Younger as managing director, had a capital of £1 million, with all of the ordinary, and the bulk of the preference, shares being held by McEwan and his family.

Devoting himself increasingly to politics, McEwan, a Gladstonian Liberal, held the Edinburgh Central seat from 1886 until 1900. Although a highly regarded constituency MP, who even managed to gain support from the temperance lobby, McEwan seems to have been happy to confine himself to the back benches in the House of Commons, except when he generated controversy by demanding government action on Irish home rule. It was a measure of his popularity in Edinburgh that at the general election in 1895 he was returned unopposed. He is said to have declined a title, remarking, 'No, I would rather be first in my own order, than be at the tail end of another', indicating his personal pride as a successful self-made businessman (Donnachie, *DSBB*, 43). He was made a privy councillor in 1907.

Apart from his association with the firm and product which still bear his name, William McEwan was a notable philanthropist, who made gifts both to the nation and to the city of Edinburgh. He acquired a valuable art collection and presented paintings to the National Gallery of Scotland. The splendid McEwan Hall at the University of Edinburgh was built (to the design of Sir Robert Rowand Anderson) at a cost to McEwan of £115,000, plus £6500 per annum for maintenance. When the hall was opened in 1897 McEwan was made an honorary LLD and presented with the freedom of the city of Edinburgh. He was a deputy lieutenant of Edinburgh for thirty years. His last

home, Polesden Lacey, Surrey, was ultimately bequeathed to the National Trust by his only child, Margaret Anderson, who later became better-known as Dame Margaret *Greville (1863–1942), the noted socialite and friend of royalty. McEwan had married her mother, Helen Anderson (1835/6–1906), widow of William Anderson, day porter at McEwan's brewery, in 1885.

McEwan died in London, at 16 Charles Street, Mayfair, on 12 May 1913, aged eighty-five, and was buried at Great Bookham, Surrey. His total estate was valued at £1.5 million, an enormous sum for the time, representing his share in the firm, and investments in other industrial, railway, and mining enterprises, both in Britain and overseas. McEwan was undoubtedly one of the most successful brewers of his generation who, by good fortune, entered the industry when it was undergoing a dramatic period of expansion. One obituary described him as 'a shrewd, hard headed, hard working businessman … one of the merchant princes of Scotland' who built up his firm from 'small beginnings to huge dimensions and world wide reputation' (Donnachie, *DSBB*). This was a fitting tribute to McEwan's enterprise and energy.   IAN DONNACHIE

Sources I. Donnachie, 'McEwan, William', *DSBB* · I. Donnachie, *A history of the brewing industry in Scotland* (1979) · A. Topen, 'William McEwan: the early years', *Scottish Brewing Archive Newsletter*, no. 23 (1994), 31–9 · J. Dallas and C. McMaster, *The beer drinker's companion* (1993) · J. Lloyd Williams, 'Ale, altruism and art: the benefactions of William McEwan', *Apollo*, 139 (May 1994), 47–53 · d. cert. · W. McEwan, notebooks and diaries
Archives U. Glas., Archives and Business Records Centre, Scottish Brewing Archive, William McEwan & Co. Ltd MSS | Polesden Lacey, Great Bookham, Surrey, papers/artefacts
Likenesses bust, 1885, Polesden Lacey, Surrey · W. W. Ouless, oils, exh. RA 1901, priv. coll. [*see illus.*] · photograph, 1907, Polesden Lacey, Surrey · photograph, *c.*1910, U. Glas., Archives and Business Record Centre, Scottish Brewing Archive · portrait, Polesden Lacey, Surrey
Wealth at death £1,501,250 18s. 11d.: confirmation, 22 July 1913, *CCI* · £35,208 17s. 2d.: eik additional estate, 17 Feb 1914, *CCI*

McEwen, Francis Jack [Frank] (1907–1994), art gallery director and promoter of British and African art, was born on 19 April 1907 in Mexico. His father was a British mining engineer; his mother was French. He spent much of his childhood in Devon, where he acquired a lifelong love of the sea; he was also impressed by carvings obtained by his father in west Africa. In 1921 he went to Mill Hill School, and in 1926 he began studying art history in Paris. Henri Focillon stimulated his interest in 'primitive' art, and also enabled him to meet Brancusi, Braque, Matisse, Picasso, and Léger. McEwen's decision to become a painter caused a breach with his father, and from 1928 he had to support himself, mainly by painting and picture restoration; in 1939 he started an artists' workshop in Toulon. A relationship with the painter Frances Wood (1899–1984) resulted in the birth of a son, but ended in or before 1937. When the Germans invaded France in 1940, McEwen escaped in a fishing boat to Algiers. Late in 1942, on the strength of his local contacts, he joined allied headquarters.

In January 1945, soon after the British Council established itself in Paris, McEwen was appointed fine arts officer. His pre-war friendships with artists and museum directors proved invaluable in organizing exhibitions in Paris of Henry Moore, Blake, Turner, Graham Sutherland, and Ben Nicholson; he was also involved in London exhibitions of modern French painting, and selected that at the Royal Academy in 1951. McEwen's contribution to British–French cultural understanding was highly esteemed by the British Council's fine arts committee, but from 1951 financial constraints caused the council to curtail its activities in France. By 1954 it was clear that McEwen could not expect to continue his work in Paris, and in any case his heart was no longer in it; he did not care for the latest trends in French painting.

At this juncture McEwen was invited to advise on the creation of a national art gallery in Salisbury, Southern Rhodesia. He was not impressed by this buoyant but distinctly philistine colony run by white settlers. The chairman of the gallery's trustees, Stephen Courtauld, assumed that it should acquire old masters. McEwen argued that the gallery could prosper only on the basis of exchanges, which meant offering locally produced art, and of this there seemed nothing worth attention. (He was always scathing about so-called 'airport art'.) Nevertheless, when the post of director was advertised, he applied, encouraged by Picasso as well as the art critic Herbert Read. He got the job, resigned from the British Council in 1955, and spent much of the next year sailing a yacht to Cape Town by way of Brazil.

When McEwen reached Salisbury, the gallery building (designed with his advice by modernist British architects) was unfinished, but he soon put the gallery on the world art map. In 1957 it displayed a loan exhibition, 'Rembrandt to Picasso', assembled from leading public collections in Europe. From 1956 to 1966 McEwen was married to Cecilia Nel, a mosaicist. During these years he began to help Africans discover their own talents as painters and especially as sculptors in local soapstone and serpentine. (In this enterprise, he followed the teaching practice of the symbolist Gustave Moreau.) This new art was often inspired by Shona beliefs in ancestral spirits. To Western eyes, this work might seem to resemble that of European artists such as Brancusi, but McEwen denied any such influence and instead stressed the impact of African art on the pioneers of cubism and abstraction. In any event, he was able to use his European contacts to arrange exhibitions and sales for Shona art abroad as well as at home. It was prominently displayed at the International Congress of African Culture held in Salisbury in 1962, and was shown in London in 1963. Commercial success reconciled gallery trustees unsympathetic to African art, and meanwhile McEwen's achievements were recognized in Britain by his appointment as OBE in 1963.

Despite his work with Africans, and his ebullient personality, McEwen sought to avoid overt political commitment, but after Southern Rhodesia unilaterally declared independence in 1965 he was officially said to have gone on sick leave—during which he adjudicated an all-African art exhibition in Dakar. He returned to Southern Rhodesia, and in 1969, with his new wife, Mary McFadden, established a new artists' workshop at Vukutu, in the eastern highlands. Shona carvings were shown in the United States in 1968, at the Musée Rodin in Paris in 1970–71, and in London in 1972. However, political tensions and waning government support induced McEwen to resign in 1973. With (Margaret) Ann Moseley, an art gallery employee whom he married in 1971, he spent more than a decade living on a yacht and sailing between the Mediterranean and Brazil. In 1986 the McEwens settled at Ilfracombe on the north Devon coast, and it was there that McEwen died on 15 January 1994. He was survived by his wife, Ann.

McEwen was not the only, or even the first, white person to encourage African artists in Southern Rhodesia, but his long experience in France enabled him to make their work known to the world at large, and he set standards of quality which helped to ensure that the skills he nurtured survived in independent Zimbabwe.   A. D. ROBERTS

Sources *The Times* (17 Jan 1994) · W. Shaw, 'Frank McEwen', *New Horizons* [British Council Retirement Association], 54 (autumn 1994), 27–9 · 'Profile: Frank McEwen', *Central African Examiner* (27 Feb 1960), 13–4 · B. Joosten, *Sculptors from Zimbabwe: the first generation* (Dodewaard, Netherlands, 2001), 16–22 · J. Russell, 'The challenge of African Art', *Apollo* (Nov 1962), 697–701 · M. Peppiatt, 'Shona sculpture: an African Renaissance', *Art International*, 16/3 (20 March 1972), 20–21, 62–3 · F. McEwen, 'In search of art in Rhodesia', *Horizon* (June 1960), 28–34 · F. McEwen, 'Art promotes racial understanding', *Museum News* [Washington DC], 39/10 (1961), 36–9 · F. McEwen, 'The National Gallery of Salisbury and its workshop school', *Museum* [UNESCO], 16/3 (1963), 174–7 · private information (2004) · d. cert.

Archives BM, department of ethnography · BM, department of ethnography, publications and artefacts (African art) · British Council, London · National Archives of Zimbabwe, Harare

Likenesses photograph, 1971, BM; repro. in J. Mack, ed., *Africa: arts and cultures* (2000), 209 · photograph, 1993, repro. in *Southern African encounter*, 1/3 (July 1994), 17 · photograph, repro. in *The Times*

Wealth at death under £125,000: probate, 22 Feb 1994, *CGPLA Eng. & Wales*

McEwen, Sir John Blackwood (1868–1948), composer and college head, was born on 13 April 1868 at East Bank manse, Hawick, Roxburghshire, the son of James McEwen, United Presbyterian minister of Sydney Place Church, and his wife, Jane Blackwood. After obtaining his MA at Glasgow University in 1888, McEwen studied music while holding choirmasterships, first at St James's Free Church and subsequently at Lanark parish church. In 1891 he travelled to London where he attended the Royal Academy of Music (1893–5) to study under Frederick Corder, Tobias Matthay, and Ebenezer Prout. Returning to Scotland in 1895 he settled in Greenock as choirmaster of South parish church and he taught composition and piano at the Athenaeum School of Music in Glasgow. In 1898 he was invited by Sir A. C. Mackenzie to become a professor of harmony and composition at the Royal Academy of Music.

By the time of his employment at the Royal Academy of Music, McEwen had completed a sizeable corpus of work—three student symphonies (now missing), a string quartet (no. 1), an overture, two choral works, and a symphony in A minor—exhibiting his considerable ambitions as a composer. His first public performance, of the string quartet no. 1 (1893), took place in 1894, and other works—the *Scene from Hellas* (1894), to words by Shelley, and the *Overture to a Comedy* (1894), given under Corder—brought his name before the public. Later works continued to raise his profile, notably the viola concerto (1901) written for Lionel Tertis, and (with a distinctive Caledonian orientation) two *Border Ballads*: 'Coronach' (1906) and 'Grey Galloway' (1908). On 20 December 1902 he married Hedwig Ethel Cole (1878/9–1949), daughter of Henry Alwyn Bevan Cole, naval architect. They had no children. His best-known work, the *Solway Symphony*, was composed in 1911, but it remained unperformed until it received an award from the Carnegie Trust, who published it in 1921. Soon afterwards, on 12 October 1922, it was given the first of at least six hearings under Dan Godfrey at Bournemouth and its first performance in London at the Philharmonic Society, under Eugene Goossens (22 February 1923). In 1923 it was the first British symphony to receive a complete recording (by the Aeolian Orchestra under Cuthbert Whitemore for Vocalion). Other works remained unperformed during his lifetime, including the large-scale *Hymn on the Morning of Christ's Nativity* (1901–5); the first *Border Ballad*, 'The Demon Lover' (1906–7); *Hills o'Heather* for cello and orchestra (1918); and *Where the Wild Thyme Blows* (1936). Though he maintained that he learned most from artistic fraternization with fellow student-composers Hermann Löhr, Charles Macpherson, and particularly his future brother-in-law, William H. Bell, McEwen shows an indebtedness, particularly in his orchestral work, to the highly coloured, post-Wagnerian palette of Strauss, Skryabin, and the late French Romantics such as Chausson, Dukas, and Charpentier (much endorsed by his teacher, Corder), a late-Romantic propensity that even extended to 'Sprechgesang' in the *Fourteen Poems* for 'inflected voice' and piano (1943). By comparison, his vast output of chamber music—including no less than seventeen string quartets written between 1893 and 1947—reveals a creative mind disposed towards more abstract, polyphonic thought.

Seemingly unconcerned about the dissemination of his own works, McEwen nevertheless did much to further the cause of British music and composers, notably as a prominent member of the Philharmonic Society after the war. He was also a founder member, first honorary secretary, and one of the chief promoters (along with Corder) of the Society of British Composers (1905–18) and of the Avison edition. As a teacher he exercised a liberal aesthetic outlook among his pupils and produced various influential textbooks including *The Elements of Music* (1910), *The Thought in Music* (1912), and *The Foundations of Musical Aesthetics* (1917), as well as primers on harmony and counterpoint. Moreover, he helped found the Anglo-French Music Publishing Company in 1916 in order to produce educational music in lieu of German publications stemmed by the war. Radically egalitarian in his views, he also produced a series of outspoken pamphlets—*Abolish Money*

and *Total Democracy*—that reveal his left-wing inclinations.

In 1924 McEwen succeeded Mackenzie as principal of the Royal Academy of Music, a position he held until 1936. Honours soon followed including an honorary DMus at Oxford (1926), a knighthood (1931), the presidency of the Incorporated Society of Musicians, honorary membership of the University of Helsinki, and an honorary LLD at Glasgow (1933). On his death at his home, 25 Abercorn Place, St John's Wood, London, on 14 June 1948 he left a substantial legacy for the promotion of new Scottish chamber music, his copyright, and the vast bulk of his manuscripts to the University of Glasgow. JEREMY DIBBLE

Sources H. G. Farmer, *A history of music in Scotland* (1948) · *DNB* · H. C. Colles, Grove, *Dict. mus.* (1927) · *New Grove* · C. Ehrlich, *First philharmonic: a history of the Royal Philharmonic Society* (1995) · b. cert. · m. cert. · d. cert.
Archives Royal Academy of Music, London, MSS · U. Glas. | FILM Royal Academy of Music, London
Likenesses R. G. Eves, oils, Royal Academy of Music, London · photographs, Royal Academy of Music, London · photographs, U. Glas., McEwen archive
Wealth at death £7074 15s. 4d.: probate, 9 Sept 1948, *CGPLA Eng. & Wales*

M'Ewen, William (1735–1762), Associate Synod minister, was born at Perth and studied theology under Ebenezer Erskine at Stirling and James Fisher at Glasgow. In 1753 he was licensed to preach by the Associate Presbytery of Dunfermline, and in 1754 he was ordained minister of the Associate congregation in Dundee. He died suddenly of a violent fever at Leith on 13 January 1762, only two days after marrying the eldest daughter of John Wardlaw, a merchant from Dalkeith. He was buried in Dalkeith churchyard. His contemporaries lamented him as a man of great promise struck down in his prime. M'Ewen's fame rests largely on two posthumous writings, *Grace and Truth* (1763), an exposition of the typology of the Old Testament, and *A Select Set of Essays, Doctrinal and Practical* (2 vols., 1767), which covers the main themes of Christian doctrine. Both works were edited by John Patison, minister of Edinburgh's Bristo Associate congregation, who also wrote a memoir of M'Ewen, prefixed to various editions of M'Ewen's works.

GORDON GOODWIN, *rev.* N. R. NEEDHAM

Sources J. Patison, preface, in W. M'Ewen, *A select set of essays, doctrinal and practical*, 1 (1767), ix–cv · J. M'Kerrow, *History of the Secession church*, rev. edn (1841) · R. Small, *History of the congregations of the United Presbyterian church from 1733 to 1900*, 2 vols. (1904) · N. R. Needham, 'McEwen, William', *DSCHT*

Macewen, Sir William (1848–1924), surgeon, was born at Woodend, a cottage near Port Bannatyne on the Isle of Bute, Scotland, on 22 June 1848, the youngest of twelve children of John Macewen (*b.* 1794), a ship's master, and his wife, Janet, *née* Stevenson. He was educated at a local school in Rothesay, and, after the family moved to Glasgow in 1860, at the collegiate school in Garnethill. A tall and athletic youth, he excelled in the gymnasium and at single stick and fencing, while showing sufficient academic talents to encourage him to go on to university.

Sir William Macewen (1848–1924), by T. & R. Annan & Sons

Macewen studied medicine at the University of Glasgow from 1865 to 1869 and graduated MB, CM. He attended the lectures of Joseph Lister, the regius professor of surgery, and acted as his dresser in the wards of the Glasgow Royal Infirmary. Like most of his fellow students, he was profoundly influenced by Lister's work on antisepsis. After graduating in 1869 Macewen served for one year as a house surgeon and house physician at the infirmary. He assisted Lister on at least one occasion, before the latter left in 1869 to become professor of clinical surgery at the University of Edinburgh. Macewen's first venture into print was a report, 'A case of transfusion under the care of Mr Lister', which was published in the *Glasgow Medical Journal* in November 1869.

In the winter of 1870–71 Macewen became the first resident medical officer at the Belvidere Fever Hospital, Glasgow, then under construction. The superintendent of the existing fever hospital, James Burn Russell, reported that Macewen 'gave his whole soul to the work, and manifested great self-reliance and genuine administrative ability' (Russell, 11). In 1871 he became casualty surgeon at the central police division as well as a district medical officer, at the same time as he began to build a flourishing private practice in the city. In 1873 he married Mary Watson Allen, daughter of Hugh Allen, of Crosshill, Glasgow, and the sister of his friend James Allen; they were to have three sons and three daughters. Also in 1873 Macewen became dispensary surgeon at the Western Infirmary, and he moved to Glasgow Royal Infirmary in that capacity two years later. In 1876 he became a teacher of forensic medicine at

the infirmary's medical school, and he subsequently became teacher of surgery in 1881, and professor of clinical surgery in 1888 after the medical school was superseded by St Mungo's College. He was also appointed one of the five visiting surgeons at the infirmary.

During his eighteen years at the Glasgow Royal Infirmary, Macewen became one of Britain's most famous surgeons. The foundation of his success lay in the development, from the early 1870s, of an effective aseptic procedure, which greatly reduced the risk of infection in surgical wounds. Macewen, aware of the limitations of antiseptic dressings, insisted that the exposed skin of the surgeon, patient, and theatre staff was cleaned before an operation began, in order to exclude bacteria from the surgical wound. He wore a sterilizable white gown in the theatre, at a time when many other surgeons continued to operate in old coats or in their shirtsleeves. Macewen also redesigned and re-equipped an operating room at the infirmary, and he used all-steel instruments of his own design which, like the ligatures, dressings, and other theatre equipment, were sterilized before each operation.

The development of a strict and highly successful aseptic procedure enabled Macewen to devise operating techniques for cases in which it had been considered too dangerous to perform surgery in the past. He began his pioneering work in brain surgery in 1879, when he became reputedly the first surgeon to remove a brain tumour and to operate on a subdural haemorrhage. Recognizing that disease of the middle ear was a cause of abscess of the brain, Macewen devised successful methods of operating on cases of mastoid disease. During the 1880s he also had some success with operations on the spinal cord.

Having demonstrated that bone grew from bone and not from the periosteum, as had been generally believed, Macewen was able to revolutionize the practice of bone surgery. He introduced a procedure for implanting grafts to replace missing sections of limb bones, and in 1879 he conducted a bone transplant, presenting a paper on the subject to the Royal Society in 1881. By 1884 he could report on 1800 operations he had performed to remove parts of bones or joints, without a single case of postoperative infection.

In 1887, disturbed by the prevalence of genu valgum (caused by rickets) among poor children in Glasgow, Macewen introduced a procedure to correct the patient's deformity by breaking the leg bones and straightening them. The operation became known as Macewen's osteotomy, and he designed his own wedge-like steel instrument—Macewen's osteotome—for the purpose. Macewen was also a pioneer of a procedure to open up the chest to surgical procedure, having proved to his satisfaction that this would not lead to the collapse of the lung, and he successfully resected the lung. Among his other successes were the development of an operating procedure for the cure of inguinal hernia, and the introduction of a process for intubating the larynx in order to keep the airway open. In 1880 Macewen published *On Osteotomy*, a study of the etiology, pathology, and surgical treatment of the bone deformities of rickets. The book met with universal acclaim, and established for Macewen an international reputation as a surgeon—a reputation reinforced by his address, 'The surgery of the brain and spinal cord', to the British Association, in 1888. Subsequent publications included *Pyogenic Infectious Diseases of the Brain and Spinal Cord* (1893), *Atlas of Head Sections* (1893), and *The Growth of Bone* (1912), which were greeted with acclaim by the world's leading surgeons.

The development of advanced surgical operation techniques, particularly in relation to cerebrospinal surgery, required careful pre-operative diagnosis and prolonged post-operative care by dedicated and trained nursing staff. At the Glasgow Royal Infirmary Macewen was assisted by the matron, Rebecca Strong, who was willing to assign nurses to his wards for longer periods than to the wards of the other surgeons. Macewen trained the nurses to observe and report accurately on the condition of patients, and he readily acknowledged their role in his achievements at the infirmary: in August 1884 he wrote to Mrs Strong, 'you are so mixed up with everything I do in the surgery way. I look on you and the nurses as part of myself, and any honour which might be conferred on me as something which should be shared in Glasgow' (Macewen to Strong, Aug 1884, Royal College of Physicians and Surgeons). Mrs Strong shared his belief that nursing should be recognized as a profession, with its own rigorous examinations and with standardized qualifications. She helped him to devise the curriculum for the world's first preliminary training school for nurses, which was introduced at the infirmary in 1893.

In 1889 Macewen had been offered the chair of surgery at Johns Hopkins University, in the USA. He had declined the post. In 1892 he succeeded George B. Macleod as regius professor of surgery at the University of Glasgow and was appointed a visiting surgeon at the Western Infirmary. His relations with the board of managers and the medical superintendent at the Western were often strained, as Macewen was impatient of bureaucracy and refused to follow regulations he considered petty or restrictive. However, the university chair gave him the opportunity to pursue his research, and his lectures and teaching influenced a generation of surgeons.

Macewen taught his students the importance of independent research, building on Lister's teachings on the value of careful deduction based on observation and experiment, and he refused to accept received medical opinion unless it could be proved in practice. His own research was painstaking and generally undertaken alone, for Macewen was not a 'team player' and had not the patience nor the capacity to delegate work. However, although he did not found his own 'school' of surgeons, his publications and teaching made a profound impression on the thinking of Glasgow students such as J. Hogarth Pringle, who spread Macewen's philosophy of scientific surgery throughout the United Kingdom and beyond.

As one of the greatest surgeons of his day, Macewen was the recipient of many honours. In 1890 Glasgow University conferred on him the degree of LLD. Other honorary degrees were conferred on him by English and Irish universities; he was also honoured by surgical societies and academies in Europe and the USA. Macewen was elected a fellow of the Royal Society in 1895, and an honorary fellow of the Royal College of Surgeons in 1900. In 1909 he was appointed honorary surgeon to the king; he served as surgeon-general in Scotland, and during the First World War he became surgeon-general to the fleet in Scotland, with the rank of rear-admiral. Macewen was also a member of the committee which was responsible for opening the Princess Louise Scottish Hospital for Limbless Soldiers and Sailors, in Erskine. He was knighted in 1902, and made a companion in the Order of the Bath in 1917. It is said that of all the honours he received, however, few gave him more pride than being awarded the freedom of the burgh of Rothesay in 1922, on the occasion of a visit he made in his capacity as president of the British Medical Association.

Contemporaries described Macewen as a giant of a man, with an erect bearing and a commanding voice. He spent long hours in the hospital and at his research, but found time to lead a happy family life and to devote some time to outside hobbies and interests. The family lived in Glasgow, but spent holidays at their holiday home, at Geraghty, on the Isle of Bute, where Macewen indulged his love of sailing, possessing a motor boat and yacht.

Macewen was generally recognized by his contemporaries as the pioneer of brain surgery. However, his development of an aseptic procedure for the operating theatre, and his meticulous scientific research methods, heralded the modern era of surgery. He died at his home, 3 Woodside Crescent, Glasgow, on 22 March 1924, and was cremated in the city's western necropolis three days later.

IAIN F. RUSSELL

Sources *Glasgow Herald* (24 March 1924), 11–12 · A. K. Bowman, *Sir William Macewen* (1942) · C. Duguid, *Macewen of Glasgow* (1957) · H. A. Macewen, *The man in the white coat* (1974) · A. Young, 'Sir William Macewen and the Glasgow school of surgery', *Surgery, Gynaecology and Obstetrics* (Dec 1926), 823 · J. Jenkinson, M. Moss, and I. Russell, *The Royal: the history of the Glasgow Royal Infirmary* (1994) · *Glasgow Medical Journal*, 101 (1924), 217–37 · *DNB* · A. Young, *Sir William Macewen: an oration* (1926) · *BMJ* (29 March 1924), 603–8 · *BMJ* (5 April 1924), 644 · J. B. Russell, *Report of the city of Glasgow fever hospitals, May 1870 – April 1872* (1873) · parish register (birth), Bute, Rothesay, 30 Oct 1848 · d. cert. · Macewen–Strong correspondence, Royal College of Physicians and Surgeons of Glasgow
Archives Royal College of Physicians and Surgeons of Glasgow, papers, corresp., and medical journals · U. Glas., Archives and Business Records Centre, corresp. and papers · Wellcome L., papers
Likenesses group portrait, photograph, 1892, Ruchill Hospital, Glasgow, Greater Glasgow health board archives · G. Paulin, marble bust, 1925, Scot. NPG · T. & R. Annan & Sons, photograph, NPG [*see illus.*] · C. R. Dowell, oils, RCS Eng. · photograph, repro. in *Glasgow Medical Journal*, 216–17 · photograph, repro. in *Glasgow Herald*, 5
Wealth at death £13,128 13s. 8d.: confirmation, 24 June 1924, *CCI*

MacFadden, James (1842–1917), Roman Catholic priest and tenant leader, was born near Carrigart, co. Donegal, the fourth of five children. His father, John, was a comfortable Catholic farmer in a region where members of the minority Church of Ireland dominated that class. Related to several influential figures in the Roman Catholic hierarchy, including Daniel MacGettigan, bishop of Raphoe (1861–70) and archbishop of Armagh (1870–87), and Michael Logue, bishop of Raphoe (1879–88) and archbishop of Armagh (1887–1923), he entered St Patrick's College, Maynooth, in 1863 and continued his education in the Dunboyne Establishment.

After his ordination in 1871 he was sent as a curate to Templecrone in west Donegal. Two years later he was appointed administrator of the neighbouring parish of Gweedore, where he became parish priest in 1875. His parishioners were predominantly Irish-speaking tenants who occupied 5 or 6 acres of poor land. The potatoes they grew on these lilliputian holdings formed the mainstay of their diet and they paid rents with seasonal earnings in the 'tattie-fields' of Scotland and the wages of children, often as young as seven, who worked as farm servants in the prosperous Laggan district of east Donegal. Despite his comfortable background, MacFadden's responsibility for his parishioners' souls did not eclipse his concern for their material well-being. While he promoted attendance at mass and prohibited 'sinful' unsupervised dances in private houses, he also sponsored the establishment of schools, lobbied for a railway extension, and attempted to improve public health. Ultimately his social concern led to political action. In 1881, following the internment of local activists, he became leader of the Gweedore branch of the Land League. Over the next twelve years he organized rent strikes, resistance to evictions, and the relief of distressed tenants. One of the most prominent priests in the land war and Plan of Campaign, he enjoyed immense popularity in co. Donegal and a high national profile. A charismatic figure, his parishioners regarded him with 'a reverence and awe scarcely credible' (Geary, 29). Although he was only a short, stocky man, they nicknamed him An Sagart Mór ('the big priest'), and the nationalist press hailed him as the Patriot Priest of Gweedore. Loyalists, however, dubbed him an 'apostle of anarchy'. He served a three-month gaol sentence in 1888 for a speech in which he encouraged the non-payment of rent and declared that he was 'the law in Gweedore'. In February 1889 the authorities sought him for a similar offence. An ill-timed attempt to arrest him after mass resulted in a riot, during which his parishioners beat District Inspector Martin to death. A controversial trial followed and, although MacFadden was acquitted, several tenants received lengthy sentences. On the Liberals' return to office in 1892, however, they were released. He published a pamphlet, *The present and past of the agrarian struggle in Gweedore with letters on railway extension in county Donegal* (1889), which gives an account of his political activities.

The land agitation over, MacFadden spent most of 1897–1901 in North America fund-raising for a cathedral in Letterkenny. On his return he was appointed parish priest of Inniskeel in south-west Donegal. Here social concern no longer compensated for his arrogant and dictatorial manner. In several novels Patrick MacGill (1890–1963) thinly disguised him as Father Devany, a greedy man, indifferent to suffering. He remained involved in nationalist politics and was a leading supporter of the Ancient Order of Hibernians and Conradh na Gaelige (the Gaelic League). He died at home at Glenties, co. Donegal, on 17 April 1917 and was buried there on the 19th. Although an important political figure, he has attracted little historical attention. BREANDÁN MAC SUIBHNE

Sources E. Maguire, *A history of the diocese of Raphoe*, 2 vols. (1920) · P. Ó Gallchobhair, *The history of landlordism in Donegal*, new edn (1975) · L. M. Geary, *The plan of campaign, 1886–1891* (1986) · L. Briody, *Glenties and Inniskeel* (1986)
Archives NA Ire., chief secretary's office, registered papers · Raphoe Diocesan Archives, Letterkenny, Ireland | NA Ire., Irish Land League MSS · NA Ire., National League MSS
Likenesses P. Kelly, photograph · caricatures, repro. in *United Ireland* (28 April 1888–12 Jan 1889) · sketch, repro. in Gallchobhair, *History of landlordism in Donegal*, cover
Wealth at death £1617 11s. 3d.: probate, 14 June 1917, CGPLA Eng. & Wales

McFadyean, Sir Andrew (1887–1974), public servant and politician, was born at Leith on 23 April 1887, the eldest of the three sons (there were also two daughters) of Sir John *McFadyean (1853–1941), professor of anatomy in the Royal (Dick) Veterinary College, Edinburgh, and later principal of the Royal Veterinary College, London, and his wife, Mara Eleanor (d. 1929), daughter of Thomas Walley, principal of the Royal Veterinary College, Edinburgh. He was educated at University College School, London, and University College, Oxford, where he took a second class in classical honour moderations (1907) and a first in *literae humaniores* (1909). He entered the Treasury in 1910. On 7 October 1913 he married Dorothea Emily, youngest daughter of Charles Keane Chute, actor. They had a son, Colin (b. 1914), and three daughters, Sybil Barbara (b. 1917), Margaret Ann (b. 1925), and Joan Eleanor (b. 1930). Between 1913 and 1917 McFadyean was private secretary to six financial secretaries, including Charles Masterman, Edwin Montagu, and Stanley Baldwin; for a time he doubled as private secretary to Sir John Bradbury, the joint permanent secretary. In 1917, at a time when Britain was becoming increasingly dependent on American credit, he accompanied Sir S. Hardman Lever on an important financial mission to the United States, and from 1917 to 1919 he served under John Maynard Keynes in the Treasury division dealing with external finance. For the final four months of the peace conference he was Treasury representative in Paris.

In 1920 McFadyean was seconded for service with the Reparation Commission, which had been set up in Paris to decide the extent of Germany's obligations. For two years he served as secretary to the British delegation, before succeeding Sir Arthur Salter as general secretary of the commission. He agreed with the conclusions drawn by Keynes in *The Economic Consequences of the Peace* (1919) and in 1924 played an important role in reducing Germany's obligations when he was secretary of the principal committee of experts, which drew up what became known as the Dawes plan. Hyperinflation had shown the need for rehabilitation of Germany's finances, and for some means by which reparations could be paid without upsetting exchange rates. Under the Dawes plan, payments were rescheduled and were to be met from new taxes to be imposed as Germany's economy recovered. The mark was stabilized on gold, restoring confidence, so that an international loan could be raised, covering the first year's instalment. Finally, reparations were to be held in a fund which was not to be converted into other currencies if that would cause depreciation of the Reichsmark. McFadyean himself held that the men chiefly responsible for the Dawes plan were Sir Josiah Stamp and the American Owen D. Young, but Stamp's letters to his wife at the time made plain that he and McFadyean worked closely and harmoniously at all stages of drafting. McFadyean was appointed one of four allied controllers to supervise payments under the plan, being based in Berlin as commissioner for controlled revenues. He was knighted in 1925. In 1929 the Young plan, with which he had no direct part, aimed at a final settlement of reparations. As he pointed out prophetically, falling prices in a world depression meant that the real burden on Germany under the Young plan was likely to be heavier, and not lighter, than its obligations under the Dawes plan, which were adjustable to such a change. McFadyean himself returned from Berlin in 1930 before there was any clear sign of default.

After eleven years abroad McFadyean decided against a return to the Treasury, and embarked on a career in the City, where his reputation for uncompromising probity made him a valuable member of a number of boards of directors, particularly of refugee firms from Germany. He was chairman of S. G. Warburg & Co. Ltd, from its foundation in 1934 (as the New Trading Company Ltd) until 1952, and a director until 1967, by which time it had become a leading merchant bank. He also turned to politics, and was the Liberal Party's joint treasurer from 1936 to 1948, president from 1949 to 1950, and vice-president from 1950 to 1960. He stood as a candidate in the 1945 and 1950 general elections (for the City of London and Finchley respectively) and, far from being discouraged by defeat, he was one of a small core who helped sustain the party in its darkest days. He described himself as an Asquithian and a whig, and his pamphlet *The Liberal Case* (1950) was a statement of classical Liberalism, tinged with wry realism: 'Those who in the last thirty years have worked for the restoration of the Liberal Party can be suspected of no worldly hope', he observed (McFadyean, *The Liberal Case*, 64). He was an advocate of proportional representation, and a supporter of the Scottish covenant.

McFadyean was a member of the council of the Royal Institute of International Affairs from 1933 to 1967, and its president in 1970, and from 1944 he was chairman of the Institute of Pacific Relations committee. As a publicist of European unity on liberal principles he translated two works by Count Richard Coudenhove-Kalergi, *The Totalitarian State Against Man* (1938), arguing against the Hegelian conception of the state, and *Europe must Unite* (1940),

calling for a European commonwealth based on a European ideal transcending, without weakening, national patriotisms. After the war he helped to found Liberal International, of which he was vice-president from 1954 to 1967, and he was a tireless advocate of the Common Market. He believed that tariffs and monopolist and restrictive practices in industry were destroying Britain's competitiveness, and he was president of the Free Trade Union from 1948 to 1959. Nevertheless, he was no dogmatic advocate of *laissez-faire*. As a member of the court of the British North Borneo Chartered Company, and of the international rubber regulation committee, he knew how producers of primary products might suffer from overproduction. In *The History of Rubber Regulation, 1934–1943* (1944), which he edited, he noted how demand might be a good deal more elastic than supply, and that the alternative to regulation had been the 'slow and cruel play of market forces' (J. McFadyean, ed., *History of Rubber Regulation*, 1944, 'Introduction'). Other causes with which he was associated included assistance to persecuted Jewry, and also to 'enemy aliens' unjustly interned during the war.

McFadyean was tall and muscular, with a long face, and a quizzical expression. He was a passionate devotee of opera and theatre. He died in London on 2 October 1974 and was survived by his wife and four children.

G. C. PEDEN

Sources A. McFadyean, *Recollected in tranquillity* (1964) · *The Times* (3 Oct 1974) · BLPES, McFadyean MSS · A. McFadyean, *Reparation reviewed* (1930) · J. Harry Jones, *Josiah Stamp, public servant* (1964), 209–31 · private information (2004) · *WWW*, 1971–80 · Burke, *Peerage*

Archives BLPES, papers | University College, Oxford, account book at University College, Oxford

Likenesses W. Stoneman, photograph, 1947, NPG · J. Oppenheim, portrait

Wealth at death £188,207: probate, 5 Dec 1974, *CGPLA Eng. & Wales*

McFadyean, Sir John (1853–1941), veterinary surgeon, was born on 17 June 1853, the younger son in the family of two sons and two daughters of Andrew McFadyean, tenant farmer, of Barrachan, Wigtownshire, and his wife, Jane McKissoch. He finished school at the Ewart Institute, Edinburgh, at the age of sixteen and worked on his father's farm, which was mainly concerned with a herd of dairy cattle, a small flock of sheep, and some pigs and horses. When high rents and falling prices threatened the farm with insolvency he decided to use the experience he had obtained with domestic animals by training to become a veterinary surgeon.

In 1874 McFadyean entered the Royal (Dick) Veterinary College, Edinburgh, and in 1876 became a member of the Royal College of Veterinary Surgeons. He was also awarded the gold medal of the Highland and Agricultural Society. From 1876 to 1891 he was lecturer in anatomy at the college, and in 1891 he was appointed dean and professor of pathology and bacteriology.

Early in his career McFadyean recognized that the study and teaching of veterinary anatomy were handicapped by the lack of detailed knowledge of the subject and the consequent inadequacy of the textbooks then in use. Having

Sir John McFadyean (1853–1941), by Elliott & Fry

considered the absence of any work on the anatomy of animals comparable with that obtained by medical students in the dissection of the human body, he decided first to obtain qualifications in medicine, and secondly to undertake his own studies in the anatomy of animals. Accordingly in 1883 he obtained his MB and BSc at Edinburgh University.

Meanwhile, McFadyean was carrying out his own investigations on the carcasses of horses, which led to the publication in 1884 of his *Anatomy of the Horse—a Dissection Guide*, followed in 1889 by *The Comparative Anatomy of the Domesticated Animals*. As his experience increased his interest turned from the study of animal anatomy to problems in the fields of bacteriology and pathology, and at the same time his reputation as a pioneer in veterinary surgery steadily increased. In 1888 he founded the *Journal of Comparative Pathology and Bacteriology*.

In 1892 McFadyean was appointed principal of the Royal Veterinary College, London, and he held that post until his retirement in 1927. In 1901, as a member of the British Congress on Tuberculosis, he created something of a sensation. Before a distinguished audience Dr Robert Koch, the eminent Berlin bacteriologist, who in 1882 had described the tubercle bacillus, stated positively in his lecture on the subject that the bacillus found in infected animals could not be transferred to human beings. At the end of Koch's discourse McFadyean took the floor, disagreed with the eminent doctor, and described his own research in which he was certain that infected cows' milk was responsible for tuberculosis in young children. His

researches, which led to the discovery of the causes and means of treatment of bovine tuberculosis, were eventually published in his *Tuberculosis as Regards Heredity in Causation and Elimination from Infected Herds* (1911).

From 1889 to 1904 McFadyean was also keenly interested in the problems of anthrax disease in animals. The importance of his work was recognized when he was knighted in 1905. He was president of the Royal College of Veterinary Surgeons from 1906 to 1910 and again in 1930–31; from 1904 to 1928 he was honorary consulting veterinary surgeon to the Royal Agricultural Society of England. In 1930 he presided at the eleventh International Veterinary Congress in London. In the course of his career he received many honours from medical, veterinary, and agricultural societies both at home and abroad, including an honorary fellowship of the Royal Society of Medicine. When he retired he had come to be regarded as the founder of modern veterinary research.

In 1883 McFadyean married Mara Eleanor (*d.* 1929), daughter of Thomas Walley, principal of the Royal Veterinary College, Edinburgh. They had three sons and two daughters. The eldest son, Andrew *McFadyean, became a Treasury official, a diplomat, and a businessman.

McFadyean spent the years of his retirement at Highlands House, Leatherhead, and died at Heatherhead Nursing Home, Hindhead, on 1 February 1941. *The Times* obituary stated, 'By his death the veterinary world has lost one of the last of the band of pioneers who successfully converted veterinarianism into the great profession which is constantly advancing both in scientific knowledge and in public esteem'.   H. F. OXBURY, *rev.*

Sources *The Times* (4 Feb 1941) · I. Pattison, *John McFadyean: a great British veterinarian* (1981)
Likenesses Elliott & Fry, photograph, NPG [*see illus.*]
Wealth at death £61,286 19*s.* 10*d.*: probate, 17 March 1941, CGPLA Eng. & Wales

Macfadyen, Allan (1860–1907), bacteriologist, born on 26 May 1860 at Glasgow, was the youngest of the four sons of Archibald Macfadyen, brass-founder, and his wife, Margaret, daughter of D. McKinlay of Stornaway. He was educated at Dr Bryce's Collegiate School at Edinburgh from 1871, and he became a student in the University of Edinburgh in 1878. He graduated MB, CM (1883), MD with gold medal (1886), and BSc in hygiene (1888), and he studied chemistry and bacteriology in Bern, Göttingen, and Munich. After returning to Britain he was a research scholar of the Grocers' Company from 1889 to 1892, and he became a lecturer on bacteriology at the College of State Medicine in London, which was subsequently amalgamated with the Jenner Institute of Preventive Medicine (afterwards the Lister Institute). Macfadyen was made director in 1891. Subsequently he was appointed head of the bacteriological department, and was its director in 1903. On 7 January 1890 he married Marie, daughter of Professor Cartleng, director of the botanical gardens at Dettingen. They had no children.

Macfadyen played a prominent role in planning and

organizing the building of the Lister Institute on the Chelsea Embankment. From 1901 to 1904 he was Fullerian professor of physiology at the Royal Institution, where he delivered lectures entitled 'The cell as the unit of life'; these were published posthumously in 1908. A fatal accident involving two of Macfadyen's assistants led to his dismissal from the institute in 1905. He left with some reluctance, and devoted himself entirely to original work, in the pursuit of which he accidentally infected himself with Malta fever and typhoid fever. He died of these at Hampstead, London, on 1 March 1907, and was buried there.

Macfadyen's chief claim to recognition is his work on the endotoxins (the intracellular juices) of pathogenic micro-organisms. He showed that it was possible to immunize animals by means of the endotoxins of the micro-organisms of diseases such as typhoid, cholera, pneumonia, and plague, and that serums of the immunized animals exhibited preventative and curative properties towards infections of the respective microbes. In much of this work he was assisted by S. Rowland. Macfadyen also investigated thermophilic bacteria, and with Sir James Dewar showed that the vital processes of some bacteria are not destroyed by temperatures approaching absolute zero. In addition to this work, he published many memoirs in medical and scientific periodicals, including the *Proceedings of the Royal Society*, in 1889, and the second volume of the *Transactions of the International Congress of Hygiene*. Macfadyen was a shy and very private man who made few enemies.

H. D. ROLLESTON, rev. TIM O'NEILL

Sources BMJ (9 March 1907), 601 · The Lancet (9 March 1907), 696–7 · R. Kohler, 'The background to Arthur Harden's discovery of cozymase', *Bulletin of the History of Medicine*, 48 (1974), 22–40 · CGPLA Eng. & Wales (1907)
Archives Wellcome L., Lister Institute MSS
Likenesses photograph, repro. in A. Macfadyen, *The cell as the unit of life* (1908)
Wealth at death £9221 12s. 2d.: administration, 22 March 1907, CGPLA Eng. & Wales

Macfadyen, Sir Eric (1879–1966), developer of tropical agriculture, was born in Whalley Range, Manchester, on 9 February 1879, the fifth and youngest son of the seven children of the Revd John Allison Macfadyen, minister of Chorlton Road Congregational Church, Manchester, and his wife, Elizabeth Anderson of Greenock. From Lynams (the Dragon School), Oxford, he won a scholarship to Clifton College, Bristol, where he was head of his house. Below average height, he was tough and self-reliant. In sport, he particularly enjoyed swimming and running.

A classical scholarship took Macfadyen to Wadham College, Oxford, for two years before he joined the imperial yeomanry and served in South Africa in 1901–2, where he was seriously injured in an accident. This left him with a damaged left eyelid, which he afterwards supported with a monocle. Invalided out with the queen's medal and three clasps, he returned to Wadham, involved himself in university politics, and became president of the union in 1902. Macfadyen inherited his father's gifts as a speaker and developed into a skilled debater, master of his brief, with an engaging wit, and the rare faculty of making his hearers believe he was presenting their own thoughts.

In 1902 Macfadyen obtained a second in *literae humaniores* and headed the list of entrants by examination to the Malayan civil service. He commented in a letter to his mother dated 24 January 1904, 'I incline to the feeling that Government services were not meant for Macfadyens' (Macfadyen). He nevertheless spent three years in various posts in Taiping, Kuala Selangor, and Kuala Lumpur before changing his career.

In association with a Chinese friend, Macfadyen went into partnership as a contractor, obtaining public tenders for road construction in the Kuala Selangor and Klang areas, opening up fresh land for agriculture. It was a natural step into planting, as at this time the new rubber-producing tree, *hevea braziliensis*, was rapidly replacing coffee production in Malaya. His experience in the Malayan civil service at Kuala Selangor district office at a time when agriculture was developing rapidly had made him well qualified to select land for planting. Macfadyen joined Jebong estate as an assistant, then, in quick succession, started his own small rubber estate, which he named Lunderston after his father's home in Scotland, and in 1906, having been promised land in the Klang district, arranged the formation of a syndicate to finance the New Crocodile River Rubber (Selangor) Company Ltd, in which he was the second largest shareholder.

Macfadyen helped to form, and became a senior partner of, Macfadyen, Wilde & Co., which became the leading firm of visiting agents (planting advisers) in Malaya. He helped to form the Planter's Association of Malaya, which he duly chaired. He was also a member of the federal council of the Federated Malay States in 1911–16 and 1919–20. After returning to England during the First World War, he enlisted in the Royal Horse Artillery and served in France, 1917–18. At the end of 1918 he joined Harrisons and Crosfield Ltd, 1–4 Great Tower Street, London, then principally East India merchants and managing agents for eastern plantation companies, and one of the largest businesses of its kind. After an extended visit to Malaya from 1918 to 1921 he supervised estate operations in Malaya from London, making frequent visits to the territory in his joint capacity of director of Harrisons and Crosfield Ltd and director and chairman of numerous plantation companies in the Harrisons and Crosfield agency group, remaining on the boards of London Asiatic, Golden Hope, and Straits Plantations after retiring from the Harrisons and Crosfield main board in 1955.

An enlightened appreciation of the importance of research and development in agriculture led Macfadyen in 1925 to acquire for Harrisons and Crosfield the Prang Besar estate in Malaya, which was pioneering the selection and bud grafting of high-yielding rubber, and which thereafter provided high-quality planting material for all companies in the agency group, as well as many other estates. In the late 1920s and early 1930s (a period of economic depression) he merged and amalgamated rubber estates into larger and more efficient units, continually encouraging scientific progress, developing agronomic techniques, and also consolidating and improving management. During and after the Second World War he planned the rehabilitation and long-term future of estates that had been neglected during the Japanese occupation and were also threatened by the new competition from synthetic rubbers. In 1947 he established the first latex bulking and shipping facility in Malaya.

Macfadyen's interest in tropical crops extended beyond rubber. He foresaw the growth in demand for edible oils and fats and led his group of estates into a new crop, oil palm, in the early 1950s; oil palm eventually overtook rubber in both scale and importance. He set up an oil palm research station at Banting, Malaya. He also initiated research into cocoa, which he built into another significant alternative to rubber production on Harrisons and Crosfield agency estates.

Macfadyen was a member of the governing body of the Imperial College of Tropical Agriculture, Trinidad, which he joined in 1928, becoming its chairman in 1937, and for his services to tropical agriculture in the colonial empire he was knighted in 1943. He was chairman of the Rubber Growers' Association and was awarded their gold medal in 1952.

In 1923 Macfadyen entered politics, when he won Devizes for the Liberals, but in the election of 1924 he lost his seat. He assisted Sir Malcolm Watson in his work for the Ross Institute and Hospital for Tropical Diseases, Putney Heath, which effectively controlled malaria in Malaya, and he was its chairman from 1946 to 1958.

In 1920, in Klang, Macfadyen married Violet Lucy Stanley, daughter of E. H. S. Champneys, of Otterpool Manor, Sellindge, Kent, and they rented a house in Kent. They had three sons and three daughters. In 1930 Macfadyen purchased Meopham Bank, Hildenborough, near Tonbridge, Kent, where he farmed hops and barley, and his wife had charge of a herd of Guernseys. He served in his third war, the Second World War, as a captain in the Home Guard at Meopham. At the age of seventy-five he made his last trip to the East at the height of the Malayan emergency, visiting every estate in his charge, and almost every field. Macfadyen died at Meopham Bank on 13 July 1966. He was survived by his wife.   GUY NICKALLS

Sources E. Macfadyen, *Eric Macfadyen* (1968) [autobiography] · *One hundred years as East India merchants, 1844–1943*, Harrisons & Crosfield Limited (privately published, London, 1943) · private information (1981) · private information (2004) · *DNB* · P. Pugh and others, *Great enterprise: a history of Harrisons & Crosfield*, ed. G. Nickalls (Harrisons & Crosfield, 1990) · d. cert.
Archives NRA, corresp.
Likenesses S. Allon, caricature, 1958, repro. in Pugh and others, *Great enterprise*, p. 127
Wealth at death £47,154: probate, 30 March 1967, *CGPLA Eng. & Wales*

McFadyen, John Edgar (1870–1933), biblical scholar, was born at 205 Caledonia Road, Glasgow, on 17 July 1870, the eldest child in the family of three sons and four daughters of James Hemphill McFadyen, manager of the publishing department of Glasgow's *Evening Citizen* and *Weekly Citizen* newspapers, and his wife, Jane McKee. He was educated at Hutcheson's Boys' Grammar School, Glasgow, and at Glasgow University. He graduated MA with a first class in classics in 1890 and then went on a scholarship to Balliol College, Oxford, where he took a second degree in *literae humaniores*, graduating in 1894. In Oxford he won the junior (1893) and the senior (1896) Hall–Houghton Septuagint prizes and the Denyer and Johnson scholarship (1897). In 1894 he returned to Glasgow as a classical scholar, in order to take the theological course at the Free Church college (later Trinity College), where he was influenced by the scholars A. B. Bruce, George Adam Smith, T. M. Lindsay, James Stuart Candlish, and Henry Drummond. He also spent a semester at Marburg during this period. In 1898 he finished his theological studies and was appointed to the chair of Old Testament literature and exegesis in Knox College, Toronto. In 1898 he married (Marianne Sophie Emilie Wilhelmine Caroline) Marie, daughter of *Amtsgerichtsrat* Wilhelm Scheffer, of Eschwege, Hesse. They had two sons and a daughter. McFadyen and his wife left in 1898 for Toronto where they remained until 1910, when he was recalled to Glasgow to take up the post of professor of Old Testament language, literature, and theology at Trinity College, Glasgow. McFadyen, who received honorary degrees from Pine Hill Divinity Hall, Halifax, Nova Scotia, in 1910 and the University of Glasgow in 1911, was also a popular and influential teacher. He remained in his post at Trinity College until his death, in Glasgow, on 24 December 1933.

In the second half of the nineteenth century, the scientific theory of evolution engendered the belief in the steady progress of human thought and made a vogue of philosophical materialism. It was inevitable that the books of the Bible should be subjected to literary and historical criticism, with the result that many generally accepted ideas were severely disturbed and the doctrine of the verbal inspiration of the holy scriptures was directly challenged. It was McFadyen's main work to be a mediator of the new learning, both to those who had been disturbed by it and to those who desired to profit by it, although now many of its methods are applied with much greater caution.

It is intelligible, therefore, that one of McFadyen's early publications was a volume of apologetic with the title *Old Testament Criticism and the Christian Church* (1903). Apart from his repeated revisions (1914–1930) of the *Introductory Hebrew Grammar* of A. B. Davidson, McFadyen did not devote himself to linguistic or philological studies; his work was predominantly exegetical, homiletical, and devotional. His translations of various books of the Old Testament into modern idiom satisfied an urgent need; exegetical studies such as *A Cry for Justice* (1912) and *The Problem of Pain* (1917) were evidence of genuine scholarship and of living faith; while in volumes such as *The Use of the Old Testament in the Light of Modern Knowledge* (1922), *The Approach to the Old Testament* (1926), and *A Guide to the Understanding of the Old Testament* (1927), he stressed the essential unity and the spiritual content of that collection of biblical texts.   JOHN MAUCHLINE, *rev.* GERALD LAW

Sources D. Lamont, *Expository Times*, 45 (1933–4), 261–4 · *Glasgow Herald* (26 Dec 1933) · W. I. Addison, *The Snell exhibitions: from the University of Glasgow to Balliol College, Oxford* (1901) · b. cert. · *CGPLA Eng. & Wales* (1934)
Wealth at death £3778 16s. 3d.: confirmation, 29 March 1934, *CCI*

McFadzean, Francis Scott, Baron McFadzean of Kelvinside (1915–1992), businessman and economist, was born on 26 November 1915 at 8 Fullarton Terrace, Troon, Ayrshire, the son of Francis Findlay McFadzean, law clerk, and his wife, Annie Scott, *née* Smith. Frank, as he was always known, developed early on a broad accent, and qualities of forthrightness and decisiveness which he never lost. He left school at the age of fourteen to go to sea and pursue the romance of travel and hazard, but after four years of washing down decks and painting hulls he reviewed his progress and made his first career change. Three months of intensive study in the Mitchell Library, Glasgow, saw him pass the entry examination for Glasgow University, where he took a first in economics and developed an appetite and talent for intellectual debate. Later a postgraduate degree in business administration at the London School of Economics (LSE) completed his academic armoury. After a short spell as a civil servant, from 1938 to 1940, in which his intellectual strength guided him through the Board of Trade into the Treasury, his career was interrupted by the Second World War. After joining the Duke of Cornwall's light infantry as a private he made his way through the ranks and through Africa, Italy, and north-west Europe finally to Malaya, where he was demobilized as a colonel.

McFadzean began his post-war career working with the Malayan government (1945–9) and then with the Colonial Development Corporation (1949–52). His strong opinions soon led him into direct conflict with Lord Reith, chairman of the latter, and their letters announcing a parting of the ways crossed in the post. McFadzean then joined the Royal Dutch-Shell group of companies, rising to become managing director of the group, a post he held from 1964 to 1976, and chairman of the committee of managing directors, from 1972 to 1976. He also chaired Shell Oil in the United States and Shell Canada. The years of his chairmanship were turbulent, with the first oil crisis in 1974 rewriting the rules for the oil industry. His resilience and decisiveness were called on heavily during these years, as they had been during the Nigerian crisis five years earlier, when he flew into the rebels' camp in Enugu to obtain the safe passage of his expatriates. On his return from Nigeria his preference for a low profile was exemplified by his whimsical willingness to speak only to the *Sunday Post*. He was knighted in 1975.

In 1976, shortly before his retirement from Shell, McFadzean was appointed chairman of British Airways by Harold Wilson. With typical clinical appreciation of his new situation he completed the integration of British European Airways and the British Overseas Airways Corporation, making considerable cost savings, but, even more importantly, winning the battle to build the airline

Francis Scott McFadzean, Baron McFadzean of Kelvinside (1915–1992), by unknown photographer

around Boeing aircraft, a base which underpinned the airline's competitive position and secured its future. These years with British Airways took their toll on his health and led to his leaving the corporation in 1979. Nevertheless, in December 1979 he was persuaded by Margaret Thatcher, who much admired his acumen, to accept the chairmanship of Rolls-Royce (which he had previously served as a non-executive director). Rolls-Royce was in major financial difficulties when he arrived. The recession in the airline industry had deepened drastically in the early 1980s, following the second oil crisis, and orders had fallen by almost 75 per cent. McFadzean tackled effectively the cost implications of this without damaging the momentum of technological development. As a result Rolls-Royce kept its place in the front rank of engine suppliers and within three years was profitable again and ready for privatization. Like British Airways, Rolls-Royce, thanks to McFadzean (by now Baron McFadzean of Kelvinside), had got its fundamentals right.

McFadzean's determination to set his own course and break the shackles of a traditional and comfortable Scottish life emerged early, with his departure from home into the rough and tumble of life at sea. During these formative four years he gained confidence in the strength of his intellect, and realized that he needed to pursue education to develop and hone his mind. His studies and his mental jousting with Alec Cairncross and others did just that. This period of education in Glasgow and later at the LSE convinced him that he had something to offer in the academic field of economics. Perhaps he saw himself in the line of Adam Smith and the other thinkers of the Scottish Enlightenment. He certainly had the practical experience to contribute. Nevertheless, it was a pity that his contribution should have taken the form of debunking another's ideas rather than of a broader statement of his own: two of his three books were attacks on the liberal economist John Kenneth Galbraith.

McFadzean's internationalism was not an academic

conversion but born of personal experience throughout the war years and his career with the Colonial Development Corporation and Shell. His respect for his associates in foreign countries was based on friendship and understanding, not on the anticipation of material gain for his company. The calculations may have been based on money, but the decisions were made on the importance of maintaining the relationship. This brought security and stability to difficult situations, and made solutions easier to find.

The origins of McFadzean's decisiveness are more elusive. His primary objective in Shell was to ensure that momentum was never stalled by indecision. He seemed to have a fear, perhaps emanating from his period of employment with the government, as a civil servant and then with a public sector corporation, that there were many ways in which a decision could be avoided and action frustrated. He contributed greatly to Shell's effectiveness in decision making, so important in the crisis years. The same was true of his time at British Airways, when he refused to be frustrated over Boeing, thus laying the proper foundation for a great airline. However, the same clarity fitted ill with the industrial relations of the 1970s. In this period agreements between employers and trade unions were labyrinthine, and there was little receptivity for broad-brush strategic moves. Agreements moved forward by inches. This fitted ill with McFadzean's background and humour, and it left a mark on his attitude and his health.

Throughout his working life McFadzean was a natural 'free trader', almost more at home in the dynamism and bustle of the Far East than in Britain itself. The excitement and the turbulence of the oil industry suited him well. Risk taking was second nature to him, and his fearlessness, born in the mountainous seas of the Atlantic Ocean, never left him. With no sense of hierarchy, he treated everyone as a colleague worth listening to and arguing with, although he knew where the buck stopped. For him a decision deferred was an opportunity lost. To those who knew him well he was straightforward and helpful. He held strong views but would welcome disagreement. His friendship was always worth having, not just for natural enjoyment but for the support it always conveyed. Nevertheless, for those who were more acquaintances than friends he could appear detached and reserved, and his gruff reactions could disturb rather than endear.

McFadzean was twice married: first in 1938 to Isabel McKenzie Beattie, who died in 1987, and second in 1988 to Sonja Lian Hoa Nio Khung. He died at his home, Woodside, Quarry Woods, Bisham, Berkshire, on 23 May 1992, of kidney and heart failure. He was survived by his second wife, and by the daughter of his first marriage, Felicity Carmen Francesca (*b.* 1946), who in 1979 married Sir Richard (later Baron) Marsh, the former Labour cabinet minister.

BOB REID

Sources personal knowledge (2004) • *The Times* (29 May 1992) • *The Independent* (1 June 1992) • WWW • *Debrett's Peerage* • b. cert. • d. cert.

Likenesses photograph, News International Synidcation, London [*see illus.*] • photograph, repro. in *The Independent*
Wealth at death £767,286: probate, 10 Sept 1992, *CGPLA Eng. & Wales*

McFadzean, William Hunter, Baron McFadzean (1903–1996), businessman, was born on 17 December 1903 in Stranraer, Wigtownshire, Scotland, the second of the three sons of Henry McFadzean (*d.* 1918), cheese merchant and travelling instructor in cheese-making, and his wife, Agnes Wylie Hunter (*d.* 1960). He was educated at Stranraer Academy and high school, and read law and chartered accountancy at Glasgow University, but graduated only in accountancy in 1922. Having been articled to McLay, McAllister, and McGibbon, chartered accountants, in Glasgow in 1922, he qualified as a chartered accountant in 1927, and moved to London to join Chalmers Wade. On 8 June 1933 he married Eileen Gordon (*b.* 1911/12), daughter of Arthur Gordon, of Blundellsands, Lancashire. They had one son and two daughters, one of whom was adopted.

McFadzean moved to Liverpool in 1932 to become the accountant of British Insulated Cables Ltd, a client of Chalmers Wade. He became financial secretary in 1937 and executive manager in 1942, playing a key role in the company's contribution to war production, and he was closely involved in planning the merger with Callender's Cable and Construction Company in 1945. He joined the board of the new company, British Insulated Callender's Cables (BICC) as executive director in 1945 and after being appointed deputy chairman in 1947, and chief executive director in 1950, he became chairman and managing director of BICC in 1954. He played an important part in its growth in the post-war years from a small cable company to an international cable and construction group. He realized that if the company was to expand, it could not confine its operations to England, and he negotiated partnerships and co-operative deals, including one with Rio-Tinto Zinc (RTZ) and British Aluminium; he was deputy chairman of RTZ/BICC Aluminium Holdings Ltd from 1967 to 1973. During his chairmanship of BICC exports and overseas sales grew from £3 million to £250 million. McFadzean retired as managing director in 1961, and chairman in 1973, when he became honorary life president.

McFadzean was knighted in 1960. He was president of the Federation of British Industries (later the Confederation of British Industry) from 1959 to 1961, and was the first chairman of the British National Export Council from 1964 to 1966, and president from 1966 to 1968. He was also a founder member of the Export Council for Europe in 1960, serving for four years, and a member of the Commonwealth Export Council from 1964 to 1966. McFadzean wanted the government to back a strong export policy for British companies. BICC was the largest employer in Huyton, Harold Wilson's constituency, and McFadzean was a friend of the prime minister, who rewarded him for his services to exports with a life peerage in 1966.

Banking was another area which interested McFadzean. He was appointed to the board of Midland Bank in 1959, and was deputy chairman from 1968 to 1977, remaining a director until 1981. During the period of his deputy chairmanship, in 1971, Midland Bank was part of a consortium that bought Thomas Cook, the travel agent business, which had been nationalized after the war. This went on to become a profitable part of the Midland Bank group. Midland Bank was one of the clearing banks that shared in the rescue of the secondary banks during the secondary banking crisis of 1974. McFadzean was also involved in the nuclear industry, as president of the British Nuclear Forum from 1964 to 1966, and later as deputy chairman of the National Nuclear Corporation from 1973 to 1980.

McFadzean, chairman of the Council of Industrial Federations of the European Free Trade Association (EFTA) from 1960 to 1963, supported Britain's entry into the Common Market, and was one of the first British businessmen to see the advantages of a political union. He made his maiden, and only, speech in the House of Lords on 26 July 1971 during the debate on the government white paper *The United Kingdom and the European Communities*. In this he described the Common Market as an 'inspiring conception' (*Hansard 5L*, 5th ser., 65–9), and talked of the tragedy of Britain's lack of involvement in the talks leading up to the treaty of Rome in 1957. Emphasizing the importance of Britain's being part of a larger economic grouping, he argued that Britain had to join the EEC, already an economic success, in order to halt the decline of its competitive position in the world, and take advantage of the great potential of a larger market. He also thought that membership would give the British people a new sense of purpose and direction.

McFadzean was created a knight of the Thistle in 1976. He died of bronchopneumonia, following a stroke, on 14 January 1996, at Bybrook House Nursing Home, Middle Hill, Box, Wiltshire. He was survived by his wife, son, and daughter, his adopted daughter having predeceased him.

ANNE PIMLOTT BAKER

Sources WWW · *The Times* (16 Jan 1996) · *The Times* (17 Jan 1996) · *The Independent* (17 Jan 1996) · *Hansard 5L* (1971), 323.65–9 · A. R. Holmes and E. Green, *Midland: 150 years of banking business* (1986) · m. cert. · d. cert. · *CGPLA Eng. & Wales* (1996) · Burke, *Peerage*
Archives U. Warwick Mod. RC, papers relating to work as president of the Federation of British Inustries
Likenesses photograph, repro. in *The Times* (17 Jan 1996) · photograph, repro. in *The Independent*
Wealth at death £409,635: probate, 27 March 1996, *CGPLA Eng. & Wales*

Macfait, Ebenezer (d. 1786), writer, details of whose parentage and upbringing are unknown, practised medicine at Edinburgh, in addition to which he published, anonymously, *Remarks on the Life and Writings of Plato, with Answers to the Principal Objections against him* (1760) and the first part of *A New System of General Geography* (1780). Macfait also contributed two papers on meteorological subjects to the first volume of *Essays Physical and Literary* (1754). He died at Alva, Stirlingshire, the seat of his friend John Johnston, on 25 November 1786.

GORDON GOODWIN, *rev.* PHILIP CARTER

Sources *Scots Magazine*, 48 (1786), 622 · Watt, *Bibl. Brit.*

McFall [*née* Clarke], **Frances Elizabeth Bellenden** [*pseud.* Sarah Grand] (1854–1943), novelist and women's rights campaigner, was born on 10 June 1854 in Donaghadee, co. Down, Ireland, the fourth of the five children of Edward John Bellenden Clarke (1813–1861), a lieutenant in the Royal Navy and coastguard, and his wife, Margaret Bell Sherwood (1813–1874). Both parents were English, and after the death of her father in 1861, Clarke and her family moved to near Scarborough, Yorkshire, to be near her mother's relatives. Educated at home until the age of fourteen, she had two years of formal schooling, first at the Royal Naval School at Twickenham, Middlesex, and then at a finishing school in Holland Road, Kensington, London. Viewing marriage as her only opportunity to continue her education, on 23 August 1870 she married David Chambers McFall (1834/5–1898), an army surgeon attached to the Indian border regiment. He was about twenty years her senior, a widower with two sons, Haldane (who was only six years younger than Clarke) and Albert. Frances McFall's only child, David Archibald Edward (Archie) McFall, who became an actor, was born on 7 October 1871. From 1873 to 1878 she travelled with her husband and son to Singapore, Ceylon, China, Japan, and the Straits Settlements. In 1879 they moved to Norwich, where David McFall was stationed, and then in 1881 moved to Warrington, Lancashire, where he retired as honorary brigade surgeon. Their marriage was not a happy one, and in 1890 she left her husband and son and moved to London to pursue her writing career.

McFall's first book, *Two Dear Little Feet*, a cautionary tale about the dangers of fashionably tight boots, was published in 1873, but after that she had little success in getting her early fiction published. In 1888 she published her first novel, *Ideala: a Study from Life*, anonymously and at her own expense. The success of *Ideala* (which was republished by Bentley in 1889) gave her the courage and the resources to live on her own. From the beginning her desire to write was inseparable from her desire to instruct and reform. Profoundly influenced by Josephine Butler's campaign against the Contagious Diseases Acts, she was intent upon educating her readers about any and all issues she felt pertinent to the well-being and advancement of women. In her novel *The Heavenly Twins*, published under the pseudonym Sarah Grand, she condemned the sexual double standard, argued for more opportunities and independence for women, and criticized gender-role socialization. But her central subject was the spread of syphilis from men to their wives and children; the disease's destructive effects are represented with clinical detail, presumably gleaned from her husband's medical textbooks. Not surprisingly the novel was rejected by numerous publishers, but when Heinemann published it in 1893 it became a sensational best-seller. It was reprinted six times in its first year and sold over 20,000 copies by its second year in print. It was condemned on moral grounds and criticized for its confusing narrative structure, but it was praised by Mark Twain and George Bernard Shaw and thrilled a reading public eager for fiction that dealt in a frank manner with sexuality and the issues of the day. It was the first of what came to be called 'new woman' novels (McFall claimed to have coined the term 'new woman') which depicted women's growing dissatisfaction with the restrictions of Victorian society.

The Heavenly Twins changed McFall's life. With it was born the persona of Sarah Grand, often called 'Madame' Grand, a self-styled 'woman of genius', who was impeccably dressed, had a charming manner, and wore distinctively large hats, and who lectured and wrote on women's issues for the next two decades. McFall's philosophy was moderate in nature: she advocated marriage and contested the sexual double standard by demanding sexual purity for men as well as women. She believed that this very moderation, combined with her witty and calculatedly feminine style, would do more for women than the militant agenda and tactics of the suffragettes. In 1901 she went on a four-month lecture tour of the United States, and from 1903 to 1912 she lectured throughout England and published numerous articles promoting women's suffrage as well as rational dress and the benefits of bicycling for women. She was a member of the Women Writers' Suffrage League and the Women Citizens' Association, and vice-president of the Women's Suffrage Society. After moving to Tunbridge Wells in 1898, she became president of the local branches of the National Council of Women and the National Union of Women's Suffrage Societies.

Although McFall continued to write fiction, none of her other novels matched the success or generated the controversy of *The Heavenly Twins*. Her autobiographical novel, *The Beth Book* (1897), contains some of her best writing in its first half, which vividly depicts the deprivations of the heroine's childhood and boldly describes the awakening of her sexuality. But like *The Heavenly Twins* it is overly long and tackles too many topics, including vivisection, lock hospitals, and the abuse of caffeine. She turned her attention to land reform and sweatshops in her last two novels, *Adnam's Orchard* (1912) and *The Winged Victory* (1916).

After women got the vote in 1918, McFall's celebrity quickly faded. By 1922 most of her books were out of print. She often responded to formal criticism of her writing by saying that matter meant more to her than manner, but by being tied so closely to the issues and controversies of her age, the matter of her novels eventually lost its relevance. In the 1970s interest in McFall's work was revived by feminist literary criticism, but her passionate and well-intentioned novels—unwieldy, proselytizing, often tiresome in their detail and length—remain of interest primarily as historical documents.

After living in Tunbridge Wells with her stepson, the artist and writer Haldane McFall, for twenty years, Frances McFall moved to Bath in 1920. There she turned her considerable energies towards civic duties, taking on the largely ceremonial post of the city's lady mayoress from 1922 to 1929 (excluding the years 1923 and 1924), serving with Mayor Cedric Chivers, a widower and businessman. When Bath was bombed in 1942, relatives persuaded her,

with difficulty, to leave her damaged home and move to Calne, Wiltshire. McFall died there at her home, The Grange, on 12 May 1943 and was buried on 15 May in Lansdown cemetery, Bath. JANE ELDRIDGE MILLER

Sources G. Kersley, *Darling madame: Sarah Grand, devoted friend* (1983) · J. Huddleston, *Sarah Grand* (1979) · *The Times* (13 May 1943) · *New York Times* (13 May 1943) · m. cert. · *CGPLA Eng. & Wales* (1943)
Archives Bath Central Library, letters, notes, and cards, BAI 5AN · BL, corresp. and MSS · NL Scot., corresp. and MSS · U. Cal., Los Angeles, corresp. and MSS | Smith College, Northampton, Massachusetts, letters to William Heinemann · U. Leeds, Brotherton L., letters to M. Betham-Edwards · University of British Columbia Library, letters to Mary Haweis
Likenesses A. Praga, oils, 1896, Victoria Art Gallery, Bath
Wealth at death £4632 6s. 6d.: probate, 21 July 1943, *CGPLA Eng. & Wales*

Macfarlan, Duncan (1771–1857), university principal, was born at Drymen, Stirlingshire, on 27 September 1771, the second of three children of Duncan Macfarlan (1706–1791) and his wife, Anne Allan (d. 1823). His father, who married late in life, was the parish minister, a doughty moderate and upholder of patronage who earned the nickname 'Duncan Rungs' from his dexterity with the stout stick or rung with which he kept order at markets and fairs; the son inherited his father's decided views on church politics and never deviated from them. He entered Glasgow University in 1783, and graduated MA in 1788, proceeding to the study of divinity. Licensed by the presbytery of Dumbarton on 28 June 1791—only two days before his father's death—he was presented as his father's successor in Drymen in September and was ordained in the following February. He married, on 28 August 1797, his cousin Anne (1778–1814), daughter of John Allan, minister of Row; they had four daughters and five sons, but only two of their children outlived their father.

Macfarlan received the degree of DD from Glasgow University in 1806 and served two spells as dean of faculties there (1806–8 and 1810–12). An unsuccessful candidate for the chair of divinity in 1814, he was also passed over in that same year when Thomas Chalmers was preferred for the Tron Church in Glasgow. In 1815 he became one of the king's chaplains. He was elected moderator of the general assembly in 1819, and became dean of the Chapel Royal in 1820. In April 1823 he was appointed principal of Glasgow University, the post to be held jointly with that of minister of the High Church (Glasgow Cathedral). His advancement was due to the influence of the duke of Montrose, who was chancellor of the university and who, as patron, had presented Macfarlan to the parish of Drymen. Opposition to the proposed settlement, on the grounds of plurality, was considerable, and was led from within the university by the divinity professor, Stevenson Macgill. It proved impossible to delay Macfarlan's installation as principal, but he was not admitted as minister until July 1824 after a vote at the general assembly had gone in his favour.

Macfarlan was the originator of the colonial mission scheme in 1835 and remained convener until 1856. He celebrated his ministerial jubilee in 1842 and the occasion was marked by a public dinner given by the citizens of Glasgow. He was prominent in the counsels of the moderate party throughout the disputes leading to the Disruption. At the assembly of 1843, after Dr David Welsh had departed with the Free Church adherents, Macfarlan occupied the moderatorial chair for a second time.

A man of distinguished appearance and gentlemanly demeanour, Macfarlan inevitably found himself involved in controversy by virtue of his prominence in the church, but it was conceded that he did not consciously provoke opposition, and neither did he give unnecessary offence in expressing strong views. His longevity and his consistency of opinion sometimes left him as the champion of outdated causes, as in the case of his upholding of religious tests in universities. It seems paradoxical that he achieved such eminence without excelling as a preacher, a scholar, a writer, or a speaker in church courts. Yet all deferred to him in the question of sagacity and sound judgement, based on his knowledge of the constitution and laws of the church. As his obituary stated 'it was nothing unusual to hear it remarked that the head of Principal Macfarlan was worth the brains of a whole Presbytery any day' (*Glasgow Herald*, 27 Nov 1857). A historian of the university considered that 'it may be questioned whether any Principal has performed the duties of the office more efficiently and to the advantage of the University than Dr Macfarlan' (Murray, 287).

Macfarlan enjoyed good health to the end of his life and even when he fractured his thigh in a fall in Helensburgh in August 1857, hopes were entertained of his recovery. He was brought back to the college where he died, father of the church, on 25 November 1857. He was buried, amid great ceremony, in Glasgow necropolis on 1 December, where a substantial monument marks his grave.

LIONEL ALEXANDER RITCHIE

Sources *Glasgow Herald* (27 Nov 1857) · *Fasti Scot.* · D. Murray, *Memories of the old college of Glasgow: some chapters in the history of the university* (1927) · J. MacLehose, ed., *Memoirs and portraits of one hundred Glasgow men who have died during the last thirty years*, 2 (1886), 189–90 · *Macphail's Edinburgh Ecclesiastical Journal and Literary Review*, 24/144 (1858), 323–37 · J. Smith, *Our Scottish clergy*, 2nd ser. (1849), 72–9 · J. G. Smith, *Strathendrick and its inhabitants from early times* (1896), 88–95 · *DNB* · J. Coutts, *A history of the University of Glasgow* (1909) · private information (2004)
Archives U. Glas., corresp. and papers | BL, corresp. with Sir Robert Peel, Add. MSS 40399–40541 · NL Scot., corresp. with John Lee · NL Scot., corresp. with William Mure
Likenesses J. G. Gilbert, oils, 1839, U. Glas. · engraving, repro. in *Memoirs and portraits of one hundred Glasgow men*, p. 189
Wealth at death £1778 13s. 5½d.: confirmation, 1859, Scotland

Macfarlan, James (1832–1862), poet, was born in Kirk Street, Calton, Glasgow, on 9 April 1832, the son of Andrew Macfarlan, a weaver turned pedlar from Augher, co. Tyrone, and his wife, Margaret Marshall. Macfarlan received rudimentary schooling at Kilmarnock and Glasgow. James Macfarlan always gave 1832 as his date of birth, suggesting that an earlier baptismal record for a child of the same name in Barony parish on 26 October 1828 may have been a sibling who died in infancy. In any event, at the age of twelve, stirred by Byron's poetry, he joined subscription libraries in towns visited in the family wanderings. At twenty, Macfarlan, then a professional pedlar, had read the principal English poets, and had himself written verse. In 1853 he walked to and from London, securing the publication of *Poems* (1854), which gave him some reputation, but little profit. For a short time subsequently he was assistant librarian in the Glasgow Athenaeum, but returned to peddling. He printed in Glasgow a second book, *City Songs* (1855), dedicated to the earl of Carlisle, but received scanty encouragement from the earl or the public. Struggling on against consumption, poverty, alcoholism, and neglect, getting and quickly losing employment, he was eventually employed as police-court reporter to the Glasgow *Bulletin*. Too erratic for this post, he successfully contributed short stories for a time to the weekly *The Workman*. On 3 August 1855 he married Agnes Miller, a steam-loom weaver from Belfast, who helped the income by dressmaking. They had four children. Dickens printed several of his poems in *All The Year Round*, including the apocalyptic 'The Ruined City', and Thackeray, hearing Samuel Lover recite 'The Lords of Labour' ('They come, they come, in glorious march!') in 1859, exclaimed that he did not think 'Burns himself could have taken the wind out of this man's sails'. Although he could be said to embody the voice of the urban oppressed, Macfarlan was not overtly political in his writing, nor did he use dialect. He is the lone artist in the teeming metropolis, despairing of fame, an archetypal Romantic poet. He sneered at convention and bit every hand that fed him. He was a paradox to his contemporaries: 'there never was such a great mind in such a vile body' (Hodgson). Exasperating as he was, he still produced some remarkable poetry.

Macfarlan took the temperance pledge about 1860, but his health grew progressively worse. A friend paid for a doctor who diagnosed pulmonary consumption. On a cold day at the end of October 1862 he collapsed after fruitlessly hawking his pamphlet *The Attic Study*. He lingered for a week and died on 6 November 1862 in his garret at 64 Drygate, Glasgow. He was buried on 10 November in Cheapside cemetery, Anderston, Glasgow. He was survived by his wife.   T. W. BAYNE, *rev.* HAMISH WHYTE

Sources H. Whyte, 'The miseries of hope: James Macfarlan (1832–1862)', *A Glasgow collection*, ed. K. McCarra and H. Whyte (1990), 137–55 [incl. transcription of Macfarlan's MS 'Sketch of my life'] · C. Rae-Brown, 'Memoir', in J. Macfarlan, *Poetical works* (1882) · [W. Hodgson], 'Occasional papers about old acquaintances, no 1: James Macfarlan, pedlar, and poet', undated newscutting, Mitchell L., Glas., Acc. no. 763715 · G. Eyre-Todd, 'James Macfarlan', *The Glasgow poets: their lives and poems*, ed. G. Eyre-Todd (1903), 377–81 · C. Rogers, *A century of Scottish life* (1871), 223–7 · A. A., 'Sketch of the author's life', in J. Macfarlan, *Lyrics of life* (1856), v–vii · 'James Macfarlane [sic]', *Tait's Edinburgh Magazine*, new ser., 25 (1858), 738–9 · *Glasgow Herald* (10 Nov 1862), 4 · *Glasgow Sentinel* (22 Nov 1862), 5 · A. C. Murdoch, 'James Macfarlan', *People's Friend* (2 June 1880), 339 · T. Bayne, 'The poetry of a Scottish pedlar', *Temple Bar*, 125 (1902), 271–8 · E. Morgan, 'Scottish poetry in the nineteenth century', *The history of Scottish literature*, ed. C. Craig, 3: *Nineteenth century*, ed. D. Gifford (1988), 337–49, esp. 342–3 · J. G. Wilson, ed., *The poets and poetry of Scotland*, 2 (1877), 482 · J. D. Young, 'Alexander Rodger (1784–1846) and James MacFarlan [sic] (1832–62): the voices of a subdued people', in J. D. Young, *The very bastards of creation* (1997),

102–41 · *The letters of Charles Dickens*, ed. M. House, G. Storey, and others, 9 (1997) · d. cert.

Archives Mitchell L., Glas., poems and papers

Macfarlan, John. *See* Macfarlane, John (*b*. before 1781, *d*. 1846).

Macfarlan, Patrick (1781–1849), Free Church of Scotland minister, was born in Edinburgh on 4 April 1781, the eleventh and youngest child of John Warden Macfarlan or Macfarlane (1740–1788), minister of the second charge, Canongate parish, Edinburgh, and his wife, Anne. He was brother of John *Macfarlane (*b*. before 1781, *d*. 1846). He was educated at Edinburgh high school and Edinburgh University, and was licensed by the presbytery of Edinburgh in December 1803. He was presented to the charge of Kippen, Stirlingshire, in 1806, transferring to Polmont in 1810. He married on 8 January 1808 Catherine, the daughter of Robert Clason, minister of Logie. They had a son, John (1815–1891), minister of Middle Free Church, Greenock, and three daughters. His wife died in 1815.

In 1824 Macfarlan succeeded Thomas Chalmers as minister of St John's, Glasgow, transferring to St Enoch's, Glasgow, in the following year. In 1832, and on Chalmers's recommendation, he was presented to the west parish, Greenock. He served as moderator of the general assembly in 1834. He was a prominent figure in the non-intrusion controversy which culminated in the Disruption of 1843, and his talents as a polemicist were well exercised. His adherence to the Free Church cause was seen as especially significant, as he then occupied the richest living in the Church of Scotland. The symbolism of his sacrifice was used in the painting of the Disruption day by David Octavius Hill, in which Macfarlan is shown in the act of signing the deed of demission, the first minister to do so. He was subsequently minister of the West Free Church, Greenock, and was moderator of the general assembly of the Free Church of Scotland in 1845. As a minister he was considered an unremarkable preacher but a good pastor. His portrait in Wylie's *Disruption Worthies* (1881) shows a bald man of slightly gaunt appearance, but with refined and striking features. One observer, writing in 1848, described 'a tall thin figure—a cranium finely chiselled, and bare as the autumn field' (Smith, 70). Although, as his output of pamphlets on subjects such as the Apocrypha controversy and the Disruption bear witness, he was a keen controversialist, his otherwise mild and gentle disposition belied this side of his nature. He was also a promoter of the Evangelical Alliance and took a keen interest in the affairs of reformed churches on the continent. He died on 13 November 1849.

LIONEL ALEXANDER RITCHIE

Sources *Fasti Scot.* · J. Smith, *Our Scottish clergy*, 2nd ser. (1849), 66–71 · W. Ewing, ed., *Annals of the Free Church of Scotland, 1843–1900*, 1 (1914), 226–7 · J. A. Wylie, *Disruption worthies: a memorial of 1843*, ed. J. B. Gillies, new edn (1881) · *Free Church Magazine*, 6 (1849), 375–6 · *DNB* · NA Scot., SC 58/42/18, p. 59

Archives NRA, priv. coll., letters to Moncrieff family · U. Edin., New Coll. L., letters to Thomas Chalmers

Likenesses D. O. Hill, oils, Free Church College, Edinburgh · lithograph, repro. in Wylie, *Disruption worthies*, facing p. 371

Wealth at death £9788 8s.: confirmation, 31 Jan 1850, NA Scot., SC 58/42/18, p. 59

Macfarlan, Robert (1733/4–1804), writer and translator, was born in Scotland and educated at Edinburgh University. He moved to England and supported himself by keeping a school at Walthamstow, Essex. In addition, he wrote reports of the parliamentary debates during Lord North's administration, contributed the first and fourth volumes of *The History of the First Ten Years of the Reign of George III*, and for a time edited the *Morning Chronicle* and *London Packet*.

As an enthusiastic admirer of James Macpherson's Ossian poems, Macfarlan published a Latin translation of one of them, *Temora*, in 1769. This was not well received, but Macfarlan persisted with his translation, based not on Macpherson's English text, but on what purported to be the Gaelic original. In 1807 it was posthumously published in three handsome volumes by the Highland Society of London, with the Gaelic and English texts on facing pages. Macfarlan was described in Sir John Sinclair's introduction as 'a scholar perfectly skilled in both languages' (Sinclair, 89). Such a translation might seem an eccentric undertaking. Macfarlan's obituary commented: 'What is there to which the schoolmasters of North Britain do not consider themselves equal?' (*GM*, 791–2). The study was in fact part of a campaign, led by Sir John Sinclair, to claim that Macpherson's work was a genuine translation from the Gaelic and deserved to be treated as an ancient classic text.

Macfarlan's other substantial translation was not into Latin but from it. This work, published in 1801, was a version of George Buchanan's *De jure regni apud Scotos* ('Of the law of sovereignty in Scotland') of 1579, an exposition of the Scottish doctrine that sovereignty rested with the people. In this case, Macfarlan justified his translation with the argument that Latin was becoming so unfashionable that it would soon be as unintelligible as Sanskrit. He was as enthusiastic for Buchanan as he was for Ossian. In his introduction he described Buchanan as 'the father of politics in modern Europe' (Macfarlan, 64) and stated that 'the existence of such a luminary in the north rationally explains why the Scots got the start of their southern neighbours in the causes of religious and civil liberty' (ibid., 80).

Although Macfarlan's school at Walthamstow had a good reputation, by 1801 he was reduced to a much smaller establishment. He included an advertisement at the end of his translation of Buchanan, in which he said that he offered board and education for six young gentlemen at £100 a year and had two vacancies. All the signs are that Macfarlan was a Gaelic-speaking highlander of strong Scottish patriotism and considerable talent who had a hard struggle to survive in the Grub Street of his day. He died aged seventy on 8 August 1804, as a result of falling under a carriage at Hammersmith during a parliamentary election.

PAUL HENDERSON SCOTT

Sources Anderson, *Scot. nat.*, 2.731–2 · *GM*, 1st ser., 74 (1804), 791–2 · J. Sinclair, 'Dissertation on the authenticity of the poems of Ossian', *The poems of Ossian*, trans. R. Macfarlan, 3 vols. (1807) ·

R. Macfarlan, 'Introduction', in G. Buchanan, *De jure regni apud Scotos*, trans. R. Macfarlan (1799)

Macfarlan, Walter, of Arrochar [of that ilk] (*d.* **1767**), antiquary and chief of clan Macfarlan, was the second son of John Macfarlan of Arrochar (*d.* 1705), chief of clan Macfarlan, and Helen (*d.* 1741), daughter of Robert, second Viscount Arbuthnott. He was born, probably at Arrochar, some time after 1689 (it is known that he was under twenty-one in 1709) and possibly not long before he succeeded his father as chief of clan Macfarlan in 1705.

From his early years Macfarlan, an enthusiastic Scottish patriot, devoted himself to antiquarian research connected with the history of Scotland. Ecclesiastical records specially attracted him, and he employed a clerk named Tait to make copies of most of the cartularies accessible to him.

Macfarlan appears to have held strict views on etiquette, particularly in relation to his own position as chief of a highland clan. 'The late laird of Macfarlan, an eminent genealogist', wrote Dr Johnson, 'considered himself as disrespectfully treated if the common addition [i.e. Mr] was applied to him. "Mr. Macfarlan", said he, "may with equal propriety be said to many; but I, and I only, am Macfarlan"' (*Johnson's Journey*, 139).

Macfarlan married Lady Elizabeth Erskine (1735–1790), daughter of Alexander, fifth earl of Kellie, in 1760; they had no children. He died at his house in Reid's Close, Canongate, Edinburgh, on 5 June 1767, and was buried at the New Kirk, Greyfriars, Edinburgh, on 8 June. He was succeeded by his brother William. His library was sold, and in 1785 the Faculty of Advocates purchased his manuscripts, of which the cartularies of Aberdeen, Arbroath, Balmerino, Dryburgh, Dunfermline, Kelso, Lindores, Melrose, Moray, St Andrews, and Scone have been printed. His genealogical and geographical collections were published by the Scottish History Society between 1800 and 1808. His printed cartularies were extensively used by Sir Robert Douglas in his *Peerage of Scotland* (1764).

A. F. POLLARD, *rev.* ALEXANDER DU TOIT

Sources J. MacFarlane, *History of clan MacFarlane* (1921) • R. Douglas and others, *The baronage of Scotland* (1798) • W. Fraser, *The chiefs of Colquhoun and their country*, 2 vols. (1869) • *Scots Magazine*, 29 (1767) • Burke, *Peerage* • W. B. Turnbull, *Catalogue of the manuscripts in the library of the Faculty of Advocates* (1869) • *Boswell's London journal, 1762–63*, ed. F. A. Pottle (1950), vol. 1 of *The Yale editions of the private papers of James Boswell*, trade edn (1950–89) • *Johnson's Journey to the western islands of Scotland*, ed. R. W. Chapman (1930)
Archives NL Scot., notes and collections | S. Antiquaries, Lond., transcripts of collections of Sir Robert Sibbald and account of the MacDonald of Glengary family
Likenesses J. T. Seton, oils, 1757, Scot. NPG • portrait, S. Antiquaries, Lond.
Wealth at death left Arrochar estate (sold for £28,000, 1784) and Edinburgh house to brother

Macfarlane, Mrs [*née* Straiton] (*fl.* **1716–1719**), murderer, was the daughter of Colonel Charles Straiton, a zealous Jacobite. An 'extreme beauty', she married the middle-aged John Macfarlane of Edinburgh, writer to the signet and law agent to Simon Fraser, Lord Lovat, when she was about nineteen.

The *Domestic Annals* record that the Macfarlanes were intimately acquainted with Captain John Cayley, commissioner of customs and son of Cornelius Cayley of York, who lodged in Parliament Close with Mrs Murray, a friend of Mrs Macfarlane's since her schooldays. Cayley appears to have boasted publicly of a liaison with Mrs Macfarlane, while John Macfarlane believed his wife's story that Cayley enlisted Mrs Murray in 'a very bad design' against her. John Macfarlane described how, on 29 September 1716, Mrs Murray invited his wife to her home and locked her in alone with Cayley who used 'barbarous force' against her. On 2 October Cayley called on Mrs Macfarlane when she was at home alone. In his account of events John Macfarlane insisted that Cayley made directly for his wife's bedchamber 'resolving to have his purpose'; according to another account, Mrs Macfarlane led him there herself. Whether to defend her honour or avenge herself on an indiscreet lover, Mrs Macfarlane fired a pair of pistols at Cayley, killing him with a shot to the heart. She immediately sent for her husband who confirmed that she wished to tell the whole story before a magistrate, his wife saying later that she had suffered 'the most unworthy provocation'. John Macfarlane, who publicly maintained his wife's 'integrity, virtue and innocence', advised against this and sent her into hiding, where she remained until at least February 1719 when, failing to appear to stand trial, she was outlawed.

Mrs Macfarlane was sheltered temporarily by the Swintons who were distant relatives. Sir Walter Scott remembered being told by his great-aunt Margaret Swinton that as a child she had met 'the enchanted queen' pouring tea in the parlour at Swinton House, but that she had vanished when the child had turned round, escaping through a sliding panel into an adjacent concealed apartment. This incident became the description of the concealment and discovery of the countess of Derby in Scott's *Peveril of the Peak* (1822).

Robert Chambers is sceptical, but Scott and Swinton believed that Mrs Macfarlane returned to live and die in Edinburgh and was not brought to trial. This is possible as her life in Edinburgh appears to have been relatively short, for her husband remarried on 6 October 1719.

T. F. HENDERSON, *rev.* BARBARA WHITE

Sources R. Chambers, *Domestic annals of Scotland from the revolution to the rebellion of 1745* (1841) • A. C. Swinton, *The Swintons of that ilk and their cadets* (1883) • *The works of Alexander Pope*, ed. W. Roscoe, 10 vols. (1824–5), vol. 9, p. 35

Macfarlane, Charles (1799–1858), historian and traveller, was born on 18 December 1799, probably in the Scottish highlands, the son of Robert Macfarlane and his wife, the daughter of John Howard and the widow of a major called Harris. From January 1816 until May 1827 Macfarlane lived in Naples; travelling throughout Italy, he became fluent in Italian and well read in Italian literature. He became acquainted with many English aristocrats and literary figures, including Henry Augustus Dillon-Lee, the thirteenth Viscount Dillon, John William Ward, the fourth Baron Dudley and Ward, and Percy Bysshe Shelley; he met the poet in the Museo Borbonico in Naples and with him visited the ruins of Pompeii. In 1827 he travelled to Turkey and spent sixteen months in Constantinople and the surrounding provinces. On returning to Britain in February 1829 he published his first book, *Constantinople in 1828*. Both a travelogue and a recent history of Turkey, this extensive work was enlivened by occasional lively descriptions of everyday events, but was imbued with Macfarlane's rampant racial prejudices against Armenians, Jews, and (to a lesser degree) Turks, which were only moderated by his obvious susceptibility to all varieties of Eastern women.

On settling in London—after a brief spell in Brighton recovering from malaria—Macfarlane earned a living by literary hack work. He must have married soon after his arrival in Britain, as his eldest son was born in July 1832; the couple had two sons and three daughters in total. Macfarlane was employed for many years on the staff of the publisher Charles Knight, and became a minor figure in the London literary world, acquainted with celebrities including Hartley Coleridge, the Wordsworths, Thomas De Quincey, Leigh Hunt, John Murray, James Mackintosh, Thomas Hood, and Anna Jameson. He had a talent for company: J. R. Planché considered him 'a most amusing companion and a warm friend' (Planché, 2.207), and Knight described him (more guardedly) as 'a most agreeable companion and an affectionate though not a safe friend' (Knight, 2.261). His residence near London, at Barnet, was brought to an end by a visit to Italy and Turkey in 1846, after which he moved to Canterbury.

Macfarlane's most significant work was probably the narrative of the civil and military history of England which he contributed to Knight's *Pictorial History of England* (1837–44), edited by G. L. Craik; an updated abridgement was published in *The Cabinet History of England* (1845–7) and it also appeared in later editions under the title of *The Comprehensive History of England* (1856–61; 1876–8). Many of his other works appeared in one or other of Knight's many series of publications, including *The French Revolution* (1844), *The Romance of Travel: the East* (1846), and *Popular Customs, Sports, and Recollections of South Italy* (1846), the last of which had originally appeared in the *Penny Magazine*. He also published biographies of statesmen and soldiers, works on contemporary politics, military matters, and histories of India, Japan, and China. His historical novels remain readable if quite extraordinarily long-winded: it seems probable that *The Camp of Refuge* (1844) was a model for Charles Kingsley's *Hereward the Wake* (1865). The ironical comment of his memorialist in *The Athenaeum*—that he was a 'voluminous—rather than a luminous—writer ... whose complete list of works astonishes by its mere extent' (*The Athenaeum*, 1625)—is largely justified.

A breach with Knight ensued in the early 1850s, probably on the grounds of their contrasting political views. Macfarlane was a diehard tory: Knight commented in his own autobiography that his contribution to *The Pictorial History*, while showing 'considerable powers of narration', was 'essentially ... partizan' (Knight, 2.261). Macfarlane, meanwhile, felt that the publisher had fallen under the liberal influence of Douglas Jerrold, Charles Dickens, and

most importantly, Harriet Martineau, whom he vituperated as an 'ill-favoured, dogmatizing, masculine spinster' (Macfarlane, 93). The sheer violence of his attack on Martineau, in his *Reminiscences* (written in the mid-1850s), seems to have been fuelled by his disappointment over *The History of the Thirty Years' Peace*, a work for which he thought he should have been commissioned but which Knight invited Martineau to write. This—and Knight's financial speculations—were blamed by Macfarlane for his poverty in the 1850s: in June 1857 he was admitted as a poor brother to Charterhouse, London, where he died on 9 December 1858.   ROSEMARY MITCHELL

Sources C. Macfarlane, *Reminiscences of a literary life*, ed. J. F. Tattersall (1917) · *DNB* · *The Athenaeum* (18 Dec 1858), 800 · C. Knight, *Passages of a working life during half a century*, 3 vols. (1864–5) · J. R. Planché, *The recollections and reflections of J. R. Planché*, 2 vols. (1872)
Archives BL, reminiscences, Add. MSS 39775–39776 · BL, travels in Turkey and Asia Minor, Add. MSS 25430–25431
Likenesses W. Brockedon, chalk drawing, 1832, NPG

Macfarlane, Donald (1834–1926), Free Church of Scotland minister, was born at Vallay, North Uist, the fourth of the six children of Donald Macfarlane, a manager of farms on the estate of Colonel Gordon of Cluny, Aberdeenshire, the proprietor of South Uist and Barra. His mother was Elizabeth Macdonald, daughter of Alexander Macdonald, Trotternish, Skye.

Macfarlane's early education was at parish schools in South Uist. In 1850 he attended a school at Uiskeva, Benbecula, which had been set up through the efforts of the Ladies' Society for the Religious Improvement of the Remote Highlands and Islands. Its first teacher was Donald Macdonald, afterwards Free Church minister of Shieldaig, who became a lifelong friend of Macfarlane's. In October 1856 a change occurred which altered the whole course of Macfarlane's life, when he was called to the Christian ministry through the preaching of Alexander MacColl of Duirinish, Skye, and afterwards of Lochalsh.

In order to raise sufficient funds to start a university course Macfarlane taught for the next seven years in three Hebridean schools. He began his college course at Glasgow University in 1863, and completed his divinity course in 1873. He studied under two distinguished professors, William Ramsay and Edmund Law Lushington. Under Lushington he made a special study of Greek. His theology course was at Glasgow Free Church College, where the principal was Patrick Fairbairn.

The spiritual and theological decline of the Free Church in the fifty years after the Disruption accelerated during the ten-year union controversy that coincided with Macfarlane's period in Glasgow. The controversy was stirred by the attempts at effecting a union between the Free Church and the United Presbyterian church. The United Presbyterians were voluntaries and were willing to tolerate an Amyraldian view of the atonement—essentially, that Christ died for all. The negotiations polarized the Free Church into two parties and divided every presbytery. Macfarlane supported the anti-unionists, led by

James Begg, and his acquaintance with theological compromise during these years left its impress on the rest of his career.

The presbytery of Skye and Uist licensed Macfarlane on 24 June 1874 at Snizort. While still a probationer at Dunoon he met John Kennedy of Dingwall, who recommended the elders of the congregation of Strathconan, Ross-shire, to call him as their minister. He was ordained and inducted at Strathconan on 20 January 1876. Three years later he received a call to Moy, Inverness-shire. While there he married Mary Morrison (d. 1928), the eldest daughter of Alexander Morrison, Sollas, North Uist. Horatius Bonar conducted the ceremony on 14 April 1880 at the Windsor Hotel, Princes Street, Edinburgh. They had no children. In 1888 Macfarlane accepted a call to Kilmallie in the Free Church Presbytery of Abertarff.

In the last quarter of the nineteenth century worldwide Presbyterianism was loosening its attachment to Calvinism and to the Westminster confession of faith. The United Presbyterian church passed a declaratory act in 1879, whose purpose was to declare or explain the confession, a dilution of the church's commitment to Calvinism. Presbyterian churches throughout the world soon followed the United Presbyterians' lead. The Free Church of Scotland set up a committee in 1889 to report on ways of 'providing relief' for those who could not give unqualified subscription to the Westminster confession. Two years later a declaratory act was approved by the general assembly, which became church law in 1892.

Before the declaratory act was passed, opposition to it had been organized by the constitutional party in the Free Church—a grouping with which Macfarlane was associated. In January 1893 Macfarlane's presbytery of Abertarff engrossed in its records a protest against the general assembly's action in approving the declaratory act. A week later, on 25 January 1893, Macfarlane's own kirk session placed a similar protest in its minutes. During the resulting turmoil Macfarlane was translated from Kilmallie to Raasay. The induction was on 25 April 1893 and he took office under a protest against the declaratory act.

The general assembly of the Free Church of Scotland of 1893 was the jubilee of the Disruption. Most major Presbyterian churches in the world sent delegates to the gathering. On 25 May the commissioners dealt with the overtures for the repeal of the declaratory act. When, through the influence of Principal Robert Rainy, the assembly refused to repeal the act, Macfarlane advanced to the clerk's table and laid on it a protest. This action led to the formation of the Free Presbyterian Church of Scotland. Macfarlane was joined by his friend Donald Macdonald (the only minister to stand with him), a group of students led by Neil Cameron, and a large number of elders and lay people, mainly in the Scottish highlands. The new church's first presbytery met on 28 July 1893, and on 14 August 1893 the presbytery adopted a deed of separation from the Free Church.

Macfarlane became the first Free Presbyterian minister of Raasay. Initially the landowner refused to grant a site for either a church or a manse. For five years Macfarlane lived in a rented house in Broadford on Skye and crossed to Raasay by boat every weekend. In 1903 he was translated to Dingwall, where he continued his ministry for a further twenty-three years. Macfarlane, together with Neil Cameron, guided the Free Presbyterian church for the first thirty years of its existence. Both vigorously opposed attempts, in 1905 and 1918, to unite the Free Presbyterian church with the section of the Free Church that refused to enter the 1900 union of the majority Free Church with the United Presbyterian church.

Donald Macfarlane believed the Bible to be the inerrant word of God. His sermons were noted for their remarkable clearness and simplicity. His published works include *Memoir and Remains of the Rev. Donald Macdonald: Shieldaig* (1903), *Sermons on the Love of God and Cognate Themes* (1918), and several pamphlets. He died at Dingwall on 4 November 1926 and was buried in the cemetery there on 9 November.   ROY MIDDLETON

Sources D. Beaton, *Memoir, diary and remains of the Rev Donald Macfarlane, Dingwall* (1929) · A. McPherson, ed., *History of the Free Presbyterian Church of Scotland, 1893–1970* [n.d.] · N. Cameron, *Ministers and men of the Free Presbyterian church*, ed. R. Middleton (1993) · [D. R. Macsween], ed., *One hundred years of witness* (1993) · J. L. MacLeod, *The second disruption: the Free Church in Victorian Scotland and the origins of the Free Presbyterian church* (2000) · K. R. Ross, *Church and creed: the Free Church case, 1900–1904, and its origins* (1988) · A. L. Drummond and J. Bulloch, *The church in late Victorian Scotland* (1978) · A. L. Drummond and J. Bulloch, *The church in Victorian Scotland, 1843–1874* (1975) · *Free Presbyterian Magazine*, 31 (1926–7), 361–70 · W. Ewing, ed., *Annals of the Free Church of Scotland, 1843–1900*, 1 (1914), 227 · *DSCHT*, 513 · *Northern Chronicle* (10 Nov 1926), 5, col. 1 · *Inverness Courier* (9 Nov 1926), 6, col. 4

Wealth at death £604 4s. 6d.: confirmation, 22 Dec 1926, Scotland, *CCI*

Macfarlane, Duncan. *See* Macfarlan, Duncan (1771–1857).

Macfarlane, (Robert) Gwyn (1907–1987), clinical pathologist and haematologist, was born on 26 June 1907 at Worthing, Sussex, the posthumous son and only child of John Gray Macfarlane (1868–1907), for many years solicitor of the high court of Bombay, India, but latterly manager of the Siamese branch of the Bombay and Burma Trading Corporation. He died of rabies at Bangkok while his wife, Eileen Montagu (b. 1888), daughter of the Revd Lancelot Sanderson, was on her way to England for the child's birth. Macfarlane attended St Nicholas day school in Southampton, progressing to Highfield preparatory school, Liphook, then to Cheltenham College, where he excelled in science and mathematics, and displayed a passionate interest in anything mechanical. However, he decided on a medical career and entered St Bartholomew's medical school in 1925. His studies were protracted by his outside interests in the humanities, music, motoring, and sailing, but in 1933 he qualified MRCS and LRCP and graduated MB BS (London).

After several short-term spells in hospitals and general practice Macfarlane moved to pathology as junior demonstrator at Barts in 1934. The following year he was awarded a fellowship by the Sir Halley Stewart Trust to undertake research on bleeding. His first published paper was on blood coagulation, a topic on which he built his career and reputation; his 1938 MD was on bleeding, with a gold medal for his thesis. There followed a period at the newly founded British Postgraduate Medical School at Hammersmith Hospital as clinical pathologist and assistant lecturer in clinical pathology, under the directorship of Janet Vaughan. There he continued his work, with Vaughan, essentially using the weakness of the clotting mechanism in haemophiliacs to study normal haemostasis. A key feature of his work was the linking of clinical cases with laboratory experiments and vice versa. His most influential publications at this time were review articles, which typically combined thoroughness and elegance with a critical edge. He assisted Vaughan in her pioneering work in organizing blood banking in anticipation of war. During the 1930s also, he explored various ways of treating haemophiliacs, including work on snake venom that eventually led Burroughs Wellcome to produce Stypven, a coagulant derived from the venom of Russell's viper.

In 1936 Macfarlane had married Hilary, daughter of Harry Arthur Hamilton Carson, surgeon, and herself a newly qualified doctor, whom he had met on a Bart's sailing club trip in Ramsgate harbour. They had four sons and a daughter and enjoyed a long and happy life together. Early in 1939 Macfarlane moved to the Wellcome Physiological Laboratories at Beckenham, Kent, as assistant bacteriologist. But finding the commercial world uncongenial he left in 1940 to become clinical pathologist at the Radcliffe Infirmary, Oxford, beginning an association that endured until his retirement in 1968. During the Second World War, in collaboration with J. R. P. O'Brien, Macfarlane developed national standards and procedures for the measurement of haemoglobin levels in the blood, he organized the local blood transfusion service, and continued to develop clinical laboratory services. He left Oxford only for war service overseas in a mobile bacteriology laboratory in 1944–5. Hilary Macfarlane worked as a general practitioner at Witney and they lived for most of the time at Downhill Farm, near Witney, surrounded by farm animals and usually with an added complement of friends.

In 1948 Macfarlane was appointed Radcliffe lecturer in haematology, moving to a readership in 1957 and a chair in clinical pathology in 1965. He was elected fellow of the Royal Society in 1956 and in 1959 his growing reputation was recognized when the Medical Research Council supported the creation of a unit concerned with blood coagulation in his department. Among his many friends at Oxford was Howard Florey, best known for his work on the development of penicillin, and Macfarlane's respected position was recognized by a fellowship at All Souls in 1963.

Macfarlane's most productive period of research had started shortly after the end of the war, when he began collaborative research with Rosemary Biggs, first on the breakup of blood clots (fibrinolysis) and the conditions that favoured the process. However, their main achievement came in the 1950s in their contribution to the revision of the accepted model of blood coagulation that required the presence of four factors. More and more factors were recognized and were given the Roman numeral system that is still used. Macfarlane's laboratory focused on factors V and X, and then factors VIII and IX. The accepted theory of coagulation suggested simply that the various factors needed to be present to react at the site of an injury for coagulation to occur. However, Macfarlane replaced this with the notion that each factor played a specific role in a sequence of reactions that produced clotting. His idea became known as the cascade hypothesis, because it explained how a small injury could, through escalating reactions, produce a major physiological response.

Throughout the 1950s the laboratory work of Macfarlane, Biggs, and other colleagues was helped by its interactions with clinical work. They developed improved methods for the diagnosis of bleeding conditions, including genetic disorders. They also made innovations in the management of haemophiliac patients, refining Mersky's idea of extracting the antihaemophilic globulin (AHG) from normal blood and giving it prophylactically to sufferers. When it transpired that one patient would need the AHG from a thousand patients for a single year's treatment, the Radcliffe Infirmary looked to animal sources. This proved to have limited value with haemophiliacs due to antigenic reactions, but it was useful clinically in surgery and was produced industrially from the late 1950s. Work continued on concentrating using human AHG, which was now known as factor VIII for use in the surgical and dental treatment of haemophiliacs.

After Macfarlane's retirement methods were developed to extract factor VIII from routine blood donations and the type of preventive service Macfarlane had envisaged for many years became possible. Through the Haemophiliac Society, Macfarlane campaigned for the establishment of blood products laboratories. However, the government response was slow and weak, with just the two laboratories in Oxford and Elstree unable to meet demand. In 1974 the government began to import factor VIII from the United States and by the early 1980s around two thirds was imported. In the early 1980s it was slowly realized that factor VIII treatment had led to many haemophiliacs becoming infected as a result of HIV contamination of blood products. Macfarlane was desperately upset that such a promising treatment had brought such a tragedy. He did all he could, with the Haemophiliac Society, to pressurize the government to introduce heat treatment of factor VIII, to establish more blood products laboratories in Britain, and to provide compensation. In 1977 Macfarlane retired to Achnasheen, Ross-shire, where, helped by his wife and a local builder, he restored a crofter's cottage, naming it, after its last owner, Mallie's Cottage. He took on new challenges, championing the cause of haemophiliacs, and writing two biographies: *Howard Florey: the Making of a Great Scientist* (1979) and *Alexander Fleming, the Man and the Myth* (1984). These were significant contributions to the history of medicine which, in the case of Fleming, led to a television documentary and sparked a re-evaluation of Fleming's work on penicillin and his scientific standing. Macfarlane died at Mallie's Cottage on 26 March 1987. MICHAEL WORBOYS

Sources G. V. Born and D. J. Weatherall, *Memoirs FRS*, 35 (1990), 211–45 · A. Robb-Smith, *The life and achievements of Professor Robert Gwyn Macfarlane* (1993) · 'Robert Gwyn Macfarlane', *The Lancet* (1987), 1.932–3 · personal knowledge (1996) [*DNB*]
Archives Wellcome L., corresp. and papers | FILM 'Microbe and mould', *BBC Horizon*, 1995 [featured Macfarlane and based on his biography of Alexander Fleming]
Likenesses photograph, repro. in Born and Weatherall, *Memoirs FRS*
Wealth at death £53,385: probate, 24 July 1987, *CGPLA Eng. & Wales*

Macfarlane, James (1800–1871). *See under* Macfarlane, John (*b.* before 1781, *d.* 1846).

Macfarlane, James (1845–1889). *See under* Macfarlane, John (*b.* before 1781, *d.* 1846).

McFarlane, James Walter (1920–1999), literary scholar, was born on 12 December 1920 at 21 Rainton Street, Sunderland, the son of James McFarlane, boiler plater, and his wife, Florence Elizabeth Todd. He was educated at Bede Grammar School, Sunderland, and went to St Catherine's Society, Oxford, to read modern languages in 1939. His university career was interrupted by the Second World War, and he served in the intelligence corps in Europe (1941–6), ending the war as a major. He married (Lillie) Kathleen Crouch (*b.* 1921/2), textile artist, on 16 September 1944; they had two sons and a daughter. McFarlane returned to Oxford, and graduated in 1947 and took a BLitt degree in the following year. He was a soccer blue at Oxford, and during the war occasionally appeared as a centre half for Sunderland.

In 1947 McFarlane was appointed lecturer in the department of German and Scandinavian studies at King's College, University of Durham (which in 1963 became the University of Newcastle upon Tyne). Having originally intended to work on German literature, he soon became absorbed in Norwegian writers, initially the great novelist Knut Hamsun, whose *Pan* he translated in 1955. His concern with Hamsun was enduring—he translated *The Wayfarers* (1980), and with Harald Naess brought out a two-volume edition of Hamsun's letters (1990, 1998). But it was to Ibsen that he devoted most of his scholarly career, beginning with the publication of *Ibsen and the Temper of Norwegian Literature* (1960), and encompassing his masterly eight-volume edition of Ibsen's prose plays. For the *Oxford Ibsen* (1960–77) McFarlane translated all the prose plays and wrote critical introductions, carrying on the early work on the reception of Ibsen by Edmund Gosse and William Archer. The enterprise was quickly recognized as a major contribution to the translation and understanding of Ibsen's genius and towering role in pioneering modernism on the European stage. It became a source of regret to him that his accurate, refined translations, informed by his wide knowledge of the writer's language and milieu, did not become the standard performing versions of the texts: others, less accurate by far, aiming to make the text 'contemporary' in a sensationalist

vein, claimed and held the stage. But McFarlane never ceased to deepen academic and public awareness of Ibsen, through his lectures and articles, culminating in his *Cambridge Companion to Henrik Ibsen* (1994), while his students traced the history of Ibsen performance in Britain and elsewhere.

In 1964 McFarlane was appointed professor of European literature at the new University of East Anglia, and became founding dean of the school of European studies (1964–8). A companionable, enthusiastic, and inspiring colleague, teacher, and dean, he led the new university towards a more open academic structure, characterized by organization into schools of study in which a number of disciplines were united, offering opportunities for comparative and interdisciplinary approaches. He preferred the title professor of European literature to the narrower professor of Scandinavian or Norwegian language and literature, and it was in this light that he breathed life and hope into the new teaching and administrative arrangements. He built up a new department (or 'sector', as it was known) of modern Scandinavian studies, which taught all three major Scandinavian languages, and he also forwarded his subject through the journal *Scandinavica*, of which he was editor (1975–90) and editor at large (1991–9). His striking bearded figure, seated before a handsome woven work of art by his wife, presided over the school as first among equals in the community he had largely formed. His constructive and forward-looking temper found an echo in others who joined the new university, and in 1976 he and Malcolm Bradbury, professor of American literature (itself a new subject in British universities) and pioneer of the creative writing MA degree, were jointly editors of a widely used book, *Modernism: a Guide to European Literature, 1890–1930*, in which McFarlane insisted on giving due weight to the Nordic, German, Italian, and Russian influences on modernism, which had often been neglected in favour of the French, British, and American.

When in the early 1980s cuts in government funding hit the universities, and in particular small language departments, McFarlane did battle to save his subject. His department was acknowledged to be the foremost British department of modern Scandinavian studies, and it was one of the four to survive. Even so, the threat was not over, and with characteristic generosity in 1982 he offered his own early retirement in return for an agreement that the department should be maintained and all the Scandinavian languages should continue to be taught. This gesture, however quixotic, ensured the survival of the department, to which he remained attached as professorial fellow (1982–6) and professor emeritus. In 1985 he was presented with a Festschrift by his colleagues in European studies, *Facets of European Modernism*, edited by Janet Garton.

McFarlane's devotion to his subject and his founding ardour were not spent, however, and in 1985, with his colleague Janet Garton, he set up Norvik Press, and became its managing editor. Norvik continues his work of making Scandinavian literature more widely known. He published his translation of Obstfelder's *A Priest's Diary* with

Norvik in 1988. Although in the 1990s the school of European studies was dissolved into the school of language, linguistics, and translation, and most of the teachers of literature were transferred to the school of English and American studies, undermining the intellectual vision that had driven the formation of the University of East Anglia, McFarlane's achievements in his subject stand. He was much honoured abroad, especially in Scandinavia: he was elected a foreign member of the Norwegian Academy of Science in 1977 and of the Royal Danish Academy of Sciences and Letters in 1983; he became an honorary member of Phi Beta Kappa in 1984, and was appointed to the Royal Norwegian order of St Olav in 1975.

Mac, as he was known to friends and colleagues, died on 9 August 1999 at his home, The Croft, Hunworth Road, Stody, near Melton Constable, Norfolk. He was survived by his wife, his children, and six grandsons.

ELINOR SHAFFER

Sources *The Independent* (25 Aug 1999) · *The Guardian* (30 Aug 1999) · *WWW* · personal knowledge (2004) · private information (2004) · b. cert. · m. cert. · d. cert.
Likenesses photograph, repro. in *The Independent* · photograph, repro. in *The Guardian*

Macfarlane [*married name* Brodie], **Jessie** (1843–1871), preacher, was born on 20 January 1843 in Edinburgh, the daughter of Archibald McFarlane, a clothier, and his wife, Mary Maxwell, *née* Turner. Her parents were presbyterians and her early religious experience was influenced by an uncle who, it appears, was a minister. In 1859 she heard Brownlow North (1810–1875), the aristocratic lay preacher, in Edinburgh, and this began an intense period of conviction of sin. Further attendance at revival meetings brought her to an evangelical conversion towards the end of 1860 during the singing of Charlotte Elliott's hymn 'Just as I am'. In January 1861, shortly after the death of a younger sister who had implored her to be religiously active, she spontaneously began extemporary preaching at a meeting for women, proving highly effective. She started preaching regularly to other women and throughout 1861 spoke at revivalist missions elsewhere in Scotland, among them one in and around Kelso, where her meetings were arranged by Horatius Bonar (1808–1889), the Free Church of Scotland minister and hymn writer, and while she was there an evangelical awakening took place. During a mission in 1862 at Gullane, East Lothian, so many men crowded around the place she was preaching that she began to admit them to her meetings.

Jessie Macfarlane's active lay ministry was controversial. The man whom she was to marry broke off their engagement because of her public preaching to mixed-gender audiences. She began the religious instruction of new converts in various places, an even more contentious issue than preaching to those deemed unconverted. She was promoted to a larger audience in Glasgow and Edinburgh by Gordon Forlong (1819–1908), an upper-class revivalist who had become convinced of the legitimacy of female preachers on eschatological grounds. In 1864 she published a pamphlet *Scriptural Warrant for Women to Preach the Gospel* (1864), in which—repeating the arguments commonly used by contemporary supporters of women preachers—she claimed that the role of prophetess had not been abolished in the church, and that seemingly negative New Testament strictures on a public role for women were the result of either mistranslation or misinterpretation.

In 1862 Jessie Macfarlane had undergone believer's baptism in an Edinburgh Baptist church, and although she remained non-denominational her views accorded with those of the (Plymouth) Brethren, whose millenarian opinions she shared. She was dependent on free-will offerings for her financial support. Her preaching, often deeply emotional, was enhanced by her 'rich full voice' (*In Memoriam*, 23). One contemporary report noted that her 'demeanour is exceedingly ladylike' (ibid., 47). Her activities were paralleled by women such as Geraldine Hooper (1841–1872), whom she met. The emergence of women preachers was made possible by the revivalist enthusiasm for converts and the egalitarian impulse often implicit within such movements. It has been argued that their activities were important at a popular level in making expanded roles for women possible in the later nineteenth century.

From 1866 onwards Jessie Macfarlane preached in many places in England, including Ipswich, Manchester, and London. On 31 October 1869 she married David Brodie, a physician from Liberton, Edinburgh. Although it had been her intention to continue preaching, she was increasingly troubled by ill health. She died childless on 18 August 1871 at Columbia Lodge, Liberton, survived by her husband. She was buried in Grange cemetery, Edinburgh.

NEIL DICKSON

Sources H. I. G., *In memoriam: Jessie McFarlane, a tribute of affection* (1872) · O. Anderson, 'Women preachers in mid-Victorian Britain: some reflexions on feminism, popular religion and social change', *HJ*, 12 (1969), 467–84 · N. Dickson, 'Modern prophetesses: women preachers in the nineteenth-century Scottish Brethren', *Records of the Scottish Church History Society*, 25 (1993–5), 89–117 · d. cert.

Macfarlane [Macfarlan], **John** (*b.* before **1781**, *d.* **1846**), lawyer, elder brother of Patrick *Macfarlan (1781–1849), was the eldest son of John Warden (1740–1788), minister of the second charge, Canongate, Edinburgh, who took the additional name of Macfarlane after marrying Anne, daughter of Hugh Macfarlane of Kirkton or Ballencleroche. John, who succeeded to the family property, was brought up to the law, and developed a good practice as an advocate. He was one of Sir Walter Scott's friends, studied German with him about 1788, and was regarded by Lockhart as a 'Kantist' (Lockhart, 1.231). He knew Dugald Stewart and Sir Henry Moncrieff, was interested in philosophy, and was a good lawyer. He is mentioned in Henry Cockburn's *Memorials* as 'an apostle, and worthy of the best apostolic age'. He published two pamphlets, *Who are the Friends of Religion and the Church?* (1838) and *The Presbyterian Empire: its Origin, Decline, and Fall* (1842). He died on 18 December 1846, leaving, with his wife, Christian, a son, **James Macfarlane** [Macfarlan] (1800–1871), who was born on 28 January 1800, qualified as an advocate, then was licensed by the presbytery of Glasgow in 1831, and became minister of Muiravonside, near Linlithgow, on the presentation of William IV, in 1834. He was a Hebrew scholar, and published in 1845 an English version of the *Prophecies of Ezekiel*. On 31 October 1837 he married Matilda Marianne Christie, daughter of Captain Christie of the 78th regiment, and granddaughter of William Morehead of Herbertshire. Their children included **James Macfarlane** [Macfarlan] (1845–1889), who was born on 6 January 1845, educated at the Edinburgh Academy (1858–61) and Edinburgh University (1861–4), and licensed as a minister. He assisted at Dundee from 1869 to 1871 when he was appointed minister of Ruthwell by the earl of Mansfield. Also in 1871 he married Helen, daughter of Professor Allan Menzies of Edinburgh University. He was an archaeologist, and in 1887 he got the runic cross of Ruthwell, on which he wrote a monograph (1885), moved to the church. He died at Foulden, Berwickshire, on 4 October 1889, leaving several children, and was buried at Ruthwell. A memorial hall was built in commemoration of his work in the parish. W. A. J. ARCHBOLD, *rev.* H. C. G. MATTHEW

Sources *Fasti Scot.*, new edn · J. G. Lockhart, *Memoirs of the life of Sir Walter Scott*, 7 vols. (1837–8) · *The letters of Sir Walter Scott*, ed. H. J. C. Grierson and others, centenary edn, 12 vols. (1932–79) · *Dumfries and Galloway Standard and Advertiser* (9 Oct 1889) · *Dumfries and Galloway Courier and Herald* (12 Oct 1889) · H. MacFarlan, *James MacFarlan* (privately printed, Edinburgh, 1892) · H. M'Farlan, *Selections from letters and journals of Ruthwell manse life, 1871–1889* (1914)

Macfarlane, John (1807–1875), minister of the United Presbyterian church, was born in Dunfermline on 1 April 1807, the third son of James Macfarlane and his wife, Grace Husband. His father exercised a collegiate ministry with his wife's father, Dr James Husband (*d.* 1821), for forty years at Queen Anne Street Church, Dunfermline, a Secession congregation. Macfarlane's mother died on 13 May 1816, shortly after giving birth to her ninth child. John was educated at the local grammar school and at Edinburgh and Glasgow universities, before entering the Divinity Hall of the United Secession church in 1825.

Macfarlane was licensed by the presbytery of Edinburgh in 1830 and was ordained in Kincardine, near Alloa, in March of the following year. His reputation as a preacher and writer were soon established. His work included many biographical memoirs of his fellow clergy. In 1832 he was at the centre of controversy when a steeple with a bell was added to his church. The parish minister obtained an interdict preventing the bell from being rung, but the legal challenge collapsed when it was found that the ringing of church bells was not the exclusive privilege of the established church. On 27 March 1837 Macfarlane married Janet Jamieson Kidston, second daughter of another Secession minister, Dr William Kidston. They had seven children, of whom four died in infancy or childhood.

In 1840 Macfarlane was called to Nicolson Street Church, Glasgow. In 1842 the congregation removed to a new, and somewhat showy, church seating 1200 in South Portland Street. The new building was called Erskine Church, in honour of Ralph and Ebenezer Erskine, leaders of the original secession of 1733. Macfarlane was awarded

the degree of LLD by Glasgow University in 1842, an unusual honour for such a prominent dissenter. He took an increasing interest in Presbyterian church extension in England, an activity generously funded by John Henderson of Park, Glasgow. The result of this was the opening of Presbyterian churches at Highbury and Clapham, London. Macfarlane was called to the latter in 1861. His ministry in London was highly successful in terms of the growth of the congregation, and much of the considerable debt incurred in building the church was cleared. He was elected moderator of the United Presbyterian synod in 1866 and of the English provincial synod in 1870. His health, however, was poor after illness in 1864, and this was compounded by the death of his wife in 1869. After a long illness he died on 7 February 1875 at his home, 14 Victoria Road, Clapham Common; he was buried on the 12th. T. B. JOHNSTONE, *rev.* LIONEL ALEXANDER RITCHIE

Sources W. Graham, *Memoir of John Macfarlane* (1876) · J. Smith, *Our Scottish clergy*, 2nd ser. (1849), 379–85 · W. Mackelvie, *Annals and statistics of the United Presbyterian church*, ed. W. Blair and D. Young (1873) · R. Small, *History of the congregations of the United Presbyterian church from 1733 to 1900*, 1 (1904), 369; 2 (1904), 62–3 · personal information (1893) · Boase, *Mod. Eng. biog.*

Likenesses E. Burton, mezzotint, pubd 1858 (after N. Macbeth), BM · photograph (in later life), repro. in Graham, *Memoir of John Macfarlane*, frontispiece

McFarlane, Kenneth Bruce (1903–1966), historian, was born on 18 October 1903 at 191 Amesbury Avenue, Streatham, London, the only child of Andrew McFarlane OBE, a civil servant in the Admiralty, and his first wife, Elizabeth Annie Stancombe. His mother died after a long illness while he was still a schoolboy, and his father remarried. After education at local preparatory schools and Dulwich College (1917–22) he won a scholarship to Exeter College, Oxford, which he entered in Michaelmas term 1922. He won the Stanhope historical essay prize in 1924, obtained a first class in modern history in 1925, and was elected to a senior demyship at Magdalen College in 1926. He became a fellow by examination in 1927 and a tutorial fellow in 1928, and remained at the college until his death in 1966. His chosen field of research was England in the fourteenth and fifteenth centuries, a period which William Stubbs had seen as constitutionally retrograde, with parliament's precocious development stifled by factional politics. More recently T. F. Tout had argued that the crown and the magnates were locked in a struggle for the control of government through the administrative offices of exchequer, chancery, and household. Tout's work extended no further than 1399, and the fifteenth century remained *terra incognita*.

McFarlane's initial impulse was to carry forward the study of the institutions of government, the council, and the exchequer with a thesis on Cardinal Beaufort. But he rejected both Stubbs's whig constitutionalism and Tout's belief in the opposition of crown and magnates. Adopting a Marxist approach he at first interpreted the period as the clash of a new moneyed and mercantile class with the old feudal order. He soon saw this to be too crude a formulation, for what impressed him was the survival, adaptability, and inclusiveness of the ruling class throughout English history. It was this that gave direction and coherence to the evolution of the English state. Having arrived at this position he set himself to investigate all aspects of this élite in his chosen period: its members and families; their lands and finances; their consumption and culture; their education and beliefs; and their service in war and politics. In this last he was much influenced by L. B. Namier's recent study of eighteenth-century English politics in terms of patronage and 'interests'. He could see a similar structure in the political society of the later middle ages, and this he delineated in two brilliant and seminal articles, 'Bastard feudalism' (1945) and 'Parliament and bastard feudalism' (1944), reprinted among his collected essays in *England in the Fifteenth Century* (1981). These introduced historians to a world of magnate retinues and affinities; service and patronage; indentures, annuities, and 'good lordship'; of shamelessly competitive ambition and floating loyalties. He thereby not only changed historians' views on the period but set a new direction for future research.

McFarlane now intensified his own investigations into the archives of the medieval aristocracy, some of them in the public records but many still remaining in stately homes (like Longleat) or on deposit in county record offices (as at Stafford and Lancaster). Hitherto none of this material had been explored, and all of it required laborious transcription before it could be interpreted and a synthesis made. A provisional exposition of his findings was presented in the Ford lectures at Oxford in 1953, a landmark in the historical study of the period. These gave a portrait of the late medieval nobility both as individuals of varying temperaments and abilities and as a class with a mentality fashioned by war and chivalric convention, financial acumen, dynastic pride, and political service. But he saw the lectures as provisional, refusing to publish them and continuing to accumulate evidence for a deeper synthesis. The text of 1953, with subsequent additions, was published posthumously as *The Nobility of Later Medieval England* (1973) and his transcriptions from the archives, comparable in value to those of Dodsworth and Dugdale, were deposited in Magdalen College.

McFarlane's short study *John Wycliffe and the Beginnings of English Nonconformity* (1952) was written, at the invitation of A. L. Rowse, for a wider audience. Though incredulous and dismissive about Wycliffe's beliefs McFarlane found the conflict between authority and heresy a valuable key to the mentality and power of the establishment; and in similar terms he went on to investigate how Wycliffite ideas penetrated the inner circles of the court of Richard II. The recovery of the covert beliefs of a group of chamber knights, a skilled piece of historical detective work, was posthumously published in *Lancastrian King and Lollard Knights* (1972). He returned to political history with the delivery of the Raleigh lecture at the British Academy (to which he had been elected in 1964) on the Wars of the Roses, a masterly analysis of the causes and nature of the collapse of political society. Alongside this historical research he had been led to re-examine the canon of Memling's paintings, prompted by perceiving the inaccurate dating of the 'Donne triptych', on exhibition in 1948. This occupied him intermittently over many years, leading him into an intensive study of the iconographical elements in Memling's paintings and the inspection of most of those in European galleries. His conclusions were published posthumously in a distilled form by Edgar Wind in *Hans Memling* (1971).

McFarlane preferred to write lectures and papers rather than books. Some were of seminal importance and all touched major problems and raised new lines of enquiry. Everything he wrote had the stamp of authority, based as it was on first-hand investigation and an instinctive distrust of received opinion. Nor did he conceal the provisional nature of some of his conclusions. His intellectual integrity and historical craftsmanship inspired the generation whose research he supervised, and their lineal successors, so that the study of late medieval England became part of the curriculum in most British universities. Partly because of his shyness and inner melancholy, and partly because of his charismatic personality, the pupils to whom he tentatively offered friendship became lifelong intimates. A volume of his letters to some of these (*Letters to Friends, 1940–1966*, ed. G. L. Harriss, 1999) reveals something of the inner man and much about his daily preoccupations and diversions. They show him as widely read, with a sharp visual sense, an intense interest in people, and a belief in the pre-eminent importance of human relationships. He had a long-standing association with Dr Helena *Wright, to whom he often turned for advice.

McFarlane never married. He died, of a stroke, while walking at Great Hampden in Buckinghamshire on 16 July 1966 and was cremated at Oxford. He had no religious beliefs and had given instructions that no memorial service was to be held. G. L. HARRISS

Sources K. J. Leyser, 'Kenneth Bruce McFarlane, 1903–1966', *PBA*, 62 (1976), 485–506 · G. L. Harriss, ed., *K. B. McFarlane: letters to friends, 1940–1966* (1999) · J. P. Cooper, 'Introduction', in K. B. McFarlane, *The nobility of later medieval England* (1973), vii–xxxvii · J. P. Cooper, 'K. B. McFarlane, 1903–1966', *Oxford Magazine* (12–19 May 1967), 326–7, 337–8; repr. in J. P. Cooper, *Land, men and beliefs: studies in early modern history*, ed. G. E. Aylmer and J. S. Morrill (1983) · M. C. Carpenter, 'Political and constitutional history: before and after McFarlane', *The McFarlane legacy*, ed. R. H. Bretnell and A. J. Pollard (1995), 175–206 · M. H. Keen, 'English political history of the late middle ages, 1272–1520', *Mediaeval Studies* [British Academy centenary volume; forthcoming] · Magd. Oxf. · b. cert. · register, Dulwich College

Archives Magd. Oxf., corresp. and MSS

Likenesses photograph, repro. in McFarlane, *Nobility of late medieval England*, frontispiece

Wealth at death £25,035: probate, 14 Oct 1966, *CGPLA Eng. & Wales*

MacFarlane, Sir (Frank) Noel Mason- (1889–1953), army officer, was born on 23 October 1889 in Maidenhead, the eldest son of Dr David James Mason (1862–1930), a Scot who later added his mother's name, MacFarlane, and his wife, Mary Blanche Anstey (d. 1947). He was educated at

Cordwalles School, Maidenhead (1896–1902), Rugby School (1902–7), and the Royal Military Academy, Woolwich (1907–9), and was posted to the Royal Artillery in 1909. War service in France, Belgium, and Mesopotamia gained him a Military Cross with two bars, two mentions in dispatches, and a Croix de Guerre. On 14 September 1918 he married Islay (1895/6–1947), daughter of Frederick Islay Pitman, stockbroker. They had a son and a daughter, though Mrs Mason-MacFarlane disliked her husband's nomadic lifestyle. He took part in the Third Anglo-Afghan War of 1919–20, and in 1920 went to the Staff College at Quetta.

In 1931 Mason-Mac, as he was commonly known, became military attaché in Vienna, with additional responsibility for Budapest and Bern. His work was commended by the British minister in Vienna, Walford Selby. Mason-MacFarlane graduated from the Imperial Defence College in 1935, and two years later secured the crucial posting to Berlin working under the ambassador, Sir Nevile Henderson.

Although Henderson liked Mason-MacFarlane, the military attaché thought the ambassador did not take a tough enough line with the Nazis. In his leisure hours Mason-MacFarlane took to writing uncomplimentary verse about his 'celibate and caustic chief' (Mason-MacFarlane MSS, 27 Aug 1938, IWM, MM 28). He was present when German troops entered Vienna in March 1938 at the time of the Anschluss, and Henderson sent him on a dangerous mission to the Prague embassy in September after the Godesberg meeting between Hitler and Chamberlain. This was to deliver a map outlining Germany's demands in the Sudetenland.

As a result of his trip through Czech defence lines, Mason-MacFarlane formed the impression that Czech army morale was poor (he had great expertise about the German army, but his opinion was not shared by the British military attaché in Prague). Mason-MacFarlane repeated this opinion on a visit to London on 27 September, eliciting a sharp response from the permanent under-secretary at the Foreign Office, Cadogan, who wrote in his diary 'What does he know about it?' (*The Diaries of Sir Alexander Cadogan*, ed. D. Dilks, 1971, 107). Foreign Office officials, in contrast with those at the War Office who trusted Mason-Mac's judgement, found him excitable and an advocate of hair-brained schemes. His biographer cites the occasion when Mason-MacFarlane told him in 1938 that he was thinking of shooting Hitler from his house on the Charlottenburger Chaussee in Berlin. He could, he claimed, 'pick the bastard off from here as easy as winking' (Butler, 75). The plan came to nothing, but no one doubted that Mason-MacFarlane had the nerve to carry it out, even if his superiors disapproved. Life in Nazi Germany became increasingly distasteful for Mason-MacFarlane, and he was relieved when, in the summer of 1939, he was posted back to Aldershot as brigadier in command in the Royal Artillery.

As director of military intelligence, with the rank of major-general, with the British expeditionary force in France in 1939, Mason-MacFarlane had knowledge of Germany and the German army which was invaluable. When the Germans broke the French Ninth Army front he improvised and commanded a scratch force to protect the British right and immediate rear. 'MacForce' was behind the French First Army, whose front never actually broke, was afterwards withdrawn to prepare the defence of Kassel, and was then disbanded. Mason-MacFarlane and other key officers were ordered back to Britain. For his work in France he was appointed DSO.

In June 1940 Mason-MacFarlane was sent as deputy governor to Gibraltar where his energy, character, and leadership, in extremely difficult circumstances, performed miracles in reorganizing the defences and maintaining morale. After a brief interlude commanding a division in Kent, Mason-MacFarlane was sent to Moscow in 1941 as head of the British military mission, with the task of maximizing the effectiveness of allied aid to Russia. Once more he came up against authority by criticizing over-optimistic promises and opposing aid without conditions. In June 1942 he returned to Gibraltar, this time as governor and commander-in-chief. He now had the invidious task of continuing preparations for defence, and maintaining morale while the risks of attack decreased. He accommodated General Eisenhower's headquarters for the invasion of north Africa and gave valuable support to these operations. In 1943 he was promoted KCB; he had been appointed CB in 1939.

Italy surrendered on 3 September 1943 and Mason-MacFarlane was asked to head a military mission to Brindisi on 13 September. Then, and subsequently as head of the Allied Control Commission, Mason-MacFarlane's task was to make a former enemy into an ally. He preferred Bonomi to Marshal Badoglio as a head of government, but this did not accord with the Whitehall view. Churchill thought Mason-MacFarlane had been weak in his new role, and Harold MacMillan wrote later that Mason-MacFarlane had made 'a complete mess' of the Italian situation. MacMillan found him 'frightfully temperamental and a regular prima donna' (H. MacMillan, *War Diaries: Politics and War in the Mediterranean*, 1984, 466, 428). He also judged Mason-MacFarlane to be lacking in political judgement, but was aware that by 1944 he had serious health problems. These forced him to resign his post, and go on sick leave. As a schoolboy he had broken his neck. Later a fall, pigsticking, injured his back, and a motor accident broke a number of ribs close to the spine. From about 1940, as a result of these injuries, he suffered increasing paralysis. By 1944 he was in constant pain. The rest of his life was a tragic tale of operations and increasing disability. Nevertheless, in the general election of 1945, moved by a long-standing lack of sympathy with the Conservative Party, he stood as Labour candidate for the constituency of North Paddington and defeated Brendan Bracken, one of Churchill's closest allies. He was mentioned as a possible secretary of state for war, but his health forced him to resign his seat in October 1946. He died on 12 August 1953 at his home, Scarlett's Farm, Kiln Green, Twyford, Berkshire.

Mason-MacFarlane has been described by one who served under him (and later became a field marshal) as a near-genius. He was a very fine fighting soldier, with an acute brain, a realistic understanding of people and events, and a gift of lucid exposition. He was also a fine linguist, speaking excellent French and German, and some Spanish, Hungarian, and Russian. He was an outstanding athlete. To his staff Mason-Mac was a most inspiring leader. He had the panache and idiosyncrasy which focus, but also the common touch which retains, the loyalty of troops. He was impetuous to the point of appearing reckless. Less well liked by contemporaries and his superiors, he was too often right, and there was a sarcastic edge to his tongue. He had, too, a full share of personal ambition. In the last resort, there was, perhaps, some lack of judgement. But of his dynamism, will-power, and courage there was never any doubt.

F. S. V. Donnison, *rev.* Peter Neville

Sources E. Butler, *Mason-Mac: the life of Lieutenant-General Sir Noel Mason-MacFarlane* (1972) · N. Henderson, *Failure of a mission* (1940) · W. Selby, *Diplomatic twilight, 1930–1940* (1953) · H. Macmillan, *War diaries: politics and war in the Mediterranean, January 1943 – May 1945* (1984) · L. F. Ellis, *The war in France and Flanders, 1939–1940* (1953) · B. Bond, *France and Belgium, 1939–40* (1971) · P. Meehan, *The unnecessary war* (1992) · D. C. Watt, *How war came* (1989) · m. cert. · private information (1971) · *CGPLA Eng. & Wales* (1953) · papers, IWM
Archives IWM, corresp. and papers | PRO, Nevile Henderson MSS, Foreign Office, 800/264–270 · U. Aberdeen, Ogilvie-Forbes MSS | FILM IWM FVA, news footage
Likenesses R. G. Eves, oils, 1940, IWM · W. Stoneman, photographs, 1940–45, NPG
Wealth at death £74,457 13s.: probate, 24 Oct 1953, *CGPLA Eng. & Wales*

Macfarlane, Patrick (1757/8–1832), Gaelic scholar, was for some time schoolmaster at Appin, Argyllshire, but towards the end of his life was resident in Glasgow. His work in Gaelic literature consisted mostly of translations published by the Society in Scotland for the Propagation of Christian Knowledge. Among the authors whose works he translated into Gaelic are Richard Baxter, Hugh Blair, John Bunyan, Philip Doddridge, and William Guthrie. He corrected the proofs of the Gaelic New Testament of 1813 and of Norman MacLeod and Daniel Dewar's *Dictionary of the Gaelic Language* (1831). He also compiled a manual for family devotion (1829) and published a small collection of Gaelic poems (1813) and *A New and Copious Vocabulary of Gaelic and English* (1815). He died aged seventy-four at Glasgow in late 1832.

J. R. MacDonald, *rev.* Philip Carter

Sources *GM*, 1st ser., 103/1 (1833), 93 · J. Reid, *Bibliotheca Scoto-Celtica, or, An account of all the books which have been printed in the Gaelic language* (1832) · D. S. Thomson, ed., *The companion to Gaelic Scotland*, new edn (1994)

Macfarlane, Robert. *See* Macfarlan, Robert (1733/4–1804).

Macfarlane, Robert, Lord Ormidale (1802–1880), judge, born on 30 July 1802, was the only son of Parlan Macfarlane, farmer, of Glen Luss, Dunbartonshire. Educated at Glasgow and Edinburgh he was later apprenticed as a writer to the signet in the offices of his future father-in-law, James Greig of Eccles. He passed as a writer to the signet in 1827 and practised as a solicitor for ten years. During this period he spent some time in Jamaica. He wrote a treatise entitled *The Practice of the Court of Session in Jury Causes* (1837), a work which brought him into considerable notice.

Macfarlane subsequently determined to practise at the Scottish bar, to which he was called on 10 March 1838. He soon took a leading place among counsel and acquired one of the largest jury practices at the Scottish bar. Although he was not one of the foremost orators of his day, his attractive combination of shrewdness, directness, and common sense enabled him to perform well before juries. He married on 21 October 1843 Grace Adinston Greig of Eccles, Berwickshire, who died on 4 June 1870. They had at least one son and two daughters.

In 1853 Macfarlane was appointed sheriff of Renfrewshire, and on 13 January 1862 he was raised to the bench of the court of session on the death of Lord Wood, taking the courtesy title of Lord Ormidale. He sat at first instance for twelve years, finally transferring to the inner house in 1874. He was a popular judge as well as a painstaking and effective one. Courteous, unaffected, and with a keen, though never inappropriate, sense of humour, his patience and consideration were particularly appreciated by young counsel.

Lord Ormidale retired from the bench in 1880 and died only a few days later, on 3 November, at Hartrigge House, Jedburgh. His most important achievement had perhaps been his advocacy of the reform of the procedure of the court of session. He delivered a famous and not uncontroversial address upon the condition of the court to the Juridical Society in 1867, which more than anything else led to the act of parliament of 1868 which remodelled the court of session and abolished many of the technicalities of Scottish pleading.

Nathan Wells

Sources *Journal of Jurisprudence*, 24 (1880) · F. J. Grant, ed., *The Faculty of Advocates in Scotland, 1532–1943*, Scottish RS, 145 (1944) · *The Scotsman* (5 Nov 1880)
Wealth at death £53,293 8s.: confirmation, 30 Nov 1880, CCI

Macfarquhar, Colin (1744/5–1793), printer and publisher, was born in Edinburgh, the son of James Macfarquhar, a wigmaker, and his wife, Margaret. On 13 December 1767 he married Jane, daughter of James Scruton, an accountant in Glasgow; they had one son and four daughters.

After an apprenticeship Macfarquhar probably became a master printer about 1767. Besides printing books he also published a number of titles, including Jean Frédéric Osterwald's English edition of the Bible (c.1770); *The Psalms of David in Meter* (1771); *Letters Written by the Earl of Chesterfield to his Son* (1774–5), in association with the paper merchant George Douglas and his friend and sometime partner the bookseller Charles Elliot; and several volumes of the *Edinburgh Magazine, or, Literary Miscellany* (1785–1803), again with Elliot. Two of these publications resulted in litigation. Alexander Kincaid, in his capacity as the king's printer in Scotland, sued Macfarquhar for infringing on his alleged monopoly of printing bibles in Scotland but withdrew his complaint. On the other hand, the London bookseller James Dodsley, who had paid for a copyright on Chesterfield's *Letters to his Son*, persevered in his suit against Macfarquhar and other Scottish publishers in the court of session. It ruled against Macfarquhar, who had to destroy hundreds of copies of his press run. Like many other British publishers Macfarquhar tested the shadowy line between legal publishing and literary piracy.

Macfarquhar proved to be not only an aggressive businessman but also an exceptionally creative and able one. This can be seen from a history of his most important publication, the *Encyclopaedia Britannica*, the first alphabetically arranged general encyclopaedia published in Scotland. The earliest edition appeared in instalments from 1768 to 1771 and as a three-volume set in 1771. Macfarquhar and his co-publisher, the engraver Andrew Bell, knew how to market their reference book: they were the first eighteenth-century British publishers to entitle their work an encyclopaedia, a word with selling power thanks to the reputation of the *Encyclopédie* edited by Denis Diderot and Jean Le Rond d'Alembert from 1751 to 1772; also they distinguished the *Britannica* from its competitors by publishing it in quarto rather than in octavo or folio and by featuring long synthesizing articles as well as short ones. In addition they kept costs down by printing the *Britannica* in Macfarquhar's printing shop and by assigning Bell the engraving of all the copperplates. The two lightened their task by choosing not to edit it themselves and instead selected William Smellie. He copied and abridged so much from other sources that this edition of the *Britannica* turned out to be undistinguished.

Macfarquhar and Bell then decided on an expanded second edition. In order to raise the capital they formed a syndicate with eight other Scottish publishers. This edition was published in instalments from 1777 to 1784 and in ten quarto volumes with imprints from 1778 to 1783. Bell remained responsible for the engravings and Macfarquhar for at least part of the printing. They named a new editor, James Tytler, who greatly improved the work by including biographies and by providing more depth on many subjects. The wholesale copying from earlier publications continued and caused threatened and actual lawsuits. Macfarquhar and Bell settled these by awarding sets to the aggrieved parties, Samuel Foart Simmons, John Murray, and George Robinson.

The third edition marks the high point of the eighteenth-century editions of the *Britannica*. Published by Macfarquhar and Bell alone and issued in instalments from 1788 to 1797, and then in eighteen quarto volumes in 1797, it was the first encyclopaedia published in Great Britain to be compiled by more than a handful of contributors. Bell kept on furnishing the engravings and Macfarquhar did some of the printing but this time Macfarquhar, a man of extensive learning despite his limited formal schooling, chose to edit the work himself. Before his death he had completed the first twelve volumes up to the article 'Mysteries'. George Gleig, who took over after that, recruited such eminent contributors as John Robison and probably John Barclay but Macfarquhar deserves recognition for helping to make this edition an exemplar of the

Scottish Enlightenment, the most informative general encyclopaedia in eighteenth-century Britain, and a bestseller with a press run reaching perhaps 13,000 sets. Still the publication of the third edition was not without difficulties. Like the second edition it resulted in a lawsuit; the farrier James Clark claimed that the sixty-one-page article 'Farriery' had been copied from two of his books. The case was dismissed on a technicality in 1804, long after Macfarquhar's death on 2 April 1793, at the age of forty-eight. He was survived by his wife. Macfarquhar's estate included the eight-room house in Buccleuch Place, near Edinburgh, in which he died and probably £12,500 or more, much of it from sales of the *Britannica*.

FRANK A. KAFKER

Sources F. A. Kafker, 'The achievement of Andrew Bell and Colin Macfarquhar as the first publishers of the *Encyclopaedia Britannica*', *British Journal for Eighteenth-Century Studies*, 18 (1995), 139–52 · G. Gleig, preface, *Encyclopaedia Britannica*, 3rd edn (1797), esp. 1.xii–xiii, xv · *Edinburgh Advertiser* (2–5 April 1793), 222 · trust, deed, and settlement of Colin Macfarquhar, recorded, 8 April 1793, NA Scot., MS RD4/253, fols. 668–86 · commission and factory by Colin Macfarquhar's trustees, recorded, 13 April 1793, NA Scot., MS RD4/253, fols. 712–17 · submission and decret arbitral between Colin Macfarquhar's trustees and his mother, recorded, 14 Dec 1793, NA Scot., MS RD4/254, fols. 1199–202 · F. J. Grant, ed., *Register of marriages of the city of Edinburgh, 1751–1800*, Scottish RS, 53 (1922), 464 · C. B. B. Watson, ed., *Roll of Edinburgh burgesses and guild-brethren, 1761–1841*, Scottish RS, 68 (1933), 99 · R. Kerr, *Memoirs of the life, writings and correspondence of William Smellie*, 2 vols. (1811); repr. (1996), vol.1, pp. 361–5 · T. Constable, *Archibald Constable and his literary correspondents*, 1 (1873), 8; 2 (1873), 311–13 · NL Scot., Gleig MS 3869, esp. fols. 11r–12v, 14r · NL Scot., Liston MSS 5526, fols. 104–5; 5527, fols. 213–14 · W. McDougall, 'Smugglers, reprinters and hot pursuers: the Irish–Scottish book trade and copyright prosecutions in the late eighteenth century', *The Stationers' Company and the book trade, 1550–1990*, ed. R. Myers and M. Harris, St Paul's Bibliographies (1997), 151–83, esp. 174–5 · W. Zachs, *The first John Murray and the late eighteenth-century London book trade* (1998) · W. M. Morison, *The decisions of the court of session*, 21 vols. (1801–5), vol. 10, pp. 8308–8310; appx, pt 1, literary property, pp. 1–7, 9–13 · John Murray copybooks, John Murray, London, archives, esp. John Murray to Andrew Blane, 14 Aug 1783; John Murray to Colin Macfarquhar, Andrew Bell, and John Hutton, 26 Aug 1783 · George Gleig to George Monck Berkeley and George Berkeley, BL, Add. MS 39312, esp. 11 April 1788, fols. 68r–68v; 20 May 1793, fol. 144r · 'Biographical memoir of the author', J. Skinner, *Theological works of the late Rev. John Skinner*, 1 (1809), lxiii, lxvii–lxviii

Archives BL, Add. MS 39312 · John Murray, London, archives · NA Scot., MS RD4/253, fols. 668–86, 712–17; MS RD4/254, fols. 1199–202 · NL Scot., Gleig MSS, MS 3869 · NL Scot., Sir Robert Liston MSS, MS 5526, fols. 104–5, MS 5527, fols. 213–14

Wealth at death probably over £12,500: trust, deed, and settlement, NA Scot., MS RD 4/253, fols. 668–86, recorded 8 April 1793

Macfarren, George (1788–1843), playwright and theatre manager, was born in London on 5 September 1788, the son of George Macfarren. He was educated chiefly at Archbishop Tenison's school in Castle Street, Leicester Square, and while there he wrote a tragedy which was privately staged by his schoolfellows, with the support of Edmund Kean, then a boy of their own age. Macfarren was also a musician, and 'could sustain either of the parts in a violin quartet', and 'had he not met with a fashionable teacher of dancing, named Bishop, who offered to make him a gentleman instead of a fiddler, he would have adopted music as his profession' (*Musical World*, 24). He was the first teacher of Oury the violinist, and while still under twenty years of age he opened a dancing academy of his own. In 1816 he visited Paris, where he had lessons in dancing from the best teachers. In August 1808 he had married Elizabeth (b. 1792), daughter of John Jackson, a book-binder of Glasgow, who had settled in London. They had six children, George Alexander *Macfarren (1813–1887), Eliza (1814–1815), John (1818–1901), Ellen (b. 1821), Basil (1824–1837), and Walter Cecil *Macfarren (1826–1905). All of the children were artistic, and George Alexander and Walter Cecil were to pursue successful musical careers.

Macfarren's natural bent was, however, towards the stage, and on 28 September 1818 his first publicly per-formed dramatic work, *Ah! What a Pity, or, The Dark Knight and the Fair Lady*, was given at the English Opera House (for the benefit of John Pritt Harley); from this date almost every year saw one of his productions performed. These included *Winning a Husband* (1819), and *Tom and Jerry in France* (1823), both comedies, and several historical dramas, including *Guy Fawkes* (1822); *Edward the Black Prince* (1823); *George III* (1824); and *The Horatii and Curiatii* (1825), all of which were performed at the Royal Coburg Theatre. Macfarren's work in adaptation was also wide-ranging, and included *Oberon* (1826), *Gil Blas* (1827), and the post-humously performed *Don Quixote* (1846), all three having been performed at Drury Lane. His work for the Royal Surrey Theatre included two dramas, *Auld Robin Gray* (1828) and *The Talisman* (1828), and a particularly successful farce entitled *March of Intellect* (1829).

In February 1831 Macfarren took over the management of the theatre in Tottenham Street, which he called the Queen's Theatre, in honour of Queen Adelaide, and here he remained until July of the following year, producing, among numerous other works, *The Danish Wife* (1831) and a dramatic version of Handel's *Acis and Galatea*, for which Cipriani Potter wrote additional accompaniments. Mac-farren seems to have laid particular stress on accuracy of detail and naturalness in staging the plays which he pro-duced. Robert Elliston, successively lessee of Drury Lane, the Olympic, and Surrey theatres, stated that 'no such per-fect pictures as he saw at the Queen's Theatre had ever been put on the stage'. None the less, the venture did not meet with pecuniary success, and Macfarren left the Queen's on being appointed stage manager of the Surrey, where, among other plays, he produced the Christmas pantomime *Harlequin Reformer* (1831). He afterwards went to the Strand, for which he wrote *Innocent Sins* (1838), a comedy. He also produced plays for the Lyceum and Hay-market theatres, and collaborated with his son George Alexander Macfarren on an *Emblematical Tribute on the Mar-riage of the Queen* in 1840. He also wrote a great many short poems, which were set to music by E. J. Loder, G. A. and W. C. Macfarren, Henry Smart (Estelle) and others. He was also a good amateur draughtsman and painter, a faculty which stood him in good stead in designing theatrical scenes.

In 1834 Macfarren visited Milan, where his daughter was studying singing, and there wrote the libretto of an opera,

Caractacus. During some years of his life Macfarren was totally blind, but a year before his death he underwent an operation for cataract and recovered his sight. While blind he devoted himself largely to literature, and he first suggested the formation of the Handel Society. In 1841 he became editor and proprietor of the *Musical World*. He died suddenly on 24 April 1843 in Castle Street, Leicester Square.   R. H. LEGGE, *rev.* REBECCA MILLS

Sources H. C. Bannister, *George Alexander Macfarren, his life, works and influence* (1891), 1–18 • private information (1893) [Walter Cecil Macfarren] • J. F. Waller, ed., *The imperial dictionary of universal biog-raphy*, 3 vols. (1857–63) • W. D. Adams, *Dictionary of English literature*, rev. edn [1879–80] • *Musical World*, 55 (6 Jan 1877), 23–4 • G. Dubourg, *The violin*, 5th edn, rev. J. Bishop (1887), 217 • W. Macfar-ren, *Memories: an autobiography* (1905)
Likenesses Davison, oils • H. Lejeune, oils

Macfarren, Sir George Alexander (1813–1887), com-poser, the son of George *Macfarren (1788–1843), a dancing-master, dramatist, and impresario, and his wife, Elizabeth, *née* Jackson (b. 1792), was born at 24 Villiers Street, Strand, London, on Shrove Tuesday 2 March 1813. In August 1820 he was sent to Dr Nicholas's school in Eal-ing, where his father taught dancing for many years. He was a delicate child, suffering especially from poor eye-sight, which was later to result in total blindness, and in 1823 was removed from school to undergo a course of eye treatment. His general education then continued at Lan-cing School for some eighteen months; his musical educa-tion he received primarily from his father until, in March 1827, he became a pupil of Charles Lucas. From 1829 he attended the Royal Academy of Music, studying compos-ition with Cipriani Potter, piano with William Henry Holmes, and, as a second instrument, trombone with Smithies. While at the academy he formed friendships with William Sterndale Bennett, James William Davison, and other musicians of the same generation who shared an interest in the most recent developments in German music. This influence made itself strongly apparent in his compositions of these years, and like Bennett he devoted himself at an early stage to symphonic music. A sym-phony in C was performed at an academy concert in Sep-tember 1830 and another in D minor was played there in December 1831. Macfarren made his first important pub-lic début as a composer with an overture in D written for the opening, under his father's management, of the Queen's Theatre in Tottenham Street in 1831, and the fol-lowing year he provided music for the play *The Maid of Switzerland*. On 24 June 1833 he received the academy's bronze medal for composition and progress in piano play-ing, and two days later another of his overtures was given at an academy concert; it was perhaps this work that appeared on the programme of Paganini's concert at Drury Lane on 17 July 1833 as 'grand overture'.

Macfarren was one of the founder members of the Soci-ety of British Musicians, which, in its early years, provided opportunities for the performance of orchestral music by British composers, and the concerts of the society at that time included his symphony in F minor (27 October 1834),

Sir George Alexander Macfarren (1813–1887), by Bassano

overture *The Merchant of Venice* (October 1835), and piano concerto in C minor (2 November 1835). His first operatic venture dates from this period, but *Caractacus*, for which his father supplied the libretto, was not performed and does not seem to have been completed; it was reportedly denied a licence by the censor of plays, T. L. Serle, on the grounds of historical inaccuracy. In 1836 he rapidly composed one of his most popular pieces, the overture *Chevy Chace* (for a piece by J. R. Planché), which Mendelssohn selected for performance at the Leipzig Gewandhaus in 1843.

After leaving the Royal Academy in 1836, Macfarren accepted a position teaching music in a school on the Isle of Man, where, with few musical resources, he concentrated on composition; the major work to which he devoted his energies during his island sojourn was an opera entitled *Craso, the Forlorn*, for which his father again provided the libretto. In 1837 he returned to London to take up a post teaching harmony and composition at the Royal Academy of Music, and at about this time wrote his overture *Romeo and Juliet*. During these years Macfarren was seen by the faction of the press which trumpeted the superiority of German over Italian music as a leading figure in the struggle to gain recognition for a serious school of British composers, particularly in the field of opera. Thus the success of his *The Devil's Opera*, written quickly during the summer of 1838 and given its première at the Lyceum on 13 August, was hailed as a significant counterweight to the tunefully vapid confections of Balfe and

others. In the wake of this success an enlarged two-act version of *Craso*, under the title *El malechor*, was accepted by Alfred Bunn for performance at Drury Lane in 1839, but the collapse of the company prevented its production, and two further offers of performance the following year, from Barnett at St James's and from Balfe at the English Opera House, came to nothing under similar circumstances. An *Emblematical Tribute*, a masque on which Macfarren collaborated with his father, was staged at Drury Lane in 1840 in celebration of Queen Victoria's marriage.

Macfarren became increasingly involved in a range of other activities around this time. He was co-editor of the first volume of Chappell's *Collection of English National Airs* (later reissued as *Popular Music of the Olden Time*), which appeared in 1838. He also began to write regularly about music, initially for the *Musical World*. In 1840 he joined the council of the newly established Musical Antiquarian Society, for which he was to edit a number of works by early English composers; and in 1844, following his father's suggestion, he founded the Handel Society and became its secretary. Although short-lived, the society produced sixteen volumes of Handel's works; Macfarren himself edited *Belshazzar*, *Judas Maccabaeus*, and *Jephtha*, and he persuaded Mendelssohn to edit *Israel in Egypt*, a task which the latter approached with a degree of scrupulous scholarship exceptional for its day.

On 27 September 1844, at Marylebone church, Macfarren married Clarina Thalia Andrae (1828–1916) from Lübeck, a contralto, who, under the name (Clara) Natalia Macfarren, became a distinguished editor and translator of operas and songs; she also published several piano pieces and, about 1868, an *Elementary Course for Vocalizing and Pronouncing the English Language*. From these years date a number of Macfarren's chamber works: they include string quartets in A and F, a piano trio in E minor, a piano quintet in G minor for the same instrumentation as Schubert's 'Trout', and his first two piano sonatas, in E♭ and A. Mendelssohn, whom Macfarren later hailed as 'my musical Godfather' (Bodl. Oxf., MS M. Deneke, xxiv, letter of 18 Dec 1846), facilitated the publication of the trio and a quartet in Leipzig in 1846. In 1844 Macfarren was appointed music director at Covent Garden, which, as he informed Mendelssohn, was 'by far the most important (professional) situation in which I have ever been placed' (Bodl. Oxf., MS M. Deneke, xx, 176 letter of 19 Nov 1844), and his duties commenced in January 1845 with the British première of Mendelssohn's incidental music to Sophocles' *Antigone*. On 9 June of the same year Macfarren enjoyed the exceptional honour, for an Englishman, of having his C♯ minor symphony (published for piano duet as the second symphony) performed at a concert of the Philharmonic Society. But, on sending his next symphony to Mendelssohn in 1846, he observed, 'except it make an extraordinary success in your country there is little or no chance of its ever being played in mine' (Bodl. Oxf., MS M. Deneke, xxiv, 87 letter of 15 Oct 1846). In 1845 he completed the opera *An Adventure of Don Quixote*, begun in 1841 to a libretto by his father, which started a successful run on 3 February 1846 at Drury Lane.

At the Royal Academy, Macfarren had come into conflict with his colleagues over his advocacy and teaching of Dr Day's controversial system of harmony, and in 1847, after a formal debate before a board of the professors, he resigned his post. By that time his eyesight had deteriorated so greatly that he went to New York to consult a leading oculist, but despite a stay of eighteen months he derived no significant benefit from the treatment. However, he employed himself in completing his opera *Charles the Second*, to a libretto by Desmond Ryan; this was highly successful when produced under E. J. Loder at the Princess's Theatre on 27 October 1849, and remained in the repertory for two seasons. His wife made her London operatic début as the page in this opera. For the National Concerts in 1850 he composed his serenata *The Sleeper Awakened*, with words by John Oxenford; and the following year he and Oxenford collaborated on the opera *Allan of Aberfeldy*, which was scheduled by Bunn for production at Drury Lane, but was permanently shelved when Bunn again became bankrupt. The cantata *Lenore*, the libretto of which was arranged from Bürger's German ballad by Oxenford, was successful under the baton of Julius Benedict at the Harmonic Union concert of 25 April 1853, and was repeated at the Birmingham festival that year. For the New Philharmonic Society in 1854 Macfarren composed another Shakespearian overture, *Hamlet*, and for the Bradford festival of 1857 the cantata *May Day*, which enjoyed greater popularity than many of his works; a cantata entitled *Christmas*, given its première by the London Musical Society under Alfred Mellon on 9 May 1860, did not prove as popular. His opera *Robin Hood*, produced at Her Majesty's Theatre (11 October 1860) with a star cast of English singers, however, gained Macfarren one of his greatest theatrical successes; his friend Davison gave it a particularly glowing review in the *Musical World*. This period also saw the publication of his *A Sketch of the Life of Handel* (1859) and his musical textbook *The Rudiments of Harmony*, which reached a sixteenth edition by 1887.

During the composition of *Robin Hood* Macfarren became virtually blind, and thereafter was compelled to dictate all his compositions and writings to an amanuensis; but within a short time he resumed his former productivity. *Freya's Gift*, a masque for the marriage of the prince of Wales, with a libretto by Oxenford, was produced at Covent Garden on 10 March 1863. Shortly afterwards he was commissioned by German Reed to compose a chamber opera, *Jessy Lea*, performed at the Gallery of Illustration on 2 November 1863, which led in 1864 to another work of the same kind, *The Soldier's Legacy*; both had librettos by Oxenford. At the same time Macfarren had completed an opera, *She Stoops to Conquer*, to a libretto by Edward Fitzball, which was produced at Covent Garden with Mellon conducting on 11 February 1864, and in the same year his four-act opera *Helvellyn*, with a libretto by Oxenford, was given there. The individual numbers of his *13 Choral Songs*, published at this time, were often reprinted.

The later 1860s saw no more important composition than the setting of Christina Rossetti's *Songs in a Cornfield* (1868), but Macfarren became very active as a lecturer in London at the City of London Institute (1866–70) and the Royal Institution (1867), the latter lectures giving rise to his book *Six Lectures on Harmony* (1867) and the former probably providing much of the material for *On the Structure of a Sonata* (1871) and *Eighty Musical Sentences* (1875). Around 1870 he turned his attention to oratorio, beginning work on *St John the Baptist* for the Gloucester festival of 1871; its première was postponed until the Bristol festival of 1873, but it was then so successful that Macfarren immediately received commissions for two further oratorios, resulting in *The Resurrection* (Birmingham festival, 1876) and *Joseph* (Leeds festival, 1877). In the midst of this activity, tenaciously returning to a genre forsaken by almost all British musicians of his generation, he composed his ninth symphony in E minor (1874).

In 1875, on the death of Sterndale Bennett, Macfarren was elected principal of the Royal Academy of Music and professor of music at Cambridge University. He received the honorary degrees of Doctor of Music at Cambridge in April 1875, at Oxford in 1876, and at Dublin in 1878, in which year he was also made an MA by Cambridge (giving him full membership of the university). His textbook *Counterpoint, a Practical Course of Study* was published in 1879. His last opera, *Kenilworth*, composed in 1880, was never staged. In 1882 he wrote music for the performance of Sophocles' *Ajax* at Cambridge, which was conducted by C. V. Stanford; in 1883 his fourth oratorio, *King David*, was given at the Leeds festival under Sir Arthur Sullivan, and in 1884 August Manns directed his St George's Te Deum at the Crystal Palace. Macfarren accepted a knighthood in 1883, after much hesitation. In his last years, although he wrote a certain amount of chamber music, which remained unpublished, he was chiefly involved with his duties at Cambridge and the Royal Academy. He also wrote biographical articles for *The Imperial Dictionary of Universal Biography* and saw through the press his *Musical History Briefly Narrated and Technically Discussed* (1885), revised from articles originally contributed to the ninth edition of the *Encyclopaedia Britannica*. A collection entitled *Addresses and Lectures* was posthumously published in 1888. On 31 October 1887, following a period of ill health, Macfarren died suddenly at his home, 7 Hamilton Terrace, St John's Wood, London. After a request for burial in Westminster Abbey had been refused, his funeral took place at Hampstead cemetery on 5 November, followed by a memorial service in the abbey. CLIVE BROWN

Sources H. C. Banister, *A life of George Alexander Macfarren* (1891) · K. Mendelssohn-Bartholdy, *Goethe and Mendelssohn*, ed. and trans. M. E. von Glahn, 2nd edn (1874), 158ff. [with additions by the ed.] · *MT*, 28 (1887), 713–5 · *DNB* · Bodl. Oxf., Mendelssohn MSS

Archives Bodl. Oxf., Mendelssohn MSS

Likenesses Bassano, photograph, NPG [*see illus.*] · Lock & Whitfield, woodburytype photograph, NPG; repro. in T. Cooper, *Men of mark: a gallery of contemporary portraits* (1881) · portrait, repro. in Banister, *Life of George Alexander Macfarren*, frontispiece · wood-engraving (after photograph by H. Watkins), NPG; repro. in *ILN* (24 April 1875)

Wealth at death £4462 9s. 10d.: probate, 2 Dec 1887, *CGPLA Eng. &
Wales*

Macfarren, Walter Cecil (1826–1905), pianist and composer, born in Villiers Street, Strand, London, on 28 August 1826, was the youngest son of the dancing master and playwright George *Macfarren (1788–1843) and his wife, Elizabeth, *née* Jackson (b. 1792), and the brother of Sir George Alexander *Macfarren. He was a choirboy at Westminster Abbey under James Turle (1836–41), and sang at Queen Victoria's coronation. When his voice broke, he thought of becoming an artist, and took some lessons in painting before serving as a salesman in a Brighton piano warehouse. In October 1842 he was persuaded by his brother to enter the Royal Academy of Music, where he learned the piano under W. H. Holmes and composition under his own brother and Cipriani Potter. In January 1846 he became a sub-professor of the piano. He remained on the staff of the Royal Academy for fifty-seven years, for many years lecturing there six times annually as well as teaching the piano. In 1852 he married Julia Fanner, the daughter of an artist; she became mentally unstable in 1878, and died childless in 1902.

Macfarren was an accomplished performer, though in later years his style was regarded as old-fashioned. He composed many small but well-written and attractive piano pieces recalling Mendelssohn and Sterndale Bennett. His vocal works included two church services and many short secular pieces; the partsong 'You stole my love' proved very successful. He produced overtures to *The Winter's Tale* (1844) and *The Taming of the Shrew* (1845) and *Beppo*, a concert overture (1847). He suffered from weak eyesight, but unlike his brother did not become totally blind. From 1873 to 1880 he conducted the concerts at the Royal Academy, and from 1877 to 1880 was treasurer of the Philharmonic Society. Having resumed the composition of large works, he produced with success at William Kuhe's Brighton festivals his *Pastoral Overture* (1878), *Hero and Leander* (1897), and a symphony in B♭ (1880); however, none was sufficiently original to retain a place in the concert repertory. In 1881 there followed a concert piece for piano and orchestra, written for his pupil, Miss Kuhe, which was his only large composition to be printed, and an overture to *Henry V*, performed at the Norwich festival.

Macfarren was appointed music critic of *The Queen* newspaper in 1862, to which he contributed articles, moderately conservative in tone, until his death. For the music publishers Ashdown and Parry (afterwards Edwin Ashdown) he edited Popular Classics, which reached 240 numbers; he also edited Mozart's complete piano works and Beethoven's sonatas. His complete *Scale and Arpeggio Manual* (1882) became a standard teaching book. After the death of his brother Sir G. A. Macfarren in 1887, he was regarded as a candidate to succeed him as principal of the Royal Academy of Music.

On the occasion of Macfarren's jubilee in 1896 he founded two prizes, gold medals for piano playing, at the Royal Academy. In 1904 he retired from all active work, apart from contributing to *The Queen*; on this occasion an illuminated address, signed by several hundreds of his friends, was publicly presented to him. He lived at 3 Osnaburgh Terrace, Regent's Park, and usually spent his vacations at Brighton. In the summer of 1905 he published *Memories*, an autobiography which was insufficiently revised. He died at home in London on 2 September 1905, and was buried in St Pancras cemetery, East Finchley, on 7 September.   HENRY DAVEY, rev. CLIVE BROWN

Sources *MT*, 39 (1898), 10–15 · *Musical Herald* (April 1893) · *Musical Herald* (Dec 1901) · *Musical Herald* (Sept 1903) · *Musical Herald* (Nov 1905) · W. C. Macfarren, *Memories* (1905) · personal knowledge (1912)
Likenesses portrait, repro. in *Musical Herald* (April 1893) · portrait, repro. in 'Mr Walter Macfarren' (Jan 1898)
Wealth at death £27,315 7s. 4d.: probate, 21 Sept 1905, *CGPLA Eng. & Wales*

Mac Fhirbhisigh, Dubhaltach Óg [Duald MacFirbis, Dudly Ferbisie, Dualdus Firbissius] (c.**1600–1671**), scribe and genealogist, was born about 1600 (not, as often suggested, in 1585), probably at Lackan (*Irish* Leacán Meic Fhir Bhisigh), co. Sligo. He was the eldest of four sons of Giolla Íosa Mór (*d. c.*1643), son of Dubhaltach Mór, who was himself an accomplished scribe, and belonged to a leading hereditary learned family of north Connaught who served as historians and poets to the Ó Dubhda (O'Dowd) chieftains of Tireragh in west co. Sligo; his mother was from the Mac Diarmada family. Contrary to what is commonly stated, he was not a direct descendant of Gilla Ísa Mac Fir Bisig (*fl.* 1392–1418), who compiled and partly wrote the important Irish manuscript called the Book of Lecan and a significant portion of the Yellow Book of Lecan. Virtually nothing is known of his early life, but he may well have received some of his education in Galway city, where he would have been a near-contemporary of John Lynch and Patrick Darcy. He may also have received more traditional training at a school run by the learned family of Mac Aodhagáin, celebrated lawyers and historians, at Ballymacegan on the shores of Lough Derg in north co. Tipperary. He Anglicized his name as Dudly Ferbisie and it was Latinized as Dualdus Firbissius, from which the commonly used form Duald MacFirbis derives.

In May 1643 at Ballymacegan (perhaps on a return visit), Mac Fhirbhisigh copied an ancient glossary called *Dúil Laithne* ('Book of Latin'). In that same year he transcribed from an old MacEgan manuscript a collection of early annalistic material from south Leinster now known as the 'fragmentary annals' of Ireland. The copy was made for 'Rev Dr John Lynch', then archdeacon of Tuam. It was probably about this time too, perhaps while still at Ballymacegan, that he transcribed a valuable early Irish legal tract, *Bretha neimheadh déidheanach*, and an important collection of early Irish annals, *Chronicum Scotorum*.

Mac Fhirbhisigh was settled in Galway by the spring of 1645, when he transcribed an ancient historico-genealogical text, *Senchas síl Ír*. His source was the late fourteenth-century manuscript called the Book of Uí Mhaine (but known to him as the Book of Ó Dubhagáin). The copy of the *Senchas*, now incorporated in his 'Book of genealogies', is of particular value since almost a third of the Síol Ír text has since been lost from the exemplar.

Towards the end of 1647 Mac Fhirbhisigh completed a translation from English into Irish (begun by others over a decade earlier) of two books containing the rule of St Clare and other documents pertaining to the order of Poor Clares, which had a house in Galway. He gives his place of writing as 'The college of Galway', that is, the collegiate church of St Nicholas or one of the attached buildings, where he continued to work over the next few years. By the spring of 1649 he was hard at work on his *magnum opus*, the monumental 'Leabhar genealach' ('Book of genealogies'), an enormous compendium of Irish genealogical lore covering the period from pre-Christian times to the mid-seventeenth century and collected from a variety of sources, some of them now lost. In August of that year he used the celebrated annals of the four masters as a source for a catalogue of the kings of Ireland, extending from prehistoric times down to the twelfth century. By the close of 1650 he had completed the main text of the 'Book of genealogies', including a detailed general index, having laboured during a particularly disturbed period of Galway's history. Already buffeted by the growing storm of war, the city was devastated in 1649–50 by the bubonic plague, which reportedly killed some 3700 of the inhabitants. In the middle of 1651 Galway came under siege from Sir Charles Coote's parliamentarian forces and underwent great privations before its capitulation nine months later. It is not known whether Mac Fhirbhisigh remained in the city during this period or whether he made his escape before the enemy closed in.

In summer 1653 at an undisclosed location (but possibly elsewhere in co. Galway) Mac Fhirbhisigh added hagiographical material to the 'Book of genealogies', some of it taken from the early fifteenth-century Leabhar Breac. By April 1656 he was back in his home area of west Sligo or north-east Mayo as a witness to the marriage of his hereditary lord, Dathí Óg Ó Dubhda (David O'Dowda), to the latter's cousin, Dorothy O'Dowd; in fact, he may have drafted the interesting 'Marriage articles' (in English). In 1656, also, he compiled a work on early Irish authors, which is now lost except for a partial copy which he commenced in May 1657. In October 1657, in Sligo town, he copied into the 'Book of genealogies' some particularly interesting early material from sources which are no longer extant. In the early 1660s he was listed as liable to pay hearth-tax on a dwelling in Castletown, some miles north of his native Lackan. About this period he is mentioned in print for the first and only time in his lifetime, in his friend John Lynch's *Cambrensis eversus*, which was published in France in 1662.

In 1664 Mac Fhirbhisigh made significant additions to the 'Book of genealogies' but gives no indication of where he found or transcribed this new material. It may have been in Dublin, which he had certainly reached by the end of the following year when he penned a bilingual genealogy of the Berminghams, barons of Athenry. About this time he found employment with the Anglo-Irish historian and antiquary Sir James Ware. During 1665 and 1666 he furnished Ware with English translations of portions of the annals of Inisfallen and of Tigernach relating to the

twelfth and thirteenth centuries and of the annals of Lecan (now lost) covering the years 1443 to 1468. He also wrote a tract in English on early Irish bishops, drawing on various documents (few of them now extant) from the archives of Clann Fhirbhisigh. During a sojourn back in Tireragh in spring 1666 he compiled a work in Irish on early Irish bishops and then set to work on an abridged version of the 'Book of genealogies'. Since his original copy of the abridgement does not survive it is not known if he ever finished it; both of the two earliest extant copies (one certainly and one possibly from the early eighteenth century) appear incomplete. He was back in Dublin for some weeks at the time of Ware's death on 1 December but then returned to Connaught for the last time. Seeking patronage from Sir Dermot O'Shaughnessy in south Galway, he composed a poem in his honour, but we do not know if it produced the desired effect. He may next have sought support from the marquess of Antrim, in Larne, co. Antrim, where he left several important manuscripts in the hands of the local learned family of Ó Gnímh. He then returned to Tireragh and in January 1671 at Doonflin, about a dozen miles east of Lackan, he was stabbed to death by one Thomas Crofton in circumstances which are unclear. He was buried in Kilglass old cemetery, co. Sligo.

Mac Fhirbhisigh's scholarly achievement was substantial. As one of the last traditionally trained members of a hereditary learned family, his labours ensured the survival of several important sources of medieval and early modern Irish history. Without his diligence as copyist, compiler, and translator, knowledge of various aspects of early and medieval Ireland would be much the poorer. It is ironic that someone who supplied so much information about others left few details about his own life; nothing is known of his personal appearance, his marital status, or extensive portions of his life.   NOLLAIG Ó MURAÍLE

Sources N. Ó. Muraíle, *The celebrated antiquary: Dubhaltach Mac Fhirbhisigh (c. 1600–1671)* (1996); repr. (2002) • N. Ó Muraíle, 'Aspects of the intellectual life of seventeenth century Galway', *Galway history and society: interdisciplinary essays on the history of an Irish county*, ed. G. Moran and R. Gillespie (1996), 149–211, esp. nn. 140–97 • W. O'Sullivan, 'The manuscript collection of Dubhaltach Mac Fhirbhisigh', *Seanchas: studies in early and medieval Irish archaeology, history and literature in honour of Francis J. Byrne*, ed. A. P. Smyth (2000), 439–47 • *DNB*

Archives BL, MSS • BL, translations and extracts, Add. MS 4799 • Bodl. Oxf., MSS • Royal Irish Acad., MSS • TCD, MSS • University College, Dublin, MSS, book of genealogies

Macfie, Robert Andrew (1811–1893), sugar refiner and politician, was born on 4 October 1811 at 52 Kirkgate, Leith, the eldest of the nine children of John Macfie (1783–1852), sugar refiner and provost of Leith, and his wife, Alison (1791–1857), second daughter of William Thorburn, also of Leith, and his first wife, Robina Scott. Educated at the high schools of Leith and Edinburgh, and at the University of Edinburgh, in 1829 he entered his father's business, the year after it was severely damaged by a fire at the underinsured sugar refinery. Despite a vocation for the Presbyterian ministry, he continued in business, moving to Glasgow in 1835 as a bill collector for the National Bank of Scotland, then to Liverpool in 1838 to establish a refinery for Macfie & Sons. This prospered, eventually replacing Greenock and Leith as the firm's centre of operations. Macfie co-operated with Leone Levi in founding the Liverpool chamber of commerce, and was elected a life trustee of the city's exchange.

On 2 January 1840 Macfie married Caroline Eliza (1813/14–1897), the eldest daughter of John Easton MD of Courance Hill, Dumfries, a retired army surgeon. They had seven children, all born in Liverpool, of whom two died in infancy. Resident between 1856 and 1871 at Ashfield Hall, an estate of 90 acres near Great Neston, Cheshire, in 1862 Macfie purchased Dreghorn Castle, south of Edinburgh. Four years after his retirement from business in October 1867, this became the family home.

Macfie was a convinced Presbyterian and, with his wife, promoter of overseas missions. In 1838 he became a director of the Glasgow Missionary Society. Active in the Evangelical Alliance from its inception in the mid-1840s, he served on its council from 1852 for many years, and on the foreign mission committee of the Presbyterian Church of England between 1848 and 1866. In 1857–8 he founded Parkgate Presbyterian Church, Neston. He played a major role in promoting an international conference on missions held at Liverpool in 1860, which was reputedly the first of its kind. His most lasting contribution to the church was his initiation and financial sponsorship of the Ante-Nicene Christian Library. In 1865 he agreed with the publishers, T. and T. Clark of Edinburgh, the publication of a cheap scholarly edition of a translation of the pre-Nicene fathers into English by Alexander Roberts and James Donaldson, and donated nearly 300 sets of the 24-volume work to missionary libraries.

Having unsuccessfully contested Leith burghs for the Liberal Party in 1859, Macfie was elected to the seat under the widened franchise in 1868. In parliament he pursued the sugar refiners' case against the loss of tariff protection under the French trade treaty of 1860, linking it with their disadvantaged position, relative to their Caribbean competitors, under the reformed patent system. A persistent advocate of the latter's abolition, proposing a system of 'national recompenses' in lieu of patents, he also agitated for the abridgement of authors' copyrights. Concern for the consolidation and defence of the empire made him a pioneer of imperial federation: he was a founding fellow of the Royal Colonial Institute and active on its council. He also spoke regularly on Scottish affairs: while a firm upholder of the union, he was concerned to maintain the independence of Scotland's educational and religious traditions, and campaigned for the improvement of Scottish coastal defences.

Macfie pursued these concerns after losing his seat in 1874. Besides letters to newspapers and speeches to conferences, he published several books on both the patent question and imperial federation, turning finally to issues of patronage and forms of worship in the Church of Scotland. Evidently he was regarded as obsessive in such matters, his obituarist commenting that 'he hammered away

at the same subject, in season and out of season … wherever he could get people to listen to him', unable to understand why others did not share his enthusiasms (*The Scotsman*, 18 Feb 1893). Fortunately he was not easily offended and remained cheerful under duress. Earnest yet amiable in manner and appearance, with a round, bearded face, Macfie was a devout worshipper and a generous contributor to religious and philanthropic causes. His commercial knowledge and reputation for integrity were valued in the local community. He served as a magistrate and commissioner of supply for Midlothian, and was elected a fellow of the Royal Society of Edinburgh in 1877.

Macfie died at Dreghorn on 16 February 1893, following several months of suffering from 'an internal malady', which had recently become acute. He was buried five days later in the family vault in South Leith churchyard.

CHRISTINE MACLEOD

Sources *The Scotsman* (4 Jan 1840) • *The Scotsman* (18 Feb 1893) • *The Scotsman* (22 Feb 1893) • *Men and women of the time* (1891), 590 • *Biograph and Review*, 2 (1879), 61–4 • 'Robert Andrew Macfie', *New Monthly Magazine*, 4th ser., 1 (1879), 936–8 • *Hansard 3* (1869–73), vols. 196–217 • 'Royal commission to inquire into … letters patent for inventions', *Parl. papers* (1864), 29.462–70, no. 3419 • 'Select committee on … letters patent', *Parl. papers* (1871), 10.800–04, no. 368 • census return for Neston, Wirral, 1861, district 460a • *WWBMP* • U. Glas., Macfie family MSS, DC 120
Archives NL Scot., letters received, Acc. 8605 • U. Glas., Archives and Business Records Centre, corresp. and papers
Likenesses A. E. Fradelle, photograph, repro. in 'Robert Andrew Macfie', facing p. 936 • photograph, U. Glas., Macfie family MSS
Wealth at death £56,753 6s. 4d.: confirmation, 14 April 1893, *CCI* • £4790: additional estate, 2 April 1894, *CCI*

MacFirbis, Duald. *See* Mac Fhirbhisigh, Dubhaltach Óg (*c*.1600–1671).

Mac Flainn, Flann [Florence Macflynn] (*d.* 1256), archbishop of Tuam, was chancellor of Tuam and sub-deacon to the pope when he was elected archbishop following the death of his predecessor about Christmas 1249. The royal assent was given on 27 May 1250 and restitution of the episcopal temporalities was ordered on 25 July, but the election may have been uncanonical since Mac Flainn went to Rome to seek papal confirmation and he was not consecrated until 25 December 1250. At his election he was described as 'faithful to the kingdom' (*Calendar … Ireland*, 1, no. 3044) and in the following year, like his predecessors, he endeavoured to obtain possession of the see of Annaghdown; he appears to have gone to England in 1252 to discuss the matter with Henry III and eventually secured possession of the see, conceding in return the 'vill' of Annaghdown 'in order that the king may there fortify a castle' (*Calendar … Ireland*, 2, nos. 77, 274). He held a synod of the clergy of Ireland at Tuam in 1251. His episcopate was marked by quarrels with neighbouring bishops and controversy regarding Armagh's claim to primacy over the province of Tuam, the pope finding in favour of Armagh in 1255. Following the ineffectiveness of an earlier complaint in 1253, he made a journey to England in 1255 to lay a statement of grievances before the king on behalf of the Irish church; namely, that the bishops and their tenants were dragged into distant courts, contrary to the ancient liberties of the church, and that they were oppressed by the sheriffs and the barons, Irishmen being prevented from bequeathing their chattels and fulfilling their crusading vows. Henry ordered such remedy as tended to the welfare of the church to be applied. Papal intervention in the matter was also sought. About May 1256 Mac Flainn seems to have made a fresh journey to England, to present a further petition on the same matter, but he died on the way, at Bristol. Leave to elect a successor was issued on 29 June. Mac Flainn is described in the annals of Connacht as a man of wisdom with a knowledge of law, and elsewhere as 'an honest, prudent, and learned man' (*Calendar … Ireland*, 1, no. 3044).

C. L. KINGSFORD, *rev.* SEÁN DUFFY

Sources H. S. Sweetman and G. F. Handcock, eds., *Calendar of documents relating to Ireland*, 5 vols., PRO (1875–86), vols. 1–2 · *CEPR letters*, vol. 1 · M. P. Sheehy, ed., *Pontificia Hibernica: medieval papal chancery documents concerning Ireland, 640–1261*, 2 (1965) · A. M. Freeman, ed. and trans., *Annála Connacht / The annals of Connacht* (1944) · W. M. Hennessy, ed. and trans., *The annals of Loch Cé: a chronicle of Irish affairs from AD 1014 to AD 1590*, 1, Rolls Series, 54 (1871) · *AFM*, vol. 3 · J. A. Walt, *The church and the two nations in medieval Ireland* (1970)

McGahey, Michael [Mick] (1925–1999), trade unionist, was born on 29 May 1925 at 110 Stane Place, Shotts, Lanarkshire, the son of James McGahey, a coalminer, and his wife, Rose Ann, *née* Ferry. His mother was a devout Roman Catholic from Derry, but his father was a founder member of the Communist Party of Great Britain and one of the miners' leaders during the general strike of 1926. The family was forced to move shortly thereafter to Cambuslang, near Glasgow, and McGahey was educated there. He left school at the age of fourteen to work at Gateside colliery as a pony driver, and spent the next quarter of a century working down the mine. He also joined the Young Communist League and the National Union of Mineworkers (NUM), becoming chairman of the local union branch when he was eighteen. On 25 November 1954 he married Catherine, a 25-year-old hosiery mender and the daughter of John Young, a builder's labourer. They had two daughters, Caroline and Elaine, and a son, also Michael.

In 1958 McGahey was elected to the NUM's Scottish executive, and eight years later he became one of the union's national executive members. In 1967 he was elected full-time president of the union's Scottish area in succession to his fellow communist Alex Moffat. As Scottish president he articulated the growing mood of militancy among the miners after nearly a decade of redundancies and pit closures as well as declining real wages. He took a highly militant line on what needed to be done, arguing that the miners had to reassert themselves if they hoped to save their jobs and the coal industry. But his bid to become national president of the union failed in 1971, when he was beaten decisively in a rank-and-file ballot by the more moderate Lancastrian Joe Gormley, whom he later described as 'in the classic tradition of the class traitor' (*The Times*). A year later, however, McGahey made a further advance when he was elected vice-president of the

Michael McGahey (1925–1999), by Maggi Hambling, 1988

union by delegates at its annual conference. It was a key post that he retained until his retirement.

During the 1972 and 1973–4 miners' strikes McGahey was strongly criticized by Edward Heath and his government for seeking to turn those industrial disputes into political struggles. On one occasion he suggested that the miners were not in conflict simply to establish decent wages and a better standard of living but to bring an end to the Conservative government and create the 'conditions for a rapid advance to Socialism' (*The Times*). 'I want the Tories to be the anvil, and I will be a good blacksmith', he also declared (ibid.). Such comments brought him rebukes from Gormley. But McGahey never attempted to distinguish between his roles as a union leader and as a communist. He described himself as but 'a product of my class and my movement' (*The Scotsman*). As a member of the Communist Party's executive after 1971, he sought to win wider support for his militant policies.

McGahey's uncompromising outlook probably cost him the presidency of the mineworkers' union. In 1980 Gormley made it clear he did not intend to retire from the top post for the time being. He thereby ensured McGahey would be ineligible to stand for the presidency under a union rule (pushed through by Gormley himself) that required any contender to be under the age of fifty-five. Admirers believed that if McGahey had been elected president instead of Arthur Scargill the union would never have been led into the disastrous strike of 1984–5 that destroyed the miners as a credible industrial force and accelerated the contraction of the coal industry, but this is mere conjecture. McGahey always believed the miners should use their collective strength to exploit their market power, and he displayed no public doubt or caution in pursuing that strategy. It was he and not Scargill who warned that the union would not be 'constitutionalized' out of calling a national strike in March 1984 by what he called 'ballotitis' (*The Guardian*), even although this meant ignoring a clear rule of the union that a majority of the miners had to agree to strike action in a secret ballot before a dispute could be called. Nor at any stage did McGahey publicly repudiate the tactics of intimidation used by the union to try to force working miners in Nottinghamshire and elsewhere in the midlands to join the strike. Whatever his private reservations might have been about picket-line violence, he was never willing to challenge Scargill's conduct of the dispute. It is true he was held in high regard by many senior managers in the National Coal Board, who recognized he could be pragmatic when it was deemed necessary. But he never seemed ready to acknowledge the need to co-operate fully in the modernization of the coal industry and defend what was becoming an increasingly vulnerable position in a highly competitive energy market. He continued to see the miners as the vanguard for the socialist advance, but by the early 1980s his implacable ideology and harsh language found few echoes in the wider workforce.

McGahey remained a communist until the party dissolved itself in 1990, although he identified himself incongruously with its Euro-communist wing in his later years (largely out of loyalty to the party leadership). But his uncritical admiration for the Soviet Union survived intact. He once described that country as 'a beacon which lit the road into the future for the working class across the world'. McGahey also once described dissident miners locked away in mental hospitals for challenging Soviet power as 'renegades'. He supported the Red Army's suppression of the Hungarian uprising in 1956, arguing that the new regime in Budapest 'did not back the tenets of Communism'. Middle-class admirers in the media may have been impressed by his love of poetry and abilities as a genial saloon-bar raconteur, but throughout his life McGahey was unflinching in his ideological commitment to the Soviet cause, despite all the twists and turns he was required to make as a result.

McGahey came to represent the unyielding, aggressive face of the miners and was even seen by some as a subversive threat to democratic government. But for his many admirers on the left he was a warm, compassionate autodidact who reflected all that was heroic about the labour movement in struggle. An outstanding orator, for many years he suffered from emphysema, a legacy of his years down the pit, aggravated by his fondness for Capstan cigarettes, which gave his voice an inimitably gravelly quality. He died at the Royal Infirmary, Edinburgh, on 30 January 1999, survived by his wife and three children. His funeral service was held at Mortonhall crematorium, Edinburgh, on 3 February 1999.   ROBERT TAYLOR

Sources *The Times* (1 Feb 1999) · *Daily Telegraph* (1 Feb 1999) · *The Guardian* (1 Feb 1999) · *The Independent* (1 Feb 1999) · *The Scotsman* (1 Feb 1999) · *Financial Times* (1 Feb 1999) · *The Herald* (2 Feb 1999) · personal knowledge (2004) · private information (2004) · b. cert. · m. cert. · d. cert.
Likenesses group portrait, photograph, 1974, Hult. Arch. · photograph, 1980, repro. in *The Independent* · photograph, 1984, repro. in *The Times* · photograph, 1984, repro. in *Daily Telegraph* · photograph, 1984, repro. in *The Guardian* · M. Hambling, portrait, 1988, Scot. NPG [*see illus.*] · photograph, repro. in *The Scotsman*

McGauley, James William (*c.*1806–1867), physicist and inventor, was the son of a carpenter and belonged to a Roman Catholic family who resided at Kilmainham in Dublin. He was educated at the Revd Michael Doyle's academy at 23 Arran Quay, Dublin, and he is also said to have received three months' tuition 'from a gentleman of Trinity College, Dublin'. In 1824 he entered St Patrick's College, Maynooth, to be trained for the Roman Catholic priesthood and in November 1826, as a student, he gave evidence before the royal commission on the college. In Maynooth he came under the influence of Nicholas Callan, the professor of natural philosophy, and in consequence he developed a deep interest in science and especially in electrodynamics. By 1835 he was a priest attached to St Mary's Church in Marlborough Street, Dublin, and in that year he read to the first Dublin meeting of the British Association a widely noticed paper on the nature and potential of magnetism. The following year, while still continuing with his pastoral duties, he became professor of natural philosophy to the board of national education in Ireland. He was allowed to operate a laboratory in the board's Marlborough Street headquarters, and between 1840 and 1854 he wrote several mediocre textbooks in algebra, architecture, arithmetic, and physics, all intended for use in Irish national schools. His relationship with the board, and especially with Robert Sullivan, was somewhat acrimonious.

Late in 1856, perhaps as a result of a decision to renounce his vows and to marry, he departed for Canada. His wife's name is not known. About 1865 he returned to live in London where he became a council member of the Inventors' Institute (founded in May 1862 with Sir David Brewster as its first president), an editor of the *Scientific Review*, and managing director of the Inventors' Patentright Association. His own outstanding invention was the trembler interrupter (1837) universally employed in electric bells. He died suddenly in London on 25 October 1867, leaving his widow and four children in impoverished circumstances. A memorial fund was established for their maintenance and some £300 was raised, including a government contribution of £60.

GORDON L. HERRIES DAVIES

Sources P. J. McLaughlin, *Nicholas Callan: priest–scientist, 1799–1864* (1965) · *Scientific Review* (1 Nov 1867), 339 · St Patrick's College, Maynooth, co. Kildare, records of St Patrick's College

MacGauran [Magauran, Mac Gauran], **Edmund** (*c.*1548–1593), Roman Catholic archbishop of Armagh, was a member of the MacGauran or McGovern family of Tullyhaw, co. Cavan, and is reputed to have been born in the lordship of the MacGuire in the Monaghan–Fermanagh region. Some references suggest that he may have been educated for the priesthood in Spain, possibly at Salamanca or at Santiago de Compostela. On 11 September 1581 Pope Gregory XIII appointed him bishop of Ardagh and entrusted him with a special mission to the Ulster Gaelic lords. He was to try to obtain their support for the Geraldine war or Desmond rebellion (1579–83), which was then raging in Munster. It is regarded as the first Counter-Reformation military crusade in Ireland. Following the reduction of Desmond, MacGauran fled to Spain in 1585 and associated with the Geraldine exiles in Lisbon such as Maurice Fitzgerald, Edmund Eustace, Charles O'Conor-Faly, and Bishop Cornelius O'Mulrian of Killaloe.

On 1 July 1587 MacGauran was translated from Ardagh to the archbishopric of Armagh in succession to the late Richard Creagh. On 7 August both MacGauran and his friend Juan de San Clemente Torquemada, archbishop of Santiago de Compostela, received the pallium in Rome. Both had requested the pallium through the same Spanish proxy and they returned to Spain together after the consistory. In an audience with Philip II, Archbishop MacGauran formed the impression that Spain would support an uprising in Ireland led by the Catholic and Gaelic lords of Ulster against Elizabeth I. In June 1591 he outlined his plans in a letter to another Geraldine exile, Oliver Eustace, an Irish officer in the army of Flanders. MacGauran asked Eustace to organize a force of Irish veterans in the Spanish service to spearhead his proposed campaign. This letter was intercepted by Lord Burghley's agents and the Elizabethan government became aware of MacGauran's intrigues. In 1592, according to Sir Richard Bingham, governor of Connaught, MacGauran corresponded with Red Hugh O'Donnell, earl of Tyrconnell, and Hugh MacGuire of Fermanagh regarding a possible uprising. Philip II apparently promised a contingent of Spanish troops to help them in the summer of that year. However, though MacGauran gained privileged access to King Philip, accompanying him on a visit to France for the marriage of the infanta to the duke of Guise, he seems to have misjudged the extent of Philip's commitment to intervention in Ireland at this time.

Some time in autumn 1592 MacGauran returned to Ireland in a ship owned by the Drogheda merchant James Fleming. Outlawed by the Tudor administration, he was protected by Hugh MacGuire who refused demands by Lord Deputy Sir William Fitzwilliam for the archbishop's surrender. In winter 1592 MacGauran presided over a council of seven bishops under O'Donnell's protection in the Franciscan friary in Donegal. This meeting proposed the formation of a Catholic confederacy or league among the nobility and clergy of Ulster and Connaught under the leadership of Tyrconnell. Archbishop James O'Hely of Tuam was sent to represent this confederacy at the court of Philip II and to liaise with the Geraldine exiles in Lisbon. Meanwhile MacGauran and the other prelates settled differences between Hugh MacGuire and Brien O'Rourke of Breifne. By spring 1593 the combined forces of MacGuire, Mac Sweeney Duff, O'Reilly, O'Donnell, and O'Rourke of Breifne had captured the strategic castle of Beleek. On 6 June 1593 Bingham informed Burghley that

MacGauran 'doth much mischief riding on his chief horse, with his staff and shirt of mail' (*CSP Ire.*, 1592–6, 103). The politico-military Catholic confederacy which MacGauran had instigated soon developed into a more potent force which by 1595 would be led by Hugh O'Neill, earl of Tyrone, and Red Hugh O'Donnell, earl of Tyrconnell. This league would formally align itself with Philip II and, with Spanish finance, arms, ammunition, and troops, would come very close to defeating Elizabethan forces in Ireland during the Nine Years' War (1594–1603). However, Archbishop MacGauran did not live to see these developments as he was killed in an encounter between MacGuire and Bingham in north Connaught on midsummer eve, 20 June 1593. DECLAN M. DOWNEY

Sources Archivio Segreto Vaticano, Acta Camerarii, XII, fol. 68 · letter of MacGauran to Idiaquez, Archivo General de Simancas, Secretaria de Estado, Legajo 839, fol. 67 · W. M. Brady, *The episcopal succession in England, Scotland, and Ireland, AD 1400 to 1875*, 1 (1876), 221, 292 · J. Linchaeo [J. Lynch], *De praesulibus Hiberniae*, ed. J. F. O'Doherty, IMC, 1 (1944), 282–3 [orig. pubd 1672] · J. J. Silke, 'The Irish appeal of 1593 to Spain: some light on the genesis of the nine years' war', *Irish Ecclesiastical Record*, 5th ser., 92 (1959), 279–90, 362–71 · *Calendar of the manuscripts of the most hon. the marquis of Salisbury*, 4, HMC, 9 (1892), 117–18 · *CSP Ire.*, 1588–96 · M. J. Connellan, 'Archbishops Edmund Mac Gauran and Malachy Ó'Queely: some circumstances of their deaths', *Irish Ecclesiastical Record*, 5th ser., 70 (1948), 48–59, esp. 51 · J. J. Silke, *Kinsale: the Spanish intervention in Ireland at the end of the Elizabethan wars* (1970), 25–7 · M. Rodriguez-Pazas, *El episcopado Gallego a la luz de documentos Romanos, i arzobispos de Santiago, 1550–1850* (Madrid, 1946), 106 · D. M. Downey, 'Culture and diplomacy: the Spanish Habsburg dimension in the Irish Counter-Reformation movement, *c*.1529–*c*.1629', PhD diss., U. Cam., 1994, 92–6

M'Gavin, William [*pseud.* a Protestant] (**1773–1832**), religious controversialist, was born on 25 August 1773 at Darnlaw, in the parish of Auchinleck, Ayrshire, the third son of James M'Gavin (1730–1789), a farmer, and his wife, Mary McMillan (*d.* 1814). He received little formal schooling, and moved with his family to Paisley in 1783. At the age of twelve he was bound apprentice as a drawboy to a weaver and he persevered in this trade until he went to work for John Neilson, a Paisley bookseller, in 1790. In 1793 he left to assist in the school run by his elder brother John. This was not to his taste and after several years he entered the business of thread manufacture. This proved an expensive failure but he was rescued by the offer of a position with David Lamb, a cotton merchant in the American trade in Glasgow. This gave him scope for rapid advancement and handsome remuneration and he was admitted a partner after seven years. M'Gavin's relationship with the Lamb family was a close one; he lodged with them and acted as tutor to their two sons.

M'Gavin had been brought up in the Anti-Burgher church and he adhered to the congregation of James Ramsay after moving to Glasgow. The two men were simultaneously drawn to Congregationalism and M'Gavin assisted Ramsay in the church they formed in 1802. He was ordained co-pastor in 1804 but withdrew in 1807, adhering instead to the congregation of Greville Ewing, though he continued as an itinerant preacher and became involved in the numerous benevolent and religious societies which were being established at that time. On 7 October 1805 M'Gavin married Isabella Campbell. They had no children.

M'Gavin achieved notoriety in 1818 following an exchange of letters in the *Glasgow Chronicle* concerning the building of a new Roman Catholic chapel in Clyde Street, Glasgow. M'Gavin's letters were signed 'A Protestant' and quickly gave rise to a weekly periodical, *The Protestant*, which, *inter alia*, repeated and embellished the charge that money for the new building was extorted from the Catholic poor. In 1821 an action for libel was brought by a priest, Andrew Scott (1772–1846). Damages of £100 and, more significantly, costs amounting to £1387 were awarded against M'Gavin, though £900 was raised by public subscription. M'Gavin engaged in further disputes with Robert Owen of New Lanark, and with William Cobbett concerning his *History of the Protestant Reformation*. He also became involved, albeit unwittingly, in the Apocrypha controversy.

In 1822 M'Gavin received the offer of the managership of the Glasgow branch of the British Linen Company's bank, which conveniently rescued him from the difficulties which had overtaken his business. He remained in this position thereafter. Alongside his business and religious concerns there was constant literary activity. In addition to numerous tracts, he edited an improved edition of John Howie's *Scots Worthies* (1827), superintended a new edition of Knox's *History of the Reformation*, and wrote the introduction for John Brown of Whitburn's *Memorials of the Nonconformist Ministers of the Seventeenth Century*.

M'Gavin died of apoplexy at his home in Queen Street, Glasgow, on 23 August 1832. He was buried in the crypt of Wellington Street Chapel on 27 August and a substantial monument was erected in the Glasgow necropolis, close to that of John Knox, in 1834.

LIONEL ALEXANDER RITCHIE

Sources W. Reid, *The merchant evangelist* (1884) · *The posthumous works of the late William M'Gavin* (1834) · Chambers, *Scots.* (1855) · Anderson, *Scot. nat.*, 732–3 · G. Blair, *Biographic and descriptive sketches of Glasgow necropolis* (1857) · *DNB*
Likenesses S. Freeman, print (after J. Campbell), BM, NPG; repro. in Chambers, *Scots.*, 1st edn · portrait, repro. in Chambers, *Scots.*; formerly in the possession of his widow

McGeachy [*married name* Schuller], **Mary Agnes Craig** (1901–1991), international civil servant, was born on 7 November 1901 at 116 Brock Street, Sarnia, Ontario, Canada, the first daughter and second of the four children of Donald McGeachy (1868–1946), evangelist, and his wife, Anna Jenet, *née* Jamieson (1867–1944). Both parents were Ontario-Scotch: her father was born in Campbeltown, on the Mull of Kintyre, and her mother was born in Ailsa Craig, Ontario.

The daughter of a gospel-hall preacher in small-town Ontario, McGeachy had no family contacts to ease her way. She attended Sarnia schools and the Sarnia Collegiate Institute before entering the University of Toronto in 1920 to study English and history. She graduated with a first-class degree in 1924, then obtained an Ontario specialists' teaching certificate at the Ontario College of Education in 1925. Active in the student Christian movement, she retained her connections for the two years that she taught history at the Collegiate Institute in Hamilton, a steel manufacturing city in Ontario. In 1927 she attended conferences in Europe and decided not to return to schoolteaching. She became the editor of a trilingual student magazine, *Vox Studentium*, in Geneva. In 1928 she obtained a position in the information section of the League of Nations, and worked there as a senior assistant until 1940, becoming acting director of her section.

In 1940 McGeachy joined the British Ministry of Economic Warfare's public relations department. Sent to Washington, she toured the United States to explain the British policy of blockade against occupied Europe. After America entered the war her work shifted to include postwar planning. In October 1942 she was made first secretary at the British embassy in Washington, with local diplomatic rank, an honour welcomed by the Federation of Women Civil Servants and the all-party Woman Power Committee in the British House of Commons. A Canadian who always travelled on a British passport, she was the first woman to be given British diplomatic rank. In 1944 she was made director of welfare in the new United Nations Relief and Rehabilitation Administration (UNRRA), responsible for the needs of women, children, and old people in the displaced persons camps of Europe. She was the only woman in an executive position in the new international organization.

On 21 December 1944 McGeachy married Erwin Schuller (1909–1967), a Viennese-born banker. Having retired from the labour force after the UNRRA position came to an end in 1946 she turned towards voluntary work. Living after the war in Johannesburg, then Toronto, and finally New York, she became involved with the International Council of Women, an organization promoting women's rights and welfare. From 1963 to 1973 she served as its president and experienced the difficulties of navigating the politics of the cold war as they affected a nongovernmental organization in its liaison with the United Nations. Meanwhile her private life was not smooth. In 1952 she and her husband adopted a daughter (*b.* 1945) and a son (*b.* 1947), but she resisted domesticity. Unbowed by the tragedy of her husband's suicide, in 1967, she remained active in old age and expanded her activities to include membership in a religious lay order, the Society of the Companions of the Holy Cross, located in Byfield, Massachusetts. In 1985 she received the title of dame of the order of St John of the Knights of Malta. She died on 2 November 1991 in the vacation house that she had bought in 1946 at Keene, in the Adirondack Mountains, in upper New York state, and was cremated at Keene on 11 November. She was survived by her two adopted children.

McGeachy's life sheds light upon the contrasting twentieth-century conventions affecting men and women. Responding in her earlier career to the idealism of international co-operation in the League of Nations and in the first international aid agency, UNRRA, she later led the work of the International Council of Women as an organization with consultative status at the United Nations. At a time when married women were expected to retire from paid work she saw voluntary work as a way for women to serve society as citizens. MARY KINNEAR

Sources NA Canada, Mary Agnes Craig McGeachy and Erwin Schuller collection, R 9369 · United Nations, Geneva, League of Nations archives · United Nations, New York, United Nations Relief and Rehabilitation Administration archives · Brussels, Archiefcentrum voor Vrouwengeschiedenis–Centre d'Archives pour l'Histoire des Femmes (AVG–CARHIF), International Coucil of Women papers · FO papers, PRO, FO/371; chief clerk, FO/366 · Women's Library, London · University of Toronto Archives, Ontario · yearbooks, 1916–20, Sarnia Collegiate Institute, Ontario · student Christian movement papers, Victoria Library, Toronto · division papers, Hamilton-Wentworth School, Ontario · *Vox Studentium* (1923–) · woman power committee, BLPES · register of births, 23 Nov 1901, Lambton county, Ontario, entry 02112 · *Sarnia Observer* [Canada] (31 Jan 1944) · *Sarnia Observer* [Canada] (15 Oct 1946) · m. cert. · private information (2004) [Janet Holmes, daughter]
Archives priv. coll. | Archiefcentrum voor Vrouwengeschiedenis–Centre d'Archives pour l'Histoire des Femmes (AVG–CARHIF), Brussels, International Council of Women papers · United Nations, Geneva, League of Nations archives · United Nations, New York, United Nations Relief and Rehabilitation Administration archives
Likenesses photographs, priv. coll.

MacGeagh, Sir Henry Davies Foster (1883–1962), lawyer, was born in Kingston upon Thames, Surrey, on 21 October 1883, the only son of Thomas Edwin Foster MacGeagh MD (*b.* 1854) of Hadlow Castle, Kent, surgeon lieutenant-colonel in the Honourable Artillery Company of London, and his wife, Fanny, daughter of Colonel Jacob Davies of Baltimore, USA. He was educated at St Paul's School and at Magdalen College, Oxford, where he rowed for his college and took a third in modern history in 1905. Called to the bar (Middle Temple) in 1906, he joined the south-eastern circuit. In 1909 he obtained a Territorial Army commission with the London rifle brigade, and following the outbreak of war he was sent to France and Flanders. In 1916, in consequence of the services' need to expand the number of military lawyers, he was appointed military assistant to the judge-advocate-general, combining the post with those of deputy assistant and then assistant adjutant-general at the War Office. In 1917 he married Rita (*d.* 1959), daughter of William Kiddle of Walbundrie, New South Wales.

On MacGeagh's appointment in 1923 as head of the newly created military and air force branch of the judge-advocate-general's office, which, separate from the judicial branch under Sir Felix Cassel, assumed responsibility for service prosecutions, he transferred to the regular army with the rank of colonel. He held that post (apart from a short spell in 1927 in Shanghai) until he succeeded Cassel as judge-advocate-general in 1934 and retired from the army. Like his predecessor he held the office for many years (twenty in his case); he served four sovereigns and advised 21 secretaries of state for war and for air during his long tenure. He could also point to a succession of lawyers appointed to his staff during and shortly after the Second World War who subsequently attained judicial office.

They included three future lord chancellors (Kilmuir, Dilhorne, and Elwyn-Jones) and numerous future Supreme Court, county court, and Scottish judges. If in other respects he had shortcomings, few could match the distinguished cast of lawyers which he had assembled for the challenge of upholding military justice during the war. He stoutly defended even his less-than-polished wartime judge-advocates whenever military commands were outraged by court martial acquittals prompted by inconvenient legal rulings that his representative delivered during trials. His indulgence towards subordinates' shortcomings, as in the Pensotti case, might, however, end in problems and embarrassment.

Before the Second World War MacGeagh regularly had to defend his office against press and parliamentary criticism regarding the alleged iniquities of military law. Press reporting of the 'Officer in the Tower' case in 1933 was followed by further controversy over the Colonel Sandford case in 1934. The Oliver committee was set up in 1938 to investigate alleged miscarriages of military justice, coinciding (but not fortuitously, according to MacGeagh) with a strong attack on the judge-advocate-general's office by a barrister, Cecil Binney, writing in *Nineteenth Century*. When the committee eventually gave his office a clean bill of health, MacGeagh told a War Office official that he could now indulge in 'blowing my Office trumpet' (Rubin, 'Status', 243). More challenges were to face his office, not least the futile attempt to prise from the office of works in 1936 a mantelpiece for his own room and, from the War Office in 1938, the retention of a self-contained switchboard not shared with other departments. He was also obliged to respond vigorously to a report in 1944 by the solicitor-general, David Maxwell Fyfe, his former judge-advocate, on alleged underemployment in his department following anonymous complaints to this effect, probably emanating from Reginald Manningham-Buller, Cyril Salmon, and Harry Hylton-Foster, at a time when the civil courts were short of quality advocates. He reasonably pointed out that the informants—he had a 'shrewd idea of the sources from which these rumours spread' (PRO, WO32/11078)—were misleadingly arguing from the specific to the general.

The decision to conduct war crimes trials presented a further challenge. Generally speaking, MacGeagh was a less-than-dynamic driver of the admittedly difficult programme of investigating and then prosecuting crimes on a scale hitherto not imaginable by his department, and where the alleged perpetrators were not the usual cast of defalcating British officers or undisciplined British squaddies. MacGeagh, 'old, pedantic and conservative, tired out by the war and totally oblivious to conditions in Europe' (Bower, 129), even turned down an offer of extra staff for the work but was none the less resolute in preventing other bodies from encroaching on his newly acquired territory. British war crimes trials in Europe were, in the event, a less than glittering achievement. Military law reform in the post-war period of the Labour government also preoccupied him. Following the recommendations of the Lewis committee of inquiry into military law in 1946–

9, a committee whose composition he had sought (legitimately) to influence, he reluctantly accepted the creation of a civilian appeal court from the decisions of courts martial. After all, the creation of the courts martial appeal court in 1951 could be viewed as reflecting society's less than complete satisfaction with the judicial and post-trial role of his department, and as an acknowledgement that all had not been well with the military justice system, especially during the demobilization period when large-scale mutinies had occurred. He was less concerned about the transfer of his own responsibilities from the service ministers to the lord chancellor and about the transfer of his military and air force departments to the army and Royal Air Force.

MacGeagh retired as judge-advocate-general in 1954. Compared with Cassel, he was somewhat plodding, unimaginative, and cautious, perhaps even indecisive. One senior colleague, Brigadier Halse, recalled that MacGeagh 'could not make up his mind about anything', and always used to discuss complicated cases with his predecessor (Halse, 9). His undoubted achievement, however, was to maintain the solid if unspectacular administration of the military law system over two decades of intense social, political, administrative, and military challenge. He can be criticized for misplaced loyalty (the Pensotti case); for a failure, though widely shared, to address problems such as institutional command influence; and for a failure determinedly to meet the moral challenge of addressing war crimes trials.

MacGeagh was appointed CBE in 1919, received a knighthood in 1930, and was made KCB in 1946 and GCVO in 1950. He took silk in 1924 and became a bencher of the Middle Temple in 1931 (perhaps not wholly in accordance with the general rules for appointment, given the unusual nature of the judge-advocate-general's responsibilities) and treasurer in 1950. None the less his contribution to the life of his inn was significant. He was a member of the council of the Society for Comparative Legislation and contributed to the 'Royal forces' title of Halsbury's *Laws of England* edited by the first Lord Hailsham. In 1953 he became chairman of the Council of Legal Education. A vice-president of the Ulster Association (London), he was also a commissioner of the Duke of York's Royal Military School. Of striking pose, with dreamy eyes and a dignified moustache, he betrayed more than a hint of Rhett Butler in his appearance. He died on 29 December 1962 at Beaumont House, Marylebone, London.   G. R. RUBIN

Sources The Times (31 Dec 1962) · WWW · Walford, *County families* (1919) · matriculation records, Oxf. UA · G. R. Rubin, 'The status of the judge advocate general of the forces in the United Kingdom since the 1930s', *Revue de droit militaire et de droit de la guerre / Military Law and Law of War Review*, 33 (1994), 243–71 · R. C. Halse, 'Forty years on', c.1978, Office of the Judge Advocate General, 22 Kingsway, London [unpublished MS] · T. Bower, *Blind eye to murder: Britain, America and the purging of Nazi Germany—a pledge betrayed* (1995) · PRO, LCO 53/166; WO 32/11078; WO 225/4 · Lord Kilmuir, *Political adventure* (1964) · G. R. Rubin, 'Court-martial jurisdiction and ex-service personnel: the 'Boydell' gap' (1948) revisited', *Journal of Legal History*, 21 (2000), 67–84 · G. R. Rubin, 'The Pensotti Royal Air Force court martial controversy, 1944–1965', *New Zealand Armed Forces Law Review*, 1 (2001), 36–41 · CGPLA Eng. & Wales (1963)

Archives PRO, military career, WO 374/44142
Likenesses photograph, repro. in Bower, *Blind eye to murder* · photograph, repro. in The Times
Wealth at death £14,878 4s. 10d.: probate, 22 Feb 1963, CGPLA Eng. & Wales

McGee, Thomas D'Arcy (1825–1868), journalist and politician in Canada, was born at Carlingford, co. Louth, Ireland, on 13 April 1825, the second son and fifth child of James McGee, a coastguard of an Ulster family, and his wife, Dorcas Catherine Morgan, daughter of a Dublin bookseller who had been involved with the United Irishmen. In 1833 James McGee obtained an appointment in the custom house at Wexford, but while moving to their new home his wife died in an accident. Thomas McGee attended a day school in Wexford, but did not receive any further education. Just seventeen years old and with no means to support himself, he emigrated to America and reached Boston in June 1842, where he became involved in O'Connell's repeal movement and received an offer of a job in the office of the *Boston Pilot*, where he worked first as a clerk, then as a contributor and editor.

In 1845 McGee was appointed parliamentary correspondent of the *Freeman's Journal* in London. When his employer realized that McGee also wrote for the Young Ireland paper, *The Nation*, he was dismissed. He then became London correspondent for *The Nation*. McGee also wrote poems under a variety of pseudonyms: Montanus, Amergin, Feargail, Sarsfield, An Irish Exile, Gilla-Eirin, Gilla-Patrick, M, and T. D. M. He also published *Historical Sketches of O'Connell and his Friends* (3rd edn, 1845), *Irish Writers of the Seventeenth Century* (1846), *Memoir of the Life and Conquests of Art McMurrogh, King of Leinster* (1847), and *A Memoir of C. G. Duffy* (1849).

In 1846 McGee returned to Ireland to work in *The Nation* office. In Young Ireland circles McGee's eloquence and powerful poetry were highly regarded. However, since he dressed carelessly, he was frequently criticized as ill-dressed, or even shabby. According to Charles Gavan Duffy, his opponents distorted his name to Darky McGee, because of his dark features (Duffy, *Four Years*, 20). In 1847 he was appointed secretary to the committee of the Irish Confederation and also became president of the Davis Confederate Club in Dublin. In the same year, on 13 July, he married Mary Theresa Caffrey, and the couple had five children, of whom only two daughters survived childhood.

Although at first interested in James Fintan Lalor's radical politics on land distribution, McGee supported Duffy's moderate policy of a co-operation with the landlords. He was opposed to John Mitchel's radical policies, which promoted revolution and the abolition of the landlord class. However the French revolution of 1848 convinced the moderate wing of the Young Irelanders that a revolution was the right policy for Ireland. McGee went on a secret mission to Scotland in order to procure arms and ammunition, and also to seize two or three Clyde steamers with the aim of landing at the coast of Sligo and starting a rebellion there. When the enterprise failed, he was hidden by Edward Maginn, the Roman Catholic

Thomas D'Arcy McGee (1825–1868), by William Notman, 1868

coadjutor-bishop of Derry, whose biography he published in 1857. He subsequently escaped to America, disguised as a priest.

In New York, McGee immediately started the *New York Nation*. The success of this paper was threatened by his clash with the Catholic clergy, especially Archbishop Hughes, over the 1848 rebellion. McGee condemned the priests for discouraging the Irish peasantry from joining the Young Irelanders' rebellion. He then went to Boston and founded another newspaper, the *American Celt*. Through his work with Irish immigrants, McGee became convinced that their Catholic faith was often their only remaining possession, and he became more spiritually committed himself. He also appears to have undergone a dramatic conversion from revolutionary republican politics, becoming a conservative constitutionalist. This reversion to his original moderate political opinions brought accusations of treachery from his comrades of 1848, in particular from Mitchel and Devin Reilly. He moved his paper first to Buffalo, where his interest in Canada awakened, and then back to New York. While in America he published various works on Irish and American history, including *Catholic History of North America* (1854) and *A Popular History of Ireland* (2 vols., 1862). He also gave many lectures on immigration and Canada.

In 1857 McGee moved to Montreal, and started another paper, the *New Era*. Within a year of his arrival in Canada he was elected to the legislative assembly as member for Montreal West. He continued to give lectures on political

and historical topics and to campaign on behalf of immigrants. In May 1862 he became president of the executive council, a position he held until 1864. During 1864–7 he was minister of agriculture, emigration, and statistics. He played an important role in the formation of the dominion of Canada and the confederation of the provinces, and his influence in accomplishing the union in 1867 was acknowledged by many of his contemporaries. He wrote a number of works on this topic, including *The Crown and the Confederation* (1864) and *Speeches and Addresses, Chiefly on the Subject of the British American Union* (1865). He was elected member for Montreal West in the first Dominion parliament in the autumn of 1867.

McGee was very well liked in political circles, and his talents as an orator were often admired. However, he became increasingly unpopular among Fenian supporters in the Irish community after he denounced their planned invasion of Canada and advocated their severe punishment. They accused him of treachery to the Irish nationalist cause. On his return from a parliamentary sitting on 7 April 1868 he was shot down in Sparks Street, Ottawa. Fenians were held to be responsible for his death, and P. J. Whelan was arrested and hanged for his murder. McGee was accorded a state funeral on 13 April 1868, and was buried in Côte des Neiges cemetery, Montreal. His widow and daughters were provided for by the Canadian government. BRIGITTE ANTON

Sources J. Phelan, *The ardent exile: life and times of Thomas D'Arcy McGee* (1951) · C. Murphy, ed., *1825 — D'Arcy McGee — 1925: a collection of speeches and addresses* (1937) · *DCB*, vol. 9 · C. G. Duffy, *Four years of Irish history, 1845–1849: a sequel to 'Young Ireland'* (1883) · C. G. Duffy, *My life in two hemispheres*, 2 vols. (1898); facs. edn (Shannon, 1969) · T. F. O'Sullivan, *The Young Irelanders*, 2nd edn (1945) · *The Nation* (1845–8) · R. Davis, *The Young Ireland movement* (1987) · D. Gwynn, *Young Ireland and 1848* (1949) · T. D. McGee, letters to J. F. Lalor, 1847, NL Ire., Lalor MSS [items 103–8], MS 340 · T. D. McGee, letter to W. S. O'Brien, 29 June 1847, NL Ire., O'Brien papers [item 1917], MS 438 · police warrant for Thomas D'Arcy McGee, 28 July 1848, NL Ire., MS 7910 · *The Times* (22 April 1868), 10 · *The Times* (25 April 1868), 12 · *The Times* (9 May 1868), 12 · I. Skelton, *The life of Thomas D'Arcy McGee* (1925)

Archives Concordia University, Montreal, Georges P. Vanier Library · NA Canada · NL Ire. | NL Ire., Ferguson MSS · NL Ire., Lalor MSS · NL Ire., Larcom MSS · NL Ire., William Smith O'Brien MSS

Likenesses D. J. Hurley, oils, 1867, NA Canada · photographs, c.1867, NA Canada · W. Notman, photograph, 1868, NA Canada [see illus.] · statue, 1925, Parliament Hill, Ottawa, Canada · J. Gogarty, memorial statue, 1991, Carlingford, co. Louth, Ireland · photograph, repro. in C. Murphy, *1825 — D'Arcy McGee — 1925* · photograph, repro. in C. G. Duffy, *Young Ireland: a fragment of Irish history, 1840–1845* (1861)

Wealth at death Canadian government made provisions for his widow and daughters; apparently only had house in Montgomery Terrace, Montreal, and no other property or savings; friends made up subscription of $6000 which wiped out debts: Phelan, *The ardent exile*, 298; *DCB*, 9.494, col. 1; *The Times* (9 May 1868), p. 12, col. 2

Macgeoghegan, James (1702–1764), historian, was born near Uisneach in co. Westmeath, Ireland, in 1702. His father is described as a substantial farmer. At an early age Macgeoghegan was sent to France for his education, studying at the college of Rheims, where he distinguished himself in philosophy, obtained first prize in the theology examination, and was ordained a Roman Catholic priest. He later studied at the University of Paris where on 15 October 1733 he obtained an MA degree. He was closely associated with the Irish College in Paris, and held posts as chaplain at the Hôtel Dieu, the hospital next to Notre Dame, and chaplain to the Irish brigade in France. In later life he was an incumbent of the church of St Merry. At some point he acquired the title of *abbé*.

In the last few years of his life Macgeoghegan published his *Histoire de l'Irlande, ancienne et moderne, tirée des monuments les plus authentiques* (Paris, vol. 1, 1758; vols. 2 and 3, 1762). Whereas the first volume obtained the necessary royal permission without any problems, he was unfortunate in seeking publication for the final volumes precisely at the time when the Seven Years' War between Britain and France was winding to a close. The French censor, who rightly suspected that Macgeoghegan had Jacobite sympathies, feared that publication might cause offence to the British, and insisted that a passage be deleted from the third volume and that it be printed without royal permission with a bogus place and date of publication of Amsterdam 1763 on the frontispiece. The *Histoire* is a patriotic text with a clear Roman Catholic and Jacobite agenda. Macgeoghegan paints a picture of the Gaelic Irish attempting for centuries to preserve their land, independence, and ultimately religion, against the predations of the English. With the accession of the Stuarts this ancient and noble people formally submitted to a dynasty deemed to have legitimate Irish roots, and combined with their old opponents, but co-religionists, the Old English settlers, into a loyal Roman Catholic nation. The weak and ungrateful Stuarts, beset by evil advisers and puritan democrats, brought nothing but sorrow to the faithful Irish who had to endure confiscation and religious persecution, culminating in the usurpation by William of Orange. Thus Macgeoghegan was able to combine into a plausible explanatory framework both Gaelic resistance to English colonization and fidelity to the disastrous Stuart dynasty. As a consequence his book became in its nineteenth-century translation a classic in the canon of Irish nationalism. Macgeoghegan died in the rue des Arcis, at the sign of the Green Monkey, Paris, on 30 March 1764.

VINCENT GEOGHEGAN

Sources R. Hayes, *Biographical dictionary of Irishmen in France* (1949) · V. Geoghegan, 'A Jacobite history: the Abbé Macgeoghegan's *History of Ireland*', *Eighteenth-Century Ireland*, 6 (1991), 37–55 · P. O'Kelly, 'Biographical sketch of the author', in Abbé Macgeoghegan, *The history of Ireland, ancient and modern* (1845), 11–14 · 'Lettres et mémoires relatifs à la librairie sous l'administration de M. de Malesherbes, D–H nos 135–142', Bibliothèque Nationale, Paris, MS 22144 du Fonds Français · 'Succession en déshérence de M. l'abbé Magherghan', Archives Nationales, Paris, MSS T 1419, Y 13957 · L. W. B. Brockliss and P. Ferté, 'Prosopography and notes to Irish clerics in France in the seventeenth and eighteenth centuries', 1987, Royal Irish Acad. · Y. Le Juen, 'The Abbé Macgeoghegan dies', *Eighteenth-Century Ireland*, 13 (1998), 135–48 · A. Cogan, *The diocese of Meath, ancient and modern*, 3 [1870], 652 · *DNB*

Archives Archives Nationales, Paris, 'Succession en déshérence de M. l'abbé Magherghan', MSS T 1419, Y 13957 · Bibliothèque Nationale, Paris, 'Lettres et mémoires relatifs à la librairie sous l'administration de M. de Malesherbes, D–H nos 135–142', MS 22144 du Fonds Français
Wealth at death 2366 livres, 12 sols, 3 deniers: 'Succession en déshérence de M. l'abbé Magherghan', Archives Nationales, Paris, MSS T 1419, Y 13957

MacGeoghegan, Roche [*name in religion* Roque de la Cruz] (1580–1644), Roman Catholic bishop of Kildare, was the sixth son of Ross MacGeoghegan, chief of the sept of the MacGeoghegans of Moycashel or Kinelfiacha, co. Westmeath, and Sheila Dempsey. This branch of the MacGeoghegan clan held between 5000 and 10,000 acres in co. Westmeath and was a prominent Gaelic Irish family, which became closely connected to the Counter-Reformation in the seventeenth century. Roche's cousin Anthony MacGeoghegan was bishop of Clonmacnoise, and two of his younger cousins, Dominic and Arthur MacGeoghegan, also became Dominican friars. Roche MacGeoghegan began his education under the tutelage of Catholic laymen, initially in co. Westmeath and then in Clonmel, co. Tipperary. At this stage he was also educated by John Power, a Catholic priest, and may have attended a state-established protestant school for six months. After courses in the humanities, in 1600 he travelled to Lisbon and entered the Dominican order. Given the name in religion Roque de la Cruz (Ross of the Cross), he also completed a further five-month course in humanities while residing at the Irish College. From 1601 he spent eight years at Salamanca, where he lectured to Irish students.

Some time between 1614 and 1617 MacGeoghegan was appointed vicar of the Irish congregation of Dominicans. He was certainly in Ireland from 1614, where he undertook the task of reorganizing the Dominican order. In the late sixteenth century the Dominicans had been virtually obliterated in Ireland, so that the order's reorganization in the seventeenth century became one important element of the Counter-Reformation drive steered by Irish clergy returning from the continent. At this stage MacGeoghegan's priorities were to facilitate the missionary activities of the Dominican clergy, and he petitioned successfully for two sets of papal faculties (1617) which enabled them to celebrate the sacraments whenever and wherever possible, to read prohibited books in order to refute heresies, and to grant marriage dispensations. He also attended the Dominican chapter at Lisbon in 1618, where he was awarded the theological decree of *praesentatus* after the requisite examination in recognition of his preaching activity in Ireland. This chapter also allowed him to present his plans for the Irish mission, which were subsequently endorsed by the order. To increase the numerical strength of the Dominican congregation, all Irish Dominicans were ordered to return to Ireland on completion of their studies, and MacGeoghegan was ascribed authority to recall all those who had already completed their studies to the Irish mission.

MacGeoghegan did not attend the 1622 chapter of the order, but was represented there by John Fox. This chapter appointed MacGeoghegan prior provincial of Ireland, a position which he held until 1627. By this time MacGeoghegan had become further involved in the provision of

Dominicans for Ireland; between 1619 and 1626 he established a noviciate in Urlar (Mayo) and spent two years there teaching novices. In 1626 he was forced to leave Ireland for Louvain after being denounced to the royal authorities by several clergy whom he had censured for indiscipline. Provision of clergy remained his priority, however, and he was instrumental in the foundation of a Dominican college at Louvain. It was MacGeoghegan who lobbied Philip II of Spain successfully so that the college was granted initial funds and annual allowances for its maintenance.

MacGeoghegan's energy and organizational prowess meant that on the death of the archbishop of Armagh, Peter Lombard, in 1625 he became a leading candidate for the vacant see. The Dominicans campaigned enthusiastically for his appointment, on the basis that it would enable the order to defend itself in its recurring disputes with the powerful Franciscans and with bishops in Ireland. MacGeoghegan himself wrote to Michael of the Holy Spirit, the Dominican procurator at Rome, that he believed Dominican bishops would protect the order from the interference of Franciscan clergy, some of whom held powerful episcopal positions. Although MacGeoghegan's nomination to Armagh was supported by Spain as well as the Dominican order, he was not appointed, largely due to the opposition of the earls of Tyrone and Tyrconnell, who argued that no palesman should become archbishop of Gaelic Ulster. In 1629, however, he was appointed bishop of Kildare in Leinster and returned to Ireland.

As he had been during his time as the architect of Dominican revival in Ireland, MacGeoghegan proved conscientious and energetic in his new role as a bishop who followed the Tridentine model of episcopal leadership as far as possible. He held regular visitations of his diocese, produced two reports *ad limina* (1633 and 1637), preached personally, and attempted to improve clerical standards through the introduction of monthly ecclesiastical conferences. He also held a number of diocesan synods, and attended the provincial synod held at Tyrchogir (Queen's county) in 1640. In his personal life he was equally strict, meditating daily and adapting the penitential practices of fasting, sleeping on bare ground, and wearing a hair-shirt and chains beneath his outer clothing.

By the early 1640s MacGeoghegan's lifestyle had taken its toll, although it is not clear whether his final decline was rapid or protracted. An older tradition claimed that he was seized with paralysis while preaching a panegyric of Saint Francis and died almost immediately, but official reports represent him as paralysed and helpless for a long time prior to his death. In either case, he died on 26 May 1644, possibly in co. Westmeath. His place of burial is also unclear; he is thought to have been buried in the same year either in the Catholic church of Kildare or in the tomb of his ancestors at the Franciscan friary of Multyfarnham. During his lifetime he had accumulated a fine library, which was divided between the Dominican order and Kildare diocese on his death, a fitting epitaph to a classic Counter-Reformation cleric who had spearheaded

Dominican revival in Ireland and who had devoted his final years to the introduction of Tridentine reform in Kildare.   ALISON FORRESTAL

Sources T. Flynn, *The Irish Dominicans, 1536–1641* (1993) • M. Comerford, *Collections relating to the dioceses of Kildare and Leighlin*, 3 vols. (1883), vol. 1 • P. F. Moran, ed., *Spicilegium Ossoriense*, 1 (1874) • C. P. Meehan, *The rise and fall of the Irish Franciscan monasteries, and memoirs of the Irish hierarchy in the seventeenth century*, 2nd edn (1869) • J. Linchaeo [J. Lynch], *De praesulibus Hiberniae*, ed. J. F. O'Doherty, 2 vols., IMC (1944) • A. Forrestal, *Catholic synods in Ireland, 1600–1690* (1998) • T. W. Moody and others, eds., *A new history of Ireland*, 3: *Early modern Ireland, 1534–1691* (1976) • *DNB*
Wealth at death extensive library divided between Dominican order and Kildare diocese at time of death: Comerford, *Collections*

Macgeorge, Andrew (1810–1891), writer, son of Andrew Macgeorge, lawyer, was born on 13 May 1810, in Glasgow. He received his school and university education at Glasgow. He was admitted into the faculty of procurators in 1836, becoming about the same time a member of his father's firm. In 1841 he married Margaret, *née* Pollock, of Whitehall, near Glasgow; they had one daughter, who married Revd Dr Alison of Edinburgh. After his father's death Macgeorge was head of the firm until 1889, when he retired.

Recognized as a sound ecclesiastical lawyer, Macgeorge was connected with some famous cases in the courts of the Church of Scotland, and was an uncompromising churchman, publishing several books on the Scottish church and the 'real character and tendency' of Free Church claims. He also wrote, under the pseudonym of Veritas, an elaborate series of articles on the principles of the free church, which were collected later for private circulation. He was skilled in heraldry, and as an antiquary he contributed important papers to the Archaeological Society of Glasgow. His love of art is illustrated by his biography of W. L. Leitch, and by many watercolour paintings and clever caricatures. For John Brown's *Rab and his Friends* (1859), he drew an illustration of a dogfight, and Thackeray highly commended some of his caricatures when shown them by Brown. He took an active interest in Glasgow, publishing two books relating to the city and supporting its public institutions, notably the Royal Hospital for Sick Children, which was founded by his exertions, and of which he was long the secretary. Glasgow University conferred on him the degree of LLD four months before his death which took place on 4 September 1891 at Row, Dunbartonshire. His wife and daughter survived him.   T. W. BAYNE, *rev.* CATHERINE PEASE-WATKIN

Sources *Glasgow Herald* (5 Sept 1891) • *Helensburgh and Gareloch Times* (7 Sept 1891) • personal knowledge (1893) • *CCI* (1891)
Archives NL Scot., volume of reminiscences • U. Glas. L., diary
Wealth at death £14,800 8s. 8d.: confirmation, 31 Oct 1891, *CCI*

McGhee, Richard (1851–1930), trade unionist and politician, was born at Lurgan in Ulster in late January or early February 1851, the eldest of three sons of protestant parents, Richard and Alice McGhee. He was baptized on 12 February 1851. His father was a poor tenant farmer on the estate of Lord Lurgan, but later opened a general store in Lurgan. After attending the local school in Lurgan, at twenty years of age Richard moved to Glasgow where he served a seven-year engineering apprenticeship. On 20 July 1880 he married Mary (1857–1949), the daughter of George Campbell, a pattern-maker, and his wife, Catherine; they had five sons and a daughter. In the same year as his marriage McGhee started an unsuccessful small engineering business with his brother George. He then became a commercial traveller in cutlery and stationery, a profitable activity that sustained him throughout his working life.

In Glasgow, McGhee became involved in radical Irish and Scottish politics and in 1879 established a lifelong friendship with Michael Davitt, the Irish nationalist and founder of the Irish Land League. Henry George, the American radical, proved to be an even greater influence and McGhee remained a committed Georgeite throughout his life, supporting a single tax on land to end the excesses of landlordism.

By the mid-1880s McGhee had established a reputation as a man of principle, acute intelligence, and singular debating skills in the cause of Irish home rule, the campaign for land reform, and the spread of Georgeite radicalism. He was a founder member of the Scottish Land Restoration League in 1884 in support of the crofters' agitation. The universality of George's message and his belief that the problems of the Irish could be solved only by alliance with the British working class encouraged McGhee to assist unorganized, unskilled workers in England and Scotland.

McGhee became involved in trade unionism during the 1880s through the American Knights of Labor, a general union which established branches in Britain. He was briefly a Knights of Labor organizer assisting the nail- and chain-makers of Cradley Heath in the midlands from 1887 and was subsequently sent to Glasgow on a recruiting campaign. It was during a waterfront dispute there in early 1889 that the National Union of Dock Labourers (NUDL) was formed and McGhee was invited to become honorary president with Edward McHugh as general secretary.

The new union rapidly established branches in Scotland, Ireland, and north-west England, surviving substantial disputes in Glasgow in 1889 and Liverpool in 1890. McGhee, unpaid and part-time, was less prominent than McHugh but he devoted considerable time and energy to the organization and policies of the new union. He played a part in developing ca'canny tactics in Glasgow and Liverpool and introduced the union 'button', a metal badge designed to fit into the lapel. These buttons were issued to paid-up members and changed quarterly: their absence identified non-members, encouraging them to enlist to avoid the hostility of fellow workers.

In 1893 both McGhee and McHugh resigned from the NUDL claiming their work had been completed, but their departure was hastened by sectional jealousies and branch indiscipline. McGhee nevertheless remained involved in the organization of waterfront workers. He was an executive council member of the International Federation of Ship, Dock and River Workers, an ambitious venture founded by Tom Mann in 1896 which, although less successful than had been hoped, was ultimately revived as the International Transport Workers' Federation. McGhee was also associated with the seamen's union for many years, helping to secure the extension of the Workmen's Compensation Act to seamen in 1906 and their inclusion in the Health Insurance Act of 1911. He attended the union's annual conferences and was elected an honorary member of the executive council and a trustee in 1911, holding the latter position until his death in 1930.

In spite of the time and energy McGhee spent in the cause of labour organization, his commitment to Irish nationalism remained unimpaired, and from the early 1890s he was involved in Irish parliamentary politics. In 1892 he was unsuccessful in securing the nationalist nomination for South Louth but, following the death of the successful candidate in 1896, he was nominated and won the seat in the consequent by-election. His campaign was based on the cause of home rule on advanced nationalist principles, the endorsement of Catholic demands on education, the complete abolition of landlordism, and support for labourers based upon his own 'humble efforts during the past ten years on behalf of the toiling masses'. He was unexpectedly defeated in the election of 1900 but was again returned to parliament as the nationalist member for Mid-Tyrone in 1910. McGhee retained his seat until 1918, when the four constituencies of co. Tyrone were reduced to three, and he did not stand in the contest.

As an MP McGhee behaved as an orthodox nationalist member. He complained of the inequity of the taxation system and condemned the British during the Second South African War. During the First World War, however, the Irish nationalist party led by John Redmond lost credibility. McGhee loyally supported Redmond in his decision in 1914 to support the British war effort and in his condemnation of the Easter rising of 1916. The brutal reaction of the British government to the rising and the unsuccessful attempt to activate the Government of Ireland Act of 1914 which would have granted some measure of home rule finally destroyed Redmond and the constitutional movement. In the circumstances it is not surprising that McGhee did not seek re-election in 1918.

McGhee died at his home, 3 Hayburn Crescent, Partickhill, Glasgow, on 7 April 1930, aged seventy-nine, and was buried in Glasgow on 10 April. He had been in indifferent health for some time and, following a visit to England on seamen's business, he became ill and died of pneumonia within a fortnight. He was survived by his wife. His youngest son, appropriately named Henry George McGhee, was Labour MP for the Peniston division of Yorkshire from 1935 until his death in 1959.

An important figure in the cause of Irish nationalism, McGhee also contributed to the development of an influential Georgeite movement in Britain during the 1880s. He believed strongly in bringing together the Irish and British working classes, whose common experience of exploitation was of greater importance than divisive factors of nationality and religion. His earlier career as a trade union organizer was also noteworthy.

ERIC TAPLIN

Sources *DLB* · private information (2004) · E. L. Taplin, *The dockers' union: a study of the National Union of Dock Labourers, 1889–1922* (1985)
Archives priv. coll., personal papers, incl. corresp. with Michael Davitt · TCD, corresp. with John Dillon
Wealth at death £600: probate, 22 May 1931, *CGPLA Eng. & Wales*

M'Ghee, Robert James (1789–1872), Church of Ireland clergyman and anti-Catholic polemicist, was born in Ireland, probably in co. Carlow, about April 1789, the son of James M'Ghee, a clergyman. He was educated at Mr Pack's school and, from 1805 to 1810, at Trinity College, Dublin (BA 1811, MA 1813). He was ordained in the Church of Ireland in 1812, but remained unbeneficed for more than twenty-five years. He married at this period and had children, including a son, also Robert James, and a daughter, Mary Letitia. In 1817, in a vigorous exchange of pamphlets with William Phelan, a more moderate apologist for the Church of Ireland, M'Ghee established himself as an advocate of an uncompromising protestant biblicism.

During the 1830s M'Ghee emerged as a particularly virulent and energetic critic of the Irish Roman Catholic church, vigorously supporting James Edward Gordon and the campaigns of the Reformation Society in Ireland. In 1835 he claimed to have discovered that the *Theologia* of Peter Dens, a mid-eighteenth-century Belgian writer, had been adopted as an authoritative text by the Irish bishops, and subsequently identified a number of other texts which he held collectively to be conclusive proof of the persecuting, subversive, and corrupting tendency of 'Romanism as it rules in Ireland'. He claimed he had uncovered a Roman Catholic conspiracy to subvert church, state, and morality. He set out his arguments and evidence at a series of high-profile public meetings all over Britain during 1835 and 1836. His efforts made an important contribution to the launching of the Protestant Association and to the prevalence of anti-Catholic attitudes in the politics of the late 1830s. His credibility was, however, significantly damaged when in July 1836 he mistook a satire by James Henthorn Todd, fellow of Trinity College, Dublin, for an authentic bull by the then pope, Gregory XVI. M'Ghee also promulgated his views through voluminous pamphleteering, and in 1840 deposited sets of 'Documents on the Crimes of the Popish Apostasy' in the Bodleian Library, Oxford, and Cambridge University Library. In extensive unsolicited correspondence he urged Wellington, Peel, and, later, Lord Derby to use this information to mount a decisive political counter-attack against Irish Roman Catholic influence.

In 1838 M'Ghee was appointed minister of the proprietary chapel of Harold's Cross church, Dublin, and in 1846 the strongly evangelical George Montagu, sixth duke of Manchester—Orangeman, student of prophecy, and first president of the Reformation Society—presented him to the living of Holywell-cum-Needingworth, Huntingdonshire. His pastoral work and some of his later writings suggested a more positive dimension of his outlook, as a zealous evangelical who believed that the future of his own church lay in the effective proclamation of the gospel and the conversion of souls to Christ. He died at Ebury Street, Chester Square, Belgravia, on 16 April 1872.

JOHN WOLFFE

Sources J. Wolffe, *The protestant crusade in Great Britain, 1829–1860* (1991) · D. Bowen, *The protestant crusade in Ireland, 1800–70* (1978) · *The Record* (19 April 1872) · *The Record* (22 April 1872) · M. O'Sullivan and R. J. M'Ghee, *Romanism as it rules in Ireland*, 2 vols. (1840) · D. M. Lewis, ed., *The Blackwell dictionary of evangelical biography, 1730–1860*, 2 vols. (1995) · Boase, *Mod. Eng. biog.* · Burtchaell & Sadleir, *Alum. Dubl.*
Archives BL, corresp. with Sir Robert Peel, Add. MSS 40181–40615, 62939 [int. Poc.: W] · Bodl. Oxf., letters to Sir Thomas Phillips · Lpool RO, letters to fourteenth earl of Derby · U. Southampton L., Wellington MSS

McGill, Alexander (c.1680–1734), mason and architect, was the son of George McGill, minister of Arbirlot in Forfarshire (c.1641–1691x1702), and his wife, Margaret Guthrie. In 1697 he was apprenticed to Alexander Nisbet, an Edinburgh mason with strong professional connections in Forfarshire. Nisbet was also married to a Mary McGill (d. 1692), which may imply some family connection. Apart from these details, McGill's early life and training are obscure.

Nisbet was a member of the trades' incorporation in Edinburgh and McGill's name might have been expected to emerge in its membership rolls by c.1703. Instead, he first appears as a mason, independent of Nisbet, as early as 1701, at Kellie Castle, near Dundee. For whatever reason, his formative years were not influenced solely by his mason's training and from an early stage in his career he made use of other connections, so that by the time he was admitted to the Edinburgh masons' lodge in 1710 it was as an 'architector' rather than a stone mason.

One possibility is that McGill's career was influenced by his connection with James Maule, fourth earl of Panmure, who was the patron of Arbirlot parish. Kellie Castle belonged to the earl's brother Harry Maule of Kellie, and McGill collaborated on alterations to this property (1699–1705) with Alexander Edward, an Episcopalian minister who was closely associated with the Panmures and who turned to architecture after the revolution of 1688. It is possible that Edward and McGill already knew each other, having lived in the same area, but the importance of the Edward connection is that the minister was also associated with Sir William Bruce of Kinross, and McGill was thus linked with this key architectural figure from an early stage of his career. In 1708 McGill worked on the latter stages of Craigiehall, a small house on the outskirts of Edinburgh designed by Bruce and an important precursor to Hopetoun House near by. McGill was also involved in Bruce's very last project, House of Nairne, Perthshire, designed partly by the countess of Atholl with advice from Bruce and Edward, and taken over by McGill after Bruce's death in 1710. In the Craigiehall project McGill worked with John Erskine, twenty-second or sixth earl of Mar, the leading aristocratic amateur architect in Scotland at that time. He continued to be associated with Mar even after the latter's exile after the Jacobite rising of 1715.

McGill was also closely associated with James Smith, another major figure in Scottish architecture in this period, who established himself as the main architectural rival to Bruce by the 1690s. McGill and Smith worked together on Yester House (Haddingtonshire) for the marquess of Tweeddale, c.1700–1715. The design for this very elaborate house is mainly credited to Smith, but McGill was responsible for a number of houses on his own that are distinctive and interesting in their own right, notably Blair Drummond in Perthshire (1715–17) and Donibristle in Fife (1719–23). McGill shared Bruce's interest in the wider setting of the house, both in the design of landscapes, for Hugh Campbell, third earl of Loudoun, at Loudon Castle in Ayrshire in 1716, and in a concern with the architectural setting of courts and pavilions around the house. At both Blair Drummond and Donibristle he combined a series of simple and functional elements to make highly formal and monumental layouts of courtyards and pavilions. At Donibristle, in particular, this includes a dramatic series of terraces between the house and the River Forth, to the south.

McGill was first city architect of Edinburgh between 1720 and 1725. It was a significant post for a number of reasons. First, the city chose someone from outside the incorporation of trades and the emphasis was on his status as an architect rather than an operative mason. Second, it connects McGill with the beginnings of the great eighteenth-century project of improvement in Edinburgh, best exemplified by the New Town, but which also involved a whole series of social and economic improvements, many of which required architectural changes to the city. One of the key figures behind this scheme was Lord Provost George Drummond, who became city treasurer in 1717 at the very time that McGill was finishing Blair Drummond for George Drummond, the namesake and kinsman of the Edinburgh treasurer. Using the proceeds of an ale tax, the treasurer set out a substantial programme of improvements with McGill as architectural adviser from 1718, before his official appointment; the architect continued to advise the city on an *ad hoc* basis even after his salary of £50 per annum became more than the city could afford and the post was suspended. His work ranged from water supply and other infrastructure improvements to a new charity workhouse and a colony of houses and workshops for French weavers brought to the city in the 1720s to initiate a trade in cambric. His most important contribution to the city, however, was undoubtedly Greyfriars Kirk: partially destroyed in an explosion in 1718, it was expanded and remodelled by McGill to provide accommodation for two congregations between 1719 and 1723.

McGill's career was ultimately eclipsed by that of William Adam, who rose to prominence in the 1720s and dominated Scottish architecture for the next thirty years. However, McGill is a significant figure as, like Adam, he represents the move towards the architectural profession and away from the craft of the mason, and because he is associated with the early impulse towards improvement in Edinburgh. He died in Edinburgh in May 1734 and was survived by his wife, Margaret Hamilton (d. 1736).

JOHN LOWREY

Sources Colvin, *Archs.* · M. Glendinning, R. MacInnes, and A. MacKechnie, *A history of Scottish architecture* (1996) · J. Macaulay, *The classical country house in Scotland* (1987) · town council minutes, Edinburgh City Archives, 48.282, 288 · town council sederunt book of sub-committee for managing the ale duty, 1710–68, Edinburgh City Archives · town council ale duty committee copy book, 1718–28, Edinburgh City Archives · *Fasti Scot.*, new edn, vol. 5 · NA Scot., Commissariat of Edinburgh · Register of Testaments: Alexander McGill and Margaret Hamilton, his relict, 28/2/1737, 28/5/1756 · J. Dunbar, 'The building of Yester House', *Transactions of the East Lothian Antiquarian and Field Naturalists' Society*, 13 (1972)
Archives Edinburgh City Archives, town council minutes, *passim*, and ale duty papers, *passim* · Mount Stuart Trust, Isle of Bute, corresp. relating to Loudoun house and gardens · NA Scot., Dalhousie MSS · NA Scot., Erskine of Mar MSS · NA Scot., Montrose MSS

MacGill, David, of Cranstoun Riddel (d. 1595). *See under* MacGill, James, of Nether Rankeillour (d. 1579).

McGill, Donald Fraser Gould (1875–1962), cartoonist, was born at 46 Park Street, Regent's Park, London, on 28 January 1875, the son of John Streeter Davenport McGill, a stationer, and his wife, Rosina Bisgood. His Glaswegian ancestors had emigrated to Canada in the eighteenth century, where they made a fortune in fur trading. One, James McGill (1744–1813), founded McGill University; Donald's grandfather was president of the Bank of Montreal and speaker of the Canadian legislative council. Donald's father did not, however, inherit the family wealth. Donald was educated at Blackheath proprietary school, and at the age of seventeen suffered an injury in a school rugby match that necessitated the amputation of his foot. Always able to draw, he joined the famous correspondence school run by cartoonist John Hassall, the New School of Art. He worked in the office of Maudsleys, naval architects, for three years from 1893; in 1897 he was apprenticed to the Thames Ironworks, Shipbuilding, and Engineering Company, where he stayed until 1907.

McGill became a 'Sunday painter', exhibiting some pictures in the window of a Sussex shop, where they were seen by Joseph Ascher, a German immigrant entrepreneur whose interests included confectionery, advertising, insurance, freak shows, Venables check-action parlour pianofortes, and also the Pictorial Postcard Company. Ascher bought the rights to some of McGill's paintings and published them as cards, but was forced to remainder them at a farthing each or five for 1d. When Ascher saw some of McGill's lighter work, however, coloured pictures of Victorian ladies showing their ankles to passing 'mashers', he instantly bought the rights for 6s. each. McGill provided six pictures a week, using as inspiration the jokes he heard at the Palace of Varieties, Edmonton, where he had free admission, since his father-in-law owned the theatre.

In December 1905 the *Picture Postcard Magazine* announced, 'The Picture Postcard Company have discovered a promising young humour artist, Donald McGill by name, in the confident expectation that comic cards of his designing will soon become widely popular'. Two years later McGill left the Thames Ironworks Company and became a partner in the card firm of Hutson Bros., leaving in 1910 to freelance his cards to Ascher's company. When Ascher was interned in 1914 as an enemy alien, McGill moved to the Inter-Art Company where he worked on the staff until 1931. After a further five years' freelance work, in 1936 he rejoined Ascher, who was now working as D. Custance. McGill was given a card corner of his own, known as the New Donald McGill Comics series. From 1952 until he retired in 1962 he was contracted to the company as director in charge of postcard design.

While personally of modest and courteous character and dapper appearance, McGill was known nationally as the king of the seaside postcard, especially between the 1920s (stylistically his best period) and the 1950s, for his once unique and later much imitated style and his extremely saucy jokes, which led on one occasion (in 1954) to a prosecution and a fine of £50, plus £25 costs. His subjects ranged through males (fat man in tight swimming costume: 'I can't see my little Willie!'), fat women (fat male nudist to fat female nudist: 'I haven't seen such sights since I was weaned!'), soldiers (girl to tommy: 'How long's your furlough?'), babies (vicar: 'What's the little boy's name?' 'It's not a boy and let go of my finger!'), spinsters (old maid to burglar: 'If you're not out of my bedroom in 24 hours I'll phone the police!'), virgins (to doctor: 'Since I slipped on my tightrope I've developed a split personality!'), and even prostitutes ('How's business, dearie?' 'Just up and down!'). In time McGill's most popular card proved to be the praying girl: 'Excuse me Lord while I kick Fido!' It sold six million copies; McGill received 6s.

It was in 1941 that the first critical attention was paid to McGill's postcard work. In Horizon George Orwell described McGill's jokes as 'the Sancho Panza view of life' (Orwell, 160) and noted that 'McGill is a clever draughtsman with a real caricaturist's touch in the drawing of faces, but the special value of his postcards is that they are so completely typical. They represent … the norm of the comic postcard' (ibid., 154). Indeed, decades after his death they were still reprinted, copied by lesser cartoonists, and collected by the thousand, while his saucy sense of humour was inherited by the makers of the Carry on films. His work was exhibited at the Brighton Festival in 1967, at the Langton Gallery, London, and at Littlehampton Museum, Sussex.

Sadly, despite his fame and popularity, McGill made very little from his huge body of work. Ascher left an estate of £40,000; McGill, only £735—saved from his regular pay of £8 per postcard and £20 a year director's fee—when he died from a gastric ulcer and diverticulitis of the colon at St James's Hospital, Balham, on 13 October 1962. His fame was recognized by the placing of a blue plaque on his home, 36 Christchurch Road, Streatham Hill, London. Examples of his work are in the Victoria and Albert Museum, London.   DENIS GIFFORD

Sources G. Orwell, 'The art of Donald McGill', Horizon, 4 (Feb 1941), 153–63 • A. Calder-Marshall, Wish you were here (1966) • F. Anderson, The comic postcard in English life (1970) • B. Green, I've lost my little Willie (1976) • A. Wykes, Saucy seaside postcards (1977) • G. Howell, Penguin book of naughty postcards (1977) • D. McGill, Stop tickling me! • b. cert. • d. cert. • E. Buckland, The world of Donald McGill (1984)
Wealth at death £735 6s.: probate, 13 Dec 1962, CGPLA Eng. & Wales

MacGill, Hamilton Montgomerie (1807–1880), minister of the United Presbyterian church, was born in Catrine, Ayrshire, and educated at Mauchline, at Glasgow University from 1827, and at the Divinity Hall of the United Secession church in Glasgow from 1831. He was licensed by the presbytery of Kilmarnock in March 1836 and ordained minister of Duke Street Church, Glasgow, in February 1837, as colleague to the aged Dr Muter. In 1840 a section of the congregation, unhappy with the operation of the collegiate arrangement, separated to form the Montrose Street Church, to which MacGill was then called. He married, in 1842, Cecilia Heugh, daughter of Dr Hugh *Heugh, a fellow Secession minister whose Life (1850) MacGill was later to write.

In 1858 MacGill left his charge to become home mission secretary of the United Presbyterian church. He had previously edited the Juvenile Missionary Magazine and now became editor of the Missionary Record. In 1868 he resigned the home secretaryship for what was thought, not in the event correctly, to be the less taxing office of foreign mission secretary. Glasgow University honoured him with the degree of DD in 1870. In 1876 he published Songs of the Christian Creed and Life, a selection of Latin and Greek hymns translated into English verse.

In appearance MacGill was said to resemble Thomas Carlyle with a 'mild, expressive and finely chiselled face—a face in which softness and spirituality hold a calm contest for the dominion' (Smith, 68). His wife remembered him as having a 'delicate poetical temperament' (MacGill, 26), as sensitive as a scientific instrument. He enjoyed great popularity as a preacher and was highly esteemed as an administrator.

At the synod of 1879 it was evident that his health was failing. His efforts to recuperate included a trip to the south of France the following year, but he got no further than Paris, where he died on 3 June. His body was brought back to Scotland, where he was buried in Glasgow necropolis, next to his father-in-law, on 11 June 1880.

LIONEL ALEXANDER RITCHIE

Sources H. M. MacGill, Memories of the Rev. Dr Hamilton MacGill, ed. [C. H. MacGill] (1880) • United Presbyterian Magazine, new ser., 24 (1880) • J. Smith, Our Scottish clergy, 1st ser. (1848), 67–71 • W. Mackelvie, Annals and statistics of the United Presbyterian church, ed. W. Blair and D. Young (1873) • R. Small, History of the congregations of the United Presbyterian church from 1733 to 1900, 2 (1904), 73 • personal knowledge (1893) [DNB]
Likenesses photograph (in later life), repro. in MacGill, Memories of the Rev. Dr Hamilton MacGill, frontispiece
Wealth at death £1925 19s. 3d.: confirmation, 22 July 1880, CCI

MacGill [Mackgill], **James**, of Nether Rankeillour (d. 1579), lawyer and administrator, was born in Edinburgh, the eldest son of James MacGill, a substantial Edinburgh merchant who was treasurer of the burgh in 1532–3

and 1545–6 and a bailie in 1549–50; and Helen Wardlaw of Torrie, in Fife. His father feued part of the common muir in 1537 and lands at Liberton, to the south of the burgh, in 1538; there is no evidence, however, to support claims that he was knighted and made lord provost of Edinburgh in the reign of James V. The younger James was educated at the University of St Andrews, where he matriculated at the 'Protestant well' of St Leonard's College in 1532. It is likely that after graduating he studied abroad, like many other law students. He was admitted a member of the Faculty of Advocates on 1 March 1550. On 4 March 1554 he was confirmed in possession of the lands of Nether Rankeillour, Fife.

On 25 June 1554, two months after parliament ratified the appointment of Mary of Guise-Lorraine as regent, MacGill became clerk register, succeeding Thomas Marjoribanks, originally a client of Cardinal David Beaton; on 20 August following he was made an ordinary lord of session. His wife, Janet Adamson, daughter of William Adamson of Craigrook and Janet, daughter of Sir Archibald Napier of Merchiston, was one of John Knox's 'dear sisters of Edinburgh'. Knox wrote to her from Lyons, probably in 1557. She came of a prominent Edinburgh family. Her father was on the town council—a bailie and dean of guild a number of times between 1527 and 1545—and her brother William Adamson was entered a burgess in 1542 and became one of the small circle of protestants in the capital in the early 1540s; William married Agnes, younger sister of John Bellenden of Auchnoull, who succeeded his father, Thomas, as justice clerk in 1547. The careers of these two crown servants, MacGill and Bellenden, both drawn from the close-knit Edinburgh establishment, were to shadow each other closely in the 1560s and early 1570s. Between October 1556 and September 1558 MacGill was one of the group of lawyers appointed presidents of the burgh, who could preside over the town council in the absence of the lord provost. He was also one of the trio of well-qualified lawyers appointed to advise the executors of the estate of Robert Reid, bishop of Orkney, who on his death in 1558 left an endowment to found a college in Edinburgh. He was one of the commissioners who negotiated the Anglo-Scottish treaty of Upsettlington (or Ladykirk) in May 1559.

Although it has been alleged that MacGill, like William Maitland of Lethington, threw his lot in with the lords of the congregation late in 1559, there is no evidence to substantiate this. Knox testifies that their friendship began only late in 1560. Yet it is likely that MacGill would by reason of his office have been involved with the organization of the Reformation parliament of August 1560. He first made contact with the English agent Thomas Randolph in the following month. It is clear that MacGill, in common with the other major office-holders of the crown, survived the revolution of 1559–60 and remained in royal service. He was confirmed as clerk register and appointed to the privy council on the return from France of Queen Mary in August 1561. In the controversy among the reformers which followed the queen's return, when the Catholic mass was said in her private chapel in Holyroodhouse, a debate was held in MacGill's house in Edinburgh in November 1561. MacGill was one of the six privy councillors present who unanimously defended the arrangement, in the teeth of opposition from Knox and other leading ministers. That meeting was recalled by MacGill in the better-known debate between Knox and Lethington in the general assembly of June 1564.

MacGill's prominence in this period is confirmed by his service on a commission, including Lethington and the earls of Moray and Morton, which devised the compromise settlement for ministers of the new church known as the thirds of benefices and approved by the privy council on 22 December 1561 though denounced by Knox. MacGill was also a member of the subsequent commission set up on 24 January 1562 which scrutinized the rentals of benefices and determined stipends of individual ministers. In August 1562 he accompanied the queen, Moray, and the bulk of the privy council on their progress to the north, which ended with the defeat and death of George Gordon, fourth earl of Huntly at Corrichie. In December 1563 MacGill again tried to act as a go-between, arranging a meeting between Knox, Moray, and Lethington at his house. By the time of the meeting of the general assembly in June 1564, however, he was firmly classed by Knox as belonging to the 'courtiers' (*History of the Reformation*, 2.102).

MacGill was not involved in Moray's rebellion in the autumn of 1565 but fled the capital on 18 March 1566, along with Bellenden and Alexander Guthrie, town clerk of Edinburgh, nine days after the murder of the queen's servant David Riccio. He was declared a rebel and deprived of his office, which was given to James Balfour of Pittendreich. His rehabilitation as early as June 1566 suggests that he may have been only marginally involved in the Riccio affair. He was nevertheless singled out by the bishop of Mondovi as 'a man of no family and contriver of all evil' who needed to be eliminated (Pollen, 278). By 1567 he was back in the queen's service, and he sat on the assize which exonerated Bothwell from involvement in the murder of Darnley. By June 1567 he had joined the confederate lords who confronted the queen and Bothwell in the field at Carberry, and after Mary was deposed he became part of the hard core of confederates who emerged as the king's party. He and Sir James Melville were chosen to represent this faction in offering the regency to Moray when he reached Berwick early in August.

In December 1567 MacGill was restored as clerk register by the new regent. His shifting allegiances in this period provoked an angry reaction in the Marian proclamation issued after the queen's escape from Lochleven in May 1568: he and Henry Balnaves of Halhill were condemned as 'oppin traitouris' and 'airis [heirs] to Judas' (Pollen, 273). Both were to be part of the formidable galaxy of intellectual and legal talent, which also included Lethington and George Buchanan, assembled by Moray to argue the case against Mary in her first trial at York in September 1568. After the York conference MacGill and Lethington were chosen for a special audience with Elizabeth; some later sources, including Calderwood, saw MacGill as the secretary's minder rather than his colleague. The divisions opening up both within Moray's administration and among the king's men as a whole over the treatment of the queen came to a head in a convention, held at Perth in July 1569, over the issue of whether to press for her divorce, an eventuality which might have made her restoration a possibility. Within the administration Bellenden and MacGill were resolutely opposed to this proposal, whereas Lethington and Sir William Murray of Tullibardine, the comptroller, favoured it. The debate was heated and acrimonious. MacGill was later one of the king's men singled out for ridicule in a series of propaganda pieces written by John and Thomas Maitland, the secretary's brothers. The assassination of Moray six months later confirmed these splits. Within a week of the murder MacGill and Morton represented the king's lords at a meeting with English commissioners in Edinburgh, at which they promised the continuance of the 'amity' in return for English military aid and support for Lennox's selection as regent. In March 1571 MacGill accompanied Morton on a mission to England, to ensure the continuing custody of Queen Mary.

Against this background of difficulties for the king's party MacGill had been appointed lord provost of Edinburgh in October 1570, at the head of a council of king's men. That body was dismissed and exiled from the burgh in June 1571, but it set up a rival administration in the nearby port of Leith. MacGill seems to have been singled out for rough treatment by the Marians in the town. Many of his goods and valuables, which he was attempting to move to safety at Pinkie, were intercepted by a Marian force from the castle in May 1571. He and his son David, also a lawyer and Edinburgh burgess, were forfeited by a Marian parliament in June 1571, and two of his houses as well as that of his son in the town were demolished by the notorious Captain of the Chimneys in 1572.

Throughout this period, in which the Leith exiles became the most militant element among the king's men, MacGill remained provost. He supervised a campaign of ruthless retribution, inflicted on more than 450 Marian sympathizers in Edinburgh through both the kirk session and the law courts after the exiles returned to the capital in July 1572 and displaced the Marian town council. He continued as a regular attender of meetings of the privy council throughout the period of Morton's regency (1572–8). After the temporary fall of Morton in March 1578, MacGill was confirmed as clerk register and charged, along with George Buchanan, with managing affairs until the next meeting of parliament. Ever the survivor, he continued on the privy council after Morton's rehabilitation. He died in Edinburgh on 16 October 1579.

With his wife, Janet Adamson, MacGill had five sons and two daughters. The eldest son was James MacGill of Rankeillour, from whom descended the MacGills, viscounts of Oxfurd. The elder James MacGill's brother was **David MacGill of Cranstoun Riddel** (d. 1595), also a graduate and prominent lawyer. He was made a burgess and guild of Edinburgh *gratis* by right of his father on 25 September 1555, became a lord of session, and was made a king's

advocate in 1582. As early as 1565 his tax assessment showed him to be among the wealthiest ten lawyers in the capital. The MacGill brothers both appeared on a protestant subscription list of 1562 for a poor hospital in the capital. But David MacGill was condemned by the radical minister and diarist James Melville for his 'contempt of the ministrie', and when he died in February 1595, after a long illness, both Andrew and James Melville were present, to witness a death-bed repentance for his years 'without all sense of God' (Melville, 135). David MacGill married twice. With his first wife, Elizabeth Forrester of Corstorphine, he had six sons and two daughters. His eldest son, also David MacGill of Cranstoun Riddel, followed his father in making his career in the law. He became a lord of session and was made a privy councillor in 1603, but died young in 1607. Elizabeth died on 16 March 1579, and her husband then married Isobel Cunningham, who survived him.

MICHAEL LYNCH

Sources M. Lynch, *Edinburgh and the Reformation* (1981) · M. Wood and T. B. Whitson, *The lord provosts of Edinburgh, 1296 to 1932* (1932) · G. Donaldson, *All the queen's men: power and politics in Mary Stewart's Scotland* (1983) · M. Lee, *James Stewart, earl of Moray* (New York, 1953) · T. van Heijnsbergen, 'The interaction between literature and history in Queen Mary's Edinburgh: the Bannatyne manuscript and its prosopographical context', *The Renaissance in Scotland: studies in literature, religion, history, and culture offered to John Durkan*, ed. A. A. MacDonald and others (1994), 183–225 · P. F. Tytler, *History of Scotland*, 3 (1829) · *Scots peerage*, 6.587–94 · J. D. Marwick, ed., *Extracts from the records of the burgh of Edinburgh, AD 1528–1589*, [2–4], Scottish Burgh RS, 3–5 (1871–82) · *Reg. PCS*, vol. 1 · *John Knox's History of the Reformation in Scotland*, ed. W. C. Dickinson, 2 vols. (1949) · T. Thomson, ed., *A diurnal of remarkable occurrents that have passed within the country of Scotland*, Bannatyne Club, 43 (1833) · R. Bannatyne, *Memoriales of transactions in Scotland, 1569–1573*, ed. [R. Pitcairn], Bannatyne Club, 51 (1836) · D. Calderwood, *The history of the Kirk of Scotland*, ed. T. Thomson and D. Laing, 8 vols., Wodrow Society, 7 (1842–9) · *Memoirs of his own life by Sir James Melville of Halhill*, ed. T. Thomson, Bannatyne Club, 18 (1827) · J. H. Pollen, ed., *Papal negotiations with Mary queen of Scots during her reign in Scotland, 1561–1567*, Scottish History Society, 37 (1901) · *CSP Scot.*, 1547–81 · G. W. T. Omond, *The lord advocates of Scotland, second series, 1834–1880* (1914) · MS register of Edinburgh testaments, NA Scot.

MacGill, James, of Cranstoun Riddel, **first viscount of Oxfurd** (d. 1663), judge and politician, was the second son of David MacGill of Cranstoun Riddel (d. 1607), king's advocate, and his wife, Marie (d. 1606), eldest daughter of Sir William Sinclair of Herdmanstoun, and his wife, Sibil. On 10 July 1619 he was served heir to his elder brother, David. By contract dated 20 December 1621 he married his first wife, Katherine, eldest daughter of John Cockburn of Ormiston. They had three sons and four daughters.

In July 1625 MacGill was named as one of the justices of the peace for Edinburghshire qualified to act as sheriff. On 22 August 1626 he accepted the sheriffship of Edinburgh, and became sheriff-principal in 1628. He was created a baronet on 19 July 1627, and was admitted an ordinary lord of session on 3 November 1629, after which the court chose him to oversee the collection of the tax of 40s. Scots in every pound land of old extent that had been granted them for their use. The heritors of Edinburghshire elected him their commissioner to the convention of the estates in 1630. In 1631 he was appointed to the commission created to survey Scotland's laws with a view to harmonizing them with those of England, and in 1632 was involved in the discussions on Charles I's plans for fishing.

It appears that MacGill was sympathetic to the covenanters, as he was a commissioner of exchequer in 1644 and 1645, on the committee of war for Edinburghshire in 1647 and 1648, and a member of the committee of estates in 1651. On 19 April that year Charles II created him viscount of Oxfurd and Lord MacGill of Cousland, but the English occupation of Scotland prevented his assuming the title. During the occupation he was among those approved by the protector's Scottish council in 1656 as a justice of the peace for Edinburghshire, and was named as a commissioner of the cess for the same county in 1655, 1656, and 1660.

Following the Restoration, Oxfurd was again appointed a judge, although he did not take up his seat, and was named a commissioner of exchequer. In 1661 he sat in parliament as Viscount Oxenford. He died on 5 May 1663, and was buried three days later in Cranston kirk. He was survived by his second wife, Christian (d. 1664), daughter of Sir William Livingston of Kilsyth, whom he had married by contract dated 8 July 1646. Although this marriage had also produced many children—five sons and four daughters—at least five of Oxfurd's sons predeceased him, and he was succeeded as second viscount by Christian's third son, Robert (1651–1705).   DAVID MENARRY

Sources *Scots peerage* · M. D. Young, ed., *The parliaments of Scotland: burgh and shire commissioners*, 2 vols. (1992–3) · *Reg. PCS*, 1st ser. · *Reg. PCS*, 2nd ser. · *Reg. PCS*, 3rd ser. · *APS*, 1625–69 · J. M. Thomson and others, eds., *Registrum magni sigilli regum Scotorum / The register of the great seal of Scotland*, 11 vols. (1882–1914) · G. Donaldson, *Scotland: James V to James VII* (1965), vol. 3 of *The Edinburgh history of Scotland* (1965–75), 218 · C. H. Firth, ed., *Scotland and the protectorate: letters and papers relating to the military government of Scotland from January 1654 to June 1659*, Scottish History Society, 31 (1899), 312 · J. Nicoll, *A diary of public transactions and other occurrences, chiefly in Scotland, from January 1650 to June 1667*, ed. D. Laing, Bannatyne Club, 52 (1836), 75, 325, 336, 355, 358 · *The diary of Mr John Lamont of Newton, 1649–1671*, ed. G. R. Kinloch, Maitland Club, 7 (1830), 203, 240 · GEC, *Peerage*, new edn

McGill, James (1744–1813), fur trader and politician in Canada, was born on 6 October 1744 in Stockwell Street, Glasgow, Lanarkshire, Scotland, the second child and eldest son of James McGill (*bap.* 1717, *d.* 1784) and his wife, Margaret Gibson. His father, grandfather, and great-grandfather James Craig were all ironsmiths and members of the Incorporation of Hammermen, the guild controlling the craft. The father prospered, and young James was not apprenticed to his father's trade but after attending Glasgow grammar school matriculated at Glasgow University in 1756. To stay until graduation would have indicated an intention to enter one of the learned professions, but he opted for something more adventurous and emigrated around 1760, probably for the tobacco plantations of the Carolinas. The first definite news of him in North America comes from 1766, when he served as factor, or agent, in the Canadian fur trade for William Grant, travelling from

James McGill (1744–1813), by Louis Dulongpré, *c.*1800–10

Montreal by canoe to Mackinac, the trading post at the junction of lakes Superior, Michigan, and Huron.

For the next nine years McGill engaged in the arduous life of an itinerant fur trader, often wintering in the frozen wilderness with native bands. He returned permanently to Montreal in 1775, just in time to experience the American occupation of the city, and was one of the signatories to the terms of surrender. But revolutionary fervour, even though expounded by Benjamin Franklin, failed to win Canadian support, and the Americans departed, leaving McGill determined never to suffer that indignity and financial loss again. On 2 December 1776 he married a French-Canadian widow, Marie-Charlotte Desrivières, *née* Guillimin (*d.* 1818), and that same year with the Irishman Isaac Todd established the fur and general merchandising company of Todd, McGill & Co. He continued in trade, less actively in his senior years, until his death, by which time he was reputed to be the richest man in Canada.

McGill was named to the magistracy in 1776, and continued to serve conscientiously when he was elevated to justice of the peace in 1796. In 1792 he was elected to the first legislative assembly of Lower Canada as a member for Montreal West; he declined to stand in 1796 but was re-elected in 1800 and 1804. He was prominent in the assembly's business because he was fluently bilingual. In 1793 he became a member of the governor-general's executive council, and continued very actively until his death. The first Canada Militia Act was proclaimed in 1777; ten years later another fur trader, Alexander Henry, wrote in a letter from Montreal: 'At my return here I found all our friends Militia Mad; James McGill is a Major and Isaac

Todd a Captain' (Alex Henry to William Edgar, 22 Oct 1787, letters and accounts of the North West Company, 1763–1803, 81). McGill worked assiduously to prepare the local forces for any second American invasion. When the Anglo-American War began his rank was that of colonel commanding the Montreal garrison. As chairman of the Montreal committee of the executive council, he was also head of civil government in the city. In that capacity he quelled a local rebellion opposing mobilization. His military rank was raised to acting brigadier-general, and it was the forces he and his friends had readied that on 26 October 1813 defeated the American army attacking from the south.

McGill died at his home on rue Notre Dame, Montreal, on 19 December 1813, a month after receiving the order to demobilize his troops; he was buried at Montreal protestant cemetery on 21 December. His will assigned the bulk of his fortune to his wife and her sons, but he bequeathed his farm, Burnside, and £10,000 for the founding of McGill College in Montreal 'for the purposes of education and the advancement of learning in this Province'. The college received a royal charter naming it a university on 31 March 1821. STANLEY BRICE FROST

Sources S. B. Frost, *James McGill of Montreal* (1995) · S. B. Frost, *McGill University for the advancement of learning*, 1 (1980) · J. Cooper, 'McGill, James', *DCB*, vol. 5 · M. S. MacSporran, 'James McGill: a critical biography', thesis, McGill University, 1930 · M. M. Quaife, *The John Askin papers*, 2 vols. (1928–31) · H. A. Innis, *The fur trade in Canada: an introduction to Canadian economic history*, rev. edn (1956) · G. F. G. Stanley, *Canada invaded, 1775–1776* (Toronto, 1973) · G. F. G. Stanley, *The war of 1812* (1983) · J. M. McGill, 'McGill family history', *c.*1960, McGill University, Montreal · letters and accounts of the North West Company, 1763–1803, Metropolitan Toronto Reference Library, Ontario · parish register (baptism), Glasgow · *Montreal Gazette* (21 Dec 1813) · will, PRO, PROB 11/1559, sig. 486

Archives McGill University, Montreal, archives, private papers | NA Canada · NA Canada, legal, parliamentary, military, and fur trade records

Likenesses L. Dulangpré, oils, *c.*1800–1810, McGill University, Montreal, McCord Museum [*see illus.*] · W. Berczy, miniature, watercolour on ivory, McGill University, Montreal, McCord Museum · two oil paintings (after L. Dulangpré), McGill University, Montreal

Wealth at death approx. £160,000; two main heirs said to have received £60,000 each; also rue Notre Dame property valued at approx. £3000; large estates of land in the Eastern Townships and Upper Canada; McGill College bequest represented some £20,000

MacGill, Patrick (1890–1963), writer, was born on 1 January 1890 at Maas, near Gweebarra Bay, west co. Donegal, the first among at least eleven children of William MacGill, a tenant farmer, and his wife, Bridget, *née* Boyle. After an early education at the Mullanmore national school and some work on his father's land, MacGill was sold as a bonded servant. Of the £5 he earned for six months' work at the age of twelve on a farm near Strabane, Tyrone, £4 15*s.* went to his parents' landlord and to their priest. He worked from 5 a.m. to 11 p.m. in what were typical hours for many such children. On 29 June 1905 he ran away on the promise of 16*s.* per week as a member of a potato digging gang in Scotland. Accompanied from time to time by companions, he tramped across Ayrshire, Clydeside, and

Argyll, helping to build the aluminium factory at Kinlochleven reservoir from 1906. Journalism provided a surplus of income but he later wrote that 'My success as a writer discomfited me a little even. I at first felt I was committing some sin against my mates.'

After leaving Kinlochleven, MacGill worked as a platelayer on the Caledonian railway. By 1911 he had enough poems and wages to publish at his own expense *Gleanings from a Navvy's Scrapbook*, which he sold from door to door in Greenock. He claimed to have sold 8000 copies. The book was saluted by Marxist and socialist reviewers but MacGill's socialism shared little with Irish nationalism and he was later blamed for seeking his destiny away from Dublin's seething pot.

MacGill's decision to accept an offer of work from C. Arthur Pearson, owner of the London *Daily Express*, found him patronage. His work with the paper from September or October 1911 to January 1912 involved interviews and on one occasion George Bernard Shaw demanded of him, 'why did you give up honest employment to take this job?' Either from such a professional meeting, or from a less formal encounter in a Turkish bath, MacGill made friends with the Anglican canon Sir John Neale Dalton, former tutor and resident mentor at Windsor Castle to George V. MacGill was given the title of Dalton's secretary and moved to 4 Cloisters, Windsor. Although no private correspondence survives, Dalton's nature was undoubtedly homosexual, which accounts for his initial interest in the slight but strongly muscular 21-year-old. MacGill's innocence probably saw little harm in some demonstrative affection and horseplay, and the relationship was probably platonic. MacGill's literary labours were strongly encouraged by the canon. The first task was to revise, augment, and refine *Songs of a Navvy*. The extent of their collaboration on *Children of the Dead End* (1914), the first of MacGill's three autobiographical novels, must remain unknown, however. When it was published in March 1914 it sold 10,000 copies in two weeks. It became a best-seller, partly because its content met the prevailing flavour for naturalism, muckraking, socialism, and iconoclasm, partly because it appeared at the high tide of pre-war labour unrest, its narrative supplying human answers to economic questions, and partly because MacGill's publisher Herbert Jenkins was a marketing genius. Reviews varied between ecstasy from the *Manchester Guardian*, *The Standard*, *Saturday Review*, and *Pall Mall Gazette* to sour regrets for the fictionalization from the *TLS* and *The Athenaeum*.

MacGill's next book, *The Rat-pit* (1915), was the woman-centred counterpart to its predecessor's male preoccupations in giving literary life to nomadic labour in Scotland. Showing insight into the female psychology of its characters, *The Rat-pit* asserted his status as a major novelist and the *New Statesman* of 10 April 1915 compared it favourably with the latest work of Virginia Woolf. By this time MacGill was a rifleman in France, having enlisted in the London Irish Rifles at the outbreak of war. He promptly began writing newspaper reports on what he saw, including even the most ironic comments from his fellow recruits.

His on-the-spot articles for the *Daily Mail* were unflinching in their commitment to the allied cause, but they showed little disposition to wallow in 'Germanophobia', and home-front reviewers complained that he did not hate the Hun enough. The articles were collected in his book *The Amateur Army* and were on sale by May 1915. While MacGill did not prettify the experience of soldiers, he conveyed the humanity, resilience, and deflationary wit of his fellow privates and non-commissioned officers. *The Amateur Army* sold 20,000 copies before the war's end and Jenkins printed a fourth edition of another 5000 in December 1918.

MacGill was wounded on 25 September 1915 at the battle of Loos while serving as a stretcher-bearer. He finished his series of articles when in hospital at Versailles two days later, despite his strafed arm. On 27 November 1915 he married Margaret-Catherine Gibbons (1887–1972), a fellow author, daughter of William Gibbons, a carriage designer and builder, and his wife, Hannah L. Grime. The wedding was paid for by Jenkins, who also acted as best man. After his marriage MacGill was seconded to military intelligence, a useful way of keeping him under surveillance. Military authorities held that his report 'Out there', published in *Pearson's Magazine*, was liable to aid the enemy by providing information on British troops; when his next book focusing on combat experience was announced, MacGill was threatened with court martial. His well-connected friends elegantly averted the crisis and his second (and somewhat censored) volume of army observations, *The Red Horizon*, appeared early in 1916. Mac-Gill followed it with his account of Loos up to his wounding, *The Great Push* (1916). *Soldier Songs* (1916) collected his war verse with a valuable preface on songs the soldiers made. MacGill's third fictionalized memoir of pre-war Ireland, *Glenmornan*, was published in 1918 but the Ireland he knew was dying as the work appeared, and post-war disillusion rejected the many Catholics like MacGill who had volunteered in the British army. He tried coming to terms with the challenge of Sinn Féin to post-war Ireland in *Maureen* (1919), but it was too uncomfortable a book for revolutionary Ireland. His account of the Australians in France, *The Diggers*, was published in 1919. While his 1921 novel *Fear!* sought to face personal problems war censorship would not permit to be aired, MacGill had waited too long to come clean: the *TLS* (12 May 1921) reflected the now widespread boredom with the war. His comic masterpiece of the Irish picaresque, *Lanty Hanlon* (1922), and revival of nomadic labour life, *Moleskin Joe* (1923), had some popular and literary success, but foretold the end of MacGill's quintessential appeal in Britain. With the death of his greatest supporter Jenkins, MacGill's future works, including *The Carpenter of Orra* (1924), *Sid Puddlefoot* (1926), and *Black Bonar* (1928), had to take their chances in a dwindling market. Although MacGill's First World War three-act play, *Suspense* (1930), was praised by the critics for its realism, the West End was not interested in soldiers, and the play ran only for two months at the Duke of York's Theatre. In New York it was performed for only one week in 1931.

Having lived for a time in Switzerland and in Kent, the MacGills stayed in the United States after a lecture tour foundered in the American depression. The sales of Mac-Gill's books, including *Tulliver's Mill* (1934), *The Glen of Carra* (1934), *The Well of the World's End* (1935), and *Helen Spenser* (1937), were disappointing. By the end of the 1930s multiple sclerosis had made MacGill an invalid. He and Margaret settled in Miami, Florida, where she sought to set up an acting school, but the Second World War killed off the venture in 1941. In an unpublished memorial essay one of MacGill's three daughters, Chris, recorded that he continued to write, but the rejection of his work was concealed from him and his wife presented her own financial returns as those for his writing. Their survival in later years was made possible only by the piecemeal selling of his library. In the end he was living utterly forgotten in Fall River, Massachusetts. Patrick MacGill died in Miami, Florida on 23 November 1963 and was buried at Notre Dame cemetery, Fall River, Massachusetts. On 25 April 1972 he was re-interred in St Patrick's cemetery. His verse was largely but not entirely collected in *The Navvy Poet* (1984): it repays reading aloud.

MacGill's victimization in Ireland because of his war service and his subsequent isolation from post-war Irish nationalism injured him in Irish letters and in due course in English markets. He summed up the sources of creativity and his credentials as he wished them to be remembered in his *Who's Who* entry under 'Recreation': 'telling stories to his wife; watching spiders; mowing Irish meadows'. A Patrick MacGill summer school has met annually in Glenties since the centenary of his birth.

OWEN DUDLEY EDWARDS

Sources O. D. Edwards, 'Patrick MacGill and the making of a historical source: with a handlist of his works', *Innes Review*, 37 (autumn 1986), 73–99 · P. O'Sullivan, 'Patrick MacGill: the making of a writer', *Ireland's histories*, ed. S. Hutton and P. Stewart (1981), 203–22 · T. G. Brand, 'A critique of the novels of Patrick MacGill', MA diss., University of Ulster, 1995 · *Irish Book Lover*, 3–12 (1911–20) · B. Aspinwall, 'Patrick MacGill, 1890–1963: an alternative vision', *The church and the arts*, ed. D. Wood, SCH, 28 (1992), 499–513 · B. Aspinwall, 'Half-slave, half-free: Patrick Macgill and the Catholic church', *New Blackfriars*, 65 (1984), 359–71 · B. Kiely, *Modern Irish fiction* (1950) · R. Greacen, '"Taking the Derry boat": Patrick Mac-Gill, novelist', *Eire-Ireland: — a Journal of Irish Studies*, 16 (spring 1981) · WW (1936) · WW (1946) · WW (1951) · J. E. Handley, *The navvy in Scotland* (1970) · private information (2004)

Archives Worcester College, Oxford, letters to J. N. Dalton

Likenesses Sasha, two photographs, 1930, Hult. Arch.

Macgill, Stevenson (1765–1840), university professor, was born at Port Glasgow on 19 January 1765, son of Thomas Macgill (*d.* 1804), a shipbuilder and devout Wesleyan Methodist. His mother, Frances Welsh (*d.* 1829), was equally godly, as befitted someone with a supposed family connection to John Knox. He was educated at the parish school before going on to Glasgow University at the age of ten. Licensed to preach by the presbytery of Paisley in 1790, he was presented to the parish of Eastwood, Renfrewshire, in September 1791. Before this he had received the offer of the chair of civil history in St Andrews, a position tenable with a small country living, but his opposition to ecclesiastical pluralities led him to refuse. He

Stevenson Macgill (1765–1840), attrib. Sir Henry Raeburn

remained at Eastwood until his translation to the Tron Church, Glasgow, in October 1797. He received a DD from Aberdeen in 1803.

In Glasgow, Macgill had extensive scope for his numerous social concerns which included prisons, lunatic asylums, and education, as well as the material welfare of his parishioners. He also promoted an association which met monthly for the purpose of literary and theological discussion. It was in this forum that he read a number of essays, later published as *Considerations Addressed to a Young Clergyman* (1809), which appeared in its enlarged second edition as *Letters to a Young Clergyman* (1820). The work advanced Macgill's claim to consideration when the divinity chair fell vacant with the death of the aged Robert Findlay in 1814. He also enjoyed powerful support from evangelicals, such as Sir Henry Wellwood Moncreiff and Andrew Thomson.

Once elected to the chair Macgill reorganized the teaching of theology. He is not remembered for any intellectual brilliance, being described by one writer as 'neither a man of high genius nor commanding eloquence' (Chambers, Scots., 5.412), rather he was an effective trainer of ministers. He was also a principled and combative foe, as he proved in his opposition to the simultaneous appointment of Duncan Macfarlan as principal of the university and minister of the High Church, Glasgow, in 1824. Macgill's struggle was of no avail on this specific occasion, but the extensive discussion of the issue effectively prevented the continuation of the practice of pluralities in the Church of Scotland.

About the same time Macgill was instrumental in the erection of a monument to John Knox in the Glasgow necropolis, its having recently been discovered that Knox had been a student at Glasgow. In 1828 he was made moderator of the general assembly, somewhat belatedly it was felt. In 1834 he was appointed chaplain-in-ordinary to William IV, and in 1835 dean of the Chapel Royal. He died at the Old College, Glasgow, on 18 August 1840, never having married, and having lived nearly all his life with his mother. He was buried in that part of the burying-ground of Blackfriars Church belonging to the university, and appropriated to professors of divinity. To the end Macgill was a man of many enthusiasms, chief among which were the work of the Society in Scotland for Propagating Christian Knowledge and the cause of missions to India and to the Jews. His biographer is perhaps justified in describing him as 'an enemy to all corruption and the staunch friend of all reform' (Burns, 323).

LIONEL ALEXANDER RITCHIE

Sources *Fasti Scot.*, 3.136, 475; 7.401–2 · R. Burns, *Memoir of the Rev. Stevenson Macgill* (1842) · S. Macgill, *Discourses … with a biographical memoir* (1844) · H. M. B. Reid, *The divinity professors in the University of Glasgow, 1640–1903* (1923), 285–309 · Chambers, *Scots.* (1835)
Archives U. Edin., New Coll. L., lectures | NRA, priv. coll., letters to Moncreiff family · U. Edin., New Coll. L., letters to Thomas Chalmers
Likenesses attrib. H. Raeburn, portrait; Christies, 2 June 1950, lot 123 [*see illus.*] · portrait (in later life), repro. in Burns, *Memoir of Stevenson Macgill*, frontispiece · portrait, repro. in S. Macgill, *Sermons* (1839)

M'Gill, William (1732–1807), Church of Scotland minister and author, was born on 11 July 1732 at Carsenestock, Penninghame, Wigtownshire, the fifth son of William M'Gill, a local farmer, and his wife, Jean Heron. He was educated at the parish schools of Minnigaff and Penninghame, and at the University of Glasgow, where he graduated MA in 1753. Licensed by the presbytery of Wigtown in October 1759 he was appointed as assistant to the minister of Kilwinning, Ayrshire, on 12 June 1760. He was ordained minister of Ayr (second charge) on 22 October 1761. On 7 November 1763 he married Elizabeth Dunlop (*d.* 1785), niece of William *Dalrymple, minister of the first charge of Ayr, with whom he had eight children. A man of erect and commanding stature, M'Gill was highly and warmly regarded by his congregation. His friends included the poet Robert Burns who praised him in his correspondence as 'my learned and truly worthy friend' and 'one of the worthiest, as well as one of the ablest, in the whole priesthood of the Kirk of Scotland' (November 1787 and December 1788, in *Letters*, 1.175, 454).

Whatever his talents as a minister it is his contribution to religious controversy for which M'Gill is now best remembered. He was an adherent of the moderate party of the Church of Scotland which supported the law of patronage in the appointment of ministers to parish charges and which tended to include theologically more liberal ministers of the kirk. Along with his colleague William Dalrymple, M'Gill was regarded as having advocated before 1780 the abolition of subscription to the Westminster confession of faith (1649) for office-bearers in the Church of Scotland. A year after receiving a DD degree from the University of Glasgow in 1785 he published *A Practical Essay on the Death of Jesus Christ*, in which he intended to restate the doctrines of the purpose of God and the person and work of Christ. M'Gill's principal motive for the book appears to have been financial. He was then in debt and poor health and sought to make provision for his large family following the death of his wife on 9 June 1785.

However, M'Gill's study, which appears to have been influenced by Joseph Priestley's *Theological Repository* (1770–71), quickly became a subject of enquiry for a much wider circle. Of particular interest was his controversial view that Christ had been afflicted by weakness at the prospect of his approaching death when he prayed in the Garden of Gethsemane, an interpretation widely regarded as implying a denial of Christ's divinity. Among his friends there was initially some unease at the content of his *Essay*. However, the relative absence of discussion soon after publication reassured associates like James Wodrow, minister of Stevenston, Ayrshire, who wrote in January 1787 that, on reflection, the book 'is as inoffensive as you can imagine' (DWL, Wodrow–Kenrick Corr., MS 24157, fol. 126, quoted in Fitzpatrick, 'Varieties', 41). M'Gill also found support from his uncle, a former moderator of the general assembly, who published his own *History of Christ*, also in 1787. Among his early critics the most significant was James Russel, whose *Reasons of Our Lord's agony in the garden, and the influence of just views of them on universal holiness* (1787) accused M'Gill of Socianism.

Even so, no action was taken against M'Gill until after his publication of a centenary sermon defending the benefits of the revolution of 1688. This followed a scathing attack by a local orthodox minister, the Revd William Peebles of Newton-on-Ayr, to whom M'Gill responded in an appendix to his sermon. Wodrow described the retort as a 'mixture of mildness and keenness which cuts like a razor ... I had no conception that the Dr had such talents for controversy' (8 March 1789, DWL, MS 21157, fol. 241, quoted in Fitzpatrick, 'Varieties', 42). M'Gill's open defence of his position was deemed unacceptable and a complaint was presented to the synod of Glasgow and Ayr accusing him of heterodox doctrine. The synod required the presbytery of Ayr to take up the matter and they in turn presented a fifty-page document which claimed that M'Gill's book contained passages 'contrary to the word of God and the confession of faith'. The general assembly of 1789 reversed the synod's decision, but instructed the presbytery to take steps to preserve the purity of doctrine of the church and the authority of its doctrinal standards. For several months the case went back and forth between the presbytery and the synod until a settlement was reached at a meeting on 14 April 1790. Here M'Gill offered an explanation and an apology for that which 'may appear improper' which the majority of the synod accepted, though Calvinist opponents of moderatism made several subsequent attempts to reignite the issue. During the controversy Robert Burns referred regularly to its impact on his friend and satirized the hard-line position of M'Gill's critics in his 'The Kirk of Scotland's Garland, or, The Kirk's Alarm' (1789):

> Doctor Mac, Doctor Mac,
> Ye should stretch on a rack,
> To strike evil-doers wi' terror;
> To join faith and sense,
> Upon any pretence,
> Is heretic damnable error.
> (Henderson, 94)

While M'Gill's position was almost certainly in breach of the Church of Scotland's doctrinal position his stress on the humanity and example of Christ—rather than on his divinity and atonement—was not consistent with the requirement of the Westminster confession. The synod's investigation was therefore conducted almost entirely on procedural grounds, demonstrating that, while willing to condemn errors of doctrine, no party within the Church of Scotland had a majority prepared to prosecute repentant perpetrators. Though exposing the limits of moderation and the vigour of Calvinist orthodoxy, notably among members of the original Secession church, the resolution of M'Gill's case suggested to James Wodrow the triumph of 'sensible men' in both parties (2 June 1790, DWL, MS 21157, fol. 154, quoted in Fitzpatrick, 'Varieties', 48). M'Gill remained at Ayr, where he died from asthma on 30 March 1807.   JOHN R. MCINTOSH

Sources DNB · *Fasti Scot.*, new edn, vol. 3 · A. McNair, *Scots theology in the eighteenth century* (1928) · J. R. McIntosh, *Church and theology in Enlightenment Scotland: the popular party, 1740–1800* (1998) · *Scots Magazine*, 51 (1789) · M. Fitzpatrick, 'Varieties of candour: English and Scottish style', *Enlightenment and Dissent*, 7 (1988), 35–56 · H. F. Henderson, *The religious controversies of Scotland* (1905) · M. Fitzpatrick, 'The Enlightenment, politics and providence: some Scottish and English comparisons', *Enlightenment and religion: rational dissent in eighteenth-century Britain*, ed. K. Haakonssen (1996), 64–98 · *The letters of Robert Burns*, ed. J. de Lancey Ferguson, 2nd edn, ed. G. Ross Roy, 2 vols. (1985)

Mac-Gilleain, Iain. *See* Maclean, John (*c*.1680–1756).

MacGill-Eain, Somhairle. *See* MacLean, Sorley (1911–1996).

McGillivray, Alexander (1750–1793), American Indian leader, was born on 15 December 1750 at Little Tallassee, a Creek Indian village on the Coosa River in Upper Creek country. He was one of the three children of **Lachlan McGillivray** (1719–1799), prominent Scottish trader and planter, and his consort, Sehoy Marchand, the daughter of a French officer and a Creek woman of the Wind clan. Various dates have been alleged for Alexander's birth; the matter is settled by a statement in the will of Lachlan McGillivray that Alexander was born on 15 December 1750.

Lachlan was a member of the clan Chattan (clan of the Cat), born at Dunmaglass in Strathnairn, Inverness-shire, Scotland. His father was William McGillivray, a drover, and his mother was Janet McIntosh. At the age of sixteen he accompanied over a hundred members of his clan to Darien, Georgia, at the invitation of Georgia's founder, James Edward Oglethorpe. A number of Scots were killed or captured in Oglethorpe's 1740 invasion of Florida, nearly depopulating Darien. Lachlan went to Charles Town, South Carolina, where a kinsman operated an American Indian trading company. In 1744 Lachlan secured a licence to trade in several villages in the Upper Creek country near the junction of the Coosa and Tallapoosa rivers. He made his residence at the village of Little Tallassee and took as his spouse Sehoy Marchand. He regarded her as his lawful wife and never married another. They had three children, Sophia, Alexander, and Jeannet (Janet). For the first six years of his life Alexander lived at Little Tallassee. During this time Lachlan McGillivray acted as intermediary between the Creek leaders and the governors of South Carolina and Georgia. The proximity of Little Tallassee to the French Fort Toulouse enabled McGillivray to keep the British governors informed of French activities.

In 1757 Lachlan McGillivray moved from Little Tallassee to Augusta; most likely his family went with him. Some time after that Lachlan took Alexander to Charles Town to reside with Lachlan's brother and to receive an education. Alexander studied at Charles Town's free school under the tutelage of George Sheed and William Henderson. By 1767, if not before, Alexander returned to his father's new residence, the rice plantation called Vale Royal outside Savannah. Sixteen-year-old Alexander signed several legal documents as witness. He secured employment in Savannah as a clerk in the mercantile house of Samuel Elbert, and later with the firm of Alexander Inglis & Co.

Although Lachlan McGillivray protested against British efforts to raise revenue in America he could not bring himself to break with the mother country. He perceived that British policy protected American Indian trade and territory whereas revolutionary Georgians coveted American Indian land. When Lachlan and other prominent loyalists were forced to leave Georgia in 1776, Alexander returned to the Creek country. The British superintendent for Indian affairs in the southern district, John Stuart, managing Indian affairs from Pensacola, realized that Alexander's intelligence as well as his membership in the Wind clan made him a valuable auxiliary in the British war effort against the rebelling colonists. Stuart appointed him deputy to veteran commissioner David Taitt. Most of the Upper Creek towns took up arms on behalf of the British. Early in 1779 Stuart ordered Taitt and McGillivray to lead a body of American Indians to Augusta to join forces with Lieutenant-Colonel Archibald Campbell's British regulars. The troops retreated from Augusta before the Creeks arrived and most of the Indians turned back, but some, led by Taitt and McGillivray, fought their way through to British-held Savannah where Alexander and his father were reunited. Alexander and his band helped defend Savannah during the unsuccessful Franco-American siege of that town in September and October 1779.

Lieutenant-Colonel Thomas Brown of the King's rangers, who succeeded John Stuart as superintendent of the Creek and Cherokee nations, retained Alexander as deputy commissioner and instructed him to lead Upper Creek warriors to defend Pensacola against a Spanish attack. McGillivray did so, but the inept British commander surrendered to the enemy in May 1781. In 1783 the Creek national council recognized McGillivray as 'Head Warrior of all the Nation'. When his British allies withdrew at the conclusion of the American War of Independence, McGillivray concluded an agreement with the Spanish government in Florida by which the Creek nation would be supplied by the Florida-based firm of Panton, Leslie & Co. From 1783 until 1790 McGillivray's warriors resisted Georgia's efforts to cross the Ogeechee River; and McGillivray disregarded treaties signed by lesser chieftains with Georgia and United States authorities. Georgia's inability to influence McGillivray explains that state's eagerness to endorse the federal constitution of 1787, which would result in support for Georgia's expansion by other states.

Finally in 1790 McGillivray accepted the invitation of President George Washington, and with a delegation of Creek headmen travelled to New York to sign a treaty with the new federal government by which he ceded the territory between the Ogeechee and Oconee rivers, far less than the Georgians wanted. Having secured treaties with both the Spanish and American governments, McGillivray looked forward to a period of peace. He constructed a new house on the site of his father's residence at Little Tallassee. He sent his son Aleck to be educated under the watchful care of Lachlan in Scotland. He is believed to have been married three times, to daughters of Jacob Moniac, Joseph Cornell, and a trader named Macrae. Alexander wrote a history of his people and sent the manuscript to the noted philosopher and historian William Robertson. Robertson died before publishing the history and the manuscript was lost. While visiting William Panton in Pensacola, Alexander contracted pneumonia and died on 17 February 1793 after a brief illness. He was buried in Little Tallassee. Panton informed the Spanish authorities that McGillivray had no papers of importance with him when he died, only a letter from his father in Scotland. Lachlan McGillivray died at Dunmaglass, the McGillivray ancestral house, on 16 November 1799, and three years later, young Aleck, for whom the Creek people had such hopes, died of pneumonia, also at Dunmaglass. After Alexander McGillivray's death, no other leader emerged who exercised the same control over the Creek nation. EDWARD J. CASHIN

Sources E. J. Cashin, *Lachlan McGillivray, Indian trader and the shaping of the southern colonial frontier* (Athens, Georgia, 1992) · E. J. Cashin, *The king's ranger: Thomas Brown and the American Revolution on the southern frontier* (1989); reprint (New York, 1999) · J. Walton Caughey, *McGillivray of the Creeks* (Norman, Oklahoma, 1938) · W. S. Coker and T. D. Walton, *Indian traders of the Southeastern Spanish borderlands: Panton, Leslie and Company and John Forbes and Company, 1783–1847* (Pensacola, Florida, 1986) · D. H. Corkran, *The Creek frontier, 1540–1783* (Norman, Oklahoma, 1967) · K. H. Braund, *Deerskins and duffels: the Creek Indian trade with Anglo-America, 1685–1815* (Lincoln, Nebraska, 1993)
Likenesses cameo, Creek Museum, Ocmulgee, Oklahoma
Wealth at death owned several plantations and indeterminate number of slaves; according to Creek custom, women relatives

claimed his possessions: *GM* (August 1793); Marie Taylor Greenslade, 'William Panton, c.1745–1801', *Florida Historical Quarterly*, 14 (1935), 107–29

Macgillivray, Charles Robert (1805/6–1867), physician and Gaelic scholar, the son of Neil Macgillivray, a crofter, and his wife, Christina, *née* McEachran, was born in Kilfinichen, Mull. He received his elementary education at the school of his native parish, and when about twenty went to Glasgow, where he found employment in a druggist's shop. He married Margaret Cameron. In 1849 he commenced business as a druggist, and in 1853 graduated MD. In 1859 he was appointed lecturer in Gaelic at the Glasgow Institution. He died on 31 May 1867 at 109 Glebe Street, Glasgow. His wife survived him.

Macgillivray was an enthusiastic Gaelic scholar, and assisted Norman Macleod the elder with his publications. In 1858 he published a Gaelic grammar, but his best-known work is a translation of Bunyan's *Pilgrim's Progress* (1869), in which he was helped by Archibald Macfadyen the hymn writer. He also translated parts of Howie's *Scotch Biography* into Gaelic, published in London in 1870–73.

J. R. MACDONALD, rev. H. C. G. MATTHEW

Sources *GM*, 4th ser., 3 (1867), 253 · private information (1893) · d. cert.

MacGillivray, Sir Donald Charles (1906–1966), colonial administrator, was born in Edinburgh on 22 September 1906, the second son of Evan James MacGillivray KC, of Wimbledon and of Ringwood, Hampshire, a Scot who lived and practised at the bar in England, and his wife, Maude, eldest daughter of Charles J. Turcan, merchant, of Leith. He was educated at Sherborne School from 1920 to 1925 and at Trinity College, Oxford, from 1925 to 1929, where he obtained third-class honours in philosophy, politics, and economics in 1928. At school and at Oxford he was well liked by his contemporaries but showed little sign of his innate talents. He entered the colonial administrative service in 1928 and underwent the normal year's training at Oxford before going out to Tanganyika in 1929.

In his first year spent in Dar es Salaam, MacGillivray was recognized as a potential 'high-flyer'. However, in accordance with the practice of the service, he was posted from 1930 to 1934 to districts in the Lake Province to obtain a thorough grounding in district administration. Although still junior he had temporary charge of districts more than once and showed interest in native affairs and customs. When he revisited this area in 1956 after an interval of twenty years he was remembered and warmly welcomed by a large assembly of African chiefs. His work was recognized by his appointment as MBE in 1936. In 1936 he married Louisa Mai, daughter of Marvyn Knox-Browne, of Aughentaire Castle, co. Tyrone; they had one son. From 1935 to 1938 he returned to Dar es Salaam to serve as private secretary to the governor, Sir Harold A. MacMichael, whom he followed to Palestine in 1938.

In Palestine, MacGillivray returned for a time to district work first in Galilee from 1942 to 1944 and then as district commissioner in Samaria. He next became under-

Sir Donald Charles MacGillivray (1906–1966), by unknown photographer, 1957 [leaving Kuala Lumpur after independence]

secretary to the Palestine government which made use of his ability as a diplomatist by posting him to duty as liaison officer first with the Anglo-American committee and then with the United Nations Special Committee on Palestine. He served as colonial secretary in Jamaica from 1947 to 1952 showing great tact and political skill in his dealings with local political leaders.

Instead of the governorship which would normally have followed his time in Jamaica, where he had on occasion acted as governor, MacGillivray was next selected for service in Malaya as deputy high commissioner to General Sir Gerald Templer. The two men arrived together on 6 February 1952. They had never met before being posted to Malaya and they presented a total contrast in temperament and professional background. It was, however, a very successful partnership. Templer was concerned mainly with the co-ordination and direction of civil and military resources in the campaign against communist insurgents in Malaya. While Templer was out and about on his cyclonic tours of the Malay states MacGillivray took over the direction and control of the complex federal government system of Malaya.

On taking office as colonial secretary in late 1951 Oliver Lyttelton had visited Malaya and reported adversely to the cabinet on a 'desk-bound central authority, clogged with paper and remote' (Stockwell, 2.324). MacGillivray did not find it necessary in 1952 to make major changes, but the appointment of a newcomer as civil deputy to Templer was resented in the higher ranks of the Malayan civil service, and led to the retirement of the chief secretary. His successor, David C. Watherston, served under MacGillivray for the five years from 1952 to independence in 1957. Both were rather reserved and introvert; it was a chilly and correct, but effective, collaboration. Throughout his time MacGillivray lacked anyone of long Malayan experience to whom he could turn for informal advice. It may not have been an utter disadvantage, but it showed in an occasional lack of 'touch', though quickly remedied if it led to a mistake. When Templer left in June 1954 MacGillivray succeeded him as high commissioner but not as military director of operations.

The greater part of Malaya comprised Malay states, with an authoritarian Anglo-Malay diarchy, and the two major communities, Malay and Chinese, were at odds over any advance towards democratic government. MacGillivray had served in Tanganyika when the limitations of 'indirect rule' through traditional authority were becoming apparent, and later in Palestine he had seen how savage inter-communal conflict could be. He found that the Colonial Office had proposed that elected district and town councils should be 'an important part in the political evolution of Malaya' (Stockwell, 3.55), but little progress had been made. Looking back in 1954 on his programme of establishing local elected councils, MacGillivray conceded that 'after an extremely promising start' there was a danger that the manoeuvres of national politicians would reduce them to 'a farce' (ibid.). It can be argued that they were simply alien to the political culture and could never have taken root. His second main initiative was to propose the institution of 'national schools' at which 'children of all races would be instructed in the medium of either Malay or English' (ibid., 3.106). However neither Malay nor Chinese leaders found the scheme acceptable and moreover it would have been very costly to build a large number of new schools. It was not put to the test of experiment.

In negotiations for a gradual transfer of power to an elected government MacGillivray showed a surer touch. By 1954 there were two leading political groups, each comprising representatives of the main communities, but under Malay leadership. Party Negara, led by Datuk Onn, was in form a conventional non-communal party, which accepted the inevitability of gradual progress. The other, the Alliance, was a coalition of communal parties, led by Tunku Abdul Rahman, which demanded more rapid progress towards the election of a majority of members of the central legislature (all of whom in 1954 were official or appointed members) with a view to independence at an early date. In his quiet, cool, courteous fashion MacGillivray was able by patient diplomacy to keep both parties within the political process. The situation might easily have gone off the rails, but to his credit it did not.

Like other observers MacGillivray had probably expected that the first federal (national) elections in mid-1955 would give minority representation to both parties, but in the event the Alliance swept the board, winning fifty-one of the fifty-two contested seats. It then took office in a diarchy by which, for the time being, certain key functions, such as defence, were reserved to the colonial power. MacGillivray had now to establish a harmonious relationship with elected ministers. Privately there were official fears that 'the natural diversity of [communal] interests' would fragment 'a highly artificial grouping' of communal parties (Stockwell, 3.390), and MacGillivray had, in 1954, thought them 'ready to put party advantage before the interests of the country' (ibid., 3.54). Moreover, as the transfer of power drew near, Abdul Rahman had insisted upon meeting the communist leader, Chin Peng, at Baling to explore the possibility of bringing the emergency to an end by negotiation—an attempt that failed. Although negotiations in London and the Reid constitutional commission reduced the significance of MacGillivray's handling of events in Malaya, it was still a delicate task, which he accomplished with skill, so that the final achievement of Malayan independence in August 1957 came in an atmosphere of general goodwill.

Kept well under wraps, since no one wished to expose the raw nerves of the problem, was the position of the Malay rulers as 'constitutional' monarchs in an independent Malaya. In commenting on the report of the Reid commission MacGillivray had written that there would be more problems in 'getting agreement between elements in Malaya than between those elements and H.M.G.' (Stockwell, 3.361). Neither the rulers nor the Alliance government wished to allow Britain to arbitrate or—worse still—to play off one against the other. Yet Britain was, if only marginally, involved, since, on winding up the Malayan Union in 1948, it had declared by treaty that each ruler was to regain 'the prerogatives, power and jurisdiction' which he had possessed on 1 December 1941. In the course of his discussions with Chin Peng, Tunku Abdul Rahman had said that 'the Rulers will become constitutional Rulers ... more like figureheads [and] will not get mixed up in politics or in the administration' (Smith, 204). That, however, was not the rulers' interpretation of being a constitutional monarch which was, in the autocratic tradition of Malay monarchy, l'état c'est moi. In the final discussions before independence there were, reported Watherston, 'some extremely sticky meetings' to discuss the powers of the rulers' state governments (Stockwell, 3.367). Abdul Rahman said that such matters were best 'left over for decision after Merdeka [independence]' and with reluctance MacGillivray and Watherston had to fall in with the idea. It was still a bone of contention forty years later.

When Malaya became independent in 1957, MacGillivray retired from the colonial service. Having been appointed CMG (1949) and KCMG (1953), he was made GCMG in the year of his retirement. Never one to rest, he bought a farm in the highlands of Kenya at Gilgil, and also became involved in public life in east Africa, serving as chairman from 1958 to 1961 of the council of Makerere College in Uganda and then of the council of the University of East Africa from 1961 to 1964. When the British government appointed a commission to report on the constitutional problems of the Federation of Rhodesia and Nyasaland in 1960 MacGillivray became its vice-chairman. Apart from holding company directorships, notably in banking, he became the director in 1964 of the United Nations Special Fund for the East African Livestock Development Survey. He thus continued to travel widely and to drive himself hard until cancer brought his working life to its end. He died in hospital in Nairobi on 24 December 1966. He was survived by his wife.

Slight of build, quiet in manner, and to those who did not know him well at times rather reserved, MacGillivray had a lively mind, a sense of humour, and a capacity—indeed a personal need—to absorb himself in the work in hand. In his successful career as a colonial administrator he was a man of his time. In the era of decolonization it was patient skill rather than drastic action, above all sympathetic and intelligent diplomacy which was needed to resolve the problems of dependent territories as they moved towards independence. In this context and in this way MacGillivray made a notable contribution.

J. M. GULLICK

Sources private information (1981) · personal knowledge (2004) · A. J. Stockwell, ed., *Malaya*, 3 vols. (1995), ser. B/3 of *British documents on the end of empire* · S. C. Smith, *British relations with the Malay rulers from decentralization to Malayan independence, 1930–1957* (1995) · J. Cloake, *Templer, tiger of Malaya: the life of Field Marshal Sir Gerald Templer* (1985) · *The Times* (28 Dec 1966) · *Sherborne School Magazine* (1967)
Archives Bodl. RH, papers relating to Malaya command · St Ant. Oxf., Middle East Centre, papers relating to Palestine | PRO, CO archives
Likenesses photograph, 1957, Hult. Arch. [*see illus.*] · photographs, repro. in N. J. White, *Business, government and the end of empire, Malaya, 1942–1957* (1996), pl. 18 · photographs, repro. in M. Sheppard, *Tunku: a pictorial biography*, 1 (1984), 139 · photographs, Hult. Arch.
Wealth at death £12,949: probate resealed, Kenya, 1968

MacGillivray, John (1821–1867), natural history collector, was born in Aberdeen in December 1821, the eldest son of William *MacGillivray (1796–1852), a distinguished Scottish naturalist and ornithologist, and his wife, Marion McCaskill (1803–1852). When he was a year old his family moved to Edinburgh following the appointment of his father as an assistant to Robert Jameson, the regius professor of natural history. During MacGillivray's teenage years the American bird artist John James Audubon was a frequent visitor to the family home. Growing up in such company the young man could hardly have become other than a naturalist, and although he began studying medicine at Edinburgh he spent most of his time collecting natural history specimens. At the age of nineteen he spent eight days on St Kilda; he subsequently published important papers on the zoology, geology, agriculture, and natural history of the island group.

In 1841 MacGillivray moved back to Aberdeen when his father was appointed to the chair of natural history at Marischal College, but after a few months he went to work for the thirteenth earl of Derby at his menagerie and museum at Knowsley, near Liverpool. In 1842 he joined the Admiralty surveying vessel HMS *Fly* as a naturalist, making collections on behalf of the earl. The *Fly* spent four years surveying in the south-western Pacific, especially around the Great Barrier Reef, and MacGillivray made important collections of mammals, birds, fishes, invertebrates, and plants. These collections were subsequently transferred to the Liverpool Museum and the Natural History Museum.

A few months after his return to England in February 1846, MacGillivray was appointed as the official Admiralty naturalist on another surveying vessel, HMS *Rattlesnake*, and he spent another four years off the north-east coast of Australia. This voyage marked the high point of MacGillivray's career. He collected widely and sent back important collections, especially of birds, many of them new species, that went to John Gould, the bird artist. He also kept a daily record of sightings of albatrosses and petrels between Rio de Janeiro and Tasmania, the first such detailed account of the distribution of seabirds at sea. MacGillivray also showed a considerable talent for communicating with the native peoples he encountered on his voyages; his notebooks contain several vocabularies and grammars of native languages.

Early in 1848 the *Rattlesnake* was in Sydney, and in March of that year MacGillivray married Williamina Gray, originally from Aberdeen. A daughter was born on 25 December 1848 and both mother and child returned to England with MacGillivray in 1850. There MacGillivray wrote the official *Narrative of the Voyage of HMS Rattlesnake*; after it was published in 1852 he spent just six months longer in England before he joined HMS *Herald* as a civilian naturalist and set sail again for Australia, to spend another four years at sea. MacGillivray's family (now three daughters) remained in London. His financial provision for them appears to have been quite inadequate, and conchologist Hugh Cuming supported the family at least until 1852.

For the first three years of the *Herald*'s voyage MacGillivray does at least appear to have been a reliable collector, sending back a steady supply of specimens. However, in the last few months of the ship's stay in Australian waters he began drinking, fell foul of the captain, Captain Denham, and was dismissed from the ship in Sydney in 1855. MacGillivray had spent an unparalleled twelve years living almost continuously in the cramped conditions of the Royal Navy ships of the day, and in the last few months on the *Herald* there had been long tedious spells of routine surveying work with few opportunities for shore collecting. It is perhaps understandable that he had had enough.

MacGillivray never returned to England and spent the remaining twelve years of his life in the Australian region. Shortly after his dismissal his family sailed for Australia, their fare paid by Sir William Hooker; his wife died on the voyage, and the fate of the three children is unknown. From 1858 to 1860 MacGillivray was in the New Hebrides, supporting himself by commercial collecting, but many of his last years remain a mystery. He had no settled work: there are some newspaper articles that he wrote in Sydney newspapers but his life ended in alcoholic obscurity in a Sydney lodging house, on 6 June 1867. He was buried in

Sydney. MacGillivray's published work is essentially trivial but, despite the failings of his later years, he is remembered for his integrity and diligence as a naturalist and collector, enduring uncomfortable, often dangerous conditions, to send back specimens on which other men made their reputations. ROBERT RALPH

Sources R. Ralph, 'John MacGillivray—his life and work', *Archives of Natural History*, 20 (1993), 185–95 · P. Beaton, 'A martyr to science', *Good Words* (1868), 425–9 · *AusDB*
Archives Admiralty Library, London, journal of HMS *Herald*, vocabularies of Pacific islands · NHM, catalogue of *radiata* and *mollusca* collected · NL Aus., notes on voyage of HMS *Rattlesnake* · RBG Kew, archives, narrative of voyage of HMS *Rattlesnake*, catalogue of botanical specimens | RBG Kew, archives, letters to Sir William Hooker
Likenesses engraving, repro. in Beaton, 'A martyr to science'
Wealth at death penniless: Beaton 'A martyr'

McGillivray, Lachlan (1719–1799). *See under* McGillivray, Alexander (1750–1793).

MacGillivray, (James) Pittendrigh (1856–1938), sculptor, was born at Port Elphinstone, Inverurie, Aberdeenshire, on 30 May 1856, the eldest son of a mason sculptor, William MacGillivray, and his wife, Margaret Pittendrigh. The family moved to Edinburgh in 1868, and in the following year, aged thirteen, MacGillivray was apprenticed to the sculptor William Brodie. On the expiry of his apprenticeship, in 1875, he moved to Glasgow, where he became an assistant to James Steel, for whom he carved the decorative sculpture on the Scotia Theatre (afterwards known as the Metropole). He then worked for John Mossman, whom he assisted on the Glasgow statues of Thomas Campbell (1877) and David Livingstone (1879). In 1882 he established an independent practice, and three years later received his first public commission, for a bronze portrait bust of General Gordon (Glasgow Art Gallery).

While in Glasgow, MacGillivray worked as a painter as well as a sculptor, and it was for his proficiency in painting that he was elected a member of the Glasgow Arts Club in 1882. In the same year he initiated the Palette Club, of which he was the first president. During the 1880s he was closely associated with the group of painters known as the Glasgow Boys, and his was a leading role in the founding and editing of the *Scottish Art Review*, the magazine of the Glasgow school. On at least one commission—the funerary monument to Alexander McCall (1888; Glasgow necropolis)—he worked in collaboration with the architect Charles Rennie Mackintosh.

From 1890 MacGillivray devoted most of his attention to sculpture, and received his first major commission—a statue of Robert Burns for Irvine—in 1893. In the same year, after a study tour to Brussels, he moved to Edinburgh, where he settled for the rest of his life. He designed his own house and studio, Ravelston Elms, which was built with the assistance of his friend and patron the fourth marquess of Bute. The most notable feature of the project, which was completed in 1896, was the adaptation of the studio for the production of large-scale sculpture. It incorporated an entrance of sufficient height and width to enable MacGillivray to wheel his monumental works

out into the open to see what effect they would have outdoors.

MacGillivray attained his greatest success in the late 1890s and the early years of the twentieth century. In this period he received at least twelve major commissions, including six statues for the façade of the Scottish National Portrait Gallery, Edinburgh. But by far the largest and most significant project was his national monument to William Gladstone (1904–13; Edinburgh), which incorporated a portrait statue 9 feet 6 inches high and eight life-size figures, each modelled from life by the sculptor. The emphasis that MacGillivray placed on technique and craftsmanship applied equally to his smaller works. He produced more than forty-five such pieces—portrait, allegorical, and narrative—in these years alone. Like his monumental works they are characterized by originality of composition and an appreciation of symbolism and decorative effect. A stylistic evolution towards increased emphasis on freedom of handling and surface texture in the manner of Rodin is clearly evident after his visit to Brussels in 1893.

In 1903 MacGillivray travelled to Europe again, visiting Rome, Florence, and Brussels. On his return to Scotland he was commissioned by the Scottish education department to prepare a report on art schools and art teaching in Scotland and to offer recommendations for the improvement of facilities. Always outspoken, he unequivocally declared the existing schools unsatisfactory and insisted that priority be given to a sound practical training in craftsmanship. One result of his report was the founding of the Edinburgh College of Art, the scheme of which, as well as the first set of plans adopted by Edinburgh town council, were also his work.

MacGillivray was a man of wide-ranging interests and talents. In 1914 he organized an exhibition of art in aid of Belgian relief. In 1920 he designed the official robes for members of the Royal Scottish Academy. He was a respected authority on the clans and their tartans and was created an honorary member of the Scottish Pipers' Society. He was an honorary fellow of the Royal Incorporation of Architects, Scotland, and an honorary member of the Aberdeen Artists' Society and of the Scottish Society of Photographic Art.

Literature also claimed MacGillivray's attention. As well as papers on varying subjects and much occasional verse he published two volumes of poetry, *Pro patria* (1915) and *Bog Myrtle and Peat Reek* (1922). The latter, a volume of sixty-one poems, many in the north- and south-country dialects of the Scots tongue, was brought out in a form that reflects MacGillivray's fastidious nature. It was printed privately in a limited edition of 300 signed copies. For the title-page he drew and engraved a heraldic design of the Scottish thistle with a bordure of entwined thistle leaves. The same thistle motif was stamped in gold on the buckram binding.

Like his prototypes of the cinquecento MacGillivray was almost universal in his range: sculptor, painter, architect, musician, orator, and philosopher. Always an ardent nationalist, he made issues of Scottish nationalism and home rule a major part of his writings and oratory. Nor was he afraid to challenge official bodies and institutions. In 'Anent the Scots Academy' (in *Bog Myrtle and Peat Reek*) he poured scorn on the Royal Scottish Academy. In 1917 he maligned the trustees of the National Gallery of Scotland for not spending a due portion of their acquisitions budget on sculpture. He publicly criticized the policy that no work by a member or associate of the Royal Scottish Academy could be accepted for the national collection until five years after the artist's death. Almost certainly his outspoken nature cost him a knighthood (Cammell, 108–9) and was a significant factor in his defeat in the election for rector of Edinburgh University in 1932 (NL Scot., MS 3901, fol. 231).

In common with the other outstanding personality of nineteenth-century Scottish sculpture, Sir John Steell, MacGillivray refused to be drawn to London, instead electing to remain in the country of his birth to advance the establishment of a national school of sculpture. His efforts were recognized in 1921, when the office of sculptor royal for Scotland, which had been in abeyance since Steell's death thirty years earlier, was revived for MacGillivray.

MacGillivray was elected associate of the Royal Scottish Academy in 1892 and member in 1901. An honorary degree of doctor of laws was conferred on him by Aberdeen University in 1909. His work was shown at the Royal Scottish Academy in 1872, 1874, 1875, and 1887, and in almost every year from 1891 to 1938. He exhibited at Paisley, Stirling, Dundee, and London, and at the Royal Glasgow Institute of the Fine Arts from 1875 to 1932, and again in 1938. He held solo artist exhibitions of his work at Glasgow in 1927 and at Edinburgh in 1930. Several pieces of his sculpture were shown at the exhibition of the work of the Glasgow Boys arranged by the Scottish Arts Council in 1971. His work was a point of focus in the National Galleries of Scotland exhibition 'Virtue and Vision: Sculpture and Scotland, 1540–1990' of 1991.

Pittendrigh MacGillivray died at his home, Ravelston Elms, 41 Murrayfield Road, Edinburgh, on 29 April 1938, and was buried in Gogarburn parish churchyard. His wife, Frieda Rettig (Röhl), by birth Polish and of French-Huguenot origins, had predeceased him in 1910, and one of his daughters, Erinna, had died in 1917. He was survived by his other daughter, Erhna Mycale, who died unmarried in 1962.   ROBIN L. WOODWARD

Sources J. P. MacGillivray, written and photographic material, NL Scot., MS Acc. 3501, nos. 1–47 [incl. correspondence, photographs, memorabilia, press cuttings, and notes] · R. L. Woodward, 'Nineteenth century Scottish sculpture', PhD diss., U. Edin., 1979 · R. Woodward, 'Pittendrigh MacGillivray', *Virtue and vision: sculpture and Scotland, 1540–1990*, ed. F. Pearson (1991), 99–104 · *The Scotsman* (30 April 1938), 17 · C. R. Cammell, *The heart of Scotland* (1956) · b. cert. · d. cert.
Archives Aberdeen Art Gallery, photographic record of work · Glasgow Art Gallery, complete set of woodcuts · NG Scot., D3990–D4037 · NL Scot., corresp. and papers, Dep 349 · NL Scot., corresp. and papers, photographs, memorabilia, press cuttings, and notes,

MS Acc. 3501, nos. 1–47 · U. Glas. L., corresp. | NL Scot., corresp. with William Skeoch Cumming
Likenesses D. Foggie, pencil drawing, 1917, Scot. NPG · J. W. Thompson, pencil drawing, 1932, Scot. NPG · B. Schotz, bronze bust, Scot. NPG · portrait, repro. in E. Gordon, *The Royal Scottish Academy of Painting, Sculpture and Architecture, 1826–1976* (1976), pl. XX · portrait, repro. in *Scotsman*, 17 · portrait, repro. in Cammell, *The heart of Scotland*, frontispiece and facing p. 96 · portrait, repro. in *The Glasgow Boys Scottish Arts Council*, part II (1971), frontispiece and p. 90
Wealth at death £969 12s. 11d.: confirmation, 23 June 1938, *CCI*

MacGillivray, William (1796–1852), ornithologist and natural historian, was born in Old Aberdeen on 25 January 1796. His father, also William (d. 1812), came from the Outer Hebrides and was a student at the local university; his mother, Anne Wishart, was a local Aberdeen girl and the two were not married. His father joined the army and was later killed in the Peninsular War, probably at the siege of Burgos in 1812. At the age of three, MacGillivray was taken to his uncle's farm in Harris and brought up there. He returned to Aberdeen in 1811 to attend the grammar school there, and in 1812 entered University and King's College, Aberdeen. He travelled to and from Harris on foot for each session, a round trip of 360 miles through the highlands. The long walks encouraged the development of his love of natural history in all its branches, but it was ornithology that became his chosen field.

In September 1819 MacGillivray walked from Aberdeen to London to see the bird collection in the British Museum. The most direct route is about 500 miles but he wanted to explore and record the natural history of parts of Scotland that he had not seen and he walked 501 miles before he crossed the border into England at Carlisle. The complete journey was 837 miles, carried out in eight weeks, and he wrote a detailed journal of some 60,000 words on the way. Shortly after this journey MacGillivray moved to Edinburgh, where he was employed by Professor Robert Jameson (1774–1854) as his assistant and secretary. He was also responsible for curating Jameson's natural history collection and museum, one of the largest of its kind. It was in this period of his life that MacGillivray began publishing, his works ranging from a weekly piece on natural history in the *Edinburgh Literary Gazette* to scientific papers in the *Edinburgh Philosophical Journal*, to books on botany. On 29 September 1820 he married Marion McCaskill (1803–1852), from Harris. They had thirteen children, four of whom died in infancy. Their eldest son, John *MacGillivray (1821–1867) spent many years on Royal Navy survey ships and was an important natural history collector.

In the summer of 1830 MacGillivray met John James Audubon—a meeting that was to lead to lifelong friendship, and to have a profound influence on ornithology in Britain and in the United States. Audubon had already published a number of plates of *The Birds of America* and was about to produce a separate text to accompany them. He was aware of his limitations—English was not his native language and he had no formal training in science—and was introduced to MacGillivray as someone who might take his field notes and observations on

American birds and turn them into an acceptable text. MacGillivray agreed to do this and the five volumes plus a synopsis of the *Ornithological Biographies* were published over the next decade.

The 1830s were also a time of extraordinary activity for MacGillivray in other spheres. In 1831 he became conservator of the museum of the Royal College of Surgeons in Edinburgh, a position he held until 1841. After first supervising the move of the collection to new premises, he spent nearly three years preparing a new catalogue. He was also publishing books, including *The Travels and Researches of Alexander von Humboldt* (1832), *Descriptions of the Rapacious Birds of Great Britain* (1836), *An Introduction to the Study of Botany* (1837), and *A Manual of British Ornithology* (1840). Between 1838 and 1840 he published three volumes of *A History of British Birds*. At the same time he was also producing life-size paintings of British birds. His intention was that they should be published to accompany *A History of British Birds* but the volumes were not a commercial success and he could never afford to have his paintings published. (Indeed, the final two volumes of his *History* were not published until shortly before his death and their true value not appreciated for several decades.) His style of painting was clearly influenced by Audubon. He also painted fish and mammals, and all 213 paintings are in the library of the Natural History Museum, London.

In 1841 MacGillivray made the final move of his career, back to Aberdeen as the regius professor of natural history at Marischal College. He was a popular teacher and insisted on his students getting out into the field and handling specimens. His writing continued at an extraordinary pace, with a book on the molluscan fauna of northeast Scotland, a textbook of conchology, a series of portraits of domestic cattle, another manual of ornithology, and the final two volumes of *A History of British Birds* (1852). He died on 8 September 1852 at his home, 152 Crown Street, Aberdeen, probably as a result of the effort of two months' field work around Lochnagar and Braemar in the previous year. The manuscript based on this work was unpublished at his death but was published for private circulation by Queen Victoria as *The Natural History of Dee Side and Braemar*. He was buried at the new Calton cemetery, Edinburgh.   ROBERT RALPH

Sources R. Ralph, *William MacGillivray* (1993) · W. MacGillivray and J. A. Thomson, *Life of William MacGillivray* (1910) · V. C. Wynne-Edwards, 'The centenary of William MacGillivray, 1796–1852', *Scottish Naturalist*, 64 (1952), 65–9 · bap. reg. Scot. (25 Jan 1796), Aberdeen, Old Machar
Archives NHM, drawings · U. Aberdeen, notebooks and diaries · U. Aberdeen L., journals and notes | Leics. RO, Harley MSS · Shetland Archives, Lerwick, corresp. with Thomas Edmonston
Likenesses W. MacGillivray, oils, repro. in Ralph, *William MacGillivray*
Wealth at death under £50: will, Edinburgh City Archives

McGillveray, Angus (1930–1996), politician, was born at Dunmaglas, 46 Main Street, East Whitburn, West Lothian, on 13 October 1930, the elder of two sons of Joseph Charles McGillveray (1900–1971), fruiterer, and his wife, Marion

Prentice, *née* Docherty (1902–1981). Educated at Whitburn primary school (1935–41) and Lindsay High School, Bathgate (1941–5), he was apprenticed to John Laughridge, a local company of painters and decorators. After his apprenticeship he worked with them for two years before establishing his own firm of painters and decorators in 1955. On 29 March 1952 he married Jean Blair Brown (*b.* 1930), florist, at the Church of Scotland, Stoneyburn, West Lothian. They had a daughter, Janice, and two sons, Charles and Colin.

McGillveray was from his early years a great exponent of the culture of Scotland. A gifted artist, he also had special interests in piping and highland dancing. He arranged many fund-raising ceilidhs for cultural societies. He was responsible for holding in Bathgate one of the biggest highland dancing competitions in Scotland. It was to raise still more funds that he created a weekly sweep, called Saltire Pools, which benefited a wide range of cultural organizations.

McGillveray joined the Scottish National Party (SNP) in 1952 when it was still a small organization with some 20 branches and a small membership. In the early 1960s the SNP began to grow. In 1962 it contested the West Lothian by-election and won over 23 per cent of the vote. The impetus given by this election boosted the SNP's national membership and prestige. It also created a power centre in West Lothian where McGillveray worked alongside the future party chairman, William Wolfe, to modernize the party. On his own initiative, McGillveray established a publications department in West Calder, which supplied leaflets, badges, and policy booklets to the party. By 1964 the SNP had 35 branches, and by 1970 the total had mushroomed to over 400. Membership had also gone through exponential growth. The whole organization was hungry for promotional material. During that period, McGillveray, by then head of the SNP's publications department, assisted by his wife, Jean, established a Scotland-wide network and sales reached into six figures. The famous *It's Scotland's Oil* leaflet (1973) sold over 1 million copies—a stupendous figure for a country with 3 million households. In 1962, again on his own initiative and at his own cost, he adapted the formula of Saltire Pools to found the SNP's own version, Alba Pools. This was a runaway success. In its first five years, it raked in £200,000. This money financed the explosive growth of the SNP and permitted the SNP at national level to set a high standard in research and publications new to Scottish politics.

McGillveray's organizational genius and marketing flair contributed critically to the emergence of the SNP as a major player in Scottish and United Kingdom politics. He was widely recognized as a mainspring of the leap forward. Additionally, he fought many local elections and served on the West Lothian district council. Although his family had lived in the lowlands for two centuries, he was proud of his highland origins and was open and welcoming by nature. He died in the house of his birth on 4 November 1996, after a courageous struggle over years against cancer, and was survived by his wife and their three children. There was a huge turn-out at his funeral, at Falkirk crematorium four days later, testifying to the affection and respect in which he was held.

GORDON WILSON

Sources *The Scotsman* (7 Nov 1996) · *The Herald* (7 Nov 1996) · private information (2004) [Jean McGillveray] · personal knowledge (2004) · b. cert. · d. cert.
Likenesses photograph, repro. in *The Scotsman*
Wealth at death £91,268: confirmation, 3 Feb 1997, *CCI*

Mac Giolla Fhiondáin, Pádraig (c.1665–1733), poet, was born in the district of the Fews, in the south of co. Armagh. His mother, Siobhán Nic Ardail, a noted female poet and repository of local history, was the great-granddaughter of Toirdhealbhach an tSeanfhoinn, a legendary musical composer who lived in the sixteenth century. Although his links with south Armagh are strongly reflected in his poetry, there have been persistent suggestions that he was a native of co. Down, and he has also been linked with co. Louth. There is, however, another tradition that would associate him with the townland of Lisleitrim in the parish of Creggan Lower, co. Armagh.

Mac Giolla Fhiondáin was a farmer who was reputed to be comfortably off and was noted for his generosity and hospitality, his house being a magnet for poets and musicians. He is said to have conducted a school of poetry at Cnoc Céin Mhic Cáinte (Killin Hill) near Dundalk and was on friendly terms with the south-east Ulster poets of his day, Mac Cuarta, Ó Doirnín, Pádraig Ó Prontaigh, Fearghus Mac Bheatha, and others, as well as with the celebrated harper Toirdhealbhach Ó Cearbhalláin. He was highly regarded by his contemporaries, both as a poet and harper, and was reputed to be learned in a number of languages; his familiarity with the classics and with early Irish literature is clear from his poetry. He was also familiar with, and somewhat influenced by, contemporary English poetry, especially in his love poems.

Some seventeen poems in Irish by Mac Giolla Fhiondáin survive, as well as one in English and one which is macaronic. It is likely that many of his compositions have not been preserved, while a number of other poems have sometimes been wrongly attributed to him. More than half the poems relate to Mac Giolla Fhiondáin's fellow poets, including one in praise of Séamus Dall Mac Cuarta and an elegy for the same poet who predeceased him by just a few weeks. A further six are love poems. His lament for Owen Roe O'Neill (d. 1649) was frequently copied by later scribes. It is noteworthy that two of his poems appeared in print before the close of the eighteenth century, one (the macaronic 'Angelical Maid') in Joseph Cooper Walker's *Historical Memoirs of the Irish Bards* (1786) and the other ('A iníon thais na mbánchíoch') in Charlotte Brooke's *Reliques of Irish Poetry* (1789).

Mac Giolla Fhiondáin died in March 1733, and was buried in Creggan graveyard. He left a son, also named Pádraig, and a daughter, Máire or Mailigh. The former was reputedly a man of some learning but the daughter was especially celebrated as the author of a number of popular songs. Some confusion is caused by the fact that a poet and

harper also named Pádraig Mac Giolla Fhiondáin was active in south Armagh—and living in Lisleitrim—in the final third of the eighteenth century and into the early nineteenth. A friend of the poet Art Mac Cumhaigh, whom he visited on the night of his death in 1773, this Mac Giolla Fhiondáin was still living in 1802 when he furnished the collector Edward Bunting with a number of Irish airs. It is highly unlikely that he is to be identified with the son of the subject of this entry, but he may well have been his grandson.

NOLLAIG Ó MURAÍLE

Sources *DNB* · S. Mag Uidhir, *Pádraig Mac a Liondain: Dánta* (1977)

Mac Giolla Ghunna, Cathal Buí (*fl.* mid-18th cent.), poet, came from the Breifne (the Cavan–Leitrim–Fermanagh) region of south-west Ulster. Nothing is known of his immediate family background, but the surname Mac Giolla Ghunna (Anglicized variously as McElgun, Kilgunn, Kildunn, Gilgun, Dunne) is found predominantly in that part of Ulster; the poet probably belonged to that region. According to folk tradition and the late nineteenth-century manuscript tradition, Mac Giolla Ghunna earned his livelihood as a pedlar hawking his wares from place to place in the northern counties and leading a somewhat dissolute life. Legends about his lifestyle and death abound in Gaelic-speaking districts. According to one of these, he had studied for the priesthood at a Catholic continental college (MacGrianna, 118), but contemporary sources do not confirm this, and indeed the total absence of contemporary references to Cathal Buí suggests that he is more a creation of the folk imagination than a real historical figure. The 'Buí' ('yellow') sobriquet to his personal name is interesting: adjectives are used not infrequently in this manner in the Irish tradition, but worth noting in this context is Cearbhall Buí Ó Dálaigh (Cearbhall O'Daly) who flourished in the first half of the seventeenth century and who was similarly 'a man of great notoriety in his day' (O'Rahilly, 102).

Sixteen songs are attributed to Mac Giolla Ghunna (Ó Buachalla, *Cathal Buí*) and these in the main celebrate the delights of drinking and the pleasures of love. The songs seem in both style and subject matter to be distanced somewhat from contemporary works. They appear to reflect a voice of dissent against the restrictions on freedoms being visited on ordinary people by both church and state. The most accomplished of these songs is 'An bonnán buí' ('The yellow bittern') (Ó Buachalla, *Nua Dhuanaire II*, 47–8). This, which is a remarkable poetic achievement, occurs frequently in the later nineteenth-century manuscripts and was effectively translated into English by Thomas Mac Donagh who captured much of the drama and the rhythms of the original. In the dead bird lying by the wayside the poet finds a correspondence which encapsulates his own emotions. For the bird has, in the frozen-over marshlands and lakes, died of thirst, and the poet affirms that in the light of this, and despite the admonitions of his lover, he will not be caught up in a plight similar to that of the yellow bittern:

O Yellow Bittern I pity your lot
Though they say that a sot like myself is curst

I was sober a while, but I'll drink and be wise
For fear I should die in the end of thirst.
(MacGrianna, 118)

Mac Giolla Ghunna, apparently towards the end of his days, wrote a poem of repentance, 'Marbhna Chathail Bhuí' ('Cathal Buí's Elegy'), which was also very popular and was written in manuscript A.39 in the Franciscan Library, Killiney, Dublin, by Father Brian Ó Cathaláin in 1773–5. Father Ó Cathaláin was parish priest in Donaghmoyne, co. Monaghan and it is in the graveyard in Donaghmoyne that Cathal Buí is reputedly buried.

DIARMAID Ó DOIBHLIN

Sources B. Ó Buachalla, *Cathal Buí Amhráin* (1975) · E. Ó Muirgheasa, *Céad de Cheoltaibh uladh* (1915) · Franciscan Library, Killiney, Dublin, MS A.39 · S. MacGrianna, *Pádraic Ó Conaire agus Aistí Eile* (1936) · B. Ó Cuiv, *Aspects of personal names* (1986) · T. F. O'Rahilly, *Irish poets, historians and judges in English documents, 1538–1615* (1922) · T. MacDonagh, *Literature in Ireland* (1926) · B. Ó Buachalla, *Nua Dhuanaire II* (1976)
Archives Franciscan Library, Killiney, co. Dublin, MS A.39

McGlashan, Alexander (*c.*1740–1797), violinist and band leader, was apparently born in Perthshire. He is first heard of in Edinburgh in 1759, where he established a reputation as the leader of the most fashionable dance band in that city. He gave regular concerts at St Cecilia's Hall, near the Cowgate, and was known as King McGlashan on account of his stately appearance and showy style of dress. The leadership of the band passed to William Gow on McGlashan's retirement about 1787. He edited, and probably contributed anonymously to, three important volumes of Scottish music, *A Collection of Strathspey Reels* (1780), *A Collection of Scots Measures* (1781), and *A Collection of Reels* (1786). He died in Edinburgh in May 1797 and was buried there in Greyfriars churchyard.

J. C. HADDEN, *rev.* K. D. REYNOLDS

Sources D. Johnson, 'McGlashan, Alexander', *New Grove* · F. Kidson, 'McGlashan, Alexander', *Grove, Dict. mus.* (1927) · M. A. Alburger, *Scottish fiddlers and their music* (1983) · J. Glen, *The Glen collection of Scottish dance music*, 2 vols. (1891–5) · R. Burns and others, *The Scots musical museum*, ed. J. Johnson, 1 (1787), 66

McGlashan, John (1802–1864), lawyer, was born on 7 November 1802 in Cannongate, Edinburgh, the eldest son of John McGlashan, auctioneer, furniture dealer, valuer, and warehouseman, and his wife, Mary, *née* Fraser. He was educated at Edinburgh high school from 1815 to 1818 before attending classes at Edinburgh University. After a period in articles to Andrew Crombie, he qualified as a solicitor in September 1824. In 1826 or 1827 at Stirling he married Isabella (*d.* 1888), daughter of William MacEwan or MacEwen of Stirling, an officer in the first Royal Scots. She is commemorated in Dunedin, New Zealand, by the place name Balmacewen. They had ten children. The eldest, Jane Gilchrist McGlashan, was born in December 1827.

In 1830 McGlashan became a member of the faculty of admiralty procurators and in 1831 he was appointed commissioner for proofs in the sheriff court of Edinburgh. He remained in this post for twenty-one years. From 1832 to 1839 he was also public examiner of the Society of Solicitors. The early onset of serious deafness disqualified him for general practice and it was as an academic lawyer that he made himself known. His contributions to the codification of Scottish law were valuable. He wrote legal texts on the Scottish sheriff courts, the law of aliment, and pawnbroking.

A dedicated member of the Free Church from 1843, McGlashan was attracted by the possibility of forming an emigrant Presbyterian community in New Zealand. In August 1847 he became secretary of the Otago Association, a post which he retained until the dissolution of the association in 1853. From 1848 to 1852 he was editor of the *Otago Journal*. In these capacities he promoted a scheme of emigration, oversaw arrangements for the dispatch of emigrants, and lobbied, with an inflexibility which some thought destructive to the interests of the association, in an attempt to ensure that Otago remained exclusively a lowland Scottish and Free Church community. Clause 78 of the 1852 Constitution Act, designed to safeguard the interests of Otago, was largely his work.

The sale of land in New Zealand was hampered by financial recession and a lack of church support. Widely publicized dissent developed within the Otago Association. Robert Cargill accused McGlashan of inefficiency and dishonesty. He was paid a substantial salary by the association and yet, according to Cargill, he was by 1849 devoting half his time to other work. As the only paid representative of the association, and as its most senior member after the departure of many of its leading figures for New Zealand in 1849, McGlashan was in a position of considerable power, which he exercised with careful regard for his own interests: from his earliest involvement with the settlement scheme he was influenced by the hope of senior legal employment in the colony.

On 14 June 1853 McGlashan sailed with his family from Gravesend for Dunedin. He became Otago's provincial solicitor and treasurer in January 1854. In 1855 he won the western district seat in the Otago provincial council, holding it until 1863. From 1855 to 1861 he was provincial secretary and solicitor and also secretary of the board of education. He was involved in the codification of the province's ordinances. He wrote the warden's court rules. In 1861 he fell under suspicion of financial malpractice during the investigation into the affairs of the disgraced superintendent, James Macandrew, and was forced to resign office. Though cleared of dishonesty and reappointed as provincial solicitor in 1862, he was censured for carelessness.

McGlashan was a sincere and influential churchman. He drew up the *Institutes of the Free Church of Otago* in 1847, was closely involved with First Church, Dunedin, and campaigned for the funding of religion through a tax on land sales. In his lectures entitled *Civilisation and Christianity* (1854) and *Colonisation* (1857) he illustrated the attitudes and aims of leaders of the Otago Free Church. He supported a close link between education and religion and saw education as a means of promoting equality. He is credited with significant responsibility for the education system which developed in Otago.

McGlashan died in Dunedin on 2 November 1864 after receiving head injuries in a riding accident. His wife survived him with nine of their children. In 1918 John McGlashan College was founded, after his daughters' gift of the family home and estate.   C. A. CREFFIELD

Sources *DNZB*, vol. 1 · A. H. McLintock, ed., *An encyclopaedia of New Zealand*, 3 vols. (1966) · A. H. McLintock, *The history of Otago: the origins and growth of a Wakefield class settlement* (1949) · T. M. Hocken, *Contributions to the early history of New Zealand* (1898)
Archives Otago Early Settlers Museum · University of Otago, Dunedin, Hocken Library
Likenesses portrait, repro. in Hocken, *Contributions to the early history of New Zealand*, facing p. 89

McGonagall, William (*c*.1825–1902), poet and actor, was born in Edinburgh, the fifth child of Charles McGonagall, a migrant Irish cotton weaver, and his wife, Margaret Maxwell. The family settled eventually in Dundee where William McGonagall also became a hand-loom weaver. On 11 July 1846 he married Jean King of Edinburgh; they had seven children. McGonagall was largely self-taught. He was passionately fond of Shakespeare and at about the age of twenty began his career as an amateur actor in the role of Macbeth. He went on to appear in minor parts in the wood-and-canvas 'penny gaffs' and to give public recitations wherever he could find a paying audience.

It was not until his early fifties that McGonagall was seized with 'a strong desire to write poetry' (McGonagall, *Poetic Gems*, 6–7). His first efforts were published in the Dundee edition of one of the leading Scottish popular papers, the *Weekly News*. He soon established his characteristic manner, with such pieces as 'The Famous Tay Whale' and 'The Tay Bridge Disaster' which remain among the best-known of all his poems. He wrote about battles, fires, shipwrecks, and disasters; processions and shows; and the deaths of public men. There were verses about tourist spots, and watering holes; heroic deeds from Scottish history, and the superior qualities of Sunlight Soap; poems in praise of temperance and love and nature; and a number of quite unsingable songs. Much of what he described he cannot possibly have seen: recycled material from newspaper columns was conjured into rhyme by an uncertain practitioner whose foremost need was to feed himself and his family.

McGonagall's diction was drawn from the high fustian of Scottish popular melodrama, and his metre from the printed poetry of the street. His control of tone was erratic, fluctuating between the lofty and bathetic, and his imagery was frequently conventional. The predominant tone was gloomily fatalistic, focusing on man's ceaseless struggle with malignant natural forces, and the manifold perils of existence. If he had been merely inept, of course, he would simply have been forgotten, like countless other proletarian versifiers. McGonagall's triumph was to forge, by some unfathomable alchemy, the commonplace effects of popular-print rhetoric into an unmistakably personal style. Nobody else has ever sounded quite like him. And he had positive strengths: a sense of wonder, a

childlike ability to enter absolutely into what he depicted, and a real gift for narrative that could shape appropriate material into racy little verse-novellas with a rough but genuine graphic power.

As the weaving trade declined, McGonagall struggled to make a living selling his poems in the streets, and performing in music-halls and pubs. These tended to be anarchic places and he often found his audiences disruptive. The writer William Power saw him in the Albion Halls in Glasgow:

> He wore a Highland dress of Rob Roy tartan and boy's size. After reciting some of his own poems, to an accompaniment of whistles and cat-calls, the Bard armed himself with a most dangerous-looking broadsword, and strode up and down the platform, declaiming … 'Give me another horse!—Bind up my wounds!' His voice rose to a howl. He thrust and slashed at imaginary foes. A shower of apples and oranges fell on the platform. Almost before they touched it, they were met by the fell edge of McGonagall's claymore and cut to pieces. The Bard was beaded with perspiration and orange juice. (Power, 285)

A number of strands of Scottish popular culture came together in McGonagall—the bellowing street-corner elocutionists, the urban broadsheet and song-slip patterers, the penny readings, which mixed entertainment with self-improvement, and, most of all, perhaps, a line of genuinely popular poetry. He was the heir not of Burns and Hogg and Lady Nairne, but of chapbook writers such as Claudero and Dougal Graham, and through them a tradition of metrical journalism going back to the broadside poets of the seventeenth century. An estimated 200,000 people were regularly writing poetry in Victorian Scotland and they found their main publication outlet in the burgeoning popular press of which the *Weekly News* was an outstanding example. It was there that 'the Great McGonagall' found much of his inspiration; there too his work first appeared in print, while the journal's heartless chronicling of his many mishaps kept him steadily before the public eye as a potential butt and object of ridicule. Unable to endure relentless persecution by local audiences, he moved briefly to Perth, and then, in 1895, to Edinburgh. As a performer of his own works he enjoyed a national reputation in Scotland but he was unable to secure engagements in the music-halls of London or New York. William McGonagall died of a cerebral haemorrhage at his home, 5 South College Street, Edinburgh, on 29 September 1902. He was buried in Greyfriars kirkyard, Edinburgh, in a pauper's grave, but a plaque was later erected to his memory there.   WILLIAM DONALDSON

Sources W. McGonagall, 'Brief autobiography', 'Reminiscences', *Poetic gems selected from the works of William McGonagall, poet and tragedian*, ed. D. W. Smith (1934); repr. (1985), 5–12, 12–18 · W. McGonagall, 'The autobiography of Sir William Topaz McGonagall, poet and tragedian, knight of the white elephant, Burmah', *More poetic gems selected from the works of William McGonagall, poet and tragedian*, ed. D. W. Smith (1969), 5–34 · D. Phillips, *No poet's corner in the abbey: the dramatic story of William McGonagall* (1971) · W. Power, *My Scotland* (1934), 284–90 · H. Henderson, 'McGonagall the what?', *Alias MacAlias: writings on songs, folk and literature* (1992), 274–94 · H. MacDiarmid [C. R. Grieve], 'The great McGonagall', *Scottish eccentrics*,

ed. A. Riach, [new edn] (1993), 57–75 • W. Donaldson, *Popular litera-ture in Victorian Scotland* (1986) • m. cert.
Archives Dundee Central Library, MSS
Likenesses photograph, *c.*1890, repro. in Phillips, *No poet's corner in the abbey* • J. Brown, chalk, 1893, Dundee Art Gallery • W. B. Lamond, oils, Dundee Art Gallery

M'Gonigle, George Cuthbert Mura (1889–1939), medical officer of health, was born on 19 February 1889 at 48 North Bridge Street, Monkwearmouth, near Sunderland, co. Durham, the only child of Canon William Alexander M'Gonigle (1849–1939) and his wife, Sarah Catherine Stobbs (*d.* 1925). William M'Gonigle came from co. Derry, Ireland, and had graduated in theology at Durham University. At the age of three George M'Gonigle contracted poliomyelitis, which left him with a limp yet also with a determination to overcome his disability and to help others similarly afflicted to do the same. He was educated at the Newcastle school of medicine and graduated MB, BS of Durham University in 1910, and MD in 1913. He gained the diploma in public health (DPH) and became bachelor of hygiene (BHy) in 1914, and showed an early determination to specialize in public health work. After first working as a house surgeon at the Royal Victoria Infirmary, Newcastle upon Tyne, he took a post as school medical officer with the Durham county health department. In the First World War he served in the Royal Army Medical Corps at home and in France and Italy with the rank of captain. It was while serving in Italy that he met and married on 15 July 1916 Dorothy Evelyn Campbell (1890/91–1980), daughter of Captain Charles Campbell, and a nurse with the Volunteer Aid Detachment. There were no children.

M'Gonigle returned to his post in Durham in 1919, and in 1924 he was appointed medical officer of health and school medical officer for Stockton-on-Tees, where he remained until his death. In Stockton he continued the work begun in Durham, investigating rickets in children. His rigorous studies revealed a high level of rickets, which M'Gonigle attributed to poor diet. He refused to accept the situation and determined to eliminate this scourge of the poor. The focus of his concern was not general under-nutrition, but rather deficiencies in essential vitamins and minerals. Whereas the Ministry of Health attributed poor nutrition almost entirely to the ignorance of working-class mothers of the most nutritious foods to buy, M'Gonigle maintained that poverty was the main factor. He made this point over and over again on conference platforms, in journal articles, and in newspapers. His inquiries showed that the poor could not afford the relatively expensive milk, butter, eggs, green vegetables, and fruit necessary for health.

M'Gonigle worked long hours at the child welfare centres in Stockton in spite of his many other duties as medical officer for the town. He promoted green vegetables and less starchy food to wean babies and persuaded his health committee to provide dried milk and cod liver oil for poorer families and vitamins for pregnant women. His indefatigable work led to a dramatic reduction in rickets in infants and a decrease in the number of stillbirths: the

results encouraged further research into child and maternal health and the local newspaper rightly dubbed him 'The housewives' champion'.

Most medical officers saw the elimination of overcrowded and insanitary dwellings as the answer to many problems of public health. In 1927 Stockton council built an estate of houses for rent and moved people into them from the slums. Because only half of the slum area was cleared, M'Gonigle saw the opportunity to study the health of both populations. In 1932 he presented his conclusions to his health committee in a report entitled 'Poverty, nutrition and the public health', which showed that the death rate was higher on the new housing estate than in the old slum area, thus challenging the received wisdom of the day. M'Gonigle claimed that the high rents of the new houses meant less money for food, which in turn affected the families' health. His report was published in the *Proceedings of the Royal Society of Medicine*. Its timing was opportune as the popular press was also asking questions about income and nutrition. The British Medical Association (BMA) responded by establishing a committee to find out the minimum cost of a diet to preserve health and invited M'Gonigle to become a member. M'Gonigle was a leading light of this committee, which used the evidence he had collected in Stockton and which caused controversy by revising upwards the Ministry of Health's standards for calorie and protein requirements and, to the great annoyance of ministry officials, claimed that a family on unemployment benefit could not afford an adequate diet. The BMA's nutrition report, issued in November 1933 in pamphlet form, was used by Labour MPs and the Trade Union Congress in their attempts to improve the lot of the unemployed and also by campaigning groups such as Eleanor Rathbone's Children's Minimum Council and Frederick le Gros Clark's Committee Against Malnutrition.

M'Gonigle's book *Poverty and Public Health* (1936) was published by Gollancz and also issued as a Left Book Club edition. Expanding on his data on the results of rehousing and the effects of malnutrition, he reiterated his view that the poor were badly fed simply because they could not afford to buy the right kinds of food. The film *Enough to Eat?* (1936), in which M'Gonigle took part, emphasized this view, as did radio broadcasts by M'Gonigle and John Boyd Orr, the head of the Rowett Institute and an influential fellow campaigner on malnutrition. After M'Gonigle's death, food rationing during the Second World War aimed to give people a balanced diet, and mothers and infants were entitled to orange juice, cod liver oil, and milk, from the child welfare centres. In spite of the shortages health statistics showed a considerable improvement during the war: in 1944 infant mortality figures were the lowest on record.

M'Gonigle died from pneumonia at his home, 86 High Street, Norton, Stockton-on-Tees, on 30 July 1939, and it was unfortunate that he did not live to see the improvements for which he had fought. He was buried on the day after his death at St Mary's parish church, Norton. His wife survived him. In 1948, under the Labour government, a film was requested by the Foreign Office to show abroad the work of a medical officer of health. The film, called *One Man's Story*, used M'Gonigle's career in Stockton to portray the ideal medical officer. Ironically, whereas the implications of his work had been consistently resisted by government during the 1930s, he had now become idealized in official propaganda.   SUSAN MCLAURIN

Sources *BMJ* (2 Aug 1939), 371 · S. McLaurin, *The housewives' champion* (1997) · S. McLaurin, 'Unemployment and health: the work of Dr G. C. M. M'Gonigle, 1924–1939', MA diss., University of Teesside, 1996 · ministry of health files, PRO, MH 56 · b. cert. · d. cert. · *Medical Directory* (1930) · Crockford (1939) · private information (2004) · F. le G. Clark, 'Medicine is no cure when it's food that's lacking', *Daily Worker* (10 Nov 1936) · C. Webster, 'Health, welfare, and unemployment during the depression', *Past and Present*, 109 (1985), 204–30 · C. Webster, 'Healthy or hungry thirties?', *History Workshop Journal*, 13 (1982), 110–29 · D. F. Smith, 'The social construction of dietary standards: the British Medical Association–Ministry of Health advisory committee on nutrition report of 1934', *Eating agendas: food and nutrition as social problems*, ed. D. Maurer and J. Sobal (1995), 279–304
Archives Cleveland Archives, Middlesbrough, medical reports and MSS · Wellcome L., papers | FILM BFI, *Enough to eat?* (1936)
Likenesses photograph, repro. in Clark, 'Medicine is no cure'
Wealth at death £1935 14s. 6d.: probate, 29 Sept 1939, *CGPLA Eng. & Wales*

McGovern, John (1887–1968), politician and moral re-armament campaigner, was born in Coatbridge, Lanarkshire, on 13 December 1887, one of six children of Thomas McGovern, steel smelter, and his wife, Agnes McInally, a textile mill worker. In 1895 the family moved to Shettleston, a mining community that was later incorporated into Glasgow. McGovern attended St Paul's (*c.*1895–1900) and St Mary's (*c.*1900–1901) schools in Shettleston, leaving school at the age of thirteen to serve an apprenticeship as a plumber and gasfitter. In 1908 he set up in business of his own and on 21 June 1910 married Mary Fenton (*d.* 1963), the couple having met through mutual enthusiasm for the church choir. Both were Roman Catholics, and McGovern gained his political grounding via the Catholic Socialist Society, founded by John Wheatley, a prominent figure in the Independent Labour Party (ILP). However, from around 1913 he lapsed from the faith, resenting the denunciation by local clergy of his socialism. Although he became reconciled with the church, his early stance was indicative of his outspoken individualism, a trait that characterized his controversial political career.

After the First World War McGovern became disenchanted with Labour orthodoxy and joined the circle surrounding Guy Aldred and his idiosyncratic brand of libertarian communism. The connection did not last, and in 1925, following a brief sojourn in Australia, he renewed his ILP commitment. His dominating personality and campaigning zeal meant that he rose swiftly to public prominence, first as a parish councillor and then as a Glasgow town councillor. In 1930 he fended off a strong Conservative challenge to win the Shettleston parliamentary by-election, called after the death of Wheatley, who had served as MP since 1922. The campaign showed that McGovern could cause hackles to rise on the left as well as the

John McGovern (1887–1968), by Lafayette, 1931

right. The communists had put up their own candidate, whose bitter personal attacks on McGovern fuelled his implacable, lifelong hostility towards the party. The constituency Labour Party then expelled him, following accusations of irregularities in the nomination process for the by-election. This meant that McGovern sat as an independent MP, although he retained ILP membership.

Reflecting remarkable political resilience, McGovern held on to Shettleston in the 1931 general election, topping the poll again in 1935 and 1945 despite official Labour Party opposition. His breach with Labour in 1930 was indicative of mounting ILP disillusion over the direction of socialism within the wider party. The climax came in 1932 when James Maxton led the disaffiliation of the ILP from the Labour Party over attempts to restrain dissension in the Parliamentary Labour Party. Thereafter, a close-knit group of Glasgow MPs, including Maxton and McGovern, ardently portrayed themselves as the uncorrupted soul of socialism at Westminster.

McGovern was suspended from the Commons on several occasions for taking a forthright stance on matters he perceived as points of principle. One episode that brought nationwide publicity occurred in July 1931, when he refused to withdraw a question to the Scottish secretary about restrictions on the right of free speech in Glasgow. He was forcibly ejected from the Commons after what the *Glasgow Herald* (3 July 1931) described as 'a fierce scuffle'. During the 1930s McGovern also became prominently associated with the National Unemployed Workers' Movement, much to the dismay of its communist leadership.

McGovern's anti-communist onslaught continued during the Spanish Civil War, and in 1937 he wrote a scathing indictment of atrocities committed against the libertarian left, *Red Terror in Spain*. However, he also gained considerable press coverage in Glasgow for his sustained attacks on the Roman Catholic church and its anti-republican stance.

McGovern's passionate peace commitment during the Second World War added to his nonconformist image. However, his views were changing. Maxton's death was the catalyst for him to rejoin the Labour Party in 1947, convinced that the ILP had become too isolated. His pronouncements became more right wing, especially after his conversion in 1954 to the Moral Re-Armament Movement, which called for class collaboration to repulse encroaching communism. He showed especial hostility to Labour's Bevanite wing, which he believed was manipulating party policy in a pro-Soviet direction. He also firmly believed that the party had been infiltrated by Soviet agents. In November 1954 he defied a directive to abstain from a Commons vote on German re-armament, and was the only Labour MP to support the measure. He argued that he had been acting in strict accordance with Labour Party conference decisions, but he lost the parliamentary whip until March 1955.

Despite concern about his views, McGovern's position as MP was so deeply entrenched that little could be done to challenge him, and he did not stand down until 1959. He died at his home, 54 Clevedon Drive, Glasgow, on 14 February 1968, acknowledged as the last of the Clydeside 'rebels'; he was cremated at Daldowie crematorium, Uddingston, on 17 February. Whatever the contradictions of his politics (and McGovern latterly urged support for the Conservatives), he tenaciously adhered to his convictions. A combative figure who embraced controversy, he was one of Scotland's most enduring politicians.

IRENE MAVER

Sources *Glasgow Herald* (15 Feb 1968) · *The Times* (15 Feb 1968) · J. McGovern, *Neither fear nor favour* (1960) · W. Knox, 'McGovern, John', *Scottish labour leaders, 1918–39: a biographical dictionary*, ed. W. Knox (1984) · 'John McGovern—politician and rebel', *The Bailie* (11 April 1936) · *Scottish biographies* (1938) · *WWW, 1961–70* · T. Gallagher, *Glasgow the uneasy peace: religious tension in modern Scotland* (1987) · J. T. Caldwell, *Come dungeons dark: the life and times of Guy Aldred, Glasgow anarchist* (1988) · J. McNair, *James Maxton, the beloved rebel* (1955) · T. Driberg, *The mystery of Moral Re-Armament: a study of Frank Buchman and his movement* (1964) · H. McShane and J. Smith, *No mean fighter* (1978) · P. Norton, ed., *Dissension in the House of Commons: intra-party dissent in the House of Commons' division lobbies, 1945–1974* (1975) · A. McKinlay and R. J. Morris, eds., *The ILP on Clydeside, 1893–1932* (1991)
Archives SOUND IWM FVA, oral history interview
Likenesses Lafayette, photograph, 1931, NPG [*see illus.*] · drawing, repro. in 'John McGovern' · photographs, repro. in McGovern, *Neither fear nor favour* · portrait, repro. in *MRA Pictorial* (1960)

McGowan, Harry Duncan, first Baron McGowan (1874–1961), chemical industrialist, was born in Glasgow on 3 June 1874, the only son and second of three children of Harry McGowan, brass fitter, and his wife, Agnes, daughter of Richard Wilson. He went to Hutchesontown School and then, on a bursary, to Allan Glen's School, both in Glasgow, and at fifteen joined Nobel's Explosives Company, Glasgow and Ardeer, as an office boy. Without capital, influential connections, or technical training of any kind, McGowan made his way as a professional manager in the firm which was the largest subsidiary of the Anglo-German Nobel–Dynamite Trust Company. It dominated the explosives trade of the British empire, secured to it by agreements between the trust and other makers in Europe and America in return for undertakings not to compete in their 'exclusive territories'. As assistant to Thomas Johnston, Nobel's powerful, ingenious, and not overscrupulous general manager, McGowan was early introduced to elaborate industrial diplomacy on a worldwide scale. In 1903 he married Jean Boyle (d. 1952), daughter of William Young, of Paisley. They had two sons and two daughters.

In Canada, between 1909 and 1911, McGowan played a large part in constructing Canadian Explosives Limited (1910), later Canadian Industries Limited (CIL), a merger of explosives firms jointly owned by Nobel's, who had control, and Du Pont, the largest American explosives business. (CIL became much the largest chemical business in Canada. The Du Pont alliance, greatly enlarged and elaborated, became at length the centrepiece of ICI's foreign policy until, in the late forties, the American authorities broke it up with the anti-trust suit *US v. ICI*.) McGowan was deeply impressed by the Du Pont business and by Pierre S. Du Pont and others of the family. Where they led, in later years, he would often follow.

The Nobel–Dynamite Trust was destroyed by the outbreak of war in 1914, leaving Nobel's Explosives much greater freedom of action, which McGowan used to carry through a merger of almost the entire British explosives industry. At much the same time he was closely concerned with moves, backed by the government, to bring about a similarly comprehensive merger of British dyestuffs businesses. In 1918 he became chairman and managing director of Explosives Trades Limited, renamed in 1920 Nobel Industries Limited and was rewarded with a KBE. In 1919 he joined the board, on its formation, of British Dyestuffs Corporation. No one had ever held so great a position in the British chemical industry.

McGowan's aim in forming Nobel Industries was to move resources out of explosives, for which, rightly, he foresaw no very bright peacetime future, into other activities, especially the motor industry and its associated trades. Influenced by Du Pont, he directed £3 million in 1920 into General Motors, alongside Du Pont's much larger investment, and considerable sums went also into Dunlop, Lucas, and other British firms servicing the motor trade. Until the crash of 1929 the General Motors investment was very successful and judicious sales provided capital for ICI's expansion in the late twenties.

Nobel Industries Limited provided the model for McGowan's largest conception: Imperial Chemical Industries Limited. The formation in Germany, in the autumn of 1925, of IG Farbenindustrie threatened to overwhelm the British chemical industry by sheer weight of concentrated industrial power, and McGowan, prodded by Reginald McKenna, proposed a defensive merger between the four largest British chemical businesses: Nobel Industries; Brunner, Mond; United Alkali Company; and British Dyestuffs Corporation. Sir Alfred Mond (later Lord Melchett) originally had plans for a different merger for his firm, including the IG and an American firm, Allied Chemical and Dye, but his scheme broke down on the refusal of the latter to come in. In New York in September 1926 Mond and McGowan agreed upon the merger which brought ICI into existence.

On 31 December 1930, after the death of Melchett, McGowan became chairman and sole managing director of ICI. It was a daunting moment. ICI was staggering under the impact of the slump on over-optimistic expansion, and by 1935 about 10 per cent of the capital of the business had been lost. McGowan's strategy for recovery depended heavily on a worldwide network of trading agreements with almost every producer of any importance at home or abroad, including Du Pont, IG, and producers of alkali in western Europe, the United States, and the USSR. Elaborate cartels regulated output, prices, selling areas, and exchange of technical knowledge in fertilizers, dyestuffs, alkali, the products of hydrogenation, and indeed nearly every article of any importance in any branch of the chemical industry. Early in 1937 he was created a baron, taking the title Baron McGowan of Ardeer.

McGowan was a dictator and his dictatorship antagonized his board. In 1937 they rebelled, taking the opportunity offered by the failure of McGowan's personal speculations, carried out on credit from brokers which at one time reached £1.9 million. In the winter of 1937 McGowan's career was apparently in ruin. He had been rescued from bankruptcy, but Sir William McLintock had advised the board that they could no longer have confidence in him, and they had chosen his successor, the second Lord Melchett. On Christmas day Melchett had a heart attack, putting him out of action for a year. The board's nerve broke, and they recoiled from dismissing McGowan. He remained chairman until 31 December 1950. He had outfaced adversity and won.

As a businessman, McGowan was not of the stature of Sir Charles Tennant, who had been one of the founders of Nobel's Explosives, of Lord Leverhulme, or even, perhaps, of his colleague, Alfred Mond. He lacked their creative flair. What he had was force, vitality, and courage, and his great appetite for power was balanced by his ability to use it and a total acceptance of responsibility. He told the second Lord Melchett that he did not accept 'the theory … that competition is essential to efficiency'. Instead, he relied on the cartel system which was characteristic of the chemical industry for many years, and he defended it in the House of Lords as 'a medium for the orderly expansion of world trade'. For success, ICI had to be strong enough to enforce the respect of foreign competitors. McGowan and Mond repeatedly said that the object of founding ICI— 'Imperial in aspect and Imperial in name'—was to make the British chemical industry strong enough in its 'natural markets'—Great Britain and the British empire—to develop the export trade and to build healthy and varied manufacturing enterprises in the United Kingdom, Canada, South Africa, Australasia, and other countries as they became capable of supporting them.

In the circumstances of the thirties, with productive capacity throughout the world running far ahead of effective demand, no such policy would have been possible without the protection of cartels, behind which the main centres of ICI's strength, in the United Kingdom, could be reorganized and modernized. McGowan's most important service to the nation was to see what needed doing in the chemical industry and to do it, which above all required will-power, his essential quality.

Florid of countenance, sanguine in expression, and fond of good living, McGowan could be brutal and was often coarse. His relations with his family were stormy and his judgement, especially in his own affairs, was sometimes faulty. But when everything has been said against him, and plenty can be said, one fact remains: he rescued the British chemical industry from the threat of extinction in the twenties, and in the thirties set it on the way to the technological revolution of the fifties and sixties. In a period chiefly remarkable for the failure of British will and nerve, McGowan's nerve never broke and his will prevailed.

McGowan died at St Mary's Hospital, Paddington, London on 13 July 1961. His elder son, Harry Wilson (1906–1966), succeeded to the title. W. J. READER, rev.

Sources W. J. Reader, *Imperial Chemical Industries, a history*, 1 (1970) · private information (1981) · d. cert.

Archives BL OIOC, letters to Lord Reading, MSS Eur. E 238, F 118 · BLPES, corresp. with Hugh Dalton · Bodl. Oxf., Monkton MSS · HLRO, corresp. with Lord Beaverbrook · Nuffield Oxf., corresp. with Lord Cherwell | FILM BFI NFTVA, documentary footage

Likenesses W. Orpen, oils, 1928, ICI House, London · W. Stoneman, two photographs, 1931–53, NPG · H. Caster, photographs, NPG · H. Knight, oils, priv. coll.

Wealth at death £207,452 14s. 5d.: probate, 4 Sept 1961, *CGPLA Eng. & Wales*

Macgowan, John (1726–1780), Particular Baptist minister, was born in Edinburgh. After receiving a good education he was apprenticed to a weaver, but subsequently settled in Bridge Street, Warrington, as a baker. He had early become a local preacher with the Wesleyans, but, impressed by the logic of the Calvinistic system of theology, he was attracted to the Independents. He finally joined the Particular Baptists and ministered at the Baptist chapel at Hill Cliff, near Warrington, from about 1751 to 1757. His energetic prosecution of his duties commended him to the church at Bridgnorth, where he served until 1766, in which year he was elected moderator of the Midland Association.

In September 1766 Macgowan accepted an invitation to preach at the Old Meeting-House in Devonshire Square, Bishopsgate, London, opened by William Kiffin in 1687, though he was not ordained to the pastorate until the following July (1767), when John Gill, Samuel Stennett, and Benjamin Wallin all took part. Here he remained until his premature death. His preaching, despite its high Calvinist emphases, was popular, described by Joseph Ivimey as 'faithful, judicious and affectionate' (Ivimey, 4.318). Walter Wilson testifies that Macgowan experienced great conflicts in the discharge of his ministerial duties because of an over-active consciousness of guilt which sometimes threatened to overwhelm him with shame when he appeared in public. Notwithstanding this he was frequently called upon to preach at ordination services. In April 1779 he conducted the opening worship in the house of Mrs Mary Hills of King's Row, Walworth, which had been registered for 'religious worship by a congregation of Protestants dissenting from the Church of England who scruple the Baptizing of Infants, commonly called Baptists' (Philcox, 362).

Macgowan was probably more effective with his pen than in the pulpit, certainly if the number of titles authored and the frequency of their reprinting be any criteria. He had a considerable following in America as well as in Britain, and his works were translated into Welsh and Gaelic. His publications, some of them published under the pseudonym the Shaver or Pasquin Shaveblock, included most significantly *The Arians and Socinians Monitor* (1761), *Priestcraft Defended* (1768), and *Dialogues of Devils* (1772). His style could be ironic and caustic, even menacing and censorious, effecting a dogmatism, that not all shared, in passing sentence on the doctrinal deviance of others beyond the scope of that allocated to humankind, who must always be ignorant of belated reformation and repentance. In his devotional writings he was criticized for being too fanciful, finding allegories 'where Paul would not' (Ivimey, 4.321).

In failing health, Macgowan administered the sacrament at Devonshire Square for the last time on 12 November 1780, and died, presumably in London, on 25 November. He was buried in Bunhill Fields, and was survived by a widow and several children.

CHARLOTTE FELL-SMITH, *rev.* J. H. Y. BRIGGS

Sources B. Wallin, *A brand pluckt from the fire* (1780) [funeral discourse] · W. Wilson, *The history and antiquities of the dissenting churches and meeting houses in London, Westminster and Southwark*, 4 vols. (1808–14), vol. 1 · J. Ivimey, *A history of the Baptists*, 4 vols. (1811–30), vol. 4 · H. N. Philcox, 'Early days at East Street, Walworth', *Baptist Quarterly*, 9 (1938–9), 362–7
Likenesses R. Houston, mezzotint, pubd 1774 (after J. Russell), BM, NPG

Macgradoigh, Augustin. *See* Magraidhin, Aughuistín (*c.*1349–1405).

McGrath, Patrick Gerard (1916–1994), forensic psychiatrist, was born in Glasgow on 10 June 1916, the only son of Patrick McGrath (1873–1960), headmaster, and his wife, Mary, *née* Murray (1874–1925), schoolteacher. He had two sisters, Sarah and Molly. His family were of Irish Catholic immigrant stock. His father, the headmaster of 'a large school in a Glasgow slum inhabited almost entirely by Irish labourers', was 'exposed to discrimination little short of persecution and was paid one tenth of the salary of [the headmaster of] a small Protestant school in the same area' (McGrath). McGrath senior was a man of great learning who carried an edition of Ovid in his pocket into

which he could dip whenever an opportunity presented. Despite the most stringent financial circumstances he saw to it that his three children were given the best available education. McGrath himself attended St Aloysius's College, a Jesuit school in Glasgow, before entering Glasgow University in 1933 to read medicine. He qualified in September 1939, coinciding almost exactly with the start of the Second World War.

McGrath volunteered immediately and was commissioned in the Royal Army Medical Corps airborne division, a small, prestigious, cloak-and-dagger unit. In 1941 he was posted to Gibraltar, where, in undisclosed circumstances, he literally fell off the Rock, sustaining injuries of such gravity that his immediate return to the UK for treatment was considered essential. He recovered satisfactorily, and when he reached the convalescent stage 'the authorities were kind enough to ask me where I wanted to work till I was fit for overseas again' (McGrath). By then he had witnessed at first hand the psychological devastation of war in both combatants and civilians, and it was this painful awareness that prompted his interest in psychiatry. He therefore unhesitatingly seized the opportunity to work at the Crichton Royal in Dumfries, a mental hospital taken over for the duration of the war for the treatment of psychiatric casualties. There he had the good fortune to work with the *crème de la crème* of British psychiatry, such as Willi Mayer-Gross, Isaiah Berliner, Dennis Carrol, and Erwin Stengel—for the latter of whom he acquired a particular respect and affection. Once fit McGrath returned to active service and to a life of incredible adventure which might have provided storylines for a library of war epics. *Inter alia* he travelled the golden road to Samarkand from one end to the other, pausing at different times to carry out operations in perilous conditions in Burma, China, and India. He ended the war with the honorary rank of lieutenant-colonel.

After demobilization McGrath took up psychiatry as his life's work, and worked at Gartnavel Hospital in Glasgow for a time before heading south to England. There he was appointed first to the staff at Peckham House, a private mental hospital in north London, and then to the staff at the Royal Eastern Counties Hospital in Colchester, Essex. He then returned briefly to Scotland as deputy medical superintendent at Glengall Hospital outside Ayr. He gained a diploma of psychological medicine from the University of Edinburgh in 1955. Meanwhile, on 25 January 1949 he had married Helen Patricia O'Brien (*b.* 1926), whom he had met at a wedding in Glasgow in 1947. They had three sons and a daughter.

In 1956, by serendipity he later claimed, McGrath joined Broadmoor as deputy to the physician superintendent, Stanley James. Soon afterwards James became ill, and in 1957 McGrath took over his position, to serve with great distinction until he retired in 1981. Modern Broadmoor as it became was undoubtedly the creation of McGrath himself. He had inherited a hospital which was, in effect, a Victorian slum, overcrowded and understaffed both in terms of nursing and, in particular, medical personnel: McGrath was the one and only qualified psychiatrist, although one psychotherapist attended on Saturday morning. There was no social worker and no psychologist. The sole pre-occupation of the staff at all levels was with custody; therapy was almost a dirty word. McGrath tackled his awesome job with the fiery integrity that had characterized his attitude to previous obstacles in his life. Aided by the opportunities offered by the revolutionary Mental Health Act of 1959, additional consultant psychiatrists were added, together with a number of junior trainees. Social workers were appointed, a psychology department was created, and a nursing school came into being which, as with all the ancillary innovations, began to flourish. As a result of these much needed innovations, the patient population began to drop. The metamorphosis Broadmoor underwent was necessarily slow, at times painfully so, but in twenty-five years of devoted and inspired service to the hospital McGrath succeeded in converting a forbidding institution into a caring, efficient psychiatric hospital. He succeeded in his herculean task not by adopting the stance of a dictator, however benevolent, but by exercising his own particular brand of paternalism: as a father he could most certainly be benevolent, but when occasion demanded he could be mightily stern. And no matter what, he was always the boss, the head of the table.

McGrath once said, with his characteristic wit, that he could discharge a quarter of Broadmoor's patients without danger to the public; but the only snag was that no one could tell him which was the safe quarter. And there was the rub: assessing dangerousness is the besetting dilemma of any forensic psychiatrist. Inevitably, particularly since the inception of a more liberal discharge policy at Broadmoor, errors of judgement were made—as for example in the notorious cases of Graham Young, the mass poisoner, and Ronald Sailes, the serial murderer: both were released to kill again. The outcry from the media was understandably deafening: McGrath's neck was on the block, although technically he was not personally responsible. Nevertheless, he supported his fellow consultants to the hilt and helped to field the flak until such time as the sound and fury subsided.

By virtue of his day-to-day clinical work at Broadmoor, McGrath was very soon accepted as an expert in forensic psychiatry. So he was an obvious choice to join the relevant subcommittee of the forensic section of the Royal Medico-Psychological Association, the precursor of the Royal College of Psychiatrists. The subcommittee was later promoted to the status of a section, which McGrath served as chairman from 1973 to 1975. He was then vice-president of the Royal College of Psychiatrists from 1978 to 1980. Further evidence of the high regard in which he was held was seen in his appointment as a member of the Parole Board, on which he served from 1982 to 1985, in company with his sister, Sarah McCabe, a distinguished criminologist. In 1960 he was awarded a Cropwood fellowship in the Institute of Criminology at Cambridge University, on whose advisory council he later served. He was appointed CBE in 1971 and CB when he retired in 1981. A newly constituted library was named after him at Broadmoor, the opening ceremony of which he attended not long before his death. He was not, unfortunately, a prolific writer: he summarized his œuvre as 'the very occasional paper and a half-a-dozen letters in The Times' (McGrath).

In 1992, McGrath was diagnosed as suffering from cancer of the stomach. This was later followed by a seemingly unrelated cancer of the throat. Surgical intervention failed to arrest the malignant conditions and slowly and inexorably, like the old soldier of legend, he faded away. He died at his home, 18 Heathermount Drive, Edgecombe Park, Crowthorne, Berkshire, on 18 October 1994; his funeral service was held at the church of the Holy Ghost, Crowthorne, on 24 October. He was survived by his wife, daughter, and three sons, the eldest of whom, also Patrick, was a novelist who drew upon his father's and his own experiences at Broadmoor to write a series of novels and short stories exploring madness in its various forms.

HENRY R. ROLLIN

Sources   *The Times* (28 Oct 1994) · *Daily Telegraph* (10 Nov 1994) · *The Independent* (16 Nov 1994) · *WWW*, 1991–5 · *Medical Directory* · P. McGrath, autobiographical notes, priv. coll. · personal knowledge (2004) · private information (2004)
Likenesses   photograph, repro. in *The Times*

McGrath, Sir Patrick Thomas (1868–1929), politician in Newfoundland and journalist, was born in St John's, Newfoundland, on 16 December 1868, the eldest son of William McGrath and his wife, Mary Birmingham. He attended Christian Brothers schools in the city until the age of fourteen, when he was apprenticed to the pharmacists McMurdo & Co. Ill health led him to seek outdoor employment and in 1891 he began work as a reporter for the *Evening Herald*. In 1894 he became Newfoundland correspondent for the London *Times* and he subsequently wrote for other newspapers and magazines in Britain, Canada, and the United States.

The path to a successful career in Newfoundland journalism, however, lay in being a spokesman for local politicians and in this field McGrath proved himself most adept. In 1893 he served as interim editor of the *Herald* during the general election, when the paper supported the tory opposition. The following year he took over the editorship and played a prominent role in helping the Conservative leader James Winter defeat the Liberal premier William Whiteway in the 1897 general election. In 1900 he supported the election of the Liberal leader Robert Bond as premier. From 1897 to 1900 he was assistant clerk in the Newfoundland house of assembly and was chief clerk from 1901 to 1911.

In 1907, when Edward Morris, St John's West member of the house of assembly, split with Bond, McGrath resigned from the *Herald* in order to start the *Evening Chronicle* in support of Morris and the newly formed People's Party. In the 1908 general election, which resulted in a tie, he did yeoman service as chief propagandist for Morris and again provided advice and editorial support when Morris won a clear victory in 1909. In 1912 Morris appointed McGrath to the legislative council, where he proved an able debater of public issues. He was president of the legislative council from 1915 to 1919 and from 1925 until his death.

In addition to the many pamphlets on Newfoundland, McGrath wrote *Newfoundland in 1911* (1911), a history and guidebook. He also contributed chapters on Newfoundland to the volume on *British America* (1923) in the Nations of To-day series edited by John Buchan, and to the second volume of Sir Charles Lucas's *The Empire at War* (1923).

During the First World War McGrath served as honorary secretary of the Newfoundland Patriotic Fund and finance secretary of the Newfoundland regiment. He helped to organize the war pensions board and was its first chairman; he also served as chairman of a government commission which investigated the high cost of living conditions. Despite being created a KBE in 1918 he felt that his public services were unappreciated in his native Newfoundland.

After resigning from newspaper life in 1920 McGrath extensively researched Newfoundland's case in the legal dispute with Canada over the location of the boundary between Quebec and Labrador. His historical researches used British, Canadian, and American archives, and he played a key role in forming the legal case of 1926–7 which resulted in the dispute being settled in Newfoundland's favour by the privy council. Although a supporter of political union with Canada, he was—as his work on the boundary dispute illustrated—a staunch defender of Newfoundland's rights, and an avid booster of its industrial development. He generally kept private his views on Canadian federation.

Despite having little formal education McGrath was both a reader and thinker, a man of infinite humour, full of good stories, and to the last had a touch of the Irish gamin. More than once his shrewd and biting tongue and pen helped to win an election, but neither in victory nor in defeat did he bear malice. He died, unmarried, at St John's, Newfoundland, on 14 June 1929.

W. L. GRANT, rev. MELVIN BAKER

Sources *The Times* (15 June 1929) · *New York Times* (15 June 1929) · *WWW* · private information (1937) · M. Baker, 'Patrick Thomas McGrath', *Newfoundland Quarterly*, 88/4 (1992–3), 37–8 · 'Articles by Sir Patrick Thomas McGrath', ed. M. Baker, typescript, 1993, Memorial University of Newfoundland, Smallwood Foundation for Newfoundland and Labrador Studies · M. Baker, ed., 'Sir Patrick Thomas McGrath: a brief bibliography of his writing', typescript, 1974, Memorial University of Newfoundland, Smallwood Foundation for Newfoundland and Labrador Studies · B. J. Pippy, 'Sir Patrick McGrath: a biographical essay', hons. diss., Memorial University of Newfoundland, 1992
Archives Memorial University, Newfoundland, Smallwood Foundation for Newfoundland and Labrador Studies | BL, corresp. with Lord Northcliffe, Add. MS 62166

MacGregor family (*per.* 1450–1604), highland chiefs, appear to have been descended from, or at least related to, a minor house of the early medieval lordship of Glenorchy. According to the earliest evidence, that of an early-fifteenth-century praise poem, the progenitor of the kindred was Donnchadh Beag, about 1300, from whose time the MacGregors possessed the lands of Glen Strae, which extended eastwards through the fertile Strath of Glenorchy and which gave them a base in the south-west highlands. There, at Sronmilchan, was the primary residence of the chief; there also lay the MacGregors' burial-ground of Diseart Chonnain, *anglice* Dalmally. The lordship of Glen Strae evidently formed part of the larger lordship of Lorne, whose overlords, the MacDougalls, were ruined by the wars of independence. This may have allowed the MacGregors a period of independence under Griogair (*fl.* 1330), the eponym of the clan, and his immediate successors. But by the end of the fourteenth century they were coming increasingly under the influence of the Campbells of Loch Awe, and eventually they became a client kindred, through the ultimate controlling influence of the earls of Argyll, of the Campbells of Glenorchy. Indeed, the latters' principal fortress, Kilchurn Castle—held for them by the MacGregors of Brackley—is only 2 miles away from Sronmilchan. The resulting alliance lasted until the mid-sixteenth century, and proved crucial for the extraordinarily successful expansion of both kindreds eastwards into highland Perthshire.

Witness lists demonstrate that until the mid-fifteenth century the MacGregors were in effect a west-coast clan. But although this placed them within the sphere of influence of the MacDonald lords of the Isles, there is abundant documentary evidence from the mid-fifteenth century to show that their most important relationship was with their Campbell overlords. Pádraig MacGregor (*d.* 1461) received papal dispensation to marry Mariota Campbell in 1441, while his son Eòin Dubh MacGregor (*d.* 1519) married as one of his wives 'Ealasaid from Glen Lyon', doubtless from the same family. Campbell patronage probably gave the vicarage of Fortingall to the notable MacGregor family, whose members compiled the valuable collection of poetry and chronicles known as the Book of the Dean of Lismore.

The MacGregors remained in the service of the Campbells of Glenorchy until 1513, when they were apparently given by the earl of Argyll to Campbell of Cawdor, before reverting again to Glenorchy after 1550. The services they rendered were primarily military, the kindred

> being used as the plasma upon which both branches fed until they themselves had become politically viable … [B]etween 1437 and 1513 the expansion of the Campbells of Glen Orchy eastwards was carried out in tandem with the MacGregors, who often seem to have been operating in the van, paving the way for the spread of Campbell of Glen Orchy influence. (MacGregor, 80)

The prosperity of the Glenorchy Campbells began with the knighthood and lands of Lawers, Perthshire, given to Cailean or Colin Campbell as a reward for capturing the murderers of James I in 1437. The kindred thereupon embarked upon nearly a century of expansion to the east. Although documentary proof is lacking that the MacGregors were in their service, the correlation of their respective settlement patterns in Breadalbane and beyond makes it clear that the two kindreds worked in tandem. A general pattern suggests itself by which the

MacGregors would establish themselves as kindly tenants on the ground, by sword-right if necessary, after which, and probably because of which, the Campbells of Glenorchy were able to secure titles and offices to the land they occupied. However, although the Campbells used Glen Dochart as their major artery to the east, the MacGregors tended to migrate through Glen Lyon further to the north, an area easily accessible from Glenorchy itself, which subsequently became another focus for clan settlement and clan sentiment. By the early sixteenth century the ascendancy of the two kindreds stretched as far as the east end of Loch Tay. As befitted their new prestigious status, the MacGregors began to derive their chiefly line from Kenneth MacAlpine, king of Scots in the mid-ninth century.

From 1513, when both Archibald Campbell, second earl of Argyll, and Duncan or Donnachadh Campbell of Glenorchy died at Flodden, the lordship of the latter kindred appears to have entered a fallow period. MacGregor power continued to grow, however, under **Eòin MacGregor** (*d.* 1528), the second cousin (albeit not necessarily the closest heir), who succeeded Eòin Dubh, possibly because he was favoured by the Campbells of Argyll as a result of his marriage to Eilidh, a daughter of Sir Cailean (Colin) Campbell of Glenorchy. The next chief, **Alasdair MacGregor** (*d.* 1548/9?), was only a child when he succeeded. The influence of his tutor, apparently the somewhat vicious **Donnchadh Làdasach** [Lordly] **MacGregor** (*d.* 1552), may be apparent in the increasingly violent methods the kindred used to take advantage of the breakdown of Menzies control over Rannoch and install themselves in that area.

It seems that between 1513 and 1550 the services of the kindred were transferred from the Glenorchy Campbells to the Cawdor line. In the latter year, however, the sixth chief of Glenorchy, Cailean Liath *Campbell (1499–1583) [*see under* Campbell family of Glenorchy], came to power. His accession late in life saw the commencing of a phase of quite extraordinary expansion, as well as dramatic changes in the policy of his lineage towards the MacGregors. Ruthless, assertive, ambitious, acquisitive, and opportunistic, Cailean Liath demanded absolute obedience, through bonds of manrent, calps, and other exactions, from the smaller kindreds about him, above all from the MacGregors, who he thought had grown too powerful. He and his son Duncan, or Donnchadh Dubh, showed themselves utterly intolerant of opposition. If legal methods failed, they did not hesitate to turn to pitiless violence.

Probably in summer 1550 Eòin Ruadh MacGregor, the new chief, son of Alasdair and his wife, a daughter of Campbell of Ardkinglas, died while still a child, owing to a mysterious arrowshot. He was succeeded by his younger brother **Griogair Ruadh** [Gregor Roy] **MacGregor** (*d.* 1570). The leadership of the kindred devolved on the violent and unruly Donnchadh Làdasach, who embarked on a brutal campaign against the Campbells. This vendetta was brought to an end with his judicial execution, along with that of his two sons, by Cailean Liath on 16 June 1552. This event led to renewed instability in the region as,

in the absence of any recognized adult leader of the kindred, Glenorchy attempted to win MacGregor loyalties. Two years later the fourth earl of Argyll gave him the ward and marriage of Griogair Ruadh. A period of relative peace ensued, during which Cailean Liath dramatically expanded his lordship to the south, a move which brought yet more MacGregor families under his hegemony. This period of peace was shattered, however, on 21 May 1562 when a band of MacGregors slew Alasdair mac Eòghain Duibh, himself a Rannoch MacGregor and a servant of Cailean Liath. Later that year Griogair Ruadh attained his majority, but Cailean Liath would infeft him in the ancestral MacGregor lands of Glen Strae only if the young chief accepted unspecified legal restrictions on his chiefship, handed over the murderers, and did homage to Glenorchy. 'The stark choice facing Griogair Ruadh was submission or defiance, and it would have to be made before 1 January' (MacGregor, 313).

The young chief chose defiance and on 7 December 1562 launched a brutal onslaught against various Campbell kindreds. For nearly eight years a bitter feud ensued, devastating much of western Perthshire. The MacGregors, acting as mobile guerrillas, were declared rebels; Cailean Liath was given full legal powers to capture and punish them. Many of the surrounding districts were caught up in the resulting violence. Despite this, perhaps even as a result of Cailean Liath's intransigence, sympathy and support for the MacGregors were widespread. In the summer of 1565 there was a brief *rapprochement* brokered by the fifth earl of Argyll as a result of Campbell involvement in the chaseabout raid, the rising against Mary, queen of Scots, during which, rather extraordinarily, Griogair Ruadh appears to have married Marion or Mór Campbell of Glen Lyon. Following Mary's downfall in 1567, however, relations between the MacGregors and Campbells once more turned sour. On the morning of 1 August 1569 Griogair Ruadh was captured, apparently by treachery. The following year, on 7 April, he was beheaded, an event commemorated in Marion Campbell's great lullaby-lament *Griogal cridhe*. The axe was wielded by Cailean Liath himself. At the end of June Cailean granted the MacGregor lands of Glen Strae not, as he had promised, to Marion Campbell and Alasdair [*see below*], the child of her marriage to Griogair Ruadh, but to his own eldest son, Donnachadh Dubh. A series of revenge attacks by MacGregors against Cailean Liath and Donnachadh Ruadh of Glen Lyon followed, possibly with the covert assistance of the earls of Argyll and Lennox. A final settlement was reached towards the beginning of winter, brokered by Griogair Ruadh's brother Eòghan. The latter was to be given the ward and non-entry of Glen Strae as tutor to his two nephews during their minority, on condition that he and his kindred gave homage to Cailean Liath.

This new relationship between the MacGregors and the Campbells of Glenorchy was by no means stable. Cailean Liath and his son steadfastly refused to infeft the MacGregor chiefs in Glen Strae, and the final two decades of the sixteenth century, especially following the death of Cailean Liath in 1583, were marked by cattle raids and increasingly widespread and vicious feuding. This cycle of violence culminated in the murder of Eòin Drummond of Drummond-Ernoch, the king's forester in Glenartney, in 1589, while he was hunting for venison for the wedding of James VI and Anne of Denmark. The hard-line policy of the crown which resulted further increased the pressure on the kindred: an act of parliament of 1594 placed the MacGregors at the head of the list of lawless clans. **Alasdair MacGregor** (d. 1604), the young chief, found himself in a quandary simultaneously trying to keep on the right side of the authorities while attempting to rein in members of an ever-fragmenting clan, not least his own brother Iain Dubh. Magnates on the highland border began to employ renegade MacGregors in feuds with their neighbours. Ironically, the Campbells of Glenorchy were thus still able to take advantage of MacGregor aggression, this time by making bonds of protection with the heads of clans on whose land the unruly kindred lived.

An incipient feud with the Colquhouns of Luss was the MacGregors' undoing. On 7 February 1603 a parley at Glen Fruin—said to have taken place following the execution of two young MacGregors who had slaughtered and roasted Sir Humphrey Colquhoun's prize *mult dubh an earbaill ghil* ('black wedder with the white tail')—went disastrously wrong. The MacGregors won the resulting battle; but a number of spectators from Dumbarton who had been taken prisoner (including thirty-seven schoolboys, according to the traditional account) were subsequently killed. A national scandal ensued. On 3 April, two days before he left for England, James VI, by act of privy council, proscribed the name MacGregor: to use it would be a capital offence. Along with the rest of his clan, Alasdair of Glen Strae turned fugitive. He was eventually caught by a stratagem of the seventh earl of Argyll, and on 20 January 1604 he was executed at Edinburgh along with eleven of his principal clansmen. He was hanged his own height above the rest.

The harrying of the MacGregors and their resetters won the Campbells political and financial benefits. However, it also resulted in widespread and lasting social instability, especially on the periphery of the Gàidhealtachd, where the majority of the broken clan found sanctuary. In 1661 the name was restored, but proscription was reimposed in 1693, and not until 1774 were members of clan Gregor legally permitted to bear their surname once more. For posterity, the extraordinarily powerful songs which describe their predicament, songs which won them sympathy and support throughout the Gàidhealtachd, constitute the greatest legacy of the pursuit of the MacGregors.

DOMHNALL UILLEAM STIÙBHART

Sources M. MacGregor, 'A political history of the MacGregors before 1571', PhD diss., U. Edin., 1989 · J. E. A. Dawson, ed., *Campbell letters, 1559–1583*, Scottish History Society, 5th ser., 10 (1997) · W. R. Kermack, *The clan MacGregor* (1979) · A. A. Whittal Ramsay, *The arrow of Glenlyon* (1932) · A. I. Macinnes, *Clanship, commerce and the house of Stuart, 1603–1788* (1996), 61 · M. Newton, *Bho Chluaidh gu Calasraid: from the Clyde to Callander* (1999), 190–210 · J. E. A. Dawson, *The politics of religion in the age of Mary, queen of Scots: the earl of Argyll and the struggle for Britain and Ireland* (2002) · A. G. M. MacGregor, *History of the clan Gregor: from public records and private collections*, 2 vols. (1898–1901)

MacGregor, Alasdair (d. 1548/9?). *See under* Macgregor family (*per.* 1450–1604).

MacGregor, Alasdair (d. 1604). *See under* Macgregor family (*per.* 1450–1604).

MacGregor, Alexander (1806–1881), Church of Scotland minister and writer of Scottish Gaelic prose, was born on 26 May 1806 at the Mission House, Dalfuil, Glengairn, near Ballater, the eldest of the four children of the Revd Robert MacGregor (1767–1846) and his wife, Janet Menzies. Robert MacGregor was a collector of Gaelic poetry and a Gaelic poet. In addition to being a missionary on the Royal Bounty, he taught at a school during the week and it was there that Alexander received his early education before proceeding to King's College, Aberdeen, from which he graduated MA in 1827, having gained prizes in natural philosophy and mathematics. He then attended the Divinity Hall at the University of Edinburgh from 1831 to 1835. On concluding his studies he rejoined his parents who were now resident in the parish of Kilmuir, Skye, to which his father had answered a call in 1822. Remaining with the established church after the Disruption of 1843, he was ordained as assistant and successor to his father in 1844. On 18 December 1846 he married Catherine MacGregor (1822–1889); they had eight children, of whom six survived to adulthood. Their eldest grandson was Sir Alasdair Duncan Atholl MacGregor (1883–1945) whose posts included appointment as chief justice of the supreme court of Hong Kong in 1934. In 1850 Alexander MacGregor accepted a call to Edinburgh's Gaelic church and in 1853 he was translated to the West Church, Inverness, where he remained until he died in 1881. After his death one writer observed that:

> his large heart, his truly catholic spirit, his boundless charity knew not the mean, selfish, repulsive creed of those that would scarcely admit to Heaven any one but those who could see eye to eye with them in matters of ecclesiastical form and ceremony. (Mackenzie, 93)

MacGregor was one of the most prolific writers in Scottish Gaelic in the nineteenth century, contributing under the pen-names Alasdair Ruadh, Sgiathanach, and S. to most contemporary periodicals which published Gaelic. He has received little attention from scholars of Gaelic literature in the past, in part because Gaelic prose is under-researched as compared with poetry and song, but equally because his use of pen-names has tended to conceal the true extent and significance of his writing. Until the nineteenth century Gaelic prose was predominantly religious in nature and tended to be translated rather than original. MacGregor's writings, along with those of the Revd Dr Norman MacLeod (1783–1862), were crucial in establishing a register for non-religious writing, and broke new ground by experimenting with new genres, most notably the prose dialogue. His Gaelic writings appeared mainly in *Cuairtear nan Gleann* (1840–43), *Fear-*

Tathaich nam Beann (1848–50), *An Gaidheal* (1871–7), and *Highlander* (1873–81).

One of MacGregor's aims was to provide useful information and morally uplifting literature for Gaels in their native language. Thus his writings cover a breadth of subjects, ranging from essays which describe North America for intending emigrants, support the abolition of slavery, explain astronomy and coral, discuss education in the highlands, and argue the need for both Gaelic and English to be used in highland schools, to moral tales which promote self-help, temperance, and thrift. His prose dialogues, of which he wrote no fewer than sixty-four, draw on similar topics to his essays, but attempt to make information accessible to readers by using more colloquial language and by using characters to lend authority to the information being conveyed. MacGregor's partiality for this genre indicates a consciousness of his audience's requirements, as he used the dialogue to facilitate the transition between an essentially oral culture and the printed word. He also wrote prose in English relating to the highlands and he undertook a number of translations from English to Gaelic. He translated texts of guidance for fishermen and mariners into Gaelic, but most notable was his translation into Gaelic of the Apocrypha, undertaken at the request of Prince Louis Lucien Bonaparte and published in 1860. MacGregor had a great interest in highland folklore and history and was described by a contemporary as 'our best Gaelic scholar, and the first authority upon all questions connected with the history, antiquities, traditions, language and literature of his countrymen' (Mackenzie, 95). In common with a number of contemporaries, such as Sheriff Alexander Nicolson, he collected Gaelic proverbs. However, instead of presenting them in the usual form of a list, he embedded them in his dialogues so as to display them in a manner more reflective of their everyday use. He wrote over thirty essays in English on highland destitution, Gaelic literature, and highland history. His contribution on the parish of Kilmuir to the *New Statistical Account of Scotland* runs to some fifty pages and contains a wealth of information. His collected essays on Flora Macdonald were published in one volume, *The Life of Flora Macdonald and her Adventures with Prince Charlie* (1882), as were some of his writings on highland folklore in *Highland Superstitions* (1891) and a lecture on highland history in *The Feuds of the Clans* (1907). He was instrumental in setting up the *Celtic Magazine* in 1876 along with Alexander MacKenzie, who was to be its editor.

MacGregor died on 19 October 1881 at his home, 4 Victoria Terrace, Inverness, and was buried five days later in the chapelyard, Inverness. An elegy to him was composed by the renowned Gaelic poet Mary MacPherson (1821–1898), 'Marbhrann don Urramach Alasdair MacGriogair' ('Elegy to the Reverend Alexander MacGregor') (Meek, 140).   SHEILA M. KIDD

Sources A. M[ackenzie], 'The Rev. Alexander MacGregor, M.A.', *Celtic Magazine*, 74 (1881), 92–9 · *Biographies of highland clergymen* (1889) · *Fasti Scot.*, new edn, 6. 463 · *Fasti Scot.*, new edn, 7. 172 · D. E. Meek, *Màiri Mhòr nan Òran*, Scottish Gaelic Texts Society, 2 (1998) · S. M. Kidd, 'The Rev. Alexander MacGregor: the writer behind the pen-names', *Transactions of the Gaelic Society of Inverness*, 61 [forthcoming]
Likenesses photograph, repro. in *Biographies of highland clergymen*
Wealth at death £8920 2s. 2d.: confirmation, 2 Dec 1881, CCI

Macgregor, Sir Charles Metcalfe (1840–1887), army officer, explorer, and military strategist, was born at Agra on 12 September 1840, the second son of Robert Guthrie Macgregor and his wife, Alexina Watson, daughter of General Archibald Watson of the Bengal army. He had eight sisters and two brothers. Macgregor was brought up in Perthshire by his grandmother and was educated at Glenalmond College, Marlborough College, and Haileybury College. In 1869 he married Frances Mary, youngest daughter of Sir Henry Durand; she died on passage to England on 9 May 1873, leaving one daughter. Macgregor married his second wife, Charlotte Mary, second daughter of Frederick W. Jardine, in February 1883; she survived him.

Macgregor was commissioned in the Indian army in October 1856 and was serving as an ensign in the 57th Bengal native infantry at the outbreak of the mutiny at Ferozepore in 1857, taking part in the pursuit of the 10th light cavalry from the cantonment. He participated in the siege of Delhi, and accompanied Colonel Gerrard's column at the capture of Rewari, at Kanaunda, and in the action of Narnaul, where he captured an enemy artillery piece. Macgregor distinguished himself in action under Sir T. Seaton's command at Gangari, Patial, and Mainpuri. He served with Lord Clyde's army throughout the siege and assault of Lucknow (where his elder brother died defending the residency). Macgregor then accompanied Sir Hope Grant's force to the north of Lucknow, where he demonstrated personal bravery and established his military reputation at Bori and in various minor skirmishes.

In August 1858 Macgregor was given command of a squadron of Hodson's Horse, and near Daryabad charged and captured a gun from the enemy, although his horse was killed and he was severely wounded. When he recovered he rejoined Sir Hope Grant's force, with which he fought at the Gogra River, at Wazirgaon, Machligaon, Bankasia, and across the Rapti River. In 1859 he led the advance guard of Sir A. Horsford's expedition, charging with the cavalry three times at Sarwaghat. Subsequently, while serving with Brigadier Holdich's column, he captured Murad Baksh, the famous rebel chief, who fired on the English women at Cawnpore. In 1860 Macgregor joined Fane's Horse and served with it in China. At Sinho he was severely wounded when he charged a force of Tartar cavalry to save an artillery battery; he was recommended for gallantry. While still suffering from his wounds, he took part in the fighting near Tungchow (Tongzhou) and the capture of Peking (Beijing).

When Macgregor returned to India in 1861 he was made second in command of Hodson's Horse, with which he served for three years while writing several studies on cavalry organization, tactics, and training. In 1864 he served with General Dunsford's column of the Bhutan field force as brigade major, and was severely wounded at the assault of Dalingkot and again at Chamorchi, Bala, and Nago. He led a reconnaissance mission from Dalina to Chirang, for which he was mentioned in dispatches. Following the campaign he was appointed deputy assistant quartermaster-general of the eastern frontier, and published a detailed study on mountain warfare.

In 1867–8 Macgregor was employed with the advanced guard of the Abyssinian expedition under Sir Robert Napier, and took an active part in the engagement at Arogee and at the capture of Magdala. In 1868 he began work on compiling the *Gazetteer of Central Asia*, containing detailed strategical and topographical information, for the Indian government. It took five years to complete and stimulated his intense personal interest in Indian defence problems, and in the course of its preparation he undertook several reconnaissance missions across the northwest frontier. Macgregor was instrumental in founding the United Service Institution of India, providing a forum for professional military study, discussion, and debate. He took a keen interest in this organization, contributing several articles to its journal. Macgregor was employed as director-general of transport during the famine in north Berar. He was appointed member of the ordnance commission in 1874, and assistant quartermaster-general of the Rawal Pindi division in February 1875.

Macgregor carried out several important explorations on the Indian frontier. In April 1875 he reconnoitred a route from the Persian Gulf to Sarakhs, within a few miles of Herat, in order to obtain information about the Afghan frontier. He proceeded to England, and was made a CSI. At Lord Salisbury's request he undertook another hazardous exploration through Baluchistan, accompanied by Captain Lockwood. Macgregor was placed on special duty in charge of the Khyber line of communications at the beginning of the Second Anglo-Afghan War in 1878, accompanying General Maude's expedition against the Zakha Khel Afridis in the Bazar valley as chief of staff. Later he was appointed chief of staff to Sir Samuel Browne, with whom he served during the advance from Jalalabad to Gandamak. After the conclusion of the treaty he made arrangements for the withdrawal of the Peshawar valley field force. He was created a CIE in January 1878 and was made a CB for the Afghan campaign.

When the second phase of the war began, Macgregor was appointed chief of staff to Sir Frederick Roberts, accompanying the advance from Ali Khel in the Kurram valley across the Shutar Gardan Pass. He took an active part in the battle of Charasia, capture of Kabul, and occupation of the Sherpur cantonment. On 11 December 1879 Macgregor recaptured from the enemy the four abandoned British guns at Kala-i-Aoshar outside Kabul. He took a leading part in the defence of Sherpur and the subsequent fighting in Maidan and Wardak. When Sir Donald Stewart arrived from Kandahar, Macgregor became his chief of staff until the defeat at Maiwand. Macgregor then commanded the 3rd infantry brigade of Sir Frederick Roberts's Kabul–Kandahar field force during the march to Kandahar, and was present at the final victory over Ayub Khan's army on the banks of the Arghandab.

Macgregor (now a brigadier-general) led a column through the Marri Country at the end of the campaign, and on his return to Simla was created KCB and was made quartermaster-general in India. He superintended the compilation of the *History of the Second Afghan War*, which was later suppressed by the Indian government as it contained a critique of Indian defence policy beyond its terms of reference.

Macgregor returned to India in 1884 and took command of the intelligence department, which he dramatically improved in efficiency, and also prepared plans to mobilize an army corps quickly in event of sudden emergency. In 1884 his comprehensive and exhaustive treatise *The Defence of India: a Strategical Study* was privately published, but its characteristically outspoken and alarmist views on British strategy in event of Russian attack led to its suppression by the imperial authorities. Macgregor was placed in command of the Punjab frontier force, but his health broke down, forcing him to return to England. A few days after his promotion to major-general he died of peritonitis at Shepherd's Hotel, Cairo, on 5 February 1887, at the age of forty-six, following exploratory surgery to examine his liver for an abscess. His body was returned to Scotland for burial in the family graveyard at Glengyle on the shores of Loch Katrine.

S. P. OLIVER, *rev.* T. R. MOREMAN

Sources Lady Macgregor [C. M. Macgregor], ed., *The life and opinions of Major General Sir Charles Metcalfe Macgregor* (1888) • A. W. Preston, 'Sir Charles Macgregor and the defence of India', *HJ*, 12 (1969), 58–77 • Biographical file, Colonel (local Major-General) Sir C. M. Macgregor, KCB, CSI, CIE Bengal Staff Corps, BL OIOC • 'The career of an Indian general: Sir Charles Macgregor', *Blackwood*, 144 (1888), 664–80 • *War in Afghanistan, 1879–80: the personal diary of Major General Sir Charles Metcalfe Macgregor*, ed. W. Trousdale (1985) • ecclesiastical returns, BL OIOC, N/1/56 fol. 136

Archives Scottish United Services Museum, Edinburgh | BL OIOC, letters to T. D. Baker, MS Eur. D 567 • NAM, letters to Lord Roberts • SOAS, letters to H. M. Durand relating to his expedition to Persia

Likenesses portrait (after photograph by Bassano), repro. in Macgregor, ed., *Life and opinions* • wood-engraving (after photograph by Suscipi of Rome), NPG; repro. in *ILN* (20 Sept 1879)

Wealth at death £2798 13s. 10d.: resworn probate, Sept 1887, CGPLA Eng. & Wales

MacGregor, Donnchadh Làdasach (d. 1552). *See under* MacGregor family (*per.* 1450–1604).

MacGregor, Eòin (d. 1528). *See under* MacGregor family (*per.* 1450–1604).

MacGregor, Sir Evan (1842–1926), Admiralty official, was born on 31 March 1842 at Fernie Castle, Fife, the third son of Sir John Atholl Bannatyne Murray MacGregor, third baronet (d. 1851/2), of Lanrick and Balquhidder, and his wife, Mary Charlotte, youngest daughter and coheir of Admiral Sir Thomas Masterman *Hardy, first baronet. The clan MacGregor had been under a ban during most of the seventeenth and eighteenth centuries, and the use of the name was forbidden by penal statutes, finally repealed in 1774. The members of the clan acknowledged General

John Murray as their chief, and he was created a baronet in 1795, resuming the name of MacGregor in 1822.

When Evan MacGregor was nine years old his father, then lieutenant-governor of the Virgin Islands, died at Tortola in the West Indies. His mother was given by Queen Victoria a residence at Hampton Court and went to live there with her young family and her twice-widowed mother. MacGregor was sent to Mr Walton's school at Hampton, and afterwards as a boarder to Charterhouse, London. On 13 August 1860 his father's first cousin, Captain the Hon. James Drummond RN, procured for him a nomination from the duke of Somerset (then first lord) to a temporary clerkship in the Admiralty.

MacGregor entered the Admiralty service thoroughly imbued with the traditions of the navy. Captain Drummond himself joined the Admiralty board as junior sea lord in June 1861, and in the following year he appointed his young cousin as his private secretary. On Drummond's going to sea in 1866 Lord John Hay and Sir John Dalrymple Hay, who in succession filled the post of junior sea lord within a few months, both appointed MacGregor as their private secretary. In January 1869 he became private secretary to the senior sea lord, Admiral Sir Sidney Dacres. During the next ten years he continued as private secretary to successive senior sea lords Sir Alexander Milne, Sir Hastings Yelverton, and Sir George Wellesley. In the meantime he advanced through the various ranks of the department until, in January 1880, he was promoted principal clerk in the secretariat and was appointed head of the military branch which dealt with fleet operations and political work, and came directly under the supervision of the senior sea lord. Having reached this important position at the early age of thirty-seven, MacGregor soon had the opportunity of proving his merit.

In 1880 a combined naval demonstration by the principal naval powers, commanded by Sir Beauchamp Seymour, was undertaken off the coast of Albania in order to compel Turkey to surrender Dulcigno to Montenegro, in accordance with the treaty of Berlin. At the end of the year the First South African War broke out, and naval assistance was rendered by the landing at Durban of a naval brigade which served throughout the war. In 1882 the British navy bombarded Alexandria, landed a naval brigade, and manned steamboats on the Nile. The headquarters' administration of all this under the direction of the Admiralty board was by MacGregor's branch, and his energy and efficiency were rewarded by a CB in 1882.

On 21 April 1884 Lord Northbrook selected MacGregor as permanent secretary to the Admiralty, and he held the office for twenty-three years under lords Northbrook, Ripon, George Hamilton, Spencer, Goschen, Selborne, Cawdor, and Tweedmouth. In 1884 he married Annie Louise (d. 1922), daughter of Colonel William Alexander Middleton; they had one daughter.

The period from 1884 to 1907 was one of immense development both in the fleet itself and in the administration of the navy. Under the Naval Defence Act (1889) of Lord George Hamilton the navy was almost entirely rebuilt, and under the Naval Works Acts from 1895 onwards new harbours, barracks, and dockyards were constructed all over the world; further, before MacGregor retired, the reforms in naval education and training and in the distribution and organization of the fleet, promoted by Lord Fisher, had been carried through, and the construction of the dreadnought fleet, which was to serve in the First World War, had begun.

During his career MacGregor saw great changes both in the navy and the Admiralty. When he joined the office, all the members of the board occupied residences in the building in Whitehall which also housed a total staff of 124, and the navy estimates amounted to £12,800,000; nearly a third of the ships afloat were still sailing ships. When he retired the navy estimates had reached nearly £32 million, while the departmental staff under his control in Whitehall had grown to 1089, and great new buildings had been constructed to house them, partly owing to the transfer of the subordinate navy departments from Somerset House.

MacGregor's early training and associations made him a faithful guardian of the interests of the naval service and a promoter of the policy of the sea lords with whom he served; he had little experience of, or interest in, finance or the civil side of his office, which he was content to leave to trusted colleagues and subordinates. He could not, in consequence, fill the role of close personal adviser to the cabinet minister at the head of the department, but his memory and experience made him an invaluable ally, especially of the first sea lords who wished to introduce any new line of policy. He wrote clearly and incisively, and his letters and minutes were models of official correspondence. With a power of concentration on the business before him, he set to his rapidly growing staff an example of punctuality and thoroughness and of devotion to the service. He was impartial in his own decisions and loyally accepted any overruling of his advice by superior authority. He neither was nor wished to be the initiator of important reforms, but his shrewd counsel and loyal assistance were of the greatest advantage to successive naval administrators with whom he served. This was especially important in the case of Lord Fisher, with whom he had been on terms of close personal friendship since the 1870s. As an insider MacGregor's influence is hard to determine, but his advice, support, and information were always at Fisher's disposal.

MacGregor was appointed KCB in 1892 and GCB in 1906, and was one of the first to receive the ISO when it was created in 1903. He intensely disliked publicity, and was devoted to his family and friends. In his early days at Hampton Court rowing had been his chief recreation, and he made many canoeing trips on the rivers of central Europe, and even to the Norwegian fjords, where in later years he went annually for salmon fishing. He retired in May 1907, having reached the statutory age under civil service regulations, and spent his retirement at his home, Aynsome, Cartmel, Lancashire, where he died on 21 March 1926. A memorial to him was erected in Cartmel

Priory. His long service as permanent secretary, in a period of dramatic change for both the navy and its administration, reflected both ability and commitment.

V. W. BADDELEY, *rev.* ANDREW LAMBERT

Sources N. A. M. Rodger, *The admiralty* (1979) · R. F. MacKay, *Fisher of Kilverstone* (1973) · J. C. Sainty, ed., *Admiralty officials, 1660–1870* (1975) · *Fear God and dread nought: the correspondence of Admiral of the Fleet Lord Fisher of Kilverstone*, ed. A. J. Marder, 3 vols. (1952–9) · *WWW* · *CGPLA Eng. & Wales* (1926)
Archives Kilverstone Hall, Norfolk, Fisher MSS
Wealth at death £38,715 14s. 7d.: probate, 3 June 1926, *CGPLA Eng. & Wales*

MacGregor, Gregor (1786–1845), soldier and adventurer, was the grandson of Gregor MacGregor Drummond who had enlisted in the forerunner of the Black Watch (then Sempill's Highlanders), served abroad with distinction, and been instrumental in obtaining the repeal of legislation which had outlawed the clan MacGregor since the seventeenth century. Gregor MacGregor was born in Edinburgh on 24 December 1786, son of Daniel MacGregor, a captain in the East India Company service, and Ann Austin, also of Edinburgh. After his father died in 1794 MacGregor's mother raised him and his two sisters with the help of cousins and guardians. He entered the army in 1803 as an ensign in the 59th foot and in 1805 purchased his captaincy and married Maria Bowater (*d.* 1811), daughter of a British admiral, at St Margaret's, Westminster. In 1808 he began studying chemistry and natural sciences in Edinburgh.

MacGregor served briefly with his regiment in the Iberian peninsula but sold up his captaincy in 1810 following a disagreement with a superior officer. He joined the Portuguese service and received a Portuguese order of knighthood after a few months. He returned to England, where his wife died soon after his arrival. Around this time he apparently met General Francisco de Miranda, the Venezuelan patriot, then living in London, as in 1811 he sailed for Venezuela to join the struggle for independence from Spain, taking with him an extensive library and a personal piper. In Caracas he became colonel and aide-de-camp to General Miranda and in 1812 married Simón Bolívar's niece, Josefa Antonia Andrea Aristiguieta y Llovera (*d.* 1838). After the first Venezuelan republic collapsed that same year, MacGregor and his wife fled to Colombia. When the patriot stronghold of Cartagena fell to Spanish troops in 1815, the MacGregors escaped to Haiti where Bolívar regrouped to attack the mainland again. In the ensuing campaign MacGregor led his troops with brilliant success. Bolívar made him a general of division and awarded him the Orden de los Libertadores, the young nation's highest decoration.

In 1816, irritated at being refused a higher command, MacGregor sailed to the United States where he hoped to wrest Florida from Spanish control. In 1817 with a small force he captured Amelia Island off Florida's east coast. When his men mutinied because he had no funds to pay them, MacGregor relinquished command to another adventurer and sailed for Nassau in the Bahamas. In late

Gregor MacGregor (1786–1845), by Samuel William Reynolds senior (after Simon Jacques Rochard)

1817 he embarked for England to recruit men for Bolívar's army. He had little difficulty enlisting unemployed, discharged servicemen in London and Dublin by promising them lavish rewards of cash and land in America. However, instead of sailing to rendezvous with Bolívar, MacGregor in 1819 launched two ill-judged independent forays against Spanish strongholds in Panama and Colombia. Each ended in disaster, with great loss of life.

Now disowned by Bolívar, MacGregor in early 1820 sailed to the Mosquito Shore of what is now Honduras. There he obtained in exchange for rum and trinkets a grant of some 8 million acres from George Frederick Augustus, king of the Mosquito Indians, a ferocious people who were descended from shipwrecked black slaves and local Sumu and Poyer Indians and who shared the English hostility towards Spain. The English in Jamaica and British Honduras had encouraged the Indians in their attacks on Spanish settlements and in 1687 had began crowning their principal chiefs as kings. MacGregor returned to England where he registered his land grant in the court of chancery and called himself Gregor I, cacique of Poyais, the name he gave his fictional country. He opened a Poyaisian legation and land office in the City from which he sold commissions in the non-existent Poyaisian navy and army as well as land in Poyais at 4s. an acre. Pamphlets and advertisements extolled the climate, soil, and mineral wealth of Poyais, the capital of which, St Josephs, boasted a bank, a cathedral, and splendid public buildings. At least two hundred men, women, and children—mostly Scots—parted with their savings and sailed from Leith and London for Poyais to find only jungles, swamps, and disease. All would have perished but for a timely rescue expedition from British Honduras.

Back in London MacGregor persuaded the respectable bankers Perring & Co. to manage a major loan for his new nation. In 1823 a £200,000 Poyais bond issue yielding five per cent per annum and authorized by 'Gregor I, sovereign prince of the independent state of Poyais' was offered at the stock exchange. The general climate of the time favoured MacGregor—after Waterloo the English government's borrowing requirements fell and therefore high-yielding foreign securities seemed particularly attractive, especially those of the newly independent Latin American nations. Given the public's hazy knowledge of geography, Poyais seemed a plausible investment. MacGregor grossed over £50,000 before his fraud was discovered.

When, in late 1823, news of the fate of the unfortunate Poyais immigrants reached London, MacGregor and his family moved to Paris. Here he soon became acquainted with several French cabinet ministers who sought his advice on South American affairs. In 1825 he sold 480,000 acres of Poyais to a French colonization company, which led to his trial and imprisonment for fraud. Acquitted on appeal in July 1826, MacGregor returned to London and for the next twelve years travelled between London, Paris, and Edinburgh selling Poyais land grants. To lend credibility to his schemes he published in 1836 a constitution for Poyais, loosely modelled on that of the USA.

In 1838 his wife died and MacGregor decided to return to Venezuela. He petitioned the Venezuelan government for citizenship and, in recognition of his services in the cause of independence, asked to be reinstated as general, with back pay and a pension. His request was granted and he was confirmed as a general of division, with a pension of one-third of his salary and a sum of 4000 pesos. He settled in Caracas, where he became a respected member of the community and died peacefully in bed on 4 December 1845; he was buried in the cathedral with full military honours, with the president of the republic, cabinet ministers, and the diplomatic corps in attendance.

FRANK GRIFFITH DAWSON

Sources D. Stewart, *Sketches of the character, manners, and present state of the highlanders of Scotland: with details of the military service of the highland regiments*, 2 vols. (1822) · M. Rafter, *Memoirs of Gregor M'Gregor* (1820) · F. Maceroni, *Memoirs of the life and adventures of Colonel Maceroni, late aide-de-camp to Joachim Murat, King of Naples*, 2 vols. (1838) · F. G. Dawson, *The Banker*, 132 (Jan 1982), 72–3 · T. Strangeways, *Sketch of the Mosquito Shore including the territory of Poyais* (1822) · J. Hastie, *Narrative of a voyage on the ship Kinnersley Castle from Leith Roads to Poyais* (1823) · T. F. Davis, *MacGregor's invasion of Florida, 1817* (1928) · G. MacGregor, *Exposición documentada*, 1838, Archivo Historico Nacional, Caracas, Venezuela · V. Allen, 'The prince of Poyais', *History Today*, 2 (1952), 53–8 · A. Hasbrouck, 'Gregor McGregor and the colonisation of Poyais', *The Hispanic American Historical Review*, 7 (1927), 438
Archives Archivo Historico Nacional, Caracas, Venezuela, Illustres Proceres—Hojas de Servicio | NA Scot., John MacGregor MSS
Likenesses S. W. Reynolds senior, mezzotint (after S. J. Rochard), BM, NPG [*see illus.*] · G. Watson, oils, Scot. NPG · portrait, repro. in

Strangeways, *Sketch of the Mosquito Shore including the territory of Poyais* · portrait, Palacio de Congreso, Caracas, Venezuela

MacGregor, Griogair Ruadh (*d.* 1570). *See under* MacGregor family (*per.* 1450–1604).

MacGregor, Sir Ian Kinloch (1912–1998), metallurgical engineer and industrialist, was born on 21 September 1912 at The Bungalow, Kinlochleven, Argyll, the third son of Daniel MacGregor, a works accountant, and his wife, Grace Alexanderina, *née* Fraser Maclean, a schoolteacher. His parents were leading lights in the United Free Church of Scotland, a strictly Calvinist denomination which emphasized the virtues of hard work and thrift, traits which remained with MacGregor throughout his life. Educated at George Watson's College, Edinburgh, and at Hillhead High School, Glasgow, MacGregor proceeded to Glasgow University to study metallurgical engineering. After the award of a first-class degree of outstanding quality, he then obtained a diploma, with distinction, from the Royal College of Science and Technology (now the University of Strathclyde).

In the mid-1930s MacGregor was recruited to the armour department of Beardmores, the distinguished Clydeside engineering concern. The Beardmore forge had provided the power base for the red Clydesider David Kirkwood, and one of MacGregor's first tasks as a junior manager was to face down a strike of overhead crane operatives. Identified by Beardmores' chairman, Sir James Lithgow, as a high-flyer, at the outbreak of the Second World War MacGregor was recruited to the Ministry of Supply, where he began work on tank designs. He soon attracted the attention of Lord Beaverbrook, and in 1940 he was sent to North America, first to Canada and then to the USA, to procure armoured metal. He was then attached to the British military mission to advise on war production, and it was here that he became acquainted with the production methods and managerial styles characteristic of the American metal and engineering industries. MacGregor married a Welsh girl, Sybil Spencer (*d.* 1996), in Washington in 1942. They had a son and daughter.

American experience At the end of the war MacGregor chose to remain in the USA. The election of a Labour government in Britain committed to a programme of nationalization was unattractive to him, while he had come to admire the way of life in the USA, with its class-free society. In 1956 the metallurgical company for which MacGregor worked took part in a merger to form American Metal Climax (later Amax). Appointed chief executive of the group in 1966 and chairman in 1969, MacGregor, increasingly concerned about the reliance of the American economy on oil, presided over a significant programme of diversification which transformed Amax into one of the world's leading mining corporations. By the middle of the 1970s the company was the third largest American coal producer. MacGregor also joined Lazard Brothers, investment bankers of Wall Street, and became chairman of the international chamber of commerce in Paris.

Sir Ian Kinloch
MacGregor (1912–
1998), by David
Mansell, 1984

By this time MacGregor had acquired a formidable reputation as an industrialist who was committed to managerial prerogatives in the face of labour unrest. He fought long and hard against recognition of the United Mineworkers of America and in so doing acquired considerable tactical experience in facing down strikes. His workaholic tendencies were legendary, as was his ability to fly almost continuously between America, Europe, and Australia in pursuit of his business affairs. He was richly rewarded by Amax: in 1975 his salary amounted to £150,000 and his shares in the company were worth nearly £2 million. Age did not diminish his energy: in his sixties he was quoted as saying, 'At my age, some men chase young girls. Some play golf. Some become vegetables. I work' (*The Independent*, 15 April 1998). Thus, as retirement from Amax approached, it is not surprising that MacGregor was in search of a fresh challenge, and at the age of sixty-five he accepted the offer of the prime minister, James Callaghan, to become a non-executive director of British Leyland (BL), acting as deputy to Sir Michael Edwardes, the company chairman.

Return to British industry Brought into public ownership in 1975 in the wake of bankruptcy, BL was afflicted by low productivity and an unenviable record of labour relations. A defining moment in MacGregor's career at BL was the dismissal of the communist shop steward, Derek (Red Robbo) Robinson from the company's Longbridge plant. MacGregor later claimed that it was he rather than the reluctant Edwardes who had initiated Robinson's sacking, although accounts differ. In any event, it was MacGregor's reputation for implacable hostility to militant trade unionism, together with his managerial capabilities, which resulted in his appointment as chairman of the British Steel Corporation (BSC) in May 1980. This position was in the gift of Sir Keith Joseph, the new secretary of state for industry in Margaret Thatcher's Conservative administration, and the announcement of Joseph's choice was received with incredulity in a House of Commons ignorant of both MacGregor's American experience and his Scottish origins. Additional controversy was caused by the terms of MacGregor's appointment—a £1.8

million 'transfer fee' payable to Lazard Brothers to secure his services. Like BL, BSC was encumbered with outdated plant, low productivity, and severe financial problems. In the year of MacGregor's appointment, the corporation employed 166,000 workers to make 14 million tons of steel: losses amounted to £1.8 billion. MacGregor's immediate response was to drive through a programme of fundamental rationalization entailing substantial plant closures and redundancies. By 1983 production was almost at the level of 1980, but BSC was employing only 71,000 workers. Although losses amounted to £256 million, a revolution in productivity was underway. By the middle of the decade BSC was profitable, highly efficient by contemporary European standards, and *en route* for privatization.

Coal industry challenges MacGregor was proud of his achievements at BSC, all the more so since the vast majority of job losses were achieved by voluntary redundancies—albeit at the cost of the desolation of numerous steel-making communities. His next appointment, therefore, at the age of seventy-one, was greeted with dismay within the wider trade-union movement and the Labour Party. MacGregor himself reputedly wished to move to the coal industry as his next challenge in the restructuring of British industry, and, as far as the prime minister was concerned, he was the ideal candidate to take on the chairmanship of the National Coal Board (NCB). Here again was an industry which, in MacGregor's view, seemed to epitomize the 'British disease'—well shielded from the market force of competition, subject to growing overcapacity in the face of changes in the energy market, and in the grip of militant trade unionism. The government had already announced a programme of pit closures which had produced an uncompromising response from Arthur Scargill, president of the National Union of Mineworkers (NUM). In the light of MacGregor's openly confessed aim to end the NCB's status as a 'social security enterprise', conflict was inevitable.

The most bitter dispute in British industrial relations began in March 1984, when the NUM executive called a national strike in response to MacGregor's announcement of pit closures. The dispute lasted for a year and was marked by increasingly violent confrontations between striking miners and the police, as well as by a rising tide of social and economic distress within mining communities. MacGregor himself was repelled by the NUM's tactic of intimidation of working miners, and early in the dispute expressed the wish to the prime minister that he could have at his side 'some of my scruffy, sometimes ill-disciplined, sometimes loud mouthed American police ... and some of the curious ways of the law to back them up' (*The Times*, 14 April 1998). It was MacGregor's intransigence in refusing successive peace overtures which led to an increasing rift with the secretary of state for energy, Peter Walker. The latter began his own discussions with key NUM officials and overrode MacGregor in securing cabinet approval for a settlement with the pit deputies' union, the National Association of Colliery Overmen,

Deputies and Shotfirers (NACODS), when strike action was threatened in the autumn of 1984. MacGregor was also criticized for his weak presentation of the NCB's case: in meeting journalists he was dour, impassive, and abrasive, habitually referring to his 'Department of Economic Warfare' and to the fact that, in war, 'a soldier has to shoot to kill. Unfortunately, I'm a soldier in that kind of war' (*The Guardian*, 14 April 1998). Thatcher found him 'strangely lacking in guile … he had no experience of dealing with trade union leaders intent on using the process of negotiation to score political points, so time and again he and his colleagues were outmanoeuvred by Arthur Scargill and the NUM leadership' (Thatcher, 342).

The coal strike ended in March 1985 with the complete rout of the NUM and the implementation of a selective pit-closure programme by the NCB. At the inception of the dispute, coal reserves were at a record high, and as it proceeded the NUM was unable to secure the support of other trade unions. Indeed, the union was fractured and fatally weakened as a result of the establishment of the rival Union of Democratic Mineworkers. Mick McGahey, the communist leader of the Scottish miners, even claimed after MacGregor's death that the end result of the dispute was 'to destroy trade unionism not only in mining, but in Britain' (*The Independent*, 15 April 1998). For MacGregor, the prime minister had obtained 'the results she paid for; in fact, much more than she paid for' from his chairmanship of the NCB (*Daily Telegraph*, 14 April 1998). His reward was a knighthood in 1986, but MacGregor felt snubbed on the appointment of his successor, the emollient Robert Haslam, who had also followed in his place when he left BSC.

After his retirement from the NCB in 1986, MacGregor rejoined Lazards as a non-executive director. His name was canvassed in the press as an 'efficiency-enhancing' head of the National Health Service and also as a board member of British Gas, but nothing came of these campaigns on his behalf. He was, however, much in demand as a 'company doctor' and took on a number of company chairmanships, including that of Goldcrest Films and the troubled property group Mountleigh. At the age of seventy-eight he was particularly disappointed at his enforced retirement from the chairmanship of two American companies.

Beyond his industrial interests, MacGregor was peripatetic, spending time in New York and commuting between his Bermuda home and his mansion on the shores of Loch Fyne. Reflecting his religious upbringing, his moralizing tendencies were confirmed by his chairmanship of Religion in American Life, an organization famous for its slogan, 'The family that prays together stays together'. On his repatriation to Britain, MacGregor lent his support to ORT—the Organization for Rehabilitation through Training. This organization was Russian and Jewish in origin and devoted its charitable activities to technical training. For MacGregor, the importance of ORT lay in its inculcation of the work ethic among its clients.

MacGregor was mentally tough and physically resilient.

A hard-bitten career industrialist with vast experience of the American corporate sector, he came to epitomize the very essence of Thatcherism in the 1980s insofar as the main aims were to reinvigorate market forces and marginalize the trade-union movement. There can be no doubt that the 'cold bath' effects of Thatcherism, as implemented by MacGregor, had favourable effects on industrial productivity. In this respect, MacGregor was the ideal instrument, and it is no surprise that he was among the leading businessmen who publicly urged Conservative MPs to back Thatcher's continuation as leader. In addition to his knighthood, he was appointed chevalier of the Légion d'honneur in 1972. He died of heart failure in Musgrove Park Hospital, Taunton, Somerset, on 13 April 1998, and was cremated.   M. W. KIRBY

Sources I. MacGregor and R. Taylor, *The enemies within: the story of the miners' strike, 1984–5* (1986) • M. Parker, *Thatcherism and the fall of coal: politics and economics of UK coal, 1979–2000* (2000) • H. Beynon, ed., *Digging deeper: issues in the miners' strike* (1985) • R. Winterton, *Coal, crisis and conflict: the 1984–85 miners' strike in Yorkshire* (1989) • P. Walker, *Staying power* (1991) • H. Abromeit, *British steel: an industry between the state and the private sector* (1986) • J. Wood, *Wheels of misfortune: the rise and fall of the British motor industry* (1985) • E. Wallis, *Industrial relations in the privatised coal industry: continuity, change and contradictions* (2000) • *Daily Telegraph* (14 April 1998) • *The Times* (14 April 1998) • *The Independent* (15 April 1998) • *The Scotsman* (14 April 1998) • *The Guardian* (14 April 1998) • WWW • b. cert. • d. cert. • M. Thatcher, *The Downing Street years* (1993)
Archives U. Glas., papers, mainly relating to business
Likenesses D. Mansell, photograph, 1984, Hult. Arch. [*see illus.*] • photographs, Hult. Arch.

MacGregor, James (*c*.1480–1551), collector of poetry and dean of Lismore, son of Dugald MacGregor of Fortingall in Perthshire, held the deanship of Lismore in Argyll. He is thought to have been educated at the University of St Andrews, and was a notary public as his father had been. His working base was probably Fortingall, at the foot of Glen Lyon, and the MacGregors had a strong presence there, owning the vicarage of Fortingall, though Campbell domination was already threatening it in the dean's lifetime.

MacGregor's place in Scottish literary history rests on his close involvement with the manuscript known as the Book of the Dean of Lismore. It is thought that this was mainly written between 1512 and 1526. The original idea is credited to Finlay, chief of the MacNabs, another prominent Perthshire clan, and he seems to have made some collection of Gaelic verse from the 'strolling bards' who used to travel through the Gaelic countryside. The tradition is that Finlay MacNab encouraged Dugald MacGregor to continue and extend this collection, and that Dugald's sons James and Duncan (himself a poet) continued and extended the work.

The resulting manuscript is the primary source for early Gaelic verse, and an important source for some Irish verse also. A more or less unified system of professional Gaelic verse using the standard literary language existed in Scotland and Ireland until the early part of the seventeenth century, and professional poets continued to circulate in both Scottish and Irish locations. The manuscript draws on the sources connected with this system, evidently using both written and oral material. In some instances it appears that more than one manuscript version of a poem has been used. The bardic styles and techniques and literary language were not totally confined to the professional poets, but were practised also by amateurs, generally by members of the leading families that used the services of professional poets. As a result of these various developments the dean's manuscript includes a wide range of Gaelic verse. There is a good representation of verse by Irish Ó Dálaigh poets (eighteen poems), including Muireadhach Albanach, who is supposed to be the founder of the related Scottish bardic dynasty of the MacMhuirichs. Strangely, the MacMhuirichs themselves are less well represented.

Work by professional bards serving the Campbell, MacDonald, and MacGregor chiefs is also represented, showing the existence of hereditary bardic families apart from that of the MacMhuirichs. Verse by 'amateurs' includes poems by the fifteenth-century poet Iseabail Ní Mheic Cailéin, connected with the earls of Argyll, and by Sir Duncan Campbell of Glenorchy (d. 1513), who is represented by nine poems that have a strong emphasis on bawdiness. There is a strong Perthshire and Argyll emphasis in the manuscript's collection, with only occasional items with other Scottish backgrounds. The manuscript includes a wide range of heroic ballads, mostly anonymous, reflecting both the pan-Gaelic popularity of this kind of verse and also some specifically Scottish instances. The collection does not include vernacular verse in non-classical language and styles, though such verse would undoubtedly be known by MacGregor.

The manuscript also includes miscellaneous items, such as a Scottish chronicle written in Latin and Scots, verses in Scots, some Latin verse about Scottish kings or the dangers of drunkenness, notes for a shopping trip to Dunkeld, and occasional notes in English. The Gaelic verse items are written in a peculiar orthography which is evidently based on that used for current Scots. This was presumably a conscious effort at 'reforming' Gaelic orthography, strongly influenced by the dean's normal writing practices as a notary public operating in a context that was often non-Gaelic. Yet is seems clear that the dean could handle the classical Gaelic language and orthography used in Gaelic manuscripts. One bonus from his orthographic decisions is that Gaelic dialectal usages (especially Perthshire ones) show up, whereas the classical usage would have obscured them.

The dean died in 1551 and was buried in the church at Inchordin. His manuscript came into the public area as a result of James Macpherson's collecting tours in 1760–61, and in 1803 was handed over by the Highland Society of London to the Highland Society of Scotland; it later moved to the Library of the Faculty of Advocates and finally to the National Library of Scotland.

DERICK S. THOMSON

Sources W. J. Watson, ed., *Scottish verse from the book of the dean of Lismore*, Scottish Gaelic Texts Society, 1 (1937) · *Poems from the book of the dean of Lismore*, ed. E. C. Quiggin and J. Fraser (1937) · D. S. Thomson, ed., *The companion to Gaelic Scotland* (1983) · *DNB*
Archives NL Scot., Book of the Dean of Lismore

MacGregor, James (1832–1910), Church of Scotland minister, was born at Brownhill, Scone, on 11 July 1832, the eldest son of James MacGregor (*b.* 1788), farmer, and his wife, Margaret MacDougall (*bap.* 1801). A malformation of his legs restricted his growth, and he was of a diminutive stature. He was educated at Scone parish school and Perth Academy before he went on to the University of St Andrews in 1847 to study for the ministry. He was licensed by the presbytery of Perth in May 1855 and became minister of the High Church, Paisley, in November of that year. In May 1862 he transferred to the parish of Monimail in Fife, but he was soon sought to be colleague to Dr James Boyd at the Tron Church, Glasgow. He moved there in March 1864, succeeding Boyd after his death in June 1865. He moved again, in January 1868, to the Tron Church, Edinburgh, where his interest in the social conditions of the parish led him to set up a parochial visitation committee, later amalgamated with the Association for Improving the Condition of the Poor. In 1870 the University of St Andrews honoured him with the degree of DD. He became senior minister at the prestigious Edinburgh charge of St Cuthbert's in 1873, where he was to remain for the next thirty-seven years. It was during his ministry that the old parish church was razed to the ground and a new building constructed.

In 1864 MacGregor married Helen King, daughter of David Robertson, a Glasgow publisher, with whom he had two daughters, both of whom died young. His wife had been consumptive even before their marriage and died on 23 January 1875. On 6 September 1892 he married his second wife, Helen, daughter of Charles Murray of Perth.

MacGregor was one of a group of Church of Scotland ministers who restored the fortunes of the established church following the bleak period immediately after the Disruption. He was acknowledged to be the outstanding preacher of his day and his rhetorical gifts were put at the service of church defence when disestablishment emerged as a political threat. He left no body of published works by which he can be judged, but the strength of his personality emerges from Balfour's biography. In 1886 he became chaplain in ordinary to Queen Victoria, an appointment renewed by her successors. In 1889 he was one of the Scottish representatives at the jubilee celebration of the Australian Presbyterian church, while in 1891 he served as moderator of the general assembly. MacGregor travelled extensively, going to Spain for his health and visiting, among other places, the Holy Land (1861). In 1881 he accompanied the marquess of Lorne, then governor-general of Canada, to the Northwest Territories. He died at his home, 3 Eton Terrace, Edinburgh, on 25 November 1910, and was buried at the city's Grange cemetery.

LIONEL ALEXANDER RITCHIE

Sources F. Balfour, *Life and letters of the Reverend James MacGregor* (1912) · *Fasti Scot.* · *WWW* · private information (1912) · *The Scotsman* (26 Nov 1910) · *Glasgow Herald* (26 Nov 1910) · *DNB*
Archives NL Scot., diaries, royal letters

Likenesses photographs, 1850–1910, repro. in Balfour, *Life and letters of the Reverend James Macgregor* · O. Leyde, group portrait, *c.*1875 · G. Reid, group portrait, 1898 · J. Bowie, portrait, session house of St Cuthbert's Church, Edinburgh · cartoon, repro. in Balfour, *Life and letters of the Reverend James Macgregor*, facing p. 392 · portrait (aged eighteen), repro. in Balfour, *Life and letters of the Reverend James Macgregor*, frontispiece
Wealth at death £14,821 17s. 5d.: confirmation, 10 Jan 1911, *CCI*

MacGregor, John (1797–1857), civil servant and free-trader, was born at Drynie, near Stornoway, the eldest son of David MacGregor and Janet Ross. He had at least two brothers. In 1803 his parents took him to Canada, where they lived in Nova Scotia before moving to Prince Edward Island three years later. He was educated at his father's school at Covehead on Prince Edward Island. While in Canada, in 1822 he was appointed high sheriff, but the lieutenant-governor dismissed him following a political clash. Among other activities he opened a store, acted as a land agent, helped to found a subscription library, and sat in the provincial legislature. After returning to England in 1827 he set up in business in Liverpool, but it failed. The following year he published the first of more than thirty books dealing with travel, commerce, and history. Of these, the earliest are considered the best, since they reflect his experiences in Canada. One of them, *Historical & Descriptive Sketches of the Maritime Colonies of British America* (1828), was reprinted as recently as 1968. In 1832 he visited France to collect commercial information. It was the first of many such inquiries, and led to work for the government. For this work he was probably recommended by James Deacon Hume, whom he had met soon after his return from Canada. He married on 30 January 1833 Anne (*d.* 1853), daughter of William Peard Jillard of Oakhill, Somerset. They had no children.

In 1836 MacGregor reported to the Board of Trade on the effects of the *Zollverein* on British trade with Germany. He attended the first conference of that body later the same year, with instructions to explore the possibilities of a tariff agreement. Both sides were willing to make concessions, but negotiations foundered. MacGregor reported that the Prussian commissioner 'took his stand upon Corn, saying the other reductions were of little consequence' (Brown, 105). In 1838 he led discussions which resulted in a commercial treaty with Austria. He met Metternich and Kolowrat, the minister of finance. Talks which he conducted with a very free hand in 1839 and 1840 led to draft treaties with Naples and Prussia. When Hume retired in 1840 MacGregor succeeded him as joint secretary of the Board of Trade (24 January 1840). He was a strong advocate of free trade. J. B. Smith recalled how 'as President of the Manchester Chamber of Commerce, I went … with a deputation and we met Mr Deacon Hume and Mr Porter at Mr MacGregor's. Many Members of the House of Commons, and other advocates of free trade, came in during the evening, and there were animated discussions upon the question which had become one of great interest' (Badham, 335). Soon after becoming joint secretary MacGregor appeared before the select committee on import duties (1840), when his dogmatic views on free trade were given full vent. This created difficulties for

John MacGregor (1797–1857), by unknown engraver, pubd 1848

him the following year, when the Conservatives returned to power. Lord Ripon told MacGregor that he could have no confidence in him in consequence of his evidence before the committee. MacGregor stood his ground and refused to resign. This is consistent with what he later told Lord John Russell: 'During Sir Robert Peel's ministry, I made it to be distinctly understood both by him and several Presidents of the Board of Trade that they must not consider me in any more favourable light than as a firm adherent of your Lordship' (Parris, 67). In December 1845, when Russell was trying to form a government, MacGregor wrote to him, offering to resign his official post if he could be promised the vice-presidency in a whig administration.

MacGregor was elected MP for Glasgow in July 1847 and gave up the joint secretaryship. He sat as a Liberal, spoke frequently on commercial, financial, and colonial matters, and voted for the ballot. While an MP he lived at 1 Princes Terrace, London, and was a member of the Athenaeum. Soon after his parliamentary début he embarked on a career in finance. In giving up his official post he had renounced an income of £1500 p.a. His seat in parliament carried, of course, no salary. However, his official experience left him with a certain standing in the world of business. He was, moreover, the representative of a major commercial city. Like that of Dickens's Mr Merdle in *Little Dorrit*, though at a humbler level, MacGregor's name had become one to add lustre to a prospectus: 'The weightiest of men had said to projectors, "Now what name have you got? Have you got Merdle?" And the reply being in the negative, had said "Then I won't look at you."' (Dickens, chap. 21).

When in 1849 the Royal British Bank received its charter, MacGregor became its paid chairman. In this role he was a party to the publication of misleading accounts and took out a substantial loan on inadequate security. In 1854 he severed his connection with the bank. Two years later it failed, and MacGregor fled to France, unable to repay more than a small fraction of what he owed. In March 1857 he gave up his seat in parliament and died on 23 April 1857 at 42 Grande Rue, Boulogne. The immediate causes of death were said to be bilious fever and paralysis. Several of his associates were tried and imprisoned in 1858. There is little doubt that MacGregor would have shared their fate had he stood in the dock with them.   HENRY PARRIS

Sources L. Brown, *The board of trade and the free-trade movement, 1830–42* (1958) · *DCB*, vol. 6 · D. M. Evans, *Facts, failures, and frauds: revelations financial, mercantile, criminal* (1859) · C. Badham, *Life of James Deacon Hume, Secretary of the Board of Trade* (1859) · H. Parris, *Constitutional bureaucracy* (1969) · *DNB* · J. B. Williams, *British commercial policy and trade expansion, 1750–1850* (1972) · *WWBMP* · J. C. Sainty, ed., *Officials of the board of trade, 1660–1870* (1974) · Gladstone, *Diaries* · d. cert. [photocopy supplied by Boulogne Public Library]

Archives BL, corresp. with Sir Robert Peel and others · NL Scot., letters to Blackwoods

Likenesses engraving, NPG; repro. in *ILN*, 12 (1848), 75 [*see illus.*]

MacGregor, John [*called* Rob Roy] (1825–1892), philanthropist and traveller, born on 24 January 1825 at Gravesend, Kent, was the eldest son of General Sir Duncan MacGregor KCB (1787–1881), inspector-general of police in Ireland. His mother was Elizabeth (*d.* 9 March 1858), the youngest daughter of Sir William Dick, bt, of Prestonfield, near Edinburgh. As a boy he was good at mechanics, read well, and was good at sports, particularly boating. His mind early took a strong religious bent, and he was with some difficulty dissuaded from becoming a missionary. His schooling was interrupted by his father's frequent changes of station, and he attended seven schools including King's School, Canterbury. In 1839 he entered Trinity College, Dublin, where he remained for a year, taking prizes for mathematics. From there he went to a tutor and, in 1844, to Trinity College, Cambridge, graduating as thirty-fourth wrangler in 1847 (MA in 1850). He was admitted to the Inner Temple in 1846, called to the bar in 1851, and devoted himself for a time to patent law; but having ample means, he gave up the law to spend his life in travel and philanthropic work, with occasional diversions into literary and mechanical investigations.

In July 1849 MacGregor started overland across Europe to the Levant, and on to Egypt and to Palestine: his tour occupied nine months. In 1851 he went to Russia, thence to Algeria and Tunis and from there to Canada and the United States. Between 1853 and 1863 he used his mathematical skills to study modes of marine propulsion. In

John MacGregor [Rob Roy] (1825–1892), by Elliott & Fry

order to investigate the claim that Blasco de Garay employed steam for purposes of marine propulsion in 1543, in the autumn of 1857 he went to Simancas and examined the Spanish archives, satisfying himself that de Garay made no such pretension.

In the summer of 1865 MacGregor launched his canoe the *Rob Roy*, and started on the first of the solitary cruises by which he is best known. He paddled along many continental rivers including the Sambre, Meuse, Rhine, Main, Danube, Aar, Moselle, and Seine and lakes Constance, Zürich, and Lucerne. Lord Aberdeen, in another canoe, joined MacGregor for part of the way. The log was published in 1866 as *A Thousand Miles in the Rob Roy Canoe*, which was widely read and encouraged the little known sport of canoeing in England. In 1866 MacGregor made a summer trip in a new and smaller canoe through part of Norway and Sweden; then to Denmark and Schleswig-Holstein, and so to the North Sea and Heligoland, publishing *Rob Roy on the Baltic* in 1867. In that year he sailed to France in a small yawl, built to his own design and also christened *Rob Roy*, again publishing an account of his voyage. In November 1868 he travelled by steamer to Alexandria, to start on the most adventurous of his canoe voyages, through the Suez Canal and down the Red Sea, and thence to Palestine, navigating the Jordan and Lake Gennesareth. His account of the trip ran to many editions.

Meanwhile MacGregor was active in philanthropic schemes in London. In 1851 he helped found the Shoeblack Brigade to provide employment for boys rescued by ragged schools, and supported Lord Shaftesbury's efforts on behalf of destitute children, becoming vice-president of the Ragged School Union. He was for several years honorary secretary of the Open-Air Mission, the Pure Literature Society, and the Protestant Alliance, and an active member of the British and Foreign Bible Society and of the Reformatory and Refuge Union. The profits from his writings and his frequent lectures about his travels were given to charity. He was elected member for Greenwich on the London school board in 1870 and 1873, and was for some time the chairman of the industrial schools committee of the board. He was also an enthusiastic volunteer soldier.

In later life, owing to failing health, MacGregor resided at Lochiel, Boscombe, Bournemouth, where he died on 16 July 1892, leaving a widow, Annie Bethia—the daughter of Admiral Sir J. Crawford Caffin, whom he had married on 4 December 1873—and two daughters; he was buried in Bournemouth cemetery.

MacGregor wrote well and always illustrated his own books. While at Cambridge as an undergraduate he sent the first of several papers to the *Mechanics' Magazine* and also sketches to *Punch*. His records of his travels were very popular in their day, but have been forgotten; he is best remembered as a pioneer of canoeing.

C. A. HARRIS, *rev.* ELIZABETH BAIGENT

Sources E. Hodder, *John MacGregor: "Rob Roy"* (1894) · *The Times* (20 July 1892) · R. Turner, letter, *The Times* (22 July 1892), 8b · Venn, *Alum. Cant.* · *CGPLA Eng. & Wales* (1892) · Boase, *Mod. Eng. biog.* · private information (1893) · Burke, *Gen. GB* · 'It all began with MacGregor', *Canoeing in Britain*, 61 (Dec 1966), 115 · m. cert.
Archives LMA, letters · NMM, corresp. and papers · Palestine Exploration Fund, London, sketchbook and notes relating to journey on the Jordan
Likenesses Butterworth & Heath, woodcut, BM; repro. in *Reformatory and Refuge Journal* (1874) · Elliott & Fry, photographs, NPG [*see illus.*] · Maull & Fox, photograph, NPG · H. Wayland, group portrait, photograph, NPG · Window & Grove, photogravure, NPG · portraits, repro. in Hodder, *John MacGregor "Rob Roy"*
Wealth at death £21,756 12s. 1d.: resworn probate, Aug 1893, *CGPLA Eng. & Wales* (1892)

McGregor, John James (1775–1834), historian and newspaper editor, born at Limerick on 24 February 1775, was brought up as a methodist, and became an ardent supporter of the Methodist denomination. At an early age he became editor of the *Munster Telegraph*, published at Waterford. Subsequently he moved to Dublin, where he became editor of the *Church Methodist Magazine*, a quarterly journal. His own publications reflected his keen historical interests and knowledge. The *History of the French Revolution, and of the Wars Resulting from that Event* (1816–27) was followed by the *New Picture of Dublin* (1821) with maps and views and *The history, topography, and antiquities of the county and city of Limerick, with a view of the history and antiquities of Ireland* (1826–7), written jointly with the Revd P. Fitzgerald, vicar of Cahercony. In the wake of his literary achievements came his appointment in 1829 to the post of literary assistant to the Kildare Place Education Society, a Church of Ireland body established in 1811 to train teachers. Subsequently, he published his final work, *True Stories from the*

History of Ireland (1829–33) in the manner of Sir Walter Scott's *Tales of a Grandfather* (1828–30). McGregor died at Ranelagh, near Dublin on 24 November 1834.

THOMPSON COOPER, *rev.* NILANJANA BANERJI

Sources J. J. McGregor, *Memoir of John James McGregor* (Dublin, 1840) · *GM*, 2nd ser., 3 (1835), 111 · W. T. Lowndes, *The bibliographer's manual of English literature*, ed. H. G. Bohn, [new edn], 6 vols. (1869) · Allibone, *Dict.*
Likenesses S. Freeman, engraving (after miniature by Purcell)

McGregor, Oliver Ross, Baron McGregor of Durris (1921–1997), social scientist and public servant, was born at Durris, Kincardineshire, on 25 August 1921, the only child of William McGregor, farmer, and his wife, Anne Olivia, *née* Ross. He was educated at Worksop College, Aberdeen University, and the London School of Economics. At the start of the Second World War he enlisted as a gunner before being seconded to the War Office and the Ministry of Agriculture and Fisheries. On 23 September 1944 he married Nellie Weate (*b.* 1918), civil servant, daughter of Harold Weate, trade union official, and his wife, Nellie, *née* Archer. They had three sons.

After demobilization McGregor graduated with first-class honours in economic history from the London School of Economics and taught briefly at Hull before his appointment to a lectureship at Bedford College, London, in 1947. He went on to serve at Bedford College as reader in social institutions from 1960 to 1964 and as professor of social institutions from 1964 to 1985, retiring shortly after Bedford College was incorporated into Royal Holloway College. As head of department between 1964 and 1977 he recruited and led a cadre of talented scholars, notably in the fields of social history, socio-legal studies, and medical sociology. McGregor was a man of prodigious intellectual energy and enthusiasm. In addition to his engagements in London University during the 1970s he was elected to a fellowship of Wolfson College, Oxford, and served as director of the Centre for Socio-Legal Studies in Oxford University, where he initiated a series of major intercollegiate research projects involving London, Bristol, and Oxford.

In March 1955 McGregor published in the *British Journal of Sociology* a pioneering article entitled 'The social position of women in England, 1850–1914: a bibliography', which stimulated much subsequent work by other authors, on the history of women in late nineteenth- and early twentieth-century Britain. In his first major work, *Divorce in England* (1957), he undertook a critical analysis of the findings of the Morton commission, and set out a number of cogent and radical proposals for the reform of the divorce laws. His next major, co-authored work, *Separated Spouses* (1970), was the first nationally representative survey of the jurisdiction of magistrates' courts over matrimony and the illegitimate child. Its findings and recommendations made a significant contribution to the debate about family law and its subsequent reform. As a member of the select committee on one-parent families, McGregor played a key role in sponsoring research and in drafting the final report (the Finer report, 1974) with Sir

Morris Finer. Their joint monograph, *The History of the Obligation to Maintain*, was a masterly historical analysis of the changing relationship between the development of the poor law and family law relating to the treatment of illegitimate children in England during the nineteenth century.

From the 1970s onwards, McGregor wrote numerous articles on issues of social and legal reform, including his contributions to such distinguished lecture programmes as the James Seth memorial, the Maccabaean in jurisprudence, the Tom Olsen, and the Hamlyn series. He combined these academic activities with continuous service as a member of committees on subjects such as the enforcement of judgement debts (1965), statutory maintenance limits (1966), and land use (1967), and as president of the National Council for One-Parent Families (1975–91) and the National Association of Citizens' Advice Bureaux (1981–6). Throughout his long career he sought both to extend the frontiers of scholarship in his fields of enquiry and to apply research findings to central issues of social reform and public service. In this respect he stood as a distinguished, representative figure in a tradition of British 'blue-book' social science which had its origins in the great reform movements of nineteenth-century social policy.

Self-regulation in the fields of advertising and the press were, taken together, the second of McGregor's abiding interests. He was a doughty and indefatigable defender of press freedom. After the death of Sir Morris Finer in 1975 he was appointed chairman of the royal commission on the press. The commission's report of 1977 set out an authoritative statement of the institutional preconditions for freedom of the press, including the reform of the then Press Council. The report also emphasized the close institutional and financial connections between newspapers and the advertising industry. McGregor's involvement in the management of advertising followed logically from his commitment to the principles of freedom and self-regulation of the press in commercial activity. During his ten years of outstanding service as chairman of the Advertising Standards Authority from 1980 to 1990 he played a key role in the revision of that industry's codes of practice in protecting the public interest and in dealing with complaints. By this time his achievements were already recognized in his election to an honorary fellowship at the London School of Economics in 1977 and the conferment of an honorary degree by Bristol University in 1986. In 1978 he was created a Labour life peer, as Baron McGregor of Durris, and he subsequently served in the House of Lords as an active reforming independent member.

In 1990 McGregor was appointed as the first chairman of the Press Complaints Commission. His three years as chairman were, at times, fraught with controversy. The commission was rocked by a series of high-profile press revelations about the private lives of the prince and princess of Wales, culminating in the publication of a book by Andrew Morton on Princess Diana. The future of self-regulation was very much in doubt. There were some tactical errors of judgement on the commission's part. Nevertheless on the key issues of principle and strategy McGregor got it right. He ensured that the industry wrote, endorsed, and gave total support to a code of practice that the commission administered. He steered the commission through its hazardous early years and restored the credibility of press self-regulation.

McGregor had a restless, inquisitive, and highly original mind. His command of nineteenth-century social history and understanding of the impact of law on the making of social policy were memorably impressive. As a public speaker, he was a master of rhetorical delivery and cadence. He loved the cut and thrust of academic and political argument. His conversation sparkled with anecdote and wit. His friendship was staunch and graced with many discreet acts of kindness and consideration. Throughout their marriage he and his wife, Nellie, were generous and welcoming hosts to a wide circle of friends at their London home in Wyldes Close, Hampstead. For many years Nellie served as a magistrate and as a leading member of the London School of Economics alumni society. She was also made an honorary fellow of the school in 1991. In his last few years, with the constant and loving support of Nellie, McGregor stoically battled against encroaching ill health. He died in London on 10 November 1997 and was buried in the family grave in the kirkyard at Durris, Kincardineshire. He was survived by his wife and three sons. A memorial gathering was held in the Great Hall, St Bartholomew's Hospital, London, on 4 March 1998. On his gravestone he was described, appropriately, as 'scholar, teacher and reformer'.   ROBERT PINKER

Sources *The Independent* (12 Nov 1997) · *The Guardian* (12 Nov 1997) · *Daily Telegraph* (12 Nov 1997) · *The Times* (12 Nov 1997) · *The Scotsman* (15 Nov 1997) · WWW · personal knowledge (2004) · private information (2004)

Likenesses photograph, repro. in *The Times* · photograph, repro. in *The Independent* · photograph, repro. in *Daily Telegraph* · photograph, repro. in *The Guardian* · photograph, repro. in *The Scotsman*

MacGregor [*later* Campbell], **Robert** [*known as* Rob Roy] (*bap.* 1671, *d.* 1734), outlaw and folk hero, was the third son of Lieutenant-Colonel Donald Glas MacGregor (*d.* 1702) and his wife, Margaret (*d.* 1691), daughter of Archibald Campbell of Gleneaves. He was born in Glengyle, northwest of Loch Katrine in the parish of Callander, and was baptized on 7 March 1671 at Inchcailloch parish church in Buchanan, Stirlingshire.

Early life: raider and trader To lowland eyes MacGregor's family was one of tenant farmers, his father renting Glengyle from the marquess of Montrose, but in their own terms they were clan gentry, descended from the chiefs of the dispersed and much persecuted clan Gregor. The remnants of the clan were struggling to maintain its identity, and indeed to subsist, and as well as being brought up to breed and trade in cattle Rob (whose red hair earned him the name Roy) was no doubt introduced early to the practices of cattle raiding and the raising of blackmail. Such fees were paid by cattle owners to protect their beasts from theft, a practice which ranged from providing a genuine security service to the extortion of protection money. His father took an active part in the Jacobite rising of 1689, and in September he and Rob were raiding cattle in Stirlingshire 'for their masters' with 140 men (NA Scot., GD 26/8/38). At the beginning of 1693 Rob married Mary MacGregor and the following year he obtained land at Inversnaid, between Loch Lomond and Loch Katrine, and built a house there. The reintroduction in the same year of old penal laws proscribing the MacGregors seems to have had little effect except to make a change in name necessary, and Rob chose the name Campbell, by which he was known for the rest of his life, thus adopting his mother's maiden name. Identifying with his new name Rob attached himself to the interests of the Campbell earl of Breadalbane to counter the enmity of those whom he raided such as Lord John Murray (son of the marquess of Atholl), who in 1695 unsuccessfully sent out a party of men to arrest Rob as the son of the man 'who cheated my father, and he and his family have continued to doe all they could against me' (MacGregor, 2.276). Later in the year, however, Breadalbane was charged with treason, and Rob hastened to switch his allegiances, signing a bond in June to behave as a loyal subject to the government and a faithful servant of Lord Murray. Once Breadalbane was freed, however, Rob reverted to accepting his protection, and in the years that followed he thrived modestly, with reliance on cattle stealing being increasingly replaced by legitimate trading. In 1701 he gained possession of the lands of Craigrostan (which included Inversnaid), and the following year, on his father's death, he became tutor (guardian) of Glengyle, near Loch Katrine, which had passed to his young nephew, James Graham. In 1703 he arranged the purchase of Glengyle from Montrose in his and his nephew's name, but agreed that, as Montrose remained their feudal superior, they would follow him as vassals in all lawful wars and expeditions.

In the decade that followed, Rob became well known as a cattle trader. His abilities brought him recognition as effective leader of the MacGregors, though not formally their chief. The status brought complications at a time when Jacobite intrigue was intense, but though Rob's sympathies were Jacobite he was anxious to avoid involvement—and indeed ready to gain credit with the authorities by passing intelligence. When approached in 1704 to take part in intrigues of the Jacobite Lord Lovat to discredit the first duke of Atholl, Rob hastened to warn him. But in 1707 he again pledged his loyalty to Breadalbane, referring to his mother's Campbell blood: 'I have the honour to have come of your Lordship's family, and shall keep my dependency suitable to the samine [same]'. All his promises to Breadalbane 'shall be keeped while I live' (Fraser, 2.446). It would be interesting to know what these promises were, for though Breadalbane's past lay in support for the government the crafty old politician was developing Jacobite sympathies. It was therefore not surprising that the authorities were alarmed when in 1710 Rob's interests turned towards arms dealing and he ordered 400–500 muskets and hundreds of pistols and swords. The arms were likely to end up in Jacobite hands,

and the government intervened to prevent most of them being delivered.

Outlaw and rebel Much of Rob's trading was carried out in conjunction with John Hamilton of Bardowie, who supplied both cash and security for credit, and in 1708 became the father-in-law of Rob's nephew. The business involved receiving advances from landowners and others to buy cattle, delivery often being due months later. In 1711–12 over-expansion or miscalculation led to disaster. The first sign of the impending crash came in autumn 1711 when a creditor sought to retrieve his money by collecting debts due to Rob by others. Rob was appalled that 'when I was on top of my bussines' action would be taken that might 'brake my credit' (NL Scot., MS 1314, fol. 3). By December Rob was anticipating disaster, for he assigned his lands of Ardress and Craigrostan to Bardowie (who was by far his largest creditor) and Graham of Glengyle for a nominal rent, thus hoping to preserve them from his other creditors. Meanwhile he continued collecting money from customers to buy cattle. Between November 1711 and April 1712 he received at least £12,500 Scots (over £1000 sterling) in this way, but the cattle were never delivered. In June the marquess of Montrose, one of his creditors, organized the publication of an advertisement denouncing Rob as a bankrupt and offering a reward for his apprehension. Rob himself 'finding that his affairs begun to go backward', retreated to remote areas of the highlands (*Third Report*, HMC, 381), and late in June 1712 he was in the Western Isles, ostensibly in pursuit of debts due to him, promising that he would spend his last groat to satisfy his creditors and go 'very near' (ibid.) to full repayment. But a hint that he might have to go to Ireland not surprisingly led his creditors to suspect that he was absconding, having 'the intention of leaving the country' (ibid.). Rumour stated that he had gathered his money and fled to join the Stuart pretender.

Rob Roy's fall was a matter of business failure, and the later tradition that it was due to a drover absconding with his money is implausible in view of the evidence that he knew months in advance that he was in trouble, and that he never himself used this as an explanation. His flight to the remote highlands, Montrose's determination to bring him to justice, and Rob's passionate belief that he had been wronged, however, converted an everyday bankruptcy into an epic story.

Pursued vindictively by one great man (as he saw it), Rob sought the protection of another, protesting to the duke of Atholl in January 1713 that Montrose was unjustly trying to ruin him. But when, at the instance of Montrose and other creditors, Craigrostan was seized from Rob it was the earl of Breadalbane who gave him refuge, renting him land in Glen Dochart. In June he wrote that he would do all he could to satisfy his creditors, giving priority to Montrose's claims, but the duke was implacable or mistrustful. However, Rob had on his side widespread sympathy, and while Montrose was seeking his arrest he was able to continue trading on a limited scale, and Breadalbane not only protected but employed him. In January 1714 Rob, 'a bankrupt Jacobite' (*Correspondence of the Rev.*

Robert Wodrow, 1.547n.), led 500 of Breadalbane's men at the funeral of his brother-in-law, Sir Alexander Campbell of Lochnell, and the earl appointed him as a bailie to hold courts to suppress disorder on parts of his estates.

The accession of George I in August 1714 led to intensified Jacobite activity aimed at restoring the Stuart dynasty, and Rob Roy saw in this a chance to restore his fortunes or at least to hit back at the Hanoverian Montrose. In October he appeared at Crieff and drank the pretender's health, and early in 1715 rumour claimed that he was enlisting men, having a Jacobite commission as a colonel. However, the Hanoverian authorities were mainly interested in Rob as a potential source of intelligence, for it was rightly believed that he was more concerned with the restitution of his lands than in national politics. By May it was known that he was supplying intelligence to the Hanoverian duke of Argyll, though whether it was reliable was doubted. Thus by the time the rising broke out in 1715 Rob was in close touch with both sides, but trusted by neither. He accepted that his nephew Glengyle was his senior in rank among the MacGregors, but he seems to have taken the initiative in raising the MacGregors in arms and organizing a raid in September which seized all the boats on Loch Lomond and then threatened Dumbarton, although he withdrew after slaughtering a herd of Montrose's deer on an island on the loch. Orders from the Jacobite commander, the earl of Mar, then sent Rob with a force to attack Argyll's castle at Inveraray, but he was diverted to the main Jacobite camp at Perth. When Mar and Argyll confronted each other at the battle of Sheriffmuir on 13 November 1715 Rob and his men were in the vicinity, but took no part in the contest: it seems likely that he was excluded from the main Jacobite army through distrust, and, as a supplier of intelligence to Argyll, he was probably happy to await the outcome of the battle on the sidelines.

After the drawn battle the Jacobite cause wilted, but Rob remained nominally committed to it, and it gave him a chance to indulge his taste for raiding. Appearing in December at Craigrostan, now in Montrose's possession, Rob forbade the tenants to pay rent to the duke (as he now was), and then (January 1716) carried out a foray into Fife during which he occupied Falkland Palace, becoming (for a few days) its deputy governor under Glengyle. Plunder evidently took precedence over a positive pursuit of the Jacobite cause, but none the less brought official retribution. He attempted to re-establish himself at Craigrostan, but was unable to resist when troops surprised him there in April 1716. His houses were burnt and his cattle and moveable goods carried off, though he and his followers, firing from cover, killed two or three soldiers and wounded others, thus gaining some revenge. But the incident evidently persuaded Rob that his position was untenable, and the following month he and his men went to Inveraray and surrendered their arms to the Hanoverians, in return for assurances that they would be allowed to live peacefully. Rob now doubtless hoped to invoke his earlier links with Argyll to gain protection, but his timing was disastrous. In June political changes in London saw Argyll dismissed from all his offices. Further, in June Rob was among the Scottish Jacobites attainted for high treason.

Rob now embarked on a campaign of raiding Montrose's estates, in the hope of gaining concessions from him. Parties of soldiers sent to track him down were thwarted by the wild terrain, the weather, and his evasive skills. In November he kidnapped Montrose's factor, John Graham the younger of Killearn, while he was collecting rents, and demanded that for his ransom Montrose cancel all his debts, pay him for his losses through the destruction at Craigrostan, and give his word that he would not trouble Rob in future. If men were sent against him Killearn would suffer for it. The demands were unrealistic, as Rob probably knew, and he had not the ruthlessness to make good his threats against his captive, whom he freed after a week or two. To Rob, no doubt, the gesture was worthwhile in so far as it showed his contempt for Montrose and humiliated him. The duke complained furiously to London of this insult done to the authority of the state, but the military was reluctant to act, believing that Rob would always succeed in slipping away when troops were sent against him—and there are indications that in any case it was feared by some that if Rob was captured he might cause political embarrassment by revealing Argyll's contacts with him and other Jacobites during the rising of 1715.

George I ordered that all efforts should be made to catch Rob, but by early 1717 Montrose inclined towards making an agreement with him, hoping to buy him off with a cash payment and promises of future good treatment, and Rob, exhausted and probably sick, was ready to consider submission. But rather than submit to Montrose he chose to deal with Atholl. On 3 June, by Atholl's account, a demoralized Rob had surrendered to him, saying he had 'not lain three nights together in a house these twelve months' (MacGregor, 2.317), but Rob was to claim that he had been tricked by being given a safe conduct to talk with Atholl that had not been honoured. Two days later he escaped from Atholl's prison at Logierait, and Atholl, who had been boasting of how he had managed to detain the notorious Rob Roy, now joined Montrose in finding that attempting to tame Rob could lead to humiliation. On 25 June from Balquhidder he issued his 'Declaration of Rob Roy to all true lovers of honour and honesty', though its circulation must have been small as it was not printed. In this Rob claimed that he was the victim of political conspiracy. Montrose and others had promised to secure his honour and fortune if he submitted, provided he agreed to accuse (falsely) the duke of Argyll of treasonable communications with the Jacobites. Atholl had been involved in the plot, and on Rob's refusal to denounce Argyll had treacherously arrested him. How much truth there was in this is impossible to know, but it is plausible that Argyll's enemies hoped Rob could provide them with damning information.

Keeping up the pressure on Montrose, in July Rob stole cattle and grain from his main residence, Buchanan Castle, and disarmed Montrose's tenants who were sent in pursuit. Plans were now being made to build barracks in

the highlands where troops could be stationed permanently, and Montrose was eager to start work on one at
Inversnaid. But attempts to organize his lowland tenants
to start on the site led Rob to threaten to burn their houses
if they did so. None the less a party of men guarded by soldiers marched to Inversnaid, Rob Roy retreating as they
advanced. In retaliation he again raided Buchanan, breaking open the duke's grain stores, cheekily leaving a receipt
for what he stole, regarding it as part of his rightful rents
from Craigrostan. He was soon forced to surrender Craigrostan, though in August 1718 he no doubt led the party of
highlanders who carried off quarriers and masons working on the new barracks, in spite of the fact that troops
were stationed there. However, he failed to prevent completion of the building, though he continued to raid, and
his attack on a party of troops and tenants of Montrose
pursuing stolen cattle in January 1719 led to a proclamation being issued offering £200 sterling for his capture.

Rob's boldness at this particular time was probably
inspired by knowledge that preparations for a new Jacobite rising were well advanced: he might not be committed
to the cause, but could hope to benefit from it. In April he
was inspired to rhetorical denunciation of his creditors,
especially 'that rebellious bugger the Duke of Montrose …
who is very far degenerate from his predecessors' (NL
Scot., MS 8494, fols. 198–9), and with alcohol inspired fervour he drew up a mock challenge to Montrose to fight
him, jeering at him for cowardice. But instead of sending
it to the duke he gave it to a friend to divert him and his
comrades 'when you are takeing your botle' (NL Scot., MS
901, fols. 142–3). Rob knew that part of the Jacobite plan
was for a Spanish expedition to land in the west highlands, but the fleet had been dispersed by storms and only
300 men, led by the marquess of Tullibardine (the son of
the duke of Atholl), reached their intended destination.
Rob and about forty of his clansmen joined Tullibardine,
though by one account they were 'auxiliaries' who served
'for their pay' rather than dedicated Jacobites (*Various Collections*, 5.241–2). They shared in the collapse of the Jacobite force in the battle of Glensheil (10 June).

Rob remained an outlaw, but the authorities seemed
inclined to ignore him rather than waste further effort
and reputation by pursuing him, though in March 1720 he
drew attention to himself by attacking a party of soldiers
unwise enough to spend a night in Balquhidder, wounding several of them. But though Rob continued to seek to
collect 'his' rents of Craigrostan, the estate had been forfeited to the crown because of his part in the '15 rising.
The government then sold it to Montrose and reached a
settlement with Rob's creditors. He must have realized
that any chance of regaining Craigrostan had been lost,
and his raiding slackened. Moreover, the settlement
solved one problem: he no longer faced legal action
against him for debt. He remained, however, a rebel.

Submission and pardon In 1725 a change in government
policy brought Rob a chance to make his peace. General
George Wade was sent to Scotland as commander-in-
chief, authorized to offer remaining rebels like Rob the

chance to receive a pardon after writing letters of submission. Rob's letter of submission was typical of the man,
arguing more forcibly than plausibly that he had never
meant to be a rebel. He begged for the mercy and favour
that Wade had procured for others in his 'unfortunate circumstances'. He had indeed been guilty of the great crime
of rebellion in 1715, he admitted, but that had only been
because he had been in debt to Montrose. His 'real inclination' had been to join the government's forces, but had
he done so he would have been arrested for debt. It had
been impossible for him to remain neutral, so he had been
forced into unnatural rebellion—but had sent all the
intelligence he could to Argyll. He and his men handed in
their arms, and on 19 October 1725 he formally submitted
to Wade at Dunkeld—and for good measure gave him
intelligence of the movements of Jacobite conspirators in
the highlands. His pardon followed, and in accordance
with his new allegiance (or his own interests) he agreed to
act as a spy for Wade in 1727, his activities leading to the
arrest of at least one Jacobite activist (James Stirling of
Keir). Two of Rob's sons were enlisted in one of the independent companies that were supposed to police the
highlands. But though outwardly Rob was now playing
the peaceful Hanoverian citizen old habits died hard. In
1729 his soldier sons were charged with cattle and horse
stealing, and only the skills of Rob's tongue saved them
and him from prosecution. His wife too was active in the
family business, being recorded in 1725 travelling round
Stirlingshire collecting blackmail protection money for
her husband.

Rob Roy spent his last years in Balquhidder on a farm
leased to him on the estate of the duke of Atholl. He died
on 28 December 1734, and was buried in Balquhidder
churchyard though he had converted to Roman Catholicism in his final years. He was survived by his wife.

Man and myth Already in his own lifetime Rob had
become a legend, and the fact that both Rob and Robin are
diminutives of Robert assisted his identification with
Robin Hood, for he was widely regarded as a humble man
who had taken to banditry to right wrongs done to him by
an arrogant magnate, and though he may not have given
to the poor, Rob acquired the image of a man who did not
steal indiscriminately, but took what was his by right
from the great while sparing poor men. Such leniency of
course, as with outlaws in many countries, was policy as
well as principle, for to survive the outlaw needed the
sympathy of the common people. That Rob had this is
clear: he was not betrayed in all his years on the run. For so
notorious a bandit he was notably unbloodthirsty, and he
had the ability to charm those who met him. A man who
was introduced to him in 1726 had 'a damnable ill opinion'
of him, but was soon converted 'for by God he's a jolly
man' (National Register of Archives for Scotland, survey
182/1/9, Scott-Kerr of Sunlaws, 2). In his deeds he sometimes showed a style, almost a sense of humour, as well as
daring, that made many ready to forgive him his sins.
Who else would leave a receipt for stolen goods? An
account (wildly inaccurate in places) of his actions

appeared in London in 1723 as *The Highland Rogue*, and 'lovable rogue' seems to sum up a widespread perception of his story—he did wrong, but you had to laugh, and the puncturing of the pride of grandees such as Montrose and Atholl appealed to many.

Traditions of his life grew and multiplied until he was credited with a quite improbable number of raids, escapes, and duels. William Wordsworth was inspired to verse by a visit to what he (wrongly) thought was his grave in 1803, hailing him as being as good as Robin Hood, and a man who had a primitive, honest morality derived from nature. But it was Sir Walter Scott's *Rob Roy* (1817) that launched Rob's international reputation. Plays, operas, and hack biographies followed, cashing in on the popularity of Scott's work, while unlikely numbers of relics of the hero were conveniently discovered—dirks, sporrans, pistols, and swords, many of which ended up in Scott's own collection at Abbotsford. But though Scott inspired much myth making, the historical introduction to his novel provides an essential starting point for the study of the serious life of the real Rob. But Rob has always appealed more to the tourist and entertainment industries than the historian. The erection of a statue of him by Benno Schotz in Stirling in 1975 indicates that, as a man who had been oppressed by the great and defied them, Rob Roy serves as a hero in a democratic age, and a Rob Roy centre in Callander encourages hero worship by tourists who mainly know of him through a 1994 Hollywood film, starring Liam Neeson, whose account of his deeds is just about as fictional as Scott's.   DAVID STEVENSON

Sources D. Stevenson, *The hunt for Rob Roy: the man and the myth* [forthcoming] · DNB · W. H. Murray, *Rob Roy Macgregor: his life and times* (1982) · *The real Rob Roy: a guide to the sources in the Scottish Record Office* (1995) · A. G. M. MacGregor, *History of the clan Gregor: from public records and private collections*, 2 vols. (1898–1901) · E. B., *The highland rogue* (1723) · W. Scott, *Rob Roy* (1817) · A. H. Millar, *History of Rob Roy* (1883) · H. Howlett, *Highland constable: life and times of Rob Roy MacGregor* (1950) · NA Scot., GD 26, 112, 220 · *The correspondence of the Rev. Robert Wodrow*, ed. T. M'Crie, 3 vols., Wodrow Society, [3] (1842–3) · K. Macleay, *Historical memoirs of Rob Roy and the clan Macgregor* (1818) · J. J. H. H. Stewart-Murray, seventh duke of Atholl, *Chronicles of the Atholl and Tullibardine families*, 5 vols. (privately printed, Edinburgh, 1908) · J. A. Smith, 'Notices of an original letter of King James II … also some documents relating to Rob Roy MacGregor', *Proceedings of the Society of Antiquaries of Scotland*, 7 (1866–8) · P. Hopkins, *Glencoe and the end of the highland war* (1986) · W. Fraser, ed., *The Red Book of Menteith*, 2 vols. (1880) · *Third report*, HMC, 2 (1872) · *Report on manuscripts in various collections*, 8 vols., HMC, 55 (1901–14), vol. 5

Archives NA Scot., letters and papers | Blair Castle, Perthshire, Stewart Murray of Atholl MSS · Stirling Council Archives, Stirling, MacGregor of MacGregor MSS

MacGregor, Sir William (1846–1919), colonial governor, was born at Hillockhead in the parish of Towie, Aberdeenshire, on 20 October 1846, the eldest son of John MacGregor, a crofter, and his wife, Agnes, the daughter of William Smith, a farmer, of Pitprone in the nearby parish of Leochel-Cushnie. He went to the village school of Tillyduke, where his ability soon attracted attention; despite working on farms as a boy, his own efforts and the help of friends enabled him to go to Aberdeen grammar school in

1865. He then went to university at Aberdeen (1867), where he studied medicine, and he continued his education at Anderson's Medical College (LFPS). He graduated MB (1872) and MD (1874) from Aberdeen and LRCP from Edinburgh.

While still a medical student, MacGregor married Mary, the daughter of Peter Thomson, on 4 October 1868. They had one son and one daughter before her death in 1877. After practising medicine for a short time in Scotland, MacGregor was appointed in 1873 assistant medical officer in the Seychelles; in 1874 resident surgeon in the civil hospital at Port Louis, Mauritius; and in 1875 chief medical officer for the colony of Fiji. During the next thirteen years, encouraged by Sir Arthur Gordon, he gained much administrative experience and showed considerable ability. He was resourceful in dealing with the epidemic of measles which decimated the population of Fiji in 1878 and in rescuing three people at once in a shipwreck near Suva in 1884, for which he was awarded the Albert medal (1884) and the Clarke gold medal of Australia (1885). In November 1883 he made a second marriage, to Mary Jane, the daughter of Captain Robert Cocks, a merchant seaman. They had two daughters. His career also began to develop as he gradually came to occupy important administrative posts and gained experience by acting as temporary administrator of the colony on more than one occasion.

In 1888 MacGregor was appointed the first administrator (receiving the title of lieutenant-governor in 1895) of British New Guinea (later Papua New Guinea), which had been proclaimed a British protectorate only a few years before, in 1884. There was much pioneer work to be done, and MacGregor, with limited resources, showed great energy in laying the foundations of sound administration. He organized an efficient native police force, insisted on strict enforcement of the laws, tackled the difficult problems of land tenure and native labour, and resisted exploitation of the Papuan people. The policy of peaceful penetration which he promoted gradually came to be tolerated by the indigenous tribes of the country and led to the exploitation of its natural resources by Papuans as well as Europeans. He was created KCMG in 1889, and in 1896 was given the founder's medal by the Royal Geographical Society for his exploration of the territory. A paper which he had read to the society, was later developed into *British New Guinea: Country and People*, which was published in 1897.

MacGregor left New Guinea in 1898 and was appointed governor of Lagos the following year. Here, too, he helped to develop a recently acquired colony, requiring the tribal chiefs to share in the work of government and making the country more accessible through the building of railways. He also campaigned actively against malaria, helping Ronald Ross to apply his discoveries into the disease.

After five years in Lagos, during which his health suffered and he had differences with the crown agents as well as disputes over policies towards inland protectorates, in 1904 MacGregor was appointed governor of Newfoundland. In this post he used his medical knowledge to attempt to prevent tuberculosis, and his tact and diplomacy contributed largely to the settlement of the difficult and immediate question of American fishing rights. He also organized and personally conducted a scientific expedition to Labrador, the aim of which was to survey its coast and investigate its natural resources. The results of this expedition were of anthropological as well as geographical and meteorological interest, and he was awarded the GCMG in 1907.

From 1909 to 1914 MacGregor served as governor of Queensland, where his reputation had preceded him from New Guinea. In Queensland he concentrated his efforts on developing education, agriculture, and medicine, and wisely kept within the constitutional limits of his powers. Largely on account of his own efforts, the University of Queensland was founded during his term of office, in 1910, and he became its first chancellor.

MacGregor retired, in July 1914, after nearly forty years' work in colonial administration, was made a privy councillor, and went to live on his estate at Chapel-on-Leader, Berwickshire. When the First World War broke out he volunteered for service, and was involved in lecturing and committee work, particularly advising on the Pacific region.

In 1918 his health began to deteriorate and, after an operation in a nursing home in Aberdeen, he died on 3 July 1919. He was buried in the churchyard at Towie, his native village.

MacGregor died with a reputation as one of the most able and well regarded of Great Britain's colonial administrators, whose successes were due largely to his own efforts. While he lacked the advantages of birth, his knowledge of languages, botany, ethnology, and medicine all helped him to become an effective administrator, and his physical strength helped him to succeed as a scientific explorer. His ability to persuade native peoples of the countries which he governed was largely a result of his determination to prevent their exploitation by Europeans, and to the tact and respect, as well as the patience, which he showed them. He was said to be reticent by nature, without boastfulness or egotism, and yet to have had 'a certain ruggedness in his character'. According to Lord Bryce, his strength and restraint made him 'a model of what a colonial governor should be'. He was made an honorary LLD of the universities of Aberdeen, Edinburgh, and Queensland, and an honorary DSc of the University of Cambridge. He presented his substantial collection of ethnological specimens from Fiji, New Guinea, Lagos, and Labrador to the University of Aberdeen.

F. P. SPRENT, rev. LYNN MILNE

Sources R. B. Joyce, 'MacGregor, Sir William', *AusDB*, vol. 5 · R. B. Joyce, *Sir William MacGregor* (1971) · R. W. Reid, 'Sir William MacGregor', *Aberdeen University Review*, 7 (1919–20), 1–14 · C. B. Fletcher, *The new Pacific* (1917)
Archives Mitchell L., NSW, corresp. and papers · Mitchell L., NSW, notebook of exploration of Owen Stanley Range · NL Aus., diaries | BL, letters to Lord Stanmore, Add. MS 49203 · Bodl. Oxf., letters to James Bryce · Bodl. Oxf., corresp. with Lewis Harcourt · NL Aus., corresp. with Alfred Deakin
Likenesses portrait, repro. in *Royal Academy Pictures* (1916)

Wealth at death £35,000: *AusDB*

McGregor, William (1847–1911), football administrator, was born in Braco, Perthshire. Little is known about him before he moved in 1870 to Birmingham, where he and his brother Peter opened a linen draper's shop at 306–7 Summer Lane, Newtown, then about a mile from the city centre. He does not seem to have been much of a football player himself, although he had played the game with other boys in Braco after they had seen the local stonemasons kicking a ball about. His interest may have been revived by meeting other Scots in Birmingham who were keen on the sport: J. Campbell Orr founded the Calthorpe team in the early 1870s and George Ramsay was a leading member of Aston Villa. McGregor was enthusiastic enough about the growing popular pastime to arrange the half-day closing of his shop for Saturday afternoons so that he could watch the games. He was invited to join the committee of Aston Villa in the late 1870s, and umpired for the club. His shop meanwhile began to sell football shirts and shorts and to become a meeting-place for local followers of the sport. At this time McGregor lived with his wife, Jesse, their daughter and son in a terraced house on Witton Road not far from the Aston Lower Grounds. Later the family moved to 8 Salisbury Road, close to Cannon Hill Park. They worshipped at the Congregational church in Wheeler Street, and like many Congregationalists McGregor was also a Liberal in politics and a teetotaller.

About this time football was developing rapidly as a spectator sport, especially in Lancashire and the midlands. Local and regional cup competitions, together with the FA cup, encouraged clubs to widen their search for good players and some, including Aston Villa, began to pay them for playing. Professionalism was legalized in 1885 but the priority given to cup ties disrupted ordinary fixture lists and often led to other supposedly competitive matches becoming one-sided friendly games which proved unattractive to paying customers. What was required was a regular programme of fixtures between the strongest teams, along the same lines as the county cricket championship. This was what McGregor proposed when he wrote to five of the leading clubs on 2 March 1888. The Football League was born at a meeting in Manchester on 17 April with six clubs from Lancashire and six from the midlands.

McGregor subsequently became chairman of the league's management committee (1888–92), president (1892–4), and a life member (1895–1911). He was also a Football Association councillor and something of a football celebrity, writing regularly on the sport in the press and giving his name to products such as the McGregor football. On 4 December 1911 he was presented with the FA's long service medal but shortly afterwards he became ill. He died at Miss Storer's Nursing Home, 70 Newhall Street, Birmingham, on 20 December 1911. Jesse had died in December 1908 and McGregor was buried next to her in St Mary's Church, Handsworth, Birmingham, on 23 December 1911.

TONY MASON

Sources A. Gibson and W. Pickford, *Association football and the men who made it*, 4 vols. [1905–6] • S. Inglis, *League football and the men who made it: the official centenary of the Football League, 1888–1988* (1988) • T. Mason, *Association football and English society, 1863–1915* (1980) • *Birmingham Gazette and Express* (21 Dec 1911) • *Birmingham Daily Mail* (23 Dec 1911) • *Birmingham Daily Post* (21 Dec 1911) • *Birmingham Mail* (2 Nov 1955)
Likenesses portrait, Villa Park, Birmingham
Wealth at death £3391 10s. 11d.: probate, 7 Feb 1912, *CGPLA Eng. & Wales*

MacGregor, William (1848–1937), Church of England clergyman and philanthropist, was born on 16 May 1848 at 26 Falkner Street, Liverpool, the second of the three sons of Walter Fergus MacGregor (1810–1863), an engineer, and his wife, Anne Jane (1820/21–1892), the daughter of Richard Moon. William's paternal grandfather, Alexander MacGregor (1772–1828), a merchant and banker in the port, seems to have been the originator of the family's wealth. His father Walter was a wealthy man—he left £100,000—and his resources allowed William to be educated at Rugby School under Frederick Temple and at Exeter College, Oxford (BA, 1871); he entered the Inner Temple in 1870.

MacGregor soon abandoned the law for the ministry, apparently influenced by Temple's brand of muscular Christianity and the broad church approach of his predecessor Thomas Arnold. He impressed Brooke Lambert, the vicar of Tamworth, who appointed MacGregor his curate for the village of Hopwas in 1872. Tamworth was a growing town with serious social problems, the remedy of which was actively opposed by the leading local landowner and MP for the town, the profligate Sir Robert Peel, third baronet, on the grounds of cost. Hopwas had a small, inadequate chapel and no clerical residence. MacGregor's private means allowed a chapel to be commenced before he left in 1876 to become curate and then vicar of the deeply impoverished Liverpool parish of St Matthias. Nevertheless, he continued his involvement in Tamworth, supplying £1000 to continue the construction of a charity hospital. The living at Tamworth was so poor as to require an incumbent with private means and so, when those of Brooke Lambert failed in 1878, MacGregor was the obvious replacement.

The new vicar attracted larger congregations, especially among working families, by shortening services and altering their timing, abbreviating sermons and making their content more 'political', beautifying the church, and having more hymns sung. MacGregor shamed the wealthy into giving more in the collection and continued the process of church extension in the town's suburbs. An ecumenical, he collaborated with nonconformists in establishing mission halls. He appointed energetic clergymen to assist him, partly paid for by his own refusal to draw a stipend. MacGregor was a radical Liberal, who believed that social improvement could be achieved only by creating the conditions where self-help could prosper, in particular through better education and public health. Despite the reluctance of many Anglicans, he actively promoted board schools, serving as unpaid secretary to the Tamworth board and personally running a penny bank;

he even offered to interview any child found walking the streets during school hours. He spent £3000 in establishing a youth club with baths and a gymnasium, revived Tamworth's library and reading room, and actively supported a coffee room and working men's clubs and institutes. In the field of public health, he employed a 'Bible woman' to visit homes and advise on nutrition.

MacGregor's social conscience led to the end of his incumbency. He campaigned against slum landlords—effectively accusing them of murder—and was the only property owner prepared to lease premises to the Tamworth Co-operative Society, of which he became treasurer in 1886. The town's shopkeepers boycotted the church, arguing that his 'Municipal Gospel' was replacing morality by materialism. MacGregor's health, which was never strong, gave him a pretext to resign in 1887.

MacGregor, a lifelong bachelor, did not desert the townspeople but lived nearby at Bolehall Manor House in Warwickshire for the remaining fifty years of his life. A freemason, he invested successfully in such socially useful concerns as the town's building society and savings bank and also in a newspaper (whose aim was to bridge Tamworth's bitter political divide); he served as chairman of all three concerns. He was a county councillor for forty years (with the best attendance record of any councillor between 1907 and 1910) and did much to promote education in Warwickshire and around Tamworth. MacGregor served as a magistrate, and his support for the miners' union helped to defuse class hostility locally. He was a leading mover in 1897 in buying Tamworth Castle and grounds as a museum and public park and gave land in Bolehall for another park. Ill health led him to holiday in Egypt, and he amassed one of Britain's best private collections of Egyptian relics. This was auctioned in 1922 in 1800 lots, when the British Museum acquired many items. From 1888 to 1930 MacGregor was a member of the committee of the Egypt Exploration Fund and was a generous patron. He was a fellow of the Society of Antiquaries and an authority on Greek pottery.

MacGregor died of old age at Bolehall Manor House on 26 February 1937 and was buried in Hopwas churchyard on 1 March. His career serves to represent those many evangelical philanthropists who did much to secure social improvement and promote political harmony in the late nineteenth and early twentieth centuries.

DAVID BROWN

Sources D. Brown, 'The Reverend William MacGregor and the improvement of Tamworth', *Midland History*, 24 (1999), 129–46 • *Tamworth Herald* (1872–87) • *Tamworth Herald* (6 March 1937) • *Tamworth Parish Magazine* (1872–87) • J. S. Harding, *History of the Tamworth Industrial Co-operative Society* (1910) • Burke, *Gen. GB* (1937) • W. R. Dawson and E. P. Uphill, *Who was who in Egyptology*, 3rd edn, rev. M. L. Bierbrier (1995) • C. H. Goodliffe, *A history of Tamworth Hospital* (1976) • R. Bolton King, J. D. Browne, and E. M. H. Ibbetson, *Bolton King: practical idealist* (1978), 18–32 • H. W. De Ath, 'The landed interest and Warwickshire county council, 1899–1928', MA diss., Lanchester Polytechnic, 1985 • Crockford (1885) • census returns, 1881, PRO, RG 11/2760, fol. 46 • [F. Temple], ed., *Rugby School register from 1675 to 1867 inclusive* (1867), 225, 230 • b. cert. • d. cert.

Archives Tamworth Public Library, Tamworth Educational Association minutes book I, RL TA edu A 84

Likenesses brass engraving, Tamworth Co-operative Society · photograph, repro. in *Tamworth Herald* (6 March 1937) · photograph, *Tamworth Herald* offices, Tamworth · photographs, *Tamworth Herald* offices, Tamworth, archives

Wealth at death £84,251 17s. 4d.: probate, 24 April 1937, *CGPLA Eng. & Wales*

MacGregor, William York (1855–1923). *See under* Glasgow Boys (*act.* 1875–1895).

McGrigor, Sir James, **first baronet** (1771–1858), military surgeon, was born at Cromdale, Inverness-shire, on 9 April 1771, the eldest of the three sons of Colquhoun McGrigor (*d.* 1800), merchant of Aberdeen, and his wife, Anne, daughter of Lewis Grant of Lathendrey in Strathspey, Inverness-shire.

Education and beginnings of army career McGrigor was educated at the grammar school at Aberdeen, and at Marischal College, where he graduated MA in 1788. He studied medicine at Aberdeen and Edinburgh, and after his return to Aberdeen in 1789, while an apprentice to George French, surgeon to the County Infirmary, he was one of the founders of a local medico-chirurgical society among the students. Wishing to become an army surgeon, he went to London, where he attended Mr Wilson's lectures on anatomy, and after the outbreak of war with France purchased the post of surgeon to De Burgh's regiment, later famous as the 88th or Connaught Rangers. His appointment was dated 13 September 1793, and his name was at first spelt MacGregor in the army list. He served with the regiment in Flanders, and in the winter retreat to Bremen in 1794–5, in which his health suffered severely. When the 88th was at Southampton soon after its return, Lieutenant-Colonel William Carr Beresford, afterwards Marshal Beresford, was appointed to the command of the regiment. Beresford quarrelled with McGrigor, blaming him for the highly insanitary condition of the regiment, although the regimental infirmary was admitted to be in excellent order, and, among other arbitrary acts, insisted on his attending all parades. McGrigor protested and applied, without success, for exchange to another regiment. However a better understanding prevailed between the two men after Beresford made a favourable report of McGrigor's services. Later in the year (1795) the regiment was ordered to the West Indies. Mistaking a sailing signal, the transport in which McGrigor had embarked set off and reached Barbados alone, long in advance of the other troops. She was thought to be lost, and a replacement was appointed to fill McGrigor's post. McGrigor accompanied a detachment of the 25th regiment to suppress the revolt in Grenada, but was shipwrecked on the way. Meanwhile the 88th had embarked with Admiral Sir Hugh Cloberry Christian but the transports were shattered and dispersed in a storm in November 1795. Only two companies of the 88th reached the West Indies, with which, after serving in Grenada and St Vincent, McGrigor came home in the autumn of 1796. In May 1799 he landed with the 88th at Bombay, proceeding with it afterwards to Ceylon, and in

Sir James McGrigor, first baronet (1771–1858), by William Ward (after John Jackson)

1801 was appointed superintending surgeon of the force of 8000 European and Indian troops sent up the Red Sea to join the army in Egypt, under Major-General David Baird. McGrigor received a commission from the East India Company, so that he might take charge of the Indian details. Baird's force landed at Quseir in May–June 1801, and after crossing the desert to Qena, descended the Nile to Rosetta. There McGrigor had to deal with a serious outbreak of the plague among the troops. When the army evacuated Egypt, McGrigor crossed the desert to Suez, and returned to Bombay and thence to England.

McGrigor was transferred to the Royal Horse Guards (Blues), and served with them at Canterbury and Windsor, where he was noticed by George III and Queen Charlotte.

Deputy inspector-general of hospitals McGrigor proceeded MD at Marischal College on 20 February 1804, and on 27 June 1805 was made one of the new deputy inspectors-general of hospitals, and placed in charge of the northern district (headquarters York), where he introduced many improvements and stimulated the officers under him through a mixture of courtesy, criticism, and advice. His talents attracted the notice of the duke of York, who transferred him to the south-western district (headquarters Winchester), subsequently placing the Portsmouth district and Isle of Wight and a part of the Sussex district under him as well. At this time McGrigor had in medical charge the counties of Sussex, Hampshire, Dorset, Wiltshire, Somerset, Gloucestershire, and Worcestershire, and south Wales; the medical organization of numerous expeditions dispatched from Portsmouth at this period was also entrusted to him. The south coast was the land-fall of troops returning from abroad. During his time in this post, McGrigor must have pondered on the problems of disposal of sick and wounded. Infectious disease was the predominant cause of sickness. On the return of troops from Corunna, heavily infected with what was then called 'fever', he declared the difficulties 'unsurmountable'. Nevertheless, he overcame them. It is not impossible that the experience gained then helped him to formulate his system of evacuation, described below.

McGrigor's reputation now stood very high. His old chief, Beresford, applied for his services as principal medical officer (PMO) of the Portuguese army, but before he could take up his posting, he was ordered to Walcheren, where the British camp site was under water and 3000 men were ill with malaria. The Walcheren campaign was one of the disasters of British military medicine. McGrigor was on board HMS *Venerable* when she was wrecked at the mouth of the Scheldt. After long delay the crew were rescued by the small boats of the fleet from Flushing. Sir Eyre Coote the younger, who had succeeded to command, testified to the important services rendered by McGrigor, who was himself infected with malaria.

Promotion and marriage After his return McGrigor was promoted inspector-general of hospitals on 25 August 1809. Not long after resuming duty, on 23 June 1810 he married Mary (1779–1872), youngest daughter of Duncan Grant of Lingeistone, Moray—sister of his old friend Lewis Grant (afterwards Sir Lewis Grant MD), of Brigadier-General Colquhoun Grant (1780–1829), and of Colonel Alexander Grant CB, Madras army—with whom he had three sons and one daughter.

On 13 June 1811 McGrigor received the sinecure position of physician to the Portsmouth garrison, but soon afterwards was promoted once more, this time to become chief of the medical staff of the Peninsular army under command of Wellington. He arrived in Lisbon on 10 January 1812 and was present with the army throughout the rest of the campaign, serving from Ciudad Rodrigo to Toulouse, including the siege of Badajoz, the terrible Burgos retreat, and the major battles of Vitoria, the Pyrenees, and Toulouse.

It was during this war that McGrigor made his name as a medical director of the first rank. Although it was George James Guthrie, the surgeon, who has the credit for introducing the Guthrie pony cart to transport wounded in the winter campaign which followed the taking of Ciudad Rodrigo to hospitals manned by regimental medical officers—so that wounded men were kept with their own comrades, and in contravention of the general order that sick and wounded be sent directly to general hospitals—it was McGrigor who instituted the 'chain of evacuation'. McGrigor had the concept of 'stages' on the 'way back', as the RAMC puts it, and his methods are still the basis of evacuation today. Thus he had field hospitals in which less severely wounded could be treated, allowing them to be returned to duty more readily, while maintaining space in

the general hospitals for those needing more major treatment and longer care. His allocation of food for the wounded was the reason for the famous exchange with Wellington, at Madrid, when the Iron Duke asked McGrigor in anger: 'Who commands the Army, Sir, I or you?'. McGrigor stood his ground. Wellington went on: 'As long as you live, Sir, never do anything without my orders' (McGrigor, 302). But he invited his medical director to dine with him the same evening. McGrigor's administrative ability, and the courage and self-reliance which enabled him to accept grave responsibility at critical moments, speedily won the confidence of Wellington, who later declared that McGrigor was 'one of the most industrious, able, and successful public servants I have ever met with' (*Dispatches of the Duke of Wellington*, 7.643). On McGrigor's representations, the services of medical officers were recognized by their being mentioned in dispatches, something never granted before. This happened first after the battle of Badajoz. It is worth recording, however, that it was not until thirty-seven years later, that he, as director-general, eventually persuaded the high command to award decorations for doctors.

Knight and director-general After the peace of 1814 McGrigor returned home, was knighted, and retired on an allowance of £3 a day. The medical officers who had served under him presented him with a service of plate valued at a 1000 guineas. He applied himself anew to his favourite subjects, anatomy and chemistry; but on 13 June 1815 he was appointed director-general of the army medical department, and held the post until 1851. The salary was £2000 a year, with the equivalent rank of major-general. McGrigor founded the Museum of Natural History and Pathological Anatomy at Fort Pitt, Chatham; its library was later moved to Netley near Southampton.

Now director-general of the Army Medical Services, McGrigor carried out six reforms of importance. The first was the inauguration of medical reports from all military stations, which twenty years later formed the basis of the *Statistical Returns of the Health of the Army*, perpetuated as the annual blue books of the army medical department. The second was assistance to widows and dependants—in 1816 he started the Army Friendly Society, for help to widows of medical officers and in 1820 the Army Benevolent Society, for assisting the orphans of medical officers. Third, he instituted research into all aspects of army health, and fourth, in connection with this, was responsible for the development of chairs of military medicine in Dublin and Edinburgh. Fifth, he enhanced the whole system of selection of men seeking commissions in the medical services, personally interviewing candidates, and later seeing that in their early careers they were well guided. And lastly, he won the honour of royal commissions for his medical officers.

After thirty-eight years in post, McGrigor retired on pension at the beginning of 1851. He died at his residence at 3 Harley Street, London, on 2 April 1858, aged nearly eighty-seven. He was survived by his wife and his son Charles Rhoderick succeeded him as second baronet.

Honours and publications McGrigor was elected FRS on 14 March 1816. He received the freedom of the cities of Edinburgh and Aberdeen. The University of Edinburgh made him an honorary LLD; Marischal College, now part of the University of Aberdeen, chose him as rector in 1826, 1827, and 1841. He was created a baronet in September 1831. He was a fellow of the colleges of physicians of London and Edinburgh, honorary physician to the queen, a fellow of the Royal Society of Edinburgh, a member of the council of the University of London, and of many learned societies at home and abroad. He was made a KCB on 17 August 1850. He had also the Turkish order of the Crescent, the commander's cross of the Portuguese Tower and Sword, and the war medal with five clasps.

McGrigor was author of a *Memoir on the Health of the 88th and other Regiments, from June 1800 to May 1801*, presented to the Bombay Medical Society in 1801; *Medical Sketches of the Expedition to Egypt from India* (1804); *A Letter to the Commissioners of Military Enquiry* (1808), a reply to animadversions on the *5th Report of the Commissioners of Military Enquiry* which had been published by Edward Nathaniel Bancroft; a memoir on the fever that appeared in the British army after the return from Corunna, in *Edinburgh Medical and Surgical Journal*, 6, 1810; a 'Memoir on the health of the army in the Peninsula', in *Transactions of the Medico-Chirurgical Society*, London, 6; also *Report of Sickness, Mortality, and Invaliding in the Army in the West Indies* (1838) and a similar report for the United Kingdom, Mediterranean, and British North America in 1839.

A memorial to McGrigor in the quadrangle of Marischal College was 'erected near the place of his education and the scenes of his youth'.

H. M. CHICHESTER, rev. J. S. G. BLAIR

Sources J. McGrigor, *The autobiography and services of Sir J. McGrigor* (1861) · private information (1893) · Chambers, *Scots.* (1835) · Burke, *Peerage* (1857) · *GM*, 3rd ser., 4 (1858), 553 · *PRS*, 9 (1857–9) · *Supplementary despatches (correspondence) and memoranda of Field Marshal Arthur, duke of Wellington*, ed. A. R. Wellesley, second duke of Wellington, 15 vols. (1858–72) · W. J. St E.-G. Rhys, 'Mentioned in despatches', *Thirty fourth international congress on the history of medicine* [Glasgow, 1994] (1994), 116 · *The dispatches of … the duke of Wellington … from 1799 to 1818*, ed. J. Gurwood, 7: *Peninsula, 1790–1813* (1837), 643 · *IGI*
Archives Aberdeen Medico-Chirurgical Society, casebooks, corresp. and reports · NRA, priv. coll., personal and family papers · Wellcome L., autobiography · Wellcome L., corresp. | BL, corresp. and papers relating to J. McGrigor · BL, letters to Lord Palmerston, Add. MSS 48429, 48431 · W. Sussex RO, letters to duke of Richmond · Wellcome L., corresp. with Sir John Hall · Yale U., Beinecke L., letters to T. J. Pettigrew
Likenesses J. Holl, stipple, 1839, Wellcome L. · plaster bust, 1858, Scot. NPG · M. Noble, bronze statue, c.1865, Royal Army Medical College, London · D. Wilkie, oils, 1893, Netley Hospital, Southampton · H. Adlard, stipple (after H. Room), Wellcome L. · T. Heaphy, watercolour drawing, NPG · W. Theed junior, bust, Royal Military College, Sandhurst · W. Ward, mezzotint (after J. Jackson), NPG, Wellcome L. [*see illus.*]
Wealth at death under £25,000: probate, 29 June 1858, CGPLA Eng. & Wales

McGrigor, James (1819–1863), army officer in the East India Company, son of Charles McGrigor or McGregor, who retired from the service as lieutenant-colonel 70th regiment and died barrack-master at Nottingham in 1841, and nephew of Sir James McGrigor bt, MD, was educated at Addiscombe College (1833–4), and in 1834 received a Bombay infantry cadetship. On 24 February 1835 he was appointed ensign in the 21st Bombay native infantry, in which he became lieutenant on 18 July 1839 and captain on 24 January 1845. At about this time he married a sister of Lieutenant-General Graeme Alexander Lockhart of Castlehill, Lanarkshire, and late of the 78th highlanders.

As a lieutenant McGrigor served under Sir Charles James Napier in the Sind War, and for a time was adjutant of the Gujarat irregular horse. He became brevet major on 28 November 1854. In September 1857 McGrigor, still a captain and brevet major, was in command of the 21st Bombay native infantry at Karachi. The Indian mutiny was at its height, and Bartle Frere had just sent away every available European and Baluch soldier either to Multan or the south Maratha country. Shortly before 11 p.m. on 16 September 1857 McGrigor was warned by two loyal sepoy officers that a mutiny and massacre of Europeans was arranged for twelve o'clock that night. Mrs McGrigor at once courageously decided to leave her husband's hands free by making her way alone to a place of comparative safety. Snatching a couple of sheets from the bed and wrapping them round her, in the guise of an ayah, she escaped unmolested. McGrigor hurried to the authorities, and a troop of the Bombay European horse artillery arrived just before the time appointed for the outbreak. When, at midnight, McGrigor ordered the 'assembly' to sound, the regiment found itself confronted by the battery, with guns loaded and ready for action. In answer to a short but forcible appeal from McGrigor the regiment laid down its arms, which were removed on the artillery wagons. The regiment was disbanded, and some of the ringleaders were tried by a court-martial of sepoy officers, and executed, not one escaping.

McGrigor received the thanks of the government, and on 20 July 1858 was appointed major of the 30th Bombay native infantry, one of the new regiments then raised in Sind. On 1 January 1862 he was promoted to lieutenant-colonel of the 15th Bombay native infantry. He had been stationed for some months with his battalion at Aden, passing much of his time on shooting excursions in Arabia, when he was accidentally drowned while bathing, on 28 June 1863, in Aden.

H. M. CHICHESTER, rev. JAMES FALKNER

Sources *Indian Army List* · *GM*, 3rd ser., 15 (1863), 247, 510 · P. Cadell, *History of the Bombay army* (1938)

McGrigor, Sir Rhoderick Robert (1893–1959), naval officer, was born on 12 April 1893 in York, the only son of Major Charles Rhoderick Robert McGrigor of the King's Royal Rifles, and his wife, Ada Rosamond, daughter of Robert Hartley Bower, of Welham, Yorkshire. Although coming from a distinguished army family Rhoderick set his heart on going to sea and was sent back to England from South Africa to prepare for entry to the Royal Naval College, Osborne, at the beginning of 1906, under the Selborne scheme. As a cadet he was bright and energetic,

Sir Rhoderick Robert McGrigor (1893–1959), by Bassano, 1947

qualities that were to serve him well for the rest of his career, and despite missing two terms because of sickness—bronchial troubles were to dog him for many years—passed out top of the Royal Naval College, Dartmouth, to join his first ship, HMS *Dreadnought* in 1910.

McGrigor was in the destroyer *Foxhound* by the time war broke out in August 1914, being promoted lieutenant in October and seeing service in the Dardanelles. Moving to HMS *Malaya* at the end of 1915 McGrigor was in the forefront of the action at Jutland. He then specialized as a torpedo officer, doing the long course at *Vernon* in 1917–18. He became torpedo officer of the battleship *Conqueror* in June 1918 and in 1919 became a fleet torpedo officer in the old cruiser *Highflyer*, flagship of the East India station. 1922 saw McGrigor return to England for duty with the submarines at HMS *Dolphin* at Gosport and his promotion to lieutenant-commander. He undertook the staff course at Greenwich in 1923–4 after which he became torpedo officer of the fifth destroyer flotilla. Appointment to the staff at *Vernon* in October 1926 marked McGrigor as one of the leading 'T' officers of his day and he was promoted commander while at the tactical school in 1927.

McGrigor became senior operations officer of the Atlantic Fleet in August 1930 and was promoted captain at the end of 1933. After joining the senior officer's course at Sheerness late because of a recurrence of illness McGrigor became deputy director of training and staff duties on the naval staff. This was invaluable experience of Whitehall at a critical time but McGrigor was pleased to return to sea in 1936 in command of the fourth destroyer flotilla. The flotilla saw service off Spain in the Spanish Civil War and

McGrigor earned the personal thanks of the first sea lord for helping save survivors from the cruiser *Baleares*. 1938 saw transfer to the China station as chief of staff in the rank of commodore and McGrigor remained in this post until the end of 1940, when he was appointed to command the battle cruiser *Renown*, flagship of Sir James Somerville's force H based at Gibraltar.

After an eventful few months that included the sinking of the *Bismarck* and the bombardment of Genoa, McGrigor received early promotion to rear-admiral in July 1941. Reluctantly, he left a sea command for more duty at the Admiralty on the board as assistant chief of naval staff. His sure understanding of technology was at a premium at a time of rapid development. He returned to the Mediterranean in 1943 to command landing forces for the capture of Pantelleria and the invasion of Sicily in July. He was awarded the DSO at the end of the year by which time he was flag officer, Taranto and Adriatic, after three months as flag officer, Sicily.

In March 1944 McGrigor took command of the Home Fleet's 1st cruiser squadron, and until the war's end acted as one of the fleet's two principal operational task-force commanders. He was involved in the passage of five Arctic convoys to Russia and several carrier attacks on the battleship *Tirpitz*, and took escort-carrier and surface-action groups to interdict German activities in Norwegian waters. On 15 April 1945, the day he was promoted vice-admiral—having been recently created second in command of the Home Fleet—McGrigor commanded its last major operation of the war, *Judgment*, a successful escort-carrier strike that took out Germany's U-boat infrastructure in Vestfiord.

As one of the service's most distinguished younger flag officers it was no surprise that McGrigor was appointed back to the Board of Admiralty as vice-chief of naval staff on 1 October 1945. He fought hard to mitigate the effects of demobilization, which had reduced the Home Fleet to a barely operational force when McGrigor took over command of it at the beginning of 1948. The commander-in-chief, promoted admiral in September, presided over the resurrection of the fleet to operational capability, leading it in the battleship *Duke of York* on flag-showing cruises and exercises. McGrigor had moved his flag to the carrier *Implacable* when he hauled it down for the last time at sea to become commander-in-chief, Portsmouth, in 1950.

In December 1951 McGrigor succeeded Lord Fraser of North Cape as first sea lord and chief of naval staff. He inherited a difficult situation with Churchill's government cutting back its predecessor's rearmament programme. McGrigor ably defended his service's position in national defence in the discussions that led to the Global Strategy Paper drawn up by the chiefs of staff in 1952, the first sea lord refusing to be intimidated by his colleagues, marshal of the Royal Air Force, Sir John Slessor, and Field Marshal Sir William Slim. Pressed harder by the government's continuing 'radical review' McGrigor and his staff had to fight hard to retain their vital aircraft-carrier programme. No one knew better than McGrigor the value of carrier-based air power, and indeed its value in northern waters where the Soviet navy was likely to be engaged. The first sea lord, a self-effacing man, was happier putting forward an argument on paper than in person, but on 5 November 1954 he appeared before the cabinet to lead the pro-carrier case. His able advocacy helped carry the day for the carriers; it was probably his finest hour as chief of naval staff.

McGrigor also supervised radical new thinking within the service to re-shape it for the thermonuclear age. The process of reconstructing the service that would be taken over by his successor Mountbatten as his own was begun at the end of 1954. Another key initiative of McGrigor's period of office was the committee on officer structure and training which altered both the structure and training of the naval officer corps. Admiral of the Fleet Sir Rhoderick McGrigor (as he had been since May 1953) thus left a strong legacy to Lord Mountbatten to whom he handed over in April 1955. The quiet and modest Wee Mac had led a strong team effort that had not just responded to governmental attacks on the service but had traced a new path for it in a fundamentally changed strategic environment.

A homely man, McGrigor had married Gwendoline, daughter of Colonel Geoffrey Glyn and widow of Major Charles Greville, Grenadier Guards, on 26 November 1931 at St Peter's, Cranley Gardens. They adopted twin boys, who followed family traditions and joined the armed services. McGrigor was appointed CB at the beginning of 1944. He was mentioned in dispatches a year later and was knighted with a KCB in June 1945. A GCB followed at the beginning of 1951 and on 1 April 1952 he was appointed first and principal naval aide-de-camp to the new queen. He spent his last years living at Tarland in rural Aberdeenshire, where he could indulge at last in his pastimes of shooting and fishing. He had been made an honorary LLD of St Andrews University in 1953 and was rector of Aberdeen University from 1954 to 1957; Aberdeen made him an honorary LLD in 1955. He died, suddenly, after an operation in Aberdeen on 3 December 1959. His wife survived him, but died soon afterwards.   ERIC J. GROVE

Sources PRO, ADM 196/55, fols. 59–60 · E. J. Grove, 'Admiral Sir Rhoderick McGrigor (1951–1955)', *The first sea lords*, ed. M. H. Murfett (1995), 249–69 · WWW, 1951–60 · DNB · CGPLA Eng. & Wales (1960)
Archives NMM, papers | PRO, Admiralty files, ADM 205 | FILM BFI NFTVA, news footage · BFI NFTVA, record footage · IWM FVA, actuality footage
Likenesses W. Stoneman, two photographs, 1942–52, NPG · Bassano, photograph, 1947, NPG [*see illus.*] · M. L. De M. Murray, oils, Royal Naval College, Greenwich

McGrory, James Edward [Jimmy] (1904–1982), footballer, was born on 26 April 1904 at 179 Millburn Street, Glasgow, one of the four sons and four daughters of Henry McGrory, gasworks labourer (1859/60–1924), and his wife, Catherine, *née* Coll (1866/7–1916). They were Irish Roman Catholic immigrants, typical of Glasgow's east end in both religion and poverty. At sixteen McGrory was earning £2 per week playing football with St Roch's juniors.

James Edward [Jimmy] **McGrory** (1904–1982), by unknown photographer, 1932

After an unsuccessful trial at Bury he signed, aged seventeen, for Celtic, the Football Club formed as a focus for Glasgow's Irish immigrants.

A disappointing first season led to a loan period with Clydebank, which ended after McGrory scored a winner against Celtic. On his return to Celtic he failed to score for three games before finally netting against Falkirk on the afternoon of his father's funeral on 30 August 1924. From then on his scoring record was phenomenal; eighty-four goals over the next two seasons as Celtic won the Scottish cup (1925) and league championship (1926). Eight games starting in December 1927 saw twenty-one goals, including eight in a 9–1 victory over Dunfermline. McGrory was short (5 feet 6 and a half inches) for a centre forward, but almost a third of all of his goals were headers (hence his nickname, the Mermaid). Watching McGrory 'hover hawk-like, then twist that powerful neck, and flick the ball as fiercely as most players could kick it' gave journalist Hughie Taylor the most 'tingling sensation' in football (Campbell and Woods, 380). While not the most skilful player, his positional sense, strength, courage, and relentless workrate were outstanding. Of his style of play McGrory himself, with characteristic modesty, said 'I was often in the right place at the right time; goalscoring is in the mind and I went looking for goals' (Campbell and Woods, 380).

Despite McGrory's success, Celtic had to wait a decade

after 1926 before again winning the Scottish league championship. During this period they lost their dominant position in Scottish football to Glasgow Rangers, who under Bill Struth were adopted by the 'respectable' protestant Scottish middle class and made a practice of having no Roman Catholic players. In the summer of 1928 Celtic accepted a £10,000 transfer bid for McGrory from Arsenal. McGrory, loyal to Celtic and doubting whether he would succeed in England, refused the move despite promises to make him a wealthy man. Although he was earning £8—the maximum wage at that time—clubs routinely found ways to pay their top players more. Arsenal obviously intended to do this for McGrory. Indeed at Celtic there seem to have been some players earning £9 per week. On 10 July 1931 he married Veronica Green (b. 1898/9).

Jimmy McGrory was often overlooked by the Scottish national side. It has been suggested that there was some anti-Celtic bias on the part of the Scotland selectors, and some successful Celtic players did have surprisingly few caps. McGrory, though, had the misfortune to be contesting with the troubled great Hughie Gallagher for the centre-forward spot. However, in his seven appearances for his country he scored six times; a late winner against England at Hampden Park, Glasgow, in 1933 gave birth to the 'Hampden roar'. As Celtic recovered in the mid-1930s McGrory had his best scoring season, with fifty goals in 1935–6. On 21 December 1935 he reached a then world record of 363 career goals. In a game against Motherwell on 14 March 1936 he scored three goals in three minutes; this was the season in which Celtic recovered the league championship, before winning the Scottish cup in the next. In his last competitive match, against Queen's Park on 16 October 1937, McGrory scored his 550th goal in top-class football, still a British record. He is Celtic's highest-scoring player ever and his 410 goals in the Scottish league remains a record.

In December 1937 Celtic released McGrory to become manager of Kilmarnock, on condition that he retired from playing. His first game in charge was a 9–1 defeat to Celtic. However, Kilmarnock recovered to avoid relegation (beating Celtic on the way) and reach the Scottish cup final. During the Second World War McGrory had to take on work as head storeman at ICI, Ayrshire, when Kilmarnock's ground was put to military use as a munitions dump. In 1945 he was appointed Celtic manager, but in 1948 he contemplated resignation as his poor side only avoided relegation by beating Dundee on the last day of the season. He remained Celtic's manager for another seventeen years, but it is accepted that for most of that time the chairman, Robert Kelly, had final say over most matters, including team selection and transfers (Campbell and Woods, 181). There were successes under McGrory: 1951 saw victories in the St Mungo cup, staged to celebrate the Festival of Britain, and the Scottish cup; a surprise win in the coronation cup (1953) led to a league and cup double under Jock Stein's captaincy in the 1953–4 season and on 19 October 1957 Celtic won the league cup in an astonishing 7–1 win over Rangers. Yet despite some

excellent players, Celtic were inconsistent; fine general play was often not converted into goals.

In 1952 McGrory sparked a crisis which almost forced Celtic from Scottish football after writing to Eamon de Valera to ask for a new Irish tricolour to replace the tattered one which flew above Celtic Park. The Scottish Football Association (SFA) demanded that Celtic take down the flag of a foreign country. Robert Kelly refused, pointing out that the SFA had no jurisdiction over which flags clubs flew. Celtic, with the support of Rangers, eventually forced the SFA to back down. Celtic won nothing between 1957 and 1964. McGrory's managerial methods were outdated and his teams lacked tactical nous. A haphazard youth policy had produced some excellent young players, but did not give them adequate training or support. To redress these failings, on 31 January 1965 Robert Kelly appointed Jock Stein as Celtic manager. McGrory was given the new post of public relations officer, which he kept until retirement. In 1975 he published his memoir *A Lifetime in Paradise*. He died of old age in Glasgow's Southern General Hospital on 20 October 1982 and was buried in Glasgow. He was survived by his second wife, Barbara Frances Agnes, née Schoning.

Jimmy McGrory is remembered not only as a brave and prolific goalscorer with Celtic but also as one who 'set the highest standards of fair play and sportsmanship that could be expected of any player' (Murray, *Glasgow's Giants*, 114). He was much loved, quiet, gentlemanly, generous, and devoutly religious. JOHN MCMANUS

Sources *A lifetime in paradise, the Jimmy McGrory story*, ed. G. McNee (1975) · T. Campbell and P. Woods, *The glory and the dream: the history of Celtic F.C., 1887–1986* (1986) · B. Wilson, *Celtic: a century with honour* (1988) · W. Murray, *The Old Firm: sport, sectarianism and society in Scotland* (1984) · W. Murray, *Glasgow's giants: 100 years of the Old Firm* (1988) · P. Burns and P. Woods, *Oh, Hampden in the sun* (1997) · b. cert. · d. cert. · d. certs. [Henry McGrory, Catherine McGrory] **Likenesses** photograph, 1932, SMG / Empics Ltd [*see illus.*] · cigarette card, 1934, repro. in J. Huntington-Whiteley, *The book of British sporting heroes* (1998) **Wealth at death** £5747.04: confirmation, 30 June 1983, *CCI*

McGuinness, James Henry (1912–1987), civil servant, was born on 29 September 1912 at 67 Parkfield Mount, Holbeck, Leeds, the only son (he had one sister) of James Henry McGuinness, commercial traveller, and his wife, Rose McManus. Both his parents were Roman Catholics from Glasgow, where his father became chief clerk at the Scotstoun works of Pilkington Brothers. He was educated at St Aloysius College, Glasgow, and Glasgow University, where he met and later (on 1 December 1939) married a fellow student, Annie Eveline Fordyce (b. 1909/10), who became a schoolteacher. In 1932 he entered Trinity College, Oxford, with an open scholarship, gaining firsts in classical moderations (1934) and Greats (1936). Though urged by Maurice Bowra to pursue an academic career he entered the civil service in 1936 and after three years in London transferred to the Department of Health for Scotland, becoming a driving force in post-war planning and economic development in Scotland. From 1944 he was associated with the Clyde Valley regional plan, one of several studies proposing post-war dispersal from congested cities. During the depression he had been deeply affected by the physical squalor and social demoralization in Glasgow. The plan, empowered by new legislation, offered regeneration and a cause to which he remained committed for the rest of his career.

The success of East Kilbride, the first of several new towns proposed in the plan, lay not as originally envisaged in creating a self-contained community of relocated industry and population but, somewhat in the manner that proved to be the case with the London new towns, in attracting entirely new industry offering high earnings and in making new housing readily available for go-ahead young Glaswegians who would otherwise have left Scotland altogether; all this while at the same time conferring and deriving benefit to and from the adjacent city and metropolitan area. By the early sixties Scotland's traditional industries were collapsing, causing dereliction, high unemployment, and massive emigration by young people to England and overseas. Hitherto regional assistance had been directed to unemployment blackspots, for social rather than economic reasons. McGuinness realized that physical and social improvement were contingent upon economic growth and that East Kilbride showed how this might be stimulated. His analysis was underpinned by knowledge of contemporary French planning and Perroux's advocacy of *pôles de croissance*, which deliberately brought together new infrastructure and interrelated and industrial developments with appropriate social services and vocational training. This thinking lay behind the Toothill report of 1961 by Scottish industrialists, economists, and businessmen. McGuinness was instrumental in setting up this group, which recommended the fostering of growth points on similar lines.

Promoted under-secretary in 1959, McGuinness was well placed, with a secretary of state in cabinet (Jack Maclay, then Michael Noble, and later William Ross) to shape regional policies to Scotland's advantage. As head of a new regional development division (within the overarching Scottish Office but outside the four Scottish departments) and chairman of the Scottish economic planning board (1965–72), he was able to focus the hitherto fragmented resources of central and local government and the private sector on this objective. Action flowing from white papers on central Scotland (Cmnd 2188, 1963) and the Scottish economy (Cmnd 2864, 1965), produced under his direction, placed the country in the forefront of United Kingdom regional development by the end of the decade, with modern infrastructure, much inward investment, and falling unemployment and emigration. By 1975 Scotland had wrested control of financial incentives from Whitehall.

McGuinness cultivated many contacts outside St Andrew's House to keep himself well informed and improve understanding of government policies, but his style did not commend him to everyone. Slim, smiling, enigmatic, playing his cards close to his chest for high stakes and generally winning—more conventional colleagues found him too clever by half. Other departments resented trespass on their territory. Professionals, unaware of the obstacles he faced, thought him over-ready to compromise. Though he never became head of a department his effectiveness was probably not diminished, but it must have been as disappointing to him as it was bewildering to outsiders that people with less drive and imagination reached the top. Those who worked closely with him knew him to be selflessly dedicated to Scottish recovery, an inspiring leader, a good listener, undoctrinaire, and tremendous fun.

McGuinness flourished at a time favourable to his talents and aims. The recession of the 1970s, the sterling crisis, and the Thatcher years made regionalism seem to some an unaffordable luxury. His successors fought hard to retain the structures he had put in place. Although some of the largest projects he had helped to win for Scotland were lost in the exceptionally difficult circumstances of the early 1980s, the fact that Scotland has become one of the more prosperous parts of the United Kingdom owes much to his achievements, which have subsequently been developed to meet new challenges.

McGuinness was widely read, a discerning traveller and gifted linguist, learning Serbo-Croat while commuting from Glasgow and enough Russian to understand what was going on when he accompanied his secretary of state to the USSR. In 1972 he became a senior research fellow in politics at Glasgow University and in 1978 was made an honorary member of the Royal Town Planning Institute. He loved music, playing the violin and piano, and after retirement, as chairman of the Scottish Baroque Ensemble and the Scottish Philharmonic Society, helped raise funds to acquire and convert a redundant Edinburgh church to create the Queen's Hall, giving the ensemble and the Scottish Chamber Orchestra a permanent home. He died at his home, 28 Falkland Street, Glasgow, on 22 May 1987 and was buried at Lambhill cemetery on 27 May. His wife survived him; they had a son and two daughters.

DEREK LYDDON and PATRICK HARRISON

Sources *Imperial Calendar* (1935–65) · *Civil Service List* (1966–73) · *WWW, 1971–80* · E. M. Wills, *Livingston: the making of a Scottish new town* (1996) · *The Scotsman* (29 April 1969) · *The Scotsman* (5 May 1972) · *The Scotsman* (5 Oct 1977) · *Glasgow Herald* (15 Feb 1973) · private information (2004) [Scottish Office colleagues] · R. Smith and U. Wannop, *Strategic planning in action: the impact of the Clyde valley regional plan, 1946–1982* (1985) · b. cert. · m. cert. · d. cert.
Archives NA Scot., files of department of health, Scotland; Scottish development department; regional development division of Scottish office, memoranda and letters; records of Scottish new towns
Likenesses photograph, repro. in *Glasgow Herald* (15 Feb 1973) · photograph, repro. in *Glasgow Herald* (5 Oct 1977) · photograph, repro. in *Glasgow Herald* (5 July 1972)

McGuinness, Norah Allison (1901–1980), painter and theatre designer, was born on 7 November 1901 at Lawrence Street, Londonderry, the daughter of Joseph Allison McGuinness, a coal merchant and shipowner, and his wife, Jessie, *née* McCleery. She studied graphic design and painting at the Metropolitan School of Art, Dublin, from

1921 to 1924. In her final year there, when she first exhibited at the Royal Hibernian Academy in Dublin, she decided to concentrate on painting rather than on book illustration, although the latter remained a source of income throughout her career. Having moved to London, she spent some months during 1924 studying art at the Chelsea Polytechnic. She also received her first important graphic design commission, to produce the illustrations for an edition of Laurence Sterne's *A Sentimental Journey through France and Italy* which was published in 1925. In the same year she married Geoffrey Phibbs, a librarian from Wicklow, who wrote poetry under the name Geoffrey Taylor. Their marriage broke up in 1929 and they were divorced in 1931.

In 1926 McGuinness began her long involvement with the theatre, designing the sets and costumes for W. B. Yeats's play *Deirdre*, first performed at the Abbey Theatre, Dublin, that year. In 1927 she designed sets and costumes for the Peacock Theatre in Dublin. The success of these projects led to many more set designs and costumes for the Abbey Theatre, as well as portraits of leading actors. On the advice of a fellow Irish painter, Mainie Jellett, McGuinness went to Paris in 1929 to study privately with the painter André Lhote; this stay of two years greatly affected her painting style, and she introduced some elements from fauvism and cubism. Her subject matter remained constant—mostly still lifes, seascapes, and landscapes, with a few portraits. As her career progressed, she found her own mature style, employing loose brushwork and a spontaneous approach to her subject. She kept her forms simple and strong, and her colours mostly subdued in range. After ending her studies with Lhote in 1931, she spent a short time travelling in France and then returned to London; she lived and worked in Hammersmith until 1937, and sent paintings to mixed exhibitions at Lucy Wertheim's Gallery, and also showed with the Seven and Five Society and the London Group. She had solo exhibitions at Lucy Wertheim's Gallery in 1933, the Zwemmer Gallery in 1934, and the Dublin Painters' Gallery in Dublin in March 1936, shortly after joining the Dublin Painters' Society. McGuinness had two further shows at this venue in 1938 and 1941 and remained a member of the society until about 1950. In her Hammersmith years she resumed her book illustration and produced fashion drawings for the magazines *Bystander* and *Vogue*.

In 1937 McGuinness returned home to Ireland, where she remained for the rest of her life. She did, however, travel to New York in 1937 and again in 1939, when she had a solo exhibition at the Paul Reinhardt Gallery, and also managed to produce some fashion illustrations for *Harper's Bazaar* and window displays for Fifth Avenue department stores, such as Bonwit Tellers. In 1943 she was one of the founder members of the Irish Exhibition of Living Art, an annual exhibition held in Dublin devoted to showing avant-garde work; its first exhibition was held in September 1943. This organization was set up in opposition to the somewhat old-fashioned outlook of the Royal Hibernian Academy in Dublin. In September 1944 McGuinness was elected chairman of the committee of the Irish Exhibition

of Living Art and in March 1948 became president, a post she held until 1972. She probably gained more praise for her diplomatic role in running this organization than she did for her paintings, and is fondly remembered for her energetic role in seeking out opportunities for living Irish artists. However, McGuinness was elected an honorary member of the Royal Hibernian Academy in 1957, the rival organization that first showed her work in the early 1920s.

In 1950 McGuinness was one of two painters, the other being Nano Reid, chosen to represent Ireland at the Venice Biennale. In the 1950s and early 1960s she showed work at the Dawson Gallery in Dublin, the leading gallery in the city for contemporary art. *Garden Green*, a major still life of 1952, is in the collection of the Hugh Lane Municipal Gallery of Modern Art, and *Shore Pools*, a moody landscape from 1965, can be seen at the Irish Museum of Modern Art, Dublin. McGuinness had a major retrospective exhibition at Trinity College, Dublin, in October 1968, and her last exhibition was at the Taylor Galleries, Dublin, in 1979. Her work is in the collection of the Ulster Museum, Belfast, the Victoria and Albert Museum, London, Sligo Museum and Art Gallery, the Hugh Lane Municipal Gallery of Modern Art in Dublin, and the Hirschhorn Museum, Washington, DC. She died at Monkstown Hospital, Dún Laoghaire, on 22 November 1980.

JUDITH COLLINS

Sources A. Crookshank, *Norah McGuinness* (1968) [exhibition catalogue, TCD, Oct 1968] · T. Bodkin, 'The art of Miss Norah McGuinness', *The Studio*, 90 (1925), 168–71 · M. Hartigan, 'The commercial design career of Norah McGuiness', *Irish Arts Review*, 3/3 (1986), 23–5 · S. B. Kennedy, *Irish art and modernism, 1880–1950* (1991) [exhibition catalogue, Hugh Lane Municipal Gallery of Modern Art, Dublin, 20 Sept – 10 Nov 1991 and Ulster Museum, Belfast, 22 Nov 1991 – 26 Jan 1992] · T. Snoddy, *Dictionary of Irish artists: 20th century* (1996) · D. Gaze, ed., *Dictionary of women artists* (1997) · b. cert. · d. cert.

McGurk, John (1874–1944), trade unionist, was born at Hoyle Mill, Barnsley, on 17 September 1874, the eldest of fifteen children of John McGurk, a miner, and his wife, Hannah (*née* Lord). Six months later the family moved to Pendlebury, near Manchester, and at the age of twelve McGurk went to work in a local colliery. He soon began to be active in the Lancashire and Cheshire Miners' Federation, and secured election as delegate to the federation's monthly conference, and then to its executive.

On 22 February 1908 McGurk was elected to the full-time post of miners' agent covering pits in north-east Lancashire from Oldham round to Burnley and Accrington. His prominence within the coalfield grew; in 1912, he sat as its representative on the executive of the Miners' Federation of Great Britain (MFGB), a position he held on five later occasions. Like almost all miners' officials he was a strong supporter of the allies during the First World War.

McGurk was typical of his generation of mining trade union officials in seeing a commitment to the Labour Party as an integral element in his work. In the general election of December 1918 he stood as the Labour Party candidate in Darwen, sponsored by the miners. His line was firmly patriotic: Germany should be made to pay and the Kaiser should be punished. Yet his revanchism incorporated a class antagonism—'it would not surprise him … to see the late heads of the German people being entertained at Buckingham Palace before twelve months was over' (*Northern Daily Telegraph*, 9 Dec 1918). McGurk finished third in the poll, as he did again in the contest of November 1922. He fought no further parliamentary contests; his one successful electoral campaign was for a seat on the Bury town council.

McGurk's address from the chair at the Labour Party conference in June 1919 involved an attack on 'direct action' and a presentation of the Labour Party and parliament as the way forward. This intervention was particularly significant in the context of debates about the use of industrial methods for political objectives. McGurk's counsel of caution came at a moment of optimism for the MFGB; two years later the federation fought a three-month lock-out in an ultimately unsuccessful attempt to protect wartime and immediate post-war gains. During this 1921 struggle, McGurk became a controversial figure with his public assertion that the MFGB had no hope of obtaining one of its principal objects, the national profits pool.

In the 1920s Lancashire as a declining coalfield could be militant on industrial issues and McGurk appeared sometimes within the MFGB as the advocate of a more forward policy. During the 1926 dispute, he played the leading part in the attempt by some of the miners' delegation at that year's TUC to shout down the locomotive men's leader, John Bromley (1876–1945), who had been critical of the MFGB leaders.

After the 1926 defeat McGurk played his part in attempting to maintain effective trade unionism in the depressed Lancashire coalfield; he also stood with the other Lancashire officials to block attempts by the Communist Party to expand their influence in Lancashire. In April 1929 he became Lancashire president; in 1932–3 he sat on the general council of the TUC.

Soon after the outbreak of war in 1939, McGurk's health began to deteriorate. He resigned the Lancashire presidency in January 1944 and his agent's post eight months later. He died at his home, 92 Haig Road, in Bury, on 22 November 1944. His wife, Eliza, an active member of the Labour Party, had died in July 1943. They had two daughters.

McGurk was a characteristic miners' leader of his generation, a hard but flexible negotiator, a thorough opponent of the left who viewed the Labour Party as the custodian of trade union interests. This pragmatic bargainer was known for his quick temper; Lancashire conferences could be subjected to what one critic described as 'language not becoming to a person of his standing' (*DLB*). His power base in a decentralized federation lay in a specific coalfield and his attitudes were influenced by its priorities.   DAVID HOWELL

Sources R. P. Arnot, *The miners: a history of the Miners' Federation of Great Britain*, 2: … *from 1910 onwards* (1953) · R. P. Arnot, *The miners: a history of the Miners' Federation of Great Britain*, 3: … *from 1930 onwards* (1961) · *Labour party conference report* (1919) [for his speech from the chair] · *Labour party conference report* (1937) [for his antipathy to intellectuals] · I. Scott, 'The Lancashire & Cheshire Miners' Federation, 1900–1914', PhD diss., University of York, 1977 · *DLB* · d. cert.

Archives National Union of Mineworkers, Hilden Street, Leigh, Lancashire area offices, Miners' Federation of Great Britain records · National Union of Mineworkers, Hilden Street, Leigh, Lancashire area offices, Lancashire and Cheshire Miners' Federation records · National Union of Mineworkers, Sheffield, Miners' Federation of Great Britain records

Wealth at death £1255 6s. 5d.: probate, 16 March 1945, *CGPLA Eng. & Wales*

Machado, Roger [Ruy] (d. 1510), diplomat and herald, was probably of Portuguese extraction and may have lived among the Portuguese merchants at Bruges in 1455.

Machado first appears as Leicester herald on missions to the Low Countries in 1478 or 1479 and in 1480. He was possibly the Leicester herald present at the marriage of Richard, duke of York, to Anne Mowbray in January 1478. As Leicester he participated in Edward IV's funeral in April 1483, an event he describes in his journal, now in the College of Arms. The following December he was in Calais assisting a William Rosse appointed by Richard III to supervise the victualling of the town. In 1484—the year of the incorporation of the College of Arms—Machado was importing wine from Spain and he may have been involved in the trading of furs and fabrics. He is known to have been married either in or before 1484, and an inventory of his household goods that year suggests a comfortable lifestyle. However, his non-payment of a debt or possibly a disagreement with the king forced him to flee the country.

From January 1485 Machado took part in various missions abroad in the service of Thomas Grey, marquess of Dorset; these may have been to the advantage of the exiled Henry Tudor. However, it is possible he betrayed Dorset's plans to desert Henry for he was certainly well rewarded by his new master in the coming months. Probably just before Bosworth, Henry, as earl of Richmond, made him his Richmond herald. Machado came over with Henry and on 21 September, as Richmond herald, was appointed searcher of customs at Southampton; no one else was to deputize for him in this role. By the end of October he was Richmond king of arms. On Christmas day he was promoted to Norroy king of arms even though the present incumbent, John More, continued in that office until his death in 1491. On 24 January 1494 Machado was appointed Clarenceux king of arms, though as both Norroy and Clarenceux he kept the title Richmond, presumably out of affection for his royal master; henceforth he was known as Richmond, Norroy king of arms, or Richmond, Clarenceux king of arms.

In June 1498 Machado and John Writhe, Garter king of arms, were granted a joint licence to make visitations, but there is no evidence that they undertook any. It may be that Machado wished to concentrate on his trading activities and diplomatic missions rather than on his heraldic duties. In 1505 he declined the king's offer of the office of Garter on the grounds that he was too old and weak. Nevertheless, henceforth he was to receive a third (20 marks) of Garter's salary (£40). It appears that Machado may also have handed over to Thomas Writhe, the new Garter, many of Clarenceux's duties. In January 1509 the two made an indenture formalizing the situation, Machado handing over substantial powers as Clarenceux. In return Garter promised to pay him £4 a year.

Machado is best remembered as an accomplished diplomat, involved in numerous missions, many of a highly sensitive nature. He described three in his journal: the first to Spain and Portugal in 1488 and 1489 and the other two both to Brittany in 1490 when he took a much larger part in the negotiations. In August 1494 he was dispatched to Charles VIII of France to discuss Charles's offer of aid to Henry should the emperor Maximilian support Perkin Warbeck's claim to the English throne. At the same time he was to offer Henry's good offices for a settlement of the dispute between Charles and Ferdinand of Spain regarding the kingdom of Naples. In January 1495 he again visited Charles, then in Italy, and in March 1496 and October 1497 he was once more in France. On the last occasion he may have had with him Warbeck's confession since he had been involved in the impostor's recent surrender. In 1501 Machado was sent to Maximilian, and he may have visited Denmark in 1502 or 1503 on a further mission. In January 1508 he entertained the French ambassador in London.

Machado knew English, French, Spanish, and Portuguese, and probably also Italian and Latin. The Milanese ambassador considered him wise, endowed with wit and discretion, a man who saw everything. He was clearly an old friend and faithful servant of Henry VII. In June 1483 Machado was described as late of Southampton and formerly of London, and from 1486 to 1497 he lived in Simnel Street, Southampton. He died on 6 May 1510.

ADRIAN AILES

Sources W. H. Godfrey, A. Wagner, and H. Stanford London, *The College of Arms, Queen Victoria Street* (1963) · M. Jones, 'Les ambassades de Roger Machado', *1491 La Bretagne, Terre d'Europe*, ed. J. Kerhervé and T. Daniel (1992), 147–60 · A. Wagner, *Heralds of England: a history of the office and College of Arms* (1967) · B. André, *Historia regis Henrici septimi*, ed. J. Gairdner, Rolls Series, 10 (1858) · R. Machado, journal, Coll. Arms, Arundel MS L1 · F. Madden, 'Documents relating to Perkin Warbeck with remarks on his history', *Archaeologia*, 27 (1838), 153–210 · early chancery proceedings, PRO, C1/66/297–300 · *CSP Milan* · M. Hemmant, ed., *Select cases in the exchequer chamber*, [2], SeldS, 64 (1948) · C. S. L. Davies, 'Bishop John Morton, the Holy See, and the accession of Henry VII', *EngHR*, 102 (1987), 2–30 · I. Arthurson, *The Perkin Warbeck conspiracy, 1491–1499* (1994) · P. Holdsworth, 'Hamwih', *Current Archaeology*, 7/8 (1981), 243–9

Archives BL, Add. MS 45133, fols. 35b–44 · Coll. Arms, Arundel MS L1

MacHale, John (1791–1881), Roman Catholic archbishop of Tuam, was born on 6 March 1791 in the village of Tubbernavine, co. Mayo, in the diocese of Killala, and was baptized a Catholic on 8 March. He was the fifth son of Patrick MacHale, a wayside innkeeper and farmer, and Mary Mulkieran.

Education and ordination MacHale received his early education at Tubbernavine and at Lahardaunm, where he learned English, his mother tongue being Irish. In 1804 he

John MacHale (1791–1881), by Alessandro Capalti, 1855

was sent to the classical school at Castlebar, where he acquired a knowledge of Greek and Latin and a taste for English literature. He proved to be such a promising scholar that the bishop of Killala, Dominic Bellew, offered him a free place in St Patrick's College, the recently established national seminary at Maynooth. He entered Maynooth in the autumn of 1807, where he pursued a distinguished academic course for seven years, after which he was ordained priest on 26 July 1814 by Daniel Murray, the coadjutor to the archbishop of Dublin. Shortly after his ordination MacHale was formally appointed a lecturer to assist the celebrated French émigré priest and professor of dogmatic theology Louis Delahogue, who was then in his seventy-fourth year and unwell. When Delahogue finally retired some six years later, on 22 June 1820, MacHale was appointed to succeed him.

Ecclesiastical career, 1820–1834 On 29 January 1820 MacHale made his début as a controversialist in the public press. For a period of more than three years, in a series of thirty-two letters under the pseudonym of Hierophilos, he attacked the protestant establishment in church and state. His letters gave great offence, less for their content than for their tone, which was ironic and contemptuous about the vaunted advantages of the British constitution. In late 1824, however, the bishop of Killala, Peter Waldron, who had been ill, requested the pope to provide him with a coadjutor with the right of succession and recommended MacHale. The pope complied in early 1825, and

MacHale was consecrated bishop of Maronia by Daniel Murray, the archbishop of Dublin, in Maynooth on 5 June 1825. He was the first Irish bishop in modern times to have been entirely educated in Ireland.

MacHale continued to serve as coadjutor until Waldron's death on 20 May 1834. During his long apprenticeship he demonstrated zeal and energy both as a pastor and polemicist. As a pastor he immediately visited every parish in the diocese, conducting missions and taking spiritual advantage of the universal jubilee granted by the pope in 1825. MacHale also decided to build a cathedral for Killala in Ballina. He collected the necessary funds and in late 1831 the cathedral, an impressive achievement, was opened for worship. MacHale continued his attacks in the press, singling out the proselytizers of the Catholic poor and those politicians he held responsible for the deplorable state of Ireland, most particularly the whig prime minister, Earl Grey. In the midst of all his labours, pastoral and polemical, MacHale managed to publish in 1828 an impressive two-volume study, *The Evidences and Doctrines of the Catholic Church*.

Shortly after the opening of his cathedral MacHale decided to make a long-deferred pilgrimage to Rome. He set out in late 1831 and remained in Rome until the following summer. He was invited to give the usual Lenten discourses to the large English-speaking community that visited Rome for the winter season. The sermons made such an impression that they were immediately translated into Italian and published. Even more importantly for his future, however, he made a very favourable impression on the new pope, Gregory XVI, and also acquired a valuable friend in the recently appointed rector of the Irish College and a favourite of the pope, Paul Cullen. On his return to Ireland in late 1832 MacHale was appalled by what he considered to be a deteriorating economic and social situation. In resuming his public letters to the prime minister he denounced the government's indifference to the worsening condition of the poor, and eventually came to the conclusion that the only solution to Ireland's manifold problems was the repeal of the Act of Union between Great Britain and Ireland.

Less than a month after he had succeeded to the see of Killala in May 1834, MacHale was nominated by the senior clergy of the archdiocese of Tuam as a candidate to succeed their recently deceased archbishop. The bishops of the province of Tuam were unanimous in recommending him for the appointment, but the British government was determined to prevent it. Gregory XVI, however, had become disturbed about the repeated interference by the British government in Irish episcopal appointments. He decided to delay the usual procedure and ordered that the speeches by MacHale that had been cited by the government as seditious be translated into Italian. On reading them he found they were not what they had been represented to be, and on 1 August 1834 appointed MacHale to Tuam.

Controversy and the struggle for power, 1834–1860 MacHale's subsequent career as archbishop of Tuam proved to be as extraordinary as it was stormy. Shortly after his succession he launched a struggle for power in the Irish church that was to continue for twenty-five years. Before making his bid for power in the national church, however, he had shrewdly consolidated his local power base among his six suffragan bishops in the province of Tuam. The occasion for this had been provided by the appointment of Francis Joseph O'Finan, his successor as bishop of Killala. MacHale's influence had been determinant in O'Finan's appointment, but hardly had the new bishop taken possession of his see when it became apparent that he was temperamentally unfit. After four years of scandals, appeals, and counter-appeals to Rome, O'Finan was finally removed. During this arduous process, MacHale provided the leadership that resulted in the consolidation of his power base among his suffragans.

As the O'Finan affair began to wind down, MacHale launched his bid for national power by challenging Daniel Murray, the venerable archbishop of Dublin, for the leadership of the Irish church. In February 1838 he published two open letters to the home secretary, Lord John Russell, denouncing the national system of primary education in Ireland, which had been established by the government in 1831, for being subversive of the faith of Irish Catholics. Not only had the Irish bishops approved the system in 1831, but as an earnest of that approval Murray had consented to serve on the public board that governed the system. The novelty of MacHale's denunciation, however, was that it involved not only a public criticism of his episcopal colleagues and Murray but also an appeal over their heads to Irish public opinion. MacHale rallied a minority of the ten bishops, which included his six suffragans and himself, in an episcopal body of twenty-seven, and in early 1839 appealed to Rome. Some two years later, in January 1841, though not before the whole issue had been bitterly fought out in the press, Rome decided to allow each bishop to deal with the national system as he thought best. Though the Roman decision proved a victory for Murray and the sixteen bishops who supported him, the harmony and unity that had characterized the Irish church under Murray's leadership had been seriously compromised by the quarrel.

Politics, O'Connell, and educational policy In the meantime MacHale had considerably enhanced his national political image by publicly endorsing in April 1840 the movement recently launched by Daniel O'Connell for the repeal of the Act of Union. Over the next five years, in public letters to the press and on the political hustings, MacHale lent the prestige of his name and his office to the cause of repeal and carried the great majority of the Irish bishops and clergy with him. Indeed, by 1845 he was, after Daniel O'Connell, the most popular man in Ireland. When Sir Robert Peel, the Conservative prime minister, in order to soften the universal demand of Catholics for repeal in Ireland, then proposed in early 1844 a programme of legislative reform to conciliate Catholics, MacHale viewed it as a political plot to divide the Catholic body. When the government introduced a Charitable Bequests Bill, designed to give greater security to legacies left by Catholics to their church, he denounced the measure in August 1844 and eventually carried eighteen of the twenty-seven Irish bishops with him on the issue. When a Roman rescript, published in November 1844, urging the Irish bishops and clergy to assume a position in politics more in keeping with their sacred office, was then followed in December by the rumour that Rome was about to establish diplomatic relations with the British government, the public uproar in the press about an English conspiracy against the Irish church that had been initiated by the Bequests Bill became a frenzy. The cumulative effect of this furore was to turn MacHale and his episcopal colleagues into national heroes, while reducing Murray and his few remaining supporters to 'castle bishops', or government tools, in the public mind.

When in early May 1845 Peel's government introduced a Queen's Colleges Bill to provide non-denominational higher education for Catholics and Presbyterians MacHale was hostile to the measure, and over the next six months initiated another donnybrook in the press. In late October 1845 MacHale rallied nineteen bishops, including himself, in a body of twenty-six, to appeal to Rome against the colleges. Some two years later, on 9 October 1847, Rome finally condemned the colleges and forbade the Irish bishops from taking any part in them. Murray and his supporters, however, reopened the whole question at Rome when the government indicated that it was prepared to make significant changes to meet the needs of Catholics. The threat was perceived to be so serious by the opponents of the colleges that they persuaded MacHale to proceed to Rome to counter the efforts being made. After an extended stay of some seven months, MacHale secured on 11 October 1848 a second condemnation of the colleges.

MacHale and Cullen On his return to Ireland MacHale began to make preparations for the holding of a provincial synod at Tuam in January 1849 to give some legislative effect to the Roman condemnations of the colleges. MacHale and his suffragans proceeded to enact legislation which they intended would prevent their clergy and laity from taking part in the Queen's College that had been established in Galway city. The bishop of Galway, however, broke ranks and objected to the proposed decrees as exceeding the terms of the Roman condemnations. When MacHale then forwarded the decrees to Rome for approval, the Propaganda authorities were not pleased with either their content or their form and declined, in effect, to act on them. MacHale's reputation and standing with the new pope, Pius IX, and the Propaganda authorities, which had been much impaired in recent years by his prominence in politics, was not improved by his obvious inability to give satisfactory legislative effect to the recent Roman rescripts condemning the colleges.

Meanwhile, MacHale and his clerical allies in Ireland had been making strenuous efforts to maintain their majority in the episcopal body by insisting that the issue of the Queen's Colleges be the test for any new appointment to an Irish see. In spite of all their efforts, however, it was apparent that their large majority was being slowly eroded. When the archbishop of Armagh, William Crolly, Murray's chief supporter in the episcopal body, died unexpectedly in April 1849, therefore, MacHale and his supporters spared no efforts to have one of their partisans appointed. Both the clergy of Armagh and the bishops of that province were much divided on the merits of the candidates proposed, and the prefect of the Propaganda, Cardinal Fransoni, finally wrote to the three archbishops on 30 July 1849 enquiring if there were a suitable candidate other than those who had been already recommended. MacHale and the archbishop of Cashel, Michael Slattery, recommended Paul Cullen, rector of the Irish College, who for many years had been very partial to the MacHale faction, and who was a personal favourite of Pius IX and the Propaganda authorities. The pope, therefore, appointed Cullen archbishop of Armagh to the great delight of MacHale and his party. Cullen was also appointed apostolic delegate of the Holy See in Ireland and instructed to convene a national synod, at which he was to preside, to restore peace and harmony to a long-distracted Irish church. The synod was convened at Thurles in August 1850, where Cullen, in alliance with MacHale, narrowly succeeded in containing Murray and his supporters in legislating the condemnation of the Queen's Colleges. MacHale had assumed a very low profile at the synod, and Cullen was very impressive in providing a comprehensive canonical frame for a thoroughgoing reform of the Irish church. Less than two years later, on the death of Murray, Cullen was translated by Pius IX on 3 May 1852 from Armagh to Dublin, the wealthiest and most important see in the Irish church.

MacHale deeply resented Cullen's emergence as the effective leader of the Irish church, and the result was yet another struggle for power that was to continue for nearly a decade. The occasion was Cullen's attempt to prevent the Catholic Defence Association, which had been founded in August 1851 in Dublin to protect the civil liberties of both British and Irish Catholics, from being turned into another political vehicle by MacHale and his supporters. Their quarrel was soon extended to who should control the recently established Catholic University and to what the appropriate political role of priests should be in the recently launched Tenant Right League. MacHale protested not only against Cullen's interference in Irish episcopal appointments and the affairs of dioceses and provinces not his own, but also against his meddling in the seminary at Maynooth and the Irish College at Paris, both of which were part of the general jurisdiction of the Irish bishops as a body. The climax finally took place in Rome in December 1854, where MacHale and Cullen had come to assist at the definition of the dogma of immaculate conception. After the definition on 8 December, the six Irish bishops present in Rome attended a series of meetings at the Propaganda under the presidency of its secretary, Alessandro Barnabò, to discuss the affairs of the Irish church. The discussions were very bitter, and at the third meeting there was a violent confrontation between MacHale and Barnabò, who immediately terminated the meetings and reported MacHale's conduct to the pope that same evening. MacHale had not only made an implacable enemy of Barnabò, but when the secretary succeeded as cardinal-prefect less than two years later MacHale's standing at Rome was irreparably damaged.

Patriot bishop, 1860–1881 From 1856 MacHale's standing declined, and by 1860 Cullen had reduced his once formidable power base among the bishops to three or four out of thirty. To compensate for the decline of his influence in the Irish church and at Rome, MacHale began systematically to undermine Cullen's public image as a patriot bishop in Ireland, while simultaneously enhancing his own as a staunch defender of the rights and privileges of the Irish church against English and Roman intrigue. By 1860 MacHale had finally succeeded in reducing Cullen in the public mind, as he had Murray in the 1840s, to a 'castle bishop'. Indeed, in the last twenty years of his life MacHale seldom lost an opportunity to cultivate his own image as the archetypical patriot bishop. During the decade of the 1860s, for example, he gave his muted blessing to the revolutionary Irish Republican (Fenian) Brotherhood. With the rise of the home-rule movement in the decade of the 1870s, moreover, MacHale was one of the few bishops who endorsed it from its inception, and as the movement became more popular in the country over time MacHale's political and national reputation grew. By the end of the decade of the 1870s, MacHale had become in the Irish popular mind a political and religious oracle and the most famous man in Ireland.

During that same decade, however, MacHale's reputation at Rome had been further impaired. At the First Vatican Council in 1870 he was among the minority of prelates who opposed the definition of papal infallibility because he believed it to be inopportune. Shortly after his return from Rome, what was left of his power base among his suffragans in Tuam was liquidated by new appointments, but not without a struggle. Though he was now reduced to a minority of one among the bishops in the Irish church, he was determined to fight to the end. In July 1875 MacHale actually requested Pius IX, as a special favour, to appoint his nephew, Thomas MacHale, professor of scripture and canon law at the Irish College in Paris, as his coadjutor with the right of succession in Tuam. The pope refused, and in the long struggle that then ensued Pius IX finally appointed the bishop of Galway, John MacEvilly, a protégé of Cullen's, on 3 February 1878 as coadjutor to MacHale. MacHale, who detested MacEvilly, refused his consent. When the Roman authorities then insisted, MacHale informed the pope and the cardinal-prefect on 28 June 1878 that if MacEvilly were forced on him he would not only resign as archbishop of Tuam but explain his reasons for doing so to the Irish people at home and abroad. The Roman authorities were not only aghast but intimidated, and after much equivocation prudently decided to leave the problem of the succession to Tuam to time and providence. MacHale died at Tuam on 7 November 1881, and was buried in the sanctuary of his cathedral on 15 November.

Achievement and significance MacHale was first and foremost a popular radical. He drew his real strength from the Irish people. He was the Lion of the Fold of Judah, the Patriarch of the West, the incorruptible defender of the imprescriptible rights of the Irish people in church and state, and the true inheritor of the political mantle of Daniel O'Connell. Like his radical political mentor, MacHale's posture was pugnacious and his tactics were confrontational. Not even O'Connell found the place in the affectionate memory of the Irish people that MacHale did, and this was so because MacHale's impact was not merely political but cultural and social as well. MacHale was the only prominent man in Irish life who kept faith with the Irish language between the demise of Young Ireland in 1848 and the emergence of the Gaelic League in 1893. MacHale not only thought, prayed, preached, and conversed in Irish, but he composed and translated in it. His translations included Thomas Moore's celebrated *Melodies* (1842–52), Homer's *Iliad* (1844–61), and the Pentateuch (1866) from the Vulgate, as well as numerous devotional and religious works translated and published between 1839 and 1859. His contribution to Irish culture and its language was seen as a token of his deep loyalty and commitment to the survival of Irish identity.

As well as understanding that man did not live by bread alone, MacHale nevertheless appreciated that man could not survive without bread. He insisted that the Irish church had a responsibility for the survival and well-being of the Irish people, through a temporal as well as a spiritual mission, and especially to the poor and defenceless. For sixty years after his Hierophilos letters, MacHale was an uncompromising champion of the poor and underprivileged, and the combination of his stand on social justice with his commitment to cultural and political nationalism explains why he was idolized as a national symbol in his own day and has been mythologized as the archetypical patriot Irish bishop since his death.

EMMET LARKIN

Sources E. Larkin, *The making of the Roman Catholic church in Ireland, 1850–1860* (1980) · E. Larkin, *The consolidation of the Roman Catholic church in Ireland, 1860–1870* (1987) · E. Larkin, *The Roman Catholic church and the home rule movement in Ireland, 1870–1874* (1990) · E. Larkin, *The Roman Catholic church and the emergence of the modern Irish political system, 1874–1878* (1996) · E. Larkin, *The Roman Catholic church and the creation of the modern Irish state, 1878–1886* (1975) · D. A. Kerr, *Peel, priests, and politics: Sir Robert Peel's administration and the Roman Catholic church in Ireland, 1841–1846* (1982) · J. F. Broderick, *The Holy See and the Irish movement for the repeal of the union with England, 1829–1847* (1951) · B. O'Reilly, *John MacHale, archbishop of Tuam, his life, times, and correspondence*, 2 vols. (1890) · U. J. Bourke, *The life and times of the Most Rev. John MacHale, archbishop of Tuam and metropolitan* (1882) · Á. Ní Cheannain, *Leon an Iarthair: aistí ar Sheán Mac Héil, árdeaspag Thuama, 1834–1881* (1983) · N. Costello, *John MacHale, archbishop of Tuam* (1939) · P. Devine, 'John MacHale, archbishop of Tuam', *Dublin Review*, 109 (1891) · *Irish Catholic Directory* (1882), 240
Archives Sacra Congregazione di Propaganda Fide, Rome, Irish corresp. | Diocesan Archives, Thurles, Slattery MSS · Irish College, Rome, Cullen MSS
Likenesses J. Cashman, engraving, c.1840, repro. in *A selection of Moore's melodies*, trans. J. MacHale (1871) [in Irish] · Bross?, engraving, c.1850, repro. in Bourke, *Life and times of John MacHale* · Hennessy Del.?, drawing, c.1850, repro. in Bourke, *Life and times of John*

MacHale · A. Capalti, oils, 1855, NG Ire. [see illus.] · A. D. Heath, engraving, 1859 (after portrait, c.1840), repro. in Larkin, *Making of the Roman Catholic church* · oils, c.1870, St Patrick's College, Maynooth, Ireland; repro. in Larkin, *Consolidation of the Roman Catholic church* · T. Farrell, statue, The Square, Tuam, Galway, Ireland · J. H. Foley, bronze statue, Tuam Cathedral, Tuam, Galway, Ireland · group portrait, coloured lithograph (*The illustrious sons of Ireland*), NPG

Wealth at death £5716 6s. 8d.: probate, 28 Jan 1882, CGPLA Ire.

MacHardy, John (*fl.* 1948). *See under* Knoydart, Seven Men of (*act.* 1948).

Machell, James Octavius (1837–1902), racehorse owner and manager, born at Etton rectory, near Beverley, Yorkshire, on 5 December 1837, was the son of Robert Machell (1797–1860), vicar of Marton in Cleveland, who was descended from an old Westmorland family, and his first wife, Eliza Mary (*d.* 1841), daughter of James Zealey and heir to the Sterne and Waines property at Little Weighton and Beverley.

After education at Rossall School, near Fleetwood, Lancashire, where he distinguished himself in athletics, particularly sprinting, Machell joined, when seventeen years old, the 14th foot (afterwards the West Yorkshire regiment) as ensign. In 1858 he was gazetted lieutenant, and in 1862 captain. For some time he was quartered in Ireland, where he had ample opportunities for indulging his love of sport and won many a bet by jumping over the mess-room table or from the floor to the mantel-shelf. He exchanged into the 59th in 1863, but retired from the service the same year, owing (it is said) to the commanding officer's refusal to permit him to go to Doncaster for the St Leger.

Thereupon Machell settled at Newmarket, taking with him a three-year-old horse called Bacchus, which he had bought for a very small sum. With this animal he at once won a big handicap, worth £1000, and he was said to have won an additional £10,000 in bets. Thus he quickly obtained a firm footing in the racing world, and was very soon one of its conspicuous figures. He made his living managing other people's turf affairs, advising them on horse purchases and race entries. He was closely connected with three Derby winners: Hermit (1867), which he persuaded Henry Chaplin to buy for £1000 as a yearling; Isinglass (1893), whose dam he obtained for Harry McCalmont; and Sir John Willoughby's Harvester (1884), whose trainer's stables were managed by the captain. He was also an owner in his own right, between 1864 and 1902 winning 540 races, worth £110,010. He was also an astute gambler. Eventually the turf brought him sufficient wealth to buy back the family's old Westmorland seat, Crackenthorpe Hall.

Machell was a good judge of horses, but less so of men. His acerbic tongue cost him the services of the leading jockeys Fred Archer and George Fordham when he accused them of not trying on horses that he had backed. He was respected rather than liked, and in his latter years he was severely depressed, tortured by gout and aware that his suspicious nature had cost him several racing

friendships. He died, unmarried, at 23 Eversfield Place, St Leonards, Sussex, on 11 May 1902, and was buried in Newmarket cemetery.

EDWARD MOORHOUSE, *rev.* WRAY VAMPLEW

Sources R. Mortimer, R. Onslow, and P. Willett, *Biographical encyclopedia of British flat racing* (1978) · R. Onslow, *Great racing gambles and frauds*, 3 (1993) · *The Sportsman* (12 May 1902) · *Pall Mall Gazette* (12 May 1902) · G. Plumptre, *The fast set: the world of Edwardian racing* (1985) · CGPLA Eng. & Wales (1902)

Likenesses Hopkins and Havell, oils, Crackenthorpe Hall, Appleby · Spy [L. Ward], cartoon, NPG; repro. in VF (3 Dec 1887)

Wealth at death £47,569 0s. 8d.: probate, 2 Oct 1902, CGPLA Eng. & Wales

Machell, Thomas (*bap.* 1647, *d.* 1698), antiquary, the second son of Lancelot Machell (*c.*1617–1681) and his wife, Elizabeth (*d.* 1701), daughter of Thomas Sleddall of Penrith, Cumberland, was born at Crackenthorpe Hall, near Appleby, Westmorland, seat of the Machell family since the twelfth century, and was baptized at St Michael's Church, Bongate, Appleby, on 20 June 1647. He went to Queen's College, Oxford, in 1664, and graduated BA in 1668 and MA in 1672; he was elected a fellow of Queen's later that year. In Oxford Machell came into contact with the leading antiquaries of the day: Sir William Dugdale and Anthony Wood, who encouraged him to compile for Cumberland and Westmorland an antiquarian account modelled on Dugdale's for Warwickshire. In 1677 Machell appears to have embarked on a systematic collection of data, writing to gentlemen and clergy in the two counties, and sending them lists of queries to answer. He set his pupils (including William Nicolson, future bishop of Carlisle) to transcribe records in the Tower.

In 1677 Machell was instituted to the rectory of Kirkby Thore, Westmorland, to which he moved and where he remained for the rest of his life. About 1680 he married Elizabeth (*d.* 1701), widow of Andrew Whelpdale, rector of Newnham, Hampshire, and daughter and coheir of William Godson, lord of the manor of Dogmersfield, Hampshire. Whelpdale, originally from Penrith, was connected by marriage to Machell's mother's family. Elizabeth brought six children to her second marriage, and she and Machell had a further two sons and five daughters. The family at Kirkby Thore rectory was thus large and tensions surfaced. Machell fell out with his sister and mother, in part over his father's will, and relations with his stepson, William Whelpdale, were strained. Machell's wife and mother-in-law later claimed that he had 'used William very unkindly' (Hindleston, 118), by demanding money from him for education and maintenance and forcing William to sell to him the advowson of Dogmersfield in 1694.

Machell meanwhile was gathering documentary materials; he travelled extensively, recording the heritage of his native county by direct observation, sketching buildings and heraldry, and noting inscriptions and information given him by local informants. He visited most parishes in northern Westmorland and, between 1691 and 1693, made three antiquarian journeys to the barony of Kendal, the southern half of the county, which lay outside Carlisle diocese.

By the end of his life the material Machell had accumulated towards a history of Westmorland (and, to a lesser extent, Cumberland) was voluminous, if neither as comprehensive nor as systematic as he originally intended. He left his papers to his wife and children, asking that they should be sent to William Nicolson, then archdeacon of Carlisle, with the intention that he should examine them and 'put them in order' (Ferguson, 4) with a view to publication. However, Nicolson considered the papers 'so imperfect, Raw and indigested, that 'twas impossible to bring them (of 'emselves) to any such Account as the good man hoped for' (Machell MSS, Cumbria AS, vol. 1, preface), and he noted that their value was compromised by being so heavily weighted towards the Machell family and the parish of Kirkby Thore. He had the papers bound into six large volumes which he deposited in the Dean and Chapter Library at Carlisle, where they became an essential quarry for later antiquaries, notably Joseph Nicolson and Richard Burn, who used Machell's material extensively in their *History of Westmorland and Cumberland* (1777), and Samuel Jefferson, who printed a summary of their contents in his *History and Antiquities of Carlisle* (1838). Machell's descriptions and sketches of churches, Roman sites, castles, and domestic buildings contain a wealth of accurately observed detail, and are of continuing value to architectural historians and archaeologists. The papers are now in Cumbria Record Office, Carlisle.

Machell's interest in architecture extended to practical involvement in building. He claimed that he and Edward Addison of Kirkby Thore were 'the first introducers of Regular building into these Parts' (Machell MSS, Cumbria AS, vol. 1, p. 538) and that he himself had carried out alterations at the bishop of Carlisle's palace at Rose Castle, the Machell family seat at Crackenthorpe Hall, and other houses in Westmorland, and had built the organ loft in St Laurence's Church at Appleby. Thomas Machell died at Kirkby Thore on 11 November 1698, aged fifty-one, and was buried on the south side of the altar in the chancel at Kirkby Thore church the following day.

ANGUS J. L. WINCHESTER

Sources J. Rogan and E. Birley, 'Thomas Machell, the antiquary', *Transactions of the Cumberland and Westmorland Antiquarian and Archaeological Society*, new ser., 55 (1956), 132–53 · J. M. Ewbank, ed., *Antiquary on horseback*, Cumberland and Westmorland Antiquarian and Archaeological Society, extra ser., 19 (1963) · E. Bellassis, 'Machell of Crackenthorpe', *Transactions of the Cumberland and Westmorland Antiquarian and Archaeological Society*, 8 (1885–6), 416–66 · R. S. Ferguson, 'Wills relating to the dean and chapter library at Carlisle', *Transactions of the Cumberland and Westmorland Antiquarian and Archaeological Society*, 4 (1878–9), 1–12 · C. R. Hindleston, 'Thomas Machell, his wife and children and his Whelpdale stepchildren', *Transactions of the Cumberland and Westmorland Antiquarian and Archaeological Society*, new ser., 70 (1970), 110–45 · R. Bowyer, 'Notes on the Kirkbythore registers', *Transactions of the Cumberland and Westmorland Antiquarian and Archaeological Society*, 4 (1878–9), 372–86 · B. Tyson, ed., *The estate and household accounts of Sir Daniel Fleming of Rydal Hall, Westmorland, from 1688–1701*, Cumberland and Westmorland Antiquarian and Archaeological Society, 13 (2001), 267

Archives Cumbria AS, Carlisle, Cumberland and Westmorland collections

Wealth at death £392; incl. £153 8s. 6d. in debts owing to testator: Ferguson, 'Wills'

Machen, Arthur Llewelyn Jones (1863–1947), writer, was born on 3 March 1863 at 3 High Street, Caerleon, Monmouthshire, the only child of the Revd John Edward Jones (1831/2–1887), rector of Llanddewi Fach, and his wife, Janet Robina Machen (1826/7–1885), whose maiden name was adopted by the family in order to please her Scottish relatives. He was educated at Hereford Cathedral school (1874–80). The splendours of the landscape surrounding Llanddewi rectory, his boyhood home near Caerleon, and his passion for romantic literature inspired him to begin writing. His début in print was *Eleusinia* (1881), a mystical poem. The mystery and wonder it expressed also characterized all his later creations.

His father's poverty prevented Machen from attending university, and his attempt at a medical career proved short-lived when he failed the preliminary examination of the Royal College of Surgeons in 1880. In 1881 he moved to London, trying unsuccessfully to enter journalism. Living in poverty, he wrote while variously employed as a tutor, publishers' clerk, and cataloguer of occult books. His early works included *The Anatomy of Tobacco* (1884), a translation of *The Heptameron* (1886), and *The Chronicle of Clemendy* (1888). On 31 August 1887 he married Amelia (d. 1899), daughter of Frederick Metcalfe Hogg, of Worthing, Sussex. After her death from cancer Machen briefly sought solace in the Hermetic Order of the Golden Dawn, an occult society, but ultimately found its teachings sterile.

In the next decade Machen translated Casanova's *Memoires* (1894) and composed some of his finest fiction. *The Great God Pan* (1894) and *The Three Impostors* (1895), his early ventures into the macabre, appeared in the Bodley Head's Keynotes series. *The Hill of Dreams*, one of the period's most lyrical and decadent novels, was completed in 1897, but remained unpublished for ten years.

Machen joined Frank Benson's Shakespeare repertory company as an actor in 1901, and subsequently toured with several theatrical companies. He resumed writing between stage engagements. His literary theories were trenchantly expressed in *Hieroglyphics* (1902), and his supernatural tales were collected in *The House of Souls* (1906). On 25 June 1903 Machen married one of the actresses in Benson's company, Dorothie Purefoy Hudleston (1878–1947), the daughter of Colonel Josiah Hudleston, formerly of the Madras staff corps. They had a son, Hilary (1912–1987), and a daughter, Janet (b. 1917).

From 1910 to 1921 Machen worked as a reporter for the London *Evening News*. Although he detested journalism, his Johnsonian manner and compelling character established him as one of Fleet Street's most charismatic figures. The *Evening News* carried several of his wonder stories, and the appearance in September 1914 of his wartime fantasy 'The Bowmen' brought him to public attention. The tale of St George and phantom archers from Agincourt aiding British troops was widely accepted as factual, and by the summer of 1915 the legend of the 'angels of Mons' had swept the country.

In the 1920s, having been neglected by the British literary establishment for forty years, Machen attracted a coterie of admirers in the United States. Writers such as Vincent Starrett and Carl Van Vechten, extolling his powerful prose, proclaimed him a mystagogue of the secrets of life and art in the tradition of Edgar Allan Poe and Nathaniel Hawthorne. Machen's reminiscences, *Far Off Things* (1922) and *Things Near and Far* (1923), movingly recaptured his youth in Monmouthshire and his struggles as a writer during the *fin de siècle*, and revealed the depth of his dedication to literature.

By the end of the 1920s, as the vogue for his books diminished, Machen encountered renewed financial hardship. He and his family moved to Amersham, Buckinghamshire, where he produced essays, reviews, innumerable letters, and a final crop of stories. In 1932 he received a civil-list pension. In old age he maintained a relish for life in defiance of tribulations and failing health, and his geniality and goodness made him the centre of a circle of faithful friends and admirers. Machen died in St Joseph's Nursing Home, Beaconsfield, Buckinghamshire, on 15 December 1947, and was buried in the municipal cemetery at Amersham.

No critical consensus regarding Machen exists. Some critics view him as a literary curiosity, while others revere him as a unique talent. Praised by writers as diverse as H. P. Lovecraft, Jorge Luis Borges, and John Betjeman, he remains a pioneering cult author in the horror and fantasy fields. Central to his artistic philosophy is the concept of the numinous underlying the ordinary: in his words, 'the sense of the eternal mysteries, the eternal beauty hidden beneath the crust of common and commonplace things' (Machen, *London Adventure*, 75). An American Arthur Machen Society was established in 1948, and was succeeded by a British appreciation society in 1986. Much of Machen's work has been kept alive in both countries by the small press. ROGER DOBSON

Sources A. Reynolds and W. Charlton, *Arthur Machen: a short account of his life and work* (1963) · W. D. Sweetser, *Arthur Machen* (1964) · A. Machen, *Far off things* (1922) · A. Machen, *Things near and far* (1923) · A. Goldstone and W. D. Sweetser, *A bibliography of Arthur Machen* (1965) · M. Murphy, ed., *Starrett vs. Machen: a record of discovery and correspondence* (1977) · private information (2004) · A. Machen, *The London adventure* (1924) · CGPLA Eng. & Wales (1948)
Archives McGill University, McLennan Library, literary MSS and press notices · Newport Central Library, Monmouthshire, corresp. · NL Wales, letters · Ransom HRC, MS of Madam Favart and notebook | BL, corresp. with Society of Authors, Add. MS 56743 · Harvard U., Houghton L., letters to Cyril Clemens and papers · Newport Central Library, Monmouthshire, letters to Leslie Millar · NL Wales, letters to A. Addams-Williams · NL Wales, corresp. with Harry Spurr · Ransom HRC, corresp. with John Lane · U. Aberdeen L., letters to J. B. Chapman | SOUND Radio Wales (?), BBC Sound Archives
Likenesses photograph, 1890–99, repro. in E. Jepson, *Memories of an Edwardian and neo-Georgian* (1937) · E. O. Hoppé, photographs, 1900–40 · Baron Scotfield, silhouette, *c*.1913, repro. in A. Machen, *The bowmen and other legends of the war* (1915) · E. Walters, oils, 1940–49, NL Wales
Wealth at death £1333 2s. 8d.: probate, 9 Feb 1948, CGPLA Eng. & Wales

Machen, Thomas (*c*.1541–1614). *See under* Machyn, Henry (1496/1498–1563).

McHenry, James (1785–1845), poet and novelist, was born on 20 December 1785 in Larne, co. Antrim, the son of a merchant there. He studied at Trinity College, Dublin, and at Glasgow, where he qualified in medicine. He practised as a doctor, first in Larne and then in Belfast. He also had strong literary interests, and his poem *Patrick* (1810) is a narrative of the uprising of 1798.

In 1817 McHenry emigrated to the United States, where he lived successively in Baltimore, Pittsburgh, and Philadelphia, where he settled in 1824, both trading and practising medicine. He continued his literary pursuits in his new home; his poem *The Pleasures of Friendship* appeared in 1822, and was reprinted with other poems at Philadelphia in 1836. In 1824 he founded and became editor of the *American Monthly Magazine*, where the novel for which he is best known, *O'Halloran, or, The Insurgent Chief* (1824), first appeared. He wrote some five other historical novels between 1823 and 1829, including *The Hearts of Steel* (1825), which, like *O'Halloran*, is written from a Presbyterian standpoint out of personal knowledge of the United Irishmen and Ulster agrarian politics. His narrative poems included *Waltham: an American Revolutionary Tale* (1823), and *The Antediluvians, or, The World Destroyed* (1839).

From 1842 until his death McHenry was United States consul in Londonderry. He died at Larne, co. Antrim, on 21 July 1845. His son James, a well-known financier, died at Kensington in 1891. His daughter Mary married Mr J. Bellargee Cox of Philadelphia.

THOMAS HAMILTON, *rev.* JOHN D. HAIGH

Sources J. G. Wilson and J. Fiske, eds., *Appleton's cyclopaedia of American biography*, 7 vols. (1887–1900) · R. Welch, ed., *The Oxford companion to Irish literature* (1996)

Macheth family (*per. c*.1124–1215), rebels, took part in revolts against four successive kings of Scots over some ninety years. Their first known representative, **Malcolm Macheth**, earl of Ross (*d*. 1168), may have rebelled in 1124 against King David I. He was certainly 'out' in 1130 with Angus, earl of Moray, who claimed the Scottish throne as a descendant of King Lulach (*d*. 1058); they were defeated, and Angus killed, at Stracathro. In 1134 Malcolm again rebelled and David I sought and may have received Norman help; in the same year Malcolm was captured and imprisoned in Roxburgh Castle, where he spent the next twenty-three years. There were no more rebellions against David I for the rest of his reign.

The ancestry of Malcolm Macheth and the reasons for his revolts have been variously explained. Orderic Vitalis describes him as the illegitimate son of Alexander I, but although Orderic is usually reliable, this seems unlikely. Ailred of Rievaulx, writing of the wars of 1138, refers to him as 'the heir of his father's hatred and persecution' (Anderson, *Scottish Annals*, 193), a phrase which has been taken to mean that he was the son of Angus of Moray. John Fordun, writing in the fourteenth century, asserts that he claimed, falsely, to be Angus's son, an assertion which misled later historians into confusing Malcolm with

*Wimund, bishop of the Isles, who undoubtedly contended that he was the son of Angus. But all these suggestions ignore the problems raised by Malcolm's patronym, and it seems more likely that he was the son of an Earl Aed (Heth; *d.* before 1130?) recorded early in the twelfth century, who may have held the earldom of Ross. A family link with Earl Angus is possible, but cannot be proved. However it was derived, Malcolm's eminence is clearly demonstrated by his marriage, in or before 1134, to a sister of *Somerled, lord of Argyll; it may also explain his later imprisonment, since the usual fate for defeated rebels was execution. David I's mercy, or political judgement, could have been decisive in this, however, for Malcolm's rebellious descendants were not treated so leniently.

Malcolm's sons (their exact number and, with one exception, names are not known) joined Somerled in his revolt against Malcolm IV late in 1154; one son, **Donald Macheth** (*fl.* 1156), was captured at Whithorn in 1156 and sent to join his father at Roxburgh. In 1157 Malcolm Macheth was reconciled with the king and was probably loyal thereafter. He was granted the earldom of Ross, which he held from 1162 at the latest until his death in 1168.

King William the Lion appointed no successor as earl; nothing more is known about Malcolm Macheth's sons except that Donald had a son, **Aed Macheth** (*d.* 1186), who kept alive the family claims. Ross was a focus of unrest, probably from Macheth activity, in 1179; by 1181 a major rising was well under way, led by Donald Ban of the *Macwilliam family, with whom the Macheths were often associated thereafter. Aed, son of Donald Macheth, took part; by now an outlaw, with an unnamed nephew and fifty-eight followers he was trapped and killed at the abbey of Coupar Angus in 1186.

After the defeat of the Macwilliams at 'Mam Garvia' on 31 July 1187 the Macheths were quiet for nearly ten years. Malcolm Macheth also had a daughter, **Hvarflod Macheth**, countess of Orkney and Caithness (*fl.* 1196), the bigamous second wife of *Harald Maddadson, earl of Orkney and Caithness (1133/4–1206). She was thus the sister-in-law of Malcolm, earl of Atholl, who had been responsible for the death of her nephew Aed in 1186; she is said to have instigated the revolt of Earl Harald against King William in 1196. In 1197 Thorfinn Haraldsson, the earl's son from his first marriage, was defeated in battle near Inverness and Harald was captured and put in Roxburgh Castle; having made his peace with the king, he then left Thorfinn as a hostage in his place. About 1201, after further troubles in Caithness, Thorfinn was blinded and emasculated and died later in prison. John and David, the sons of Harald and Hvarflod, were recognized as earls of Orkney and Caithness after Harald's death. Perhaps warned by Thorfinn's fate, neither pressed any claims based on their Macheth blood. David died, apparently childless, in 1214; John (*d.* 1231) succeeded as sole earl, and King William in the last months of his reign went to Moray and received John's (unnamed) daughter as a hostage. Her fate is not known; nor is the date of death of her grandmother Hvarflod.

The Macheths may have been responsible for the invitation from the lords of Ross which encouraged Guthred Macwilliam's invasion in 1211. If so, at least one survived Guthred's defeat in 1212, since Aed's son, **Kenneth Macheth** (*d.* 1215), took part in the next Macwilliam rising in 1215, when the rebels invaded Moray (more likely Ross). They were defeated in May or June and their severed heads, including Kenneth's, were presented to Alexander II on 15 June 1215. Nothing more is known of the family thereafter; a conjecture that they were the ancestors of clan Mackay is no more than that. If any were still alive their claims to Ross were denied when the earldom was granted to Farquhar Mactaggart, who had put down the rebellion of 1215, some time between 1221 and 1226.

W. W. SCOTT

Sources A. O. Anderson, ed. and trans., *Early sources of Scottish history, AD 500 to 1286*, 2 vols. (1922); repr. with corrections (1990) · A. O. Anderson, ed., *Scottish annals from English chroniclers, AD 500 to 1286* (1908); repr. (1991) · G. W. S. Barrow, *Kingship and unity: Scotland, 1000–1306* (1981) · G. W. S. Barrow, ed., *Regesta regum Scottorum*, 1–2 (1960–71) · W. Bower, *Scotichronicon*, ed. D. E. R. Watt and others, new edn, 9 vols. (1987–98), vols. 4–5 · A. C. Lawrie, ed., *Annals of the reigns of Malcolm and William, kings of Scotland* (1910) · R. L. G. Ritchie, *The Normans in Scotland* (1954)

Macheth, Aed (*d.* 1186). *See under* Macheth family (*per.* c.1124–1215).

Macheth, Donald (*fl.* 1156). *See under* Macheth family (*per.* c.1124–1215).

Macheth, Hvarflod, countess of Orkney and Caithness (*fl.* 1196). *See under* Macheth family (*per.* c.1124–1215).

Macheth, Kenneth (*d.* 1215). *See under* Macheth family (*per.* c.1124–1215).

Macheth, Malcolm, earl of Ross (*d.* 1168). *See under* Macheth family (*per.* c.1124–1215).

Machim [Robert Machin] (*supp. fl.* 14th cent.), supposed adventurer, is said to have lived in the fourteenth century, and is claimed, in sixteenth-century writings and works derived from them, as the discoverer of the island of Madeira.

Three traditions refer to him or to a similar character of similar name. What may be the earliest is represented by part of a work headed *Descripçao de Ceuta e norte de Africa* in a compilation of maritime interest known as the Valentim Fernandes manuscript. No author or year is given for the *Descripçao*, but internal evidence suggests the date 1507, which is borne by another work in the same compendium. Here Machym is said to be an exiled English knight, bound for Spain with his unnamed mistress and blown to the island of Porto Santo, where he sights Madeira to the south-west. While he explores the interior of the latter island, most of his crew, fearful of the place and covetous of his goods, make off in the ship. After shipwreck on the African mainland the survivors are enslaved. The mistress, who has remained on Madeira, dies, and her lover builds an oratory over her grave. Encouraging his remaining crew 'like a good knight', he escapes with them in a craft of their own manufacture (Bensaúde and Baião,

107). Wrecked and enslaved on the African coast, they encounter their old shipmates and attack them murderously. Separated by Moors, who upbraid Christians for fighting each other, they tell their story, which local officials communicate to the king of Fez. The adventurer is sent on by the latter to the court of a King Juan of Castile, where he dies. Goats he released on Porto Santo fill the island.

António Galvão, the lay Apostle of the Molucas, included an almost identical story in his *Tratado dos descobrimentos*, published posthumously in 1563. He attempted to give it a historical setting first by introducing the outward voyage of the protagonist, whom he calls Machim, immediately after describing events of 1344, with the words, 'They say that in this same time the isle of Madeira was discovered' (Galvão, 114); and second by claiming that a Castilian expedition of 1393 was inspired 'by the information which Machim gave of this island' (ibid., 116). Thanks to a translation published by Richard Hakluyt in 1601, Galvão's version later became well known to English readers.

A second tradition derives from a work said to have been written by a squire of the household of the Portuguese infante Dom Henrique (Henry the Navigator), variously called Francisco de Alcoforado or Gonçalo Aires Ferreira. Two seventeenth-century manuscripts of such a work survive under Alcoforado's name, but the tradition they represent must already have been in place by 1579, when Jerónimo Dias Leite, canon of Funchal, used it in a work of his own and sent a copy to Gaspar Fructuoso, the resident historian of the Azores. In this version, the hero is a good knight called the Machim, and his mistress is named as Ana de Arfet or Harfet. While adding much circumstantial detail, this version makes two important departures: Machim dies on Madeira and is buried alongside Ana; the survivors tell their story to a Castilian fellow captive in Morocco called Juan Damores, who, after his ransom, falls into Portuguese hands and inspires Dom Henrique to mount an expedition in search of the island c.1419.

Most later writings on the subject combined this version with that derived via Galvão. The most influential was a mawkish account of Roberto o Machino by Francisco Manuel de Melo, written in 1654, which prompted French and English translations. The latter, published in 1675, introduced the names Lionel Machin and Arabella Darcy.

A third tradition, started in writing by Count Giulio Landi (*d*. 1579?), who visited Madeira in 1530, gives the name il Macino to a French merchant, who, blown to Madeira—this time without a mistress—returns, after adventures in which he is enslaved and ransomed, to colonize the island. Though diffused in works published in 1574 and 1599, this apparent rationalization of a romance lacked the appeal of the rival versions.

Elements of these traditions are common in late medieval chivalric fiction: the amorous imbroglio, the seaborne setting, the interventions of the wind, the romantic island, the changes of fortune, the interplay of treachery and fidelity, the exemplary conduct of the model knight,

the generous Moors. The historical discovery of Madeira is undocumented, but the island appears recognizably in sea charts dated from 1339 onwards.

FELIPE FERNÁNDEZ-ARMESTO

Sources J. Bensaúde and A. Baião, *O manuscrito 'Valentim Fernandes'* (1940) · A. Galvão, *Tratado dos descobrimentos*, ed. V. de Lagoa and E. Sanceau (1944) · G. Fructuoso, *As saudades da terra: historia das ilhas do Porto Sancto, Madeira, Desertas e Salvagems*, ed. A. R. de Azevedo (1873) · A. A. G. Rodrigues, *Don Francisco Manuel de Melo e o descobrimento de Madeira* (1935) · J. D. Leite, *Descobrimento da ilha da Madeira e discurso da vida e feitos dos capitães da dita ilha*, ed. J. F. Machado (1947) · G. Landi, *La descrittione dell' isola de la Madeira*, trans. A. Fino (1574) · M. Constantino, *História da ilha da Madeira*, ed. and trans. J. B. de Afonseca and F. A. da Silva (1930) · F. M. de Melo, *Epanáforas de varia história portuguesa*, ed. J. Serrão (1977) · F. M. de Melo, *Epanáfora amorosa*, ed. J. M. de Castro (Lisbon?, [n.d., 1975?]) · F. Fernández-Armesto, 'Inglaterra y el atlántico en la baja edad media', in A. B. Massieu, *Canarias e Inglaterra a través de la historia* (1995), 11–28 · F. Fernández-Armesto, 'Medieval Atlantic exploration: the evidence of maps', in G. D. Winius, *Portugal the pathfinder* (1995), 41–70 · F. M. de Melo, *Epanáforas*, ed. E. Prestage (1931) · A. Galvão, *The discoveries of the world*, trans. R. Hakluyt (1601)

Machin, Arnold (1911–1999), sculptor, was born on 30 September 1911 at 793 London Road, Oakhill, Stoke-on-Trent, Staffordshire, the ninth child among the eight sons and four daughters of William James Machin, a pottery modeller, and his wife, Sarah Ann, *née* Walker. He was educated at Trent Vale Church of England school, and in 1925 began an apprenticeship as a china painter with Minton's in Stoke-on-Trent, while studying part-time at Stoke School of Art from 1927. In 1933 he moved to Derby to take up a job as a painter at the Old Derby china works, and attended Derby School of Art in the evenings until 1935, when he became a full-time student.

Awarded a scholarship by the Royal College of Art in 1937, Machin studied sculpture, working mainly in terracotta, and as the top sculpture student won the silver medal in 1940, and a travelling scholarship for sculpture, which the war prevented him from taking up. He moved back to the Potteries, where Josiah Wedgwood & Co., on the recommendation of the Royal College of Art, employed him to design 'English' figures for the American market. He also taught part-time at Stoke School of Art before moving to London in 1942 to work for Voluntary Service for Peace. He spent a year in Wormwood Scrubs prison as a conscientious objector until 1943, when Wedgwood gave him a job as a figure modeller. He remained with Wedgwood throughout the 1940s, creating more than twenty figures, including the very successful *Taurus* (1945), decorated with the signs of the zodiac. At the same time he was sculpting terracotta figures: in 1944 the Tate Gallery bought his *John the Baptist* and *The Annunciation* through the Knapping fund, and in 1947 the Royal Academy, through the Chantrey bequest, acquired *Spring*, a life-size seated terracotta nude in the classical Italian style. He liked the spontaneity of modelling in clay: 'I think that I was born a terracotta modeller … Whereas in stone-carving the sculpture is produced by cutting away and destroying the original stone, in work with clay one is building up and creating from the earth itself' (*The Life and Times of Arnold Machin*, 48). On 26 April 1949 he married

(Beryl) Patricia Newton (*b.* 1920/21), a flower painter, daughter of Lieutenant-Colonel Henry Newton, an inventor and electrical engineer: they had one son. While continuing to live in Staffordshire, Machin taught in the ceramic school of the Royal College of Art in London from 1951 to 1958, and was master of sculpture at the Royal Academy schools from 1958 to 1967.

Machin's design for a new effigy of the queen was chosen in 1964 for the obverse side of the new coinage to be launched in 1968 in preparation for decimalization in 1971, and by 1985, when it was superseded by Raphael Maklouf's effigy, the Royal Mint had produced 17 billion coins bearing this design. He also won the commissions to design the royal silver wedding commemorative crown in 1972 and the silver jubilee crown in 1977. He was one of five artists invited in 1965 by the royal mail to submit designs for a new portrait of the queen to replace Dorothy Wilding's for the definitive British postage stamp, and it was his design, inspired by the simplicity of the portrait of the young Queen Victoria on the penny black stamp, that was chosen. As with his design for the coinage, he modelled the head in clay as a sculpted relief, working from pencil sketches, before photographing it in different lighting conditions. The final design, introduced in 1967, remained unchanged into the twenty-first century, reputedly being reproduced more times than any other image in history.

After the success of his coinage and stamp designs, Machin was commissioned by Wedgwood to design several bas-relief portraits of the royal family, including one to commemorate the wedding of Princess Anne in 1973, and he was also asked to design porcelain figures for Royal Worcester, including figures of the *Four Seasons* in 1968. He first became interested in garden design in the early 1970s, and in the old fields round his home, Offley Rock, near Eccleshall, Staffordshire, he created a garden with loggias, grottoes, waterfalls, and fountains, full of ornaments and sculptures. As well as designing garden seats, summer houses, gates, and garden ornaments, his work included the design of a grotto fountain (1986) at Henbury Hall for Sebastian de Ferranti.

Machin was elected an associate of the Royal Academy of Arts in 1947, and a full member in 1956. In the last decade of his life he was a regular exhibitor at the RA summer exhibition. Disapproving of the direction in which modern British art was going, he was one of the leading protesters against the Royal Academy's 1997 Sensation exhibition. He was appointed OBE in 1965. He died on 9 March 1999 at his home near Eccleshall, Staffordshire. Before he died he dictated his memoirs, which were published as *Artist of an Icon* (2002).   ANNE PIMLOTT BAKER

Sources *The life and times of Arnold Machin* (2001) [catalogue of the retrospective exhibition at the RA schools] · J. Skinner, ed., *The connoisseur catalogue of Machin stamps and decimal definitives* (1977) [10th edn, 1995] · *The Times* (10 March 1999) · *Daily Telegraph* (10 March 1999) · *The Independent* (15 March 1999) · private information (2004) [son] · b. cert. · m. cert. · d. cert. · *WW* · A. Machin, *Artist of an icon* (2002)
Archives Royal Mail Heritage, London · royal mint archives

Likenesses photograph, 1947, repro. in Machin, *Artist of an icon* · Wesley, photograph, 1967, Hult. Arch. · photograph, 1967, repro. in *Daily Telegraph*
Wealth at death £385,356—gross: probate, 2001, *CGPLA Eng. & Wales*

Machin, Henry. See Machyn, Henry (1496/1498–1563).

Machin, John (1624–1664), clergyman and ejected minister, was born on 2 October 1624 at Seabridge, Staffordshire (now a suburb of Newcastle under Lyme), and baptized the same day at Newcastle, the only surviving son of John Machin (*d.* 1653) and his wife, Katherine Vernon (*d.* 1664). The family had held the estate at Seabridge since the 1530s. Machin was educated first by Mr Orme at Newcastle under Lyme and subsequently by John Ball at Whitmore, Staffordshire. After school he spent some years engaged in husbandry, but in December 1645 was admitted to Jesus College, Cambridge, where he graduated BA in 1649 and proceeded MA in 1653. At Cambridge he came under the influence of puritan teachers and organized meetings for scholars to discuss religion. He subsequently viewed his early life, which seems to have consisted of an addiction to cock-fighting, as dissolute.

Machin was ordained by the Whitchurch, Shropshire, classis in 1649, and after ordination chose not to have any settled cure, apart from preaching on alternate Sundays in Ashbourne, Derbyshire, and, in early 1651, lecturing at Atherstone in Warwickshire. He saw his calling to minister in as wide a theatre as possible, and declared: 'O that whole Staffordshire and Cheshire might be saved!' (Newcome, *Life and Death*, 15). About this time he met Henry Newcome, upon whom he was to have considerable influence. Machin's home at Seabridge became the focus for private days of devotion for a circle of men, including Newcome and Thomas Leadbeater of Holmes Chapel. Their time was spent in discussion, preaching, and prayer, and meetings continued to take place at intervals over the next few years.

In early 1653 Machin inherited the Seabridge estate on his father's death. This enabled him to finance a monthly lecture circuit throughout the towns of Staffordshire, which continued until 1660. On 29 September 1653 in Uttoxeter, Staffordshire, he married Jane (*d.* 1707), the daughter of John Butler of Mickleover, Derbyshire. They had five children: Samuel (*b.* 1654), Lydia (*b.* 1656), John (*b.* 1658), and Sarah (*b.* 1660)—all born at Astbury, Cheshire—and Esther, born at Whitley, Cheshire, in 1663.

By the spring of 1654 Machin was joint minister, with George Moxon, of Astbury in south-east Cheshire. There he stayed until 1661 when he became curate at Whitley in the parish of Great Budworth, Cheshire. He appears an intense character, and a rousing preacher 'which made one of his Kindred say, that he liked his cousen Machin well, but that he made his house a chapel when he came to him' (Newcome, *Life and Death*, 20). He also developed the habit of carving texts on trees or the walls and mantelpieces of homes he visited. Nevertheless, he was a generous man, giving alms to the poor and financial aid to friends in straitened circumstances. He was ejected from

Whitley in 1662, and returned, deeply distressed, to Seabridge, where he died of fever on 6 September 1664. He was buried at Newcastle under Lyme on 8 September. His will was proved at Lichfield in July 1665, with the estate valued at £120 10s.

Little is known of Machin, other than what is recorded by Henry Newcome in his autobiography and *A Faithful Narrative of the Life and Death of ... Mr. John Machin* (1671), which Matthew Henry attributed to Newcome. (In his autobiography Newcome suggests that both he and Thomas Leadbeater collaborated, about 1665 or 1666, on the text, a version of which appears in Samuel Clarke's *Lives of Sundry Eminent Persons*, 1683.) Nevertheless, in his day, Machin was well known to the godly community in the north-west. On his death Matthew Henry described him thus:

> A worthy instrument in Gospel work. Laborious, faithful and successful above his fellows, taken away in the midst of his days. The first candle I have heard of put out by God, among the many hundreds put under a bushel by men. (Henry, 1.268)

Nevertheless, Machin's influence persisted. His house at Seabridge was licensed in Jane Machin's name as a presbyterian meeting-house in 1672. She was buried at Mickleover on 24 June 1707. The Machins' eldest son, Samuel, inherited the estate and in time became a supporter of the presbyterian community in Newcastle under Lyme.

CATHERINE NUNN

Sources [H. Newcome], *A faithful narrative of the life and death of ... Mr. John Machin* (1671) · *The autobiography of Henry Newcome*, ed. R. Parkinson, 2 vols., Chetham Society, 26–7 (1852) · *The diary of the Rev. Henry Newcome, from September 30, 1661, to September 29, 1663*, ed. T. Heywood, Chetham Society, 18 (1849) · M. Henry, *The life of Philip and Matthew Henry*, 2 vols. (1828); repr. (1974) · *Calamy rev.* · G. L. Turner, ed., *Original records of early nonconformity under persecution and indulgence*, 2 (1912) · C. M. Nunn, 'The ministry of Henry Newcome: presbyterianism in south-east Cheshire, 1648–1662', MPhil diss., University of Manchester, 1998 · will and inventory, 1665, Lichfield Joint RO

Wealth at death £120 10s.: *Calamy rev.*; will and inventory, Lichfield Joint RO

Machin, John (*bap.* 1686?, *d.* 1751), astronomer, was possibly the son of John and Mary Machin who was baptized on 17 October 1686 at St Botolph without Bishopsgate, London. Nothing is known of his early years or his education, but he was elected a fellow of the Royal Society on 30 November 1710 and served as its secretary from 1718 to 1747. He was on the society's committee set up to adjudicate the priority dispute between Newton and Leibnitz over the invention of the calculus, which vindicated Newton, and he was one of those charged to edit the relevant documents, published in 1712 as the *Commercium epistolicum*. His application for the professorship of astronomy at Gresham College in 1713 was naturally supported by Newton, who stated that he knew Machin to be proficient in Latin and mathematics, and that he had prepared Flamsteed's observations for the press, and also by the Savilian professor John Keill, Edmond Halley, and James Pound. He was duly appointed on 16 May 1713, and held the post until his death.

Machin was considered an able mathematician, and several of his papers were published in the *Philosophical Transactions*; however, his attempt to rectify Newton's lunar theory in his *Laws of the Moon's Motion According to Gravity*, which was appended to a 1729 translation of Newton's *Principia*, was considered a poor performance, while his computation of the value of π to 100 decimal places by Halley's method was merely a testimony to perseverance. Having made amendments to the lunar tables, he asserted unsuccessfully his claim to a share of the parliamentary reward for the discovery of longitude. He left unfinished a major work on lunar theory begun in 1717.

In October 1726 Machin was at Broxmouth, Roxburghshire, the seat of the duke of Roxburghe, where he observed a brilliant and spectacular aurora, later described to the Royal Society. On another occasion he took issue with the reasons given by Sir John Clerk for the ability of geese and other birds to migrate over vast distances, apparently without food or rest. Machin strenuously disputed Clerk's assertion that the birds flew at a great height to escape the friction of the air, and that they coasted as the earth rotated beneath them. In his later years Machin was in poor health and attended infrequently at the society; hence he was not re-elected in 1747. A resident of the parish of St Peter-le-Poer, Old Broad Street, he was unmarried, and his only relative was a second cousin, Mary Tasker. He died, aged sixty-four, in London, on 9 June 1751 and was buried at St Botolph without Bishopsgate on 12 June. He left no will and, as Mary Tasker renounced, the administration of his estate was granted to a creditor, John Thompson. ANITA McCONNELL

Sources C. R. Weld, *A history of the Royal Society*, 2 vols. (1848), vol. 1, p. 410 · Nichols, *Illustrations*, 4.23 · BL, Add. MS 6194, 210–12 · *GM*, 1st ser., 21 (1751), 284 · *London Magazine*, 20 (1751), 284 · *Scots Magazine*, 13 (1751), 309 · S. P. Rigaud and S. J. Rigaud, eds., *Correspondence of scientific men of the seventeenth century*, 1 (1841), 280 · C. Hutton, *Tracts on mathematical and philosophical subjects*, 1 (1812), 266 · W. Jones, *Synopsis palmariorum matheseos, or, A new introduction to the mathematics* (1706), 243 · *Reliquiae Galeanae, or, Miscellaneous pieces by the late learned brothers Roger and Samuel Gale* (1781), no. 2, pt 1 [3/2] of *Bibliotheca topographica Britannica*, ed. J. Nichols (1780–1800), 267 · administration, PRO, PROB 6/127, fol. 227v · parish registers, St Botolph without Bishopsgate, London · *DNB*

Archives BL, corresp. and papers · RS

Machin, Lewis (*fl.* 1608), playwright, is believed to have collaborated with Gervase *Markham on a play *The Dumbe Knight*. The only evidence of his existence is a prefatory letter in the first quarto of 1608, signed 'Lewes Machin'. There are two variant issues of this quarto, one whose title-page describes the play as a 'pleasant Comedy ... written by Iarvis Markham', and another, also dated 1608, which describes it as a 'historicall Comedy' and bears no author's name, though both bear the same epistle. As Markham is known to have spelt his first name variously as Jarvis or Jervis, even Iervis (following the early editions of some of his other books), and as the two names written in Elizabethan secretary hand would have a marked resemblance to each other, it is quite possible that 'Lewes

Machin' is no more than a compositor's misreading of Jervis Markham. Machin's name is not found in any other work or source.

However, it is a principle of editing that the lesser-known word is more likely to be mistaken for the familiar, and therefore an unknown Lewis Machin may have paid the penalty for obscurity and had his signature mistaken for the better-known and prolific Markham. If a Lewis Machin existed, he may have been, as Chambers suggests, related to the Richard Machin who was listed as an actor in Germany from 1600 to 1606.   JULIA GASPER

Sources G. Markham and L. Machin, 'The dumbe knight', variant quartos, 1608, Bodl. Oxf., MSS Malone 219 (3) and 4 T39 (2) Art · G. Markham and L. Machin, 'The dumbe knight', BM edn, 1608, STC film no. 17399 · G. Markham and L. Machin, *The dumbe knight* (1633) · G. Markham, *The English arcadia* (1607), preface · G. Markham, *Markham's methode* (1636), preface · G. Markham and W. Sampson, *Herod and Antipater* (1622) · T. May, *The heire: an excellent comedy* (1622) · R. Brome, *The northern lasse* (1632) · E. K. Chambers, *The Elizabethan stage*, 4 vols. (1923); rev. edn (1951) · F. N. L. Poynter, *Bibliography of Gervase Markham, 1568?–1637* (1962) · *STC, 1475–1640*

Machlinia, William de. *See* Maclyn, William (*fl.* 1482–1490).

Machon, John (1602?–1679/80), Church of England clergyman, was the eldest son of John Machon (1571/1572–1638?), incumbent first of Aston-next-Birmingham, and later of Rugeley and of Longdon, Staffordshire. His mother was Anne, daughter of John Jones MD and rector of Tretham, near Rotherham, Yorkshire. He had two known brothers and two sisters. Like his father he was educated at Magdalen Hall, Oxford, where he matriculated on 26 June 1621 aged eighteen. He graduated BA on 7 February 1624 and proceeded MA on 15 June 1626.

Presumably through Thomas Morton, bishop of Coventry and Lichfield, on 9 September 1631 Machon gained the Wellington prebend of Lichfield Cathedral. On 24 September 1632 he became vicar of Hartburn, Northumberland, worth £100, and also in the gift of Thomas Morton, by then bishop of Durham. In 1636 he resigned Hartburn when presented to Christ's Hospital, Sherburn, co. Durham, since it was stipulated that the master must be a preacher with no other cure. He was responsible for thirty poor 'brothers': the foundation income was about £240. This charity was supervised by the bishop of Durham, still Thomas Morton. At an unknown date Machon married Deborah, daughter of William Blakiston of the city of York; they had two known sons and three daughters.

During the civil war Machon was in 1642 violently ejected from Sherburn Hospital by Sir William Armine and other Scottish commissioners. The family retreated to Staffordshire, where he had inherited an estate, probably at Longdon where his father had bought land. He petitioned the council of state vainly for reinstatement in 1653 and 1657, and was only restored by the sheriff on 12 March 1661. By 1666 his coat of arms was recorded, as Machon of Sherborne. His son Thomas (1642–1673) was educated at Hart Hall, Oxford, graduating BA in 1659 and proceeding MA in 1662. He became chaplain to Prince

Rupert of the Rhine. In 1671 John Machon resigned Wellington prebend in favour of his son, who died on 6 February 1673 and was buried at Sherburn. John Machon remained master there until his death, and was buried in the chapel of the hospital on 22 January 1680.

ELIZABETH ALLEN

Sources R. Surtees, *The history and antiquities of the county palatine of Durham*, 1/2 (1816), 142–3 · *Reg. Oxf.*, 2/2.182, 392; 2/3.180, 407 · J. Foster, ed., *Pedigrees recorded at the visitations of the county palatine of Durham* (1887), 218 · *Walker rev.*, 142 · *The injunctions and other ecclesiastical proceedings of Richard Barnes, bishop of Durham*, ed. [J. Raine], SurtS, 22 (1850), 8 · *VCH Berkshire*, 2.116–17 · *Collections for a History of Staffordshire*, William Salt Archaeological Society, new ser., 10 (1907), 46, 58 · Foster, *Alum. Oxon.* · H. M. Wood, ed., *Durham protestations*, SurtS, 135 (1922), 140 · J. C. Hodgson, ed., *North country diaries*, 2, SurtS, 124 (1915), 161 · *DNB* · W. P. W. Phillimore, *Calendars of wills and administrations … of the bishop of Lichfield and Coventry, 1516–1652*, British RS, 7 (1892), 468 · B. Willis, *A survey of the cathedrals of York, Durham, Carlisle … Bristol*, 2 vols. (1727); repr. (1892), 468

Wealth at death well off: Surtees, *Durham*, vol. 1, pt 2, 142–3; *VCH Durham*

Machray, Robert (1831–1904), archbishop of Rupert's Land, Canada, born in Aberdeen on 17 May 1831, of highland ancestry, was son of Robert Machray, advocate of Aberdeen, and his wife, Christian Macallum. His parents were Presbyterians. After early education at Nairn Academy and at Coull parish school, he graduated MA from King's College, Aberdeen, in 1851, being head of his year and winning the Simpson and Hutton prizes. Proceeding in 1851 to Sidney Sussex College, Cambridge, he graduated there in 1855 as thirty-fourth wrangler, and was elected to a fellowship (and to an honorary fellowship in 1865). He proceeded MA in 1858, and was dean of his college in the same year. Meanwhile he had joined the Church of England, and was ordained deacon in 1855 and priest the following year. He became vicar of Madingley, near Cambridge, in 1862. In 1865 Machray was Ramsden preacher at Cambridge and also accepted the bishopric of Rupert's Land, as successor to David Anderson, the first bishop, being consecrated at Lambeth on 24 June 1865. He proceeded DD of Cambridge, and was made honorary LLD of Aberdeen in the same year.

Machray's diocese covered 2 million square miles of territory, with headquarters at Winnipeg, then a hamlet with a population of 150. To assist him in the administration of the diocese he had only eighteen clergymen. In 1866 he made a difficult tour of inspection of the Native American missions and held a first conference of the diocese on 30 May 1866. A first diocesan synod met on 29 May 1867. Machray was active in introducing new methods of education. He renewed and reorganized the disused St John's College, Winnipeg, securing John Maclean, later first bishop of Saskatchewan, as warden and theological tutor; he himself lectured in ecclesiastical history and liturgiology as well as in mathematics. He also formed a college school for boys, of which he took charge. In 1878 he founded Machray exhibitions at the college for sons of clergymen and contributed to the foundation of St John's Ladies' College. When the University of Manitoba was constituted in 1877, Machray became chancellor, holding the office until his death. St John's College was made a constituent college of the university. He was also chairman successively of the provincial board of education and the advisory board, and exerted in that capacity constant influence upon the educational development of the province.

Meanwhile Machray was faced by great difficulties in organizing his diocese. Frequent destruction of the crops by locusts and the rebellion of Riel in 1870 interrupted progress. At the same time the population was growing, and Machray did all in his power to organize the diocese on lines likely to serve the future. In the course of time the bishopric was subdivided into eight sees (Moosonee, 1872; Mackenzie river, 1874; Saskatchewan, 1874; Athabasca, 1884; Qu'Appelle, 1884; Calgary, 1888; Selkirk, 1891; Keewatin, 1901). Some 190 clergy and numerous lay readers were enlisted in church work. In 1875 Machray became metropolitan of Canada under the primacy of the archbishop of Canterbury, and on the union of the Canadian Anglican churches in 1893 he was created archbishop of Rupert's Land and primate of all Canada. He aided in the formation of the general synod of the dominion which met in that year, when he was also created prelate of the Order of St Michael and St George. Machray attended the Lambeth conferences in 1878 and 1888, and in the latter year preached before Cambridge University. He received the honorary degree of DD from Manitoba University in 1883 and from Durham in 1888, and that of DCL from Trinity College, Toronto, in 1893. He died unmarried at Winnipeg on 9 March 1904. A state funeral was decreed, and he was buried in the cemetery of St John's Cathedral.

PELHAM EDGAR, *rev.* H. C. G. MATTHEW

Sources R. Machray, *Life of Archbishop Machray* (1909) · C. H. Mockridge, *The bishops of the Church of England in Canada and Newfoundland, being an illustrated historical sketch* (1896) · O. R. Rowley, *The Anglican episcopate of Canada and Newfoundland* (1928) · Venn, *Alum. Cant.* · W. B. Heeney, *Leaders of the Canadian church* (1920) · W. S. Wallace, ed., *The dictionary of Canadian biography* (1926)

Archives LPL, corresp. with E. W. Benson · LPL, corresp. with A. C. Tait

Likenesses C. Forbes, portrait, 1882 · photograph, NPG

Wealth at death £3466 7s. 4d.: Canadian probate sealed in London, 9 Dec 1904, *CGPLA Eng. & Wales*

Machtig, Sir Eric Gustav Siegfried (1889–1973), civil servant, was born on 21 August 1889 at 46 Merton Road, Wimbledon, the son of Friedrich Gustav Mächtig, a professor of music, and his wife, Pauline Petronella, *née* Schneider. Both parents were German born.

After attending St Paul's School, London, where he was a scholar, Machtig proceeded (also as a scholar) to Trinity College, Cambridge, where he obtained a first-class degree (second division) in the classical tripos in 1911. He entered the Colonial Office in October 1912 where he worked in the east African department and then in the Tanganyika and Somaliland department. He was promoted to first-class clerk in 1917 and was made a principal in 1920. In 1930 he transferred to the Dominions Office as assistant secretary. In 1934 he became head of the department dealing with the high commission territories in southern Africa and in 1936 rose to be assistant under-

secretary. In 1939 he felt slighted when, despite being next in line, he was not made permanent under-secretary. He served as acting permanent under-secretary until Sir Cosmo Parkinson arrived from the Colonial Office on 1 February 1940, at which time Machtig was given the newly invented title of deputy under-secretary. However, in May 1940 Parkinson was recalled to the Colonial Office and Machtig succeeded him.

Machtig was a pragmatic, honourable, clear-thinking man who cultivated his ministers. He was good at administration. But he was also conservative in all senses, disliked change and, although his placatory instinct was valuable in maintaining reasonable relations with Éire during the Second World War, he was unsuited to head the Dominions Office at a time of rapid transition in the Commonwealth. Moreover, his shyness and dislike of mixing with (or even seeing) people prevented him networking effectively in Whitehall or establishing close relations with dominion leaders and their representatives. He ran the Dominions Office in the manner of a remote, authoritarian Victorian father, centralizing work in his own hands and projecting his own meticulous ways in sometimes petty bureaucratic procedures. Even the war could not alter his office routine: at 5 p.m. prompt he retreated to catch the train to the wartime haven in Peaslake, Surrey, that he shared with his aged mother. After his marriage on 22 March to Nora Marguerite Friend (1892/3–1943) of North Cray, Kent, the 48-year-old daughter of a merchant, his wife also shared this house. However, she fell seriously ill in 1942 and died in 1943. Utterly desolate, Machtig retreated further into himself and his rigidities became more marked.

When the Dominions Office and the India Office were merged into the new Commonwealth Relations Office in 1947, they initially remained in most respects separate departments under one roof, with Machtig retaining his old responsibilities and having little to do with the Asian side under its permanent under-secretary, Sir Archibald Carter. To bring the office together called for someone with an outgoing personality, organizational drive, readiness to innovate, and (preferably) experience of working overseas. Added to this, Machtig proved incompatible with Philip Noel-Baker, the secretary of state appointed to take charge of the new ministry. After much resistance Machtig left the Commonwealth Relations Office on assignment for special duties in December 1948. He retired in 1949. He was appointed MBE in 1918, OBE in 1926, CMG in 1935, KCMG in 1939, KCB in 1943, and GCMG in 1948.

Machtig had a satisfying retirement and particularly enjoyed travelling as a director of Barclay's Bank (DCO) from 1949 to 1969. He chaired the working committee of the Lord Mayor's National Thanksgiving Fund in 1950, was chairman of the Sister Trust from 1950 to 1965, and a vice-chairman of the Victoria League from 1950 to 1962.

Machtig was of average height and fair complexion. He presented an overall impression of roundness with, owing to his thick glasses, an owlish look. He spoke clearly but sounded as if he had catarrh. He was a keen musician, a skilful violinist, and an enthusiastic and competent squash player. He died, childless, of cerebral thrombosis at his home, 11 Belvedere Drive, Wimbledon, on 24 July 1973.   LORNA LLOYD

Sources J. Garner, *The commonwealth office, 1925–1968* (1978) • private information (2004) • *WW* (1962) • *WWW, 1971–80* • correspondence with Sir Harry Batterbee, 1939–45, Bodl. RH • *Colonial Office List* • PRO, Machtig MSS, DO 121 [1940–48] • *The Times* (25 July 1973) • Kelly, *Handbk* (1973) • b. cert. • m. cert. • d. cert. • *CGPLA Eng. & Wales* (1973)
Archives PRO, DO 121 | Bodl. RH, corresp. with Sir Harry Batterbee
Wealth at death £98,619: probate, 27 Sept 1973, *CGPLA Eng. & Wales*

Machyn [Machin], **Henry** (1496/1498–1563), chronicler, was born on the Wednesday after Whitsun in a year which Machyn himself, reporting his own birthday, inconsistently gives as both 1496 and 1498. His parentage and place of birth are uncertain, but it is likely that he was born in north Leicestershire, since John Machyn, miller, eldest son of his eldest brother John Machyn, was of Hoby in that county, and a Machyn family using the names John, Henry, and Christopher had existed in that region for at least a century. Henry went to London in his youth. He was certainly established there by 1530 since he was admitted to the Merchant Taylors' Company that year, his brother Christopher (d. 1550) being admitted to the same company shortly afterwards. Henry Machyn married at least twice. One wife, Joan, died in childbirth in August 1548. She was possibly the mother of William (d. 1548), and Machyn's two surviving children: Jane, who married John Browne of All Hallows-the-Great in 1563, and John, who is named as Machyn's heir in his will. On 18 January 1549 Machyn married Dorothy Lawe or Lowe of the parish of St Dionis Backchurch; they had three daughters, Mary, Katheryn and Awdrey, all of whom died in infancy.

Machyn was a clerk of his small parish of Holy Trinity-the-Less. In this capacity he attended—and sang at—many funerals which had elaborate heraldic trappings, including some of those for which he independently provided escutcheons and hearse cloths. As a parish clerk he also was responsible for keeping the original copy of the parish register, entries from which are preserved in the late sixteenth-century copy in the London Guildhall Library. Probably inspired by this, he began in 1550 to record details of heraldic funerals in his own 'chronicle'. In February 1551 he recorded Bishop Gardiner's committal to the Tower, and afterwards increasingly interspersed his descriptions of funerals with other contemporary news, such as political and religious events, crimes, criminals' executions, proclamations, strange occurrences, and ceremonies such as the lord mayor's show. The earnestness of his religious views, which tended towards Catholicism, provoked him to slander Jean Veron, the French protestant preacher, for which he records that he did penance at Paul's Cross on 23 November 1561.

One of Machyn's last chronicle entries, in July 1563, refers to an outbreak of plague in London, and it is probable he succumbed to this disease. He was buried on 11 November. In his will, dated two days earlier, he made his wife his executor. She survived the epidemic, and in 1564 married Nicholas Hearne of the parish of St Mildred, Bread Street. Machyn bequeathed his chronicle to William Hervy, Clarenceux king of arms. It was later acquired by Sir Robert Cotton, and was damaged in the fire at Ashburnham House in 1731. It then lay unbound for a century, was pieced together by Sir Frederick Madden in 1829, and was edited for the Camden Society by J. G. Nicholls in 1848, under the somewhat misleading title *The Diary of Henry Machyn, Citizen and Merchant-Taylor of London, from A.D. 1550 to A.D. 1563*. The manuscript is now Cotton MS Vitellius F.v in the British Library.

It used to be thought that Henry Machyn was in some way connected with a Gloucestershire family with the same name, but this is implausible. A distinguished member of the latter family was **Thomas Machen** (c.1541–1614), a merchant who was three times mayor of Gloucester. The son of Henry Machen (d. 1566) and his wife, whose surname may have been Baugh or Brayh, he was possibly the Thomas Machin who in 1562 supplicated for his MA at Oxford, where three of his sons were later educated. Successful in business and politics, with his son-in-law Thomas Rich he was the leader of a godly faction in the corporation of Gloucester, and in 1613 he was elected MP for the city. By 1566 he had married Christian Baston (c.1546–1615); they had seven sons and six daughters. He died on 18 October 1614 leaving much property, including the manor of Condicote, which he bought in 1599, and bequeathing more than £4000 to his family and to various Gloucester charities. His monument survives in Gloucester Cathedral, representing him kneeling in his mayoral robes.   IAN MORTIMER

Sources I. Mortimer, 'Tudor chronicler or sixteenth-century diarist? Henry Machyn and the nature of his manuscript', *Sixteenth Century Journal*, 33/4 (2002), 983–1001 • *The diary of Henry Machyn, citizen and merchant-taylor of London, from AD 1550 to AD 1563*, ed. J. G. Nichols, CS, 42 (1848) • R. M. Wilson, 'The orthography and provenance of Henry Machyn', *Early English and Norse studies*, ed. A. Browne and P. Foote (1963), 202–16 • printed and MS catalogues of the Cotton collection, 1629–1802, BL • GL, Merchant Taylors' Company MSS [microfilm] • will, GL, archdeaconry of London will register 3, fols. 49v–50r; commissary court register 12 • S. Rudder, *A new history of Gloucestershire* (1779) • *VCH Gloucestershire*, vols. 4, 6 • J. Maclean and W. C. Heane, eds., *The visitation of the county of Gloucester taken in the year 1623*, Harleian Society, 21 (1885) • will, PRO, PROB 11/49, fols. 111v–113v [Henry Machin (d. 1566), father of Thomas Machin] • will of Thomas Machen, PRO, PROB 11/124, fols. 460v–462r [Thomas Machen] • Foster, *Alum. Oxon., 1500–1714*, 3.957 • parish register, Holy Trinity-the-Less, 18 Jan 1549 [marriage to Dorothy Lawe] • parish register, Holy Trinity-the-Less, 11 Nov 1563 [burial] • tombstone, Gloucester Cathedral [Thomas Machen]
Archives BL, diary, MS Cotton Vitellius F V
Likenesses memorial tomb effigy (Thomas Machen), Gloucester Cathedral
Wealth at death at least two freehold tenements: will, GL archdeaconry of London will register 3, fols. 49v–50r • probably more than £10,000; Thomas Machen: will, PRO, PROB 11/124, fols. 460v–462r

Mac Iain Deòrsa. *See* Hay, George Campbell (1915–1984).

Maciain, Alasdair. *See* Macdonald, Alexander, of Glencoe (d. 1692).

McIan [*née* Whitaker], **Frances Matilda** [Fanny] (*c*.1814–1897), painter and design school superintendent, was born at 20 Westgate Street, Bath, and baptized on 21 June 1820 at St Mary's Chapel, Queen Square, Bath. She was the third of five children of William Whitaker (d. 1836) and Sarah Hawkins (d. 1849), cabinet-makers. Nothing is known of her education.

Whitaker eloped with Robert Ronald McIan [*see below*] on 21 February 1831 and married him (as Robert Jones, his stage name), at Sts Philip and Jacob, Bristol. She subsequently taught him to paint, and they often mirrored each other's subjects: for instance her *Slave's Dream* (exh. RA, 1847) depicted a 'vision' as did his *Scene in Lochaber*, exhibited at the British Institution the same year. W. P. Frith also records watching Fanny teach John Leech to paint in oils in their studio. She first exhibited at the Royal Academy in 1836, a portrait, *Red Star of the Evening and Diving Mouse*, co-performers in the play *Rifle-Shot* with her husband. But her first success came in 1837 with *The Escape of Alaster Macdonald*, exhibited at the Society of British Artists. In 1842 she presented Charles Dickens with *Nell and the Widow*, a watercolour. He thanked her with a bound copy of *The Old Curiosity Shop*, writing that she had 'beautifully perpetuated' it (*Letters of Charles Dickens*, 3.4). She also illustrated F. B. C.'s *Quadruped's Picnic* for Dickens's son. Other illustrations were made for *The Book of British Ballads* (1842) and *Sketches of Irish Character* (1844), edited and written by her friends Mr and Mrs S. C. Hall.

In October 1842 Fanny McIan became the first superintendent of the Female School of Design, Somerset House: her 'qualifications as an artist, and fitness in every respect for the situation' were considered 'very satisfactory', despite possible objections as to her husband's connections with the stage (*Minutes of the Council of the Government School of Design, 1836–1847*, 1.120). The *Art Union* praised her for her 'energy of mind', 'amiability of temper', and 'uprightness of conduct', and felt her eminently suited to teach middle-class girls to design for industry and thus enlarge the field of employment for women (*Art Union*, 4, 1842, 82).

In the summers of 1843 and 1844 Fanny McIan visited Sèvres, 'to improve her knowledge of ornamental art in order to teach porcelain painting to her students', and subsequently reported in detail to the school's council (*Minutes of the Council of the Government School of Design, 1836–1847*, 2.73–5). Ill health caused frequent absences from school: on one such occasion in 1843 William Macready, the actor, was touched to find her at home painting *The Empty Cradle* (exh. RA, 1843). She had no children. Despite turmoil at the Male School, Somerset House, and frustrations at the Female School, McIan determinedly pursued her way, successfully encouraging her students to win prizes against their male counterparts. Sarah King Peter, when founding the first American Female School of Design in Philadelphia in 1848, consulted her. That year the London Female School was 'unceremoniously' moved to a soap manufacturers' premises in the Strand; Dickens

criticized the poor conditions. Fanny gave a spirited account of these, and her aims for the school, to the select committee of 1849. Under her leadership the Female School gained several prizes at the Great Exhibition of 1851 (Great Exhibition, *Reports of the Juries*, section III, class 18, exhibits 85, 86, 94, 97) and in 1852 the students embroidered the duke of Wellington's funeral pall.

Throughout her time at the school McIan continued to exhibit. *Soldiers' Wives Awaiting the Results of Battle* (priv. coll.) was shown at the 'Free exhibition', Hyde Park, in 1849 and Henry Cole, in his capacity as head of the department of practical art, noticed her ambitious last work, *Highland Emigration, 1852* (exh. Royal Scottish Academy, 1852) while visiting the relocated Female School at Gower Street. On 7 April 1854 Fanny was elected an honorary associate of the Royal Scottish Academy (proposed by Robert Scott Lauder, seconded by J. Noël Paton). With members of her school she made an important contribution to the first exhibition of the Society of Female Artists in 1857.

From 1853 on, Fanny's husband Robert McIan began to suffer a painful mental illness. Despite school duties she nursed him with such devotion that at his death in December 1856 friends feared for her own life. In May 1857 she retired, with a state pension of £100 per annum, but remained a lifelong patron of the school. She was married, briefly, to Richard James Unwin (d. 1864), a man of independent means, of London and Argyllshire, and instead of painting collected objets d'art. She died, intestate, at 14 Cambridge Street, Edgware Road, London, on 7 April 1897 and was buried in Kensal Green cemetery.

Robert Ronald McIan (1803?–1856), actor and illustrator, was by his own account the son of Robert McIan, a sheep farmer of Inverness-shire. Baptized a Roman Catholic, he was educated in Liverpool and Shropshire. He abandoned apprenticeships to become, as Mr Jones, an actor and scene-painter in Glasgow, and afterwards toured with Belville Penley's company. In 1827 he joined the Theatre Royal, Bath, where he made his début as Dougal in *Rob Roy*: Sir Walter Scott thought 'the character stepped from the novel on to the stage' (*The Era*, 11).

On moving to London in 1834 'Jones' claimed the name Ronald McIan, and descent from the McIans of Glencoe. A passionate highlander and member of the Club of True Highlanders, he pursued careers in acting and painting with equal energy and enthusiasm, making his London début as Lo Zingaro at the English Opera House on 6 October 1834 and following it with *Rifle-Shot*. On the stage he was noted for his agility and swordsmanship.

Between 1835 and 1842 McIan divided his acting career between the English Opera House, Theatre Royal Covent Garden, and Drury Lane. The summers of 1841–3 were spent directing and acting at the Adelphi, Edinburgh. Dickens, seeing him there as Robin Oig in *Twa' Drovers*, thought him 'quite wonderful, and most affecting' (letter to John Forster, 30 June 1841, *Letters of Charles Dickens*, ed. Dexter, 2.316). The end of McIan's stage career in 1843 coincided with the death by drowning of his fellow actor, Elton. Through McIan's intervention Dickens became chairman of the Elton Fund for his orphans, though Dickens considered McIan as secretary as 'unfurnished in two commodities: judgment and discretion' (*Letters of Charles Dickens*, ed. Dexter, 1.561).

From 1835 to 1856 McIan was a frequent exhibitor at the Royal Academy and elsewhere. He was an exquisite colourist, and an early painter of scenes from highland history, *A Highland Feud* (exh. British Institution, 1843; Tatton Park, Cheshire), and *A Highland Coronach* (exh. Royal Scottish Academy, 1850) being two examples. His illustrations for *Clans of the Scottish Highlands*, and *Gaelic Gatherings, or, The Highlanders at Home*, by James Logan (first published in parts, 1843–7 and 1847–9, and later bound) are his best-known work. He also illustrated Eliza Ogilvy's *Highland Minstrelsy* and books by Mr and Mrs S. C. Hall. S. C. Hall gave an entertaining account of McIan's enthusiastic guiding during tours of the highlands (Hall, *Retrospect of a Long Life*). McIan assisted his wife at the Female School of Design between 1847 and 1852. Though he was made an associate of the Royal Scottish Academy in 1852, rules of residence thwarted his hopes of becoming a full academician.

McIan's last paintings were military in character: four major ones showing the 79th Cameron Highlanders on duty in Edinburgh, 1852, were commissioned by Colonel the Hon. Lauderdale Maule (Regimental Museum, Fort George, Inverness-shire). Maule's death in the Crimea before their exhibition at the Royal Scottish Academy in 1855 coincided with the onset of McIan's own painful mental illness. Despite it, in 1855 he successfully designed new uniforms for the Ross-shire militia (Regimental Museum, Fort George, Inverness-shire). He died at his home, 4 Heath Mount, Hampstead, London, on 13 December 1856, leaving estate of £1000, and was buried at Highgate cemetery. His friends mourned a 'warm-hearted honourable man' (*Literary Gazette*, 20 Dec 1856, 1025).

BELINDA MORSE

Sources *Reports*, Royal Female School of Art (1868–1905) · 'Select committee on the school of design', *Parl. papers* (1849), 18.115–22, 498, no. 576 · *Minutes of the council of the Government School of Design*, 3 vols. (1846–9) · *The letters of Charles Dickens*, ed. M. House, G. Storey, and others, 3–4 (1974–7) · W. P. Frith, *John Leech: his life and work*, 2 (1891), 4–5 · *The diaries of William Charles Macready*, ed. W. Toynbee, 2 (1912), 201–2 · 'The Female School of Design in the capital of the world', *Household Words* (15 March 1851), 577–81 · *Art Union*, 4 (1842), 82 · *Art Union*, 9 (1847), 361 · *Art Journal*, 12 (1850), 362 · *Art Journal*, 19 (1857), 62 · H. Cole, diary, 19 April 1852, V&A NAL · B. Morse, *A woman of design, a man of passion: the pioneering McIans* (2001) · exhibition catalogues (1835–41) [Society of British Artists] · The exhibition of the Royal Academy (1836–47) [exhibition catalogues] · exhibition catalogues (1836–56) [Manchester] · exhibition catalogues (1837–52) [National Institution] · *Catalogue of the works of British artists in the gallery of the British Institution* (1836–54) [exhibition catalogues] · exhibition catalogues (1840–55) [Royal Scot. Acad.] · exhibition catalogues (1848–9) ['Free Exhibition', Hyde Park, London] · *Actors by Gaslight*, 24 (29 Sept 1838), 186 · S. C. Hall, *Retrospect of a long life: from 1815 to 1883*, 2 (1883), 268–77 · *The Times* (11 Sept 1838), 5f · D. Macdonald, *The mountain heath* (1838) · *Literary Gazette* (20 Dec 1856), 1025 · *The letters of Charles Dickens*, ed. W. Dexter, 3 vols. (1938) · playbills · *The Era* (21 Dec 1856) · church register (baptism), 21 June 1820, Som. ARS · private information (2004) · m. cert. · d. cert.

Archives Royal Scot. Acad.

Likenesses F. McIan, chalk drawing, *c*.1854 (Robert McIan), Scot. NPG · J. G. Tunny, photograph, *c*.1854 (Robert McIan), Scot. NPG · R. R. McIan, sketch, priv. coll. · F. Stone, oils (Robert McIan), Scot. NPG

Wealth at death £1000—Robert McIan: administration, PRO, PROB 6/233

McIan, Robert Ronald (1803?–1856). *See under* McIan, Frances Matilda (*c*.1814–1897).

McIlquham [M'Ilquham; *née* Medley], **Harriett** (1837–1910), local politician and suffragist, was born on 8 August 1837 at 41 Brick Lane, Old Street, London, the daughter of Edward Medley, master baker, and Harriet Medley, *née* Sanders. She spent her early life in London, and was reared in a Unitarian family in an atmosphere conducive to freedom of thought. Encouraged to take an interest in public questions, she read advanced literature, attended lectures by eminent Victorian radicals, and, like other young women with a social conscience, turned to parish visiting. Her liberal upbringing and exposure to radical thought thus sowed the seeds of a life devoted to progressive social reform and the political emancipation of women. Upon marriage to James Henry McIlquham (*b*. 1832/3), surveyor to the Cheltenham improvement commissioners, on 23 September 1858, in the Finsbury Chapel, London, she moved to Gloucestershire, where she resided for the rest of her life. Their union produced two sons, Gilbert and Harold, and two daughters, Mary and Harriett. After an initial stay in Cheltenham, in 1869 Harriett purchased an estate at nearby Staverton, which she personally managed as a working farm. For the next forty years she gave her considerable energies to raising the children, managing the estate, and a life of public work that encompassed pioneering service in local government and a vigorous commitment to women's emancipation.

McIlquham's initial encounter with women's suffrage occurred upon hearing George Jacob Holyoake lecture in 1856, and she was also present in the House of Commons when the first women's suffrage bill was talked out by opponents. Her main organizational activities centred on Gloucestershire: with Henry's assistance and support she assiduously promoted the issue at innumerable public meetings, and was a key member of the Cheltenham Women's Suffrage Society in later years. However, she also contributed to the great demonstrations of 1880–81 in both Birmingham and Bristol, working with activists such as Lilias Ashurst and Helen Blackburn. Her speaking gifts, and later her writings, helped to make her a national figure. The division in the suffrage movement in the 1880s over strategy saw her take a leading role in the formation of the London-based Women's Franchise League (WFL) in 1889, which was uncompromising in its insistence that every suffrage bill should specifically include married women; Harriett firmly believed that their exclusion would render coverture a statutory disability. Other members included Elizabeth Wolstenholme Elmy, a close friend, with whom she helped to establish the Women's Emancipation Union in 1892 after a split with the WFL, and shared an interest in reform of marriage and the divorce laws; her article 'Marriage: a just and honourable partnership' appeared in the *Westminster Review* (157, April 1902).

In the field of local government Harriett McIlquham was a true pioneer. In 1881 she was elected by a large majority as poor-law guardian for Boddington in the Tewkesbury Union, thus becoming the first married woman guardian in the country. Local government law *vis-à-vis* the position of women was full of anomalies: although the clerk of the union refused to allow her to vote in respect of her own property because she was married, he none the less let her nomination go forward. When the result was contested, the Local Government Board ruled that on the question of the election of married women it saw no reason why Mrs McIlquham should not 'lead the way'. Many other women, married and unmarried, followed in her footsteps, although not until the Local Government Act of 1894 were the rights of married women both to vote and serve enshrined in statute. Harriett continued to blaze a trail: she was subsequently appointed an overseer for the parish of Staverton, a unique position for a woman to hold, became the first chair of Staverton parish council in 1894, and served as returning officer at the second parish council election. She also acted as rural district councillor for Boddington, served on the Boddington and Staverton school board, and after the 1902 Education Act sat on the board of management of the education committee. In 1888 she was one of four women selected by campaigners to test the eligibility of women to sit on the new county councils: she stood unsuccessfully as an independent in the central ward of Cheltenham, which proved to be the only failure in a distinguished career in which she 'abundantly vindicated women's claim to a share in every branch of local government work' (*Cheltenham Chronicle*).

In the 1890s Harriett McIlquham worked with other campaigners in the National Union of Women Workers, the Women's Local Government Society, and the Women's Emancipation Union, publishing under its aegis several pamphlets on the themes of women's work in local government and the franchise, such as *Women's Enfranchisement: an Ancient Right, a Modern Need* (c.1892). A well-known figure at conferences, she read papers on suffrage, local government, and the poor law. She also contributed articles to the *Westminster Review* and the *Nineteenth Century*, including a series of original and scholarly essays on the history of feminist writing, an example being 'Mary Astell: a seventeenth century advocate for women' (*Westminster Review*, 149, April 1898).

Harriett McIlquham remained an active radical in later life, embracing new ideas and new movements. She joined the Cheltenham branch of the Women's Freedom League, became a loyal supporter of the local Independent Labour Party, and was a leading light of the Cheltenham Ethical Society, for which she had prepared a paper only days before her death. She died of heart failure on 24 January 1910 at Staverton House and was buried three days

later in Staverton parish church. Her life was marked by great generosity to friends and colleagues, and by a vigorous belief in the political emancipation of women.

LINDA WALKER

Sources *Cheltenham Chronicle and Gloucestershire Graphic* (29 Jan 1910) · *Women's Penny Paper* (1889–92) · *Women's Suffrage Journal* (1880–90) · *Report* [Women's Emancipation Union] (1892–9) · *Annual Report* [Women's Local Government Society] (1893) · H. Blackburn, *Women's suffrage: a record of the women's suffrage movement in the British Isles* (1902) · L. Bland, 'The married woman, the "new woman" and the feminist: sexual politics of the 1890s', *Equal or different: women's politics, 1800–1914*, ed. J. Rendall (1987), 141–64 · Women's Library, London, box 86 · b. cert. · m. cert. · P. Hollis, *Ladies elect: women in English local government, 1865–1914* (1987) · S. S. Holton, *Suffrage days: stories from the women's suffrage movement* (1996)
Archives Women's Library, London, autograph letters collection · Women's Library, London, box 86 | BL, Elizabeth Wolstenholme Elmy collection, Add. MSS 47449–47455
Likenesses photograph, repro. in *Cheltenham Chronicle and Gloucestershire Graphic*
Wealth at death £5996: resworn probate, 9 May 1910, *CGPLA Eng. & Wales*

McIlroy, Dame (**Anne**) **Louise** (1878–1968), obstetrician and gynaecologist, was born at Lavin House, co. Antrim, Ireland, daughter of James McIlroy, general practitioner of Ballycastle, co. Antrim. Her sister, Janie Hamilton McIlroy, became a specialist in ophthalmology. Louise McIlroy graduated MB ChB at Glasgow University in 1898, going on to receive an MD with commendation in 1900. Her postgraduate work took her to Dublin (LM 1901), London, Vienna, and Berlin, and she obtained a DSc from Glasgow University in 1910. McIlroy was appointed resident house surgeon at the Samaritan Hospital For Women, Glasgow, in 1900 and in 1906 she succeeded Elizabeth Pace as gynaecologist at the city's Victoria Infirmary. Her first prestigious post came in 1911, when she was appointed first assistant to the Muirhead professor of obstetrics and gynaecology in Glasgow, Professor J. M. Munro Kerr, who was to have a strong influence on her later work.

On the outbreak of the First World War McIlroy gave up her promising career in Glasgow to work for the war effort. She was one of the founders of the Scottish Women's Hospital for Foreign Service. Appointed surgeon-in-chief, she served in France, Serbia, and Salonika, and became surgeon at the Royal Army Medical Corps hospital at Constantinople. In recognition of her services she was awarded the Croix de Guerre in 1916, and became OBE in 1920. On her return to Britain she published a book describing her wartime experiences, *From a Balcony on the Bosphorus* (1924).

In 1921 McIlroy was appointed consulting obstetrician and gynaecological surgeon at the Royal Free Hospital and became the first woman professor of obstetrics and gynaecology at the Royal Free Hospital school of medicine, University of London. Her appointment was seen by some as an unwelcome experiment, not only because she was a woman, but also because she had trained and worked outside London. Yet McIlroy came to be renowned for her teaching as well as for her prolific research and writing. She is remembered particularly for her book *The Toxaemias of Pregnancy* (1936), and for her work on the relief of pain in childbirth and the management of asphyxia of the newborn, but her numerous British and American journal articles dating from 1904 to 1951 also cover social issues such as 'the problem of the working mother' (*Index Medicus*, 1922). In 1929 McIlroy was promoted to DBE and also elected as a founder fellow of the Royal College of Obstetricians and Gynaecologists, if only because her male colleagues 'thought it necessary to have a representative of the women' (Shaw, 47). In 1932 she gained the MRCP.

Dame Louise McIlroy took early retirement in 1934, but continued to practise at 115a Harley Street, London, and as consultant to the Bermondsey Medical Mission, the Thorpe Coombe Maternity Hospital, and to the boroughs of Finchley and Walthamstow. She obtained a second DSc, this time from the University of London, in 1934, and obtained the LLD at Glasgow University the following year. She also received a number of honorary degrees, and was elected FRCP in 1937. During the Second World War she again made a significant contribution by helping to organize the emergency maternity services in Buckinghamshire and by acting as consultant gynaecologist to the Women's Royal Naval Service in Plymouth. She was considered by her contemporaries to have 'great personal charm' and a 'puckish sense of humour', but also to be 'devastating in criticism if warranted' and to enjoy nothing better than 'a wordy battle with her male colleagues' (*BMJ*, 451). Dame Louise McIlroy died on 8 February 1968 in Glasgow Hospital. She was commemorated at the Royal Free Hospital by having a gynaecological ward named after her. SUSAN J. PITT

Sources *BMJ* (17 Feb 1968), 451 · W. F. Shaw, *Twenty-five years: the story of the Royal College of Obstetricians and Gynaecologists* (1954) · *Index Medicus* (1903–51) · D. Bank and A. Esposito, eds., *British biographical index*, 4 vols. (1990) · J. Peel, *The lives of the fellows of the Royal College of Obstetricians and Gynaecologists, 1929–1969* (1976) · *The medical who's who* (1917–18) · E. Martell, L. G. Pine, and A. Lawrence, eds., *Who was who among English and European authors, 1931–1949*, 3 vols. (1978)
Likenesses J. S. Sargent, portrait, Royal Free Hospital, London; repro. in *BMJ*
Wealth at death £4391.69: confirmation, 8 Sept 1972, CCI

Macilwain, George (1797–1882), surgeon, was the son of an Irish country surgeon who had been a pupil of John Abernethy. In 1814 he was likewise sent to study under Abernethy at St Bartholomew's Hospital, London, and was admitted a member of the Royal College of Surgeons on 4 September 1818; he was elected honorary fellow in 1843. He was surgeon to the Finsbury Dispensary for twenty years, and to the Fever Hospital temporarily, and was appointed consulting surgeon on his retirement. He was also consulting surgeon to schools of the St Anne's Society, and surgeon to the City of London Truss Society. In practice he was opposed to non-essential amputation and the use of violent purgatives. He was also an uncompromising opponent of vivisection. In 1871 Macilwain gave up his chambers in the Courtyard, Albany, Piccadilly, London, where he had lived since November 1853, and retired to Matching, near Harlow, Essex.

Macilwain was a member of the Royal Institution, a fellow and for some time vice-president of the Royal Medico-Chirurgical Society, and a member of the Royal Irish Academy. In 1853 he published his rambling but entertaining *Memoirs of John Abernethy* (2 vols.). The third edition (1 vol., 1856) contains important additions.

Macilwain's chief medical writings are: *A Treatise on Stricture of the Urethra* (1824; 2nd edn, entitled *Surgical Observations on … Diseases of the Mucous Canals of the Body*, 1830); *Remarks on the Unity of the Body* (1836); *Medicine and Surgery, one Inductive Science* (1838); *Remarks on Vivisection* (1847); *Remarks on Ovariotomy* (1863); and *Vivisection: being Short Comments on … the Evidence Given before the Royal Commission* (1877).

Macilwain died in Matching on 22 January 1882, survived by his wife, Maria Margaret. Their daughter, Anna Maria, was the mother of the historian Hugh Macilwain *Last (1894–1957).

GORDON GOODWIN, rev. MICHAEL BEVAN

Sources *The Lancet* (28 Jan 1882), 159 · *Medical Times and Gazette* (28 Jan 1882), 107 · G. Macilwain, preface, *Memoirs of John Abernethy*, 2 vols. (1853) · *London and Provincial Medical Directory* · CGPLA Eng. & Wales (1882)
Wealth at death £6745 12s. 11d.: probate, 1 March 1882, CGPLA Eng. & Wales

McIlwraith, Sir Thomas (1835–1900), entrepreneur and politician in Australia, the son of John McIlwraith, a plumber, and his wife, Janet Hamilton, the daughter of John Howat, was born at Ayr, Scotland, on 17 May 1835, and educated at Watson's school and the Wallacetown Academy in Ayr, after which he joined his father's plumbing business. In 1854 he followed his elder brother John to Victoria, Australia, and first obtained employment as a surveyor and engineer on the Victorian railways. He then assumed a partnership with the well-known contractors Cornish and Bruce. In 1861, having gradually taken up eight runs in the Maranoa district in south-west Queensland, he began to live there part of the time, and in 1870 he moved to his station at Merrivale, about 300 miles west of Brisbane. On 6 June 1863 he had married Margaret Whannell, the sister of his brother John's wife. They had three daughters, but she, disliking rural life, lived in Brisbane and, after her heavy drinking had been discovered, in Scotland. His attempts to separate her from her daughters failed. She died on 14 October 1877. McIlwraith had another daughter, born in 1865 from his liaison with Victoria Findlay. McIlwraith's pastoral business was also beset with problems arising from drought, overexpenditure, and recession. He transferred from wool to meat and later shared in his brother Andrew's schemes for shipping refrigerated meat and butter to England (1879–80).

In 1870 McIlwraith had been elected to the legislative assembly of Queensland, where he sat for various constituencies with brief interruptions until 1895. A strong advocate of assisted immigration and railway development financed by land grants to the construction companies, in January 1874 he became minister for public works and mines under Arthur Macalister, but resigned in

Sir Thomas McIlwraith (1835–1900), by Elliott & Fry, pubd 1900

October after a dispute over the land-grant railway policy. In opposition he consolidated his party, and, after winning the elections in late 1878, in January 1879 became premier and colonial treasurer. His vigorous development programme and his reform of local government brought short-term prosperity to the colony, lionizing in Britain, which he visited in 1879–80, charges of corruption in 1880 (from which a royal commission exonerated him the following year), and a KCMG in 1882. On 4 April 1883 he ordered the annexation of eastern New Guinea to Queensland, partly to ensure labour for the sugar industry and partly to anticipate foreign intervention nearby. This aroused great enthusiasm throughout Australia but much criticism in Britain. Gladstone's government disallowed it in July, though in September 1884 it claimed a protectorate over the southern part.

McIlwraith's wish to introduce Indian coolies for the sugar plantations and his land-grant railway policy won him many enemies but did encourage considerable line construction and settlement. He also funded rapid development through government and private debt deals, in some of which he had a personal interest. Having lost support in the legislative assembly, he resigned office in November 1883. In 1884 he visited Britain again, but on his return, facing difficulties from the drought-induced pastoral depression, he turned his attention to speculation in mining and city real estate. He resigned from parliament in June 1886, but made a comeback at the general election in 1888, in which he led the new National Party to victory and then became premier, colonial secretary, and treasurer. He fought and won a battle with the governor, Sir Anthony Musgrave, insisting that the premier should exercise the crown's prerogative of mercy. In October he disagreed with the imperial government over the appointment of a governor, but lost his case. On 30 November ill health forced McIlwraith to resign as premier, though he remained in the cabinet. However, in September 1889 he left the ministry after a dispute with his colleagues on questions of finance. The following year he joined his former opponent Sir Samuel Griffith, and in August 1890 he became colonial treasurer in Griffith's

ministry. He criticized Griffith's federation proposals at the 1891 convention, but his influence was seen in 1891–2 in measures to break the great shearers' strike and to undermine white working-class poor in the sugar-cane industry by repealing the ban on recruiting Pacific Islanders (Kanakas). In 1892 he was charged with fraud over loans advanced by his Queensland Investment and Land Mortgage Company, but after a rather inconclusive outcome he managed to regain the office of premier in March 1893, when Griffiths was appointed chief justice.

McIlwraith's tenure was short-lived. Investigations into the Queensland National Bank, of which he was a director, revealed spectacular professional incompetence and considerable personal indebtedness. In October 1893 he resigned as premier, though he remained chief secretary until March 1895, despite having left for Britain in January, to recruit his health and hinder investigations into his financial affairs. In 1895 he declined the position of agent-general but remained nominally a member of the legislative assembly and minister until 1897. He died on 17 July 1900 at 208 Cromwell Road, London, and was buried at Ayr. He was survived by his second wife, Harriette Ann, the daughter of Archibald Mosman (1799–1863), a pioneer Sydney businessman and pastoralist, of Armidale, New South Wales, whom he had married on 14 June 1879. Five daughters also survived him.

McIlwraith was a burly 6 foot womanizer with the instincts of a gambler. His ebullient character and preference for large-scale if risky ventures coloured both his private business dealings and his ministries' policies. Neither proved sustainable, but they marked him out from his more sober contemporaries.

ELIZABETH BAIGENT

Sources AusDB · D. J. Murphy and R. B. Joyce, eds., Queensland political portraits, 1859–1952 (1978) · D. B. Waterson, A biographical register of the Queensland parliament, 1860–1929 (1972) · R. C. Thompson, Australian imperialism in the Pacific (1980) · T. A. Coghlan, Labour and industry in Australia, from the first settlement in 1788 to the establishment of the commonwealth in 1901, 4 vols. (1918) · C. A. Bernays, Queensland politics during sixty years, 1859–1919 [1919] · F. Adams, The Australians: a social sketch (1893) · DNB · d. cert.

Archives Australian National University, Canberra | State Library of Queensland, South Brisbane, John Oxley Library, Palmer MSS

Likenesses Elliott & Fry, photograph, pubd 1900, NPG [see illus.] · wood-engraving, NPG; repro. in ILN (30 Dec 1882)

Wealth at death £2,297 17s. 4d.: administration, 24 Nov 1900, CGPLA Eng. & Wales

McIndoe, Sir Archibald Hector (1900–1960), plastic surgeon, was born in Dunedin, New Zealand, on 4 May 1900, the second of the four children of John McIndoe, printer, and his wife, Mabel Hill. He received his early education at Otago high school and university, graduating MB ChB in 1924 and winning the junior medicine and senior clinical surgery prizes. Awarded the first New Zealand fellowship of the Mayo Foundation, McIndoe left for the United States to continue his postgraduate training. At the Mayo Clinic in New York he had a brilliant career and was considered one of the most promising of its younger group. Lord Moynihan was so impressed with his surgical skill that he suggested a permanent career for him in England. With an MS (Rochester) added to his list of degrees, McIndoe arrived in London in the winter of 1930, but found to his consternation that there was no appointment and no remuneration available to him.

Fortunately McIndoe's cousin, Sir Harold *Gillies, the plastic surgeon, came to his rescue. McIndoe had unusual skill as an abdominal surgeon and was already an authority on the surgery of the liver and biliary passages. He now lost no time in adapting himself to the meticulous plastic surgery practised by his cousin. He passed his FRCS (England) in 1932 and soon afterwards was appointed to the Hospital for Tropical Diseases as a general surgeon. In 1934 he obtained the fellowship of the American College of Surgeons.

By the outbreak of war in 1939 McIndoe was a plastic surgeon of great promise and had added to the literature of plastic surgery with a number of papers on general aspects of the work. In order to shed some of his responsibility, Gillies arranged for McIndoe to become the consultant in plastic surgery to the Royal Air Force. He also sent him to East Grinstead in Sussex to make arrangements for a centre which would serve the south-east of London and receive air-raid casualties with facial injuries and burns. McIndoe was a strong and determined man who had the knack of getting what he wanted, even if it meant treading on other people's toes. His advice to a colleague on receiving his fellowship was: 'Well, now you can put on your heaviest pair of boots and tread on anybody who gets in your way.' McIndoe did just that, and achieved the impossible. At the tiny Queen Victoria Hospital he built up a centre which rapidly became a model to the country and which by careful publicity on behalf of the Royal Air Force became widely known. He treated several hundred severely burned airmen, fought to achieve better pay and conditions for them until they were rehabilitated, saw to their rehabilitation himself, and even lent them money to set them up in civilian life. He did this by never sparing himself or those around him and by very wisely refusing to be put into uniform, thus being able to talk directly to those at the top. The air staff with whom he had to deal were particularly able and enlightened and he met with few of the tribulations and vexations which other pioneers in organization, such as Florence Nightingale, had to suffer in their time. As a result of the combined efforts of McIndoe, the Air Council, and others, every airman going into action knew that behind him there was a first-class medical service to take care of him, however severely injured he might be. Those who did become patients at East Grinstead were so skilfully handled psychologically that they were not self-conscious about their mutilations; they founded their own club, 'McIndoe's Guinea Pigs', which continued to meet annually after the war to follow up the health and welfare of its members.

'Archie' McIndoe's success during the war can be attributed to the fact that the right person was in the right place. There were only three other experienced plastic surgeons available in 1939 and McIndoe's personality and independent outlook, together with his American training, put him in a unique position. He was a first-class surgeon, a striking administrator, and a powerful personality—so powerful that there was no share of the limelight even for his immediate colleagues. But it was his personality which pulled the airmen through.

McIndoe was appointed CBE in 1944 and was knighted in 1947, and he received numerous foreign decorations. His last years were spent largely in the service of the Royal College of Surgeons, on whose council he served from 1948. As chairman of the finance committee he is reported to have raised over 2.5 million pounds for the college, of which he was vice-chairman in 1957–9. After 1945 he also increased the facilities at East Grinstead and appointed a number of consultant staff who helped with the training of plastic surgeons from all over the world. He helped to found the British Association of Plastic Surgeons and was its third president, in 1949. He also ran an extremely busy and remunerative private practice and found time to travel abroad and write articles on his own subject. Although he will not be remembered particularly for his writings, or for his original thinking in his speciality, he made certain contributions to the treatment of burns and on surgical technique which were accepted as authoritative. In 1953 he took part in the formation of the first Hand Club of Great Britain. Further recognition of his work came from abroad with a number of honorary doctorates and fellowships. He was widely liked and admired in the United States, where he was a frequent visitor, and he was given a second, honorary, fellowship of the American College of Surgeons in 1941.

In 1924 McIndoe married Adonia Stella, daughter of Thomas Aitken of Dunedin; they had two daughters. The marriage was dissolved in 1953. On 31 July 1954 he married Mrs Constance Belchem (b. 1916/17), daughter of John Hutton, a member of Lloyd's. McIndoe died at his home, 84 Albion Gate, London, on 12 April 1960; his ashes were buried in the Royal Air Force church of St Clement Danes in the Strand, London, an honour unique to a civilian doctor from his combatant colleagues. He was survived by his second wife. RICHARD BATTLE, rev. H. C. G. MATTHEW

Sources L. Mosley, *Faces from the fire* (1962) · H. McLeave, *McIndoe: plastic surgeon* (1961) · *WWW* · personal knowledge (1971) · private information (1971) · Burke, *Peerage* (1959) · m. cert. [Constance Belchem]
Archives U. Oxf., Kilner Library of Plastic Surgery, professional papers and corresp.
Likenesses M. Eason, oils, Queen Victoria Hospital, East Grinstead · E. Halliday, oils, RCS Eng. · C. Mann, oils, priv. coll. · M. McIndoe, oils, priv. coll.
Wealth at death £142,901 13s. 4d.: probate, 22 July 1960, CGPLA Eng. & Wales

MacInnes, Colin (1914–1976), novelist and essayist, was the second child and younger son (a daughter died in infancy) of the novelist Angela Margaret *Thirkell (1890–1961) and her first husband, James Campbell McInnes (1874–1945), the baritone lieder singer. He was born at 20 The Grove, The Boltons, London, on 20 August 1914, changing the spelling of his name to MacInnes when he became a professional writer. Through descent from a

Colin MacInnes (1914–1976), by John Deakin, 1950s

Wesleyan minister, the Revd George Browne Macdonald (1805–1868), his maternal great-grandfather was the painter Sir Edward Burne-*Jones (1833–1898), and Rudyard Kipling and Stanley Baldwin were his grandmother's cousins. Often mistakenly thought to be Australian, for he was brought up in Melbourne, on his mother's side he was entirely British.

When MacInnes was only three his parents divorced, and in 1918 his mother married George Thirkell, an Australian engineer. In 1919 he and his elder brother, Graham, sailed with their mother and stepfather to Australia. The boys adopted the name Thirkell and were enrolled in the Scotch College at Melbourne. When MacInnes was fourteen his mother's second marriage collapsed, and she departed for England with Lance, her son with George Thirkell, leaving her two eldest boys to finish their schooling in Australia.

MacInnes freely admitted that he never loved his mother, nor she him, and that there was no human contact whatsoever with his stepfather. Yet despite these privations MacInnes always claimed to have enjoyed a happy childhood, relishing Australia, his school and schoolfriends, and the holidays spent on sheep stations and fruit farms in the Australian bush.

In 1931 MacInnes paid visits to France and Germany and, declining the opportunity to attend university in Australia, he remained on the continent, taking a job in Belgium with the Imperial Continental Gas Company, an incongruous choice of occupation which nevertheless he endured for five years. Having had no contact with his father since he was an infant, in 1934 he again met up with James McInnes, and both Colin and his elder brother reverted to

their original surname, Colin later adapting the spelling to MacInnes.

Eventually determined on a career as an artist, in 1937 MacInnes became a student at the Chelsea Polytechnic, transferring the following year to the Euston Road School of Drawing and Painting. His studies were disrupted, however, by the outbreak of the Second World War. In 1940 he joined the Wiltshire regiment, being posted a year later to the intelligence corps, with whom he spent two years in Gibraltar before being employed in Germany with the rank of sergeant interrogating spies and Nazi sympathizers. By the end of the war he had decided his future lay as a writer rather than a painter; in an attempt to combine both interests, in 1947 he joined *The Observer* as art critic, employment that was abruptly terminated after only six months.

MacInnes had a mercurial temperament. He functioned best alone, and he wisely got down to work on his first novel, *To the Victors the Spoils*, a semi-autobiographical account of his work in the intelligence corps. Published in 1950, it was nominated Book of the Month by the *Daily Graphic*. His second novel, *June in her Spring*, published two years later, remained his own favourite among his novels but was largely ignored when it came out, for it dealt to some extent with homosexuality, in 1952 still a taboo subject.

In searching for his own authentic voice MacInnes was doubly handicapped: he strongly disliked his mother as a person and despised her as a novelist. The feeling was mutual, and although Angela Thirkell died a wealthy woman she cut MacInnes out of her will. He found her work 'able in execution' but in content 'totally revolting', and was aghast whenever referred to as Angela Thirkell's son. He once admitted that he found her death a liberation, and that some of the themes he had chosen to write about recommended themselves precisely because they were ones that would disgust her.

Those themes were the very stuff of MacInnes's contemporary London: drugs, prostitution, race riots, and the teenage revolution, all of which feature in the trilogy of London novels for which he is best remembered, *City of Spades* (1957), *Absolute Beginners* (1959), and *Mr Love and Justice* (1960). In the events about which he wrote, MacInnes more or less took an active part. In 1955 he was arrested in an East End gambling club, and subsequently acquitted on a drugs charge; three years later, having failed to pay any income tax for several years, he was declared bankrupt; by 1961 he was a self-proclaimed 'anarchist sympathizer'; and in 1966 he was recognized as propagandist for the British Black Power leader Michael X. On a British Council tour of Africa in 1971 his behaviour was so outrageous that the tour had to be abandoned.

MacInnes contributed to a wide variety of periodicals, including *The Spectator*, *New Society*, *Encounter*, the *New Statesman*, *Queen*, and *Gay News*, for whom he wrote perceptively and at length about Arthur Rimbaud. MacInnes was almost entirely self-educated, and in his essays he adopted a light and entertaining style that belied considerable erudition. Some of his aphorisms rivalled those of Oscar

Wilde: 'If chastity were not considered a virtue it would be quite attractive'; 'Only the rich can afford to be mean'.

In 1969 MacInnes published the first of two historical novels, *Westward to Laughter*, a satire on R. L. Stevenson's *Treasure Island*. A second historical novel, *Three Years to Play*, appeared the following year, but although written with verve and authenticity neither of these books achieved the popular success of the three 'London novels'. These remain important source material for MacInnes's own times, and were rediscovered by a young readership in the mid-1980s, resulting in the generally ill-received film adaptation of *Absolute Beginners* (1986). In 1973 he published an extended essay on bisexuality, *Loving them both*, and in 1974 his last novel, *Out of the Garden*, a questionable impression of England in decline. In 1976 cancer of the oesophagus was diagnosed, and very shortly before he died MacInnes wrote an unsentimental article for *New Society* about his decision to undergo surgery. Only sixty-one, he died on 22 April 1976 at his home, 74 Marine Parade, Hythe, Kent, of a massive haemorrhage, and was buried at sea off Folkestone a week later. He was predominantly homosexual and never married.

MICHAEL DE-LA-NOY

Sources T. Gould, *Absolute MacInnes* (1985) · T. Gould, *Inside outsider* (1983) · *The Times* (24 April 1976) · d. cert. · b. cert.
Archives BL · U. Sussex, corresp. and literary papers · University of Rochester, New York, Rush Rhees Library, corresp., literary MSS and papers
Likenesses J. Deakin, photograph, 1950–59, NPG [*see illus.*] · D. McCullin, photograph, 1962, Hult. Arch.
Wealth at death £4995: probate, 24 June 1977, *CGPLA Eng. & Wales*

McInnes [*married name* Highet], **Helen Clark** (1907–1985), novelist, was born at 224 Armadale Street, Glasgow, on 7 October 1907, the only child of Donald McInnes, foreman joiner, and Jessica Cecilia Sutherland, *née* McDiarmid. When she was five years old her parents moved to Helensburgh, Dunbartonshire, where she attended the Hermitage School. She passed the entrance examination for the University of Glasgow at the age of sixteen, but postponed her entry and attended the Glasgow High School for Girls for one year, before matriculating in 1925. Her family moved back to Glasgow when she went up to university. She played tennis for the university, and was actively involved in the annual student charities' week events. In her final year she undertook part-time work in the university library, where she helped catalogue early printed books. Her interest in books continued after graduation (MA in French and German, 1928), when she was appointed special cataloguer to the Ferguson Collection at Glasgow University Library (1928–9). From 1929 to 1930 she was employed by Dunbartonshire education authority, selecting books for county libraries. In 1930 she enrolled at University College, London, where she was awarded a diploma in librarianship in 1931.

On 22 September 1932 Helen married Gilbert Arthur Highet (*d.* 1978), a classicist, whom she had met when they were both students at Glasgow. The marriage ceremony took place in the recently opened University of Glasgow

memorial chapel. They moved to Oxford upon his appointment as a don at St John's College. Their son, Keith, was born in 1933 and Helen combined the roles of wife and mother with active participation in university life. She took a keen interest in amateur dramatics, and acted in several plays produced by St John's College, the Oxford University dramatic society, and the Experimental Theatre Club. She also travelled extensively in Europe, financing these trips by translating books from German. In 1937 Gilbert Highet was invited to lecture for one year at Columbia University, New York. The family moved to New York in 1938, when he was offered a permanent post as professor of Latin and Greek. New York became the family's home and in 1952 both Helen and Gilbert took American citizenship. Gilbert Highet was appointed Anthon professor of Latin at Columbia. In America, as in Europe, they loved to travel and spent their holidays exploring many parts of the United States, especially enjoying the rugged mountain areas.

Helen began writing novels in 1939, her first book, *Above Suspicion*, being published in 1941 under the name Helen MacInnes. This book, the story of a young British couple looking for an anti-Nazi agent in Bavaria, was apparently based on her honeymoon in Bavaria. It later became a film, released in 1943 and starring Joan Crawford and Fred MacMurray. The success of this first novel launched her on a career which would lead to her being acclaimed by her publishers, Collins, as the Queen of Spy Writers. She wrote a total of twenty-one novels, which had sold 23 million copies and had been translated into twenty-two languages by the time of her death. Her work was noted for its high literary standard and descriptive accuracy, and for her obvious understanding of complex political situations and knowledge of current affairs. This may in part have been due to the fact that she kept a diary of important political events in the countries she visited. Her extensive personal experience of European travel must also have contributed to the vividness and accuracy of description of the geographical settings, culture, and customs of the regions in which her novels were set. However, her obituary in *The Times* mentions that some people were concerned that the literary quality of her novels was in danger of being overshadowed by her political standpoint.

In addition to *Above Suspicion*, film adaptations were made of the novels *Assignment in Brittany* (1943), *The Venetian Affair* (1967), and *The Salzburg Connection* (1969). In 1966 Helen was awarded the Columbia prize in literature by Iona College, New Rochelle, New York. In 1969 she was the subject of a BBC radio programme entitled *Home this Afternoon*, in which she was interviewed about her life and work by Jack Singleton. In 1973 both she and Gilbert Highet received the Wallace award of the American-Scottish Foundation, awarded annually to Scottish-Americans distinguished in the fields of education, journalism, literature, and diplomacy.

Following Gilbert Highet's death in 1978 Helen continued to write, and divided her time between her apartment in New York city and her country home on Long Island. Her last book, *Ride a Pale Horse*, was published in

1984, and appeared in the paperback best-seller list of the *New York Times* on the day before her death. A number of her books were reprinted after her death. Having suffered a stroke a few weeks earlier, Helen McInnes died in hospital in Manhattan, New York, on 30 September 1985.

VIRGINIA RUSSELL

Sources C. Primrose, ed., *St. Mungo's bairns: some notable Glasgow students down the centuries* (1990), 52–3 · matriculation album, 1925–6, U. Glas., Archives and Business Records Centre, alumni records, R8/5/46/12, record no. 337 · register of members of the general council of the university, 1973, U. Glas., Archives and Business Records Centre, alumni records, DC183/11/97 · graduation roll, 21 Feb 1928, U. Glas., Archives and Business Records Centre, alumni records, R1/1/2, p. 30 · particulars of registration of marriages of women graduates, Feb 1929–March 1933, U. Glas., Archives and Business Records Centre, alumni records, R12/5, record no. 1049 · *Glasgow Herald* (3 Oct 1985) · *The Times* (3 Oct 1985) · *New York Times* (1 Oct 1985) · private information (2004) [Greene and Heaton, literary agents] · 'Helen MacInnes, American crime and spy writer', *Annual Obituary* (1985), 470–72 · *WWW* · B. Benstock and T. F. Staley, eds., *British mystery and thriller writers since 1940: first series*, DLitB, 87 (1989) · b. cert.

Archives Princeton University Library | U. Glas., corresp. with William Collins Sons & Co., UGD 243/11/1/11/24/1 | SOUND BBC Sound Archive, London, *Home this afternoon*, Helen McInnes interviewed about her life and work by Jack Singleton; broadcast 30 July 1969

Likenesses photograph (in youth), repro. in Primrose, ed., *St. Mungo's bairns*, 52 · photograph, repro. in H. McInnes, *Ride a pale horse* (1984), jacket · photograph, Greene and Heaton Limited, 37 Goldhawk Road, London

Macintosh, Charles (1766–1843), manufacturing chemist and inventor of mackintosh waterproof fabrics, was born in Glasgow on 29 December 1766, the son of George Macintosh (d. 1807) of Glasgow, merchant, and his wife, Mary Moore (d. 1808). His maternal uncle was John Moore (1729–1802), the father of Lieutenant-General Sir John Moore (1761–1809). Macintosh was educated at a Glasgow grammar school and afterwards at a school in Catterick Bridge, Yorkshire. Although placed for training in a Glasgow counting house, his spare hours were devoted to science. Initially interested in botany, he subsequently turned to chemistry, and he often attended the lectures of William Irvine in Glasgow, and later those of Joseph Black in Edinburgh. He embarked upon a successful business career before he was twenty. In 1786 he introduced from the Netherlands the manufacture of sugar of lead—lead (II) acetate—and about the same time he commenced making acetate of alumina. In 1797 he started the first alum works in Scotland and subsequently became connected with the St Rollox bleaching powder works, near Glasgow. Seven years earlier, in 1790, he had married Mary (d. 1844), daughter of Alexander Fisher of Glasgow, merchant and the claimed distant descendant of certain kings of Scotland.

During a long business career Macintosh either invented or introduced from abroad a variety of chemically based processes with distinct commercial applications. In addition to the manufacture of sugar of lead these included a new method for calico printing, a variety of methods for dyeing cloth (particularly with Prussian blue), a valuable method of bleaching using dry chloride

Charles Macintosh (1766–1843), by unknown engraver

of lime, a method for preserving citric acid during ocean voyages, a manufacturing process for yeast, and a variety of inventions relating to iron and steel. However, it was about 1820, while experimenting with the by-products of coal gas, that he came upon or rediscovered the method of sealing a layer of rubber in between layers of cloth that still carries his name (quickly modified by the public to mackintosh). The waterproof fabric thus created, although subject to deterioration in extremes of cold or heat, was commercially successful for making garments, medical devices, nautical equipment, tents, and other products requiring flexibility and impermeability.

Macintosh was not the first to devise a way of using rubber to make fabrics waterproof but his chemical method (using cheap coal oil as a solvent) was well suited to large-scale, economical manufacturing and he and his business partners possessed considerable skill as well in devising and then promoting a very large variety of rubber goods which could be mass-produced using his method. It is likely that his method led to the first rubber products widely used by the general public for everyday purposes.

A patent for his waterproofing process was obtained by Macintosh in June 1823 and, based upon it, Macintosh, in partnership with Thomas *Hancock, established and then expanded a successful manufacturing and marketing business in Glasgow and Manchester. Many practical difficulties had to be overcome, but the material soon came into wide use, and as early as April 1824 Macintosh was in correspondence with the ill-fated explorer Sir John Franklin on the subject of a supply of waterproof canvas bags, air-beds, and pillows for use on an Arctic expedition. The waterproof fabric trade of Macintosh & Co. fell off after the introduction of railways, when travellers were not as much exposed to the weather as in stagecoaches or on horseback, but the rest of the business continued to grow and prosper. Macintosh was tireless in his efforts to promote his business interests, carrying on an extensive commercial correspondence in English and French (in which he was fluent) and travelling numerous times to France, Germany, and Sardinia, as well as continuing to keep up to date with developments in chemistry; he attended lectures at the University of Glasgow until he was over fifty.

In 1836 Macintosh's waterproofing patent was infringed by a London firm of silk mercers called Everington & Son, leading to a trial, celebrated in its day, in which the patent was enthusiastically vindicated by the jury (even before the lord chief justice had completed his summing up for them) and the inventor's name then passed almost immediately into the English language, having first been used generically, it seems, in a private letter written in 1836 by the painter William Powell Frith, of *Derby Day* fame, and at least as early as 1840 in America by the poet Longfellow.

In 1825 Macintosh had obtained a patent for converting malleable iron into steel, by exposing it at a white heat to the action of gases charged with carbon, such as coal gas. Macintosh took great interest in the manufacture of iron and he rendered considerable practical assistance to James Beaumont Neilson in 1828 in bringing the latter's 'hot-blast' process into use. Neilson assigned to him a share in the patent and Macintosh thus became a party to the ensuing litigation (concerning the levy of a licence fee from users of the process), which was only brought to a close in May 1843, a few months before his death.

Macintosh's connection with the commercial applications of rubber has somewhat obscured his contemporary fame as an innovative chemist. His discoveries in that branch of science led to his election in 1824 as a fellow of the Royal Society. He died at Dunchattan, near Glasgow, from an intestinal malady, on 25 July 1843. Macintosh was survived by two of his three children, one of whom, George, wrote a detailed memoir of his father's life and business career.

R. B. PROSSER, *rev.* GEOFFREY V. MORSON

Sources G. Macintosh, *Biographical memoir of the late Charles Macintosh of Campsie and Dunchattan* (1847) • T. Hancock, *Personal narrative of the origin and progress of the caoutchouc or India-rubber manufacture in England* (1857) • H. Schurer, 'The macintosh: the paternity of an invention', *Transactions* [Newcomen Society], 28 (1951-3), 77-87 • N. Clow and A. Clow, 'George Macintosh, 1739-1807, and Charles Macintosh, 1766-1842 [*sic*]', *Chemistry and Industry* (13 March 1943), 104-6 • W. Woodruff, *The rise of the British rubber industry during the nineteenth century* (1958), 2-6, 225-6 • *Abstracts of the Papers Communicated to the Royal Society of London*, 5 (1843-50), 486-8 • 'Report of case of *Macintosh v. Everington*', *Mechanics' Magazine*, 24 (1836) • L. Day and I. McNeil, eds., *Biographical dictionary of the history of technology* (1996) • S. S. Pickles, 'Production and utilization of rubber', *A history of technology*, ed. C. Singer and others, 5: *The late nineteenth century, c. 1850 to c. 1900* (1958), 752-75 • G. Babcock, *History of the United States Rubber Company* (1966), 6-8, 13-14 • Chambers, *Scots.*, rev. T. Thomson (1875) • J. Fisher, *The Glasgow encyclopedia* (1994), 275 • 'Mackintosh', *The Oxford English dictionary*, ed. J. A. H. Murray and others, 12 vols. (1933) • 'Mackintosh', *The Oxford English dictionary*, ed. J. A. Simpson and E. S. C. Weiner, 2nd edn, 20 vols. (1989)
Archives Mitchell L., Glas., Strathclyde regional archives, Macintosh company archives
Likenesses R. C. Bell, steel engraving (in old age; after J. Graham Gilbert), repro. in Macintosh, *Biographical memoir of the late Charles Macintosh of Campsie and Dunchattan* • E. Burton, mezzotint (after J. G. Gilbert), BM • engraving, NPG [*see illus.*]

Macintosh, Donald (1743-1808), Scottish Episcopal clergyman and Gaelic scholar, was born at Orchilmore, near Killiecrankie, Perthshire, the son of a tenant farmer. After attending the parish school he went to Edinburgh, where he worked from 1774 as a penny postman. He subsequently became a copying clerk and tutor to the family of Stewart of Gairntuilly. In 1785 he began work in the legal office of the deputy keeper of the signet and became honorary clerk (1785-9) for the Gaelic language to the Society of Antiquaries in Scotland. In the same year he published his *Gaelic Proverbs*, which laid the foundations for all later collections and which remains a valuable contribution to Celtic literature.

On the death of Prince Charles Edward in 1788 Macintosh aligned himself with the tiny ranks of nonjurors who still clung to the Jacobite cause, saw Cardinal Henry of York as the rightful king, and refused to accept the Repeal Act (1792) requiring a public oath of loyalty to the Hanoverians. In 1789 he was ordained as deacon and priest by James Brown of Montrose, the only presbyter to refuse the Repeal Act, who himself had been consecrated as a bishop, despite the apparent irregularity of that act. It is also possible that Brown, in the interests of sustaining a nonjuring apostolic succession, may have consecrated him a bishop. Macintosh, while on his travels gathering Gaelic manuscripts, ministered to scattered nonjuring remnants in the north of Scotland, though his base was at Baillie Fyfe's Close, Edinburgh. In 1794 he raised an unsuccessful action in the Scottish court of session against those who managed the funds for the relief of Episcopalian clergy and had deprived him of his meagre salary of £9. He argued that he had 'a preferable right as the only nonjuring clergyman remaining' (Scot. RO, CH 12/12), but the lord president threw out his petition, 'at a loss whether to frown at the audaciousness or to smile at the high pitch of folly at his advisers. What! a person glorying in his disloyalty to the best of kings' (Nicolson, 420).

Laughed out of court as a nonjuror, Macintosh retained his dignity as a scholar. In 1801 he was appointed keeper of manuscripts and translator of the Gaelic language to the Highland and Agricultural Society of Scotland at a salary of £10. As a fieldworker he scoured the countryside for Gaelic manuscripts, recovering among others the medical manuscripts of the Episcopalian John MacLachlan of Lorn, Argyll. He also prepared a catalogue of Gaelic manuscripts owned by the Highland Society, which he published in 1806. His good handwriting enabled him to make legible copies of poor transcripts, though he cannot have felt happy at a society resolution declaring its unanimous loyalty to the Revolution Settlement of 1688. As one of a handful of men in Scotland who could read a classical Gaelic manuscript, he was appointed by the Highland

Society to a small committee to test the authenticity of James Macpherson's translations of the poems of Ossian. *The Report* (1805), which remains a primary source for the study of the learned orders of Gaelic Scotland, concluded that Ossianic poetry existed but gave only a guarded approval to Macpherson's translations. Macintosh also served on a Highland Society committee investigating the possibility of publishing the *Highland Gentlemen's Dictionary* though the project came to nothing in his lifetime.

Macintosh died, unmarried, in Edinburgh on 22 November 1808, the last survivor of the Scottish nonjuring clergy, and was buried in Old Greyfriars churchyard. Two legacies, totalling £250, had helped him financially through the years from 1794 onwards and in his will he left £318. He bequeathed his two thousand books and manuscripts to the town of Dunkeld, though the books were later housed in the Sandeman Library, Perth.

GERALD M. D. HOWAT

Sources D. Macintosh, *A collection of Gaelic proverbs and familiar phrases*, ed. A. Nicolson (1881) • R. I. Black, 'The Gaelic Academy', *Scottish Gaelic Studies*, 14/2 (1986), 1–38; 15 (1988), 103–22 • W. Stephen, 'Donald Macintosh', *Episcopal Magazine*, 14 (1836), 189–92 • J. Skinner, *Annals of Scottish episcopacy* (1818) • G. Grub, *An ecclesiastical history of Scotland*, 4 vols. (1861) • J. D. G. Davidson, ed., *The Royal Highland and Agricultural Society of Scotland: a short history* (1984) • *Scots Magazine and Edinburgh Literary Miscellany*, 70 (1808), 958 • NA Scot., CH 12/12

Archives Royal Highland and Agricultural Society, Edinburgh, letters and inventory of MSS | NA Scot., petition to court of session, 1797

Wealth at death £318 5s. 4d.: will, Edinburgh commissary court books, NA Scot., SC 70/1/1

McIntosh, Hugh (1768–1840), civil engineering contractor, was born on 4 December 1768 at Milntown of Kildrummie, Nairn, the second son of David McIntosh (*c.*1730–1790) and Margaret Tolmie. The family had an agricultural background. After a brief education at Inverness he went south in search of work with the canal contractor Alexander Mackenzie (1769–1836). His career began as a navvy on the Forth and Clyde Canal, then in its final stage of construction under Robert Whitworth. The first contracts which McIntosh took in his own name were on the Lancaster Canal, where the engineer was John Rennie.

In 1797 McIntosh began work on a succession of contracts on the Grand Trunk Canal system. On 10 December 1798 he married Mary (1773–1833), the daughter of William Cross (1744–1827), an agent of the canal company, at Cheddleton, Staffordshire. Here, where their home was a contractor's hut, their only surviving child, David (1799–1856), was born. In 1803 they moved to Poplar to enable McIntosh directly to supervise the massive East India Dock excavations. Within ten years he had built up a national organization and his prosperity led to the opening of an office in Bloomsbury. His son attended Glasgow University, from 1814 to 1817, before starting to work for his father on the Edinburgh and Glasgow Union Canal.

McIntosh's contracts are too numerous to detail. While the Grand Trunk Canal works were in progress he took other contracts on the Kennet and Avon, Croydon, Thames and Medway, and Regent's canals. With his son he took contracts on the Great Western, Thames and Severn, and Gloucester and Berkeley canals, and on Sharpness docks. He remained a canal contractor throughout his career; among his final works were contracts on the Aire and Calder Navigation and the Grand Junction Canal. Meanwhile, he was heavily involved in the construction of new docks and their associated roads in London, carrying out works for almost all the docks companies. Other road contracts included Highgate Archway and Vauxhall Bridge Road in London and turnpikes near Manchester and Brighton. He became an important contractor for gas and waterworks companies in the London and Bristol areas, and laid sewers around London.

McIntosh's ability was rewarded by substantial government contracts. In addition to enormous works at Pembroke, Plymouth, and Portsmouth dockyards, he built the North Hyde Canal and mounds. He carried out much work for the royal parks and palaces. He was the contractor at Chetney Hill lazaretto near Sheerness. He was also possibly the first British contractor to work overseas when he undertook demolition work at Flushing for Lord Liverpool. He carried out harbour works at Shoreham, Whitstable, Dover, Hull, and Southampton, and various sea defence works, most notably at Dymchurch.

McIntosh built bridges at Harmondsworth, Brentford, and Northampton, widened Clopton Bridge, Stratford upon Avon, and repaired Rochester Bridge. He was contractor for Telford's Mythe Bridge near Tewkesbury, and he built floating bridges over the Itchen and at Portsmouth. In 1821 he gave evidence to the House of Commons on London Bridge, and he carried out site investigations for the new bridge; his son provided evidence on the new bridge's stability in 1831 and also repaired Blackfriars Bridge (1834–42).

McIntosh embraced the opportunities offered by the railway boom of the 1830s, and built the London to Greenwich railway. His son was responsible for extensive works on the London and South Western and Midland Counties railways, Dutton Viaduct on the Grand Junction, and smaller contracts on the Northern and Eastern, and Birmingham and Derby Junction railways, and together they also took eight contracts on the Great Western Railway. Their claims for payment were turned down by Isambard Kingdom Brunel, who refused to settle McIntosh's account until David McIntosh's accounts were submitted, and refused also McIntosh senior's demand for an independent arbitrator. One factor was probably the precarious finances of the railway company at the time, and it emerged that Brunel had never properly certified the work actually carried out by the contractors, concealing its true cost. Their claims were pursued through chancery and finally settled in their favour in 1866. McIntosh suffered an eye infection while working on the Gloucester and Berkeley Canal in 1826, and this resulted in blindness. This may in part explain why many of the later contracts, particularly the railway contracts, were taken in his son's name, although McIntosh remained active until his death and kept a tight control on site visits by asking detailed questions.

McIntosh was one of the key individuals in developing the British civil engineering industry. He relied on his family, chiefly his brother James and his own son, to manage his works, but many famous contractors worked under him—the Airds, the Betts, the Ross and Radford families, William Henderson, James Leishman, and William Mackenzie. They enabled McIntosh to establish himself as the first contractor with a nationwide organization. McIntosh died of apoplexy on 31 August 1840, while meeting his agents for his contracts on the North Midland Railway and Manchester and Leeds line, at the Strafford Arms Hotel, Wakefield. He was buried in the family vault at St Matthias Church, Poplar. He left a considerable fortune of £300,000, more than any civil engineer to that date, and had acquired numerous properties in the East End of London and Essex.   MIKE CHRIMES

Sources M. M. Chrimes, 'Hugh McIntosh, 1768–1840', *Transactions* [Newcomen Society], 66 (1994–5), 175–92 · *PICE*, 16 (1856–7), 162–3 · D. Brooke, 'The equity suit of *McIntosh v. the Great Western Railway*: the "Jarndyce" of railway litigation', *Journal of Transport History*, 3rd ser., 17 (1996), 133–49 · T. Nicholson, *Strictures on a pamphlet published at the request of the Manchester Statistical Society* (1846) · A. W. Skempton, 'Engineering in the port of London, 1789–1808', *Transactions* [Newcomen Society], 50 (1978–9), 87–108 · A. W. Skempton, 'Engineering in the Port of London, 1808–1834', *Transactions* [Newcomen Society], 53 (1981–2), 73–96 · *GM*, 2nd ser., 14 (1840), 441 · *The life of Thomas Telford: civil engineer, written by himself*, ed. J. Rickman (1838), 257–8 · J. S. Abernethy, *The life and works of James Abernethy* (1897), 64–5 · *Railway Times* (12 Sept 1840), 773 · *Wakefield Journal* (4 Sept 1840) · S. Porter, ed., *Poplar, Blackwall and the Isle of Dogs: the parish of All Saints*, 2 vols., Survey of London, 43–4 (1994) · parish register (burial), 8 September 1840, London, Poplar, St Matthias · *IGI* · d. cert.
Archives LMA, records of London gas and water companies, sewer commissions · Museum of London, dock company minutes, etc. · PRO, dockyard records · PRO, railway and canal records | Inst. CE, Mackenzie Collection · Inst. CE, Rennie Collection · Inst. CE, Telford Collection · Ironbridge Gorge Museum, Telford MSS · Gloucester and Berkeley canal · University of Bristol, MSS relating to *McIntosh v. Great Western Railway* lawsuit
Wealth at death £300,000: PRO, death duty registers, IR 26/1555, no. 706

McIntosh, Lachlan (1727–1806), planter and revolutionary army officer in America, was born on 5 March 1727 at Badenoch, Inverness-shire, the son of John Mohr McIntosh (*c*.1700–1761), and his wife, Marjorie Fraser. In 1735 Lachlan accompanied his parents and over a hundred Scots of clan Chattan to establish the town of Darien on Georgia's southern frontier. The Scots came to fight the Spanish in Florida and they had their opportunity when Colonel James Oglethorpe invaded Florida in 1740. Unfortunately the unwary Scots were surprised by a night attack on their outlying post and most were killed or taken prisoner. Among the latter was Lachlan's father. Fatherless, Lachlan and his sister Anne went to George Whitefield's famous Bethesda Orphan House in Savannah, where he received an education. Two years later, as a Spanish invasion threatened Georgia, fifteen-year-old Lachlan joined Oglethorpe's regiment at Frederica and took part in the repulse of the enemy.

At the age of twenty-one McIntosh went to Charles Town, South Carolina, to work as a merchant and formed a lasting friendship with the wealthy Henry Laurens, future leading American patriot, who thereafter acted as McIntosh's mentor. On 1 January 1756 McIntosh married Sarah Threadcraft of Charles Town and returned to the Georgia coastal area. With the advice and financial backing of Laurens, he acquired valuable rice lands as his family grew by six sons and two daughters. Between 1763 and 1776 he obtained over 14,000 acres.

Except for one term in the Georgia Commons house in 1770, McIntosh avoided politics until 12 January 1775 when he headed a parish committee and issued resolutions supporting the measures of the continental congress. When British warships threatened Savannah a year later, Georgia's provincial congress appointed McIntosh colonel of the local battalion, and ordered him to defend the town. The British made away with what they came for—a number of vessels loaded with rice—and McIntosh wrote to George Washington that the invasion had been turned back. Until this time McIntosh had remained above party bickering, but the radical faction, headed by Button Gwinnett, began a campaign of criticism about McIntosh's failure to protect the Georgia borderlands and his friendship with known loyalists. Antagonism deepened when McIntosh criticized the radically democratic Georgia constitution of 1777, crafted by a committee headed by Gwinnett. Finally, after a failed American invasion of loyalist Florida, during which Gwinnett, as commander of the militia, refused to co-operate with McIntosh who was then the newly appointed general of the Georgia continentals (part of the regular American army), the two settled their differences in a duel. Both were wounded; Gwinnett died, McIntosh recovered. But in the resulting hue and cry of Gwinnett's followers, congress transferred McIntosh to Washington's command and he spent an uncomfortable winter at Valley Forge. Washington assigned McIntosh the important task of securing the Northwest Territory and capturing British-held Detroit. Congress confused matters by also ordering him to pacify hostile American Indians on the Pennsylvania frontier. With enormous difficulty troops under McIntosh managed to construct forts McIntosh and Laurens in the Ohio country, solidifying patriot American claims to the region, but criticism from his subordinates made his life miserable. He requested and received a transfer to Georgia in 1779, after British forces had reoccupied its low country and restored royal government.

McIntosh served under General Benjamin Lincoln in the failed Franco-American siege of Savannah in October 1779. With the withdrawal of Count d'Estaing's French forces, McIntosh returned to Augusta where a radical faction and a conservative faction had each established a government claiming to represent Georgia. Elections in November gave the radical group control of the assembly and that body instructed Governor George Walton to dispatch a message to congress requesting McIntosh's second removal from the state. McIntosh had already joined Lincoln in the defence of Charles Town when he was notified that congress had suspended him from command.

Charles Town fell to the British on 12 May 1780 and the captured McIntosh was exchanged and sent to Philadelphia, where he persuaded congress to repeal his suspension.

After the British evacuation of Georgia in 1782, McIntosh demanded an investigation of the letter calling for his suspension. William Glascock, whose name as speaker was subscribed to the letter, denied having seen it. George Walton admitted having the clerk sign the letter because the speaker had left town. The assembly denounced the forgery and vindicated McIntosh, but in a show of even-handedness elected George Walton chief justice. Congress made amends by promoting McIntosh to the rank of major-general.

After the war McIntosh served on various commissions, notably that which concluded a treaty with South Carolina in 1787 establishing the boundary between the states in the northern reaches. He was honoured by election to the presidency of the Georgia Society of the Cincinnati, an honorary society of officers who served in the late war. In 1793 the old Darien district was named McIntosh county. McIntosh might have enjoyed the honours conferred on him and the respect of his countrymen more if his last years had not been burdened by a crushing debt. He died at his Savannah home on 20 February 1806. He was buried in the colonial cemetery, Savannah.

EDWARD J. CASHIN

Sources H. H. Jackson, *Lachlan McIntosh and the politics of revolutionary Georgia* (1979) · L. Hawes, *Lachlan McIntosh papers in the University of Georgia libraries* (Athens, GA, 1968) · L. Hawes, 'The papers of Lachlan McIntosh', *Collections of the Georgia Historical Society*, 12 (1957) · Georgia Historical Society, Savannah, Georgia, Margaret Davis Cate collection · K. Coleman and C. S. Gurr, eds., *Dictionary of Georgia biography*, 2 vols. (Athens, GA, 1983)
Archives New York Historical Society, papers · NYPL, Thomas Addis Emmet collection, papers | South Carolina Historical Society, Charleston, Henry Laurens papers
Likenesses C. W. Peale, oils, *c*.1782, Independence National Historical Park, Philadelphia, Pennsylvania
Wealth at death personal effects amounted to $206; left wife the lot in Savannah where they resided, unspecified shares of US bonds, Duboy Island in the Altamaha River, and four household slaves; held extensive land grants and left them to surviving son, his two daughters, and sons-in-law: probate court records, Chatham county courthouse, Savannah

Macintosh, Sir Robert Reynolds (1897–1989), anaesthetist, was born on 17 October 1897 in Timaru, New Zealand. Baptized Rewi Rawhiti (Maori names being popular at the time), he was the youngest in the family of two sons and one daughter of Charles Nicholson Macintosh, newspaper editor, businessman, farmer, and mayor of Timaru in 1901, and his wife, Lydia Beatrice Thompson. He spent part of his childhood in Argentina, but returned to New Zealand when he was thirteen years old. He was educated at Waitaki Boys' High School in the South Island, where he shone academically and athletically, and was head of school. In December 1915 he travelled to Britain and was commissioned in the Royal Scots Fusiliers. After a short period in France he was transferred to the Royal Flying Corps, for which he had originally volunteered. He was mentioned in dispatches, but was shot down behind enemy lines on 26 May 1917 and taken prisoner. There followed a remarkable series of attempted escapes from various prisoner-of-war camps, which have been documented in H. E. Hervey's *Cage-Birds* (1940).

After the First World War Macintosh entered Guy's Hospital medical school, qualifying MRCS LRCP in 1924. While working for the FRCS (Edin.), which he obtained in 1927, he undertook anaesthetic sessions in Guy's dental school. His skills were soon recognized and within a few years he had built up a large West End dental anaesthetic practice.

In February 1937 Macintosh was appointed to the first Nuffield chair of anaesthetics in Oxford and was awarded the DM (Oxon.). Since he had never received any formal academic training in anaesthesia, he spent some months visiting other departments, including that run by the only other professor of anaesthesia, Ralph Waters, in Madison, Wisconsin. Later in 1937 he anaesthetized for an American plastic surgeon who had volunteered to treat the wounded in the Spanish Civil War. The experience of working under wartime conditions with very primitive equipment convinced Macintosh that there was a need for a simple, portable vaporizer, which would deliver known concentrations of ether when used under field conditions. When he returned to Oxford he invoked the aid of physicists in the Clarendon Laboratory, who produced the prototype Oxford vaporizer no. 1. Between 1941 and 1945 several thousand vaporizers were produced in the Morris car factory in Cowley, many being used in the armed services and, later, in economically underdeveloped countries. More sophisticated vaporizers and other items of equipment (such as the Macintosh laryngoscope) were subsequently developed and these, together with the superbly illustrated textbooks written by Macintosh and other members of department, had a major impact on the practice of anaesthesia.

During the Second World War Macintosh became an air commodore in the Royal Air Force in 1941, with responsibility for the anaesthetic services, but he retained his Oxford connections. The department provided training courses for many anaesthetists from the armed services and elsewhere, and was also deeply involved in hazardous physiological research into the provision of respirable atmospheres in submarines, survival during parachute descent from high altitudes, and the evaluation of life-jackets, using an anaesthetized volunteer submerged in a swimming-pool.

Macintosh's modesty and keen interest in his staff induced great personal loyalty. He delighted in his fellowship of Pembroke College (from 1937) and supported the college generously, later being made an honorary fellow (1965). He had great personal courage and did not hesitate to confront his colleagues over a matter of principle. He was one of the first to press for inquiries into the causes of death under anaesthesia and later travelled the world demonstrating simple but safe anaesthetic techniques. These tours resulted in his acquisition of a vast circle of friends, who regularly made the pilgrimage to Oxford.

Macintosh was knighted in 1955, and received many other distinctions, including honorary doctorates from the universities of Buenos Aires (1950), Aix-Marseilles (1952), Wales (1962), Poznan (1968), and the Medical College of Ohio (1977), and honorary fellowships of the Royal Society of Medicine (1966), the Royal College of Obstetricians and Gynaecologists (1973), the Royal College of Surgeons (1989), and three faculties of anaesthesia. He retired in 1965.

Macintosh was a skilled boxer in his youth, continued to take a keen interest in sport throughout his life, and remained very active in retirement. He was of average height and had a rubicund complexion and suntanned bald pate. He wore thick spectacles and had a soft voice. He rarely talked about himself, but interrogated dining companions kindly, if somewhat relentlessly. On 16 September 1925 he married Rosa Emily May (b. 1894/5), daughter of Ernest William Medway Henderson, builder; they had no children and Rosa died in 1956. In 1962 Macintosh married Ann Francis, daughter of Robert William Manning, an army officer. She had two sons from a previous marriage to Dennis Vincent Wilson Francis, who was employed in the motor industry. Macintosh, who lived latterly at 326 Woodstock Road, Oxford, suffered a fall while walking his dog and died in the Radcliffe Infirmary, Oxford, on 28 August 1989.   KEITH SYKES, *rev.*

William Carmichael M'Intosh (1838–1931), by unknown artist

Sources H. E. Hervey, *Cage-birds* (1940) · J. Beinart, *A history of the Nuffield department of anaesthetics, Oxford, 1937–1987* (1987) · m. cert. · *CGPLA Eng. & Wales* (1990) · personal knowledge (1996) · private information (1996) [Ann Francis, Guy Francis] · R. Bryce-Smith, J. V. Mitchell, and J. Parkhouse, *The Nuffield department of anaesthetics, Oxford, 1937–1962* (1963) · M. K. Sykes, 'Macintosh: from Timaru to Timbuktu', *Annals of the Scottish Society of Anaesthetists*, 35 (1995), 9–14 · R. Trubuhovich, 'Sir Robert Macintosh and intensive care', *Intensive Care Medicine*, 16 (1990), 472–3 · *The Times* (8 Sept 1989) · *Daily Telegraph* (7 Sept 1989) · A. C. Smith, *The Guardian* (11 Sept 1989) · M. K. Sykes, *The Independent* (12 Sept 1989) · A. C. Smith, *BMJ* (30 Sept 1989), 851 · R. Bannister, *BMJ* (30 Sept 1989), 1097 · M. K. Sykes, *The Lancet* (30 Sept 1989), 816 · *Anaesthesia*, 44 (1989), 951–2 · M. K. Sykes, *Pembroke Record* (1989), 18–20 · C. McK. Holmes, *Royal Australian College of Surgeons Bulletin* (Nov 1989), 42–3 · C. McK. Holmes, *New Zealand Society of Anaesthetists Newsletter* (March 1990), 8–11 · T. B. Boulton, *Proceedings of the History of Anaesthesia Society*, 8b (1990), 97–109
Archives Wellcome L., corresp., lectures, notes, papers relating to the Nuffield Department of Anaesthetics, clinical and research notes, etc. |FILM Radcliffe Infirmary, Oxford, videos |SOUND priv. coll., interviews conducted by J. Beinart
Likenesses photograph, 1988, repro. in W. D. A. Smith and G. M. C. Paterson, eds., *A tribute to Professor Sir Robert Macintosh on his 90th birthday* (1988) · G. Kelly, oils, Radcliffe Infirmary, Oxford, Nuffield department of anaesthetics
Wealth at death £1,343,103: probate, 9 Jan 1990, *CGPLA Eng. & Wales*

M'Intosh, William Carmichael (1838–1931), zoologist, was born at St Andrews on 10 October 1838, the only son and fourth of six children of John M'Intosh (1804–1897), builder and town councillor of St Andrews, and his wife, Elizabeth (Eliza; 1801–1881), third daughter of Robert Mitchell, linen manufacturer. His youngest sister, Roberta (1843–1869), married the zoologist Albert Günther (1830–

1914); she was a gifted artist and executed many of the illustrations for her brother's works.

M'Intosh was educated at Madras College, St Andrews and St Andrews University. He then transferred to Edinburgh where he studied medicine. He graduated MD with distinction and gold medal in 1860 and specialized in the study of mental disease. In 1863 he became medical superintendent of Perth District Asylum at Murthly, a post which he held for the next twenty years.

From his boyhood M'Intosh had been interested in natural history, and at Edinburgh he was especially influenced by John Goodsir, the anatomist, and G. J. Allman, the zoologist, the latter of whom he accompanied on dredging excursions in the Firth of Forth. He then began a long series of faunistic papers which were continued until the last years of his life. A number of these papers were reprinted in *The Marine Invertebrates and Fishes of St. Andrews* (1875) with a supplement, *Additions to the Marine Fauna of St. Andrews* (1927). His most important work in pure zoology was his great *Monograph of the British Marine Annelids*, published by the Ray Society (4 vols., 1873–1923). The first two parts of this work, published in 1873 and 1874, dealt with the nemertine worms (a group now included in the phylum Nemertini). Work on the remainder of the monograph did not begin until 1900; it was finally completed in 1923. Also important was M'Intosh's report on the polychaete worms obtained by the *Challenger* expedition, which appeared in two volumes in 1885.

In 1882 the chair of natural history in the University of St Andrews became vacant and M'Intosh, fulfilling a long-term ambition, returned to his native city as professor of zoology, a position which he occupied until his retirement in 1917. In 1883 he was appointed to conduct investigations on behalf of a royal commission on Scottish sea fisheries (the trawling commission), and as part of this work set up one of the country's first marine laboratories at St Andrews. These researches were summarized in *Life Histories of British Marine Food-Fishes* (with Arthur Thomas Masterman, 1897) and *The Resources of the Sea* (1898).

M'Intosh was elected FRS in 1877 and was awarded a royal medal in 1899. He was also elected FRS (Edinburgh) in 1869, having been awarded the Neill medal in 1868; he was vice-president from 1927 to 1930. In 1924 he received the Linnean medal of the Linnean Society. He was president of the Ray Society from 1913 until his death. He received honorary degrees from the universities of St Andrews, Edinburgh, Oxford, and Durham. He was primarily a descriptive zoologist, and his writings on the polychaete and especially the nemertine worms provide a classic account of these groups. In fishery research he was one of the pioneers, and although many of his conclusions (such as his belief that human activity would not seriously deplete marine resources) are now outdated, he had a clearer conception of the broad outlines of marine ecology than many of his contemporaries.

M'Intosh's passion for science left little time for other interests, but he was active in the temperance movement. He never married and died at St Andrews on 1 April 1931.

W. T. CALMAN, rev. MARGARET DEACON

Sources A. E. Gunther, *William Carmichael M'Intosh, M.D., F.R.S.* (1977) · W. T. C. [W. T. Calman], *PRS*, 110B (1932), xxiv–xxviii · D. Merriman, 'William Carmichael M'Intosh, nonagenarian', *Proceedings of the Royal Society of Edinburgh*, 72B (1972), 99–105 · E. E. Prince, *A great Scottish naturalist* (1893) · W. T. Calman, 'Prof. W. C. M'Intosh', *Nature*, 127 (1931), 673–4 · *List of works, memoirs and papers by William Carmichael M'Intosh* (1926) · 'Professor M'Intosh, the doyen of marine zoology', *The Times* (2 April 1931) · private information (1949)

Archives NHM, corresp. and papers · U. St Andr. L., corresp. and papers · U. St Andr. L., papers relating to the royal commission on trawling, 1884 | Linn. Soc., typescripts relating to his life and work by A. E. Gunther · NHM, notes on A. E. Gunther's *William Carmichael M'Intosh*

Likenesses J. Caw, oils, c.1880, Linn. Soc. · photographs, U. St Andr., M'Intosh collection · portrait, Linn. Soc. [*see illus.*]

Wealth at death £3816 13s. 2d.: confirmation, 1931, Scotland

Macintyre, Donald (1831–1903), army officer, born at Kincraig House, Ross-shire, on 12 September 1831, was second son of Donald Macintyre of Calcutta and his wife, Margaret, daughter of John Mackenzie of Kincraig House, Ross-shire. Educated at private schools in England and abroad, he was at Addiscombe College from 1848 to 1850, and obtained his first commission in the Bengal army on 14 June 1850.

With the 66th Gurkhas Macintyre served under Sir Colin Campbell in the two expeditions of 1852 against the hill peoples on the Peshawar frontier, including the destruction of the fortified village of Prangarh and the action at Ishkakot. He also joined the expeditionary force against the Bori Afridis in November 1853. In 1856 he took part with the 66th Gurkhas in the expedition under Sir Neville Chamberlain to Kurram valley, Afghanistan. He

was made lieutenant on 23 November 1856. During 1857 and 1858, when engaged in raising an extra Gurkha regiment (subsequently the 4th Gurkhas), he took part in protecting the hill passes on the Kalee Kumaon frontier from the Rohilkhand rebels and in keeping the district in order. He was promoted captain in June 1862, served with the Doaba field force in Peshawar valley in 1864, and became major on 14 June 1870. He served with the Lushai expedition in 1871–2, was mentioned in dispatches, and was promoted brevet lieutenant-colonel on 11 September 1872. For his gallantry at the storming of the stockaded village of Lalgnoora on 4 January 1872 he received the Victoria Cross. Macintyre, who was serving as second in command to Colonel Herbert Macpherson, commanding the 2nd Gurkhas, while leading the assault was the first to reach the stockade, which was 8–9 feet high. Macintyre sprang over the burning stockade and the village was successfully stormed under heavy fire.

Macintyre, who became lieutenant-colonel on 14 January 1876 and colonel on 1 October 1887, commanded the 2nd Prince of Wales's Own Gurkhas at the occupation of Cyprus and also with the Khyber column, directed against the Zakha Khel Afridis, in the Anglo-Afghan War of 1878–9. He was also in both expeditions to the Bazar valley under Lieutenant-General Sir Francis Maude. He retired with the rank of major-general on 24 December 1880, and subsequently lived at Mackenzie Lodge, Fortrose, Ross-shire.

Macintyre, who was a traveller and sportsman, published an account of his experiences in *Hindu Koh: Wanderings and Wild Sports on and beyond the Himalayas* (1889). He married Angelica Alison, daughter of the Revd T. J. Patteson of Kirmettees, Forfar; she survived her husband. Macintyre was a JP for Ross-shire and a fellow of the Royal Geographical Society. He died at Mackenzie Lodge, Fortrose, on 15 April 1903 and was buried in Rosemarkie churchyard.

H. M. VIBART, rev. JAMES FALKNER

Sources Army List · Hart's Army List · Indian Army List · The Times (17 April 1903) · T. E. Toomey, *Heroes of the Victoria Cross* (1895) · W. H. Paget, *A record of the expeditions against the north-west frontier tribes, since the annexation of the Punjab*, rev. A. H. Mason (1884)

Likenesses A. Bassano, photograph, c.1880, repro. in Toomey, *Heroes of the Victoria cross*, 197

Macintyre, Donald George Frederick Wyville (1904–1981), naval officer and historian, was born on 26 January 1904 in Dehra Dun, India, the younger son (there were no daughters) of Lieutenant-Colonel Donald Charles Frederick Macintyre, Indian army, and his wife, Maud, daughter of Colonel George Strahan, of the Royal Engineers. Macintyre entered the Royal Navy on 15 September 1917 and was educated at the Royal Naval College at Osborne and Dartmouth.

After initial sea service in destroyers Macintyre became a fleet fighter pilot in 1927 and for the next six years served in squadrons based in aircraft-carriers. This phase of his service was ended by medical unfitness for flying in 1935 and he returned to small ships, gaining his first command, HMS *Kingfisher*, soon afterwards. The outbreak of the Second World War found him in home waters in command of HMS *Venomous*.

Macintyre's experience as a destroyer officer made him a natural choice for fleet tasks but his instinct was more for the convoy war developing in the Atlantic and it was here that he spent most of his immensely distinguished war career. He was an early leader in the development of the escort group concept, where a mixed group of destroyers, frigates, and corvettes worked up and worked together under an experienced senior officer and, by their well-practised procedures and knowledge of each other's characteristics, were able to give much better support to a convoy than any *ad hoc* formation.

Macintyre's first success against the U-boats came on 16 March 1941, and it was a highly dramatic one, for in HMS *Walker*, with the *Vanoc* in company, he sank the submarines of two noted German aces—Schepke and Kretschmer—in a single action. For this he was appointed to the DSO.

After a brief spell ashore Macintyre returned to sea in HMS *Hesperus*. He measured his success in this ship and the escort group he commanded in two ways: by the number of U-boats sunk by the group but, equally important in his eyes, by the fact that he lost only two ships from convoy in nearly two years. Macintyre regarded this trade-off as a vindication of convoy as both an offensive and a protective measure. Notable successes during this period were the destruction of *U-357* by ramming in December 1942 and of *U-191* and *U-186* in April and May 1943 respectively. For these actions Macintyre was awarded two bars to his DSO. The tide had now turned decisively against the U-boats. Macintyre remained at sea until mid-1944, with one further success in May of that year when HMS *Bickerton* under his command sank *U-765*, HMS *Bligh* in company. He was awarded the DSC for this action. He was also, for his service to the USA during the war, made an officer of the Legion of Merit.

Macintyre had been promoted commander at the end of 1940 and spent the rest of the war in that rank. He was promoted captain at the end of 1945 and his service for the next decade was mainly ashore, though he commanded the third training flotilla between 1948 and 1950. He was placed on the retired list in July 1955.

Macintyre then turned his energies to writing, beginning with an account of his own war in *U-Boat Killer* (1956) and following up with almost one book a year for the next decade and a half. Most of his books were on the recent history of maritime war, though from time to time he went further back with, for example, a biography of Admiral Lord Rodney. With their lack of footnotes, references, and bibliography, and their graphic and sometimes colourful language, Macintyre's books represented the 'popular' end of history and were not in the style of heavy scholarship fashionable twenty years later. But on analysis they remain admirably accurate and show tremendous grasp of the essentials of sea power and of the naval art. Macintyre's researches were undoubtedly aided by his association with the Naval Historical Branch, which he

joined in August 1964 and from which he retired in December 1972.

Burly and somewhat bear-like in appearance and gruff in manner, Macintyre could be daunting on first acquaintance, but it needed only the briefest of conversations to convince him one knew one's job and he was then the most kind and helpful of men. Considering his analytical powers and skill with words, it is astonishing that use was not made of him in the Admiralty during his service as a captain; but perhaps his outspokenness was not regarded as an asset in those years.

In 1941 he married Monica Josephine Clifford Rowley, daughter of Roger Walter Strickland, gentleman; they had a son and a daughter. Macintyre died in Ashford, Kent, on 23 May 1981. He was survived by his wife.

RICHARD HILL, *rev.*

Sources *The Times* (11 June 1981) · D. G. F. W. Macintyre, *U-boat killer* (1956) · *CGPLA Eng. & Wales* (1981) · private information (1990) **Archives** FILM IWM FVA, news footage **Wealth at death** £76,405: probate, 21 Aug 1981, *CGPLA Eng. & Wales*

Macintyre, Duncan Bàn [Donnchadh Bàn Mac an t-Saoir] (1723?–1812), poet, was born in Druim Liaghart, on the southern shore of Loch Tulla, Argyllshire; he was probably the Duncan Macintyre, son of Donald, who was baptized in the parish of Lochgoilhead on 28 July 1723. He was involved in the battle of Falkirk (1746), apparently serving as a substitute for a local farmer, Fletcher of Crannach Farm; he lost Fletcher's sword on this occasion, and recorded the event in a poem. He fought on the Hanoverian side, but later seemed to show some embarrassment over this allegiance, which was no doubt imposed on him by his connection with Campbell landlords. He became a forester in the service of the earls of Breadalbane shortly after the Jacobite rising of 1745, operating in Glen Lochay (near Killin); later he worked at Dalness and in Mamlorn. Some of these localities surface prominently in his early verse—for example, Coire Cheathaich at the upper reaches of Glen Lochay and Ben Doran in the vicinity of Glenorchy.

Macintyre's verse writing began early, and he continued to compose throughout his life; he was known by the Gaelic nickname Donnchadh Bàn nan Oran (Fair-haired Duncan of the Songs). Some of his earlier poems are in the well-established praise-song tradition, his subjects being members of the Campbell aristocracy; they include Lord Glenorchy, who was to become the third earl of Breadalbane in 1752; John Campbell, a grandson of the first earl and closely involved with the Royal Bank in Edinburgh; Captain Duncan Campbell, who despite his reputation did not carry out the barbaric instructions of the duke of Cumberland in the post-Culloden period; and Colin Campbell of Glenure, who was murdered in 1752 (the 'Appin murder'). Lochtayside, and especially Killin, connections feature strongly in these poems, which are very competent examples of the genre. Macintyre had made the acquaintance of James Stewart, the Killin minister who translated the New Testament into Gaelic (1767), and his son, John, who was to see the poet's first edition of his poems through the press in 1768. It is reported that Donald MacNicol, minister of Lismore, had already written down many of Macintyre's poems, for he was not himself literate. It seems very probable that Macintyre was introduced to Alasdair Mac Mhaighstir Alasdair's poems by these friends after their publication in 1751, and there are clear signs of their influence on his work. This is especially clear in the case of 'Oran an t-samhraidh' (Song of summer), and the extended praise of a corrie in Mac Mhaighstir Alasdair's 'Allt an t-siùcair' (The sugar brook) must have influenced Macintyre's poem in praise of Coire Cheathaich. The metre of Mac Mhaighstir Alasdair's 'Moladh Mòraig' (The praise of Morag) also shows in Macintyre's 'Moladh Beinn Dòbhrain' (The praise of Ben Doran), which similarly uses the succession of movements and rhythms associated with classical pipe music or *ceòl mòr*.

Macintyre's early songs describe aspects of the rural life of the 1740s–60s: singing and drinking in local inns, hunting expeditions, the pleasure of using guns, and romantic associations, including a song addressed to Màiri Bhàn Og, his young bride, Mary, from Inveroran. Cupid intrudes briefly into this song, but its atmosphere remains local, personal, sensuous, and generous. The Ben Doran poem and several others develop Macintyre's fascination with the landscape inhabited by the deer, and with the deer themselves in their many varieties and idiosyncrasies. Here he achieves his most individual, sensuous, and skilfully crafted work, without a hint of sentimentality. Other poems reveal his disillusion with rural developments, by which sheep edge out the deer, and the fact that the lifestyle he loves is gradually disappearing in the face of economic pressures from outside the rural society. He made his final visit to his beloved mountains in 1802, when he composed the haunting 'Cead deireannach nam beann' (Final farewell to the mountains).

In 1767 Macintyre and his family moved to Edinburgh, when he enrolled in the city guard, in which he seems to have served for many years. Much later, from 1793 to 1799, he served with the Breadalbane fencibles, moving about Scotland. He continued to compose songs; one, for example, celebrating the fencibles, together with some drinking songs, and a series of songs in praise of Gaelic and of the bagpipes associated with piping competitions run by the London Highland Society and held at Falkirk between 1781 and 1789. These are somewhat repetitive, and generally his work after his move to Edinburgh is low-key and of limited interest. Macintyre died in 1812 and was buried in Greyfriars churchyard in Edinburgh.

There can be no doubt that Macintyre's finest work dates from about 1750–68. On one level it gives us a vivid and authentic picture of rural life in Argyllshire and Perthshire at this period, while the best of his work combines great metrical skills with a finely honed sensitivity to natural scenery and the animal life that brought so much additional excitement to his enjoyment of that landscape. Several editions of his poems appeared during his lifetime (in 1768, 1790, and 1804), and reprints continued throughout the nineteenth century. In 1912 George Calder published an edition with a useful biographical introduction, and verse translations, which are pedestrian. About 1929 Donald James MacLeod published an edition of the poems, with a French introduction and translation; this was his doctoral thesis at the University of Rennes. The definitive edition was edited by Angus MacLeod and published by the Scottish Gaelic Texts Society in 1952. This has a carefully edited text and extensive textual annotation. The translations here are in prose, and are very accurate, though somewhat ponderous. Several more poetic translations appeared in subsequent decades, including Iain Crichton Smith's translation *Ben Dorain* (1969). DERICK S. THOMSON

Sources *The songs of Duncan Bàn Macintyre*, ed. A. MacLeod (1952) · *The Gaelic songs of Duncan Macintyre*, ed. G. Calder (1912) · D. S. Thomson, *An introduction to Gaelic poetry*, 2nd edn (1990) · D. S. Thomson, *Gaelic poetry in the eighteenth century: a bilingual anthology* (1993) · W. Gillies, 'The poem in praise of Ben Dobhrain', *Lines Review*, 63 (1977) · Iain Crichton Smith, *Ben Dorain* (1969) · parish register (baptism), 28 July 1723, parish of Lochgoilhead, Argyllshire · d. cert.
Archives U. Glas., McLagan MSS

Macintyre, John (1857–1928), laryngological surgeon and radiologist, was born on 2 October 1857 in the slum area of 343 High Street, Glasgow. His father, Donald Macintyre, had migrated from his native Argyll to Glasgow in search of work, and became a journeyman tailor there. His mother, Margaret, *née* Livingston, was a relative of David Livingstone. Macintyre had a somewhat heavy build, humorous but sententious speech, grey-hazel eyes, and dark brown hair which marked him as a Celt of highland origin. After a brief school attendance curtailed by ill health, he was self-educated. Macintyre later obtained a job as temporary electrician at the Glasgow Royal Infirmary and graduated MB, CM from Glasgow University in 1882. He was then engaged as a ship's surgeon, and gained postgraduate experience in London, Paris, and Vienna, before returning to Glasgow as assistant surgeon to the Lock Hospital.

During 1885 Macintyre returned to the infirmary as full-time medical electrician and set out to equip the hospital with electrical current for medical and surgical purposes. In the same year he obtained positions at the two extramural schools of medicine attached to the infirmary: dispensary surgeon at Anderson's College and demonstrator of anatomy at the infirmary school of medicine. He later became professor of surgery at Anderson's. In 1886 he was appointed assistant surgeon in the throat department of the infirmary. He developed a large consulting practice in Glasgow, from 1891 in his rooms at 179 Bath Street. Many of Macintyre's patients and visitors were famous actors, singers, or musicians. He owned a very early phonograph and liked to collect recordings of his callers. He had become council member of the British Laryngological and Rhinological Association in 1889, and vice-president in 1890. In 1891 he became co-editor of the *British Journal of Laryngology* (and later joint proprietor and chief editor). Macintyre became president of the association in 1893 and was appointed surgeon in charge of the infirmary's ear, nose, and throat department. He always considered himself to be an ear, nose, and throat surgeon with an interest in X-rays, and only forty-five of his 111 published papers were on X-rays. However, in 1887 he had overseen the establishment of a separate electrical department in the infirmary, which included equipment built and donated by the aristocratic technologist Lord Blythswood.

The medical uses of electricity, which was initially used only for the illumination of body cavities, had by 1887 expanded to include therapeutic applications. The professional corollary was the evolution of the post of hospital medical electrician from that of a mere technician to one suitable for a trained clinician with a scientific bent. The further expansion of the electrical department in 1894 meant that the hospital was in a unique position to exploit the discovery of X-rays by Röntgen in November 1895. Clinicians who were also medical electricians were one of the conduits through which the new X-ray technology first entered hospitals and became used in diagnosis and therapy.

Röntgen had pre-circulated details of his experiments to international scientists, including Kelvin in Glasgow. Kelvin passed the paper to his nephew, J. T. Bottomley, of the Glasgow University Physical Laboratory, who, in turn, passed it on to his fellow members of the Philosophical Society of Glasgow, Lord Blythswood and Macintyre. These men began experimenting with X-rays. The Glasgow group benefited from the input of a range of expertise and assistance, which, as well as Macintyre's experience, included Kelvin's electrical equipment and knowledge, Blythswood's technical knowledge of machines, and the co-operation of local electrical and manufacturing firms. Macintyre persuaded the infirmary managers to further expand his electrical department and to include an X-ray unit in February 1896. Macintyre moved his experiments from Bath Street to the hospital. This was the first such unit in any British hospital, and, perhaps, in the world. A. A. C. Swinton claimed to have produced the first X-ray of a human hand in Britain on 13 January 1896; on 5 February Macintyre, Blythswood, and Bottomley gave a paper and demonstration on the new rays to the Philosophical Society entitled 'On the Röntgen rays, or, The new photography' (*Proceedings of the Royal Philosophical Society of Glasgow*, 27, 1896, 156–64). Here both Röntgen's original images and the Glasgow group's repetitions were shown depicting the frog and the human hand, forearm, and skull. During 1896 Macintyre published eighteen papers on technical developments in X-ray photography; he produced the first instantaneous X-ray (with the fluorescent screen cryptoscope which he believed would ultimately replace photographs); the first X-ray of a renal stone; of the spine; of the interior of the cranium; the heart, lung, and contents of the middle intestine; and of a foreign body in the oesophagus.

In March 1896 Röntgen wrote to Macintyre for details of his technique for X-raying soft tissues. Macintyre's greatest technical achievement came in the second half of 1896 when his advances in reducing exposure time allowed

him to produce the first X-ray cinematograph of a frog's legs, which paved the way for later developments in radiography. The number of referrals to the infirmary X-ray unit he received was so large that the managers were again approached to build an extension, and the new electrical pavilion was opened in 1902. Reflecting the growing status of the medical use of electricity, Macintyre had been appointed consulting electrician to the infirmary in 1900. He was quick to realize the potential harmful effects of exposure and insisted early on protection for himself and his staff. By the end of the nineteenth century he was using X-rays therapeutically on tumours, and his first published paper on this was in 1902, 'Recent electrotherapeutic work in medicine and surgery' (*Transactions of the Medico-Chirurgical Society of Glasgow*, 4, 1901–3, 131–52).

Macintyre was elected president of the British Laryngological and Rhinological Association for a second time in 1900, and in 1901 he became president of the Röntgen Society. In 1915 he was made a knight of grace of the order of St John of Jerusalem, and was elected to the fellowship of the Royal Faculty of Physicians and Surgeons of Glasgow in 1918. He married Agnes Jean (*d. c.*1926), the daughter of H. R. Hardie, in 1892. They had two children: one became a radiologist and served on the Glasgow Royal Infirmary staff. Macintyre died at his home, 179 Bath Street, Glasgow, on 29 October 1928 after suffering from chronic blood poisoning for some months.

ANDREW HULL

Sources A. L. Goodall, 'John Macintyre pioneer radiologist, 1857–1928', *Surgo*, Whitsun (1958), 119–26 · *Glasgow Medical Journal*, 90 (1928), 363–7 · Christopher Smith, 'Medical radiology: its practical application', in O. Checkand and M. Lamb, *Healthcare as social history: the Glasgow case* (1982), 100–15 · b. cert. · d. cert.
Archives Mitchell L., Glas., Greater Glasgow Health Board archives, corresp. and ephemera incl. press cuttings and family scrapbook, HB86 | Royal College of Physicians and Surgeons, Glasgow, two X-ray tubes | FILM Royal College of Physicians and Surgeons Archive, Glasgow, X-ray cinematograph of frog's legs
Likenesses photograph, Mitchell L., Glas., Greater Glasgow health board archives
Wealth at death £18,847 9s. 8d.: confirmation, 1929, CCI · £865 1s. 7d.: additional estate, 1932, CCI

McIntyre, Robert Douglas (1913–1998), Scottish nationalist and medical practitioner, was born in Dalziel, near Motherwell, on 15 December 1913, the third son of the Revd John E. McIntyre and his wife, Catherine Morison. Educated at Hamilton Academy and Daniel Stewart's College, McIntyre went on to study medicine at the universities of Edinburgh and Glasgow, where he specialized in public health. It was at university that he became interested in politics and joined the Labour Party in 1936.

By the advent of the Second World War, McIntyre had become disillusioned with the Labour Party's commitment to Scottish home rule and had joined the Scottish National Party (SNP). He had already formed the core of his political beliefs, which were broadly centrist. He believed in the primacy of community, had a distrust of large-scale bureaucracy, and had a passionate belief in the rights of individuals. The acceptance of the totalitarian Soviet regime by many Labour activists had been a factor in his growing disillusionment with the Labour Party. Steeped in Scottish history and Scottish culture, he refused to accept the idea of British national identity. He believed in the right of small nations to self-government and was active in supporting nationalist groups within the Soviet Union. As SNP membership secretary from 1940, he set about revitalizing the party's organization and encouraged new members to join. McIntyre gravitated towards the radical wing of the party, and in the split of 1942 he backed the anti-conscription leader Douglas Young against the moderate John MacCormick. McIntyre was himself a conscientious objector. Following the defection of John MacCormick, McIntyre set to work to rebuild the party's electoral strategy and this paid dividends in the Kircaldy by-election of 1944, when Douglas Young was only narrowly defeated by the Labour candidate.

In the Motherwell by-election in April 1945 McIntyre beat the Labour candidate to become the SNP's first member of parliament. Even though it lasted only twenty-one days, his victory was a watershed in the history of the SNP, as it demonstrated the party could attain its goal of Scottish independence by winning elections to secure an electoral mandate. This policy was enshrined in the SNP constitution of 1946, which McIntyre largely composed along with Arthur Donaldson, and which has become the basic template for nationalist policy ever since. McIntyre was party chairman from 1948 to 1956. He also worked hard to give the SNP a political identity separate from the other main British parties. By choosing a broadly social democrat basis for nationalist policies, it was hoped that the SNP would be able to distinguish itself from Labour and the Conservatives in socio-economic policies. Although the nationalists made little headway in the 1950s and early 1960s, McIntyre worked hard to keep the SNP to its principles of contesting elections as a separate and distinctive political party in order to secure an electoral mandate for independence. This policy was borne out by the failure of the national convention in the early 1950s, which largely gave the SNP a monopoly of nationalist political activity. In 1959 McIntyre married Latitia MacLeod, a psychiatrist.

A shrewd political operator, McIntyre insisted on discipline in the party and recognized that there would be no quick fix for attaining independence. Consequently, much time was spent in the 1950s and early 1960s on organizational matters, building up an electoral machinery, and recruiting new members. McIntyre was keen to present the SNP as a moderate and reasonable party, and was largely responsible for expelling those who promoted anti-English sentiment and violent or illegal tactics. He practised what he preached, and was one of the few nationalist candidates to stand at a general election in the 1950s. Yet it was through such tenacity that the SNP was able to increase its number of parliamentary candidates from three in 1950 to twenty-three by the general election of 1966. McIntyre's efforts to build up the party infrastructure paid dividends in the mid-1960s, when an influx of new members was able to meld into a mature party organization; it took advantage of growing dissatisfaction with

the Labour government to secure a by-election win in Hamilton in 1967 and make sweeping gains in local government in 1969. It was another facet of McIntyre's strategy to contest elections at local government level. He was provost of Stirling from 1967 to 1975 and argued that the best way that the SNP could convince voters that the party was a serious organization was to demonstrate that they could exercise power in a responsible manner. McIntyre made great play with the fact that as provost he was able to play an important role in securing new housing, municipal facilities, and a university for the town of Stirling. His position within the community was further enhanced by his work as a local doctor.

The period from 1974 to 1979 was tumultuous in Scottish politics and McIntyre, as SNP president (1958–80), worked hard to steer the party through many difficult obstacles. Ever the pragmatist, he tried to ensure the SNP would stick to its key objective of securing an electoral mandate for independence. He was suspicious of attempts to move the party to the left in an endeavour to capture disaffected Labour supporters, and opposed endeavours by nationalist militants to take direct action following the defeat of the 1979 referendum on devolution. He favoured expelling militants who, he argued, were diverting the party from its key objectives.

Although he resigned the party presidency in 1980, McIntyre still continued to play an active part in politics by contributing to policy debate, working for his constituency party and canvassing at elections. Unlike the SNP leadership, he lent his support to the Scottish convention in 1989, arguing that the party should not be dogmatic in its attitude about co-operating with others for home rule. Given the subsequent success of the convention, it proved to be a remarkably prescient observation. More than anybody, he is credited as the father of modern Scottish nationalism. McIntyre died at the Royal Infirmary, Stirling, on 2 February 1998 and was buried four days later at St Thomas cemetery, Stirling. His wife survived him.

RICHARD J. FINLAY

Sources NL Scot., McIntyre MSS · R. J. Finlay, *Independent and free: Scottish politics and the origins of the Scottish national party, 1918–1945* (1994) · *WW* · *The Scotsman* (5 Feb 1998) · *Glasgow Herald* (5 Feb 1998)
Archives NL Scot., political corresp. and papers | NL Scot., Donaldson MSS | SOUND BBC WAC
Likenesses portrait, Stirling Region Archives
Wealth at death £301,436.29: confirmation, 28 April 1998, *CCI*

MacIver, David Randall- (1873–1945), archaeologist and anthropologist, was born in London on 31 October 1873, the only son of John MacIver (*d.* 1875), shipowner, and his wife, Eliza Mary Rutherford. His father died a young man and his mother later married Richard Randall, barrister, whose name MacIver added to his own. He was educated at Radley College and was elected a scholar of Queen's College, Oxford, where he obtained a first class in *literae humaniores* in 1896.

While at Oxford MacIver also found time to investigate the subject of anthropology, and was much influenced by E. B. Tylor. His first ambition was to follow up this interest by work in Yucatán. This project, however, came to nothing and instead, having obtained an introduction to Flinders Petrie, he went to Egypt. From 1899 to 1901 he excavated at Abydos for the Egypt Exploration Fund (later Society), and from 1900 to 1906 he was Laycock student of Egyptology at Worcester College, Oxford. In Egypt he included measuring skulls among the other duties of an excavator and thus added a new and highly important item to the essential data to be compiled by a field worker. He undertook an anthropometrical study of this craniological material under the supervision of the anatomist Arthur Thomson. Their results were published as *The Ancient Races of the Thebaid* (1905). His many excavations during these years, and his able and prompt publication of reports on these early works, were of invaluable use to his successors in the field. Many of the major names in Egyptology in the first half of the twentieth century owed much to his pioneering work.

In 1905 Randall-MacIver went to Rhodesia at the invitation of the British Association and the Rhodes Trustees to excavate at Zimbabwe and other sites. Although much had been written about the immense antiquity of these ruins, MacIver was able to suggest in his book *Mediaeval Rhodesia* (1906; repr., 1971) a revised date of AD 1200 to 1500 (subsequently extended back to AD 1000 by others). In 1907 he was elected a fellow of the Society of Antiquaries of London.

After his Laycock studentship expired, Randall-MacIver, assisted by C. L. Woolley, directed (1907–11) an archaeological expedition in Nubia for the University Museum in Philadelphia, funded by a coal magnate, E. B. Coxe jun. His *Areika* (1909) described the Meroitic civilization of the black nations to the south of Egypt during the period of the Roman empire. In 1911 he married Joanna (*d.* 1931), daughter of W. H. Davidge, of New York, whom he had met through the Coxe family. In the same year he became librarian of the American Geographical Society, but in 1914, on the outbreak of the First World War in Europe, he returned immediately to England and served on the intelligence staff in both France and Macedonia.

After the war Randall-MacIver settled in Rome and this period was perhaps the most fruitful in his long and varied career. His publication of *Villanovans and Early Etruscans* (1924), which was produced during these years and which was perhaps his main achievement, was at the time an essential source for any student on the subject. To this period also belong other well-known books on Italian archaeology including *The Iron Age in Italy* (1927), *Italy before the Romans* (1928), and *Greek Cities in Italy and Sicily* (1931). Following his wife's death he continued to live in Rome, making visits to Rhodes, Syria, Cyprus, and the Balearic Islands, spending summers in the USA. In 1936 he married Mabel, daughter of Edward S. Holden, of St Louis, USA, and widow of George Tuttle, of New York.

In 1938 Randall-MacIver was elected FBA, an honour which greatly pleased him. He was in the United States on the outbreak of the Second World War in 1939 and although unable to take an active part in the war he nevertheless found activities of a quieter kind to employ his wide experience. Among these was his invaluable assistance to those charged by the United States war department with listing Italian monuments to be protected from destruction.

In the archaeological world Randall-MacIver was a much beloved and fascinating figure. His appearance throughout his life was extremely striking for he was very tall with bright blue eyes and wavy fair hair; to this was added a smiling sparkling charm of speech which gave a peculiar interest to everything he said and served to kindle in others his own unfailing enthusiasm and optimism. He was a worker with very high standards and he expected others to hold equal standards. Although he was intolerant of slipshod work or thought in any form, and never hesitated to denounce such weaknesses when he found them, he was also full of encouragement and interest in the efforts of others, and always ready to do anything within his power to help young students on the threshold of their own careers.

Randall-MacIver was always exceedingly proud of his highland origin. He was a complete stranger to any form of narrow nationalism and spent his life with equal serenity in England, Italy, or America. He died on 30 April 1945 at his residence in New York. His second wife survived him, but both marriages were childless.

T. C. HENCKEN, rev. S. STODDART

Sources personal knowledge (1959) · private information (1959) · D. Ridgway, 'David Randall-MacIver, 1873–1945', *PBA*, 69 (1983), 559–77 · W. R. Dawson and E. P. Uphill, *Who was who in Egyptology*, 3rd edn, rev. M. L. Bierbrier (1995)

Archives Queen's College, Oxford, autobiographical notes and papers | Bodl. Oxf., corresp. with J. L. Myres

Likenesses W. Stoneman, photograph, 1939, NPG · M. Heide, photograph, repro. in Ridgway, 'David Randall-MacIver, 1873–1945', facing p. 259

MacIver, Robert Morrison (1882–1970), political theorist and sociologist, was born on 17 April 1882 at North Beach Street, Stornoway, Isle of Lewis, the third child of Donald MacIver, a successful tweed merchant and a devout member of the Free Church of Scotland, and his wife, Christina Morrison. MacIver was schooled at the Nicholson Institute, Stornoway. His early childhood was happy, and he delighted in the outdoor life of the island, but in adolescence he concluded that he could not subscribe to his father's puritanical brand of Christianity, and began to feel oppressed by the piety of his home. His longing for escape was satisfied when, at the early age of sixteen, he won a scholarship to Edinburgh University. He took a first in classics in 1903. He then moved on to Oriel College, Oxford, where he took a first in Greats in 1907, in spite of having spent the week before his final examinations playing golf at Huntercombe.

Although his undergraduate studies had been in classics, MacIver's real interest lay in political theory and sociology, and in 1907 he became a lecturer in political science at Aberdeen. Here he began to develop his political ideas in a series of articles and in a book, *Community* (1917). MacIver was critical of the idealist school, which still dominated British political philosophy at this time, arguing that its exponents, in particular Bernard Bosanquet, had made dangerously inflated claims for the power of the state. He warned that the idealist state threatened to engulf other forms of human association. Instead MacIver advanced an alternative theory of the state, insisting that it was merely a subordinate organ of the wider community, and that its remit was thus strictly limited. He developed this idea of the state more fully in *The Modern State* (1926).

MacIver's thought was a notable contribution to the wider attack on the idealist theory of the state made around the time of the First World War. In this respect his ideas resembled those of pluralist authors such as Harold Laski and J. N. Figgis, and MacIver was sometimes wrongly bracketed with them. But whereas the pluralists disowned any idea that society had a common purpose, MacIver's theory of community emphasized its harmony and common purpose. His writings were notable for their optimistic belief in social progress and in the identity of interest between individual and society.

In 1915 MacIver accepted a chair in political science at Toronto. He was vice chairman of the Canadian War Labour Board from 1917 until 1919. He spent the rest of his career in North America, which he greatly preferred to what he saw as the class-ridden society of Britain. Paradoxically, though, it was in Britain that his writings were most acclaimed; among British champions of his ideas were James Bryce, George Unwin, Ernest Barker, and Archbishop William Temple.

In 1927 MacIver moved to Columbia University, where, as Lieber professor of political philosophy and sociology from 1929 until 1950, he sought to develop the teaching of sociology. He produced several more books, among them *Society: a Textbook of Sociology* (1937), *Leviathan and the People* (1939), and *The Web of Government* (1947). But his writings lost their vogue after the Second World War. His interdisciplinary approach and his optimism about society seemed dated, and he felt increasingly at odds with the direction taken by academic sociology, deploring its obsession with quantitative method. His versatility meant that he was nevertheless still in great demand as the author of official reports. He published research studies on academic freedom, race relations, the United Nations, and juvenile delinquency. Between 1963 and 1966 he was successively president and chancellor of the New School for Social Research in New York. He received eight honorary degrees, and was a fellow of both the Royal Society of Canada and the American Academy of Arts and Sciences and a corresponding fellow of the British Academy.

On 14 August 1911 MacIver married Ethel Marion Peterkin (*b*. 1884/5), who had been one of his students at Aberdeen. In his autobiography, *As a Tale that is Told* (1968), he described this as a very happy union, though he also alluded to some extramarital affairs. MacIver had three children, of whom one son predeceased him. He died at the Columbia Presbyterian Medical Center, New York, on 15 June 1970. MATTHEW GRIMLEY

Sources R. M. MacIver, *As a tale that is told* (Chicago, 1968) [autobiography] • *The Scotsman* (17 June 1970) • *Oriel College Record* (1970–

71) • J. M. Jordan, 'MacIver, Robert Morrison', *ANB* • *WWW* • b. cert. • m. cert.
Archives Col. U., MSS

MacKail [MacKaile], **Hugh** (1640/41–1666), Church of Scotland minister and martyr, was born at Liberton, near Edinburgh, the son of Matthew MacKail (*fl.* 1620–1674), a minister of the Church of Scotland who was deprived of his living and expelled from his parish at Bothwell in 1662. Raised in a family of clergymen, steeped in the uncompromising traditions and principles of lowland presbyterianism, Hugh proved—from the very first—to be an exceptionally gifted child, renowned for his precocious talents, strong religious calling, and deep-seated learning. Having been sent away to Edinburgh to live with his uncle, also Hugh MacKail (*d.* 1660), he studied divinity at the university there under the close supervision and direction of Thomas Crawford. Having graduated in 1658, he took up an influential position, first as tutor and then as chaplain, in the household of Sir James Stewart of Coltness and Kirkfield, the then lord provost of Edinburgh. Had it not been for the Restoration, and the re-establishment of the prelacy, it seems likely that MacKail would have been well placed to have enjoyed a prominent, though perhaps less remarkable, career at the heart of the established kirk.

In the winter of 1661 the presbytery licensed MacKail to preach in Edinburgh. However, even though his sermons won him a considerable following in the city, and the support of an enthusiastic congregation, his own ministry was to prove to be remarkably short-lived. His last sermon was preached at St Giles's Cathedral in September 1662, on the sabbath immediately before the 8 September deadline set by the authorities for the removal of those ministers from Edinburgh who had refused to accept the episcopalian remodelling of the church government. In his sermon he powerfully denounced those statesmen and prelates who had deprived Christ's flock of trusted shepherds. God's people, he concluded, were sometimes to be persecuted 'by a Pharaoh upon the Throne, sometimes by a Haman in the State, [and] sometimes by a Judas in the Church'. The stark analogy drawn between these biblical figures and Charles II, the earl of Rothes, and Archbishop Sharp, respectively, could not have been clearer or more devastatingly couched, and the sermon was neither overlooked nor afterwards forgiven by those at whom its censure had been aimed (MacKail, 3–25). A troop of horsemen was immediately dispatched to Kirkfield House, which lay on the outskirts of the city, with an order for the chaplain's arrest. However, with the probable connivance of the family and servants of his wealthy patron, MacKail effected a rapid escape and took refuge at his father's house in Bothwell. He spent the next three years in exile in the Low Countries, probably including some time at or near Rotterdam, in the company of other Scottish exiles and foreign protestant theologians working out of the university there. He certainly devoted his time to prayer and biblical study, and won a formidable reputation among his peers for both his keen intellect and the charismatic style of his preaching.

MacKail slipped back into Scotland and was active in the

west of the country immediately before the outbreak of the Pentland rising, and joined the main body of the insurgents on 18 November 1666. However, his scholarly frame was not cut out for the rigours of military life, and the hard conditions in camp on the open moorlands effectively served to break his health. During the march through Ayr he had to be supported in the saddle by his friends, and at Colinton, on 27 November, the day before battle was finally joined with the government forces, he was forced to withdraw from the field. His departure could not have been worse timed, as the covenanter host was already beginning to break up, as the anticipated general rising in the west did not materialize, and as desertions were becoming a daily occurrence. Heading across open country towards Liberton parish, in search of refuge at his father's temporary home, while still bearing arms he was seized by local scouts loyal to the government and in the pay of General Thomas Dalyell, and was taken into custody close to the promontory of Braids Crags. Even then MacKail might have saved himself and talked his way out of danger, but his refusal to answer the most basic of questions as to his identity and intentions quickly brought him to the notice of an officer of dragoons, who had him conveyed to Edinburgh under guard.

Once inside the city walls MacKail was thoroughly searched by the authorities for any secret correspondence which might have revealed the intentions of the rebel army. When nothing was found, he was committed to the Tolbooth to be brought before the earl of Dumfries and the other members of the Scottish privy council the very next morning. He was interviewed on 28 November, just as General Dalyell's soldiers were advancing upon Rullion Green in order to engage the insurgents in a decisive battle, and it is this timing, given the uncertainty of the authorities as to the outcome of this engagement, which may satisfactorily explain their particular zeal in mounting an unprecedentedly harsh and gruelling interrogation of their young victim. At this point MacKail's refusal to accept the authority of those present to try him, and his continued reluctance to say anything at all in his own defence, served to arouse both the hatred and suspicion of the council, who now came to expect 'vast Discoveries' from him about a major plot linking the activities of the Scottish rebels with those of English radicals and Dutch republicans (Wodrow, 1.259). Having been wrongly identified as one of the guiding lights behind the Pentland rising, MacKail was interviewed again the next day. He sought to present the rebellion primarily as an act of self-defence in response to the free quartering of troops and the enforcement of fines for nonconformity upon the citizens of Dumfries and Galloway. On 3 December he was once again brought before the council, with the earl of Rothes and the marquess of Montrose assuming a pivotal role in the increasingly brutal manner in which he was treated. Having refused to incriminate any of his friends, or to name any rebel sympathizers still at large within the city of Edinburgh, he was shown a pair of iron boots and threatened with torture by them unless he confessed all

he knew and turned king's evidence against his former comrades.

The passage of the night failed to break MacKail's resolve, and on 4 December he was duly 'tortured and examined in the bootes' (*Reg. PCS*, 231), which were tightened ten or eleven times. Wedges were driven into his shin bone, and his leg was shattered by their continual application. Unable to walk, or even to stand, he was laid low by fever, and on 11 December he argued for a delay in his trial so that he might have space to recover from his injuries. Indeed, so serious had been his experience under torture that Bishop Gilbert Burnet believed him to have died from it. MacKail's family and supporters were not idle in attempting to gain him a reprieve, and appeals for his release were directed towards many courtiers and the womenfolk of the influential Douglas clan. His cousin, Matthew *MacKail, a well-known Edinburgh apothecary, sought out and petitioned Archbishop James Sharp, first at his residence in the Scottish capital and then at his seat in St Andrews. However, Sharp recalled only too well the sermon delivered against him from the pulpit of St Giles's, and refused point-blank to add his voice to the chorus demanding a pardon. On 18 December, though still unrecovered, Hugh MacKail was examined by Lord Renton, the justice clerk, and by Sir William Murray. Even though he had left the ranks of the insurgents before fighting had commenced, it was judged that his presence on the march through Ayr, Ochiltree, and Lanark—where he had been 'seen on horseback … carrying a sword with the rebels'—was more than enough to secure his conviction for high treason. On the announcement that he was to be executed at the Mercat Cross, in Edinburgh, on Saturday 22 December 1666, a large crowd turned up outside the courtroom to voice its support for him, and it was with some difficulty that his escort bore him back to his cell in the Tolbooth.

According to his contemporary biographer, Sir James Stewart, it was in the last days and hours of his life that MacKail's strength of character showed itself most forcefully. While in prison he passed his time composing Latin epigrams, and distinguished himself by both his stoical acceptance of his fate and by his good humour, in consistently trying to revive the spirits and harden the resolve of his fellow captives. He was determined to make his progress to the gallows a memorable and instructive occasion for all of those who still sought to adhere to the principles of the Scottish national covenant. His youth, frail physique, and delicate beauty excited comment and compassion from the spectators, and, having surrendered his hat and cloak to his guards, he prayed on the scaffold before ascending the ladder, exclaiming to the crowds below that every rung brought him 'a degree nearer heaven' (Stewart, 270). Perched atop the cross beams of the gallows, Bible in hand, he read to them from the last chapter of the Revelation of St John, and told them that they should not blame the judges or executioners, but the prelates who had brought ruin upon the land. The unprecedented freedom he was allowed in addressing his supporters was due in part to the generous bribes handed out by his family to the executioner, and, when he came to be turned off the gallows, the hangman permitted his cousin to break through the lines of soldiers to pull down upon his legs and thereby end his agony. The payment of bribes also ensured that MacKail's body was laid out in the Magdalene Chapel and dressed there for burial, and, even though he was still interred in the corner of the east dyke at Grey-friars churchyard normally reserved for criminals, 'a great company of honest men' and sympathizers was permitted to accompany his corpse, either that evening or the next day, to the graveside (*Memoirs of Mr. William Veitch and George Brysson*, 37n.).

Though guileless and little suited to a world of violence—he almost betrayed a comrade unwittingly by a spontaneous display of emotion upon seeing him again in the streets of Edinburgh, following the collapse of the Pentland rising—MacKail was seen to be morally and physically courageous at times of the grimmest adversity. By the manner of his exemplary death he helped to establish a pattern of self-conscious martyrdom enacted throughout the lowlands by numerous Scottish covenanters during the 'killing times' of the 1670s and 1680s. Despite MacKail's being dead long before the events described, there is good evidence that Sir Walter Scott based his character Ephraim Macbriar, in *Old Mortality*, partly upon him: the young preacher, half invalid, who underwent vigils, rigours, and imprisonment for the sake of his cause and in the name of personal faith, without once breaking under torture and surrendering his friends up to the hangman's noose.   JOHN CALLOW

Sources J. Stewart, *Naphtali, or, The wrestlings of the Church of Scotland for the kingdom of Christ* (1667); repr. (1845) • H. MacKail, *The last publick sermon, being a faithful and free one, preached by Mr. Hugh Mac-Kaile, preacher of the gospel at Edinburgh, in the Old Church there* (1749) • *Memoirs of Mr. William Veitch and George Brysson*, ed. T. M'Crie (1825) • W. McGavin, ed., *Memoirs of John Brown of Priesthill and the Rev. Hugh MacKail* (1839) • *Bishop Burnet's History*, vol. 1 • R. Wodrow, *The history of the sufferings of the Church of Scotland, from the Restauration to the revolution*, 1 (1721) • *Reg. PCS*, 3rd ser., vol. 2 • *Memoirs of Rev. John Blackader*, ed. A. Crichton (1823) • C. S. Terry, *The Pentland rising and Rullion Green* (1905) • J. K. Hewison, *The covenanters: a history of the church in Scotland from the Reformation to the revolution*, 2nd edn, 2 (1913) • W. H. Carslaw, preface, in J. Howie, *The Scots worthies*, ed. W. H. Carslaw, [new edn] (1870), ix–xv • Anderson, *Scot. nat.*, vol. 3

Wealth at death could not have been considerable; property declared forfeit following conviction for treason, 18 Dec 1666, and acted upon following execution 22 Dec: *Reg. PCS*, 3rd ser., 2.236

Mackail, John William (1859–1945), classical scholar, literary critic, and poet, was born at Ascog in the parish of Kingarth, Isle of Bute, on 26 August 1859, the only son and second child of the Revd John Mackail, a Free Church minister who, after service in Malta and Calcutta, had retired in 1852 owing to ill health, and his wife, Louisa Irving, youngest daughter of Aglionby Ross *Carson, rector of Edinburgh high school. He was educated at Ayr Academy, where the rector was James Macdonald, father of Sir George Macdonald with whom Mackail formed a close friendship. In 1874 he entered Edinburgh University and was greatly influenced by W. Y. Sellar, then professor of humanity, by whose advice he sat for a scholarship at

John William Mackail (1859–1945), by Elliott & Fry

Balliol College, Oxford. He was elected to the Warner exhibition (1877) with the rank of honorary scholar.

Benjamin Jowett was then master of Balliol and Mackail's tutors were Evelyn Abbott, R. L. Nettleship, and J. L. Strachan-Davidson, with whom he maintained a lasting friendship. Mackail obtained first classes in classical moderations (1879) and *literae humaniores* (1881), won the Hertford (1880), Ireland (1880), Craven (1882), and Derby (1884) university scholarships, and was without question the most brilliant undergraduate scholar of his time. He was also awarded the Newdigate prize in 1881 for a poem on Thermopylae. He joined with H. C. Beeching and Bowyer Nichols in producing three volumes of verse entitled *Mensae secundae* (1879), *Love in Idleness* (1883), and *Love's Looking-Glass* (1891), and contributed to the series of college epigrams known as *The Masque of B-ll--l* (1881), on which he wrote an article in *The Times* in 1939.

In 1882 Mackail was elected to a fellowship at Balliol, but instead of pursuing the academic career which lay open to him, in 1884 he accepted a place in the education department of the privy council, which later became the Board of Education. Appointed assistant secretary in 1903, he took a prominent part in the establishment of a system of secondary education under the act of 1902, and in organizing the inspection voluntarily sought by many of the public schools. When in 1919 he resigned from the board his official life was over.

Meanwhile side by side with his work in the office Mackail was developing the life of a writer and critic, in which he was destined to reach high distinction, if not a wide popular appeal. His writings fall naturally into three main classes: those on classical poetry, those on general literature, and biographies. At first, as was natural, Greek and Latin literature claimed his attention and that interest was never lost. In 1885 he published a translation in prose of Virgil's *Aeneid*; its manner was traditional and, apart from an occasional brilliant phrase, it was not striking. Virgil (he insisted that this was the correct English spelling of the name) remained always his main interest among Latin poets. He completed his prose translation by versions of the *Eclogues* and *Georgics*, published together in 1889, wrote of him in his *Latin Literature* (1895) and in articles included in subsequent books, and in 1923 contributed a volume entitled *Virgil and his Meaning to the World of To-Day* to the American series Our Debt to Greece and Rome. The culmination of his work in this field was reached in 1930, when he published an edition of the *Aeneid*; in this he purposely excluded detailed comment on text, grammar, and metre, and treated it as a great work of poetry, noting points of diction and expression passed over by previous editors, often suggesting the exact English equivalent, and insisting upon the structure of the whole poem and its individual books.

Mackail's best-known contribution to the study of Latin in general was the volume entitled *Latin Literature*. His works on Greek, if not so numerous, are substantial and important. In 1890, at the age of thirty, he published a remarkable edition of *Select Epigrams from the Greek Anthology*. The poems are accompanied by neat prose translations and the notes treat them as living expressions of vital experience. In 1903, 1905, and 1910 appeared three volumes of a translation of the *Odyssey*, this time not in prose but in a rhyming quatrain; the verse runs smoothly, but most readers have probably felt that the vehicle does not aptly reproduce Homer. In 1910 Mackail also published a volume of *Lectures on Greek Poetry*; he treats it as a continuous whole, regarding Homer as 'medieval', Sophocles as fully classical, and the Alexandrians as the Romantics in the first stages of decline.

In 1906 Mackail was elected professor of poetry at Oxford, and in the five years of his tenure of the chair attracted large audiences and covered a wide field. Three volumes resulted: the *Lectures on Greek Poetry* have already been noticed, but in the other two he passed outside the classics into his second field and revealed his knowledge of the poetry of other languages and in particular of English. *The Springs of Helicon* (1909) is devoted to studies of Chaucer, Spenser, and Milton; he sets each in his own background and regards them as constituting a progressive development. In the *Lectures on Poetry* (1911), a more miscellaneous collection, Mackail included not only Dante, but Arabic poetry, regarded as the precursor of French ballad epics. There are also two lectures on Shakespeare, who held for Mackail in English poetry the place occupied in Latin by Virgil, and to him he returned in 1930

in his *Approach to Shakespeare*, which includes an enlightening analysis of each of the plays. *Studies of English Poets* (1926) and *Studies in Humanism* (1938) are collections of essays and lectures written at different times.

The third field of Mackail's activity was that of biography. *The Life and Letters of George Wyndham*, which he published with Guy Wyndham in two volumes in 1925, and the memoir of his old tutor Strachan-Davidson (1926), are both sympathetic portraits, but the *Life of William Morris* (1899) is an important study, although Mackail's undisguised dislike of Morris's revolutionary convictions resulted in an inadequate treatment of his later political activities and writings.

In 1888 Mackail married Margaret, only daughter of the painter Edward Burne-*Jones; they had one son and two daughters. The son, Denis Mackail (1892–1971), and the elder daughter, Angela *Thirkell, made reputations as novelists.

Many honours came to Mackail. He was president of the Classical Association, which he helped to found, in 1922–3; he was also president of the English Association in 1929–30 and of the newly formed Virgil Society in 1945. In 1914 he was elected FBA and served as president from 1932 to 1936. In 1924 he was appointed professor of ancient literature in the Royal Academy. He received honorary degrees from the universities of Edinburgh, St Andrews, Oxford, Cambridge, London, Belfast, and Adelaide. He was elected an honorary fellow of Balliol in 1922. In 1935 he was appointed OM.

Mackail was a tall man and always good-looking; in later life his white hair added a dignity and beauty to his face. He had a fine voice and a meticulously clear enunciation, enhanced by a trace of Scottish intonation. He was suave and courteous and always an interesting talker, but reticent as to his own beliefs and feelings. He died at his home, 6 Pembroke Gardens, Kensington, London, on 13 December 1945.   CYRIL BAILEY, rev. RICHARD SMAIL

Sources C. Bailey, 'John William Mackail, 1859–1945', *PBA*, 31 (1945), 245–55 · *The Times* (14 Dec 1945) · *CGPLA Eng. & Wales* (1946) · *WWW*

Archives Balliol Oxf., notebooks · NRA, corresp. and literary papers · William Morris Gallery, Walthamstow, notes for *Life of William Morris* | Balliol Oxf., corresp. with J. L. Strachan-Davidson and literary MSS · BL, corresp. incl. family corresp. with Sir Sydney Cockerell, Add. MS 52734 · BL, corresp. with Macmillans, Add. MS 55127 · Bodl. Oxf., corresp. with Robert Bridges · Bodl. Oxf., letters to various members of the Lewis family · Bodl. Oxf., corresp. with Gilbert Murray · Bodl. Oxf., corresp. relating to Society for Protection of Science and Learning · JRL, letters to Samuel Alexander · NL Wales, letters to T. E. Ellis · RS, letters to the Royal Society

Likenesses Elliott & Fry, photograph, NPG [*see illus.*] · photograph, repro. in *PBA*

Wealth at death £12,662 13s. 11d.: probate, 6 June 1946, *CGPLA Eng. & Wales*

Mackail, Matthew (*fl.* **1657–1696**), apothecary and physician, was the son of Hew Mackail (d. 1660), a clergyman who was appointed minister of Percietown in 1633 and was subsequently translated to Irvine and Trinity College Church, Edinburgh, and Sibilla Stevenson (d. 1665/6). He became an apothecary in Edinburgh, where he achieved the status of burgess and guildbrother on 11 November

1658. During the previous year he had spent some time at the instigation of James Sharp, the future archbishop of St Andrews, in London, where he wrote a number of papers on matters of religion and the church. When his cousin Hugh Mackail was imprisoned in the tolbooth of Edinburgh in 1666 for covenanting activities Matthew Mackail appealed on his behalf to Archbishop Sharp, but to no avail, as his cousin was subsequently hanged; Mackail apparently endeavoured to ease his cousin's suffering by pulling his legs while he hung from the gallows in order to hasten death. Mackail then moved to Aberdeen, where he practised medicine, and obtained the degree of MD from King's College on 14 July 1696. Mackail was a prolific author on medical and scientific—particularly chemical—matters. Among his many publications were: *Descriptio topographico-spagyrica fontium mineralium Moffatensium in Annandia Scotiae* (1659), which was subsequently translated into English and published in Edinburgh in 1664 'with a Description of the City Well at Saint Catherine's Chapel in the parish of Libberton, together with the Description of a monstrous Child, born and living in Caithness' (Robertson, 320); *Moffet-Well* (Edinburgh 1664), with 'a Character of Mr Culpepper and his writings' (ibid.); *Noli me tangere tactus, seu, Tractatulus de cancre curatione* (Rotterdam, 1675); *Macis macerata, or, A Short Treatise Concerning the Use of Mace* (Aberdeen, 1677); *The Diversitie of Salts and Spirits* (Aberdeen, 1683); *Terrae prodromus theoricus* (Aberdeen, 1691). The publications have a clear chemical bias, which reflects Mackail's background as an apothecary. The poll tax records for 1696 reveal him as living in Aberdeen with his wife and son. A portrait of Mackail is in the possession of Marischal College. The date of Mackail's death is unknown.

A son, **Matthew Mackail** (1691/2–1733), graduated MA from Marischal College, Aberdeen, in 1708; he subsequently matriculated as a student of medicine at the University of Leiden on 9 December 1712 at the age of twenty and gained his MD degree from the University of Rheims on 15 July 1713. He returned to Aberdeen and on 8 October 1717 was appointed professor of medicine of Marischal College, replacing Patrick Chalmers, who had been expelled by the commission of visitation for participation in the Jacobite uprising of 1715. On 15 November 1729 Mackail was appointed regent in philosophy in addition to his chair of medicine, and gave his inaugural lecture, comparing Copernican and Newtonian philosophies, on 4 December 1729. He died in May 1733, and his inventory, recorded on 19 March 1734, revealed assets, including books, valued at £352 sterling. The inventory also records that he had three children, William, James, and Isobel.

[ANON.], *rev.* HELEN M. DINGWALL

Sources J. Robertson, *Book of bon accord, or, A guide to the city of Aberdeen* (1839) · J. D. Comrie, *History of Scottish medicine*, 2nd edn, 2 vols. (1932) · E. H. B. Rodger, *Aberdeen doctors at home and abroad* (1893) · C. Innes, ed., *Fasti Aberdonenses ... 1494–1854*, Spalding Club, 26 (1854) · C. B. B. Watson, ed., *Roll of Edinburgh burgesses and guild-brethren, 1406–1700*, Scottish RS, 59 (1929) · R. W. Innes Smith, *English-speaking students of medicine at the University of Leyden* (1932) · Wing, *STC* · *Fasti Scot.*, new edn · J. Stuart, ed., *List of pollable persons in the shire of Aberdeen, 1696*, Spalding Club (1844)

Likenesses portrait, Marischal College, Aberdeen

Wealth at death £352—Matthew Mackail (1691/2–1733): NA Scot., commissariot court register of testaments CC 1/6/15, 19 March 1734

Mackail, Matthew (1691/2–1733). *See under* Mackail, Matthew (*fl.* 1657–1696).

Mackarell [Makkarell], **Matthew** (*d.* 1537), abbot of Barlings, was probably of Scottish descent, and born to parents in the service of the first duke of Norfolk. He had entered the Premonstratensian abbey of Cockersand in Lancashire as a novice by 1497, and was professed as a canon, ordained priest, and appointed sacristan there by 1500. He clearly asked for a licence to study at Cambridge, to which he went early in the sixteenth century, and had obtained his BTh degree by 1510. From Cambridge he probably proceeded to Freiburg-im-Breisgau, where he gained his doctorate in theology before returning to England about 1516. By 1519 he was abbot of Alnwick, Northumberland, and by 1529 of Barlings, Lincolnshire. By 1524, he was a bishop-suffragan first in the diocese of York, then of Lincoln, with the title of bishop of Chalcedon.

Mackarrell's was not the quiet life that his bare biographical details suggest. He was the chosen preacher (perhaps because of a family affiliation) at the funeral of the second duke of Norfolk in May 1524, and such was his sermon on death that the congregation was said to have fled the church, leaving it to the preacher and the corpse. As abbot of Barlings he played a somewhat ambiguous role in the Lincolnshire rebellion of 1536, itself the precursor to the Pilgrimage of Grace. He would later claim that the common people intimidated him, but in view of his previous record that is unlikely, and clearly he regarded the dissolution of the lesser monasteries in 1536 as daylight robbery. Accordingly, he seems to have taken precautions to dispose of some of the wealth of his house, sensing that it would not be too long before the greater monasteries went the way of the lesser. There is much evidence to suggest that he provided the rebels with food and hospitality. He was accused by Edward Dymock and other gentlemen that on 'dyvers tymes' he had urged the rebels 'to goo forwarde' (PRO, E 36/118, p. 1). It seems unlikely that he was uninvolved, but some of the accusations against him by interested parties, notably that he had plundered the house of John Freeman, are improbable. The anticlericalism of the courts he faced at Lincoln and London, and the suggestion of Scottish ancestry possibly conveyed by his name and early residence near the border, may have made Mackerell a man of few friends. In any event, he was executed as a traitor at Tyburn on 29 March 1537 and buried the same day at Pardon churchyard, London. Judged by the letter of the law he appears to have been guilty; had he not been a canon, probably a Scot, and a theologian, he might have fared better.

MARGARET BOWKER

Sources H. M. Colvin, *The white canons in England* (1951) · M. H. Dodds and R. Dodds, *The Pilgrimage of Grace, 1536–1537, and the Exeter conspiracy, 1538*, 2 vols. (1915); repr. (1971) · F. A. Gasquet, ed., *Collectanea Anglo-Premonstratensia*, 3 vols., CS, 3rd ser., 6, 10, 12 (1904–6), nos. 308, 309 · Venn, *Alum. Cant.*, 1/3.124 · G. Brenan and

E. P. Statham, *The house of Howard*, 1 (1907) • M. Bowker, 'Lincolnshire, 1536: heresy, schism or religious discontent', *Schism, heresy and religious protest*, ed. D. Baker, SCH, 9 (1972), 195–212 • exchequer, treasury of receipt, miscellaneous books, PRO, E 36/118, p. 1

Mackarness, John Fielder (1820–1889), bishop of Oxford, eldest son of John Mackarness, a West India merchant of Elstree House, Bath (*d.* 2 January 1870), who married on 8 June 1819 Catherine, daughter of George Smith Coxhead MD, was born at Islington, London, on 3 December 1820. He was educated at Eton, a pupil of Dr Okes, later provost of King's College, Cambridge, and was a king's scholar from 1832. He matriculated from Merton College, Oxford, in 1840, and was postmaster from that year until 1844. At Eton he was captain of the football club; he rowed in the Merton boat, and was president of the Oxford Union. In 1843 he took a second class in classics, graduating BA in 1844. He was ordained deacon by Bishop Bagot in 1844, and priest by Bishop Pepys of Worcester. His subsequent degrees were MA (1847) and DD (1869).

On 30 June 1844 Mackarness was elected to a fellowship at Exeter College, which he vacated on 11 August 1846 after receiving preferment in the church. From 11 August 1845 to 1855 he held the vicarage of Tardebigge in Worcestershire, and was presented by Bishop Pepys on the recommendation of Bishop Selwyn as an honorary canon of Worcester Cathedral, a post he held from 1854 to 1858. He married at Ottery St Mary, Devon, on 7 August 1849, Alethea Buchanan, youngest daughter of Sir John Taylor *Coleridge. They had three sons and four daughters.

On the nomination of William Courtenay, eleventh Earl Devon, Mackarness was appointed to the rectory of Honiton, Devon, in 1855. In Honiton he was responsible for the management of Honiton grammar school, and for building a new national school and a chapel for the workhouse. He developed the Honiton Church Association and served as a diocesan inspector of schools. He remained at Honiton until his appointment to the episcopal bench, holding with it from 1858 a prebendal stall in Exeter Cathedral, and from 1867 the adjoining vicarage of Monkton. In 1865 he was elected as proctor in convocation for that diocese, but lost his seat in 1869 through declining to oppose the disestablishment of the Irish church. Mackarness saw it as a political question which would not be helped by clerical interference.

On the recommendation of Gladstone, Mackarness was appointed to the see of Oxford; he was consecrated bishop on 25 January 1870 and invested as chancellor of the Garter on 5 February 1870. Personally a high-churchman, Mackarness supported a high conception of the responsibilities of the ministerial office and the authority of the church. He supported sisterhoods and guarded use of private confession, but recognized that excessive ceremonial was objectionable to some. As a bishop he did not require everyone to share his views. His love of peace led him to wish for the dissolution of party organizations such as the English Church Union and the Church Association, and to establish a diocesan conference to promote greater unity in the diocese.

John Fielder Mackarness (1820–1889), by Walter William Ouless, 1881

Mackarness was unwilling to become party to the lawsuits against ritualists under the Public Worship Regulation Act. When an attempt was made to force him to take proceedings against Thomas Thellusson Carter, the rector of Clewer, he argued the case for the right of episcopal veto in person before the judges of the Queen's Bench Division. Judgment went against him, but on carrying the case to the Court of Appeal it was given in his favour, and this decision was confirmed by the House of Lords (1880). He saw it as a bishop's duty to deal with clerical discipline, not to satisfy an aggrieved third party.

A Liberal in politics, Mackarness voted in the Lords against the Anglo-Afghan War and the Public Worship Regulation Act. He supported the Burial Laws Amendment Act in 1880, and approved the removal of religious tests in the universities, saying that they did harm to the causes of religion. He came to fear the spread of anti-Christian views at Oxford, denouncing in his second charge to the clergy (1875) the creed of hedonism and Materialism which he detected in Walter Pater's *Studies in the History of the Renaissance* (1873). On surrendering to the ecclesiastical commissioners the management of the Oxford bishopric estates, Mackarness paid them £1729, his estimation of the surplus he had made from them.

Mackarness was the author of numerous sermons and charges, and until his elevation to the see of Oxford he regularly contributed to *The Guardian*. His chief publications were *A Few Words to the Country Parsons on the Election for Oxford University* (1847), in support of Gladstone, and *A Plea for Toleration, in Answer to the No Popery Cry* (1850), when he was the only clerical opponent in the Worcester diocese of the Eccesiastical Titles Bill. With the Revd Richard Seymour he edited in 1862 a volume called *Eighteen years of a clerical meeting, being the minutes of the Alcester Clerical Association, 1842–60*. A sermon by him on the death of Lord Lyttelton, to whom he was honorary chaplain, 1855–69, appeared in *Brief Memorials of Lord Lyttelton* (1876). Failing health compelled him to retire in August 1888, his resignation taking legal effect on 17 November 1888. Mackarness died at Angus House, Granville Road, Eastbourne, on 16 September 1889, and was buried on 21 September in Sandhurst churchyard, Berkshire. He was survived by his wife.

W. P. COURTNEY, *rev.* ELLIE CLEWLOW

Sources C. C. Mackarness, *Memorials of the episcopate of John Fielder Mackarness* (1892) • C. W. Boase, ed., *Registrum Collegii Exoniensis*, new edn, OHS, 27 (1894) • J. Bentley, *Ritualism and politics in Victorian Britain* (1978) • P. T. Marsh, *The Victorian church in decline: Archbishop Tait and the Church of England, 1868–1882* (1969) • J. F. Mackarness, 'May or must': a letter to the venerable Alfred Pott, archdeacon of Berks, on a recent case in the court of the queen's bench*, 2nd edn (1879) • W. Ince, *A memory of Bishop Mackarness: a sermon preached in the cathedral church of Christ in Oxford, 22 Sept 1889* (1890) • O. Chadwick, *The Victorian church*, 2nd edn, 2 vols. (1970–72) • Foster, *Alum. Oxon.* • *The Guardian* (25 Sept 1889) • J. S. Reynolds, *The evangelicals at Oxford, 1735–1871: a record of an unchronicled movement*, [2nd edn] (1975) • Boase, *Mod. Eng. biog.*
Archives BL, corresp. with W. E. Gladstone, Add. MSS 44422–44493 • LPL, corresp. with A. C. Tait
Likenesses W. W. Ouless, oils, 1881, Cuddesdon College, Oxford [*see illus.*] • Hill & Saunders, photograph, repro. in Mackarness, *Memorials of the episcopate of John Fielder Mackarness* • bronze plaque with portrait medallion, Christ Church Oxf. • portrait, repro. in *Church Portrait Journal*, 3 (1882), 65 • portrait, repro. in *Illustrated Times* (26 Jan 1870), 73 • wood-engraving (after photograph by W. T. & R. Gowland), NPG; repro. in *ILN*, 56 (1 Jan 1870), 13–14
Wealth at death £16,470 4s. 7d.: probate, 5 Nov 1889, *CGPLA Eng. & Wales*

Mackarness [*née* Planché], **Matilda Anne** (1825–1881), children's writer, born on 23 November 1825, was the younger daughter of the playwright James Robinson *Planché (1796–1880) and of Elizabeth St George (1796–1846), also a playwright. From an early age Matilda Anne Planché wrote novels and moral tales for children. As a novelist she took Dickens for her model and cited *The Chimes* as the inspiration for *Old Joliffe*, published in 1845, and *A Sequel to Old Joliffe* (1846). In 1849 she published the work on which her reputation chiefly rested, *A Trap to Catch a Sunbeam*, a brightly written little tale emphasizing the value of domestic virtues. It was composed some three years before the date of publication, and went through forty-two editions, the last appearing in 1882, and was translated into many foreign languages, including Hindustani.

On 21 December 1852 Matilda Anne Planché married, at Holy Trinity Church, Brompton, London, the Revd Henry S. Mackarness, son of John Mackarness (*d.* 1870), a West India merchant, and Catherine Smith. He was the brother of John Fielder Mackarness, bishop of Oxford, and of George R. Mackarness, bishop of Argyll and the Isles. The couple settled in his first parish at Dymchurch, Hythe, Kent. They afterwards went to Ash-next-Sandwich, Kent, where Mackarness was vicar, until his death on 26 December 1868. He left very slender provision for his widow and her seven children; four others had died in infancy. She went to live with her father in London, first at Chelsea, and afterwards at Clapham.

Matilda Anne Mackarness wrote more than forty books for children, averaging at least one publication per year from 1849 to the time of her death. Many of her books were successful in America as well as in Britain. She also contributed to the *Magnet Stories* (1860–62), wrote a collection of 'ballad stories' for the *Girl's Own Paper*, edited *The Young Lady's Book* (1876), and edited and contributed several stories to a publication called *Lights and Shadows* (1879). Some of her tales were collected and published as the Sunbeam Series.

Matilda Anne Mackarness died on 6 May 1881 at 1 Royal Crescent, Margate, Kent. She was buried beside her husband in Ash-next-Sandwich churchyard. One more work, *A Woman without a Head* (1892), was published posthumously from a manuscript which had been lost for twelve years.

ELIZABETH LEE, *rev.* VICTORIA MILLAR

Sources *The Athenaeum* (28 May 1881), 720–21 • private information (1893) [Mrs Mackarness's daughter] • J. R. Planché, *The recollections and reflections of J. R. Planché*, 2 (1872), 149 • Allibone, *Dict.* • H. G. Adams, ed., *A cyclopaedia of female biography* (1857) • Boase, *Mod. Eng. biog.* • BL cat. • IGI

Mackay, Aeneas James George (1839–1911), legal and historical writer, born at Edinburgh on 3 November 1839, was the only son of Thomas George Mackay, writer to the signet, and his wife, Mary, daughter of John Kirkcaldy of Baldovie, Forfarshire. He was educated at Edinburgh Academy, and proceeded to King's College, London, where he gained distinction in divinity and history. He continued his study at University College, Oxford, where he matriculated on 28 April 1858 and graduated BA in 1862, with a second in the school of law and history; he proceeded MA in 1865. He then went to Heidelberg, and finally he completed his legal education at Edinburgh University, where he was one of the first to obtain the degree of LLB.

Mackay was called to the Scottish bar on 1 December 1864, and soon acquired a considerable practice, being sought rather for his written opinions than for his powers of oratory. He devoted much time to further study in law and history, and in 1874 he succeeded Cosmo Innes as professor of constitutional law and history at Edinburgh University. While he occupied this chair he brought out his greatest work, *The Practice of the Court of Session* (2 vols., 1877–9) which was still a standard authority in the early twentieth century. In 1881 he was appointed advocate-depute by Lord Balfour, then lord advocate, and he resigned his chair at Edinburgh on 31 July of that year.

In 1886 Mackay was made sheriff-principal of Fife and Kinross, an office which he filled with distinction for fifteen years. Since a sheriffdom was not an exclusively judicial office, Mackay was able to take silk in 1897. Nominated by Lord Robertson (who was at that time lord president), he was one of the first Scottish barristers in private practice to become queen's counsel, an honour which until then had been available in Scotland only to law officers, former law officers, and deans of the Faculty of Advocates.

Aeneas James George Mackay (1839–1911), by John Henry Lorimer, 1890

Mackay wrote prolifically on both legal and historical matters, especially during the tenure of his sheriffdom. Besides his work on practice at the Court of Session, he prepared an elaborate and exhaustive account of pre-union legislation, issued as a blue book, in connection with the revision of Scottish statute law, and wrote many articles on Scottish subjects for the *Dictionary of National Biography* and for the *Encyclopaedia Britannica*. He wrote a number of books on literature and history, including works on the poet William Dunbar and on the history of Fife and Kinross. Mackay was one of the founders of the Scottish History Society, which was established in 1885. Mackay contributed 127 articles to the *Dictionary of National Biography*, mostly on medieval subjects. They included entries on all the Scottish kings from Fergus I to James V, and on many of the leading members of the Scottish nobility. By later standards he was over-reliant upon chronicle sources at the expense of record evidence, and like most late nineteenth-century historians he was inclined to regard strong kingship as an absolute good, and barons as almost by definition violent and factious. But within the restrictions imposed by his terms of reference, his articles were wide-ranging and based upon detailed research, either his own or, as he was scrupulous in acknowledging, that of others.

Mackay was made LLD of Edinburgh in 1882, and was a fellow of King's College, London. On 21 July 1891, he married Lilian Alina (d. 1919), daughter of Colonel Charles W. St John, of the 94th regiment. They had no children. In 1901 Mackay was compelled to resign his sheriffdom on the grounds of ill health, and during the last ten years of his life illness condemned him to inactivity. He died at his home, Balgreen, Gorgie, Edinburgh, on 10 June 1911.

A. H. MILLAR, *rev.* NATHAN WELLS

Sources *The Times* (12 June 1911) · *Scots Law Times: News* (17 June 1911) · F. J. Grant, ed., *The Faculty of Advocates in Scotland, 1532–1943*, Scottish RS, 145 (1944) · *The Scotsman* (12 June 1911) · *Scottish Law Review*, 27 (1911), 159 · Foster, *Alum. Oxon.* · *CCI* (1911)
Likenesses albumen print, *c.*1851–1859, NPG · J. H. Lorimer, pencil drawing, 1890, Scot. NPG [*see illus.*] · W. G. Boss, pencil drawing, Scot. NPG
Wealth at death £53,458 3*s.* 3*d.*: confirmation, 1 Sept 1911, *CCI*

Mackay, Alexander (1808–1852), journalist, born in Scotland, was in early life a journalist in Toronto, Canada. After working in Canada for several years, and travelling widely there and in the United States, he returned home and joined the staff of the London *Morning Chronicle*. He revisited the United States in 1846 to report the debates in Congress on the Oregon question, for the *Chronicle*. Mackay was called to the bar from the Middle Temple on 7 May 1847. In 1848 he wrote *Electoral Districts … an Inquiry into the Working of the Reform Bill*, and in 1849 he published *The Western World, or, Travels in the United States* (3 vols.), dedicated to Richard Cobden, and for a generation a standard description. He ended his connection with the *Morning Chronicle* in 1849 because of its opposition to the Rebellion Losses Bill of Canada. In that year he published *The Crisis in Canada … in Reference to the Rebellion Losses Bill*. In 1851 the chambers of commerce of Manchester, Liverpool, Blackburn, and Glasgow sent him to inquire into the cultivation of cotton in India and the condition of the cultivators of the soil, more especially within the presidencies of Bombay and Madras. After staying for about a year in India, Mackay was forced by ill health to return to Britain. He died at sea on 15 April 1852. His *Western India* (reports for the chambers of commerce) was published posthumously in 1853, edited by James Robertson, with a preface by Sir Thomas Bazley.

GORDON GOODWIN, *rev.* H. C. G. MATTHEW

Sources *GM*, 2nd ser., 37 (1852), 634 · *Law List* (1852)
Likenesses C. S. Hervé, lithograph, BM

Mackay, Alexander (1815–1895), geographical writer and Free Church of Scotland minister, born in Thurso on 15 November 1815, was the youngest of the eight children of Murdoch Mackay, farmer, of Latheron, Caithness. On his father's second marriage young Mackay went to Aberdeen, where he studied at King's College, and graduated MA in 1840. In 1844 he became the first Free Church minister of Rhynie in Aberdeenshire, the established minister of which had been one of the seven clergymen of Strathbogie deposed by the general assembly of the Church of Scotland. Mackay married in November 1846 Anna Margaret Lillie, daughter of Alexander Lillie of Banff. They had five sons, all of whom died before their father; one of them was the missionary in Uganda, Alexander Murdoch *Mackay. Mackay's geological studies, chiefly concerned with rare fossils found in the Old Red Sandstone in a quarry near Rhynie, led him to correspond with Hugh Miller, Sir Andrew Ramsay, of the Geological Survey, Sir

Roderick Murchison, and Keith Johnston the elder, who recommended him as a fellow of the Royal Geographical Society in 1859.

In 1861 Mackay published a *Manual of Modern Geography*, which ran to twelve editions and was followed by *Outlines of Modern Geography* in 1865. In 1866 the degree of LLD was conferred on him by King's College, Aberdeen. By 1867 Mackay was finding the charge of a congregation less congenial than literary work; he resigned his pastorate and went to Edinburgh and thence to Ventnor in the Isle of Wight in 1878, where he spent his time writing, producing four further geography books as well as a biography and two other works. He died suddenly of cardiac failure, compounding chronic bronchitis, at Prospect House, Grove Road, Ventnor, on 31 January 1895.

Mackay's works had a very large circulation, and are characterized by the relentless repetition of facts. His moment of inspiration came in his *Rhyming Geography* (1873). As his obituarist remarked, 'Some of the stanzas … once read, are difficult to forget' (*Geographical Journal*, 1895, 276). His most tortuous piece of work was a mnemonic system for remembering numbers, described in *Facts and Dates* (1869).

GEORGE STRONACH, *rev.* ELIZABETH BAIGENT

Sources *GJ*, 7 (1895), 276–7 · private information (1901) · d. cert. · *CGPLA Eng. & Wales* (1895)
Wealth at death £557 10s. 2d.: probate, 13 May 1895, *CGPLA Eng. & Wales*

Mackay, Alexander (1833–1902), educationist, was born in Bonar Bridge, Sutherland, on 22 February 1833. He was son of William Mackay, tailor and clothier, of Bonar Bridge, and his wife, Elizabeth Macgregor. Educated at Bonar Bridge parochial school, Mackay passed to St Andrews University, where he was a prizeman. He graduated MA, and in 1891 was admitted to the honorary degree of LLD.

After a short engagement as a teacher at Cameron in Fife Mackay moved to Torryburn, where he was parish schoolmaster for twenty-six years. There he carried on the best Scottish teaching traditions and made a special effort to train boys for the colonies. From 1862 until his death he was an elder of the established church. In 1863 he married Jane Watt, who, with a son and four daughters, survived him.

On the passing in 1861 of the Parochial and Burgh Schoolmasters Act, which refashioned the old system of Scottish education, Mackay devoted himself to the development of educational methods and administration and to the organization of the teaching profession. He became a chief contributor to a weekly paper, *Educational News*, established at Edinburgh on 1 January 1876 by William Ballantyne Hodgson and other educational leaders as the official organ of Scottish teachers. On 1 July 1878 he undertook its editorship, at first without salary. He improved the financial position of the paper, and received a salary from 1881. Under his control the paper, in which he wrote on a wide range of themes, did much to increase the efficiency of the statutory system of education and to improve the position of the teaching profession. From 1876 until his death Mackay was treasurer of the Educational Institute of Scotland. He was its president in 1881, and greatly extended its influence. In 1897 he was elected a member of the school board of Edinburgh and was re-elected in 1900. He was also convener of the evening school committee.

A Conservative in politics, Mackay possessed much force of character, independence of mind, and clarity of judgement. He published several works of value in the teaching profession including *Foreign Systems of Education*, *Aesthetics in Schools*, *A History of Scotland*, *A Plea for our Parish Schools*, and *Free Trade in Teaching*. He died at his home, 13 Warriston Crescent, Edinburgh, on 4 December 1902.

J. E. G. DE MONTMORENCY, *rev.* C. A. CREFFIELD

Sources *The Times* (8 Dec 1902) · *The Scotsman* (5 Dec 1902) · *Educational News* (13 Dec 1902)
Likenesses portrait, repro. in *Educational News*
Wealth at death £1412 1s. 9d.: confirmation, 2 Feb 1903, *CCI* · £90: additional estate, 20 Nov 1903, *CCI*

Mackay, Alexander Murdoch (1849–1890), missionary, son of Alexander Mackay LLD, Free Church minister of Rhynie, Aberdeenshire, was born in the manse there on 13 October 1849. After receiving tuition from his father to the age of fourteen and from 1864 to 1867 at Aberdeen grammar school, he entered the Free Church Training College for Teachers in Edinburgh in the autumn of 1867. He then decided to become an engineer. For a further three years he studied the necessary subjects in Edinburgh University, and gained a practical knowledge of engineering by spending his afternoons at the works of Messrs Miller and Herbert, in Leith. His mornings he occupied in teaching at George Watson's College. In November 1873 Mackay went to Germany to learn the language, working as a draughtsman with an engineering firm in Berlin. In his leisure he translated Lübsen's work on differential and integral calculus, and constructed an agricultural machine of his own invention, which won first prize at the Breslau Exhibition. This led to his promotion to the position of chief of the locomotive department in the firm.

Mackay resided at Berlin with the family of Hofprediger Baur, one of the ministers of the cathedral there. Under Baur's influence Mackay's fascination in missionary life led to his determining to go as a missionary to Madagascar, and he began to study the Malagasy language. In April 1875 he was an unsuccessful candidate for the Church Missionary Society's post of lay superintendent for a settlement of liberated slaves near Mombasa. The firm with which Mackay worked at Berlin was dissolved in September 1875, and he became draughtsman in a similar business at Kottbus, 60 miles south-east of Berlin. When H. M. Stanley, the explorer, in a letter to the *Daily Telegraph*, challenged Christendom to send missionaries to Uganda, Mackay offered his services to the Church Missionary Society (CMS) in its proposed mission to Victoria Nyanza. The offer was accepted on 26 January 1876, and he returned to England in March.

On 27 April 1876 Mackay and four other missionaries set sail from Southampton. After arriving at Zanzibar on 30

Alexander Murdoch Mackay (1849–1890), by Georges Henri Manesse, pubd 1891

May he remained at the coast to engineer a road to Mpwapwa, and reached Uganda only in November 1878. There he remained for most of the time until his death in 1890. His knowledge of practical mechanics was of immense service to the kings of Buganda in making flag masts and lead coffins, and in mending guns as well as maintaining boats and presses for the CMS. With King Mutesa he formed a friendly alliance until a reaction by traditional cult leaders cut off most of his ties with the court. Thereafter he concentrated on translating Bible portions and teaching individuals at the CMS compound.

Before his access to court circles was curtailed, in 1879 Mackay had started to attract younger courtiers to protestant Christianity by his debates with Simeon Lourdel, one of the first Roman Catholic missionaries to Buganda. He had also attracted others through his engineering expertise. After the death of Mutesa in October 1884, the new king, Mwanga, at first encouraged both CMS missionaries and the White Fathers in their work. But then his attitude seemed to change: the new CMS leader, Bishop James Hannington, was murdered on his orders in neighbouring Busoga. In June 1886 thirty-two protestant converts and thirteen Catholic readers, among others, were slaughtered by royal edict. Mwanga was driven from his throne in September 1888 by a palace coup engineered by Muslim and Christian courtiers, but by this time Mackay had been banished to the southern end of Lake Victoria for more than a year. Mwanga's successor, Kiwewa, regarded the Christians as well as the Muslims with suspicion. Kiwewa was ousted by the Muslims and then Mwanga was reinstated by the Christians (he had become a Christian himself in the interval). On 4 February 1890, just before

the Christian Buganda triumphed, Mackay caught malarial fever. Four days later he died at Usambiro, on 8 February 1890; he was buried there, the last survivor of the little band that set out for Uganda in 1876, and was reburied at Namirembe, Uganda, outside the Anglican cathedral, in 1927.'During the whole period of nearly fourteen years', the minutes of the committee of the CMS for 22 April 1890 record, Mackay 'never once left the shores of Africa, and for the great part of that time he was in Uganda itself.'

Mackay was at times a difficult man to work with. He quarrelled constantly with his fellow CMS missionaries as well as with the Catholic priests. He ignored repeated instructions made by the CMS committee in Britain to abandon Buganda, and he never returned to Zanzibar to defend himself for shooting one of his coastal porters in the foot. He was a stubborn man. Yet he is remembered in Uganda as one of the most successful propagators of Christianity there in the late nineteenth century.

A. H. MILLAR, *rev.* MICHAEL TWADDLE

Sources [A. Harrison], *A. M. Mackay: pioneer missionary of the Church Missionary Society in Uganda* (1890) · D. A. Low, 'Alexander Mackay', *Makerere Journal* (1959), ii, 50–56 · J. M. Waliggo, 'The religio-political context of the Uganda martyrs and its significance', *African Christian Studies*, 2/1 (1986), 3–40 · M. Twaddle, *Kakungulu and the creation of Uganda* (1993) · E. Stock, *The history of the Church Missionary Society: its environment, its men and its work*, 3 (1899)
Archives U. Birm. L., corresp. and journals
Likenesses G. H. Manesse, engraving, repro. in Harrison, *A. M. Mackay*, 2nd edn (1891), frontispiece [*see illus.*]
Wealth at death £1350 2s. 3d.: administration, 19 Aug 1891, *CGPLA Eng. & Wales*

Mackay, Andrew (1758–1809), teacher of navigation, one of four sons and three daughters of Hugh Mackay (*c.*1731–1789) of Melness in Sutherland and his wife, Alison Mudie (*c.*1725–1789), was born on 17 October 1758 in Long Acre, Aberdeen, where his father was a dancing-master. He attended the grammar school but in 1790, in a letter of introduction from Patrick Copland, professor of mathematics at Marischal College, to William Herschel, whom Mackay longed to meet, he is described as completely self-taught in mathematics, navigation, and astronomy. Although he attended no classes Marischal College made him an honorary MA and in 1781 he was appointed keeper of the university's observatory on Castle Hill, but without a salary. His notebook of routine observations up to 1789 survives: he corrected the latitude of Aberdeen, estimated the longitude by comparing timings of Jovian satellite phenomena with Greenwich, and rated chronometers. Meantime he earned his living teaching mathematics, geography, navigation with lunars, surveying, and fortification. He married Margaret Younger in Aberdeen on 16 October 1791; they had four sons and five daughters. In 1792 he was teaching a wide range of mathematical subjects at Fortrose Academy, and the following year was back in Aberdeen with his own 'Naval Academy'; also about this time he was superintendent of the harbour.

Mackay was awarded the LLD by Marischal College in 1786 and by King's College in 1795, was an honorary member of the Literary and Philosophical Society of Newcastle upon Tyne, and was elected a fellow of the Royal Society of

Edinburgh in 1793, to which he contributed an account of the position of the Aberdeen observatory. He failed to obtain the vacant chair of mathematics at King's in 1800 despite these accomplishments, his publications, and the support of Alexander, fourth duke of Gordon, patron of science and chancellor of the college. The principal, Roderick McLeod, gave his casting vote for Copland, who declined the chair; Copland's supporters then produced William Duncan, a writing-master, who was elected. Mackay and his supporters were incensed: in 1802 he brought an unsuccessful action in the court of session against the college. He moved to London in 1804 to continue teaching navigation, astronomy, geography, mathematics, natural philosophy, architecture, and engineering, latterly in his house in George Street, Trinity Square. He was also examiner in mathematics for the East India Company, Trinity House, and Christ's Hospital.

Mackay published *The theory and practice of finding the longitude at sea or on land: to which are added various methods of determining the latitude of a place by variation of the compass* (2 vols., 1793), for which he received the thanks of the boards of longitude of England and France; the second edition (1801) contains his portrait. Between 1796 and 1804 Mackay had numerous other works on navigation and mathematics published, several of which went to second editions. He contributed articles on navigation to Abraham Rees's *Cyclopaedia* (1819), and 'Navigation', 'Parallax', 'Pendulum', 'Projection of the sphere', 'Shipbuilding', and 'Tactics' to the third edition of *Encyclopaedia Britannica* (1797). He revised the twelfth edition of James Ferguson's *Astronomy* (1808). Francis Maseres discussed the work of this 'very able Mathematician' in volume six of his *Scriptores* (Maseres, 6.i–x), which contained a further two papers by Mackay on Halley's problem and computations of the sines and tangents of very small angles. His navigation texts were rather too rigorously mathematical for the average seaman and did not enjoy the popularity of those of John William Norie and John Hamilton Moore.

Described as 'a little, bustling, bandy-legged man with eyes of jet and a countenance of much intelligence and animation' (*Aberdeen Journal Notes and Queries*, 8, 1915, 159), Mackay had a kindly and obliging nature, and was highly esteemed by his pupils. He died at his home in George Street, Trinity Square, London, on 3 August 1809, probably of a brain haemorrhage brought on by overwork, and was buried at All Hallows Barking by the Tower.

DAVID GAVINE

Sources R. M. Lawrance, 'Andrew Mackay, LLD, a distinguished nautical author', *Aberdeen Book Lover*, 2 (Nov 1916), 49–54 • A. Mackay, *The book of Mackay* (1906), 327 • *Aberdeen Journal notes and queries*, 8 (1915), 159 • F. Maseres, *Scriptores Logarithmici*, 6 (1809), i–x, liii–lxxxiv • *Fasti academiae Mariscallanae Aberdonensis: selections from the records of the Marischal College and University, MDXCIII–MDCCCLX*, 1, ed. P. J. Anderson, New Spalding Club, 4 (1889), 450 • P. J. Anderson, ed., *Officers and graduates of University and King's College, Aberdeen, MVD–MDCCCLX*, New Spalding Club, 11 (1893), 65, 113 • *European Magazine and London Review*, 56 (1809), 157 • *Edinburgh Annual Register* (1809), 328 • E. G. R. Taylor, *The mathematical practitioners of Hanoverian England, 1714–1840* (1966), 317–18 • P. Copland to W. Herschel, RAS, Herschel MSS, C21 • minute book of the court of session, 21, 1802, 230 • parish records, Aberdeen

Archives NMM, corresp. and papers • U. Aberdeen, observation book
Likenesses J. Heath, stipple (after A. Robertson), NPG; repro. in Mackay, *Book of Mackay*

MacKay, Angus (1813–1859), collector and editor of highland bagpipe music, was born on 10 September 1813, probably on the Isle of Raasay, Scotland. He was the third of four piping sons of John MacKay of Raasay (1767–1848), the leading composer and teacher of his generation, and his wife, Margaret MacLean. As a boy he was piper to Sara Drummond, Lady Gwydir, and, as his adult career progressed, successively to Davidson of Tulloch, Campbell of Islay, and, from 25 July 1843, Queen Victoria. He married Mary Russell in Edinburgh on 25 May 1841; they had two sons and two daughters.

MacKay's development was precocious. In 1826 he took fourth prize at the Edinburgh competitions run by the Highland Societies of London and Scotland, and in 1835, aged just twenty-one, he won the prize pipe for first place. Even more significant, perhaps, was his prize in 1825 for setting a collection of pipe tunes in modern 'scientific' staff notation, which the Highland Societies were keen to promote. He went on to become the most influential collector and editor of pipe music in nineteenth-century Scotland.

MacKay lived at a time of rapid change in the piping world. His father had been a traditional family piper until late in his career, but Angus moved in a more individualistic and entrepreneurial market, in which the piper was more mobile, success in competition the marker of professional eminence, and a published collection the acme of a good career. Traditional oral methods of instruction—where it was said that seven years went into the making of a good piper and seven generations of knowledge before that—were coming under pressure. The needs of the army as an employer of pipers meant accelerated, and therefore cheaper, training, demanding standardized settings of tunes and fixed written scores.

MacKay's *Collection of Ancient Piobaireachd or Highland Pipe Music* (1838) appeared under the auspices of the Highland Society of London, a powerful institution with wide influence in Scottish cultural affairs. It contained sixty-one tunes written in staff notation. The extensive introduction and notes described the leading piping dynasties, such as the MacCrimmons, the MacArthurs, and the MacKays of Gairloch, and gave the history of the Highland Societies of London and Scotland's competitions from their inception in 1781 to 1838. The volume was issued under Angus MacKay's name, and derived its subsequent authority from his immense personal standing, but the extent of his contribution remains unclear. The Highland Society may well have determined the selection of tunes, and its under-secretary, James Logan (author of *The Scottish Gael*, 1831), is now thought to have written the letterpress sections, which were highly influential in determining how piobaireachd was to be interpreted in the wider non-Gaelic-speaking world during the nineteenth and early twentieth centuries.

The prospectus stated: 'The leading object of the Editor

the manuscript or to give financial acknowledgement to the compiler.

Angus MacKay's manuscripts are a major source for subsequent published collections of piobaireachd. And yet his later editors have, while invoking his name, frequently compromised his text, by using notational procedures which obscured his clearly expressed musical intention, thereby creating widespread uncertainty about timing and expression among modern performers.

MacKay had to give up his royal appointment in 1854. He became violently insane, probably as a result of tertiary syphilis, and was confined in the Crichton Royal Hospital, near Dumfries. On 21 March 1859, he was drowned in the River Nith while attempting to escape. The body was never recovered.

It is impossible to overstate MacKay's influence on the culture of the highland bagpipe. The story of his reputation in the century and a half which followed his death is virtually synonymous with the history of piping itself.

WILLIAM DONALDSON

Sources W. Donaldson, *The highland pipe and Scottish society, 1750–1950* (2000) · A. Mackay, *A collection of ancient piobaireachd or highland pipe music* (1838) · N. T. McKay, 'Angus Mackay (1812–1859) and his contribution to highland music', *Transactions of the Gaelic Society of Inverness*, 55 (1986–8), 203–16 · P. Cooke, 'Changing styles in pibroch playing', *International Piper*, 1/2 (1978), 12–14 · J. A. Maclellan, 'Angus Mackay of Raasay', *Piping Times*, 18/6 (1965–6), 10–14 · W. Donaldson, 'Change and invariance in the traditional performing arts', *Northern Scotland*, 17 (1997), 33–54 · D. MacDonald, *A collection of the ancient martial music of Caledonia* (c.1819) · J. MacDonald, *A compleat theory of the Scots highland bagpipe* (1803) · *Oban Times* (1861–1950) · R. D. Cannon, *A bibliography of bagpipe music* (1980) · R. D. Cannon, *The highland bagpipe and its music* (1988) · clinical notes on patient 'no. 738 Angus Mackay', Crichton Royal Hospital · d. cert. **Archives** NL Scot.
Likenesses W. Wyld, watercolour, c.1852, Royal Collection [*see illus.*] · portrait, oils, Caledonian Club, London

Angus MacKay (1813–1859), by William Wyld, c.1852

is to preserve in its native simplicity and purity the ancient music of the country, by furnishing a fixed standard for future performers.' The collection attempted to fix a stable repertory for competitive and instructional purposes, to substitute for fluid oral variants a standard authoritative written text, and to lay down a more uniform and simplified style of ornamentation. MacKay's settings were more prescriptive than those of his predecessors, Joseph and Donald MacDonald (*A Compleat Theory of the Scots Highland Bagpipe*, 1803, and *A Collection of the Ancient Martial Music of Caledonia*, c.1819), which had tended, typically, to assume a degree of performer choice.

Three editions of the work were published during the nineteenth century (1838, 1839, 1899) and it rapidly became the standard text. Its expense (a guinea and a half) meant that it was not, as has frequently been claimed, 'the pipers' bible', but, with the rise of the competition circuit as the major arena for piobaireachd playing, and the bookish orientation of most piping judges, MacKay's printed text frequently dictated what was heard in public and how it was played into the following century.

In 1841 MacKay completed an extensive manuscript collection of piobaireachd, drawn from his father's playing and other sources. It numbered 183 tunes in all, written out in fair copy, and was obviously intended for publication. But at this point the Highland Societies drew back. They concluded, quite wrongly, that the best tunes were in the published volume of 1838, and declined to acquire

Mackay, Angus (1824–1886), journalist and politician in Australia, was born at Aberdeen on 26 January 1824, the son of Murdoch Mackay of the 78th highlanders and his wife, Elizabeth Macleod. His father on receiving his pension in 1827 emigrated with his family to New South Wales.

Mackay was educated for the Presbyterian ministry at the Australian College in Sydney. He taught there for a time and became headmaster of a Sydney Presbyterian school. By then he had turned his attention to journalism, and before he was twenty he was a contributor to the *Australian Magazine* and Robert Lowe's *The Atlas*, of which he became editor in 1847. In 1849 he was honorary secretary of the Constitutional Association, assisting Henry Parkes in agitating for universal suffrage and land reform and opposing convict transportation. The following year he migrated to Geelong, Victoria, to manage a general business for Parkes, but in 1851 he returned to journalism in New South Wales, first on the *People's Advocate*, then as a special goldfields correspondent for Parkes's new radical paper *The Empire*, and finally as that paper's political reporter. In 1853 he was again in Victoria as a digger. He took a leading part in the agitation against the mining licence fee, and in October headed a deputation to Melbourne and gave important evidence before the committee of inquiry on the goldfields. He then became the Bendigo correspondent of *The Argus*. In 1854 at Melbourne he married Margaret O'Shaunasy: they had three sons and three daughters. The following year Mackay became a proprietor and the editor of the *Bendigo Advertiser*, where he helped to form the Working Miner's Protection Society and campaigned for an eight-hour day. In 1863 he and his co-owners established the *McIvor Times* and later bought the *Riverine Herald*. In 1879 Mackay returned to Sydney, and was part of a syndicate which launched the *Sydney Daily Telegraph*.

In 1868, after repeated invitations, Mackay stood for and won the seat of Sandhurst Boroughs (Bendigo), Victoria, which he represented as a moderate liberal in three successive parliaments. From 1871 to 1875 he was minister of mines in three successive ministries, and in 1874–5 he was also minister of education. His speeches as a minister were businesslike and straightforward. His Regulation of Mines Act of 1873 enforced an eight-hour work limit and made employers responsible for accidents—which about halved the number of accidents. He pushed successfully for completing the Coliban irrigation scheme to bring water to Bendigo and for the enactment of compulsory and secular education.

Mackay was a lover of sports and the theatre and was a member of the cricket team which in 1865 played against the first All England eleven to visit Australia. In 1874 his first wife died, and on 15 July 1875 in Melbourne he married Annie Leslie Anderson, who survived him.

Mackay moved to Sydney in 1879 to become the founding editor of the *Daily Telegraph*, but returned in 1883 and in May was again elected for Sandhurst. He died there on 5 July 1886, leaving an estate worth £6722, and was buried in Sandhurst cemetery on 7 July. A monument to his memory was erected in Bendigo.

C. A. HARRIS, *rev.* ELIZABETH BAIGENT

Sources *AusDB* • *The Argus* [Melbourne] (6 July 1886) • *The Argus* [Melbourne] (7 July 1886) • *Year Book of Australia* (1886) • R. L. Knight, *Illiberal liberal* (1966) • G. Serle, *The golden age: a history of the colony of Victoria, 1851–1861* (1963) • G. Blainey, *The rush that never ended: a history of Australian mining* (1963) • *Victorian parliamentary debates* (1873), 17.2098ff
Wealth at death £6722: probate, Australia

McKay, Archibald (1801–1883), poet and topographer, was born at Kilmarnock, the son of Alexander McKay, farmer, and his wife, Janet, *née* McGill. After receiving a rudimentary education he was apprenticed to a hand-loom weaver, but subsequently became a bookbinder. He also operated a circulating library in King Street, Kilmarnock, and on 2 November 1820 he married Elizabeth McGill. He also wrote verse, and his *Poems* appeared in 1830. It was soon followed by another collection entitled *Recreations of Leisure Hours* (1832; 2nd edn, 1844). His poems attracted considerable attention, and some of the pieces, such as 'My First Bawbee', 'My Ain Couthie Wife', and 'Drouthy Tam' (first published in 1828) gained great popularity. McKay was also interested in local history and topography, and in

1848 published *A History of Kilmarnock*, which ran into two further editions. After the death of his first wife McKay married Margaret Buchanan on 5 March 1867. She was to predecease him; McKay died at 19 Titchfield Street, Kilmarnock, on 14 April 1883.

GORDON GOODWIN, *rev.* SARAH COUPER

Sources C. Rogers, *The modern Scottish minstrel, or, The songs of Scotland of the past half-century*, 5 (1857), 85 • Boase, *Mod. Eng. biog.*, 2.618 • Irving, *Scots.* • *The Times* (27 April 1883), 12 • *The Athenaeum* (28 April 1883), 543 • d. cert. • IGI

Mackay, Charles (1812–1889), poet and writer, was born in Perth, Scotland, on 26 March 1812, the son of George Mackay, a bandmaster in the Royal Artillery, and his wife, Amelia, *née* Cargill. His mother died when Charles was very young, and he was raised by his father, who had contracted malaria and had returned to Scotland, invalided out as a half-pay lieutenant. His early childhood was spent in a 'lonely house' by Newhaven, on the Firth of Forth. Then, probably in 1822, with his father 'knocking about the world' (Mackay, *Forty Years*, 1.15), he was sent to live with a Royal Artillery veteran named Threlkeld who was settled as a tailor in Woolwich, and whose wife, Grace Stuart, of Perth, taught the boy a huge repertory of Scots songs. When Charles was ten, his father withdrew him from his Woolwich dame-school to continue his education in London, under the care of John Lees, a Church of Scotland minister. Andrew Robertson, the portrait painter, and a friend of Charles's father, encouraged the boy's writing, and showed his verses to the charismatic Scottish preacher Edward Irving. The experience of hearing Irving read them aloud, according to Mackay, 'moulded my future career, and made me a man of letters' (ibid., 1.26)—though elsewhere he wrote of how he loathed the hell-fire sermons which Irving preached to packed audiences at his chapel in Cross Street, Covent Garden, and completely eschewed the gloomy Calvinist theology. At the age of thirteen, Mackay saw his verse first published in a penny periodical called *The Casket*.

Charles Mackay's father settled comfortably in Brussels, where his half pay stretched further than in Britain and he could augment it by language teaching (his pupils included the sons of the prince of Orange). Charles's great-uncle Major-General Robert Mackay was in the service of the East India Company, and it seems that he elected to pay for Charles's education on the understanding that he would go to India as a cadet. At the age of fourteen, Charles joined his father in Brussels, where he went to a school in the boulevard de Namur. He became proficient not only in French and German, but also in Spanish and Italian. However, when his 'poor, proud father' quarrelled with his 'rich, proud uncle' (Mackay, *Through the Long Day*, 1.18), the Indian deal fell through, and Charles Mackay went as secretary to the retired ironmaster William Cockerill, whose sons still carried on his foundry near Liège. He submitted journalism in French and verse in English to local journals, and when his father wanted him to enter the iron business, Mackay's insistence that he must live by his pen prevailed. They returned to London in 1832, and Mackay established an important connection by tutoring in Italian a young Jewish lawyer, Benjamin Lumley, who would later be a noted theatrical manager. One of Lumley's Jewish friends, Henry Russell, was a singer and composer and he set several verses by Mackay to music. One song, 'Some love to roam o'er the dark sea foam', became extremely popular and 'was to be heard for many months on all the barrel-organs' (ibid., 1.46). The publisher cleared hundreds of pounds, but Mackay got nothing.

After briefly working for *The Sun*, a Liberal evening paper, Mackay joined the *Morning Chronicle*, *The Times*'s leading rival, then under the editorship of John Black. George Hogarth, a gifted Scot, worked under him, and Hogarth's future son-in-law Charles Dickens was one of the parliamentary reporters. Mackay soon beat no less a rival than Thackeray for the post of sub-editor, which 'chained' him to a desk 'nearly all night for six nights in the week'. Mackay's energy was remarkable. By the time he was thirty he had published, beside contributions to various periodicals and three volumes of verse, *A History of London* (1838); a two-volume guide to *The Thames and its Tributaries* (1840); a novel, *Longbeard, Lord of London* (1841); and a very successful collection of essays entitled *Memoirs of Extraordinary Popular Delusions, and the Madness of Crowds* (3 vols., 1841).

In 1844, tired of ceaseless subbing, Mackay accepted the editorship of the *Glasgow Argus* and became a leading figure in Glasgow liberal life. Agitation against the corn laws was reaching a peak, and Mackay's remit was to support that cause. In 1846 Dickens tried to poach Mackay for the recently founded *Daily News*, but Mackay agreed only to contribute a dozen sets of anti-corn law verses to the paper. These were gathered and published with immense success as *Voices from the Crowd* in 1847. Mackay resumed what he came to see as a Faustian compact with Russell, whose setting of 'There's a good time coming, boys', as sung by himself, sold 400,000 copies worldwide.

Most of Mackay's ideas were in line with those of his Scottish contemporary Samuel Smiles, who was also at this time an active journalist in the anti-corn law cause. Mackay extolled the values of self-help, temperance, and 'independence'. Freed from want by cheaper corn, the working man could educate himself in the fine fruits of human intellect and the wonders of God's universe as revealed by science. Mackay talked freely about equality and democracy, but, in the dangerous era of Chartism, stressed that the British working man need not take to the barricades to achieve them:

> We've won without such aid before,
> *And so we shall again.*

Meanwhile, he encouraged emigration as a solution for those many workers who despaired of a better life in Britain. One of his most popular songs was 'Cheer boys! cheer!', projecting the emigrants' hopes:

> The star of empire glitters in the west.
> Here we had toil and little to reward it,
> But there shall plenty smile upon our pain,

> And ours shall be the mountain and the forest,
> And boundless prairies ripe with golden grain.

For the fifth reprint of *Voices from the Crowd*, published in 1857, Mackay wrote a preface explaining that in the era of anti-corn law agitation he had 'written his songs as plainly as possible, that they might express the general sentiment of the toiling classes in phraseology broad, simple, and intelligible as the occasion'. His grander aspirations in verse were represented in his lengthy philosophical work, *Egeria, or, The Spirit of Nature*, published with other poems in 1850. But Mackay in this and other ambitious productions remained a fatally facile writer who could never spurn a cliché or decline the prospect of an easy rhyme.

Made an LLD of Glasgow University in 1846, Mackay resigned the editorship of the *Argus* in 1847, after feud broke out in Glasgow's Liberal circles. In 1848 he joined the *Illustrated London News*, hired to give it 'a voice on all the political, social, and literary questions of the time' (Mackay, *Through the Long Day*, 1.353). Circulation rose from 40,000 to 60,000 copies in less than a year. From December 1851, at the proprietor's suggestion, the paper issued a series of musical supplements, each containing an original song by Mackay adapted to an old English melody arranged by Sir Henry Bishop. The composer's death in April 1855 curtailed the series, but eighty lyrics (of the hundred originally projected) were published as *Songs for Music* in the following year, with enormous success.

From 1857 to 1858 Mackay undertook a tour of North America, where he lectured on 'Songs National, Historical and Popular', and hobnobbed with soldiers, politicians, and the writers Henry Wadsworth Longfellow, Ralph Waldo Emerson, William Hickling Prescott, and Oliver Wendell Holmes. He left the *Illustrated London News* in 1859, and launched an unsuccessful periodical, *London Review*, from which he resigned after six months. His first wife, Rose Henrietta Vale, whom he had married in Glasgow about 1845, died in 1859, and on 27 February 1861 he married Mary Elizabeth Mills (1830/31–1876), the widowed daughter of John Kirtland. They had already had a daughter, Mary *Mackay (1855–1924), who was later to become a novelist under the name Marie Corelli. From February 1862 to December 1865, during the American Civil War, he acted as *The Times*'s correspondent in New York. This was not an easy time for him, as, although his copy was published anonymously, everyone in New York public life knew from the outset what he was doing in the city. His once straightforward liberalism was now contorted by his sense of Britain's national interests, and many northerners resented his belief that, while slavery was abhorrent, the north should not war with the south over it. More agreeably, through an Irish acquaintance, he was the journalist who 'scooped' the story of the existence of the Fenian conspiracy by Irish nationalists based in the United States, which was later responsible for 'outrages' in Britain.

Mackay eventually quarrelled with *The Times*, and thereafter freelanced, writing for many noted periodicals, leaving himself 'leisure for other work that did not pay, but that ministered to my enjoyment, the increase of my knowledge, and the education of my mental faculties' (Mackay, *Through the Long Day*, 2.395). True to the spirit of 'self-help', he took on the experts in the field of historical philology. He argued that they had ignored the Celtic roots of much European vocabulary—that 'the apparently unmeaning choruses of many popular English and French songs and ballads, which Dr. Johnson would have treated as "gibberish", such as "Fal lal la", "fol de rol", "Hey, nonnie nonnie"' were 'desecrated remnants of Hymns to the Sun, sung by the Druids … more than two thousand years ago, all distinctly traceable to the Keltic' (ibid., 2.399). He worked for more than five years on his book *The Gaelic and Celtic Etymology of the Languages of Western Europe*, published in 1878 by subscription, and was more than £300 out of pocket as a result. He could not find a publisher for a work in French entitled *Origines celtiques de la langue française*. In a book entitled *Obscure Words and Phrases in the Writings of Shakespeare and his Contemporaries* he tried to score more Celtic points off Dr Johnson. His very last work was a *Dictionary of Lowland Scotch* (1888). Charles Mackay died at his home, 47 Longridge Road, Brompton, London, on 24 December 1889, survived by his daughter and at least one son, Eric Mackay. He was buried on 2 January 1890 at Kensal Green cemetery.

Charles Mackay's passionate erudition and urbane, unaffected prose style contributed to make him one of the chief figures in the establishment of Victorian journalism as a dignified profession. His two overlapping sets of memoirs remain full of interest, as he associated with many important people, and was a frequent guest at the famous breakfasts given by the poet Samuel Rogers. In America he met Abraham Lincoln, and later, in 1869, showed Jefferson Davis, former president of the Southern Confederacy, around the Scottish highlands.

The Chandos Classics edition of Mackay's *Poetical Works*, published thirteen years before his death, ran to 626 closely printed pages. Mackay believed passionately that poetry conveyed truths superior to those of political economy, had an exalted view of his own calling as poet, and, looking back on his career in 1887, wrote that he was 'painfully conscious' that his 'worst' literary work had been the most popular while the best had received 'slight or no recognition' (Mackay, *Through the Long Day*, 2.394). His vogue as the 'Poet of the People' had already passed. While James Grant Wilson had continued to acclaim him as such when introducing a generous selection of his work in what became a standard anthology, *The Poets and Poetry of Scotland* (1877), Alfred H. Miles, in the relevant volume of his compilation, *The Poets and the Poetry of the Nineteenth Century*, published three years after Mackay's death, could muster only faint praise for his song lyrics and observed that 'his longer efforts in verse have lost whatever interest they may once have excited'. In the twentieth century, no one sought to revive, by biography or criticism, the reputation of a man admired greatly by distinguished and lowly contemporaries alike.

ANGUS CALDER

Sources DNB · C. Mackay, *Forty years' recollections of life, literature and public affairs, from 1830–1870*, 2 vols. (1877) · C. Mackay, *Through the long day, or, Memorials of a literary life through half a century*, 2 vols. (1887) · d. cert. · m. cert., 1861 · bap. reg. Scot. · CGPLA Eng. & Wales (1890)

Archives BL, corresp. relating to English songs, Add. MS 29905 · Hunt. L., letters · London Library, MSS · Morgan L., papers · Perth Museum and Art Gallery, papers, corresp., and literary MSS · Shakespeare Birthplace Trust RO, Stratford upon Avon, corresp. and papers · Southern Illinois University, Carbondale, papers | BL, letters to Royal Literary Fund, loan 96 · BL, letters to Alfred Wallace, Add. MSS 46440–46441 · Herts. ALS, corresp. with Lord Lytton · NL Scot., letters to Dr L. C. Alexander · NL Scot., corresp. with Blackwoods · NL Scot., corresp. with George Combe · U. Aberdeen L., letters to Peter Buchan

Likenesses H. Watkins, albumen print, 1855–9, NPG · C. Cook, stipple (after J. O. Murray), NPG · P. Naumann & R. Taylor & Co., wood-engraving, BM, NPG; repro. in *ILN* (14 May 1892) · W. Roffe, stipple (after photograph by C. Watkins), NPG

Wealth at death £2718 6s. 9d.: resworn probate, Aug 1890, CGPLA Eng. & Wales

Mackay, Donald, first Lord Reay (1591–1649), army officer in the Danish–Norwegian and Swedish service, was born in February or March 1591, the eldest son of Uisdean dubh (or Hugh) Mackay (1561–1614) of Farr, Sutherland, and his wife, Lady Jean (or Jane) Gordon, eldest daughter of Alexander Gordon, eleventh earl of Sutherland. Mackay had a brother, Thomas, and two sisters, Anna and Mary.

Early life Mackay, along with his father, became a justice of the peace for Inverness-shire and Cromarty in June 1610, and two years later he was a commissioner of the peace for Sutherland and Strathnaver. Mackay and John Gordon of Embo were involved in a case with George Sinclair, fifth earl of Caithness, when the latter's nephew James was killed, but all charges against them were dropped in 1613. In December that year Mackay was given a commission of fire and sword, along with George Gordon, first marquess of Huntly, and others, against Cameron of Lochiel.

Mackay married Barbara Mackenzie, the daughter of the first Lord Kintail in 1610. With her he had six children, including John Mackay, later second Lord Reay [*see below*], and Angus, who followed his father into Danish–Norwegian service. Mackay succeeded as head of the clan Mackay in 1614, this making him a leading power in the Strathnaver area of Sutherland. He was knighted in April 1616 by James VI. Soon after this a struggle with the house of Sutherland began, which was to run the course of his life. Mackay's marriage deteriorated; in 1617 his wife complained to the Scottish privy council of his ill treatment of her through his dalliance with Lady Mary Lindsay, the daughter of David, eleventh earl of Crawford. Mackay not only had an illegitimate son with her, but also brought her to live with him in his home when Barbara had just delivered a child. Mackay was put to the horn and ordered to the Tolbooth in Edinburgh, the first of several spells in prison. In June 1620 he was fined 2000 merks for his adultery.

This behaviour did not damage Mackay's status and on 20 August 1623 the Scottish privy council appointed him and his brother justices of the peace for Sutherland and Strathnaver. The following year he bought the lands of Reay, Sandside, Darochow, Borlum, Easald, Achatrescar, Auchamerland, and Showarie from Alexander, Lord

Forbes. He also bought the Little Isles of Strathnave from William Macallan, and 27 merklands of Moidart and 24 merklands of Arisaig from John McRonald, chief of clan Ronald.

Service in the Thirty Years' War Notwithstanding his interests in Scotland Mackay looked abroad for his future and came to play a major role in the Thirty Years' War. In 1626 he went to London to ask Charles I for permission to raise a regiment for the anti-Habsburg forces, and joined the army of the protestant military entrepreneur Ernst, count of Mansfeld. Two warrants were issued within four months. The first, dated 3 March 1626, authorized the levy and transport of 2000 men; the second, on 21 July, was for 3000 men. Recruitment was neither an easy nor straightforward task. Mackay had to sell his lands of Moidart and Arisaig to the earl of Seaforth to fund these levies. He was specifically ordered not to harbour Robert Monro of Fowlis among his recruits, as Fowlis was a fugitive from the law at the time. Desertion was a constant threat and by July 1000 recruits had disappeared, mostly because of the lack of pay. However, by August 1626 Mackay had apparently gathered 3600 men and sought permission to transport them.

Mansfeld wanted these men divided into fifteen companies of about 200 men each. Although Mackay had permission to enlist 5000, he only raised about 3000 at first, and of these Alexander, Lord Forbes, provided about 800 men. The troops embarked from Cromarty in October 1626, though Mackay himself was too ill to accompany them until January 1627. The regiment was transferred to the service of Christian IV of Denmark upon Mansfeld's death at the end of 1626. While Mackay was abroad Charles I created him a baronet of Nova Scotia on 18 March, or May, 1627.

Mackay's regiment distinguished itself by its actions. First, four companies under Major Dunbar staunchly resisted the imperial army's attack on Boitzenburg. Second the regiment held the pass of Oldenburg for nine hours while their German allies retired in disorder; Mackay himself was wounded in this effort, and less than 1000 of his men survived. When the command was given for all the Danish forces to retire Mackay's troops were the only ones to return to Denmark–Norway; the rest had surrendered to the imperial forces.

Conditions for Mackay's men were far from ideal. Not only had he never been paid for their shipment, but he also complained to the elector palatine of the lack of victuals for his men on 25 July 1627. He was reappointed colonel of his Scottish regiment in July 1627. He obliged himself to levy a further 1000 men of foot in October 1627, for which authorization was given by the privy council of Scotland on 31 March 1628.

On 19 January 1628 Charles I provided Mackay with a charter for the lands which had been resigned to him by Alexander, Lord Forbes. On 19 February Mackay received a third commission, to levy an additional 1000 men. He had also been made a peer of Scotland, as Lord Reay, on 20 June 1628. Towards the end of the year Reay travelled to Copenhagen, probably to install three of his sons, including

John, at the Academy of Sorø in Denmark on 29 September.

Following Christian IV's peace with the emperor, Reay's regiment was reformed on 3 September 1628 to consist of 1000 men in five companies. Although the regiment was transferred to Swedish service in the summer of 1629, Reay himself moved his family—including his mother, servants and whole retinue—to Denmark. Reay returned to Denmark with more recruits early in 1630, and accompanied Gustavus Adolphus of Sweden to Pomerania.

Treason, trial by combat, and bigamy Just a few months later the Scottish privy council authorized Reay to levy 2000 men for the use of the Swedish king. At the same time James Hamilton, marquess of Hamilton, received a commission from Gustavus Adolphus to raise 6000 men, and sent his lieutenant David Ramsay to Britain to recruit. On the ship off Elsinore—Reay claimed later—Ramsay told him that Hamilton's recruits were actually going to be used against Charles I. In England Reay charged Ramsay with treason: with Reay the only witness to the conversation the case would have failed under common law, which required two witnesses, so he challenged Ramsay before the court of chivalry in November 1631. The court appointed the two men to meet in single combat before the king the following April, each armed with spear, long and short swords, and dagger. In the event the duel never took place, as the king concluded that Ramsay was guilty of no more than seditious words rather than treason and that Hamilton was entirely innocent of the charges made against him by Reay and Lord Ochiltree. Ramsay and Reay were both sent to the Tower of London in May pending sufficient sureties not to act against each other, and were released in August.

Although Reay never returned to active service in Sweden his regiment continued to play an important role in the Swedish campaigns in Germany, its campaigns recorded in the account of another Robert Monro, the author of *Monro his Expedition with the Worthy Scots Regiment (called Mac-Keyes Regiment)* (1637). Monro acted as an itinerant ambassador to the Stuarts on behalf of Sweden, by bringing progress reports from the war. In 1634 Reay was issued with a commission to apprehend 'sorners', implying that he was perhaps levying troops for Swedish service again. By February 1637 Mackay was listed among the Scottish officers paid off by the Swedes and received 600 riksdaler.

By this time Reay's marital affairs had become even more complicated. He seems to have progressed from adultery to bigamy, taking out a warrant in 1631 against Rachel Winterfield, or Harrison, who claimed that he had married her and that she had borne him at least one child, Donald. About this time Reay's first wife died and he married Elizabeth Thomson (d. 1641), daughter of Robert Thomson, keeper of the queen's wardrobe. They had one daughter, Anne. Rachel Winterfield pursued her case for maintenance for years. Reay continued to contradict her claims, arguing that the marriage had been nullified upon the discovery that she had married bigamously and that she had used forged documents to continue her case against him. The court of delegates in London found the marriage valid, and in Scotland he was ordered to pay past and future maintenance. Reay sold his lands of Reay to William Innes and signed over the rest of his estates to his son John. He applied for leave to travel abroad to call in debts he was owed; on 1 April the king wrote to inform the Scottish privy council that permission was conditional upon Reay's making due provision for 'her who is now found to be his wife' (*Reg. PCS*, 2nd ser., 6.440). On 1 August the Scottish privy council raised the maintenance due to her to £2000 sterling for arrears and for the future £400 sterling per annum (to be reduced to £300 if he brought up his son). Reay continued to be evasive and recalcitrant, and in July 1642 he was gaoled in Blackness Castle for non-payment of alimony to Rachel Winterfield. His wife, Elizabeth, died in June 1641, and some time after that he married Mary Sinclair, daughter of Francis Sinclair of Stirkoke, Caithness.

The British civil wars, Denmark–Norway, and death   Like many royalist sympathizers Reay signed the covenant in April 1638 under duress. The very next year the covenanters captured a ship belonging to Reay, loaded with arms and treasure, when it was blown off course into Peterhead harbour. Presumably to allay suspicions, Reay then raised a regiment for service in the army of the covenant, joining George Mackenzie, second earl of Seaforth—a fellow covert royalist—and 4000 men to form the northern covenanter forces in May 1639. Reay and Seaforth signed a secret royalist bond that summer, and the next year the pair of them were warded in Scotland suspected of supporting the king. By 1643 the authorities appear to have ordered him not to stray beyond his own estates, where, according to Sir John Gordon of Embo, 'he tyrannizes as if there were no king nor law to putt order to his insolencies' (*Reg. PCS*, 2nd ser., 7.406–7). In November of that year Reay levied a regiment of 1000 foot at the request of Christian IV and embarked for Denmark–Norway. While there Reay commanded the regiment of his son, Colonel Angus Mackay. In 1644 Reay returned to Britain with a ship loaded with £20,000 Scots worth of arms and goods, and landed at Newcastle just before the army of the solemn league and covenant laid siege to the town. He and Lord Crawford held on to Newcastle garrison until October, when they were captured. They were sent to Edinburgh and imprisoned for the next year and a half. During this time the Scottish estates proscribed Reay's lands. Christian IV intervened personally in May 1645 and obtained his release. The Scottish estates remained distrustful of Reay and authorized the earl of Sutherland to send a force to Strathnaver and obtain his submission in October 1647.

Christian IV still sought reliable troops from Reay, who was obliged to fulfil this obligation before his Danish pension would be paid to him. Reay must have realized that his situation in Scotland was hopeless and he returned to Denmark–Norway in 1648. Frederick III of Denmark–Norway provided Reay with a warrant for 500 daler in January 1649. Reay's last letter was dated 2 February 1649 at Copenhagen, and referred to his plans to raise a new regiment for Swedish service. However, he appears to

have died by 10 February. Some sources say he died at Copenhagen, others at Bergen, where he had been appointed governor. The Danish–Norwegian king apparently chartered a frigate to take Reay back to Scotland, and he was buried at Kirkiboll church at Tongue in Strathnaver.

Mackay's royalist son John Mackay, second Lord Reay (*c*.1612–1680), royalist army officer, was the eldest surviving son of Donald Mackay, first Lord Reay, and his first wife, Barbara Mackenzie, daughter of the first Lord Kintail. Little is known of his early life, though he attended Sorø Academy in Denmark in September 1628 along with two of his brothers. He returned to Scotland and in 1636 he married Isabella Sinclair, daughter of George Sinclair, earl of Caithness, with whom he had two children, George and Jane.

Mackay, like his father, was a staunch royalist. In 1639 Montrose captured him, along with the marquess of Huntly, when Aberdeen fell to the covenanters. Although Mackay was sent to Edinburgh he was quickly released when he signed the covenant. From 1644 he harboured the marquess of Huntly, who had fled Aberdeenshire, for two years. On the death of his father in February 1649 he succeeded to the peerage. That month he joined Sir Thomas Urquhart of Cromarty and Mackenzie of Pluscarden with 700 men in taking Inverness. Although this force retired it re-emerged to take Inverness in May. Reay was captured once again, this time at Balveny Castle, and sent to Edinburgh, where he remained a prisoner until 1650. Meanwhile the Scottish parliament helped the earl of Sutherland to acquire Reay's lands and to build a stronghold in Strathnaver.

Reay apparently escaped from his Edinburgh prison in 1650, though his wife, Isabella, is also said to have pleaded with Cromwell for his release. He remained a supporter of Charles II and in 1653 was proposed as a committee member to help run the government in Scotland. Reay joined Glencairn's uprising in 1654 and took the opportunity to lay waste the lands of his enemy Sutherland. With the failure of the rising Reay was forced to sign an agreement with General Monck in May 1655 to hand over his weapons and provide a bond of £2000 for security; nevertheless he kept his estate. After the death of his first wife Reay married Barbara Mackay, the daughter of Hugh Mackay of Scourie. They had six children: Donald (*b*. 1657/8), Angus, Robert, Joanna, Anna, and Sibylla.

After the Restoration Reay enjoyed royal favour. He attended parliament as second Lord Reay in 1661. Two years later he was appointed justice of the peace for Sutherland. He signed the declaration against the national covenant and solemn league and covenant in February 1664. Although Charles II offered in the same year to compensate Reay for all his losses incurred on the king's behalf, he never received the money. Charles also recommended him to Frederick III of Denmark–Norway, perhaps in the hope that Reay could obtain some funds there. Mackay, like his father before him, signed over his estate to his son at some point during his life. He became involved in a local feud between the Munros of Eriboll and the Sinclairs of Dunbeath. In 1668 Reay, along with the Munros, was granted a royal letter of fire and sword against the Sinclairs, who had unjustly attacked the Munros. At a later point the Sinclairs paid a fine of 50,204 merks to Reay. In 1669 he received his first summons from the Scottish privy council to appear before it annually to renew his band to keep peace in the highlands. He was again given a commission of fire and sword in 1672 in order to rid the country of insurgents. After this Reay appears to have lived peacefully at his home in Durness, and he died, probably at home, in 1680. His eldest son, Donald, had been killed earlier that year while on a hunting expedition when a barrel of gunpowder he was standing beside blew up. The title passed to Donald's only son, George Mackay (1678–1748).   A. N. L. GROSJEAN

Sources Riksarkivet, Stockholm, Svenska armén, militära chefer, 1620–1840; anglica · military muster rolls, Krigsarkivet, Stockholm, 1629/11, 14, 18, 20; 1630/22–8, 36–8; 1632/28 · NA Scot., Reay papers, GD 84 · S. Hedar, *Kammarkollegiets protokoll med bilagor*, 1 (Stockholm, 1934) · *Reg. PCS*, 1st ser., vols. 9–13 · *Reg. PCS*, 2nd ser., vols. 1–6 · *Reg. PCS*, 3rd ser., vols. 1, 3, 4 · *CSP dom.*, 1631–3 · G. Lind, *Danish officers, 1614–1662* [computer database, Danish data archives 1573] · J. C. W. Hirsch and K. Hirsch, eds., 'Fortegnelse øver Dansu ou Norske officerer med flere fra 1648 til 1814', 12 vols., unpublished MS, 1888–1907, Rigsarkivet, Copenhagen, vol. 7 · *Sixth report*, HMC, 5 (1877–8) · *The manuscripts of the duke of Hamilton*, HMC, 21 (1887) · *APS*, 1643–60 · T. Riis, *Should auld acquaintance be forgot … Scottish–Danish relations, c.1450–1707*, 2 (1988) · R. Monro, *Monro his expedition with the worthy Scots regiment (called Mac-Keyes regiment) levied in August 1626* (1637); new edn, with introduction by W. S. Brockington (1999) · J. Mackay, *An old Scots brigade* (1885) · J. Mackay, 'Mackay's regiment', *Transactions of the Gaelic Society of Inverness*, 8 (1878–9), 128–89 · A. Mackay, *The book of Mackay* (1906) · I. Grimble, *Chief of Mackay* (1965) · E. M. Furgol, *A regimental history of the covenanting armies, 1639–1651* (1990) · H. Marryat, *One year in Sweden including a visit to the Isle of Gotland* (1862) · *GEC, Peerage* · *Scots peerage* · S. Murdoch, *Britain, Denmark–Norway and the house of Stuart, 1603–1660* (2000) · *State trials*, 5.426–520 · G. D. Squibb, *The high court of chivalry* (1959)
Archives NA Scot., corresp. and papers relating to levying of troops for Gustavus Adolphus, GD 84
Wealth at death in receipt of yearly pension of 2000 daler from Denmark–Norway in 1649: Riis, *Should auld acquaintance*

Mackay, Donald James, eleventh Lord Reay and Baron Reay (1839–1921), administrator in India and educational administrator, was born at The Hague, the Netherlands, on 22 December 1839, the elder son of Aeneas, Baron Mackay of Ophemert, Holland, tenth Lord Reay (1807–1876), and his wife, Mary Catherine Anne Jacoba Fagel (d. 1886), the daughter of Baron Fagel, privy councillor of the Netherlands. His ancestor Donald Mackay, first Lord Reay, raised a regiment among his clansmen and served at its head with the Danish and Swedish armies during the Thirty Years' War. Mackay was educated at the University of Leiden (1856–61), where he graduated in laws with a thesis in colonial policy and administration. On entering the Dutch foreign office he was attached to the Dutch legation in London, but was transferred the same year (1861) to the Dutch Colonial Office. In 1871 he entered the chamber of representatives as a member of the Left (Liberal) Party.

In 1875 Mackay left the Netherlands and settled in England, succeeding to his father's Scottish title in 1876 and becoming naturalized in 1877. He married in the latter year Fanny Georgiana Jane (d. 1917), the daughter of Richard Hasler, of Aldingbourne, Sussex, and the widow of Alexander Mitchell MP, of Stow, Midlothian. In 1881 he was created Baron Reay in the peerage of the United Kingdom, and in 1885 Gladstone appointed him governor of Bombay, a post which he held until 1890. Throughout his career Reay paid close attention to international law and politics and to colonial administration. He was a liberal, convinced of the necessity of binding together the colonies and India with the mother country. Domestically his main interests lay in education, and he promoted the cause of popular and especially technical education.

Reay was a vigorous, self-reliant, and enlightened governor who took a warm interest in the various sectors of the Indian community and exerted himself in promoting education, especially technical training. He also paid much attention to the development of internal communications, especially of the railway system. In 1888 his honour and nerve were tested in the case of a British commissioner charged with corruption. A full indemnity was offered to witnesses, but his action was overruled by the viceroy and described in the House of Lords by the secretary of state as ill-advised. His offer of resignation was not accepted. He was made GCIE in 1887 and GCSI in 1890. In 1894 Reay was appointed under-secretary of state for India, but he held the office for only fifteen months, the Liberal ministry of Lord Rosebery having terminated in summer 1895. During this period the expedition to Chitral was organized and successfully concluded.

In 1897 Reay was elected chairman of the London school board, and he retained that office until the abolition of the board in 1904. He also enjoyed a long association with University College, London, which led to his serving as vice-president of its council from 1892 and president from 1897. He became closely involved in moves to reform the University of London and enlarge its powers (the Association for Promoting a Teaching University for London was founded in his house). After University College became incorporated in the reorganized university in 1907 he continued until his death in 1921 to serve as chairman of the college committee.

Another long-lasting connection was with the Royal Asiatic Society, of which Reay was president from 1893 until 1921. This involved him in the movement to establish the British Academy, and he found himself included in the list of the original fellows. When Lord Rosebery declined the invitation to become the new academy's first president, Reay's name was substituted, and he served in that capacity from 1902 to 1907. Although he was not himself a scholar, he had generous intellectual sympathies, and he made a suitable figurehead. The ambitious plans for the new academy which he put forward in his first presidential address in 1903 were, unfortunately, largely unfulfilled. He was as cosmopolitan in his international connections, and his successor as president paid tribute to him 'as our ambassador accredited to all the learned bodies of the Continent'—including the Académie des Sciences Morales et Politiques in Paris, of which he was elected a foreign associate in 1906.

His involvement with these three bodies gave Reay a key position in the long campaign to found a school of oriental studies in London. Eventually, in 1908, after leading a deputation to the prime minister, he was appointed to chair a Treasury committee which recommended the establishment of a school as a constituent college within the University of London, although it was not until 1917 that the school opened its doors to admit its first students. Reay served on its governing body until his death.

Reay took an active part in the proceedings of the Institut de Droit International, of which he was elected an associate (1882) and member (1892), serving as vice-president at Venice (1896) and at Brussels (1902), and as president at Edinburgh (1904). In spite, however, of his interest in questions of international law he never published any work on the subject.

In 1907 Reay was appointed third British delegate to the second peace conference at The Hague, where he served as member of the second commission on the laws and customs of war on land. He read a closely reasoned explanation of the definition of fleet auxiliaries, delivered important speeches proposing the abolition of contraband, and presented the new British draft on the subject of delays of grace.

Reay was sworn of the privy council in 1906, created KT in 1911, and served as lord lieutenant of Roxburghshire from 1892 to 1918. He was rector of St Andrews University from 1884 to 1886 and held honorary degrees from the universities of Edinburgh and Oxford.

In January 1917 an accident, which resulted in a broken thigh bone, confined Reay thenceforth to an invalid's chair, but this did not prevent him from attending meetings of University College, the British Academy, and the Royal Asiatic Society. He died at Carolside, Earlston, Berwickshire, on 31 July 1921. His wife had predeceased him in 1917, and they had no children.

Reay was a devout Presbyterian, of simple tastes and habits. He took an active part in the foundation and opening (1883) of St Columba's Presbyterian Church, Pont Street, London. A statue of him commemorating his services as governor of Bombay was erected in Bombay in 1895.   E. M. SATOW, rev. P. W. H. BROWN

Sources Bryce, 'Lord Reay, 1839–1921', *PBA*, 10 (1921–3), 533–9 · *WWW* · W. Wilson Hunter, *Bombay, 1885–1890: a study in Indian administration* (1893) · S. Simmonds and S. Digby, *The Royal Asiatic Society: its history and treasures* (1979) · C. H. Philips, *The School of Oriental and African Studies, University of London, 1917–1967* (1967) · N. B. Harte, *The University of London, 1836–1986: an illustrated history* (1986) · *CGPLA Eng. & Wales* (1922) · Burke, *Peerage* (2000) · personal knowledge (1927)
Archives NA Scot., speeches at the second international peace conference · Nationaal Archief, The Hague, corresp. and papers · SOAS, papers as governor of Bombay | BL, letters to Sir Henry Campbell-Bannerman, Add. MSS 41232–41242 · BL, letters to T. H. S. Escott, Add. MS 58785 · BL, letters to Herbert Gladstone, Add. MS 46017 · BL, letters to Mary Gladstone, Add. MS 46242 · BL, letters to W. E. Gladstone, Add. MSS 44463–44789 · BL, letters to Arthur Godley, MS Eur. F 102 · BL, letters to Sir Edward Walter Hamilton, Add. MS 48617 · BL OIOC, corresp. with Lord Cross, MS Eur. E 243 · BL OIOC, letters to first Viscount Morley, MS Eur. D 573 · Bodl. Oxf., letters to Lord Kimberley · CAC Cam., corresp.

with Lord Randolph Churchill · CUL, corresp. with Lord Hardinge · King's AC Cam., letters to Oscar Browning · NL Scot., corresp. with Lord Rosebery · NL Scot., corresp., incl. with Lord Rosebery and Sir Patrick Geddes · NRA, earl of Kimberley papers · PRO, corresp. with Sir Ernest Satow, PRO 30/33/11/11–18
Likenesses H. R. Pinker, statue, *c*.1895, Bombay · A. Gilbert, bust, Bombay · J. Russell & Sons, photograph, NPG · A. A. Van Anrooy, oils (in old age), British Academy, London · wood-engraving (after photograph by Elliott & Fry), NPG; repro. in *ILN* (17 Feb 1883)
Wealth at death £83,500 16s. 10d.: probate, 17 March 1922, *CGPLA Eng. & Wales*

Mackay, (William) Fulton Beith (1922–1987), actor, was born on 12 August 1922, at 19 Underwood Lane, Paisley, Renfrewshire, son of William McKay, who worked in the Navy, Army, and Air Force Institutes (NAAFI), and his wife, Agnes Scott McDermid. Orphaned at an early age, he was brought up by a widowed aunt in Clydebank, where he attended Elgin Street primary school, Whitecrook primary, and then Clydebank high school. A bright pupil with a good singing voice and considerable ability at football, he had begun his training as a quantity surveyor when war broke out in 1939. After his experiences as a young volunteer air-raid warden in the Clydebank blitz, in 1941 he joined the Black Watch, serving abroad for five years.

Mackay decided to become an actor and trained at the Royal Academy of Dramatic Art in London. While a student, he saw the Glasgow Citizens' Theatre Company in the West End in *Let Wives Tak Tent*, Robert Kemp's Scots adaptation of *L'école des femmes*. The acting style of the company, particularly that of Duncan Macrae, so fired his imagination that he resolved to work at the Citizens. He achieved his ambition, playing there from 1949 to 1951 and from 1953 to 1958 alongside such stalwarts as Roddy MacMillan, Stanley Baxter, Andrew Keir, and that same Duncan Macrae who became his mentor and lifelong friend.

Fulton Mackay soon made his mark in many varied roles. He was King Humanitie in *Ane Satyre of the Thrie Estaites* by Sir David Lindsay (1490–1555) in the Edinburgh Festival of 1949; he gave 'a fine, insolent performance' (*Glasgow Herald*) as the unscrupulous student tenor in Kemp's eighteenth-century Scots comedy *The Scientific Singers*. In James Bridie's *The Queen's Comedy*, dealing with the Olympian gods' interference in the Trojan wars, he gave a fluid, flaccid performance as Sleep, and in 1958, he made a memorable Jimmy Porter in John Osborne's *Look Back in Anger*.

In 1962 Mackay moved to London and worked in distinguished companies including the Old Vic, as Solveig's Father in Ibsen's *Peer Gynt*, and as Dapper in Tyrone Guthrie's production of Ben Jonson's *The Alchemist*. At this time he married the Irish actress Julia Philomena (Sheila) Manahan and they set up home in Chelsea. He was fond of Ibsen's plays and directed *The Wild Duck* for the Scottish Actors' Company in 1969. In 1971 he played Dr Wangel in Ibsen's *The Lady from the Sea* at Greenwich. In 1972 at the Royal Lyceum Theatre, Edinburgh, he played in Bill Bryden's *Willie Rough*, creating the one-legged, bibulous war veteran Hughie Frizzell, repeating this inspired tragicomic performance in the Shaw Theatre in London, where in 1976 his performance as Davis in Harold Pinter's *The Caretaker* also won him acclaim. He played the alcoholic screen writer in Bill Bryden's play *Old Movies* at the National and the possessive father in Eugene O'Neill's *Anna Christie* in 1979. Of this performance Eric Shorter's review in the *Daily Telegraph* in 1979 noted that here was an actor capable of matching the strength of O'Neill's writing.

Mackay was happy to acknowledge the part television played in his career. In the 1960s he played the chief of police in *Special Branch*; but the role that gained him the admiration of millions was that of the ferocious, pompous prison warder Mr Mackay in *Porridge*, where his verbal exchanges with Ronnie Barker's Fletcher made superb television comedy. His most notable film was Bill Forsyth's *Local Hero*, where his gentle, philosophical old beachcomber was an engaging creation.

He enjoyed a quiet home life with his wife, Sheila. Under the pen name of Aeneas MacBride he wrote four television plays for BBC Scotland, including *The Girl who Wore Flowers in her Hair*. He was also a talented artist. In 1981 the Royal Scottish Academy of Music and Drama gave him an honorary fellowship and in 1984 he was appointed OBE.

Playing the gaoler in *Die Fledermaus*, Strauss's opera, in the Coliseum was a great delight to Mackay. His last appearance on stage was as Dr Ridgeon in G. B. Shaw's *The Doctor's Dilemma* at the Theatre Royal, Bristol, in March 1987. In the same year on 6 June, his death occurred at 42 Nottingham Place, Westminster, from post-operative complications after minor surgery. In an obituary Allen Wright wrote that 'his enthusiasm for the art of acting inspired respect and warm admiration' and recalled how, of his hard-fought dramatic career, Mackay would often modestly say, using an expression of his old friend Roddy McMillan, that 'It's better than working' (*The Scotsman*).

HELEN MURDOCH

Sources U. Glas. L., special collections department, Scottish Theatre Archive · personal knowledge (2004) · private information (2004) · *Glasgow Herald* (2 May 1950) · A. Wright, *The Scotsman* (8 June 1987) · *CGPLA Eng. & Wales* (1987) · *The Times* (8 June 1987) · will of Fulton Mackay · b. cert. · d. cert.
Archives U. Glas., Scottish Theatre Archive | FILM BFI NFTVA, performance footage | SOUND BL NSA, performance recordings
Likenesses photographs, U. Glas., Scottish Theatre Archive · photographs, Hult. Arch.
Wealth at death £340,277: probate, 16 Sept 1987, *CGPLA Eng. & Wales*

Mackay, Helen Marion McPherson (1891–1965), paediatrician, was born on 23 May 1891 in Inverness, Scotland, the second of three children and only daughter of Duncan Lachlan Mackay, of the Indian Civil Service, and his wife, Marion Gordon Campbell Mackay (*née* Wimberley), the daughter of Douglas Wimberley JP of Inverness. Her early years were spent in Burma, where she was educated at home. She entered Cheltenham Ladies' College at the age of fifteen and went on to study medicine at the London School of Medicine for Women (Royal Free Hospital) and qualified MRCS, LRCP, and MB BS (London) in 1914. It was very difficult at that time for a woman to pursue a career

in a medical speciality but there were some opportunities in paediatrics and she managed to obtain an appointment as house physician and surgeon at the Queen Elizabeth Hospital for Children in Hackney. She belonged to a generation of paediatricians who took part in the development of paediatrics as a speciality distinct from adult medicine and was one of the first women to be appointed as a hospital consultant in any speciality. She became MRCP and MD (London) in 1917.

In 1920 Mackay became the first woman to be appointed as physician to the Queen Elizabeth Hospital. Soon after her appointment she went to Vienna with a team of British scientists from the Lister Institute for Preventive Medicine, led by Harriette Chick, to research into the cause and prevention of rickets, an extremely common disease in the famine which occurred in the aftermath of the First World War. This study provided important evidence for the role of cod liver oil and sunlight in the prevention and cure of rickets in childhood. The Medical Research Council's Special Report 77 summarized their work in Vienna. While in Vienna Mackay observed that anaemia was even more common than rickets and became interested in finding the cause. Having found that many of the anaemic infants in Vienna improved with iron therapy, she returned to London and made further studies on anaemia in childhood. Using the same scientific rigour that characterized the study on rickets and working with a medical statistician, Major Greenwood, she became the first person to show that iron deficiency is the commonest cause of anaemia in children, to study its epidemiology, and to draw attention to the importance of its prevention. Her *Nutritional Anaemia in Infancy* was published in 1931, and the findings of her studies still summarize fairly accurately much of our present day knowledge of iron deficiency anaemia in infancy.

Mackay worked as a consultant paediatrician to the Mother's Hospital, Clapton, and to Hackney Hospital until her retirement in 1959 and made many research contributions into the nutrition of new-born babies and young children. In 1934 she became the first woman to be made a fellow of the Royal College of Physicians. Her widest reputation came from her research work but the deep respect and affection with which she was held locally came from her unfailing commitment to her clinical work in the East End of London. She encouraged and inspired many young paediatricians, notably Ciceley Williams, who described the nutritional disorder of kwashiorkor. Mackay recognized the importance of social factors in child health and was one of the first paediatricians to take paediatric care outside hospital into the community. She leaned to the left in her political views but was not politically active. She had no conspicuous religious beliefs.

Dressed in the familiar brown suit and tie she wore every day, and sometimes sporting a trilby hat, Mackay had a somewhat severe physical presence but her smile was warm and kind. She had an engaging honesty and lack of self-importance. She was reserved, with a quiet voice, and had little small talk but could be firm and show disapproval when necessary. She never married. Lorel

Goodfellow (*d.* 1988), a laboratory scientist, with whom she wrote one of her first papers on anaemia, became her lifelong companion. Visitors to their home were amused to find that they always called each other 'Mackay' and 'Goodfellow'. Outside medicine, her abiding interest was ornithology and she belonged to more societies concerned with this pursuit than with medicine. Mackay died of a stroke in the Elizabeth Garrett Anderson Hospital in London on 17 July 1965 and was buried on the 20th at Golders Green crematorium.   DAVID STEVENS

Sources *BMJ* (7 Aug 1965), 367 · *The Lancet* (31 July 1965), 248 · Munk, *Roll* · H. Mackay, biographical details, RCP Lond. · D. Stevens, 'Helen Mackay and anaemia in infancy—then and now', *Archives of disease in Childhood*, 66 (1991), 1451–3 · D. Stevens, 'Helen Mackay, another iron lady', *BMJ* (20 July 1991), 147–8 · Richard Dobbs funeral address, priv. coll. · Theodore Fox funeral address, priv. coll. · Ciceley Williams funeral address, priv. coll. · private information (2004) · *WWW*
Likenesses photographs, Royal College of Physicians Library
Wealth at death £52,001: probate, 14 Oct 1965, *CGPLA Eng. & Wales*

Mackay, Hugh (*d.* 1692), army officer, was the third son of Colonel Hugh Mackay (*d.* 1662) of Scourie in Sutherland, and Ann, daughter of John Corbet of Arkboll, Ross.

Military service, 1660–1688 In 1660 Mackay, 'a Scotch gentleman, very large in his person' (Bernardi, 18), took an ensign's commission in Lord George Douglas's regiment (later the Royal Scots), then in French pay, and served against the Dutch. He succeeded to the family estates in 1668 after both his elder brothers were murdered in separate incidents in Caithness. Rather than return home, in 1669 he volunteered to fight the Turks as an auxiliary with the emperor's force in Candia (Crete), for which he received a medal from the Venetian republic. In his absence his brothers' murderers, William and John Sinclair, obtained remission by representing that they had acted in self-defence. On his return from Candia (Crete) Mackay petitioned the king to have this decision reversed, but to no effect.

Mackay returned to his regiment and as a captain in 1672 took part in the French occupation of Gelderland. He was stationed in Bemmel, where he was billeted on the family of Clara de Bie, whom he married. They had a son and three daughters. His marriage prompted a change of loyalty in that he resigned his commission in the French service and joined the Dutch army. Through the influence of Adjutant-General Colyear, another Scot in the Dutch service, in 1674 Mackay was given the command of ten independent English companies then serving at the siege of Grave. He was promoted to colonel of a regiment in 1677, and in 1685 commanded the brigade of English and Scottish regiments when it was ordered to England during Monmouth's rebellion. King James promoted him to major-general of the forces in Scotland, but once the emergency was over Mackay returned to the Netherlands. When James recalled the brigade again in 1688, he refused to return to England. On being ordered a second time to return, he relented and 'went to take leave of the Prince of Orange and the States; but being there let into the secret, as was supposed, of the intended Revolution, he changed

Hugh Mackay (*d.* 1692), by William Barnard (after Seeman?)

his mind' (*Historical Account*, 63) and stayed in the Netherlands. In November 1688 he sailed back to England as part of the prince of Orange's invasion force.

Commander-in-chief in Scotland After the revolution William III appointed Mackay commander-in-chief of the army in Scotland. He was ill for the first few weeks of 1689 and did not arrive in Edinburgh until late March. Although the city was in safe hands, the castle was held by the Jacobite duke of Gordon while John Graham, Viscount Dundee, was attempting to raise the highlands for King James. Mackay's first act was to detach men to secure Stirling Castle against the Jacobites. Once he was satisfied that Edinburgh was out of danger, he set off in pursuit of Dundee. Despite 'being thirty years a stranger to that kingdom' (H. Mackay, 45), he displayed a confident and remarkable knowledge of highland warfare. He spent the next four months harrying Dundee's highland army. He avoided a battle because his own men were mostly new recruits whom he hoped to train on the march, and because he had only 'a small number [of men] whereof, as afterwards appeared, a considerable part was traitors' (ibid., 11). He solved the second problem by having a number of his dragoons officers arrested before the campaign was over.

After marching to Inverness, where he left a garrison, Mackay had only 650 men against Dundee's 3000. 'But God, who overrules all the actions of the creatures, preserved singularly that small handful of men beyond all expectation' (H. Mackay, 35). His careful positioning along the eastern fringe of the highlands kept Dundee confined to the hills as any descent into the plain would put the highlanders at risk of being massacred by Mackay's horsemen. He returned to Edinburgh, where the castle had surrendered to Sir John Lanier in his absence, and on 4 July

1689 he was appointed a privy counsellor for Scotland. While in Edinburgh he learned that Blair Castle, a stronghold belonging to the marquess of Atholl, had been seized for Dundee and was being sieged by Lord John Murray, the marquess's son.

Mackay marched his reinforced army from Perth to Dunkeld on 26 July 1689 and on the next day set out for Blair Castle. Five miles from his objective he was met at Killiecrankie by Dundee's army. The highlanders lined the ridge above his position, with their backs 'to a very high hill, which is the ordinary maxim of Highlanders who never fight against regular forces upon any thing of equal terms, without a sure retreat at their back, particularly if their enemies be provided of horse' (H. Mackay, 51). As the highlanders charged down the slope, Mackay, accompanied by his servant, cut his way through them and turned to survey the scene. The highlanders had pierced through the line 'so that in a twinkling of an eye, our men, as well as the enemy, were out of sight being got down pell mell to the river where our baggage stood' (ibid., 57). Although his inexperienced battalions 'behaved lyck the vilest cowards in nature' (ibid., 255), the three regiments that stood their ground did great execution:

> The enemy lost on the field six for our one, the fire to our right having been continued and brisk, whereby not only Dundee, with several gentlemen of quality of the counties of Angus and Perth, but also many of the best gentlemen among the Highlanders, particularly of the MacDonalds of the Isles and Glengarie were killed.   (ibid., 59)

Mackay's army was nevertheless shattered, the greatest losses being not on the field of battle but in the pursuit of those who fled. As night fell, while the highlanders were still distracted by the plunder of the baggage train, he led off the remnants of his force and marched them for two days and nights across a hostile country to Stirling. The experience of Killiecrankie inspired him to replace the old plug bayonet with a bayonet of his own design which was fixed by two rings alongside, rather than in, the muzzle, so that when facing a charge, 'the soldiers may safely keep their fire till they pour it into their breasts, and then have no other motion to make but to push as with a pike' (ibid., 52).

After Killiecrankie In Stirling Mackay was far from despondent and, as he had not been pursued, he struck out northwards 'to chase those highland barbarians again to their hilly confidence and refuge' (H. Mackay, 255). Before setting out, he dismissed the thousands of west country Presbyterians who had gathered in the hope that he would arm them to fight the highlanders. He would, he wrote, 'rather make use of any succour than see the enemies of the gospel fortify themselves in the kingdom' (ibid., 63). Four days after his defeat at Killiecrankie, he surprised Perth and directed his dragoons to attack a group of 300 highlanders outside the town, killing 120 of them. 'They were all Athole-men and were so opiniater or stupefied that not one of them called for quarters. We lost but one man in the action' (ibid., 64). He then marched to Forfar and on to Aberdeen after Dundee's successor, Alexander Cannon,

> who, not daring to meet such a body of horse in the plain country, retired to the hills, marching round the skirts of the Highlands while Mackay attended him in the plain below and daily in sight of each other and exchanging bravadoes to fight; but the one durst as little march up the high grounds as the other descend to the low.   (Balcarres, 49)

Nevertheless, Cannon managed to slip away from Mackay to attack the Cameronian regiment which had garrisoned Dunkeld. There, on 21 August 1689, Cannon's army suffered a defeat from which it never recovered. Three days later Mackay took Blair Castle, after which the weather made any further campaigning impossible. The highland army dispersed until the spring, Cannon set up winter quarters in Lochaber, and Mackay returned to Edinburgh. There he was frustrated by the government's failure to implement his plans for building a fort at Inverlochy to control the western highlands. The infighting in Scotland between the various factions and religious groups gave Mackay 'a real distaste of the country and service' (H. Mackay, 77). His frustration was compounded by orders from London to disband some of the dragoons, which Mackay saw as being essential, and making Lord Leven, 'tho' but a colonel and a youth without service', senior to him on the commission to remodel the army for the spring campaign. Mackay 'nevertheless dissembled his displeasure, lest by any such disputes the hands of the enemys might be strengthened' (ibid., 83).

During the winter Thomas Buchan arrived to take over the command of King James's highland army from Cannon. Mackay's response was to detach 600 men to the frigates stationed along the west coast with instructions 'to make a diversion, allarme the rebells coasts, cut their communication with the Islanders now in rebellione against their Majesties authoritie, and to take away or burn all their boats' (H. Mackay, 323). The effect was that when Buchan finally began his campaign in late April, he was unable to raise 1000 men from among the highlanders as the rest were intent on guarding the shore against raids from the frigates. Mackay's best commander, Sir Thomas Livingstone, surprised Buchan's army at Cromdale on 1 May and killed and captured 400 of the fleeing highlanders without the loss of any of his own men.

In July 1690, although frustrated by shortages of supplies, Mackay built Fort William at Inverlochy in eleven days and garrisoned it with 1000 men under the command of Lieutenant-Colonel John Hill. He remarked that whatever 'I can doe to a dispersd lurcking enemy, the governour of Inverlochy can doe it much more effectually within three months: that is to burn their houses and destroy their corns' (H. Mackay, 331). He then marched off in pursuit of Buchan, whom he dogged for the rest of the summer, frustrating attempts on Aberdeen and Inverness. As the season wore on, the position of the Jacobites became desperate. By September the only clansmen willing to join Buchan were 'some few loose fellows upon the hope of plunder' (ibid., 354), and by October the rebellion had all but petered out.

Lieutenant-general in Ireland Mackay travelled to the Netherlands, where he spent the winter with his family. In the following spring he received a commission to serve in Ireland as a lieutenant-general under General Ginckel. The campaign of 1691 opened with General St Ruth's Irish army west of the Shannon, and Ginckel's army east of it. After taking the Irish outpost of Ballymore, Ginckel reached Athlone on 19 June and two days later had captured that part of the town on the east bank of the Shannon. The Irish-occupied west bank of the town was separated from the east bank by a narrow bridge which had been broken at the western end. After wasting a week in trying to repair the bridge under heavy fire from the Irish troops, Ginckel held a council of war. Thomas Tollemache proposed an attack through the Shannon itself. Mackay opposed the idea as the attacking troops would then be swept out by the entire Irish army that was camped on the far side of the town. He was overruled.

Ginckel's system was to have his subordinate generals command by rota. As Mackay was due to command on the day of the assault, Ginckel suggested suspending the rota so that Tollemache could put his own plan into effect. Mackay refused to be superseded. 'I added that although I did not approve of the attack, I would press ahead with it, with God's help' (H. Mackay, 153). At six in the evening on 30 June, on a signal given by a church bell, 1500 grenadiers leapt out of their trenches and charged into the Shannon under cover of a sudden barrage from Ginckel's artillery. While the pioneers and infantry charged along the broken bridge, Mackay led the second wave of grenadiers through the river. The attack was

> executed by Mackay with so much resolution, that many ancient officers said it was the most gallant action they had ever seen. They passed the river and went through the breaches into the town, with the loss of only fifty men, having killed above a thousand of the enemy; and yet they spared all that asked quarter. (*Burnet's History*, 339)

As his troops secured the town, Mackay told them 'that they had more reason to fall upon their knees and thank God for the victory, and that they were brave men, and the best of men if they would swear less' (Story, 108). The expected counter-attack never came. St Ruth had ignored advice to tear down Athlone's western defences, and the victors found themselves protected from the Irish army by the town's walls. Mackay later wrote that 'The hand of God was clearly visible because to force this passage defied all the rules of war and policy' (H. Mackay, 144).

St Ruth retreated to the west but, determined to face the Williamites in open battle, he allowed Ginckel to catch up with him at Aughrim on 12 July 1691. The Irish army took up prepared positions along Kilcommodon Hill overlooking the road to Galway. The battle began in the late afternoon.

> By the advice of Major-General *Mackay*, it was agreed to begin the fight on the enemies Right thereby proposing to draw part of their strength from *Aghrim* Castle near to where their main Body was posted, so that the Right Wing of the *English* might have easier Passage over to attack their left, and then the whole *English* Army might have the opportunity to

engage, which was otherways impossible which Advice had its desired end. (Boyer, 262)

While the battle was still in doubt, Mackay directed a large body of horse to break through on the left of the Irish line. The Irish left wing collapsed, and the battle, which proved to be the bloodiest in Irish history, became a rout.

The Williamite army reached Galway on 19 July. On that night Mackay commanded those troops who crossed the Corrib in tin boats to prevent any reinforcements from reaching the town. On the following day the governor called for a ceasefire and began negotiating terms. At the siege of Limerick Mackay led on 25 August 1691 one of the first wave of troops to occupy the high ground overlooking the city. After a month of bombardment he and Tollemache were left in charge of the troops on the co. Limerick side of the Shannon when Ginckel moved his headquarters with the rest of the army across the pontoon bridge into co. Clare. On 23 September 1691 Sarsfield asked for a ceasefire. Mackay took part in the ensuing negotiations, and signed the civil articles of the treaty of Limerick (3 October 1691) as a witness. He left Ireland at the beginning of November 1691 and returned to his family in the Netherlands for the winter.

Last days In the spring of 1692 Mackay rejoined the army in Flanders, where he served under Count Solms against the French. At the battle of Steenkerke on 3 August 1692, 'being ordered to a post that he saw could not be maintained, he sent his opinion about it; but the former orders were confirmed; so he went on saying only, "The will of the Lord be done"' (*Burnet's History*, 348). He was killed.

Burnet wrote of Mackay:

> He was a man of such strict principles that he would not have served in a war that he did not think lawful. He took great care of his soldiers' morals and forced them to be both sober and just in their quarters; he spent all the time that he was master of in secret prayers and in reading of the Scriptures. It was observed that when he had full leisure for his devotions, he acted with a peculiar exaltation of courage. (*Burnet's History*, 349)

He left detailed accounts of his campaigns in Scotland and Ireland, which have been published, together with an account of the siege of Candia and a treatise on the wars of Julius Caesar, which have not. His military manual, *The Rules of War for the Infantry* (1693) contains twenty-three articles on the drill and preparation necessary on the day of battle. The last of these begins:

> Lastly, when all dispositions are made, and the army waiting for the signal to move towards the enemy, both officers and soldiers ought seriously to recommend (together with their souls and bodies) the care and protection of the cause for which they so freely expose their lives, to GOD.

PIERS WAUCHOPE

Sources H. Mackay, *Memoirs of the war carried on in Scotland and Ireland*, ed. J. M. Hog and others, Bannatyne Club, 45 (1833) · J. Mackay of Rockfield, *The life of Lieutenant-General Hugh Mackay of Scoury* (1836) · G. Story, *A continuation of the impartial history of the wars of Ireland* (1693) · *An abridgement of Bishop Burnet's History of his own times*, ed. T. Stackhouse (1906) · *A supplement to Burnet's History of my own time*, ed. H. C. Foxcroft (1902) · *An historical account of the British regiments employed … in the formation and defence of the Dutch republic* (1794) · C. Lindsay [earl of Balcarres], *Memoirs touching the revolution* *in Scotland*, ed. A. W. C. Lindsay [earl of Crawford and Balcarres], Bannatyne Club (1841) • A. Boyer, *The history of King William III*, 3 vols. (1702–3), vol. 2 • J. Bernardi, *A short history of the life of Major John Bernardi written by himself* (1729)

Archives BL, memoirs of campaigns in Ireland and Crete, Add. MS 33264 • BL, memoirs of campaigns in Scotland and treatise on Julius Caesar's wars, King's MSS 227, 245, 246 • Nationaal Archief, The Hague, papers • NL Scot., memoirs and corresp.

Likenesses W. Barnard, engraving (after E. Seeman?), NPG [*see illus.*]

MacKay, Iain Dall (1656?–1754), piper, composer, and bard, was born at Meikle Talladale, Loch Maree, in the parish of Gairloch, Wester Ross, the only child of Ruairidh MacKay (*c*.1590–1689), piper to MacKenzie of Gairloch. The name of his mother is unknown; she is said to have been a daughter of the first Lord Reay, chief of MacKay. Ruairidh left Sutherland for Gairloch in the early seventeenth century.

Smallpox deprived Iain of his sight when he was seven. His father was not blind, and the condition was not hereditary. Nothing is known of Iain's physical appearance; he was left-handed, and information in his poems indicates that he may have been manic depressive. He was illiterate because of his blindness. A contemporary said: 'From his agreeable manners [he] added more to the conviviality of a company than any man I know' (A. MacKay, 12).

About 1678 Iain was sent to Skye to study piping and composition under Patrick Og MacCrimmon, and he remained there until about 1685. During these years he composed *The Blind Piper's Obstinacy*, *Pronnadh nam miall* ('Squashing of lice'), *Am port leathach* ('The half-finished tune'), and *The Hen's March*. He also learned to compose bardic verse, possibly without formal training other than in conversation with the Talisker circle, a group of poets and musicians in Skye.

After returning to Gairloch Iain became piper and bard to the laird. Little of his poetic work has survived, but there is enough to show his mastery of the genre. *Corrienessan's Lament* (1697), the earliest extant piobaireachd poem, is a fine example of Gaelic nature poetry. Two stanzas survive of his *Elegy* for Sir Kenneth MacKenzie (1703), and five lines of his *Song of Welcome* for Sir Alexander MacKenzie (1720). His long celebratory poem *A Poet's Blessing* on the marriage of Sir Alexander (1730) seems to be complete. Two poems made in Skye are the *Song to Hector MacLean, Laird of the Island of Muck*, dating from between 1730 and 1733, and the stately *Ode of Consolation* for Sir Alexander MacDonald of Sleat (1734).

Iain lived in Engadal, above the laird's house, until moving in his old age to Badachro on Loch Gairloch. In the 1690s his cousin was paying him a small allowance, and he later came under the patronage of Robert Munro, chief of the Munros of Foulis, who also was blind. Robert encouraged Iain to compose piobaireachd in honour of both Munros and MacKays. Between 1697 and 1729 Iain composed *Munros' Salute* (*c*.1698), *The Battle of Glenshiel* (1719), *The Unjust Incarceration* (*c*.1720), *The Lament for the Laird of Anapool* (in honour of Iain's second cousin; 1720s?), *The Lament for Lady Anapool* (1720s?), *The Lament for the Laird of Contullich* (1726), and *The Lament for Donald Duaghal MacKay*

(in honour of Iain's grandfather, first Lord Reay; the authorship of this work is disputed). It was said in 1841 that Iain had composed 'numberless strathspeys, reels and jigs' (J. MacKenzie, *Sar-obair*, 108), but these have not survived, apart from two reels, *Cailleach liath Raasaidh* ('The old grey-haired woman of Raasay') and *Cailleach a'mhuilleir* ('The miller's old woman').

In 1720 Iain's absentee chief returned to Gairloch, and Iain's new prosperity enabled him to marry. The name of his wife is not known for certain; local tradition suggests she was a Fraser from Talladale. There were two sons, John (who emigrated to Nova Scotia) and Angus (*b. c*.1723), who succeeded his father as piper to Gairloch, and a daughter, whose son was the Gaelic poet William *Ross. The last of the piping MacKays in Gairloch was Angus's son John Roy, who emigrated in 1805.

Probably in the 1720s Iain composed his masterpiece, *The Lament for Patrick Og MacCrimmon*, supposedly after hearing a false rumour of Patrick's death. Iain died, probably at his home, Leas an Rosaich, Badachro, Gairloch, in 1754, aged, according to tradition, ninety-eight. He was buried beside his father in the old burial-ground at Gairloch. The grave is now unmarked, but a stone was 'noted by earlier writers but not found in 1985' (Beattie and Beattie, 28).   BRIDGET MACKENZIE

Sources 'Squire' J. MacKay, 'Reminiscences of a long life', MS, 1868, Public Archives, Halifax, Nova Scotia, MG 20 [pub. in *Oban Times* (1935)], 674/7 • A. MacRae, 'The MacKays of Gairloch', in *Proceedings of the Piobaireachd Society conference, 1982*, Piobaireachd Society, 1–16 • B. Mackenzie, 'Iain Dall MacKay, the blind piper of Gairloch: the man and his work', in *Proceedings of the Piobaireachd Society conference, 1994*, Piobaireachd Society, 1–29 • B. Mackenzie, 'Where did the blind piper live? New discoveries about the MacKay family in Gairloch', *Piping Times*, 45/12 (1992–3), 17–25; 46/4 (1993–4), 26–32; 46/5 (1993–4), 17–23 • W. Matheson, ed., *The blind harper / An clarsair dall*, Scottish Gaelic Texts Society, 12 (1970) • J. H. Dixon, *Gairloch, and guidebook to Loch Maree* (1886) [repr. 1974] • J. G. Gibson, 'Piper John MacKay and Roderick MacLennan: a tale of two immigrants and their incomplete genealogy', *Nova Scotia Historical Review*, 2/2 (1982) • W. MacGill, *Old Ross-shire and Scotland from the Tain and Balnagowan documents* (1909) • J. MacKenzie, *Pigeon holes of memory*, ed. C. Byam Shaw (1988) • O. MacKenzie, *A hundred years in the highlands* (1921) • A. G. Beattie and M. H. Beattie, *Pre-1855 gravestone inscriptions in Wester Ross, Gairloch old burial ground* (1985) • J. Mackenzie, ed., *Sar-obair nam bard Gaelach: the beauties of Gaelic poetry*, new edn (1907) • A. MacKay, *A collection of ancient piobaireachd or highland pipe music* (1838) [republished 1972]

Archives NL Scot., Smith MS 14876, fol. 36 a–b • U. Glas., MacDiarmaid MS • U. Glas., MacLagan MS

McKay, Ian John (1953–1982), soldier, was born on 7 May 1953 at Chapeltown maternity home, Sheffield, the eldest of the three sons of Kenneth John McKay (1929–1998), a pyrometrical observer in the steelworks, and his wife, Freda Doreen Hargreaves (*b*. 1933). He was educated at Blackburn primary school (1957–8), Roughwood infant and junior school (1958–64), and Rotherham grammar school (1964–70). Although he did well academically at school, he was best remembered as a keen sportsman. He won junior titles and awards in local championships for cricket, tennis, athletics, and badminton. However, his talents as a footballer were such that at the time he joined the army he was training with Sheffield United Football Club.

McKay left school at seventeen determined to join the Parachute regiment, against the advice of his father. It was suggested he try to gain entry to the Royal Military Academy, Sandhurst, for officer training as he was well educated and a successful sportsman. He rejected the idea of further study as he was impatient to start soldiering, and felt he would prefer to work his way up through the ranks. He enlisted on 3 August 1970 and six months later was a qualified paratrooper, posted to the 1st battalion, the Parachute regiment (1 Para).

In March 1971, while still only seventeen, he went with his battalion to Northern Ireland. Shortly after his arrival three young Scottish soldiers were killed by the IRA in a single incident, which caused great public disquiet as they were under eighteen. McKay was sent home until after his birthday. He rejoined his battalion in time for the event known afterwards as 'bloody Sunday'. He was involved in the clash between the battalion and illegal marchers and IRA gunmen that resulted in 1 Para killing thirteen men aged between seventeen and forty-one. A fourteenth man, aged fifty-nine, died later. He subsequently gave evidence at Lord Chief Justice Widgery's inquiry. For safety reasons McKay and others involved were subsequently excused further service in Northern Ireland.

A former commanding officer described McKay as bright, cheerful, enthusiastic, outgoing, and utterly dedicated to his profession, with a very determined streak. He hated to lose. On 4 December 1976 he married a dental nurse, Marica Coffey, née Vickers (b. 1948), and they had a daughter, Melanie Jane McKay, who was born on 5 August 1977. During his twelve years' service before going to the Falkland Islands he worked his way up the promotion ladder to the rank of sergeant, proving himself an excellent instructor of recruits.

In April 1982 he sailed for the Falklands as the platoon sergeant of 4 platoon, B company, 3 Para, having only recently joined that battalion. The first major engagement for his unit was the attack on Mount Longdon, one of several key features about 8 miles west of the capital, Stanley. The struggle of 3 Para to secure Mount Longdon on the night of 11–12 June took ten hours of vicious infantry fighting in the dark, involving frequent hand-to-hand encounters with bayonet and boot among the rocks and bunkers. Near the summit the 4 platoon commander fell wounded and McKay took command. He realized that a heavy machine gun only about 35 yards away was holding up the attack. He gathered four soldiers, arranged covering fire, and led the rush forwards. Two were cut down instantly. The others reached some cover and grenaded the enemy. McKay and Corporal Bailey again moved forward but this time Bailey was hit so McKay continued the assault on his own. The exact circumstances of his death are not known. His body was found within a few feet of a bunker with several dead Argentinians near by. His supreme gallantry earned him the posthumous award of the Victoria Cross. Although initially buried in the Falklands McKay's body, along with sixty-three other bodies,

was brought home, and on 26 November 1982 McKay was buried again with full military honours at Aldershot military cemetery.   MARK ADKIN

Sources M. Adkin, *The last eleven?* (1991) · J. Thompson, *No picnic* (1985) · M. Arthur, *Above all courage* (1985) · private information (2004) [F. D. McKay, mother]
Archives FILM IWM FVA, news footage · IWM FVA, *ITN news*, 9 Oct 1982, FAL 17337
Likenesses photograph, repro. in Adkin, *Last eleven?*, facing p. 178

Mackay, Isabella Gordon [Bella] (1777/8–1850), philanthropist and religious activist, was probably born at her parents' home near Brora in Sutherland, the youngest daughter of John Gordon of Carrol and Isabella McLeod of Geanies. Although her father's estate was small, Bella, as she was known, enjoyed 'highly respectable connexions' (Mackay, p. xliv), most notably family ties to Donald McLeod (1745–1834), sheriff-depute of Ross. On 3 May 1803 she married John Mackay of Rockfield (1762–1841), eldest son of the Revd Thomas Mackay, one-time minister of Lairg. A graduate of the University of Edinburgh, Mackay served briefly as clerk in the Indian Civil Service until blindness forced him into early pensioned retirement.

Devout Presbyterians, this childless couple had the advantage of modest affluence and prominent social standing. Moving in urbane circles, the Mackays numbered as acquaintances such illuminati as Thomas McCrie, Dugald Stewart, and Thomas Thomson. Between 1803 and 1823 they sojourned in Cromarty, Lairg, London, Edinburgh, Devon, and Shinness in the highlands of Scotland, taking up permanent residence in Edinburgh in 1823. During the summer months, they often migrated to Rockfield, an estate formerly called Little Tarrel in the parish of Tarbat, Easter Ross, which they had purchased in 1804. As principal landowners in Tarbat, the Mackays were credited with 'extensive and judiciously conducted improvements' (*Statistical Account*, 14.465).

Isabella Gordon Mackay was an exemplary helpmeet, acting as her husband's amanuensis and sharing in his humanitarian interests, particularly the Gaelic Schools' Society and Edinburgh Auxiliary Bible Society, as well as the welfare of orphans and indigent blind. In 1842 she became his biographer, celebrating his life in a laudatory memoir which was included in a reprinted edition of his *Life of Lieut.-Gen. Hugh Mackay of Scoury*. Although devoted to her husband, her interests extended far beyond the home into the public sphere of benevolence where she demonstrated a singular talent for awakening the sympathies of others in her own good works.

Two forces shaped Isabella Gordon Mackay's life—her Scottish patriotism and her Christian faith. Touched by the 'Spirit of grace', she was motivated to 'consecrate' hand, head, and heart to the 'salvation of souls' and a variety of humanitarian causes (*A Brief Sketch of the Cape Breton Mission*, 18). Her primary interest was the Presbyterian mission field in the British North American colony of Nova Scotia. As a zealous supporter of the Glasgow Colonial Society she was the prime mover behind the organization of several itinerating libraries established in Merigomish,

Middle River, Baddeck, and Margaree by 1830. In 1832 she resolved to focus her energies: she mobilized the Edinburgh Ladies' Association and devised a comprehensive blueprint for the placement of clergy, schoolteachers, and catechists in Cape Breton, Nova Scotia. The specific aim of this association was to alleviate the spiritual and educational destitution of Cape Breton's scattered highland Presbyterian population. Isabella Mackay and the association were practically synonymous: she became the leading publicist and lobbyist for the Cape Breton mission by organizing bazaars and drafting brochures and circulars. She explored every avenue to gain patronage and profile for her cause by corresponding with statesmen and divines alike, including Lord Aberdeen, Lord Glenelg, Sir George Grey, the Revd Thomas Chalmers, and the Revd Robert Burns. Many of the early nineteenth-century Presbyterian clergy who came to Cape Breton were sponsored by the Edinburgh Ladies' Association; indirectly Isabella Mackay moulded the island's distinctive brand of Presbyterianism. She recruited men of piety, physical stamina, and fluency in Gaelic to serve in this mission field; by the 1850s the association furnished stipends for five ministers, eight catechists, three teachers, and three students. The Boularderie Academy opened there in 1837 owing in large measure to her financial and moral support. Based on Lancastrian pedagogical principles, the academy offered courses in grammar, geography, Latin, algebra, and navigation; it also served as a preparatory school for teachers. Bridging spiritual and secular concerns, Isabella dispatched school books, medical supplies, scissors, and cloth, along with tracts and bibles, to Cape Breton's Scottish immigrants. She was also a benefactor to the Free Church College in Halifax, Nova Scotia, contributing over one-third of its library holdings and financing bursaries for deserving Cape Breton students training for the ministry at the college.

Described by one contemporary as 'slightly built' with 'round-ruddy cheeks' and 'great liveliness and energy' (diary of the Revd Murdoch Stewart), this dynamic woman was an outspoken personality who eschewed demure gentility, luxury, and leisure. The words 'indomitable' and 'indefatigable' seem too anaemic for Isabella. In her letters she disparaged young ministers for their materialism, chided the Revd Chalmers for his apathy towards the Cape Breton mission, and harped at the Revd Burns for trespassing on the activities of the Ladies. After her husband's death she chose to live frugally as a boarder, thereby enabling her to contribute more liberally to 'the cause of Christ' (ibid.). By the late 1840s Isabella's interest in Cape Breton was eclipsed by concerns closer to home. The political crisis within the Church of Scotland and widespread poverty in the highlands and islands monopolized her attention. She collected food and clothing for those regions devastated by potato crop failures, and extended relief to the ministers and schoolmasters who had suffered financial hardship by the Disruption.

Isabella Gordon Mackay died in Edinburgh on 15 November 1850. As her final act of Christian patriotism, she left a generous bequest to the Free Church of Scotland to supplement the stipends of ministers stationed in various Sutherland parishes. Both she and her husband were buried in St Cuthbert's churchyard, Edinburgh.

LAURIE C. C. STANLEY-BLACKWELL and
JEAN M. MACLENNAN

Sources I. Mackay, 'Brief sketch of the life and character of John Mackay, esq. of Rockfield', in J. Mackay, *Life of Lieut.-Gen. Hugh Mackay of Scoury*, 2nd edn (1842) · inventory of Isabella Gordon Mackay, NA Scot., SC 70/1/72, 53–7 · will of Isabella Gordon Mackay, NA Scot., RD 5/869, 188–216 · Glasgow Colonial Society correspondence, Victoria University, Toronto, United Church archives · *A brief sketch of the Cape Breton mission with a notice of the late Mrs Mackay of Rockfield … (1851)* · *Annual Report of the Glasgow Colonial Society* (1826–36) · U. Edin., New Coll. L., Rev. Thomas Chalmers MSS, CHA · *Presbyterian Witness* (18 Jan 1851) · D. Sage, *Memorabilia domestica* (1889) · L. Stanley, *The well-watered garden: the Presbyterian church in Cape Breton, 1798–1860* (1983) · diary of the Revd Murdoch Stewart, Public Archives of Nova Scotia, Halifax, Canada, MG1, vol. 1471A · A. Fraser and F. Munro, *Tarbat: Easter Ross, a historical sketch* (1988) · *Sketch of missionary proceedings at Cape Breton, from August, 1833, to December, 1837* [1837?] · *Statistical account of Scotland: Inverness, Ross and Cromarty*, 14 (1845) · *Fasti Scot.*, new edn, vol. 7 · private information (2004) [Mrs H. C. S. Mackenzie; Mrs K. MacLennan] · Public Archives of Nova Scotia, Colonial Office papers, CO 217/157, 159, 162–3, 168–70 · A. Mackenzie, *History of the Macleods* (1889)
Archives Public Archives of Nova Scotia, Halifax, Colonial Office MSS · U. Edin., New Coll. L., Revd Thomas Chalmers MSS · University of Toronto, Victoria University, United Church archives, Glasgow Colonial Society correspondence
Wealth at death £10,141 5s. 4d.—in Scotland, incl. generous legacy to Free Church; plus £1000 owing to her: confirmation, NA Scot., SC 70/1/72, pp. 53–7

Mackay, James Lyle, first earl of Inchcape (1852–1932), shipowner, was born in Bank Street, Arbroath, Forfarshire, on 11 September 1852, the youngest of four children of James Mackay, shipmaster and owner of small barques, of Arbroath, and his wife, Deborah, daughter of Alexander Lyle, of Canada. From his earliest years he lived in the world of shipping; at the age of eight he accompanied his father on a voyage to Archangel, narrowly escaping death by drowning. In 1862 his father was drowned crossing the Atlantic, and his mother died two years later. Mackay was then at Elgin Academy and cared more for the sea than for books. He left school at the age of fourteen and he was employed for a few months as scrivener in a lawyer's office, then he was apprenticed to a rope maker in Arbroath; at nineteen he went to London as a clerk, earning £50 a year with Gellatly, Hankey, Sewell & Co., a shipping agency, and it was his work there and at Gravesend which brought him into daily contact with the seaborne commerce of London. He had a legacy of £100 a year as patrimony.

In 1874 Mackay was appointed to the staff of Mackinnon, Mackenzie & Co., of Calcutta, agents of the British India Steam Navigation Company (BISN). In 1878 the failure of the City of Glasgow Bank ruined the Bombay agents of BISN. In the same year Mackay was chosen by Mackinnon Mackenzie to act in their place. Within two years he was given a partnership with an interest in the Bombay firm. Bombay was not only the port of entry to India, but also was the centre of a vast entrepôt trade extending

James Lyle Mackay, first earl of Inchcape (1852–1932), by Philip A. de Laszlo, 1921

undoubtedly contributed to the establishment of Indian currency on the gold standard. By the time he left India, he was senior partner in the firms of Mackinnon, Mackenzie & Co. and of Macneill & Co., and through his reorganization of Binny & Co., of Madras, his field of enterprise embraced the jute, tea, and coal industries of Bengal, the cotton and wool industries of Madras, the seaborne trade between India and Burma, the Persian Gulf and east Africa, and many ancillary companies in the hinterland of these areas.

In 1893, on the death of Sir William Mackinnon, Mackay returned to Britain to take charge of the London office of the British India Company. Having been impressed by Mackay's contribution to debates at the intersection of administration and trade in India, Lord Lansdowne, as foreign secretary, appointed him special commissioner and plenipotentiary in 1901 to obtain a commercial treaty with China in the aftermath of the Boxer uprising. Uncharacteristic patience, flexibility, and tolerance of delay were demonstrated as progress was gradually made on the dismantling of *likin*, or internal customs, even if the treaty of Shanghai of September 1902 failed to live up to expectations. Lansdowne commended his tenacity and thereafter Mackay's expertise in trade and shipping was regularly sought.

Mackay became a government-nominated director of the Suez Canal Company in 1904 and vice-president of the board and president of the London committee in 1922. Through a similar process he became director of the Anglo-Persian Oil Company, resigning in 1925. As president of the chamber of shipping in 1903, and subsequently in 1918–20, he joined a committee of inquiry into the consular service. In relation to the domestic economy he scrutinized the role of government workshops, 1905–7, with much scepticism. His membership of the war risks advisory committee, 1906–7, marked the more direct application of his expertise; it considered the advisability of a national indemnity for ships and cargo in time of war and this work assumed strategic significance eight years later.

In the Edwardian era Mackay became the government's authority on commercial relations between Britain and India. From 1897 to 1911, an unusually long period, he was a member of the Council of India, and after 1906 he was in regular contact with Lord Morley, who infelicitously offered him the viceroyalty of India in 1909 before obtaining cabinet approval. Mackay came as close as any businessman could to this prized office of imperial diplomacy. In 1907 Mackay represented India (with Morley) at the Imperial Conference, which proved contentious as his free trade outlook hardly accorded with protectionist feeling in the Indian empire. In 1911 he visited India to arbitrate on the disputes on railway regulation, having chaired a committee on the financing of Indian railways in 1907. On his retirement from the Council of India in 1911 he received a barony.

Mackay's supervision of BISN led him to visit Australia in 1900–01 to inspect and reorganize the coastal fleet of

from Durban to Basrah and from Suez to Colombo. Mackay made personal visits to the trading agents to build up a local knowledge of the conditions in the Persian Gulf, which was put at the disposal of the British government in the First World War. His knowledge thus acquired, cemented by his unusually tenacious memory, was of immense value in his task, which included the carriage of troops and stores in connection with the Russo–Turkish War of 1877–8 and the Anglo-Zulu War of 1879. A service from Aden to Zanzibar, established in 1873, led to the emergence by Sir William Mackinnon of the British East Africa Company in 1888, and the emergence of the British east African possessions.

Mackay married on 10 July 1883 Jane Paterson (d. 1937), daughter of James Shanks of Rosely, Arbroath, a leading Scottish engineer. Mackay returned to Calcutta in 1883 and became sheriff in 1892 and president of the Bengal chamber of commerce, from 1890 to 1893. He was confronted with the burning question of the Indian currency. From 1891 to 1893 he served on the legislative council, and in 1892, soon after Mackay was elected president of the Indian Currency Association, the viceroy, H. C. K. Petty-Fitzmaurice, Lord Lansdowne, who had picked him out from the British merchant community, selected him to put their views before the Indian currency committee sitting in London under Lord Herschell. His evidence the Australian Steam Navigation Company. Beyond shipping, his growing presence in British banking and railway interests was exemplified by his directorships of the National Provincial Bank (he was later chairman) and of the East Indian Railway Company. He also became a director of the Great Western Railway (GWR) in 1918. On becoming chairman of British India in 1913 he negotiated amalgamation with the Peninsula and Oriental Steam Navigation Company (P. & O.). In 1914 Inchcape obtained the chairmanship of the P. & O., yet the distinctive identities and autonomy of the two companies were deliberately preserved. The sphere of geographical operations of these companies was extended by the acquisition of the New Zealand Shipping Company and the Federal Steam Navigation Company in 1916. In the immediate post-war period large holdings were obtained in the Orient Line and the short-sea trading General Steam Navigation Company.

Consequently, Inchcape's significance as the most prominent figure in British shipping after 1914 grew with each successive year, most notably illustrated by his chairmanship of the committee which established rates of hire, or 'blue book rates', for vessels chartered by the government, 1914–19. During the First World War he advised the Foreign Office on trading with the enemy, the Board of Agriculture and Fisheries on refrigerated ships carrying meat from Australia, the Board of Trade on congestion at British ports, and the War Office on the transport of troops from India.

But Inchcape always retained a liberal sense of the proper activities of government. He was an early critic of the national shipbuilding yard at Chepstow and drew attention to the menacing possibilities of government control of shipping before the war ended. In his letter writing to the press he campaigned against great schemes for the reconstruction of civil society and urged that industry should be allowed to get on with its business. His forceful condemnation of universal post-elementary education in 1921 was based on a minimal-state perspective which took explicit form when he was president of the Increased Tax Payers Society. As a member of the committee on national expenditure his input was barely second to the chairman, Sir Eric Geddes, and meetings for drafting the report took place at Glenapp Castle, Inchcape's estate in Ayrshire. By June 1922 Inchcape had sold 196 government standard ships and 418 ex-enemy steamers by private sale and quickened the winding up of the Ministry of Shipping at minimum cost. His commitment to anti-waste, espousal of individual business effort, demand that the government should leave trade 'severely alone', and hostility to state interventionism were reinforced by his membership of Lord Cunliffe's influential committee on currency, in 1918, which sought the early restoration of pre-war fiscal policy. In 1922–3 Inchcape gained a direct opportunity to implement the quest for balanced budgets as chairman of the Indian retrenchment committee. In these circumstances it was hardly surprising that he declined the offer of the crown of Albania in 1921, for the new ruler was required to initiate the construction of railways, roads, and schools in the kingdom.

Inchcape did not initiate great enterprises but was chosen to develop firms which already existed, first Mackinnon, Mackenzie & Co. and second P. & O. After 1913 his prime concern was the management of a shipping conglomerate and the restoration of tonnage lost during the war. In the inter-war years 130 ships were built for the fleet. In addition, he acquired a shareholding in banking, marine insurance, and trading companies, which included the interests of the Mackinnon family. After his death these holdings formed the basis of the Inchcape group of companies. He also willingly undertook government work, provided the separation of politics and business remained intact, not least for the purposes of free trade. He finally adopted protectionism in 1931. Inchcape's sympathies for the Liberal Party were tested in the early 1920s, and in 1926 he switched to the Conservative benches in the House of Lords. He never regarded himself as a politician. His relentless, strenuous, orderly, brusque quest for business efficiency was implemented alongside a generous sympathy for estate workers in the demanding context of the times. He was self-made, but not from impoverished conditions, and his enormous commitment to work was not supported by a religious outlook. His attachment to the sea formed a significant leisure pursuit. His yacht, *Rover*, of 700 tons and with a crew of over thirty, was used for Mediterranean voyages. He was appointed honorary captain RNR in 1927. In 1928 his increasing pessimism was heightened by the death of his daughter Elsie on a pioneering transatlantic flight. Her assets were given to the Treasury.

Inchcape was appointed KCIE in 1894, GCMG in 1902, KCSI in 1910, and GCSI in 1924; he was advanced to the degree of a viscount in 1924 and to that of earl of Inchcape and Viscount Glenapp in 1929. He died at Monaco, on board his yacht, *Rover*, on 23 May 1932, and was succeeded as second earl by his son, Kenneth Mackay (1887–1939).

KEITH GRIEVES

Sources S. Jones, *Trade and shipping: Lord Inchcape, 1852–1932* (1989) • H. H. Bolitho, *James Lyle Mackay: first earl of Inchcape* (1936) • Lord Inchcape [J. L. Mackay], 'Shipowners and shipbuilders', *Brassey's Naval and Shipping Annual* (1923), 224–30 • S. Jones, *Two centuries of overseas trading: the origins and growth of the Inchcape Group* (1986) • S. Jones, 'British mercantile enterprise overseas in the nineteenth century: the example of James Lyle Mackay, first earl of Inchcape', *Studies in British privateering, trading enterprise and seamen's welfare*, ed. S. Fisher (1987), 79–97 • J. Turner, *British politics and the Great War: coalition and conflict, 1915–1918* (1992) • K. O. Morgan, *Consensus and disunity: the Lloyd George coalition government, 1918–1922* (1979) • B. Cage, ed., *The Scots abroad: labour, capital, and enterprise, 1750–1914* (1985) • G. Blake, *B. I. centenary, 1856–1956* (1956) • P. Griffiths, *A history of the Inchcape Group* (privately printed, London, 1977) • *DNB* • Bonar Law MSS, HLRO • *The Times* (24 May 1932) • G. Stow, 'Mackay, James Lyle', *DBB* • Burke, *Peerage* • *CGPLA Eng. & Wales* (1932)

Archives BL OIOC, material on the legistlative council and retrenchment committee • GL, Inchcape plc, archives • NMM, letter-books and files, BIS/8/4–7 • NRA, priv. coll., papers | Bodl. Oxf., corresp. with Lewis Harcourt • CUL, corresp. with Lord Hardinge • HLRO, corresp. with Andrew Bonar Law • PRO, corresp. with Sir E. M. Satow, PRO 30/33/7/12 • U. Newcastle, corresp. with Walter Runciman

Wealth at death £552,809 0s. 6d.: Scottish confirmation sealed in London, 28 Sept 1932, *CGPLA Eng. & Wales*

Mackay, James Townsend (1775–1862), botanist, was born on 29 January 1775 at Kirkcaldy, Fife. After being educated at the parish school he was trained as a gardener, and having filled several posts in Scotland went to Ireland in March 1804 as assistant botanist and gardener assistant to the professor of botany at the University of Dublin, Dr Robert Scott. In July 1806 the university leased land at Lansdowne Road, Ballsbridge, and Mackay was charged with creating there a new botanical garden, the fourth formed by the university. Mackay, an outstanding horticulturist, began planting in 1808 and soon established the richest and most varied collection of exotic plants in Ireland.

Mackay was an excellent field botanist; during his career he visited most parts of Ireland and discovered numerous plants new to the country. In his publications on native species he reported several for the first time including the eponymous *Erica mackaiana*, a native heather. His first paper was 'A systematic catalogue of rare plants found in Ireland' (*Transactions of the Dublin Society*, 5, 1806, 121–84). This was substantially enlarged into *A Catalogue of the Indigenous Plants of Ireland*, first published in the *Transactions of the Royal Irish Academy* (14, 1825, 103–98) and separately issued in Dublin in 1825, and a decade later he compiled *Flora Hibernica* (1836), with contributions from Dr Thomas Taylor (*d.* 1848) on bryophytes, and William Henry Harvey (1811–1866) on algae. Mackay also published several accounts of cultivated plants.

Mackay was elected a member of the Royal Irish Academy about 1825 and an associate of the Linnean Society of London in 1806, and was a member of the botanical societies of Edinburgh and London. The University of Dublin bestowed on him the honorary degree of LLD in 1850. He remained curator of Trinity College Botanic Gardens, although partly paralysed about 1860, until his death from bronchitis on 25 February 1862 at his home, Dawson Grove, Dublin. He never married. *Zygopetalum mackaii*, a tropical orchid, and several cryptogams including *Jungermannia mackaii* and *Fucus mackaii* were named after him. *Mackaya*, a South African shrub, is the only one of several genera named after Mackay that is still accepted. He was buried on 1 March 1862 at Mount Jerome cemetery, Harold's Cross, Dublin.   E. CHARLES NELSON

Sources *DNB* · P. W. Jackson, *The story of the Botanic Gardens of Trinity College Dublin, 1687–1987* (1987) · E. C. Nelson, '"Reserved to the fellows": four centuries of gardens at Trinity College, Dublin', *Trinity College Dublin and the idea of a university*, ed. C. H. Holland (1991), 185–222 · Desmond, *Botanists*, rev. edn · records (burial), Dublin **Archives** Linn. Soc., papers · National Botanic Gardens, Glasnevin, Dublin, catalogue of Irish plants; MSS, some herbarium specimens · RBG Kew, MSS · TCD, department of botany, MSS, herbarium | PRO NIre., Foster-Massereene MSS **Likenesses** M. Scott, pencil?, repro. in Nelson, 'Reserved to the fellows'

Mackay, John, second Lord Reay (*c.*1612–1680). *See under* Mackay, Donald, first Lord Reay (1591–1649).

Mackay, John (1724–1783), coal owner and industrialist, was born on 16 December 1724, the only son of John Mackay of Inverness, merchant, and his wife, Jean, *née* Barbour, of Aldourie. Nothing is known of his early life, but he moved to London before 1757 and married Millicent Neate, who brought him £3000, at St Andrew's, Holborn, on 12 May 1759; they had at least one son and a daughter. In 1761, while still in London, he joined Jonathan Greenall of Parr in a patent for an improved method of salt refining and was later involved with him in a steam engine project. Mackay moved to Belfield in Cheshire before 1763, when he turned his attention to south-west Lancashire, which was the source of coal for Cheshire's salt refining after the Sankey Canal was opened in 1757.

Mackay introduced a new process for the manufacture of stained and enamelled glass in Liverpool and pursued coal rights at Croxteth (the nearest mines to Liverpool), but his main interests were the large collieries he acquired in the early 1760s—at Parr, in proximity to the Sankey Canal, and at St Helens, where he was in partnership with Thomas Leigh. The former probably produced just under 30,000 tons a year, the latter about one-third as much. His Ravenhead and Thatto Heath workings, developed with £16,500 borrowed in London (£12,000 of it from David Garrick), came fully on stream in 1770 and 1771. They had a capacity of about 40,000 tons a year which, with Parr and St Helens, made Mackay the largest coal producer in Lancashire, and among the largest in Britain.

According to Sir Peter Legh, Mackay 'love[d] his own conjectures' (Sir Peter Legh to Richard Orford, 28 May 1768, Legh MSS, box 56), and his schemes were undoubtedly more complex and much grander than those of his rivals. On entering the coal trade in 1763 he proposed to supply Dublin by a Sankey cartel in which he would provide twice as much coal as other coal masters. After the failure of the proposal, attempts were made to limit production on the Sankey and there were continual bitter price wars. At first 'the Gentile Men Colliars [Sir Peter Legh and Sir Thomas Gerard] was Injureing them selves Very Much by selling Coal as they did' (letter of Thomas Leigh, 2 Jan 1765, Legh MSS, box 51). By 1768 Mackay was proving exasperatingly difficult to deal with. One of his proposals to Legh was 'so long and so full of Invective I had neither patience to read it nor sufficient knowledge to understand it' (Legh to Orford, 23 April 1768, Legh MSS, box 56). He continually refused to raise his prices, being 'a whimsical Man and not a little positive', 'convinced of sticking too long to his own conceits' (Legh to Orford, 30 April 1768, 28 May 1768, Legh MSS, box 56) and irrational because of his bitter hatred of Sarah *Clayton, whose reserves he bought after her bankruptcy in 1778.

Although Mackay's Ravenhead and Thatto Heath collieries were badly located at the head of the canal, he cleverly recognized the peculiar qualities of the seams they tapped, especially the Rushy Park, which became renowned for glass smelting. To initiate cast plate-glass manufacture in Britain, over £50,000 was raised in 1773 by a numerous company (of peers, prominent East India associates, and two glass makers from St Gobain), and a further £60,000 was raised before 1792. Mackay was a partner and brought the works to Ravenhead to benefit from concessionary rates on his special fuel. When construction finished in 1776 the casting hall was the largest industrial building in existence. In 1779 Thomas Williams (1737–1802) of the Parys Mine Company built a copper smelter at Ravenhead. His main reason for choosing the site was Mackay's offer of concessionary rates on fire-clay (which lies beneath some of the deepest coal seams) and coal, and he gave him a monopoly of supply by specifying fuel from the Ravenhead Main Delf seam. Mackay had a similar agreement with the Stanley copper works, eastward along the Sankey Canal.

Mackay built a large mansion in the new Gothic style at Ravenhead, to which the canal was extended in 1773. He probably introduced the longwall mining technique into Lancashire, and also provided cottages with gardens for his colliers. When Mackay died in 1783 at Buxton Spa, aged fifty-eight, his enormous collieries had apparently secure markets, but the Ravenhead glass works were teetering on the edge of ruin and he was in heavy debt. His son John died before him and his businesses passed to Colonel James Fraser of the East India Company, who married Mackay's daughter, Millicent, in 1783; the businesses were administered for Fraser after 1787 by Mackay's brother-in-law, Admiral Philip Affleck, also of the East India Company. After Mackay's death competitive and innovative turmoil was succeeded on the Sankey by calm, steady consolidation. Williams's copper interests thrived on the export of ingots to the Far East through the East India Company and the production of sheets to copper-bottom the English fleet; they were worth £800,000 in 1799, with an estimated profit of over £29,000 in 1784 at Ravenhead. The glass works produced 7279 plates worth £90,000 in 1801; that year profits were £15,000, and they doubled in the next ten years. These large factories, which were initiated by Mackay, had come to dominate British glass and copper production by 1800 and were in large part responsible for the rapid growth of St Helens as an industrial centre.   JOHN LANGTON

Sources T. C. Barker and J. R. Harris, *A Merseyside town in the industrial revolution: St Helens, 1750–1900* (1954) · T. C. Barker, *Pilkington Brothers and the glass industry* (1960) · J. Langton, *Geographical change and industrial revolution: coalmining in south west Lancashire, 1590–1799* (1979) · Legh MSS, JRL, boxes 51, 56 · National Index of Parish Registers
Archives Derbys. RO, Wrightington MSS · JRL, Legh MSS · Pilkington Bros., St Helens, Ravenhead deeds

Mackay, John Alexander (1889–1983), theologian and Hispanic scholar, was born on 17 May 1889 in Inverness, Scotland, the eldest of the five children of Duncan Mackay (1859–1948), a tailor and clothier, and his wife, Isabella Macdonald (1869–1933).

Mackay received an MA in 1912 with first-class honours in philosophy from the University of Aberdeen. He studied theology with the tutor of the theological school of the

Free Presbyterian church, first in Inverness (1910–11) and then in Wick (1912–13). He transferred his membership to the Free Church in 1913. In 1915 he received a bachelor of divinity degree from Princeton Theological Seminary in the United States. During the following year he studied at the University of Madrid, where he was deeply influenced by Miguel de Unamuno.

Ordained to the ministry of the Free Church on 1 August 1916, Mackay was sent by the denomination as a missionary to Lima, Peru. His partner in those labours was Jane Logan Wells (1886–1987) whom he married in Aberdeen on 16 August 1916; the couple had four children. In Lima, Mackay founded the Anglo-Peruvian College (later called Colegio San Andrés) in 1917 and served as its principal for eight years. Mackay studied at the National University of Peru (Lima) from which he received a DLitt for a thesis on Unamuno (1918). During 1925 he served there as professor of metaphysics and the history of philosophy. From 1926 to 1932 Mackay was a special lecturer for the South American Federation of Young Men's Christian Associations, and travelled extensively throughout Latin America. In 1932, having written several books in Spanish, he published in English *The other Spanish Christ*, which traced the coming of Spanish Catholicism to South America. Arguing that the dominant Catholic tradition offered an inadequate view of Jesus Christ, Mackay also contended that an alternative, more vital Catholic tradition existed among Spanish thinkers such as Ramon Lull, Teresa of Avila, John of the Cross, and Unamuno. As the work of an English-speaking protestant Mackay's book was remarkable for its informed appreciation of the literature, culture, and thought of Latin America and Spain.

In 1932 Mackay became secretary for Latin America and Africa of the board of foreign missions of the Presbyterian church in the United States of America. From his office in New York, Mackay continued his advocacy of Latin American concerns. In *That other America* (1935), for example, he prefaced a study of the religious situation in Latin America with criticism of the United States' military intervention in the region, and reminded his North American readers 'that there is another America which is militantly jealous of its rights to the continental name' (p. 1).

In 1936 Mackay became president and professor of ecumenics at Princeton Theological Seminary. The seminary and the Presbyterian church with which it was affiliated had recently passed through the so-called fundamentalist controversy. In 1929 a reorganization of the seminary had prompted the withdrawal of several of the most conservative professors. Mackay rejuvenated and unified the institution and set it on a path transcending what he perceived as the sterile categories of both fundamentalism and modernism. In 1944 he founded the quarterly journal *Theology Today* and was its editor until 1951.

Mackay served in numerous ecclesiastical capacities. At the Oxford conference (1937), where he coined the often-quoted dictum 'Let the church be the church', he headed the commission on the universal church and the world of nations. In 1948 he played a leading role in Amsterdam at the organizing assembly of the World Council of Churches and served on the organization's central committee until 1954. President of the World Presbyterian Alliance (1954–9), he was also moderator of the general assembly of the Presbyterian church in the USA (1953–4). As moderator he wrote 'A letter to Presbyterians' sent by the denomination's general council to all Presbyterian pastors in November 1953. At the height of the McCarthy era the letter warned that inordinate fear of communism was encouraging inquisitorial tactics, the violation of citizens' rights, and a tendency to equate conscientious dissent with treason.

Mackay's religious views were the product of diverse influences. Shaped by both the Christocentric piety and the doctrinal rigour of the Free Presbyterian church, he also appreciated the theological precision of the older conservative Princeton seminary tradition represented by his professor, Benjamin B. Warfield. In Spain he encountered the existentialism of Unamuno, who introduced him to Spanish mysticism as well as to the writings of Dostoyevsky and Kierkegaard. By the 1930s Mackay resonated with themes of protestant neo-orthodoxy. Based in part on his experience in Latin America, Mackay also appreciated the contribution of the Pentecostal movement to Christian life and thought. Mackay's breadth of vision was expressed in three abiding beliefs: that the centre of Christianity is devotion to Jesus Christ, not to a theological system; that the churches needed to manifest more fully their unity; and that this unity would be discovered only as they engaged in common mission. These convictions are apparent in such works as *A Preface to Christian Theology* (1941), *Heritage and Destiny* (1943), *God's Order* (1953), *The Presbyterian Way of Life* (1960), *Ecumenics* (1964), and *Christian Reality and Appearance* (1969).

Mackay wrote thirteen books, delivered more than twenty named lectureships, and earned numerous honorary degrees. After retiring from the Princeton seminary he served as adjunct professor of Hispanic thought at the American University in Washington, DC, in 1961–4. In 1961, as the Joseph Cooke lecturer, he travelled extensively through Asia, preaching and delivering lectures. In 1964 the government of Peru conferred on him las palmas magisteriales del Peru in recognition of his services to national education. He died in Hightstown, where he was living in New Jersey, USA, on 9 June 1983, and was buried in the Princeton cemetery on 13 June.

JAMES H. MOORHEAD

Sources 'Memorial minute: John Alexander Mackay, 1889–1983', *Theology Today*, 40 (Jan 1984), 453–6 • E. J. Jurji, ed., *The ecumenical era in church and society: a symposium in honor of John A. Mackay* (1959) • G. W. Gillette, 'John A. Mackay: influences on my life', *Journal of Presbyterian History*, 56 (spring 1978), 20–34 [interview] • J. H. Smylie, 'Mackay and McCarthyism, 1953–54', *Journal of Church and State* (1964), 352–65 • H. McKennie Goodpasture, 'The Latin American soul of John A. Mackay', *Journal of Presbyterian History*, 48 (winter 1970), 265–92 • R. R. Curlee and M. R. Isaac-Curlee, 'Bridging the gap: John A. Mackay, Presbyterians, and the charismatic movement', *American Presbyterians*, 72 (autumn 1994), 141–56 • J. L. Garrett, 'John A. Mackay on the Roman Catholic Church', *Journal of Presbyterian History*, 50 (summer 1972), 111–28 • D. Lewis, 'Type of the wise … John A. Mackay and our witness to the gospel today',

Reformed World, 38 (1984), 177–81 • 'In memoriam: John A. Mackay, 1889–1983', *International Review of Mission*, 72 (Oct 1983), 672–3 • private information (2004) • records, Princeton Theological Seminary, New Jersey, USA

Archives Princeton Theological Seminary, New Jersey, MSS | SOUND Princeton Theological Seminary, New Jersey, archives
Likenesses D. A. Walter, oils, 1993, Princeton Theological Seminary, New Jersey

Mackay, Kenneth James William, third earl of Inchcape (1917–1994), businessman, was born on 27 December 1917 at Uckfield, Sussex, the second child and eldest son in the family of three sons and one daughter of Kenneth Mackay, Viscount Glenapp, later second earl of Inchcape (1887–1939), businessman and army officer, and his first wife, Joan (d. 1933), youngest daughter of John Francis Moriarty, lord justice of appeal in Ireland. He was known by the courtesy title of Viscount Glenapp from 1932 until succeeding to the earldom on 21 June 1939. He was educated at Eton and Trinity College, Cambridge, from where he graduated in law. On the outbreak of war he was commissioned a lieutenant in the 12th lancers. He saw active service in the retreat from Dunkirk, and was one of the last to be evacuated. He then served in Italy with the 27th lancers, under Sir Andrew Horsbrugh-Porter. He ended the war as a major, and was demobilized in 1946. On 12 February 1941 he had married Aline Thorn Hannay, widow of Flying Officer Patrick Claude Hannay and only daughter of Sir Richard Arthur Pease, second baronet. They had a daughter, Lucinda Louise (b. 1941), and two sons, (Kenneth) Peter Lyle (b. 1943) and James Jonathan Thorn (b. 1947). The marriage was dissolved in 1954 and on 13 February 1965 Mackay married Caroline Harrison, dressage rider, and eldest daughter of Cholmeley Dering Harrison, of Emo Court, co. Laois, Ireland. With his second wife he had two more sons, Shane Lyle (b. 1973) and Ian Cholmeley (b. 1976), and adopted another, Anthony Kenneth (b. 1967).

On demobilization Inchcape joined his family's business. This traced its origins to his grandfather James Lyle *Mackay, first earl of Inchcape (1852–1932), who by the 1890s was senior partner of Mackinnon, Mackenzie & Co., a leading agency house based at Calcutta. The Inchcape family went on to accumulate significant partnership interests in many leading British-owned agency houses operating in particular in India, the Persian Gulf, east Africa, and London. They also had major shipping interests including P. & O. Steam Navigation Co., of which the first earl of Inchcape was chairman. For long these agency businesses flourished, bringing great wealth, prestige, and influence to the Inchcapes but, faced with the decline of empire and its traditional structures, a hostile fiscal environment at home, changing patterns of trade, and weakened family management, they looked especially vulnerable by the late 1940s. Initially Inchcape went out to India to work with Mackinnon Mackenzie, but he returned in 1948 to take charge of the family's increasingly disparate network of loosely linked shareholdings. He gradually reshaped these businesses and in 1958 chose the only feasible route to secure their long-term future: he unified most of them within a holding company, Inchcape

& Co. Ltd, which was floated on the London stock exchange with 25 per cent of the equity being offered to the public. At a stroke he solved his family businesses' inherent fiscal and funding problems, obtained a market value for them, and at the same time preserved family control and leadership under the Inchcape name.

Inchcape was chairman and chief executive of the new company and in the next twenty-five years managed it with considerable skill. By sticking to the principle of 'new place old business, new business old place', and permitting a full measure of local autonomy and independent operation, the company was remarkably prosperous. Along the way it acquired other British businesses trading internationally—not least the Borneo Company in 1967, and the Anglo Thai Corporation in 1975. Inchcapes' market capitalization rose from £2.6 million in 1958 to £400 million in 1980; in 1977 it was the twenty-eighth largest British company in terms of market value. In this transformation Inchcape's contribution was vital—'the use of the single word "Inchcape" could be used interchangeably as the Group and the man' (Jones, *Two Centuries*, 283), surmised Inchcapes' official historian in 1986. Inchcape retired in 1982 from what had become a highly respected and firmly based international business services group, albeit one in which family influence was inevitably greatly diluted; he was appointed life president. Thereafter he managed his family's considerable private wealth through chairmanship of Inchcape Family Investments Ltd and Glenapp Estate Company Ltd.

Inchcape was also a force in the British shipping industry. In 1957 he renewed his family's close connection with P. & O. by joining its board and from 1973 until 1983 he was its chairman. He set in hand a programme of modernization that contributed to the company's survival as the last UK shipping company of significant size. In 1976–7 he was elected president of the General Council of British Shipping. He held directorships of many other leading companies, including British Petroleum Company Ltd, Royal Exchange Assurance, National Provincial Bank Ltd, and Burmah Oil Company Ltd. He was a tough and shrewd businessman. His strength of character and business acumen were no more clearly shown than in 1972 when, as a director of P. & O., he provoked a boardroom crisis by resisting the company's proposed merger with the construction company Bovis, claiming it offered poor value. He won full shareholder support and in 1974, having been appointed chairman, he acquired Bovis for a fifth of its 1972 valuation. In 1982 he took a close personal interest in the arrangements under which P. & O. shipping (including the P. & O. flagship, the 45,000 ton liner *Canberra*) was requisitioned and sent, along with some 850 merchant seamen and civilian staff, to the Falkland Islands as part of the British task force.

Inchcape was of short, stocky build, and was by nature quiet and somewhat shy. Yet he was also pugnacious, which at an early age enabled him to excel at the Eton wall game. He listed his recreations in *Who's Who* as 'all field sports'; he was a particularly keen fox-hunter. He was

president of the Royal Society of India, Pakistan and Ceylon from 1970 to 1976, and was prime warden of the Shipwrights' Company in 1967 and of the Fishmongers' Company in 1977–8. He died on 17 March 1994, survived by his second wife and the children of both marriages. He was succeeded as fourth earl of Inchcape by the elder son of his first marriage. A memorial service was held in Southwark Cathedral on 3 May 1994.   JOHN ORBELL

Sources S. Jones, *Two centuries of overseas trading: the origins and growth of the Inchcape Group* (1986) · P. Griffiths, *A history of the Inchcape Group* (privately printed, London, 1977) · *The Times* (21 March 1994) · *The Independent* (26 March 1994) · D. Howarth and S. Howarth, *The story of P & O* (1986) · S. Jones, *Trade and shipping: Lord Inchcape, 1852–1932* (1989) · S. Jones and D. E. Salamie, 'Inchcape Plc', *International directory of company histories*, ed. T. Grant, 16 (1997) · *WWW, 1991–5* · Burke, *Peerage* (1999)
Archives GL, Inchcape plc archives
Likenesses D. Anderson, oils, P. & O., London · photograph, repro. in *The Independent*
Wealth at death £3,012,018: administration with will, 1994, *CGPLA Eng. & Wales*

Mackay, Mackintosh (1793–1873), Free Church of Scotland minister and Gaelic scholar, was born at Eddrachillis, Sutherland, on 18 November 1793, the son of Alexander Mackay, tacksman of Duartbeg and a captain in the Reay fencibles, and his wife, Helen, eldest daughter of Alexander Falconer, minister of Eddrachillis. He was educated at Tongue parochial school, then at Mr Pollock's academy, Ullapool, before going in 1815 to St Andrews and from there in 1820 to study at the theological hall of Glasgow University. Between university sessions he taught at Bowmore, Laggan, and Portree. He was ordained and inducted to Laggan on 28 September 1825. As a nineteen-year-old W. F. Skene (1809–1892) studied Gaelic under him at Laggan manse: Mackay thus formed a bridge between older traditional study and later scholarship.

Mackay had been engaged by the Highland Society of Scotland to set in order its collections for a Gaelic dictionary. The *Dictionarium Scoto-Celticum: a Dictionary of the Gaelic Language* was published in two large volumes by Blackwood in Edinburgh in 1828. Its preface praises Mackay's 'indefatigable labours … philological acuteness and learning'. A proposal for an abridgement seems to have come to nothing. In the following year Mackay published a (bowdlerized) edition, with memoir, of the works of 'Rob Donn', Robert Mackay (1714–1778). His distinction as a Gaelic scholar led to the award of a Glasgow LLD in 1829. On 22 February 1828 he married Frances (*d.* 1877), daughter of Francis Burton of Edinburgh; they had one son (born and died 1829).

Between 1828 and 1831 Mackay frequently corresponded with and visited Sir Walter Scott, to whom he sent many documentary illustrations of highland history, including anecdotes of Rob Roy and an account of the battle of Mulroy for use in *Tales of a Grandfather*. An uncompleted set of Mackay's *Reminiscences* of Scott (undated but written after 1850) was printed. Scott reckoned 'my Celtick friend' Mackay 'a simple learned man and a highlander who weighs his own nation justly, a modest and estimable person' (13 May 1831, *The Journal of Sir Walter*

Scott, ed. D. Douglas, 2 vols., 1891) and encouraged him in his search for a living less remote than Laggan.

Mackay obtained through the duke of Argyll's patronage the sizeable living of Dunoon and Kilmun, to which he was admitted on 19 April 1832. He was very active as minister and preacher throughout his widespread parish, twice enlarging his main church, building a new one at Kilmun, and setting up two chapels of ease. In 1843 he seceded from the Church of Scotland and joined the new Free Church; he travelled widely to explain the Disruption to congregations and to organize the Free Church in the highlands. He acted as convener of the Free Church highland committee, and in 1849, as moderator of the Free Church, he urged the needs of highland congregations on its annual assembly.

Mackay moved to Australia in 1854 to become minister of the Gaelic church in Melbourne and thereafter of St George's Presbyterian Church in Sydney where he remained from 1856 to 1861. This unexpected emigration was actuated by a call to minister to the needs of his countrymen in Australia, and by the hope that prosperous parishioners might assist their impoverished ancestral territories. He returned to Scotland in 1862 and became Free Church minister of Tarbert, Isle of Harris, retiring on grounds of age and health in 1868. Mackay died at Portobello, Edinburgh, on 17 May 1873, and was buried at Duddingston.

Mackay published a number of sermons, and addresses commemorating deceased clerical colleagues, and contributed a history of the church in Scotland as introduction to the Gaelic version of Howie's *Scots Worthies* (1872). He wrote in English a good account of Dunoon and Kilmun for the Argyll volume of the *New Statistical Account of Scotland*. Between 1846 and 1850 he edited the thirty-six issues of the Free Church Gaelic periodical *An fhianuis* ('The witness'). He was recalled as being tall and dignified, a fine ministerial presence, but reserved in manner to the point of austerity. He was energetic with his pen, but prosy as a writer in English. His early lexicographical work and pioneering edition of Rob Donn are remembered in the development of Gaelic studies.

ALAN BELL

Sources *Fasti Scot.* · J. Kennedy, *Disruption worthies of the highlands* (1879), 79–88 · *Celtic Monthly*, 16 (1908), 214 · D. S. Thomson, ed., *The companion to Gaelic Scotland*, new edn (1994) · NL Scot., Scott MSS · NA Scot., SC 70/1/163/43–7
Archives NL Scot., Irish genealogies · NL Scot., papers relating to the highlands · Royal Highland and Agricultural Society of Scotland, Edinburgh, letters relating to Gaelic dictionary | NL Scot., Blackwood MSS · NL Scot., Scott letter-books · U. Edin., New Coll. L., letters to Thomas Chalmers
Likenesses photograph, repro. in Kennedy, *Disruption worthies of the highlands*
Wealth at death £546 2s. 5d.: confirmation, 25 June 1873, NA Scot., SC 70/1/163/43–7

Mackay, Mary [*pseud.* Marie Corelli] (1855–1924), novelist, was born on 1 May 1855 at Gloucester Terrace, Bayswater, London, the illegitimate child of Charles *Mackay LLD (1812–1889), journalist and writer of Scottish songs, and Mary Ellen Mills, *née* Kirtland (d. 1876). In 1859 Charles

Mackay's wife died, and two years later he married Mills, and the family left London to settle at Fern Dell, Box Hill, Surrey. Mary was educated at home, and her precocious talent as a pianist was particularly encouraged by her neighbour, the novelist George Meredith. She spent her late teens in a convent school in France. In 1876 Mrs Mackay died, and Bertha Vyver (c.1855–c.1930), Mary's childhood friend, came to live at Fern Dell. Vyver remained Mary Mackay's lifelong companion, assisting with her career and running her household.

The household moved to 47 Longridge Road, Kensington, London, in 1883, where they were joined by Eric Mackay, Mary's half-brother, twenty years older than her and heavily encumbered by debts. The move to London prompted the beginnings of Mary's career. She had devised the pseudonym Marie Corelli as a stage name for a planned career as a concert pianist and singer, but after several indifferently received performances in London, Edinburgh, and various provincial towns during the early 1880s, she did not pursue her music. Turning to journalism, in July 1885 she published her first article in *Temple Bar* magazine, 'One of the World's Wonders', signed Marie Corelli. Meanwhile, she was at work on her first novel, *A Romance of Two Worlds*, published in February 1886 by George Bentley. The novel was a judicious blend of mysticism, pseudo-science, and pseudo-religiosity, appealing to a contemporary interest in the occult. While her ideas were roundly ridiculed in the literary press, *A Romance* sold well, and found an unlikely admirer in Oscar Wilde, who wrote to her: 'I have read the book over again … you certainly tell of marvellous things in marvellous ways' (Vyver, 58).

Mary Mackay was a swift and diligent writer, and, again as Marie Corelli, produced a successor within months. *Vendetta* (1886) was a melodramatic family saga set during the Naples cholera epidemic, and it too achieved sales respectable enough to delight Bentley. It established her pseudonym for good, and brought her welcome fame and financial independence. It was *Thelma* (1887), however, set in Scandinavia, which laid the foundations of her sustained popularity and literary fortune. It was in turn followed by *Ardath: the Story of a Dead Self* (1889), which won her the admiration and lasting friendship of William Gladstone. With *Wormwood* (1890), Mackay turned from her established themes of spiritualism and psychic phenomena to address the contemporary problem of addiction to absinthe. That same year she published *My Wonderful Wife*, another 'issue' novel which satirized the emerging spectre of the 'new woman' from the perspective of a man married to an anti-heroine who smokes, shoots, and dresses in men's clothes.

In 1889 Dr Mackay died, and Mary stayed for six months in Eastbourne with her brother Eric and Bertha Vyver, to recover from nervous exhaustion and depression. Soon, however, she was writing again, and the anonymously published *The Silver Domino* (1892), foretelling the arrival of a novelist destined to outsell all her competitors, alienated many of her professional contacts. *The Soul of Lilith* (1892) was more kindly received, although the story, a reworking of *Frankenstein* which centred upon the mystical powers of an Arabian fakir, El-Rami, provoked understandable mirth from reviewers. However, in 1893 Marie Corelli broke into the ranks of the best-seller with *Barabbas: a Dream of the World's Tragedy*, a daring fictionalization of the crucifixion story rejected by a nervous George Bentley, but published by the newly established Algernon Methuen. She called the novel a 'passion play in prose', and its melodramatic religiosity proved such a success with the public, if not the critics, that it ran to fourteen editions in three years.

The success of *Barabbas* fortified Mackay against the scourges of literary London, prompting her to deliver her next novel to Methuen only on condition that no review copies were to be released to the press in advance. *The Sorrows of Satan* (1895) thus gained lucrative advance notoriety, and it achieved an immediate sale greater than that of any other English novel at that time, although its popularity was perhaps due to an accident in publishing history, since it was one of the first novels to appear in a single sixpenny edition following the collapse of the three-decker. The story tantalizingly combined a semi-sacred theme with prurient descriptions of the vices of the rich. *The Sorrows of Satan* was in many respects the climax of Mackay's career, establishing Marie Corelli as the most popular novelist in Britain for the next dozen years. However, since *The Sorrows of Satan* had as its heroine a woman writer, Mavis Clare, whose serene personality and mystical gifts are the main challenge to the devil on earth, the novel also secured a view of Mackay as a self-regarding eccentric, a reputation she was unable to live down.

The next year saw the publication of *The Murder of Delicia*, with a very similar heroine to Mavis Clare, more divine than human, and critical amusement turned to open mockery. Meanwhile, a rift between Mary Mackay and her brother Eric had been occasioned by Eric's production of a dramatic version of *The Sorrows of Satan*, without his sister's consent. The play was a failure, and when Eric died the following year, her distress was accentuated when she discovered that he had spread a rumour that he was the real author of Marie Corelli's novels. Mackay privately printed and distributed a controversial pamphlet accusing her brother of slander, and her actions were widely perceived as an unforgivable attempt to libel the dead.

In 1899 Mary Mackay and Bertha Vyver left London for good, moving to Mason Croft in Stratford upon Avon, the town's associations with Shakespeare explaining its appeal. There Mackay contributed to a wide range of middle-class women's journals, including the *Ladies' Home Journal*, *Good Housekeeping*, and *Harper's Bazaar*. She cultivated an eccentric reputation and appearance, becoming embroiled in local controversies and reacting against the 'rational dress' movement with her exaggeratedly feminine, flower-strewn costumes. In 1900 she released a *Birthday Book*, a collection of sentimental quotations and illustrations from her novels, capitalizing upon her reputation as a literary celebrity.

The Master Christian appeared in June 1900, a narrative of the second coming of Christ, and its vehement attack upon the Catholic church offended many. It was followed by *Temporal Power* (1902), a thinly disguised and unflattering portrait of the court of Edward VII, which still further alienated Mackay's remaining friends in London society. However, her popularity with the general public was undiminished, and by 1901 it was estimated that each of Marie Corelli's novels made £10,000, a figure supplemented by high fees for her journalism. By this time, more than half of her books were worldwide best-sellers, many translated into almost all the European languages. *Treasures of Heaven* (1906) sold 100,000 copies on its first day of publication.

In 1907 Mary Mackay began a romantic friendship with Arthur Severn, a happily married Royal Academician, and she became heavily involved in promoting Severn's paintings. The two collaborated on *The Devil's Motor* (1910), which once more focused upon characters from Christian mythology. Her affection for Severn perhaps inspired her to direct her vehement dislike of turn-of-the-century feminism against the suffrage movement. She campaigned for the Anti-Suffrage League during the second half of the decade, publishing articles such as 'Woman— or suffragette?' (July 1907) in *Harper's Bazaar*, which insisted that suffrage would deprive women of their influence over their menfolk.

By 1910 the friendship with Severn was at an end, and Marie Corelli's literary reputation was also in decline. *The Devil's Motor* failed to share in the success of her earlier works, and *The Life Everlasting* (1911), elaborating upon a theory of eternal youth, similarly failed to capture the public imagination. From 1914, Mackay threw herself into the war effort, appealing at public meetings to men to enlist, offering her home as a military hospital, and donating large sums of money to the Red Cross. Her reputation was sullied in 1917, when she was prosecuted for food hoarding, and although she protested that a large donation of sugar from her friend Sir Thomas Lipton was for jam-making, and the jam for public consumption, she was convicted. Shortly before the armistice, Mackay began work on her final long novel, *The Secret Power* (1921). However, public taste for her work had altered immeasurably since the war, and while her sales were still respectably high, they were far below those she commanded before 1914. In January 1924 she collapsed from a heart complaint, and three months later died on 21 April 1924 at Mason Croft; she was buried at the Evesham Road cemetery, Stratford upon Avon. Bertha Vyver published her memoirs of Marie Corelli in 1930.

KATHERINE MULLIN

Sources E. Bigland, *Marie Corelli: the woman and the legend* (1953) • B. Vyver, *Memoirs of Marie Corelli* (1930) • G. Bullock, *Marie Corelli: the life and death of a best seller* (1940) • A. Federico, 'Marie Corelli and literary celebrity', *Nineteenth-Century Studies*, 11 (1997) • Blain, Clements & Grundy, *Feminist comp.* • J. Casey, 'Marie Corelli and *fin de siècle* feminism', *English Literature in Transition, 1880–1920*, 35 (1992), 163–76 • *CGPLA Eng. & Wales* (1924) • T. Ransom, *The mysterious Miss Marie Corelli* (1999) • A. Federico, *Idol of suburbia: Marie Corelli and late-Victorian literary culture* (2000)

Archives BL, letters [copies] · Bodl. Oxf., letters · Claremont Colleges, California, Honnold/Mudd Library, papers · Col. U., Rare Book and Manuscript Library, papers · Detroit Public Library, papers · Folger, papers · Kensington Central Library, London, letters, MSS incl. letters to her secretary, and literary papers · Morgan L., papers · NYPL, papers · Ransom HRC, corresp. and literary papers · Shakespeare Birthplace Trust RO, Stratford upon Avon, corresp. and papers; letters; literary proofs, papers, miscellanea; MS of *Sorrow of Satan* · University of Illinois, Chicago, papers · University of Iowa Libraries, special collections, papers · Yale U., Beinecke L., papers | BL, corresp. with R. Bentley & son, Add. MSS 46622–46646 · BL, letters to F. H. Fisher [copies] · BL, letters to W. E. Gladstone, Add. MSS 44507–44509 · BL, corresp. of subject and her executors with Society of Authors, Add. MS 56683 · Bodl. Oxf., letters to Sidney Lee · CAC Cam., letters to W. T. Stead · Keats House, Hampstead, London, letters to W. E. Doubleday · Richmond Local Studies Library, London, corresp. with Douglas Sladen · Shakespeare Birthplace Trust RO, Stratford upon Avon, letters to Archibald Flower and papers · Shakespeare Birthplace Trust RO, Stratford upon Avon, letters to Anna Nairne · Shakespeare Birthplace Trust RO, Stratford upon Avon, letters to Frederick C. Wellstood · Theatre Museum, London, letters to lord chamberlain's licensee **Likenesses** H. Donald-Smith, oils, 1897, NPG · G. Gabell, photogravure, 1906, NPG · photographs, repro. in Bigland, *Marie Corelli: the woman and the legend*
Wealth at death £24,076 17s. 4d.: probate, 8 July 1924, CGPLA Eng. & Wales

MacKay, Peter Carl [*called* Ras Prince Monolulu] (1881?–1965), racing tipster, claimed to have been born in Addis Ababa, Abyssinia (now Ethiopia), the son of a chieftain of a Jewish tribe. It is possible, however, that he was born in the Caribbean or Guiana, of mixed race. On a marriage certificate in 1931 he gave his father's name as William McKay, described as a contractor. He told Sidney White, who helped compile his autobiography, that he was intrigued by missionaries' tales and decided to find out more about the white man's world. Making his way to the African coast, he was shanghaied on board a British ship and gave his name as Prince Monolulu, mistakenly hoping thereby to be well treated. The ship was wrecked on the Portuguese coast, whence he made his way to New York. Finding that religion paved the way to food and shelter, he associated himself with the Salvation Army. A Scot taught him to preach, and—he claimed—baptized him with the name Peter Carl MacKay. He took a variety of jobs ashore and at sea, visiting many ports between Brazil and Canada. Eventually he worked his passage on the cattle boat *Minnetonka* and landed in Tilbury in 1902.

While in New York, MacKay had already made for himself the 'Abyssinian' costume, an embroidered silk jacket and baggy pantaloons, in which he became a familiar sight in England. As Monolulu, he found less colour prejudice in London, although his remarkable appearance and manner naturally attracted abuse, both good-natured and hostile. Infinitely adaptable, he had no difficulty in getting work; he danced in the chorus of *In Dahomey*, sang patriotic songs in the streets during the Second South African War, and first went to Epsom on the day when Rock Sand won the Derby (1903). He worked at first with an Irish tipster, acting as his shouter to attract people, before deciding to go into business for himself. He then adopted

the plumed headdress which made him more visible in a crowd. After hearing the religious revivalist Gypsy Daniels attracting crowds with his shout of 'I've got heaven', Monolulu adopted his own slogan 'I've gotta horse', sometimes alternating with 'Black man for luck'. Travelling round the country, he worked the local markets selling anything from tawdries to quack remedies, and, along the way, calling in at racing stables, gradually amassing the knowledge which helped him as a tipster.

Never one to stay long in one place, Monolulu then went to St Petersburg with an American negro show, then on to Moscow, where he attended race meetings and claimed to have met the tsar. He went to Germany, a country which he did not like, admitting that as a teetotaller he found it difficult to make friends with the beer-drinking population. He joined a circus; he went to Italy; he crossed into southern France, then Switzerland, then Belgium. He was in Königsberg when the First World War broke out, and was sent along with other British people to the prison camp at Ruhleben, ironically located on a racecourse near Berlin. Freed, he travelled to Denmark, from where he made his way back to London in 1919.

Monolulu's big success came in 1920 when he tipped Spion Kop to win the Derby. He put £25 of his own money on the horse which won at 20:1, his winnings augmented by gifts from grateful punters. Ten years later he had a similar success with Blenheim, but he was robbed on the way home and arrived at his Camden Town lodgings to admit to his expectant wife, who had heard the good news on the radio, that he had only threepence to his name. Blessed with a loud voice and a large vocabulary, Monolulu was frequently in court for using bad language, or for fortune-telling, but he was always able somehow to pay his fines and never saw the inside of a prison. He seems generally to have maintained friendly relationships with the police and magistrates, who knew him well.

According to his own account, Monolulu was married six times, the first marriage taking place in 1902 in a Jewish ceremony in Moscow. His wife was taken away by the police, and a year later he married a German girl in a Catholic ceremony. She left him and was subsequently killed in a car accident. He met another German girl, whom he brought to England. They married at Lambeth and had a son, but she died three years after the marriage. In 1920 he met a girl in Stratford; they married, and had two sons, but divorced in 1928. One of his sons died in Copenhagen trying to save a small boy from drowning in an ornamental pond. The fifth marriage may have been in 1930 to a girl he met in Brighton. He was recorded as being divorced from Rhoda Mary, *née* Carley, when he married, at St Pancras register office on 21 August 1931, Nellie Amelia (*b.* 1908/9) of Edmonton, the daughter of Edward Adkins, a helmet maker. This wedding attracted more publicity than the earlier ones, for by now Monolulu was a well-known figure throughout Britain.

Monolulu's colourful persona and his way with words brought him before the microphone and the ciné camera on many occasions. On 6 June 1936 the BBC invited him for the 100th performance of the radio programme *Saturday Magazine*; he was in *In Town Tonight* in 1938; he was on TV in *Picture Page* in October 1936; he appeared with Doris Hare in the popular radio show *Shipmates Ashore* at the Merchant Navy Club during the Second World War, and in *Navy Mixture* with Bonar Colleano and Benny Lee. He filmed in Ireland on *The Sport of Kings* (1931) with Leslie Henson, and on *Wings of the Morning* (1937), and made a nuisance of himself during the Irish elections by offering to tip the winners. He was a guest at a Foyle's literary lunch at Grosvenor House, where he introduced the speakers.

A handsome and well-built figure, Monolulu was inevitably brought by his presence at the sport of kings into contact with royalty, the Aga Khan, and peers of the realm, as well as with the common man eager to venture 'a bob each way'. Money flowed into his pockets and out again nearly as fast, for on several occasions he was robbed as he made his way home, or beaten up by gangs of toughs maddened by their inability to find the money hidden within his clothes.

When Monolulu arrived in New York on 11 September 1951 for the fight between Ray Robinson and Randolph Turpin, the *New York Times* described 'this 6-ft Ethiopian in his plumes and red jacket adorned with green shamrock, star of David … round his neck a lion's claw, a real horseshoe, and binoculars' (12 Sept 1951, 38, col. 4). The Ethiopian embassy, on the other hand, put out a notice saying that he was not a prince (*New York Times*, 15 Sept 1951, 9, col. 5). Monolulu collapsed at Epsom just before the Derby in June 1964 and was taken to Epsom District Hospital. He revived, but was unwell in October that year and died in hospital in London on 15 February 1965. His colourful jackets are preserved in the National Racing Museum. He was commemorated by two public houses, the Prince Monolulu in the West End, and The Abyssinian in Hornsey, north London, whose sign shows him in his finery, holding up a race card.   ANITA MCCONNELL

Sources S. H. White, *I gotta horse: the autobiography of Ras Prince Monolulu as told to Sidney H. White* (1950) · *New York Times* (12 Sept 1951), p. 38, col. 4 · *New York Times* (15 Sept 1951), p. 9, col. 5 · *New York Times* (16 Feb 1965), p. 28, cols. 4–6 · *The Times* (4 June 1964), 8g · *The Times* (15 Feb 1965), 10b · m. cert., 1931
Likenesses G. Woodbine, photograph, 1931, National Museum of Photography, Film and Television, Bradford; repro. in *Daily Herald* · photographs, repro. in White, *I gotta horse*

Mackay, Robert [called Rob Donn] (1714–1778), Scottish Gaelic poet, was the son of Donald Mackay (Domhnall Donn) born at Allt na Caillich, in Strathmore, which lies between the north coast of Sutherland and the inland Ben Hope. The earliest work ascribed to him is a neat quatrain said to have been composed when he was three years old that pokes fun at the tailor who had made him a garment that buttoned at the rear, out of his reach. This was a fitting start for an œuvre that was to include much fun and satire.

At a very early age (seven, according to the *Memoir* in the 1829 edition of his poems) Robert was taken into the family of John Mackay (Iain Mac Eachainn), a tacksman who

was a distant cousin of Lord Reay. Here Rob Donn helped to herd calves and he joined in the activities of a family with an ear for poetry. Throughout his life he worked as herdsman, drover, and gamekeeper, for some time directly employed by Lord Reay near Durness. This allowed him to observe at close quarters the mores of the ruling class, and to make the acquaintance of the Revd Murdo MacDonald, who began his long ministry in Durness in 1726. MacDonald's successor, John Thomson, encouraged his own daughter to write down many of Rob Donn's poems from the bard's dictation, for he had never learned to write. He was married to Janet Mackay (1714–1777), from Strathmore, Sutherland.

The very different modes and influences that Rob Donn experienced coalesce in his poetry: rural society and natural scenery, the excitement of the chase and occasional trips to cattle marts in the south, a spell in the Sutherland fencible regiment between 1759 and 1763, the folk heritage of verse and story and glimpses of the work of sophisticated writers such as Alexander Pope and Alasdair Mac Mhaighstir Alasdair, his own family life and the rather foreign world of the local aristocracy. These are all viewed through the eyes of a man who was a keen observer, something of a philosopher, a humorist, and a satirist. This varied experience has left us an unrivalled picture of society in Gaelic Sutherland in the eighteenth century. He is credited also with having composed airs for many of his songs.

Natural description surfaces in some of the poems and songs. In 'Cead fhir Bhìoguis don fhrìth' ('Bighouse's Farewell to the Deer-Forest') Rob Donn recalls nostalgically his deer-hunting experiences in his observation of 'the yellow-skinned one lithely running down the hill, with the hounds in full chase, playing with its pelt'. As a curiosity there is his poem on winter, which consists largely of clever inversions of Alasdair Mac Mhaighstir Alasdair's poem on summer, implying an impressive feat of memory and concentration for a man who did not read or write.

Rob Donn's poems are, however, mainly about people and human relationships. There are one or two early love poems, such as one to Ann Morrison (this romance ended but one of his grandchildren and one of Morrison's grandchildren were later married). During his period with the fencibles he composed an interesting mock love poem for a girl, Sally, who was the officers' favourite. On a more serious and sustained level he composed a number of elegies for prominent members of the Sutherland society, including his early patron Iain Mac Eachainn; the Revd Murdo MacDonald; Donald, fourth Lord Reay; and the earl of Sutherland. He contrasts Iain Mac Eachainn with those who hoard their wealth and property, and at the end of the poem he contrasts his heartfelt praise rather wryly with the sycophancy of many elegists.

The attraction of humour and satire can sometimes invade even the territory of Rob Donn's elegies. In a poem dated to 1754 he relates the death of Prime Minister Pelham to the approaching death of an old acquaintance, Ewen. In an address to Death he says:

your view takes in high and low
you snatched Pelham from greatness
and Ewen from Polla
('"S tric thu, Bhàis, cur an cèill dhuinn', first line; *Songs and Poems*, ed. Morrison, 46–8)

The best-known of his humorous/satirical elegies is that for the Rispond misers, two brothers who died, as did their housekeeper, within the same week. Religious, philosophical, and political views also surface in this poem:

The High King in his providence
wisely left some men short,
to test the sense and charity
of those who have a lot;
these should surely give a part
of all the wealth they 've got
to poor folk who are ready
to increase their meagre stock
(ibid., 49–51)

Some of Rob Donn's satire is directed against more prestigious targets, such as where he exposes Lady Reay's plot to arrange a marriage for a servant girl who had been made pregnant by one of the nobility. There is a refreshing lack of sycophancy in a number of his poems, and one could wish that he had survived to comment on the activities of landlords and factors in the generation after his death in Sutherland in 1778 (the era of Patrick Sellar). A similar independence of judgement shows in his attitude to the Jacobite rising of 1745, where his Jacobite (or perhaps simply highland) sympathies contrast with those of the local nobility.

Rob Donn's poetry is variable in quality. Much of it is of fairly limited parochial interest, laced with community fun and scandal, but poems and passages surface repeatedly that rise well above the parochial norm. This unique quality in his work was most strikingly identified by Ian Grimble in his book *The World of Rob Donn* (1979). The earliest edition of the poems appeared in 1829, with two subsequent editions in 1899 (one by Hew Morrison, another by Adam Gunn and Malcolm MacFarlane). There has been some interference in early editions with dialectal usages, and a new critical edition of the work is required.

DERICK S. THOMSON

Sources M. Mackay, 'Memoir', in *Songs and poems in the Gaelic language by Robert Mackay*, ed. M. Mackay (1829) · H. Morrison, 'Memoir', in *Songs and poems in the Gaelic language by Rob Donn*, enl. edn, ed. H. Morrison (1899) · I. Grimble, *The world of Rob Donn* (1979) · D. S. Thomson, *An introduction to Gaelic poetry*, 2nd edn (1990)
Archives U. Glas., McLagan MS

Mackay, Robert William (1803–1882), philosopher and theologian, was born on 27 May 1803 in Piccadilly, London, the only son of John Mackay. He was educated at Winchester College and matriculated at Brasenose College, Oxford, on 15 January 1821; he graduated BA in 1824 and proceeded MA in 1828, and won the chancellor's prize for Latin verse. In 1824 he was among the founding members of the Athenaeum. On leaving Oxford he entered Lincoln's Inn in 1828, but after planning and partly writing a treatise on equity he conceived a dislike to the subject, and turned to theology and philosophy.

Mackay wrote three major works: *The progress of the intellect, as exemplified in the religious development of the Greeks and Hebrews* (published in 1850); *A Sketch of the Rise and Progress of Christianity* (1853); and *The Tübingen school and its antecedents: a review of the history and present condition of modern theology* (1863). Using a great deal of historical material, all of them develop the same basic argument about the intrinsically corrupting effect on religion of religious establishments. Mackay borrows his argument about the self-serving nature of religious establishments from Enlightenment thought, but pushes it in the direction of a radical religious individualism. For Mackay the influence of churches in 'superseding individual thought in the highest problems of human concernment, and supplying a ready-made solution at the cheapest rate of obedience and unreflecting assent' (*The Tübingen School*, 5) is simply an example of the 'essentially utilitarian and immoral' (ibid., 10) nature of all forms of government. Establishments inhibit 'the mental energy which is the soul of political independence' (ibid., 7), according to Mackay, because their static nature contradicts 'the principle of progressive improvement alone suited to imperfect human nature' (ibid., vii). Mackay's insistence on the 'essentially individual' (ibid., 4) nature of religion leads in *The Tübingen School* to his welcoming unreservedly the critical theology of F. C. Baur, originator of the historical hypothesis that the books of the New Testament witness to a conflict between the Judaizing strain of Christianity associated with Peter and the hellenistic universalism of Paul. The 'progressive character' (ibid., 12) of Baur's theology is seen by Mackay as restoring the 'true Protestantism' whose spirit had been compromised by association with church establishments. This emphasis suggests that Mackay's popularization of German critical theology was directed against the Catholicizing tendencies of the Oxford Movement. Mackay's later translations of Plato testify to an enthusiasm for a Christian hellenism in which he remains close to figures such as Thomas Arnold.

Mackay formed part of the freethinking circle associated with John Chapman's editorship of the *Westminster Review*; unsurprisingly, his first book received an enthusiastic review (attributed to George Eliot) in that journal (*Westminster Review*, 54, 1851, 353–8). The review suggests that Mackay's value as a writer consists above all in his eloquence, and laments that this is all too often submerged by a cumbersome erudition. Later commentators, on the other hand, regard Mackay's work chiefly as a useful popularization and digest of the prolix writings of the Tübingen theologians, with the more rhetorical passages being an embarrassment. This suggests that Mackay's reputation may have suffered as a result of the mid-nineteenth-century move towards more scientific styles of scholarship. A close friend, Philip Gilbert Hamerton, characterized Mackay as an unworldly figure, someone who had forfeited 'that keen and clear sense of present reality that common folks have by nature' through 'excessive culture' and who suffered as a writer from being 'overpowered by the immense masses of his materials'

(Hamerton, 147). Mackay died at his home, 41 Hamilton Terrace, St John's Wood, London, on 23 February 1882. He was survived by his wife, Frances Maseres Mackay.

GAVIN BUDGE

Sources DNB · P. G. Hamerton, *An autobiography, 1834–1855, and the memoir by his wife, 1854–1894* (1897) · [G. Eliot], 'Review of *The progress of the intellect* by Robert William Mackay', *Westminster Review*, 54 (1850–51), 353–8 · A. W. Benn, *The history of English rationalism in the nineteenth century*, 2 vols. (1906) · J. M. Wheeler, *A biographical dictionary of freethinkers of all ages and nations* (1889) · CGPLA Eng. & Wales (1882)
Archives UCL, letters to W. Sharpe
Wealth at death £49,846 13s. 6d.: resworn probate, May 1882, CGPLA Eng. & Wales

Mackay, Thomas (1849–1912), social theorist, was born in Edinburgh on 10 December 1849, the eldest son of Aeneas John Mackay, a former major in the 16th regiment Bengal native infantry, and his wife, Eleanor Roberts. Mackay's mother died in 1855, leaving one brother, James. In 1864 both brothers were sent to Trinity College, Glenalmond, from where Thomas went in 1868 to New College, Oxford, where he took thirds in classical moderations and *literae humaniores*. He was admitted to the Inner Temple in 1871. In 1874, the same year in which he was called to the bar, he became engaged to Beatrice Baillie (d. 1899), the daughter of the Hon. and Revd John Baillie, canon of York. His prospective father-in-law appears to have doubted Mackay's ability to support a wife and family as a young barrister, and instead persuaded him to go into business. He thus became a partner in the wine business of Charles Kinloch, a first cousin of his father.

The offices of Kinloch and Mackay were situated in London's East End, a location that gave a practical stimulus to Mackay's interest in social and economic questions. He became a member, and then secretary, of the local committee of the Charity Organization Society (COS), an office he retained for twenty-five years; he also served as vice-chairman of the COS national council for eleven years. The COS worked to supplement the basic relief provided by the 1834 poor law with organized, charitable giving to the 'deserving' poor, and Mackay's leading role in the society provided the bedrock for his subsequent investigations into the principles and methods of poor relief.

In 1885 Mackay's partnership with Kinloch ended, but he had acquired a sufficiently large fortune to enable him to devote his energies to a study of social problems. His first work, *The English Poor*, was published in 1889; its argument for the strict application of the 1834 poor law draws heavily upon the writings of Herbert Spencer, especially in support of the view that poor relief is the cause rather than the cure of social problems. Like Spencer, Mackay was committed to the principles of individualism, the doctrine which resisted the extension of the activities of the state beyond those necessary to protect liberty and property, and he became a member of the Liberty and Property Defence League. In 1891 he edited *A Plea for Liberty*, intended as the league's riposte to the *Fabian Essays in Socialism*. Mackay himself contributed the chapter on 'Investment', and Auberon Herbert and Wordsworth Donisthorpe also provided chapters. Herbert Spencer

wrote the introduction. Three years later this volume was followed by another, also edited by Mackay, under the title of *A Policy of Free Exchange*.

Mackay continued to publish on social topics throughout the 1890s. An anonymous pamphlet, *The Great Coalition: an Adventure in Statecraft* (1893), satirized the efforts of social reformers. More substantial was *Methods of Social Reform* (1896), a collection of review articles, and *The State and Charity* (1898), which appeared in the English Citizen series. In 1899 Mackay published his chief work, *A History of the English Poor Law from 1834 to the Present Day*, which was technically a continuation of the *History* begun by Sir George Nicholl. In all these writings Mackay emphasized the debilitating effects on the character of the poor of state benefits and indiscriminate charity, and argued that the solution to social problems must reside in self-help and voluntary action.

Mackay edited the autobiography of Samuel Smiles (1905) and was also the author of biographies of the engineer Sir John Fowler (1900) and of Albert Pell (1908), a friend who shared many of his social views. He contributed frequently to the leading reviews and to *The Spectator*. In 1894 he was awarded an honorary degree by the University of St Andrews.

Mackay's first wife died in 1899, leaving him childless, and in 1905 he remarried, his second wife being the eldest daughter of James Augustus Grant, the African explorer. She died in 1907, leaving an infant son who did not long survive her. Mackay himself died at his London home, 89 Iverna Court, Kensington, of heart failure on 23 February 1912.

M. W. TAYLOR

Sources *Charity Organisation Review*, new ser., 31 (1912), 174–82 · E. Bristow, 'The Liberty and Property Defence League and individualism', *HJ*, 18 (1975), 761–89 · M. W. Taylor, *Men versus the state* (1992) · J. W. Mason, 'Thomas Mackay: the anti-socialist philosophy of the Charity Organisation Society', *Essays in anti-labour history*, ed. K. D. Brown (1974), 290–316 · b. cert.
Wealth at death £30,769 1s. 7d.: resworn probate, 1 April 1912, CGPLA Eng. & Wales

McKean, Thomas (1734–1817), revolutionary politician in America, was born on 19 March 1734 in New London township, Chester county, Pennsylvania, the second of four children of William McKean (1707–1769), an unsuccessful farmer and innkeeper, and his first wife, Letitia (c.1710–1742), daughter of Robert and Dorothea Finney. His parents were immigrants from Ulster of Scottish lineage. At the death of their mother McKean—pronounced McCain—and his elder brother, Robert (1732–1767), were placed in the home of a neighbour, the Revd Francis Alison, a learned Presbyterian minister, where they formed part of the first class in an academy that eventually became the University of Delaware. In 1750 Thomas began to read law with his cousin David Finney in New Castle, the legislative seat of the Three Lower Counties on the Delaware.

Admitted to the bar in 1754, McKean soon enjoyed a thriving law practice (which quickly expanded into Pennsylvania), as well as a promising political career. After his first election to the Lower Counties assembly in 1762 he was re-elected annually, one year excepted, until 1779. The respect won by his intellect and vigour was demonstrated by his choice as speaker of this body in 1772 and 1773. His first introduction to intercolonial politics came in 1765 when he was one of a small delegation sent to the Stamp Act congress, called to protest against British legislation. Thereafter he frequently served on committees of correspondence designed to keep Delaware (as the Lower Counties were being called) in touch with the action of its neighbours. In 1774 he was chosen in a delegation of three to attend the continental congress, where he began an exceptionally long service that lasted, with one break, until 1783. In 1774 McKean also moved his principal residence from New Castle to Philadelphia following the death of his first wife, Mary Borden (1744–1773), whom he had married on 21 July 1763 and with whom he had six children. With his second wife, Sarah Armitage (1747–1820), whom he married on 3 September 1774, he had five more children, of whom two died in infancy.

McKean was one of two Delaware delegates present on 1 July 1776, when the subject of independence was debated in congress. Finding himself at odds with his more conservative colleague George Read, McKean sent for the third Delaware delegate, Caesar Rodney, who joined him in time to cast Delaware's vote with eleven other colonies (one abstained) for independence. All three men subsequently signed the declaration adopted on 4 July. Later that month McKean, as colonel, led a battalion of Pennsylvania militia to join forces facing the British at New York, but no serious action occurred. He soon hurried back to Delaware to participate in a convention that wrote a state constitution for this small colony. In the autumn of 1776 Delaware voters punished McKean and Rodney for their line in July by removing them from the congressional delegation. He continued, however, to serve in the Delaware assembly, and in September 1777, when British forces entered Delaware and carried off the chief executive, McKean temporarily assumed the vacant position.

Though McKean was not pleased with Pennsylvania's radical constitution (adopted in 1776), in the following year he accepted the post of its chief justice and sought to establish a strong and independent court system. Retaining at the same time a seat in congress, to which he was restored by Delaware in December 1777, he assumed a heavy, if ambitious, burden in serving two states. The acme of his career in congress came in 1781, when from July to November he was its president, the highest civil post in the country.

In twenty-two years as chief justice, McKean won respect for his independence and his moderation, though this approach disappointed every faction at some time or other. Along with the lawyer and politician James Wilson, he led the movement to have Pennsylvania ratify the federal constitution (the second state to do so) in 1787; their arguments were printed in London as *Commentaries on the Constitution of the United States* (1792). He was also active in the movement for a second, more conservative Pennsylvania constitution in 1789–90. In the 1790s McKean's sympathy with the French Revolution aligned him with

Thomas Jefferson and the republicans, who made him their candidate for governor of Pennsylvania in 1799 and again in 1802. After his electoral successes his introduction of the spoils system in political appointments and particularly his partiality for members of his own family helped arouse opposition, as did his refusal to accept legal and judicial reforms desired by a radical wing of his party. When he sought a third term in 1805, his party split, but he prevailed, with help from many of his former federalist opponents.

After 1808 McKean retired from active politics, devoting time to family affairs and to an estate comprising more than 10,000 acres in Pennsylvania and Delaware, as well as a splendid mansion in Philadelphia. Vain and often intemperate, he was respected for his learning, as well as for the services he had performed for his country in perilous times. He died in Philadelphia on 24 June 1817 and was buried in the cemetery of the First Presbyterian Church, though later his body was moved to the more elegant Laurel Hill.   JOHN A. MUNROE

Sources G. S. Rowe, *Thomas McKean: the shaping of an American republicanism* (1978) · G. S. Rowe, 'McKean, Thomas', *ANB* · J. Coleman, *Thomas McKean, forgotten leader of the revolution* (1975) · G. S. Rowe, ed., 'Thomas McKean's *Biographical sketches*', *Delaware History*, 26 (1994–5), 125–37 · R. Buchanan, *Genealogy of the McKean family … and life of the Hon. Thomas McKean* (1890) · P. H. Smith and others, eds., *Letters of delegates to congress, 1774–1789*, 26 vols. (1976–2000) · G. S. Rowe, *Embattled bench: the Pennsylvania supreme court and the forging of a democratic society, 1684–1809* (1994) · J. Munroe, *Colonial Delaware—a history* (1978) · H. Tinkcom, *The republicans and federalists in Pennsylvania, 1790–1801* (1950) · S. Higginbotham, *The keystone in the democratic arch: Pennsylvania politics, 1800–1816* (1952)
Archives Hist. Soc. Penn., papers | Hist. Soc. Penn., Simon Gratz collection and others · Historical Society of Delaware, Wilmington, H. F. Brown collection · Historical Society of Delaware, Wilmington, Rodney collection · L. Cong., William Atlee papers
Likenesses C. W. Peale, oils, *c*.1776, Westmorland Museum of Art, Greensburg, Pennsylvania · C. W. Peale, double portrait, oils, 1787 (with his son), Philadelphia Museum of Art · C. W. Peale, oils, 1791, Smithsonian Institution, Washington, DC, National Portrait Gallery · J. Sharples, pastel drawing, 1796–7, Independence Hall, Philadelphia · C. W. Peale, oils, 1797, Independence Hall, Philadelphia · attrib. R. Peale ?, oils, *c*.1802 (after G. Stuart), Historical Society of Delaware, Wilmington · G. Stuart, oils, 1802, priv. coll. · D. Edwin, engraving, *c*.1803 (after G. Stuart), Smithsonian Institution, Washington, DC, National Portrait Gallery · J. Lambdin, oils, *c*.1830–1852 (after G. Stuart), Hist. Soc. Penn.
Wealth at death over 10,000 acres of land in Pennsylvania and Delaware; three-storey brick mansion at Third and Pine, Philadelphia: Rowe, *Thomas McKean*, 393; will, Buchanan, *Genealogy*, 115–16

McKechnie, William Sharp (1863–1930), historian, was born at Paisley on 2 September 1863, the third and youngest son of William McKechnie MD, of Paisley, and his wife, Helen Landale Balfour. He was educated at Greenock Academy, and at sixteen entered the University of Glasgow, where he graduated MA in 1883 with first-class honours in philosophy. Destined for the legal profession, he served his apprenticeship at Glasgow in the office of Sir James Roberton, whom he ultimately succeeded in the chair of conveyancing at Glasgow University. In 1887 he proceeded to the degree of LLB. Forgoing his original intention of being called to the Scottish bar, he set up in business in Glasgow with a friend as solicitors under the name of McKechnie and Gray, a partnership which lasted from 1890 to 1915.

McKechnie's interests, however, were more academic, and in 1894 he was appointed lecturer in constitutional law and history at Glasgow University. His students were drawn from the two faculties of law and arts. He helped to establish an honours group in history by offering an honours course in his own subject of constitutional law.

In 1916 the chair of conveyancing at Glasgow fell vacant, and McKechnie was persuaded to stand for it. His election meant the abandonment of his work in constitutional law, although he never gave up the hope of returning to it in retirement. A considerable part of the duty of his chair was that of acting as a kind of official referee in cases of disputed interpretations of deeds of conveyancing. McKechnie's lectures were prepared with exemplary care, but he had never built up a large practice or specialized in the intricacies of the Scottish land law. His anxious nature suffered under the strain, he fell into ill health and resigned the chair in 1927. On his retirement the university conferred on him the degree of LLD.

McKechnie's published work falls into three categories. First, as a student of political philosophy his earliest book, *The State and the Individual*, written as a thesis for the degree of doctor of philosophy which was conferred on him in 1895, was published in 1896 and was very favourably received. In 1906 he made another excursion into the same domain with an article on George Buchanan's tractate *De jure regni*, contributed to *George Buchanan: Glasgow Quatercentenary Studies*. Second, holding strong political views, he felt that a historian of the British constitution should express an opinion on the important constitutional question at issue in 1908–9. A series of articles contributed to the *Glasgow Herald* (there was a later series in the *Morning Post*) appeared in book form in 1909, entitled *The Reform of the House of Lords*. It was admitted even by opponents of his views to be an informing and suggestive little book. In 1912 his alarm at the alteration in the balance of the British constitution wrought from him a confession of political faith in a book entitled *The New Democracy and the Constitution*.

Third, there is *Magna Carta*, the work for which McKechnie is best remembered, first published in 1905 and heavily revised in 1914. For many years this was the standard work on the subject, and was not wholly replaced by Holt's *Magna Carta* (1965; 2nd edn, 1992). The great bulk of the book, especially the first edition, was made up of a learned commentary on the charter, chapter by chapter. This reveals all McKechnie's learning as a constitutional lawyer and his steady open-mindedness in evaluating the opinions of others. Good sense is its prime quality. He was a little uncertain in handling the intricate detail of the related documents, and was inclined here and there to outline the differing views of his contemporaries and leave it at that (see, for example, the discussion in 'Unknown charter', 2nd edn, 171–5). This was more marked in the second edition than in the first, which in some ways is the better book. In his discussion of events before and at Runnymede the work is overtaken by that of Cheney and Holt, and there are many other areas where modern opinion depends on sources (for example, the pipe rolls of the reign of John) not available in print when McKechnie wrote. Nevertheless *Magna Carta* still merits consultation.

McKechnie was modest and retiring by nature and, although a man of decided opinions, never made himself prominent in public life. He often corresponded with scholars in his own subject at home and abroad, but felt most at home in a small circle of intimate friends. He married in 1894 Elizabeth Cochrane, daughter of John Malloch JP, of Elderslie, Renfrewshire, and they had one son and one daughter.

From 1879 McKechnie lived in Elderslie. Before he retired he moved to near the university in Glasgow, where he died on 2 July 1930, survived by his wife. He was buried in Woodside cemetery, Paisley.

D. J. Medley, *rev.* J. C. Holt

Sources *The Times* (5 July 1930) · personal knowledge (1937) · private information (1937) · C. R. Cheney, 'The eve of Magna Carta', *Bulletin of the John Rylands Library*, 38 (1956), 311–41 · J. C. Holt, 'The making of Magna Carta', *EngHR*, 72 (1957), 401–22 · J. C. Holt, *Magna Carta* (1965); 2nd edn (1992)
Wealth at death £23,463 17*s*. 7*d*.: confirmation, 1930, *CCI*

McKellar, John Campbell (1859–1941), architect and builder, was born on 1 November 1859 in Glasgow, the son of Robert McKellar, bleacher, dyer, and property developer, of Newlandsfield, Pollokshaws, Glasgow. He left Queen's Park Collegiate School in 1875 to start an apprenticeship with James Munro, the Glasgow architect, later becoming Munro's chief assistant.

In 1883 McKellar set up his own architectural practice. He soon began to employ contractors himself to build tenements to his own design, many of which he kept as an investment and source of income, and by 1896 he had built eighty-nine, mainly in Crossmyloof in south Glasgow, and in Kelvindale and Maryhill in the north-west of the city. He also designed churches, including the Hood Memorial Church in east Glasgow, a Congregational church.

By 1896 McKellar had expanded enough to form a limited liability company, with capital of £40,000, increased in 1899 to £100,000. He was chairman of the new company, and kept his architectural practice, John C. McKellar, separate. The new company gradually sold off the older properties, while building new ones for rent and sale, mainly in Kelvindale, and buying up land for development. It also bought tenements in Troon, a seaside resort on the west coast, and began to acquire office buildings, such as Gresham House in Glasgow, bought for £24,000 in 1903. It continued to build tenements, including, in 1906, a block near where the new Yarrow shipyard was to be built. Between 1900 and 1906 nearly a hundred tenements were built.

McKellar was badly hit by Lloyd George's 'people's budget' and the Finance Act of 1909, which imposed heavy duties on builders' profits. In 1906 the company had embarked on building a development of small houses for sale on the Hillington Park estate to the south-west of Glasgow city centre, building thirty in the first stage, hoping to attract buyers by widespread advertising and instalment-plan buying schemes, but the houses proved difficult to sell, as owner-occupation was rare in Glasgow, and company profits fell from £2449 in 1909 to £266 in 1910. Eventually, the rest of the Hillington land was sold to Glasgow corporation, and the plan was abandoned. With the introduction of rent restriction during the First World War income from rents fell, and the company moved much of its capital out of property and into other forms of investment.

McKellar was a Conservative, opposed to government and municipal intervention in the housing market. He gave evidence to the royal commission on housing in Scotland in 1913, arguing against government subsidies for local authority building, which enabled local councils to let houses at uneconomic rents, thereby hitting private builders and landlords. In his speech at the company's annual general meeting in 1934 he attacked 'the Hitlerite rule of unreasonable and unfair Socialists and Communists, who aim at the confiscation and theft of property that cannot be removed out of their reach' (*DSBB*, 2.153). Unlike some of his competitors, who managed very successfully to combine working on local authority contracts with private house building, McKellar failed to appreciate the direction in which the construction industry was moving.

McKellar remained managing director of John C. McKellar Ltd until shortly before his death on 27 March 1941, in Glasgow. He had been married to Jessie Nisbet (d. 1925), daughter of the Revd Robert Hood of Muslin Street, Glasgow, and had one son. His leisure time was taken up with sailing and golf.   ANNE PIMLOTT BAKER

Sources N. J. Morgan, 'McKellar, John Campbell', *DSBB*
Likenesses photograph, repro. in Morgan, 'John Campbell McKellar', vol. 2, p.151

Mackellar [*née* Cameron], **Mary** (1834–1890), poet, was born at Fort William on 1 October 1834, the daughter of Allan Cameron (d. c.1845), baker at Fort William. Her father died young and Mary kept his little shop from 1845 to 1849, going to school every other day. The family left the district in 1849. Being brought up in the Lochaber district, she acquired wide knowledge of the local Gaelic and its traditions. She married at a young age John Mackellar, captain and joint owner of a coasting vessel, with whom she sailed for several years, visiting many places in Europe, and being twice shipwrecked. Mackellar settled in Edinburgh in 1876, and shortly afterwards obtained a judicial separation from her husband.

Mackellar lived by her pen and published her poems in Gaelic and English in many periodicals. These were collected into *Poems and Songs, Gaelic and English* (1880). She was equally eloquent in both languages, although her Gaelic poetry is considered superior. She also wrote *The Tourist's Handbook of Gaelic and English Phrases for the Highlands* (1880), and her translation of Queen Victoria's second series of *Leaves from our Journal in the Highlands* was rendered in forcible and idiomatic Gaelic. Her *Guide to Lochaber* gives many traditions and historical incidents nowhere else recorded. She held the office of 'bard' to the Gaelic Society of Inverness, in whose *Transactions* much of her prose appeared. Mackellar was granted £50 from the Royal Bounty Fund in 1885.

Mary Mackellar died in Edinburgh on 7 September 1890 and was buried in Kilmallie, Argyll, where a monument was built to her memory by public subscription.

J. C. HADDEN, *rev.* SAYONI BASU

Sources D. H. Edwards, *Modern Scottish poets, with biographical and critical notices*, 2 (1881) · 'Mary Mackellar—the Lochaber bard', *Scots Magazine* [Perth], 7 (1890–91), 451–63 · C. Kerrigan, ed., *An anthology of Scottish women poets* (1991) · M. Mackellar, 'Legends and traditions of Lochaber', *Transactions of the Gaelic Society of Inverness*, 16 (1889–90), 267–76 · A. Murdoch, *Recent and living Scottish poets* (1890) · D. S. Thomson, ed., *The companion to Gaelic Scotland* (1983)
Archives NL Scot., letters to Blackwoods

Mackellar, Patrick (c.1717–1778), military engineer, was born at Maam, Argyllshire, the child, probably the eldest, of John Mackellar (*fl.* 1717–1740) of Maam, a minor laird and tacksman to the duke of Argyll, and his wife, Isobell Campbell. Mackellar was appointed clerk-extraordinary under the Board of Ordnance at Woolwich on 1 July 1735 and after a short time there was promoted to clerk of the works and sent to Minorca, where he commenced his new employment in August 1736. He was appointed practitioner engineer on 7 September 1742 and on 8 March 1743 was promoted to engineer-extraordinary, bypassing the rank of sub-engineer. In the same March he became draughtsman to Captain John Hargrave, the chief engineer in Minorca, and was further promoted to engineer-in-ordinary in Minorca (local rank) on 2 January 1747. Mackellar was present at Minorca for a substantial period when significant work was being done to strengthen the fortress of St Philips and its subterranean defences.

On 2 January 1746 Mackellar gained a commission as ensign in Wynyard's (17th) foot, a commission he resigned on 18 March 1749 when the regiment left Minorca. In January 1750 he was granted permission to return to Britain to look after his private affairs, mentioning in support of his request that he had been at this duty in Minorca for thirteen years. While in Scotland he was given an introduction to Archibald Campbell, third duke of Argyll, whose brother, the second duke, when master-general, had given Mackellar his start with the Board of Ordnance. He was promoted to engineer-in-ordinary on the establishment from 31 July 1751, by which time he was at Sheerness by order of the board, carrying out a survey there the following year. In 1753 he was granted leave of absence.

War in North America In 1754 Mackellar was appointed to join the expeditionary force to North America under Major-General Edward Braddock. Mackellar was one of four engineers appointed to serve under the expedition's chief engineer, James Montresor, who landed sick in Ireland and missed the campaign. Arriving at Hampton, Virginia, in February 1755 Braddock intended to attack the French at Fort Duquesne, near to present-day Pittsburgh, a considerable march which commenced in mid-April. Mackellar was in charge of the advance party that formed a road for the main body of the army across the Allegheny Mountains through a wild and little-known territory. On 9 July, having just crossed the Monongahela River, a few miles from Fort Duquesne, the army was attacked by a strong force of French and Indians and was cut to pieces. Braddock was mortally wounded; Mackellar was also wounded and lost his horse and baggage.

Early in 1756 Mackellar was ordered to Oswego by Braddock's replacement, Governor William Shirley. He was to survey the fort and make such additions as seemed to him necessary. Arriving there on 16 May, Mackellar found the old fortifications in poor state while the new works were not well advanced. The defence of Oswego depended on a naval superiority on the lake so as to prevent an attacking force from being able to transport large ordnance. The urgent building of craft for the lake took most of the available labour and impeded work on the forts. When Montcalm, with a much superior force, invested Fort Ontario on 11 August, the inadequacy of the fortifications was immediately apparent. The garrison evacuated Fort Ontario on 13 August, surrendering Oswego shortly after, and the survivors were taken prisoner. Mackellar was held briefly at both Montreal and Quebec. He was courteously treated and was back in England in November on parole.

Mackellar was employed for a time during 1757 in repairing castles, forts, and batteries in Scotland. On 14 May 1757 the corps of engineers was given military rank in the army; the equivalent for Mackellar, as engineer-in-ordinary, was the rank of captain. On 4 January 1758 he was advanced to sub-director and major.

Mackellar was second to Colonel Bastide in the engineer contingent on the Louisbourg expedition which sailed from Halifax, Nova Scotia, under Major-General Jeffrey Amherst on 28 May 1758. The attack on Louisbourg, an important and well-fortified garrison commanding the entry to the Gulf of St Lawrence and, thus, to Montreal, Quebec, and the Canadian hinterland, was, if successful, to open the way for a British take-over of French Canada. The expedition landed at Cape Breton on 8 June, not without heavy resistance. On 8 July Bastide was wounded and the remainder of the siege operations were handed over to Mackellar who broke ground before the fortress on 12 July. This was the turning point of the operation and the besieging batteries gradually took their toll of the fortress walls and ramparts. The French surrender came on 27 July. Despite the evident contribution Mackellar's work made, Brigadier James Wolfe, whose first experience as a senior commander this was, criticized the general conduct of the siege and some of his colleagues, including the engineers, without whose mistakes he thought Louisbourg could have been taken in ten days. In October 1758 Mackellar

was assigned to survey the defences at Halifax, Nova Scotia, but after his report in April 1759 his work on strengthening them was interrupted when he was ordered to accompany Wolfe to Quebec as chief engineer. Mackellar had more experience of North America than most other senior engineers and had been prisoner at Quebec, a factor that would have pointed to him as particularly suitable, notwithstanding Wolfe's poor opinion of engineers in general.

Wolfe's army arrived before Quebec on 26 June 1759, effecting a landing at Isle d'Orléans, Mackellar's recommended point of disembarkation. In the first days of July Mackellar began the construction of batteries on ground across the river opposite Quebec at Pointe aux Pères. By 12 July these batteries began a bombardment of the upper and lower towns that was to last throughout the many weeks of stalemate while Wolfe struggled to find the key to the conquest of a city the French were convinced was impregnable. Mackellar's opinion was that storming the lower town, even if successful, would serve no purpose as it would not facilitate the conquest of the upper town. Mackellar was wounded severely during Wolfe's failed attack of 31 July. Eventually, on the night of 12 September, with Admiral Charles Saunders warning that his ships could not stay much longer owing to the impending onset of winter ice, Wolfe's army found a way up to the Plains of Abraham, and so to the capture of the city some days later. Mackellar remained as chief engineer following the capitulation, under the command of Brigadier-General James Murray. On 22 September he presented a report on the state of the fortifications in which he showed that those on the landward side could not resist cannon for more than a few days and could not be put in condition to do so in under twelve months. He outlined seven measures to be taken to secure Quebec against assaults and surprises. The French attempted to retake Quebec in April 1760 and Mackellar was dangerously wounded in this action, but was well enough by September to accompany Murray to Montreal where the combined British armies forced the surrender of French Canada.

Martinique and Havana Shortly after the surrender of Montreal, Mackellar was ordered to return to Halifax, where he arrived on 24 October to work on designs for fortifications. He maintained a correspondence with Amherst, the commander-in-chief in North America, who ordered him to New York in 1761. He arrived in late July, carrying with him new plans for Halifax to discuss with Amherst. However, Amherst now appointed Mackellar chief engineer with the expedition to be directed against Martinique under the command of Lieutenant-General Robert Monckton. With the fleet under the command of Admiral George Rodney the expedition set sail on 19 November and arrived before the island on 7 January 1762, but was unable to effect a landing until 16 January at Point Negro, a few miles from Fort Royal. Mackellar conducted the siege, which was troublesome and costly in terms of casualties, and Fort Royal was stormed and captured on 4 February. This was followed by the capitulation of the whole island of Martinique as well as the other islands in the possession of the French.

Mackellar was promoted to lieutenant-colonel on 3 January 1762 and on 18 March delivered to Monckton a detailed survey of the state of the fortifications at Fort Royal with proposals for dealing with them. On 1 April he wrote to the board requesting leave to come home, having made a similar request from Quebec. The ball that wounded him at Quebec was still inside him and could not be removed, the surgeons saying his only chance of successful treatment was to return to England. On 25 April the expedition under George Keppel, third earl of Albemarle, bound for Havana, put in at Port Royal with orders for Mackellar to join as chief engineer.

Mackellar prepared a detailed report on the options open to the invading forces, and the landing was made on 7 June at Coximar with some opposition, but by 10 June troops were before the fortress of El Morro and on high ground opposite the city. Under Mackellar's direction preparations were made for a siege, but the ground was extremely hard and lack of earth for sandbags hindered construction. Lack of fresh water was to be a continuing problem, as was regular fire from the fortress and from ships in the harbour. Roads were constructed to bring all the necessary equipment and stores from the landing place to the batteries. The first of the batteries opened fire on 20 June, with more on 1 July. Sickness, which was to take a heavy toll of the troops and was a regular threat to Europeans in these climes, had already begun to have alarming effects, and shortage of manpower became a serious problem. Further batteries were opened through July and were taking their toll of El Morro's walls and gradually silencing the Spanish guns. On 17 July Mackellar began a trench so that the batteries could be moved closer to the fortress; despite continued Spanish counter-attacks the British finished mining the walls and stormed the fortress on 30 July.

After the capture of El Morro attention turned to the city of Havana, with more batteries being directed against its walls, a major bombardment beginning on 11 August. The governor realized the hopeless position of the city and soon asked for terms of surrender. The whole island of Cuba thus came into British hands including nine sail of the line in Havana harbour. It has been stated that Mackellar was severely wounded at the very end of the siege of Havana but evidence for this has not been found. Mackellar had the distinction of a major role in what Syrett has referred to as 'the most difficult siege undertaken by the British army between the great sieges of Marlborough's campaigns and those of the Peninsular War' (Syrett, xxxiv). He showed great skill and resource and enjoyed a corresponding rise in his reputation as well as a share in the prize money amounting to £564 14s. 6d. Mackellar's journal of the siege was included by Albemarle in his official dispatches and was published in the *London Gazette*.

Chief engineer for Minorca In September the Board of Ordnance at last allowed Mackellar's return to England. Besides the continuing effects of his Quebec wound he

had also suffered the debilitating climate of Martinique and of Cuba, as well as exerting himself during two sieges, one of them long and difficult. On his return to London he worked with a draughtsman completing plans that he had brought from North America, intended for the map room at the Tower of London. The board, sitting on 9 February 1763, received another request from Mackellar for leave of absence to recover his health. This they refused saying it was not known how soon he might be wanted. Soon thereafter he was appointed chief engineer for Minorca, which had been lost to France in 1756 and was returned to Britain under the terms of the treaty of Paris. He was sent out to settle details of the hand-over with the French commandant prior to the arrival of the British garrison, and arrived on 29 May. As was customary on that station, Mackellar was given an extra 30s. per day out of the revenues of the island.

Mackellar set himself to the task of repairing the fortifications and to resolving the long-standing problem of barracks at St Philips. The town of St Philips, which provided barracks for soldiers as well as homes for inhabitants, had always stood too close to St Philips Castle, the main fortification of the island. The French besiegers in 1756 had made good use of the buildings, erecting some of their most useful batteries there; Mackellar estimated they had shortened the siege by three weeks. In February 1764 Mackellar put forward a well-reasoned proposal for re-siting the town further along the harbour on the road to Mahón near Cala Font on ground lower than the fortress. At length his plan was approved, and work began in 1771 on what was to be called Georgetown, later renamed Villa-Carlos by Spain, and then, after catalanization, Es Castell. The present-day town with its grid of streets stands much as Mackellar planned it, particularly the barracks square, a fitting memorial to the engineer who probably spent more years on the island than any other.

Mackellar's last years at Minorca were dogged by ill health. The ball lodged in his body at Quebec could never be extracted and caused him great discomfort. He took the waters at a spa in France in 1770. In 1776 he was given leave to return to Britain after stating to the board that 'without his presence in England next summer he shall be a considerable sufferer in his private affairs' (PRO, WO47/87, fol. 75). On 18 November of that year he was granted a warrant as colonel of foot in the island of Minorca only and on 29 August 1777 he was promoted to the rank of director of engineers and colonel in the army. He died at Minorca on 22 October 1778, the second most senior engineer in the service, and was probably buried there.

Mackellar made a will at Edinburgh on 7 September 1776 in which he acknowledged and made provision for two sons 'begotten by me on the body of Mrs Elizabeth Lezain of Mahon, widow' (PRO, PROB 11/1055). Elsewhere in published material she is referred to as Miss Elizabeth Basaline. The sum of £6000 was left to be equally shared between the boys, the younger of whom was six years old when Mackellar died. The elder son, John (1766–1854), entered the navy and attained the rank of admiral. The younger, Neil (1772–1829), made a career in the army, achieving the rank of colonel.

Mackellar's progression in his career was almost entirely due to his own merit. In the *History of the Corps of Royal Engineers*, Porter records that he received no mark of favour, distinction, or honour and that his promotions were gained slowly and by seniority. After a long and distinguished career he attained only the rank of colonel. Mackellar was not a man to suffer any snub and was ever jealous of the status of the corps to which he belonged. His enthusiasm in this respect could occasionally be injudicious, as in his joint letter with the commander of the artillery on the Havana expedition in 1762 concerning baggage allowances, which drew the reply 'that the master-general doth not understand what they mean by the word dissatisfaction which approaches too near to mutiny to be mentioned' (PRO, WO47/60 fol. 59). The engineers at this period often found themselves being treated with scant regard by officers of the army, and Mackellar resisted such a situation when at Minorca in 1765 he asserted his right, as the most senior officer present, to assume command of the island in the governor's absence when officers of regiments of foot denied that an engineer was eligible. George, first Marquess Townshend, who had served with him at Quebec and later became master-general of the ordnance, wrote to Lieutenant-General James Murray stating that Mackellar was a 'meritorious and indefatigable officer' whom they both had equal reason to applaud (PRO, WO46/9, fol. 23). Murray, when governor of Quebec, wrote that Mackellar's zeal for and knowledge of the service were well known.

PAUL LATCHAM

Sources D. Beaton, 'The clan Mackellar', *Journal of the Clan Campbell Society (North America)*, 23/3 (1996) [pt 1] · D. Beaton, 'The clan Mackellar', *Journal of the Clan Campbell Society (North America)*, 24/3 (1997) [pt 2] · D. Beaton, 'The clan Mackellar', *Journal of the Clan Campbell Society (North America)*, 24/4 (1997) [pt 3] · J. W. S. Connolly, 'Notitia historica of the corps of royal engineers', MS, c.1860, Royal Engineers Corps Library, Chatham · D. Gregory, *Minorca, the illusory prize* (1990) · C. Hibbert, *Wolfe at Quebec* (1959) · J. P. Hudson, 'The original reconnaissance map for the battle of Quebec', *British Library Journal*, 1 (1975), 22–4 · I. G. Lindsay and M. Cosh, *Inveraray and the dukes of Argyll* (1973) · P. Mackellar, 'A short account of the expedition against Quebec, commanded by Major-General Wolfe in the year 1759 by an engineer upon that expedition', *Royal Engineers Corps Papers*, 1 (1849–50), 1–20 [signed P. M. and wrongly attributed to Major Moncrief; repr. in A. Doughty and G. W. Parmelee, *The siege of Quebec and the battle of the Plains of Abraham*, 6 vols. (1901), 5.33–58 (where it is likewise attributed to Moncrief)] · P. Mackellar, Journal of the siege of Havana, 1762, PRO, CO/117/1, fols. 110–18 [Mackellar's journal *London Gazette* (11 Sept 1762) *London Gazette Extraordinary* (30 Sept 1762)] · T. Mante, *History of the late war in North America* (1772) · S. M. Pargellis, *Lord Loudoun in North America* (1933) · W. Porter, *History of the corps of royal engineers*, 2 vols. (1889) · C. P. Stacey, *Quebec, 1759: the siege and the battle* (1959) · D. Syrett, ed., *The siege and capture of Havana, 1762*, Navy RS, 114 (1970) · R. Wright, *The life of Major-General James Wolfe* (1864) · *GM*, 1st ser., 48 (1778), 607 · will, PRO, PROB 11/1055, fols. 200–02 · board of ordnance minutes, PRO, WO47 *passim* · ordnance letter book, Halifax, PRO, WO55/1820; WO55/1821 · PRO, Amherst papers, WO34/012–015 · Minorca, original correspondence, PRO, CO174 · ordnance out letters, PRO, WO46/9–10 · ordnance establishments and commission books, PRO, WO54, *passim* · letters to James Gabriel Montresor, Hunt. L.

Archives BL, plans for Quebec and St Philips, Minorca · PRO, plans for Georgetown, Minorca; Havana, El Morro, Cuba

Wealth at death £6000 to be shared between two illegitimate sons: will, PRO, PROB 11/1055, fols. 200–02

Mackelvie, William (1800–1863), minister of the United Presbyterian church, was born in Edinburgh on 7 March 1800. His father died soon after, and Mackelvie grew up in Leith, where he became a draper's apprentice. He severed his early connection with the established church in order to join the Associate Secession congregation of Kirkgate, Leith. He was enthusiastic in his new loyalty and went on to study for the ministry at Edinburgh University and at the Divinity Hall of the United Secession church, Glasgow. In March 1827 he was licensed to preach by the presbytery of Stirling and Falkirk. He supplied at the Albion Chapel, London, before moving to Balgedie, Kinross-shire, where he performed the same service for the ailing minister, William Gibson. On Gibson's death Mackelvie was called to the charge, to which he was ordained in August 1829. On 6 May 1836 he married, at St Cuthbert's, Edinburgh, Ann Sarah Margaret (b. 1800), daughter of Dr John M'Intosh of London, with whom he had two sons. She survived him. In becoming a Secession minister Mackelvie had fulfilled his highest ambition, and he was largely content in that role. He did, however, play a prominent role in promoting the union between the Secession and Relief churches, which took place in 1847. He was honoured with the degree of DD from Hamilton College, New York, in 1846 and appointed moderator of the United Presbyterian synod in 1856, although by this time he was somewhat deaf and ailing.

John Macfarlane's memoir of Mackelvie (published with Mackelvie's sermons in 1865) suggests a reserved character, much influenced by his childhood hardships. His difficult nature emerges more vividly from the pages of W. Graham's biography of Macfarlane, where Mackelvie is described as 'sententious, reflective, moody, with a pronounced and at any time prepared disposition to assert himself' (Graham, 59). Mackelvie published several works, including, in 1837, a biography of a local poet, Michael Bruce. His great work, however, appeared only after his death, as *Annals and Statistics of the United Presbyterian Church* (1873). This project had absorbed his time and energies for many years, but it became apparent that his health would not allow him to complete it. He underwent a serious operation in 1860 and, for two years before his death on 10 December 1863 at Balgedie, he was unable to undertake his ministerial duties. The task of completing the volume fell to a church committee under the editorship of Dr William Blair of Dunblane.

LIONEL ALEXANDER RITCHIE

Sources W. Mackelvie, *Sermons … with memoir of the author* by J. Macfarlane (1865) · *United Presbyterian Magazine*, new ser., 3 (1864) · W. Mackelvie, *Annals and statistics of the United Presbyterian church*, ed. W. Blair and D. Young (1873) · W. Graham, *Memoir of John Macfarlane* (1876), 59–63 · R. Small, *History of the congregations of the United Presbyterian church from 1733 to 1900*, 1 (1904), 395

Likenesses engraving (in middle age ?), repro. in Mackelvie, *Sermons*, frontispiece

Wealth at death £1041 14*s*. 11*d*.: inventory, 5 Feb 1864, NA Scot., SC22/44/5, 269

Macken, John [*pseud.* Ismael Fitzadam] (1784?–1823), poet, was the eldest son of Richard Macken, merchant, of Brookeborough, near Enniskillen, co. Fermanagh. In early manhood, he claimed to have spent some years as a sailor in the navy, and to have been present at the bombardment of Algiers, before returning to conduct business at Ballyconnell, co. Cavan. He later settled in Enniskillen, where, with his brother-in-law, Edward Duffy, he established, co-edited, and contributed to the *Erne Packet*, also known as the *Enniskillen Chronicle*. The first number was published on 10 August 1808.

In 1818 Macken went to London, and published at his own cost a volume of poetry, *The Harp of the Desert*, recounting his experiences at Algiers. He dedicated the poems to Lord Exmouth, the hero of the battle, who snubbed him by ignoring the compliment, and the volume failed. While in London, Macken began a close friendship with Henry Nugent Bell, the genealogist, who introduced him to William Jerdan, the editor of the *Literary Gazette*. Jerdan became an influential friend, and Macken contributed many poems to the *Literary Gazette* under the pseudonym Ismael Fitzadam. In 1821 Macken published *Lays on Land* under this pseudonym with the aid of Jerdan, who promoted the collection vigorously in his magazine, describing the poems as 'combining Scott and Byron most admirably together' (Jerdan, 40). Yet, despite Jerdan's best efforts, this third volume met with little success.

After working with Henry Nugent Bell on the *Huntington Peerage* (1821), Macken returned, disheartened, to Ireland. He resumed his post as co-editor of the *Enniskillen Chronicle*, but his health was failing. He died at Enniskillen on 7 May 1823, aged thirty-nine and was buried in Aughaveagh parish church, Enniskillen, where there is a memorial to him. After his death, Letitia Elizabeth Landon wrote an elegy for him in the *Literary Gazette*, and William Jerdan published several of Macken's poems in the magazine as a tribute. Some poems appeared in Alaric Watt's *Poetical Album* (1828), together with a largely apocryphal autobiographical letter. A poem, 'Napoleon moribundis' was mistakenly attributed to him, and several correspondents to the third series of *Notes and Queries* praised him highly on its account: however, it was in fact the work of Thomas McCarthy.

GORDON GOODWIN, rev. KATHERINE MULLIN

Sources D. J. O'Donoghue, *The poets of Ireland: a biographical and bibliographical dictionary* (1912) · A. J. Webb, *A compendium of Irish biography* (1878), 162 · K. Newmann, *Dictionary of Ulster biography* (1993) · *GM*, 5th ser., 5 (1870) · W. Jerdan, *The autobiography of William Jerdan: with his literary, political, and social reminiscences and correspondence during the last fifty years*, 4 vols. (1852–3), vol. 3, pp. 39–45

Mackendrick, Alexander (1912–1993), film director, was born in Boston, Massachusetts, on 8 September 1912, the only son of Francis Robert (Frank) Mackendrick (*d.* 1918), shipbuilding draughtsman and civil engineer, and his wife, Martha, *née* Doig. Both parents were Scottish. His

Alexander Mackendrick (1912–1993), by John Deakin, *c*.1954

father died in the influenza epidemic of 1918, and his mother, attempting to establish a career as a dress designer, agreed to Alexander's returning to Scotland with his grandfather. He was educated at Hillhead School, Glasgow, until 1926, when his outstanding drawing talents enabled him to enrol at the Glasgow School of Art. He left in 1929 without taking his degree, and travelled to London to work for the advertising agency J. Walter Thompson. He rose to become one of the agency's top art directors, but his fascination with the cinema led him to collaborate with his cousin Roger MacDougall on a script, 'War on Wednesday', that was filmed in 1937 as *Midnight Menace*. For J. Walter Thompson he scripted and storyboarded five Horlicks commercials, which were filmed by the Hungarian animated film-maker George Pal. Meanwhile, on 24 March 1934, he married Eileen Ashcroft (*b.* 1914/15), a women's magazine journalist.

During the Second World War Mackendrick made propaganda films for the Ministry of Information, and in 1943 joined a psychological warfare unit headed by the future Labour minister Richard Crossman. In 1944 he was given the task of monitoring film production in Italy, giving official approval to Roberto Rossellini's *Rome—Open City* (1945) and organizing documentary reportage of the uncovering of the Fosse Ardeatine massacre for *Giorni di gloria* (1945). When the war was over he spent a brief period with MacDougall making Ministry of Information documentaries and then joined Ealing Studios as a scriptwriter and sketch artist. After storyboarding and co-scripting Basil Dearden's *Saraband for Dead Lovers* (1948) and Charles Crichton's *Another Shore* (1948) he was given the opportunity to direct a low-budget comedy, *Whisky Galore!* (1949), filmed on the island of Barra in 1948. The film was only modestly successful in Britain but was hugely popular in both America (as *Tight Little Island*) and France (as *Whisky à Gogo*). His first marriage having ended in divorce in 1943, Mackendrick married Hilary Lloyd (*b.* 1924/5), a film publicity worker, on Christmas eve 1948, while the success of *Whisky Galore!* was still uncertain.

After acting as second unit director on Basil Dearden's *The Blue Lamp* (1950) and Charles Crichton's *Dance Hall* (1950) Mackendrick began work on his second film as director, *The Man in the White Suit* (1951), based on an unperformed play by Roger MacDougall about a man who invents a material that never gets dirty and never wears out. Though it failed to emulate the international success of *Whisky Galore!* it was generally well received, and its satirical attack on the timid obscurantism of British industry contradicts the idea of Ealing comedy as cosy, nostalgic, and reassuring. Three further films followed at Ealing: *Mandy* (1952), *The Maggie* (1954), and *The Ladykillers* (1955), all projects over which Mackendrick was able to exert considerable personal control and all confirming him as a talented and original director.

In October 1955 Ealing Studios was sold to the BBC, and Mackendrick went to Hollywood to make an adaptation of Bernard Shaw's *The Devil's Disciple*. When casting problems delayed production he was assigned a tough New York black comedy, *The Sweet Smell of Success* (1957). Putting Tony Curtis in a role that destroyed his matinée-idol image did little for the film's commercial prospects but Mackendrick won critical admiration for his evocation of a dark, slick, sleazy world, and the reputation of the film has continued to grow. He returned to England for the filming of *The Devil's Disciple* (1959) but disagreements with the film's two leading actors, Kirk Douglas and Burt Lancaster, led to his being replaced. Further disappointment followed when he was ousted as the director of the expensive wartime epic *The Guns of Navarone* (1961). What had seemed an extremely promising career now looked in jeopardy. He was rescued by his mentor at Ealing, Michael Balcon, who entrusted him with *Sammy Going South* (1963), an ambitious Technicolor epic about a ten-year-old boy's journey through Africa from Port Said (where his parents have been killed in a British bombing raid) to Durban. The film is unique in its uncondescending picture of Africa in the last days of British colonialism, but in 1963 it seemed irrelevant to the new world of the Beatles and Mary Quant, and failed to arouse much interest.

After making an episode of the American television series *The Defenders* ('The hidden fury', 1964) Mackendrick worked with John Osborne on a version of *Moll Flanders* and with Tony Hancock on an adaptation of Eugene Ionesco's *Rhinoceros*. Neither project prospered, but a long-standing ambition to film Richard Hughes's novel *A High Wind in Jamaica* was unexpectedly realized in 1965. Mackendrick had proved his ability to inspire fine performances from children in *Mandy*, *The Maggie*, and *Sammy Going South*, and was a natural choice for a story that centred upon a group of children being kidnapped by pirates. Unfortunately what the film's backer, Twentieth Century Fox, wanted was a Disney-like adventure story that would ignore the sinister intimations of Hughes's novel, and Mackendrick needed all his patience, guile, and persistence to make a film that remained true to the spirit of the book. Twentieth Century Fox took their revenge by cutting the film down from 135 to 103 minutes, but it remained a disturbing, significant, and visually sophisticated film.

Mackendrick's next—and last—feature film, *Don't Make Waves* (1967), also suffered from producer interference, but here the script was much weaker and Mackendrick himself regarded it as irredeemable. In 1969, after his plans for a personal and idiosyncratic version of the Mary, queen of Scots, story was aborted by the abrupt withdrawal of American financial support from British film production, he accepted the post of dean of the California Institute of the Arts film school. He remained as dean until 1978, and after stepping down continued to teach there until his death, in Los Angeles on 22 December 1993. He was survived by his wife, Hilary.

Mackendrick was always reluctant to regard himself as a victim, and blamed his inadequacy as deal-maker for his difficulties. He told one interviewer that:

> To spend, say 50 per cent of your time trying to get the job, and 50 per cent of your time doing the job—that's a fair break. If you spend 95 per cent of your time trying to get the job, and only five per cent doing it, you're in the wrong business. (Kemp, *Lethal Innocence*, 236)

It remains a matter of shame and regret that a director of his stature should abandon film-making. But his decision to quit meant that for over twenty years he enjoyed a second career as a teacher of film, which brought both him and his pupils immense satisfaction.

The variety of Mackendrick's work and the fact that his best-loved films—*Whisky Galore!* and *The Ladykillers*—were comedies has militated against his being considered one of the great film directors. He himself never made the mistake of not taking comedy seriously, arguing that 'To be frivolous about trivial things is childish—but to make fun of things that really scare you, that if you like is the basis of truth in comedy' (Kemp, 'Saving grace', 149). Even his most congenial comedy, *Whisky Galore!*, has a sharp edge, and the affection for the quaint and eccentric in *The Ladykillers* masks a thrillingly macabre story. Once they are set against a wider framework than that offered by Ealing, Mackendrick's comedies, together with *Mandy*, *The Sweet Smell of Success*, *Sammy Going South*, and *A High Wind in Jamaica*, can be seen as part of a body of work that is full of insight, wisdom, and humanity.　　　ROBERT MURPHY

Sources P. Kemp, *Lethal innocence: the cinema of Alexander Mackendrick* (1991) · C. Barr, *Ealing Studios* (1977) · 'Tavernier on Mackendrick', *Sight and Sound* (Aug 1994), 16–21 · P. Kemp, 'Saving grace: Mackendrick at Quimper', *Sight and Sound* (summer 1990), 149 · P. Kemp, 'There are no rules: the film teaching of Alexander Mackendrick', *Metro*, 113/114 (1998), 91–5 · 'Alexander Mackendrick', *Film Dope* (June 1987), 35–7 · C. Barr, 'Projecting Britain and the British character: Ealing Studios, part 2', *Screen*, 15/2 (summer 1974), 126–63 · A. Mackendrick, 'A film director and his public', *The Listener* (23 Sept 1961), 482–3, 489 [transcript of talk given on the Home Service, 15 Sept 1961] · P. Goldstone, 'The Mackendrick legacy', *American Film*, new ser., 4 (March 1979), 66–9 · 'Mandy: daughter of transition', *All our yesterdays*, ed. C. Barr (1986),

335–61 • P. Kemp, 'Mackendrickland', *Sight and Sound* (winter 1988–9), 48–52 • *The Independent* (28 Dec 1993) • *The Independent* (1 Jan 1994)

Archives NL Scot., corresp. with James Kennaway | FILM 'Scope: Alexander Mackendrick', interview with A. M. on career in film industry and teaching at California Institute of the Arts by W. Gordon Smith, BBC 1, Scotland, 17 March 1975, dir. / prod. W. Gordon Smith • 'Mackendrick: the man who walked away', survey of A. M.'s career, incl. interviews, Scottish TV, 21 August 1986, prod. Russell Galbraith, dir. Dermot McQuarrie • 'Typically British', dir. Stephen Frears, Channel 4, 2 Sept 1995, includes comments from Mackendrick on British cinema

Likenesses R. McLean, drawing, 1939, repro. in *The Independent* (1 Jan 1994) • photographs, 1948–57, Hult. Arch. • J. Deakin, photograph, *c*.1954, NPG [*see illus.*]

McKendrick, Anderson Gray (1876–1943), mathematician, epidemiologist, and army officer, was born on 8 September 1876 at 1 Chester Street, Edinburgh, youngest of the five children of John Gray *McKendrick (1841–1926), professor of physiology in Glasgow, and his wife, Mary Souttar (1842–1896), eldest daughter of William Souttar, Great North of Scotland Railway accountant, and his wife, Mary Mearns. His second forename carried forward in the family the name of his father's benefactor when a student in Aberdeen.

McKendrick was educated at Kelvinside Academy, Glasgow (1882–91), studied at Jena University, Germany (1894–5), and completed medical studies at the University of Glasgow in 1900, graduating MB ChB with high commendation. With a first on the entrance examination, he entered the Indian Medical Service (IMS) and trained in military and tropical medicine at the Army Medical School, Netley, where he studied under the bacteriologist Almroth Wright.

In June 1901 McKendrick was dispatched to Sierre Leone on the fifth Liverpool malarial expedition to study anti-malarial techniques with Ronald Ross, whose example profoundly influenced the direction of McKendrick's life work. Ross impressed on the young physician lieutenant, not yet trained in mathematics, the tremendous power of mathematical methods in medical research.

McKendrick saw distinguished military service in the Somaliland campaign (1903–4), then, posted to India, was appointed in 1905 to the research department of the Government of India Pasteur Institute at Kasauli, the provincial bacteriological and pathological laboratory for the Punjab. There he concentrated on investigating the disease of rabies, treating patients, preparing vaccine, and conducting experimental work, with evenings reserved for study of J. W. Mellor's *Higher Mathematics, for Students of Chemistry and Physics* (1902).

On 3 February 1910 McKendrick married Mildred Macleod Wylie (1886–1952), daughter of Major-General Henry Wylie, former resident of the Gurkha state of Nepal. They had two sons and two daughters. His son Gordon was a naval officer, related by marriage to Admiral Andrew Browne Cunningham; his other son, John Gray, was an army officer (died of wounds in 1945).

During his forty-year research career McKendrick made many important contributions to biology, medicine, epidemiology, demography, mathematics, and statistics, and

to the intricate embroidery that weaves these fields together. In an early statistical study in immunology (with W. F. Harvey, 1907), McKendrick showed that the quantity of virus and the length of time over which it is administered are the critical factors in anti-rabic immunization. In time he became the acknowledged British authority on rabies, publishing important critical reviews of rabies literature in the *Tropical Disease Bulletin* (1924–34) and influential annual reviews of rabies treatment statistics for the League of Nations (1927–37).

For some years McKendrick searched for a theoretical way of comparing different anti-malarial measures. He succeeded by mathematically modelling the interaction between infected humans and infected mosquitos ('The rise and fall of epidemics', 1912), showing that when the ratio of the size of the mosquito population to the human is large, quinine prophylaxis gives better results, whereas if it is small, anti-mosquito measures are more efficient.

In 1912, in a letter to his mentor Ronald Ross, McKendrick reported a mathematical breakthrough related to leukocyte effectiveness, later published in *Science Progress* ('The physical aspect of the opsonic experiment', 1914). McKendrick had derived a differential–difference equation satisfied by the distribution function of the number of bacteria neutralized by each leukocyte. Amazingly, in solving this equation McKendrick independently discovered the important Poisson distribution, and his equation may well be the earliest characterization of the Poisson process by a differential–difference equation. In a subsequent paper ('Studies on the theory of continuous probabilities, with special reference to its bearing on natural phenomena of a progressive nature', 1914), McKendrick derived and studied equations for a stochastic process now called the pure birth process and for a particular birth–death process, which appears to be the earliest treatment of these processes in probability theory. This paper foreshadowed McKendrick's later extraordinary work on mathematical epidemiology, having in it his first mathematical model of an epidemic.

On home leave in 1913, McKendrick finally undertook formal training in mathematics at Aberdeen, but was recalled to the Pasteur Institute in 1914, where he served for six years as its director. In 1920, for health reasons, McKendrick was forced to give up his post in India to return to Scotland, initially leaving his family in India. In the same year he was appointed superintendent of the Royal College of Physicians' laboratory, Edinburgh, where he actively pursued his research until retirement. While in Edinburgh he was an elder of the Pleasance church and lived in Succoth Gardens, Murrayfield.

McKendrick was awarded the DSc degree by the University of Aberdeen in 1927. His pathbreaking dissertation in 1926, 'Applications of mathematics to medical problems', contains the first formulation of a partial differential equation for the age distribution of a population and the first stochastic treatment of an epidemic. It is a *tour de force*, cited continually.

This work was followed by five major papers (with W. O. *Kermack) on a deterministic theory of epidemics, in which several fundamental problems in epidemiology were addressed. For example: what starts an epidemic and what brings it to an end? One of the celebrated results is the classic Kermack–McKendrick threshold theorem: if a contagious disease confers permanent immunity to a survivor, introduction of infectious cases into a closed population of susceptibles (no births, immigration, or emigration) will give rise to an epidemic if and only if the density of susceptibles is above a certain critical value (threshold). The epidemic ends when the susceptible density is about as far below the threshold as it was above it initially. This result was extended, with appropriate modifications, when there is a continuous supply of new susceptibles, and immunity is partial.

In addition to his pioneering work in mathematical epidemiology, McKendrick also made contributions of lasting consequence to the development of mathematical analysis in demography, especially on generation mortality projection and applications, showing in particular that the important factor in lifetime health is the environment up to age fifteen, with obvious implications for health policy (W. Kermack, A. McKendrick, and P. McKinlay, 'Death-rates in Great Britain and Sweden: expressions of specific mortality rates as products of two factors and some consequences thereof', *Journal of Hygiene*, 34, 1934, 433–57).

McKendrick was a truly Christian gentleman, a tall and handsome man, brilliant in mind, kind and modest in person, a skilful counsellor and administrator who gave of himself and knew how to enable others. He was fluent in German and French and a fine musician who played the cello, organ, piano, and ocarina. He was a fellow of the Royal Society of Edinburgh and a fellow of the Royal College of Physicians, Edinburgh. He was awarded the Cullen prize by the Royal College of Physicians in 1934.

In 1941, due to poor health, McKendrick retired to Carrmoor, Carrbridge, Inverness-shire. He was an elder of the Church of Scotland there, but also sometimes attended Free Church services. He died at Carrmoor of coronary heart disease on 30 May 1943 and was buried in Carrbridge cemetery.   WARREN M. HIRSCH

Sources W. F. H., *Edinburgh Medical Journal*, 3rd ser., 50 (1943), 500–06 [incl. list of publications] · *Year Book of the Royal Society of Edinburgh* (1942–3), 23–4 · *BMJ* (19 June 1943), 771–2 · *Glasgow Medical Journal*, 140 (1943), 21–2 · *The Lancet* (10 July 1943), 59 · J. Aitchison and G. S. Watson, 'A not-so-plain tale from the Raj: A. G. McKendrick, IMS', *The influence of Scottish medicine*, ed. D. A. Dow (1988), 113–28 · J. Gani, 'The early use of stochastic methods: a historical note on McKendrick's pioneering papers', *Statistics and probability: essays in honor of C. R. Rao*, ed. G. Kallianpur, P. R. Krishnaiah, and J. K. Ghosh (1982), 263–8 · J. O. Irwin, 'The contributions of G. U. Yule and A. G. McKendrick to stochastic process methods in biology and medicine', *Stochastic models in medicine and biology*, ed. J. Gurland (1964), 147–65 · F. Yates, *Memoirs FRS*, 17 (1971), 416–20 [appx to J. N. Davidson, obit. of W. O. Kermack] · J. G. McKendrick, *The story of my life* (1919) · R. Ross, *Memoirs* (1923), 434–54 · J. O. Irwin, 'Mathematics in medical and biological statistics', *Journal of the Royal Statistical Society: series A*, 126 (1963), 18–29 · F. A. Haight, *Handbook of the Poisson distribution* (1967), 102–121 · F. C. Hoppensteadt, 'Some influences of population biology on mathematics', *Essays in the history of mathematics*, ed. A. Schlissel (1984), 25–9 · M. S. Bartlett, *Stochastic population models* (1960), 54–61 · W. Feller, *An introduction to probability theory and its applications*, 3rd edn (1968), 450 · M. S. Bartlett, *An introduction to stochastic processes, with special reference to methods and applications*, 3rd edn (1978), 58 · private information (2004) [Joyce Matthew]
Archives Royal College of Physicians of Edinburgh, MSS | London School of Hygiene and Tropical Medicine, Ross MSS · UCL, Karl Pearson MSS · Wellcome L., Ross MSS
Wealth at death £6116 8s. 3d.: confirmation, 24 Sept 1943, *CCI*

McKendrick, John Gray (1841–1926), physiologist, was born on 12 August 1841 in the Hardgate, Aberdeen, the only son of James MacKendrick, a silk merchant, of Braco, Perthshire, and his wife, Elizabeth, *née* Smith, of Laurencekirk. The key elements in his life were his fascination with natural processes, humanity, and the Christian faith. It is remarkable that a long struggle with poverty should have produced a man so driven by idealism. His mother contracted tuberculosis and could look after him for only his first three or four months. His father died aged twenty-nine after his business in Aberdeen failed; he entrusted his son to a Mrs Gray, a milliner, who became the guiding spirit of McKendrick's early years. For a while she looked after the boy in Aberdeen, but he liked the country, so she left him with his grandparents in Braco. The summer of 1854 was a formative one. Long days in the countryside employed as a 'herd laddie' made a deep impression, and, as McKendrick later explained, 'My mind awoke about this time' (McKendrick, *Story of my Life*, 11). Meanwhile, Mrs Gray obtained an apprenticeship for him with a firm of advocates in Aberdeen. Through the kindness of friends he was introduced to the possibilities of education, and to his future wife, Mary Souttar. His interest in natural history, especially marine zoology, was encouraged by an anatomist, Peter Redfern, who arranged for McKendrick to exhibit an aquarium at the British Association meeting of 1859, attended by John Gould, Richard Owen, T. H. Huxley, and Roderick Murchison. Redfern suggested that McKendrick should study medicine, and in 1861, aged twenty, he passed the examinations to enter the medical faculty of Aberdeen University.

McKendrick's first year went well, bringing him the comparative anatomy prize, and honours in chemistry, but then disaster struck. His employer asked him to return for work one Saturday afternoon, but he stayed too long at a concert to hear Jenny Lind sing, and was dismissed for being almost thirty minutes late. He found work in Edinburgh in a newspaper office, learnt anatomy from John Goodsir, whom he regarded as the father of British physiology, and won Goodsir's gold medal. But he suffered another frightening setback when he coughed blood. W. T. Gairdner, later a pioneer in public health, diagnosed tuberculosis and advised rest in the country. McKendrick soon recovered, and with further training in Aberdeen and Edinburgh graduated MD, ChB in 1864. After posts in Chester and Whitechapel, London, he got a well-paid position as house surgeon in Belford Hospital, Fort William, and on 21 August 1867 was able to marry Mary Souttar (1842–1896), daughter of William Souttar, a railway clerk, and his wife, Mary, *née* Mearns. They had two daughters and three sons, including Anderson Gray *McKendrick (1876–1943), medical statistician.

John Gray McKendrick (1841–1926), by Olive Edis

In 1869 McKendrick by chance met Hughes Bennett, professor of physiology in Edinburgh University, who offered him an assistantship. Acceptance reduced his salary, but opened the door to science as a profession. Bennett's frail health gave McKendrick the opportunity to stand in for the professor during the winter sessions, lecturing also to some formidable women pioneers, such as Sophia Jex-Blake. McKendrick also began research. From observing the effects of removing portions of the brains of pigeons he concluded that the deeper parts of the corpora striata are concerned with movement. He was intrigued to know what part of the brain gave these birds their individual characters; for this reason, years later, he set up a lectureship in experimental psychology in Glasgow University. His most significant research was with the physical chemist James Dewar. They discovered that light falling on the retina elicited an electric signal in the retina and optic nerve; the same effect was demonstrated in many species. Light shining on one retina affected optic lobes on both sides of the head. Unhappily, unknown to them, Holmgren of Uppsala had already published similar findings. McKendrick and Dewar also collaborated in pharmacological experiments; their work on chinoline and piridine bases laid the foundations for antipyrine therapy. These experiments made McKendrick's reputation. He later made observations on many subjects—measurements of the cochlea, improvements to apparatus, anaesthetics, respiration—but none had the impact of these earlier studies in Edinburgh. In 1873 Bennett resigned, but

William Rutherford, not McKendrick, was elected to succeed him. Initially this was another setback—Lister called round to sympathize—but McKendrick quickly recovered financially by extramural teaching, and in 1876 became professor of physiology in Glasgow University.

McKendrick's predecessor, Andrew Buchanan, who discovered fibrinogen, left a department seriously behind the times. McKendrick bought equipment from the continent, initially at his own expense. By the time of his retirement he had raised about £20,000 for the department and provided his successor with spacious accommodation. He wrote textbooks for medical students, first a single volume, then two volumes, and a biography of Hermann von Helmholtz (1899). Although McKendrick was a founder member of the Physiological Society, his research activities focused on the Royal Institution, where Dewar was now director. As Fullerian professor there (a post held conjointly with his regius chair), he gave public lectures, including Christmas lectures to children. The text of the 1892 series survives, confirming his reputation as one of the best popular lecturers of his time. In addition, he was in demand to lecture on the relation between science and religion (he was a strong Congregationalist). The Combe lectures drew audiences of a thousand. McKendrick later expressed remorse that he had allowed all this intense activity to direct his attention away from original research. However, in his favourite topic, acoustics, experimental methods were still too primitive for real progress.

In 1906 McKendrick retired to Stonehaven, Aberdeenshire, and was elected provost in 1910. He was elected FRSE and FRCP Edin. (1871) and FRS (1884), and received an honorary LLD from Aberdeen (1882), and Glasgow (1907). He died at his home, 10 Rosslyn Terrace, Glasgow, on 2 January 1926, and was buried at the chapel of St Mary's between Muchalls and Stonehaven.

MARGARET H. GLADDEN

Sources J. G. McKendrick, *The story of my life* (1919) · D. N. Paton, *PRS*, 100B (1926), xiv–xviii · R. Bayliss, 'John Gray M'Kendrick, physiologist (1841–1926)', *Medical History*, 17 (1973), 288–303 · J. G. McKendrick, *Valedictory address* (1906) · R. C. Garry and M. H. Gladden, 'The physiological training of Victorian medical students in Glasgow', *Journal of Physiology*, 329 (1982), 6P · m. cert. · *CCI* (1926)
Archives RS · U. Glas., special collection | Hunterian Museum and Art Gallery, Glasgow, physiological equipment
Likenesses J. H. Lorimer, portrait, 1908, U. Glas., West Medical Building · O. Edis, photograph, NPG [*see illus.*] · photographs, T. & R. Annan & Sons, photographers, Glasgow · photographs, Wellcome L.
Wealth at death £5402 18s. 4d.: confirmation, 14 April 1926, *CCI*

McKenna, Andrew Joseph (1833–1872), journalist, was born in co. Cavan on 1 November 1833, third son of Joseph McKenna and his wife, Esther, *née* Young. He was educated at Kilmore Academy in co. Cavan and at St Patrick's College, Maynooth (where he matriculated in August 1853), though he was not ordained. His early life is obscure but he wrote poetry for *The Nation* and other newspapers under various pseudonyms. In 1862 he became the first editor of the Belfast *Ulster Observer*, a paper founded by the Ulster Catholic Publishing Company to advocate free trade, civil and religious liberty, and a measure of reform. In 1865 the bishop of Down and Connor, Patrick Dorrian, launched a mission in Belfast to revive the Catholic church. McKenna's liberal stance as the editor of a professedly Catholic paper was unacceptable to Dorrian, who pressed to have him removed. In 1868 McKenna left the *Observer* (which almost immediately ceased publication) and founded the *Northern Star*, advertising it as a 'liberal Catholic journal holding advanced views'. Its first editor was a Father Cahill. Almost immediately his new paper was attacked by Bishop Dorrian and by a Belfast newsagent, Owen Kerr. On McKenna's death in April 1872 the paper ceased publication and was taken over by Bishop Dorrian's allies, Owen Kerr and Kevin and T. E. Fitzpatrick, who then founded the *Ulster Examiner*.

McKenna was said by his obituarist to have been 'an eloquent speaker and a ready and forcible writer' (*The Nation*). In 1865 he was admitted to the Irish bar, and it was claimed that, had he lived longer, his new career as a lawyer would have been as distinguished as his career in the Irish press. McKenna married a Miss McHugh and they had a daughter who died in 1871. Her death apparently hastened his own, and he died on 4 April 1872 at Millbank House, Holywood, co. Down. He was buried in Friar's Bush cemetery, Belfast.   MARIE-LOUISE LEGG

Sources A. A. Campbell, *Belfast newspapers past and present* (1921) • D. J. O'Donoghue, *The poets of Ireland: a biographical and bibliographical dictionary* (1912); repr. (1970) • *Belfast News-Letter* (5 April 1872) • *The Nation* (13 April 1872) • E. Keane, P. Beryl Phair, and T. U. Sadleir, eds., *King's Inns admission papers, 1607–1867*, IMC (1982) • P. J. Hamell, *Maynooth: students and ordinations index, 1795–1895* (1982) • *CGPLA Ire.* (1872)
Wealth at death under £2000: administration, 8 May 1872, *CGPLA Ire.*

Mackenna, John (1771–1814), army officer in Chile, son of William Mackenna of Willville, co. Monaghan, and his wife, Eleanor, daughter of Philip O'Reilly of Ballymorris, was born at Clogher, co. Tyrone, on 26 October 1771. He was fourth in lineal descent from Major John Mackenna, Jacobite high sheriff of co. Monaghan, who was killed by William III's troops at Drumbanagher on 13 March 1689. His education was entrusted to his kinsman, Alexander O'Reilly (1730–1794), a general in the Spanish service, who had been governor of Louisiana (1767–9), commanded against Algiers in 1775, and was at the time of his death commander of the army of Catalonia.

By O'Reilly's directions Mackenna left Ireland in 1784, entered the Royal Military Academy of Mathematics at Barcelona, and in 1787 was appointed cadet in the Spanish engineers. He served under O'Reilly during 1787–8 in the garrison at Ceuta, and during 1794 in the campaign of Rousillon against the French republic. His service was distinguished, but his promotion being delayed he determined to seek his fortune in the New World, and, against his family's wishes, he sailed for Peru in October 1796. He carried with him recommendations to the Spanish viceroy, Ambrosio O'Higgins, won his spurs as an engineer by reconstructing the important bridge of Rimac, and was on 11 August 1797 appointed governor of Osorno. As such he

encouraged colonization and built a road, in the face of great natural obstacles, from Osorno to Chiloé, before in 1808 being recalled to erect fortifications against the supposed threat of a French invasion. Mackenna married in 1809 Josefa Vicuña Larraín, and they had a daughter, Carmen; she married a cousin, Pedro Felix Vicuña, and had a son, Benjamin Vicuña Mackenna (1831–1886), a distinguished historian.

Like many other Chilean *peninsulares* Mackenna decided in 1810 to join the party of revolution, being employed by the new government as its chief military adviser. In this capacity, as well as continuing his work of fortification, he drew up plans for a new army and a military academy, and was in the following year appointed governor of Valparaiso. However, his innate conservatism and sense of order soon caused him to become dissatisfied with the aftermath of the revolution—as he complained, 'Everyone wants to talk, nobody to listen; everyone wants to command, nobody to obey'—and he therefore decided to throw in his lot with the ambitious *criollo* adventurer José Miguel Carrera. The scion of a powerful local family, Carrera had since 1808 been fighting as a volunteer in the Peninsular War, but, on hearing the news of the Chilean revolution, he had come home determined to advance the interests of his clan. His dare-devil bravado and promise of a strong administration appealing to many military men, he was in September 1811 able to overthrow the junta in Santiago and replace it with a new one of which Mackenna was a member. Discovering that in doing so he had only succeeded in advancing the interests of the even more powerful Larraín family, into which Mackenna had married in 1809, Carrera launched a second coup two months later and established a personal dictatorship. Mackenna was arrested, accused of plotting Carrera's assassination, and banished to Rioja. There he remained until April 1813 when the successes achieved by the loyalist expeditionary force dispatched from Peru to reconquer Chile compelled Carrera to recall him and appoint him his chief of staff.

In the campaign that followed Mackenna fought bravely, especially at the siege of Chillán, but his advice was disregarded and his relations with Carrera, whom he had come to regard as ignorant, immoral, and dangerously anticlerical, went from bad to worse. With the patriot forces on the point of collapse, Mackenna therefore seized on the opportunity provided by Carrera's defeat at the River Roble on 17 October 1813 to persuade the junta established by the dictator to govern Chile during his absence at the front to replace Carrera with the future 'liberator', Bernardo O'Higgins, with whom he had become close friends. Having been rewarded by O'Higgins with the command of part of the army, Mackenna succeeded in defeating the loyalists at Membrillar, where he was slightly wounded, helped check their march on Santiago, and took part in negotiations for the short-lived peace of Lircay that followed. At this point Carrera reappeared on the scene; having been captured by the loyalists shortly after his replacement by O'Higgins, he was now released and made his way to Santiago where he promptly launched another coup on 23 July 1814 and re-established himself as dictator. Mackenna was arrested and banished once again, and settled in Mendoza.

During Mackenna's absence the loyalists resumed hostilities, and secured a decisive victory over O'Higgins (who had suppressed his fury at Carrera's latest coup in the interests of national unity) and Carrera at Rancagua, the entire patriot leadership then fleeing across the Andes to Mendoza. Violent quarrels immediately broke out between the supporters and opponents of Carrera and both sides sent embassies to Buenos Aires to obtain the support of the government, these being headed by Mackenna and Carrera's younger brother, Luis. Encountering Mackenna in Buenos Aires, Luis Carrera challenged him to a duel, this taking place in the small hours of 21 November 1814. Mackenna was mortally wounded when hit in the throat by his opponent's second shot. He was buried in the cloister of the convent of Santo Domingo at Buenos Aires, where an inscription was placed to his memory in 1855. THOMAS SECCOMBE, rev. CHARLES ESDAILE

Sources V. Mackenna, *Vida de D. Juan Mackenna* (1859) · D. B. Arana, *Historia general de Chile* (1891) · P. P. Figueroa, ed., *Diccionario biografico general de Chile, 1550–1889* (1889) · private information (1893) [P. Mackenna] · R. Tellez Yañez, *El General Juan Mackenna, héroe del Membrillar* (1952) · L. Nicholson, *The liberators: a study of independence movements in Spanish America* (1969) · J. Lynch, *Caudillos in Spanish America, 1800–1850* (1992) · L. Bethell, ed., *The Cambridge history of Latin America*, 3 (1985) · J. Lynch, *The Spanish American revolutions, 1808–1826* (1973) · S. Collier, *Ideas and politics of Chilean independence, 1808–1833* (1967)

McKenna [*née* Cnockaert], **Marthe** (1892–*c*.1969), spy, was born in Westrosebeke, Belgium, one of five children of Felix Cnockaert, farmer, and his wife. Although many details of her family remain obscure, it appears that both parents were Belgian and that she had three brothers and one sister.

Prior to the outbreak of the First World War Marthe studied at the medical school of Ghent University. Her education was interrupted by the invasion of Belgium by German forces in 1914, which occurred while she was visiting her family. Marthe remained with her parents and was in Westrosebeke when it was overrun by enemy forces. She volunteered her services as a nurse at an emergency hospital set up in the village to treat German and allied soldiers, and was allowed to remain there even after all other villagers had been removed from the area. Marthe was especially valued by the German authorities for her ability to speak fluent English and German, as well as French and Flemish.

Early in 1915 Marthe was sent to Roeselare, north-east of Ypres, where she was reunited with her parents and where she continued to work as a nurse at a military hospital. At this time she was approached by an old family friend, Lucelle Deldonck, who revealed herself as an agent for British intelligence and who wanted to recruit Marthe into espionage work for the allies. For almost two years Marthe used her position in the hospital and her proximity to German soldiers in a café in Roeselare purchased by her parents to gather information on troop movements, artillery concentrations, locations of supply dumps, and

other strategic concerns. This information was then passed on through a network of Belgian agents, a number of whom were women. In many cases these women, Marthe included, also aided in the escape of allied prisoners.

After being involved in the destruction of an ammunition dump Marthe was arrested on espionage charges in November 1916 and sentenced to death. This sentence was later commuted to life in prison when it was discovered she had been awarded the Iron Cross by the German government for her nursing services. She then spent the remainder of the war in very poor conditions in a prison in Ghent.

All of Marthe's immediate family survived the war, although two of her brothers were permanent invalids due to war injuries. While Marthe herself was recovering from her ordeal in prison she learned that she had been mentioned in dispatches on 8 November 1918 by Field Marshal Sir Douglas Haig in recognition of her intelligence work; for this she was given a certificate by the British government noting her 'gallant and distinguished services in the Field' and signed by the secretary of state for war, Winston Churchill (McKenna, 4). The French and Belgian governments both made her a member of the Légion d'honneur. After receiving her demobilization papers and prison pay from British intelligence Marthe returned to Westrosebeke for the first time after the war, where she met a British army officer, John McKenna (d. *c*.1962), whom she married shortly thereafter.

Marthe McKenna and her husband apparently moved to Manchester following the war, but later returned to Belgium, settling in the rebuilt family home in Westrosebeke. In 1931 an English writer travelling in Belgium happened upon the McKennas and, hearing about her war work, encouraged Marthe to record her story in English for publication. The result was the memoir *I was a Spy!*, ghost-written by her husband and published in 1932, with a glowingly complimentary forward written by Churchill. It was subsequently made into a popular film by Victor Saville, which starred Madeleine Carroll as Marthe.

Following this well-received volume and a collection of espionage anecdotes published in 1934, the McKennas switched to producing spy fiction under Marthe's name—publishing over a dozen novels and numerous short stories between the mid-1930s and the early 1950s. Ironically (but perhaps not surprisingly) while the details of these stories often drew on Marthe's wartime experiences, the plots tended to stick to the more familiar format of the day in which the hero was typically male (and English) and women appeared as loyal sidekicks and love interests, damsels in distress, or seductive villains.

It is difficult to determine the extent to which Marthe McKenna was personally responsible for the numerous works of spy fiction published under her name. Given the nature of the prose and their stylistic similarity to other popular contemporary British thrillers, it is likely that John McKenna was largely responsible for the actual writing. The absence of any publications under Marthe's name after 1951 appears to coincide roughly with the point at which their marriage ended unhappily. Marthe McKenna then lived a secluded life in Westrosebeke until her death, which took place about 1969.

Although details about many aspects of her life are scarce and her status as an author is uncertain, Marthe McKenna should be recognized for her contributions as an intelligence agent during the First World War, when most modern intelligence services were still in their infancy. Completely inexperienced in such work, she pursued her activities under undeniably dangerous circumstances and paid a heavy price when caught. Her efforts put her in the company of a select group of women agents of the period whose achievements and experiences are only beginning to receive serious attention within the broader field of the history of intelligence operations.

DEBORAH E. VAN SETERS

Sources M. McKenna, *I was a spy!* (1932) · D. McCormick, *Who's who in spy fiction* (1977) · E. Martell, L. G. Pine, and A. Lawrence, eds., *Who was who among English and European authors, 1931–1949*, 2 (1978) · P. Craig and M. Cadogan, *The lady investigates: women detectives and spies in fiction* (1981) · R. Seth, *Encyclopedia of espionage* (1974) · P. Webster, 'The spy they put out in the cold', *The Guardian* (13 Nov 1998) **Likenesses** photograph, c.1914, repro. in McKenna, *I was a spy!* · photograph, c.1932, repro. in McKenna, *I was a spy!*

Mackenna [McCannadh]**, Nial** (*fl.* **1700**), Irish-language poet and harpist, was born in the Fews, co. Armagh, Ireland. He afterwards settled in Mullaghcrew, co. Louth, where he wrote poems and songs. He was the author of the words (the music being far older) of a song well known throughout the north of Ireland from Louth to Mayo, 'Sheela bheag ni Choindhealbham' ('Little Celia Conlan'). He also wrote 'Mo mhile slan duitse sios a Thriucha' ('A thousand healths to thee down at Thriucha'), a well-known song to a local tune, 'Ainnir dear ciuin' ('Pretty, gentle damsel'), and 'Ni measama fein' ('I do not think myself'). NORMAN MOORE, *rev.* STUART HANDLEY

Sources E. O'Reilly, *A chronological account of nearly four hundred Irish writers with a descriptive catalogue of their works*, Transactions of the Iberno-Celtic Society (1820), 203–4

McKenna, Reginald (1863–1943), politician and banker, was born in Kensington, London, on 6 July 1863, the fifth son and youngest child of William Columban McKenna (1819–1887), a civil servant with the Inland Revenue, and his wife, Emma (*d.* 1905), daughter of Charles Hanby. McKenna's father, a Roman Catholic from co. Monaghan, Ireland, was distantly related by marriage to Daniel O'Connell, who in 1838 helped him to obtain a civil service post in London. Later W. C. McKenna converted to protestantism, and his children were raised as protestants. Reginald identified himself as a Congregationalist.

Because of W. C. McKenna's financial difficulties, arising from the Overend Gurney bank failure in 1866, his family was broken up, the two eldest sons remaining in London with their father to work while Emma McKenna, the daughters, and the youngest sons lived inexpensively in France. Reginald received a European primary education, in St Malo, France, until 1874, and subsequently at Ebersdorf, Germany, until 1877, becoming fluent in French and German. While the family was briefly

Reginald McKenna (1863–1943), by George Charles Beresford, 1909

reunited in England in the late 1870s, he attended King's College School, London. Winning a scholarship at Trinity Hall, Cambridge, he was ranked among the senior optimes in the mathematical tripos list of 1885. In 1916 he became an honorary fellow of Trinity Hall. He gained distinction from rowing in the Cambridge University crews who beat Oxford in the 1887 boat race and who won the Grand Challenge Cup in 1886 and the Stewards' Cup in 1887 at Henley.

Early political career McKenna was called to the bar by the Inner Temple in 1887 and built up a thriving practice. In 1892 he stood unsuccessfully as Liberal candidate for Clapham, and in 1895 was returned as a Liberal for North Monmouthshire—for which he sat until 1918. In the House of Commons he joined a small group of young radicals mentored by the veteran politician Sir Charles Dilke. Guided by Dilke, McKenna and his allies became accomplished parliamentarians who regularly interpellated Conservative ministers. He was especially close to Dilke, being labelled in the press as his Man Friday. Taking his patron's advice, the young MP chose a special subject, tariffs, in which he became an expert.

McKenna, representing a Welsh constituency, was also active in the house on behalf of Wales, attacking the Conservative government's Education Bill of 1897 and other legislation offensive to nonconformists. Although much less provocative and nationalistic than his fellow MP David Lloyd George, McKenna was on cordial terms with him and they worked closely together. In 1898 Lloyd

George declined his nomination to succeed the recently deceased chairman of the Welsh parliamentary group, Sir George Osborne Morgan.

Like Lloyd George, but less demonstratively, McKenna was critical of aspects of the Second South African War (1899–1902). While objecting to the Chamberlain family's connection with war contracts, he also demanded that the families of fallen soldiers be compensated as generously as if they had met with factory accidents—a proposal which Lloyd George seconded. Participating in the Liberals' wartime feud between radicals and imperialists, he stood behind the party leader, Sir Henry Campbell-Bannerman, against the imperialists led by Lord Rosebery, H. H. Asquith, and R. B. Haldane.

With peace restored, McKenna joined Lloyd George and other radical, Welsh, and nonconformist MPs in contesting the Balfour government's Education Bill of 1902. As one of the Liberal MPs best informed about tariffs, he fought vigorously against Joseph Chamberlain's protectionist crusade. In 1903 he helped to found the Free Trade Union. His attack (1904) on the discriminatory tobacco duties of the chancellor of the exchequer, Austen Chamberlain, was a masterful performance, reinforcing his claim to ministerial office when the Liberals assumed power. He also strengthened his credentials as a Welsh and radical MP by fighting the government's anti-temperance Licensing Bill of 1904, alongside Lloyd George and the new Liberal recruit, Winston Churchill. He was among the radicals—including Dilke, Lloyd George, and Henry Labouchere—who were critical of the slackness of parliamentary Liberalism, and in 1904–5 canvassed the possibility of forming a radical caucus to ginger the party.

At the Treasury and the Board of Education When Campbell-Bannerman formed his Liberal government in December 1905 McKenna was among the backbenchers slated for junior ministerial office. His appointment as financial secretary of the Treasury, one of the most prestigious junior posts, offered him valuable training for an eventual cabinet ministry. He was befriended by his superior, Asquith, the chancellor of the exchequer, his adversary during the Second South African War but with whom he had already worked during the anti-protectionism campaign. He became indispensable to Asquith for his enterprise, quick thinking, and analytical skills. He aided Asquith in creating the distinction in income tax between earned and unearned income, and developing a graduated tax.

When the presidency of the Board of Education became vacant in January 1907 Campbell-Bannerman had to choose between McKenna and the flashier Winston Churchill, parliamentary under-secretary at the Colonial Office. McKenna's knowledge of Wales, a hot spot of 'Church v. Chapel' agitation over education, as well as his very successful record at the Treasury, secured his promotion to cabinet rank—the first since the formation of the ministry.

McKenna's tenure at the Board of Education was constructive but unspectacular. The government's Education Bill of 1906, intended to rectify nonconformist grievances

with the 1902 act, had been vetoed by the House of Lords, and less controversial bills introduced by McKenna in 1907 and 1908 had to be dropped because of nonconformist objections. Establishment of a Welsh department in the Board of Education in 1907 was popular in Wales, but disagreement over appointments to it and over enforcement in Wales of the hated 1902 act produced the first significant disputes between McKenna and Lloyd George. Among McKenna's innovations was the creation of a school medical service which carried out the compulsory physical examination of schoolchildren.

First lord of the Admiralty Asquith's succession to the prime ministership in April 1908 resulted in several new cabinet appointments. Asquith—who had warmed to McKenna while they were colleagues at the Treasury and admired his forthrightness and precision in cabinet—chose him to head the Admiralty, once more in preference to Churchill. There is some evidence that Asquith would have liked McKenna to succeed him as chancellor of the exchequer, but Lloyd George's claim to this high office was too strong.

After a brief engagement, McKenna on 3 June 1908 married the youthful Pamela Jekyll (1889–1943), younger daughter of Sir Herbert Jekyll. Pamela McKenna was a friend of Herbert and Margot Asquith, and one of several young women with whom Herbert Asquith carried on a platonic flirtation. Pamela's relationship with the Asquiths, especially the prime minister, drew her husband into their social circle and enhanced his political status.

McKenna's service at the Admiralty overlapped the last years as first sea lord of Sir John (later Lord) Fisher, who quickly reached an understanding with his much younger political chief. The new first lord was immediately drawn into the tempestuous admiral's fight to strengthen the British navy, as well as the latter's professional and personal quarrels with rivals, particularly Lord Charles Beresford.

McKenna forcefully championed Fisher against the latter's enemy, Admiral Beresford, who was critical of the first sea lord and his policies to the point of insubordination. The popular Beresford had many admirers, so it was not until March 1909 that McKenna—over resistance from some of his cabinet colleagues—was able to terminate Beresford's command of the Channel Fleet and effectively retire him. Beresford struck back by charging that under Fisher the navy was badly prepared for war because of poor distribution of the fleets and lack of a planning staff. McKenna ably defended Fisher in the spring of 1909 before a subcommittee of the committee of imperial defence, which generally upheld the first sea lord against Beresford's charges.

Economical radicals both within and outside the cabinet had expected that McKenna—hitherto an advocate of retrenchment in defence appropriations—would resist Fisher's costly naval construction plans, especially for the phenomenally expensive dreadnought class battleships. Fisher, however, convinced his superior that legitimate supremacy over Britain's chief naval adversary, Germany, and survival in a future war, depended on building state-of-the-art warships on a grand scale. McKenna, as a radical, belonged to the blue water school, which based British defence policy on a 'wall of ships', obviating continental military commitments. Although always economy-conscious, McKenna as navy minister viewed timely warship construction as a patriotic necessity.

During early 1909 McKenna was embroiled in a bitter quarrel within the cabinet over naval construction. On the basis of what later proved to be faulty intelligence, the sea lords had convinced McKenna that Germany was accelerating its building programme, and that to stay ahead Great Britain must appropriate for six dreadnoughts annually in 1909–12 instead of the previously scheduled four. McKenna's expanded estimates brought him into conflict not only with the radical 'economists' in the cabinet, but with Lloyd George, Churchill, and other ministers hoping to spend substantially for social reforms. The struggle within the cabinet had as its backdrop a Conservative-inspired naval scare in parliament and the press. Eight new dreadnoughts were demanded immediately with the cry 'We want eight and we won't wait'. Supported by Asquith, McKenna was able to arrange for the building of eighteen of the giant warships by the end of 1912.

The fight over the dreadnoughts, and subsequently over the land taxes (which McKenna opposed) in Lloyd George's 1909 'people's budget', added to the deepening antagonism between the two ministers—based upon personality differences and perceived slights. McKenna had come to dislike Lloyd George's pragmatism, opportunism, and—he believed—lack of principles, while Lloyd George was irritated by his former political ally's self-assertiveness, didacticism, and stubbornness. There was similar but less intense ill feeling between McKenna and Churchill, at this time an ambitious social reformer.

The Agadir crisis of 1911 between France and Germany, in which Great Britain went to the brink of war with Germany, created a situation in which McKenna's loyalty to his professional staff, and his confidence in their judgements, told against him. During the crisis Lloyd George and Churchill claimed—like Admiral Beresford two years earlier—to be disturbed by the navy's unpreparedness for war. R. B. Haldane, the war minister, was troubled by the refusal of Admiral Arthur K. Wilson, Fisher's successor as first sea lord, to sanction a naval war staff comparable to the army's.

These problems came to a head at the 23 August 1911 meeting of the committee of imperial defence. The War Office's plans to send an expeditionary force to Europe to fight beside the French army were articulately outlined by General Henry H. Wilson. They contrasted positively with the Admiralty's less defined plans to defend the British Isles, dominate British seaways, and destroy the German fleets, rather inarticulately explained by Admiral Wilson. McKenna's own blue water views, which he asserted with his usual forthrightness, were challenged by Haldane, Lloyd George, and Churchill.

The committee of imperial defence meeting was followed by a series of conversations between these ministers and Asquith, who was persuaded that McKenna's cocksureness and unwillingness to bend were unacceptable in a service minister at a critical time. In October 1911 the prime minister ordered McKenna to exchange offices with the home secretary, Churchill. Happy in his Admiralty post and unwilling to leave it, McKenna blamed Lloyd George and Churchill for his predicament. After briefly considering an alternative appointment as permanent secretary of the Treasury, the premier civil service position, he opted for the Home Office.

At the Home Office McKenna's tenure at the Home Office was the nadir of his political career, although he could claim some solid legislative accomplishments including the Mental Deficiency Act (1913) and the Criminal Justice Administration Act (1914). The Welsh Church Disestablishment Bill, over which he and Lloyd George had a temporary *rapprochement*, occupied a disproportionate amount of the home secretary's time and energy between 1912 and 1914. Under a Parliament Act deadline, he had to guide the complex legislation session by session through parliamentary traps set by embittered Conservatives. Finally, as a concession to party unity at the beginning of the First World War, promulgation of the controversial bill was postponed for the duration.

McKenna's use of soldiers and police in labour disputes, many of them in the Welsh coalmines, was more restrained than his predecessor's. His stern measures to deal with suffragette agitators were unpopular with many Liberals, especially the despised Discharge of Prisoners (or 'Cat and Mouse') Act (1913) which allowed police to release and later rearrest prisoners staging hunger strikes. He urged the government to take a firmer line against Sir Edward Carson's Ulster resistance movement (1912–14). In the Marconi affair (1913) he contended that Lloyd George and other ministers accused of misusing inside information for personal gain should resign.

After leaving the Admiralty McKenna kept up with defence issues and lost no opportunity to voice his blue water convictions. In 1912 he opposed Churchill's plan, as part of a deal with the French, to move British warships from the Mediterranean to the North Sea. Early in 1914 he condemned Churchill's naval estimates as unnecessarily costly, largely because—he argued—the first lord was concentrating too many ships in home waters. On the eve of war in July–August 1914 he was in close touch with events on the continent through family members and acquaintances. He was certain that the inevitable German invasion of Belgium would bring Great Britain into the war, but he believed that British intervention should be limited to naval warfare. As in 1911, he opposed sending an army expeditionary force to the continent. Once the decision was made to dispatch troops, he wanted to leave the war in the hands of military and naval professionals and—as far as possible—continue with 'business as usual'.

McKenna, whose department was in charge of internal security, was sharply criticized in parliament and the press for his lenient treatment of enemy aliens, few of whom the home secretary believed endangered public safety. His refusal to take seriously a press-inspired spy scare, and his discouragement, through the Home Office's press bureau, of atrocity stories about enemy troops led to charges that he was pro-German. Along with the German-educated Lord Haldane, he was a favourite scapegoat of the right-wing press. During the government reorganization of May 1915 it was widely predicted that he would be dropped. Nevertheless McKenna not only survived, but in the new coalition cabinet was promoted to the Treasury to replace Lloyd George, who was appointed munitions minister.

Chancellor of the exchequer and after In contrast to the disappointing years at the Home Office, when his political career seemed to be in eclipse, McKenna as chancellor was at the height of his powers. His two budgets, of September 1915 and April 1916, attempted through judicious mixes of taxation and borrowing to pay for the war without crippling Great Britain's economic future. The 1915 budget included sharply increased income taxes, an unprecedented excess profits tax, and the 'McKenna duties' on luxury consumer goods—attacked by many Liberals as a major crack in free trade. McKenna defended these tariffs as necessary and temporary war measures, although they were fated to become permanent. Both McKenna budgets distributed the tax burden between the middle and working classes more evenly than before the war.

In July 1915, with the value of the pound against the dollar falling rapidly, McKenna boldly negotiated new loans from the British government's American bankers secured by collateral advanced by the Prudential Assurance company. This incident confirmed his fear that the war's enormous costs were dangerously weakening Great Britain's international financial position, especially *vis-à-vis* the United States.

In late 1915 McKenna and most of his Liberal cabinet colleagues strenuously fought demands for military conscription by Lloyd George and the Conservative ministers. In contrast to the other Liberal ministers, who simply denounced conscription as violating Liberal principles, McKenna and the Board of Trade president, Walter Runciman, asserted that it would ruin the economy, and possibly lose the war, by stripping British industry of manpower. McKenna's conviction that Germany would eventually be defeated by the British naval blockade ran counter to the position of Lloyd George and the War Office that a large British army was needed to sustain France and Russia in the war. McKenna threatened resignation, but stayed on after conscription was adopted.

In the political crisis of December 1916 McKenna joined most Liberal ministers in urging Asquith to call Lloyd George's bluff when the war minister demanded the establishment of a small executive war committee headed by himself. The failure of this strategy, and Lloyd George's success in forming a new coalition ministry, meant loss of office for McKenna and his Liberal colleagues. During the rest of the war McKenna sat with Asquith and other Liberal former ministers on the front

opposition bench, where they rather ineffectually criticized Lloyd George's war policies. A major parliamentary confrontation in May 1918 between the Asquithians and the government, the 'Maurice debate', in which the opposition challenged Lloyd George's veracity about the strength of British forces in Europe, contributed to the prime minister's decision to split the Liberal Party. In the December 1918 election McKenna and other Asquithian former ministers lost their seats.

Chairman of the Midland Bank In April 1917 McKenna had become a director of the Midland Bank, with the understanding that if his political career went into abeyance he would be the next chairman of the bank. In 1919 he succeeded to the chairmanship, a post he would occupy for the rest of his life. In the financial world of inter-war London, McKenna's acumen was highly respected. His annual addresses to the Midland's shareholders—a selection of which were published in 1928 as *Post-War Banking Policy*—were lucid examinations of current economic issues.

Twice a return to political office, as chancellor of the exchequer, failed to materialize. After the fall of Lloyd George in 1922 the new Conservative prime minister, Andrew Bonar Law, possibly hoping to establish an alliance with the Asquith Liberals, offered posts to McKenna and another Liberal; but the former declined as he doubted that Bonar Law would win the forthcoming election. McKenna in 1923 provisionally accepted a similar offer from Bonar Law's successor, Stanley Baldwin, but this time his demand for a safe seat representing the City of London could not be granted. It was speculated that had he taken office on either occasion, he might have gone on to become prime minister. During the twenties he was sporadically mentioned in the press as prime ministerial material. He still described himself as a Liberal.

Although no longer a professional politician, McKenna throughout the twenties and thirties remained active in public affairs. He was in regular communication with the economist John Maynard Keynes, whose innovative theories gradually modified McKenna's Gladstonian concepts. He advised the Bonar Law government about its debt negotiations with the United States in 1922–3, and accepted, while disliking it, the settlement achieved by Stanley Baldwin, the chancellor of the exchequer. He was critical of British reparations policy as too burdensome upon Germany, and in 1924 chaired a committee of the revisionist Dawes commission. When his old adversary, Winston Churchill, became chancellor in 1925, he was consulted by him about restoration of the gold standard; McKenna's view was that the policy was unsatisfactory but unavoidable.

McKenna was in frequent demand for advice and committee service to the Labour governments of 1924 and 1929–31, notably service on the Macmillan committee on finance and industry (1930–31), which subjected Montagu Norman, the governor of the Bank of England, to searching examination. He was also consulted by Lord Beaverbrook, a friend for many years, during the press magnate's empire crusade in 1930. McKenna no longer believed that free trade was sacrosanct, but remained convinced that

British prosperity depended on international networks of trade and earnings. In the thirties he thought that nothing was to be gained from treating the communist and fascist powers as outcasts, but shared Churchill's distaste for appeasement.

McKenna was of medium height, but his spare build and athletic physique, even in old age, made him look taller. To correct a tendency to stammer, he began each day by declaiming famous orations. Assertive and waspish in public, possibly as a defence against shyness, he was genial and kindly in private, relaxing especially among family and friends. People who found him distant on early acquaintance often were charmed once his barriers were down. He mellowed considerably after leaving politics. He rowed, swam, golfed, and walked for physical recreation, enjoyed chess, and was an accomplished bridge player. He was a client of the architect Edwin Lutyens.

Suffering from various ailments from time to time during his earlier years, McKenna in later life was in good health until almost eighty. After a short illness he died in his London residence, above the Midland Bank's 70 Pall Mall branch, on 6 September 1943, and his ashes were buried near his country house at Mells Park, Somerset. Pamela McKenna only briefly survived her much-loved husband, dying the same year. The elder of their two sons predeceased them.

Historians have viewed McKenna as an elusive figure, partly because he left behind few personal papers and never wrote a memoir. His permanent officials, and even so hostile a colleague as Lloyd George, praised his administrative competence, which was carried over into his banking career. McKenna's political ability was less impressive, and its impact less positive. His inflexibility handicapped him severely. It resulted in the loss of his Admiralty post, and—in the form of bad advice to Asquith in December 1916 and after—contributed to the downfall of the Liberal Party. On the other hand, his breadth of vision was greater than that of most of his contemporaries, not least respecting the outcome and effects of the First World War.

D. M. Cregier

Sources S. McKenna, *Reginald McKenna, 1863–1943: a memoir* (1948) · *DNB* · *The Times* (7 Sept 1943) · A. J. Marder, *From the Dreadnought to Scapa Flow: the Royal Navy in the Fisher era, 1904–1919*, 5 vols. (1961–70) · R. S. Churchill and M. Gilbert, *Winston S. Churchill*, 2–3 (1967–71) · Lord Riddell, *The Riddell diaries, 1908–1923*, ed. J. M. McEwen (1986) · *Inside Asquith's cabinet: from the diaries of Charles Hobhouse*, ed. E. David (1977) · *H. H. Asquith: letters to Venetia Stanley*, ed. M. Brock and E. Brock (1982) · Lord Beaverbrook, *Politicians and the war, 1914–1916*, 1 vol. edn (1960) · *Lady Cynthia Asquith: diaries, 1915–1918*, ed. E. M. Horsley (New York, 1969) · J. A. Spender, *Life, journalism and politics*, 1 (1927), 111–113, 162–5, 228–9, 240–3 · P. J. Grigg, *Prejudice and judgment* (1948), 101–05, 116–19, 182–5 · F. Stevenson, *Lloyd George: a diary*, ed. A. J. P. Taylor (1971) · A. Fitzroy, *Memoirs*, 2 vols. [1925] · *A liberal chronicle: journals and papers of J. A. Pease*, ed. C. Hazlehurst and C. Woodland (1994) · B. B. Gilbert, *David Lloyd George: a political life*, 2 vols. (1987–92) · D. W. Bebbington, *The nonconformist conscience: chapel and politics, 1870–1914* (1982), 148–51 · R. F. Harrod, *The life of John Maynard Keynes* (1951); repr. (1972), 247–8, 487–9, 500–02 · K. Middlemas and J. Barnes, *Baldwin: a biography* (1969), 175–7 · R. Thurlow, *The secret state: British internal security in the twentieth century* (1994), 54–7 · K. Burk, 'The treasury: from impotence to power', *War and the state: the transformation of British government, 1914–1919*, ed. K. Burk (1982), 84–107, esp. 84–96 · A. Offer, *The First World War: an agrarian interpretation* (1989), 266–9, 276–309 · J. Wilson, *CB: a life of Sir Henry Campbell-Bannerman* (1973), 588–91 · selected documents, CAC Cam., McKenna MSS · E. Green, 'McKenna, Reginald', *DBB* · D. French, *British strategy and war aims, 1914–1916* (1986)

Archives CAC Cam., corresp. and papers | BL, letters to Sir Charles Dilke, Add. MSS 43915–43920 · BL, corresp. with Lord Northcliffe, Add. MS 62157 · BL OIOC, letters to Lord Reading, MSS Eur E 238, F118 · BLPES, letters to A. G. Gardiner · Bodl. Oxf., corresp. with Herbert Asquith · Bodl. Oxf., corresp. with Lord Selborne · CAC Cam., Churchill MSS · CAC Cam., corresp. with Lord Fisher · CAC Cam., letters to A. Hurd · CUL, corresp. with Lord Hardinge · HLRO, corresp. with Lord Beaverbrook · HLRO, letters to David Lloyd George · HLRO, corresp. with Andrew Bonar Law · HLRO, corresp. with John St Loe Strachey · HSBC Group Archives, London, Midland Bank archives · King's Cam., Keynes MSS · NL Aus., corresp. with Alfred Deakin · PRO, corresp. with Lord Kitchener, 30/57, WO 159 · U. Newcastle, Robinson L., letters to Walter Runciman | FILM BFI NFTVA, propaganda film footage

Likenesses G. C. Beresford, photograph, 1909, NPG [*see illus.*] · J. Russell & Sons, photograph, 1915, NPG · J. Gunn, oils, 1935, HSBC Group Archives, London, Midland Bank archives; repro. in McKenna, *Reginald McKenna* · Matt, caricature, repro. in Lord Birkenhead, *Contemporary personalities* (1924), 214 · Owl, mechanical reproduction, NPG; repro. in *VF* (23 April 1913) · B. Partridge, cartoon, NPG; repro. in *Punch* (22 April 1908–21 May 1928) · Spy [L. Ward], lithograph, NPG; repro. in *VF* (31 Oct 1906) · photograph, Admiralty; repro. in Marder, *From Dreadnought to Scapa Flow*, pl. II, facing p. 11 · photograph, repro. in *New York Times* (7 Sept 1943), 23 · sixty cartoons, repro. in *Punch* (1906–18); repro. in McKenna, *Reginald McKenna*

Wealth at death £89,948 1s. 4d.: probate, 2 Dec 1943, *CGPLA Eng. & Wales*

McKenna, Siobhan (1923–1986), actress, was born in Belfast on 24 May 1923, the daughter of Owen McKenna, professor of mathematics, and his wife, Margaret O'Reilly. She was educated at St Louis Convent, Monaghan, and the National University of Ireland. A red-haired beauty, in 1948 she married the actor Denis O'Dea (1905–1978); they had one son. An accomplished linguist, Siobhan McKenna alternated regularly throughout her career between playing in English and in Gaelic; her first professional engagement, while aged eighteen and still at university, was at the An Taibhdheare Theatre in Galway where she played Lady Macbeth in Gaelic. By 1943 she was playing at the Abbey Theatre, Dublin, again in both languages.

McKenna's first appearance on the London stage was at the Embassy Theatre on 3 March 1947, in Paul Vincent Carroll's *The White Steed*, playing the part of Nora Fintry. From 1947 onward she was regularly seen in London, Dublin, and (from 1955) New York. Several critics, right from the start, commented on her evident power as a young actress. J. C. Trewin, for example, reviewing the first production of James Forsyth's *Héloïse* at the Embassy Theatre in 1951, wrote that

> Siobhan McKenna is an actress of vision who can be as poignant in her silences as in her speech. I have seen her this year dominating a stage in such parts as Pegeen Mike (easy enough to dominate there) [in J. M. Synge's *The Playboy of the Western World*] and—far less easy—the girl Regina in *Ghosts*.

Siobhan McKenna (1923–1986), by unknown photographer

> Always she makes us feel that Héloïse is about to become the woman of our imagining. It does not happen because the author has kept a too earnest guard upon his text ... *Héloïse* is not framed theatrically and it strangely lacks passion.
> (Trewin, 136)

Kenneth Tynan, commenting on the same production, noted that 'Siobhan McKenna, flinty of mien, offers a pinched Héloïse which, in its pallor and intensity, recalls the spooky lady in Charles Addams' drawings' (Tynan, 16).

It was Kenneth Tynan who at an early stage spotted McKenna's capacity for adding an element of greatness and artistic intensity not immediately apparent in the original text. It was on these grounds that he praised her performance of the title part in Bernard Shaw's *Saint Joan* in 1954. Shaw's St Joan, he argued, suffered as 'a dramatic creation from the weakness of having no weaknesses. A divinely illuminated simpleton, she is incapable of change or development'. However, 'this actress lets us see life stripping Joan down to her spiritual buff' (Tynan, 83).

Siobhan McKenna played the part again in 1956, in new productions of the play at the Sanders Theatre in Cambridge, Massachusetts, and the Phoenix Theatre in New York. The following year she was highly praised for a most distinguished rendering of Viola in *Twelfth Night* at Stratford, Ontario, another role which she repeated with renewed distinction at Cambridge in 1959. These two parts—St Joan and Viola—became the performances by which she is chiefly remembered, and the period 1954–9 (which also included her first Broadway appearance, as Miss Madrigal in Enid Bagnold's *The Chalk Garden* in 1955),

is recalled as the time of her chief glory. In 1957 Tynan singled her out as a possible successor to Dame Sybil Thorndike and Dame Edith Evans (Tynan, 187), the recognized *doyennes* of British theatre.

At the Cambridge (Massachusetts) Drama Festival, in November 1957, McKenna played Lady Macbeth, repeated her triumph as Viola, and played Margaret Hyland in *The Rope Dancers* (Wishengrad). At the Dublin Festival of 1960 she again played Pegeen Mike, and then toured Europe with that production before appearing in the same part at the Piccadilly and St Martin's theatres in London in November 1960. In 1961 at the Dublin Festival she portrayed Joan Dark in Bertolt Brecht's *St Joan of the Stockyards*, which she repeated in London in 1965. Along with Peter O'Toole and Jack McGowran she starred in Sean O'Casey's *Juno and the Paycock* in 1966 at the Gaiety. Her Juno, according to *The Times*, was 'unpretentious and universal!'.

McKenna extended her theatrical range somewhat at the Dublin Festival of 1962 by presenting a 'one-woman show', *An Evening with Irish Writers*. This was very well received and led on to other solo recitals later, notably *Here are Ladies*, first seen at the Playhouse, Oxford, in April 1970 and repeated many times later in London, New York, and elsewhere. She played Madame Ranevsky in Chekhov's *The Cherry Orchard* at the 1977 Dublin Festival and in the same year appeared at the Guelph Spring Festival (Canada) in Eric Salmon's production of John Murrell's *Memoir*, a full-length play with only two characters, in which she played the part of the ageing Sarah Bernhardt.

McKenna's seemingly triumphant career nevertheless peaked too early; and from the late 1960s and through the 1970s her work increasingly showed signs of self-indulgence and lack of discipline. Though she went on playing, offers of striking leading parts became fewer and she developed a quarrelsome streak, with more than a touch of arrogance. Realizing—for she was both sensitive and intelligent—that she was missing crucial opportunities, McKenna quarrelled, drank, and fought—all to excess—and, sadly, became a kind of caricature Irishwoman. Her principal performance, in other words, was given off-stage. She once boasted in 1977 that she had the reputation of being the Broadway player with the greatest and most potent talent for disrupting a rehearsal and bringing it to a complete and destructive standstill.

Yet even in those final years McKenna did—even if only sporadically—valuable work in keeping Irish drama alive in the theatre. Several of the great Irish roles she repeated many times in many parts of the world. In 1973 she directed three Irish plays for the Toronto Arts Festival (and, reportedly, fell out with everyone in sight). She translated several English plays into Gaelic, including Shaw's *Saint Joan*, J. M. Barrie's *Mary Rose*, and W. B. Yeats's *The Countess Cathleen*. In 1975 she was appointed to the council of state of the Republic of Ireland. Her acting career effectively finished in 1980 and she died in Dublin on 16 November 1986 at the age of sixty-three.   ERIC SALMON

Sources I. Herbert, ed., *Who's who in the theatre*, 17th edn, 2 vols. (1981) · K. Tynan, *Curtains* (1961) · J. C. Trewin, *A play tonight* (1952) · personal knowledge (2004) · *The Times* (17 Nov 1986) · records, St

Louis Convent, Monaghan · records, National University of Ireland · Actors' Equity Association
Archives FILM BFI NFTVA, *Generations*, Channel 4, 23 March 1987 · BFI NFTVA, performance footage | SOUND BL NSA, documentary recordings · BL NSA, performance recordings
Likenesses Y. Karsh, bromide print, 1957, NPG · F. Daniels, photograph, repro. in *Three plays* (1956) · photograph, BFI [*see illus.*] · photographs, Hult. Arch.

Mackenna, Theobald (*d.* 1808), political writer, was trained as a barrister. Prior to December 1791 he acted as the secretary to the Catholic Committee in Ireland, but upon the secession of Valentine Browne's anti-democratic party, he became the mouthpiece of the seceders, whose fears were aroused by recent events in revolutionary France. A unionist who was also eager for Catholic emancipation and parliamentary reform, Mackenna voiced strongly his repugnance to Wolfe Tone's republican and separatist policy in a 1793 pamphlet, as he felt Tone's policy would lead to unequivocal evil for Ireland. He continued to write on behalf of the English government in the early 1790s, believing that, once the union was achieved, England would bring prosperity to Ireland.

Impressed by Mackenna's moderate unionist views, Thomas Lewis O'Beirne, the bishop of Meath, recommended Mackenna to Lord Castlereagh, who hired him to write on his behalf in bringing through the Act of Union. When the union was followed by neither religious concessions nor political reforms, however, Mackenna was bitterly disappointed, and devoted much of the rest of his life to writing pamphlets calling public attention to the government's broken pledges, and to the unjust conditions suffered by Irish Catholic clergy and believers alike, suggesting as a remedy that the government support the Catholic church in Ireland and provide stipends for its clergy. Mackenna died in Dublin on 31 December 1808. His reputation as a polemical essayist survived well into the early twentieth century.

G. P. MORIARTY, *rev.* JASON EDWARDS

Sources W. E. H. Lecky, *A history of England in the eighteenth century*, 8 vols. (1879–90), vols. 7–8 · W. B. S. Taylor, *History of the University of Dublin* (1845), 467 · *GM*, 1st ser., 79 (1809)

Mackennal, Alexander (1835–1904), Congregational minister, was born in Truro on 14 January 1835, the third of seven children of Patrick Mackennal, an immigrant from Galloway, and his wife, Gertrude, a Cornish woman. The family moved in 1848 to London, where Alexander continued his education in the school of William Pinches, off Lombard Street; two of his fellow pupils were Henry Irving and Edward Clarke. In 1851 he entered Glasgow University. Here he was active in the Dialectic Society and in Liberal politics. He left without graduating in 1854. He had resolved to train for the ministry and entered Hackney College the same year, completing his course there and his BA at University College, London, in 1857. As a student he was greatly influenced by T. T. Lynch and by F. D. Maurice's liberal theology. He served first at Burton upon Trent (1858–61). There he was not happy, as the more conservative section of his flock broke away to form an orthodox presbyterian church: his ministry in the village church at

Alexander Mackennal (1835–1904), by Ernest H. Mills

Branstone was more rewarding. In 1861 he moved to Surbiton, where he stayed nine years (1861–70). In this rising town a church had been gathered by the Revd R. H. Smith and was meeting in a large hall. Soon Mackennal had increased the congregation to the point where a church building was deemed necessary: he largely designed this himself. In 1867 he married Fanny (*d.* 1903), daughter of Dr Hoile of Montrose and widow of Colin Wilson. The couple were to have three sons and two daughters. In the same year, with Dean Stanley and others, he produced a volume entitled *Addresses to Working People*.

In 1870 Mackennal received a call to Gallowtree Gate Congregational Church, Leicester, in succession to the theologically advanced J. A. Picton. He remained there until 1877. He threw himself eagerly into the work of the Leicester and Rutland Congregational Union, of which he became secretary, of the Leicester Literary and Philosophical Society, of which he became president, and into educational politics in the town, though he was not happy with the act of 1870 and refused to stand for the Leicester school board. He steered clear of the Leicester conference of advanced Congregational ministers in 1877, though he had by now adopted universal restorationism and a radical kenotic Christology.

In 1877, having rejected calls to London and elsewhere, Mackennal accepted the pastorate of Bowdon Downs church (built 1848), a smart suburban congregation standing in a similar relationship to Manchester as Surbiton had to London. He remained here until his death. Bowdon Downs responded to the dynamic, liberal preaching of this stocky, red-faced, and enormously learned man. The church thrived: soon Mackennal's stipend rose to £1000 a year; he sent his sons to Rugby, and his daughters married the sons of wealthy chapel-goers. Bowdon Downs's giving to Mansfield College, Oxford, where Mackennal was a frequent visitor and preacher, and whose council chairman he became in 1891, was second only to Carr's Lane, Birmingham. In 1888 Mackennal was elected chairman of the Congregational Union: it fell to him to deliver a veiled rebuke to Spurgeon over the 'down-grade'.

It was in the 1890s that Mackennal really came into his own. He gave valuable advice to the widow of John Rylands over the founding of the famous library in Manchester. He was active in the Forward Movement of the London Missionary Society to reawaken its pristine enthusiasm. He encouraged one of his deacons, Frank Crossley, in his important social enterprises. He orchestrated the International Congregational Council, which first met in 1891, with himself as co-secretary. He was the inspiration behind the first Free Church congress in Manchester in 1892, and when the fourth congress of 1896 became the National Council of the Evangelical Free Churches he was recognized as one of its leaders, serving as its secretary from 1892 to 1898 and its president in 1899. With C. A. Berry he helped organize the Grindelwald Home Reunion conferences of 1891–6, and edited their organ, the *Review of the Churches*. He was in fact the linkman between Grindelwald, the congresses, and the International Congregational Council. In 1893 he produced the *Story of the English Separatists*, which took up the themes of R. W. Dale and J. A. Macfadyen (whose biography he also wrote) that the evangelical revival had brought an unhealthy individualism into Congregational life, the antidote for which was not a switch to collectivism but 'a pure and disciplined' church life such as had characterized the puritans. This was also the salt which savours a healthy democracy.

The Second South African War brought to an end this remarkable decade of Mackennal's career. An active member of the Peace Society, he had been able to justify the Crimean and American Civil wars but not this 'sinful' conflict. He was accused of being a pro-Boer, one or two pamphlets were written against him, and a few church members resigned, especially when in 1900 he took his anti-militarism to the point of envisioning Britain as a 'sacrificial nation', disarming herself as an example for others to follow. In July 1901 he was a signatory to the Congregational ministers' manifesto demanding an end to the war, a general amnesty, and the granting of self-rule to the Boer republics.

Mackennal emerged from this turmoil an aged and disillusioned man: he averred in his *Sketches of Congregationalism* of 1901 that he was 'sick of class churches'. His wife died in 1903; he himself died at Coombe House, Hampstead Lane, Highgate, Middlesex, on 23 June 1904 and was buried at Bowdon. IAN SELLERS

Sources D. Macfadyen, *Alexander Mackennal, life and letters* (1905) • *Congregational Year Book* (1905) • C. Binfield, *So down to prayers: studies in English nonconformity, 1780–1920* (1977) • *Altrincham Guardian* (29 June 1904) • *Altrincham Guardian* (6 July 1904) • *The Times* (14 Jan 1904) • *The Times* (26–7 June 1904) • *CGPLA Eng. & Wales* (1904) • *Royal Cornwall Gazette* (24 Jan 1835)

Likenesses wood-engraving, c.1891 (after photograph by Martin and Sallnow), NPG; repro. in *ILN* (31 Oct 1891) • E. H. Mills, photograph, repro. in Macfadyen, *Alexander Mackennal* [see illus.]

Wealth at death £2755 14s. 5d.: probate, 19 Aug 1904, *CGPLA Eng. & Wales*

Mackennal, Sir (Edgar) Bertram (1863–1931), sculptor, was born in Fitzroy, Melbourne, Australia, on 12 June 1863, the second son of John Simpson Mackennal (1832–1901) and his wife, Annabella Hyde. His father was an architectural sculptor, who was born in Ayrshire and, after being articled to a Liverpool sculptor, emigrated in 1852 to Melbourne, where he worked at his original profession from the 1850s to the 1890s. Bertram Mackennal studied first under his father and at the National Gallery of Victoria School of Design in Melbourne. At the age of eighteen he went to London, encouraged by Marshall Wood, chiefly to study the Elgin marbles, and entered the Royal Academy Schools on 4 December 1883. Dissatisfied with the routine there, he left after a short time and went to Paris, where he worked in several studios and met Auguste Rodin and Alfred Gilbert. He returned to England and secured a position as head of the art department in a pottery at Coalport, Shropshire. Mackennal married in 1884 Agnes Eliza (d. 1947), daughter of Henry Spooner, of London, with whom he had a daughter. He first exhibited at the Royal Academy in 1886, and in 1887 he won the competition for the façade decoration of Parliament House, Melbourne. This took him back to Australia, but in 1891, largely following the advice of Sarah Bernhardt, he returned to Paris, where he gained his first great success with the bronze figure *Circe* (National Gallery of Victoria, Melbourne) which received an honourable mention in the salon of 1893. In the following year *Circe* was a *scandale d'estime* at the Royal Academy owing to its supposed erotic qualities. Mackennal's lost polychrome work treating the subjects of prostitution and the assertive new woman in an allegorical format, *For she Sitteth on a Seat in the High Places of the City* (1895), was at the forefront of contemporary British sculptural radicalism. A major surviving work of this period is the art nouveau marble portrait bust of an American socialite, Grace Lopthorpe Dunham (1896; National Gallery of Australia, Canberra), commissioned by the sitter. The life-size figurative group in marble for the Springthorpe memorial, Boorondaro cemetery, Melbourne (1897–1900), marks the zenith of his contribution to the symbolist vein of the New Sculpture.

Mackennal's marble female nude *Oceana* (1897) commissioned by the Union Club of Sydney; the Second South African War memorial for Islington (1903); the memorials to Queen Victoria for Lahore, Blackburn, and Ballarat, Australia (1900); the pediment of the Local Government Board office, Westminster; and the medals for the 1908 London Olympics, some of which were adapted for the 1948 games as well, followed at intervals. In 1910 Mackennal was called upon to design the coronation medals of George V and Queen Mary, and also the obverse of the new coinage, to supersede the Edwardian design of G. W.

Sir (Edgar) Bertram Mackennal (1863–1931), by James Russell & Sons

De Saulles. He also collaborated upon designs for postage stamps for the new reign. In recognition of his services to the royal family, Mackennal was appointed MVO in 1912. He was then commissioned, with Edwin Lutyens as architect, to execute a series of memorials to Edward VII. He also sculpted the figures of Edward and Alexandra for their tomb in St George's Chapel, Windsor, completed in 1927. His major London equestrian statue of George V in Waterloo Place was unveiled in July 1921, when he was made KCVO. Among other important works by Mackennal are the national memorial to Gainsborough at Sudbury, Suffolk; the tomb of Sir Redvers Buller in Winchester Cathedral; the nude male figure *Here am I* for Eton College playing fields; the war memorial to members of both houses of parliament in the porch of St Stephen's Hall; and the large bronze *Phaeton Driving the Chariot of the Sun* (1923) for Australia House (Strand, London). In the last year of his life Mackennal was commissioned by King George to execute a portrait in marble of Queen Alexandra to be placed on the wall of Sandringham church. He was elected an associate of the Royal Academy in 1909 and Royal Academician in 1922, but he did not exhibit at the academy after 1929, in which year he exhibited the realist figures of a soldier and a sailor for the cenotaph, Martin Place, Sydney. The Tate collection holds his *Earth and the Elements*, a small group of four figures in marble, and *Diana Wounded*, a life-size marble figure, both purchased by the terms of the Chantrey bequest in 1907 and 1908 respectively. These two acquisitions made in successive years

were considered a singular honour. Mackennal revisited Australia in 1901 and again in 1926, when the sales at an exhibition of his work established a record for an Australian sculptor.

Mackennal was a capable sculptor of graceful figurative compositions and an important associate figure in the New Sculpture movement. In Australia Mackennal is remembered for his success in Britain, the first Australian artist to be elected to the Royal Academy, to have a work purchased for the Tate, and to be knighted. In the context of British art, his role as reliable and efficient sculptor to the Edwardian and Georgian establishment should be acknowledged, even if the decorative and imaginative richness that marked his work pre-1900 was later subsumed under a blander, more anonymous style. Most of his intimate cabinet-sized bronzes, reflecting turn-of-the-century radical interest in 'sculpture for the home', have been collected by Australian museums and remain relatively unknown in Britain, whence many have been exported back to Australia. Those in British collections include *Salome* (bronze, 1897; Harris Museum and Art Gallery, Preston) and a miniature *Circe* (bronze, c.1893; Birmingham Museum and Art Gallery). A small collection of Mackennal's works at the Ashmolean Museum, Oxford, includes a marble *Sappho* (1909) and a miniature *Diana Wounded* (bronze, c.1905). Spielmann noted that Mackennal's work 'gives evidence of a good sense of design and has great refinement of movement and nervousness of treatment, somewhat daring in conception and handling, it is always sculpturesque' (Spielmann, 135). Further examples of Mackennal's work are in the National Gallery of Australia, Canberra; the Art Gallery of New South Wales, Sydney; Ballarat Fine Art Gallery, Victoria; and Boorondaro cemetery, Kew, Melbourne. Even when his art was out of favour in the 1940s Mackennal was pronounced to have been a brilliant '"all round" sculptor and a master of his craft, particularly in the treatment of marble, with poetical imagination and a peculiar elegance of style'. Mackennal died suddenly at his home, Watcombe Hall, Watcombe, Torquay, Devon, on 10 October 1931. He was buried in Torquay.

CHARLES MARRIOTT, rev. JULIET PEERS

Sources J. Peers, 'A gift to us from Australia', *The Medal*, 23 (1993), 29–33 · J. Peers, 'Angels, harlots and nymphs: some themes in Australian art nouveau sculpture', *Art and Australia*, 25/2 (1987) · R. Jope-Slade, 'An Australian quartette', *Magazine of Art*, 18 (1894–5), 389–94 · W. K. West, 'The sculpture of Bertram McKennal', *The Studio*, 44 (1908), 262–7 · M. H. Spielmann, *British sculpture and sculptors of to-day* (1901) · N. Penny, ed., *Catalogue of European sculpture in the Ashmolean Museum, 1540 to the present day*, 3 (1992), 119–24 · S. Beattie, *The New Sculpture* (1983) · D. Edwards, *Stampede of the lower gods: classical mythology in Australian art, 1890s–1930s* (1989) [exhibition catalogue, Sydney Art Gallery of New South Wales] · J. Peers, *The new sculpture in Australia: Australian art nouveau sculpture, 1880–1920* (1987) [exhibition catalogue, McClelland Gallery, Langwarrin, Victoria, 3 May – 5 June 1987] · N. Hutchison, 'Temptress imperious: Bertram Mackennal's *Circe*', *Creating Australia: 200 years of art, 1788–1988*, ed. D. Thomas (1988) [exhibition catalogue, 'The great Australian art exhibition', Brisbane and elsewhere, May 1988 – July 1989] · W. Moore, *The story of Australian art* (1934) · W. K. Parkes, *Sculpture of today* (1921) · *The Times* (12 Oct 1931) · *AusDB* · B. Read, *Victorian sculpture* (1982) · G. Popp and H. Valentine, *Royal Academy of*

Arts directory of membership: from the foundation in 1768 to 1995, includ-ing honorary members (1996) · roll books, National Gallery of Victoria, school of design
Archives CUL, corresp. with Lord Hardinge · Henry Moore Institute, Leeds · National Gallery of Australia, papers, artist's files
Likenesses A. Altson, sketch, 1894, repro. in Jope-Slade, 'An Australian quartette' (1895) · photograph, 1920?–1929?, repro. in Moore, *Story of Australian art*, vol. 2 · W. Stoneman, photograph, 1924, NPG · J. Russell & Sons, photograph, NPG [*see illus.*]
Wealth at death £17,208: probate, 20 Nov 1931, *CGPLA Eng. & Wales*

Mackenzie family of Kintail (*per. c.*1475–1611), highland chiefs, though for a time they claimed to be of Norman origin, almost certainly shared native ancestry with the Mathesons on the north-west coast of Scotland. They held land from the earls of Ross, but in the fifteenth century are said to have consistently opposed them. After the forfeiture of Earl John in 1475 they gradually emerged to become, by the end of the following century, the leading power in Ross with a web of cadet families established from east to west of the region.

Alexander Mackenzie (d. 1477×88), called Ionraic (Upright), was chief of the Mackenzies. In 1477 he was confirmed by the crown in Strathconon, Strathgarve, and Strathbraan, lands in the centre of Ross which he had held there from the earl. It is suggested that he had been settled there under the eye of the earl almost as a hostage for the good behaviour of his relations in the west. Alexander, who had been sent by James I to be educated in the lowlands in Perth, was not wholly loyal to the earl although he married his son Kenneth to Finvola, daughter of the earl's brother Celestine. Family tradition has it that the charter which he received from the earl in 1463 was a reward for making peace between the king and the earl. Alexander lived on an island in Loch Kinellan, near the modern Strathpeffer, where he died between 1477 and 1488. He was followed as chief for a short time by his son Kenneth (d. 1492), who fought against the MacDonald claimant to the earldom of Ross at the battle of Park in 1491. He was the first of the family to be buried at Beauly Priory, where on his tombstone he is described as Kenneth Mackenzie of Kintail (the region in the western highlands on either side of Glen Shiel), a designation used thereafter by Mackenzie chiefs. A second Kenneth (d. c.1502), who may have been his son and brief successor, got into trouble with the crown for ravages in east Ross and was imprisoned in Edinburgh Castle. Lamed in escaping over the ramparts he was killed resisting recapture in the Torwood, near Stirling.

John Mackenzie of Kintail (d. 1561), called John of Killin from his birthplace or base near Garve, was the son of the elder Kenneth and his second wife, Agnes Fraser of Lovat. A minor when he succeeded either his father or half-brother, in 1501 he complained to the lords of council about the behaviour of his tutor and uncle Hector Mackenzie. In 1509 probably with backing from his Fraser relatives he received a royal charter of all the lands previously held by the family, including Kintail, and also the castle of Eilean Donan, at the head of Loch Duich, traditionally associated with the Mackenzies but lost by them

by the early fourteenth century. John, who is said to have fought at both Flodden in 1513 and Pinkie in 1547, also supported the crown nearer home against the rebels in the isles. He began the steady expansion of his clan lands into Lochalsh, Lochbroom, and Lochcarron, to the north of Kintail, which included much of the rough bounds towards the centre of the country. On the death of their last MacDonald owner in 1519 those lands had been divided between his two sisters, one of whom had married Dingwall of Kildun and the other Macdonell of Glengarry. Between 1543 and 1579 the Mackenzies acquired by exchange or purchase all the Dingwall half, but the Glengarry part took longer and was not so easily come by. Meanwhile, lands in the east were also falling to the family through the 1530s and 1540s, including Brahan, near Dingwall, which was later to become the chief's home. John married Elizabeth, daughter of John Grant of Freuchie, and they had at least two sons. He died in Invercarron on 26 January 1561. The elder of his sons was his successor, Kenneth (d. 1574), whose short chiefship was notable for his prosecution of feuds with, among others, the MacDonalds of Sleat and the Munros of Foulis. He married Elizabeth, daughter of John Stewart, second earl of Atholl, and they had three sons and six daughters, most of the latter being usefully married to local lairds.

Kenneth was succeeded by his second but eldest surviving son, **Colin Mackenzie** (d. 1594), called Cam, meaning one-eyed or crooked, who continued the expansion of the lands and influence of his clan. He was described as wise and judicious in the laws of the country but physically 'a tender feeble man' and in practice he relied on the strong arm of his brother Roderick (c.1574–1626?), who acted for him 'in the fields' (Warrand, 11). Between them they added to their territory from various sources. Church lands, made available after the Reformation, were acquired near the east coast and on the Black Isle, and gave rise to a serious clash with the Munros at Chanonry in 1572. The Mackenzies faced a brief challenge in their domination of east Ross from William and Andrew Keith, courtiers who were attracted by the profits from that fertile country and in the 1580s collected extensive feus there. But the challenge evaporated when Andrew died and William, turning his attention elsewhere, sold off his holdings, which some fifty years later came to the Mackenzies. On the west the latter added the church lands of Applecross, and the Glengarry half of Lochalsh, Lochbroom, and Lochcarron, partly through Colin's marriage with Barbara Grant of Freuchie, whose family had held them since 1546, and partly as the result of much bloodshed and 'manie more skirmishes' with the Macdonells of Glengarry, ending in the siege and destruction of Strome Castle in 1602 (Macphail, 49). Even further west the Mackenzies found themselves involved in the chaotic affairs of the Macleods of Lewis through the marriage of John of Killin's daughter Janet with Roderick *Macleod. She bore a son who her husband claimed was not his, and he divorced Janet. The boy was known as Torquil Cononach from having been brought up by his mother's people in Strathconon. Roderick remarried and had another son, who was drowned in

1563, leaving a disputed succession in which Colin supported Torquil Cononach and was given custody of the Lewis family charters and a grant of his lands of Assynt and Coigach on the mainland. The 'ewill trowbles of the Lewes' were to haunt his son also (ibid., 265). Colin died in Redcastle, Black Isle, on 14 June 1594 having made his mark locally as a landowner and nationally, being appointed a privy councillor in 1593. With his wife, Barbara Grant, he had six sons and five daughters.

Colin was followed by his eldest son, **Kenneth Mackenzie** (*d.* 1611), who carried forward his father's work in the highlands and islands, and also in Edinburgh, where he was made a privy councillor and very soon became chief agent for the crown in the highlands. In 1609 he was made a peer as Lord Mackenzie of Kintail. He was immediately drawn into the affairs of Lewis, which would dominate his time as chief. Roderick Macleod died in 1596, leaving, besides two young sons, Torquil Dubh and Tormod, by a third marriage, five acknowledged illegitimate sons. During the turmoil among them Torquil Cononach's son John was killed and his younger son died of fever, Torquil Dubh was killed by one of his half-brothers, and Kenneth Mackenzie abducted Tormod from school in the lowlands and imprisoned him. Meanwhile, James VI had decided to 'civilize' Lewis by establishing a fishery there, and encouraged a group of gentlemen known as the Fife Adventurers to undertake it. Kenneth appeared to support them but also stirred up trouble and released Tormod to join in the opposition. In 1605 Tormod gave himself up to the crown and was exiled. At the same time Torquil Cononach's daughter and heir, Margaret, was married to Kenneth's immediate younger brother Roderick, later to be notorious as the tutor of Kintail. The Mackenzies finally benefited from the chaos in Lewis when, in 1610, following much harassment of the surviving Fife Adventurers, they were able to buy them out and take possession of the island, which they were to hold for more than two centuries. They developed the port of Stornoway with Dutch assistance. Kenneth, who was married twice, first to Jean (*d.* 1604), daughter of George Ross of Balnagown, and second to Isobel (*d.* 1617), daughter of Sir Gilbert Ogilvie of Powrie, had seven sons and three daughters. On his death on 27 February 1611 he was followed by his eldest son, Colin *Mackenzie, who in 1623 was created first earl of Seaforth.   R. W. MUNRO and JEAN MUNRO

Sources D. Warrand, *Some Mackenzie pedigrees* (1965) · A. Mackenzie, *History of the Mackenzies, with genealogies of the principal families of the name*, new edn (1894) · W. Macfarlane, *Genealogical collections concerning families in Scotland*, ed. J. T. Clark, 2 vols., Scottish History Society, 33–4 (1900) · *Scots peerage* · I. F. Grant, *The MacLeods: the history of a clan, 1200–1956* (1959) · D. Gregory, *The history of the western highlands and isles of Scotland* (1836) · W. Malkeson, *Traditions of the Mackenzies*, Transactions of the Gaelic Society of Inverness (1963) · J. R. N. Macphail, ed., *Highland papers*, 2; Scottish History Society, 2nd ser., 12 (1916)
Archives NL Scot., estate corresp. and papers

Mackenzie, Agnes Mure (1891–1955), historian and novelist, was born on 9 April 1891 at 24 South Beach Street, Stornoway, Isle of Lewis, the eldest of the three children of

Agnes Mure Mackenzie (1891–1955), by Bassano, 1934

Murdo Mackenzie, physician and surgeon, and his wife, Sarah Agnes Drake. Following an attack of scarlet fever in childhood which severely damaged her sight and hearing, she was educated at home until the age of fourteen, thereafter attending the local secondary school, the Nicholson Institute, Stornoway. From there she went to the University of Aberdeen (MA, 1913) gaining a first-class honours degree in English literature (1921), and a DLitt for a thesis on Shakespeare (1924). She became the first woman editor of the university magazine *Alma Mater*, and an active suffragette. Her witty and vivid personality made her a memorable companion, although her deafness restricted her in general society.

Agnes Mure Mackenzie taught as an assistant lecturer in English at Aberdeen University (1915–18) and at Aberdeen Training Centre (1914–18), and after the war worked for a time for James Hastings, then editing the *Encyclopaedia of Religion and Ethics* (13 vols., 1908–26). But her real ambition was to become a writer. This meant residence in London, which became her home for the next thirty years. Although she disliked its artifice and the false cleverness of the London literati, it possessed two major assets: 'blessed invisibility' (Shepherd, 138), and the library of the British Museum. She obtained a part-time lectureship in English literature at Birkbeck College, from which she was painfully dismissed after five years of fulfilling work, following a student complaint that her lectures were inaudible. Thereafter she made her living wholly by the pen, writing reviews, doing editorial work, and acting as a publisher's reader. By 1930 she had seven delicately written historical novels to her credit and three works of criticism, including a pioneering feminist study, *The Women in Shakespeare's Plays* (1924), the subject of her Aberdeen DLitt. Although there was critical acclaim, there was little money; yet she allowed the Society of Authors to fight a test case in her name against irregular payment for commissioned pieces, well knowing what effect this might have upon her ability to attract future work.

An invitation to give a series of adult education lectures on Scottish literature signalled a new direction in her research and led to her most important work of criticism, *An Historical Survey of Scottish Literature to 1714* (1933). It also introduced her to the publisher Alexander MacLehose, who had an important influence on her later writing. Their shared interest in Robert the Bruce led to a commission for a historical work which would re-examine the currently negative interpretation of Bruce's career. This was published as *Robert Bruce, King of Scots* (1934) and proved to be merely the first instalment of what was to grow over the following decade into an ambitious six-volume history of Scotland, with an additional single-volume summary and related textbooks for schools. It was strongly revisionist in stance, marked by a determination to rescue Scottish historiography from its characteristic parochialism, defeatism, and presbyterian bias (the writer was a devout Scottish Episcopalian). It became the standard work in its field during the mid-twentieth century. The final volume, *Scotland in Modern Times, 1720–1939* (1941) was particularly influential, offering an account of Victorian and twentieth-century Scotland which shaped the thinking of a whole generation. Although not explicitly nationalist, it delivered a shattering indictment of the Union in economic, social, and cultural terms. The series revealed keen insight into human motive and an instinctive political grasp of the ways (and waywardness) of institutions. It was shaped by its writer's sense of the central importance of history to the interpretation of the present, and was distinguished by cosmopolitan breadth, cultural sophistication, and conspicuous elegance of style.

In 1940 Agnes Mure Mackenzie was appointed as an adviser to the Scottish education department, and in 1942 made an honorary president of the Saltire Society. In 1945 she was made a CBE for services to Scottish history, and in 1951 an LLD at the University of Aberdeen. She settled in Edinburgh in 1951 and continued her busy schedule of lecturing and writing.

Amid such a wealth of well-written prose, it is perhaps a little curious that one of the best known of Agnes Mure Mackenzie's works should be a poem, the brief lyric 'To People who have Gardens', one of a set of graceful verses written while she was a student at Aberdeen. It holds the laconic and the lissom in such characteristically delicate balance that, later set to music by Marjorie Kennedy-Fraser, it became one of the classic songs of modern Scotland:

For day's work and week's work
As I go up and down

There are many gardens
All about the town.

One that's gay with daffodils,
One where children play,
One white with cherry-flower,
Another red with may.

A kitten, and a lilac-bush,
Bridal white and tall,
And later, crimson ramblers,
Against a granite wall …

I have passed your railings
When you never knew,
And, People who have Gardens,
I give my thanks to you.
(Mackenzie and Shepherd, 43; Kennedy-Fraser, 83–87)

Agnes Mure Mackenzie was slightly built, elegant in her dress, and—although she considered herself 'an ugly divil' (Shepherd, 135)—strikingly featured, with a determined square jaw, and long aristocratic lip. She never married, and lived with her lifelong companion and sister Jean. She suffered a coronary thrombosis at her home, 19 Lonsdale Terrace, Edinburgh, and died at the Royal Infirmary, Edinburgh on 26 February 1955.

WILLIAM DONALDSON

Sources N. Shepherd, 'Agnes Mure Mackenzie …: a portrait', *Aberdeen University Review*, 36 (1955–6), 132–40 · *The Scotsman* (28 Feb 1955) · A. M. Mackenzie and A. Shepherd, eds., *Alma Mater anthology, 1883–1919* (1919) · M. Kennedy-Fraser and K. Macleod, eds., *Songs of the Hebrides*, 3 (1921) · T. Watt, ed., *Roll of the graduates of the University of Aberdeen, 1901–25* (1935) · A. M. Mackenzie, *The process of literature* (1929) · b. cert. · d. cert.
Archives NL Scot., corresp. and papers · U. Aberdeen L., lecture notes, papers | NL Scot., letters to Alison Cairns · U. Aberdeen L., Queen Mother Library, letters to Nan Shepherd
Likenesses D. Young, photograph, 1932, Scot. NPG · Bassano, photograph, 1934, NPG [*see illus.*] · photograph, repro. in Shepherd, 'Agnes Mure Mackenzie', facing p. 136
Wealth at death £10,150 2s. 1d.: confirmation, 20 April 1955, CCI

Mackenzie, Alexander (d. 1477×88). *See under* Mackenzie family of Kintail (*per. c.*1475–1611).

Mackenzie, Sir Alexander (1763/4–1820), explorer, was born at Luskentyre House, Stornoway, Isle of Lewis (where a plaque was later erected to mark his birth), the third of four children of Kenneth Mackenzie (d. 1780) of Melbost Farm near Stornoway, and Isabella Maciver. His mother died when he was a young child and in 1774, faced with a depression at home, Kenneth took his own two sisters and Alexander to join his brother John in New York. The American War of Independence broke out shortly after their arrival and Alexander was sent first to Johnstown in the Mohawk Valley and in 1778 to Montreal. After having attended school in that city, in 1779 Mackenzie joined the firm of Finlay and Gregory (from 1783 Gregory, MacLeod & Co). The company traded fur and other goods and Mackenzie showed both enjoyment of and skill in trading; by 1785 he was offered a share in the company provided he would serve in a post in the far west. Mackenzie accepted the challenge with enthusiasm.

Mackenzie entered into the partnership when the fur

trade in the west of Canada was undergoing considerable change and in 1787 Gregory, MacLeod & Co. amalgamated with the much bigger North West Company. One of the North West Company's aims was to win for itself trading privileges by undertaking to explore and open to trade the north-west parts of the country, much of the geography of which was either not known at all or erroneously set down in contemporary maps and descriptions. Mackenzie began trading first from headquarters in Athabasca and in 1788 moved west to be based at the first Fort Chipewyan, on the southern shore of Lake Athabasca.

From Fort Chipewyan Mackenzie set out on his first journey on 3 June 1789, hoping to discover new routes and open up new areas to the fur trade. The party made slow progress along the Slave River with its many rapids and they were delayed by ice on the Great Slave Lake, but once they entered what has subsequently become known as the Mackenzie River they made rapid progress. Contemporaries believed that the Mackenzie River went due west and would thus provide a route across the continent, but it rapidly became clear that the river turned to go due north. Mackenzie followed it until he reached the Arctic Ocean when the party turned and made for home. They reached Fort Chipewyan on 12 September having covered over 3000 miles in some 100 days. Mackenzie had clarified a major misunderstanding in the geography of the region but his discovery attracted little notice since it rather frustrated than helped the company's trading aims.

Although the Mackenzie River did not answer to the purpose, Mackenzie was determined to find a route west to the Pacific. When he set off for his second expedition in 1792 he knew well enough how great was the task. In the interval between his two expeditions the true longitude for Fort Chipewyan had been discovered and, by comparing this with James Cook's measurement of longitude of the western coast of Canada, Mackenzie knew that the distance between the two was much greater than had originally been thought. On 10 October 1792 he left Fort Chipewyan and travelled up the Peace River, overwintering at Fort Fork (later Peace River Landing). In the following spring, on 9 May 1793, he set off again following the Peace River and later the Parsnip River, where the going proved much more difficult. At last on 18 June he began his descent of the McGregor River and reached the Fraser River, travelling down it as far as what was later Fort Alexandria, having been named after him. There Indians advised him to go back up the Fraser until he got to the West Road River and follow the latter river westward. He followed that advice and in July reached the Bella Coola Gorge, following the river down to the Pacific Ocean. This was the first journey across North America north of Mexico. On 23 July Mackenzie set off for home, reaching Fort Chipewyan on 24 August, thus keeping up his record for exceptional speed in the 2300 miles he had travelled. As in his first journey he had brought his whole party home safely and had added very considerably to the knowledge of the geography of the country, but his discoveries again brought little prospect of increased trade, since the rugged routes could never become a servicable trade route.

Mackenzie spent the winter of 1793–4 at Fort Chipewyan and in a restless and disconsolate mood decided to leave the west of the country for Montreal. In September 1794 he outlined to John Graves Simcoe, lieutenant-governor of Upper Canada, his plans that the North West Company, the Hudson's Bay Company, and the East India Company should co-operate in opening up the fur trade in both the interior and western parts of Canada and on the Pacific coast. Having settled in Montreal, Mackenzie was offered a partnership in McTavish, Frobisher & Co. in 1795, but he was not altogether in sympathy with his partners, and when his partnership expired on 30 November 1799 he left suddenly for England.

Having reached London, Mackenzie's priority was to publish his *Voyages from Montreal to the Frozen and Pacific Ocean* (1801). It is likely that the general information it contains on the history of the fur trade is provided by Roderick Mackenzie, Alexander Mackenzie's cousin, who worked with him in the trade. The rest of the work contains Alexander Mackenzie's journals and finally his proposals for co-operation between the North West Company, the Hudson's Bay Company, and the East India Company. The book attracted considerable attention, and on 10 February 1802 Mackenzie was knighted.

Mackenzie returned to Montreal in 1802 hoping to re-enter the fur trade. Since 1800 he had been acquiring shares in the New North West Company—so much so, that by 1802 it was sometimes known as Sir Alexander Mackenzie & Co. When Mackenzie reached Montreal in 1802 he hoped to unite the new and original North West companies, but his antagonism with Simon McTavish of the original North West Company prevented this. The two companies did eventually join, but the resultant company excluded Mackenzie, who had come to be regarded as something of a maverick.

Mackenzie decided to enter politics and on 16 June 1804 he was elected to represent the county of Huntingdon in the house of assembly of Lower Canada. He sat until 1808, but his heart was not in it and he was in London from the autumn of 1805 onwards.

By 1808 Mackenzie's mind was turning to a new project. He hoped that by buying shares in the Hudson's Bay Company he would be able to secure the use of the bay for Montreal fur traders. At the same time Lord Selkirk was buying shares to further his project of colonizing the Red River country. Initially Selkirk and Mackenzie were on good terms, but when Mackenzie realized the scale of Selkirk's project he opposed it—in vain, as it was approved by the Hudson's Bay general court in 1811. This failure was followed by his renewed failure to interest the government in his plans for reorganizing the fur trade.

Disillusioned, Mackenzie decided to retire to Scotland where in 1812 he married Geddes (*b.* 1797/8), one of the twin daughters of George Mackenzie (*d.* 1809). She was fourteen years old and Mackenzie forty-eight. Geddes and her twin sister had inherited the estate of Avoch and after their marriage the Mackenzies usually spent the season in London and lived for the rest of the year at Avoch. They had a daughter (*b.* 1816) and two sons (*b.* 1818 and 1819). By the time of his last son's birth Mackenzie was in poor health, and in January 1820 he died in an inn at Mulnain, near Dunkeld.

Mackenzie's fame rests squarely on his two remarkable voyages. His career thereafter was something of an anticlimax, though his scheme for reorganizing the fur trade was prescient and was adopted in some respects after his death.   ELIZABETH BAIGENT

Sources *The journals and letters of Sir Alexander Mackenzie*, ed. W. Kaye Lamb, Hakluyt Society, extra ser., 41 (1970) · W. Kaye Lamb, 'Mackenzie, Alexander', *DCB*, vol. 5 · PRO, PROB 6/196, fol. 52v

Archives BL, journal, Stowe MS 793 · McGill University, Montreal, McLennan Library, journal · NA Canada, business records [copies]

Likenesses P. Condé, stipple (after T. Lawrence), BM; repro. in A. Mackenzie, *Voyages* (1801) · T. Lawrence, oils, National Gallery of Canada, Ottawa, war memorials collection; repro. in *Journals and letters*, ed. Lamb

Wealth at death property in Scotland and previously substantial shareholdings in Canadian ventures: PRO, PROB 6/196, fol. 52v

Mackenzie, Alexander (1822–1892), prime minister of Canada, was born on 28 January 1822 at Logierait, near Dunkeld in Perthshire, the third of the ten sons of Alexander Mackenzie (1784–1836), a shipbuilder and carpenter, and his wife, Mary Stewart Fleming (1795–1861), the daughter of a local schoolmaster. He attended schools in Perth and Moulin (near Pitlochry), then Dunkeld. Before his father died he had to give up his education: when he was thirteen he and his two elder brothers had to work to provide food for his mother and seven younger brothers. He was apprenticed to a local builder, where he learned stonecutting and masonry, and by the age of twenty was a journeyman mason, working on the new railway being built between Glasgow and Ayr. He boarded with another stonemason family, the Neils, in Irvine, and there met the 17-year-old Helen Neil (1826–1852). He emigrated with the Neil family to Canada in April 1842, and arrived in Montreal on 6 May.

The Neils and Mackenzie moved up-country to Kingston, Canada West, where they were joined by Hope Mackenzie, an elder brother, in 1843. Mackenzie married Helen Neil on 28 March 1845. To one part of the wedding vows the 23-year-old bridegroom objected; neither his brother nor the clergyman could induce him to say, 'with this body I thee worship' (Thomson, 22). Mackenzie seems to have thought it both sacrilegious and indecent. There were three children of this marriage, of whom one, Mary, survived.

In 1847 the Mackenzie group moved westward to Port Sarnia, at the very western edge of the province on the St Clair River, on the water route between Lake Huron and Lake Erie, and just across from the busy little American town of Port Huron, Michigan. In Sarnia Mackenzie found his niche, and there he remained, a well-respected stonemason, then builder and contractor. There was plenty of opportunity for a young man of talent and integrity, driven by his own inner gospel of work. In his spare time he strove to make up for deficiencies in his grammar and

arithmetic; he had a quick mind, a retentive memory, and an inclination, perhaps Scottish, to get to the bottom of whatever he tackled. There was always to be a plumb-line, utilitarian set to his mind, and he tended to judge others by the same square-cut, stonemason's standard. Subtle he was not.

In 1852 Mackenzie's wife died, and on 17 June 1853 he married a second time. His new wife, Jane Sym (*b*. 1833?), soon took charge of his household and the bringing up of Mary, the daughter of his first marriage. There were no children of this second marriage.

Being an instinctive reformer and liberal, Mackenzie had always taken to politics, a natural extension of his desire for the improvement of society and of the men and women in it. The very first issue of his new Sarnia newspaper, the *Lambton Shield*, set this out: the paper would be a constitutional but unflinching advocate of progressive reform, 'to secure civil and religious equality' (Thomson, 32).

Mackenzie's political leader then, and for the next thirty years, was George Brown, the outspoken, restless, Free Kirk Scot who edited the Toronto *Globe*, and whose biographer Mackenzie later became. Mackenzie's own political work began in 1851, and in 1861 he was elected to the provincial assembly for Lambton county as a Reformer in the party of George Brown. He soon established himself as a man of direct speech and strong opinions. That, combined with an almost innate sense of parliamentary footwork, made him a valuable lieutenant.

After confederation in 1867, Mackenzie was elected to the Canadian House of Commons, and slowly began gathering about him like-minded men from the other new provinces of Canada under a party that came to be called Liberal. Brown went out of politics to devote himself to *The Globe* and to stock farming, and in March 1873 the Liberal Party elected Mackenzie as leader. Within six months the Canadian Pacific Railroad scandal had brought down the Conservative government of Sir John Macdonald, and on 7 November 1873 Mackenzie was sworn in as prime minister. He himself took on the heavy portfolio of minister of public works. He called a general election in January 1874 and his party wiped the floor with the Conservatives. Of the 206 seats in the House of Commons, Liberals won 138, the Conservatives only sixty-seven; there was one independent.

Even with that big majority Mackenzie's administration was riddled with difficulties. The most intractable one was the Pacific Railway, agreed to by the previous government with British Columbia to bring that far western colony into confederation in 1871. The railway to the Pacific was to be commenced on 20 July 1873 and finished by 20 July 1881. It was an impossible timetable; at the time of confederation few had any notion of the problems of getting a railway through the Rocky Mountains, to say nothing of the other ranges further west. When the surveys began and the obstacles were discovered, Mackenzie, his party, and the Ontario constituencies, where lay much of their electoral support, baulked at the enormous price to be paid building a huge and probably profitless 2000 mile railway to the west coast to satisfy a few thousand British Columbians.

Mackenzie wrestled with solutions to that and other problems throughout his ministry, sometimes with the help, not always welcomed by Mackenzie, of the governor-general, Lord Dufferin, who made a difficult trip to British Columbia via San Francisco, to try to soften British Columbia's attitude. Mackenzie carried a tremendous burden especially as minister of public works, under whose aegis the Pacific Railway work was proceeding. He worked extremely hard; in fact he worked too hard. And there was something hectoring and schoolmasterish about his administration; he enjoyed ferreting out weakness and wickedness, and tended to judge his subordinates by how much work they got done, or how well posted they were on departmental business. The department of public works gradually became well run. But Mackenzie, in effectively running his department, ruined his government. *Grip*, the Toronto comic weekly, was jocular but right:

> He was sitting, you remember, like a clerk … when it would have been better for the party had he been seeing people and wining, dining and poking bartenders in the ribs, jovially, like John A. [Sir John A. Macdonald]. But he could never be taught these little arts … There was no gin and talk about MAC. (*Grip*, 3 April 1880)

And what really ruined his administration was an extraordinary run of bad economic times that affected both the United States and Canada from 1873 to 1878.

Mackenzie went to the polls in 1878 and was defeated by almost as large a majority as the one by which he had won in 1874. He was stunned and bitter. 'Canada', he lamented to Charles Black on 15 October 1878, 'does not care for rigid adherence to principle in the government. I administered her affairs with a more scrupulous regard to economy and justice than I would shew in my own affairs' (Mackenzie MSS, National Archives of Canada). He had also ruined his health. He was never quite the same after 1878, and it soon began to show. In April 1880 he was approached by a group of senior Liberals and asked to step down as leader. He was even more aggrieved at that.

Mackenzie remained in parliament, however, through the 1880s, being continuously re-elected for East York by grateful and appreciative constituents. He was watchful and shrewd in debates, interjecting biting comments on the failings of the Conservative government, which held power all through his last years. His health gradually deteriorated despite occasional trips abroad to try to restore it. There was degeneration in his voice that increasingly made it difficult for him to speak. He had a slight stroke in 1882, but Conservative ministers still watched and worried in the House of Commons if they saw Mackenzie pull himself to his feet. He died at his home, in Wellesley Street, Toronto, on 17 April 1892, from the effects of a fall, and was buried on 20 April at Lakeview cemetery, Sarnia.

The conventional view of Mackenzie was that he was dogged, dour, and humourless, a grey mixture of prudery and porridge. That does him great injustice; his hard work, his integrity, and his fearless no-favours-to-anyone way of politics were in great need in a political world still rife with patronage. Mackenzie had wit, though with a caustic edge. He wrote to his daughter Mary on 25 September 1879, about a vice-regal reception when Toronto society was presented to the Princess Louise and Lord Lorne, the governor-general:

> Lady Howland went through in grand style curtseying so low that everyone wondered how the whole of that 300 pound woman ever got up again. Another stupendous woman a head taller than me and three times as thick went through with the preliminary movement to a curtsey. The officer immediately behind stepped back hurriedly evidently seized with a sudden apprehension of what might become of his family if the curtsey should fail in the recovery. Some one whispered, 'Is that whole woman to be presented at once …?' (Mackenzie MSS, Queen's University Archives)

Canada has probably never had a more sober and scrupulous prime minister, though Mackenzie often felt ill-requited for those exemplary virtues. Wilfrid Laurier remarked in parliament after his death, 'He strove for the right as he saw the right' (House of Commons debates, 19 April 1892). There are worse things to be remembered for.

P. B. Waite

Sources NA Canada, Alexander Mackenzie collection · Queen's University Archives, Kingston, Ontario, Alexander Mackenzie MSS · D. C. Thomson, *Alexander Mackenzie: clear grit* (1960) · B. Forster, 'Mackenzie, Alexander', *DCB*, vol. 12 · *Grip* (3 April 1880) · *The Dufferin-Carnarvon correspondence, 1874–1878*, ed. C. W. De Kiewiet and F. H. Underhill (1955)
Archives NA Canada, Mackenzie MSS · Queen's University, Kingston, Ontario, Mackenzie MSS | Bodl. Oxf., corresp. with Lord Kimberley · National Archives of Canada, Ottawa, George Brown MSS · PRO NIre., corresp. with Lord Dufferin · Public Archives of Ontario, Toronto, Edward Blake MSS · Public Archives of Ontario, Toronto, Sir Richard Cartwright MSS
Likenesses photograph, 1873, NA Canada · chromolithograph, NPG
Wealth at death modest circumstances: Thomson, *Alexander Mackenzie*; Forster, 'Mackenzie'

Mackenzie, Sir Alexander (1842–1902), administrator in India, born at Dumfries on 28 June 1842, was the eldest son of the eleven children of John Robertson Mackenzie (1811–1877), Presbyterian minister, and Alexandrina, fourth daughter of Dr James Christie of Huntly. The family moved to Birmingham in 1847, and Mackenzie was educated there, at King Edward VI's School, and afterwards at Trinity Hall, Cambridge, where he did well in college examinations, but did not take the classical tripos as he could not subscribe to the Anglican test for a fellowship. He took the Indian Civil Service examination in July 1861, and came second.

Mackenzie arrived in India in December 1862. The following year he married Georgina Louisa (d. 1892), youngest daughter of Colonel W. Bremner of the Madras army. He served as assistant magistrate and collector in Bengal, becoming under secretary and junior secretary of the local government in 1866. He had charge of the political correspondence of the province, which at that time included Assam. At the request of Sir William Grey, he wrote a report entitled *Memorandum on the North-East Frontier of Bengal* (1869) which he later brought up to date in his

History of the relations of government with the hill tribes of the north-east frontier of Bengal (1884). A particularly candid account, the work was for many years a standard authority. He afterwards served successively as secretary of the board of revenue (1875–6), as magistrate and collector of Murshidabad (1876–7), again as secretary of the board (1877), and as financial secretary of the Bengal government (1877–82). Concurrently with the last appointment, from January 1879 he was a member of the provincial legislative assembly. Appointed home secretary of the executive council in April 1882, he identified himself closely with the plans of the viceroy, Lord Ripon, for the extension of local self-government and for the encouragement of capital and private enterprise. He was also much involved in shaping the Bengal Tenancy Act and Rent Law of 1885. In 1886 he was made a CSI.

Mackenzie went to the Central Provinces as chief commissioner in 1887, but his plans for reform were hindered by disagreement with the military members of the provincial commission. In December 1890 he was transferred to Burma as chief commissioner, and was promoted KCSI in the following month. He suppressed the raids of the hill tribes by sending out some seventeen or eighteen expeditions of military police; by 1892 he reported complete tranquillity and proposed reducing the numbers of military police. His wife died in 1892, and he spent the next two years on leave in Britain, during which period he married, on 15 August 1893, the twenty-four-year-old Mabel Elizabeth, daughter of Ralph Elliot, engineer. They had a son and a daughter. In April 1895 he joined the government of India as temporary member, and in December he became lieutenant-governor of Bengal.

Mackenzie's connection with Lord Ripon assured him a welcome from the Indian press; but nationalist sentiments were alienated when he initiated a bill to amend the Calcutta Municipal Act. His government took the view that Europeans 'ought to have a predominant influence in the affairs of the town', as against the 'educated middle class Hindu' into whose hands municipal power had passed under the existing act (Indian Municipalities Proceedings, 1898, nos. 28–35). When the bill—modified by Lord Curzon even more drastically in favour of official and European commercial representation—was passed in 1899, soon after Mackenzie's retirement, the elected commissioners resigned in a body from the corporation in an unprecedented demonstration of nationalist solidarity.

Meanwhile, Mackenzie sought to protect Bengal from the financial demands of the government of India, likening the province to a lamb thrown on its back and close-sheared for the benefit of the central administration. He passed an act in 1896 to enlarge the powers of municipalities outside the capital. He speeded the progress of the important land settlement operations which his predecessor, Sir Charles Elliott, had inaugurated in Bihar and Orissa. Mackenzie was prevented by ill health from exercising personal supervision in the field during the severe famine of 1896–7, but he directed the policy, and the economic results were due to him. The plague posed more problems, but his arrangements kept the disease out of Bengal until April 1898, nearly two years after its appearance in Bombay. Mackenzie's health broke down under the various strains, and he resigned in April 1898. In none of the three provinces in which he ruled was Mackenzie's high promise fulfilled. He was 'stronger in office work and on paper than in active administration' (*Pioneer Mail*, 26 April 1912). Although in Anglo-Indian circles he was thought to be one of the ablest men of his time, Bengal nationalists had no fond memory of his administration.

On his return to England, Mackenzie became a director of several companies, spoke on missionary platforms, and took an active part in the work of the Marylebone Presbyterian Church. In 1901 he was adopted as a Liberal candidate for Plymouth, but had to withdraw because of ill health. He died at his residence, Radnor, Holmbury St Mary, near Dorking, Surrey, on 10 November 1902, and was buried at Ewhurst church. He was survived by his second wife, who subsequently married Noel Farrer, second son of the first Baron Farrer.

F. H. BROWN, rev. RAJAT KANTA RAY

Sources C. E. Buckland, *Bengal under the lieutenant-governors*, 2nd edn, 2 vols. (1902) · L. Fraser, *India under Curzon and after* (1911) · J. Nisbet, *Burma under British rule and before* (1901) · R. K. Ray, *Social conflict and political unrest in Bengal, 1875–1927* (1984) · R. Ray, *Urban roots of Indian nationalism: pressure groups and conflict of interest in Calcutta city politics, 1875–1939* (1979) · *The Times* (11 Nov 1902) · *Calcutta Stateman* (12 Nov 1902) · *Pioneer Mail* (21 Nov 1902) · *Pioneer Mail* (26 April 1912) · *Presbyterian* (20 Nov 1902) · m. cert. [A. Mackenzie ad M. E. Elliot] · *Indian Mirror* (14 Nov 1902) · *Hindu Patriot* (13 Nov 1902) · Burke, *Peerage* (1939) · Indian Municipalities Proceedings, 1898, BL OIOC

Archives BL, letters to Lord Ripon, Add. MS 43581

Wealth at death £58,119 18s. 2d.: probate, 10 Jan 1903, CGPLA Eng. & Wales

McKenzie, Alexander (1869–1951), chemist, was born at Dundee on 6 December 1869, the eldest of the six surviving children of Peter Mitchell McKenzie, a schoolmaster, and his wife, Isobel Buchanan, the daughter of a farmer at Lochgoil. He received his early education in his father's schools at Dundee and later at Tealing, where he was well grounded in the classics. In 1882 he entered the high school at Dundee, where one of the teachers, Frank Young, interested him in chemistry. In 1885 he was awarded the Edinburgh Angus Club medal in Latin, and entered the United College in the University of St Andrews, graduating MA four years later. He went on to take his BSc, specializing in chemistry and natural philosophy, in 1891. He later claimed, perhaps in jest, that his interest in chemistry stemmed from his forebears, who were alleged to have had an illicit still in Glen Shee.

In 1891–3 McKenzie was chemistry lecture assistant to Thomas Purdie at St Andrews, thereby gaining experience in lecturing, and in performing the lecture bench demonstrations which later became a great feature of his own first-year courses. In 1893–8 he was a university assistant. To further his chemical research work he next went to Berlin, where under the supervision of Marckwald he graduated PhD in 1901. In Berlin he acquainted himself with the local scientific and cultural scene and became a fluent speaker and writer of German. Returning to Britain in 1901 he spent one year on a research studentship from the Grocers' Company working under Arthur Harden at the Jenner Institute for Preventive Medicine, London. In 1902 he became assistant lecturer in chemistry at the University of Birmingham. In 1905 he returned to London as head of the chemistry department in Birkbeck College, where teaching duties were very heavy and he could do his research work only in his leisure hours. His final move was in 1914 to the chair of chemistry at Dundee. With smaller classes and no evening teaching, and after completion of important wartime work, he built up a vigorous organic research school. In 1906 McKenzie married Alice Helene Sand, a sister of Henry Julius Salomon Sand, a well-known writer on electrochemistry. They had one son, Duncan Buchanan McKenzie, who became an electrical engineer.

McKenzie's main topics of research lay in the fields of optical activity and stereochemistry. A skilled experimenter of originality and resource, he was distinguished for his use of the Grignard reaction, and for his fundamental work on asymmetric synthesis. He carried out important studies of the phenomenon of racemization, and detailed investigations of the Walden inversion. He was particularly associated with mandelic acid and its derivatives. During the First World War his laboratory made important contributions to the synthesis of vital products and to the preparation and study of arsenical war gases. In all he published, alone and with his co-workers, 122 papers, most of which appeared in the *Journal of the Chemical Society* and the *Berichte* of the German Chemical Society.

McKenzie was elected a fellow of the Royal Society in 1916 and was a fellow and council member of the Chemical Society. He belonged to the Institute of Chemistry and the Deutsche Chemische Gesellschaft, and was a secretary of the chemistry section of the British Association in 1908. In 1932 he was elected to the Kaiserlich Deutsche Akademie der Naturforscher zu Halle, and in 1939 was awarded an honorary degree of LLD by St Andrews. He lectured in Berlin in 1931 at the invitation of the Kaiser Wilhelm Gesellschaft, and later in the same year delivered a course of six invitation lectures at the University of Basel. He was a man of wide interests, highly regarded by his colleagues, friends, and students for his honesty in thought and action.

McKenzie was an enthusiastic golfer, and continued to play an excellent game until stopped by ill health. Although holding a life appointment, after developing asthma he retired from the Dundee chair in 1938 in the interests of the department. He continued to take an active interest in chemistry, reading the monthly journals and making notes for the use of his former colleagues and research students. He died at Barnhill, Angus, on 11 June 1951, survived by his wife.

I. A. SMITH, *rev.* K. D. WATSON

Sources J. Read, *Obits. FRS*, 8 (1952–3), 207–28 · H. Wren, *JCS* (1952), 270–71 · *Nature*, 168 (1951), 143–4 · election certificate, RS
Archives University of Dundee

Likenesses W. Stoneman, photograph, 1932, NPG · Russell & Sons, photograph, RS
Wealth at death £6008 6s. 0d.: confirmation, 15 Aug 1951, *CCI*

Mackenzie, Sir Alexander Campbell (1847–1935), composer and conductor, was born in Nelson Street, Edinburgh, on 22 August 1847, the eldest son of Alexander Mackenzie and his wife, Jessie Watson Campbell. Musical talent ran in his family, his great-grandfather having been a member of the Forfarshire militia band, his grandfather a professional violinist, and his father leader of the orchestra at the Theatre Royal, Edinburgh, and editor of the *National Dance Music of Scotland* (1859).

From the age of eight, Mackenzie regularly played the violin in his father's orchestra. When he was ten, after leaving Hunter's School, Edinburgh, he was sent to study music at Schwarzburg-Sondershausen in Thuringia. He lived with his teacher, the Stadtmusiker August Bartel, attended the Realschule, and studied the violin under K. W. Ulrich and theory with Eduard Stein; in 1861 he joined the ducal orchestra as second violinist. In 1862 he moved to London and entered the Royal Academy of Music, shortly afterwards winning the king's scholarship, and studied violin with Prosper Sainton, composition with Charles Lucas, and piano with Frederick Bowen Jewson. During this time he supplemented his income by playing in various London theatre orchestras, including the Strand Music Hall, where he accompanied well-known variety stars.

Having completed his training in 1865, Mackenzie settled in Edinburgh, where he remained until 1881, and became known as a violinist. He gave chamber concerts, at one of which in 1870 Schumann's piano quartet and quintet were played for the first time in Scotland. In October 1870 he was appointed organist of St George's Church, Charlotte Square, and in 1873 became conductor of the Scottish Vocal Music Association. He played in the orchestra at the Birmingham festivals of 1864, 1867, 1870, and 1873, and gave piano lessons at the Edinburgh Ladies' College for up to six hours a day, teaching eight pupils simultaneously on eight instruments. In 1874 he married Mary Malina (*d.* 1925), daughter of John Burnside, of Edinburgh. They had a daughter, Mary. In addition, Mackenzie found time to compose a piano trio and a string quartet, as well as an accomplished piano quartet in E♭, op. 11, published by Kahnt at Leipzig and performed in London on 4 March 1875. Hans von Bülow, who had seen the proof sheets of this work, later made the composer's acquaintance. It was through this meeting that Mackenzie's overture *Cervantes*, performed at Schwarzburg-Sondershausen in 1877, was produced at Glasgow two years later under von Bülow's direction. Soon after, two other orchestral works appeared, *Rhapsodie Ecossaise* and *Burns* (his second Scottish rhapsody), played at Glasgow in 1880 and 1881 respectively, and conducted by August Manns.

But overwork began to undermine Mackenzie's health. After a period of rest abroad (1879–80) he soon recovered and decided to remain in the warmer climate of Italy. Save for just over a year in England (1885) he made Florence his headquarters for seven years (1881–8), where he spent

Sir Alexander Campbell Mackenzie (1847–1935), by Walery, pubd 1888

much time at the house of Carl Hillebrand in the company of Liszt. In Florence he settled down to compositions of larger scale. Besides purely instrumental works he wrote operas and choral works, including the cantata *The Bride* (performed to acclaim at the Worcester festival of 1881), the cantata *Jason* (for the Bristol festival, 1882), the opera *Colomba* (first produced at Drury Lane, London, by the Carl Rosa company, 9 April 1883), and the oratorio *The Rose of Sharon* (one of the successes of the Norwich festival of 1884). These works established Mackenzie's reputation as one of Britain's leading composers. A violin concerto written for Pablo Sarasate was played at the Birmingham festival of 1885 and six pieces for the violin (including *Benedictus*) were a feature of Monday Popular Concerts at the St James's Hall (1888), with Lady Hallé as soloist. During the season of 1885–6 Mackenzie returned to England as conductor of the Novello Oratorio Choir in London, and met Gounod and Dvořák. Liszt paid his final visit to England primarily in order to hear his *Saint Elisabeth* performed under Mackenzie's direction at the Royal Academy of Music in 1886. Mackenzie's opera *The Troubadour* (1886) was a near disaster, but Liszt was working on a piano fantasia based on themes from it at the time of his death the same year.

Following the death of Sir George Macfarren in October 1887, Mackenzie was appointed to succeed him as principal of the Royal Academy, a position which he held from 22 February 1888 until his retirement in 1924. At the time the academy faced strong competition from the recently opened Royal College of Music and Guildhall School of Music and the standard of its teaching had been criticized in the press. Mackenzie's first task was to set his house in order. Supported by royal patronage and by a sympathetic board of directors and committee of management, reforms were initiated. The professorial staff became a more cohesive body. Generous donors gave sums of money to found scholarships and student numbers increased. The scope and influence of Mackenzie's own experience broadened the musical education which the academy was meant to provide. He established links with the Royal College, which, with the friendly co-operation of Hubert Parry, culminated in the formation in 1889 of the Associated Board of the Royal Academy of Music and the Royal College of Music—an examining body, later known as the Associated Board of the Royal Schools of Music.

From 1892 to 1899 Mackenzie was conductor of the Philharmonic Society's concerts, which brought him into close personal touch with composers, conductors, and performers of international repute, including Saint-Saëns, Grieg, Strauss, Busoni, and Joachim. He conducted the first English performances of Tchaikovsky's sixth symphony (28 February 1894) and Borodin's second symphony (27 February 1896). His intimate knowledge of German and Italian, coupled with his cosmopolitan musicianship, eminently fitted him to be president of the International Musical Society, a post he held from 1908 to 1912; he presided over congresses at Vienna (1909) and London (1911), the latter of which featured British music.

In the 1860s and 1870s Mackenzie had produced several collections of traditional Scottish songs arranged for piano or violin and piano, and in 1903 he undertook a six-week tour of Canada at the invitation of Charles Harriss in order to study the possibilities of Canadian folk-song. Many contemporary British works then introduced by Mackenzie gave impetus to choral festival competitions throughout Canada and eleven new choral societies were founded as a result. At the academy he taught composition, conducted the students' orchestra, and lectured, besides attending to his administrative work. The move in 1911 from Tenterden Street to the new building at York Gate, Marylebone Road, and the centenary celebrations (1922), with a performance of his opera *The Cricket on the Hearth* (first performed in 1914), provide ample testimony to his gifts of organization. Many students, who went on to become distinguished members of their profession, remembered his genial friendship and wise leadership with gratitude.

In his day Mackenzie was regarded as the finest ever Scottish musician, and many of his programmatic works are based on Scottish subjects, but his music is cosmopolitan in style and somewhat old-fashioned for its period, displaying influences of French and German composers, including Bizet, Gounod, Schumann, and Wagner. Particularly attractive is his imaginative and colourful use of the orchestra. In addition to the works already mentioned, Mackenzie composed a one-act opera, *The Eve of St John* (1924), three comic operas, incidental music to six dramas, orchestral works, including a 'Scottish' concerto for piano (1897), the suite *London Day by Day* (1902), and the *Canadian Rhapsody* (1905), instrumental music, and more than 150 songs and partsongs. He also wrote books on Verdi (1913) and Liszt (*c*.1920). In his *A Musician's Narrative* (1927), a lively account of his musical experiences, he was proud to describe 'a lifetime spent, boy and man, in the service of British music' (Mackenzie, 262).

Mackenzie was knighted in 1895 and appointed KCVO in 1922. His many academic distinctions included the honorary degree of doctor of music of the universities of St Andrews (1886), Cambridge (1888), Edinburgh (1890), and Oxford (1922), the honorary LLD of Glasgow (1901) and Leeds (1904), and the honorary DCL of McGill University (1903). He was also a member of the Royal Swedish Academy (1898) and received the gold medals for arts and sciences of Hesse (1884) and Saxe-Coburg and Gotha (1893). He died at his house in London, 20 Taviton Street, Tavistock Square, on 28 April 1935, and his remains were cremated at Golders Green on 2 May, after a funeral service at St Marylebone parish church. A memorial service took place at St Paul's Cathedral, on 9 May 1935.

MOIR CARNEGIE, rev. ROSEMARY FIRMAN

Sources MT, 39 (1898), 369–74 · MT, 76 (1935), 497–503 · J. Spencer, 'Mackenzie, Sir Alexander Campbell', *New Grove* · C. Willeby, *Masters of English music* (1893), 103–72 · Brown & Stratton, *Brit. mus.* · F. Corder, *A history of the Royal Academy of Music from 1822 to 1922* (1922) · P. A. Scholes, *The mirror of music, 1844–1944: a century of musical life in Britain as reflected in the pages of the Musical Times*, 2 vols. (1947) · A. Loewenberg, *Annals of opera, 1597–1940*, 3rd edn (1978) · *The Times* (29 April 1935) · D. J. Barker, 'The music of Sir Alexander Campbell Mackenzie, 1847–1935: a critical study', PhD diss., U. Durham, 1999 · D. J. Barker, 'Mackenzie, Sir Alexander Campbell', *New Grove*, 2nd edn · d. cert. · m. cert. · A. C. Mackenzie, *A musician's narrative* (1927) · *CGPLA Eng. & Wales* (1935)

Archives BL, musical compositions, Add. MSS 65509–65520 · FM Cam. · NL Scot., corresp. | BL, letters to Percy Pitt, Egerton MS 3305 · NL Scot., letters to Nicolas Kilburn

Likenesses photographs, *c*.1859–1898, repro. in 'Alexander Campbell Mackenzie', 39 (1 June 1898) · Walery, photograph, pubd 1888, NPG [*see illus.*] · W. Stoneman, photograph, 1922, NPG · R. de l'Hôpital, oils, 1923, Royal Academy of Music, London · R. Haines, photograph, 1930–39, repro. in 'Alexander Campbell Mackenzie', 76 (June 1935) · W. & D. Downey, woodburytype photograph, NPG; repro. in W. Downey and D. Downey, *The cabinet portrait gallery* (1894), vol. 5 · H. Furniss, pen-and-ink sketch, NPG · F. Lion, pencil drawing, NPG · J. Russell & Sons, photograph, NPG · Spy [L. Ward], caricature, repro. in *VF* (14 Jan 1904) · Vandyk, double portrait, photograph (with Edward German), NPG

Wealth at death £22,718 4*s*.: probate, 7 June 1935, *CGPLA Eng. & Wales*

MacKenzie, Alister [Alexander] (1870–1934), golf course architect and medical practitioner, was born at The Orchard, Normanton, near Leeds, on 30 August 1870, the second of six children of Dr William Scobie MacKenzie (*c*.1820–1917), medical practitioner, and his wife, Mary Jane Smith. The family came from Lochinver, Sutherland, where Dr William's father, Alexander (Meal Mhor), managed the duke of Sutherland's Assynt estates. The Scottish connection remained strong and, though baptized Alexander, MacKenzie adopted the Gaelic form Alister.

After schooling, probably at Queen Elizabeth Grammar School, Wakefield, MacKenzie went to Gonville and Caius College, Cambridge, in 1888, intending to study medicine, probably under paternal pressure. He obtained his BA in 1891, with a third in the natural sciences tripos. After moving to Leeds medical school, he showed his unconventionality by extending his undergraduate career to seventeen years. In 1895 he obtained the MRCS and LRCP, which permitted him to practise medicine, but he took only desultory advantage of this. He obtained the Cambridge MB, BCh, in 1897 but in 1905 he was still registered as a Leeds undergraduate and concluded his aimless degree collecting with the Leeds MB, ChB. That year he married Edith Wedderburn; it was a childless union which ended in divorce in 1929.

MacKenzie served in the Second South African War as 'civil surgeon' with the Somerset light infantry, but became more interested in the way that the Boers repeatedly confused the British by intelligent camouflage than he was in any medical matters. On returning to Leeds to study and, occasionally, to practise medicine he started experimenting with golf course design, an activity with many similarities to camouflaging. In August 1914 he won a *Country Life* competition to design a hole for a course on Long Island, New York. A nascent career was, however, stalled almost immediately by the outbreak of the First World War.

As a territorial major, MacKenzie served with the Royal Army Medical Corps in Flanders from the outset, but again it was camouflage rather than medicine which interested him. In *Country Life* (6 March 1915) an article on military entrenchments gave MacKenzie's views on camouflage, criticizing the officers responsible. Court-martial might have resulted; instead he was transferred to the engineers to work on camouflage, albeit at the reduced rank of lieutenant. This marked the end of his transient medical career, though he continued to enjoy using the prefix Dr.

From 1918 MacKenzie's true career, golf course design, blossomed. He was convinced of the enormous medical, social, and cultural benefits of golf, and was an early champion of municipal golf in England: in his book *Golf Architecture* (1920) he wrote that municipal golf courses 'would help enormously in increasing the health, the virility, and the prosperity of the nation, and would do much to counteract discontent and Bolshevism' (p. 119). Contracts came from both sides of the Atlantic and the balance of his work gradually shifted to America. Much of it was done in co-operation with his younger brother Charles, who supervised construction. In 1926 MacKenzie made a remarkably productive trip to Australia, where he left his mark with many distinguished courses, none more so than Royal Melbourne.

In 1929 MacKenzie moved permanently to California and in 1930 he married Hilda (*née* Sykes), widow of Edgar Haddock. They had been friends as students and she brought him two stepsons. His remaining years combined great happiness and achievement. They established a home on the edge of Pasatiempo, one of his own courses. As with Sir Harry Lauder, then popular in American music-halls, American life suited him and he it. Kilted, they flaunted their Scottishness and shared a penchant for pawky but rather feeble jokes.

MacKenzie designed over 100 new courses in all, the majority in California, including the wonderful links at Cypress Point on the Monterey peninsula, which opened in August 1928. It was the latter which brought MacKenzie's work to the attention of Robert Tyre (Bobby) Jones, the greatest of all amateur golfers and controller of a new development at Augusta, Georgia. Jones contracted MacKenzie to design the course, and the undulating Augusta site, which had been established a century earlier as a private estate with many and varied trees and shrubs, gave MacKenzie a unique opportunity to combine the preservation and creation of beauty—his benchmark in all his architectural work.

MacKenzie died from coronary thrombosis at his home, 70 Hollins Drive, Pasatiempo, on 6 January 1934, before the first playing of what would come to be called the masters' championship over the US national course at Augusta. His second wife survived him. He wished to be buried in the family grave at Nedd, near Lochinver, but circumstances precluded this and his ashes were scattered over Pasatiempo course. His name is now on the family stone. Two publications appeared posthumously, *Military Engineer* (on camouflage) and *The Spirit of St Andrews* (on golf).

How great was MacKenzie's achievement? He has been compared to Holbein, to Rembrandt, and to Picasso but perhaps a more apt and appropriate comparison is with another artist of the landscape, Capability Brown. As golf has developed, so has an appreciation of the unique blend of aesthetic, technical, and commercial sensibilities embodied by the best course designers, of whom there has been none greater than Dr Alister MacKenzie.

JAMES S. SCOTT

Sources J. S. Scott, T. Doak, and R. M. Haddock, *Dr Alister MacKenzie and his courses* [forthcoming] • Venn, *Alum. Cant.* • A. MacKenzie, *Golf architecture* (1920) [repr. 1982] • b. cert. • d. cert.
Archives Light Infantry regimental headquarters, Winchester | Stanford University, Hoover Institution
Likenesses I. Bacon, photograph
Wealth at death £184 5s. 9d. in England: probate, 26 Nov 1934, CGPLA Eng. & Wales

McKenzie, Andrew [pseud. Gaelus] (**1780–1839**), poet, was born at Dunover, co. Down, the second son of a small farmer. One of a family of six, his parents struggled to raise and educate him. He attended a local school for a brief period, and at the age of fourteen he began an apprenticeship as a linen weaver. He developed a passion for books, not only reading poetry but also composing verses at the loom. At the age of twenty he began to publish his verses in the *Belfast News-Letter*, under the pseudonym Gaelus. His contributions were well received: he began to establish a reputation in Belfast literary circles and was acclaimed by his fellow weaver poets as 'the Bard of Dunover'.

McKenzie exchanged poetic epistles with Robert Anderson, the Cumberland Bard (1770–1833), who was employed as a calico print designer in Doagh and Carnmoney, co. Antrim, between 1808 and 1818. Anderson, who had himself published *Ballads in the Cumberland Dialect* in 1805, encouraged McKenzie to write in Ulster Scots. In 1810 McKenzie published his first collection, *Poems and Songs, on Different Subjects*, which attracted more than 2000 subscribers, and was favourably reviewed. It earned him over £200.

McKenzie bought a fishing boat and built a cottage at Dunover, which he called Mount Gaelus. Yet catastrophe followed: the fishing boat was wrecked, and he narrowly escaped drowning; and he was evicted from his cottage, because he had failed to secure a lease. He, his wife, and six children found themselves homeless and destitute. He eventually found employment in Belfast as a seller of religious tracts, but never again enjoyed financial security. Despite his poverty, McKenzie published a second collection in 1832, *The Masonic Chaplet*, largely through the support of several lodges of freemasons, of which society he was an enthusiastic member. However, both his health and his fortunes continued to decline. He died in Belfast in extreme poverty on 10 May 1839, and was buried in the Shankill graveyard on 13 May.

McKenzie belongs to the group of Ulster poets known as the rhyming weavers, who wrote in both standard English and vernacular Ulster Scots. His work reveals a tension between his desire for wider literary recognition and his position as a local folk-poet, articulating the hardships, fears, and aspirations of the rural working class. In 'Gannaway Burn' (*Masonic Chaplet*, 34–5) he succeeds in combining pastoral idyll with the use of Ulster Scots to evoke the lost rural landscape of his youth.   IVAN HERBISON

Sources J. Fullarton, 'Sketches of Ulster poets: Andrew McKenzie', *Ulster Magazine*, 2/21 (1861), 374–8 • J. Hewitt, *Rhyming weavers and other country poets of Antrim and Down* (1974) • B. Walker, 'Country letters: some correspondence of Ulster poets of the nineteenth century', *An uncommon bookman: essays in memory of J. R. R. Adams*, ed. J. Gray and W. McCann (1996), 119–39 • I. Herbison, 'A sense of place: landscape and locality in the work of the rhyming weavers', *The poet's place: Ulster literature and society. Essays in honour of John Hewitt, 1907–1987*, ed. G. Dawe and J. Wilson Foster (1991), 63–75 • A. Gailey, 'The Ulster poets and local life', *An uncommon bookman: essays in honour of J. R. R. Adams*, ed. J. Gray and W. McCann (1996), 159–74 • F. J. Bigger, 'Robert Anderson, the Cumberland bard: some notes on his connection with Belfast and Carnmoney, 1808–1818', *Ulster Journal of Archaeology*, new ser., 5 (1898–9), 100–04 • A. McKenzie, *Poems and songs, on different subjects* (1810) • A. McKenzie, *The masonic chaplet, with a few other poems* (1832)
Likenesses engraving, repro. in McKenzie, *Poems and songs*, frontispiece
Wealth at death died in extreme poverty: Fullarton, 'Ulster poets', 378

Mackenzie, Anna [known as Lady Anna Mackenzie], **countess of Balcarres and countess of Argyll** (*c.*1621–1707), noblewoman, was born presumably at Brahan Castle, near Dingwall, the second daughter of Colin *Mackenzie, first earl of Seaforth (d. 1633), and his wife, Lady Margaret (1599–1630), daughter of Alexander Seton, first earl of Dunfermline. Her parents both died when she was a child, and she was sent to live with her cousin Lord Rothes at Leslie in Fife. It was there that she met and fell in love with another cousin, Alexander *Lindsay, master of Balcarres

(1618–1659), a handsome, auburn-haired young man, high-spirited and intelligent. They married in April 1640, despite some opposition from her uncle, the second earl of Seaforth, who would have preferred her to bring him new allies by finding a husband outside the family. Dark and pretty, with large brown eyes, Lady Anna had, according to her father-in-law, a 'mild nature and sweet disposition' (Lindsay, *Memoir*, 14). She also proved to be a devoted wife. In 1641, on the death of his father, her husband inherited his title of Lord Lindsay of Balcarres. Soon afterwards he went to fight in the civil war, initially on the covenanting side, before becoming a supporter of the young Charles II. Lady Lindsay remained at Balcarres, where her first two short-lived sons were born. Soon after Charles II's Scottish coronation in 1651, in connection with which her husband was created earl of Balcarres, she received a visit from the king. He agreed to be godfather to her expected child, a third son, who was subsequently named after him and baptized on 7 February 1651.

Balcarres ruined himself financially by his support of the royal cause, suffering sequestration by parliament, and Countess Anna sold her jewels and her personal possessions to help him. In 1653, although ill, he went to the highlands to try to raise a rebellion against Cromwell. Richard Baxter, the famous presbyterian divine, later told how the countess went with her husband and, 'through dearness of affection, had marched with him and lain out of doors with him on the mountains' (Lindsay, *Memoir*, 34). When Charles II summoned Balcarres to France, to seek his advice about a further expedition to Scotland, Countess Anna went too. Leaving their children at Balcarres, they undertook the perilous journey in disguise, accompanied by their friend Sir Robert Moray, and reached Paris in May 1654. The next few years were spent at the court of the exiled queen mother, Henrietta Maria, but in 1657 they moved to The Hague when Anna was appointed governess to Princess Mary of Orange's small son, the future William III. This gave them some means of maintaining themselves, but by now the earl was seriously ill. His wife nursed him tenderly, but he died in her arms on 30 August 1659. Describing his death, she told a friend, 'I stayed by him and dressed him all myself, which he expected from me—for a month before that he would not eat nor drink but that I gave … At last I closed those dear eyes and that dear mouth I never in all my life heard make a lie' (Lindsay, *Memoir*, 43).

Countess Anna's young son Charles Lindsay was now earl, and in an effort to have the sequestration lifted from his estates she paid a brief visit to London before returning to Balcarres for her husband's burial, which took place on 12 June 1660. Charles II now having been restored, she went south again, spending almost two years in London where, said Baxter, 'her great wisdom, modesty, piety and sincerity made her accounted the saint at the Court' (Lindsay, *Memoir*, 52). Even so, she accomplished little, telling a friend despairingly, 'I am not the present mistress of sixpence' (ibid., 57). Ill with anxiety, she went home again and in October 1662 her troubles were compounded by the death of her son the earl at the age of eleven. He was

succeeded by his younger brother, Colin *Lindsay (1652–1721). Sustained by her strong religious faith and a circle of close friends, Countess Anna struggled on. The king authorized payment of pensions to her in 1664, but she had to wait for at least two years before receiving the money. By then her situation was improving, however, and she gave up claims made by her son to the Seaforth estates in exchange for 80,000 marks (about £4500 sterling). With patient determination, she eventually succeeded in putting the Balcarres finances on a sound basis before making a significant change to her life. While she had been with her husband in the highlands in 1653, one of their companions had been Archibald *Campbell, Lord Lorne (1629–1685). Now ninth earl of Argyll, he had been widowed in 1668. Drawn together by longstanding friendship and shared grief, they decided to marry. The ceremony took place on 28 January 1670 and Countess Anna went to live with her new husband at his castle of Inveraray in Argyll and in his mansion in Stirling, Argyll's Lodging.

When on 19 December 1681 Argyll was sentenced to death for high treason in the wake of his refusal to subscribe to the Test Act, and was imprisoned in Edinburgh Castle, he only escaped execution when Countess Anna's daughter Sophia, who had married one of his sons, smuggled him out of the castle disguised as her page. He managed to slip away to Holland, but his estates were forfeited under attainder, and his wife found herself once more in grave financial difficulties, all her revenues cut off except for a small income from the jointure agreed in her first marriage contract. Sympathetic to her plight, the king granted her 7000 merks (nearly £400) from the Argyll estates, but she lived in straitened circumstances, constantly anxious about her exiled husband. In December 1683 she was summoned before the privy council, who questioned her about some cipher letters apparently implicating him in the Rye House plot. When, in the spring of 1685, he landed in Argyll with an invasion force in support of the duke of Monmouth's rebellion, Anna was immediately arrested and held prisoner in Edinburgh Castle. Very soon afterwards the earl himself was captured and taken there. Countess Anna was allowed to see him briefly for one last time, and his cheerful resolution only faltered when they said goodbye to each other. He was beheaded under his original sentence of death on 30 June 1685.

Released shortly afterwards, Countess Anna continued her undaunted efforts for her family, and played a significant role in keeping the Argyll interest together until the revolution of 1688. Within weeks she was travelling to London on behalf of her exiled son-in-law Sir Duncan Campbell, and she took up once more her all too familiar battle to maintain the Balcarres estates. Her son Colin, the third earl, was imprisoned in 1688 as a leading supporter of James VII and II, and on his release the following year he withdrew to the continent, leaving behind enormous debts. His mother moved to Balcarres, dealt with his financial problems with experience and efficiency, and stayed on after his return in 1700. Six years later, she suffered a

series of strokes and died in the spring of 1707 at the age of about eighty-six. She was buried at Balcarres on 29 May 1707.
                                                            ROSALIND K. MARSHALL

Sources Alexander, Lord Lindsay [A. Lindsay], *A memoir of Lady Anna Mackenzie, countess of Balcarres and afterwards of Argyll, 1621–1706* (1868) · Lord Lindsay [A. W. C. Lindsay, earl of Crawford], *Lives of the Lindsays*, [new edn], 2 (1849) · *The Lauderdale papers*, ed. O. Airy, 3 vols., CS, new ser., 34, 36, 38 (1884–5) · *Scots peerage* · GEC, *Peerage*
Archives BL, Lauderdale corresp.
Likenesses D. Scougal, oils · engraving (after portrait), Scot. NPG

Mackenzie, Anne (1813/14–1877). *See under* Mackenzie, Charles Frederick (1825–1862).

Mackenzie, Basil William Sholto, second Baron Amulree (1900–1983), physician and geriatrician, was born at 57 Harcourt Terrace, Kensington, London, on 25 July 1900, the elder child and only son of William Warrender *Mackenzie, first Baron Amulree (1860–1942), barrister and industrial arbitrator, and secretary of state for air in Ramsay MacDonald's second government, and his wife, Lilian (d. 1916), elder daughter of William Hardwick *Bradbury (1832–1892) of Whitefriars, publisher and printer. After attending Lancing College, Sussex, and Gonville and Caius College, Cambridge (MA, 1925), he qualified MRCS, LRCP, at University College Hospital (UCH), London, in 1925, MRCP in 1928, and MD in 1936. He was assistant pathologist at the Royal Northern Hospital, and later at University College Hospital, before in 1936 joining the Ministry of Health. There he was concerned first with cancer services, and then with the care of the 'chronic sick' in public institutions. Thenceforth the care of old people became his enduring professional concern. Amulree worked with clinicians such as Marjory Warren at the West Middlesex Hospital, J. H. Sheldon in Wolverhampton, Trevor Howell in Croydon, Lionel Cosin in Oxford, and a small group of other pioneers who in 1947 founded the Medical Society for the Care of the Elderly. He was the first president of this society and, until 1973, of its successor, the British Geriatrics Society.

In 1949 Amulree returned to University College Hospital as physician in geriatric medicine (which had become a specialty in the then new National Health Service). At its St Pancras branch, with the help of gifted assistants such as Norman Exton-Smith he established the first teaching hospital geriatric unit in the world. Later, along with Max Rosenheim, he helped to raise funds for the establishment at UCH of the first chair of geriatric medicine in London. Exton-Smith became foundation professor in 1972.

Well before Amulree's retirement in 1966, geriatric medicine had become famous as a British invention. It soon spread across the world, attracting many visitors to the UK. Despite changes in public policy, for the better and for the worse, the essential philosophy of geriatric medicine as set out in Amulree's *Adding Life to Years* (1951) has endured: careful diagnostic and functional assessment of even the most 'unpromising' patients, appropriate treatment, and multi-professional rehabilitation, whenever possible helping old people to stay in their own homes,

alongside good long-stay care for those who need it. Amulree's qualities and his standing (and, as he used to say, his seat in the House of Lords) resulted in his becoming chairman or president of the Attendance Allowance Board, the Association of Occupational Therapists, the Society of Chiropodists, the Association of Welfare Officers, the Society for the Study of Medical Ethics, the London county division of the British Red Cross, and the London Medical Group. He became FRCP in 1946, and later honorary FRCGP, as well as an honorary member of the Faculty (later Royal College) of Radiologists. In 1977 he was made KBE for services to health and welfare. In the Lords he was Liberal whip from 1955 to 1977. He was a keen European and spoke excellent French.

A bachelor, Amulree lived in some style at 18 Egerton Terrace, London, where he was a generous host. Around him were his books—including the copy of William Harvey's *De motu cordis* that had belonged to his uncle, Sir James *Mackenzie (1853–1925), who famously analysed the irregularities of the pulse—and his pictures and ceramics. He knew Picasso and Graham Sutherland, and his collection included works by them, and by Braque, Monet, and Matisse, along with drawings by Guercino and Tiepolo, most of which he later bequeathed to galleries around the world. Shy and modest, he was forceful when it came to causes which mattered to him. Amulree was devoted to his friends, who enjoyed his conversation, especially on his beloved Impressionists. He mastered a stammer, especially when he was among his friends. George Adams, another pioneer of geriatrics, described him in appearance as 'something of a Lord Peter Wimsey': tall, erect, with monocle, he had a shock of very fair—later white—hair falling over his forehead. Always his eyes were kindly.

Amulree retired to Cranbrook, Kent, and continued to take an interest in health and welfare. A hobby was his research on monastic infirmaries before 1700, and he wrote on hygiene conditions in ancient Rome. He remained a writer of letters, to friends and to *The Times*: in the latter he suggested in 1978 that Buckingham Palace might occasionally be opened to the public—a proposal that was firmly put down in a riposte from a court official. In this as in other things he was forward-looking.

Amulree died on 15 December 1983, of colon cancer, in the Kent and Sussex Hospital, Tunbridge Wells. The barony became extinct. His substantial residuary estate he left to causes to do with old people, and to University College Hospital for an Amulree travelling studentship, stipulating that 'no person to whom a grant shall be made shall be under any obligation to make any report on what he or she has done during his or her travel abroad', and that 'the Trustees of the Fund are not to be unduly influenced by the athletic prowess of the person selected' (will, 1983). There were also bequests to the Amulree ward at the Ipswich and East Suffolk Hospital and to the Amulree Day Hospital at St Mary's Hospital, Portsmouth.

                                                            TOM ARIE

Sources private information (2004) · Munk, *Roll* · personal knowledge (2004) · British Geriatrics Society, London, Amulree MSS ·

DNB · *BMJ* (7 Jan 1984), 156 · *The Lancet* (7 Jan 1984) · *The Times* (16 Dec 1983) · b. cert. · d. cert. · *CGPLA Eng. & Wales* (1984) · will, proved Brighton, 1983 · *WWW*
Archives British Geriatrics Society, London, cuttings and letters
Likenesses R. Piper, oils, British Geriatrics Society, London
Wealth at death £1,267,932: probate, 9 April 1984, *CGPLA Eng. & Wales*

Mackenzie, Charles Frederick (1825–1862), bishop of central Africa, born at Harcus Cottage, Portmore, Peeblesshire, on 10 April 1825, was youngest child of Colin Mackenzie (*d.* 1830) of Portmore, a clerk of session, an Episcopalian, and one of Scott's friends and colleagues. His mother was Elizabeth, daughter of Sir William *Forbes, sixth baronet (1739–1806), of Pitsligo. William Forbes *Mackenzie (1807–1862) was his brother. After his father's death in 1830 he was brought up by his eldest sister, Elizabeth, attending first a private school and then Edinburgh Academy and, from 1840, the Grange School, Bishopwearmouth, near Sunderland, where he revealed a talent for mathematics. He went into residence as a pensioner of St John's College, Cambridge, in October 1844, but, finding that he would as a Scot be disqualified from holding a fellowship there, moved the next May to Gonville and Caius College. He read diligently, and in January 1848 was placed second wrangler in the mathematical tripos, Isaac Todhunter being senior. He graduated BA in 1848 and MA in 1851. From 1848 to 1862 he was fellow of and became a tutor there. Tall, well made, and muscular, he delighted in athletic exercise, was an oarsman and cricketer, and rowed and played cricket with the undergraduates of the college after his election as fellow. In May 1848 he was appointed one of the secretaries to the Cambridge board of education, and held that office until 1855. He was ordained deacon on Trinity Sunday 1851, and from October 1851 to 1854 was curate at Haslingfield, Cambridgeshire, while continuing his college work. In 1852 he was an examiner for mathematical honours, and was moderator in 1853–4, publishing in 1854 with William Walton *Solutions of the Problems and Riders Proposed in the Senate-House Examination for 1854*.

Although anxious to become a missionary Mackenzie yielded to friends' advice, and in 1853 refused an invitation to join the Delhi mission, but in December 1854 accepted the offer of John William Colenso, bishop of Natal, to take him to Natal as his archdeacon. Accompanied by his elder sister Anne he embarked with Colenso on 7 March 1855. For about a year and a half he acted as parish priest to the English settlers at Durban, meeting strong opposition from his congregation, who disapproved of his use of the surplice—'preaching in a surplice appeared to some to be only Popery in disguise' (Goodwin, 124)—and other changes made in accordance with Colenso's wish. An opposition service was started, conducted by a layman. His sister Alice joined him in 1857, and after taking part in the Umlazi mission he was established at a post on the Umhlali River about 40 miles north of Durban, where he worked hard ministering to the scattered English settlers, the soldiers quartered in the neighbourhood, and a small

Charles Frederick Mackenzie (1825–1862), by unknown photographer, late 1850s

congregation of Africans. He was appointed salaried chaplain to the troops in 1858. In the church conference held at Pietermaritzburg in April he advocated the right of black congregations to an equal voice with white congregations in the proposed church synod, and being defeated retired from the conference. After a severe attack of illness he returned to England in the summer of 1859. In November after David Livingstone's appeal in speeches at Oxford and Cambridge universities, he accepted the invitation of the delegates of the new Universities' Mission to central Africa to be head of their mission. The upper house of convocation having in June 1860 approved the appointment of missionary bishops, and desiring that Mackenzie be ordained bishop by the bishop of Cape Town and his comprovincials, he sailed from England—with a presentiment that he would never return—on 6 October, arriving at the Cape on 12 November, and was consecrated bishop of central Africa in Cape Town Cathedral on 1 January 1861.

After a visit to Natal Mackenzie met Livingstone at Kongoni, and was persuaded by him to ascend the Rovuma, in an attempt to reach the Shire district without passing through territory claimed by the Portuguese. The river proved unnavigable and he finally ascended the Zambezi and Shire rivers. Marching into the Shire highlands under Livingstone's conduct, they encountered a party of eighty-four slaves, mainly women and children, being driven for sale in the Zambezi valley. On Livingstone's initiative the group was liberated and presented to the bishop as his first congregation. This intervention, followed by others which over the next few days brought the number under his protection to 177, determined in two ways all else that befell the mission. First, in a region torn by wars generated by the Indian Ocean slave trade, it committed Mackenzie to use force in defence of his clients. No sooner had their party been settled by Livingstone at Magomero, they were persuaded by a council of Mangania chiefs and headmen to protect Mangania territory from incursions by Yao slavers. After binding the chiefs not to enslave any captives they might make, and to discourage slavery, Mackenzie and his party joined in the war. Their help enabled their allies to win two victories which added more refugees to their settlement.

The second consequence of such a beginning was that Mackenzie and his party were themselves widely believed to be slavers. The bishop interpreted the wars as 'tribal' and understood his own actions as giving support to the secular authority of his diocese. In practice, the whole region had passed under the control of warlords, who fought with each other irrespective of 'tribe', and whom the missionaries by seizing clients and building a stockade appeared to be imitating. Their numbers dropped as their people, fearing to be sold as slaves, abandoned Magomero. In December, when three of his party were exploring a shorter route to the Shire, they were attacked under the impression that they were slavers at the village of Mangasanja and two men and some goods seized. Mackenzie engaged the help of the Makololo people, and set out on 23 October 1861 to punish those he believed to be the aggressors, burnt Mangasanja, and recovered the missing men. He then had to hasten to the confluence of the Ruo and the Shire, where Livingstone had arranged to meet him with stores on 1 January 1862. On their way he and his companion, an ordained missionary, lost their medicines by the upsetting of a boat, and Mackenzie pushed on without them. He arrived too late to meet Livingstone, and died at Malo Island of a fever on 31 January. He was buried on Malo Island. In January 1863 Livingstone visited Mackenzie's grave and erected a cross over it. A fund raised in Mackenzie's memory was applied to the establishment in 1870 of the see of Zululand.

Mackenzie was nearly 6 feet in height, with a pleasant expression, rather small eyes, and a forehead which, naturally large, appeared larger owing to early baldness. In manner he was winning and gentle, unselfish, and full of vigour. The controversies which drove him from Natal anticipated many of the conflicts between visiting missionaries and the settler church which have dogged Anglicanism in South Africa until recently. In the Shire highlands, his actions show him to have been profoundly innocent of the problems of the region and the complexities of his position.

Charles Mackenzie's elder sister **Anne Mackenzie** (1813/14–1877) for several years accompanied him, and 'her life entwined itself around his work' (Awdry, 3). Born presumably in Edinburgh or at Harcus Cottage, Portmore, Peeblesshire, she was educated at home and 'attended classes'. An invalid, 'always ailing, often very ill … there seemed no special niche in life for her' (Awdry, 33). After her mother's death she lived mainly in lodgings, sometimes in Edinburgh, sometimes at the seaside, with her maid.

In 1854, advised for her health to live in a milder climate, Anne Mackenzie accepted her brother Charles's invitation to accompany him to Natal. She was never a professed missionary, and was initially unenthusiastic about missionary work and did not consider being a missionary 'as quite a gentleman's profession' (Awdry, 35). A conventional middle-aged spinster—at forty-two reportedly one of the oldest European women in the colony—she found colonial life difficult. White ants destroyed property, Africans put rancid grease on their skins, and 'the Kafir smell, as she calls it, made her sick, or faint' (ibid., 64), and African girls were 'sad romps, knowing nothing of the duty of modesty' (ibid., 56). Nevertheless she kept house for her brother, 'made him a comfortable home' (Goodwin, 134), and tried to maintain her 'dainty ways'. She helped with his pastoral tasks, preferring to work with settlers rather than Africans. In 1857 they were joined by their sister Alice, and in 1859 Anne and her brother returned to England. In 1860 they went back to the Cape. In 1861 he went to Magomero while she remained in Cape Town intending to join him later.

In December 1861 Anne Mackenzie and Mrs Burrup, the young bride of Henry Burrup, Mackenzie's fellow missionary, with their maids, travelled on a brig to join Mackenzie's party. After delays and vicissitudes, at Kongoni, at the mouth of the Zambezi, they met Livingstone, later than planned. He did not want them to come—he wrote that 'most high church people lean on wives or sisters' (Jeal, 302)—and he was 'rather abrupt and ungracious' (Awdry, 232) to Miss Mackenzie. They started up the Zambezi in Livingstone's boat, the *Pioneer*. The journey was unhappy. Dr John Kirk considered Miss Mackenzie 'an old invalid who had followed him [her brother] through some sort of fanatical infatuation' (Jeal, 306). She disliked Mary Livingstone—Livingstone's embittered, heavy-drinking wife—as she considered Mrs Livingstone's criticism of missionaries an attack on her brother. There were quarrels, Livingstone was angry, and the sailors got drunk and enjoyed African women. Miss Mackenzie and Mrs Burrup transferred to a naval open gig under Captain Wilson RN, of the paddle-frigate *Gorgon*, who was helping the expedition. Miss Mackenzie was ill with fever. On 3 March she learned her brother had died. She returned ill to Cape Town and thence to Edinburgh.

Anne Mackenzie resided with friends at Havant, Hampshire. She collected funds for Bishop Gray's Zululand 'Mackenzie mission', named after her brother, and published an edition of her late friend Mrs Robertson's letters, *Mission Life among the Zulu-Kafirs: Memorials of Henrietta Robertson* (1866). From 1866 she edited a small missionary periodical, *The Net*. She also taught Sunday school. 'A person of very decided opinions … a fair fragile lady, tenderly refined, and old rather with sorrow than with years' (Awdry, 257–8), she died aged 62 on 12 February 1877 at Woodfield, Havant.

WILLIAM HUNT, *rev.* LANDEG WHITE

Sources H. Goodwin, *Memoir of Bishop Mackenzie*, 2nd edn (1865) • O. Chadwick, *Mackenzie's grave* (1959) • L. White, *Magomero: portrait of an African village* (1987) • Venn, *Alum. Cant.* • Boase, *Mod. Eng. biog.* • *Manchester Guardian* (2 July 1862) • F. Awdry, *An elder sister: a short sketch of Anne Mackenzie, and her brother the missionary bishop* (1878) • T. Jeal, *Livingstone* (1975) • d. cert. [Anne Mackenzie]
Archives Bodl. RH
Likenesses photograph, 1856–9, Bodl. RH [*see illus.*] • Dalziel, woodcut, BM • Richmond?, oils, Gon. & Caius Cam. • engraving, repro. in Goodwin, *Memoir* (1865)

Mackenzie, Colin (d. **1594**). *See under* Mackenzie family of Kintail (*per. c.*1475–1611).

Mackenzie, Colin, of Kintail, first earl of Seaforth (*c.***1597–1633**), nobleman, was the eldest son of Kenneth *Mackenzie, first Lord Mackenzie of Kintail (*d.* 1611) [*see under* Mackenzie family of Kintail], and his wife, Jean (*d.* 1604), daughter of George Ross of Balnagowan. Following the death of his father, on 27 February 1611 his minority was dispensed with 'by royal precept', and he inherited estates in the Isle of Lewis and Ross-shire. On 5 June 1614 his political connections were secured by his marriage to Lady Margaret Seton (1599–1630), daughter of Alexander *Seton, first earl of Dunfermline (1556–1622), lord chancellor of Scotland, and his first wife, Lilias Drummond. In August 1616 he was appointed JP for Elgin, Forres, and Nairn, a commission renewed on 20 August 1623. He sat as a lord of the Scottish parliament in June 1617 and August 1621, when he voted against ratifying the five articles of Perth.

Having been created earl of Seaforth on 3 December 1623, he continued to serve as justice and to improve the administration of his estates in Lewis, Kintail, Lochalsh, Lochcarron, Strathconnon, and Lochbrune. He generated controversy in June 1628 when he proposed that Stornoway in Lewis be converted into a royal burgh: this plan was vigorously challenged and defeated by the convention of royal burghs, on the grounds that Seaforth was illegally employing Dutch colonists instead of lowland Scots. His other development projects were less provocative. Reputed to have been 'a most religious & vertuous Lord' (NL Scot., Adv. MS 34.6.27, fol. 27r), committed to kirk plantation and ministerial maintenance in the highlands, by the end of his life he had built churches in each of his baronies, and endowed Chanonry with 4000 merks Scots to establish a grammar school.

Seaforth attended the king at Whitehall in 1629, and was again summoned to court on 3 December 1630, remaining until at least 14 July 1631, when he complained that his brother-in-law Lord Reay had falsely accused him of criticizing the earl of Menteith; despite this accusation, Charles permitted him to travel to Essex to recuperate from an undisclosed sickness, and further bolstered his reputation by proclaiming him 'the best archer in Britain' (Mackenzie, 246). After a long illness Seaforth died at his family seat in Chanonry, Ross-shire, on 15 April 1633, and

was buried at Chanonry church on 28 May, having been predeceased by his wife (1630) and son, Alexander (1629). His daughters, Jean and Anna *Mackenzie, were declared his heir-portioners on 29 November 1636, while his title passed to his half-brother, George *Mackenzie, second earl of Seaforth (*d.* 1651).   J. R. M. SIZER

Sources A. Mackenzie, *History of the Mackenzies, with genealogies of the principal families of the name*, new edn (1894) • *Scots peerage* • D. Warrand, *Some Mackenzie pedigrees* (1965), 15–16 • GEC, *Peerage* • *Reg. PCS*, 1st ser., 10.619; 12.558n.; 13.349 • *Reg. PCS*, 2nd ser., 1.60–61, 426; 2.336–7, 357, 396–7; 3.479–80; 4.106–7 • 'History of the Mackenzies', NL Scot., Adv. MS 34.6.27, fol. 27r • NA Scot., Seaforth MSS, GD 46/18/138 • NL Scot., Adv. MS 24.2.12, fol. 167 • NL Scot., MS 7002, fol. 29 • *APS*, 1593–1625, 525 • M. Lee, *The road to revolution: Scotland under Charles I, 1625–1637* (1985), 102–3 • F. J. Grant, *Index to genealogies, birthbriefs and funeral escutcheons recorded in the Lyon office*, Scottish RS, 31 (1908), 49
Archives NA Scot., Seaforth muniments, GD 46 | NL Scot., Advocates MSS, 34.6.27
Wealth at death eroded by litigation with earl of Argyll over 'the superiority of Moidart and Arisaig': Mackenzie, *History*, 241–2

Mackenzie, Colin (1753–1821), military engineer and surveyor, was born at Stornoway, Isle of Lewis, in the Outer Hebrides, one of four children of Murdoch Mackenzie, merchant and postmaster, and his wife, Barbara. Little is known of his early life. His friend Alexander Johnston (1775–1849), referred to his mathematical skills and to his interest in 'Oriental researches' (Phillimore, 1.349), and to the patronage of Lord Seaforth and of Johnston's maternal grandfather, Lord Napier. Mackenzie was appointed comptroller of customs in Lewis, but took leave (to January 1783), seeking service in India. A Colin Mackenzie is reported sailing on the *Deptford*, which reached India in 1782, and Johnston refers to a visit to Madura early in 1783, but official records and his own account suggest that he did not arrive in India until August 1783, on the *Argos*. He was appointed ensign in the East India Company's infantry on 16 May 1783 and almost at once transferred to the engineers. He was promoted lieutenant (1789), captain (1793), major (1806), brevet lieutenant-colonel (1809), regimental lieutenant-colonel (1810), and full colonel (1819).

Johnston attributes Mackenzie's historical interests to his meeting Hindu scholars in Madura, through Johnston's mother, Hester. Mackenzie was 'methodical to the last degree', often to the detriment of his health, and 'never to be hurried' (Phillimore, 2.421). Being 'stiff but estimable' (ibid., 427), he had 'little … inclination for social life, though he had a large circle of friends' (R. H. Phillimore, 'Introduction', W. C. Mackenzie, *Colonel Colin Mackenzie, First Surveyor-General of India*, 1952, ix). His tact and loyalty were particularly evident with Indian assistants.

After surveying in Dindigul (1784) and Nellore (1787), in 1788 Mackenzie conducted a survey of roads across a large tract of the northern Carnatic, at his own expense. The chief engineer called for 'a mark of approbation and compensation' (Phillimore, vol. 1), thus setting a precedent. Attached to General Medows's troops in the Third Anglo-Mysore War (1790–92), Mackenzie breached forts he later surveyed, and was several times mentioned in dispatches.

Colin Mackenzie (1753–1821), by Thomas Hickey, 1816

He was appointed engineer and surveyor in Hyderabad, and for much of the 1790s worked towards a map of the Deccan, interrupted by the siege of Pondicherry (1793) and the expedition to Ceylon (1795). He gathered a small team of assistants, including several Indians, mostly paid by himself. In 1798–9, in the last war against Mysore, Mackenzie's knowledge of the country, plus his advance surveying, quickened the Hyderabad army's long march to join Arthur Wellesley. At Seringapatam a near ambush cemented his friendship with Wellesley, who claimed he 'never saw a more zealous, a more diligent, or a more useful officer'. Mackenzie's 'bravery and *sangfroid* in action were proverbial' (Phillimore, 1.351), and his engineering played a crucial part in the defeat of Tipu Sultan.

Mackenzie then argued that effective government needed a fundamental survey. Set the task, he spent six months in preparation, helped by John Mather, a pioneering surveyor of Baramahal and Salem. Mackenzie's design was both mathematical (using astronomical observations and triangulation, in advance of but in co-operation with William Lambton's trigonometrical survey) and physical, meaning historical, natural-historical, social, political, and economic. The resulting Mysore survey (1799–1808), was a struggle against climate, illness, local conditions, inadequate staff, lack of funds, and fickle backing. Mackenzie persevered doggedly, even ruthlessly, confident he

would be vindicated by results. In its mathematical aspect the Mysore survey was surpassed by Lambton's broad, superficial measurement. In its physical elements, in method, range and depth, it was the model for the future.

Mackenzie held a sinecure in Madras, to arrange and analyse his materials and prepare maps and reports (1808), and was appointed Madras surveyor-general in 1810, with overall control despite a disagreement over military surveying with the quartermaster-general, Valentine Blacker. In 1811 he was chief engineer to the expedition to Java, and personally reconnoitred landing-places; tall (6ft 2in.) and energetic, he once outpaced pursuers under fire. After the fall of Java he prepared, with some Madras staff, a characteristically thorough geographical and statistical report (1811–13). On 18 November 1812 he married Petronella Jacomina Bartels, a Dutch woman born in Ceylon, and then took his first and only period of long leave, setting up house in Calcutta with his wife and her sister. He also travelled, without his wife, across northern India in 1814, viewing the Himalayas (which he immediately wanted to survey), taking his usual copious notes and collecting manuscripts, coins, and inscriptions.

Mackenzie returned to Madras in 1814, but in 1815 was appointed surveyor-general of India. Until 1817 he delayed returning to Calcutta, while he planned the new office, organized work in Madras, and arranged for assistants to accompany him. He found Calcutta debilitating, and was increasingly unwell, but defined and defended his office energetically. He completed a general report on fifty years' surveying. He sought centralization while insisting on delegation, though he failed to incorporate the trigonometrical survey (finally brought in under George Everest in 1830). Mackenzie's vision of the survey was continued, despite a brief interregnum under Blacker, by the appointment as surveyor-general of John Hodgson, whom Mackenzie had met and praised in 1814.

Mackenzie often felt undervalued, and spent much time claiming allowances and expenses he believed due to him; but his personal interest was often hard to separate from his institution-building. Some of his problems were caused by retrenchment, some by misunderstanding, notably by James Rennell (1742–1830), a great surveyor but one who, advising the company in London, failed to appreciate Mackenzie's (and Lambton's) new standards and ambitions. Mackenzie succeeded by preparation and organization, by completeness, standardization, and record-keeping, and by professionalism, training, and creating formal structures. During the Mysore survey, as his staff were withdrawn, he made effective use of India-born European or Eurasian apprentices from the Madras surveying school founded by Michael Topping in 1794. Like Topping, but unlike Lambton, he saw them as starting a cadre of trained surveyors. In Bengal, until Mackenzie took charge, the employment of Indian, Eurasian, or India-born European surveyors was forbidden. Several of his Madras apprentices, and, under his influence, many from the orphanage at Kidderpore, Bengal, had successful careers in the service.

Mackenzie's concerns with surveying in depth and with history and religion, and his lack of Indian languages, brought him into close contact with Indian informants and collaborators. He wrote that it was only after returning from Ceylon in 1796 that he found the means of undertaking historical work. A young Brahman scholar, Kavali Venkata Boriah (d. 1803), introduced him to 'Hindu knowledge'; his brothers, especially K. V. Lakshmaiah, were remembered in Mackenzie's will. Mackenzie claimed credit for discovering the distinctiveness of Jainism, subdivisions of other religious sects, the usefulness of inscriptions (particularly to understand land tenures), and the significance of ancient stones, trophies, and burial mounds, publishing his findings in a number of journals, including *Asiatick Researches* and the *Journal of the Royal Asiatic Society*. Mackenzie's collections in Madras (especially modern Indian languages), and at the British Library (classical and European languages), comprise thousands of inscriptions, tracts, and artefacts which are invaluable for studying Indian and Javanese history and culture. Much was sent to England during his lifetime, and after his death, near Calcutta, on 8 May 1821, the company purchased his remaining materials for Rs 100,000 (about £10,000). He was buried in the south cemetery, Park Street, Calcutta. His wife survived him.

Although he produced historical memoirs, catalogues, notes, drawings, and paintings, Mackenzie and his collaborators did not publish much. Among others, Arrowsmith's *Atlas* (1822), and that of John Walker (1825), incorporated Mackenzie's work. His chief contributions were the preservation of materials, and the development of the survey as an important institution of government.

P. G. ROBB

Sources R. H. Phillimore, ed., *Historical records of the survey of India*, 1–3 (1945–54) • M. H. Edney, *Mapping an empire: the geographical construction of British India, 1765–1843* (1997) • D. Hill, 'Biographical sketch of the literary career of the late Colonel Colin Mackenzie', *Journal of the Royal Asiatic Society of Great Britain and Ireland*, 1 (1834), 333–64 • W. C. Mackenzie, *Colonel Colin Mackenzie, first surveyor-general of India* (1952) • P. Robb, 'Completing "our Stock of Geography", or an object "still more sublime": Colin Mackenzie's survey of Mysore, 1799–1810', *Journal of the Royal Asiatic Society of Great Britain and Ireland*, 3rd ser., 8 (1998), 181–206 • N. B. Dirks, 'Colonial histories and native informants: biography of an archive', *Orientalism and the postcolonial predicament: perspectives on South Asia*, ed. C. Breckenridge and P. van der Veer (1994), 279–313 • N. B. Dirks, 'Guiltless spoilations', *Perceptions of South Asia's visual past*, ed. C. B. Asher and T. R. Metcalfe (1995), 211–32 • T. V. Mahalingam, *Mackenzie manuscripts*, 1 (1972) [in Government Oriental Manuscripts Library, Madras] • 'Biographical sketch of the literary career of the late Colonel Colin Mackenzie', *Madras Journal of Literature and Science*, 2 (1835), 262–90; 354–69 [extracted from *Journal of the Royal Asiatic Society for Great Britain and Ireland*, 1, (1835)] • H. M. Vibart, *The military engineer in India*, 1 (1881) • Lord Teignmouth [C. J. Shore], *Reminiscences of many years*, 2 vols. (1878) • J. Blakiston, *Twelve years of military adventure in three quarters of the globe*, 1 (1829) • DNB • *Register of graves of the Mission, Tiretta, North and South cemeteries in Park Street, Calcutta* (Calcutta, 1900)

Archives BL OIOC, MS collection • Church of Scotland foreign mission committee, Edinburgh, MSS, deed box 2 • Government Oriental Manuscripts Library, Madras | BL, Add. MSS 9868, 9871, 13582, 13660, 13663, 14380, 26102B • Bodl. Oxf., MS Add. C. 91 • National Archives of India, New Delhi, Survey of India memoirs • NL Scot., corresp. with John Leyden • NL Wales, Clive MS 50

Likenesses T. Hickey, oils, 1816, BL OIOC [*see illus.*]

Wealth at death over RS72,000: Phillimore, ed., *Historical records*, vol. 3 • over £30,000: Phillimore, ed., *Historical records*, vol. 3

Mackenzie, Colin (1806–1881), army and political officer in India, born in London on 25 March 1806, was the penultimate son of Kenneth Francis Mackenzie (1748–1831) and his wife, Anne, *née* Townsend (d. 1846). His father, of the Redcastle branch of Mackenzies, was a barrister, plantation owner, and attorney-general of Grenada, where he lost much during the slave rebellion of 1795–6. Colin was educated at a school in Cumberland, at Dollar Academy, and at the Revd Dr Donne's school in Oswestry, and in 1825 he was appointed a cadet in the Madras army. He served in the 10th and later the 48th Madras native infantry.

One of Mackenzie's brothers became secretary of the Polish Association and in 1831 Mackenzie, on leave, attempted unsuccessfully to join the Polish rising. In May 1832 he married Adeline (b. 1812), eldest daughter of James Pattle of the Bengal civil service. They had three daughters, and she died in May 1836. Mackenzie was Church of Scotland then, following the Disruption, Free Church, and from about 1836 a committed evangelical, a friend of missionaries and converts and 'every free and evangelical church' (Smith, 196).

Mackenzie served successfully in the 1834 Coorg campaign, partly as deputy assistant quartermaster-general. In 1836 he volunteered to accompany Captain Chads on HM frigate *Andromache* to the Malacca straits to suppress Malay piracy. Although he was officially a 'passenger', his bravery earned the praise of Chads and afterwards of Lord Auckland, governor-general of India, who in 1840 selected him for service in British-occupied Afghanistan.

Mackenzie was first an assistant political agent under George Clerk at Peshawar. From there he went to Kabul, where he joined the sappers raised by his friend George Broadfoot. In October 1841 Mackenzie accompanied the advance guard of Sale's brigade as far as Khurd Kabul, then returned to Kabul, where he commanded a very weak detached godown fort on the outskirts of the city, containing the commissariat grain of Shah Shuja's troops. During the Kabul insurrection in November, unreinforced, he bravely defended it for two days then, short of ammunition, he and his garrison at night fought their way back to the cantonments. Sir John Kaye called their defence 'one of the most honourable incidents of the war' (Kaye, 2.194).

On 23 December Mackenzie, as one of Sir William Macnaghten's political agents, attended the meeting between Macnaghten and Akbar Khan. Mackenzie and Eldred Pottinger, suspecting treachery, had tried to dissuade Macnaghten from attending. Macnaghten was shot by Akbar, and Mackenzie and George Lawrence were taken prisoner and later freed. During the 1842 retreat from Kabul, Mackenzie tried to stimulate the efforts of the senior officers. It was agreed that hostages be given to Akbar, and Pottinger selected Mackenzie: so from 8 January he was one of Akbar's prisoners. This probably saved his life, as almost everyone who continued on the retreat died. Because of his religious life the Afghans called him the English Mullah and trusted him. While a hostage he was twice sent by Akbar with letters to Sir George Pollock at Jalalabad. On these missions he had narrow escapes, and after the second he almost died from typhus. He was subsequently carried off by Akbar with the other prisoners, and they were being taken over the Hindu Kush to be sent to Bukhara and there sold as slaves when, owing to Akbar's defeat and flight in September, the Afghan in charge of them was induced by a promise of a large sum to release them. Later in September Mackenzie took part in the capture of the fort of Istalif, then in October returned with Pollock's army to India. Like others (except the Jalalabad garrison) connected with the Anglo-Afghan War, Mackenzie incurred the hostility of the new governor-general, Lord Ellenborough. He was refused the Kabul medal and the accompanying six months' pay, and it was not until 1853 that, through the intervention of Lord Dalhousie, it was granted to him.

In November 1843 Mackenzie married Helen Catharine (b. c.1819), eldest daughter of Admiral John Erskine Douglas. She shared his religious convictions, and wrote *Life in the Camp, the Mission and the Zenana* (1853), the biography of her husband, *Storms and Sunshine of a Soldier's Life* (1884), and other works. She survived him.

Mackenzie was subsequently employed at Ludhiana on the north-west frontier to raise and train a Sikh regiment (the 4th), with which he kept peace on the border during the Anglo-Sikh War of 1848–9. He met Lord Dalhousie, who valued his conduct in the Anglo-Afghan War, his character, and talents, and 'always showed Mackenzie marked friendship' (Mackenzie, 2.46). Reportedly on his advice Dalhousie decided against ceding to Afghanistan the country between the Indus and the Sulaiman range. Mackenzie urged that Peshawar was the gate of India, and so should not be given up. He was still a regimental captain when, in 1850, he was appointed by Dalhousie brigadier-general commanding the Ellichpur division of the Hyderabad contingent. The nizam's payment for the Hyderabad contingent being in arrears, Dalhousie ordered that Berar be taken under British control. Mackenzie achieved this in 1853, peacefully, effectively, and, according to Dalhousie, 'without shedding a drop of blood or losing a rupee of revenue' (Mackenzie, 2.86).

At Bolarum in September 1855, during the Muharram religious festival, 3rd cavalry sepoys, defying orders, processed noisily past Mackenzie's house. He went out unarmed and was attacked, sabred, and dangerously wounded. The government acknowledged his bravery but condemned his action as 'intemperate'. This controversial judgment adversely affected his career. He was compelled by his wounds to go to England, was there when the mutiny began, and returned to India in December 1857. From 1858 to 1862 he held the political appointment of governor-general's agent with the nawab nazim of Bengal at Murshidabad, but in difficult relations with the nawab did not receive from government the support he believed

due; the government disapproved of his conduct and dismissed him. Disappointed in his career, he was, inappropriately, from 1862 to 1864 superintendent of army clothing. He hoped for another appointment but was again disappointed. When he requested a Madras divisional command the commander-in-chief refused on the ground of the censure over the Bolarum case. Francis, Lord Napier, governor of Madras, disapproved of the decision and referred it to the secretary of state, who declined to intervene. Mackenzie was made CB in 1867.

In 1873 Mackenzie finally left India and returned to England. He resided in Kensington and, despite illness, devoted himself to religious and philanthropic causes including the Bible Society, the Evangelical Alliance, the Lord's Day Observance Society, the Anti-Slavery Society, and Frances Power Cobbe's Victoria Street anti-vivisection society; she described him as 'a noble old hero' (*Life*, 647). In 1878 he opposed, in the *Daily News* and elsewhere, the government's intervention in Afghanistan (which led to the Second Anglo-Afghan War). A devout Christian and a brave soldier, Mackenzie died at The Hitchel, St Margaret's Road, Edinburgh, on 23 October 1881, and was buried at the nearby Grange cemetery.

A. J. ARBUTHNOT, *rev.* ROGER T. STEARN

Sources H. Mackenzie, *Storms and sunshine of a soldier's life*, 2 vols. (1884) · G. Smith, *Twelve Indian statesmen* (1897) · J. W. Kaye, *History of the war in Afghanistan*, 3rd edn, 2 (1874) · G. Lawrence, *Reminiscences of forty-three years in India* (1874) · J. A. Norris, *The First Afghan War, 1838–1842* (1967) · P. Macrory, *Signal catastrophe: the story of a disastrous retreat from Kabul, 1842* (1966); repr. as *Kabul catastrophe* (1986) · H. M. Durand, *The First Afghan War and its causes* (1879) · *ILN* (12 Nov 1881) · *Life of Frances Power Cobbe as told by herself*, [another edn] (1904) · *CGPLA Eng. & Wales* (1882) · R. T. Stearn, '"Most noble Colin": Colin Mackenzie, 1806–81', *Soldiers of the Queen*, 81 (1995)
Likenesses photogravure, repro. in Mackenzie, *Storms and sunshine of a soldier's life*, vol. 1, frontispiece · wood-engraving (after photograph by Bassano), NPG; repro. in *ILN*, 79, 464
Wealth at death £8341 0s. 9d.: confirmation, 27 Aug 1882, *CCI*

Mackenzie, Sir (Edward Montague Anthony) Compton (1883–1972), writer, was born on 17 January 1883 at West Hartlepool, co. Durham, the eldest in the family of two sons and three daughters of Edward Compton Mackenzie (1854–1918) [see Compton, Edward], the founder and actor–manager of the Compton Comedy Company, and his wife, Virginia Frances *Bateman (1853–1940) [see under Bateman, Hezekiah Linthicum], daughter of Hezekiah Linthicum *Bateman of Baltimore. Edward Compton was the son of Henry *Compton (1805–1877), the actor, whose real name was Charles Mackenzie. One of Compton Mackenzie's sisters was Fay *Compton (1894–1978), the actress, who was a star in the plays of J. M. Barrie in the 1920s.

Monty, as he became known, was an imaginative and sensitive child, and the theatrical and bohemian milieu in which he grew up had a profound effect in determining both his flamboyant personality and his life. His prodigious output as a writer was in large part the result of his formidable powers of memory: he claimed to have total

Sir (Edward Montague Anthony) Compton Mackenzie (1883–1972), by Robert Heriot Westwater, 1962

recall of his life from the age of four onwards. He was educated at St Paul's School (1891–1900) and at Magdalen College, Oxford. He graduated with second-class honours in modern history in 1904, and a year later, on 30 November 1905, he married Faith Nora Stone (1878–1960), an actress. In 1907 his first book, a volume of poetry, was published. He abandoned his training for the English bar in the same year to pursue his ambition to write for the stage, but success eluded him until he turned to prose fiction. With the publication in 1911 of his first novel, *The Passionate Elopement*—based on his first play, *The Gentlemen in Grey*—he embarked upon a long and prolific career.

Life behind the scenes of a variety theatre, and the *commedia dell'arte*, provided Mackenzie with the raw material for his successful second novel, *Carnival* (1912), but it was the publication of his masterpiece, *Sinister Street* (1913–14), which made him a literary celebrity. A semi-autobiographical and intensely detailed and atmospheric account of childhood and education, the novel was described by Ford Madox Ford as 'possibly a work of real genius' (Ford, 353–4), Edmund Gosse compared it favourably with Proust, while Henry James concluded that its author was the most promising English novelist of his generation. Banned by some circulating libraries on account of its perceived sexual frankness, *Sinister Street* furthermore introduced Mackenzie to a notoriety which was seldom absent from his diverse activities.

The intervention of the First World War was to make Mackenzie's eminence as an Edwardian literary celebrity short-lived. He attempted unsuccessfully to obtain a commission in the Seaforth Highlanders, but thanks to the influence of General Ian Hamilton, who admired *Sinister Street*, Mackenzie became a lieutenant in the Royal Marines in 1915. He served with the Royal Naval division in the Dardanelles campaign of 1915, describing the conflicting experiences of romantic adventure and exposure to the horror of industrialized slaughter as that of 'a butterfly in a graveyard' in the first of his war memoirs, *Gallipoli Memories* (1929). In 1916 he became military control officer in Athens, and the following year moved to a leading role as director of the Aegean intelligence service in Syria, recounted in *Extremes Meet* (1928). His colourful career as a spy provided further material for *Athenian Memories* (1931) and *Greek Memories* (1932—withdrawn; reissued, 1940), the latter leading to his prosecution under the Official Secrets Act and his famous—frequently farcical—trial at the Old Bailey.

After the First World War, Mackenzie returned to the Neapolitan island of Capri, which he had discovered in 1913 as a spiritual home, and rejoined the extraordinary diaspora of expatriate artists and intellectuals who found refuge there, including Norman Douglas, D. H. and Frieda Lawrence, Somerset Maugham, Axel Munthe, E. F. T. Marinetti, and Maksim Gorky. Capri, portrayed in his bittersweet novels *Vestal Fire* (1927) and *Extraordinary Women* (1928) as a microcosm of European culture, was to prove decisive in Mackenzie's life, for it was there that he was received into the Catholic church in 1914, and where a lifelong love affair with islands began.

Mackenzie, like so many of his generation, lost direction in the early 1920s as his Edwardian aesthetic lost favour, and he became more of a jobbing writer, and less of a literary purist, largely as a result of financial necessity. Sickened by the First World War, which had also taken its personal toll on his first marriage, he found himself—in political and cultural terms—increasingly 'at an angle to English society' (Wilson, 539–40). It was in Scotland, stirring under the new cultural and political mood of the Scottish Renaissance, that he identified an atavistic destiny which accorded perfectly with his childhood Jacobite dreams, his readiness to identify with the politics of minorities and the oppressed, and his need for rootedness. From 1925 onwards Mackenzie continued a process of reorientation towards the country, establishing an important relationship with Christopher Murray Grieve (Hugh MacDiarmid). Along with MacDiarmid and R. B. Cunninghame Graham, he was a founder member of the National Party of Scotland in 1928, and in 1932 Mackenzie was elected as the first nationalist rector of Glasgow University.

Mackenzie's, like Cunninghame Graham's, was a romantic nationalism—a matter of emotion as opposed to abstract political theorizing—but it was not, like MacDiarmid's, predicated upon anti-English hostility. For this reason his contribution to the nationalist movement has been greatly misunderstood. Through radio, Mackenzie found another outlet for his oratorical powers, declaring in a famous broadcast in 1929 that 'an English voice and a Scottish heart is a better combination than a Scottish voice and an English heart' (Mackenzie, 'Soul', 2–21). He had identified the vast potential of new media at a very early stage, having founded a magazine devoted to broadcasting, *Vox*, in 1926, and *The Gramophone* in 1923, which he edited until 1961. He was a literary critic with the *Daily Mail* from 1931 to 1935.

By the time Mackenzie had established himself in 1933 on the Hebridean island of Barra, where he later built his famous house Suidheachan ('the sitting-down place'), he had made a conscious decision to bring his involvement in Scottish political and cultural affairs to bear upon his fiction. *The Four Winds of Love*, published in six volumes between 1937 and 1945 and containing almost 1 million words, is one of the most ambitious Scottish novels of the twentieth century, an enormous historical odyssey which anatomizes the politics of peripheral nationalism both throughout Europe and in Britain, again through semi-autobiographical character development. The novel's concluding vision of a Catholic Christian confederation of small Celtic nations encapsulates the author's eccentric political romanticism perfectly.

After the Second World War, Mackenzie became one of Scotland's best loved authors for a decidedly less Olympian view of history in his series of light-hearted comedies (or 'farces' as he preferred to call them) of the highlands, featuring the blimpish Anglo-Scottish laird Ben Nevis, or affectionate fictional portrayals of Barra as the island of Todday. The Todday comedies in particular domesticated a deeply serious theme—the right of small communities to self-determination in the face of larger, frequently ignorant, interfering forces, most famously in *Whisky Galore* (1947). Here Mackenzie fictionalized a real incident, the sinking of the SS *Politician* off Eriskay with thousands of cases of whisky, and the islanders' desperate attempts to salvage their providential gift of liquid gold from the sea. Aided by the brilliant Ealing Studios film of 1948, shot on Barra itself and in which Mackenzie himself plays the skipper of the stricken ship, the story's permanent place in twentieth-century folklore is assured.

Although Mackenzie's output of novels (including delightful books for children), essays, criticism, history, biography, autobiography, and travel writing was prolific—a total of 113 published titles—it can truly be said that if he had never written a word he would still have been a celebrity. He had a personality as exhibitory and colourful as his writing, and remained throughout his life a gregarious man with a brilliant sense of comedy. Flamboyant, a raconteur and mimic, he was no less memorable as the formidable scourge of politicians, bureaucrats, and governments, and the passionate defender of the ostracized, the shunned, and the wronged. His support for the anti-monarchist faction in Greece during the First World War, and afterwards for Greek independence, won him from the population a pseudo-Byronic adulation. He maintained a ruthless discipline as a truly professional writer, keeping faith with publishers and editors, often at grave risk to his health, and in defiance of the excruciating bouts of sciatica which plagued him all his life. He never

saved money, and his extravagant lifestyle provoked recurring financial crises which he would avert more often than not through frenetic feats of composition, writing all night sustained by Ovaltine and gramophone records, and sleeping by day. Whenever threatened with financial ruin, he would react immediately by purchasing an expensive suit.

A liberal with what his friend MacDiarmid detected as an inclination to the left (as a younger man Mackenzie had been attracted to Christian socialism), he was anti-capitalist, but not pro-communist, and, as the 1920s progressed, increasingly pro-Irish and Scottish, but never anglophobic. Beneath the political activism there was an equally reclusive and ascetic leaning: the private man who sought refuge from time, and other tyrannies of the twentieth century, first on the channel islands of Herm and Jethou, and later the even more remote Barra; havens for the cloistered scholar capable of interminable periods of intensive research and composition.

It is the theatricality of Mackenzie's career, however, that will remain his strongest legacy. If the stage is never far from his prose—especially in his superb ear for dialogue—it is most conspicuous in the self-dramatizing flair with which he conducted his life. Arguably Mackenzie's greatest production was himself, a prolonged performance of alternating—and sometimes conflicting—roles. He described himself as 'Protean', capable of assuming the characteristics of everything, and everyone, with whom he became involved. He was magnetically drawn towards the centre of things, and temperamentally repelled by the sidelines.

Island exiles had already ended for Mackenzie when he purchased an elegant residence in Edinburgh's Georgian New Town in 1952, the city where forty-five years earlier his first play was produced at the Lyceum Theatre. Dividing his time between his Drummond Place flat and the south of France, Mackenzie relished his role as something of an elder statesman of Scottish letters. Whether pronouncing upon weighty matters literary and political, or appearing in whisky commercials, he was equally at ease as both intellectual and entertainer. There was a remarkable coda to his career as a novelist: *Thin Ice*, published in 1956, was a terse, sombre, and restrained study of scandal in the life of a homosexual politician, and a poignantly elegiac recapitulation of his early Edwardian preoccupation with the restrictions of English society. Mackenzie's twilight literary undertaking, and in many ways his most remarkable achievement, was the monumental *My Life and Times*, published in ten 'octaves' (eight years per volume) between 1963 and 1971, containing an astonishing amount of exhaustively detailed reminiscence. On 23 January 1962 he married Christina (Chrissie) MacLeod MacSween (1909–1963) of Tarbert, Harris, who had been the author's companion, housekeeper, and wife in all but name since 1929. She died in 1963, and on 4 March 1965 he married her younger sister, Lilian (Lily) Mackenzie MacSween (*b*. 1918/19).

Mackenzie died at his home, 31 Drummond Place, Edinburgh, on 30 November 1972, from cancer of the prostate.

A year before, at the age of eighty-eight, he was almost totally blind, but had begun writing a new novel, using a board with wires stretched across the paper to guide his pen. Mackenzie's productivity never deserted him at the end; nor did the penchant for drama. When his body was flown to the island of Barra for burial, 82-year-old Calum Johnston, a friend from before the Second World War, was waiting to pipe the body to its final resting place. As the rituals came to a close, Johnston collapsed and died.

Mackenzie was appointed OBE in 1919 and knighted in 1952. He was CLit (1968), FRSL, honorary RSA, and honorary LLD of Glasgow and St Francis Xavier University.

GAVIN WALLACE

Sources C. Mackenzie, *My life and times*, 10 vols. (1963–71) • C. Mackenzie, 'The soul of the nation', *Scots Independent* (Dec 1929), 20–21 [transcript of BBC broadcast, 'What's wrong with Scotland?', 5 Nov 1929] • G. Wallace, 'English voice, Scottish heart: a critical study of the fiction of Compton Mackenzie', PhD diss., U. Edin., 1986 • A. Linklater, *Compton Mackenzie: a life* (1987) • P. V. Brooks, *A bibliography of and about the works of Anthony Edward Montagu Compton Mackenzie: Sir Compton Mackenzie, 1883–1972* (1984) • [F. M. Ford Hueffer], 'Literary portraits: Mr Compton Mackenzie and *Sinister Street*', *The Outlook*, 33 (13 Sept 1913) • E. Wilson, *The bit between my teeth: a literary chronicle of 1950–1965* (1965) • m. cert. [Faith Nora Stone] • m. cert. [Christina Macleod MacSween] • m. cert. [Lilian Mackenzie MacSween]

Archives NL Scot., MSS • Ransom HRC, MSS • U. Edin., MSS |FILM BFI NFTVA |SOUND BBC sound archives

Likenesses photographs, c.1910–1972, Hult. Arch. • G. C. Beresford, photograph, 1912, Hult. Arch., NPG • A. L. Coburn, photograph, 1914, NPG • M. Katz, bronze head, 1919, U. Texas • P. Evans, crayon drawing, c.1920–1929, NPG • D. Foggie, pencil drawing, 1933, Scot. NPG • H. Coster, two photographs, 1934–54, NPG • Elliott & Fry, photograph, c.1949, NPG • R. Adler, photograph, c.1950–1959, NPG • R. H. Westwater, oils, 1954, U. Texas • R. H. Westwater, oils, 1962, Scot. NPG [*see illus.*] • H. Wilson, pastel drawing, 1963, NPG • W. Bird, photograph, 1965, NPG • E. Arnold, photograph, 1972, NPG • W. O. Hutchison, oils, Scot. NPG • R. S. Sherriffs, ink and wash caricature, NPG • F. Topolski, portrait, NPG

McKenzie, Donald Francis (1931–1999), bibliographer and literary scholar, was born on 5 June 1931 in Timaru, South Canterbury, New Zealand, the eldest of the five children of Leslie Olson McKenzie (*b. c.*1910), a bootmaker, and his wife, Millicent Irene, *née* Last (*b.* 1911). His parents' family backgrounds were in Somerset and Wiltshire. His father was restless, and McKenzie's early education was accordingly peripatetic as the family moved from place to place. His last school was Palmerston North Boys' High School, where his part in a local radio programme about politics drew attention to his unusual abilities. After leaving in 1948 he was recruited to the post office in Wellington as a cadet or trainee. Like many others of his generation he enrolled part-time at Victoria University College. Among his teachers there was Keith Maslen, also from Canterbury, who kindled an interest in literature and its printing. Maslen had a formative influence on McKenzie's career.

McKenzie married Dora Mary Haigh, the daughter of recent immigrants; she fostered his interest in theatre and cinema, and introduced him to wider cultures. Their son, Matthew Arthur, was born on 23 December 1956. On graduating in 1954, and following this with a diploma in journalism, McKenzie was appointed to a short-term post in the university's English department, then headed by Ian Gordon. Soon afterwards he won a scholarship for postgraduate study at Cambridge, and in October 1957 he arrived at Corpus Christi College. His supervisor was Philip Gaskell, and his subject was the working conditions of printers in the age of Shakespeare. This proved relatively unproductive. Then, after a year's research, he was introduced to the unexploited and richly detailed archives of Cambridge University Press in the late seventeenth and early eighteenth centuries. McKenzie found himself in a world that eventually provided the evidence for re-evaluating most of his predecessors' work. The archives showed that early printing houses were by no means coherently organized, that books were set and printed concurrently, often with long (not always explicable) gaps in production, and that work was often shared haphazardly, whether for composition or at press. No other printing house in Britain of this date afforded such detail of how a printing business was run. Inevitably, what was recorded so clearly in Cambridge was also applied to earlier printing in London, particularly to a century or so earlier and to plays in particular. McKenzie's work overturned many bibliographical and editorial theories; henceforth it was impossible not to take account of his findings. They were published as *The Cambridge University Press, 1696–1712: a Bibliographical Study* (2 vols., 1966). Some of the scholarly world was slow to acknowledge it, or to understand it, and through a subsequent series of articles McKenzie worked for a better appreciation of what he had uncovered.

McKenzie's research had also taken him to the archives of the Stationers' Company, and hence to the national centre of the British book trade. Here, reading through the records of apprentices, he was able to extend his interest in the trade's prosopography. The resulting three volumes of *Stationers' Company Apprentices*, covering the years 1605 to 1800 (published by the Bibliographical Society of the University of Virginia and the Oxford Bibliographical Society, 1961–78), offer a resource unmatched by any other manufacturing industry.

On completing his PhD, McKenzie returned in 1960 to a permanent appointment in the English department at Victoria, where in 1969 he was appointed professor. With a view partly to teaching and partly to printing the work of local authors, he established the Wai-te-ata Press, and persuaded Cambridge University Press to lend to it an iron hand-press made in the early nineteenth century. Other old printing equipment was also gathered in. Authors included the poets Peter Bland, Alistair Campbell, Iain Lonie, and Bill Manhire. Music publishing was added a little later. McKenzie also took a leading part in establishing Downstage Theatre (a professional company based in Wellington), served on the indecent publications tribunal, founded Victoria University Press, and became increasingly involved in the activities and government of the National Library of New Zealand and the Alexander Turnbull Library.

In all his work on printed books (the term to be taken to include pamphlets, newspapers, periodicals, broadsides, and other slighter materials), McKenzie insisted on the importance of the original artefact. This led naturally to concerns for the future of libraries, their collections, their staffing, and their financing. As a leading theorist on the history of the book, he sought also to relate print to other media, including theatre, manuscript, radio, film, and electronic texts. One did not supersede another; it existed alongside, and, like different editions, offered new interpretations. It followed that the surrogate, though perhaps valuable in itself, could never serve as the original. In his inaugural series of Panizzi lectures (1985), delivered at the British Library, McKenzie pursued this theme, insisting also on the place of the reader as interpreter. He summed up part of his argument with the remark that 'bibliographers should be concerned to show that forms effect meaning'. The lectures were published as *Bibliography and the Sociology of Texts* (1986).

For years, McKenzie divided his life between duties in Wellington and research leave in England. Emotionally, he did not find it easy. In 1984 he reduced his commitment at Victoria University to part-time in order to work on a new edition of William Congreve for Oxford University Press. Meanwhile, the position of reader in textual criticism at Oxford had been left unfilled since the retirement of David Foxon in 1982. McKenzie was an obvious candidate, and in 1986 he was appointed, also becoming fellow of Pembroke College; three years later he was appointed to a chair in the subject. In McKenzie's hands the subject was transformed. He encouraged study of the textual implications of media of all kinds—by no means only manuscript and print. He had been elected a corresponding fellow of the British Academy in 1980 and a fellow in 1986.

In 1976 McKenzie delivered the Sandars lectures in bibliography at Cambridge and in 1988 the Lyell lectures at Oxford. In both, he explored the seventeenth-century book trade, and the ways in which printers, publishers, and authors worked together to establish meaning through typography: Ben Jonson and Congreve stood at opposite poles chronologically, but the printed editions of their works showed similar concerns. In 1988 McKenzie was elected an honorary fellow of the Australian Academy of the Humanities, and in 1990 he was awarded the gold medal of the Bibliographical Society.

Though he was divorced in 1989, and seemed settled in Britain—on 5 August 1994 marrying Christine Yvonne Ferdinand (*b.* 1949), a fellow of Magdalen College—he never ceased to regret his absence from New Zealand. In 1983 he sought to contribute a bibliographical perspective to the debates over the treaty of Waitangi; his intervention was not generally welcomed by New Zealand historians, though the relevance of his questions could hardly be set aside. When in 1997 Victoria University awarded him an honorary degree, he valued it all the more—as a general acknowledgement of what he had tried to do for his university, for his subject, and for his country.

In his last years, McKenzie launched plans with Cambridge University Press for a *History of the Book in Britain*. In 1997 he used his Clark lectures (Trinity College, Cambridge) to address some of the more literary issues arising from his edition of Congreve, though the edition itself was left unfinished at his death. He underwent major heart surgery, but refused to modify his pace, and he died of heart failure in the library of the Taylor Institution in Oxford on 22 March 1999. His ashes were scattered in the sea off the small North Island holiday town of Paikakariki.

Though not especially tall, McKenzie possessed great presence, his sharp, bright blue eyes conveying a sense of immediate engagement with whatever subject or person was to hand. Generous with his own time, he had a natural gift for friendship. With age, his abundant hair (generally worn slightly long) went white, and he became still more striking. A well-developed sense of humour, coupled with firmly held beliefs and a scrupulous sense of fairness, could make him a formidable advocate or foe, whether in his research or in the innumerable meetings which crowded his life. His students, recognizing his belief in them, responded to his enthusiasm and helped make his work widely influential. DAVID MCKITTERICK

Sources WW · personal knowledge (2004) · private information (2004) · m. cert. [Christine Ferdinand] · d. cert. · PBA [forthcoming] · *The Independent* (25 March 1999) · K. Coleridge, *New Zealand Libraries*, 49 (Sept 1999) · K. Maslen, *Bulletin*, 23/1 (1999), 3–10 [Bibliographical Society of Australia and New Zealand]
Archives priv. coll. | NL NZ, Wai-te-ata Press
Likenesses photograph, repro. in *The Independent*; priv. coll.

Mackenzie, Dugal (*supp. c.*1545–1588?), author and teacher, cannot be traced in contemporary records. Thomas Dempster, in the early seventeenth century, refers to 'David [*sic*] Makynius Aberdonensis' as the author of *In sibyllina oracula*—not now to be found, but published in Paris in 1578, according to George Mackenzie writing in the early eighteenth century. By this latter account Dugal Mackenzie was born at Kishorn in Wester Ross, the son of Dugal Mackenzie and 'a Brother Daughter' of Macleod of Harris, 'in the Beginning of the reign of Queen Mary'— that is, in the mid-1540s (Mackenzie, 2.476). His father was the illegitimate son of John Mackenzie of Kintail (*d.* 1561). From school in Ross-shire at Chanonry (by Rosemarkie Cathedral), Mackenzie went to King's College, Aberdeen, and (allegedly) to Paris, for further study. George Mackenzie takes substantially from Dempster the account of an illness, caused by excessive study and characterized by a persistent discharge from the eyes and nostrils, for which Mackenzie sought a cure in the Low Countries. Thence (or from Paris) he returned home 'and devoted himself to the education of youth' (*Historia ecclesiastica*, 2.498). George Mackenzie claims that Dugal became a regent at King's College, Aberdeen: the records do not confirm this, but are too incomplete to exclude it. However, one nineteenth-century clan historian suggests that Dugal Mackenzie taught in the Chanonry school he had himself attended; and this may be a more plausible interpretation of Dempster's statement. Mackenzie's date of death—garbled in Dempster—seems to have been 1588.

J. H. BURNS

Sources *Thomae Dempsteri Historia ecclesiastica gentis Scotorum, sive, De scriptoribus Scotis*, ed. D. Irving, rev. edn, 2, Bannatyne Club, 21 (1829), 498–9 · G. Mackenzie, *The lives and characters of the most eminent writers of the Scots nation*, 2 (1711), 476 · A. Mackenzie, *History of the clan Mackenzie* (1879), 116

Mackenzie, Duncan (1861–1934), archaeologist, was born on 17 May 1861 in the crofting village of Aultgowrie on the Fairburn estate, Ross-shire, Scotland, the fourth of nine children born to Alexander Stuart Mackenzie (1827–1885), a gamekeeper, and his wife, Margaret (1834–1895), *née* Kennedy. He attended primary school in the nearby village of Marybank, where he was a pupil teacher from 1876 to 1880. From 1880 to 1882 he studied at Raining's School in Inverness, run by the Society in Scotland for Propagating Christian Knowledge. In 1882 he became a student of the arts faculty of the University of Edinburgh, and graduated with an MA in philosophy in 1890. Subsequently he studied philosophy and classical archaeology at the universities of Munich, Berlin, and Vienna. In 1895 he received a doctorate from Vienna with a thesis on the west frieze of the 'heroon' at Gölbasi, ancient Trysa, in Lycia, supervised by the distinguished archaeologist O. Benndorf.

Between 1896 and 1899 Mackenzie was a student at the British School at Athens, participating in its various projects, notably the excavations of Phylakopi on Melos, one of the key prehistoric sites in the Aegean. His contribution was crucial: he effectively directed the excavations from their very beginning, and was the only archaeologist present throughout their duration. His own records of the excavation, or daybooks, were therefore indispensable for subsequent studies and publications.

Early in 1900 Mackenzie moved to Rome to continue his archaeological studies. In mid-March, however, his plans were disrupted by a momentous telegram sent by Arthur J. Evans, inviting him to superintend his excavations at Knossos in Crete. Mackenzie accepted immediately, and on 23 March 1900 began his work on the famous site of the 'palace of Minos'. During the next decade he excavated there for four to five months almost every year. While not engaged in his Cretan work, Mackenzie lived in Rome, pursuing various archaeological researches. Between 1903 and 1906 he held a Carnegie Trust fellowship in history, and between 1906 and 1909 he travelled and recorded prehistoric monuments in Sardinia. In December 1909 he was appointed explorer of the Palestine Exploration Fund, and in 1910 he started the fund's excavations at ʿAin Shems (biblical Beth Shemesh). Clashes with his new employers, however, led to the termination of his contract in 1912.

In 1913 Mackenzie worked in the Sudan for Henry Wellcome on the excavations at Dar al-Mek and Saqadi, and during the First World War he resumed his collaboration with Evans: by June 1915 he had moved to Evans's residence near Oxford, and was helping with the publication of his employer's *magnum opus*, *The Palace of Minos at Knossos* (1921–35) as well as with the reorganization of the Aegean collections in the Ashmolean Museum, Oxford. In 1920 Evans sent Mackenzie to inspect Knossos, work on the finds, and conduct some soundings, and in 1922 embarked on a new series of excavation and restoration work at Knossos. Mackenzie resumed his role of right-hand man until 1929. In 1924 Evans donated all his personal Knossian properties to the British School at Athens, and in 1926 Mackenzie became the school's first Knossos curator. He held this post until 1929, when Evans had him sacked and banished from Knossos for excessive drinking. After this Mackenzie's physical and mental health rapidly deteriorated. His younger sister Christina, who had followed him to Rome, had married an Italian, and continued to live in Italy, took charge of him. He spent his last years in a nursing home in the Adriatic town of Pesaro, where he died on 25 August 1934, mad and forgotten; he was buried at Pesaro.

Mackenzie was one of the first professional field archaeologists, and the unsung hero of the famous excavations at Knossos. His relative obscurity was partly due to the fact that he was overshadowed by his more flamboyant and charismatic employer, and partly to the fact that, unlike Evans, he was not a prolific or gifted writer. His most important published works are the chapter 'The successive settlements at Phylakopi in their Aegeo-Cretan relations' in T. D. Atkinson and others, *The Excavations at Phylakopi in Melos* (1904), 238–72; the two articles 'The pottery of Knossos' (*Journal of Hellenic Studies*, 23, 1903, 157–205) and 'The Middle Minoan pottery of Knossos' (*Journal of Hellenic Studies*, 26, 1906, 243–67); the four articles on Cretan palaces in *Annual of the British School at Athens*, 11–14 (1905–8); and his reports on the excavations at ʿAin Shems published in *Palestine Exploration Fund Annual*, 1 and 2 (1911, 1913). His daybooks of the excavations at Phylakopi, ʿAin Shems, Dar al-Mek, Saqadi, and especially Knossos, are his most significant contribution to archaeology. They formed the basis of important publications by others, notably Evans's. Moreover, they not only contain precious, often unpublished, information on these important sites, but also show a precision in the recording of excavations, and an attention to problems of methodology and interpretation, which are remarkable for the period.

NICOLETTA MOMIGLIANO

Sources N. Momigliano, *Duncan Mackenzie: a cautious canny highlander and the palace of Minos at Knossos* (1999) · **Archives** British School at Athens · British School at Rome · Palestine Exploration Fund, London · U. Oxf., Griffith Institute | AM Oxf., Evans archive · **Likenesses** P. de Jong, cartoon, priv. coll.; repro. in R. Hood, *Faces of archaeology in Greece* (1998)

Mackenzie, Eneas (1777–1832), topographical writer, was born in Aberdeen on 12 January 1777, the son of a shoemaker. His parents moved to Newcastle upon Tyne when he was three years old. After an attempt at the Baptist ministry and an unsuccessful venture as a shipbroker in Sunderland, he returned to Newcastle and opened a private school. An Eneas Mackenzie, probably he, married Elizabeth Patterson at All Saints, Newcastle, on 21 November 1805. In 1810 he formed a business partnership with the printer John Moore Dent, with premises in St Nicholas

Churchyard. The firm specialized in educational and historical works, many compiled by Mackenzie himself, for sale in parts by door-to-door travellers.

Mackenzie was a strong radical, a secretary of the Northern Political Union, and the leading founder of the Newcastle Mechanics' Institute in 1824. His publications (all from Newcastle) contain much statistical information aimed at providing grounds for local self-improvement. They include *An Historical and Descriptive View of the County of Northumberland* (2 vols., 1811, revised as 'historical, topographical and descriptive' to 2 vols. quarto, 1825); *A Descriptive and Historical Account of the Town and County of Newcastle-upon-Tyne* (2 vols., 1827); and *An Historical, Topographical and Descriptive View of the County Palatine of Durham* (1834), which had been completed after Mackenzie's death by Metcalf Ross. His other writings included compilations on the history of Egypt (1809), on the life of Napoleon (1816), and on modern geography (1817). More substantially there was *An Historical, Topographical, and Descriptive View of the United States of America, and of Upper and Lower Canada* (1819, with a second edition the same year); this encouraged emigration by including letters from recent settlers in North America. Mackenzie died of cholera on 21 February 1832 at Newcastle. His son, also named Eneas, started an unsuccessful radical newspaper there in 1832.

ALAN BELL

Sources C. J. Hunt, *The book trade in Northumberland and Durham to 1860: a biographical dictionary* (1975), 63–4 · R. Welford, *Men of mark 'twixt Tyne and Tweed*, 3 vols. (1895) · *DNB* · *IGI*

Mackenzie, Sir Francis Alexander, of Gairloch, fifth baronet (1798–1843). *See under* Mackenzie, John (1803–1886).

Mackenzie, Francis Humberston, Baron Seaforth and Mackenzie of Kintail (1754–1815), army officer and colonial governor, was born on 9 June 1754, the second son of William Mackenzie (*d.* 1770), a major in the army, grandson of the Jacobite peer Kenneth, fourth earl of Seaforth, and Mary (*d.* 1813), daughter and heir of Matthew Humberston of Humberston, Lincolnshire. His elder brother was Thomas Frederick Mackenzie *Humberston. At twelve years of age a violent attack of scarlet fever permanently destroyed his hearing and for a time deprived him of speech. He nevertheless grew up distinguished by his extensive attainments and great intellectual activity. On 22 April 1782 he married Mary (1754/5–1829), daughter of the Revd Baptist Proby, dean of Lichfield, and first cousin of John Joshua Proby, first earl of Carysfort, with whom he had four sons and six daughters. On the death of his brother in 1783 he succeeded to the Seaforth estates and chiefship, becoming the twenty-first *caber feidh* or hereditary chief of the clan Mackenzie. But for the attainder of 1716 he would have become the ninth earl of Seaforth.

Mackenzie successfully restored the Seaforth interest in Ross-shire, where he was returned to parliament in 1784 partly thanks to a number of fictitious votes. He supported the opposition to Pitt, but became encumbered by debts and did not stand in 1790.

His opposition to the ministry notwithstanding, Mackenzie offered to raise a Highland regiment for service in India in 1787. The offer was accepted, but the Seaforth recruits were taken to complete the 74th and 75th foot. He repeated the offer at the time of the Nootka Sound difficulty (in May 1790), but it was declined. It was repeated once more in 1793 and accepted. Mackenzie, now considering himself a supporter of the ministry in the face of revolutionary France, then raised the 'Ross-shire Buffs', which was enrolled as the 78th foot, the third Highland regiment bearing that number, and the first regiment added to the army during the war with revolutionary France. The regiment later became the 2nd Seaforth (late 78th) Highlanders. Mackenzie was appointed lieutenant-colonel commandant. He raised a second battalion for the regiment in 1794, which was amalgamated with the 1st battalion at the Cape in 1795. Mackenzie, who had never joined the regiment, resigned the command in that year, and was appointed lord lieutenant of Ross-shire. On 1 May 1794 he had returned to the Commons as MP for Ross-shire, this time voting with Pitt's government. In order to accommodate an ally of Henry Dundas, Sir Charles Lockhart Ross, he did not stand in 1796. By way of reward, on 26 October 1797 he was created 'Lord Seaforth, Baron Mackenzie of Kintail' in the peerage of Great Britain. On 23 April 1798 he was appointed colonel of the newly formed 2nd North British, or Caithness, Sutherland, Ross, and Cromarty militia, subsequently the Highland rifle militia, and then the 3rd or militia battalion of Seaforth Highlanders. He became colonel in the army on 3 May 1796, major-general on 29 April 1802, and lieutenant-general on 25 April 1808.

On 26 November 1800 Lord Seaforth was appointed governor of Barbados, arriving there early in 1801 and, with the exception of a part of 1803, when he was on leave, remaining until 1806. He vigorously took up the inquiry into the slave trade, and in a letter addressed to John Jeffreys Pratt, second Earl Camden, secretary of state for war and the colonies, on 13 November 1804, gave, on the authority of unimpeachable witnesses, including the colonial attorney-general, details of atrocities committed against slaves in the island. Under Seaforth's influence the assembly of the island in the following year passed a partial reform of the law whereby any one wilfully and maliciously killing a slave, whether the owner or not of such slave, on being convicted on the evidence of white witnesses, was to suffer death. The evidence of slaves or free coloured persons was excluded. Nevertheless previously the punishment had been a fine of £15, which was rarely imposed. The planters were keen to counter the arguments of British abolitionists and the slavery laws were further consolidated in 1817 and 1825. When the French fleet under Villeneuve arrived in the West Indies in 1804, Seaforth proclaimed martial law in the island, without consulting the assembly, who protested against this violation of their liberties. The British government supported him, and the assembly appears to have altered its tone. Seaforth was entertained at a grand dinner at Bridgetown before his departure from the island, which took place on 25 July 1806.

Seaforth was made a fellow of the Royal Society on 26 June 1794 and took a lively interest in science and art. In 1796 he lent £1000 to Thomas Lawrence, then a struggling artist, who had applied to him for aid, and he commissioned Benjamin West to paint one of his huge canvases depicting the first chief of Seaforth saving King Alexander of Scotland from the attack of an infuriated stag. West later bought back the picture for exhibition at the price paid for it—£800. Between 1804 and 1806 Seaforth compiled a long list of West Indian plants (BL, Add. MS 28610, fol. 20ff.).

Unhappily, Seaforth's closing years were darkened by calamities and personal suffering. Mismanagement of his estates and his own extravagance involved him in inextricable embarrassments. When he wanted to sell the estate of Lochalsh his tenants offered to pay his debts if he would come and reside among them. But his improvidence rendered the expedient useless. Part of the barony of Kintail, the 'gift-land' of the house, was next put up for sale, a step the clansmen sought to avert by offering to buy it in, so that the lands might not pass to strangers. In deference to this feeling, the intended sale was postponed for two years. Seaforth's third son, William Frederick, was the only one to survive into adulthood, and became MP for Ross-shire in 1812, but died unmarried on 25 October 1814. Seaforth himself died, heartbroken and paralysed in mind and body, at Warriston, near Edinburgh on 11 January 1815. His widow died in Edinburgh on 27 February 1829. The Seaforth title became extinct; the chiefship passed to Mackenzie of Allengrange; the estates went by act of entail to Seaforth's eldest daughter, Mary Elizabeth Frederica Stewart-*Mackenzie (1783–1862), who married, first, Admiral Sir Samuel *Hood, and second James Alexander Stewart (later Stewart-Mackenzie) MP, sometime governor of Ceylon, and lord high commissioner of the Ionian Islands, who died in 1845.

The history of the last Seaforth was believed to fulfil a prophecy that in the days of a deaf mute *caber feidh* the 'gift-land' of the house should be sold, and the male line of Seaforth come to an end. The prophecy, dating from the time of Charles II, was said to have been uttered by Kenneth Mackenzie (Coinneach Odhar), who was reported to have been put to a cruel death, *c*.1670, by the Lady Seaforth of the time.   H. M. CHICHESTER, rev. JONATHAN SPAIN

Sources Scots peerage · GEC, Peerage · A. Mackenzie, History of the clan Mackenzie (1879) · A. Mackenzie, The prophecies of the Brahan seer (1877) · T. Southey, Chronological history of the West Indies, 3 vols. (1827); facs. edn (1968) [3] · F. A. Hoyos, Barbados: a history from the Amerindians to independence (1978) · A. Swinson, A register of the regiments and corps of the British army (1972) · H. Davidson, History and sources of the 78th highlanders (the Royal-Buffs), 1793–1881, 2 vols. (1901) · E. Haden-Guest, 'Mackenzie, Francis Humberston', HoP, Commons, 1754–90 · D. G. Henry and D. R. Fisher, 'Mackenzie, Francis Humberston', HoP, Commons, 1790–1820

Archives BL, lists of West Indian plants sent to England, Add. MS 28610 · NA Scot., corresp. and papers | NL Scot., corresp. with Lord Melville

Likenesses T. Lawrence, portrait, repro. in Davidson, History and sources of the 78th highlanders · J. S. Stuart, ink drawing (with the third titular duke of Perth; after unknown artist), Scot. NPG · B. Thorvaldsen, pencil drawing, Thorvaldsen Museum, Copenhagen

Mackenzie, Frederick (*c*.1787–1854), watercolour painter and architectural draughtsman, was the son of Thomas Mackenzie, a linen draper. A pupil of the architect John Adey Repton, the son of Humphrey Repton, the landscape gardener, Mackenzie first exhibited at the Royal Academy in 1804 when he was sixteen. Soon afterwards he was working for John Britton, who had a talent for finding artists able to convey his own enormous enthusiasm for his antiquarian publications. Britton employed Mackenzie to make drawings for *The Beauties of England and Wales*, *Architectural Antiquities of Great Britain* (1807–9), and *Cathedral Antiquities* (1814–21). The drawings were engraved by John and Henry Le Keux, and Britton's obituarist in the *Illustrated London News* stated that 'Even the faithful Hollar is faithless when compared with Mackenzie and Le Keux' (10 Jan 1857).

From 1813 Mackenzie began to send watercolour drawings to the Society of Painters in Water Colours. He eventually contributed ninety-seven pictures to its exhibitions, a modest total; the early pictures were almost exclusively of Oxford or Cambridge colleges, while later ones were usually of English cathedrals or churches. There is a letter from Mackenzie to the society, dated 22 June 1815, giving detailed instructions for the disposal of his pictures at the end of that year's exhibition; he writes with great good humour asking for expenses for 'caravans, tumbrils, diligences, horses, neddys, mules, camels, coachmen' to be taken into account and 'all other things proper to be remembered on these scribleritical occasions' (Royal Watercolour Society, J107/198). In 1822 Mackenzie was elected an associate of the society and he became a full member the following year. From 1831 until his death he served as its treasurer during years in which the society was beginning to enjoy both prestige and prosperity. His drawing for the 1834 exhibition, *The principal room of the National Gallery, formerly the residence of John Julius Angerstein, esq, lately pulled down*, was praised in the *Literary Gazette* as a 'marvellous picture in every respect—a National Gallery in itself. The perfection with which he has copied the old Masters in frames the size of dominos, and the effect of the whole, are quite extraordinary' (Hardie, 3.18). The picture was bought at Christies for the South Kensington Museum (now the V&A) in 1887 for £110. (Mackenzie had originally asked 150 guineas for it, an exceptional price even at the time, for his drawings usually sold for less than £60.) His work, which was attractively coloured, was highly praised for its accuracy and sense of perspective.

Most of Mackenzie's output, signed 'F. Mackenzie', continued to be done for publication. His work included a collaboration with Augustus Pugin in *Specimens of Gothic Architecture* (1821), Rudolph Ackermann's *Histories of Oxford and Cambridge* (1814–15), and James Ingram's *Memorials of Oxford* (100 plates, 1837). Mackenzie himself published *Etchings of Landscape for the Use of Students* in 1812 and books on St Stephen's Chapel, Westminster, in 1844 and King's

College, Cambridge, in 1846. With the invention of the calotype or early photograph, the occupation of architectural draughtsman was more or less superseded, however: Mackenzie's circumstances in later years seem to have been considerably straitened.

On 15 June 1843, at the age of about fifty-six, Mackenzie married a widow, Mary Hine. In 1847 he moved to 43 Stanhope Street, Regent's Park, where he died from heart disease on 25 April 1854. J. L. Roget records that Mackenzie was much loved by the fellow members of the Society of Painters in Water Colours and its minutes record that they provided a mourning coach for his funeral at Highgate cemetery. It was found after his death that most of the benefit that Mackenzie's widow would have received from the society had already been signed away in a post-obit bond for £60 to the artist William Henry Hunt; to replace it, members subscribed £110 towards the purchase of an annuity for Mary Mackenzie and her disabled daughter. A six-day sale by Sotheby and Wilkinson of Mackenzie's notable collection of pictures and illustrated books was held in March 1855; the 1236 lots included hundreds of etchings from continental and English schools.

SIMON FENWICK

Sources Bankside Gallery, London, Royal Water Colour Society MSS · J. L. Roget, *A history of the 'Old Water-Colour' Society*, 2 vols. (1891) · M. Hardie, *Water-colour painting in Britain*, ed. D. Snelgrove, J. Mayne, and B. Taylor, 3 vols. (1966–8) · *The Royal Watercolour Society: the first fifty years, 1805–1855* (1992)
Archives Bankside Gallery, London, Royal Water Colour Society MSS

Mackenzie, George, second earl of Seaforth (d. 1651), chief of clan Mackenzie, was the second son of Kenneth Mackenzie (d. 1611), chief of clan Mackenzie and from 17 November 1609 first Lord Mackenzie of Kintail, and his second wife, Elizabeth or Isabel (d. in or before 1617), daughter of Sir Gilbert Ogilvie of Powry, Forfarshire; his birth date is unknown, but his parents were married after 9 May 1604 and before 12 March 1607. Following the death of his brother Alexander in 1614, he became the male heir to his half-brother Colin *Mackenzie (d. 1633), second Lord Mackenzie of Kintail and from 1623 first earl of Seaforth. He married, by a contract dated 22 and 23 January 1628, Barbara (b. 1607), eldest daughter of Arthur Forbes, Lord Forbes, and his wife, Jean Elphinstone. When the first earl died on 15 April 1633, Mackenzie succeeded as second earl of Seaforth. The following year he became a justice of the peace for the shires of Elgin, Nairn, Forres, and Inverness, and in 1637 the king appointed him to the Scottish privy council.

From 1638 Seaforth adhered to the covenanting party, but his royalist feelings significantly modified his presbyterian leanings, and a strong regard to his own interests led him to take an inconsistent political line. He was one of those who on 17 February 1639 assembled to prevent George Gordon, marquess of Huntly, from garrisoning the castle of Inverness. While loyalty to the covenanting cause may have been one motivation for his part in this first blow against the king's cause in Scotland, the earl may also have desired to maintain his local dominance

rather than share it with a lowlander covenanter garrison. None the less, on 9 April he arrived in Aberdeen to offer his services to the covenanter general Alexander Leslie. In May, at the head of 4000 men of various clans beyond the Spey, he attempted to join the army of Montrose at Aberdeen, perhaps heading the levy to prevent the spread of violence to his region, but he was resisted by the Gordons and others, and it was finally agreed that both parties should withdraw to their homes. The concordat cast doubt on his loyalty to the covenanter cause because it represented the only case of a major truce between covenanters and royalists.

Seaforth attended the general assembly which met at Aberdeen on 20 July 1640, and was one of the committee appointed to try certain doctors and ministers for not subscribing the covenant. On 5 August he headed a party of noblemen and gentlemen who destroyed various images and crucifixes in the churches of Aberdeen. Nevertheless he shortly afterwards signed, along with Montrose, the bond of Cumbernauld. In July 1641 he came under suspicion of having communication with the king's army, and one of his servants, who was bringing letters to him from Edinburgh, was apprehended. On learning of this Seaforth went south to Edinburgh, but after trial nothing was found against him. He attended the meeting of the estates in October, and was nominated by the king to the privy council, his nomination being approved by the estates on 13 November.

When Alasdair MacColla landed in Morvern from Ireland in the summer of 1644, expecting to raise a force of highlanders for the king, Seaforth refused to join the general, but agreed not to bar his passage south into Atholl, where MacColla joined Montrose. Charles nominated Seaforth 'chief justice general of the Isles', but he declined on account of the 'malignancy of the times' (Gordon, 64). After Montrose's victory at Aberdeen in September, Seaforth and his co-commander the earl of Sutherland, heading a force of northern and Moray covenanters, prevented the royalist general from crossing the Spey, forcing him to retreat to Badenoch in order to escape the earl of Argyll, who was advancing with a superior force. After ravaging Argyll's country, in January 1645 Montrose went to Loch Ness, intending to give battle to Seaforth, who by this time was commander of an army guarding the north end of the loch, but learning of Argyll's preparations in the south, returned instead to Inverlochy, where he defeated Argyll on 2 February. In the meantime Seaforth had disbanded his army, so when Montrose turned again towards Inverness both Seaforth and the committee of estates, sitting in mid-February at Elgin, fled northwards. Their flight was shortlived, however, and returning to Elgin, Seaforth was 'seized' by Montrose and freed only after he had signed the Kilcumin bond. He and others accompanied Montrose on his march from Elgin to the Spey, where he extracted from them a solemn oath never to draw arms against the king, and on their parole to return as soon as possible to take Inverness for the king, they were permitted to leave for their estates. Instead of fulfilling his promise, Seaforth wrote almost immediately to the Earl Marischal at Aberdeen that he had yielded to Montrose only through fear, and intended to remain 'by the good cause till his death' (Spalding, 2.450). He indeed joined the covenanter Major-General Sir John Hurry with the Mackenzies and their allied clans shortly before the battle of Auldearn on 9 May, but although many of his kinsmen and clan supporters were subsequently slaughtered by Montrose's victorious forces, Seaforth made his escape, 'being well mounted' (Gordon, 127). He then joined Montrose at Inverness, simultaneously quartering his men on the lands of his covenanter allies the Lovat Frasers. Yet despite his apparent conversion, or reversion, to the king's cause, no evidence exists of the earl supporting Montrose during the ensuing royalist siege of Inverness. Instead, following the covenanter Major-General John Middleton's relief of the burgh, Seaforth renewed the Kilcumin bond with Montrose. As Middleton's victorious campaign continued, Lady Seaforth surrendered Fortrose Castle to him and Seaforth rendered himself to the mercy of the covenanter general.

In June 1646 Seaforth was excommunicated by the general assembly of the kirk for lending countenance to Montrose by signing the Kilcumin bond and by issuing his own pro-royalist remonstrance. After Charles I had put himself in the hands of the Scots at Newark, Seaforth approached Middleton, made terms with the committee of the estates, and did public penance for his apostasy in St Giles's, Edinburgh. By the end of 1646 Seaforth and all the former royalist Mackenzie lairds had been pardoned. During the engagement the earl supported the effort to aid Charles I, but did not raise any troops. Following the king's execution, Seaforth joined Charles II in the Netherlands, and was nominated by him as principal secretary of state for Scotland. He was included in the act of 19 May 1650 which excluded 'persons from entering within the kingdom from beyond sea with his Majesty, until they give satisfaction to the church and state' (Balfour, 4.14), but on 27 December the act of banishment against him was recalled. However, he proved, as Edward Nicholas observed to the duke of Ormond, 'a faithful Scotsman' (*Ormonde MSS*, new ser., 1.223), and remained abroad. He died at Schiedam in the Netherlands about 14 October 1651.

Seaforth was survived by his wife, Barbara, who was still living in 1666. They had four sons, Kenneth [*see below*], George (a biographical writer), Colin, and Roderick, and three daughters, Jean (who married first John Erskine, earl of Mar, and second Andrew, Lord Fraser), Margaret (who married Sir William Sinclair of Mey), and Barbara (who married Sir John Urquhart of Cromarty). Seaforth also had an illegitimate son, John, first of the family of Gruiard.

Kenneth Mackenzie, third earl of Seaforth (1635–1678), army officer and politician, was known as Lord Kintail until his father's death. He studied from 1641 to 1650 under the Revd Farquhar Macrae, chief of that name, hereditary chamberlain of Kintail and constable of Eilean Donan Castle for the Mackenzies. In 1650 he entered King's College, Aberdeen, but the tumultuous times

quickly ended his academic career. On 20 December the estates nominated Kintail colonel of foot for his clan and allies. Ably assisted by his uncle and other relatives, Kintail raised over 1000 men. He and his regiment served in the Worcester campaign. He was captured during the battle and languished in prison during the English rule of Scotland. Having succeeded his father, his prospects remained grim: in 1654 Cromwell excepted the earl from his Act of Grace. However, the Restoration brought freedom and a position as one of the chief royal agents in the highlands. About 1660 he married Isabel (d. 1715), daughter of Sir John Mackenzie of Tarbat and his wife, Margaret Erskine. On 23 April 1662, in recognition of his regional power, he was made sheriff of Ross. He became a privy councillor for Scotland in 1674, and was a commissioner to suppress conventicles in 1676. He died on 16 December 1678 at Chanonry, Ross-shire, and was buried on 23 January 1679.   T. F. HENDERSON, *rev.* EDWARD M. FURGOL

Sources A. Mackenzie, *History of the clan Mackenzie* (1879) · APS · J. Balfour, *Works*, 4 vols. (1823–5) · P. Gordon, *A short abridgement of Britane's distemper*, ed. J. Dunn, Spalding Club, 10 (1844) · J. Spalding, *Memorialls of the trubles in Scotland and in England, AD 1624 – AD 1645*, ed. J. Stuart, 2 vols., Spalding Club, [21, 23] (1850–51) · *Scots peerage* · GEC, *Peerage* · D. Stevenson, *Revolution and counter-revolution in Scotland, 1644–1651*, Royal Historical Society Studies in History, 4 (1977) · *The letters and journals of Robert Baillie*, ed. D. Laing, 3 vols., Bannatyne Club, 73 (1841–2) · J. Fraser, *Chronicles of the Frasers: the Wardlaw manuscript*, ed. W. Mackay, Scottish History Society, 1st ser., 47 (1905) · J. Rushworth, *Historical collections*, new edn, 8 vols. (1721–2) · *Calendar of the manuscripts of the marquess of Ormonde*, new ser., 8 vols., HMC, 36 (1902–20), vol. 1

Mackenzie, George, first earl of Cromarty (1630–1714), politician and polymath, was born at Innerteil, near Kinghorn, Fife, the eldest son of Sir John Mackenzie (d. 1654) of Tarbat, Ross-shire, baronet, and his wife, Margaret, daughter of Sir George Erskine of Innerteil, Lord Innerteil, a lord of the court of session. He was educated at the University of St Andrews and King's College, Aberdeen, from where he graduated in 1646. These years laid the foundations for his formidable and various intellectual achievements as a naturalist, geographer, historian, and theologian. Nevertheless, the troubled politics of this era inevitably impinged on Mackenzie, who at this stage seems to have been a conventional cavalier, though George Lockhart of Carnwath later claimed that Mackenzie had 'complyed with all the opposite governments that had been on foot since the year 1648' (Lockhart, 42). At any rate, in 1653 Mackenzie joined the earl of Glencairn's expedition on behalf of Charles II, and with its failure fled first to the highlands. Later, Mackenzie went into exile on the continent, where he remained until the Restoration, employing much of his enforced leisure in the study of law. In the interim, following his father's death on 10 September 1654, he had succeeded to the family estates. That year he married Anna (d. 1699), daughter of Sir James Sinclair of Mey and his wife, Elizabeth Leslie; they had four sons.

Mackenzie's career in government commenced at the Restoration, and he rapidly became addicted to the intrigues of political life. 'Never', according to Lockhart, 'was there a more fickle, unsteady man in the world' who

George Mackenzie, first earl of Cromarty (1630–1714), by Michael Dahl, c.1708

served governments of a variety of different hues 'till he got what he aimed at, though often he did not know what that was'. Indeed, 'so extreamly maggoty and unsettled' was he 'that he was never much to be relyed upon or valued' (Lockhart, 42–3). According to Gilbert Burnet, Mackenzie was 'a young man of great vivacity of parts, but full of ambition, and had the art of recommending himself to all sides and parties by turns' (*Burnet's History*, 97). Mackenzie's politics remain as hard to fathom now as they were to his perplexed—and equally exasperated—contemporaries, though they were clear enough at the start. A protégé of John Middleton, first earl of Middleton, he was described by his kinsman Sir George Mackenzie as a 'passionate Cavalier' (Mackenzie, 27), and on 14 February 1661 he was nominated a lord of session with the judicial title of Lord Tarbat. Nevertheless, Lockhart alleged that Tarbat was 'full of projects, and never rejected one, provided it was new'.

According to Sir George Mackenzie, Tarbat was the principal begetter of the Act Rescissory (which rescinded all legislation passed in the covenanting parliaments). He is also credited with the leading role in a notorious underhand scheme—the billeting affair—which brought about the downfall of his patron, Middleton, and temporarily sidetracked Tarbat's own political ambitions. The intended victim of the billeting ploy was Middleton's rival John Maitland, second earl of Lauderdale, who, along with eleven other figures, was to be declared incapable of holding office by a secret vote of the estates recorded on private papers, or billets. However, the king rejected the act

of billeting out of hand and was not mollified by Tarbat's special pleading 'that he design'd nothing in that affair beside the serving of his royal interest' through 'the prevention of that ruin which the cavaliers of Scotland were like to suffer by Lauderdale's influence' (Mackenzie, 77). Instead both Middleton and Tarbat lost their own offices, with the latter deprived of his seat on the judicial bench on 16 February 1664.

A long semi-retirement ensued until Tarbat 'changed his side, and solicited earnestly for Lauderdail's favore' ('Memorandum', 333). Lauderdale was disinclined at first to display any mercy, though 'when the House of Hamiltoune became heavie upon Lauderdaile, he passed from his prejudice against Tarbat' (ibid.). Archbishop James Sharp had also pressed the case for rehabilitation, which resulted in 1678 in Tarbat's winning appointment as lord justice general, along with a royal pension, admission as a privy councillor, and, most importantly, a letter of pardon from the king for his involvement in the billeting affair. On 1 October 1681 Tarbat became lord clerk register and was later readmitted as a lord of session. Tarbat made himself useful to the regime as 'a notable deviser of mischief' (ibid.) against the Presbyterians, and was fully implicated in the persecutions of the killing time. His continued rise was assured with the decline of Lauderdale, and the accession of James VII and II led to his creation in 1685 as Viscount Tarbat and Lord Macleod and Castlehaven in the peerage of Scotland.

Despite his proximity to James and his logistical involvement in the defeat of Argyll's rebellion in 1685, at the revolution Tarbat was quick to dissociate himself from the old order. Indeed, spotting the necessity of conciliating William of Orange, he appears to have helped to gull James Drummond, earl of Perth—a Jacobite loyalist—into disbanding the militia. Yet so 'possessed with terrour' was Tarbat at the rapid change of circumstances, that, it is alleged, he

> stood up in Parliament confessing his sins, and that he had been ane ill man; crying out, was there no mercy for a penitent siner? and proffering to confine himself at home for the rest of his days, provyding the Parliament would but spare his life and fortune. ('Memorandum', 334)

Tarbat need not have worried. William saw the value of experienced pre-revolution ministers, and, at any rate, trusted Tarbat's Presbyterian cousin George Melville, Lord Melville, whose life Tarbat had saved in 1683. As a result, Tarbat managed to obtain an exoneration in April 1689 for the part he had played in the former administration, though it seems that he had still not been fully exonerated by January 1690.

Accommodating himself to the new politics, Tarbat began to project himself as a revolution tory, while also maintaining links with Jacobites. Nevertheless, there were also signs—perhaps deliberately deceptive, perhaps only the hard-nosed Erastianism of a *politique*—that the partisan cavalier was mellowing into an eirenic statesman. A latitudinarian approach to religious differences seemed to inform Tarbat's politics. In his 'Memorial in relation to the church', which he submitted to the new ministry in 1689, Tarbat traced the political turbulence experienced by Scotland over the previous century to disputes over church government. How could one build a durable polity when 'Episcopacy appears unsufferable by a great party, and Presbitry is as odious to [the] other' (Melville, 125)? The solution required a charitable spirit of reconciliation and some ingenuity in the framing of a new model for the Church of Scotland. Tarbat's proposed experiment involved uniting the loyal Williamite clergy of both churches in a national church embracing two types of church courts—properly presbyterian synods and quasi-episcopal synods with permanent moderators whose stipends would be paid out of the former bishops' rents. In reality, the Church of Scotland was re-established in 1690 on a narrowly presbyterian base, which alienated—as Tarbat's memorandum predicted—a substantial body of Episcopalians, many of whom were loyal Williamites, whose cause Tarbat was to appear to champion. Tarbat also suggested at a very early stage that bribes ought to be dispensed to the highland clans to ensure stability in that region. Although slow to recognize the wisdom of Tarbat's advice for a relaxed highland policy, whose provenance might have been a deeper crypto-Jacobite double game, the government did employ him as a negotiator with the clans in the pacification of the highlands.

On 5 March 1692 Tarbat once more became lord clerk register, and returned to his old ways. On 16 May 1693 Secretary Johnstone reported to William Carstares that Tarbat had been caught 'grossly malversing in his office, both in publick and private business in parliament', the principal offence being repeated falsification of its minutes for his own ends (McCormick, 173). Tarbat's roguery was so brazen that although nobody 'had so much as one word to say in his defence' he survived:

> This is the third tyme my Lord Tarbat has been catched, and the thing always so gross, that he lost countenance, and gave over defending himself; yet still he relapses. The truth is, all men were so ashamed of him, that they spared him.   (ibid.)

Nevertheless, Tarbat was forced to step down in early 1696. On the accession of Queen Anne, however, Tarbat was appointed one of the secretaries of state, and on 1 January 1703 he was created earl of Cromarty. In 1704 he resigned the office of secretary, and on 26 June 1705 became lord justice general, a post he held until 1710. Meanwhile, his first wife having died in 1699, on 29 April 1700 he married Margaret Wemyss, *suo jure* countess of Wemyss (1659–1705), widow of James Wemyss, Lord Burntisland. She died five years later, and was buried on 1 June 1705 at East Wemyss.

Cromarty's impenetrable politics continued to irritate his contemporaries across the political and religious spectrum. Lockhart, a Jacobite commentator, alleged that Cromarty

> pretended to favour the Royal Family [the exiled Stuarts] and the episcopal clergy, yet he never did one act in favour of any of them, excepting that when he was secretary to Queen Anne he procured an act of indemnity and a letter from her recommending the episcopal clergy to the Privy Council's protection.   (Lockhart, 42)

On the other hand, the Reverend Robert Wodrow, an arch-Presbyterian, accused Cromarty of 'spiriting up the Episcopall people, that there might be an occasion to grant them a Tolleration, and to pave the way for the Pretender' (Wodrow). Yet Lockhart claimed that, when Queen Anne abandoned the tories, Cromarty 'turned as great a Whig as the best of them, joined with Tweedale's party to advance the Hanoverian succession in the parliament [of] 1704, and was at last a zealous stickler and writer in favour of the Union' (Lockhart, 42–3).

Cromarty's stance was more consistent than it seemed. Contrary to his reputation as a shameless opportunist, he always supported incorporating union from the publication of his pamphlet *Paraneisis pacifica* in 1702, and was its most persuasive and sophisticated advocate. In particular, Cromarty's unionist commitments sat easily with his latitudinarian outlook, and he hoped that union would ameliorate the position of his fellow Episcopalians. Moreover, the obvious differences in church government between Scotland and England pertained only to 'praeter-fundamentals' (*Paraneisis*, 18), Cromarty believed, and should not stand in the way of union. Unusually for his time, he welcomed the notion of an inclusive pan-British identity: 'May wee be Brittains, and down goe the old ignominious names of Scotland, of England' (Fraser, 2.2). A sentimental attachment to names should not stand in the way of the vital objective of Anglo-Scottish union. Cromarty dared to ridicule the 'sophisms' of false patriots who 'would rather have a piece of Britain under their patrocinie, than it should be in a whole, and thereby in the state of a durable life' (*Second Letter on the British Union*, 1706, 18). In particular he used his satirical creation Mr Con in the pamphlet *Trialogus* (1706) as a mouthpiece for the tired old slogans of Scottish patriotism, exposing these as inadequate substitutes for a calculation of the national interest. Union did not mean the surrender of Scottish sovereignty, which had effectively been lost already. Indeed, full incorporation into a new British nation, Cromarty argued, was very much in Scotland's interests. 'Unless wee be a part each of other', he wrote to John, earl of Mar, 'the union will be as a blood puddin to band a catt, i.e. till one or the other be hungry, and then the puddin flyes' (Fraser, 2.1).

Cromarty's unionism was predicated upon an unsentimental analysis of international power politics. In a Europe of powerful territorial and maritime empires, with the War of the Spanish Succession currently being waged to prevent the realization of a Franco-Spanish universal monarchy, Cromarty understood that Anglo-Scottish incorporation had become a strategic necessity for the maintenance of the European balance of power. Once the Union had been achieved Cromarty continued to agitate for further measures of British integration, most notably in *Several Proposals Conducing to a Farther Union of Britain* (1711). In particular he objected to the continuing Presbyterian persecution of Scottish Episcopalians. Here and elsewhere Cromarty challenged the Presbyterian appropriation of Reformation principles, arguing that the

Scottish Reformation had at first involved church government by superintendents quite distinct from the later democratic innovations of modern Presbyterians.

At times Cromarty presented himself as a self-conscious and reluctant participant in the sectarian battles of his age, in one case tracing confessional disputation back to its original source, the Devil, who had used theologians to introduce metaphysical abstractions and points of contention into the primitive simplicity of Christ's message. Described by one otherwise ill-disposed commentator as 'well accomplished in all kinds of learning' (Lockhart, 43), by another observer as 'a great Master of Philosophy, and much esteemed by the Royal Society of London' (*Memoirs of the Secret Services*, 188), Cromarty stood on the cusp of the Scottish Enlightenment. His world-view represented a curious blend of the old theology and the new science. Typically, the emergence of the deists provoked Cromarty into constructing a bizarre defence of the fundamental truths of Christian revelation. Only prophecy, he argued, provided a reliable defence of the Bible. Some critics might scoff at miracles, for instance as mere natural effects, or argue that their short-lived impact could convince only direct witnesses. However, Cromarty believed that the system of synchronic prophecy which he outlined in his *Synopsis apocalyptica* (1708), where biblical prophecies were carefully calibrated against chronological computations, provided a secure basis for the defence of the divine authority of scripture. Cromarty also maintained an interest in the second sight, a phenomenon which he had experienced at first hand in the Scottish highlands during the early 1650s and for which he hazarded an environmental explanation. Several of his writings on natural history were published in the *Transactions* of the Royal Society.

In general Cromarty maintained his political and intellectual interests in separate spheres. Indeed, his undoubted fascination with religion appears to have been theoretical rather than character-forming; Burnet perceived that he 'had great notions of virtue and religion, but they were only notions, at least they have not had great effect on himself at all times' (*Burnet's History*, 97). Yet, he clearly possessed an abundance of charm. Lockhart described Cromarty as 'a good-natured gentleman, master of an extraordinary gift of pleasing and diverting conversation' (Lockhart, 43), a verdict endorsed by John Macky, who noted that he 'hath a great deal of Wit, and is the pleasantest Companion in the World' (*Memoirs of the Secret Services*, 188). Past seventy years old Cromarty was described as one who 'hath been very handsom in his Person; is tall, fair complexioned' (ibid.). He died at New Tarbat, Ross-shire, on 17 August 1714 and was buried, not as he had directed beside his second wife at Wemyss, but beside his ancestors at Dingwall.   COLIN KIDD

Sources W. Fraser, *The earls of Cromartie: their kindred, country and correspondence*, 2 vols. (1876) · 'Memorandum anent the viscount of Tarbat', *Culloden papers: comprising an extensive and interesting correspondence from the year 1625 to 1748*, ed. H. R. Duff (1815), 333–5 · W. H. L. Melville, ed., *Leven and Melville papers: letters and state papers chiefly addressed to George, earl of Melville … 1689–1691*, Bannatyne Club, 77 (1843) · *State papers and letters addressed to William Carstares*, ed. J. M'Cormick (1774) · [G. Lockhart], *Scotland's Ruine: Lockhart of Carnwath's memoirs of the Union*, ed. D. Szechi (1995) · *Memoirs of the secret services of John Macky*, ed. A. R. (1733), 187–8 · G. Mackenzie, *Memoirs of the affairs of Scotland from the Restoration of King Charles II A.D. MDCLX* (1821) · *Bishop Burnet's History of his own time*, new edn, 2 vols. (1838) · R. Wodrow, *Analecta, or, Materials for a history of remarkable providences, mostly relating to Scotch ministers and Christians*, ed. [M. Leishman], 3, Maitland Club, 60 (1843), 147 · P. Hopkins, *Glencoe and the end of the highland war* (1986) · *Scots peerage*, 3.73–7 · W. Ferguson, *Scotland's relations with England: a survey to 1707* (1977) · 'A succinct accompt of my Lord Tarbott's relations, in a letter to the Honourable Robert Boyle, esquire, of the predictions made by seers', R. Kirk, *The secret commonwealth of elves, fauns and fairies* (1893), 39–51 · C. Innes, ed., *Fasti Aberdonenses … 1494–1854*, Spalding Club, 26 (1854), 468 · *DNB* · J. Robertson, 'Andrew Fletcher's vision of union', *Scotland and England, 1286–1815*, ed. R. Mason (1987) · J. Robertson, ed., *A union for empire: political thought and the union of 1707* · P. W. J. Riley, 'The formation of the Scottish ministry of 1703', *SHR*, 44 (1965), 112–34, esp. 117 · P. W. J. Riley, *The Union of England and Scotland* (1978) · P. W. J. Riley, *King William and the Scottish politicians* (1979) · A. L. Murray, 'The lord clerk register', *SHR*, 53 (1974), 124–56, esp. 141–3 · GEC, *Peerage*

Archives NA Scot., corresp. · NL Scot., legal corresp. | BL, letters and memoranda to earl of Godolphin, Add. MS 39953 · BL, letters to duke of Lauderdale and Charles II, Add. MSS 23114–23117, 23242–23246, *passim* · BL, corresp. with Lord Nottingham, Add. MSS 29588–29589, 29595, *passim* · NA Scot., corresp. with Lord Leven and Lord Melville · NA Scot., corresp. with earl of Mar · NL Scot., letters to Forbes family · U. Edin., letters to duke of Lauderdale · W. Sussex RO, letters to marquess of Huntly

Likenesses M. Dahl, oils, *c*.1708, Parliament Hall, Edinburgh, Faculty of Advocates [*see illus.*] · attrib. J. B. Medina, oils, Scot. NPG · J. Smith, mezzotint, BM · P. Vanderbank, line engraving (after J. B. Medina), BM

Mackenzie, Sir George, of Rosehaugh (1636/1638–1691), judge and politician, was born in Dundee either in 1636, as most sources assert, or in 1638, as his own works suggest. He was the eldest son of Simon Mackenzie (*d*. 1666) of Lochslin and his first wife, Elizabeth (*d*. before 1650), daughter of Peter Bruce, principal of St Leonard's College, St Andrews; George *Mackenzie, second earl of Seaforth (*d*. 1651) was his uncle. In 1650 he entered King's College, Aberdeen, where he studied for several years before moving to St Leonard's College, St Andrews, from where he graduated on 13 May 1653. From 1656 Mackenzie studied law at the French University of Bourges, which he later described as 'that Athens of the Jurists' (Mackenzie, *Works*, 1.7), and graduated on 24 October 1658 with a diploma *in utroque*, denoting competence in both civil and canon law. In his petition to join the Faculty of Advocates in Edinburgh the following year, however, he claimed to have been studying the law 'these six yeares past' at universities in both France and the Netherlands, suggesting that he may also have attended a Dutch university for some time between 1653 and 1656 (NL Scot., Adv. MS 25.2.5(i), fol. 324*r*).

Early career To coincide with Charles II's restoration in 1660, Mackenzie published his first work, entitled *Aretina, or, The Serious Romance*, often regarded as 'the first Scottish novel'. Defending the didactic value of romance-writing as serving to show 'what should be done', he proceeded to

Sir George Mackenzie of Rosehaugh (1636/1638–1691), by Sir Godfrey Kneller, in or before 1686

incorporate a thinly veiled allegorical account of the recent civil wars within his tale (preface, 7). Having been admitted to the Faculty of Advocates on 18 January 1659, following the Restoration he was readmitted on 5 June 1661 before being promoted to the office of justice-depute on 25 July 1661 with an annual salary of £50. He had already acquired early prominence for his courageous pleading as a member of the defence counsel unsuccessfully attempting to save the first marquess of Argyll from treason charges earlier that year. Aware that an argument 'might escape us which might be interpreted in itself as treason' (Mackenzie, *Memoirs*, 35), Mackenzie nevertheless contended that, with no Act of Indemnity passed in Scotland, regarding Argyll's former compliance as perfidious established a dangerous precedent, since all Scots had been 'forc'd to be the idle Witnesses' of the usurpation, even by paying Cromwellian taxes ('Fifteenth pleading', Mackenzie, *Works*, 1.80). A post-nuptial contract dated 8 December 1662 indicates that Mackenzie had recently married Elizabeth (d. 1669), daughter of John Dickson of Hartree, a lord of session; they subsequently had at least one son and two daughters. As justice-depute, Mackenzie became involved in the notorious series of trials staged during one of the largest witch-hunts in Scottish history, when, in sixteen months between 1661 and 1662, over 600 people were accused of acts of sorcery and diabolism. While not denying witchcraft's existence, Mackenzie was disturbed by the ways in which he believed 'poor Innocents die in Multitudes by an unworthy Martyrdom, and Burning comes in fashion', and he therefore insisted on the strictest degrees of judicial rigour and impartiality to dispel popular superstition and hysteria (ibid., 'Sixteenth

pleading', 1.89). He resigned as justice-depute on 8 December 1663, though remuneration was not received until 2 March 1668.

Amid recrudescent religious sectarianism, Mackenzie published *Religio stoici* (1663), attacking 'those mad-cap Zealots of this Bigot Age' (sig. A2r). Reprinted eight times during the Restoration, his tract denounced religious persecution, arguing that to punish 'the body for that which is a guilt of the soul' was as unjust as penalizing one family member for the crime of a relative (ibid., sig. A6r). In 1665 Mackenzie's *Moral Essay Preferring Solitude to Publick Employment* attracted the attention in London of Abraham Cowley, who allegedly 'sent all about town in vain to get the author' (Vickers, x) before John Evelyn penned a devastatingly skilful rejoinder rejecting Mackenzie's showy elevation of leisure over business. In the same year Mackenzie was chosen as advocate for Dundee, and in 1666, when it was resolved that treason trials could occur in the absence of the accused, participated in prosecutions relating to the covenanters' Pentland rising. Having been knighted in 1666, he subsequently took his title from his estate at Rosehaugh in the Black Isle, which he purchased from the bishop of Ross in 1668. In addition to Rosehaugh, he also resided at the Shank in Edinburghshire. Despite regarding Edinburgh as 'the most unwholesome and unpleasant town in Scotland' (Mackenzie, *Memoirs*, 223), when in the capital he lived in what became known as Rosehaugh's Close in the High Street, now Strichen's Close. Following his first wife's death in August 1669, on 4 January 1670 he married Margaret Halyburton (d. 1713), daughter of James Halyburton of Pitcur; they had one son.

Having been elected to the Scottish parliament for Ross-shire in 1669, Mackenzie was initially regarded as 'that factious young man' (Mackenzie, *Memoirs*, 223) by the parliamentary high commissioner, the earl of Lauderdale, but he survived attempts to deprive him of his seat on technical grounds. Staunchly patriotic, he responded to Charles II's overtures to appoint commissioners to treat for an incorporating Anglo-Scottish union in 1670 by insisting in his maiden speech to parliament that any 'Union should be a national Act; and the way to make it so is, that all its steps should be nationally concluded' (ibid., 152). Notwithstanding, he denied the right of parliamentary commissioners to 'extinguish, or innovate the Constitution of the Parliament of Scotland' unless agreed unanimously, since each commissioner's right 'cannot be taken away without his own Consent, tho' all these who are in the Society with him should Renounce what is theirs' (Mackenzie, *Works*, 2.669). This argument that the Scottish parliament was not entitled to legislate itself out of existence by a majority vote acquired especial resonance nearly forty years later amid negotiations for Anglo-Scottish union in 1707, when Mackenzie's opinions were revived by anti-unionist pamphleteers.

Mackenzie as lord advocate Re-elected to the parliaments of 1670, 1672, and 1673, Mackenzie gradually relinquished his role as opposition defender of popular liberties, becoming a committed supporter of the earl (later duke) of Lauderdale, who evidently 'trusted him thereafter with all affairs of the greatest importance and secrecy' (Mackenzie, *Memoirs*, 259–60). When Charles II refused to sanction parliamentary appeal for a judgment of the session, the so-called advocates' strike erupted, and on 24 November 1674 Mackenzie was formally debarred from practice. According to Archbishop John Paterson of Glasgow, however, he thereafter proved a 'good instrument' (NA Scot., CH 12/12/1370) in ensuring that the dispute was eventually resolved, and, as the first 'outed advocate' who 'clearly returned to his duty', Mackenzie was the first to be readmitted on 29 June 1675 (NA Scot., CS 1/7). Despite having earlier turned down the unsalaried post of justice-general, on 28 June 1676 he was appointed as 'understudy' to the lord advocate, Sir John Nisbet of Dirleton, with an annual salary of £100. On 23 August 1677 Mackenzie succeeded Nisbet as lord advocate and was formally received into the office on 4 September, resolving immediately to 'give the world ane experiment of his justice' by discharging those prisoners 'his predecessor had left him, because no money had been offered' to initiate prosecutions (*Historical Notices*, 1.174, 180). On 5 January 1682 he was elected dean of the Faculty of Advocates, and was re-elected on 30 January 1685 on account of the 'beginning and considerable advancement' he had made in informally founding a faculty library (Pinkerton, 58, 69). As dean, Mackenzie insisted that new entrants be required to purchase volumes for the library, thus ending the 'bad custome' which had hitherto prevailed, whereby successful petitioners held feasts for their examiners (ibid., 75–6).

As civil unrest intensified across Scotland, however, Mackenzie acquired the unenviable popular sobriquet Bluidy Mackenzie for his vigorous prosecution of prominent covenanters, including James Mitchell, Sir Hugh Campbell of Cessnock, Robert Baillie of Jerviswood, and the ninth earl of Argyll. In September 1680 the extremist covenanter Richard Cargill 'excommunicated' Mackenzie from 'the true Church' for his 'constant pleading against, and persecuting to death, the people of God', as well as for his 'ungodly, erroneous, phantastic, and blasphemous tenets, printed to the world in his pamphlets and pasquils' (Thomson, 509–10).

As lord advocate, Mackenzie was known for being forthright in his professional and personal dealings: as he informed Lauderdale in 1680, 'I always tell my opinion & if it please not I serv others according to ther inclination' (Airy, 3.195). Referring to Mackenzie's notorious irascibility in the courtroom, Lauder of Fountainhall observed how 'finding he had mistaken himself, he raged and swore, and railed' during a trial in 1682 (*Historical Notices*, 1.366). When complaints were lodged that vociferous presbyterians were disrupting the earl of Cessnock's trial in 1684, another covenanter, John Erskine of Carnock, recalled how the court decided 'there was none there shouted more than my Lord Advocate himself, which the Advocate said he had done, but that it was his part to do so' (*Journal of John Erskine*, 54). Having acquired a distinguished reputation for forensic eloquence, Mackenzie

himself believed that the 'Scottish Idiom of the British Tongue' was better suited to legal pleading than were native English or French speakers on account of the 'fiery, abrupt, sprightly and bold' qualities of the Scottish character ('Pleadings', Mackenzie, *Works*, 1.17). During the trial of James Mitchell for the attempted murder of Archbishop James Sharp in 1678, however, the English clergyman George Hickes described Mackenzie as 'almost the only great man of this country' who pursued Mitchell 'like a gallant man and a good Christian' (Ellis, 2nd ser., 4.29). Further eloquent testimony was supplied by the radical covenanter Alexander Shields, who regarded the lord advocate as 'a man that could give advice', following Mackenzie's indication that he was 'willing to conference upon it when I pleased' when Shields himself was prosecuted for treason in 1685 (NA Scot., JC 39/73/1).

In addition to holding high public office as lord advocate, Mackenzie also sustained an extensive published output that encompassed jurisprudence, imaginative literature, moral philosophy, and political theory. As he himself once acknowledged, 'being bred to the Law … requires a whole Man and his whole Age' (Mackenzie, *Works*, 2.574), and his reputation as a jurist was pre-eminent. His *Institutions of the Law of Scotland* (1684) went through nine editions before being replaced as the main textbook for teaching Scots law by John Erskine's *Institutions* (1758). Concerned to locate the sources of authority within Scots law, Mackenzie accorded priority to statutes that he deemed 'the chief Pillars of our Law', clearly promulgated by a sovereign lawgiver (*Observations*, sig. A2r). Believing that the Scottish statutes should be publicly accessible, in 1686 he issued his *Observations on the Acts of Parliament from the Time of James I &c.*, insisting that monarchs were as obliged to laws as subjects. Similar concerns for legal transparency had also underpinned Mackenzie's *Laws and Customs of Scotland in Matters Criminal* (1678), which provided the first systematic and detailed exposition of Scots criminal law. Prioritizing the authority of penal statutes, Mackenzie's aspiration was 'that nothing were a Crime which is not declared to be so, by a Statute', since that would render 'Subjects inexcuseable, and prevent the arbitrariness of Judges' (*Laws and Customs*, 1.1.3). With regard to incipient crimes and criminal intention, however, he differentiated between the severity appropriate for public crimes and the potential for leniency in private transgressions. As he conceived it, an individual who allegedly 'designed to commit a [public] crime, should be punished as if he had committed it; if he was only letted by accident, because the Common-wealth cannot otherwise be secure' (ibid., 1.1.4).

The preservation of order nevertheless remained Mackenzie's priority in the aftermath of the mid-century civil wars. As domestic unrest escalated from the late 1670s onwards, he privately advised Charles II that, as an absolute sovereign ruling in exceptionally volatile circumstances, he was 'not oblieged to shew a Law for what yow doe' (BL, Add. MS 23244, fol. 20v). As Mackenzie confirmed in *A Vindication of his Majesties Government and Judicatures* (1683), whatever measures were required to ensure civil peace were rendered lawful, since 'the Necessity of State is that supereminent Law, to which upon occasions all particular Acts must bow' (Mackenzie, *Works*, 2.350). He was also compelled to justify dispensing with various legal niceties in his capacity as lord advocate. When the admissibility of auxiliary evidence was challenged during the trial of Robert Baillie of Jerviswood in 1684, for example, Mackenzie warned the jury to avoid 'encouraging a civil war, Wherein your selves and your Posterity may bleed', by finding 'the least difficulty' in a case where there were 'Proofs which are stronger than witnesses' (*Tryal ... of Jerviswood*, 36).

Royalism As lord advocate, Mackenzie's published output extended beyond the legal sphere to include works of political theory that later came to denote the apotheosis of royalist political sentiment in the twilight years of Stuart absolutism in Scotland. In 1684, for example, he composed *Jus regium, or, The just and solid foundations of monarchy in general, and more especially of the monarchy of Scotland*, directed against the resistance theories expounded by post-Reformation presbyterians and Jesuits alike. Incensed that writers such as George Buchanan 'should have adventur'd upon a debate in Law' without legal training and 'should have written Books upon that Subject, without citing one Law, Civil, or Municipal, *pro* or *con*', Mackenzie insisted that the sovereign authority of the Scottish monarch was divinely ordained, absolute, and irresistible (p. 6). Defending ancient constitutionalist arguments that the Scottish monarchy had been originally founded in 330 BC by the legendary Fergus I, he upheld notions of natural subjection, rejecting those 'Jesuitical and Fanatical Principles, that every man is born free, and at Liberty to choose what form of government he pleaseth' (ibid., 24). Mackenzie also defended absolute monarchy's qualitative superiority, for though 'a mixt monarchy may seem a plausible thing to Metaphysical Spirits and School-men, yet to such as understand Government and the World, it cannot but appear impracticable' (ibid., 42). Since the Scottish monarchy was also hereditary, he denounced whig exclusionist attempts to deprive the duke of York from succeeding to the English throne in the late 1670s, declaring that such attempts served only 'to allow that Arbitrariness against our Kings, which we would not allow in them to us' (G. Mackenzie, *Lawful Successor*, 1684 175–6).

Evidence of the influential reception of Mackenzie's royalist ideas is provided by the resolution passed by the convocation of Oxford University in June 1684 thanking him 'for the service he had done his Majesty in writing and publishing *Jus regium*' (*Life and Times of Anthony Wood*, 3.96). Having recently received a copy of *Jus regium* and various other volumes as gifts from Mackenzie, in May 1686 the Dutch stadholder, William of Orange, responded that he greatly esteemed 'le zèle que vous continuez de temoigner pour l'honneur & la gloire de la Maison Royale, & pareillement l'affection que vous conservez à mon égard' ('the zeal you continue to demonstrate for the honour and glory of the royal house, and equally the affection

you have for me'; Mackenzie, *Works*, preface). The uncompromising character of Mackenzie's royalist ideology subsequently moved the nineteenth-century historian Frederic Maitland to affirm that nowhere in the history of political thought was the belief 'that we perceive intuitively that hereditary monarchy is at all times and in all places the one right form of government' defended more comprehensively than in *Jus regium* (*The Collected Papers of F.W. Maitland*, ed. H. Fisher, 3 vols., 1911, 1.8).

Concern to defend the Scottish monarchy's integrity also entailed Mackenzie's involvement in a historiographical dispute with William Lloyd, the Anglican bishop of St Asaph, whose claim that Scotland had not been settled until the sixth century fatally undermined Scottish claims to be the oldest monarchy in the world. Seeking to demonstrate, as one contemporary put it, 'how injurious the Bischop is, not only to our wholle nation, but to our kings', in 'loping of 45 of ther royall ancestors' (Lauder, *Historical Observes*, 155), Mackenzie published *A Defence of the Antiquity of the Royal Line of Scotland* (1685). Following Bishop Edward Stillingfleet of Worcester's entry into the debate on Lloyd's side, Mackenzie issued *The Antiquity of the Royal Line of Scotland Further Cleared and Defended* (1686), observing that both senior clerics were 'angry at me, tho' the King's Advocate, for daring to say that this was a Kind of Lèse-Majesté', though he conceded that he had intended the term 'in a rhetorical, and not in a legal Sense' when attacking their historical researches (Mackenzie, *Works*, 2.400). In the aftermath of the establishment of the Scottish record of arms in 1672, Mackenzie reinforced the monarch's dignity in *The Science of Heraldry*, which insisted on armigerous scruples being observed, since an improper use of royal arms could denote a treasonable claim to sovereignty, and 'he who usurps a Prince's Arms, loses his Head' (ibid., 2.583).

Mackenzie also remained firmly opposed to the claims of religious conscience being fraudulently used as a pretext for political resistance. His own religious convictions appear to have been essentially latitudinarian, eirenic, and *politique*: as one contemporary confirmed, 'speaking of religion, he loved not to stand on pin points with God' (*Journal of John Erskine*, 24). Such ecumenicism was, however, circumscribed by an Erastian commitment to enforce outward conformity. As he once warned Charles II, 'Remember, remember, that such pretexts borrowed from libertie and conscience grew up in the last age to a rebellion' (BL, Add. MS 23244, fol. 27v).

Mackenzie's considerable efforts on behalf of the Stuart monarchs were not unreciprocated. In December 1678 Charles II publicly endorsed his conduct as lord advocate, grateful for 'the care and faithfulness with which he had maintained the royal prerogative' (*CSP dom.*, 1678, 274). Mackenzie was not, however, without enemies. The previous year he had been assaulted by a gang of angry political adversaries and had suffered a broken leg, the effects of which caused him to limp permanently thereafter, earning him the nickname Vulcan in popular pasquils. But, as he protested to Archbishop James Sharp of St Andrews, apart from bodily harm, he doubted his enemies' ability to break his resolve, given his own 'secret pleasur in serving the King' (BL, Add. MS 23138, fol. 53*v*).

The Williamite revolution Mackenzie's instinctive inclination to serve the Stuart cause was, however, severely tested following the accession of James VII and II in 1685. The following February, Lauder of Fountainhall observed that Mackenzie's 'fall is intended, because he would not be for taking off the penal statutes' (*Chronological Notes*, 160), and on 17 May 1686 Mackenzie was indeed forced to demit office as lord advocate because of his failure to support James's plans to enact religious toleration. Despite travelling to London, he returned 'without seeing the king' and was thus obliged to 'put on his gown as ane ordinary Advocat' when the session resumed that autumn (ibid., 189, 201). Ironically, he thereafter proved successful at defending several prominent covenanting rebels from treason charges initiated by his successor, Sir John Dalrymple, before being reappointed himself as lord advocate on 31 January 1688.

On 15 March 1689 Mackenzie is thought to have delivered the inaugural speech at the formal opening of the Advocates' Library, which he envisaged as 'a modern Lyceum and a new Stoa where brilliant wits will be exercised in harmless encounters' (G. Mackenzie, *Oratio inauguralis in aperienda Jurisconsultorum Bibliotheca*, ed. J. Cairns and A. Cain, 1989, 64) and which in 1925 became the National Library of Scotland. On 16 March, however, the convention of estates 'resolved to take the poynt of securitie into consideration' (*APS*, supplement, 48), following Mackenzie's claims that fears for his personal safety were preventing him from attending the convention as an elected member for Forfarshire. On 4 April he did attend as one of a minority of five who opposed the convention's decision to declare the Scottish throne vacant following the flight of James VII and II to France.

Electing to leave Scotland, Mackenzie recognized in April 1689 that 'My bigotrie for the Royall familie & for Monarchie is & has been very troublesom to me' (BL, Add. MS 34516, fol. 63). Regretting that he had now become the target of assassination plots by former covenanters, he nevertheless ventured that 'it may seem reasonable to suffer mee to live, for in conscience all the Lawyers now alyv in Scotland put together, know not how to resolve one sure rule' (ibid., fols. 61–2). For his part he acknowledged that he thereafter intended 'to live peaceably and with great satisfaction under the present new elected King, for tho' I was not clear to make a King, yet I love not civill wars nor disorders & wee owe much to him' (ibid.). Together with his cousin George *Mackenzie, Viscount Tarbat, Mackenzie did, however, petition William of Orange in 1689 to remember that 'Episcopacy is necessary for the support of Monarchy'. Moreover, William should also disregard popular pressure to re-establish Presbyterianism as it had not been hitherto possible to discern 'one Ace of difference between the two' systems in practice (Mackenzie and Mackenzie, *A Memorial for his Highness the Prince of Orange, in Relation to the Affairs of Scotland*, 1689, 5, 8).

Following Mackenzie's arrival in England, John Evelyn recorded dining with 'the famous Lawyer' Mackenzie and Bishop Edward Lloyd in London in March 1690, recalling how all three authors had variously opposed one another in print, but were 'now most friendly reconciled' (Evelyn, *Diary*, 921). Having settled in Oxford thereafter, Mackenzie was admitted a student member of the university's Bodleian Library on 2 June 1690. During a visit to London he suffered a haemorrhage, and on 8 May 1691 died in lodgings in St James's Street, Westminster. His corpse was returned to Edinburgh and lay in the abbey church at Holyroodhouse, before being buried in Greyfriars churchyard on 26 June 'in great State and pomp' in an elaborate vault which he himself had designed, attended by 'so great a concourse of people that hath not yet been seen on such an occasion' (Wood, *Ath. Oxon.: Fasti*, 2.413). Mackenzie's surviving son from his second marriage, George, succeeded to his father's entailed estates in October 1691 but died childless in 1707, whereupon succession to the estates was successfully contested by Mackenzie's second daughter from his first marriage, Elizabeth, by then married to Sir James Mackenzie of Royston.

Mackenzie's reputation In Sir Walter Scott's novel *Redgauntlet* (1824), retrospective allusion is made to the 'Bluidy Advocate MacKenyie, who, for his worldly wit and wisdom, had been to the rest as a god' (W. Scott, *Redgauntlet*, ed. G. A. M. Wood and D. Hewitt, 1997, 96). Widely regarded among his peers as 'the brightest man in the nation' (*Chronological Notes*, 161), Mackenzie's prominent public service and prolific printed oeuvre indeed ensured a lively contemporary and posthumous reputation. Having published over twenty volumes on a heterogeneous range of subjects, at his death Mackenzie left an unfinished commentary on Justinian's *Digest* which indicated his wish for 'time to make a scheme of Law and vertues' (BL, Add. MS 18236, fol. 6*r*). Edited by Thomas Ruddiman, Mackenzie's collected works appeared in two volumes in 1718 and 1722. Adorning the title-page was a quotation from Pliny admiring those individuals whose noble actions were remembered by posterity, as well as those whose works were read by succeeding generations. Pliny's contention, however, that 'most happy' were those individuals 'who have done both' rendered his aphorism a fitting epithet to Mackenzie's own achievements. In 1822 Thomas Thomson published the surviving portions of Mackenzie's *Memoirs of the Affairs of Scotland from the Restoration of King Charles*. As Mackenzie had confirmed in the opening to these political *Memoirs*, while not offering 'an account of the fate of great monarchies … the events I relate were the products of as much hate, and of as many thoughts in the actors, as actions of much greater splendour' (p. 4).

When reviewing the character of Mackenzie's private thoughts and actions, however, biographical material remains sparse: much surviving correspondence from Mackenzie concludes with the injunction 'Burn this letter I entreat yow'. As he confessed on one occasion, 'at this distance & in this confusion no man knowes what to writ' (BL, Add. MS 34516, fols. 61–2). His diligence as a correspondent had, however, been challenged by John Grahame of Claverhouse, who complained in 1682 of the lack of political information he was receiving from Edinburgh, particularly from 'my good friend, the Advocat', who 'wreats to me very kyndly; but … ordinarily loses the letter and forgats the business befor he have the tyme to make any return' (*Buccleuch MSS*, 1.268). Despite his preoccupations, Mackenzie had evidently been regarded as a crucial political ally or foe. For John Drummond of Lundin he remained 'the oddest man in the world' and 'as humorsome as the winde'. Nevertheless, while in London in 1683, Drummond had acknowledged that 'people hear seis only his best side, and that is so good, he has mor influence on men's mynds that will hear him then can be imagined' (*Buccleuch MSS*, 2.144, 156).

Mackenzie's reputation thus extended widely. In a professional capacity, two of his former law tutors from Bourges, Robert Tuillier and Gaspard Thaumas de la Thaumassière, had deemed his *Idea eloquentiae forensis hodiernae* of 1681 superior to any account of legal rhetoric previously published. In a spirit of critical generosity John Dryden remembered 'that Noble Wit of Scotland, Sr George MacKenzy', whose advice on poetic style Dryden had found profitable (J. Dryden, *Works*, ed. A. B. Chambers and W. Frost, 1974, 4.96). The Utrecht historian Johannes Graevius promoted the continental publication of several of Mackenzie's works in Jena, Leipzig, and Coburg, and sent a copy of Mackenzie's *Antiquity of the Royal Line of Scotland* to John Locke in 1690. For Graevius, Mackenzie was indeed not only 'a man both of the highest honour and of the highest genius and learning', but also an individual 'distinguished no less for his services in government than for the outstanding monuments of his genius' (Mackenzie, *Works*, preface).   CLARE JACKSON

Sources A. Lang, *Sir George Mackenzie, king's advocate, of Rosehaugh: his life and times, 1636(?)–1691* (1909) • G. Mackenzie, *Memoirs of the affairs of Scotland from the Restoration of King Charles A.D.M.DC.LX.*, ed. T. Thomson (1822) • *The works of that eminent and learned lawyer, Sir George Mackenzie of Rosehaugh*, ed. T. Ruddiman, 2 vols. (1718–22) • J. W. Barty, *Ancient deeds and other writs in the Mackenzie–Wharncliffe charter chest* (1906) • J. W. Cairns, 'Sir George Mackenzie, the Faculty of Advocates and the Avocates' Library', in G. Mackenzie, *Oratio inauguralis in aperienda Jurisconsultorum Bibliotheca*, ed. J. Cairns and A. Cain (1989), 18–35 • J. C. L. Jackson, 'Royalist politics, religion and ideas in Restoration Scotland, 1660–1689', PhD diss., U. Cam., 1998 • F. S. Ferguson, 'A bibliography of the works of Sir George Mackenzie', *Edinburgh Bibliographical Society Transactions*, 1 (1935–8), 1–60 • G. W. T. Omond, *The lord advocates of Scotland*, 2 vols. (1883) • BL, Add. MS 18244, fols. 20–28 • *Historical notices of Scotish affairs, selected from the manuscripts of Sir John Lauder of Fountainhall*, ed. D. Laing, 2 vols., Bannatyne Club, 87 (1848) • J. Lauder, *Historical observes of memorable occurrents in church and state, from October 1680 to April 1686*, ed. A. Urquhart and D. Laing, Bannatyne Club, 66 (1840) • *Chronological notes of Scottish affairs, from 1680 till 1701, being chiefly taken from the diary of Lord Fountainhall* (1822) • *Journals of Sir John Lauder*, ed. D. Crawford, Scottish History Society, 36 (1900) • B. Vickers, ed., *Public and private life in the seventeenth century: the Mackenzie–Evelyn debate* (New York, 1985) • *Wood, Ath. Oxon.: Fasti* (1820) • *The life and times of Anthony Wood*, ed. A. Clark, 3, OHS, 26 (1894) • J. W. Cairns, 'The moveable text of Mackenzie: bibliographical problems for the Scottish concept of institutional writing', *Critical studies in ancient law, comparative law and legal studies*, ed. J. W. Cairns and O. F. Robinson (2001), 235–48 • O. Airy, ed., *The Lauderdale papers*, 3 vols. (1884–5) • *Report on the Laing manuscripts*, 2 vols., HMC, 72 (1914–25) • D. Warrand, *Some Mackenzie pedigrees* (1965) • *The tryal and process of high-treason and doom of forfaulture against Mr. Robert Baillie of Jerviswood, traitor* (1685) • *The journal of the Hon. John Erskine of Carnock, 1683–7*, ed. W. MacLeod (1893) • C. Lindsay [earl of Balcarres], *Memoirs touching the revolution in Scotland*, ed. A. W. C. Lindsay [earl of Crawford and Balcarres], Bannatyne Club (1841) • J. Thomson, ed., *A cloud of witnesses for the royal prerogatives of Jesus Christ, being the last speeches and testimonies of those who have suffered for the truth in Scotland, since the year 1680* [n.d.] • J. M. Pinkerton, ed., *The minute book of the Faculty of Advocates*, vol. 1 (1976) • *CSP dom., 1678, with additions, 1674–9* • J. R. N. MacPhail, ed., *Papers from the collection of Sir William Fraser*, Scottish History Society, 3rd ser., 5 (1924) • T. I. Rae, 'The origins of the Advocates Library', *For the encouragement of learning: Scotland's national library, 1689–1989*, ed. P. Cadell and A. Mathieson (1989), 1–22 • P. J. Anderson, ed., *Roll of alumni in arts of the University and King's College of Aberdeen, 1596–1860* (1900) • *APS* • *Reg. PCS*, 3rd ser., vol. 1 • C. Jackson, 'The paradoxical virtue of the historical romance: Sir George Makenzie's *Aretina* (1660) and the civil wars', *Celtic dimensions of the British civil wars*, ed. J. Young (1997), 205–25 • D. Havenstein, '*Religio* writing in seventeenth-century England and Scotland: Sir Thomas Browne's *Religio Medici* (1634) and Sir George Mackenzie's *Religio stoici* (1663)', *Scottish Literary Journal*, 25/2 (1998), 17–33 • *The manuscripts of his grace the duke of Buccleuch and Queensberry … preserved at Drumlanrig Castle*, 2 vols., HMC, 44 (1897–1903) • H. Ellis, ed., *Original letters illustrative of English history*, 2nd ser., 4 vols. (1827) • 'Letter from [Alexander] Shields in the Tolbooth [to John Forbes, Rotterdam] 9 April 1685', NA Scot., JC 39/73/1 • 'Letter from Robert Tuillier and Gaspard Thaumas de la Thamaussière to Mackenzie, 1681', NA Scot., RH 9/2/20 • NL Scot., Adv. MS 25.2.5(i), fol. 324r • 'Sir George Mackenzie to Archbishop Sharp [August or September 1677]', BL, Add. MS 23138, fol. 53 • Episcopal Church records, NA Scot., CH 12/12/1370 • books of sederunt, NA Scot., CS 1/6/1, fol. 473, and CS 1/7 • commissary court records, NA Scot., CC 8/8/83 and CC 8/8/86 • graduation lists, U. St Andr., MS UY 305/3, fol. 31 • matriculation lists, University of Bourges, France, Archives du Cher, D.9

Archives NL Scot., corresp. • NL Scot., letters • NL Scot., memoirs of affairs of Scotland | BL, letters to duke of Lauderdale and duchess of Lauderdale, and Charles II, Add. MSS 23135–23137, 23242–23249 • Buckminster Park, Grantham, corresp. with duke of Lauderdale • U. Edin., genealogical papers relating to Scottish families

Likenesses G. Kneller, oils, in or before 1686, Faculty of Advocates, Parliament Hall, Edinburgh [*see illus.*] • R. White, line engraving, 1686 (after G. Kneller); BM; version, Bodl. Oxf. • J. Beugo, line engraving (after G. Kneller), BM • J. Beugo, wash drawing (after G. Kneller), Scot. NPG • J. Rogers, line engraving (after G. Kneller), BM • P. Vanderbank, line engraving (after G. Kneller), BM, NPG • oils (after G. Kneller), Scot. NPG • silhouette, NPG

Mackenzie, George (1669–1725), physician and biographer, was born in Ross-shire on 10 December 1669, son of the Hon. Colin Mackenzie, soldier, second son of George *Mackenzie, second earl of Seaforth, and Jean Lawrie (*d.* 1670/71), daughter of Dr Robert Lawrie, dean of Edinburgh and bishop of Brechin. An Episcopalian, Mackenzie first attended university in Aberdeen, graduating from King's College in 1682, before moving to continue his education in Oxford and thereafter in Paris where he spent several years studying medicine. Returning to Aberdeen, he graduated MD from King's College in 1696 and was subsequently elected a fellow of the Royal College of Physicians of Edinburgh in 1704. The following year he was elected physician to Heriot's Hospital, but after attacking the hospital's Presbyterian governors in a printed pamphlet, his appointment was rescinded in 1711 and, following further investigations, he was formally dismissed in 1714.

Between 1708 and 1722 Mackenzie published a series of three substantial volumes comprehending *The Lives and Characters of the most Eminent Writers of the Scots Nation*, evidently concerned that although 'our Nation has produc'd as Great Men as any other', no written commemoration of Scotland's great authors had hitherto been attempted ('Preface' to *Lives and Characters*, 1, 1708, i). Acknowledging a debt to contemporary French encyclopaedic historians, he vigorously defended the didactic purpose of his undertaking, declaring that '[t]he Moral and Intellectual Conduct of Men's Lives, is, in a great Part, Owing to the Observations which they make, either upon the Vertues or Failures of Others' (ibid., 2, iii). Regarding questions of historical objectivity, Mackenzie remained, however, somewhat equivocal, observing that since 'all Parties misrepresent Facts ... it is an infinite Trouble to sift out the Truth' (ibid.) or to establish conclusively the veracity of ancient historical documents. Consequently, while his venture was undoubtedly ambitious, it was also frequently imprecise and inaccurate. Despite owning Mackenzie to be 'my very intimate Acquaintance' the antiquary Thomas Ruddiman, for instance, later acknowledged that 'he was sometimes too credulous' (Ruddiman, 126). Likewise, according to Robert Wodrow, although Mackenzie had also been 'a crony' and frequent drinking companion of another physician and writer, Archibald Pitcairne, when Pitcairne read Mackenzie's biographies 'he declared they were not worth a button' (Wodrow, 1.69). Mackenzie was also responsible for composing the brief biography which was prefixed to the collected works of his kinsman, the former lord advocate Sir George Mackenzie of Rosehaugh (1636–1691). In the sphere of genealogical research, he prepared a manuscript history of the Mackenzie of Seaforth dynasty, together with an account of the familial relationships between the Mackenzies and Fitzgeralds from AD 1000 onwards.

Mackenzie was also interested in contemporary developments in natural philosophy and, in 1722, he sent a detailed account of the dissection of a Brazilian coatimundi to the English scientist Sir Hans Sloane; this was subsequently included in the *Philosophical Transactions* of the Royal Society. On 28 November 1725 Mackenzie died at Fortrose in Ross-shire and was buried a week later, amid great ceremony, alongside other distinguished members of the Mackenzie of Seaforth family. Although he was married, nothing is known of his wife or of any descendants (BL, Add. MS 39188, fol. 77).   CLARE JACKSON

Sources *Caledonian Mercury* (16 Dec 1725) • *Scots peerage* • W. Steven, *Memoir of George Heriot* (1845) • T. Ruddiman, *A vindication of Mr George Buchanan's paraphrase of the book of Psalms* (1745) • R. Wodrow, *Analecta, or, Materials for a history of remarkable providences, mostly relating to Scotch ministers and Christians*, ed. [M. Leishman], 4 vols., Maitland Club, 60 (1842–3) • P. J. Anderson, ed., *Officers and graduates of University and King's College, Aberdeen, MVD–MDCCCLX*, New Spalding Club, 11 (1893) • W. S. Craig, *History of the Royal College of Physicians of Edinburgh* (1976) • K. Hulton, G. Shaw, and R. Pearson, eds., *The Philosophical Transactions of the Royal Society of London, from 1713 to 1723*, 6 (1809) • correspondence, BL, Sloane MSS
Archives BL, corresp., Sloane MSS

Mackenzie, George, styled third earl of Cromarty (*c*.1703–1766), Jacobite army officer, was the eldest son of John, second earl (*c*.1656–1731), and his second wife, Mary (*b*. 1681, *d*. before 1717), eldest daughter of Patrick Murray, third Lord Elibank. His father was tried in the high court of justiciary in August 1691 for the murder at Leith of Elias Poiret, sieur de la Roche, but was acquitted. On 23 September 1724 Mackenzie married Isabella Gordon, 'Bonnie Bell' (1704/5–1769), eldest daughter of Sir William Gordon, bt, of Dalpholly, with whom he had three sons, including John *Mackenzie, Lord Macleod, who rose to be Count Cromarty and commandant of the sword in the Swedish service, and seven daughters. From his birth, Mackenzie bore the title master of Macleod, and in 1714 he became Lord Tarbat; on the death of his father on 20 February 1731 he succeeded to the earldom. In 1737–8 he was grand master of freemasons.

When the 1745 rising began, although he received an approach from Charles Edward Stuart, Jacobite prince of Wales, on 8 August, Cromarty equivocated for a while, asking advice of his neighbours, particularly Forbes of Culloden and Lord Lovat, to whom he was very close. It was argued after the 'Forty-Five that pique at his son's not being given charge of commissions in the independent companies to be raised for the crown led him to join the rising, but in any case Cromarty had been one of those who had engaged to support the prince in 1740. After the battle of Prestonpans, Lord Tullibardine, as commander-in-chief in Scotland, wrote to Cromarty on 28 September asking him to rise. He did so shortly thereafter, raising around 300–400 men, who were mainly engaged in shadowing Loudoun's forces and raising money, particularly the Fife cess: they were operational only north of the Forth. On 31 December he received orders to join the main army, and in January 1746 Cromarty's regiment supervised the transport of artillery across the Forth for the siege of Stirling before taking part in the battle of Falkirk, where he appears to have commanded a brigade. Subsequently he undertook a number of operations in the north, which had mixed success, before the arrival of the duke of Perth to take overall command of them in March. With the Jacobite army in desperate need of money, Cromarty was dispatched north to recover the arms and over £15,000 seized from the *Prince Charles* by Lord Reay, who had also taken prisoner almost 200 picquets. Cromarty's battalion, failing either to recover these funds or collect new ones (such as the Orkney moneys raised by Sir James Stewart of Burray), was surprised and defeated at Dunrobin on 15 April by the earl of Sutherland's militia. Cromarty shut himself and his officers in the castle, whence he was shortly taken either by stratagem or by being dragged out from behind a chair-hanging, beneath which his foot was visible. He was sent to the Tower, and brought to trial with the earl of Kilmarnock and Lord Balmerino before the House of Lords on 28 July. Despite a humiliating *mea culpa* before his judges on the 30th, on 1 August he was sentenced to death and his estates and title forfeited. On the 9th, nine days before the execution of the other lords, he was saved by the intercession of his wife and a number of magnate supporters, including Augusta princess of Wales and possibly Frederick prince of Wales: Cromarty's father-in-law had been her husband's private secretary.

On 18 February 1748 Cromarty was permitted to leave the Tower, and thereafter lodged in Ladyhill, Devon, and later in Northcote, near Honiton. The countess was granted a pension from the Cromarty estates on 26 February 1749, and when this went unpaid repeated efforts were made to secure it: payments to Cromarty's family were later doubled to £400. Cromarty's pardon in October 1749 was conditional on his residing where directed, and he spent the rest of his life in southern England. Despite his wife's pension, Cromarty was 'miserable' with 'loads of debts' (GEC, *Peerage*, 3.546). His son, Lord Macleod, redeemed first the family finances by becoming a soldier of fortune, and then the family honour in the eyes of the government by serving with the army in India: he composed both an account of the 'Forty-five and of his service in the Seven Years' War. Despite his forfeiture in England, Cromarty was named to the French ministers as a potential supporter of the attempt of 1759, but he appears to have taken no further part in Jacobite conspiracy up to the time of his death in Poland Street, Westminster, on 28 September 1766. He was buried at St James's, Westminster, on 5 October.

Lord Cromarty was apparently an amiable man, but of little consequence as a soldier or politician. His status rests entirely on his willingness to use his authority as a local magnate to raise a battalion for the Jacobite army, to which otherwise he contributed little. Horace Walpole described him at his trial as an 'indifferent figure, much dejected, and rather sullen' (GEC, *Peerage*, 3.546).

MURRAY G. H. PITTOCK

Sources DNB · W. Fraser, *The earls of Cromartie: their kindred, country and correspondence*, 2 vols. (1876) · *Scots peerage* · GEC, *Peerage*, new edn · *A Jacobite source list: list of documents in the Scottish Record Office relating to the Jacobites* (1995) · F. J. McLynn, *Charles Edward Stuart: a tragedy in many acts* (1988) · A. Livingstone, C. W. H. Aikman, and B. S. Hart, eds., *Muster roll of Prince Charles Edward Stuart's army, 1745–46* (1984) · K. Tomasson and F. Buist, *Battles of the '45* (1962) · intelligence reports on the rebellion, NL Scot., MS 17514 · E. Cruickshanks, ed., *Ideology and conspiracy: aspects of Jacobitism, 1689–1759* (1982) · S. Reid, *1745: a military history of the last Jacobite rising* (1996) · C. Humphreys, *A letter sent to the late Lord Balmerino* (1746)
Archives NA Scot., annexed estate papers, E746 · NA Scot., corresp. · NA Scot., Cromartie muniments, GD 305 · NL Scot., legal corresp.
Likenesses engraving, repro. in Humphreys, *Letter*, frontispiece · portrait, repro. in Fraser, *Earls of Cromartie*, ccx

Mackenzie, George (1741–1787). *See under* Mackenzie, John, Lord Macleod, and Count Cromarty in the Swedish nobility (1727–1789).

Mackenzie, George (1777–1856), meteorologist and army officer, was born in Sutherland, where his relatives were thriving farmers. In his early days he was tacksman and farmer at Cyderhall, near Dornoch, but after a lawsuit with the factor, in which he won £500 damages, he gave up farming and enlisted in the militia, becoming lieutenant of the Caithness legion regiment of fencibles, captain of the Caithness Volunteers, and lieutenant of the Royal Perth militia, in which he continued until it was disbanded. He was then retained on the staff, and awarded a pension of half a crown a day.

In 1802 Mackenzie began to keep a register of meteorological observations, making these successively at Edinburgh, Dover, London, Haddington, Plymouth, Newcastle, and Leith. Eventually he settled at Perth, where he lived for his last thirty years. He is reputed to have spent only two hours a day in bed, the remainder of his time being occupied in maintaining a continuous weather register.

Mackenzie formulated a primary cycle of winds in 1819. He concluded that weather occurred in cycles, publishing his findings in: *The System of the Weather of the British Isles* (1818); *Manual of the weather for the year 1830, including a brief account of the cycles of the winds and weather* (1829); *Elements of the Cycles of Winds, Weather, and Prices of Corn* (1843); and in annual reports of his observations. His work was reviewed in 1818 by Professor Robert Jameson in the *Edinburgh Review* and Sir David Brewster in *Blackwood's Magazine*, while the English board of agriculture accorded thanks. A copy of Mackenzie's 1818 publication was presented to the French Académie des Sciences, which charged Baron von Humboldt with producing a report on it.

Mackenzie was keenly interested in politics of the most liberal character. Apparently he never married. In his later years he was noted as a kind-hearted old man, possessing a fund of humour. In January 1855 he was taken ill with asthma, followed in 1856 by slight paralysis and shock. He died at County Place, Perth, on 13 May 1856.

GORDON GOODWIN, *rev.* JIM BURTON

Sources *Perthshire Advertiser* (15 May 1856) · J. Woods, *The elements and influence of the weather* (1861) · *GM*, 2nd ser., 45 (1856), 667
Wealth at death financially comfortable: *Perthshire Advertiser*

Mackenzie, Sir George Steuart, seventh baronet (1780–1848), chemist, geologist, and antiquary, was born in Edinburgh on 22 June 1780, only surviving child of Sir Alexander Mackenzie, sixth baronet (c.1741–1796), a major-general in the Bengal army, and Katherine (d. 1829), daughter of Robert Ramsay of Camno, Leith merchant. The family seat was Coul House at Contin, near Dingwall, Ross-shire.

Mackenzie matriculated at the University of Edinburgh in chemistry, attending the sessions 1796–7 and 1798–9. He was elected to the Society of Antiquaries of Scotland in 1798 and, on the proposal of Sir James Hall, John Playfair, and T. C. Hope, to fellowship of the Royal Society of Edinburgh in 1799. In February 1800 he read a paper to that society on experiments on the combustion of diamond (published in Nicholson's *Journal of Natural Philosophy*, 4, June 1800, 103–10). The identity of diamond with carbon was established by experiments on the formation of steel.

In 1801 Mackenzie was admitted to the Highland Society and returned to the university to attend classes in the 1802–3 session under Andrew Coventry in agriculture and Alexander Monro secundus in anatomy. On 8 June 1802 he married Mary (d. 1835), the fifth daughter of the agricultural improver Donald McLeod of Geanies (c.1746–1834). Following his marriage Mackenzie became 'one of the most robust and uncompromising of improvers' (Richards and Clough, 184). Influenced by Sir Joseph Banks and others he became a proponent of merino sheep and purchased from the king's flock in 1807. (His views on the animals were summarized in his *Treatise on the Diseases and Management of Sheep*, 1809). His report for the board of agriculture—*General View of the Agriculture of the Counties of Ross and Cromarty* (1813)—has been described as 'a substantial description and indictment of the older forms of life in the Highlands, and a prescription for a new society and economy' (ibid.). On his own estate he 'evicted every crofter' (Shaw, 196), which made him unpopular among highlanders.

Mackenzie was influenced towards Huttonian geology by his chemistry teachers Joseph Black and T. C. Hope, who were friends of James Hutton, and by publication of John Playfair's *Illustrations of the Huttonian Theory of the Earth* (1802). He later attended the natural history class in the university where Robert Jameson's mineralogical teaching would be valuable, although his Wernerian stance was at odds with Mackenzie's convictions. Contact with an Icelandic medical student, Ólafur Loptsson, led Mackenzie to consider visiting Iceland in 1809. The journey was delayed because of hostilities with Denmark, but in 1810 an order in council liberated trade between Iceland and the ports of Leith, London, and Liverpool; Mackenzie set sail with the physicians Henry Holland (1788–1873) and Richard Bright (1789–1858). *Travels in the Island of Iceland during the Summer of 1810* was published in 1811 and described the natural history of the island and the history, literature, and diseases of the people. (Bright and Holland made significant contributions—both had read papers on Iceland to the Geological Society of London in 1811.) Mackenzie's *Iceland* long remained a key publication but he had drawn on Holland's manuscript, and Holland objected to Mackenzie's misrepresentation of his geological observations. For the second edition (1812) Holland drew a distinction between recorded observations, for which he was to be given credit, and Mackenzie's Huttonian interpretations. Lyell admired Mackenzie's 'magnificent collection of mineralogical treasures' from Iceland (*Life, Letters and Journals*, 1.186), part of which later went to Glasgow University. Mackenzie's melodrama *Helga*, based on Holland's précis of an Icelandic saga, was staged in Edinburgh in January 1812 but was howled off the boards by Wernerian opponents. In that year Mackenzie and Thomas Allan visited the Faeroe Islands. Summaries by Mackenzie of these islands appeared in Brewster's *Edinburgh Encyclopaedia* (Faeroe, 1815; Iceland, 1817).

Mackenzie was later attracted to the study of Scotland's more recent geological past. He sympathized with James Hall's débâcle (great sea-flood) hypothesis and, while accepting J. D. Forbes's evidence for the glaciation of the Cuillins, he rejected the possibility of a former ice age and clung to the outdated Huttonian view of the Alps. He also studied vitrified forts in the north of Scotland and believed vitrification was due to accidental fire arising from the use of such forts as beacons. His work was communicated to, and eventually published by, the Society of Antiquaries of Scotland and his position argued in his 'Forts vitrified' in *The Edinburgh Encyclopaedia* (1815).

Mackenzie was active in many organizations. He did much for the Royal Society of Edinburgh and revivified the Society of Antiquaries of Scotland. He was elected FRS in 1815. When George IV visited Edinburgh in 1822 Mackenzie, as president of the Astronomical Institution, was instrumental in gaining the title 'Royal' for the Edinburgh observatory. He urged the importance of relationships with overseas academies and was made an honorary member of the royal commission for antiquities of the Royal Society of Copenhagen in 1815, and was a member of the Icelandic Literary Society of Copenhagen.

Sir George was described by Dr John Mackenzie (1803–1886), who knew him, as being always short of money and one who would 'part with his temper in a hurry but can't be bothered keeping up a quarrel' (Shaw, 196). Sir Charles Lyell thought him 'very gentlemanlike and intelligent and full of information' with good taste (*Life, Letters and Journals*, 1.156).

Following the death of his first wife in 1835, Mackenzie married, on 27 October the next year, Catherine (d. 1857), widow of Captain John Street RA and daughter of Sir Henry Jardine. The couple had one son (Mackenzie also had seven sons and three daughters from his first marriage). Mackenzie died of stomach cancer at his home, Kinellan House, Murrayfield, Edinburgh, on 26 October 1848 and was buried at Coul in the family burial-ground of Preas Mairi.

CHARLES D. WATERSTON and H. S. TORRENS

Sources bap. reg. Scot. · matriculation records, U. Edin. L., special collections division, university archives · H. Holland, correspondence, NL Scot., Acc. 7515 · letter, G. S. Mackenzie to J. Russell, 8 Nov 1848, NA Scot., RD5/820, fols. 338–40 · H. A. Brück, *The story of astronomy in Edinburgh* (1983) · Burke, *Peerage* (1999) · H. B. Carter, *Sir Joseph Banks, 1743–1820* (1988) · W. R. Dawson, *The Banks letters* (1958) · J. Laskey, *A general account of the Hunterian Museum* (1813) · *Life, letters and journals of Sir Charles Lyell, Bart.*, ed. K. M. Lyell, 2 vols. (1881) · E. Richards and M. Clough, *Cromartie: highland life, 1650–1914* (1989) · C. B. Shaw, *Pigeon holes of memory: the life and times of Dr John Mackenzie, 1803–1886* (1988) · R. B. K. Stevenson, 'The museum, its beginnings and its development', *The Scottish antiquarian tradition*, ed. A. S. Bell (1981), 31–85 · C. D. Waterston, *Collections in context* (1997) · A. Wawn, '*Gunnlaugs saga ormstungu* and the Theatre Royal Edinburgh 1812: melodrama and Sir George Mackenzie', *Scandinavica*, 21 (1982), 139–51 · *The Iceland journal of Sir Henry Holland, 1810*, ed. A. Wawn, Hakluyt Society, 2nd ser. 168 (1987) · V. C. P. Hodson, *List of officers of the Bengal army, 1758–1834*, 3 (1946), 153 · C. D. Waterston, 'Late Enlightenment science and generalism: the case of Sir George Steuart Mackenzie of Coul (1780–1848)', in P. Wood, *Science and medicine in the Scottish Enlightenment*, ed. C. W. J. Withers (2002), 301–26

Archives Hunterian Museum, Glasgow, geological specimens · NA Scot. · National Museum of Scotland, Edinburgh, antiquarian specimens · NHM · NL Scot. · RBG Kew · Royal Society of Edinburgh · Society of Antiquaries of Scotland, Edinburgh · U. Edin. | BL, letters to Lord Aberdeen, Add. MSS 43231–43233, 43243 · NL Scot., corresp. with George Combe · NL Scot., corresp. with Archibald Constable · NL Scot., corresp. with Sir Walter Scott · U. St

Andr. L., corresp. with James David Forbes · UCL, letters to Society for the Diffusion of Useful Knowledge **Likenesses** H. Raeburn, oils, *c.*1796 · H. Raeburn, oils, *c.*1810–1813, priv. coll. **Wealth at death** £11,952 19*s.* 4*d.*: NA Scot., SC 70/1/70 Commissariat of Edinburgh, record of inventories 1849/50, 760

Mackenzie, Sir George Sutherland (1844–1910), explorer and businessman, was born at Bolarum, India, on 5 May 1844, the third son of Sir William Mackenzie, inspector-general of the Madras medical service, and his wife, Margaret, daughter of Edmund Prendergast, of Ardfinnan Castle, co. Tipperary. Educated at Clapham under Dr Charles Pritchard, he went into business, joining the firm of Gray, Dawes & Co., East India merchants, in London, and agents for the British India Steam Navigation Company. As a partner in the firm, Mackenzie was closely connected with the British India Steam Navigation Company, of which he was made a director. In 1866, at twenty-two years of age, he went to the Persian Gulf as the representative of his firm, and after some time at Bushehr was sent into the interior to establish agencies at Shiraz and Esfahan. In 1869 Mackenzie opened a branch at Basrah and expanded trade by steamer services on the Tigris and Euphrates; and in 1875 he travelled from Esfahan through the Bakhtiari country by way of Shustar to the head of the gulf. Though unarmed and with three attendants only, he was never attacked, and by his tact made friends with the chiefs of the tribes. In 1878 he made the reverse journey, starting from Muhammarah, steaming up the Karun River, and then proceeding by way of Shustar. At his death Mackenzie was called 'the doyen of Persian explorers' (*GJ*, 6, 1910, 738). The Foreign Office drew on his experience and the advice of his close associate Sir William Mackinnon to urge railway construction on the shah of Persia in 1886, a plan which foundered on prevarication and financial problems. Mackenzie also revived the idea of steam navigation on the Karun and in 1888 drafted a concession agreement; it was rejected by the shah. On 10 July 1883 Mackenzie married Eliza Mary (d. 1904), the daughter of Major William Cairns Armstrong, of 28 Hogarth Road, London. They had no children.

After the Anglo-German agreement of 1886, in May 1887 the British East African Association, of which Mackenzie was a member, obtained from the sultan of Zanzibar a concession of the coastline of east Africa between the Umba River and Kipini, near the mouth of the Tana. A founders' agreement, dated 18 April 1888, in which Mackenzie figures as a contributor of £5000 and a director, was followed by a royal charter which, on 3 September 1888, incorporated the association under the name of the Imperial British East Africa Company. At the same time, the agency house of Smith, Mackenzie & Co. at Zanzibar acted as importers for the company and for the government of the East Africa Protectorate from 1895.

In October 1888 Mackenzie arrived at Zanzibar to take over, as managing director, the coast leased to the company, and then went on to Mombasa. The time was critical. The African nations in the German sphere were rising against the German East African Company. A joint blockade of the whole east African coast by Great Britain and Germany was found necessary. In the British sphere the Arabs were on the eve of an armed rising owing to runaway slaves being harboured at the mission stations. Mackenzie averted this danger, and paid Arab slave owners compensation for the fugitive slaves at the rate of $25 a head, the gross sum amounting to £3500. Sir Charles Euan-Smith, British consul-general at Zanzibar, described this act as one of 'unparalleled generosity and philanthropy', and bore the strongest testimony to Mackenzie's 'tact and good judgment'. The admiral on the station, Fremantle, commented on his 'tact, care and discretion', and reported that 'he has literally won golden opinions, the Arabs spontaneously giving him a feast' (*Parl. Pap. Africa*, no. 1, 1889, August 1889, pp. 13, 17, 21, 36, etc.). By further gifts and cash he created a company network of Swahili Arabs in the interior and co-operated with potential Indian and Arab rivals by financing caravans.

Mackenzie paid a visit to England in 1889, but returned to Mombasa again in December of that year accompanied by Captain F. D. Lugard, who wrote of 'the personal affection which Mackenzie inspired in all who served under him'. By way of developing east Africa he introduced Persian agriculturists and improved Mombasa town and harbour, but was less successful in recruiting staff to run departments or man interior posts. Mackenzie sent Lugard, commissioned to the company, to survey the route to Machakos; when this failed he was instrumental in directing this initiative towards Uganda, a policy continued by his successor, Sir Francis de Winton. He was also of assistance to the Italians in negotiating treaties for them with the Somali, and received the grand cross of the crown of Italy. Mackenzie returned to Britain in May 1890. There he continued to urge further British expansion into Uganda and directed Lugard's publicity campaign against company evacuation in November 1892.

Mackenzie must bear some of the responsibility for the failure of the Imperial British East Africa Company, which lost its charter in 1895. Like other directors he placed too much confidence in Mackinnon and allowed his imperial patriotism to override his business acumen—a mistake he had never made in Persia. Mackenzie continued to direct the affairs of Gray, Dawes & Co. profitably, and made large investments in the Indian textile factories of Binny & Co. Ltd. He was made CB in 1897 and KCMG in 1902. He also held the grand cross of the Brilliant Star of Zanzibar. He was a member of the council of the Royal Geographical Society from 1893 to 1909 and vice-president in 1901–5. On 14 July 1905, the year after his first wife's death, he married Mary Matilda, the widow of Archibald Bovill and daughter of Hugh Darby Owen, in Chelsea. They had no children. He died suddenly at 157 Winchester House, Old Broad Street, London, on 1 November 1910, and was buried at Brookwood cemetery, Surrey. A photograph of a portrait which belonged to his sister Mrs Mackinnon, of 10 Hyde Park Gardens, was left to the Royal Colonial Institute, of which Mackenzie was a prominent member.

C. P. LUCAS, *rev.* COLIN NEWBURY

Sources R. L. Greaves, *Persia and the defence of India* (1959) · J. S. Galbraith, *Mackinnon and east Africa, 1878–1895: a study in the new imperialism* (1972) · S. Jones, *Two centuries of overseas trading: the origins and growth of the Inchcape Group* (1986) · *DSBB* · m. certs. · *CGPLA Eng. & Wales* (1910) · d. cert.
Archives SOAS, corresp. relating to British East African Company business | Bodl. RH, corresp. with F. D. Lugard · Inchcape Group, London, archives · PRO, Foreign Office confidential print
Likenesses portrait, priv. coll. · wood-engraving, NPG; repro. in *ILN* (24 Aug 1889)
Wealth at death £104,004 19s. 6d.: probate, 16 Dec 1910, *CGPLA Eng. & Wales*

Mackenzie, Georgina Mary Muir [*married name* Georgina Mary Sebright, Lady Sebright] (**1833–1874**), traveller and writer, was the eldest of the nine children of Sir John William Pitt Muir Mackenzie, second baronet, of Delvine, Perthshire, and his wife, Sophia Matilda Johnstone. In 1855, for health reasons, she, with her mother and sisters, moved to London. In 1858, with Adeline Paulina Irby, she began a two-year tour of the Austro-Hungarian empire, during which they were arrested as spies with 'pan-Slavistic tendencies'. They thereafter embarked on extensive journeys across Turkey in Europe, examining the conditions of the Slav Christians under Turkish rule and the position and education of Christian women and girls. In 1864, for health reasons, they returned to England.

The first account of their travels, including the spy incident, was published anonymously in 1862 as *Across the Carpathians*. In 1864 Georgina Muir Mackenzie presented a paper at the British Association for the Advancement of Science (the only woman speaker), which was then published as *Notes on the south Slavonic countries in Austria and Turkey in Europe containing historical and political information added to the substance of a paper read at the British Association at Bath, 1864*. The following year she and Paulina Irby spoke at the association's meeting on the characteristics of the Slavonic people. In 1867 the full extent of their knowledge and experiences was published in *Travels in the Slavonic Provinces of Turkey-in-Europe*, with the authors identified as G. Muir Mackenzie and A. P. Irby. The book was substantial and authoritative, and included an account of the most hazardous of their journeys undertaken in 1863. The order of the names on the title-page indicated the balance of authorship between the two women, and Muir Mackenzie can be considered the principal author and the scholar. The factual and historical appendices showed the depth of research that had been undertaken in its preparation. The book was well received, W. E. Gladstone, in his introduction to the second edition, calling it 'the best English book I have seen on Eastern matters'.

In 1871 Georgina Muir Mackenzie started a new life, marrying, on 24 November Sir Charles Sebright (1807–1884), consul-general of the Ionian Islands, whom she had met in 1862 and 1863 when visiting those islands, and who had gone to live in Corfu. On 24 January 1874 she died in Corfu and was buried in its military cemetery.

DOROTHY ANDERSON

Sources D. Anderson, *Miss Irby and her friends* (1966) · [G. M. M. Mackenzie and A. P. Irby], *Across the Carpathians* (1862) · G. M. Mackenzie and A. P. Irby, *The Turks, the Greeks, and the Slavons: travels in the Slavonic provinces of Turkey-in-Europe* (1867); 2nd edn as *Travels in the Slavonic provinces of Turkey-in-Europe* (1877) · Burke, *Peerage* · Boase, *Mod. Eng. biog.* · Gladstone, *Diaries*
Archives NL Scot., estate and family MSS
Likenesses portrait, priv. coll.
Wealth at death under £1000: administration, 8 Sept 1874, *CGPLA Eng. & Wales*

Mackenzie [*née* Spence], **Dame Helen Carruthers** (1859–1945), educationist and public health campaigner, was born on 13 April 1859 at Mortlach, Banffshire, the daughter of William Spence, merchant tailor and provost of Dufftown, and his wife, Mary McDonell. She was educated at the local village school, where she became a pupil teacher, and completed teacher training at the Church of Scotland Training College, Aberdeen. Her early career was as a teacher at various schools in Aberdeen.

On 12 February 1892 Helen Spence married Dr (William) Leslie *Mackenzie (1862–1935), shortly to become the first medical inspector of schools at the Local Government Board for Scotland. Their subsequent careers were dedicated to the improvement of the physical condition of Scottish schoolchildren and jointly they were influential in the early twentieth-century movement to improve the health of children. In 1902, on behalf of the royal commission (Scotland) on physical training, they conducted a pioneering investigation into the physical state of Edinburgh schoolchildren. The study, organized by Helen, involved the examination of 600 children drawn from four schools deliberately chosen to enable comparison between children from middle-class and working-class areas of the city. Helen was present while her husband checked each child and she also wrote the findings. The study demonstrated that children from the poorer areas were smaller, lighter, and less healthy than children from wealthier homes. The children from Canongate School in the heart of the Old Town were especially unhealthy, with many suffering from significant medical defects; and their conclusion was that the principal factors responsible were bad housing and inadequate and unsatisfactory diets. On the basis of their study they projected that almost 30 per cent of children in Edinburgh were severely malnourished. They called for the systematic medical inspection of school children and the training of teachers in matters of health and hygiene.

In 1904 Helen Mackenzie, giving evidence before the interdepartmental committee on physical deterioration, argued that part of the problem was the ignorance of many women in respect of nutrition, hygiene, and the care of infants. She demanded changes to the education system to enable instruction for girls in these areas. The subsequent Education (Scotland) Act (1908) required school boards to organize the medical inspection of schoolchildren, to provide meal services for poor children, and to provide domestic instruction for girls. The Mackenzies also co-operated in promoting the establishment of a number of special schools for mentally handicapped children, and campaigned for the effective treatment of children suffering minor ailments such as scabies and ringworm.

A member of the school board for Edinburgh and of the departmental committee on industrial schools, Helen Mackenzie also campaigned for an extension of day and evening continuation classes for young women. She was an original member of the East of Scotland Provincial Committee for the Training of Teachers and a governor of the Royal Institution for Deaf and Dumb Children, and she became a member of the council of the Edinburgh College of Domestic Science. Her association with the college (subsequently Queen Margaret College) extended over thirty years and she chaired the council in 1943–5.

Helen Mackenzie was also interested in social work and particularly in the problems of female factory workers. She was secretary of the industrial section of the National Union of Women Workers and also of the Edinburgh branch of the Industrial Law Committee. Before the First World War, she lectured on this subject in the Edinburgh College and during the war assisted on a training course for welfare supervisors appointed by firms employing female labour. After the war she continued to lecture at the University of Edinburgh.

Helen Mackenzie was also active in relation to mental health, female health, and rural district nursing. She was a governor of what became the Royal Scottish National Hospital for the permanent care of mentally handicapped people, and was at different times a member of the health services commission and the Mental Welfare Association. A close friend of Dr Elsie Inglis, she assisted in obtaining better maternity hospital facilities in Edinburgh. She also joined her husband in the promotion of the Highlands and Islands Medical Service which was based on peripatetic district nurses. This latter initiative achieved worldwide recognition, and similar organizations were established elsewhere, notably the Frontier Medical Service in Kentucky.

Helen Mackenzie was a gifted public speaker, her speeches being 'marked by directness and candour, and spiced with a characteristic humour that gripped attention' (*The Scotsman*, 26 Sept 1945). She acquired the title Lady Mackenzie when her husband was knighted in 1919 (though she was universally referred to as Lady Leslie Mackenzie). She was appointed DBE in 1933 and received an LLD from the University of Edinburgh in 1937. She was also a fellow of the Educational Institute of Scotland. For many years an active member of the Woman Citizens' Association, she tended to stress the widening opportunities open to women and also their duties as citizens.

The Mackenzies had no children, but they were devoted to one another, and it was a heavy blow for Lady Leslie Mackenzie when her husband died in 1935. She died at 14 Belgrave Place, Edinburgh, on 25 September 1945, and was cremated on 28 September at Warriston crematorium. The principal of the Edinburgh College of Domestic Science wrote of 'her courage' and of 'her vigorous common sense, her shrewdness, her trenchant comments, her energy, her humour, her sincerity' (*ECDS Magazine*, 7).

TOM BEGG

Sources T. Begg, *The excellent women: the origins and history of Queen Margaret College* (1994) · 'Inter-departmental committee on physical deterioration: list of witnesses and evidence', *Parl. papers* (1904), 32.54, 275–8, Cd 2186 [evidence of Charles Booth, Mrs Leslie Mackenzie] · 'Royal commission on physical training (Scotland)', *Parl. papers* (1903), vol. 30, Cd 1507–8 · *Edinburgh College of Domestic Science Magazine* (Oct 1945), 6–7 [bound vol. 1933–45] · *The Scotsman* (3 July 1937) · *The Scotsman* (26 Sept 1945) · b. cert. · m. cert.
Wealth at death £6153 16s. 6d.: confirmation, 20 Oct 1945, CCI

Mackenzie, Henry (1745–1831), writer, was born in Edinburgh on 26 July 1745, the son of Joshua Mackenzie, a prosperous physician, and his wife, Margaret Rose of Kilravock, eldest daughter of the sixteenth baron of Kilravock. Dr Mackenzie was directly descended from the eighth baron of Kintail, chief of clan Mackenzie. Henry Mackenzie was educated at Edinburgh high school and, from 1758 to 1761, at the University of Edinburgh. He was articled clerk to George Inglis of Redhall, king's attorney in exchequer, but left for London in 1765 to complete his studies in English exchequer practice, which as regulated by the Act of Union was also the law of the exchequer of Scotland.

Mackenzie returned to Scotland in 1768 and became a partner of George Inglis. He also began writing his sentimental novel *The Man of Feeling*, which was published anonymously in 1771. His London years furnished some of the material for his protagonist's adventures, which are described in a series of loosely linked fragments. Harley, with his ideal sensibility, frequently sheds tears over the misfortunes of the people he meets, and his innocence is constantly contrasted with the worldliness of others. The novel became the most popular of its decade. The first American edition was published in 1782, and by the 1820s the novel had appeared in nine different editions. It was reprinted several times and translated into French, German, Polish, and Swedish. Labelled a 'man of feeling' after the novel's publication, Mackenzie was indeed a man of extraordinary sensibility, and he is generally known as the arch-sentimentalist of Scottish literature. However, there were two sides to Mackenzie's character. While he was a man of taste and sentiment, he was also a pragmatic professional lawyer. Such a dualism reveals a specific Scottish trait evident in his writings as well as in his life. He was a prolific letter-writer, even by eighteenth-century standards, his correspondents ranging from literary acquaintances to politicians and diplomats in Britain and France. Members of his own large family also received his witty and insightful epistles.

The Man of Feeling was followed in February 1773 by *The Man of the World*, in which Sindall, a seducer and villain, is intended as a striking contrast to Harley. In that year Mackenzie succeeded Inglis in the crown practice for the board of customs and excise in the court of the exchequer, while his play *The Prince of Tunis*, a romantic tragedy, was first performed at the Theatre Royal in Edinburgh on 8 March. His other plays were *Shipwreck* (a version of Lillo's *Fatal Curiosity*), *The Force of Fashion, a Comedy*, and *The White Hypocrite*.

Henry Mackenzie (1745-1831), by Sir Henry Raeburn, c.1810

On 6 January 1776 Mackenzie married Penuel Grant, daughter of Sir Ludovick Grant of Grant and granddaughter of the earl of Findlater and Seafield. They had eleven children. His epistolary novel, *Julia de Roubigne*, appeared in 1777. Mackenzie's professional legal career reached its zenith when he was appointed comptroller of taxes for Scotland in 1779, having been recommended for the post by Henry Dundas, Viscount Melville. Meanwhile, he continued his literary pursuits by editing two periodicals: *The Mirror* (1779-80) and *The Lounger* (1785-7). Following the example of Addison's *Spectator*, they were the first Scottish weeklies of their kind. Mackenzie contributed most of the essays and focused on life and society, advocating a way of life based on natural sentiment and harmony. The balance between egotistic and altruistic motives was very much a tenet of the Scottish Enlightenment. Mackenzie's essays 'On novel-writing' and 'Criticism on the character and tragedy of Hamlet' are good examples of the literary analysis to be found in *The Mirror* and *The Lounger*.

Publishers often took Mackenzie's advice before accepting a manuscript. He supported Robert Burns by writing a favourable and influential review of the Kilmarnock poems, and he gave Sir Walter Scott a start on the ladder towards literary fame. He later became one the first writers 'of any literary reputation to admire Byron' (Thompson, 323).

On 21 April 1788 Mackenzie read his 'Account of the German theatre' to the Royal Society of Edinburgh, of which he was a founder member. The lecture was the result of his unflagging endeavours to acquaint himself with German literature and German theatre. It inspired Scott to attempt translations of ballads by Gottfried August Burger and of Goethe's *Götz von Berlichingen*. Mackenzie himself tried his skill at adaptations for the British stage with the help of French translations of the original texts.

In 1790–91 there appeared, in a series of articles, Mackenzie's 'Letters of Brutus to certain political characters', strongly Pittite in tone and written for the *Edinburgh Herald*. Yet his elaborate 'Review of the principal proceedings of the parliament of 1784' (1792) was the only one of his numerous political writings which he subsequently acknowledged.

From 1789 Mackenzie was active in the Highland Society of Scotland. He was one of its directors and edited its *Transactions*. In 1797 he was asked to convene and chair a committee of the society charged with inquiring into the authenticity of the poems of Ossian, as 'translated' by James Macpherson. A *Report*, published in 1805, collected various pieces of evidence and explained the decision taken by the commission. It defended Macpherson against fabricating the poems altogether, but conceded that he inserted passages, deleted others, and refined the language. To all appearances, however, the report satisfied, at least partially, the desire of the Scottish literati to claim the heritage of a national epic dating back to an ancient civilization.

From 1801 to 1810 Mackenzie was a trustee of the Edinburgh Theatre Royal, together with Sir Walter Scott and William Erskine. As the grand old man of letters in Edinburgh, Mackenzie was commissioned by Constable to edit the works of John Home, whose tragedy *Douglas* had caused much controversy. In his biographical introduction to the three-volume edition (1822), he draws upon his insider knowledge and fund of literary anecdote. The unique position Mackenzie occupied in society and the great influence he exercised in all matters literary coincided with Edinburgh's cultural and intellectual heyday in the final quarter of the eighteenth and first two decades of the nineteenth century. A unifying, if not solitary, element in a rapidly changing cultural landscape, Mackenzie links the age of David Hume and Adam Smith to that of Robert Burns, John Galt, James Hogg, and Walter Scott.

Henry Mackenzie died in Edinburgh on 14 January 1831, and was buried in Greyfriars churchyard, Edinburgh. The *Edinburgh Evening Courant* observed in its obituary: 'We cannot but with feelings of regret, notice the departure of almost the last of that eminent class of literary men, who, about fifty years ago, cast such a lustre on our city … there have been few authors more distinguished'.

H. W. Drescher

Sources Chambers, *Scots.* (1856) · H. W. Thompson, *A Scottish man of feeling: some account of Henry Mackenzie, esq. of Edinburgh* (1931) · H. W. Drescher, *Themen und Formen des periodischen Essays im späten 18. Jahrhundert* (Frankfurt am Main, [1971]) · *Literature and literati: the literary correspondence and notebooks of Henry Mackenzie*, ed. H. W. Drescher, 2 vols. (1989-99) · H. W. Drescher, *Lexikon der englischen*

Literatur (1971) · Highland Society of Scotland, *Report of the committee of the Highland Society of Scotland* (1805)

Archives Folger · Hunt. L. · NA Scot., letters · NL Scot., corresp., literary MSS, and papers · NL Scot., corresp. and literary MSS relating to his life of Hume · U. Edin. L., financial papers | NA Scot., letters to Grant family · NA Scot., letters to George Home · NA Scot., letters to Lord Melville · NL Scot., letters to *Blackwoods* · NL Scot., corresp. with Constables · NL Scot., corresp. with Robert Liston · NL Scot., letters to Anne Ord · NL Scot., corresp. with Sir Walter Scott · NRA, priv. coll., letters to John Swinton · NRA, priv. coll., corresp. with William Creech

Likenesses H. Raeburn, oils, *c*.1810, NPG [*see illus.*]

Mackenzie, Henry (1808–1878), bishop-suffragan of Nottingham, the fourth and youngest son of John Mackenzie, merchant, descended from the Mackenzie clan of Torridon in Ross-shire, was born in King's Arms Yard, Coleman Street, City of London, on 16 May 1808. He was educated at the Merchant Taylors' School under Dr Cherry. Owing to the death of his father he left school aged twelve and worked in a merchant's counting-house. In 1830 he matriculated from Pembroke College, Oxford, where he had Dr Jeune, subsequently bishop of Peterborough, as his tutor, and formed a lifelong friendship with John Jackson (1811–1885), later bishop of Lincoln and of London. He took an honorary fourth class in *literae humaniores* in 1834, graduating MA in 1838 and DD in 1869.

In 1834 Mackenzie was ordained to the curacy of Wool and Lulworth, on the south coast of Dorset, by the bishop of Rochester for the bishop of Bristol. In 1835, having been ordained priest by the archbishop of Canterbury, he accepted a temporary engagement as assistant chaplain to the English residents at Rotterdam. It was while there that he first came to the notice of Charles James Blomfield, bishop of London. On returning to England in 1836 Mackenzie became curate of St Peter's, Walworth, from where he moved in 1837 to the mastership of Bancroft's Hospital, Mile End, where he was also secretary to the committee for the erection of ten new churches in Bethnal Green. In 1840 he was made perpetual curate of the densely populated riverside parish of St James's, Bermondsey. While at Bermondsey he gained the friendship of Frederick Denison Maurice, then chaplain of Guy's Hospital. Maurice recommended him to Dean Pellew of Norwich for the cure of Great Yarmouth, to which he was appointed in 1844. Mackenzie was recalled to London by Blomfield in 1848 as rector of St Martin-in-the-Fields, where Gladstone was one of his admiring parishioners. It was his experience in London which led Mackenzie to express support for a church–state alliance at parochial level, suggesting a system of home visitation under the joint direction of the clergy, the board of guardians, and the police in order to rationalize the distribution of charity.

In 1855 Mackenzie was appointed by Lord Chancellor Cranworth to the well-endowed living of Tydd St Mary, in the fens of Lincolnshire, near Wisbech. While there he claimed to have built the first mission church in Lincolnshire (*c*.1857), in response to the proliferation of dissenting chapels. He became known as the father of mission houses in south Lincolnshire. His college friend Bishop Jackson, who in 1853 had succeeded Bishop Kaye in the see of Lincoln, made him one of his examining chaplains in 1855, and in 1858 collated him to the prebendal stall of Leighton Ecclesia, once held by George Herbert. As bishop's chaplain he delivered courses of lectures on pastoral work to the candidates for holy orders, which were published in 1863. The lectures reflected his interest in the position of the clergy in society. He depicted the clergy as officers in the kingdom of the Redeemer and believed that effective ministry was possible only if both pastor and parishioners were of the same social class. On the elevation of Dr Jeremie to the deanery of Lincoln in 1864 he succeeded him as subdean and canon residentiary, and on the death of Archdeacon Wilkins in 1866 was appointed to the archdeaconry of Nottingham, exchanging the lucrative living of Tydd for the poorly endowed rectory of South Collingham, near Newark, in order that he might become resident within his archdeaconry. As a member of the chapter Mackenzie tried to make the cathedral the centre of spiritual life; for example, as subdean he held communion weekly instead of monthly. In 1869 he became honorary chaplain to the bishop of London.

In 1870 the long-dormant office of bishop-suffragan was revived in him on the nomination of Bishop Christopher Wordsworth, Bishop Jackson's successor in the see of Lincoln, and he was consecrated as bishop-suffragan of Nottingham at St Mary's, Nottingham, by Bishop Jackson on 2 February 1870. The revival of the office of bishop-suffragan, after more than three centuries' suspension, was not at first popular. Mackenzie had to work hard to overcome local sensitivity to being put in the care of a 'curate bishop' and to ensure that he gave due respect to his diocesan. On one occasion he got into trouble for signing himself Henry Nottingham. In 1871 he exchanged Collingham for the perpetual curacy of Scofton, near Worksop, which he also resigned in 1873 to devote himself exclusively to his episcopal duties. These he continued to fulfil until growing years and infirmities led to his resignation at the beginning of 1878. Mackenzie was married twice: first to Elizabeth, daughter of Robert Ridley of Essequibo, with whom he had one daughter, and secondly to Antoinette, daughter of Sir James H. Turing, formerly consul at Rotterdam, with whom he had six sons and five daughters. On his retirement, Nottinghamshire gave Mackenzie a sum of money to be invested in Mrs Mackenzie's name for the benefit of their family.

In convocation, of which Mackenzie became a member by election in 1857 and by office in 1866, few men did more varied and more useful work. He was also a prominent figure at several church congresses, especially that at Nottingham, and served on a number of committees, including one establishing a board of missions. Besides sermons, charges, and occasional pamphlets, he also published *The Life of Offa, King of Mercia* (1840), *A Short Commentary on the Gospels and Acts* (1847), and a collection of hymns and verses. Mackenzie died at the subdeanery, Lincoln, on 15 October 1878 and was buried on 19 October at South Collingham.

EDMUND VENABLES, *rev.* ELLIE CLEWLOW

Sources *The Guardian* (23 Oct 1878) · B. Heeney, *A different kind of gentleman: parish clergy as professional men in early and mid-Victorian England* (1976) · Foster, *Alum. Oxon.* · O. Chadwick, *The Victorian church*, 3rd edn, 2 vols. (1971–2) · Crockford (1878) · *The Times* (16 Oct 1878) · *The Times* (18 Oct 1878) · Gladstone, *Diaries*
Archives BL, corresp. with W. E. Gladstone, Add. MSS 44356–44443 · LPL, corresp. with A. C. Tait and related papers
Likenesses portrait, repro. in *ILN*, 24 (1854), 401 · wood-engraving (after photograph by Maull & Co.), NPG; repro. in *ILN* (26 Oct 1878) · wood-engraving (after photograph by J. Watkins), NPG; repro. in *ILN*, 56 (5 March 1870), 253
Wealth at death under £8000: probate, 15 Nov 1878, *CGPLA Eng. & Wales*

Mackenzie, Sir Hugh Stirling (1913–1996), naval officer, was born in Inverness on 3 July 1913, the youngest of the three sons, in the family of three sons and one daughter, of Dr Theodore Charles Mackenzie (1877–1951), medical superintendent of the Inverness District Asylum, and his wife, Margaret (Madge) Wilson (1879–1962). He was educated at Cargilfield School, and then entered the Royal Naval College, Dartmouth, as a cadet in 1927. As a midshipman he served in the battleship *Resolution* and the destroyer *Achates* in the Mediterranean. He joined the Submarine Service in 1934. His first submarine was *Rainbow*, in which he enjoyed two years on the China station. He came home in 1937 to be first lieutenant of *Seahorse* and then *Osiris*. He found life in submarines full of incident. During a fleet exercise in September 1938 *Seahorse* was rammed and had her periscope standards knocked over by the destroyer *Foxhound*. *Osiris*, an aged submarine, sprang a serious leak at maximum depth and just managed to struggle to the surface.

After war was declared in September 1939 *Osiris* went out to the Mediterranean, where Mackenzie (nicknamed 'Rufus' Mackenzie, to distinguish him from another submarine commanding officer A. J. 'Black' Mackenzie) did three patrols. *Osiris* had an early success by sinking the Italian torpedo boat *Palestro* in the strait of Otranto on 22 September 1940. Mackenzie was then selected for the submarine commanding officers' qualifying course (the 'Perisher'), which he passed early in 1941. His first command was the training boat *H.28*, based at Londonderry, followed by *H.43*, the training boat for Atlantic convoy escorts working up at HMS *Western Isles*, Tobermory. He was appointed in command of the large T class boat *Thrasher* in October 1941, and took her out to the Mediterranean.

On Friday 13 February 1942 *Thrasher* sailed from Alexandria on her eighth war patrol, her fourth under Mackenzie's command. On 16 February, forewarned by ULTRA special intelligence, *Thrasher* was off Suda Bay, on the north coast of Crete, waiting to ambush an axis supply ship of some 3000 tons. Mackenzie torpedoed and sank the target when it duly arrived, but it was strongly escorted by five anti-submarine vessels who counter-attacked, with bomb and machine-gun support from aircraft, dropping 33 depth charges, some of them very close indeed. *Thrasher* got clear, and surfaced after dark that evening to recharge batteries and head for her next patrol position in the Gulf of Taranto. Clearing the land *Thrasher*

began to roll in the swell and Mackenzie, asleep in his cabin, was woken by what he called 'a rhythmic banging immediately overhead' (Mackenzie, 3). Silence was vitally necessary for the submarine's safety, so Mackenzie ordered the bridge watch to investigate. They reported that there was a 3 foot long bomb lying on the casing beneath the muzzle of the 4 inch gun, and there was also a jagged hole in the casing, where it seemed a second bomb had penetrated. The first lieutenant, Peter Roberts, and Petty Officer Thomas William (Nat) Gould volunteered to remove the bombs. They could not throw the first bomb off the casing because it would fall on the saddle tank below and might explode. They wrapped it in sacking and manhandled it 100 feet forward to the bows and dropped it overboard, while *Thrasher* went full astern. They then climbed down and began gingerly to manoeuvre the second bomb along the cramped and restricted space below until they could hoist it up onto the casing. After forty minutes, during which Mackenzie might well have had to dive the submarine and drown them both, they dragged the bomb forward and dropped it overboard.

Mackenzie did not make much of this incident in his patrol report, merely saying 'I should like to bring to your notice Lt Roberts and PO Gould for their excellent conduct when acting as "bomb disposal party"'. But when he returned from patrol Mackenzie was ordered by the commander-in-chief, Admiral Sir Andrew Cunningham, to render full recommendations for an award for Roberts and Gould. 'Several months passed, and with them several exciting patrols', Mackenzie recalled,

> the events of February 16/17th were almost forgotten when we were shaken, I think that is the right word, by the news that Roberts and Gould had each been awarded the Victoria Cross. A great personal honour to themselves and as they and I felt also to their fellow submariners, which I am sure was the reason behind ABC's decision to make a special mark of the affair. (Mackenzie, 5–6)

In June 1942 *Thrasher* sank Mussolini's yacht *Diana*, but was herself attacked by a 'friendly' Fleet Air Arm Swordfish and only just managed to limp back to Alexandria. Mackenzie was awarded the DSO and bar for his twelve war patrols in *Thrasher*, when he was credited with sinking 40,000 tons of enemy shipping. His last command of the war was *Tantalus*, in the East Indies fleet. She sailed from Fremantle, Australia, on 3 January 1945 for a patrol in the South China Sea, where Mackenzie sank a variety of small shipping. Target prospects seemed so good that he requested, and was granted, a ten-day patrol extension. On 11 February he sighted the fighting tops of two capital ships, the battleships *Ise* and *Hyuga*, making their escape back to Japan. He tried desperately hard to get ahead of them, but was hampered by the air escort, detected, bombed, forced to go deep, and was unable to attack. However, he was the only British submarine commanding officer ever to sight Japanese battleships through his periscope. *Tantalus* returned to Fremantle on 26 February after a patrol of fifty-five days (thirty-nine in the patrol area) and 11,692 miles—the longest patrol of any British submarine in the war. Mackenzie was awarded the DSC in 1945. On 10

August 1946 he married Third Officer Helen Maureen Bradish-Ellames WRNS (*b.* 1922), elder daughter of Major J. E. M. Bradish-Ellames. They had one son and two daughters.

After the war Mackenzie was appointed as teacher, in charge of the 'Perisher' course, commander in the depot ships *Forth* and *Montclare*, and then executive officer of the cruiser *Liverpool*, flagship of the 1st cruiser squadron in the Mediterranean. Promoted to captain, he commanded the Underwater Detection Establishment at Portland from 1952 until June 1954, when he took command of *Chevron* as captain, 1st destroyer squadron. His next appointments, from 1954 to 1961, were in HMS *Dolphin*, the submarine base at Gosport, as chief staff officer to the flag officer (submarines), and in command of HMS *Ganges*, the boys' training establishment at Shotley, Harwich. Promoted to rear admiral, he hoisted his flag as flag officer (submarines) in July 1961.

Mackenzie had a 'pierhead jump' when, on new year's day 1963, he was appointed chief Polaris executive, with a budget of £350 million and the task of making Polaris operational within five years. He was given *carte blanche* to pick his staff and soon gathered a nucleus of very able officers, by no means all submariners. But Polaris was an undertaking of immense complexity. Mackenzie had to deal with other ministry departments (some of them hostile towards Polaris), the Atomic Weapons Research Establishment, several local authorities, the shipbuilders Vickers and Cammell Lairds, and, most important of all, the Americans, without whom the Polaris project would have been impossible. The Americans were quickly charmed and impressed by Mackenzie's competence, enthusiasm, and energy. Nevertheless he had to surmount innumerable manpower and material difficulties, the abolition of the Admiralty as a separate organization, the election of a Labour government which reduced the number of Polaris submarines from five to four, and a severe bout of double pneumonia. It had been decided in 1963 that the first Polaris test firing would take place off Cape Canaveral at 11.15 on 15 February 1968. HMS *Resolution* duly fired her first A3 missile at the required place and time. The Polaris programme was thus accomplished on time and within budget—an unprecedented (and unrepeated) achievement in modern British naval history. Mackenzie was promoted to KCB in 1966, having been appointed CB in 1963.

Mackenzie retired in 1968 and was chairman of the Navy League from 1969 until 1974, and director of the Atlantic Salmon Research Trust from 1969 until 1979, and chairman following its relaunch as the Atlantic Salmon Trust until 1983. Having survived so many submarine incidents he had a very bad crash on the M1 in July 1982, when his car caught fire. Despite suffering severe burns himself, he managed to rescue his wife from their blazing car. This was another instance of the sword of Damocles, which he thought had always hung over him all his life. His memoirs, an entertaining and informative account of his wartime career and his Polaris experience, and a very valuable addition to modern naval history, were published by the Royal Navy Submarine Museum under that title, *The Sword*

of Damocles, in 1995. On 28 March 1996 Mackenzie attended a ceremony at HMS *Neptune*, the Faslane submarine base, to mark the decommissioning of *Repulse*, the last of the Resolution class of Polaris submarines, whose deterrent task was taken over by the Vanguard class of Trident armed submarines. He could thus fairly claim to have seen the whole Polaris project through from start to finish.

With his open cheerful features and his genial manner, Rufus Mackenzie was one of the best-known and most highly respected personalities in the Submarine Service. One of his 'Perisher' students, Johnnie Coote, later commented that his 'ready smile and infectious sense of fun concealed a shrewd observant mind'. After his death, Nat Gould said of him:

> Rufus Mackenzie was the best CO I ever served under. He was a very generous man in thought, word and deed. He was ice-cool in action. He would pass you a sandwich in the middle of an attack. He was firm but honest and very fair. I never expected to get the VC. When we came down from the casing that night, we were soaking wet. All he said was 'You'd better get yourself dried'. (*Daily Telegraph*)

Mackenzie died of a heart attack at home, Sylvan Lodge, Puttenham, near Guildford, Surrey, on 8 October 1996, and was cremated. His ashes were buried near Inverness. He was survived by his wife, son, and two daughters. A service of thanksgiving was held in Guildford Cathedral on 8 February 1997.   JOHN WINTON

Sources H. Mackenzie, *The sword of Damocles: some memories of Vice Admiral Sir Hugh Mackenzie KCB, DSO*, DSC* (1995) · P. Nailor, *The Nassau connection: the organisation and management of the British Polaris project* (1988) · J. E. Moore, ed., *The impact of Polaris* (1999) · E. J. Grove, *Vanguard to Trident: British naval policy since World War II* (1987) · J. Winton, *The Victoria cross at sea* (1978) · J. Coote, *Submariner* (1991) · *Daily Telegraph* (10 Oct 1996) · *The Times* (11 Oct 1996) · *The Independent* (18 Oct 1996) · *The Guardian* (29 Oct 1996) · Navy List · WWW · Royal Navy submarine records, Royal Navy Submarine Museum, Gosport, Hampshire · private information (2004)
Archives Royal Navy Submarine Museum, Gosport, Hampshire, Royal Navy submarine records
Likenesses photograph, repro. in *Daily Telegraph* · photograph, repro. in *The Times* · photograph, repro. in *The Independent* · photograph, repro. in *The Guardian* · photographs, repro. in Mackenzie, *Sword of Damocles*
Wealth at death £207,227: probate, 4 March 1997, *CGPLA Eng. & Wales*

Mackenzie, James (1682?–1761), physician, was probably born in Scotland. He studied medicine at Edinburgh University and enrolled at the University of Leiden on 15 March 1700. He graduated MD from King's College, Aberdeen, on 12 December 1719, and was elected an honorary fellow of the Royal College of Physicians, Edinburgh, in 1755. He practised medicine in Worcester for many years, and became friends with several learned and influential individuals, including E. M. da Costa and Lady Mary Wortley Montagu, who was noted for promoting smallpox inoculation. The bishop of Worcester, Isaac Maddox, and Philip Doddridge consulted Mackenzie about the foundation of the Worcester Infirmary, and Mackenzie served as attending physician to this institution from its establishment in 1745 until his retirement from practice in 1751, when he settled in Kidderminster.

Mackenzie is best known for his book, *The History of Health and the Art of Preserving it*, dedicated to Isaac Maddox, and first published in Edinburgh in 1758. The book was divided into two parts. The first part discussed man's diet before the fall and medical opinions concerning diet and health in subsequent historical epochs from antiquity to the modern era; contemporary writers discussed included John Arbuthnot and Richard Mead. The second part was arranged topically and covered basic medical subjects, including the different temperaments, periods of life, prophylaxis, and rules of health. In part due to his friendship with Lady Mary Wortley Montagu, the third edition of the book, published in 1760 in Edinburgh, included an appendix entitled 'A short and clear account of the commencement, progress, utility, and proper management of inoculating the small pox as a valuable branch of prophylaxis'. The appendix provided a brief history of inoculation in Britain and a detailed account of how to inoculate individuals. Mackenzie advocated a less invasive technique than had been used earlier in the century, and indicated that inoculation was widely accepted as a beneficial practice. There were two French editions of this book. Mackenzie died at Sutton Coldfield, Warwickshire, on 7 August 1761.

ANDREA RUSNOCK

Sources R. W. Innes Smith, *English-speaking students of medicine at the University of Leyden* (1932) · *GM*, 1st ser., 31 (1761), 382 · *DNB* · W. H. McMenemey, *A history of the Worcester Royal Infirmary* (1947)

Mackenzie, Sir James (1853–1925), physician and medical researcher, was the second son and one of the seven children of Robert Mackenzie (1816–1898), a farmer, and his wife, Jean Campbell Menzies (d. 1892). He was born at his father's farm of Pictstonhill at Scone, Perthshire, on 12 April 1853. His parents were stern adherents of the United Presbyterian church; James was to become an agnostic. William Warrender *Mackenzie, later first Baron Amulree (1860–1942), was his brother. James Mackenzie left Perth Academy at fifteen to become apprenticed to a pharmacist, by whom four years later he was offered a partnership. Mackenzie chose instead to study medicine at the University of Edinburgh, where he graduated (1878) and was awarded his MD degree (1882).

In 1879 Mackenzie joined a general practice at Burnley, Lancashire, and was appointed physician to the Victoria Hospital. At Burnley he married on 13 September 1887 Frances Bellamy (b. 1864/5), daughter of George Jackson of Boston, Lincolnshire; they had two daughters. While at Burnley he began the patient, exact, and exhaustive clinical studies which were to be continued until his death.

Mackenzie's earliest work was upon herpes zoster (shingles); he made use of the phenomena displayed by this disease to map out areas of the skin supplied by the spinal nerves. Out of these observations in large part grew his later observations upon pain and tenderness, and on referred pain and pain as symptom; these were collected in *Symptoms and their Interpretation* (1909). From the same basal observations he developed his studies and views of angina pectoris, published in a book of that title in 1923. His reputation rests on his long continued researches into the nature of irregularities of the heart's rhythm. He

Sir James Mackenzie (1853–1925), by unknown photographer

graphically recorded the movements of the jugular veins and used these records in conjunction with others in an elaborate and acute analysis of the movements of the heart's separate chambers. His 'polygraph', an instrument devised to take his records, was invented with the aid of a Lancashire watchmaker, Mr Shaw. Mackenzie's book *The Study of the Pulse* (1902), in which the earlier observations were collected, gave the impetus to much work of the same kind by others. The fuller studies of the pulsations, his rich experience of cardiovascular disease from other points of view, and the general philosophy underlying his work, were displayed in *Diseases of the Heart* (1908), a book which quickly ran through several editions, and which, like *Symptoms and their Interpretation*, was translated into several languages. Mackenzie provided striking examples of exact observation of patients, and of simple and accurate deductions from these. He was intensely interested in the mechanism of disease, of the symptoms displayed by disease, and the relation of heart action to disorders in other organs. He did more, perhaps, than any other medical practitioner before him to place upon a rational basis forecasts of the course of heart disease in individual patients, and the treatment of heart disease by digitalis.

Mackenzie's first recognition came from Canada, the United States, and the continent. In 1907 he moved to London, where he became a notable consultant. He became consulting physician to the London Hospital (1913), was elected a fellow of the Royal Society (1915), was knighted (1915), and received many other honours. During the First World War he acted as consultant to the Military Heart Hospital, an institution formed chiefly at his suggestion. He ascribed soldiers' 'disordered action of the heart' to general undiagnosed infections rather than to specific physical or mental damage. In 1918 Mackenzie went to St Andrews to found the Institute of Clinical Research. He involved local general practitioners in long-term exact recording of patients' symptoms and illnesses. The conception of the institute outran its resources, and Mackenzie returned to London in 1924.

Mackenzie, who was 6 feet 2 inches tall, physically powerful, and gaunt, had a vigorous and impressive personality, a combative argumentation, and a clear vision of essentials, which combined to make him a great teacher. An uncommon faculty of criticism and a deep distrust of authoritative statement gave him a rare discrimination between the known and the unknown; this, associated in unusual degree with originality, a retentive memory, and determined purpose, underlay his success as an investigator. He remained an outsider, brilliant in his diagnoses and exact observation, and denunciatory of laboratory research, narrow specialists, and slack panjandrums. As he grew older he inclined to a holistic, vitalist concept of life and disease. Privately, he was a fierce radical-Liberal.

A true appreciation of Mackenzie's character and work can be obtained only if it is remembered that his chief discoveries were made in time snatched during the routine of a heavy industrial practice, and that during the last fifteen years of his life he suffered much from angina pectoris, which he had done so much to elucidate. He eventually died of the condition at his home, 53 Albert Hall Mansions, Knightsbridge, London, on 26 January 1925. He was survived by his wife.   F. B. SMITH

Sources A. Mair, *Sir James Mackenzie, M. D., 1853–1925: general practitioner* [*c*.1986] · parish register, Scone, Perth, 12 April 1853 [birth] · m. cert. · d. cert. · *WWW* · personal knowledge (1937) [*DNB*]
Archives U. Edin. L., corresp. and papers · Wellcome L., notebooks and papers
Likenesses H. Sedcole, mezzotint (after D. Mackenzie), Wellcome L. · monument, Burnley, Lancashire · photographs, repro. in Mair, *Sir James Mackenzie* · photogravure, repro. in R. McNair Wilson, *The beloved physician: Sir James Mackenzie* (1926) [*see illus.*] · two photographs, Wellcome L.
Wealth at death £39,416 13*s.* 1*d.*: confirmation, 7 April 1925, *CCI*

Mackenzie, James Stuart (1719–1800), politician and astronomer, was born on 23 February 1719, the younger son in the family of two sons and four daughters of James Stuart, second earl of Bute (*c*.1690–1723), royal servant, and his wife, Anne (1692–1736), daughter of Archibald Campbell (later first duke of Argyll). In 1723, on his father's death, he assumed the surname and estate of his great-grandfather Sir George Mackenzie of Rosehaugh, baronet, also acquiring property in Forfarshire, Perthshire, and London. He was educated at Eton College (1728–32) and, after the grand tour, in Leiden (1737). An impetuous young man, he became infatuated with the dancer Barberoni and was summoned home from Europe. His family had him safely married to his first cousin Lady Elizabeth Campbell (1721/2–1799), fourth daughter of John, second duke of Argyll, on 16 February 1749. Their two children died in infancy.

Mackenzie represented Argyll (1742–7), Buteshire (1747–

James Stuart Mackenzie (1719–1800), by Thomas Bardwell, 1752

54), Ayr burghs (1754–61), and Ross-shire (1761–80) in parliament. He attended regularly but never spoke. In 1758 he was made envoy-extraordinary to the king of Sardinia, living 'in a most splendid stile' in Turin and very popular. The death of the third duke of Argyll in 1761 left the management of Scotland at the disposal of his nephew John *Stuart, third earl of Bute, Mackenzie's elder brother, who became chief minister. Although desiring a diplomatic posting to Venice, Mackenzie was recalled to take over Scottish affairs from Sir Gilbert Elliot. In 1763 he was sworn of the privy council and made lord privy seal for Scotland, with considerable powers of patronage. Although an amiable and scrupulously honest man, he was tactless, politically naïve, and, like Bute, doctrinaire. He was unfortunate to have been in office when George III's association with the earl of Bute brought unpopularity to his whole family. The intimacy of the Stuart brothers with George III was much disliked by the House of Commons.

In 1762 Mackenzie was involved in the clash between moderate and evangelical factions over appointments of clergy to Edinburgh charges, and his well-meaning attempts to secure the best-qualified candidates and to appease all sides provoked further animosity over civil and judicial promotions. With the final removal of Bute from the king's advisers in 1765 George Grenville also forced out Mackenzie, but in the administration of Chatham in 1766 he was reinstated as lord privy seal for Scotland for life, at the same £3000 salary but without power.

In 1780 Mackenzie left politics to devote himself to agricultural improvements and amateur science on his Belmont estate in Perthshire. Triangulations on distant hills were attempted, weather records kept, and there was an astronomical observatory. An obsessive bureaucrat, he listed the numerous instruments of his scientific friends, but published nothing. He knew Giuseppe Piazzi, Nevil Maskelyne, and probably James Bradley, and was an early member of the Royal Society of Edinburgh. His wife died in Mayfair on 16 July 1799 and Mackenzie died of grief, also in London, on 6 April 1800, and his estate passed to his brother's son, James Archibald Stuart-*Wortley, later first Baron Wharncliffe.   DAVID GAVINE, rev.

Sources R. Douglas, *The peerage of Scotland*, 2nd edn, ed. J. P. Wood, 2 vols. (1813) · E. Haden-Guest, 'Stuart-Mackenzie, Hon. James', HoP, *Commons, 1754–90* · D. Gavine, 'James Stewart Mackenzie (1719–1800) and the Bute MSS', *Journal for the History of Astronomy*, 5 (1974), 208–14 · A. Murdoch, *'The people above': politics and administration in mid-eighteenth-century Scotland* (1980) · J. S. Shaw, *The management of Scottish society, 1707–1764: power, nobles, lawyers, Edinburgh agents and English influences* (1983) · GEC, *Peerage*, new edn
Archives Bute archive, Mount Stuart, Isle of Bute, scientific and administrative MSS | BL, corresp. with earl of Liverpool, Add. MSS 38200–38213, 38304–38306, 38469 · Glamorgan RO, Cardiff, letters and papers · NL Scot., corresp. with William Mure
Likenesses T. Bardwell, portrait, 1752, Buccleuch estates, Selkirk [see illus.] · J. Nollekens, relief, Westminster Abbey · portrait, Mount Stuart, Isle of Bute

Mackenzie, John, of Kintail (d. 1561). *See under* Mackenzie family of Kintail (per. c.1475–1611).

Mackenzie, John (1646/7–1696), Presbyterian minister and pamphleteer, was born at Lowcross, near Cookstown, co. Tyrone, of parents who are unknown. He graduated MA from Edinburgh University in 1669 and was licensed to preach by the meeting (presbytery) of Down. In 1673 he was ordained minister of the congregation of Derryloran (Cookstown). Along with seven other Presbyterian clergymen he took refuge in Londonderry during the celebrated siege of 1688–9. He was invited to become chaplain in the regiment of George Walker, one of the city governors, and the contemporary poem, *Londerias*, describes a 'Master Mackenzie' who 'taught the Army to fear God's great Name' (Aickin). On one occasion he was also chosen as one of six commissioners to enter into negotiations with the Jacobite forces.

Mackenzie is best known, however, for his part in the brief pamphlet war that followed the appearance of George Walker's *True Account of the Siege of London-Derry* on 13 September 1689. Walker, who had been fêted in Scotland and England as the hero of the conflict, produced a best-selling memoir that marginalized the role of Presbyterians in the defence of the city. The issue was a particularly sensitive one, since Irish protestants were deeply divided along denominational and political lines, divisions which quickly resurfaced as the Catholic military threat receded. As the largest nonconformist group the Presbyterians had high hopes for some amelioration of their legal position under the new Williamite regime; conversely members of the Church of Ireland feared that their monopoly over public worship was no safer under the Calvinist William III than it had been under the Catholic James II. At a Presbyterian meeting held in Belfast on 5 November 1689 it was decided to send a deputation to London to provide an 'impartial' version of events. Without waiting for formalities, Mackenzie set out for England.

Mackenzie's *Narrative of the Siege of Londonderry*, the fullest reply to Walker, emphasized the role of the Presbyterian clergy and gentry in the resistance to James II, claiming that the Presbyterians in Derry had outnumbered episcopalians by as many as fifteen to one. In Mackenzie's version of events it is the Presbyterian Colonel Adam Murray who figures as the hero of the conflict. Walker's role is belittled: it is claimed that his authority as a 'governor' was confined to the care of provisions, and that he had been suspected both of treating with the Jacobites and embezzling the stores. Further pamphlets followed, as the episcopalian interpretation was backed up by an anonymous pamphleteer, probably Dr John Vesey, archbishop of Tuam, and Mackenzie and Walker both published vindications of their positions.

The *Narrative of the Siege of Londonderry* remains an indispensable historical source, but it did not prevent the re-establishment of a narrow episcopalian ascendancy in Ireland. Mackenzie returned to London in 1694 to complain to the king of the harassment of Presbyterian clergymen by the diocesan courts. He died at Cookstown two years later, in 1696, aged forty-nine, and was buried that year in Derryloran churchyard; he is not known to have married. There is a pocket book of his manuscript sermons, preached to various congregations in Derry, co. Tyrone, Armagh, and Down in 1681–2, preserved in the Presbyterian Historical Society of Ireland, Belfast. He appears in George Folingsby's painting, *The Relief of Derry*, now in the Guildhall, Derry.   I. R. MCBRIDE

Sources J. Aickin, *Londerias, or, A narrative of the siege of London-Derry* (1699) · *An apology for the failures charg'd on the Reverend Mr George Walker's printed account of the late siege of Derry, in a letter to the undertaker of a more accurate narrative of that siege* (1689) · J. MacKenzie, *A narrative of the siege of London-Derry* (1690) · J. Mackenzie, *Dr Walker's invisible champion foyl'd, or, An appendix to the late narrative of the siege of Derry* (1690) · *Reflections on a paper, pretending to be an apology for the failures charged on Mr Walker's account of the siege of London-Derry* (1589) · [J. Vesey?], *Mr John Mackenzyes narrative of the siege of London-Derry a false libel: in defence of Dr George Walker* (1690) · G. Walker, *A true account of the siege of London-Derry* (1689) · G. Walker, *A vindication of the true account of the siege of Derry* (1689) · W. D. Killen, ed., *Mackenzie's memorials of the siege of Derry including his narrative and its vindication* (1861), introduction · I. McBride, *The siege of Derry in Ulster protestant mythology* (1997) · J. S. Reid and W. D. Killen, *History of the Presbyterian church in Ireland*, new edn, 3 vols. (1867) · T. Witherow, *Derry and Enniskillen in the year 1689: the story of some famous battlefields in Ulster* (1873) · T. Witherow, *Historical and literary memorials of presbyterianism in Ireland, 1623–1731* (1879) · DNB
Archives Presbyterian Historical Society of Ireland, Belfast, notebook with MS copies of sermons
Likenesses G. Folingsby, portrait (*The relief of Derry*), Guildhall, Derry

Mackenzie, John, Lord Macleod, and Count Cromarty in the Swedish nobility (1727–1789), Jacobite sympathizer and British army officer, was the eldest of the twelve children of George *Mackenzie, third earl of Cromarty (c.1703–1766), and Isabella Gordon (1704/5–1769), daughter of Sir William Gordon of Invergordon. Mackenzie, styled Lord Macleod, was privately educated by a succession of tutors who were all subsequently ordained as ministers of the Church of Scotland. On the outbreak of the last Jacobite rising in 1745 the lord president, Duncan Forbes of Culloden, offered Lord Macleod the command of an independent company, but instead, despite their firmly Presbyterian background, both Macleod and his father eventually declared for Charles Edward Stuart, the Young Pretender, and raised a small regiment from among their Mackenzie clansmen.

In company with a battalion of Frasers commanded by Lord Lovat's son, Simon Fraser, the regiment joined Lord John Drummond's forces at Perth and remained there until 1 December 1745, when they were sent forward to Dunblane and afterwards took possession of Bridge of Allan. Further progress was then halted by a small mixed brigade of regular and loyalist troops covering the Forth crossings. However, when the return of Prince Charles Edward's army from Derby forced the retreat of this brigade to Edinburgh, Macleod met the prince at Glasgow on 12 January 1746 and subsequently took part in the battle of Falkirk on 22 January. In common with a substantial part of the Jacobite army, most of Macleod's men appear to have run away, but he himself, separated from his father, later claimed to have found the prince sheltering in a small hut at the end of the battle. Afterwards Macleod took part in more successful operations in the north of Scotland against a loyalist army commanded by John Campbell, earl of Loudoun.

On 25 March 1746 a French blockade-runner carrying £12,000 in gold was forced ashore near Tongue in Caithness and most of the gold was promptly seized by loyalist militia. Cromarty's regiment was part of an expeditionary force sent to recover the gold, but was returning to Inverness empty-handed when it was ambushed and defeated by the loyalists at Embo on 15 April 1746. At the time Macleod and Cromarty were absent, paying their respects to Lady Sutherland at Dunrobin Castle, and when summoned to surrender they initially refused. However, on leaving the castle, the loyalist officer sent to negotiate with them told the rebel sentry at the gate that they had in fact done so. Consequently he was allowed to re-enter the castle with some of his men and arrest both Cromarty and Macleod without further resistance. Father and son were taken first to Inverness, where the duke of Cumberland had won the battle of Culloden on the 16th, and then to the Tower of London. A true bill for high treason was found against Macleod on 23 August 1746, and he subsequently pleaded guilty at his trial on 20 December and threw himself on the king's mercy. Although his father was found guilty, had his estates forfeited, and was condemned to death, some very determined lobbying by the countess of Cromarty won a remittance of the death sentence on condition that the earl thereafter resided in Devon. Consequently, Lord Macleod was also pardoned on 22 January 1748, on condition of conveying all his rights and claims on the estates of the earldom of Cromarty to the crown within six months of attaining his majority.

Having done so, in April of the following year Macleod travelled to Hamburg and then on to Berlin. His original intention may have been to take service in the Prussian army, but instead he obtained letters of introduction there to the Swedish court from another estranged Jacobite, Field Marshal James Keith. After serving for a time as a volunteer, Macleod obtained command of a company in Major-General Hamilton's regiment in June 1750, and in April 1755 became major in 'an old Swedish regiment'. Two years later he finally obtained leave to join the Prussian army as a volunteer, served in Bohemia as an aide-de-camp to Marshal Keith, and took part in the battle and siege of Prague. However, when Sweden subsequently joined in the war against Prussia, he had to return. Then, rather than fight against his erstwhile colleagues, Macleod obtained leave to go to England instead. There he discussed the possibility of transferring to the British service, but when negotiations proved abortive he returned to Sweden. In 1762 he was made a knight of the order of the North Star, and on the death of his father in 1766 he was created Count (Greve) Cromarty in the Swedish nobility and also made a commandant of the order of the Sword of Sweden.

Shortly after the outbreak of the American War of Independence Macleod again applied to join the British army. During the previous war a number of former Jacobites, headed by Macleod's former colleague Simon Fraser, had rehabilitated themselves by raising and leading a highland regiment. Having seen Fraser successfully regain his family estates and raise another regiment, Macleod now took the opportunity to emulate him by doing the same. On 19 December 1777 he was granted letters of service for the raising of his regiment and within a few weeks succeeded in gathering in some 840 highland recruits and 236 others from further afield. Inspected at Elgin in April 1778 and passed as fit for service, the regiment was embodied as the 73rd highlanders, and Macleod was at the same time authorized to raise a second battalion. This battalion, commanded by Macleod's younger brother, George Mackenzie [see below], served throughout the war in Gibraltar, but Macleod himself with the 1st battalion 73rd highlanders embarked for India early in 1779.

Delayed by the need to occupy Goree and refit at the Cape of Good Hope, Macleod and his men did not land at Madras until 20 January 1780. On 20 July the territory of the Madras presidency was invaded by Mysorean troops led by Haider Ali, and as the senior king's officer Macleod was ordered by the presidency council to concentrate both his own and the East India Company's troops at Poonamallee. Having done so he was then directed to march on Conjeeveram, but protesting as to the inadequacy of his forces took up a position at St Thomas's Mount instead. On 25 August he was superseded there by Sir Hector Monro, who ordered the march on Conjeeveram to be resumed, with the intention of linking up there with another force led by Colonel William Baillie. In the event Baillie's detachment, which included both flank companies of the 1st battalion 73rd highlanders, was attacked and destroyed before the junction could be effected. Monro made no attempt to assist his colleague although the sounds of battle, just a few miles away, could clearly be heard in his camp. Instead he retired in some haste to Madras, where he in turn was superseded by Sir Eyre Coote. Macleod, on the other hand, distinguished himself during the retreat and served on under Coote until August 1781, when, as a result of a dispute with the general, he returned home and, although seeing no further service, was himself promoted major-general in 1782. In the meantime, also, he became MP for Ross-shire in 1780, holding the seat until 1784 when, in consequence of his military services, he was allowed to redeem his forfeited estates in return for a payment of £19,000 to cover any outstanding debts and expenses incurred by the forfeited estates commissioners. Thereafter he devoted himself to the improvement of the estates. On 4 June 1786 he married Margery (1761/2–1842), eldest daughter of the sixteenth Lord Forbes, but died at Edinburgh on 2 April 1789 and was buried alongside his mother in the old Canongate churchyard. As he had no children and his brother George had predeceased him, the Cromarty estates devolved on his cousin, Kenneth Mackenzie of Cromarty.

George Mackenzie (1741–1787), army officer, was born at Tarbat House, Ross-shire. The younger brother of Lord Macleod, he was only five when his father was convicted of treason and therefore escaped any awkward Jacobite associations. Consequently he entered the British army long before his brother and was already serving in the 1st (or Royal) regiment in 1778 when he was appointed lieutenant-colonel of the 2nd battalion 73rd highlanders. He commanded the 2nd battalion throughout the siege of Gibraltar, and when the battalion was afterwards disbanded at Stirling in October 1783, he went out to India to take over the 1st battalion—which, consequent upon the disbandment of Fraser's Highlanders, was renumbered as the 71st highlanders (afterwards the Highland light infantry) in 1786. He died of fever, unmarried and without children, at Wallajabad on 4 June 1787, where he was buried the same day.   STUART REID

Sources DNB · W. Fraser, *The earls of Cromartie: their kindred, country and correspondence*, 2 vols. (1876) · Burke, *Peerage* (1999) · D. Stewart, *Sketches of the character, manners, and present state of the highlanders of Scotland: with details of the military service of the highland regiments*, 2 vols. (1822) · W. B. Blaikie, ed., *Origins of the 'Forty-Five and the papers relating to that rising*, Scottish History Society, 2nd ser., vol. 2 (1916) · L. B. Oatts, *Proud heritage: the story of the highland light infantry* (1952) · S. Reid, *1745: a military history of the last Jacobite rising* (1996) · E. Haden-Guest, 'Mackenzie, John', HoP, *Commons, 1754–90* · gravestone, Canongate cemetery, Edinburgh
Archives NA Scot., corresp.

Mackenzie, John (1803–1886), physician and landowner, was born in Scotland on 23 November 1803, the fourth of the five sons of Sir Hector Mackenzie of Gairloch, fourth baronet (1758–1826), and his second wife, Christian, *née* Henderson. He was educated at Edinburgh University, graduating as a physician (DM) in 1824, and as a surgeon in 1825; he became a lifelong friend of William Pulteney Alison, the poor-law reformer. In 1826 he married Mary Jane (Dulcinea) Inglis (*d.* April 1897), daughter of Dr John *Inglis, minister of Forteviot, and his wife, Maria. They

John Mackenzie (1803–1886), by J. Collier, 1867

had three sons and five daughters. After practising in London (where he attended Edward Irving's Catholic Apostolic church), Dover, and Norwich in the army medical department and trying private practice in Edinburgh, he abandoned medicine in 1832 to become a tenant farmer, first at Strathpeffer on the estate of Sir George Mackenzie of Coul, later in the Isle of Ewe, Gairloch. He farmed until 1856, never making less than 20 per cent per annum on his outlay of £1000. Mackenzie was unusual in this success and, recognizing the plight of his Scottish farming contemporaries, set out to educate them and improve their methods so as to reduce emigration; his *Improvements to Highland Crofts* (1842) and his *Croft Cultivation—by an Old Crofter* (1885), written in English and Gaelic, which he spoke fluently, set out his views. He became trustee and factor of the large family estates at Conan on the death of his brother, **Sir Francis Alexander Mackenzie of Gairloch**, fifth baronet (1798–1843), who had embarked on utopian plans for estate improvement which left the estate almost bankrupt. Sir Francis published *Hints for the Use of Highland Tenants and Cottagers by a Proprietor* (1838) and was married to Mary, daughter of Osgood Hanbury, a Quaker brewer in Essex. Once in charge of the estate, John Mackenzie developed his reforming ideas, essentially an attempt to develop crofting as an alternative to sheep farming and evictions. He visited Belgium to study small-farming methods and to attend an international agricultural conference in 1848. His *Letter to Lord John Russell* (1851) attacked Sir John M'Neill's report supporting highland clearances and established Mackenzie's reputation as a reforming landlord and factor, though this was questioned by some of the witnesses to the Napier royal commission on crofting in 1883. From 1844 he had a house in Inverness and from 1867 until 1873 he was the town's lord provost. A Freechurchman and (from 1860) a total abstainer from alcohol, Mackenzie tried, with some success, to modernize the town of Inverness and to prevent its river from flooding; he had less success in controlling the citizens' drinking habits. When he received Queen Victoria on her visit in 1872, she found him 'a fine-looking old man in a kilt, with very white hair and a long white beard' (More Leaves, 181). He died at his house, Eileanach, in Inverness on 18 December 1886 and was buried in the family vault at Beauly.

Throughout most of his adult life Mackenzie kept a diary and in 1882 began his autobiography, an important source for the social history of the highlands. It was published in *Pigeonholes of Memory: the Life and Times of Dr John Mackenzie*, edited by Christina Byam Shaw (1988), but it was earlier known through the poorly edited extracts used by his nephew for his influential book, *A Hundred Years in the Highlands* (1921, rev. edn by Mrs Sawyer, 1949). This nephew was **Osgood Hanbury Mackenzie** (1842–1922), gardener and author, son of Sir Francis Alexander Mackenzie and his wife, Mary, and eventual heir to the Inverewe estate. Osgood Mackenzie's book was, in fact, dictated to a ghost writer; his real achievement was as a gardener, for he founded in 1865 the famous garden at Inverewe, the estate given him by his mother in 1862, which his daughter, Mairi Sawyer, presented to the National Trust for Scotland in 1951.

H. C. G. MATTHEW

Sources C. Byam Shaw, ed., *Pigeon holes of memory: the life and times of Dr John Mackenzie, 1803–1886* (1988) · Queen Victoria, *More leaves from the journal of a life in the highlands, from 1862 to 1882* (1884) · M. Cowan, *Inverewe: a garden in the north-west Highlands* (1964) · Burke, *Peerage*
Archives priv. coll.
Likenesses J. Collier, photograph, 1867, unknown collection; copyprint, NPG [*see illus.*] · photographs, repro. in Byam Shaw, ed., *Pigeon holes of memory*
Wealth at death £944 12s. 7d.: confirmation, 2 Aug 1887, CCI · £600: eik additional estate, 8 Dec 1887, CCI

Mackenzie, John (1806–1848), collector of Gaelic verse, was born on 17 July 1806 at Meallan Theàrlaich in the parish of Gairloch, Ross-shire. His father, Alasdair, was closely related to the Mackenzie lairds of Gairloch, and his mother, Margaret Mackenzie, was a granddaughter of a famous minister, James Robertson of Loch Broom.

John Mackenzie became an apprentice joiner, and developed his hobbies of playing musical instruments and collecting Gaelic songs. In 1823 he had a bad accident at work, and eventually had to give up the joinery trade, allowing him to concentrate more fully on his collecting activities. The first important result was the noting down of the poems of William Ross from the oral recitation of Ross's old friend Alasdair Campbell. He is said to have spent twenty-one evenings writing down these poems. They were published in 1833 (though 1830 is the date on

the title-page), with a second edition in 1834. In 1836 Mackenzie moved to Glasgow, taking up a clerical position in Glasgow University's printing office. After several years he moved to Edinburgh, to work for MacLachlan and Stewart, publishers and booksellers. There his main work was in translating English works into Gaelic, and proofreading such works, mainly of a religious kind and including several of John Bunyan's works. In all he wrote, translated, or edited about thirty books.

Mackenzie is thought to have had a significant input into the monthly periodical *Cuairtear nan Gleann* (1840–43), and in 1844 he published a Gaelic history of Charles Edward Stuart's involvement in the Jacobite rising of 1745 (in part at least a translation of an anonymous author). In 1845 he published an English–Gaelic dictionary, which continued to be reprinted until the 1970s.

Mackenzie's most influential work was his collection of Gaelic verse, first published in 1841 under the title *Sar-obair nam bard Gaelach, or, The Beauties of Gaelic Poetry*. This contains poetry attributed to thirty-six authors (of whom two or three are fictitious) and a short selection of anonymous songs. There are extensive selections of several famous poets such as Iain Lom, Alasdair Mac Mhaighstir Alasdair, Rob Donn, and Donnchadh Bàn, with biographical introductions. Despite various inaccuracies of ascription and detailed text, and some suspect biographical elements, the collection was a notable achievement, and was highly popular in Gaelic circles. The texts are at times based on earlier collections or editions of individual poets, but have some input from alternative oral versions.

In 1848, in severely declining health, Mackenzie returned to Ross-shire, and died at Inverewe on 19 August 1848. In 1878 a memorial cairn was placed close to the Gairloch graveyard in which he was buried.

DERICK S. THOMSON

Sources [T. M. Murchison], 'Iain MacCoinnich, Clach air a Chàrn', *An Gaidheal* (Aug 1948), 125–8 · *Celtic Magazine* (1877) · J. Mackenzie, ed., *Sar-obair nam bard Gaelach, or, The beauties of Gaelic poetry* (1841)

Mackenzie, John (1835–1899), missionary in Africa, was born in Knockando in Moray, Scotland, on 30 August 1835, the son of a small farmer. He was educated at local schools and then apprenticed to a newspaper. Having been brought up in the Church of Scotland, at about the age of eighteen he underwent a conversion experience in a Congregationalist church and soon after sought to become a missionary. After undergoing theological training in Bedford, England, he was accepted by the nondenominational London Missionary Society (LMS), ordained, and sent to South Africa in 1858. In the same year he married Ellen Douglas (d. 1925); they were to have ten children, one of whom wrote his biography.

Mackenzie was to have gone to work among the Kololo in central Africa, but instead he remained at the established missionary centre of Kuruman on the 'missionaries' road', acting for Robert Moffat. From 1862 he was stationed further north at the Ngwato capital Shoshong, in what became Bechuanaland. While on leave in Britain

John Mackenzie (1835–1899), by unknown photographer

in 1869–71, he wrote *Ten Years North of the Orange River* (1871). Shoshong remained his base until 1876, when he moved back to Kuruman so as to be able to continue teaching in the Moffat institution for training African teachers.

Mackenzie was a humanitarian imperialist, who believed in the extension of British rule in order to protect African peoples from European encroachment. After clashes occurred north of the Cape Colony in 1878, Sir Bartle Frere, the British high commissioner, invited him to become British commissioner for Bechuanaland south of the Molopo River. Mackenzie refused because he did not wish to stop working for the LMS. While he continued working as a missionary, he spent much of his time campaigning for British annexation of the land west of the Transvaal, as Boer encroachment increased after the Pretoria Convention of 1881. Another threat came from Cecil Rhodes and other Cape politicians who wanted to see the area become part of the Cape. Mackenzie took his campaign for direct British rule to Britain in 1882, where a South African committee was formed to promote his ideas. A few years later the LMS agreed that he might accept the post of deputy commissioner in the Bechuanaland protectorate. Although Rhodes forced him to vacate it after only four months, Mackenzie accompanied the expedition led by Sir Charles Warren to Bechuanaland in 1885, and he was present when Warren announced the

establishment of a British protectorate over Bechuanaland.

With the withdrawal of the Warren expedition, Mackenzie returned to Britain where he continued his campaign, now to ensure the continuance of direct British rule and the primacy of African interests in Bechuanaland. In 1887 he published *Austral Africa: Losing it or Ruling it*, an account of events in the area from 1878. Although he failed to prevent Rhodes from getting his own way with the founding of the British South Africa Company, Mackenzie's pressure on the British government was undoubtedly important in the final decision in 1895 to maintain direct rule over Bechuanaland north of the Molopo River. He must therefore be acknowledged as one of the founders of the later state of Botswana.

In 1891 Mackenzie returned to South Africa to take up an appointment as the LMS missionary at Hankey, near Port Elizabeth. He continued to work there until shortly before his death, from a stroke, at the home of his son in Kimberley on 23 March 1899. He was buried in Kimberley on 25 March. CHRISTOPHER SAUNDERS

Sources A. Sillery, *John Mackenzie of Bechuanaland* (1971) · *Papers of John Mackenzie*, ed. A. J. Dachs (1975) · W. D. Mackenzie, *John Mackenzie, South African missionary and statesman* (1902) · A. J. Dachs, 'Missionary imperialism: the case of Bechuanaland', *Journal of African History*, 13 (1972), 647–58 · A. Sillery, 'Mackenzie, John', *DSAB* · K. Shillington, *The colonisation of the Southern Tswana, 1870–1900* (1985) · J. A. I. Agar-Hamilton, *The road to the north: South Africa, 1852–1886* (1937) · D. M. Schreuder, *Gladstone and Kruger* (1969) · D. M. Schreuder, *The scramble for southern Africa, 1877–1895* (1980) · J. Mackenzie, *Ten years north of the Orange river* (1871) · J. Mackenzie, *Austral Africa: losing it or ruling it* (1887)
Archives University of the Witwatersrand, Johannesburg, South Africa | Bodl. RH, Aborigines Protection Society MSS · Cape Archives, South Africa, various collections · PRO, Colonial Office corresp. · SOAS, Council for World Mission, London Missionary Society MSS
Likenesses photograph, NPG [*see illus.*] · photograph, repro. in Sillery, *John Mackenzie of Bechuanaland* · photograph, repro. in Dachs, ed., *Papers of John Mackenzie* · photograph, repro. in R. Lovett, *The history of the London Missionary Society* (1899)

McKenzie [M'Kenzie], **Sir John** (1839–1901), land reformer in New Zealand, was born at Brae Tolly on the Ardross estate, Easter Ross, Scotland, on 6 October 1839, the second son of John McKenzie, a small tenant farmer noted for his progressive farming methods on the estate, and his wife, Catherine Munro. As a second son, he had little chance of advancing beyond the lot of a crofter. Although his family was never cleared off their land, when he was only five McKenzie saw evicted farmers sheltering in the graveyard at Croick, and determined to prevent such abuses happening again. His family's membership of the Free Church of Scotland, which aimed in the highlands to end landlord domination of religious life, reinforced this determination.

McKenzie was educated at the local parish school at Rosskeen, where he became literate in Gaelic. After leaving school at the age of fifteen he worked as a shepherd until a number of factors persuaded him to emigrate. His father married and his marriage to a much younger woman proved uncomfortable for the reconstituted family. When McKenzie's lover became pregnant and refused to travel with him to New Zealand, he signed a bond to support his child, engaged in a whirlwind courtship with Annie Munro (*b.* 1833), the daughter of a nearby tenant farmer, married her at Dingwall on 23 May 1860, and left for New Zealand the following day on the *Henrietta*.

McKenzie soon found work as a shepherd on the Puketapu run of the ex-whaler 'Johnny' Jones. He was promoted to manager and saved enough to buy his own 76-acre farm near Palmerston in 1865. In 1874 he moved to a rough, 1000-acre leasehold property near Dunback, but did not achieve any degree of financial security until he purchased an 800-acre farm north of Palmerston in 1888.

McKenzie taught himself English and threw himself into politics. His career on local bodies and as a backbench parliamentarian was not especially distinguished, but he learned much about the business of politics and the importance of compromise on the Bushey road board (1865–70), the Palmerston school committee (1867–9), the Otago provincial council (1871–6), the Waikouaiti county council (1877–82), and the Waihemo county council, which he helped create (1882–7). He was elected to parliament for Waihemo in 1881, and also served on both the Otago education and land board during the 1880s. He was an effective junior whip in the Stout–Vogel government of 1884–7, and became a specialist on land matters. This specialization won him the portfolio of lands in the Liberal government which came to power in 1891.

Initially McKenzie encountered difficulties. The premier, John Ballance, was more interested in using land reform to solve problems of urban unemployment than in restructuring New Zealand's farming industry. After 1892, however, McKenzie became more dominant, and introduced the lease-in-perpetuity, or 999-year lease without revaluation, and established a department of agriculture to satisfy the demands of the small-farmer faction within the Liberal Party. The economic viability of the lease-in-perpetuity has been debated ever since, but it was a clever compromise which satisfied the powerful freehold section within the Liberal Party.

In 1893 McKenzie used a clause in Ballance's Land and Income Assessment Act to purchase New Zealand's largest freehold property, the 84,000-acre Cheviot estate. This was a much better deal for trustees than government, but it was also a political master stroke which won a large mandate at the 1893 election. This electoral support enabled McKenzie to introduce compulsory repurchase under his Land for Settlements Act of 1894. Although seldom applied, this was still a very radical measure (aimed at making land available to genuine settlers, as opposed to speculators, at a fair price) which was not introduced in any other colony in Australasia. Borrowing was required to ensure the success of subdivision and forced the Liberal Party to move away from its earlier efforts at achieving self-sufficiency. The estates broken up under this scheme generally worked well and brought benefit to those farmers with capital who operated middle-sized units. The land-reform programme did not solve urban unemployment but, when combined with the regulatory activities of the department of agriculture and the provision of cheap credit under the Advances to Settlers Act, helped to hasten the triumph of the family farm over the great estate system.

McKenzie also passed and administered several pieces of legislation to speed up the purchase of Maori land in an endeavour to win the support of rural North Island electorates. The reintroduction of virtually full crown pre-emption enabled the government to buy up nearly 3 million acres at a low price. This land was then utilized by the emerging dairy industry. McKenzie seemed little concerned at the irony of a highlander being responsible for such dispossession.

After the death of Ballance in 1893 McKenzie proved a very effective lieutenant to Richard Seddon in the Liberal ministry. He was forced to resign on 27 June 1900 by an incurable cancer of the bladder, but lingered on, and became the first man in the empire to be knighted in a railway carriage, on 25 June 1901. He died on 6 August 1901 at Heathfield, his farm near Palmerston, and was buried at Palmerston. He left his wife, Annie, two sons and three daughters, and a legacy of active state involvement in the development of New Zealand's farming industry. This contribution, and the securing of so much Maori land so quickly and so cheaply, far outweighed the importance of his tenurial experiments. TOM BROOKING

Sources T. Brooking, *Lands for the people? The highland clearances and the colonisation of New Zealand: a biography of John McKenzie* (1996) · T. Brooking, 'On writing a biography of New Zealand's most famous land reformer', *Historical News*, 56 (1988), 6–10 · T. Brooking, 'On writing a biography of New Zealand's most famous land reformer', *Historical News*, 62 (1991), 6–10 · T. Brooking, 'On writing a biography of New Zealand's most famous land reformer', *Historical News*, 64 (1992), 6–10 · T. Brooking, 'McKenzie, Sir John', *DNZB*, 294–7, vol. 2 · T. Brooking, '"Busting up" the greatest estate of all: liberal Maori land policy, 1891–1911', *New Zealand Journal of History*, 26 (1992), 78–98 · R. M. Burdon, 'Sir John McKenzie', in R. M. Burdon, *Some New Zealand notables*, 2nd ser. (1945), 67–109 · D. McKenzie, 'Sir John McKenzie', *The advance guard*, ed. G. Griffiths, 2 (1974), 5–40 · *Parliamentary debates* (*Hansard*), New Zealand Parliament, House of Representatives (1881–1901) · 'Annual reports of the department of lands', *Appendix to the Journal of the House of Representatives*, C1 (1891–1900) · W. P. Reeves, *State experiments in Australia and New Zealand*, 1 (1902) · A. Siegfried, *Democracy in New Zealand*, trans. E. V. Burns (1904) · W. J. Gardner, *A pastoral kingdom divided: Cheviot, 1889–1894* (1992) · C. D. R. Downes, 'Lands for the people: the life and work of Sir John McKenzie, 1838–1901', MA diss., University of Otago, 1954 · will, supreme court, Dunedin, 1901 · parish register (birth), Rosskeen parish, Easter Ross, 6 Oct 1839 · parish register (marriage), Dingwall, Ross-shire, 23 May 1860 · *Otago Daily Times* (7 Aug 1901) · *Otago Witness* (14 Aug 1901) · J. P. McAloon, 'Colonial wealth: the rich of Canterbury and Otago, 1890–1914', PhD diss., University of Otago, 1993

Archives Archives New Zealand, Wellington, Seddon MSS · NL NZ, Turnbull L., Robert Stout, W. P. Reeves MSS |SOUND Radio New Zealand Archives, Christchurch

Likenesses V. Hunt, caricature, NL NZ, Turnbull L. · tinted photograph, Oamora Early Settlers Museum

Wealth at death £1000 split between two married daughters; £200 to wife and unmarried daughter; Heathfield farm to sons; but family claim cash never materialized

MacKenzie, John Bàn (*c.*1797–1864), piper and composer, was born at Achilty, near Strathpeffer, Ross-shire. One of a family of at least three sons and one daughter, he was probably the eldest son of William MacKenzie, farmer, and his wife, Mary MacKay. The births of the children were not registered. William's brother Kenneth was piper to Lord Breadalbane at Ardmaddy Castle, Argyll, where he lived with his sister Christie, but the MacKenzies were a Ross-shire family. Mary MacKay's family is said locally to have come to Achilty from the Isle of Raasay.

John Bàn was sent for piping tuition to Donald Mór Mac-Lennan of Moy, a well-known piping teacher, at the expense of a local benefactor. Later he was taught by John Beag MacRae, piper to the earl of Seaforth, at Brahan Castle. About 1817 he went to Raasay for lessons with John MacKay, acknowledged as the authority on piobaireachd at that time as he had learned from the MacCrimmons in Skye. Other than piping tuition, John Bàn had no formal education and was illiterate all his life, unable even to sign his name. A fluent and knowledgeable Gaelic speaker, he was hesitant in speaking English.

In 1820 John Bàn was engaged as estate piper by George MacKenzie, at Allangrange, in the Black Isle, and the following year went to Tulloch Castle, near Dingwall, as piper to Duncan Davidson. For the royal visit to Edinburgh in 1822 John Bàn was one of the pipers who played before the king, and he competed regularly in the Edinburgh competitions, held every four years until 1841.

In 1832 Duncan Davidson, a married man with eight children, began to pay court to a young heiress, Maria MacKenzie (*c.*1807–1881) of Applecross. He used John Bàn as his go-between to urge Maria to elope with him. Maria, however, eloped with John Bàn. The couple fled south to Crieff, where they were married legally under Scots law by public declaration. Their first son, Donald, was born there later that year. In 1833 John Bàn was engaged by the marquess of Breadalbane to be his piper at Taymouth Castle, near Aberfeldy, a post which he held for the next twenty-eight years. He had a family of eight children. Two of the four boys died in infancy in 1847, and one of the girls was born mentally handicapped; the two surviving sons joined the army.

John Bàn won the prize pipe for piobaireachd at the Northern Meeting at Inverness in 1849, and, in 1852, the gold medal for former winners, the highest honour in piping at that time. In 1840 Queen Victoria visited Taymouth. Impressed by John Bàn's playing, she invited him to become her personal piper. He declined, and the contemporary story is that when the queen exclaimed 'But where else will I find as good a piper as yourself, and one so handsome?', his reply was 'Madam, I fear your search will fail on both counts.'

John Bàn was a tall, well-built man, known for his good looks. His hair and beard were blond, which gave rise to his byname, Bàn ('white, fair'). It remained appropriate all his life, as his hair went white when he was in his fifties. He is said to have had 'clean-cut knees' which had an effect on the society ladies at Taymouth house parties; family tradition says that he had difficulty in evading their advances, but prudently managed to preserve his good name. He was known for his strong character, and at the Disruption of the churches, he went over to the Free Church of Scotland.

In 1861 John Bàn left Taymouth to retire to the Black Isle, and lived at Greenhill Cottage, Munlochy. Two years later his eldest son, Donald, an excellent piper who had won the prize pipe at the age of fourteen, died from smallpox. John Bàn, already suffering from cancer, was deeply affected by his son's death. In the months that followed he composed his finest piobaireachd work, 'His Father's Lament for Donald MacKenzie'. John Bàn died from cancer of the bladder and rectum on 23 April 1864 at his home in Munlochy. He was buried beside his three sons in the Kinettas burial-ground, Strathpeffer. His importance to the piping world lies in the high standard of his playing that continued the traditions of the MacCrimmons which he learned from John MacKay. John Bàn, Donald Cameron, and Calum MacPherson were the giants of piping in the nineteenth century. BRIDGET MACKENZIE

Sources parish register, Contin, Ross-shire, General Register Office for Scotland, Edinburgh · parish register, Crieff, Perthshire, General Register Office for Scotland, Edinburgh · parish register, Weem, Perthshire, General Register Office for Scotland, Edinburgh · parish register, Kilbrandon, Argyll, General Register Office for Scotland, Edinburgh · N. Macrae, *Dingwall's history of a thousand years* (1923) · gravestones, Kinettas burial-ground, Strathpeffer, Ross-shire · gravestones, Walton cemetery, Liverpool · d. cert. · C. M. Robertson, account of John Bàn's elopement, NL Scot., MS 46713 · A. A. Fairrie, *The Northern Meeting, 1788–1988* (1988) · census returns for Achilty, Ross-shire, for Munlochy, Ross-shire, and for Weem, Perthshire, 1841, 1851, 1861 · private information (2004) [family] · letters from Maria MacKenzie to the Northern Meeting committee, priv. coll., Inverness
Likenesses D. O. Hill and R. Adamson, photograph, 1840–1849?, Scot. NPG; repro. in W. Donaldson, *The highland pipe and Scottish society, 1750–1950* (2000) · photograph, *c.*1850, priv. coll. · photograph, 1850–1859?, Royal Scottish Pipers Society, Edinburgh
Wealth at death £87 2*s.* 2*d.*: confirmation, 16 June 1864, NA Scot., 25/44/8, 191–3

Mackenzie, John Kenneth (1850–1888), medical missionary, born at Great Yarmouth, Norfolk, on 25 August 1850, was the younger son of Alexander Mackenzie, a native of Ross-shire, and his wife, Margaret, a member of a Brecknockshire family. His parents soon moved to Bristol. After being educated at a private school there, he entered a merchant's office as clerk in 1865. He countered the defects of his education by private study, and devoted all his leisure time to evangelical work among the poorer classes in Bristol. Soon abandoning commercial life, he studied medicine with the intention of becoming a medical missionary. In October 1870 he entered the Bristol medical school, and in 1874 obtained medical diplomas from London and Edinburgh. For a time he attended the Royal Ophthalmic Hospital in London.

In 1875 the London Missionary Society appointed Mackenzie superintendent of a newly founded medical station at Hangchow (Hangzhou), China, where he arrived on 8 June after an adventurous voyage. A mission had been established there in 1861, and a hospital was founded in

1867, connected with the new medical station. He worked energetically, made excursions into the surrounding district, and gained the confidence of the Chinese by his skill as a doctor, and especially by his cure of the wife of Li Hongzhang, the viceroy of the area. The unhealthy climate forced him to move, and in March 1879 he went to Tientsin (Tianjin), where a hospital had been established ten years before. Here, as at Hangchow, he speedily gained a high reputation among the Chinese, and he obtained funds for the erection of a new hospital, which was opened on 2 December 1880. One of his most important works in Tientsin was the founding of a medical school for Chinese students. Owing to the illness of his wife he returned to London in February 1883, but arrived at Tientsin again on 25 September 1883. He died there on 1 April 1888 of smallpox, contracted while attending a Chinese patient. A. H. MILLAR, rev. H. C. G. MATTHEW

Sources M. I. Bryson, *John Kenneth Mackenzie: medical missionary in China* (1891) · K. S. Latourette, *A history of Christian missions in China* (1929); repr. (1967) · *CGPLA Eng. & Wales* (1889)

Mackenzie, John Stuart (1860–1935), philosopher, was born at Springburn, Glasgow, on 29 February 1860, the younger son of Thomas McKenzie, and his wife, Janet Brown. He and a brother three years his senior comprised the whole family of Thomas McKenzie, an intrepid but not, in the worldly sense, specially successful Scot who, after having been in business in some branch of the clothing trade in Glasgow, emigrated in 1868 with his family to South America, where he was overtaken by disaster. Within a short time of their arrival his wife, and, some months afterwards, he himself, died; and the children had to be brought back to Scotland to the care of relatives. The elder boy went into engineering in which he did well, while John was sent to the Glasgow high school and then to Glasgow University, where he had a brilliant career and graduated MA in 1882. Having been awarded the Shaw fellowship at the University of Edinburgh, he found himself urged by his chief philosophical teacher, Edward Caird, to take up the subject of social philosophy, in preference to the study of Hegel, which for him had lain 'nearer to the heart's desire'. Thus it happened that his Shaw lectures, delivered during his tenure (1884–9) of the fellowship, constituted an 'Introduction to social philosophy', and were published under that title in 1890.

Meantime, in 1886, Mackenzie had entered Trinity College, Cambridge, as a scholar. He obtained a first class in the moral sciences tripos of 1889. But much more important than any gaining of distinctions at Cambridge were the friendships which he contracted there; in particular that of J. M. E. McTaggart, a youth of kindred tastes, six years junior to him, whom he found much absorbed, as he had himself once been, in Herbert Spencer. Not uncharacteristically, Mackenzie seems to have urged McTaggart towards the Hegelian researches from which he himself had been led to abstain. J. M. E. McTaggart's later influence on his own pupils gave the impetus to much in the early development of those tendencies in philosophy which

during the first half of the twentieth century were especially associated with Cambridge.

In 1890 Mackenzie was elected into a fellowship at Trinity which he held until 1896. In 1895 he was appointed professor of logic and philosophy at University College, Cardiff, a post from which he retired in 1915 at the early age of fifty-five, in order, chiefly, 'to have time to write'.

It is not implied, of course, that Mackenzie had not already written. Besides his Shaw lectures, his *Outlines of Metaphysics* (1902), and his *Lectures on Humanism* (1907), he had produced, as far back as 1893, a *Manual of Ethics* which seemed, somewhat to his astonishment, to have made his name familiar almost wherever ethics were taught and English was spoken. It was still in print, in its sixth edition, in 1948. He was president of the Moral Education League from 1908 to 1916.

What Mackenzie would probably have regarded as his chief works were published during and after the First World War. They were *Elements of Constructive Philosophy* (1917), *Outlines of Social Philosophy* (1918), *Fundamental Problems of Life* (1928), and, finally, a small but comprehensive volume, entitled *Cosmic Problems* (1931). His *Arrows of Desire* (1920) is a collection of occasional essays on 'our national character and outlook'. The University of Glasgow conferred upon him the honorary degree of LLD in 1911 and he was elected a fellow of the British Academy in 1934.

As a representative of the later phase of the neo-Hegelian school of British idealistic philosophy, Mackenzie invites comparison, as a teacher and writer, with McTaggart. Their ultimate metaphysical faith was the same; but Mackenzie had nothing of that intense need for precise statement and rigidly concatenated argument which characterized McTaggart. Mackenzie was not a 'dry light', as Caird had once remarked to him. He held the universe to be, indeed, an order; but creative imagination must be the key to it rather than logic. And this seems in later years, although the personal link was never broken, to have drawn him rather away from McTaggart's thought, and to have led him to see the chief promise for the future of philosophy in such thinkers as, for example, the mountaineer-philosopher (Edward) Douglas Fawcett (1866–1960) who, although groping rather more in the dark, appealed to him as perhaps pointing nearer to the dawn.

Mackenzie married in 1898 Hettie Millicent (1863–1942), daughter of Walter William Hughes, of Bristol. Herself an educationist and writer, she was head of the department for the training of teachers at Cardiff. They had no children. She edited his autobiography, published in 1936. Mackenzie died at his home, Upfield Cottage, Brockweir, near Chepstow, on 6 December 1935.

J. W. SCOTT, rev. MARK J. SCHOFIELD

Sources H. M. H. Mackenzie, ed., *John Stuart Mackenzie* (1936) · J. H. Muirhead, *PBA*, 21 (1935) · personal knowledge (1949) · *CGPLA Eng. & Wales* (1936)
Archives CUL, letters to G. E. Moore · JRL, letters to Samuel Alexander · NL Scot., corresp. with Sir Patrick Geddes
Wealth at death £13,253 15s.: probate, 6 May 1936, *CGPLA Eng. & Wales*

Mackenzie, Kenneth, Lord Mackenzie of Kintail (d. 1611). *See under* Mackenzie family of Kintail (*per. c.*1475–1611).

Mackenzie, Kenneth, third earl of Seaforth (1635–1678). *See under* Mackenzie, George, second earl of Seaforth (d. 1651).

Mackenzie, Kenneth, fourth earl of Seaforth and Jacobite first marquess of Seaforth (*bap.* 1661, *d.* 1701), clan chief, was baptized at Kinghorn, Fife, on 8 December 1661, the eldest son of Kenneth *Mackenzie, third earl of Seaforth (d. 1678) [*see under* Mackenzie, George], and Isobel (d. 1715), daughter of Sir John Mackenzie of Tarbat; he had three brothers and four sisters. Nothing is known of his early life or education. He succeeded as fourth earl on 16 December 1678 and was served heir to his great-grandfather in 1681. His mother's brother Sir George *Mackenzie of Tarbat (1630–1714) and other relatives, by buying up debts, obtained legal ownership of the estate to forestall outside creditors, and temporarily transferred it to her.

James, duke of York, eager to convert the Mackenzie chiefs to Catholicism and prevent their family's financial ruin, evidently arranged Seaforth's next, unprecedented, steps. Moving to England, the earl, who was already the father of an illegitimate son, married, by contract of 1 May 1684, Frances (1660–1732), second daughter of William *Herbert, first marquess of Powis, the moderate leader of the Catholic aristocracy. Seaforth turned Catholic, for life; his two surviving brothers temporarily also converted. The earl and countess had two children, William *Mackenzie, later fifth earl (d. 1740), and Mary (d. 1740). Under the marriage contract, Powis was to maintain the Seaforths' household for three years (in practice, five) in England, where Powis's favour in James's reign was reflected upon the earl. Seaforth became, in his absence, a Scottish privy councillor in November 1686 and a knight of the Thistle on 6 June 1687.

At the revolution Seaforth and his family were captured trying to escape in a yacht, but then crossed to France with William's pass. In March 1689 Seaforth accompanied James (and Powis) to Ireland. Late in 1689, after James had to send away the unpopular earl of Melfort, Seaforth served informally as secretary of state for Scotland.

Seaforth's main mission was to cross to the highlands and raise his clan for James, as his uncle Colin Mackenzie had tried to do since late 1689. Early in January 1690 he sailed from Galway, but strong winds drove back his damaged ship. He was suffering increasingly from attacks of the stone (which restricted his later activities, exacerbated his imprisonments, and probably killed him), and over the next few months his strong enthusiasm ebbed. To revive it, James created him (Jacobite) marquess of Seaforth and major-general, shortly before he sailed in April from Dublin with a shipload of troops and supplies. But he also carried a Williamite friend, Sir Thomas Southwell, condemned by the Irish courts for treason, as the only certain means of preventing his execution, and therefore had one major adviser constantly urging surrender. Landing on 20 May 1690 at Eilean Donan, his west highland castle, Seaforth made contact with the Jacobite commander Major-General Thomas Buchan. Dismayed, however, by the recent defeat at Cromdale, he did not raise the Mackenzies, and negotiated all summer through Tarbat and Colonel John Hill for his submission on terms.

The Jacobites blamed Seaforth for their failures, and in late August, when Major-General Hugh Mackay pursued Buchan past Inverness, he raised the highland Mackenzies of west Ross-shire, 800–900 strong. He probably considered joining Buchan until he belatedly heard of the defeat at the Boyne, but claimed soon afterwards that his intention was to defend his clan from both sides; characteristically, he did just enough to alienate both. Mackay, thinking he might easily be influenced into active rebellion, threatened to ravage the Mackenzie country indiscriminately. Seaforth made a secret agreement with him to be captured collusively, but then, fearing for his health if imprisoned, unwisely broke it. Mackay's renewed threats against his clan forced Seaforth to disband his men on 2 September and surrender himself next day. He was imprisoned at Inverness and, from November, in Edinburgh Castle. Tarbat protested that this would discourage further Jacobite submissions.

On 7 January 1691 Seaforth was bailed, and remained free in Edinburgh and its vicinity on giving his word not to plot, though he kept in contact with Buchan, for whom Colin Mackenzie again garrisoned Eilean Donan until the highlanders' submission. Much of Scottish society acknowledged Seaforth's (and later his son's) Jacobite marquessate. However, when Seaforth fled from Edinburgh on 6 May 1692 during the French invasion threat, apparently motivated only by vague hopes, and groundless fears of torture, he alienated the Scottish government. Recaptured ten days later, he was again imprisoned in Edinburgh Castle. William ordered his prosecution for treason, which began in the 1693 parliament, but was then remitted to the justice court and finally abandoned in 1697. The privy council, relenting, was about to recommend his release in August 1695 when he escaped again. He was not thought dangerous or pursued, and, having surrendered at Inverness in September 1696, was bailed in March 1697.

However, Seaforth's family's vast private debts and arrears of public dues now threatened him, and Tarbat and other leading Mackenzies had become unscrupulously hostile. Since 1690 Seaforth had continued the clan's imprisonment of a profligate apostate Catholic priest in various western isles. Now he failed to produce him in time upon the privy council's order—his last, and ruinous, major mistake. Another imprisonment in Edinburgh Castle from July 1698 was prolonged by private influences until March 1700. Returning to his home, Brahan Castle in the Black Isle, he died there, before he could set his complex affairs in order, in March 1701. Prolonged financial disputes between his mother, impoverished by standing his surety, and his widow began at his deathbed. Countess Frances in late 1701 sent her children to France to be reared as Catholics, despite the Mackenzie gentry's protests, helping ensure that the family would remain Jacobite and marginalized for another quarter-century. Mary married in 1712 John Caryll, son of Alexander Pope's friend, and later Francis, second (Jacobite) Lord Sempill. Countess Frances died in Paris on 16 December 1732.   PAUL HOPKINS

Sources P. A. Hopkins, *Glencoe and the end of the highland war* (1986); rev. edn (1998) · D. Warrand, *Some Mackenzie pedigrees* (1965) · NL Scot., Delvine MSS 1356, 1360, 1329, 1333 · Seaforth MSS, Add. MSS 28251, 28239, BL · register of the Scottish privy council, NA Scot., PC1/47–52 · H. Mackay, *Memoirs of the war carried on in Scotland and Ireland*, ed. J. M. Hog and others, Bannatyne Club, 45 (1833) · D. Warrand, ed., *More Culloden papers*, 5 vols. (1923–30), vol. 1 · J. Fraser, *Chronicles of the Frasers: the Wardlaw manuscript*, ed. W. Mackay, Scottish History Society, 1st ser., 47 (1905) · GEC, *Peerage* · W. H. L. Melville, ed., *Leven and Melville papers: letters and state papers chiefly addressed to George, earl of Melville … 1689–1691*, Bannatyne Club, 77 (1843) · E. W. M. Balfour-Melville, ed., *An account of the proceedings of the estates in Scotland, 1689–1690*, 2 vols., Scottish History Society, 3rd ser., 46–7 (1954–5) · *Scots peerage* · BL, Melfort MSS, Lansdowne MS 1163A–C · *State trials*, vol. 13
Archives BL, family MSS, Add. MS 28251 · Mitchell L., Glas. | NL Scot., Delvine MSS
Likenesses R. White, line engraving (after his pencil drawing), BM, NPG · R. White, pencil drawing on vellum, BM · oils, Fortrose town hall, Highland
Wealth at death large estates in Ross-shire, but private debts and arrears of public feu duties and taxes may have outweighed them in value: NL Scot., Delvine MSS

Mackenzie, Kenneth [later Sir Kenneth Douglas, first baronet] (1754–1833), army officer, was born at Dundee, the son and heir of Kenneth Mackenzie of Kilcoy, Ross-shire, and his wife, Janet, daughter of Sir Robert Douglas, baronet, author of the *Scots Peerage*, and sister of Sir Alexander Douglas of Glenbervie, last baronet. On 26 August 1767, aged thirteen, Mackenzie joined the 33rd regiment as an ensign. Having been promoted lieutenant in 1775, he transferred to the 14th regiment in 1783, with which he served in the West Indies until 1791 and thereafter in the Netherlands campaign, during which, as a senior lieutenant, he commanded a company. He was wounded at the ill-fated siege of Dunkirk, but his prowess as an officer caught the attention of Thomas Graham of Balgowan (later General Lord Lynedoch), who, when raising the 90th regiment in 1794, asked for Mackenzie's services. The latter, appointed first captain and then major in the new unit, which was considered a light infantry battalion and drilled accordingly, accompanied it to the Île Dieu, Gibraltar, and, in 1796, Portugal. Here, under Sir Charles Stuart, Mackenzie headed and instructed an improvised battalion comprising the light companies of the various regiments in Stuart's force. Accompanying Stuart's expedition to Minorca, he served as deputy adjutant-general and was made lieutenant-colonel when the island fell in October 1798.

Sir Ralph Abercromby superseded Stuart and, after landing in Egypt, defeated General Menou at Abu Qir on 20 March 1801. Mackenzie, with the 90th, saw heavy fighting, during which not only Abercromby but also Lieutenant-Colonel Ogilvie of the 44th was killed. Mackenzie took command of that unit in his stead, and remained with it in Egypt and Gibraltar until 1803, when he was recalled and attached to a training camp at Shorncliffe, Kent.

Shorncliffe was under the jurisdiction of General Sir John Moore, commander of the southern military district. Moore realized that because, over the preceding decades, afforestation, enclosure, and urbanization had transformed the south of England and numerous other areas of the European terrain, military tactics were in a state of flux; and light troops, once confined to a subordinate role on the periphery of armies, were now playing an ever greater part in set-piece battles, with the French fielding thousands of *tirailleurs*, *voltigeurs*, and *chasseurs*. Encouraged by the duke of York, the commander-in-chief, Moore wanted to transform some regiments of the line into permanent bodies of light infantry which, suitably equipped and trained, would be capable of fighting, not only in the customary close-order formations of the period but also as free-thinking, free-firing skirmishers. However militarily prudent this might seem, it was a somewhat controversial proposal at the time, since it involved liberating troops from both the physical and psychological constraints of orthodox linear tactics, and to encourage common soldiers to show initiative was regarded by many as potentially destabilizing.

The first regiment converted to light infantry was Moore's own, the 52nd, which was officially retitled on 18 January 1803. Mackenzie was appointed its lieutenant-colonel because of his particular talent for training skirmishers, and he played a pivotal role in the instruction of the new unit. An accomplished marksman whose principal pastime was shooting, he applied some of the practices of the hunt to the battlefield, educating his troops in fieldcraft and in the work of the scout. He also devised a new tactical drill and manual exercise, together with a more natural style of marching which enabled the soldiers to move more rapidly and with less fatigue. This was the famous 'Shorncliffe system' of drill, of which Mackenzie was the principal architect. He also promoted a more relaxed form of discipline woven from strands of Enlightenment thinking: the common soldier was no longer treated like an automaton, to be flogged and drilled into obedience, but more like a member of a family in which his seniors were encouraged to take on a paternal role.

By July 1803 the 43rd foot had also been redesignated as a light regiment. Brigaded together with the 95th (rifles), they and the 52nd had plenty of time to hone their new skills while awaiting Napoleon's expected invasion of southern England. Mackenzie, however, was seriously injured—suffering 'a very severe concussion of the brain' (*GM*, 443)—in a fall from his horse in November 1803. He had to take sick leave during the summer of 1804, but on 18 December at Hythe, Kent, he married Rachel, only child of Robert Andrews of Shorncliffe; they had six sons and a daughter. Promoted colonel on 25 April 1808, he accompanied Graham to Cadiz in 1810 and took command of a brigade. His health remained precarious, however, and he soon returned to Britain to recuperate. His convalescence continued until 1811, when, in June, he was promoted major-general and subsequently placed in charge of another light infantry training camp, at Brabourne Lees, east Kent.

During 1813 he accompanied Sir Thomas Graham to the Netherlands and had command of the 2nd division before being incapacitated by another fall from his horse. He was made governor of Antwerp in 1814 but, appointed to command and train new light troops in England, was recalled just before Waterloo. Thereafter he retired to Hythe, where he took a keen interest in local affairs and became a jurat. He was promoted lieutenant-general on 19 July 1821, made colonel of the 58th regiment on 1 March 1828, and created a baronet on 30 September 1831, assuming by royal licence in October 1831 the name and arms of Douglas of Glenbervie, the baronetcy of which was dormant since the death of his wife's brother, Alexander Douglas, seventh baronet (1738–1812). He died at Holles Street, Cavendish Square, London, on 22 November 1833 and was buried at Hythe. He was succeeded as second baronet by his son Robert Andrews Douglas (1807–1843), army officer.   DAVID GATES

Sources D. Gates, *The British light infantry arm, c.1790–1815* (1987) · W. S. Moorsom, ed., *Historical record of the fifty-second regiment (Oxfordshire light infantry), from the year 1755 to the year 1858* (1860) · G. T. Napier, *Passages in the early military life of General Sir George T. Napier: written by himself*, ed. W. C. E. Napier (1884) · W. F. P. Napier, *Life of General Sir William Napier*, ed. H. A. Bruce, 2 vols. (1864) · J. Philippart, ed., *The royal military calendar*, 3rd edn, 3 (1820), 181–5 · *The diary of Sir John Moore*, ed. J. F. Maurice, 2 vols. (1904) · A. M. Delaroye, *Life of Thomas Graham, Lord Lynedoch* (1880) · C. T. Atkinson, ed., *Supplementary report on the manuscripts of Robert Graham esq. of Fintry*, HMC, 81 (1940) · *GM*, 2nd ser., 1 (1834), 441–3

Archives NL Scot., manuscripts division, military corresp., Acc. 10458 | NL Scot., manuscripts division, corresp., mainly with Thomas Graham and Sir John Moore, 8028 · NL Scot., manuscripts division, letters to Lord Lynedoch, MSS 3595–3620

Mackenzie, Kenneth Augustus Muir, Baron Muir Mackenzie (1845–1930), civil servant and politician, was born on 29 June 1845 at Delvine, Perthshire, the fourth son of Sir John William Pitt Muir Mackenzie, second baronet, and his wife, Sophia Matilda, daughter of James Raymond Johnstone. He was educated at Charterhouse and at Balliol College, Oxford, where he graduated BA in 1868, having taken a second in *literae humaniores*. Called to the bar by Lincoln's Inn in 1873, he undertook pupillages with both the future lords Bowen and Davey and began practice at the bar. On 26 February 1874 he married Amy Margaret (d. 1900), daughter of William Graham, MP for Glasgow, and sister of a Balliol contemporary. She later became aunt to the future lord chancellor, the first Lord Hailsham.

In 1880, at the age of thirty-five, Muir Mackenzie was to suffer a remarkable change of career. The Judicature Act of 1873 and the Appellate Jurisdiction Act of 1876 had reformed the court structure and established a clear hierarchy of judges. The judicature commission (1867–72) was urged to establish a ministry of justice to run the system, staffed by civil servants professionalized under the Northcote–Trevelyan reforms. That was unattractive to the judges and the profession, who were not enthusiastic admirers of utilitarian reforms. It was agreed therefore

Kenneth Augustus Muir Mackenzie, Baron Muir Mackenzie (1845–1930), by Walter Stoneman, 1917

that the lord chancellor, in addition to his work as politician and judge, should take over the executive and administrative functions relating to the judges, the profession, and the higher courts.

Thus began the Lord Chancellor's Office (later known as the Lord Chancellor's Department). A small office had been established as early as 1874, but its real founding occurred when Muir Mackenzie was appointed by Lord Selborne, the Liberal lord chancellor, as clerk of the crown in Chancery in 1880. He was also referred to as principal secretary, although in 1882 the two offices were merged. The appointment was not an established civil service one, and it was unclear whether Muir Mackenzie would stay when Selborne left. By 1882, however, Selborne was arguing that:

> the new Judicature System has thrown around the Chancellor such a network of departmental business … that … it will not be possible to prevent serious inconvenience to the public business on a change in the Great Seal … without a really efficient Permanent Secretary. (Selborne to Cairns, 29 March 1882, LCO 2/262)

In August 1883 Selborne persuaded Cairns, the former Conservative lord chancellor, to make a joint approach to the Treasury for a permanent establishment, 'in fact, a Permanent Secretary of the Ministry of Justice' (Selborne to Cairns, 16 Aug 1883, LCO 2/262). The Treasury surprisingly easily conceded that such support was needed, and that the lord chancellor should have a 'political' private secretary (a post to which Lord Wolmer was appointed) and a permanent secretary, a post to which Muir Mackenzie was appointed in May 1884.

The office continued to operate mainly outside the regular civil service, staffed, at least until the 1960s, only by lawyers. For most of Muir Mackenzie's time, however, the office was sparsely staffed. There was Adolphus Liddell secured from the parliament office and the assistant serjeant-at-arms from the House of Lords who acted as Muir Mackenzie's secretary. In addition, there were two secretaries and an odd-job man. While Muir Mackenzie claimed only to be the lord chancellor's 'postman', in fact he was a powerful force as administrator of the judiciary and the courts—and the *éminence grise* of the legal profession. His was the hand behind the implementation of the court reforms and the modernization of procedure. His successor, Lord Schuster, powerfully described his performance, acknowledging his 'subtle brain and keen wit', his hatred of waste or disorder, and his incredible industry, but noting that 'he was a man naturally secretive, unwilling to trust to his subordinates either his plans or their execution, and though an advanced Radical in politics, he was in many matters exceedingly conservative'. He, for example, detested the use either of shorthand or of typewriting. Schuster recalled that he 'wrote his letters himself, keeping no copies, made no record of agreements to which he was a party, and was unwilling or unable to delegate' (Schuster, Memorandum, 31 Jan 1943, LCO 2/3630). Muir Mackenzie was, however, a strong man. As Schuster later commented (Schuster to Coldstream, 12 July 1955, LCO 2/5233) while discussing the number of law lords, 'Muir Mackenzie was completely unscrupulous in interpreting a statute and disregarded its provisions if they did not suit him.'

Muir Mackenzie became disenchanted by Halsbury's reluctance to champion reform, but when the long period of Conservative rule finally ended in 1905, there were the Liberal chancellors, Loreburn and Haldane (whom Muir Mackenzie particularly liked) to serve, and important reforms—for instance, in the county courts, on the appointment of JPs, and in the judicial committee of the privy council—to undertake. Moreover, during these years Muir Mackenzie played an important role in depoliticizing the appointment of the judges, at least in the High Court and Court of Appeal. Created KCB in 1898, he was made GCB in 1911 and a privy councillor in 1924. He served as warden of Winchester College from 1904 to 1915, and treasurer of Lincoln's Inn in 1917. With the appearance of Lord Buckmaster in May 1915, Muir Mackenzie ceased to be permanent secretary. Lord Haldane had, however, arranged for him to be made a peer (29 June 1915), prompting Muir Mackenzie to remark, 'I don't care a d— whether I am baron or barren' (Heuston, 226). For someone aged seventy, retirement might have seemed appropriate—not for Muir Mackenzie. He served as a lord-in-waiting in both the first and the second Labour administrations, dying in office at his London home, 27 Cumberland Terrace, Regent's Park, on 22 May 1930, aged eighty-five, reputedly the oldest minister in the twentieth century. After cremation at Golders Green, his remains were buried at Westminster Abbey on the 27th. Since he had no male heir (he had three daughters and a son, who predeceased him in 1901), his peerage died with him.

ROBERT STEVENS

Sources R. Stevens, *The independence of the judiciary: the view from the lord chancellor's office* (1993) · R. F. V. Heuston, *Lives of the lord chancellors, 1885–1940* (1964) · R. Stevens, *Laws and politics: the House of Lords as a judicial body, 1800–1976* (1978) · WWW · A. G. C. Liddell, *Notes from the life of an ordinary mortal* (1911) · PRO, Lord Chancellor's Office MSS · GEC, *Peerage* · I. Elliott, ed., *The Balliol College register, 1833–1933*, 2nd edn (privately printed, Oxford, 1934) · *Debrett's Peerage*
Archives PRO, lord chancellor's office MSS | BL, letters to W. E. Gladstone, Add. MSS 44297–44498, *passim* · BL, letters to Lord Halsbury, Add. MS 56370 · BL OIOC, letters to Lord Reading, MSS Eur. E 238, F 118 · LPL, corresp. with Archbishop Benson · NL Scot., corresp. with Lord Haldane
Likenesses W. Stoneman, photograph, 1917, NPG [*see illus.*] · portrait, NPG · portrait, lord chancellor's office, London
Wealth at death £1436 6s. 9d.: probate, 31 Oct 1930, CGPLA Eng. & Wales

Mackenzie, Kenneth Douglas (1811–1873), army officer, born on 1 February 1811, was the only son and eldest child of Donald Mackenzie and his wife, the daughter of T. Mylne of Mylnefield, Perthshire; he was the nephew of General Sir Kenneth *Mackenzie. On 25 November 1831 he was appointed ensign in the 92nd highlanders, becoming lieutenant in 1836 and captain in 1844, all by purchase. He served with the regiment in the Mediterranean, West Indies, and at home. During the Irish trouble of 1848 he acted as brigadier-major of the flying column under Major-General John Macdonald (d. 1869), to whom he had been adjutant in the 92nd. On the arrest of William Smith O'Brien at Thurles railway station on 5 August 1848 Mackenzie, to avoid a possible rescue attempt or a blockage of the line, stopped a passenger train, in which to convey O'Brien to Dublin. The engine driver refused to co-operate until Mackenzie held a pistol to his head and threatened to shoot him. Sir George Grey stated in the House of Commons that Mackenzie's conduct had been commended by the commander-in-chief, the duke of Wellington.

Mackenzie soon after received the appointment of deputy assistant adjutant-general in Dublin, which he held until 1854. He went to the Crimea as brigade major of Codrington's brigade of the light division, and was present at the Alma, Inkerman, and Sevastopol. He was made brevet major on 12 December 1854 and brevet lieutenant-colonel on 2 November 1855. From the beginning of 1855 to the end of the war he served first as deputy assistant quartermaster-general, then as an assistant adjutant-general at the headquarters at Sevastopol, and later as assistant quartermaster-general at Balaklava. Lord Raglan praised his efficiency, and he was awarded the fifth class of the Mejidiye and the Légion d'honneur (fifth class). After the war he went back to Dublin as deputy assistant adjutant-general. He became major in the 92nd in 1857, accompanied the regiment to India in January 1858, served in the central India campaign, and was made an assistant adjutant-general in Bengal. In June 1859 he was sent to quell a mutiny in the 5th Bengal European infantry at Berhampore, for which he was thanked by the governor-general in council, and by the secretary of state. In 1860 he was deputy quartermaster-general and head of the department in the expedition to China, and was made a CB. In 1861 he married Mary, daughter of General G. T. Colomb; she survived him.

Mackenzie was promoted to a lieutenant-colonelcy unattached in 1861, serving as deputy quartermaster-general in Canada. He was assistant adjutant-general in Dublin during the Fenian disturbances of 1865–6, and became brevet colonel on 1 April 1869. On 1 April 1870 he was appointed assistant quartermaster-general at the Horse Guards, and took an active part in organizing the first autumn manoeuvres, which were held on Dartmoor in 1873. While driving out from the camp to dinner at a nearby country house on Sunday, 24 August 1873, Mackenzie and his brother-in-law, Captain Colomb, attempted, near Roborough, to ford the River Meavy, which was flooded with recent rains; the horse was swept off his legs, the gig upset, and the occupants with difficulty reached the bank. Mackenzie died immediately afterwards of syncope induced by exhaustion.

H. M. CHICHESTER, rev. JAMES FALKNER

Sources Army List · The Times (26 Aug 1873) · Army and Navy Gazette (30 Aug 1873) · Hart's Army List · Boase, Mod. Eng. biog.
Likenesses silhouette, c.1845, priv. coll. · Maull & Fox, photograph, 1861
Wealth at death under £6000: probate, 15 Sept 1873, CGPLA Eng. & Wales

Mackenzie, Sir (William) Leslie (1862–1935), health administrator, was born on 30 May 1862 at Shandwick Mains, a small farming community on the coast of Easter Ross, the son of James Mackenzie, the local grieve, and his wife, Margaret, née Bain. Until the age of fourteen he attended the neighbouring board school, in a one-roomed thatched cottage, where he was taught by an elderly teacher and his university-educated son. Between the ages of eleven and fourteen he served as a pupil-teacher, the traditional activity for bright children from modest homes. Mackenzie then moved to Aberdeen and entered the grammar school, where he remained until he was sixteen. He then spent some time teaching at a private girls' school. In 1883 he graduated from Aberdeen University with an MA in philosophy (first class) and classics (second class), winning prizes and scholarships to the value of £80 and £100, each for two years. He then spent a term studying at Edinburgh University. At Aberdeen, Mackenzie came under the influence of Alexander Bain, the professor of logic and English literature, and a one-time associate of Edwin Chadwick.

Mackenzie decided to enter medicine and was awarded a bursary to study at Aberdeen, where he graduated with MB, CM (with honours), in 1888. He became the resident assistant physician at Aberdeen Royal Infirmary and also an assistant to Matthew Hay, professor of physiology at the university. In 1890 he obtained a diploma in public health and became the assistant medical officer at Aberdeen, transferring the following year to become the county medical officer of health for Kirkcudbrightshire and Wigtownshire, the first such appointment under the 1889 Local Government (Scotland) Act. On 12 February 1892 Mackenzie married Helen Carruthers Spence (1859–1945) [see Mackenzie, Dame Helen Carruthers], the daughter of William Spence, clothier. There were no children. His wife pursued an independent political life, on Edinburgh's school board and in other public institutions, and in 1936 she became a member of the Scottish health committee, where her views on a reformed health service closely resembled Labour's post-1945 scheme.

In 1895 Mackenzie obtained highest honours from Edinburgh for his MD on rural water supplies, having in the previous year been appointed Leith's first full-time medical officer, after the burgh had failed to deal with an outbreak of smallpox. At Leith he introduced the immediate disinfection of homes following an outbreak of tuberculosis, rigorously attended to outbreaks of diphtheria, and called for the regular medical inspection of schoolchildren and for the supply of milk to expectant mothers. In 1901 he was appointed the Scottish Local Government Board's first medical inspector (after complaints from MPs on the state of medical provision in the highlands), and the following year he conducted the survey of 600 schoolchildren for the royal commission (Scotland) on physical training, which demonstrated the poor condition of inner city children. His report was debated in parliament during discussion of the Second South African War and led to MPs demanding the introduction of a school meals' service and medical inspection. In 1902, at a meeting in Edinburgh of the Medico-Chirurgical Society, he vigorously disagreed with the Scottish medical establishment on the infectivity of TB; Mackenzie suggested environmental factors, which could be controlled through compulsory notification and hospital treatment, while Sir Henry Littlejohn and others blamed individual habits.

In 1904 Mackenzie was appointed the medical member of the Scottish Local Government Board (during a Conservative government), and between 1913 and 1919 he was a member of the Highlands and Islands Medical Service Board (whose administrative scheme he largely drafted). He gave evidence to the royal commission on the care and control of the feeble-minded (1908), largely against the eugenics movement, and to the royal commission on the poor laws (1909), where he called for a preventive health service, run by the local authority and removed from the stigma of pauperism. Mackenzie served on a number of other government and medical commissions, the most important being the royal commission on housing (Scotland) between 1913 and 1917. He personally drafted the topics each witness was asked to address and took an active interest in drafting the 1919 Housing Bill. Mackenzie considered the introduction of state-subsidized council housing the most important issue in which he played an effective part. His knighthood in 1919 was awarded on the personal recommendation of Lloyd George. He was a medical member of the Scottish board of health between 1919 and 1928. In the 1920s the plans he laid down for the Highlands and Islands Medical Service were followed by governments in Canada, the USA, and South Africa; the most notable scheme, in Kentucky, was opened by Mackenzie in 1928. He wrote widely in medical journals, but is best-known for *The Medical Inspection of Schoolchildren* (1904), *The Health of the School Child* (1906), *Health and Disease* (1911), and *Scottish Mothers and Children* (1917).

Mackenzie's contemporaries regarded him with awe, as a radical philosopher who saw medicine not as a palliative nor a means for private gain, but as an instrument of social development, firmly rooted in the validity of human experience. He was one of the first to realize the limitations of the post-Chadwickian school of public health and the need, if health was to improve, for the movement to acquire new arguments and a different strategy. Public health in the nineteenth century was orientated towards controlling environmental factors of disease; Mackenzie saw the new movement as the production of personal fitness. In that respect his publications (and legislative imprint) on behalf of the schoolchild, the TB victim, the sick pauper, the expectant mother, and the slum tenant, embodied the heart of new Liberalism—social advancement through positive intervention.

Mackenzie had a natural courtesy, linked to a pawky humour, but few, it was said, could escape his strong personality and withering contempt for administrative or professional incompetence. Although his writings often suffered from 'dialectical embellishment', his background in philosophy and medicine greatly strengthened his power of persuasion; it was difficult for other officials convincingly to marshal a countervailing argument.

Mackenzie died on 28 February 1935, in Edinburgh, after a long illness, and was cremated on 2 March. His wife survived him. IAN LEVITT

Mary Elizabeth Frederica Stewart-Mackenzie, Lady Hood (1783–1862), by Samuel William Reynolds senior (after Sir Thomas Lawrence, 1808)

Sources *Sanitary Journal of Scotland* (1891–1901) · A. M., *Edinburgh Medical Journal*, 3rd ser., 42 (1935), 231–2 · *The Lancet* (9 March 1935), 577–8 · *BMJ* (9 March 1935), 506–7 · *The Scotsman* (1 March 1935) · *The Lancet* (6 Dec 1902), 1545–6 · *Annual Report* [Scottish Board of Supervision] (1891–4) · *Annual Report* [Scottish Local Government Board] (1895–1919) · *County and Municipal Record* (1901–15) · *Journal of the Royal Sanitary Institute*, 42 (1921–2), 11–17 · *WW* · b. cert. · *CCI* (1935) · I. Levitt, 'The state, the family and the Scottish health problem, the work of Dr Leslie Mackenzie, 1891–1928', *Northern Scotland*, 17 (1997), 55–72
Archives NA Scot., Scottish home and health department MSS
Likenesses photograph, repro. in I. Levitt, *Poverty and welfare in Scotland, 1890–1948* (1988)
Wealth at death £7949 15s. 3d.: confirmation, 11 April 1935, *CCI*

Mackenzie, Louisa Caroline Stewart-. *See* Baring, Louisa Caroline, Lady Ashburton (1827–1903).

Mackenzie, Mary Elizabeth Frederica Stewart-, Lady Hood (1783–1862), chief of clan Mackenzie, eldest of the six daughters and coheirs of Francis Humberston *Mackenzie, Baron Seaforth (1754–1815), and Mary (1754/5–1829), daughter of Baptist Proby, dean of Lichfield, and brother of Lord Carysfort, was born at Tarnadale on 27 March 1783. In 1801 she went with her family to Barbados, where her father was governor; she met there, and married at Bridgetown, on 6 November 1804, Sir Samuel *Hood (1762–1814), vice-admiral of the white. They returned to Britain, where Lady Hood established a firm friendship with Sir Walter Scott, despite her whig sympathies; he described her as having 'the spirit of the chieftainess in every drop of her blood' (Lockhart, 306). In 1814 she accompanied her husband to the East Indies on his appointment as commander-in-chief. She travelled extensively in India, and claimed to be the first British woman to shoot a tiger in that country. Sir Samuel Hood died on 24 December 1814, and in the following year his widow succeeded to the family estates on the death of her father, his four sons having predeceased him. She thus became the chief of clan Mackenzie. The failure of the male line when there should be a deaf clan chief had been predicted in an old curse, and was apparently fulfilled in this generation.

On 21 May 1817 Lady Hood married James Alexander Stewart of Glasserton (1784–1843), elder son of Admiral Keith Stewart (d. 1795), third son of Alexander Stewart, sixth earl of Galloway. On their marriage the name Mackenzie was added to that of Stewart. They had three sons and three daughters. Her husband was MP for Ross and Cromarty from 1831 to 1837, governor of Ceylon in 1837–40, and lord high commissioner of the Ionian Islands from 1840 to 1843.

Ill health and the financial difficulties which threatened to overwhelm the Seaforth estates prevented Mary Stewart-Mackenzie from leading the Mackenzies at Scott's pageant to welcome George IV to Scotland in 1822. Her financial difficulties were resolved only on the marriage of her third daughter, Louisa, to William Baring, second Lord Ashburton, in 1858 [see Baring, Louisa]. She died at Brahan Castle, Ross-shire, on 28 November 1862, her second husband having died in 1843; a lengthy procession of mourners, led by pipers, followed her coffin for the 20 miles to Fortrose Cathedral where she was buried.

T. F. HENDERSON, rev. K. D. REYNOLDS

Sources *Familiar letters of Sir Walter Scott*, ed. D. Douglas, 2 vols. (1894) · *GM*, 3rd ser., 12 (1862), 379–80 · J. Prebble, *The king's jaunt: George IV in Scotland, August 1822* (1988) · V. Surtees, *The Ludovisi goddess: the life of Louisa, Lady Ashburton* (1984) · J. G. Lockhart, *Memoirs of the life of Sir Walter Scott*, [new edn] (1845) · GEC, *Peerage*
Archives NA Scot., corresp. and papers, GD46 | Department of National Archives, Sri Lanka, MSS of second husband relating to Ceylon · NL Scot., corresp. with Sir Walter Scott, MSS 3878–3918
Likenesses T. Lawrence, oils, exh. RA 1808, Castle Abbey, Northamptonshire · S. W. Reynolds senior, engraving (after T. Lawrence, 1808), BM [see illus.] · portrait (after oil painting by T. Lawrence), Ross and Cromarty District Council; repro. in Prebble, *King's jaunt*
Wealth at death £12,314 14s. 10d.: confirmation, 14 March 1863, NA Scot., SC 25/44/7, 643–87

Sir Morell Mackenzie (1837–1892), by Walery, *c.*1888

Mackenzie, Sir Morell (1837–1892), physician and laryngologist, was born on 7 July 1837 at 742 High Road, Leytonstone, London, the eldest of the nine children of Stephen Mackenzie (1803–1851), a general practitioner, and his wife, Margaret Frances (*d.* 1877), daughter of Adam Harvey, a wine merchant of Lewes and Brighton. He was descended from the Scottish family of Mackenzie of Scatwell in Ross-shire. His education at Dr Greig's school in Walthamstow was terminated when he was sixteen, following the death of his father, who had fallen from his gig. Aware that his duty was to help provide for his family Mackenzie joined the Union Assurance Company and attended evening classes in natural history and chemistry at King's College, London. It became clear that Mackenzie wanted to study medicine; his aunt, Miss Harvey, who kept a girls' school in Notting Hill, came to his rescue, and financed not only his successful undergraduate career at the London Hospital, but also his postgraduate travel to Europe. Mackenzie qualified in 1858 with the diplomas of membership of the Royal College of Surgeons and licentiateship of the Society of Apothecaries. After house posts he visited Paris, Vienna, Pest; and, briefly, Berlin and Italy.

It was in 1859 in Pest that Mackenzie was taught the use of the laryngoscope by Professor Johann Czermak. Laryngoscopy with a mirror was first successfully demonstrated by Manuel García in 1854. The technique was applied clinically by Professor Ludwig Türck of Vienna,

but he was able to use the mirror only in daylight. Czermak's contribution was to employ artificial light. Returning to London in 1860 Mackenzie determined to become a physician laryngologist and successfully graduated MB in 1861 and MD in 1862. He was awarded the Jacksonian prize of the Royal College of Surgeons in 1863 for his three-volume essay, 'On the pathology and treatment of diseases of the larynx: the diagnostic indications to include the appearances as seen in the living person', illustrated by his own fine watercolours. He was appointed assistant physician to the London Hospital in 1866 and full physician in 1873 (a post which because of his increasing practice of laryngology he resigned a few months later).

In 1862 Mackenzie started a private practice at 64 George Street, Hanover Square, and leased premises at 5 King Street behind Regent Street, where in 1863 he opened the Metropolitan Free Dispensary for Diseases of the Throat and Loss of Voice, which in two years was moved to 32 Golden Square, and renamed the Hospital for Diseases of the Throat, the first of its kind in the world. In 1883 the hospital was rebuilt and was finally closed in 1985. In 1863 Mackenzie gave a paper to the annual meeting of the British Medical Association, published as *The treatment of hoarseness and loss of voice by the direct application of galvanism to the vocal cords*, in which he originated the terms 'abductors' and 'adductors' for the two sets of muscles which open and close the larynx. In the same year he married Margaret, daughter of John Bouch, of Bickley Park, Kent.

Mackenzie became a member of the Royal College of Physicians in 1864 and the following year published *The Use of the Laryngoscope in Diseases of the Throat*, which ran to three editions and was translated into French, German, and Italian. His *Essay on Growths of the Larynx* appeared in 1871; and in 1880 the first volume of his greatest work, *Manual of Diseases of the Throat and Nose*, was published (second vol. 1884). This huge work was translated into German by Felix Semon and into French by E. J. Moure. It became 'the laryngologist's bible'. Morell Mackenzie had developed an exceptional dexterity and had adapted the German laryngeal instruments by altering their angle from a wide curve to a right angle. In the days before the introduction of cocaine Mackenzie relied solely on the patient sucking ice immediately before the operation and taking the occasional inhalation of chloroform or bromides. In 1887 Mackenzie supported R. Norris Wolfenden in the foundation of the monthly *Journal of Laryngology and Rhinology*. The following year he founded the British Rhino-Laryngological Association, which in 1907 amalgamated with the Laryngological Society (founded by Felix Semon in 1893) to become the section of laryngology of the Royal Society of Medicine.

Mackenzie was self-willed and ambitious, but possessed an artistic and extravagant temperament, and a kindly and generous nature. The Mackenzies frequently entertained people from all facets of London social life. He was an ardent 'first nighter' and a great friend of many actors and singers. Mackenzie freely passed on his new technical knowledge to many physicians, some of whom, through professional jealousy, later repaid him poorly, by lack of support when he most needed it. For recreation Mackenzie loved his house and garden in Wargrave, Berkshire, which he planned and built. He cruised the Thames in a gondola, rode, and played tennis and chess.

In 1887 Mackenzie's skill as a laryngologist led to his involvement in the sad case of Crown Prince Frederick of Germany, who had married the eldest daughter of Queen Victoria, the princess royal, and who was suspected of suffering from laryngeal cancer. Mackenzie rightly insisted on biopsy, but was unable on three separate occasions to get sufficient material, and the biopsies, examined by Professor Virchow, were all negative. Mackenzie's treatment involved the intra-laryngeal removal of the growth, causing the *British Medical Journal* to proclaim that 'Dr Mackenzie's fellow-countrymen cannot but feel a certain pride in his having so well upheld the credit of English medicine abroad' (Bartrip, 84). Unfortunately it became clear within a few months that the royal patient had cancer and a palliative tracheotomy was performed by Dr Bramann. Two months later the aged Kaiser died and the crown prince succeeded as Frederick III. He reigned for ninety-nine days and died on 15 June 1888. His death was blamed by the Germans on Morell Mackenzie, but the patient himself held his English doctor in great esteem, decorating him with the grand cross and star of the Hohenzollern order; and at his request, Queen Victoria honoured him with a knighthood in 1887. Mackenzie had served his patient well and had protected his interests both medically and socially so assiduously that he himself suffered physically and mentally from the long ordeal. He also had to bear constant criticism from his medical colleagues and the world press. Mackenzie received death threats, became involved in a public quarrel with members of the German medical profession, and instigated libel actions against two newspapers which had accused him of professional incompetence (Bartrip, 85). Perhaps unwisely, he sought to protect himself by publishing an angry book, *The Fatal Illness of Frederick the Noble* (1888), which was received unfavourably, and led to censure of him by the Royal College of Surgeons and the British Medical Association, and his resignation from the Royal College of Physicians.

Mackenzie, who had been an asthmatic since the age of eighteen, died on 3 February 1892 of influenzal pneumonia in his home at 19 Harley Street, London, at the age of fifty-four, leaving his wife, two sons, Kenneth and Harry, his daughters, Ethel, Olga, and Hilda, and his brothers, Alfred and Sir Stephen *Mackenzie (1844–1909). He was buried in St Mary's churchyard, Wargrave. While the saga of Frederick served to draw public attention to Mackenzie's career, it must never be forgotten that he was truly the father of British laryngology, the first English laryngologist, the founder of the first hospital for diseases of the throat in the world, and the author of the first standard textbook on diseases of the throat, as well as the man who, single-handed and in the face of overwhelming opposition, sought to prolong the life and effected the accession of Frederick III.   NEIL WEIR

Sources R. S. Stevenson, *Morell Mackenzie: the story of a Victorian tragedy* (1946) · H. R. Haweis, *Sir Morell Mackenzie, physician and operator: a memoir* (1893) · *Journal of Laryngology, Rhinology and Otology*, 6 (1892), 95–108 · *The Times* (16 Oct 1888), 6 · *DNB* · P. Bartrip, *Mirror of medicine: a history of the British Medical Journal* (1990), 84–7 · P. A. Grace, 'Doctors differ over the German crown prince', *BMJ* (19–26 Dec 1992), 1536–8
Archives Wellcome L., corresp. and papers | CAC Cam., letters to W. T. Stead
Likenesses Walery, photograph, c.1888, NPG [*see illus.*] · Ape [C. Pellegrini], cartoon, NPG; repro. in *VF* (15 Oct 1887) · Byrne and Co., photograph, Wellcome L. · Elliott & Fry, photograph, Wellcome L.; repro. in *Journal of Laryngology, Rhinology and Otology*, 94 · H. Mendelsohn, photograph, repro. in Haweis, *Sir Morell Mackenzie, physician and operator*, frontispiece · Walery, photograph, Wellcome L. · oils, RCP Lond. · oils, Royal Society of Medicine, London · photogravure, Wellcome L. · photomechanical print, Wellcome L. · wood-engraving, NPG; repro. in *ILN* (24 Sept 1887) · wood-engraving (after photograph by Elliott & Fry), NPG; repro. in *ILN* (13 Feb 1892)
Wealth at death £23,500 4s. 2d.: resworn probate, Nov 1894, *CGPLA Eng. & Wales* (1892)

Mackenzie [McKenzie], **Murdoch, the elder** (c.1712–1797), hydrographer, was born in Orkney, the third son of James Mackenzie of Groundwater (d. 1723), writer (lawyer), notary public, and town clerk of Kirkwall, and Marion (née Traill), who were married in 1709. Murdoch's paternal grandfather was the Revd Thomas Mackenzie (c.1652–1688) and his great-grandfather was Murdoch Mackenzie, bishop of Orkney (1600–1688). He matriculated at Edinburgh University in 1729, where he was instructed in mathematics by Professor Colin Maclaurin, and from 1734 to 1739 he was schoolmaster at Kirkwall grammar school. By 1743 he had acquired surveying expertise, possibly from assisting Alexander Bryce (also a former pupil of Maclaurin) in Bryce's 1740 survey of the north coast of Scotland because Mackenzie later used this outline in *Orcades*, his volume of sea charts.

After advertising in April 1743 for subscribers, Mackenzie surveyed Orkney and its coasts from 1744 to 1747, and briefly surveyed Lewis in 1748. His principal patron was James Douglas, fourteenth earl of Morton, and he was also supported by subscriptions from the East India Company and a loan of instruments from the Admiralty. In 1749 he laid a paper on 'The state of the tides in Orkney' before the Royal Society (*Philosophical Transactions*, 1749, 149–60) and in 1750 he published *Orcades, or, A Geographical and Hydrographical Survey of the Orkney and Lewis Islands* which included five charts of the Orkney Islands and three, less detailed, charts of Lewis. Following the success of *Orcades* the Admiralty commissioned Mackenzie as a civilian to survey the west coast of Scotland from 1751 to 1757, and then the west coast of Britain and Ireland, first in the smack *Culloden* and later in the sloop *Bird*. Many of these manuscript charts still survive at the beginning of the twenty-first century in the United Kingdom Hydrographic Office, Taunton. After retiring from active surveying in 1771 he prepared these charts for publication in the two volumes of *A Maritim Survey of Ireland and the West of Great Britain*, with sailing directions in two smaller volumes, *A Nautical Description of the West Coast of Great Britain* and *Nautical Descriptions of the Coasts of Ireland* (1776).

In 1774 Mackenzie was elected a fellow of the Royal Society and his certificate, describing him as 'well-acquainted with mathematical and philosophical learning', was signed by Sir Joseph Banks, Daniel Solander, Thomas Pennant, and others. In the same year he published *A Treatise of Maritim Surveying* which remained a standard work on hydrographic surveying for over half a century. This work is notable for the first description of a station pointer, an instrument which made fixing the position of a survey ship at sea much more accurate and quicker, although the paucity of soundings in his charts suggests Mackenzie himself did not make use of the device. He withdrew from the Royal Society in 1796.

Mackenzie set new standards for hydrographic surveying in Britain, by recognizing the importance of a good land survey using triangulation as the foundation of accurate marine surveying. Given the limitations of his instruments, and the size of the task which he undertook, he concentrated on identifying and recording routes of safe passage, rather than detailed surveys. Although Mackenzie was subjected to acrimonious criticism in 1785 mariners came to his defence with the claim 'he who has McKenzie's charts … needs no pilot' (John Clerk of Eldin, *Justification of Mr Murdoch M'Kenzie's Nautical Survey of the Orkney Island and Hebrides*, 1785, 8). Mackenzie did not marry, but was greatly involved in supporting his many nephews and nieces. After his retirement he lived in London until 1795 when he moved to Minehead, Somerset, under the care of his nephew Lieutenant Murdoch *Mackenzie, who had succeeded him as Admiralty surveyor and with whom he is often confused. He was buried in Minehead on 16 October 1797.   DIANA C. F. WEBSTER

Sources D. C. F. Smith, 'The progress of the *Orcades* survey, with biographical notes on Murdoch Mackenzie senior (1712–1797)', *Annals of Science*, 44 (1987), 277–88 · D. C. F. Webster, 'A cartographic controversy: in defence of Murdoch Mackenzie', *Togail tir; Marking time: the map of the Western Isles*, ed. F. Macleod (1989), 33–42 · A. H. W. Robinson, *Marine cartography in Britain: a history of the sea chart to 1855* (1962) · Royal Scottish Geographical Society, *The early maps of Scotland to 1850*, ed. D. G. Moir, 3rd edn, 2 vols. (1973–83), vol. 1., pp. 89–91, vol. 2., pp. 1–2, 14–17 · R. W. St Clair, ed., Orcadian Families series, unpublished typescript, Orkney Archives · S. Fisher, 'The origins of the station pointer', *International Hydrographic Review*, 68 (1991), 119–26 · B. H. Hossack, *Kirkwall in the Orkneys* (1990) · A. H. W. Robinson, 'The early hydrographic surveys of the British Isles', *Empire Survey Review*, 11 (1951), 60–65 · A. H. W. Robinson, 'Marine surveying in Britain during the 17th and 18th centuries', *GJ*, 123 (1957), 449–56 · L. S. Dawson, *Memoirs of hydrography*, 2 vols. [n.d., 1883?] · E. Bray, 'The charting of the seas: Murdoch Mackenzie', *The discovery of the Hebrides: voyagers to the Western Isles, 1745–1883* (1986), 58–69 · A. Robinson, 'Murdoch MacKenzie and his Orcades sea atlas', *Map Collector*, 16 (1981), 24–7
Archives Hydrographic Office, Taunton, MSS sea charts | NL Scot., John Mackenzie of Delvin MSS · Orkney Archives, Kirkwall, survey method
Wealth at death under £600: will, PRO, PROB 11/1300, sig. 46

Mackenzie [McKenzie], **Murdoch, the younger** (1743–1829), naval officer and hydrographic surveyor, was born on 28 February 1743, the son of Thomas Mackenzie (*fl.* 1709–1760), a landowner, of Groundwater, Orkney, and his wife, Elizabeth (*née* Blaw). Murdoch Mackenzie probably attended Kirkwall grammar school where his uncle, Murdoch *Mackenzie the elder, had been a schoolmaster from 1734 to 1739. Murdoch the younger joined the smack *Culloden* on 23 October 1759, and served in her as an able seaman and midshipman, but also as assistant surveyor to Murdoch Mackenzie the elder, who was employed at the time surveying the west coasts of the British Isles. On 27 February 1763 Murdoch the younger was discharged sick and on 26 May he married Ann (also known as Anna) Saxon (1746/7–1786) in St Peter's Church, Liverpool. On 21 June 1764 he sailed as a midshipman in the *Tamar* (Captain Patrick Mouat), consort to the *Dolphin* during John Byron's voyage round the world; he returned to England in June 1766. Subsequently Mackenzie served for three months in the yacht *Charlotte* before passing for lieutenant on 9 December. On 8 May 1767 he became a midshipman in the sloop *Bird* in which his uncle was continuing his survey. On 24 May 1771 he was appointed to succeed his uncle as Admiralty surveyor with orders to start work in the Bristol Channel, thence to the Downs and so on to Cape Wrath. He began his survey in June 1771 in the *Bird*, serving in her as a supernumerary, and by 1774 he had surveyed the north coast of the Bristol Channel from Worms Head to the entrance to the River Severn, the north coasts of Somerset and Devon, and the north and south coasts of Cornwall. Later that year, at the request of Trinity House, Mackenzie was ordered to survey the channels leading into the Thames estuary between North Foreland and the Nore. During this survey Mackenzie found a new channel north of Margate Sand, named Queen's Channel, which was buoyed by Trinity House with Mackenzie's assistance. On 12 March 1775 Mackenzie published his chart of the Queen's Channel in which the buoys were depicted (a chart of Queen's Channel on a smaller scale without the buoyage having been engraved earlier), accompanied by a small book of sailing directions. When sailing on his third voyage Captain Cook was among the earliest captains to use this channel. During this survey Mackenzie appears to have used a station pointer for the first time and as a result the number of soundings that he was able to insert on his surveys increased significantly. Mackenzie completed his survey of the Thames estuary in 1776 in the yacht *Queenborough*. This enabled him to publish a further chart, depicting the whole area covered by his survey and with sixteen views drawn along its top and bottom borders. In 1777, 1778, and 1779 he surveyed Plymouth Sound and its eastern approaches in the sloop *Peterel*. In 1779, when the combined French and Spanish fleets appeared off Plymouth, all the marks were withdrawn, and Mackenzie's surveying boats were used to indicate their sites to the British ships. During this year Mackenzie was sent by Admiral Lord Shuldham, commander-in-chief, Plymouth, on special services to Jersey and other places, including Tor Bay, which he surveyed. On 5 August 1779 he was promoted lieutenant, but he continued to serve in the *Peterel* as a supernumerary until 11 June 1780 when he was appointed in command at his own request. In 1780 he returned to the Thames estuary to survey the channel between the Isle of Sheppey and the mainland, suspicions having arisen that the Dutch, with whom Britain was then at war, might attempt to get into the Medway again by this passage. In 1781 he surveyed the Needles at the request of Trinity House, and in the next three years he followed this with detailed surveys of Southampton Water, Portsmouth, and Langstone harbours, and the important anchorage of Spithead. In 1785 Mackenzie was engaged in surveying the western entrance to the Solent and from there westwards as far as Poole harbour. The following year he continued his survey eastwards as far as Bognor Regis. On 31 October 1786 Mackenzie's wife died, possibly on board the *Peterel*, while he was surveying Chichester harbour. She was buried on 6 November in St Nicholas's Church, West Itchenor. In 1787 he resumed his survey westwards from Poole to Bridport. On 27 November 1787 he married Sarah Ann Cox (1753–1826) in St Michael's Church, Minehead. About this time his eyesight began to fail, but he continued to act as chief surveyor to the Admiralty until he was ordered to cease survey operations on 18 June 1788, whereupon he was succeeded as Admiralty surveyor by his cousin and former assistant, Graeme Spence. Mackenzie's charts remained unpublished until 11 March 1802 when his survey of Falmouth was engraved,

followed by his chart of the Owers, Chichester, and Emsworth harbours on 19 November 1804. It seems probable that many of his other surveys were issued in proof form for use by selected ships of the Royal Navy at about the same time. Mackenzie's sailing directions and surveys, particularly his early ones, were revised between 1804 and 1811 by Graeme Spence, working in the hydrographic office on his own retirement from active surveying, but Mackenzie's extensive collection of sailing directions were never published. Mackenzie's remaining surveys were finally published by Thomas Hurd in 1811 in an atlas titled *Charts of the English Channel*, which was issued only to ships of the Royal Navy. It was not until 1821 that Admiralty charts were offered for sale, enabling the general public to make use of Mackenzie's surveys. Mackenzie was promoted commander on 31 January 1814. He died on 27 January 1829 in Minehead and was buried on 3 February in St Mary Magdalene Church, Exford, next to his second wife, who had died on 26 July 1826. There is a memorial tablet to Mackenzie and his wife in this church. In addition a stained glass window was erected to his memory in Chiddingfold parish church, Surrey, by his nephew Robert Hodson, who benefited under his will.

ANDREW C. F. DAVID

Sources PRO, ADM MSS · L. S. Dawson, *Memoirs of hydrography* (1885); repr. (1969) · A. H. W. Robinson, *Marine cartography in Britain: a history of the sea chart to 1855* (1962) · G. S. Ritchie, *The Admiralty chart: British naval hydrography in the nineteenth century*, new edn (1995) · S. Fisher, 'The origins of the station pointer', *International Hydrographic Review*, 68/2 (1991), 119–26 · A. C. F. David, 'Alexander Dalrymple and the emergence of the admiralty chart', *Five hundred years of nautical science, 1400–1900*, ed. D. Howse (1981), 153–64 · *GM*, 1st ser., 99/1 (1829), 188

Archives BL, charts, Maps M.T.11.h.2 (3), (4), (6) · GL, nautical descriptions, MS 30152 · Hydrographic Office, Taunton, Admiralty Library, nautical descriptions, MSS 65–70 · Hydrographic Office, Taunton, MS surveys and nautical description of the Bristol Channel, OD 189 · PRO, Adm 7/846 · Trinity House, London, nautical descriptions

Wealth at death approx. £5000–£10,000: will, 1829, PRO, PROB 11/1751, sig. 95

Mackenzie, Osgood Hanbury (1842–1922). *See under* Mackenzie, John (1803–1886).

Mackenzie, Robert (1823–1881), journalist and writer, born on 27 September 1823, son of William Mackenzie and his wife, Margaret *née* Millan, at Barry, Forfarshire, where his father was parish schoolmaster, was educated by his father and at a school at St Andrews. The family moved to Dundee, and Mackenzie was apprenticed as a clerk in a merchant's office. He served in various posts, but about 1843 became reporter to the *Northern Warder* in Dundee, which he afterwards sub-edited.

Mackenzie left journalism for commerce, and became a partner in the firm of Mackenzie, Ramsay & Co., Dundee, which failed after the crisis of 1857. He returned to journalism in 1875, frequently visited America, and wrote several books, including *The United States of America: a History* (1870), *The Nineteenth Century: a History* (1880), and *America: a History* (1882). In 1883 Mackenzie also edited with notes an incomplete edition of *Gulliver's Travels*.

Mackenzie married twice, first to a daughter of John Home Scott, and second to a daughter of William Cunningham (1805–1861); three sons and one daughter survived him. Just before his death he was actively engaged as agent for the Westinghouse Brake Company, and completed a contract between this company and the directors of the Caledonian Railway. However, Mackenzie's career was cut short by ill health. He died at his house in Magdalen Yard Road, Roseangle, Dundee, on 2 February 1881.

W. A. J. ARCHBOLD, *rev.* JOANNE POTIER

Sources *Dundee Advertiser* (3 Feb 1881) · *Northern Warden* (4 Feb 1881) · Boase, *Mod. Eng. biog.* · D. Griffiths, ed., *The encyclopedia of the British press, 1422–1992* (1992), 392 **Wealth at death** £1311 13*s*. 1*d*.: confirmation, 21 May 1881, *CCI* · £69 0*s*. 2*d*.: additional inventory, 30 Dec 1884, *CCI*

Mackenzie, Robert Shelton [*pseud.* Sholto] (1809–1880), writer and journal editor, born at Drews Court, co. Limerick, on 22 June 1809, was the second son of Captain Kenneth Mackenzie, an army officer and author of a volume of Gaelic poetry, published in Glasgow in 1796. Robert Mackenzie was educated at a school in Fermoy, co. Cork, where his father was postmaster after his retirement from the army, and at the age of thirteen he was apprenticed to an apothecary in Cork. He seems to have opened a school in Fermoy after completing his apprenticeship, and in 1825–6 was still in that town, writing poems for the *Dublin and London Magazine* and other journals, using the pseudonym Sholto. About 1828 he acted for a short time as editor of a paper at Hanley, Staffordshire. His first book, a volume of poems, *Lays of Palestine*, was published in London.

After 1830 Mackenzie went to London, and wrote for various journals, including the *Lady's Magazine* and the *London Magazine*. He contributed biographies to the *Georgian Era* (1832–4), and was on the staff of several London newspapers. In 1834 he was awarded an honorary LLD degree by Glasgow University. From 1834 he was the first European correspondent for the American press, writing for the *New York Evening Star*. Besides writing for the *Dublin University Magazine* (1837–8), he edited the *Liverpool Journal*. In 1852 he was declared bankrupt in the Manchester bankruptcy court and lost his positions. He went to America to start afresh, settled in Philadelphia, and by 1857 was book and foreign editor of the *Philadelphia Press*. He died there on 30 November 1880.

Mackenzie was a prolific author, his works on the whole competent but of little lasting value. While in England he edited works by J. S. Knowles (1838), wrote a life of Guizot as the foreword to a translation, *Democracy and its Mission* (1846), and published a work on commercial law (1847) and a collection of stories, *Mornings at Matlock* (3 vols., 1850). Once in America, he became a prolific editor of European authors, with a special eye to the growing American market for Irish literature and history, editing (among many) William Maginn's *Miscellaneous Writings* (5 vols., 1855–7), Lady Morgan's *O'Briens and O'Flaherties* (2 vols., 1857), and *Father Tom and the Pope* (1868), his preface erroneously attributing Samuel Ferguson's sketch to John Fisher Murray. He also published there lives of Dickens

(1870) and Scott (1871). He was a correspondent of Elizabeth Barrett Browning. He left three works in preparation: 'The poets and poetry of Ireland', 'Men of '98', and 'Actors and actresses'.

D. J. O'DONOGHUE, *rev.* H. C. G. MATTHEW

Sources Boase, *Mod. Eng. biog.* · Allibone, *Dict.* · U. Glas. L. · D. B. Green, 'Elizabeth Barrett Browning and R. Shelton Mackenzie', *Studies in Bibliography*, 14 (1961), 245–50 · *Law Times* (30 Oct 1852) · F. S. Drake, *Dictionary of American biography, including men of the time*, new edn (1876) **Archives** Hunt. L., letters | BL, corresp. with Sir Robert Peel and Lady Peel, Add. MSS 40551, 40560, 40566 · Bodl. Oxf., letters to Harriet Pigott · NL Scot., letters to Blackwoods · UCL, letters to Lord Brougham

McKenzie, Robert Trelford (1917–1981), political scientist and radio and television broadcaster, was born on 11 September 1917 in Vancouver, Canada, the only child of William Meldrum McKenzie, grocer, and his wife, Frances, *née* Chapman. He was educated at King Edward High School, Vancouver, and at the University of British Columbia (BA 1937), where in 1937 he became a lecturer, and where he developed what became a lifelong passion for politics. He joined the CCF, the Canadian equivalent of the British Labour Party, but later assumptions that this marked him down as 'left-wing' were exaggerated. He was careful to conceal his own views but they were in fact only mildly to the left of centre, and firmly anti-Marxist: he battled with communists in both Vancouver and London.

In 1943 McKenzie joined the Canadian army, serving in the artillery until seconded to current affairs education; in 1944 war service took him for the first time to London, where he was destined to spend the rest of his working life. He never ceased to be a Canadian, in both outlook and accent, and his affection for Britain was tinged with exasperation at what he regarded as its social affectations, but he came to love the country and to be fascinated by its politics. He arrived in London with an introduction to G. R. Strauss, and through him started with a full entreé to lively Labour Party circles.

When McKenzie left the Canadian army (as a captain) in 1946, he was persuaded by Professor Harold Laski to join the London School of Economics (LSE) and work for a doctorate. The result was of importance to any study of twentieth-century British politics. His doctoral thesis was the basis of a book published in 1955—*British Political Parties: the Distribution of Power Within the Conservative and Labour Parties*. McKenzie's meticulous analysis led him to see the Conservatives as more professional, and more ruthless, than popularly supposed, while the Labour Party he found to be crucially skilled in circumventing the extra-parliamentary bias in its constitution. The book created as great an impact as any work on British politics published since 1945.

McKenzie's judgements became widely accepted, and remained influential, although his work was to some extent outdated by such changes as the emergence of a strong third party, and the shift of power within the structure of the Labour Party. In 1968 McKenzie published, with Allan Silver, a further book—*Angels in Marble: Working*

Class Conservatism in Urban England. This did not attract the same interest as the earlier work, but was an original and enduring contribution to political history and analysis.

McKenzie's academic work was of lasting importance, but paradoxically the wider public knew him largely through his appearances on television. The viewers identified him above all with a device he called the 'swingometer'. This was shaped like a large, inverted metronome and, standing alongside it every election night from 1964 to 1979, McKenzie pushed it to left or right, marking the percentage swing in votes to one side or the other. McKenzie became in time rather too obsessed with the device, the function of which was overtaken by computer analysis, but it served its turn as a way of educating an uninformed public on how the swing in votes is exaggerated into a disproportionate shift in parliamentary seats.

It is perhaps typical of television that McKenzie should be remembered for a few bravura performances with the swingometer rather than for his many more substantial appearances, particularly his political commentary and interviewing on radio and television, which was generally regarded as the best-informed and most penetrating heard or seen up to that time. He was equally skilled when interviewing a truculent Viscount Hailsham at the height of the Profumo affair in 1963, or gently leading a benign Harold Macmillan through a series of reminiscences.

McKenzie sometimes felt that the academic world did not give him sufficient credit for his television work, because to him they were different sides of the same coin, spreading political understanding to divergent audiences. Since 1949 he had been a lecturer in the LSE sociology department and he was particularly pleased when in 1964 the LSE made him professor of sociology (with special reference to politics) and later chairman of the sociology department. He had earlier been a visiting lecturer on politics at Harvard and Yale (1958–9), and in 1969 he received an honorary degree from Simon Fraser University in his native Vancouver.

To television viewers, McKenzie appeared a chubby figure, rather intimidating behind heavy spectacles, but with a lurking sense of humour. Politicians respected his wide knowledge and recognized that, however sharp his questioning, he was never discourteous. Although rather a private man—he never married—McKenzie had a wide circle of friends, with whom he delighted to argue, and to entertain at his little house on an island in the Thames, where he was able to exercise his love of gardening.

McKenzie died of cancer on 12 October 1981 at University College Hospital, London. The next day Harold Macmillan wrote: 'Apart from his great charm he had a quite remarkable knowledge of political history over the last hundred years or more. The depth of his learning he concealed under a light touch.'

IAN TRETHOWAN, *rev.* DAVID BUTLER

Sources *The Times* (14 Oct 1981) · personal knowledge (1990) · private information (1990) · *WWW*
Archives FILM BFI NFTVA, performance footage | SOUND BL NSA, performance recordings
Likenesses two group photographs, 1965–74, Hult. Arch.

Wealth at death £122,434: probate, 5 Feb 1982, *CGPLA Eng. & Wales*

Mackenzie, Samuel (1785–1847), portrait painter, was born in the parish of Kilmuir, Ross-shire, on 28 December 1785 and baptized on 31 December, when his name was omitted from the parish register. His parents were William Mackenzie, a fisherman in Portlich, Ross-shire, and his wife, Ann. Family information records that his father died when Samuel was eight years old and the young lad worked as a herd-boy for an uncle.

The year of Mackenzie's arrival in Edinburgh is not recorded but he was employed in the city by Dalziel, a marble-cutter in Leith Walk. The arms over the entrance to the Bank of Scotland and the sphinxes in Charlotte Square were carved by Mackenzie and John Marshall. Deeply impressed by the paintings of Raeburn, he began, at the age of about twenty-five, to study as a portrait painter. His portraits gained him the painter's friendship and he worked in Raeburn's studio. In 1812, when he was residing in Shakespeare Square, he contributed a portrait of a gentleman to the Exhibition of Associated Artists, Edinburgh, and he continued to exhibit with the association from 1814 to 1816. He was patronized by George Gordon, fifth duke of Gordon, and James Innes Ker, fifth duke of Roxburghe, and for a time visited the north annually to paint portraits. In 1821 Mackenzie exhibited his full lengths of the duchess of Roxburghe and the marquess of Bowmont at the Royal Institution, Edinburgh. His contributions to the Royal Institution's exhibitions from 1825 to 1829 included a group portrait with Mrs Burns, widow of the poet, engraved by William Holl in *The Land of Burns*. He also painted a portrait of Lord Brougham.

Mackenzie was one of the twenty-four artists who in 1829 were admitted as members of the Scottish Academy, which obtained its royal charter in 1838. With the single exception of the year 1842 he exhibited every year until 1846, showing mainly portraits. In 1830 he exhibited a portrait of the writer and traveller James Silk Buckingham. Mackenzie painted the portrait of the Revd Dr David Dickson (1780–1842) and modelled the head in Alexander Handyside Ritchie's monument to Dickson in St Cuthbert's burying-ground, Edinburgh. He also exhibited a few genre subjects such as *The Beggar Girl* (1839) and *The Sailor's Orphan Boy* (1841). He was considered especially successful in his female portraits, and he painted some fancy heads, several of which were engraved. Examples of his art remain at Floors Castle and Gordon Castle. Mackenzie was a man of considerable culture and a good mathematician. He was particularly interested in horology and constructed sundials for every latitude.

He died in Edinburgh on 23 January 1847, and was buried in the Warriston cemetery.

J. M. GRAY, *rev.* LUCY DIXON

Sources J. L. Caw, *Scottish painting past and present, 1620–1908* (1908); repr. (1975) · W. D. McKay and F. Rinder, *The Royal Scottish Academy, 1826–1916* (1917) · P. J. M. McEwan, *Dictionary of Scottish art and architecture* (1994) · J. Halsby and P. Harris, *The dictionary of Scottish painters, 1600–1960* (1990) · H. Smailes, *The concise catalogue of the Scottish National Portrait Gallery* (1990) · Edinburgh and Leith postal directories, 1820–44 · D. Irwin and F. Irwin, *Scottish painters at home and abroad, 1700–1900* (1975) · D. Thomson, *'Raeburn': the art of Sir Henry Raeburn, 1756–1823* (1997) [exhibition catalogue, Royal Scot. Acad., 1 Aug 1997 – 5 Oct 1997, and NPG, 24 Oct 1997 – 1 Feb 1998]

Mackenzie, Sir Stephen (1844–1909), physician, born on 13 October 1844 at Leytonstone, Essex, was the seventh child of the four sons and five daughters of Stephen Mackenzie (d. 1851), who, in addition to his medical practice at Walthamstow, Essex, had a large establishment for the treatment of hysterical patients. His mother, Margaret Frances (d. 1877), was the daughter of Adam Harvey, a wine merchant of Lewes and Brighton. Sir Morell *Mackenzie (1837–1892), the laryngologist, was the eldest child. An uncle, Charles Mackenzie, known as Henry Compton (1805–1877), was a Shakespearian actor. Of Mackenzie's sisters, Agnes Marian was the mother of George Albert Cooke (1865–1939), regius professor of Hebrew and canon of Christ Church, Oxford, while Margaret Elizabeth was mother of Sir Francis Arthur Aglen (1869–1932), inspector-general of Chinese maritime customs. Mackenzie's father was killed in a carriage accident in 1851, leaving his family in somewhat straitened circumstances. Stephen Mackenzie, after education at Christ's Hospital (1853–9), began his medical career as apprentice to Benjamin Dulley of Wellingborough, Northamptonshire, whose daughter Helen he married in 1879. They had one daughter and three sons.

Mackenzie entered the medical school of the London Hospital in 1866, and became MRCS in 1869. After holding a number of resident appointments at the London Hospital, he lived for a year at Aberdeen, and there graduated MB with highest honours in 1873 and MD in 1875. He became MRCP in 1874 and FRCP in 1879. After working at the Charité Hospital, Berlin, in 1873, he returned to the London Hospital, and was appointed in succession medical registrar (1873), assistant physician (1874), physician to the skin department (1875–1903), physician (1886), and consulting physician (1905). In 1877 he was appointed examining physician to the London Orphan Asylum; in the same year he became lecturer on pathology (jointly with H. G. Sutton), and in 1886, lecturer on medicine in the medical school. He was a fellow or member of at least nine London medical societies.

Mackenzie was distinguished not only as a general physician, but for his special knowledge of skin diseases, to which he made many original contributions, and of ophthalmology, which by his teaching he did much to introduce into general medicine. He was physician (1884–1905) and consulting physician to the Royal London Ophthalmic Hospital (Moorfields), and wrote on changes in the retina in diseases of the kidneys. In 1891 he delivered the Lettsomian lectures before the Medical Society of London, on anaemia. He also made some original observations on the distribution of the filarial parasites in human blood in relation to sleep and rest. He employed glycerinated calf lymph for vaccination, thus reviving the practice instituted by Dr Cheyne in 1853.

Mackenzie wrote numerous articles in Richard Quain's *Dictionary of Medicine*, T. C. Allbutt's *System of Medicine*, the *British Medical Journal*, *The Lancet*, and other medical publications, but published no independent treatise. He was knighted in 1903, and soon afterwards resigned his hospital appointments, owing to increasing asthma. For the same reason he spent the winters in Egypt for the last few years of his life.

Mackenzie died on 3 September 1909, at his home, 9 Rose Hill, Dorking, Surrey, and was buried on 8 September at Dorking. He was survived by his wife.

H. D. ROLLESTON, *rev.* HUGH SERIES

Sources 'In memoriam Sir Stephen Mackenzie', *London Hospital Gazette*, 16 (1909–10), 6–10 · *BMJ* (11 Sept 1909), 732–3 · *The Lancet* (18 Sept 1909), 898 · *Men and women of the time* (1899) · *CGPLA Eng. & Wales* (1909)
Likenesses H. Gibbs, oils, 1882, priv. coll. · O. Edis, photograph, NPG · O. and K. Edis, photograph, repro. in 'Sir Stephen Mackenzie', *BMJ* · photograph, repro. in 'In memoriam Sir Stephen Mackenzie'
Wealth at death £10,181 8s. 7d.: probate, 29 Oct 1909, *CGPLA Eng. & Wales*

McKenzie, (Robert) Tait (1867–1938), expert in physical education and sculptor, was born at Ramsay, Ontario, Canada, on 26 May 1867, the second of the three sons of William McKenzie, who had arrived in Canada from Scotland in 1858, and his wife, Catherine Shiells, also originally from Scotland. His father, a minister of the Free Church of Scotland, was shortly to move to nearby Almonte, a community which continued to look after his widow and her sons after his death in 1876. Tait McKenzie was educated at Ottawa Collegiate Institute where he obtained a BA in 1889 and McGill University where he was conferred MD in 1892 and where he built himself up to become a sufficiently good athlete to allow him to take the post of assistant instructor at the gymnasium in 1891, and the following year to take charge of physical training at the university. After appointments as house surgeon at Montreal General Hospital (1893) and as a ship's surgeon (1894), he settled in practice in Montreal where he was for a year house physician to the earl of Aberdeen, governor-general of Canada (1895–6). McKenzie continued to be associated with McGill, holding university posts and recommending new practices on campus, such as physical training for all freshmen (following the American model) and the treatment of deformity by exercise. In 1904 he was appointed professor of physical education at the University of Pennsylvania. In 1907 he married Ethel O'Neil of Hamilton, Ontario. From the 1890s McKenzie regularly wrote articles on athletics and in 1910 he published *Exercise in Education and Medicine*. He was president of the Society of Directors of Physical Education in Colleges (1912) and of the American Physical Education Association (1913–15). In 1915, impatient to have news of a suitable war posting, he sailed to England where he served in the Royal Army Medical Corps within the division of physical training and bayonet fighting, working with men in the camps before their posting, and in the hospitals thereafter, becoming involved with the work of Sir Robert Jones in the army's orthopaedic centres. McKenzie returned to Philadelphia and thence to Canada in the winter of 1916–17 and worked with shell-shocked and paralysed soldiers in the command depots of both Canada and the United States.

Tait McKenzie's intensive study of physical form and its relation to health and prowess is closely connected to the way in which he began his career as a sculptor. Though he had taught anatomy to artists, McKenzie made no sculpture until *c*.1900, when his studies in violent effort, breathlessness, and fatigue, later published as an article, led him to create four masks of physical expression, which were later refined and widely reproduced. His interest in the recently introduced 'crouch' start, and in the average dimensions of successful runners, led to *The Sprinter* (bronze statuette, 1902; copy in Fitzwilliam Museum, Cambridge), shown at the Society of American Artists in New York and at the Royal Academy in London in 1903, and at the Paris Salon in 1904. From a field of 400 Harvard students he took a sample of fifty from whose dimensions he developed his *Athlete* of 1903 (bronze statuette; copies in Ashmolean Museum, Oxford, Museum of Natural History, New York, and Toronto Art Museum, Canada), seen as a modern equivalent to a Greek work. In 1904 he essayed his first non-tabulated figure, and went on to make a series of single- and double-figure pieces representing a variety of sports during that decade. His bronze relief *Joy of Effort* was shown at the 1912 Olympic games and set into the wall of the stadium in Stockholm, Sweden. In 1911 he received his first commission, to make a bronze statue of Benjamin Franklin (University of Pennsylvania), and after the war he was uniquely well placed to undertake a number of memorials to its victims, some of them in Britain. A 1920 exhibition at London's Fine Art Society (which included the *Franklin*) led to the *Homecoming* for Cambridge, and as a past president of the St Andrews Society of Philadelphia he was chosen for *The Call*, the Scottish–American war memorial in Edinburgh (1924–7). The diamond jubilee of Canadian federation in 1927 unlocked funds for a memorial to General Wolfe which had lain dormant for twenty years; McKenzie's sketches were completed that year and the statue unveiled at Greenwich in 1930. Three other portrait statues occupied the post-war years, two at the University of Pennsylvania and one at Princeton. In the post-war period McKenzie's models of contemporary athletic stars sold in sizeable editions, evidence of the enthusiasm for physical training and the belief in the correlation between athleticism and aesthetic beauty. He also produced a number of medals. He died in Philadelphia on 29 April 1938. He had no children. Examples of his work are in the J. William White Collection, University of Pennsylvania, Philadelphia.

PENELOPE CURTIS

Sources C. E. C. Hussey, *Tait McKenzie: a sculptor of youth* (1929) · K. Parkes, *The art of carved sculpture*, 1 (1931), 136–41 · *DNB* · P. Attwood, 'McKenzie, Robert Tait', *The dictionary of art*, ed. J. Turner (1996) · B. Read and P. Skipwith, *Sculpture in Britain between the wars* (1986), 108–9 [exhibition catalogue, Fine Art Society, London, 10 June – 12 Aug 1986]

Mackenzie, Thomas, **Lord Mackenzie** (1807–1869), judge, son of George Mackenzie, shoemaker, of Cromwell Park, Perth, was born on 16 April 1807 at Cromwell Park.

He was educated at Perth Academy and, after studying two years at the University of St Andrews, went on to Edinburgh. There he worked as a clerk while studying for the Scottish bar, to which he was called on 8 December 1832. Mackenzie enjoyed considerable success at the bar, owing partly to the patronage of the lord advocate, Andrew Rutherford, to whom he acted as junior, but also to extreme hard work. He amassed an almost unparalleled knowledge of case law, and could digest any amount of legal papers; he also had an impressive ability to advise with great accuracy on the outcome of a case by discerning the tone and temper of the courts and juries of the time. His cases were argued with pluck and vigour, and expressed moral courage and a sense of natural justice.

In June 1851 Mackenzie was appointed to the sheriffdom of Ross and Cromarty, and on 11 January 1855 he was appointed solicitor-general for Scotland in Viscount Palmerston's first administration. Only eighteen days later he was raised to the bench of the court of session, taking the courtesy title of Lord Mackenzie. There he displayed those qualities of unremitting industry and exhaustive research which had stood him in such good stead at the bar. His judgments, the product of very thorough and patient study, were for the most part a model of lucidity: he would state the law clearly and concisely, following this with a summary of the material facts, as readily comprehensible as it was comprehensive, and with a pithy, straightforward conclusion.

Although Mackenzie was not to sit in any legal *cause célèbre* during his years on the bench, he was credited with having drafted the Bankruptcy Act of Scotland 1856. He also wrote *Studies in Roman Law, with Comparative Views of the Laws of France, England and Scotland* (1862), a thorough, pellucid work which was much used as an examination text in Cambridge and at the inns of court in London and Dublin. In his later years on the bench Mackenzie had a tendency to become irritable, and at times he would fail properly to comprehend the arguments put to him by counsel. Convinced that his health would not permit a continuation of his strenuous labours, he retired from the bench in November 1864. He died five years later, on 26 September 1869 at his home, Inverleith House, Heriot Row, Edinburgh.

Mackenzie appeared to contemporaries as a cold and impersonal figure, whose only life was his work. According to his obituary in *The Scotsman* (29 September 1869),

> No warm friendships had he, no wife, no public explosions of benevolence, no quarrels. He toiled on to the end like a machine. Labour of the brain had become to him a sort of second nature, and in it he found the chief and almost only pleasure in life.

[ANON.], *rev.* NATHAN WELLS

Sources *Journal of Jurisprudence*, 13 (1869) · *The Scotsman* (29 Sept 1869) · F. J. Grant, ed., *The Faculty of Advocates in Scotland, 1532–1943*, Scottish RS, 145 (1944) · Ward, *Men of the reign* · NA Scot., SC 70/1/146/305
Wealth at death £80,430 12s. 11d.: inventory, 23 Dec 1869, NA Scot., SC 70/1/146/305

Mackenzie, William, fifth earl of Seaforth (d. 1740), Jacobite army officer, known in Gaelic as Uilleam Dubh (Black William), was the eldest son of Kenneth *Mackenzie, fourth earl of Seaforth (bap. 1661, d. 1701), and his wife, Lady Frances Herbert (d. 1732), second daughter of William, first marquess of Powis. A Catholic Jacobite, he was, according to Peggy Millar, warded in Edinburgh Castle by Queen Anne during the abortive Jacobite attempt of 1708 and within his own castle shortly after the accession of George I in 1714. He attended the hunt of 27 August 1715 which John Erskine, earl of Mar, used to plan a Jacobite rising; on 6 September he was present when Mar raised the standard at Braemar. Seaforth was at Sheriffmuir and was appointed lieutenant-general and commander-in-chief of the northern counties for the Jacobite forces. By 13 September he was forced to return north to oppose government forces under John Sutherland, sixteenth earl of Sutherland. Seaforth challenged Colonel Sir Robert Munro of Fowlis to fight, forcing him to withdraw and allowing Seaforth to install Sir John Mackenzie of Coull as Jacobite governor of Inverness Castle with 400 men. Initially he tried to negotiate with Sutherland for the security of his lands but spent some time trying to secure the Inverness and Nairn region before marching off to join the earl of Mar at Perth; he was back north after only a week and on his own lands by 1 December. On 27 December he opened up negotiations with Lord Lovat who threatened his lands. With his mother acting as an intermediary, Seaforth apparently agreed to disarm his people and retire quietly to his lands but, finding excuses, remained in arms throughout January 1716. George I accepted Seaforth's submission, but he now crossed to the Isle of Lewis in order to raise more of his tenants, and, evading government forces, crossed back to Ross and took ship to France in February. During March, Lord Lovat and Major-General Joseph Wightman tried to disarm and frighten the lowland Mackenzies. On 7 May, Seaforth was attainted by act of parliament and his estates forfeited.

In French exile Seaforth became involved in difficulties over money which the exiled King James had sent to Scotland, and which was now held by Seaforth's mother. Seaforth complained he was living in poverty because the allowance granted to him by James was in arrears. In November 1718, attempting to head off criticism, he submitted a long memorial to the earl of Mar detailing his services to the exiled Stuarts and blaming the marquess of Huntly for the failure of the rising. By March 1719 it was apparent Seaforth belonged to the Mar faction opposed to the duke of Ormond, a situation which contributed to the failure of the next rising.

In 1719 Seaforth was reluctant to leave Paris or to call out his tenants on the Isle of Lewis until King James had first committed a force to invade England. Nevertheless, once established on the Scottish mainland he took an active part; at the battle of Glenshiel on 10 June Seaforth contributed some 500 men from Kintail. He held position at the left of the Jacobite forces on the side of a hill called Scour Ouran with 200 men and bore the brunt of the fighting; he sent twice to be reinforced but had to give way and was badly wounded in the arm. With difficulty he escaped to France. General Wightman took the opportunity to burn out Seaforth's tenants in the aftermath of the conflict. Seaforth wrote to James from Scotland in August that year complaining that only his men were engaged at Glenshiel and that each man was left to 'shift' for himself (Dickson, 273).

In 1718 Seaforth's aunt, Lady Carrington, stated he received not a shilling from his lands, but Colonel Donald Murchison, chamberlain to Seaforth, was by 1719 collecting his rents from tenants; in 1721 Murchison and 300 clansmen fought briefly with the commissioners appointed to administer the forfeited estates at Ath-na-Muileach in Glen Affric. According to William Mackay, Seaforth, after he was pardoned, treated Murchison with 'gross ingratitude' (MacKay, 12). Seaforth allowed his followers to conform to the disarming act of 1725 and, largely through the good offices of General George Wade, a pardon was obtained for him despite opposition by the duke of Argyll. The attainder was reversed by letters patent of 12 June 1726, allowing him to return home, but the forfeiture remained in force. Subsequently George II granted him arrears of feu duties assigned to the crown from the forfeited Seaforth estates. In 1726 the rents of Seaforth, from Lewis and Ross, amounted to the not inconsiderable sum of £2216 sterling.

On 22 April 1715 Seaforth married Mary (d. 1739), only daughter and heir of Nicholas Kennet of Coxhow, Northumberland, and they had three sons: Kenneth, Lord Fortrose, who was MP for the Inverness burghs and Ross, supported the government during the 1745 rising, died on 19 October 1761, and was buried in Westminster Abbey; Ronald, who died unmarried; and Nicholas, who drowned at Douai. Seaforth had one daughter, Frances, who married John Gordon of Kenmure. Both James, first duke of Liria, and Lady Carrington describe Seaforth as a brave and honourable man, but his propensity for recrimination and trouble over money matters reveal a more complex character. Seaforth died on 8 January 1740 in the island of Lewis and was buried there, among the MacLeods, in the chapel of Ui.   DAVIE HORSBURGH

Sources Calendar of the Stuart papers belonging to his majesty the king, preserved at Windsor Castle, 7 vols., HMC, 56 (1902–23), vols. 5, 7 · A. MacBean, 'Memorial concerning the highlands', Origins of the 'Forty-Five and other papers relating to that rising, ed. W. B. Blaikie, Scottish History Society, 2nd ser., vol. 2 (1916), 71–92 · The Jacobite attempt of 1719: letters of James Butler, second duke of Ormonde, relating to Cardinal Alberoni's project for the invasion of Great Britain on behalf of the Stuarts, and to the landing of a Spanish expedition in Scotland, ed. W. K. Dickson, Scottish History Society, 19 (1895) · W. Fraser, ed., The Sutherland book, 3 vols. (1892) · W. MacKay, 'Donald Murchison and the forfeited estates commissioners', Transactions of the Gaelic Society of Inverness, 19 (1893–4), 1–12 · J. R. N. Macphail, ed., 'Papers relating to the estates of the Chisholm and the earl of Seaforth forfeited in 1716', Highland papers, 2, Scottish History Society, 2nd ser., 12 (1916), 290–343 · P. Millar, James (1971) · M. A. Murchison, 'Notes on the Murchisons', Transactions of the Gaelic Society of Inverness, 39/40 (1942–50), 262–93 · C. Sinclair-Stevenson, Inglorious rebellion: the Jacobite risings of 1708, 1715 and 1719 (1971) · C. S. Terry, ed., The Jacobites and the union (1922) · GEC, Peerage

Archives NRA, priv. coll., papers relating to debts to Lord Annandale

Mackenzie, William (1791–1868), surgeon, was born in Queen Street, Glasgow, on or shortly before 25 April 1791, the only son of James Mackenzie (d. 1800), a muslin manufacturer, and his wife, Isabella Dick. He was educated at Glasgow grammar school and matriculated at Glasgow University in 1803. He then devoted himself to theology, intending to become a minister of the Church of Scotland, but in 1810, abandoning divinity, he began the study of medicine at the university and at Glasgow Royal Infirmary. In 1813 he was resident clerk to Dr Richard Miller at the infirmary, and in 1815 he obtained the diploma of the Faculty of Physicians and Surgeons of Glasgow. After a short stay in London, where he attended the lectures given by John Abernethy at St Bartholomew's Hospital, he resided in Paris, Pavia, and Vienna. In Vienna he studied under Von Beer, who encouraged his early bias towards surgery of the eye. Early in 1818 he returned home. On 1 May of that year he became a member of the Royal College of Surgeons, London, and set up in Newman Street, Westminster, hoping to establish a practice there.

Failing in this intention, however, Mackenzie returned to Glasgow in 1819, and in the same year he took the additional diploma of fellow of the Faculty of Physicians and Surgeons of Glasgow. He also commenced general practice, and lectured upon a variety of medical subjects in Anderson's College, the extra-academical school of medicine in Glasgow. In conjunction with George Monteath he founded the Glasgow Eye Infirmary in 1824, and in 1828 he was appointed Waltonian lecturer in the University of Glasgow 'on the structure, functions, and diseases of the eye'. In 1833 he proceeded MD at Glasgow; he was appointed surgeon-oculist to the queen in Scotland in 1838, and in December 1843 he was one of the surgeons upon whom the newly instituted fellowship of the Royal College of Surgeons in London was conferred *honoris causa*. Mackenzie married, on 12 December 1854, Sophia Christina (b. 1819), daughter of William Napier of Edinburgh; she and a son survived him.

Mackenzie's scientific attainments were illustrated by his *Practical Treatise on the Diseases of the Eye* (1830), which remained the standard book on its subject until the introduction of the ophthalmoscope in 1851 effected a radical change in the diagnosis and treatment of intraocular disease. The book ran through four editions up to 1854; it was translated into German in 1832; into French in 1844, an edition criticized by Mackenzie for its omission of all bibliographical references, and in an authorized version in 1856; a supplement was produced in 1866. It was especially important for the explicit test of hardness of the eye to distinguish between glaucoma and cataract. Mackenzie wrote numerous other works on the eye and its diseases, and was editor of the first two volumes of the *Glasgow Medical Journal*.

Mackenzie combined a keen intellect with an amazing memory and unlimited perseverance. Small in stature but powerfully built, while still young he became nearly bald, with his remaining hair grey, so that at the peak of his career he already looked old. He continued to teach until his death, though in his later years a disease of the trachaea prevented him from speaking loudly and obliged him to rely on others to deliver his lectures. He died of angina pectoris at his home, 1 Oakfield Terrace, Hillhead, Glasgow, on 30 July 1868. Mackenzie's widow and son donated his medical library to the Faculty of Physicians and Surgeons of Glasgow, and his collection of preparations of the eye were given to the medical school of St Mungo's College.   D'A. POWER, *rev.* ANITA MCCONNELL

Sources A. M. W. Thomson, *The Glasgow Eye Infirmary, 1824–1962* (1963) · G. Rainey, *Glasgow Medical Journal*, new ser., 1 (1868), 6–15 · *The Lancet* (29 Aug 1868), 300 · J. C. E. N. Warlomont, *Annales d'Oculistique*, 60 (1868), 110–16 · J. Hirschberg, *The history of ophthalmology*, trans. F. C. Blodi, 8b (1988), 3–45 · W. I. Addison, *A roll of graduates of the University of Glasgow from 31st December 1727 to 31st December 1897* (1898), 387 · bap. reg. Scot.
Archives Royal College of Physicians and Surgeons of Glasgow, letters
Likenesses A. Keith, oils; in possession of Mrs Mackenzie, 1893 · D. Macnee, oils; at Glasgow Eye Infirmary in 1893 · lithograph, repro. in Warlomont, *Annales d'Oculistique* · oils (after A. Keith), Faculty of Physicians and Surgeons of Glasgow

Mackenzie, William (1794–1851), civil engineer, was born on 20 March 1794 at Marsden Chapel, Nelson, Lancashire, the eldest of the eleven children of Alexander Mackenzie (1769–1836), contractor, and Mary Roberts (d. 1828). His father had moved south from Muirton, Ross-shire, working as a navvy on the Forth and Clyde Canal, and as a contractor on the Leeds and Liverpool Canal, for both of which Robert Whitworth was engineer. Following a peripatetic childhood linked to his father's contracts around Lancashire, William began an apprenticeship with a Blackburn weaver, but abandoned this for civil engineering. In 1811 he became a pupil of Thomas Clapham, a lock carpenter on the Leeds and Liverpool Canal. He then worked for John Clapham on a dry dock at Troon harbour before joining John Cargill, one of Thomas Telford's favourite contractors, on Craigellachie Bridge. He completed his early training as an agent for his father's old friend, Hugh McIntosh, on the Edinburgh and Glasgow Union Canal from 1816 to 1822. On 9 November 1819 he married Mary (1789–1838), daughter of James Dalziel, a Glasgow commission agent.

In 1822 Mackenzie assisted McIntosh in estimating for the completion of the Gloucester and Berkeley Canal, becoming one of the agents when McIntosh was awarded the contract. Soon after he was appointed resident engineer on Telford's Mythe Bridge, Tewkesbury. Mackenzie described this work in a paper published in the *Transactions* (2.1) of the Institution of Civil Engineers, which he had joined in 1828. Before the bridge was completed Mackenzie was appointed resident engineer, again under Telford, on the Birmingham Canal improvements. This involved the supervision of some of the largest excavations ever built on a British canal. On its completion Mackenzie returned to contracting, and in 1832 successfully tendered for the tunnel works on the Liverpool and Manchester Railway between Edge Hill and Lime Street. The work proved profitable. As the 1830s progressed Mackenzie took other profitable contracts on the Grand Junction, north Union, Midland Counties, and Glasgow, Paisley, and Greenock railways. He took other, less successful, contracts on the London and Birmingham, and Glasgow, Paisley, Kilmarnock, and Ayr lines, combining this with consultancy work for canal and waterworks companies, and more general contracting such as the Liverpool Haymarket and the Manchester and Sheffield Junction Canal. Some of his outstanding works were on the Shannon navigation (1841–7), where he was the only contractor who did not become involved in litigation with the commissioners.

Despite the personal setbacks of the loss of his father in 1836 and the death of his first wife in December 1838, Mackenzie's business prospered. He had already had a small staff while working on the Birmingham Canal, notably his brother-in-law William Dalziel, and Francis Jenkins. His youngest brother, Edward (1811–1880), joined him in 1834, and George Woodhouse in 1840.

Mackenzie's experience and reliability led to an approach by Joseph Locke (1805–1860) in the summer of 1840 about a tunnel contract at Rolleboise on the Paris to Rouen railway. After visiting France, Mackenzie agreed with Thomas Brassey (1805–1870) later that year to tender jointly for works on the line. Construction began in 1841, when Mackenzie moved to Paris, and over the next decade Mackenzie and Brassey became the dominant force in European railway contracting. Following the successful completion of the Paris to Rouen line in 1843 Mackenzie was approached by capitalists from all over Europe. In France he was heavily involved with the companies which obtained the Orléans to Bordeaux and Tours to Nantes railway concessions, as well as several other companies which failed or had their concessions revoked in the 1848 period. In Spain, which he visited twice, he was involved in several schemes including a railway from Madrid to Bilbao, improvements to the Ebro navigation, and organizing surveys on behalf of railway promoters, such as Salamanca. He was active in the Italian states. In Belgium he was a major shareholder in the concession for the Tournai to Jurboise and Landen to Hasselt railways, and tendered for other works.

As contractors Mackenzie and Brassey built the Rouen to Le Havre railway and its extension to Dieppe, the Abbéville to Boulogne section of the Amiens–Boulogne line, the Orléans–Bordeaux railway, and part of the Rhine and Marne Canal. They also built the first line in Spain, between Barcelona and Mataro. In Britain they built the Eastern Union Railway, part of the Chester and Holyhead Railway, the North Staffordshire Railway, the north Wales mineral lines extension to Shrewsbury, the Liverpool and Ormskirk Railway, the Trent valley railway, and the Lancaster and Carlisle and the associated line to Kendal and Windermere. They built the massive railway system associated with the Caledonian Railway, including subsidiary lines such as the Scottish Midland and Scottish Central railways. Dock and harbour work was carried out at Greenock and Birkenhead. Many of the British contracts

were carried out in partnership with John Stephenson (c.1794–1848) beginning with the Lancaster and Carlisle Railway in 1844. Contracts were taken in a variety of names: William Mackenzie & Co., Mackenzie and Brassey, John Stephenson & Co., Thomas Brassey & Co.

Mackenzie had other investments outside railways. He was one of the original shareholders in the scheme to revive Brymbo ironworks with other former associates of Hugh McIntosh. With Brassey he took shares in the Allcard and Buddicom works near Rouen, and, less successfully, ironworks at Evreux and Pont-Audemer. In Liverpool, in association with Henry Edwards, a local architect and builder, he began to develop land for housing. He also acquired estates at Craigs, Newbie, and Auchenskeoch in Scotland.

For most of his life Mackenzie had followed work around the country. From 1832 he maintained a home and offices in Liverpool and from 1841 in Paris. In 1843 he moved to 74 Grove Street, Liverpool, and began to improve it extensively, no doubt influenced by the fashionable standards of Paris. Like other distinguished engineers such as Telford he surrounded himself with images of engineering. He commissioned illustrations of his own works, and he bought or commissioned portraits of other engineers whom he knew such as Telford, John Woodhouse, and Alexander Mackenzie Ross. The portrait of Mackenzie by T. H. Illidge was presented to his second wife, Sarah Dewhurst (1807–1867), whom he had married on 31 December 1839, at a banquet in Paris in January 1846. It portrays a commanding stout figure, with receding hair, dominating the landscape. Mackenzie was then at the height of his powers and influence.

Mackenzie was, with Thomas Brassey, the leading European contractor in the 1840s. He had far more experience than most of the engineers and contractors working at the time, which contributed to the rapid and successful expansion of the network in the years of railway mania. His financial resources, enormous by the standards of previous generations, enabled him to invest in plant to a greater extent than before. He was the first contractor to purchase locomotives for moving spoil, in 1832, and in the 1840s pioneered the use of steam excavators on the Rouen to Le Havre railway. In January 1848 he fell seriously ill from gangrene. This coincided with serious problems arising from the near bankruptcy and subsequent death of John Stephenson, and the general financial and political crisis of 1848. Although Mackenzie recovered, and was active for a further eighteen months until he again fell ill at the end of 1849, Brassey decided to end the partnership. By separate agreements in February and October 1850 concerning their British and continental contracts the responsibility for completing the majority of the contracts was passed to Brassey, with the exception of the Orléans to Bordeaux line, which Mackenzie was to complete with his brother Edward. By the arbitration of Robert Stephenson and Alexander Mackenzie Ross, Mackenzie received a payment for his share in the profits of the outstanding British contracts, which included several, such as the Great Northern Railway, which Brassey claimed were carried out using his capital alone.

Although Mackenzie continued to conduct business until his death on 29 October 1851 he never fully recovered his health, having lost his left foot in 1850. He died at his home, 74 Grove Street, Liverpool. Both his marriages were childless, and although his widow continued to live in the family house until her death in 1867, he left almost his entire estate of £341,848 to his youngest brother, Edward, including his interest in the Orléans to Bordeaux contracts, which Edward completed. Edward went on to die a millionaire. In 1868 he erected a monument to William Mackenzie at the Scottish church of St Andrew, Rodney Street, Liverpool, where he had been buried.

MIKE CHRIMES

Sources M. Chrimes, M. K. M. Murphy, and G. Ribeill, *Mackenzie: giant of the railways* (1994) · M. K. M. Murphy, 'New insights from the Mackenzie collection', *Perceptions of great engineers*, ed. D. P. Smith (1994), 85–91 · *PICE*, 11 (1851–2), 102–5 · *Journal des chemins de fer* (8 Nov 1851) · A. Mackenzie, 'Mackenzies of Fawley Court and Farr', *History of the Mackenzies, with genealogies of the principal families of the name*, new edn (1894) · W. Mackenzie, diaries of William Mackenzie, 1840–57, Inst. CE, Mackenzie MSS · E. Mackenzie, diaries of Edward Mackenzie, 1839–53, Inst. CE, Mackenzie MSS · d. cert.
Archives Bucks. RLSS · Inst. CE, archives, diary, letter-book, notebooks, daybook, sketchbook · priv. coll. | Inst. CE, work on French railways with T. Brassey · Ironbridge Gorge Museum, Telford MSS · NA Scot., railway and canal records · PRO, railway and canal records
Likenesses rock cutting, landscape, 1841, Ironbridge, Shropshire, Elton Collection · T. H. Illidge, group portrait, oils, 1845–6 (with his family) · G. R. Ward, engraving (after T. H. Illidge, 1845–6), Inst. CE
Wealth at death £341,848: will

Mackenzie, Sir William (1849–1923), Canadian railway builder and financier, was born in Eldon township, Victoria County, Upper Canada (now Ontario), on 30 October 1849, the fifth son of John Mackenzie, farmer, and his wife, Mary, daughter of John Maclaughlin, who had come after their marriage from Inverness-shire, Scotland. He was educated at Kirkfield primary school and at the Lindsay grammar school.

In his early days Mackenzie was a primary school teacher, but soon became a carpenter and lumber-merchant, and ultimately in 1871 a railway contractor, laying down rails from Maine to the vast Canadian prairies. After entering into a partnership with Donald Mann, he constructed the Regina–Calgary and Calgary–Edmonton lines for the Canadian Pacific Railway (CPR) in the 1880s. In the early 1890s Mackenzie and Mann introduced electrified street railways to Canadian cities such as Toronto, Montreal, and Winnipeg. After that they went to Britain. Failing in their proposal for greater London, Mackenzie and Ross incorporated the City of Birmingham Tramways Company in 1895. They then moved on to Latin America and the Caribbean, where they promoted and financed a number of power and tramway enterprises around the turn of the century.

In 1896 Mackenzie, along with Mann, purchased his first railway line, the Lake Manitoba Railway and Canal Company, which was soon joined to other prairie lines. By 1905 Mackenzie and Mann owned or built railway lines that extended from Port Arthur on Lake Superior to Edmonton, all known as the Canadian Northern Railway (CNR). From its incorporation in 1899, Mackenzie and Mann's CNR competed vigorously with the CPR, cutting rates and obtaining political favour in the form of dominion and provincial guarantees for their enormous bond issues. Mackenzie's downfall lay in his decision to create a transcontinental railway like the CPR after 1905. His northern prairie railway, carrying grain to the lakehead and immigrant settlers west was a viable system, but the cost of building through the Rocky Mountains to Vancouver, and through the northern Ontario wilderness, combined with low volumes of traffic after construction, used up virtually all his fortune, despite large government subsidies. It was a testament to Mackenzie's skills as a financier that he succeeded in selling £65,000,000 worth of CNR bonds in Great Britain, despite the fact that perhaps only one-half that amount was guaranteed by the Canadian or provincial governments. From 1900 until 1915 railway mileage doubled in Canada, and no one person more exemplified the speculative boom than Mackenzie with his unbounded optimism concerning the future of the country and his railway.

In 1903 the Grand Trunk Railway entered into arrangements with the Liberal government under Sir Wilfrid Laurier to build in co-operation the Grand Trunk Pacific and National Transcontinental railways. An attempt was made to bring together Mackenzie and the Grand Trunk directors, but this failed through the fault of the grandees of the older company, who greatly underestimated the ability and constructive genius of Mackenzie. In 1911, disappointed in his attempt to obtain from Laurier the promise of a subsidy for his Rocky Mountains section, Mackenzie threw all his weight into Robert Borden's Conservative Party, and was partly responsible for the defeat of Laurier in the general election of that year. With Borden as prime minister, the subsidy was granted.

Just as Mackenzie was seeing his ambition fulfilled, however, disaster struck. First, the recession of 1913 dealt a staggering blow to the share value of his enterprises, including the CNR, and next the outbreak of the First World War stopped the flow of capital and settlers from Europe. The profits of the prairie section of the line, although considerable, were insufficient to carry the vast expense of the mountain section, and in 1917–18 the Canadian Northern was taken over by the Dominion government and eventually merged with the Grand Trunk Railway and the Intercolonial Railway to form the Canadian National Railway. British bondholders were fully compensated in the railway nationalization but Mackenzie was paid far less than he felt the shares were worth, and he lived out his remaining years with far less, in terms of wealth and reputation, than he felt he deserved for all of his efforts.

Mackenzie married in 1872 Margaret (d. 1917), the daughter of John Merry, of Kirkfield, Ontario; one son and six daughters survived him, and two other sons predeceased their father. He and his partner, Mann, were created knights bachelor on 1 January 1911.

No man in Canadian life has been more variously judged than Mackenzie. By his enemies he was accused of never hesitating either to bribe a newspaper or to corrupt a legislature. Yet to his friends he was the trail-blazer and a nation-builder. One of the great railway builders of North America, Mackenzie died at Avenue Road Hill, Toronto, from a heart attack on 5 December 1923. He was buried at Kirkfield, Ontario.   GREGORY P. MARCHILDON

Sources R. B. Fleming, *The railway king of Canada: Sir William Mackenzie, 1849–1923* (c.1991) · T. D. Regehr, *The Canadian Northern railway: pioneer road of the northern prairies, 1895–1918* (1976) · G. R. Stevens, *Canadian national railways*, 2 vols. (1960–62) · D. McDowall, *The light: Brazilian Traction, Light and Power Company Limited, 1899–1945* (1988) · C. Armstrong and H. V. Nelles, *Southern exposure: Canadian promoters in Latin America and the Caribbean, 1896–1930* (1988) · C. Armstrong and H. V. Nelles, *Monopoly's moment: the organization and regulation of Canadian utilities, 1830–1930* (1986) · *The Canadian encyclopedia*, 2nd edn (1988) · G. D. Taylor and P. A. Baskerville, *A concise history of business in Canada* (1994) · M. Bliss, *Northern enterprise: five centuries of Canadian business* (1987) · W. K. Lamb, *History of the Canadian Pacific Railway* (1977) · J. A. Eagle, *The Canadian Pacific Railway and the development of western Canada, 1896–1914* (1989)
Archives CPR Corporate Archives, Montreal, Canadian Pacific railway MSS · NA Canada, Porteous MSS · Public Archives of Ontario, Toronto, Whitney MSS
Likenesses photographs, repro. in Fleming, *Railway king of Canada*, centre plates · photographs, repro. in Stevens, *Canadian national railways*, centre plate
Wealth at death approx. $800,000 in Canada: Fleming, *The railway king*, 247

Mackenzie, William Bell (1806–1870), Church of England clergyman, second son of James Mackenzie, was born on 7 April 1806 in Sheffield, and was educated at the grammar school there. When his father and mother died in 1822, Mackenzie was withdrawn from formal education and he began to study law. He took up tuition work to compensate for his lack of private means, but with the help of exhibitions from the father of a pupil and from the Clerical Education Society he was able to proceed to university. He was admitted sizar at St John's, Cambridge, on 9 July 1829, but migrated to Magdalen Hall, Oxford, on 26 June 1830, graduating BA in 1834 and MA in 1837. An evangelical, he was a Sunday school teacher under W. W. Champneys while an undergraduate.

Mackenzie was ordained deacon in 1834 and became curate of St James's, Bristol, where he became involved in Bible classes and visiting the poor; he also developed his interest in the doctrines of reformers and early puritans. From 1838, as incumbent of St James's, Holloway, Mackenzie took an interest in building schools and visitation, and gradually collected a large congregation. He advocated the cause of the Moravian church, and was among the first to start special services in St Paul's Cathedral. He also preached at the Church Missionary Society. Mackenzie's interest in his parishioners was reflected in his published work, which included *Bible Studies for Family Reading* (1867) and *Married Life, its Duties, Trials and Joys* (1861).

Mackenzie married Maria Cowper, youngest daughter of Harman Visiger of Bristol, on 11 April 1840. Their children included three sons, Henry, Walter, and Arthur, two of whom predeceased their father. Mackenzie died at Ramsgate on 22 November 1870, and was buried on 30 November at Highgate cemetery; he was survived by his wife.

A. F. POLLARD, *rev.* ELLIE CLEWLOW

Sources G. Calthrop, *Memorials of the life and ministry of the Rev. W. B. Mackenzie, MA* · Venn, *Alum. Cant.* · Foster, *Alum. Oxon.* · J. S. Reynolds, *The evangelicals at Oxford, 1735–1871: a record of an unchronicled movement*, [2nd edn] (1975) · *CGPLA Eng. & Wales* (1870)
Likenesses T. H. Maguire, lithograph (after L. Stocks), BM · engraving, repro. in Calthrop, *Memorials of the life and ministry of the Rev. W. B. Mackenzie, MA*
Wealth at death under £12,000: probate, 21 Dec 1870, *CGPLA Eng. & Wales*

Mackenzie, William Forbes (1807–1862), politician and temperance reformer, born on 18 April 1807 at Portmore, Peeblesshire, was the third and eldest surviving son of Colin Mackenzie, writer to the signet in Edinburgh, deputy keeper of the signet, and a friend of Sir Walter Scott. His mother was Elizabeth, daughter of Sir William *Forbes of Pitsligo, bt; Charles Frederick *Mackenzie was his brother. The family was descended from the Mackenzies of Balmanully, a younger branch of the Mackenzies of Gairloch, who claimed as their progenitor Hector, son of Alexander, sixth baron of Kintail. Forbes Mackenzie (as he was known) was educated for the law, and was called to the bar in 1827. In March 1830 he married Helen Anne (*d.* 1870), daughter of Sir James Montgomery, second baronet, and his first wife, Lady Elizabeth *née* Hamilton. They had a son, Colin, and a daughter, Elizabeth Helen, who died young.

Forbes Mackenzie succeeded to the estate of Portmore on the death of his father in September 1830, and in 1831 was appointed deputy lieutenant of the county of Peebles. He also sat in the House of Commons as member for that county in 1837–41, 1841–7, and 1847–52. From 26 April 1845 until 11 March 1846 he was a junior whip, resigning over corn-law repeal. From February 1852 until January 1853 he was Disraeli's parliamentary secretary at the Treasury. He was elected for Liverpool in July 1852 but lost his seat on petition in June 1853. He stood unsuccessfully for Derby in 1857. Unusually for a Conservative, he was an ardent temperance reformer, his chief achievement being to originate the Act for the Regulation of Public Houses in Scotland (16 & 17 Vict. c. 67) known as the Forbes Mackenzie Act, which provided for the closing of public houses on Sundays and at 10 p.m. on weekdays. From 1859 he was chairman of the Scottish lunacy commissioners. Forbes Mackenzie died suddenly while on a visit to The Glen, Peeblesshire, on 24 September 1862.   H. C. G. MATTHEW

Sources Burke, *Gen. GB* · Boase, *Mod. Eng. biog.* · N. Gash, *Sir Robert Peel: the life of Sir Robert Peel after 1830* (1972) · J. C. Sainty, ed., *Treasury officials, 1660–1870* (1972) · B. Harrison, *Drink and the Victorians: the temperance question in England, 1815–1872* (1971)
Archives BL, letters to Lord Hardwicke, Add. MSS 35788–35807 · Lpool RO, letters to fourteenth earl of Derby
Likenesses A. Edouart, silhouette, 1830, Scot. NPG

Mackenzie, William James Millar (1909–1996), political scientist, was born in Edinburgh on 8 April 1909, the only child of Laurence Millar Mackenzie (*d.* 1933), writer to the signet, and his wife, Anna Marion *née* McClymont (1879–1958). His parents adopted a daughter when he was nineteen. He was educated at Edinburgh Academy and at Balliol College, Oxford, where he was awarded a first in moderations in 1929 and another in Greats in 1931. Expected to follow his father in the family law firm, he then read law at Edinburgh University and served an apprenticeship for a year. But through sheer brilliance he was able to launch himself independently into an academic career. With the physical confidence of a rugby player and the intellectual satisfaction of one who had won both the Craven and the Ireland scholarships he was elected in 1933 a fellow of Magdalen College, Oxford, switching from classics to politics in 1936. This was symptomatic of his reluctance to be confined by the boundaries of disciplines. All his colleagues remarked on the range of his reading and on his familiarity with the methods of different disciplines. His approach was to ask the right questions rather than to give a set of answers.

In 1939 a Magdalen colleague, Thomas Dewar (Harry) Weldon, also a tutor in politics, brought Mackenzie into the air secretariat of the Air Ministry, which served the chiefs of the air staff and the Air Council. He met there another Oxford graduate, Pamela Muriel Malyon (*b.* 1919), a psychiatric social worker, whom he married on 24 July 1943; they had a son and four daughters. His financial investments were made with advice from his brother-in-law, through whom he became a member of Lloyds. In 1942–3 he was sent for six months to the RAF delegation in Washington, DC, to succeed Weldon as deputy director of administration and finance, and on his return he was promoted assistant secretary in charge of the secretariat. From this position he came close to the controversies about the use of Bomber Command and to the Linemann/Tizard debate, which gave him a lifelong fascination with the workings of bureaucracy. He became a natural enthusiast for organization theory, and made a number of key personal contacts which stood him in good stead in later years, when he wished to promote public administration training. On his return to Magdalen College after the war he was invited to be the historian of an organizational puzzle, the Special Operations Executive. This official history remained classified as secret until after his death.

Mackenzie was a pioneer in establishing political science as a discipline in British universities, having accepted the new chair of government in the University of Manchester in July 1948. From that base he created a network of contacts, sought to encourage talent, and appointed a body of staff who were well trained to move out into other universities at the time of the expansion in the early 1960s. A special feature of the Manchester faculty of economic and social studies was the high degree of mutual respect between the senior professors, such as Ely Devons, W. Arthur Lewis, Michael Polanyi, and Max Gluckman. He was a founder member of the Political Studies Association in 1950, and, as the head of one of the few political science departments in the country, became widely known overseas, especially in the United States and Europe. He took a special interest in Africa and in the conditions necessary for free elections. In some respects he acted as a mediator between American political science and British political studies. Apart from his *Politics and Social Science* (1967), written on leave of absence in Norway in 1966, he tended to prepare articles, seminar papers, and 'think pieces' rather than books, although upon retirement he wrote in rapid succession *Power, Violence, and Decision* (1975), *Political Identity* (1977), and *Biological Ideas and Politics* (1978). Several papers from 1951 to 1968 were brought together in *Explorations in Government* (1975), which also contained an autobiographical introduction. He became the first chairman of the politics committee of the Social Science Research Council created in 1965, and therefore a key figure in the initiation of British academics into the subtleties of judgement about research applications. His 1958 paper called 'The conceptual framework and the cash basis' had a unique appeal. He remained at Manchester until 1966, when he moved to the University of Glasgow, first as James Bryce professor of government (1966–70), then as Edward Caird professor of politics (1970–74).

The flow of invitations to advise government began principally after Mackenzie became constitutional adviser to Tanganyika in 1952, when that mandated territory was considering a system of regional councils elected on a special franchise. This venture brought him into contact with the Colonial Office and with English local authorities, which were at the time being used as models for training colonial peoples in democratic practice. There were then few senior academics with interests in the relationship between local and central government. In 1957 he was invited to be a member of the royal commission on local government in Greater London, which recommended the creation of the Greater London council, and in 1964 of the Maud committee on management in local government. In 1959–60 he became constitutional adviser on Kenya to the secretary of state who recommended him to the governor as 'a very cautious but very sound Scot who is apt to appear a little gauche at first meeting, but … remains detached and avoids emotional involvement' (CO 822/1474: Alan Lennox-Boyd to Sir Evelyn Baring, 27 June 1959); in 1961 he declined to play a similar role on Mauritius. He was active in getting the Colonial Office to consider the public administration training necessary for the Africans who were succeeding Europeans, and was one of the principal instigators of the committee on training in public administration for overseas countries (1961–3), of which he was vice-chairman. He also served on the committee on the remuneration of ministers and members of parliament in 1963–4, and on the committee on university libraries in 1964–7, and was active in local public service in both Manchester and Glasgow. In Manchester he was co-opted onto the city education committee and then became a member in 1965 of the North West Regional Economic Planning Council; he was also a member of the British Wool Marketing Board. In Glasgow he chaired the children's panel advisory committee. He died of pneumonia at the Western Infirmary, Glasgow, on 22 August 1996; he was cremated at Clydebank crematorium on 2 September, and his ashes scattered at Balquhidder where he had a holiday home. He was survived by his wife and five children. J. M. LEE

Sources B. Chapman and A. Potter, eds., *William James Millar Mackenzie: political questions* (1974), 1–23 · R. Rose, 'William James Millar Mackenzie, 1909–1996', *PBA*, 101 (1999), 465–85 · W. J. M. Mackenzie, *Explorations in government* (1975), 9–36 · *The Independent* (27 Aug 1996) · *The Guardian* (30 Aug 1996) · *The Times* (2 Sept 1996) · I. Elliott, ed., *The Balliol College register, 1900–1950*, 3rd edn (privately printed, Oxford, 1953) · *WWW* · private information (2004) [M. Earnshaw] · history of RAF delegation to Washington DC, 1941–4, PRO, cabinet office records, CAB 102/639 · history of special operations executive, PRO, cabinet office records, CAB 102/649–53 · minute of 14/12/1951, PRO, colonial office records, CO 822/606 · letter of 27/6/1959, PRO, colonial office records, CO 822/1474

Archives U. Glas., Archives and Business Records Centre, corresp. and papers · U. Glas. L., papers | Bodl. Oxf., corresp. with third earl of Selborne · JRL, letters to *Manchester Guardian* · PRO, cabinet papers, CAB 102/639, 649–53 · PRO, Colonial Office papers, CO 822/606, 1474

Likenesses photograph, repro. in Chapman and Potter, eds., *William James Millar Mackenzie*, frontispiece · photograph, repro. in *The Times* · photograph, repro. in *The Independent*

Wealth at death £308,455.33: confirmation, 1996, *CCI*

Mackenzie, William Lyon (1795–1861), journalist and politician in Canada, was born on 12 March 1795 at Springfield, Dundee, the only child of Daniel Mackenzie (*c*.1767–1795), a weaver, and Elizabeth Chalmers (*c*.1749–1839), *née* Mackenzie. After leaving school he held several jobs, and by 1814 he and his mother were operating a general store and circulating library. Its collapse gave him a lifelong sympathy for the indebted and a deep suspicion of the monied and privileged.

In 1820 Mackenzie migrated to Upper Canada, to be joined two years later by his mother, his illegitimate son, James, and Isabel Baxter (1805–1873), whom Mrs Mackenzie had chosen as his wife. He and Isabel married in Montreal on 1 July 1822 and had thirteen children together. In May 1824 Mackenzie began publishing the *Colonial Advocate* at Queenston, but soon moved the paper to the provincial capital, York. Political life in the province was increasingly polarized between supporters and critics of the local oligarchy. Mackenzie sided with the critics. Stung by his highly personal attacks, a gang of young tories ransacked his office in 1826 and flung his type into the harbour. The diminutive Mackenzie won a sizeable court settlement, a reputation as a martyr, and, in 1828, election to the assembly. There he demanded investigations into matters great and small, showing particular dislike for monopolies, limited liability, and paper money. He returned from a journey to the United States in 1829 impressed with the economies, enterprises, and institutions of the republic.

The tory majority in the new assembly elected in 1830 ejected 'Little Mac' in December 1831 for allegedly offending the dignity of the house. Re-elections and re-expulsions followed. In April 1832 he took his grievances, and those of the reformers generally, to England, where he met with sympathetic parliamentarians and recounted his concerns to the colonial secretary, Lord

William Lyon Mackenzie (1795–1861), by John Wycliffe Lowes Forster, 1931

Goderich. The following year he presented his critique of Upper Canada's 'extravagant church and state establishments' to the British public in *Sketches of Canada and the United States*. When Goderich urged conciliation on the assembly, its tory members expelled Mackenzie a fourth time. Goderich's attempt to chastise two ringleaders was overturned by his successor, Lord Stanley. A disappointed Mackenzie returned to Canada. Lieutenant-Governor Colborne ended the farce by demanding that the tories yield. This sorry episode helped convince Mackenzie that

> Our government is one of the meanest which it is possible to conceive … Individuals are lifted up high in society in these colonies, whom our farmers, if aware of their real character, would not permit to associate with the dogs of their flocks. (*The Constitution*, 28 June 1837)

In 1834 York became a city, taking the name of Toronto, and Mackenzie became its first mayor. A divided council and an inadequate tax base bedevilled his efforts, leading to accusations, then and since, that his was an unsuccessful administration. Whatever his reputation as mayor, he retained popularity with provincial voters, and formed part of the reform majority returned to the assembly in October 1834. Here, he chaired a committee probing the colonists' grievances. His report was exhaustive, documenting all kinds of injustices. The new lieutenant-governor, Sir Francis Bond Head, who arrived in 1836, came with instructions prompting him to be conciliatory but not to yield to demands for constitutional reform.

When a storm blew up over the call for responsible government, Head prorogued the assembly and called an election. Government supporters, aided by official interference, won easily. A distraught Mackenzie lost his seat.

The troubles of Upper Canada paled into insignificance beside those in Lower Canada, where the British government suspended the normal operation of government in 1837. Mackenzie, who had begun a new paper, *The Constitution*, on 4 July 1836, advised 'Agitation! agitation! agitation!' (*The Constitution*, 13 Sept 1837). He urged the formation of political unions and the summoning of a convention of delegates from the two Canadas. He stumped the countryside, his flaming red wig proclaiming his presence, his fiery oratory fuelling anger. In November 1837 rebellion broke out in Lower Canada. 'Little Mac' saw his opportunity. He did not manufacture the grievances which produced discontent, but he was instrumental in translating ill-feeling into action. He told his audiences that a move on Toronto would overawe the government. On 15 November he published a draft constitution based on American models. A co-conspirator, John Rolph, summoned the rebels being mustered into Toronto on 4 December, earlier than planned. Mackenzie tried unsuccessfully to stay the change. Collapsing under the pressures of the moment, he dallied with his men at the north end of the capital, giving the government time to marshal its forces. On 7 December a much larger loyalist force routed his 500 followers. He, Rolph, and most other leaders escaped to the United States. A minor outbreak to the west of Toronto was put down a week later with ease. December also saw the dispersal of the rebel forces in Lower Canada.

Shortly after arriving in Buffalo, Mackenzie helped organize an unsuccessful expedition to Navy Island in the Niagara River. He decided to further the cause of the 'patriots', as those who sought to overthrow the Upper Canadian government from the United States were known, by publishing *Mackenzie's Gazette*, but the fortunes of both paper and 'patriots' foundered. In June 1839 publisher Mackenzie was found guilty of violating America's neutrality laws, and was fined $10 and ordered to gaol for eighteen months. He served almost a year of his sentence. In June 1842 he took his family to New York city, where he was, first, librarian and actuary of the mechanics' institute, then a customs clerk. He resigned this latter post in June 1845, but not before copying or absconding with papers which, published, helped produce a political scandal implicating former president Van Buren and the existing state administration.

Though Mackenzie had assumed American citizenship in 1843, he wished the freedom to return to Canada. The reformers of the Canadas were in the ascendant. This was signified by the achievement of responsible government, which many have insisted was due in no small part to Mackenzie and 'his' rebellion. This seems overdrawn. Even if rebellion was a necessary prelude to responsible government, the Lower Canadian uprising would have sufficed. Nevertheless, the changed situation produced a general amnesty in 1849 which included Mackenzie. In 1850 he settled in Toronto. Ever short of money, he wrote for various papers. In the spring of 1851 he was elected to the assembly. As an Independent Reformer, he fought entrenched interests. In the legislature and in *The Message*, which he began in 1852, he jousted with enemies old and new. Keen to retain his independence, he would make no alliances in an age when political combinations were in flux. He made little or no contribution to the emergence of the large Reform grouping which took shape in the late 1850s, since he was especially eager to denounce those many Reformers whose principles were less fixed than his own. He was concerned about both political and economic currency, and led the successful fight for the introduction of the dollar; with less effect, he badgered for the introduction of the sort of democratic devices he had seen adopted in 1846 at the state constitutional convention at Albany, which he had covered for Horace Greeley's *New York Tribune*. He was increasingly disillusioned with the corruption of an age where politics and economic development were ever closer entwined. As chairman of the finance committee of the assembly in 1854–5, he was well placed to observe and publicize the peculations of the day. Ill, and feeling that the age had failed him, he resigned his seat in the assembly in August 1858; his continued political commentary flirted with the allied notions of independence and annexation before settling on a transatlantic union of Britons.

Mackenzie's virtues were many. He was an inveterate opponent of privilege and cant, battling against those who argued that democratic devices were dangerous or irresponsible. He championed the small, the overtaxed, the under-represented. Public fiscal prudence, hard money, and unlimited liability were his economic mantras. Democratic institutions would allow the independent farmer to flourish and fashion a more egalitarian society. Here, he had a 'decided' policy. Yet, on one important score he was an enigma without variation: he could not work within existing structures to produce change. His instincts were to overturn, to discombobulate, to flee. One suspects that when death came, as it did on 28 August 1861, at his home in Bond Street, Toronto, from 'softening of the brain' (Gates, *After the Rebellion*, 342), it was a final, blessed flight. Mackenzie was buried three days later in the Toronto necropolis.   COLIN FREDERICK READ

Sources C. Lindsey, *The life and times of Wm. Lyon Mackenzie: with an account of the Canadian rebellion of 1837, and the subsequent frontier disturbances, chiefly from unpublished documents* (1862) • F. H. Armstrong and R. J. Stagg, 'Mackenzie, William Lyon', *DCB*, vol. 9 • L. F. Gates, *After the rebellion: the later years of William Lyon Mackenzie* (1988) • *The Constitution* (4 July 1836–6 Dec 1837) • C. Read and R. J. Stagg, eds., *The rebellion of 1837 in Upper Canada* (1985) • F. H. Armstrong, 'William Lyon Mackenzie, first mayor of Toronto: a study of a critic in power', *Canadian Historical Review*, 48 (1967), 309–31 • L. F. Gates, 'The decided policy of William Lyon Mackenzie', *Canadian Historical Review*, 40 (1959), 185–208 • W. D. LeSueur, *William Lyon Mackenzie: a reinterpretation*, ed. A. B. McKillop (1979) • J. E. Rea, 'William Lyon Mackenzie—Jacksonian?', *Mid-America: An Historical Quarterly*, 50 (1968), 223–35 • R. A. MacKay, 'The political ideas of William Lyon Mackenzie', *Canadian Journal of Economics and Political Science*, 3

(1937), 1–22 • F. H. Armstrong, 'William Lyon Mackenzie: the persistent hero', *Journal of Canadian Studies*, 6 (1971), 21–36 • F. H. Armstrong, 'Reformer as capitalist: William Lyon Mackenzie and the printers' strike of 1836', *Ontario History*, 59 (1967), 187–96 • W. Kilbourn, *The firebrand: William Lyon Mackenzie and the rebellion in Upper Canada* (1956) • D. Flint, *William Lyon Mackenzie: rebel against authority* (1971) • *The Globe* [Toronto] (29 Aug 1861)

Archives NA Canada | Dundas Historical Society Museum, Ontario, Lesslie MSS • NA Canada, John Neilson MSS • Public Archives of Ontario, Toronto, Mackenzie-Lindsey MSS

Likenesses J. W. L. Forster, oils, 1931, NA Canada [*see illus.*] • Forster, portrait, Queen's Park Legislature, Toronto, Canada • Forster, portrait, Toronto City Hall, Canada • Forster, portrait, Mackenzie House, Toronto, Canada • A. Sandham, portrait, NA Canada, c3918 • portrait, NA Canada • portrait (after engraving by E. B. Hullis), Archives of Ontario, Toronto, S13290 • portrait (after pen-and-ink by L. M. Kerr), NA Canada, c28754 • two busts, Queen's Park Legislature, Toronto, Canada

Wealth at death owed $3000, but owned house, which had been given to him by supporters

Mackenzie, William MacArthur [Billy] (1957–1997), popular singer and songwriter, was born on 27 March 1957 at Dundee Royal Infirmary, the eldest of the six children of Jim Mackenzie, and his wife, Lily Agnes O'Phee Abbott (*d.* 1996). His family were of Irish, Scottish, and Romany descent. Mackenzie was educated at St Mary's Forebank primary school and St Michael's comprehensive school, both in Dundee. After a spell in London he travelled to America. There, early in 1975, he was married in Las Vegas to Chloe Dummar, sister of Melvin Dummar, who later achieved fleeting fame as a result of his claim to be the part heir of the billionaire recluse Howard Hughes. It appears that the marriage was, at least on Mackenzie's part, a 'green card' arrangement—to enable him to stay in America—and did not last. Later he claimed to have children living in America, but this may exemplify his capacity for inventing myths about himself.

Returning to Scotland, Mackenzie—who had sung since childhood—teamed up with Linlithgow-based guitarist Alan Rankine (*b.* 1958). They played local social clubs and settled on the name of The Associates. They gained some notoriety from their first, self-released single—a cover of David Bowie's 'Boys keep Swinging'—not least over royalty payments. They were signed to the London-based record-label Fiction, and made an album, *The affectionate punch* (1980), which was critically acclaimed. The band subsequently released a series of singles on the independent label, Situation Two—notable among them 'Tell me Easter's on Friday' and 'White Car in Germany'—that were also well received. These were later collected on an album, *Fourth drawer down*, whose title referred to the hiding place of the band's drug of choice at the time—an over-the-counter herbal soporific.

In 1982 The Associates—bolstered by the addition of former Cure bassist Michael Dempsey, John Murphy on drums, and Martha Ladly on backing vocals—signed to WEA and released what is generally regarded as their finest album, *Sulk*. From it came their first hit and best-known song, 'Party Fears Two', whose distinctive keyboard riff was later used as the theme music to the BBC Radio 4 satirical programme *Week ending*. This was followed into the singles charts by 'Club Country'—a deconstructive critique of the golf club set. Mackenzie's lyrics were often oblique and sometimes surreal; his eccentricity also surfaced in the musical instructions he issued to producers and colleagues—'It's got to sound like Abba meets Bet Lynch on acid' being one such injunction (Lester). The band is often discussed in the context of the dandified 'new romantic' movement of the early 1980s; Mackenzie had always been fashion-conscious, and owned a clothes shop in Dundee for a time, but they were not a part of what was essentially a metropolitan trend.

Like many pop acts of the era, The Associates played synthesizers and used studio technology to the maximum. What set them apart from many of their contemporaries—and gave their music greater longevity—were the complexity of their arrangements, the imaginative use of 'found' sound, and the use of inventive, sometimes bizarre studio techniques (such as singing through a vacuum-cleaner tube). Another distinguishing feature of their music—at a time when a deadpan, even robotic vocal style was in favour—was Mackenzie's remarkable voice; he had a five-octave range and his style verged on the operatic. Their overall recorded sound was lush and opulent—among their acknowledged influences were the 'Krautrock' of German electronic-based acts such as Kraftwerk and Can; the west-coast American electronic pioneers Sparks; the British glam rock survivors David Bowie and Roxy Music, as well as the Tamla Motown sound. Live, The Associates' were arguably a less exciting proposition, and Mackenzie's growing stage fright was a large factor in his split with Alan Rankine in 1983.

Rankine went on to record three solo albums; Mackenzie kept The Associates' name and released *Perhaps* (1984) and *Wild and lonely* (1990). These were not great commercial successes and their recording was fraught, partly owing to Mackenzie's perfectionism and free-spirited compulsion to experiment in the studio. *Perhaps* had to be entirely re-recorded after the first attempt was deemed unsuitable for release by his record company. The same fate befell a 'lost' album from 1988 entitled *The glamour chase*, which was finally issued in 2002. Mackenzie made two albums under his own name: *Outernational* (1992), and the posthumously released *Beyond the sun* (1997). In the mid-1990s he found himself without a record company, and collaborative efforts with Paul Haig, formerly of Josef K (*Memory palace*) and with Steve Aungle (*Eurocentric*) saw the light of day only after his death. An attempt to link up again with Alan Rankine in 1993 came to nothing, though their demo recordings later appeared on another posthumous album of out-takes and rarities, *Double hipness* (2000). Other notable collaborations included an appearance on B. E. F.'s albums of classic covers, *Music of quality and distinction* (1982, 1991); a link-up with Shirley Bassey under the aegis of the Swiss electronic dance music pioneers Yello (1987), and a vocal credit on Barry Adamson's acclaimed *Oedipus schmoedipus* (1996).

Upset by the death of his mother, Billy Mackenzie sank into a depression late in 1996. He was found dead in a shed at his father's home in Auchterhouse, near Dundee, from an overdose of prescriptions drugs on 22 January 1997. He left a note. It was widely noted that *Sulk* had included a version of 'Gloomy Sunday', a song whose association with suicides became so notorious that it had earlier been banned by the BBC. The professional frustrations of the 1990s had undoubtedly taken their toll on him; his personal life, about which he was guarded (he was widely assumed to be bisexual) appears not to have given him an anchor or a refuge. His funeral was held on 27 January in Dundee.

Billy Mackenzie was 5 feet 7 inches tall, with dark, chiselled features. For a time a beret—worn originally to cover a misjudged haircut—was his visual trademark; latterly he adopted elaborate coiffures and, occasionally, a hairpiece to cover hair loss. He bred whippets as a sideline, and once hired a hotel suite (at the expense of his record company) to house two pups. The word that crops up most often in critical descriptions of his talent is 'mercurial'. Interest in his work has grown since his death, as evidenced by a remarkable number of posthumous releases and reissues, and the publication of a full, thoroughly researched biography.   H. J. SPENCER

Sources T. Doyle, *The glamour chase: the maverick life of Billy Mackenzie* (1998) · P. Lester, 'Goodbye Mr Mackenzie', *Uncut* (June 1997); see online at www.billymackenzie.com, July 2002 · G. Blecken, interview, *Record Collector* (July 1994); electronic repr. destinationpop. com/THEASSOCIATES.html, July 2002 · Jonas Wårstad, *discography*, www.billymackenzie.com · CGPLA Eng. & Wales (1997)
Likenesses photographs, repro. in Doyle, *Glamour chase* · photographs, repro. in www.billymackenzie.com [consulted July 2002]
Wealth at death under £180,000: administration, 24 Feb 1997, CGPLA Eng. & Wales · under £180,000: probate, 24 Feb 1997, CGPLA Eng. & Wales

Mackenzie, William Warrender, first Baron Amulree (1860–1942), lawyer and industrial arbitrator, was born at Pickston Hill, Scone, Perthshire, on 19 August 1860, the fourth son of Robert Mackenzie (1816–1898), farmer, and his wife, Jean Campbell (d. 1892), daughter of Basil Menzies, who was also a farmer. He was educated at Perth Academy and at Edinburgh University, where he graduated in 1885. He was called to the bar by Lincoln's Inn in 1886 and, as a barrister on the northern circuit, established a reputation as a specialist in matters affecting local authorities. Although he was not a great advocate, the judges before whom he appeared respected him for his thorough knowledge of the law. He edited several editions of Pratt's *Law of Highways*, was one of the editors of Halsbury's *Laws of England*, and was responsible for other legal works, including many editions of the *Overseers' Handbook* and Paterson's *Licensing Acts*. He married in 1897 Lilian (d. 1916), elder daughter of William Hardwick *Bradbury, publisher and printer, of Whitefriars; they had one son and one daughter.

Mackenzie took silk in 1914 and appeared set to become a judge. Soon after the outbreak of war, however, he was appointed the arbitrator in a number of wages disputes and spent the next eleven years almost exclusively involved in industrial arbitration. From the outset he displayed the qualities and personality demanded of an independent arbitrator with the result that in 1917 he was appointed one of the chairmen of the committee on production—the principal arbitration tribunal operating under the Munitions of War Act. In this capacity he helped to resolve many of the problems government faced in the regulation of wartime labour, and especially the upward adjustment of wages in a variety of competing industries in line with rising prices.

In 1919 Mackenzie was appointed the first president of the industrial court, created under the act of 1919. He remained in that office until 1926. Like the committee on production, on which it was modelled, the industrial court was based on the then novel principle of panels composed of independent members and representatives of employers and workers. The court had initially been planned as the agency for the active development of a body of case law which would bring more order to Britain's voluntaristic system of industrial relations. This was an objective which Mackenzie shared. However, opposition from both sides of industry and eventually Whitehall denied it the necessary powers. Reference of disputes to the court, for example, were voluntary and its awards could not be enforced. Within these limitations, the court played a valuable role in the downward adjustment of wages in the depression of the early 1920s, handling over a hundred cases a year until 1926.

Whether, in more propitious circumstances, Mackenzie would have left a more lasting legacy is open to debate. Under considerable pressure from Whitehall (Lowe, 101), he accepted that the level of wages should be based on the conventional market criterion of 'value of work done' rather than on social need, the cost of living, or industrial profitability. He later wrote in *Industrial Arbitration in Great Britain* (1929) that the court should be 'in the rear rather than the van of reform. Its function is rather to peg down and make secure gains which have been won in the march of progress and not itself lead the advance' (p. 186). On a fact-finding mission to the USA with Ernest Bevin in 1926, he referred to the latter's investigations on the shopfloor rather than in the boardroom as searching 'in the gutter' (Lowe, 92).

While president of the industrial court, Mackenzie chaired several politically sensitive inquiries such as those into the 1922 engineering dispute and the dismissal of striking policemen (in 1919) and prison officers (in 1924). He was referee under the Electricity (Supply) Acts of 1919 and 1922. He also chaired many bodies set up by employers and trade unions to resolve their disputes independently of government such as the railway national wages board (1920–26) and the tramway tribunal of Great Britain (from 1924). After leaving the industrial court, he continued to be appointed the chairman of many commissions and committees. These included the royal commissions on licensing (1929–31) and on Newfoundland (1933) and the committee on holidays with pay (1937–8). In 1937 and 1938 he was chairman of the council of the Royal Society of Arts.

Mackenzie was appointed KBE in 1918 and GBE in 1926 and raised to the peerage as Baron Amulree, of Strathbraan, Perthshire, on 22 July 1929. Between October 1930 and November 1931 he served under Ramsay MacDonald in the Labour and National governments as secretary of state for air and was sworn of the privy council. His term of office was undistinguished. Thereafter he was an active member of the House of Lords. He died at Upper Close, Winterbourne Stoke, Wiltshire, on 5 May 1942 and was succeeded as second baron by his son, Basil William Sholto *Mackenzie.   RODNEY LOWE

Sources DNB · The Times (6 May 1942) · H. Wilson, 'William Warrender MacKenzie, Baron Amulree of Strathbraan; his influence on industrial relations', Journal of the Royal Society of Arts, 94 (1945–6), 106–13 · personal knowledge (1959) [DNB] · R. Lowe, Adjusting to democracy: the role of the ministry of labour in British politics, 1916–1939 (1986) · E. Wigham, Strikes and the government, 1893–1974 (1976) · Burke, Peerage (1967) · GEC, Peerage · CGPLA Eng. & Wales (1942)
Archives Bodl. Oxf., corresp., diary, and papers
Likenesses W. Stoneman, photograph, 1936, NPG · P. F. S. Spence, portrait; in family possession in 1959
Wealth at death £162,644 1s. 7d.: probate, 5 Oct 1942, CGPLA Eng. & Wales

Mackenzie-Stuart. For this title name see Stuart, Alexander John Mackenzie, Baron Mackenzie-Stuart (1924–2000).

McKeown, Thomas (1912–1988), medical historian and exponent of social medicine, was born on 2 November 1912 in Portadown, northern Ireland, the third in the family of three sons and one daughter of William McKeown, preacher, builder, and officer in the Salvation Army, and his wife, Matilda Duff, also a Salvation Army officer. The family later moved to Vancouver, Canada. McKeown was educated in Vancouver at Burnaby South high school. He went to the University of British Columbia, obtaining a first-class degree in chemistry (1932) at the age of nineteen. He then obtained a national research scholarship to McGill University and a first doctorate (1935) at the age of twenty-two. He proceeded to Trinity College, Oxford, as a Rhodes scholar, gaining his DPhil in 1938. He became Poulton research scholar and demonstrator in physiology at Guy's Hospital medical school, carrying out research in endocrinology. In 1940 he married Esme Joan Bryan, daughter of Thomas William Widdowson, a London dentist; they had a son and a daughter. He achieved his MB BS in 1942, and then was engaged for a while during the Second World War under Solly Zuckerman, on behalf of the Ministry of Home Security, investigating the effects of bombing.

In 1945 McKeown was appointed to the new chair of social medicine at the University of Birmingham where he remained until his retirement in 1977, acting as the university's pro-vice-chancellor in 1974–7. He was awarded a Birmingham MD in 1947 and became a member (1952) and then a fellow (1958) of the Royal College of Physicians. From 1950 to 1958 he was joint editor of the British Journal of Preventive and Social Medicine. He was the author of

many scientific papers, which applied the broadening discipline of epidemiology to chronic as well as infective disease, the physiology and pathology of growth, nutrition and development, the growth of populations, and the evaluation and planning of health services. It was in this last field that he made his chief mark, forcing a realistic reappraisal of the origins of health improvements. He challenged the belief of many doctors that health changes, and the reductions in mortality during the previous century, had sprung from clinical practice, arguing rather that they were due to social, economic, public-health engineering, and dietary improvements. These ideas were developed with colleagues over a period of many years and gave rise to papers written jointly with R. G. Brown ('Medical evidence related to English population changes in the eighteenth century', Population Studies, 9, 1955) and with R. G. Brown and R. G. Record ('An interpretation of the modern rise of population in Europe', Population Studies, 27, 1972). These analyses eventually found a unified expression in McKeown's books. It was to the benefit and credit of medicine that this reappraisal should come from within the discipline rather than from outside. The social medicine movement (of which he was a founder), and the application of scientific analysis to health-care planning (of which he was the leading exponent), led the way to changes in public health practice in Britain and elsewhere. His books included An Introduction to Social Medicine (1966, jointly with C. R. Lowe), The Modern Rise of Population (1976), and The Role of Medicine (1979).

McKeown's reformulation of the role of medicine was often treated with suspicion, enmity, and misrepresentation. These ideas were too heretical, competing over-forcefully with fixed attitudes to planning, and with traditional pathways towards administrative power and professional status-building. It was therefore understandable if it took the medical and political worlds some time to catch up, and if they never quite made it. Yet, by the time he retired, McKeown was not so far in advance as to justify the disgraceful denial of civil honours. He became honorary FFCM (Ireland, 1980) and honorary FACP (1982), and was given an honorary DSc by McGill University (1981).

McKeown was a gifted writer, and a polished and incisive speaker. He was an impressive lecturer, tall, slim, and good-looking, and he was always so much in command of his subject that he would never refer to notes. His interests covered walking, music, opera, and literature, and he had a special love of poetry, wine, and English puddings. He died from cancer on 13 June 1988 in Birmingham, survived by his wife.   E. G. KNOX, rev.

Sources The Independent (21 June 1988) · The Times (20 June 1988) · personal knowledge (1996) · private information (1996) · CGPLA Eng. & Wales (1988)
Wealth at death £140,426: probate, 5 Oct 1988, CGPLA Eng. & Wales

Mackerell, Benjamin (bap. 1685, d. 1738), antiquary and librarian, was baptized on 15 April 1685 at St Peter Mancroft, Norwich, the youngest son of Alderman John Mackerell (1643–1723), mercer, and Anne Browne (1646–1711), daughter of Elias Browne. His father's family were of

Huguenot stock, and Benjamin Mackerell had independent, albeit limited, means. During the 1720s he lived close to Chapelfield House, and in the 1730s in the Market Place, Norwich. He married his first wife, Ann (d. 1733), c.1708; they had ten children. Following her death, in March 1733, he married Lydia Knights at St Peter Mancroft on 15 November 1733.

Mackerell began his antiquarian career by copying hundreds of shields, crests, and mottoes, from windows, monuments, hatchments, and carriage doors. Other church notes and antiquarian manuscripts were painstakingly compiled, systematically arranged, and indexed. His father was granted arms on 10 April 1718, and in 1722 Mackerell was introduced to Peter Le Neve, Norroy king of arms. He joined Le Neve's 'little Society of Icenian Antiquaries', which included Thomas Tanner and Thomas Kirkpatrick, who were collecting materials for the history of Norfolk (Nichols, 3.433). Mackerell hoped that Le Neve would use his influence to secure him a post in the College of Arms, but the latter died in 1729 before doing so.

Mackerell completed accounts of St Stephen's parish in 1729–30 and St Peter Mancroft in 1735–6, and began to compile a detailed history of Norwich. He also claimed to have been the draughtsman of *A New and Accurate Map of Norfolk* (1731), which was largely copied from James Corbridge's map of 1730.

Mackerell was librarian of the Norwich Public Library from 1724 following two decades of its decline and neglect, which he remedied by enforcing the regulations, enlarging the membership, and encouraging donations. John Kirkpatrick bequeathed 200 early printed books and manuscripts together with his collection of coins and medals in 1728. This gave rise to Mackerell's compiling *A New Catalogue of the Books in the Public Library of the City of Norwich* (1733), which was financed by the Norwich assembly. It was to have been followed by an illustrated catalogue of Kirkpatrick's coin collection, but this was never published.

Mackerell expected the library to benefit from a far larger bequest from Le Neve. However, the terms of the will were ignored and Le Neve's collections remained with his executor Thomas Martin, who moved them to Palgrave. Mackerell was most upset when in July 1733 he read proposals for a history of Norfolk, based upon Le Neve's collections, issued by Martin's friend Francis Blomefield. Mackerell alerted the Norwich mayor's court to Martin's malversation, but they took no action. In October 1735 Mackerell introduced himself to Blomefield and they shared a brief acquaintanceship before quarrelling in 1737. Mackerell justifiably felt that the task was too great for Blomefield alone and that he himself should compile the histories of Norwich and King's Lynn, using Le Neve's materials. Blomefield rejected this suggestion, but Mackerell decided to proceed nevertheless, relying upon his own collections. Mackerell's *History and Antiquities of … King's Lynn* appeared early in 1738, almost entirely copied from manuscript histories compiled by John Green, c.1724, and Henry Bell, c.1710. Green had primarily described the monuments in the various churches and religious houses, which Mackerell interspersed with Bell's description of the town, municipal and other buildings, charters, and civic regalia. The whole was a crude pastiche with little of Mackerell's own work. Its publication was a paltry means of retribution against Blomefield, rather than a serious attempt to write the history of one of the foremost ports in England.

Of more concern to Blomefield, however, was Mackerell's detailed history of Norwich, then nearing completion. Unlike the account of King's Lynn, Mackerell's 'Norwich' was primarily his own work, although he may have incorporated some material from Kirkpatrick. The larger of the two manuscript volumes begins with a historical account of the city and the foundation of the cathedral priory and other monasteries and religious houses. This is followed by an account of the parish churches and their funeral monuments. The second volume covers the topographical and municipal history, including accounts of streets and lanes, various office holders, rights and privileges, public buildings, and institutions. He also added a contemporary description of the city and wrote about notable events in its history, such as Kett's uprising.

In October 1735 Mackerell described himself as 'infirm, and unfitt for everything' (*Correspondence*, 99) and during the winter of 1737 his health began to fail. The last six months of his life were spent in a race to complete the history of Norwich. He died at his home in the Market Place, Norwich, on 29 March 1738 and was buried in St Stephen's Church on 1 April; his executors announced that they would publish his work, but never did so. The manuscript history of Norwich, now in the Norfolk Record Office, is detailed, accurate, and well organized; its publication would have secured Mackerell's reputation as a historian.

DAVID STOKER

Sources D. Stoker, 'Benjamin Mackerell, antiquary, librarian, and plagiarist', *Norfolk Archaeology*, 42 (1994–7), 1–12 • E. M. James, 'Thomas Preston's manuscript of Henry Bell's "Antiquities of King's Lynn", and its use by Benjamin Mackerell', *West Norfolk Local History Society Journal*, 1 (1981), 291–303 • *The correspondence of the Reverend Francis Blomefield, 1705–52*, ed. D. Stoker, Norfolk RS, 55 (1992), 99, 234–5 • private information (2004) [unpublished genealogical notes compiled by Mrs E. Mathias of the subject] • Nichols, *Illustrations*, 3.433 • D. Stoker, 'The ill-gotten library of "Honest Tom" Martin', *Property of a gentleman: the formation, organisation and dispersal of the private library, 1620–1920*, St Paul's Bibliographies (1991), 90–112 • G. A. Stephen, *Three centuries of a city library* (1917) • F. Johnson, 'John Kirkpatrick, antiquary', *Norfolk Archaeology*, 23 (1927–9), 285–304 • [J. Chambers], *A general history of the county of Norfolk*, 2 (1829), 1079 • F. Blomefield and C. Parkin, *An essay towards a topographical history of the county of Norfolk*, [2nd edn], 11 vols. (1805–10), vol. 4, pp. 208–9 • *DNB* • *IGI* • parish register, Norwich, St Peter Mancroft, 15 April 1685 [baptism] • parish register, St Stephen's, Norwich [marriage]

Archives BL, account of church of St Peter Mancroft, Norwich, and notes on Norfolk churches, Add. MSS 9370, 23011, 12525–12526 • Norfolk RO, armorial probably by Mackerell • Norfolk RO, heraldic papers • Norfolk RO, heraldic papers relating to Norfolk • Norfolk RO, list of Norfolk parishes and MS History of Norwich

Wealth at death several houses and other properties in Norwich and Blickling, Norfolk; jewellery; plate; library; valuables: will

McKerrow, John (1789–1867), minister of the United Presbyterian church and historian, was born in Mauchline, Ayrshire, on 15 May 1789, the third son of John McKerrow and his wife, Margaret, in a family of six sons and four daughters. His father, a cloth merchant, died while he was still a boy and his mother died during his first session at Glasgow University, which he attended from 1803. In 1807 he entered the Associate Synod Divinity Hall, where he studied under Dr George Lawson. Licensed by the presbytery of Kilmarnock in 1812, he was ordained colleague and successor to the Revd William Fletcher (d. 1815) at Bridge of Teith, Perthshire, on 25 August 1813; this was in preference to another call from a congregation at Ecclefechan, Dumfriesshire.

While a diligent pastor, a competent preacher, and a scrupulous attender of church courts, McKerrow's fame derived from his writings. His *Life and Correspondence of the Late Revd Henry Belfrage DD of Falkirk* (1837), prepared in collaboration with John Macfarlane, was followed by the *History of the Secession Church* (1839), a revised and enlarged edition of which appeared in 1841. His treatise *The Office of Ruling Elder in the Christian Church* (1846) won him a prize of £50. He was a frequent contributor to, among others, the *Christian Repository*, the *Edinburgh Theological Magazine*, and the *United Secession Magazine*. His final work, the *History of the Foreign Missions of the Secession and United Presbyterian Church* (1867), was published only weeks before his death. This was a fitting end to his exertions as, in the early days of his denomination's missionary activities, he had conducted all the synod's business on the subject.

McKerrow married, on 30 August 1840, Mary Lindsay of Ayr whose brother, William Schaw Lindsay (1816–1877), later achieved fame and fortune as a shipowner and MP. In 1841 McKerrow received the degree of DD from Washington College in the USA and on his ministerial jubilee in 1863 his congregation presented him with 600 sovereigns. What appeared to be a mild attack of influenza proved more serious and McKerrow died at his home at Bridge of Teith on 13 May 1867, suddenly but peacefully, as he prepared to attend the United Presbyterian church synod.

T. B. JOHNSTONE, rev. LIONEL ALEXANDER RITCHIE

Sources *United Presbyterian Magazine*, new ser., 11 (1867), 406–11 · R. Small, *History of the congregations of the United Presbyterian church from 1733 to 1900*, 2 (1904), 678–9 · J. Smith, *Our Scottish clergy*, 3rd ser. (1851), 297–303 · parish register (marriage), Ayr, 30 Aug 1840

Wealth at death £1991 8s. 9d.: confirmation, 1867, Scotland

McKerrow, Ronald Brunlees (1872–1940), bibliographer and literary scholar, was born at Putney, Surrey, on 12 December 1872, the only son of Alexander McKerrow, civil engineer, and grandson of William *McKerrow, one-time moderator of the Presbyterian Church of England. His mother was Mary Jane, elder daughter of Sir James Brunlees, one-time president of the Institution of Civil Engineers. From Harrow School McKerrow proceeded to King's College, London, and then to Trinity College, Cambridge, where he won the chancellor's English medal in 1895 and graduated in medieval and modern languages in 1897. After three years (1897–1900) as professor of English in the Government School of Foreign Languages at Tokyo, and having mastered Japanese and the operation of a small hand printing press, he settled in London. Once there, McKerrow engaged in literary and critical work, and became a director of the publishing firm of Sidgwick and Jackson in 1908 and an honorary secretary (jointly with Alfred William Pollard) of the Bibliographical Society in 1912.

Throughout McKerrow's life the society remained one of his chief concerns. For it he produced two exhaustive illustrated monographs, *Printers' and Publishers' Devices in England and Scotland, 1485–1640* (1913) and *Title-Page Borders used in England and Scotland, 1485 to 1640* (with Frederic Sutherland Ferguson, 1932). McKerrow's edition of the works of the Elizabethan writer Thomas Nash, undertaken at the suggestion of A. H. Bullen, appeared in five volumes between 1904 and 1910, and was at once recognized as setting a standard in English editing. Although McKerrow was over age for military service, during the First World War he joined the Royal Naval Volunteer Reserve and was attached to a searchlight unit in London. On 29 March 1915 he married Amy (b. 1876/7), daughter of William Bonnet of Conwy; they had twin sons.

McKerrow lectured in English at King's College until 1919. In 1925 he founded the *Review of English Studies*, which he continued to edit until his death, combining the task from 1934 to 1937 with the editorship of *The Library*, the organ of the Bibliographical Society. He was perhaps best known for his often reprinted *Introduction to Bibliography for Literary Students* (1927), an authoritative guide to everything in the material production of printed books that relate to the study and editing of English literature. It served as the basis of the extensive efforts in the field performed by W. W. Greg and Fredson Bowers.

The last ten years of McKerrow's life were devoted to the great critical edition of Shakespeare that he undertook for the Clarendon Press. A substantial portion of it, comprising most of the early plays, was prepared for publication, but the only part published before his death was the slender but important volume *Prolegomena for the Oxford Shakespeare* (1939), in which he laid down what he considered to be the principles of text construction and explained his methods of applying them. In this and other works McKerrow probably accomplished more than anyone else in placing the editing of English literature upon a scientific basis. In fact, this achievement was his ultimate aim throughout his career. His powers of observation, memory, and inference in bibliography combined to give him a sure insight into mechanical processes. Still, for him this insight, and much else, was ancillary to the critical study of literature, for which he ungrudgingly provided his wide knowledge and experience at the service of others. If, as some thought, McKerrow's intolerance of speculation (where certainty was admittedly unattainable) led him to impose too severe a curb on the liberty of an editor, he kept his invaluable criticism sane and informed, and based it firmly on recognized and clearly defined principles.

McKerrow was the Sandars reader in bibliography at

Cambridge University (1928–9) and was awarded the gold medal of the Bibliographical Society in 1929. He was also elected a fellow of the British Academy in 1932 and received the honorary degree of PhD from Louvain University in 1927. Considered by many to be the father of twentieth-century descriptive bibliography, McKerrow died at Picket Piece, Wendover, Buckinghamshire, on 20 January 1940, and was buried in the local parish church. He was survived by his wife.

W. W. GREG, *rev.* JOHN V. RICHARDSON JR.

Sources *The Times* (22 Jan 1940), 1 · [H. H. Child], *TLS* (27 Jan 1940), 46 · W. W. Greg, 'Ronald Brunlees McKerrow', *PBA*, 26 (1940), 488–515 · F. C. Francis, 'A list of the writings of Ronald Brunlees McKerrow', *The Library*, 4th ser., 21 (1940–41), 229–63 · Venn, *Alum. Cant.* · *WWW* · m. cert. · d. cert. · *CGPLA Eng. & Wales* (1940)
Archives Trinity Cam., personal MSS | Bodl. Oxf., corresp. with Graham Pollard
Likenesses W. Stoneman, photograph, 1933, NPG · portrait, repro. in W. W. Greg, 'Ronald Brunlees McKerrow'
Wealth at death £9512 7s. 7d.: probate, 17 April 1940, *CGPLA Eng. & Wales*

McKerrow, William (1803–1878), minister of the Presbyterian Church of England and educationist, was born on 7 September 1803, the son of William and Elizabeth (*née* Muir) McKerrow of Kilmarnock. His parents were keen supporters of the Burgher section of the Secession church, and after his education at Kilmarnock Academy he attended Glasgow University (1817–23), entered the Divinity Hall of the United Secession church in 1821, and was licensed to preach in 1826. He received two calls, to Cumbernauld and to Lloyd Street, Manchester (the only Presbyterian church in the city at that time), and acceded to the latter on 24 May 1827. He was ordained on 7 September of that year. On 6 March 1829 he married Anne, daughter of John Begg of Banff House, Rusholme.

McKerrow stayed in the Lloyd Street pastorate all his life and his significance in the history of Manchester and south-east Lancashire is twofold. Firstly, as a Presbyterian minister he saw the successful transfer in 1858 of the Lloyd Street congregation to a new building in Brunswick Street, which became one of Manchester's most influential churches. Born into a small schismatic sect, McKerrow worked tirelessly for wider Presbyterian unity, and helped found a number of new churches, notably one at Blackburn. He aided the formation of the Lancashire presbytery of his church in 1831, the creation of the United Presbyterian church in 1847, the formation of an English synod of the same in 1863—becoming its moderator in 1866–7—and finally the all-important union of 1876 which gave rise to the Presbyterian Church of England. McKerrow was chosen moderator of this body in 1877–8, a singular tribute to his standing within the denomination.

Secondly, from his arrival in Manchester, McKerrow was closely associated with radical causes. Lloyd Street Chapel was situated in a needy area opposite the town hall, and he was moved by a sense of political and social injustice. A fierce controversy with Hugh Stowell, the most aggressive of the local evangelical Anglican clergy, in the *Manchester*

William McKerrow (1803–1878), by unknown photographer

Courier and *Manchester Times* in 1834 on the question of dissenting grievances led to the formation of a United Committee of Manchester Dissenters (1834) and the Manchester Voluntary Church Association (1839), founded in the vestry of Lloyd Street Chapel, a body which subsequently threw in its lot with Edward Miall and *The Nonconformist* newspaper. McKerrow led a local agitation for the civil registration of births, marriages, and deaths in 1837, and the following year was one of the seven men (six of them from Lloyd Street) who founded the Manchester Anti-Corn Law Association. He was one of the promoters (maybe the original inspirer) of the Ministerial Anti-Corn Law Convention in August 1841.

Prominent in the agitation against the educational clauses of Graham's Factory Bill (1843), McKerrow protested the following year against the Maynooth grant, though in this campaign the local running was made by the Congregationalists. Throughout the rest of the 1840s he was concerned with the Peace Society and the United Kingdom Alliance, while in 1846 he founded the *Manchester Examiner* to be the organ of local radicalism as against the more temperate Liberalism of *The Guardian*. In 1848 *The Examiner* was merged with Archibald Prentice's *Manchester Times*. In 1847 McKerrow broke with the voluntaryism of the past and, in recognition of the need he saw all around him, helped found (again in the vestry of Lloyd Street Chapel) the Lancashire Public School Association (widened by McKerrow and his friend Richard Cobden into a national association in December 1850). He also helped promote a model secular school in Jackson's Row,

Manchester. He took part in deputations to parliament and gave evidence to a parliamentary committee on education in 1853, but his educational hopes were dashed when Sir John Pakington's permissive bill of 1857 was lost. This same year he took part in the general election campaign, deputizing for Cobden, who was ill, in support of John Bright and Milner Gibson, pacifist/radical candidates for Manchester. In the bellicose atmosphere of the times both were defeated.

In 1861 McKerrow was lecturing for the Liberation Society, which led to a spirited clash with the Revd James Bardsley, rector of St Anne's, of the Church Defence Association. He was also, as a promoter of the Union and Emancipation Society, concerned with famine relief in Manchester during the cotton famine of the early 1860s. A little later he was a member of the Manchester Education Aid Society, which strongly influenced the contents of the Forster act of 1870. That year he was elected to the Manchester school board at the head of the list of 'unsectarian' candidates, securing re-election in 1873 and 1876. He was made chairman of the board's sites committee and founded, out of the money given to him at his ministerial jubilee dinner, a scholarship to enable board-school children to proceed to secondary education.

Small, powerfully built, and dynamic, McKerrow was an earnest expository preacher. He was awarded the degree of DD by Heidelberg University in 1851. He went into semi-retirement in 1869 and resigned his pastorate in 1871. He had moved to Bowdon, Cheshire, in March 1870, and he died there of congestion of the lungs on 4 June 1878. He was buried in Ardwick cemetery, Manchester. His wife had predeceased him in 1863. They had eight children, of whom the two best-known were the Revd James Muir McKerrow, his father's biographer, and Alderman John Begg McKerrow of Salford.   IAN SELLERS

Sources *Weekly Review* (8 June 1878) · *Weekly Review* (15 June 1878) · W. Graham, 'The late Dr William M'Kerrow, Manchester', *United Presbyterian Magazine*, new ser., 22 (1878), 356–61 · J. M. McKerrow, *Memoir of William McKerrow, DD* (1881) · W. E. A. Axon, ed., *The annals of Manchester: a chronological record from the earliest times to the end of 1885* (1886) · newspaper cuttings, Man. CL [microfilm]

Likenesses photograph, repro. in McKerrow, *Memoir* [see illus.]

Wealth at death under £18,000: probate, 25 July 1878, *CGPLA Eng. & Wales*

Mackeson, Frederick (1807–1853), army officer in the East India Company, son of William and Harriett Mackeson, was born at Hythe, Kent, on 28 September 1807. He was educated at the King's School, Canterbury, and in France, and in 1825 received a Bengal cadetship. On 4 December 1825 he was appointed ensign in the 14th Bengal native infantry, in which he became lieutenant in 1828 and captain in 1843. In 1831, and for several years afterwards, his regiment was stationed at Ludhiana. The foreign officers employed by the Sikh ruler, Ranjit Singh, used frequently to visit the British political agent, Sir Claude Martin Wade, on which occasions Mackeson's proficiency in French was useful. He was thus brought into notice, despite his modest disposition. In 1837 he accompanied Sir Alexander Burnes to Kabul. He was afterwards sent to Bahawalpur as

agent for the navigation of the Indus, in which capacity he was employed in surveying the river and keeping note of the complicated politics of the Punjab. In 1838–9 he rendered valuable services in connection with the lines of communication of the army of the Indus at the onset of the First Afghan War. These services were recognized in 1840, when he was still a subaltern, by a brevet majority to qualify him for his appointment as CB, which was made on 24 December 1842. After the final withdrawal of the British troops from Afghanistan, he was appointed acting superintendent of Buttee, and assistant to the political agents in Rajputana and at Delhi.

During the First Anglo-Sikh War Mackeson was with Sir Harry Smith's division and was at Aliwal. On 16 March 1846 he was appointed superintendent of the Cis-Sutlej territory. As governor-general's agent he was with Hugh Gough, first Viscount Gough, in the Punjab campaign of 1848–9, and was commended by lords Dalhousie and Gough. After the battle of Chilianwala, Brigadier Burn's brigade was in danger of being turned by a Sikh force, and Mackeson offered to warn of the Sikh approach. He found the Jhelum—the widest and most dangerous river in the Punjab—in full flood. He swam the river with difficulty, delivered his message, and saved the brigade. He became local lieutenant-colonel in 1849, and in 1851, being then senior captain of his regiment and a brevet lieutenant-colonel, was appointed commissioner at Peshawar, in succession to George St Patrick Lawrence. For the next two years Mackeson attempted to bring the peoples of the frontier into order. He was assassinated when sitting on his veranda, on 10 September 1853, by a man from Koner, who handed him a petition and then attacked him with a large knife. It was generally believed that a price had been set on Mackeson's head, although the government denied that it was the case. His assassin was tried, and on 1 October 1853 was hanged. By the advice of John Lawrence the murderer's body was burned and the ashes thrown into a running stream, so that there might be no opportunity of making the burying-place a shrine. Mackeson was a bold and efficient officer who favoured tough measures on the frontier, and paid the price for doing so.

H. M. CHICHESTER, *rev.* JAMES FALKNER

Sources *Indian Army and Civil Service List* · *East-India Register* · S. Cotton, *Nine years on the north-west frontier of India, from 1854–1863* (1868) · *GM*, 2nd ser., 41 (1854), 200–01 · R. B. Smith, *Life of Lord Lawrence*, 2 vols. (1883)

Archives NA Scot., corresp. with Lord Dalhousie, GD 45

Mackesy, Pierse Joseph (1883–1956), army officer, was born on 5 April 1883 in Dublin, reportedly in Merrion Square, the younger son of Lieutenant-General William Henry Mackesy (1837–1914), Bengal staff corps, a veteran of the Indian Mutiny and the Crimean and Afghan wars, of 65 Albert Hall Mansion, London, and his wife, Teresa (d. c.1922), daughter of Pierse Creagh of Mount Elva, co. Clare. Mackesy's mother was Roman Catholic, his father a Catholic convert; Mackesy was brought up a Catholic but later became an Anglican. Mackesy's elder brother was Colonel

John Pierse Mackesy (1873–*c*.1943), Royal Engineers, educated at Stonyhurst College and the Royal Military Academy, Woolwich, who served in Sierra Leone and the Second South African War and on the western front, and retired in 1923.

Mackesy was educated at St Paul's School, Hammersmith (May 1897 to December 1899), where he was a capitation scholar, and at the Royal Military Academy, Woolwich (1900–02). His nickname, Pat, probably originated from his time at Woolwich. He was commissioned second lieutenant, Royal Engineers, in August 1902, and was promoted lieutenant in March 1905. In 1911 he was appointed to Colonial Office survey duty in the Gold Coast, and made surveys of Ashanti and the northern territories. In August 1913 he was promoted captain and appointed deputy director of surveys, Gold Coast. At the outbreak of war in 1914 he was ordered to acquire horses to mount police and others for the invasion of the German colonies of Togoland and Cameroon. He served with the expedition until he fell ill at the end of the year, and was sent back to Accra and invalided to England. He served in France with the 15th (Scottish) and 1st divisions, winning an MC, was promoted major in August 1917, and was awarded a DSO in January 1918. In spring 1918 he attended the staff course at Cambridge, returning to France soon after the German March offensive, as GSO2 at 6th corps then at general headquarters.

Promoted brevet lieutenant-colonel in December 1919, Mackesy served with distinction as a staff officer with the British force at Murmansk, and following the withdrawal from north Russia, joined the military mission to General Anton Ivanovich Denikin in southern Russia. He returned home in 1920 and attended the staff college at Camberley. On 26 June 1923 he married Leonora Dorothy Rivers (1902–1972)—called Marjorie by her husband and friends—only daughter of James Cook of Enfield, Cults, Aberdeenshire; they had two sons and she survived her husband. She was a romantic novelist with the pen names Leonora Starr and Dorothy Rivers, and published impressions of everyday life in Southwold. One son was Dr Piers Gerald Mackesy (*b.* 1924), fellow of Pembroke College, Oxford, and military historian.

Mackesy taught as a GSO2 at the staff college in Quetta, Baluchistan, India (1927–30)—where his students included Slim, the future field marshal, who praised his teaching—then commanded the depot battalion of Royal Engineers at Chatham. From spring 1935 he commanded the 3rd infantry brigade at Bordon, Hampshire, then in Palestine during the Arab rebellion, and he was promoted major-general in October 1937. He returned to England early in 1938 to command the 49th (West Riding) division, Territorial Army (TA), and was made a CB. In 1938 he attended the Pacific defence conference in Australia then, at its request, advised the New Zealand government on its forces. He returned to England and at the beginning of the Second World War was embodying and training his TA division.

Late in 1939 and early in 1940 the British government considered intervention in Norway—strategically important, but weakly defended and neutral—to interdict German iron-ore supplies from Sweden, which were exported through Norway, and to help Finland against the Soviet invasion (from November 1939). Military preparations were started and Mackesy was designated commander of the force to occupy Narvik—the ice-free port in northern Norway within the Arctic Circle, crucial to the iron-ore export—then advance along the railway to capture the Gallivare ore fields in Sweden and assist the Finns. He had grave doubts: on 8 March he wrote to the War Office that 'the plan as it now stands may result in a dangerous if not disastrous situation' (Kersaudy, 33). General Sir Edmund Ironside, chief of the Imperial General Staff, commented 'a more unmilitary show I have never seen' (ibid.). The British vacillated and delayed and their intelligence failed. On 9 April 1940 the Germans seized the initiative by their audacious surprise invasion of Norway, despite British naval superiority, and captured the Norwegian ports, including Narvik. Churchill, first lord of the admiralty, wrote, 'we have been completely outwitted' (Gilbert, 224).

The British government decided on operation Rupert to capture Narvik in co-operation with the French, and Mackesy was appointed commander of 'Rupertforce', 'an independent command directly under the War Office' (Derry, 248). His written instructions from Ironside, dated 10 April 1940, stated that the force's objective was to 'eject the Germans from the Narvik area and to establish control of Narvik itself' (ibid., 247), that 'it is not intended that you should land in the face of opposition … the decision whether to land or not will be taken by the Senior Naval Officer in consultation with you' (ibid., 248), and that his initial task was to establish his base at Harstad. However, Ironside also wrote separately to him the same day, 'You may have a chance of taking advantage of naval action and you should do so if you can. Boldness is required' (ibid., 249). Already convinced that the plan was inept and the expedition badly mounted, Mackesy sailed from Scapa Flow on 12 April, reached Norway on 14 April, and established his base at the small port of Harstad, on the island of Hinnoy, about 35 miles direct from Narvik but much further by sea.

Churchill later called the Norwegian venture 'this ramshackle campaign' (Marder, 163). Hastily improvised, with inadequate intelligence, planning, and preparation, it was muddled from the start. Although the principles of joint command were well understood and stated in official manuals, in the crisis the chiefs of staff ignored them. The naval and military chiefs acted independently without consulting each other, and issued separate unharmonized orders: 'thus was confusion worse confounded' (Moulton, 149). There was no combined headquarters and initially no single overall commander. The transports had not been packed tactically, and the British lacked landing craft, motor transport, and artillery, but received a railway unit, 1000 office personnel, and large quantities of office furniture. Harstad with its inadequate facilities was soon chaotically congested. The Germans had air superiority.

The naval commander, the veteran admiral of the fleet William Henry Dudley Boyle, twelfth earl of Cork and Orrery (1873–1967), was selected by Churchill, the cabinet protagonist of the Narvik operation, for his aggressive spirit. He did not meet Mackesy before they left Britain, on the same day but separately, and was not given written instructions but was briefed verbally by Churchill and others. On 15 April, Mackesy and Cork finally met. Witnesses of their meeting recognized the instant antagonism between them. Cork was astonished to learn that Mackesy was not ready for immediate operations and an opposed landing, and that 'the General and myself left the U.K. with diametrically opposite views as to what was required' (Connell, 91). Cork proposed an immediate improvised direct attack to capture Narvik, exploiting naval success off Narvik on 13 April, but Mackesy refused. Both Major-General J. L. Moulton (1906–1993), himself an amphibious warfare expert, and T. K. Derry, the official historian of the campaign, later considered that Cork's proposed attack, though risky, might have succeeded then, but thereafter its chance of success declined. Mackesy claimed that an attack would result in the 'snows of Narvik being turned into another version of the mud of Passchendaele' (Derry, 152). Moulton later wrote that this was 'strange and hysterical language for a military commander, and symptomatic of long-suppressed fears and doubts … springing from Gallipoli as well as from Passchendaele' (Moulton, 225–6). Mackesy was unconciliatory and intellectually intolerant and failed (unlike Auchinleck later) to effectively handle Cork. They had different temperaments, there was mutual antipathy, and they failed to liaise adequately. Mackesy, with his Russian experience, concerned at the limitations of his force and the problems of snow and ice, refused to be hurried and intended to act surely and slowly, waiting until the snow had melted. Churchill, who pressed for action, wrote on 17 April, 'we were taken aback by General Mackesy's proposal to sit down in front of Narvik, and convert the operation into a kind of siege' (Gilbert, 251). Mackesy claimed that he delayed because of insufficient troops, artillery, and mortar ammunition, and the snow. He believed a premature attack would be disastrous.

On 27 April, at Churchill's instigation, Cork was appointed commander of all the forces in the Narvik area. However, he was unwilling to overrule, or was convinced by, Mackesy and his army officers. Cork planned a naval bombardment to force the Germans at Narvik to surrender. Mackesy opposed this, claiming it would harm 'thousands of Norwegian men, women and children' (Marder, 165). Churchill told Cork, 'If this Officer appears to be spreading a bad spirit … do not hesitate to relieve him or place him under arrest' (ibid.). On 24 April the battleship *Warspite* and other warships bombarded. The Germans did not surrender nor did the British land. Cork, pressed by Churchill, wanted a landing near Narvik, but Mackesy, fearing an 'Arctic Gallipoli' (Kersaudy, 197), wanted a slow enveloping operation. More British disagreement and

inaction followed. Moulton later alleged that Mackesy 'seemed intent to erect every argument against action' (Moulton, 225).

Late in April 1940 a French force under *général de brigade* Antoine Marie Béthouart landed at Harstad. He wanted a landing at Bjerkvik to capture the Oyjord peninsula as a springboard to Narvik. Mackesy (who intended to capture the peninsula by a different route) advised against this then acquiesced. On 13 May, with British naval firepower support, the French Foreign Legion and light tanks made a successful opposed landing and captured Bjerkvik and later Oyjord. This successful operation was for Churchill proof of Mackesy's incompetence. Moulton later wrote that 'the first landing under fire in the Second World War had succeeded. The ghost of Gallipoli, if not laid, was in retreat' (Moulton, 225). Béthouart, he also wrote, showed 'moral courage and energy sadly lacking in the British military command' (ibid., 227). Meanwhile the chiefs of staff had decided to send Lieutenant-General C. J. E. Auchinleck (1884–1981) ostensibly to report but in fact to replace Mackesy, with a secret document authorizing him to assume command. He had known Mackesy at the staff college in Quetta, and reportedly had a high opinion of his intelligence and ability. Auchinleck reached Norway on 11 May. He soon decided that the personal relations between Cork and Mackesy precluded their effective co-operation and so, on 13 May after the Bjerkvik landing, assumed command. Mackesy was recalled to Britain. Narvik was finally captured on 28 May but, following the fall of France, was evacuated on 7 June, and 'this small, ill-starred campaign' (Derry, 246) ended.

Mackesy was placed on the retired list in August 1940, then was employed at the War Office for the rest of the year. In spring 1941 he was appointed to the offices of the war cabinet and, with a small tri-service staff, made a study of possible enemy operations: his last official employment. From 1941 to 1947 he was *Daily Telegraph* military correspondent. He retired to his home at Lane End, Southwold, Suffolk, and was active as an independent in local government: borough councillor (1946–53), mayor (1949–52), and county councillor (1949–55). He published a pamphlet, *Southwold Guns* (1950), on the cannons at South Green, Southwold. He was the honorary county treasurer of the Soldiers', Sailors' and Airmen's Families Association and 'the mainspring of all S. S. A. F. A.'s work in the county' (*The Times*, 14 June 1956). Latterly he suffered from painful arthritis. He died suddenly on 8 June 1956 at Osborne House, East Cowes, Isle of Wight.

Described as a 'man of trained intelligence', Mackesy was a 'soldier of wide experience' who had a 'full career of successful achievement' until he came to public prominence as commander of the land forces at Narvik (*The Times*, 11 June 1956). Some writers on the Second World War gave less favourable accounts of the latter phase of his career; his conduct of the Narvik campaign was criticized in Churchill's influential memoirs *The Second World War*, volume 1, *The Gathering Storm* (1948). However, his son Dr Piers Mackesy, military historian, published articles in the *Journal of the Royal United Service Institution* (1970) and *History*

Today (1985) arguing that in the Narvik campaign Mackesy was right, and that Churchill's version was flawed by inaccuracy, innuendo, and inconsistency resulting from 'the author's profound emotional involvement' (Mackesy, 'Churchill on Narvik', 32), and unfairly made Mackesy the scapegoat. Mackesy had, claimed his son, 'probably saved the army and Churchill himself from another Gallipoli massacre which might have prejudiced the development of combined operations in later years' (*History Today*, 19).

ROGER T. STEARN

Sources *The Times* (11 June 1956) · *The Times* (14 June 1956) · private information (2004) [P. Mackesy, son] · *WWW*, 1897–1915 · *WWW*, 1951–60 · *WW* (1938) · *WW* (1942) · *WW* (1943) · *WW* (1944) · *WW* (1945) · *WW* (1955) · R. B. Gardiner, ed., *The admission registers of St Paul's School, from 1876 to 1905* (1906) · *Hart's Army List* (1913) · *Army List* (1919–38) · *The Journal* [Southwold] (15 June 1956) · T. K. Derry, *The campaign in Norway* (1952) [official history] · J. L. Moulton, *The Norwegian campaign of 1940: a study of warfare in three dimensions* (1966) · J. Connell, *Auchinleck: a biography of Field-Marshal Sir Claude Auchinleck* (1959) · A. J. Marder, *From the Dardanelles to Oran: studies of the Royal Navy in war and peace, 1915–1940* (1974) · M. Gilbert, *Winston S. Churchill*, 6: *Finest hour, 1939–1941* (1983) · W. S. Churchill, *The Second World War*, 1 (1948) · F. Kersaudy, *Norway 1940* (1990) · P. Mackesy, 'Churchill on Narvik', *Journal of the Royal United Service Institution* (1970) · P. Mackesy, 'Churchill as chronicler: the Narvik episode', *History Today* (March 1970), 14–20 · Earl of Cork and Orrery [W. H. D. Boyle], *My naval life, 1886–1941* [1942]

Likenesses W. Stoneman, photograph, 1937, NPG · photograph, repro. in *History Today* (March 1985)

Wealth at death £1010 10s. 4d.: probate, 11 Sept 1956, CGPLA Eng. & Wales

---

McKewan, David Hall (1816–1873), watercolour painter, was born on 16 February 1816 in London, one of at least two sons of David McKewan, manager to Messrs Hall of Custom House quay, Lower Thames Street, London, and his wife, Matilda. He is thought to have been a pupil of David Cox, as he knew this artist before he began exhibiting at the New Watercolour Society in 1848, and his watercolours were similar to those of Cox.

McKewan became a full member of the society in 1850 and contributed 498 works to its exhibitions, mainly views of Welsh streams and waterfalls, and scenes of the coast of north Wales. He also painted landscapes in Scotland, Ireland, and Kent, and it is likely that he travelled to the Middle East in the late 1850s, as there are a number of watercolours of Middle Eastern subjects, including several of the Ottoman Railway. In the late 1860s he concentrated on painting country-house interiors, including those of Knole in Kent and Haddon Hall in Derbyshire. As well as working in full colour, he painted brown wash studies of trees and woods. Two of his landscapes, *Ancient Aqueduct across the River Meles, Smyrna* and *Glen Callater, Aberdeenshire*, are in the Victoria and Albert Museum, London. He published *Lessons on Trees in Water-Colours* (1859) and produced drawings for R. P. Leitch's *Landscape and other Studies in Sepia* (1870). McKewan died on 2 August 1873 at his home, Oakfield House, 11 Upper Park Road, Haverstock Hill in north London. He seems to have combined his painting career with working as a printer.

ANNE PIMLOTT BAKER

Sources Mallalieu, *Watercolour artists*, vols. 1–2 · S. Wilcox and C. Newall, *Victorian landscape watercolors* (1992), 80, 104 [exhibition catalogue, New Haven, CT, Cleveland, OH, and Birmingham, 9 Sept 1992 – 12 April 1993] · Graves, *RA exhibitors* · J. Johnson, ed., *Works exhibited at the Royal Society of British Artists, 1824–1893, and the New English Art Club, 1888–1917*, 2 vols. (1975) · Wood, *Vic. painters*, 3rd edn · L. Lambourne and J. Hamilton, eds., *British watercolours in the Victoria and Albert Museum* (1980) · *DNB* · *CGPLA Eng. & Wales* (1873)

Wealth at death under £30,000: resworn probate, May 1874, CGPLA Eng. & Wales (1873)

Mackgill, James. *See* MacGill, James, of Nether Rankeillour (*d.* 1579).

Mackie, Alastair Webster (1925–1995), poet and teacher, was born at 42 Baker Street, Aberdeen, on 10 August 1925, the son of Frank Mackie (1901–1978), a quarry worker, and his wife, Anne Webster Ross (1900–1961). He was educated at Skene Square primary school from 1930 to 1937 and won a scholarship to Robert Gordon's College, Aberdeen. Immediately after finishing school in 1943 Mackie joined the forces, and served for a few months in the RAF. He then transferred to the Royal Navy, and became a telegraphist on a minesweeper in the Mediterranean. He was demobilized late in 1946 and went directly to Aberdeen University, where he graduated in 1950 with a first-class honours degree in English.

On 11 August 1951 Mackie married Elizabeth Coutts (Bet) Law (*b.* 1929), a library assistant and daughter of Alexander Law (1901–1990), an engineer, and Louisa Lumsden Coutts (1906–1997). They had two daughters. In the same year he became a teacher at Stromness Academy, Orkney. In 1954 George Mackay Brown lent him a copy of Hugh MacDiarmid's *Sangschaw*. Mackie described the experience of 'digesting this key work' as 'like absorbing a mind-bending chemical' (King and Crichton Smith, 79). He began to write poetry in Scots, in the dialect of his Aberdeen childhood. Two of his poems were published in the *Saltire Review* in 1956, but he knew that his range was limited and that he needed 'to extend the word-hoard. I became an archaeologist' (ibid., 80). He trawled an old Scots dictionary, looking for words that 'could be pressed into the service of poetry … [to produce] the paradoxical effect of being at once alien and irreplaceable' (ibid., 80).

In 1959 Mackie was appointed an English teacher at Waid Academy, Anstruther, East Neuk of Fife. Many of his students went on to be writers and journalists, and by all accounts he was 'a teacher of unparalleled inspirational ability' (*The Scotsman*). His poetry meanwhile appeared in issues of *Lines Review* in 1959 and in 1960. For a time, however, discouraged by his lack of success in publication, Mackie gave up writing in Scots in favour of translation from French, Italian, German, and Russian. His first pamphlet, *Soundings* (1966), contained sixteen poems, fourteen in English and two in Scots, written in the late 1950s. Early in August 1967 he began to write original poems in Scots once more. While the first period of his Scots poems was characterized by short, traditional lyrics the second contained sequences of much larger scope. From the publication of *Soundings* his work continued to appear in various periodicals and collections, including

Akros (1967 and 1969), *Contemporary Scottish Verse, 1959–69*, and *The Akros Anthology of Scottish Poetry, 1965–1970*. In May 1972 Mackie published his second collection of poems, *Clytach*, all of which were in Scots. His sequence about a highland journey, *At the Heich Kirk-Yard*, appeared in 1974. *Back-Green Odyssey and other Poems*, accompanied by drawings by his daughter Frances, was published in 1980. In 1983 he took early retirement from teaching. Frances illustrated another collection, *Ingaitherins: Selected Poems* (1987), and a number of his translations were included in *European Poetry in Scotland* (1989), edited by Peter France and Duncan Glen.

Mackie fought an ongoing battle against anxiety and depression; his poems are often gritty and frequently pessimistic, but they can also be comic, and display his talent for the speaking voice. They reflect too his range of learning, his grounding in classical and European as well as British literature. Among his best poems are 'Pieta' and 'Mongol Quine'. 'Scots Pegasus' is only one of many that assert his feelings on the state of Scots as a popular as well as a literary language. In an early article for the Edinburgh University review, *Gambit*, Mackie wrote that 'the question of language is concerned inevitably with the state of Scots culture. A necessary concomitant of writing in Scots is to become aware of what one is, what are one's roots and allegiances' (Mackie, 7). In all his writing he endeavoured to 'extend the scope of Scots poetry as far as it was given to accomplish … it is not by chance that my hero is Odysseus' (King and Crichton Smith, 80). Lines from the first sonnet of *Back-Green Odyssey* display his breadth of vision as well as his down-to-earth, debunking sense of humour:

Ulysses-
dominie, I cast aff the thether-tow
and steer my boat sittin on my doup-end.

Alastair Mackie died at Victoria Hospital, Kirkcaldy, Fife, on 3 June 1995 and was cremated on 8 June 1995. His ashes were interred at Anstruther cemetery. His wife survived him.

JANE POTTER

Sources *The Independent* (11 July 1995) · b. cert. · m. cert. · d. cert. · L. Mason, *Two north-east makars: Alexander Scott and Alastair Mackie: a study of their Scots poetry* (1975) · A. Mackie, 'Och I wish ye hadn't come right now', *Gambit: Edinburgh University Review* (autumn 1965), 6–9 · C. King and I. Crichton Smith, eds., *Twelve more modern Scottish poets* (1986) · *The Scotsman* (15 June 1995) · private information (2004)
Archives NL Scot., corresp. and literary papers, Acc. 11262 | SOUND BL NSA, documentary recording

Mackie, Charles (1688–1770), historian and university teacher, was born at Limekilns, near Dunfermline, Fife, on 31 March 1688, the son of William Mackie (d. 1699), then minister at Portmoak, Kinross-shire, and his wife, Christine (d. 1688), daughter of Magnus Aytoun, clerk at Burntisland. Mackie's mother died when he was six months old, and his father subsequently married Margaret, sister of William Carstares, principal of the University of Edinburgh. Following his father's death in 1699 Mackie is said to have become an intimate in the Carstares household, and his uncle may have overseen his university education,

at Edinburgh, where he matriculated in 1702 and graduated in 1705; at Groeningen, from 1707 to 1708; and at Leiden, in 1715 and later. On 3 February 1726 Mackie married Ann (d. 1770), daughter of Henry Hamilton, an Edinburgh surgeon, and reputed to be the Hamilla of the song 'To Mistress A. H.' in the *Tea Table Miscellany*. They had thirteen children, all of whom died in childhood, the last in 1747.

On 28 August 1719 Edinburgh town council appointed Mackie the first professor of universal history in the university, at a salary of £50 per annum. Initially the appointment was to last only until 1723, but it was permanently extended in 1722. Mackie's duties were extensive and included responsibility for Western history as well as for the history of Scotland, and for Greek, Roman, and British antiquities. Manuscript copies of some of his courses survive. Despite his continuing to lecture in Latin at a time when some others in Scotland were beginning to use English his courses were popular, his annual salary and fees averaging a comfortable £185 during his best years. Mackie taught until 1753, when because of his bad state of health he requested that the town council appoint John Gordon to be his colleague. Within a year, however, Gordon himself resigned, but he was soon replaced by William Wallace, which finally allowed Mackie at least to retire from teaching. In 1765 Wallace became professor of Scots law and Mackie retired completely, leaving sole possession of the chair to his friend John Pringle.

Mackie left no published works that can be certainly identified as his, though there is evidence that he may have written *Antiquitatum romanarum brevis descriptio*. This work possibly was published in the early 1740s, but the only surviving copies are from 1759. A basic set of notes intended for antiquities students, it covers in factual outline Roman religious, civil, and military antiquities, and its topics generally parallel those of a surviving manuscript of Mackie's antiquities lectures ('On Roman antiquities', Edinburgh University Library, MS La.III.758). Throughout his career Mackie was fascinated by chronology. His surviving papers contain numerous chronological notes and schemes, ranging from meticulous lists of the dates of death of public figures (for example, his 'Commonplace book and obituary, 1737–1749', ibid., MS La.III.537), to summaries of Newton's thinking on the subject ('Miscellaneous manuscripts', Edinburgh University Library, MS La.II.37), to his own 'Chronological whim', in which he speculates that important historical events occur in complementary pairs that are equidistant from a central point in time, the birth of Christ ('Miscellaneous notes', MS La.III.253, fol. 2). He seriously considered publishing for his students a table of chronology to supplement N. Lenglet du Fresnoy's *Tablettes chronologiques de l'histoire universelle* (1729), but the project was abandoned in the 1740s. As a working historian Mackie laid greatest emphasis on accuracy, fidelity, and impartiality; 'Truth', he declared in one of his commonplace books, 'is the very soul of history' ('Commonplace books kept', MS Dc.5.24^2). His notes suggest that his approach to history involved the critical examination of sources, the careful evaluation of evidence, and wariness about subjective bias. Perhaps his most typical discussion is 'On the sources of vulgar errors in history' ('Miscellaneous manuscripts', MS La.II.37, fols. 92–104), a paper delivered in 1741 in which he analyses historical prejudices and distortions in light of Francis Bacon's 'idols of the mind'. Mackie does not seem to have given much attention to the construction of historical narrative or to the graces of style, matters that would be left to the next generation, particularly one of his most famous students, William Robertson.

Yet despite this somewhat traditional approach to history Mackie contributed to the more liberal educational atmosphere that emerged in Edinburgh during the 1730s and 1740s. He was a mason of the Canongate-Kilwinning lodge, a member of the Old Revolution Club, and, perhaps most importantly, a member of the Rankenian Club (indeed a copy of William Wishart's inaugural address as principal of the University of Edinburgh survives in Mackie's 'Miscellaneous manuscripts'). Here he joined others besides Wishart—such as Robert Wallace, Colin MacLaurin, and John Stevenson—to help to create a programme of study that would appeal to landed gentlemen, not just clergymen, and emphasize polite learning, civil history, and civic virtue. His long and intimate friendship with Alexander Melville, fourth earl of Leven (which is documented in a large collection of letters), his extensive correspondence with travellers and residents on the continent, plus a list of students that included John Home, Sir Gilbert Eliot, George Dempster, John Erskine of Carnock, Sir Robert Murray Keith, and Sir Andrew Mitchell—all demonstrate Mackie's participation in the evolution occurring in Edinburgh intellectual life.

Mackie died in Edinburgh on 11 September 1770, following his wife, who had died on 1 January. His rather unorganized papers went primarily to Edinburgh University Library, although he also left some money, books, and manuscripts to Joseph Maccormick, 'whom he had patronized and assisted' (Mackie, 'Notebook').

JEFFREY R. SMITTEN

Sources L. Sharp, 'Charles Mackie, the first professor of history at Edinburgh University', *SHR*, 41 (1962), 23–45 · P. Jones, 'The Scottish professoriate and the polite academy, 1720–1746', *Wealth and virtue: the shaping of political economy in the Scottish Enlightenment*, ed. I. Hont and M. Ignatieff (1983), 89–117 · 'Notebook kept by Charles Mackie', U. Edin. L., MS Dc.1.47 · 'Commonplace books kept by Charles Mackie', 2 vols., U. Edin. L., MS Dc.5.24(1), 5.24(2) · 'Letters to Charles Mackie', U. Edin. L., MS La.II.91 · 'Letters to Charles Mackie from Alexander Melville', NA Scot., GD 26/13/602 · C. Mackie, 'Lectures on universal history', U. Edin. L., MS La.III.237 **Archives** NL Scot. · U. Edin. L., corresp. and papers | NA Scot., Melville MSS

McKie, Douglas (1896–1967), historian of science, was born on 15 July 1896 at Ebbw Vale in Monmouthshire, the elder son of James McKie, a Scottish soldier and farmer, and his wife, Janet Moseley. He was educated at Tredegar grammar school and he chose the army for his career. In 1915 he entered the Royal Military College, Sandhurst, for a shortened wartime course and was later commissioned in the South Wales Borderers with whom he served for eighteen months in France until he was severely wounded at Passchendaele in 1917. After many months in hospital he rejoined his regiment at home and was with them in the army of occupation in Germany when he was selected for a staff college course. However, in view of his physical handicap due to his wound he decided to leave the army in 1920. He then entered University College, London, where he read chemistry under F. G. Donnan. While at University College, in 1922, he married Mary, second daughter of Thomas Smith, of Kirkby-la-Thorpe; she had been his wartime nurse. (Their only child, Dr Duncan McKie, a mineralogist, became a fellow of Jesus College, Cambridge.)

After taking his BSc with first-class honours in 1923 McKie spent several years in research at University College, gaining the Ramsay memorial medal (1925) and a PhD (1928). This grounding in experimental scientific research made his subsequent historical studies of the work of the old masters of chemistry realistic and sympathetic. In 1925 he became a part-time assistant to Professor Abraham Wolf in the department of the history and philosophy of science in which he was to spend the next forty years. Later under McKie's stimulating leadership it became the leading centre of that subject in Britain. McKie became lecturer in 1934, reader in 1946, and succeeded to the chair in 1957, retiring as an emeritus professor in 1964.

McKie was never a narrow specialist. He read widely and with his retentive memory and interest in individuals he got a broad perspective of the history of science from the seventeenth century to recent times, and he left an impressive record of books and papers. In spite of their wide coverage they are never superficial as McKie had a quick eye for the significant and for those episodes which played a crucial part in progress. The strength of the school he developed owed much to the example he set in his lectures and writings.

In 1935 McKie published (with N. H. de V. Heathcote) *The Discovery of Specific and Latent Heats*, which led to his lifelong study of the chemist Joseph Black. In the same year there also appeared his *Antoine Lavoisier: the Father of Modern Chemistry*. This led, twenty years later, to his membership of the committee of the French Académie des Sciences responsible for the editing and publishing of Lavoisier's correspondence and laboratory records. McKie devoted much time to the planning of this work, for which he was made a chevalier of the Légion d'honneur in recognition of his services to France. His second book on Lavoisier in 1952 dealt with his public work as an administrator and economist and with his contribution to education as well as with his scientific work. In his last years he was still at work on Lavoisier, collecting material for a definitive life and preparing for publication Lavoisier's laboratory notebooks; both these projects he left unfinished.

In 1936 McKie founded the *Annals of Science*, a journal he edited with scholarly care until his death. Between 1937 and 1939, with J. R. Partington (and in parallel with his early work on Lavoisier's chemistry), he published a series of papers in that journal on phlogiston theory. At this period too, he became involved in a study of a remarkable precursor of Lavoisier and eventually published in 1951 a facsimile reprint, with critical introduction, of *The Essays of Jean Rey*.

Shortly before his death McKie published his edition of Thomas Cochrane's *Notes from Doctor Black's Lectures on Chemistry, 1767/8* (1966). The various manuscript versions of Black's lectures had been the subject of a series of papers, part of the material which McKie had been collecting for years for the first full-length portrait of the influential Scottish chemist. McKie had traced Black's missing correspondence and all the background work had been done when illness overtook him.

McKie's rich store of knowledge and his critical judgement were always available to his friends. The planning of the tercentenary volume *The Royal Society: its Origins and Founders* (1960) owed much to his advice. He contributed to it the opening article, 'The origins and foundation of the Royal Society of London'. He also contributed the chapter on science and technology to the *New Cambridge Modern History*.

McKie's services to the history of science were manifold. Many historians were trained under his watchful eye. He was proud of his Scottish ancestry and his election into the Royal Society of Edinburgh in 1958 gave him special pleasure. He was also a fellow of University College, London, of the Royal Institute of Chemistry, of the Royal Society of Arts, and of the Society of Antiquaries. In 1963 the division of the history of chemistry of the American Chemical Society gave McKie the Dexter award in recognition of his international eminence as a scholar. McKie had a serious operation in 1964 and died in London on 28 August 1967.   HAROLD HARTLEY, rev.

Sources WWW · CGPLA Eng. & Wales (1968) · Annals of Science, 24 (1968), 1–5 · The Times (31 Aug 1967) · private information (1981) · personal knowledge (1981)

Wealth at death £22,693: probate, 29 May 1968, CGPLA Eng. & Wales

M'Kie [McKie], **James** (1816–1891), publisher, was born at Kilmarnock, Ayrshire, on 7 October 1816, reputedly the illegitimate son of James M'Kie, carpet weaver, and Elizabeth Boyd (later Elizabeth Brown). He was apprenticed to the publisher Hugh Crawford, the successor of John Wilson, printer of the Kilmarnock edition of Burns's poems. In 1839 he set up business for himself, publishing *The Ayrshire Inspirer*, a weekly periodical devoted to poetry; priced at a penny, it ran for ten numbers. In 1842 he gathered material from Kilmarnock's leading literary figures and published at his own expense a literary annual, *The Ayrshire Wreath*, which continued for three years, with a circulation between 1000 and 1500, and which intensified his 'hobby for local literature' (M'Kie, *Title Pages*, i). On 8 March 1844 he married Agnes Jane Crawford (or Drennan), and in that year he acquired Hugh Crawford's business and began to develop his own career as a publisher, embarking as proprietor of a series of newspapers, including the *Kilmarnock Journal* (1846) and the *Kilmarnock Weekly Post* (1856–65). His business empire also included more lucrative regular printing contracts, including titles such as *The Kilmarnock and Riccarton Directory*, *Names of Paupers: Kilmarnock Town and Parish*, and *Kilmarnock Sabbath School*

Union, as well as annual reports of charitable institutions such as the ragged school and the fever hospital in Kilmarnock.

In 1866 M'Kie turned his attention to his growing interest in the literary works of Robert Burns and, feeding off the passion for Burns's poetry throughout Britain, published a facsimile of the Kilmarnock edition, which proved to be a great commercial success. In addition to the 'standard' trade edition of the facsimile, he issued, in partnership with the London booksellers Willis and Sotheran, a large-paper edition of the facsimile, at 2 guineas, which was issued together with the first catalogue of his own substantial collection of Burnsiana, *Title Pages (and Imprints) of the Books in the Private Library of James M'Kie, Kilmarnock* (1867). In 1871 he further capitalized on the interest in Burns, issuing the Kilmarnock 'popular' edition and, in 1886, the Kilmarnock 'centenary' edition. As a collector of Burnsiana in his lifetime, M'Kie was without equal. He began collecting in 1843 and soon had to enlarge his house to accommodate the books, and he soon began to attract visitors interested in making use of the collection. In 1882 the local Burns Club made a move to purchase it, and the library was duly acquired from M'Kie and deposited in the Museum of the Burns Monument in Kilmarnock. The collection has since been partially dispersed, but a large portion remains in the Dick Institute, Kilmarnock. After his first wife's death he married Dorothy Tyson, who survived him. He died in Kilmarnock on 26 September 1891, having lived latterly at Alpha Cottage, West Park Lane, Kilmarnock.   RICHARD OVENDEN

Sources D. Sneddon, ed., Catalogue of the M'Kie Burnsiana Library (1909) · J. M'Kie, Title pages (and imprints) of the books in the private library of James M'Kie, Kilmarnock (1867) [privately printed] · Catalogue of the McKie Burnsiana Library with a list of the subscribers (privately printed, Kilmarnock, 1883) · Bibliotheca Burnsiana (1866) [privately printed] · m. reg. Scot. [J. McKie and A. J. Crawford] · bap. reg. Scot. · register of deaths

Archives Dick Institute, Kilmarnock, collection

Likenesses albumen print, c.1867, NL Scot.; repro. in M'Kie, Title pages, frontispiece

Wealth at death £264 4s. 2d.: confirmation, 30 Nov 1891, CCI

Mackie, James (1864–1943), manufacturer of textile machinery, was born on 6 October 1864 at Belfast, the eldest of the four children of James Mackie (d. 1887), a manufacturer of linen machinery, and his wife, Mary (née Millar). His father was Scottish, his mother Irish. James senior had come to Ireland from Forfar in 1845 to install a steam engine in a linen mill in Drogheda. His work impressed the foreman, James Scrimgeour, and when the latter established a foundry and engineering works in Belfast, Mackie became manager. Later Scrimgeour offered him a partnership, which he declined, deciding simply to invest money in the business; so when the firm went bankrupt in 1858 Mackie was not liable for its debts. Although he lost money, he managed to purchase the company's Albert Street premises and some of its equipment and began repairing machinery. With the cotton famine of the 1860s there was an increase in linen production and a consequent rise in demand for new machines and for the servicing of existing stock. Thus when the younger James was born his father's business was expanding. However, when the boom ended in the 1870s, the firm survived only by rigid economies.

James Mackie received only an elementary education, at Belfast model school on the Falls Road. He entered the business in 1874, and continued his education at Queen Street Mechanics' Institute (later to become Belfast College of Technology). The firm remained small, specializing in mill machinery renovations and accepting contracts for dismantling and re-erecting textile plants. In 1884 James became a junior partner in the business and, when his father died in 1887, he succeeded in partnership with his younger brother Thomas (1870–1956). Shortly afterwards James married Elizabeth Pringle (d. 1940); they had five sons and a daughter. In the business, Thomas supervised the production side, while James was responsible for sales. He travelled widely in central and eastern Europe gaining orders and in 1895 established contacts in Russia. Increasingly the Mackies moved from repair work towards the manufacture of a wide range of linen machinery. In 1893 the company acquired a site on Belfast's Springfield Road, which, although greatly enlarged after 1919, remained its location until 1992. The business expanded steadily, producing wet-spinning frames and flax-preparing machinery. In 1897 Mackies became a limited company and in 1902 it took over Clonard foundry, bringing in John Horner, the previous owner, to the board. Together Mackies and Horner developed a revolutionary hackling machine, embodying a differential drive and grouping of metal pins to comb the flax.

In the pre-war boom the company expanded rapidly. In 1907 it was one of the first firms in the city to electrify and in 1911, together with Sir Otto Jaffe, linen merchant and former lord mayor of Belfast, diversified by acquiring McTears' spinning works in east Belfast. Later, as the Strand Spinning Company, this became wholly owned by Mackies. At this time the firm employed around 350 men. After 1914 the company went over to making munitions; its labour force rose to 650 and its premises were extended. From 1920 the linen industry declined and the business looked to other markets. It experimented in producing jute machinery, building a mill on its Springfield site to test the products; this also provided additional income as the resulting yarn was exported. By 1929 jute equipment was Mackies' most important product.

The business was highly export-orientated; by the end of the 1930s its overseas staff totalled 110 in a workforce of 2000, and covered 52 countries. This complex operation was headed by James Mackie. The firm became one of the world's leading suppliers of sisal and hard-fibre spinning machinery, and were pioneers in developing a complete range of products for processing jute. It was among the first to adopt package arrangements for establishing factories overseas, taking responsibility for planning, supplying, and installing equipment, and starting up production.

After 1939 the firm moved again into munitions, such as armour-piercing shells, hand grenades, and aircraft parts. In certain specialized projectiles, nine per cent of national requirements came from Mackies. The firm expanded dramatically. By 1944 the labour force, hitherto almost exclusively male, had increased to 12,000, 7200 of them women; another 8000 worked in associated Mackie organizations. That year the company's nominal capital was still £156,000, a figure bearing no relation to the firm's true value.

Throughout its development Mackies remained a private family controlled company. James continued as managing director until his death, although by 1939 Thomas Mackie (appointed CBE in 1942) was primarily responsible for the day-to-day running of the firm. Mackies' success was based on both technical awareness, prudent finance, and the reinvestment of profits. The brothers lived frugally (their sons, for example, received further education at Belfast Technical College rather than at university). The company's finances also benefited greatly from the two wars. After 1945 the business continued to prosper, with markets in both eastern and western Europe moving from jute towards machinery for wool and man-made fibres.

James Mackie had many outside business interests, particularly through directorships in the linen industry, in firms such as the Ulster Spinning Company and the Rosebank Weaving Company. His public offices were few: deputy lieutenant for Belfast, JP for co. Antrim, and for six years a member of Belfast Harbour Board. He died at a nursing home, The Retreat, Armagh, on 12 April 1943, and was buried at Belfast city cemetery on the 14th. He was succeeded as managing director by his brother Thomas, and by his sons James and John. DAVID JOHNSON

Sources A. S. Moore, 'A history of the Belfast engineering firm of Jas. Mackie & Sons Ltd., written to celebrate its centenary', 1946, Belfast City Library, A. S. Moore Collection, G1 · Belfast City Library, A. S. Moore Collection · *Belfast News-Letter* (13 April 1943) · *Northern Whig and Belfast Post* (13 April 1943) · *Belfast and Northern Ireland Directory* (1897–1943) · W. E. Coe, *The engineering industry of the north of Ireland* (1969) · B. Whyte, 'Mackies, the myth and the millions', *Belfast Telegraph* (15 Dec 1976) · Registrar general (NI) · Belfast city council, cemetery department
Archives Belfast City Library, A. S. Moore collection
Wealth at death £111,155: will, PRO NIre., no. 1125

Mackie, John (1748–1831), physician, the eldest of a family of fifteen children, was born at Dunfermline Abbey in Fife. He was educated by his uncle Andrew Donaldson and also studied under Dr John Stedman. In 1763 he began studying medicine at Edinburgh, and after leaving the university he settled at Huntingdon. In 1784 he married Dorothea Sophia Des Champs (d. 1819), the eldest daughter of John Des Champs, rector of Rilesden, Dorset, and chaplain to the queen of Prussia; they had a son and a daughter. Dorothea translated the *Letters of Madame de Sévigné* into English (1802).

About 1792 Mackie moved to Southampton, and practised there with great success until 1814, when he left for a ten-year tour of the continent. During his travels he practised medicine only occasionally, but numbered among his patients the queen of Spain, the former king of the Netherlands, and other persons of rank. In 1819 he printed anonymously at Vevey for private distribution a *Sketch of a New Theory of Man*, which was translated into French, and reprinted in English in 1822. On his return to England, after passing several winters in Bath, he moved to Chichester, where he died on 29 January 1831 at the age of eighty-three. He was buried in the village churchyard of West Hampnett, near Chichester.

Mackie was a religious man and a dedicated member of the Church of England, notwithstanding his Scottish parentage and education. He was described as being generous to his patients, and while at Southampton he showed great kindness to numerous French emigrants. He was fond of reading, and was very popular in society. The novelist Laetitia-Matilda Hawkins, in her *Memoirs, Anecdotes, Facts and Opinions* (1824), considered him to be a pleasant conversationalist.

W. A. GREENHILL, *rev.* KAYE BAGSHAW

Sources *GM*, 1st ser., 101/2 (1831), 276–80 · L.-M. Hawkins, *Memoirs, anecdotes, facts and opinions*, 2 vols. (1824), vol. 1, p. 310
Likenesses G. Engleheart, miniature, 1784 · Slater, watercolour drawing, 1808 · S. Freeman, stipple, 1830 (after M. Moore, 1830), Wellcome L. · M. Moore, portrait, 1830 · G. Glaser, stipple (after A. Penley), Wellcome L.

Mackie, John, Baron John-Mackie (1909–1994), farmer and politician, was born on 24 November 1909 at North Ythsie, Tarves, Aberdeenshire, one of six children and the second of three sons of Maitland Mackie, farmer, and his wife, Mary Ann, *née* Yull. His father came from a prosperous Scottish farming family, with extensive holdings in Aberdeenshire and Essex. After Aberdeen high school, Mackie went to the North of Scotland College of Agriculture, where he concurrently gained practical experience as a grieve on both arable and mainly stock family farms. On 6 June 1934 he married Jeannie Inglis Milne (*b.* 1910/11), daughter of Robert Milne, farmer, of Farnell, Angus. They had three sons and two daughters. In 1939 Mackie was elected a member of the Aberdeen and Kincardine agricultural executive committee, and in 1942 he was made a governor of the North of Scotland College of Agriculture. For the next twenty-two years, until he became a minister of the crown, college policy was one of his central interests; in particular, he was a protagonist in the cause of allocating resources to the study of diseases in livestock. In 1949 he was made a governor of the National Institute of Agricultural Engineering.

Mackie's political career was ignited in 1952, when he scored a memorable success at the Labour Party conference in Morecambe by delivering a passionate plea for land nationalization. Morecambe was one of Labour's most depressing conferences, and Mackie's speech was one of the few moments which produced real enthusiasm. Along with a group of other big farmers, such as Wilfred Cave and Henry Walston, Mackie was committed both to socialism and to applying modern methods to farming. In this campaign they carried much credibility with the rank and file of the Labour Party, as it became known that they paid those who worked on their farms wages substantially above the going rate.

Having been a token Labour candidate in October 1951 in the hopeless North Angus and Mearns constituency, Mackie was chosen to be Labour's standard-bearer in Lanark, which had been Jennie Lee's seat. He lost to Patrick Maitland at the general election of 1955 by 958 votes. Mackie almost despaired of ever finding a Labour seat. However, both his interest in health—he had been chair of the Aberdeen and Kincardine health executive committee (1948–51)—and the fact that he had fought their beloved Lanark, brought Mackie into friendship with Aneurin Bevan and his wife, Jennie Lee, who had acquired a small farm in Buckinghamshire, about which Mackie gave them a lot of good advice. Their public endorsement helped to win him the nomination for the safe Labour seat of Enfield East, which he won in October 1959.

Mackie's views were not simply vaguely Labour, as was the case with a number of rich contemporaries, but determinedly left-wing socialist. In 1958, in a much discussed Fabian pamphlet, he argued the case for land nationalization. He contended that few of the old estates were still functioning really well. There was the problem of new landlords, such as investment trusts and insurance companies. There was entailed land, held by solicitors on behalf of far-off relations of the previous owners. A lot of land was held by wealthy businessmen purely to save death duties; it was usually badly managed. Mackie's credo was that it should be let by the state to those who could farm it well. One reason for state ownership was to get full production from the land, and this, Mackie contended, could only be achieved if farmers were adequately trained. In the late 1950s such thinking was appealing to the vast majority of active members of the Labour Party.

Mackie served as joint parliamentary under-secretary at the Ministry of Agriculture, Fisheries and Food throughout the first and second Wilson governments, from October 1964 to June 1970. He and his fellow under-secretary James Hay were among the very few junior ministers who were not involved in the ministerial merry-go-round. They were perceived as round pegs in round holes. Mackie travelled widely on official business, and his good humour was widely credited with defusing tensions with Argentina in March 1968, after the Reid committee had blamed Argentine mutton, imported into Britain, for a virulent outbreak of foot-and-mouth disease. Mackie became an opposition spokesman on agriculture following the Conservative election victory in June 1970. Deeply pro-European, he was one of 69 Labour MPs who accompanied Ted Heath into the pro-Common Market lobby on 28 October 1971. In the act of voting against his party, Mackie was literally in tears. Differences with his constituency activists over Europe were one factor in his decision to retire from parliament at the February 1974 general election.

Mackie served as a successful chairman of the Forestry Commission, from 1976 to 1979, but was replaced by the incoming Conservative government. He was made a life peer in 1981, as Baron John-Mackie of Nazeing. In the House of Lords—where he joined his younger brother George, Baron Mackie of Benshie (*b.* 1919), who had briefly served as Liberal MP for Caithness and Sutherland, from 1964 to 1966—he was an opposition whip and spokesman on agriculture from 1983 to 1988. He died of heart failure at his home, Harold's Park Farm, Nazeing, Essex, on 26 May 1994. He was survived by his wife and their five children.   TAM DALYELL

Sources *The Independent* (27 May 1994) · *The Times* (27 May 1994) · *WWW*, 1991–5 · personal knowledge (2004) · private information (2004) · b. cert. · m. cert. · d. cert.
Archives NRA, priv. coll., papers in private possession
Likenesses photograph, repro. in *The Independent* · photograph, repro. in *The Times*

Mackie, John Leslie (1917–1981), philosopher, was born on 25 August 1917 in Sydney, New South Wales, Australia, the younger of the two children of Alexander Mackie (1876–1956), principal of Sydney Teachers' College, and his wife, Annie Burnett Duncan (1888–1973), a schoolteacher. He was educated at Knox grammar school, Sydney, and the University of Sydney (1935–8), where he gained first-class honours in Greek and Latin, with a high distinction, and the G. S. Caird scholarship in philosophy. Winning the Wentworth scholarship, he went to Oriel College, Oxford (1938–41), where he was awarded first-class honours in *literae humaniores*.

After war service in the Royal Electrical and Mechanical Engineers (REME) in the Middle East and Italy (he was mentioned in dispatches), Mackie joined the department of moral and political philosophy in the University of Sydney as lecturer in 1946; he was promoted to senior lecturer in 1951. In 1947 he married Joan Armiger Meredith (*b.* 1925), a Sydney graduate and civil servant; they had three daughters and two sons. In 1955 he became professor of philosophy in the University of Otago, New Zealand, but returned to Sydney in 1959 as Challis professor of philosophy in succession to his former teacher John Anderson. He left Australia in 1963 to take up an appointment as the first occupant of the chair of philosophy in the University of York, which he held until 1967, when he was elected a fellow of University College, Oxford, as praelector (tutor) in philosophy, and from 1978 as professorial fellow in conjunction with his appointment to an *ad hominem* readership in Oxford University. He also held a visiting appointment at the University of Minnesota. He was a Radcliffe philosophy fellow in 1971–3, and he was elected a fellow of the British Academy in 1974.

Mackie had an enormous breadth of philosophical concerns; almost nothing was outside his scope, from ancient philosophy to decision theory. It was characteristic of him that, having been given Richard Dawkins's *The Selfish Gene* as a suitable Christmas present for someone with general intellectual interests, he worked up an article about it. He wrote many papers, on a great range of philosophical topics; some of them were collected after his death in two volumes of *Selected Works* (1985). His first book, *Truth, Probability, and Paradox* (1973), is essentially still in the article mode, though the essays that comprise it are linked not only in subject matter but also methodologically, by a faith in the power of 'fairly simple, common-sense, perhaps old-fashioned ways of thinking' to resolve philosophical difficulties, and a suspicion that technical procedures in philosophy are more likely to confuse than to illuminate. Mackie was here characteristically resisting

an American-inspired trend in the philosophy of language; his faith in plain, untechnical common sense shaped all his philosophical work. *The Cement of the Universe* (1974) is an elaboration and defence of a fundamentally empiricist conception of causation. *Problems from Locke* (1976) works sympathetically through a number of central issues discussed by a philosopher whose 'plain man' stance Mackie found congenial. In *Ethics: Inventing Right and Wrong* (1977), perhaps his most widely known work, Mackie argues that ordinary ethical thinking embodies a false conception of values and obligations as real denizens of the world, found rather than—as the subtitle indicates that we should suppose—invented. The book's main aim is to give an account of how ethical thinking should proceed, once disabused of this metaphysical error, but most of the attention it has attracted has been focused on the metaphysical thesis itself; the work has been influential in giving new life to the question of truth in ethics, which had gone out of fashion under the influence of emotivism and prescriptivism. *Hume's Ethical Theory* (1980) gives a reading of Hume as a precursor of Mackie's own approach to moral philosophy. His last book, *The Miracle of Theism* (1982), was in press when Mackie died: it contains a critical treatment of a number of standard positions in the philosophy of religion, as viewed from the standpoint of Mackie's own uncompromising empiricism.

The main strengths and weaknesses of Mackie's philosophical work can be directly linked to his sympathy for empiricism, his faith in common sense, and the shining clarity of his thinking. Any suggestion that philosophy can be intractably difficult aroused his suspicion; such conceptions struck him as probably indicative of someone's being led astray by his own means of expression or, less innocently, of someone's trying to give an illusory impression of depth. Mackie's own writing is fluent and unpretentiously lucid; it puts everything in the open. Philosophical activity as he conceives it aims to get problems straightforwardly formulated, and to solve them by applying rational powers that belong to, or at least are continuous with, common sense. This yields work that is a model of clear reasonableness and intellectual honesty. But such an approach is better suited to some areas of philosophy than to others. Even within empiricism, there are strands in Hume that are alien to a conception of philosophy according to which all difficulties can in principle take the form of questions answerable by a sober exercise of rationality. And in spite of Mackie's catholicity of philosophical interests, it is hard to imagine him setting out to write books called *Problems from Kant* or *Problems from Wittgenstein*. He did discuss both those philosophers, but he was constitutionally less at home with them than with Locke and the more Lockean side of Hume.

Mackie was short in stature and slight in build, and typically quiet, even reserved, in demeanour, though philosophical discussion could excite him into a staccato 'But, but, but!' He was a private person, and few outside his family thought they knew him well. He was a patient and conscientious teacher, and a wise and selfless colleague. He had no interest in academic politics, but dutifully did his part in keeping the several institutions he belonged to running smoothly. His increasing eminence in philosophy made no difference to his unassuming style; he was apparently without vanity. He was a tireless participant in philosophical argument, on virtually any topic. He died in Oxford, of cancer, on 12 December 1981, and was cremated in Oxford after a funeral service in University College. His wife survived him.   JOHN McDOWELL

Sources J. McDowell, 'John Leslie Mackie', *PBA*, 76 (1990), 487–98 · personal knowledge (2004) · private information (2004) · G. L. Cawkwell and S. Blackburn, 'Memorial addresses', *University College record* (1982) · *CGPLA Eng. & Wales* (1982)
Likenesses photograph, British Academy; repro. in McDowell, 'John Leslie Mackie', 488
Wealth at death under £25,000: administration with will, 5 Feb 1982, *CGPLA Eng. & Wales*

Mackie, Sir Peter Jeffrey, first baronet (1855–1924), distiller, was born on 26 November 1855 at Corsepatrick, St Ninians, Stirlingshire, son of Alexander Mackie (1821–1884), farmer, grain merchant, and distiller, and his wife, Janet Simpson-Brown. His grandfather and great-grandfather had been proprietors of the Dunmore Park estate in Stirlingshire; other earlier Mackies had worked in the wine and spirit trades. James Logan Mackie, an uncle, co-owned the Lagavulin distillery in Islay, and it was to his firm, James L. Mackie & Co., that Peter Mackie was recruited in 1878, some years after the end of his formal education at Stirling high school.

Lagavulin, a dark, island malt of great distinction, sold well as a 'self' (or unblended) whisky. It was, however, through blending—the dilution of taste and cost through mixing partly malted grain spirit with traditional wholly malted barley liquor—that wider marketing lay. In the mid-1880s Peter Mackie became a partner in the new firm of Mackie & Co., which had offices in London with the objective of increasing sales of Lagavulin and other producers' blends. The two businesses amalgamated in 1890 to form Mackie & Co. (Distillers), and made the critical decision to use Lagavulin (with additional purchased malts) for a blend of their own—called White Horse after an inn on the Edinburgh Canongate, adjacent to property owned by the Mackie family since the seventeenth century. In 1895, on J. L. Mackie's retirement, the firm became a private limited company under Peter Mackie's chairmanship. He remained in charge until his death in 1924, his last years being marked by an abortive bid (1920–23) to unite with Buchanan-Dewar, and the decision (1924) to convert to a public company, White Horse Distillers Ltd.

In a conservative trade like whisky, with premiums on tradition and predictability, success lay less with technical innovation (where Mackie certainly experimented) than with effective organization and marketing. Mackie remained cautious organizationally, favouring independent status and related opportunities for personal authority and family recruitment. In sales promotion, however, he worked with vigour, widening the range of blends (Gaelic Old Smuggler, Logan's Perfection, Greyhound, and others), building a name for quality and reliability, and

coming to rank in the industry's 'big five'. The company declared in 1914 that it 'never … used nor ever will use second-rate materials' (*Field*, 14 Feb 1914), refusing to 'cater for the cheap trade' (*Daily Mail*). Mackie's efforts, aided by costly advertising, were particularly successful in imperial markets, most of which he inspected for himself. He also extended his distilling base, adding an old-fashioned malt mill at Lagavulin, and moving into Speyside, where he took control of Craigellachie-Glenlivet between 1890 and 1900 and secured half-ownership of Craggenmore in 1921. The Hazelburn distillery at Campbeltown, Argyll, and Holloway's gin distillery at Kennington, London, were bought shortly after the First World War. More extreme diversifications—all abandoned when 'restless Peter' died—produced carragheen seaweed, tweed, concrete slabs, and BBM (brain, bone, and muscle) flour.

Outside the whisky business, and in line with his paternal ancestry, Mackie assumed the perspectives of the landed classes. In 1889 he married his cousin, Jessie Lockett Abercrombie, and their two surviving daughters, Isobel and Mary, took husbands from the lesser aristocracy (Logan, their only son, was killed in action outside Jerusalem in 1917). Estates (and accompanying magistracies) were acquired at Corraith, near Symington, Ayrshire, and Glenreasdell, in north Kintyre, the one at Corraith holding a modest library and an art collection of catholic taste. In 1903, with A. Stodart Walker and some additional contributors, he produced *The Keeper's Book*, a substantial volume on the duties of a gamekeeper, which had gone through fourteen editions by 1920. Since his Islay days Mackie had maintained a strong interest in highland affairs, inclining towards tariff reform as a means of checking depopulation. He was a determined tory, serving briefly as president of the Scottish Unionist Association. Socialism he dismissed as 'a clever device of weaklings and dupes of Society, whose heart instead of their head rules their actions' (*DSBB*). In 1909 he rounded on Lloyd George's raised duties on spirits, and later held office in both the Whisky Association and the Licensed Victuallers' Association. Imperial sentiment underlay his gift of pedigree cattle to Rhodesia and his sponsorship of the Mackie anthropological expedition to central Africa. In 1920 he was awarded a baronetcy.

Peter Mackie was a tall, sparely built man, favouring highland dress at home and a monocle and 'low-crowned "topper" of a slightly rakish cut' in London (*Evening News*). Robert Bruce Lockhart describes him as a mix of genius, megalomania, and eccentricity. By his own testimony, 'efficiency' was his motto, 'grit' his favourite word, and 'hard and long work' his explanation for White Horse's success (*Daily Sketch*; Walker, 9; Distillers Co. Ltd, 45). He died at Corraith on 22 September 1924 after a long illness.   W. M. MATHEW

Sources White Horse MSS, United Distillers Archive, Leven, Fife · *Daily Mail* (7 Feb 1914) · *The Field* (14 Feb 1914) · *Evening News* (8 June 1920) · *Daily Sketch* (13 July 1920) · N. J. Morgan, Heritage notes: the Mackie family, Peter Mackie, and the development of the White Horse brand, 25 Sept 1991, United Distillers Archive, Leven, Fife ·

United Distillers Archive, Leven, Fife, Photocopies of Mackie family letters and photographs · White Horse sales figures, United Distillers Archive, Leven, Fife · M. Moss, 'Mackie, Sir Peter Jeffrey', *DSBB* · A. S. Walker, *James Logan Mackie Younger of Glenreasdell, lieutenant Ayrshire yeomanry: a memoir* (1919) · A. S. Walker and P. J. Mackie, *The keeper's book: a guide to the duties of a gamekeeper* (1903) · Distillers Company Ltd, *DCL and Scotch whisky* (1966) · Sir R. B. Lockhart, *The whisky of Scotland in fact and story* (1951) · B. Spiller, *The chameleon's eye: James Buchanan & Company Limited, 1884–1984* (1984) · R. Weir, 'Rationalization and diversification in the Scotch whisky industry, 1900–1939: another look at "old" and "new" industries', *Economic History Review*, 2nd ser., 42 (1989), 375–95

Archives United Distillers Archive, Leven, Fife, White Horse MSS

Likenesses photographs, 1901–12, repro. in Walker, *James Logan Mackie Younger of Glenreasdell, lieutenant Ayrshire yeomanry*, 7 · photographs, United Distillers Archive, Leven, Fife, White Horse MSS

Wealth at death £525,641 14s. 1d.: confirmation, 18 Dec 1924, *CCI*

McKie, Sir William Neil (1901–1984), church musician, was born on 22 May 1901 in Melbourne, Australia, the second son (the first died in infancy) in the family of three sons and three daughters of the Revd William McKie, vicar of St Philip's, Collingwood, and his wife, Mary, daughter of James Doyle, journalist. His mother was one of the earliest women graduates of Melbourne University, which gave degrees to women before Oxford and Cambridge began to do so. Both parents were Australian-born, but all four grandparents had emigrated from Ireland in the 1850s, after one of McKie's grandfathers had been imprisoned, with other members of the Young Ireland party, on a charge of sedition, of which he was acquitted.

At Melbourne grammar school McKie was taught by Arthur Nickson, a pupil of Sir Walter Parratt. In 1921, after a year at the Royal College of Music under Henry Ley, he won the organ scholarship at Worcester College, Oxford, of which he was later to be an honorary fellow (1954). He gained his BMus in 1924.

During vacations McKie used sometimes to act as assistant to Noel Ponsonby at Ely Cathedral, where he gained his first insights into the disciplines of cathedral music. An even stronger influence, however, was that of Sir Hugh Allen, at the time sceptical about cathedral music, and inclined to channel his abler apprentices into school music, or administration, rather than church music. McKie, accordingly, after a short probationary period at Radley College (1923–6), went to Clifton College (1926–30) for five years as director of music. By nature, however, he was a performer rather than an administrator, and in 1931 he decided to return as city organist to Melbourne, where he soon won recognition as an outstanding player and personality.

In 1938, on the retirement of H. C. Stewart, McKie was appointed to succeed him as organist of Magdalen College, Oxford, where he stayed for two years, devoting himself almost exclusively to college music and to the development of his own skills, particularly as choir trainer, in which he excelled. His standards were exacting and his methods rigorous, but he won the affection of his choristers and he was happy in the work, except for occasional brushes with college dons, notably C. S. Lewis, who disapproved of the choral services and resented the cost of their upkeep.

In 1941, after Ernest Bullock was bombed out of Westminster, McKie was called to take his place. It was a tragic time for Westminster Abbey. The music establishment had been dispersed, its future was uncertain, and McKie himself was of military age, due to be absent until further notice with the Royal Air Force Volunteer Reserve. Not until 1946 was he able to begin the great task of rebuilding the abbey's musical tradition. His main aim, in this single-minded effort, was to maintain unvaryingly high standards in the daily services, and to modernize the technique, style, and repertory of the choir. Such was his perfectionism that he was known to cancel an anthem moments before the beginning of a service if its rehearsal displeased him. He was successful in his efforts, in spite of some opposition and frequent disruption of his plans by the obligation to provide, sometimes at short notice, music for royal and state occasions. Of these the most demanding was the coronation of 1953, whose music (including Vaughan Williams's anthem 'O taste and see', commissioned for the occasion by McKie) was well chosen, brilliantly performed, and highly praised. It was largely in recognition of this achievement that McKie was knighted that year. Some years earlier, in 1944, Oxford had made him an honorary DMus, and in 1948 he was appointed MVO. He was also FRSCM, FRCM, FRCO, FTCL, and honorary member of the Royal Academy of Music.

The claims of his work at the abbey did not prevent McKie from taking an active part in London music. He taught at the Royal Academy of Music (1946–62), and in 1956–8 served as president of the Royal College of Organists. He also composed some unpretentious but distinguished church music, and greatly helped many young musicians who came within his influence.

McKie was a fine-looking man, masterful in bearing, with strong features and a jutting chin that gave the impression of formidable authority and self-confidence. But the cost of sustaining this appearance was high for, especially in early life, McKie was diffident, anxious, and liable to severe depression. More than once, in his time at the abbey, he admitted to being close to breakdown. But his unexpected marriage on 5 April 1956, at the age of nearly fifty-five, greatly strengthened him. His wife, Phyllis, daughter of John Wardrope Ross, of Montreal, and widow of Gerald Walker Birks, a Canadian businessman, was a lady of great charm and character, under whose influence his social life broadened. He became more confident and relaxed, better able to believe that he was admired and indeed loved. Even so, he remained what he had always been, a shy and reserved man, most at home in the company of a few friends, preferably male, as critical as himself, and not necessarily musicians.

After retirement from the abbey in 1963 the McKies went to live in Ottawa where Lady McKie had many connections, and for a time William continued to take part in musical activities. But his health was declining, and some time before his wife's death in 1983, he was admitted to hospital suffering from Alzheimer's disease, from which he died in Ottawa on 1 December 1984. There were no children. THOMAS ARMSTRONG, *rev.*

Sources personal knowledge (1990) · private information (1990, 2004) · *The Times* (14 Dec 1984) · *New Grove* · m. cert.
Likenesses group portrait, photograph, 1947, Hult. Arch. · B. Hardy, photograph, 1953, Hult. Arch.

McKillop [*née* Seward], **Margaret** (1864–1929), scientist and university teacher, was born on 22 January 1864 at 23 Church Street, Wigan, Lancashire, the daughter of James Seward, a schoolmaster at the Liverpool Institute, and his wife, Sarah Jane Woodgates. She was educated at Blackburne House school, Liverpool, and Somerville Hall, Oxford, where she held the Gilchrist exhibition and the Reinagle scholarship, jointly worth £80 a year, which enabled her to complete her studies. She lacked neither social confidence nor academic ability, and a Somerville contemporary, Frances Elizabeth Sheldon, remembered her as 'our calm, sensible but witty Miss Seward, the smartest girl in England' (Sheldon, letter to her mother, 2 Feb 1883). In October 1884 she became the first woman at Oxford entered for the honour school of mathematics, gaining a second class; and in 1885 she became the first to gain a first class in the final honour school of natural science (chemistry). As Oxford women were not yet permitted to graduate, she proceeded to her MA in 1905 at Trinity College, Dublin, which had admitted women to full membership in the previous year.

By then Seward had been teaching for twenty years. After her final exams in 1885 she stayed on as a resident science tutor at Somerville. Her duties included chaperoning undergraduates, a convention taken very seriously in the early days of women at Oxford. Some male dons found the practice as unwelcome as did the chaperones themselves, and when the eminent Christ Church chemist A. G. Vernon Harcourt made known his strong objections, Seward carried out her own research elsewhere in his laboratory, while her charge, Miss Florence Rich, attended his class. In 1887 Seward took up the post of lecturer in chemistry at Royal Holloway College, where she remained until 1891, when her marriage to John McKillop, a civil engineer, entailed a move to Singapore. After three or four years they returned to England with their only child, Alasdair. She next taught at Bradford Girls' Grammar School and Roedean School before, in 1897, becoming lecturer in chemistry at the ladies' department of King's College, in the University of London (renamed the women's department in 1902, and becoming King's College for Women in 1908). She was made a fellow in February 1911 and remained at King's until 1915.

In June 1899 McKillop represented theoretical science as a profession at the International Congress of Women, held in London. She recognized a natural tendency among the scientists present 'to exalt one's own 'ology as the very one for women' and also a 'general and hearty appreciation of the kindness received by women students from scientific men'. She nevertheless came away with a poor view of her subject 'as offering "openings" for college women students' (*Somerville Students' Association Report*,

Nov 1899, 20). Her determination to change this was given full scope at King's, where she played an important part in the development of 'home and social science' as an academic discipline, modelled on the professional training given in medicine, agriculture, and engineering. The progress of 'domestic science' was given impetus by the Edwardian interest in reform of the home as a social institution, and by the increasing demand for women teachers, school and factory inspectors, and health visitors. In 1908 a three-year course in 'home and social science' was begun at King's, and in the following year McKillop contributed a short article on its progress to the Somerville Students' Association annual report, citing the demand from headmistresses for the 'new sort of domestic science teacher' (*Somerville Students' Association Report*, Oct 1909, 48). McKillop defined this as someone who taught science applicable to the home, a 'practical-minded woman' who was also a good form teacher, but she accepted that headmistresses were 'a little inclined to expect a first class chemist combined with a first class cook, who can also take odd sciences and other subjects throughout the school!' (ibid., 48). The subject's growing academic standing was acknowledged in 1916 when the University of London instituted a diploma in household and social science; in 1920 the course was recognized with the degree of bachelor of science.

With Mabel Atkinson, who taught economics and ethics at King's from 1908 to 1914, McKillop wrote *Economics: Descriptive and Theoretical* (1911), an undergraduate textbook. She left King's in 1915 and in the following year published *Food Values: what they are and how to Calculate them*, a straightforward approach to the complex subject of nutrition intended for anyone involved in cookery, whether at a professional or a domestic level. In 1917 she undertook war work with the information and statistical department at the Ministry of Food. Through her son, Alasdair, like his father a civil engineer, she became interested in theories of industrial efficiency and scientific management reaching Britain from the United States. Together they wrote *Efficiency Methods: an Introduction to Scientific Management* (1917), which welcomed a sea change in attitudes to industry brought about by the war, when 'to be inefficient has become a national crime'. The 'business man', they noted with approval, was at last being 'respectfully treated by the governing class' (p. 197). The change was timely since nobody associated with British industry could ignore the new work practices being pioneered in America, which were certain to be taken up by Britain's industrial competitors, notably Germany and Japan. *Efficiency Methods* is in effect a manual showing British industry how to increase production and eliminate waste. Among the illustrations is a series of photographs showing the old and new methods for loading sixteen boxes onto a truck. Trade unionists were certain to be alarmed by this time and motion study, but the McKillops saw efficiency methods as a way of benefiting everyone: greater productivity, they reasoned, would result in improved welfare for the workers.

After the war McKillop, who was created MBE in 1919,

worked with the Fabian Society women's group to raise the status and public perception of domestic work. While at King's she had acted as assistant librarian, in 1914, and she ended her career as the librarian of the Sociological Society (1921–9). She died on 29 May 1929 at St Mary's Nursing Home, Burlington Lane, Chiswick, London, her husband having predeceased her; she was survived by her son.   MARK POTTLE

Sources Somerville College register, 1879–1971 [1972] · MSS register Students Somerville Hall, Somerville College, Oxford · Somerville Students' Association Report (Sept 1890); (Sept 1891); (Sept 1893); (Nov 1899); (Oct 1901); (Oct 1909) · typescript letters, F. E. Sheldon, 1880–83, Somerville College, Oxford · N. L. Blakestad, 'King's College of Household and Social Science and the origins of dietetics education', Nutrition in Britain: science, scientists, and politics in the twentieth century, ed. D. F. Smith (1997), 75–98 · P. Adams, Somerville for women: an Oxford college, 1879–1993 (1996) · C. Law, Suffrage and power: the women's movement, 1918–1928 (1997) · N. Marsh, The history of Queen Elizabeth College: one hundred years of university education in Kensington (1986) · H. Sillitoe, A history of the teaching of domestic subjects (1933) · The Times (6 Oct 1913) · S. Rawson, 'Where London girls may study: II. King's College, Kensington Square', Girl's Realm, 1/12 (Oct 1899), 1201–7 · TLS (22 June 1916), 298; (15 Nov 1917), 557 · b. cert. · d. cert.

Likenesses portrait, Somerville College, Archives, photo album marked '1879–1889'

Wealth at death £1198 1s. 2d.: probate, 26 June 1929, CGPLA Eng. & Wales

MacKillop, Mary Helen [name in religion Mary of the Cross] (1842–1909), Roman Catholic nun, was born on 15 January 1842 in Brunswick Street, Fitzroy, Melbourne, the eldest of eight children of Alexander MacKillop (1812–1868), failed businessman, politician, gold-seeker, and farmer, and his wife, Flora MacDonald (1816–1886). Her parents had emigrated to Australia from the Lochaber district of Inverness-shire and retained the Catholicism of their ancestors. Alexander had studied for the priesthood in Rome for six years and this background equipped him to add a richer dimension to the education which Mary received in one private school. The family depended on relatives and friends, given her father's gullibility and ineptitude in worldly matters. Mary was obliged to work as a shopgirl, governess for her relatives, and teacher in a Catholic school at Portland. She had striking grey eyes and a dignified presence.

In 1860 Mary MacKillop first met the London-born Julian Tenison Woods. A Catholic priest, a scientist, and an obstinate but innocent idealist, Woods perceived her qualities of character and potential as a leader. He encouraged her to open a Catholic primary school in his parish of Penola, South Australia, in 1866. The school was to take children irrespective of the ability of the parents to pay. He also intended the teachers to become a religious community named 'The Sisters of St Joseph of the Sacred Heart'. Its members were to devote themselves to the education of poor children and, possessing neither money nor property, share the people's lifestyle. Taking her vows on 15 August 1867, Mary became the first member and co-founder of the new institute, authorized by Bishop Sheil (Adelaide) who approved Woods's rule of life for the sisters in 1868.

The rapid development of the Josephites in South Australia created tensions and jealousies among some of the clergy who persuaded Sheil, unwell and ever mindful of his episcopal authority, that Mary was disobedient. He solemnly excommunicated her on 22 September 1871. Her sisters were mostly disbanded and many of her schools closed. Restored to a healthier frame of mind, Sheil lifted the excommunication on 23 February 1872. He died a week later.

This crisis caused Mary to visit Europe and the United Kingdom in 1873–4. Although frequently ill, she travelled widely seeking advice on teaching methods, and in Ireland recruited young women for her sisterhood. In Rome Pius IX received her kindly while Vatican officials widely amended Woods's rule and allowed the sisters to own some property in the dioceses in which they worked. They also approved of the centralization of authority in the institute under its elected superior general rather than in the hands of local bishops. Woods was bitterly disappointed at Mary's seeming lack of resistance to the change on the ownership of property. The ensuing breach between them, painful to Woods, but more especially to Mary who regarded him as her father in God, became irrevocable.

Writing to the authorities while in Rome in 1873 Mary began: 'It is an Australian who writes this', and it was later said of the sisters that they were 'as much a part of the colonial scene as the drovers, shearers and bullock drivers' (Gardiner, 25). The sense of nationality and independence then growing among native-born Australians became part of the ethos of the sisters under Mary's guidance, and the institute was neither Irish nor Roman, but Australian. Concepts of class divisions among the members, or with those in whose orbit they moved, never gained a foothold.

Rapid and widespread development of the institute soon followed, eventually spreading throughout the Australian mainland and New Zealand. The question of local episcopal jurisdiction over her sisterhood plagued Mary for many years. Several Irish bishops, notably the Quinn brothers of Brisbane and Bathurst, refused to allow her institute to work in their dioceses unless subject to their authority. Even Bishop Reynolds, Sheil's successor and early champion of the sisters, eventually drove Mary from Adelaide with the intention of depriving her of the role of mother general. Rather than preside over the virtual dismemberment of her beloved institute by bishops to whom episcopal control was an absolute, Mary courageously stood by the Roman decision on central government, first made in 1874 and confirmed in 1888. The mother house of the institute was transferred from Adelaide to Sydney in 1889.

Rarely pausing to restore the energy she depleted in constant travels to the institute's houses throughout Australia, Mary suffered a stroke in 1901 in New Zealand. She retained her mental faculties, however, and worked until her death from a cerebral haemorrhage on 8 August 1909 at the mother house, the Convent of Sisters of St Joseph, Mount Street, north Sydney. Buried two days later at nearby Gore Hill, her remains were returned in 1914 to the Mary MacKillop Memorial Chapel, where they lie in a simple tomb.

Mary's leitmotif was to do the will of God. To her the Bible was 'a dear book which I am never tired of reading' and in it she seemed to discern that will with greater clarity than some of her adversaries (Gardiner, 128). While she was firm and even authoritative when the purpose of her work was in jeopardy, none doubted her devotion to the poor and destitute. Some contemporary ecclesiastics, including Cardinal Patrick Moran, archbishop of Sydney, stood in awe of her spiritual gifts. To the Catholic people, especially to the poor of the Sydney Rocks area and similar abandoned places throughout Australia, Mary was revered as both mother and saint. The first step towards her canonization was taken in Sydney in 1925. On the Randwick racecourse, Sydney, Pope John Paul II proclaimed her blessed during pontifical mass on 19 January 1995. Blessed Mary MacKillop is the first native-born Australian to bear that distinction.   JOHN N. MOLONY

Sources P. Gardiner, *An extraordinary Australian: Mary MacKillop, the authorised biography* (Sydney, 1994) · M. M. Press, *Julian Tenison Woods* (Sydney, 1979) · O. Thorpe, *Mary MacKillop*, 3rd edn (Sydney, 1994) · archives of Sisters of St Joseph, Mount Street, north Sydney · archives of the Pontifical Irish College, Rome · bap. cert. · d. cert. · d. cert. [Alexander MacKillop, father]

Archives archdiocese of Adelaide, South Australia, archives · Irish College, Rome, archives · Sacra Congregazione di Propaganda Fide, Rome, Propaganda Fide archives · Scots College, Rome, archives · Sisters of St Joseph, Mount Street, Sydney, archives

Likenesses photographs, Sisters of St Joseph, Mount Street, Sydney

Mackinder, Sir Halford John (1861–1947), geographer and politician, was born at Elswitha Hall, Clask Gate Street, Gainsborough, Lincolnshire, on 15 February 1861, the eldest among the six children of Draper Mackinder (1818–1912), medical doctor, and Fanny Anne (1831–1905), daughter of Halford Wotton Hewitt of Lichfield, also a medical doctor.

Early life and education Mackinder developed an early interest in geography. As a boy he went frequently into the surrounding countryside, often accompanying his father on his medical rounds. His father, as medical officer of health, studied medical geography and attempted to relate diseases to environmental conditions. The Mackinder household was Anglican, Liberal, well stocked with books, and open to visitors. Mackinder attended Queen Elizabeth Grammar School, Gainsborough, between 1870 and 1874 and Epsom College between 1874 and 1880. The college offered a good scientific education, and Draper Mackinder wanted his son to be a doctor. Instead, in 1880 Mackinder was elected to a junior studentship in physical science at Christ Church, Oxford, for five years. He studied under Henry Moseley in the laboratories at the university museum and gained a first-class degree in natural science (1883). In his fourth year at Oxford, Mackinder read modern history, curious to discover whether ideas on evolution, which had dominated his studies of the natural world, could be applied to human development. He was

Sir Halford John Mackinder (1861–1947), by Sir William Rothenstein

placed only in the second class (1884), not least because he was simultaneously preparing to compete for the Burdett-Coutts scholarship in geology, to which he was elected in 1884, and studying anthropology and economics. Mackinder was active at the Oxford Union, and was elected its treasurer, secretary, and then president in 1883. He was also a member of the university's junior scientific society, its war games club, and rifle volunteers.

In 1885 Mackinder began to read law, and in 1886 he was called to the bar from the Inner Temple. In his autobiographical notes, compiled towards the end of his life, Mackinder recalled defending, successfully, at least one case on the midland circuit, but the law never commanded his interest.

Geography at Oxford, Reading, and London At the Oxford Union, Mackinder was associated with a group, led by Michael Sadler, that wanted to broaden educational opportunities in Britain. In 1885 Sadler was appointed secretary of the extension lectures subcommittee of the Oxford local examinations delegacy, after 1892 the delegacy for the extension of teaching beyond the limits of the university. Sadler greatly expanded its activities, bringing in young lecturers, including Mackinder. From 1886 Mackinder offered courses, including some in the 'new geography', at several extension centres. In addition he was frequently in London for his law studies, and while there made contact with leading figures at the Royal Geographical Society (RGS).

At the time reformers within the RGS were promoting the teaching of geography in schools and universities, conscious that Britain lagged behind continental Europe and particularly Germany. Scott Keltie was appointed the society's inspector of geographical instruction. When Mackinder visited Keltie's exhibition (1885–6) of geographical teaching materials, the two men exchanged ideas. Mackinder came into increasing contact with Keltie, Henry Bates, Francis Galton, James Bryce, Clements Markham, and Douglas Freshfield, all leading reformers at the RGS who wanted to complement the society's long-standing promotion of exploration with encouragement of 'scientific geography' and geographical education. They had heard of Mackinder's extension lectures and wanted to harness his talents to their cause. Bates, at Francis Galton's suggestion, asked that Mackinder prepare a paper 'On the scope and methods of geography'. In it Mackinder lamented geography's condition, dominated by the compilation of isolated facts. What it needed was a unifying methodology based on a search for causal relations to be achieved by defining geography as the science of the interaction between society and the environment. Thus united, geography was to bridge the gap between the sciences and the humanities. He rejected environmental determinism while placing the physical environment at the heart of geographical studies. The paper delivered to the society on 31 January aroused strong feelings, both for and against; it was published in the *Cambridge Review* (2 March 1887) and in the *Proceedings of the Royal Geographical Society* (vol. 9, 1887, 141–60).

Mackinder's 'Scope and methods' paper was widely regarded as critical to the success of the RGS's campaign to promote the teaching of geography in universities. Shortly after the paper was delivered, the RGS and the delegates of the common university fund at Oxford agreed to establish a readership in geography at Oxford, with the society and the fund each paying half the annual salary of £300. Professor Moseley successfully argued for the appointment to the readership of Mackinder, his former pupil, though he was only twenty-six, and Mackinder began delivering lectures in Michaelmas term 1887. His lectures on human geography were well attended by historians, for the material was part of an examination syllabus. Ironically, given Mackinder's insistence on the centrality of the subject, his physical geography lectures attracted few undergraduates as the matter lay outside all examination syllabuses.

On 3 January 1889 Mackinder married Emilie Catherine (*b.* 1869/70), second daughter of Christian David *Ginsburg, Old Testament scholar, and his wife, Emilie. The couple married at Christ Church, Virginia Water, and lived at 1 Bradmore Road in north Oxford. A son was born to them on 1 January 1891 but lived for only a few hours. About 1900 the couple separated, after which Bonnie, as she was known, lived in Capri. There was no divorce and the couple remained in contact until the end of Mackinder's life, though he felt the failure of his marriage keenly.

Mackinder continued to lecture for the University of Oxford extension delegacy throughout England. In 1890 Sadler and Mackinder saw the opportunity of using government technical education funds to create a university extension centre outside Oxford. They published a short book, written in a week, entitled *University Extension: has it a Future?* (1890). Sadler interested Christ Church, of which he was steward, in using the school of science and art at Reading as the basis for an extension college. In 1892 Christ Church elected Mackinder to a studentship and offered his services to Reading as principal of the extension college, which opened in 1892 and grew rapidly, thanks to Mackinder's enthusiasm, energy, and willingness to bend rules. In 1902 Reading became a university college and Mackinder served as principal until 1903.

In 1895 Mackinder proposed the creation of a London institute of geography. Eventually Clements Markham, by then president of the RGS, endorsed the idea, but full funding could not be found. Markham then approached the University of Oxford with a proposal that the society and the university pay half the cost of an Oxford school of geography. Early in 1899 the university accepted the plan and agreed to create a diploma in geography. The school was founded with Mackinder as the director of what was the earliest British university geography department.

Before the school opened Mackinder spent summer 1899 in east Africa, leading an expedition that made the first recorded ascent of Mount Kenya, perhaps to prove that he was not 'merely' a scientific geographer and to head off reputed German contenders for the summit. As well as scaling the peak his expedition did survey work, took photographs, and collected specimens.

On his return Mackinder established the Oxford school with characteristic vigour and enthusiasm, appointing staff, including A. J. Herbertson, admitting women, and ensuring that his students succeeded in university and other careers. Mackinder recognized the need to establish a secure base for university geography by promoting school geography. He was a successful author of school geography textbooks (which provided him with badly needed royalties); he began summer schools for teachers, who came to Oxford's school of geography to improve their knowledge and teaching of the subject; and he chaired the meeting at Oxford in 1893 at which the Geographical Association (for the teaching of geography in schools) was founded. He was the association's chairman 1913–43. By 1903 Mackinder was directing the school of geography and the London School of Economics (LSE). Some Oxford colleagues resented this and he resigned in 1905, simultaneously relinquishing his Christ Church studentship. Freed of his commitments in Oxford and Reading, he focused on his London activities.

The London School of Economics and Political Science was established in 1895, and from the start Mackinder delivered lectures there. He was appointed reader in economic geography in 1900. In 1902 he was appointed full-time lecturer in economic geography at London University, with responsibility for advising on the organization of a department of geography at LSE. In 1903 he was appointed the second director of LSE, simultaneously resigning as principal of Reading and giving up his Oxford extension work. He held the directorship until 1908. From 1906 to 1914 Mackinder organized at LSE an annual course for army officers—the Mackindergarten, as it was known.

Entry into politics At LSE, Mackinder came into contact with influential politicians, academics, and business leaders. In 1902 Beatrice and Sidney Webb established the Co-Efficients, a dining club whose purpose was, in Mackinder's words, to study the 'aims, policy and methods of imperial efficiency at home and abroad' (Parker, 30). Its early members included L. S. Amery, Sir Edward Grey, W. A. S. Hewins, Mackinder, L. J. Maxse, H. G. Wells, and Michael Sadler. The Compatriots Club was founded in 1904 by Mackinder, Hewins, and Amery, and other pro-tariff reform imperialists. Mackinder's paper (*National Review*, 45, 1905, 136–43) and book (*Money-power and Man-power*, 1906) on 'man-power' (a term he coined) originated in a paper given to the Compatriots on the theme of national and imperial resource endowment.

In 1900 Mackinder stood (unsuccessfully) as the Liberal Imperialist candidate at Warwick and Leamington. Three years later Amery persuaded Mackinder, after Joseph Chamberlain had abandoned free trade for imperial preference and protective tariffs, to join the Conservatives. In 1908 Alfred Milner and Amery found funds to provide Mackinder with an income for a few years while he established himself in politics. In June 1908 Mackinder resigned the directorship of LSE and, retaining his readership at London University, went to Canada to deliver lectures in support of imperial unity. (He later identified Canada as the centre of a future, modernized British empire; *Geographical Journal*, 33, 1909, 462–76.) In 1909 he fought a by-election at Hawick Burghs as a Conservative, but lost. He was then adopted as the Conservative and Unionist candidate by the Camlachie division of Glasgow; he won the seat in January 1910 and retained it until 1922.

As an MP Mackinder spoke on economic issues, Scottish questions, and imperial themes. He was active in the First World War, helping recruitment in Scotland and serving on the Montague War Savings Committee. He served on royal commissions on income tax (1919), awards to inventors (1919), and food prices (1925). In 1919 Mackinder was appointed British high commissioner to South Russia, and sent by Lord Curzon to find ways of checking Bolshevik expansion. He visited General Denikin's White Russian forces in January 1920. On his return he made a report to the cabinet advocating British support for anti-Bolshevik forces from Poland to the Black Sea, but won no support for the proposed policy at a time when anti-interventionism held sway and the White Russians were in retreat. Mackinder chaired the imperial shipping committee between 1920 and 1945. The committee produced a number of reports, mostly written by Mackinder, who was convinced of the empire's need of good sea communication. He also chaired the Imperial Economic Committee from 1925 to 1931. Though characteristically busy as an MP, Mackinder failed to achieve the ministerial rank which influential friends expected of him, at least in part because he moved from the Liberal to the Conservative Party.

Mackinder was a visionary imperialist. As early as 1900 he declared at Leamington that the empire should become a league of democracies with a common defence policy. He advocated an imperial tariff system and more widespread economic development in the empire. From 1903 Mackinder worked with the visual instruction committee of the Colonial Office to develop illustrated lecture programmes to encourage understanding of the cultural diversity found within the empire. Throughout his political career Mackinder was associated with imperial unity and organizations, such as the Victorian League, that promoted co-operation between peoples in the empire.

Mackinder needed to secure an additional income from business ventures. He had an interest in Electro-Bleach, established in 1913, which was absorbed into Brunner Mond in 1920. Such ventures brought him some income but he was not conspicuously successful.

Geopolitics Mackinder is best remembered for his writings in 'geopolitics', a term which he disliked and did not use but which has come to encompass his ideas about how physical and human geography forms the basis of political power. The textbook *Britain and the British Seas* (1902) showed a clear grasp of the strategic and imperial implications of the position and resource endowment of the British Isles. The latter part of the book dealt with Britain in an imperial setting, seeing London as a global financial and commercial centre. 'The geographical pivot of history', published in the *Geographical Journal*, 23, 1904, 421–37, set out the basic fear in Western international relations: that one power, or alliance of powers, could gain control of Eurasia and use the resources of the region to dominate the world. *Democratic Ideals and Reality* (1919), written in haste for the Versailles conference, developed the ideas of his 'Geographical pivot' paper. He analysed the weakness of the post-war world and argued that power was being centralized within large states. Mass political movements were emerging, but populations would be manipulated by ruthless organizers controlling state machinery. Mackinder favoured creating new nation states from the territory of defeated empires, but he saw that the middle tier of states—for example, Poland, Czechoslovakia, and Hungary—which were created between Germany and Russia, would be vulnerable and become a battleground. In his famous pronouncement:

Who rules East Europe commands the Heartland:
Who rules the Heartland commands the World-Island:
Who rules the World-Island commands the World.
(*Democratic Ideals and Reality*, 194)

On publication the book made little impact in Britain and America. While President Wilson in 1919 took the political geographer Isaiah Bowman to Versailles, the British government did not consult Mackinder. The book was noticed in Germany, however, and when in 1938–9 Nazi Germany and the USSR started to divide the middle tier and then Germany attacked the Soviet Union, commentators assumed to his dismay that Mackinder's ideas were the inspiration for Nazi strategy. It is true that the German geopolitician Karl Haushofer admired Mackinder's analysis and advocated an alliance between Germany and the USSR in order to defeat the maritime powers. But Hitler's view, which predated *Democratic Ideals and Reality*, saw the USSR not as an ally but as a region to be plundered for resources. Hitler was not influenced by Mackinder, but his view that Germany should control the wheat fields of the Ukraine, the minerals of the Urals, and the forests of Siberia, and use the resources as the basis for world domination, paralleled closely Mackinder's fear that the heart of Eurasia could become a global power base.

As the USA was drawn into the war, *Democratic Ideals and Reality* was reread and republished. Much of what Mackinder said was incorporated into N. J. Spykman's *America's Strategy in World Politics* (1942), which was widely quoted in policy debates about the post-war world. Mackinder's views on the world after the war are in 'The round world and the winning of the peace' (*Foreign Affairs*, 21, 1943, 595–605). He saw that the Soviet Union would have firm control of the heartland in the post-war world but still feared Germany.

Last years Mackinder was knighted in 1920 and was sworn of the privy council in 1926. He was made titular professor at the University of London in 1923, two years before he retired from the institution. He was honoured by numerous geographical societies, including the American Geographical Society (Daly gold medal, 1943) and the RGS (patron's medal, 1945). He was disappointed not to be given an honorary degree by the University of Reading (formerly the University College of Reading) after its charter was granted in 1926.

Mackinder had moved from Oxford to London about 1904 and stayed there until the approach of the Second World War, when he moved to Parkstone in Dorset to live with his brother the Revd Lionel Mackinder and sister-in-law Eleanor. He died on 6 March 1947 at 4 Cambridge Road, Bournemouth. He was cremated. A memorial service was held on 17 March 1947 at the church of St Mary the Virgin, Reading. He left little money, having in his lifetime had to borrow from his family in the absence of a secure income.

Influence and reputation Mackinder's distinction in a number of fields—university teaching, university administration, politics, school geography—is evident. Laying the foundations of Reading University and broadening the programmes at LSE were of major importance; however, in no field did he achieve all that his supporters had hoped. Sometimes this was due to factors beyond his control, such as his party's exclusion from office; sometimes it was because he started many things and his energies were thinly spread. Late in life Mackinder declared geography to have been his vocation, confounding those who have interpreted his career as an abandonment of geography for politics. In truth his political and geographical aims were inseparable: he wanted to create a new scientific geography which could be pressed into the service of imperialism. As early as 1887, in his 'Scope and methods' paper, Mackinder declared that his new geography was designed 'to attract minds of an amplitude fitting them to be rulers of men' (p. 143).

As a geographer Mackinder succeeded in establishing the teaching of the subject at Oxford, London, and Reading universities, and helped establish the subject in British schools. As an imperialist he failed to gain support for his vision of a unified and modernized empire to counterbalance the new continental powers. As a geopolitician, however, he is still widely read and his work commands considerable interest nearly 100 years later.

In 1971 the University of Oxford established a Halford Mackinder professorship of geography in his memory.

BRIAN W. BLOUET

Sources B. W. Blouet, *Halford Mackinder: a biography* (1987) • P. Coones, *Mackinder's 'Scope and methods of geography' after a hundred years* (1987) [research paper, school of geography, University of Oxford] • P. Coones, 'The centenary of the Mackinder readership at Oxford', *GJ*, 155 (1989), 13–22 • W. H. Parker, *Mackinder: geography as an aid to statecraft* (1982) • H. J. Mackinder, *The first ascent of Mount Kenya*, ed. K. M. Barbour (1991) [ed. with an introduction and notes by K. M. Barbour] • R. Symonds, *Oxford and empire: the last lost cause* (1986) • R. Walford, 'Mackinder, the GA in wartime and the national curriculum', *Geography*, 78/2 (1993), 117–23 • E. W. Gilbert, '"Seven lamps of geography": an appreciation of the teaching of Sir Halford Mackinder', *Geography*, 36 (1951), 21–43 • E. W. Gilbert, *British pioneers in geography* (1972) • B. W. Blouet, *Sir Halford Mackinder, 1861–1947: some new perspectives* (1975) [research paper, school of geography, University of Oxford] • D. N. Livingstone, *The geographical tradition* (1992) • *WWW* • *Hist. U. Oxf. 8: 20th cent.* • G. Kearns, 'Halford John Mackinder, 1861–1947', *Geographers: biobibliographical studies*, 9, ed. T. W. Freeman (1985), 71–86 • B. W. Blouet, *Geopolitics and globalization in the twentieth century* (2001) • H. C. E. Matthew, *The liberal imperialists* (1973) • L. S. Amery, *My political life*, 1: *England before the storm, 1896–1914* (1953) • b. cert. • m. cert. • d. cert. • R. Dahrendorf, *LSE: a history of the London School of Economics and Political Science 1895–1995* (1995)

Archives Bodl. RH, notebooks and journals relating to ascent of Mount Kenya • PRO, corresp. relating to Russia, FO 800 • University of Oxford, corresp. and MSS | BLPES, corresp. relating to National Theatre • RGS, letters to Royal Geographical Society

Likenesses M. R., oils, 1908, U. Reading • W. Rothenstein, drawing, 1933, London School of Economics • W. Rothenstein, sanguine and chalk drawing, NPG [*see illus.*]

Wealth at death £5165 0s. 5d.: probate, 20 May 1947, *CGPLA Eng. & Wales*

MacKinlay, Antoinette Sterling (1843×50–1904), singer, was born at Sterlingville, New York, the daughter of James Sterling, an ironmaster; she claimed descent from William Bradford, one of the Pilgrim Fathers. Her date of birth is contested: several sources give 23 January 1843 and others give 1850, while her death certificate suggests that she was born in 1846 or 1847. As a child, she imbibed strongly anti-British prejudices, and, stirred by stories of the Boston Tea Party, resolved never to drink tea, which resolution she kept all her life.

Sterling had a voice of considerable range and volume, and took lessons from a Signor Abella in New York. When her father was ruined by the reduction of import duties and died in 1857, she went to Mississippi as a teacher and later gave singing lessons. She returned to the north in the summer of 1862 as a result of the civil war. About 1866 she became a church singer and was engaged in Henry Ward Beecher's church at Brooklyn.

In 1868 Sterling went to Europe for further training; she sang at Darlington in Handel's *Messiah* on 17 December, and took some lessons under W. H. Cummings in London before going to Germany. There she studied in Cologne with Mathilde Marchesi and in Baden with Pauline Viardot, and finally returned to London, where she was a pupil of Manuel García. In 1871 she went back to America and became a prominent concert singer. Her voice had developed into a contralto of exceptional power and richness. She was again in England at the beginning of 1873, but almost immediately returned to America, where she toured with Theodore Thomas's orchestra; she gave a farewell concert in Boston on 13 May.

Sterling's first engagement in London was at the Covent Garden Promenade Concert on 5 November 1873, where she sang 'Schlafe, mein Liebster' from Bach's Christmas oratorio and some classical lieder. She had a great popular success, and enthusiastic receptions on her appearances at the Crystal Palace, the Royal Albert Hall, Exeter Hall, and St James's Hall quickly followed. In February 1874 she sang in Mendelssohn's *Elijah* on two consecutive nights at Exeter Hall and the Royal Albert Hall. At this stage her repertory consisted entirely of oratorio and lieder. Not all criticism was favourable: 'her style is wanting in sensibility and refinement. Excellence of voice is not all that is required of the art of vocalisation' (*Athenaeum*, 14 March 1874). But her popularity was undeniable, and she was engaged for the Three Choirs festival at Hereford. On Easter Sunday 1875 she was married at the Savoy Chapel to John MacKinlay (*d.* 1893), a Scottish-American. They settled in Stanhope Place, London, and her husband soon assumed control of the management of her career, which then took a change of direction.

Engagements for high-class concerts gradually ceased, but she still sang in oratorio and her taste remained faithful to the German repertory, including Wagner. In 1877 she found her vocation: Sullivan's 'Lost Chord' exactly suited her, and attained unprecedented popularity, being long associated with her name. She restricted herself more and more to simple, sentimental ballads, especially those with semi-religious words: 'Caller Herrin'' was also extremely popular, and in later years she favoured Behrend's setting of Tennyson's 'Crossing the Bar'.

MacKinlay had always been viewed as eccentric, refusing to wear a low-necked dress, and obtained permission to dress in her usual style at a command performance before Queen Victoria in 1874. She never wore corsets. She was a sometime vice-president of the World's Women's Christian Temperance Union. After belonging to various religious organizations she finally became an ardent Christian Scientist. In 1893 she made a tour of Australia, during which her husband died at Adelaide. In 1895 she revisited America, but did not settle there and returned to London. In the winter of 1902–3 she made her farewell tour; her last appearance was at East Ham on 15 October 1903, and the last song which she sang was 'Crossing the Bar'. She died at 70 Belsize Park Gardens, Belsize Park, on 10 January 1904 and was cremated at Golders Green. She was survived by a son, Malcolm, who became a popular singer, and a daughter, Jean, who became an actress.

HENRY DAVEY, *rev.* JAMES J. NOTT

Sources M. S. MacKinlay, *Antoinette Sterling and other celebrities* (1906) · M. S. MacKinlay, *Garcia the centenarian and his times* (1908) · *MT*, 45 (1904), 114–15 · Grove, *Dict. mus.* · *Baltzell's dictionary of musicians* (1911) · private information (1874, 1912) · d. cert.
Likenesses L. V. Blandy, chalk drawing, 1880, NPG · J. D. Penrose, oils, 1891, Royal Society of Musicians, London · Barraud, photograph, NPG; repro. in *Men and women of the day*, 1 (1888) · Walery, photograph, NPG · lithograph, BM · photographs, repro. in M. S. MacKinlay, *Antoinette Sterling and other celebrities* · prints, Harvard TC · wood-engraving (after photograph by Fradelle & Marshall), NPG; repro. in *ILN* (24 April 1875)

McKinlay, John (1819–1872), explorer in Australia, the third son of Dugald McKinlay and his wife, Mary, *née* McKellar, was born on 16 August 1819 at Sandbank, on Holy Loch, Argyll, Scotland. He was educated at Dalinlongart School and emigrated with his brother Alexander in 1836 to New South Wales, where his uncle was a landholder at Goulburn. After 1840 he moved to the Victorian side of the Murray/Darling area, from where he explored the country in New South Wales and South Australia towards Lake Frome and earned a reputation as an expert bushman. He took up a number of pastoral leases in this area.

McKinlay was the South Australian government's choice to lead an expedition to ascertain the fate of Robert O'Hara Burke and William Wills, who had failed to return from their expedition to cross Australia south to north. McKinlay's party left Adelaide on 16 August 1861. It consisted of ten men, with horses, bullocks, and camels, as well as sheep for food. McKinlay pushed through the dry lakes country of Cooper Creek and found, on 21 October, the remains of William Gray, whom Burke and Wills had buried on 17 April 1861. Because the Aborigines had told him that white people had been killed here (possibly confusing this with the earlier massacre considered to be of the explorer Ludwig Leichhardt at Wantata waterhole, a little further north), he named it Lake Massacre. Also because the Aborigines had emptied the grave and roughly reburied the body nearby, McKinlay at first believed that Burke and Wills had been killed here. Later (after learning that Alfred William Howitt had found Burke's and Wills's graves in September 1861) he realized it was Gray's body which he had discovered.

McKinlay proceeded to explore the country to the north, eventually, on 19 May 1862, reaching the Gulf of Carpentaria at the mouth of the Albert River, becoming the first after Burke and Wills to traverse the continent from south to north. He then returned about 50 kilometres and proceeded east to cross the Great Dividing range, move down the Burdekin River, cross it, and struggle towards the coast. His exploration finished in early August at the Bowen River, from where he moved to Port Denison (later Bowen). All his party had survived, but they had been reduced to great straits, having had to eat most of the camels and horses. McKinlay had discovered good grazing land and had proved himself a most competent explorer. His journal of the expedition was published by the Victorian government as part of its account of the Burke Relief Expedition (*c.*1873).

A giant of a man, McKinlay was able to overcome all obstacles. His resourcefulness was again demonstrated when, in September 1865, he was invited by the South Australian government to make an exploration in the Northern Territory in the area of the South Alligator River. He was beset by floods and other perils from which he again, with his extraordinary ingenuity, extricated his party. A further visit to the Northern Territory was made in 1870.

Between and after his explorations McKinlay remained a pastoralist. He married Jane (Jeannie), the daughter of his friend James Pile, on 17 January 1863 at St George's Church, Gawler. He died, worn out but greatly honoured, on 31 December 1872, and was buried at Willaston cemetery, Gawler.   ALAN E. J. ANDREWS

Sources J. Davis, *Tracks of McKinlay and party across Australia: by John Davis one of the expedition*, ed. W. Westgarth (1863) · W. Howitt, *History of discovery in Australia and New Zealand*, 2 (1895) · G. C. Morphett and others, 'Gray's grave at Lake Massacre', *Proceedings of the Royal Geographical Society of Australasia, South Australian Branch*, 40 (1938–9), 12–42 · E. H. J. Feeken, G. E. E. Feeken, and O. H. K. Spate, *The discovery and exploration of Australia* (1970) · *AusDB*, vol. 5 · W. J. Wills, *A successful exploration through the interior of Australia ... from the journals and letters of William John Wills*, ed. W. Wills (1863) · G. Connell, *The mystery of Ludwig Leichhardt* (1980) · P. Serle, *Dictionary of Australian biography*, 2 vols. (1949)
Likenesses portrait, Gawler Institute, South Australia · woodengraving, NPG; repro. in *ILN* (14 Jan 1865)

Mackinnon, Daniel (1791–1836), army officer and historian, was the son of William Mackinnon (son of William Mackinnon, chief of clan Mackinnon) and his wife, Harriet, *née* Frye. William Alexander *Mackinnon was his elder brother, and Daniel Henry *Mackinnon was his first cousin. On 16 June 1804 he was appointed ensign in the Coldstream Guards, in which his uncle, Henry *Mackinnon, who fell as a major-general at Ciudad Rodrigo in 1812, was then a lieutenant-colonel. He became lieutenant and captain in the regiment in 1808, captain and lieutenant-colonel on 25 July 1814, junior major in 1826, senior major in 1829, and regimental lieutenant-colonel and colonel in 1830. He served with his regiment at Bremen in 1805, at Copenhagen in 1807, in the Peninsula from 31 December 1808 to August 1812, and in the Netherlands from August to December 1814. He was captain of the grenadier company and acting second major of his battalion at Waterloo, when he was dispatched in the afternoon of 18 June with the grenadier and no. 1 companies to reinforce Hougoumont after Foy had put the Nassau troops to flight. He received a severe wound in the knee, had his horse shot under him, lost his sword, and seized another from a French officer. When lieutenant-colonel of the regiment he compiled the *Origin and History of the Coldstream Guards* (2 vols., 1832), which continues to be highly regarded.

About 1826 Mackinnon married Miss Dent, daughter of John Dent, MP for Poole; they had no children and she survived him. Dan Mackinnon, as he was known, was remarkable for his extraordinary agility and daring in climbing, vaulting, and similar exercises. Many stories were told of his athletic feats and practical jokes. Gronow relates many anecdotes of him, and states that Joe Grimaldi often said, 'Colonel Mackinnon had only to put on

Daniel Mackinnon (1791–1836), by George Dawe

the motley, and he would totally eclipse me' (*Reminiscences*, 1.61). Gronow describes Mackinnon as the constant companion of Byron when the poet was at Lisbon during the Peninsular War. A well-built, handsome man, a *bon viveur* and witty raconteur, he was in later years a well-known figure about town. Mackinnon died at his residence in Hertford Street, Mayfair, Westminster, on 22 June 1836.

H. M. CHICHESTER, *rev.* JAMES FALKNER

Sources *Army List* · Burke, *Gen. GB* · *GM*, 1st ser., 103/1 (1833), 240 [review] · *GM*, 2nd ser., 6 (1836), 208 [review] · *The reminiscences and recollections of Captain Gronow*, 2 (1900)
Likenesses G. Dawe, portrait; Sothebys, 9 March 1988, lot 58 [*see illus.*] · D. Dighton, portrait, repro. in *Royal Catalogue*, 433 (*c*.1821) · engraving, repro. in J. MacInnes, *Brave sons of Skye* (1899) · engraving, repro. in *Household Brigade Magazine* (spring 1965)

Mackinnon, Daniel Henry (1813–1884), army officer, was born on 18 September 1813, youngest and last surviving son of Daniel Mackinnon (*d.* 1830) of Binfield, Berkshire, barrister, and Rachel Yeamans, youngest daughter and eventual heir of Captain Eliot of the 47th regiment. The army officer Daniel Mackinnon and the politician William Alexander Mackinnon were his first cousins. He graduated BA at Trinity College, Dublin, where he was classical prizeman in 1834 and seventh moderator in 1836. On 1 July 1836 he was appointed cornet in the 16th lancers, in which he became lieutenant in 1838 and captain in 1847. He served in Afghanistan in 1838–9, was present at the capture of Ghazni, in the Anglo-Sikh War of 1845–6, where he had a horse shot under him at Badiwal, and at Aliwal and Sobraon. He afterwards exchanged to the 6th dragoon guards (Carabiniers), and retired on half pay unattached. Mackinnon married in 1847 Caroline, youngest daughter of Thomas Robert, Baron Dimsdale; they had at least one child, and she survived him. While on half pay he was for a time paymaster of the 43rd light infantry, and afterwards staff officer of pensioners at various stations, from February 1854 until his retirement on full pay, with the brevet of major-general, in 1878. Mackinnon published *Military Services and Adventures in the Far East* (2nd edn, 2 vols., 1849) and *British Military Power in India* (1858). He died at his residence, 66 Warwick Square, London, on 7 January 1884.

H. M. CHICHESTER, rev. JAMES LUNT

Sources Hart's Army List · Broad Arrow (14 Jan 1884), 788 · Burke, *Gen. GB* [MacKinnon of MacKinnon] · H. Graham, *History of the sixteenth, the queen's, light dragoons (lancers), 1759–1912* (privately printed, Devizes, 1912) · Boase, *Mod. Eng. biog.* · Kelly, *Handbk*
Wealth at death £12,756 13s. 1d.: probate, 17 July 1884, CGPLA Eng. & Wales

MacKinnon, Donald MacKenzie (1913–1994), philosopher and theologian, was born in Oban, Argyll, on 27 August 1913, the son of Donald MacKenzie MacKinnon (*d.* 1930), procurator fiscal, and his wife, Grace Isabella Rhind. An Anglicized Scot, MacKinnon was educated at Cargilfield School, Edinburgh (1921–6), Winchester College (1926–31) to which he won a scholarship, and New College, Oxford (1931–5), where he also held a scholarship and graduated in both Greats and theology. He served as A. E. Taylor's assistant in moral philosophy at Edinburgh University (1936–7) during which time he met Lois (*b.* 1915), daughter of a distinguished Church of Scotland minister Oliver Dryer. Their marriage, begun in 1939, lasted almost fifty-five years until MacKinnon's death. They had no children.

After Edinburgh, MacKinnon, having won the John Locke scholarship, became fellow and tutor at Keble College, Oxford (1937–47), and held the Wilde lectureship in natural and comparative religion (1945–7). During this period he confirmed his reputation as a philosopher of unusual range and scholarly acumen. Never willing to swim with the currents of intellectual fashion, he resisted the anti-metaphysical strains of linguistic philosophy while insisting upon the relevance of theological issues. An Anglo-Catholic with socialist sympathies—he was a member of the Labour Party—MacKinnon's thought was generally at odds with the times. This, coupled with an imperious if eccentric style, made him a speaker, essayist, and radio broadcaster in high demand. Despite his earlier pacifist leanings MacKinnon's abhorrence of national socialism prompted him to volunteer for war service in 1939. Although turned down on medical grounds he continued teaching philosophy throughout the war to naval and air force cadets. He was one of very few who quickly recognized the awful significance of the shoah for Christian theology, a theme to which he constantly returned in subsequent writings on the atonement and tragedy. He dedicated considerable energy in wartime Oxford to assisting Jewish refugee scholars. In later years he was much exercised by the nuclear problem and became a supporter of the Campaign for Nuclear Disarmament.

At the age of thirty-four MacKinnon was appointed to the regius chair of moral philosophy in Aberdeen University (1947–60). As a teacher of large ordinary classes in his subject, he influenced generations of undergraduates. He completed an important monograph, *A Study in Ethical Theory* (1957), before taking up the Norris–Hulse chair of divinity in Cambridge (1960–76). This was held concurrently with a fellowship at Corpus Christi College. For fifteen years MacKinnon dominated Cambridge theology. Although trained originally as a philosopher, he was astonishingly well read in most areas of theology and biblical scholarship. While he remained of strong Episcopalian leanings, he displayed an impressive awareness of Roman Catholic and Reformed theology. An Oxbridge don, he was unusually engaged with continental and Marxist philosophy and travelled frequently to the European continent, though never to the USA. His willingness to learn from Marxist thought is evident in *Christian Faith and Communist Faith* (1953) while his frequent tilting at the trappings of ecclesiastical office is apparent in a devastating critique, *The Stripping of the Altars* (1969).

Successive generations of the ablest students were deeply influenced by MacKinnon's thought and style in Oxford, Aberdeen, and Cambridge; his formative impact upon Iris Murdoch has recently been described by her biographer, Peter Conradi. Collections of essays appeared as *Borderlands of Theology* (1968), *Explorations in Theology* (1979), and *Themes in Theology, the Three-Fold Cord* (1987). Much in demand as a conference speaker, MacKinnon travelled extensively and served *inter alia* on the theological commission charged with drafting papers for the general assembly of the World Council of Churches in 1954. Together with his wife, he found the world of the Cambridge college somewhat cramped, and long vacations were spent at their home in North Connel, Argyll, near MacKinnon's birthplace. Here he continued his writing while Lois was able to devote herself to landscape painting. His eventual decision to receive communion at a Church of Scotland service on Easter Sunday in Rhugarbh revealed a growing ecumenical openness partly under the influence of his wife's Presbyterianism.

MacKinnon's genius resided in his ability to connect themes in analytic philosophy, Christian doctrine, literature, and politics. His work was habitually in an interrogative mode, questioning easy certainties and a premature closure on vital problems. His thought is difficult to summarize, doubtless because MacKinnon always resisted categorization. However, several emphases stand out. These include a lifelong affinity with Kantian moral philosophy, philosophical and theological realism, the classical formulations of the Trinity and the incarnation, the urgency of theological reflection upon the shoah, the nuclear threat, and the significance of the tragic in relation to human experience and the atonement. Though his sympathies were with doctrinal orthodoxy, he relished the struggle with ancient and modern problems and was at his most severe in the face of anything resembling a theological shibboleth. His Gifford lectures delivered in 1965/6 were not released for publication until 1974, as *The Problem of Metaphysics*. His large physical presence was matched by a towering intellect haunted by intellectual and moral enigmas. At times, this could manifest itself in remarkable eccentricities which were widely celebrated and recounted in sundry 'MacKinnon stories'. Scarcely concealed here was a deep personal anguish known best to his wife whose patient, practical support was indispensable to his health and work.

MacKinnon's renown as a speaker was demonstrated by invitations he accepted to deliver named lecture series in Cambridge, Exeter, Aberystwyth, the London School of Economics, Newcastle, and Stirling. He served as president of the Aristotelian Society (1976–7) and president of the Society for the Study of Theology (1981–2). After retiral from Cambridge in 1976 he taught in St Andrews for one session during the interregnum in the chair of divinity, before returning to Aberdeen. There he became a kenspeckle figure in and around King's College, participating regularly in philosophy and theology seminars while continuing his work as an essayist and reviewer. Two Festschriften were published in his honour: *The Philosophical Frontiers of Christian Theology* (ed. B. Hebblethwaite and S. Sutherland, 1982) and *Christ, Ethics and Tragedy* (ed. K. Surin, 1989). The former volume contains a full bibliography of his writings until 1980; the latter is based upon a Cambridge conference dedicated to the study of his work. MacKinnon was elected a fellow of the British Academy in 1978 and a fellow of the Royal Society of Edinburgh in 1984. He was awarded honorary degrees by the universities of Aberdeen, Edinburgh, and Stirling. Following a sudden heart attack, he died in Aberdeen Royal Infirmary on 2 March 1994; his cremation took place in Aberdeen on 7 March. Memorial services were held in his honour in Aberdeen and Cambridge.   DAVID FERGUSSON

Sources WW (1994) · *The Guardian* (5 March 1994) · private information (2004) [Lois MacKinnon] · D. M. MacKinnon, *Borderlands of theology* (1968) · D. M. MacKinnon, *Explorations in theology* (1979) · D. M. MacKinnon, *Themes in theology, the three-fold cord: essays in philosophy, politics and theology* (1987) · G. Steiner, 'Tribute to Donald MacKinnon', *Theology*, 98 (1995), 2–9 · P. Conradi, *Iris Murdoch: a life* (2002)
Archives priv. coll., corresp. and MSS |SOUND BL NSA, performance recording
Likenesses photographs, priv. coll.
Wealth at death £461,358.65: confirmation, 16 May 1994, NA Scot., SC/CO 756/152

Mackinnon, Doris Livingstone (1883–1956), protozoologist, was born on 30 September 1883 at 4 Forest Road, Aberdeen, the eldest of five children of Lachlan Mackinnon (1855–1948), advocate and consular agent for France and Belgium, and his wife, Theodora Thompson of London. Her interest in science was stimulated by her father (an amateur ornithologist, botanist, and astronomer) and by her acquaintance with the geologist Maria Ogilvie Gordon, who encouraged her to study science seriously. Mackinnon graduated BSc from Aberdeen University in 1906,

at a time when few women were studying science. She gained a special distinction in botany and geology, and submitted her thesis 'Studies on protozoa' for the degree of DSc in 1914. She was awarded an honorary LLD by the university in 1943.

After graduation Mackinnon received a Carnegie scholarship and spent a year in the laboratory of Richard Hertwig in Munich. She also spent a few months at the biological station at Roscoff in Brittany (where she worked on protozoological research with M. F. Vlès) and at the Quick Laboratory in Cambridge—under the supervision of Professor G. H. F. Nuttall. In 1908 Mackinnon returned to Aberdeen as personal assistant to Professor J. Arthur Thomson at the university; she collaborated with him on several papers. In 1909 she moved to Dundee as assistant to Professor W. D'Arcy Thompson; she was promoted to lecturer in 1916. It was at University College, Dundee, that Mackinnon gained her reputation as a brilliant lecturer and protozoologist specializing in the parasites of insects.

In 1916 Mackinnon was introduced to the study of amoebic dysentery by Clifford Dobell. From then, until 1918, she took a leave of absence to do war work as a protozoologist in military hospitals, including the 1st Western General Hospital, Liverpool, and University War Hospital, Southampton. During this period she published several papers and reports with colleagues concerning *Entamoeba histolytica* (the bacteria responsible for amoebic dysentery in humans). She returned to Dundee in 1918, where, for some months, she ran the zoology department singlehandedly, D'Arcy Thompson having accepted a position at St Andrews. In 1919 she was appointed lecturer in zoology at King's College, University of London, later being promoted to reader (1921) and professor (1927). Mackinnon remained at King's until her retirement in 1949, at which time she was elected an emeritus professor and an honorary research associate of University College, London.

Doris Mackinnon was the author of about forty scientific papers, chiefly on parasitic protozoa. A talented writer and artist, with a good knowledge of German and music, she brought a wide perspective to her writing and teaching. While in Dundee she often lectured for a popular audience, as well as publishing a series of articles about children and childhood memories in periodicals and in the *Manchester Guardian*. Later she gave a course of broadcast talks for schools which formed the basis of her book *The Animal's World* (1936), a revised and expanded edition of which was published in 1950. Her early training in German enabled her to produce in 1926 a translation of Jacob von Uexküll's *Theoretische Biologie* and, three years later, of Paul Mies's *Die Bedeutung der Skizzen Beethovens zur Erkenntnis seines Stiles* (as *Beethoven's Sketches: an Analysis of his Style, Based on his Sketchbook*). Her artistic ability is suggested by her illustrations of specimens. Doris Mackinnon was remembered as an outstanding lecturer who never repeated a lecture in thirty years of teaching. Her colleague Ben Dawes wrote that she was

> an inspiring teacher, rapid but always lucid in exposition, she had a natural dignity and touch of the grand manner

which at all times commanded respect and attention and which could, on occasions, give devastating force to a well deserved reprimand. (*The Times*)

Doris Mackinnon corresponded with many of her students after graduation, offering them advice and guidance in their careers. During the Second World War she sent news and gifts of books to those who were serving abroad. Following her retirement she began work on a textbook for undergraduates. Frequently interrupted by illness, in the spring of 1956 she invited R. S. J. Hawes of University College, London, to collaborate with her. In that June, however, she suffered a severe stroke, and died at her Chelsea home, 44 St Leonard's Terrace, three months later, on 10 September 1956. *An Introduction to the Study of Protozoa*, which was edited and completed by Hawes, was published in 1961.　　　FERNANDA HELEN PERRONE

Sources *Nature*, 178 (1956), 1093–4 · *The Times* (20 Sept 1956), 14b · *Aberdeen University Review*, 37 (1957–8), 101–2 · R. S. J. Hawes, 'Preface', in D. L. Mackinnon, *An introduction to the study of protozoa* (1961) · Department of special collections and archives, U. Aberdeen, King's College · M. Shafe, *University education in Dundee* (1982) · L. Moore, *Bajanellas and Semilinas: Aberdeen University and the education of women, 1860–1920* (1991) · T. Watt, *Roll of graduates of the University of Aberdeen, 1901–1925* (1935) · J. MacKintosh, *Roll of the graduates of the University of Aberdeen, 1926–1955* (1960) · M. D. Allardyce, ed., *Roll of Service in the great war*, Aberdeen University Studies, 84 (1921), 282 · *The women's who's who, 1934–5: an annual record of the careers and activities of the leading women of the day* (1934) · b. cert. · d. cert.

Archives U. Aberdeen, King's College

Likenesses photograph, c.1914, repro. in Shafe, *University education in Dundee*

Wealth at death £18,730 15s. 11d.: probate, 19 Nov 1956, CGPLA Eng. & Wales

MacKinnon, Sir Frank Douglas (1871–1946), judge and writer, was born in London on 11 February 1871, the eldest son of Benjamin Thomas Mackinnon, a Lloyd's underwriter of Lingfield, Surrey, and his wife, Katherine, daughter of Joseph Edwards, a mahogany broker. After attending Highgate School he won an open exhibition to Trinity College, Oxford, where he gained a first in classical moderations (1892) and a second in *literae humaniores* (1894). For the rest of his life he maintained a close connection with Trinity, regularly donating books and fine art to the college.

In 1897 MacKinnon was called to the bar by the Inner Temple. Along with Robert Alderson Wright, he became a pupil of Thomas Edward Scrutton, a notable commercial lawyer (and later one of the most outstanding Court of Appeal judges). When Scrutton took silk in 1901, MacKinnon acquired a large part of his master's junior commercial practice, an acquisition enhanced by the young barrister's family connections with Lloyd's, of which his brother Sir Percy Graham Mackinnon (1872–1956) was chairman on a number of occasions. The world of commercial litigation was thus familiar territory for the young practitioner and he rapidly built up a considerable business. In 1906 he married Frances, daughter of William Henry Massey of Twyford, Berkshire, with whom he had two children. In 1914 he took silk and after the outbreak of the First World War was able to exploit the rapid growth

in prize-law cases, which often entailed appearances before the judicial committee of the privy council. The war generated many new commercial disputes which MacKinnon handled with patience and adroitness, for example, in respect to the doctrine of frustration of contract, on which he published a pamphlet, *The Effect of War on Contract* (1917). He began to establish a reputation as a scholar, assisting his mentor in preparing later editions of the authoritative *Scrutton on Charterparties and Bills of Lading*. Later writings included a lecture entitled *Some Aspects of Commercial Law* (1926) and a paper on the 'origins of commercial law' in the *Law Quarterly Review* (1936). The latter, his presidential address to the Association of Average Adjusters, drew attention to the seminal role of Lord Mansfield in the creation of mercantile law in the late eighteenth century. It was a hint of his emotional identification with that century which would inspire a number of his future publications.

High Court judge MacKinnon's elevation to the bench in 1924 (the only judicial appointment during the first Labour government) followed the death of the commercial judge Sir Clement Bailhache. The appointment was greatly welcomed within the profession and the mercantile community. For by then MacKinnon had proved himself to be a jurist of distinction and on many occasions had advised the government on questions of mercantile law policy, especially in relation to international codes. An interesting feature of his promotion was the desire of the lord chancellor, Haldane, to have the appointment announced quickly after Bailhache's death. In particular, although MacKinnon's nomination had no political significance (he did not engage in party politics and Haldane's predecessors, Birkenhead and Cave, both approved of his elevation) the lord chancellor was extremely anxious at the beginning of October 1924 to avoid the appearance of an appointment being made 'in the last agony of the [first Labour] government's existence' (PRO, LCO6/861). For it was not thought within the Lord Chancellor's Office that, following the mishandling of the Campbell case, the government's life would endure for another week. By the time Cave had returned to the woolsack on 7 November, MacKinnon was still awaiting the customary knighthood and Sir Claud Schuster had to remind the new prime minister's private secretary, Lieutenant-Colonel Sir Ronald Waterhouse, a few days later to rectify an omission which had no doubt been overlooked in 'the exciting events of the last few weeks' (PRO, LCO6/861). MacKinnon eventually got his knighthood just before Christmas that year.

As planned, MacKinnon frequently sat in the commercial court but also went on circuit. Yet despite the reputation which he had already acquired he did not quite succeed, in respect to his judicial role, in emulating the prodigious industry and the vast erudition of his commercial law mentor, Scrutton. He was none the less quick to see the point in cases before him and his judgments were always scholarly. Although he had never gone on circuit as a barrister and had hardly ever addressed a jury while at the bar, as a judge he was none the less at ease with juries.

One of the leading criminal trials over which he presided was that of Mrs Harriet Crouch at Chelmsford who was acquitted in 1926 of the murder of her husband whom she had suspected of having an affair with their domestic servant. In the same year he chaired a committee appointed by Lord Chancellor Cave to examine the law relating to arbitration. Reporting in January 1927, the committee concluded that the Arbitration Act of 1889 had worked well but that a number of amendments, which did not in most cases involve any common principle, were desirable. The recommendations of the committee were only partially taken into account in the Arbitration Acts of 1928 and 1934.

Court of Appeal In 1937 MacKinnon was promoted to the Court of Appeal and was sworn of the privy council. He pointed out to Schuster at the time that when he had previously been sworn in as a judge of the King's Bench in 1924 he had worn the robes of Mr Justice Shearman (who had in fact previously been an outstanding athlete). However, that apparel had been too large for him. Therefore on this occasion he would wait to hear from Schuster as to whose attire he would wear. 'Otherwise I will assume that I need only be dressed like a gentleman' (PRO, LCO6/913). As a Court of Appeal judge he made only a limited contribution to doctrine. The most celebrated is probably his 'officious bystander' test to determine the existence of implied terms in contract, a test known to generations of law students (*Shirlaw* v. *Southern Foundries Ltd* [1939]). He was also partial to the occasional expression of dry humour on the bench. He noted, for example, that the regular political shifts in the Rent Acts which the county court judges were charged with enforcing were hastening many of them to their graves in trying to interpret the legislation. He also, on a celebrated occasion, poked fun at the judicial omnipotence of the House of Lords, whom he dubbed in *Salisbury* (*Marquess*) v. *Gilmore* ([1942]), as the 'voices of infallibility'. This was a reference to the Lords' ruling in the nineteenth-century case of *Jorden* v. *Money* (1854) which laid down that estoppel was confined to representations of existing fact. Thus despite his own inclination (and the advocacy of Tom Denning KC) MacKinnon in the Court of Appeal was constrained from extending the doctrine to promises on which the promisee had relied to his detriment (needless to say Tom Denning approved the new doctrine in the famous *High Trees* decision four years later: see *Central London Property Trust Ltd* v. *High Trees House Ltd* [1947]). On another occasion during a workmen's compensation hearing he remarked that, 'If by some happy catastrophe the vast mass of reported cases had been wholly destroyed … I should be of opinion that this appeal should succeed' (see *Noble* v. *Southern Railway Co* [1939]). The House of Lords took the hint and promptly overruled the offending authorities.

As a Court of Appeal judge, MacKinnon's pragmatic qualities were widely recognized and his contribution to doctrine, though not extensive, was appreciated. Had he eschewed his practice as a judge of first instance of not reserving judgment, it is possible that his judicial reputation would have been greater. He had been talked about as a potential House of Lords replacement in 1938 but the call never came and Lord Porter was in fact appointed. He was prone, like some other judges, to display remoteness from 'real life'. For example in a famous libel case in 1943 following the publication in the magazine *Lilliput* of a photograph of a famous male milliner to the queen, juxtaposed next to the picture of a pansy, MacKinnon had to turn to the lord chief justice, Goddard, for enlightenment. Having once remarked (presumably in jest) that 'he is the best judge whose name is known to fewest readers of the *Daily Mail*' (MacKinnon, *On Circuit*, 27), he would have been in danger, in less deferential times, of exposing his ignorance to the yellow press.

Indeed MacKinnon was himself nothing if not sensationalist when it came to describing (fortunately deceased) judicial colleagues. For he considered that judges were as much a suitable subject for the judgement of history as any other public figures. Thus in 1944 he noted that Sir John Compton Lawrance had been, 'a stupid man, a very ill-equipped lawyer and a bad judge', though he regarded Sir Edward Ridley as the worst judge that he had appeared before: 'Ridley had much better brains than Lawrance, but he had a perverse instinct for unfairness that Lawrance could never approach' (Shetreet, 242). As to the unfortunate McCardie (who committed suicide over debts), he observed that 'the future student of Law Reports will [not] infer from his prolix disquisitions that McCardie was a great judge' (MacKinnon, *Law Quarterly Review*, 238). Yet of other judges he would be much kinder. In his *Dictionary of National Biography* entry on Lord Sumner—one of several legal subjects on whom he wrote—he praised the latter's judgments and admired his (as he thought) magnetic personality. Mr Justice Talbot, another *Dictionary of National Biography* subject for his sharp pen, was his ideal judge, especially as his name was 'unknown to the readers of cheap newspapers' (ibid.).

Literary and antiquarian interests MacKinnon was a student of literature as well as of law, and had a particular interest in eighteenth-century writers. For many years he was a member of the Johnson Club and contributed a fine essay entitled 'The law and the lawyers' to the collection *Johnson's England* (1933), edited by A. S. Turberville. The lucidity and the acuteness of observation in that essay could still be recognized decades later when the 'new social history' of crime and the criminal law was influencing academic writing on the eighteenth-century 'bloody code'. Similar remarks might also be made regarding his monograph, *Grand Larceny* (1937), which described the trial in 1800 at Taunton assizes, for the capital offence of stealing from a shop, of Jane Leigh Perrot, an aunt of Jane Austen. Other works of literature by MacKinnon (some of which were contained in a collection, *Inner Temple Papers*, published in 1948 after his death) include annotations to Charles Lamb's 'The old benchers of the Inner Temple' (1927); a scholarly edition of Fanny Burney's *Evelina* (1930); and, most significantly, *On Circuit: 1924–1937* (1940). Part travelogue, this volume captured well the atmosphere surrounding the English assize system, describing in diary form the day-to-day life of an itinerant judge. But it also contained much useful legal, historical, literary, and architectural detail, emphasizing MacKinnon's antiquarian interest in the physical as well as in the intellectual world of the past. His sadness at the damage caused to the Inner Temple library by 'Hitler's Havoc' is evident in the elaborate memorandum *The Ravages of the War in the Inner Temple*, which he wrote in 1945. Yet the project for restoring and renovating an inn to which he was devoted and to which he (sometimes anonymously) donated books and fine art (including a portrait of Sir Francis Page, the eighteenth-century 'hanging judge' who dealt harshly with the 'Berkshire blacks') received his enthusiastic approval. For he had always been highly critical of what he considered the vandalism of Victorian architects. Dogmatic in matters of literary and artistic taste, he roundly condemned the Victorian 'Restorers' of the Temple Church whom he identified as:

> Smirke, Cottingham, Willement, and the rest of the gang … To have got rid of their awful stained glass windows, their ghastly pulpit, their hideous encaustic tiles, their abominable pews and seats (on which alone they spent over £10,000) will be almost a blessing in disguise. (G[oodhart], 139)

He looked forward to the inn becoming once more, in the words of Lamb, 'the most elegant spot in the metropolis' (*DNB*).

MacKinnon's views on Victorian architects were characteristic of his strong opinions on cultural artefacts. Towards the end of his life he announced triumphantly in a Court of Appeal case concerning broadcasting that he did not possess a wireless, nor intended to obtain one. No doubt the protestation spoke to MacKinnon's genuine love of eighteenth-century culture but perhaps it also spoke to an intellectual snobbery. Indeed psychoanalysts might even advance a different kind of interpretation, pointing to a fundamental unhappiness with his twentieth-century cosmopolitan existence (his remarkable and prolonged devotion to his old college as well as to his inn, perhaps sanctuaries from the harsh realities outside the cocoon, surpassed the norm). 'Rather more than most people', noted Norman Birkett:

> he [MacKinnon] loved old things, old buildings, old books, old pictures … In a very special sense he lived in the past [and] … He never seemed quite reconciled to having been born in the age in which he lived, and he did his very best to try and live in another. (Birkett, 380)

MacKinnon was apparently more content to be remembered as a historian, literary critic, jurist and treatise writer, judicial biographer, antiquary, and architectural historian, than as an eminent Court of Appeal judge. While there is no indication that he did not perform his judicial duties in any other than a conscientious manner, he seemed to throw himself into his extra-curricular activities with peculiar enthusiasm, perhaps as an escape from the real world. This is what made him more interesting and indeed more important to subsequent generations than many of his contemporary judicial colleagues. But perhaps it also limited his judicial fame for posterity.

Although not political in the 'party political' sense, MacKinnon indulged his enthusiasms by holding office in legal and antiquarian organizations. As well as his presidency of the Average Adjusters' Association (1935), he was president of the Johnson Society of Lichfield (1933), president of the Buckinghamshire Archaeological Society, chairman of Buckinghamshire quarter sessions, a member of the Historical Manuscripts Commission, and a fellow of the Society of Antiquaries. He was a bencher of the Inner Temple (1923) and treasurer in 1945. He was also made an honorary fellow of Trinity College, Oxford, in 1931.

In appearance MacKinnon possessed bushy eyebrows, penetrating eyes, a pronounced angular nose, and firm mouth. A keen walker, he climbed Snowdon on two consecutive icy days in January 1931 when nearly sixty. His last years were saddened by the loss of his daughter, son-in-law, and young grandchild when their ship the *Almeda Star* was torpedoed in the Atlantic in 1941. Walking to work at the law courts, which was his regular practice, he suffered a heart attack and died soon afterwards at Charing Cross Hospital, London, on 23 January 1946. His wife and son, who became bursar of Eton College, survived him.

G. R. RUBIN

Sources DNB · N. Birkett, review of *Inner Temple papers*, *Law Quarterly Review*, 65 (1949), 380–84 · A. L. G[oodhart], 'F. D. M., 1871–1946', *Law Quarterly Review*, 62 (1946), 139–40 · *The Times* (24 Jan 1946) · PRO, LC06/861; LC06/913; LC02/1789 · S. Shetreet, *Judges on trial* (1976) · F. D. MacKinnon, *On circuit: 1924–1937* (1940) · F. D. MacKinnon, 'An unfortunate preference', *Law Quarterly Review*, 61 (1945), 237–8 · Lord Denning, *The discipline of law* (1979) · F. Bresler, *Lord Goddard* (1977) · P. Polden, *A history of the county court, 1846–1971* (1999)
Likenesses W. Stoneman, photograph, 1927, NPG · G. Kelly, pencil drawing, U. Birm., Holdsworth Club
Wealth at death £79,804 2s. 2d.: probate, 5 June 1946, CGPLA Eng. & Wales

MacKinnon, Henry (1773–1812), army officer, was born on 15 July 1773 at Longwood, near Winchester, the youngest of the four sons (there were also four daughters) of William MacKinnon, scion of an ancient Scottish family, and his wife, Louisa, daughter of James Vernon. He was educated at the military college of Tournai in Languedoc, France. In his youth, while his family was living in the Dauphiné, he reputedly knew Napoleon Bonaparte, who courted his sister.

On 31 May 1790 MacKinnon was commissioned into the 43rd foot, but he transferred into the Coldstream Guards in 1793. He first saw active service under Frederick, duke of York, in Flanders in 1794, and in 1798 was brigade major to Major-General George Nugent during the 1798 Irish uprising. He participated in the 1801 expedition to Egypt, and served in Hanover in 1805 and at the taking of Copenhagen in 1807. He married Catherine, daughter of Sir John *Call, first baronet, military engineer. They had two sons, George and Donald, who both joined the army.

MacKinnon saw distinguished service in the Peninsular War in Portugal from 1809 under Sir Arthur Wellesley (later first duke of Wellington). After participating in the Talavara campaign he was put in command of the 2nd brigade of the 3rd division from October 1809, and on 25 October he was gazetted a colonel. More distinguished service in Portugal ensued, including some at Busaco (1810), but he became sick in late June 1811 and was absent from his unit until 31 October.

On new year's day 1812 MacKinnon was promoted major-general; during the bitter winter siege of Ciudad Rodrigo, he led his brigade with great courage. At the storming of the fortress on 19 January 1812 he was blown up at the head of his brigade when a French magazine exploded, killing 108 men. His blackened body was recovered and buried by his nephew, Daniel *MacKinnon, Coldstream Guards. Wellington wrote in his dispatch: 'Major-General MacKinnon was unfortunately blown up by the accidental explosion of one of the enemy's expense magazines, close to the breach.' Major-General Thomas Picton wrote on 25 January that he was 'a most gallant, intelligent officer and estimable man'. A monument was erected in St Paul's Cathedral.   D. G. CHANDLER, rev.

Sources R. Southey, *History of the Peninsular War*, 2 (1827) · *GM*, 1st ser., 82/1 (1812), 190 · H. J. Rose, *A new general biographical dictionary*, ed. H. J. Rose and T. Wright, 12 vols. (1857), vol. 9 · private information (1993)

Mackinnon, Sir (**William**) **Henry** (1852–1929), army officer, was born in London on 15 December 1852, the younger son of William Alexander Mackinnon (1813–1903) of Acryse Park, Kent; his father was the son of William Alexander *Mackinnon (1784–1870) and the thirty-fourth chief of clan Fingon (Mackinnon), and served as Liberal MP for Rye (1852–3) and for Lymington (1857–68). His mother was Margaret Sophia, only daughter of Francis Willes. Mackinnon was educated from 1866 at Harrow School, and while still there was appointed to the Grenadier Guards in 1870 (ensign and lieutenant, by purchase, June 1870; lieutenant and captain, August 1872). From 1876 to 1880 he was adjutant to the 2nd battalion. From 1884 to 1885 he was military secretary to the governor of Malta (General Sir John Lintorn Simmons), and from 1885 to 1887 private secretary to the governor of Madras (Sir Mountstuart Grant Duff). Promoted colonel in February 1889, from July 1893 to 1898 Mackinnon was assistant adjutant-general, London district. When the Second South African War began in October 1899 he returned to the appointment as a temporary expedient.

The City of London Imperial Volunteers (CIV), with which Mackinnon's name became associated, was formed in December 1899, and, despite Volunteer officers' resentment at the appointment of a regular, Mackinnon was made colonel-commandant. The unit was raised and equipped by the City of London, and enlisted from members of the Honourable Artillery Company and of the Volunteer battalions of London and the adjoining counties, in civilian life largely clerks. The CIV, comprising an infantry battalion, mounted infantry, and a field artillery battery, went to South Africa in January 1900, and took part in engagements in the Orange Free State and the Transvaal. The mounted infantry, attached with other units as divisional troops to the 9th division, played a minor part in the movements which led to the relief of Kimberley on 15 February 1900, and assisted in the capture of Jacobsdal, which was held as a strategic position in the investment of

General Piet Cronje's laager. In March the same detachment fought in the action at Karee siding, which restored to the British the use of the railway bridge over the Modder River. During the advance from Bloemfontein to Kroonstad the City Imperial Volunteers was in support of the 21st brigade, and, in the advance from Kroonstad to Pretoria, it led the way in the battle of Doornkop on 29 May, capturing a hill after a sharp fight and putting to flight about 500 of the enemy. In June it attacked Klein-fontein Ridge as a preliminary to the battle of Diamond Hill. With the help of the Royal Sussex regiment, the ridge was captured on 11 June, and next day Diamond Hill itself was carried. In western Transvaal the CIV formed part of the force commanded by Horace Smith-Dorrien in pursuit of the elusive General Christiaan De Wet, while in the Orange Free State its battery assisted in the holding of Bloemfontein; it was represented in July at the action of Bakenkop, where it was heavily engaged. The mounted infantry, still with Smith-Dorrien's brigade, took part in the advance to Komati Poort in September, while in the previous month the battalion arrived for the third time at Pretoria.

The most outstanding CIV experiences were the battles of Doornkop and Diamond Hill, but all its achievements justified Mackinnon's faith, and his own reputation was enhanced by its exploits. The CIV left South Africa early in October 1900, and on reaching England received a tumultuous mass welcome—in which two persons were crushed to death in Ludgate Circus—on its march through London to a thanksgiving service at St Paul's Cathedral. Mackinnon was mentioned in dispatches and created CB; he published *The Journal of the CIV in South Africa* (1901).

Mackinnon, now a major-general, on returning to England was appointed to command the imperial yeomanry at Aldershot in 1901. In 1904 he was made director of auxiliary forces. He advised on the formation of the Territorial Force, and in 1908 became its director-general and was promoted lieutenant-general. With his tact and experience of Volunteers, he alleviated the problems of the new force. In 1910 he went to the western command as general officer commanding-in-chief. He was promoted full general in 1913. In February 1916 he was appointed director of recruiting at the War Office, but was replaced by Sir Auckland Geddes the following May.

Mackinnon, whose honours included the CVO (1903), KCB and KCVO (1908), GCB (1916), and the colonelcy of the King's regiment (Liverpool) 1916–23, retired in 1919, but continued active in a number of philanthropic organizations and movements in which he had a long-lasting and deep interest. He was chairman of the Heatherwood Hospital, Weybridge, and of the Royal Soldiers' Daughters' Home, Hampstead; vice-president of the Officers' Association, British Legion; a member of the councils of the United Service Fund, the Royal United Kingdom Beneficent Association, and the Gordon Boys' Home; a trustee of the Guards' Home; and the senior churchwarden of the guards' chapel, Wellington barracks. Possessing high ideals, and incapable of meanness or unkindness, he had a simple, unassuming, and charming personality.

Mackinnon married on 15 December 1881 Madeleine Frances (*d.* 1926), daughter of Lieutenant-Colonel Villiers La Touche Hatton (Grenadier Guards) of Clonard, co. Wexford, and they had one daughter. He died at his London home, 14 Evelyn Mansions, Carlisle Place, Westminster, on 17 March 1929.　　　C. V. OWEN, *rev.* ROGER T. STEARN

Sir William Mackinnon, baronet (1823–1893), by Eveleen Myers

Sources *The Times* (18 March 1929) · *Household Brigade Magazine* (spring 1929) · W. H. Mackinnon, *The journal of the CIV in South Africa* (1901) · T. Pakenham, *The Boer War* (1979) · R. Price, *An imperial war and the British working class: working-class attitudes and reactions to the Boer War, 1899–1902* (1972) · I. F. W. Beckett, *The amateur military tradition, 1558–1945* (1991) · E. M. Spiers, *Haldane: an army reformer* (1980) · P. Dennis, *The Territorial Army, 1906–1940*, Royal Historical Society Studies in History, 51 (1987) · J. H. Stogdon, ed., *The Harrow School register, 1845–1925*, 4th edn, 2 (1925) · Venn, *Alum. Cant.* · *WWBMP* · *Hart's Army List* (1891) · *WWW* · *Debrett's Peerage* · Burke, *Gen. GB* · Kelly, *Handbk* · Burke, *Peerage*
Archives Lpool RO, corresp. with seventeenth earl of Derby
Likenesses W. Stoneman, photograph, 1917, NPG · Spy [L. Ward], chromolithograph caricature, NPG; repro. in *VF* (7 Feb 1901) · photograph, repro. in P. J. Haythornthwaite, 'The Boer War', *Uniforms Illustrated*, 19 (1987), 35
Wealth at death £51,253 1s. 5d.: administration, 1 May 1929, *CGPLA Eng. & Wales*

Mackinnon, Sir William, baronet (1823–1893), shipping entrepreneur and imperialist, born at Campbeltown, Argyll, on 31 March 1823, was the son of Duncan Mackinnon (*d.* 1836) of Campbeltown and his wife, Isabella (*d.* 1861), daughter of John Currie of the same town. He was educated at Campbeltown, and was trained to the grocery trade there. Early in life, however, he came to Glasgow, and was employed in a silk warehouse and afterwards in the office of a merchant engaged in the Eastern trade. In 1847 he went out to India and joined his old schoolfellow Robert Mackenzie, who was engaged in the coasting trade in the Bay of Bengal. Together they founded the firm of Mackinnon, Mackenzie & Co. On 12 May 1856 Mackinnon married Janet Colquhoun (*d.* 1894), elder daughter of John Jameson of Woodside Crescent, Glasgow. They had no children.

On 29 September 1856 the Calcutta and Burmah Steam Navigation Company was founded mainly through Mackinnon's efforts. It was renamed the British India Steam Navigation Company on 8 December 1862. The company began with a single steamer plying between Calcutta and Rangoon, but under Mackinnon's direction it became one of the greatest shipping companies in the world, developing, and in many instances creating, a vast trade around the coast of India and Burma, the Persian Gulf, and the east coast of Africa, besides establishing subsidiary lines of connection with Britain, the Dutch East Indies, and Australia. He was careful to have his ships constructed in such a manner that they could be used for the transport of troops, thus relieving the Indian government from the necessity of maintaining a large transport fleet and ensuring employment for his vessels. His great business capacity did not override the humanity of his disposition: on learning that during a famine in Orissa his agents had made a contract with the government for the conveyance of rice from Burma at enhanced rates, he at once cancelled the agreement, and ordered that the rice should be carried at less than the ordinary price.

About 1873 the company established a mail service between Aden and Zanzibar. Mackinnon gained the confidence of the sultan, Seyyid Barghash, and in 1878 he opened negotiations with him for the lease of a territory extending 1150 miles along the coastline from Tungi to Warsheik, and extending inland as far as the eastern province of the Congo Free State. The district comprised at least 590,000 square miles, and included lakes Nyasa, Tanganyika, and Victoria Nyanza. The British government, however, declined to sanction the concession, which, if ratified, would have secured for Britain the whole of what became German East Africa. In 1886 Lord Salisbury, the foreign minister, used Mackinnon's influence to secure the coastline from Wanga to Kipini as a British sphere of influence, but declined to become directly involved in east Africa. Mackinnon formed the British East Africa Association, to promote the formation of a company; £250,000 was subscribed. A charter was granted, and the Imperial British East Africa Company was formally incorporated on 18 April 1888, with Mackinnon, who had subscribed 10 per cent of the shares, as chairman. The company acquired a coastline of 150 miles, including the excellent harbour of Mombasa, and extending from the River Tana to the frontier of the German protectorate. The company, which included among its principles the abolition of the slave trade, the prohibition of trade monopoly, and the equal treatment of all nationalities—and among its subscribers

Sir Thomas Fowell Buxton and the husband of Angela Burdett-Coutts—found itself seriously handicapped in its relations with foreign associations, such as the German East African Company, by the strenuous support which they received from their respective governments. The British government, on the other hand, was debarred by the principles of English colonial administration from offering similar assistance. The territory of the company was finally taken over by the British government on 1 July 1895 in return for a cash payment.

Mackinnon had a great part in promoting Sir H. M. Stanley's expedition for the relief of Emin Pasha. In November 1886 he addressed a letter, urging immediate action, to Sir James Fergusson, under-secretary of state for foreign affairs, and followed this by submitting to Lord Iddesleigh, the foreign secretary, a memorandum suggesting the formation of a small committee to send out an expedition. He and his friends subscribed more than half the sum of £29,000 provided for the venture, the rest being provided by the Egyptian government.

Mackinnon had contacts with Leopold, king of the Belgians. When, however, the awful condition of African forced labour in the Congo became known—the 'red rubber' scandal—Mackinnon became a prominent member of the anti-slavery campaign.

Mackinnon was for some time a director of the City of Glasgow Bank, and assisted in extricating the concern from its earlier difficulties. In 1870, finding that he could not approve the policy of the other directors, he resigned his seat on the board. On the failure of the bank in 1878 the liquidators brought a claim against him in the Court of Session for about £400,000. After protracted litigation Mackinnon, who had peremptorily declined to listen to any suggestion of compromise, was completely exonerated by the court from the charges brought against him, and it was demonstrated that the course taken by the directors was contrary to his express advice.

Mackinnon was an active supporter of the Free Church of Scotland. Towards the end of his life, however, the passage of the Declaratory Act, of which he disapproved, led to some difference of opinion between him and the leaders of the church, and he materially assisted the seceding members in the Scottish highlands. In 1891 he founded the East African Scottish Mission.

In 1882 Mackinnon was nominated CIE, and on 15 July 1889 he was created a baronet. He died in London, in the Burlington Hotel, on 22 June 1893, leaving an estate worth more than half a million pounds. He was buried at Clachan in Argyll on 28 June. The baronetcy became extinct with his death. Mackinnon possessed great administrative ability. When Sir Bartle Frere sent Sir Lewis Pelly to the Persian Gulf in 1862 he said, 'Look out for a little Scotsman called Mackinnon; you will find him the mainspring of all the British enterprise there.'

E. I. Carlyle, *rev.* John S. Galbraith

Sources J. S. Galbraith, *Mackinnon and east Africa, 1878–1895: a study in the new imperialism* (1972) · R. Oliver and G. Mathew, *History of East Africa*, 1 (1963) · *The Scotsman* (23 June 1893) · *The Scotsman* (29 June

1893) · *Glasgow Herald* (23 June 1893) · *The Times* (23 June 1893) · *CCI* (1893)
Archives SOAS, corresp. and papers relating to Africa, British India Steam Navigation Company, City of Glasgow bank, and Scottish estates | NL Scot., letters to Duncan Mackinnon · NRA, priv. coll., letters from the ninth duke of Argyll · PRO, FO 2, FO 83 (Africa) · PRO, FO 84 (slave trade)
Likenesses E. Myers, photograph, NPG [*see illus.*] · photograph, repro. in Galbraith, *Mackinnon and east Africa*, frontispiece · wood-engraving, NPG; repro. in *ILN* (24 Aug 1889)
Wealth at death £560,563 7s. 10d.: confirmation, 18 Oct 1893, *CCI*

Mackinnon, William Alexander, of Mackinnon (1784–1870), politician and chief of clan Mackinnon, born on 2 August 1784 in Dauphiné, France, was the eldest son of William Mackinnon and his wife, Harriet, daughter of Francis Frye of Antigua. Daniel *Mackinnon (1791–1836) was his younger brother. He matriculated at St John's College, Cambridge, in 1800 and graduated BA in 1804 and MA in 1807; he then became a student of Lincoln's Inn, but was not called to the bar. In 1809 he succeeded his grandfather, William Mackinnon, as chief of clan Mackinnon and inherited his estates. He was already wealthy from his father's success in the West Indies and used some of his money to buy back Mackinnon lands in Scotland. On 3 August 1812 he married Emma Mary (d. 1835), only daughter of Joseph Budworth *Palmer of Palmerstown, co. Mayo, who was a great beauty and an even greater heiress; they had three sons and three daughters. In due course he inherited the Palmer estates.

In 1819, with the support of the Barne family, Mackinnon was returned for Dunwich as a tory; he did not stand in 1820. He was elected for Lymington in 1831, but lost the seat in 1833 because of his tory speech on the Reform Bill on 20 March 1832, which was published. He was re-elected for Lymington in 1835 and retained the seat until 1852. When his son William Alexander Mackinnon (1832–1903) was unseated on petition, in 1853, for Rye, Mackinnon was returned for that borough without opposition, and he was re-elected in 1857 and 1859. In 1865 he finally retired. During the many years that he sat in parliament he proved himself a hard-working and useful member. Though classed as a Conservative, he was from the mid-1830s at the least a liberal conservative, and a free-trader. He brought in bills for the amendment of the patent laws, to prevent intramural interments in populous cities and towns (1842), and to abate the smoke nuisance; he also obtained select committees on the removal of Smithfield market and later promoted measures relating to turnpike trusts and the establishment of a rural police (1855). Mackinnon was an unpaid colonization commissioner for South Australia and, in 1842, chairman of the UK Insurance Office and of the Society Against Cruelty. Elected a fellow of the Royal Society in 1827, he was also a fellow of the Royal Geographical and Asiatic societies and of the Society of Antiquaries. Besides some tracts, he published anonymously in 1828 a treatise *On Public Opinion in Great Britain and other Parts of the World*, which passed through two editions. It was subsequently rewritten in two volumes, as *History of Civilisation* (1846).

Mackinnon had seats in co. Mayo, Kent, Hampshire, and Surrey, in addition to his Scottish estates. He died at one of his properties, Belvedere, Broadstairs, on 30 April 1870 and was buried at another, Acrise Park, Kent. His son William, a Liberal MP, succeeded him as chief of the clan. Another son, Daniel Lionel Mackinnon, was killed at the battle of Inkerman. His grandson Sir (William) Henry *Mackinnon served as an army officer in southern Africa.

H. C. G. MATTHEW

Sources *The Scotsman* (3 May 1870) · *The Times* (3 May 1870) · *Dod's Parliamentary Companion* · Venn, *Alum. Cant.* · HoP, *Commons* · **Archives** BL, corresp. with Sir Robert Peel, Add. MSS 40418–40594 · **Likenesses** lithograph (after unknown artist), BM, NPG · **Wealth at death** under £100,000: probate, 17 May 1870, *CGPLA Eng. & Wales*

Mackintosh family (*per. c.*1491–1606), clan chiefs, occupied strategic lands to the south and east of Inverness which they held from the earls and bishops of Moray, together with parts of Badenoch held from the earls of Huntly. By inheritance they were superiors of lands in Lochaber occupied by Camerons and MacDonalds who remained loyal to their own chiefs. The head of the Mackintosh family was chief of his own clan and also captain of the clan Chattan, a loose confederation of some dozen smaller clans in the area, who kept their own identity but supplied him with fighting men and looked to him for protection. **Farquhar Mackintosh** (*d.* 1514) was the only surviving son of Duncan Mackintosh (*d.* 1496) and Lady Florence, daughter of Alexander *MacDonald, third lord of the Isles and earl of Ross [see under MacDonald family (*per. c.*1300–*c.*1500)]. During his father's lifetime Farquhar supported Alexander MacDonald of Lochalsh in his rebellion, was captured in 1495 and imprisoned until after the death of James IV in 1513. While in prison Farquhar is said to have written an account of the family which formed the basis of later histories. He died within a year of his release, leaving two illegitimate sons. During Farquhar's imprisonment the clan was led by his cousin and eventual successor, William Mackintosh (*d.* 1515), who undertook several revenge raids into Rannoch, Appin, and Glencoe, and finally moved against the Camerons in Lochaber. He resisted joining the next MacDonald rising in 1503–6, remaining loyal to the king. He made an important marriage with Isabel McNiven, coheir of the lands of Dunachton in Badenoch, which he held alone after buying out his wife's sister. His successors as chiefs used the designation Mackintosh of Dunachton for nearly a century.

William Mackintosh was murdered in Inverness by a rival for the chiefship, and his brother Lachlan Mackintosh (*d.* 1524) was murdered while hunting, leaving a three-year-old son **William Mackintosh** (*c.*1521–1550). Lachlan had married Jean, daughter of Sir Alexander Gordon and Janet Kennedy, mistress of King James IV and mother of James Stewart, earl of Moray (*d.* 1544). This marriage brought the clan into the web of raids, alliances, and jealousies which surrounded Moray, and especially involved it in the rivalry between the earls of Huntly and

Moray, from both of whom the Mackintoshes held land. Moray took charge of his young nephew, but the clan was then led by Farquhar's bastard son Hector, who unsuccessfully tried to make himself chief and attacked Moray's lands. In 1540 William took over control of his clan, at first with the support of Moray. The latter's death in 1544 left Mackintosh at the mercy of Huntly at a time when ownership of the Lochaber lands also brought him into conflict with MacDonald of Clanranald and Cameron of Lochiel. In 1549 Huntly was given the earldom of Moray and became sole superior of Mackintosh and the clan Chattan. William was forced into reluctant dependence on Huntly but the earl apparently feared the power that Mackintosh could command within his territory and accused him of conspiracy to murder him. William was tried in Aberdeen and beheaded at Strathbogie on 23 August 1550. His estates were forfeited.

William Mackintosh was succeeded by his son **Lachlan Mackintosh** (*c.*1543–1606), who was brought up by Kenneth Mackenzie of Kintail, whose daughter he later married, while the clan was led by a cousin, Donald 'Williamson'. Huntly's action was declared illegal in 1557, and Lachlan, with his estates restored, was free to join the court of Mary, queen of Scots. In 1562, with the clan Chattan, he was in the royal army at the battle of Corrichie where Huntly was defeated and died. The following years saw many changes of fortune for Lachlan's superiors. Huntly had lost the earldom of Moray to the queen's half-brother, and his successors sought to strengthen their base in Badenoch by rebuilding Ruthven Castle and trying to undermine the loyalty of part of clan Chattan. In the famous feud between Huntly and Moray which culminated in the murder of Moray in 1592, Mackintosh supported the latter, who was a protestant, and at the battle of Glenlivet in 1594 fought under the earl of Argyll against the victorious 'Catholic earls'. Though he lived at a time of much fighting Lachlan was essentially a man of peace, but his son Angus, who led the clan on several occasions, wanted a stronger policy. When he failed to persuade his father to such action he departed for the continent and died at Padua in 1593. Lachlan died in September or October 1606 and was the first chief to be buried at Petty, near Inverness, thereafter the family mausoleum. He left a grandson, Lachlan, to lead the clan in the following century. That the Mackintoshes were involved in much of the turmoil of the sixteenth century owed more to the position of their lands than to their size. They were courted by greater men who looked for their support and they formed bonds and alliances with many of their neighbours, some of which lasted while others were quickly rejected as they struggled to maintain themselves in their clan territory.

R. W. MUNRO and JEAN MUNRO

Sources A. M. Mackintosh, *The Mackintoshes and clan Chattan* (1903) · W. Macfarlane, *Genealogical collections concerning families in Scotland*, ed. J. T. Clark, 2 vols., Scottish History Society, 33–4 (1900) · H. Paton, ed., *The Mackintosh muniments, 1442–1820* (1903) · M. Mackintosh of Mackintosh, *The history of the clan Mackintosh and the clan Chattan* (1997) · **Archives** NA Scot., GD 176

Mackintosh, Sir Aeneas [Angus], baronet (1751/2–1820), author, chief of clan Mackintosh, and captain of clan Chattan, was the only son of Alexander Mackintosh, and his wife, Janet Davidson (or Davison).

Aeneas (sometimes Anglicized as Angus) succeeded as chief of clan Mackintosh in 1770 following the death of his uncle, also Aeneas, who died childless. He raised a company in 1775 for the 2nd battalion of Fraser's Highlanders, which later became the 71st regiment. The following year he sailed with his company for America, to fight in the War of Independence under the command of the Hon. Simon Fraser, son of Lord Lovat. The company was called into action while crossing the Atlantic when its ship was attacked by an American privateer. Once in America, Mackintosh fought in the battle of Brooklyn and was involved in campaigns between 1777 and 1781. With the surrender of Lord Cornwallis in 1781 his military exploits came to a close, after which he and the company were held prisoners of war and did not return home until 1783, after hostilities had ceased.

Mackintosh married Margaret Grant, the youngest daughter of Sir Ludovic Grant of Dalvey on 5 November 1785. He then spent much of his time on his estate at Moy, Inverness-shire, which he set out to improve and consolidate. In addition to planting many trees he built a new residence, Moy Hall, at the northern end of Loch Moy. He entailed the family estates for his successors, and although he did much to improve his lands and allowed tenants to live on his estate rent free in times of hardship, he is perhaps best remembered for his work as an author.

Mackintosh's two works, *Notes Descriptive and Historical, Principally Relating to the Parish of Moy in Strathdearn* and *The Mackintoshes and Clan Chattan*, were both published posthumously. The latter was published in Edinburgh in 1903. *Notes Descriptive and Historical* was probably begun about 1774 and not completed until the author's return from America in 1783. The book was privately published in London in 1892 and was the more important of his works. It has served as an invaluable historical source on account of its vivid and entertaining descriptions of local concerns, highland customs, superstitions, and life in Inverness during the late eighteenth and early nineteenth centuries. Writing within living memory of the 1745 Jacobite uprising he curtailed the legend that had grown up around the activities of his aunt, wife of the twenty-second chief. Colonel Anne, as she was known, was said to have ridden a white horse at the head of her Jacobite regiment in the battlefield. His version of events was that she had simply managed to persuade 700 of the clan to take up arms for the Stewart cause by her agreeable conversation and insinuation. The book also includes numerous drawings and plans, and a map of the district. According to a historian of clan Mackintosh, A. M. Mackintosh, parts of the book concerning earlier family history reveal a certain misinterpretation of original sources.

Amiable and kind, Mackintosh was generally respected and well loved. His considerable powers of observation were complemented by his education and intelligence. As a mark of his position in the highlands he was made a baronet by George III in 1812. He died, aged sixty-eight, at the family seat, Moy Hall, on 21 January 1820. Being childless, his baronetcy died with him, and he was succeeded as clan chief by his second cousin, Alexander Mackintosh. Following a public breakfast at Moy Hall, the funeral procession of more than forty carriages and a large gathering of people on foot and horseback proceeded 16 miles to the parish of Petty, where he was interred at the family burying-place. A sumptuous dinner was later held at Cant's Hotel, Inverness, for the many gentlemen who wished to pay tribute to his memory. In 1824 his wife erected, at the cost of almost £1000, a 70 foot high obelisk of granite on the island in Loch Moy as a mark of her affection and regard for his memory.   CHRISTINE LODGE

Sources *Inverness Journal* (4 Feb 1820) · A. Mackintosh-Shaw, *Historical memoirs of the house and clan of Mackintosh and of the clan Chattan*, 2 vols. (1880) · A. M. Mackintosh, *The Mackintoshes and clan Chattan* (1903) · I. F. Grant, *Along a highland road* (1980) · private information (2004)
Likenesses portrait, priv. coll.

Mackintosh, Sir Alexander (1858–1948), political journalist, was born in Turriff, Aberdeenshire, on 3 February 1858, the son of William Mackintosh, station agent, and his wife, Catherine, *née* McGrigor. He was educated at Macduff and at Aberdeen University, and began his career in journalism at the age of nineteen as a reporter on the *Banffshire Journal*. In 1879 he joined the *Aberdeen Free Press*, where he was to remain until 1922. In 1881, when the press gallery of the House of Commons was opened to provincial journalists for the first time, the *Aberdeen Free Press* sent him to London to join the parliamentary staff. He arrived at Westminster just in time to hear and report Disraeli's last speech in the Lords, and to see Gladstone and Bright side by side on the Treasury bench in the Commons, and Lord Randolph Churchill and Arthur Balfour on the opposition side. In 1884 he married Annie, daughter of Andrew Bannerman of Bendigo, Victoria. They had a son and a daughter.

Mackintosh's reporting of parliament soon established a reputation for him, and he was made the London editor of the *Aberdeen Free Press* in 1887. His daily writings, first as sketch writer and later as lobbyist, displayed a good sense of political history and judgement in his interpretation of the policies and activities of members of parliament. He soon became known in political circles and was taken into the confidence of many leading political figures of the day, perhaps helped by the reputation which he established for himself through his *Joseph Chamberlain: an Honest Biography* (1906), which was thought empathetic as well as well researched. Even Asquith, who usually disliked journalists, sought his help when compiling his memoirs, and referred to his knowledge of politics as both wide and accurate. In 1894 he served as chairman of the parliamentary journalists' lobby committee and in 1927 as chair of the press's gallery committee. In 1923 he became the political correspondent for the *Liverpool Daily Post*, where he was to remain for fifteen years, gradually establishing a reputation as the doyen among political journalists. He was knighted in 1932 during the premiership of Ramsay MacDonald, who was a close personal friend.

Mackintosh left the press gallery in 1938, but maintained his interest in parliamentary affairs. He was present for every budget speech between 1881 and 1947 and contributed regular political notes to the *British Weekly* for over forty years. To his gossipy reminiscences of the house, *From Gladstone to Lloyd George* (1921), he added *Echoes of Big Ben* (1945). He died at his home, 57 Union Road, Clapham, London, on 15 April 1948, having continued to listen to all the major parliamentary debates until just before his death.   CHANDRIKA KAUL

Sources *DNB* · A. Mackintosh, *Echoes of Big Ben* (1945) · *WWW*
Archives HLRO, parliamentary press gallery records
Wealth at death £7143 15s. 7d.: probate, 28 Aug 1948, *CGPLA Eng. & Wales*

Mackintosh, Allan Roy (1936–1995), physicist, was born on 22 January 1936 in Nottingham, the younger of the two sons of Malcolm Roy Mackintosh and his wife, Alice, *née* Williams. His brother, Ian, was born in 1927. According to Mackintosh's own account,

> The family lived in a working-class neighbourhood of very good type, with honest and helpful people. My father joined the Royal Air Force when I was four years old, and thereafter I scarcely saw him again, because my parents were divorced at the end of the war. Thereafter we were very poor, but I nevertheless had a very happy childhood, largely due to my mother, whose support and deep belief in education, together with the availability of scholarships, allowed me to attend an excellent school and an excellent university. … My brother always set an excellent example, and it was largely through his influence that I became a physicist like him. (Bleaney, 323)

After attending Haydn Road primary school, Nottingham, he went as a foundation scholar to Nottingham high school from 1947 to 1954. From there he won a scholarship to Peterhouse, Cambridge, to read physics. He graduated with first-class honours in 1957, and won the Tait prize for physics both that year and in 1958. From 1957 to 1960 he continued his studies at the Royal Society Mond Laboratory in Cambridge where, supervised by Professor Brian Pippard, he investigated the Fermi surface of metals. He gained his PhD in 1960 for his dissertation, 'Ultrasonic attenuation in metals'.

While at Cambridge, Mackintosh met a young Danish woman, Jette Stannow, the daughter of Erik Stannow, industrial manager, and his wife, Ida, *née* Lyng. They married on 30 August 1958 at Birkerød, near Copenhagen. They had two daughters, Anne Karen (*b.* 1959) and Ida Alys (*b.* 1964), and a son, Paul Erik (*b.* 1962). In 1960 Mackintosh accepted an appointment as associate professor of physics at Iowa State University, Ames, where he continued his study of the electronic structure of metals by a variety of sophisticated techniques. He pioneered the use of positron annihilation and magneto-acoustic effects on liquid and solid metals. He also contributed to the theoretical understanding of various metals, including tungsten, gallium, and mercury.

At Ames, Professors F. W. Spedding and S. Legvold had begun separation of the lanthanide (rare earth) metals.

Because the chemical properties of these metals are very similar this was difficult. As soon as pure samples of the metals had been prepared the magnetic susceptibility and electrical resistivity were studied. Early measurements of the heat capacity at low temperatures in Oxford started with the lighter elements, moving on to terbium, which has a large hyperfine structure. Attempts at Ames to interpret preliminary measurements by neutron scattering on polycrystalline metals showed that single crystals were needed. The first samples of sufficient size for a range of measurements were prepared there in the late 1950s. They revealed that the magnetic properties are unusually complicated through the interplay of exchange and crystal field interactions. Clearly, further investigations would form a challenge to the inquisitive physicist. Mackintosh took this up and established himself as the leading expert in this new field. Following a sabbatical year (1963–4) at the Danish National Laboratory, Risø, he realized that neutron scattering could provide precise information on the magnetic and lattice dynamics of the lanthanide metals.

Mackintosh and his family moved permanently to Denmark in 1966. After four years as research professor at the Technical High School (later renamed the Technical University of Denmark) he was appointed professor of physics at Copenhagen University. In 1971 he became director of the National Laboratory at Risø, near Roskilde. Mackintosh had taken with him some single crystals of rare earth metals. On these, using a new reactor and novel techniques for neutron scattering experiments, with Hans Bjerrum Møller and others he made the first measurements on spin waves and magnetic structures. After the lighter lanthanide elements he studied some alloys and found that the interactions were anisotropic and again very complicated. In addition to his own work he provided the motivation and encouragement for many others, in England as well as in Denmark. He remained as director of the Danish National Laboratory until 1976, when he returned to his chair in Copenhagen.

In later years Mackintosh turned his attention to the history of physics, including the first use of computers for calculations. At a conference, in an after-dinner speech later published as a posthumous paper in *Notes and Records of the Royal Society of London* (1997), he compared the work of Ernest Rutherford and Niels Bohr. His title, 'The crocodile and the elephant', alluded to the crocodile carved on the wall of the Royal Society Mond Laboratory in Cambridge, and the order of the Elephant, one of the highest Danish national honours, awarded to Bohr. An earlier publication of the Royal Danish Scientific Society, in 1980, showed that Mackintosh had mastered the Danish language—the title (in English) was 'From chaos to order: solid state physics in the twentieth century'. He drew attention to the little-known doctoral thesis by Niels Bohr, entitled 'Studies of the electron theory of metals' (1911). At Cambridge, Bohr had attempted to interest Sir Joseph Thomson in it, without success because it was in Danish. Somewhat disappointed, Bohr turned his attention to other phenomena—'a loss for metal physics, but a great step forward for atomic physics' (Bleaney, 327).

Mackintosh was a firm believer in international co-operation in science. He was president of the European Physical Society from 1980 to 1982 and served on many committees in Brussels, being particularly influential in the development of the EU large installation programme. He was a member of the Danish planning committee for research from 1982 to 1985 and director of the Nordic Institute for Theoretical Physics from 1986 to 1989. With Jens Jensen he wrote *Rare Earth Magnetism: Structures and Excitations* (1991), which soon became a classic text. He was appointed a knight of the Dannebrog order in 1975, and received the F. H. Spedding award in 1986. He was elected a member of the Danish Academy of Technical Sciences in 1972, the Royal Danish Academy of Science and Letters in 1977, and FRS in 1991. He died in Roskilde, Denmark, following a car accident on 20 December 1995. He was survived by his wife and three children. A memorial symposium was held in Copenhagen on 26–9 August 1996; the proceedings were published by the Royal Danish Academy of Science and Letters in 1997.   BREBIS BLEANEY

Sources H. B. Møller, 'Allan R. Mackintosh', address at memorial gathering, Copenhagen, 26–9 Aug 1996 · B. Bleaney, *Memoirs FRS*, 43 (1997), 323–31 · *The Independent* (11 Jan 1996) · *WWW*
Likenesses photograph, repro. in Bleaney, *Memoirs FRS*, 321

Mackintosh [*née* Farquharson], **Anne** [*nicknamed* Colonel Anne], **Lady Mackintosh** (1723–1784), Jacobite campaigner, was the eldest daughter of John Farquharson of Invercauld, Braemar, Scotland, who had himself been (coercedly) 'out' in the 1715 rising (for which he was subsequently pardoned). In February 1741 Anne married Aeneas (or Angus) Mackintosh of Mackintosh (*d.* 1770), whose seat, Moy Hall, some 12 miles from Inverness, was on the edge of Drumossie or Culloden Muir, where the Jacobite cause would suffer decisive defeat on 16 April 1746. While clan Chattan, of which Aeneas was captain, was predisposed to come out on the Jacobite side in 1744, Aeneas himself was less obviously committed, holding, from December 1744, a commission in one of three new companies which he had raised for the Hanoverian government's regiments. In January 1746 he raised a full company in the government Highland regiment. In character a vacillator, whether Mackintosh connived in his wife's later actions or whether Anne acted on her own initiative is unclear; such apparently divided allegiances might be less ideological than pragmatic. What is certain is that Anne raised, personally, some 600 men for the Stuart cause. Of these, 300 were retained for the protection of the Moy estate, the remainder joining Lord Lewis Gordon at Perth and thence Charles Edward Stuart's forces at Stirling.

Lady Mackintosh's other direct involvement in the Jacobite rising of 1745 occurred on Sunday 16 February 1746. Having received Prince Charles Edward and an escort of some thirty highlanders at Moy Hall, she contrived their escape on being warned of the approach of government forces commanded by John Campbell, fourth earl of Loudoun, from the garrison at Inverness, whence they would

Anne Mackintosh, Lady Mackintosh (1723–1784), by Allan Ramsay, *c.*1748

return following the rout of Moy, a successful tactical ambush by five of Lady Mackintosh's men. Following the larger defeat of the Highland regiment near Dornoch on 20 March, Lady Mackintosh was given charge of her husband and it was in their exchange on this occasion that, apocryphally, she acquired the title Colonel Anne. In the aftermath of Culloden she was imprisoned at Inverness for six weeks. Contrary to some accounts she was not taken to London, which she would not visit until 1748, when, like Flora Macdonald, she would find herself 'caressed' by sympathetic 'ladys of quality' (Sir Aeneas Mackintosh, quoted in MacDonald, 16). In 1763 she was elected 'burges freewoman and guildsister' (ibid.) of Inverness. Following the death of her husband, in 1770, she removed to the Edinburgh port of Leith, where she died on 2 March 1784 after a five-month illness, 'presenting the use of her reason to the last' (ibid., 19). She had no children.

Colonel Anne was the victim both of the instant accretion of mythology surrounding the 'Forty-Five and of prevalent concepts of femininity—those of her own day and of the nineteenth century in which the Jacobite era would be represented. She has thus been variously idealized as a 'Highland Joan of Arc' (W. D. Norie, *The Life and Adventures of Charles Edward Stuart*, 1901, 3.102)—from the erroneous idea, significantly taken up by nineteenth-century painters and illustrators, that she actually led in person at the battle of Falkirk the 300 men she had contributed—and demonized in the contemporary whig press in Edinburgh but especially London as an Amazonian figure, a masculine, armed 'woman of monstrous size'. A surviving portrait by Allan Ramsay, dated *c.*1748, bears out the contemporary observation of her husband's nephew, Sir Aeneas *Mackintosh, of 'a very thin girl' (Macdonald, 7); her alleged size and masculinity may be taken as the corollary of her masculinity of independent initiative. This was, in fact, limited. According to Sir Aeneas she 'never saw the men but once, and was at her own house' (ibid.) during times of military engagement. Lady Mackintosh's surviving correspondence suggests a conventional domesticity and familial concern, in keeping with the cockade-sewing hinted at by the expenditure on white ribbon documented in the Moy household accounts for 8 and 11 April 1746. She was buried in North Leith: the inscription on the 1820 stone makes no reference to her Colonel Anne persona.

EIRWEN E. C. NICHOLSON

Sources F. Macdonald, 'Colonel Anne': Lady Anne Mackintosh (1987) · M. Craig, 'Damn' rebel bitches': the women of the '45 (1997)
Likenesses A. Ramsay, oils, c.1748, Moy Hall, Inverness [see illus.] · J. Macardell, mezzotint (after A. Ramsay), BM, NPG

Mackintosh, Charles Fraser- (1828–1901), author and politician, was born at Inverness on 5 June 1828, the younger son of Alexander Fraser (1764–1834) of Dochnalurg and his wife, Marjory (d. 1865), daughter of Captain Alexander Mackintosh. By royal licence on 18 September 1857, in accordance with the will of his maternal uncle, Eneas Mackintosh, he assumed the additional surname of Mackintosh. At the age of fourteen he began his legal apprenticeship in Inverness and in 1849 he was sent to Edinburgh to continue his legal studies at the university where he attended classes in civil and Scots law, conveyancing, and rhetoric. In 1853 he established his own legal practice in Inverness. He retired from legal practice in 1867, and from 1869 to 1873 acted as commissioner on the Mackintosh estates, himself owning small estates outside Inverness. On 12 July 1876 he married Eveline May (d. 1925), only child of Richard David Holland, of Kilvean, Inverness-shire.

Fraser-Mackintosh began his political career in November 1857 when he was elected to the Inverness town council, serving until his resignation in 1862. During the 1860s he was responsible for a series of improvements in the town of Inverness. In February 1874, standing as an independent liberal, he was elected MP for the Inverness burghs seat, defeating the sitting Liberal member, Eneas W. Mackintosh of Raigmore. In his campaign Fraser-Mackintosh was supported by the more radical of the Inverness newspapers, the Advertiser and John Murdoch's Highlander. During the 1870s he was active in a range of causes, especially that of the Gaelic language. After the Education (Scotland) Act of 1872 a campaign to demand a place for Gaelic in the Scottish curriculum was initiated. This was promoted by the Gaelic Society of Inverness, of which Fraser-Mackintosh was one of the founding members in 1871. Minor concessions for the language were secured in the 1870s. Fraser-Mackintosh was also prominent in the successful campaign to endow a chair of Celtic in the University of Edinburgh. During the period from 1874 to 1885 he was popularly known as the Member for the Highlands owing to his popularity among the crofters

of the highland counties who were not enfranchised until 1885.

In 1882, along with Donald H. MacFarlane, the member for co. Carlow in Ireland, Fraser-Mackintosh called for the establishment of a royal commission to inquire into the crofting issue. When that commission was appointed (1883) under the chairmanship of Lord Napier, Fraser-Mackintosh was appointed as a member. The Napier commission toured the highlands in 1883 taking evidence and reported the following year. Although few of its recommendations were implemented in later legislation the commission was central in giving greater publicity to the cause of the crofters. In 1885 Fraser-Mackintosh accepted the nomination to stand as a crofter candidate in Inverness-shire, the Scottish county electorate having been greatly expanded by the reforms of 1885. When the Liberal Party divided over the issue of Irish home rule in 1886, Fraser-Mackintosh, alone among the crofter MPs, became a Liberal Unionist. Although a radical on land issues, he was sometimes described as an 'imperialist'. His belief in the repopulation of the highlands stemmed from his awareness of the martial tradition of highlanders and his desire to harness it for the British empire. At the general election of July 1892 he was opposed by a crofter candidate, Dr Charles MacGregor, and defeated.

Fraser-Mackintosh was also a noted historian and genealogist. His primary interest was clan genealogy and the history of Inverness and the surrounding region. His historical columns in the Inverness Advertiser and The Highlander were collected as Antiquarian Notes, published in 1865, reprinted in 1897, and with a second edition in 1913. Invernessiana: Contributions toward a History of the Town and Parish of Inverness, from 1160 to 1599 was published in 1875 and his third major work, Letters of Two Centuries Chiefly Connected with Inverness and the Highlands, from 1616 to 1815, was published in 1890. In addition, Fraser-Mackintosh was a frequent contributor to the Transactions of the Gaelic Society of Inverness. He was awarded the honorary degree of doctor of laws by the University of Aberdeen in 1897 for his contribution to the literature of the highlands. Fraser-Mackintosh died in Bournemouth on 25 January 1901 and was buried in Kensal Green cemetery, London. He was survived by his wife; they had no children.

EWEN A. CAMERON

Sources I. M. M. MacPhail, The crofters' war (1989) · K. MacDonald, 'Life of the author', in C. Fraser-Mackintosh, Antiquarian notes: a series of papers regarding families and places in the highlands, 2nd edn (1913) · Inverness Courier (29 Jan 1901) · J. Hunter, The making of the crofting community (1976) · E. A. Cameron, Land for the people (1996) · Burke, Gen. GB · CCI (1901) · CGPLA Eng. & Wales (1901) · E. A. Cameron, 'The political career of Charles Fraser Mackintosh, 1874–1892', Transactions of the Gaelic Society of Inverness, 60 (1996–8), 70–119 · E. A. Cameron, The life and times of Fraser Mackintosh, crofter MP (2000) · Oban Times (2 Feb 1901)
Archives Inverness Library, Fraser-Mackintosh Library · NA Scot.
Wealth at death £7281 10s. 0d.: confirmation, 26 July 1901, CCI · additional estate, 3 Aug 1907

Mackintosh, Charles Rennie (1868–1928), architect, decorative artist, and watercolour painter, was born on 7 June

Charles Rennie Mackintosh (1868–1928), by James Craig Annan, 1893

1868 at 70 Parson Street, Glasgow, the fourth of the eleven children of William McIntosh (*c*.1837–1908), a clerk in the Glasgow police force, and his first wife, Margaret Rennie (*c*.1837–1885). He was educated at Reid's Public School and Allan Glen's Institution, both in Glasgow, between 1875 and 1884, and from 1884 to 1889 he was an articled pupil in the office of a local architect, John Hutchison. From 1889 he worked as a draughtsman with Honeyman and Keppie, one of the leading architectural firms in Glasgow, where he remained for most of his architectural career. It was in the office of Honeyman and Keppie, at first as a draughtsman and from 1901 as a partner, that he designed his finest buildings for sites in and around Glasgow and much of his remarkable decorative work. He was extraordinarily creative but his career was uneventful, at least until it started to go wrong. For many years it was simply the story of his work.

Early work in Glasgow While training as an architect in professional offices, Mackintosh also attended Glasgow School of Art between 1883 and 1894. He was one of a group of talented students there, mainly young middle-class women, who called themselves The Immortals. Herbert McNair, a colleague from Honeyman and Keppie, was also part of the group and in the mid-1890s he and Mackintosh worked closely with the sisters Margaret and Frances Macdonald, painting complex watercolours and designing posters and works of decorative art. Symbolism, the arts and crafts movement, and art nouveau are all influences on this work. Mackintosh's experiences at

Glasgow School of Art and the friendships he made there seemed to settle the shape of his career, with its interplay of architecture, decorative art, and painting, and he learned a good deal about himself and his abilities. Hardworking, voluble, kind, sometimes moody, and above all talented, he moved easily among these women despite his working-class origins. A photograph of 1893 by James Craig Annan shows him as he learned to see himself, dressed in the style of an artist of the 1890s rather than in the dark suit and stiff collar of the professional architect which he wore at Honeyman and Keppie. In a way, his whole life was lived between the identities of architect and artist.

When Mackintosh began work, progressive architects in Britain were playful and eclectic. They mixed several styles in a single building, handled masses freely, and focused attention on individual details. The high academic styles, classical and Gothic, no longer had authority over them. In Scotland eclecticism was combined with a specifically nationalist enthusiasm for a style derived from Scottish castles and tower houses and known as Scottish Baronial. This spirit of freedom and Scottishness informed much of Mackintosh's architectural work, though it was less obvious in his work as a decorative artist. It can be seen in the earliest building which can be confidently attributed to him, an addition to the printing office of the *Glasgow Herald* newspaper at 68–76 Mitchell Street in the centre of Glasgow (1894–95; now a centre for architecture and design). Here there is a dramatic corner tower and the upper stages break out into elaborate detail like a Scottish tower house. Indeed, it is hard to imagine an atmosphere more congenial to an architect of such determined originality as Mackintosh than this eclecticism. Later, when progressive architects turned to new ideals of formal composition and rational planning, it was a question whether Mackintosh could follow them.

In 1896 a competition was held for the design of a new building for Glasgow School of Art, to be built in the centre of the city. Honeyman and Keppie won the competition with a design by Mackintosh, which laid out studios and workshops in two ranges of equal length on either side of a centrepiece with tall wings at either end. For lack of funds, only the eastern part and the centrepiece were built in 1897–9, with the rest left to be completed later. Glasgow School of Art is an enigmatic and endearing building. It looks bare, as if the design had been generated only by its functions. But careful contemplation reveals Mackintosh's purely compositional skill. He handled parts of the building, bays, wings, whole façades, with a freedom and expressiveness most architects achieve only in their handling of detail. The freedom of eclecticism, which amounted to little more than playfulness in the hands of Mackintosh's British contemporaries, is here taken to an extreme, suggesting ambiguities and dislocations between the different parts, between inside and outside, between what seems to be the case and what is. The self-consciousness would be mannerist if Mackintosh had been working with rules that could be seen to be broken, but he was not. His design engages not with a stylistic code but with his own activity as a designer and with the perceptions of those who use and look at the building: it is a commentary upon itself.

In the years that Glasgow School of Art was being built, Mackintosh was also working at Honeyman and Keppie on Martyrs' Public School (1895–8; now in museum use), Queen's Cross Church (1897–9; now the headquarters of the Charles Rennie Mackintosh Society), and Ruchill Street Free Church Halls (1898–9). This was typical work in a respected architectural practice in a thriving industrial city at the end of the nineteenth century. Less typical was the decorative work which Mackintosh was beginning to do, some of it probably in his own name. In 1897 he designed stencilled decorations for Miss Cranston's Buchanan Street tea-rooms and in 1898 furniture for her Argyle Street tea-rooms. His first domestic interiors were a bedroom in Westdel, a middle-class house in Glasgow (1898?), and a dining-room in Munich for the publisher Hugo Bruckmann (1898?); the Buchanan Street decorations have been destroyed, but some furniture from the other interiors survives. It was work such as this which first brought Mackintosh to the notice of the public, for his architectural work was necessarily done in the name of Honeyman and Keppie. In 1897 the influential art magazine *The Studio* published two articles by Gleeson White on Mackintosh, the Macdonalds, McNair, and their associate Talwin Morris; this was followed in 1898 by an article of similar scope in the German magazine *Dekorative Kunst*.

When Mackintosh designed an interior he usually also designed furniture for it, and this was always a significant part of his production, running alongside larger projects. It was not unusual for progressive late Victorian architects to design furniture, but Mackintosh was peculiar in that he would almost always create new designs for each interior, so strong was his appetite for formal invention, so acute his sense of the wholeness of interiors. Conversely, he rarely designed furniture without a specific interior in mind, and never for any kind of industrial production. His work was, in this sense, bespoke.

Within each interior the furniture helped to create a harmonious and exclusive atmosphere. Some of the more ambitious pieces also played a subsidiary architectural role, articulating the space. The high-backed chairs which Mackintosh designed for the Argyle Street tea-rooms, for instance, created an intimate enclave when gathered round a table. The backs of these chairs have tall, tapering uprights with an oval headpiece slotted through them; they manage to combine a Japanese simplicity of construction with a weird sense of authority, as if they were creatures from another world. Furniture designed in this way might be expected to look odd once removed from its original setting, but it is a curious truth, and a tribute to the strength of Mackintosh's visual imagery, that his furniture designs, many of which are now widely available in reproduction, are not diminished when seen by themselves. The high-backed chairs, in fact, seem to grow in stature.

The busiest years On 22 August 1900 Mackintosh married Margaret Macdonald (1864–1933) [*see* Mackintosh, Margaret Macdonald] in the episcopal church at Dumbarton. (Herbert McNair had married Frances Macdonald, (1874–1921) in the previous year.) Their marriage set the seal on a personal and creative relationship that had been developing for some time, and the story of their life together and the nature of their work both suggest its profound importance for Mackintosh: he once told Macdonald that she was half, if not three quarters, of the inspiration for his architectural work. But Mackintosh's life is relatively poorly documented and the true, and no doubt changing, nature of their relationship cannot be firmly established for lack of evidence. It seems obvious that they would have collaborated on the decoration and furnishing of the flat at 120 Mains Street in the centre of Glasgow into which they moved when they got married, and this interior can be read as an intimate expression of their relationship. The dining-room was spare and dark, the drawing-room spare and light, in a heightened, aesthetic version of the gender code which divided contemporary middle-class interiors into dark masculine and light feminine areas. With the bedroom at Westdel, the Mains Street flat introduces a sequence of interiors very different from Mackintosh's earlier architectural work: stone gives way to softer, more ephemeral materials, the powerful but somehow conflicted intellect that expressed itself in the dislocations of Glasgow School of Art gives way to strong and simple emotion.

The first of these interiors was the ladies' luncheon room at Miss Cranston's Ingram Street tea-rooms, on which Mackintosh and Macdonald were working at the time of their marriage. Glasgow was famous for its tearooms, places of light refreshment serving good cheap food in pleasant surroundings. (In other cities they might be called cafés, tea shops, or refreshment rooms. In all such places alcohol was not served, thanks to the influence of the temperance movement.) Kate Cranston was well known among Glasgow tea-room proprietors for the quality of her establishments, the homely and artistic interiors of which catered particularly for middle-class women. In the 1890s she had employed a number of architects and designers, including Mackintosh, but now she began to give him all her work. At Ingram Street Mackintosh created a silvery-white interior with gesso panels of dreaming women in the frieze, one designed and made by him, the other designed and made by Macdonald. (The Ingram Street tea-rooms no longer exist, but the interiors have been partly reconstructed by Glasgow Museums.) Three years later he remodelled an entire building in Sauchiehall Street as the Willow Tea Rooms, on the first floor of which he and Macdonald created the most visually sumptuous of their feminine interiors, the Salon de Luxe. Although these interiors were quite unlike other tearooms in Glasgow or elsewhere, they worked well: the mixture of art and domesticity which Mackintosh and Macdonald had created for themselves at 120 Mains Street fitted Miss Cranston's needs exactly when transposed to a place of public refreshment.

Late in 1900 Mackintosh and Macdonald travelled to Vienna to supervise the installation of their work, and that of Frances Macdonald and Herbert McNair, at the eighth exhibition of the *Wiener Sezession*, the leading avant-garde art group in the city. Their work was not altogether well received by the critics, but they enjoyed good relations with the leaders of the *Sezession*, especially Josef Hoffmann, who seemed to be working along the same lines. Soon afterwards Mackintosh entered a German competition to design a *Haus eines Kunstfreundes* ('a house for an art-lover'). The remarkable designs, partly attributable to Macdonald, were unsuccessful, but they were lavishly published in Germany in 1902. In that year also, Mackintosh designed a music-room for Fritz Waerndorfer, one of the principal patrons of progressive decorative art in Vienna, again with contributions from Macdonald. Work and contacts such as these, together with the advocacy of the German architect and critic Hermann Muthesius in books and articles, gave Mackintosh something of a reputation in Europe, especially in Germany and Austria, and much has been made of this since his death. It has to be remembered that progressive British architecture and decorative art as a whole was very influential in Germany and Austria at the turn of the century; and Mackintosh was not, in fact, as widely known as some of his contemporaries. But his reputation was enough to make it painful for him, when demand for his work in Glasgow began to fall off, to reflect on the difference between his reception at home and abroad.

The favourite building type of progressive British architects at the turn of the century was the detached middle-class house in the suburbs or in the country: it could be so informal, and so traditional ('cottage', 'manor house'). Mackintosh designed several such houses, of which the most important were Windyhill in the village of Kilmacolm, west of Glasgow (1900–01), and the Hill House, Helensburgh, on the banks of the Clyde (1902–4; National Trust for Scotland). Both present a sequence of controlled but apparently artless and irregular façades clothed in harling (which the English call roughcast). With typical complexity, Mackintosh used harling both to create proto-modern abstract details and to locate his work within Scottish traditions, for harling was the usual covering for Scottish houses of the lesser gentry in the sixteenth and seventeenth centuries. At Windyhill the interior was relatively plain, in keeping with the tastes of the client, but at the Hill House, Mackintosh's full decorative repertory was brought into play. Spaces were defined by the pattern of carpets on the floor. The walls were stencilled with organic ornament as if the house was a garden. And all over the house pieces of coloured glass, worthless in themselves, were set into doors, light fittings, and balusters, so that as the light moves round the house they glow like jewels. With its plain, harled exterior and its jewelled, decorative interior, the Hill House presents one of the most telling examples of dislocation in Mackintosh's work.

By the time the Hill House was completed in the spring of 1904, a change was coming over Mackintosh's work. At Glasgow School of Art he had been all playfulness and dislocation. At Scotland Street School (1903–6; now a museum), a building of a similar type, he was calm and rational: the elevations clearly express the orderly plan, except that a pair of semicircular stair towers noticeably do not contain spiral stairs. He knew that progressive architects in Britain, and especially in Glasgow, were moving away from eclecticism towards ideals of order and efficiency. Beaux-Arts training in Paris, the classical tradition, and steel-framed office buildings in America: these were their enthusiasms, and Mackintosh hoped perhaps to share them. His decorative art did not always march in step with his architecture, but it underwent a similar change at this time. At Hous'hill (dem.), an old house on the outskirts of Glasgow which he decorated and furnished in 1904–5 for Kate Cranston and her husband, John Cochrane, a shift can be seen away from organic ornament, sensuousness, and hints of symbolism towards clarity, rectilinear forms, and the decorative use of squares.

Scotland Street School and Hous'hill are outstanding works, and yet there was perhaps a loss of nerve mixed up in these changes. Around 1905 the flow of work which had kept Mackintosh busy and creative for eight or nine years showed signs of drying up. Normally he prided himself on his creative independence, but in 1906 he designed a house in a broadly conventional Cotswold style (Auchinibert, Killearn, 1906–8), simply because that was what the client wanted.

Later work in Glasgow Then, early in 1907, Honeyman, Keppie, and Mackintosh were asked to complete the building of Glasgow School of Art. Between 1907 and 1909 the west range was completed broadly to the original design and the west wing was completely recast. Mackintosh treated the wing as a sheer tower up the west face of which run three immensely tall oriels, 63 feet of stone, iron, and glass, a treatment derived from the canted bays which lit the rear elevations of contemporary, American-inspired office buildings in Glasgow. Mackintosh was borrowing from the new progressives here, but only for certain effects, not in the design of the building as a whole. It is not rationality which makes the west wing remarkable, but its vertical drama, and elsewhere he created contradictions as remarkable as any in the 1896–9 phase. In the library, the principal interior of the west wing, the wooden gallery is a rectilinear forest of quasi-constructional timber. On one side it runs right across the face of Mackintosh's great oriels, cancelling out their light. Glasgow School of Art is Mackintosh's masterpiece, and the west wing and the library are its most masterly parts, but they were designed in the spirit of 1890s' eclecticism. By the time the building was finished it was out of date. The magazine of the architecture students at the school, among whom the new progressivism ruled, described it as 'bizarre'.

Between the completion of Glasgow School of Art in 1909 and the outbreak of war in 1914, Mackintosh had only six new jobs, none of them large, though the Chinese Room and the Cloister Room at Miss Cranston's Ingram Street tea-rooms, of 1911–12, are both powerful designs.

His career was beginning to fall apart, but it is not clear exactly why. The office records of Honeyman, Keppie, and Mackintosh suggest that the firm's workload fell by half in 1910 and half again in 1911, and recovered only in 1914. John Keppie, Mackintosh's active partner, seems to have suffered equally in these fallow years, and the loss of work was not peculiar to Mackintosh. But it was probably complicated in his case by a habit of heavy drinking and a tendency to depression, for both of which there is good evidence. At all events, he seemed to lose his grip professionally. In 1913 he was responsible for the firm's entry in a competition for a teacher-training college in Glasgow. As the deadline approached, he had almost nothing to show and the job was taken away from him. Shortly afterwards he left the partnership and opened an office of his own; so far as is known, he got no work.

Wanderings In the middle of July 1914 Mackintosh and Macdonald went on holiday to the seaside village of Walberswick in Suffolk. About three weeks later war broke out. They decided to stay on in Walberswick and, as things turned out, Mackintosh never went back to Glasgow except to visit. His parting from his native city, with which so much of his creative life was bound up, was thus casual and accidental. While they were staying at Walberswick, Mackintosh painted more than forty delicate watercolours of flowers in the precise style of botanical illustrations but with an eye, as always, to decorative effect. He had used watercolour before, not only to embellish sketches he made from nature but also as the chosen medium for his earliest substantial experiments as a painter, the symbolic and decorative watercolours he created alongside McNair and the Macdonalds in the 1890s. Now its simplicities acted as a kind of healing. By January he seemed to Macdonald much improved. But then he was reported to the military authorities on suspicion of spying. This absurd idea arose from his Glasgow accent, his sketching, his habit of taking long solitary walks at dusk, and the real fear of invasion on the east coast. It seemed to be confirmed in early May, when the military authorities found letters from Germany (all some years old) among his belongings. Mackintosh was asked to leave the area, and went to London; Macdonald followed soon after. In August they found two studios to rent, next door to each other in Glebe Place, Chelsea.

Mackintosh and Macdonald spent the next eight years in Chelsea, with little money and little prospect of work in a strange city during wartime. Late in 1915, as if in a fairy story, W. J. Bassett-Lowke, a manufacturer of scale models and an ardent modernist, asked Mackintosh to remodel a small house for him in Northampton, 78 Derngate (1916–19). Mackintosh's vivid, Viennese-inspired interiors show that he had regained his creative nerve, as do the dozen or so watercolour still lifes he painted at this time and the textile designs which he and Macdonald produced in their hundreds and sold to manufacturers to make ends meet. In the watercolours and textiles particularly, Mackintosh drew freely and fruitfully on Post-Impressionist and Fauve work, and on Bakst and the Ballets Russes. With these progressives, at least, he was in tune. But the couple were continually short of money and, as in Glasgow, it is not easy to catch the tenor of their lives. They had good friends among the artists of Chelsea—they could call themselves bohemians now, and put a bold face on their adversity—but stories of Mackintosh's depression recur. In photographs of this date he looks saddened. After the war he was asked to design studio-houses and studio-flats in and around Glebe Place, and for a few months in 1920 he had as much work on his drawing-board as in his busiest Glasgow days. But almost all the commissions fell through, and all that was built was one studio-house, 49 Glebe Place (1920–21), much altered from his original design.

In 1923 Mackintosh and Macdonald went to the south of France for a holiday that turned into something much longer. They stayed in the Roussillon region, where the Pyrenees meet the Mediterranean, a quiet, expatriate couple moving from place to place, living in hotels, and depending greatly on each other. They were probably most often in Port Vendres, a busy little town where the cargo boats unloaded from Algeria. Mackintosh now painted with a steady purpose, producing a series of more than forty watercolours, mainly views of rocks, buildings, and landscapes rendered in a stylized, geometrical manner and drenched with colour. In leaving Britain he had given up any hope that he might practise again as an architect, and painting was now at the centre of his life. These late watercolours were much more ambitious than most of those he had painted in Glasgow or Walberswick. His letters at this time show him scrutinizing the landscape, struggling to adapt the medium to his purposes. When they were exhibited in Glasgow after his death, the late paintings startled his contemporaries. But at the same time they grew out of his earlier skills: line, plane, and perspective are handled just as they were in his most sophisticated architectural work in Glasgow. The artist and the architect in Mackintosh had found a new relationship.

Death and conclusion In May 1927 Macdonald went back to London for six weeks for medical treatment and Mackintosh wrote to her almost every day. Almost at the end of his life these letters show us a Mackintosh impossible to know from looking at his work: down-to-earth, funny, slightly defeated, stumbling in the expression of his love. In one of the letters he wrote that his tongue felt swollen, and blamed it on his American tobacco. (At this time, America stood for everything he disliked in the modern world.) In fact, he had cancer of the tongue. He became seriously ill in the autumn of 1927 and was taken back to London. After radium treatment at Westminster Hospital he lived for some months unable to speak, before dying at 26 Porchester Square on 10 December 1928. The funeral was held the next day at Golders Green crematorium.

The large collection of Mackintosh's drawings and designs, together with furniture and archival material, which was still in his possession at his death passed, after Macdonald's death in 1933, into the hands of their friend and client William Davidson, and thence to the Hunterian

Art Gallery at the University of Glasgow. Together with the furniture from 6 Florentine Terrace (Mackintosh and Macdonald's last house in Glasgow) which was also given by the Davidson family, it constitutes the Mackintosh estate and collection at the Hunterian.

The standard account of Mackintosh's life and work is Thomas Howarth's *Charles Rennie Mackintosh and the Modern Movement* (1952), which, as its title suggests, presented Mackintosh's work as part of the development of twentieth-century architectural modernism, with its belief in functionalism and its turning away from the past. Howarth described Glasgow School of Art as the first major building of the movement, and he shaped Mackintosh's career so that it fitted neatly into the larger narratives of modernism, arguing that he was not fully understood in Glasgow, and only properly appreciated in the proto-modern circles of Vienna. More recent work on Mackintosh has not been so obviously modernist in spirit, but it has tended to revise or supplement Howarth without displacing his general account. The decorative element in Mackintosh's work, which Howarth had rather deplored, was brought forward in the 1960s and 1970s, and Roger Billcliffe's *catalogue raisonné*, *Charles Rennie Mackintosh: the Complete Furniture, Furniture Drawings, and Interior Designs* (1979), is the most enduring product of this phase. In the 1980s and 1990s writers have questioned the isolation in which Mackintosh has been placed, drawing attention to the richness of architectural and decorative talent in Glasgow at the turn of the century, and particularly to the importance of Margaret Macdonald and the two artists' shared creativity. Meanwhile Mackintosh has become more popular than almost any other architect in British history. His admirers are struck by the qualities of light and space in his work and by an originality that seems uncannily up to date. Thinking of the 'clutter' of the nineteenth century and the 'clean lines' of the twentieth, they see Mackintosh as Howarth saw him, a man ahead of his time.

In his own day Mackintosh's reputation was that of an architect and decorative artist of extreme originality. This reputation was strongest between about 1900 and 1910 and in progressive artistic circles. But anyone outside those circles, asked who was the most important architect in Glasgow, would have given the name of John James Burnet, whose work is more skilled and varied than Mackintosh's but not so strangely original. Even within progressive artistic circles in Britain, Mackintosh's work was much less widely publicized and less influential than that of the architect–designers C. F. A. Voysey and M. H. Baillie Scott. And though he seems to have been much talked about in parts of Europe, it is hard to find evidence of the influence of his work on his European contemporaries, beyond the borrowing of motifs. His work was essentially strange, and isolated in its strangeness.

Today Mackintosh is ranked, not with Voysey or Baillie Scott, but with a handful of architect–designers of great originality and international reputation, particularly Antoni Gaudí in Barcelona and Frank Lloyd Wright in Chicago. Like the modernist version of Mackintosh, this account can do violence to history, for Mackintosh, Gaudí, and Wright worked in different and separate worlds. But it has this merit: that, by placing Mackintosh in a position of relative isolation, it reflects the strangeness of his work, the self-conscious dislocations of his architecture, and the intensity of feeling in his interiors, qualities not paralleled in the work of his contemporaries.

ALAN CRAWFORD

Sources T. Howarth, *Charles Rennie Mackintosh and the modern movement*, 3rd edn (1990) · *Charles Rennie Mackintosh: the architectural papers*, ed. P. Robertson (1990) · R. Billcliffe, *Charles Rennie Mackintosh: the complete furniture, furniture drawings, and interior designs* (1979) · R. Billcliffe, *Charles Rennie Mackintosh: textile designs* (1993) · P. Robertson, *Charles Rennie Mackintosh: art is the flower* (1995) · A. Crawford, *Charles Rennie Mackintosh* (1995) · W. Kaplan, ed., *Charles Rennie Mackintosh* (1996) · D. Brett, *C. R. Mackintosh: the poetics of workmanship* (1992) · I. Paterson, 'In search of the Mackintosh family: a preliminary study', typescript MS, 1990, priv. coll. · Mitchell L., Glas., Strathclyde regional archives, dean of guild court MSS

Archives Glasgow Museum and Art Gallery · Glasgow School of Art, collection · Hunterian Museum and Art Gallery, Glasgow, corresp. and diary · U. Glas. L., corresp. and papers · University of Strathclyde, Glasgow, MSS and drawings

Likenesses J. C. Annan, photograph, 1893, Glasgow School of Art [*see illus.*] · T. & R. Annan, photographs, 1893, T. & R. Annan & Sons, Glasgow · F. Newbery, oils, 1914, Scot. NPG · E. O'Hoppé, photographs, *c.*1920, Glasgow School of Art · E. O'Hoppé, photographs, *c.*1920, Glasgow, Hunterian Museum and Art Gallery

MacKintosh, Elizabeth [*pseuds.* Josephine Tey, Gordon Daviot] (1896–1952), novelist and playwright, was born in Inverness on 25 July 1896, the eldest of the three daughters (there were no sons) of Colin MacKintosh (*d.* 1950), a fruiterer, and his wife, Josephine Horne, a former teacher. She was educated at Inverness Royal Academy, and, from 1914 to 1917, at the Anstey Physical Training College in Erdington, Birmingham. (Her 1946 thriller, *Miss Pym Disposes*, was set in such a college.) She taught briefly in schools in Liverpool, Oban, and Eastbourne, and for a longer period in Tunbridge Wells, Kent, but in 1923 returned to Inverness to nurse her dying mother and then to keep house for her invalid father, whom she outlived by only two years.

MacKintosh's first detective novel, *The Man in the Queue*, a highly accomplished piece of work for a beginner, was published in 1929 under the pseudonym of Gordon Daviot—the name by which she preferred to be known, in both public and private—though for her seven other works in this genre she took the name Josephine Tey. She always preferred her plays, referring wryly to her novels as her 'yearly knitting' (Gielgud, 1.x), but they are classics of their kind, deftly constructed with strong characterization and a meticulous prose style. Five of them feature as their main character Inspector Alan Grant, a gentleman police officer 'not coarse like a bobby' (*The Man in the Queue*, 118) and with independent means 'to smooth and embroider life' (ibid., 39). A later novel, *A Shilling for Candles* (1936), became Alfred Hitchcock's favourite of his English films, as *Young and Innocent* (1937). It is Grant who, in MacKintosh's most original story, *The Daughter of Time* (1951), while immobilized in hospital, satisfies himself by reading and reason that the infamous Richard III of Shakespeare, school history books, and folk memory, is a Tudor fabrication. Her case for the defence is notably restrained, unlike her treatment of the same subject in *Dickon*, a play published posthumously in 1953. *The Franchise Affair* (1948), a story of two women wrongly accused of kidnapping, and based on an eighteenth-century *cause célèbre*, was another popular work, later to be made into a film.

MacKintosh's plays, while well crafted and with shrewdly observed characters, lack the pace and tension of her thrillers. Her first, *Richard of Bordeaux*, was the most successful. It shows Richard II as an idealist, charming but wilful and immature. His speeches about the futility of war, and the pro-war arguments of his associates, reflect her own bitterness about the First World War. John Gielgud, who became a lifelong friend, took the title role and persuaded her to revise it considerably before its production in London's West End in 1932. It was enthusiastically received and ran for a year. Her later plays, however, fell below this promise. *The Laughing Woman* (1934), about the sculptor Henri Gaudier-Brzeska, was a failure. It was followed in the same year by *Queen of Scots*, with Laurence Olivier as Bothwell. This was more successful, though Gielgud, who had helped her rework it, felt that she made too much of the romantic Mary Stuart and failed to show her as intriguer and harlot also. *The Stars Bow Down*, with its biblical theme of Joseph and his brothers, was published in 1939, though it was another ten years before it was performed, at the Malvern festival. Another biblical play, *The Little Dry Thorn*, based on the story of Abraham and Sarah (published posthumously in *Plays* in 1953), received its first public performance in Glasgow in 1946.

In both her biblical plays and her historical ones MacKintosh made a point of making her characters speak in colloquial, even slangy, modern idiom. 'They have some of the romantic glamour of the old historical melodramas, without the pseudo-period dialogue and fustian sentiment', said John Gielgud in his preface to the 1953 edition of her plays. She was, he said, an elusive character who shunned photographers and publicity of all kinds and who gave no interviews to the press, was deeply reserved, and was 'proud without being arrogant, and obstinate, though not conceited' (Gielgud, 1.ix–xii). During the last year of her life, when she knew that she was mortally ill, she resolutely avoided all her friends. Her last work, *The Privateer* (1952), was a romantic novel based on the life of the buccaneer Henry Morgan. Among her other works are a number of short plays written for broadcasting, and a biography, *Claverhouse* (1937). Her main interests were the cinema (which she preferred to the theatre) and horse-racing; she drew upon her knowledge of the latter in *Brat Farrar* (1949), a novel featuring a false claimant to an estate. She died, unmarried, of cancer of the liver at her home, 235 Covington Way, Streatham, London, on 13 February 1952.   GILLIAN AVERY

Sources *The Times* (15 Feb 1952) · *Inverness Courier* (15 Feb 1952) · private information (2004) [Society of the White Rose] · J. Gielgud, foreword, in G. Daviot, *Plays* (1953) · *WW* · d. cert. · *CGPLA Eng. & Wales* (1952)
Likenesses Sasha, two photographs, 1934, Hult. Arch.
Wealth at death £24,323 18s. 8d.: confirmation, 13 Aug 1952, CCI

Mackintosh, Farquhar (d. 1514). *See under* Mackintosh family (*per. c.*1491–1606).

Mackintosh, Harold Vincent, **first Viscount Mackintosh of Halifax** (1891–1964), confectionery manufacturer and public administrator, was born in King's Cross Lane, Halifax, Yorkshire, on 8 June 1891, the eldest of three sons, all destined to enter the confectionery business founded by their father, John *Mackintosh (1868–1920), of Scottish descent, and his wife, Violet, daughter of James Taylor, of Clover Hill, Halifax.

Mackintosh was educated in Halifax, first at a dame-school, then at the board school, and finally at Halifax New School, a private grammar school, where he became head boy and captain of the hockey and cricket teams. On leaving school in 1909, he went to Germany, working at the family's factory there for two years to learn both the manufacturing and selling side of the business. He was appointed a director in 1913. On the death of his father in 1920 he became chairman of the family firm, having meanwhile served during the First World War in the Royal Naval Volunteer Reserve. In 1916 Mackintosh married Constance Emily (1891–1975), daughter of Edgar Cooper Stoneham OBE, an accountant in the civil service; she was born on the same day as Mackintosh. It was an intensely happy marriage. They had a daughter and one son, John (b. 1921).

Mackintosh was eventually able to implement business expansion plans delayed because of the war, and in March 1921 John Mackintosh & Sons Ltd was floated as a public company. New production technology, managerial reorganization, and the systemization of employment policies transformed a company that became in the 1920s Britain's premier manufacturer of toffees. By 1925–6, the labour force had reached twice its pre-war level. The acquisition of A. J. Caley of Norwich in 1932 (subsequently managed by Harold's brother Eric) enabled Mackintosh to enter less price-sensitive markets, in which it could exploit its recently acquired specialism in chocolate-toffee products. Quality Street and Rolo were two notable branding successes of the 1930s, and others followed in the post-war years. By 1956, Mackintosh & Sons employed some 4000 people. Its achievements stemmed from an insistence on product quality, and a long and highly effective marketing tradition. Mackintosh's enthusiasm for advertising led to his presidency of the Advertising Association (1942–6), of the National Advertising Benevolent Association (1946–8), and, from 1949, to a great deal of organization for the International Advertising Convention, over which he presided in 1951.

Business interests apart, Mackintosh recorded that he worked throughout his life for three causes—thrift, Sunday schools, and medical research. He was involved in the negotiations which brought about the amalgamation of the two building societies in Halifax, the Equitable and

Harold Vincent Mackintosh, first Viscount Mackintosh of Halifax (1891–1964), by Walter Bird, 1961

the Permanent, into the Halifax in 1928, and it was through his work for the building society movement that he came to join the board of Martins Bank. His connection with the savings movement began when he became a trustee of York County Savings Bank and vice-president of the Trustee Savings Banks Association. In 1941 he was elected Yorkshire member of the National Savings Committee, and was then appointed vice-chairman. Two years later he succeeded John Seely, Baron Mottistone, as chairman of the committee, and in 1946 he became head of the savings movement on the retirement of Robert, first Baron Kindersley. Mackintosh was responsible for the publicity for wartime saving, based on 'War Savings Weeks' which progressively changed their theme: War Weapons Week, Warships Week, Wings for Victory, Salute the Soldier, and Thanksgiving were among the many causes. After 1945 Mackintosh continued to lead the National Savings movement. He travelled more than 20,000 miles a year in its cause, and was very popular with the movement's voluntary workers. The general public knew him well through his broadcasts and public appearances. Newspapermen liked his frankness, his unfailing good humour, and his accessibility. The National Savings Committee benefited greatly by his wide experience of advertising and modern publicity methods. One important innovation was his introduction of premium savings bonds in 1956, which, despite the condemnation of the archbishop of Canterbury, quickly became a national institution.

Mackintosh's second interest sprang from his early upbringing in the Methodist church, of which he was a staunch supporter. He was chairman of its central board of finance, a director of the Methodist Central Buying Association, and joint treasurer of the Home Missionary Committee and of Ashville College, Harrogate. He was president of the National Sunday School Union (1924–5) and of the World Council of Christian Education and Sunday School Associations (1928–58), continuing as chairman until his death, and as honorary treasurer of the

British committee. He was also a vice-president of the national council of the YMCA. In 1926 Mackintosh became secretary of a campaign started in Yorkshire for cancer research, and in 1936 he became its chairman. His flair for publicity was put to good use in raising money, and Yorkshire cancer research centres were established at the universities of Leeds and Sheffield.

In 1947 Mackintosh made his home in Norwich, partly because the bombed Caley factory at Norwich was being rebuilt, and partly to be within easier reach of London and his work for National Savings. He became interested in the proposals for the new University of East Anglia; he was chairman of the promotion committee in 1959, and became its first chancellor in 1964, though he died before his ceremonial installation.

Beneath a brusque exterior Mackintosh had a warm, friendly, and generous nature. He was one of the most popular after-dinner speakers in the country, with a fund of stories told in his rich Yorkshire brogue. One of his recreations was farming, and his herd of Jersey cows won him trophies in all big agricultural shows. He was president of the Yorkshire Agricultural Society (1928–9) and in 1960 president of the Royal Norfolk Agricultural Society. Another hobby was the collection of early Staffordshire pottery, and in 1938 he published a book entitled *Early English Figure Pottery*. He had also a fine collection of paintings, particularly works of the Norwich school. In 1959–64 he was a member of the Arts Council.

Mackintosh was appointed a JP in 1925, deputy lieutenant for the West Riding of Yorkshire in 1945, an honorary freeman of the county borough of Halifax in 1954, and an honorary LLD of Leeds University in 1948. He was knighted in 1922, created a baronet in 1935, baron in 1948, and viscount in 1957. He sat in the House of Lords as an independent member, despite his Liberal Party leanings. He died on 27 December 1964 at his home, Thickthorn Hall, Hethersett, near Norwich, following a stroke. He was survived by his wife. His son, John, succeeded as second viscount.   INMAN, *rev.* ROBERT FITZGERALD

Sources R. Fitzgerald, *Rowntree and the marketing revolution, 1862–1969* (1995) · Viscount Mackintosh of Halifax, *By faith and work* (1966) · E. D. Mackintosh, *Norwich adventure: an account of events at Chapel Field* (privately printed, Norwich, 1947) · D. J. Jeremy, 'Chapel in a business career: the case of John Mackintosh (1868–1920)', *Business and religion in Britain*, ed. D. J. Jeremy (1988), 95–117
Archives Borth. Inst.
Likenesses W. Bird, photograph, 1961, NPG [*see illus.*] · portrait, repro. in MacKintosh, *By faith and work* · portrait, repro. in W. H. Beable, *The romance of great businesses* (1926) · portrait, Rowntree, York · portrait, Borth. Inst.
Wealth at death £218,404: probate, 26 Jan 1965, *CGPLA Eng. & Wales*

Mackintosh, Hugh Ross (1870–1936), Church of Scotland minister and theologian, was born in Paisley on 31 October 1870, the fourth child of Alexander Mackintosh (*d.* 1880), minister of the Gaelic Free Church in Paisley, and his wife, Jannet Ross. Both parents having died by 1880, the Mackintosh children were brought up by their aunt, wife of the Free Church minister at Edderton, Ross-shire.

Hugh was dux of Tain Royal Academy at sixteen, then distinguished himself at George Watson's College, Edinburgh (1886–8) before entering that city's university. He gained a first in philosophy (and the Ferguson scholarship, 1893), and a second in classics.

Then came divinity studies at the Free Church college, New College (1893–7), under such eminent scholars as Robert Rainy, A. B. Davidson, and Marcus Dods. Other professors who influenced Mackintosh included James Denney of Glasgow and Wilhelm Herrmann of Marburg. During student days Mackintosh spent brief periods also at the universities of Halle and Freiburg, benefiting from the thinking of Friedrich Loofs, Johannes Weiss, and Martin Kähler.

In 1897 Mackintosh was ordained in the Free Church of Scotland and inducted to its charge at Queen Street, Tayport. In that same year he earned an Edinburgh doctorate in philosophy, for a thesis on Albrecht Ritschl's *Theory of Value-Judgments*. Two years later, on 8 June 1899, he married Jessie Air, third daughter of David Air, a prominent Dundee businessman. In 1900 he co-edited with A. B. Macaulay *The Christian Doctrine of Justification and Reconciliation*, translated from Ritschl's original. In 1901 Mackintosh was inducted to the newly formed Beechgrove church, Aberdeen, but a fruitful ministry there soon ended on his appointment as professor of systematic theology at New College, Edinburgh, a post he held from 1904 to 1936. A collection of his Tayport and Aberdeen sermons was published as *Life on God's Plan* (1909).

Mackintosh's distinguished tenure at New College was marked by a 'sincere attempt to understand and accept modern thought-forms without jettisoning the evangelical faith' (Redman, 10). His lectures in dogmatic theology, painstakingly prepared and regularly revised in light of the most recent developments in critical scholarship, attracted postgraduate students from around the world. But perhaps his most appreciative audience was found among those preparing for parish ministry, to whom he 'often declared that the test of theology is whether it will preach well' (Gardiner, 225). His bibliography reveals an energetic response in published reviews, essays, and monographs to the most important theological currents of his time. In addition to those books which he co-edited—with F. Loofs, *Anti-Haeckel: an Exposure of Haeckel's View of Christianity* (1903); with A. Caldecott, *Readings in the Literature of Theism* (1904); with J. Wendland, *Miracles and Christianity* (1911); and with J. S. Stewart, the translation from a work by F. D. E. Schleiermacher, *The Christian Faith*—he also wrote several well received books of his own: *The Person of Christ* (1913); *Studies in Christian Truth* (1913); *Immortality and the Future* (1915); *The Originality of the Christian Message* (1920); *The Divine Initiative* (1921); *Some Aspects of Christian Belief* (1923); and *The Christian Apprehension of God* (1928). Two additional volumes of sermons were published: *The Highway of God* (1931) and *Sermons* (posthumous, 1938), to which Macaulay's 'Memoir' served as preface. However, it is chiefly because of a handful of books that he is remembered today; his magisterial, *The Doctrine of the Person of*

Jesus Christ (1912), a soteriological study, *The Christian Experience of Forgiveness* (1927), and his survey, *Types of Modern Theology: from Schleiermacher to Barth* (posthumous, 1937) remain important restatements of Christian doctrine, the last of which demonstrates a subtle appreciation of Søren Kierkegaard and Karl Barth. In addition to his earned degrees Mackintosh received the honorary DD from New College, Edinburgh (1908), and from Oxford (1929).

While Mackintosh frequently preached and taught in churches, and took his share of ecclesiastical responsibility, according to D. M. Baillie he kept himself aloof from church politics. In response to a request by the United Free Church of Scotland he served as chairman of the committee on the testimony of the church. The committee produced its 'Brief statement of the church's faith', which was received by the general assembly of 1921. After the union of the United Free Church of Scotland and the Church of Scotland in 1929 Mackintosh was asked to preside over a committee of the Church of Scotland to write a 'Short statement of the church's faith', which was issued in 1935.

Mackintosh was elected in 1932 moderator of the general assembly of the Church of Scotland, a role he assumed with characteristic energy, attending to ceremonial receptions and visiting related ecclesiastical bodies across Europe. Macaulay states that it was during his year as moderator, and especially because of the anxiety Mackintosh felt over the implications of the rise of national socialism in Germany, that 'he undoubtedly lost ground in health' (Macaulay, 18). Mackintosh continued to teach, however, and to speak for various church events. Indeed, it was while he was speaking at a conference for lay missionaries in Stornoway that he became fatally ill, dying there on 8 June 1936. His funeral was held on 11 June, at Barclay Church, Edinburgh; he was buried in the Morningside cemetery. He was survived by his wife and four children.   MICHAEL JINKINS

Sources *Fasti Scot.*, new edn, vol. 9 · J. A. Lamb, ed., *The fasti of the United Free Church of Scotland, 1900–1929* (1956) · A. B. Macaulay, 'Memoir', in H. R. Mackintosh, *Sermons* (1938) · *DNB* · H. Watt, *New College Edinburgh: a centenary history* (1946) · R. R. Redman, jun., *Reformulating reformed theology: Jesus Christ in the theology of H. R. Mackintosh* (1991) [bibliography] · T. W. Gardiner, 'Tribute to Professor H. R. Mackintosh', *Scottish Journal of Theology*, 5 (1952), 225–36 · J. G. Riddell, 'The late Very Reverend Professor H. R. Mackintosh', *Expository Times*, 48 (1936–7), 6–11 · T. F. Torrance, 'H. R. Mackintosh: theologian of the cross', *Scottish Bulletin of Evangelical Theology*, 5 (1989), 160–173 · D. F. Wright and G. D. Badcock, eds., *Disruption to diversity: Edinburgh divinity, 1846–1996* (1996) · *Beechgrove church, Aberdeen: a record of fifty years, 1900–1950*, Beechgrove church [1950]

Archives U. Edin., New Coll. L.

Likenesses F. H. Newbery, portrait, Scot. NPG · photograph, repro. in H. R. Mackintosh, *Sermons* (1938), frontispiece · photograph, repro. in Watt, *New College Edinburgh*, following p. 224 · photograph, repro. in *Beechgrove church*, following p. 38 · photograph, U. Edin., New College

Wealth at death £4649 3s. 3d.: confirmation, 1 Aug 1936, *CCI*

Mackintosh, Sir James, of Kyllachy (1765–1832), political writer and politician, was born on 24 October 1765 at

Sir James Mackintosh of Kyllachy (1765–1832), by Sir Thomas Lawrence, exh. RA 1804

Aldourie on the banks of Loch Ness, 7 miles from Inverness, the eldest of the three children of John Mackintosh (d. 1788), army officer, and Marjory (1739–1780), daughter of Alexander MacGillivray. John inherited Kyllachy, a small estate that had been in his wife's family for two centuries.

Early years and education With his father away with his regiment, first in Antigua and then in Dublin, James was brought up by his mother. In 1775 he was sent to school at Fortrose, Ross-shire. He was remembered locally to have shown strong intellectual abilities from an early age, reading a great deal and taking a keen interest in the politics of the American War of Independence while at school. In the playground he liked to act out parliamentary debates with his peers, preferring the role of his hero Charles James Fox for himself (he later named his first son, who died in infancy, Charles James Fox Mackintosh). In 1778, aged thirteen, he precociously declared himself a whig. In the following year Marjory Mackintosh joined her husband in Gibraltar, leaving James in Scotland. She died in June 1780, and in October of that year James went to King's College, Aberdeen. He attended lectures there over four winters and stayed with his grandmother during the summers. It was at Aberdeen that he began to read Cicero, an author who was to have a considerable influence on Mackintosh's own writing career. He also gained a reputation as a poet, based in part on a collection of verse he brought to the university, and became interested in 'speculation', inspired by the writings of Joseph Priestley, William Warburton, and James Beattie, then professor of moral philosophy at

Marischal College, Aberdeen. While at the university Mackintosh formed a lasting friendship with Robert Hall (1764–1831), later famous as a preacher, with whom he established a debating society, the Hall and Mackintosh Club. At this time James also fell in love with a Miss Scott, who became the object of his courtship and poetic talents for about four years. His family were impoverished, however, and he was deeply concerned at this time to secure a financial and professional settlement that would form the basis for a marriage proposal. To this end, Mackintosh hoped to become a professor at Aberdeen—a not unreasonable plan—but it came to nothing. Ultimately Miss Scott married an Inverness physician.

Too poor to enter the Scottish bar, Mackintosh decided on a career in medicine, having received his first degree in March 1784. He began his medical studies at Edinburgh University in October and was there given to a somewhat dissipated lifestyle, with contemporaries recalling his fondness for drinking and dancing. None the less he remained a diligent pupil: 'whatever might be the inconstancy of his other amours', wrote a fellow student, John Fleming, 'the love of knowledge never once deserted him' (O'Leary, 12). Nor clearly was he without ambition. A year after his arrival at the university he put himself forward as a candidate for the chair of moral philosophy vacated by Adam Ferguson. Ferguson is said to have treated him 'kindly', but the post went to the common-sense philosopher Dugald Stewart. Mackintosh also became involved in the dispute between rival schools of medical science centred on the professor of practical medicine, William Cullen, and Cullen's former secretary, John Brown (bap. 1735, d. 1788). The latter promoted a more progressive form of medicine to which Mackintosh was attracted, having been cured of a fever by a friend employing 'Brunonian' methods. He supported 'Brown's heresy' at weekly meetings of the Royal Medical Society, of which he was subsequently elected president. He was likewise president of the Speculative Society and spoke against the slave trade at his first address. Friends from this time included the judge Charles Hope, later Lord Graton, the historian Malcolm Laing, the political activist Thomas Addis Emmet, and the author Benjamin Constant. In autumn 1787 he received his diploma on the strength of his dissertation, 'De motu musculari'.

London and politics In spring 1788 Mackintosh moved to London, where he took up residence with a maternal cousin, Mr Fraser, in Clipstone Street. He planned to move to St Petersburg and went as far as obtaining a letter of introduction from Dugald Stewart, whom he had met in London in June 1788, though the proposal came to nothing. That year saw the death of both Mackintosh's academic mentor, John Brown, and his father, who had returned to Scotland from Gibraltar five years earlier. On his father's death James inherited the family estate and became known as Mackintosh of Kyllachy. On 8 April 1789 he married Catherine Stuart (d. 1797) at St Marylebone, London, to the annoyance of both families, who considered their union irresponsible. The couple toured the Low Countries, where James practised French. During the trip he finally abandoned all plans for a medical career in favour of political commentary, and at Liège gained first-hand knowledge of the emerging revolution in France. Mary (d. 1876), their first child, was born later that year, and the family returned to England in 1790.

Mackintosh's emergence as a prominent political writer, and as a defender and then critic of the French revolutionaries, occurred during the 1790s, which he spent predominantly in London. In need of money he turned to journalism as a means of raising funds and assisting the whig cause. His early contributions focused on George III's mental health and suitability to reign. Like Charles James Fox, Mackintosh believed the king insane, and called for him to be replaced by the prince of Wales. On 11 December 1788 his Foxite contribution appeared as an article in *The Gazetteer*, and it was probably through the paper's editor, James Perry, that Mackintosh met James Boswell at this time. His support for the prince was subsequently reprinted as *Arguments Concerning the Constitutional Right of Parliament to Appoint a Regency* (1788). In autumn 1790 he became foreign editor, for a short period, of *The Oracle*. He also contributed articles—including a complimentary sketch of the Jacobin count de Mirabeau—to the *Morning Chronicle*, of which he had become joint owner and editor and to which he sent letters under the pseudonym the Ghost of Vandeput. Through his promotion of the revolutionary cause he became an associate of radicals such as Thomas Brand Hollis and John Horne Tooke, whom he supported in the parliamentary election of June 1790, despite Horne Tooke's candidacy being against his childhood hero, Fox.

Responses to the French Revolution Late in 1790 critics of events in France were bolstered by the publication of Edmund Burke's *Reflections on the Revolution in France*, which prompted a series of radical retorts. Of these the two most significant were Thomas Paine's *Rights of Man* and Mackintosh's *Vindiciae Gallicae: a Defence of the French Revolution and its English Admirers*. Paine himself had been less than impressed by the latter's contribution to the debate, informing Mackintosh via a mutual friend that 'he will come too late unless he hastens, for after the appearance of my reply [to Burke] nothing more will remain to be said' (O'Leary, 22). In the event Paine's response appeared first, but in some circles exceeded the wishes of its readers by advocating reforms that ran too close to democracy, and in doing so confirmed Burke's warnings of impending domestic revolution. Published in April 1791, Mackintosh's study 'redressed the balance' (ibid., 25), providing moderate supporters of the revolution with an eloquent statement on the need for reform in Britain as well as France. While not condemning the methods used in France, Mackintosh did not believe them suitable or yet necessary for effecting change in Britain: 'We desire to avert revolution by reform; subversion by correction'. According to the poet Thomas Campbell, *Vindiciae Gallicae* established its author as the 'apostle of liberalism' among 'a class ... to whom the manner of Paine was repulsive', while matching Burke 'in the tactics of moral science, and in the beauty of style and illustration' (ibid., 22, 25). It had

actually been Mackintosh's intention not to rival but to undermine the *Reflections* by exposing the weakness of Burke's argument and evidence behind his flamboyant and showy prose. In truth Mackintosh's engagement with Burke is in a style not dissimilar to that of its target, a fact acknowledged by Burke himself and by Patrick O'Leary, Mackintosh's most recent biographer. For others, among them Conor Cruise O'Brien, the deficiencies of Mackintosh's writing were secondary in a study which made him 'the most acute of Burke's early critics' (introduction to *Reflections*, 1969, 50).

In 1791 Mackintosh began a friendship with Samuel Parr, and together they toured the scene of July's Church and King riots in Birmingham, an event which he condemned in the third edition of *Vindiciae Gallicae*. He had himself been master of ceremonies at a dinner similar to that targeted by the rioters. Following the passing of the Libel Act (1792) Mackintosh was associated with a circle which went on to found the Friends to the Liberty of the Press, and, following a proposal from Horne Tooke, was offered honorary membership of the Society for Constitutional Information. In the same year—in connection with Charles Grey, Thomas Brand Hollis, Richard Brinsley Sheridan, and Samuel Whitbread—he became involved with a new pressure group, the Society of Friends of the People, whose purpose was to canvass for parliamentary reform, including an extension of the franchise and more frequent elections. Opposition to reform within the Commons prompted Mackintosh to attack the prime minister in his *Letter to the Right Honourable William Pitt*, signed 'An Honest Man', in which he drew attention to an important and recurring theme of his political philosophy: that it was only through significant concessions that violent revolution would be avoided.

Mackintosh's second daughter, Maitland (d. 1861)—named after Lord Lauderdale, the trustee for his Kyllachy estate—was born on 1 June 1792. Later that year Mackintosh travelled to the continent to collect material for his journalism. However, this was a time when events in France were beginning to undermine support for the revolution, and Mackintosh was among those who became increasingly disillusioned with its violent turn. While in Boulogne he heard of the death of Theobald Dillon, the Dublin-born general of the French army, at the hands of his own troops. The infamous Paris massacre of September was likewise deeply shocking for this early sponsor of the revolution and continued to feature prominently in his later writing; Mackintosh's journal entry for 2 September 1811, for example, reads 'nineteen years from the massacre in the prisons of Paris' (O'Leary, 30). However, his conversion appears to have been gradual, since he accepted a certificate of honorary citizenship of the French Republic from the revolutionary government's minister on his return to London.

New responses to Burke In January 1795 Mackintosh was elected to the Whig Club after a delay due to fears that his views might prove too extreme for existing members. In July he began to write for the *Monthly Review* while under financial pressure and during a period of intensive study for his law examinations. He was called to the bar later that year. Evidence of his disappointment with events in France was clearly evident by 1796, when he visited his former adversary Edmund Burke. He had read Burke's *Two Letters on a Regicide Peace* and reviewed them favourably for the *Monthly Review*. Though still in disagreement over Burke's view of the 'present politics of Europe', he maintained that he had come to approve of 'the general principles' of one whom he now held in the 'most affectionate veneration' (Ayling, 266–7). He wrote to Burke asking if they could meet to tell him so in person. Though suspicious of Mackintosh's 'supposed conversion', Burke invited him to stay at Beaconsfield, which he did for a few days shortly after Christmas 1796. Mackintosh later recalled 'the astonishing effusions' of Burke's conversation and his use of the 'sublimest images mingled with the most wretched puns' (ibid., 277). By 1799 Mackintosh had reversed his original stance to the extent that he could speak of the recently deceased Burke as 'the most eloquent of men, the perpetual force and vigour of his arguments being hid from vulgar observation by the dazzling glories in which they were enshrined' (Cruise O'Brien, 414).

Catherine, Mackintosh's first wife, died in April 1797. On 10 April 1798 he married Catherine Allen (*d.* 1830), sister-in-law of Josiah and John Wedgwood, who brought him into contact with the Wedgwood family. Later that year he was offered a partnership with Daniel Stuart, his first wife's brother, on the *Morning Post*. He bought shares in the paper but appears to have sold these soon afterwards, and agreed to write for it on a salaried basis. In February 1798 Mackintosh and his friends—among them the City merchant Richard 'Conversation' Sharp and James Scarlett, later Lord Abinger—formed a club based on their circle. Dubbed the King of Clubs by Robert 'Bobus' Smith, the society remained an exclusive gathering of, according to Thomas Campbell, 'the reigning wits of London', dedicated to literary debate and for twenty years serving as a 'lineal descendant of the Johnson, Burke and Goldsmith Society' (O'Leary, 47). In November 1798 Mackintosh proposed a lecture series to the Honourable Society of Lincoln's Inn in which he would make public his change of opinion towards Burke. However, like Burke, certain benchers remained wary of a speaker previously associated with Jacobinism. As a result Mackintosh rushed *A Discourse on the Law of Nature and Nations*, which contained the substance of his first lecture, through the press. It was well received, eliciting a complimentary response from another former object of his criticism, William Pitt. After some canvassing on Mackintosh's behalf by George Canning—then speaker of the Commons and, despite political differences, a friend from the early 1790s—and an intervention from Lord Loughborough, he was given permission to deliver the lectures between February and June 1799. His subsequent attack on 'perfectibilist speculations' which he identified as 'part of the dangerous disease associated with the spread of the "new philosophy" since the French revolution' was implicitly directed at William Godwin and provoked a quarrel (Winch, 273–4).

Mackintosh himself now became a target for radicals such as Samuel Taylor Coleridge (who had previously sought his advice on matters of finance) objecting to his attack on Godwin's political philosophy. Mackintosh delivered the lectures for a second time in 1800 and once more asserted his disillusionment with the course of recent French history; it was, as he wrote to the Irish lawyer George Moore, an 'extraordinary revolution … which has rooted up every Principle of Democracy in that country and banished people from all concern in government' (O'Leary, 54).

Shrinking attendance at, and fees from, the second series of lectures now prompted Mackintosh to seek, again with Canning's help, a position as a judge in India. However, news of these initial efforts became public and he was lampooned by Charles Lamb as a place-seeker. During 1802 he met both George III and Napoleon, though in the following year he defended Jean Peltier, the French royalist refugee, against the French emperor. Peltier had been accused of attempting to incite the assassination of the first consul in his newspaper *L'Ambigu*. Although the charge was justified, in January 1803 Mackintosh unsuccessfully defended Peltier on the grounds of British press freedom. Later that year he finally received, through Canning's influence, a post as judge in Bombay. Former friends, including Samuel Parr, were further alienated by his acceptance of the position from a tory government, but Mackintosh was adamant that his appointment would not prompt him to support the administration.

India and parliamentary career Mackintosh's new office brought with it a knighthood (21 December 1803), and it was as Sir James that, having sailed for India with his family on 14 February, he assumed his post as recorder of Bombay on 26 May 1804. He soon made clear his determination to adjudicate in a fair manner, disregarding differences in race and status. He hoped to reform the police, the administration of penal law, and, in particular, the prison system. In the spirit of Beccaria and Bentham he sought to use prison as the principal instrument of punishment, and offended the resident British community by resisting the use of the death penalty. In 1805 he further upset the local establishment by taking a stand against corruption. In the previous November he had also founded the Bombay Literary Society, through which he hoped to encourage cultivation of 'philosophically' minded contemplation of oriental culture and history. In 1806, prompted by an interest in international law, he took up the additional post of judge in Bombay's vice-admiralty court, a body principally charged with determining the fate of captured vessels. That year also saw the birth of a son, the only one to outlive him, and in January 1808 his eldest daughter, Mary, married an East India Company servant, Claudius James *Rich (1786/7–1821); in September of the following year his daughter Maitland married William *Erskine (1773–1852), who later achieved fame as a Persian scholar and historian of India. In 1808 Mackintosh was awarded an honorary doctorate from Aberdeen, and also that year had his first bout of serious illness with a chest complaint.

Lady Mackintosh left for England in February 1810 and was followed by Sir James in November 1811, when he resigned his post as recorder. Before departure Mackintosh had been required to make one exception to his refusal to pass the death sentence when, in July 1811, a British soldier was hanged for the murder of an Indian on Goa.

On returning to Britain, Mackintosh received overtures from Spencer Percival and the prince regent to become a supporter of the tory party. Instead, in 1813 he became a leading spokesman for the whigs when he was elected MP for Nairn and took up writing for the *Edinburgh Review*. At this time he established friendships with Lord Byron and Mme de Staël, whom he encountered in whig circles centred on Holland House. Having been elected to the Royal Society in 1813, in the following year he joined The Club, founded by Samuel Johnson. He championed freedom for Poland and visited Paris. During this trip he was consulted by the duke of Wellington over the slave trade, and he completed his tour with a visit to Switzerland. In 1815 he made a powerful critique in the Commons of the government's attitude towards America, to which he admitted a 'partiality', in the wake of the Anglo-American War (1812–14). He received a second honorary doctorate, this time from Oxford, in 1815, and a third, from Harvard, in 1822; in 1818 he became professor of law and general politics at East India College, Haileybury. In 1819 he was elected MP for Knaresborough, a seat he held for the rest of his life, and in 1827 he was sworn of the privy council. Following the death of Sir Samuel Romilly, Mackintosh emerged as the leading advocate of law reform, and carried the Commons vote in favour of ending capital punishment for aspects of forgery (with the exception of Bank of England notes). As in India he made clear his preference for alternative punishments in all cases, but equally realized that progress was possible only through compromise.

In 1823 Mackintosh beat Sir Walter Scott to become rector of Glasgow University, a post he held for two years. In that year his daughter Kitty, who had married Sir William Saltonstall Wiseman in 1811, involved the family in scandal when she eloped to Jamaica and her husband began divorce proceedings; though highly newsworthy, the event neither was used by Mackintosh's political enemies nor required him to abandon his belief in press freedom. It was on this subject that he spoke in January 1823 in a tribute to Charles James Fox which demonstrated his ongoing support for established reform causes: reducing cases of war, suspensions of the constitution, and violations of personal liberty, while limiting crown prerogatives. Most pointed was his support for parliamentary reform, Catholic emancipation, and Irish grievances. Other causes championed at this time include Latin American claims for independence and, drawing parallels with British policy in Ireland, the defence of French Canadian rights when the union of Upper and Lower Canada was proposed. A co-founder of the Athenaeum in 1824, in the following year he joined William Warburton on the committee of the body which later became the Royal Society for the Prevention of Cruelty to Animals.

Histories and reputation Mackintosh had long desired to write a history of England, but in August 1828 he gave priority to a history of ethical philosophy proposed by Macvey Napier, editor of the seventh edition of the *Encyclopaedia Britannica*. The central thesis of his *Dissertation on the Progress of Ethical Philosophy* (1830), that ethics rest solidly on the primacy of conscience, opposed the views of utilitarians and prompted the Benthamite James Mill's hostile *Fragment of Mackintosh* (1835). To other reviewers the *Dissertation* was evidence of Mackintosh's extraordinarily wide reading, culture, and love of knowledge as he assembled a study drawing on Aristotle, Aquinas, Bacon, Hobbes, Locke, Liebnitz, Shaftesbury, Butler, and, of course, Cicero—a writer whose work he read repeatedly and quoted frequently, and to whom he was often compared for his learning and eloquence. Alexander Hill Everett spoke for many acquaintances when he wrote after Mackintosh's death of 'the beautiful union of talents, virtues and graces, that distinguish the character of the illustrious Roman orator, to which his own bore in its leading traits a marked resemblance' (O'Leary, 194).

During 1829 Mackintosh returned to his historical study which he began to publish, a year later, as a *History of England from the Earliest Times to the Final Establishment of the Reformation* in Dionysius Lardner's Cabinet Cyclopaedia. In compiling the work Mackintosh drew on his extensive research for a second account, *History of the Revolution in England in 1688*, on which he progressed no further before his death than James II's abdication. Mackintosh's notes were in time passed to Thomas Babington Macaulay, with whom Sir James had become intimate through the Holland House circle. Macaulay himself drew heavily on Mackintosh's material for his own history, which reached 1701 (the end point of his friend's research), and wrote warmly in the *Edinburgh Review* of Sir James's contribution to an essentially English form of scholarship which understood the proximity of law and history and, as with Mackintosh's own career, the fruitful combination of lawyer and historian. Above all Mackintosh's history was characterized by tolerance and fairness. 'He was', wrote Macaulay, 'singularly mild, calm, and impartial, in his judgements of men and parties ... He had a quick eye for the redeeming parts of a character, and a large toleration for the infirmities of men exposed to strong temptations' (O'Leary, 200). Sir James's last major parliamentary act was to participate in debates over Lord John Russell's Reform Bill during which he returned to a familiar theme—the need for reform as a bulwark to revolution—and quoted Cicero's *De legibus* on the merits of making concessions to popular politics. Mackintosh died on 30 May 1832 at his home at Langham Place, Clapham, having been in a weakened condition since doctors earlier that year failed for some days to detect a chicken bone lodged in his throat. He was buried on 4 June at Hampstead; Lady Mackintosh, who had died of a stroke on 6 May 1830, had been buried with her daughter Elizabeth at Chene. Sir James is commemorated by William Theed's monument in Whigs' Corner, Westminster Abbey, and by a relief bust on the former India Office, now part of the Foreign and Commonwealth Office, London.

Somewhat unfairly Mackintosh is now best remembered for his move away from an early commitment to the French Revolution and from his critique of Burke's *Reflections*. According to the editor of a recent edition of his work, 'few turncoats have made their recantation as public as James Mackintosh' (Jonathan Wordsworth, introduction to *Vindiciae Gallicae*, 1989). However, Sir James's development, as both a political writer and a politician, is better understood in terms of his ongoing advocacy of reasonable reform. His desire for liberal and democratic reform remained consistent throughout his adult life, and is as evident in his early assertion of the 'rights of man' as in his attack on later revolutionary excess or his promotion of national freedoms and animal rights in the 1820s, or an extension of the franchise during the Reform Bill debates of 1831. Thus, for Hugh Trevor-Roper, Mackintosh exists alongside John Millar and Macaulay in the 'succession of historians through whom Whigs of the Holland House circle effected a reconstruction of the Whig views of politics and history' (introduction to Macaulay's *History of England*, 1979, 12–13). Participation in the intellectual construction of whiggism was married to an active participation in whig politics, particularly on his return from India at a time when many critics expected him to be drawn towards tory circles. For Richard B. Sher he is one of the figures who 'kept the intellectual reputation of Scotland and her capital on a high plane until well into Victorian times' (Sher, 308), while J. G. A. Pocock considers him a 'representative of Scottish scientific Whiggism' (Pocock, 297). Away from politics Mackintosh's liberalism was evident in his open-mindedness and contemporary, catholic tastes communicated with an eloquence reminiscent of Roman oratory. George Ticknor, Harvard academic and visitor to Holland House, believed that he had never met with anyone 'whose conversation was more richly nourished with knowledge, at once elegant and profound … What is best in modern letters and culture seems to have passed through his mind and given a peculiar raciness to what he says' (O'Leary, 148).   CHRISTOPHER J. FINLAY

Sources P. O'Leary, *Sir James Mackintosh: the whig Cicero* (1989) · R. B. Sher, *Church and university in the Scottish Enlightenment: the moderate literati of Edinburgh* (1985) · J. G. A. Pocock, 'The varieties of whiggism from exclusion to reform: a history of ideology and discourse', *Virtue, commerce and history* (1985) · L. Reid, *Charles James Fox: a man for the people* (1969) · D. Winch, *Riches and poverty: an intellectual history of political economy in Britain, 1750–1834* (1996) · S. Ayling, *Edmund Burke: his life and opinions* (1988) · C. Cruise O'Brien, *The great melody: a thematic biography and anthology of Edmund Burke* (1992) · E. P. Thompson, *The making of the English working class* (1991) · I. S. Ross, *Adam Smith: a life* (1995) · J. C. D. Clark, *English society, 1660–1832*, 2nd edn (2000)

Archives BL, journals, corresp., and historical collections, Add. MSS 34487–34526, 51653–51657, 52436–52453 · BL, papers · BL OIOC · Hunt. L., letters · NA Scot. · NL Scot., corresp. and historical papers | BL, corresp. with John Allen, Add. MS 52182 · BL, letters to Lord Grenville, Add. MS 58964 · BL, corresp. with Lord and Lady Holland; MS account of Holland House, Add. MSS 51653–51657 · BL, letters to Macvey Napier, Add. 34613–34614 · NL Scot., letters to

Archibald Constable · NRA, priv. coll., letters to William Adam · University of Keele, Wedgwood archives

Likenesses T. Lawrence, oils, exh. RA 1804, NPG [*see illus.*] · I. W. Slater, lithograph, pubd 1824 (after J. Slater), BM, NPG · F. W. Wilkin, chalk drawing, 1824, Scot. NPG · W. Heath, caricature, coloured etching, pubd 1829 (*Keeping the child quiet*), V&A · W. Ridley, stipple (after J. Opie), BM, NPG; repro. in *Monthly Mirror* (1804) · C. Smith, oils, Scot. NPG · A. Sparrow, miniature (after F. W. Wilkin, 1837), AM Oxf. · W. Theed junior, monument, Westminster Abbey · J. Thomson, stipple (after W. Derby), BM, NPG; repro. in *European Magazine* (1824) · C. Turner, mezzotint (after bust by H. B. Burlowe), BM, NPG · bust, Gov. Art Coll.

Wealth at death £8000–£9000 but only £863 after payment of debts: P. O'Leary, *Sir James Mackintosh: the whig Cicero* (1989), 207

Mackintosh, James Macalister (1891–1966), public health teacher and administrator, was born in Kilmarnock on 17 February 1891, the younger son of James Dunbar Mackintosh, solicitor, and his wife, Janet Macalister. He was educated in Glasgow at the high school and at the university, and graduated MA in 1912. He then commenced medical studies, which were interrupted in 1914 by the outbreak of war; he served in France with a commission in the 6th Cameron Highlanders. After being wounded at the battle of Loos he returned to Britain and graduated MB ChB in 1916. He went back to France as a captain in the Royal Army Medical Corps in 1918. In 1919 he married Marjorie, daughter of David Strathie, chartered accountant, of Glasgow; they had one son and two daughters.

After the war Mackintosh decided on a career in public health. He took his DPH in 1920, obtained his MD in 1923 with high commendation, and in 1930 was called to the bar from Gray's Inn, London. In 1920 he began the movement from post to post which was the career pattern of the public health officer of those days. Four years in Dorset were followed by two in Burton upon Trent and three in Leicestershire. In 1930 he became county medical officer of Northampton, where he spent perhaps the happiest years of his professional life. He soon established himself as an expert on rural housing and his reports on that subject are a permanent contribution to social history. His interest was not limited to the siting, construction, and sanitary amenities of rural cottages, but included the lives, habits, and financial resources of their inhabitants. The influence of housing on health was one of his abiding interests. In 1952 he published *Housing and Family Life*, in which he argued for comfort and function (as in the provision of indoor toilet facilities, indoor hot and cold running water, and central heating) as primary desirables in all types of housing.

In 1937 Mackintosh was appointed chief medical officer in the Department of Health for Scotland, and he was there for four years. Arriving shortly after the publication of the Cathcart committee's report on the Scottish health services, Mackintosh looked forward to presiding over the developments which would give effect to its recommendations; but the war clouds were gathering and he devoted himself to the task of organizing the Emergency Medical Service in Scotland, the system of hospital provision designed to deal with the expected civilian air-raid casualties. He also served on the Feversham committee, which in 1939 recommended the amalgamation of the voluntary mental health services and led to the eventual formation of the National Association for Mental Health.

Mackintosh found central government a disappointing experience and welcomed the opportunity in 1941 of becoming professor of public health in his old university of Glasgow. Three years later he moved south to become professor of public health in the University of London and dean of the London School of Hygiene and Tropical Medicine. Wartime tenants occupied a large part of the school building, a sixth of which, including the department of public health, was a derelict ruin through bomb damage. All teaching, except some courses in tropical medicine, had been in abeyance for five years, and most of the pre-war staff had disappeared. Mackintosh gave up the deanship after five years to devote himself to the department, but in those five years he had directed the rebuilding of the bomb-damaged part of the building, completely reorganized and restarted the course for the DPH, and set the school on its feet again.

Mackintosh was as well known internationally among public health workers as he was in his own country. His interest in international public health started in 1941 with a prolonged visit to the United States. He was appointed a general adviser on civil defence, advising on air-raid precautions, for example, and on arrangements for dealing with casualties, and he toured almost every state of America. This was the first of Mackintosh's many visits to the United States. His greatest activities in the international field were carried out under the World Health Organization. He was invited to take part in meetings of experts on public health administration and to act as a consultant on rural housing. His advice was also sought on such matters as public health teaching, and with Professor Fred Grundy he carried out an important study detailed in *The Teaching of Hygiene and Public Health in Europe* (1957). His introduction to the first report on the world health situation, published in 1959, was a notable contribution on the theory and practice of international public health. After retiring from his chair in 1956 Mackintosh directed the World Health Organization division of education and training, from 1958 to 1960. He then returned to the United States for two years as an adviser to the Avalon and Milbank foundations. After he finally retired he continued to write despite his failing health, and his essays under the title *Topics in Public Health* were published in 1965, the year before his death. In 1943 Mackintosh had been elected FRCP of London and Edinburgh. He had also received the honorary LLD of Glasgow in 1950 and of Birmingham in 1961.

Despite suggestions to the contrary, Mackintosh was an able, practical, and flexible administrator. Nevertheless, his greatest contribution was as a teacher and interpreter of public health. Both his speaking and his writing were clear, attractive, and persuasive. He had a keen interest in the origins and trends of social policy and institutions. His interest in social attitudes and his feel for their importance in determining trends in health through changing individual behaviour were unique in his day. He was a social philosopher and diagnostician whose sensitive awareness of the importance of public opinion and individual behaviour in public health was conveyed most clearly in his Heath Clark lectures, 'Trends of opinion about the public health, 1901–51' (1951). Mackintosh has been described as the poet of public health and indeed published privately a slim volume of verse under the title *Airs, Waters and Places* (no date). His frail and diffident appearance belied his resilience, charm, and immense capacity for friendship. He was reflective, original, genial, and warm of heart. It was typical that in middle age he wrote an admonitory letter to himself to be opened on retirement. Mackintosh died in Southmead Hospital, Bristol, on 20 April 1966.

J. H. F. BROTHERSTON, *rev.* ANNE HARDY

Sources *The Lancet* (30 April 1966), 988–90 · *BMJ* (30 April 1966), 1118–9 · personal knowledge (1981) · private information (1981) · *CGPLA Eng. & Wales* (1966)

Wealth at death £11,997: probate, 16 Sept 1966, *CGPLA Eng. & Wales*

Mackintosh, John (1833–1907), historian, son of William Mackintosh, a private soldier, was born at Aberdeen on 9 November 1833. He was educated at Botriphinie parish school, Banffshire, and at an early period settled in Aberdeen as stationer and newsagent. Mackintosh was self-taught as a historian. In 1878 he brought out the first volume of a *History of Civilisation in Scotland*, which was in 1888 completed in four volumes, a new edition appearing 1892–6. He also wrote *The Story of Scotland* (1890), a *History of the Valley of the Dee* (1895), and *Historical Earls and Earldoms* (1898). In 1880 he received the degree of LLD from the University of Aberdeen, and in 1900 a civil-list pension of £50. He died at Aberdeen on 4 May 1907.

T. F. HENDERSON, *rev.* H. C. G. MATTHEW

Sources *WWW* · *The Scotsman* (6 May 1907) · *Glasgow Herald* (6 May 1907)

Mackintosh, John (1868–1920), confectionery manufacturer, was born in Dukinfield, Cheshire, on 7 July 1868, the son of Joseph Mackintosh, cotton spinner, and his wife, Mary Jane, *née* Burgess. Three months later, Joseph moved to Halifax to become a foreman at the cotton spinners Bowman Brothers, which was managed by his brother, John. Mary Mackintosh, having taught at her own father's school and at the Methodist New Connexion Sunday school, Queen's Road, Halifax, had to undertake the education of her son, John, who at the age of ten began work as a half-timer at Bowman Brothers. Halifax was a stronghold of the small Methodist New Connexion church, and the Mackintoshs were active and founding members of the Queen's Road congregation. By 1881, at the age of thirteen, John Mackintosh was employed full-time on doubling machines, twisting yarn into thread.

In 1890 Mackintosh married a confectioner's assistant and fellow member of his chapel, Violet Taylor, the daughter of a carpet weaver. In the same year they used their joint savings of £100 to open a pastry shop at Kings Cross Lane, Halifax, Violet running their small enterprise, while

John Mackintosh (1868–1920), by unknown photographer

John continued to work at the cotton mill. Mackintosh began to search for a speciality which would distinguish his shop and attract custom on the Saturday half-holiday, and Violet developed a recipe which blended the traditional, brittle English butterscotch with caramel, a softer confectionery mainly imported at the time from the USA. They called their new line Mackintosh's Celebrated Toffee, and it was Mackintosh's success that ultimately transformed popular understanding of the term 'toffee', previously a description of any sugar or boiled sweet. When his father died in 1891, aged only forty-eight, Mackintosh had to take responsibility for his mother, five sisters, and a brother, in addition to his wife, but by the middle of the year sales of Celebrated Toffee enabled him to resign from his job at the cotton mill. When new bus routes ceased to carry customers past his house, he responded by setting up a stall at Halifax market, while his wife continued to supervise the shop. By 1894 he had established a trade outside his home town, and he began to rent a small warehouse in Bond Street, Halifax, and, one year later, bigger premises at Hope Street, where he could make his toffee on a larger scale.

The firm was converted into a limited liability company, John Mackintosh Ltd, in 1899. Mackintosh wanted to build a new works at Queen's Road, the site of his Methodist congregation, but could only raise £11,000 of the £15,000 needed. With much difficulty, he persuaded his sceptical bank manager to lend the shortfall, and the company failed to pay dividends for many years. Mackintosh was determined to reinvest his profits, and his expansion plans remained ambitious. In 1909 the Queen's Road factory was burnt down, and Mackintosh used the insurance money of £20,000 to buy the empty Albion Mills. The Queen's Road factory was rebuilt, undertaking the manufacture of chocolate in 1912, and by 1914 John Mackintosh Ltd employed some 1000 people. The scale of Mackintosh's ambition is especially revealed by his overseas activities. In 1904 he began production in a factory at Astbury Park, New Jersey, but the venture soon faltered, causing large financial losses and forcing Mackintosh to restore his fortune. He nevertheless opened a works at Crefeld, near Düsseldorf, in 1906, later sending his son to

Germany in order to learn the language. By 1914 he had also established manufacturing operations in Australia and Canada.

Mackintosh was deeply influenced by his religion and local chapel life. These associations moulded his moral outlook, his charitable gifts, and his belief in the work ethic. He owed his education, his earliest insights into organization, the management of people, and, possibly, advertising to the Methodist New Connexion. His sect encouraged lay leadership, and as a result Mackintosh emerged at an early age as a key figure within his local congregation. In 1884, when fifteen years old, he sat on his chapel's Band of Hope committee. The Sunday school had some 600 members and 60 officers in the 1880s, and Mackintosh served continuously as a staff member for almost thirty years. He was its librarian from 1886 to 1889, its minute secretary from 1889 to 1895, and superintendent from 1895 to 1914. In addition he acted as secretary to the chapel's trustees from 1899 to 1920. Between 1900 and 1909 he was circuit secretary for West Halifax and circuit treasurer from 1909 to 1914, the New Connexion having become part of the United Methodists in 1907. He was a regular delegate to the annual denominational conference, but from 1914 failing health forced him to relinquish his regional and national offices.

Mackintosh was a physically large, modest, and unpretentious man, who never forgot his origins, and his life and emotional commitment revolved around his family, his business, and the Queen's Road chapel. Although he assisted individual members of his congregation financially, he ensured that the chapel remained independent of his wealth. He gained a reputation for his support of local causes. At his factories he exhibited the characteristics of Christian paternalism, and during the First World War he provided £10,000 to the families of employees on active service. He found no calling to public life until his election as a Liberal member of Halifax town council in 1913, and, and, belatedly, in 1918 he was appointed a borough magistrate.

It was marketing which enabled Mackintosh to establish his toffee as a leading British consumer product. When he first produced his Celebrated Toffee in 1891 he issued handbills, in the same way he would have done to advertise a chapel meeting, and he was soon utilizing newspapers and posters. Through his religious connections he may already have acquired an ease with public speaking and a facility for dealing with people, but he also possessed an innate flair for and understanding of publicity. He emphasized the uniqueness and quality of his toffee, wrapping and selling it in attractive containers. As early as 1896 Mackintosh was calling himself the 'Toffee King'. In 1902 he introduced a consumer and coupon competition, the prize being a model cottage worth £250, and he followed this with two scholarships of £30 per annum and with the forwarding of free samples. He came to appreciate the power and advertising value of the popular media, and in 1903 his products began to appear on the front page of the *Daily Mail*.

During the First World War the number of employees

fell from 1000 to 250, and the German factory was sequestered. In 1917 Mackintosh Ltd developed a line, Toffee-De-Luxe, that was to emerge as its lead product over the next decade, and in 1919 it introduced an employee bonus scheme of £1 for each year of service. By 1920 the company had assets of £350,512. Mackintosh himself was made a director of the Halifax Equitable Bank in 1916, later becoming its vice-chairman as well as vice-chairman of the Equitable Building Society. He was the president of several sports clubs, and had a keen interest in bowling, football, and cricket. When John Mackintosh & Sons Ltd was restructured as a public company in 1921, employee numbers had been restored to their pre-war levels, and output was sixty times the volume achieved in 1899, the year it first became a limited company. Its capital of £750,000 was fully subscribed, with 90 per cent of the ordinary shares controlled by the family. In pursuit of his business interests John Mackintosh was widely travelled, but he continued to live at his modest terraced house in Halifax, the base of his manufacturing operations, and the venue of his religious, charitable, and temperance work. Regarded as unaffected and sympathetic, and as mindful of obligations to his community, he was a man who on several occasions risked his whole fortune to establish a business and one of Britain's most recognizable product lines. He suffered from bad health and died from a heart attack at his house at Greystones, Savile Park, Halifax, on 27 January 1920, aged fifty-one. He was survived by his wife and three sons, the eldest of whom, Harold Vincent *Mackintosh, became chairman of the family firm on his father's death. ROBERT FITZGERALD

Sources G. W. Crutchley, *John Mackintosh: a biography* (1920) · Viscount Mackintosh of Halifax [H. V. Mackintosh], *By faith and work* (1966) · D. J. Jeremy, 'Chapel in a business career: the case of John Mackintosh (1868–1920)', *Business and religion in Britain*, ed. D. J. Jeremy (1988), 95–117 · 'The late Councillor John Mackintosh, J.P.', *Confectionery Journal* (5 Feb 1920), 787–8 · W. H. Beable, *Romance of great businesses*, 2 vols. (1926)
Archives Borth. Inst., Rowntree archives
Likenesses photograph, Halifax Courier Ltd, Halifax, Yorkshire [*see illus.*] · portrait, repro. in Crutchley, *John Mackintosh*
Wealth at death £254,563 11s. 2d.: probate, 1 April 1920, CGPLA Eng. & Wales

Mackintosh, John Pitcairn (1929–1978), politician and university teacher, was born in Simla, India, on 24 August 1929, the elder of two brothers. He spent his first eleven years in British India where his mother, Mary Victoria Pitcairn, taught at a teacher training college. Her husband, Colin M. Mackintosh, had gone to India to sell cotton piece goods; then he represented McCallum's Perfection Whiskey, finally transferring to insurance work. Later, John Mackintosh used to recall how one of his earliest childhood memories was the image of demonstrators lying round the lorries carrying Lancashire piece goods, so that they could not move. The campaign of M. K. Gandhi to protect Indian home industry was, perhaps, Mackintosh's introduction to his lifelong concern with overseas issues and the problems of the developing world.

At the beginning of the Second World War the Mackintosh family returned to Edinburgh, sending the boys to Melville College. Mackintosh was to speak with affection of individual teachers, and of unhappy times at the school. He progressed to Edinburgh University, where he achieved a first-class honours degree in history (1950), and then to Balliol College, Oxford, to read philosophy, politics, and economics, in which he achieved a second class in 1952.

At Oxford certain lifelong scars were inflicted. Whereas Scottish undergraduates, straight from school or national service, tended to enjoy Oxbridge, those already having a degree from a Scottish university often returned disenchanted. Mackintosh held that Balliol men were very arrogant: 'I resented them very much. They said that a first class honours degree at a Scottish University meant that one was probably fit to come up to Oxford as an undergraduate'. This early encounter with the English establishment possibly sowed the seed of lifelong scepticism about mandarin-level civil servants, and caused his concern with Scottish devolution and an assembly in Edinburgh. The Oxford experience might also partially account for Mackintosh giving vent to witty irreverence towards so many of the products of Oxbridge, something that was to disadvantage him in later life when his political preferment was being contemplated. His malicious tongue was more wounding than perhaps he realized, and therefore sour jokes at his expense were well received both among his university colleagues and MPs. For example, the story went the rounds that Harold Wilson, in 1967, commented to the long-serving secretary of state for Scotland: 'You had better keep an eye on that man Mackintosh, Willie. He wants your job.' 'No, Harold,' came Ross's reply. 'He wants yours!'

This rather too obvious and impatient ambition, dangerously allied with an incapacity to suffer fools gladly, may have been developed by an American influence, fostered during postgraduate work at Princeton, where Mackintosh was Sir John Dill memorial fellow in 1952–3. Brash, Mackintosh was not. Insensitive, as to how he could grate on other less gifted men, he certainly was.

Mackintosh's first job was that of a junior lecturer in history at Glasgow University (1953–4), followed by seven years as lecturer at Edinburgh University between 1954 and 1961. His many pupils testify to the brilliance of his lecturing and his capacity to inspire undergraduates. He was entertaining and articulate to the point of being envied by his colleagues, and he displayed a genuine concern for his students. In 1957 he married one of his history students, Janette, daughter of J. D. Robertson; they had a daughter and a son. Having unsuccessfully contested the Pentlands division of Edinburgh as Labour candidate in the 1959 general election, in 1960 a parliamentary career seemed open to Mackintosh when he had the all-powerful backing of the general secretary of the Scottish Trades Union Congress, George Middleton, in a by-election for the Paisley seat. At the last moment Mackintosh declined to go forward, and departed to take up a professorial post at the University of Ibadan in Nigeria. It was in this period that he was to publish his book *The British Cabinet* (1962), which, in the eyes of Richard Crossman, who reviewed the volume of this still obscure academic, initiated the concept of prime ministerial government and placed Mackintosh in the same league as Walter Bagehot. It was indeed a seminal thesis. The irony is that, had Mackintosh gone to parliament as MP for Paisley in 1960, he could hardly have been denied a post in the 1964 Labour government, leading to a cabinet position before the end of the first Wilson administration in 1970. He would then doubtless have written about the myth and the reality of cabinet government in the light of experience.

In 1963 Mackintosh returned to be senior lecturer in politics at Glasgow University, and, to the dismay of his friends, his marriage to Janette Robertson, willing hostess to a generation of undergraduates, was dissolved. In that year he married Catherine Margaret Una Maclean, a lecturer in social medicine, the daughter of the Revd C. Maclean of Scarp, Harris; they had a son and a daughter.

In 1965–6 Mackintosh was professor of politics at the University of Strathclyde, working on *The Devolution of Power: Local Democracy, Regionalism and Nationalism*, which was to be published in 1968. This was the intellectual furniture of much of the Scottish devolution campaigns of the 1970s—though Mackintosh himself, shortly before his death, was scathing about the opportunism and unworkability of the proposals embodied in the Labour government's Scotland Bill in 1977–8. With some justice, he supposed that any prime minister really concerned to allow devolution, other than for reasons of sheer short-term political expediency, would have given him the post of minister of state in the Cabinet Office, responsible for the devolution proposals.

Mackintosh was elected Labour MP for Berwick and East Lothian in 1966. The fact that so talented a man, who was arguably the most compellingly persuasive parliamentary orator of his generation, never achieved ministerial office requires some explanation. One clue is to be found in his maiden speech, a dazzling performance, which lingers in the memory of all who heard it. His tribute to his defeated opponent, Sir William Anstruther-Gray, former deputy chairman of ways and means and chairman of the 1922 committee, was one of the handsomest ever heard:

> It is perhaps not well known to hon. Members that Sir William was one of the men who returned from the Front in May, 1940, and persuaded 32 of his back bench colleagues to go into the Lobby against their own Government—against the leadership of Neville Chamberlain—thus helping to bring down that Government. On that occasion he was a true patriot. Like my predecessor, I hope to represent efficiently the constituency which has elected me. I shall work hard on its behalf. (*Hansard 5C*, 9 May 1966, col. 77)

This Mackintosh did, prodigiously, with a six-month interregnum in 1974, when he was defeated in February and returned the same October. At the memorial meeting in the House of Commons, Gerald O'Brien, the full-time agent of the Berwick and East Lothian constituency Labour Party, moved an ultra-sophisticated audience by claiming that the Lammermuir hills wept when Mackintosh died; and, on the way to his funeral, little groups of constituents from the farming areas could be observed all along the route of the cortège paying their last respects to a politician who had come to be loved by those for whom he worked. In dealing with constituents' problems Mackintosh was patient, caring, and charming, a different person from the one who, in London, chastised the Wilsons and the Callaghans with his acerbic wit. Moreover, the very point which Mackintosh selected in Anstruther-Gray's career for favourable mention was, with hindsight, to be a trailer for his own rebellions, too numerous to chronicle. Among the more remembered must be that hectic night in November 1976 when Mackintosh and Walden abstained on the Docks Bill, which was consequently lost, to the consternation of the hierarchy of Labour ministers.

Mackintosh's interest in constitutional and procedural questions was put to immediate use when he entered parliament by his appointment to the select committees for the oversight of government, and he served on experimental committees on agriculture (1967–8) and Scottish affairs (1968–70), forerunners of the departmentally related committee system introduced in 1979. Never was there a more spectacular, intellectual, verbal clash of arms than when Mackintosh bearded Richard Crossman, then leader of the house, on the proposal to terminate the activities of the embryonic agriculture committee. After a Wagnerian battle Mackintosh lost, but won the war of select committees. He delighted in arguing questions of parliamentary reform with his colleagues and the clerks of the house, and was generous with his time in exposition of the practicalities of parliamentary government to those outside. He gave valuable help to the Commonwealth Parliamentary Association and to the Hansard Society, of which he was chairman from 1974 until his death.

No picture of Mackintosh can be complete without an attempt to convey his demonic energy—apparent whether playing with his children, stepchildren, or the children of others; or pouring out polished, provocative articles for *The Times*, *The Scotsman*, the *Political Quarterly*, and a host of other newspapers and journals; or fascinating Königswinter conferences; or electrifying the special conference of the Labour Party, a largely hostile audience, when speaking on entry to the European Economic Community in the Central Hall, Westminster, from an unusual and even physically hazardous position in the front row of the gallery, leaning over a balcony. There was also the extraordinary courage and self-discipline which he exercised during the last year of his life, when he knew he was fatally ill, but kept the knowledge to himself, seeking no pity and working with frenetic effort. He died in the Western General Hospital, Edinburgh, on 30 July 1978. He was buried in the churchyard at Gifford, East Lothian.

TAM DALYELL, *rev.*

Sources personal knowledge (1986) · *WWW* · *The Times* (31 July 1978) · R. Jenkins, *The Times* (10 Aug 1978) · P. Cosgrave, *The Spectator*

(5 Aug 1978) · *The Observer* (6 Aug 1978) · D. Marquand, 'John Mackintosh: social democrat', *The Listener* (2 Nov 1978), 571–2
Archives NL Scot., corresp. and papers | FILM BFI NFTVA, documentary footage
Likenesses photograph, repro. in *The Times*
Wealth at death £104,356.97: confirmation, 24 Nov 1978, *CCI*

Mackintosh, Lachlan (*c*.1543–1606). *See under* Mackintosh family (*per. c*.1491–1606).

Mackintosh, Lauchlan [Lachlan], of Torcastle (*bap.* 1639, *d.* 1704), chief of clan Mackintosh and captain of clan Chattan, was baptized on 17 October 1639 in Inverness, the son of William Mackintosh (*d.* 1660), chief of the Mackintoshes and captain of clan Chattan, and his wife, Margaret (*d.* 1674), eldest daughter of David Graham, laird of Fintray. After attending schools in Inverness and Elgin, he studied philosophy for two years at King's College, Aberdeen, and later at St Leonard's College, St Andrews. Shortly after the death of his father on 22 November 1660 he succeeded as chief.

Mackintosh's chiefship saw the cessation of a 300-year-old feud between the Mackintoshes and clan Chattan and the clan Cameron over the lands of Glenlui and Locharkaig in Lochaber, to which the Camerons claimed a right through highland custom and the Mackintoshes claimed a right through law. A reconciliation finally occurred in 1665. Mackintosh also had to deal with the reassertion of independence by the Macphersons in 1664. He tried to dispel this with a renewal of the 1609 bond of union, but while most of the leading men of the clan signed, Andrew Macpherson of Cluny, head of that family, did not. Macpherson determination to break away from the Mackintosh chief was realized when in 1672 Duncan, who had succeeded Andrew, applied for a coat of arms for the name of Macpherson, distinct from that of Mackintosh. However, a compromise was reached with the help of Lauchlan Mackintosh of Kinrara, uncle of the chief, and it was decided that Duncan was responsible for those of his name, but '[without] prejudice always to the Laird of M'Intosh … who are his vassals' (*Loyall Dissuasive and other Papers*, 56–7). The chief's authority in the locality was upheld against the marquess of Huntly, whose lands in Lochaber were under the Mackintoshes' stewardry, and who, jealous of Mackintosh's legal right to hold courts, tried with the earl of Moray to prevent him from fulfilling his duties. Mackintosh, however, held court throughout Lochaber, and was granted further powers to deal with lawless elements as he wished.

On 23 July 1667 Mackintosh married Magdalene (or Margaret), only daughter of John Lindsay of Edzell, with whom he had a son, Lauchlan. Some months after her death he married, on 25 August 1677, Anne, daughter of Sir George Munro of Culrain and widow of Donald, master of Reay, with whom he had a daughter, Christian, who later married David Dunbar of Dunphail. In 1702, for reasons of old age, he transferred the clan estate to his son, Lauchlan. He died two years later, at Dalcross Castle, on 9 December 1704, and was buried at Petty after having lain in state until mid-January. ALISON CATHCART

Sources H. Paton, ed., *The Mackintosh muniments, 1442–1820* (1923) · L. Mackintosh, 'Epitome of the origin and increase of the Mackintoshes, 1679', in W. Macfarlane, *Genealogical collections concerning families in Scotland*, ed. J. T. Clark, 1, Scottish History Society, 33 (1900), 1 · A. M. Mackintosh, *The Mackintoshes and clan Chattan* (1903) · C. Fraser-Mackintosh, *An account of the confederation of clan Chattan: its kith and kin* (1898) · *Scots peerage* · Charles, eleventh marquis of Huntly, earl of Aboyne, ed., *The records of Aboyne MCCXXX–MDCLXXXI*, New Spalding Club, 13 (1894) · *The loyall dissuasive and other papers concerning the affairs of clan Chattan: by Sir Æneas Macpherson, knight of Invereshie, 1691–1705*, ed. A. D. Murdoch, Scottish History Society, 41 (1902)
Archives Highland Regional Archives, Inverness · NA Scot., King's College special collections · NL Scot., MS 9854 | priv. coll., family papers

Mackintosh, Margaret Macdonald [*née* Margaret Macdonald] (1864–1933), watercolour painter and designer, was born on 5 November 1864 in Tipton, Staffordshire, the second of the five children of John Macdonald (1825–1895), engineer and colliery manager, and his wife, Frances Grove Hardeman (1838–1912), daughter of Joseph Hardeman, counting house clerk, and his wife, Harriet Moore. Her father was from Glasgow, her mother from Cradley Heath, Staffordshire. Her younger sister **Frances Eliza Macdonald** (1873–1921), artist, was born on 24 August 1873 in Ravenscliff Road, Kidsgrove, Stafford. Margaret was educated at Orme Girls' School in north Staffordshire until she was sixteen and attended an art school in Germany in her late teens or early twenties. In 1890 after her father's retirement and subsequent move to 9 Windsor Terrace, Glasgow, Margaret and her sister Frances immediately began attending classes at the Glasgow School of Art. Four years after her father's death in 1895, Margaret moved with her mother to live with her brother Charles at Dunglass Castle, Bowling, near Glasgow.

Macdonald's watercolour drawings and designs attracted attention in Glasgow in 1894, the year she completed her studies, because of her tendency to distort and elongate the human form. A poster advertising a Glasgow Institute of the Fine Arts Exhibition (1895) made with her sister Frances and the architect and designer (James) Herbert McNair (1868–1955) signalled Macdonald's appreciation for a collaborative art-making practice. After 1896 she established her reputation as a metalworker. The clock she designed and made with Frances Macdonald and her own beaten metal panel *The Annunciation* (exh. London Arts and Crafts Exhibition Society, 1896) received accolades from London's prestigious art journal *The Studio* while, at the same time, the journal acknowledged the 'eccentricity' of the work that deserved its nickname 'the spooky school' (*The Studio*, 9, 1896, 202). The Macdonald sisters along with their future husbands, Charles Rennie *Mackintosh (1868–1928) and (James) Herbert McNair (who married Frances on 14 June 1899 at the Scottish Episcopal church in Dumbarton), would come to be called the Glasgow Four by later critics and art historians; the art they made became part of the regionally defined Glasgow style. Frances Macdonald's work featured in several art journals including *The Studio* and the *Yellow Book*. She died on 12 December 1921 aged forty-eight at 50 Gibson Street,

Glasgow. Most of her work was destroyed by her husband, together with his own.

In 1898 Margaret was elected a member of the Royal Scottish Society of Painters in Watercolour. She exhibited intermittently with them until 1922, becoming a member of their council from 1907 to 1909 and again from 1911 to 1913, and remaining a member of the society until 1924. Her watercolour pictures, for example *Mysterious Garden* (1911; priv. coll.), most frequently represent aloof or mysterious women either with elongated, emaciated bodies or with bodies hidden by diaphanous garments which resemble flowers in full bloom. However, Margaret made her most exciting and well-known work for interiors designed by Charles Rennie Mackintosh. It is this work that is now most frequently seen in exhibitions, for example, in the highly praised '"Glasgow Girls": Women in Art and Design, 1880–1920' (Glasgow, 1990) and 'Charles Rennie Mackintosh' (Glasgow, New York, Chicago, Los Angeles, 1996 and 1997), and is on permanent display in the reconstructed Mackintosh–Macdonald house in the Hunterian Art Gallery, Glasgow.

On 22 August 1900 Macdonald married the architect Charles Rennie Mackintosh in the Scottish Episcopal church at Dumbarton near Glasgow. The couple lived at 120 Mains Street, Glasgow, until 1906 when they moved into their personally decorated flat at 6 Florentine Terrace. While the couple lived in Glasgow, Margaret designed a number of gesso panels for Mackintosh interiors including *The May Queen* for the Ingram Street tea rooms (1900; Glasgow Museums and Art Galleries), *O ye who Walk in Willowwood* (1903; Glasgow Museums and Art Galleries) for the Willow tea rooms in Sauchiehall Street, and the *Seven Princesses* (c.1906; Österreichisches Museum für Angewandte Kunst, Vienna) for the home of the Viennese financier Fritz Wärndorfer. All the panels, like the watercolour paintings, depict women. They demonstrate Macdonald Mackintosh's ability to introduce an exquisitely sophisticated linear design into the sumptuous texture so characteristic of gesso work.

During the summer of 1914 the couple holidayed in Walberswick, Suffolk; then, rather than returning to Glasgow, the Mackintoshes moved to London where both kept studios in Chelsea. In 1923 the Mackintoshes left for France, staying first in Collioure then in Port Vendres, where they were able to live on their modest income. They returned to London in 1927, when Charles Rennie Mackintosh received treatment for cancer. When her husband died in 1928, Margaret stayed for a time at 12 Porchester Square, London, returned briefly to France, and then based herself in her Glebe Place studio in Chelsea. She died at 39 Royal Avenue, Chelsea, London, on 7 January 1933 and was cremated at Golders Green on 10 January. Much of her work can be viewed in the Hunterian Art Gallery, Glasgow.

JANICE HELLAND

Sources J. Helland, *The studios of Frances and Margaret Macdonald* (1996) · P. Robertson, *Margaret Macdonald Mackintosh, 1864–1933* (1983) · J. Helland, 'The critics and the arts and crafts: the instance of Margaret Macdonald and Charles Rennie Mackintosh', *Art History*, 17 (1994), 205–23 · J. Helland, 'Collaborative work among The Four', *Charles Rennie Mackintosh*, ed. W. Kaplan (1996), 89–112 · J. Burkhauser, ed., *The Glasgow girls: women in art and design, 1880–1920* (1990) · *The Times* (9 Jan 1933), 1 · b. cert. · b. cert. [Frances Eliza Macdonald] · registration books, Glasgow School of Art [Frances Eliza Macdonald] · d. cert. [Frances Eliza Macdonald] · m. cert. [Frances Eliza Macdonald] · d. cert. · J. Helland, 'A sense of extravagance: Margaret Macdonald's gesso panels, 1900–1903', *Visual Culture in Britain*, 2/1 (2001), 1–15
Archives Hunterian Museum and Art Gallery, Glasgow
Likenesses T. & R. Annan, photograph, c.1900, Hunterian Museum and Art Gallery, Glasgow

Mackintosh, Robert (1858–1933), Congregational minister and theologian, was born on 23 May 1858 at Dunoon, Argyllshire, one of seven children of the evangelical Calvinist Charles Calder Mackintosh (1806–1868) and his wife, Annie, second daughter of Robert Brown of Fairlie, Ayrshire. His father was Free Church of Scotland minister at Dunoon. Following her husband's death his mother moved with the family to Glasgow, where they came under the influence of Alexander Whyte, then assistant minister of Free St John's, and later of Free St George's, Edinburgh, with which church the Mackintoshes subsequently became associated.

Mackintosh won a scholarship to Oxford, but his mother persuaded him not to take it up. Instead he went to Glasgow University (1872–7), where he graduated with first-class honours in philosophy and second-class honours in classics. Of all his teachers Edward Caird impressed him most, though he subsequently found cause first to repudiate and later to modify his teacher's idealism. Theological studies at New College, Edinburgh, followed, and the family moved to Edinburgh. Whyte was very supportive of Mackintosh, who was already reading Erskine of Linlathen and struggling with such doctrinal issues as the eternity of punishment, which assailed his conscience but was affirmed in his church's Westminster confession. Of his theological teachers A. B. Davidson was the most inspiring, while he later dismissed James MacGregor, professor of doctrine, as an arch-Calvinist.

On graduating BD, Mackintosh pursued further studies in Jena and Marburg and then, during a missionary assistantship to Dr Walter Smith at Edinburgh, he contracted scarlet fever. A recuperative trip to New Zealand followed, during which Mackintosh worked on his first book, *Christ and the Jewish Law* (1886). He visited the south of France and Palestine, all the while 'fighting for life as a Christian, and for liberty as a preacher from the fetters of a seventeenth-century creed' (*Christianity and Sin*, 1917, 107). He supported Robert Rainy's campaign for a declaratory act, designed to clarify the free church's relation to the Westminster confession of faith; but this alone did not suffice to ease his distaste for the confession. On the other hand he drew small comfort from the emotional revivalism which was becoming popular at the time (though he later said that he owed his conversion to Dwight Lyman Moody and Ira David Sankey). Hence his provocatively entitled pamphlets, *The Obsoleteness of the Westminster Confession of Faith* and *The Insufficiency of Revivalism as a Religious System*. These were bound with his *Essays towards a New Theology* (1889), his other themes being 'The atonement morally viewed', 'The biblical doctrines of judgment and immortality', 'Internal evidence for the truth of holy scripture', and 'The Calvinist conception of grace'. Far from being mere academic exercises, here was Mackintosh struggling to come to terms with topics which had tormented him for years. In the year in which this book appeared, Mackintosh was awarded the degree of DD by Glasgow University.

In the same year Mackintosh went to Withington Presbyterian Church, Manchester, as assistant to Benjamin Bell. His sojourn was brief, for on 11 December 1890 he was ordained and inducted to the pastorate of Dumfries Congregational Church. Mackintosh later said that he came to Congregationalism as a refugee from narrow Calvinistic confessionalism. While at Dumfries, on 22 May 1894 he married Mary Wilson Robb (1871–1924), daughter of James Henderson Robb, a trader of that town. They had four daughters and two sons. One of the latter was stillborn; the other, to his father's bewilderment, became a priest of the Church of England.

In 1894 Mackintosh was called to be professor at Lancashire Independent college, Manchester, and thus began the family's long association with Withington Congregational Church. Mackintosh served under four principals: Caleb Scott, W. F. Adeney, W. H. Bennett—for whom he had a particular affection—and A. J. Grieve, the last of whom delivered Mackintosh's funeral oration; in it he expressed his great respect for his colleague's saintliness and scholarship, while noting that where teaching was concerned, 'his gifts were not of the "popular" order'— though there is evidence that Mackintosh's children's addresses in church were well received.

Mackintosh's teaching duties were at first weighted towards philosophy and sociology, and later towards theology, and this is borne out by the progression of his books: *From Comte to Benjamin Kidd* (1899), *A First Primer of Apologetics* (1900; 2nd edn, 1904), *Hegel and Hegelianism* (1903), *Christian Ethics* (1909), *Christianity and Sin* (1913), *Albrecht Ritschl and his School* (1915), *Historic Theories of Atonement* (1920), *Values* (1928), and, after his retirement, *Some Central Things* (1932). Away from his main academic lines were a biography, *Principal Rainy* (1907), and a commentary, *Thessalonians and Corinthians* (1909) in the Westminster New Testament series. He also contributed biblical papers to *The Expositor*, and 'Galatians' to A. S. Peake's *A Commentary on the Bible* (1919). He wrote substantial articles—'Apologetics', 'Theism', and 'Theology' among them—for the eleventh edition of *Encyclopaedia Britannica*, and a shorter piece on apologetics for its successor edition. He contributed articles and reviews to a number of other journals.

A lecturer in the faculty of theology of the University of Manchester from its inception in 1904, Mackintosh owed his appointment, as he thought, to the professor of philosophy, Samuel Alexander. In 1908 Mackintosh presented a 'masterly' paper at the International Congregational Council (ICC) meeting in Edinburgh which 'paralyzed, overpowered' some of the able representatives (*Proceedings of the International Congregational Council*, 1908, 124). In 1918 he chaired the Lancashire Congregational Union and

in 1920, in the absence through ill health of P. T. Forsyth, he presented the report 'The contribution of British Congregationalism to religious thought' at the ICC assembly in Boston, USA. In 1924 he attended the Conference on Politics, Economics and Citizenship in Birmingham. Mackintosh retired in June 1930 and moved to Whaley Bridge. In 1933 he suffered a heart attack and died on 12 February at 22 York Place, Chorlton upon Medlock, Manchester. The funeral service was held three days later at Lancashire Independent college, followed by interment at Taxal churchyard.

Mackintosh was a man of utter integrity. Regarded by some as austere, even aloof, he was capable of great kindness and, for all his scholarship, had a childlike simplicity. He loved music, enjoyed singing, loathed gardening. With his pointed humour expressed in memorable sentences he could slay intellectual giants, but he had every sympathy with those who faced the trial of faith as he had done. His own words constitute his most appropriate epitaph: 'For one's own part, one would thankfully spend one's whole life till one was spent out, for the privilege of removing a single obstacle from the path of hearts that are seeking God' (*Albrecht Ritschl and his School*, 4).

ALAN P. F. SELL

Sources A. P. F Sell, *Robert Mackintosh: theologian of integrity* (1977) · *Proceedings of the International Congregational Council* (1908–20) · m. cert. · d. cert. · *CGPLA Eng. & Wales* (1933)

Likenesses photograph, repro. in Sell, *Robert Mackintosh* · photograph, repro. in *Proceedings of the International Congregational Council* (1908)

Wealth at death £13,880 15s. 1d.: resworn probate, 22 April 1933, *CGPLA Eng. & Wales*

Mackintosh, William (*c*.1521–1550). *See under* Mackintosh family (*per. c*.1491–1606).

Mackintosh, William, of Borlum [called Uilleam Dearg] (*c*.1657–1743), Jacobite army officer, was the eldest of the eight sons of William Mackintosh (*d*. 1717), laird of Borlum, and Mary, daughter of William Baillie of Dunain. Probably raised in the Scottish Episcopal church, Mackintosh entered King's College, Aberdeen, in 1672, graduating MA in July 1677. He appears as a captain in the Scottish regiment of Colonel Henry Gage serving in the Spanish Netherlands in 1681. During the 1690s he resided mostly in Hertfordshire, but was engaged in the service of the exiled James VII (James II in England) in France, Ireland, and Scotland. By February 1698 he was back in Scotland when he formed part of a commission of fire and sword granted by the privy council to Lachlan Mackintosh of that ilk against the Macdonalds of Keppoch.

In 1707 Mackintosh (also known as Borlum during and after his father's lifetime, and by his Gaelic nickname Uilleam Dearg, Red William) is described as a colonel. He was in French service by autumn 1714, when he returned to Scotland to enlist support for the Jacobite cause. In 1715 he persuaded Mackintosh of that ilk to join the Jacobites and, under the pretence of a troop review, they marched on Inverness in the early hours of the morning of 13 September with some 400 men. After seizing the king's officers and any stores, Borlum himself proclaimed James VIII and

III (James Francis Edward Stuart) at the market cross before marching off to seize Culloden House. Having failed in this venture he returned to Inverness, fortified it with extra men sent by William Mackenzie, fifth earl of Seaforth, and then marched south with several hundred men on 20 September to join the earl of Mar at Perth. Borlum and Mackintosh of that ilk arrived at Perth on 5 October, where they were organized into a regiment of thirteen companies, of which the vast majority of the officers—27 out of 32—were Mackintoshes. This regiment was 'reckoned to be the best the Earl of Mar had' (Terry, 84).

Borlum now marched to secure south-east Scotland against George I's forces. At this time Lockhart says Borlum began to be styled brigadier. Based at Burntisland, he moved his troops into the burghs of the east neuk of Fife, and, taking those boats which he could find, organized the crossing of the Firth of Forth on the night of 12 October; during this time British men-of-war bombarded him at Burntisland without success. Of the 2500 troops intended for the crossing some 1600 made it across to Haddingtonshire; others never embarked because of contrary winds or were captured.

However, Borlum now secured Leith and, marching his troops to the borders, arrived at Kelso on 22 October, where he 'appeared very well' in contrast to the fatigue of his troops (Terry, 197). During a council of war, held on 27 October, he supported the plan to join with the Jacobites of Argyll and march on Glasgow and Dumfries. Instead the decision was taken to march on England. One witness, Peter Clarke, described the entry of the Mackintoshes into Kendal on 5 November with Borlum dressed in highland garb and armed to the teeth ('Journall', ed. Paton, 1.514).

All the while Borlum was shadowed by Hanoverian troops from Newcastle under General Carpenter, whom he wanted to engage, but Borlum and the Jacobite general Thomas Forster could not agree on a plan of action. Borlum fortified Preston. When the Hanoverian general Sir Charles Wills attacked, his forces were cut to pieces in a crossfire directed by troops Borlum had hidden around the town. Unfortunately for Borlum, Forster allowed them to be surrounded by the joint forces of Wills and Carpenter and they were forced to surrender on 16 November.

Borlum was given as a hostage along with Lord Derwentwater, and, with his brother John Mackintosh, was lodged in Newgate prison. During their incarceration, it is said Borlum and Forster had time to quarrel loudly over the failure of the campaign. While exercising in the prison yard on 4 May 1716, the day before his trial for high treason, Borlum charged the turnkeys and led a daring breakout; although some were recaptured, Borlum and his brother had escaped to Paris by September. A reward of £200 was offered by the corporation of London for his capture, to which the government added a further £1000.

Borlum returned to Scotland in May 1719 and met with the Earl Marischal and others at Loch Long and, together with the 'Spanish Collonell', commanded the forces to the right of William, earl of Seaforth, at the battle of Glenshiel. Borlum was unable to reinforce Seaforth during the critical part of the battle. In the aftermath he again escaped to France but returned to Scotland in 1722 and 1724 before he was finally captured, probably in Caithness, by government troops in November 1727. He was sent a state prisoner to Edinburgh Castle, where he remained for the rest of his life.

During his imprisonment Borlum wrote *An essay on ways and means of enclosing, fallowing, and planting lands in Scotland, and that in sixteen years at farthest* (1729). He states in this work that some of the ideas were suggested by Robert Boyle, with whom he was acquainted in England. Prior to 1715 Borlum had already promoted afforestation on his own lands at Borlum, Benchar, and Raits, Inverness-shire, cumulatively assessed at just over £1160 Scots in the sheriffdom valuation roll of 1644. In his *Essay* Borlum now recommended the same policy to other Scottish landowners. In his second work, *A Short Scheme* (1742), he discussed at some length the need to combat reiving in the central highlands. Another work, entitled *An Essay on the Husbandry of Scotland* (1732), is occasionally, but incorrectly, attributed to him.

Borlum was a complex character; sometimes he was portrayed as a hardened soldier and at other times as one of the new breed of improving eighteenth-century landlords. He was evidently a clever military strategist—as his crossing of the Forth demonstrates—which appears to contradict the comment by James, Jacobite duke of Liria, that Borlum was stupid but loyal. One eyewitness refers to Borlum's 'grim countenance' which, combined with the handbill advertising the reward for his arrest in 1716, suggests a striking appearance: 'a tall, raw-boned man, about sixty, fair-complexioned, beetle-browed, grey-eyed, speaking with a broad Scotch accent' ('Journall', ed. Paton).

Mackintosh of Borlum married in 1688 Mary, daughter of Edward Reade of Ipsen House, Oxfordshire, who was maid of honour to Princess Anne, later Queen Anne. Mary died in 1712. They had six children: Lachlan, the heir, who gained control and sold off most of the family lands and drowned at sea in 1723; William and Richard, who both died young; Winwood, who married Roderick Mackenzie of Fairburn, Ross-shire, in 1710; Helen, who is said to have married an Inverness merchant; and Forbes Mary. Borlum died in Edinburgh Castle on 7 January 1743, aged about eighty-five.

DAVIE HORSBURGH

Sources A. M. Mackintosh, *Brigadier Mackintosh of Borlum, Jacobite hero and martyr* (1918) · C. Petrie, *The Jacobite movement*, 3rd edn (1959) · W. Fraser, ed., *The Sutherland book*, 3 vols. (1892) · 'A journall of severall occurences in 1715 by Peter Clarke', ed. H. Paton, *Miscellany … I*, Scottish History Society, 15 (1893), 513–22 · A. MacBean, 'Memorial concerning the highlands', *Origins of the 'Forty-Five and other papers relating to that rising*, ed. W. B. Blaikie, Scottish History Society, 2nd ser., vol. 2 (1916), 71–92 · *The Jacobite attempt of 1719: letters of James Butler, second duke of Ormonde, relating to Cardinal Alberoni's project for the invasion of Great Britain on behalf of the Stuarts, and to the landing of a Spanish expedition in Scotland*, ed. W. K. Dickson, Scottish History Society, 19 (1895) · C. S. Terry, ed., *The Jacobites and the union* (1922) · B. Lenman, *The Jacobite risings in Britain, 1689–1746*, new edn (1995) · J. Bayne, *The Jacobite rising of 1715* (1970)

Likenesses portrait, 1707, repro. in Mackintosh, *Brigadier Mackintosh of Borlum*

Mackirdy, Olive Christian. *See* Malvery, Olive Christian (1876/7–1914).

Macklin [Melaghlin, MacLaughlin], **Charles** (1699?–1797), actor and playwright, was probably born in Culdaff, co. Donegal, Ireland, the son of William Melaghlin (or McLaughlin; *d.* 1704), a publican, and his wife, Agnes, *née* Flanagan (*c*.1660–1759). His origins and early years have been the subject of myth, speculation, and biographical fantasy. Macklin's earliest biographer, Francis Aspry Congreve, records that the actor was born in the barony of Innishoven about 1699 in circumstances which were 'indigent in the extreme', and tells the story of a 'late Irish Judge' remembering him as 'a very inferior servant in Trinity College, Dublin' (Congreve, 10–11). According to James Kirkman, Macklin was descended from landed gentry, his father having lost his estates as a result of misguided loyalty to King James during the events of the revolution of 1688 (in this account, Macklin was born two months before the battle of the Boyne—that is, early in 1690). The Melaghlins moved to Dublin in the early 1700s and William died in 1704; in February 1707 Agnes married another supporter of King James, who had subsequently turned publican, Luke O'Meally.

Education and early career Charles was sent to board at a school in Islandbridge, a village just west of Dublin, where he was taught by a Scotsman by the name of Nicholson— reportedly 'a compendium of all those gloomy, brutal passions which constitute the systematic tyrant' (Kirkman, 1.23), who was to instill into the boy a hatred of the Scots which was to last a lifetime. Macklin's first recorded stage appearance was (surprisingly, in view of his rasping voice, sturdy build, and rugged countenance) in the female role of Monimia in a school production of Thomas Otway's tragedy *The Orphan*, an event which provided an outlet for his dangerously undisciplined energies, and from which 'he always dated his first disposition to become an actor' (Kirkman, 1.25).

About 1708 Macklin left Dublin for England, and he spent the next few years in a series of menial jobs (possibly serving as a waiter or tapster). At some point between then and 1720 he took to the theatre, appearing with a succession of touring companies in Wales, the midlands, and in the Bath and Bristol area. Macklin himself later stated that he 'came to reside in Westminster in 1720' and 'first trod the stage' three years later (Appleton, 247), although no record of this exists; Congreve alludes to an unsuccessful appearance at Lincoln's Inn Fields in 1725 as Alcander in Dryden's and Lee's *Oedipus*, 'in which he spoke with so little of the then tragic cadence' (Congreve, 12) that he was dismissed from the company. Macklin's view was that his 'familiar' pattern of delivery was at odds with the '*hoity-toity* tone of the tragedy of that day' (Cooke, 13)—a perception of the relations between regional and class accent, theatrical diction, and his own version of realism which was to underpin his work as a performer and as a trainer of actors.

Charles Macklin (1699?–1797), by John Opie, *c*.1792

For the next three years Macklin was on tour in the west country. In 1733, however, came his first significant opportunity as a result of the actors' revolt, led by Theophilus Cibber, against John Highmore's chaotic management of the Drury Lane theatre. The precipitate departure of the major part of Highmore's company for the Haymarket left the hapless patentee desperate for actors, and Macklin duly stepped forward into an array of substantial roles which he might otherwise have waited for years to acquire, including Brazen in George Farquhar's *The Recruiting Officer*. From the end of October 1733 to March 1734, when the Haymarket rebels returned to Drury Lane, Macklin enjoyed some success at the theatre; between March and May he was seen intermittently at the Haymarket and Lincoln's Inn Fields. During this period he also entered into a permanent relationship with the actress Mrs Ann Grace, and a daughter, Maria, was born in the summer of 1733. Although Ann later adopted Macklin as her surname, it appears that the couple never formally married. Like Charles she was of Irish descent, but her origins, her early years, and even her name are relatively indeterminate. In Kirkman's account she was 'the widow of a very respectable hosier in Dublin' (Kirkman, 1.174); according to Cooke, her maiden name was Grace Purvor (Cooke, 76). The family settled in Covent Garden. In Cooke's account, Macklin's early forties saw his conversion from Roman Catholicism to protestantism:

as he was strolling one day through Lincoln's Inn Fields, he saw a little book upon a stall called *The Funeral of the Mass* … the consequence of which was, that he deserted his mother church, and became a convert to the Protestant religion. (Cooke, 75)

Drury Lane, on trial, and Shylock During the summer of 1734 Macklin was again on tour, possibly in Chester, Wales, and Bristol. His daughter Maria was baptized in Portsmouth on 1 September 1734. On 24 September, at the invitation of Drury Lane's new manager, Charles Fleetwood, he signed articles as a regular member of the company. He took on a wide range of second-rank parts and rapidly made himself indispensable both as an actor and as Fleetwood's associate. On the evening of 10 May 1735 Macklin's short temper led to an incident which might well have curtailed not only his acting career but also his life. On the night before, Macklin had worn a certain property wig in the farce *Trick for Trick*; however, Hallam attempted to claim it for that evening's performance. Hallam surrendered the wig, but Macklin continued verbally to abuse him. When Hallam eventually retorted, Macklin leapt out of his chair and shoved his stick at his face. The thrust caught Hallam in the eye, and, in the words of the surgeon who was called to his assistance, 'the flick had passed through the thin bone, that contains the eye, into the brain' (Kirkman, 1.200). According to his own testimony, Macklin instantly regretted his action (although he also hinted that Hallam had brought his fate upon himself, claiming that 'his left side was then towards me; but he turned about unluckily') and threw the stick into the fire. Hallam ordered Thomas Arne's son, who was sitting by, costumed as a girl for the part of Estifania, to 'Whip up your clothes, you little b-h, and urine in my eye' (Kirkman, 1.202); when young Arne proved unable to comply with the request, Macklin himself duly obliged. Despite this attempt to provide a natural antiseptic, Hallam died the next morning. Indicted for wilful murder on 13 May, Macklin surrendered himself voluntarily. The case came to trial at the Old Bailey on 12 December. Since he was not entitled to legal representation, Macklin used the intervening period to prepare his own defence, an experience which gave him a taste for litigation that lasted for the rest of his career. Under Macklin's cross-examination a succession of witnesses concurred that the killing was accidental rather than premeditated; moreover, Macklin asserted in his own mitigation that the wig itself was *absolutely necessary* for my part, as the *whole force* of the *poet's wit* depends on the *lean, meagre looks* of one that is in want of food' (Kirkman, 1.201). The jury quickly returned a verdict of manslaughter, and Macklin's sentence was 'to be branded on the hand and discharged' (Appleton, 33). By the end of January 1736 Macklin was back at Drury Lane.

The 1740–41 season saw two key events in Macklin's stage career. The first was his appearance on 15 April 1740 in David Garrick's afterpiece *Lethe, or, Esop in the Shades*, inaugurating a friendship that later turned to bitter rivalry. The second was his sensational début as Shylock, which afforded the first significant demonstration of his systematic, almost forensic, approach to character-building. *The Merchant of Venice* had rarely been staged since the seventeenth century, and the role of Shylock had been associated with *commedia dell'arte*-derived traditions of low comedy. Macklin's conception of the part was informed by rather more detailed research and sympathetic observation than had hitherto been the case, his essential reference points being Josephus' *History of the Jews* and his daily visits to The Exchange and the adjacent coffee houses, 'that by a frequent intercourse and conversation with the unforeskinned race he might habituate himself to their air and deportment' (Appleton, 46). The play opened on 14 February 1741; in Macklin's account, he was 'in such a cause, to be tried by a *special jury*'; appropriately enough, the trial scene 'wound up the fulness of my reputation: here I was well listened to; and here I made a silent yet forcible impression on my audience, that I retired from this great attempt most perfectly satisfied' (Cooke, 92–3). Despite its commitment to verisimilitude, the characterization was not designed to solicit sympathy. Macklin's Shylock was a monstrous, scornful, coldly malign force, and hugely popular with audiences; he was to continue to play the part for fifty years. Much later, according to legend, he not only afforded George II himself a sleepless night after attending a performance, but also provoked him to urge Sir Robert Walpole to threaten one of his more recalcitrant parliaments by 'sending them to the theatre to see that Irishman play Shylock' (Highfill, Burnim & Langhans, *BDA*, 10). As far as contemporary audiences were concerned, Macklin's rendition was authentically Shakespearian, as it was commemorated in a couplet often attributed to Pope:

This is the Jew
That Shakespeare drew.

With Shylock it appeared that Macklin had transformed himself from a modest success into the leading light of the London stage. But in October 1741 his triumph was overshadowed by the equally spectacular reclamation of one of Shakespeare's tragic protagonists, in Garrick's début performance as Richard III. Macklin initially celebrated his friend's success, and they performed together at Drury Lane through the 1742–3 season. During this period Garrick and the actress Peg Woffington moved into the Macklins' house in Bow Street, Covent Garden—an arrangement which has given rise to speculation about a possible *ménage à trois*. Towards the end of the season, however, events at Drury Lane led to a break between Macklin and Garrick which was never fully healed. Even with Garrick, Macklin, Woffington, Kitty Clive, and Hannah Pritchard in the company, Fleetwood was mired in debt and unable to pay his actors' salaries. In May 1743, under Garrick's leadership, the company staged a walk-out, while petitioning the lord chamberlain to allow them to form a new company. Given the terms of the 1737 Licensing Act, the attempted coup was doomed from the outset, and the rebels were forced to go back to Fleetwood to negotiate for re-engagement. The manager agreed to reinstate the entire company—apart from Macklin, whom he regarded as the most treacherous and ungrateful of all. To no effect, Garrick pleaded Macklin's case, volunteering cuts in his own salary to secure his fellow actor's engagement; he then attempted to persuade Macklin by offering to pay him himself. Macklin refused the offer. As Garrick returned to the Drury Lane stage in

December (under significantly better terms than before), Macklin's supporters took up the cudgels. A pamphlet was issued denouncing Garrick (who replied in kind), and Macklin's friends pelted the actor off stage. Although the row subsided, and a year later the two actors were publicly reconciled, Macklin harboured a grudge towards Garrick for the rest of his life.

Banished from Drury Lane, Macklin set up a short-lived experiment at the Haymarket wherein he recruited a scratch company of amateurs, whom he intended, without significant success, to school in his new art of plain, 'natural' acting. By the summer of 1744 he was on the Kentish circuit. He was accompanied by Mrs Macklin and their daughter, Maria, who had made her own stage début two years previously. **Maria Macklin** (1733–1781) was one of her father's pupils who went on to enjoy some success as an actress. Her first appearance was as the young Duke of York in *Richard III* at Drury Lane on 20 December 1742; for the next thirty years she played at Drury Lane and Covent Garden, mostly in middle-ranking roles. She was fortunate enough to enjoy the continued support of Garrick despite her father's continued animosity towards the actor, and her talents were generally recognized by contemporaries, but her personal and professional relationship with her father was complex and, as time went on, increasingly distant. She was unusually pious for a member of the theatrical profession at that time, and remained unmarried. She died on 3 July 1781, outlived by her father, her brother, and her stepmother.

In 1744, in fairly desperate financial circumstances, Macklin sent begging letters to Fleetwood. Fortunately, Fleetwood's own financial difficulties were also catching up with him, and before the end of the year he retired to France, leaving the Drury Lane patent to pass to James Lacy. Macklin triumphantly returned to the stage on 19 December 1744, as Shylock. The performance included a conciliatory prologue in which Macklin somewhat optimistically promised to:

> take no part; no private jarrs foment
> But hasten from disputes I can't prevent.

He also undertook to 'meddle not with State affairs' (Kirkman, 1.297), but the events of the Jacobite rising of 1745 prompted a response from him which belied this oath of self-censorship as well as inaugurating a second element in his theatrical activities: playwriting. On 18 January 1746 Drury Lane attempted to exploit the current mood of anti-Catholic patriotism with the première of Macklin's cod-Shakespearian tragedy *Henry VII, or, The Popish Imposter*. Although the play's loyal stance ensured that it was not hissed from the stage, it was taken off after two unsuccessful performances. Disappointed by his play's failure, Macklin none the less persisted with his authorial efforts and wrote a two-act farce, *A Will and No Will*, which was produced on 23 April 1746.

Dublin, London, and retirement For the 1746–7 season Garrick was engaged by John Rich for Covent Garden, and his place was taken by the young Irish player Spranger Barry, who became one of Macklin's close friends. During 1747 Garrick entered into partnership with James Lacy as joint owner and manager of the Drury Lane theatre. After the cool reception of his adaptation of John Ford's *Love's Melancholy* and his own farce *The Fortune Hunters*, Macklin accepted Thomas Sheridan's offer of two seasons at the Smock Alley Theatre in Dublin. However, the mutual competitiveness of the two actors rapidly turned to rancour, and by the end of March 1750 the Macklins were dismissed. At some point between 1748 and 1750 Macklin's son, John, was born. Between 1750 and 1752 he enjoyed steady success as part of John Rich's company at Covent Garden. He was, however, growing tired of the theatre: his range of roles was narrowing, and his authorial efforts failed to impress. In 1753, after an unhappy appearance in Samuel Foote's *The Englishman in Paris*, and with his daughter, Maria, now firmly established as an actress in her own right, Macklin announced his retirement. Taking advantage of the current vogue for debating societies and coffee-house rhetoric, he drew upon his training and teaching experience to establish in Covent Garden's north piazza what he called 'a Magnificent Coffee-Room and a School of Oratory … the great desideratum of our Country' (Appleton, 98), which was to be graced by a series of public lectures by himself. Macklin's ambitious plans for a forum for enlightened political, religious, legal, and literary debate were thwarted as the initially buoyant custom of 'The British Inquisition' rapidly diminished, his debts mounted, and his staff took to dipping into the takings; his own lectures merely provided the opportunity for mockery and the trading of drunken insults. In January 1755 he was listed as bankrupt.

Macklin now negotiated with Spranger Barry over plans to establish a new theatre in Dublin, on the site of the Crow Street Music Hall. Thomas Sheridan was sufficiently provoked by this potential challenge to the Smock Alley monopoly to start to issue pamphlets denouncing his old rival, to which Macklin was characteristically quick to respond. Macklin's participation in the project foundered amid acrimony between himself and Barry, and when the Crow Street Theatre opened in October 1758 he was back in London. In the meantime Mrs Macklin had fallen ill, leading to her death on 28 December 1758. Macklin established a relationship with one of his servants, Elizabeth Jones (*d.* 1806), who was the same age as his daughter; they were later married. During this period Macklin wrote his most successful stage play, the satirical comedy *Love à-la-Mode*, which he managed to persuade a reluctant Garrick to produce. On 12 December 1759 his brief retirement ended with a reappearance at Drury Lane as Shylock, and as Sir Archy Macsarcasm in his own play, presented as the afterpiece. It was an immediate hit, and remained popular with actors and audiences for the next fifty years, providing numerous opportunities for Macklin to indulge in his taste for litigation, in actions against unauthorized performances or publication.

After the failure of his *The Married Libertine* in January 1761, Macklin took up Barry's invitation of a season at Crow Street, but once again became embroiled in legal wrangling with its proprietors over payment. In late spring 1762 he tried, unsuccessfully, to persuade Garrick to enter into an arrangement whereby he would divide his time between Drury Lane and Dublin. From 1762 to 1767 he appeared at Crow Street in the winter, with occasional excursions to London. Macklin's playwriting efforts finally won critical and commercial acclaim with the comedy *The Man of the World*, first performed (under the title *The True Born Scotchman*) at Smock Alley on 10 July 1764. He joined Colman's company at Covent Garden in the autumn of 1767. A dispute had arisen between the Covent Garden managers over Colman's arrogation of authority, and Macklin naturally became involved, 'with as much seeming spirit and alacrity, as if he had been the solicitor instead of the client' (Cooke, 271); the conflict came to an abrupt end in July 1769 when one of the parties suddenly died of a chill on a cricket field. For the best part of the next decade Macklin acted in Dublin, London, and on tour in England, while also inculcating young performers in his 'science' of acting. His protégés included Henrietta Leeson, to whom he was strongly (and hopelessly) attracted.

Macbeth and later career At the end of 1773 Macklin returned to Covent Garden, which was still under Colman's management, to make what would be his last substantial theatrical innovation. After months of careful planning and research, Macklin's production of *Macbeth* opened on 23 October. It marked the beginnings of a major shift in the theory and practice of Shakespearian staging in Britain. Costumed in 'the old Caledonian habit', Macklin's Macbeth broke with the custom of playing Shakespeare in contemporary costume by introducing a sense of place and period; instead of the 'suit of scarlet and gold, a tail wig etc' of the 'modern military officer', Macklin appeared in 'tartan stockings … wearing a Balmoral bonnet' (Highfill, Burnim & Langhans, *BDA*, 19). His experiment was largely judged a success, and it subsequently proved to foreshadow the Shakespearian staging methods of the nineteenth century. In the short term, however, the performance provided the occasion for yet another damaging squabble. Macklin's first entry was greeted with isolated hissing; seated in the audience, Mrs Macklin confronted the alleged perpetrators, James Sparks and the actor Samuel Reddish (an antagonist from Macklin's time in Dublin). Macklin pursued the allegation in the press, and subsequent performances were marred by violent demonstrations in and around the auditorium by pro- and anti-Macklin factions. On 18 November matters came to a head during *The Merchant of Venice*. At Sparks's instigation, the performance was halted amid calls for Macklin to be dismissed. With the rioters tearing up the seats and smashing chandeliers, Colman acceded to the demand, and announced that Macklin was discharged forthwith.

In June the following year, incensed by his (unproven) suspicion that Garrick had been behind the disturbances, Macklin pressed charges of riot and conspiracy against five known participants. He pursued the action himself with his usual enthusiasm, and the trial commenced on 24 February 1775. The case against the defendants was unanswerable, and guilty verdicts on the charge of riot were promptly returned. It was then that Macklin executed another bold stroke that fully redeemed his reputation in the eyes of a fiercely attentive public. Instead of insisting upon full settlement of damages (to which he was entitled) he exercised leniency, urging that the guilty men should do no more than meet his legal costs and pay £300 towards his own and Maria Macklin's benefit. Praising Macklin for this display of magnanimity, the presiding judge, Lord Mansfield, said 'You have met with great applause today. You never acted better' (Kirkman, 2.256).

It was Macklin's last major legal and histrionic triumph, although he continued to pursue lawsuits and to act at Covent Garden, on tour, and in Dublin until the middle of the following decade. These were not the happiest of times: he was increasingly afflicted by deafness and absent-mindedness, and he became alienated from Maria, who had never really emerged from her father's shadow and who died at the age of forty-eight in July 1781; he was also disappointed by his son John's persistent failure to secure lasting or settled employment. Some comfort came from the fact that in 1781 Macklin finally persuaded the lord chamberlain to allow *The Man of the World* on to the English stage. Having judiciously toned down the ferocious anti-Scots polemic and biting topicality, Macklin found success for a play which would remain popular well into the next century. In 1777 he and Elizabeth Jones had moved to lodgings at 6 Tavistock Row, Covent Garden. The couple married on 13 February 1778. Macklin occupied himself with acting tuition and periodic forays into the theatre. His final appearance was on 7 May 1789 in *The Merchant of Venice*. After stumbling through two or three speeches he informed the audience that 'he was unable to proceed in the part', an apology received 'with a mixed applause of indulgence and commiseration' (Cooke, 317). He spent the years after this abrupt retirement in poor health and in financial difficulties. Macklin died at his home in Tavistock Row on 11 July 1797, and was buried at St Paul's, Covent Garden, five days later. He was survived by Elizabeth Macklin, who struggled on under the burden of her husband's bankruptcy at his death. She died in April 1806.

If Macklin's bitter legacy to his second spouse is a sad reflection of his personal decline in his final years, posterity has been somewhat kinder to the actor himself. The complexities of his personality, which were not unrelated to his ambivalent status as a socially mobile Irishman of mysterious origins, afforded material for several contemporary biographies of varying reliability, by Congreve in 1798, Kirkman in 1799, and Cooke in 1804, although only one major account of his life (Appleton's *Charles Macklin: an Actor's Life*, 1961) has appeared since. Macklin continues to be associated with Garrick as one of the key innovators in eighteenth-century English theatre; those inclined to see its history in terms of a natural progression from the artifice of the post-Restoration period to the realism of the Victorians tend to credit Macklin with the reforms that made the latter possible. But Macklin's pursuit of a 'natural' style as a performer and teacher, and his attempts to apply the principles of the Enlightenment to the science of acting, might also be placed in the context of his incessant, troubled shuttling between the theatres of London and Dublin, the centre and the periphery of eighteenth-century English culture. It is also worth reflecting upon the fact that Macklin's most celebrated achievement was in the part of a maligned outsider who none the less wields enormous power at the very heart of the society that both vilifies and depends upon him. Like Shylock, Macklin spent much of his career in and on trials of various kinds. Whatever extremes of admiration and loathing he inspired in his own lifetime, the verdict of history on the scale and significance of his accomplishments has been largely favourable. ROBERT SHAUGHNESSY

Sources W. W. Appleton, *Charles Macklin: an actor's life* (1961) · F. Congreve, *Authentic memoirs of the late Mr Charles Macklin* (1798) · J. T. Kirkman, *Memoirs of the life of Charles Macklin*, 2 vols. (1799) · W. Cooke, *Memoirs of Charles Macklin, comedian* (1804) · E. Parry, *Charles Macklin* (1891) · Highfill, Burnim & Langhans, *BDA*
Archives Folger, papers · Harvard U., Houghton L., papers · Hunt. L., papers | Harvard TC · Liverpool Central Library, papers relating to quarrel with George Colman
Likenesses J. Zoffany, oils, *c*.1768, Royal National Theatre, London · J. Zoffany, group portrait, oils, *c*.1768–1775, Tate collection · S. De Wilde, oils, *c*.1770, NG Ire. · engraving, 1773 · attrib. J. Zoffany, oils, *c*.1775, National Theatre Collection, London · J. Roberts, drawing, 1778, BM · T. Cook, line engraving, 1779 (after J. Roberts), BM; repro. in J. Bell, *Bell's British theatre* (1779) · J. Walker, line engraving, pubd 1779 (after D. Dodd), NG Ire. · S. De Wilde, oils, *c*.1781, NG Ire.; version, Garr. Club · J. C. Lochée, Wedgwood medallion, 1784, Wedgwood Museum, Stoke-on-Trent · J. H. Ramberg, Indian ink wash and pen drawing, 1784, BM · J. Corner, line engraving, 1787 (after J. C. Lochée), BM, NPG; repro. in *European Magazine* (1787) · J. Opie, oils, *c*.1792, NPG [*see illus.*] · W. Ridley, stipple, pubd 1796 (after W. Beechey), BM, NPG · engraving, 1798, repro. in Congreve, *Authentic memoirs of the late Charles Macklin* · H. Brocas the elder, stipple (after J. Opie or stipple by J. Hopwood, 1808), NG Ire. · T. Cook, line engraving (after J. H. Ramberg), BM

Macklin, Maria (1733–1781). *See under* Macklin, Charles (1699?–1797).

Macklin, Thomas (1752/3–1800), printseller and picture dealer, may have been the son of 'the Reverend Garrard Macklin of the Kingdom of Ireland' mentioned in the will of Thomas Wilson, prebendary of Westminster, from whom Thomas Macklin inherited considerable property in 1784. His friend the engraver John Landseer said that Macklin had been an 'Irish cabin boy' and later a frame gilder who had learned stipple engraving from Francesco Bartolozzi (Landseer, *Algernon Sidney's Letter*, 22). In 1777 he married Hannah Kenting (*d.* 1808). In 1779 he began business as a printseller at 1 Lincoln's Inn Fields, London, and in 1782 moved to 39 Fleet Street. In the same year he enjoyed considerable success with his print of the recently deceased Rear-Admiral Richard Kempenfelt, which sold 7000 copies. Two years later he inherited half of Thomas Wilson's £20,000 estate, and not long thereafter he began the print speculations which were to make him famous.

On 1 January 1787 Macklin announced his plan to commission 100 paintings illustrating the works of the English poets to be published as engravings at monthly intervals between February 1790 and January 1795. In the event the progress of *Macklin's English Poets*, better known as *The Poets' Gallery*, was inhibited by the war with France (which closed the continent to the extensive British export trade in prints) and by the death of his sleeping partner Edward Rogers (1750–1795) of Liverpool who had invested £11,000. Even with this assistance the project remained prohibitively expensive. The considerable sum of £500 was paid for Sir Joshua Reynolds's *Cottagers*, also known as *The Macklin Family* on account of its depiction of Macklin's wife and their daughter Maria. Between 1788 and 1799 only six parts (each containing four prints) were published. In addition to work by Reynolds, these parts included paintings by Henry Fuseli, Thomas Gainsborough, Angelica Kauffmann, Thomas Stothard, and Francis Wheatley, with most of the engravings being undertaken by Bartolozzi. Like his rival printsellers, John Boydell and Robert Bowyer, Macklin held annual exhibitions, the first of which opened in Pall Mall on 14 April 1788.

In 1789 Macklin announced plans for an illustrated folio Bible in three (eventually six) volumes to promote 'the glory of the English school' of painting and engraving and 'the interest of our HOLY RELIGION'. New type (cut by Joseph Jackson and Vincent Figgins) and new paper were created for the venture, and the historic paintings were to be 'finished in a style of elegance [and magnificence in Paper, Printing, and Engraving] of which there is not in Europe or the world any example' (Macklin's *Holy Bible* prospectus, 1789). Macklin initially proposed sixty prints (eventually seventy-two) plus vignettes. The largest number of paintings (sixteen, in addition to 111 vignettes) were undertaken by Philippe Jacques de Louthenbourg; Hugh Douglas Hamilton produced a further twelve paintings and John Opie seven. Other artists included Richard Cosway, Benjamin West, and Richard Westall, as well as Fuseli, Kauffmann, Reynolds, and Stothard, and the subscription list for 703 copies at £46 1s. apiece was headed by the king, the queen, and the prince of Wales. Macklin's project was again ambitious and costly. He paid Reynolds £500 for his *Holy Family* and William Sharp £700 for its engraving; the average cost for forty-five of the Bible's other engravings was £220 and the total cost of the publication was an estimated £30,000. Macklin's resulting indebtedness required him to sell some of the Poets' Gallery paintings by lottery in 1797, but with the financial assistance of John Wilson of Liverpool work on Macklin's *Holy Bible* was finally brought to its triumphant conclusion. The last engraving was finished just five days before his death, aged forty-seven, at Fleet Street on 25 October 1800, and the last of the vignettes was completed six weeks later. The Macklin Bible endures as the most ambitious edition produced in Britain, often pirated but never rivalled.

A major force in the florescence of book illustration in England in the 1790s, Macklin also spent possibly as much as £300,000 as a patron of the arts. His widow continued the Poets' Gallery until 1801 when, on 27–30 May, the remaining paintings were sold. Another, unsuccessful, auction was held after her death on 12 January 1808. Macklin's second daughter, Hannah, was left in such financial dolour that appeals were made to the Royal Academy for her living expenses in 1821 and her funeral in the following year. 　　　　　　　　　　　　　　G. E. BENTLEY JUN.

Sources *GM*, 1st ser., 54 (1784), 317–18 · *GM*, 1st ser., 70 (1800), 1014 · *GM*, 1st ser., 78 (1808), 92 · J. Landseer, review of E. Forster, *The British gallery of engravings*, *Review of Publications of Art*, 1 (1807), 281 · A. Sidney [J. Landseer], *Algernon Sidney's letter to Thomas Wyse* (1843) · I. Maxted, *The London book trades, 1775–1800: a preliminary checklist of members* (1977) · *Monthly Magazine*, 7 (1799), 54 · *Monthly Magazine*, 10 (1800), 369 · *The statutes at large, from the thirty-fifth year of the reign of King George the third, to the thirty-eighth year* (1798), 663 · 'Press cuttings from English newspapers on matters of artistic interest, 1686–1835', 6 vols., V&A · T. Clayton, *The English print, 1688–1802* (1997) · T. S. R. Boase, 'Macklin and Bowyer', *Journal of the Warburg and Courtauld Institutes*, 26 (1963), 148–77 · will, PRO, PROB 11/1351, fols. 199v–205r

Mackmurdo, Arthur Heygate (1851–1942), architect and social reformer, was born on 12 December 1851 in Edmonton, Middlesex, the eldest child and elder son (there was at least one daughter) of Edward Mackmurdo, chemical manufacturer, of Edmonton, and his wife, Anne *née* Jones. He was educated at Felsted School, Essex. Apprenticed to the architect T. Chatfield Clarke, he moved in 1873 into the offices of James Brooks. Brooks attended to every detail of his churches and Mackmurdo later acknowledged his debt to him as an exemplar of methodical thoroughness.

During these years Mackmurdo absorbed the main aesthetic and moral influences that were to guide him through his life, not so much from immediate masters as from the writings of John Ruskin, Herbert Spencer, and Auguste Comte. Ruskin's *Fors Clavigera* (1871–4) was probably Mackmurdo's greatest single inspiration, and he modelled his first pamphlet, *The Immorality of Lending for Payment of Interest or of any Usurious Gain* (1878), on Ruskin's *Unto this Last* (1862). Most accounts of Mackmurdo's early life state that he travelled with Ruskin in Italy in 1874, but no mention of this appears in any contemporary writings. Study of Mackmurdo's character reveals a strong vein of the mountebank and many of his claims seem to have little basis in fact. He was largely self-taught through wide reading and attendance at public lectures. None of this seriously detracts from his achievement as an architect and designer during the 1880s and 1890s: a fruitful diversion from his lifelong obsession with monetary reform. In whatever he did he displayed a strong didactic tendency and was always guided by his self-proclaimed precept that every 'social organism must possess a definite physical structure'.

Mackmurdo set up his own architectural practice at 20 Southampton Street, the Strand, London, in 1875 and moved to 20 Fitzroy Street, Bloomsbury, in 1888. He was an associate of the RIBA from 1882 to 1885. Apart from a cold-storage warehouse in Charterhouse Street in the City of London, his architectural output was limited to a handful of houses in London and the Manchester area, including

25 Cadogan Gardens, Chelsea, in partnership with George Hornblower, for the Australian artist Mortimer Menpes. Interesting as these houses are individually, they barely begin to support Mackmurdo's reputation, which rests principally upon the foundation and achievements of the Century Guild.

The Century Guild was founded in 1882 'to render all branches of Art the sphere no longer of the tradesman but of the Artist' as Mackmurdo wrote in April 1882 in the first number of the guild periodical, the *Hobby Horse*. The Guild was employed in cabinet-making, decorative metalwork, and the designing of wallpaper and fabrics involving many craftsmen. Mackmurdo's own designs are noted for their sinuous patterns based on plant and bird forms. The frontispiece of his book *Wren's City Churches* (1883), with its swirling pattern, is one of the precursors of English art nouveau, as is his famous chair of similar date with its fretted back with a design of subaqueous plants. A major collection of the guild's work is in the William Morris Museum, Walthamstow. Unlike C. R. Ashbee and other confrères within the guild revival movement, Mackmurdo was less than generous in acknowledging the contributions of others. During the six years that the Century Guild existed its output was modest, though its participation in public exhibitions, notably in London at the Health Exhibition (1884), and Inventions Exhibition (1885), at the Liverpool International Exhibition (1886), and the Manchester Jubilee Exhibition (1887), gave it a considerable influence. Sadly, the underlying amateurishness of the organization could not stand the strain and the guild disintegrated in 1888. Mackmurdo was also involved at this period with several other pioneer reform movements, such as the Society for the Preservation of Ancient Buildings, the Home Arts and Industries Association, and the Art for Schools Association.

In 1902 Mackmurdo married Eliza, daughter of the musician Richard Carte. He retired from architectural practice in 1906 and concentrated once again on his utopian schemes for social and economic reform. His major book on the subject, *The Human Hive: its Life and Law*, was published in 1926. He died at Beacon Hill, Great Totham, Essex, on 15 March 1942, having been predeceased by his wife, and was buried at Wickham Bishop, Essex. There were no children of the marriage.

　　　　　　　　　　　　　　PEYTON SKIPWITH, rev.

Sources N. Pevsner, 'Arthur H. Mackmurdo', *ArchR*, 83 (1938), 141–3 · A. Vallance, 'Mr Arthur H. Mackmurdo and the Century Guild', *The Studio*, 16 (1899), 183–92 · T. Price, 'Curious Mr Mackmurdo', BArch diss., U. Newcastle, 1981 · *Catalogue of A. H. Mackmurdo and the Century Guild collection* (1967) [exhibition catalogue, William Morris Gallery, London, 1967] · *CGPLA Eng. & Wales* (1942)
Archives Colchester Museums · William Morris Gallery, London, corresp. and papers | Bodl. Oxf., corresp. with Selwyn Image
Wealth at death £415 14s. 2d.: probate, 11 June 1942, *CGPLA Eng. & Wales*

Mackness, James (1804–1851), general medical practitioner, was born on 31 March 1804 at Wellingborough, Northamptonshire, the elder of the two sons of Thomas Mackness (*d.* 1829), an unsuccessful lace trader, and his wife, Beulah Gent (*d.* 1847). He attended a day school in

Wellingborough where he was severely chastised, as he also was by his father. When he was eight years of age his parents moved to Edinburgh where, at the age of twelve or thirteen, he joined them. After another year or two of schooling, his father entered him in the drapery trade. Mackness disliked this occupation and determined to pursue a medical career. Fearful that he might run away to sea if thwarted, his mother supported him in this ambition. At the age of seventeen he embarked upon his medical studies having 'had nothing more than an ordinary English education' (Howard, 8). At the same time, though also required to supervise his father's ailing business, he set about learning Latin and French.

After attending lectures at Edinburgh University between 1822 and 1824, Mackness qualified as a member of the Royal College of Surgeons, at his second attempt, on 22 December 1824. He then spent a short time as a medical assistant to a general practitioner in Great Yarmouth. He did not like this position and soon moved to a similar one at Saxmundham in Suffolk. He remained there until July 1827, at which point he set up on his own at Turvey in Bedfordshire where, following the death of his father on 11 March 1829, he lived with his mother. On 5 January 1830 he married Maria Whitworth (1800/01–1895), of Turvey, the second daughter of John Whitworth. The marriage was childless, but the couple were generous to the children of Mackness's brother. In March 1831 Mackness moved to Northampton where his wife had relatives. There he gradually built up an extensive, though poorly remunerated, practice.

From the early 1830s Mackness's health began to fail and in 1837 he found it necessary to give up his practice. He then spent about two years travelling in England and on the continent. In order to qualify himself for less strenuous practice, he took an MD degree, on 15 May 1840, at St Andrews University. In the same month, leaving his mother in Northampton, he settled in Hastings, Sussex, the climate of which he thought would be good for his health. There he occasionally took in residential patients. In November 1840 he was appointed physician to the town's dispensary. Mackness became a licentiate of the Royal College of Physicians in January 1843; a month later, his deteriorating health having made it difficult to perform his duties as dispensary physician, his appointment was converted into a home-based, consulting position. Mackness became a member of the Provincial Medical and Surgical Association (British Medical Association from 1855) in 1843. He was a council member from 1844 and a regular attender of the anniversary meetings. He sat on the association's medical ethics committee in 1849; in 1851, but for his death, he would have read a paper on the medical topography of the Sussex coast at that year's annual meeting in Brighton.

Mackness was an enthusiast for public health, public service, and schemes for working class 'improvement'. He helped to found a mechanics' institute and a friendly society in Northampton and a mutual assurance society in Hastings. In Hastings he served as an alderman; he was also involved in the Health of Towns movement. As his own health declined and he found medical practice more difficult, he took to writing on medical and other subjects. In 1842 he published *Hastings Considered as a Resort for Invalids* (1842), which went into a second edition in 1850. Among his other works were *The Moral Aspects of Medical Life* (1846), which incorporated a translation of K. F. H. Marx's *Akesios* (1844), and *Dysphonia clericorum, or, Clergyman's Sore Throat: its Pathology, Treatment and Prevention* (1848).

Mackness's recreations included chess, for which he had a passion and, especially in his youth, the theatre. An enthusiast for self-improvement, in later life he taught himself German. After suffering from neuralgia for many years Mackness died of pneumonia at his address in Wellington Square, Hastings, on 8 February 1851. He was buried on 14 February in St Mary's cemetery, Hastings, where a tomb was erected to his memory through a subscription by his friends and patients. His wife survived him.

P. W. J. BARTRIP

Sources M. M. Howard, *Memorials of James Mackness Esq, M.D.* (1851) · Boase, *Mod. Eng. biog.* · *The Lancet* (23 Aug 1851), 180 · *The Lancet* (15 Feb 1851), 196 · *London and Provincial Medical Directory* (1852), 647 · *Annual Register* (1851) · DNB · *Provincial Medical and Surgical Journal* (19 Feb 1851), 112

Macknight, James (1721–1800), biblical scholar, was born at the manse, Irvine, Ayrshire, on 17 September 1721, the third of seven children of William Macknight (1685–1750), Church of Scotland minister of Irvine and a native of Ireland, and his wife, Elizabeth Gemmil (*d.* 1753). He was educated at Irvine and at the universities of Glasgow (MA, 1742) and Leiden. Licensed by the presbytery of Irvine, he was first attached to a chapel of ease in Gorbals, then worked as assistant at Kilwinning before he was ordained to the parish of Maybole, in Ayrshire, on 10 May 1753. On 30 April 1754 he married Elizabeth M'Cormick (*d.* 1813) with whom he had four sons.

While still a student Macknight had begun to collect the materials for his first publication, *A Harmony of the Four Gospels* (1756); the favourable reception encouraged him to prepare a second, amended, edition in 1763, and a fifth edition was published in 1819. He also published *The Truth of Gospel History* in 1763. His work attracted the attention, and the criticism, of the patristic scholar Nathaniel Lardner. Macknight was honoured with the degree of DD from Edinburgh University in 1759. In 1769 he was elected moderator of the general assembly of the Church of Scotland and, later that year, he was translated and admitted to the parish of Jedburgh, Roxburghshire, on 30 November. He was again translated, to Lady Yester's Church, Edinburgh, on 21 July 1772. His final move was to the collegiate charge of the Old Church, Edinburgh, to which he was translated and admitted on 26 November 1778, his colleague being the historian Robert Henry. While a moderate in church politics, Macknight nevertheless in 1782 moved the declaratory act of assembly which reaffirmed the practice of the church in requiring a call from the parishioners in addition to the patron's presentation. In 1784 he was made joint collector of the Ministers' Widows' Fund.

Intensive study, however, was the characteristic of

Macknight's life. For over thirty years he was engaged in the preparation of his final and most substantial work, *A New Literal Translation from the Original Greek of All the Apostolic Epistles*, which appeared in four volumes in 1795; it continued to be published in various editions into the middle of the nineteenth century. A work of painstaking labour, the entire manuscript had been written five times in his own hand. This work was preceded by *The Translation of the … Epistles to the Thessalonians* (1787), a foretaste of his *magnum opus*. Study engrossed him for up to eleven hours a day and, even when he took his walks, it involved shuffling round the Meadows in Edinburgh with his nose in a book. Lord Cockburn remembered 'his large, bony visage, his enormous white wig, girdled by many tiers of curls, his old snuffy black clothes, his broad flat feet, and his threadbare blue great-coat' (*Memorials … by Henry Cockburn*, 53). His literary work concluded, despite having enjoyed robust health throughout his life, Macknight began to fail and he died of pneumonia in Edinburgh on 13 January 1800. He was survived by his wife, who died on 10 March 1813. Their youngest son, Thomas Macknight (1762–1836), pursued his father's calling in several Edinburgh charges and with some distinction. He is chiefly remembered, however, as the candidate unsuccessfully advanced by the city's moderate clergy, in opposition to the supposedly heterodox John Leslie, for the chair of mathematics in Edinburgh University in 1805 in what was a *cause célèbre*.

LIONEL ALEXANDER RITCHIE

Sources J. Macknight, *A new literal translation from the original Greek, of all the apostolical epistles … to which is prefixed, an acccount of the life of the author*, 4th edn, 1 (1809), iii–xxiv · 'Account of the life and character of Dr MacKnight', *Scots Magazine and Edinburgh Literary Miscellany*, 69 (1807), 105–9, 177–81 · *Fasti Scot.*, new edn, 1.72 · *Memorials of his time, by Henry Cockburn* (1856), 53–4 · Allibone, *Dict.* · Chambers, *Scots.* (1835), 3.525–9 · Anderson, *Scot. nat.* · *DNB* · W. I. Addison, *A roll of graduates of the University of Glasgow from 31st December 1727 to 31st December 1897* (1898), 391

Macknight, Thomas (1829–1899), political writer and newspaper editor, was born at Gainsford, co. Durham, on 15 February 1829, the son of Thomas Macknight, and his wife, Elizabeth. After being educated at Dr Bowman's school at Gainsford, he became a student in the medical faculty at King's College, London, which he entered on 28 September 1849. Macknight had a distinguished career at college, winning a number of prizes and becoming president of the King's College Literary and Scientific Union. He also edited a short-lived college literary and scientific magazine. The most important effect of his time there, however, was the lasting influence of the Christian socialist, F. D. Maurice. Macknight's later approach to the problems of Ulster politics was attributed to Maurice's 'breadth of religious view and truly Catholic charity' (*Northern Whig*, 20 Nov 1899).

Macknight left college in 1851, and began his career by writing leaders for a number of London daily papers. At the same time, he wrote an anonymous critical biography of Disraeli, followed by a defence of the foreign policies of Aberdeen and Palmerston in the years leading up to the Crimean War. His major work during this period was a life

of Edmund Burke. Some time between 1856 and 1859 Macknight married the actress and theatre manager Sarah *Thorne (1836–1899). They had two children, Edmund (b. 1860) and Elizabeth (b. 1862), but chose to live separately after only a short period.

In January 1866 Macknight was appointed to succeed Frank Harrison Hill as editor of the Belfast *Northern Whig*, where he remained for thirty-three years. He committed the newspaper to the policies of Gladstonian Liberalism, and his articles on the disestablishment of the Church of Ireland were believed to have been crucial to its success. His approach to Ulster sectarianism was clear-sighted and even-handed. In the 1868 general election the newspaper supported both Thomas McClure, a Liberal, and William Johnston, an extreme protestant, who had been imprisoned under the Party Processions Act, as members for Belfast. Macknight was deeply sympathetic to the problems of tenant farmers, and regarded the land question as 'the first plank in an enlightened unionist policy'. Thus he opposed Gladstone's proposals for home rule, believing that Ireland's problems could only be remedied by legislation from Westminster.

Macknight was a devout man who read the New Testament in Greek every day. His memoirs, *Ulster as it is, or, Twenty-Eight Years' Experience as an Irish Editor* (1896), are an important record of Ulster policies and personalities of the period. Macknight died at his home at 28 Wellington Park, Belfast, on 19 November 1899, and was buried on 21 November 1899 in the Belfast city cemetery.

MARIE-LOUISE LEGG

Sources *Northern Whig* (20 Nov 1899) · *Northern Whig* (21 Nov 1899) · T. Macknight, *Ulster as it is, or, Twenty-eight years' experience as an Irish editor*, 2 vols. (1896) · private information (2004) · *The Times* (19 Nov 1899)
Archives BL, corresp. with W. E. Gladstone, Add. MSS 44379–44462
Wealth at death £855 13s. 0d.: probate, 13 Dec 1899, *CGPLA Ire.*

Mackonochie, Alexander Heriot (1825–1887), Church of England clergyman, was born at Fareham, Hampshire, on 11 August 1825, the third son of George Mackonochie (1775/6–1827), a retired colonel in the East India Company, and his wife, Isabella Alison. Brought up in an austere and pious household, he was educated at private schools in Bath and Exeter. After attending lectures at Edinburgh University he matriculated from Wadham College, Oxford, in June 1844 and graduated BA in 1848, MA in 1851. At Oxford, Mackonochie lived a frugal and rather retired life, though he made friends with a wide range of other students. Politically Conservative, he was held to be low church in his religious opinions by a contemporary; although close to Charles Marriott, he does not seem to have adopted Tractarian views in these years.

Mackonochie was ordained in Lent 1849, and took a curacy at Westbury in Wiltshire; in October 1852 he became a curate at Wantage, Berkshire, where the Tractarian W. J. Butler was pursuing a pattern pastoral ministry. Mackonochie worked hard in the church schools, and took special charge of Charlton, a rural district outside Wantage. Here his preaching style, though initially stilted, seems to have made some impact: a sexton later recalled that 'He'd rumple himself up to give it 'em straight and plain till he were red in the face' (Towle, 37). Despite his harsh voice Mackonochie's sermons became striking in their practical emphasis and forceful sincerity. In 1858 he became a curate at St George-in-the-East, London, a church which was the focus in the following year of a series of anti-ritualist riots; he served with C. F. Lowder in a pioneering mission to the dockland slums of east London.

On 3 January 1862 Mackonochie was ordained as perpetual curate at St Alban the Martyr, Holborn, London, a church newly built at the expense of J. G. Hubbard, a merchant and MP. He had accepted the cure with some hesitation, perturbed by his patron's opposition to ritualist views. In a letter of March 1860 he had outlined his own theological position to Butler: while equivocal over the ritualist extremes of John Purchas, he was clearly committed by this date to a radical position on eucharistic doctrine similar to that of G. A. Denison. Holding that ritual was the outward clothing of a sound faith, at St Alban's he proceeded to introduce daily communion, with Gregorian chants and ceremonial (despite, paradoxically, his own indifference to such aesthetic aids to worship). These innovations attracted much attention, some of it unfavourable: the staunchly protestant Lord Shaftesbury, who visited the church in July 1866, noted that 'In outward form and ritual [the service] is the worship of Jupiter or Juno' (Towle, 133). Another visitor, A. P. Stanley, was apparently less indignant and more prescient: he reputedly told A. C. Tait, bishop of London, that he had seen 'three men in green, and you will find it difficult to put them down' (Russell, 49).

In 1867 John Martin—instigated by the ultra-protestant Church Association—brought a lawsuit against Mackonochie under the Church Discipline Act of 1840: the trial took place in the court of arches on 15 June and Mackonochie was charged with elevating the host above his head, using a mixed chalice and altar lights, censing things and persons, and kneeling during the prayer of consecration. The judgment, delivered on 28 March 1868, decided two points against Mackonochie and three in his favour, and omitted to rule on costs. Mackonochie declared his intention to comply with the judgment, but the opposition appealed to the privy council, which decided the three points against Mackonochie and ordered him to pay all costs. Further monitions and judgments followed in 1869–70, as the Church Association held that he was continuing the condemned practices, until, on 25 November 1870, Mackonochie was suspended from his office for three months. In the spring of 1869 he had been inhibited from preaching in the diocese of Ripon; in the same year Hugh McNeile refused to speak at the Liverpool church congress because Mackonochie's name also appeared on the programme.

Mackonochie's involvement in ritualistic controversy took place within the context of a busy pastoral ministry. Tall, spare, and austere in appearance, with a downwardly dropping mouth, he was the image of the earnest and hard-working ritualist slum priest (and a natural target for caricaturists, including 'Ape'). With the assistance of a band of lay workers and two dedicated curates, Arthur Stanton and Edward Russell, Mackonochie founded a plethora of parochial associations, including a working men's club, mothers' meetings, schools, a soup kitchen, a cricket club, and a clothing fund. The 'three-hour devotion' was first observed in St Alban's on Good Friday 1864; the parish was one of the first to hold a harvest festival; confessions were openly held (Mackonochie specialized in hearing the confessions of women); and St Alban's participated fully in the high-church London missions of 1869 and 1874. In addition to his parochial duties, from 1867 Mackonochie held the chaplaincy of the Anglican sisterhood of St Saviour; sisters from this order, as well as the Clewer community of St John the Baptist, seem to have worked in the parish. Mackonochie also served as master of the Society of the Holy Cross (the Societas Sanctae Crucis or SSC), a priestly fraternity inspired by Pusey and founded in 1857, in the years 1863–75, 1879–81, and 1885. He played an important role in devising the society's constitution and directing its activities: wholly clerical in its membership and fairly extreme in its ecclesiastic politics, this rather secretive body came to shape both the ritualist movement and public perception of it. During the 1877 controversy in parliament over J. C. Chambers's *The Priest in Absolution* (which the society had sponsored) Mackonochie staunchly opposed several concessionary measures intended to mollify the bishops.

In March 1874 a new lawsuit was brought against Mackonochie by the Church Association: to the original charges were added new ones, including the use of processions with the crucifix, the Agnus Dei, and the eastward position. The judgment of 12 June 1875 found against him on most counts and imposed a six-week suspension. Although heroically stubborn and not averse to a little legal hair-splitting (witness his distinction between kneeling, genuflecting, and bowing), Mackonochie was wearied by the controversies surrounding him; he became an advocate of the disestablishment of the Church of England, joining Edward Miall's Liberation Society and publishing an article on the subject in *Nineteenth Century* in June 1877. In March 1878 Martin appealed to the dean of arches to uphold the 1875 judgment, which he claimed Mackonochie had disobeyed; in June 1878—now in the court created by the 1874 Public Worship Regulation Act—Mackonochie was suspended *ab officio et beneficio* for three years. A fresh round of legal proceedings was interrupted in 1882 by his resignation of his cure at the request of Tait, now archbishop of Canterbury.

Mackonochie's submission to this stroke of archiepiscopal 'moral blackmail' (Reynolds, 252)—Tait's request was made from his deathbed—did not secure him from further prosecution in his new parish of St Peter, London Docks; here he served for one unhappy year before resigning in December 1883 to return to St Alban's as a freelance assistant. Declining in health and mind, he spent much time with his friend Alexander Chinnery-Haldane, bishop of Argyll and the Isles. While out walking near the bishop's home in Ballachulish, Argyll, on 14

December 1887, he was lost in the Forest of Mamore, and was found dead two days later. He was unmarried. After a well-attended funeral at St Alban's on 23 December he was buried in the cemetery at Woking on the same day. A cross was erected on the spot where his body was found, and a chapel dedicated to his memory was added to St Alban's in the 1890s.   ROSEMARY MITCHELL

Sources [E. A. Towle], *Alexander Heriot Mackonochie: a memoir*, ed. E. F. Russell (1890) · M. Reynolds, *Martyr of ritualism: Father Mackonochie of St Alban's, Holborn* (1965) · G. W. E. Russell, *Saint Alban the Martyr, Holborn: a history of fifty years* (1913) · J. Embry, *The Catholic movement and the Society of the Holy Cross* (1931) · B. Palmer, *Reverend rebels: five Victorian clerics and their fight against authority* (1993), 65–115 · G. Rowell, *The vision glorious* (1983), 116–40 · J. Bentley, *Ritualism and politics in Victorian Britain* (1978) · *CGPLA Eng. & Wales* (1888)
Archives LMA, letter-book, with papers relating to Mackonochie | LPL, corresp. with A. C. Tait and related papers
Likenesses photograph, *c.*1850–1859, repro. in Reynolds, *Martyr of ritualism*, frontispiece · sketch, 1867, NPG · Ape [C. Pellegrini], chromolithograph caricature, repro. in *VF* (31 Dec 1870) · R. T., wood-engraving, NPG; repro. in *ILN* (31 Dec 1887) · A. Venables, oils, repro. in Russell, *Saint Alban the Martyr*, frontispiece · S. A. Walker, carte-de-visite, NPG
Wealth at death £2113 16s.: probate, 16 April 1888, *CGPLA Eng. & Wales*

McKowen, James (1814–1889), poet and bleachworks finisher, was born at Lambeg, near Lisburn, co. Antrim, on 11 February 1814, and received an elementary education at a local school. In his youth, he was said to walk regularly from Lambeg to Belfast to go to the theatre. After working in Barbours, a thread manufacturers in Hilden, co. Antrim, McKowen entered Richardson, Sons, and Owden Bleachworks in Belfast, where he remained for the rest of his working life, eventually receiving a pension.

About 1840 McKowen had begun to contribute lively poems to the *Northern Whig* and other Ulster papers, generally under the pseudonym of Kitty Connor, and he also wrote a little for *The Nation*, using the signature of Curlew. He became a household favourite, and one of his poems, 'The Old Irish Cow', became very popular throughout Ulster; another, 'The Ould Irish Jig', has remained popular in Ireland for over a hundred years. He died at Beechside, Lisburn, on 23 April 1889, and was buried at Lambeg. He was survived by his widow, Rebecca. McKowen's poems were written in Ulster Scots dialect. They were never published in book form, but appeared in several anthologies of Irish verse. Nine appeared in *The Harp of Erin* (1867; 2nd edn, 1869) edited by Ralph Varian, and two in Daniel Connolly's *Household Library of Ireland's Poets* (1889), where his name is misspelt McKeown.

D. J. O'DONOGHUE, *rev.* KATHERINE MULLIN

Sources A. M. Brady and B. Cleeve, eds., *A biographical dictionary of Irish writers*, rev. edn (1985) · K. Newmann, *Dictionary of Ulster biography* (1993) · D. Connolly, ed., *Household library of Ireland's poets* (1889) · R. Varian, ed., *The harp of Erin*, 2nd edn (1869) · D. J. O'Donoghue, *The poets of Ireland: a biographical dictionary with bibliographical particulars*, 1 vol. in 3 pts (1892–3) · Boase, *Mod. Eng. biog.* · *Northern Whig* (24 April 1889) · *CGPLA Ire.* (1889)
Wealth at death £523 10s. 9d.: probate, 3 July 1889, *CGPLA Ire.*

Mackreth, Sir Robert (*bap.* 1727, *d.* 1819), speculator and politician, obscured his origins from contemporaries, but was almost certainly from Kendal, Westmorland (he left £50 to the poor there, as well as some property and a bequest to a female relative). The only indication from local records has him baptized at Greyrigg Chapel, Kendal, on 27 November 1727, the son of William Mackreth of Whinfell, who apparently married Agnes Jackson at Longsleddale Chapel on 6 May 1724. An elder brother, Thomas (1726–1787), was for forty years master of the Kendal Hospital and charity school. Mackreth's will names another brother, John, whose grandson Henry Williams was the chief beneficiary. By about 1750 Mackreth had moved to London, and it is certain that he worked as a billiard marker and waiter, and later as the manager, in Arthur's Coffeehouse, Piccadilly, which became White's Club. After saving enough to acquire a vintner's shop in St James's Street, he remained manager and became engaged to his employer's only surviving daughter and heir Mary Elizabeth. Robert Arthur died on 6 June 1761, and Mackreth inherited the club on marrying Mary Arthur (*c.*1744–1784) on 22 October 1761. The couple had no children, and Mackreth did not remarry after his wife's death on 3 June 1784. He handed the management of the club over to a kinsman on 5 April 1763 and betook himself to speculation: moneylending, bookmaking in the City, and estate agency. He bought the Ewhurst estate on the Hampshire–Surrey border about 1763.

Mackreth's first brush with politics may have been in 1768, when he reputedly did well taking bets on John Wilkes's prospects in the London election. In October 1774 he was himself returned to parliament for the pocket borough of Castle Rising by his business client George Walpole, third earl of Orford, who was evidently in debt to him. Orford, not yet certified insane, left £300 to Mackreth, then living in Cork Street, and made him his executor in a will dated 4 December 1776. Horace Walpole, the earl's uncle, believed that his nephew could not hope to clear the debt until his mother's death. Mackreth's Commons membership at once excited ridicule, and the *London Chronicle* (8–10 November 1774) supplied a burlesque speech of thanks to his constituents: 'I shall ever think it my duty to *wait upon you* on all occasions, so I shall not suffer a single *bill* to be *brought in* without my inspection.' Mackreth, who later claimed that Orford owed him £6000, retained his seat, and in 1784 transferred to Ashburton, another small borough with Orford as patron. Horace Walpole had joked when Mackreth first took his seat that Wilkes would propose 'Bob' as speaker (Walpole, 29.221). He was no speaker in the house, and generally voted with the North ministry. In lists of 1780 and 1783 he is given as a follower of Richard Rigby. He broke with North after his fall, and voted for Shelburne over the peace in 1783 and against Fox's East India Bill in 1783, being himself an investor in company stock. He later supported Pitt's administration.

Mackreth fell foul of the law in 1786 when James Fox Lane, a young buck who frequented White's, charged him with cheating him of his inheritance while a minor. Fox Lane obtained a £20,000 compensation order from the master of the rolls, and Mackreth, against whom costs were awarded, appealed in vain to the lord chancellor and the Lords. Resenting the conduct of John Scott, later Lord Eldon, who had been Fox Lane's counsel, he verbally abused him when they met in Lincoln's Inn Fields in November 1792, and challenged him to a duel for an alleged insult during the trial. In the action for assault brought by Scott, Mackreth was sentenced to six weeks' imprisonment and fined £100 for breach of the peace. He wrote from prison protesting, but his complaints and later requests for favours from Pitt were ignored. When, after all, he was knighted, on 8 May 1795, it was because, as a freeman, he presented a loyal address from Westminster to the king on the prince of Wales's marriage. This honour was doubtless calculated to mollify a disgruntled Mackreth, who had only ten days before written to Anthony Hamond, a fellow executor of Orford's will, deploring the extravagance of the younger royal family. Mackreth participated in the sale of Orford's Ashburton property to Robert Trefusis, later seventeenth Baron Clinton, who thereby became his new parliamentary patron. As part owner of a plantation and slaves in Grenada, Mackreth voted against abolition of the slave trade on 15 March 1796. He was a critic of Pitt's tax proposals and suggested alternatives involving the sale of crown lands on 4 December 1797, but at their third reading he voted with government on 4 January 1798. His new patron's death in 1797 further jeopardized his future as an MP, as did a long illness from late 1798 until early in 1800, when he wrote disparagingly about the cost of Pitt's war aims. He did not seek re-election in 1802.

Mackreth died in London, where his residence was then 3 St James's Place, on 6 February 1819, allegedly aged ninety-four, but more probably ninety-one. He was buried at Ewhurst on 13 February. In his will of 12 December 1818 he insisted he had led an honest and upright life, and proposed to benefit less fortunate relatives, for he had hopes of recovering £25,000 in chancery. Before he died he disposed of the Ewhurst estate, which changed hands from its purchaser John Symmons to Sir Peter Pole in 1824 and again to the duke of Wellington in 1829. His great-nephew Henry Williams and his heirs, enjoined to take the surname of Mackreth, were left the London and Grenada properties. No likeness of Mackreth is known. Jeremy Bentham recalled of him: 'Mackreth's great ambition was to be considered a gentleman, and to be admitted among the quality, but he often was disappointed' (*Works of Jeremy Bentham*, 10.48).   ROLAND THORNE

Sources HoP, *Commons* · Walpole, *Corr.* · PRO, PROB 11/1619 · *GM*, 1st ser., 89/1 (1819), 282 · *The works of Jeremy Bentham*, ed. J. Bowring, [new edn], 11 vols. (1843–59), vol. 10, pp. 48–50 · *Leeds Intelligencer* (18 Jan 1791) · parish register, Greyrigg Chapel, Kendal, Westmorland, 1726–7 [baptism] · parish register, Longsleddale Chapel, Longsleddale, Westmorland, 1724 [marriage] · W. H. Manchée, *The Westminster city fathers (the Burgess Court of Westminster), 1585–1901* (1924), 173–4 · E. Bellasis, *Westmorland church notes*, 2 (1889), 41 · *Annual Register* (1793), 22 · Norfolk RO, Hamond papers

Archives Norfolk RO, Hamond MSS · PRO, Chatham MSS, PRO 30/8/154

Wealth at death under £18,000: PRO, death duty registers, IR 26/791; will, PRO, PROB 11/1619

Mackworth, Humphrey (1603–1654), government official and politician, was born on 27 January 1603, the eldest of three children and only son of Richard Mackworth (d. 1617) of Betton Strange, Shropshire, and his wife, Dorothy, daughter of Lawrence Cranage of Keele. The family held property just south of Shrewsbury and elsewhere in Shropshire. Humphrey was educated at Shrewsbury School (from January 1614), Queens' College, Cambridge (from Easter 1617), and Gray's Inn (from October 1621). In 1624 he came into his estates, control of which had been acquired by his widowed mother after his father's death. Around 1624 he married his first wife, Ann, daughter of Thomas Waller of Beaconsfield. Thereafter, Mackworth practised law and was called to the bar in the early 1630s. He divided his time between London and Shropshire—he collected reports on cases in common pleas and king's bench during 1626–31, while in the 1630s he acted as 'learned council' to Shrewsbury, with lodgings in the town. His growing family—at least three sons and two daughters were baptized between 1626 and the death of his first wife in May 1636—resided nearby at his principal house in Betton Strange. In July 1638 he married secondly Mary (d. 1679), daughter of Thomas Venables of Cheshire; from this marriage he had a son, who died in childhood, and a daughter.

During the 1630s Mackworth was prominent in the affairs of Shrewsbury. In 1635 he became an alderman, a position confirmed in the new charter of 1638 prompted by Archbishop Laud's *quo warranto* action, in which Mackworth represented Shrewsbury. He also appears several times as one of a group opposed to the king's religious policies—in 1633 he was criticized by the curate of St Chad's for refusing to bow at the name of Jesus, and in 1637–8 he supported the 'godly' side in a bitter dispute over the appointment to the then vacant curacy of St Chad's. In 1640 he reportedly played a leading role in advancing a Shropshire petition against episcopacy.

Despite connections with several royalist families, Mackworth's religion probably inclined him against the king, and from the outbreak of war he was a parliamentarian. He was one of several Shrewsbury men condemned for high treason by royal proclamation in October 1642. During 1643–4 he was appointed by parliament to a string of Shropshire committees, though the county was then largely royalist. As a captain in the army, in late 1643 he was active in and around Wem, working to secure the area for parliament. However, during 1643–4 he was also in Coventry, where he held a stewardship, and in London, lobbying for Shropshire and preparing for and giving evidence at Laud's trial. Despite an intermittent military career, by 1645 Mackworth was a colonel, and after the capture of Shrewsbury in February he became its governor, an appointment confirmed by parliament and held until his death. In August 1648 he suppressed royalist activity in the area and in August 1651 he firmly rebutted the entreaties of Charles Stuart and his army. He was recorder of Shrewsbury from November 1645, of Wenlock from September 1647, and of Bridgnorth by 1653. He was named to all the parliamentary committees for Shropshire from 1646 until his death. In 1648 he was appointed an attorney-general for north Wales and vice-chamberlain of Chester, and in 1649 he became deputy chief justice of the Chester circuit, in which capacity he presided over the trials of James Stanley, seventh earl of Derby, Sir Timothy Fetherstonhaugh, and John Benbowe in October 1651. His surviving correspondence indicates support for the regicide and loyalty to parliament, the army, and the new republic.

On 2 February 1654 the council of state of the protectorate recommended that Mackworth be added to its number; with Oliver Cromwell's approval, he took his seat on 7 February. No surviving evidence reveals why or upon whose initiative he was made a councillor, nor is there evidence of earlier connections between Mackworth and Cromwell. He brought substantial legal and administrative experience to the council, and he proved very dedicated, attending all but a handful of recorded meetings between 7 February and 5 December. He was also on many council committees, and chaired the committee that excluded some members of the first protectorate parliament. Mackworth was returned as MP for Shropshire, his only parliamentary experience; he was active in the house, nominated to at least sixteen committees between September and December.

Mackworth died suddenly and intestate in December 1654 at the lodgings in the mews at Whitehall that he held as a protectoral councillor. He was buried in Westminster Abbey on the night of 26 December. In 1660 his was one of a number of corpses disinterred and dumped in a pit near St Margaret's Church. His eldest son, Thomas (MP for Ludlow from 1646 and for Shropshire in 1656 and 1658), subsequently secured administration of his estate. A younger son, Humphrey (MP for Shrewsbury in all three protectorate parliaments), succeeded him as governor of Shrewsbury. His widow, who survived him by a quarter of a century, eventually obtained from the protectoral government both payment to cover Mackworth's funeral expenses and a pension.   PETER GAUNT

Sources B. Coulton, 'Humphrey Mackworth: puritan, republican, Cromwellian', *Cromwelliana* (1999), 7–23 · J. B. Blakeway, 'History of Shrewsbury hundred or liberties [pts 1–2]', *Transactions of the Shropshire Archaeological and Natural History Society*, 2nd ser., 1 (1888), 93–128, 311–406, esp. 380–96 · J. E. Auden, 'Shropshire and the royalist conspiracies … 1648–60', *Transactions of the Shropshire Archaeological and Natural History Society*, 3rd ser., 10 (1910), 87–168 · H. T. Weyman, 'Shropshire members of parliament', *Transactions of the Shropshire Archaeological Society*, 4th ser., 11 (1927–8), 153–84 · H. Johnstone, 'Two governors of Shrewsbury during the great civil war and the interregnum', *EngHR*, 26 (1911), 267–77 · H. Owen and J. B. Blakeway, *A history of Shrewsbury*, 2 vols. (1825) · J. B. Blakeway, *Sheriffs of Shropshire* (1831) · E. C. Hope-Edwards and others, eds., *The register of St Chad's, Shrewsbury*, 3 vols. (1913–18) · JHC · CSP dom., 1653–9 · BL, Add. MS 35962 · PRO, SP 18; SP 25; SP 28; C 142; Ward 5; Ward 7; PROB 11; PROB 12 · Shrops. RRC, 6000; LB7
Archives NL Wales, family deeds and documents · Shrops. RRC, leases, mortgages, note of administration of estate to son, etc. | Shrops. RRC

Mackworth, Sir Humphry (1657–1727), industrial entrepreneur and politician, was born in January 1657 at Betton Strange or Grange, Little Betton, Shropshire, the second son of Thomas Mackworth (*c*.1628–1696), landowner, and his wife, Anne, daughter of Richard Bulkeley of Buntingsdale, Shropshire. The Mackworths were originally from Derbyshire and had settled at Little Betton in 1553. Humphry Mackworth was educated at Oxford, matriculating as a member of Magdalen College on 11 December 1674, and at the Middle Temple, London, where he was admitted on 10 June 1675. He was called to the bar on 26 May 1682 and subsequently became a master of the bench there. On 15 January 1683 he was made knight bachelor, by which time he resided at Tardebigge, Worcestershire.

In 1686 Mackworth married Mary (*b*. *c*.1660, *d*. in or before July 1696), daughter and sole heir of Sir Herbert Evans of Gnoll, Neath, Glamorgan, and his wife, Anne Morgan of Pencraig, Monmouthshire. They lived at the Evanses' mansion, the Great House, in the borough of Neath, and had three sons, the eldest of whom, Herbert (1689–1765), succeeded his father. After 1715 Mackworth resided at Gnoll House, a newly built mansion on his estate. Mackworth was the constable of Neath Castle in 1703 and 1709, and in 1715 he purchased the lordships of Neath and Afan outright. He was MP for Cardiganshire in 1701, 1702–5, and 1710–13; and for Totnes, Devon, in 1705–8.

Mackworth brought to Gnoll a legal expertise and a belief in providence which drove him to develop its resources, most notably by reorganizing the colliery ventures at Melincryddan and elsewhere around Neath. As early as 1695 he began to smelt copper ore imported from Cornwall and Cardiganshire, and in an agreement with the Neath burgesses in September 1697 he succeeded in co-ordinating all its mining activities, bringing forward major employment, transportation, and technological innovations, and transforming the Welsh industrial scene.

Mackworth's Cardiganshire associations were strengthened when he joined the Company of Mine Adventurers of England at Esgair Hir and other mines, extracting and smelting lead, silver, and copper. The concern had become moribund but through its manager, William Waller, Mackworth was persuaded to buy out the share of Edward Pryse of Gogerddan, which, paid by instalments, eventually totalled £16,440 13*s*. 10*d*. by 1703. He recapitalized the concern by raising new funds, up to £125,000, from a lottery share arrangement. The company was incorporated in October 1698, with Mackworth becoming deputy governor for life. Several of his Neath agents were employed with Waller, and the Mine Adventurers leased Mackworth's smelter. Mackworth invested £16,900 at Neath between 1698 and 1708, integrating mining, refining, and casting activities, manufacturing chemicals, and improving dock facilities.

After 1705 the Mine Adventurers were overtaken by production and cash-flow problems which Mackworth tried to resolve by dubious share launches and unbacked bills, as well as by expanding into Flintshire. A directors' investigation into mismanagement in 1708–9 led to Waller's dismissal, and bankruptcy proceedings against Mackworth ensued in 1710. Waller's counter-charges of misappropriation of funds by Mackworth and his officials William Shiers and Thomas Dykes led to a Commons inquiry in 1709–10 which found them culpable. Legislation was proposed to restrict their movements but the prorogation of parliament saved them. Mackworth's fellow directors cleared him of dishonesty but creditors and shareholders elected a new board which overthrew Mackworth and found fault with his conduct, though not fraud.

In 1713 Mackworth organized a new joint-stock company, the Mineral Manufacturers of Neath, with himself as cashier-general, and by concentrating on brass production he built a prosperous undertaking. Supporters within the Mine Adventurers tried to restore his membership in 1720, exonerating him from past accusations, but Mackworth overextended his hand by attempting to influence the election of a new governor. A shareholders' petition to parliament led to further censure. By then Mackworth's Neath operation was also in difficulties. The final years saw him embroiled in a court action over the fraudulent sealing of a document and a customs' investigation into the importation of contraband. His personal finances were such that, at his death, his debts and legal costs exceeded his credits by as much as £2657 15s. 2d.

Politically Mackworth was a tory who had been loyal to James II. His nomination for Cardiganshire by the Mine Adventurers in 1701 was typical of a trading concern's political ambitions. The adventurers were noted for their high-church toryism and Mackworth proved an assertive upholder of their principles and protestantism in parliament and through pamphlets. His loyalty to the Anglican church was marked by his support for the Occasional Conformity Bill in 1703, when he objected to toleration and defended the pre-eminence of the Commons over the Lords, and for the tack in 1704. He was suspected of promoting the controversial *Memorial of the Church of England* (1705), via William Shiers. His anti-whig and anti-court views led to his attacks on the king's ministers in 1701 and on Robert Harley as speaker in 1704–5. He was critical of the succession question and the Regency Bill of 1706.

Mackworth held views about clearing the public debt and creating a central bank, and attended parliamentary committees examining bills on economic reform and local development, including in Wales. Ironically, given his business record, he attended committees to consider legislation against fraud and, in 1710, to regulate bankruptcy. He worked on legal-administrative issues but made his greatest mark in social and moral reform, which many of his political and religious persuasion saw as conjoined. As befitted the scion of a Cromwellian family, Mackworth possessed highly puritanical attitudes and believed in legislating against social evils. His main campaign was to secure useful employment for the poor. He introduced several related bills in 1703–7 but none passed the Lords. Even out of parliament he campaigned for moral improvement among the lower orders—against mug-houses, for example, in 1717.

Mackworth inexplicably sought election for Oxford in 1705 but stronger contestants kept him out. He lamented his loss but found a seat at Totnes. In 1708 his return for Cardiganshire was thwarted by landed interests and he was out of parliament fighting the Cardigan Boroughs by-election when his business affairs came under scrutiny. He lost but regained the county seat in November 1710. This became his last campaign. Thereafter he retired, occasionally emerging with forays into pamphleteering.

Mackworth's involvement in Glamorgan's local politics derived from his rivalry with the predominant Mansell family of Margam, who regarded Mackworth as a 'tyrant' (P. Jenkins, 148) wishing to bend the county to his own economic power, and who resented his attempts to establish control over the borough of Neath. Conflicts occurred between their supporters, culminating in rioting, destruction of property, and attacks on Mackworth workers in 1705. Protracted legal action ensued and a parliamentary inquiry blamed the Mansells. Ideological considerations also played their part. The Mansells were followers of Harley, while Mackworth's high toryism linked him with Jacobite interests such as the second duke of Beaufort and, in Cardiganshire, Lewis Pryse of Gogerddan. Through these ties Mackworth consolidated his family's long-term political power.

Mackworth's Anglican moral piety led to his being among the five initiators of the Society for the Promotion of Christian Knowledge (SPCK), most having Welsh associations, who first met in London on 8 March 1699. With many of the same people Mackworth also established in 1701 the Society for the Propagation of the Gospel in Foreign Parts. Although less prominent in the SPCK after 1703 he strove to provide popular schooling at Neath and in Cardiganshire.

Mackworth's paternalism also extended to building workers' houses and establishing a fund to maintain sick and injured employees and their families. Consequently he was held in high esteem by many dependants. At the height of his disgrace in 1710 he was acclaimed in popular Welsh verse as 'Ceidwad Cymru' ('the maintainer of Wales') for his altruism (Rhys Phillips, 735, stanza 14). Mackworth died on 25 August 1727 and was buried two days later.   WILLIAM P. GRIFFITH

Sources D. Rhys Phillips, *The history of the Vale of Neath* (1925) · W. Rees, *Industry before the industrial revolution*, 2 (1968) · M. Ransome, 'The parliamentary career of Sir Humphry Mackworth, 1701–1713', *University of Birmingham Historical Journal*, 1/2 (1948), 232–54 · G. Eaton, *The Mackworths of the Gnoll: a century of domination* (1990) · E. Jenkins, ed., *Neath and district: a symposium* (1974) · *The parliamentary diary of Sir Richard Cocks, 1698–1702*, ed. D. W. Hayton (1996) · W. A. Speck, ed., 'An anonymous parliamentary diary, 1705–6', *Camden miscellany, XXIII*, CS, 4th ser., 7 (1969), 29–84 · P. Jenkins, *The making of a ruling class: the Glamorgan gentry, 1640–1790* (1983) · A. Hopkins, 'A Bodleian manuscript and Mackworth supremacy in Neath, 1722–25', *Transactions of the Neath Antiquarian Society* (1988–9), 69–78 · M. Clement, ed., *Correspondence and minutes of the SPCK relating to Wales, 1699–1740* (1952) · *JHC*, 15 (1705–8) · *JHC*, 16 (1708–11) · S. Evans, 'An investigation of Sir Humphrey Mackworth's industrial activities', MA diss., U. Wales, 1953 · *DNB* · Burke, *Peerage* (1845)

Archives NL Wales, MS 14362 E. · NL Wales, diary · U. Wales, Swansea, family and professional papers | Bodl. Oxf., MS Rawl. C390 · NL Wales, corresp. with Mansell family · West Glamorgan

RO, Swansea, Eaglesbush Estate collection, D/D RE · West Glamorgan RO, Swansea, Gnoll collection, D/D Gn

Mackworth [Macworth], **John** (*c*.1375–1450), dean of Lincoln, was born about 1375, a date inferred from his later career, into an undistinguished landowning family from Mackworth in Derbyshire. It is highly likely that he owed his advancement to a connection between his family and John of Gaunt, duke of Lancaster, whose use of Tutbury Castle in neighbouring Staffordshire for hunting and recreation resulted in the employment in Tutbury of local residents, and in the use of its revenue to increase Lancastrian influence in Derbyshire. Thomas Mackworth, John's brother, would become receiver at Tutbury in 1425. When Gaunt's son usurped the throne as Henry IV, John Mackworth himself was among those who benefited. In May 1401 he received his first benefice, Great Dunmow in Essex (in the king's hand through the crown's wardship of the young Edmund Mortimer), while in the following October he was one of the small group that constituted the household of Henry, prince of Wales, to whose council he became chancellor, certainly by 1406 but possibly earlier.

Although Mackworth owed his promotion to the Lancastrians, their insecurity after 1399, even in their areas of influence, may account for the number of his appointments which were disputed, or even blocked, most notably the Lincoln canonry and prebend of Empingham in 1404 (only secured in 1412), the archdeaconry of Norfolk in 1408 (resigned by July 1412 and perhaps never held), and the Salisbury canonry and prebend of Preston in 1412 (only secured after an inquiry ordered by the pope). His tenure of the deanery of Lincoln, to which he was appointed in 1412, was confirmed only three years later, while his way to the bishopric of Lincoln, to which he was elected early in 1431, following the death of Richard Flemming, was blocked altogether, William Gray (or Grey) being translated from Salisbury.

An unusual educational background necessitated dispensations to allow Mackworth to proceed to his canon-law degrees in middle age. He was a master of arts by 1407, probably at Oxford, but his canon law was not completed until some fifteen years later. His legal skills sharpened his argumentative nature, and the experience of the house of Lancaster made him all too ready to surround himself with retainers, usually drawn from Derbyshire families. He claimed to have been assaulted at Cromer by a mob, and, learning the lesson, he took retainers to Lincoln on occasions to sit in chapter and intimidate resident canons, or to sit in the Galilee court in the cathedral and put pressure on its decisions. On 28 June 1435, the eve of the feast of Sts Peter and Paul, two of his Derbyshire friends and his notary attacked the chancellor of Lincoln in the cathedral, to the horror of pilgrims and canons alike. He and his henchmen likewise went to the aid of his widowed sister-in-law, and threatened Lord Cromwell's servants with violence if they collected disputed rents in 1446.

Mackworth's intransigence did not depend entirely on strong-arm tactics. He blatantly ignored episcopal summonses, causing Bishop Gray to complain: 'You have taken no care to certify us of your proceeding' (Thompson, 1.70). He caused such distress at Lincoln that bishops Flemming, Gray, and Alnwick were consecutively called on to settle disputes, all three of which ran on for a number of years. He thrived on litigation: papal letters of 1434 record that he had apparently excommunicated canons of the cathedral for an unnamed reason. He clearly delighted in shocking the canons, whether, in 1437, by the size of his train (worn to upstage the bishop), by walking out of order and disrupting processions, by arriving late or early for mass or office and insisting on celebrating mass no matter who had been scheduled, or by regarding the deanery of Lincoln (to which he rarely came) as a sort of court, where he built stables to the ruin of the fabric and where his servants had the run of close and town.

Mackworth's disputes arose mainly because he glimpsed power as a poor man and had not the funds to emulate the household of a young prince who had given him a new opening on the world. He sought all the financial breaks that a fifteenth-century cleric might aspire to: by holding a licence not just to hold incompatible benefices but dignitaries; by farming the fruits of his deanery; by steadily building up landholdings, within Derbyshire and elsewhere; and supremely at Lincoln, by being a non-resident dean and yet receiving all the perquisites of residence; and by not paying to the common fund his 'septisms', or that seventh of the income of prebends in which he did not reside. Bishop Flemming left it to his conscience to pay his arrears but ordered future payment, and Mackworth's debts to the cathedral were a constant part of his fight with the chapter: he refused to give hospitality while wanting personally to admit to office the lower cathedral clergy; he appointed inadequate deputies for himself or none, and yet he wanted to correct the faults of others and visit the prebends of non-residents. In all his seemingly disparate disputes with the chapter, Mackworth's pursuit of fees is the most usual, yet concealed.

Bishop Alnwick shrewdly saw the point. Alnwick's award at Lincoln of June 1439, based on some forty-two complaints by the canons against Mackworth, and some fourteen by him against them, ignored the infighting and the dean's flamboyant eccentricities. Concentrating instead on defining the constitutional relationships between the dean and the chapter, it became, despite Mackworth's protests, part of the lasting customs of Lincoln to which subsequent generations would refer. John Mackworth died probably at Tredington, Worcestershire in the summer of 1450 and there, not at Lincoln, he is buried. His legacy is Bishop Alnwick's award.

MARGARET BOWKER

Sources H. Bradshaw and C. Wordsworth, eds., *Statutes of Lincoln Cathedral*, 3 vols. (1892–7), vol. 2, pt 2 · *The award of William Alnwick, bishop of Lincoln, AD 1439*, ed. and trans. R. M. Woolley (1913) · Emden, *Oxf.*, 3.2193–4 · A. H. Thompson, ed., *Visitations of religious houses in the diocese of Lincoln*, 1, Lincoln RS, 7 (1914) · A. H. Thompson, *The English clergy and their organization in the later middle ages* (1947) · W. R. M. Griffiths, 'The military career and affinity of Henry, prince of Wales, 1399–1413', MLitt diss., U. Oxf., 1980 · S. M. Wright, *The Derbyshire gentry in the fifteenth century*, Derbyshire RS, 8

(1983) • S. Walker, *The Lancastrian affinity, 1361–1399* (1990) • *Fasti Angl., 1300–1541*, [Lincoln]
Archives Lincs. Arch., dean and chapter muniments

Macky, John (d. 1726), writer and spy, was a Scot of obscure birth, parentage, and education. He fled from France to London in the summer of 1692 with the first news of the intended French and Jacobite invasion from La Hogue. Although he was initially disbelieved, he was vindicated, informed on several Scottish Jacobites, and was rewarded with an appointment as a coastal inspector between Harwich and Dover of treasonable correspondence with France. He was employed in counter-espionage work, and helped to apprehend several individuals involved in the plot in 1696 to assassinate William III. With the re-establishment of postal services to France following the peace of Ryswick, on 1 January 1698 Macky was placed in charge of the packet-boat and royal express service from Dover to Calais, Ostend, and Nieuwpoort. By his own testimony, he financed this endeavour with the portion secured upon his marriage in 1697 to a daughter of Sir William Spring, bt, of Pakenham, Suffolk. The surveillance of disaffected Jacobites remained his responsibility. After the start of the War of the Spanish Succession the Post Office terminated the service (12 August 1702), and in the following year Macky was awarded a pension at half pay. Shortly thereafter he left England for the island of Zante, to manage an estate bequeathed in part to him by his deceased wife. *En route* he unsuccessfully sought an audience with Sophia, electress of Hanover, in October 1703, and delivered to her a copy of his 'characters' of the British political élite. Although he later stated that his vivid character sketches were composed at the electress's request, most can be dated from internal evidence to about 1700, with revisions up to 1704 in the version which appeared as *Memoirs of the Secret Services of John Macky* (1733), published by his son, Spring Macky. He appears to have returned to England before the end of 1705.

The conquest of the Southern Netherlands after the battle of Ramilles in May 1706 opened the door to the resumption of the packet-boat route from Dover to Ostend. Although John Churchill, duke of Marlborough, distrusted Macky as a client of his rival Charles Talbot, duke of Shrewsbury, Macky secured appointment as an independent Post Office contractor, beginning work in July 1706 and concluding in May 1713. He speedily re-established an espionage network for surveillance of Jacobites and French naval and privateering activity at Dunkirk. This, the largest and most successful British spy ring of the war, was instrumental in uncovering James Stuart's attempted invasion of Scotland in February and March 1708. It was also Macky, a whig sympathizer and zealous anti-Catholic, who detected the secret peace mission of Matthew Prior and François Gaultier in July 1711, creating a political crisis at home and abroad. In so doing, he appears unwittingly to have assisted the secretary of state, Henry St John, in his efforts to destroy Robert Harley's broad-based ministry.

The loss of his Post Office contract in 1713 exposed Macky's extensive indebtedness, and he fled in that year

to Flanders to escape his creditors. Appeals by him to enter Harley's service went unheeded. Comments made in his *Memoirs*, written in 1723, on the vindictiveness of St John and Harley and his imprisonment until the accession of George I are mistruths; in common with all his memorials, the statements are self-serving and hyperbolic. Macky's credit and contemporary reputation never recovered from the events of 1713. After returning to London in 1714 he found meagre support from the whig ministry. An attempt to manage the Dublin packet-boats produced additional debt. Macky turned to travel writing, and produced the first volume of his popular *A Journey through England in Familiar Letters* in 1714. This was frequently reprinted, and was followed by a second volume (1722), *A Journey through Scotland* (1723), and *A Journey through the Austrian Netherlands* (1725). The writings established for Macky a minor literary reputation, although he was best known to contemporaries for his posthumous 'characters' and his propagandist tract *A View of the Court of St Germains from the Year 1690 to 1695* (1696), which he stated sold 30,000 copies. Following his release from a debtor's prison in March 1722 by George I's principal British minister, Charles Spencer, earl of Sunderland, Macky exploited governmental concern over the Francis Atterbury plot to resurrect his career as an espionage agent in the years 1723–5. His *Journey through the Austrian Netherlands* of April to September 1724 (undertaken instead of a promised volume on Ireland) probably masked his espionage work in the territories. Macky died at Rotterdam in 1726.

J. D. ALSOP

Sources *Memoirs of the secret services of John Macky*, ed. A. R. (1733) • J. D. Alsop, *British espionage, propaganda and political intrigue during the war of the Spanish Succession* [forthcoming] • J. D. Alsop, 'The detection of Matthew Prior's peace mission of 1711', *British Journal for Eighteenth-Century Studies*, 7 (1984), 61–7 • P. H. Scott, 'The secret services of John Macky', *Scottish Literary Journal*, 6/1 (1979), 72–80 • P. S. Fritz, 'The anti-Jacobite intelligence system of the English ministers, 1715–1745', *HJ*, 16 (1973), 265–89 • *Calendar of the manuscripts of the marquis of Bath preserved at Longleat, Wiltshire*, 5 vols., HMC, 58 (1904–80), vol. 3 • *The manuscripts of his grace the duke of Buccleuch and Queensberry ... preserved at Drumlanrig Castle*, 2 vols., HMC, 44 (1897–1903), vol. 2 • *The manuscripts of his grace the duke of Portland*, 10 vols., HMC, 29 (1891–1931), vol. 5 • W. A. Shaw, ed., *Calendar of treasury books*, [33 vols. in 64], PRO (1904–69) • J. Redington, ed., *Calendar of Treasury papers*, 6 vols., PRO (1868–89) • PRO, SP 34/9, 16, 17, 19, 21, E 351/2770–2789 • BL, Add. MSS 7077, 28883, 28893, 32686, 40771–40772, 40775, 61400, 61546, 61562–61563, 61567, 61579, 61597, 61601, 70024, 70029, 70031, 70191, 70248 • CUL, Cholmondeley (Houghton) MSS • CKS, MS u 1015/c 45
Archives BL, corresp. and petitions, Add. MSS | BL, letters to John Ellis, Add. MSS 28882–28894 • BL, letters to James Vernon, Add. MSS 40771, 40772, 40775 [copies] • CUL, letters to Sir Robert Walpole
Wealth at death see *Memoirs*; BL, Add. MS 61597

McLachlan, Donald Harvey (1908–1971), journalist and intelligence officer, was born in London at Flat 6, 23 Cathcart Hill, Islington, on 25 September 1908, the only child of David James McLachlan, a hotel manager, and his wife, Elizabeth Hine. From the City of London School he won a scholarship in French at Magdalen College, Oxford, where he took a first in modern Greats in 1930. He held a Laming fellowship at Queen's College, Oxford, in 1932–3.

Two sisters called Harman, daughters of Nathaniel Bishop Harman, a surgeon, who were at Lady Margaret Hall, Oxford, resolved to marry their two brightest contemporaries. Elizabeth married the future seventh earl of Longford; Katherine (1909/10–1997), known as Kitty, married McLachlan on 12 May 1934. It was a close and happy marriage, to which three sons and a daughter were born.

By the time it began McLachlan was on the staff of *The Times* as its correspondent in Warsaw. He was standing in for the Berlin correspondent, who was on holiday, on the night of the Reichstag fire, 27 February 1933. His dispatch on this was so telling that he was brought back to London to write leading articles. He happened to be in charge of the paper the night that news came in, at 8.45 p.m., that Albert I of Belgium had died; he went to press at 9.22 with a news article, a leading article, and a complete obituary, the last ten years of which he had also just written. Yet he found the work less interesting than being a foreign correspondent, and in 1936 he left for two years as an assistant master at Winchester College, where he taught German, Russian, and current affairs—the last two hitherto untaught subjects. As an agnostic he was in a difficulty in compulsory divinity classes: instead of instilling Christianity, he taught ethics out of lives of Socrates and Voltaire. He was a stimulating teacher, encouraging his pupils to think for themselves, and sharing with them his knowledge of European personalities as well as his gift for languages. *The Times* lured him back with the offer of the editorship of the *Times Educational Supplement*, which he ran in 1938–40.

In spite of his defective eyesight—he wore heavily horn-rimmed spectacles—McLachlan was accepted by the army, with an emergency commission as a second lieutenant, general list, on 8 July 1940. After a brief intelligence course at Swanage he was posted to the intelligence branch of southern command, where he served until late October, while German invasion was thought imminent. He was then attached to the Duke of Cornwall's light infantry for training.

From this McLachlan was rescued by the director of naval intelligence, J. H. Godfrey, who had him posted probationary lieutenant in the special branch of the Royal Naval Volunteer Reserve on 31 December 1940. He served no sea time; he worked in the naval intelligence department, at first on U-boat tracking. Later in 1941 he moved to naval intelligence division (NID) 17 Z. NID was now only cover for him: in fact, though in naval uniform, he joined the political warfare executive, running black broadcasts under the aegis of Sefton Delmer of the *Daily Express*, who had known him before the war. His rank, from 1942 to 1945, was acting temporary lieutenant-commander.

McLachlan's task was to run Kriegswellensender Atlantik, an ostensibly German short-wave station that aimed at rotting the morale of U-boat crews, partly by scabrous accounts of what their wives and girlfriends were doing while they were at sea. No one has ever been able to establish what impact it had. In March 1944 he again moved, to the psychological warfare branch of Supreme Headquarters, Allied Expeditionary Force, where he worked, still under Delmer, against the morale of the German army; again without precisely assessable results. Authority was satisfied with him, and he was appointed OBE in 1945.

After the war McLachlan returned to journalism and served from 1947 to 1954 as joint foreign editor of *The Economist* with Barbara Ward, under Geoffrey Crowther's editorship. He took, as always, a sternly rationalist line about foreign policy, attacking the sentimentality of the left as sharply as he opposed any tendencies towards tyranny of the right. In 1954 he moved to the *Daily Telegraph* as deputy editor. It was he who wrote the article headed 'The smack of firm government' early in 1956 that so much annoyed Sir Anthony Eden. He alternately exhilarated and alarmed his colleagues, because of the many bright ideas he put before them. He was a tall, thin, clean-shaven man, thin-lipped, decisive in manner, and noticeably helpful to anyone he thought promising. He was a visiting fellow of Nuffield College, Oxford, in 1960–68, and sat on the BBC's General Advisory Council from 1961 to 1965.

For its first five years, from 5 February 1961, McLachlan edited the *Sunday Telegraph*, intended to 'fill the gap'—as he put it on its first page—between the two quality Sunday papers, *The Observer* and the *Sunday Times*, and the more popular ones. He meant to make it readily readable in a single day, and yet to include plenty of hard news and commentary as well as many cultural features, but never escaped from the quip that the gap it filled was between Saturday's *Telegraph* and Monday's *Telegraph*.

In 1966 McLachlan resigned, because he wanted to write books instead of articles. First he produced *Room 39* (1968), a long and original account of wartime naval intelligence, studded with asterisks (inserted whenever he wanted to refer to most secret sources, still then unavowable, to which he had himself been privy in NID). It remains one of the leading texts on practical intelligence work.

McLachlan then wrote *In the Chair*, a life of R. W. Barrington-Ward, the wartime editor of *The Times*, a sympathetic biography which appeared after its author's death. He also wrote a novel, *No Case for the Crown* (1972), about the secret world, in which a principal character is removed by the counter-espionage service by being forced to drive into a tree. He next began a life (never finished) of Kurt Hahn, the headmaster of Gordonstoun, the Scottish public school on the Moray Firth. He went there early in 1971 to pursue research. On long journeys, he and Kitty normally shared the driving; she happened to have a broken wrist, and he went alone. On 10 January, early on the way back, he drove into a tree and died at once. His ashes were scattered, close to his country home, on the Hanger near Selborne, Hampshire; friends put up trees there to his memory.　　　　　M. R. D. Foot

Sources *Navy Lists* (1941–5) · D. H. McLachlan, *Room 39* (1968) · S. Delmer, *Black boomerang* (1952) · R. D. Edwards, *The pursuit of reason* (1993) · *Daily Telegraph* (11 Jan 1971) · *Sunday Telegraph* (17 Jan 1971) · *The Times* (11 Jan 1971) · *WWW, 1971–80* · personal knowledge (2004) · *Oxford University Calendars* (1929–34) · *Army List* (1940) · b. cert. · m. cert.

Archives CAC Cam., papers relating to history of naval intelligence | BL, corresp. with Society of Authors, Add. 63287 · King's Lond., Liddell Hart C., corresp. with Sir B. H. Liddell Hart
Likenesses photograph, repro. in *Daily Telegraph* · photograph, repro. in *The Times*
Wealth at death £28,322: probate, 16 July 1971, *CGPLA Eng. & Wales*

MacLachlan, Ewen (1773–1822), poet and Gaelic scholar, was born at Torracaltin, Nether Lochaber, the son of a weaver. After attending the parish school at Kilmallie, he worked as private tutor to several prominent local families. Financial assistance from the chief of the clan Glengarry allowed him to attend King's College, Aberdeen, where he distinguished himself in the classics and wrote verse in Greek and Latin. He contributed poems in Gaelic to Allan MacDougall's *Orain Ghaidhealacha* (1798).

On graduating AM in 1800 MacLachlan won a royal bursary and entered the Divinity Hall at Aberdeen. Deciding against the ministry, he was appointed librarian at King's College and a master at Old Aberdeen grammar school. His *Metrical Effusions* appeared in 1807 and in an expanded edition in 1816; it contained verse in Greek, Latin, Gaelic, and English, and included a metrical paraphrase of the book of Revelation. He was engaged by the Highland Society of Scotland to assist on their *Gaelic Dictionary* which was published in two volumes in 1828, but his most substantial work in Gaelic was a translation of books i–vii of the *Iliad*, which went unpublished until the appearance of John MacDonald's *Ewen MacLachlan's Gaelic Verse* in 1937. Derick Thomson has described the translation as 'a steady rather than an exciting performance', with 'touches of exuberance' (Thomson, 179). MacDonald's collection also contained poems on the seasons and a popular song, 'Gur gile mo leannan' ('Fair is my love').

About 1811 MacLachlan made an unsuccessful attempt to become professor of Gaelic at the University of Edinburgh. In 1819 he was appointed headmaster at Aberdeen grammar school. His physical health was never strong; he was still hard at work on the *Gaelic Dictionary* when he died in Aberdeen on 29 March 1822. He was buried in his native glen at Lochaber. DOUGLAS BROWN

Sources D. S. Thomson, ed., *The companion to Gaelic Scotland*, new edn (1994) · N. MacNeill, *The literature of the highlanders* (1892) · Anderson, *Scot. nat.*
Archives NL Scot., analyses and transcripts of MSS and other papers · Royal Highland and Agricultural Society of Scotland, Edinburgh, corresp. relating to Gaelic matters · U. Aberdeen L., papers

McLachlan, Herbert (1876–1958), historian of nonconformity and college head, was born on 22 August 1876 at Dulesgate, near Todmorden, the second son of John McLachlan (1840–1899), cotton mill manager, and his wife, Sarah Gladwell (b. 1849). His early board school education was cut short in 1889 when he joined his father's newly acquired oil and dry-salter's business at Ardwick, Manchester, an occupation he found uncongenial.

Herbert's academic promise was already clear, and his religious interests developed as a Sunday school teacher at the Unitarian church at Newchurch in Rossendale. In 1896 he decided to train for the Unitarian ministry, and began to attend evening classes; in due course he matriculated at the Victoria University of Manchester, the university with which he was uniquely associated for decades, and from which he graduated on no fewer than six occasions.

Having also entered the Unitarian Home Missionary College, Manchester in 1899, McLachlan carried off numerous university and college prizes, which included a double first, an MA, and in 1906 a BD with distinction. He was much influenced by the then principal, Alexander Gordon, whose knowledge of the oddities of dissent in Britain and Europe was unique. McLachlan later wrote his biography (1932), an endearing picture of a similar spirit equally devoted to hard work and painstaking research. Then followed his only period in the ministry, serving churches in Yorkshire at Leeds and Bradford for five years before returning to the college he had so recently left, as tutor and warden. While at Leeds he married Mary Jane Taylor (1872–1940) on 5 November 1906; she later became matron of the Manchester Unitarian College for a while. They had one child, Herbert John (b. 1908), who followed his father as a Unitarian minister, a leading historian of nonconformity, and principal of a theological college (Manchester College, Oxford) from 1949 to 1951.

Numerous books and articles on biblical criticism and nonconformist history flowed from McLachlan's pen over succeeding decades, despite a heavy teaching load and active denominational involvement. In 1915 he became lecturer in Greek in the university, and principal of the Unitarian College in 1921. He was awarded a DD in 1920 for biblical research into the third gospel, the first in the university for twenty-one years. Between 1925 and 1927 he was dean of the faculty of theology.

However it is as a historian of eighteenth- and nineteenth-century nonconformity that McLachlan is remembered, and for the significant contribution he made to the historiography of dissent. His book on the nonconformist academies, *English Education under the Test Acts* (1931), remains the key and most oft quoted work on the subject. McLachlan's studies of Unitarian and radical dissenting history remain works that have to be consulted by historians of the period, in particular *The Methodist Unitarian Movement* (1919), *The Unitarian Movement in the Religious Life of England* (1934), and *Warrington Academy: its History and Influence* (1943). While the presentation of his scholarship may not be to modern standards, the originality and breadth of its content is undeniable. His bibliographic work over decades on the original material on early radical dissent held in the Unitarian College collection (later incorporated in the John Rylands University Library of Manchester) has ensured that his contribution to the story of this period is a permanent one.

McLachlan was widely respected, particularly by his more able students, but was often detested by the rest. Considered by many a martinet, and a stickler for detailed observance of university rules, as college principal for twenty-three years and senior figure within the faculty of theology he had an indelible effect on generations of Unitarian ministers and other students. Many found him stern and unbending, and even one of his favourite students concluded: 'not always did his officers and students see eye to eye with him, but many have since felt that what he planned and expected of them was far more to their benefit than they thought at the time' (Kenworthy, 116). Limited experience as a minister did not prevent his being very clear as to what the profession needed and required of its members. McLachlan finally retired from the university in 1944 and was awarded a DLitt, but remained as examiner in Greek for another two years. On 11 September 1942 he married Jane (*b.* 1886/7), daughter of Daniel McWilliam, a master mariner, and he spent his last years living at 11 Sydenham Avenue, Liverpool, dying in that city on 21 February 1958 at 241 Westminster Road, Kirkdale. His last major work, *Essays and Addresses* (1950), brought together disparate strands of his researches assembled over nearly half a century. It demonstrated that he had not lost his touch in clearly explaining the history of dissent from the seventeenth to the twentieth century to the non-specialist but intelligent reader.　　ALAN RUSTON

Sources J. McLachlan, *The wine of life: a testament to vital encounter* (privately printed, Sheffield, 1991) • F. Kenworthy, *Transactions of the Unitarian Historical Society*, 11/4 (1955–8), 113–16 • *WWW*, 1951–60 • *General Assembly of Unitarian and Free Christian Churches Year Book* (1959), 102–3 • H. McLachlan, *Unitarian College Manchester: register of students, 1854–1929* (privately printed, 1929), 58–9 • *The Inquirer* (1 March 1958), 72 • *The Inquirer* (8 March 1958), 76–7 • personal knowledge (2004) [former students] • H. McLachlan, *The Unitarian Home Missionary College* (1915), 102 • *CGPLA Eng. & Wales* (1958) • m. cert. • d. cert. • private information (2004)
Archives JRL, Unitarian College collection
Likenesses photograph, 1941, repro. in McLachlan, *Wine of life*, 63 • photograph, repro. in McLachlan, *Unitarian Home Missionary College*, facing p. 102 • photograph, repro. in *Unitarian and Free Christian Churches Year Book* (1937), frontispiece • portrait, JRL, Unitarian College collection
Wealth at death £11,481 2s. 6d.: probate, 16 June 1958, *CGPLA Eng. & Wales*

McLachlan, Jean Olivia. See Lindsay, Jean Olivia (1910–1996).

Maclachlan, Lauchlan (1688–1746), Jacobite army officer and chief of clan Lachlan (Lachlainn), was born at Castle Lachlan, Argyll, the son of Lachlan Maclachlan (*d.* 1719), chief of the ancient, but minor, Argyll clan Lachlan (Lachlainn). On 23 September 1719 he became chief of the clan following his father's death. The Maclachlans controlled territory in Cowal, Argyll, and on the western shores of Loch Fyne, south of Inveraray. Since the fifteenth century, until the forfeiture of James VII, the family had allied itself to the Campbells; during the Jacobite risings of 1689 and 1715, however, the clan Lachlan turned out in support of the Stuarts. In 1719 the Revd John Maclachlan of Kilchoan ensured his kinsmen's loyalty to the exiled Stuarts by successfully fostering nonjuring episcopalianism.

Aside from his own episcopalianism and his marriage to Mary, daughter of Robert Stewart of Appin (in or before 1735; she eventually outlived him), little is known of Lauchlan Maclachlan before his involvement in the Jacobite rising of 1745. After Charles Edward Stuart's landing in August 1745 Kenneth Maclachlan of Keilaneuchanich

mustered the clansmen in the western clan lands near Dunadd. In mid-September Lauchlan Maclachlan, having gathered 260 men, marched north-east from Castle Lachlan to join the prince. With the majority of the clansmen away with the Jacobite army, the Hanoverian Argyll militia occupied Castle Lachlan. Meanwhile Maclachlan and his men had joined Prince Charles's army and helped defeat the government forces under Sir John Cope at Prestonpans. Following the fall of Carlisle to the Jacobites in mid-November the prince sent Maclachlan with sixteen horsemen to Perth to speed the departure of the 3000 recruits gathered there. However, the governor, William Drummond, fourth Viscount Strathallan, refused to allow the men to march because, as a French officer serving with the Jacobites, he had orders not to advance from Scotland while the Hanoverians still garrisoned fortresses there. Maclachlan and his men served at the siege of Stirling Castle and contributed to the victory over Hawley's forces at Falkirk. He was made commissary of the army while at Inverness.

At Culloden on 16 April 1746 Maclachlan commanded 115 of his kinsmen and 182 Macleans from Mull in a composite battalion, stationed in the centre of the Jacobite army's first line between the Farquharsons and the Chisholms. He was killed by a cannonball during the Jacobite attack and buried on the battlefield. After the battle the Argyll militia destroyed the chief's castle and his property when they ended their occupation. At the intercession of the duke of Argyll, Maclachlan's fourteen-year-old son Robert was restored to the clan lands on 18 November 1749. However, by the termination of heritable jurisdiction in the previous year, his power as a clan chief was considerably circumscribed.　　EDWARD M. FURGOL

Sources R. Forbes, *The lyon in mourning, or, A collection of speeches, letters, journals … relative to … Prince Charles Edward Stuart*, ed. H. Paton, 3 vols., Scottish History Society, 20–22 (1895–6) • W. B. Blaikie, ed., *Origins of the 'Forty-Five and other papers relating to that rising*, Scottish History Society, 2nd ser., 2 (1916); facs. repr. (1975) • S. Reid, *Like hungry wolves: Culloden Moor, 16 April 1746* (1994) • A. I. Macinnes, *Clanship, commerce, and the house of Stuart, 1603–1788* (1996) • G. S. Maclachlan, 'Rights of council', *Clan Lachlan*, 17 (Oct 1987), 29 • D. McLachlan, letter, *Clan Lachlan*, 18 (1988), 10 • G. S. MacLachlan, 'A matter of opinion', *Clan Maclachlan*, 19 (Oct 1988), 22–3 • *APS*, 1670–95; 1702–7 • *Reg. PCS*, 3rd ser., vol. 7 • G. Black, *The surnames of Scotland*, repr. edn (1996) • F. Adam, *The clans, septs and regiments of the Scottish highlands*, rev. T. Innes, 8th edn (1970)
Archives Castle Lachlan, Strathlachlan, Argyll | Inveraray Castle, Inveraray, Argyll, Argyll MSS

McLachlan, Laurentia Margaret (1866–1953), abbess of Stanbrook and scholar, was born on 11 January 1866 at Coatbridge, Lanarkshire, and baptized Margaret at St Margaret's Church, Airdrie, the youngest of the seven children of Henry McLachlan (1828–1890), accountant, and his wife, Mary McAleese (1828–1900). From her father, a highlander, and a Huguenot born grandmother, McLachlan inherited French wit and charm; from her Irish mother, practicality and an ability to organize. These traits fused and developed into the extraordinary capacity for friendship and government she was to show as nun and abbess, inviting comparison with the twelfth-century Cistercian

Laurentia Margaret McLachlan (1866–1953), by unknown photographer, 1923

abbot, Ailred of Rievaulx, on the eve of whose feast she had been born. Like Ailred, Margaret did not enjoy robust health. Frail as a child (her father nicknamed her Bodle after the Scottish coin worth less than a ha'penny), her formal education was intermittent: spells at a dame-school in Coatbridge, and convent schools in Bothwell and Edinburgh comprised her primary schooling, while her secondary education was almost entirely at home directed by her clerical brother, James. Hers was not, however, an overly pious upbringing—she later described herself in a letter to Sydney Cockerell as 'terribly fond of pleasure' (*In a Great Tradition*, 93) and, at the time of starting school at Stanbrook Abbey, near Worcester, on 6 September 1881, a 'hater of nuns' (ibid., 81). Exactly four years later she became a nun of that same Stanbrook Abbey, an enclosed Benedictine community where she would spend the next seventy years. The reasons for such a volte-face are not clear. 'The why is God's secret', she wrote in *Ad quid venisti*, her 1934 pamphlet on vocation. Her mother excepted, the family initially resented the decision from which, she said, her father never fully recovered. But there was no estrangement. She had entered the noviciate on 2 February 1884, receiving the name Laurentia after the martyr St Laurence and, more proximately, Father Laurence Shepherd, Ampleforth monk and from 1863 to 1885 chaplain and great benefactor of Stanbrook.

Interest in Gregorian chant sown in childhood, given impetus on a visit to the French Benedictine abbey of Solesmes in 1883, and nurtured in the daily singing of the divine office, flowered by 1914 when Dame Laurentia was widely acknowledged as the foremost authority on plainsong in English speaking countries. Organist from 1892

and precentress from 1893, she had caught the tide of nineteenth-century liturgical revival spearheaded at Solesmes and projected to Stanbrook by Laurence Shepherd, and became, herself, instrumental in that revival. In 1890 she had been asked to visit the nuns at Princethorpe Priory, the first of five such missions to foster the singing of plainsong. In touch with leading figures in plainsong such as Dom Mocquereau (Solesmes), she maintained an independent, pragmatic approach, detached from the musical controversies of the day. Her first published work, *Gregorian music, an outline of musical palaeography. Illustrated by facsimiles of ancient manuscripts* (1897) by the Benedictines of Stanbrook, is far more than an epitome of Dom Mocquereau's work in the volumes of *Paléographie musicale*, the material restructured to suit the English temperament. In 1899 she began research on the thirteenth-century Worcester antiphoner, later published as the introduction to volume 12 of the *Paléographie musicale* (1922–5). Of more widespread influence was *A Grammar of Plainsong* (1905), written to implement Pius X's 1903 *Motu proprio* on church music. Translated into French, German, and Italian and running to four editions, the *Grammar* was prefaced by an autograph letter from Pius X in recognition of Stanbrook's work for the restoration of the chant. That work permeated to grassroots through *Plainsong for Schools* (1930). In 1927 Dame Laurentia was elected a vice-president of the Plainsong and Mediaeval Music Society and, from its inception in 1929, supported the Society of St Gregory, being listed among their patrons in 1937. However, the crowning achievement had come on 6 September 1934 when she was awarded the *bene merenti* by Pius XI for her work in church music.

Historical scholarship was an early interest: Dame Laurentia published *St Egwin and his Abbey of Evesham* (1904); *Stanbrook Abbey: a Sketch of its History, 1625–1925* (1925) and, in 1929, contributed an article to the *Journal of Theological Studies* (30, 174–6) on St Wulfstan's prayerbook. Such study grew alongside liturgical work, for which she often consulted original manuscripts, lent to Stanbrook through the good offices of friends like Canon Wilson, librarian of Worcester Cathedral, and Sir Sydney Cockerell, director of the Fitzwilliam Museum, Cambridge. She brought to their study discipline, liturgical knowledge, and a certain monastic insight. From the rubrics in the Worcester antiphoner, she was able to reconstruct details of the medieval cathedral later confirmed by archaeology. To the six articles on medieval and musical subjects she published between 1904 and 1937 should be added the significant identification of an eighth-century fragment in Worcester Cathedral Library as the earliest manuscript of Paterius's *De expositione novi et veteris testamenti*.

The demands of the abbatial office, to which Dame Laurentia was elected on 24 November 1931, left little time for study; even so, in 1933 she became first woman vice-president of the Henry Bradshaw Society (founded in 1890 to edit rare liturgical texts) and helped produce two volumes for their proceedings in 1936 and 1937, her final contribution in this field—a contribution none the less sufficient to elicit from Francis Wormald the encomium, 'a true daughter of St Benedict and Dom Jean Mabillon' (*The Times*, 24 Aug 1953).

There was little surprise at Dame Laurentia's being chosen abbess (she had been subprioress 1910–25 and prioress 1925–31), despite advanced years and increasing frailty. Some hold that such drawbacks, on the material plane, lent to her abbacy a deep spirit of trust, on her part, and an equally profound response of love from the community. In 1931 she was involved in reformulating the constitutions of the nuns of the English Benedictine congregation, while at Stanbrook she encouraged flexibility and personal initiative and recognized the need for leisure, allocating free time and an outdoor recreation area. To qualities of leadership she added those powers of sympathy and affection which had gained her a wide circle of friends, making her accessible to even the youngest sister. She is remembered giving correction with a twinkle in the grey-green eyes! Her last publications, six treatises based on conferences given to the nuns, bear witness to her spiritual wisdom. At her death, on 23 August 1953 in the abbey, she left a community remarkable for its unity and diversity—a final echo of Ailred's Rievaulx and testament to her own influence.

That influence has extended through the story of her friendships with Sir Sydney Cockerell and George Bernard Shaw, told in *In a Great Tradition* (1956) by the Benedictines of Stanbrook, revised as *The Nun, the Infidel and the Superman* by Dame Felicitas Corrigan (1985), reprinted in 1990 as *Friends of a Lifetime*. Since 1988 she has been even more widely known through Hugh Whitemore's play, *The Best of Friends*, which, after a long West End run and national tour, enjoyed phenomenal success into the 1990s, touring eleven countries on four continents. The televising of the play brought the enclosed figure of Dame Laurentia into millions of homes. Such popularity suggests a shift in perception of her place in the national memory. Research on the chant has progressed and Dame Laurentia's contribution, historically significant as it will remain, plays little part in her enduring appeal. This lies rather in the 'enclosed nun with the unenclosed mind', as George Bernard Shaw described her (Corrigan, *Friends of a Lifetime*, 8), whose greatness of personality matched the stature of the medieval abbesses described by Bede. She was buried on 26 August 1953 at Stanbrook Abbey.

LAURENTIA JOHNS

Sources In a great tradition (1956) [tribute to Dame Laurentia McLachlan, abbess of Stanbrook, by the Benedictines of Stanbrook] · F. Corrigan, *The nun, the infidel and the superman* (1985) · F. Corrigan, *Friends of a lifetime* (1990) · *Daily Mail* (24 Aug 1953) · *The Times* (24 Aug 1953) · *Berrow's Journal* (28 Aug 1953) · L. M. McLachlan, *Ad quid venisti* (1934) · Stanbrook Abbey, Worcestershire, archives · private information (2004)

Archives Stanbrook Abbey, Worcestershire
Likenesses four photographs, 1884–c.1950, repro. in *In a great tradition* · photograph, 1923, Stanbrook Abbey, Worcestershire, archives [*see illus.*] · etched window, 2000, Worcester Cathedral

McLachlan, Robert (1837–1904), entomologist, was born at 17 Upper East Smithfield, London, on 10 April 1837, one of five children of Hugh McLachlan (*d.* 1855) and his wife, Hannah Thompson, of Northamptonshire. His father was a native of Greenock who settled in early life in London and became a successful chronometer maker; in the latter part of his life, his father lived on a small farm or country house in Hainault Forest, Essex.

McLachlan was educated at Ilford in Essex, probably at a private school. After an engagement was broken off he made a voyage, in 1855, at the age of eighteen, to Australia and China. On his travels he collected much botanical material, which was examined and identified by Robert Brown, keeper of the botanical department of the British Museum. McLachlan's acquaintance with the natural history publisher John Van Voorst (1804–1898) probably steered his interests towards entomology; later, prompted by the writings of Hermann August Hagen, he began work on elucidating British and foreign families of Neuroptera. His first paper on this order appeared in the *Entomologist's Annual* in 1861; it was followed by various important monographs. His *Catalogue of British Neuroptera* was published by the Entomological Society in 1870. He wrote his earliest works on Neuroptera while living in Forest Hill, Kent, with his mother.

A zealous collector, McLachlan brought together an unequalled series of specimens and maintained a voluminous correspondence at home and abroad relating to the study. He was also a careful and thorough scientist. He became the pioneer of the world fauna of Trichoptera, and his greatest work was considered to be his *Monographic revision and synopsis of the Trichoptera [caddis-flies] of the European fauna* (1874–84). This work, originally published in nine parts, was illustrated by nearly 2000 of his own detailed drawings, made under the camera lucida. For the *Encyclopaedia Britannica* (9th edition), he wrote the article 'Insects'.

McLachlan was a member of many English and foreign scientific societies. He was elected a fellow of the Linnean Society in 1862, and served on its council (1879–83). He was also made FRS on 7 June 1877 (being supported by Charles Darwin and George Bentham), and gave valued honorary assistance for several years in editing the society's *Catalogue of Scientific Papers*. He became a member of the Entomological Society in 1858 and filled the offices of secretary (1868–72), treasurer (1873–5, 1891–1904), and president (1885–6). On the establishment of the *Entomologist's Monthly Magazine* (1864) he acted as its first editor, eventually becoming proprietor (1902) without relinquishing his editorial work. He was also a member of the Zoological Society, the Royal Horticultural Society, and the council of the Ray Society.

McLachlan suffered from insomnia for many years, and it is believed that he never properly recovered from the death of two nephews. He died, unmarried, on 23 May 1904, at his home, West View, 23 Clarendon Road, Lewisham, London, and was buried five days later in the Tower Hamlets cemetery, London. His collection of Neuroptera was the most impressive of his time in the British Isles; after his death it was inherited by his nephew.

T. E. JAMES, *rev.* YOLANDA FOOTE

Sources E. S., 'Robert McLachlan, 1837–1904', *PRS*, 75 (1904–5), 367–70 · *Catalogue of scientific papers*, Royal Society, 19 vols. (1867–

1925) · *Transactions of the Entomological Society* (1904) [presidential address] · *Proceedings of the Entomological Society* (1886) [presidential address] · *Entomologist's Monthly Magazine*, 40 (1904), 145–8 · *Entomological News* (Sept 1904) · E. Saunders, *Proceedings of the Linnean Society of London*, 117th session (1904–5), 42–3 · *Proceedings of the Royal Horticultural Society*, 29 (1904) · *Nature*, 70 (1904), 106 · *Men and women of the time* (1899) · E. O. Essig, *A history of entomology* (1931) · R. F. Smith, T. E. Mittler, and C. N. Smith, eds., *History of entomology* (1973) · *CGPLA Eng. & Wales* · *IGI*
Archives NHM, corresp. and notebooks; drawings · Oxf. U. Mus. NH, Hope Library, corresp., drawings, and papers · Royal Entomological Society of London, corresp. and papers | Oxf. U. Mus. NH, letters to Sir E. B. Poulton; corresp. with J. O. Westwood · Royal Entomological Society of London, letters to C. J. Wainwright
Likenesses black and white photograph, 1904 (after P. P. Calvert), repro. in Essig, *History of entomology*
Wealth at death £25,893 11s. 3d.: resworn administration, 2 July 1904, *CGPLA Eng. & Wales*

McLachlan, Thomas Hope (1845–1897), landscape painter, the second son of Thomas McLachlan and his wife, Jane Hope, was born on 16 March 1845 at Darlington, where his father was manager of the National Provincial Bank. Educated at Merchiston Castle School, Edinburgh, and Trinity College, Cambridge, where he graduated BA in 1868 and was bracketed first in the moral science tripos, he entered Lincoln's Inn on 27 October 1865 and was called to the bar on 17 November 1868. In 1870 he married Jean, the youngest daughter of William Stow Stowell of Faverdale; they had a son and a daughter. McLachlan practised for several years in the court of chancery but he did not care for the work and had few briefs. He wanted to be a painter and, encouraged by the Edinburgh-born painter John Pettie and others who believed in his gifts, he gave up law in 1878 and took to art.

McLachlan had no academic training to begin with and the short time that he spent in the studio of Carolus Duran at a later date was of little account; but he studied the early English landscape painters and later was considerably influenced by the work of the French romanticists and by Cecil Gordon Lawson. His work was always individual and interesting, for he had a poetic apprehension of nature and was happiest in the expansive and comparatively barren landscapes of the north. His painting was 'peculiarly sensitive to the grave and impressive emotions which belong to twilight, night, and solitude' (Caw, 316), and if his technique was somewhat faulty he designed with dignity and was a refined and powerful colourist. He also made a number of highly expressive etchings, several of which were reproduced in the *Magazine of Art*.

McLachlan exhibited at the Royal Academy and the Grosvenor Gallery, and later at the New Gallery and the Institute of Painters in Oil Colours, of which he was a member. In 1894 the academy accepted four of his works; he nevertheless remained largely unknown outside a circle of fellow artists and art connoisseurs. This comparative neglect prompted an article in the *Magazine of Art* in December 1894, accompanied by reproductions of six of his best paintings, including *Idleness*, *An October Storm*, and *A Wind on the Hill*, the last depicting a storm-buffeted peasant in the style of Jean-François Millet. The article praised McLachlan's sensitivity to landscape, commenting on his ability 'to render the effects of airiness and movement in the sky' while conveying also 'a sense of solidity, of actual physical weight, in the earth beneath it' (p. 62).

It was not until 1896, when McLachlan became associated with five other painters in the landscape exhibition at the Dudley Gallery, that the beauty of his work, there seen more in a mass and in more congenial surroundings, drew the attention it deserved. He lived to share in only one other exhibition, for on 1 April 1897 he died at his home, Birkwood, in Weybridge, Surrey; he was survived by his wife. The following June a collection of his pictures was brought together in the studios of his friends Leslie Thomson and R. W. Allan. It was perhaps only with this memorial exhibition that his talent became properly appreciated, and afterwards some admirers presented a characteristic work, *Ships that Pass in the Night*, to the National Gallery, London. Another work, *Isles of the Sea*, a sunset piece, was presented to the Guildhall Collection, London.   J. L. CAW, rev. MARK POTTLE

Sources J. L. Caw, *Scottish painting past and present, 1620–1908* (1908) · Wood, *Vic. painters*, 2nd edn · P. J. M. McEwan, *Dictionary of Scottish art and architecture* (1994) · *Art Journal*, new ser., 17 (1897) · J. Johnson and A. Greutzner, *The dictionary of British artists, 1880–1940* (1976), vol. 5 of *Dictionary of British art* · *Saturday Review*, 83 (1897), 655–6 · *Magazine of Art*, 18 (1894–5) · private information (2004) [J. L. Caw] · J. Foster, *Men-at-the-bar: a biographical hand-list of the members of the various inns of court*, 2nd edn (1885) · S. Image, preface, *Thomas Hope McLachlan* [exhibition catalogue] · *CGPLA Eng. & Wales* (1897)
Likenesses E. R. Hughes, red chalk, repro. in *Art Journal* · portrait, repro. in *Magazine of Art*
Wealth at death £759 18s. 5d.: probate, 27 April 1897, *CGPLA Eng. & Wales*

Maclagan, Sir Andrew Douglas (1812–1900), physician and expert in forensic medicine and public health, born on 17 April 1812 in Ayr, was the eldest of seven sons of David Maclagan and his wife, Jane, daughter of Philip Whiteside, a medical practitioner of Ayr. Maclagan's father was serving as physician to the forces in Portugal at the time of his son's birth and did not see him until 'he was eating a mutton chop'. Of the six siblings, two entered the medical profession and William Dalrymple *Maclagan (1826–1910) became the archbishop of York. Maclagan entered Edinburgh high school in 1818. He studied medicine at the University of Edinburgh and graduated MD in 1833. He became a licentiate of the Royal College of Surgeons of Edinburgh in 1831 and a fellow in 1833. After further study in Berlin, Paris, and London, he was elected assistant surgeon to the Edinburgh Royal Infirmary.

In 1845 Maclagan's interest in chemistry led him to take up extramural teaching of the subject at Surgeons' Hall, Edinburgh. His forensic career began as a medical witness for the defence of Madeleine Smith on the charge of poisoning her lover, Emil L'Angelier, in 1859, when Robert Christison appeared for the crown. The charge was not proven. Christison and Maclagan became great friends and often appeared together for the crown. Maclagan appeared for the crown with Henry Littlejohn in the trial of Dr Pritchard for the murder of his wife and mother-in-law by poisoning (Glasgow, 1865) and in the trial of

Eugene Chantrelle for the drugging and gassing of his wife (Edinburgh, 1878). Both defendants were found guilty and hanged. Maclagan became a leading authority on the analysis of poisons and published important works on the subject, such as *Contributions to Toxicology, Cases of Poisoning* (1849).

In 1862 Maclagan was appointed regius professor of forensic medicine and public health at Edinburgh University, succeeding Thomas Trail. He was instrumental in raising the profile of medical practitioners in Scottish public health administration, and immediately entered into the task of instructing undergraduate medical students in the basic rules of public hygiene. He introduced postgraduate teaching in 1875. The BSc in public health, open only to medical graduates, was timely, as Scottish medical officers of health were struggling for the status and recognition given to that office in England and Wales under the 1875 Public Health Act. Both lecture courses took the English approach to public health, Scottish practice being dealt with separately. The degree examinations consisted of chemistry, medicine, practical sanitation, and sanitary law. The BSc was followed by the establishment of a DSc degree in 1877. Maclagan's postgraduate courses attracted many doctors who took up responsible posts in English public health administration, for example Edward Hope, medical officer of health for Liverpool. At a time when medical practitioners working in Scottish public health were pressing for recognition (they were eventually acknowledged in the 1897 Public Health Act, Scotland), Maclagan's public health qualifications formed an essential part of the successful argument.

When Maclagan was appointed regius professor he automatically became one of the professors of clinical medicine, and during the later years, when he became the senior professor, he lectured almost entirely on dermatology. It is due to him that a department for skin diseases was formed in the Edinburgh Royal Infirmary. Maclagan retired from the chair of forensic medicine and public health in 1897. The university bestowed upon him the degree of LLD, an honour accorded to him also by Glasgow University in 1881. He was elected president in Edinburgh of both the Royal College of Surgeons (1859–60) and the Royal College of Physicians (1884–7), a distinction shared only with his father. He served a period as president of the Royal Society of Edinburgh, and in 1886 he was knighted by Queen Victoria.

Maclagan was married to Elizabeth Allan Thompson. He was an excellent amateur musician and poet, his most notable contribution being 'Nugae canorae medicae', and was a fellow of the Harveian and the Aesculapian societies, delighting the membership with his ballads. He died at 28 Heriot Row, Edinburgh, on 5 April 1900, after a short illness. He was buried four days later in Dean cemetery, Edinburgh. Among the pall bearers were his son, Robert Craig Maclagan, and his brother William. His wife had predeceased him. BRENDA M. WHITE

Sources *BMJ* (14 April 1900), 935–7 · *The Lancet* (14 April 1900) · *The Scotsman* (6 April 1900) · W. B. Hole, *Quasi cursores: portraits of the high officers and professors of the University of Edinburgh at its tercentenary festival* (1884) · W. S. Craig, *History of the Royal College of Physicians of Edinburgh* (1976) · T. Jesse, ed., *The trial of Madeleine Smith*, Notable British Trials (1921) · W. Roughead, *The trial of Doctor Pritchard*, Notable British Trials (1906) · calendars, 1862–97, U. Edin. · *Medical Directory* · parish register (birth), 17 April 1812, Ayr · d. cert.

Wealth at death £8114 10s. 11d.: confirmation, 12 May 1900, CCI

Maclagan, Christian (1811–1901), archaeologist, was born at Underwood, near Denny, Stirlingshire, the daughter of George Maclagan (d. 1818), distiller and chemist of good education, and his wife, Christian, daughter of Thomas Colville, printer, of Dundee. Her great-great-grandfather Alexander Maclagan (1653–1722) was parish minister of Little Dunkeld, Perthshire, and was succeeded in that charge by his only son, Alexander Maclagan (1694–1768), a strong Hanoverian in a Jacobite parish. Her grandfather Frederick Maclagan (1738–1818), who just outlived her father, was ordained parish minister of Melrose in 1768, and she was engaged on a biography of him at her death.

Christian Maclagan was brought up by her mother at Underwood, and at Braehead Farm, Stirlingshire. After the Disruption in 1843 she joined the Free Church, and built a mission church in St Mary's Wynd, Stirling; but having quarrelled with Dr Beith, the Free Church minister, she joined the established church, and transferred the building to that denomination; it became *quoad sacra* parish church.

In later life Christian Maclagan lived at Ravenscroft, near Denny, and devoted much time and money to the removal of slums in Stirling, providing houses for the working classes outside the burgh. Her father and grandfather had both been interested in Roman forts in Scotland, and this subject engrossed the greater part of her long life. Her researches in prehistoric remains in Scotland were in general unacceptable both to her contemporaries and to posterity: her belief that stone circles were the remains of large buildings has not found favour. She was made a lady associate of the Society of Antiquaries of Scotland in 1871, and her name remained on the roll until her death, although she wished to withdraw because the society refused her the rights of a fellow. She was an artist of ability, although her right hand was rendered useless by a bone disease and she could employ only her left hand. She devised a special method for taking rubbings from sculptured stones, and exhibited the results of her work at the Glasgow exhibitions of 1888 and 1901, but she never disclosed the secret of her plan. In consequence of her dispute with the Society of Antiquaries of Scotland, she sent all her rubbings from stones to the British Museum.

Christian Maclagan's published works were all on prehistoric subjects and included *The Hill Forts, Stone Circles, and other Structural Remains of Ancient Scotland* (1875), *Chips from Old Stones* (published privately, 1881), *What Mean these Stones? with Plates of Druidic Stones in Scotland* (1894), and *A Catalogue Raisonné of the British Museum Collection of Rubbings from Ancient Sculptured Stones* (1895; the annotated copy in the British Library discloses her factual errors). She contributed papers to the Stirling Natural History and Archaeological Society in 1882 and 1893, showing rubbings of sculptured stones at Islay and Ardchattan Priory, prepared by her method. She died, unmarried, at Ravenscroft, Stirling, on 10 May 1901, and was buried in Stirling cemetery. She left an unpublished autobiography, no longer extant. Maclagan might be presented as a victim of injustice and unmitigated male prejudice but in fact she was a poor scholar.   A. H. MILLAR, *rev.* H. C. G. MATTHEW

Sources *The Scotsman* (13 May 1901) · *The Sentinel* [Stirling] (14 May 1901) · *The Athenaeum* (18 May 1901), 634–5 · private information (1912)

Archives BL, rubbings of Scottish sculptured stones, Add. MSS 34798, 35165A–D

Maclagan, Sir Eric Robert Dalrymple (1879–1951), museum director, was born in London on 4 December 1879, the only son of William Dalrymple *Maclagan (1826–1910), bishop of Lichfield, later archbishop of York, and his second wife, Augusta Anne, daughter of William Keppel Barrington, sixth Viscount Barrington. He had a sister and two half-brothers. Educated at Winchester College, he read classics at Christ Church, Oxford, where he obtained a third class in honour moderations (1900) and a fourth in *literae humaniores* (1902). He joined the staff of the Victoria and Albert Museum in 1905 as assistant in the department of textiles, and in 1907 produced *A Guide to English Ecclesiastical Embroideries*. From textiles, Maclagan was transferred in 1909 to the department of architecture and sculpture, where he rearranged the collection of Italian sculpture, and published the *Catalogue of Italian Plaquettes* (1924). In 1913 Maclagan married Helen Elizabeth (1879–1942), daughter of Commander Frederick Canning Lascelles, second son of the fourth earl of Harewood. They had two sons, the younger of whom was killed in action in 1942.

In 1916 Maclagan was transferred temporarily to the Foreign Office and later to the Ministry of Information. He became head of the ministry's bureau in Paris and its controller for France in 1918, a post for which his fluent French especially fitted him. In 1919 he was attached to the British peace delegation and was present at the signing of the treaty. For his services in France, Maclagan was appointed CBE in 1919.

On the retirement of Sir Cecil Harcourt-Smith in 1924, Maclagan was appointed director of the Victoria and Albert Museum. During his twenty-one years in office the museum further increased its reputation as a centre for research and learning, to which Maclagan's monumental *Catalogue of Italian Sculpture*, produced in 1932 in collaboration with Margaret Longhurst, then assistant keeper in the department, bears witness. But the director's scholarly approach did not deflect him from an awareness of the growing interest of the general public in the resources of the museum. Under his influence important advances towards the popularization of the museum were made, not only in the increase of inexpensive publications such as a series of sixpenny picture books, including his own *Children in Sculpture* and *Portrait Busts*, and the organization of free public lectures, but also in various ways in which

Sir Eric Robert Dalrymple Maclagan (1879–1951), by Howard Coster, 1937

the vast collections could be made more accessible to people of general rather than specialized knowledge. A welcome innovation was the placing in the entrance hall each Monday of the 'object of the week'. Among the number of the learned articles, catalogues, and other erudite material which he produced, Maclagan was the author of one best-seller: an essay entitled *The Bayeux Tapestry*, published as a King Penguin in 1943. He was the first to envisage the system of rearranging the museum according to primary and secondary collections, thereby making the task of obtaining some impression of the museum as a whole a less formidable proposition for the general visitor. This reorganization proved impracticable in the financial climate of the thirties and was not realized until Sir Leigh Ashton reassembled the collections after 1945, when a new field of opportunity was opened and a fresh emphasis was placed upon the whole question of museum display.

During Maclagan's term of office, fresh interest was focused on the museum either by the acquisitions or by the series of distinguished exhibitions which he personally organized. These reflected the fastidious precision of his scholarship and the wide range of his perceptions as a connoisseur. Among the most outstanding were the exhibitions of works of art belonging to the livery companies of the City of London (1926), of English medieval art (1930), a landmark in its time, the William Morris centenary exhibition (1934), the exhibition of the Eumorfopoulos collection (1936), and the exhibition of sculptures which had been removed from Westminster Abbey during the Second World War (1945). Maclagan was knighted in 1933, and in 1945 he was appointed KCVO.

Maclagan held important appointments both at home and abroad. In 1927–8 he was Charles Eliot Norton professor at Harvard, his lectures, published in 1935 as *Italian Sculpture of the Renaissance*, representing, perhaps, his most important general work. He was vice-president of the Society of Antiquaries (1932–6), president of the Museums Association (1935–6), and chairman of the National Buildings Record. He was also appointed to lectureships at Edinburgh, Belfast, Dublin, and Hull, and was given honorary degrees at Birmingham (LLD, 1944) and Oxford (DLitt, 1945). As chairman of the fine arts committee of the British Council from 1941 Maclagan organized many exhibitions sent abroad by the council after the war, and went on several lecture tours abroad, including one to Canada in 1948 and one to South Africa in 1950. He was a gifted lecturer, was proficient in French and German, and until the end of his life read Greek and Latin for pleasure.

Maclagan's interests were varied and extended well beyond the confines of his specialization in the field of early Christian and Italian Renaissance art. He admired many modern artists and had in his possession a bust of himself by Meštrović. He was one of the first private collectors to buy the work of Henry Moore and unveiled the painting of the crucifixion by Graham Sutherland in the church of St Matthew at Northampton. A keen churchman and, after his retirement, a member of the church assembly, he took a prominent part in the affairs of the Anglo-Catholic movement; and he performed much public service on behalf of the church through the Cathedrals Advisory Council and the Central Council for the Care of Churches, which then had its headquarters in the Victoria and Albert Museum. Maclagan's knowledge of literature, especially of poetry, was profound; he could quote extensively, and at times amusingly, from poets both good and bad. He made several translations of the work of French poets, especially of Rimbaud and Valéry and, while an undergraduate, published a volume of poems, *Leaves in the Road* (1901), for which he designed the jacket. He also made a special study of Blake's *Prophetic Books* and with A. G. B. Russell published editions of *Jerusalem* (1904) and *Milton* (1907). He took an interest in book production and was one of the first to recognize the genius of Edward Johnston, on whose formal script he based his own handwriting. He designed several bookplates, including one for his friend Bernard Berenson.

Maclagan was an enthusiastic traveller. It was perhaps fitting that he should have died, suddenly, on 14 September 1951, in Spain, when making the ascent to see the church of Santa Cristina Pola de Lena. He was buried at the British cemetery at Bilbao.

TRENCHARD COX, rev. ANNE PIMLOTT BAKER

Sources *The Times* (17 Sept 1951) · *The Times* (22 Sept 1951) · *The Times* (25 Sept 1951) · *The Times* (11 Oct 1951) · Burke, *Peerage* · *WWW* · private information (1971) · personal knowledge (1971) · *CGPLA Eng. & Wales* (1951)

Archives Harvard U., letters to Bernard Berenson and Mary Berenson · Tate collection, corresp. with Lord Clark · U. Glas., letters to D. S. MacColl

Likenesses H. Coster, photograph, 1937, NPG [*see illus.*] · W. Stoneman, photograph, 1940, NPG · F. Dodd, charcoal drawing, 1944, V&A · H. Coster, photographs, NPG

Wealth at death £23,336 9s. 4d.: probate, 7 Dec 1951, *CGPLA Eng. & Wales*

McLagan, James (1728–1805), folklorist, was born at Ballechin, in Strathtay, Perthshire, in 1728. The birth or baptism of James, son of Donald McClagon, is recorded in the parish of Moulin, Perthshire, on 8 September 1728. He matriculated at the University of St Andrews in the 1750/51 session, and was ordained by the presbytery of Dunkeld in 1760. His first charge was the chapel of ease in Amulree, Perthshire. In 1764 he was appointed chaplain to the 42nd regiment (the Black Watch), which had originally been raised at Aberfeldy, Perthshire. He continued as chaplain until 1788; he served in the Isle of Man and was involved in the American War of Independence. The freedom of Glasgow was conferred on him in 1776. In 1788 he was admitted to the charge of Blair Atholl and Strowan, Perthshire, which he held until his death. In 1784 he married Catherine Stuart, daughter of James Stuart, the minister of Killin, who translated the New Testament into Gaelic (1767). She was half her husband's age in 1784, and they had a family of four sons and three daughters. Their eldest son, James, became professor of divinity at King's College, Aberdeen.

McLagan's great achievement was the collecting of Gaelic poems and songs, and Perthshire became the focus of this work. When he was interviewed in 1800 by John Leyden, the author of *Journal of a Tour in the Highlands and Western Islands of Scotland* (pp. 258–61), McLagan told him that he had made collections of Ossianic ballads while still at school and college. This suggests that his interest in Gaelic verse started before 1750, and may have been in part a reaction to the failure of the Jacobite rising of 1745, which had strong nationalist implications for some highlanders, including James Macpherson, the Ossianic poet. McLagan corresponded with Macpherson in 1760 and 1761, Macpherson having been told that McLagan had a good collection of the kind of ballads in which he was interested; in 1800 McLagan recalled that he had given Macpherson 'about thirteen poems'. In 1760–63 Macpherson published his supposed translations of ancient Gaelic heroic balladry.

McLagan was one of a group of men, mainly from Perthshire and Argyll, who made a sustained effort to record Gaelic poetry and song in the second half of the eighteenth century. Part of this effort was encouraged by the publicity and opposition engendered by Macpherson's publication. It is clear, however, that there was an earlier positive drive in addition to the post-1760 reactive one. Adam Ferguson, McLagan's predecessor as chaplain to the Black Watch, and later professor of philosophy at the University of Edinburgh, had shown some interest in Gaelic material, and put Macpherson in touch with Edinburgh friends who shared this interest. Jerome Stone collected ballads in the early 1750s; Donald MacNicol made a large collection of Gaelic poetry. Other close contemporaries, such as Joseph Macintyre from Glenorchy, Archibald Mac-Arthur from Glenlyon, and John Stuart from Killin (McLagan's brother-in-law), were also involved in Gaelic collection and writing, and sometimes collaborated with McLagan in such work.

McLagan maintained his interest in collecting Gaelic verse throughout his life. Just over a century after his death his collection, which had been preserved by his descendants, was given to Glasgow University Library. The surviving materials consist of 1650 pages, comprising some 630 separate items, largely anonymous and ascribed verse, with a small number of prose items. There are occasional Latin items, a small number of non-Gaelic verse items, a few prose items, genealogies, prayers, and so on. In many instances these manuscripts contain the earliest, or the only, examples of particular poems or songs, and they provide a highly valuable source. McLagan's material was drawn partly from indigenous Perthshire sources, including some manuscripts which are older than 1750. He also used his contacts, both ministerial and military, to acquire versions of poems and songs from other parts of Gaelic Scotland, such as Argyll with its islands, Ross-shire, Inverness-shire, Skye and the outer isles, and districts in Aberdeenshire and elsewhere that were still Gaelic-speaking in his time. Although this collection of manuscripts has been used by various editors over the years, at the end of the twentieth century much of it still remained to be fully exploited.

Publication of secular Gaelic writing may be said to have begun as late as 1751, with the appearance of Alasdair Mac Mhaighstir Alasdair's poems, and no doubt this was an additional stimulus for eighteenth-century collectors and writers. It is likely that McLagan provided some material for the book *Clan Feuds and Songs*, published by John Gillies in 1780, and he was closely involved with the same publisher's book of 1786, known generally as the *Gillies Collection*, though Gillies himself had little or no Gaelic expertise. In 1792 an article by McLagan on the parish of Blair Atholl and Strowan appeared in the *Statistical Account*, volume 2, in which he voiced warnings about the perceptible weakening of Gaelic in that area. It is indeed fortunate that he personally preserved so much of the verse tradition while it was still available. McLagan died at Blair Atholl on 3 May 1805. DERICK S. THOMSON

Sources memorandum in McLagan MSS., U. Glas., no. 252 · J. Leyden, *Journal of a tour in the highlands and western islands of Scotland*, ed. T. Girton (1903) · A. Cameron, *Reliquiae celticae* (1892) · D. S. Thomson, 'A catalogue and indexes of the Ossianic ballads in MacLagan MSS', *Scottish Gaelic Studies*, 8/2 (1958), 177–224 · D. Thomson, 'The McLagan MSS in Glasgow University Library', *Transactions of the Gaelic Society of Inverness*, 58 (1992–4), 406–24 · b. cert. · m. cert.
Archives U. Glas.

Maclagan, Myrtle Ethel (1911–1993), cricketer and soldier, was born on 2 April 1911 in Ambala, India, the elder daughter and second of four children of Robert Smeiton Maclagan (1860–1931), army officer, and his wife, Beatrice Ethel, *née* Duperier. She moved to Britain in 1919 and lived at Haileybury College, where her father became bursar

following his retirement as a colonel in the Royal Engineers. The family had a long connection with the Indian army. Both her grandparents, Robert Maclagan and Henry William Duperier, were generals. Maclagan was also a cousin of Sir Charles Oman, the historian. She was educated at the Royal School, Bath, from 1922 to 1929, captaining and playing in numerous sports teams. She was the youngest and smallest pupil there, but this did not inhibit her in any way. In a school cricket match against Cheltenham Ladies' College she took five wickets in five successive balls. She also won the senior and middle school maths prizes and the knitting prize. In 1929 she went on to the Harcombe House Domestic Science College, where she won a first-class certificate with the Devon board.

In 1931 Maclagan went to the Colwall cricket week and took ten wickets for 22 runs in her first match. Two years later she played for England against the rest and was selected for the first women's cricket team to tour Australia and New Zealand in 1934–5. On 7 January 1935 in Sydney she scored the very first women's test match century, reaching a total of 119. It was the second test of the series against Australia. During the first, in Brisbane the previous month, she had taken seven Australian wickets for just 11 runs, a record which stood until 1958. She also scored the first test match century in England, at Blackpool, when Australia made the return visit in 1937. She went on to become a legend of the game. In fourteen test matches she scored 1007 runs at an average of 41.9, and her 51 wickets came at a cost of 16.9 runs each. She became the first player to score 1000 runs and take 50 wickets in women's test match cricket. Also a brilliant fielder, she took twelve catches in tests. Although never happy in the role, she also captained England in two test matches in 1951, when Molly Hide was injured.

Maclagan's qualities were many but, as a batsman, she was a tower of strength and particularly difficult to dislodge. She saw it as her duty to be there when the first 50 of the innings was posted; in the twenty-five innings she played in test match cricket, she herself passed 50 eight times. She played her county cricket for Surrey, and was an imposing, perhaps daunting, figure. Her strength of character was exemplified when, at the age of fifty-two and having been retired from cricket for eleven years, she emerged to play for the combined services against the Australian touring side of 1963. It was, of course, no idle whim; Maclagan made 81 not out.

Maclagan, who had served in the ATS between 1939 and 1945, rejoined the army in 1951, and was appointed supervising officer for physical training, eastern command. In 1963 she was promoted major and stationed in Aldershot as inspector of physical training, Women's Royal Army Corps. She played hockey, cricket, tennis, squash, and badminton for the army. Army squash champion for six years, badminton champion for five, she captained the army and the combined services cricket elevens between 1952 and 1963.

In retirement Maclagan lived in Camberley, Surrey, and applied herself vigorously to her many hobbies, which included carpentry, metalwork, and gardening. Her way of life was spartan and she made no concession to age. She had a constant stream of visitors from all over the country and on her eightieth birthday so many people turned up to congratulate her that she had to make a speech from the top of a stepladder. This she announced with the blast of a whistle. She did not marry. She died of cancer at the Phylis Tuckwell Hospice, Farnham, Surrey, on 11 March 1993. There was a memorial service at the Royal Military Academy, Sandhurst, on 22 April 1993.

CAROL SALMON

Sources Women's Cricket Association · R. H. Flint and N. Rheinberg, *Fair play: the story of women's cricket* (1976) · J. L. Hawes, *Women's test cricket: the golden triangle, 1934–84* (1987) · A. Stanford and M. R. Collin, *99 not out: scorecards and statistics of women's test matches, 1934–1996* · *The Independent* (17 March 1993) · *The Times* (20 March 1993) · private information (2004) [sister] · *CGPLA Eng. & Wales* (1993)

Likenesses photograph, repro. in *The Independent* · photograph, repro. in *The Times*

Wealth at death £276,642: probate, 7 July 1993, *CGPLA Eng. & Wales*

Maclagan, William Dalrymple (1826–1910), archbishop of York, born in Edinburgh on 18 June 1826, was the fifth son of Dr David Maclagan, described as 'physician to the forces', who served with distinction as a medical officer in the Peninsular War, and was president of Royal College of Physicians and of the Royal College of Surgeons at Edinburgh. His mother was Jane, daughter of another physician, Dr Philip Whiteside, and granddaughter of Dr William Dalrymple of Ayr ('D'rymple Mild'). His eldest brother, Sir Andrew Douglas *Maclagan (1812–1900), also had a distinguished medical career.

William, after education at the Edinburgh high school, attended law classes in the university, and in 1846 became a pupil in the law office of Messrs Douglas & Co. In 1843 he left the presbyterianism of his family for the Scottish Episcopal church. After deciding not to pursue a legal career he sailed for India in February 1847, and in April landed at Madras, where he joined the 51st regiment of Madras native infantry. He retired in October 1849, when, having attained the rank of lieutenant, he came home invalided. He drew his modest military pension to the last. In later periods of his life there were signs of his training as a soldier and of the habit of both expecting and giving obedience which it had engendered.

In 1852 Maclagan went into residence at Peterhouse, Cambridge, graduating BA in 1857 as a junior optime in the mathematical tripos of the previous year. Among his college contemporaries was his lifelong friend George Thomas Palmer (1836–1908; later canon); out of college he was intimate with Henry Montagu Butler (later master of Trinity College, Cambridge). On Trinity Sunday 1856 he was ordained and was licensed to the curacy of St Saviour's, Paddington. From 1858 he served as curate at St Stephen's (Avenue Road), Marylebone, until 1 January 1860, when he became organizing secretary of the London Diocesan Church Building Society, in which capacity his power of organization first found scope. Shortly before this he had issued a popular tract, *Will you be Confirmed? A Word to the Young. By a London Curate* (1859). In April 1860 he married Sarah Kate (*d.* July 1862), daughter of George

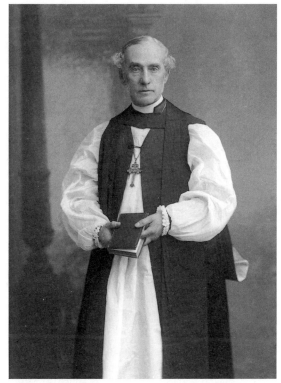

William Dalrymple Maclagan (1826–1910), by Bassano, 1895

Clapham; they had two sons. From 1865 to 1869 he was curate-in-charge at Enfield, where some of the first parochial missions were held during his tenure of office.

In September 1869 Maclagan was appointed by the lord chancellor, Lord Hatherley, to the rectory of the large south London parish of Newington, where he remained until 1875. His predecessor had been non-resident, and Maclagan's determination to recover the lapsed right of the rector to chair meetings of the vestry brought him into conflict with many parishioners, among whom dissenters were numerous. A dispute concerning compensation to the church arising from a road-widening scheme exposed him to personal attack. His labours in Newington were commemorated by an east window in the little mission church of St Gabriel, the building of which on the site of the old parish church had at first aroused local controversy. Always a moderate high-churchman, Maclagan in 1870 and 1872 edited with Archibald Weir, vicar of Forty Hill, Enfield, two series of essays entitled *The Church and the Age*, treating of the 'principles and position' of the Church of England. To the earlier series Maclagan contributed an essay, 'The church and the people', which is distinguished by its candid and optimistic tone, but still more by a characteristic determination to apply direct and practical remedies to the alienation of the working classes from the church and her services. In 1873 he visited Rome and Naples with Weir in the interests of his health. In 1875 he was transferred to the living of St Mary Abbots, Kensington, where his renown as a parish clergyman and as the organizer of parochial religious agencies rapidly rose. In

1876 he declined Lord Beaconsfield's offer of the bishopric of Calcutta, but in 1878, after being named a prebendary of St Paul's Cathedral and chaplain-in-ordinary to Queen Victoria, he accepted the bishopric of Lichfield, vacant by the death of George Augustus Selwyn.

Maclagan was enthroned at Lichfield Cathedral on 11 July 1878, and married later in that year the Hon. Augusta Anne Barrington, youngest daughter of William Keppel Barrington, sixth Viscount Barrington. His wife's powers of organization well matched his own. Practical work and efficient discharge of pastoral duties distinguished his episcopate. He brought his clergy together in synods and retreats, and directed the aid of the laity into various concurrent channels. In the late 1880s his diocese was one of the first to adopt the Mothers' Union as one of its organizations. He was also keen to establish diocesan missions. He issued many letters to the diocese in the *Lichfield Diocesan Magazine*, the most important of them being a series addressed 'Ad clerum'. *Pastoral Letters and Synodal Charges*, a volume published by him in 1892, notably illustrates his general spirit of moderation and gentle sympathy. In October 1887, at the request of Archbishop Benson and in company with John Wordsworth, bishop of Salisbury, he attended a conference of Old Catholics at Bonn, where he had an interview with Döllinger. In 1890 he testified in a different way to his desire for unity among Christians by welcoming a body of nonconformists to his palace and to the cathedral service, a proceeding which in 1895 he repeated at Bishopthorpe. Similarly, in an address on Christian brotherhood in 1904, he advocated the admission of nonconformists to holy communion. He showed himself to be conservative, however, in the matter of biblical criticism in 1889–90, and in 1894 publicly supported the widening of church defence efforts.

In 1891 Archbishop William Connor Magee died after only two months' tenure of the see of York, and Lord Salisbury offered the archbishopric to Maclagan. He was confirmed at St George's, Hanover Square, and was enthroned in the minster on 15 September 1891. At York he worked on the same lines which he had followed at Lichfield. He introduced the same regulations restricting the preaching of deacons which he had promulgated there; he also established guilds of youths inclined to pastoral life. In 1892 he established at York a training college for clergy under the name of Scholae Episcopi and presided over the first house of laity in the convocation of his province, though the laity had actually been summoned to attend by his predecessor, Archbishop Magee. From 1892 onwards he spent much time in visiting his clergy, and within three years became personally acquainted with the 650 parishes of his diocese. He was generous in diocesan gifts, more especially to the Poor Benefices Fund, which he started; on two occasions—in 1897 and in 1906—he offered to surrender £2000 of his annual income in order to facilitate the subdivision of his diocese. He discouraged advanced ritualistic usages, from the practisers of which his chief troubles as a bishop proceeded. In 1889 and 1890 he took part in the hearing at Lambeth of the charges against Edward King, bishop of Lincoln, and was

in full accordance with the policies of both Archbishop Benson and his successor, Archbishop Frederick Temple. A protracted struggle with Sir Edmund Beckett, Lord Grimthorpe, vicar-general of his province and chancellor of his archdiocese, who insisted on the issue of licences to guilty divorcees, ended only in 1900 when Grimthorpe was succeeded in these offices by Sir Alfred Cripps.

Maclagan was responsible, with Archbishop Temple, for the substance if not for the form of the 'Responsio' made in 1896 to the bull *Apostolicae curae*, in which Pope Leo XIII had denied the validity of Anglican orders. In the following year, accompanied by W. J. Birkbeck, he paid a private visit to Russia, where he was cordially received by the authorities of the Russian church as well as by the Tsar Nicholas II and the tsarina.

In 1899–1901 he and Archbishop Temple met at Lambeth Palace and issued the Lambeth judgment. This, an attempt to reduce extreme ritualistic practice in the Church of England, declared that the use of incense and reservation of the sacrament were illegal in that church. While it was not without effect, the archbishops' judgment did little to quieten the liturgical turmoil which had produced it and which continued for some years after it.

At the coronation of Edward VII in 1902 Maclagan crowned Queen Alexandra, although it was decided that this function appertained to the archbishop of York by grace rather than by right. In 1906 Maclagan celebrated the eightieth year of his life, and the fiftieth of his ministry, by a special offering of £2000 for charitable purposes. But his physical powers—especially those of memory—were then declining, and in the autumn of 1908, after taking a passive part in the Lambeth conference and many meetings incidental to the Pan-Anglican Congress, he resigned his archbishopric (thereby setting a precedent). At the beginning of 1909 he made his home at 15 Queen's Gate Place, London, where, after a short illness, he died on 19 September 1910. He was buried in Bishopthorpe churchyard. His wife and (from this marriage) a son, Eric Robert Dalrymple *Maclagan, and a daughter survived him, together with Revd Walter Douglas Dalrymple Maclagan (1862–1929), a son of his first marriage.

Maclagan's pastoral activity was notable. Although his literary style was pure and clear, and he published a considerable number of theological and pastoral addresses and essays, he never attained great renown as a preacher. Late in life he prefixed a brief essay to an edition of *The Grace of Sacraments* (1905) by Alexander Knox, a forerunner of the Tractarians. In 1855 he published for private circulation a small volume of sonnets and other short poems. But those of his writings which have lived longest are his hymns. Among them is the beautiful hymn for All Saints' day, 'The Saints of God', and two Good Friday hymns which are in *Hymns Ancient and Modern*. He also composed the tunes of a number of hymns in the same volume.

A. W. WARD, *rev.* IAN MACHIN

Sources F. D. How, *Archbishop Maclagan: being a memoir of William Dalrymple Maclagan DD, Archbishop of York* (1911) · *The Times* (20 Sept 1910), 11 · O. Chadwick, *The Victorian church*, 2nd edn, 2 vols. (1970–

72) • G. I. T. Machin, *Politics and the churches in Great Britain, 1869 to 1921* (1987) • *VCH Staffordshire*, 3.81–9 • private information (1912)
Archives Borth. Inst., official corresp. and papers | Borth. Inst., corresp. with second Viscount Halifax • LPL, corresp. with E. W. Benson • LPL, corresp. with A. C. Tait • LPL, corresp. with Frederick Temple • LPL, letters to F. A. White
Likenesses H. von Herkomer, oils, exh. RA 1892, Diocese of Lichfield; replica, Bishopthorpe Palace, York • Bassano, photograph, 1895, NPG [*see illus.*] • Maull & Fox, photograph, 1901, repro. in How, *Archbishop Maclagan* • A. U. Soord, oils, 1903, St William's College, York • J. Collier, oils, 1909, Peterhouse, Cambridge • E. A. Abbey, group portrait, oils (*The coronation of King Edward VII, 1902*), Royal Collection • E. A. Abbey, oil study (for the *Coronation of Edward VII*, 1904), Yale U. • S. P. Hall, group portrait, watercolour (*The bench of bishops, 1902*), NPG • Lock & Whitfield, woodburytype photograph, NPG; repro. in T. Cooper, *Men of mark: a gallery of contemporary portraits* (1881) • W. Richmond, portrait • Rotary Photo, postcard, NPG • Spy [L. Ward], cartoon, repro. in *VF* (5 Sept 1891) • photographs, repro. in How, *Archbishop Maclagan*
Wealth at death £17,541 19s. 8d.: resworn probate, 12 Oct 1910, CGPLA Eng. & Wales

McLaglen, Victor Andrew de Bier (1886–1959), film actor, was born on 10 December 1886 at 505 Commercial Road, Mile End, London, the eldest of the eight sons of an Anglican clergyman, Andrew Charles Alfred McLaglen, later bishop of Clermont, South Africa, and his wife, Lily Marian Adcock. Several of his brothers also appeared in films, with varying success. In 1900, lying about his age but impressing with his size, he joined the Life Guards, hoping to fight in the Second South African War. He did serve for some time but without leaving England, even becoming regimental boxing champion, before his father bought his release. He went to Canada where he worked as a labourer, a wrestler, a railroad policeman, and a professional prize-fighter. McLaglen graduated to exhibition boxing in circuses, vaudeville, and Wild West shows when touring in the United States—once going six rounds with world heavyweight champion Jack Johnson. He went to Australia and joined the Kalgoorlie gold rush, travelled to Tahiti, Fiji, and Ceylon, and was physical training instructor to the raja of Akola in India. Early in 1914 he went to South Africa where his father was bishop of Clermont, near Durban. At the outbreak of war he returned to Britain and joined the Irish fusiliers. With a lieutenant's commission he served in the Middle East. McLaglen was wounded twice, led the British espionage organization in Baghdad, and became the city's assistant provost marshal. He was demobbed with the rank of captain.

In 1919 McLaglen returned to Britain where on 28 October he married Enid Mary (d. 1942), daughter of Albert Charles Lamont, a stock exchange clerk. They had a son, the film director Andrew V. McLaglen (b. 1920), and a daughter. McLaglen returned to boxing but after being seen by a producer in a bout at the National Sporting Club, London, he was offered the lead in a film, *The Call of the Road* (1920). This comedy romance was the best British picture of the year, and McLaglen, who had accepted the part 'for fun', became an instant success. Over a dozen films followed (1921–3) and he quickly became one of Britain's most popular stars. After a slump in the British film industry in 1924 he was pleased to receive a Hollywood offer to appear in *The Beloved Brute*. 'It was thus, afterwards, that publicity depicted him: He was a big, grinning man, typecast throughout a long career as a tough NCO with a heart of gold' (Shipman, 387). Several successful films at different studios followed, but *The Winds of Chance* (1925) won him a contract at First National. That year, although on loan to Fox in a supporting role, he made his first film for the director John Ford, *The Fighting Heart*. On loan again, this time to Paramount Studios, he appeared in *Beau Geste* (1926), but another loan-out to Fox, for Raoul Walsh's *What Price Glory?* (1926), made him a star. The film was based on the play by Maxwell Anderson and Laurence Stallings, the amorous exploits of McLaglen as Captain Flagg and Edmund Lowe as Sergeant Quirt replacing the play's anti-war sentiments, and it was a big success. As a result Fox bought his contract although he only featured in his next film, *Mother Machree* (1927, released 1928), again for John Ford.

McLaglen's next big success was *A Girl in Every Port* (1928), directed by Howard Hawks. Two more films directed by John Ford, *Hangman's House* (1928) and *Strong Boy* (1929), followed, and it was for Ford that McLaglen made his first talkie, *The Black Watch* (1929). Although this was a good film, his next, Raoul Walsh's *The Cock-Eyed World* (1929), a 'Flagg and Quirt reunion', was a huge success, the year's third highest grossing film. But more formula films followed, and although von Sternberg's *Dishonored* (1931), with Marlene Dietrich, was notable, another Flagg and Quirt film, *Women of All Nations* (also 1931), was not. Nor were McLaglen and Lowe's next teamings, *Guilty as Hell* (1932) and the last Flagg and Quirt film, *Hot Pepper* (1933). Although McLaglen had starred with Jeanette MacDonald in *Annabelle's Affairs* and with Elissa Landi in *Wicked* (both 1931), it seemed that his career was suddenly on the slide.

McLaglen became an American citizen in 1933, but after leaving Fox he soon found himself in Britain as the eponymous 'hero' in *Dick Turpin* (1933). John Ford offered a lifeline, casting him as the one survivor of *The Lost Patrol* (1934), one of his best roles. Although it helped to re-establish him, there was nothing special about the films which followed. These included *No More Women* (1934), *The Great Hotel Murder*, and *Under Pressure* (both 1935), all co-starring Lowe. Lewis Milestone's *The Captain Hates the Sea* (1935) was also disappointing. Again it was Ford who came to the rescue, casting McLaglen in *The Informer* (1935), based on Liam O'Flaherty's novel. He played Gypo Nolan, a man torn between greed and loyalty during the Irish rising of 1922. Although he never liked the role, it won him an Academy award as best actor. But better roles which followed, in *Professional Soldier*, with Freddie Bartholomew, Walsh's *Klondike Annie*, with Mae West, and *Under Two Flags*, with Ronald Colman (all 1936), *This is My Affair*, with Barbara Stanwyck, and Ford's *Wee Willie Winkie*, with Shirley Temple (both 1937), were punctuated by *The Magnificent Brute* (1936), *Sea Devils* and *Nancy Steel is Missing* (both 1937), and *The Battle of Broadway* and *The Devil's Party* (both 1938).

In Britain again, McLaglen co-starred in Gracie Fields's

first international venture, *We're Going to be Rich* (1938), but it was disappointing. For the next ten years the majority of his films were also either disappointing or average, although he loved the part of Sergeant MacChesney in the excellent *Gunga Din* (1939). Other highlights of this period were his role in *Captain Fury* (1939), and guest appearances in the star-studded *Forever and a Day* (1943) and in *The Princess and the Pirate* (1944). In the later 1940s McLaglen was again cast by John Ford. He played a tough but lovable Irish sergeant in Ford's splendid US cavalry trilogy, *Fort Apache* (1948), *She Wore a Yellow Ribbon* (1949), and *Rio Grande* (1950). These were followed by Ford's *The Quiet Man* (1952) in which his role as Red Will Danaher won him an Academy award nomination as best supporting actor.

In 1943 McLaglen married his secretary, Suzanne M. Brueggeman; they were divorced in 1948. In that year he married Margaret Pumphrey. In 1936 he had formed a semi-militaristic riding and polo club, the Light Horse brigade, and a similarly styled precision motorcycle team, the Victor McLaglen Motorcycle Corps. His claim that they could be considered a 'government unit' in the event of war led to accusations of his being pro-fascist, although facts proved otherwise. McLaglen strongly supported the Motion Picture and Television Fund, which catered for the industry's sick and needy. He owed $250,000 in unpaid taxes in 1945, but successfully fought his way back from bankruptcy. At the McLaglen ranch at Clovis near Fresno in the San Joaquin valley, California, he raised horses and farmed, particularly fruit trees and grapevines. *Express to Hollywood* (1934), his autobiography, depicted his early film career.

McLaglen's final films included a cameo appearance in *Around the World in Eighty Days* (1956) and the lead in one of his son's first films, *The Abductors* (1957). By now McLaglen was having difficulty remembering his lines. His last film was *Sea Fury* (1958), made in Britain; he was Stanley Baker's rival for Luciana Paluzzi, forty-five years his junior. He died in Newport Beach, California, of a heart attack on 7 November 1959, and was interred at Forest Lawn Memorial Park, Glendale, California. McLaglen's third wife survived him.   ROBERT SHARP

Sources D. Shipman, *The great movie stars: the golden years* (1970) · S. Lesser, 'McLaglen, Victor', *DAB* · *The Times* (9 Nov 1959), 14 · E. Katz, *The international film encyclopedia* (1982), 758 · b. cert. · m. cert. [Enid Mary Lamont]
Archives Academy of Motion Picture Arts and Sciences, Beverly Hills, California, Margaret Herrick Library, collection of clippings and press releases
Likenesses photographs, Hult. Arch.

Maclaine, Archibald (1722–1804), Presbyterian minister and historian, was born in Monaghan, Ireland, the elder son of Thomas Maclaine (d. 1740), Presbyterian minister, and his wife, Elizabeth (d. c.1735), daughter of James Milling. James *Maclaine (1724–1750), the 'gentleman highwayman', was his younger brother. In 1739 Maclaine matriculated at the University of Glasgow in the second year of the recognized course of classics, philosophy, and theology that was taken by students intending to enter

the ministry. He attended the prelections of the philosopher Francis Hutcheson and would have heard the theological lectures of William Leechman, a protégé of Hutcheson who became professor of divinity in 1743. He graduated MA in 1746 and became assistant to his uncle Robert Milling, who was minister of the Scots Presbyterian church in The Hague. The following year he became his colleague and on Milling's death in 1752 he succeeded as sole minister in charge of the congregation. He remained in this post until compelled by ill health to retire on 28 June 1796. On 23 April 1758 he married Esther Wilhelmina (1736–1789), daughter of Charles Chais (1701–1785), minister of the Walloon congregation in The Hague and a native of Geneva. Maclaine collaborated with his father-in-law, a scholarly man, in several bibliographic and literary projects. Chais may have provided openings for Maclaine to both royal and scholarly circles in The Hague: for a time Maclaine gave English lessons to the crown prince, later William III, and to his mother, Princess Wilhelmina; he also corresponded with the director of the 'cabinet for natural history and art' of the stadholder, Arnot Wosman.

Maclaine's primary contribution to scholarship centred on his work as a translator of theological and philosophical works. In 1753 he published at London his translation, *Dialogues on some Important Subjects Drawn up after the Manner of Socrates*, of the work by J. J. Vernet. More significant was his translation of Johann Lorenz von Mosheim's *Institutiones historiae ecclesiasticae antiquae et recentioris*, the first definitive edition of which had been published at Helmstadt in 1755. Maclaine was attracted to the modern, pragmatic method that Mosheim brought to his history of the Christian church, and in the dedication and preface to his translation he praises Mosheim for discarding the 'unhappy Spirit of Fanaticism' and for his 'impartiality' in a work that 'breathes a spirit of moderation and freedom' (A. Maclaine, *An Ecclesiastical History, Ancient and Modern from the Birth of Christ to the Beginning of the Present Century ... Translated from the Original*, 2 vols., 1765, vii, viii, xiii). Maclaine quickly made a name for himself with the translation, first published in London in 1765, and republished many times subsequently, and he was awarded a DD from his own university within two years of its publication. Maclaine did not, however, aim to provide a merely literal translation of Mosheim's ground-breaking work for he incorporated a number of annotations, both to qualify and to amplify the author's statements. Maclaine's annotations, which amply demonstrate his own considerable knowledge of the primary material, aroused great interest in Europe and were incorporated into the German, French, and Dutch translations of the history.

Maclaine's thorough knowledge of contemporary philosophy is evident in several of his other publications, such as *A Series of Letters Addressed to Soane Jenyns esq. on Occasion of his View of the Internal Evidence of Christianity* (1777), in which he discusses the problems arising from biblical miracles, and the *Discourses on Various Subjects Delivered in the English Church at The Hague* (1799). His acceptance of a rational and 'enlightened' approach to religious belief did not, however, lead to a rejection or even a weakening of his adherence to the protestantism in which he had been brought up and educated. In the first of three appendices which he added to the second edition (1768) of his Mosheim translation, he refutes the charge of fanaticism laid against the Reformation by David Hume in his *History of England*, by maintaining that, as a consequence of its essential principles, the Reformation had introduced religious liberty to all as a natural right as well as establishing for all the 'unalienable right of private judgment' (A. Maclaine, *An Ecclesiastical History*, new edn, 2 vols., 1842, 2.522). He praises the protestant reformers for having recourse to reason and argument, to the rules of sound criticism, and to the authority and light of history. In his view, they had exhorted Christians to judge for themselves, to search the scriptures, and to assert the liberty of conscience.

The second of Maclaine's appendices was published in response to Francis Blackburne's *The Confessional* (1766) and sets out his observations on the positive influences of the contemporary 'improvements in philosophy and science' on the propagation and advancement of protestantism (A. Maclaine, *An Ecclesiastical History*, 1842, 2.525). The third appendix was also prompted in part by Blackburne, who had cast aspersions on Archbishop William Wake's correspondence with certain Gallican divines. Although he was principally concerned to correct Mosheim's inaccurate account of this correspondence, Maclaine was supplied with Wake's letters by Archbishop Thomas Secker in order to defend Wake's position.

That Maclaine was, in his day, as highly regarded in Europe as in Britain as a scholar is amply demonstrated by the fact that his translation formed the basis of other vernacular translations and that his notes were incorporated in these works. He enjoyed good relations with Jean Neaulme, the French publisher and bookseller in The Hague and Amsterdam who had published J.-J. Rousseau's *Émile* and invited Maclaine to prepare a critical edition of the work in 1762, which he declined to undertake for family reasons.

After fifty years in The Hague, Maclaine retired to Bath where he died on 25 November 1804. He was buried in the abbey, later that month, where a memorial plaque, repositioned in the Victorian period inside the north-west door, describes him as 'Ingenius, Eruditus, Pius, aeque suavitate morum, ac fama Scientiae praeclara, fuit Ornatus'.

JAMES K. CAMERON

Sources A. De Groot, 'Maclaine, Archibald', *Biografisch lexicon voor de geschiedenis van het nederlandse protestantisme*, ed. D. Nauta and others, 1 (Kampen, 1978), 149–50 · A. J. Van der Aa, *Biographisch woordenboek der Nederlanden*, Haarlem (1869), vol. 12, pp. 37–8 · *Fasti Scot.*, new edn · M. M. Kleerkoper and W. P. van Stockum, *De boekhandel te Amsterdam, voornamelijk in de 17e eeuw*, 13 pts in 2 vols. (The Hague, 1914–16) · P. C. Molhuysen and P. J. Blok, eds., *Nieuw Nederlandsch biografisch woordenboek*, 10 vols. (Leiden, 1911–37) · W. I. Addison, *A roll of graduates of the University of Glasgow from 31st December 1727 to 31st December 1897* (1898) · W. I. Addison, ed., *The matriculation albums of the University of Glasgow from 1728 to 1858* (1913) · J. Coutts, *A history of the University of Glasgow* (1909) · J. D. Mackie, *The University of Glasgow, 1451–1951: a short history* (1954) · N. Sykes, *From Sheldon to Secker* (1959) · memorial plaque, Bath Abbey · J. S. Oyer, 'Mosheim, Johann Lorenz von (1694/5–1755)', *Theologische Realenzyklopädie*, ed. G. Krause, G. Müller, and S. Schwertner, 23 (Berlin, 1994), 365–7 · E. Stöve, 'Kirchengeschichtesschreibung', in G. Müller, *Theologische Realenzyklopädie*, ed. G. Krause and S. Schwertner, 18 (Berlin, 1989), 540–50 · *DNB*

Archives University of Leiden, letters | Kon. Huis archiv, The Hague, letters to the princess and crown prince · priv. coll., letters to Lord Lansdowne

Likenesses C. H. Hodges, mezzotint, 1796, BM

Maclaine [Maclean], **James** (1724–1750), highwayman, was born in Monaghan, Ireland, youngest son of the Revd Thomas Maclaine (d. 1740), a Presbyterian minister of 'very honourable' highland Scottish descent, and Elizabeth, *née* Milling (d. c.1735), daughter of a reputable local family (*Complete History*, 5). James was the black sheep of an otherwise unexceptionable family: at the time of his execution his sister, Anne Jane, was a spinster 'living in repute' (*Complete History*, 5) in Monaghan, while his elder brother, Archibald *Maclaine, was a distinguished Calvinist minister and later a scholar of some note. James, in contrast, though educated to be a merchant, evinced such an 'Aversion to mechanic Employment' (ibid.) that after his father's death in November 1740 he soon squandered an inheritance which, while modest, was sufficient to have procured him a place in a Dutch counting-house.

Accounts of the next few years of Maclaine's life are often suspiciously picaresque and repetitious, involving numerous schemes to marry heiresses or to inveigle money from relatives or unnamed benefactresses. However, there is general agreement that within two years of his father's death Maclaine was left with no other recourse but to hire himself out, first, as a footman, and later as a butler to one Colonel Tonson of Dunkettle. We are told that the former situation accorded so ill with Maclaine's notion of his own quality that master and man soon parted ways; as for the latter, Maclaine was dismissed after 'making too free with the Colonel's Cellar' (*Complete History*, 10; *Genuine Account*, 6). Maclaine then spent some months out of place, subsisting on occasional remittances from his brother until he was able to prevail upon his old master, Tonson, to allow him to accompany him to England.

According to Maclaine's own account he arrived in London around the summer of 1743, ostensibly with the intention of enlisting in the military, and, reputedly, he obtained a small sum from the colonel on condition that he join the Horse Guards. Maclaine's martial ardour cooled immediately, and, after supposedly raising a 'charitable Contribution of 50 pounds under pretence of shipping himself to the West Indies'—a sum which was invested instead in 'fine Cloathes'—James successfully 'made Suit' to one Miss Maclogen, the daughter of a substantial innkeeper and horsedealer, with a fortune of £500 (*The Ordinary of Newgate's Account*, 87). They married some time in late 1744 or early 1745, setting up a grocer's shop in Welbeck Street.

For the next several years Maclaine enjoyed the reputation of an honest tradesman, even if his taste for finery and display gradually 'obliged him to encroach upon his Capital' (*Complete History*, 13). After his wife's death about 1748, James—after consigning his two daughters (only the

The Ladies Hero or the Unfortunate James McLeane Esqr

James Maclaine (1724–1750), by unknown engraver

elder of whom would survive him) to the care of his mother-in-law—left off trade, sold what was left of his stock, and, taking fashionable lodgings in Dean Street, Soho, set up for a fine gentleman. Indeed, Maclaine made such a figure that he was obliged to move his quarters to Hyde Park Corner when his mother-in-law began to enquire how he lived and suggest that he contribute to his children's maintenance (*Genuine Account*, 9; *Complete History*, 14).

Some six or eight months after his wife's death Maclaine was again reduced to begging for handouts from his brother, who 'raised sixty guineas by Subscription to fit him out for Jamaica' (*Complete History*, 16). But on the eve of his departure Maclaine sealed his doom when he attended a masquerade and lost all his money at the gaming tables (Allen, 26). Ashamed to show his face he yielded to the persuasion of William Plunket, an equally 'necessitous' journeyman apothecary, to go 'upon the Highway for a recruit' (*Complete History*, 17, 18; Allen, 14; *Genuine Account*, 9). The pair donned Venetian masks and robbed a grazier on Hounslow Heath; over the course of the next six months they went on to commit fifteen or sixteen robberies on the outskirts of London (*Complete History*, 21). Maclaine would later claim that Plunket was the 'acting Person' in all their undertakings, as his own conscience rendered him unable to 'utter a Word, nor to draw his Pistol' (*Genuine Account*, 11; Allen, 5; *Complete History*, 18).

Such was hardly the case on the evening of 8 November 1749, when the pair stopped Horace Walpole's coach in Hyde Park and Maclaine's pistol accidentally went off near Walpole's cheek, 'scorching his face' (*Daily Advertiser*, 10 Nov 1749). When Walpole advertised a reward of 20 guineas for the return of his watch and seals, Maclaine sent him a letter 'compounded of threats and apologies', offering to sell back his things for 40 guineas, and appointing the gallows at Tyburn for their meeting; Walpole declining terms and 'rendezvous' alike, Maclaine returned the items for the sum originally advertised (Walpole, *Corr.*, 13.23n., 40.65; *The World*, 19 Dec 1754, 317).

Maclaine had in the meantime taken 'handsome Lodgings' in St James's Street, where he 'passed for an Irish gentleman of £700 a year'—mixing so freely with polite society (including many 'Women of Fortune and Reputation') that, as Walpole drily noted, his face 'was as known … as any gentleman's who lives in that quarter' (*GM*, 20, Sept 1750; *The Ordinary of Newgate's Account*, 88; Walpole, *Corr.*, 20.168). As late as spring 1750 Maclaine still had hopes of retrieving his fortunes by marriage; however, he was thwarted in his designs on a 'young Lady of Fortune of Chelsea' (where he kept a 'country lodging') when an officer acquainted her family with 'Mac's Character' (*Genuine Account*, 16, 15). The said captain then refused to fight a duel with the irate Maclaine on the grounds that he was no gentleman—a point the latter failed to carry even after producing a letter testifying to 'his being born a Gentleman' (ibid.).

Maclaine would soon face exposure of a more dramatic kind. In the small hours of 26 June 1750 he and Plunket robbed the passengers of the Salisbury stagecoach of their money and trunks; and later that same night relieved Lord Eglinton of his purse and blunderbuss. Maclaine was then 'so infatuated' (*Complete History*, 52) as to sell some of the clothes they had robbed from Josiah Higden, a passenger on the Salisbury coach, even after the latter had published descriptions of the stolen items. After a narrow escape from a lacemaker who recognized some gold lace which he had himself, coincidentally, sold to Higden, Maclaine was apprehended when Higden identified his belongings in the shop where Maclaine had not only sold them, but had inexplicably left his name and address. On 27 July Maclaine was arrested at his lodgings and committed to the Westminster Gatehouse. A search of his rooms revealed a pair of loaded pistols, a wealth of stolen items—including '21 purses of various kinds … all crammed into one'—and (it was rumoured) 'a famous kept Mistress' (*London Magazine*, August 1750; Walpole, *Corr.*, 20.169).

The conversation of the town was suddenly engrossed by the so-called 'gentleman highwayman' who, according to Walpole, generated 'as many prints and pamphlets [as] the [Lisbon] earthquake' (*Genuine Account*, iv; Walpole, *Corr.*, 20.188). The newspapers described Maclaine as a 'tall handsome, well-made man', 'very genteel … and very gay in his dress'; less sympathetic observers demoted him to 'middle Size', noting his pockmarked, if 'broad open Countenance' (*London Magazine*, August 1750; *Whitehall Evening-Post*, 26–8 July 1750; *The Ordinary of Newgate's Account*, 84). On 1 July, despite having been cautioned that he needed to impeach two or more accomplices to be eligible for a pardon, Maclaine none the less delivered a fulsome confession to Justice Thomas Lediard, implicating only Plunket and himself in many robberies (one newspaper quoted the number as thirty-three). While recounting the Walpole robbery Maclaine wept and appeared so concerned that many of the 'Persons of Distinction' who had crowded in to hear his examination were moved to tears, 'especially the Ladies'—one of whom later claimed that Maclaine 'had often been around her House, and she never miss'd any Thing' (*GM*, September 1750; *Whitehall Evening-Post*, 31 July–2 Aug 1750; *Genuine Account*, 22–3). Upon Maclaine's pleading poverty, moreover, 'several Persons [made] him considerable Presents' (*Genuine Account*, 23).

Maclaine was removed to Newgate on 7 September, and tried at the Old Bailey on the morning of 13 September for robbing Josiah Higden. Maclaine, who had retracted his earlier confession, presented but a feeble defence, claiming that the stolen goods found in his lodgings had been given to him by Plunket in repayment of a loan (Plunket himself remained at large). Maclaine called to the bar 'nine gentlemen of credit, who gave him a very good character'; without leaving the court the jury brought in a verdict of guilty (*Proceedings*, 12–14 Sept 1750). Several newspapers reported pathetically on the fact that before being sentenced to death Maclaine attempted to speak but 'his excessive Grief … deny'd him Utterance' (*London Evening-Post*, 18–20 Sept 1750).

After his condemnation thousands of curious visitors thronged to Newgate to view the gentleman highwayman; none the less, public opinion seemed to be hardening against Maclaine. Some commentators dismissed his pretensions to gentility as impudence and affectation; his tears of remorse as cowardice rather than sensibility (*The Ordinary of Newgate's Account*, 89). Maclaine was held up by moralists as a warning to those 'in humbler Stations … not to affect a Taste and Appearance above themselves', and by satirists as an illustration that 'true politeness'—that is, 'the art of reducing vice [to]' a 'civil commerce'—had made such advances in England that thieves and gentlemen had become indistinguishable (*Complete History*, 54; Allen, 25; *The World*, 19 Dec 1754).

According to all accounts Maclaine cut a better figure as a penitent than he had as a highwayman. On 3 October 1750, while being drawn in the cart from Newgate to Tyburn, he remained 'stedfast in his Devotion' despite the 'Gaze of the Multitude'. After reaching the place of execution Maclaine 'went through the whole awful Scene with a manly Firmness, join'd with all the Appearances of true Devotion' (*Complete History*, 64; Allen, 24). His body was buried two days later at Uxbridge. A representation of Maclaine's body appeared in February 1751 as a skeleton hanging opposite that of the pugilist and criminal James Field in William Hogarth's depiction of the Royal College of Physicians from the final plate of *The Four Stages of Cruelty*. ANDREA MCKENZIE

Sources DNB · *Daily Advertiser* [London] (10–11 Nov 1749) · *Daily Advertiser* [London] (13 Nov 1749) · *Daily Advertiser* [London] (18 Nov 1749) · *GM*, 1st ser., 20 (1750) · *London Evening-Post* (6–8 Sept 1750) · *London Evening-Post* (13–15 Sept 1750) · *London Evening-Post* (18–22 Sept 1750) · *London Evening-Post* (27–9 Sept 1750) · *London Magazine*, 18 (1749), 526 · *London Magazine*, 19 (1750), 474 · *Penny London Post* (27–30 July 1750) · *Penny London Post* (30 July–1 Aug 1750) · *Penny London Post* (15–17 Sept 1750) · *Penny London Post* (26–8 Sept 1750) · *Penny London Post* (3–5 Oct 1750) · *Penny London Post* (5–8 Oct 1750) · *Read's Weekly Journal, or, British Gazetteer* (22 Sept 1750) · *Read's Weekly Journal, or, British Gazetteer* (5 Oct 1750) · *Whitehall Evening-Post, or, London Intelligencer* (26–8 July 1750) · *Whitehall Evening-Post, or, London Intelligencer* (31 July–2 Aug 1750) · *Whitehall Evening-Post, or, London Intelligencer* (11–20 Sept 1750) · *Whitehall Evening-Post, or, London Intelligencer* (25–7 Sept 1750) · *Whitehall Evening-Post, or, London Intelligencer* (2–4 Oct 1750) · F. Allen, *An account of the behaviour of Mr. James Maclaine* (1750) · *A complete history of James Maclean, the gentleman highwayman* [1750] · *A genuine account of the life and actions of James Maclean, highwayman* [1750] · *The proceedings … at Justice Hall at the Old Bailey* (12 Sept 1750), 122–4 · [J. Taylor], *The ordinary of Newgate's account of the behaviour, confession, and dying words of the twelve malefactors who were executed at Tyburn on Wednesday the 3d [sic] of October 1750* (1750) · A. Fitz-Adam, 'The "visiting highwayman"', *The World* (19 Dec 1754), 313–18 · Walpole, *Corr.*
Likenesses engraving (aged twenty-six; after drawing by L. P. Boitard), repro. in *Complete history of James Maclean*, frontispiece · engraving, NPG [*see illus.*]
Wealth at death £80–£300: *Complete history*; *Genuine account*

McLaren [Maclaren], **Alexander** (1826–1910), Baptist preacher, was born in Glasgow on 11 February 1826, the youngest of six children of highlander David McLaren (1785–1850), merchant for a Perth-based manufacturer, and his wife, Mary Wingate. From childhood McLaren was somewhat solitary, at ease in his family circle but averse to meeting strangers. An able student, he attended Glasgow high school before studying Latin then Greek at Glasgow University from 1838 to 1840. His parents influenced him greatly: his father had been groomed for the Church of Scotland ministry, but his beliefs had led him first to join a Congregational then a Baptist fellowship. From 1823 to 1836 (when he left to spend four years in Adelaide as manager of the newly formed South Australian Company) David McLaren was joint lay pastor of the Scotch Baptist church at Morrison's Court (later in Portland Street, then John Street). McLaren warmly recalled his father's preaching, which was deeply rooted in the Bible and personal experience, and Sundays devoted to worship, prayer, Bible reading, and teaching. Other childhood influences included the Revd David Russell (later his brother-in-law), a Congregational minister whose Bible class McLaren attended. Some words of Russell sparked his conversion, and he was baptized by the Revd James Paterson on 17 May 1840 at Hope Street Baptist Church, Glasgow.

In 1841 the McLaren family moved to London where, in what seemed a natural progression, Alexander began training for the Baptist ministry at Stepney College in 1842. At college McLaren was aloof but well respected. He was also independent-minded, attending the first meeting of the Liberation Society, against college instructions that students should stay away. McLaren preached his first sermon at the college on his seventeenth birthday: nervous of his boyish appearance, the college initially declined to let him preach elsewhere. Much influenced by the college principal, Dr Benjamin Davies, a distinguished

Hebrew scholar, he developed a lifelong habit of reading the Bible daily in its original. He studied the techniques of famous preachers, notably Thomas Binney and Dr Melville. He also developed a love of literature, particularly Carlyle, Scott, Thackeray, and Browning, which showed in his later sermon style. In October 1845 he gained his London University BA, winning prizes in the scripture examination, Hebrew, and Greek.

In March 1846, his MA still incomplete, McLaren agreed to become minister of Portland Chapel, Southampton, first for three months, then permanently. The church had a troubled recent history and was struggling, with only twenty members. McLaren became a popular lecturer and spent time preparing his Sunday school teachers. His main focus was preaching, however, and he prepared for this intensively. A keen observer of nature, he delighted in walks on the Isle of Wight or in the New Forest, alone or with friends including Edward Miall. On 27 March 1856 he married Marion Ann McLaren (1828–1884), one of several Edinburgh-based cousins with whom he had grown up. The couple had four daughters and a son. Well educated and cultured, Mrs McLaren brought a calming, socializing influence to his life.

Despite his natural diffidence McLaren's reputation spread, and in May 1858 he accepted an invitation to become minister of Union Chapel, an open membership Baptist church then in the suburbs of Manchester, on Oxford Road. His Sunday and mid-week sermons quickly drew a packed and influential congregation including bankers, merchants, and manufacturers, among them Frank Crossley, the inventor turned philanthropist, MPs, writers, artists, students and fellow ministers, artisans, and clerks. An imposing new chapel (with rose window, bell-tower, and thirty rooms including a lecture hall) was opened in November 1869 about a quarter of a mile down Oxford Road, and (despite McLaren's continuing self-doubt) quickly filled to its 1800 seat capacity. Schoolrooms were added in 1880. Mission work in Gorton led to a schoolroom (1867), then a chapel (1876), then another off-shoot in Birch Street. Other missions followed in Hulme (Wilmott Street, 1870; Canning Street, 1903) and Rusholme (1872—later the McLaren Jubilee People's Institute). The church also lent powerful support (in money, leaders, and workers) to mission and charity work being carried out by other people across the city and beyond.

As in Southampton, McLaren concentrated on preaching. Partly from reserve, and partly from conviction that preaching was the minister's main task, he left routine pastoral visitation to others and avoided social and platform engagements whenever possible. Betraying Quaker tendencies, he also downplayed the sacraments of baptism and communion. From early days he preached extempore, captivating listeners with his flashing blue eyes and expressive features, his nervous energy and spare, poetic style. 'His dress was unclerical and his ways unconventional; Spurgeon thought him a "dangerous man"' (DNB). Above all he was known for dissecting and interpreting biblical texts with an originality that made him difficult to pigeonhole. Notable sermons included

Ahab & Elijah (1859), those at the old Surrey Chapel on behalf of the Baptist Missionary Society (1864) and the London Missionary Society (1870), and his 1901 Baptist Union address, Evangelical Mysticism. Many of his sermons were published, starting with three volumes of Sermons Preached in [Union Chapel,] Manchester (1859, 1869, 1872), while later sermons were reproduced almost weekly in the Christian Commonwealth and The Freeman. Reflecting his scholarship and focus, McLaren's other publications, under the name Maclaren, include over forty volumes of Bible expositions, from The Life of David as Reflected in his Psalms (1880) to his thirty-two volume Expositions of Holy Scripture (1904–10). Other writings include: a pamphlet and a lecture on religious equality (1862, 1871); an address to the students at Rawdon College, The Student, his Work and the Right Preparation for it (1864); A Spring Holiday in Italy (1865), an account of his travels in which McLaren displayed his love of early Italian painters; The Union Psalter [1878]; Week-Day Evening Addresses (1877); and (overcoming his distaste for printed prayers) Pulpit Prayers (1907, 1911). From 1885 to 1906 McLaren also contributed a weekly 'International lesson' to the American Sunday School Times.

On the wider Baptist stage McLaren helped found the Manchester and Salford Baptist Union and became influential in the Lancashire and Cheshire Baptist Association. He was in demand to preach on big occasions, and was sought out for advice—one of a powerful triumvirate with Hugh Stowell Brown of Liverpool and Charles Williams of Accrington. He was Baptist Union president in 1875 and again in 1901, using his early presidential addresses to urge the need to evangelize the masses, preserve village nonconformity, and provide decent ministerial stipends, and helping to pave the way for a Union Annuity Fund. He represented the English Baptist Union at the Victoria jubilee celebrations in Australia in September 1888, led appeals for Baptist church expansion, and chaired the first Baptist World Congress in 1905. During the 'downgrade controversy' which rocked the Baptist Union in 1887–8 he stayed on good terms with all parties. The great breakfast held in his honour in 1896, and his re-election as union president, showed his high standing with fellow Baptists. Beyond the denomination he staunchly supported Wesleyan Central Missions, became the first minister of another denomination to preach the Congregational Union sermon, and was proud to have helped originate the Free Church Council movement. Pursuing his interest in education he was a governor of the John Rylands Library, advising the library on the purchase of theology books. He was also governor of Owens College, then the Victoria University of Manchester from 1900 to 1905, warmly supporting the pioneering 'undenominational' theology faculty introduced at the university in 1904 and serving on the faculty's advisory committee. His links to the Victoria University were cemented with the award of an honorary LittD in 1902. McLaren also received honorary DDs from the universities of Edinburgh (1877) and Glasgow (1907).

McLaren remained minister at Union Chapel until June 1903, in spite of bouts of ill health, the crushing blow of his wife's sudden death on 21 December 1884, and several tempting offers including (in 1885) a pressing invitation to become professor of Hebrew at Regent's Park College. From 1882 he was assisted first by the Revd John G. Raws, and from 1890 by the Revd J. Edward Roberts. In retirement he became pastor emeritus. During his forty-five-year tenure he became one of Manchester's leading citizens, the speaker of choice at public and religious gatherings, and until his wife's death a familiar figure at Hallé concerts. Always well informed about the state of trade, he was known widely as 'McLaren of Manchester'. His close association with the city was reflected in the portrait by Sir George Reid FRSA (president of the Royal Scottish Academy), paid for by subscription and presented to the City Art Gallery in 1897.

In retirement McLaren managed to preach less often than he had hoped but he revelled in the discipline of spending part of each day writing and preparing publications. In 1909, with the encroachments of suburbia threatening his tranquillity, he gave up his house in Fallowfield, Manchester, and presented his library to the Baptist college there. After his regular holiday in his beloved highlands, he went to live in Edinburgh, at 4 Whitehouse Terrace. He died there on 5 May 1910 after some weeks' illness. On 9 May, following a simple funeral at Union Chapel, his ashes were interred at Brooklands cemetery, near Manchester.

By the time of his death McLaren had outlived many of his contemporaries. Long before then, his was a voice against the tide. Convinced that the preacher's role was to proclaim eternal truths authoritatively, drawing on God's revelation in the Bible and on experience, he deplored the search for 'topicality' and the airing of doubts in the pulpit. His preaching was aimed at bringing individuals to Christ rather than expounding a 'social gospel'. Confident that the fundamental truths of the gospel were beyond questions of date or authorship, he rarely engaged publicly with issues raised by higher criticism. His powers of biblical interpretation, vividly expressed and enriched by a deep personal spirituality were, however, widely acknowledged. Commentators ranked him as one of the greatest preachers of the nineteenth century, and a formative influence on how future generations of preachers crafted and delivered their sermons.

ROSEMARY CHADWICK

Sources E. T. McLaren, *Dr. McLaren of Manchester, a sketch* (1911) • D. Williamson, *The life of Alexander Maclaren … preacher and expositor* [1910] • J. C. Carlile, *Alexander Maclaren, D.D., the man and his message* (1901) • *Baptist Times and Freeman* (13 May 1910) [suppl.] • J. E. R., 'Memoirs of deceased ministers and missionaries', *Baptist Hand-Book* (1911), 490–92 • *Manchester Guardian* (6 May 1910) • *The Times* (6 May 1910) • A. McLaren, 'David McLaren', *Scottish Baptist Magazine* (May 1897), 59–61 • I. Sellers, 'Other times, other ministries: John Fawcett and Alexander McLaren', *Baptist Quarterly*, 32 (1987–8), 181–99 • J. Stuart, 'The Rev. Alexander Maclaren', *Baptist Magazine*, 88 (1896), 249–54 • 'Dr McLaren's jubilee commemoration: presentation to the city', *Manchester Guardian* (16 Jan 1897) • R. Jones, 'The standard life of Dr. Alexander Maclaren of Manchester, 1826–1910', unpublished MSS, Regent's Park College, Angus Library • C. A. Insko, 'The biblical preaching of Alexander Maclaren', thesis submitted to the Faculty of the Southern Baptist Theological Seminary, 1950 • 'Dr Maclaren and disestablishment', *Baptist Magazine*, 86 (1894), 148 • T. H. Martin, 'Rev. Alexander Maclaren, D.D., an appreciation', *Scottish Baptist Magazine* (June 1910), 89–91 • *The calendar of Owens College, Manchester, 1900–1901* • *The Victoria University of Manchester, calendar, 1904–05* • *DNB*

Archives Man. CL, Union Chapel church meeting minutes and manuals, M499

Likenesses photographs, 1896, Regent's Park College, Oxford, Angus Library • G. Reid, oils, 1897, Man. City Gall. • F. L. Bridell, portrait • E. Martineau, portrait (in later life) • five copper printer's blocks, Regent's Park College, Oxford, Angus Library • portrait (as a young man), Regent's Park College, Oxford • portrait (as an old man), Regent's Park College, Oxford

Wealth at death £29,469 12s. 4d.: probate, 8 Sept 1910, CGPLA Eng. & Wales

Maclaren, Archibald (1755–1826), playwright, was born in the highlands of Scotland on 2 March 1755. He entered the army at a very early age, and served in the American War of Independence under generals Howe and Clinton. While his regiment lay in winter quarters he took advantage of the available time to publish several poems in the Philadelphia and New York papers. When the fighting resumed he sustained a wound in his head that reportedly reduced him to a state of insanity whenever he touched alcohol.

Maclaren's regiment returned to Scotland to recruit, and in 1783 Mr Jackson's company produced his farce *The Coup de main, or, The American Adventurers* at Edinburgh. On the conclusion of the war he was discharged, and joined Ward's itinerant troop of players at Montrose. He is said to have been a bad exponent of English roles because of his strong Scottish accent but to have performed slightly better as Scottish, Irish, and French characters. He was at his best in his own play *The Highland Drover*, which premiered in Inverness and was published in 1790; Maclaren claimed that it toured the highlands 'with universal approbation!' (Hook, 203). Its comedy arises from the fact that the drover speaks only in Gaelic, while the rest of the characters speak English.

In 1794 Maclaren enlisted as a sergeant in the Dunbartonshire Highlanders, and went with them to Guernsey, where he was engaged to act as prompter in the theatre and where several of his pieces were performed. His regiment then proceeded to Ireland and helped to suppress the rising. While there he wrote another farce, *What News from Bantry Bay?*, but it was not immediately produced because it touched upon the United Irishmen, who were at that time making secret preparations for the rising. He also published two records of his experiences in Ireland: *A Minute Description of the Battles of Gorey, Arklow, and Vinegar Hill* (1798) and *An Account of the Insurrection in Ireland* (1800).

After the battle of Vinegar Hill, Maclaren was discharged and went to London, receiving a small pension as a result of two further wounds that he had suffered. He had hopes of seeing two of his interludes, which were then in preparation, on the stage but neither came to anything. At some point he married a woman named Helen, with whom he had eleven children, but only four survived him. He lived at a series of addresses in Soho and survived on his pension and on the proceeds of over eighty publications. Most of his works were dramatic pieces but none really achieved much fame. The best-known were *The Siege of Perth* (1792), *The Siege of Berwick* (1807), *The Slaves* (1807), and *The Battle of the Dandies, or, The Half-Way House* (1818). He also published three volumes of poetry, *The Repository* (1811), *Coll and Rotha* (1812), and *Poetical Trifles* (1825). Among those who honoured his subscription lists with their names were the prince and princess of Wales, the dukes of York, Kent, Cumberland, Sussex, and Gloucester, and many other members of the nobility and the gentry. In spite of their patronage Maclaren was only ever able to afford precarious support for his family; he died, after a long illness, in 1826. A. E. J. LEGGE, *rev.* JAMES HOW

Sources D. E. Baker, *Biographia dramatica, or, A companion to the playhouse*, rev. I. Reed, new edn, rev. S. Jones, 3 vols. in 4 (1812) · R. Inglis, *The dramatic writers of Scotland* (1868) · *Memoir of Archibald Maclaren, dramatist* (1835) · A. Maclaren, *A minute description of the battles of Gorey, Arklow, and Vinegar Hill* (1798) · C. Craig, ed., *The history of Scottish literature*, 2: 1660–1800, ed. A. Hook (1987)
Wealth at death probably very little

MacLaren, Archibald (1819?–1884), teacher of physical education and author, was born at Alloa, Clackmannanshire, Scotland. The details of his early life are obscure. He was brought up a Presbyterian. At about the age of sixteen he went to Paris and studied fencing, gymnastics, and medicine but became most interested in physical training. He settled in Oxford as a fencing master some time after 1840, and on 2 July 1844 he married Charlotte Wheeler (d. c.1847), daughter of David Alphonso *Talboys, the bookseller. In 1858 he erected the 'university gymnasium' at the corner of Bear Lane. William Morris and Edward Burne Jones, as undergraduates, frequented both the gymnasium and MacLaren's home in Summertown and both men also shared his wider cultural interests. Burne Jones drew a set of illustrations for MacLaren's *The fairy family: a series of ballads and metrical tales illustrating the fairy mythology of Europe*, published in 1857, albeit without those illustrations.

In 1860 MacLaren was asked to develop a new system of physical training for the army and in 1861 twelve NCOs were selected to attend a six-month course under him at Oxford. An army training school was established at Aldershot and a gymnasium modelled on that at Oxford was completed there before the end of 1861. To enable MacLaren's methods to be more widely practised Her Majesty's Stationery Office produced *A Military System of Gymnastic Exercises for the Use of Instructors* in 1862. A general order had been issued in February 1862 that MacLaren's system, 'having been approved by the General Commanding in Chief', was to be adopted in all suitable military gymnasia. Dumb-bells, bar-bells, climbing ropes, horizontal bars, vaulting horses, and climbing walls, as well as running and free-standing exercises were brought into general use.

MacLaren was a far-sighted teacher. In an article entitled 'National systems of bodily exercise' he compared ancient and modern systems of gymnastics. None of them satisfied him. He was particularly critical of the Swedish system which was being introduced to Britain at this time. He thought that it was suitable for invalids only. 'Chicken broth may yield ample nutriment to the invalid' he wrote, 'but the soldier would make but a poor day's march upon it; you must give *him* the chicken too' (*Macmillan's Magazine*, 7, 1863, 280). He analysed also the Prussian and French systems of bodily exercise and condemned them in nationalistic terms, although MacLaren's own view of the fundamental aim of gymnastics was not very different from those which he criticized. He believed that by exercises suitably devised and arranged the body could be prepared for any task. In *Training in Theory and Practice* (1866) he applied his principles in detail to a single sport, rowing. This he judged to be 'an art of considerable intricacy … involving the possession … of both muscular and respiratory power, to promote which is the object of all training' (p. 2).

MacLaren's best-known work was *A System of Physical Education, Theoretical and Practical* (1869). In it he wrote 'all exercise may be classed under two distinct heads, Recreative and Educational'. This dichotomy within physical education was fundamental to its development in Britain and reappeared in many subsequent government documents and other treatises on education. In ten appendices to the book MacLaren showed how anthropometry should be used in physical education. He had himself carefully taken measurements of his military trainees before, during, and at the end of their course. A second edition of the book was published in 1885.

In 1851 MacLaren married a second time, to Gertrude Isabel Frances Talboys (1833–1896), sister of his deceased first wife. A good classical scholar, in 1864 she founded Summer Fields in Summertown, north Oxford, which became a well-known preparatory school. They had a family of three daughters and two sons, the second of whom, Wallace, produced a revised edition of *A System of Physical Education* in 1895. After suffering from diabetes for many years MacLaren died at Summer Fields, on 19 February 1884. He was buried in Summertown churchyard three days later. PETER C. MCINTOSH

Sources *Oxford Chronicle and Berks and Bucks Gazette* (23 Feb 1884) · *Oxford Magazine* (27 Feb 1884) · F. E. Leonard and G. B. Affleck, *A guide to the history of physical education* (1947) · E. A. Oldfield, *The history of the Army Physical Training Corps, 1860–1945* (1945) · J. Christian, introduction, in A. MacLaren, *The fairy family* (1985) · P. C. McIntosh, *Physical education in England since 1800* (1952) · N. Aldridge, *Time to spare? A history of Summer Fields* (1989) · d. cert.
Archives Army Physical Training Corps Museum, Aldershot · Oberlin College Archives, Fred E. Leonard MSS, series 6, subseries 3, box 9
Likenesses C. Eccles Williams, photograph, 1878; in possession of Eccles Williams, 1913 · F. E. Leonard, photograph (after photograph by C. Eccles Williams, 1878), Oberlin College Archives, Fred E. Leonard MSS, RG 30/47
Wealth at death £13,649 4s. 6d.: probate, 20 Aug 1884, CGPLA Eng. & Wales

MacLaren, Archibald Campbell [Archie] (1871–1944), cricketer, was born at Moss Side, Manchester, on 1 December 1871, the second of seven sons of James MacLaren (d.

1900), cotton merchant, and his wife, Emily Carver. His later career as a cricketer was encouraged at an early stage by his father, who was treasurer to the Lancashire County Cricket Club. Archie was sent to Elstree preparatory school, renowned for its cricket coaching, and subsequently to Harrow, where he represented the school against Eton at Lord's (1887–90). He was soon selected for his début in county cricket when Lancashire played Sussex at Brighton in August 1890. The eighteen-year-old made a chanceless and magnificent innings of 108, when the rest of the powerful and experienced Lancashire team were struggling on a poor pitch.

After this dazzling start, MacLaren's cricket career marked time during the next few seasons. Family finances did not allow him to go on to university, so he made the first tentative steps into what became an inventive but largely unsuccessful business career. Over the years he was to pursue a bewildering succession of jobs, business ventures, and other schemes to secure an income commensurate with his genteel aspirations. Many of these ideas were cricket-related but others included owning a hotel, advertising, working as a salesman, journalism, and acting as a racehorse bloodstock agent. For a number of years he was personal secretary and travelling companion to Prince Ranjitsinhji.

By 1894 MacLaren was able to find time for a full season's cricket and was duly selected as a member of A. E. Stoddart's team to tour Australia the following winter. The fast wickets suited his batting style and he left a lasting impression on the Australian public, scoring 228 against Victoria and 120 in the fifth test match victory which decided the series in England's favour.

On returning to England in triumph, MacLaren's first priority was to earn his living, and he became a preparatory school teacher and coach. Having missed eight Lancashire games he returned at the end of term to captain the county against Somerset at Taunton in July 1895, watched by his proud father. After winning the toss he proceeded to play one of the most remarkable innings in cricket history. By the time he was dismissed the following day, he had amassed the total of 424, including sixty-five boundaries, and eclipsed W. G. Grace's long-standing record of 344. This remained the highest individual score in first-class cricket until W. H. Ponsford made 429 at Melbourne in 1923 and was beaten as the highest innings in England only when Brian Lara made 501 not out for Warwickshire nearly 100 years later.

The next ten years saw MacLaren reach his peak as a batsman and he was, when available, an automatic choice as England's opening batsman. He built a special relationship with the Sydney ground in Australia, and scored seven hundreds in all there, only one fewer than at his home ground of Old Trafford. He toured Australia again with England in 1897–8, at the end of which he married (Kathleen) Maud Power at Toorak, Melbourne. Maud, a notable socialite, was the second daughter of Robert Power, a wealthy director of the Dalgety pastoral empire. They had two sons.

Early in his career MacLaren became the natural choice to captain any eleven in which he played and he led Lancashire from 1894 (when only twenty-two years old) to 1896, and again from 1899 to 1907. He learned much from A. N. Hornby and A. E. Stoddart, and when in 1899 it finally came time for England to replace W. G. Grace as skipper, the honour went to MacLaren. He went on to captain his country in the Ashes series of 1901–2, 1902, and 1909; his total of twenty-two matches as captain against Australia has not been exceeded before or since. But he experienced little luck and only occasional success. In between these series P. F. Warner and F. S. Jackson had, however, led England to win the rubber in 1903–4 and 1905. History has generally attributed this disappointing record to MacLaren's pessimistic view of life, but some credit must go to the great strength of the Australian sides of the period. Despite his mixed record, his captaincy was accorded almost legendary status by many of those who played under him, in particular by his Lancashire team whom he led to the county championship of 1904. He was one of the first captains to study tactics with an almost scientific rigour, although this sometimes led him to appear controversial or inflexible. His tendency towards original thinking brought MacLaren an unexpected triumph when he discovered an unknown bowler, S. F. Barnes, and immediately chose him for the tour of Australia in 1901–2. Judged foolhardy by sections of the press, his judgement was marvellously vindicated and Barnes went on to become one of the greatest bowlers of all time.

The immediate years leading up to 1914 were ones of steady decline for MacLaren on the cricket field, though he toured Argentina with Lord Hawke's MCC side in 1912. He received a commission in the Royal Army Service Corps in 1914, and took part in recruitment work in the Manchester area until invalided out in 1917. The public probably felt they would not see him play again after the war. There was one final spectacular gesture. Throughout the season of 1921 he had written that he knew how to beat Warwick Armstrong's all-conquering Australians, and at the end of the season he was given his chance when he led an invited all-amateur eleven against them at Eastbourne. Against all the odds he inflicted the tourists' first defeat with a brilliant combination of tactical awareness and team selection. Encouraged by this swansong, he accepted MCC's invitation to take a non-test match team to Australia and New Zealand during 1922–3. In the first representative match against New Zealand, MacLaren, now aged fifty-one, scored a magnificent 200 not out in what proved to be his final first-class innings.

As a batsman, MacLaren became known as the pinnacle of style. Sir Neville Cardus wrote often and memorably of his schoolboy hero: 'Magnificence was enthroned at the wicket when MacLaren took his stand there' (Down, 164). When preparing to receive the ball, he stood upright with bat raised aloft, much in the style of Graham Gooch nearly a century later. The resultant full swing of the bat was memorable when driving, but MacLaren was perhaps best-known for the power and bravery of his hook and pull shots. Most significantly, he always set out to dominate the bowler. In total he made 22,236 runs, at an average of 34.15. He was also a fine and athletic fielder, in the out-field when a young man and later as an expert slip catcher. In general appearance MacLaren was handsome, dominat-ing, and confident even to the point of arrogance.

In MacLaren's later years his wife inherited some of her family's fortune. He was at last able to live in the style for which he had always yearned. The couple bought a large estate, Warfield Park, near Bracknell, Berkshire, where MacLaren died of cancer on 17 November 1944. His wife survived him. MICHAEL DOWN

Sources M. G. Down, *Archie: a biography of A. C. MacLaren* (1981) · N. Cardus, *Autobiography* (1947) · *Wisden* (1895–1945) · *DNB* · *CGPLA Eng. & Wales* (1945)
Likenesses A. C. Tayler, lithograph, 1905 (after photograph by G. W. Beldam), NPG · G. Reynell, oils, Old Trafford cricket ground, Manchester · photographs, repro. in G. W. Beldam and C. B. Fry, *Great batsmen: their methods at a glance* (1906)
Wealth at death £6535 15s. 1d.: administration, 25 Jan 1945, CGPLA Eng. & Wales

Maclaren, Charles (1782–1866), newspaper editor, son of a small farmer and cattle dealer and his second wife, Chris-tian M'Kell or Meikle (1736/7–1829), was born at Ormiston, East Lothian on 7 October 1782. He received some educa-tion at Fala and Colinton, but was mainly self-taught. On moving to Edinburgh, where he served as clerk and book-keeper to several firms, he joined the Philomathic Debat-ing Society, where he made the acquaintance of John Ritchie, William Ritchie, and others of advanced whig views.

In August or September 1816—in the face of the Conser-vative reaction at Westminster and elsewhere—Maclaren and Ritchie discussed the founding of a newspaper which would reflect radical values, and on 30 September 1816 they published their prospectus, declaring an especial but not exclusive interest in Scottish affairs and an openness to contributors (save those who would be abusive or libel-lous). The first number of *The Scotsman* (initially a weekly paper) appeared on 25 January 1817. Maclaren was joint editor and proprietor until 1845, though from later in 1817 until 1820 he was a custom-house clerk, with J. R. M'Culloch acting as editor while the paper became finan-cially established. From 1823 it appeared twice weekly. Maclaren wrote leaders—an innovation for the Scottish press, which had hitherto often reprinted the leaders of London newspapers—championed political reform, and supported radical politics, but not with such vehemence as to estrange the larger whiggish constituency. He imme-diately appreciated the advantages and scope of railways (see his paper of 1825 in Cox and Nicol). From an early stage Maclaren supported disestablishment and cam-paigned against pluralism in the church. Until the Disrup-tion the paper was sceptical of the evangelicals, but from 1843 formed something of a bond with Thomas Chalmers and the Free Church. Maclaren was an active churchgoer, joining the Free Church in 1843 and latterly attending Old Greyfriars Church.

Maclaren was, Adam Black, the publisher, thought, 'a sterling honest man, aimiable in his disposition, fair and

courteous to all. … His style was pure and simple Saxon' (*The Glorious Privilege*, 12). But Maclaren was also disputa-tious, and well able to hold his own in the vigorous rows that permeated Edinburgh life. In 1829 he fought a duel with James Brown, editor of the tory *Caledonian Mercury*, with which Maclaren conducted an abusive campaign of denigration (energetically reciprocated) over many years; neither duellist was hurt.

In 1820 Archibald Constable employed Maclaren to edit the sixth edition of the *Encyclopaedia Britannica*, published in 1823, and to revise its historical and geographical art-icles. Like many of the self-taught Scots of his time, Mac-laren was much interested in geology. He was a fellow of the Royal Society of Edinburgh from 1837 and of the Geo-logical Society of London from 1846, and he was president of the Geological Society of Edinburgh from 1864 until his death. He published *A Sketch of the Geology of Fife and the Lothians* (1839; rev. edn, 1866) and *A Dissertation on the Topo-graphy of the Plain of Troy* (1822), reissued in 1863 as *The Plains of Troy Described* after he had visited what he believed to be the site.

On 27 January 1842 Maclaren married Jean Veitch, daughter of Richard Somner of Somnerfield, East Lothian, and widow of David Hume (1757–1838), judge and nephew of the philosopher. In 1845 he was succeeded as editor by Alexander Russel, whom he had brought on as sub-editor. Maclaren died from a stroke at his home, More-land Cottage, Grange Loan, Edinburgh, on 10 September 1866 and was buried in the Grange cemetery, Edinburgh. William Brodie's bust (1860) shows him to have been a handsome man, with sharp, rather chiselled features. He was of medium height, 'of somewhat slender make, but well proportioned' (Cox and Nicol, 1.28).

H. C. G. MATTHEW

Sources *DNB* · *Select writings political, scientific, topographical, and miscellaneous of the late C. Maclaren*, ed. R. Cox and J. Nicol, 2 vols. (1869) · [M. Magnusson and others], *The glorious privilege: the history of The Scotsman* (1967) · R. M. W. Cowan, *The newspaper in Scotland: a study of its first expansion, 1815–1860* (1946) · *Proceedings of the Royal Society of Edinburgh*, 6 (1866–9), 27–9 · *GM*, 4th ser., 2 (1866), 562
Archives Hornel Library, Broughton House, Kirkcudbright, let-ters | Man. CL, Manchester Archives and Local Studies, letters to J. B. Smith · Mitchell L., Glas., Glasgow City Archives, corresp. with John Strang · NL Scot., corresp. with George Combe
Likenesses W. Brodie, marble bust, 1861, Museum of Science and Art, Edinburgh · J. Hutchison, marble bust, 1889 (after bust by W. Brodie), Scot. NPG · photograph, repro. in Cox and Nicol, eds., *Select writings … of the late C. Maclaren*, vol. 1 · photograph (after bust by W. Brodie), repro. in Cox and Nicol, eds., *Select writings … of the late C. Maclaren*, frontispiece · portrait, repro. in *Glorious privilege: the history of The Scotsman*
Wealth at death £6608 8s. 2d.: confirmation, 12 Oct 1866, NA Scot., SC 70/1/131/777–783

McLaren, Charles Benjamin Bright, first Baron Aber-conway (1850–1934), barrister and industrialist, was born at Edinburgh on 12 May 1850, the elder son of Duncan *McLaren (1800–1886), member of parliament for Edin-burgh, and his third wife, Priscilla Bright *McLaren (1815–1906), daughter of Jacob Bright, of Green Bank, Rochdale, and sister of John Bright, the radical statesman, after whom he was named. His elder half-brother John *McLaren became, as Lord McLaren, a judge.

Educated at Edinburgh University, McLaren graduated from there in 1870 with first class honours in philosophy and won the Ferguson and Hamilton scholarships. After completing his education at the universities of Bonn and Heidelberg he took to journalism in Edinburgh and contributed numerous leading articles to *The Scotsman*. Soon, however, he turned to the English law and was called to the bar by Lincoln's Inn in 1874, developing in due course a solid chancery practice.

In view of his family associations it was natural that McLaren should be attracted to the Liberal cause in politics, and he entered the House of Commons at the general election in 1880 as member for Stafford. In 1886 he voted for Gladstone's Home Rule Bill, but he was defeated at the ensuing general election. In 1892 he was returned for the Bosworth division of Leicestershire, a constituency for which he sat continuously until 1910, when he was succeeded there by his elder son, Henry Duncan *McLaren (1879–1953).

On 6 March 1877 McLaren married Laura Elizabeth [*see* McLaren, Laura Elizabeth (1854–1933)], only daughter of Henry Davis *Pochin (1824–1895), industrialist and radical MP, of Bodnant, Denbighshire, and his wife, Agnes *Pochin, *née* Heap (1825–1908). The couple had two sons and two daughters. Pochin, who was to be sometime mayor of Salford and an associate of both McLaren's father and his uncle, John Bright, worked in the early 1860s as a manufacturing chemist in Manchester. Together with other local businessmen he was instrumental in providing capital for the flotations by David Chadwick, a Manchester accountant, of a number of joint-stock companies in the coal, iron, and engineering industries, including John Brown & Co., the Sheepbridge Coal and Iron Company, the Tredegar Iron and Coal Company, Bolckow Vaughan, and the Staveley Iron Company. Involved with these companies from the outset, Pochin often became either a director or chairman. On his death in 1895 he left an estate of £16,173 gross and, having cut his son out of his will, his interest in these and other concerns passed to his only daughter, Laura.

Although keenly interested in business affairs, the inheritance of her father's many industrial interests created logistical problems. These were solved in 1897 when McLaren, despite having been made a QC only that year, gave up his law practice to devote himself solely to helping to run his wife's business affairs. He had previously been connected with a number of the concerns before 1895, for example becoming a director of John Brown in 1882, but following his father-in-law's death he took on many of the roles which the latter had formerly occupied. In 1895 he became chairman of Tredegar, retaining this position until his death, and in 1897 he became deputy chairman of John Brown, eventually becoming chairman (1906–34) on the death of John Devonshire Ellis (1824–1906). At various times he was also chairman of Palmers Shipbuilding and Iron Company and Sheepbridge, as well as of the Metropolitan Railway Company (1904–33).

In 1902 McLaren's services to both politics and industry were recognized through a baronetcy. In 1908 he was sworn of the privy council and in 1911, on Asquith's recommendation, was raised to the peerage as Baron Aberconway of Bodnant. As a businessman, however, McLaren was noted for his pragmatic approach to business problems. He was very much concerned with the supervisory and financial aspects of the companies of which he was chairman, leaving the day-to-day management in the hands of others. Nevertheless he became widely regarded as an expert on general industrial problems, his chairman's address at the annual general meetings of John Brown usually including a survey of the current state of the heavy industries. He also wrote articles for the engineering supplement of *The Times*. His widespread knowledge of the iron, steel, and engineering industries, gained from his vantage point as chairman or director of several important manufacturing concerns, and his interest in the historical development of this sector, were reflected in his well-known study, *The Basic Industries of Great Britain* (1927).

McLaren was a man of abundant energy, of genial temperament and considerable charm. He and his wife both enjoyed entertaining at their Belgrave Square home in London, but also spent much time at Bodnant. Although it was his wife, together with their elder son, Henry, who was responsible for the development of the gardens both at Bodnant and their villa at Cap d'Antibes in the south of France, McLaren was not without his own hobbies, including shooting, forestry, and photography. He also found time to be magistrate, at various times, for Denbighshire, Flintshire, Middlesex, and Surrey.

McLaren died at his London home, 43 Belgrave Square, on 23 January 1934, from pneumonia and other health complications. His wife, Laura, had predeceased him on 4 January 1933, leaving an estate of £750,000 gross.

TREVOR BOYNS

Sources G. Holmes, 'McLaren, Charles Benjamin Bright', *DBB* · P. L. Cottrell, *Industrial finance, 1830–1914: the finance and organization of English manufacturing industry* (1980) · *The Times* (24 Jan 1934) · m. cert. · d. cert.
Likenesses B. Stone, two photographs, 1906, NPG · W. Stoneman, photograph, 1924, NPG · P. de Laszlo, portrait, Bodnant Garden, Conwy · G. F. Watt, portrait, Bodnant Garden, Conwy
Wealth at death £15,043 7s. 9d.: probate, 10 April 1934, *CGPLA Eng. & Wales*

McLaren, Duncan (1800–1886), politician, son of John McLaren, farmer, and his wife, Catherine, *née* McLellan, was born at Renton, Dunbartonshire, on 12 January 1800. At the age of twelve he was apprenticed for four years to a draper at Dunbar. From Dunbar he removed to Haddington, and thence in 1818 to Edinburgh, where the whole of his subsequent life was passed. Here he was employed by John Lauder & Co., in the High Street, until 1824, when he began in business as a draper, in a shop opposite St Giles's Church. He later diversified into railway management and banking with only partial success. In 1833 he became member of the town council of Edinburgh, and he was successively baillie, treasurer, and finally provost from 1851 to 1854. When he was appointed treasurer the city was almost bankrupt, but he made satisfactory arrangements with the creditors, including the imperial Treasury.

In 1852 McLaren unsuccessfully contested Edinburgh as a Liberal, and in connection with the contest received from *The Scotsman*, in an action for libel, the sum of £500, which he gave away to charity. In 1865 he was elected for Edinburgh, and continued to represent the city for sixteen years, acquiring in the House of Commons a position of so much authority on Scottish questions that he used to be called 'the member for Scotland'. He took part in passing the Act for the Commutation of the Annuity Tax, a local church rate peculiar to Edinburgh and Montrose. He also helped to pass the Burgess Act and the Irish Sunday Closing Act. An energetic Free Churchman, he was anti-drink, anti-establishment, anti-trade union, and anti-home rule, and 'represented sectarian individualism at its narrowest' (Harvie, 87). In 1873 the Edinburgh Trades Council called a huge meeting to protest against his support for the Criminal Law Amendment Act's picketing clause. However, on his retirement in 1881 he received a testimonial from his fellow MPs, and his portrait by Sir George Reid, president of the Royal Scottish Academy, was placed in the council chamber in Edinburgh. (A replica is in the National Portrait Gallery, Edinburgh.) He most prided himself on the establishment, in 1836, of the Heriot Free Schools, with the surplus funds of the trust; but his efforts failed to prevent the transference of these schools to the school board in 1884.

McLaren was thrice married: first, in 1829, to Grant, youngest daughter of William Aitken, a Dunbar merchant (she died on 23 April 1833, having borne one son, John *McLaren, one son and one daughter); second, in 1836, to Christina Gordon, daughter of William Renton of Edinburgh (she died on 1 November 1841, having given birth to one son and two daughters). His third wife, whom he married on 6 July 1848, was Priscilla [see McLaren, Priscilla Bright (1815–1906)], daughter of Jacob and sister of John Bright; with her he had a daughter and two sons, the first of whom, Charles Benjamin Bright *McLaren, became first Baron Aberconway; the second, Walter Stowe Bright *McLaren [see under McLaren, Eva Maria], became Liberal MP for Crewe. She died on 5 November 1906. McLaren published several pamphlets and speeches, especially on annuities. He died at his home, Newington House, Edinburgh, on 26 April 1886.

G. C. BOASE, rev. H. C. G. MATTHEW

Sources J. B. Mackie, *The life and work of Duncan McLaren*, 2 vols. (1888) · C. Harvie, *Scotland and nationalism* (1977) · C. Smout, *A century of the Scottish people, 1830–1950* (1986) · *The Times* (27 April 1886) **Archives** NL Scot., corresp. and papers; letters | BL, corresp. with W. E. Gladstone, Add. MSS 44376–44468 · NL Scot., corresp. with George Combe · NL Scot., letters to John Lee · NL Scot., Rutherford MSS · W. Sussex RO, corresp. with Richard Cobden **Likenesses** C. Smith, portrait, 1838, repro. in Mackie, *Life and work of Duncan McLaren* · photographs, 1862–76, repro. in Mackie, *Life and work of Duncan McLaren* · E. J. Gregory, oils, 1891 (after portrait, 1880), Scot. NPG · G. Reid, ink drawing (after portrait, 1882), Scot. NPG **Wealth at death** £33,013 14*s*. 4*d*.: confirmation, 14 July 1886, *CCI*

McLaren [*née* Müller], **Eva Maria** (1852/3–1921), social reformer and political activist, was the younger daughter of William Müller, a wealthy German businessman, and an English mother, Maria Henrietta. She spent her early life in Valparaiso, Chile, and was educated by a governess and at school in London. The family travelled widely, eventually settling in Hertfordshire, with a London residence in Portland Place. She was much influenced by her mother's interest in progressive issues and by her elder sister, Henrietta *Müller, founding editor of the *Women's Penny Paper* and *Woman's Herald*, who was elected to the London school board in 1879. Both sisters led unusually active lives, unshackled by Victorian convention and no doubt helped greatly by their personal wealth; as young women they mountaineered in the Swiss Alps and continued to travel in later years, for example, to India and the United States. Drawn initially to organized philanthropy, at the age of twenty Eva Müller worked with Octavia Hill in Marylebone, where her duties were to collect rents and to look after the welfare of tenants. She subsequently accepted a nurse training post at Brownlow Hill workhouse infirmary in Liverpool, but returned to London to take care of her ailing father.

Eva's marriage to **Walter Stowe Bright McLaren** (1853–1912) on 18 April 1883 introduced her to the politically influential Bright–McLaren family, with its extensive connections to the Liberal Party and the Victorian women's movement. Walter was born in Edinburgh, the youngest son of Duncan *McLaren (1800–1886), lord provost of Scotland and MP for Edinburgh, and Priscilla Bright *McLaren (1815–1906), president of the Edinburgh National Society for Women's Suffrage and sister to John and Jacob Bright. Charles Benjamin Bright *McLaren was his brother, and John *McLaren his half-brother. After an education at Craigmount School and Edinburgh University, Walter entered into business as a worsted spinner in the firm of Smith and McLaren in Keighley, and in later years became a director of numerous companies. However, his heart lay in politics, and he was subsequently elected Liberal MP for Crewe (1886–95).

Eva and Walter were remarkably close in political outlook and aspirations, and devoted much of their married life to the attainment of women's rights. Greatly influenced by his maternal relations, Walter had written a pamphlet on women's suffrage in 1874 and was instrumental in attempting to make it part of the Liberal Party's policy on electoral reform as early as 1883. He and Eva joined the executive committee of the Manchester Society for Women's Suffrage while living in Bradford, serving from 1884 to 1895. When his parliamentary career took them to London they became increasingly involved with the central committee of the National Society for Women's Suffrage, of which Eva was already a member, with her sister, Henrietta. Walter served as joint secretary of the all-party committee of the Parliamentary Supporters of the Women's Franchise Bill, which Helen Blackburn called 'an authoritative nucleus of action' (Blackburn, 173). Although keenly aware of the legal disabilities of married women, they shared the view of the central committee that any successful women's suffrage bill, even a restricted measure which enfranchised only widows and spinsters, would be better than none. This was a fiercely contested issue within the suffrage movement, which split the Bright family into two camps. On the equally divisive matter of affiliation of political associations, they were instrumental in pressing for change: Walter chaired the special general meeting of the central committee in 1888 which led to the formation of the Central National Society for Women's Suffrage on whose executive committee he and Eva served for a number of years. In the same period Eva became a leading member of the Women's Liberal Federation: she was its first honorary treasurer (1887–1914), honorary secretary of the Welsh Union of Women's Liberal Associations from 1894, and inaugurated several Women's Liberal Associations (WLAs), serving as president of Southport WLA and as vice-president of Crewe WLA in the 1890s. A member of the progressive faction during the split over suffrage in 1891, Eva believed that the federation's first aim should be to achieve electoral rights for women, and supported the implementation of the test question policy which obliged parliamentary candidates to declare themselves in favour of women's suffrage before they could obtain the crucial electoral assistance of constituency WLAs. She was active in a series of suffrage pressure groups within the WLA: the Union of Practical Suffragists, the Forward Suffrage Union, and the Liberal Women's Suffrage Union. She was author of *The History of the Women's Suffrage Movement in the Women's Liberal Federation* (1903).

Both McLarens were active members of the movement to extend women's rights in local government. Eva had been elected to the Lambeth board of guardians about 1882, and after her marriage served as poor-law guardian for the Horton district of Bradford; she continued to work for improvements in the poor law and for better conditions in workhouses. They campaigned for Lady Sandhurst and Jane Cobden in their attempt to become the first women elected to the new London county council in 1889. In the same year Eva became treasurer of the Society for Promoting the Return of Women as County Councillors, while Walter took a leading part in the affairs of its successor, the Women's Local Government Society. He introduced a successful clause into the 1894 Local Government Act to the effect that a woman should not be disqualified by marriage from being on the local government register of electors, provided that husband and wife were not qualified in respect of the same property. This was to be a significant landmark in improving the rights of married women. The McLaren marriage was clearly an egalitarian one—insofar as the law would allow—and both disliked the remnants of coverture which were still the hallmarks of a wife's legal subordination. A keen feminist, Eva rejected the conventional title of Mrs Walter McLaren and

was known throughout her political career as Mrs Eva McLaren, on the grounds that 'it is more important to know who a woman is than whose wife she is' (*Women's Penny Paper*, 1 June 1899). They were attracted to the advanced views of Edward Carpenter on the simplification of life and were drawn to many of the social reform issues of the day. They worked with Josephine Butler in the campaign for the repeal of the Contagious Diseases Acts, Eva serving as secretary and then chair of the London branch of the Ladies' National Association (LNA). This led to an interest in the lives of Indian women—child marriage and the effects of the Contagious Diseases Acts were of growing concern to a number of feminists in Britain—and in 1888 Eva co-sponsored the studies of an Indian woman student at the London school of medicine, while Walter worked with other MPs to rescind the acts governing the state regulation of prostitution in India in 1888. Members of a peace society in London in the late 1880s, they advocated the concept of a court of arbitration to settle international disputes. They attended, as delegates of the LNA and central committee of the National Society for Women's Suffrage, a French government Congress on the Civil Rights of Women in 1889, and Eva subsequently published a pamphlet on this subject in 1891. Typical of many of the Liberal suffragists of the time, she also became involved in the temperance movement. Walter was the nephew of Margaret Bright Lucas, founder of the British Women's Temperance Association (BWTA), in which Eva came to national prominence as vice-president (1894–1900). She fully supported Lady Henry Somerset's successful, albeit divisive, attempt to steer the BWTA away from a narrow crusade against drink and towards a broad platform of social reform, and served as superintendent of the Department of Work Among Municipal Women Voters.

During his first spell in the Commons from 1886 to 1895 Walter had immersed himself in legislation which chiefly affected women. In addition to suffrage and local government he had spoken favourably on the appointment of police matrons, opposed the sex discrimination implicit in the Deceased Wife's Sister Bill, and drafted an unsuccessful amendment to defeat the Shop Hours Bill of 1892 on the grounds of equality. In practice he became an unofficial whip on behalf of the late Victorian women's movement, and his removal from parliament after the general election of 1895 was a serious loss, although he remained active in a number of organizations, including the Men's League for Women's Suffrage, serving as a member of the executive committee and as a vice-president after 1907, and the Women's Local Government Society. His re-election in 1910 for Crewe Division brought renewed activity, cut short by his death from heart failure on 29 June 1912. An enormously popular MP, he had worked particularly for those interests which reflected the industrial nature of his constituency. A firm believer in conciliation in industrial disputes, he had taken a prominent part in the Miners' Conciliation Board and had helped to bring in the Minimum Wage Act. His support for the coalowners during the south Wales miners' strike, however, caused him to lose favour. Eva retired from the national spotlight, although she continued to represent the Home Counties Union on the Women's Liberal Federation executive committee in 1913–14. When war broke out she took the courageous step of resuming her belated nursing career, and worked at a base hospital in France during the winter of 1914–15. She subsequently experienced a severe breakdown in health, and died from chronic Bright's disease and uraemia on 16 August 1921 at Great Comp Cottage, Borough Green, Kent, survived by her adopted daughter, Mary Florence Campbell McLaren.

LINDA WALKER

Sources S. A. Tooley, 'Social reforms: an interview with Mrs Eva McLaren', *Woman's Signal* (31 May 1894), 370–71 · *Women's Penny Paper* (1 June 1889) · *Women's Penny Paper* (1889–91) · *Woman's Herald* (28 Nov 1891) · *Woman's Herald* (1891–3) · *Liberal Year Book* (1887–1914) · *Federation News* (Oct 1921), 38–9 · *The Times* (20 Aug 1921) · *The Times* (2 July 1912), 10 [obit of Walter Stowe Bright McLaren] · *The Times* (4 July 1912) · H. Blackburn, *Women's suffrage: a record of the women's suffrage movement in the British Isles* (1902) · WW · WWW · L. Walker, 'Party political women: a comparative study of liberal women and the Primrose League, 1890–1914', *Equal or different: women's politics, 1800–1914*, ed. J. Rendall (1987), 165–91 · A. Burton, *Burdens of history: British feminists, Indian women, and imperial culture, 1865–1915* (1994) · d. cert. · m. cert. · E. Crawford, *The women's suffrage movement* (1999)
Archives Man. CL, Manchester suffrage MSS · NL Scot., Rutherford MSS
Likenesses D. White, double portrait, photograph (with Walter Stowe Bright McLaren), repro. in Tooley, 'Social reforms: an interview with Mrs Eva McLaren' · photograph, repro. in Tooley, 'Social reforms: an interview with Mrs Eva McLaren'
Wealth at death £48,329 4s.: probate, 31 Oct 1921, CGPLA Eng. & Wales · £16,798 1s. 4d.—Walter Stowe Bright McLaren: probate, 18 July 1912, CGPLA Eng. & Wales

McLaren, Henry Duncan, second Baron Aberconway (1879–1953), industrialist, was born on 16 April 1879 at Barnes, Surrey, the eldest of four children (two sons, two daughters) of Charles Benjamin Bright *McLaren, first Baron Aberconway (1850–1934), industrialist, and his wife, Laura Elizabeth (1854–1933) [see McLaren, Laura Elizabeth], daughter of Henry Davis *Pochin (1824–1895), chemical manufacturer and radical MP, of Bodnant, Denbighshire, and Agnes *Pochin, née Heap (1825–1908). He was educated at Eton College, where he became captain of the Oppidans, and at Balliol College, Oxford, where he obtained a second in modern history (1902). Following graduation he travelled for a year or two before being called to the bar by Lincoln's Inn in 1905, though he never practised.

McLaren inherited a strong Liberal background from his parents and grandparents and after he had acquired some business experience, mainly in the enterprises of his maternal grandfather, he entered the House of Commons in 1906 as Liberal member for West Staffordshire. Until 1910 he was parliamentary private secretary to Lloyd George, for whose intellect he formed and kept the liveliest admiration. The year 1910 proved to be an eventful one for McLaren. In January he was defeated in the parliamentary election. His marriage to Christabel Mary Melville (1890–1974), daughter of Sir Melville Macnaghten, chief of the Criminal Investigation Department took place on 19

July 1910. She was a gifted woman who shared his artistic interests, and he depended greatly upon her companionship and judgement. They had three sons and two daughters. In December 1910 McLaren was elected as MP for the Bosworth division of Leicestershire, the seat given up by his father.

During the First World War, McLaren acted as director of area organization at the Ministry of Munitions, being appointed CBE in 1918 in recognition of his work. He continued as MP for Bosworth until defeated in the 1922 election, when, due to his increasing business commitments, he decided not to attempt to seek re-election. McLaren's business connections included directorships of a number of companies with which his family were associated, especially in the iron and steel, coal, and engineering industries, including John Brown & Co., Bolckow Vaughan, Palmer's Shipbuilding, and the Tredegar Iron and Coal Company Ltd. Following his father's death in 1934 McLaren succeeded not only to the peerage but also to the chairmanship of John Brown, the Sheepbridge Coal and Iron Company, Cortonwood Collieries, Yorkshire Amalgamated Collieries, and Tredegar. Although McLaren, despite his arts background, had acquired an insight into industrial techniques in his early adult years, his role in these companies, like that of his father before him, was essentially an organizational and supervisory one.

During his business career McLaren also served as a director of the National Provincial Bank and of London Assurance; but it was in the field of china clay that he was most knowledgeable. From an early age he had been closely associated with one of the family companies, H. D. Pochin & Co. In 1932 he was instrumental in bringing about an amalgamation of this company and two other major china clay manufacturers, English China Clays Ltd and Lovering China Clays Ltd, to form English Clays Lovering Pochin & Co. Ltd. McLaren became the first chairman of the new concern and exercised a considerable managerial influence over it until his death in 1953.

It is clear that McLaren's business interests were widespread, reflecting his prodigious energy. A man of considerable creative intellect, capable of switching his mind from one subject to another with remarkable agility, he drove both himself and others hard. Often considered by contemporaries to be autocratic and difficult to approach, he nevertheless respected sound arguments put forward by others. Imaginative and forward-looking, McLaren resolutely maintained the view that his companies should remain in the forefront of technical progress.

The range of McLaren's other interests may well have reduced his overall effectiveness as a businessman. An enthusiastic and splendid shot, he enjoyed travelling, and liked to drive himself in open Rolls-Royce cars, of which he had a succession. He was a JP and served as chairman of the Denbighshire quarter-sessions. He was a keen and knowledgeable collector of antique furniture, ornaments, and pictures, but plants and gardening were his great love. Encouraged by his mother, Laura, and taking advantage of the site and the lie of the land, McLaren laid out with great skill and taste a magnificent series of terraces, and fashioned a wonderful wild garden at the family estate at Bodnant in north Wales. He planted a wide range of shrubs and was particularly known for his planting and hybridization of rhododendrons. In 1949 the gardens at Bodnant were handed over to the National Trust together with a generous endowment for their upkeep. McLaren's gardening expertise made him a well-known and most distinguished president of the Royal Horticultural Society from 1931 until his death. McLaren died at Bodnant on 23 May 1953. He was survived by his wife.

ABERCONWAY, rev. TREVOR BOYNS

Sources G. Holmes, 'McLaren, Henry Duncan', DBB · m. cert. · d. cert.
Likenesses O. Birley, oils, c.1948, Royal Horticultural Society, London · O. Birley, portrait, John Brown, London · P. de Laszlo, portrait, Bodnant Garden, Conwy
Wealth at death £242,251 19s. 3d.—save and except settled land: probate, 1 Oct 1953, CGPLA Eng. & Wales · £23,525—limited to settled land: probate, 5 Nov 1953, CGPLA Eng. & Wales

Maclaren, Ian. See Watson, John (1850–1907).

McLaren, John, Lord McLaren (1831–1910), lawyer and politician, was born in Edinburgh on 17 April 1831, the only son of Duncan *McLaren (1800–1886), draper and radical politician, and his first wife, Grant (d. 1833), daughter of William Aitken, a merchant in Dunbar. Delicate health meant that John's schooling was interrupted by frequent periods abroad in places such as Madeira, Italy, and Jamaica. This broken school life did not, however, prevent him going on to Edinburgh University in the late 1840s. He was thereafter admitted to the Faculty of Advocates in December 1856. McLaren married Ottilie Augusta Schwabe (1835–1914), eldest daughter of Hermann Levy Schwabe, a merchant in Glasgow and Bridge of Allan, on 14 December 1868. They had a family of three sons and three daughters. The eldest daughter, Katherine, married McLaren's nephew, the polemicist Frederick Scott *Oliver. The youngest, Ottilie, established a reputation as a sculptor and married the composer William Wallace (1860–1940).

McLaren's career as an advocate was impeded by poor health, and he made his name largely through his legal publications. A Collection of Noble General Statutes and Acts of Sederunt, which related to procedure and evidence in Scottish courts, appeared in 1861. This was followed by A Treatise on the Law of Trusts and Trust Settlements in 1863, later revised under the titles of The Law of Scotland in Relation to Wills and Succession (1868), and The Law of Wills and Succession as Administered in Scotland (1894). This established McLaren as a leading authority in the field, and founded his reputation as an author. McLaren also edited the 1870 edition of Bell's Commentaries. Helped by his reputation his practice grew, and what his court pleading style lacked in power, it made up for in subtlety and ingenuity.

McLaren had been brought up in a family at the centre of mid-nineteenth-century radical Liberalism and religious dissent: his father's struggle to create an independent Liberalism in Edinburgh and to break the hold of the Parliament House whigs on the constituency was well known. As a sick schoolboy at home, McLaren by his own account was given his father's correspondence about Edinburgh politics to look over. He also witnessed the anti-corn law agitation in the city at close quarters: his second stepmother (Duncan McLaren married three times) was Priscilla Bright [see McLaren, Priscilla Bright], sister of John Bright, the radical MP. Among his half-brothers were Sir Charles Benjamin Bright *McLaren and Walter Stowe Bright *McLaren [see under McLaren, Eva Maria], both at one time MPs. For his part John McLaren stood between the radical tradition, and the whig establishment that his father had so bitterly opposed. In a sense his career kept step with the passage of urban middle-class liberal families into the mainstream of the Liberal Party and then beyond it. Whereas his father was a United Presbyterian dissenter, John McLaren was a generous contributor to the Church of Scotland. Like his father he opposed Irish home rule from 1886 and privately supported the Liberal Unionists.

McLaren's initial attempt to obtain a public appointment in 1862, which involved an intervention by W. E. Gladstone with Lord Advocate James Moncreiff, failed partly on account of his father's unacceptability to the Scottish whig Liberal establishment. In 1869 he was appointed sheriff of chancery, an office he held until 1880, by which time his father's opposition to the repeal of the laws on picketing had earned him the opposition of working men and the support of his erstwhile whig enemies.

In the late 1870s McLaren became very actively involved in the attempts, associated especially with William Patrick Adam, to improve the organization of the Liberal Party in Scotland. He was particularly associated with schemes to register votes in the Midlothian constituency and took part in the organization of the campaign that W. E. Gladstone mounted there in the run up to the 1880 election. McLaren himself was elected for Wigtown burghs, and appointed as lord advocate in the new Liberal administration. This was, however, to be the high point of his brief enjoyment of political office: he failed to be re-elected for Wigtown burghs in May 1880, following his appointment (though the election was later declared void following a petition). In July 1880 McLaren stood for Berwick upon Tweed, and was again narrowly defeated. In January 1881 his father resigned his Edinburgh seat in favour of McLaren, who was elected without trouble. However, in parliament his problems continued. The home secretary, Sir William Harcourt, who remained responsible for much Scottish business until the creation of the position of Scottish secretary in 1885, was necessarily in frequent contact with McLaren. Friction between them developed, in which Harcourt, a whig, may have given vent to resentment at McLaren's political background. Whatever the precise reason, and despite intervention by his step-uncle John Bright, McLaren bowed to pressure from Gladstone, and accepted a vacant position in the outer house of the Scottish Court of Session, resigning his Commons seat in August 1881.

McLaren himself, after three recent election struggles, may have resented his treatment, but it was widely felt that he was more suited to be a judge than a politician. He had lacked the constitution for oratory and public debate. As a judge he could insist on reasoned argument and indulge his taste for subtlety and distinction. In nearly thirty years on the bench he earned a reputation as an able dispenser of justice that leaned to equity rather than strict application of legal principles. His opinions were lucid, his summings-up dispassionate. Unlike his model, John Inglis, he had limited confidence in juries and he also did not share Inglis's apparent reluctance to overrule a bad precedent. He was moved to the first division of the court and became a lord of justiciary in 1885, though the criminal cases which the latter position involved were not much to his taste.

McLaren's sense of humour saved his judgments from the suspicion of condescension to the layman. In private this humour could be pungent and was mixed with carefully selected language, a studied manner, and a punctuating characteristic cough. His health precluded active recreation and he turned instead to science, especially astronomy, mathematics, and botany. In 1869 he became a fellow of the Royal Society of Edinburgh and, in addition to publishing various papers, was elected a member of council in 1883 and served three times as its vice-president. Royal Society business brought him into contact with William Thomson, Lord Kelvin, who was frequently his guest when in Edinburgh. McLaren was also a president of the Scottish Meteorological Society, a director of the Ben Nevis observatory, and was active in organizing the setting up of the Royal Observatory on Blackford Hill, Edinburgh. Honorary degrees from the universities of Edinburgh (1882), Glasgow (1883), and Aberdeen (1906) indicated public recognition of McLaren's work.

During a leave of absence caused by ill health John McLaren died of influenza at Brighton on 6 April 1910; he was buried in the Grange cemetery in Edinburgh on 9 April. He was survived by his wife, who died in 1914, a son, Duncan, who emigrated to Canada, and their three daughters. GORDON F. MILLAR

Sources The Scotsman (7 April 1910) · The Times (7 April 1910) · N. J. D. Kennedy, 'Lord McLaren', Juridical Review, 22 (1910), 181–96 · C. G. Knott, Proceedings of the Royal Society of Edinburgh, 31 (1910–11), 694–5 · J. B. Mackie, The life and work of Duncan McLaren, 2 vols. (1888) · G. W. T. Omond, The lord advocates of Scotland, second series, 1834–1880 (1914), 316–48 · WWW, 1897–1915 · The Scotsman (8 April 1910) [letters on McLaren] · The Scotsman (9 April 1910) [letters on McLaren] · The Scotsman (11 April 1910) [funeral report] · BL, James Moncreiff to W. E. Gladstone, 4 Feb 1862, Add. MS 44398, fols. 87–92 · S. P. Walker, The Faculty of Advocates, 1800–1986 (1987), 113 · F. J. Grant, ed., The Faculty of Advocates in Scotland, 1532–1943, Scottish RS, 145 (1944), 138 · WWBMP, vol. 1 · J. Foster, Members of parliament, Scotland ... 1357–1882, 2nd edn (privately printed, London, 1882), 234–5 · DNB

Archives NL Scot., corresp. and papers · RAS, letters · Royal Observatory, Edinburgh, corresp. and astronomical notes | Bodl. Oxf., corresp. with Lord Kimberley · NL Scot., F. S. Oliver MSS, corresp. and family corresp., incl. letters from his father D. McLaren and his step-uncle John Bright, Acc. 7726, 7841

Likenesses O. Wallace, marble bust, 1920, Parliament Hall, Edinburgh · J. Hutchinson, bronze bust; fomerly in possession of his widow · J. Lavery, oils, Scot. NPG · O. Leyde, oils; formerly in possession of his widow, 1912 · M. Wright, oils; formerly in possession of Charles Benjamin Bright McLaren, 1912

Wealth at death £15,907 19s. 7d.: confirmation, 13 Aug 1910, CCI · £1708 14s. 9d.: additional estate, 28 Nov 1913, CCI

McLaren [née Pochin], **Laura Elizabeth**, Lady Aberconway (1854–1933), campaigner for women's rights and horticulturist, was born at Camp Street, Broughton, Lancashire, on 14 May 1854, the only surviving daughter of Henry Davis *Pochin (1824–1895), industrial chemist and MP, and his wife, Agnes *Pochin, née Heap (1825–1908), an activist for women's rights. Her parents were radical Liberals, and on 6 March 1877 at the old Westminster meeting-house, with John Bright as a witness, Laura Pochin married Charles Benjamin Bright *McLaren (1850–1934), elder son of Priscilla Bright *McLaren and Duncan *McLaren, members of the same political and social network. Charles McLaren was a barrister at the time of their marriage, became Liberal MP for Bosworth in 1892, and was later actively involved in running steel, iron, and colliery undertakings, many linked with the Pochin inheritance. Although her husband was a Quaker, there is no evidence that Laura, whose parents were Unitarians, adopted his faith. They had four children who survived infancy: two sons, the younger of whom was killed in action in 1917, and two daughters.

Although no details are known of Laura Pochin's education, it is certain that considerable attention would have been paid to it. She was brought up by parents who thought that women had the right to equal treatment with men, both politically and legally. Her mother had specifically written that women should receive an education to fit them for a career. Laura McLaren's obituarist in The Times was to write that she was 'a capable woman of business, with the ready grasp and the courageous power of decision that enabled her to weigh big problems with the brain of a man', and it would appear that this was the view taken by her father, because, her surviving brother proving unsatisfactory, she was made her father's heir.

Laura McLaren was proud of the fact that, as a child, she had attended the country's first public women's suffrage meeting, at which her mother had spoken. Immediately after her marriage she became a member of the executive committee of the London National Society of Women's Suffrage; she became a member of the finance committee, and was treasurer in 1885. Later she served on the executive committee of the Central National Society for Women's Suffrage and was president of the South Kensington Women's Liberal Association: about 1890 she prepared a summary of the evidence presented to the House of Lords on the sweating system of labour, on behalf of the Women's Liberal Federation. In 1908 Fisher Unwin published her pamphlet 'Better and happier': an answer from the Ladies' Gallery to the speeches in opposition to the Women's Suffrage Bill, February 28, 1908. In it she puts cogently the well-rehearsed arguments that she and her fellow suffragists had broadcast for the previous forty years. Responding to Herbert Gladstone's suggestion that women must

Laura Elizabeth McLaren, Lady Aberconway (1854–1933), by James Tissot, 1878

of the order of St John of Jerusalem. After the war, the suffrage issue having been settled, she carried on her interest in feminist issues as a member of the Open Door Council.

Laura McLaren inherited the Bodnant estate above the River Conwy from her father in 1895; her husband was ennobled as Baron Aberconway in 1911. She was a very keen gardener, both in Wales and at her much-loved villa in the south of France. She fostered a love of plants in her son, Henry Duncan *McLaren, to whom in 1901 she entrusted the day-to-day care of the Bodnant garden. She was especially interested in spring and summer herbaceous plants, roses, peonies, and the native flora, and was particularly involved in developing the semi-formal borders around the house. She was continuously consulted over the long process of creating the magnificent series of terraces to the west of the house, and it was as an active partner with her son that she was long remembered at Bodnant. *The Times* obituarist described her as one of the foremost horticulturists in Europe and a painter of merit. Lady Aberconway died on 4 January 1933 at the Château de la Garoupe, her villa near Antibes, leaving an estate valued at £0.75 million, and was buried at the Bodnant mausoleum, The Poem.   ELIZABETH CRAWFORD

Sources H. T. Milliken, *The road to Bodnant: the story behind the foundation of the famous north Wales garden* (1975) · *The Times* (12 Jan 1933), 14 · private information (2004) · b. cert. · m. cert. · *CGPLA Eng. & Wales* (1933)
Likenesses J. Tissot, portrait, 1878, Bodnant, Conwy [*see illus.*] · P. de Laszlo, oils, after 1918, Bodnant, Conwy
Wealth at death £750,639 4s. 11d.: probate, 25 Feb 1933, *CGPLA Eng. & Wales*

get out to convert the electorate to their viewpoint, she writes

> men who suggest this spade-work do not know at what cost to women it is done. In the first place women are miserably poor; the wives of rich men have often nothing but their dress allowance; … half the women of this country work for a wage which a Royal Commission declared to average not more than 1s a day; married women are busily occupied with their homes and with their children … to do spadework—to carry on political agitation—needs a lifetime of leisure. … How often have we tramped along the muddy lanes, how often have we gone round from door to door, often receiving rebuffs and unkindness. Well do we remember dreary railway stations at midnight, the last train gone, and snow upon the ground. (L. E. McLaren, *'Better and Happier'*, 1908, 17)

She was the author of a very practical document, *The Woman's Charter of Rights and Liberties—Preliminary Draft* (1909), which was undertaken as the result of a decision made at the fifth congress of the International Woman Suffrage Alliance to present simultaneously in 1910 to all the parliaments of the world a comprehensive statement or charter detailing the legal injustices and legislative needs of women. By 1913 she was a vice-president of the non-party National Political League for Men and Women. During the First World War she ran a nursing home for officers in her London home, 43 Belgrave Square, for which she was appointed CBE and was made lady of grace

McLaren, (William) Norman (1914–1987), film director, was born on 11 April 1914 at 21 Albert Place, Stirling, the youngest of three children of William McLaren, a master house painter, and his wife, Jeanie Cross Wilson Smith. Little is known about his early life and education. He studied art and interior design at the Glasgow School of Art (1933–6), but soon found his enthusiasm fired more by college film society screenings of work by Soviet directors V. Pudovkin and S. Eisenstein. He saw film as an exciting new artistic medium and the abstract films of the European avant-garde appealed to his interest in synaesthesia: even as a schoolboy some of his paintings had aspired to represent music visually. Like many artists he realized film was a way to make created images move. His student films, such as the delightful experimental documentary of a student ball, *Camera Makes Whoopee* (1935), aroused attention, local newspapers proclaiming him 'the young genius of Glasgow School of Art' (Cutler). He also became, briefly, politicized, making *Hell Unlimited* (1936) an anti-capitalist, anti-war film with Scottish sculptor Helen Biggar, and he worked as cameraman on a Spanish civil-war documentary.

John Grierson, a seminal figure in British documentary film-making, and then head of the General Post Office film unit, spotted the young McLaren's talent at a Scottish Amateur Film Festival, and in 1937 he invited his fellow countryman to join him in London. Also at the unit—then a focus for innovative film-making—was Len Lye. Lye's

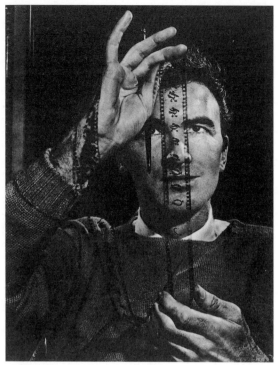

(William) **Norman McLaren** (1914–1987), by Yousuf Karsh, 1957

work was a direct precursor to McLaren's own experiments in painting directly onto film, and he rekindled McLaren's interest in animation. He also experimented with drawing sound directly on film. McLaren later wrote that

> animation is not the art of moving drawings, but of the drawn movement: the key is not what one finds in a drawing, but what is created between the drawings linked in a series. (Solomon, 11)

After working on sponsored documentary films, in 1939 McLaren moved to the United States. On arrival in New York he obtained work through friends, painting murals in luxury private homes. He then made some short abstract films with support from the Guggenheim Foundation. In 1941 he was again given a job by Grierson, who was now in Canada heading the new national film board (NFB), a government initiative to help the Canadian war effort. McLaren made propaganda films, experimental in form but with general appeal. In 1943 McLaren was asked to organize an animation department at the NFB in Ottawa. After the war the NFB's remit changed and they made history, ethnic, creative, and experimental films. McLaren had found a perfect haven, allowing him almost total freedom and security to pursue his own artistic goals.

For the next forty years Norman McLaren never ceased to experiment and to invent new techniques. He is most usually associated with the direct, or cameraless, method, which involved working directly onto the film stock, and for his many developments of that technique. But his interests were wide-ranging and this is reflected in the

variety of his films, all of which aspired to achieve coherence of the visual rhythm with the rhythm of sound. Like a latter-day Leonardo, he considered science, art, technique, and style as one whole. He often developed techniques before finding a suitable film subject for them. Sometimes his experiments left him dissatisfied, but he would return to them years, even decades, later to successful effect. Process was important to him: he took from the surrealists a belief in the creative role of the unconscious. McLaren's closest collaborator at the NFB until the 1970s was Evelyn Lambart, who had a background in mathematics and science. Together they made *Begone Dull Care* (1949), an exuberant abstract film that was accompanied by a jazz score by Oscar Peterson. It enthused Pablo Picasso, who commented, 'Finally, something new!' (Bendazzi, 116), and their vibrancy and appeal have endured.

In 1949 McLaren went to China on a UNESCO mission to teach local artists visual communication for health education programmes. He was caught up in the civil war there and on his return to Canada he made *Neighbours* (1952). This pixilated allegory of how humankind's territorial instincts lead to mutual destruction won an Oscar in 1953. McLaren's reply to a congratulatory telegram was typical: 'Thanks, but who is Oscar?' His stay in India that year, working on another government education project, saw the structure of his own films become influenced by Indian classical music—gradually developing a simple theme and increasing in complexity and tempo.

The late 1950s and early 1960s saw McLaren return to experiments with abstraction, particularly with geometric forms. A growing interest in how film could represent dance was manifest in the later 1960s. *Pas de deux* (1967) began with a desire to see images multiply in a stroboscopic way and it revived E. J. Marey's technique of chronophotography to recreate the movement of two dancers; it was the first of a series of dance films.

McLaren was an intensely private man, and when he was asked to introduce the 1960 Montreal film festival, shyness led him to animate himself on film instead—also a demonstration of his sense of fun. He was generous with his knowledge and he duplicated technical notes on all of his films in response to enquiries from around the world about his methods. Some critics have questioned McLaren's status as an abstract artist, given the tendency to figuration and narrative suggestion in many of his films, but for others that tendency is precisely their appeal. The dance series often divided opinion. It is perhaps the earlier films that continue to have the strongest impact, but the body of his work as a whole is rich enough to sustain enduring interest. Although he retired in 1984 McLaren continued to experiment with film-making. He died, unmarried, in Montreal on 26 January 1987.

JAYNE PILLING

Sources V. T. Richard and N. McLaren, *Manipulator of movement: the National Film Board years, 1947–1967* (1982) · G. Bendazzi, *Cartoons: one hundred years of cinema animation* (1994) · A. Bastiancich, *L'opera di Norman McLaren* (Torino, 1981) · D. Williams, *Norman McLaren: the creative process* (National Film Board of Canada, 1993) [video documentary] · W. Moritz, 'Norman McLaren and Jules Engel', *A reader in animation studies*, ed. J. Pilling (1997), 104–11 · C. Solomon, ed., *The*

art of the animated image: an anthology (Los Angeles, CA, 1987) • M. E. Cutler, 'Unique genius of Norman McLaren', *Arts Canada*, 22 (May 1965), 10 • *The Times* (28 Jan 1987)
Archives National Film Board of Canada, Montreal, MSS | NL Scot., corresp., mainly with Florence Russell | FILM BFI NFTVA, performance footage • La Cinémathèque Québécoise, Montreal, Canada • National Film Board of Canada, Montreal | SOUND National Film Board of Canada, Montreal, Norman McLaren archives
Likenesses Y. Karsh, photograph, 1957, priv. coll. [*see illus.*]

McLaren, Priscilla Bright (1815–1906), campaigner for women's rights, was born on 8 September 1815 at Greenbank, Rochdale, Lancashire, the fifth of the eleven children of Jacob Bright (1775–1851), bookkeeper and owner of a cotton spinning business, and his second wife, Martha, *née* Wood (1788/9–1830). The politicians John *Bright and Jacob *Bright were her brothers. She was educated at Hannah Wilson's school, South Parade, York, and at Hannah Johnson's school in Liverpool. As a girl she visited Newgate prison with her fellow Quaker Elizabeth Fry, 'and her upbringing gave her a keen and active interest in politics which she never lost until the end of her life' (*Englishwoman's Review*, 59).

After John Bright's first wife, Elizabeth, died in September 1841, leaving an eleven-year-old daughter, Priscilla Bright moved into her brother's Rochdale home, One Ash, until he remarried in June 1847. As well as assisting Bright with fund-raising and canvassing, she ran his household and brought up his daughter, to whom she remained very close and with whom—as Helen P. Bright Clark—she worked closely in campaigning activities. In 1842 Priscilla met the recently widowed Scottish Presbyterian Duncan *McLaren (1800–1886) while he was on a visit to her brother at One Ash. Freed from her domestic responsibilities on Bright's remarriage, she and McLaren were themselves married on 6 July 1848; they had one daughter and two sons, Charles Benjamin Bright *McLaren, first Baron Aberconway, and Walter Stowe Bright *McLaren [*see under* McLaren, Eva Maria]. She also took on responsibility for five stepchildren, the eldest of whom was seventeen. They shared the same broad political interests: for both of them, their Liberal convictions veered strongly towards radicalism. Alike in party politics and single-issue agitation, Priscilla McLaren and her husband were equal partners, though they disagreed from time to time on matters of tactics and policy.

McLaren inherited from her father a disciplined exactness in the use of words, and from her mother an abiding love of poetry. She had perhaps a lighter touch than her husband and a broader range of cultural interests: a stepson described her as 'a powerful influence … in strengthening and refining the character of my father' (*Annual Monitor*, 115).

When in 1870 Josephine Butler began her social purity and women's equality campaign against the Contagious Diseases Acts of 1864 and 1866, the McLarens were her vigorous supporters. On 30 March 1871 Duncan McLaren presented to parliament a petition from 250,000 women calling for repeal of the acts. John Bright was cautious in the matter but his extended family included active repealers,

Priscilla Bright McLaren (1815–1906), by unknown photographer

including (in parliament) his brother Jacob, as well as Duncan McLaren and later his sons, while the Ladies' National Association had the support of Bright's sister Margaret Bright Lucas and his first wife's sisters Margaret Tanner, Anna Maria Priestman, and Mary Priestman, who were among Josephine Butler's close friends. Helen Bright Clark and her husband, William Stephens *Clark, were similarly active in this, as in other campaigns for women's rights in the political sphere and over access to higher education. Between 1869 and 1872 the McLarens were both active in the campaign to admit women medical students to the University of Edinburgh.

Priscilla McLaren became disillusioned at what she regarded as the complacency of many men in her political circle over the Contagious Diseases Acts, and became an advocate of women-only meetings within the association: 'women meeting women—I mean *ladies*—at which we can speak freely of the false idea of morality in which our *gentlemen* are educated and in which they live'. She wanted meetings for working-class women also, but believed that it was incumbent upon the middle classes to take the lead: 'we require [that] the ladies of the country [be] plainly told how their male friends live and what they believe' (Holton, 33).

McLaren found her instinctive pragmatism sorely tested on other issues of women's rights. She told a conference of the Married Women's Property Committee in 1880 that their struggle was 'a question of power. They could not bear that the wife should have power' (Holton, 54). On women's suffrage too she was radicalized by running into a brick wall of male indifference. Both she and her husband supported John Stuart Mill's amendment to the 1867 Reform Act in favour of female suffrage, and she became the first president of the Edinburgh Society for Women's Suffrage in 1870, her stepdaughter Agnes being joint secretary with Eliza Wigham. She gave full support to her brother Jacob Bright, who took on the leadership of the suffragists in parliament following Mill's failure to gain re-election in 1868. But John Bright was out of sympathy with his sister's suffrage activities ('She, dear creature, is almost too passionate and enthusiastic to reason on such a question'). Her view, given in a letter written to Helen Bright Clark after his death, was that 'he could never *bear* women to assert themselves' (Robbins, 219, 233). Nor was her brother the only object of McLaren's ire on this score; later, when the Liberal Party leadership came out against women's suffrage early in 1881, she complained bitterly of 'how badly the men are behaving', and after 'a most insulting' speech on the subject by Gladstone, she wrote that her husband 'looks very sorrowful for us. But every man's mouth is shut' (Holton, 66). Later she broke with Gladstone over home rule and became a Liberal Unionist. Like her husband she advocated an imperial parliament with representation for the colonies. Not long before she died, she signalled her acceptance of a place for suffragette militancy by signing a letter of sympathy for the activists imprisoned in October 1906.

Activity in the anti-slavery movement brought Priscilla McLaren into touch with the Garrisonian Elizabeth Pease Nichol, who had moved to Glasgow on her marriage in 1853. Later she often reminded her great-niece Alice Clark that she had been born on the anniversary of the emancipation of slaves. Both Priscilla and Duncan McLaren were also active in temperance work, and in both campaigns she worked alongside Eliza Wigham.

At the time of her marriage to Duncan McLaren, Quaker marriage was restricted to members and she had scruples about 'hireling priests'; they were perforce married before the superintendent registrar. For this she was disowned by Marsden monthly meeting, a step she regarded as so unjust that she never reapplied for membership. She consented, however, to her membership being restored to her in 1887 at the monthly meeting's initiative. Ten years later she was rejoicing that Friends were getting to grips with biblical criticism and the social implications of the gospel.

Priscilla McLaren was an indefatigable and (certainly within the family where, to Helen Clark and her children, she was their beloved Aunt Tilla) an entertaining letter-writer. Unlike some campaigners she had a great feeling for individuals and was a good listener. Her judgements were sometimes impatient, but she 'could look with a smile upon her own strong convictions and impulses' (*British Friend*, 310). She died from pneumonia at home at Newington House, Blacket Avenue, Edinburgh, on 5 November 1906, and was buried beside her husband (who had died on 26 April 1886) in St Cuthbert's churchyard, Edinburgh on 9 November. EDWARD H. MILLIGAN

Sources J. B. Mackie, *The life and work of Duncan McLaren*, 2 vols. (1888) • J. T. Mills, *John Bright and the Quakers*, 2 vols. (1935), esp. vol. 1, pp. 274–82, 293–317 • *Annual Monitor* (1907), 112–22 • *The Friend*, new ser., 46 (1906), 824 • *British Friend*, new ser., 15 (1906), 309–10 • S. S. Holton, *Suffrage days: stories from the women's suffrage movement* (1996) • *Englishwoman's Review*, 38 (1907), 59–60 • K. Robbins, *John Bright* (1979)

Archives NL Scot., corresp. and papers

Likenesses H. G. Gubbins?, portrait, *c*.1840, repro. in G. M. Trevelyan, *The life of John Bright* (1913) • photograph, 1884, repro. in Mackie, *Life and work*, vol. 2 • photograph, NPG [*see illus.*]

Wealth at death £2574 7*s.* 6*d.*: confirmation, 27 Feb 1907, *CCI* • £19 0*s.* 5*d.*: eik additional estate, 6 Aug 1908, *CCI*

McLaren, Walter Stowe Bright (1853–1912). *See under* McLaren, Eva Maria (1852/3–1921).

McLaren, William (1772–1832), poet, was born at Paisley, became a handloom weaver, and at one period went to Ireland as a manufacturer but had to return because he expressed his political opinions too vigorously. When he inherited money and property from his mother, whose surname was Scadlock, he went to Glasgow with the intention of attending the university. However, it is not clear whether he ever matriculated. Latterly he opened a public house in Paisley, married, and started a family.

McLaren, who developed an early taste for literature, became intimate with Robert Tannahill, with whom in 1805 he founded the Paisley Burns Club. Tannahill's volume of verse published in 1807 was dedicated to him. In 1815 he edited, with a memoir, *Poems and Songs* by Tannahill; and in 1818, also with a memoir, the posthumous poems of his half-brother James Scadlock. He collected his own verse in two volumes, entitled respectively *Emma, or, The Cruel Father* (1817) and *Isabella, or, The Robbers* (1827). He also wrote several pamphlets of ephemeral interest.

Towards the end of his life McLaren was forced through improvidence to return to the loom. He died in Paisley on 2 May 1832, a victim of the terrible plague then visiting the country. J. C. HADDEN, *rev.* JAMES HOW

Sources R. Brown, *Paisley poets, with brief memoirs of them, and selections from their poetry*, 2 vols. (1889) • C. Rogers, *The modern Scottish minstrel* (1857)

Wealth at death probably nothing

MacLauchlan, Henry (1792–1882), surveyor, was born at Landguard Fort, Felixstowe, Suffolk, on 26 April 1792, the elder son of Andrew MacLauchlan, Board of Ordnance storekeeper, and his second wife, Martha Haywood. Following his father's death in 1795, Henry went with his mother to her family in Chichester, and about 1804 became a cadet in the Royal Corps of Military Surveyors and Draftsmen at the Tower of London. He trained as a military surveyor, spending several years in Cork, but along with most other draughtsmen was placed on half pay when the corps disbanded in 1817. In 1823–4 MacLauchlan was employed by the Ordnance Survey in Gloucestershire, south Wales, and Bedfordshire.

In 1835, as one of the few surveyors with geological knowledge, MacLauchlan was seconded to work with Henry De la Beche to add geological data to the Cornish Ordnance Survey sheets. MacLauchlan had been elected a fellow of the Geological Society in 1832 (he read papers in

1833 and 1842) and was acknowledged by W. D. Conybeare and G. B. Greenough, both eminent geologists of the day. By 1839 he had transferred back to routine survey work, in which he continued until he retired in November 1844, though his cartographical opinion on future scales of ordnance maps and contouring was sought by a parliamentary commission in 1854. He favoured the use of hill shading over contouring, which he considered less informative and less beautiful.

On retirement MacLauchlan returned to Cornwall with the assessionable manors commission, surveying hill forts and linear earthworks. His work culminated in six papers published between 1847 and 1853 in the annual reports of the Royal Institution of Cornwall. By 1848 MacLauchlan was conducting a similar survey of ancient remains in the North Riding of Yorkshire for the keen amateur archaeologist Algernon Percy, Lord Prudhoe, later fourth duke of Northumberland. On its successful completion and publication (*Archaeological Journal*, 1849), the duke commissioned MacLauchlan to undertake further field surveys of Watling Street, Hadrian's Wall, the eastern branch of Watling Street, and other remains in Northumberland, all of which were carried out and published between 1850 and 1867.

MacLauchlan not only recorded with precision details of many ancient monuments, some of which have since been destroyed, but also provided texts to accompany his (largely sound) observations. His work was accorded little recognition until the 1950s and 1960s, but later scholars working on Roman and prehistoric remains in the north of England freely acknowledge their debt to his draughtsmanship and accuracy. His particular contribution concerned the derivation of place names.

MacLauchlan never married, lodging in the Lambeth and Clapham areas of London when not engaged on archaeological work. He died on 27 January 1882 at 14 Liston Road, Clapham, London.   J. C. DAY, *rev.*

Sources B. Charlton and J. Day, 'Henry MacLauchlan: surveyor and field archaeologist', *Between and beyond the walls*, ed. R. Miket and C. Burgess (1984), 4–37 · D. B. Charlton and J. C. Day, 'The archaeological field sketches of Henry MacLauchlan', *Archaeologia Aeliana*, 5th ser., 13 (1985), 147–61
Archives BL · Ordnance Survey HQ, Southampton, letters, 461 1&2 | Alnwick Castle, archives · NMG Wales, Henry De la Beche MSS · Tyne & Wear Museums, J. C. Bruce collection
Likenesses photograph, *c.*1860, Tyne & Wear Museums, J. C. Bruce collection
Wealth at death over £4100: Charlton and Day, 'Henry MacLauchlan'

Maclauchlan, Margaret (1621/2–1685). *See under* Wilson, Margaret (1666/7–1685).

Maclauchlan, Thomas (1816–1886), Free Church of Scotland minister and Gaelic scholar, was born on 29 January 1816 at Moy, Inverness-shire. He was the fourth child of James Maclauchlan, minister of Moy, and his second wife, Catherine Fraser. He was educated initially at home and then at the University of Aberdeen from 1829, graduating MA in 1833. He subsequently studied divinity at Aberdeen

and Edinburgh, and was licensed by the Church of Scotland Presbytery of Inverness on 27 June 1837. After a brief spell in Daviot, he was appointed to be his father's colleague and successor at Moy on 19 April 1838. Maclauchlan was married three times: on 22 March 1848 to Eliza Mackay; on 30 July 1857 to Margaret Hunter Geddes; and on 25 February 1869 to Fanny Leach Fraser.

Maclauchlan's ministry in the Church of Scotland began in the middle of the bitter 'ten years' conflict' that preceded the Disruption of 1843, and in this dispute he, along with his brother Simon, was a firm supporter of the evangelical party that would eventually leave the church. He was present at the momentous general assembly of 1843, and was one of those who walked out to form the Free Church. 'There seemed to be on all', he said, 'a feeling of awe' (Leask, 57). This action led to him being deprived of both church and manse, and, indeed, on the first weekend after the Disruption his congregation met for worship outside in a wood. As a Free Church minister, he moved to Stratherrick in 1844 and then to St Columba's, the Gaelic Free Church of Edinburgh, in 1849. This was to be his congregation until his death. He served as moderator of the Free Church general assembly in 1876.

Maclauchlan was deeply interested in his native highlands, studying and writing on such topical subjects as depopulation, destitution, and land use, as well as on the educational work of the Free Church in that part of Scotland. He served on the Free Church highland committee for many years, and was its tireless convenor for almost thirty years from 1855 until ill health forced his resignation in 1882. He was deeply committed to Celtic studies and to the Gaelic language at a time when it was under considerable threat, and once commented that 'for a Highland minister, Gaelic is more important than Greek' (*Proceedings and Debates*, 1875, 192). He taught Gaelic at New College for thirty years, unpaid, but his greatest contribution to the language was probably the deciphering, translating, and editing of the sixteenth-century manuscript 'Dean of Lismore's book', a very significant early collection of Gaelic poetry. This, and his other contributions to Celtic studies, earned him a fellowship of the Society of Antiquaries for Scotland in 1856 and the degree of LLD from Aberdeen in 1864. Maclauchlan, however, was not afraid to deal with more controversial issues. In 1857 he was highly critical of what he called 'the fallacy and absurdity of the whole doctrine of race'. As one of the excuses for the highland clearances, he believed that racism had been one of the notions most damaging to the Gaelic population of the highlands (Maclauchlan, 14–15).

After some years of failing health, Maclauchlan died in Edinburgh on 21 March 1886, and was buried in the Grange cemetery, Edinburgh. He was survived by his third wife and at least two sons.   JAMES LACHLAN MACLEOD

Sources W. K. Leask, *Dr Thomas Mclauchlan* (1905) · T. Maclauchlan, *Celtic gleanings* (1857) · W. G. Blaikie, *After fifty years* (1893) · T. Brown, *Annals of the Disruption*, new edn (1893) · W. Ewing, ed., *Annals of the Free Church of Scotland, 1843–1900*, 2 vols. (1914) · A. L. Drummond and J. Bulloch, *The church in Victorian Scotland, 1843–1874* (1975) · *Proceedings and Debates of the General Assembly*

of the Free Church of Scotland (1843–86) • N. Walker, *Chapters from the history of the Free Church of Scotland* (1895) • *IGI* • *CCI* (1886)
Likenesses D. O. Hill, group portrait (*The first general assembly of the Free Church of Scotland*), Free Church College, The Mound, Edinburgh
Wealth at death £6,393 1s. 10d.: confirmation, 6 May 1886, *CCI*

McLaughlin, (Florence) Patricia Alice (1916–1997), politician, was born in Downpatrick, co. Down, on 23 June 1916, the only daughter of Canon F. B. Aldwell, Church of Ireland clergyman. She was educated at Ashleigh House, Belfast, and Trinity College, Dublin, where she read modern languages. From her schooldays she was a supporter of the Ulster Unionist Party, and she held student political office at university. In 1937 she married (William) Henry Wood McLaughlin, civil engineer and director of McLaughlin and Harvey Ltd, a large firm of building contractors with operations in London, Belfast, and Dublin. They had one son and two daughters. As a comfortable housewife she had considerable time for politics. She became active in the Unionist Society, a liberal and relatively intellectual ginger group within the Unionist Party, serving as chairman of the society from 1953, and was also secretary and treasurer of the Mid-Down Unionist Women's Association.

McLaughlin's relative moderation made her an attractive Unionist candidate for the cockpit constituency of West Belfast. West Belfast had been narrowly won by twenty-five votes in 1951 by the left-wing nationalist Jack Beattie in a straight fight between his Irish Labour Party and the Ulster Unionists. Four years later, in May 1955, with a Sinn Féin candidate also standing, the nationalist vote was split and McLaughlin was returned with a majority of more than 18,000. She thus became Northern Ireland's second female MP (the first being Patricia Ford, later Lady Fisher).

In parliament McLaughlin lobbied strongly for the textile industry, claiming that she wore nothing but Irish linen (despite its trade name, largely a product of Northern Ireland). She was not prominent on gender issues, although she did join Barbara Castle in campaigning for a ban on turnstiles in women's public lavatories. She was honorary secretary to the parliamentary home safety committee (1956–64) and a delegate to the assemblies of the Council of Europe and the Western European Union (1959–64), but her contribution with most resonance was establishing a women's Orange lodge at Westminster.

The final stage of McLaughlin's parliamentary career was dogged by controversy over Newry-based Seenozip Industries, which manufactured zips. The company defrauded the Northern Ireland ministry of commerce of £30,000 before going bankrupt in 1964, and as a result two men were gaoled. McLaughlin, a director, had facilitated contacts between her fellow directors and the ministry. Although she resigned her own directorship in September 1962, her involvement with the company tarnished her reputation, and she was eventually criticized by a Northern Ireland watchdog committee in October 1964 for not revealing that she had been given free shares in the company worth £698. The scandal seemed all too emblematic

(Florence) Patricia Alice McLaughlin (1916–1997), by unknown photographer

of the dog-days of Lord Brookeborough's premiership. The Northern Ireland Labour Party made much of ambiguous ethical standards in public life and the potential for corruption in Stormont's strategy of featherbedding declining industries through the Industrial Development Acts (NI) of 1945–53. Terence O'Neill, Stormont prime minister from March 1963, introduced a cabinet code of conduct in May 1963, discouraging the holding of directorships simultaneously with public office. He also switched the emphasis of public investment from employment support to developing infrastructure such as motorways and new towns. New standards of political ethics had implications for the coherence of the Unionist Party, leading indirectly to the resignation of a senior Stormont cabinet minister, Harry West, in 1967.

On 1 September 1964 McLaughlin announced her intention not to contest the West Belfast seat again, owing to ill health. In the final years of her tenure the local Unionist association had been increasingly infiltrated by supporters of the Revd Ian Paisley, much against her liberal instincts, and her successor as Unionist candidate, James Kilfedder, relied upon their support both in securing the Unionist Party nomination and in mobilizing electoral support. His subsequent election campaign was marred by rioting in the constituency, the worst in Northern Ireland since 1935. Kilfedder won the seat, though with a reduced majority, but in 1966 he lost it to the nationalist Gerry Fitt. A readjustment of the constituency's boundaries in 1966 made it a safe nationalist seat.

McLaughlin attempted to return to politics when she was chosen to fight Central Wandsworth for the Conservative Party in 1970, but she failed to win the marginal seat. She worked ceaselessly for voluntary and consumer associations, including the Royal Society for the Prevention of Accidents (of which she was vice-president from 1962 to 1985), and was the first general secretary of the Foundation for Marriage Education. A committed Christian, she was a frequent diocesan delegate at Anglican conferences. She was appointed OBE in 1975. She died of bronchopneumonia and chronic obstructive airways disease at the

Dower House Nursing Home, Headbourne Worthy, Hampshire, on 7 January 1997. She was survived by a son and a daughter, her husband and one daughter having predeceased her.

Patricia McLaughlin was an Ulster patriot, sincere if unimaginative in her sympathy for the social ills of her deprived constituency. She was typical, in all but her gender, of an upper middle-class and gentry élite that dominated Unionist politics from the 1920s to the 1960s. The inglorious Seenozip episode signified growing discontent with the perceived amateurishness and self-serving of an élite excessively accustomed to untrammelled authority. She was replaced by an MP in many ways typical of a new generation, a lawyer committed to aggressive modernity and populist demagogy. Her commitment to the public good was thereafter expressed through voluntary service.   MARC MULHOLLAND

Sources M. Mulholland, *Northern Ireland at the crossroads: Ulster Unionism in the O'Neill years, 1960–9* (2000) · *Belfast Telegraph* (12 Dec 1963) · *Belfast Telegraph* (20 Dec 1963) · *Belfast Telegraph* (1 July 1963) · *Belfast Telegraph* (13 Oct 1963) · *New Statesman* (3 Jan 1964) · *The Guardian* (14 Jan 1964) · *Daily Telegraph* (20 Jan 1997) · *The Independent* (24 Jan 1997) · WWW · d. cert.
Likenesses photograph, 1956, repro. in *Daily Telegraph* · photograph, 1956, repro. in *The Independent* · photograph, News International Syndication, London [*see illus.*]

MacLaurin, Colin (1698–1746), mathematician and natural philosopher, was born in Kilmoden, Argyll, Scotland, in February of 1698, the third son of John MacLaurin (1658–1698), a minister in the Scottish church, and his wife, Mary, daughter of John Cameron. He lost both his parents in childhood, his father dying only six weeks after Colin's birth. After his mother's death in 1707, his uncle Daniel MacLaurin, also a minister, undertook the care of Colin and his elder brother John *MacLaurin, the second brother, Daniel, having died young. John was sent to the University of Glasgow, and became a minister in that city. Colin in 1709 followed his brother to the University of Glasgow, where he continued the classical education he had begun in the parish schools, and began mathematical studies under the direction of Robert Simson (1687–1768). The influences of Simson's interest in the history of mathematics, his enthusiasm for classical Greek methods, and his piety can all be seen in MacLaurin's subsequent career.

In 1713 MacLaurin defended a thesis on the power of gravity, and was awarded the degree of master of arts. In this thesis he refuted a number of theories as to the cause of gravity and argued that it can only be accounted for as the direct result of divine will; he demonstrated in the manner of Isaac Newton's *Principia* that the observed law of terrestrial gravity suffices to explain lunar and planetary motion; and he argued from the evident grandeur and fitness of the creation to the omnipotence and benevolence of the creator. At about this same time, MacLaurin began a correspondence with Colin Campbell (1644–1726), something of a Mersenne figure for Scottish and English mathematicians and natural philosophers in this period. In 1714 MacLaurin sent Campbell several mathematical

papers, in one of which he provided fluxional demonstrations to a number of propositions from the *Principia*, and another entitled *De viribus mentium bonipetis*. In this latter paper, MacLaurin applied the method of fluxions to the analysis of the forces with which our minds are attracted to various goods, in a manner analogous to the mathematical analysis of celestial mechanics.

MacLaurin spent another year at the university after earning his master's degree, reading divinity. He left the university in 1714, and continued his studies independently at the home of his uncle in Kilfinan, where he lived until 1717, when, at the age of nineteen, he was appointed to the chair of mathematics at Marischal College in Aberdeen.

Mathematical career Colin MacLaurin was a younger contemporary, and to some extent a protégé of Isaac Newton, and he wrote the first thorough, systematic, axiomatic development of the method of fluxions, the Newtonian version of the calculus. However, his relative isolation in Scotland—and his heavy teaching duties, about which he persistently complained—denied him the fame commensurate with his stature. He came to the attention of Newton's circle in London early in his career when he published two papers on the construction and mensuration of curves in the *Philosophical Transactions* for 1718 and 1719. Edmond Halley, then secretary of the Royal Society, invited him to go to London in 1719. He was admitted to membership in the Royal Society (1719), and often visited Newton, who encouraged him to publish the rest of his work on the description of curves. MacLaurin did so in his first major book, the *Geometria organica*, which was published under Newton's imprimatur in 1720. In its dedication and preface MacLaurin praises his patron Newton for having determined the proper relationship between mathematics and natural philosophy, and he defends and justifies the pursuit of pure geometry. He asserts the dependence of natural philosophy, the ultimate purpose of which is to reveal God's work, on mathematics, and argues that mathematics and mathematical relationships underlie not only attempts to investigate nature, but nature herself.

MacLaurin's *Geometria organica* is organic in the sense of instrumental; it treats curves from the point of view of their theoretical construction by means of abstract instruments. MacLaurin uses this method to generalize the Newtonian organic generation of conics to all orders of curves, and applies it to the classification of curves on the model of Newton's *Enumeratio linearum tertii ordinis*. Among other things in this treatise, he invents pedal curves, he states Cramer's paradox, thirty years before Cramer published it and attributed it to MacLaurin, he describes many of the particular curves thought to have been discovered in the nineteenth century, and he treats many applications to mechanics, including problems of centripetal forces and motion in resisting media. The influence of *Geometria* can be seen in the work of the later geometers Poncelet, Chasles, Steiner, Grassmann, and Salmon. Also in 1720, MacLaurin published *De linearum geometricarum proprietatibus*, in which he studies the curvature and harmonic properties of curves, and properties of their tangents and secant lines. Poncelet was to make extensive use of this work in his *Traité des propriétés projectives des figures* (1822).

MacLaurin in 1721 made his second trip to London, where he was engaged by Lord Polworth, the king's ambassador to the Congress of Cambrai, as a tutor and travelling companion for his son, who was to accompany his father to Cambrai and then set off in the following spring on a tour of France. MacLaurin returned to Aberdeen to finish the year's teaching and to obtain a leave of absence, but he left at the beginning of the summer vacation in May without such permission, and, apparently with no further correspondence with the university officials, stayed away for three years.

MacLaurin continued his mathematical work during this time—he wrote an important treatise on the percussion of bodies for a prize-contest on the subject set up by the Paris Académie Royale des Sciences, and he also carried on research which was to figure later in the MacLaurin–Braikenridge controversy. Despite significant competition MacLaurin won the Académie Royale's contest, thereby giving a considerable boost to the forces of Newtonianism on the continent. In 1724 MacLaurin's charge was overcome by a fever and died at Montpellier in southern France. Thus deprived of his patron, MacLaurin returned to his job in Aberdeen. He was there in January 1725, when he expressed regret for his long unexcused absence and was accepted back. In January of 1726, however, the governors of Marischal College learned 'by the publick newsprints' (Tweedie, 135) that he had accepted a position at the University of Edinburgh, and his position in Aberdeen was declared vacant.

MacLaurin had been appointed at Edinburgh the previous November as a deputy for James Gregory (1666–1742), who had become too infirm to carry out his teaching duties. There was some difficulty about funds for a second professor of mathematics, since Gregory was to retain the income from the professorship for the rest of his life, more or less as a pension. The appointment was apparently secured for MacLaurin by the intervention of Newton, who offered to pay £20 a year toward MacLaurin's salary if that would facilitate his appointment. MacLaurin had to pay Gregory a considerable sum for consenting to his appointment, and then Gregory failed to die as quickly as expected, surviving and depriving MacLaurin of the full salary until 1744.

MacLaurin taught a three-year course from elementary to advanced mathematics, beginning with arithmetic and Euclid, and working up to the *Principia* and the method of fluxions. He also taught experimental philosophy, surveying, fortification, geography, theory of gunnery, astronomy, and optics. He wrote his *A Treatise of Algebra* at this time for use in his courses, although it did not appear in print until after his death. On its publication the *Treatise* became a popular textbook, going through many editions and remaining in use through the rest of the century.

In 1726 MacLaurin published 'A letter ... concerning equations with impossible roots' in the *Philosophical Transactions*. In this paper he extended Newton's rules for determining the number of impossible, that is, complex roots of polynomial equations. George Campbell published a paper in the 1728 *Philosophical Transactions* carrying the same methods further than MacLaurin had done in 1726; Campbell's results seemed to grow directly out of MacLaurin's 1726 paper, or worse, to have been taken from MacLaurin's teaching at Edinburgh, where Campbell had been a private teacher at least since 1719. MacLaurin hastened to publish the continuation of his 1726 piece, 'A second letter ... concerning the roots of equations', in the 1729 *Philosophical Transactions*, in which he delivered and proved several propositions that Campbell had given without proof in his paper, and several that went far beyond Campbell.

Defence of Newtonian philosophy Some time after Newton died in 1727 John Conduitt asked MacLaurin to collaborate in the writing of his biography; the project lost momentum with Conduitt's death in 1737 but MacLaurin continued with his part in it and the work was published posthumously in 1748 as *An Account of Sir Isaac Newton's Philosophical Discoveries*. MacLaurin discusses Newton's method of investigation and of 'philosophizing', as well as his discoveries, and begins with a long history of natural philosophy since the ancients, in which he again asserts the importance for religion of sound natural philosophy. Though a number of other general expositions of Newton's thought were published during the eighteenth century, MacLaurin's *Account* has long been recognized as the leading authoritative statement of mainstream Newtonianism. As with his prize-winning *Treatise on Percussion* of 1724, one of the priorities of his *Account* was to combat the rival natural philosophy promulgated by the followers of Leibniz.

On 18 July 1733 MacLaurin married Anne Stewart, the daughter of the late solicitor general for Scotland, Walter Stewart. They had seven children, four daughters and three sons; two of them, Barbara and Walter, died in 1739, but John *MacLaurin (later Lord Dreghorn), Colin, and three daughters survived their father.

In the same year William Braikenridge published *Exercitatio geometrica de descriptione linearum curvarum*, and in the January–March 1735 issue of the *Philosophical Transactions*, a continuation under the title, 'A general method of describing curves, by the intersection of right-lines; moving about points in a given plane'. *Exercitatio geometrica* contained what has come to be called the Braikenridge–MacLaurin theorem. The *Philosophical Transactions* article treats the construction of cubics and quartics along the lines pursued by MacLaurin in his *Geometria organica*. These publications gave rise to a priority dispute and to charges of plagiarism, both apparently originated by Braikenridge. MacLaurin responded by publishing a paper dated 27 November 1722, which he declared he had written while *en route* for Cambrai. This paper contains the Braikenridge–MacLaurin theorem, and carries its generalization much further than Braikenridge had done.

MacLaurin's theorem contains Pascal's theorem on a hexagon inscribed in a conic as a special case.

MacLaurin was one of two co-secretaries of the Edinburgh Philosophical Society on its foundation in 1737. It was originally the Edinburgh Society for Improving Medical Knowledge, but on MacLaurin's urging the plan was expanded to include natural philosophy and antiquities, and it became the Royal Society of Edinburgh in 1783.

In 1734 George Berkeley had published *The Analyst, or, A Discourse Addressed to an Infidel Mathematician, wherein it is Examined whether the Object, Principles, and Inferences of the Modern Analysis are More Distinctly Conceived, or More Evidently Deduced, than Religious Mysteries and Points of Faith*. The main point of Berkeley's pamphlet was that it is wrong for freethinkers to complain of the incomprehensibility of religion, and to throw up mathematics as the model of right reasoning, since mathematical doctrines are also incomprehensible and, not being susceptible of rigorous demonstration, are accepted on faith. As an example, Berkeley fixed on 'the modern analysis', that is, the Newtonian method of fluxions and the Leibnizian differential and integral calculus. Besides objecting to particular demonstrations and procedures, Berkeley's criticism of the method of fluxions amounted to the well-substantiated assertion that it was founded inescapably either on infinitesimals or on a shifting of hypotheses, both of which were logically indefensible.

MacLaurin's magnum opus, the *Treatise of Fluxions*, published in 1742, was begun as a response to Berkeley's *Analyst*. MacLaurin founded the method of fluxions on a limit concept drawn from the method of exhaustions in classical geometry, avoiding the use of infinitesimals, infinite processes, and actually infinite quantities, and avoiding any shifting of the hypothesis. In addition, he went on in this treatise of over 760 pages to demonstrate that the method so founded would support the entire received structure of fluxions and the calculus, and could deal effectively with all of the challenge problems then being exchanged between British and continental mathematicians.

MacLaurin's response to Berkeley was informed by his belief that mathematics, properly understood, is necessarily based on real, actually existent entities, which belief made it impossible for MacLaurin—as for Berkeley—to accept a system based on infinitesimals, and by his ideas about the role of mathematics in religion, both directly, as 'the surest bulwark against the skeptics' (letters, Aberdeen University, MS 206), and by way of natural philosophy, the ultimate purpose of which is to support natural religion. These ideas led MacLaurin both to emphasize the importance of sound foundations in such a vital enterprise, and to be offended by the suggestion that mathematics is dangerous to religion, or that mathematicians are liable to lead men to infidelity. He stresses the value of the methods of the ancients, especially their insistence on deduction from clear and distinct principles. He describes geometry's fall from grace with the introduction of indivisibles and infinitesimals—an introduction of mysteries into a science where there should be none—and its salvation at the hands of Newton, who placed these systems on a sound basis with the method of fluxions.

The Jacobite rising and death MacLaurin took a leading role in preparing the defence of Edinburgh against the highland army of Prince Charles Edward Stuart in the Jacobite rebellion of 1745. MacLaurin was supervising the loading of cannon on 16 September when he heard the news that 'a packed meeting' (*Collected Letters*, 126) (the volunteers, organized to defend the city, were all out manning the walls) had voted to capitulate. When Edinburgh was occupied MacLaurin fled south into England where he was invited to stay with Thomas Herring, a zealous whig and the archbishop of York. He returned to Edinburgh on 16 November, after the Jacobites' departure, having travelled for three days from York. It is generally reported that MacLaurin arrived back in Edinburgh mortally ill, after a difficult journey both ways on horseback, including a fall and exposure to unpleasant weather. He was, however, able to return to his duties, although, as he reports in a letter of 9 December, he had caught 'the most dangerous cold' (*Collected Letters*, 132) he had ever had, from which, he said, he was then recovering. He apparently did not recover entirely, and a dropsy of the belly was diagnosed, but resisted treatment; he died on 14 June 1746. He continued to dictate the concluding chapter of his *Account of Sir Isaac Newton's Philosophical Discoveries*, 'Of the supreme author and governor of the universe, the true and living God', until a few hours before his death, and he remained the natural philosopher to the end, asking his friend and eulogist, the anatomy professor Alexander Monro, to account for various phenomena he experienced as his body failed.

MacLaurin was buried in Greyfriars churchyard, Edinburgh; his tombstone is set in the exterior south wall of the church. His wife and family were left financially insecure, and put Patrick Murdoch in charge of editing MacLaurin's writings, which resulted in the appearance in 1748 of the *Account of Sir Isaac Newton's Philosophical Discoveries* and *A Treatise of Algebra*, the former published 'for the author's children' with a large subscription.

ERIK LARS SAGENG

Sources P. Murdoch, 'An account of the life and writings of the author', in C. Maclaurin, *An account of Sir Isaac Newton's philosophical discoveries*, ed. P. Murdoch (1748); repr. with introduction and index of names by L. L. Laundan (1968) [repr. 1968] • C. Tweedie, 'A study of the life and writings of Colin MacLaurin', *Mathematical Gazette*, 8 (1915–16), 133–51; 9 (1917–19), 303–6; 10 (1920–21), 209 • H. W. Turnbull, *Bicentenary of the death of Colin Maclaurin* (1951) • C. Maclaurin, 'Journall of what pass'd relating to the defence of Edinburgh from the monday September 2d till monday September 16', NL Scot., MS 1342 • C. Maclaurin, letters, 1720–43, and journal, 1722–4, U. Aberdeen L., MS 206 • *The collected letters of Colin MacLaurin*, ed. S. Mills (1982) • 'A short account of the University of Edinburgh, the present professors in it, and the several parts of learning taught by them', *Scots Magazine*, 3 (1741), 371–4 • marriage contract, Dalry office, register of deeds, 1 July–31 Dec 1746, vol. 160

Archives BL, papers relating to spheroids and *Nugae Poeticae*, Add. MSS 4437, 52247 • NL Scot., journals and letters • RS, papers • U. Aberdeen L., MSS and letters • U. Edin. L., special collections division, lecture notes and papers • U. Glas. L., notebooks and letters | NA Scot., letters to Sir John Clerk • NRA, priv. coll., letters to James Stirling • U. Glas. L., special collections department, papers relating to projected biography by J. C. Eaton • U. Glas. L., special collections department, letters to James Spreull, etc. [copies]

Likenesses C. Metz, oils, 1746?; in possession of Jessie Maclaren, Hartwell House, Moffat, Dumfriesshire in 1954 ; negative, U. Glas. L. • McLaron Young, photograph, 1959 (after C. Metz), U. Glas. • Earl of Buchan, pencil and chalk drawing (after J. Ferguson), Scot. NPG • S. Freeman, stipple (after model by Percey), NPG, RS • Page, stipple, NPG • Trotter, stipple, NPG

MacLaurin, John (1693–1754), Church of Scotland minister and theologian, was born in October 1693 at Glendaruel, Argyll, the son of John MacLaurin (1658–1698), the minister of Kilmodan, and his wife, Mary (d. 1707), daughter of John Cameron, the minister of Campbeltown. In the year after his birth the synod of Argyll published a metrical translation of the Psalms in Gaelic, which was partially translated and edited by his father. In March 1698 the elder John MacLaurin died, just six weeks after the birth of his only other surviving child, Colin *MacLaurin (1698–1746), who became a famous mathematician and professor at the University of Edinburgh. After their mother died in 1707 John and Colin were raised by their uncle, Daniel MacLaurin, the minister of Kilfinan, Argyll. John graduated MA from the University of Glasgow on 14 November 1712. He continued his education by studying divinity at Glasgow and the University of Leiden and was licensed by the presbytery of Dumbarton on 2 June 1717. On 7 May 1719 he was ordained to the parish of Luss, on the banks of Loch Lomond, in Dunbartonshire. Two years later he married Lilias (d. 1747), daughter of John Rae of Little Govan, with whom he had nine children, including a daughter, Elizabeth (d. 1754), who married John *Gillies, a prominent evangelical minister in Glasgow from 1742 until his death in 1796. MacLaurin remained at Luss until his translation to the Northwest or Ramshorn Church in Glasgow on 3 January 1723. At Glasgow he was active in helping to establish in 1733 the Glasgow Town Hospital, which became a model for the treatment of the poor and insane; he is believed to have had 'a chief hand in composing the printed account of that excellent institution' (Gillies, iii) that was prefixed to *The Regulations of the Town's Hospital at Glasgow* (1735). A Gaelic speaker, he was strongly committed to Glasgow's 'four or five hundred Highlanders who do not understand the English' (*Correspondence of … Wodrow*, 2.676), and his concern for them led him to espouse the cause of poor-law and social reform. These concerns are reflected in an anonymous pamphlet of 1729, *The Case of the Poor Consider'd*, which is thought to be his earliest publication.

In spite of prejudices against his 'Highland accent, which disgusted a nice ear' (*Scotland and Scotsmen*, 1.286), MacLaurin was regarded as one of the greatest Scottish preachers of his day, and his sermon on Galatians 6: 14, 'Glorying in the Cross of Christ', is recognized as a model of eighteenth-century Scottish evangelical preaching. It was first published posthumously in Glasgow in 1755 in *Sermons and Essays*, which contained two other sermons as well as essays on prejudices against the gospel, Christian piety, and the scripture doctrine of divine grace. A biographical memoir by the editor, John Gillies, was prefixed to the book, which generated a second edition in London

in 1772. In 1773 another large volume of MacLaurin's sermons and essays appeared in Edinburgh called *An Essay on the Prophecies Relating to the Messiah*. The title essay of that work, reflecting MacLaurin's strong interest in prophecy, may have circulated privately before publication, for it is said to have influenced a popular work that Bishop Richard Hurd published in 1772, *An Introduction to the Study of the Prophecies Concerning the Christian Church*. Another piece in the 1773 collection, 'A philosophical inquiry into the nature of happiness', shows an affinity to work on that subject by the New England theologian, Jonathan Edwards, for whom MacLaurin helped to raise money after Edwards was dismissed from his congregation at Northampton, Massachusetts, in 1750. Like Edwards, Thomas Prince, and other American clergymen with whom he corresponded, MacLaurin was committed to evangelicalism, and during the early 1740s he was deeply involved in the Cambuslang revival near Glasgow. He also shared Edwards's philosophical approach to theology, drawing upon contemporary secular thought concerning the operation of the human mind and the will.

In 1740 MacLaurin was a candidate for the professorship of divinity at the University of Glasgow but lost the chair to Michael Potter. When Potter died in November 1743 MacLaurin tried again in a three-way race with William Leechman, the minister of nearby Beith, and William Craig, the leading moderate minister in Glasgow. MacLaurin appeared to have the advantage until Craig withdrew and gave his support to Leechman, who was the close friend and protégé of the professor of moral philosophy, Francis Hutcheson. Although Leechman's admiring biographer, James Wodrow, admitted that MacLaurin had the support of almost the entire town, the election was in the hands of the faculty, who were evenly divided, and on 13 December the tie was broken in Leechman's favour by the casting vote of the university rector. The outcome was a victory for Hutcheson and the proponents of politeness and enlightenment, but for the advocates of orthodoxy it represented a bitter defeat, and it put an end to MacLaurin's academic aspirations.

Colin MacLaurin had supported John's contest with Leechman with some reluctance because of his belief that his brother was 'really over Orthodox' (Mills, 86–7). Three years later, on 14 June 1746, Colin died suddenly, and this was followed on 16 December 1747 by the death of MacLaurin's wife. Thirteen months later, in January 1749, MacLaurin married Margaret (1702–1784), daughter of Patrick Bell, of Cowcaddens, with whom he had one son who died young.

In 1753 and 1754, when party differences in the Church of Scotland ran high, MacLaurin either wrote or helped to publish several polemical pamphlets in opposition to lay patronage in the selection of parish ministers, including *A Loud Cry for Help to the Struggling Church of Scotland*, *The Terms of Ministerial and Christian Communion Imposed on the Church of Scotland by a Prevailing Party*, and *The Nature of Ecclesiastic Government, and of the Constitution of the Church of Scotland Illustrated*, and he penned the introduction to *An Inquiry into the Powers Committed to the General Assemblies of the*

Church by the Revd John Adam of Falkirk. These works draw upon a wide range of continental theologians and English deists, as well as political and philosophical writers, in an attempt to provide a coherent interpretation of the popular party position on the nature of Presbyterian church polity.

MacLaurin died in Glasgow on 8 September 1754. A mural monument was subsequently placed in the church at Kilmodan, in memory of John, Colin, and their father.

RICHARD B. SHER

Sources DNB · W. H. Gould, ed., *The works of the Revd John MacLaurin* (1810) · *Fasti Scot.*, new edn · J. Macleod, *Scottish theology in relation to church history since the Reformation*, [3rd edn] (1974) · J. Coutts, *A history of the University of Glasgow* (1909) · J. Gillies, 'Some account of the life and character of the author', in J. MacLaurin, *Sermons and essays* (1755) · A. Fawcett, *The Cambuslang revival: the scottish evangelical revival of the eighteenth century* (1971) · T. D. Kennedy, 'William Leechman, pulpit eloquence and the Glasgow Enlightenment', *The Glasgow Enlightenment*, ed. A. Hook and R. B. Sher (1995), 56–72 · J. R. McIntosh, *Church and theology in Enlightenment Scotland: the popular party, 1740–1800* (1998) · *The collected letters of Colin MacLaurin*, ed. S. Mills (1982) · *Scotland and Scotsmen in the eighteenth century: from the MSS of John Ramsay, esq., of Ochtertyre*, ed. A. Allardyce, 2 vols. (1888) · W. R. Scott, *Francis Hutcheson: his life, teaching and position in the history of philosophy* (1900) · J. Wodrow, 'Account of the author's life and of his lectures', in W. Leechman, *Sermons*, 2 vols. (1789) · R. Wodrow, *Analecta, or, Materials for a history of remarkable providences, mostly relating to Scotch ministers and Christians*, ed. [M. Leishman], 4 vols., Maitland Club, 60 (1842–3) · *The correspondence of the Rev. Robert Wodrow*, ed. T. M'Crie, 3 vols., Wodrow Society, [3] (1842–3)

MacLaurin, John, Lord Dreghorn (1734–1796), judge and writer, eldest son of Colin *MacLaurin (1698–1746), professor of mathematics in Edinburgh University, and his wife, Anne Stewart, was born in Edinburgh on 15 December 1734. After his father's death he, his mother, a brother, and three sisters were reliant on the income from a small estate in Berwickshire which 'yielded no more than a bare competence for the education and maintenance of the family' (*Works*, vi). MacLaurin went to Edinburgh high school for five years, going on to Edinburgh University, as was often the case in those days, at too early an age to derive the full benefit from his attendance. A career in the church was not one that suited his lively personality and he chose law instead, being admitted advocate on 3 August 1756. In June 1762 MacLaurin married Esther Cunninghame (d. 1780), with whom he had ten children, although only two sons and a daughter survived him.

MacLaurin developed a talent for poetry early in life, a trait which he shared with his eccentric sister Mary. Youthful exuberance and biting satire were evident in *The Philosopher's Opera* (1757), in which his targets included David Hume and John Home, author of *Douglas*. Like many of his early works this was produced anonymously, often by his own hand, for private circulation and it was hardly surprising that it and other plays and poems were excluded, on grounds of taste, from the collection of his serious works, prepared and published by his son Colin in 1798.

MacLaurin gained much practice at the bar of the general assembly of the Church of Scotland. This was an ideal showcase for the talents of an aspiring advocate but

in MacLaurin's case it was also the result of personal conviction. His appearances were to argue the case against lay patrons in disputed presentations and his views on the question were published in 1766 as *Considerations on the Right of Patronage*.

In appearance MacLaurin was tall and spare, his voice rendered somewhat monotonous by a want of teeth, yet it is clear that he was a lively and interesting figure. 'His learning introduced him into the society of the grave, his vivacity recommended him to the company of the gay: domestic distress indeed made him become retired and abstemious' (*Works*, xv). He was one of the earliest fellows of the Royal Society of Edinburgh, to which he contributed an essay arguing that ancient Troy was not taken by the Greeks. A keen classical scholar, MacLaurin also studied the language and literature of France. This, together with sympathies inclined to reform, was not altogether a happy combination in the highly-charged political atmosphere of his later years and was a further reason for his withdrawal from society.

MacLaurin became a senator of the college of justice, as Lord Dreghorn, on 17 January 1788, through the interest of Henry Dundas. His title was derived from his residence, Dreghorn Castle, just outside Edinburgh. He died, probably at Dreghorn Castle, 'of a putrid fever' (*Works*, xiii) on 24 December 1796 and was buried in Greyfriars churchyard, Edinburgh, in his father's grave.

LIONEL ALEXANDER RITCHIE

Sources *The works of the late John Maclaurin esq. of Dreghorn*, 2 vols. (1798), v–xxxii · G. Brunton and D. Haig, *An historical account of the senators of the college of justice, from its institution in MDXXXII* (1832) · F. J. Grant, ed., *The Faculty of Advocates in Scotland, 1532–1943*, Scottish RS, 145 (1944) · *Scots Magazine*, 58 (1796), 865 · *N&Q*, 3rd ser., 10 (1866), 392, 443, 503 · *N&Q*, 3rd ser., 11 (1867), 261, 424–5 · DNB
Archives NL Scot., corresp.
Likenesses engraving, repro. in *Works of the late John Maclaurin esq. of Dreghorn*

Maclay, John Scott, Viscount Muirshiel (1905–1992), businessman and politician, was born on 26 October 1905 at 13 Park Terrace, Glasgow, the youngest child in the family of five sons and two daughters of Joseph Paton *Maclay, first Baron Maclay (1857–1951), shipowner and public servant, and his wife, Martha (d. 1929), daughter of William Strang, muslin manufacturer, of Glasgow. His father was chairman of Maclay and McIntyre, shipowners, a friend of Andrew Bonar Law, and a very successful controller of shipping under Lloyd George during the First World War. Of his four brothers, the two eldest, Ebenezer (1891–1918) and William (1895–1915), were killed in action during the First World War; the third, Joseph (1899–1969), was Liberal MP for Paisley from 1931 to 1945, and succeeded his father as second Baron Maclay and chairman of Maclay and McIntyre; the fourth, Walter (1901–1964), was an eminent psychiatrist and sometime honorary physician to the queen.

John Maclay was educated at Winchester College and at Trinity College, Cambridge, where he was in the crew that beat Oxford in the 1927 boat race, before joining the family shipping firm. On 16 October 1930 he married Betty

John Scott Maclay, Viscount Muirshiel (1905–1992), by Hay Wrightson

L'Estrange Astley (1902–1974), younger daughter of Major Delaval Graham L'Estrange Astley, of Wroxham, Norfolk. There were no children of the marriage. On the outbreak of the Second World War he served briefly as a captain in the 57th Searchlight regiment of the Royal Artillery, before being seconded to the Ministry of War Transport and sent to Washington as deputy to Sir (James) Arthur Salter, head of the British merchant shipping mission there. He succeeded Salter as its head in 1944, and was gazetted CMG in the same year.

Maclay had been elected unopposed as National Liberal MP for Montrose Burghs in July 1940, and on his return from Washington he was briefly parliamentary secretary to the Ministry of Production in Churchill's 'caretaker' ministry of May–July 1945. Following the Labour victory in the general election of that year he kept largely to commercial life, serving as chairman of the British committee of the international chamber of commerce from 1947 to 1951, but he also took part very effectively in Commons debates on shipping and trade. After the abolition of the Montrose Burghs constituency he stood successfully as National Liberal and Conservative candidate for West Renfrewshire, which he represented for the next fourteen years. Between 1957 and 1967 he was president of the National Liberal council (the National Liberals had six Scottish MPs), a not utterly fictive role in view of his preference for consensual policies. In October 1951 Churchill made him minister of transport and civil aviation, without a seat in cabinet, but his health was poor and a crisis

over increased fares for London transport in May 1952 brought about his resignation. He served briefly as president of the assembly of the Western European Union in 1955–6 (and later expressed regret that Britain had not played a more constructive role in the early stages of European integration) before returning to office under Sir Anthony Eden as minister of state for the colonies in October 1956. While there, he was (albeit briefly) closely involved in formulating the British response to developments in Cyprus and Ghana.

In January 1957, on replacing Eden as premier, Harold Macmillan appointed Maclay secretary of state for Scotland in place of James Stuart. A shy personality and somewhat quavering delivery made him an unobtrusive presence as secretary of state, yet he presided tactfully over a considerable expansion in the capabilities of the post. He later recollected of his time in office that 'Secretaries of State were now being judged by the performance of the Scottish economy', with traditional British departments such as the Board of Trade being regarded as marginal. Stuart, a friend and confidant of Churchill, had not regarded industry as a priority, though he developed the social and infrastructural responsibilities of the Scottish Office in response to the nationalist pressure of John MacCormick's covenant movement and the Balfour commission of 1953–5. But, as an inquiry by Alexander Cairncross had disclosed in 1953, the country's economy was still archaically dependent on the traditional capital goods and textile industries. Already suffering from under-investment, these industries were thrown into crisis both by the post-Suez depression and by the technical changes enforced by the canal's closure: giant tankers and containerization. Macmillan himself took a direct interest in the country which had produced his publishing forebears, and made common cause with leaders of Scottish business, notably Lord Polwarth of the Scottish Council (Development and Industry) and George Middleton, general secretary of the Scottish Trades Union Congress. National policy on developmental assistance was still, however, determined by unemployment levels, not by entrepreneurial potential, and in real terms less was being spent on industrial policy than twenty years earlier. Urgency was underlined by the general election of October 1959, in which—against the British trend—the right-wing vote in Scotland fell from 51.1 per cent to 47.2 per cent and seats from 36 out of 71 to 31.

This disaffection was tackled by Macmillan, now with Cairncross as his chief economic adviser and his former assistant and ghost writer Allan Young as Board of Trade controller in Scotland, by sweeping moves of industrial direction in the steel and automotive industries. In 1959 came the decision—against the advice of the industry's leaders—to site a new integrated steelworks and strip mill at Ravenscraig, near Motherwell, and in 1960 Macmillan followed this with his Local Employment Act. As a result, Maclay joined with the Scottish council to create a committee on future strategies for Scottish industry, under J. N. Toothill, managing director of Ferranti's Scottish operation. As well as the co-ordination of regional development bodies and a shift towards the encouragement of diversified industries based on 'growth points' in the new towns, the Toothill report (substantially drafted by the committee's secretary, Dr Tom Burns, later professor of sociology at Edinburgh) recommended 'a new department which should bring together the present industrial and planning functions of the Scottish departments'. Accordingly in 1962 the Scottish Office changed from having, besides agriculture and fisheries, a home department, and a health department, to a new structure of an 'economic' development department plus a 'social' home and health department. This was to cope with the opening of the Ravenscraig strip mill and two motor plants—Rootes Cars at Linwood, near Paisley, and British Motor Corporation Vans at Bathgate—which were seen as inaugurating a new era of Scottish consumer-goods manufacturing. Counsels were fatally divided, however, between the advocates of diversification and the remaining heavy industrial magnates, who favoured a huge littoral steel-and-ships development on the Clyde estuary. Nobody then realized how useful the latter course would have been in coping with the challenge of North Sea oil.

Despite considerable achievements, including the initiation of construction of the Forth and Tay road bridges, the inauguration of Scotland's first nuclear power station, and of the Glasgow redevelopment plan, important measures of rating reform, improvements to hospitals, the licensing laws, and the fishing fleet—and the fateful decision in the Housing (Scotland) Act of 1957 to encourage high-rise building with a special subsidy of £40 per flat, which revolutionized, if it did not exactly improve, the Scottish urban landscape—Maclay came under increasing criticism. In 1961 the inquiry of Dr Beeching into the railway network was under way, with its recommendations likely to involve extensive line closures in rural Scotland. The railway modernization programme of 1955 had singularly failed to save Scotland's greatest railway manufacturer, the North British Locomotive Company, chaired by Viscount Reith; it went under in 1961. In 1962 Maclay was in confrontation with the miners and the Labour Party over the National Coal Board's plans to close twenty pits over a four-year period (he secured a favourable price-hike for otherwise uneconomic Scottish coal, but this did him little good) and with the teaching profession (once a pillar of the Scots bourgeoisie but now going swiftly left) over pay. Wishing to spend more time with his wife, who was now confined to a wheelchair, he offered his resignation early in 1962, but was persuaded to stay on. Then on 13 July 1962, along with a third of the cabinet, he was axed. Macmillan replaced him with Michael Noble, MP for Argyll, to little avail. Despite the remarkable popularity of Macmillan's successor, Sir Alec Douglas-Home, the number of Scottish tory MPs fell to twenty-four in 1964 and twenty in 1966.

In 1962 Maclay was made a Companion of Honour, like Walter Elliot and Tom Johnston before him. He went to the Lords in 1964 as Viscount Muirshiel of Kilmacolm, and became a knight of the Thistle in 1973. Between 1967 and 1980 he was lord lieutenant of Renfrewshire. He occupied his retirement from politics as a director of the National Provincial Bank, the Peninsular and Oriental Steamship Company, and the Clydesdale Bank, and also as a trustee of the National Galleries of Scotland (1966–76) and founder chairman of the Scottish Civic Trust (1967–89). He received honorary degrees from the universities of Edinburgh (1963), Strathclyde (1966), and Glasgow (1970). He died of heart failure at his house, Knapps Wood, Kilmacolm, Renfrewshire, on 17 August 1992. His wife predeceased him. A memorial service was held at Kilmacolm Old Kirk on 16 September 1992. Of his well-meant projects, the Linwood and Bathgate motor works were closed in 1981, and Ravenscraig steelworks were closed in 1992.

Maclay's career was enigmatic. From occupying only minor office—and without enjoying any great success in it—he became, during his five-year tenure of the Scottish secretaryship, the essential creator of the institution as it was to preside over Scottish affairs between then and the creation of a Scottish parliament forty years later. A modest and unpretentious man, he was motivated by a strong sense of public duty, and was described by a former parliamentary private secretary as 'the most saintly character I knew in politics' (*The Times*, 29 Aug 1992).

CHRISTOPHER HARVIE

Sources *Herald* (21 Aug 1992) · *Herald* (1957–62) · *The Times* (21 Aug 1992); (29 Aug 1992); (23 Sept 1992) · *Daily Telegraph* (21 Aug 1992) · *The Independent* (21 Aug 1992) · *WWW* · Burke, *Peerage* · b. cert. · d. cert. · G. Pattinger, *The secretaries of state for Scotland* · *Scotland* [monthly of the Scottish Council: Development and Industry] (1957–62) · Sir Douglas Haddow, former permanent secretary, Scottish Office, interview, 1986
Archives U. Glas., Archives and Business Records Centre, corresp., papers, and press cuttings | NA Scot., Scottish Office papers | FILM BBC Scotland, Glasgow, BBC TV news footage
Likenesses photograph, 1946, repro. in *The Independent* · photograph, 1985 (with Willie Ross, Gordon Campbell, Bruce Millan, and George Younger), repro. in Hawie and Jones, *The road to home rule* (2000) · J. Gunn, portrait, Dover House, Whitehall, Scotland Office · H. Wrightson, photograph, NPG [*see illus.*] · photograph, repro. in *The Times* (21 Aug 1992)
Wealth at death £725,954.92: confirmation with corrective inventory, 30 July 1993, *CCI* (1992)

Maclay, Joseph Paton, first Baron Maclay (1857–1951), shipowner and shipping controller, was born at Glasgow on 6 September 1857, the third son of Ebenezer Maclay, master upholsterer, and his wife, Janet, daughter of Joseph Paton, of Paisley. Maclay, whose ancestors had for several generations lived in Glasgow, was educated there as a boy and began business as a clerk. In 1885 with Thomas Walker McIntyre (father of Lord Sorn) he established the trampship firm of Maclay and McIntyre, which became one of the largest shipping concerns on the Clyde. In 1914 they owned fifty cargo vessels and Maclay was the chief partner in the firm.

He served on the Clyde Trust and the Glasgow town council, and as a magistrate. A Liberal in politics, he was a strong advocate of temperance and was active in the evangelical and philanthropic life of Scotland; and for his services he was created a baronet in 1914.

In December 1916 Sir Joseph Maclay reluctantly became

minister of shipping, and was appointed to the privy council as one of the new businessmen-in-government appointed by David Lloyd George. Andrew Bonar Law knew Maclay well, and was primarily responsible for his translation from a Glasgow shipping magnate to the head of a new department in Whitehall, which occupied the drained lake in St James's Park. As shipping controller Maclay took charge of shipping movements for priority war materials and foodstuffs, government relations with shipowners, the expansion of merchant shipbuilding output, and the purchase and supervision of foreign shipping. These new developments were received with deep hostility at the Admiralty, which firmly retained control of naval ship construction, and opposed the emergent idea of convoys after the onset of the German unrestricted submarine offensive in February 1917. The 'concordat' between Maclay and Sir Edward Carson, first lord of the Admiralty, obtained in the same month, recognized the importance of merchant shipbuilding, and increased completion rates of vessels under construction were obtained in the first quarter of 1917, despite the obstructionist fatalism of the sea lords.

In May 1917 Maclay lost control of merchant shipbuilding when Admiralty supply departments were placed under civilian experts in a further initiative to diminish Carson's sphere of responsibilities. Maclay considered resignation but the changes which he demanded at the Admiralty 'from the top downwards' followed Carson's departure in July 1917. Maclay repeatedly drew Lloyd George's attention to the shipmasters' lack of confidence in the Admiralty, which culminated in his warning of 28 June that without reforms 'we shall have these men refusing to go to sea' (Beaverbrook, 170). In his *War Memoirs* Lloyd George noted that Maclay 'repeatedly pressed that convoys should be given a trial' (Lloyd George, 1938, vol. 1, 688).

At the Ministry of Shipping Maclay requisitioned the remaining uncontrolled merchant ships in 1917, and obtained more efficient use of available tonnage by the restriction of non-essential imports. This measure reflected the willingness of new ministers to contemplate the condition of emerging total war in a way that was barely apparent at the Board of Trade in 1916. However, Maclay had few pretensions to corporatist bias. He argued that although a centralizing bureaucracy of shipping control brought better co-ordination of supply movements for naval and military operations, national shipbuilding plans in 1917 should not copy the schemes for shell production of 1915 because 'we had to deal with a great industry, probably our premier industry, old established, highly organized, possessing within itself immense potentialities, having a tradition and a reputation' (HL F/35/2/46). The strength of Maclay's Liberalism was still apparent late in the war in his frequently stated respect for the individual effort of the shipbuilder, through the generations, whose expertise was relegated by policy on 'lines predetermined in Whitehall'. Consequently, his participation in the enlarging role of the state was only justified by the temporary exigencies of large-scale war, which blurred the distinction between operational and manufacturing activity. Maclay constantly experienced the interplay of military and civilian activity at close hand. During 1918 he cogently demanded the return of troops from France for the crucial purposes of merchant shipbuilding and coal production.

Maclay became an authoritative voice in the debates on coal output for home, Admiralty, and allied consumption. In September 1918 the lack of coal at coaling stations and bunkers in home ports detained ships, and caused chaos to the movement of men and materials. In these circumstances the transport of American troops to Europe, largely in British ships, was a remarkable logistical feat, which illustrated one of the most important ways in which civilian experts contributed to allied victory. In August 1918 Lloyd George described him as a 'truly wonderful man' (Riddell, 350).

As an owner and manager of capital Maclay was critical of the government's concessions on pay to trade unions and he opposed the nationalization of shipping. Alongside other businessmen-in-government his competence provided substance for Lloyd George's energizing rhetoric as war leader, but provided no foundation for an alternative centrist party. Maclay was impatient of coalition politics, avoided a seat in the House of Commons throughout his ministerial term, and depended on the political support proffered by Bonar Law. He was not enthused by reconstructionist politics, and obtained the early decontrol of shipping in 1919. However, the dismantling of the Ministry of Shipping was a protracted process, ending in 1921, and involved the sale of government standard ships built during the war and ex-enemy ships allocated to Britain by the reparations commission. Maclay was cautious in his dealings with the 'interest' from whence he came, and he avoided extended and open-ended debates with shipowners and shipbuilders, who distrusted any statement short of returning the industries to their position in 1914. He was not a mouthpiece of the industries in peace, and as his wartime *raison d'être* ended, Maclay's old Liberal equilibrium was restored. In the virulent atmosphere of 'anti-waste' he accepted a final role to assist the politically debilitated prime minister. He became a member of the committee on national expenditure, 1921, which was dominated by Scottish businessmen, and confirmed the post-war quest for economic orthodoxy. Maclay was created a baron in 1922, in Lloyd George's resignation honours list, received the freedom of the City of Glasgow in the same year, and was deputy lieutenant for the county of Renfrewshire. He left public life, except for membership of the royal commission on coal supplies, the committee on property and endowments (Church of Scotland) 1922, and the committee of inquiry on reformatory and industrial schools in Scotland. His philanthropic work continued, most notably, as president of the Orphan Homes of Scotland. His one publication was indicative of a simple piety. *The Starting Place of the Day* was published in 1918. As a book of prayers, which he compiled for family worship, it was designed 'to overcome the difficulty which heads of households encounter in offering extempore prayer'

(Maclay, 5). In the general election of 1923 Maclay was the host for Lloyd George's party during his celebrated 'Liberal Reunion' visit to Paisley to support Asquith's campaign (Jenkins, 498–9).

Both Lord Beaverbrook and Lord Riddell remarked on Maclay's honest, direct approach, firmness of resolve, and expertise on shipping issues. He was a tireless contributor to policy development at the intersection of naval and mercantile spheres, and expressed confidence that supply problems could be overcome, even in the crisis months of 1917, which endeared him to Lloyd George. *The Times* obituary remarked on a 'hardness and gentleness curiously mingled' (*The Times*, 25 April 1951). In his sixtieth year Maclay took on an exhausting ministerial role of central significance to allied strategic policy. He provided the war cabinet with stark scenarios, and, if hesitant in presentation, he was transparently clear in his requirements of other departments in fulfilment of shipping plans.

In 1889 he married Martha (*d.* 28 Sept 1929), daughter of William Strang, muslin manufacturer, of Glasgow. They had five sons and two daughters. Two sons were killed in the First World War, and in their memory the parents presented to the University of Glasgow (of which he had been made an honorary LLD in 1919) a student hostel, Maclay Hall. Lord Maclay died at his home, Duchal, Kilmacolm, Renfrewshire, on 24 April 1951 and was buried at the Orphan Homes of Scotland church, Bridge of Weir, Renfrewshire, on 27 April. He was succeeded by his son, Sir Joseph Maclay KBE (1899–1969).   KEITH GRIEVES

Sources D. Lloyd George, *War memoirs*, new edn, 2 vols. (1938) · *The Times* (25 April 1951) · *The Times* (28 April 1951) · S. W. Roskill, *Hankey, man of secrets*, 1 (1970) · G. A. Riddell, *Lord Riddell's war diary, 1914–1918* (1933), 350 · S. Armitage, *The politics of decontrol of industry: Britain and the United States* (1969) · J. Turner, *British politics and the Great War: coalition and conflict, 1915–1918* (1992) · M. A. Beaverbrook, *Men and power, 1917–1918* (1956), 170 [J. Maclay to D. Lloyd George, 28 June 1917] · HLRO, Bonar Law MSS · HLRO, Lloyd George MSS · K. O. Morgan, *Consensus and disunity: the Lloyd George coalition government, 1918–1922* (1979) · J. A. Salter, *Allied shipping control* (1921) · C. E. Fayle, *Seaborne trade*, 3 vols., History of the Great War (1920–24) · J. P. Maclay, *The starting place of the day: a book of prayers for family worship* [1918], 5 · *DNB* · R. Jenkins, *Asquith* (1964), 498–9

Archives NRA, priv. coll., corresp. and papers | Bodl. Oxf., corresp. with Viscount Addison · HLRO, corresp. with Andrew Bonar Law · HLRO, corresp. with David Lloyd George

Wealth at death £1,179,554 14s. 3d.: confirmation, 18 May 1951, *CCI*

Maclean family of Duart (*per.* 1493–1598),

highland chiefs, were heads of the most powerful branch of the clan Gillean. In the fourteenth century they rose to prominence in the Hebrides as stewards to MacDonald lords of the isles, who rewarded them with land in Mull, Morvern, Tiree, Islay, Jura, and Lochaber. The forfeiture of John MacDonald in 1493 meant that the leading Maclean chiefs now held their land directly from the Scottish crown, and a struggle for the leadership of the isles followed.

The chief of Duart at this crucial period was the formidable **Lachlan Cattanach Maclean of Duart** (*c.*1465–1523), who most likely owed his sobriquet Cattanach to his having been fostered with the clan Chattan. Like several of his contemporaries he is a larger-than-life figure about

whom several traditional stories, unusually unflattering caricatures, survive. Although Lachlan had royal support to become Maclean of Duart, and certainly received a crown charter in 1496, he subsequently resisted James IV's efforts to bring the isles under royal control. By the end of 1503 he was in revolt and devastated Badenoch, and on 18 March 1504 he was forfeited for treasons, which included proclaiming Donald Dubh MacDonald, John's illegitimate grandson, to be the lord of the isles. The king responded by sending a fleet to western waters, which captured Maclean's castle of Cairn-na-Burgh (Carnaburg), west of Mull. The fortress was handed over to the first earl of Argyll, and by June 1504 Maclean had submitted and was reconciled to the king. A further rebellion in 1515 was also suppressed, and thereafter Lachlan became a follower of the earl of Argyll. It was a policy followed by successive Macleans of Duart, with significant interruptions, over the next hundred years.

This alliance was cemented by marriage. Lachlan Maclean 'married' a daughter of the second earl of Argyll whose name is variously recorded as Janet and Katherine. He had at least five other wives or mistresses. According to tradition he and Argyll's daughter 'did not agree behind the curtain' (Crossapol MS, in writer's possession), and she tried to poison him. Lachlan retaliated by having Argyll's daughter put on a rock on the Sound of Mull, from which she was rescued just before it became submerged at high tide. To avenge his sister's treatment Sir John Campbell of Cawdor had Lachlan murdered in Edinburgh on 10 November 1523.

Hector Mor Maclean of Duart (*fl.* 1527–1570), Lachlan Maclean's eldest son and successor, was a staunch supporter of the fourth and fifth earls of Argyll. In 1545 Hector Mor joined Donald Dubh MacDonald in his rebellion, but he may have done so only to destroy it for when the rebellion failed Maclean was well rewarded. He obtained more land in Islay, and, even more significantly, married his daughter Katherine, 'in face of holy kirk', to Argyll (Argyll transcripts, V, 102). This was a major coup. The earls of Argyll might give their daughters in marriage to island chiefs; they themselves had hitherto invariably married the daughters of their fellow lowland magnates.

Hector Mor reinforced his links with Argyll in 1557, when Lady Janet Campbell, Argyll's eldest daughter, described as being 'in her pure virginity', married Hector Og (*d.* 1575), Duart's eldest son (Argyll transcripts, V, 79). As the marriage contract was witnessed by two Campbell prelates who were leading members of the 'protestant' party, it is probable that the Macleans had committed themselves to the reformed religion by that date. It is unlikely that so fervent a reformer as the fifth earl of Argyll would have allowed his sister to marry a papist.

It is uncertain whether Hector Mor himself, who is last recorded in 1570, ever became a protestant, but his grandson and ultimate heir **Sir Lachlan Mor Maclean of Duart** (1558–1598) certainly did. Lachlan Mor succeeded his father in 1575. His youth was dominated by his uncle the sixth earl of Argyll, and by the latter's protégé Hector Allansoun Maclean of Gigha, who was Lachlan's foster father. Their dominance ended in 1577, when Maclean of Gigha was surprised by Lachlan Mor's supporters, imprisoned, and beheaded. Lachlan Mor compounded the insult to his uncle by marrying Margaret Cunningham, the daughter of Argyll's rival the fifth earl of Glencairn. Argyll retaliated by siding with the MacDonalds in their bloody feud with the Macleans which tore the Hebrides apart in the 1580s. It was a feud which increasingly had an international dimension as both clans were drawn into Ulster politics. In Ireland the English were attempting to put down Hugh O'Neill's rebellion. Lachlan Mor (who was knighted in 1596) had control of 3000 fighting men, and since he could have tipped the balance in favour of whichever party he supported he was courted by both sides. In the event his men never went to Ireland, and Sir Lachlan was killed at Tràigh Ghruinneart in Islay on 5 August 1598—in battle with the men of Kintyre by some accounts, by treachery according to others—to prevent his interfering in Ulster. Queen Elizabeth never paid him the money she had promised him, and from the cost of maintaining so many fighting men in readiness to intervene in Ulster stemmed the debts that eventually ruined the family.   NICHOLAS MACLEAN-BRISTOL

Sources NL Scot., MS 3018 · NL Scot., MS 28.3.12 · N. D. Campbell, tenth duke of Argyll, Argyll transcripts, Inveraray Castle, Argyll · G. Burnett and others, eds., *The exchequer rolls of Scotland*, 23 vols. (1878–1908), vol. 12 · *LP Henry VIII*, vol. 1, pt 20, no. 21 · *CSP Scot., 1595–7* · NA Scot., GD 39/94/104 · N. Maclean-Bristol, *Warriors and priests* (1995) · N. Maclean-Bristol, *Murder under trust* (1999) · J. R. N. Macphail, ed., *Highland papers*, vol. 1; Scottish History Society, 2nd ser., 5 (1914) · *Registrum secreti sigilli regum Scottorum, 1488–1548*, vols. 1–3; *1424–1513*; *1513–46* · *AFM*, 3rd edn · N. Macdougall, *James IV* (1989) · *Scots peerage* · A. Macdonald, *The Macdonald collection of Gaelic poetry*, ed. A. Macdonald (1911) · D. D. MacKinnon and A. Morrison, *The Macleods* [n.d.], section 1

Maclean, Alexander (1840–1904), genre painter, was born on 22 November 1840 in the parish of Gorbals, Glasgow, the son of David McLean, a manufacturer, and his wife, Margaret McGregor. He was educated at Helensburgh and Edinburgh, and was in business at Glasgow until 1861. He then studied painting in Rome, Florence, and Antwerp before moving to London. He exhibited ten pictures at the Royal Academy between 1872 and 1904, including *Covent Garden Market* (1874), *Looking Back* (1876), and *At the Railings, St Paul's, Covent Garden* (1877). He also exhibited *Finis* at the Royal Scottish Academy in 1878 and four paintings at the Society of British Artists between 1872 and 1893. Maclean died on 30 October 1904 at St Leonards, Sussex.

L. H. CUST, *rev.* ANNE PIMLOTT BAKER

Sources J. Johnson, ed., *Works exhibited at the Royal Society of British Artists, 1824–1893, and the New English Art Club, 1888–1917*, 2 vols. (1975), 305 · P. J. M. McEwan, *Dictionary of Scottish art and architecture* (1994), 375 · Graves, *RA exhibitors* · Boase, *Mod. Eng. biog.* · bap. reg. Scot. · private information (1893)

Maclean, Alistair Stuart (1922–1987), novelist, was born on 21 April 1922 in Shettleston, Glasgow, the third of four sons (there were no daughters) of the Revd Alistair Maclean, Church of Scotland minister, of Glasgow and Daviot, Inverness-shire, and his wife, Mary, daughter of Archie Lamont, warehouseman, of Possil Park, Glasgow. He

Alistair Stuart Maclean (1922–1987), by Snowdon, 1981

spent the first fourteen years of his life in the highland districts of Daviot and Dunlichty, where his father was ministering. At home in the manse only Gaelic was spoken, a curious restriction when the father both wrote and delivered the English language with a fine eloquence and must have known that his children would require it later in life. Maclean was educated at Daviot School, Inverness Royal Academy, and Hillhead high school in Glasgow, and Glasgow University, from which he graduated MA in 1950. In 1983 he was awarded an honorary DLitt by Glasgow University. He served in the Royal Navy from 1941 to 1946, much of the time as a leading torpedo operator on HMS *Royalist*, on the notorious Russian convoys to Murmansk.

From 1946 until 1956 Maclean taught English, history, and geography at Gallowflat School, Rutherglen, Glasgow. After winning a short-story competition run by the *Glasgow Herald* he came to the attention of Ian Chapman, who worked at the Collins publishing house. Chapman persuaded him to write *HMS Ulysses*, which was published in October 1955. It was an instant best-seller, with 250,000 copies sold in the first six months. *HMS Ulysses* was a Book Society choice, as was *The Guns of Navarone* (1957); they were followed by *Ice Station Zebra* (1963). Maclean then left his native Scotland and became a tax exile in Switzerland. In his subsequent nomadic life, he moved back to England and then to the south of France, California, and Yugoslavia. During these years he completed a total of thirty-two books, of which twenty-six were novels; they brought him gross earnings of around £20 million. Many of the books became films, notably *The Guns of Navarone* (1961), *Ice Station Zebra* (1968), *Where Eagles Dare* (1969), and *When Eight Bells Toll* (1971). The books were fast-moving thrillers, without great literary stature. Women rarely featured in them.

Maclean was of spare build and about 5 feet 7 inches tall. He had sleek dark hair, with a middle parting: he was not unattractive, but was not an imposing figure. He had a thick Scottish highland accent, which at times made him difficult to understand. He was highly intelligent, with a fascination for medical science in general and cancer research in particular. His life was greatly influenced by the early death of his brother, Lachlan, while a 21-year-old medical student at Glasgow University. He was a very complex character, full of inhibitions and strange moods, with a wry sense of humour which only appeared when he was relaxed in the company of friends. He was introverted and shy and, although his behaviour could be boorish, he was extremely generous, not only with his material possessions but in his willingness to encourage and help other writers in their careers. His charitable acts were never flamboyant or publicized.

On 2 July 1953 he married Gisela Heinrichsen, of Schleswig-Holstein, Germany. They had two sons of their own and adopted a third. Whether it was because, as a very shy and guilt-ridden man, Maclean found his success difficult to cope with or because of a growing drink problem, his marriage latterly was unhappy, and ended in divorce in 1972. In the same year he married, at Caxton Hall, London, Mary Marcelle Georgius (1934/5–1985), daughter of Georgius Guibourg, a well-known French music-hall entertainer. Marcelle wasted his money on attempted film productions and other extravagant enterprises and a lifestyle which was in total contrast to Maclean's very modest and unspectacular way of life. She died of cancer in Los Angeles in 1985, aged fifty and penniless, in spite of having had a substantial divorce settlement in 1977.

Maclean returned to England in the mid-1960s, having bought Jamaica Inn on Bodmin Moor. But restlessness soon took him to Geneva where he spent most of the early 1970s. He died on 2 February 1987 at University Hospital, Munich, during a winter holiday with his first wife, Gisela, in the Black Forest. He had been controlling his hard drinking, and his death followed a series of strokes. He lived the last eight years of his life alone in a rented villa just outside Dubrovnik, overlooking the Adriatic, with a view which reminded him of his Scottish west-coast origins. The landlord kept his apartment as a shrine after his death, but the typewriter, books, and other symbols of his writing den were plundered by federal troops during the breakup of Yugoslavia in 1991.   IAN CHAPMAN, rev.

Sources J. Webster, *Alistair Maclean* (1991) · *The Independent* (7 Feb 1987) · *The Bookseller* (20 Feb 1987), 591 · *The Times* (3 Feb 1987) · *CGPLA Eng. & Wales* (1987) · private information (1996) · personal knowledge (1996)
Likenesses Snowdon, photograph, 1981, NPG [*see illus.*] · Snowdon, photograph, repro. in Webster, *Alistair Maclean*
Wealth at death £73,347 in England and Wales: probate, 6 Nov 1987, *CGPLA Eng. & Wales*

Maclean, Allan (1725–1798), army officer, was born at Torloisk, Isle of Mull, Argyllshire, the son of Donald Maclean of Torloisk and his wife, Mary Campbell. Little is known of his early life. He fought in the Jacobite army at Culloden in 1746, and after the collapse of the Stuart cause fled to the Netherlands. There he joined the Scots brigade as a subaltern and fought in the defence of Bergen op Zoom in 1747. Taken prisoner, he was at once paroled by the French

commander, Marshal Löwendahl. When George III granted amnesty to Scottish rebels in 1750 Maclean returned home, and on 8 January 1756 he was appointed a lieutenant in the 62nd (later the 60th) regiment, the Royal Americans.

During the Seven Years' War Maclean was severely wounded at Fort Carillon in 1758 and again wounded at Fort Niagara in 1759. Having been promoted captain-lieutenant on 27 July 1758, he was appointed captain of the New York independent company on 16 January 1759, and in that capacity served under James Wolfe at the capture of Quebec. He returned to Scotland, and was appointed major-commandant of a corps of highlanders to be raised as the 114th Royal Highland volunteers (Maclean's Highlanders). After short service in America the regiment was disbanded, and Maclean was placed on half pay. He received a land grant on St John Island (Prince Edward Island) for his services but apparently did not live there. On 7 February 1771, at St Martin-in-the-Fields, Westminster, he married Janet Maclean; they had no children. He was promoted brevet lieutenant-colonel on 25 May 1772.

In June 1775 Maclean was commissioned lieutenant-colonel-commandant of a provincial corps, the Royal Highland Emigrants, which he raised from discharged highland soldiers who had settled in America at the end of the previous war. When the Americans invaded Canada in the autumn of 1775 he marched from Quebec with the highlanders and other reinforcements for Guy Carleton at Montreal. Compelled to retreat, he preceded Carleton to Quebec, arriving on 13 November, just before enemy forces under Benedict Arnold. He was joined by Carleton on 19 November, but Quebec was besieged by a rebel army that vastly outnumbered the defenders. Although pessimistic about holding the city he was encouraged by Carleton, who appointed him second in command. When the Americans attacked the place on 31 December, Maclean defeated them with heavy losses. On 6 May 1776, when reinforcements arrived at Quebec, Maclean sortied from the city in command of the highlanders and the Royal Fusiliers. He routed the rebels and compelled them into headlong retreat, but was disgusted when Carleton, for political reasons, did not press the Americans with vigour. Maclean remained in Quebec to hurry along other reinforcements as Carleton chased the rebels out of Canada.

In the summer of 1776 Maclean travelled to England seeking justice for himself and the Royal Highland Emigrants; he arrived on 1 September. Notwithstanding his and his men's conduct at the siege of Quebec, and an earlier promise that his corps would be made a permanent regiment, neither he nor the highlanders had received recognition. Despite his efforts the corps was not received until 1 April 1779, when it was brought into the line as the 84th, or Royal Highland Emigrants, regiment. Nor was Maclean appointed its colonel, for that honour went to Sir Henry Clinton. Maclean had returned to Quebec in 1777, and in June was appointed by Carleton military governor of Montreal with the local rank of brigadier-general. In late

September he reinforced Fort Ticonderoga, and a month later, after John Burgoyne's surrender at Saratoga, New York, he fell back to St Jean in preparation for an American attack that never materialized. He was stationed at Quebec in the winter of 1778, organizing amateur theatricals, and three years later was posted at Niagara. He was commissioned a brevet colonel on 17 November 1782.

Maclean returned to England in 1783, and retired; he died on 18 February 1798 at his home in Argyle Street, London. A grizzled, hard-fighting Scottish soldier, he is remembered as a hero among descendants of the Royal Highland Emigrants in the Canadian maritime provinces.　　　　　　　　　PAUL DAVID NELSON

Sources J. P. McLean, *An historical account of the settlement of Scottish highlanders in America prior to the peace of 1783* (1900) · F. Parkman, *Montcalm and Wolfe*, 2 (1884) · R. S. Allen, ed., *The Loyal Americans* (1983) · M. B. Fryer, *King's men: the soldier founders of Ontario* (1980) · P. D. Nelson, *General Sir Guy Carleton: soldier-statesman of early British Canada* (2000) · J. H. Smith, *Our struggle for the fourteenth colony: Canada and the American Revolution*, 2 vols. (1907) · R. M. Hatch, *Thrust for Canada: the American attempt on Quebec in 1775–1776* (1979) · 'Letterbook of Captain Alexander McDonald, of the Royal Highland Emigrants, 1775–1779', *Collections of the New York Historical Society*, 15 (1883) [whole issue] · G. F. G. Stanley, *Canada invaded, 1775–1776* (Toronto, 1973) · Fortescue, *Brit. army*, vol. 3 · G. F. G. Stanley, 'Maclean, Allan', *DCB*, vol. 4 · *GM*, 1st ser., 68 (1798), 354–5 · *DNB*
Archives BL, letters to Sir Frederick Haldimand and others, Add. MSS 21732–21865

McLean, Archibald (1733–1812), Scotch Baptist minister, was born on 1 May 1733, at East Kilbride, Lanarkshire, and was the son of a farmer, a highlander descended from Brolus, eldest son of Duart, chief of the clan of the McLeans, and a Miss Struthers, a farmer's daughter. In his infancy he spent about six months on the island of Mull, where he acquired a knowledge of Gaelic. On his return he was educated first at Cathcart, and afterwards at Cowcaddens, and in 1746 was apprenticed to a printer in Glasgow. In 1759 he married Isabella (1733–1790), youngest daughter of William Moore, merchant, with whom he obtained a small property, enabling him to set up as a bookseller and printer in Glasgow in 1760. He relinquished his business seven years later and, after living for a short time in London, he acted from 1767 to 1785 as overseer of Donaldson & Co., printers, in Edinburgh.

McLean had been raised in the Church of Scotland, but in 1762 he joined the Glasites, or Sandemanians. In 1763 he left them for the Baptists, taking with him many Glasite customs and views of doctrine, and in June 1768 he was chosen as an elder in the Edinburgh Scotch Baptist church. Thenceforth he was an ardent advocate of his new creed. He visited centres in Scotland and England where the principles of the Scotch Baptists had gained access, formed associations, and aided the regulation of their affairs. He was a friend of Andrew Fuller and an energetic supporter of the Particular Baptist Missionary Society, and also promoted mission work in Scotland. For many years he rarely omitted an annual journey into England, during which he visited London, Hull, Beverley, Chester,

Nottingham, and Liverpool. In 1785 the church in Edinburgh awarded him a stipend to allow him to concentrate on preaching and writing.

McLean was a voluminous writer on many scriptural and controversial subjects. His most influential works included *Letters to Mr Glas in Answer to his Dissertation on Infant Baptism* (1767), which is the first Scottish defence of the baptism of believers by immersion, and *The Commission Given by Jesus Christ to his Apostles Illustrated* (1786), which sets out Scotch Baptist beliefs in full. In addition, he contributed an essay on 'Baptists in Scotland' to Rippon's *Annual Register* (1795), and a commentary on the epistle to the Hebrews (rev. edn 1820) was long valued. McLean died in Edinburgh on 21 December 1812 and was buried in the city's St Cuthbert's churchyard. Collected editions of his works appeared in 1823 (edited by William Jones) and as 7 volumes in 1847–8.

THOMPSON COOPER, *rev.* DEREK B. MURRAY

Sources W. Jones, 'Memoir', in *The works of Archibald McLean*, ed. W. Jones, 6 vols. (1823) · D. W. Bebbington, ed., *The Baptists in Scotland: a history* (1988) · D. B. Murray, 'McLean, Archibald', *DSCHT* · R. D. Mitchell, 'Archibald McLean, Baptist pioneer in Scotland', PhD diss., U. Edin., 1950
Archives NA Scot., corresp. and papers | Bodl. Oxf., letters to Ralph Griffiths
Likenesses G. Watson, oils, c.1810, Scot. NPG · stipple, pubd 1815, V&A · C. Turner, oils, Scot. NPG; copy, British Baptist Church, Edinburgh

Maclean [*formerly* Macleane], **Arthur John** (1858–1943), Scottish Episcopal bishop of Moray, Ross, and Caithness, and Syriac scholar, was born on 6 July 1858 at 15 Springfield Place, Bath, the last of ten children of A. J. Macleane (1811/12–1858), clergyman and Latin scholar, and his wife, Sarah, daughter of R. S. Hutchings, clergyman and orientalist, and his wife, Elvina. Maclean (he dropped the final 'e' after university) belonged to a branch of the Macleanes of Ardgour which migrated to India after the Jacobite rising of 1745 and achieved great prominence there. His father, after a short period in the Indian Civil Service, settled in England but died two months before Maclean's birth. In 1865 Maclean was sent, with his brother Douglas, to live with his sister Flora and her husband, the Revd James Cholmeley, in Lincolnshire. Like his surrogate father Maclean was a gifted mathematician. Educated first in Huntingdon, he then went to Eton College in 1873 as a king's scholar, and then in 1876 to King's College, Cambridge, where he gained a first-class degree, ninth wrangler, in mathematics (1880) and until 1883 was college mathematical lecturer (as he was also at Selwyn College). His vacations from Cambridge were spent in his beloved Scottish highlands (he later claimed to have seen the Loch Ness monster), and especially on the island of Cumbrae where he learned to read and speak Gaelic and was inspired by the teachings of the Oxford Movement. In December 1882 he was ordained deacon, and in June 1883 was priested in the Scottish Episcopal church. From 1882 to 1886 he was priest-in-charge of Portree, Skye, where he began by building a parish church, St Columba's.

In 1886 Maclean travelled to Orumiyyeh, in the Azerbaijan province of Persia, as the first head of the archbishop of Canterbury's mission to the Assyrian Christians which had as its purpose not conversion, which its statutes forbade, but the strengthening of faith and religious practice. He oversaw the establishment, by 1891, of an upper school for young clergy, four high schools for boys, and seventy-eight village schools. The mission press acquired Syriac type and printed liturgical and other works. In 1890 a house of Anglican Sisters of Bethany was founded in Orumiyyeh with an associated girls' school. He learned to speak modern Syriac, and later published an important grammar (1895) and dictionary (1901) of the language, as well as learning classical Syriac which he employed in several significant liturgical studies.

In March 1891 Maclean left Persia for Portree, his former parish. In 1892 he co-authored an account of the Assyrian Christians and in the same year he was honoured by being appointed canon of Cumbrae and dean of Argyll and the Isles. He built a rectory, and married Eva Maclean (d. 1951), daughter of John Maclean MD, on 14 June 1894; they had no children. After a period as rector of St John's, Selkirk (1897–1903), where he became a central figure in the campaign for lay representation in the Episcopal church, he was appointed Pantonian professor and principal of the Episcopal Theological College in Edinburgh. He spent only five terms at the college but his energy, devotion, and financial skills saved it from near ruin. He was consecrated as bishop of Moray, Ross, and Caithness in December 1904 (in the same year he received the degree of DD from Cambridge and from Glasgow) and resigned as principal at Easter 1905. He then took up residence in Eden Court, Inverness, where he remained for the rest of his life, actively involved in diocesan affairs and a central figure in the production of the Scottish prayer book of 1929. On 8 February 1935 he was elected primus of the Scottish Episcopal church, which he represented at the coronation of George VI in 1937. He resigned just a fortnight before his death, at his home, Eden Court, Inverness, on 24 February 1943. He was buried on the 27th in Tomnahurich cemetery, Inverness.   D. G. K. TAYLOR

Sources W. G. S. Snow, *Arthur John Maclean, bishop of Moray primus* (1950) · J. F. Coakley, *The church of the East and the Church of England: a history of the archbishop of Canterbury's Assyrian mission* (1992) · A. J. Maclean and W. H. Browne, *The catholicos of the East and his people* (1892) · Crockford (1937) · *The Times* (26 Feb 1943) · *The Times* (1 March 1943)
Archives NRA, priv. coll., corresp. and papers
Likenesses photograph, 1886, LPL; repro. in Coakley, *The church of the East*, 105 · photograph, 1904?, repro. in Snow, *Arthur John Maclean* · photograph, 1920, repro. in Snow, *Arthur John Maclean*
Wealth at death £5350 14s. 2d.: confirmation, 14 July 1943, CCI

McLean [*married name* Beaton], **Catherine** [Kate] (1879–1960), trade unionist, was born on 6 January 1879 at 16 Henderson Street, Glasgow, the daughter of Murdoch McLean, grain store keeper, and his wife, Mary. She was the fourth of six children, and attended Bishop Street and Gorbals schools until the age of twelve.

Kate McLean, as she was known, lived for most of her life in Glasgow, and was deeply involved in its labour movement from 1908, when she joined the Women's Labour League. By 1909 she was a delegate to Glasgow

Trades Council from the National Federation of Women Workers (NFWW). Kate McLean was to remain involved with the trades council for a number of years, and was a member of the parliamentary committee of the Scottish Trades Union Congress (STUC). She remained an active STUC delegate until her marriage in 1914.

Kate McLean was an organizer for the NFWW in Scotland and was involved in recruiting members to it, and forming branches, as well as supporting women in particular struggles. She was a key figure in a number of disputes, including the 1911 strike at the dyeworks in the Vale of Leven, the United Turkey Red combine, and the 1913 networkers' strike in Kilbirnie, Ayrshire, the longest recorded strike of women workers in the pre-war years, which lasted from April to September 1913.

In 1914, at the age of thirty-five, Kate McLean married Duncan Burns Beaton, a twenty-eight year-old coalminer from Cowdenbeath. Her husband was also active in the labour movement, although not to the same extent, and was secretary of Cowdenbeath Trades Council (1916–17). By the early 1920s, however, the couple were resident in Glasgow. Duncan Burns was on the education committee of the Glasgow Trades Council in 1922–3, by which time Kate was contesting local council wards in Glasgow for the Independent Labour Party. As Kate Beaton, she stood for the Glasgow Sandyford ward in 1920 and 1921, and in 1923 was elected unopposed in the Hutchisontown ward in a by-election caused by the election of the sitting councillor, George Buchan, as MP. Re-elected in 1925, she held the seat until 1949 when she declined to stand. During her time on the council she served on virtually all the committees, was elected bailie and magistrate, and was convener of the welfare committee in 1944–5.

Kate Beaton was also very active in the co-operative movement in Glasgow, first joining the Co-op in 1921. Her service to the movement, and particularly to the St George Society, lasted twenty years, during which time she worked her way up from delegates' secretary to director in 1929 and vice president in 1931. She went on to become the first woman to hold the post of president in 1948. Duncan Burns Beaton died in a nursing home in 1959 at the age of seventy-three from general thrombosis and pneumonia. Kate Beaton died on 21 October 1960 of heart failure and senility at 20 Burnbank Terrace, Glasgow. She was cremated at Glasgow crematorium on 25 October.

A woman of small stature which belied her energy, Kate McLean was active for most of her adult life in the labour movement in the west of Scotland. Working alongside Mary Macarthur, she was an important figure in the NFWW and within the Labour Party of the 'red Clydeside' era.   GEORGE RAWLINSON

Sources Glasgow Trades Council, minutes and annual reports, 1909–46, Mitchell L., Glas. · A. Tuckett, *The Scottish Trades Union Congress: the first 80 years, 1897–1977* (1986) · E. Gordon, *Women and the labour movement in Scotland* (1991) · *Forward* (1910) · *Forward* (1911) · *Forward* (1912) · *Evening Times* [Glasgow] (1910–60) · *Scottish Co-operator* (31 Jan 1948) · *Scottish Co-operator* (14 Aug 1948) · *Scottish Co-operator* (29 Oct 1960) · A. Robinson, 'A study of women workers in the Vale of Leven cotton finishing industry', BA diss., Strathclyde University, 1994 · S. Lawenhak, 'Women in the leadership of the STUC, 1897–1970', *Journal of the Scottish Labour History Society*, 7/4 (July 1973) · b. cert. · d. cert.

Likenesses photographs, repro. in *Scottish Co-operator* (7 Feb 1948) · photographs, repro. in *Scottish Co-operator* (14 Aug 1948)

Maclean, Charles (*fl.* 1788–1824), physician and writer on politics, about whose early life nothing is known, entered the service of the East India Company and in 1788 was surgeon of the *William Pitt*; afterwards he served similarly on the *Northumberland* and the *Houghton*—all were East Indiamen. In this capacity he visited Jamaica and made several voyages to India. About 1792 he settled in Bengal, where he had charge of a hospital, apparently at Calcutta. However, his name does not appear on any Bengal medical list. In 1795 he deserted from the *Houghton* and was ordered to return to England. He ignored these orders and was still in Calcutta three years later. He also served before 1798 as medical officer to troops in Batavia and at Bencoolen.

Maclean's travels gave him exceptional facilities for the study of fevers, and in 1796 he published in Calcutta his results in *Dissertation on the Source of Epidemic Diseases*, which argued that epidemics arose not from contagion but from miasmata, atmospheric phenomena, and the cumulative effects of scarcity and famine. In the spring of 1798, in an Indian newspaper Maclean made an insinuation against Jacob Rider, a magistrate, which the government objected to; Maclean was ordered to leave India by the new governor-general, Marquess Wellesley. After some resistance Maclean submitted, and was deported to Europe in the *Busbridge*. An intention to visit Spain in 1800 in order to study the fevers prevalent there was frustrated by the war, but in the same year he managed to acquire an MD degree from Marischal College, Aberdeen. In 1801 he was at Hamburg, and on the conclusion of peace he travelled to Amsterdam, Rotterdam, and Paris, to advocate an international institution at Constantinople for the study and treatment of the plague. He was one of the prisoners forcibly detained by Napoleon in 1803, but was allowed to leave Bordeaux on 13 December 1803, on proving that he had not visited England for ten years.

In April 1804 Maclean applied for a post on the hospital staff for the British army. He was placed in the York Hospital, Chelsea, London, where he remained until 15 January 1805, when he was ordered to Chelmsford. His theory that epidemics were not contagious does not seem to have inspired the authorities with much confidence in him, and the delay in his promotion led him to tender his resignation, which was not accepted. After an unsuccessful application for a post on Sir James Craig's Mediterranean expedition, Maclean left the service, and his name appeared in the *Hue and Cry* as a deserter. No further steps were taken against him, but he became a bitter opponent of the government. In 1806 he made a virulent attack on Marquess Wellesley in a series of letters, entitled *The Affairs of Asia Considered in their Effects on the Liberties of Britain*, which soon reached a second edition. He was supported in the House of Commons by his friend James Paull.

In 1809 Maclean applied for a post on the Walcheren expedition, without success. Soon after he became lecturer on the diseases of hot climates to the East India Company, and he championed the company's cause against the proposals of the government to throw open the trade to India in his *View of the Consequences of Laying Open the Trade to India* (1810). He also published a pamphlet on smallpox vaccination entitled *On the State of Vaccination in 1810* (1810), which denounced Jennerian vaccination as a 'splendid delusion'. Maclean claimed that the returns of the national vaccine establishment compiled by Sir Lucas Pepys, physician-general to the army and president of the Royal College of Physicians, were fraudulent, and that there was much evidence to show that vaccination did not work.

From 1815 to 1817 Maclean travelled in Spain, Turkey, and the Levant, and he studied the plague at the Greek Pest Hospital at Constantinople, in the service of the Levant Company. His experiences in the Levant and in India provided the basis for his most important medical work, *The Results of an Investigation Respecting Epidemic and Pestilential Diseases* (1817). Here Maclean restated his opposition to the theory that epidemic diseases were contagious, adding that the quarantine measures then imposed routinely in most Mediterranean ports against vessels sailing from the Levant had no basis in medical fact. In this, and in another work entitled *Suggestions for the Prevention and Mitigation of Epidemic and Pestilential Diseases* (1817), Maclean argued that plague had spread and declined at similar rates in all countries, regardless of whether they operated a system of quarantine. It was on these grounds that he called on the British government to abandon its own system of quarantine, but the government and the Royal College of Physicians, which Maclean charged with a flagrant abandonment of public duty, refused to adopt his recommendations or repay his expenses.

In 1818 Maclean resumed his lectures in England and planned a series of volumes entitled The Archives of Health, which never appeared. However, he did publish a digest of his lectures to surgeons of the East India Company, entitled *Practical Illustrations of the Progress of Medical Improvement* (1818), in which he expounded his unorthodox views on the treatment of acute diseases such as fevers. Maclean advocated a modified version of the 'excitation' doctrine popularized in the eighteenth century by the Edinburgh physician John Brown. Like Brown, Maclean believed that many diseases were caused by diminished vitality and that the body could be restored to health by the use of 'stimulants' such as wine. Brunonian ideas had been fashionable in radical circles in Britain and among surgeons employed by the East India Company, but they were increasingly denounced by influential Anglo-Indian practitioners such as James Johnson. Maclean was no stranger to controversy and claimed that Brunonian doctrines had been grossly vilified and misunderstood, accusing his critics of lacking even the smallest comprehension of the subject. Nor did he cease his attacks on the body politic. In 1820, in *Specimens of Systematic Misrule*, he attacked the 'holy alliance' and the tory government of England, and in the same year he published *The triumph of public opinion, with proposed articles of impeachment against the ministers of the crown in the case of Caroline, queen of England.*

In 1821 Maclean made what was to be his last trip overseas, having been commissioned by the Spanish government to investigate the nature and causes of a fever epidemic which had ravaged Barcelona. For his services he received the accolades he had been denied in Britain, being made a knight of the order of Charles III and a member of several Spanish academies of medicine. Maclean's visit to Spain provided the occasion for a renewed attack upon the system of quarantine. In his *Remarks on the British Quarantine Laws* (1823) he repeated many of his earlier arguments against what he described as this 'most gigantic, extraordinary, and mischievous superstructure'. This was followed by a lecture on the same subject at Liverpool, in the following year, which was also published. His death occurred soon afterwards.   MARK HARRISON

Sources D. G. Crawford, *A history of the Indian medical service, 1600–1913*, 2 (1914), 60–61 · *DNB*

Archives BL, letters to Lord Glenville, Add. MS 59265

Maclean, Charles Hector Fitzroy, Baron Maclean (1916–1990), courtier and chief scout, was born in London on 5 May 1916, the youngest of the three children and only surviving son of Major Hector Fitzroy Maclean (1873–1932), Scots Guards, and his wife, Winifred Joan Wilding (d. 1941). On his father's death he became heir to his grandfather, Sir Fitzroy Donald Maclean, tenth baronet, of Duart and Morven, and twenty-sixth chief of clan Maclean, whom he succeeded in 1936. Charles Maclean—or Chips, as he was invariably called—was educated at Canford School, Dorset, and served in the Scots Guards during the Second World War. He saw action in France, Belgium, Holland, and Germany, and was mentioned in dispatches. On 7 June 1941 he married (Joan) Elizabeth Mann (b. 1923); they had a son and a daughter.

Maclean retired from the army after the war and moved to the family home, Duart Castle, on the Isle of Mull, where he devoted himself to breeding highland cattle and blackface sheep. He was appointed lord lieutenant of Argyll in 1954 and a JP in the following year. He held many other public and charitable offices in Scotland. These included being a brigadier in the Royal Company of Archers, president of the Territorial and Auxiliary Forces Association of Argyll, and vice-president of the Highland Cattle Society of Scotland. As a young boy Maclean had been a cub scout; he had not moved on to the boy scouts, but in 1954 he became chief commissioner for Scotland of the Boy Scouts Association, and in 1959 became chief scout of the UK and overseas branches, and chief scout of the Commonwealth. He relinquished the former post in 1971, the latter in 1975. He was quick to reform a movement that had become something of an anachronism: 'We must do more to show that scouting is really swinging and "with it"', he told the movement (*The Times*, 9 Feb 1990). By the time he retired from the organization it had been revitalized: it dropped 'Boy' from its title, shorts were

replaced by long trousers in the uniform, and new activities such as caving and gliding were added to the old repertory of model making, camping, and angling. The reforms were not universally welcomed, and a breakaway organization, the Baden-Powell Scouts Association, was formed in 1970 to perpetuate the traditional model of scouting. Maclean was appointed KBE in 1967 and a knight of the Order of the Thistle in 1969.

In 1971 Maclean was given a life peerage as Baron Maclean, of Duart and Morven, appointed GCVO, sworn of the privy council, and appointed lord chamberlain, succeeding Lord Cobbold. He took over shortly after publication of the report of the select committee on the civil list (22 November 1971), which had opened the finances of the royal household to public scrutiny. As lord chamberlain he oversaw all ceremonial (but not state) occasions, a task he relished. His first challenge was the lying-in-state and funeral of the duke of Windsor at Windsor in June 1972. It was the correct etiquette that he should bid farewell to the widowed duchess of Windsor when she flew back to Paris. Again correctly, he did not bow, since she was not a royal highness. Some felt that it would have been kinder had a member of the royal family accompanied her to Heathrow Airport, though the entire royal family were at her car to bid her farewell at Windsor Castle. He also oversaw the funerals of Prince William of Gloucester (in 1972), the duke of Gloucester (1974), Earl Mountbatten of Burma (1979), and Princess Alice, countess of Athlone (1981). He presided over the celebrations for the queen's silver wedding (1972), the marriage of Princess Anne (1973), the silver jubilee (1977), and the wedding of the prince of Wales and Lady Diana Spencer in 1981. These spectacles were Maclean's forte. He was widely liked in the royal household, and his approach was less confrontational than that of either his predecessor or his successor, Lord Airlie. Behind his deadpan face there was an impish sense of humour. Robert Runcie, the archbishop of Canterbury, said of him: 'Nobody was less ponderously dutiful or less formidably distinguished' (private information). He retired as lord chamberlain in 1984, was appointed a permanent lord in waiting, and received the Royal Victorian Chain. In 1985 he became chief steward of Hampton Court Palace. Part of the palace was destroyed by fire on Easter Monday 1986. Lord Maclean died at his home in the palace on 8 February 1990, shortly before the restoration work was completed. He was succeeded in his baronetcy by his son, Lachlan.   HUGO VICKERS

Sources *The Times* (9 Feb 1990) · Burke, *Peerage* (1999) · private information (2004) [Sir Lachlan Maclean, son; General Sir Michael Gow] · *WW* · B. Pimlott, *The queen* (1996)

McLean, David (1833–1908), banker, was born on 4 February 1833 at Scotswalls Farm, Crossgates, near Dunfermline, Fife, Scotland, the fifth of the six children of James McLean (1791–1851), farmer, and his wife, Isabel (1790–1882), daughter of James Pettie and his wife, Jannet Reddie. As the son of a poor farmer, McLean's early education was erratic, but he became apprenticed to William Beveridge, manager of the Dunfermline branch of the Western Bank of Scotland, from whom he learned his banking and with whom he established a lasting personal relationship. When the Western Bank failed in 1857, McLean determined to follow his elder brother to New Zealand. On reaching London, however, he checked with the Oriental Bank Corporation (then the most important British overseas bank), to which he had written previously, and learned that a position in India or China had just been offered him. Abandoning his plans (and passage money), he accepted the China offer and, after training, went east to Hong Kong, where in 1862 he became acting manager. Transferred to Shanghai, he became acting manager of that branch in 1864.

The promoters of the Hongkong Bank were impressed by McLean and attempted to poach him, but he initially could not be tempted. Months later, however, McLean, convinced that he would not be confirmed manager by the Oriental Bank, applied to become, and in 1865 was appointed as, the Hongkong Bank's first Shanghai manager. There, he was particularly successful, both professionally and personally. The board of directors offered McLean the chief managership of the bank in 1870, but he considered managing the Shanghai branch of virtually equal importance.

Despite sending regular remittances to support his mother and other members of his family, McLean had been able to save £50,000, and in 1873 he returned to Britain, accepting the sub-managership of the bank's London office. Within a few months he had uncovered improper transactions by the manager; and in consequence McLean was appointed to replace him. In 1874 he returned to Scotland to marry Elizabeth Livingston (1852–1929), daughter of John Manson, banker, of Fingask, and Elizabeth Livingston Blaikie, and sister of Sir Patrick Manson. The McLeans had four children.

By 1874 the Hongkong Bank was in difficulty, and McLean was once again offered the top executive position. Now fully settled in London, he declined, but agreed to act as inspector to reassure shareholders. In this he was successful, and was able to ensure that his protégé, Thomas Jackson, became the new chief manager. McLean continued to act as virtual tutor, not only to Jackson but also to other, more isolated, managers; and the surviving correspondence constitutes a major source for an understanding of the intricacies of exchange banking. In addition, McLean had a positive effect on recruitment policy. Banks on the China coast had on occasion employed local 'Europeans' with dangerously mixed results; but McLean developed a 'service' of young British staff, trained in London and sent east as needed, with the intention of lifetime careers with the bank.

The Scottish McLean was in no way awed by the City of London and its financial institutions. The Hongkong Bank acted from time to time as agent for the Chinese government, and McLean in 1874 successfully introduced the first public China loan on the London market. With the advice of the London and County Bank, and through Panmure Gordon & Co., McLean gained confidence. In 1885, during the Sino-French War, the Hongkong Bank was prepared to act as agent for the Chinese 6 per cent gold loan of £757,000. Barings, and Matheson & Co., were also agents for a second loan; intent on retaining market control, they urged McLean to permit them to issue both, but without mention of the Hongkong Bank. After obtaining authority from head office, McLean refused. Quietly, he had prepared his own prospectus; it was ready for mailing, and the Hongkong Bank's loan was, in fact, oversubscribed. In 1887 McLean turned down a proposal from Rothschild's that the Hongkong Bank join with a German group, but the concept was in any case premature. McLean would first establish his bank's independence and prove its capabilities. This in turn would provide the experience and credibility necessary for its later key role in China's public borrowing.

In 1889 McLean retired from the London management to make way for the return—temporary as it turned out—of Thomas Jackson, accepting instead membership of the bank's London consultative committee. McLean had been an expert witness before the royal commission on gold and silver in 1886, but he now seriously underestimated the long-run weakness of silver by accepting a directorship in the newly formed Trust and Loan Company of China, Japan, and the Straits, a company established to finance China's anticipated modernization. Suitable projects did not materialize; the company, with its funds in the East, speculated as silver continued its fall. As the company did not itself operate in the London–China exchanges, McLean, although remaining on the Hongkong Bank's London Committee, saw no conflict of interest, but in 1893 the Trust and Loan Company, reorganized as the Bank of China, Japan, and the Straits, changed policy. McLean, deciding that his honour required his remaining with the failing enterprise, severed all connections with the Hongkong Bank.

In 1889 there were two innovative companies with complementary products—the financially liquid Lamson Store Service Company, and the expanding, but capital-short Paragon Check Book Company. The chairman of Lamson, John M. Kelly, had known David McLean in the East and now sought his advice. Together they obtained a majority interest in Paragon, and in 1889 established through merger the Lamson Paragon Supply Company Ltd, with a registered capital of £30,000. McLean was a director until his resignation in 1907, by which time the company had become a successful multinational with a capital of £400,000; his son Alan became chairman in 1912.

David McLean remained a director of the Imperial Bank of Persia and a successful venture capitalist, with interests in rubber and tin. An enthusiastic sportsman, he rented in 1884 a shooting estate, Littlewood Park, above Kirkton of Forbes, near Alford, Aberdeenshire, where he was noted for his prizewinning herd of Aberdeen cattle. He retired there, and he died on 18 June 1908 at Littlewood Park. He was buried in the cemetery of Kirkton of Forbes.

David McLean was one of the most important overseas bankers of his generation. As Shanghai manager, first of the Oriental Bank Corporation and then of the newly established Hongkong and Shanghai Banking Corporation, McLean successfully developed the techniques of exchange banking and related trade finance in the most commercially important 'treaty port' on the China coast. On return to London as manager for the Hongkong Bank, he proved that the bank, although based in Hong Kong, was competent to act as agent for the issue of Chinese government loans. His system of executive staff recruitment for service in the East was an influential model, which prevailed at least until the 1950s. By the time of his retirement the Hongkong Bank had become the largest British overseas bank.   FRANK H. H. KING

Sources F. H. H. King and others, *The history of the Hongkong and Shanghai Banking Corporation*, 4 vols. (1987–91) · G. Jones, *The history of the British Bank of the Middle East*, 1: *Banking and empire in Iran* (1986) · F. H. H. King, ed., *Eastern banking: essays in the history of the Hongkong and Shanghai Banking Corporation* (1983) · D. W. Evans, *1886–1936: a narrative of fifty years* (privately printed, 1936?) · T. E. Elias, *A half century of Paragon progress* (privately printed, London, 1937) · 'Royal commission to inquire into … relative values of the precious metals: final report', *Parl. papers* (1888), 45.285, C. 5512; 45.455, C. 5512-I · m. cert. · will · d. cert. · private information (2004)
Archives SOAS, McLean MSS | HSBC Group Archives, London · HSBC Group Archives, London, Midland Bank archives · HSBC Group Archives, London, Hongkong Bank Group archives, especially 'personalities' file
Likenesses photograph, 1873, repro. in King, *History of The Hongkong and Shanghai Banking Corporation*, 280 ff., no. 8 · G. Reid, portrait, priv. coll. · photograph (as director of Paragon), repro. in Evans, *1886–1936: a narrative of fifty years*, vol. 1, p. 14 · photographs, priv. coll. · photographs, HSBC Group Archives, London, Hongkong Bank Group archives · photographs, HSBC Group Archives, London, Midland Bank archives
Wealth at death £252,489 6s. 3d.: confirmation, 19 Aug 1908, CCI

McLean, Sir Donald (1820–1877), land commissioner and politician in New Zealand, was born on 25 October 1820 at Kilmaluaig, on Tiree, Inner Hebrides, the third child of John McLean and his wife, Margaret McColl. His father is described as a tacksman, with a large lease from the duke of Argyll, and the young Donald was born into gentry life. But Argyll subdivided his estate, dispossessing John McLean. Donald was then educated by his mother's brother, the Revd Donald McColl, and began studying for the Presbyterian ministry. In 1838, however, he emigrated to Sydney. There he worked for merchants who, in 1840, sent him to New Zealand, where he engaged in timber cutting, managed a trading schooner, and acquired a knowledge of Maori. In 1844 he secured a post as clerk and interpreter in the protectorate of aborigines, and was soon made sub-protector in the Taranaki district.

In Taranaki, McLean assisted in land purchases and mediated between Maori and settler, especially over the disputed purchase of Taranaki land by the New Zealand Company. He mixed socially with the Taranaki gentry and sympathized with them when Governor FitzRoy overturned the purchase.

When Governor Grey abolished the protectorate of aborigines in 1846 McLean continued as police inspector in Taranaki, working effectively with the chiefs and recruiting Maori police. From 1847 Grey used McLean as a land purchase commissioner. In 1850 McLean was made resident magistrate, partly in order to prosecute settlers illegally leasing land from Maori and thereby encouraging Maori not to sell the freehold to the government. On 28 August 1851 McLean married Susan Douglas, the daughter of Robert Strang, a Wellington official. She was a warm and humanizing influence on the earnest, self-righteous McLean, but she died in December 1852, soon after the birth of their son, Douglas. McLean later helped two of his sisters and two brothers emigrate to New Zealand.

In 1853 McLean became chief land purchase commissioner. He sought to overcome the resistance of the native people to selling by dealing with the more compliant chiefs and fostering their support by gifts and offers to register portions of the land as their personal estates. Although he was criticized for this by local missionaries, McLean persisted, and his methods led to fighting in Hawkes Bay as one land-selling nation encroached on the interests of another. McLean blamed the increasing resistance to land selling on the interference of the King movement (*kingitanga*), a combination of nations under an elected king, centred on the Waikato district.

In 1859 McLean attempted to break through continued Maori resistance to land selling in Taranaki by advising Governor Gore Browne to accept an offer of land on the Waitara River from a local leader against the opposition of the acknowledged senior chief of the Te Atiawa people. Attempts to force the survey through under military protection led to war, in which Maori warriors from the King movement joined.

McLean, like most settlers, felt that Maori nationalism was futile in the face of British settlement and had to be met and overcome promptly. But the Colonial Office believed that he and Browne had been misguided in the Waitara purchase; Browne was transferred, and McLean lost office and retired to Maraekakaho, the estate he was acquiring in Hawkes Bay. In 1863 he was elected superintendent of that province.

Governor Grey, however, in his second term of office, failed to come to terms with the King movement, and when war resumed in Taranaki he ordered the invasion of the Waikato. McLean was made agent of the general government in Hawkes Bay with wide powers. He mobilized the settler militia and used his influence with local chiefs to keep them neutral or take the government side. When emissaries of the politico-religious Pai Marire (hauhau) movement, more radical than the King movement and involved in violence, entered the district in 1865, he took a hard line, demanding cessions of land from nations who supported them and exiling to the Chatham Islands those believed to have collaborated with the Pai Marire. Some of these exiles, led by Te Kooti, escaped in 1868 and launched a series of devastating raids on east coast settlements.

In 1866 McLean had been elected to the house of representatives for the Napier seat. Provided that Maori did not obstruct settlement, McLean hoped to assist their advancement in the new society. He helped secure laws providing for Maori parliamentary representation and schools in Maori villages. In June 1869 he became native minister and defence minister, posts he held almost continuously for seven years. McLean had learned that land confiscation and tough measures only provoked more Maori resistance, and his policies were henceforward marked by careful diplomacy. Chiefs were encouraged to accept posts in district administration, to take roading contracts, and to establish schools in their area. McLean resisted settler pressure to renew attacks on the King movement, but he refrained from any formal recognition of that movement. Te Kooti and other wanted men were allowed to shelter in the 'King Country'.

McLean also oversaw the native land court, which replaced customary Maori tenure with crown titles, listing the names of the individual owners. Although some Maori were expected to become farmers, the individuals listed on titles were easy targets for private and crown agents seeking to acquire their interests. For thus promoting the peaceful acquisition of Maori land and the advancement of settlement, McLean was made KCMG in July 1874. Illnesses and exertions over the years had weakened his heart, and he resigned office in December 1876. He died at Napier, Hawkes Bay, on 5 January 1877, aged fifty-six, and was buried there on 8 January. Because of his command of their language and protocols, McLean had great influence with Maori, and was much less crass and racist than many of his colleagues. His diplomacy and assiduous toil prevented a renewal of serious violence, despite incidents on the King Country frontier. He is celebrated in early histories as a bringer of peace, but he was above all a determined agent of settlement; it is now recognized that his policies contributed to war in the 1860s, and the legacy of his land purchase methods underlies Maori protest in modern New Zealand.   ALAN WARD

Sources NL NZ, Turnbull L., McLean MSS · K. Sinclair, *The origins of the Maori wars* (1957) · R. W. S. Fargher, 'Donald McLean, chief land purchase agent (1846–61) and native secretary (1856–61)', MA diss., University of Auckland, 1947 · B. Parr, 'The McLean estate: a study of pastoral finance and estate management in New Zealand, 1853–91', MA diss., University of Auckland, 1970 · A. Ward, *A show of justice: racial 'amalgamation' in nineteenth century New Zealand* (1974) · W. Gisborne, *New Zealand rulers and statesmen, 1840–1885* (1886) · J. Cowan, *Sir Donald McLean* (1940) · DNZB, vol. 1 · J. Belich, *Making peoples* (1996)
Archives Archives New Zealand, Wellington, MA series, AGG-HB series · NL NZ, Turnbull L.
Likenesses photograph (as native minister), repro. in Ward, *Show of justice*, 177 · photographs, Archives New Zealand · photographs, NL NZ, Turnbull L.
Wealth at death under £47,000: affidavit of only child, R. D. D. McLean, NL NZ, Turnbull L., McLean MSS, folder 899

Maclean, Sir Donald (1864–1932), politician, was born at Farnworth, Lancashire, on 9 January 1864, the elder of two sons of John Maclean, a master cordwainer, and his wife, Agnes Macmellin (1833–1924). Both parents were Presbyterians, a faith to which Maclean remained actively attached; his mother was a Gaelic-speaking Scottish highlander and his father a native of the Hebrides. The family eventually settled in Carmarthen, and Maclean was educated at Haverfordwest and Carmarthen grammar schools. In 1887 he was admitted as solicitor, a profession

he continued to practise until his death. On 2 October 1907 he married Gwendolen Margaret, eldest daughter of Andrew Devitt of Oxted, Surrey, a colonial broker in the City of London. They had one daughter and four sons.

Practising as a solicitor first in Cardiff, Maclean later moved to London, where he retained his Welsh connections. In the 1920s he was a member of Church, Rackham & Co. of Lincoln's Inn Fields and was elected to the council of the Law Society, to whose vice-presidency he was nominated in 1932. He began involvements in provincial business, as director of the Great Northern Coal Company Ltd. He was also active in social campaigns. A teetotaller, he spoke for the temperance movement and became a director of the United Kingdom Temperance and General Provident Institution. He was among the founders of the National Society for the Prevention of Cruelty to Children, acting as secretary of its Cardiff branch and later as its national solicitor.

With such antecedents and associations, Maclean's politics were deeply ingrained. He had 'Liberalism in his bones' (*Political Diaries of C. P. Scott*, 436), a quality which did not bring him ministerial posts during the Liberal Party's Edwardian dominance, but which commanded special admiration and authority amid its parlous condition after 1918. As parliamentary candidate for the double-member constituency of Bath, he was defeated at the 1900 election but headed the poll at the 1906 election. The Liberal whips soon made use of his legal experience. When the party acquired control of the *Westminster Gazette* in 1908 Maclean was made company secretary, and in 1912 he was nominated as a party shareholder of the *Birmingham Daily Gazette*. He was defeated at the January 1910 election, but at the December election of that year returned as MP for Peebles and Selkirk.

As deputy chairman of ways and means from 1911 to 1918 Maclean's efficient yet patient chairmanship of innumerable House of Commons committees, especially during the war years, made him a respected Westminster figure. From May 1915 he served on a quasi-judicial Home Office committee assessing interned enemy aliens. He was chairman of a Treasury committee on enemy debts in 1916, of the London Appeal Tribunal from 1916 to 1918, and of a reconstruction committee on local government from July to December 1917, which accepted Beatrice Webb's arguments for replacing the poor law authorities by county and borough councils, eventually achieved in 1929. In 1924 he chaired a committee on registration of dock labour, which reconvened in 1920 to settle further registration disputes, and in 1926 an interdepartmental committee on the effect of social insurance on migration. He was sworn of the privy council in 1916 and made KBE 1917.

Maclean remained loyal to Asquith's leadership rather than following Lloyd George during the wartime Liberal Party ruptures. When at the 1918 election Asquith was defeated Maclean was among the few independent Liberals returned (for the redrawn constituency of Peebles and South Midlothian) and was propelled into public prominence. He insisted upon the depleted Asquithian Liberal group of fewer than thirty MPs—disparagingly labelled the Wee Frees—forming a regular opposition to Lloyd George's coalition government. As chairman of the Liberal parliamentary party from January 1919 and acting leader of the whole party, he was an unexpected success. After Asquith won the Paisley by-election in February 1920 Maclean continued as parliamentary chairman, and some colleagues wished he could have remained overall party leader. Not only did he lead a vigorous assault on the coalition government's Liberal claims, he also helped to resuscitate the party organization in the country and to consolidate control of sympathetic national and provincial newspapers, achieved with the formation in 1920 of the Westminster Press Ltd, of which he became a director.

As a standard-bearer of retrenchment, free trade, and Liberal high-mindedness, and a bitter critic of Lloyd George, Maclean remained through the 1920s at the heart of an Asquithian Liberal group which on occasion was more Asquithian than Asquith himself. Doubtful of Asquith's diligence and wider appeal, in 1921 they considered replacing him as leader by Lord Grey, as part of a proposed opposition alliance with Lord Robert Cecil's dissident Conservatives. When the coalition government eventually fell, however, Maclean could not participate in the new parliamentary opportunities. He was defeated in three successive elections, losing his seat in 1922 and failing to win at Kilmarnock in 1923 and East Cardiff in 1924.

Out of parliament, Maclean supplemented his income from legal work and newspaper boards with directorships of the Cardiff Exchange and Office Ltd and Hudson and Kearn's Ltd, of which he became chairman in 1926. As president of the National Liberal Federation from 1922 to 1925 he helped negotiate the Asquithian Liberals' reluctant reunion with Lloyd George's Liberals under the pressure of Baldwin's protectionist campaign in late 1923. During 1924, however, he found new complaints against Lloyd George as he tried, with minimal success, to extract money for an insolvent party organization from Lloyd George's opulent political fund. After the Liberal vote collapsed at the 1924 election Maclean was prominent in presenting Lloyd George's strategic gyrations and personal fund as the chief explanation for the party's decline and the main obstacle to its revival, and the Asquithians as the guardians of consistent, uncorrupted, Liberalism. With other Asquithian members of the Liberal shadow cabinet he pressed a reluctant Asquith to ostracize Lloyd George, only to find that, when Asquith finally forced a break in May 1926 over the party's attitude towards the general strike, Lloyd George commanded a majority of the party's support.

After Asquith retired in September 1926 and Lloyd George captured control of the party organization, Maclean became a founder member of the Liberal Council, created under Lord Grey's presidency to preserve a Liberalism independent from, and obsessively hostile to, that of Lloyd George. He was nevertheless among the beneficiaries of Lloyd George's revival of the Liberal Party, when

at the 1929 election he was returned as MP for North Cornwall, a seat he retained until his death. At first he remained a dissident, but with Liberal MPs holding the parliamentary balance of power he increasingly supported Lloyd George's preference for a free trade Labour government over the protectionist Conservatives, and by early 1931 was again active in the Liberal shadow cabinet. He was still, however, a stern advocate of government retrenchment. With Lloyd George incapacitated by illness, during the August 1931 financial and political crisis Maclean accompanied Sir Herbert Samuel in negotiations between the three party leaderships, joining Conservatives in insisting upon expenditure cuts and, as the Labour cabinet disintegrated, pressing for an emergency all-party coalition government under MacDonald's premiership.

Ministerial office at last came, with Maclean's appointment as president of the Board of Education in the National Government formed in August 1931. He did as much as anyone could in soothing angry teachers and administrators suffering reductions in expenditure on salaries and schools. As the Liberal Party dissolved into three sections in the autumn of 1931 over the prospects of the emergency government's continuing as a permanent coalition, Maclean stayed with the main 'Samuelite Liberal' group, reluctantly acquiescing in the Conservative ministers' insistence upon an early election but trying to defend the free trade cause amid a protectionist deluge. Retaining his North Cornwall seat at the October 1931 general election, he was elevated to the cabinet in November 1931. He was among the four free trade ministers who opposed the introduction of the Import Duties Bill in January 1932 and who agreed to remain in office only when their Conservative colleagues accepted an extraordinary suspension of collective cabinet responsibility—the 'agreement to differ'—allowing them to express public dissent. In the early summer of 1932 Maclean suffered heart trouble, and he died suddenly at his London home, 6 Southwick Place, on 15 June 1932. He was buried at Penn, Buckinghamshire. His wife and their five children survived him; the third son, Donald Duart *Maclean, was the diplomatist and Russian spy.   PHILIP WILLIAMSON

Sources DNB · *The Times* (16 June 1932) · *The Times* (18 June 1932) · *The Times* (27 Aug 1932) · *Directory of Directors* (1914–32) · T. Wilson, *The downfall of the liberal party, 1914–1935* (1966) · *The political diaries of C. P. Scott, 1911–1928*, ed. T. Wilson (1970) · S. E. Koss, *The rise and fall of the political press in Britain*, 2 (1984) · P. Williamson, *National crisis and national government: British politics, the economy and empire, 1926–1932* (1992) · M. Bentley, *The liberal mind, 1914–1929* (1977) · *CGPLA Eng. & Wales* (1932)

Archives Bodl. Oxf., corresp. and papers | BL, corresp. with Lord Gladstone, Add. MS 46474 · Bodl. Oxf., corresp. with Herbert Asquith · HLRO, corresp. with Herbert Samuel · Sci. Mus., Pearson (first Lord Cowdray) MSS · U. Newcastle, Robinson L., corresp. with Walter Runciman

Likenesses J. Russell & Sons, photograph, c.1915, NPG · W. Stoneman, photograph, 1925, NPG

Wealth at death £24,126 17s. 4d.: probate, 23 Aug 1932, *CGPLA Eng. & Wales*

Maclean, Donald Duart (1913–1983), diplomatist and spy, was born in London on 25 May 1913, the third of four sons

Donald Duart Maclean (1913–1983), by Ramsey & Muspratt, 1930s?

and five children of Sir Donald *Maclean (1864–1932), Liberal politician and cabinet minister, and his wife, Gwendolen Margaret, eldest daughter of Andrew Devitt JP of Oxted, Surrey. He, like his two elder brothers, was educated at Gresham's School, Holt, where the headmaster, J. R. Eccles, enforced the so-called 'honour system' with the aim of maintaining the highest moral standards. It may well be supposed that this system, allied to a strict upbringing at the hands of Sir Donald, a non-smoker, temperance advocate, and severe sabbatarian, may have brought out in his son the tendency both to rebel and to deceive authority.

In October 1931 Maclean went up to Trinity Hall, Cambridge, with an exhibition in modern languages. He soon joined those on the extreme left who aimed to reanimate, and dominate, the university socialist society; this group included Guy *Burgess, Anthony *Blunt, and H. A. R. (Kim) *Philby. Maclean, handsome, standing 6 feet 4 inches tall, was prominent both physically and intellectually among his contemporaries. He at first made no secret of his communist sympathies; but in mid-1934 he abandoned open political activity and announced his intention to enter the diplomatic service. This move coincided with his recruitment by the NKVD (later KGB) of the Soviet Union. In June 1934 he graduated with first class honours in part two of the modern languages tripos, having gained a second class in part one in 1932. He entered the diplomatic service in 1935, serving in the League of Nations and western department of the Foreign Office.

In 1938 Maclean was appointed third secretary at the Paris embassy. There he met an American student, Melinda Marling, eldest daughter of Francis Marling, a Chicago businessman, whose wife had divorced him in 1928 to marry a New England property owner, Hal Dunbar. Donald (who was bisexual) and Melinda were married in Paris on 10 June 1940 at the time of the evacuation of the city. Back in London he was promoted second secretary and employed in the general department until April 1944, when he was transferred to the Washington embassy, and

soon after promoted first secretary. An indication that his credit with the NKVD was as high as with the Foreign Office is provided by the Soviet decision to transfer to Washington Maclean's London case officer ('control'). For some months in 1946 Maclean was acting head of chancery; but his most important duties, from the NKVD's viewpoint, were connected with the development of the atom bomb. Early in 1947 he became joint secretary of the Anglo-American-Canadian Combined Policy Committee, a post that gave him access to the American atomic energy commission at a time when the American government was making maximum efforts to prevent leakage of information about nuclear weapons.

Two sons were born to the Macleans in the Washington years. When Maclean left in September 1948, on promotion to counsellor and head of chancery in Cairo, he was the youngest officer in his new grade. In Cairo, however, an all-round deterioration set in, culminating in a drunken spree that caused him to be sent back to London and subjected to psychiatric examination. The Foreign Office, believing that he had recovered, appointed him in November 1950 to be head of the American department. This was a sensitive post, because of tensions resulting from the Korean War. Meanwhile the investigation of earlier leakages in Washington began to point to Maclean as prime suspect. Through Philby and Burgess he became aware of this and on 25 May 1951 defected with Burgess to the USSR. Soon afterwards his wife gave birth to a daughter in London. She later moved with her children to Switzerland and in September 1953 left secretly to join her husband. In 1967 she had an affair with Philby in Moscow.

In Moscow, Maclean taught graduate courses in international relations and published *British Foreign Policy since Suez* (London, 1970). An expanded Russian edition led to his award of a doctorate of the Institute of World Economics and International Relations. By 1979 his former wife and children had left and gone to the West. He died on 6 March 1983 in Moscow and was cremated there. His ashes were taken by his elder son and buried in the family plot at Penn, Buckinghamshire.

There has never been any official assessment on the British side of the damage done by Maclean as a spy; opinions differ concerning the benefit derived by the USSR from his undoubted insight into American nuclear capacity in the crucial years before the first Soviet atomic test in 1949. A report prepared in 1955 by American military intelligence, however, is unambiguous in attributing very grave damage to the combined activities of Maclean and Burgess. In the long term the most lasting damage was probably that suffered by Anglo-American relations, much of it arising from American criticism of the laxity of British security. ROBERT CECIL, *rev.*

Sources R. Cecil, *A divided life: a biography of Donald Maclean* (1988) · *The Times* (17 March 1983) · *CGPLA Eng. & Wales* (1983) **Archives** FILM BFI NFTVA, current affairs footage **Likenesses** Ramsey & Muspratt, 1930?–1939, NPG [*see illus.*] · photograph, c.1935, Hult. Arch. · group portrait, photograph, 1951, Hult. Arch. · photographs, 1951, Hult. Arch. · photographs, repro. in Cecil, *Divided life*

Wealth at death £4997: administration with will, 23 June 1983, *CGPLA Eng. & Wales*

Maclean, Sir Fitzroy Hew Royle, first baronet (1911–1996), army officer and politician, was born in Cairo on 11 March 1911, the only son of Major Charles Wilberforce Maclean (*b.* 1875) and his wife, Frances Elaine, *née* Royle (*d.* 1954). The name Maclean indicates 'the sons of Gillean of the Battle-Axe', Gillean being a thirteenth-century chieftain who held sway over the territories of Duart, Lochbuie, and Ardgour. Over the centuries the Macleans frequently distinguished themselves in battle (often for the Jacobite cause), a tradition which continued when Maclean's father, an officer in the Queen's Own Cameron Highlanders, was appointed DSO in the First World War.

Fitzroy Maclean's early life was spent in Scotland and Italy, where his mother imbued him with a love and facility for languages, of which he spoke several fluently. He was educated at Heatherdown preparatory school, Ascot, and Eton College, from where he won a scholarship in 1928 to study modern languages at King's College, Cambridge. Before going to Cambridge he spent a year in Germany, where he studied Latin and Greek. On his return he decided to switch to classics, and won a first in his classical tripos. He then switched again, to history, and was awarded a second in part two in 1932.

Diplomatist On leaving Cambridge Maclean passed the examination for the diplomatic service, which he joined in November 1933. He was swiftly marked down as 'one to note' (*The Independent*, 19 June 1996). At the Foreign Office he acquired the nickname Fitzwhiskers, to distinguish him from his contemporary Donald 'Fancy Pants' Maclean, who subsequently betrayed secret information to the Soviet Union before eventually fleeing there.

Maclean's early career began at the Foreign Office in London and then in the British embassy in Paris, when he was transferred as a third secretary in October 1934. In February 1937 he was transferred to the British embassy in Moscow, where he was promoted second secretary in November 1938. His choice of this somewhat unglamorous posting—he had volunteered for it instead of taking a more attractive assignment in Washington—revealed uncanny foresight, for he was able to observe the great purge trials of the period. He was also able to make many unorthodox, and often uncomfortable, journeys into remote parts of the Soviet Union; he was trailed by the Russian secret service, though, as he pointed out firmly both at the time and later, the trips were purely for interest. They undoubtedly helped him to perfect his knowledge of everyday Russian. Owing to his contacts he was not surprised by the announcement of the Nazi-Russian pact, which stunned the rest of the world on 31 August 1939, and indicated Russian approval for the Nazi invasion of Poland.

By then Maclean was already back at the Foreign Office in London, working at the Russian desk. He found his task tedious and irksome over the next two years, as everyone he knew seemed to be joining the services in one capacity or another. As the descendant of a martial family he spent

Sir Fitzroy Hew Royle Maclean, first baronet (1911–1996), by Elliott & Fry, 1954

much time and energy trying to discover a means of leaving what was classed as a 'reserved occupation' (prohibiting the holder from joining the armed forces). In 1941 his efforts were rewarded when he discovered a regulation which said that if a Foreign Office employee were elected an MP he would have to resign his official post. By exercising every ounce of his personal charm and diplomatic skills he managed to get himself adopted as the Conservative candidate for Lancaster, and on the strength of this he promptly resigned his Foreign Office appointment and enlisted in the Cameron Highlanders as a private soldier. He recalled, 'At meal times we threw ourselves on our food like a pack of wolves and wherever we were given a chance we slept, indoors, out of doors, in broad daylight, in the middle of a room full of men, shouting, singing, swearing' (*Daily Telegraph*, 18 June 1996). He was soon commissioned a second lieutenant (August 1941), but the Foreign Office, furious that he had not yet become an MP, tried to extract him from the army and take him back into service. Happily for Maclean a by-election came up in Lancaster in October 1941 and, after spending a few days' leave canvassing, he was astonished and delighted to be elected (defeating Fenner Brockway of the Independent Labour Party by a large margin).

Soldier Before he could take his seat in the House of Commons the army sent Maclean on a mission to Cairo. There he encountered David Stirling, who had recently formed the Special Air Service (SAS) in order to raid installations deep in enemy-held territory. Maclean joined the 1st SAS regiment in January 1942, as a lieutenant. Although originally trained to be dropped by parachute the SAS had found it more effective to penetrate the depths of the desert in trucks or jeeps armed with grenades, time-bombs, and machine-guns. On one of these expeditions Maclean and some others, including Randolph Churchill, went into Benghazi with the intention of creating havoc in the harbour. At the entrance they were challenged by an Italian sentry. In this distinctly awkward situation Maclean decided to turn defence into attack and, after rebuking the sentry for his slowness in challenging them, demanded to see the guard commander, to whom he gave a severe dressing-down in fluent Italian. Maclean informed him they were staff officers (and were presumably thought to be Germans) and had been in the area for several hours without being challenged. Maclean warned the guard commander, 'For all you know we might have been British saboteurs carrying explosives', an idea which the guard commander thought quite incredible (*Daily Telegraph*, 18 June 1996). Soon afterwards on another expedition Maclean was badly injured in a car crash caused by Stirling's reckless driving—he later expressed the view that 'David Stirling's driving was the most dangerous thing in World War Two' (*The Independent*, 19 June 1996)—but recovered in time to take part in yet another raid on Benghazi. At the end of the desert campaign he was selected by General Sir Henry Maitland (Jumbo) Wilson to arrest the pro-Nazi governor-general of Esfahan, General Zahidi, which he succeeded in doing. He was promoted captain in September 1942 and lieutenant-colonel in 1943.

In July 1943 Churchill decided that Maclean, with his record as a man of action, linguist, and diplomat, would be the right man to send to Yugoslavia as the head of a military mission to Tito, who since 1941 had been harassing the Germans, forcing them to deploy whole divisions on anti-guerrilla work. Unfortunately there was bitter rivalry in Yugoslavia between General Draza Mihailovic, who was a royalist and commanded the Chetniks, and Josip Broz (Tito), who was a communist and commanded the partisans. The Foreign Office was distinctly suspicious of Tito, who they thought would establish a communist government if successful militarily, but to many Tito seemed a more reliable ally than the Chetniks, who were accused (by Tito) of co-operating with the Germans instead of attacking them. Meanwhile SOE (Special Operations Executive), in general charge of overseas subversive activities, thought it should be in entire control of operations in Yugoslavia and also resented Maclean's appointment. Churchill, not concerned with diplomatic niceties, simply wished to find out who was killing the most Germans and assist them to kill more.

Maclean, somewhat uncritically, accepted Tito's view of Mihailovic's Chetniks, and developed whole-hearted admiration for Tito's skills and powers as a guerrilla leader. His two-year command, as a rapidly promoted brigadier, was far from easy, for he had to make certain that Tito received the material he needed during a period when supplies were easily delayed, misrouted, of the wrong type, or generally inadequate, that his efforts were not frustrated by contemporaries jealous of his own rapid promotion, that an attached Soviet military mission did not try to nullify or belittle his achievements, and that his own team co-operated rather than quarrelled. Randolph Churchill was a member of the mission, and brought in the erratic novelist Evelyn Waugh. They were the sort of people Maclean did not need: Randolph Churchill was stubborn and quarrelsome; Waugh, loathing communism and contemptuous of the Official Secrets Act, irresponsibly and ludicrously put forward the idea that Tito was a woman. Apart from the diplomatic requirements of his job, Maclean had to impress physically and militarily in an area where chaos and hardship were always present and daunting. Fortunately he was equal to the challenge.

Although Maclean's preference for Tito over Mihailovic caused some criticism, particularly after the war when Tito was powerful enough to execute his rival, there seems little doubt that Tito was the more effective guerrilla fighter, and that Maclean's support had helped to build up his self-confidence sufficiently for him to defy Stalin four years later in 1948, and put him in a position to keep Yugoslavia intact and independent for thirty-five years. It seems unlikely that the Chetniks would have been able, or even willing, to keep the Soviet army from the Adriatic coast. Maclean's wartime honours included the Croix de Guerre in 1943, the CBE (military) in 1944, and the (Yugoslav) Partisan star (first class) in 1945. He was appointed to the order of merit (Yugoslavia) in 1969 and the order of the Yugoslav Star with ribbon in 1981. He was one of only three foreigners allowed to own property in Yugoslavia under Tito, and holidayed frequently at his villa on the island of Korcula.

Politician and author At the end of the war Maclean was given the local rank of major-general and put in charge of the special refugee commissions in Austria, Germany, and Italy. On completing this assignment he returned to take up his parliamentary seat. On 12 January 1946 he married the Hon. Veronica Nell (*b.* 1920), second daughter of Simon Joseph Fraser, fourteenth Lord Lovat (sixteenth but for an attainder), and widow of Lieutenant Alan Phipps, naval officer, second son of Sir Eric Phipps, diplomatist. Maclean became stepfather to the son and daughter of his wife's first marriage, and he and his wife had two further sons.

Unfortunately Maclean was a poor speaker and made little impact in parliament, though in October 1954 Churchill, anxious to reward Maclean for his loyalty and long service in parliament, made him parliamentary undersecretary of state for war. He remained in this post through Churchill's resignation in April 1955, and through the Suez debacle in 1956, but he was removed by Macmillan following the latter's assumption of office in January 1957. Macmillan described him as 'so hopeless in the house that he is a passenger in office … a great pity as he is so able' (*Daily Telegraph*, 18 June 1996). Maclean was recompensed by being made a baronet in July 1957. However, he served on as an MP for another seventeen years, representing Lancaster until the general election of October 1959, and Bute and North Ayrshire from then until February 1974. He was a member of the British delegation to the North Atlantic Assembly from 1962 to 1974 (chairman of its military committee, 1964–74) and a member of the British delegation to the Council of Europe and Western European Union from 1972 to 1974.

Maclean soon found plenty to do apart from being a back-bench MP. He spent much time at the family seat of Strachur in Argyll and ran a hotel on the shores of Loch Fyne. In 1949 he had published his enormously successful autobiography *Eastern Approaches* and in 1957 he produced the first of sixteen more books, including *Jugoslavia* (1969), *Tito* (1980), and several books about Russia, notably *Holy Russia* (1979), *Portrait of the Soviet Union* (1988), and *All the Russias* (1992). His interest in the history of his native land resulted in *A Concise History of Scotland* (1970), *The Isles of the Sea* (1985), *Bonnie Prince Charlie* (1988), and—his last book—*Highlanders* (1995). None of these, however, achieved the success of *Eastern Approaches*.

During the 1960s Maclean also made a new career as a performer and producer in television, though he was not sufficiently relaxed to be a success on the screen. However, his visits to unknown areas of Russia produced interesting documentation, and he was also able to use these visits to make various investigations on behalf of the British government. In 1985 he advised Margaret Thatcher to cultivate close relations with Mikhail Gorbachov. He also gave the Russians some unsolicited advice on their policies, pointing out that many of their activities were alienating potential well-wishers. He was appointed a knight of the Thistle in 1993.

Maclean was a man of legendary courage and great charm, and a strong sense of humour, who is said to have been the inspiration for his friend Ian Fleming's James Bond. He was, in fact, more like John Buchan's Richard Hannay. He enjoyed good food and drink, conversation, and the company of women, whom he treated with old-fashioned courtesy rather than as victims for predatory approaches. He managed to be at ease at all levels of society from private soldiers and peasant partisans to peers and persons of renown. He said what he thought was right, telling Winston Churchill, for example, that his Fulton speech about an 'iron curtain' was ridiculous, and Alec Douglas-Home that his action in expelling ninety Russian diplomats was pointless and silly. But his less publicized suggestions on moves to allay Russian suspicions of western policies were undoubtedly constructive. It may not be too much to claim that Maclean's advice began the process that helped to end the cold war.

Towards the end of his life Maclean was much crippled by arthritis, which caused his 6 foot 3 inch frame to stoop, but he remained alert and determined to the end. He fulfilled a lifetime's ambition in 1995 by travelling from London to Paris on a Eurostar train through the channel tunnel: he remembered a particularly stormy crossing of the channel at the age of eight, when his grandmother told him that one day he would be able to travel the whole way by train. He died at Clouds Hill, Offley, Hitchin, Hertfordshire, on 15 June 1996, and was survived by his wife, two stepchildren, and two sons. He was succeeded as second baronet by his elder son, Charles Edward (*b.* 1946).

PHILIP WARNER

Sources F. Maclean, *Eastern approaches* (1949) · *The Times* (18 June 1996) · *Daily Telegraph* (18 June 1996) · *The Scotsman* (18 June 1996) · *The Independent* (19 June 1996) · *The Independent* (26 June 1996) · Special Air Service archives, Hereford · WWW · Burke, *Peerage* · *Debrett's Peerage*
Archives BL OIOC, corresp. with F. M. Bailey
Likenesses photograph, 1943, Hult. Arch. · group portrait, photograph, 1951, Hult. Arch. · Elliott & Fry, photograph, 1954, NPG [*see illus.*] · photograph, repro. in *The Times* · photograph, repro. in *Daily Telegraph* · photograph, repro. in *The Scotsman* · photograph, repro. in *The Independent* (19 June 1996)
Wealth at death £1,295,850.84: confirmation, 6 Dec 1997, *CCI*

McLean, Sir Francis Charles (1904–1998), broadcasting engineer, was born on 6 November 1904 at 5 Back 45, Friston Street, Ladywood, Birmingham, the son of Michael McLean, a railway porter, and his wife, Alice. After gaining first-class honours in electrical engineering at the University of Birmingham, McLean joined the Western Electric Company in Birmingham, working on the design of high-power radio transmitters. In 1928 he was sent to work at the Standard Telephones and Cables research laboratories in Paris, where he learned to speak excellent French, a skill which stood him in good stead at international conferences later in his career. For several years he travelled all over Europe, designing high-power equipment for broadcasting stations in Czechoslovakia, Hungary, Italy, Switzerland, and France. He married Dorothy Mabel Blackstaffe in 1930; they had one son and one daughter. Back in England in 1932, he worked on the design of the short- and medium-wave transmitters used by the BBC, and in 1937 he was asked to join the BBC as head of the radio section of the station design and installation department, where he was in charge of transmitter design.

With the outbreak of war McLean became involved in the expansion of BBC monitoring stations, and the extension of short-wave broadcasting, and he designed mobile transmitters for the war reporting unit. One of five BBC engineers seconded to the psychological warfare division of the Supreme Headquarters Allied Expeditionary Force (SHAEF) in 1943, McLean was appointed chief engineer, in charge of planning the rehabilitation of broadcasting stations in the liberated areas of Europe. He entered Paris in August 1944, and after getting some of the French transmitters back on the air he moved on to Luxembourg in September to restart the Radio Luxemburg transmitter, so that it could be used for psychological warfare against the German army. As the invading armies moved through Germany, McLean and his engineers repaired transmitters, or replaced those that had been destroyed with mobile equipment. They also installed public address systems so that the military authorities could distribute information to the local populations.

Back at the BBC in 1945, McLean was involved in expanding the overseas services, and was sent to Singapore in 1946 to plan the Far East Relay System. He was also an adviser to the new Radio Pakistan after partition. He represented the BBC at an increasing number of international conferences: he was at the European regional conference in Copenhagen in 1948 convened to discuss the reallocation of wavelengths because of the congestion in the medium-wave band after the war, and in 1950 he was principal BBC representative in Florence for the meeting of the technical committee of the International Telecommunications Convention, which met to discuss high-frequency bands. He rose rapidly in the engineering division, and as deputy chief engineer from 1952 he led BBC delegations to conferences on frequency modulation (FM) broadcasting, stereo broadcasting, and colour television. With the coming of commercial television, McLean was offered the job of chief engineer by the Independent Television Authority (ITA) in 1954, but he refused, although by September 1955 nearly 200 engineers had left the BBC to join the commercial television companies.

Appointed deputy director of engineering in 1960, McLean succeeded Sir Harold Bishop as director of engineering in 1963. His period as director was dominated by planning the introduction of colour television. He had already been the driving force behind developing a 625-line ultra-high frequency network for the second television channel, BBC 2, launched in 1964, but colour television was the most complex of all the technical problems ever tackled by the BBC. The BBC had been experimenting with colour since 1950, and in 1953 McLean had read a paper to the British Association entitled 'The application of colour to television broadcasting'. By the early 1960s there were three rival systems to choose from: in North America the Americans had developed NTSC; in Europe the French and most of the eastern European countries favoured SECAM; while Germany and most other European countries preferred PAL. McLean represented Britain at discussions of the European Broadcasting Union on colour television from 1962 to 1964 in the hope of reaching agreement on a uniform colour system for Europe, and he lectured widely in Britain and abroad, giving the Faraday lecture in 1966 on colour television, and the Granada lecture for 1966 on telecommunications in the next ten years. In the absence of an agreement on an international system, Britain opted for PAL in 1966, and it seemed that the exchange of programmes between the different systems would be impossible. But the design department of the BBC developed the electronic standards converter, which made it possible to convert programmes from other systems, and its success was demonstrated by the transmission of colour pictures from the Olympic games in Mexico in 1968 to homes all round the world. Colour television was launched in Britain on BBC 2 in July 1967, in which year McLean was knighted.

McLean retired from the BBC in 1968. Chairman of the British Standards Institution telecommunications standards committee since 1960, he continued to serve until 1977. In his retirement he was also technical director of a company set up to develop video technology, and a director from 1961 of Oxley Developments, making electronic components. In 1974 he chaired the royal commission on FM broadcasting in Australia. He bought a small farm near Newbury where he raised sheep, and took an interest in local history as president of the Newbury District Field Club.

McLean died on 19 December 1998 at a nursing home, Newbury Dalecare, Stockcross, Newbury, Berkshire. He was cremated at Basingstoke crematorium on 29 December. ANNE PIMLOTT BAKER

Sources A. Briggs, *The history of broadcasting in the United Kingdom*, rev. edn, 5 vols. (1995), vols. 3–5 · E. Pawley, *BBC engineering, 1922–1972* (1972) · *The Independent* (28 Dec 1998) · *The Times* (20 Jan 1999) · *WW* · engineering archives, BBC WAC · b. cert. · d. cert.
Archives BBC WAC, engineering archives
Likenesses group portrait, photograph, 1944, repro. in *The Independent* · photograph, repro. in Pawley, *BBC engineering*, pl. 25 · photograph, repro. in *The Times*

Maclean, George (1801–1847), colonial administrator, was born in Keith, Banffshire, on 24 February 1801, the second son and fifth child in the family of four daughters and three sons of James Maclean, a Church of Scotland minister, and his first wife, Elizabeth Tod. All that is known of his education or early years is that from 1815 to 1817 he served as an ensign in the 27th foot then in the 91st foot, from which he had to retire in poor health in 1821. In 1826 he became a lieutenant in the Royal African Colonial Corps.

In 1828 Maclean arrived in the Gold Coast just as Britain abandoned its administration of coastal forts, transferring them to a merchants' committee, which appointed Maclean as its 'president of the council' in 1829. Maclean, lacking any sovereign authority, quickly established an informal influence by arbitrating disputes among the small Fante kingdoms. Soon he began to preside over African courts, administering African law, persuading local kings to co-operate against the menace of the Asante from the north, to outlaw human sacrifice and kidnapping, and to change their laws about debts. The result was that trade expanded with the spread of this informal *pax*.

In June 1838, while on leave in England, Maclean married Letitia Elizabeth *Landon (1802–1838), a popular romantic poet often known as L. E. L.; she was the daughter of the Revd Whittington Landon, dean of Exeter. Soon after arriving at Cape Coast Castle she was found dead (15 October 1838), an empty bottle of prussic acid in her room. Her dramatic death led to much gossip and speculation, including the entirely false rumour that she had been poisoned by an African woman said to be Maclean's common-law wife and mother of several children by him. It is probable that L. E. L. in fact died from a heart attack.

These slanders focused newspaper attention on the hitherto unnoticed Gold Coast and attracted humanitarian interest, then at its peak in Britain. Maclean was further embarrassed in 1839 when anti-slavery interests discovered that British merchants in the Gold Coast were selling supplies to illegal slave-trading vessels. This led in

1842 to a Colonial Office investigation by Dr Richard Madden, followed by a parliamentary select committee, both of which stressed that Maclean lacked any legal authority to suppress slaving, and praised the way he had created an informal judicial *pax*. Both inquiries demanded that the Colonial Office take over the administration of the Gold Coast forts, and take effective measures against slave trading.

Respect for Maclean's methods lay behind the passage of the Foreign Jurisdiction Act of 1843, which permitted Britain to assume judicial functions in protected territories as if they were ceded colonies. With these provisions the Colonial Office appointed Governor H. W. Hill to the Gold Coast in 1843, with Maclean as judicial assessor. Maclean laid the basis for the series of treaties with coastal rulers who acknowledged British judicial powers which came to be known as the Bond of 1844. Maclean died of dysentery at Cape Coast on 22 May 1847, and was buried there.

Maclean's achievements were considerable. His skills as an impartial arbitrator won him the respect of Africans. Asked by Madden if Africans were an 'inferior race', Maclean replied that they were inferior in civilization, but potentially equal; for the time this was a liberal view. His activities made possible the early development of peaceful commerce with Britain and led directly to the establishment of colonial rule. In a longer perspective, Ghanaian nationalists would later cite Maclean's judicial system and the Bond of 1844 as historical evidence that the Gold Coast was never a conquered colony, but a territory that came peacefully and voluntarily under British rule, and could move to independence in the same manner.

JOHN FLINT

Sources G. E. Metcalfe, *Maclean of the Gold Coast* (1962) · J. D. Fage, 'The administration of George Maclean on the Gold Coast, 1830–1844', *Transactions of the Historical Society of Ghana*, part 4 (1955), 104–20 · 'Select committee on the west coast of Africa', *Parl. papers* (1842), vol. 11, no 551

Archives PRO, CO MSS

Maclean, Sir Harry Aubrey de Vere (1848–1920), army officer, the eldest son of Andrew Maclean (*d.* 1908) of Drimnin, Argyllshire, inspector-general in the Army Medical Service, and his wife, Clara, daughter of Henry Holland Harrison, was born at Chatham on 15 June 1848. He first served as a clerk in the Privy Council Office, but joined the 69th regiment in 1869. At the time of the Fenian border raid into Canada in April 1870 the 69th formed part of the Huntingdon field force under Colonel Bagot which attacked and defeated the Fenians at Trout River, not far from Montreal. From Canada he went with the 69th to Bermuda in 1870, and in 1873 to Gibraltar.

In 1876 Maclean retired from the army. The following year Mawlay Hasan, the ambitious reforming sultan of Morocco (*r.* 1873–94), sent 100 men to be trained at Gibraltar in order to act as instructors to the army of 10,000 men which he proposed to raise. He asked for a British officer to accompany them back to Morocco, and Maclean accepted the appointment. He first served as drill instructor at Tangier, but was shortly after promoted to be

Sir Harry Aubrey de Vere Maclean (1848–1920), by W. & D. Downey

kaid of 400 *asakir* (infantry) and instructor of the forces attached to the court. His pay was 200 francs a month, with the promise of an increase when he had learned sufficient Arabic to drill his men without an interpreter. About three months after his appointment he had fulfilled this condition. Eventually he learnt to speak Arabic fluently, but he never acquired a good accent, and Mawlay Hasan used to laugh at his strange pronunciation. His pay was raised to £30 a month, with a horse, and a house wherever the sultan resided. To instruct the army was, however, frustrating work; the sultan would not allow his soldiers to learn too much, nor to have proper musketry instruction, for fear they might become dangerous as rebels.

Mawlay Hasan and his successor, Abdul-Aziz, both liked Maclean and confided in him, and he accompanied the court wherever it went. But his position at first was not easy. The ministers were jealous, and in 1881 obtained his dismissal. In 1882, however, he was restored and accompanied Mawlay Hasan on an expedition to the Sus province. A long time had elapsed since any sultan had ventured on such an expedition, but it was quite successful, and they traversed the Sus almost as far as Cape Juby. Maclean accompanied the sultan on many other journeys, visiting Tafilelt—then a city barred to Europeans—as well as all the other chief towns of Morocco. He was partly responsible for the successful concealment of the news of the death of Mawlay Hasan in 1894 until the grand vizier could take the necessary steps for assuring the succession of the sultan's favourite son, Mawlay Abdul-Aziz (r. 1894–1908). Maclean was popular with his men, to whom he was considerate, though firm. Of powerful physique, he was able to deal summarily with insubordinate individuals. His chief function was advisory, but in 1892 he was entrusted with the command of a force suppressing an insurrection of the Anjera people. To the British legation at Tangier Maclean was very helpful, acting as its unofficial agent at the sultan's court; but he was not the Machiavelli of intrigue that some foreign legations alleged. His position at court depended on his loyalty to the sultan, but his relations with the British legation did much to smooth the conduct of business. His services were rewarded by a CMG in 1898, and in 1901, when he came with a Moroccan mission to the coronation of Edward VII, he was created KCMG.

In 1904 Maclean narrowly escaped being kidnapped near Tangier by the followers of the rebel sharif, Ahmad al-Raisuni; his escape was due to the resource of Mr Carleton, the British consular agent at Alcazar, who happened to be with him. In July 1907, while negotiating with Raisuni on behalf of the Makhzen, he was kidnapped and held to ransom. For seven months he was a captive, and although he endured the hardships with courage and coolness they seriously undermined his health. Raisuni at first was exorbitant in his terms, even demanding the governorship of Tangier, but gradually he was persuaded to moderate them by the efforts of Sir Herbert White, the British chargé d'affaires, and Maclean was eventually released, following payment of £20,000. In 1908 Abdul-Aziz was deposed; his successor, his rebel brother Mawlay Abdul-Hafiz, although wanting to retain Maclean's services, would not offer acceptable terms, and in 1909 Maclean resigned. After his retirement he lived partly at Richmond and partly at Tangier.

Maclean was twice married; first, in 1882 to Catharine, daughter of Thomas Coe of Gibraltar, with whom he had one son and three daughters, and whom he divorced in 1905; secondly, in 1913 to Ella, daughter of Sir Harry *Prendergast, who, with one daughter, survived him. Maclean in his Moroccan uniform was always an imposing figure, and he was famous for his hospitality to British visitors at the court. He devoted much of his spare time to the bagpipes, the piano, the guitar, and the accordion. He was an amateur inventor, but none of his inventions was commercially successful. Maclean died at his residence, Drimnin House, The Marsham, Tangier, on 4 February 1920.

[ANON.], rev. ROGER T. STEARN

Sources The Times (6 Feb 1920) · H. B. Hill, 'Stories of Kaid Maclean, by his daughter "Babs"', Country Life, 47 (1920), 796–7 · Hart's Army List (1871) · private information (1927) · WWW · Kelly, Handbk · J. M. Abun-Nasr, A history of the Maghrib (1971)
Likenesses W. & D. Downey, photograph, NPG [see illus.] · Spy [L. Ward], cartoon, NPG; repro. in VF (25 Feb 1904) · pencil drawing, Scot. NPG
Wealth at death £71,411 17s. 5d.: probate, 20 April 1920, CGPLA Eng. & Wales

Maclean, Hector Mor, of Duart (fl. 1527–1570). See under Maclean family of Duart (per. 1493–1598).

Maclean, Ida Smedley (1877–1944), biochemist, was born in Birmingham on 14 June 1877, the second daughter of William T. Smedley, businessman and philanthropist, and his wife, Annie Elizabeth Duckworth, daughter of a Liverpool coffee merchant. Her sister Constance married Maxwell *Armfield. Ida Smedley grew up in a cultured and progressive home. She was taught by her mother until she was nine, when she entered King Edward VI High School for Girls, Birmingham. An accomplished pianist and actress, she had little time to pursue these interests in later years. She was a student at Newnham College, Cambridge, from 1896 to 1899, obtaining a first class in part one of the natural sciences tripos (1898) and a second class in part two (1899). From 1901 to 1903 she held a Bathurst studentship, doing postgraduate research under H. E. Armstrong at the Central Technical College, London. She served as demonstrator in chemistry at Newnham College in 1903 and 1904 and was a research fellow at the Davy–Faraday Laboratory of the Royal Institution from 1904 to 1906. She received a DSc from London University in 1905.

In 1906 Smedley was appointed assistant lecturer in the chemistry department of Manchester University, the first woman to hold a staff position in that department. She remained there for four years, during which time she conducted researches on the optical properties of organic compounds. In 1910 she returned to London and began her work in biochemistry, which was to continue for the rest of her life. She held one of the first Beit research fellowships (1910–14), and worked at the Lister Institute for Preventive Medicine with Arthur Harden. In 1913, in recognition of her early biochemical work, she received the Ellen Richards prize, an award presented by the American Association of University Women for outstanding research by a woman scientist. She became a staff member of the Lister Institute in 1932. In 1913 she married Hugh Maclean (1879–1957), later professor of medicine at the University of London and St Thomas's Hospital. He was the son of Hector Maclean. They had one son and one daughter.

During the First World War, Maclean worked at the Admiralty on various projects of national importance, including the large-scale production of acetone from starch by fermentation. Her special interests included fat synthesis from carbohydrates, and the biochemical function of the fatty acids in the animal body. About thirty papers on this work, much of it collaborative, appeared in the Biochemical Journal between 1920 and 1941. Her monograph The Metabolism of Fat, published in 1943 as the first of Methuen's monographs in biochemistry, summarized her views on the field, in which she was by then a recognized authority.

Ida Smedley Maclean was instrumental in advancing the professional status of university women. She was one of the founders of the British Federation of University Women, from which grew the International Federation of University Women. From the start of the movement in 1907 she held high office, and later served as president (1929–35). The federation now administers a research fellowship for women graduates in her name. She was also a leader in the protracted struggle for the admission of women to fellowship in the London Chemical Society, which finally succeeded in 1920. She was the first woman to be formally accepted into the society and was a member of its council (1931–4). In 1918 she became a fellow of the Institute of Chemistry. From 1941 to 1944 she served on the Cambridge University women's appointments board.

Ida Smedley Maclean died on 2 March 1944 in University College Hospital, London, and was cremated at Golders Green.   MARY R. S. CREESE, *rev.*

Sources *JCS* (1946), pt1, pp. 65–7 · *Newnham College Roll Letter* (1945), 50–51 · [A. B. White], ed., *Newnham College register, 1871–1950*, 2 vols. (1964) · private information (1993) · *WW*
Wealth at death £3374 9s. 5d.: administration, 23 Aug 1944, *CGPLA Eng. & Wales*

Maclean, James Mackenzie (1835–1906), journalist and politician, was born on 13 August 1835 at Liberton, near Edinburgh. His father, Alexander Maclean, who was from the Hebridean island of Uist, spent some years in Jamaica before settling at Liberton, where he died in 1839. His mother belonged to the Biagrie family and was of French descent. Maclean was educated first at Circus Place School, Edinburgh, then at Dr Bruce's Grammar School, Newcastle upon Tyne, where his mother moved with her two sons on her husband's death. In 1845, after a year at a preparatory school in Hertford, he entered Christ's Hospital as a foundationer and attained the coveted distinction of becoming a 'Grecian'. He was unable to go to Trinity College, Cambridge, as he had once hoped, because of lack of money.

Having contributed a few articles to *The Leader*, Maclean began his journalistic career in earnest in 1854 when he joined the editorial staff of the local *Newcastle Chronicle*, then a weekly paper. He was editor from 1855 to 1858. On the recommendation of Alexander Russel, the editor of *The Scotsman*, he became a leader writer for the *Manchester Guardian* for two years, and at the end of 1859 Russel's influence again helped him secure the editorship of the *Bombay Gazette* in western India. Disagreements with the proprietor led him to resign early in 1861 but, persuaded by friends to remain in Bombay, he founded the *Bombay Saturday Review*, which, although modelled on its London prototype, gave more prominence to commercial affairs. Maclean gathered round him many eminent contributors, including the vice-chancellor of Bombay University, Sir Alexander Grant, the authority on Indian art Sir George Birdwood, the politician Thomas Chisholm Anstey, and occasionally even the governor, Sir Bartle Frere. The advertisement revenue benefited from the share mania (1861–5) arising from the American Civil War and the consequent expansion of the Bombay cotton trade.

In 1864 Maclean purchased the principal share in the *Bombay Gazette*, of which he resumed the editorship, and before long became the sole proprietor. He now devoted his energies to the *Gazette*, and discontinued the *Bombay Saturday Review*. His candour and independence infused new vigour into the discussion of public affairs in western India, and while severely criticizing the political aspirations of the Indian population, he was at times equally opposed to the policies of the British government. His vituperative style, which extended the circulation of his paper, appealed particularly to the younger generation of Indians, and he set the model of licence which the west Indian press was to adopt wholeheartedly in the years of agitation for independence. He also helped to galvanize public opinion in Bombay to many charitable ends. Sir George Birdwood pronounced him to be 'the ablest publicist we ever had in India' (*Royal Society of Arts Journal*, 14 June 1901).

Appointed in 1865 to the bench of justices, which had a general supervision of municipal affairs, Maclean initiated the agitation which resulted in the creation of a semi-elective municipal corporation (1872). In 1867 he married Anna Maria (d. 1897), daughter of Philip Whitehead of the *Bombay Gazette*. As chairman of the Bombay town council he read in 1875 the address of welcome to the prince of Wales. On this occasion he compiled an authorative *Guide to Bombay* (1875), which was reissued annually for many years. He was made a fellow of Bombay University.

At the close of 1879 Maclean sold the *Gazette* in order to participate in politics in Britain, although he was not successful when he stood as a Conservative for the Elgin burghs at the general election of 1880. For a time he associated himself with Lord Randolph Churchill, and helped secure his election to the chairmanship of the National Union of Conservative Associations (February 1884). But an estrangement followed when it seemed to Maclean that Churchill was seeking to supplant Lord Salisbury as party leader. A motion which Maclean submitted to the council (2 May 1884) with a view to restoring harmony in the party was carried, and led Lord Randolph to resign the chairmanship and to withdraw for the time from the political arena (Churchill, vol. 1, chap. 7).

At the general election of 1885 Maclean was elected as MP for Oldham, and retained his seat in the elections of 1886. Lord Randolph, now leader of the house, became reconciled to him, and he seconded the address in October 1886. Maclean soon won a reputation as an effective speaker and a fierce critic. He notably offended trade unionists and bimetallists, and in the election of 1892 lost his seat.

In 1882 Maclean had acquired a large stake in the *Western Mail*, Cardiff, to which he contributed for many years a weekly political column. He stood for the borough in 1895, and, defeating Sir Edward James Reed, became the first Conservative member for Cardiff for forty years. While maintaining his reputation as a parliamentary debater, he developed a distrust and dislike of Joseph Chamberlain, which ultimately ruined his parliamentary career. He opposed the Conservative government on many critical questions, chiefly the retention of Chitral, the negotiations leading up to the Second South African War, and the imposition in 1899 of countervailing sugar duties in India. In this connection he seconded on 15 June 1899 a no confidence motion moved by the opposition, and owing to the angry interruptions on his own side he crossed the floor of the house to finish his speech. The Cardiff Conservatives withdrew their support. He disposed of his interest in the *Western Mail* and retired from parliament in 1900. In the same year, on 23 July (his first wife having died in 1897), he married a widow, Sara Kennedy, the third daughter of Dr D. Hayle of Harrogate. There were no children of either marriage.

An ardent free-trader, Maclean spoke and wrote against Chamberlain's tariff reform campaign. In a paper read to the Indian section of the Royal Society of Arts (10 December 1903), he emphasized the objections from the Indian point of view (cf. his *India's Place in an Imperial Federation*, 1904). He resumed writing for Liberal journals, such as the *Manchester Guardian* and the *South Wales Daily News*; some of these contributions were revised and collected as *Recollections of Westminster and India* (1902).

An original member of the Institute of Journalists, he was president of the conference at Cardiff in 1899. He revisited India at the end of 1898, and was received with enthusiasm in Bombay. After suffering a stroke he died at Seaborough, Southbourne, Bournemouth, on 22 April 1906, survived by his wife. He was buried at Chiswick.

F. H. Brown, *rev.* Chandrika Kaul

Sources W. S. Churchill, *Lord Randolph Churchill*, 2 vols. (1906) · *The Times* (24 April 1906) · *Manchester Guardian* (24 April 1906) · *Times of India* (25 April 1906) · *Cardiff Times* (28 April 1906) · *Stalybridge Standard* (28 April 1906) · *Bombay Gazette* (28 April 1906) · *Oldham Chronicle* (30 April 1906) · H. W. Lucy, *A diary of the Salisbury parliament, 1886–1892* (1892) · H. W. Lucy, *A diary of the Unionist parliament, 1895–1900* (1901) · WWW
Likenesses S. Maclean, pastel
Wealth at death £1291 0s. 7d.: probate, 14 May 1906, CGPLA Eng. & Wales

Maclean [Macklier, Makeléer], **John** [Hans; styled Sir John Maclean, baronet] (*d.* **1666**), merchant in Sweden, was born in Scotland in the early 1600s, the son of Hector Maclean, laird of Duart, and his wife, Isabella Acheson, daughter of Sir Archibald Acheson of Gosford. Known as Iain Dubh in his youth, little is known of Maclean's early life, though he is sometimes described as having been in Stuart naval service and sometimes as a merchant and trader in Germany. In 1623–4 he was a royal supplier to Queen Maria Eleanora in Stockholm, where his trading partner James had been a burgess since 1609. He married James's wife's sister, Anna Gubbertz (*d.* 1653), in 1629 and had fifteen children with her, though only ten survived to adulthood. First recorded in Göteborg in 1628, he became a burgess there the following year. His main trade was in iron bars and timber, but included shipbuilding materials, salt, herrings, spirits, and English coal. His success allowed him to build up a small fleet of his own. He represented Göteborg in the 1632 Swedish parliament, and from 1635 to 1650 he served as a town councillor, taking an active role in ecclesiastical, educational, customs, and building activities. He entertained the Swedish regent, Chancellor Axel Oxenstierna, and the state marshal, Jakob de la Gardie, on their visit to Göteborg in 1639.

During the bishops' wars in Scotland, Maclean supplied the covenanters with ships and weapons from Sweden. He also funded the Irish 'wild geese' who settled in Göteborg

in 1640–47 to receive military training from the Ulfsparre family. From 1643 to 1645 he played a vital role in defending Göteborg from Danish attack by supplying the Swedish crown with food and clothing on credit and by furnishing warships and privateers. He organized and funded a reconnaissance mission to Copenhagen in 1644. He also called on the personal fleet of his friend the Walloon financier Louis de Geer, to protect Göteborg harbour from the Danes. Maclean's business success continued as he and his associates established a rope and sail factory in Göteborg on 20 May 1646. He again represented Göteborg at the parliament in 1649. He was ennobled under the name of Macklier (sometimes written Makeléer) on 20 May 1649 and formally introduced into the Swedish house of nobility in 1652. When the Stuart envoy Colonel John Cochrane was sent to Scandinavia in 1649 to obtain military support for Charles II, Maclean provided James Graham, marquess of Montrose, with ships and weapons at his own expense, though two shipments appear to have been intercepted by the English Commonwealth fleet. The exiled Charles II created him a baronet on 13 April 1650, though no patent was ever issued; this honour was perhaps in lieu of the 1350 riksdaler Charles owed him and which Maclean never received. His involvement with Montrose may be explained by the marriage of his eldest son, Jacob (Jakob), to Cochrane's daughter Catherine.

In 1653 Maclean married, as his second wife, Lilian Hamilton (*d.* 1658). He met the Cromwellian ambassador Bulstrode Whitelocke several times during Whitelocke's embassy to Sweden in 1653–4, presumably in the capacity of a civic official for Göteborg. In 1658 he received three royal donations of land in Halland, Sweden. That year he was married for the third time; his wife was Anna Gordon (*d.* 1677), daughter of another Scot in Sweden, Colonel Thomas Thomson, and his wife, Catherine Murray, and widow of Johan Gordon, colonel in the Swedish army. In 1660 he received the title of 'commissary'. He still sought the repayment of his money and goods lost in Montrose's campaign and sent Charles II a bill for £9112 at 8 per cent to be paid over the following decade, but to no avail. His sons had varied careers. The eldest, Jacob (1632–1663), became a gentleman-in-waiting to Charles II and a colonel in the Stuart army. Johan (1636–1696) became the president of the court of justice in Göteborg, while Gustav (1641–1701) and Peter (1644–1697) both became colonels in the Swedish army. David (1646–1708) became the first Baron Maclean in Sweden, serving as an assistant to the Swedish ambassador to Britain in 1674, and becoming a colonel and governor in the Swedish army. John Maclean died in Göteborg on 7 July 1666 and was buried in the German church there on 16 August. A. N. L. Grosjean

Sources Göteborg Landsarkiv, ref. 801, Göteborgs Drätselkammare 1638, nos. 90, 92, 97 · NA Scot., GD 40/10/4; 220/6/2085; 220/6/2985 · E. B. Grage, 'Makelier, Hans', *Svenskt biografiskt lexikon* · N. A. Kullberg, S. Bergh, and P. Sondén, eds., *Svenska riksrådets protokoll*, 18 vols. (Stockholm, 1878–1959) · G. Elgenstierna, *Svenska adelns ättartavlor*, 9 vols. (1925–36), vol. 5 · GEC, *Baronetage* · H. Almquist, *Göteborgs historia, grundläggningen och de första hundra åren* (1935) · W. Berg, *Samlingar till Göteborgs historia* (1890) · H. Fröding and B. Andersson, *Göteborgs historia:*

näringsliv och samhällsutveckling (1996) • H. Fröding, *Berättelser ur Göteborgs äldsta historia* (1908) • S. Skarback, *Göteborg på 1600 talet* (1992) • *Svenska män och kvinnor*, 5 (1949) • T. Fischer, *The Scots in Sweden* (1907) • H. Marryat, *One year in Sweden including a visit to the isle of Gotland* (1862) • J. P. Maclean, *A history of the clan Maclean from its first settlement at Duard Castle, in the isle of Mull, to the present period* (1889) • J. N. M. Maclean, *The Macleans of Sweden* (1971)

Archives Göteborg Landsarkiv, Sweden, Ref. 801, Göteborg Drätselkammare 1638, nos. 90, 92, 97 • NA Scot., gifts and deposits, GD 40/10/4 • NA Scot., gifts and deposits, GD 220/6/2085 • NA Scot., gifts and deposits, GD 220/6/2985 • Riksarkivet, Stockholm, Biographica collection

Wealth at death wealthy; owned three royal donations of land in Halland, Sweden, and had bought an estate for 10,000 thaler in 1652: Grage, 'Makelier, Hans'; Elgenstierna, *Svenska adelns ättartavlor*; Fischer, *The Scots*

Maclean, John [Iain Mac-Gilleain] (*c*.1680–1756), Gaelic poet and Church of Scotland minister, was the son of Ewen Maclean, laird of Treshnish, a group of Hebridean isles 5½ miles south-east of Coll and 3 miles west of the entrance of Loch Tuadh on the Isle of Mull. The Treshnish Macleans formed the second branch of the family of the Macleans of Ardgour. Sinclair states that Ewen Maclean had two natural sons named John and Lachlan (Sinclair, *Clan Gillean*, 330–35). He married Margaret, daughter of Neil Maclean of Drimnacross on Coll, and they had two sons, Hector and a second boy named John. The poet John is said by Sinclair to have been Ewen's eldest son (ibid. and Sinclair, *The Maclean Bards*, 221–34). John Patterson Maclean, however, refers to him as Ewen's third son (J. P. Maclean, 275–8). Whatever their order of birth, it was the other John who succeeded Ewen as the last Maclean of Treshnish. Their brother Hector Maclean became the minister of Coll.

Maclean married Isabella, daughter of Charles Neil Bane Maclean, and had one son and three daughters. On 25 February 1702 he was licensed to preach and on 13 September 1702 was inducted to the pastoral charge of Kilninian and Kilmore on Mull. His predecessor, John Beaton, had become a prey to a feud between the Macleans of Duart and the Campbells of Ardnamurchan, and as a result was forced out of his charge. Beaton was the learned last member of the famous Mull medical family and had recorded the contents of the family's manuscript library. In Coleraine, in the north of Ireland, probably in February 1700, Beaton met Edward Lhuyd, the renowned Welsh polymath and keeper of the Ashmolean Museum, who, backed by subscribers, was making a grand tour of Celtic countries in search of archaeological, botanical, historical, and linguistic material, including Gaelic dialects.

Lhuyd later compiled a list of twelve questions, the answers to which would assist him with his researches. The questions related, *inter alia*, to information about Gaelic grammar, dictionaries, or vocabulary; fashions and customs of the highlanders; old coins, utensils, or arms; burrows or artificial mounds; old highland poets, historians, and physicians; Gaelic Christian names, and so on. On 13 April 1701 they were sent to John Maclean by the Revd Robert Wodrow, an ecclesiastical historian, with the request that he put them to Beaton, whom Wodrow had unsuccessfully tried to contact directly. Maclean succeeded in meeting Beaton and obtained informative responses to nine of the questions. Maclean's reply to Wodrow of 20 April 1702, written at Inveraray, was printed in *Analecta Scotica: collections illustrative of the civil, ecclesiastical and literary history of Scotland* (1st ser., 1834, 121–5) and is reproduced in *Edward Lhuyd in the Scottish Highlands, 1699–1700* by J. L. Campbell and Derick Thomson (1963, 25–36).

In 1704 Edward Lhuyd published his *Archaeologia Britannica*, containing a Gaelic–English vocabulary. In 1707 a second edition was issued containing complimentary poetical addresses from highland ministers, including one from John Maclean. A translation of this poem from the original Gaelic is contained in *The Literature of the Highlanders* by Nigel Macneill (2nd edn, 1929, 271–2). Very few of Maclean's poems in Gaelic survive. Four, including his tribute to Lhuyd and an elegy for his wife, Isabella, appear in the Revd A. Maclean Sinclair's book *The Gaelic Bards: from 1715 to 1765*, and these four together with another, about the marriage of his daughter Anna, are printed in the first part of the same author's volumes *Na baird leathanach*.

As a minister Maclean was testified by the presbytery of Mull to be a man of great zeal for the interest of religion and the dignity of the ministerial character. He died on 12 March 1756 in the fifty-fourth year of his ministry, and was buried beside his father in Kilninian. He was succeeded as minister of Kilninian and Kilmore by his only son, Alexander.   RICHARD D. JACKSON

Sources A. M. Sinclair, *The clan Gillean* (1899), 330–35 • A. Maclean of Ardgour, *A brief genealogical account of the family of McLean* (privately printed, Edinburgh, 1872), 68–74 • J. P. Maclean, *A history of the clan Maclean from its first settlement at Duard Castle, in the isle of Mull, to the present period* (1889), 275–8, 382–5 • *Fasti Scot.*, new edn, 4.115 • A. M. Sinclair, *The Gaelic bards from 1715 to 1765* (1892), 54–68 • A. M. Sinclair, *The Maclean bards*, 1 (Charlottetown, 1898), 221–34 • W. J. Watson, *Bardachd Ghaidhlig: Gaelic poetry, 1550–1900*, [new edn] (1976), 155–7 • E. Lhuyd, *Archaeologica Britannica, giving some account additional to what has been hitherto publish'd of the languages, histories and customs of the original inhabitants of Great Britain* (1707) • Seneachie [J. C. Sinclair], *An historical and genealogical account of the clan Maclean from its first settlement at Castle Duart in the isle of Mull to the present period* (1838), 283–7 • J. N. M. Maclean, ed., *Clan Gillean* (1954) • D. Thomson, ed., *The companion to Gaelic Scotland* (1994), 193

Maclean, Sir John (1811–1895), antiquary, son of Robert Lean of Trehudreth Barton, in Blisland, Cornwall, and his wife, Elizabeth, daughter of Thomas Every of Bodmin, was born at Trehudreth on 17 September 1811. He married at Helland church, Cornwall, on 5 December 1835, Mary (*b.* 1813), elder daughter and coheir of Thomas Billing, of Blisland and St Breward. In 1845, having traced his ancestry to the Macleans of Dochgarroch, he assumed the prefix of Mac.

Maclean entered the ordnance department of the War Office in 1837, was keeper of the ordnance records in the Tower of London from 1855 to 1861, and deputy chief auditor of army accounts from 1865 to 1871. In that year he retired on a pension, and on 14 January 1871 was knighted at Osborne. While engaged in official life he resided at Pallingswick Lodge, Hammersmith, and as an active churchman he took much interest in the ecclesiastical administration of the parish of St John, Hammersmith. After his retirement he lived at Bicknor Court, near Coleford, Gloucestershire, and from about 1887 at Glasbury House, Richmond Hill, Clifton, Bristol.

Maclean's great undertaking was the culmination of twenty years' work, the three-volume *Parochial and Family History of the Deanery of Trigg Minor*, a rural deanery of east Cornwall. It comprised the topographical particulars of twenty parishes, the principal of which was Bodmin, and contained elaborate pedigrees of many of the leading families in the county. It came out in parts between 1868 and 1879. His other publications included historical biographies, genealogical works, and numerous edited texts, many for the Camden Society and for the Harleian Society, of which he was a founder. He co-operated with H. H. Drake and J. L. Vivian in editing *The Visitation of … Cornwall in the Year 1620* (1874).

While living in London, Maclean shared with enthusiasm in the work of its chief antiquarian societies. He was elected FSA on 15 December 1855, and was for many years a member of the council. He frequently attended the meetings of the Royal Archaeological Institute, supplied articles to the journal, and completed the general index to its first twenty-five volumes. He also helped to found the Bristol and Gloucestershire Archaeological Society, and contributed many papers to its *Transactions*, volumes 3–16 of which he edited. Many articles by him appeared in the publications of the Clifton Antiquarian Club, the Somerset Archaeological and Natural History Society, and the Royal Institution of Cornwall, of which he was president in 1892.

Maclean died at his home, Glasbury House, on 6 March 1895. He was survived by his wife.

W. P. COURTNEY, *rev.* CHRISTINE NORTH

Sources Boase & Courtney, *Bibl. Corn.*, 1.332–4, 2.973, 1273 · G. C. Boase, *Collectanea Cornubiensia: a collection of biographical and topographical notes relating to the county of Cornwall* (1890) · *Journal of the Royal Institution of Cornwall*, 13 (1895–8), 24–6 · W. P. Courtney, *The Academy* (16 March 1895), 237 · *Transactions of the Bristol and Gloucestershire Archaeological Society*, 19 (1894–5), 168–9 · *Dod's Peerage* (1894)
Archives Exeter Central Library, West Country Studies Library, Cornwall and Devon antiquarian notes and extracts · Royal Institution of Cornwall, Truro, Brooks collection, papers | U. Newcastle, Robinson L., letters to Sir Walter Trevelyan
Wealth at death £4420 8s. 6d.: probate, 22 April 1895, *CGPLA Eng. & Wales*

Maclean, John (1828–1886), bishop of Saskatchewan, was born on 17 November 1828, the son of Charles Maclean, a merchant of Portsoy, Banffshire, and his wife, Jannet, *née* Watson. In 1847 he gained a bursary to read classics and science at King's College, Aberdeen, and in 1851 he gained his MA.

After graduation Maclean moved to London to work for a firm managed by an uncle; he later took charge of the company's foreign correspondence. It was in London that he became interested in the Church of England Young

Men's Society and decided to become a member of the Church of England. His friendship with Robert Machray, a fellow student at Aberdeen, was probably influential both in this decision and in his desire to become ordained. He was also influenced by Isaac Hellmuth, secretary of the Colonial and Continental Church Society in British North America, who persuaded him to emigrate to Canada.

Maclean was duly ordained deacon by the bishop of Ripon, on 1 August 1858, and priest on 15 December 1858 by Dr Cronyn, bishop of Huron, who appointed him chaplain to the garrison and assistant curate of St Paul's Cathedral in London, Ontario, where he remained until 1866. In 1861 he married Kathleen Wilhelmina, daughter of the Revd Richard Flood; they had ten children.

In 1866 the bishop of Rupert's Land, Maclean's old friend Robert Machray, invited him to move into his diocese. Maclean was appointed in Winnipeg as professor of divinity and warden of St John's College, and rector of St John's Cathedral; examining chaplain to the bishop of Rupert's Land; and archdeacon of Assiniboia. He worked hard, particularly as the population was increasing greatly with the growth of Winnipeg and in the country districts consisted of very poor settlers. Both Maclean and Machray urged moderation during the Red River disturbance of 1869–70, and they advised participation in the convention which Louis Riel proposed holding in January 1870. Maclean's work was recognized in 1871 by the award of honorary degrees from Kenyon College, Ohio; Bishop's College, Lennoxville, Quebec; and Trinity College, Toronto.

In 1873 Maclean visited Britain in order to raise an endowment for a new diocese of Saskatchewan, to be formed out of the extensive diocese of Rupert's Land. The area of 420,000 square miles was sparsely settled by Europeans and no large subscriptions could be relied upon from the inhabitants. By the time he returned to Canada £6200 had been invested, and £2092 had been granted by the Society for the Propagation of the Gospel, with the promise of an annual allowance to the bishop from the society. Maclean was consecrated bishop of Saskatchewan by the archbishop of Canterbury on 3 May 1874 at Lambeth Palace, and he returned to Canada in August of the same year.

En route for his new diocese Maclean held visitations and confirmations on behalf of the bishop of Rupert's Land, and he arrived in Prince Albert, a settlement of about 500 people, in February 1875. It was from Prince Albert that Maclean engaged in the task of building up the diocese, both physically and spiritually. He travelled over 1000 miles every winter by dog sled 'with no roads, no bridges, and no houses for one or two hundred miles at a stretch in some parts' (Pascoe, 180c), organizing missions among the settlers and the Indians, as well as ministering to the mounted police.

In 1879 Maclean established Emmanuel College at Prince Albert, primarily for the training of Native American clergy but also to act as a high school for the Northwest Territories. By 1882 there were twenty-nine mission stations in the diocese, six of whose clergy had been trained at Emmanuel College. The following year Emmanuel College was incorporated as the University of Saskatchewan. Work among the Indians, and people of mixed race, was put under some strain by the Northwest rebellion under Louis Riel in 1885. Prince Albert itself was cut off from communication with Winnipeg and crowded with refugees.

In August 1886 Maclean was able to make a visitation to Calgary and Edmonton in the west of the diocese, and it was here that he met with the accident that caused his death. He was thrown from the wagon in which he was travelling and brought back to Edmonton so seriously injured that, to avoid further damage, he was forced to return to Prince Albert by boat, accompanied by his fifteen-year-old son. The journey of 500 miles along the north Saskatchewan River took twenty-two days and Maclean lingered a further eighteen days before he died on 7 November. He was survived by his wife. Maclean was buried in St Mary's churchyard, Prince Albert, mourned as a man of great administrative talent, strong-willed, and impatient of opposition, who nevertheless 'lived and laboured nobly and with a whole heart for the work which he was consecrated to do' (*The Record*).

CLARE BROWN

Sources DCB, vol. 11 · C. F. Pascoe, *Two hundred years of the SPG*, rev. edn, 2 vols. (1901) · *Men of the time* (1884) · *The Record* (12 Nov 1886), 1116 · *The Times* (15 Nov 1886), 7f · *The Guardian* (17 Nov 1886), 1720 **Archives** Bodl. RH, Society for the Propagation of the Gospel · Saskatoon, records of the synod of the diocese of Saskatchewan

Maclean, John (1835?–1890), actor, was born in London. He began his career giving dramatic recitations, and made his first appearance on the stage at the Theatre Royal, Plymouth, in 1859, playing the King to the Hamlet of Charles Kean. After acting in Jersey, Guernsey, and Birmingham, he performed in London on 7 September 1861 at the Surrey, as Peter Purcell in *The Idiot of the Mountain*. In May 1863 at the Olympic he was the original Mr Gibson in *The Ticket-of-Leave Man*, adapted by Tom Taylor from *Léonard*, by Brisebarre and Nus. In July 1867, at the Princess's, he was the original Saunders, an old Scottish servant, in W. G. Wills's *The Man o' Airlie*. On the opening night of the Gaiety Theatre (21 December 1868), under the management of John Hollingshead, Maclean created the part of Sir Gilbert Ethelward in *On the Cards*, a version by Alfred Thompson of *L'Escamoteur*, by D'Ennery and Brésil. At the same house in 1869 he was the original Duke of Loamshire in T. W. Robertson's *Dreams*, the first Marquis de Fontenelle in *The Life Chase*, an adaptation by John Oxenford and Horace Wigan of Adolphe Belot's *Le drame de la rue de la Paix*, and Sir Tunbelly Clumsy in *The Man of Quality*, an alteration by John Hollingshead of Vanbrugh's *The Relapse*. At the Princess's, in June 1871, he was Mr Clifford in the production of Edmund Falconer's *Eileen Oge, or, Dark's the Hour Before the Dawn*. He then returned to the Gaiety, where he played Polonius to the Hamlet of Walter Montgomery. Among very numerous parts in which he was seen at the Gaiety may be mentioned Sneer in *The Critic* and the Earl of Bareacres in F. C. Burnand's *Jeames* (1878).

When the Olympic opened under John Hollingshead's management, Maclean returned to that house and performed there until 1881, when he was seen at the Vaudeville as Martin Chuzzlewit in the piece of that name and as Dr Lattimer in H. J. Byron's *Punch*. In 1884 he joined the Prince's Theatre, subsequently the Prince of Wales's, under Edgar Bruce; on the opening night (18 January) he took part in a revival of W. S. Gilbert's *The Palace of Truth*, and in March he appeared in *Breaking a Butterfly*, adapted from Ibsen's *A Doll's House* by H. A. Jones and Henry Herman. In a revival at the St James's of *As You Like It*, in January 1885, he played Adam, and in September 1887 he was Camillo in the revival of *The Winter's Tale* at the Lyceum by Mary Anderson, whom he accompanied to America.

After his return Maclean was little seen onstage. His last appearance was at an afternoon performance at the Strand of *My Brother's Sister*, in which, under the management of Minnie Palmer, he played an old French nobleman. Maclean, who was a mason, died on 15 March 1890, at his lodgings at 14 Percy Street, Tottenham Court Road, London, and was buried on 19 March at Paddington cemetery.

A sound and trustworthy actor, Maclean never rose to eminence. He was capable of playing in a respectable fashion most parts in comedy and was generally satisfactory, but was seldom assigned a role of any distinguishing feature. His chief success was in elderly parts, often Scots or Irishmen; however, he won recognition owing to the want of any very formidable rival.

JOSEPH KNIGHT, rev. NILANJANA BANERJI

Sources *The Era* (22 March 1890) · C. E. Pascoe, ed., *The dramatic list* (1879) · C. E. Pascoe, ed., *The dramatic list*, 2nd edn (1880) · *The life and reminiscences of E. L. Blanchard, with notes from the diary of Wm. Blanchard*, ed. C. W. Scott and C. Howard, 2 vols. (1891) · *The Theatre* · *The Athenaeum* · *Sunday Times* · *Era Almanack and Annual* · d. cert. · CGPLA Eng. & Wales (1890) · personal knowledge (1893) **Wealth at death** £753 5s. 4d.: probate, 9 April 1890, CGPLA Eng. & Wales

Maclean, John (1879–1923), revolutionary socialist, was born in Pollokshaws, Glasgow, on 14 August 1879, the sixth child of Daniel Maclean, a potter, and his wife, Annie McPhee, a weaver, who were members of the strictly sabbatarian Original Secessionist church. Maclean was eight years old when his father died, and he was brought up by his mother and maternal grandmother. Despite financial difficulties, he entered the Free Church Teacher Training College in 1898 and qualified as a teacher in 1900. He was then employed by the Govan school board until dismissed during the First World War, effectively on account of his wartime political activities. His commitment to educational self-improvement led him to pursue a course of part-time academic study at Glasgow University, from which he graduated with an MA degree in 1904.

Maclean was already actively involved in Marxist politics, having joined the Social Democratic Federation (SDF) in late 1902 or early 1903. His principal contribution was to build up a Marxist education programme for working-class and socialist activists in and around Glasgow. His classes in Marxism attracted the largest audiences of their kind in Europe before the war and put Maclean into contact with many of the militants who were to emerge in the influential Clyde Workers' Committee in 1915.

Maclean was also active throughout the period 1903–14 as a peripatetic propagandist, travelling regularly across Scotland and northern England during each summer vacation. As well as participating in SDF activities, he was engaged within the co-operative movement, trying to move it towards a more explicitly political alignment with the broad labour movement. His marriage to Agnes Wood, a nurse, in 1909 and the subsequent birth of two daughters, Jean (in May 1911) and Agnes (in April 1913), did little to deflect him from his political activities. Contact with a Russian political émigré Peter Petroff in 1907 strengthened his commitment to internationalism and led him to become more explicitly critical of the path which the SDF, now recast as the British Socialist Party (BSP), was taking under the direction of its leader, Henry Hyndman, in the years preceding the outbreak of war. Hyndman's support for British government rearmament and anti-German sentiment was opposed by Maclean as representing a fundamental deviation from Marxist orthodoxy as expressed through the Second International.

The outbreak of war in August 1914 divided the BSP, and Maclean emerged as an active opponent of the war. His earliest anti-war activity took the form of regular anti-recruiting meetings held opposite the principal recruiting office in Glasgow, which resulted in his first arrest in September 1915 and brief imprisonment in November. He was also prominent in the Clyde rent strike of 1915 and by early 1916 was arrested by the authorities in a pre-emptive strike against targeted militants, among them Willie Gallacher, Jimmy Maxton, and John Muir. Maclean was convicted in May 1916 on six counts, including incitement to strike against conscription and appealing to soldiers to lay

down their arms. He received an 'exemplary' sentence of three years' imprisonment in Peterhead prison, where the physical and psychological effects of the ordeal led to suggestions that he suffered a severe mental breakdown.

Maclean was released on parole on 30 June 1917 following representations to Lloyd George by George Lansbury concerning his mental state. He went to Hastings to recuperate and met Georgy Chicherin, later the Soviet foreign minister, in London. After he returned to Glasgow in the autumn of 1917 Maclean's Marxist education classes expanded to involve some 1300 regular attenders, including almost 300 coalminers. Encouraged by the success of the Bolshevik Revolution he now began to advocate a revolutionary solution to the war, and called on British workers to emulate the Bolshevik success with Glasgow as the British Petrograd. Gallacher described Maclean in the winter of 1917–18 as a 'driving dynamo of energy', and his appointment by the Bolsheviks as an honorary president of the Petrograd Soviet and the Soviet consul in Glasgow added to his prestige as a revolutionary socialist while drawing him again to the attention of the British authorities.

In February 1918, at a time when the German army was mounting its last great offensive of the war, the general officer commanding the army in Scotland argued that action be taken against Maclean, either by revoking his parole or by laying a fresh prosecution against him. Maclean was perceived as more dangerous than other militants because, while they focused more narrowly on industrial grievances, he consistently linked such grievances to a revolutionary political end. On 15 April, with the German offensive at its height, Maclean was arrested for sedition, mainly for calling on workers to deliver a revolutionary blow on May day. His arrest meant he was absent from the May day demonstrations in Glasgow, but

John Maclean (1879–1923), by unknown photographer, 1919 [centre, with David Kirkwood (far left), at a workers' demonstration in Glasgow]

he used his trial, on 9 May, to issue an impassioned denunciation of the war as a capitalist-imperialist adventure: 'I come here not as the accused but as the accuser of capitalism dripping with blood from head to foot.' Sentenced to five years' penal servitude in Peterhead prison, he immediately commenced a hunger strike, protesting that his food was doctored. The authorities took steps to have him certified insane, but Dr Gilbert Garrey, the medical officer at Peterhead, refused to sign such a certificate, for he found that 'Mentally he is quite clear and alert and does not show any sign of insanity.' In October, as part of the campaign to gain his release, Maclean was adopted as the official Labour Party parliamentary candidate for the Gorbals constituency, held by George Barnes, a coalition-Labour member of the government, and was released from prison in November 1918 following the end of the war. Although he contested the ensuing general election, Maclean played little active part in the campaign, effectively conducted by Gallacher, who considered that Maclean was too confused mentally to participate. In the event Maclean polled 7436 votes against the victorious Barnes.

By early 1919 Maclean was sufficiently recovered to undertake a propaganda tour of northern England, and he remained initially confident that the opportunity for revolution on an international and domestic scale remained open. His hopes for a British revolution were based on the expectation that unrest in the engineering and textile industries could be linked to the growing unrest in the mining industry to spark off a general strike, which would be the prelude to a revolutionary take-over. However, by the end of 1919 Maclean's confidence and influence was waning. His domestic life was disrupted when his wife left him because of his refusal to abandon his political activities. Realignments on the revolutionary left served to marginalize him politically.

The principal political event on the Marxist left in 1920 was the attempt to unify the disparate parties and groups into a unified Communist Party. The main participants in the discussions to create a single British Communist Party, in line with the requirements of the Communist Third International, were the BSP, the Socialist Labour Party (SLP), and the Workers' Socialist Federation. In the wake of the Bolshevik Revolution the leadership of the BSP, the largest of the Marxist organizations and the one of which Maclean was a member, was transformed. Those unwilling to accept the principles of Bolshevik party organization were removed, and new figures emerged, such as Colonel L'Estrange Malone and Francis Meynell. Much of the reorganization was orchestrated by Theodore Rothstein, a veteran Marxist and an unofficial Bolshevik representative. Maclean was profoundly suspicious of Malone and Meynell and the other 'johnny-come-latelys' to the revolutionary cause. He questioned also Rothstein's role as arbiter of revolutionary integrity, contrasting Rothstein's current position with his anonymous role during the war, when he had kept a deliberately low profile.

At his most extreme Maclean publicly discerned the hand of the British authorities manipulating events and

believed the kind of personnel being recruited into the new Communist Party—'poets, sentimentalists, syndicalists with a sprinkling of Marxists'—ensured it could not become a genuinely revolutionary party. The vehemence of his critique of the emerging party and its leading personalities served to confirm, for many, Maclean's alleged mental instability and led to his effective exclusion from the process of Communist Party formation. His attempt to pre-empt the creation of the Communist Party of Great Britain (CPGB) by forming a specifically Scottish communist organization in 1920 failed largely through the intervention of his erstwhile associate Gallacher, who, fresh from a visit to Moscow, relayed the Bolshevik instruction that a British party be formed. Relations between Maclean and Gallacher, already strained, broke down irretrievably when Gallacher attributed Maclean's political behaviour to mental instability.

The formation of the CPGB consigned Maclean to the political margins. He failed to enlist the support of the Bolsheviks through his 'Open letter to Lenin', which painted a more pessimistic picture of the immediate prospects for revolution in Britain than that offered by the communists. During the remainder of his life Maclean spent two periods in prison for political activity and was briefly a member of the rump SLP. His final political initiative was the creation of the Scottish Workers' Republican Party (SWRP) in February 1923. For Maclean the SWRP was not based upon a higher commitment to a Scottish nation; rather it was a mechanism for attacking political opponents and furthering a revolutionary internationalism by specifically challenging the British empire. The party's political rhetoric thus dwelt less on Scottish national identity than on its 'red' credentials in contrast to the 'pinks' of the CPGB and the Labour Party. The birth of the SWRP coincided with Maclean's physical decline and financial destitution. He died in Glasgow of pneumonia on 30 November 1923 and was buried in Eastwood cemetery on 3 December.

Maclean's life ended in personal failure and his political legacy was obscured. Ironically enough it was initially claimed by the CPGB, principally through the various memoirs of Gallacher and the biography written by Tom Bell. Communists appropriated Maclean by claiming his wartime exploits, while explaining his final political conduct in terms of mental instability caused by imprisonment. In the 1960s and 1970s Maclean was claimed by a Scottish new left through John Broom's biography, in which he was represented as a Scottish revolutionary socialist. The biography by Nan Milton, Maclean's daughter, and the publication of a collection of his writings, *In the Rapids of Revolution* (1978), brought him to the attention of Trotskyist groups. A John Maclean Society exists to propagate his memory, and in December 1973 a monument in the form of a large cairn was unveiled in his honour in Pollokshaws, on the fiftieth anniversary of his death.   JOHN McHUGH

Sources B. J. Ripley and J. McHugh, *John Maclean* (1989) • J. Broom, *John Maclean* (1973) • N. Milton, *John Maclean* (1973) • N. Milton, ed.,

In the rapids of revolution (1978) • D. Howell, *A lost left* (1986) • W. Kendall, *The revolutionary movement in Britain, 1900–21* (1969) • T. Bell, *John Maclean: fighter for freedom* (1944) • NL Scot., Maclean MS Acc. 4251 • *DNB* • W. Knox, ed., *Scottish labour leaders, 1918–39: a biographical dictionary* (1984) • *CGPLA Eng. & Wales* (1924)

Archives NL Scot., ACC 4251 | NA Scot., prison file, HH 16/132/26385 | FILM BFI NFTVA, 'The revolutionaries', BBC1, 16 July 1980

Likenesses portrait, 1916, NA Scot., HH 16/132 • photograph, 1919, Scot. NPG [*see illus.*]

Wealth at death £215 10s. 3d.: confirmation, 15 Jan 1924, *CCI*

Maclean, Lachlan Cattanach, of Duart (c.1465–1523). *See under* Maclean family of Duart (*per.* 1493–1598).

Maclean, Sir Lachlan Mor, of Duart (1558–1598). *See under* Maclean family of Duart (*per.* 1493–1598).

McLean, Lex [*real name* Alexander McLean Cameron] (1907–1975), comedian, was born on 30 April 1907 at 6 Rosebery Place, Clydebank, Dunbartonshire. He was the son of Donald (Daniel) Cameron (c.1871–1951), ironmoulder, and his second wife, Mary Howe McLean (1876–1948), greengrocer. After secondary education at Clydebank high school he began an apprenticeship at John Brown's shipyard when he was fourteen. He left in 1924 for his first professional appearance as a pianist in a theatre orchestra in Clydebank. Also an accomplished accordionist, saxophonist, and clarinettist, his versatility earned him bookings in local theatres and with seaside concert parties. In the late 1920s and early 1930s he toured Scotland with a group, the Meltonians, and became a foil for comics such as Jack Radcliffe and George West. He married Grace Isabella Dryburgh (1910–1980), a dancer, on 2 June 1939. There were no children from the marriage.

In 1948 Lex McLean put together his own roadshow and went out as a solo comic. His reception justified the opinion he had always held of his ability. By 1950 he could command £80 for a week at the Glasgow Metropole and in 1955 exceeded all records with a nineteen-week summer season at the Aberdeen Tivoli. Similar success followed in Edinburgh and Dundee and he did not hesitate when asked to take over the prestigious summer shows at the Glasgow Pavilion. This was McLean's breakthrough. From the outset he was a smash hit and went on to fill the theatre twice nightly, six nights a week, between May and September for the next fifteen years.

McLean was also the top box-office draw in Edinburgh, Dundee, and Aberdeen. He had a self-confidence, which to some bordered on arrogance, concerning his ability and knowledge of what audiences wanted on a night out. He thought it wrong and a betrayal to try to educate them as he said they came because 'they want to laugh and they go away feeling happy' (Somerville). His comedy was brash, boisterous, and bawdy and the targets were familiar: nagging wives, mothers-in-law, and work-shy husbands. From the first moment he burst on stage in one of his outrageous baggy suits, loosing volleys of one-liners and castigating unfortunate latecomers, the audiences were with him for the rest of the show. Undoubtedly McLean's material was nearer the bone than that of his predecessors but he stoutly denied accusations that he was 'blue' or

suggestive. He was too clever to use bad language or be offensive but he knew how to deliver a *double entendre* and challenge the audience to see something untoward in anything said or done on stage.

A strong, well-balanced supporting cast was always a feature of a Lex McLean show. He chose the acts himself, insisted on high standards, and was not slow to dismiss those whom he considered unprofessional or not making sufficient impact. His famous exhortation was 'Keep it bright!' The tempo was never allowed to flag, with McLean working harder than anyone to keep the show moving along. Although his four television series between 1968 and 1972 were popular, his active, noisy style did not really suit the medium, with which he never seemed truly happy.

Off-stage McLean was the opposite of his loud, extrovert stage character. Always soberly suited, his only concession to showmanship was a polka-dotted bow tie. He was a quiet, very private individual who lived with his wife in their large seafront house in Helensburgh, where his favourite relaxation was sailing his cabin cruiser on the Firth of Clyde. As well as control over the cast, McLean's contracts gave him a generous percentage of box-office takings and this undoubtedly made him the highest-earning performer in Scotland in the 1960s. Despite this he always gave the impression of being worried and unsure about the future, and from 1971 he was dogged by illness. Lex McLean died at his home, 2 Cumberland Avenue, Helensburgh, from pneumonia on 23 March 1975, and was cremated at Clydebank crematorium on 26 March. He was the outstanding Scottish comedian of his generation, and was content to remain in Scotland, seeing no advantage in giving up his pre-eminent position with absolute control over his career to work for someone else.   ARCHIE L. FOLEY

Sources J. Somerville, 'When Lex was king', *Scots Magazine*, 140 (1994), 273–84 • J. House, *Music hall memories* (1986) • J. H. Littlejohn, *Aberdeen Tivoli* (1986) • *The Scotsman* (24 March 1975) • *Glasgow Herald* (24 March 1975) • private information (2004) • b. cert. • m. cert. • d. cert.

Archives U. Glas. L., special collections department, Scottish Theatre Archive, programmes, Revels of 1950, STA A.E. Box 2/24 • U. Glas. L., special collections department, Scottish Theatre Archive, programmes, The Lex McLean Show, STA BMC 4/34; F.n. Box 1/3; F.A. Box 7/17; F.A. Box 10/84; F.n. Box 1/4; F.B. Box 8/37; A.E. Box 9/7G | FILM BBC WAC | SOUND BL NSA, performance recordings

Likenesses photographs, BBC WAC

Wealth at death £79,565.59: confirmation, 4 May 1976, *CCI*

McLean, Neil Loudon Desmond (1918–1986), intelligence officer and politician, was born on 28 November 1918 at 80 Astley Gardens, London, the elder son of Neil Gillean McLean (c.1880–1963), a prosperous East India merchant, and his wife, Grace Audrey (d. 1969), daughter of Patrick Kearns, and a direct descendant of 'Gillean of the Battle-Axe', the thirteenth-century father of the clan Maclean.

Later known by all as Billy, McLean was educated at West Hill Park, Hampshire, and Eton College. He was a keen sportsman, and his holidays were often spent hunting and fishing for salmon on his father's estate at Glencalvie. Later he rode several point-to-point winners at the Royal Military College, Sandhurst, from where he was commissioned into the Royal Scots Greys in August 1938.

In January 1941, having served in Palestine since 1939, McLean joined the Special Operations Executive (SOE). For the rest of 1941 he served under Colonel Orde Wingate in Abyssinia, commanding a joint force of Abyssinian and Eritrean irregulars (known unofficially as McLean's Foot) against the occupying Italians. After a series of SOE staff jobs in Cairo, Syria, and Palestine, and a spell working for MI9 in Istanbul, he was then selected to lead the first SOE mission to Albania. Promoted major and in command of a four-man team, in April 1943 he parachuted into northern Greece, crossed the border into occupied Albania, and made contact with the partisan resistance.

Under McLean's skilled guidance the mission oversaw the creation, training, and armament of the Albanian 1st partisan brigade, which later formed the spearhead of the partisan war effort against the Germans. After being evacuated from Albania in November 1943, McLean received the DSO for his 'example of coolness and courage under conditions of extreme physical difficulty … often under heavy enemy fire' (private information). But his work in the country was not yet done.

As civil strife in Albania between nationalist bands and communist-led partisans threatened to weaken the power of the Albanian resistance, SOE and the Foreign Office in London put their weight behind a plan of McLean's to bring nationalists and partisans together in a combined struggle against the Germans. With this aim in mind McLean, now twenty-five and a lieutenant-colonel, returned to Albania in April 1944. Despite his best efforts, however, the nationalists refused to move. Indeed, the presence of his mission served to worsen SOE's relations with the partisans, who were suspicious of Britain's motives for dealing with their right-wing opponents. In the end, anxious to appease the partisans, the only movement actively fighting the common enemy, Britain resolved to support and recognize them alone. McLean and his team, which included the young Julian Amery, were withdrawn from Albania in October 1944. For the rest of their lives McLean and Amery thought the British had been mistaken in so strongly backing the partisans.

McLean next volunteered for SOE work in the Far East, and in the spring of 1945 he became military adviser to the British consul in Kashgar, Chinese Turkestan (Xinjiang). When the war ended he travelled extensively in Asia and the Middle East before returning to London and resigning his commission. In the late 1940s he became involved in the ill-fated attempt by British and American intelligence services to overthrow Enver Hoxha's new communist regime in Albania.

In 1949 McLean married Daška Kennedy, née Ivanović-Banac (b. c.1915), of Dubrovnik, Yugoslavia, becoming stepfather to her four young children. Soon afterwards he attempted to enter politics, twice standing unsuccessfully for election for Preston South (1950 and 1951), on the first occasion losing by only sixteen votes. Eventually, at a by-election in 1954, he became Conservative MP for Inverness, a seat he held for ten years.

Both in and out of parliament McLean was passionately interested in international politics and a lifelong defender of what he viewed as Britain's interests abroad. Although his opinions did not always accord with those of the government (he was an enthusiastic member of the Suez group and later, with Julian Amery, of the 'Pinay cercle'), they were confidently held and adeptly argued. He spent time in Indochina and Algeria, fact-finding and writing for newspapers at home. For five years from 1962 he was closely involved in helping Imam al-Badr resist President Nasser's attempt to install a republican president in North Yemen. Recruited by the royalists as their principal military adviser, McLean spent much time in the region and played a decisive role in Britain's refusal to recognize the communist-backed government. Xan Fielding, his friend and biographer, considered this McLean's 'crowning achievement' (Fielding, 156).

After leaving parliament in 1964 McLean continued to indulge his love of adventure and taste for politics on trips to Asia, north Africa, and the Middle East, where his political contacts in the Muslim world were extensive. Writing of his discreet dealings with foreign heads of government, Fielding describes McLean as acting as a sort of 'unofficial under-secretary' of the Foreign Office (Fielding, 170). Harold Macmillan wrote respectfully to him in 1979: 'You are one of those people whose services to our dear country are known only to a few' (Fielding, 208).

Billy McLean was tall and handsome, slim in his youth, with fair hair brushed back from a broad forehead. He was calm and considered in thought and deed, even in moments of gravest danger, and his charm, kindness, and humour endeared him to his many friends. A highlander at heart, later in life he derived great pleasure from membership of the exclusive queen's bodyguard for Scotland, the Royal Company of Archers. His delight in outdoor pursuits never waned and he particularly enjoyed spearfishing for moray eel off the northern coast of Majorca.

Weakened by diabetes and septicaemia, McLean died from heart failure at King Edward VII Hospital, London, on 17 November 1986; he was buried in London.

RODERICK BAILEY

Sources X. Fielding, *One man in his time: the life of Lieutenant-Colonel N.L.D. ('Billy') McLean, DSO* (1990) · *Daily Telegraph* (20 Nov 1986) · *The Spectator* (22 Nov 1986) · *The Times* (19 Nov 1986) · private information (2004) [SOE adviser] · b. cert. · *CGPLA Eng. & Wales* (1987)
Archives IWM, papers relating to service with Scots Greys and special operations executive
Wealth at death £190,405: probate, 16 March 1987, *CGPLA Eng. & Wales*

McLean, Norman (1865–1947), semitic and biblical scholar, was born at Lanark on 2 October 1865, the eldest son of the Revd Daniel McLean, a minister of the United Presbyterian Church of Scotland in Lanark from 1865, and his wife, Grace Millar. He was educated in Edinburgh at the Royal High School and then at Edinburgh University, where he took his MA degree in 1885 with first-class honours in classics and philosophy. In 1887 he entered Christ's

College, Cambridge, as a scholar. He obtained first-class honours in part one of the classical tripos (1888) and in the Semitic languages tripos (1890), gained the Jeremie Septuagint prize (1890) and the Mason prize for biblical Hebrew and the Tyrwhitt Hebrew scholarship (both 1891), and was elected a fellow at Christ's (1893). William Robertson Smith was also then a fellow of Christ's, and McLean as his pupil became heir to the highest traditions in Semitic learning. He was simultaneously appointed lecturer in Hebrew at Christ's, and in 1903 university lecturer in Aramaic, an office which he held until 1931. In addition McLean was a pupil of William Wright, after whose death in 1889 McLean revised for separate publication his article on Syriac literature in the ninth edition of the *Encyclopaedia Britannica* (as *A Short History of Syriac Literature*, 1894, repr. 2001) and completed his unfinished edition of *The Ecclesiastical History of Eusebius in Syriac* (1898). He contributed his own articles on Syriac literature to the eleventh edition of the *Encyclopaedia Britannica*: 'in these articles— as in his lectures—he succeeded in making "dead bones live"' (*The Times*, 21 Aug 1947).

McLean found his life's work in 1895, when, with Alan England Brooke and later also Henry St John Thackeray, he was entrusted by Cambridge University Press with the preparation of what is generally known as the larger Cambridge Septuagint (*The Old Testament in Greek*, 9 pts, 1906–40), a full critical edition utilizing the ancient versions and patristic quotations. To this immense task he devoted forty years, among other things learning Ethiopic, continuing the work to within a few years of his death.

In 1896 McLean married Mary Grace, the daughter of Colonel Charles R. Luce JP, of Halcombe, Malmesbury. There were no children, and her early death in 1905 was 'the one great sorrow of his life' (*The Times*, 21 Aug 1947).

McLean held several offices at Christ's, and from 1927 he was master of the college. His influence alike in the college and in wider university affairs won him not only respect for his wisdom but a wealth of affection. Although he was a man of strong personality, his mind was not self-centred but was directed outwards by interest in and regard for others. As a teacher he was most stimulating because he was so eager to share his knowledge, and so concerned for his students individually. They rewarded Daddy McLean, as they called him, with devotion. He sought honours for his pupils, but not for himself; those which came to him were therefore all the more gratifying: the mastership at Christ's, the honorary degrees of LLD from Edinburgh (1931) and DLitt from Oxford (1936), and his election as FBA in 1934. He was a lifelong Liberal, and had deep religious belief, although he rarely talked about it, and his friendship was quiet and unvarying.

McLean's health was poor after a serious operation in the mid-1920s and suffered serious breakdowns in 1930 and 1933. As a result he was not able to accept the post of vice-chancellor of Cambridge when it rotated to him, and he had to retire early as master of Christ's in 1936. He died in a Cambridge nursing home on 20 August 1947, leaving as his legacy—apart from the Syriac *Eusebius*, which remains the standard edition—his contribution to the Cambridge Septuagint. This was only half-finished (Genesis to Tobit) at his death, and no one could be found to complete it (Thackeray had died in 1930 and Brooke in 1939), but it remains an invaluable complement to the later Göttingen Septuagint.

W. A. L. ELMSLIE, *rev.* R. S. SIMPSON

Sources personal knowledge (1959) · private information (1959) · *The Times* (21 Aug 1947), 7 · J. Peile, *Biographical register of Christ's College, 1505–1905, and of the earlier foundation, God's House, 1448–1505*, ed. [J. A. Venn], 2 (1913), p. 731 · *Oxford University Calendar* (1937) · private information (2004) [Dr Sebastian Brock]
Wealth at death £12,895 14s. 4d.: probate, 16 Oct 1947, CGPLA Eng. & Wales

Maclean, Patrick (*fl.* 1538–1565), Roman Catholic bishop-elect of the Isles, was the illegitimate son of Lachlan Cattanach *Maclean (c.1465–1523) and an unidentified Katherine Hay. Several times referred to as 'brother germane to Lord Maclane' (*LP Henry VIII*, 20/2, no. 4), that is, to Hector Maclean of Duart, he owed his influence to his relationship to that formidable chief. Nothing is known of his early life, but as he is invariably described as Master Patrick he was evidently a university graduate. He may have been the 'Dom Patrick Mauchlyne, chaplain' who received £5 from the revenues of Haddington in 1531, and for several years thereafter (*Exchequer Rolls 1529–1536*, 59), but his first certain appearance in the records comes in 1538, when he accounted at the exchequer for crown revenues from the Isles received by his brother. By 1545 he was bailie of Iona and justice clerk of the South Isles.

In 1544 Donald Dubh, the last MacDonald lord of the Isles, escaped from prison and fled to his homeland. The islanders under Duart's leadership rose in revolt, at a time when Henry VIII was making strenuous efforts, abetted by the fourth earl of Lennox, to force the Scots to break their alliance with France and marry their infant queen Mary to Prince Edward of England. In a politically confused situation Donald saw advantage in an alliance with Lennox and England, and employed Patrick Maclean as one of his agents. In March 1545, having already been with Lennox, Maclean proceeded to Westminster, from where the privy council soon sent him back to Donald with promises of money. The result was that on 28 July, 'with the advice of his barons and council of the Isles' (among whom Duart was named first), Donald made Maclean one of his commissioners to negotiate an alliance with the English king. An essential component in any agreement was Donald's ability to raise fighting men in Ireland, and to expedite this Maclean visited Dublin in mid-August, but was back at Westminster by the 23rd. On 5 September the privy council reported that articles had been agreed whereby the English would pay the wages of 3000 of Donald's men and assist him with a further 2000 men under the command of the ninth earl of Ormond.

Donald Dubh died at the end of 1545 and the uprising collapsed. It has been argued that it was also betrayed by Duart, who was certainly in favour with the pro-French Scottish party later in 1546. Patrick Maclean was in Ireland in February 1546, endeavouring to revive the islemen's alliance with England, but he too subsequently made his peace with the Scottish government, for on 7 August, following the death of Bishop Farquhar MacEachan, he received 'the temporalite of all landis … quhilkis [were] pertinentis of the bischoprik of the Iles and abbacy of Colmkill' (*Registrum secreti sigilli*, 3, no. 2367).

For nearly twenty years there was confusion in the sequence of bishops of the Isles. Maclean was not without rivals, and, indeed, neither then nor later was he formally made bishop, but was styled only bishop-elect. He seems to have claimed papal provision, but in 1551 one Roderick Maclean began an action to deprive Patrick of the abbey of Iona, perhaps all he actually held, and a year later the lords of council ordered him to hand the abbey over, on the grounds that he had failed to demonstrate his provision. Roderick Maclean was dead by 26 November 1553, to be succeeded by Alexander Gordon, but again without confirmation. One John Campbell was referred to as bishop-elect in 1560, but Patrick Maclean once more obtained crown nomination to the see, and on 22 April 1562 Gordon resigned to him his rights in Iona. Maclean's second tenure of Iona and the Isles was short-lived, however. On 12 January 1565, still only 'elect of the Iles', he acknowledged 'the impotence of his awne bodie' and resigned all his rights to John Carswell, an active reformer supported by the fifth earl of Argyll. Carswell promised him 'ane yeirlie pensioun for his intertenement' (*Registrum secreti sigilli*, 5, no. 1885). No further reference to Maclean survives, and he probably died soon afterwards.

NICHOLAS MACLEAN-BRISTOL

Sources NL Scot., MS 3018 · M. Dilworth, 'Iona Abbey at the Reformation', *Scottish Gaelic Studies*, 12/1 (1971), 77–109 · N. Maclean-Bristol, *Warriors and priests: the history of the clan Maclean, 1300–1570* (1995) · *Registrum secreti sigilli regum Scottorum*, 3 (1936); 5 (1957) · R. K. Hannay, ed., *Acts of the lords of council in public affairs, 1501–1554* (1932) · *LP Henry VIII*, vols. 20–21 · *CSP Ire.*, 1509–73 · J. Bain, ed., *The Hamilton papers* (1892) · D. Gregory, *The history of the western highlands and isles of Scotland*, 2nd edn (1881) · K. A. Steer and J. W. M. Bannerman, *Late medieval monumental sculpture in the west highlands* (1977) · D. E. R. Watt, ed., *Fasti ecclesiae Scoticanae medii aevi ad annum 1638*, [2nd edn], Scottish RS, new ser., 1 (1969), 205–6 · M. Merriman, *The rough wooings: Mary queen of Scots, 1542–1551* (2000) · G. Burnett and others, eds., *The exchequer rolls of Scotland*, 17 (1897) · Vatican Archives, resignations, 212, fol. 96 [Burnett's microfilms, Glasgow]

MacLean, Sorley [Somhairle MacGill-Eain] (1911–1996), poet, was born on 26 October 1911 at Oscaig, Raasay, Inverness-shire, the second of the seven children of Malcolm MacLean (1880–1951), a tailor, and his wife, Christina (1886–1974), daughter of Sorley Nicolson of Braes, Skye, and his wife, Isobel.

Early years and education MacLean received his early education at Raasay primary school (1918–24) and then at Portree High School, on Skye (1924–9), where he had a very good grounding in such subjects as Latin (he became a great lover of Virgil) and French (including Corneille, Racine, Villon, and Verlaine). Much seventeenth- and eighteenth-century poetry in Gaelic was read, and he also took a great interest in English and history.

However, as with many poets and other writers it was not what he was taught in school that influenced MacLean's work (though of course it was important); he was

Sorley MacLean (1911–1996), by Alexander Moffat, 1978

also greatly influenced by the historical evidence of the clearances, and communicated especially by oral tradition. He had been born into a family of traditional singers and pipers. The first great artistic impression on MacLean was made by his father's mother, who sang some of the very greatest of Gaelic songs. His father, too, had a fine voice and was very interested in Gaelic poetry. Other relatives were also good singers and his brother John was a player of pibroch. Thus the poet grew up in an environment that was rich with Gaelic culture of all kinds, particularly song. This had an immense influence. Indeed so great an impression did these songs have on MacLean that he later wrote: 'Even to this day, I sometimes think that if I had been a singer I would have written no verse, but perhaps if I had been a singer I would have tried to create original melodies' (MacLean, 9). These great songs of the sixteenth and seventeenth centuries had for him, above all, intense passion—of love and grief and hate and other emotions—and they were a powerful influence.

MacLean was brought up in the Presbyterian Free Church of Scotland which, according to him, believed that 'not only were the secular arts dangerous vanities but also that the great bulk of humanity, and the great bulk of Free Presbyterians as well, were to spend an eternity of physical and mental torture' (MacLean, 10). The small number of the elect who could be saved made MacLean anti-élitist. In a letter to Douglas Young written in 1941 he stated:

Perhaps my obsession with the 'cause' of the unhappy, the unsuccessful, the oppressed comes ultimately from this. I preferred the multitude of my friends who [were] certain to be 'lost' to those few who were to be saved. In fact there was no-one of my own family who on form showed any potentiality for salvation. I disliked many of the obvious 'elect' not because of their good fortune, but because most of them were unlovable people and I regarded their preoccupation with salvation much as I regard the careerist at present.   (Whyte, 141)

Even so MacLean was influenced constructively by his Free Presbyterian background, admitting that he was 'very familiar with Seceder metaphysics and imagery and vocabulary' (ibid., 3). The theme of choice, with free will pitted against constricting circumstances, which generates much of the creative tension in MacLean's work, can perhaps be seen as a reflex of the religious debate about election. He was also ready to acknowledge his debt to the great Gaelic preachers within the Free Presbyterian tradition, like the Revd Ewen MacQueen, whose powerful rhetoric moved him. He also retained warm friendships with clergymen of different churches throughout his life. Although he is sometimes regarded as antipathetic to the church in the highlands his views need to be read carefully. His well-known poem 'Ban-ghaidheal' ('Highland woman'), in which he condemns Christ and his church for failing to address the oppression of highland women, weighed down by burdens in their creels and the demands of the rent, should not be taken as a blanket dismissal of the whole church in the highlands. It is a comment on the church's general lack of social conscience. MacLean's indictment foreshadows the critique at the heart of 'liberation theology' in Latin America, Africa, and the Third World in the second half of the twentieth century.

From sixteen or so MacLean had been writing some verse in English and in Gaelic. Moreover from the age of twelve he had been 'an idealist democratic revolutionary' (MacLean, 9), fancying his future as a politician who would help to change the world. In his later teens 'a dichotomy' took him: 'my pure aesthetic idols of old Gaelic songs, and my humano-aesthetic idols of Blake and Shelley' (ibid., 10). His English verse became more influenced by Donne, Eliot, and Pound. Though he came from a thoroughly Gaelic environment it seemed economically sensible to study English. The great Herbert Grierson, who was doing so much to make Donne influential, was professor at Edinburgh University when MacLean began his studies there aged seventeen.

In 1933 MacLean met James B. Caird, who introduced him to the poetry of Christopher Murray Grieve (known as Hugh MacDiarmid, 1892–1978). So overwhelmed was he by that poet's early lyrics that it almost destroyed his chance of writing poetry himself. MacDiarmid's work seemed to him to be 'the unattainable summit of the lyric, and the lyric is the summit of all poetry' (MacLean, 11). In it he found a combination of timeless and modern sensibility. MacDiarmid's *A Drunk Man Looks at the Thistle* also suggested to him the idea of a song medley with lyric peaks, an idea that would bear fruit later in his long poem *An Cuilithionn* (*The Cuillin*, 1939). Caird recalls discussions with MacLean that ranged over Greek, Latin, French, English, and Scottish poetry; he describes MacLean as passionate and eloquent when his interest was aroused. They were both devoted to MacDiarmid and to Yeats. At this time MacLean was becoming discontented with his own poems in English, feeling that they did not express his authentic self, and in 1932 he wrote a Gaelic poem, 'The Heron', which shows quite clearly that a new poetic power had entered Gaelic literature. This is the first work in his *Collected Poems* (1989) and shows that he himself felt that it was here that he found his voice. It is a very modern poem, troubled in its thought but decisive in the expression of that thought.

After four years at Edinburgh University, where he achieved a first-class honours degree in English, MacLean undertook a year of teacher training at Moray House College of Education, in Edinburgh. By 1934 he had met MacDiarmid, and the two men remained in close contact thereafter. Together with George Campbell Hay (1915–1984), MacLean and MacDiarmid formed part of a literary circle whose presiding genius was Douglas Young (1913–1973), himself a poet and a lecturer in Latin and Greek at several Scottish universities before his emigration to Canada and, later, the USA. Young's passionate commitment to Scottish nationalism and to a modern renaissance of Scottish verse encouraged all within the group: 'He cemented the relationships between Hugh MacDiarmid and Sorley MacLean' (Byrne, 3).

MacLean's professional life was spent as a teacher, beginning at Portree High School, on Skye, in 1934 and ending at Plockton High School, Ross-shire, where he was headmaster until his retirement, in 1972. He could not be a 'professional poet' and wrote only when intensely moved to do so. His life in education, first as teacher, then principal teacher of English, and finally headmaster, prevented him, as he himself would say, from writing poetry for long periods.

Dàin do Eimhir agus dàin eile: work of the 1930s Though not published until 1943 the poems in *Dàin do Eimhir agus dàin eile* ('Poems to Eimhir and Other Poems') were mostly written in the thirties. They are for the most part love poems set against the background of the Spanish Civil War. The Eimhir of the title is the name of the wife of the Ulster hero, Cú Chulainn, and it covers the identity of four young ladies who attracted MacLean's attention to varying degrees and who had a catalytic role in the creation of the poems. MacLean wrote:

My mother's long illness in 1936, its recurrence in 1938, the outbreak of the Spanish Civil War in 1936, the progressive decline of my father's business in the Thirties … made these years for me years of difficult choice and the tension of these years confirmed self-expression in poetry not in action. (MacLean, 12)

Thus MacLean did not go to the Spanish Civil War, because he was needed to support his family. However, what comes across in *Dàin do Eimhir* is a conflict between private love and public duty: it seems that he did not go because of a passionate and, in historical terms, selfish love affair. In effect what we have here is the key book of Gaelic twentieth-century poetry in the same way as *A Drunk Man Looks at the Thistle* and Eliot's *The Waste Land* are key texts in Scots and English, respectively. Many of the poems have a lovely musical quality, as one would expect from a poet who loved the great Gaelic songs of the sixteenth and seventeenth centuries, but this is at the same time infused with an urgent political content. It was unusual to find, in Gaelic, poetry that dealt so urgently with contemporary issues that lay outside the highlands, an issue that was in fact at the centre of history. MacLean had himself been dismissive of nineteenth-century Gaelic poetry: 'in the main, [it] is an expression of a somewhat romantic nostalgia for a hopelessly gone past rather than a realist examination of the change' (MacLean, 45). It had for the most part not faced the clearances directly. His own poetry in *Dàin do Eimhir* certainly has an urgent political tone.

However, it is MacLean's love poetry that makes the greatest impact. Behind it is the influence of William Ross, the great eighteenth-century Gaelic love poet, and almost certainly of Yeats. The influence of Donne can perhaps be found in 'The Selling of a Soul'. In these poems there are references to the doomed miner of Spain fighting 'the brute and brigand at the head of Europe'. Sometimes, as in 'The Choice', the poet shows contempt for himself that he did not fight in Spain. There are references to Francis Cornford, Julian Bell, and Federico Garcia Lorca.

From a Marxist standpoint there are attacks in the love poems on the bourgeoisie and on religion. A whole complex of ideas is brought together in a longish work, 'Prayer', which describes the agony of seeing Spain 'lost' while MacLean himself did nothing. Should he ask that his 'heart be purified' from the 'weakness' of his 'pure-white love' so that he could become as 'brave as Dmitrov or Connolly'? He calls his own life 'the death-like life' because he preferred 'a woman to crescent History'. He recognizes that his prayer is not sincere and that his spirit is not 'one-fold'. There are poems with metaphysical imagery and ones of surrealism. Such poetry was quite new in Gaelic, but these works were to be found alongside lovely lyrical poems like 'Under Sail'. All the love poems, however, resonate from a common centre and with the same intensity and personal rhythm. There is a mixture of the traditional and the new, as this Marxist highlander is remade by an existential experience.

An Cuilithionn (The Cuillin) *An Cuilithionn* is the long poem that MacLean started in 1939. The idea for it had probably been generated by a reading of MacDiarmid's *A Drunk Man Looks at the Thistle*. He had left Portree High School in 1937 and gone to teach in Mull, and that island, with its desolation, had made him aware of the highland clearances. He was also obsessed with the approaching war and the idea that Nazism and fascism would conquer Europe. The poem stopped in late May or June 1939 and was not resumed until late October or November of that year; it was concluded in December.

The 'Cuilithionn' are the Cuillin mountains of Skye, which in the poem become a symbol for a human ideal. The poem has much in it about the highland clearances, which are combined with the sufferings of Spain. In the poem MacLean was able to see, by means of Marxist theory, the clearances as part of a European capitalist aggrandizement. Other highland poets had been more naïve and not equipped with that analysis. In this long poem MacLean attacks the bourgeoisie, and Scotland itself, among many other nations including England, France, and of course Germany. They are all part of the morass at the foot of the Cuillins—the quagmire that has swallowed so many of the poor and oppressed. This morass even swallowed the French Revolution, and swallowed the heroism of Spain. The poet has no hope of ever ascending 'to the high hunting ground of the moorland'. He says that there is so much of the morass in his spirit that his 'courage has taken the grey hue'. It may be that this hatred of the self came about because he did not fight in the Spanish Civil War.

Under the personification of Clio, the muse of history, there is a long catalogue of the sufferings of populations, beginning in Skye and spreading outwards to Ireland, England, Spain, France, Italy, Greece, Germany, India, and China. However, as well as mention of these sufferings there is mention of heroes who fought for freedom—Connolly and Pearse, Wat Tyler and John Ball, Spartacus, Nehru and Gandhi, among others—as well as writers such as Rousseau, Voltaire, and Cobbett.

Two particular men stand out in the catalogue of the heroic. One is John MacLean, a man of his own clan of whom he felt very proud and to whom he dedicated a poem. John MacLean was a schoolmaster and member of the Social Democratic Federation. He believed passionately in workers' education. He was anti-militarist and was imprisoned four times between 1911 and 1921. He died at the age of forty-four. The other outstanding figure was Dmitrov, a Bulgarian communist who was arrested in 1933 on a trumped-up charge of having set fire to the Reichstag. He conducted his own defence, making a fool of Goering, his prosecutor.

An Cuilithionn is not as fine a poem as *A Drunk Man Looks at the Thistle*. There is not enough variation of tone nor are there any of the comic passages and philosophic bravura with which MacDiarmid enlivened his poem. MacLean's best poetry has always been passionately lyrical, for he does not have the same interest in ideas as MacDiarmid. What we get from *An Cuilithionn* is the passionate cry of a sensitive mind against deeply felt oppression.

MacDiarmid and MacLean continued to encourage one another, MacLean by providing translations of eighteenth- and nineteenth-century Gaelic verse for MacDiarmid's *Golden Treasury of Scottish Verse* (1940) and MacDiarmid by saluting and affirming MacLean's verse when his first volume, *Seventeen Poems for Sixpence*, produced in collaboration with the poet Robert Garioch, who hand-printed it, was published in 1940. MacDiarmid found MacLean's support invaluable in his ongoing crusade against parochialism and Anglocentrism.

War service, marriage, and further poems, 1940–1946 MacLean volunteered for the army in September 1939 but, having learned that he would lose his teaching salary, he waited for conscription, which came in September 1940, when he was enlisted into the signal corps. In the meantime he taught evacuees at Hawick between October 1939 and June 1940. His army training took place at Catterick Camp, Yorkshire, and from there he corresponded with Young on the preparation of *Dàin do Eimhir* for publication. Young typed and edited the drafts, checking every difficult point with MacLean. In December 1941 MacLean was sent to Egypt on active service. He wrote to MacDiarmid:

> My fear and hatred of the Nazis [is] even more than my hatred of the English Empire ... I support the British Empire because it is the weakest and therefore not as great a threat to Europe and the rest of the world as a German victory. (Ross and Hendry, 27)

He served in north Africa and was wounded three times. The last time was in 1942, during the battle of El Alamein. He was seriously injured when a land mine exploded near him, shattering many of the bones in his feet and heels. The following nine months he spent in military hospitals, until his discharge from Raigmore Hospital, Inverness, in August 1943. For many years parts of *An Cuilithionn* were published here and there in magazines and journals. When MacLean was invalided out of the army he says that there was some talk of publishing it in full, but production was delayed until 'the behaviour of the Russian government to the Polish insurrection in 1944 made me politically as well as aesthetically disgusted with most of it' (S. MacLean, *Collected Poems*, 1989, 63).

It seems that MacLean lost his faith in the USSR as the political saviour of the working classes, and in 1946 he was writing to MacDiarmid that he was 'utterly at sea in politics these days, having for the past year and a half, come to the conclusion that the Communist Party is no use for me' and that he had gone back to 'social democracy and swithering between Labour and S.N.P' (Ross and Hendry, 28).

In 1944 he met (Catherine) Renee Stewart Cameron (*b.* 1920), whom he married on 24 July 1946. They had three daughters: Ishbel, Catriona, and Mary.

Six poems from the war period are to be found in MacLean's *Collected Poems*. 'Going Westwards' shows his general attitude to the war and the enemy. However, he says there is no avoidance of the struggle and he reflects in the last verse on his own heroic ancestors. 'Heroes' is an interesting poem in which he describes an Englishman who fought with him in Egypt. Unlike the handsome highland chiefs commemorated in Gaelic poetry this is:

> a poor little chap with chubby cheeks
> and knees grinding each other,
> pimply unattractive face.

Nevertheless this is 'a lion against the breast of battle'. Though he was killed while firing into the German tanks he did not receive any medals. One of the most powerful of the war poems is 'Death Valley', where the poet finds a dead soldier:

> a boy with his forelock down about his cheek
> and his face slate-grey.

As he observes the 'flies about grey corpses' he wonders about the 'right and joy' that this German got from his *Führer* and whether the boy had in his lifetime abused the

Jews or communists. In 'Autumn Day' there is an interesting reference to the Free Presbyterian doctrine of the elect. Six men are killed beside MacLean quite suddenly. He concludes:

> One Election took them
> and did not take me,
> without asking us
> which was better or worse.

Of MacLean's other poems one might single out the lovely 'The Woods of Raasay', in some ways one of his most traditional pieces, with its many adjectives, such as one finds for instance in the great eighteenth-century poem 'Ben Dorain', by Duncan Ban Macintyre. However, though 'The Woods of Raasay' has a lovely freshness it is also shot through with sexual imagery, disturbances, and anguished reflections on love. Another poem, 'Hallaig', about one of the cleared villages in Skye, may be his best single poem. The tone is quiet and eerie, elegiac and gentle. He sees the dead people in the shape of a wood going up beside the stream. He writes of the young girls going to church as they did when they were alive. But now it is a 'Sabbath of the dead'. It is a heart-breaking poetic vision in which MacLean reaches the very heart of the highland experience of desolation and lost community and beauty, Hallaig's ghostly history and its suffering. And yet it is also a resurrection.

Two of MacLean's poems about Ireland are worth mentioning: first, 'The National Museum of Ireland', a poem about the great Irish hero Connolly, on whose shirt the poet sees 'the rusty red spot of blood'. Connolly is the hero 'who is dearest to me of them all'. In the other poem, 'At Yeats' Grave', MacLean says that 'courage and beauty had their flagpoles through your side'. Another fine poem is his elegy on his brother Calum (1915–1960), who died of cancer and by whose bravery in enduring the disease MacLean was greatly struck. Calum was a very distinguished folklorist who had done a spectacular thing, being converted to Catholicism from Free Presbyterianism. MacLean writes:

> You dearly bought the pride
> that we bought in your death.

MacLean also spent a long time on the poem 'The Cave of Gold'. Apart from 'The Woods of Raasay' all these poems were written during that period, one of which is called 'Screapadal'. Screapadal is a deserted township in the north of Raasay, which like Hallaig was cleared of its people. Screapadal is again threatened, this time by a new enemy, a submarine off the sound of Skye. The poet imagines the 'sudden holocaust' and the 'poisonous bracken'.

Ris a' bhruthaich: critical writing and later years *Ris a' bhruthaich* ('Up the brae') is subtitled 'The criticism and prose writings of Sorley MacLean'. It consists of occasional papers and articles, and three Gaelic short stories, and was published in 1985. The papers were given to the Gaelic Society of Inverness and published in their *Transactions*. Other criticism and articles written by MacLean between 1934 and 1976 were published in magazines such as *Scottish Art and Letters*, *Gairm*, and *Chapman*. MacLean's criticism was of foundational importance in the Gaelic context, since very little in the way of properly critical analysis of Gaelic literature had been attempted previously. Much of what existed tended to summarize and to affirm the literature, often in a romantic vein. A critical engagement that assessed the weaknesses as well as the strengths of the material was hardly known; Gaelic scholars of the time tended to be more concerned with language than literature. MacLean was not, however, alone in reacting against the prevailing shallowness and the worship of romantic idols. MacDiarmid had reacted in a similar manner to the romantic reconstructions of Marjory Kennedy Fraser in the 1920s. A Lewisman, Murdo Murray (1890–1964), also began to assess nineteenth-century Gaelic literature in a critical light at much the same time as MacLean, and independently of him. Both MacLean and Murray reacted against the type of romanticism found in the songs and verse of Neil MacLeod and other nineteenth-century sentimentalists, and both wrote critical essays that rehabilitated the verse of Mary MacPherson (Màiri Mhòr nan Oran; 1821–1898), the poet of the highland land agitation of the 1870s and 1880s. MacPherson's verbosity and unvarnished realism offended the romantic practitioners of the late nineteenth century and the earlier twentieth century, including MacLean's maternal uncle Alexander Nicolson, who dismissed her verse on Skye as a 'glorified tourist guide'.

MacLean, like MacDiarmid, attacked the 'Celtic twilight' idea, and much of his criticism was in praise of the great sixteenth- and seventeenth-century songs. The best Gaelic poetry, MacLean pointed out, is hard and clear and objective: 'Great poetry may cry in despair for one thing that exists or that it would like to exist, but it never assumes the existence of something which it knows perfectly well doesn't exist' (MacLean, 17). Again and again in the best Gaelic poetry he showed either the existence of real passion or authentic detail as well as sharp visual imagery. However, he found nineteenth-century poetry 'flabby and anaemic: it lacks power, gusto, spontaneity, joie de vivre' (ibid., 57). He wrote a seminal paper, 'The poetry of the clearances', and he found with some notable exceptions that such poetry suffers from 'intellectual weakness' (ibid., 61). To some extent MacLean overstated his case, and his criticism has helped to darken the pall that still hangs over nineteenth-century Gaelic verse. Nevertheless his analysis demonstrated some of the real strengths of the period, displayed notably in the work of John Smith of Lewis, Mary MacPherson of Skye, and William Livingston of Islay. All three poets had voiced disapproval of the status quo of their own time, and to an extent MacLean's affirmation of their political robustness echoed the sentiments of Hugh MacDiarmid, although it also reflected his admiration for the stand of highland crofters against landlordism in the 1870s and 1880s and the radical socialism that had shaped his own world view in the 1930s. Moving beyond the Gaelic world, MacLean sometimes compared Gaelic poets to English ones. Thus, while Wordsworth infected nature with philosophy, Duncan Ban Macintyre had physical exactness. Similarly he

preferred the eighteenth-century love poet William Ross to Keats. Here too what now appears to be a deliberate and probably over-argued attempt to rescue Gaelic literature from the thrall of English perspectives can be detected, reminiscent of MacDiarmid's campaign. Nevertheless MacLean's essays provided the first consistent body of modern analytical writing that took Gaelic literature seriously and applied critical yardsticks to it. There is therefore a clear parallel between his work as a poet who brought Gaelic verse firmly into the twentieth century and as a critic who laid new foundations for Gaelic literary criticism.

Though by their occasional nature these essays tend to be repetitive they are valuable in that they show quite clearly MacLean's grasp of the strengths and weaknesses of Gaelic poetry, and the prolific examples he quotes undoubtedly strengthen his case. Also, to him, the visual and audible were very important, as was 'the great lyrical cry' that he found time and again in the passionate songs that he admired. (It is interesting, for instance, that in connection with the Spanish Civil War his favourite poem was Cornford's 'Heart of the Heartless World', a poignant love lyric, rather than, for example, anything by Auden.) In their enthusiasms and clear-headedness these essays show quite clearly the influences on MacLean's poetry.

In appearance Sorley MacLean was tall and well-built. Indeed he himself says in his poem 'Going Westwards':

And be what was as it was,
I am of the big men of Braes,
of the heroic Raasay Macleods.

In his youth he played much shinty and was a university blue. He restarted shinty in his period as headmaster at Plockton High School and was a highly competitive instructor to the pupils. He writes too of rowing when he was young and having political arguments with an aunt as he rowed the boat. Later the Cuillins seduced him from the sea.

MacLean admired heroism, and was very proud of his clan and of Gaelic culture, about which he was very knowledgeable. He had a very strong memory and was extremely interested in genealogy. He was friendly and approachable, very much appreciated wit in others, and had a highly developed sense of humour, which was never revealed in his writing. The fact was that as he became older he sometimes fell asleep in company. He did this once, late at night, in the company of fellow poet Norman MacCaig, and to excuse himself he said 'he had now got to the stage that he could not guarantee keeping awake, even if he had the company of Voltaire on one side, and Helen of Troy on the other' (private information). One could imagine him passionate in argument in his youth, one whom the ills of the world would not let rest.

MacLean was in great demand as a reader of his poetry from the time that he retired from teaching, in 1972. He read often in Scotland, England, Wales, Ireland, and in Europe. His wife, Renee, accompanied him to many of his readings. He read with passion, though it often seemed that he did not regard his translations very highly in comparison with the original poems. Often in Ireland, MacLean was venerated there as a great Celtic poet. In 1973 he made an album recording of a selection of his poems, *Barran agus Asbhuain*, while acting (to 1975) as creative writer in residence at Edinburgh University.

MacLean's final *Collected Poems* (1989) contains 313 pages composed of Gaelic poems with English translations. His output therefore is not large; he was one of those poets who wrote only under compulsion. As a teacher he was highly conscientious, and it was perhaps because of this that he wrote so little in his latter years. He received many honours, including honorary degrees from eight universities as well as prestigious prizes, especially the queen's medal for poetry. He was also made a freeman of Skye and Lochalsh. *Somhairle: dàin is deilbh: a Celebration on the 80th Birthday of Sorley MacLean* was published in 1991. Yet in spite of all this recognition he was rooted in Skye. It inspired much of the subject matter and the symbolism of his poetry, and it is this rootedness that gave his work most of its authenticity.

Sorley MacLean died on 24 November 1996 at Raigmore Hospital, Inverness, of a stroke, and was buried on 28 November at Portree, on the Isle of Skye. By the time of his death his reputation went far beyond Scotland. Increasing interest in his work is evidenced by the numerous articles and critical assessments in academic journals and studies of Scottish and Gaelic literature. A corrected edition of *From Wood to Ridge*, containing both English and Gaelic versions of the poems, was published in 1999. In 2002 Christopher Whyte reconstructed the creation of *Dàin do Eimhir* as a sequence of sixty-one poems, *Somhairle MacGill-Eain*. He examines in detail the emotional, intellectual, and contextual processes that determined its shape, and he provides many insights into the pressures (and not least the poet's own reservations) that affected its presentation in different collections and editions. Even in the first edition, of 1943, twelve poems were missing from the original sequence, and in Whyte's reconstruction one (no. 7) is still lacking. MacLean's personal view of the sequence was at times despairing, as he indicated to Young, and he himself was prepared to publish only certain parts of it. Latterly he took an aversion to it, and denied as lately as 1989 that it was 'really a sequence' (Whyte, 1). It is interesting to consider whether MacLean would have been content with the recreation and restoration of the sequence and the 'original' forms of the texts. Whatever the poet's personal inhibitions it is beyond doubt that *Dàin do Eimhir* represents a remarkable literary achievement. The edition is a major scholarly contribution to the understanding of MacLean's mind and of the literary world in which he operated in the 1930s and 1940s.

IAIN CRICHTON SMITH and DONALD E. MEEK

Sources R. Ross and J. Hendry, *Sorley MacLean: critical essays* (1986) · W. Gilles, ed., *Ris a' bhruthaich: the criticism and prose writings of Sorley MacLean* (1985) · M. Byrne, 'Tails o the comet'?: MacLean, Hay, Young and MacDiarmid's renaissance', *ScotLit*, 26 (2002), 1–3 · C. Whyte, ed., *Somhairle MacGill-Eain / Sorley MacLean: Dàin do Eimhir* (2002) · private information (2004) · personal knowledge (2004)

Archives NL Scot., notebook, corresp., and literary MSS | SOUND BL NSA, performance recordings

Likenesses oils, 1908, U. Reading · W. Rothenstein, drawing, 1933, London School of Economics · A. Moffat, drawing, 1978, Scot. NPG [*see illus.*] · W. Rothenstein, sanguine and chalk drawing, NPG

Maclear, George Frederick (1833–1902), writer on theology, born at Bedford on 3 February 1833, was the eldest son of the Revd George Maclear MA, chaplain of Bedford county prison (1832–69), and his wife, Isabella Ingle. Educated at Bedford grammar school, he matriculated at Trinity College, Cambridge, in 1851, won a scholarship in 1854, and had a distinguished academic career. He won the Carus Greek Testament prize in 1854 and 1855, and after graduating BA with a second class in the classical tripos of 1855, he was placed in the first class in the theological tripos of 1856 (its first year). He gained the Burney prize in 1855, the Hulsean in 1857, the Maitland in 1858 and 1861, and the Norrisian in 1863. All five prize essays were published. His Maitland essay of 1858, *The Christian Statesman and our Indian Empire*, reached a second edition. That of 1861, 'Christian missions during the middle ages', was recast as *Apostles of Mediaeval Europe* (1869), and was the first of a series of volumes on missionary history. Maclear proceeded MA in 1860, BD in 1867, and DD in 1872. Ordained deacon in 1856 and priest in 1857, he held curacies at Clopton (1856–8), and St Barnabas, Kennington (1858–60). He was assistant preacher at Curzon Chapel, Mayfair (1860–65), reader at the Temple (1865–70), select preacher at Cambridge (1868, 1880, and 1886) and at Oxford (1881–2), and Ramsden preacher at Cambridge in 1890. He delivered the Boyle lectures at Whitehall in 1879–80, published as *On the Evidential Value of the Holy Eucharist* (1883; 4th edn, 1898).

Meanwhile Maclear was an assistant master at King's College School, London (1860–66), and headmaster (1866–80). He showed great ability as teacher and organizer, doubled the numbers, and greatly raised the standing of the school. While headmaster he declined an offer of the see of Colombo in 1875. Eventually he accepted the post of warden of St Augustine's Missionary College, Canterbury, in 1880, and held it until his death. In this capacity he worked untiringly as preacher, lecturer, and adviser on foreign mission work. In 1885 he was made an honorary canon of Canterbury Cathedral.

Maclear was twice married: first, on 10 June 1857, to Christiana Susan, daughter of J. Campbell, rector of Eye, Suffolk (she died on 31 May 1874, being predeceased by an only daughter), and second, on 27 December 1878, to Eva, eldest daughter of William Henry D'Olier Purcell, vicar of Exmouth; she died on 1 March 1890, leaving three sons and a daughter. Maclear died at St Augustine's College, after a long illness, on 19 October 1902, and was buried in St Martin's churchyard, Canterbury.

Maclear enjoyed a wide reputation as a theological writer. His lucid and well-arranged textbooks, which were long in general use, include the *Class Books of Old and New Testament History* (1862), the *Class Book of the Catechism* (1868), and *An Introduction to the Articles* (1895; new edn,

1909), written with the Revd Watkin Wynn Williams. To missionary history he contributed, besides the work mentioned, *The Conversion of the West* (4 vols., 1878) and *St Augustine's, Canterbury: its Rise, Ruin, and Restoration* (1888), and he wrote on missions in the *Encyclopaedia Britannica* (9th edn). Maclear also published several devotional and liturgical books. *Lectures on Pastoral Theology*, a selection from his unpublished manuscripts, was edited by the Revd R. J. E. Boggis in 1904.

G. Le G. Norgate, *rev.* H. C. G. Matthew

Sources *King's College School Magazine* (Dec 1902) · *The Guardian* (22 Oct 1902) · *Church Times* (24 Oct 1902) · *The Times* (20 Oct 1902) · *The Times* (23 Oct 1902) · *Kentish Observer* (23 Oct 1902) · F. J. C. Hearnshaw, *The centenary history of King's College, London, 1828–1928* (1929) · Venn, *Alum. Cant.*
Archives Canterbury Cathedral, archives, notebooks | LPL, letters to E. W. Benson · LPL, letters to A. C. Tait
Likenesses S. P. Hall, oils, 1902, King's College School, Wimbledon
Wealth at death £12,997 10s. 8d.: probate, 26 Nov 1902, *CGPLA Eng. & Wales*

Maclear, John Fiot Lee Pearse (1838–1907), naval officer, son of Sir Thomas *Maclear (1794–1879), astronomer royal at the Cape of Good Hope, and his wife, Mary, *née* Pearse (*d.* 1861), was born at Cape Town, Cape Colony, on 27 June 1838. Educated at a private school in the Cape, he entered the navy in September 1851 as a cadet on the frigate *Castor*, then bearing the broad pennant of Christopher Wyvill, commodore in command on the Cape of Good Hope station. In her he saw service during hostilities on the eastern frontier of Cape Colony in 1851, and afterwards, as a midshipman of the *Algiers*, served in the Crimean War in the Baltic and the Black Sea from 1854 to 1856. He passed his examination in July 1857, and served on board the *Cyclops* in the Red Sea as mate during disturbances at Jiddah in Arabia in 1858. On 19 May 1859 he was promoted lieutenant, and shortly afterwards was appointed to the *Sphinx*, in which he served on the China station until 1862, being present at several engagements during the Second Opium War, including the Taku (Dagu) forts. In 1863 he went to the *Excellent* to qualify as a gunnery lieutenant, and in February 1864 was appointed to the *Princess Royal*, flagship on the China station. He returned home in her, and in October 1867 was chosen first lieutenant of the frigate *Octavia*, flagship of Commodore Heath [see Heath, Sir Leopold George] in the East Indies. In her he took part in the Abyssinian expedition in 1868, earning promotion to commander (dated 14 August 1868).

In 1872 the *Challenger* was commissioned by Sir George Nares, with Maclear as his commander, for a voyage of scientific discovery circumnavigating the world. Maclear returned home in her in 1876 and was promoted captain on 14 August. On 4 June 1878 he married Julia, sixth daughter of Sir John Frederick William *Herschel. In 1879 he succeeded Nares in command of the sloop *Alert* and remained in her until 1882, completing the survey of the Strait of Magellan. From 1883 to 1887 he commanded the *Flying Fish* on surveying service, carrying out other valuable scientific work during the same time. On 20 June 1891 he reached flag rank, and two months later he retired. He

was promoted vice-admiral on the retired list in 1897, and admiral in 1903. After leaving the sea Maclear assisted in the compilation of several volumes of the official sailing directions, especially those for the Indonesian archipelago (1890, 1893), for the west coasts of Central America and the United States (1896), for the Bering Sea and Alaska (1898), as well as for the *Arctic Pilot* (2, 1901; 3, 1905). He was also a fellow of the Royal Geographical and Royal Meteorological societies. He died of heart failure in a hotel at Niagara on 17 July 1907, and his body was brought back to England for burial.

L. G. C. Laughton, *rev.* Roger Morriss

Sources *The Times* (19 July 1907) · *GJ*, 30 (1907), 447 · *Quarterly Journal of the Royal Meteorological Society*, 34 (1908), 135–6 · C. W. Thomson, *The voyage of the Challenger*, 2 vols. (1877) · W. J. J. Spry, *Cruise of HMS Challenger* (1876) · A. Day, *The admiralty hydrographic service, 1795–1919* (1967) · E. Linklater, *The voyage of the Challenger* (1974) · G. S. Graham, *The China station: war and diplomacy, 1830–1860* (1978) · WWW
Archives NMM, corresp. and papers

Maclear, Sir Thomas (1794–1879), astronomer, was born on 17 March 1794 at Newtownstewart, co. Tyrone, Ireland, the eldest son of James Maclear. After refusing his father's wish that he enter the Anglican church, he was dismissed at the age of fifteen to the care of his maternal uncles, Sir George and Dr Thomas Magrath, who supervised his medical education at Guy's and St Thomas's hospitals, London. A brilliant student, admitted to the Royal College of Surgeons in 1815, he was appointed house surgeon at Bedford Infirmary. There he met Admiral William Henry Smyth (1788–1865), one of a group of astronomical enthusiasts, with whom Maclear studied the subject. He built a small observatory and attained a professional standard of competence. In 1823 he went into partnership with his uncle at Biggleswade, Bedfordshire, and in 1825 married Mary, the daughter of Theed Pearse, clerk of the peace for that county. The Royal Observatory at the Cape of Good Hope had been founded in 1820 as a southern counterpart to Greenwich, but had had a chequered history. On the resignation of Thomas Henderson, the government astronomer, in 1833, Maclear was appointed to replace him. He arrived at the Cape observatory on 5 January 1834 with his wife and five daughters (by 1846 he would have ten children, including John Fiot Lee Pearse *Maclear). John Herschel, with his family, arrived ten days after Maclear, and during his four-year stay gave the latter technical support and encouragement.

The imposing stone observatory building, resembling that at Cambridge, stood isolated on a barren unfenced knoll between two flood-prone rivers. Maclear's Admiralty letter of appointment enumerated wide-ranging duties, including tidal and meteorological observations and the provision of a time service to shipping, but only allowed him one assistant and a labourer. Staff troubles had been chronic, and his first reliable assistant, who arrived on 9 October 1835, was Charles Piazzi Smyth (1819–1900), a sixteen-year-old genius, not yet eccentric, the second son of Admiral Smyth. An additional assistant, William Mann, who later married Maclear's daughter

Caroline, arrived in 1839. Maclear appointed his son George William Herschel Maclear to the staff in 1852.

For Maclear's primary task, the determination of precise positions of southern stars, a transit circle and a mural circle, the latter unreliable, were incorporated in the building structure. The mural circle was replaced in 1847, and both by an up-to-date transit circle in 1855. The diminutive Maclear, known to his staff as the Emperor, drove his staff and himself hard at meridian observations, but could not also speedily complete the tedious reductions needed for publication. He was criticized for these delays, and most of his observations were published by his successors.

In 1752 the visiting French astronomer Nicolas Louis de Lacaille had surveyed an arc of latitude, a degree and a quarter in length, north from Cape Town, and found an anomalous value of the earth's ellipticity in the south. Having been enjoined to repeat the measure, Maclear first made a practice measurement of a base-line, using home-made equipment, on the Grand Parade in Cape Town in December 1837.

The zenith sector used by James Bradley in his studies of aberration was sent to the Cape from Greenwich for precise determination of the latitudes of geodetic stations. It was 12½ feet tall, and never designed for field work, but was nevertheless so used until 1847. All traces of Lacaille's base-line having disappeared, Maclear measured a new one 8 miles long in the flat country midway between the ends of the arc, assisted by a squad from the garrison, using manufactured measuring bars sent from England. The results confirmed the traditional view of the form of the earth in the southern hemisphere. Lacaille's erroneous result was attributed to gravitational deflection of the vertical close to mountains. After this initial work the survey was extended up to 1847, northwards into Nama Land and south to Cape Point, with the energetic assistance, often under hazardous conditions, of Smyth and Mann. The results of the survey, edited by George Airy and published in 1866, brought Maclear the Lalande prize of the Institute of France and a royal medal of the Royal Society, of which he had been a fellow since 1831. He also received other European honours.

In 1836 Maclear installed a time ball at the observatory, which freed the astronomer from the nightly duty of discharging a signal pistol from its roof. Later time balls operated by telegraph were installed at Port Elizabeth and at the naval base at Simonstown. Maclear reobserved Alpha Centauri and confirmed Henderson's pioneer parallax determination. After receiving a 7 inch refractor in 1847, he diligently observed comets and published seventeen notes. He was active in many civic and intellectual projects in the colony, including the establishment of standard weights and measures and the provision of lighthouses. As an intimate friend and consultant to David Livingstone, he was an enthusiast for exploration of central Africa. He was knighted after a visit to Britain and parts of Europe in 1860. In 1861 he was devastated by the death of his wife, who, though so deaf she had to use an ear trumpet, charmed all who knew her. She was buried in

the observatory grounds. In 1870 Maclear retired, reluctantly, from the now consolidated and landscaped observatory to the care of a daughter in the nearby suburb of Mowbray. He became totally blind in 1876, and died on 14 July 1879. He was buried alongside his wife. On 17 July the Cape house of assembly passed a resolution of regret and appreciation of his many public services.

DAVID S. EVANS

Sources [D. Gill], *Monthly Notices of the Royal Astronomical Society*, 40 (1879–80), 200–04 · *DNB* · D. Gill, *A history and description of the Royal Observatory, Cape of Good Hope* (1913) · B. Warner, *Astronomers at the Royal Observatory, Cape of Good Hope* (1979) · B. Warner, *Charles Piazzi Smyth, astronomer-artist: his Cape years, 1835–45* (1983) · T. Maclear, *Verification and extension of Lacaille's arc of meridian*, ed. G. B. Airy, 2 vols. (1866) · B. Warner, ed., 'The Maclear commemorative symposium', *Transactions of the Royal Society of South Africa*, 50 (1995), 59–94
Archives Cape archives department, Cape Town, corresp. and papers · CUL, corresp. and papers · RGS, coast surveys of South Africa | Bucks. RLSS, corresp. with John Fiott Lee · National Library of South Africa, Cape Town, letters to Sir George Grey · NL Scot., corresp. with David Livingstone · RS, corresp. with Sir John Herschel

Macleay, Alexander (1767–1848), entomologist and civil servant in Australia, was born in Ross-shire, Scotland, on 24 June 1767, the son of William Macleay, provost of Wick and deputy lieutenant of Caithness. He received a good education but where is not known. In 1788 he moved to London and formed a partnership with William Sharp, a London wine merchant. Three years later, on 15 October 1791, he married Elizabeth Barclay (1769–1847) at St Dunstan's Church, London. In 1795 he became chief clerk in the prisoner of war section of the transport office. He was appointed head of the correspondence department in 1797 and from 1807 was secretary to the board.

Besides gaining administrative experience, Macleay occupied public positions, including that of director of the British Fisheries Association, and won high repute as a scientist. Elected fellow of the Linnean Society in 1794, he served as secretary between 1798 and 1825. In 1808 he was elected fellow of the Royal Society and in 1824 joined its council. He was a corresponding member of several European learned societies and published several monographs; in 1814 he was presented with a diploma by the Royal Academy of Science in Stockholm. He won particular renown for his collection, principally of insects, which was considered one of the finest in Europe.

In March 1817 Macleay was retired on pension following the abolition of the transport board. He possessed other assets, including those in a family bank in Wick, which he had to sell in mid-1825 after the bank experienced difficulties. His income, however, proved insufficient for the needs of himself and his growing family, and in 1825 he accepted an offer from Earl Bathurst to become colonial secretary in New South Wales.

Macleay reached Sydney with his wife and six daughters on 5 January 1826, and formed a friendly relationship with Governor Ralph Darling and Henry Dumaresq, the governor's private secretary and brother-in-law. The three men worked so closely together that they were regarded as an 'inner cabinet'. Macleay handled official correspondence, liaised between governor and colonists, and sat on both the executive and legislative councils. He proved adept at his task, worked long hours, and provided constructive advice that helped Darling to overhaul the public service. He shared the governor's conservative outlook and incurred opprobrium for taking his side in the political conflicts of 1826–31. Macleay was unjustly accused by Darling's opponents of having used his position to further his own interests. Criticism, personal and political, persisted during the administration of Darling's successor, the urbane, liberal-minded Sir Richard Bourke. Macleay's relationship with the new governor, originally harmonious, deteriorated, and on 2 January 1837, tired of the struggle, he was eased out of office by Bourke, who appointed as replacement his own brother-in-law, Edward Deas Thompson. Macleay believed he had been wronged and took steps to defend his reputation. After Bourke's recall in 1838 he eventually received £1750 in commutation of his pension. In July 1843, following the coming of representative government, he was elected to the legislative council and in August he became the first speaker, a post he occupied until May 1846.

While performing his duties as colonial secretary, Macleay had become a landed proprietor. He received a grant of 54 acres overlooking Elizabeth Bay where, in 1837, he built a splendid Georgian-style mansion. Outside Sydney he acquired grazing properties at Byalla, Brownlow Hill, and Uladulla, as well as leases on the Murrumbidgee and Richmond Rivers. By 1844 he owned more than 9600 acres, 2600 by grant, the rest by purchase. Despite this, he experienced recurrent financial problems and was saved from insolvency only by the managerial skills of his eldest son, William Sharp *Macleay, one of seventeen children.

Throughout, Macleay maintained his scientific interests and continued to enlarge the collection he had brought from England. He kept in contact with the Royal and Linnean societies and worked on horticulture and natural history. In the Darling period, he became vice-patron of the Agricultural Society and made an important contribution to its work. He was also a strong supporter of the botanic gardens and of the Australian Museum, which he served as president. He helped promote cultural life through membership of the board of the subscription library from 1826, and he worked for the disadvantaged by assisting the Benevolent Society and the Sydney Dispensary.

On reaching Sydney, Macleay had been criticized by the judges Stephen and Dowling, among others, for 'ungentlemanly' looks, a 'vulgar Scotch dialect', and being 'too much stiffen'd in official life' to make a 'good government secretary'. Macleay proved his critics wrong and won deserved respect as colonial secretary and a distinguished scientist and public figure. His premature death, on 18 July 1848, at Elizabeth Bay House, Sydney, following a carriage accident, was widely regretted. He was buried at St James's Church, Sydney. Elizabeth Bay House and the Macleay Museum, which houses the collection he

started and his descendants enlarged, stand as further testaments to his work.

His third son, **Sir George Macleay** (1809–1891), pastoralist and traveller, was educated at Westminster School. After going out to Australia in 1827 he accompanied Charles Sturt in one of his exploring expeditions down the Murray River. He acquired substantial grazing interests. He was involved in politics and sat on the legislative council (1851–6) and in the legislative assembly (1856–9). Macleay was also a scientist and collector. He was created a CMG in 1869, and in 1875 became KCMG. After 1859 he travelled widely in Europe and the Near East. He was convivial and his wide circle of friends included politicians and scientists. He was married twice, first, in 1842, to Barbara St Clair (d. 1869), the daughter of Major James Innes of Scotland, and second, in 1890, to Augusta (d. 1919), the daughter of W. Sams of Launceston, Tasmania. Macleay died childless at Chalet des Rosiers, Menton, France, on 24 June 1891, while away from Pendell Court, Blechingley, Surrey, his home since about 1860.

G. S. BOULGER, *rev.* BRIAN H. FLETCHER

Sources Macleay volumes, Mitchell L., NSW, Macarthur MSS · Macleay MSS, Linn. Soc. · Norton Smith MSS, Mitchell L., NSW · colonial secretary's MSS, State Archives of New South Wales, Sydney · Mitchell L., NSW, Linnean Society of New South Wales MSS · NL Aus., Barker MSS · H. King, 'Man in a trap: Alexander Macleay, colonial secretary of New South Wales', *Royal Australian Historical Society Journal and Proceedings*, 68 (1982), 37–48 · H. King, *Richard Bourke* (1971) · B. H. Fletcher, *Ralph Darling: a governor maligned* (1984) · A. McMartin, *Public servants and patronage: the foundation and rise of the New South Wales public service* (1983) · *AusDB*
Archives Linn. Soc., corresp. and papers · Mitchell L., NSW | Linn. Soc., corresp. with Sir James Smith; letters to William Swainson · Mitchell L., NSW, Norton Smith and Linnean Society of New South Wales MSS · NL Aus., Barker MSS · State Archives of New South Wales, Sydney, colonial secretary's MSS
Likenesses T. Lawrence, oils, *c*.1825, Linn. Soc. · C. Fox, line engraving (after T. Lawrence), BM, NPG · portrait, State Library of New South Wales, Sydney, Dixson Gallery
Wealth at death £85,719 18*s*.; Sir George Macleay: probate, 1891

Macleay, Sir George (1809–1891). *See under* Macleay, Alexander (1767–1848).

Macleay, James Robert (1811–1892). *See under* Macleay, William Sharp (1792–1865).

MacLeay, Kenneth, the elder (*fl.* 1789–1829). *See under* MacLeay, Kenneth, the younger (1802–1878).

MacLeay, Kenneth, the younger (1802–1878), painter, was born in Oban, Argyll, on 19 July 1802 and baptized there on 21 July. He was the second of the three sons of Kenneth MacLeay the elder [*see below*] and his second wife, Flora (*b.* 1773), daughter of the Revd Patrick *Macdonald (1729–1824), musicologist, composer, and minister of the parish of Kilmore and Kilbride, in Argyll. **Kenneth MacLeay the elder** (*fl.* 1789–1829), self-styled surgeon and antiquary, is first recorded as a 'student of physic' and / or apothecary in Edinburgh in 1789, the year of his marriage to Agnes Dawson. By 1800 MacLeay, who may never have graduated as a surgeon, had settled in Oban, where he contracted a second marriage, to Flora Macdonald. The five children of

Kenneth MacLeay the younger (1802–1878), by David Octavius Hill and Robert Adamson, 1843–8

this marriage included the painters Kenneth MacLeay the younger and MacNeill MacLeay (1806–1883). While employed as a surgeon to the 3rd regiment of militia in Oban in 1810 the elder MacLeay published an informative geological account of the Spar cave recently discovered on Skye. Soon after 1813 he moved to Crieff, and in 1818 to Glasgow, in quest of improved prospects, both medical and literary. In 1817 he contributed to *Blackwood's Magazine* an account of Rob Roy MacGregor, which, when issued independently with a memoir of Lady Grange, enjoyed a notable if controversial success. In 1829, when nearly destitute, he appealed to Sir Walter Scott for financial assistance to take up an unspecified appointment in Inverness. Thereafter MacLeay disappears into obscurity.

While the family were at Crieff the younger MacLeay began copying engravings, and at Glasgow he probably received some rudimentary instruction in miniature painting. His earliest surviving miniatures, a self-portrait and a group portrait of Lady Sitwell of Renishaw and her eldest daughter, were both executed in watercolours on ivory in 1821. Over the winter of 1821–2 MacLeay moved permanently to Edinburgh and was admitted to the Trustees' Academy, with the Perthshire sculptor Laurence Macdonald, to study under the landscape painter Andrew Wilson.

Within his inaugural year MacLeay established a professional portrait practice, rapidly attaining financial self-sufficiency. In 1826, during the period when he exhibited as a miniaturist with the Institution for the Encouragement of the Fine Arts in Scotland, he painted an important Lawrentian miniature of Jane Baillie Welsh (Scot. NPG) shortly before her marriage to Thomas Carlyle. MacLeay's unchallenged supremacy among miniaturists then resident in Scotland was acknowledged by his election that year as a founding associate of the Scottish Academy, and in 1829 by his promotion to academician. From 1828 he became a prolific and annual supporter of the exhibitions of the academy, which latterly he also served as a visitor to the life class.

On 1 July 1840 MacLeay married Louisa Campbell (1817–1868), the eldest child of the fourth marriage of Colonel James Callander, or Campbell, of Craigforth, who had inherited by entail the estates of Ardkinglas. MacLeay had four daughters with Louisa Campbell, and two (or possibly three) sons. His growing professional ascendancy and relative financial security during the previous decade had been underpinned by his opportunistic exploitation of cabinet portraiture in watercolours as a fashionable alternative to miniatures. This genre, introduced into Edinburgh by William Nicholson, conformed to the compositional conventions of full-scale portraiture in oils and was developed by MacLeay in two equally popular and complementary styles. His decorative 'finished' manner, characterized by elaborately contextualized landscape or architectural settings, was epitomized by his 1847 portrait of the Revd Thomas Guthrie (Scot. NPG), and his allusively 'sketchy' manner by his 1844 full-length watercolour portrait of Helen Faucit, Lady Martin (Royal Scottish Academy, Edinburgh).

MacLeay's clientele for this type of portraiture encompassed both the middle-class social and intellectual élite of Edinburgh and the landed gentry and aristocracy of the west of Scotland. His bankruptcy in 1859 was occasioned, by his own testimony, by the advent of photography, which effectively destroyed his business as a portrait miniaturist and watercolourist. In 1858 he acquired the Edinburgh studio of the Hungarian photographer Iván Szabó. Until 1861 MacLeay exhibited as a photographer with the Photographic Society of Scotland, specializing in collodion portraits tinted with watercolour, but without enduring success (he is represented both as miniaturist and as photographer in the Scottish National Portrait Gallery).

In 1863 MacLeay's miniatures were especially commended by Prince Alfred at the exhibition of Scottish art staged in honour of the Social Science Congress in Edinburgh. The following year, on the recommendation of Noël Paton, Queen Victoria commissioned a miniature of the prince and watercolours of the princes Arthur and Leopold (Royal Collection). Her related commission in 1865 for a series of costume portraits of her favourite retainers at Balmoral evolved into an ambitious pictorial survey of the highland clans. This was completed in 1869 and published by royal command in 1870 as *The Highlanders of Scotland*, with chromolithographic reproductions after MacLeay's original watercolours. As a documentary record of contemporary tartan the publication was unrivalled and of considerable ethnological importance.

Royal patronage and public acclaim ultimately failed to relaunch MacLeay's career as a miniaturist. From 1830 to 1840 he had shared two successive studios in Edinburgh with his younger and less accomplished brother, the landscape painter MacNeill MacLeay (1806–1883). About 1848 MacNeill MacLeay made a tactical retreat to Stirling, following a scandal, probably of a financial rather than a personal nature, which also precipitated his resignation from associate membership of the Royal Scottish Academy. Kenneth MacLeay's independent experimentation with landscape painting in oils—both pure landscape and landscape imbued with literary and / or historical associations—dominated his exhibited work during his final decade as a strategy for professional survival. (As landscape painters both brothers are represented in Perth Museum and Art Gallery.)

MacLeay died of haematomesis on 3 November 1878 at his home, 3 Malta Terrace, in Edinburgh. After a funeral of Episcopalian rite he was buried in the 'West churchyard' (St Cuthbert's) on 7 November. In 1879 the queen purchased further drawings from his daughter Millicent, who in 1880 was awarded a civil-list pension for MacLeay's services to Scottish art. HELEN E. SMAILES

Sources H. Smailes, Kenneth MacLeay, 1802–78 (1992) · D. Millar, The highlanders of Scotland: the complete watercolours commissioned by Queen Victoria from Kenneth MacLeay of her Scottish retainers and clansmen (1986) · The Scotsman (4 Nov 1878) · The Scotsman (8 Nov 1878) · Edinburgh Evening Courant (4 Nov 1878) · Kenneth MacLeay's sequestration process and sederunt book, NA Scot., CS 318/5/227 · records of the Photographic Society of Scotland, NA Scot., GD 356 · J. Lawson, 'Bankruptcy through the lens: the case of Kenneth MacLeay', Bulletin of the Scottish Society for the History of Photography (spring 1986), 25–7 · C. B. de Laperriere, ed., The Royal Scottish Academy exhibitors, 1826–1990, 4 vols. (1991), vol. 3 · NL Scot., Blackwood MS 4003, fols. 148, 150, 152, 154, 156, 158; Blackwood MS 4004, fol. 196; Blackwood MS 4005, fols. 198–200 · NL Scot., Airth MS 10958, fol. 200 · K. MacLeay, letter to W. Scott, 7 Dec 1829, NL Scot., MS 3911, fol. 118 · K. MacLeay, letter to Sir Robert Peel, 6 Dec 1825, BL, Peel papers, Add. MS 40383, fol. 256 · bap. reg. Scot. · Fasti Scot., new edn, 4.95 · P. R. Drummond, Perthshire in bygone days (1879), 128 · m. reg. Scot. [Louisa Campbell; Agnes Dawson] · W. D. McKay and F. Rinder, The Royal Scottish Academy, 1826–1916 (1917)

Archives NA Scot., her sequestration process and sederunt book, CS 318/5/227 · priv. coll., MSS notebook 'Notes on the colours and mixture of colours in painting on ivory on paper and in oil' · Royal Scot. Acad., exhibition corresp. | BL, Peel MSS [Kenneth MacLeay the elder] · NA Scot., records of the Photographic Society of Scotland, GD 356 · National War Museum of Scotland, Edinburgh, 'A list of the officers of the local militia of Great Britain' (1811), p. 9 [Kenneth MacLeay the elder] · NL Scot., Airth MSS [Kenneth MacLeay the elder] · NL Scot., Blackwood MSS [Kenneth MacLeay the elder] · Royal Arch., corresp. relating to 'The highlanders of Scotland' commission, RA Y/167/21, RA Z/200/65, PP Vic 22184, PP Vic 17728, Add. MSS T (94)

Likenesses K. MacLeay, self-portrait, miniature, watercolour on ivory, 1821, priv. coll. · J. Gibson, oils, c.1829, Scot. NPG · D. O. Hill and R. Adamson, calotype photographs, c.1843–1847, Scot. NPG · D. O. Hill and R. Adamson, photograph, 1843–8, NPG [see illus.] · J. G. Tunny, photograph, c.1854, Royal Scot. Acad., J. G. Tunny album · J. M. Barclay, oils, c.1870, Royal Scot. Acad. · L. Ghémar, lithograph,

Scot. NPG · K. MacLeay, self-portrait, watercolour, NG Scot., MacLeay album, D. 4874, fol. 62 B · P. Park, bust (plaster model for marble); formerly at Royal Scot. Acad.; missing, presumed destroyed, 1990

Wealth at death £364 7s.—personal estate and effects at residence, 3 Malta Terrace: inventory, sheriff court, Edinburgh, NA Scot., SC 70/1/193, p. 877ff.

Macleay, Sir William John (1820–1891), naturalist and politician in Australia, was born on 13 June 1820 at Wick, Caithness, the second son of Kenneth Macleay (1765–1826) of Keiss, and his wife, Isabella (d. 1837), the daughter of J. Horne of Stirkoke, Caithness. He was educated at the Edinburgh Academy (1834–6) and began, but discontinued, studies at the University of Edinburgh. In 1839, on advice from his uncle Alexander Macleay in Australia, the orphaned William emigrated and settled in New South Wales.

Macleay worked initially on the family's pastoral holdings; by 1848 he had taken over a large property at Mulberrygong, on the Murrumbidgee River, and by 1857 he held six runs, totalling 314,000 acres. Under the influence of his uncle and his cousins William Sharpe and George Macleay, all noted naturalists in the colony, he also began to take a keen interest in natural history.

In 1855 Macleay was elected to the legislative council and in the following year to the newly formed legislative assembly, for Lachlan and Lower Darling; later he sat for the Murrumbidgee district, which he represented until 1874. In June 1857 he married Susan Emmeline (c.1839–1903), the daughter of Sir Edward Deas *Thomson, former New South Wales colonial secretary. They had no children.

In parliament Macleay chaired a large number of select committees, mainly as a result of the 'unusual tactic' (Hoare and Rutledge) he employed to press his own views by calling for the establishment of a committee and then ensuring his selection at its head. He was a committed and active promoter of protectionism. He was appointed to the legislative council in 1877.

The contribution for which Macleay is most noted was his support for scientific endeavours, in particular those of the Entomological (later Linnean) Society of New South Wales, of which he was the first president. The society noted that without Macleay's 'example and influence … and by his benefactions' (Fletcher, 567) over many years it might not have existed. He gave financial support to numerous specimen-collecting and scientific expeditions, and also published widely on insects and animals in the colonies. His valuable collections were donated on his death to the University of Sydney, along with a large endowment to ensure their upkeep. The Linnean Society received the bulk of his £81,000 estate.

Macleay was knighted in 1889. He died at his home at Elizabeth Bay, Sydney, on 7 December 1891, and was buried at Waverley cemetery, Sydney. MARC BRODIE

Sources J. J. Fletcher, 'The society's heritage from the Macleays', Proceedings [Linnean Society of New South Wales], 45 (1920), 567–78 · M. Hoare and M. Rutledge, 'Macleay, Sir William', AusDB, vol. 5 · *Fanny to William: the letters of Frances Leonora Macleay, 1812–1836*, ed. B. Earnshaw, J. Hughes, and L. Davidson (1993) · C. N. Connolly, *Biographical register of the New South Wales parliament, 1856–1901* (1983) · S. G. Foster, *Colonial improver: Edward Deas Thomson, 1800–1879* (1978) · DNB

Archives Linnean Society of New South Wales · Mitchell L., NSW | Mitchell L., NSW, Macarthur MSS · University of Sydney, log of the Chevert

Likenesses photographs, Mitchell L., NSW · portrait, repro. in T. S., *Australian portrait gallery* (1885) · portraits, repro. in P. Stanbury and J. Holland, eds., *Mr Macleay's celebrated cabinet* (1988)

Wealth at death over £81,000: AusDB

Macleay, William Sharp (1792–1865), entomologist, was born in London on 31 July 1792, the eldest son of the seventeen children of Alexander *Macleay (1767–1848), entomologist, colonial secretary (1825–36), and speaker (1843–6) of the first legislative council of New South Wales, and his wife, Elizabeth (1769–1847), daughter of James Barclay of Urie. After attending Westminster School (1806–10), in Michaelmas 1810 William matriculated at Trinity College, Cambridge, where he graduated BA (1814) and MA (1818). His father had amassed one of the largest private entomological collections in England, and he imparted his passion for natural history to his son, whose passion was fuelled by meeting leading French naturalists when he served as attaché to the British embassy in France (1814) and then as secretary to the board for liquidating British claims on the French government following the peace of 1815.

By his own account Macleay struck upon his unique 'quinarian' approach to taxonomy in 1817, claiming to have discovered a regularity in nature based on series of five. He published part 1 of *Horae entomologicae, or, Essays on the Annulose Animals* in 1819, and initially intended to study, according to a 'natural system', a particular grouping of beetles, Linnaeus's genus *Scarabaeus*, of which some 1800 species were in his father's cabinet. He sought to wed rigorous study of morphology and physiology to a symmetrical system worthy of 'the plan of creation itself, the work of an all-wise, all-powerful Deity' (Macleay, *Horae entomologicae*, xiii). Although he rejected the notion of an 'essential character', he struggled with the 'ignorance of physiological entomology' (ibid., xxv); the functions of few parts of insects were understood. Consequently, analogies of functions in Vertebrata were difficult, if not impossible, to discern when considering insects. Following J. C. Fabricius and C. De Geer, he argued that the one exception might be the mouthparts. But such heavy reliance on a single feature threatened to push him into the camp of the 'artificial systems' that he rejected. His solution was to emphasize the additional importance of an understanding of affinities, or variations, within similar organisms. By stressing 'variation in structure' (affinity) over 'difference in structure' (analogy), his chosen study of entomology became more relevant: the sheer number and diversity of insects promised the greatest hope of discerning a systematic chain of continuity in nature.

Macleay's quinary system was a response to French temporal progressionism and German *Naturphilosophie*. He asserted that to be truly natural groupings the series had to return to themselves or form circles, which, founded on relationships of affinity, were linked to other circles through relationships of analogy. This system permitted him to construct a chain of continuity based on gradation structure, but divorced from Lamarckian notions of 'order of formation' or a temporal process. Possessing an intimate knowledge of French zoological comparative anatomy, and aware of the revolutionary implications of the Lamarckian temporalization of the chain of being, Macleay responded with a curious mixture of comparative anatomy, British natural theology, and a classicist's reverence for the natural perfection of the circle.

Part 2 of *Horae entomologicae* (1821), published in the same year that Macleay was elected a member of the Linnean Society of London, aspired to extend the quinary system to the entire animal kingdom. However, most of the print run of part 1 was destroyed by fire, while copies of part 2 were damaged by flood. Macleay later speculated that fewer than 100 copies of the complete book remained in circulation. Nevertheless, quinarianism received considerable attention. The formation of the Zoological Club of the Linnean Society in 1822 provided Macleay's ideas with a forum, principally the *Zoological Journal*. Contributing approximately two dozen papers to the *Transactions of the Linnean Society*, the *Zoological Journal*, the *Philosophical Magazine*, the *Transactions of the Zoological Society*, and the *Annals and Magazine of Natural History*, Macleay devoted nearly his entire literary output to the defence and elaboration of quinarianism. The passions that his system aroused in natural history circles proved long-lived. H. E. Strickland's assessment (1844) was perhaps most accurate historically: 'Alchemy was the parent of chemistry, astrology of astronomy, and quinarianism has at least been one of the foster-parents of philosophical zoology' (Strickland, 172). Writing in late 1859, Charles Darwin informed both T. H. Huxley and Richard Owen that he feared publication of the *Origin of Species* would precipitate a 'case like Macleay's Quinarian system' (*Correspondence, 1858–1859*, 430). Specifically, he recalled Macleay's clash with the Revd John Fleming, and quoted some of the burning invective from Macleay's *Letter on the Dying Struggle of the Dichotomous System* (1830).

Macleay deployed his quinarian system in his *Annulosa Javanica* (1825), a systematic description of insects collected in Java between 1812 and 1817 by Thomas Horsfield under the auspices of the East India Company and Sir Stamford Raffles. On 1 August 1825 he was appointed commissioner of arbitration to the mixed British and Spanish court of commission for the abolition of the slave trade, and he moved to Guanabacoa, Cuba, where he cultivated orchids in his leisure hours. This posting restricted his active involvement in London's scientific circles for the next decade. On 20 February 1830 he became a commissary judge in the court of commission, and on 9 April 1836 he became judge of the mixed British and Spanish court of justice. He left Cuba for England later that year, and paused in the United States to meet and collect with

American naturalists. He was later elected a corresponding member of the Academy of Natural Sciences of Philadelphia. On 1 February 1837 he retired from public service on a pension of £900 per annum.

Back in England, Macleay rapidly reintegrated into London's scientific community. In 1837 he was elected to the councils of the Linnean Society, the Zoological Society, the Entomological Society of London, and the British Association for the Advancement of Science, and he served as president of section D at the association's annual meeting in Liverpool in September. Informally, he was equally influential: he implored Darwin to publish his zoological researches from the *Beagle* voyage. Macleay himself published *Illustrations of the Annulosa of South Africa* (1838), a systematic description of the Annulosa collected between 1834 and 1836 during an expedition, under the direction of Andrew Smith, funded by the Cape of Good Hope Association for Exploring Central Africa. He contended that his experience in the tropics and his recent acquisition of M. Verreaux's collection of South African Annulosa and manuscript notes fitted him admirably for the task.

After his years in the tropics, Macleay had difficulty readjusting to the English climate. Consequently, he decided to visit Australia, where his father and family had emigrated. Leaving England with his cousins, William and John, in late 1838, he arrived in Sydney in March 1839. Having originally intended to stay for three or four years, he remained for the rest of his life. He was in time to retrieve Alexander Macleay from the brink of insolvency. In the process he purchased Elizabeth Bay House to offset debts (1844–5), and irrevocably damaged relations with his parents.

Unfortunately, however, Macleay missed a possible reunion with his younger brother **James Robert Macleay** (1811–1892). Born on 15 April 1811, James was also educated at Westminster School, and was a king's scholar (1825). In Australia he and his elder brother George *Macleay [*see under* Macleay, Alexander] were in charge of their father's property at Brownlow Hill and the farm at Glendarewel attached to it. Shortly before leaving Australia to embark on a career in the Foreign Office, James joined the 22-week voyage of the *Comet* to Pitcairn Island to relocate the islanders to Otaheite in early 1831. He returned to England in 1837 and married Amelia Savage (*d.* 1887) in London. The following year he was appointed secretary to the legation in Chile, and from 1843 to 1858 he was secretary and registrar to the mixed British and Portuguese commission for the suppression of the slave trade at the Cape of Good Hope. He retired on an annual pension of £166 on 1 May 1858, and died at 49 Queen's Gate Gardens, Kensington, London, on 28 October 1892.

Renowned for its gardens and its occupants, the Macleay house at Elizabeth Bay acted as a magnet for local and visiting intellectuals. John Gould, J. D. Hooker, William Swainson, and T. H. Huxley all paid visits there to William Sharp Macleay. The latter's strongest and most enduring friendship was with Robert Lowe and his wife, to each of whom he bequeathed £1000 in his will. Lowe remembered Macleay as unparalleled in conversational powers:

> He was an excellent classical scholar, he knew more of modern history and biography than anyone with whom I was ever acquainted, and in addition to all this he was a profoundly scientific man. … An excellent companion, with a store of caustic wit, he reminded me continually of the best part of Scott's *Antiquary*.   (Martin, 1.41)

Macleay played a minor role in Sydney's public life: in 1848 he was a commissioner of national education and in 1855 he served on the executive council under Sir William Denison. An architect of the act to establish and endow the Australian Museum, he served on its committee (1841–53) and as an elective trustee (1853–62). He published little in Australia after 1839: four papers in the *Annals and Magazine of Natural History*, two letters to the *Sydney Morning Herald*, and the occasional contribution to the *Atlas*. In a letter to Lowe, dated May 1860, he wrote about the *Origin of Species*, and confessed his inability to part with cherished religious beliefs that seemed to clash with Darwin's theory:

> This living cell of matter … has been constantly and actively sprouting forth by natural selection into all forms of animals and vegetables that ever have existed or will hereafter exist. All special interference of a Creator with it Darwin repeatedly denies. I am myself so far a Pantheist that I see God in everything: but then I believe in His special Providence, and that He is the constant and active sole Creator and all-wise Administrator of the Universe. (Martin, 2.206)

Four years later Macleay was writing to inform his friends of his declining health. With the onset of diabetes in 1862 and persistent visitations of gout, he found himself considerably weakened: 'I never was what you would call a decided beauty; but if you were to see me now, you would not know the ugly, lanky, thin, scraggy, toothless individual' (Martin, 2.235). In the late afternoon of 26 January 1865 he slipped into unconsciousness, and died at seven o'clock in the evening at Elizabeth Bay House. A funeral service was held two days later, when Macleay was buried in the family vault in what was then known as Camperdown cemetery, near St Stephen's Church, Newtown, Sydney. In addition, a cenotaph to his memory was placed in St James's Church, King Street. A lifelong bachelor, he left the majority of his estate to his brother George. In accordance with an agreement dated 24 May 1863, the combined insect collection of Alexander and William Sharp Macleay, which totalled 100,000–150,000 specimens, was bequeathed to his cousin and entomological protégé, Sir William John Macleay. After making his own additions to the collection, Sir William faithfully adhered to the terms of the bequest and donated it to the University of Sydney, where in 1888 it became the core of the Macleay Museum.   J. F. M. CLARK

Sources *The Zoologist*, 23 (1865), 9584 · *Proceedings of the Linnean Society of London* (1864–5), ci–ciii · *The Times* (15 April 1865), 11 · J. J. Fletcher, 'The society's heritage from the Macleays', *Proceedings of the Linnean Society of New South Wales*, 45 (1920), 567–635 · *AusDB* · J. J. Fletcher, ed., *The Macleay memorial volume* (1893) · A. Patchett Martin, *Life and letters of the Right Honourable Robert Lowe, Viscount Sherbrooke*, 2 vols. (1893) · Venn, *Alum. Cant.*, 2/4.278 · *The correspondence* of *Charles Darwin*, ed. F. Burkhardt and S. Smith, 2 (1986) · *The correspondence of Charles Darwin*, ed. F. Burkhardt and S. Smith, 7 (1991) · L. Huxley, *Life and letters of Thomas Henry Huxley*, [new edn], 1 (1913) · A. Desmond, 'The making of institutional zoology in London, 1822–1836', *History of Science*, 23 (1985), 153–85, 223–50 · D. S. Horning jun., 'The Macleay insect collection', *Antenna*, 8 (1984), 172–5 · J. Holland, 'Diminishing circles: W. S. Macleay in Sydney, 1839–1865', *Historical Records of Australian Science*, 11 (1996–7), 119–47 · A. T. Gage and W. T. Stearn, *A bicentenary history of the Linnean Society of London* (1988) · W. Swainson, *Taxidermy: bibliography and biography* (1840) · M. P. Winsor, *Starfish, jellyfish, and the order of life: issues in nineteenth-century science* (1976) · P. F. Rehbock, *The philosophical naturalists: themes in early nineteenth-century British biology* (1983) · D. Ospovat, *The development of Darwin's theory: natural history, natural theology, and natural selection, 1838–1859* (1981) · *Fanny to William: the letters of Frances Leonora Macleay, 1812–1836*, ed. B. Earnshaw, J. Hughes, and L. Davidson (1993) · P. Stanbury and J. Holland, eds., *Mr Macleay's celebrated cabinet: the history of the Macleays and their museum* (1988) · W. S. Macleay, *Horae entomologicae, or, Essays on the annulose animals* (1819–21) · W. S. Macleay, 'Remarks on the comparative anatomy of certain birds of Cuba, with a view to their respective places in the system of nature or to their relations with other animals', *Transactions of the Linnean Society of London*, 16 (1833), 1–46 · H. E. Strickland, 'Report on the recent progress and present state of ornithology', *Report of the British Association for the Advancement of Science*, 14 (1845), 170–221

Archives Linn. Soc., corresp. and papers · University of Sydney, Macleay Museum, insect collection and MSS | Oxf. U. Mus. NH, Hope Collection, F. W. Hope and J. O. Westwood MSS and insects **Likenesses** C. Summers, marble bust, 1870, Linn. Soc. · lithograph, Linn. Soc.; copies, Australian Museum and Macleay Museum, Sydney, Australia · medallion on cenotaph, St James's Church, Sydney, Australia

Maclehose [*née* Craig], **Agnes** (1758–1841), letter writer and poet, was born in Glasgow on 26 April 1758, the third of four daughters of Andrew Craig (*d.* 1782), a surgeon, and his wife, Christian (*d.* 1767), daughter of John *Maclaurin, a minister of the Scottish church. She later attributed her piety to the religious training that she received from her mother during her early childhood. She had little formal education, although her father did send her to a boarding-school in Edinburgh for six months when she was fifteen, by which time all her siblings were dead. It was on a journey to Edinburgh that she met James Maclehose (*c.*1754–1812), a lawyer from Glasgow, whom she married on 1 July 1776. According to a story told at the time, he saw her in Glasgow and was so struck by her beauty that he booked all the other seats on the coach on which she was travelling so that he could be alone with her on the ten-hour journey. The marriage proved to be very unhappy, and they formally separated in December 1780. James Maclehose took custody of their two sons (a third son had died in infancy), both under three at the time; he later took custody also of their youngest child, born a few months after the separation. Agnes Maclehose remained with her father until his death, in 1782, when she moved to Edinburgh. By that time James Maclehose had gone to London—where he eventually ended up in a debtors' prison—and Agnes had recovered her children; she supported herself and them on a small annuity left by her father, and subsequently with the help of a cousin, William Craig, later Lord Craig.

Agnes Maclehose (1758–1841), by John Miers, 1788

During her time in Edinburgh, Agnes Maclehose cultivated literary interests and friendships and, as she started writing poetry herself, she became passionately interested in the poetry of her contemporaries. In December 1787 she arranged to be introduced to Robert Burns at the house of a mutual friend. On Christmas eve she sent him the verses 'When first you saw Clarinda's charms', and thereafter she and Burns corresponded, using the pseudonyms Clarinda and Sylvander. It is this correspondence for which Agnes Maclehose became known. Most of the letters date from the winter of 1787–8 and were written in the fashionable, sentimental style of the 1780s; in one of her early letters Maclehose described the correspondence as 'the effusion of a benevolent heart upon meeting one similar to itself' (Barr, 25). On 3 January 1788 she sent Burns a poem beginning 'Talk not of Love! It gives me pain'. Burns thought that the second half of the first stanza was worthy of Sappho, and sent the verses with some alteration and an additional stanza for publication in Johnson's *Musical Museum*, where they were set to the air 'The Banks of Spey'. On 19 January Maclehose sent Johnson lines 'To a Blackbird Singing on a Tree', with an additional stanza by Burns, which were also published in the *Museum*. Despite being reminded by Maclehose that she was a married woman Burns proclaimed himself devoted to her, declaring at one point 'I esteem you, I love you, as a friend, I admire you, I love you as a woman, beyond any one in the circle of creation' (ibid., 157–8). She meanwhile insisted that while never 'were there two hearts formed so exactly alike as ours' she was nevertheless 'shock[ed]' by Burns's 'avowal of being an enemy to Calvinism' (ibid., 58) and deeply troubled by the potential 'criminality' of their friendship (ibid., 122). Her main hope in writing to him, she insisted repeatedly, was to make him 'embrace the Gospel' (ibid., 83) and 'feel a little of the genuine gospel humility' (ibid., 114) that she drew from her strong Calvinist faith—a goal which she clearly failed to achieve.

Unsurprisingly the correspondence lapsed following Burns's marriage to Jean Armour in August 1788. Agnes Maclehose apparently heard of the marriage from their mutual friend Robert Ainslie; though her letter to Burns on that occasion does not survive it is clear from his response that she indignantly broke off the correspondence. While they did exchange some letters in the early 1790s, in which Maclehose enclosed lines on 'Sympathy', they met only once more, in December 1791, shortly before Agnes Maclehose set off to join her husband, then in Jamaica, in a final effort to salvage her marriage. Her departure in February 1792 was the incident that led Burns to compose 'Ae Fond Kiss'—perhaps the most famous of the poems inspired by Clarinda. The journey to Jamaica was an utter failure—James Maclehose did not even bother to meet his wife when she landed—and Agnes remained there less than three months. By August 1792 she was back in Edinburgh, explaining that poor health prevented her from remaining in a tropical climate, although in a memoir written after her death her grandson claimed that James Maclehose's mistreatment of his slaves—and his wife's discovery that he kept a slave mistress—were the decisive factors in her departure. For much of the rest of her husband's life Agnes Maclehose attempted to claim court-ordered support payments for the education of her one surviving son, but she received almost no money from him and remained dependent on her cousin Lord Craig (who died in 1813) and, later, on her son, who became a writer to the signet in Edinburgh. After her return from Jamaica she spent the rest of her life in Edinburgh, enjoying what social life she could in her relatively straitened circumstances. Later in her life she was apparently sought out by Burns's admirers as a living link with the poet; she seems to have encouraged such interest and to have remembered fondly her relatively brief friendship with him. In December 1831 she noted the fortieth anniversary of their final meeting in her diary, and, according to one account, even in her old age she 'never wearied of telling the story of her flirtation with Burns' (Ross, 224).

However much she might have enjoyed reminiscing about the affair in her old age Agnes Maclehose was careful to retain control of the letters after Burns's death. In negotiations with his biographers Alexander Cunningham and John Syme she offered to select passages from his letters to her in exchange for the return of her own; she eventually succeeded in recovering the manuscripts, and only a few passages from Burns's side of the correspondence were published during her lifetime. The result was that there was considerable speculation about the relationship among Burns's biographers and admirers; Clarinda's reputation was both attacked and defended for years afterwards. Cunningham himself wrote slightingly of her that 'for aught I know [she] may be as chaste as Diana, but ... [she] bears a quisquis character in the World' (McIntyre, 406). In his biography of Burns, John Gibson Lockhart scarcely mentions Clarinda, except to dismiss the published excerpts of Burns's side of the correspondence as a regrettable lapse on his part into 'bad taste, bombastic language, and fulsome sentiment' (Lockhart, 121). Even the biographer and memoirist Robert Chambers, a friend and admirer of Agnes Maclehose who met her long after Burns's death, thought it 'almost necessary to have

known the woman' to appreciate the 'perfect innocence of [her] nature' (Chambers, 358–9).

Agnes Maclehose died at her home at Calton Hill, Edinburgh, on 22 October 1841. Soon afterwards her grandson published, for the first time, both sides of the correspondence—minus some of her letters, which she had apparently destroyed, and some passages from Burns's letters, which according to the preface had been destroyed by frequent handling as Agnes Maclehose showed them to visitors or cut pieces out for autograph hunters. Once in print the letters encouraged admirers of Burns to romanticize the affair; as one Victorian writer proclaimed in a volume of tributes to her, 'among the heroines of Burns, Agnes M'Lehose is not the least deserving of honour as an honest, a beautiful, and a gifted woman' (Ross, x).

PAM PERKINS

Sources J. MacKay, *Burns* (1992) · A. J. Barr, ed., *Sylvander and Clarinda* (New York, 1917) · J. D. Ross, ed., *Burns' Clarinda* (1897) · I. McIntyre, *Dirt and deity* (1995) · J. G. Lockhart, *Life of Burns* (New York, 1907) · R. Chambers, *Traditions of Edinburgh, 1824* (1967) · *Annual Register* (1841)
Likenesses J. Miers, silhouette, 1788, Scot. NPG [*see illus.*] · A. Banks, engraving (after Miers), repro. in W. S. Douglas, ed., *The works of Robert Burns* · woodcut (aged forty; after silhouette), repro. in W. S. Douglas, ed., *The works of Robert Burns*

MacLehose, James (1811–1885), bookseller and publisher, was born in Govan, near Glasgow, on 16 March 1811, the eldest son of Thomas MacLehose, a weaver, and Jean McLean. When he was twelve he was apprenticed for seven years to a relative, George Gallie, a bookseller and stationer in Glasgow. While with him he became a close friend of a fellow apprentice in the book trade, Daniel Macmillan. In 1833 he went to London to gain experience with Seeley & Co., booksellers in Fleet Street. When Macmillan was unable to find employment in the south, MacLehose got him a position with Seeleys and they remained close friends for the rest of their lives. MacLehose returned to Glasgow in 1838 and went into business with Robert Nelson. The partnership was dissolved in 1841 and MacLehose continued in business alone, opening a circulating library—the Western Book Club—in the same year.

This was a period of intense religious debate in Scotland and in 1843 MacLehose began publishing religious tracts for seceders. His authors included Dr Hugh Heugh and Dr W. L. Anderson. In 1849 he moved his shop to St Vincent Street, which soon became 'the centre round which gathered almost daily, most of the literary and intellectual talent of his city' (MacLehose, *Glasgow University Press*, 246). His book trade concentrated on the ancient world and European theological and literary works, many of which were purchased through London agents. He also acted as bookseller to the Faculty of Physicians and Surgeons of Glasgow and the Glasgow Faculty of Procurators. He expanded his publishing business to include local and Scottish titles, for example the works of Jemima Blackburn, the wife of the professor of mathematics at the University of Glasgow, and Thomas Annan, the celebrated

Glasgow photographer. A fine bindery was opened in Glasgow during 1862 and two years later MacLehose was appointed bookseller to the university. Macmillan, by then a very successful publisher, offered him a partnership in 1865, which he refused, opening instead a printing shop in Ayr in partnership with his brother Robert McPhail MacLehose (1820–1910), a bookseller in that town. Macmillan's immediately began to patronize the new works.

With his connections in Glasgow, James MacLehose was well placed to succeed Charles Griffin as printer to the University of Glasgow in 1871. His first publication for Professor Hugh Blackburn and Professor Sir William Thomson was a new edition of Newton's *Principia mathematica* published in that year. He soon began publishing textbooks and monographs for university staff, numbering among his authors the brothers John and Edward Caird, William Leishman, John Nichol, and John Veitch. The university press of George Richardson in Glasgow was acquired in 1872 and the printing business, which traded as Robert MacLehose, moved from Ayr.

On 18 July 1850 MacLehose had married Louisa Sing, *née* Jackson; they had three sons and four daughters. He took his two eldest sons, Robert and James, into partnership in 1881. Two of his sons, James and Norman, cemented relations with the Macmillans by marrying daughters of Alexander. Although well known in Glasgow, MacLehose never played an active part in public affairs. He died in Glasgow on 20 December 1885 and his widow died on 13 June 1898.   MICHAEL S. MOSS

Sources C. M. MacLehose, genealogical notes supplied by Lord MacLehose (1997) · *Books published by James MacLehose from 1838 to 1881 and by James MacLehose & Sons to 1905 presented to the library of the University of Glasgow* (1905) · *Catalogue of books published by James MacLehose & Sons* (1887) · J. MacLehose, *The Glasgow University Press, 1638–1931: with some notes on Scottish printing in the last three hundred years* (1931) · C. Morgan, *The house of Macmillan, 1843–1943* (1943)

MacLehose, (Crawford) Murray, Baron MacLehose of Beoch (1917–2000), diplomatist and colonial administrator, was born on 16 October 1917 in Partick, Glasgow, the second son of Hamish Alexander MacLehose (1886–1962), master printer, of Glenmilne, Campsie Glen, Stirlingshire (who was then serving as a major in the 8th battalion, Scottish Rifles), and his wife, Margaret Bruce Black. His parents were both Scottish. He followed his father to Rugby School (1931–6), where he was captain of fives and winner of the king's medal for a prize essay on Talleyrand, and Balliol College, Oxford (1936–9), where he read modern history (BA 1939).

Having joined the Malayan civil service in 1939, MacLehose was sent in 1940 to learn the Hokkien dialect in south-east China, attached to the British consulate in Amoy (Xiamen). The advancing Japanese interned him from December 1941 to October 1942. After repatriation, he returned to China in February 1943 as a lieutenant in the Royal Naval Volunteer Reserve (1942–5), running an intelligence operation with Chinese guerrillas behind Japanese lines. For these services in China, carried out in the face of severe hardship, he was appointed MBE (military)

in 1946. He served as acting consul in Fuzhou in 1944–6 and joined the foreign service in May 1947. On 24 June 1947 he married Margaret Noël (Squeak) Dunlop, the daughter of Thomas Charles Dunlop, newspaper proprietor. Their twin daughters, Elfrida and Sylvia, were born in 1949.

MacLehose was sent again to China for consular service in Hangchow (Hangzhou) (1947–9). He returned in January 1950 to the Foreign Office in London, then between 1951 and 1959 he served as first secretary in Prague, head of chancery in Wellington, and commercial secretary in Paris. Promoted counsellor in 1959, he was seconded to the Hong Kong government as political adviser to the governor, Sir Robert Black. This was followed by service as head of the Far Eastern department in the Foreign Office (1963–5). In 1964 he was created CMG. He was then principal private secretary (1965–7) to two temperamentally quite different foreign secretaries, Michael Stewart and George Brown. The latter referred appreciatively to him in his memoirs as 'my gloomy Scot' (*In my Way*, 1971, 128). Two ambassadorships followed. In the early days of the Vietnam War MacLehose was accredited to the government of South Vietnam (1967–9), from where he transferred to Denmark (1969–71). To his sadness, he had to leave Copenhagen early, compensated by the honour of a KCMG on his appointment as governor and commander-in-chief of Hong Kong (1971–82).

Although he was the first of a new breed of governors chosen from the Foreign Office rather than from colonial ranks, MacLehose was one of the most outstanding under British rule, governing Hong Kong firmly with vision and great distinction for ten and a half years. The wide experience he had gained in his early career was good training for the challenge of the governorship. Independent action as a young man behind Japanese lines, working knowledge of Asian and Soviet communism, experience of both Commonwealth and colonial practices, and being private secretary to two foreign secretaries all gave him insight into the problems of modern government, Britain's place in the post-imperial world, and the complex relations between China and the West.

MacLehose succeeded in changing the image of Hong Kong from that of a conservative crown colony to that of a modern, prosperous, international commercial and financial centre living at peace with, and of value to, China in its post-Mao reforms. With the help of an American consultancy firm, he reformed the outdated colonial administration; he assaulted an endemic problem through the setting up of the independent commission against corruption, even though it meant confronting a subsequent police-force mutiny; he gave the administration a caring image through a ten-year housing scheme and massive progress in education; he made the government of Hong Kong more responsive to public opinion by reforming local councils and introducing district boards. He dealt successfully in his usual practical style with the problems of illegal Chinese immigration and Vietnamese boat people. The Hong Kong arts festival was conceived at his insistence. In these manifold directions, he created a flourishing, confident Hong Kong with an international reputation.

An austere, tall, and gaunt figure, MacLehose towered over his colleagues both physically and mentally. His somewhat aloof presence concealed a warm heart and ready sense of fun. He was a man of great integrity. Though often blunt, he was never afraid to admit error, and his innate kindness and the ability to connect with the common people of Hong Kong inspired huge public respect. He loved paddling about in a little boat (part of a love of the sea which went back to crewing in a yacht for the Seawanhaka cup in 1938). He also enjoyed walking in the hills of the New Territories. Villagers were often surprised to see the tall governor appear in remote areas, asking how things were in their district and clearing up rubbish on their beaches. The local expatriates, equally surprised by his vigour and resource, referred to him with affectionate respect as Jock the Sock or the Big Mac. He was later criticized at home and by pressure groups in Hong Kong for not trying to introduce a more democratic form of government. But, with pragmatic realism, he understood the danger of alarming Beijing into thinking that Hong Kong was being set on a path to independence, something no Chinese government could ever countenance. As a mark of respect and in tune with their new 'opening-up' policy of economic reform, the Chinese government invited him to visit Beijing in 1979, making his the first official visit by a governor since the communist take-over in 1949. The visit was memorable as the first step on the path to discussions on the future of Hong Kong after 1997. The visit enabled Deng Xiaoping to give the helpful reassurance through the governor that the Hong Kong people should 'put their hearts at ease', thus indicating the Chinese government's willingness to see capitalism continue in Hong Kong for a long time after 1997 while socialism was maintained in China.

MacLehose was one of the last great British pro-consuls. When he left in early 1982, having been the longest-serving governor, the *South China Morning Post* issued a special supplement, 'The MacLehose years', in which the editorial conclusion was that he was 'the right man at the right time'. He was appointed knight of St John (1972), KCVO (1975, after the memorable first visit by a British monarch to Hong Kong), and GBE (1976). On retirement he was created a life peer as Baron MacLehose of Beoch (his much loved Beoch farm was near his father's home in Ayrshire). In 1983 the queen honoured him as a knight of the Thistle.

With characteristic energy and public spirit, MacLehose continued to work hard after retirement. He was a deputy lieutenant of Ayr and Arran. He was a director of the National Westminster Bank (1982–8), and chaired the Scottish Trust for the Physically Disabled (1982–90) and the Margaret Blackwood Housing Association (1982–90). He was also president of the Great Britain–China Centre (1982–93) and chairman of governors of the School of Oriental and African Studies, London University (1985–90). The universities of York, Strathclyde, and Hong Kong

awarded him honorary degrees (in 1983, 1984, and 1990 respectively). He played a full part in the House of Lords, sitting on the cross-benches, offering experience and common sense on the future of Hong Kong. This was particularly valuable during the run-up to the resumption of Chinese sovereignty in 1997. Being apprehensive about the potential consequences of the political reforms proposed by Governor Patten in 1992, he warned in the House of Lords against making the Hong Kong people 'heroic pawns' in Sino–British quarrels and made the point that 'the power, reasonable expectation and rights of the Chinese Government' could be disregarded 'only at the peril of Hong Kong' (*Hansard 5L*, vol. 54, col. 221, 9 Dec 1992). Throughout his life MacLehose was most loyally supported by his wife. He died peacefully in Ayr Hospital on 27 May 2000, survived by his wife and their two daughters. A memorial service was held on 13 July 2000 at St Margaret's, Westminster.   ALAN DONALD

Sources *The Times* (1 June 2000) · *Daily Telegraph* (1 June 2000) · *The Guardian* (2 June 2000) · *The Independent* (2 June 2000) · *The Scotsman* (2 June 2000) · *The Scotsman* (8 June 2000) · Burke, *Peerage* · WWW · *International who's who* · *Rugby School register* · *Balliol College register* · personal knowledge (2004) · private information (2004) [Lady MacLehose, Lord Wilson of Tillyorn] · b. cert. · m. cert. · d. cert.
Archives NRA priv. coll., papers
Likenesses photograph, 1967, repro. in *The Times* · photograph, 1971, repro. in *Daily Telegraph* · photograph, *c*.1982, repro. in *The Guardian* · photograph, *c*.1982, repro. in *The Scotsman* (2 June 2000) · photograph, repro. in *The Independent* · photographs, priv. coll.

MacLellan, Angus [Aonghus Beag mac Aonghuis 'ic Eachainn 'ic Dhomhnaill 'ic Chaluim 'ic Dhomhnaill, Aonghus mac 'ill' Fhialain] (1869–1966), storyteller and farm worker, was born at Poll Torain, Loch Eynort, South Uist, Inverness-shire, on 7 July 1869, the youngest son of Angus MacLellan, grass-keeper, and his wife, Mary, *née* Wilson. The younger Angus was one of the last great traditional Gaelic storytellers of South Uist, Inverness-shire, a crofter–fisherman and a skilled farm worker with horses and sheep; his sister, Mrs Neil Campbell, who lived to be 100, was said to have been the last monoglot Gaelic speaker on South Uist, and was herself the teller of pithy anecdotes and a singer of Gaelic ballads and old waulking songs.

A collection of forty-five of MacLellan's stories, including his version of *Fionn saga* and a number of international folk tales, was published in translation in 1961 as *Stories from South Uist*. Many other stories which he recorded have still to be transcribed and translated. His story of Conall Gulbann was published in volume 44 of the *Transactions of the Gaelic Society of Inverness* as a Gaelic text with English précis by J. L. Campbell. His version of the 'Cattle Raid of Cooley' was published by Dr Calum MacLean in *Arv* (20. 160–80).

Much historical and sociological interest attaches to MacLellan's autobiography, published in 1962 in translation as *The Furrow Behind Me*. Taken from a recording, the Gaelic text was published in the *Norsk Tidsskrift for Sprogvidenskap* in 1972 and entitled *Saoghal an treobhaiche* ('The ploughman's world'). It is the longest text in colloquial Scottish Gaelic and includes his memories of life as a farm worker for Robert Menzies at Tirinie (1889–93) and Thomas MacDonald at Borenich (1893–4) (both farms in Perthshire), for Edward Kane at Rowardennan on Loch Lomondside (1895–7), and for Duncan Fraser at Dalmally, Argyll (1898–1900), in the days when farm workers in the highlands signed on to work for six months for about £15 and potatoes and milk.

Later MacLellan went home to help his parents in Uist, and in 1908 he obtained the official status of a crofter there. His stories and his memories are told with a wealth of dialogue and characterization which would do credit to a professional novelist. MacLellan was made MBE in 1965 for his great contribution to the preservation of Gaelic oral literature and was also an honorary chieftain of the Gaelic Society of Inverness. He died unmarried at 6 Frobost, South Uist, on 19 March 1966 and was buried at Hanlainn on that island.   J. L. CAMPBELL

Sources personal knowledge (2004) · A. McLellan, *Saoghal an Treobhaiche* (1972) · A. McLellan, *The furrow behind me* (1962) · B. R. S. Megaw, 'Finding the hidden Scotland', *TLS* (9 April 1964) · b. cert. · d. cert.
Archives SOUND c/o J. L. Campbell, Island of Canna, Canna collection of recordings on ediphone, wire, and tape of Gaelic oral tradition from South Uist, Barra, and Nova Scotia, made between 1937 and 1968
Likenesses photographs, priv. coll.
Wealth at death small flock of sheep

McLellan, Archibald (1795/1797–1854), art collector and local politician, was born in Glasgow, the son of Archibald McLellan (1746/7–1831), a coachbuilder, and his wife, Christian Shillinglaw (*fl. c.*1774–1832). He was educated in Glasgow, at the grammar school from 1804 and afterwards at the University of Glasgow, where he matriculated in 1808. McLellan joined his father's firm and, after learning the trade, became a partner. He entered the trades house and local politics as a young man. As a tory he was often challenged by the *Reformers' Gazette*, a radical magazine published in Glasgow in the 1830s. He opposed the Reform Bill of 1832, but supported the Scotch Municipal Reform Bill which ensured that Glasgow's trades and merchants houses retained their involvement in municipal affairs.

McLellan was closely involved in a number of Glasgow's cultural and educational institutions. He joined the Glasgow Dilettanti Society in 1825 and became its president in 1834. At one of the society's meetings he read an essay on the poor condition of the city's St Mungo's Cathedral which resulted in the publication of *An Essay on the Cathedral Church of Glasgow* (1833) and the building's subsequent restoration. He was appointed a trustee of Anderson's University in 1840, served on the Glasgow Art Union's management committee, supported the scheme to establish an institute of the fine arts, and was president of the City of Glasgow Fine Art Association at its foundation in 1853. McLellan was also a book collector and an accomplished musician. He strongly believed in supporting native talent and was one of a number of Glasgow citizens opposed to Archibald Alison's motion to commission a foreign artist to produce an equestrian statue of the duke of Wellington for the city. McLellan set out his argument against the proposal in *A Letter to Archibald Alison*

which was published about 1840 for private circulation. He and his fellow objectors were unsuccessful and the work was undertaken by Carlo Marochetti.

McLellan is best-known for his large collection of old master paintings and for the gallery constructed to house them on Glasgow's Sauchiehall Street; it was part of a commercial development, one of several property interests that he had in the city. The collection, to which he devoted thirty years, and which included the Dutch, Flemish, Italian, French, and British schools, was discussed in Gustav Waagen's *Treasures of Art in Great Britain* (1854); he found in McLellan 'a most ardent lover of the arts' (Waagen, 286). McLellan wanted his collection and gallery to be open to the public and appointed trustees to administer them for the people of Glasgow. However, he died from heart disease at his country residence, Mugdock Castle, Stirlingshire, on 22 October 1854, before the building work was finished.

At his death, McLellan's finances were in disarray, presenting the trustees with serious problems. However, the McLellan Gallery did open to the public in 1855, and in the following year, after a long and difficult debate, the Glasgow corporation agreed to buy the buildings and pictures for a total of £44,500. Glasgow then possessed the country's first civic-funded art gallery and the basis of one of the finest public art collections (now housed in the city's Kelvingrove Art Gallery and Museum). McLellan's pictures include Sandro Botticelli's *Annunciation*, Bernard van Orley's *Virgin and Child by a Fountain*, Jacob Jordaens's *Fruit Seller*, and Giorgione's *The Adulteress Brought before Christ*.

Archibald McLellan was a highly regarded public figure, influential in Glasgow's business and cultural life. While the radical *Reformers' Gazette* challenged his social conscience, his obituary in the *Glasgow Courier* described him as 'warm, impetuous and irascible' as well as 'generous, open-hearted, kind and hospitable' (*Glasgow Courier*, 24 Oct 1854). He never married but had two children: Archibald, with Isabella Hutcheson (*fl. c.*1825–c.1911), and Christina, with Elizabeth Park. He was buried in the new churchyard at St Mungo's Cathedral on 27 October 1854.

GEORGE FAIRFULL SMITH

Sources *Glasgow Courier* (24 Oct 1854) · *Glasgow Herald* (27 Oct 1854) · J. MacLehose, ed., *Memoirs and portraits of one hundred Glasgow men who have died during the last thirty years*, 2 (1886) · M. Park, 'The McLellan bequest', *Scottish Art Review*, 17 (1991), 22–5 · J. Morrison, 'Victorian municipal patronage', *Journal of the History of Collections*, 8 (1996), 93–102 · E. Gallie, 'Archibald McLellan', *Scottish Art Review*, 5/1 (1954), 7–11 · *Reformers' Gazette* (1832–6) · *The McLellan Gallery: catalogue of pictures bequeathed to the people of Glasgow by the late Archibald McLellan* (1855) · J. Paton, *The fine art collection of Glasgow* (1906) · 'Profiles of former directors: Archibald McLellan', *Glasgow Chamber of Commerce Journal*, 55/6 (June 1970), 296–7 · G. F. Waagen, *Treasures of art in Great Britain*, 3 (1854), 286–91 · wills and testaments of Archibald McLellan, NA Scot., 966/375/137, 966/377/137 · trust disposition and settlement and deed of bequest, NA Scot., 966/362/137, 966/355/136 · Glasgow grammar school classbooks, Mitchell L., Glas., MS 140/16/2 and 3 · 'Estate of the late Archibald McLellan', *Glasgow Courier* (10 Feb 1855) · *The Post Office directory* [annuals] · bur. reg. Scot.

Likenesses stipple, pubd 1815, V&A · E. Robertson, watercolour miniature, 1834, Glasgow Museums, Glasgow, Scotland · J. Graham Gilbert, oils, 1839, Trades' Hall of Glasgow, Glasgow, Scotland · R. C. Crawford, bust (after portrait by J. Graham Gilbert, 1839), Glasgow Museums, Glasgow · W. Graham, photograph (after silhouette by A. Edouart, 1831), Mitchell L., Glas., William Graham collection

Wealth at death sequestrated estate of the late Archibald McLellan; art gallery and picture collection purchased by the city for £44,500: *Glasgow Courier* (10 Feb 1855)

Maclellan, John (1609–1650), Church of Scotland minister, was born in Kirkcudbright, the son of Michael Maclellan, a burgess of that town. He graduated MA from Glasgow University in 1629. Shortly afterwards he emigrated to Ireland and soon distinguished himself as an able schoolmaster at Newtownards, co. Down, inspiring his pupils and coaching 'several hopeful youths' for university entrance (Livingstone, 'Memorable characteristics', 1.331). Possessed of a strong religious calling he was ordained minister in Down by fellow Scottish presbyterian ministers and began to preach regularly at their kirks, though it does not appear that a regular parish was settled upon him. Following active resistance to the growing power of the episcopate, however, in 1636 he was officially deposed from his ministry by the bishop of Down and excommunicated from the church. On 9 September he set out from Loch Fergus on the *Eagle's Wing* with 140 other religious dissidents bound for America, but a storm struck the vessel half way between the Irish coast and the banks of Newfoundland. Maclellan, untroubled by seasickness, continued to preach and minister to the sick. On 3 November the *Eagle's Wing* limped back to port in Ireland and the scheme for settlement was quietly abandoned on account of it, being 'made evident to us, that it was not [part of God's] Will' (Livingstone, *Life*, 19).

Maclellan then toured the counties of Donegal and Tyrone, preaching covertly in private houses, but the unwelcome attention of the authorities compelled him to return to Scotland in disguise. On his arrival in 1638 he was called to serve as the minister of Kirkcudbright and in October that year he attended the general assembly of the Church of Scotland at Glasgow. About this time he delivered a sermon in which he attacked the meddling of King Charles I in the affairs of the kirk and concluded 'that the king had no mor to doe with ther General Assemblyes, then they had to doe with his Parliamentes' (Gordon, 1.145). At the general assembly of 1640 he was censured for encouraging private evening prayer meetings in his parish but he avoided a major confrontation over the issue, seeking clarification instead of the church's position upon personal devotional study. His subsequent appearances at the commissions of assembly of the church in 1642, 1643, 1648, and 1649 were far less controversial and he was active in co-ordinating the local covenanter war effort in Dumfriesshire throughout the 1640s. In 1642 and 1643 he was dispatched by the commissions of assembly on preaching tours of northern Ireland, for four and three months respectively.

At an unknown date Maclellan married Marion Fleming, daughter of an Edinburgh merchant and sister-in-law of the Revd John Livingstone. Following her death in 1640 or 1641, after 1641 he married Isobel, whose other name is unknown. Both marriages were childless. Meanwhile, a protracted struggle with the magistrates of Kirkcudbright over Maclellan's salary was resolved only by the intervention of his patron, Lord Kirkcudbright, and by the magistrates' decision, in 1640, to award both him and his wife one sixteenth of the yield of hay from the town's meadows. It was undoubtedly the memory of this conflict which led him to appeal, in a letter to Kirkcudbright of 20 February 1649, for the central funding of the clergy and the removal of patronage which 'will be found a great Plague to the kirk and an Obstacle to the Propagation of Religion' ('Just copy', 45).

Famed for having a gift of prophecy, Maclellan allegedly foresaw the execution of Charles I, the defeat of Hamilton's army at the battle of Preston, and the ruination of the entire Scottish nobility. However, his fierce defence of the link between the Scottish people and the presbyterian church, as exemplified by the national covenant, led him to attack both the growth of new sects and the English 'Model of a Platoniek Republick' ('Just copy', 46, 48). By late 1649 he was looking forward to an alliance between royalists and covenanters, and welcomed the prospect of the future restoration of Charles II.

'A most straight and zealous man', Maclellan was energetic and diligent in his ministry, but lacked tact and the human touch (Livingstone, 'Memorable characteristics', 1.331). In October 1639 he so enraged one of his parishioners, Gilbert Reid, that the man threatened to shoot him and had to be gaoled in order to ensure the minister's continued safety. Moreover, in May 1642 he publicly humiliated another of his congregation, Janet Creichton, by making her stand at the church door while wearing a paper that proclaimed her fault in contradicting him. It was doubtless during such a dispute, concerning Maclellan's authority, that he came to be cursed by a 'witch'. His brother-in-law, the Revd John Livingstone, certainly believed that this incident hastened his end, but Maclellan's final sickness appears to have been protracted and in his last writings he showed his preoccupation with his own mortality. Before his death in Kirkcudbright at the beginning of 1650 he wrote his own epitaph in verse. In it he rejected the world: 'I lived to die, but now I die to live' (Nicholson, 219), and gave thanks for his 'Faith in fruition, hope in having ends' (ibid.). His account of the physical geography of Galloway, written in Latin, was posthumously published by Bleau in his *Atlas Scotiae* in 1662, and reveals Maclellan to have been a capable linguist and scholar. Isobel survived her husband and subsequently married Thomas Hall, minister of Larne, Ireland; Maclellan's sister Elizabeth Mulean acted as executor of his estate.   JOHN CALLOW

Sources J. Nicholson, ed., *Minute book kept by the war committee of the covenanters in the stewartry of Kirkcudbright in the years 1640 & 1641* (1855) · J. Livingstone, *A brief historical relation of the life of Mr John Livingston, minister of the Gospel* (1727) · J. Gordon of Rothiemay, *History of Scots affairs, from MDCXXXVII to MDCXLI*, 1–2 (1841) · *Fasti Scot.*, new edn, vol. 2 · 'The just copy of a letter, written by Mr John

M'Clelland … to John Lord Kirkcudbright 20 Feb. 1649', in P. Gillespie, *Rulers sins* (1723), 45–8 • [R. Baillie], *Letters and journals*, ed. R. Aiken, 2 vols. (1775) • J. Livingstone, 'Memorable characteristics', *Select biographies*, ed. W. K. Tweedie, 1, Wodrow Society, 7/1 (1845), 293–348 • T. Murray, *The literary history of Galloway* (1822) • J. S. Reid and W. D. Killen, *History of the Presbyterian church in Ireland*, 3 vols. (1834–53) • A. Stevenson, *History of the church and state of Scotland*, 3 vols. (1753–7) • A. Ford, J. McGuire, and K. Milne, eds., *As by law established: the Church of Ireland since the Reformation* (Dublin, 1995) • A. Ford, *The protestant reformation in Ireland, 1590–1641* (Frankfurt, Bern, New York, and Nancy, 1985)

Archives NL Scot., Wodrow MSS, Anal, Fol, Lett; Adv MS 27 6 2 • U. Edin., Wodrow corresp. and papers, Dc 8 1 110; LA ii 690; iii 116 263 355 • U. Glas., Wodrow MSS, MS Gen 1197–1218

MacLellan, John Archibald (1921–1991), piper and composer, was born on 9 July 1921 in Dunfermline, Fife, the eldest of the three sons of William MacLellan (1894–1985), estate gardener, and his wife, Christina MacDonald (1887–1967). Both parents were of west highland origin, and of the Roman Catholic faith. This led them to seek work in Dalreichart, Glen Moriston, Inverness-shire, and then in Fort Augustus, where the boys attended St Columba's School. MacLellan left school at fifteen in 1936, to join the army as a boy piper in the Queen's Own Cameron Highlanders. In 1941, he became the youngest pipe major ever appointed in the British army, in the 9th battalion Seaforth Highlanders, at nineteen.

After his war service MacLellan went on the full pipe major's course at Edinburgh Castle, under Pipe Major Willie Ross, who awarded him a certificate with distinction at the end of his six months. He also attended a course on piobaireachd with John MacDonald of Inverness. He then became pipe major of, successively, the 2nd Seaforth, the 1st Seaforth, the lowland brigade, and the 11th Seaforth, gaining first-class grades in his certificates of education throughout his army career. Lacking opportunity for further promotion, he left the pipe band, and was promoted to warrant officer I with the appointments of regimental sergeant-major of the 1st and 11th Seaforth until in 1959 his career took an unexpected turn: he was appointed to replace Willie Ross at Edinburgh Castle. The army piping class was restructured as the Army School of Piping, with MacLellan as its first instructor. He was then the senior pipe major in the army.

In 1963 MacLellan was appointed MBE 'for his contribution to the improvement of army piping', and five years later was appointed to a commission in the Queen's Own Highlanders with the rank of captain. Having reorganized the Army School of Piping, he now became the first director of army bagpipe music. He retired from the army in 1976, after forty years of service, and devoted himself to teaching and writing. He also became a judge at all the major competitions, respected for his wide knowledge of piping, and for his integrity.

During his army career MacLellan was competing as a solo piper. He won the gold medal for piobaireachd at the Argyll gathering in 1957, and at the Northern Meeting, Inverness in 1959; and he twice won the gold clasp for former winners at Inverness, in 1958 and 1963, the highest award in solo piping. This established him as one of the leading pipers in the world.

On 26 June 1946 MacLellan married Christine (Bunty) Murray (b. 1925), from Rogart, Sutherland, whom he courted when the Seaforths were in camp at Achany in 1942. They had two children, a son, Colin, later a leading piper, and a daughter, Kirsteen. When the appointment to the castle was confirmed, the MacLellans were able to buy their first permanent home, after twenty-three years of married life. They moved to 14 Dean Park Crescent, Edinburgh, in 1970. There they launched a new magazine, the *International Piper*. It was short-lived (1978–81), but had considerable impact, and copies are still sought by piping enthusiasts.

MacLellan was writing about piping, lecturing, teaching, composing, and playing. He began a campaign lasting nearly five years to have the bagpipe accepted as a musical instrument by the Scottish education department. His aim was to enable young pipers to take music in their O level and higher level examinations, with the pipe as their chosen instrument, which had never been allowed before. He also wanted to organize piping tuition in Scottish schools as part of the normal school curriculum. He worked with Seumas MacNeill to achieve these aims, but it is to John MacLellan that the credit must go for their eventual success. The immediate result was that more than 2000 children took up the pipes, and piping, especially in the highlands, took on a new lease of life. MacLellan followed up this triumph with regular visits, encouraging the youngsters with his enthusiasm. Not only the children but all pipers owe him a debt for his work in establishing the respectability and dignity of piping in the eyes of officialdom.

Another great achievement was the Institute of Piping, established to provide a standard of playing which could be rewarded with diplomas and certificates, all over the world. At MacLellan's suggestion, the Army School of Piping, the College of Piping, and the Piobaireachd Society combined to form the institute, and he organized the setting-up and operation of the scheme, to the benefit of many overseas players.

MacLellan's extensive publications and compositions for the pipes included *Music for the Highland Bagpipe* (1961), *The Piper's Handbook* (1966), and *Notation and Tuning of the Highland Bagpipe* (1982); he also published a guide to teaching canntaireachd and he completely revised the 1963 edition of *Logan's Tutor*. He collaborated with Lieutenant-Colonel David Murray to produce the *Queen's Own Highlanders' Standard Settings of Pipe Music* (1962). In addition, he amassed a personal collection of manuscripts and rare early editions of pipe music. His own compositions included some *ceòl beag*, mainly marches, and several piobaireachd works, including 'Salute to the Queen's Own Highlanders'. The best-known is 'The Phantom Piper of Corrieyairack', which won him a Saltire award in 1969.

After he retired from the army, MacLellan became the honorary secretary of the music committee of the Piobaireachd Society, responsible for all the society's publications of pipe music. He rapidly became an authority on piobaireachd, and initiated seminars for judges and for other enthusiasts, created a judges' committee, and organized the publication of the last volumes of the society's piobaireachd series. He was commissioned to compose the piobaireachd 'Salute to the Piobaireachd Society', and was a familiar and respected figure at the society's conferences.

John MacLellan was a tall, well-built man, with a strong-featured face and an intimidating manner—until he recognized a fellow piping enthusiast. His single-mindedness sometimes made him brusque, especially if he was on the trail of a piece of piping memorabilia; but he is remembered with affection by his many pupils, in Scotland, Canada, the USA, and South Africa. In 1989, the piping world paid tribute to his achievements by awarding him the Balvenie medal for services to piping.

John MacLellan collapsed at his home in Edinburgh on 26 April 1991, and died in the Royal Infirmary, Edinburgh. He was cremated at Warriston cemetery, Edinburgh, on 30 April and his ashes were scattered at Inveran, Sutherland, where in the 1940s he used to play piobaireachd beside the River Shin with his friend Angus MacPherson. In his tribute in the *Piping Times* for June 1991, Seumas MacNeill wrote 'John's death is a blow from which piping will not readily recover ... a giant has departed from our world'. In recognition of his achievements, a room in the refurbished School of Bagpipe Music in Edinburgh Castle has been called the John MacLellan Room, and the Piobaireachd Society has given a bench, suitably inscribed, for the use of visitors to the castle.   BRIDGET MACKENZIE

Sources b. cert. · d. cert. · priv. coll., MacLellan MSS · *Piping Times*, 43/9 (1990–91) · *Piping Times*, 45/7 (1992–3) · D. Murray, *Music of the Scottish regiments* (1994) · R. D. Cannon, *A bibliography of bagpipe music* (1980) · B. Mackenzie, *Piping traditions of the north of Scotland* (1998) · private information (2004) [family]
Archives NRA, priv. coll., books and MSS, pipes | FILM Army School of Bagpipe Music, Edinburgh Castle, sound recording (teaching tapes) | SOUND Army School of Bagpipe Music, Edinburgh Castle, teaching tapes · BL NSA, performance recording · priv. coll., reel-to-reel tapes and old 78 rpm records · U. Edin., School of Scottish studies, sound recordings (teaching tapes)
Likenesses photograph (with Yehudi Menuhin), repro. in *Daily Express* (Aug 1963) · photographs, Edinburgh Castle · photographs, Royal Scottish Pipers' Association Rooms, Rose Lane, Edinburgh · photographs, Edinburgh Academy · photographs, U. Edin., school of Scottish studies
Wealth at death £78,524.60: confirmation, 23 May 1991, *CCI*

MacLellan, Maud Lilburn (1903–1977), commanding officer of the FANY, was born on 6 October 1903 at 37 Athole Gardens, Kelvinside, Glasgow, one of two daughters of the three children of Walter Thomas MacLellan (1858–1931), iron merchant, and his wife, Jane Adair Whyte (1868–1947). Her grandfather Walter MacLellan (1815–1889) was a founder member of P. and W. MacLellan, iron founders and suppliers for much imperial bridge building in the nineteenth century.

In 1929 MacLellan, known as Mac, joined the Glasgow section of the First Aid Nursing Yeomanry, the FANY. This had been formed in 1907 by a former cavalry sergeant-major, Edward Baker, as an all-female mounted ambulance unit. As a self-financing and therefore independent organization, the FANY had survived the mass disbanding of women's units which followed the armistice. Despite the prevailing mood of disarmament and appeasement, the FANY continued recruiting and training throughout the twenties and thirties and was thus well placed to supply the first 1500 driver-mechanics for the newly formed women's Auxiliary Territorial Service (ATS) in 1938. Although promised administrative independence within the new service by the War Office, the hostility of the ATS director, Dame Helen Gwynne-Vaughan, forced the FANY drivers within months into choosing between enrolment in the ATS or abandoning the fledgeling organization altogether. Many FANYs were outraged at this breach of agreement and feelings ran high. MacLellan, by then a senior officer, in what she saw as the best interests of the country at such a critical time, led by example and in November 1938 accepted command of the 4th Scottish motor company, ATS. She became group commander of the Scottish motor transport companies in August 1940 and established excellent relations with the military commanders of Scottish command, overcoming much hostility towards the new women's service.

A contemporary volunteer later recalled how MacLellan imposed military discipline in 1939 on a group of women who were unruly and not very military-minded. 'She achieved it by her personal example, integrity and a great sense of humour. We all loved her' (H. Clark, *FANY Gazette*, 1977). In May 1944 MacLellan took command of the motor transport training centre at Camberley where the then Princess Elizabeth trained as a junior officer. MacLellan returned to the FANY at the end of the war, and in September 1947 became corps commander on the retirement of Mary Baxter Ellis. In the early post-war years the FANY faced an uncertain future. On the one hand, its involvement in so many theatres of war, and especially with the Special Operations Executive, was becoming public knowledge. On the other, the decision of the War Office in 1947 to establish a permanent women's service, the Women's Royal Army Corps, seemed to leave no role for the FANY. However, MacLellan believed that their future was dependent on their own interpretation of what patriotism demands from the individual and that their best hope lay in cultivating a number of specialist skills and powerful patrons. 'She was a woman of vision and believed that after the War the Corps should remain available to serve the country' (H. Clark, *FANY Gazette*, 1977). She pursued this vision with tenacity. Now known as the FANY (Princess Royal's Volunteer Corps), the organization has continued to provide specialist communications for the civil and military authorities. It has remained an independent, all-women voluntary organization.

MacLellan was made an OBE in the queen's birthday honours in 1957, the fiftieth anniversary of the founding of the FANY corps. A small, dark-haired woman, she was called by her FANY peers Wee Maudie. She was a lifelong resident of Helensburgh, travelling tirelessly to London on a regular basis to fulfil her role as FANY commanding officer. She retired in 1965. She never married, and her great love was fishing, a hobby she pursued throughout

Scotland and Ireland. She died on 21 May 1977 at 9 East Abercrombie Street, Helensburgh, of arteriosclerosis, and was cremated at Cardross crematorium.

LYNETTE BEARDWOOD

Sources *FANY Gazette* (1929) · *FANY Gazette* (1939) · *FANY Gazette* (1947) · *FANY Gazette* (1965) · *FANY Gazette* (1977) · Duke of York's headquarters, London SW3, FANY archives · I. Ward, *FANY invicta* (1955) · H. Popham, *FANY: the story of the women's transport service* (1984) · private information (2004) [Donald MacLellan, cousin] · b. cert. · d. cert.

Archives Duke of York's headquarters, London, Women's Transport Service (FANY), FANY archives

Likenesses S. Morle, oils, 1997, FANY, London

Wealth at death £124,186.06: corrective inventory, 23 Sept 1977, *CCI*

Maclellan, Robert, first Lord Kirkcudbright (d. 1639), landowner, was the son of Thomas Maclellan of Bombie (d. 1597) and Grizel Maxwell, daughter of John, fourth Lord Herries. On his father's death Sir William Maclellan became his tutor (guardian) for the remainder of his childhood. In 1632 Maclellan stated that he was aged forty 'or thereabouts' (Maxwell, 100), but it seems that he was significantly older, for the contracts for his first marriage (to Agnes, daughter of Hugh Campbell, first Lord Campbell of Loudoun) are dated October 1603. Moreover, he served as provost of Kirkcudbright in 1606–10 and 1611–12, and was knighted on 3 October 1607. In 1608–9 he was involved in feuding with local rivals, and was imprisoned for attacks on opponents in Kirkcudbright and Edinburgh.

Maclellan's main interests soon switched from Scotland to Ireland. In 1610 he was one of the nine Scottish 'chief undertakers' chosen to organize the plantation of Ulster, being granted the precinct of Boylagh and Banagh in co. Donegal. Since he had no known influential political or court connections the reasons that he was chosen for this privilege are unknown, though the lands he was granted in the plantation were recognized as among the least promising for settlement. In the event he made no attempt to settle colonists in Donegal, selling his lands there in 1616. In their place he leased land in co. Londonderry. His continuing interest in Ulster was no doubt encouraged by the fact that, after the death of his first wife, he had in 1614 married Mary, daughter of Sir Hugh Montgomery (later Viscount Montgomery of the Great Ardes), and her dowry included lands in co. Down. Maclellan was active in attracting settlers to his Londonderry lands but soon ran into financial difficulties, not least because many of his tenants, having believed the lands they were to occupy would be measured in Irish acres, discovered that the smaller English acre had been used. Hiring 150 men from Scotland to resist a feared Spanish invasion in 1625 cost him £4200 sterling, which was only repaid by the crown in 1629. None the less, already by 1622 Maclellan's Scots settlement in Londonderry was regarded as the strongest and best able to defend itself in the county.

Though in 1628 Maclellan described Ireland as 'where his residence has been this long tyme bygane' (Young, 2.446) he maintained close contact with Scotland. In 1621 he sat in parliament for Wigtownshire, demonstrating his support for the king by voting to ratify the five articles of Perth. Appointment as a justice of the peace for Kirkcudbrightshire and Wigtownshire followed in 1623. In 1631 he was evidently created a baronet, and on 25 June 1633, while Charles I was in Scotland for his coronation, he was created Lord Kirkcudbright, doubtless as a reward for his services in Ulster. Following the death of his second wife he married, in September 1636, the twice-widowed Mary, daughter of Robert Gage, of Raunds in Northamptonshire; her previous husbands had been John Rowley of Castle Roe, co. Londonderry, and Sir George Trevelyan. She died seven months after her husband, on 7 August 1639.

Kirkcudbright died in Ulster on 18 January 1639. An allegation that a few weeks before he had sat in the general assembly of the Church of Scotland and supported the covenanters in opposing Charles I's religious policies is erroneous, as is the story that he had served as a gentleman of the bedchamber to both James VI and Charles I. He was succeeded by his nephew Thomas Maclellan.

DAVID STEVENSON

Sources *Scots peerage* · M. P. Maxwell, *The Scottish migration to Ulster in the reign of James I* (1973) · M. D. Young, ed., *The parliaments of Scotland: burgh and shire commissioners*, 2 vols. (1992–3) · GEC, *Peerage* · *DNB* · GEC, *Baronetage* · N. Canny, *Making Ireland British, 1580–1650* (2001)

McLellan, Robert (1907–1985), playwright, was born at Kirkfieldbank in Lanarkshire on 28 January 1907, the son of John McLellan, a compositor, and his wife, Elizabeth, *née* Hannah. His maternal grandparents had a fruit farm in the Clyde valley, where he spent many childhood holidays and which provided the background for the short stories collected under the title *Linmill* (1977). McLellan attended secondary school in Bearsden, a well-to-do suburb to the north of Glasgow, but his university studies in philosophy were cut short by a bout of ill health, and he never completed his degree.

On 1 October 1938 McLellan married Kathleen Heys (b. 1912/13), whom he had met while leading summer climbs in the Lake District, and settled with her in a cottage at High Corrie on the island of Arran in the Firth of Clyde, where he remained for the rest of his life. They had two children, Kathleen and John. From the time that he moved to Arran, McLellan supported himself by his writing, something which has proved very difficult in Scotland unless the individual concerned has been able to achieve success beyond his or her native land. As to the apparent remoteness of his home, and its distance from professional theatrical activity, McLellan commented in a magazine article: 'I can never be quite sure where the centre of things is … more often than not, though I keep the feeling to myself for fear of ridicule, it seems to be in High Corrie.' He also felt that too close an involvement in the theatre 'can lead to a restricted view of human nature. Actors are, in no unkind sense of the word, a peculiar people' (McLellan, 35–6).

The development of a Scottish dramatic tradition in the twentieth century was somewhat erratic. In the latter part of the nineteenth century the native element in the theatre north of the border consisted largely of adaptations of the novels of Walter Scott, of original pieces on other well-worn historical themes, and of music-hall sketches. But in the first years of the twentieth century the Glasgow Repertory Company (1909–14), an organization funded by subscribing citizens of the city, offered apprentice Scottish dramatists the chance to expand their artistic horizons and to see their work alongside a range of contemporary playwrights. Several availed themselves of the opportunity, but by the time McLellan came to write the principal outlets for the indigenous dramatist in Scotland were a number of amateur companies, such as the Scottish National Players and the Curtain Theatre. From 1933 to 1940 the Curtain offered programmes, principally of new plays, in a converted drawing-room in the west end of Glasgow, and then in the small Lyric Theatre. In January 1934 it presented as one of a triple bill of one-act pieces McLellan's *Jeddart Justice*. This was followed by several other one-act plays and a number of full-length ones, including *Toom Byres* (1936) and *Jamie the Saxt* (1937). This latter piece is generally regarded as McLellan's finest work; the title role was originally played by Duncan Macrae, a Scottish actor of distinction who, like so many of his generation, came into the professional theatre via the amateur one. Nevertheless, McLellan always had reservations about Macrae's approach to the part, reservations which were heightened when the piece was revived in 1956 as part of a season of mainly Scottish plays in Edinburgh and Glasgow, and the actor cut speeches wholesale in order to secure the comic effects at which he had become so adept.

The founding of professional repertory theatres in Scotland during and after the Second World War provided McLellan and others of his generation with opportunities that had not been available to them in their native land until that point. Unlike O. H. Mavor (James Bridie), whose wit and urbanity suited audiences outside Scotland, McLellan wrote in a form of lowland Scots that does not travel very well, and so the West End route which Bridie pursued with alacrity was not open to him. McLellan was adamant throughout his career that the Scots he employed had none of the artifice of the Lallans found in the poetry of C. M. Grieve (Hugh MacDiarmid), but stemmed from the variety of the language he had heard as a child growing up on the edge of rural lowland Scotland. Ruefully McLellan recalled that whenever he had a success on the stage he was encouraged to write in English, something he did not wish to do. Indeed, it is striking that, when he does employ both languages, for instance in plays such as *The Hypocrite* or *Young Auchinleck*, the passages in Scots move with vivacity, while the English ones tend to limp along. Given McLellan's linguistic position, the appearance in his own country of a number of theatres which were actively seeking plays by indigenous writers was absolutely crucial to the later development of his writing. Indeed, he was associated with most of the important companies in Scotland in the period immediately after the war: Glasgow Unity Theatre premièred

Torwatletie in 1946 and *The Flouers o' Edinburgh* in 1948, the Glasgow Citizens' staged *Mary Stewart* in 1951, and Edinburgh Gateway gave *Young Auchinleck* its first performance in 1962. McLellan continued to work as a dramatist until 1967, when *The Hypocrite* was presented by the Royal Lyceum Company in Edinburgh.

Of McLellan's plays the two which have been most frequently revived are *Jamie the Saxt* and *The Flouers o' Edinburgh*. The continued popularity of these pieces is easy to explain. One presents a most appealing picture of James VI as a very canny individual, who skilfully outwits those who seek to undermine his position at the Scottish court, then reaps his reward in the shape of the prospect of the throne in England. The other explores the issue of Scottish identity through a dramatization of the controversy which arose in the post-Union Edinburgh of the eighteenth century as to whether people with serious social aspirations should abandon their 'barbarous' native tongue in favour of English; this issue and related aspects of national consciousness are hardy perennials in the Scottish context.

Most of McLellan's plays are historical dramas, and his few forays into the modern world—such as the early *Portrait of an Artist* (the Curtain, 1939), which is set in 'bohemian' Glasgow, and *The Road to the Isles* (Glasgow Citizens', 1954), which tries to engage with the problem of highland regeneration—are not successful. McLellan is at his happiest and most effective when he is recreating Scotland's past: he once offered the view that he was, in a sense, writing some of the plays which would have been written if Scotland had continued to have a vigorous drama after the departure of the court for London in 1603, and if the depredations visited on the theatre by the Presbyterian reformers had never taken place. For the most part McLellan's view of Scotland's past is devoid of the sentimentality and nostalgia which have permeated Scottish culture: even in comedy, violence and sudden death are never very far away. McLellan's great strength, however, is in the creation of lively action and of character. He was particularly concerned, as he saw it, to 'fix' in dramatic form aspects of the Scottish character which he considered to be important, and in this he is often very successful.

McLellan's skilled use of the Scots language to create character on the stage is paralleled by its employment to suggest particular place and circumstance in much of his occasional verse, but particularly in the stories republished as *Linmill*, many of which were originally written to be broadcast on BBC radio. McLellan also produced a popular guide to his adopted home, *The Isle of Arran* (1976). He took an active part in the affairs of the community: he was a member of Arran district council for a number of years and became chairman of the Association of District Councils of Scotland, the body which represented these second-tier authorities prior to local government reorganization in 1975. He was made an OBE in 1978. McLellan died at his home in Arran on 27 January 1985 of a cerebral haemorrhage, and was buried in Sannox cemetery on the island on 30 January.

There is a certain heroism about McLellan's dogged pursuit of what he saw as his proper path as a dramatist, despite the meagre financial returns and the limited number of productions of his work. It is perfectly understandable that he chose to do what he knew he could do best, but it is none the less a matter of regret that in his writing his engagement with the modern world is oblique rather than direct. DAVID HUTCHISON

Sources *Arran Banner* (2 Feb 1985) · *Glasgow Herald* (29 Jan 1985) · *The Scotsman* (29 Jan 1985) · *The Times* (2 Feb 1985) · R. McLellan, 'Living in Scotland today', *Scottish Field* (Dec 1956), 35–6 · D. Hutchison, *The modern Scottish theatre* (1977) · I. Campbell, 'Introduction', in R. McLellan, *Jamie the Saxt* (1970) · personal knowledge (2004) · m. cert. · d. cert.
Archives NL Scot., corresp. and papers | NL Scot., letters to A. K. Annand · NL Scot., letters to Alexander Reid
Likenesses photographs, NL Scot.

McLennan, George Stewart (1883–1929), player and composer of highland bagpipe music, was born on 9 February 1883 at 105 St Leonard Street, Edinburgh, the eighth child in the family of seven sons and two daughters of John McLennan, superintendent of police and editor of bagpipe music (1843–1923), and his first wife, Elizabeth Stewart (*d.* 1889). The McLennans were one of the leading piping dynasties of Scotland, tracing their descent from Murdoch McLennan, town piper of Inverness in the early sixteenth century. One of them had played at Culloden, another at Waterloo. A collateral branch came down through Donald Mór McLennan of Moy (*b. c.*1783), who had taught the famous pipers Donald Cameron (1810–1868) and John Bàn MacKenzie (1796–1864).

G. S. McLennan began his musical instruction with his father at the age of four. Later he had lessons from his uncle Pipe-Major John Stewart, and in highland dancing from his gifted cousin William McLennan (1860–1892). He was a child prodigy, playing before Queen Victoria by royal command at the age of ten and winning amateur competitions while barely into his teens.

Alarmed by McLennan's ambition to become a sailor, his father enlisted him as a boy piper in the 1st Gordons in October 1899. By 1905 he was pipe-major, one of the youngest ever in the British army. He served in Cork, in Aldershot, and in Colchester where, on 3 April 1912, he married Nona Lucking. They had two sons, George (1914–1996) and John (1916–1940). McLennan was stationed at the Gordons' depot at Aberdeen from 1913 until early in 1918, when he joined the 1st battalion in France as a Lewis gunner. Although military service restricted his opportunity to compete, he won all the top awards, including the gold medal at the Argyllshire Gathering in 1904, the gold medal at the Northern Meeting at Inverness in 1905, and the clasp, the highest award for *ceòl mór*, in 1909, 1920, and 1921. His style as a piobaireachd player was strongly influenced by the ideas set forth in his father's book *The Piobaireachd as MacCrimmon Played it* (1907), which argued that under the twin influences of competition and dubious theorizing, playing had become too slow and rhythmically loose.

Like his father, he placed a high value on the musical autonomy of the player. Almost alone among the master pipers of the day, he refused to teach the 'official' scores prescribed by the Piobaireachd Society of Scotland for purposes of competition, although these were widely criticized (even by the players paid to teach them). As a consequence the society declined to employ him as an instructor.

G. S. McLennan was noted for his melodious pipe and outstanding technique. His fingers were so strong that spectators could distinctly hear their slap on the chanter as he marched round the boards. In the light music of the pipe (marches, strathspeys, reels, and jigs) he pioneered the faster and more heavily decorated style that developed during the opening decades of the twentieth century. He was also the most gifted composer of highland bagpipe music of his generation, indeed many would say of the whole twentieth century. Selections of his tunes were published in his father's book *The Piobaireachd as Performed in the Highlands for Ages, till about the Year 1808* (1924) and in his own collection, *Highland Bagpipe Music* (1929), published in the year of his tragically early death. Some of the compositions for a planned further volume were eventually published in *The Gordon Highlanders Pipe Music Collection* (1983–5).

McLennan's style as a composer was highly original and inventive. Tunes such as 'Pipe Major John Stewart', 'Mrs MacPherson of Inveran', 'The Jig of Slurs', and 'The Little Cascade' were quickly recognized as classics. 'The Little Cascade' in particular, with its unique tonality and jazzily syncopated rhythms, was hailed as one of the wonders of modern Scotland. Perhaps more than any other single composer, G. S. McLennan was responsible for developing the light music of the pipe into a mature and sophisticated form, rivalling piobaireachd in technical difficulty and far outstripping it in creative vigour. Yet his own original piobaireachd compositions were as fresh and innovative as his achievement in *ceòl beag*, though not all had been published by the end of the twentieth century.

G. S. McLennan had great personal presence. He was a dapper figure, short but well knit, whose boyish good looks were complemented by a neatly waxed military moustache, and whose kindness and personal integrity won him much affection and esteem.

On retiring from the army in 1921, McLennan set up as a bagpipe maker at 2 Bath Street, Aberdeen. He was the focus of a lively musical circle in the city which included the fiddle virtuoso James Scott Skinner (who dedicated a march tune 'The Gordon Highlanders' to him) and the prominent piping judge Alfred E. Milne. But as a result of war service he developed a serious lung condition and died shortly before midnight on 31 May 1929 at his home at 48B Powis Place, Aberdeen. The highland dancer Mary Aitken ran 10 miles through the night to the village of Blackburn to bring the news of his death to Alfred Milne.

At McLennan's funeral on 4 June the gun carriage was preceded by forty pipers, and 20,000 people lined the route to Aberdeen station. His remains were interred at Echobank cemetery in Edinburgh. McLennan's wife,

Nona, survived him. In 1996 a major international invitational piping competition was established in San Diego, California, to commemorate him.

WILLIAM DONALDSON

Sources W. Donaldson, *The highland pipe and Scottish society, 1750–1950* (2000) · P. Graham and B. MacRae, eds., *The Gordon highlanders pipe music collection*, 2 vols. (1983–5) · G. S. McLennan, *Highland bagpipe music* (1929) · J. McLennan, *The piobaireachd as MacCrimmon played it: with instructions how to read and understand music* [1907] · J. McLennan, *The piobaireachd as performed in the highlands for ages, till about the year 1808* [1924] · A. Fairrie, *The Northern Meeting, 1788–1988* (1988) · J. Campbell, *Highland bagpipe makers* (2001) · W. Donaldson, 'Change and invariance in the traditional performing arts', *Northern Scotland*, 17 (1997), 33–54 · W. Donaldson, 'Manuscript material in the University of Aberdeen for the study of piping', *Northern Scotland*, 20 (2000), 167–78 · private information (2004) · d. cert. · b. cert.
Likenesses photographs, repro. in Graham and MacRae, eds., *Gordon highlanders*
Wealth at death £380 4s. 11d.: confirmation, 31 Aug 1929, *CCI*

McLennan, Sir John Cunningham (1867–1935), physicist, was born at Ingersoll, Ontario, Canada, on 14 April 1867, the son of David McLennan (d. 1897), from Aberdeenshire, miller and grain dealer, and Barbara (d. 1915), daughter of John Cunningham of Stewarton, Ayrshire. The family moved to Clinton, Ontario, where McLennan attended the Collegiate Institute. Having failed to obtain a post with the railway, he qualified as a teacher at the Stratford model school in 1884. He then taught for three years to obtain funds to study at the University of Toronto; he enrolled there in 1889. After graduating as head of his class in physics in 1892 he served for six years as assistant demonstrator in that subject. In the summer of 1896 he visited major physics laboratories in Europe. In 1898–9 he studied at Cambridge under J. J. Thomson at the Cavendish Laboratory. Lack of funds brought him back to Toronto after a year, and there he increasingly took on the superintendence of the physics laboratory. He was responsible for introducing practical laboratory courses, and original investigations for undergraduate as well as graduate students. He was a vigorous and early advocate for university research. He became demonstrator in 1899, associate professor in 1902, and director of the physics laboratory in 1904. He assumed the chair of physics in 1907. He had guided the Alumni Association from around 1900; one of its achievements was a new physics building, with a laboratory which was one of the best equipped anywhere in McLennan's day; the physics laboratory at Toronto later became the McLennan Laboratory.

McLennan's first scientific paper, on electrical conductivity in gases traversed by cathode rays, was published in 1900 by the Royal Society of London, and, in translation, in the *Zeitschrift für Physikalische Chemie*. Other early papers were on radiation in the atmosphere (which he did not identify as penetrating radiation, or cosmic rays). In 1910 his research shifted from radioactivity to spectroscopy. In the same year he married Elsie Monro Ramsay (d. 1933), daughter and heir of William Ramsay, whisky merchant, of Bowland, Midlothian; they had no children.

Then came the First World War. McLennan was one of a dozen scientists invited to advise the Canadian government on the development of industrial research. He was also invited by the (UK) board of inventions and research to determine the helium content of natural gas in Canada, and to pursue experiments for its purification and production. He proposed the use of helium in airships. Other major work included advisory work for the Admiralty, including what Rutherford described as work of outstanding importance in combating the submarine menace. Shortly after the armistice he was invited to become scientific adviser to the chief of the naval staff, but when the cabinet decided against a new naval laboratory McLennan declined and returned to the University of Toronto.

There, having acquired a good supply of helium, McLennan set himself to equip his laboratory for spectroscopic investigations, and to create in it a cryogenic branch. He succeeded in liquefying helium in 1923 (this had already been accomplished by Kamerlingh Onnes at Leiden). He worked on low temperature superconductivity of metals, and in 1925, with Gordon Merritt Shrum, he discovered that the origin of the auroral green line was due to excited oxygen. This earned him the royal medal of the Royal Society of London in 1927. He also continued with his spectroscopic researches, most notably on the metals, and the hyperfine structure of their spectral lines.

McLennan's reputation, and that of his department, attracted graduate students from around the world. His emphasis upon research, and the success of his advocacy, led to his appointment as dean of graduate studies. He sought to centralize research and research funding, but was frustrated by the autonomy of departments, and resigned after two years, in 1932. He had been a member of a royal commission in Ontario on the treatment of cancer, exploring the use of radium since 1931. Following his retirement from the University of Toronto, he removed to England with his wife, built a house in Surrey, and continued to work on radiation therapy. A special laboratory and clinic were established for him.

McLennan was an eminent physicist, one of the best known and most productive outside Europe and the USA. 'Clear-sighted, swift in decision and energetic in action, his qualities stood him in good service, and many stories are current in illustration of his driving power and almost ruthless disregard of persons and difficulties that stood in his way' (Lord Rutherford, cited in Langton, 49). Most of his research was undertaken with students, and many of them went on to distinguished careers, including Shrum, Eli F. Burton (McLennan's successor at Toronto), and David Keys at McGill. He supplemented his abilities as a teacher and his commitment to research with a notable gift for the popularization of science. As president of the Royal Canadian Institute, he was a prime mover in the successful campaign for the establishment at Ottawa of the laboratories of the National Research Council; he was chair of its associate committee on physics and engineering physics from 1919 to 1931. In politics he was a strong Conservative and imperialist.

McLennan had been appointed OBE in 1917 for his wartime scientific services. In 1935 he was made KBE. He was elected to the Royal Society of Canada in 1903, was its president in 1924, and received its Flavelle medal in 1926. Elected FRS in 1915, he gave its Bakerian lecture in 1928, and was vice-president in 1933–4; he was president of the Royal Canadian Institute in 1915–16. He was author and co-author of some 250 scientific papers. He died suddenly, near Abbeville, France, on 9 October 1935, while returning by train from Paris to London; he was on his way back to England from a meeting of the International Bureau of Weights and Measures.   TREVOR H. LEVERE

Sources H. H. Langton, *Sir John Cunningham McLennan: a memoir* (1939) · A. S. Eve, *Obits. FRS*, 1 (1932–5), 577–83 · *DSB* · Y. Gingras, *Physics and the rise of scientific research in Canada*, trans. P. Keating (1991) · *Proceedings and Transactions of the Royal Society of Canada*, 3rd ser., 30 (1936), vi–x
Archives University of Toronto, Thomas Fisher Rare Book Library, corresp. and papers | CUL, letters to Lord Rutherford · McGill University, Montreal, letters to Lord Rutherford · University of Copenhagen, Niels Bohr Institute for Astronomy, Physics, and Geophysics, corresp. with Niels Bohr
Likenesses Lafayette Ltd, photograph, 1920, RS · W. Stoneman, photograph, 1933, NPG · A. John, oils, University of Toronto, McLennan Physics Building · three photographs, RS
Wealth at death £9732 14s. 8d.: administration with will, 2 June 1936, *CGPLA Eng. & Wales*

McLennan, John Ferguson (1827–1881), social anthropologist, born at Inverness on 14 October 1827, was the eldest of three sons of John McLennan, insurance agent, of Inverness, and Jessie Ross, his wife. He was educated at Inverness and at King's College, Aberdeen, where he graduated MA in 1849. He subsequently entered Trinity College, Cambridge, where in 1853 he obtained a wrangler's place in the mathematical tripos. After leaving Cambridge University without a degree, he spent two years in London writing for *The Leader*, then edited by George Henry Lewes, and other periodicals. On returning to Edinburgh he was called to the bar in January 1857. He took an active part in the agitation which led to the Court of Session Act of 1868, and became secretary to the Scottish Law Amendment Society. He married on 23 December 1862 Mary Bell, daughter of John Ramsay *McCulloch, with whom he had a daughter. In 1870, following the death of his wife earlier that year, he moved to London and in 1871 he accepted the post of parliamentary draughtsman for Scotland.

In 1857 appeared McLennan's first considerable literary effort, the article on 'Law' in the *Encyclopaedia Britannica* (8th edn). In the course of the researches into ancient institutions which it involved, McLennan was led to speculate on the origin of the curious custom of marriage by collusive abduction, which obtained in historic times, both at Sparta and at Rome, and conjectured that it was a relic of an archaic custom of marriage by actual abduction, or 'capture'. Further research led him to the conclusion that primitive society consisted of miscellaneous hordes, recognizing no ties of kinship, practising promiscuous sexual intercourse and female infanticide, and thus compelled to prey upon one another for women. Hence

was established within each horde a custom of having sexual intercourse with none but alien women (exogamy), which acquired a religious or quasi-religious sanction, and survived into historic times. In course of time uterine—but at first only uterine—kinship came to be recognized, and with its recognition abduction gave place to the more peaceful practice of the reception of sexual partners by women under the maternal roof, which, from its prevalence among the Nairs, McLennan termed Nair polyandry. Among more evolved peoples this was succeeded by polyandry of the type found in Tibet, where several brothers have a wife in common. This practice gave rise in turn to patriarchal monandry, polygamous or monogamous according to circumstances.

In support of this very bold hypothesis McLennan marshalled a considerable mass of evidence in his *Primitive Marriage* (1865). Although anticipated to some slight extent by the Swiss jurist Bachofen (in *Das Mutterrecht*, 1861), McLennan's work was the result of altogether independent thought and research. Although his ideas on social evolution, like those of his contemporaries, were soon rejected, the questions he asked and his sociological approach to ethnographic material, earned him a place as one of the founding fathers of modern British social anthropology. In particular, his influence on William Robertson Smith, and the latter's influence on Durkheim, ensured that his methodology passed into the mainstream of anthropological thought.

Lack of leisure combined with ill health to frustrate McLennan's long-cherished intention of rewriting *Primitive Marriage*. He continued, however, his investigations into the subject until shortly before his death. In 1866 he discussed the Homeric evidence in two articles on 'Kinship in ancient Greece' in the *Fortnightly Review*, and contributed a slighter paper on 'Bride catching' to *The Argosy*. He broke entirely new ground in a brief article on 'Totemism' in the supplement to *Chambers's Encyclopaedia* (1868), followed by a series on the same subject, entitled 'The worship of animals and plants', in the *Fortnightly Review* (1869–70). The essays on Greek kinship and *Primitive Marriage* together with new material, including an examination of Morgan's theory of classificatory kin terms, appeared in McLennan's *Studies in Ancient History* (1876). An article in the *Fortnightly Review* (1877) on 'The levirate and polyandry', an attempt to deduce the former institution from the latter, provoked a reply from Herbert Spencer. Besides his work on anthropology, McLennan published a *Memoir of Thomas Drummond, Under-Secretary in Ireland* (1867). He received from the University of Aberdeen the degree of LLD in 1874. On 20 January 1875 he married his second wife, Eleonora Anne, daughter of Francis Holles Brandram, JP for the counties of Kent and Sussex; she died in 1895 or 1896.

To clear the way for a comprehensive work which he projected on the evolution of the idea of kinship, McLennan began in 1880, but did not live to complete, a critical examination of Henry Maine's patriarchal theory, with the view of proving it to be a historical anachronism. His health, however, was already thoroughly undermined by consumption, and while wintering in Algeria he suffered from repeated attacks of malarial fever. He returned to Britain in the spring of 1881, and died later that year, after some months of complete prostration, at his house, Hawthorndene, Hayes Common, Kent, on 16 June.

The fragment on the patriarchal theory, edited and completed by McLennan's brother Donald, who had helped in its composition, was published in 1885. For the projected work on kinship McLennan left considerable materials, the arrangement of which, begun by Donald McLennan, but interrupted by his death in 1891 and then by that of Professor Robertson Smith, was completed by McLennan's widow and Arthur Platt and published in 1896.

J. M. RIGG, rev. PETER RIVIÈRE

Sources P. Rivière, introduction, in J. F. McLennan, *Primitive marriage*, ed. P. Rivière (1970) · P. Rivière, 'William Robertson Smith and John Ferguson McLennan: the Aberdeen roots of British social anthropology', *Proceedings of the William Robertson Smith Congress* (1994) · *The Scotsman* (20 June 1881) · *The Athenaeum* (25 June 1881), 851 · *Encyclopaedia Britannica*, 9th edn (1875–89) · J. S. Black and G. W. Chrystal, *The life of William Robertson Smith* (1912) · E. E. Evans-Pritchard, *A history of anthropological thought* (1981)
Likenesses J. Hutchinson, marble bust, 1892, Trinity Cam.
Wealth at death £240 1s.: probate, 28 March 1882, *CGPLA Eng. & Wales*

MacLeod. For this title name *see* individual entries under MacLeod; *see also* Mackenzie, John, Lord Macleod, and Count Cromarty in the Swedish nobility (1727–1789).

MacLeod, Alexander (1817–1891), minister of the Presbyterian Church of England, was born at Nairn on 17 October 1817, the son of Alexander MacLeod, excise officer, and Mary, his wife. He was educated at Nairn Academy and at Carlton School, Glasgow, and attended the Carlton Relief church. He studied at Glasgow University from 1835 to 1838 and at the Relief Theological Hall from 1839 to 1844. On 20 February 1844 he was ordained and inducted to the Relief congregation at Strathaven, Lanarkshire, where he stayed for eleven years. He married in 1845 Elizabeth Mackie (d. 1911): they had eight children. MacLeod was minister of the John Street United Presbyterian Church, Glasgow, from 1855 to 1864, when he was inducted to the ministry of Trinity United Presbyterian Church, Birkenhead. This church had been built, largely by James Stitt, to serve the growing Scottish community of the new town of Birkenhead, and especially its Claughton suburb. MacLeod, a passionate, energetic, and formidably learned highlander, inspired his congregation to start a Sunday school and a city mission in Brassey Street, and imparted to them an interest in the foreign mission field, particularly China. His pulpit style was lively, and he had a special rapport with young people. The church prospered: by the 1870s the minister's salary was £700 per annum. He received a Glasgow DD in 1865, launched Trinity's own magazine, *Our Church News*, in 1878, and in 1889 was elected moderator of the Presbyterian Church of England. His publications included *Christus consolator* (1870), *Talking to the Children* (1872), *Days of Heaven upon Earth* (1878), *William Logan* (1879), *The Children's Portion* (1884), and (posthumously) *A Man's Gift and Other Sermons* (1895). MacLeod died on 13 January 1891, and was buried in Flaybrick Hill cemetery, Birkenhead.

T. B. JOHNSTONE, rev. IAN SELLERS

Sources A. G. Fleming, 'Memorial sketch', in A. MacLeod, *A man's gift and other sermons* (1895) · *Presbyterian Church of England Year Book* (1892) · *Presbyterian Messenger* (3 May 1889) · A. Herschel, *History of Trinity Presbyterian Church* (1910) · R. S. Archer, *Trinity Presbyterian Church, Claughton* (1938) · R. Jones, *A portrait of Trinity with Palm Grove* (1988)
Likenesses portrait, repro. in Jones, *Portrait of Trinity with Palm Grove*
Wealth at death £869: probate, 16 Feb 1891, *CGPLA Eng. & Wales*

MacLeod, Allan (d. 1805), political writer, presumably a native of Scotland, lived in London, where he edited the *London Albion Journal*. In addition, between 1796 and 1805 he published a number of pamphlets on political and religious themes which indicate that his opinions changed considerably during this time. The early works are favourable to radical ideas and attack Edmund Burke and Bishop Watson of Llandaff, both of whom had criticized the political and religious principles of the French Revolution. However, after 1803 a change is noticeable. His later pamphlets are characterized by their strong support for the British government's policy of war with France and Spain, and are critical of those whig politicians who opposed the conflict. Judging by his early work, Macleod was sympathetic to Thomas Paine and inclined towards an anti-monarchical position. The rise of Napoleon and his construction of a despotic regime may therefore have been the cause of Macleod's changing political outlook. As well as titles such as *Letters on the Importance of the Present War* (1803) and *A Review of Papers on the War with Spain* (1805), Macleod published critical comments on the work of the bookseller James Lackington and on the dangers of a boarding-school education for girls. He appears to have given up journalism and retired to Edinburgh in 1805, where he died at his lodging on 17 September of that year. GORDON GOODWIN, rev. ALEXANDER DU TOIT

Sources Watt, *Bibl. Brit.*, 2.631 · *GM*, 1st ser., 75 (1805), 973

MacLeod, Catherine [Kitty; Ceit NicLeòid] (1914–2000), Gaelic singer, was born on 4 September 1914 at Kasauli, near Simla, India, the elder daughter and eldest of three children of Kenneth MacLeod (Coinneach NicLeòid, d. 1937), soldier, formerly of Eorrabaidh, Lewis, and his wife, Anna, *née* MacLeod (Anna NicLeòid), primary school-teacher, formerly of Tongue, Stornoway, Lewis. Just before the First World War her mother had gone out to India in order to be with her husband, regimental provost sergeant of the Seaforth Highlanders. However, following the capture of her husband by the Turks at the siege of Kut in Mesopotamia, from where he was reported as missing, presumed killed, she and her infant daughter were sent back to Britain. The ship in which they were travelling was torpedoed and sunk in the Mediterranean. After some time in a lifeboat they were eventually rescued, taken to Marseilles and from there to the Pool of London, Tilbury, where they experienced a Zeppelin air raid. Mrs MacLeod then became a teacher, first in Mangersta, Lewis, then at Skigersta, Ness. At that time, conscious efforts were being made by the education authorities to eradicate the Gaelic language, and any children heard to be speaking *Gàidhlig* were punished. Anna MacLeod rigorously resisted this policy and encouraged the use of Gaelic in her classes. After two years it was discovered that her husband had been found alive in Alexandria, Egypt, though having been badly treated by the Turks and unable to speak. However, when housed in the Royal Victoria Military Hospital at Netley, Hampshire, on seeing his infant daughter, he miraculously regained his speech and was eventually well enough to study horticulture at Aberdeen University, and then to work as a market gardener at Skigersta, where the couple had two more children, Kenneth Angus and Marietta (*d.* 1983).

Kitty MacLeod and her siblings were raised in an environment in which Gaelic was the everyday language. Her parents were both musical, her brother took up piping, and her sister became a singer and composer. Kitty was enabled, through grants, to enrol at Edinburgh University, where she studied under Dr W. J. Watson, the distinguished Celtic scholar, in 1935 winning the Elizabeth Hamilton prize for the most outstanding woman student in philosophy. Among her contemporaries were Sorley MacLean, the Isle of Rasaay bard, and Calum Iain MacLeod, later head of the Gaelic College at St Ann's, Cape Breton, Nova Scotia. She graduated in Celtic and philosophy in 1936. In Edinburgh she frequently took part in concerts given by Commun Tir Nam Beann (the Society of the Land of the Hills), in 1934 winning the Tir Nam Beann medal. In 1936, having been encouraged to enter the national Mòd, the main Gaelic music festival, in Inverness, she won both the gold medal and the James Grant memorial award for the best performance of a song chosen by the singer herself. The type of unaccompanied solo singing she performed was in marked contrast to the more romanticized and frequently accompanied songs as represented in the arrangements of Marjorie Kennedy-Fraser and Sir Hugh Robertson, but gradually displaced the latter as the dominant form of Gaelic singing.

Following the death of MacLeod's father in 1937, the family was obliged to move to Glasgow, where her mother was able to obtain a better-paid teaching post. Kitty, too, became a teacher, first in Manchester, then in Glasgow where she taught for some time at Abbotsford School in the Gorbals. In 1938 she made a trip to the Barra Isles, where she learnt many of the songs for which she later became famous, both in performance and recordings. The songs 'An ataireachd ard' ('The high swelling of the sea') and 'Fliuch an oidche' ('Wet [is] the night') were later sung in many different versions, 'Fliuch an oidche' appearing in the pop charts in the 1990s as sung by the Celtic rock band Capercaillie under the title 'Coisich a ruin' ('Walking [with my] love'). MacLeod also carried out investigations into the history of the old Celtic songs. The lament 'O, Ailein duinn shiuibhlainn leat' ('Oh, brown-haired Allan, I would go with you') was based on the story of the tragic

death of Allan Morrison, a son of the minister at Barvas, who was drowned in the Minch in 1768 on the eve of his wedding to Anna Campbell of Scalpay, Harris. The lament, composed by Anna, is one of a group of 'blood-drinking' songs, in which was commemorated the old Celtic tradition whereby the drinking of a lover's and a friend's blood symbolized the highest love and respect. Another blood-drinking song, 'Grigol chridhe' ('Gregor of my heart'), was a lament dating from the 1570s, in which Marion McGregor's husband was beheaded by her own Campbell kinsmen. Other songs collected in Barra included 'Latha dhomh am beinn a' cheathaich', 'O, mhic iarla nam bratach bana', and 'Caisteal a' ghlinne'. On Eriskay, she discovered that the 'Eriskay love-lilt', immortalized by Marjorie Kennedy-Fraser, had no connection with either Eriskay or Barra, having been brought to the Western Isles by fishermen from Lewis, where it was known as 'Gradh geal mo chridhe' ('The fair desire of my heart').

In 1940 MacLeod appeared in a film about the work in wartime of Hebridean women entitled *The Western Isles*. She and her sister Marietta were subsequently invited to sing on the BBC Third Programme, as well as at concerts organized by highland and island societies. Both singers made recordings for BBC archives and for the school of Scottish studies at Edinburgh University. In August 1951 an invitation was received from Hamish Henderson for them to sing at the Edinburgh people's festival ceilidh, in which they sang some of the songs collected on Barra. This concert marked the beginning of the Edinburgh festival fringe, the songs she sang later being issued in the United States by Allan Lomax on a Columbia Masterworks recording entitled *The Highlands and the Lowlands*. In 1953 Kitty and Marietta, who had now become a successful actress, appeared in the royal command film performance of the film *Rob Roy: the Highland Rogue*, starring Richard Todd, Glynis Johns, and James Robertson Justice, in which the sisters sang a *purt-a-beul* composed by Marietta for the wedding scene. Kitty was also screen-tested for the part of Flora MacDonald in the film *Bonnie Prince Charlie*, featuring David Niven, but was not selected—perhaps fortunately, since the film was neither a critical nor a commercial success. For the next few years Kitty appeared very rarely in public, being anxious to protect her work from unscrupulous commercial interests. However, in 1961 she recorded for Gaelfonn Records, one of her songs being 'Leòdhas mo ghràidh' ('Lewis of my love').

With the death of her brother and mother, Kitty MacLeod moved to East Lothian, where she was headmistress of a primary school until her retirement in 1974, when she settled in Ormiston. Following the death of her sister Marietta in 1983 she helped establish America's own national Mòd, held annually in Ligonier, Pennsylvania, this being done in conjunction with her brother-in-law, Donald MacDonald, and Catriona Parsons, who had been born on Lewis. The main award for female singers is the Marietta MacLeod memorial quaich. In 1993 Kitty MacLeod's life story was celebrated in a television programme entitled *Born to Sing*, presented by Neen McKay and broadcast on

BBC2. She was described by Magnus Magnusson as 'the doyenne of Scotland's Gaelic singers' (*The Scotsman*).

Kitty MacLeod married twice, her first husband being Murdoch Dubh (Murdo) MacLennan from Lochs, a wallpaper manufacturers' marketing director, whom she divorced, and her second husband being Dr Ernest Renaud Lewtas Gregson (*b.* 1918), a widower and Edinburgh doctor, whom she married on 26 February 1998. She died of cancer of the pancreas at Hilton Lodge Nursing Home, Haddington, East Lothian, on 7 May 2000, and was survived by her second husband. A memorial service was held in Edinburgh on 11 May, in which Gaelic melodies were played by the organist. At the end of the service a recording of Kitty MacLeod's voice was heard singing her version of 'An ataireachd ard'.   G. R. SEAMAN

Sources S. MacLean, *Ris a'bhruthaich* (1985) · J. MacDonald, 'My turn', www.naaclt.org/News/news2.2.html [10th ICCS Report: the tenth international congress of Celtic studies at U. Edin. from 23–29 July 1995] · *The Scotsman* (9 May 2000) · *The Guardian* (17 May 2000) · *The Guardian* (27 May 2000) · K. Hunt, 'News—June 2000', www.dissidenten.com/ken/ken2006.html, March 2002 · 'Kitty Macleod, "The Lewis nightingale"', *Eilean an Fhraoich Annual* [n.d., 2000/01], 11–14 · m. cert. [Ernest Renand Lewtas Gregson] · d. cert.
Archives SOUND BBC archives · U. Edin., School of Scottish Studies
Likenesses photograph, 1940–49, repro. in *The Scotsman* · photograph, repro. in 'Kitty Macleod, "The Lewis nightingale"', 11

MacLeod, Donald (1916–1982), player and composer of highland bagpipe music, was born at 5 Newton Street, Stornoway, Isle of Lewis, on 14 August 1916, one of two sons and three daughters of Donald MacLeod (*c.*1880–*c.*1954), labourer, and his wife, Donaldina, *née* MacDonald (*c.*1880–*c.*1959). He married Winifred May Garden in September 1942: they had two daughters.

His musical education began at the age of four with his father, who was pipe-major of the Lewis pipe band, then continued with pipe-majors Willie Ross and John MacDonald of Inverness, the foremost instructors of their generation. Eventually he went for more than twenty-five years to MacDonald, whom he later described as a martinet, and a wonderful teacher.

MacLeod enlisted as a piper in the 2nd battalion Seaforth Highlanders in 1937. On the outbreak of war he went with his battalion to France and was captured when the 51st Highland division was surrendered at St Valéry in May 1940. He managed to escape, responding in Gaelic when challenged, and made his way back to Scotland. He dismissed the episode afterwards with a characteristically ironical reference to his slight stature, saying, 'Ach, the Germans threw the tiddlers back.' He returned to France as pipe-major of 7th Seaforth, and eventually piped them across the Rhine in the spring of 1945. John MacDonald sought anxiously for news of MacLeod during the war years, commending his musical integrity and predicting that he would be one of the mainstays of the art in the coming generation.

Donald MacLeod became one of the most successful competing pipers of the twentieth century. He won the gold medals for piobaireachd at Inverness (1947) and Oban

(1954), and eight clasps for former winners at the Northern Meeting between 1948 and 1964. He also gained eight silver stars, the foremost award for march, strathspey and reel playing, between 1952 and 1959. He was acknowledged to be the best player and teacher in the army, but he was not appointed as Willie Ross's successor at the Army School of Piping, although he had conducted the course successfully in 1958–60, when Ross was taken suddenly ill. On retiring from the army in 1962, he became partner in Grainger and Campbell, bagpipe manufacturers in Glasgow; its back shop at 1103 Argyle Street became a rendezvous for pipers from all over the world. He gave lessons and recitals in America, Canada, Sweden, South Africa, Rhodesia, New Zealand, and Australia. A generous and encouraging teacher, he pioneered the use of taperecorded lessons and his radio broadcasts for the BBC included a series called *Piobaireachd for the Beginner*. Seven of his pupils won gold medals at the Northern Meeting. In 1978 he was appointed MBE for services to piping.

MacLeod's outstanding achievement was as a composer and arranger. He began composing at the age of twelve and by the time of his death had published six volumes of light music and one of original piobaireachds, leaving a projected publication of '1001 tunes', plus material for at least another four or five books of light music. MacLeod was not merely prolific; his work was of almost unvaryingly high quality. His stringent musical standards were a byword among colleagues; one of them recollected that he would hear his pipe-major working over some, to the listener's ear, delightfully promising material, only to find that it had been consigned to the waste-paper basket by the following morning. While a great admirer of the work of G. S. McLennan, Peter MacLeod, John MacColl, and William Laurie, he was also influenced by the traditional fiddle, accordion, and song repertories. His melodic invention was exceptional. It is said that one year at the Northern Meeting he had written only two parts of his jig 'The Seagull' out of the four required, but entered the tune expecting inspiration to strike in the meantime. In the event, he had to improvise the final two parts on the platform, not only a considerable feat in itself, but especially tricky on the repeat, when he had to remember what he had done the first time round. His range was remarkable—there was no genre of pipe music to which he did not make a significant contribution. Although some found his piobaireachd compositions rather slight, their sweetness and wit (as in his 'Cabar Féidh gu Bràth', dedicated to the Seaforth, which turned out to be a veiled parody of the familiar march tune 'Highland Laddie'), swept through the staid *ceòl mór* scene like a breath of fresh air. Few would dispute that he was the finest all-round composer of bagpipe music in the twentieth century.

Donald MacLeod died at his home at 44 Cardonald Gardens, Glasgow, on 29 June 1982. He was cremated at Linn crematorium and buried at Linn cemetery, Glasgow. In 1994 the Lewis and Harris Piping Society introduced an annual invitational competition to honour his achievement.   WILLIAM DONALDSON

Sources A. J. MacLellan, 'P/M Donald MacLeod', *Proceedings of the Piobaireachd Society Conference*, 17 (1990), 1–13 • A. J. MacLellan, 'Tribute to Donald MacLeod', *Pipeline*, BBC Scotland, 2001 • D. Murray, 'Pipe Major Donald MacLeod MBE', *Piping Times*, 52/10 (2000), 11–19 • D. MacLeod, 'Some memories of John MacDonald', *Piping Times*, 14/6–8 (1962), 6–7, 14–15 • W. Donaldson, *The highland pipe and Scottish society, 1750–1950* (2000) • NL Scot., Piobaireachd Society MSS; music committee minutes, Acc. 9103/3; correspondence, 1951–4, Acc. 9103/10; correspondence, 1955–7, Acc. 9103/11 • A. Fairrie, *The Northern Meeting, 1788–1988* (1988) • C. Morrison, 'Honour when due', *Piping Times*, 53/2 (2000), 47–9 • private information (2004) • b. cert. • d. cert.
Likenesses photograph, repro. in *Oban Times* (25 March 1933), 5 • photographs (in later life), repro. in Murray, 'Pipe Major Donald Macleod MBE', 11, 17
Wealth at death £18603.82: confirmation, Scotland, 15 Sept 1982, *CCI*

McLeod, Sir Donald Friell (1810–1872), administrator in India, was born at Fort William, Calcutta, on 6 May 1810, the second son of Lieutenant-General **Duncan McLeod** (1780–1856) and his wife, Henrietta Caroline Lestock, *née* Friell (1781/2–1830), who was descended on her mother's side from a Huguenot family, the Boileaus of Castelnau. Duncan McLeod, of the McLeods of Assynt, had joined the Bengal Engineers in 1794 and eventually became chief engineer for Bengal. Among his creations were the Murshidabad palace and the iron bridge over the Gumti River at Lucknow. Returning to England in 1841, he became a director of the Agra Bank. He died in London on 8 June 1856.

In 1814 Donald was sent home to his grandfather at the family seat of Gleanies in Ross-shire. In 1819 he entered Edinburgh high school and thereafter Dr Glennie's school at Dulwich and Dr Carmalt's school at Putney. In 1826 his father secured him a writership in the East India Company's service and he joined the East India College, Haileybury. John Lawrence, a Haileybury contemporary, became a firm friend.

McLeod arrived in Calcutta in December 1828 and, after a period at Fort William College, was posted to Monghyr. There he attended sermons preached by a Baptist missionary, A. Leslie, and in 1831 sought baptism from him. Previously a Presbyterian, after his conversion McLeod remained friendly to the kirk and indeed to any Protestant endeavour which he thought likely to aid the Christianization of India.

Shortly after his baptism McLeod was transferred to William Sleeman's thuggee and dacoity department at Saugor. He did not find the arrest and execution of Sleeman's 'thugs' congenial work and was greatly relieved in 1835 to be transferred to Seoni district in the Saugor and Nerbudda territories in central India. Although it was not a prestigious posting, McLeod was happy there. The landscape reminded him of Scotland and he relished the opportunities for proselytization among the Gonds, the aboriginal people of that region. In 1840 he was given charge of Jubbulpore district and in the following year, frustrated by British missionaries' lack of interest in the area, he paid for Pastor Gossner of Berlin to send out five German artisans and farmers with their families to establish an agricultural community near Amarkantak under J. Loesch of the Basel missionary society. The missionaries were well received by the Gonds, but in mid-July 1842 cholera killed all but two of them. McLeod was disappointed but he never lost faith in his dream of Christianizing the Gonds and was still promoting it after the uprising of 1857.

In 1843 McLeod was appointed magistrate of Benares. His years there were calm—one of the greatest recommendations for a district officer—and in 1849 John Lawrence selected him for the commissionership of Jullundur in the Punjab. In 1854 he was promoted to financial commissioner. In the same year, on 10 October, he married Frances Mary (Fanny), the nineteen-year-old daughter of his colleague and friend Robert Montgomery, but she died barely ten months later, in August 1855. During the 1857 uprising, although incapacitated by ill health, McLeod served as one of Lawrence's most reassuringly stable advisers, and Montgomery credited him with the policy of separating loyal from mutinous sepoys in suspected regiments.

After the rising Montgomery became lieutenant-governor of the Punjab and in 1865 McLeod succeeded him. Sir Charles Wood had been reluctant to appoint an evangelical to the post, but Lawrence, as viceroy, declared that he would 'go bail' for him. The position suited McLeod's philanthropic tendencies admirably and he used his patronage to boost vernacular education, primary health care, and agricultural innovation. He founded the university college of Lahore, and established over 300 native municipalities, the most extensive and unniggardly of the early experiments in local self-government. He had a reputation for indiscriminate courtesy and gentility and, far from handicapping him politically, his devoutness actually raised his standing among some Indians. During his time in office, cheap coloured lithographs circulated in Lahore showing him seated as a holy man being venerated by Sikh ascetics. Whatever his popularity, however, McLeod was no sentimentalist and he believed that some of his younger administrators, men such as Lepel Griffin, took an overly romantic view of the potential for close British-Indian relations.

As an administrator, McLeod was less conspicuously successful. Lawrence thought him inefficient, and he himself found the work of officialdom boring and, at times, overtaxing. When confronted with the Punjab's looming issue of tenancy protection McLeod confessed to Lawrence that he hoped to avoid the legislative discussions for which he had 'no aptitude or relish'. He was at a loss to understand his administrators' passion for polemic and ideology, asking plaintively why a middle course could not be steered between the extremes of the absolute rights of occupancy and eviction.

McLeod was appointed KCSI in 1866 and retired in 1870, returning to Britain for only the second time in forty years. In retirement he was unusually dependent on his service pension, having given most of his salary away as he earned it. One beneficiary was the Revd Lal Bihari De of the Free Church of Scotland who received his early education at McLeod's expense. In London McLeod became chairman of the Sind, Punjab and Delhi Railway and supported numerous charities, including the East London Mission, the Christian Vernacular Education Society and the Baptist Missionary Society.

On 28 November 1872 McLeod slipped between the platform and a train at Gloucester Road underground station in London. He died from his injuries later the same day, at St George's Hospital, and was buried on 5 December at Kensal Green cemetery.   KATHERINE PRIOR

Sources E. Lake, *Sir Donald McLeod, CB, KCSI: a record of forty-two years' service in India* (1873) [(1873?)] • *The Times* (4 Dec 1872), 12 • *The Times* (30 Nov 1872), 4 • BL OIOC, MS Eur. F90 • ecclesiastical records, BL OIOC • [A. Raynor], ed., *Mutiny records* (1911) [from Punjab government records] • *The Times* (7 Dec 1872), 5 • *DNB* • *CGPLA Eng. & Wales* (1873)
Archives BL OIOC, John Lawrence collection
Likenesses group portrait, photograph, 1860–69, BL OIOC • group portrait, photograph, 1865, BL OIOC, 211(55) • group portrait, photograph, 1865, BL OIOC • black and white portrait (after lithograph), BL OIOC, Montgomery Collection • wood-engraving, NPG; repro. in *ILN* (14 Dec 1872)
Wealth at death under £10,000: administration, 27 Jan 1873, *CGPLA Eng. & Wales*

McLeod, Duncan (1780–1856). *See under* McLeod, Sir Donald Friell (1810–1872).

Macleod, Evelyn Hester, Baroness Macleod of Borve (1915–1999). *See under* Macleod, Iain Norman (1913–1970).

MacLeod, Fiona. *See* Sharp, William (1855–1905).

MacLeod, Dame Flora Louisa Cecilia (1878–1976), chief of clan MacLeod, was born on 3 February 1878 at 12 Downing Street, Westminster, London, the elder of the two daughters of Sir Reginald MacLeod of MacLeod (1847–1935), twenty-seventh chief, and his wife, Agnes Mary Cecilia (d. 1921), daughter of Sir Stafford *Northcote, chancellor of the exchequer. Her younger sister was Olive Susan Miranda *Temple (1880–1936). Flora was born at the chancellor's official residence, her mother having returned there for the birth. Her early years were spent in London before moving to Edinburgh when her father was under-secretary for Scotland. Agnes MacLeod was an invalid for thirty-two years, and partially blind, but as a child Flora led an active life, playing croquet and cricket and displaying a fondness for music: she played the viola and piano and performed with the Edinburgh Ladies' Orchestra. Her interest in politics and literary matters was stimulated by her father, who was accustomed to play intellectual games with his family and guests. In 1896 she was presented at Buckingham Palace. She spent the summer of 1904 in India with her aunt Alice Northcote, and learned some Hindustani as she could not bear not to be able to ask for what she wanted.

Flora married on 5 June 1901 Hubert (1870–1933), the ninth son and tenth child of John *Walter (1818–1894), chief proprietor of *The Times* and his second wife, Flora MacNabb. They had two daughters: Alice (1902–1980) and Joan (1905–1977). In 1907 Flora accompanied her husband to Brussels when he was a correspondent for *The Times*; her

language skills enabled her to assist him (notably she sent the telegram stating that Belgium had taken the Congo, as Hubert was in the press gallery at Westminster at the time), and two years later they moved on a posting to Berlin. In 1914 she accompanied her father to Canada and the USA. He lived with Flora after her mother died, and she acted as his hostess on the four annual visits to Dunvegan.

The family lived first in Devonshire Terrace, moving in 1916 to 19 Cheyne Place, Chelsea. The marriage was not particularly happy, as Flora was far more able and ambitious than Hubert, although he was known as a sparkling raconteur. During the First World War, Flora served as a voluntary aid detachment nurse and in the infant welfare service. She was chairman of Chelsea welfare service, medical secretary of a school in Battersea, and secretary of Chelsea war savings committee. She also became involved in local politics, being asked by Sir Samuel Hoare MP to chair a women's auxiliary branch, and she was one of six women elected to Chelsea borough council. She was a founding member of Chelsea Housing Improvement Society and later chairman of the Chelsea branch of the League of Nations. From 1921 she spent more time on Skye and became aware of the harsh living conditions for the local people. She started an egg depot in Dunvegan and a tweed industry among settlers from the outer isles in Portnalong. In 1929 she was elected a district councillor for Skye, and was co-opted onto the education and public health committees of Inverness county council and of the county nursing association. By 1931 Flora had given up her work in Chelsea and was committed to Skye. She had been brought up as an episcopalian but now joined the Church of Scotland. In 1932 she was elected county councillor for Bracadale.

In 1929 Flora resumed her maiden name, and on her father's death in 1935 she succeeded to the chiefship of clan MacLeod as well as to the estate of Dunvegan and Dunvegan Castle. This was in accordance with the terms of the entail stating that should the male line fail, the estate should pass to the eldest daughter of the last chief. The lord Lyon approved her change of name to MacLeod of MacLeod in 1935. She was accepted as chief by the Clan MacLeod Society in 1936 and in the following year met 200 clansmen in Edinburgh, welcoming some 300 overseas clansmen at the castle in 1937 as part of the coronation celebrations. A serious fire destroyed the south wing of the castle in 1938, but swift action by local people saved its treasures and the rebuilding programme, completed by Christmas 1940, incorporated some modernization.

During the Second World War, Flora offered the castle for the rehabilitation of wounded servicemen but it was not accepted, as Skye was part of the exclusion zone. She was, however, able to entertain many MacLeod servicemen on leave, and wrote to many others held as prisoners of war. A branch of the Home Guard was formed, and Flora was responsible for an emergency store of food in the castle, to be distributed locally in the event of a German invasion. Flora's elder daughter, Alice, married to Archie MacNab, changed her name to MacLeod in 1943 as she was Flora's heir; however, it was discovered that the entail could easily be broken, and this was done in favour of Flora's second grandson, John, son of Joan and Robert Wolrige Gordon (whereupon the MacNabs reverted to their original name).

After the war Flora laboured to boost tourism on Skye; she joined the Scottish Tourist Board in 1950 and worked with Major Iain Hilleary to set up Skye Week in late May to extend the tourist season. She made several high-profile visits to Canada and the USA, founding clan societies and generating publicity for tourism. These contacts proved useful when, shortly after her return from the USA in 1953, the roof of Dunvegan Castle was found to be in a very bad condition and an American Dunvegan foundation was set up to help raise money for repairs. Also in 1953 she became DBE. Flora then departed for Australia and New Zealand, where again she founded several clan societies, bringing all these together as a worldwide clan organization. This became the most important thing in her life—and became her memorial.

To celebrate the coming of age of her twin grandsons, John and Patrick, in August 1956 Flora laid on a generous hospitality programme, coinciding with the first clan parliament and a lunch for Elizabeth II and representatives of the distant clan societies. She featured in several television documentaries, and in 1967 portrayed her ancestor in a BBC film about Boswell and Johnson. She continued to travel abroad almost every year, and in the 1960s accompanied Peter Howard, leader of Moral Re-Armament. These tours were interrupted briefly by a spell in hospital following a car accident. In 1965 she made over the castle and estate to John, her heir, but the castle remained her home, where she was cared for by her daughter Joan. By 1972 this had become too difficult for her and she moved to Ythan Lodge in Aberdeenshire, although still living in London for much of the year. On 4 November 1976 she took her usual daily walk from Ythan, and having reached the far point she sat down on a bank and died.

JOHN DAVIDSON KELLY

Sources The Times (5–6 Nov 1976) · WWW · private information (2004) · b. cert. · m. cert. · A. W. Gordon, Dame Flora: the biography of Dame Flora MacLeod (1974) · I. F. Grant, The MacLeods: the history of a clan, new edn (1981) · A. Morrison, The chiefs of clan MacLeod (1986) · Clan MacLeod Magazine [Clan MacLeod Society of Scotland from 1935; Associated Clan MacLeod Societies from 1974]
Archives Dunvegan Castle, Skye, papers | SOUND Clan MacLeod Society of Scotland, tapes of the proceedings of Clan MacLeod parliaments, made by W. Cowe Esq.
Wealth at death £5607.63: confirmation, 8 June 1977, CCI

MacLeod, George Fielden, Baron MacLeod of Fuinary (1895–1991), Church of Scotland minister and founder of the Iona Community, was born on 17 June 1895 at 4 Park Circus Place, Glasgow, the younger son and youngest of the three children of Sir John Mackintosh MacLeod, first baronet (1857–1934), an accountant and Unionist MP for Glasgow Central (1915–18) and Kelvingrove (1918–22), and his wife, Edith, née Fielden (d. 1942), daughter of Joshua *Fielden, a wealthy Unitarian mill owner and Conservative MP for the West Riding of Yorkshire (1868–80). MacLeod, commonly known simply as George, was among the

George Fielden MacLeod, Baron MacLeod of Fuinary (1895–1991), by Maurice Ambler, 1955

most flamboyant and charismatic Scottish church leaders of the twentieth century, and possibly the most influential. He belonged to a distinguished lineage of highland ministers of the established Church of Scotland, stretching back for several generations and including a remarkable number of moderators of the general assembly, royal chaplains, and doctors of divinity. He was very much aware of this ministerial heritage, and of his highland and Celtic roots, although his own upbringing and education made him a thoroughly Anglicized Scottish aristocrat. From early on he felt a destiny to be a leader of men. He inherited from his mother's side of the family considerable personal wealth, and was for most of his life a prominent Christian socialist, with a remarkable ability to relate to all sorts of people—borstal boys at the Iona Community's centre at Camas, unemployed men on the streets of Govan, or students on campuses throughout Britain, North America, and Australia. He was a passionate patrician, and his enthusiasm and commitment were infectious; several generations of young Scots, and many others as well, fell under the spell of his preaching, with its imaginative and romantic weaving of words, and its call to costly and relevant discipleship.

The pacifist warrior After education at Cargilfield School, Edinburgh, Winchester College, and Oriel College, Oxford (where he passed the examination in classical moderations), at the start of the First World War MacLeod enlisted in the Argyll and Sutherland Highlanders. He served with enthusiasm, courage, and distinction in Greece and on the western front, becoming captain and adjutant, and being gazetted MC in 1917 and awarded a Croix de Guerre with palm in 1918. He seems at the time never to have questioned the morality or necessity of the war, or of the way it was being waged in the trenches. Indeed his war diary was peppered with unqualified jingoism, as in the entry for 21 June 1918: 'A Battalion in our Brigade did a splendid show last night, and killed 80 Bosche, taking 19 prisoners! This is the spirit that will "Win the War"' (MacLeod papers, folder 37).

From the later 1930s MacLeod was a prominent pacifist, but the story that his pacifism was the result of horror at what he had experienced in the trenches is a myth, one which MacLeod was not beyond encouraging himself. As late as 1928, in a published sermon on the occasion of the funeral of Field Marshal Earl Haig, there was no hint of unease at war as such, at the First World War, or indeed at the way that war was fought. Haig 'was not only valiant, he was Valiant for Truth'; and without qualification MacLeod cited 'The Lord your God, it is he that hath fought for you' (G. F. MacLeod, *Earl Haig, KT*, 1928, 7, 9).

MacLeod was a member of the Fellowship of Reconciliation from 1934, but it was only by 1937 that he had 'come out' as an absolute pacifist. Early in the Second World War John White, at that time the dominant figure in the Church of Scotland, expressed great concern that the Iona Community under MacLeod's leadership had become 'a nursery of pacifists'. Throughout the Second World War, and the cold war that followed, MacLeod adopted a thoroughgoing pacifist stance, which was sometimes divisive in the community he founded, and after the Second World War led to annual ritual debates in the general assembly, when a pacifist motion proposed by MacLeod was regularly rejected. Only in 1986 did the assembly adopt a motion proposed by MacLeod, in the following terms: 'As of now this General Assembly declares that no church can accede to the use of nuclear weapons to defend any cause whatever. They call on Her Majesty's government to desist from their use and stop their further development' (Ferguson, *George MacLeod*, 409).

The making of the minister MacLeod's experience of the First World War may not have made him a pacifist, but it undoubtedly stimulated the young man who had intended to make a career in the law to recognize instead that he had what was almost hereditary in his family—a vocation to the ministry of the Church of Scotland. After graduating BA from Oxford under war regulations in 1919, he returned to Scotland to study theology at Edinburgh University. Then, as throughout his later life, MacLeod was rather impatient with academic theology, preferring a few simple truths that spoke to the heart and were relevant to the needs of the world, to the work of careful scholarship. Working in Edinburgh slums such as the Pleasance was for him, as for many others, formative in developing his passion for justice and his ability to communicate with all sorts and conditions of people. From

Edinburgh he went for a year to Union Theological Seminary in New York, then a bastion of the social gospel. Thus started MacLeod's long love affair with North America, which he later visited frequently, mesmerizing students in campuses all over the United States and arousing much enthusiasm and support for his various projects, particularly the Iona Community.

While he was in America MacLeod encountered 'Tubby' Clayton, the founder of Toc H. Clayton recruited MacLeod to establish Toc H in America, and eventually to direct Toc H work in Glasgow. Clayton's personality deeply influenced MacLeod, and Toc H reminded him of the depth of fellowship he had enjoyed during the war. In 1924 he was ordained by the presbytery of Glasgow to be a full-time Toc H padre in Glasgow.

After returning to Scotland from America in 1922, MacLeod was first assistant in St Giles's, the High Kirk of Edinburgh, at the heart of a huge slum parish. He was tireless and ebullient in his ministry, particularly with boys from the slums, and quickly recognized as a notable preacher. In 1926 he was called to be the collegiate minister of St Cuthbert's, a society church in central Edinburgh. There his preaching attracted large congregations, and the handsome bachelor was commonly known as 'the Rudolph Valentino of the Edinburgh pulpit'. So far, MacLeod was following with some distinction the conventional *cursus honorum* of 'princes' of the Church of Scotland.

A new beginning The break came in 1930, when MacLeod accepted a call to Govan old parish church, where his great-uncle John MacLeod had had a remarkable ministry in the late nineteenth century. Unlike St Cuthbert's, Govan was basically a working-class parish; even more than St Cuthbert's it maintained a high-church tradition of worship. MacLeod arrived as minister in the depths of the depression, with a huge incidence of unemployment, much poverty, and hardship for most families in the parish. He developed a ministry to the whole parish, very much in the tradition of Thomas Chalmers, and indeed of his grandfather Norman MacLeod at the Barony, and of his great-uncle in Govan. He was outraged at the poverty with which he was surrounded; it made him an outspoken Christian socialist. His Govan ministry was like a whirlwind, as he initiated a huge programme of social action, service, and open-air preaching, culminating in an immensely successful parish mission in Holy Week 1934. He really believed in the parish system, and was convinced that the future of the Church of Scotland depended on its revival. He ran his parish like a military campaign, always leading from the front, and being the first to 'go over the top'.

But even MacLeod, with his superabundant energy and his apparently total confidence, had his breaking point. In 1932–3 he had a prolonged period of depression which, as it were, mirrored in his inner life the poverty and hopelessness by which he was surrounded in Govan. He was completely exhausted, physically and spiritually. Out of this depression, and in particular as a consequence of a profound experience in Jerusalem in Holy Week 1933, he returned to Govan with an enlarged vision and a new surge of energy.

The birth of the Iona Community MacLeod's move from Govan to realize his vision and establish an Iona community in 1938 seemed to some people another abrupt change of direction. It was, however, a coming together of his war experience, his struggles to make the faith a relevant reality in conditions of great hardship during the depression of the 1930s, his romantic and inventive attachment to the tradition of 'Celtic Christianity', and his own very strong and personal spirituality, strengthened by his own period of depression. He never tired of telling the story, in numerous versions, of how the Iona Community emerged out of his ministry in Govan. He was summoned to visit in hospital a man who was dying of starvation. The man turned out to be Archie Gray, who had heckled MacLeod while he was preaching in the open air. Archie 'was bitter about the Church, not because it was preaching falsehoods, but because it was speaking the truth and did not mean what it said'. 'Archie Gray', George announced, 'was the real founder of the Iona Community' (Ferguson, *George MacLeod*, 137).

From the beginning of the Iona Community, MacLeod saw himself as a kind of latter-day Columba, directing a campaign for the re-evangelization of Scotland from the ancient holy centre of Iona. But he behaved like a military commander, or another Ignatius of Loyola, leading a disciplined army in the service of the Lord. From the beginning, rebuilding the ruined abbey was at the heart of the community's activity. At a time of unemployment and social division, craftsmen, ministers, and divinity students together discovered in the labour of rebuilding the dignity of creative work; budding ministers learned how to communicate with ordinary folk; shared and lively worship, drawing particularly on what was imagined to be a living tradition of Celtic spirituality, renewed the worship of the Church of Scotland. MacLeod freely invented 'ancient Celtic' beliefs and practices, and often seems to have convinced even himself that they were authentic. For a time at least, he embraced Rudolph Steiner's theories about the spiritual significance of the Celts, and was also much attracted to the way in which Steiner and his associates understood community, cared for the disadvantaged, and believed that the physical world was charged with spiritual significance. In *The Coracle* (November 1939) he solemnly reported that 'It was a practice of the Celtic Clergy to bathe in the sea EVERY DAY OF THE YEAR'. He thus justified his own frequent practice of inveigling young members of the community to join him in an early morning swim. From early on, alongside the rebuilding work, there were youth camps and varied conferences on Iona, attracting a wide constituency to the island where, as MacLeod was wont to say, the veil between time and eternity was very thin.

In April 1944 MacLeod succeeded his nephew Captain Sir Ian Francis Norman MacLeod as fourth baronet, although he did not use the title. On 28 August 1948 he married his cousin Lorna Helen Janet Macleod (d. 1984), elder daughter of the Revd Donald Macleod, of Balvonie of Inshes, Inverness. They had a daughter, Eva Mary Ellen (b. 1950), and two sons, (John) Maxwell Norman (b. 1952) and Neil David (b. 1959).

The pen as a sword The ideology behind the rebuilding of the abbey and the work of the Iona Community was outlined by MacLeod in his book *We Shall Re-Build: the Work of the Iona Community on Mainland and Island* (1944). The purpose was to revitalize the Church of Scotland and, more broadly, the Presbyterian family of churches. This was to be achieved through recovering the centrality of mission and reinvigorating the parish and the congregation. Twelve years later MacLeod's Cunningham lectures, published as *Only One Way Left* (1956), presented a broader and less ecclesiastical agenda, concerned with nuclear warfare, justice, and the environment—all encompassed in a passionate commitment to the cosmic Christ. MacLeod was not a disciplined or original thinker, and his writings were not of lasting significance, but at the time he had a rare and exciting capacity to kindle the heart and elicit commitment. Apart from his Warrack lectures on preaching, published as *Speaking the Truth in Love: the Modern Preacher's Task* (1936), he published a large number of sermons in collections such as *Govan Calling* (1934) or individually, and a stream of manifestos and tracts for the times. But the best way to trace how his thinking developed is through the Iona Community's journal, *The Coracle*. In the early days it was almost entirely written by MacLeod, and it continued while he was leader of the community to be his major workshop of ideas.

The maturing community At the beginning the Iona Community consisted entirely of men, most of them young ministers, or 'licentiates', straight out of the Scottish theological colleges, with MacLeod and a few older ministers to lead them, together with a handful of craftsmen. In the winter the ministers in the community went to work in 'community parishes' on the mainland, mostly in the inner cities and housing estates, while the craftsmen and a few others continued the rebuilding work on the island. The rebuilding was a romantic project, in part an attempt to recover the Celtic heritage, in part a symbol of the renewal and rebuilding of the church as a whole that was required. It continued throughout the war, with MacLeod almost miraculously charming money and materials for the reconstruction from rich donors. The project was a sign of hope in dark days, and an affirmation of the future. Its completion in 1965 was a massive achievement, duly celebrated, but it brought into the open what many people had suspected: neither MacLeod nor the community as a whole had a very clear idea of what to do with the now reconstructed abbey. MacLeod shortly afterwards demitted his post as leader with a note of bitterness, as he strongly opposed the plans supported by the majority of the community for the future use of the buildings. The community wanted the abbey to be a centre of spirituality, study, and meeting all the year round; MacLeod wanted it to be a centre for applied theology attached to the four Scottish divinity colleges.

Especially at the beginning, the Iona Community was

seen as a strictly disciplined, military-style body of men, a brotherhood. Even after his own marriage MacLeod resolutely set his face against any involvement by women or wives in the life of the community. It was to be 'an experiment in the technique of Fellowship'. Community members had a uniform—dark blue suits, shirts, and ties, supposedly the dress of ordinary Scots working men—which they were expected to wear while on the island. Everyone was to attend all services, and meals were taken in common. From this base the discipline of the community developed, involving a commitment to peace and justice (though not necessarily to pacifism), a daily practice of prayer and Bible reading, and an economic discipline.

The fifteen years after the Second World War were the great days of the Iona Community, and the high point of MacLeod's career. The community grew larger, and without ever ceasing to be controversial it became regarded as one of the greatest gifts of the Church of Scotland to the world church, for as it grew it became thoroughly ecumenical and well regarded all over the Christian world. Iona Abbey became, and continues to be, a major centre of spiritual renewal and lively and relevant worship.

As the buildings neared completion and the community developed a will of its own on a number of issues, MacLeod's energies began to turn in other directions, and he became more freelance in his activities. After serving as moderator of the general assembly of the Church of Scotland in 1957–8, from 1958 he was convener of the church extension committee of the Church of Scotland, a position in which he gave typically vigorous leadership, wiping out a huge deficit incurred by the construction of new churches to serve the housing estates which had sprung up all over Scotland. In the same year he became convener of a special committee on central Africa, and in 1959 the general assembly responded enthusiastically to his call to support the opposition to the Central African Federation: 'Someone must speak for the Africans, and that someone will be the General Assembly of the Church of Scotland', he said.

'I joy'd when to the House of Lords …' In 1967, two years after the great Pentecost service to celebrate the completion of the rebuilding of Iona Abbey, MacLeod was made a life peer, as Baron MacLeod of Fuinary. Now he prepared for new battles and a different campaign. He resigned as leader of the community, becoming a general without an army who none the less could still excite new generations with his passionate oratory and calls to action. For some years he had shown himself to be increasingly restless, spending long periods on overseas preaching and speaking tours, and clearly looking for new projects and new battles to fight for the kingdom of God.

MacLeod's membership of the House of Lords was not a success. His speeches were few, and his pulpit oratory fell rather flat in the lords' chamber. His successors as leaders of the community were rather different in style, and he bombarded them with advice and warnings, feeling that without his leadership the community was adrift. He set up abortive or short-lived initiatives, such as 'The new

breakthrough in Christ', which was unambiguously pacifist, and 'The new reformation'. He tried unsuccessfully to establish a new community at his family seat of Fuinary in Morven, Argyll. Even as a peer of the realm, an ex-moderator of the general assembly, a rector of Glasgow University (1968–71), and chaplain to the queen, MacLeod in his later years remained a rebel with many a cause, an aristocratic radical who was a constant irritant to the establishment of which he was so much a part. His greatest critics came to respect the old warrior, while continuing to disagree with him. He was a soldier and a romantic, whose infectious, imperious vision challenged and enriched the life of church and society in Scotland and far beyond. His great legacy was the Iona Community, which continues to flourish, to disturb, and to transform.

The spirituality of George MacLeod MacLeod was one of the greatest preachers of his day, but no theologian. Leading theologians of the time, such as the Baillie brothers, Archie Craig, David Cairns, Garth Macgregor, and Charles Raven, supported him and the work of the community enthusiastically, but his own theological thinking was (according to his friends) mystical and Celtic, and (according to his critics) confused sloganizing. He argued that the natural order was the garment of Christ, and that the central problem of the modern world was the division between the spiritual and the material. From this polarization all the evils of the modern age flowed, but it had been already definitively overcome in the incarnation. In sacramental life the wound that kept the material and the spiritual apart was healed, but those who took the sacraments seriously must work out their reality in the life of the world.

MacLeod was a man of intense and moving piety. His prayers, like his sermons, invited people to encounter reality at a new depth, and challenged them to go and transform the world. He was the joint recipient of the Templeton prize for progress in religion in 1989, and the recipient of a number of honorary doctorates from universities in Britain and North America. He died at his home, 23 Learmonth Terrace, Edinburgh, on 27 June 1991; he was cremated and his ashes were partly scattered on Iona and partly interred beside his wife's grave in Inverness. He was survived by his daughter and two sons, the elder of whom succeeded to the baronetcy.

DUNCAN B. FORRESTER

Sources R. Ferguson, *George MacLeod: founder of the Iona Community* (1990) · G. F. MacLeod papers, NA Scot., accession list 9084 · *The Coracle*, 1– (1938–) · R. Ferguson, *Love your crooked neighbour* (1999), 46–57 [funeral sermon] · T. R. Morton, *The Iona Community: personal impressions of the early years* (1977) · R. Ferguson, *Chasing the wild goose: the Iona Community* (1988) · D. E. Meek, *The quest for Celtic spirituality* (2000) · Burke, *Peerage* · *WWW*, 1991–5 · personal knowledge (2004) · private information (2004)

Archives NL Scot., corresp. and papers | Bodl. RH, corresp. relating to African Bureau · Scott Bader Company Ltd, Wellingborough, corresp. with Ernest Bader

Likenesses M. Ambler, photograph, 1955, Hult. Arch. [see illus.] · D. Bisset, bronze bust, 1956, Iona Abbey · D. A. Donaldson, portrait, 1967, Iona Abbey · photograph, repro. in Ferguson, *Love your*

crooked neighbour, 34 • photographs, repro. in Ferguson, *George Mac-Leod*
Wealth at death   £305,379.84: confirmation, 7 Jan 1992, NA Scot., SC/CO 336/18

Macleod, Sir George Husband Baird (1828–1892), surgeon, was born at Campsie, Stirlingshire, the third son of Norman *Macleod (1783–1862), Church of Scotland minister, and his wife, Agnes Maxwell. He was the brother of Norman *Macleod (1812–1872), who too was a minister of the Church of Scotland.

After graduating MD from Glasgow University in 1853, Macleod set out on a yachting tour, during which he made an unsuccessful attempt to reach the Crimea. However, following a personal request from Mrs Campbell of Garscube, whose son George had been wounded in the fighting, Macleod succeeded in reaching the Crimea, where he rescued Campbell; he then transferred him to hospital in Scutari and later accompanied him home. Macleod then met the minister of war and informed him of the conditions he had experienced in the Crimea. He soon afterwards volunteered as a civil surgeon and on 25 February 1854 was appointed surgeon-in-charge and superintendent of the civil hospital at Smyrna. Macleod spent fifteen months in this post before travelling to the Crimea, where he was awarded the honorary rank of major. He returned home in 1856, after visiting Palestine, Egypt, and Paris on the way.

Back in Glasgow, Macleod established himself in practice and in 1856 published a series of articles in the *Edinburgh Medical Journal* about his work in the Crimea. These were followed two years later by a book, *Notes on the Surgery of War in the Crimea*. About this time he became a lecturer in surgery in the Glasgow Royal Infirmary and lecturer in military surgery at Anderson's University. In 1859 Macleod published a series of articles on syphilis in the *Glasgow Medical Journal*, which led to his appointment as acting surgeon at the city's Lock Hospital. In the same year he also published an article in the *Glasgow Medical Journal* entitled 'Reasons why sanatoria should be established on the Clyde for the sick poor'.

On 27 April 1859 Macleod married Sophia (*b.* 1836/7), daughter of William Houldsworth, merchant, and his wife, Mary Trueman. They had four sons and two daughters. According to a contemporary profile of Macleod, 'he never … never suffered indolence to overcome him so far as to interfere in the slightest degree with his business prominence' (Bevan, 89). Personal qualities also seem to have assisted his rise in the medical profession. The profile went on to note that Macleod's:

> good looks have certainly been no bar in the way of his advancement. Good looks are always an advantage to medical men. They are something in the position of drapers' assistants. Ladies like to be attended by gentlemen who are nice-looking and pleasant in both appearance and manner, just as men like to have among their surroundings women who are gentle and graceful. Dr George is handsome and knows it. (ibid., 90)

In 1869 Macleod succeeded Sir Joseph Lister as regius professor of surgery at Glasgow University. He also became surgeon in the Glasgow Infirmary, and, later,

senior surgeon at the Western Infirmary. Macleod was known as a 'neat and skilful operator' (*The Lancet*) but had little interest in the newer scientific developments in surgery. He received many honours, including an appointment as surgeon-in-ordinary to the queen in Scotland. He also served as deputy lieutenant and JP for Dunbartonshire. Macleod was knighted in 1887. His *The Four Apostles of Surgery* (on Hippocrates, Galen, Paré, and John Hunter) was published in 1877.

Macleod was taken ill a few days before his death, which occurred at his home at 10 Woodside Crescent, Glasgow, on 31 August 1892. He was buried at Campsie after John Caird (1820–1898) had conducted a funeral service for him at Park Church, Glasgow. His wife survived him.

MICHAEL BEVAN

Sources   H. Conway, 'The Glasgow medical faculty, 1869–1892: from Lister to Macewen', *Journal of the Royal College of Physicians of Edinburgh*, 32 (2002), 52–8 • *The Lancet* (10 Sept 1892), 641 • m. cert. • d. cert. • M. Bevan, 'The social context of medical practice: gynaecology in Glasgow, 1850–1914', PhD diss., University of Essex, 1992

Macleod, Henry Dunning (1821–1902), economist, born at Moray Place, Edinburgh, on 31 March 1821, was the second son and youngest child of Roderick Macleod (1786–1853) of Cadboll and Invergordon Castle, lord lieutenant of Cromarty and for several years MP successively for the county of Cromarty, the county of Sutherland, and the Inverness burghs. His mother was Isabella (*d.* 1878), daughter of William Cunninghame of Laimshaw, Ayrshire. He was called Dunning after his great-uncle John Dunning, the first Lord Ashburton. He had one brother, Robert Bruce Aeneas (1818–1888), fifth of Cadboll, and three sisters.

Macleod was educated first at Edinburgh Academy, then at Eton College. He matriculated at Trinity College, Cambridge, in 1839, graduated BA in 1843 as senior optime in the mathematical tripos, and proceeded MA in 1863. On 5 May 1843 he was admitted a student of the Inner Temple. He was abroad for the greater part of the next two years, and then read as a pupil (1846–8) in the chambers of Edward Bullen, special pleader, before being called to the bar on 26 January 1849. His subsequent legal career was intermittent. He established a certain reputation as a mercantile lawyer, joined the midland circuit in 1863, and was employed by the government from June 1868 until March 1870 in preparing a digest of the law of bills of exchange.

Macleod's life was mainly devoted to the study of political economy. In 1847, while still a law student, he acted as chairman of a committee formed in Easter Ross, a district in which his father was the largest landowner, to devise an improved system of poor-law relief. His plan was adopted with success in Easter Ross, and was described in the report issued by the Board of Supervision for the relief of the poor in 1852. It was subsequently imitated extensively throughout Scotland. Macleod remained for six years in Easter Ross supervising its working, and during that time he was also active in advocating free trade at the elections of 1847 and 1852.

In 1853, the year of his marriage to Elizabeth Mackenzie, eldest daughter of Hugh J. Cameron, sometime provost of Dingwall, Macleod went to London. He resided at Kensington for the rest of his life. He had suffered severely from bank failures and afterwards was often in straitened circumstances. Soon after settling in London he was engaged in a law case in which he successfully contested the claim of the Board of Trade to prohibit a joint-stock bank, founded under Sir Robert Peel's act of 1845, from increasing its capital. Macleod expounded the general conclusions to which the litigation brought him in his first work, *The Theory and Practice of Banking* (1856; 5th edn, 1892–3; Italian translation). Less successful was his return to the law courts in 1856, with his fellow directors, on a charge of conspiracy to defraud. His conviction for this offence was not quickly forgotten, although how much it added to the difficulties of his subsequent career is hard to say. From 1860 to 1868 he acted as coach in political economy to selected candidates for the Indian Civil Service. He also lectured on banking at Cambridge in 1877, at King's College, London, in 1878, and at Edinburgh and Aberdeen in 1882, and he read many papers on the subject before learned societies.

Macleod, who agreed in the main with Richard Whately's views, regarded value as consisting in exchangeability, not as dependent on utility or cost of production. He quoted Whately's dictum that the diver was employed because the pearl was desired and thus valuable: the pearl was not valuable on account of the cost of the diver. He was the first writer to give due stress to the power of interest rates to lure the world's gold across national boundaries; and the first to give a detailed account of the process by which bank credit is created. His insistence that the quantity of credit, not the quantity of notes and coin, was the driving force in the economy was common enough for his time; but unlike most of those who held it, Macleod remained a stern opponent of inflationary finance. In his *Elements of Political Economy* (1858; re-issued in 1872–5 as *The Principles of Economical Philosophy*, and again in 1881–6 as *The Elements of Economics*) he enriched the economic vocabulary with the term 'Gresham's law'. This he first applied to the well-known principle of currency that 'bad money drives out good', or that 'where two media come into circulation at the same time, the more valuable will tend to disappear'. Macleod did not assume that this conclusion was first reached by Sir Thomas Gresham when seeking to restore the debased coinage of Queen Elizabeth's reign, for it was well understood before the sixteenth century. Macleod's term was universally adopted by writers on currency. The *Dictionary of Political Economy* (1858), of which only one volume appeared, was the attempt of one man to do what was afterwards accomplished by R. H. I. Palgrave with collaborators.

Macleod's views and attainments were not much regarded by orthodox economists; the feeling was mutual. During his career his subjective notion of value went from being a footnote in economics to a barely challenged orthodoxy: Macleod took no notice and went on attacking the reigning fashion, oblivious that it had caught up with him. He was an unsuccessful candidate for the chairs of political economy at Cambridge in 1863 and again in 1884, at Edinburgh in 1871, and at Oxford in 1888. As his idea of candidature was abuse of Ricardo and John Stuart Mill followed up by self-praise for having created the 'science of economics' single-handed, and given his aversion to submitting testimonials from anyone remotely likely to be regarded as an economist, his lack of success is not surprising. On the continent and in America he was treated with more respect than in Britain. He was elected a fellow of the Cambridge Philosophical Society on 25 February 1850, and was corresponding member of the Société d'Économie Politique of Paris and of the Real Academia de Jurisprudencia y Legislación, Madrid.

In 1887 Macleod drew up, at the request of the gold and silver commission, a memorandum on the relation of money to prices. His last book, *The History of Economics* (1896), showed he had lost none of his appetite for invective, nor his contempt (Adam Smith always excluded) for the classical economists. He died at Norwood, London, on 16 July 1902, and was buried at Norwood cemetery. He had been in receipt of a civil-list pension of £100 since 20 June 1892. Two of his sons, Roderick Henry and Keith William Bruce, were officers in the Indian and Ceylon civil services respectively. One daughter, Mary, was a successful writer of books for children.

S. E. FRYER, *rev.* JOHN MALONEY

Sources *The Times* (18 July 1902) · *Economic Journal*, 12 (1902), 583–4 · E. R. A. Seligman, ed., *Encyclopaedia of the social sciences*, 15 vols. (1930–35) · J. Maloney, *The professionalisation of economics* (1991) · review, *QR*, 194 (1901), 345–71 · H.D. Macleod, statement and testimonials of Henry Dunning Macleod, candidate for the chair of commercial and political economics and mercantile law, U. Edin., 1871 · H. D. Macleod, 'An address to the board of electors to the professorship of political economy in the University of Oxford', 1888 · Burke, *Gen. GB* · J. Foster, *Men-at-the-bar: a biographical hand-list of the members of the various inns of court*, 2nd edn (1885) · *Law List* · Allibone, *Dict.* · private information (1912)
Archives NRA, corresp. and papers · priv. coll.? | UCL, corresp. with Sir Edwin Chadwick

McLeod, Herbert (1841–1923), chemist and bibliographer, was born on 19 February 1841 in Stamford Hill, north London, the eldest child of Bentley McLeod (1808–1870), brewer, and Louisa Jane, *née* Cristall (1811–1901). McLeod received his initial education at Stockwell grammar school and at a private school in Deal, to where the family had moved in 1853. In 1855 he went to the (short-lived) Panopticon in Leicester Square, London, where he studied chemistry under George Frederick Ansell. The following year he entered the Royal College of Chemistry, London, to study under August Hofmann. In 1858 he became a junior assistant in the college, and in 1860 assistant chemist. In 1865 Hofmann was appointed professor of chemistry at Berlin. McLeod served as his assistant there during his first semester before returning to the Royal College of Chemistry as assistant to Hofmann's replacement, Edward Frankland. In 1871 McLeod was appointed professor of experimental science at the Royal Indian Engineering College at Coopers Hill, a post which he held (later as professor of chemistry) until his retirement in 1901. In 1888 he married Amelia Sarah (Minnie) Woodley (1862–1945); they had three sons and two daughters.

McLeod was elected a fellow of the Chemical Society in 1868, served on its council from 1871 to 1874 and again from 1880 to 1884, and was vice-president from 1887 to 1890 and from 1901 to 1904. He was elected a fellow of the Royal Society in 1881 and was on the council from 1887 to 1889. He was president of the chemistry section of the British Association in 1892. He received an honorary degree of LLD from St Andrews University in 1907.

As a chemist, McLeod's chief contribution was the invention in 1874 of an instrument for measuring very low pressures on an absolute scale; the 'McLeod gauge' is still a standard part of the equipment in chemistry and physics laboratories. In 1878, with George Sydenham Clarke, he devised an instrument for determining the speed of machines. In 1880 he showed that ozone was formed in the slow oxidation of phosphorus in air, and in 1884 he invented a sunshine recorder using ferrocyanide paper. From 1888 McLeod read the proofs of the Royal Society's *Catalogue of Scientific Papers*, published in the nineteenth century, and from 1902 to 1915 he undertook the direction of this catalogue, giving the later volumes an accuracy not achieved earlier.

McLeod was devoutly religious throughout his life, belonging to the Anglo-Catholic wing of the Church of England. As Alexander Taylor, his chief at Coopers Hill, expressed it, McLeod was 'A High Churchman and a Tory, and, in all paths of life, a follower of the most orthodox of the strictest sects of orthodoxy' (A. C. Taylor, *General Sir Alex Taylor*, 1913, 2.257). He was thus deeply disturbed at the way in which science (which was, after all, his profession) and religion were beginning to be placed by some in opposition to each other. Especially problematic in the mid-1860s was the outcome of the trials of some of the contributors to *Essays and Reviews* (1860) and of Bishop Colenso, which demonstrated that the Anglican church had very little power over what its members believed. The writings both of the essayists and of Colenso did contain some arguments drawn from modern science, the existence of which prompted McLeod and a few others at the Royal College of Chemistry in 1864 to write and promulgate *The Declaration of Students of the Natural and Physical Sciences*. This asserted 'that it is impossible for the Word of God, as written in the book of nature, and God's Word written in Holy Scripture, to contradict one another, however much they may appear to differ'. The *Declaration* was circulated throughout the British scientific community and when it was published in May 1865 it had been signed by 717 individuals or about 15 per cent of the community, including sixty-six fellows of the Royal Society (11.1 per cent of the fellowship). The *Declaration* attracted strong criticism from some leaders of the scientific community, including Charles Daubeny, John Herschel, William Rowan Hamilton, and Augustus De Morgan. Although the *Declaration* has ever since been used as evidence that science and religion are not necessarily in conflict, McLeod, disliking controversy entirely, played down his role in its creation, and indeed none of his obituary notices refers to it.

McLeod died of cerebral thrombosis, at his home, 109 Church Road, Richmond, Surrey, on 1 October 1923. The most meticulous of men, as his chemical and bibliographical work illustrate, he kept a daily diary from the first day of 1860 until he went into a coma three days before his death; it ran to 174 volumes. All commentators agree that he was a clear lecturer who spent much effort in devising lecture demonstrations. Although not a great chemist in the way that Thomas Graham or William Crookes were, nevertheless McLeod's career is representative of the emergence of the chemical profession in the second half of the nineteenth century. FRANK A. J. L. JAMES

Sources *Chemistry and theology in mid-Victorian London: the diary of Herbert McLeod, 1860–1870*, ed. F. A. J. L. James (1987) [microfiche] · H. F. Morley, *JCS*, 125 (1924), 990–92 · W. H. Brock and R. M. Mcleod, 'The scientists' declaration: reflexions on science and belief in the wake of *Essays and reviews*, 1864–5', *British Journal for the History of Science*, 9 (1976), 39–66 · T.E.T. [T. E. Thorpe], *PRS*, 105A (1924), x–xi
Archives CUL, corresp. relating to the *Declaration*, Add. MS 5989 · ICL, Archives, diaries and notebooks | Bodl. Oxf., *Declaration*, with signatures, Add. MS C.102 · CUL, letters to Sir George Stokes, Add. 7342
Likenesses group portrait, photograph, 1880–89 (with his family), repro. in James, *Chemistry and theology in mid-Victorian London*
Wealth at death £4407 16s. 6d.: probate, 10 Nov 1923, *CGPLA Eng. & Wales*

Macleod, Iain Norman

Macleod, Iain Norman (1913–1970), politician, was born on 11 November 1913 at Clifford House, Skipton, Yorkshire, the second child and eldest of three sons of Norman Alexander Macleod (1879–1947), doctor, and his wife and second cousin, Annabella (1880–1970), daughter of Rhoderick Ross, a doctor on the Scottish island of Lewis, and his wife, Isabella. Norman Macleod, himself the son of a Lewis fish-curer and general merchant, had settled in Skipton in 1907. He was a well-respected general practitioner in the town, with a substantial poor-law practice.

The early years, 1913–1950 In 1920 Dr Macleod bought for £1000 a Lewis property, Scaliscro, comprising a lodge and 8600 acres of well-watered moorland. During summer holidays at Scaliscro the youthful Iain Macleod hiked, fished, and shot, and was taught by his father to play bridge. Macleod's attachment to the Western Isles was central to the romantic sense of his own Scottishness that he would maintain throughout his London-based career.

After a brief attendance at St Ermysted's, Skipton's grammar school, Macleod was sent in 1923 to the somewhat spartan St Ninian's, a Dumfriesshire preparatory school which served as a feeder for the fee-paying Fettes College in Edinburgh. During his four years at St Ninian's and five at Fettes, Macleod showed no great academic talent but did develop an enduring love of literature, especially poetry, which he read and memorized in great quantity, while also beginning to write poetry himself. In addition he proved an effective debater. His real passion however was for sport. Small for his age but tough, he was a wicket-keeper and a scrum-half, albeit perennially in the seconds.

Iain Norman Macleod (1913–1970), by Walter Bird, 1962

In 1932 Macleod proceeded to Gonville and Caius College, Cambridge. He read modern history, but not very attentively. He steered clear of student politics. Having no eye for pictures and being tone-deaf he was not much attracted to the arts, although he did a little acting. What he mainly did was live the good life, in particular the good night life. This he financed largely through gambling, for example at nearby Newmarket but more especially at the bridge table. Macleod founded the Cambridge bridge club with himself as president, and spent a great deal of his time in Crockford's and other West End gaming clubs. It was through bridge, rather than his academic studies, that he honed his intellect and developed his formidable powers of memory and concentration.

It was also at bridge that Macleod met the chairman of Thomas De La Rue, a firm which specialized, appropriately enough, in printing playing cards and banknotes. Following Macleod's graduation in 1935 with a lower second, De La Rue gave him office work at £3 a week. But his interest and energy continued to flow into his life after hours. He became a professional bridge player: an international by 1936 (playing for England, not Scotland), and co-inventor of the Acol bidding system in 1937. His nights at the table often left him too tired to work during the day; De La Rue showed much forbearance but eventually, in 1938, let him go. He then enrolled at the Inner Temple in a short-lived attempt—perhaps intended to appease his father—to read for the bar. His life in this period was convivial, apolitical, and well supported by his bridge earnings. But it was not noticeably purposive.

The playboy life ended abruptly in September 1939. Macleod joined the Royal Fusiliers as a private. After being commissioned as a subaltern in the duke of Wellington's regiment in April 1940 he was sent to France to join the retreating British expeditionary force. Near Neufchatel he was involved in setting up a road block. A German armoured car burst through it, sending flying a log which fractured Macleod's thigh. He was evacuated to a hospital in Exeter, from which he eventually emerged with a permanent slight limp.

On 25 January 1941 he married Evelyn (Eve) Hester Mason [see below]. She had been Macleod's interviewer when, upon first joining up, he had applied to be an ambulance driver. A son, Torquil, and a daughter, Diana, were born in 1942 and 1944.

During the middle war years Macleod was posted to a series of army stations in England. One night in 1941, while serving with the 46th division in Wye, a thoroughly inebriated Staff Captain Macleod demanded that his friend and senior officer Alan Dawtry play stud poker with him. Dawtry declined and retired to his room, whereupon Macleod fetched his revolver and fired several shots through Dawtry's door. Remarkably, their friendship remained unaffected. Had he shot Dawtry, Macleod would later remark, Dawtry 'would never have become Town Clerk of Westminster and I should never have become a member of the Cabinet' (Shepherd, 30).

In 1943 Macleod entered the Staff College, Camberley, for advanced officer training. Under the stimulus of first-class competition in an intensely hard-working environment he realized, for the first time, the extent of his abilities. A new found sense of purpose crystallized into political ambition: he would aim at becoming a Conservative MP, and ultimately prime minister. But war service had to come first. As a major and assistant quartermaster with the 50th Northumbrian division he landed at Normandy on D-day, an experience he would later recount in a memorable article (The Spectator, 5 June 1964). He served in France until his division returned to Yorkshire in November 1944. His final army posting was in Norway in 1945–6.

Macleod was on leave in Scaliscro when the general election of 1945 was announced. Since no Conservative organization existed in the Outer Hebrides, Macleod and his father—a liberal, but an admirer of Winston Churchill—promptly created one, and at a meeting attended only by themselves, nominated Macleod as candidate. Macleod came bottom of the poll, but his 2756 votes out of nearly 13,000 was a respectable result for a Conservative candidate in the Hebrides; as he put it, 'I've got a lot of cousins in the Western Isles' (Fisher, 56).

Demobilized in January 1946, Macleod secured an interview with David Clarke, director of the Conservative parliamentary secretariat. This was a new organization whose main function was to produce debating briefs for the decimated parliamentary party. Macleod was recruited and in due course found himself handling the portfolios of Scottish affairs, labour and health. From the beginning he was a strong supporter of Beveridge-style social security, including a national health scheme; a level of social concern on his part which can plausibly be traced back to his Skipton childhood when he would sometimes accompany his father on doctor's rounds among the poor. But Macleod also insisted that there could be no social services without economic growth to pay for them. He impressed the Conservative Research Department chairman, R. A. Butler, with his energy and lucidity, as well as his liberal political views, and when in 1948 the secretariat was merged with the research department he was put in charge, first jointly and then solely, of home affairs. In that capacity he was a major drafter of the social services section of the party's policy document *The Right Road for Britain* (1949).

Like his fellow secretariat recruits Reginald Maudling and Enoch Powell, Macleod never intended his backroom service to be anything other than a springboard into parliament. In 1946 he won Conservative endorsement for Enfield. He bought a house in the constituency; paying off the mortgage was made a little easier by his continuing prowess at the bridge table and the writing of a weekly bridge column for the *Sunday Times*. An electoral redistribution in 1948 made his seat, now Enfield West, a winnable one.

Rising star, 1950–1959 Macleod entered parliament in February 1950 with a majority of over 9000. One of a famously glittering Conservative intake, he soon joined with eight other 'new men', who included Enoch Powell, Edward Heath, and Angus Maude, to form the 'one nation' group, apostles of a social and conciliatory toryism. ('Tory', not 'Conservative', was always Macleod's self-description.) He and Maude were chiefly responsible for the group's manifesto, *One Nation*, in 1950, while with Powell he went on to write the pamphlet *The Social Services: Needs and Means*, which the party published in January 1952. His concern for the needy did not translate however into any belief in state-engineered equality. Rather, Macleod believed that the objective should be 'to see that men had an equal chance to make themselves unequal' (Fisher, 79). And while he favoured an ameliorative state, he drew a firm distinction between that and what he would later disparage as 'the nanny state'—a term of his coinage, signifying Whitehall bossiness and intrusiveness into people's lives. Macleod's increasing workload in politics meant that his bridge playing career was now virtually over. Effectively it ended in 1952, the year he published his successful *Bridge is an Easy Game*.

With the Conservatives' return to office in October 1951 Macleod became chairman of the party's back-bench health and social services committee. An opportunity to make his mark in his new role soon came, in the form of a debate on the National Health Service Bill in March 1952. In fact it turned into a much greater opportunity than Macleod had anticipated, for he was called to speak not third, after the shadow health minister Edith Summerskill, but fifth, after Aneurin Bevan, architect of the National Health Service (NHS) and the opposition's finest speaker. As he sat listening to Bevan, who was in bombastic mode, Macleod rapidly composed a new version of his speech. He then led off with the arresting sentence: 'I want to deal closely and with relish with the vulgar, crude and intemperate speech to which the House of Commons has just listened' (*Hansard 5C*, vol. 498, col. 886, 27 March 1952). What enhanced Macleod's opportunity even further was that Churchill was in the chamber, having come in to hear Bevan. Churchill was preparing to leave when Macleod began; his attention caught, Churchill stayed. Macleod's speech was a *tour de force* of argument, deft handling of interjections including Bevan's, and wit—a debate on the NHS without Bevan would be like *Hamlet* 'with no one in the part of the First Gravedigger' (ibid., col. 889)—all buttressed with facts and figures memorized from his years in the research department. Nigel Fisher, sitting immediately behind Churchill, heard him ask the chief whip, Patrick Buchan-Hepburn, who this speaker was (Fisher, 82). On 7 May Macleod was summoned to Downing Street. Half expecting a reprimand over another matter—his refusal to spend a second term at the Council of Europe, which he found boring—he was stunned to find himself appointed minister of health. Emerging from no. 10 he had to ask Eve to drive him to a telephone booth so that he could find out the ministry's address.

Under the Conservatives the minister of health did not sit in cabinet, but Macleod was clearly a coming man: the first of his cohort to achieve ministerial rank and a privy councillorship. It was sadly ironic that his own health was not good. He suffered, and would do so for the rest of his life, from ankylosing spondylitis, a painful arthritic condition which attacked his spine and made it progressively more difficult for him to move his back and neck. For her part Eve Macleod was stricken by meningitis and polio in June 1952 and thereafter could walk only with the aid of sticks. Thus Macleod's work as minister of health was informed by an exceptionally clear understanding of ill health, and by compassion for those who suffered it.

Macleod was hard-working and competent, but not spectacular, in the portfolio. He saw neither need nor budgetary opportunity for innovation, legislation, or organizational reform. Rather his task was to consolidate the NHS, administer it well, and ward off efforts by the Treasury to prune its budget. In essentials his health policy differed little from Bevan's. Macleod did have to contend with the continuing dislike of many Conservatives, more especially on the party's right wing, for the NHS. But the electoral popularity of the service helped ensure that there was no intra-party challenge to his policy.

In December 1955 the prime minister, Sir Anthony Eden, brought Macleod into the cabinet as minister of labour. Macleod's predecessor, the affable Sir Walter Monckton, had been charged by Churchill with maintaining peace with the unions and on the whole he had done so, but at the price of several inflationary settlements. Macleod sought at first to achieve a greater measure of wage restraint. Meeting strong resistance from the TUC he proposed a workers' charter which specified rights, including rights against unfair dismissal, in exchange for a contract of service. This idea, however, soon foundered. Strikes were frequent, and Macleod came increasingly to accept his department's view that conciliation was the best course. But the major industrial dispute during his time, the London busmen's strike of 1958, brought him into a prolonged confrontation with the general secretary of the Transport and General Workers' Union, Frank Cousins. During the seven weeks it took to reach a settlement Macleod gained a reputation for toughness and became a national figure.

Within his party Macleod's standing was further enhanced during this episode by a withering parliamentary attack on Hugh Gaitskell. It was one of the paradoxical features of Macleod the politician that he could share many of Labour's views on social policy yet be bitterly partisan in parliamentary politics. As Roy Jenkins has suggested, he seemed to have a special dislike for those on the other side (such as Gaitskell and Jenkins) whom he saw as his competitors for the central ground (Jenkins, 40).

Macleod was too junior a cabinet minister in 1956 to be privy to Eden's machinations over Suez; he was uneasy at the movement of events, but not sufficiently involved to resign. But in his next ministerial office he would demonstrate that he had very little time indeed for the sorts of imperialist assumptions that had driven Suez policy.

Colonial secretary, 1959–1961 Eden's successor, Harold Macmillan, had a high regard for Macleod's abilities, as was apparent from the assignments which he pushed Macleod's way. In the lead up to the 1959 election Macleod was a key member of the steering committee which planned Conservative campaign strategy, and immediately after it Macmillan appointed him colonial secretary—a post which Macmillan himself called 'the worst job of all' (Macleod and Kirkman, 1).

Macleod had no previous experience in overseas policy and indeed had never set foot in a colonial territory. But his very lack of experience enabled him to think colonial policy afresh. This he did in accordance with his conviction—reinforced earlier in 1959 by the Hola Camp deaths in Kenya and the disturbances in Nyasaland—that

> we could no longer continue with the old methods of
> government in Africa and that meant inexorably a move
> towards African independence ... although it was extremely
> dangerous to move quickly it would have been far more
> dangerous to try and hold back the tide of African
> nationalism. (Macleod and Kirkman, 2, 7)

More succinctly he told Peter Goldman of the Conservative Research Department that he intended to be the last colonial secretary (Shepherd, 161).

In retrospect Macleod perceived himself as having 'telescoped events rather than created new ones' (Macleod and Kirkman, 3). His telescoping was done with the general support of the prime minister, who during 1960 was often to be seen in parliament with an arm around Macleod's shoulders; although at times Macmillan was startled by Macleod's speed, and he did not always take Macleod's side in the disputes over central Africa which Macleod had with his 'balancer', the much more cautious Commonwealth secretary, Duncan Sandys.

Surveying his 'dismal inheritance' (Macleod and Kirkman, 8) in October 1959, Macleod decided that he must grasp the nettle immediately in Kenya and central Africa, where political and racial tensions were running high. He made his first significant policy breakthrough at a Kenya conference early in 1960 by securing the agreement of the African delegates and the more liberal European delegates (whose number included his brother Rhoderick) to a constitution which opened the way to an eventual African majority in the legislature. The tactic of working through political centrists in Kenya was, he knew, 'a policy that couldn't last for very long ... But that doesn't mean in my view that it was necessarily wrong at the time' (ibid., 27). As for central Africa, Macleod decided at the outset that the key to making political progress was to bring forward the release of the Nyasaland leader Hastings Banda from detention. His insistence on early release ran counter to the advice of the governor of Nyasaland, the protests of the central African settler politicians, and the views of some of his colleagues, including for a time Macmillan. Indeed, Macleod got his way in cabinet only after threatening resignation. Banda was out within weeks, and the move towards African rule in Nyasaland had effectively begun.

Northern Rhodesia followed. Macleod's dispensation for this territory was, in his own words, 'incredibly devious and tortuous', but 'easily the one I am most proud of' (Macleod and Kirkman, 49, 47). The Macleod constitution was designed to establish racial parity in the legislature, at least for a time; an arrangement disliked by both Europeans and Africans, but one which, in Macleod's judgement, served to forestall a possible European coup while buying time for further negotiations towards a majoritarian outcome. In the process, of course, the structure of the European-ruled Central African Federation was being steadily weakened.

Macleod's colonial policy made him a much-admired figure among liberal Conservatives, but deeply antagonized the Conservative right. The antagonism became especially apparent during the long battle over the Northern Rhodesian constitution in the first half of 1961. Lord Salisbury famously attacked him as 'too clever by half', and as seeking to outwit the settlers by bridge table trickery rather than negotiating in good faith (*Hansard 5L*, vol. 229, col. 307, 7 March 1961). The attack stung, but as Macleod put it, 'I took the brutal, but I think practical view that this was an omelette that you couldn't make without breaking eggs and one couldn't be friends with everybody' (Macleod and Kirkman, 37).

Macleod's work necessitated constant informal discussions and dealings, mainly with visiting colonial politicians, and for this reason he and Eve moved from Enfield to a flat in Sloane Court West. Macleod was never wealthy, and the burden of providing so much hospitality left him considerably out of pocket. Still, his investment hastened many a political deal. One such, which he made with Julius Nyerere, concerned the general shape of a constitution for Tanganyika. Macleod was especially anxious to accelerate the pace in Tanganyika in order to demonstrate that a territory at peace could move just as rapidly as one where violence was threatened.

The demands of east and central Africa meant that Macleod was seldom able to turn his attention to other parts of the colonial empire. He did not play a major part in shaping events in the Far East, the Pacific, south Arabia, or the Mediterranean. Indicatively, he never met the Maltese leader Dom Mintoff. He did, however, develop an interest in the Caribbean, and was for a time persuaded that federation offered the best framework for decolonization there. Later he acknowledged his misjudgement on this issue; 'I regard the Caribbean as my main area of failure' (Macleod and Kirkman, 91).

In October 1961 Macmillan moved Macleod from the Colonial Office. By that time the most difficult decisions had been taken and the key precedents set. Further, from Macmillan's point of view it had become more important to restore party consensus than to go on backing a sometimes irritatingly inflexible Macleod against the right wing. Macleod departed gracefully, with a memorable party conference oration in which he presented what he described as his personal declaration of faith: 'I believe quite simply in the brotherhood of man—men of all races, of all colours, of all creeds. I think it is this that must be in the centre of our thinking' (Conservative Party archive, 1961 conference report, 25).

Macleod's successor at the Colonial Office was his old Conservative Research Department colleague Reginald Maudling. Appointed by Macmillan to bring a steadying influence into colonial policy Maudling disconcerted the prime minister by proving instead to be an enthusiastic decolonizer. His tenure effectively demonstrated the strength of Macleod's legacy: after Macleod, there could be no holding back.

The historian Roger Louis considered that 'Macleod was to Africa as Mountbatten had been to India' (quoted in Shepherd, 256). Certainly the acceleration of Britain's peaceful withdrawal from Africa stands as Macleod's greatest political achievement, securing his reputation as 'perhaps second only to Joseph Chamberlain' (*DNB*) among the reforming colonial secretaries.

The last decade, 1961–1970 Macleod was transferred to a trinity of posts: chancellor of the duchy of Lancaster (a sinecure), leader of the House of Commons, and chairman of the Conservative Party Organization. Not lacking in either ambition or ruthlessness, he had actively sought the latter two positions even though their incumbent was his old research department chief, Butler, who had no wish to relinquish the leadership of the house at least. In his new positions he looked more than ever like a potential leader of the party. But things were not so simple; for whereas his work at labour had made him naturally popular throughout the party, his radical initiatives at the Colonial Office had cost him a degree of support not only in the parliamentary party but also out in the constituencies.

Shortly after his move *Neville Chamberlain* was published, a work bearing Macleod's name although in fact he had written only its first half (Peter Goldman had written the second). Chamberlain had preceded Macleod at health, and the book enabled Macleod to express his admiration for Chamberlain's social reforms. Its somewhat revisionist view of Chamberlain's foreign policy caused a degree of annoyance in the party. Indeed it was an act of bravery on Macleod's part to put his name to it. But the book made little impact: it sold poorly and was soon forgotten.

Of his two jobs the leadership of the house required Macleod to work in relatively non-partisan style to keep parliamentary business running smoothly while the chairmanship of the party required him to press partisan interests to the utmost—tasks which were sometimes difficult to keep in balance. Over time it was the party work which made the greater demands on his energies. He was committed to modernizing the party, and for that reason urged upon Macmillan in mid-1962 the need for a major cabinet reshuffle—only to see Macmillan, in what looked like an act of desperation, sack a third of his cabinet, with disastrous impact on party morale. Macleod's misfortune, as it turned out, was to hold the exposed position of party chairman in a period of deeply unpopular economic policy, recurrent ministerial scandals, and attendant by-election disasters. He remained an inspirational orator at party gatherings, mastered television, and was a fount of ideas for electoral strategy. But none of this could alter the fact that the party slumped ever lower in the polls during his chairmanship. Quite largely for this reason, supplemented by the right's enduring animosity towards him, he was not in a strong position to challenge for the leadership when, in October 1963, the opportunity came.

Macmillan's resignation in fact caught all the pretenders by surprise. In a low mood at the time—partly perhaps because of his daughter's severe illness—Macleod saw himself as at best a dark horse candidate who might emerge if the leadership campaigns of Butler and Lord Hailsham ran out of steam. He understood Lord Home to have declared himself not a candidate, and his political antennae quite failed to register Macmillan's behind-the-scenes role in building support for Home. Once Home began to emerge Macleod bitterly opposed him: partly because he believed that leadership by Home would prove disastrous at an election, partly because he disliked Home's right of centre politics, partly because he believed that in a modernizing party a leader should necessarily come from the Commons. He threw his weight behind Butler, but too late to halt Home's momentum. He then refused (as he had earlier said he would) to serve in cabinet under Home. Only Powell joined him in refusing to serve. 'One does not expect', Macleod remarked, 'to have many people with one in the last ditch' (*DNB*). None of this did him much good in the party.

Macleod's ministerial career might have halted, but other employment soon came his way. His friend and fellow Conservative MP Ian Gilmour, owner of *The Spectator*, offered him the paper's editorship, which he accepted, and Lombards Bank appointed him a non-executive director, which gave him the important perquisite of a chauffeur-driven car (his spinal condition prevented him from driving). At *The Spectator* he was for two years a lively and industrious editor. He made no attempt to hold his writers to any political line; not even Alan Watkins, later of the *New Statesman*. In his own contributions—his weekly column written under the pseudonym of Quoodle, his editorials, his signed articles—he commented pungently on the political scene, defended his record on Africa, canvassed his enthusiasms (mainly sporting), and mounted spirited attacks on various pet hates ranging from the BBC to Harold Wilson. Most notably, in an article of 17 January 1964 on the Conservative leadership succession, he vigorously denounced the privileged Etonian 'magic circle' within his own party which had delivered the prize to Home. This in an election year.

Yet Macleod did not entirely burn his bridges. After the election defeat in October he accepted Douglas-Home's invitation to join the shadow cabinet, and set out to rehabilitate himself politically. Initially he was given the steel industry as his subject but this turned out to be of little political value to him since the Labour government, nursing its tiny majority, chose to shelve its plans for renationalization. Within the party he knew he still had much distrust to dispel, and partly for that reason reached a decision not to stand for the leadership when next it fell vacant. This it did with Douglas-Home's resignation in July 1965. The contest was between Macleod's long-time colleagues Maudling and Heath. While personally closer to Maudling, Macleod saw Heath as tougher and more aggressive and supported him accordingly. The victorious Heath rewarded Macleod with the shadow chancellorship, an appointment which marked the end of his penance and his return to the inner leadership group. It was clear that there could be no further shy at the leadership itself, for Macleod's health was worsening and Heath was four years younger than he. But Macleod was in any case enthused by the prospect of the chancellorship, on which he now set his sights.

Macleod was no economist, did not propose to become one, and did not see much point in trying to construct macroeconomic policy in opposition. His favoured project was tax reform, and on this he did do a great deal of preparatory work. Otherwise he concentrated on attacking a government that was in fairly continuous economic difficulty. Jenkins, as chancellor, did not find him 'an amiable "shadow" … No doubt he was in pain … Perhaps he also had a premonition that time was running out for him. He desperately wanted to be Chancellor' (Jenkins, 36).

Throughout these opposition years Macleod remained an enthralling platform speaker, especially at the party's annual conferences. Resonant-voiced and striking in appearance—he was small, bald of dome, and piercing of gaze—he knew how to entertain, to move, and above all to arouse his audience. The romantic side of his nature, and especially his love of poetry, helped inform his spoken language with both beauty and passion. Indeed there was a consensus among his contemporaries on both sides of politics that Macleod belonged in the exalted company of Churchill and Bevan among the political orators of the modern era (*DNB*; Jenkins, 36).

But Macleod's extraordinary effectiveness as a politician rested on much more than his gift for communication. His phenomenal powers of recollection and concentration,

allied with his extreme quickness of intellect and his ability to focus on essentials, almost always kept him on top of the issues and made him ultra-efficient in the dispatch of business. His conviviality and natural wit found their place in his political armoury, although so too did an occasional abrasiveness and an impatience with those he regarded as fools. The clarity with which he conceived his policy goals and the sheer determination with which he worked towards them counted for much. As one biographer put it, 'Macleod finessed, dummied and bodyswerved as a negotiator, but in his central purpose he drove a straight line' (Pearce, 304). And this points to the most important factor of all: the strength with which he held to his convictions. It showed up most notably in his time as colonial secretary, and was on view again in 1968 when, contrary to the decision of the shadow cabinet, he voted against the Labour government's Commonwealth Immigration Bill, seeing it as a betrayal of pledges which the Conservative government had earlier made to the Kenyan Asians.

It showed up too, of course, in Macleod's 1963 resignation. Jenkins speculates that there was 'some quality of self-destructiveness' in him (Jenkins, 49). His was a complex personality that embraced a number of opposing tendencies—he was both romantic and hard-headed, both consensual and partisan—so it is conceivable that his ambitiousness also had its obverse side. But it is just as conceivable that Macleod was someone who held his convictions so strongly that he was prepared to act upon them even when they cut across his ambitions. Not just the resignation but also the colonial secretaryship would seem to indicate this.

At the election of June 1970 the Conservatives were returned to power, and on 20 June Edward Heath appointed Macleod chancellor of the exchequer. On 7 July Macleod experienced severe abdominal pain, but insisted on attending the Commons to deliver a scheduled speech on the economy. Later in the day he was taken to St George's Hospital where he underwent an operation for a ruptured pelvic diverticulum. He returned to 11 Downing Street on 19 July, after what had appeared to be a satisfactory recovery. But late in the evening of the 20th he suffered a heart attack there and died. He was buried on 24 July at Gargrave, Yorkshire, a few miles from his Skipton birthplace, in the churchyard where his mother (who had died just seven weeks earlier), father, and sister were also buried.

Macleod's early death deprived party, government, and nation of a major politician who was at once brilliant, courageous, and controversial. His old 'one nation' colleague Robert Carr strikingly described him as 'our trumpeter … any party, any government, needs a great trumpeter' (Ramsden, *Winds of Change*, 321). Yet he was detested as well as loved within his own party, which meant that he could probably never have become leader. 'They'll never have the sense to choose him', was Harold Wilson's way of putting it (Fisher, 206). What is not in doubt is that he was the leading liberal tory of his era. He fought to sustain humane political values and to consolidate post-war social security. But it is for his role as the principal architect of

African decolonization that he is, and is likely to remain, best remembered.

Macleod's wife, **Evelyn Hester** [Eve] **Macleod** [*née* Blois], Baroness Macleod of Borve (1915–1999), public servant, was born on 19 February 1915 in Worcestershire, the eldest daughter of the rector of Hanbury, Worcestershire, the Revd Gervase Vanneck Blois (1881–1961)—youngest son of Sir John Ralph Blois, eighth baronet, who claimed descent from the sister of William I—and his wife, Hester Murray, *née* Pakington (1893–1973), youngest daughter of Herbert Perrott Murray Pakington, third Baron Hampton. Blue-eyed and attractive, Eve Blois was educated at Lawnside boarding-school, Great Malvern, was presented at court, rode, enjoyed county society, and played tennis for Worcestershire. On 3 July 1937 she married Mervyn Charles Mason (1907–1940), second son of Alwyne Mason of Foxley Manor, Malmesbury, Wiltshire. During the Second World War she worked for the London ambulance service. On 8 August 1940 Mason, then a lieutenant with the pioneer corps, died when his ship was torpedoed off Ireland. Following her marriage to Macleod she supported his political career, doing much constituency work when he was a minister. In 1952 she contracted meningitis, then polio; subsequently one leg remained paralysed. When Macleod was colonial secretary she was much involved in entertaining various conference delegates: she said she felt as if she had all Africa walking through her drawing-room. She was a magistrate and founder chairwoman, later president, of the National Association of Leagues of Hospital Friends. In 1967 she was a co-founder of Crisis at Christmas, and when a widow she was a trustee and expanded the organization. In 1971, on Heath's recommendation, she became a life peer, taking as her title that which Macleod himself had said he would take if ever he were elevated to the peerage. In the Lords she spoke on penal policy and in defence of widows' pensions. In 1976 she launched the National Association of Widows. She was a member of the Independent Broadcasting Authority (1972–5) and a very successful first chairwoman of the National Gas Consumers' Council (1972–7). She died on 17 November 1999, and was survived by her two children.

DAVID GOLDSWORTHY

Sources R. Shepherd, *Iain Macleod* (1994); repr. (1995) · N. Fisher, *Iain Macleod* (1973) · E. Pearce, *The lost leaders: the best prime ministers we never had* (1997) · I. Macleod and W. P. Kirkman, interview (transcript), 29 Dec 1967, Bodl. RH, MS Afr.s.2179 · R. Jenkins, *Portraits and miniatures* (1993); repr. (1994) · *The Times* (22 July 1970) · *DNB* · J. Ramsden, *The winds of change: Macmillan to Heath, 1957–1975* (1996) · J. Ramsden, *The age of Churchill and Eden, 1940–1957* (1995) · J. Vaizey, *In breach of promise* (1983) · Bodl. Oxf., conservative party archive · *CGPLA Eng. & Wales* (1970) · *WWW* [Eve Macleod] · Burke, *Peerage* (1967); 1 (1999) [Eve Macleod] · *The Times* (19 Dec 1999) · *The Independent* (24 Dec 1999) · *Daily Telegraph* (19 Dec 1999) · *WW* (1998) [Eve Macleod] · Burke, *Gen. GB* (1937) · Venn, *Alum. Cant.* · *Army roll of honour, World War II* (2000) [CD-ROM] · Commonwealth War Graves Commission, www.cwgc.org [debt of honour register]
Archives Bodl. Oxf., corresp. with Lord Monckton · Bodl. RH, corresp. with Sir R. R. Welensky · CAC Cam., corresp. with P. G. Buchan-Hepburn | FILM BFI NFTVA, party political footage | SOUND Bodl. RH, oral history interview
Likenesses W. Bird, photograph, 1962, NPG [*see illus.*] · N. Colvin, pen-and-ink, NPG · M. Cummings, pen-and-ink, NPG · A. James, portrait, Constitutional Club, London; posthumous · V. Weisz, pen-and-ink, NPG
Wealth at death £18,201: probate, 23 Dec 1970, *CGPLA Eng. & Wales*

MacLeod, John (1756/7–1841), Church of Scotland minister and Gaelic scholar, was born on the Isle of Skye and educated at the University of Aberdeen where he graduated in 1776. He was licensed by the presbytery of Aberdeen on 16 April 1778. After assisting Principal Campbell in Aberdeen he became parish minister of Harris on 10 April 1779. In 1795 he was granted a DD degree from Aberdeen and prior to 1804 was appointed deputy lieutenant of Inverness-shire. A sermon which he preached before the synod of Glenelg in 1799 was published later that year under the title *Caution Against the Philosophy of the Times*. On 16 April 1806 he was transferred to Kilmodan, Argyll, on 23 November 1809 he moved to Kilmarnock, and on 5 February 1816 to Dundonald, Ayrshire, where he remained for the rest of his life. He was twice married, first to Janet Campbell (*d.* 1821) and, second, to Ann Macdonald, with whom he had two children.

MacLeod took a deep interest in education in the highlands and islands. After acting as the superintendent of the schools in Glenelg for the Society in Scotland for Propagating Christian Knowledge, he was elected in 1816 by the Church of Scotland's general assembly as one of the committee appointed to publish a Gaelic Bible for pulpit use. The work, completed largely under his guidance, was published in Edinburgh in 1826. He was also the general editor of the two-volume *Gaelic Dictionary* (1828) published by the Highland Society of Scotland, and wrote a useful and informative article on Harris for Sir John Sinclair's *Statistical Account of Scotland*. He died at Dundonald on 6 February 1841 aged eighty-four.

J. R. MacDonald, *rev.* Roderick MacLeod

Sources *Fasti Scot.*, new edn · *GM*, 2nd ser., 15 (1841), 549
Archives Royal Highland and Agricultural Society of Scotland, corresp. and papers relating to Gaelic dictionary

McLeod, John (*c.*1777–1820), naval surgeon and author, was said to have been born in the parish of Bonhill, Dunbartonshire, in 1782, but was probably born five or six years earlier. After qualifying as a medical practitioner, and serving some time in the navy as a surgeon's mate, he was promoted surgeon on 5 February 1801.

During 1801 and 1802 McLeod served on small craft in the channel, and being left by the peace without employment, half pay, or a practice on shore, he accepted an appointment as surgeon of the ship *Trusty* (Davidson, master), bound from London to the coast of Africa, in the slave trade, which sailed in January 1803. At Ouidah, he was left in charge of a depot for purchasing slaves, while the *Trusty* went on to Lagos. Shortly afterwards McLeod learned from a Liverpool privateer that war had broken out again in Europe. He immediately sent on word to Lagos, whereupon Davidson, assisted by the masters of three or four other British ships at that port, attacked and captured a large French slaver, the *Julie*, which had been spoiling their market. The *Julie* was sent to the West Indies, to be sold for—it was estimated—£30,000. At Barbados, however, the capture was declared invalid. The ship was condemned as the prize of the man-of-war *Serapis*, which took possession of her, and when, some little time afterwards, the *Trusty* arrived, an officer of the vice-admiralty court boarded her, and, putting the broad arrow on her mainmast, arrested the ship and all on board as pirates. Subsequently the charge was allowed to drop, and the decision of the Barbados prize court was reversed, with the result that McLeod was awarded a part of the prize, which he received in 1820. But at the time, disappointed of his share, and disgusted at being stigmatized as a pirate, he took a passage for Jamaica, where, his leave being expired, Sir John Duckworth, the commander-in-chief, appointed him to the *Flying Fish*, a small cruiser under the command of a young lieutenant, which, for the next year, roamed the Caribbean, attacking the enemy.

McLeod afterwards served two years more on the Jamaica station, as surgeon of the frigate *Pique*, and from 1807 to 1814 was in the Mediterranean in the *Volontaire* (Captain Charles Bullen), the *Tigre* (Captain Benjamin Hallowell, afterwards Carew), and the *Warspite* (Captain Sir Henry Blackwood). From May to August 1815 he was in the *Ville de Paris*, the flagship of Lord Keith, in the channel and in December 1815 was appointed to the frigate *Alceste*, then fitting to carry out Lord Amherst as ambassador to China. McLeod continued in her during the whole voyage, until she was wrecked near Pulo Leat on 18 February 1817; he returned from Batavia with the other officers and the ship's company, in the hired ship *Caesar*. On the way home he wrote *Narrative of a Voyage in his Majesty's Late Ship Alceste*, which was published the same year.

On 4 July 1818, on the recommendation of Sir Gilbert Blane and James Wood MD, St Andrews University conferred the MD on McLeod. In July 1818 he was appointed surgeon of the yacht *Royal Sovereign*, and in 1819, encouraged by his book's success, he put together a short account of his experiences as a slaver, which was published in 1820 as *A Voyage to Africa, with some Account of the Manners and Customs of the Dahomian People*. McLeod was still surgeon of the *Royal Sovereign* at his death on 8 November 1820.

J. K. LAUGHTON, rev. ROGER MORRISS

Sources J. McLeod, *Narrative of a voyage in his majesty's late ship Alceste … with an account of her shipwreck in the straits of Gaspar* (1817) · J. McLeod, *A voyage to Africa, with some account of the manners and customs of the Dahomian people* (1820) · *GM*, 1st ser., 90/2 (1820), 476 · admiralty pay books, PRO · *Navy List* · private information (1893)

Macleod, John (1872–1948), biblical scholar and Free Church of Scotland minister, was born on 25 March 1872 at Lundavra House, Fort William, son of Alexander Newton Fraser Macleod (1836–1910), preventive man, Inland Revenue excise branch, and his wife, Isabella (1834–1889), daughter of John MacMaster, SPCK teacher in Stornoway, and his wife, Mary, both natives of Kilmallie in Lochaber. After early education at Fort William public school he enrolled in the grammar school of Old Aberdeen in 1885 and was dux in 1887. At Aberdeen University he graduated (aged nineteen) in 1891 with first-class honours in classics

and was Simpson prizeman in Greek. Declining a Ferguson classical scholarship to Oxford or Cambridge, he entered New College, Edinburgh, as a Free Church divinity student.

In 1892 the passing of the liberalizing Declaratory Act (preliminary to merging the Free Church with the United Presbyterian church) dissuaded Macleod from continuing at New College and, with a view to perfecting his Gaelic, he accepted the post of classics teacher at the Nicolson Institute, Stornoway. In 1894 he enrolled at Belfast Theological College, where he completed his training in divinity preparatory to being ordained as a minister of the Free Presbyterian Church of Scotland, formed in 1893 by a secession from the Free Church.

In 1897 Macleod became minister of the Free Presbyterian church at Ullapool and also clerk of synod, the premier administrative post in the new denomination. In Ullapool he met and on 26 April 1898 married Margaret Macleod Matheson (1863–1932), postal worker; they had three sons and two daughters, four of whom were to qualify as medical practitioners. In 1901 he moved to Kames, Argyll.

The residual Free Church minority, their claim to be the Free Church of Scotland having been upheld by the House of Lords, approached the Free Presbyterian synod with a view to reunion in 1905. Although the synod rebuffed this approach, some of its ministers—among them their clerk of synod—felt that there was no justifiable basis for continued separation from the Free Church.

In 1905, while still a Free Presbyterian minister, Macleod responded to an appeal from the diminished Free Church College in Edinburgh to assist in its teaching programme. Later that year he rejoined the Free Church and in May 1906 he was appointed professor of Greek and New Testament exegesis. In 1913 he accepted a call to the Free North Church in Inverness, a congregation numbering some 2000 people. While there he served as chairman of Inverness-shire education authority.

Macleod received an honorary DD from the University of Aberdeen in 1927 and that same year he was elected principal of the Free Church College, Edinburgh. He returned to Edinburgh as professor of apologetics in 1930. Ill health from Parkinson's disease forced his resignation in May 1942. He died at 3 Rillbank Terrace, Edinburgh, on 11 July 1948 and was buried in the Grange cemetery on 13 July.

Macleod had a massive intellect, but he did not assert his intellectual superiority. Although he was well informed on contemporary trends in theological thinking, he was disinclined to engage with rationalistic scholarship. His conviction that scripture is the infallible word of God and that reformed theology faithfully systematizes its teaching was such that he saw little need to engage in the polemical defence of either. Content to leave that task to others, he saw his own duty as simply the proclamation of scriptural truth. His teaching was impressive both in its scope and in its authority. His sermons were delivered extempore and with great fluency. His pulpit prayer was also extempore and although repetitive it charmed the ear and warmed the heart with its dignified diction, its familiar phrases, and its scriptural language.

Macleod delighted in the highways and byways of Scottish church history. The lectures he delivered at Westminster Seminary, Philadelphia, and published as *Scottish Theology in Relation to Church History* (1943) are typical of his discursive style and provide a rich source of information and comment. Some of his vast store of knowledge on the highland church, partly gleaned from personal contact with the oral tradition, may be found in his *Bypaths of Highland Church History* (1965). Much of his garnering he passed to others to publish without attribution, such self-effacement being typical of his generous nature. He donated almost 1000 books and pamphlets to the library of Westminster Seminary, Philadelphia. These items, many of unique importance and rarity, represented the cream of a collection amassed during a lifetime of enthusiastic and informed book-hunting.

Overall, although a scholar of the first rank, Macleod's achievements failed to do justice to his ability largely because for conscience's sake he cast in his lot with a church that was on the periphery. Even so his learning, his piety, and his unpretentiousness (allied, it should be said, to a certain *fierté*), all adorned his Christian testimony and left their mark on the Scottish church.

IAN R. MACDONALD

Sources G. N. M. Collins, *John Macleod, DD* (1951) · P. W. Miller, 'The late Rev Principal-Emeritus John Macleod, MA, DD', *The Monthly Record of the Free Church of Scotland* [Edinburgh] (Aug 1948), 147–9 · D. Macleod, 'The Free Church College, 1900–1970', *Disruption to diversity: Edinburgh divinity, 1846–1996*, ed. D. F. Wright and G. D. Badock (1996), 229–33 · J. F. M. Macleod, 'A boyhood in Gearasdan: notes by the late John Macleod', *Transactions of the Gaelic Society of Inverness*, 57 (1993), 224–74 · private information (2004) [J. F. M. Macleod, grandson]
Likenesses D. Foggie, oils, Free Church College, Edinburgh
Wealth at death house at 3 Rillbank Terrace, Edinburgh; also library largely divided between Westminster Seminary, Philadelphia, USA, and Free Church College, Edinburgh

Macleod, John James Rickard (1876–1935), physiologist and biochemist, was born at the Free Church manse, New Clunie, near Dunkeld, Perthshire, on 6 September 1876, the son of Robert Macleod (1846–1927), Free Church minister of New Clunie, and his wife, Jane Guthrie McWalter. He was educated at Aberdeen grammar school and from 1893 at Marischal College, Aberdeen, where he graduated MB ChB with honours in 1898 and was awarded the Anderson travelling fellowship. He worked for a year at the Physiology Institute in Leipzig, and in Berlin, and on his return was appointed demonstrator of physiology at the London Hospital Medical College under Sir Leonard Hill. In 1901 he was appointed to a Mackinnon research studentship of the Royal Society, and the following year he became a lecturer in biochemistry at the London Hospital. On 22 July 1903 he married Mary Watson McWalter, daughter of Robert McWalter of Paisley; they had no children. In the same year he was appointed professor of physiology at the Western Reserve University, Cleveland,

Ohio, where he remained until 1918 when he became professor of physiology at Toronto. During his last two years at Cleveland he had been engaged in various war duties and had acted for part of the winter session of 1916 as professor of physiology at McGill University, Montreal. In 1928 he was appointed regius professor of physiology at Aberdeen, a post which he held in spite of steadily increasing disability until his death.

Macleod's name will always be associated with the discovery of insulin. His interest in diabetes began in 1905, and before the discovery of insulin in 1921 he had published some thirty-seven papers on problems connected with the metabolism of carbohydrates. Like many other workers in the field Macleod believed that there was probably an internal secretion of the pancreas which prevented the accumulation of sugar in the blood. In October 1920 Frederick Grant *Banting came to him with a request for assistance in an attempt at the extraction of the hypothetical pancreatic secretion. Macleod recognized the feasibility of the proposed experiments, and in May 1921 gave Banting the use of a laboratory with experimental animals and the services of an assistant. Banting, in co-operation with Charles Herbert Best, obtained in a few months a promising extract which did exert a beneficial effect on experimental diabetes. The original idea which started this particular fundamental research was certainly Banting's, but without the facilities, advice, and co-operation provided by Macleod and others it is doubtful if the investigation would have reached such early success. With a group of workers attacking various problems under Macleod's direction, clear-cut and speedy results were obtained, and the value of insulin in the control of diabetes was fully established. Macleod was responsible for the adoption of the name insulin, a name that had been suggested by E. A. Sharpey-Schafer about 1916 for what at that time was the hypothetical secretion of the pancreas.

In an attempt to throw some light on the mode of action of insulin Macleod reverted to a line of research which had attracted him almost at the outset of his career. In 1908, stimulated by Claude Bernard's theories, he had studied the possible role of the nervous system in the causation of hyperglycaemia. His last serious research, published in the *Proceedings of the Royal Society* in 1932, was concerned with the possible existence of a diabetogenic centre in the brain. Macleod also carried out much research in other fields. His earliest paper, in 1899, was on the phosphorus content of muscle, and was followed by papers on such diverse subjects as compressed air sickness, the biochemistry of carbamates, lactic acid metabolism, chemistry of the tubercle bacillus, electric shock, purine bases, and the physiology of respiration. Between 1899 and 1933 he published, sometimes alone, but more often in collaboration, nearly two hundred papers, and those of his pupils, working under his direction, amounted to another hundred. He was the author of several books on physiology and diabetes including *Practical Physiology* (1903), *Diabetes, its Pathological Physiology* (1913), and *Physiology and Biochemistry in Modern Medicine* (1918), which reached its 7th edition in 1935.

Macleod was deeply interested in medical education and acted as associate dean of the medical faculty at Toronto and as dean at Aberdeen. His greatest achievement was as a teacher and director of research. His engaging personality and cheery optimism in the face of many trials inspired the affection and devotion of all who worked with him. He had many interests outside the laboratory, being well read and devoted to the arts, particularly painting; he was also a keen gardener and golfer.

Macleod's share in the discovery of insulin was recognized by the award of many honours. In 1923 he shared the Nobel prize for medicine jointly with Banting. Macleod divided his share of the prize with Professor James Bertram Collip, and Banting divided his with Best. Macleod was Cameron prizeman at Edinburgh (1923), Beaumont lecturer at Detroit (with Banting, 1923), Vanuxen lecturer at Princeton (1928), and Herter lecturer at Johns Hopkins University (1933). He was president of the American Physiological Society (1922–3) and of the Royal Canadian Institute (1925–6); he was elected FRS of Canada (1919), of London (1923), and of Edinburgh (1923), and FRCP (London), under the special by-law, in 1930. He was an honorary member of many learned societies and institutions at home and abroad. He received honorary degrees from the universities of Aberdeen, Pennsylvania, Toronto, and Western Reserve and the Jefferson medical college.

Macleod died at his home at Craigievar, Bieldside, near Aberdeen, on 16 March 1935, as a result of pneumonia complicated by heart problems. After a funeral service in the chapel of King's College, University of Aberdeen, he was buried at Allenvale cemetery three days later. He was survived by his wife.

W. J. BISHOP, *rev.* CAROLINE OVERY

Sources M. J. Williams, 'J. J. R. Macleod: the co-discoverer of insulin', *Proceedings of the Royal College of Physicians of Edinburgh*, 23 (1993), suppl. · *The Times* (18 March 1935) · *The Lancet* (23 March 1935) · *BMJ* (23 March 1935), 624 · E. P. Cathcart, *Obits. FRS*, 1 (1932–5), 585–9 · J. B. C., *Biochemical Journal*, 29 (1935), 1253–6 · *Quarterly Journal of Experimental Physiology*, 25 (1935) · M. Bliss, *The discovery of insulin* (1982)
Likenesses E. Hahn, bronze medallion, 1928, University of Toronto, Medical Sciences Building · W. Stoneman, photograph, 1931, NPG · portrait, repro. in Cathcart, *Obits. FRS* · portrait, repro. in Williams, 'J. J. R. Macleod: the co-discoverer of insulin' (1993)
Wealth at death £5660 11s. 6d.: confirmation, 29 May 1935, *CCI*

Macleod, Sir John Macpherson (1792–1881), East India Company servant, was born on 14 January 1792 at Ardarden, Dunbartonshire, the eldest son of Donald Macleod of St Kilda, formerly a colonel in the Madras army, and his wife, Diana, daughter of Donald Macdonald of Tormore in Inverness-shire. He was educated at Canongate grammar school, Edinburgh, and, from 1805 until 1809, at Edinburgh University, where he attended classes in Greek, Latin, mathematics, and natural history. In 1809 he obtained a writership for the East India Company's service in Madras and joined the East India College at Haileybury.

Macleod arrived in Madras in 1811. In 1814 he was appointed second assistant, and afterwards first assistant, in the civil departments and in 1816 became a member and secretary of the committee for revising the customs laws. In 1820 poor health occasioned his return to Britain and while there, in 1822, he married Catharine, daughter of William Greig of Thornhill in Stirlingshire. There were apparently no children of the marriage.

On returning to India in 1823, Macleod was appointed secretary to the government in the financial and general departments. His linguistic abilities having impressed his superiors, he was made Tamil translator to the government in 1825 and Persian translator in 1826. In the following year he became secretary to the government in the revenue and judicial departments and in 1829 joined the board of revenue. In June 1832 he was appointed commissioner for the government of Mysore, a nominally independent state which in the previous year had been brought under direct British supervision; it fell to Macleod, therefore, to 'clean up' and reorganize Mysore's financial and political administration to suit contemporary British ideals of governance.

On 19 February 1835 Macleod was appointed Madras member of the Indian law commission, presided over by T. B. Macaulay; his contributions to the original draft of the Indian penal code, drawn up by the commission, are preserved in *The Indian penal code as originally framed in 1837 with notes by T. B. Macaulay, J. M. Macleod, G. W. Anderson and F. Millet* (1888). An appointment to Macaulay's committee for revising the system of prison discipline throughout India automatically followed. Here too, as in the work on the penal code, he shared the committee's dominant Benthamite perspective.

In the latter part of 1836 Macleod's health broke down completely and in July 1838 he returned to Britain, eventually retiring from the service in 1841. He retained his interest in Indian legal questions and in 1848 published *Notes on the report of the Indian law commissioners, dated 23rd July 1846, on the Indian penal code*, followed in 1857 by a pamphlet, *Observations on the Legislature at Calcutta*, which challenged the supposed autonomy of the governor-general's legislative council.

Macleod was a member of the general council of the University of Edinburgh and a magistrate and deputy lieutenant for Inverness-shire. In 1866 he was nominated KCSI and in 1871 was sworn of the privy council. He died on 1 March 1881 at his London residence, 1 Stanhope Street, Hyde Park.   E. I. CARLYLE, *rev.* KATHERINE PRIOR

Sources C. C. Prinsep, *Record of services of the Honourable East India Company's civil servants in the Madras presidency from 1741 to 1858* (1885) · *The Times* (3 March 1881), 1, 7 · BL OIOC, Haileybury MSS · F. C. Danvers and others, *Memorials of old Haileybury College* (1894)
Archives BL OIOC, letters to Sir J. P. Grant, MS Eur. F 127 · Bodl. Oxf., Napier MSS
Wealth at death under £30,000—effects in England: probate, 25 April 1881, *CGPLA Eng. & Wales*

MacLeod, Kenneth (1871–1955), Church of Scotland minister and folklorist, was born at Sandareg on the island of

Eigg on 6 February 1871. He was the son of Donald Mac-Leod, parochial schoolmaster of Eigg, and his wife, Jessie, *née* Humphrey, and was the youngest but one of a family of two sons and six daughters, none of whom married. Brought up by his paternal aunt Janet MacLeod after his mother died in 1877, he absorbed the MacLeod traditions from her and the MacDonald traditions from the Gaelic storytellers and traditional singers of Eigg. He published his first article connected with this, 'The fairy snuff box', in the *Celtic Magazine* of November 1887. The magazine was edited by Alexander MacBain, whose pupil MacLeod was at Raining's school, Inverness, from 1885 to 1888; his leaving certificate proclaimed that, 'His strong point is his Gaelic; he speaks and writes the best Gaelic I know of; he is full of Gaelic lore and folk literature'.

MacLeod matriculated in the arts faculty of Glasgow University in the autumn of 1888; he was an active member of the university's Ossianic Society, and pressed for the creation of a Celtic lectureship at Glasgow. His university career ended in a breakdown in health in 1893, which prevented his taking a degree. In search of recovery he made a voyage to Australia on the *Merkara*, serving as an unpaid assistant purser in the winter of 1895–6. He then became a lay missionary for the Church of Scotland and worked in many places in the highlands and islands in that capacity, including South Uist, where he got to know Father Allan McDonald in 1897. In 1902–3 he attended Professor Donald MacKinnon's Celtic class at Edinburgh University for a session. From 1905 to 1916 he contributed many articles in Gaelic and English to the *Celtic Review*, edited by Ella Carmichael.

In 1917 MacLeod petitioned the general assembly of the Church of Scotland to be given the status of a licentiate minister. This was granted, and his first parish was the islands of Colonsay and Oronsay. In 1932 he was given an honorary DD by Aberdeen University. His last parish was the island of Gigha with Cara, from which he retired in 1947. He spent the rest of his life in Edinburgh, where he died at 42 East Claremont Street on 9 July 1955. He was buried in the Muckairn parish graveyard at Taynuillt in Argyll.

MacLeod is best known for his indispensable collaboration with Marjory Kennedy-Fraser on the collection of Gaelic songs published under the title *Songs of the Hebrides* (2 vols., 1909–17), for which he was chosen by Professor MacKinnon. MacLeod's help extended from mending broken stanzas in the verses of old songs which Kennedy-Fraser recorded on a primitive dictaphone, to making translations, and sometimes to providing Gaelic words for tunes. Convinced (though erroneously) that Hebridean folk tunes could not be taken down in musical notation as actually sung, MacLeod himself had no musical training, and did not know about modes. His association with Kennedy-Fraser's romantic pseudo-Celticism rather unfairly compromised his reputation as a serious folklorist. Kenneth MacLeod was a true ecumenical Christian endowed with a sense of humour, and loved by all who knew him. J. L. CAMPBELL

Sources personal knowledge (2004) · T. M. Murchison, *Sgriobhaidhean Choinnich Mhic Leoid: the Gaelic prose of Kenneth MacLeod* (1988) · A. Carmichael, *Carmina Gadelica* (1992) **Archives** NL Scot., papers **Wealth at death** £251 8s. 9d.: confirmation, 9 Dec 1955, *CCI*

MacLeod, Malcolm Neynoe (1882–1969), surveyor, was born on 23 May 1882, probably in Rajpur Chumparan, Bihar, India, the eldest son of Malcolm Neynoe MacLeod, who was in charge of an indigo factory in Bihar, and his wife, Eliza Agnes. He attended Aird House School, Edinburgh (1887–95), and then Rugby School (1896–8). At the age of sixteen he passed into the Royal Military Academy, Woolwich. Although he was the youngest cadet in his term, he passed out first in 1900, gaining the Pollock and Queen Victoria gold medals and prizes for military topography and geometrical drawing. He was commissioned in the Royal Engineers on 2 May 1900.

MacLeod was posted to India in May 1902 and spent three years at the military works services at Jubbulpore and in the office of the director-general military works at Simla before in 1905 he joined the survey of India. While there he suffered an onslaught of enteric fever from which he never fully recovered. After the first of three periods of six months' sick leave he returned to India to work on the surveys of the Khyber and Malakand passes, and in the Central Provinces and the Punjab. He was promoted captain in May 1910 and then transferred to the headquarters of the survey of India in Calcutta. Following another bout of fever he was sent to the healthier climate of the trans-frontier mapping office at Simla.

In 1914 MacLeod returned to England on a year's leave to improve his health. At the beginning of 1915 he was ordered to Buxton to raise and train the 145 army troops company of the Royal Engineers. He took this company, now part of the 11th corps, to France in September 1915. In 1916 he raised the 4th field survey company for the newly formed Fourth Army, which was to deliver the great Somme offensive. MacLeod's survey company was to develop new survey methods, of which the most important was 'predicted artillery fire', the technique of firing at pre-selected, accurately surveyed targets without making preliminary range-finding shots, which at once destroyed all element of surprise and revealed the allied gun positions. MacLeod considered this technique to have been decisive in the victories of Cambrai in 1916 and after. Predicted artillery bombardment came to constitute the real attack, while the infantry advance became the supporting operation, a reversal of the traditional roles of the two arms. MacLeod was promoted major in 1916, and acting lieutenant-colonel in 1918, was twice mentioned in dispatches, and was awarded the DSO and MC. In 1919 he formed and commanded the 1st survey company of the Royal Artillery. He then went as chief instructor (survey) to the School of Artillery, Larkhill, where he initiated the technical side of artillery survey.

In early 1923 MacLeod joined the Ordnance Survey at Southampton. On 9 January 1924 he married Elsie May (*b.* 1892/3, *d.* after 1978), the daughter of William Edward Gould of Wootton, New Milton. They had no children. He

Malcolm Neynoe MacLeod (1882–1969), by Walter Stoneman, 1939

remained at the Ordnance Survey for six years. In 1929 he became general staff officer in 1 MI4, the geographical section of the general staff (GSGS), whose main duties were the provision of maps for war, the collection of geographical and topographical information of the empire and foreign countries, and the co-ordination of all survey organizations in the empire. MacLeod considered that survey allied to artillery fire would be critical in any future conflict. He therefore proposed a programme to provide maps at scales of 1:250,000 for strategic moves, 1:50,000 for mobile phases, and 1:25,000 for set-piece battles. MacLeod's view that artillery was the key to future warfare was publicly contested by proponents of tank theories such as J. F. C. Fuller and Basil Liddell Hart. MacLeod promoted his ideas by writing papers in the *Royal Engineers Journal* and the *Journal of the Royal United Services Institution*, and authority was eventually given for the formation of the 19th field survey company of the Royal Engineers to produce MacLeod's maps in war.

In February 1935 MacLeod was appointed director-general of the Ordnance Survey, with the rank of brigadier. The war, post-war urban expansion and road building, and financial retrenchment had brought the Ordnance Survey to its knees, and, just as the government was passing legislation such as the Town and Country Planning Act (1932) which could not be put into effect without up-to-date plans, the survey lacked the manpower to meet numerous demands made upon it. A departmental committee was appointed in 1935 to address the national mapping crisis. MacLeod had already initiated the retriangulation of Great Britain, and now he seized the opportunity to transform the large-scale Ordnance Survey plans from their nineteenth-century format of county maps, many based on different meridians, into a homogeneous national series. It was with difficulty that his strong views on the necessity of a metric grid, the kilometre-square 1:2500 format, the survey of urban areas at the scale of 1:1250, continuous revision, and the introduction of the 1:25,000 map prevailed. However, he can be considered the architect of the structure of post-war Ordnance Survey cartography, and it was with justification that he claimed that the final report of the committee, published in 1938, amounted to a new charter for the Ordnance Survey.

More staff were recruited to implement MacLeod's proposals, and the increased responsibilities borne by the director-general led to the position's being upgraded from brigadier to major-general, to which rank MacLeod was promoted in March 1939 (he was later created CB). Civilian mapping, however, took second place to military mapping during the Second World War. As director-general MacLeod was responsible for the training and mobilization of the field survey units of the field army. On mobilization he was created inspector of survey units.

When MacLeod retired on 1 June 1943 the Ordnance Survey had printed 100 million maps for military use. He had also recast the mapping of Great Britain on new sheet lines and introduced enamelled metal plates in place of paper as the original drawing support for the large-scale plans and the systematic use of air photography for the revision of the 1:2500 plans. In retirement MacLeod became second in command of the 12th battalion Hampshire Home Guard. After the war he undertook several unpaid and semi-public duties, including the chairmanship of the Ministry of Labour's Disablement Advisory Committee. In 1946 he advised the Iraqi government on their surveys. He had been aide-de-camp to Edward VIII and George VI from 1936 to 1939, and was colonel commandant from 1941 to 1950.

MacLeod was a tall man of strong character, with great kindness and charm. The junior civilian staff at the Ordnance Survey remembered him affectionately for his approachability and willingness to stop and talk. When young he was an accomplished athlete. He served on the council of the Royal Geographical Society three times in the 1930s, and was vice-president from 1939 to 1941. In retirement he continued to interest himself in professional and scientific matters. He was an honorary member of the Royal Institution of Chartered Surveyors and chairman of the Field Survey Association.

MacLeod died on 1 August 1969 of heart failure at his home, Littlehaven, Beaulieu Road, Dibden Purlieu, Hampshire, survived by his widow.　　　YOLANDE HODSON

Sources M. N. MacLeod, 'Autobiographical notes', 1950x59?, Ordnance Survey Library, Southampton · *Royal Engineers Journal*, new ser., 83 (1969), 322–6 · R. C. A. Edge, 'Major-General M. N. MacLeod',

GJ, 135 (1969), 642–3 · Y. Hodson, 'MacLeod and the Davidson committee', *A history of the Ordnance Survey*, ed. W. A. Seymour (1980), 257–67 · private information (2004) · *CGPLA Eng. & Wales* (1969) · m. cert. · d. cert.

Archives PRO, Ordnance Survey class
Likenesses W. Stoneman, photograph, 1939, NPG [*see illus.*] · photograph, 1940–44, Ordnance Survey, Southampton · photograph, 1940–1949?, repro. in *Royal Engineers Journal*, 323
Wealth at death £64,594: probate, 22 Oct 1969, *CGPLA Eng. & Wales*

MacLeod, Mary. *See* Màiri nighean Alasdair Ruaidh (*c.*1615–*c.*1707).

MacLeod, Murdo Allan (1926–1996), Free Church of Scotland minister, was born on 5 September 1926 at Glendale, Skye, the second of four children of John MacLeod (1893–1971), then a postman, and his wife, Christina MacLeod (1897–1972).

Some of MacLeod's earliest years (1930–39) were spent in Glasgow, where the family was then resident. In 1939 they moved to Inverness, where the parents owned and managed the Kingsmills House Hotel. MacLeod was educated at the Dingwall Academy (1939–42), and then at the Inverness Royal Academy on leaving which in 1945 he began to train for a career in accountancy. Being persuaded of a call to the Christian ministry, however, he entered the University of Edinburgh and undertook an arts degree (1948–52). He then studied theology in the Free Church of Scotland college (1952–5). While in Edinburgh he met and on 11 September 1954 married Nancie Margaret Johnstone (*b.* 1930), a science graduate of the University of Edinburgh and a school teacher. There were four children of this marriage, two sons and two daughters.

In 1955 MacLeod was ordained to the Christian ministry and inducted as Free Church of Scotland minister in Tarbert, Argyll. This ministry lasted until 1963, when he transferred to Crouch End, London, as minister of the Free Church congregation there. Having had a long interest in Christian missionary work directed to the Jews, in London MacLeod became a member of the council of management of the International Society for Jewish Evangelism (IJS). When in 1970 the directorship of the society became vacant he was appointed to that position and so began what became his most significant life's work, extending over the next twenty-two years.

As director and general secretary of the IJS, MacLeod negotiated a union with the Barbican Mission to the Jews; the new society adopted the name Christian Witness to Israel. For a few years he was a joint director of the new society, but upon the death of the other joint director, the Revd Stephen Levinson, he assumed sole responsibility. Under his leadership the society adopted a reformed basis of belief and formed significant alliances with other groups worldwide, notably Jews for Jesus, whose board MacLeod joined, as also that of the German Evangeliumdienst für Israel. This involved almost constant journeys to Europe, the USA, Hong Kong, Australia, New Zealand and, of course, Israel. The work in Israel had a special place in his interest and effort. One of his colleagues there later noted that:

Murdo transformed the Society into a purpose orientated Society in which direct evangelism was a clear goal. He guided the work of the Society in Israel away from an emphasis on social and medical work toward a Society that had as its goal the strengthening of the local Churches in Israel in the work of evangelism. He made room for local leadership and supported local initiatives. (private information)

A significant part of local initiative was in the founding of a publishing house to supply Christian literature in Hebrew. A bookshop had earlier been instituted and handed over to the local church.

Murdo MacLeod became well known in the international scene as a leader in planning missionary strategy. From 1983 to 1991 he was international president of the Lausanne Consultation on Jewish Evangelism. He was a signatory of the Willowbank declaration on the Christian gospel and the Jewish people, a document drawn up by an international group after, as they declared, 'several days of intense consultation' and commended to the churches.

Over the years MacLeod contributed articles to many books and journals. In 1984 he was elected moderator of the general assembly of the Free Church of Scotland. He retired from the leadership of Christian Witness to Israel in 1992, suffering from heart disease which had necessitated bypass surgery. Heart failure caused his death on 26 April 1996 at his home, 11 St Martins Drive, Eynsford, Dartford, Kent. He was buried in Union Church cemetery, Crockenhill, Kent, on 2 May. CLEMENT GRAHAM

Sources personal knowledge (2004) · private information (2004) [Donald MacLeod] · *CGPLA Eng. & Wales* (1996) · tombstones of his parents, Fortrose old cemetery
Wealth at death £180,000: probate, 8 July 1996, *CGPLA Eng. & Wales*

Macleod, Neil (d. 1613). *See under* MacLeod, Roderick (d. 1595).

Macleod, Neil, of Assynt (1627/8?–*c.*1697), clan chief, was the son of Neil Macleod, tenth laird of Assynt, and Florence, daughter of Torquil Macleod of Lewis. His clan was struggling to survive in the face of internal feuding and pressure from the expanding Mackenzies, who had already dispersed the Macleods of Lewis and Coigach, and whose chief, the earl of Seaforth, was feudal superior of the lands of Assynt. Neil's father died in 1633, but his grandfather, Donald Mor, lived on as chief until the 1640s. On Donald Mor's death the lands passed to his son Donald Og, and when he died, about 1647, they passed to his brother Hugh. When Neil came of age in 1649 Hugh transferred the lands to him.

In the civil wars of the 1640s the men of Assynt seem to have taken their lead from George Mackenzie, second earl of Seaforth, who supported the covenanters until, in 1646, he temporarily changed sides and joined the royalist marquess of Montrose in besieging Inverness. Some of the Assynt men took part in the siege, and Neil Macleod is said to have stayed at Castle Brahan as a friend of Seaforth. He may, however, have been under duress, for Seaforth also sent men to ravage Assynt. Macleod had some time before been appointed sheriff-depute of Assynt by the earl of Sutherland, the covenanter sheriff of Sutherland, and may have sought to continue to serve his cause. In view of later allegations, it should be stressed that there is no evidence whatever that he was a friend and supporter of Montrose in the 1646 campaign. Macleod's covenanter inclinations were again indicated when, about 1647, he married Christian, daughter of Sir John Monro (Munro) of Lumlair, a covenanter. When he took possession of his lands in 1649 he wadset (a type of mortgage, whereby interest on the loan was repaid out of the revenues of the land) them to his father-in-law for £10,000, an indication of his financial problems and perhaps also an attempt to give Monro a claim to the lands to counter Mackenzie claims that they already had a right to them through an earlier wadset.

Montrose had gone into exile soon after the 1646 attack on Inverness, but he returned to Scotland to lead a new rising in 1650. After his defeat at Carbisdale (on 27 April) he fled into the highlands. Traditions of what precisely happened next vary, but it seems most probable that the fugitive was misled by some of Macleod's men, who had been sent out to hunt for him, into thinking they were leading him to safety. In fact they took him to Ardvreck Castle on Loch Assynt, where Macleod's wife held him prisoner until Macleod, who had been away from home, returned. He then handed Montrose over to the covenanters, and he was taken to Edinburgh and executed, while Macleod hastened to claim the reward due for his services. Almost immediately he was accused by royalists of treachery, he having betrayed an old comrade. Montrose had come to him for help, but Macleod had sold him to his enemies. Within months of his death Montrose had become a hero not only to royalists but, as political allegiances changed and Charles II came to Scotland, to many former covenanters. National embarrassment at Montrose's execution required a scapegoat to divert attention from others involved in the deed, and an obscure highland chieftain with no influential friends was ideal for the part.

The charge of treachery was to haunt Macleod for the rest of his life. The covenanters awarded him £20,000 Scots (about £1660 sterling) for his services, though he may never have received anything more than 400 bolls of grain—which highland tradition triumphantly claimed turned out to be mainly bad. The 'greedy wretch' (Fraser, 353) got his just deserts. 'Son of Neil from dreary Assynt,' sang a highland poet, 'The death shroud should be about you, despicable one, for you have sinfully sold the truth for Leith meal, most of which had gone sour' (*Orain Iain Luim*, 58–9).

English conquest and occupation largely spared Macleod from immediate royalist vengeance, though his estates were again ravaged by Kenneth Mackenzie, third earl of Seaforth, in 1654 during a royalist rising. After the restoration of monarchy in 1660 he was arrested and imprisoned in the Tolbooth of Edinburgh. His claim that he had not been directly responsible for Montrose's arrest was not a relevant defence, as he had certainly handed him over to his enemies, but his plea that indemnities issued by Charles II in 1650 and after 1660 protected him from prosecution were well grounded. In October 1663 the Scottish parliament sought instructions from Charles as to whether to proceed with prosecution or abandon the case. In December the privy council released him from imprisonment, on his binding himself to remain in Edinburgh, after considering certificates from physicians stating that he would die unless he was freed. In November 1664 he was permitted to return home until the following May to look after his estates. Stories that while in prison he had 'struck up to a high pitch of vice and impiety, and gave great entertainments' (*Bishop Burnet's History*, 1.230) reflect royalist determination to discredit him rather than reality. Finally, in February 1666 the king ruled that as he was covered by indemnities the case against him should be abandoned. Gilbert Burnet denounced the 'gross iniquity' of his friends' winning freedom for so base a man (ibid.), but what saved him was not friends in high places but fears by former covenanters of the implications of allowing the king to make exceptions to the Acts of Indemnity.

Macleod's troubles were not over, however, for Seaforth pursued his claims to Assynt and obtained power to eject him. When this was resisted, Seaforth obtained a commission of fire and sword in 1672 and took possession by force, scattering the several hundred men Macleod had raised to defend his clan lands. He was again imprisoned in Edinburgh, and brought to trial before the justiciary court in February 1674. The first two charges related to the betrayal of Montrose and his resistance to Seaforth in 1654. As these were accusations which it had already been agreed were covered by indemnities, their presence was simply intended to stir up feelings against the prisoner. As a lawyer remarked, attempts to punish him over Montrose having failed 'now it was hoped he might smart for it, tho on another cause' (J. Lauder, *Historical Notices*, 2 vols., 1848, 1.86). The other charges related to the events in Assynt in 1669–72, but, surprisingly, he was cleared on the grounds of insufficient evidence. Avoiding conviction on criminal charges, however, brought him no nearer to retrieving his lands, now in Mackenzie hands. He struggled on for many years, without success. In 1681 he assigned most of his (nominal) lands to Ian Macleod of Dunvegan in return for a pension of 400 merks (about £22 sterling) a year, and by about 1690 he had accepted that he would never regain Assynt. He died about 1697.

The end of the Macleods of Assynt is a familiar story— the lands of a small clan swallowed up by a greater neighbour, with family in-fighting, financial incompetence, and the ruthless manipulation of land law and political events by enemies all contributing. In the Assynt case, however, enemies had a unique advantage—that Neil Macleod was hated as the man who had betrayed Montrose. The story lingered on for centuries. In 1760 a visitor to Sutherland was told that as the result of the betrayal the Macleods of Assynt had 'become infamous, dwindled to nothing, and are no more'. Neil Macleod, he was earnestly assured, was the only Scot who had ever betrayed a countryman (R. Pococke, *Tours in Scotland*, ed. D. W. Kemp,

1887, 114–15). In the nineteenth century new force was given to the image of Neil's infamy by W. E. Aytoun's vastly popular *Lays of the Scottish Cavaliers*:

A traitor sold him to his fate
O deed of deathless shame.
(Aytoun, 34)

DAVID STEVENSON

Sources *DNB* · D. Mackinnon and A. Morrison, *The MacLeods: the genealogy of a clan*, 5 vols. (1968–77), vol. 5 · 'Montrose', *QR*, 79 (1846–7), 48–9 · W. Mackay, 'How the Macleods lost Assynt', *Transactions of the Gaelic Society of Inverness*, 16 (1891) [reprinted in W. Mackay, *Sidelights on highland history* (1925)] · 'The trial of Neil Macleod of Assynt', *Letters and papers illustrating the relations between Charles the Second and Scotland*, ed. S. R. Gardiner, Scottish History Society, 1st ser., 17 (1894) · W. G. Scott-Moncrieff, ed., *The records of the proceedings of the justiciary court, Edinburgh, 1661–1678*, 2 vols., Scottish History Society, 48–9 (1905) · 'Did Neil Macleod betray Montrose?', G. Wishart, *Memoirs of James, marquis of Montrose*, ed. A. D. Murdoch and H. F. M. Simpson (1893) · G. Gordon, 'Continuation', in R. Gordon, *Genealogical history of the earldom of Sutherland* (1813) · Bishop Burnet's History of his own time: with the suppressed passages of the first volume, ed. M. J. Routh, 6 vols. (1823) · B. Jay [S. B. Johnson], *Three centuries of falsehood exposed* (1970) · J. Fraser, *Chronicles of the Frasers: the Wardlaw manuscript*, ed. W. Mackay, Scottish History Society, 1st ser., 47 (1905) · *Orain Iain Luim: songs of John Macdonald, bard of Keppoch*, ed. A. M. Mackenzie (1973) · W. E. Aytoun, *Lays of the Scottish cavaliers, and other poems*, 2nd edn (1849)

MacLeod, Niel, of Gesto (*c.*1754–1836), collector and editor of highland bagpipe music, was the only son, in a family of three children, of John MacLeod of Gesto, head of Clann mac mhic Thormoid (a cadet branch of the MacLeods of MacLeod), whose lands lay in Bracadale in Skye, and his wife, Annabella MacKinnon of Borreraig, Strath. Niel MacLeod married Flora MacKinnon of Corry: they had six sons and seven daughters.

MacLeod succeeded his father at Gesto in 1787. He became a lieutenant in the 116th regiment of foot in 1794. Later he was a half-pay captain of Independents, and a justice of the peace. But his main significance is as an editor of piobaireachd, the classical music of the highland bagpipe. He was a friend of the leading master players in Skye, including Donald MacDonald and Iain Dubh MacCrimmon, whose pupil Alexander Bruce was Gesto's personal piper. MacLeod had a keen ear and a large repertory, and his house was a centre of highland musical culture. His daughter Ann (*b.* 1797) recollected that she had 'frequently been wakened at four in the morning by John MacCrimmon's pipes' (MacDonald, 'Bagpipes'). Gesto was himself a player until a lung condition forced him to stop and he taught the pipes to four of his sons, as well as teaching his daughter Janet (1799–1882) to play ''A Ghlas Mheur, and many other pibrochs' on the piano, at which art she was 'far and away the best in Skye' (MacDonald, 'Secrets', July 1912). When Alexander Campbell (1764–1824) visited Gesto in 1815, gathering material for his traditional music and song collection *Albyn's Anthology* (1816–18), he recorded Gaelic songs from Janet and Ann MacLeod and their mother, Flora, as well as piping material from Gesto himself.

However, relations with the chief were bad; Gesto's name was not on the list of tacksmen acting as guarantors for the Dunvegan family's gambling and political debts. Niel MacLeod fought and won a bitter lawsuit about the boundaries of his lands but John MacLeod of MacLeod refused to renew the tack in 1825, and Gesto had to leave the lands which his family had occupied for 400 years and flit to a rented house at Stein in Waternish.

The lawsuit took Gesto frequently to Edinburgh, where he was a familiar figure. A contemporary described him as

a tall, gaunt, thin-faced man, with long nose, grey hair, white hat, tartan trousers, and plaid. … He knew … almost every piobaireachd in existence—the names, the composers, their origin, and the causes for composing them … he very frequently called on, and sat for hours with old John Macdonald, the father of Donald Macdonald … He would make Donald … play 'piobaireachds' to him, all of which he himself could articulate with his pliant lips in the MacCrimmon noting style. (Donaldson, 139)

This refers to canntaireachd, a system of verbal notation where melody notes are represented by vowels and gracenotes by consonants. Gesto's 1828 collection *Pibereach or pipe tunes, as taught verbally by the McCrimmen pipers in Skye to their apprentices* was the first publication in this medium. It contained a sample of twenty pieces from Gesto's manuscript collection, described by his amanuensis, Revd Alexander MacGregor (*b.* 1806), as comprising some 200 tunes, some of its pages faded with age. The collection marked the first appearance in print of 'The Lament for the Union', 'In Praise of Morag', and other famous tunes. Its general consistency suggests that the Gesto canntaireachd was already a developed system. However, it does not always distinguish intervals clearly, except by context, which is not an unfailing guide to interpretation. Here is the opening sequence of 'The Lament for the Union':

I indro dieliu hiechin,
hindro hindrie hiachin,
biedrio dravi hiechin,
hiendo, hindo, hien hin …
(p. 13)

Staff notation was becoming the dominant mode in written pipe music and Gesto's collection appears to have had little contemporary impact. When syllabically notated scores again became an issue during the twentieth century, it was the larger and more systematic collection of Colin Mór Campbell of Nether Lorn which was to hold the field.

Growing Anglicization of the Scottish élite meant that Niel MacLeod of Gesto was among the dwindling number of highland gentlemen who could interact on an equal footing with master pipers on a basis of shared knowledge, language, and cultural outlook. Yet his family remained prominent in highland musical life for several generations. His grandson Keith Norman MacDonald (*b.* 1834) was editor of *Puirt-a-Beul* (1901). His great-grandson the painter Somerled MacDonald (1869–1948) was the leading amateur piper of his generation and during the 1930s mounted a despairing defence of the traditional style against the scores imposed on competing players by the Piobaireachd Society of Scotland. Niel MacLeod died at

Stein, in Waternish, Isle of Skye, on 21 December 1836, and was buried in the old churchyard at Struan in Bracadale.   WILLIAM DONALDSON

Sources W. Donaldson, *The highland pipe and Scottish society, 1750–1950* (2000) · D. Mackinnon and A. Morrison, *The MacLeods: the genealogy of a clan* (1970) · K. N. MacDonald, 'The bagpipes and how the MacCrimmons played them', *Oban Times* (4 July 1896) · K. N. MacDonald, 'The secrets of the canntaireachd', *Oban Times* (15 June 1912); (13 July 1912) · J. McLennan, 'The secrets of canntaireachd', *Oban Times* (15 June 1912) · N. MacLeod, 'Remarks by Captain MacLeod, as far as he has been informed by the late John Maccrimmon, piper, Dunvegan, Isle of Skye', *Celtic Magazine*, 8 (1883), 434–5 · NL Scot., Highland Society of London papers, Dep. 268 · F. Buisman, 'Canntaireachd and Colin Campbell's verbal notation: an outline', *Piping Times*, 50/3–4 (1997–8), 24–30, 28–33 · A. MacKenzie, *History of the MacLeods* (1889) · R. D. Cannon, *A bibliography of bagpipe music* (1980) · F. Collinson, *The traditional and national music of Scotland* (1966) · I. F. Grant, *The MacLeods: the history of a clan, 1200–1956* (1959)

Likenesses engraving, repro. in Collinson, *Traditional and national music of Scotland*

Macleod, Sir Norman, of Berneray (*c*.1606–1705), royalist army officer, was born in the island of Berneray, Inverness-shire, the third son of Sir Ruairidh Mor (Roderick) *Mac Leoid (Macleod) (*c*.1562–1626), and Iseabal Nic-Dhòmhnaill, daughter of Donald MacDonald, chief of Glengarry. A marble slab on the ruined castle reads 'Hic natus est illustris ille Normannus MacLeod de Berneray' ('Here is born the illustrious Norman Macleod of Berneray'). On 8 October 1614 his father fostered him to John Campbell of Hushinish, Harris. In 1631–3 he attended Glasgow University. He then entered upon the life-rent of the farm Berneray with its outliers in the Sound and Isle of Harris. On 20 December 1650 the estates appointed him lieutenant-colonel to the clan regiment of foot of his elder brother Roderick of Talisker, tutor of Macleod. The regiment mustered at least 600 men, perhaps as many as 900, and marched with the Scottish army under Charles II into England in 1651. At the battle of Worcester on 3 September the regiment held the confluence of the rivers Severn and Teme against the forces of Lambert and Fleetwood. So great was the slaughter of the Macleods on this occasion that the neighbouring clans agreed to leave them unmolested until they had time to recover their losses. Macleod was taken prisoner and tried for high treason in London. The erroneous designation of him as a Welsh ap Lloyd in the indictment saved his life, and he was sent back to prison. On 27 August 1652 he petitioned for his freedom, and was offered it on condition that he took an oath of allegiance to Cromwell. This he refused and remained in confinement in the Tower until he managed to escape and returned to the highlands.

Macleod joined William Cunningham, ninth earl of Glencairn, in the highlands in the spring of 1653, and the chiefs who met at Glenelg on 21 April to devise means for advancing the interests of the Stuarts entrusted Macleod with a message to Charles, then in Paris, promising support. That summer Macleod successfully completed his mission. Charles made him a lieutenant-colonel, and gave him a letter to the highland chiefs, dated 31 October 1653. On his way home to Scotland Charles requested him to call at The Hague and to acquaint General John Middleton with the condition of affairs in the highlands. This he did, and brought with him to Scotland a supply of arms and ammunition from the Dutch government. During the winter he was busy with the insurrection in the highlands, and (according to the *Mercurius Politicus*, no. 193) he led an unsuccessful attack upon Stornoway, then held by the friends of Cromwell. After the defeat at Lochgarry (26 July 1654) had scattered the royalists, General Middleton and other fugitives spent some time under the protection of Macleod at Dunvegan and Berneray before escaping to the continent. He received a testimonial from three royalist generals on 31 March 1655 for his assistance. When the young chief of the clan reached his majority and induced Cromwell to restore the forfeited estates, Norman and Roderick were specially excluded from the deed of restoration and pardon in the treaty of 20 May 1655. The chief received Norman Macleod's estates as part of the settlement.

Norman Macleod then seems to have joined Charles on the continent. The English demanded a bond of £400 for his peaceable behaviour on 11 October 1656, raised to £600 on 15 January 1657. In 1659 he was sent by Charles to the king of Denmark to negotiate for help for the royalist cause in England. He succeeded in getting a promise of 10,000 men, and preparations were being made for their equipment when news of the Restoration came. Shortly after Charles returned, the brothers Macleod were knighted in London, Roderick being the founder of the Macleods of Talisker, Norman of the Macleods of Berneray and Muiravonside. Sir Norman then retired to Berneray, but the wars had ruined him, and he appeared at court in 1662 to present a petition in which he narrated his services and losses. Charles readily granted him the estate of Macleod of Assynt, who had betrayed Montrose and had otherwise assisted the king's enemies; but when Assynt subsequently claimed pardon under the Act of Indemnity, the Scottish courts decided that his estates had not been forfeited, and Sir Norman had to remain in his straitened circumstances.

Macleod was twice married: first, to Margaret, daughter of John Mackenzie of Lochslin, and granddaughter of Kenneth, first lord of Kintail, with whom he had one son, John, who succeeded to the title. As dowry he received Dunglas, Balblair, Knockterd, and part of Balnain; secondly, to Catherine, eldest daughter of Sir James Mor Macdonald of Sleat, with whom he had two sons—William of Luskinder, who married Margaret, daughter of Captain Alexander Mackenzie of Suddy, and Alexander, who became lord advocate and was knighted; and three daughters—Isabel, who married Roderick MacNeil of Barra; Marian, who married Donald Maclean of Coll; and Catherine, who married Alexander Macleod of Raasay and Angus Macdonald of Scothouse.

The handsome, blue-eyed, blond-haired, ruddy-cheeked Norman Macleod served as a patron of Gaelic culture. He took a deep interest in its antiquities and history, but especially in the poetry. He served as patron to the poet Mary MacLeod, and to bards, tale tellers, harpists, and pipers.

His monetary resources remained limited, even with a promised dowry of 20,000 marks from the father of his second wife. Until 1698 he held part of the island of North Uist in lieu of the money. In that year he received the dowry money and used it to purchase a wadset of lands in Harris from Roderick Macleod of Macleod, the 19th chief. He died at an advanced age on 3 March 1705, and was buried in St Clement's Church, Rodel, on Harris.

J. R. MacDonald, rev. Edward M. Furgol

Sources NA Scot., PA.7.8, fols. 47–48; PA.11.11, fol. 32v; PA.16.5, fols. 105, 107 · APS · F. D. Dow, *Cromwellian Scotland, 1651–1660* (1979) · C. H. Firth, ed., *Scotland and the Commonwealth: letters and papers relating to the military government of Scotland, from August 1651 to December 1653*, Scottish History Society, 18 (1895) · C. H. Firth, ed., *Scotland and the protectorate: letters and papers relating to the military government of Scotland from January 1654 to June 1659*, Scottish History Society, 31 (1899) · R. Douglas and others, *The baronage of Scotland* (1798) · D. Mackinnon and A. Morrison, *The MacLeods: the genealogy of a clan*, 5 vols. (1968–77) · D. Mackinnon and A. Morrison, *Macleod chiefs of Harris and Dunvegan* (1969) · CSP dom., 1651–60
Archives Dunvegan Castle, Skye, MacLeod of MacLeod MSS
Wealth at death substantial lands

MacLeod, Norman, of Dunvegan (1705–1772), politician and chief of clan MacLeod, was born on 29 July 1705 in Perth, the younger son of Norman MacLeod of Dunvegan (c.1685–1706) and Anne Fraser, daughter of Hugh, Lord Lovat, and his wife, Lady Amelia Murray. Though known in his own family as the Red Man, from the red tartan that he wears in his portrait by Allan Ramsay, at the family seat in Skye, he was better known to his tenants and indeed to posterity as An Droch Dhuine (the Bad Man). He succeeded his elder brother, John (1704–1706), when only a year old, following his father's untimely death. His mother subsequently married Peter Fothringham, of Powrie, Forfarshire, in 1708 and, in 1717, the somewhat feckless John Mackenzie, second earl of Cromarty. He therefore suffered a somewhat rootless childhood, with his education seemingly 'much neglected' under his governor, John Macrae.

During MacLeod's minority some £90,000 Scots of longstanding debt on the vast MacLeod estate was apparently liquidated by the factor John MacLeod of Contullich and his brother Alexander, the clan lawyer. Nevertheless their traditionally-minded administration, as well as an ill-concealed Jacobitism, left them in a somewhat vulnerable position. When the chief came of age in 1724, at Cromarty's urging he initiated legal proceedings against the previous administration on grounds of dishonesty. His eventual success came at no small cost to his personal reputation.

About 1726 MacLeod married Janet, daughter of Sir Donald MacDonald, fourth baronet, of Sleat (Domhnall a' Chogaidh). The match was far from happy and they separated in 1733. The young chief revealed a rather dangerous penchant for meddling, finding himself caught up in the Lady Grange affair when in 1732 he assisted in the kidnap of Rachel, wife of James Erskine, Lord Grange [see Erskine, Rachel, Lady Grange]. Seven years later he was seriously implicated in the notorious *Long nan Daoine* (Ship of the

Norman MacLeod of Dunvegan (1705–1772), by Allan Ramsay, 1747–8

People) scheme when over a hundred of MacLeod's tenants and their children were forcibly abducted to be sold into slavery in American plantations. The ship being stormbound in Donaghadee, co. Down, some of the prisoners escaped to raise the alarm. The resulting scandal was hushed up with the help of Duncan Forbes, lord president of the court of session.

Forbes became something of a father figure to MacLeod, reconciling him with his wife, and, together with Simon Fraser, Lord Lovat, engineering his election as MP for Inverness-shire in 1741 as a supporter of the Argyll interest. Though not above Jacobite intriguing in his early years, after the rising of 1745 MacLeod employed brazenly duplicitous delaying tactics against Lord Lovat to keep the latter's Frasers at home during the crucial first few months. The chief's loyalty won him commissions to raise four independent companies for Loudon's regiment, and he supposedly tricked his own clansmen into marching against the Jacobite army. On 23 December 1745 they saw action at Inverurie. Though MacLeod himself showed great personal bravery, his forces were required to retreat before a superior Jacobite contingent, eventually ending up back in Skye. MacLeod's loyalties caused widespread animus against him in the aftermath of Culloden, his situation exacerbated by the government's tardy repayment of the £2500 that he had spent on his companies and by the death of Forbes in December 1747.

MacLeod's wife had died in April 1743. In October 1748 he married Anne, daughter of William Martin of Braes, Skye. Considerably younger than her husband, she is said to have encouraged him in his growing extravagance, a lifestyle that he was increasingly unable to afford following his retirement from parliament in 1754. Indebtedness and an increasing addiction to gambling and drink meant that he had to leave London; he subsequently settled in the Whitehouse estate, near Edinburgh, then in the modest house of Park, near St Andrews. Rents on the MacLeod estate had already been raised significantly, and for many tacksmen and tenants the widespread famine of the early 1770s proved the final straw. With mass emigration looming, rents were lowered and the estate placed in the hands of trustees. Racked by sores, gout, and stomach pains Norman MacLeod of Dunvegan died at Strathtyrum House, St Andrews, on 21 February 1772. He was buried in the churchyard of St Andrews Cathedral.

From his first marriage to Janet MacDonald, MacLeod had three children: John, his heir, who predeceased him in 1767, Ann, and Emilia. From his second marriage to Anne Martin he had three daughters: Elizabeth, Anne, and Rich Mary. He also fathered two illegitimate sons: Alexander, 'whose mother is said to have been an Edinburgh lady', and Norman. He was succeeded as chief by his grandson Norman *MacLeod (1754–1801). He well merits his somewhat evil reputation. Extravagant and boorish, with a taste for intrigue, his chief interest to historians is in his spanning of two eras in the history of the Gàidhealtachd, being the model of a new type of landlord whose future lay not so much with his clanspeople but rather in the wider British political and financial sphere. He appears to have been the first of the MacLeod chiefs not to have spoken Gaelic, and it is notable that, rather uniquely, no praise-poem for him has come down in the oral tradition of the Isle of Skye.

DOMHNALL UILLEAM STIÙBHART

Sources I. F. Grant, *The MacLeods: the history of a clan*, new edn (1981) · R. C. MacLeod, ed., *The book of Dunvegan*, 2 vols. (1939) · Dunvegan Castle, Skye, MacLeod of MacLeod MSS · E. Cruickshanks, 'MacLeod, Norman', HoP, *Commons, 1715–54*
Likenesses A. Ramsay, oils, 1747–8, Dunvegan Castle, Skye [*see illus.*]

MacLeod, Norman, of MacLeod (1754–1801), army officer and politician, was born on 4 March 1754 at Brodie Castle, Forres, Moray, the only son of John MacLeod (*d.* 1767) and Emilia Brodie (*b.* 1730), daughter of Alexander *Brodie of Brodie, lord Lyon king of arms. He was educated privately, principally in Edinburgh under the care of Professor George Stuart, and then at the University of St Andrews (1769) and University College, Oxford (1770). In 1772 he succeeded his grandfather Norman *MacLeod as chief of clan MacLeod.

For the proud head of an ancient family that claimed descent from Danish royalty, MacLeod's inheritance was a singularly unhappy one. Ruin stared him in the face. The estates were buried under a mountain of debt, numerous relatives had to be provided for, creditors were pressing for payment, and the tenantry (who were struggling to pay their rents) were considering mass emigration to America. The young chief met the crisis head on. Meetings were arranged with the tenantry, and, by promising to live among them, temporarily reduce their rents, and attend to their interests, he dissuaded most from emigrating. The response of the clan's middle and lower ranks to MacLeod's appeals convinced him of their attachment, and may have prepared him psychologically for the subsequent adoption of quasi-democratic political opinions. MacLeod's determination to live among his clan, however, was short-lived. Strict economy and attention to estate management were uncongenial and offered little hope of significantly reducing his debts, while life in the remote fastness of Dunvegan Castle was unappealing to an ambitious young man impatient to prove himself on a bigger stage.

The approach of war in America offered MacLeod a chance of escaping from the gloom that had enveloped him on Skye, and in 1775 he was commissioned with the rank of captain into the 71st regiment. While undertaking training at Inverness, he met and, on 25 March 1776, married Mary MacKenzie (*d.* 1784), daughter of Kenneth MacKenzie of Suddie, Ross-shire. Taken prisoner *en route* to the front, he never saw active service in America, but his early experience of military life did not sour him and, shortly after his return in 1779, he was appointed lieutenant-colonel of the 2nd battalion of the 42nd regiment.

In March 1781 the battalion sailed for the Cape of Good Hope, but, to MacLeod's delight, it was diverted to India, where the prospects of fame and fortune were far brighter. In 1782, shortly after his arrival, he was placed in command of a small force which defeated the vastly more numerous army of Tipu Sahib at Panniani. Ever prickly about matters of honour, MacLeod reacted furiously when a lieutenant-colonel in the East India Company army was given command over him. Honour and prospects were restored when, in April 1783, he was awarded the brevet rank of brigadier-general and placed in command of his own army. The subsequent campaign on the Malabar coast enhanced his military reputation and added significantly to his wealth.

Following the death of his first wife on 20 February 1784, MacLeod married in the same year Sarah Stackhouse (*b.* c.1767), daughter of Nathaniel Stackhouse, second in the council at Bombay. In 1785 his spirits rose when he was transferred to Bengal and appointed second in command of the army there, a post worth £6000 a year. His hopes, however, were seemingly blasted in 1788, when a general order was issued depriving all British army officers of brevet rank in India. The mortified MacLeod lobbied hard to have the order rescinded, but to no avail. Determined to seek redress and to revive his stalled career, he returned home in 1789.

Since boyhood MacLeod had entertained thoughts of a parliamentary career, and during his absence abroad his political ambitions had been ably nursed. Armed with a conditional endorsement from Henry Dundas, he worked hard to cultivate the Inverness-shire freeholders and successfully negotiated an agreement with the crucially important Fraser interest, in return for whose support in the 1790 election he would push a Fraser candidate in the one following. The duke of Gordon's hated army of 'parchment barons' (whose qualification to vote rested upon legal technicality rather than the law as traditionally understood) was thus outmanoeuvred, and Gordon was brought reluctantly to back MacLeod, who was then returned unopposed.

MacLeod supported Pitt's administration to the best of his limited parliamentary abilities until 7 May 1791, when a meeting with Dundas went so disastrously wrong as to ignite MacLeod's explosive temper and cause him to cross the floor of the house. The breach, which was apparently occasioned by Dundas's refusal to accede to MacLeod's demand for a specific appointment before agreeing to return to India, was bitter and permanent. He attached himself firmly to the opposition and the cause of political reform. Long opposed to 'fictitious' votes, MacLeod now argued for extending the county franchise. He attended the county reformers' convention, held at Edinburgh in July 1792, and proposed that the franchise should be vested in those owning land worth an annual valued rent of £100. His ideas were not adopted, but his optimism was undimmed.

A member of the London Society of the Friends of the People since May 1792, MacLeod had found on his return to Scotland that numbers of gentlemen were discussing the formation of a Scottish association based on the same principles. Although he attended the Scottish burgh reformers' convention, where he urged the burghs to co-operate with the London Friends by organizing petitions in favour of parliamentary reform, he was not actively involved in the establishment of the Scottish Association of the Friends of the People. He had no qualms, however, about supporting this plebeian organization.

MacLeod addressed the delegate meetings of the local societies in both Glasgow and Edinburgh, advocating equal representation and short parliaments, and urging petitions as the proper constitutional means of obtaining reform. Having returned to London in December, he did not attend the first national convention of the Scottish Friends of the People, but the growing conservative alarm at the radical reform movement's progress only convinced him of the need to increase his support for the Scottish radicals. On his arrival in Edinburgh in January 1793 he again addressed the local societies, stressing his confidence in them and their cause, while his morale-raising pamphlet *Letters to the People of North Britain* (1793) was serialized in the radically inclined *Edinburgh Gazetteer*. He presented the Edinburgh petition in support of Grey's reform motion of May 1793 and voted with the minority, but by then he was losing interest in the reform movement. The formal breach did not come until November, but as early as February he had turned his attention to the

opportunities offered by the outbreak of war with France.

Numerous approaches for military employment over the next four years were rebuffed, but given that MacLeod continued vigorously to oppose the government's policies, arguing in his *Considerations on False and Real Alarms* (1794) that the war was both misconceived and ruinously expensive, the wonder is that he persevered in his applications. With no prospect of retaining his Inverness-shire seat, he fired off a violent valedictory and sought refuge in the venal constituency of Milborne Port. The expenditure of £15,000 failed to convince the electors there of his merits, and MacLeod retreated north to spend his declining years in reduced circumstances, bad health, and low spirits. A jaunt to Ireland in 1800 provided only temporary relief from his depression. A cruise was arranged to restore his health, but he died at Guernsey on 16 August 1801. J. D. BRIMS

Sources R. C. MacLeod, *Norman Magnus MacLeod* (1930) · Dunvegan Castle, Skye, MacLeod of MacLeod MSS · I. F. Grant, *The MacLeods: the history of a clan*, new edn (1981) · HoP, *Commons, 1790–1820* · R. C. MacLeod, ed., *The Book of Dunvegan*, 2 vols., Third Spalding Club, 9 (1938–9) · Burke, *Gen. GB* (1937)
Archives Dunvegan Castle, Skye · NRA, priv. coll., corresp. and papers

Macleod, Norman (1783–1862), Church of Scotland minister and Gaelic scholar, was born in December 1783, the son of Norman Macleod, who was ordained in 1774 minister of Morven, Argyll, and his wife, Jean, granddaughter of William Morrison, minister of Tiree in the Hebrides. Licensed by the presbytery of Mull on 23 June 1806, he was for a short time minister at Kilbrandon, Argyll. In December 1807 he was presented by George William Campbell, sixth duke of Argyll, to the parish of Campbeltown, Argyll, where he was admitted on 12 June 1808. Marriage in 1811 to Agnes Maxwell of Aros brought them five sons and six daughters. In September 1821 he was presented to Kilmorie in Bute, but withdrew his acceptance; having been presented by George IV to Campsie, Stirlingshire, in January 1825, he was admitted there in the following August. On 30 July 1827 he obtained the degree of DD from the University of Glasgow. On 31 October 1835 he was elected by the managers minister of the Gaelic chapel of ease (St Columba's), Glasgow, and was admitted in December. He was moderator of the general assembly of the Church of Scotland which met on 18 May 1836, and in 1841 he was appointed chaplain in ordinary to the queen, and one of the deans of the Chapel Royal.

Macleod is described in the *Memoir* written by his son Norman as a 'remarkably handsome man, with a broad forehead, an open countenance full of benevolence, and hair which from an early age was snowy white' (D. Macleod, 1.4). Besides attaining some eminence as a popular preacher, especially to Gaelic audiences, he interested himself in schemes for the welfare of the highlands. It was through his action, in directing attention to the insufficient provision for elementary education in the highlands and islands, that the church was induced in 1824 to set up its own Gaelic schools. During a period of exceptional distress in the highlands Macleod made a very successful visit to England to collect subscriptions; as a result of his exertions during the potato famines of 1836–7 and 1846–7 he became known as Caraid nan Gaidheal (Friend of the Gaels). He also frequently undertook protestant evangelizing tours in Ireland, preaching to the Irish in their native language, which he had thoroughly mastered, and publishing in 1836 an Irish version of the metrical psalms.

Macleod was a Gaelic scholar of major importance. In 1826 he played a part in the publication of a large-format edition of the Bible in Gaelic and he edited anthologies for use in the new Gaelic schools. With Daniel Dewar he compiled a *Dictionary of the Gaelic Language* (1831). He established and edited two Gaelic periodicals—*An Teachdaire Gae'lach* (1829–31) and *Cuairtear nan Gleann* (1840–43), both of which survived longer than other similar publications. Macleod's Gaelic prose style was important in the extension and development of the language; in broadening its base 'he was a highly industrious and successful pioneer' (MacDonald, 532). He also published on the Old Testament.

Macleod died in Glasgow on 25 November 1862. His eldest sons, Norman *Macleod (1812–1872) and Donald, became ministers of the Church of Scotland; the third son was Sir George Husband Baird *Macleod (1828–1892), a surgeon.   H. C. G. MATTHEW

Sources J. N. Macleod, *Memorials of the Rev. Norman Macleod* (1898) · C. Ó Baoill, 'Norman Macleod, "Caraid nan Gael"', *Scottish Gaelic Studies*, 13/2 (1981), 159–68 · K. D. MacDonald, 'Macleod, Norman', *DSCHT* · D. Macleod, *Memoir of Norman Macleod, D.D.*, 2 vols. (1876) · *Fasti Scot.*

Wealth at death £4626 3s. 8d.: probate, 1862, *CGPLA Eng. & Wales*

Macleod, Norman (1812–1872), Church of Scotland minister and journalist, the eldest child of Norman *Macleod (1783–1862) and his wife, Agnes, daughter of Maxwell of Aros, chamberlain of the duke of Argyll, was born at Campbeltown, Argyll, where his father was parish minister, on 3 June 1812. His early education was at Campbeltown burgh school. At the age of twelve he was sent to board with the schoolmaster of Morven, of which parish his grandfather (another Norman) was minister. In 1825, on the removal of his father to Campsie, Stirlingshire, he became a pupil at the parish school there. In 1827 he entered Glasgow College, where his career was not especially distinguished, logic being the only subject in which he gained honours. In 1831 he went to Edinburgh University to study divinity under Thomas Chalmers and David Welsh, and was much influenced by the former. On Chalmers's recommendation he was appointed tutor to the only son of Henry Preston of Moreby Hall, Yorkshire, which post he held for three years, sometimes living at Moreby, sometimes travelling with his pupil on the continent, and finally bringing him with him to Edinburgh, when he returned there to study.

In October 1835 Macleod resumed work at Glasgow College; in May 1837 he became a licentiate of the Church of

Norman Macleod (1812–1872), by Ralston & Sons

Scotland, and on 15 March 1838 was ordained parish minister of Loudoun, Ayrshire, being presented by the dowager marchioness of Hastings. He quickly gained the affection of his parishioners, and his church became crowded. In the non-intrusion controversy, he was one of 'the forty' who advocated the adoption of a middle course between the 'evangelicals' and 'moderates', such as was afterwards embodied in Lord Aberdeen's bill, which declared that presbyteries might decide on whether presentees were suitable for the parishes to which they were presented. In 1843 Macleod published a pithy pamphlet on the controversy, entitled *Cracks about the Kirk for Kintra Folk*, which had a large circulation, and was followed by two similar pamphlets. When the Disruption took place in 1843 he remained in the Church of Scotland, and was offered various parishes left vacant by the secession. He accepted Dalkeith, and was inducted there on 15 December 1843. In addition to very active and successful parochial work, he now began to take a prominent part in the general business of the church, especially in foreign missions. He was one of the founders of the Evangelical Alliance in 1847. From 1849 to 1860 he was editor of the *Edinburgh Christian Instructor*, in which many of the papers which he afterwards wrote for *Good Words* first appeared in an embryo form. Throughout his life he maintained a steady stream of copy, supported by a variety of books, including *Reminiscences of a Highland Parish* (1862) and *Character Studies*

(1872). His correspondence was often enlivened by skilful caricatures.

In July 1851 Macleod became minister of the Barony parish, Glasgow, and on 11 August married Catherine Ann, daughter of the late William Mackintosh of Geddes and sister of Macleod's closest friend, John Mackintosh, whose biography, *The Earnest Student*, he published in 1854. Macleod threw himself into the work of the Barony with great energy. He devised many schemes for assisting the poor, establishing the first congregational penny savings bank in Glasgow; opening refreshment rooms for working men, where they would be free from the temptations of the public house; and building new schoolhouses and a mission church for the poor, to whose services only those were admitted who came in working clothes. He was soon known as one of the most eloquent preachers in Scotland, and in 1857 was appointed chaplain to Queen Victoria, with whom, as with the royal family, he became a great favourite. The queen admired his preaching (see her *Leaves from the Journal of our Life in the Highlands*, 1867, 147). In 1858 the University of Glasgow conferred on him the degree of DD. In 1860 *Good Words*, a monthly magazine mainly, although not exclusively, devoted to religious topics, was established in London, with Macleod as editor, and quickly achieved success. He wrote for it many papers, stories, and sketches, which afterwards appeared in book form. In 1864 he was appointed convener of the India mission of the Church of Scotland, in which he had for years taken a deep interest. In the same year, in company with his brother and his publisher, Alexander Strahan, he toured Egypt and Palestine, publishing his account, *Eastward* (in 1866).

In 1865 Macleod challenged the extreme Sabbatarianism then characteristic of Scotland, arguing that its thoroughgoingness was unscriptural. This provoked a violent reaction and an extended pamphlet/sermon war. It was then with some relief that Macleod accepted the general assembly's request in 1867 that he and the Revd Dr Watson of Dundee should visit Scottish mission stations in India. On returning he delivered a speech on the subject in the general assembly of 1868, publishing it as *An Address on Missions*. Another result of the tour was 'Peeps at the Far East', which first appeared in *Good Words*, and was separately published in 1871. He seems never to have entirely recovered from the fatigues of this journey. In 1869 Macleod was moderator of the general assembly, and did much to help the movement for the abolition of patronage in the Church of Scotland, leading a deputation to W. E. Gladstone, the prime minister. He also supported disestablishment of the Irish church that year. In 1871 his health seriously declined, and on Sunday, 16 June 1872, he died in his house at 204 Bath Street, Glasgow. He was buried at Campsie.

A. P. Stanley thought Macleod 'the chief ecclesiastic of the Scottish church' in the generation after Thomas Chalmers (Macleod, 2.305). He was undoubtedly prominent, but he was not characteristic of the mid-Victorian kirk, as the Sabbatarian controversy showed. His ecumenical initiatives towards the Free Church, his friendships with broad churchmen such as John Tulloch, his contacts with the court, and his journalism which reached a British, rather than a merely Scottish, audience were all steps towards making the kirk more open-minded and integrative. *Good Words* anticipated the non-Anglican national press later developed by W. Robertson Nicoll. Several monuments were raised to his memory. His mission church in Glasgow was made the Macleod Parish Church. The Barony congregation built a Macleod Memorial Missionary Institute in a destitute part of the parish. A statue of him was set up in Glasgow, and Queen Victoria placed two beautiful memorial windows in Crathie church, where he had often preached before her.

THOMAS HAMILTON, *rev.* H. C. G. MATTHEW

Sources D. Macleod, *Memoir of Norman Macleod, D.D.*, 2 vols. (1876) · *Fasti Scot.* · J. Wellwood, *Norman Macleod* (1897) · A. C. Cheyne, *The transforming of the kirk* (1983)
Archives U. Glas., Archives and Business Records Centre, journal, journal extracts | NL Scot., corresp. with Donald Macleod · U. St Andr. L., corresp. with James David Forbes
Likenesses T. Knott, oils, 1848, Scot. NPG · J. Mossman, statue, 1881, Glasgow · W. & D. Downey, carte-de-visite, NPG · Elliott & Fry, carte-de-visite, NPG · Ralston & Sons, photograph, NPG [*see illus.*] · T. Rodger, carte-de-visite, NPG · R. & E. Taylor, woodcut (after Ralston & Sons), NPG; repro. in *Illustrated Review* (15 June 1872) · photograph, repro. in Macleod, *Memoir of Norman Macleod, D.D.* · stipple, NPG · wood-engraving (after photographs by Elliott & Fry), NPG; repro. in *ILN* (29 June 1872) · woodcut, BM; repro. in *Great Thoughts* (1887)
Wealth at death £8849 18s.: confirmation, 1872, *CCI* · £433 6s. 4d.: additional inventory, 20 Dec 1912, *CCI*

MacLeod, Roderick (*d.* 1595), highland chief, was the son of Malcolm MacLeod of Lewis (*d. c.*1528) and his wife, Christine Urquhart of Cromarty. His family, which owned Assynt and Coigeach on the Scottish mainland together with the island of Lewis, had been closely connected with the lords of the isles, and when Donald Dubh MacDonald, the last of that line, escaped from prison in 1501 it was to Torquil MacLeod of Lewis, his uncle by marriage, that he turned for help. For his part in Donald's rising Torquil's lands were forfeited to the crown in 1506, but five years later they were returned to his brother Malcolm. Having succeeded his father, Roderick continued the family tradition of support for MacDonald claimants to the lordship of the isles in 1539 and again in 1545. Summoned for treason he failed to appear, and in 1554–5 the fourth earl of Argyll besieged Stornoway Castle. Although it withstood Argyll's artillery, Roderick submitted and was pardoned.

Roderick MacLeod carried on feuds with many of his neighbours, but most of his later life was overshadowed by turmoil within his own family. He was married three times, to Janet Mackenzie, daughter of John *Mackenzie of Kintail [*see under* Mackenzie family of Kintail], to Barbara Stewart of Avondale in 1541, and to Janet Maclean of Duart. When a son, Torquil, was born to Janet Mackenzie, Roderick claimed that he was the child of Hugh Morrison, breve of Lewis, and divorced her. Torquil was brought up by his mother's people in Strathconon and was consequently known as Torquil Cononach. With Barbara Stewart, Roderick had another son, Torquil Oighre (the Heir), who, however, was drowned about 1563. Some ten years later Roderick married Janet Maclean and they had two sons, Torquil Dubh and Tormod. He also had five acknowledged illegitimate sons.

The death of Torquil Oighre saw the start of the long and complicated tale of the 'ewill trowbles of the Lewes' (Macphail, 265). Roderick MacLeod had appeared to accept Torquil Cononach as his heir, but went back on this in favour of Donald Gormson MacDonald of Sleat, whose father had married a daughter of Roderick's brother Torquil. Torquil Cononach captured his father and held him prisoner for three years. On his release Roderick complained to the privy council of his 'evill handling captivite feir of my life perell of hunger and cauld and manifest compulsione' (ibid., 282). On his release he made his third marriage and had his two younger sons. In 1576 Torquil Cononach again captured his father at Stornoway together with the family charters, and handed the latter over to his uncle Mackenzie of Kintail for safe keeping. Meanwhile the five illegitimate sons divided, with Donald, Rory Og, and Neil supporting their father, and Tormod and Murdoch backing Torquil Cononach. During the ensuing turmoil the latter's eldest son was killed by Rory Og, while Donald killed Tormod but was himself captured and beheaded by Torquil Cononach, who never lost the support of his Mackenzie relatives with their considerable influence at court.

Roderick MacLeod died in 1595, in nominal possession of Lewis and with the young Torquil Dubh as his heir. In August 1596, however, Torquil Cononach received a royal charter for the lands and barony of Lewis and the lands of the mainland, and after the death from fever of his second son he named Kenneth Mackenzie of Kintail as his heir. A year later Torquil Dubh invaded Coigeach but was captured and killed by Torquil Cononach, while Kintail abducted the dead man's brother Tormod from school in the lowlands and held him prisoner for several years. After his release Tormod saved the life of Torquil Cononach when the latter was captured by John MacHutcheon MacLeod of Sanday. In 1605 Torquil's daughter and heir, Margaret, married Roderick or Rory, the brother of Kintail, who gave him a charter for Coigeach while reserving a life-rent for Roderick's father-in-law. Torquil Cononach was dead by 1609, when Roderick was granted a crown charter for the lands.

Neil MacLeod (d. 1613), who in the meantime had gained control of Lewis and of Torquil Dubh's three young sons, proved to be by far the most effective of Roderick's sons. However, he was now to be involved in a struggle of a different kind. In 1598 James VI formed a plan to 'civilize' Lewis and contracted with ten Fife gentlemen, calling themselves the Fife Adventurers, to establish a fishing colony at Stornoway 'for the public good and the king's profit' (Reg. PCS, 1592–9, 463). This was greeted with alarm by many in the highlands, and Neil led the initial opposition in Lewis. At first he was supported by his brother Murdoch, but later they fell out, and Neil handed his brother over to the Adventurers, one of whose leaders Murdoch had captured, and he was hanged at St Andrews in 1599. During the next six years the settlers were harassed by Neil MacLeod, who had the covert support of Mackenzie of Kintail, even though the latter was ostensibly backing the royal experiment. In 1605 Neil took Stornoway Castle. Two years later Mackenzie was given a royal charter to recapture it and to help the settlers generally, but he managed to warn Neil of the arrival of a supply ship for them, which Neil took.

Finally, in 1610, after he had been made a peer for his good service in Lewis, Mackenzie was instructed to allow Neil to negotiate, a process apparently forwarded when Neil by treachery seized and handed over an English pirate ship. But MacLeod's opposition to the Adventurers was reinvigorated when Mackenzie died in February 1611. In spite of having by now lost most of the island of Lewis he withdrew with his 'infamous byke of lawles and insolent lymmaris [ruffians]' to the rock of Berisay, at the mouth of Loch Roag in the west of Lewis, and there turned to piracy (Reg. PCS, 1610–13, 3). They eventually surrendered to Roderick Mackenzie after a threat to drown their women and children, and Neil was executed in Edinburgh on 13 March 1613; he was reported to have died 'verie christianlie' (Mackenzie, 258).

Neil MacLeod left two sons, Donald and Rory Dubh, who were released in 1613 on the promise of good behaviour but returned to Lewis to make trouble; Rory was killed there while Donald was captured and banished to England, from where he went to Holland. The three sons of Torquil Dubh also all disappear from the record around 1613, while his brother Tormod was exiled. Neil's brother Rory Og, who died after escaping from Duart Castle, left three sons, of whom William and Rory were executed as rebels while Malcolm, after years of piracy, died in Ireland. Thus ended a line which was subsequently described as 'the stoutest prettiest men, but a bloody wicked crew whom neither law nor reason could guide or moddell, destroying one another till in the end they were all expelled of that country' (Mackay, 265). The heir male of the family was MacLeod of Raasay, but the lands of Lewis, Assynt, and Coigeach were inherited, after so much 'ewill trowble', by the Mackenzie descendants of Torquil Cononach's daughter.

R. W. MUNRO and JEAN MUNRO

Sources I. F. Grant, *The MacLeods: the history of a clan, 1200–1956* (1959) • D. Mackinnon and A. Morrison, *The MacLeods: the genealogy of a clan*, 5 vols. (1968–77), vol. 4 • W. C. Mackenzie, *History of the Outer Hebrides* (1903) • 'The ewill trowbles of the Lewes', *Highland Papers*, ed. J. R. N. Macphail, 2; Scottish History Society, 2nd ser., 5 (1916) • W. Mackay, ed., *Chronicle of the Frasers: the Wardlaw manuscript*, Scottish History Society, 1st ser., 47 (1905) • *Reg. PCS*, 1st ser., vols. 5, 9

MacLeod, Roderick. See Mac Leòid, Sir Ruairidh, of Harris and Dunvegan (c.1562–1626).

Macleod, Roderick (1795–1852), physician and medical editor, was baptized in the parish of Old Machar, Aberdeen, on 15 September 1795, which was possibly also the date of his birth. He was one of the nine children of Roderick Macleod, principal of the University and King's College, Aberdeen, and his wife, Isabella, née Chrysty, or Christie. He was educated at the University of Aberdeen, from which he graduated MA on 28 March 1812. On 1

August 1816 he graduated MD at the University of Edinburgh, his thesis being 'De tetano' ('On tetanus'). After a brief career as an assistant surgeon in the army, from which he retired from active service on half pay, he settled in London, where he built up a 'fair share of practice' (*Medical Times and Gazette*, 626), and embarked on a career in medical journalism. On 2 January 1822 he married Margaret Sambier, daughter of the rector of St Anne's, Westminster. The marriage produced at least one child. Macleod became a licentiate of the Royal College of Physicians on 22 December 1821 and a fellow on 9 July 1836. He delivered the Goulstonian lectures at the college in 1837, and in 1839 he became consiliarus. He spent virtually his entire working life in London where he held several hospital appointments. By 1822 he was physician to the Westminster General Dispensary, the Infirmary for Children, and the Scottish Hospital in London. On 13 February 1833 he was appointed physician at St George's Hospital, retaining the post until ill health forced his retirement in 1845. He also had a professional association, much derided by *The Lancet*, with the Asylum for the Recovery of Health in St Marylebone. Although Macleod wrote extensively in the medical press he published only one book. This comprised an expanded version of his Goulstonian lectures: *On rheumatism in its various forms, and on the affections of internal organs, more especially the heart and brain, to which it gives rise* (1842).

Macleod's main professional importance lay in his editorship of two metropolitan medical journals. Between July 1822 and 1828 he edited the *London Medical and Physical Journal* (formerly the *Medical and Physical Journal*). In this endeavour John Bacot MD assisted him until 1826. The *London Medical and Physical Journal*, which *The Lancet* dubbed the 'yellow fungus', on account of the colour of its cover, was not a commercial success. In 1827 'the happy thought was conceived' by a 'coalition of almost all the leading Physicians and Surgeons' in London to establish 'an imitation of that successful journal THE LANCET,—an imitation in all respects but its principles' (*The Lancet*, 16 May 1835, 237; Clarke, 153). The idea was to counter *The Lancet*'s 'evil influence' and the journal in question was launched in December 1827 as the *London Medical Gazette*. Macleod agreed to become editor in return for a small salary, a share in the advertising profits, and an appointment at St George's Hospital. Thomas Wakley's *Lancet* reviled Macleod as an editor. This was partly because of Wakley's irrational dislike of Scottish doctors and hospital surgeons, and partly because Macleod, an avowed conservative, was a diehard opponent of medical reform. However, much of the antipathy is probably explained by the fact that both the journals that Macleod edited were direct competitors of *The Lancet*. Over a period of about ten years from the late 1820s Wakley missed few opportunities to criticize and ridicule 'Roderick the Goth' who was also described as 'ignorant', a 'fool', 'the greatest quack alive' (largely on account of his appointment as physician to the Asylum for the Recovery of Health), 'a toad-eating hack' and much more (*The Lancet*, 17 Oct 1835, 115; Clarke, 153). In 1827 Macleod brought a libel action against Wakley. When

the case was heard, in February 1828, the jury found in his favour, but Macleod's victory was Pyrrhic, since damages were assessed at a mere £5 and *The Lancet*'s campaign against him continued unabated.

Macleod was an 'upright, courteous, and kind-hearted man' (*Medical Times and Gazette*). James Fernandez Clarke considered him 'a gentleman and a scholar' who was ill-equipped to grapple with the combative Wakley. Clarke wrote that the *Gazette's* contents 'were reviewed in such a spirit of harshness and ridicule that it frightened the timid and disgusted the bold' (Clarke, 153). He believed that the *Gazette* published 'many valuable lectures and papers' (ibid., 280) but also that its aspirations of 'quality' and 'high breeding' made for an 'insipid and tame' journal which provided little serious competition to *The Lancet*.

Little is known about the last fifteen years or so of Macleod's life, beyond the fact that 'attacks of an epileptic character', which became both more frequent and severe, eventually compelled his complete retirement from professional duties (*Medical Times and Gazette*). He died at Chanonry, Old Aberdeen, on 7 December 1852, his wife having predeceased him. *The Lancet* virtually ignored his passing. P. W. J. BARTRIP

Sources *Medical Times and Gazette* (18 Dec 1852), 625–6 · Munk, *Roll* · J. F. Clarke, *Autobiographical recollections of the medical profession* (1874) · *DNB* · *The Lancet* (16 May 1835), 237 · P. J. Anderson, ed., *Officers and graduates of University and King's College, Aberdeen, MVD-MDCCCLX*, New Spalding Club, 11 (1893), 28 *passim* · Boase, *Mod. Eng. biog.*, 2.658 · S. S. Sprigge, *The life and times of Thomas Wakley* (1897) · *GM*, 1st ser., 92 (1822), 82 · *London Medical Directory* (1845) · PRO, PROB 11/2167, fol. 205v · census returns, 1841 · bap. reg. Scot.

McLeod, (James) Walter (1887–1978), bacteriologist, was born on 2 January 1887 at Dumbarton, near Glasgow, the second of three sons of John McLeod, a successful Scottish architect, and his wife, Lilias Symington, daughter of James McClymont, a gentleman farmer of Borgue House, Kirkcudbrightshire. After early schooling in Switzerland, where his mother had moved after the death of his father, McLeod was educated at Mill Hill School, London. He did well there, and in 1903 at the age of sixteen he became a medical student at the University of Glasgow, where in 1908 he graduated MB, ChB with commendation. He was an enthusiastic sportsman, playing rugby and cricket and also gaining a blue for athletics. He held two house appointments in Glasgow and, after a trip to India as a ship's surgeon, he was made a Coates scholar in 1909, and a Carnegie scholar in 1910–11 in the department of pathology, Glasgow, under Robert Muir. Here he studied streptococcal haemolysins under Carl H. Browning.

In 1912 McLeod moved to London to become assistant lecturer in pathology at Charing Cross medical school, where he continued his work on streptococci and also studied spirochaetes. In June 1914 McLeod married Jane (Jean) Christina (d. 1953), daughter of Thomas Garvie, a Scot who was a director of the Żyrardów textile factory in Poland. There were two sons and five daughters of this marriage. One son died as a result of an accident at the age of four.

When war broke out in 1914 McLeod joined the Royal

Army Medical Corps as a temporary lieutenant, and he later became captain in charge of the 8th mobile laboratory. He was mentioned in dispatches four times and was appointed military OBE (1919). During his military service he worked on trench fever, trench nephritis, bacillary dysentery, and influenza. In 1919 he became the first lecturer in bacteriology in the department of pathology at Leeds, and in 1922 he became the first Brotherton professor of bacteriology at Leeds. He remained in Leeds until he retired with the title of professor emeritus in 1952.

During the 1920s McLeod worked primarily on bacterial metabolism, but an outbreak of diphtheria in Leeds directed his attention to the diagnostic problems of this disease, and it is for his work on defining its different forms that he is best known as a microbiologist. He described different colonial forms of diphtheria bacilli and defined new media that were capable of distinguishing pathogenic from less pathogenic organisms. When sulphonamides became available he studied their action on bacteria, and later he was involved in early studies on penicillin.

In 1953, following his retirement and his wife's death, McLeod moved to Edinburgh and returned to laboratory work with support from the Scottish Hospital Endowments Research Trust, initially in the department of surgery at Edinburgh, then at Edenhall Hospital, Musselburgh. In 1956 he married Joyce Anita Shannon, daughter of Edgar Frederick Shannon, office equipment manufacturer, and his wife, Anita Lily (née Frost). In 1963 McLeod joined the central microbiological laboratory at the Western General Hospital, Edinburgh, supported by the Royal Society and the Medical Research Council. During this period much of his work was on urinary tract infections, with special reference to prostatectomy and paraplegia, and on staphylococcal toxins. It was not until his eighty-seventh year that failing health obliged him to give up laboratory work.

In 1928 McLeod was made a corresponding member of the Société de Biologie, Paris, and in 1933 he was elected FRS. He became an honorary member of the Scottish Society for Experimental Medicine and a fellow of the Royal Society of Edinburgh in 1957. He became an honorary member of the Pathological Society of Great Britain and Ireland in 1961, and an honorary fellow of the Royal College of Pathologists in 1970. He was president of the Society for General Microbiology in 1949–52. He received honorary degrees from the universities of Dublin (ScD) in 1946 and Glasgow (LLD) in 1961.

McLeod was a large man, a teetotaller, something of a puritan, with a deep Christian faith. He was an effective elder of the Presbyterian church and an active Boys' Brigade officer for half a century. He combined this with a great sense of fun and capacity for enjoyment. McLeod died in the Royal Victoria Hospital, Edinburgh, on 11 March 1978.   JAMES S. PORTERFIELD, *rev.*

Sources G. W. Wilson and K. S. Zinnemann, *Memoirs FRS*, 25 (1979), 421–44 · H. I. Johnstone, *Journal of General Microbiology*, 109 (1978) · personal knowledge (1986) · private information (1986) **Archives** U. Leeds, Brotherton L., Oakley MSS

Likenesses black and white photograph, *c*.1950, repro. in Wilson and Zimmerman, *Memoirs FRS*

Mac Leòid, Sir Ruairidh, of Harris and Dunvegan [Roderick MacLeod; *called* Ruairidh Mòr] (*c*.1562–1626), clan chief, was the second son of Tormod Mac Leòid (*d*. 1585) and his wife, Sìleas NicGilleathain, daughter of Eachann Mòr, Maclean of Duart. Ruairidh, called Mòr ('great') 'not so much from his size … as from the strength of his parts' (Mackenzie, 59), was from 1590 tutor (in effect a regent) to his nephew, the chief of Sìol Tormoid, the MacLeods of Harris and Dunvegan. As such he led mercenary forces to support his fellow Gaels in Ulster fighting the English in 1594–5 and afterwards was involved in war with other clans. By 1596 he had become chief himself and about 1598 married Iseabal NicDhòmhnaill (*d*. after 1654), daughter of Donald MacDonald of Glengarry; their son, Norman *Macleod of Berneray, became a royalist army officer. His career symbolizes the great changes that occurred in the highlands about 1600, from the semi-independence of the sixteenth-century clan chiefs to the tightening of James VI's control. He came to accept inevitable change and, in the years after his signing of the 1609 statutes of Iona, he became more acceptable to the king, whom he visited in London to receive a knighthood in 1613. He was given the freedom of the city of Edinburgh in 1623, and died in 1626, some time before 22 July, at Fortrose in the Black Isle, where he was buried.

COLM Ó BAOILL

Sources I. F. Grant, *The MacLeods: the history of a clan, 1200–1956* (1959) · A. Mackenzie, *History of the Macleods, with genealogies of the principal families of the name* (1889) · D. Mackinnon and A. Morrison, *The MacLeods: the genealogy of a clan*, 5 vols. (1968–77), vol. 1 · R. C. MacLeod, ed., *The Book of Dunvegan*, 2 vols., Third Spalding Club, 9 (1938–9) · G. A. Hayes-McCoy, *Scots mercenary forces in Ireland (1565–1603)* (1937) · J. Macdonald, 'An elegy for Ruaidhrí Mór', *Scottish Gaelic Studies*, 8/1 (1955–8), 27–52 **Wealth at death** wealth or property nowadays regarded as his was probably then regarded as the clan's: Dunvegan papers, analysed MacLeod, ed., *Book of Dunvegan*, vol. 1, pp. 263–4, 269–70

MacLiammóir, Micheál [*formerly* Alfred Lee Willmore] (**1899–1978**), actor and playwright, was born on 25 October 1899 at 150 Purves Road, London, the fifth child and only son of Alfred George Willmore (1863–1934), forage buyer, and his wife, Mary Elizabeth Lee (1867–1918); he was given the names Alfred Lee. A child actor who began working professionally at the age of ten, Willmore worked with Sir Herbert Beerbohm Tree's company and was cast, with the young Noël Coward, in the hugely successful J. M. Barrie's *Peter Pan* which ran from 1911 until 1914. After some acting work in films, Alfred Willmore turned to art and drawing, and in 1915 he enrolled at the Slade School at London University. However, he failed to complete this course and instead moved to Ireland in 1917. Alfred Willmore had no Irish connections but his interest in the writings of W. B. Yeats, the plays of the Abbey Theatre, and the Irish language led him to re-invent himself as Irish.

By 1927 Willmore had resumed his acting career with the travelling company of his brother-in-law, the actor–

Micheál MacLiammóir (1899–1978), by Paul Joyce, 1977

manager Anew McMaster and, on tour that summer in the south of Ireland, he met another young English actor, Hilton *Edwards (1903–1982), who was to become his life partner. When the tour finished that autumn, Willmore and Edwards decided to settle in Dublin, with the purpose of setting up their own theatre. As part of this process, Alfred Willmore gaelicized his surname to MacLiammóir (Liam being the Irish version of William) and his first name to Micheál. The newly created Micheál MacLiammóir chose Cork city, Ireland, as his birthplace and all of his autobiographical writings were to maintain the fiction that he was indeed Irish. As the Irishman Micheál MacLiammóir, Alfred Willmore lived and wrote and acted for the next fifty years. This remade nationality was never questioned and his Cork antecedents were never investigated and indeed reprints of his plays up to the 1990s still gave Cork as his birthplace.

MacLiammóir and Edwards's Dublin Gate Theatre opened with the first Irish production of Ibsen's *Peer Gynt* in October 1928 and over the next fifty years their Gate Theatre company presented a programme of European and experimental dramas by Wilde, Ibsen, Coward, Shaw, and many others. Central to this programme was MacLiammóir himself, as he took many of the leading parts, designed the sets, and even wrote some of the plays. He was an arresting and charismatic actor and also a designer of great originality. The Gate Theatre staged the work of new Irish dramatists, most notably Denis Johnston, and encouraged new actors including Orson Welles, who joined the Gate Theatre in the autumn of 1931. Later MacLiammóir was to play Iago to Welles's Othello in his 1952 film.

The cosmopolitan atmosphere of the Gate Theatre contrasted with Celticism of the Abbey Theatre and the two Dublin theatres were affectionately dubbed 'Sodom and Begorrah'. This public acceptance of MacLiammóir's sexuality and the recognition of his life partnership with Hilton Edwards was remarkable in a conservative, overwhelmingly Catholic country like Ireland, where homosexuality was criminalized until 1993. It was due, in part, to MacLiammóir's popularity as an actor and the confidence and ease of his public persona. The publication of successive volumes of autobiography, *All for Hecuba* (1946), *Each Actor on his Ass* (1961), and *Enter a Goldfish* (1977) further increased his visibility and popularity in Ireland and England. MacLiammóir's prose writings include a substantial body of work in Irish and his work as a playwright owed much to the dramas of W. B. Yeats, particularly his 1935 *Diarmuid agus Grainne*. However, a late play, *Prelude on Kasbeck Street* (1973), was a more personal exploration of homosexuality. MacLiammóir's greatest theatrical success came in 1960 with the première of his one-man Oscar Wilde show *The Importance of being Oscar*, a play on Wilde's life and writings, devised by MacLiammóir and Edwards. MacLiammóir was the ideal actor to interpret Wilde and his one-man play was important in the rehabilitation of Wilde's literary reputation. *The Importance of being Oscar* had a successful European and American tour, recorded in MacLiammóir's 1968 memoir, *An Oscar of No Importance*, and was later recorded for television for RTE. MacLiammóir died at 4 Harcourt Terrace, Dublin, on 6 March 1978. As a measure of the public acceptance of the MacLiammóir–Edwards partnership, the president of Ireland attended Micheál's funeral, two days later, at St Fintan's, Howth, Dublin, and paid his respects to Hilton Edwards as chief mourner. EIBHEAR WALSHE

Sources E. Walshe, 'Sodom and Begorrah: inventing Michael MacLiammóir', *Sex, nation and dissent in Irish writing*, ed. E. Walshe (1997) · C. Fitz-Simon, *The boys: a double biography* (1994) · M. O'H. Aodha, *The importance of being Micheál* (1990)
Archives Northwestern University, Chicago, Illinois, Dublin Gate Theatre Archive | FILM BFI NFTVA, performance footage · RTE, Dublin, RTE Television Archive | SOUND BBC WAC · BL NSA, 'Death or a kind of gentleman', BBC Radio 4, 26 Dec 1991, B8943/1 · BL NSA, performance footage · RTE Radio, Dublin, RTE Archives
Likenesses photograph, 1936 (as Byron), Northwestern University, Chicago, Dublin Gate Theatre archive · two photographs, 1952, Hult. Arch. · photograph, 1960, Hult. Arch. · P. Joyce, photograph, 1977, NPG [see illus.]
Wealth at death £24,051: probate, 1978, Ireland

McLintock, Sir William, first baronet (1873–1947), accountant, was born in Glasgow on 26 September 1873, the eldest son of Thomson McLintock, chartered accountant, and his wife, Jeannie, daughter of William Marshall, merchant seaman. William McLintock's mother died during his infancy and his father remarried soon after. McLintock was brought up in Sanquhar with his two younger half-brothers and sisters and attended Dumfries Academy and, following the family move to Glasgow, Glasgow high school. He appears to have had a happy childhood and his devotion to his stepmother is reflected in the fact that he visited her regularly towards the end of her life.

All three of Thomson McLintock's sons entered the accounting practice which he had founded in Glasgow in 1877. His son William achieved membership of the Glasgow Institute of Accountants and Actuaries in 1896, though only after several failures in the final examination, and became a partner in his father's practice in 1901. In the same year McLintock married Margaret Jane Fanny, daughter of Henry Lyons of Sligo. They had three daughters and one son, Thomson McLintock, who qualified as a chartered accountant and entered the firm for a time.

There is some suggestion that in the years immediately following William's admission to partnership, it proved necessary for him 'to curb his energies in such a way as to comply with the now elderly Thomson McLintock' (Winsbury, 28). The opportunity for William to exploit his full potential arose as the result of Thomson McLintock being appointed liquidator of the then London-based Northern Equitable Insurance Company. An office was established in London principally for the purpose of performing this work, with William McLintock in charge.

While most contemporary accounting firms continued to rely heavily on auditing work, the expansion of Thomson McLintock's London office was substantially based on William's reputation both as a tax expert and as an adviser on the amalgamation and reconstruction of companies. In the latter field McLintock played a pre-eminent role during the inter-war period. His initial reputation as a tax expert was based on negotiations undertaken in 1914 on behalf of the Lancashire coal owners with the Inland Revenue to secure uniform rates for depreciation on coal wagons. There followed in 1916 a Treasury invitation to become a member of the board of referees which had been set up, under the legislation to determine duty payable on excess profits, both to fix profit standards for each trade and industry and to hear appeals from taxpayers. McLintock quickly recognized the potential of taxation work for an ambitious accountancy practice, and in 1920 'brought or even some say bought' F. J. Cooksey from the Inland Revenue to run the tax department (Winsbury, 34). The move proved highly successful, both because the tax department itself grew at a phenomenal rate and because taxation proved to be a significant breeding ground for audit work.

The inter-war period saw the reconstruction of companies and industries in order to help eliminate overcapacity and to achieve reorganization along more modern business lines. Among McLintock's most notable achievements was the part he played in the creation of the Explosive Trades Ltd in 1918, the British Dyestuffs Corporation in 1919, and Cable and Wireless Ltd in 1929. McLintock worked jointly with Harry Peat when advising on the merger of the explosives companies, and the 'Nobel scheme' (involving the rationalization of explosives manufacturers) has been described as the forerunner of the big business in company mergers which were such a feature of William McLintock's activities in the period following the First World War. Other important involvements included the attempts to rationalize the Scottish

steelmakers in the 1930s, the receivership of Gamages in 1931, serving as a financial adviser to the government in the complex negotiations which resulted in the creation of the London Passenger Transport Board in 1933, and the reconstruction of the Lancashire Cotton Corporation in 1936.

Through the auspices of Sir Sydney Armitage-Smith, financial adviser to the Persian government, McLintock was appointed accountant to that government. His role was initially to examine the method of calculating royalties paid by the Anglo-Persian Oil Company under the terms of its concession; and in his first report, made in 1920, McLintock revealed errors which had resulted in the payment of royalties far less than those stipulated. Thereafter McLintock's firm carried out this task annually; and in recognition of his services he received the order of the Lion and the Sun. One occasion when McLintock's golden touch deserted him was in the setting up of investment trusts in the 1920s, since these entities were to be badly affected by the depression of the early 1930s.

McLintock also played a central part in business dramas of the inter-war period. When the creditors of the ailing Royal Mail Steam Packet Company rejected the reconstruction scheme prepared by Gilbert Garnsey for the group's chief executive, Owen Cosby Philipps, Lord Kylsant, the Treasury called in McLintock to investigate. His report, which made public the group's financial predicament, provoked banner headlines. It was on the basis of McLintock's findings that the firm was reconstructed, thereby reducing investor loss by an estimated £50 million. The report also led to the prosecution of Kylsant and the company's auditor, Harold Moreland of Price Waterhouse, for publishing a balance sheet which was false and fraudulent. Both parties were acquitted on the grounds that the published accounts complied with strict legal requirements, and one of the outcomes of this episode was that certain leading accountants, including McLintock, urged their colleagues to recognize an ethical responsibility to ensure that shareholders were properly informed.

About this time, McLintock also locked horns as auditor with the top management of Imperial Chemical Industries. McLintock objected to the draft published accounts for 1931 because of reservations concerning the value placed by the board on the company's Billingham assets. The crisis was resolved when the board backed down and, between 1931 and 1934, £4.5 million was written off Billingham's asset value.

Shortly after the First World War McLintock was called in to overhaul the finances of the royal household, and in recognition of this service he was appointed CVO, in 1922, and in the same year KBE. His later advancement to GBE in 1929 and to baronet in 1934 may well have reflected further recognition of his outstanding contribution to business and public service during this period. In the public domain his involvements included membership of the industrial arbitration court, the Racecourse Betting Control Board (1928–33), and the Economic Advisory Council, in 1929. He served on several government commissions, including the unemployment insurance committee (1927), the public utilities advisory committee (1930), the committee on main line electrification (1931), and the committee on company law amendment (1925). McLintock was also a member of various government committees: the committee on financial risks, in 1918; the royal commission on income tax, in 1919; and the committee on the simplification of income tax and surtax forms and the committee on national debt and taxation in 1924.

McLintock's great strengths included a keen business sense, allied to a sociable nature: he knew how to make friends with the right people and had an exceptional gift for attracting able people to work for him. McLintock is believed to have 'loved the limelight' and 'held court' at the Savoy Hotel in the Strand, which 'became something of a club to him' (Winsbury, 41). It was therefore something of a contrast when, in 1929, following a bargaining session on the London transport arrangements, he should have accompanied the Labour politician Herbert Morrison to a Lyons tea shop in the Strand for a meal. Partly through such social activities, Sir William was responsible for 80 per cent of the new work that came into the office between 1919 and 1939.

McLintock was extremely keen on music, being a member of the Orpheus Club in Glasgow and an enthusiastic participant in Gilbert and Sullivan operas. His sporting interests spanned tennis, golf, and shooting. He gave help to many philanthropic causes, and was especially interested in the Royal Caledonian schools and the Royal Scottish Corporation. He was a member of the Church of Scotland and made a significant contribution to the rebuilding of St Columba's Church, Pont Street, London, after it was bombed in May 1941. From the mid-1930s McLintock's health showed significant decline. He suffered from chronic bronchitis and had a kidney removed in 1934. McLintock died at the Royal Bath Hotel, Bournemouth, on 8 May 1947, and was survived by his wife.

JOHN RICHARD EDWARDS

Sources DNB · R. Winsbury, *Thomson McLintock & Co.: the first hundred years* (1977) · M. Bywater, 'McLintock, Sir William', *DBB* · *The Accountant* (24 May 1947) · W. J. Reader, *Imperial Chemical Industries, a history*, 2 vols. (1970–75) · P. L. Payne, *Colvilles and the Scottish steel industry* (1979) · H. Barty-King, *Girdle round the earth: the story of Cable and Wireless and its predecessors to mark the group's jubilee, 1929–1979* (1979) · *The Times* (9 May 1947) · d. cert.
Archives U. Newcastle, Robinson L., corresp. with Walter Runciman
Likenesses J. A. A. Berrie, portrait; family possession, 1959 · F. May, gouache caricature, NPG
Wealth at death £430,005 5s. 9d.: probate, 17 Sept 1947, CGPLA Eng. & Wales

McLintock, William Francis Porter (1887–1960), geologist and museum director, was born on 2 February 1887 in Edinburgh, the third child and elder son of Peter Buchanan McLintock, cashier, and his wife, Jane (*née* Porter). He was educated at George Heriot's School and Edinburgh University, graduating BSc with special distinction in 1907. In the same year he became assistant curator in the Museum of Practical Geology, London. There he worked on the mineral and gemstone collections, producing studies of datolite (1910) and beryl (1912), and the *Guide to the Collections of Gemstones* (1912), which became widely used as a textbook of gemmology and, with later revisions, remained in print for over seventy years.

In 1911 McLintock became curator of geology in the Royal Scottish Museum, Edinburgh, where he carried out research on the zeolites of the Tertiary lavas of Mull for which he received the DSc degree of Edinburgh University in 1915. With colleagues he described the properties and preparation of the archaeological pigment Egyptian blue (1914). He was elected FRSE in 1916. While in Edinburgh he lectured in geology as part of his duties in the museum and to evening classes in the Heriot-Watt College. During the First World War McLintock found scope for his skill in precision instrumentation in the devising, preparation, and testing of gauges for use in munition factories. In 1917 he saw the flight of a meteorite which passed as a brilliant fireball over Edinburgh, and the following day retrieved the biggest of four fragments (9.9 kg) from Blairgowrie, Perthshire for the Royal Scottish Museum. His research into its nature (1922) gave him the unique distinction, for a mineralogist, of having observed the flight of a meteorite which he collected, described, and analysed. In 1921, he returned to the Museum of Practical Geology in London as curator; while working there he first identified the rare mineral petalite as a British species.

At the invitation of the Anglo-Persian Oil Company, (later BP), McLintock went to Persia with James Phemister in 1926, to make an important assessment of the application of newly developed geophysical surveying methods to exploring geological structure. On their return an important series of papers on the use of the torsion balance in Persia and Britain was published together with investigations of magnetic anomalies, which showed abnormal polarities in basic rocks. McLintock also reported the first natural occurrence of a high-temperature form of the mineral wollastonite from rocks in south-west Persia where sediments were baked in prehistoric times by burning hydrocarbons.

In the early 1930s McLintock's most important duty was the planning of the new Geological Museum at South Kensington and the transfer of the library and collections from the dilapidated building in Jermyn Street. With the director of the geological survey, Sir John Flett, he visited many European museums, and developed revolutionary ideas towards the popular exposition of a science largely unknown and without apparent appeal to the general public. The new museum was opened in 1935. Laid out as McLintock had conceived it, the gemstone collection formed the centrepiece, supported by illuminated dioramas of practical geological interest. The exhibition was immediately and progressively successful.

In 1939 McLintock married Maude Alice, widow of James McLean Marshall and daughter of Major-General W. L. Dalrymple. When war came McLintock, deputy director of the Geological Survey and Museum since 1937, became responsible for the administrative side of its war effort. He initiated the organizations dealing with strategic materials, underground storage, and geological issues in military and economic warfare. Appointed director in 1945, his first task was to undo the chaos caused by wartime occupation of the building by civil defence; in 1947 his museum was the first of the national museums to reopen. He also reorganized the geological survey to peacetime activities, which were greatly expanded by official recognition of the need for geological advice on underground water, nationalized coal, and hydroelectric schemes, as well as discovery and evaluation of new sources of the raw materials of atomic energy. His programme for the post-war development of the survey was accepted, preserving its integrity as the organ of official geology and ensuring that the appropriate government agencies had the most experienced and balanced advice.

McLintock was vice-president of the eighteenth International Geological Congress, held at the museum headquarters in 1948, and was vice-president of the Geological Society. In 1946 he led a group of British geologists to report upon geological research in Germany, notably in the *Geologisches Landesamt*, and led the British delegation to the United Nations conference on the conservation of mineral resources at Lake Success in 1949. He served for many years on the board of Overseas Geological Surveys, the geological advisory panel of British Petroleum Ltd, and the Iron and Steel Board.

McLintock retired from the directorship in 1950 and was appointed CB in 1951. Tall, spare, and of distinguished appearance, he was always elegantly dressed. A keen golfer and trout-fisher, he enjoyed also riding and shooting. He was a ready, illuminating, and gifted raconteur who enjoyed membership of the Caledonian Club. Some years after retirement to his home at Rosemount, Blairgowrie, Perthshire, he suffered a serious heart attack from which he apparently recovered, but on a visit to Edinburgh he collapsed and died on 21 February 1960.

JAMES PHEMISTER, *rev.* PETER A. SABINE

Sources C. F. Davidson, *Year Book of the Royal Society of Edinburgh* (1959–60), 23–6 · *Proceedings of the Geological Society of London*, 1582 (1959–60), 141–2 · *The Times* (23 Feb 1960) · *The Scotsman* (23 Feb 1960) · *Nature*, 186 (1960), 200 · J. Smith Flett, *The first hundred years of the geological survey of Great Britain* (1937) · private information (1971, 2004) · personal knowledge (1971, 2004)

Archives BGS

Likenesses photograph, BGS

Wealth at death £14,046 14s. 4d.: confirmation, 21 May 1960, CCI

Maclise, Daniel (*bap.* 1806, *d.* 1870), painter, was the son of Alexander McLeish or McClise (1777–1861), a soldier of Scottish parentage who served in the Elgin fencibles in Ireland, and married Rebecca Buchanan in Cork on 24 December 1797. After leaving the army in 1801 he ran a tanning yard and shoemaking business supplying army contracts at Nile Street, where Maclise was born. Maclise's baptism was recorded on 2 February 1806 in the register of the Presbyterian church, Prince's Street, Cork. There were five other surviving children of the marriage: Joseph and William, who both became medical practitioners; Alexander, who remained in Cork; Anna, who married Percival

Daniel Maclise (*bap.* 1806, *d.* 1870), by William Lake Price, *c.*1858

Banks, a London barrister; and Isabella, who kept house for the painter later in London. After 1835 Daniel spelled his name Maclise in place of other forms.

Education and early career Maclise received a good basic classical education in Cork, where he displayed his interest in drawing rather than academic pursuits. His talent was noticed in his father's shop about 1820 by Margaret Spratt, a local lady who introduced him to George Newenham, a Cork banker, amateur artist, and collector, who provided him with his first experience in oils. He was also introduced to William Penrose, a prominent Cork collector whose home was at Woodhill. Maclise worked for a few months in 1820 as a clerk in Newenham's bank but left to study at the Cork drawing academy from the collection of plaster casts of the Vatican marbles which had been presented by Pope Pius VII to the prince regent and had been taken to Cork in 1818. He also attended the lectures in anatomy for artists given by Dr Woodroffe at the Royal Cork Institution. Woodroffe had a medical school in Parnell Place, and later practised surgery in Jervis Street Hospital, Dublin. Drawings by Maclise displayed in his father's shop attracted the attention of the antiquary and coin collector Richard Sainthill (1787–1870), who became his most important early patron: he gave Maclise the use of a room as a studio in his house in Nelson Place, and introduced him to antiquarian and romantic literature. In 1820 Maclise met S. C. Hall who, as the editor of the *Art Journal*, was a strong supporter of the painter in its pages. Through Sainthill he also met Thomas Crofton Croker (1798–1854), a pioneer of Irish folklore research, whose *Fairy Legends and Traditions of the South of Ireland*, vol. 1, appeared in 1825; Maclise contributed some whimsical scenes of Irish life to the edition of 1826. At Sainthill's request he later made drawings of ancient Irish gold objects which Sainthill sent to Croker in London; Croker in return sent paints to Maclise. On 9 August 1825 Sir Walter Scott, on a tour of Ireland, visited Bolster's bookshop in Cork, where Maclise made outline portrait drawings.

From these he worked up an elaborate profile portrait drawing of Scott which was lithographed in Dublin, bringing him his first public success. This enabled him to open his own studio in late 1825 in Patrick Street, Cork, making portrait drawings in an elegant linear style influenced by the neo-classical manner of the Cork-born painter Adam Buck. Maclise made a number of portrait drawings of officers and professional people, such as Richard Sheares and his niece Alice (1826), and the Revd Richard Hopkins Ryland (c.1827); both portraits are now in the British Museum. In 1826 Maclise visited Dublin, where he portrayed Colonel John Townshend of the 14th light dragoons and other officers of the regiment. In the summer of that year, he went on a walking tour of co. Wicklow as far as Avoca and made a large number of drawings of well-known views, inspired by the ideals of the 'picturesque tour'. He visited Donnybrook fair, Dublin, and then headed for Cork, drawing the Rock of Cashel, and travelling along the Blackwater to Lismore. In autumn 1826 he resumed his portrait practice in Cork. His sketchbooks in the Victoria and Albert Museum have large numbers of studies of Irish peasants, women and children, and scenic views.

Encouraged mainly by Sainthill, Maclise prepared a drawing for admission as a probationer student at the Royal Academy Schools. He left Cork travelling via Bristol to London, where he arrived on 18 July 1827. Sainthill entrusted him to Croker's care and gave him letters of introduction to C. R. Leslie, William Wyon, and a wide literary circle. He lived first in Newman Street, then in 1828 at 12, and in 1829 at 14 Charles Street; in 1831 he moved to 63 Upper Charlotte Street and in 1837 to 14 Russell Place, where he remained until he moved finally to 4 Cheyne Walk, Chelsea, in the early 1860s. In addition, in the early 1860s, he had a first-floor apartment in Brighton.

Maclise established his reputation in London as a portrait draughtsman with a lithograph of the début of Charles Kean (published on 1 October 1827) at Drury Lane; similarly he had a drawing lithographed of the London début of the celebrated violinist Niccolò Paganini on 3 June 1831, and published by T. McLean that year. Through Croker he was introduced to the literary world, including Thomas Moore and Benjamin Disraeli. Maclise became a regular visitor at the Disraeli family home, where he mixed with fashionable society; he made portraits of the Disraelis and their relations, the Lindoos, and Disraeli's friends Sarah and Benjamin Austin.

Maclise served as a probationer student at the Royal Academy in 1827–8, and was finally enrolled on 20 April 1828 as a painting student. He received a silver medal for antique drawing in 1829 (the year in which he first exhibited at the Royal Academy summer exhibition) and silver medals and prizes for life drawing and for a copy of Guido Reni in December 1830. His Royal Academy nudes of 1830

and 1831 (V&A) display careful cross-hatching and powerful draughtsmanship; he also portrayed academy teachers, such as John Constable. The culmination of his studies came with the gold medal for history painting, awarded for his *Choice of Hercules* (priv. coll.) in December 1831. However, he declined the travelling scholarship to Italy which was part of the prize. He had already visited Paris for some months in 1830, studying in the Louvre, the Luxembourg, and at Versailles; he also planned to go to Spain but had to return because of illness.

Maclise went to Ireland in autumn 1832 stopping off *en route* at various sites in the English midlands and north Wales. In Cork, the Society for the Promotion of the Fine Arts awarded gold medals to Maclise and John Hogan (then back from Rome) on 1 October 1832; Maclise went on to Killarney and made drawings of antiquities there. With Croker, he attended a Hallowe'en party given in Blarney by Father Matthew Horgan, a fellow antiquary: this resulted in *Snap Apple* or *All Hallows Eve* (exh. RA, 1833; priv. coll.), which shows the influence of the Cork painter Nathaniel Grogan and of David Wilkie. Also arising out of his Irish experience was *The Installation of Captain Rock* (exh. RA, 1834), whose subject was drawn from the rituals of Irish agrarian secret societies. His only other certain return visit to Ireland was in September 1837, when he stayed at the Imperial Hotel, Cork. He portrayed Irish rural scenes in his illustrations to Francis Mahony's *Reliques of Father Prout* (1836) and John Barrows's *Tour around Ireland through Sea Coast Counties in the Autumn of 1835* (1836). *Ireland: its Scenery and Character*, 1 (1841) by S. C. Hall and Anna Hall carried two of his illustrations of Irish customs, and Anna Hall's *Sketches of Irish Character* (1842) carried six of his idealized images of Irish women.

Literary connections Through Croker, Maclise was introduced to William Maginn, also of Cork origin, the editor of *Fraser's Magazine* from its inception in 1830 to 1836. During this period Maclise, under the pseudonym Alfred Croquis, contributed eighty-one lithographed drawings of eminent literary or political figures—one to each issue, with two final ones in 1838. These caricatures, accompanied by Maginn's texts, describing each individual, show an interdependence of word and image characteristic of early Victorian journalism and nice touches of humour, satire, and sharp comment. Edited by William Bates, the series was collected and published as *The Maclise Portrait Gallery* in 1874, 1883, and 1898. Among the subjects were Coleridge, Wordsworth, Goethe, Carlyle, Moore, Scott, Bulwer-Lytton, Disraeli, Croker, Leigh Hunt, Charles Lamb, Faraday, Lord John Russell, William Cobbett, Daniel O'Connell, Talleyrand, George Cruikshank, and John Soane. Exhibiting great elegance and economy of line, these drawings established Maclise's reputation in the 1830s and were singled out for extensive praise by the Pre-Raphaelite D. G. Rossetti: 'I suppose no such series of the portraits of celebrated persons of an epoch, produced by an eye and hand of so much insight and power, and realised with such a view to the actual impression of the sitter, exists anywhere' (*The Academy*, 15 April 1871, 217–18). Through *Fraser's*, Maclise met the Irish-born countess of

Blessington and her lover Count d'Orsay and he contributed illustrations of pretty girls to the annual *Heath's Book of Beauty* (vols. 3–5, 1835–7), which were edited by the countess. He had a brief flirtation with the poet Letitia Elizabeth Landon, who was admired by the *Fraser's* circle, and in 1836 he had a liaison with Lady Henrietta Sykes, who had previously been Disraeli's mistress; the affair resulted in abortive divorce proceedings against Maclise by her husband Sir Francis Sykes in 1838. A more pleasing result of Maclise's relationship with Henrietta was his very fine watercolour portrait of the Sykes family in medieval dress (c.1837, Sykes collection).

Maclise was thoroughly at home in the world of writers and literary culture, and in 1827 he met the novelist W. H. Ainsworth at Croker's home in London. He became a regular visitor to Ainsworth's house, Kensal Lodge, and painted his portrait on two occasions. At Ainsworth's parties he first met John Forster, probably in 1834; they dined together at the Garrick Club. This was to be a lifelong friendship: it was through Forster that so many of Maclise's drawings, paintings, and letters found their way to the Victoria and Albert Museum after the painter's death. In 1836, when Forster met Dickens, he introduced Maclise to the novelist and they all met frequently at the Parthenon Club, St James's Square. In May 1835 Maclise was introduced to W. C. Macready, the leading actor of the day, whose productions inspired his paintings on Shakespearian themes; Maclise, Dickens, and Forster often met Macready backstage in the late 1830s. Maclise painted a celebrated portrait of Dickens in 1839 (NPG), and during 1840 his friendship with Dickens was at its height. In April he accompanied Dickens to Richmond and on to Stratford and Lichfield; they also took walks together in the Hampstead area of London. In July 1841 Maclise visited Dickens at his seaside residence at Broadstairs and in November 1842 he accompanied Dickens, Forster, and Stanfield on a tour of Cornwall. One result of this close friendship was *Girl at the Waterfall at St. Nighton's Kieve* (exh. RA, 1843; V&A), which shows Georgina Hogarth, Dickens's sister-in-law. Maclise's warm and care-free character appealed greatly to Dickens, although in subsequent years they drifted apart.

History painter The beginnings of Maclise's career as a history painter can be seen in his *The Choice of Hercules* (1831), an example of a conservative eighteenth-century approach. Maclise was, however, part of a new movement to describe historical subjects with historical accuracy and an emphasis on the human story; his involvement was first evident in *The Interview between Charles I and Oliver Cromwell* (1836, National Gallery of Ireland, Dublin). He was much attracted to the tory Young England movement of Disraeli with its idealization of medieval social customs; this influence was evident in *Merry Christmas in the Baron's Hall* (1838, National Gallery of Ireland, Dublin), which is stylistically dependent on Netherlandish seventeenth-century painting. His love of the panoply of medievalism is revealed, too, in the *Chivalrous Vow of the Ladies and the Peacock* (1835), inspired by Scott's *The Lay of the Last Minstrel*. He was also deeply influenced by the exoticism of contemporary romantic literature: *The Veiled Prophet of Khoressan* (1832; known through watercolours in the V&A), was an oriental fantasy inspired by Moore's *Lallah Rookh*. An instant success, it brought him much public attention, and when it was exhibited in Liverpool in 1832, gained him a prize of 80 guineas. His success was recognized by the Royal Academy, which made him an associate in 1835 and a full member in 1840 after he deposited *The Wood Ranger* as his diploma piece; it epitomizes his Netherlandish style of the 1830s.

Maclise distinguished himself as a book illustrator of texts by British writers, illustrating both Edward Bulwer-Lytton's *Pilgrims of the Rhine* (1834) and his *Lelia, or, The Siege of Granada* (1839)—an orientalist romance—and Milton's 'L'allegro' and 'Il penseroso' in S. C. Hall's *Book of Gems* (1836). For Dickens he contributed illustrations to a number of books: *The Old Curiosity Shop* (1840), *The Cricket on the Hearth* (1846), *The Chimes* (1845), and *The Battle of Life* (1846), mainly depicting fairy fantasies on the frontispieces. His finest achievement in book illustration was his work for *The Irish Melodies* (1845) by his fellow Irishman, Thomas Moore, which shows the strong influence of contemporary German illustrated books; similarly Germanic were his illustrations for G. Bürger's *Leonora* (1847). Two of his illustrations were for 'Morte d'Arthur' in the 1857 Moxon edition of Tennyson's *Poems*; he also completely illustrated Tennyson's *The Princess* (1860). A very large number of his oils were based on literature, such as his *Scene from Undine* (1843) purchased by Queen Victoria and still in the Royal Collection. He also painted subjects from Goldsmith's *Vicar of Wakefield*, Lesage's *Gil Blas*, and Lady Morgan's *Life of Salvator Rosa*, and individual fancy pictures like *The Falconer* (1853; Crawford Art Gallery, Cork).

Maclise's lifelong interest in the theatre is evident in his paintings of Shakespearian scenes, where he reflected the theatrical move to greater historical accuracy of costume and setting, as in the productions of Charles Kean and W. C. Macready. This trend is apparent in *Malvolio and the Countess* (1840; National Gallery of Ireland, Dublin), and in two major pieces: *The Banquet Scene from Macbeth* (1840; Guildhall, London) and *The Play Scene from Hamlet* (1842; Tate collection). There is a strongly theatrical quality about them in the depiction of gesture and expression. Compositionally he was also influenced by the engraved Shakespearian outlines of the contemporary German illustrator Moritz Retzsch. *Hamlet* drew strong praise from most critics (although not from Ruskin), and went originally to the Vernon Gallery. These Shakespearian subjects from *Macbeth* and *Hamlet* display a new seriousness in Maclise's work, confirmed in a set of drawings, the 'Seven Ages of Man' from *As You Like It*, engraved by the Art Union (1850). His lighter side can be appreciated in *Orlando and the Wrestler* (1854, Forbes magazine collection, New York) with its Pre-Raphaelite detail of plants. Also arising from his involvement with the theatre were his portraits of *Macready as Werner* (1850) and *Foster as Kitely* (exh. RA, 1848)—both in the Victoria and Albert Museum—painted as tokens of friendship.

His work for Westminster Palace formed the centre-piece of Maclise's career. He submitted a drawing, *The Knight*, to the competition of 1844 and was one of the artists who were invited to paint trial murals in the Garden Pavilion of Buckingham Palace, on the initiative of Prince Albert. Following those experiments, he was selected to enter a further competition for the House of Lords murals; to prepare himself he travelled to Paris with his brother Dr Joseph Maclise in 1844. He stayed near the Luxembourg and was deeply impressed by contemporary French art, especially the *Hemicycle* of Delaroche in the École des Beaux-Arts; the visit helped to reorientate his career to monumental painting. He was in Paris again in 1845, with Dickens and other friends on a social visit. In July 1845, in Westminster Hall, he exhibited a cartoon, sketch, and fresco specimen of *The Spirit of Chivalry*, one of the designated themes for the House of Lords, in a Gothic style influenced by German Nazarene art: it was approved and the fresco was completed in 1848. He painted the companion fresco, *The Spirit of Justice* in 1849. The House of Lords frescoes drew strong critical approval from the *Athenaeum* and from Gustav Waagen. Closely related in style was his portrait (in oil) of the actress *Caroline Norton as Erin* (1846; priv. coll.) painted in a Nazarene manner with a gold background. However, his physical and mental health suffered from his prolonged fresco painting.

Maclise had a 'great men of history' approach to the past, probably influenced by Carlyle, and during the 1850s he painted a series of monumental narrative subjects. Influenced by the German *Illustrated Bible* (Cotta, 1846) he painted *The Sacrifice of Noah* (RA, 1847; Leeds City Art Gallery), one of his most fluently painted works with strong Germanic and Netherlandish tendencies combined. Inspired by Bulwer-Lytton's novel *The Last of the Barons*, he painted *Caxton's Printing Office* (1851; priv. coll.), an allegory of moral progress through the invention of printing; it was followed by another historical workshop scene, *Peter the Great at Deptford Dockyard* (1857; Royal Holloway College, Surrey). During the 1850s, affected by the rising tide of Irish cultural nationalism and now a member of the Irish Society in London, he was particularly interested in Hiberno-Saxon themes celebrating the rights of different, mainly Celtic, groups, in the face of military conquest. He criticized the military invader in *King Alfred and the Camp of the Danes* (exh. RA, 1852; Laing Art Gallery, Newcastle upon Tyne), *Edward I Presenting his Infant Son* (*the First Prince of Wales*) *to the Welsh People* (1848–58; squared drawing, V&A), and *The Marriage of Strongbow and Eva* (exh. RA, 1854; National Gallery of Ireland, Dublin). The latter, with its Celtic revivalist ideology, is a summation of his approach to history painting and a testimony to his Irish origin. Finally, his *Norman Conquest* series of drawings inspired by Bulwer-Lytton's *Harold the Last of the Saxon Kings*, was exhibited in 1857 and published as an album of engravings in 1866.

The culmination of the narrative histories and of Maclise's career came with the commission for *The Meeting of Wellington and Blücher* and *The Death of Nelson* for the Royal Gallery of Westminster Palace. Originally these were to be accompanied by sixteen other subjects from the history of the United Kingdom: he offered to undertake all of these works and was commissioned in 1858. He exhibited a cartoon, 45 feet long, of *Wellington* in May 1859 which drew the admiration of a number of his fellow artists, who presented him with a gold porte crayon. The *Athenaeum* and the *Art Journal* praised the work, although there was public controversy over the historicity of the moment depicted. Maclise conducted extensive research for the military details; faced with the difficulty of painting it in fresco, he sought to resign the commission but was dissuaded. In order to familiarize himself with the new 'waterglass' technique he visited Berlin, Munich, and Dresden in autumn 1859, studying the work of Wilhelm von Kaulbach and his pupils. The mural was completed in December 1861 and drew favourable comment, especially from F. G. Stephens in *The Athenaeum* (2 November 1861, 1775, 585–6). From 1863 to 1865 he worked on *The Death of Nelson*, which involved extensive naval research. Following the death of Prince Albert, who was a strong supporter of Maclise, the decorative programmes were cut back and his contract for the remaining works was cancelled, to his great distress.

In his last years Maclise returned to the subjects of his youth, scenes from Shakespeare and also new subjects reflecting Pre-Raphaelite influence: *Madeleine after Prayer* from Keats (exh. RA, 1868; Walker Art Gallery, Liverpool) and *King Cophetua and the Beggar Maid* (exh. RA, 1869). He recapitulated his genre scenes of the 1830s in *A Winter's Night Tale* (exh. RA, 1867; Manchester City Galleries); his last painting, *The Earls of Ormond and Desmond* (exh. RA, 1870), was, appropriately, taken from Irish history.

Professional standing and family life In his career Maclise also made designs for the applied arts—a bracelet design for Henry Cole in 1848, the prize medal for the international exhibition of 1862, and the Royal Academy Turner gold medal in 1859. He was active in the life of the academy, serving on its council and deputizing for the president in 1869, and teaching regularly in the schools during the 1850s. He served as a juror at the Paris Universal Exhibition of 1855; also travelling during that year to Lyons and Naples with his brother Joseph. He became a member of the Athenaeum in 1841. A confirmed bachelor, on the death in 1850 of his brother-in-law, P. W. Banks, Maclise took over the responsibility of supporting his sister Anna Banks and her family; his sister Isabella, who kept house for him, died in 1865, leaving him bereft. In his last years his heart deteriorated and he was largely confined to his home at Cheyne Walk. Maclise died there on 25 April 1870 of pneumonia and was buried in Kensal Green cemetery, London. At the Royal Academy dinner of 30 April 1870 Dickens paid a fulsome tribute to his old friend. As a young man, Maclise was tall, handsome, and well-built, and he loved swimming. Charming and excellent company in the 1820s and 1830s, he later tended to overwork and was prone to depression and withdrew into himself.

Maclise's greatest strengths as an artist were his figure draughtsmanship and pictorial composition, talents that enabled him to deal with complex narrative subjects on a large scale. He could combine great detail with clear pictorial structure and his drawings and illustrations have a linear precision which is retained in the oil paintings. His weakness lay in a tendency to pile on descriptive detail with insufficient attention to the harmonizing possibilities of tone and colour. In the characterization of his figures, he tended to rely on stereotypes with insufficient individualism. His painting style is harsh and lacks painterly effect.

Nevertheless, he was one of the few painters in the history of British and Irish art who could paint monumental narrative scenes with success. This was his principal achievement. In common with other nineteenth-century painters of historical subjects, such as Paul Delaroche, he aimed at factual reconstructions of period costume, setting, and story—notably in his narrative subjects of the 1850s and 1860s. Equally, however, he believed with his contemporaries that history painting was a moral teacher, that by focusing on significant events and personalities of the past, he was able to encapsulate political and social change. These two imperatives in history painting—the factual and the moralistic—could be contradictory and Maclise's historical scholarship was often inaccurate and his ideological narratives over-simplifications of history. As an Irish artist, he made a culturally nationalist statement in *The Marriage of Strongbow and Eva* (exh. RA, 1854; National Gallery of Ireland, Dublin), which was a pointer to the Celtic revival of the late nineteenth century. Like a historical novelist, he created grand monumental and imaginative narratives on British and Irish history, reflecting the romantic ideals of the nineteenth century towards the past.　　　JOHN TURPIN

Sources E. Kenealy, 'Daniel Maclise: our portrait gallery', *Dublin University Magazine*, 29 (1847), 594–607 · W. J. O'Driscoll, *A memoir of Daniel Maclise* (1871) · Redgrave, *Artists*, 282–3 · A. Cunningham, *The lives of the most eminent British painters*, rev. Mrs C. Heaton, 3 (1880), 406ff · Graves, *Artists* · W. G. Strickland, *A dictionary of Irish artists*, 2 (1913); facs. edn with introduction by T. J. Snoddy (1969), 64–79 · M. M. H. Thrall, *Rebellious Fraser's: Nol Yorke's magazine in the days of Maginn, Thackeray, and Carlyle* (1934) · R. Ormond, *Burlington Magazine*, 110 (1968), 685–93 · J. Turpin, 'The Irish background of Daniel Maclise', *Capuchin Annual* (1970), 177–94 · R. Ormond and J. Turpin, eds., *Daniel Maclise, 1806–1870* (1972) [exhibition catalogue, NPG, 3 March – 16 April 1972; NG Ire., 5 May – 18 June 1972] · R. Ormond, 'Daniel Maclise: a major figurative painter', *The Connoisseur*, 179 (1972), 165–71 · J. Turpin, 'The lure of the Celtic past in the art of Daniel Maclise', *Ireland of the Welcomes*, 21/1 (May–June 1972), 32–6 · J. Turpin, 'German influence on Daniel Maclise', *Apollo*, 97 (1973), 169–75 · J. Turpin, 'Daniel Maclise and his place in Victorian art', *Anglo-Irish Studies*, 1 (1975), 51–69 · A. Crookshank and the Knight of Glin [D. Fitzgerald], *The painters of Ireland, c.1660–1920* (1978) · J. Turpin, 'Daniel Maclise and Cork Society', *Journal of the Cork Historical and Archaeological Society*, 2nd ser., 85 (1980), 66–78 · J. Turpin, 'Daniel Maclise, Disraeli, and Fraser's Magazine', *Éire–Ireland*, 15/1 (1980), 46–63 · J. Turpin, 'Maclise as a Dickens illustrator', *The Dickensian*, 76 (1980), 67–77 · J. Turpin, 'Daniel Maclise and Charles Dickens: a study of their friendship', *Studies* [Dublin], 73/289 (spring 1984), 47–64 · J. Turpin, 'Maclise as a book illustrator', *Irish Arts Review*, 2/2 (1985), 23–7 · P. MacEvansoneya, 'Daniel Maclise and a bankrupt patron', *Irish Arts Review Yearbook*, 12 (1996), 128–9 · F. G. Stephens, 'Interview between Wellington and Blucher after Waterloo', *The Athenaeum* (2 Nov 1861), 585–6 · J. Turpin, 'The life and work of Daniel Maclise, 1806–1870', PhD diss., Courtauld Inst., 1973 · N. Weston, 'The development of Irish nationalism in the art and life of Daniel Maclise', PhD diss., University of Southern California, 1991 · N. Weston, *Daniel Maclise: Irish artist in Victorian London* (2001) · register, Presbyterian Church, Prince's Street, Cork, 2 Feb 1806 [baptisms]

Archives RA, autobiographical notes · TCD, letters and memoranda · V&A NAL, letters | Herts. ALS, Bulwer-Lytton MSS · Hunt. L., letters to Charles Dickens and others · RA, minutes of council of a general assembly · V&A, C. L. Eastlake, official corresp., MS 86 0 8 · V&A NAL, letters to J. N. Forster

Likenesses D. Maclise, self-portrait, pencil and watercolour, 1829, NG Ire.; repro. in O'Driscoll, *Memoir of Daniel Maclise*, frontispiece · D. Maclise, self-portrait, watercolour, 1829, Museum of Fine Arts, Boston · C. Stanfield, group portrait, watercolour and body colour, 1842, V&A · T. Bridgford, pencil drawing, 1844, NG Ire.; repro. in Kenealy, 'Daniel Maclise: our portrait gallery' · C. H. Lear, two chalk drawings, 1845, NPG · E. M. Ward, oils, 1846, NPG · C. W. Cope, pencil drawing, *c*.1846–1849, Palace of Westminster, London · C. Bauginet, lithograph, pubd 1857, BM, NPG · C. B. Birch, pencil drawing, *c*.1858, NPG · W. L. Price, photograph, *c*.1858, RA [*see illus.*] · J. Thomas, marble bust, 1859, NG Ire.; replica, NG Ire. · C. G. Lewis, group portrait, mixed engraving, pubd 1864 (*The intellect and valour of Great Britain*), NPG · E. Davis, marble bust, 1870, RA · A. B. Wyon, medal, 1878, NPG; repro. in *Art Union* · M. Jackson, woodcut (after T. Scott), BM · D. Maclise, self-portraits, sketches, V&A · attrib. Maull & Polyblank, photograph, NPG · M. L. Menpes, drypoint, BM, NPG · D. J. Pound, stipple and line engraving (after photograph by Mayall), BM, NPG; repro. in D. J. Pound, *Drawing room portrait gallery of eminent personages* (1859–60) · cartes-de-visite, NPG · lithograph (after drawing; repro. in *Fraser's Magazine*), BM; repro. in *Maginn's gallery of illustrious literary characters* (1873) · photograph, NPG

Wealth at death under £40,000: probate, 12 May 1870, *CGPLA Eng. & Wales*

Mac Lochlainn [Ua Lochlainn], **Muirchertach** (*d.* 1166), high-king of Ireland, was the son of Niall, son of Domnall Mac Lochlainn. He was king of the Cenél nEógain (whose land, Tír Eoghain, gave its name to modern Tyrone), and his province–kingdom extended from the plains in the vicinity of the primatial city of Armagh to the Inishowen peninsula in Donegal. The family took its surname from Muirchertach's great-great-grandfather, Lochlainn (*d.* 1023), who was in turn almost certainly the great-great-grandson of Domnall, son of Áed Findliath (*d.* 879), king of Ailech. Muirchertach succeeded to the kingship following the death of his uncle, Conchobar, in 1136. He defeated the petty kings of the northern Cenél nEógain in 1139 and 1142, though in the latter he was severely wounded and was deposed in the following year. In 1145 he recovered the kingship of Cenél nEógain with the aid of the Airgialla and Cenél Conaill. Having secured his position in Tír Eoghain he was victorious in battle against the east Ulster kingdom of Ulaid in 1147. In the following year he replaced the reigning king of Ulaid with a more acceptable kinsman and secured the hostages of Ulaid, Airgialla, and Cenél Conaill at an assembly at Armagh, a gesture of submission that made him the paramount king throughout the north of Ireland. In 1149 he reasserted control over Ulaid and led a cavalry march south to receive the hostages of Bréifne and Mide; he then went to Dublin to receive the submission of the Ostmen (its Hiberno-

Scandinavian rulers) and the hostages of their overlord, Diarmait Mac Murchada of Leinster.

This success made Mac Lochlainn a contender for the high-kingship of Ireland, a position then occupied by the ageing Connacht king, Toirrdelbach Ua Conchobair. In 1150 Mac Lochlainn obtained the hostages of Connacht, divided Mide in three, and in the following year launched an invasion of Connacht, again obtaining hostages as a sign of his supremacy. In 1152 he and Ua Conchobair, having made peace, joined forces and again partitioned Mide. However, Muirchertach and Ua Conchobair soon found themselves at war again. In 1153 Mac Lochlainn routed the forces of Connacht led by Toirrdelbach's son, Ruaidrí, while in the following year the Connacht fleet scored only a limited success in a major naval encounter off the Inishowen coast, primarily because Muirchertach had assembled a fleet from Galloway, Kintyre, and Man in order to withstand it. Although his forces suffered losses, Muirchertach was now in a sufficiently strong position to parade his armies through Connacht and Bréifne, and when he reached Dublin the Ostmen proclaimed him as their king; he then granted them twelve hundred cows as *tuarastal* or wages, a sign of his overlordship. Implicitly, this deed secured him the high-kingship of Ireland, though his reign is generally dated from the death of Toirrdelbach Ua Conchobair in 1156.

Mac Lochlainn invaded Osraige in alliance with Diarmait Mac Murchada in 1156. A year later he was in Munster, which he repartitioned, and having laid siege to Limerick was granted its kingship by the Ostmen. It may have been in commemoration of this circuit of Ireland that the propagandist poem known as 'Móirthimchell Éirenn Uile' was composed. His reign did not go unchallenged, however. Ruaidrí Ua Conchobair attacked Tír Eoghain in 1157 and 1158, and in the next year he and his allies, Ua Ruairc and Ua Briain, challenged Muirchertach to battle at Ardee, in Louth, but were severely routed. Mac Lochlainn then ravaged Bréifne, billeted his troops on Mide for a month, and raided Connacht; and in 1161, having taken the hostages of Bréifne, he accepted the formal submission of Ruaidrí Ua Conchobair and Diarmait Mac Murchada and was declared by the annals 'king of Ireland without opposition'.

As king, Mac Lochlainn was a munificent benefactor of the church. The Book of Kells contains a document by which he granted the church of Ardbraccan in Mide freedom from the exactions of secular rulers. Gill Meic Liac, head of the church of Armagh, made a circuit of Tír Eoghain in 1150 and 1162 and received tribute. In the same year Muirchertach gave the abbot of Derry, Flaithbertach Ua Brolcháin, a gold ring and other gifts and allowed him too to make a circuit of Tír Eoghain. In 1162 both king and abbot began an extensive building programme in Derry, culminating in 1164 in the erection of a ninety-foot-long church. In this same year, Muirchertach joined with the archbishop of Armagh in opposing the appointment of Flaithbertach to the abbacy of Iona. He was present at the consecration of the Cistercian abbey of Mellifont in 1157, at which he not only granted to the monks cows and gold

but lands in the kingdom of Mide. At about the same time he issued a charter to the Cistercian house of Newry, Down, in which he styled himself *rex totius Hiberniae* ('King of all Ireland') and by which he made a grant of lands in the vicinity to this house too.

Mac Lochlainn sought something akin to territorial ownership of the lands he conquered. In 1163, Diarmait Ua Máel Sechlainn paid him 100 ounces of gold for the kingship of western Mide. When Muirchertach invaded Ulaid in 1165, not only did he temporarily banish its king, Eochaid Mac Duinn Sléibe, but gave away lands in the latter's kingdom to Donnchad Ua Cerbaill of Airgialla and the church of Saul, in Down. In the following year, however, he treacherously blinded Eochaid, which incident brought about his own downfall. Tír Eoghain was invaded by the forces of Airgialla and Bréifne and, in a battle in south Armagh, Muirchertach was slain and was buried in the 'mausoleum of the kings' at Armagh (at which the churchmen of Derry took grave offence). His death greatly weakened the Mac Lochlainn family and ultimately paved the way for the restoration of the Uí Néill to power in Ulster. He was succeeded as high-king of Ireland by Ruaidrí Ua Conchobair of Connacht, and, because Muirchertach's demise left exposed his ally, Diarmait Mac Murchada, who was thereupon banished overseas, his death indirectly precipitated the Anglo-Norman invasion of Ireland.   SEÁN DUFFY

Sources AFM, 2nd edn · W. Stokes, ed., 'The annals of Tigernach [8 pts]', *Revue Celtique*, 16 (1895), 374–419; 17 (1896), 6–33, 119–263, 337–420; 18 (1897), 9–59, 150–97, 267–303, 374–91; pubd sep. (1993) · W. M. Hennessy and B. MacCarthy, eds., *Annals of Ulster, otherwise, annals of Senat*, 4 vols. (1887–1901) · D. Murphy, ed., *The annals of Clonmacnoise*, trans. C. Mageoghagan (1896); facs. edn (1993) · Cormcan Eigeas, 'The circuit of Ireland by Muirchertach Mac Néill, prince of Aileach: a poem written in the year 1442', ed. and trans. J. O'Donovan, *Tracts relating to Ireland*, Irish Archaeological Society, 1 (1841), 1–68 · G. Mac Niocaill, ed., *Notitiae as leabhar Cheanannais, 1033–1161* (1961), 34–6 · S. Ó Ceallaigh, *Gleanings from Ulster history*, 2nd edn (1994) · J. Hogan, 'The Irish law of kingship, with special reference to Aileach and Cenel Eóghain', *Proceedings of the Royal Irish Academy*, 40C (1931–2), 186–254 · J. Hogan, 'The Ua Briain kingship of Telach Óc', *Féil-Sgríbhinn Eoin Mhic Néill*, ed. J. Ryan (1940), 406–44 · D. Ó Corráin, *Ireland before the Normans* (1972)

Maclonan, Flann. *See* Flann mac Lonáin (d. 891x918).

McLoughlin [nic Lochlainn; *married name* Norton], **Katherine** (*fl.* 1671–1679), Quaker preacher, was born to wealthy parents in or near Coleraine, co. Londonderry. She may have been related to and even the sister of Dúnal 'Gorm' ('Blue') Mac Lochlainn, a protestant minister of Clonmany parish 20 miles north of Londonderry, and also of Peadar 'Caoch' ('Blind') who was a Roman Catholic priest. Katherine was sent to Londonderry for an education, including instruction in the Gaelic language. When she was sixteen years of age she went to Barbados, where she married a Mr Norton. In 1671 George Fox, William Edmundson, and other members of the Religious Society of Friends (Quakers) visited the island as part of their mission to establish the religious movement in the West Indies. Katherine met Fox, was convinced by the ministry, and became an 'able minister' (Rutty and Wight, 129). From the beginning, while women Friends could not usurp authority over the men but had to 'be in subjection in all things, for the man is head of the woman and Christ is head of the church', there was a role for both male and female in the church (Edmundson, 17). A truly inspired and gifted woman could, like a man, preach and travel both at home and abroad.

Katherine had returned to Ireland by 1676 'on truth's service' (Rutty and Wight, 129). She was determined to become part of the Gaelic-speaking community and minister to the existing English-speaking settlers who were Friends. She visited Friends' houses, held public meetings, and indeed preached in Gaelic on a number of occasions, notably in Lurgan on market day, which was unusual. Undoubtedly the language barrier prevented the advancement of Quakerism among the native Irish community. However, during meetings near Coleraine where her relations lived, there were several disputes 'on account of truth' (ibid., 129). But these did not deter her, and she held successful meetings throughout co. Armagh, co. Cavan, co. Westmeath, and co. Dublin.

In spring 1676 Anthony Sharp, the prominent Quaker wool merchant and commercial figure in Dublin, was host to twenty visitors, including Katherine, some of whom were preparing to sail to England or to America. Throughout his life Sharp provided hospitality for visiting Friends. Katherine reflected warmly on Sharp's 'tenderness and Godly simplicity' (Greaves, 263). She devoted the following two years to preaching and wrote to Sharp on 30 March 1678 that at meetings in the northern counties, she was 'very well refreshed and comforted amongst the Lord's innocent people, for I can say that they are as innocent a plain people as I have been amongst'. In July 1677 Sharp considered her ministry to have been 'of great service', converting a number of people including Mrs Simmons, the wife of a prominent judge, and attracting large attendances to her meetings (Kilroy, 'Women and the Reformation', 184–5). Katherine had left for England by 1679, and Rutty, writing in 1751, concluded that she was 'well qualified for the service, being of a sound judgement, large in testimony, of a good utterance, had her own to distribute and did not make the gospel chargeable' (Rutty and Wight, 129). Her fate in England is unknown, but her reputation as a preacher in Ireland was noted during her lifetime. By 1701 the number of Friends' meeting places in Ireland had increased from thirty in 1660 to fifty-three and the community numbered between 5500 and 6500.
                                                BERNADETTE WHELAN

Sources J. Rutty and T. Wight, *A history of the rise and progress of the people called Quakers in Ireland from the year 1653 to 1700*, 2nd edn (1800) • W. Edmundson, *An epistle containing wholesome advice and councel to all Friends. Grounded upon ancient examples recorded in the scriptures of truth* (1701) • R. L. Greaves, *Dublin's merchant–Quaker: Anthony Sharp and the community of Friends, 1643–1707* (1998) • R. S. Harrison, *A biographical dictionary of Irish Quakers* (1997) • P. Kilroy, 'Women and the Reformation in seventeenth-century Ireland', *Women in early modern Ireland*, ed. M. MacCurtain and M. O'Dowd (1991), 179–96 • M. J. Wigham, *The Irish Quakers: a short history of the Religious Society of Friends in Ireland* (1992) • Anthony Sharp MSS, Religious Society of Friends, Dublin, S.5, p. 15; S.4, p. 73 • A. G. Chapman, *History of the Religious Society of Friends in Lurgan* (1997) • P. Kilroy, *Protestant dissent and controversy in Ireland, 1660–1714* (1994) • J. Randall, *A brief account of the rise, principles and disciples and discipline of the people called Quakers* (1785) • *From our half years meeting in Dublin, the 9th, 10th and 11th days of the 9th month 1691: address to all Friends in this nation of Ireland or elsewhere*, Religious Society of Friends (1691) • *A second dissertation on the liberty of preaching granted to women by the people called Quakers: in answer to a late dissertation on that subject* by John Rutty (1738) • *A summary of the doctrines, discipline and history of Friends written at the desire of the meeting for sufferings in London*, 5th edn (1792)

Archives Religious Society of Friends, Dublin, letters to Anthony Sharpe

McLoughlin, Mary (*d.* after **1904**). *See under* Knock, visionaries of (*act.* 1879).

Maclure, Edward Craig (1833–1906), dean of Manchester, born in Upper Brook Street, Manchester, on 10 June 1833, was the eldest son of John Maclure, merchant, from his marriage with Elizabeth, daughter of William Kearsley, also a merchant. Educated at Manchester grammar school (1844–50), he won a Hulmeian scholarship at Brasenose College, Oxford, and matriculated there on 28 January 1852. He graduated BA in 1856 and proceeded MA in 1858, being created BD and DD in 1890. Taking holy orders, he was curate of St John's, Ladywood, Birmingham (1857–61), and St Pancras, London (1861–3), and vicar of Habergham Eaves, Burnley (1863–77). In the public life of Burnley he took a prominent part, becoming chairman of the school board. James Fraser, bishop of Manchester, appointed him in 1877 to the important vicarage of Rochdale, in 1878 to an honorary canonry of Manchester, and in 1881 to the rural deanery of Rochdale. He carried out great improvements at Rochdale parish church, for which he raised £10,000, as well as on the vicarage estate. In 1887 he acted as honorary secretary of the church congress at Manchester.

Designated archdeacon of Manchester in 1890, Maclure was before his induction appointed dean of Manchester on the death of John Oakley, being installed on 28 October. As dean Maclure won the goodwill of all classes by his broad sympathies, humour, and love of fair play. Through his incessant care the daily service in the cathedral increased in dignity and beauty, and the Sunday evening services grew to be an important element in the religious life of the city. To his energy was due the rearrangement of the boundaries of the old churchyard and the building of the western annexe and the new vestries and library at the north-east corner of the cathedral.

Maclure devoted his abundant energy to promoting popular education of a religious kind. He was elected a member of the Manchester school board in 1891, and was unanimously appointed chairman. That position he held until the board was abolished in 1903 by the Education Act of the previous year. He was afterwards deputy chairman of the education committee of the city council until his death, and was also a member of the Salford education committee. He was a member of the royal commission on secondary education in 1894 and in 1899 joined the consultative committee of the Board of Education. From 1895 to 1902 he was chairman of the School Board Association of England and Wales. He was also principal of the Scholae Episcopi at Manchester, and a governor of Owens College, Manchester University, of Manchester grammar school, of Chetham's Hospital, and of Hulme's Trust. He was made an honorary LLD at the Victoria University, Manchester, in 1902.

Maclure married on 7 May 1863 Mary Anne (d. 17 Oct 1905), daughter of Johnson Gedge of Bury St Edmunds, and had three sons (of whom William Kenneth took holy orders) and three daughters. He died at 26 York Place, Manchester, on 8 May 1906, and was buried at Kersal church, near that city. A monumental brass was placed in the chancel of the cathedral, and another memorial in the grammar school. He is fairly described as a high-churchman.

His brother, **Sir John William Maclure**, first baronet (1835–1901), born at Manchester on 22 April 1835 and educated at Manchester grammar school, was a successful merchant and manufacturer, specializing in railway development and cotton. He married on 13 December 1859 Eleanor (d. April 1910), second daughter of Thomas Nettleship of East Sheen, Surrey, with whom he had three sons and four daughters. He came into prominence as honorary secretary to the committee of the Lancashire Cotton Relief Fund, instituted in 1862 for the relief of the operatives thrown out of work through the stoppage of supplies of cotton during the American Civil War. The fund raised over £1,750,000 and Maclure received a public testimonial. He was an enthusiastic volunteer, becoming major of the 40th Lancashire rifles. As churchwarden of Manchester (1881–96) he was instrumental in collecting large sums of money for a thorough restoration of the cathedral. A strong churchman, he was in politics a Conservative, and was elected in 1886 MP for the Stretford division of Lancashire, which seat he retained until his death. His cheery temperament made him popular in the House of Commons. On 7 April 1892 he and three other directors of the Cambrian Railways were admonished by the speaker by direction of the house for a breach of privilege in dismissing a stationmaster on account of his evidence before the committee on the hours of railway servants. Maclure was created a baronet on 1 January 1898. He died on 28 January 1901, and a tablet to his memory was placed in Manchester Cathedral.

C. W. SUTTON, rev. H. C. G. MATTHEW

Sources Manchester Guardian (9 May 1906) · The Times (9 May 1906) · Manchester Courier (14 May 1906) · Guardian (30 May 1906) · C. H. Drant, Distinguished churchmen (1902) · Crockford (1906) · Dod's Parliamentary Companion (1900) · M. Hennell, The deans and canons of Manchester Cathedral, 1840–1948 [1988] · A. Boutflower, Personal reminiscences of Manchester Cathedral, 1854–1912 (1913)
Likenesses M. E. Luxmore, oils, 1895, Man. City Gall. · W. Rothenstein, lithograph, BM · wood-engraving (after photograph by Russell & Sons), NPG; repro. in ILN (26 July 1890) · portrait, repro. in Manchester Guardian · portrait, repro. in Drant, Distinguished churchmen

Wealth at death £14,975 1s. 11d.: probate, 5 June 1906, CGPLA Eng. & Wales

Maclure, Sir John William, first baronet (1835–1901). See under Maclure, Edward Craig (1833–1906).

Maclyn [de Machlinia], **William** (fl. 1482–1490), printer, was usually referred to by the Latin form Machlinia; he signed himself 'William Maclyn' in a yearbook, and was presumably known in London by that name, indicating that he came from Malines in Brabant. He first appears as a printer, with John Lettou, in the colophon of Littleton's Tenores novelli, which was printed near All Saints' Church, London, probably in 1482–3. It is in law French, and Maclyn was probably a native French speaker. Five other books are attributed to Maclyn and Lettou in 1482–3; three are yearbooks, and law books in French remained a significant part of Maclyn's output. Presumably he learned how to print from Lettou.

Between 1483 and 1490 Maclyn issued at least twenty-two books as sole printer. None are dated, though several contain his name and place of printing, London. They were printed at two locations there, Fleet Bridge and Holborn. The former, and probably earlier (c.1483–6), group includes: two Latin texts by Albertus Magnus; a reprint of Littleton's Tenores, and the Nova statuta, in French; a proclamation of the marriage of Prince Charles of France with Princess Elizabeth of England, and the Revelation of St Nicholas to a Monk of Evesham [Eynsham], in English; the Anglo-Latin Vulgaria Terentii; and a book of hours. The Holborn group (c.1486–90) contains three editions of the English version of Jacob's Treatise on the Pestilence, a reprint of the Chronicles of England, two yearbooks, a bull of Innocent VIII, the statutes for 1 Richard III, and grammatical and religious works including John Wotton's Speculum Christiani published for Henry Frankenberg, a merchant of St Clement's Lane dealing in printed books. One edition of the Treatise on the Pestilence is the first English book with a title page. Nothing further is known about Maclyn.

N. F. BLAKE

Sources E. G. Duff, The printers, stationers, and bookbinders of Westminster and London from 1476 to 1535 (1906) · H. R. Plomer, Wynkyn de Worde and his contemporaries from the death of Caxton to 1535 (1925) · E. G. Duff, Early printed books (1863) · G. Vine, A litil boke the whiche traytied and rehersed many gode thinges necessaries for the Pestilence … Reproduced in facsimile from the copy in John Rylands Library (1910) · E. G. Duff, 'Early chancery proceedings concerning members of the book trade', The Library, new ser., 8 (1907), 408–20

MacLysaght, Edward Anthony Edgeworth [Ned] (1887–1986), historian and Irish nationalist, was born on 6 November 1887 at Flax Bourton near Nailsea, Somerset, the elder of two sons of Sidney Royse Lysaght (1856–1941) and his wife, Kathrine (c.1860–1953), youngest daughter of Joseph Clarke of Waddington, Lincolnshire. S. R. Lysaght, a civil engineer and son of a Cork architect, had joined an uncle's iron and steel firm in Bristol while retaining close links with Ireland. Though married in the Church of England in Bognor Regis, the sceptical and idiosyncratic S. R. did not share Kathrine's sturdy Anglican orthodoxy. Ned Lysaght's Irishness was fostered by childhood holidays in

Cork and most significantly co. Clare, where the minor Dalcassian sept of MacLysaght had once held sway around Kilfenora. Enchanted by this element in his hybrid lineage, he reimagined himself as a child of Catholic Ireland, repeatedly denying his English birth, deprecating his protestant origins, and assuming the Gaelic prefix Mac in 1920.

Ned's upbringing was unsettled, as his father's business entailed prolonged visits to Australia and South Africa as well as frequent changes of address around Bristol. He spent three unhappy years (1902–5) as a boarder at Rugby School, along with the historian Philip Guedalla and the poet Rupert Brooke (son of Ned's housemaster). In 1907 'Edgeworth Lysaght' matriculated at Corpus Christi College, Oxford; but after two terms he 'left the place abruptly in a disreputable atmosphere of whiskey and horses' (MacLysaght, *Changing Times*, 13). Thus ended his formal education, though he eventually secured the degrees of MA (1937), DLitt (1941), and LLD (1972) from the National University of Ireland in recognition of his published historical research.

Lysaght's farming career began in 1909, when after a brief apprenticeship in England he became manager of Raheen Manor, a derelict house and neglected property of about 660 acres near Scariff in east co. Clare, which his father had acquired with the intention of eventually becoming an Irish country gentleman. Ned thus became the occupant, and eventually the owner, of a mansion with twenty-six rooms, twenty-four outhouses, twelve front windows, and three resident servants (census schedule, 1911). This was enough to secure his nomination to the Clare County Club, a haven of the former 'ascendancy' into which he had the temerity to introduce Colonel Maurice Moore, the Catholic home ruler, as a temporary member. Moore's name was expunged from the register, and Lysaght terminated his subscription. His reincarnation as a Catholic nationalist culminated in marriage to Mabel ('Maureen') Elizabeth Pattison (c.1882–1954), the South African superintendent of a Dublin hospital where he had recently surrendered his appendix. The wedding occurred in Brompton Oratory on 4 September 1913, following his conversion to Catholicism after a period of agnosticism (he was one of the few Irishmen to record his religion as 'none' in the 1911 census). Maureen's witty friends in and about Dublin's United Arts Club initiated Ned into the mysteries of fashionable 'Irish Ireland', though he had already joined the Gaelic League in co. Clare and begun to learn the Irish language. By 1917 he had acquired the *fáinne* and a strong desire to write and think in Irish.

Lysaght's attempts to tame the land and its inhabitants, and his increasing infatuation with rural Irish life and the dying Irish language, assumed fictional expression in *The Gael* (1919). Though seemingly down-to-earth and straightforward, this autobiographical novel characteristically presents its author as the product of a resolutely Catholic and Irish family escaping exile from an alien England. MacLysaght's quest for Irishness in co. Clare had already

generated *Irish Eclogues* (1915), whose earthy language, flat tone, and focus on farming suggest some affinity with the early Seamus Heaney. Heaney, however, would not have rhymed 'thirsty heifers' with 'summer zephyrs' (p. 11). Raheen was the setting for a series of social and economic experiments which, often unsuccessful, marked the development of Lysaght's practical vision of Ireland's future. A workers' co-operative was established, and Irish speakers were imported in the vain hope of creating a local Gaeltacht within which the English language would be unheard. He was a paternalist employer, paying far more than the market wage but refusing to fire non-unionized workers. Upon returning to Raheen after his marriage in 1913 he had been greeted by his twenty-seven employees as 'an ideal Christian master' and 'an indulgent father in their trials and troubles'. While threatened with a strike over union recognition in April 1919 he became dangerously ill, only to be presented on his recovery by an address in Irish, framed in oak crafted by members of the union (Fitzpatrick, 195, 206). Cattle breeding was soon combined with tree farming and a nursery business, but poor returns eventually forced surrender of much of the property to state agencies for reafforestation. S. R. Lysaght had meanwhile secured possession of Hazlewood, his uncle William's small estate near Mallow, co. Cork, midway between Old Twopothouse and New Twopothouse. Hazlewood became the centre of the family's nursery business, later extended to Blackrock, the suburb of Dublin where MacLysaght lived for most of the second half of his long life. Yet Raheen remained his second residence, imagined home, and declared address, even after he had assigned the property to his son William in 1961.

Lysaght's 'economic' nationalism made him a natural ally for the circle loosely surrounding Sir Horace Plunkett, whose *Noblesse Oblige* (1908) had called upon the Irish gentry to commit their talents to Ireland's social and economic regeneration. Lysaght wrote an admiring if uninformative biography of Plunkett in 1916. He also became a close friend of Plunkett's chief associate in the co-operative movement, the poet, artist, and mystic George Russell (AE), who was staying at Raheen when news came of the Easter rising in April 1916. Lysaght's support for constitutional nationalism had been unshaken by Redmond's commitment to the British war effort, though in retrospect he affirmed his indifference to the war and recollected early separatist stirrings. Lysaght had accepted Colonel Maurice Moore's invitation to become county organizer of the Redmondite National Volunteers in Clare, arranging a training camp at Raheen in early 1915 (Moore MSS, NL Ire., MS 10547/5). His voluminous diaries provide vivid testimony to the intellectual and emotional turmoil generated by the rising and the subsequent coercion. Though disgusted by the government's conduct and convinced that nationalism needed new leaders and policies, he advocated a national forum to formulate the terms of a settlement by compromise rather than revolution. Like Plunkett he initially contemplated dominion home rule, only gradually drifting towards self-determination and de Valera's Sinn Féin. Helped by a subvention from the Catholic archbishop of Dublin he published *Thoughts for a Convention* (1917); and along with Russell he informally represented Sinn Féin in the Irish convention inaugurated by Lloyd George in July 1917 and chaired by Plunkett. Erskine Childers, seconded from the Royal Naval Air Service to act on the secretariat, found him 'a very interesting young man—landlord—Sinn Feiner' (diary, 8–16 Aug 1917, IWM, MS 80/36/1). Prompted by his Sinn Féin advisers he resigned from this hopelessly divided assembly in January 1918. Yet, a year later, he still found it hard to declare in his diary that he had become 'a Sinn Féiner absolutely' (Fitzpatrick, 134).

Lysaght was not only a debater, pamphleteer, and occasional journalist, but a publisher of Irish and 'national' books. In January 1916, after his ever generous and novel-writing father had invested £300 in a failing publishing house, Lysaght became a director of Maunsels and manager of its Irish Book Shop, which soon shared a building with his farm produce shop in Lower Baggot Street, Dublin. As the struggle for independence intensified Lysaght's involvement rapidly expanded. He participated in Dáil Éireann's commission of inquiry into the resources and industries of Ireland in 1919, provided his Raheen office for use by the adjutant of Michael Brennan's East Clare brigade (Irish Volunteers), and endured twenty-seven raids and searches at Raheen by 'crown forces'. His disaffection with British rule deepened after 21 November 1920 (Bloody Sunday), when his clerk and friend Conor Clune, a co. Clare Gaelic Leaguer no longer connected with the volunteers, was shot in reprisal for the multiple extinction of alleged intelligence officers by Michael Collins's 'squad'.

MacLysaght's support for the Anglo-Irish treaty of December 1921 was rewarded by his election in December 1922 to the first Seanad of the Irish Free State, in twenty-fourth place among the thirty candidates elected by the Dáil. Under pressure from Eamon de Valera, republican member for County Clare, he had withdrawn as an independent candidate for Dáil Éireann in June 1922. Though involved in important commissions on railway and primary education MacLysaght was confessedly an unimpressive senator: his occasional insistence on addressing an uncomprehending Seanad in Irish helped make him a figure of fun among ex-Unionist colleagues. In 1925 he came thirtieth among the seventy-six candidates for nineteen vacancies, most of his first preferences coming from Clare and Cork. Despite defeat his local support in a nationwide constituency enabled him to easily outscore Douglas Hyde, the revered founder of the Gaelic League and future president of Éire. By 1926 this local influence had secured his nomination to the governing bodies of two university colleges (Galway and Cork). Yet his political career proceeded no further, undermined by irrepressible indiscretion, impulsiveness, and lack of gravitas. These attractive qualities may have contributed to his failures in business, though the collapse of Maunsels in 1923 and the recurrent losses at Raheen also reflected civil strife and recession. Between 1928 and 1935 he managed his father's

nursery business at Hazlewood, thus remaining in effect a dependant into his late forties.

MacLysaght's troubles were compounded by the collapse of his marriage in the mid-1920s, leading to divorce in 1936. Along with their children, Fergus Patrick and Moira Bridget (born in 1917 and 1919), Maureen continued after the breakdown to live with Sidney and Kathrine Lysaght at Hazlewood. Fergus reverted to the surname Lysaght and served as a major in the Royal Artillery in the Second World War, inheriting Hazlewood from his grandfather. MacLysaght's second wife was Mary Frances Cunneen (*c.*1911–1990), daughter of the head gardener at Hazlewood. Mamie, as she was known, bore three sons (William Xavier, Patrick, and Brian, born in 1937, 1940, and 1943). Shortly before their marriage on 1 September 1936 MacLysaght had begun his third long trip to South Africa, working as a journalist. In 1938, professedly disgusted by Afrikaner anti-Catholicism, he returned to London and subsequently Dublin, to begin a scholarly career.

MacLysaght was already well known to Gaelicists as editor of the monthly *An Sguab* ('The Broom', 1922–4) and author of *Cursaí Thomáis* (1927; translated as *The Small Fields of Carrig*, 1929) and *Toil Dé* ('God's will', 1933). His interest in Irish history was already evident in 1921, when he asked James Hogan (an intelligence officer of the East Clare brigade who professed history at University College, Cork) to accept him as a part-time research student. With characteristic economy MacLysaght recalled that 'my proposal was accepted: some years later I submitted my thesis and in due course obtained my M.A. degree' (MacLysaght, *Changing Times*, 151–2). In fact, his first-class degree for 'independent research' was not awarded until sixteen years later, after publication in 1935 of *A Short Study of a Transplanted Family* (the MacLysaghts). This was followed after four years by the often reprinted *Irish Life in the Seventeenth Century*, for which he was eventually awarded a doctorate. Further major scholarship emerged from appointments as the first inspector for the Irish Manuscripts Commission (1940–43) and first keeper of manuscripts at the National Library of Ireland (1949–54). He roamed from big house to castle and episcopal palace throughout southern Ireland, listing and abstracting documents, editing *The Kenmare Manuscripts* (1942) and two volumes of *Analecta Hibernica* (1944), and multiplying the National Library's collection of listed manuscripts from 900 to 9000 items.

MacLysaght's invaluable work as an archivist was interrupted by six unsatisfying years as successor to the Ulster king of arms, perhaps the last office under the Union to be surrendered to the Dublin government. Though neither an experienced nor an enthusiastic armorist he successfully asserted the chief herald of Ireland's entitlement to issue arms, battling spiritedly against the condescension of his fellow heralds and the bogus claims of pretended princes. His *Irish Families* (1957), *More Irish Families* (1960), *Supplement to Irish Families* (1982), and *The Surnames of Ireland* (1969), remain essential works of reference for genealogists. After retirement from the National Library he was chairman of the Irish Manuscripts Commission (1956–73), presiding affably over the dormant office with its blazing turf fire in Merrion Square, Dublin. Thereafter his unabated energy was exhibited in digging a potato patch in the family nursery at Blackrock, and revising his long-suppressed, quirky, and sometimes unreliable reminiscences. First self-deprecatingly entitled *Master of none*, these were issued in 1978 as *Changing Times*, the chapter on his private affairs having prudently been excised. In the same year he published *Leathanaigh ó mo dhialann* ('Leaves from my diary'). Small and wiry, increasingly deaf in old age, blind in one eye since boyhood, ever recognizable by his beetle brows and military moustache, he remained a familiar presence in the National Library into his late nineties.

On 4 March 1986, in his ninety-ninth year, MacLysaght succumbed to myocardial degeneration and arteriosclerosis at his home, 30 Proby Square, Blackrock, Dublin. In accordance with his will he was buried two days later at Tuamgraney, co. Clare, with his beloved son Patrick, who had drowned in Lough Derg in 1956. Though one of the two residual beneficiaries of his father's estate (amounting to almost £67,000 in 1942), MacLysaght had long since given away most of his assets including his houses at Raheen and Blackrock. His liberality had been well directed, helping William to transform Raheen into a thriving business at last. His property at death was initially valued at only £3732 net, an amount increased by £38,000 after revaluation of a shop in Cork. MacLysaght's riches resided in his mind rather than his pocket. Though indeed suggesting a jack of all trades, his varied undertakings and accomplishments amounted to an original and ingenious life, a triumph of personal transplantation.

DAVID FITZPATRICK

Sources E. MacLysaght, *Changing times: Ireland since 1898* (1978) · C. Lysaght, *Edward MacLysaght, 1887–1986: a memoir* (1988) · D. Fitzpatrick, *Politics and Irish life, 1913–1921: provincial experience of war and revolution* (1998) · E. MacLysaght, diaries, priv. coll. · NL Ire., MacLysaght MSS, MSS 2649–51, 4750, 8560 · *The Times* (6 March 1986) · *Irish Times* (5 March 1986) · *Irish Times* (8 March 1986) · *Irish Independent* (7 March 1986) · *WW* · private information (2004) [Dr MacLysaght, friends and contemporaries] · revision books for Clare and co. Cork, Valuation Office, Dublin · b. cert.
Archives NL Ire., papers · priv. coll., diaries | NL Ire., Maurice Moore MSS, MS 10547
Likenesses T. Ryan, coloured charcoal, 1969, priv. coll.; repro. in Lysaght, *Edward MacLysaght*, cover · D. Lysaght, pencil, *c.*1970–1979, priv. coll.; repro. in MacLysaght, *Changing times*, 124 · T. Ryan, oils?, Genealogical Office, Dublin · photographs, repro. in MacLysaght, *Changing times* · photographs, repro. in Lysaght, *Edward MacLysaght*
Wealth at death £41,732: revised probate, 1993, *CGPLA Éire*

Mac Maghnusa, Cathal Óg [Charles MacManus, Cathal Óg Mac Maghnusa Mhéig Uidhir, Charles MacManus Maguire] (1439–1498), historian, was the son of Cathal Óg Mac Maghnusa (*d.* 1480) and, presumably, of his wife, Gráinne (*d.* 1462), the daughter of Tomás Óg Mág Uidhir, king of Fermanagh (*d.* 1480), and grandson of Cathal Mór Mac Maghnusa (*d.* 1433). He is best known as the compiler of the annals of Ulster. He was born in February 1439 and in 1488 he was inaugurated as head of the Mac Maghnusa sept, distant relations of the Mág Uidhir dynasty, the greater part of whose royal mensal lands were held by the

Mic Mhaghnusa, 'free from all common charges and contributions of the country, because they yielded a large proportion of butter and meal and other provisions for M'Guire's table', as Sir John Davies observed in 1607 (Morley, 368). The hereditary Mac Maghnusa title was *biatach* ('food-provider') or *brughaidh* ('hospitaller'), referring not only to their obligations towards the king of Fermanagh, but also to their provision of public hospitality by maintaining a guest house for travellers, and especially for bardic troops, a customary charity in medieval Ireland.

Mac Maghnusa's estates were centred on Belleisle (Seanadh Mic Mhaghnusa) on Lough Erne, but he also entered the church (the bishop of Clogher diocese from 1448 to 1483 was his maternal uncle). He became parson of Iniskeen on Lough Erne, canon choral of Armagh and Clogher cathedrals, rural dean of Lough Erne (a deanery containing twelve churches), and episcopal vicar-general for the same area during a period of vacancy and disputed succession in Clogher diocese from 1483 to 1498. An eighteenth-century tradition that he held these ecclesiastical posts as a layman may be based on his being the proud father of a number of children: these included two daughters called Catherina (*b.* 1475 and 1477) and one named Gráinne (*d.* 1497), sons Cathal Óg (1476–1494), Edward (*b.* 1479), Cormac (*b.* 1482), Cúchonnacht (*b.* 1485), and Magonius (Mathghamhain or Maghnus; *b.* 1486), and his heir, Tomás Giolla-Baodáin, the 'official', or ecclesiastical judge, of Clogher diocese. However, approving references to 'wives' and children of the higher clergy abound in Mac Maghnusa's own annals and either he himself or his son Tomás was married to Siobhán (*d.* 1515), daughter of Bishop Mág Brádaigh of Kilmore diocese.

Apart from its frank and detailed record of society in fifteenth-century Fermanagh, the original manuscript of the annals of Ulster (Trinity College, Dublin, MS H.1.8), whose entries begin with the first century of the Christian era and continue after the death of Mac Maghnusa to 1504, is remarkable for its comparatively accurate dates and the scrupulous care taken to distinguish between the text of a series of annal entries of early Christian origin and additional material derived from later sources—an enormously useful decision. An entry for 1497 records Mac Maghnusa himself destroying the cave of St Patrick's purgatory in response to papal orders. The complaints about extortions from pilgrims which gave rise to this decree may include Mac Maghnusa among the accused, though it erroneously refers to the 'bishop' (rather than vicar-general) of the vacant see of Clogher. Predictably, the notice of his death (from smallpox) as it appears in the brief continuation of his own annals for 23 March of the following year, gives him an elevated character quite incompatible with this suggestion.

KATHARINE SIMMS

Sources W. M. Hennessy and B. MacCarthy, eds., *Annals of Ulster, otherwise, annals of Senat*, 4 vols. (1887–1901), vol. 3 · A. Gwynn, 'Cathal Mac Maghnusa and the Annals of Ulster', *Clogher Record*, 2 (1958–9), 230–43, 370–84 · A. Gwynn, *The medieval province of Armagh, 1470–1545* (1946), 163–76 · M. Haren, 'The close of the medieval pilgrimage: the papal suppression and its aftermath', *The medieval pilgrimage to St Patrick's Purgatory*, ed. M. Haren and Y. de

Pontfarcy (1988), 190–201 · *Ann. Ulster*, viii · K. Simms, 'Guesting and feasting in Gaelic Ireland', *Journal of the Royal Society of Antiquaries of Ireland*, 108 (1978), 72 · H. Morley, ed., *Ireland under Elizabeth and James the First* (1890)
Archives TCD, MS H.1.8

MacMahon, Sir Charles (1824–1891). *See under* MacMahon, Sir William, first baronet (1776–1837).

McMahon, Charles Alexander (1830–1904), army officer and geologist, born at Highgate, Middlesex, on 23 March 1830, was the son of Captain Alexander McMahon of Irish descent, formerly in the Indian service, and his wife, Ann, daughter of Major Patrick Mansell of the British army. After education at a private school, he obtained a commission in the 39th Madras native infantry on 4 February 1847, but after eight years' service in that regiment became a member of the Madras staff corps, and was transferred in 1856 to the Punjab commission, on which he served for thirty years, holding the rank of commissioner for the last fourteen. At the outbreak of the mutiny, McMahon, then a lieutenant and assistant commissioner of the Sialkot district, in which troops were quartered, was in charge owing to his superior's illness. On 9 July 1857 the Indian troops rose, and after murdering some Europeans, including four of their officers, decamped to join the rebels. McMahon contrived to send a note to General John Nicholson, who restored order at Sialkot so completely that McMahon was able a few days later to force the surrender of some 140 refugee rebels, most of whom were executed.

In 1857 McMahon married Elizabeth, daughter of Lieutenant-Colonel Charles Franklin Head, 93rd highlanders; she died in 1866, and in 1868 he married Charlotte Emily, daughter of Henry Dorling of Stroud Green House, Croydon. During this time he was acknowledged to be an able judge, when faced with a controversial case in 1865.

While commissioner of Hissar in 1871 McMahon began serious study of geology, and in 1877 published his first important paper in the *Records of the Geological Survey of India*. This and its successors dealt with a group of crystalline rocks, some of which, after examination with the microscope, he maintained to be volcanic. Subsequently, in 1879, while on leave in England, with the rank of lieutenant-colonel, he became a student at the Royal School of Mines. On returning to India he renewed his geological studies. He retired in 1885 with the rank of colonel, becoming major-general in 1888 and lieutenant-general in 1892. He settled in London and devoted himself to petrology, publishing nearly fifty papers in the journals of geological societies, to add to the twenty-one he had published while in India. Most dealt with Indian topics, but he also worked in the west country of England. He is regarded as a pioneer in petrology for his conclusion, as early as 1881, that the degree of metamorphism affords an indication of the relative age of ancient rocks. A further important conclusion was reached in 1884 when he claimed that foliation in certain crystalline rocks was due to a flowing of the mass while it was still viscid or partly crystallized. He became a fellow of the Geological Society in 1878 and was awarded its Lyell medal in 1899. He was president of the Geologists' Association in 1894–5 and of the geological section of the British Association in 1902. In 1898 he was elected fellow of the Royal Society.

McMahon died at his London house, 20 Nevern Square, Earls Court, on 21 February 1904, leaving his second wife and, from his first marriage, a daughter and a son, Colonel Sir Arthur Henry *McMahon, KCIE, CSI, of the Indian army and also a distinguished geologist who had collaborated with his father. McMahon's scientific work was characterized by scrupulous accuracy in microscopy. His ideas gained wide acceptance and still form fundamental guiding principles in the late twentieth century, although their limitations in certain circumstances, for example, the comparison of metamorphosis between areas, have become apparent.

T. G. BONNEY, *rev.* ELIZABETH BAIGENT

Sources T. G. B. [T. G. Bonney], *PRS*, 75 (1905), 363–6 · T. G. B. [T. G. Bonney], *Quarterly Journal of the Geological Society*, 61 (1905), l–lii · *Geological Magazine*, new ser., 5th decade, 1 (1904), 192, 237–9 · private information (1912) · personal knowledge (1912)
Wealth at death £15,129 17s. 2d.: resworn probate, 9 April 1904, CGPLA Eng. & Wales

MacMahon, Heber (1600–1650), Roman Catholic bishop of Clogher, was born in the barony of Farney in co. Monaghan, and was probably the son of Tirlogh MacMahon, brother of Sir Patrick MacArt Moyle MacMahon, and his wife, Eva O'Neill. His forename is sometimes given as Ever or Emer, and his name was Latinized as Emerus Mattheus. His father was much straitened in the aftermath of the flight of the earls, living in poverty near Killybegs, co. Donegal. MacMahon was probably educated by the Franciscans of Monaghan. About the end of 1617 he entered the Irish College at Douai, later progressing to the pastoral college at Louvain, where he studied under Hugh MacCaghwell on a bursary for students from the diocese of Clogher founded by Eugene Matthews, archbishop of Dublin, of which MacMahon was the first beneficiary. He was ordained priest at Louvain and became college superior. It is said that here he met Owen Roe O'Neill for the first time, and there are some grounds to suspect his involvement in a plot to contrive a French invasion of Ireland in 1628.

MacMahon returned to Ireland in 1633 and worked for many years in his native diocese of Clogher, where he became vicar-general. According to the earl of Clarendon, in 1634 he apparently also sought a pardon for his role in the plot of 1628, although this may have been a ploy to mask his activities on behalf of the O'Neill, for whom he supposedly enlisted 3000 Irish in the course of 1635 alone. It has been said that, in common with the rest of the Catholic church hierarchy in Ireland, MacMahon played no part in planning the rebellion of 1641. But members of his family certainly did. Hugh Oge Mac Mahon, who helped organize, and then fatally compromised, the conspiracy of Connor, or Cornelius, Lord Maguire, to surprise Dublin Castle, was his first cousin once removed. Moreover, according to the confessions of the chief Dublin Castle conspirators MacMahon was intimately aware of the plans for the rebellion, and as vicar apostolic of Clogher he had been appointed to act as Owen Roe O'Neill's envoy, with the intention of negotiating for the assistance of Catholic potentates on the continent. But in the event he stayed in Ireland, and was present at the head of a troop of cavalry to meet O'Neill on his return to his homeland.

On 10 February 1642, at the behest of Hugh O'Reilly, archbishop of Armagh, and at the instance of Cardinal Barberini, MacMahon obtained appointment to the vacant see of Down and Connor, in which capacity he attended the provincial synod at Kells in March 1642, the general congregation of the clergy at Kilkenny in May, and the supreme council of the confederate Catholics thereafter. But he was not consecrated until on 2 June 1643 he was translated to Clogher, which he obtained from Rome at the behest of the supreme council, on the grounds that his see was under protestant control, and that MacMahon commanded significantly more support within the new diocese, of which he was a native. From the outset MacMahon was in the van of those who sought more than merely the vindication of Catholic rights in Ireland. A French agent in Ireland at the time described him as 'one of those who desire war, and the devotion of Ireland to Spain' (*DNB*). He was a loyal supporter of the papal emissary, Scarampi, who landed in Ireland in July 1643, adhering to him in opposing the cessation of arms concluded with the king's lord lieutenant, the marquess of Ormond, in September 1643. Subsequently MacMahon was among those whom the nuncio Giovanni Rinuccini was under instruction to cultivate, which he did to good effect, despite initially distrusting the Ulster faction.

MacMahon helped to effect the reconciliation between Owen Roe O'Neill and Sir Phelim O'Neill which made possible the confederate victory at Benburb in 1646. MacMahon joined in the excommunication of all who had a hand in or gave their support to the treaty agreed the same year between Ormond and a majority in the supreme council at Kilkenny, not least because it held out no hope of the restoration of confiscated lands and made only uncertain concessions on religion. In February 1647 MacMahon lobbied the pope for the nuncio's promotion to cardinal. After Ormond's departure from Ireland in July 1647 he was one of the minority who adhered to Rinuccini's waning fortunes. The majority, eager to be rid of an opponent, ordered that MacMahon be sent to Paris with Viscount Muskerry and Geoffrey Browne to negotiate with the queen, Henrietta Maria. But he scornfully refused to go, saying that he spoke neither French nor English, that he was odious to his intended host for his involvement in the outbreak of rebellion, and that his life would be in danger, since lords Jermyn and Digby had both threatened him. In the wrangle that followed Thomas Preston, the Anglo-Irish commander of the Leinster army, demanded the bishop's imprisonment for contempt. But a hollow reconciliation between the factions followed, and Antrim was appointed to go to Paris in MacMahon's place.

A little later Bishop MacMahon was intriguing against the confederates with Colonel Michael Jones, who had assumed control of Dublin from Ormond on behalf of the English parliament. In April 1648 he joined in the denunciation of the truce under discussion between the supreme council and Lord Inchequin, and was instrumental the following month in the pronouncement of Rinuccini's second censure. MacMahon was now proclaimed a traitor, along with Owen Roe O'Neill, by the supreme council of the confederates. The pair held aloof from the second Ormond peace, offering their services independently to the new king on 20 February 1649. In March MacMahon fell temporarily into the hands of Ulster Ormondists under Sir Phelim O'Neill. Later that spring O'Neill reached agreement with several parliamentarian commanders in Ulster, an act of mutual preservation in the face of attempts to revive the royalist interest in Ireland. By the following autumn circumstances had changed once more and O'Neill's party entered into alliance with Ormond in order to face the threat from England; MacMahon was closely involved in the negotiations.

When O'Neill died shortly afterwards MacMahon effectively inherited his mantle as the leader of the old Irish Catholic interest in the north. Years before, Rinuccini had commented on the fervour of MacMahon's commitment to the Catholic cause, but had also noted that he was 'entirely swayed by political rules and motives' (Moore). MacMahon now became a most compliant and outwardly loyal servant of the king's cause in Ireland, and many years later was complimented by Ormond as the only Catholic bishop the lord lieutenant had ever had cause to trust. But MacMahon had probably come to the realistic conclusion that the only hope for Catholic Ireland now lay in expedient alliance with the representative of the crown. The bishop was probably the moving spirit behind the meeting of the Catholic bishops at Clonmacnoise in December 1649, and probably the 'principal architect' (Moody and others, 3.344) of the calls for unity in the face of the English invasion which emanated from it—an aspiration which flew in the face of outstanding differences within the Catholic hierarchy concerning the 1648 censure. But Ormond was the only source from which to rearm the Ulstermen, so MacMahon used his influence to damp down the wranglings among his brother bishops. He also worked hard to promote the sense of unity so conspicuously absent in the ranks of the old Irish. According to the late O'Neill's protestant nephew, Daniel O'Neill, it was MacMahon's presence alone which could ensure a peaceable succession to the command of the Ulster army shortly after the death of its undisputed leader. But so divisive did the matter prove that in March 1650 the bishop himself was appointed, and commissioned accordingly by the lord lieutenant. MacMahon wrote to Rinuccini excusing his acceptance of the commission, which he claimed to have done against his will, and to avoid the appointment of someone in whose hands the cause might be dissipated entirely.

Despite his eminence and ability the bishop was 'quite unfitted for military command' (Moody and others, 3.346). Supposedly against the advice of his officers, principally the former commander's son, Hugh O'Neill, MacMahon committed his forces to battle against Sir Charles Coote, lord president of Connaught, at Scarriffhollis on 21 June. The Ulster army was routed and the bishop was captured near Enniskillen. Badly wounded in the process he was said to have survived several months' imprisonment, although his death was reported in *Mercurius Politicus* under the date 5 July. In spite of promises of quarter and the safety of his life, he was hanged at Enniskillen by order of Coote, who, less than a year earlier, had been in covert alliance with the Ulster army. He was buried at Devenish Island. One bardic tribute hailed him as 'the warlike lion … the most upright-hearted of the Gaels' (Gilbert, 3.194). MacMahon was among the list of ninety-two priests killed between 1649 and 1655 whose names were submitted to be considered for beatification in 1914.

RICHARD BAGWELL, *rev.* SEAN KELSEY

Sources J. T. Gilbert, ed., *A contemporary history of affairs in Ireland from 1641 to 1652*, 3 vols. (1879–80) · S. P. Moore, 'Ever Mac Mahon, soldier bishop of the confederation of Kilkenny', *Studies: an Irish Quarterly Review*, 40 (1951), 323–33; 41 (1952), 91–8 · T. W. Moody and others, eds., *A new history of Ireland*, 3: *Early modern Ireland, 1534–1691* (1976) · J. Casway, *Owen Roe O'Neill and the struggle for Catholic Ireland* (1984) · T. ó hAnnracháin, 'Rebels and confederates: the stance of the Irish clergy in the 1640s', *Celtic dimensions of the British civil wars*, ed. J. M. Young (1997)

McMahon, Sir (Arthur) Henry (1862–1949), army officer and colonial governor, was born on 28 November 1862 in Simla, India, the eldest surviving son of Lieutenant-General Charles Alexander *McMahon (1830–1904), a soldier, geologist, and former commissioner in the Punjab, and his wife, Elizabeth (*d.* 1866), daughter of Lieutenant-Colonel C. F. Head. McMahon was educated at Haileybury College and the Royal Military College, Sandhurst, where he passed out with the sword of honour in 1882.

Commissioned second lieutenant in the 8th regiment (the King's Liverpool) on 10 March 1883, McMahon transferred to the Indian Staff Corps in July 1885 and joined the 1st Sikh infantry in the Punjab frontier force. In October 1886 he married Mary Evelyn (*d.* 1957), daughter of Francis Christopher Bland of Derryquin Castle, co. Kerry. They had two daughters. In 1887 McMahon joined the Punjab commission and three years later he transferred to the Indian political department in which he served for the next twenty-four years.

Nearly all of McMahon's early service was spent on the north-west frontier of India, where he demonstrated considerable ability in winning the trust and confidence of the various independent tribes that inhabited the tribal hinterland between India and Afghanistan. He served as political officer with the Kundar and Sherani punitive expeditions, and was political agent for Zhob (1891–3) and for Thal-Chotiali in 1892. In 1893 McMahon accompanied the Durand mission to Kabul, beginning a long friendship with the amir and later also with his two successors. He was made CIE the following year. As a British commissioner McMahon demarcated the boundary between Afghanistan and Baluchistan in 1894–6, for which he was made a CSI. He served as political agent to Gilgit (1897–8),

Sir (Arthur) Henry McMahon (1862–1949), by John Collier, 1915

and to Dir, Swat, and Chitral (1899–1901), and he was revenue and judicial commissioner in Baluchistan between 1901 and 1902.

McMahon served as the arbitrator on the boundary between Persia and Afghanistan in Sistan and as British commissioner on the Sistan mission during 1904–5 for which he was made a KCIE in 1906. In 1907 he served as chief officer in charge of the visit of the amir of Afghanistan to India and was created an Afghan sirdar first class. In January 1905 he was appointed agent to the governor-general in Baluchistan. In 1911 McMahon was selected by Lord Hardinge, the viceroy, for the important post of foreign secretary to the government of India, an appointment he held for three years. He served as master of ceremonies in 1911 during the visit of George V and Queen Mary to India, during which he was made GCVO. McMahon's diplomacy was tested to the fullest when he was British plenipotentiary for the treaty regarding Tibet between Britain, China, and Tibet in 1913–14. This conference resulted in the unsigned Simla convention, a trade agreement and the demarcation of the McMahon line delineating the boundary between Tibet and China.

On leave in England when the First World War broke out, McMahon was appointed first high commissioner for Egypt under the British protectorate, despite having no Middle East experience, on the advice of Lord Kitchener. Sir Ronald Storrs described him at this point as 'slight, fair very young for 52, quiet, friendly, agreeable, considerate and cautious' (Storrs, 191). Nevertheless McMahon lacked any knowledge of Arabic and was forced to deal with a complex political situation. In the event he was quite out of his depth, overseeing difficult political relations with the Arabs. Indeed he delegated a large part of his authority to subordinates.

Between 1915 and 1916, without closely consulting the British government, Sir Henry conducted secret correspondence with the sharif of Mecca, encouraging an Arab uprising against the sultan-caliph. In return for an Arab rebellion McMahon loosely promised independence in certain areas of the Middle East, but he failed precisely to stipulate which parts of former Turkish territory he was prepared to hand over to Arab control. The extreme vagueness of the often confused and ambiguous correspondence between McMahon and Hussein, particularly that of 24 October 1915, caused almost immediate controversy between the Arabs and the British empire over its differing interpretations, especially about whether it included Palestine. This discord heightened twenty years later as disagreement increased over the future of Palestine. The British government denied there was any inconsistency between the McMahon–Hussein correspondence and the Balfour declaration. However, the situation was further complicated by the failure to publish the full correspondence until the later 1930s for fear of its effect upon the wider Muslim world, particularly India. It was first published in English by George Antonius in *The Arab Awakening* (1938).

McMahon was created GCMG in 1916 and at the end of the year his appointment was abruptly terminated. He returned to England and in 1919 served as the British commissioner on the Middle East internal commission at the peace conference in Paris. Following his retirement McMahon pursued his wide range of personal interests and was active in the Royal Society of Arts, the Society of Antiquaries, and the Zoological Society. A fellow of the Royal Geographical and Geological societies, he also served as president of the Young Men's Christian Association. He was chairman of the Fellowship of the British Empire and was chairman of the management committee (and member of the board) of the British Empire Exhibition (1920–25). Throughout his life McMahon was an enthusiastic freemason, founding several lodges in India that accepted Indians as members, and rose to be grand senior warden of the grand lodge of England, grand commander of the temple, and sovereign grand commander of the supreme council 33°. An enthusiastic yachtsman, he was keen on fishing and other outdoor pursuits.

McMahon died in London on 29 December 1949. Despite a long and successful career in India his name will be remembered primarily as a signatory of the McMahon–Hussein correspondence.   T. R. MOREMAN

Sources C. E. Buckland, *Dictionary of Indian biography* (1906) · *WWW, 1941–50* · *DNB* · *Quarterly Indian Army List* (Jan 1911) · E. Kedourie, *In the Anglo-Arab labyrinth: the McMahon–Huseyn correspondence and its interpretations, 1914–1939* (1976) · BL OIOC, McMahon MSS · I. Friedman, 'The McMahon–Hussein correspondence and the question of Palestine', *Journal of Contemporary History*, 5 (1970), 83–122 · A. Toynbee, 'The McMahon–Hussein correspondence: comments and a reply', *Journal of Contemporary History*, 5 (1970), 185–201 · R. Storrs, *Orientations* (1943) · G. Antonius, *The Arab awakening:*

the story of the Arab nationalist movement (1938) · R. I. Khalidi, *British policy towards Syria and Palestine, 1906–1914* (1980) **Archives** BL OIOC, corresp. and papers, MSS Eur. B 228, F 101 | Bodl. Oxf., corresp. with Aurel Stein · CUL, corresp. with Lord Hardinge · U. Durham L., corresp. with Sir Reginald Wingate | FILM IWM FVA, documentary footage **Likenesses** double portrait, photograph, 1893 (with Shahbagh Khan), BL OIOC, 483/3(10) · group portrait, photograph, 1912, BL OIOC, 355/8(59) · group portrait, photograph, 1913, BL OIOC, McMahon MSS · J. Collier, portrait, 1915, NAM [*see illus.*] · W. Stoneman, photograph, 1920, NPG **Wealth at death** £26,918 0s. 2d.: probate, 13 March 1950, *CGPLA Eng. & Wales*

Mac Mahon [MacMahon], **Hugh Oge** (1606/7–1644), conspirator, was a younger son of Sir Brian MacHugh Oge Mac Mahon, the lord of Dartrey in co. Monaghan, and Lady Mary O'Neill, daughter of Hugh O'Neill, third earl of Tyrone. Mac Mahon served as a mercenary officer in the Thirty Years' War in Germany, military service abroad being a common career for non-inheriting younger sons. On the death of his older brother, his father's son and heir, Mac Mahon returned to Ireland about 1640 to take possession of the now diminished family estate.

The motive for Mac Mahon's involvement in the 1641 plot to seize Dublin Castle was probably discontent at the declining social and political status of the native landowners of Ulster and, allegedly, because 'he was mightily troubled with the proud and haughty carriage' of a British neighbour (deposition of Owen O'Connolly, fol. 1). It is difficult to understand how Mac Mahon could have been so foolish as to recruit Owen O'Connolly into the plot on 22 October 1641. O'Connolly had rejected a previous invitation some months before, was a convert to presbyterianism, and, above all, was a servant of Sir John Clotworthy. The latter was closely linked to the emergent, and extremely anti-Catholic, parliamentary party in England. The fact that Mac Mahon and O'Connolly were foster brothers may have been the key; in Ireland this was 'so firm a tie of natural affection, as their being born of the same parents could not have been esteemed a greater' (*Irish Confederation*, ed. Gilbert, 1.8). Mac Mahon, allegedly befuddled with drink, let O'Connolly slip away to disclose the plot to Lord Justice Sir William Parsons. The following morning, 23 October 1641, Mac Mahon was arrested at his lodgings and brought to Dublin Castle along with Lord Connor Maguire. He was initially defiant: 'I am now in your hands, use me as you will, I am sure I shall be shortly revenged' (*Contemporary History*, 1.355). In a later statement 'taken at the rack' in 1642, Mac Mahon, aged thirty-five, cast the net of guilty foreknowledge very widely to include 'all the parties who were parliament men [MPs] ... about May last that were papists' ('Examination of Hugh Oge McMahon', fol. 5).

The English parliament was slow to start the case against Mac Mahon and Maguire. Along with Colonel John Reade they were imprisoned in the Tower of London in July 1642. Mac Mahon now changed his line of defence and claimed that he had been duped into believing that the *coup d'état* had royal sanction and that he met Maguire 'only by chance' (*Contemporary History*, 1.562). Using smuggled saws the three prisoners escaped from the Tower in August 1644 with the assistance of two priests attached to the Spanish embassy. They remained at large in London for over a month until 'one of them looking out of the window or balcony to call a woman that cried oysters, it happened at that instant a servant of Sir John Clotworthy's espied him' (Fitzpatrick, 149). There was a suspicious neatness about the escape and recapture, not least the ubiquity of Clotworthy's servant, perhaps O'Connolly himself. The escape may have been connived at as part of a diplomatic deal which then fell through. Mac Mahon was arraigned before the court of king's bench in November 1644 and, after a quick trial, was convicted of high treason. He was executed at Tyburn on 22 November 1644.

PÁDRAIG LENIHAN

Sources J. T. Gilbert, ed., *A contemporary history of affairs in Ireland from 1641 to 1652*, 1 (1879), 353–9, 560–62, 609–29 · *History of the Irish confederation and the war in Ireland … by Richard Bellings*, ed. J. T. Gilbert, 1 (1882), 7–11 · P. Livingstone, *The Monaghan story: a documented history of the county from the earliest times to 1976* (1980), 111 · B. Fitzpatrick, *Seventeenth-century Ireland: the war of religions* (1988), 133–8 · deposition of Owen O'Connolly, TCD, MS 840, fols. 1–4 · examination of Hugh Oge McMahon, TCD, MS 840, fol. 5 · T. Ó Donnchadha, ed., 'Cín Lae Ó Mealláin', *Analecta Hibernica*, 3 (1931), 1–61, esp. 5 · W. A. Shaw, *The knights of England*, 2 vols. (1906)

McMahon, Sir John, first baronet (*c*.1754–1817), politician, was born in Ireland, the only son of John McMahon (*d.* 1789), butler to Robert Clements, first earl of Leitrim, and his first wife, who was a fellow servant. His father became comptroller of the port of Limerick and married in 1771 his second wife, Mary Stackpole, who was the daughter of James Stackpole, a merchant in Cork. They had two sons, William and Thomas, who both eventually became baronets thanks to their half-brother. McMahon's education was elementary: after three years in a Dublin school, he was allegedly a kitchen boy in Dublin at nine. As ensign in the 44th foot he went to North America in 1775, becoming barrack-master at Charles Town until 1782, then captain in the 48th foot. His military patron was Francis Rawdon, later second earl of Moira. On his return he married, about 1782, Elizabeth Ramsay (*d.* 1815) of Bath. Scandalmongers alleged that the duke of Clarence had admired her, but had been diverted by McMahon to Dorothy Jordan.

Outwardly unprepossessing, small, and pock-marked, McMahon made up for his appearance by obliging manners. Retiring on half pay in 1786, he joined the Whig Club and remained a member until 1792. In 1794 he served in Flanders, as lieutenant-colonel of the 87th foot, but returned home ill. Rather than serve in Ireland he left the army in 1796. Known as 'Colonel McMahon' or 'Mac', he was useful to Moira as a political go-between with Fox in 1797, but he soon found a more significant role as public relations officer to the prince of Wales, who had deserted his wife. The prince made him his vice-treasurer in 1800, and a member of the duchy of Cornwall council in 1802. The duke of Northumberland bought him a seat in parliament, for which Moira provided his property qualification: he thus sat for Aldeburgh from 1802 to 1812. Late in 1803 he became secretary to the prince, keeper of his privy purse and seal, and duchy auditor. In the Commons he voted with the prince's friends, and when the whigs took office in 1806 became principal storekeeper of the ordnance for a year. Despite the prince's political neutrality he found no other office until February 1811, when he became unsalaried private secretary to the prince as regent.

In August the regent induced the premier to appoint McMahon paymaster of army widows' pensions, a sinecure ripe for abolition. Opposition motions against this were defeated on 9 January and 22 February 1812, when McMahon defended himself, but nevertheless he was voted out, on 23 February. In 1812 the regent provided for him in making him private secretary and keeper of the privy purse, with a privy councillorship granted on 20 March. He vacated Aldeburgh with hopes of another seat. The regent, however, resisted McMahon's attempts to reconcile him with the whigs. McMahon, overwhelmed by the task of countering adverse publicity for the regent, longed for retirement. His health was worsening and on 2 August 1815 his wife died, leaving him a considerable fortune in jewels. He had been receiver-general of the duchy for a year when, a disconsolate widower resorting to alcohol and opium, he resigned, obtaining a baronetcy on 7 August 1817. The regent avoided bidding him farewell in person but secured McMahon's papers. Denied a British peerage, McMahon planned retirement to Falmouth, but died at Bath *en route*, on 12 September 1817. At his death he was worth £90,000, and as he had no children his baronetcy passed to his younger half-brother, Colonel Thomas McMahon.

ROLAND THORNE

Sources HoP, *Commons* · *The correspondence of George, prince of Wales, 1770–1812*, ed. A. Aspinall, 8 vols. (1963–71) · *The letters of King George IV, 1812–1830*, ed. A. Aspinall, 3 vols. (1938) · *Annual Biography and Obituary*, 2 (1818), 312–17 · R. Huish, *Memoirs of George IV*, 2 vols. (1830–31), 1.404 · *GM*, 1st ser., 85/2 (1815), 278 · *GM*, 1st ser., 87/2 (1817), 370–71 · A. Aspinall, *Politics and the press, c.1780–1850* (1949), 91, 169, 215 · Burke, *Peerage*
Archives BL, letters to Lord Liverpool and others, Add. MSS 38242–38320 · BL, letters to Robert Peel and others, Add. MSS 40191–40266 · CUL, corresp. with Spencer Perceval · Mount Stuart Trust, Isle of Bute, letters to Lord Moira
Wealth at death £90,000: PRO, death duty registers, IR 26/717; *GM*, 1st ser., 87/2, 370

MacMahon, John Henry (1829–1900), Church of Ireland clergyman and classical scholar, was born at Dublin, the son of John MacMahon, a barrister. He was educated at Enniskillen, and on 1 July 1846 entered Trinity College, Dublin. He graduated BA in 1852, being senior moderator and gold medallist in ethics and logic, and proceeded MA in 1856. He took holy orders in 1853, and was curate of Termonamongan, co. Tyrone, under William Alexander, later bishop of Derry and primate of all Ireland. Between 1855 and 1888 he served successively in the cures of All Saints', Grangegorman, co. Dublin, St Werburgh's, Dublin, and St Philip's, Dublin, during which period he also studied law, taking his LLB and LLD from Trinity College, Dublin, in 1874. He afterwards became chaplain to the lord lieutenant and, from 1887, to Mountjoy prison.

MacMahon married Frances, the daughter of Thomas

Snagge of Dublin; they had a son and daughter. MacMahon published a number of scholarly works, contributing to Bohn's Classical Library the *Metaphysics of Aristotle, Literally Translated from the Greek, with Notes, Analysis, Questions, and Index* (1857) and to Clarke's Ante-Nicene Library *The Refutation of All Heresies by Hippolytus, Translated* (1888). He was also author of *A Treatise on Metaphysics, Chiefly in Reference to Revealed Religion* (1860) and of *Church and State in England: its [sic] Origin and Use* (1873). He died at his home, 10 Winton Road, Leeson Park, Dublin, on 21 May 1900.

J. M. RIGG, *rev.* DAVID HUDDLESTON

Sources J. B. Leslie, *Derry clergy and parishes* (1937), 298 · *The Times* (24 May 1900) · J. B. Leslie, biographical succession list of clergy for the diocese of Dublin, PRO NIre., T 1075/1 · [J. H. Todd], ed., *A catalogue of graduates who have proceeded to degrees in the University of Dublin, from the earliest recorded commencements to … December 16, 1868* (1869), 392 · Burtchaell & Sadleir, *Alum. Dubl.*, 2nd edn · CGPLA Ire. (1900)

Wealth at death £2857 2s. 8d.: probate, 13 June 1900, CGPLA Ire. · £75 (in England): Irish probate sealed in England, 30 July 1900, CGPLA Eng. & Wales

MacMahon, Percy Alexander (1854–1929), mathematician, was born on 26 September 1854 in Malta, the second son of Colonel Patrick William MacMahon and his wife, Ellen, daughter of George Savage Curtis, of Teignmouth. He was sent to Cheltenham College, and in 1871, at the age of sixteen, he entered the Royal Military Academy, Woolwich. He joined the Royal Artillery at Madras in 1873 as lieutenant, and was promoted captain in 1881 and major in 1889. His battery took part in 1877 with the Punjab frontier force in a punitive expedition against the Jawaki Afridis, penetrating into their country and capturing several villages.

MacMahon left India on medical certificate in 1877, was posted to the 9th brigade at Dover, and in 1882 returned to the Royal Military Academy as instructor in mathematics. This post brought him into contact with George Greenhill, then professor of mathematics at the Artillery College, Woolwich, whose friendship changed the course of MacMahon's life. In 1890 he was appointed professor of physics at the Ordnance College, and he held this post until 1897. In that year the eminent mathematician J. J. Sylvester died and MacMahon, who shared Sylvester's interests in number theory, was considered a possible successor to the Oxford Savilian chair of geometry. He retired from the army in 1898 (as was customary, taking the title 'major' into civilian life), and thereafter devoted himself to mathematical and scientific pursuits. From 1904 to 1920 he was deputy warden of the standards under the Board of Trade, a post which brought membership from 1920 onwards of the Conférence Générale and of the Comité Internationale des Poids et Mesures which were held in Paris. For twelve years (1902–14) he was one of the general secretaries of the British Association. His clarity of expression in extempore discussions of mathematics made him a welcome and prominent member of learned societies. He was elected a fellow of the Royal Society in 1890, and received the society's highest honours, the royal medal (1900) and the Sylvester medal (1919). The London Mathematical Society, of which he was president in 1894–6,

awarded him the De Morgan medal in 1923, and he received honorary degrees from several universities. All these honours came to a man with no first degree and who, in his youth, had been associated with no university. He followed the notable Cambridge mathematicians Arthur Cayley and J. W. L. Glaisher in the tradition of pure mathematicians who took a keen interest in astronomy and who became presidents of the Royal Astronomical Society. He was its president (1917–18) and a member of the permanent eclipse committee. He was also a member of the council of the Royal Society of Arts.

On his return to Woolwich in 1882 MacMahon entered into a mathematical heritage peculiarly fitted to his powers. The theory of algebraic forms was in the full flight of development owing to the activities of Arthur Cayley and James Joseph Sylvester, and this was the one predominantly British domain in the mathematics of the time. From the outset MacMahon was captivated: he was attracted by the lightness of touch and daring playfulness, combined with an abiding sense of form, that the subject demanded. His military friends were proud of one of their number's making a reputation in such an abstract subject and one which they could not fathom. They cheerfully chaffed him as 'a good soldier spoiled'. MacMahon burst on the mathematical scene by making a direct correspondence between invariant theory and the theory of partitions, a branch of number theory. Cayley hailed MacMahon's discovery as 'very remarkable' and from that moment his mathematical reputation was assured. In the years that followed, Cayley enlisted MacMahon's help in some difficult problems in invariant theory. The theory of algebraic forms was MacMahon's speciality and he derived many results. One notable example is his master theorem, a way of analysing permutations using determinants.

MacMahon's work is mainly linked to combinatorics, a branch of abstract algebra in which he occupies a special niche. This area of mathematics grew significantly in the twentieth century. MacMahon's work was republished in an edition of his *Collected Papers* (2 vols., 1978–86). They show him to be no crabbed specialist. 'I do not believe in any branch of science being destitute of connexion with other branches', he said at a meeting of the British Association for the Advancement of Science in Glasgow (1901). This isolation was particularly characteristic of a certain tract of pure mathematics which appeared to be in a 'forlorn condition'. The timeliness of MacMahon's masterly rescue of this branch of mathematics became more evident as the twentieth century advanced, in its significance for the theory of groups and the quantum theory. At the same Glasgow meeting he illustrated a historical turn of mind by drawing attention to the London Spitalfields Mathematical Society, founded in 1717 and absorbed into the Royal Astronomical Society in 1845. In 1915 MacMahon brought together the substance of his principal discoveries in a two-volume work *Combinatory Analysis*, a ripe and penetrating account of a favourite theme, which retains throughout the impress of his personality. There followed *An Introduction to Combinatory Analysis* (1920) and

New Mathematical Pastimes (1921). This last is in lighter vein, a book which gives the geometrical by-products of his characteristic algebra, as manifested in the construction of repeated patterns.

For many years MacMahon lived in London. On 9 February 1907 he married Grace Elizabeth, daughter of C. R. Howard, of 32 Gloucester Place, London; they had no children. His charming personality, his human sympathy, and the hospitality at his home at 27 Evelyn Mansions, Carlisle Place, Westminster, endeared him to a wide circle of friends. He encouraged many younger mathematicians by his infectious enthusiasm for algebra. He was also an expert billiards player at the Athenaeum. In 1922 MacMahon retired to Cambridge, becoming a member of St John's College, to which he had become attached in 1904 on receiving the university's honorary degree of ScD. Although his absorption in scientific problems became more pronounced in later life, he mixed very willingly in social gatherings until ill health compelled his retirement to Bognor; he died there at his home, Springfield, Normanton Avenue, on Christmas day 1929.

H. W. TURNBULL, *rev.* A. J. CRILLY

Sources H. F. Baker, 'Percy Alexander MacMahon, 1854–1929', *PRS*, 127A (1930), x–xix · *Nature*, 125 (1930), 243–5 · H. H. T. [H. H. Turner], *Monthly Notices of the Royal Astronomical Society*, 90 (1929–30), 373–8 · *The Times* (28 Dec 1929) · *The Times* (31 Dec 1929) · E. K. Lloyd, 'Redfield's proofs of MacMahon's conjecture', *Historia Mathematica*, 17 (1990), 36–47 · m. cert. · d. cert.
Archives St John Cam.
Likenesses W. Stoneman, photographs, 1926, NPG · photograph, repro. in Baker, 'Percy Alexander MacMahon'
Wealth at death £2753 16s. 5d.: probate, 20 Feb 1930, CGPLA Eng. & Wales

MacMahon [M'Mahon], **Thomas O'Brien** (*fl.* **1774–1777**), political writer, was born in co. Tipperary, the son of a Mr MacMahon and his wife, *née* O'Brien. No further details of his life are known, and he is now remembered as the author of three polemical treatises strongly critical of the claims of a contemporary English and Scottish Enlightenment tradition. The first of these works, *An Essay on the Depravity and Corruption of Human Nature* (1774), attacked a series of writers—among them Shaftesbury, Hume, and Sterne—whom MacMahon identified as misguided apologists for modern, supposedly humane, social relations. By contrast MacMahon proposed a far bleaker picture, the aim of the work being to 'establish the actual baseness of the heart of man, to explore its causes, and lay open the melancholy consequences that are to be apprehended' (p. ii). Eschewing the notion of a progressive, morally coherent enlightenment, MacMahon identified himself with a separate intellectual tradition 'after the example of Hobbes and Mandeville ... who, however sincerely they may love their fellow-creatures and themselves, refuse nonetheless to flatter them at the expense of the glory of their Creator's grace' (pp. 5–6).

The *Essay* began by demonstrating how man, having rejected God's love, and now inherently evil, sought satisfaction from his own actions and through a quest for 'self-applause' at the expense of the liberty of other men, the happiness and security of women and children, and the

well-being of animals, who become the victims of a rage fuelled by man-made dissatisfactions. MacMahon went on to demonstrate how the pursuit of power filled the void left by man's godless state, and set out the means by which social relations were manipulated to this end by politicians and private individuals alike. A final chapter considered the innate duplicity of modern forms of sociability, such as weeping and displays of 'fine feeling', made popular by the vogue then current for sensibility and sentimental expression. 'Tears are frequently the forerunners of, if not attendants on, obduracy and barbarity, upon occasions that demand benevolence and mercy', was MacMahon's judgement on modern manners: 'tender-eyed' did not mean 'tender-hearted' (*Essay*, 173–4).

Appraised in the *London Magazine* and the *Monthly Review* and *Critical Review*, the *Essay* was soundly condemned in a fashion which MacMahon had earlier predicted, his views being, he believed, 'sufficient to expose the writer to the public resentment, like the late *Mandeville*' (*Essay*, vii). For the *Critical Review*, the *Essay*, based on a misreading of the scriptures, offered a self-fulfilling prophecy, since:

> nothing contributes more to extinguish virtue in the breast of man, than degrading and odious pictures of the human species ... Instead of growing better, they easily grow worse, and gradually become vicious, merely through a persuasion that they were originally created under an inability of doing any thing but what is base and villainous. (*Critical Review*, 38.348)

Undaunted, MacMahon continued his attack first with a supplement, *Man's capricious, petulant, and tyrannical conduct towards the irrational and inanimate part of the creation* (1775), and then, two years later, in his ironically titled *The candour and good-nature of Englishmen in their deliberate, cautious, and charitable way of characterising the customs, manners, constitution and religion of neighbouring nations*. MacMahon's principal focus in this latter work was English hostility to the Irish and Roman Catholicism, prejudices which he identified as central to the criticisms he had earlier suffered in the review press. The study, intending to show that the 'general character of the English nation is ... ill-manners, abuse, malevolence, oppression of states dependent on them, and irreligion' (p. vi), contained a series of dialogues initiated by a 'good natured Englishman' who accused the Irish in general and MacMahon in person of being thieves, outcasts, murderers, and enemies of liberty. Having soaked up Anglican vitriol for over 250 pages, MacMahon finally hit back with a catalogue of his own complaints about an English nation characterized by its lust for blood sports and violence, its preponderance of alcoholics and gluttons, and its tendency towards 'proverbial, creeping and vulgar speech'. The study was subsequently reprinted in Dublin in 1792 under the strikingly benign title *Remarks on the English and Irish Nations*. Details of MacMahon's later career and death are unknown.

PHILIP CARTER

Sources *DNB* · *Critical Review*, 38 (1775), 347–50 · Watt, *Bibl. Brit.*

McMahon [MacMahon], **Sir Thomas Westropp, third baronet** (**1813–1892**), army officer, born on 14 February 1813, was the eldest son of General Sir Thomas McMahon, second baronet (1779–1860), who served in the Portuguese army in the Peninsula, and became adjutant-general in India and commander-in-chief at Bombay. His mother was Emily Anne (d. 11 May 1866), daughter of Michael Roberts Westropp. His father's elder brother, Sir John *McMahon (c.1754–1817), was private secretary and keeper of the privy purse to the prince regent, afterwards George IV; he became a privy councillor and was created a baronet on 7 August 1817, with remainder in default of his own male issue to McMahon's father, Thomas.

The young Thomas obtained a cornetcy in the 16th light dragoons on 24 December 1829, and transferred to the 6th Inniskilling dragoons in 1830, in which regiment he became lieutenant on 2 December 1831 and captain on 9 June 1838. On 22 April 1842 he was transferred as captain to the 9th lancers, and served with it, under the command of Sir James Hope Grant, in India during the Sutlej campaign and at the battle of Sobraon on 10 February 1846. He was promoted to a majority unattached on 13 July 1847. He served in Turkey and the Crimea as assistant quartermaster-general of the cavalry division, and was present at the battles of the Alma, Balaklava, and the Chernaya, and at the siege of Sevastopol. He was created CB (5 July 1855) and the fifth class of the Mejidiye. While in the Crimea, on the promotion of Sir James Yorke Scarlett, he became lieutenant-colonel in the 5th dragoon guards from 12 December 1854, and commanded that regiment until he went on half pay in 1861. He succeeded his father as third baronet in 1860. He became a major-general on 6 March 1869, commanded the cavalry brigade at Aldershot and was inspector-general of cavalry from 1871 to 1876, and became lieutenant-general in 1877 and general in 1880. In 1874 he received the honorary colonelcy 18th hussars, and in 1885 was transferred to that of his former regiment, the 5th dragoon guards.

McMahon married: first, on 7 October 1851, Dora Paulina (d. 23 Sept 1852), youngest daughter of Evan Hamilton-Baillie; secondly, on 13 January 1859, Frances Mary (d. 14 April 1867), daughter of John Holford; and thirdly, on 14 August 1888, Constance Marianne (d. 19 Sept 1893), widow of John Brooking. With his second wife he had four sons, who all entered the army, and one daughter. After a long illness McMahon died at The Sycamores, Farnborough, Hampshire, on 23 January 1892.

H. M. CHICHESTER, rev. JAMES FALKNER

Sources Army List · Broad Arrow (30 Jan 1892) · Hart's Army List · E. S. Jackson, The Inniskilling dragoons: the records of an old heavy cavalry regiment (1909) · Burke, Peerage · Boase, Mod. Eng. biog.
Likenesses oils, c.1870

MacMahon, Sir William, first baronet (1776–1837), judge, was born in Dublin on 12 July 1776, the second son of John MacMahon, patentee comptroller of the port of Limerick, and his second wife, Mary, daughter of James Stackpoole, a merchant from Cork. Although brought up a Catholic, MacMahon converted to protestantism just before his call to the Irish bar at the King's Inns in the summer of 1799. He studied at Trinity College, Dublin, from November 1791, and he obtained his BA in 1796 and his MA in 1799. He joined the Munster circuit on 23 April 1805.

A contemporary of Daniel O'Connell, MacMahon was initially an unattractive speaker and was not regarded as a popular member of the circuit. However, on 23 April 1806 he was made third serjeant, on 3 December 1813 second serjeant, and on 1 March 1814 master of the rolls. He was made a baronet on 6 May 1814.

MacMahon married on 16 May 1807 Frances Burton; they had two sons. Frances died on 9 February 1813 and on 1 September of the following year MacMahon married Charlotte Shaw; they had five sons and three daughters.

MacMahon remained master of the rolls until his death, and between the years 1815 and 1825 he was one of the commissioners of the great seal. He died in Dublin on 13 January 1837 and was buried nearby at Rathfarnham on 21 January. MacMahon was remembered as a sound and impartial judge. He was appointed at a very young age, partly because his brother was secretary to the prince regent.

Sir Charles MacMahon (1824–1891), the third son of Sir William and his second wife, Charlotte, was born at Fortfield, co. Dublin, on 11 July 1824. He entered the army in 1842 and served with the 71st (Highland) light infantry in Canada and with the 10th hussars in India. He retired with the rank of captain, in 1851, and in 1853 he joined the Melbourne police force, of which he was later appointed chief commissioner. MacMahon was married to Sophia Campbell, and, later, to Clara Ann Webster, the daughter of J. D. Webster of Yea, Victoria. He retired in 1858 and from 1861 to 1863, 1871 to 1877, and 1880 to 1886 was a member of the legislative assembly. He was created a knight bachelor in 1875 and died in East Melbourne, Australia, on 28 August 1891.

J. M. RIGG, rev. SINÉAD AGNEW

Sources F. E. Ball, The judges in Ireland, 1221–1921, 2 vols. (1926), 256, 265, 276, 327, 335 · J. R. O'Flanagan, The lives of the lord chancellors and keepers of the great seals of Ireland, 2 (1870), 546–56 · GM, 2nd ser., 7 (1837), 428 · Burtchaell & Sadleir, Alum. Dubl. · J. S. Crone, A concise dictionary of Irish biography, rev. edn (1937), 142 · J. Foster, The register of admissions to Gray's Inn, 1521–1889, together with the register of marriages in Gray's Inn chapel, London (1889), 401 · 'Wilson's Dublin directory', Treble almanack (1802), 121 · J. Haydn, The book of dignities: containing lists of the official personages of the British empire, ed. H. Ockerby, 3rd edn (1894) · C. J. Smyth, Chronicle of the law officers of Ireland (1839), 48–9, 79, 199, 202 · J. R. O'Flanagan, The Munster circuit: tales, trials and traditions (1880), 160
Wealth at death large fortune; £13,000 p.a. to eldest son; plus £300 p.a. to Lady MacMahon; residue (£200,000–£300,000) distributed among other children: GM, 7.428

Mac Maíll Shechnaill, Niall. See Niall mac Maíll Shechnaill (d. 1061).

MacManus [née Johnston], **Anna Isabel** [pseud. Ethna Carbery] (1866–1902), poet and journalist, was born in Ballymena, co. Antrim, on 3 December 1866, the elder daughter of the two daughters and one son of Robert Johnston (1836–1937), a wealthy timber merchant and prominent member of the Irish Republican Brotherhood. The family later lived in Donegall Park, Belfast. Anna Johnston had begun to publish poetry under her own name by 1886, contributing to nationalist journals and newspapers

Anna Isabel MacManus [Ethna Carbery] (1866–1902), by unknown photographer

including the *Irish Monthly* and *United Ireland*. She also established contacts with literary and nationalist circles in Dublin, in particular the circle around Katharine Tynan. In October 1895 she co-founded a radical journal, the *Northern Patriot*, with her friend the poet and nationalist Alice Milligan (1866–1953); however they lost editorial control in December 1895 after a disagreement with the Belfast Workingmen's Club, the journal's sponsor. The friends then founded a rival journal, the republican *Shan Van Vocht*, which ran from January 1896 to April 1899. The editors supplied much as Iris Olkyrn and Ethna Carbery (Anna Johnston contributed over forty signed poems and stories) and they were also responsible for production and distribution. The *Shan Van Vocht* provided a digest of Irish radical and cultural nationalist activities in the period; it published early writings by James Connolly. The literary content was also impressive, including poetry by Lionel Johnson, Douglas Hyde, and Nora Hopper.

Anna Johnston was a sincere nationalist, but, unlike Alice Milligan, was opposed to amnesty for dynamitards. She had links with the Irish National Alliance, a revolutionary movement, and was a member of the Ulster '98 Centenary Committee: in 1899 Dublin Castle linked her to anti-recruiting groups in Ireland. Anna Johnston's most conspicuous contribution to Irish cultural nationalism was in 1899, when she played Princess Eithne in the first Irish-language play performed in Ireland. At the time of her death she was vice-president of Inghinidhe n hEireann, the Irish women's organization.

An early and regular contributor to the *Shan Van Vocht* was Seamus MacManus (1869–1960), a Donegal schoolmaster from a farming background, who, as Mac of Glen Ainey, had begun to publish verse and folk sketches in the *Donegal Vindicator*. MacManus rapidly became a friend of both women and his aggressive nationalism gave him easy entry to Anna Johnston's home. In early September 1899 she went on a political-cultural propaganda tour of Donegal with Alice Milligan and other nationalists, including MacManus, with whom she had fallen in love. She was profoundly shocked to discover that he was about to emigrate to the United States. MacManus left Ireland in late September 1898, and subsequently claimed that he had been financed by the French government to raise Irish-American support for a war against Great Britain. MacManus made good use of his time in the United States, placing his folk tales and Donegal anecdotes in magazines and securing book contracts. He returned to Ireland in spring 1899 and by then was probably aware of Anna Johnston's feelings, already expressed in 'Paistin Fionn', published by 'E. D. M.' in the *Shan Van Vocht* on 7 November 1898. They married in spring 1901 and lived at Mount Revelinn House, Revlin, co. Donegal, where Anna MacManus died of gastritis on 2 April 1902; she was buried two days later in the Catholic churchyard at Frosses, co. Donegal. Her death was deemed to be 'almost a national calamity' (Ryan, 181) and nationalist papers printed lengthy eulogies of Ethna Carbery.

Anna MacManus's writing focused on the Irish past, on folklore and mythology, although she also published political verse, such as 'The Suppliant', an attack on Queen Victoria's visit to Ireland, published in the *United Irishman* in April 1900. Her verse is most successful when she works within a folk tradition; her love poems addressed to Seamus MacManus, such as 'Mo Bhuachaill Cael-Dubh' and 'Paistin Fionn' follow folk-song models, but infuse them with fresh emotion. Her mythological-historical poems influenced by Sir Samuel Ferguson, such as 'Niall Glondubh to Gormlai', and her historical-patriotic poems influenced by Thomas Davis, such as 'The Erin's Hope', are less compelling. Seamus Macmanus collected her poems as *The Four Winds of Eirinn* in 1902. The volume was remarkably successful, going through ten editions in 1902 and fifteen editions by 1905—Anna MacManus's melancholy looks and her early death enhanced her stature. MacManus skilfully managed her reputation, enlarging the volume, adding a highly charged memoir to the 1918 edition and family photographs to the 1934 edition. MacManus collected his wife's historical and legendary fictions as *In the Celtic Past* (1904) and her love stories, influenced by 'Fiona MacLeod', as *The Passionate Hearts* (1903).

MacManus's assertion that 'Ethna Carbery' was 'the Irish poet of … the Revival period … she reached the Irish heart as it has not been reached by any Irish poet in a century' (*Four Winds*, 158–9) is not just a widower's piety. Mary Colum summed up Anna MacManus's popularity:

> Every one of the numerous mothers who had a son or daughter in America was pierced to the heart by her ['Paistin Fionn'] … she was probably the most widely read poet in Ireland, and I should not be surprised if her death was not more mourned throughout the country than the death of Yeats. (Colum, 115–16)

DEIRDRE TOOMEY

Sources *The four winds of Eirinn: poems by Ethna Carbery*, ed. S. MacManus (1918) · S. MacManus, *The rocky road to Dublin* (1947) · M. F. Ryan, *Fenian memories*, ed. T. F. O'Sullivan (1945) · *Irish News and Belfast Morning News* (8 April 1902) · *Donegal Vindicator* (5 April 1902) · *United Irishman* (12 April 1902) · *The collected letters of W. B. Yeats*, 2, ed. W. Gould, J. Kelly, and D. Toomey (1997), 452–3 [1896–1900] ·

M. Colum, *Life and the dream* (1947) · d. cert. · R. Hogan, ed., *Dictionary of Irish literature*, rev. edn, 2 vols. (1996) · *Catholic Bulletin* (1937) **Likenesses** photograph, NPG [*see illus.*]

McManus [Macmanus], **Terence Bellew** (1811/12–1861), revolutionary, was born in Tempo, co. Fermanagh, the eldest of three children of Philip McManus and his wife, Alice Bellew. Both parents were of Catholic gentry families but Philip squandered his inheritance. After a fragmented education, including a spell (1827–1830/31) at Urbleshanny chapel school, co. Monaghan, Terence was apprenticed to a drapery business in Monaghan town and soon became a foreman. In 1836 he left for Dublin and about 1840 he set up in business in Manchester, before moving in 1842 to Liverpool. He established an agency for Irish importers of English textiles and prospered thereby. He set up home in the fashionable resort of Seacombe in Cheshire with his sister Isabella as hostess. He was never to marry.

McManus promoted the repeal campaign in Lancashire. Throughout 1847 he rallied support for the Irish Confederation in Liverpool and he was party to the plans for a rising adumbrated from early summer 1848 by the Dublin leaders of the confederation. He arrived in Dublin on 25 July 1848 and within a few days he had caught up with Smith O'Brien at Ballingarry; it appears that he was one of the more forceful and clear-minded of the group of Young Ireland gentlemen who attempted in vain to foment a rising in the days that followed. Subsequently, McManus set about escaping to America and was on board a ship about to sail from Queenstown when he was arrested. He stood trial at Clonmel, was convicted on a charge of high treason, and on 23 October 1848 was sentenced to death along with Smith O'Brien, Thomas Francis Meagher, and Patrick O'Donoghue. Not without some legal difficulty, the government, unwilling to make martyrs, commuted the sentences to transportation for life. McManus and his comrades left Dublin on board the *Swift* on 9 July 1849 and reached Van Diemen's Land (now Tasmania) on 27 October. He escaped from the colony in early March 1851. On 5 June 1851 he arrived in San Francisco, where he set about rebuilding a commercial career. He had little success in this and following a period of ill health he died in St Mary's Hospital, San Francisco, on 15 January 1861; he was buried the next day in Calvary cemetery, San Francisco. Months later, against a background of Irish American political intrigue, his remains were disinterred for reburial in Ireland. The coffin reached New York on 15 September 1861 and was the focus of religious and political solemnities. Its arrival in Ireland on 30 October was followed by a lying-in-state and procession in Cork and another lying-in-state in Dublin before a huge funeral procession to Glasnevin cemetery on 10 November. Behind the massive funeral lay a general sense of respect for a patriotic figure, effectively manipulated by James Stephens and his active young followers, soon to be known to the world as the Fenians.   R. V. COMERFORD

Sources T. G. McAllister, *Terence Bellew McManus, 1811(?)–1861* (1972) · R. Davis, *The Young Ireland movement* (1988) · C. G. Duffy, *Young Ireland: a fragment of Irish history, 1840–1845*, 2nd edn (1880) · M. Doheny, *The felon's track* (1849)

Archives Clogher Diocesan Archives, Monaghan, Clarke MSS · NL Ire., Larcom MSS **Likenesses** lithograph, pubd 1848 (after daguerreotype), NG Ire.; copy, NG Ire. · lithograph (after lithograph by L. Gluckman), NG Ire.; repro. in *Supplement to the Irish fireside* (1885) · photograph, repro. in Doheny, *Felon's track*, facing p. xvi

Mac Maol Íosa, Nicholas (*d.* 1303), archbishop of Armagh, was a native of the diocese of Ardagh. He was elected to the archbishopric of Armagh in the summer or autumn of 1270 and travelled to Rome for consecration by Pope Gregory X, who returned from the Holy Land early in 1272. He set out for England from Italy in July of that year and did homage to Henry III before the end of September. On 27 October 1272 the temporalities of the archdiocese were restored to him. He probably attended the Council of Lyons in 1274.

Mac Maol Íosa's episcopate was notable for the extensive litigation in which he engaged in defence of what he considered to be his rights as archbishop. In 1300–01, for instance, he was involved in nearly thirty separate pleas. He contested with both the English and Irish lords of his diocese, and also with Edward I, and in return was accused of serious misconduct more than once. In 1284 he was accused of harbouring relatives who had been present at the killing of Nicholas and John de Verdon, sons of John de Verdon, by the ÓFergail family in 1272. In 1285 he was reported to have usurped the king's rights to temporalities during episcopal vacancies in the province of Armagh and the king was advised that 'it would be expedient … that no Irishman should ever be an archbishop or bishop [?], because they always preach against the king and always provide their churches with Irishmen' (*Calendar of Documents Relating to Ireland, 1285–1292*, 10). In fact Nicholas was a committed supporter of the English order in Ireland and the particular incident which provoked this outburst was his resistance to the election of Thomas St Leger as bishop of Meath. He wished to see the bishopric go instead to Walter of Fulbourn, dean of Waterford and brother of the justiciar and bishop of Waterford, Stephen of Fulbourn. In 1287 the pope decided in favour of St Leger. Nicholas was not afraid, however, to defend the rights of the church against the crown and in 1291 at Trim persuaded all the bishops of Ireland—including Thomas St Leger of Meath and Nicholas le Blund of Down, with whom he had also been in dispute—to bind themselves by mutual oath to resist pressure from the lay power. Edward was later able to recover a great deal of property from the archbishop under the provisions of the Statute of Mortmain.

Nicholas received many grants of land from the English settlers in Louth and married members of his family into local English gentry families such as those of Burgess, de Repenteny, and Napton. The acquisition of English law for his relatives and friends was a consistent policy on his part, as was the acquisition of office: Christopher Mac Maol Íosa became a canon of Derry, while Denis Mac Maol Íosa seems to have served as dean of Armagh. He was hostile to the Irish lords who intruded on church property. In

1278 he urged Edward I to build a castle at the archiepiscopal manor of Iniskeen in Monaghan on the grounds that it would increase the security of the march and because it was situated *in medio perverse gentis* ('in the midst of a perverse people'), by whom he meant either the Mac Mathgamna family or possibly that of the Ó Cearbaill. He took the opportunity of preaching the bull *Clericis laicos* in Monaghan in 1297 to threaten the Mac Mathgamna and their sub-chieftains with excommunication should they neglect to obey its provisions. On this occasion the most powerful of the Irish chiefs of Ulster, Domnall Ó Néill, swore to obey the provisions of the bull. Nicholas's death in 1303 was noted in both Irish and Anglo-Irish annals.

B. SMITH

Sources A. Gwynn, 'Nicholas Mac Maol Íosa, archbishop of Armagh', *Féil Sgríbhinn Eoin Mhic Néill*, ed. J. Ryan (1940) · J. Watt, 'English law and the Irish church: the reign of Edward I', *Medieval studies presented to Aubrey Gwynn*, ed. J. A. Watt, J. B. Morrall, and F. X. Martin (1961), 133–67 · D. Mac Íomhair, 'Primate Mac Maol Íosa and county Louth', *Seanchas Ardmhacha*, 6 (1971–2) · K. W. Nicholls, 'The register of Clogher', *Clogher Record*, 7 (1971–2), 361–431 · H. S. Sweetman and G. F. Handcock, eds., *Calendar of documents relating to Ireland*, 5 vols., PRO (1875–86), vol. 3, p. 10

MacMhuirich family (*per.* 13th–18th cent.), Gaelic poets, the leading Scottish bardic dynasty, was closely associated with the clan MacDonald, at an early stage with the MacDonald lords of the Isles, and latterly with the Clanranald MacDonalds who controlled considerable territories both in the outer isles and on the west mainland of Scotland.

Both Gaelic Scotland and Gaelic Ireland had a developed system of highly trained professional poets who served the leaders in their societies (in the case of Scotland the chiefs of the more powerful clans). They were often propagandists for their patrons, but their function also included the recording and publicizing of historical, genealogical, and legendary lore attached to these patrons. There were professional bardic schools which could be attended for periods up to seven years (the 'year' apparently consisting of six months in the calendar year), with strict curricula and a variety of attainable grades. These schools are mainly attested in Ireland, and Scottish poets often did part of their training there. A good number of bardic 'textbooks' survived in manuscript form in Ireland, and a substantial body of this classical verse has survived. It became the norm for bardic office to pass from father to son or to another close relative.

The founder of the MacMhuirich dynasty is said to be Muireadhach *Ó Dálaigh (*fl.* 1213) [*see under* Ó Dálaigh family], a prominent member of a long-lasting Irish bardic dynasty. He fled to Scotland in the second decade of the thirteenth century, apparently settling in Lennox initially, then visiting the Holy Land, and returning to Scotland for a time and establishing his family there. He became known as Muireadhach Albanach (Scottish Muireadhach), and the MacMhuirich surname derives from him. The MacMhuirichs came to hold office in the MacDonald of the Isles court, and had close associations with Kintyre and Islay, at least until the middle years of the sixteenth century. Thereafter the main branch is associated

with South Uist and Benbecula, but subsidiary lines survived elsewhere, for example in Argyll, and the poetic vein continued to surface in descendants in Canada in the twentieth century.

Two poems with specific Scottish locations (in these cases Lennox) are ascribed to Muireadhach, and about twenty poems, including a moving elegy for his wife, survive. His Scottish line of bardic descendants and practitioners is a long one, extending to eighteen generations if we follow the line to 1800. Not all the individuals can be identified, though the last eight are named in a late eighteenth-century genealogy by a descendant. The name Cathal appears in thirteenth-century records, and surfaces again in the seventeenth century with one of the finest poets of this line. A brief résumé of identified MacMhuirich poets, with some indication of their range of poems, follows.

A curious work, described as a *brosnachadh catha* ('incitement to battle'), apparently composed at the time of the battle of Harlaw (1411), a battle fought between Alexander Stewart, earl of Mar, and Donald, lord of the Isles, survives in two manuscript sources, and is ascribed in one of these to Lachlann Mor MacMhuirich aos-dana Mhic Dhomhnuill (Big Lachlan, or the elder Lachlan MacMhuirich, MacDonald's professional poet). The MacDonald fighters are described in a series of couplets, each containing four alliterating adverbs and proceeding through the alphabet, for example:

> Gu mearghanta, gu mór-chneadhach,
> Gu meanmnach, gu míleanta
> ('spiritedly, inflicting great wounds, stout-heartedly, martially').

It was probably a grandson of the 1411 poet who appears as a witness to a charter in 1485, under the designation *Lacclannus mc muredhaich archipoeta*. In the last decade of the fifteenth century another poet is referred to as Giolla Coluim mac an Ollaimh (Giolla Coluim, or Malcolm, son of the high poet; *fl.* 1490), and he laments the decline in the MacDonalds' standing at that time.

A contemporary of Giolla Coluim was John MacMhuirich (*d. c.*1510), dean of Knoydart in the first decade of the sixteenth century, and he probably was one of the dean of Lismore's sources for his collection of poetry. Another John is referred to in a rental of 1541 as *Johannes Mc Murech Albany*, and this may imply both that he was a descendant of Muireadhach and the chief poet, or *ollamh*, of his family. The dean of Lismore has three items ascribed to him, and an anonymous elegy for two Clanranald chiefs killed in 1509 and 1514 may be his also.

Three MacMhuirich poets are associated with the seventeenth century. Niall Mór MacMhuirich (*b. c.*1550) may have been the first of the dynasty to be born under the Clanranald regime. One of his surviving poems describes a lengthy spree on the occasion of the wedding in 1613 of John of Moydart and Marion MacLeod, daughter of MacLeod of Dunvegan, but his most famous poem is 'Soraidh slán don oidhche a-réir' ('A lasting farewell to last night'), a chaste and lyrical love poem. More survives of the work of two later seventeenth-century MacMhuirich poets, Cathal and Niall. **Cathal MacMhuirich** (*fl. c.*1615–1649) succeeded Niall Mór as chief MacMhuirich poet, perhaps as a result of the failure of Niall Mór's son to take up the succession. Cathal appears as a witness to various Clanranald transactions in 1629, 1630, and 1634, and is sometimes described as Clanranald's secretary. A rift seems to have developed between him and Clanranald, and Cathal may have transferred his main allegiance to MacDonald of Sleat. About a dozen of Cathal's poems survive, and he and Niall were both involved in the writing of the Books of Clanranald, which include history, legend, and genealogy as well as poetry. Cathal's surviving poems are mostly elegies and eulogies, but his vivid and inventive language supports the claim that he was the most original of the seventeenth-century MacMhuirichs. **Niall MacMhuirich** (*d.* 1726) was born in the 1630s, the son of Dòmhnall Geàrr. He succeeded Cathal, and continued to write into the second decade of the eighteenth century. He has two elegies in the vernacular style on Allan of Clanranald, who died in 1715, and a classical elegy for Allan also.

The final active member of this classical bardic dynasty was Niall's son **Dòmhnall** [Donald] **MacMhuirich** (*fl.* 1707–1740s), who was granted the tack of half the bardic lands of Stadhlaigearraidh in 1707. He seems to have died in the 1740s, leaving a few rather undistinguished poems. It was in 1800 that another Lachlann MacMhuirich made his famous declaration regarding the MacMhuirich dynasty. This claimed that he was eighteenth in the line of descent from Muireadhach. His statement was printed in the report on Ossian presented to the Highland Society of Scotland in 1805.   DERICK S. THOMSON

Sources books of Clanranald, National Museum of Antiquities of Scotland, Edinburgh, MCR 39–40 · [J. MacGregor], Book of the dean of Lismore, NL Scot. · D. S. Thomson, 'The MacMhuirich bardic family', *Transactions of the Gaelic Society of Inverness*, 43 (1960–63) · D. S. Thomson, *An introduction to Gaelic poetry*, 2nd edn (1990) · D. S. Thomson, 'Gaelic learned orders and literati in medieval Scotland', *Scottish Studies*, 12 (1968) · D. S. Thomson, 'The poetic tradition in Gaelic Scotland', *Proceedings of the 7th International Congress of Celtic Studies* (1983) · D. S. Thomson, 'Three seventeenth century bardic poets', *Bards and makars*, ed. A. J. Aitken, M. P. McDiarmid, and D. S. Thomson (1975) · B. Ó Cuív, 'Eachtra Mhuireadhaigh Í Dhálaigh', *Studia Hibernica*, 1 (1961) · D. S. Thomson, ed., *The companion to Gaelic Scotland*, new edn (1994)
Archives NL Scot., MSS | National Museum of Antiquities of Scotland, Edinburgh, books of Clanranald · U. Glas., McLagan MSS

MacMhuirich, Cathal (*fl. c.*1615–1649). *See under* MacMhuirich family (*per.* 13th–18th cent.).

MacMhuirich, Dòmhnall (*fl.* 1707–1740s). *See under* MacMhuirich family (*per.* 13th–18th cent.).

MacMhuirich, Niall (*d.* 1726). *See under* MacMhuirich family (*per.* 13th–18th cent.).

MacMichael, Sir Harold Alfred (1882–1969), colonial governor, was born on 15 October 1882 at Rowtor, Birchover,

Sir Harold Alfred MacMichael (1882–1969), by Bassano, 1935

Derbyshire, the eldest son of the Revd Charles MacMichael (*d.* 1905), and his wife, Sophia Caroline (1857–1929), eldest daughter of the Revd Alfred Nathaniel Holden Curzon, fourth Baron Scarsdale, and sister of George Nathaniel *Curzon, the future Marquess Curzon of Kedleston. MacMichael was educated at King's Lynn, moving to Bedford grammar school when his father was preferred to a living near Bedford. He distinguished himself both at games (winning the public schools fencing championship in 1901) and also academically. Awarded an open scholarship to Magdalene College, Cambridge, he took first-class honours in the first part of the classical tripos in 1904. Through a chance contact he became interested in the Egypt and Sudan civil service, which he joined in 1905 after obtaining a first class in the Arabic examination. He spent most of the next three decades in Sudan, where he made his name as a professional administrator and amateur historian.

Only seven years after the Anglo-Egyptian 'reconquest' of Sudan, the British service there was still largely military, and what would later be known as the Sudan political service was still in its infancy. MacMichael's first provincial posting, to Kordofan, the wild and varied territory west of the Nile, was ideally suited to his temperament and interests. Administrative work was highly personal, and involved much travel and contact with nomadic peoples; time was available for private pursuits, and MacMichael became a keen student of the ethnography of northern Sudan. His first book, *The Tribes of Northern and Central Kordofan*, was published in 1912 to favourable reviews, and, together with lesser pieces, won Mac-Michael an instant reputation as an expert on that little-known region.

In Sudan as elsewhere, the First World War ironically thrust young civilians into positions of greater responsibility. After a posting in Khartoum in 1913–14 MacMichael served as political officer on the Red Sea patrol and then, in 1915, as acting governor of Khartoum province. When Ali Dinar of Darfur, an autonomous sultanate west of Kordofan, threatened common cause with Britain's Ottoman enemies, MacMichael's expertise was in demand. The governor-general of Sudan, Sir Reginald Wingate, methodically prepared for war, and in this MacMichael played an important role in political intelligence. When Wingate launched an invasion in March 1916 MacMichael served as political officer with the Darfur field force, and with it entered al-Fasher, Ali Dinar's capital, on 23 May.

Just as British officials in Cairo and London had conjured up condominium in 1898 as an inexpensive way of governing Sudan, so in 1916 it fell to MacMichael to recommend ways of administering this latest accretion of unremunerative territory. In calling for decentralization MacMichael laid the foundations for what, after the war, would develop into a fully-fledged, country-wide policy of indirect rule. In its several Sudanese versions this policy indeed became closely associated with MacMichael, whom, however, some students of the period have incorrectly seen as a reactionary ideologue. In Darfur, as in southern Sudan in the early 1930s, MacMichael was conservative and pragmatic, even unimaginative and detached, but never dogmatically convinced of the genius of local institutions or an inherent majesty of tribal leaders.

The demilitarization of the Sudan government during and after the war (and especially after the departure of Wingate at the end of 1916) led to civilian promotion to the highest posts. After secondment to the Paris peace conference for consultations over Anglo-French border arrangements in the central Sahara, MacMichael became assistant civil secretary in 1919. Under colourless superiors he soon dominated what was already emerging as the most important department of the government, and by the time he succeeded as civil secretary in 1926 Mac-Michael was, after the governor-general himself, the dominant personality in the Sudan government. His high standards and attention to detail, in everything from legal briefs to Anglo-Sudanese etiquette, became legendary.

Under MacMichael the civil secretary's department evolved in all but name into a ministry of the interior with, indeed, a multiplicity of responsibilities that in other colonial governments resided elsewhere. Mac-Michael left his mark in several ways. Temperamentally cautious, in political affairs he dominated debate through intellect and a reputation for expertise born of his experience in the provinces; he acted in fact as a brake on indirect rule, when younger, more radical officials, spurred by a romantic and imperfect understanding of conditions in Northern Nigeria, demanded bold experiments. In his attitude towards the political claims of Western-educated

Sudanese, MacMichael's caution was indistinguishable from colonialist bias; his tenure in the civil secretary's office witnessed reaction against the aspirations and diminution of the authority of this class. MacMichael's sympathies in the religio-political struggle between Sayyid Ali al-Mirghani, Sudan's premier Sufi leader, and Sayyid ʿAbd al-Rahman al-Mahdi, the son and heir of the Sudanese Mahdi, were firmly with the former, whose reticence and modesty struck a sympathetic chord. Finally, in inaugurating the famous southern policy by which the south would be shielded from outside influences while education and development were brought to its indigenous peoples, MacMichael tried to apply practically the principles of indirect rule to Sudan's most backward regions. Ironically, a policy he rightly saw as cautious but progressive became reactionary and high-handed in practice, and has since been seen as a cause of later civil war.

Separate from the colonial service, the Sudan political service offered even its most eminent members no clear path of preferment outside the country. By the early 1930s MacMichael had long been ready for greater responsibility, but bureaucratic rules and departmental jealousies rendered ineffective the efforts even of high-placed patrons. Finally, in 1934 MacMichael was made governor and commander-in-chief in Tanganyika, a country where his talents as an Arabist and interests in the material culture of the ancient Near East found little scope. His administration there was competent, lacklustre, and, in retrospect, a disagreeable interlude before a more suitable position. This came in 1937, when MacMichael was appointed, in succession to Sir Arthur Wauchope, high commissioner and commander-in-chief in Palestine, a post he would occupy until 1944. His tenure thus began (in March 1938) during a crisis of Arab rebellion against the mandatory regime and Jewish settlers, and encompassed almost the entire period of the Second World War. Immediately suspected by both Arabs and Jews, MacMichael found himself with responsibility but not authority, a lightning rod for a British policy with which he often disagreed. Although an Arabist, he arrived pragmatically at the view that only partition offered long-term prospects of successful resolution of the Palestine question. On 8 August 1944 the Stern gang of Jewish terrorists failed in an attempt to assassinate MacMichael, whose term of office was in any case about to end. He left Palestine in September 1944. There followed a series of special missions. In 1945–6 MacMichael helped to draft a constitution for Malaya, and in 1946 went to Malta to negotiate reforms in the island's relations with Britain. He remained a member of the advisory council of the joint east African board, and continued to lecture and write on issues of colonial and imperial interest.

MacMichael's reputation as a scholar, founded on *The Tribes of Northern and Central Kordofan*, was enhanced by publication in 1913 of *Brands used by the Chief Camel-Owning Tribes of Kordofan* and especially, in 1922, of his two-volume *History of the Arabs in the Sudan*. In 1934, shortly after he had left Sudan for Tanganyika, *The Anglo-Egyptian Sudan* was published, and in 1954 he published *The Sudan*. The titles of these successive books perhaps reflected the changes in the country's political status over the half century of Mac-Michael's association with it. MacMichael also published many articles, notably in *Sudan Notes and Records*, the important journal of which he was a founder in 1918, on a variety of ethnographic, geographic, and even veterinary aspects of western Sudan especially. He wrote the introduction for *Sudan Political Service, 1899–1956*, a synopsis (published in the 1950s) of the service of that élite corps of which he was a principal member and defender. Although seriously flawed and now long outdated, his major works on Sudan were for many years considered definitive, and they continue to be cited as classics of a certain genre.

On 3 June 1919 at St Martin-in-the-Fields, London, Mac-Michael married Agnes De Sivrac Edith (Nesta; *d.* 1974), daughter of Canon J. O. Stephens. They had two daughters. Many honours and awards were bestowed on Mac-Michael: he was made DSO (1916), CMG (1927), KCMG (1931), and GCMG (1941), and was awarded the Burton memorial medal of the Royal Asiatic Society (1928). He was made a knight of the order of St John of Jerusalem in 1938, and held orders also of Egypt and Ethiopia. In 1939 he was made an honorary fellow of Magdalene College, Cambridge, where he had been an undergraduate. In retirement MacMichael continued to pursue lifelong interests in Sassanian seals, stamps, and books, and he often lectured and contributed explanatory pieces to the press on a variety of Near Eastern subjects. Late in life he and his wife moved from Teynham, Kent, to Folkestone, living latterly at the Princes Hotel. He died in Folkestone, on 19 September 1969.   M. W. DALY

Sir John McMichael (1904–1993), by Sir William O. Hutchison, 1968

Sources U. Durham L., department of palaeography and diplomatic, Sudan archive · *The Times* (22 Sept 1969) · *Sudan political service, 1899–1956* · M. W. Daly, *Empire on the Nile* (1986) · *DNB* · *Sudan Notes and Records* · *CGPLA Eng. & Wales* (1970)

Archives Bodl. RH, corresp. and papers · St Ant. Oxf., Middle East Centre, corresp and papers; papers relating to partition of Palestine · U. Durham L., corresp. and papers | Bodl. Oxf., letters to O. G. S. Crawford · U. Durham L., corresp. with Sir Reginald Wingate | FILM IWM SA, news footage

Likenesses W. Stoneman, photograph, 1932, NPG · Bassano, photograph, 1935, NPG [*see illus.*] · photographs, U. Durham L., Sudan archive

Wealth at death £31,419: probate, 17 March 1970, *CGPLA Eng. & Wales*

McMichael, Sir John (1904–1993), cardiologist, was born on 25 July 1904 at the High Street, Gatehouse of Fleet, Kirkcudbrightshire, the third son and fifth child of James McMichael (1854–1933), and his wife, Margaret Livingstone Sproat (*d.* 1929). His father was a butcher and small-time farmer who struggled to make ends meet but was, to use his son's words, 'a gentle God-fearing man of the kindest nature'; both parents were committed to the moral precepts of the Church of Scotland and this had a strong influence on his early life.

McMichael's first teacher at Girthon School was William Learmonth, father of Professor Sir James Learmonth, the distinguished Edinburgh surgeon. It was he who recognized McMichael's intellectual qualities at an early age and convinced his parents that he should go on to Kirkcudbright Academy—where he was dux in 1921—then,

supported by local and Carnegie scholarships, to Edinburgh University, where he graduated in medicine in 1927. After a period in junior posts he was appointed as first assistant to Professor Stanley Davidson, who held the regius chair of medicine in the University of Aberdeen. On 3 June 1932 he married Joan Katherine Macpherson (1906–1989), then a medical practitioner at Crichton, Midlothian. They had two sons, who were evacuated to Canada during the Second World War, but the marriage ended in divorce and on 7 April 1942 McMichael married Sybil Eleanor Blake (1914–1965), a radiographer, with whom he had another two sons.

In 1932 McMichael went to London as Beit memorial fellow to work in Professor T. R. Elliott's department at University College Hospital. There he met the leading clinical research worker of that era, Sir Thomas Lewis. He was helped by a fellow Scot, John W. McNee, who made his remarkable collection of spleens available to him, and he wrote his MD thesis on liver and spleen fibrosis (1933). This won him a gold medal from Edinburgh University, to which he returned as a lecturer in human physiology under Professor I. de Burgh Daly. He was now to work on the physiology of the heart, a lifelong interest. In 1937 he moved back to clinical work, being awarded the Johnstone and Lawrence research fellowship by the Royal Society. This assured his appointment as assistant physician to the Royal Infirmary, Edinburgh.

In 1938, however, Professor Francis Fraser, a remarkable talent scout who was the first director of the department of medicine at the newly established British Postgraduate Medical School at Hammersmith Hospital in London, had the foresight to appoint McMichael as his reader. With the outbreak of war a year later Fraser left to direct the Emergency Medical Service in London so that McMichael became effectively the director of the department. There were major contributions to clinical research at Hammersmith during those war years. Crush injuries and their sequels, suffered by air-raid casualties, were described by Eric Bywaters and his colleagues. McMichael worked closely with Peter Sharpey-Schafer, grandson of the Edinburgh physiologist Sir Edward Sharpey-Schafer, who had been his teacher. Together they introduced cardiac catheterization in Britain for the study of the circulation and the effects of blood loss directly in man, an important topic in times of war. McMichael also introduced percutaneous liver biopsy for the first time in Britain for investigating jaundice, a common problem for the military. He was assisted in this work by a new recruit from Edinburgh, Sheila Sherlock, who thus took her first steps towards a remarkable career in hepatology.

The introduction of these invasive methods of clinical investigation, soon to become routine procedures, required great courage on McMichael's part, for they were not welcomed with enthusiasm in the traditional teaching hospitals in London. In those days, however, before the introduction of ethical committees to supervise research, the clinical investigator made his own judgements and McMichael was not to be deterred.

In 1946 McMichael succeeded Fraser as professor of medicine at Hammersmith. By now, within little more than a decade of the foundation of the Postgraduate Medical School, his department had achieved an international reputation for its outstanding if controversial research, for its encouragement of dissident views in a world of medical conformity and for the challenging nature of its teaching. Through those years, every aspiring clinical research worker from the Commonwealth and beyond came to Hammersmith. McMichael himself continued to work on mechanisms of heart failure and the mode of action of digitalis. In later years, he turned his attention to treating high blood pressure.

McMichael's major achievement, however, was to create a clinical research environment, then unique in Britain, of free discussion and debate in which all, whatever the position they held, might join. It was, however, a freedom that was never allowed to degenerate into licence. He greatly encouraged the young, making the memorable comment at a meeting of the Association of Physicians of Great Britain and Ireland (of which he was then president) that 'we must have the young upon our shoulders, not trample them under our feet'. He was a fearless leader. Never afraid of the unconventional in medicine, he took the unfashionable view that anticoagulants should not be used to treat coronary attacks and in later life was never convinced that cholesterol was important as a cause of heart disease. He was elected FRS in 1957 and knighted in 1965.

Following the death of his second wife, on 1 October 1965 McMichael married Sheila Mary, née Howarth (1920–2000), widow of his former colleague Peter Sharpey-

Schafer. McMichael left Hammersmith in 1966, by which time he had become a towering figure in international cardiology and medicine. He now became director of the Postgraduate Medical Federation, responsible for all the postgraduate medical institutes in London. At the same time he was an influential Wellcome trustee. He had succeeded Sir Henry Dale in 1960 and until his retirement in 1977 he played a major role in ensuring that clinical research would be effectively supported.

McMichael could be ruthless when necessary, but he always retained a Churchillian magnanimity in his dealings with his colleagues. He revealed little of his inner thoughts and emotions to his associates, yet his toughness was tempered with compassion and he always felt that his department and the medical school that he served with such devotion was an extended family. His support for those who had worked with him was legendary. He remained a Scot throughout his life, always faithful to his Scottish origins and upbringing. It was at Gatehouse of Fleet that in 1982 he suffered the stroke that left him hemiplegic, dysphasic, and dyslexic during his last years. He faced with courage and fortitude the afflictions of those years and in all his vicissitudes he retained that twinkle of the eye that was one of his most endearing characteristics. He died at Manor House, Merton, a nursing home near Oxford, on 3 March 1993, and was cremated at Headington, Oxford. The memorial service, held on 18 May 1993 at St Columba's Church of Scotland, Pont Street, London, was attended by numerous family members and representatives from most of London's medical establishments and societies.   CHRISTOPHER C. BOOTH

Sources *The Times* (25 March 1993) · C. Dollery, *Memoirs FRS*, 41 (1995), 283–96 · personal knowledge (2004) · private information (2004) [family] · *CGPLA Eng. & Wales* (1993) · b. cert. · d. cert. **Archives** Wellcome L., corresp. and papers incl. autobiographical notes | SOUND Hammersmith Hospital, London, Library of Imperial College School of Medicine, audio tape **Likenesses** W. O. Hutchison, oils, 1968, unknown collection; copyprint, NPG [*see illus.*] · oils, Hammersmith Hospital, London, board room of Imperial College School of Medicine **Wealth at death** £313,982: probate, 10 Sept 1993, *CGPLA Eng. & Wales*

Macmichael, William (1783–1839), physician and author, was born on 30 November 1783 at Bridgnorth, Shropshire. He was the fourth son of the nine children of William Macmichael (*d.* 1807), a Bridgnorth banker, and his wife, Susannah Dukesil Baker. Both parents came from Dumfries; Macmichael's father suffered financial collapse about 1800. Macmichael attended Bridgnorth grammar school and then, in 1800, on the strength of a scholarship, entered Christ Church, Oxford, where he graduated BA (1805), MA (1807), and MB (1808). From 1808 to 1811 he studied medicine in Edinburgh. He was elected a Radcliffe travelling fellow in 1811, and between 1812 and 1817 he made several journeys in Greece, Russia, Bulgaria, Turkey, and Palestine; these were vividly described in his *Journey from Moscow to Constantinople in the Years 1817, 1818* (1819; 2nd edn, 1820), which was illustrated with engravings taken from his sketches.

Macmichael had undertaken research in chemistry and

mineralogy in Stockholm in 1813–14, but on his return from his travels he took up medical practice, motivated in part by the collapse of his bankers, with whom his property was entrusted. He graduated MD in 1816 and was elected a fellow of the Royal Society in 1817, and of the Royal College of Physicians in 1818. His medical practice in London, where he lived for the rest of his life, was never especially large or prosperous, but he served as physician to the Middlesex Hospital from 1822 to 1831. Through the patronage and friendship of Sir Henry Halford, Macmichael was appointed, in 1829, physician-extraordinary to George IV. In 1830 he was librarian, and in 1831 physician-in-ordinary, to William IV. He held a number of posts at the Royal College of Physicians, including that of censor in 1820 and 1832, and of registrar from 1824 to 1829, and was always loyal to the college. He enjoyed moving in élite circles and was well suited to the literary and social aspects of college life.

Macmichael was the author of four medical pamphlets: *A New View of the Infection of Scarlet Fever* (1822), *A Brief Sketch of the Progress of Opinion on the Subject of Contagion, with some Remarks on Quarantine* (1825), *Is the Cholera Spasmodica of India a Contagious Disease?* (1831; trans. Paris, 1831), and *Some Remarks on Dropsy, with a Narrative of the Last Illness of the Duke of York* (1835). However, his main claim to fame as an author rested on his medical biographies, in particular *The Gold-Headed Cane* (1827; 2nd edn, 1828). The cane of the title has on it the arms of five physicians—John Radcliffe, Richard Mead, Anthony Askew, William Pitcairn, and Matthew Baillie—and had been given to the Royal College of Physicians by Baillie's widow. The cane, anthropomorphically realized by Macmichael, begins its recollections of its owners as it sits in a display cabinet in the college library. The book adopts an elegiac and wistful tone towards its subjects, and retains a certain period charm. Macmichael's classical education and social aspirations are apparent in its urbane and witty style, although his ideals, bred within the cosy oligarchies of the London royal colleges, had little in common with the competitive, overcrowded medical profession of the 1830s, then clamouring to expand college membership. A further edition of the book was published, with additions by William Munk, in 1884. It has continued to be published, with further editions (London, 1919, 1923, 1965; New York, 1915, 1919, 1920, 1922) and a facsimile edition of the 1827 edition (London, 1968). An anonymous poetic epitaph on Macmichael summed up his legacy well:

> Here, ripe in years, in wisdom mellow
> Reposeth one most learned 'Fellow'
> Who drew an intellectual feast
> From musty tomes in Pall-Mall east
> Then wrote a book to prove his knowledge
> And praise the fellows of the College.
> (J. Murch, *Bath Physicians of Former Times*, 1882, 16–17)

In 1830 Macmichael designed and wrote seven of the eighteen *Lives of the British Physicians* (1830; reissued 1846; 2nd edn with additions, 1857), which was a popular book, though lacking the style of its more famous predecessor.

Macmichael married Mary Jane, only daughter of the Revd Thomas Freer, rector of Handsworth, on 15 February 1827 at Handsworth in Staffordshire. They had one daughter, Mary Jane, born in 1829.

Macmichael was genial in nature and prepossessing in appearance; his authorship and character traits marked him as an aspiring literary physician–gentleman. Sir Thomas Watson concluded that he 'was fertile in various and amusing anecdote, and was wont to mix, with a certain natural ease and grace, in lively and interesting discourse', all qualities to be found in *The Gold-Headed Cane* (Munk, *Roll*, 3, 1878, 182–3). Macmichael suffered a stroke in 1837, and retired from practice. He died at his home, 12 Lyon Terrace, Maida Hill, London, on 10 January 1839 and was buried at All Saints' cemetery, Kensal Green.

MARTEN HUTT

Sources Munk, *Roll*, 3.182–3 · T. C. Hunt, 'William Macmichael, MD, FRS: author of *The gold–headed cane*', *Journal of the Royal College of Physicians of London*, 2 (1968), 372–80 · DNB · H. S. Robinson, 'William Macmichael MD: his life, his works and his editors', *Medical Life*, 34 (1927), 468–88 · M. Hutt, 'Medical biography and autobiography in Britain, c.1780–1920', DPhil diss., U. Oxf., 1995, 78–81 · parish register, Baptist chapel, Bridgnorth, Shropshire, PRO, RG/1605 [birth]

Archives RCP Lond., annotated copies of books

Likenesses W. Haines, watercolour, 1823, RCP Lond.; repro. in Hunt, 'William Macmichael', 374

Macmillan family (*per. c.*1840–1986), publishers, began as Scottish farmers and came to prominence when two brothers, **Daniel Macmillan** (1813–1857) and **Alexander Macmillan** (1818–1896), entered the London publishing world in the early 1840s. The original family seat appears to have been Dunmore, in Argyll, where a tongue of land known as North Knapdale belonged to the clan. At the end of the seventeenth or early in the eighteenth century the family migrated to the island of Arran off the western Scottish coast.

Early history About Daniel Macmillan, great-grandfather of Daniel and Alexander Macmillan, little is known other than that he was industrious and staunchly religious. His son, Malcolm, was described as a kindly man, although austere; at some point he moved his family to Cork farm, where they continued for thirty years. He served as an elder in the established church. Of his ten children, the two eldest sons served on board the king's cutter in the preventive service, and a third, Duncan (1770–1823), married Katherine Crawford (1772–1835) and inherited a small farm in Upper Corrie on the island of Arran from his father-in-law. It was here that Daniel Macmillan was born, on 13 September 1813. In or about 1816, however, Duncan Macmillan moved his family, which would eventually consist of twelve children, to Irvine in Ayrshire on the Scottish mainland, and Alexander Macmillan was born here on 3 October 1818. At times Duncan Macmillan kept cattle and cultivated a small portion of land; at others he was a carter, usually carrying coal from the pits to the Irvine harbour. He was kind to children, cared greatly for his family, and was deeply religious.

Although Daniel was but nine and Alexander only four when their father died, they ever after remembered and honoured his memory. Henceforth, they would look to their elder brothers, Malcolm (*d.* 1840) and William (*d.* 1838) for guidance and kindness. It was the boys' mother, however, who was to have the greatest influence over their lives, particularly Daniel's. Although there is no record of her education, she was literate, reading to them from her Bible and teaching them from strong religious principles. She also had a pleasantly musical voice with which she sang native ballads and hymns to her children by the hearthside. Almost forty years after her death Alexander wrote: 'She had a very noble sweet nature and a certain serenity and clearness of mind that I have hardly ever met with in any other human being' (Graves, *Life and Letters of Alexander Macmillan*, 6).

With no education beyond that which four or five years at the village school could provide, along with what he gleaned from Bible reading, Daniel nevertheless set out to make his way in life through the world of books. On 1 January 1824, at the age of ten, he bound himself to Maxwell Dicks, an Irvine bookseller and bookbinder, for a 'wage of 1*s.* 6*d.* per week for the first year, with a rise of 1*s.* a week for each of the remaining six years' (Hughes, 5). His contract was completed successfully on 14 February 1831, with high recommendations from his employer. He next went to Glasgow to work in Mr Atkinson's bookshop, a fine business in the literary heart of the city. This promising career was to be interrupted, however, by the onset of severe illness which left him coughing up blood, and required him to return to Irvine for nursing by his mother. This was the first manifestation of the tuberculosis which would ultimately kill him.

Even before his recovery Daniel was exploring, with his Glasgow friend James MacLehose who had by then moved to London, the possibility of finding a situation for himself in the metropolis. By September 1833 he was well enough to travel, and spent a few days in London where he was unable to find suitable employment. At length he compromised and accepted an offer from a Mr Johnson of Cambridge to work in his shop at an annual salary of £30. Daniel would be able to board with the Johnsons and attend Baptist church services with the family. Here he remained for the next three years, his salary inching up to £35 in the third, while he mastered the business, made valuable contacts among Cambridge dons, and lost no opportunity to read widely as he pursued a programme of self-education. Still he longed to make the leap to London. In the absence of an offer he took ship to Scotland but on the voyage, through exposure to the cold, he became seriously ill. He stopped in Edinburgh, where the mother of his friend George Wilson nursed him in her home. Finally, through the intervention of MacLehose, he received an offer to work at Messrs Seeley in Fleet Street at £60 per year.

Meanwhile his younger brother Alexander was floundering. It is a confusing time in his history and solid facts are few. He taught at various country schools in the Irvine neighbourhood, including a three-month stint where he filled in for the headmaster at Scott's School, at the age of fifteen or sixteen. Later he worked as assistant to George Gallio, a bookseller in Glasgow, but left, disgusted at his employer's disapproval of novel-reading. For a while he worked for a Mr Atkinson in Glasgow. At one point he considered entering either the medical or the nautical profession. In 1836 disillusionment and despair caused him to become a sailor and ship to America, at the end of which time he landed back in Glasgow, penniless. Finally, owing to Daniel's success at Seeleys, the firm agreed to extend an offer to Alexander, also at £60; he arrived to take up his duties on 3 October 1839, his twenty-first birthday. Henceforth the brothers' partnership in the book business remained unbroken until Daniel's death in 1857.

Daniel and Alexander: getting started Both Macmillan brothers were now well positioned in London. They were hard workers, and gave satisfaction to their employers, but were also ambitious and looking for new opportunity. Realizing that their lack of formal education was a handicap, they seized every spare moment to read widely, in the classics and among such authors as P. B. Shelley, Thomas Carlyle, and Alexander Scott. Scott brought Daniel into correspondence with Julius Charles Hare, archdeacon of Lewes, and this resulted in a friendship which would later prove most useful. Hare introduced Daniel to F. D. Maurice, the Christian socialist, who became one of the Macmillans' closest associates.

By the autumn and winter of 1842 the Macmillan brothers began to think of establishing their own bookshop, together with a small publishing house. In February 1843 they occupied space at 57 Aldersgate Street and their first two titles were published later the same year: *The Philosophy of Training* by A. R. Craig, and *The Three Questions: What Am I? Whence Came I? And Whither do I Go?* by William Haig Miller, the latter published for the Religious Tract Society. The first work dealt with training for teachers of the middle class, while the latter took a hopeful view of mankind's destiny. These early books established trends in Macmillan publishing philosophy which would influence their lists far into the future: sincere interest in education and profound religious belief.

Once established, the Macmillans moved swiftly. With the help of a loan of £500 from Archdeacon Hare, the brothers purchased, also in 1843, the bookshop of a Mr Newby at 17 Trinity Street, Cambridge; the plan was for Daniel to preside over the Cambridge shop while Alexander remained in London. In the end this was not feasible and by late in the year both brothers settled in Cambridge. By 1845 the opportunity arose to purchase, from Thomas Stevenson, a larger shop, in a better location, which was prestigious for having been established in the eighteenth century. To do so they had to take the distasteful step of acquiring a partner, a Mr Barclay, a wholesale druggist, who invested £6000, despite knowing nothing about either the book or the publishing business. Temporarily the firm became Macmillan, Barclay, and Macmillan, but later, when they retired the debt, it quickly reverted to Macmillan & Co.

Early years During the years 1845–57 the Macmillan brothers laid the foundation for the future of the company. Their list addressed serious subjects, such as education, Christianity, and classical literature, but was also early in recognizing growing public interest in science and mathematics. Because of their location in a university town they published syllabuses for Cambridge courses, educational guides and companions, and handbooks for student use such as *A Short and Easy Course of Algebra* (1850), *Arithmetic: Rules and Reasons* (1850) by J. H. Boardman, and *Arithmetic Examples* (1851). In fact, by 1852, of the 131 titles so far published by Macmillan, seventy-five, or three-fifths, concerned either Cambridge scholarship or Cambridge classes. Libraries in the various Cambridge colleges offered opportunities for publishing bibliographies and lists of manuscript collections. Contemporary events, such as the death of the duke of Wellington, prompted publication of numerous sermons and sonnets reflecting on his great service to the nation. During this time of conservative growth, and despite a severely limited list, Macmillan was very early in finding places for two books by women: *Hours of Reflection* (1845) by Ellen Taylor Hudson and *Sketches of Character* (1849) by Anna T. Potts. The young firm also took considerable risk in publishing such periodicals as the *Cambridge Mathematical Journal* (1846); the *Journal of Classical and Sacred Philology* (1854); and *Academia: an Occasional Journal* (1858). These were not successful ventures, largely because the firm had not enough capital to sustain the journals until they achieved sufficient circulation to pay for themselves.

Because the Macmillans had a clear understanding of the importance of the personal element in publishing, they saw to it that 1 Trinity Street was a place for easy and convivial exchange of ideas. They cultivated acquaintance with both university dons and townspeople, and welcomed bright young students, all of whom were free to meet for conversation in an upper common room reserved for that purpose. They also began a practice, which continued through the years, of offering generous terms to their authors. Three maxims—interest in education, belief in religion, and generosity in business— became the bedrock of the Macmillan family company.

By 1850, with business prospering, the Macmillan brothers contemplated marriage. Frances Eliza Orridge (1821–1867), the daughter of a chemist who was also a Cambridge magistrate, became Daniel's wife on 4 September 1850, and Alexander married Caroline Brimley (d. 1871), eldest sister of his friend George Brimley, librarian of Trinity College, on 15 August 1851. The first Macmillan union produced four children: Frederick Orridge Macmillan [*see below*], Maurice Crawford (1853–1936), Katherine (b. 1855), and Arthur (1857–1876). Alexander and his wife had five children: Malcolm Kingsley (1852–1889), George Augustin (1855–1936), Margaret (b. 1857), Olive (b. 1859), and William Alexander (1864–1966).

In F. D. Maurice, whom Alexander referred to as their prophet, the Macmillans found their first truly prolific author. Maurice, professor of English literature and modern history at King's College, London, chaplain of Guy's Hospital, London, and author of the influential *Kingdom of Christ* (1838), was a well-known figure in academic circles. He appeared on Macmillan's list initially in 1844 with an introduction to a reprint edition of Mandeville's *Fable of the Bees* (1714). He wrote three items each in 1853 and 1854 and fifteen publications in 1855. These were largely either collections of sermons or long open letters on topics of current importance. While the Macmillans had no intention of allowing their list to become top-heavy with one author or one subject, they also knew that Maurice was an influential figure in Cambridge who might well serve as a magnet to draw other scholars to the young firm. This he certainly did, but perhaps his greatest contribution was to introduce his publishers to Charles Kingsley, rector of Eversley, in Hampshire, and a former pupil of Maurice.

Using the pseudonym Parson Lot, Kingsley was first published by Macmillan in 1850 in a pamphlet, *Cheap Clothes and Nasty*, in which he attacked the shocking working conditions in the London tailors' trade. *Phaeton, or, Loose Thoughts for Loose Thinkers* (1852) was next to appear, followed by his lectures *Alexandria and her Schools* (1854), originally delivered to the Philosophical Institution of Edinburgh. His fascination with marine biology led to the very successful *Glaucus, or, Wonders of the Shore* (1855) which was reprinted ten times by 1887. Kingsley brought excellent profits from his work but he was also responsible for a major shift in publishing policy when the firm brought out his *Westward Ho!* (1855), Macmillan's first venture into fiction. That Daniel was cognizant of the influence of Mudie's circulating library in determining the success of novels is shown by his assurance to Kingsley that Mudie would advertise *Westward Ho!* in both London and Manchester newspapers to ensure that other libraries would buy it. An Elizabethan romance, it introduced the notion of 'muscular Christianity' and was intended as a spur to Victorian society to fight the evils in its midst. That it coincided with Victorian dismay and disenchantment over conduct of the Crimean War only added to its message and it became a best-seller. As a three-decker, it had an initial print-run of 2000 (500 more than usual); the 6s. edition sold 50,000 copies by 1880; and the 6d. edition of 1889 sold 500,000 copies. *The Water-Babies* (1863) was equally popular and earned huge profits for the firm.

The Macmillans were fortunate to find another popular novelist, Thomas Hughes, also a good friend, to continue the novel tradition. Hughes proposed a book based on a schoolboy's exploits at Rugby when Thomas Arnold was headmaster. *Tom Brown's School Days* (1857), first published anonymously, sold 11,000 copies (at a time when the usual first printing was 1500) before the year's end, with a sixth edition appearing in 1858. The new policy of publishing fiction proved enormously profitable for both the Macmillans and their authors.

Daniel's death: Alexander's new responsibilities Daniel and Alexander complemented one another smoothly as a team. The older brother was restless, always seeking new opportunities, pushing for excellence. While Alexander was not lacking in these qualities, he was more stolid, very intuitive about the business, and congenial in society.

Unfortunately, all through the 1840s and 1850s Daniel suffered recurring health problems. It was in 1841 that consumptive symptoms first overtook him, and early in 1844, shortly after he moved to Cambridge to supervise the business, he suffered a violent haemorrhage and was forced to spend time recuperating. Because the brothers worked unusually long hours at the shop, and sometimes denied themselves even modest comforts, Daniel's health broke down time after time, forcing him to go to Torquay for sea air and rest. During his wedding journey in 1850 he suffered from the cold in Scotland and spent the final two weeks in Torquay resting and fighting his disease. There was a spell in 1855 that was particularly worrisome and left him a semi-invalid the rest of his life.

As Daniel's health weakened, more and more responsibility for building the Macmillan business fell on Alexander's shoulders. Their letters show that the younger brother was always careful to consult Daniel, but inevitably some decisions could not wait and the burdens and worries were borne by Alexander alone. Daniel's letters show his patience under suffering, but also his frustration that he could no longer be active in the business. On 7 May 1857 an attack of pleurisy added to his problems, and soon a throat ulcer left him unable either to eat or to drink. At length the blow fell, and Daniel died at his Cambridge home on 26 June 1857, after terrible suffering; he was buried in the Mill Road cemetery, Cambridge, on 1 July. His last child, Arthur, was not yet two months old. As Alexander contemplated the future, he saw clearly that it belonged to him for the present, but ultimately to the next generation, to Daniel's and his own sons, and from that moment he began to prepare.

Alexander's first thought was for Daniel's family, which he now took under his own roof, raising Daniel's children as his own. He was very compatible with his sister-in-law, Mrs Daniel, as he called her; she became valuable to him in business matters and he came to trust her judgement implicitly. Next he set about establishing a London branch of the company, a move Daniel had contemplated as early as 1852 but had been unable to accomplish. A nephew, Robert Bowes, was placed in charge of the premises at 23 Henrietta Street, Covent Garden. With a new London headquarters, Alexander began his practice of coming to town on Thursdays to host an informal gathering of authors and friends, which came to be known as his 'Tobacco Parliaments'. Men of such diverse tastes and talents as Alfred Tennyson, Herbert Spencer, T. H. Huxley, Francis Turner Palgrave, Coventry Patmore, F. D. Maurice, Charles Kingsley, and Thomas Hughes gathered for a light supper, followed by tobacco and spirits, to engage the topics of the day in this leisurely setting.

The imprint for Macmillan changed with the new location. 'Macmillan & Co.' now became either 'Cambridge: Macmillan & Co.', or 'Cambridge: Macmillan & Co. and 23 Henrietta Street, Covent Garden, London'. Changes also occurred in the Macmillan list, reflecting both shifts in contemporary taste and the more metropolitan location. While books on education, religion, mathematics, sermons, and university affairs were never discontinued, new material was explored. David Masson's two works *Sketch of the British Novelists* (1859) and *The Life of John Milton* (1859) were the first examples of literary criticism, of which more would follow. James Clerk Maxwell's *Essay on the Stability of the Motion of Saturn's Rings* (1859) reflected the general public's growing interest in astronomy. Macmillan's first woman novelist appeared, Margaret Oliphant, writing *Agnes Hopetoun's Schools and Holidays: the Experiences of a Little Girl* (1859), as did an anonymous *Out of the Depths: the Story of a Woman's Life* (1859).

Macmillan's Magazine A good deal of talk at the Tobacco Parliaments was given over to the possibility of Macmillan joining the trend of the 1850s among publishing houses and establishing a shilling magazine of its own. During the course of 1859 Alexander Macmillan, after careful consideration, decided to proceed, and the first issue of *Macmillan's Magazine* appeared on 1 November 1859, with a celebratory dinner that evening at Henrietta Street. David Masson was the first editor and the following men contributed articles for the first number: Masson, Hughes, George Wilson, F. G. Stephens, Franklin Lushington, and J. M. Ludlow.

During the planning phase Alexander Macmillan's old friend Ludlow had argued forcefully that a publishing house with a journal, which could publish novels first serially and later in volume form, would vastly increase the profits to both author and publisher. Although acceptance as a serial did not automatically guarantee publication in book form, Macmillan did go on to publish many of his serials, such as Hughes's *Tom Brown at Oxford* (November 1859 – July 1861); Charles Kingsley's *The Water-Babies* (August 1862 – March 1863); Oliphant's *A Son of the Soil* (November 1863 – April 1865); Charlotte Mary Yonge's *The Dove in the Eagle's Nest* (May 1865 – December 1865); Anthony Trollope's *Sir Harry Hotspur of Humblethwaite* (May 1870 – December 1870); William Black's *Strange Adventures of a Phaeton* (January 1872 – November 1872); Annie Keary's *Castle Daly* (February 1874 – July 1875); Henry James's *The Portrait of a Lady* (October 1880 – November 1881); and Thomas Hardy's *The Woodlanders* (May 1886 – February 1887). Royalties for serials were determined by the editor, while royalties for books were negotiated individually, determined to some degree by the previous popularity of the serial.

During its early years, 1859–1874, *Macmillan's* was notable for the opportunities it offered to women journalists. In its first fifteen years sixty-three women made contributions, including 11 serials, 61 pieces of poetry, and 120 prose articles. Christina Rossetti was a steady contributor, as were Frances Power Cobbe, Dinah Maria Craik, the Hon. Mrs Caroline Norton, Lady (Lucie) Duff-Gordon, Millicent Garrett Fawcett, and Octavia Hill. Even more importantly, the women wrote, not on fashion or cookery, but on substantial matters of the day, such as evolution, the death of Prince Albert, the American Civil War, justice for downtrodden Egyptians, education for women, and the Franco-Prussian War. Almost without exception the women boldly signed their names, contrary to contemporary custom.

Alexander at mid-life The years 1860 to 1872 were ones of enormous accomplishment for Alexander Macmillan, as he inaugurated one new publishing series after another, began new ventures, and moved the firm's headquarters from Cambridge to 16 Bedford Street, London. In doing so, he displayed a talent for innovation, although always tempered by a cautious business sense, and he built Macmillan into one of London's leading publishing houses.

Alexander Macmillan's interests were wide and varied. First and foremost, of course, was his responsibility for managing the business and overseeing its list of publications. His interest in things American led to his strong support for the North during the civil war. He worried about the problems of international copyright. When the publisher John W. Parker failed, he arranged to secure for Macmillan the already published early works of Kingsley, Maurice, Archbishop Trench, and C. M. Yonge. After moving the headquarters to London he took a spacious home in Upper Tooting, suitable for the two families under one roof, and named it Knapdale after the ancestral property. Here he was free to offer expansive hospitality, in the Macmillan tradition, to friends and authors. In 1863 Macmillan undertook some special projects for Oxford University, an appointment which continued until 1880, at which time he was awarded an honorary MA degree out of gratitude for his services.

One of Alexander Macmillan's foremost new ventures began with F. T. Palgrave's *Golden Treasury of the Best Songs and Lyrical Poems in the English Language* (1861), where the author brought together a selection of what he considered the best songs and poems. This technique served to encourage the growth of a new genre, the anthology. It is possible to argue with Palgrave's judgement; he rejected the poetry of John Donne, William Blake, and Emily Brontë, and made only limited selections from the work of Coleridge, Henry Vaughan, Richard Crashaw, and George Herbert. But one cannot argue with the fact that this approach became enormously popular with the British public. Showing its chief's usual caution, Macmillan initially ordered a printing of only 2000 copies. Popular demand, however, was such that by 1888 there had been twenty-three new editions and reprints.

Sensing that this was an important new approach, Alexander Macmillan at once set out to commission new works in what became the Golden Treasury series. Some of the more popular selections, out of the many titles which eventually comprised the series, included Roundell Palmer's *Book of Praise* (1862); William Allingham's *Ballad Book* (1864); and C. M. Yonge's *Book of Golden Deeds of All Time* (1864), *Book of Thoughts* (1865), and *Book of Worthies Gathered from Old Histories* (1869). Some enduring volumes in the series were Patmore's *Children's Garland* (1862), M. C. Aitken's *Scottish Song* (1874), Matthew Arnold's selections from William Wordsworth (1879) and Lord Byron (1881), and T. H. Ward's *The English Poets* (1880). Other books by Palgrave included *Songs and Sonnets by William Shakespeare* (1865), *Essays on Art* (1866), *Hymns* (1867), *Lyrical Poems* (1871), and

Chrysomela (1877), a selection from the lyrics of Robert Herrick. (The last volume in this series was not published until 1961.)

A new venture, begun in 1864, was the *Statesman's Year Book*, first edited by Frederick Martin; it was a fresh concept which provided a 'statistical, genealogical, and historic account of the states and sovereigns of the civilized world' (VanArsdel, 183). It proved to be an invaluable political and diplomatic tool, which was still in publication at the end of the twentieth century.

In the mid-1860s, with business complexities mounting, Alexander Macmillan felt keenly the need for additional help he could rely on. His first step was to appoint a partner to the firm, whose job would be to supervise the day-to-day operations. For this post, after consulting with MacLehose, he chose a fellow Scotsman, George Lillie Craik, who came to work in 1865 and stayed, a valued and trusted employee, until he died in 1905. Next Macmillan drew about him a group of several men whose judgement he could trust to serve as advisers, people with whom he could consult on difficult questions. These included John Morley, George Grove, and Norman Lockyer. Nor was he idle himself. Among works he initiated or supported were Alexander Gilchrist's biography of the then-neglected poet William Blake (1863); William Allingham's *The Ballad Book* (1864); and the very popular *Jest Book* (1864) by Mark Lemon, featuring a collection of anecdotes and sayings. There was a selection of poetry suitable for children to read on Sundays by Mrs C. F. Alexander, *The Sunday Book of Poetry* (1864); and Alexander Smith's edition of Robert Burns (1865). In addition Macmillan began commissioning textbooks on botany, chemistry, and geology for children in elementary schools, in keeping with the firm's original commitment to education.

An important series of books for children and young adults began appearing in the 1860s, beginning with Georgina M. Craik's *My First Journal: a Book for the Young* and Dinah Maria Craik's *Our Year: a Child's Book in Prose and Verse* (both 1860). Westland Marston's novel *A Lady in her Own Right* (1860) was followed by more novels in 1861: May Beverley's *The Moor Cottage*; Oliver Wendell Holmes's *Elsie Venner*; and Hughes's *Tom Brown at Oxford*. In 1862 there were Arthur Hugh Clough's *Poems with a Memoir*, Christina Rossetti's *Goblin Market and other Poems*, and Caroline Norton's *The Lady of La Garaye*. J. E. Cairnes's *The Slave Power* (1863) attempted to analyse the issues behind the American Civil War. The first Macmillan book by Matthew Arnold appeared in 1864, *A French Eton*, followed by *Essays in Criticism* in 1865. Also in 1865, Lewis Carroll's *Alice's Adventures in Wonderland* was published, at 7s. 6d., complete with forty-two illustrations by John Tenniel: second, third, fourth, and fifth editions followed each year for the next four years. *Through the Looking-Glass and What Alice Found There* appeared in 1872, with fifty Tenniel illustrations, and was reprinted twelve times up to 1887. Carroll was a difficult author to deal with, being unusually fussy about textual matters, but Alexander Macmillan treated him with much understanding. He went to great lengths, repeatedly, to do Carroll personal favours, even procuring special pantomime tickets for the author's young relative. But the publisher's forbearance paid off, for Carroll had a long association with Macmillan, and gave the firm, among many works, such future successes as *The Hunting of the Snark* (1872), and *Alice's Adventures Underground* (1886).

Alexander Macmillan also proposed, in 1865, a series to be called the Sunday Library for Household Reading which would consist of children's books published in monthly parts. As editors he suggested two Macmillan readers for educational and devotional books, C. M. Yonge and Frances Martin. The first to appear were Yonge's *Pupils of St. John the Divine* (1868); George Macdonald's *Pioneers and Founders: England's Antiphon* (1868); and Annie Keary's *Nations Around* (1870). Other titles were by Kingsley, Hughes, Archdeacon Frederic William Farrar, and Mrs Oliphant.

The year 1867 marked a new enterprise for the company: after a visit to the United States, Alexander decided that a New York branch would be feasible. He sent George Brett to open it in 1869, who was so successful that two years later Frederick Macmillan, Daniel's eldest son, was sent to receive training there.

Alexander continued to be interested in the work of women, as first demonstrated in the 1840s, and was fortunate to secure the early work of a number who would later be prominent in the struggle for women's rights. Some of these works were Sophia Jex-Blake's *Some American Schools and Colleges* (1867); Josephine Butler's *The Education and Employment of Women* (1868); Harriet Martineau's *Biographical Sketches* (1869) and *A Letter to the Deaf* (1869); *Woman's Work and Woman's Culture* (1869) edited by Butler; and Millicent Garrett Fawcett's *Political Economy for Beginners* (1870). Although Lady (Mary Anne) Barker was not a women's rights activist she nevertheless produced an unexpected success in her *Station Life in New Zealand*, which went through four editions between 1870 and 1883, and was reprinted in 1887.

One of the jewels in the firm's crown, and a truly original project for its time, was due entirely to Alexander Macmillan's far-sighted vision. An uncommonly fine edition of *The Works of William Shakespeare* was being produced, under the general editorship of W. G. Clark, the public orator of Cambridge, and John Glover, the librarian of Trinity. Using, among other sources, the Capell collection of quartos housed in the library of Trinity College, eventually the project would grow to nine volumes, but when the first one appeared in 1863 it sparked Alexander Macmillan's thinking. Although the original edition, known as *The Cambridge Shakespeare*, was designed primarily for Shakespearian students and scholars, and unusual care had been taken with the textual editing, Macmillan saw it another way, as well. Why not a popular edition, using the same text, but priced for the general consumer? Thus was born the *Globe Shakespeare* (1864). The publisher described it as 'immeasurably the cheapest, most beautiful and handy book that has appeared of *any kind, except the* Bible' (Graves, *Life and Letters of Alexander Macmillan*, 223), and ordered a first printing of 50,000 copies priced at 3s.

6d. As with the Golden Treasury books, success of the first volume inspired another series produced similarly and sold cheaply for the general reading public. The format of large print and special size, the Globe octavo, and the popular price were retained to produce volumes on Robert Burns (1868), Oliver Goldsmith (1869), Alexander Pope (1869), Edmund Spenser (1869), William Cowper (1870), John Dryden (1870), Virgil (1871), Horace (1873), and Milton (1877).

Macmillan journals Although Macmillan & Co. had no success with its first journals, in 1869, on the strong recommendation of Norman Lockyer, a respected astronomer and spectroscopist, the firm founded *Nature*, a weekly scientific paper designed to appeal to the general public as well as to offer a means for scientists to communicate with one another. It captured an audience because of growing interest in science among the lay population and also because it had the backing of such prominent Victorian scientists as Thomas Huxley, Charles Darwin, John Tyndale, and Henry Enfield Roscoe. Lockyer, the first editor, remained at his post for a remarkable fifty years (until 1919) and succeeded in building a journal respected worldwide. Other journals founded by Macmillan in the nineteenth century included: the *Journal of Physiology* (1878); *Brain* (1878); and the *Economic Journal* (1891). A nonscientific journal, the *English Illustrated Magazine* (1883), coincided with the growing trend towards magazine illustration and was sustained by such leading illustrators as Hugh Thomson, A. D. McCormick, Herbert Railton, Joseph Pennell, and Walter Crane. Some of its contributors also published their work in *Macmillan's Magazine*, including Henry James, Robert Louis Stevenson, and Rudyard Kipling, while others, such as George Meredith and Algernon Swinburne, contributed only to the illustrated publication. The first editor of the *English Illustrated Magazine* was Joseph William Comyns Carr, who was succeeded by Sir Clement Kinloch-Cooke; after ten years of dwindling circulation ownership was transferred to another publisher and it continued until 1913.

Publishing events of the 1870s Although the business continued as varied and as briskly as ever, three particular publishing events distinguished the 1870s for Macmillan & Co.: J. R. Green's history; the English Men of Letters series; and the Grove dictionary of music.

In 1874 Green's *Short History of the English People* appeared in one volume of 847 pages, and brought an entirely new philosophy to the recording of history. Green had originally contacted Alexander Macmillan five years earlier about this project and the publisher had offered much encouragement. Originally intended as a school manual or handbook, it focused on the social, economic, and intellectual aspects of history, eschewing accounts of atrocity, war, and conquest. Green's aim was to chart the growth of a society, using a broad approach and simple style, and the book became instantly, enormously, and unexpectedly popular, going on to achieve a remarkable publishing history. The British people were fascinated and the book sold 35,000 copies in eighteen months. It was reprinted with corrections fifteen times in the next twelve years. A second edition was called for in 1887, also reprinted several times, and another version appeared in parts in 1889, with analysis by C. W. A. Tait. Meanwhile Green prepared another, expanded, version, which appeared in four volumes between 1877 and 1880. Alexander Macmillan, always generous with his authors, rewrote Green's contract after he realized how successful the book would be. Originally, the firm had offered him £350 outright, with another £100 after the sale of 2000 copies; later they substituted a royalty arrangement which was much more profitable for the author. In a sense his history made both a fortune and a career for Green, who had been only marginally successful; he had large profits and Macmillan chose him to edit two new series, Literary Primers and Historical Primers, which ran to seven and eleven titles respectively.

John Morley, then editor of the *Fortnightly Review* and a rising London man of letters, approached Alexander Macmillan in 1877 with a scheme for a new series, to which he originally gave the title Short Books on Great Writers. Macmillan knew Morley well; he had befriended him ten years earlier, when as a young Oxford man he was making his way in the city, by publishing an early work, *Edmund Burke* (1867). Morley now had wide contacts among fellow literary men and for some time past had been lining up possible authors for the subjects he proposed. Writing to his son, Malcolm Macmillan, Alexander reported: 'He has got [R. H.] Hutton for Sir Walter Scott, Goldwin Smith for Wordsworth [in actuality the work was done by F. W. H. Myers], Symonds for Shelley, Pattison for Milton, Leslie Stephen for Johnson, Morrison for Gibbon'. He also told Malcolm: 'The idea is a sort of essay—biographical and critical … about twice as long as a *Quarterly* article, and in a little volume to sell at half-a-crown' (Graves, *Life and Letters of Alexander Macmillan*, 342).

The title finally settled on was English Men of Letters and it became one of the most distinguished and influential series Macmillan & Co. would ever publish. To begin, scholars of the first rank were selected to do the work, which gave the books authority, and made them suitable either for the general reader or as a point of departure for specialists. It was an idea whose time had come, in an era when the standard three-volume testamentary lives underwritten by grieving families did not provide really reliable information about their subjects. In more recent years scholars have worked to produce new, 'definitive' portraits, but for their time the English Men of Letters studies were reliable, well produced, and for nearly fifty years set the standard for critical and biographical texts.

In 1878 five volumes began the series: *Gibbon* by James Cotter Morison; *Goldsmith* by William Black; *Johnson* by Leslie Stephen; *Scott* by Richard H. Hutton; and *Shelley* by John Addington Symonds. Nine volumes followed in 1879, among them *Milton* by Mark Pattison and *Thackeray* by Anthony Trollope. Eight further volumes appeared between 1880 and the end of 1881; seven more were published in 1882, including Edmund Gosse's *Gray*, and Alfred Ainger's *Lamb*. Nine additional volumes were to be printed, at irregular intervals up to 1892, at which time the series was complete.

The third significant venture of the 1870s for Macmillan & Co. was George Grove's *Dictionary of Music and Musicians* published in four volumes (1877, 1880, 1883, and 1889), a major English reference work. Grove had had a varied life, beginning his career as a civil engineer, a post which took him to the West Indies. He was also a biblical scholar as well as a first-class music historian. He served as editor of *Macmillan's Magazine* from 1868 to 1883, leaving when he became director of the Royal School of Music in 1883, the year in which he also received his knighthood. His dictionary was not the first attempt at musical compilation in the language, but was by far the most comprehensive and was another set of Macmillan volumes to have a distinguished publishing history. Although there are no sales records of the first edition of Grove because it was originally envisaged as a part-work (the first volume was issued in parts), there was a second edition in five volumes (1904–10), edited by J. A. Fuller Maitland, which sold 7000 sets. A third edition edited by H. C. Colles appeared in 1927; Colles also supervised the 1940 fourth edition, which added a supplement to the revised five-volume set. By 1980 a sixth edition, edited by Stanley Sadie and entitled *The New Grove Dictionary of Music and Musicians*, ran to twenty volumes. The enduring popularity of this reference work reflected a steadily growing interest on the part of the public in musical scholarship and history which had its origins squarely in late Victorian England.

The interesting point which links the three foregoing projects is the tremendous impact which each had on the public and its perception of Macmillan & Co. Both generalist and specialist readers as well as scholars showed their confidence by purchasing record numbers of copies; if it had not been before, Macmillan was certainly now a dominant London publishing house. The projects succeeded because of the strong faith Alexander Macmillan had in each. Two readers for the firm expressed decidedly adverse opinions about the Green history, but Alexander's faith never wavered and was in the end fully justified. There were similar reservations among some about committing so much of the company's financial resources to the English Men of Letters series, which proved to be long-term substantial sellers. Again, the Grove project involved a large financial risk with no indication of the possible market for such an ambitious reference work. However, it initiated a work, *Grove's Musical Dictionary*, which was visionary for its time, yet went on to be a world leader in its field throughout the twentieth century. In each case, Alexander's intuition about public response succeeded in guiding Macmillan along the course of prudent finance and innovative publishing.

Second-generation Macmillans Despite the many successes, Alexander Macmillan's life was now undergoing many changes. In 1871 his wife, Caroline, died after an extended illness, during which her husband was unfailingly attentive. On 24 October 1872, he married a family friend, (Jeanne Barbe) Emma Pignatel, with whom he had two additional children, Mary (*b.* 1874) and John Victor (1877–1956). Although Alexander Macmillan certainly remained active in the business, he was beginning to plan ahead for the eventual succession of Daniel's and his own sons. Daniel's eldest, **Sir Frederick Orridge Macmillan** (1851–1936), was born at 29 Regent Street, Cambridge, on 5 October 1851, and had been educated at Uppingham School under Edward Thring, the well-known headmaster, and had then chosen to learn the retail bookselling business under his cousin Robert Bowes, at Cambridge, where he also studied printing technologies. In 1871 he was dispatched to the New York branch, where he remained for five years. On 15 April 1874 he took an American bride, Georgiana Elizabeth Warrin (1846–1943), daughter of Thomas Warrin of New Town, Long Island. The couple had no children. By 1876 he returned to London and entered the business as a partner.

Alexander Macmillan's eldest son, Malcolm Kingsley (1852–1889), was talented in literature and the arts, but seemingly had no head for business. He attended Marlborough College briefly, then King's College School, and after a gap entered Balliol College, Oxford, where it was said he made many valuable contacts; but he was destined for a tragic end. In July 1889, while hiking with a friend on Mount Olympus, he disappeared mysteriously and was never heard of again. A full investigation was conducted, but no body was ever found. It was a terrible blow to his father, who bore up bravely, but never really recovered from the shock.

Maurice Crawford (1853–1936), Daniel Macmillan's second son, attended Uppingham School, where he won a scholarship in 1867, and graduated from Christ's College, Cambridge, taking a first in the classical tripos, 1875. He was classics master at St Paul's School, 1875–83, during which time he published the first 'Macmillan family' book, *First Latin Grammar* (1879) which by 1886 had been reprinted three times. At the end of 1883 he entered the family firm. On 24 November 1884 he also took an American bride, Helen Artie Tarleton Hill (1856–1937) (a widow), daughter of Joshua Tarleton Belles MD of Spencer, Indiana, and they had three sons. The couple toured extensively in Australia and India (1884–5), when Maurice first began to sense the importance of a broader overseas base, an opportunity for expansion that would be so important to the second Macmillan generation. His lifelong special interests were scholarship, the classics, the British empire, and the Far East.

George Augustin (1855–1936), Alexander Macmillan's second son, was educated at Eton College, as a king's scholar, 1868, and entered the firm in 1874. In July 1879 he married Margaret Helen Lucas and they had one son and one daughter. He became chairman of Stainer and Bell, music publishers, where he served for many years; he was a founder and honorary secretary of the Hellenic Society (1879–1919), and honorary treasurer until 1934. He also served as the honorary secretary of the British School at Athens (1886–97). Because of his wide contacts many important books came to Macmillan in archaeology, classical art, history, and literature. The firm began publishing the *Journal of Hellenic Studies* (1880) because of his influence, but perhaps his greatest achievement was bringing in Arthur Evans's *The Palace of Minos at Knossos* (1922–35), the fascinating account of his excavations on the island of Crete.

By the mid-1880s, after working together for more than a decade, the Macmillan cousins had developed into a smoothly efficient team. Frederick supervised general business matters, fiction, poetry, art, and American ties. Maurice presided over India, education, the classics, and foreign expansion. George was in charge of Greek literature, archaeology, and music. Mention must also be made of William Jack, who served, during the 1870s, as a partner and adviser on mathematics until he left in 1879 to accept the chair in mathematics at the University of Glasgow. The boundaries of responsibility were fluid, however, and each of the cousins might develop and supervise any title in which he became interested. They established a working relationship that was as flawless and as understanding as the original partnership between Daniel and Alexander.

With new and younger men now directing the company, publishing trends were certain to change. There were new titles on a wide range of fresh subjects: Pater's *Studies in the Renaissance* (1874); Lady Barker's *First Lessons in the Principles of Cooking* (1874); in the same year, R. Jardin's *Elements of Psychology*; and Rhoda and Agnes Garrett's *Suggestions for House Decoration* (1876). Practical business concerns dictated, after passage of the 1870 Education Act, that texts, readers, and primers should proliferate. The younger Macmillans were not slow to recognize this new market, in the same way their forebears had profited from the Cambridge connection.

Accordingly, books appeared on a wide range of topics including algebra, anatomy and physiology, arithmetic, astronomy, calculus, chemistry, and classics. G. Eugene Fasnacht prepared no fewer than seventeen texts on teaching and learning the French and German languages; and he edited ten volumes of literary classics in those languages, together with biographical notes, historical introduction, glossary, and scholarly notes for each volume. Charles Colbeck edited a series, Foreign School Classics, in twenty-one volumes, as well as geology and geography primers and sketches. Several other important professional textbooks were added to the list: Henry Sidgwick's *Principles of Political Economy* (1883); James Fitzjames Stephen's *A Digest of the Criminal Law: Crimes and Punishments* (1883–87); and *A Text-Book of Pathological Anatomy and Pathogenesis* by Ernst Ziegler and Donald MacAlister (1883–7).

New names began to appear on the list, for which the Macmillan cousins shared the responsibility. Louis Pasteur published *Studies in Fermentation* with Macmillan in 1879. Joseph Henry Shorthouse came to the firm upon the recommendation of Mrs Humphry Ward. His *John Inglesant* (1881), a historical novel set in the English civil war, had first been published privately by the author, but now became a surprise best-seller for Macmillan, with six editions by February 1883, including one in the Globe series in two volumes. George Saintsbury, eventually to be one of the period's best-known literary critics, first became acquainted with Macmillan as a contributor to *The English Poets* (1880), edited by T. H. Ward, and remained because of his admiration for Frederick. They published his *Dryden* (1881), reprinted in the English Men of Letters series, and his influential study *History of Elizabethan Literature* (1887). An American expatriate, F. Marion Crawford, although difficult to deal with in royalty matters, nevertheless between 1882 and 1909 published all but three of his forty novels with Macmillan, including *Zoroaster* (1885), *A Tale of a Lonely Parish* (1886), *Sant' Ilario* (1889), and *Don Orsino* (1892).

From earliest days Alexander Macmillan and Alfred Tennyson had known and respected each other. Macmillan and David Masson visited the poet and his wife for three days in October 1859, at their home on the Isle of Wight. Despite their friendship the poet had been elusive about joining the Macmillan family of authors. Instead, he rotated among such houses as H. S. King, Alexander Strahan, and Kegan Paul, on short, five-year contracts. Finally, in 1884, as both men were nearing the end of their careers, Tennyson came to Macmillan but at the cost of a hard bargain. He insisted on a guarantee of £4000 plus any additional royalties earned beyond that, but the two old friends were together at last.

Macmillan's Colonial Library was inaugurated in 1886, under the direction of Maurice Macmillan, who had long envisioned this type of expansion for the firm. It was a natural augmentation of his father's 1875 scheme of a Text-Books for Indian Schools series. The idea was developed as an attempt to satisfy the reading needs of India and the other colonies, and also to make use of the copyrights of standard works and popular fiction which Macmillan already owned or others which they could acquire cheaply. Several methods of supply were employed: some books from the regular list were shipped out; some were specifically planned for India but manufactured in London; others were actually published abroad. To accomplish this branches of Macmillan were established in Bombay in 1901, in Calcutta in 1907, and in Madras in 1912; there were agencies in Bangalore, Colombo, and Rangoon. Macmillan was not the first British company to publish in India; it was preceded by John Murray, Bentley, and Routledge, but these other firms' lists were composed chiefly of history, travel, biography, and memoirs, whereas 94 per cent of Macmillan's selections were fiction. The families of Indian middle classes had, since the India Act of 1835, been exposed to English in their schools and they had now come to enjoy literature for itself, primarily fiction. Macmillan also published in its Colonial Library some of Fasnacht's teaching texts for French and German, some Greek and Latin readers, and a few textbooks for Indian schools, but it was their fiction that carried the day. Between 1886 and 1916, 640 titles were published, a high percentage being novels, including works by Crawford, Mrs Oliphant, Yonge, Thomas Hardy, Lady Barker, and

Hugh Conway. Ironically, a colonial author was added to the Colonial Library when Macmillan published an Australian classic previously published by Remington & Co., *Robbery under Arms* (1889) by Alexander Browne, a police magistrate of New South Wales who used the pseudonym Rolf Boldrewood. Two of his three-deckers followed: *Miner's Right* and *The Colonial Reformer* (both 1890). Australia was another profitable market for the Colonial Library and, indeed, in both countries British expatriates, as well as the native population, were eager purchasers.

Although Thomas Hardy's early novels had been rejected by Macmillan, he first established contact there when *The Woodlanders* was accepted by *Macmillan's Magazine* in 1886; it was published in book form in three volumes in 1887 and followed by *Wessex Tales* (1888). In 1886 Maurice Macmillan secured *The Mayor of Casterbridge* for the Colonial Library, while in 1893 Macmillan successfully acquired a dozen Hardy novels, but for the Colonial Library only, including *Tess of the d'Urbervilles*, which had first been published by Osgood McIlvaine in 1891. Hardy transferred all his books to Macmillan in 1902, which also published *The Dynasts* in three parts (1904–8). Hardy continued to send work to the firm for the next twenty years.

James G. Frazer, a rising young Cambridge scholar and fellow of Trinity College, wrote to George Macmillan in 1889, proposing a book based on his work over the last five years, to be entitled *The Golden Bough*, where he would offer a comparative study of the beliefs and institutions of mankind, in order to study the progress of thought from the magical, to the religious, to the scientific. The book would look at customs such as fertility rites, the sacrificial killing of kings, the dying god, and the scapegoat, in an attempt to analyse the primitive mind. George, and his reader John Morley, realized immediately that this would be a unique contribution to social anthropology and they accepted the idea at once, not realizing they were initiating an enterprise that would last more than forty years. Publication proceeded slowly, the first two volumes appearing in May 1890; the second edition in three volumes in 1900. The third edition (still in print) began publication in 1906, and was completed in twelve volumes in 1915. *Aftermath: a Supplement* followed in 1936, making the thirteen-volume set, which is the definitive edition. Each edition was an enlargement of its predecessor. A one-volume abridged edition appeared in 1922 of which 30,000 were in print by 1933, and it thus influenced a much larger reading public. A huge correspondence remains in the Macmillan archives, including letters to and from Frazer's wife, Lilly, who edited several French schoolbooks for Macmillan. While Frazer's methods and many of his conclusions have been rendered unacceptable by more modern research, nevertheless his book stirred public imagination and he was widely considered as one of the founders of modern anthropology. Macmillan published Frazer's other works as well, including his translations, with commentaries, of *Pausanias* (1898) and the *Fasti* (1929). Because of his success with *The Golden Bough* many other books on anthropology, myth, and comparative religion were offered to George, including

Edvard Westermarck's *History of Human Marriage* (1891) and *Marriage Ceremonies in Morocco* (1914); Arthur Evans's *The Mycenaean Tree and Pillar Cult* (1901); and W. W. Skeat's and C. O. Blagden's *Pagan Races of the Malay Peninsula* (1906).

Towards the end of the 1880s Alexander Macmillan was less and less involved with the company. He was in his seventies, after a life of hard work, and was devastated by the death of his eldest son, Malcolm, but work continued with the second generation of the family. Alexander Macmillan died on 26 January 1896 at his home, 21 Portland Place, London, and was buried in the Bramshott churchyard, Haslemere. After his death Macmillan & Co. became a limited company, with Frederick Orridge Macmillan as its first chairman.

During the pre-war years, literary observers sometimes suggested that Macmillan & Co., and particularly its readers, failed to stay abreast of the new trends in fiction during the years 1890 to 1914. Critics were puzzled to note that the company rejected H. G. Wells's *Ann Veronica* (1909) and *The New Machiavelli* (1910); the same was true for books by George Bernard Shaw, Arnold Bennett, and Somerset Maugham. In his brash way, Wells spoke out: 'I don't think you advertise well and I think you are out of touch with the contemporary movement in literature ... On the other hand, you are solid and sound and sane' (Morgan, 147). The firm did, however, publish his *Twelve Stories and a Dream* (1903), *The Food of the Gods and how it Came to Earth* (1904), *Kipps* (1905), *In the Days of the Comet* (1906), *Tono-Bungay* (1909), *Marriage* (1912), *The Passionate Friends* (1913), *The Wife of Sir Isaac Harman* (1914), *The World Set Free* (1914), and *The Research Magnificent* (1915). Macmillan also published Maurice Hewlett's *The Forest Lovers*, a romantic novel set in the middle ages and a best-seller of 1898. The firm's American novelists included Winston Churchill, Gertrude Atherton, and Owen Wister (*The Virginian*, 1902). As with so many others, Rudyard Kipling first came to the publisher through *Macmillan's Magazine*, where eight of his stories appeared between December 1889 and January 1893 (see *Wellesley index*, 1.633–42), beginning with 'The Incarnation of Krishna Mulvaney'. His enormous early popularity with the reading public resulted in a large number of collected editions of his work, under such labels as Uniform, Pocket, Deluxe, and School.

Early in 1890 Frederick Macmillan stepped forward to offer leadership in a bitter controversy dividing the publishing and bookselling world. The trouble had been brewing for years because booksellers ignored the price fixed on a book by a publisher, in favour of their own discounted one, thus instigating cut-throat competition. Frederick Macmillan suggested what became known as the net book agreement, whereby there would be two classes of books, with different kinds of prices: the 'net' price fixed by the publisher and adhered to by all, for which, if accepted by a bookseller, the bookseller would receive a set discount, and the 'subject', where booksellers would be free to set their own selling price. Frederick began his campaign for reform with a letter to *The Bookseller* (6 March 1890), outlining his plan, and provoking

spirited discussion in the trade. As a test case, he selected, in July 1890, an important book, *Principles of Economics* by Alfred Marshall, and 'fixed' the price, declaring, 'If a book is good enough, a bookseller cannot afford to be without it' (Morgan, 179). The dispute was so heated and so sensitive, however, that no compromise seemed possible until January 1899, when the Publishers' Association was finally able to send to the Associated Booksellers a proposal that proved acceptable.

Frederick Macmillan again stepped forward as a leader in 1905 when *The Times* introduced a scheme seemingly designed to subvert the net book agreement. It offered membership in a new Times Book Club to its annual subscribers, the club to serve as a lending library for current books. Soon officials of the club were found to be selling as 'used' books volumes that had been circulated only once or twice, and setting their own prices. The result was a bitter struggle between publishers and *The Times*, which would only be resolved after ownership of the newspaper changed hands. The new owner, Lord Northcliffe, paid Frederick Macmillan a secret visit to enlist his help in settling the dispute. Even with the best efforts of both men to avert a book war, it was not until the end of the year that *The Times* retreated. Macmillan served as president of the Publishers' Association from 1900 to 1902, and again from 1911 to 1913. He received a knighthood in 1909, not for his services to publishing, but for his work as chairman, from 1903, of the board of management of the National Hospital for the Paralysed and Epileptic, Queen Square, London.

The years 1897 and 1898 were marked by two important events for Macmillan. The first was construction of a new building for the firm's headquarters in St Martin's Street between Leicester Square and the National Gallery. Designed and equipped specially for publishing needs, it served for many years as Macmillan's principal place of business. The second event, purchase of all the stock and possessions of Richard Bentley & Son, of 8 New Burlington Street, had a far-reaching impact on Macmillan's family of authors. The firm had originally been founded by Charles Colburn about 1806, and underwent various changes in ownership until it became Richard Bentley in 1832, and ultimately Richard Bentley & Son from 1871 to 1898. For the sum of £8000 Macmillan acquired a quantity of unwanted stock, the steel and copperplates of the illustrators George Cruikshank, John Tenniel, and George Du Maurier, plus a number of fine old portraits, all of which were sold to finance the purchase. What Macmillan kept resulted in a dramatic addition to their list. The firm gained R. H. Barham's *Ingoldsby Legends* (1840–46) and *Life and Remains of Thomas Hook* (1849); Theodore Mommsen's *History of Rome* (1862–75); Frederick Courtney Selous's *Hunter's Wanderings in Africa* (1881); Edward Fitzgerald's *Letters to Fanny Kemble* (1895); and Harold Fielding-Hall's *The Soul of a People* (1898). A number of female novelists were added: Mrs W. K. Clifford, Mrs Annie Edwards, Rhoda Broughton, Helen Mathers, Mary Cholmondeley, Jessie Fothergill, Florence Montgomery, Rosa N. Carey, and Mrs

Henry Wood. Male novelists acquired were Anthony Trollope, Joseph Sheridan Le Fanu, and Marcus Clarke. Two periodicals were also included: *The Argosy* and *Temple Bar*.

The early to mid-twentieth century: the third generation The early years of the twentieth century brought a mixed group of publishing events to Macmillan. John Morley's long-awaited *Life of Gladstone* (1903) was a critical success, and sold 25,041 copies in the first year, but was only a token success financially; the Gladstone family had published on commission and reaped the profit. Some early Irish writers appeared. Sidney Royse Lysaght brought *Poems of the Unknown Way* (1901) and *Horizons and Landmarks* (1911); and Stephen Gwynn, *Old Knowledge* (1901), *John Maxwell's Marriage* (1903), *The Masters of English Literature* (1904), and *Robert Emmet* (1909). A new English Men of Letters series was also begun at this time, under the editorship of J. C. Squire. It ran to twenty-five titles between 1902 and 1919, including: *George Eliot* (1902) by Leslie Stephen, *Robert Browning* (1903) by G. K. Chesterton, and *Jane Austen* (1919) by F. Warre Cornish. The eminent Bengali poet, critic, and short fiction writer Rabindranath Tagore also joined Macmillan with his free-verse re-creations of his Bengali poems modelled on a medieval Indian devotional lyric, *Gitanjali: Song Offerings* (1913), which won the Nobel prize for literature, the first for an Asian writer.

Two third-generation Macmillans joined the board in 1911: William Edward Frank (1880–1954), known as Will, George's son, and **Daniel de Mendi Macmillan** (1886–1965), the eldest son of Maurice Crawford Macmillan and his wife, Helen Artie (Nellie) Tarleton, *née* Belles. Daniel de Mendi Macmillan was born on 1 February 1886 at Middleton House, Wandle Road, Wandsworth, London. He was educated at Eton College (where he was Newcastle scholar) and Balliol College, Oxford (1904–8). He joined the army in 1914, and was invalided the following year; towards the end of the war, on 5 April 1918, he married Margaret (1889/90–1957), the daughter of Louis Matthews (they were to have no children). He returned to publishing soon after, and acted as chairman of the company from 1936 to 1965. His brother, (Maurice) Harold *Macmillan, later earl of Stockton (1894–1986), entered the firm in 1920 as a director, and continued except for times when serving as a government minister; he was deputy chairman from 1936 to 1940, and from 1945 to 1951. He served as the British prime minister from 1957 to 1963, but after his term of office was concluded he succeeded his brother as chairman. William, a musician and director of Stainer and Bell, was a good classical scholar and a historian; Daniel, also a classical scholar, continued development of the Indian branch and the educational lists and supervised the continuity of the firm's publications. Mention must also be made of Thomas Mark Macmillan, who joined the firm in 1913 as secretary to the board and became a director in 1944.

Despite the obvious difficulties and hardships posed in the years of the First World War, the Macmillan partners struggled to prevent any major disruption of the firm's publishing schedule. Many books dealt directly with the wartime situation. Some of these were Owen Wister's *The Pentecost of Calamity* (1915), F. S. Oliver's *Ordeal by Battle* (1915), Mabel Dearmer's *Letters from a Field Hospital* (1915), Winston Churchill's *The Fighting Line* (1916), and Edith Wharton's *The Marne* (1918); and three volumes from Kipling, *France at War*, *The New Army in Training*, and *Fringes of the Fleet*, all in 1915. Others emphasized the 'business as usual' philosophy, in order to divert people's minds, with titles such as Henry Clay's *Economics: an Introduction for the General Reader* (1916), Morley's *Recollections* (1917), Edmund Gosse's *Life of Charles Algernon Swinburne* (1917), and Saintsbury's *History of the French Novel* (1917–19). The cousins also recognized that spiritual topics were important in wartime, hence William Temple's *Studies in the Spirit and Truth of Christianity* (1914), J. R. Illingsworth's *The Gospel Miracles* (1915), H. B. Swete's *The Holy Catholic Church* (1915), and Hensley Henson's *Christian Liberty* (1918). Important works of scholarship also found a place: P. M. Sykes's *History of Persia* (1915), Thomas Watts Eden's and C. H. J. Lockyer's *New System of Gynaecology*, and Frazer's *Folk-Lore in the Old Testament* (1918). Some room was found, even in wartime, for literary works: there were two collections of Hardy's poetry, *Satires of Circumstance* (1914) and *Moments of Vision and Miscellaneous Verse* (1917); and Wilfrid Scawen Blunt's *Poetical Works* (1914).

An infusion of new blood from William and Daniel de Mendi Macmillan brought change to the manuscript selection process. The venerable John Morley was replaced as senior reader in favour of Charles Whibley, a younger man of more modern tastes and outlook. An immediate consequence of this move was a marked increase in the recognition of Irish writers. James Stephens, an engaging writer of Irish fantasy, published his first novel, *The Charwoman's Daughter* (1912), with the firm, and remained with it for four more: *The Crock of Gold* (1912), *The Demi-Gods* (1914), *Songs from the Clay* (1915), and *The Adventures of Seumas Beg* (1915). A. E. (George William Russell), a leader in the Irish literary renaissance, came at roughly the same time, and Macmillan published his collected verse over the next twenty years: *Gods of War* (1915), *Candle of Vision* (1918), *Voices of the Stones* (1925), *Vale and other Poems* (1931), *The House of Titans and other Poems* (1934), and *Selected Poems* (1935). In a reader's report for 1900 John Morley had said of William Butler Yeats: 'The work does not please the ear, nor kindle the imagination' (Morgan, 221). By 1916 Macmillan thinking was so changed that the firm published his *Responsibilities* and *Reveries over Childhood*: in the same year company executives acquired, through failure of Yeats's publisher, A. H. Bullen, thirteen volumes published earlier, and Yeats remained a Macmillan author until his death in 1939. Yeats supervised revision of two volumes published posthumously, and delayed by the Second World War: *The Poems of W. B. Yeats* (1949) and *The Collected Plays of W. B. Yeats*, a revision and expansion of the collection of 1934.

By securing Yeats the third-generation Macmillans opened the floodgates of Irish literature over the next twenty-five years. Padraic Colum published *The King of Ireland's Son* (1916) and during the next ten years fifteen more titles. Sean O'Casey brought two plays in 1925, *Juno and the*

Paycock and *The Shadow of a Gunman*, and henceforth Macmillan published all his plays. In addition, they published a collection of his articles on theatre, *The Flying Wasp* (1937), six volumes of his autobiography between 1939 and 1963, and two editions of his collected plays (1939 and 1951). A veritable parade of Irish literati now published with Macmillan: Alice Stopford Green (*History of the Irish State to 1914*, 1925); Eimar O'Duffy (his satire *King Goshawk and the Birds*, 1926); F. R. Higgins (*The Dark Bread*, 1927, and *Gap of Brightness*, 1940). Esme Stuart Lennox Robinson, for nearly fifty years a playwright, manager, and director connected with Dublin's Abbey Theatre, published his collected plays in 1928. *Collected Poems* (1930) by Katharine Tynan and George Shiels's *Two Irish Plays* (1930), remained on the list for the next fifteen years; Frank O'Connor (Michael O'Donovan) published many collections of his short stories, including *Guests of the Nation* (1931); John Eglinton (pseudonym for William Kirkpatrick Magee) offered *Irish Literary Portraits* (1935) and *Memoir of A. E.* (1937); Paul Vincent Carroll published his important play *Shadow and Substance* (1938), and Joseph Hone's biography *W. B. Yeats* was issued in 1942.

At the close of the First World War, with third-generation Macmillans William and Daniel de Mendi firmly in control of the company and cousin Harold about to join it (1920), they set about consolidating their list over the next twenty years. A series of collected editions was planned: the thirty-seven volume Mellstock edition of Thomas Hardy's works (1919–20); John Morley's collected work in fifteen volumes (1921); W. E. Henley in five (1921); and Henry James in thirty-five volumes (1922–33). (James had first come to Macmillan with a volume of essays, *French Poets and Novelists*, published in 1877. Although not a profitable author for the firm, it nevertheless published most of his subsequent books as well as the New York edition of his novels.) Aside from the Hardy set, these were not financially successful. Apparently the public, while strong book buyers, wanted eclectic choice rather than collections.

Macmillan titles in history and science proved more popular. John Fortescue, the military historian, published his monumental thirteen-volume *History of the British Army* (1899–1930), as well as *The Correspondence of George III* (1927) which sold well, as did *The Greville Memoirs* (1938), edited by Lytton Strachey and Roger Fulford. Lewis Namier, the distinguished historian, brought to the company *The Structure of Politics at the Accession of George III* (1929) and *England in the Age of the American Revolution* (1930). J. L. Garvin's *The Life of Joseph Chamberlain* appeared in 1932, and Emily Anderson edited *The Letters of Mozart and his Family* (1938).

During the 1920s and 1930s the younger Macmillans saw the need to revise and update the firm's very successful teaching tools, something which had become a strong part of the business. The Modern French and the Modern German texts appeared, along with the Modern Classic series as an addition to the Elementary Classics. E. J. S. Lay produced *Teaching in Practice for Infant Schools: Projects and Pictures* (1934–7), which addressed contemporary concerns about the methodology of teaching. It was a predominant text in its field for the next thirty years, providing a complete teaching programme for infant schools as well as suggestions for primary and secondary syllabuses.

Early in the period following the First World War the young Macmillans had begun to develop an especially strong list of economic and political titles. John Maynard Keynes, the noted economist, and Daniel de Mendi began at Eton what was to be a lifelong friendship, so it was natural that the firm should publish his *Economic Consequences of Peace* (1919), written in strong opposition to the provisions of the Versailles peace conference, which he attended as a representative of the government, accompanied by Daniel. *A Treatise of Probability* (1921) followed soon after, and later his two great works *A Treatise on Money* (1930) and *General Theory of Employment, Interest and Money* (1936); in 1940 he published *How to Pay for the War*. Keynes served as Daniel's adviser on other economic works, including Alfred Marshall's *Industry and Trade* (1919), Arthur C. Pigou's *Economics of Welfare* (1920), and E. H. Carr's *International Relations since the Peace Treaties* (1937) and *The Twenty Years' Crisis, 1919–1939* (1939). He also edited the *Economic Journal* for Macmillan from 1912 to 1945. Because of Keynes's reputation many other economists came to the firm, including G. D. H. Cole, George Peel, Norman Crump, Paul Einzig, Colin Clark, Sir Cecil Kisch, Lord Stamp, Lionel Robbins, and Joan Robinson.

Fiction was one highly successful venture for Macmillan in the twenty years between the world wars. Hugh Walpole first came to the firm in 1918 and by the thirties had developed the *Herries Chronicle*, a four-novel sequence set in Cumberland: *Rogue Herries* (1930); *Judith Paris* (1931); *The Fortress* (1932); and *Vanessa* (1933). This was a strong commercial success, with *Judith Paris* selling 20,000 copies in the first two weeks. Another popular novelist of the era was Mazo de la Roche, whose publications *Jalna* (1927), transferred from Little, Brown, and *Whiteoaks* (1929) combined to produce the Jalna/Whiteoaks series of sixteen novels, similar in popularity to the *Herries* volumes. In the late 1920s and early 1930s Macmillan also acquired novels from E. M. Delafield, Richard Crompton, Edward Shanks, John Collier, Edward Thompson, A. G. Macdonell, Charles Morgan, and Naomi Royde Smith. Vera Brittain came to the firm with *Testament of Friendship* (1940).

It remained, however, for one British man and one American woman to provide Macmillan with two runaway best-sellers in the space of a little over a decade. James Hilton's *Lost Horizon* (1933), an evocative novel set in Shangri-La, a Tibetan lamasery where inhabitants never grow old, was a great success in both Britain and America, winning the Hawthornden prize in 1934. Hilton subsequently became a fiction reader for the firm. In 1936 Margaret Mitchell surprised everyone with her blockbuster *Gone with the Wind*. The Macmillan partners misjudged its appeal to the public, initially printing only 3000 copies; soon they needed 30,000, and ultimately they printed in runs of 100,000. Clearly, the investment made by the third-generation Macmillan cousins in fiction was a shrewd move.

In 1936 the Macmillan family and the Macmillan business suffered sad losses in the deaths of the three senior partners, George on 3 March, Maurice on 30 March, and Frederick on 1 June 1936. As in the past, the transfer of power had already been made and the family members were in place to ensure no outward confusion or interruption to the routine of business. Will retired, and Daniel de Mendi and Harold now assumed the major leadership roles, with Daniel as chairman and Harold as his deputy.

The Sitwell family became Macmillan authors with Osbert's *Penny Foolish* (1935), a volume of essays, and a volume of lectures by all three, Edith, Osbert, and Sacheverell, *Trio* (1938). Such well-known poets as Sturge Moore, Edward Shanks, and Edmund Blunden came to Macmillan in the 1930s and early 1940s, after having first published elsewhere. For Lawrence Binyon the firm published several volumes of poetry and then his *Collected Poems* (1931).

With the advent of the Second World War the Macmillan family faced a crucial decision: should they move the firm's stock and offices out of London to avoid damage from bombing, or should they sit tight and tough it out? Harold Macmillan was credited with making the decision to stay put, based on the security and deep basement of the company's building. Careful preparations were made for gas masks, drills were conducted, and the structure was fitted out in case of a long siege. It withstood whatever assault the Germans mounted and at the war's end had the proud record that no one had been injured at Macmillan, and business had been conducted as usual.

1945 to the present At the conclusion of the war Macmillan, in common with other British publishers, faced a severe paper shortage; the question was whether to expend its short supplies on new works, or to attempt to restore the existing list to normality. The Macmillan family decided on the latter course, in keeping with their long-standing policy of treating authors fairly. Texts, for both school and university, had top priority. Classics in their field, such as *The Golden Bough*, were continued. Living authors, and the estates of deceased writers which relied on royalties for income, also had priority. Even the opportunity to publish such a potentially important and profitable work as Winston Churchill's war memoirs was sacrificed in light of this policy.

As publishing conditions improved, four new series were inaugurated: the Casebook series, providing critical commentary on general authors for undergraduates; the Companion series, providing critical commentary for the general reader; and the Master series, supplying textbooks directly to students. By far the biggest seller, however, was the Macmillan Crime Fiction series, which published forty to fifty titles each year.

In the decades following 1945 many important novelists, poets, critics, historians, and other scholars were added to the Macmillan list. The philosopher A. J. Ayer, Leon Edel, Rumer Godden, Rupert Hart-Davis, Frank O'Connor, A. L. Rowse, C. P. Snow and his wife, Pamela Hansford Johnson, Muriel Spark, Hugh Trevor-Roper, and J. W. Wheeler-Bennett were but a few of these new Macmillan authors. The year 1951 saw the sale of the New York

branch of the firm, while St Martin's Press became the focus of Macmillan interests in the United States.

Always strong in reference works, the modern Macmillan list included such major works as *The New Grove Dictionary of Music and Musicians* (1980); *The New Palgrave: a Dictionary of Economics* (1987); and *The Dictionary of Art* (1996). *The Macmillan Encyclopedia* (annually since 1980) was praised by Harold Macmillan for containing 'ideas which we need to understand in order to appreciate the intellectual currents of our time'. Other reference works included *The Macmillan Nautical Almanac* (annually since 1980); *British Archives* (1982), a useful location list of British manuscript archives; the Macmillan Literary Companions (from 1968); and *The Macmillan Dictionary of Women's Biography* (1989), a pioneering work in its field.

In the years following the retirement of Harold Macmillan from the premiership in 1963, his energies were redirected towards publishing. He took over as chairman from his brother Daniel in 1963, and the company embarked on a period of rapid expansion, with the opening of overseas offices, mainly in African and Asian countries, and the development of educational publishing on a much more ambitious scale than ever before. Daniel de Mendi Macmillan died of heart failure at his home, 3 Grosvenor Square, Westminster, London, on 6 December 1965.

The Macmillan family's active participation in the company continued. Maurice Victor Macmillan (1921–1984), Harold's only son, an MP for many years and a minister in the Douglas-Home government, divided his time between publishing and politics, and was one of the founding fathers of Pan Books, the pioneer of quality paperback publishing in the post-war era. His eldest son, Alexander (*b*. 1943), abandoned a successful career in journalism to join the company. In 1986, upon the death of Harold Macmillan, by this time the first earl of Stockton, management of the publishing interests had largely passed to non-family directors. Following the disposal by the family trusts of the majority of the shares to Verlagsgruppe Georg von Holtzbrinck in 1995, Alexander Macmillan, now the second earl, had embraced a challenging career as a member of the European parliament.

Conclusion As one looks back over the one and a half centuries of the Macmillan family as publishers, one sees that each incarnation of the family brought its own individual qualities to ensure the firm's growth and success. Daniel Macmillan, although cut off in his prime, had the dream and the vision to foresee success in a publishing venture. He brought the traditionally Scottish traits of honesty, hard work, and fair dealing with authors. He was also shrewd in developing the Cambridge connection in the early days of the business.

When the responsibility fell on Alexander Macmillan, he saw the need for steady growth and innovation. His contributions were enormous, when one considers that he moved the business to London, conceived the idea of publishing in series, and then inaugurated one important idea after another: the Golden Treasury; the Globe; the English Men of Letters. He founded a magazine, *Macmillan's*, that prospered for almost fifty years, and another,

Nature, which is still a respected publication today; he founded the American branch; he published significant scholarly journals; he launched a musical dictionary that remains a valued source in its revised edition. Perhaps most remarkable, with only the education a village school, plus wide reading, could provide, he moved on terms of equality and respect among the foremost men of his time; and he had an uncanny ability to sense what would prove popular with the general public.

The second generation, in particular through the work of Sir Frederick Orridge Macmillan, provided continued growth and established Macmillan unquestionably as one of the world's leading publishing houses. But possibly, for long-term impact, the most important accomplishment was the establishment of the Macmillan presence overseas. That would result in the 1990s in the firm having offices, not only in the United States and Canada, but also in most of the world's capitals.

The third generation moved the company from the Victorian era to the modern age. New, contemporary authors were added to the list, reflecting changes in the literary climate. Books on the science of economics became a major commitment. This generation had to survive the two world wars, while doing business as nearly normally as possible. Clearly, each generation of the Macmillan family has made its own significant contribution to the leadership, prosperity, and success of the company.

ROSEMARY T. VAN ARSDEL

Sources E. L. Graves, *The life and letters of Alexander Macmillan* (1910) · *Letters of Alexander Macmillan*, ed. G. Macmillan (1908) · T. Hughes, *Memoir of Daniel Macmillan* (1882) · C. Morgan, *The house of Macmillan* (1943) · R. T. VanArsdel, 'The Macmillan Company', *DLB* (1991) · H. L. Dickson, *The house of words* (1963) · P. V. Blake-Hill, 'The Macmillan archive', *British Museum Quarterly*, 36 (1972), 74–80 · *A bibliographical catalogue of Macmillan and Co.'s publications from 1843 to 1889* (1891) · F. Macmillan, *The net book agreement 1899 and the book war, 1906–1908: two chapters in publishing history* (1924) · C. L. Graves, *The life and letters of Sir George Grove* (1903) · J. S. Hagen, *Tennyson and his publishers* (1979) · 'One hundred years of Macmillan history', *Publisher's Weekly* (9 Oct 1943) · A. J. Gurr, 'Macmillan's Magazine', *Review of English Literature*, 6 (1965), 39–55 · *WWW* · I. Elliott, ed., *The Balliol College register, 1900–1950*, 3rd edn (privately printed, Oxford, 1953) · *The Times* (7 Dec 1965)

Archives BL, corresp. and papers, Add. MSS 54786–56035, 61894–61896; Add. Ch. 75725 · U. Reading, corresp. and papers | Bodl. Oxf., corresp. with J. L. Myres [Frederick Macmillan] · CUL, letters to Arthur Westcott [Frederick Macmillan] · King's Cam., letters to John Maynard Keynes [Daniel de Mendi Macmillan] · NL Scot., letters to Alexander Campbell Fraser [Alexander Macmillan] · U. Birm., corresp. with Harriet Martineau [Alexander Macmillan] · U. Edin., letters to Sir Archibald Geikie [Alexander Macmillan] · U. Edin., corresp. with W. E. Gladstone [Alexander Macmillan] · U. Glas., corresp. with F. O. Bower [Frederick Macmillan]

Likenesses portrait, 1881 (Alexander Macmillan), repro. in Graves, *Life and letters of Alexander Macmillan*, facing p. 371 · H. von Herkomer, portrait, exh. RA 1887 (Alexander Macmillan), repro. in Graves, *Life and letters of Alexander Macmillan*, facing p. 277 · L. Dickinson, portrait, 1889 (Alexander Macmillan), repro. in Graves, *Life and letters of Alexander Macmillan*, facing p. 385 · R. Lutyens, lithograph, c.1961–1962 (Daniel de Mendi Macmillan), NPG · F. E. Jackson, lithograph (Frederick Orridge Macmillan), BM · C. H. Jeens, stipple (Daniel Macmillan; after L. Dickinson), BM; repro. in Hughes, *Memoir* · portrait (Daniel Macmillan), repro. in Hughes, *Memoir*, frontispiece · portrait (Alexander Macmillan; after photograph by O. G. Rejlander, 1860–70), repro. in Graves, *Life and letters of Alexander Macmillan*, frontispiece

Wealth at death £179,644 19s. 7d.—Alexander Macmillan: probate, 26 Feb 1896, CGPLA Eng. & Wales · £202,224 4s. 7d.—Frederick Orridge Macmillan: probate, 7 Aug 1936, CGPLA Eng. & Wales · £7201—Daniel de Mendi Macmillan: probate, 17 Jan 1966, CGPLA Eng. & Wales

Macmillan, Alexander (1818–1896). *See under* Macmillan family (*per. c.*1840–1986).

McMillan [Macmillan], **Angus** (1810–1865), explorer and colonist in Australia, was born in Glenbrittle, Isle of Skye, Scotland, on 14 August 1810, the fourth son of Ewan McMillan. Angus emigrated from Greenock to New South Wales to find work, arriving in January 1838. After working on several sheep stations, he took employment under Lachlan Macalister in 1838 at Clifton station, Camden.

In February 1839 McMillan was appointed by Macalister to be manager at Currawang, in the Maneroo or Monaro country. In May that year he set out to explore with an Aborigine, Jimmy Gabber, for companion. Four days later he climbed Mount McLeod, or the Haystack, from the top of which he had a bird's-eye view of the country which he wished to explore. Jimmy Gabber, however, threatened his life, and he turned back without making any decisive discovery. But Macalister encouraged him to persevere, not least as new pastures were desperately needed by the colonists, and in December 1839 McMillan started again. He got as far as Sale, moving south-west-by-west, crossing the rivers draining south from the Great Dividing Range. He reported enthusiastically to Macalister about the pasture and water supply and in 1840 claimed stations for Macalister and himself on the River Avon. Finally, after two unsuccessful attempts, on 9 February 1841 McMillan made a further effort to discover a route to the sea and on 13 February succeeded, reaching Corner Inlet on Wilson's Promontory.

Meanwhile, Paul Strzelecki's expedition was following in McMillan's tracks, guided by Matthew Macalister, the son of McMillan's employer. Strzelecki renamed many features already named by McMillan and it was his name 'Gippsland' which was adopted for the whole area in preference to McMillan's 'Caledonia Australis'. Matthew Macalister and Strzelecki's companion McArthur later disputed in newspapers whether the later party knew the extent of McMillan's discoveries: certainly Strzelecki made no mention of him in his reports and McMillan bitterly resented the fact that he got little or no credit for the discovery of the new land.

McMillan settled on his station at Bushy Park on the Avon where he was a successful pastoralist, leader of the Scottish community, and president of the Caledonian Society of Victoria. In 1857 he married Christina MacDougald (*d.* in or after 1865) and they had at least two sons. Fire and speculation, however, led to the loss of all but one of his properties in 1861.

In 1864 McMillan was asked by the government to lead the alpine expedition to open tracks in the mining areas of Omeo, Dargo and Matlock. Battling through thick scrub and against ill health, and with inadequate support from the government, he cut 220 miles of track. However, in May 1865 a pack-horse rolled on him, leaving him with severe internal injuries from which he died at Gellion's Hotel, Iguana Creek, near Bairnsdale, on 18 May 1865. He was buried in Sale cemetery after a Presbyterian service. His family were left destitute until relieved by a government grant of £2000. McMillan has belatedly received more of the credit due to him for his discovery and opening up of Gippsland, but his reputation has remained eclipsed by that of Strzelecki.   ELIZABETH BAIGENT

Sources K. Cox, *Angus McMillan: pathfinder* (1973) · C. Daley, *The story of Gippsland* (1960) · A. E. J. Andrews, 'Strzelecki's route 1840 from the Murray River to Melbourne', *Royal Australian Historical Society Journal and Proceedings*, 77 (1992), 50–62 · C. Daley, 'Angus McMillan', *Victorian Historical Magazine*, 11/3 (March 1927)
Archives State Library of Victoria, Melbourne, La Trobe picture collection, Shillinglaw MSS
Likenesses oils, shire of Alberton chambers, Yarram, Victoria

Macmillan, (Jessie) Chrystal (1872–1937), barrister and political activist, was born on 13 June 1872 at 8 Duke Street, Edinburgh, the only daughter in the family of nine children of John Macmillan, a wealthy tea merchant and past master of the Edinburgh Merchant Company, and his wife, Jessie Chrystal Finlayson. She was educated at St Leonard's School, St Andrews, and in 1892 was among the first women admitted to Edinburgh University, where in 1896 she took a BSc with first-class honours in mathematics and natural philosophy. She then attended the University of Berlin, before taking her MA in mental and moral philosophy at Edinburgh in 1900.

Chrystal Macmillan worked for the women's suffrage campaign in Scotland, as a member of the Scottish Federation of Women's Suffrage Societies, under the leadership of Sarah Siddons Mair. She was honorary secretary of the Women Graduates of the Scottish Universities (Parliamentary Franchise) Committee, which in 1906 initiated a court case over the rights of their members to the parliamentary franchise. Under legislation of 1868 the Scottish universities had four MPs; the electorate was the general councils of the universities, which included all their graduates. Macmillan, along with Elsie Inglis, Frances Melville, Margaret Nairn, and Frances Simson, argued through lawyers at the Court of Session that the word 'person', used throughout the statute, included women. The case was rejected, as was their appeal. In 1908 the case was taken to the House of Lords, where Macmillan argued it in person before the lord chancellor. Not herself a lawyer at this time, she showed considerable skill in presenting her case, but the case was rejected. Perhaps inevitably, the popular press dubbed her Portia. She moved to London, where she served on the executive of the National Union of Women's Suffrage Societies (NUWSS), and became active in the International Woman Suffrage Alliance, serving as secretary from 1913 to 1920. In this capacity she was in contact with the outstanding feminists of every country of the world, and was among the international compilers of *Woman Suffrage in Practice* (1913). She had also published two pamphlets, *The Struggle for Political*

(Jessie) **Chrystal Macmillan** (1872–1937), by unknown photographer, *c.*1912

Liberty (1909) and *Facts versus Fancies on Woman Suffrage* (1914).

Chrystal Macmillan was a committed internationalist, believing that what all people had in common was more important than the frontiers that divided them. Immediately before the outbreak of war, she helped draft an international manifesto of women, signed by the representatives of twelve million women, and delivered it to the foreign secretary, Sir Edward Grey, and the European ambassadors in London on 31 July 1914. The manifesto entreated them to attempt conciliation and arbitration to avert 'the threatened unparalleled disaster'. After the fall of Antwerp, Chrystal Macmillan and Mary Sheepshanks negotiated money guarantees from the Belgian ambassador, and then took the first food convoy across the U-boat patrolled North Sea to Flushing. As an opponent of the war, Chrystal Macmillan resigned from the NUWSS. In December 1914 she proposed to Dr Aletta Jacobs, the leader of the Dutch suffrage movement, that an international women's congress be held at The Hague to 'discuss the principles on which peace should be made and, if so agreed, to act internationally'. The conference was held in April 1915, with Chrystal Macmillan one of only three British women able to attend: the British government had closed the North Sea to shipping, but Chrystal Macmillan was already in Holland. The congress elected delegates to carry its resolutions in person to the heads of belligerent and neutral governments, to petition them to negotiate an end to the war. Chrystal Macmillan was sent to make the case for a peace mediated by neutral countries to Scandinavia and Russia, without success. Later she visited the United States, assisting the opposition to America's entry into the war. In May 1919 she was a delegate to the International Congress of Women in Zürich, which issued the first public criticism of the punitive terms of the treaty of Versailles. Together with other leading international feminists, she then took the women's resolutions on disarmament and economic co-operation to the victorious allies at the Paris peace conference, only to be ignored once more.

After the war, with the vote won, and the legal profession opened to women for the first time, Chrystal Macmillan entered the Middle Temple, and was called to the bar on 28 January 1924, one of the first generation of women barristers. 'She was the right kind of lawyer', wrote Cicely Hamilton in *Time and Tide* (16 October 1937):

> one who held that Law should be synonymous with Justice … Her chief aim in life—one might call it her passion—was to give every woman of every class and nation the essential protection of justice. She was, herself, a great and very just human being … She could not budge an inch on matters of principle but she never lost her temper and never bore a grudge in defeat.

An equal rights feminist and a Liberal in politics, in 1923 she was one of the founders of the Open Door Council, which campaigned to remove legal restrictions on the employment of women and opposed protective legislation. She served on the executives of the National Union of Societies for Equal Citizenship and the Association for Moral and Social Hygiene (which continued Josephine Butler's work for the civil rights of prostitutes and opposed the state regulation of prostitution). She gave expert evidence to various parliamentary committees, including that on the guardianship of children, and to the royal commission on unemployment insurance. She was particularly interested in the right of women to retain their own nationality on marriage to a foreigner, giving evidence to the select committee investigating it in 1922, and leading a deputation on the issue at The Hague in 1930. An expert on the legal status of women, she wrote the article on that topic for the fourteenth edition of the *Encyclopaedia Britannica*.

In June 1937 Chrystal Macmillan had to have a leg amputated. She died from heart disease at 8 Chalmers Crescent, Edinburgh, on 21 September 1937, and was cremated on 23 September in Edinburgh. In her will she left bequests to the Open Door International for the Economic Emancipation of the Woman Worker, and to the Association for Moral and Social Hygiene. A memorial prize is awarded annually in her name by the society of the Middle Temple to the highest placed woman student in the bar's final examinations.   SYBIL OLDFIELD

Sources O. Banks, *The biographical dictionary of British feminists*, 2 (1990) · *A biographical sketch of Chrystal Macmillan* [publ. by the Middle Temple for the Chrystal Macmillan Memorial Prize] · A. Wiltsher, *Most dangerous women: feminist peace campaigners of the First World War* (1985) · *The Times* (22 Sept 1937) · *The Times* (23 Sept 1937) · *Time and Tide* (2 Oct 1937) · C. Hamilton, *Time and Tide* (16 Oct 1937) · *Manchester Guardian* (23 Sept 1937) · *Manchester Guardian* (25 Sept 1937) · *Manchester Guardian* (2 Oct 1937) · *Daily Telegraph* (21 Feb 1938) · Lord Alness, *The Scotsman* (Sept 1937) [in Fawcett archive] · *News Chronicle* (22 Sept 1937) · L. Leneman, *A guid cause: the women's suffrage movement in Scotland* (1991) · *WWW* · b. cert. · d. cert.
Archives University of Colorado at Boulder, Jane Addams MSS · Women's Library, London, Women's Obituary archives
Likenesses photograph, *c*.1912, Women's Library, London [*see illus.*] · photograph, repro. in *The Common Cause* (1 Feb 1912), frontispiece
Wealth at death £14,527 14*s*. 3*d*.: resworn probate, 6 Dec 1937, *CGPLA Eng. & Wales*

Macmillan, Daniel (1813–1857). *See under* Macmillan family (*per. c.*1840–1986).

Macmillan, Daniel de Mendi (1886–1965). *See under* Macmillan family (*per. c.*1840–1986).

Macmillan, Douglas (1884–1969), civil servant and charity founder, was born on 10 August 1884 at 12 Cumnock Terrace, Castle Cary, Somerset, the seventh of eight children of William Macmillan (1844–1911), horsehair weaver and alderman of Somerset, and his wife, Emily (1843–1937), daughter of Benjamin White of Gillingham, Dorset. He was educated at Sexey's School, Bruton (1894–7), the Quaker Sidcot School, Winscombe (1897–1901), and then at the Birkbeck Literary and Scientific Institute, London (1901). Macmillan entered the civil service in London in 1902 and worked in the Board of Agriculture and, later, the Ministry of Agriculture and Fisheries, retiring as a staff officer in 1945. For his support to young civil servants during the Second World War, when he and his section were evacuated to St Anne's, Lancashire, he was appointed MBE in 1944.

On 28 March 1907, in London, Macmillan married Margaret Fielding Miller (1868–1957), a property owner from Stonehaven, Scotland; they had no children. Macmillan's family were Congregationalists with pacifist sympathies. However, in 1901 his wife had introduced him to the Strict Baptists, which led to an estrangement with his parents. For the next ten years both he and his wife were evangelical supporters of this sect, organizing bible classes in their home. Macmillan wrote numerous protracted biblical expositions and edited a minority religious magazine, the *Better Quest*, but from 1911 his interest in religion began to fade.

The death of his father from cancer, in 1911, left a deep impression on Macmillan, and the following year he founded the Society for the Prevention and Relief of Cancer. Its wide aims included establishing the cause and treatment of cancer, as Macmillan believed that this lack of knowledge had caused his father's death. He campaigned vigorously against the established cancer research organizations and chided them in the press for doing little to help cancer sufferers. In 1913 he started the *Journal of the Society for the Prevention and Relief of Cancer*, one of the first publications of its kind, but this ceased publication in 1922 because of limited support. Macmillan's early objectives included the training of nurses to specialize in cancer and the construction of a purpose-built hospital for the care of such patients, but these plans did not materialize, in part because of public ignorance and fear of the disease. Macmillan published some of the earliest statistics showing that deaths from cancer varied throughout England and Wales, and in 1912 he predicted that they would overtake those from tuberculosis—a view that was dismissed by the government. His acerbic and minority views, however, such as his aversion to surgery, delayed recognition of his good ideas. In 1924 the society almost ceased to exist. Although it survived it was renamed the National Society for Cancer Relief and given a new focus: to provide for the care of cancer patients.

Macmillan and his wife ran the society from their home in Ranelagh Road, Pimlico, London, which the organization continued to use after the Macmillans moved in 1924 to Sidcup, Kent. In the early years almost all the financial support was provided by Margaret Macmillan from the rents and sale of her properties, and she was the first fundraiser. For the first twelve years she and her husband ran the society single-handedly, and only later appointed an unpaid assistant, the first paid staff joining the charity in 1930. The following two years saw the first successful house-to-house collection by volunteers and the employment of two full-time 'nurse-visitors' to befriend families in London and York, the forerunners of what later became known as Macmillan nurses. With increasing numbers of volunteers local branches were established in 1931 to collect funds, and in 1935 was the first flag day. The following year saw the offices move to Victoria Street.

A tall, slim man with a small moustache, who lost his dark hair in adult years, Macmillan was fit and agile, fond of the countryside and, particularly, of hill walking. A teetotaller, non-smoker, and vegetarian, he had an early interest in animal welfare and was an ardent antivivisectionist. He had a formal manner and, though diffident in public, his determination and tenacious energy, which was sometimes regarded as obstinacy, allowed him to achieve his aims. He was also interested in the folklore and antiquities of Somerset. He edited the *Somerset Year Book* (1922–32) and started a small publishing concern, the Folk Press; this published volumes on folklore, including one by himself, on Castle Cary, and another, on folk song and dance. Later he edited and distributed the *Folk Magazine*, a publication of the English Dialect Society. He was also author of many articles and poems.

After his retirement from the civil service in 1945 Macmillan gave increased energy to his society, of which he became chairman four years later. In 1951, at the age of nearly seventy, he wrote *The Book of Cancer Relief*; this was one of the first publications that set out to explain the details of the disease for ordinary men and women. Following the death of his wife Macmillan married, secondly, Nora Primrose Owen, on 27 September 1958. He retired from the society in 1966, due to ill health, and returned to the town of his birth. Douglas Macmillan died at his home, Carylande, Ansford, Castle Cary, Somerset, on 9 January 1969, having himself fallen victim to cancer of the stomach; he was buried at Castle Cary cemetery on 14 January. He was survived by his second wife.

TIMOTHY J. HUNT

Sources *Somerset Year Books* (1901–39) · *Castle Cary Visitor* (1896–1915) · *Journal of the Society for the Prevention and Relief of Cancer* (1913–22) · *Annual Report* [Society for the Prevention and Relief of Cancer] (1912–24) · *Annual Report* [National Society for Cancer Relief] (1925–81) · *Western Gazette* (1900–69) · *Good News of the Coming of Age* (1907–9) · *Better Quest* (1911) · private information (2004) · b. certs. [Douglas Macmillan, Margaret Fielding Miller] · m. certs. · d. certs. [Douglas Macmillan, Margaret Fielding Macmillan] · *CGPLA Eng. & Wales* (1969)

Archives priv. coll., collected papers

Likenesses R. R. Tomlinson, oils, 1964, Macmillan Cancer Relief, London · photographs, priv. coll.

Wealth at death £16,902: probate, 16 April 1969, *CGPLA Eng. & Wales*

Macmillan, Sir Frederick Orridge (1851–1936). *See under* Macmillan family (*per. c.*1840–1986).

Macmillan, (Maurice) Harold, first earl of Stockton (1894–1986), prime minister, was born on 10 February 1894 at 52 Cadogan Place, London, the youngest of the three children (all boys) of Maurice Crawford Macmillan (1853–1936), publisher, and his wife, Helen Artie Tarleton (Nellie), née Belles (1856–1937), the only surviving daughter in the Methodist family of Joshua Tarleton Belles (1826–1896), surgeon, of Spencer, Indiana, USA, and his wife, Julia, née Reid (1836–c.1860). This was Nellie Belles's second marriage: her first husband, Mr Hill, a young painter, had died in November 1874, five months after their marriage. About 1876 she made her way to Paris, where she moved in artistic circles. In 1884 she married for the second time. Maurice Crawford Macmillan was the second son of Daniel Macmillan (1813–1857), co-founder of the publishing firm of Macmillan, and his wife, Frances Eliza, née Orridge (1821–1867). Following Daniel Macmillan's death, Maurice and his siblings were brought up in the household of their uncle, Alexander Macmillan (1818–1896), who established the firm as one of the leading London publishers [*see* Macmillan family].

Though both publishing and the United States were to be central to Macmillan's career, his mother seems to have made little of her Indiana connections, her son not visiting the state until 1956 when he was foreign secretary (on the other hand, childhood visits to Arran and the family croft, from which Daniel Macmillan had set out, aged ten and very much a 'lad o'pairts', made a strong impression on the youthful Harold). Nellie Macmillan certainly retained, however, the thrusting ambition for her children characteristic of some mid-western mothers, and was not afraid to make a fuss on their behalf. Her son recalled, 'This was sometimes embarrassing both to my father and us' (*Winds of Change*, 56). She was also strongly anti-Catholic. Her fluent French was passed to her sons. The young Harold suffered from an English diffidence which belied his American origins and the Scottish background he later made so much of, and at his dancing class he 'first experienced my distaste for any form of joint performance' (*Winds of Change*, 32). His retiring, distant father and

(Maurice) Harold Macmillan, first earl of Stockton (1894–1986), by Arnold Newman, 1954

dominant, omnipresent mother provided an unbalanced and rather uncertain parental background for a shy and sensitive child.

Macmillan attended Mr Gladstone's day school near Sloane Square from the age of about six until he was nine. The school was connected with Summer Fields, a preparatory school in Summertown, Oxford, which he attended from 1903 until 1906. From there he won a scholarship to Eton, the chief purpose for which Summer Fields existed.

Eton and Oxford The young Macmillan had little of the inevitability of success about him. At Summer Fields he was always sent to bed early instead of doing evening preparation and in his first half at Eton he was near death from pneumonia. His body grew too fast, his heart was thought to be overstrained, and he left the school through ill health after three years, spending many months in bed. His lifelong hypochondria dated from this time, initially with justification. At Eton he none the less made important lifelong friendships, including with Henry Urmston Willink, Harry Frederick Comfort Crookshank, and Julian Lambart. He played in the Eton wall game in the year a goal was scored—an unusual event—but he was not a notably affectionate old boy, rarely visiting the college, even when his son was there.

Macmillan's parents were intent on his attending Oxford University and to this end he was privately tutored at home, first by (Alfred) Dilwyn Knox, who proved cold and unsympathetic, and then by his brother Ronald Arbuthnott *Knox (sons of the bishop of Manchester). Ronnie Knox was an Eton and Balliol contemporary of Macmillan's eldest brother, Daniel. Harold Macmillan's

relationship with Knox was among the most rewarding of his life. Knox was then an Anglo-Catholic, later to be ordained priest in the Church of England (he converted to Rome in 1917). He quickly moved into the moral role of a tutor and encouraged his charge to consider his religious beliefs, taking him to a neighbouring Anglo-Catholic church. 'Catholic' to Mrs Macmillan meant Roman Catholic (like many protestants she thought the Anglo-Catholic version more pernicious than the 'real' thing) and her reaction was sharp. It was perhaps the swifter for the intensity of the relationship which had developed between Macmillan and his tutor: the latter was, as he wrote in November 1910, 'by now extremely (and not quite unreturnedly) fond of the boy' (Waugh, 106; Evelyn Waugh's biography of Knox, published in 1959 when Macmillan was prime minister, described him and his mother as 'C' and 'Mrs C'). Knox was peremptorily dismissed. Macmillan won the Williams classical exhibition to Balliol College, Oxford, a less glittering prize than his brother Daniel, who had earlier won the top scholarship: 'I jogged along behind; but, still, I jogged' (Horne, 1.21).

Macmillan matriculated from Balliol in October 1912. He took a first class in classical moderations in Trinity term 1914, but his war service prevented him taking greats. His two years at Balliol and Oxford were a liberating experience for him, but not as liberating as for many, for his mother maintained a brooding and intrusive presence in his life. He took his first, vital steps into politics in the Oxford Union, being elected secretary in November 1913 and treasurer in March 1914 (president in June 1914 for the autumn term would have been the natural consequence). Given his diffidence about public speaking, this showed considerable political intention, an intention otherwise absent in his youth. He recorded as lifelong friends met at Oxford, Geoffrey Madan, Victor Mallet, Alan Herbert, Lord Cranborne (later fifth marquess of Salisbury), (Benedict) Humphrey Sumner, and Vincent Massey. But these were the survivors of the war: Macmillan and Sumner were the sole survivors of the scholars and exhibitioners of their year. Knox was Anglican chaplain at Trinity College, next door to Balliol, and their relationship resumed. Rather like that of W. E. Gladstone and A. H. Hallam at Eton a century earlier, it had an intense quality with sexual overtones but almost certainly without sexual fulfilment. Like J. H. Newman, Knox had a circle of which he was the dominant intellectual and emotional focal point; like Newman, when Knox 'poped' some followed and others did not. Macmillan, by then at war, was in the latter group, and he remained a devout Anglican for the rest of his life.

For Macmillan, those two years at Oxford later took on a golden hue. Though he always faced the future bravely and was not a nostalgic tory, his good fortune as a surviving representative of that *jeunesse dorée* impressed him throughout his life, suffused, perhaps, with the guilt which such survivors often felt. In the inter-war years he would only visit Oxford reluctantly: it was for him a 'city of ghosts' (*Winds of Change*, 98).

The First World War Recovery from an operation for appendicitis in July 1914 prevented Macmillan immediately joining up, as he wished to do. He then joined the Artists' Rifles, drilling at the inns of court, and was commissioned second lieutenant in the King's Royal Rifle Corps. His mother got him transferred to the prestigious and clubbable Grenadier Guards in March 1915, and in July he joined its new battalion. He first saw action at the battle of Loos in September 1915, being wounded lightly in the head and seriously in the right hand. Such was his bravery on this occasion that, as a contemporary later recalled, 'during the next two years or so anything brave was described by the Guardsmen as "nearly as brave as Mr. Macmillan"' (*The Times*, 9 Jan 1987). After convalescence, he returned in April 1916 to the 2nd battalion, being stationed at the Ypres salient, and was lightly wounded on 19 July when encountering a German patrol during a reconnaissance mission to approach the German lines and listen. At the battle of the Somme in mid-September 1916 he was seriously wounded in the pelvis and left thigh, though without any bone being fractured, for the bullet was slowed by his water bottle. He lay for a day in a shell hole in no man's land: 'I had in my pocket Aeschylus's *Prometheus* in Greek. It was a play I knew very well, and seemed not inappropriate to my position … I read it intermittently'. He also feigned dead to deceive a German patrol (Macmillan, *Winds of Change*, 88). He was rescued at darkness by Company Sergeant-Major Norton, but had to make his own way, in a state of panic, to the dressing station, where his wounds were dressed but not drained, allowing abscesses to form. On his return to London his mother, sensing his imminent death, short-circuited medical protocol and, in Macmillan's opinion, saved his life. He spent the rest of the war in and out of hospital, and unable to return to France. The war left Macmillan with 'a limp handshake, a dragging gait, and sporadic pain' (*DNB*).

Macmillan and Clement Attlee are the only British prime ministers to have been seriously wounded in battle, and to both of them it gave compassion, resilience, and perspective. Macmillan realized he was lucky to be wounded; he wrote of his war: 'It was sharp. But it was short' (*Winds of Change*, 91). He admired those who had had to stick it out, despised the contempt for life which he believed some generals had shown, and also felt 'a certain contempt' (in both wars) for those who did not join up (*Winds of Change*, 99). He was initially supportive of Asquith's premiership—'Mr. Asquith's "Wait & see" is after all the watchword of Nelson, of Wellington & of Pitt. They waited for nearly 20 years, amid disloyalty & impatience at home, until the final moment came' (letter to his mother from the front, 29 April 1916, Bodl. Oxf., Macmillan MSS d 2/2, fol. 24)—but he readily transferred his loyalty to the Lloyd George coalition, believing that Asquith 'had tolerated too long the mistakes of the High Command', and that Lloyd George was 'the man who would get things done' (*Winds of Change*, 96–7). Despite his wounds, he found army life fulfilling, especially 'the knowledge one gets of the poorer classes' (*Winds of Change*, 100). His war service and war wounds were of great advantage to him in tory politics, for until the 1960s to have had 'a good war', and especially to have been wounded, counterbalanced many an intellectual and political eccentricity. Macmillan did not play the patriotic card; his body played it for him.

Marriage, publishing, and a start in politics While convalescing, Macmillan broadened and deepened his already well-read mind (he was with Asquith one of the best-read twentieth-century prime ministers). Nevertheless, at the end of the war he had no wish to complete his studies at Oxford (he was awarded an MA for his war-shortened course in 1933), and little inclination to enter the family firm: he sought experience of the world by travel, and hoped the army might provide this. After a series of unsuccessful applications he joined, through his mother's influence, the staff of the ninth duke of Devonshire, then governor-general of Canada. In Canada, in what he recalled as a time 'of almost unalloyed enjoyment' (*Winds of Change*, 115), he wooed Lady Dorothy Evelyn Cavendish (1900–1966), the third of five daughters and fourth among the seven children of the duke and duchess of Devonshire. She was the first woman to whom Macmillan had been seriously attracted, and was his only love. Said by some to be a shrewd judge of character, she sought, perhaps, a wider intellect than the aristocratic youths among whom she grew up provided. He wrote to her on the eve of their wedding: 'I shall always be your lover', and remained true to his word (Horne, 1.57). His wife's position was to be very different.

Macmillan married into the Devonshires in a society wedding at St Margaret's, Westminster, on 21 April 1920—the bride's side packed with peers, the groom's with publishers and authors who wrote for Macmillans, including six OMs led by Henry James and Thomas Hardy. After the marriage Macmillan left the army and entered the family firm as junior partner to his brother Daniel and cousin George. Authors for whom he was directly responsible included Rudyard Kipling, Thomas Hardy, J. G. Frazer, W. B. Yeats, Hugh Walpole, and Sean O'Casey. J. M. Keynes was a close friend and contemporary of Daniel Macmillan, and Harold recruited several distinguished economists including G. D. H. Cole and Lionel Robbins, and later, among many others, the historian Lewis Namier (who had graduated from Balliol the year before Macmillan arrived there).

There was thus a sharp contrast between Macmillan's professional and domestic *milieux*. Within the family, he became friendly with the duke of Devonshire, who enjoyed his conversation, but he was patronized by many of his aristocratic relatives and in the early years of his marriage was rather uneasy at Chatsworth. He bridged the gap somewhat by making himself into a competent shot and playing his part on the grouse moors. He lived during the week at his parents' home in Chester Square and at weekends at Birch Grove, the family home in Sussex, his wife usually living there rather than in London. In 1921 the Macmillans' first child, Maurice Victor (*d.* 1984) was born, followed by (Ann) Caroline in 1923 and by Catherine (d. 1991) in 1926. From 1930 their family included a third girl, Sarah (d. 1970). Birch Grove (which was rebuilt in 1926) was shared until their deaths in 1936 and 1937 with Maurice and Nellie Macmillan. Dorothy Macmillan's children remembered finding their mother sticking pins in a wax effigy of Nellie (Horne, 1.81).

Macmillan's interest in politics led him, and his family connections enabled him, to stand at the general election of 1923 as a Conservative (with protectionist overtones) for the industrial northern town of Stockton-on-Tees, an area with which he had hitherto no contact and of which he knew little. He was defeated by a margin of seventy-three votes in a seat traditionally Liberal but always closely contested. Benefiting from the collapse of the Liberal vote, he won the seat in 1924 with a majority of 3215. He was from the first an assiduous constituency MP, his archive being an unusually rich source for the north-east, and he developed a considerable affection for the people of Stockton. He remained an active partner in the family firm, and, like his publisher colleague John Buchan, attended the Commons from the mid-afternoon on. This somewhat distanced him from the increasing specialization of politics, and gave him independence of position. His business experience gave him authority when he wrote on business and the economy. Though he was keen for ministerial office, he had no need to toe the line, and he did not. He made his maiden speech on the budget on 30 April 1925, supporting its social innovations. Though he never seems to have considered joining any other party than the Conservatives, he was soon seen by the tories as something of a maverick. In 1927, with Robert Boothby, Oliver Stanley, and John Loder, he published *Industry and the State: a Conservative View*. Influenced in different ways by both Alfred Milner, who had died in 1925, and David Lloyd George, they sought a 'middle land' between 'unrestricted individualism' and socialism, with the chief branches of industry organized by self-regulating industrial associations (Ritschel, 39). Less systematic but similar views were held by many Conservatives in the inter-war period. Macmillan proposed to Winston Churchill (the chancellor of the exchequer) a scheme for alleviating industry by derating; Churchill took it up and it was enacted in the Derating Act, passed in February 1928, a very remarkable achievement for a young back-bencher. It also indicated what was to be Macmillan's position for the rest of the inter-war years: an ideas man, but not an executive politician.

Marital and political failure 1929 was a disastrous year for Macmillan. In the general election he lost his seat to the Labour candidate, Frederick Riley, and about the same time his wife embarked on an affair with the bisexual tory maverick, Robert *Boothby. Sarah Macmillan, born in August 1930, was later claimed by Dorothy Macmillan to be Boothby's child (she was not recognized in Burke's *Peerage* as one of Macmillan's children; though she was registered by Dorothy Macmillan with Macmillan as the father, the birth was not registered until six weeks after the event, on the last legal day for registration; Sarah was not

named on the certificate, nor by the standard procedure for later naming). Boothby accepted responsibility for Sarah, though with considerable doubts of his own. It may be that Dorothy Macmillan hoped her claim would encourage her husband to sue for divorce. Macmillan considered divorce (then a disaster for a politician) but, perhaps because of his mother's influence, and more certainly because of his religions convictions and his continuing love for his wife, did not pursue the matter: 'She filled my life; I thought in everything I did of her', he later told Alastair Horne in a poignant interview (Horne, 1.89). A *modus vivendi* was agreed, which lasted until Dorothy's death in 1966 (Boothby being briefly married to Dorothy's cousin in the interim): Dorothy was to be an impeccable and very effective political wife, Harold a celibate and unenquiring husband. For him it was a dismal lot, but one which in due course settled into something like convenience, bearable since he was not a strongly sexed man, and since he had the consolation of knowing, as he told Horne, that Boothby was 'a hopeless fellow' from whom his wife needed a degree of protection. Lady Dorothy's affair with Boothby was well known among the social and political élite, but was, remarkably, never publicized until after her death. With the start of her liaison, and a recurrence of trouble from his war wounds, Macmillan suffered 'what in fact seemed to have been a full-scale nervous breakdown' (Horne, 1.98). He was for several months in a sanatorium at Neu Wittelsbach, near Munich.

Planning and inter-party co-operation in the 1930s In 1931 Macmillan easily recaptured Stockton at the general election in a straight contest with the Labour candidate (again Frederick Riley), and he held it in 1935 by a majority of 4068 in a three-cornered fight. He continued his publishing work and became one of those most prominent in seeking inter-party solutions to Britain's apparently intractable economic malaise. He had written to *The Times* on 27 May 1930 supporting Sir Oswald Mosley's famous memorandum on the economy and after Mosley's resignation from the Labour government had had close contact with him; he did not, however, join Mosley's New Party, though he sympathized with some of its economic objectives. Disillusioned with the National Government of 1931, which he had hoped would provide the sort of integrated approach he sought, he wrote *Reconstruction: a Plea for a National Policy* (1933) and formed, with Henry Mond, second Baron Melchett, the Industrial Reorganization League to promote 'industrial self-government' and 'orderly planning' of the economy (Ritschel, 195). The league received wide support from both industrialists and financiers. In 1934 Melchett introduced the Industrial Reorganization (Enabling) Bill in the Lords, and Macmillan introduced it in the Commons in 1935 (in 1934 he had carried a motion in its favour at the tory conference, against the platform's opposition). The bill was 'perhaps the one single instance of an attempt to legislate a corporatist economy in Britain' (Ritschel, 209), and it exposed the difficulties of genuinely integrating capital, labour, and government. Macmillan feared that inaction would make revolution possible and perhaps inevitable. He became associated with

Reginald Clifford *Allen, Baron Allen, a National Labour supporter. Their plans for a political journal failed but they published, together with A. Barratt Brown, principal of Ruskin College, *Liberty and Democratic Leadership* (1934) and *Liberty and Democratic Leadership: a Further Statement* (1934), advocating all-party agreement. Other pamphlets followed, such as *Planning for Employment* (1935), drafted by Macmillan, though in fact marking something of a retreat from central planning.

This movement reached its zenith in *The Next Five Years: an Essay in Agreement* (1935). As Daniel Ritschel has shown, this was in its specific recommendations much less corporatist than in its general tone. Macmillan tried unsuccessfully to encourage the National Government, of which he was still a supporter, to accept Lloyd George's 'New Deal' and he spoke from the platform when Lloyd George launched his council of action in July 1935. Lloyd George in return called for a parliament 'filled with Macmillans' (Ritschel, 277). Macmillan fought the 1935 election as one who both supported the National Government and pursued the objectives of the Next Five Years group. He voted against the government's Unemployed Insured Bill and kept in close touch with Keynes, whose *General Theory* had recently been published by Macmillans, and whose views, with some reservations, Macmillan commended to the Commons in May 1936. The group around Macmillan was in fact the best political base for Keynesianism, and Macmillan and G. D. H. Cole worked to advance the idea of a popular front against unemployment. But, as with the Derating Bill in the 1920s, sectional interests prevented united action, and the front collapsed.

Macmillan developed his ideas in *The Middle Way*, published in 1938. Whereas Keynes's *General Theory* aimed at a non-technical statement of a theoretical critique, *The Middle Way* tried to offer a reasoned programme of action, Keynesian in character—'a kind of popular version of some of Keynes's ideas' (*Winds of Change*, 490)—but with a much stronger emphasis on industrial policy than Keynes had offered. It was intended to offer a middle way politically as well as in terms of policy. It was much the most cogent work on the state and the economy published by any of those who became prime ministers in the twentieth century. It left Macmillan still uncertain in his intellectual and political relationship to his party, while, ironically, staking out much of what was to be the tory party's position after 1945. In the late 1940s the book's case against socialism and in favour of a managed capitalism seemed to many tories self-evidently sensible, though in 1938 many saw it as dangerously interventionist.

Foreign policy in the 1930s Macmillan always favoured linking economic intervention with an interventionist foreign policy. This was one of the difficulties between himself, Clifford Allen, and many of the Labour members of his various groups in the 1930s, not in the case of hostility to the Hoare–Laval pact—he resigned the government whip when sanctions against Italy were dropped in June 1936 (the only back-bencher to do so), though he resumed it when Neville Chamberlain replaced Baldwin as prime minister in May 1937—but rather over policy towards Germany. In 1936 he established links with Churchill, despite his reservations about Churchill's views on India, and helped to organize the 'Arms and the Covenant' meeting at the Albert Hall on 3 December 1936. Baldwin's revival and Churchill's odd behaviour over the abdication of Edward VIII spoilt this movement, but from then on Macmillan moved on the fringes of the Churchill circle (though less directly involved in it than his wife's lover, Boothby). He was more directly associated with the group centred on Anthony Eden after February 1938, known by the whips as 'the glamour boys'. Macmillan was a useful go-between with the Labour Party as it moved towards a more active anti-fascist position. He recalled: 'I thought, as did many with me, that we ought to have fought at Munich' (*Winds of Change*, 579). Hesitant up to that point—like most members he had cheered Chamberlain's announcement that Hitler had agreed to a four-power conference—and anti-interventionist on Spain, he now became 'a violent partisan' (*Winds of Change*, 583). He campaigned for national service and against Quintin Hogg in the Oxford by-election in October 1938, and wrote *The Price of Peace*, which was privately circulated. He was also active in the parliamentary committee on refugees and put up Jews fleeing from Germany and Czechoslovakia at Birch Grove. In 1939 he published *Economic Aspects of Defence* (with his earlier pamphlet as an appendix), in the compilation of which Thomas Balogh assisted. In March 1939, after Hitler's coup, he wrote to *The Times* (21 March) advocating 'a National Government on the broadest possible basis', a prelude to the Commons' motion of 29 March which marked the appearance of a tory anti-appeasement group willing to vote against the government.

The start of the Second World War thus found Macmillan in a curious position. His plans for domestic reform, the focus of his political efforts over fifteen years, had come to no direct effect; his recent association with Churchill was soon to bring him close to the heart of government. He had not acted accommodatingly in his economic reform proposals, in the sense that a less strident tone might well have brought him ministerial office, and his association with Churchill was likewise unrelated to short-term political ambition. But not for the last time, a quite dramatic political move placed him in line for power.

The Second World War Churchill and Eden were at once given office by Chamberlain at the outbreak of war, but not their followers. Nevertheless Macmillan was chosen to lead, with the elderly David Davies, first Baron Davies, a fact-finding mission to Finland in January 1940. Finland had been invaded by Russia following the Hitler–Stalin pact, but defended itself effectively. Britain, which had entered the war to defend Poland from a similar sort of attack, was in an awkward position, since for the Finns Russia (not Germany) was the enemy power. Macmillan assessed the Finns' position as bad but not hopeless, and telegraphed Chamberlain and Churchill for support. Anglo-French support was promised, but arrived too late, and the possibility of the allies fighting Russia as well as

Germany was avoided. In the Commons debate in March 1940, Macmillan wounded Chamberlain through the effectiveness of his criticism. He noticed that neither Churchill nor Eden was present, taking this to imply support for his criticism of the prime minister; but it might have implied embarrassment on their part at the victory of Russia as a necessary evil. He was one of forty-three Conservative MPs who voted against Chamberlain on 8 May 1940, leading to the end of his government.

In Churchill's coalition government Macmillan became parliamentary secretary to Herbert Morrison, minister of supply, a rather lowly appointment but one which reflected Macmillan's reputation as a go-between (Morrison being a Labour minister). His private secretary was John *Wyndham (later first Baron Egremont), who was closely associated with him politically and personally until his death in 1972. Macmillan remained at supply until February 1942, with Sir Andrew Duncan and Max Aitken, Lord Beaverbrook, also successively his ministers. Beaverbrook was not in the Commons, so Macmillan handled ministry business there from June 1941. He wisely felt that with Beaverbrook it was sensible to maintain 'a certain aloofness, for there were aspects of his character which I found distasteful' (*The Blast of War*, 85). Macmillan made a potentially difficult relationship work, and Beaverbrook, when they later had political differences, gave Macmillan an easy ride in his papers. The ministry gave Macmillan the opportunity (backed by government fiat) to introduce the planning he had so long advocated. He did this with some success, though he felt that top-level disputes, especially between Beaverbrook and Ernest Bevin, the minister of labour, unnecessarily complicated matters. His memorandum of 28 October 1941 led eventually to a restructuring of the department, and the creation of a new Ministry of Production, initially under Beaverbrook. Since Beaverbrook was not to have a parliamentary secretary, and since the Ministry of Supply was now to be downgraded in importance, Churchill agreed to find Macmillan a new post.

On 4 February 1942 Macmillan became under-secretary at the Colonial Office. It felt, he wrote, 'like leaving a madhouse in order to enter a mausoleum' (*The Blast of War*, 161). He was simultaneously sworn of the privy council, an unusual honour for a junior minister. With Lord Moyne and Lord Cranborne successively as his ministers, Macmillan continued to speak for his department in the Commons. Working with Cranborne was pleasant for Macmillan: they were already doubly connected by marriage and that year Maurice Macmillan married one of Cranborne's nieces. Macmillan dealt with colonial economic and trade questions and his energy generated a good deal of planned economic development in the colonies, especially in rubber and tin production. He oversaw conscripted labour in certain colonies. With others, he established the colonial research committee, the start of what under the Attlee government became a Fabian-led policy of colonial economic development.

To Macmillan's dismay he found himself in November 1942 with a new chief, Oliver Stanley, and with his own rather autonomous position, with its Commons responsibilities, potentially circumscribed. There was a possibility that Macmillan might be given a peerage, to speak for the Colonial Office in the Lords. However, on 22 December Churchill invited him to become minister resident at allied forces headquarters in Algiers, with a roving commission, not very clearly spelt out, to act as political adviser to the supreme allied commander, north Africa (General Eisenhower), and to represent the British government in the development of allied policy in north Africa and the Mediterranean by travelling in the area and liaising with the American and French generals. He was to report directly to Churchill rather than via the Foreign Office, an arrangement which Eden, as foreign secretary, resented. He immediately found himself an important go-between at the Casablanca conference in January 1943, with special responsibility for liaising between the French generals Giraud and de Gaulle, Macmillan having considerable sympathy for the position of the latter. Soon after, when taking off from Algiers for Cairo, Macmillan's plane crashed; he extricated himself from the burning fuselage, but with wounds to his legs, his face badly burnt, and his eyes saved only by his spectacles. A French admiral who had lost his hat remarked in shock, 'Ma casquette! J'ai perdue ma casquette'; Macmillan replied, showing the droll humour which was becoming his hallmark: 'I don't care a damn about your casquette. J'ai perdu my bloody face' (*The Blast of War*, 271). Macmillan in fact suffered from shock as well as his wounds, but recovered remarkably quickly, being back at work within a fortnight, against his doctor's advice. He was then also affected by delayed shock, and it was not until early March 1943 that he was fully operative, and he suffered periodically from depression for some time afterwards.

Macmillan's tasks in summer 1943 were to negotiate the incorporation of the portion of the French Vichy fleet under Admiral Godfroy with that of the allies, and to arbitrate further between de Gaulle, Giraud, Churchill, and Eisenhower. Both of these he did with skill, discreetly protecting the angular de Gaulle from his exasperated colleagues, and gaining in the process the respect and friendship of his French equivalent, Jean Monnet. On several occasions his diplomacy saved the day. The upshot was the recognition of de Gaulle and Giraud as joint leaders of the French committee of national liberation (a provisional government) and a certain irritation with Macmillan on the part of Churchill, who thought he was 'much too pro-French' and helpful to de Gaulle (*The Blast of War*, 442). Macmillan, in the midst of this, accompanied the king on his visit to Malta in June 1943, in which month he was also given a degree of responsibility for liaising on Italian as well as French policy. From July 1944 he was based at the palace of Caserta, near Naples. He successfully negotiated with the Italian exiles and, after the invasion of Italy, with the king of Italy, Victor Emmanuel III, to gain agreement for a provisional government of Italy, led by Badoglio, one of whose members was Benedetto Croce, the historian, whom Macmillan had published in translation, and whom he went to visit at Sorrento. Macmillan was a strong supporter of operation Armpit (an advance on Austria through Trieste and the Ljubljana gap, with the effect of allowing immediate Anglo-American access to the Balkans and eastern Europe) and succeeded in gaining Churchill's enthusiasm for it; but the plan was rejected by the Americans in favour of operation Anvil (landings in the south of France to accompany those in Normandy). Macmillan believed that the American insistence on landings in southern France was a mistake which let the Russians dominate eastern Europe and was 'one of the sad turning points of history' (*The Blast of War*, 511).

Throughout this period Macmillan was able only indirectly to influence events and policies: his effectiveness depended on his capacity to persuade. His donnish manner and resolutely civilian appearance emphasized his oblique role in a central theatre of the war. He used the strengths and weaknesses of his position cannily, and, with the exception of his sally into grand strategy over operation Armpit, with a good deal of success (and on that, the defeat was ultimately Churchill's, not Macmillan's). He had become, as John Wyndham dubbed him, 'Viceroy of the Mediterranean' (*DNB*). He also developed a close relationship with General Alexander, and they disconcerted their London colleagues by frequently sending joint telegrams and reports.

On 10 November 1944, Churchill gave Macmillan executive authority, as acting president of the allied commission for Italy (though this was by no means a dictatorial role, for a chief purpose of the commission was gradually to hand over control to the provisional Italian government). He was also given responsibility for liaising between the Foreign Office and the army on Balkan and Greek questions. In Greece, British influence was by agreement with Russia to be predominant. It was Greece, rather than Italy, which in fact took up most of his time. Following the German withdrawal from Greece, he spent several weeks during the winter of 1944–5 in Athens, for much of the time under sniper fire in the besieged British embassy with Reginald (Rex) Leeper, the ambassador, and Osbert Lancaster, the press attaché. To prevent a communist victory, Macmillan controversially (and initially against the wishes of King George II) supported the appointment of Archbishop Damaskinos as regent, a proposal which annoyed but finally convinced Churchill during his visit at the end of December 1944.

Macmillan superintended the political arrangements for the German surrender in Italy on 29 April 1945, and on 26 May he ceased to be minister resident in the Mediterranean and acting president of the allied commission for Italy. During those last weeks of the war he was involved in a series of what became highly controversial issues. Though in Italy and Greece his chief political purpose had been to exclude the communists as far as possible from power in the post-war settlement, in Yugoslavia different conditions obtained: there, Tito and the communist partisans were firmly in control. In north-eastern Italy, Macmillan and Alexander went beyond their instructions in proposing two zones—the eastern one under Tito and the western one under allied military government, though

with Yugoslav participation. The purpose was to avoid a further campaign in which British troops would have to fight against the Yugoslav partisans. Macmillan noted: 'Neither British nor American troops will care for a new campaign in order to save Trieste for the "Eyeties". On the other hand, to give in completely may be a sort of Slav Munich' (*Tides of Fortune*, 12). After a period of considerable anxiety caused by the intransigence on the one hand of Tito and on the other of the American president, Macmillan and Alexander's proposal was eventually accepted, and formed the basis of the territorial settlement agreed in 1954.

It was in the context of possible further military action against the Yugoslavs that Alexander and Macmillan had to deal with the problematic fate of non-German troops who had been fighting for the Nazis, whether willingly or by compulsion. The surrender of Germany left large numbers of these in allied hands, as well as surrendered Germans. There was also the question of British prisoners formerly in German but now in Russian hands. The Yalta agreement established categories of troops to be returned to the Russians, with (as it transpired) an all too certain fate awaiting them. Macmillan discussed the question with General Charles Keightley, commander of 5th corps, at Klagenfurt on 13 May 1945. He advised General Keightley to hand over to the Russians about 40,000 'Cossacks and "White" Russians, with their wives and children', as he called them in his diary (*War Diaries*, 756). 'We have decided to hand them over', Macmillan noted, suggesting that the decision was a joint one, though technically he was the political adviser, Keightley the officer in charge (*War Diaries*, 757). Most of these were exchanges within the Yalta categories, but they included a considerable number, including White Russians, who fell outside them (notably through having left Russia before the Soviet Union was established). Also handed over to Tito, though Macmillan was only obliquely associated with the relevant decisions, were 'anti-partisans' (that is Yugoslavs, many of them Chetniks and Ustashi, who had supported the Germans). Macmillan, in the pressure of events in May–June 1945, was party to a process of prisoner exchange which the Anglo-American leadership soon attempted to stop. He may or may not have been aware of the likely fate of the prisoners, but he knew the importance of the Yalta agreement which determined allied policy and action, and he laid considerable personal emphasis on the importance of the simultaneous rapid recovery of British prisoners from the Russians. He was not duplicitous (the charge that he deceived his friend and close colleague Alexander has been disposed of by Alistair Horne), but his priorities were not those of close distinctions between the different domiciles of non-German troops who until a month before had been fighting with the Germans. Moreover, Macmillan advised the military; he was not responsible for giving orders, and it was not he who killed the troops who were handed over to the Russians or to the partisans. A little-noticed episode at the time and in the context of the Europe-wide unravelling of the Second World War, Macmillan's advice to Keightley and their decision to 'hand them over' was, more than thirty years later, to become a point of major controversy.

Macmillan's war thus had a curious circularity. In 1940 he had found himself advocating assistance to the Finns in their war against the Russians; by 1945 he found himself blocking the Russians as best he could 1000 miles to the south. In between, he had played a notable role in the defeat of German Nazism, by managing expertly the balance between military and political considerations in the Mediterranean and south-east Europe. He finished the war with his political reputation clearly enhanced within the political and military élite, though necessarily not much with the public, for his function was to work discreetly behind the scenes. He now stood in a powerful position in British politics: his pre-war experience had made him an important figure in the Keynesian approach to the economy which during the war gained much ground, and his wartime experience had given him great diplomatic experience and extensive contact with many of those who were to be central figures in the post-war world, particularly Eisenhower, Monnet, and de Gaulle. Together with R. A. Butler (whose career was the obverse of Macmillan's: a Foreign Office appeaser before the war and a domestic reformer during it), it would be fair to say that Macmillan by 1945 was one of Britain's best-equipped all-round tory politicians.

Post-war politics Macmillan returned to Britain on 26 May 1945 and became secretary of state for air and for the first time a member of cabinet, in Churchill's caretaker government, pending the outcome of the general election held on 5 July, its result being announced on 26 July. In September 1944 Duff Cooper had offered to arrange for Macmillan to succeed him in his very safe seat, St George's, Westminster. After initially accepting privately, Macmillan, motivated by 'fondness' for his constituency and by a desire not 'to give up Stockton without even a fight', and encouraged by Lord Beaverbrook, eventually decided to stand again for Stockton (*Tides of Fortune*, 30). He nevertheless 'had little hope of success' (*Tides of Fortune*, 31). Beaverbrook had offered the assurance of a safe vacancy should Macmillan be defeated at Stockton, as indeed he was, heavily, by George Chetwynd. However, the death of Sir Edward Campbell (before the Stockton result was declared) created a safe vacant seat at Bromley, for which Macmillan was selected (Randolph Churchill withdrawing his candidacy). He was comfortably elected on 16 November 1945. He sat for Bromley, a predominantly middle-class suburban seat in south London, for which he never felt the same affection as for Stockton, for the rest of his time in the Commons. How far this change of constituency itself affected Macmillan's political style and domestic policy in the post-war years cannot be known: it certainly made easier the emergence of a tory gent, inter-war in style and dress, making speeches which sometimes seemed embarrassingly mannered. Although the policies of *The Middle Way* now had a much clearer run, the politician who had promoted them seemed, in style if

not in substance, somewhat distanced from their modernizing intentions. This may have been an intentional insurance against right-wing tory hostility—Macmillan's toffishness emphasized what many Conservatives thought were impeccable tory qualifications to lead—but it may have reflected a genuine change in emphasis. The need to disguise the failure of his marriage—his wife's affair with Boothby continued—and the will needed to maintain his composure during an exhausting and often quite solitary war, may have made it impossible for him to avoid a fusion between political acting and his own character. The personality which Macmillan presented from the mid-1940s remained remarkably consistent for the rest of his life.

At that time the tory opposition did not mimic government with specifically assigned shadow ministers: Churchill as leader decided who should speak on which subject. Macmillan thus spoke for the opposition in both domestic and foreign policy debates. Churchill made R. A. Butler head of the Conservative Research Department, but Macmillan's writings were a fertile influence on it and he was involved in drafting the tories' *Industrial Charter*, published in May 1947, which committed the party to full employment and strategic control of the economy, and accepted the Labour government's nationalization of coal, the railways, and the Bank of England as irreversible. In his memoirs, published in 1969 at the end of a later Labour government, Macmillan wrote that nationalization was

> pure State capitalism. However, I accepted the fact that this controversy must now be settled ... the achievements of the Labour Party in this Parliament [1945–50] have stood ... [but] as time has passed, this classical form of State capitalism seems out of date. (*Tides of Fortune*, 73–5)

Though Macmillan became an effective political sniper in the late 1940s, he did not seriously question the new economic and welfare structure the Labour Party put in place—indeed his complaint with coal nationalization was that it was insufficiently radical in changing management practices with respect to the welfare of the staff. Despite his acceptance of Labour's achievement, Macmillan also argued that free enterprise still had a vital role to play, and that 'socialism' (as he believed the Labour Party to be promoting) was a dangerous threat. To meet it he suggested in 1946 that the tories and Liberals combine. He proposed a 'New Democratic Party' and suggested proportional representation in large cities (Horne, 1.298–9). These ideas—essentially a continuation of his 1930s tactics—were strongly disliked by some sections of his party, who wanted a free market rhetoric and only a tacit acceptance of Labour's achievements. Nevertheless he believed 'that with the exception of the extreme Right of the Conservative Party and the extreme Left of the Labour Party, there was a general acceptance of something like the Middle Way which I had preached so long' (*Tides of Fortune*, 81).

Macmillan's war years had placed him in a position where the vulnerability of Britain's position as a world power was increasingly apparent. But like most of his contemporaries he was slow to draw any conclusions from this. In the post-war world he initially sought no basic reappraisal of Britain's aims, though he visited India in February–March 1947 and did not dissent from the British government's policy—announced while he was returning to Britain—of an end to British rule by July 1948, though it was clearly bolder than he himself would have advocated. He followed Ernest Bevin (Labour's foreign secretary) and Churchill in their view of the USSR. Bevin was, in Macmillan's view, 'the strongest figure in the Labour Government' (*Tides of Fortune*, 137). Macmillan suspected that Churchill's 'iron curtain' speech at Fulton, Missouri, might be an over-simplification—but, with respect to the facts, 'who could resist his battering-ram of argument?' (*Tides of Fortune*, 107). Macmillan argued in his memoirs that

> following the example of India, Burma and Ceylon, the 'wind of change' soon began to blow rapidly through the whole Colonial Empire. The course, therefore, was already set by the time the Conservative Party came into power in 1951. (*Tides of Fortune*, 277)

This was true, but the link between the end of the Indian empire and rapid decolonization elsewhere was not one made by most members of the Conservative Party (including, in the late 1940s and early 1950s, Macmillan himself), nor, indeed, by most members of the Labour government.

Macmillan, influenced in part by his wartime discussions with Jean Monnet, was an early enthusiast for Churchill's united Europe movement (and was on its managing committee from 1947). He attended the Congress of Europe at the Hague in 1948, from which developed the Council of Europe at Strasbourg, from 1949, of which he was a founder member, sitting on its consultative assembly for three years. He thought the British government's decision not to join the discussions in June 1950 which arose from the Schuman plan for a European coal and steel community marked 'a black week for Britain; for the Empire; for Europe; and for the peace of the world' (*Tides of Fortune*, 191). Schuman's initiative 'may well be a major turning-point in European history. It is certainly a turning-point in the fortunes of the Tory Party. This issue affords us the last, and perhaps only, chance of regaining the initiative' (*Tides of Fortune*, 193). But he did not at this stage see any incompatibility between this view and the belief that (as he put it in 1949) 'the Empire must always have first preference for us' (*DNB*).

300,000 houses Churchill formed his third government in October 1951 following what Macmillan felt was a disappointingly narrow tory victory in the general election. Churchill appointed and announced his nine core cabinet posts before inviting Macmillan to be minister of local government and planning (the ministry also including housing), or failing that, president of the Board of Trade. Macmillan was not much attracted to either post but after some hesitation accepted local government and planning (which was renamed housing and local government). It was a high-risk choice, for the 1950 party conference had adopted the building of 300,000 houses a year as a Conservative government's target. This was difficult to achieve,

and implied possible distortion of industrial investment, an increase in inflation, and even some effect on supplies for rearmament and the Korean war. Macmillan set about his task with relish; it was unusual for a minister to be given such a constructive role, the 300,000 target being seen as a major test of the government's effectiveness. It gave him the authority to badger the Treasury to an exceptional extent, a privilege of which Macmillan took persistent advantage. He set up regional housing boards, on the advice of Sir Percy Mills, reduced the mandatory proportion of new private (as opposed to municipal) houses from one in ten to one in two, reduced the minimum required size of houses, and introduced the sale of municipal houses. A new Town and Country Planning Bill was enacted in November 1954.

Energetically supported by his parliamentary secretary, Ernest Marples, and by the civil servant Dame Evelyn Sharp, Macmillan reached the annual target in December 1953, and in fact faced the prospect in 1954 of building too many houses. The building programme was accompanied by rent increases, proposed in his white paper 'Houses—the next step' in November 1953 and enacted in the Repairs and Rent Act (1954): its aim was the reduction of slum buildings by the raising of rents for houses in good repair—a controversial and politically sensitive matter. Macmillan came to think that Aneurin Bevan's criticism—that the additional rent would be insufficient inducement to landlords—was 'probably right … Nevertheless our plan broke the ice of rigid rent control' (*Tides of Fortune*, 458). The critics were indeed right: rents went up but landlords made little progress in slum clearance or housing improvement. The aftermath of this policy was the rent scandals of the late 1950s and early 1960s, which did the tories' reputation considerable harm. Rent questions apart, Macmillan's housing achievements were substantial: they showed what a determined government could achieve with a proactive domestic policy, if it so chose. Macmillan, aware of the tension between tory anti-state rhetoric and the policies of his ministry, presented the housing programme in the context of *ad hoc* wartime-style crisis management. But they were a peacetime achievement, even so, and Macmillan looked back on this period as 'in many ways the happiest and most rewarding of my time as a Minister' (*Tides of Fortune*, 373).

Macmillan's formidable task at housing to an extent marginalized him with respect to the government's other actions. He found Eden's caution over Europe depressing and he contemplated resigning in March 1952 when the cabinet showed little interest in the question; but he circulated a further paper on Europe in March 1953 opposing a federal Europe as against Britain's national interest. In September 1954 he successfully persuaded Eden to offer a way out of the impasse created by France's rejection of the European Defence Community (the 'Pleven plan') by means of a solution based on West Germany's adherence to the Brussels treaty—thus earning, temporarily at least, the gratitude of Britain's continental neighbours. Macmillan hoped for the Foreign Office, but, with Churchill prevaricating about his retirement and Eden ensconced in the Foreign Office until that time, there was no immediate prospect of it.

In October 1954 Churchill moved a reluctant Macmillan to the Ministry of Defence, a post whose holder the premier regarded as almost personally responsible to him. (Indeed, Churchill had held the post in conjunction with the premiership for the first six months of his administration.) Macmillan found himself rather in his wartime relationship to Churchill, but with the latter no longer at the height of his powers. Macmillan had already decided that Churchill ought to resign, and, especially after Churchill's second stroke in June 1953, had played a leading role in encouraging him to fix a date. He did so partly on the ground that in Eden there was a worthy successor being unfairly denied advancement. His approaches to Churchill were much more direct than those made to Gladstone in the somewhat analogous case of 1894. Nevertheless Macmillan's forthright behaviour did not diminish Churchill's respect for him. In the meantime, Macmillan encouraged a review of the over-bureaucratic structure of NATO and defended Britain's decision to develop her own hydrogen bomb. He had already become a convinced supporter of the independent British nuclear deterrent and of the view that its possession implied a considerable reduction in conventional forces.

Foreign secretary and chancellor of the exchequer Churchill finally retired in April 1955. When Eden succeeded him as prime minister he put Macmillan in his own former position as foreign secretary, another post whose holder was seen as personally responsible to the prime minister— whether Churchill, Eden, or in due course Macmillan himself. The relationship between Eden and Macmillan was by no means as close as this appointment and Macmillan's earlier representations to Churchill about Eden seemed to suggest. Eden would have preferred Lord Salisbury as his foreign secretary but (remembering Chamberlain's unhappy experience after appointing Lord Halifax as foreign secretary in 1938) was unwilling to cause a row by having his foreign secretary in the Lords, or to shoulder the extra burden it might have meant for him in the Commons. (Ironically, Macmillan would later appoint a foreign secretary from the House of Lords, Lord Home.) Macmillan had worked in tandem with Eden at various points since 1942, but the relationship was by no means always easy, and Macmillan differed quite strongly with Eden on Europe, while admiring his diplomatic gifts. Serving as foreign secretary, with a premier whose only government experience was in the Foreign Office, was difficult.

As with defence, Macmillan's time at the Foreign Office—which he stated in his memoirs to be 'the summit of my ambitions' (*Tides of Fortune*, 582)—was uneasy. On almost all the issues, he found Eden had left a clear policy in place. Some such policies—for example, that Britain should play no part in the Messina conference from which derived the Spaak committee, which in turn designed the treaty of Rome—were not those Macmillan would have devised. He got the cabinet to agree that Britain should send a 'representative' to the meetings of the Spaak committee (Russell Bretherton; Macmillan would have preferred a 'delegate'), but the critical moment was missed. In missing it, Macmillan was acting no differently from the rest of the Foreign Office, where questions such as those of Cyprus and Egypt seemed of central importance. Macmillan spent much time on the Cyprus question, and even more on Egypt, the traditional area of imperial strategic concern.

Macmillan was getting into his stride as foreign secretary when Eden—perhaps precisely because of that— moved him on 21 December 1955 to the chancellorship of the exchequer. Macmillan strongly resented this move, which could not but be seen as a comment on his tenure of the foreign secretaryship (though Eden emphasized how important it was that R. A. Butler should have a strong successor at the Treasury). Macmillan in return held out against Butler being given the title of deputy prime minister and, consequently, in favour of the establishment of his own claim to the premiership on a basis of parity with Butler (Eden's health was already unpredictable). This was his most decisive move towards the premiership, and it worked well; moreover, Butler, now merely lord privy seal and leader of the house, no longer had a government department.

The move to the exchequer to an extent unleashed Macmillan: Eden had no special standing on financial matters, and Macmillan was soon using an authoritative, even officious, tone in letters to Eden impossible during his Foreign Office days. Macmillan, in the budget due for March 1956, wished to increase taxation, including income tax, to reduce purchasing power. He wished to link this to cuts in government expenditure, particularly in defence (in line with his view that an independent nuclear deterrent made units such as Fighter Command redundant). Eden, however, prevented both of these. Macmillan's first (and it turned out only) budget, on 17 April 1956, was chiefly notable for the introduction of premium bonds (redeemable bonds whose interest was distributed by lot in the form of prizes) and the start of a vigorous ecclesiastical row over whether the government was encouraging gambling.

Suez In 1956, Macmillan as chancellor found himself in a situation of exceptional complexity, involving the future relations of Britain with Europe and America, the traditional question of imperial suzerainty in Egypt, and that regular phenomenon of post-war Britain, a sterling crisis.

Macmillan, like almost everyone in British politics, underestimated the capacity and determination of the west European states to progress towards union. But he realized that, whatever the process under way was, Britain was not sufficiently part of it. He worked with Peter Thorneycroft (at the Board of Trade) to propose British association with the Spaak plan through an industrial free-trade area (thus preserving preferential access to the British market for Commonwealth agricultural products and raw materials). Just as this was being proposed, Egypt's nationalization of the Suez canal company in July 1956 (contrary to previous assurances) brought to the boil the long-simmering issue of what, if any, role Britain had in Egypt and in the running of the canal (the British military presence in Egypt had ended in June 1956, having lasted since 1882). Macmillan was a member of the Egypt committee established by Eden to deal with the situation, and took a forceful line in encouraging Eden to move towards military intervention. Macmillan seems to have been among the first to suggest encouraging Israeli involvement and though he had reservations about the tactical aspects of the initial invasion plans, he took the lead in August 1956 in developing them, so much so that Eden reined him in. Macmillan used analogies of Nasser with Hitler and Mussolini as energetically as any of the other tory leaders.

With the sterling reserves already depleted, Macmillan visited the USA at the end of September 1956, receiving an honorary degree from the University of Indiana and visiting his mother's home town of Spencer before proceeding to Washington. A conversation with President Eisenhower on 25 September was understood by Macmillan to have established that Eisenhower distrusted the United Nations and wished to 'get Nasser down' without UN permission being necessary (*Riding the Storm*, 134). Other accounts, by both British and Americans, later stated that Macmillan had seriously misunderstood Eisenhower's position. Roger Makins, who had been Macmillan's assistant at allied forces headquarters, Mediterranean, in 1943–4, and was now the British ambassador in Washington and the only witness to the conversation, recalled: 'I was expecting Harold to make a statement, say something important on Suez—but in fact he said nothing … Nor did Eisenhower say anything. I was amazed' (Scott Lucas, 211). Making the assumption of Eisenhower's sympathy was an important error, as Eden was emboldened and reassured by Macmillan's subsequent dispatch, and Macmillan himself failed to take the sort of financial precautions made by the French, Britain's ally in invasion. Macmillan's error was the more remarkable, given that his international career had been built on just this sort of diplomacy, and that Robert Murphy, the American diplomatist with whom he had worked for most of his time in north Africa, was among those he saw both in Washington and in London. Though the Americans may be blamed for not making clearer their hostility to British–French–Israeli military action, it was for the protagonists to be sure that they had clearance, or at least benevolent neutrality, especially as they were clients rather than equals of the USA in financial and military power.

When the Americans reacted strongly against the Anglo-French invasion (following Israel's co-ordinated attack on Egypt on 29 October), Macmillan moved quickly to reverse British policy. He belatedly requested a loan from the International Monetary Fund and urgently advised a ceasefire to gain it. 'First in, first out' was Harold Wilson's jibe (*Riding the Storm*, 163), to which there was no effective response. Macmillan recalled to Alistair Horne that Suez was 'a very bad episode in my life' (Horne, 1.447). So it undoubtedly was, but Macmillan had the capacity, and the political time, to learn lessons from it. Eden had neither.

Prime minister   Eden resigned the premiership through ill health on 9 January 1957, making no recommendation to the queen as to his successor, but suggesting she ask Lord Salisbury to consult with leading tories. With Lord Kilmuir, the lord chancellor, Lord Salisbury took soundings ('Well, which is it, Wab or Hawold?' (Earl of Kilmuir, *Memoirs: Political Adventure*, 1962, 285)) and on 10 January Macmillan, rather than the widely anticipated R. A. Butler, was summoned to Buckingham Palace and kissed hands on being appointed prime minister and first lord of the Treasury. (Among those whom Salisbury consulted was Churchill, who unhesitatingly supported Macmillan.) He took office in unpropitious circumstances, both for him and his party. He had held three major offices in as many years, with the quality of his performance quite severely questioned with respect to each, and especially the two most recent. His record on Suez was transparently bad, with both his diplomatic and his political judgement seriously questioned. His earlier reputation as a cross-party sort of person had been replaced, largely through his own political tone, by one of toffish arrogance, good-humoured but energetically partisan. His party had enjoyed the advantages of the post-war recovery and of the Labour Party's internal strife. It had won the general elections of 1951 and 1955 with increasing majorities. Yet the Conservative Party of the 1950s was ill at ease with respect to foreign, imperial, and Commonwealth policy, the very area in which it had always claimed special authority. The new prime minister's recent career was almost a personification of that unease.

Macmillan's distribution of cabinet posts was shrewd. Lord Salisbury was persuaded to stay on as lord president and leader of the House of Lords. Mindful that 'there would be plenty of gossips and ill-wishers who would try to make trouble between us' (*Riding the Storm*, 185), Macmillan offered Butler a free choice of post; he chose the home secretaryship. This enabled Macmillan to retain Selwyn Lloyd as foreign secretary. Peter Thorneycroft, a pro-European, was promoted from the Board of Trade to the Treasury. Duncan Sandys was made minister of defence, to oversee the necessary expenditure cuts. Julian Amery (Macmillan's son-in-law), hitherto an outspoken Suez rebel, was given a junior post, but charges of nepotism were deflected by the voluntary resignation of James Stuart (Macmillan's brother-in-law). The new prime minister put on a brave face to the Commons and to the public; with the party rallying to him, encouraged by the chief whip, Edward Heath (whom Macmillan retained), he avoided what some thought might be a rapid failure of his government.

The immediate post-Suez confusion in which Macmillan took office made long-term planning difficult and, though he had not discounted becoming premier, he was not prepared for the office in the sense that he would have been if in opposition. Mending fences was necessarily his first task, and it was some time before the grand reorientation of British policy which was to be his chief achievement became apparent, even to him. At the Bermuda conference with Eisenhower in March 1957, fair relations with America were restored. Macmillan probably deceived himself as to the extent that the Americans believed there was a 'special relationship' to restore; nevertheless Eisenhower agreed to pursue revision of the restrictive McMahon Act in order to resume the sharing of nuclear technology with Britain (agreements signed by Eisenhower and Macmillan on 3 November 1957 and ratified on 3 July 1958 enabled Britain to gain uniquely privileged access to American nuclear technology) and the USA moved towards taking direct responsibility in the Middle East—so that during the 1958 crisis involving Iraq, Jordan, and Lebanon, Britain and America acted in harmony. However, the wooing of the USA into the Middle East was in fact an admission that Britain, even with France, could not act without American backing.

A vital decision was the acceptance of the defence white paper drafted by Duncan Sandys and published in April 1957, which gave a greater emphasis to independent nuclear deterrence and made a consequent reduction in conventional forces (one result was the phasing out of national service). This had profound implications for Britain's foreign, economic, and scientific policies as well as for her defences, perhaps more than Macmillan at the time realized. It was also to have significant domestic political consequences. Though much British research was given over to nuclear development, with considerable distortion to the British scientific community, the British were not in fact in a position to implement Sandys's policy. Britain could make nuclear weapons, and had made important technical progress in the 1950s, but she lacked adequate means of getting them to the target area, especially as the effectiveness of the bomber force was by the later 1950s declining. The upshot was that Macmillan spent much time persuading the Americans to supply the means of delivering the nuclear weapons to their targets. His aim was to gain a British deterrent which was as independent as possible. He pursued this objective, ironically, at just the time that the American government became more favourable to sharing nuclear technology with Britain and when British policy became in practice dependent on the purchase of American systems.

Macmillan earned the gratitude of his party by refusing any inquiry into the Suez débâcle and in the debate on Suez in May 1957 only fourteen tories abstained in the Commons. Encouraging the dissidents was Lord Salisbury, who had resigned from the government in March 1957 over the release of Archbishop Makarios of Cyprus. Despite family connections and a long friendship, Salisbury's resignation was accepted with some alacrity by Macmillan, in the same spirit that a previous Salisbury had 'lanced a boil' by gratefully accepting the resignation of Lord Randolph Churchill in 1887. Macmillan's acceptance of Salisbury's resignation emphasized his political strength, his 'unflappability', and his determination to pursue a bold course in colonial policy; it may also have

represented, as Alistair Horne suggested, 'a triumph over all the slights and humiliations at the hands of Cecil and Cavendish grandees that Macmillan had suffered in the 1920s and 1930s—a kind of break with the past' (Horne, 2.39).

Letting Salisbury go was a risky tactic: the tory right was to be a vociferous though never very effective force throughout Macmillan's government. Much more serious was the resignation of the whole of his Treasury team on 6 January 1958 (Thorneycroft, the chancellor, Nigel Birch, the economic secretary to the Treasury, and J. Enoch Powell, the first secretary). Thorneycroft had demanded cuts of £153 million in the civil estimates for 1958. Some £100 million of spending cuts were agreed, but Macmillan thought it neither financially necessary nor politically possible to insist on the remainder (Eden had overruled him as chancellor on much the same grounds). Macmillan was committed intellectually and emotionally to economic expansion, in which he was encouraged by his private economic adviser, Sir Roy Harrod, who was even more expansionist than Keynes, whose friend and biographer he was. With some aplomb Macmillan famously dismissed the resignations as a 'little local difficulty' (he was leaving for a tour of the Commonwealth at the time). He later recorded it as his opinion that Thorneycroft had been led into resignation by Birch and Powell, who 'seemed to have introduced into the study of financial and economic problems a degree of fanaticism which appeared to me inappropriate' (Riding the Storm, 372). But to have dissident retrenchers as well as dissident imperialists in his party was becoming dangerous.

Macmillan, however, remained his party's best hope for a general election. Unemployment was at its lowest level since 1945 (though it was shortly to rise again) and Macmillan spoke the truth when he remarked on 20 July 1957 to a large meeting in Bradford, 'Let's be frank about it; most of our people have never had it so good' (Horne, 2.64). The Labour opposition made such capital as they could with incidents such as the Hola camp episode (the deaths from beating of eleven Mau Mau prisoners in March 1959 in Kenya, which led to the setting up of an Africa committee of the cabinet and to considerable alarm on Macmillan's part; he later described it as 'an anxious, if minor, incident' (Riding the Storm, 735)). The Devlin report on riots in Nyasaland was a serious indictment of British policy, and was rejected by the government in July 1959, an alternative report being rapidly written and accepted. Already tarred with the brush of defending the Suez episode, Macmillan's government began to seem much more a defender of 'imperial' positions than was in the long run to prove the case. Though the opposition made some impact with these and other imperial issues— attempting to link them to the general charge of incompetence which Suez permitted—they were never likely to be issues which could damage the government in a fundamental way. Macmillan was an able television interviewee, and his public persona was if anything enhanced by his depiction as 'Supermac' by the left-wing cartoonist, 'Vicky'. Sustained by the long 1950s boom, and well-led in the campaign by the prime minister, who chose the autumn rather than the spring to go to the country, the tories at the general election in October 1959 gained their highest-ever vote (13,749,830), and an increase in their majority from 58 to 100. This was a notable defeat for Labour, who—in the immediate aftermath of Suez—had expected to regain office.

Macmillan and Britain's reorientation in the world order
With his political flanks to left and right now apparently secure, Macmillan gained a breathing space. Between 1959 and 1961 occurred a series of decisions and initiatives of profound importance for Britain's place in the world. The extent to which these policy changes were intentionally related remains uncertain, but of their adjacent significance there can be no doubt. That Macmillan was already thinking in grand terms was shown by an all-day meeting he summoned at Chequers on 7 June 1959, to discuss 'what is likely to happen in the world during the next ten years': this led to the appointment of a committee 'to draw up a paper—for the use of the next Government' (diaries, 7 June 1959). The review, chaired by Norman Brook, was completed in February 1960, its report (drafted by Patrick Dean) circulated as 'Future policy study, 1960–1970' (PRO, CAB 129/100, C(60) 35, 24 Feb 1960). The report recognized that Britain was 'slipping backwards in relative economic power' and that her 'relative power in the world will certainly decline, though it does not follow that our status need necessarily do the same'. It anticipated that the Commonwealth would become 'less of an *economic* unit'. The general assumption of the report was that while Britain's economic and political power base was diminishing, she should none the less maintain 'a leading position among the Powers and a higher place in their counsels than our material assets alone would strictly warrant'. With respect to Europe: 'It is impossible to be sure that Western Europe will continue along its present path towards integration. Our tactics must, therefore, be adjusted to suit the needs of the moment'. Though the report was made for Macmillan rather than by him, its criteria and findings accorded closely with his views at this time. The pursuit of an influence and a status which were greater than the capacity to sustain them (or playing the cards above their value, as Macmillan described it) was an abiding objective of his years as prime minister, and his diaries frequently recorded the extent to which Britain was noticed as a participant, rather than the achievement of the policy objective.

The pursuit of status was not, however, a chief determinant of colonial policy. After the election Macmillan made Iain Macleod colonial secretary. There was a considerable fear that retention of colonies by force would open them to Soviet influence (the 1959–60 review considered the main area of future conflict would be in the underdeveloped world, requiring 'sustained and expensive' aid and political activity to keep such countries in the 'non-Communist world'). Under Alan Lennox-Boyd's tenure of the Colonial Office Ghana had become independent in 1957, and steps had been taken towards self government in Nigeria and elsewhere. Nevertheless Macleod greatly

accelerated the movement towards independence of colonies and protectorates; Jomo Kenyatta and Hastings Banda were released from gaol, and conferences arranging independence were almost forced on some of the colonies and protectorates involved. By the end of Macmillan's government most of British Africa bar Southern Rhodesia was independent within the Commonwealth. This was a remarkable achievement, and especially for a Conservative prime minister, whose party rhetoric had for so long rested on an imperial bass line. The complicating factor was the Central African Federation, and the possibility of the deterioration of Southern Rhodesia into a British Algeria. At the end of a long tour of rather surprised African nations in January–February 1960, Macmillan visited Southern Rhodesia and South Africa. In Southern Rhodesia he reiterated the government's support for the federation (finally dissolved during R. A. Butler's mission in 1964), but in South Africa, on Monday 3 February in Cape Town, he delivered a very carefully prepared and instantaneously famous speech, in which he told the South African parliament:

> the most striking of all the impressions I have formed since I left London a month ago is of the strength of this African national consciousness. In different places it takes different forms, but it is happening everywhere. The wind of change is blowing through this continent, and, whether we like it or not, this growth of national consciousness is a political fact. (*Pointing the Way*, 156)

The speech infuriated the Salisbury wing of the tory party, for whom 3 February was in every sense 'Black Monday', and led to the formation of the Monday Club. South Africa was effectively driven out of the Commonwealth at the prime ministers' meeting in March 1961, when (despite Macmillan's efforts to dissuade them) other member countries made clear that they would not allow South Africa to renew its membership, which it was obliged to apply to do following a plebiscite in favour of a republican constitution in October 1960.

Side by side with decolonization went two other streams of external policy: negotiations with the Soviet bloc and Britain's first application to join the European Common Market. Macmillan believed that he and Britain had a major role to play in the politics of nuclear détente—a role underpinned by Britain's status as a nuclear power, but also made more urgent by the difficulties encountered in maintaining that status. He devoted much energy to promoting the summit meeting held in Paris on 16 May 1960 and felt 'disappointment amounting almost to despair' when it broke down despite his series of personal interviews with the other participants (*Pointing the Way*, 213). Britain's chief nuclear weapon, the Blue Streak, was developed in the face of the hostility of the British chiefs of staff, but in February 1960 their opposition to its inflexibility led to the abandonment of its development. During his visit to Washington in March 1960 (chiefly to prepare the ground for the summit), Macmillan gained from Eisenhower an agreement that the USA would allow Britain to use either Skybolt missiles (fired from bombers) or Polaris missiles (fired from submarines). The British chose Skybolt, the Americans gaining in return a submarine base for Polaris submarines at Holy Loch in Scotland. Macmillan's search for a British nuclear deterrent was persistent, but the cancellation of Blue Streak made Britain dependent on American delivery systems, however much they might be presented as under British control. Perhaps ironically, given his emphasis on upgrading Britain's nuclear weapons, Macmillan took especial pride in negotiating an agreement for strict control of their testing, the nuclear test ban treaty being agreed on 10 August 1963, following an ambassadorial conference in Moscow (Kennedy had rejected Macmillan's wish for a summit meeting) and signed by Lord Home (who had replaced Lloyd as foreign secretary) on 10 October 1963.

Macmillan increasingly found himself stretched by three competing forces: the USA, the Commonwealth, and the European Economic Community (for, despite the experiment of the introduction of the European Free Trade Association in 1959–60, he perceived the gradual elimination of other possibilities). On 9 July 1960 he wrote in his diary:

> Shall we be caught between a hostile (or at least less and less friendly) America and a boastful, powerful 'Empire of Charlemagne'—now under French but later bound to come under German control. Is this the real reason for 'joining' the Common Market (if we are acceptable) and for abandoning (a) the Seven [European Free Trade Association or EFTA countries] (b) British agriculture (c) the Commonwealth? It's a grim choice.   (*Pointing the Way*, 316)

Macmillan had in his career recognized better than most the tension that these forces created. His difficulty, perhaps, was that he had a sentimental and a political sympathy for each of them. It was also the case that no leader of a large British party could have a sole commitment to any one of them.

In 1961 Macmillan developed close ties with the new American president, John F. Kennedy, skilfully avoiding the mistakes other tory leaders made when dealing with a Democrat in the White House and exploiting to the full his personal and family connections. Kennedy was a relative by marriage, as a brother-in-law of Dorothy Macmillan's late nephew, Lord Hartington. Macmillan sent as ambassador to Washington David Ormsby-Gore, the brother of Maurice Macmillan's wife, Katie, and an intimate long-term friend of Robert Kennedy, the president's brother. Macmillan's attempt to re-forge the 'special relationship' was thus underpinned by close personal relations.

Despite his success in restoring Anglo-American relations, Macmillan was haunted by the prospect that the EEC (now successfully established, and enjoying growth rates significantly higher than Britain's) would supplant Britain as America's key partner in Europe. EFTA, though much trumpeted as a 'bridge' to the EEC, was clearly not viewed as such by the six member countries of the latter, nor indeed by the United States, which regarded it as embodying all of the economic disadvantages and none of the political advantages of the EEC. It was therefore partly to maintain Britain's standing with America (and its usefulness to the Commonwealth), as well as to regain its influence in Europe, that Macmillan reluctantly came to the conclusion that Britain must attempt to join the European Communities (the European Coal and Steel Community and Euratom were not merged with the European Economic Community until 1967). He appears to have taken this decision by May 1960. In July that year he reshuffled his cabinet to ensure that pro-Europeans were in key positions—Sandys as secretary of state for Commonwealth relations, Christopher Soames as minister of agriculture, and Heath as lord privy seal, charged with the conduct of negotiations. Butler, the leading potential dissident, was later effectively neutralized by being given the task of liaising with the National Farmers' Union. Macmillan announced in the House of Commons on 31 July 1961 (just before the summer recess) that Britain would be seeking negotiations, and Britain's application was formally tabled on 10 August 1961.

In announcing his decision to the House of Commons, Macmillan emphasized that Britain would join the European Communities only if satisfactory arrangements could be made for the Commonwealth, EFTA, and British agriculture. These three issues dominated the subsequent negotiations, and the public debate in Britain. While Heath and Macmillan were upbeat in reporting the progress of negotiations in Brussels, it gradually became clear that the Europeans were in no mood to contemplate significant concessions. Future arrangements for the Commonwealth proved a particularly intractable and emotive issue. In 1956 Macmillan had gone on record as saying that Britain could never agree 'to our entering arrangements which, as a matter of principle, would prevent our treating the great range of imports from the Commonwealth at least as favourably as those from the European countries' (*Hansard 5C*, 26 Nov 1956, cols. 37–8). Nevertheless, with a few small exceptions, the most that the EEC countries would offer was a gradual imposition of the external tariff. The hostility of Commonwealth countries to any British application had been made clear during a tour of Commonwealth capitals undertaken by Heath, Sandys, and others in July 1961. The Commonwealth prime ministers' meeting in London in September 1962 passed off better than Macmillan had feared, but nevertheless resulted in a communiqué expressing disquiet at the extent to which Commonwealth interests had not been met. The prime ministers' meeting was also the occasion for Gaitskell to come out against membership of the EEC on the terms then likely; and it emboldened Macmillan's opponents within the Conservative Party, who were increasingly well organized through the Anti-Common Market League.

Despite Heath's and Macmillan's willingness to compromise, the negotiations were also overshadowed by the antipathy of de Gaulle. Even before the announcement of Britain's application, Macmillan had been advised that de Gaulle was highly unlikely to agree to British membership. In de Gaulle's view, Britain was insufficiently 'European' and would, if admitted, use its influence within the EEC to derail the European project; in particular, he regarded Britain as akin to an American 'Trojan horse'. His views were not altered by a series of personal discussions with Macmillan at the Château des Champs in June 1962. Macmillan then recorded: 'I am not at all sure how far de Gaulle and the French really feel it to be in France's interest to have us in' (*At the End of the Day*, 121). Nevertheless, he continued to hope that he could either win over or out-manoeuvre de Gaulle. In this he was undoubtedly over-optimistic.

Intervening, largely unexpectedly and certainly so with regard to the sphere of action (an attack on Berlin was considered more likely), was Khrushchov's attempt to site Soviet missiles on the island of Cuba. Kennedy kept Macmillan informed from early on in the crisis (though after he had taken 'my first decision on my own responsibility'). With Ormsby-Gore playing an active role in the discussions in the White House, Macmillan offered advice and support to Kennedy in phone calls, sometimes three a day and, shortly before Russia's climb-down in November 1962, telegraphed Khrushchov supporting the American demand that the missiles be taken out of Cuba. The upshot, Macmillan believed, was that 'We were "in on" and took full part in (and almost responsibility for) every American move' (*At the End of the Day*, 216). He perhaps overestimated Britain's standing with the USA, for whom Cuba was an essential national interest irrespective of the views of allies, but at the personal level Kennedy found his telephone discussions with Macmillan a helpful way of clearing his mind, given the variety of views about Cuba among the White House staff, and he was grateful for Britain's firm support.

The dominant tensions in British foreign policy again came into play between December 1962 and January 1963. Macmillan visited de Gaulle at Rambouillet, near Paris, on 15–16 December 1962; the talks left him with no doubt that de Gaulle intended to block Britain's application to join the EEC. Two days later, Macmillan met Kennedy in the Bahamas and after considerable difficulty persuaded the Americans to allow the British to change from Skybolt (which the Americans wished to phase out) to Polaris submarines, with a British right to use the weapons independently 'for supreme national interest' (*At the End of the Day*, 361). A month later (and undoubtedly influenced by this evidence of British dependence on America), on 14 January 1963, de Gaulle announced France's veto to Britain's EEC application, citing irreconcilable differences between the interests of Britain and those of the EEC member states. In public, Macmillan put on a brave face, suggesting that the negotiations had been broken off 'not … because the discussions were menaced with failure', but 'because they threatened to succeed' (*At the End of the Day*, 377). In his diaries, though, he recorded his despair: 'All our policies at home and abroad are in ruins … We have lost everything, except our courage and determination' (*At the End of the Day*, 367).

In the context of rapid, deliberate, and for the most part voluntary decolonization, Macmillan's government undertook a remarkable confluence of foreign policy initiatives. Frustrating though their pursuit often seemed at the time, Macmillan gained from them a quasi-

independent nuclear deterrent which lasted the rest of the century, and, despite the failure of the first application, he set the United Kingdom on the road to Europe: the choice might be 'grim', but Macmillan's decision was not one from which any subsequent British cabinet, regardless of party, seriously dissented.

More local difficulties A considerable portion of Macmillan's time was devoted to foreign and Commonwealth policy-making and activity, and his memoirs on the period of his government were largely about such questions. His peregrinations as prime minister recalled the constant movements and meetings of his war years. He probably travelled more during his premiership than any other British peacetime prime minister. At home his government was not noted for legislative proposals, and was chiefly concerned with administrative and economic matters. Macmillan had four chief domestic objectives: full employment, stable prices, a favourable balance of payments, and economic expansion. But to ride these horses he appointed what Robert Blake called 'two singularly mediocre chancellors of the exchequer [Derick Heathcoat Amory and Selwyn Lloyd]' (*DNB*). Macmillan's natural political tendency was to be expansionist, and in this he was encouraged by Sir Roy Harrod, who acted as an unofficial economic adviser. An incomes policy was established to try to maintain price stability while also encouraging growth. Unemployment rose from 500,000 to about 800,000, which genuinely shocked the prime minister as well as calling into question the tories' claim to be the party of prosperity. He became convinced, on not much evidence, that there was 'a real risk of a world deflation' (*At the End of the Day*, 89).

Lloyd was by this stage tired; he had allowed various aspects of domestic economic policy to go awry; and Macmillan resented having to take personal charge of incomes policy. Macmillan determined both to replace Lloyd and to use the occasion of his replacement for a thorough pruning of the dead wood in his government: he thought it better to introduce new ministers while his party was in power, even though it might soon lose it, and he blamed A. J. Balfour for not having done this in 1905. On 12–13 July 1962 he accordingly dismissed or accepted the resignations of the chancellor of the exchequer and six other cabinet members (one-third of his cabinet), followed by numerous junior ministers. Known immediately as 'the night of long knives', this was the most extensive reconstruction of a cabinet by a prime minister since MacDonald formed the National Government in 1931, but it did not provide the same bonus for the tory party. The party was confused, the public mocked, members of the government sensed panic in the prime minister, and the Labour opposition was considerably encouraged. Several ministers (notably Lord Kilmuir, the lord chancellor, and Lord Mills, minister without portfolio) had earlier asked to resign. It was also true that few of those sacked were missed. Macmillan nevertheless concluded that he 'was led into a serious error' by adding other changes to the essential one, the replacement of Selwyn Lloyd (*At the End of the Day*, 92). Coincidentally, Hugh Gaitskell's death in

January 1963 produced in Harold Wilson an opposition leader whose gifts were well-suited to exploiting tory weaknesses. The sackings occurred at a time when a general anti-establishment feeling was gaining ground, reflected in the BBC programme *That Was The Week That Was* and in Peter Cook's satirical depiction of Macmillan in *Beyond the Fringe*. As Robert Blake remarked, 'It was not exactly pro-Labour, but it was certainly anti-Conservative' (*DNB*).

The reputation of Macmillan's government was thus already considerably eroded when he had to meet a series of spy and sex scandals. These culminated in the spring of 1963 with the 'Profumo affair', when the secretary of state for war first denied in the Commons 'any impropriety' with Christine Keeler (who, as Macmillan put it, 'was said to share her favours with the Russian Naval Attaché, a certain Ivanov'), and then admitted that he had lied to the Commons. Profumo resigned on 6 June 1963. The trial and suicide of Stephen Ward, supposedly Keeler's procurer, created a remarkable, febrile atmosphere, particularly in London, in the summer of 1963. Other governments had suffered bouts of scandals, but those of 1962–3 would have seemed fantastic in a novel, and indeed—as the makers of *Scandal* (1989) discovered—were hard to depict on screen.

Macmillan's old-fashioned manner, so carefully cultivated and so often effective, was now a liability, for it now seemed reality rather than an act. De Gaulle's veto of Britain's application for Common Market membership demanded serious national self-appraisal, but in spring and summer 1963 the wider context was quickly forgotten. Macmillan had set a fast pace throughout his government and was tired. He took a holiday in May 1963, but the Profumo affair spoiled it. The party conference due in October could not but be an embarrassing occasion. Preparing for it, Macmillan contemplated retiring. He told the queen he would announce both that there would be no election in 1963 (one was due in 1964) and that he would not lead his party at the next election.

The ground for his resignation early in 1964 was thus quite well prepared, when on 7 October 1963 Macmillan changed his mind: he would stay on to fight the next election. Next day, however, he was admitted to hospital for an operation on his prostate gland. Before entering hospital, he dictated a minute for Lord Home (coincidentally chairman of the conference as well as foreign secretary) to read to the imminent party conference, announcing his intention to resign. Despite pain and post-operative fatigue and trauma, Macmillan was determined to play an active and decisive role in selecting his successor. Senior party members were to take soundings and report to him: he would then make a recommendation to the queen. This reversed the procedure followed at the time of Eden's resignation (who resigned recommending that soundings be then taken), for it placed the sick premier at the centre of events. In circumstances of considerable drama Macmillan resigned on 18 October in his hospital bed, the queen unprecedentedly coming to receive his resignation and his advice (which was to send for Lord Home, as she then did). Macmillan need not have so precipitately

resigned, for his health soon recovered. He appears to have believed that his prostate gland was cancerous (which his doctors had told him was at least possible). It may be that his operation caused him to return to his abandoned view of September 1963 (that he should resign) and that illness offered a convenient occasion. It was also a factor that both he, and Eden (in 1957), believed they should learn from the last months of Churchill's peacetime premiership and resign rather than linger in post. Macmillan's role in the choice of his successor was later much criticized, and was held by some to have denied Butler the premiership.

A long retirement Macmillan did not stand for the Commons at the general election in October 1964. He declined the earldom traditionally offered to prime ministers on leaving the Commons (partly, at least, because he did not wish to stymy his son Maurice's political career), and also declined the Garter, but he recommended a barony for John Wyndham, his private secretary throughout his premiership (he wrote Wyndham's memoir for the *Dictionary of National Biography*, appositely comparing him to Montagu Corry, Disraeli's secretary). It is possible that Macmillan hoped in due course to return to office as leader of an all-party coalition.

One dignified office continued to be his. In 1960 he was elected chancellor of the University of Oxford in a stiff contest with Oliver Franks. Franks was the 'official' candidate of the university establishment, and Macmillan, though prime minister, stood as something of an outsider, his campaign being organized with ruthless cunning by H. R. Trevor-Roper (whom Macmillan had controversially appointed regius professor of modern history in 1957). While prime minister, Macmillan's activities as chancellor were necessarily circumscribed, but in his long retirement he transformed the office, being frequently present in the university and making amusing speeches. He dined in all the colleges and notably favoured several which were regarded as unfashionable. With his ability to recall the supposedly golden years of Oxford before the First World War he fascinated the young and the middle-aged. He proved an effective fund-raiser in the USA and elsewhere. In retirement he continued to travel widely, including to China in 1979.

Macmillan's other focus of activity was publishing. He remained active in the family firm, and his publishing nose remained as keen as ever. He had already taken over the chairmanship from his brother Daniel in 1963, and following his retirement from politics he oversaw a period of substantial expansion in Africa and in Asia, and the development of educational publishing. He was especially involved in promoting the *New Grove Dictionary of Music* and the *Dictionary of Art*. (On his death, the management of the firm largely passed to non-family directors and in 1995 the family sold its majority stake to the German publishers Holtzbrinck.) He also devoted much time to the preparation of his memoirs, published between 1966 and 1972. His journals and diaries, kept systematically from the early 1940s, were from the start intended to form the basis of memoirs: he had observed Churchill's habit of preserving documents especially for this purpose, but in his case a diary was the preferred method. The diaries were candid in a controlled way, and clearly intended for posterity. There were gaps, notably during the crucial period of the Suez crisis. Intended as three volumes, the memoirs spread into six, for the author was his own publisher. But the expansion should not be regretted: the volumes are an unusually candid account of a political life, in the sense that they follow very closely the contemporary diaries (even when the latter are not being quoted). Even more unusually for a prime minister's memoirs, they admit mistakes. He also published his *War Diaries* (1984) which, among others matters, set in context the meeting on 13 May 1945 which became the focus of intense scrutiny in the mid-1980s as a result of the allegations by Count Nicolai Tolstoy, summarized in his *The Minister and the Massacres* (1986), with respect to Macmillan's responsibility for the return of prisoners of war to the Soviet Union in 1945—a controversy which gave Macmillan intense private distress, though he made no public riposte. He also published *The Past Masters: Politics and Politicians, 1906–1939* (1975), a nod towards Churchill's *Great Contemporaries*.

Unsurprisingly the diaries and consequently the memoirs are discreet about Macmillan's personal and family life. Though reconciled with his wife, especially from 1960 onwards—indeed, their later married years turned into something of an Indian summer—Macmillan was to the end scarred by her affair with Boothby. He even suggested to his biographer, Alistair Horne, that the Boothby affair played a part in his erratic behaviour at the time of his resignation (Horne, 2.542). Lady Dorothy's death in 1966 left Macmillan bereft. His son Maurice overcame alcoholism and his modest political success was a joy to his father. Sarah Macmillan was also an alcoholic. Whether or not he was her father, Macmillan showed her special affection and, after Lady Dorothy's death, devoted much time to helping Sarah and looking after her two adopted sons; she died in 1970.

Especially after the death of his wife, Macmillan saw Oxford, and London clubland, as places of conviviality, and he quite often appeared without much notice. When visiting Oxford he frequently stayed at nearby Garsington Manor with his friend the historian Sir John Wheeler-Bennett, or at All Souls with the warden, John Sparrow. He enjoyed the company of women 'who make me feel safe' (Horne, 2.606), including Ava Waverley, Ruth Wheeler-Bennett, Lady Diana Cooper, and Eileen *O'Casey. The last—the widow of the playwright Sean O'Casey, and herself a noted actress—claimed after Macmillan's death that their friendship had included a romantic element (though of the nature of their relationship she gave varying accounts). Throughout his life Macmillan was shy in dealing with forceful women, and he made a mortal enemy of Dame Rebecca West after turning his back on her at a literary luncheon and speaking to Diana Cooper throughout.

Without membership of either house of parliament, Macmillan's political presence after 1964 was at best marginal. He assisted behind the scenes, but effectively ceased to be a force in national politics. He remained, however, an occasional presence through television programmes and after Margaret Thatcher's monetarist tendencies had become apparent (he was initially rather favourable to her leadership of the tory party and was consulted by her in the early stages of the Falkland crisis, recommending to her the establishment of a small war cabinet, as subsequently adopted) he used television with some effect to voice critical views (notably in *The Way Ahead*, made with Robert Mackenzie). He had accepted the Order of Merit in 1976, but no other public honours. However, on his ninetieth birthday, 10 February 1984, it was announced that he was to become earl of Stockton, the first hereditary peerage for a generation. (His son Maurice was by then extremely ill, and died a month later.) After his maiden speech on 13 November 1984 he became a frequent attender at the House of Lords, often making anti-monetarist comments. But it was in a speech to the Tory Reform Group on 8 November 1985 that his remark (subsequently repeated in the House of Lords) that the government's privatization policy amounted to 'selling the family silver' hit a raw nerve. It made no difference to government policy, but the remark stung, especially as it cleverly used the same simplistic language of domestic finance commonly employed by Mrs Thatcher to justify her policies.

Though Macmillan lived at Birch Grove in Sussex all his life, he played no special role in county life. The staff at Birch Grove had mostly served there most of their working lives; he was well known among them for endearing behaviour. In old age, he became something of a national treasure. He played the part well. A lone survivor of the wartime government, he had no difficulty, when he chose, in upstaging the pedestrian characters of British politics in the 1980s.

Despite his war wounds, his many operations, and his own fear of physical decline, Macmillan's body stood up remarkably well. But by 1985 he suffered not merely from the long-term afflictions which had kept him in pain for much of his adult life, and which in his latter years caused constant insomnia, but now also from pleurisy, shingles, and gout. His last Oxford appearance was in November 1986. On 29 December 1986 he died at Birch Grove. He was buried on 5 January 1987 next to his wife and Sarah in the nearby churchyard of St Giles, Horsted Keynes, Sussex. On 10 February 1987 a memorial service was held in Westminster Abbey. He was succeeded as second earl by his grandson, Alexander Daniel Alan Macmillan (*b.* 1943).

Iconography, biography, and assessment Macmillan seemed a gift for an artist or cartoonist, but proved easier for the latter. His strong features, languid moustache, and fine head of hair gave him, especially in his later years, a powerful physical presence. The donnish element so obvious in wartime photographs (deliberately contrasting with the surrounding uniforms) was subsumed into the character of the 'gent' which Macmillan so sedulously exploited. Bryan Organ's double portrait for Oxford University (1980) brilliantly captures this aspect of his character, but other portraits, which include that of James Gunn

(1962, Balliol College, Oxford) of Macmillan in his chancellor's robes, are for the most part pedestrian, as is the bust by Angela Conner (1973, NPG). The cartoons by Vicky depicted Macmillan in various guises, often on the 'Supermac' theme, and remain powerful images.

Though Macmillan's memoirs staked out the biographical ground on his own terms, he was the subject of a striking study, *Macmillan: a Study in Ambiguity*, by Anthony Sampson (1967). Macmillan chose Alistair Horne as his official biographer, and gave Horne many interviews which, together with the full version of the diaries, played a central part in Horne's well-researched two-volume life (1988–9), especially with respect to Macmillan's complex personal life. His was not the first prime-ministerial biography to be commissioned during the subject's lifetime, but it was unusual in the extent to which it was prepared with the help of the subject, particularly through extensive interviews. Several members of the Macmillan circle published recollections, including Lord Egremont (John Wyndham), *Wyndham and Children First* (1968), and Harold Evans, Macmillan's press secretary, *Downing Street Diary: the Macmillan Years* (1981). Numerous biographies and political studies followed, especially after the papers of the Macmillan government were made available to researchers at the Public Record Office under the thirty-year rule. Macmillan's private papers and diaries were deposited in the Bodleian Library, Oxford, after the completion of Horne's biography.

Macmillan's premiership was a decisive period in terms of Britain's self-appraisal as a world power and the decisions consequent on that appraisal. But he took care to play down the extent of changes in British policy, and to disguise some of the more disquieting conclusions which arose. In personal terms, Macmillan tried to distance himself from the all-consuming embrace of professional politics. He read widely and was genuinely erudite on a wide range of subjects, often disguising his erudition until a suitable tactical moment in the conversation. His complex personality puzzled and sometimes unsettled his colleagues. His old-world manner was in some respects a perfect cover for modernization, but it was never clear how seriously either the manner or the modernization was to be taken.

Macmillan handed over to Lord Home, a man apparently in his own style of Conservatism. But this, like so much else that Macmillan did, was an uncertain message. Macmillan was not in fact a county tory, for all his love of the grouse moors and his Devonshire relations. In his two constituencies he represented working-class and then suburban Britain, and in doing so he followed the character of his century. He had a better grasp of economic issues than any prime minister of the century, with the possible exception of Harold Wilson; and, unlike Wilson, he combined wide reading and theoretical understanding with practical knowledge of the running of a business. He co-ordinated with skill, cunning, and a certain degree of deception Britain's retreat from world power status. He was sometimes unwilling to do more than hint to his

party and his nation the direction in which he was leading, but this was perhaps because he saw that the Britons of his day could not and would not face the facts.

H. C. G. MATTHEW

Sources DNB · H. Macmillan, *Winds of change, 1914–1939* (1966) [vol. 1 of autobiography] · H. Macmillan, *The blast of war, 1939–1945* (1967) [vol. 2 of autobiography] · H. Macmillan, *Tides of fortune, 1945–1955* (1969) [vol. 3 of autobiography] · H. Macmillan, *Riding the storm, 1956–1959* (1971) [vol. 4 of autobiography] · H. Macmillan, *Pointing the way, 1959–1961* (1972) [vol. 5 of autobiography] · H. Macmillan, *At the end of the day, 1961–1963* (1973) [vol. 6 of autobiography] · H. Macmillan, *War diaries: politics and war in the Mediterranean, January 1943 – May 1945* (1984) · Macmillan diaries, Bodl. Oxf. · A. Sampson, *Macmillan: a study in ambiguity* (1967) · G. Hutchinson, *The last Edwardian at no. 10* (1980) · N. Fisher, *Harold Macmillan* (1982) · A. Horne, *Macmillan*, 2 vols. (1988–9) · J. Turner, *Macmillan* (1994) · R. Lamb, *The Macmillan years, 1957–1963: the emerging truth* (1995) · R. Aldous and S. Lee, eds., *Harold Macmillan and Britain's world role* (1996) · R. Aldous and S. Lee, eds., *Harold Macmillan: aspects of a political life* (1999) · J. Charmley, 'Harold Macmillan and the making of the French committee of liberation', *International History Review*, 4 (Nov 1982), 475–627 · J. P. S. Gearson, *Harold Macmillan and the Berlin wall crisis, 1958–62* (1998) · L. V. Scott, *Macmillan, Kennedy and the Cuban missile crisis* (1999) · J. Tratt, *The Macmillan government and Europe: a study in the process of policy development* (1996) · D. Ritschel, *The politics of planning* (1997) · A. N. Porter and A. J. Stockwell, *British imperial policy and decolonization, 1938–64*, 2 vols. (1987–9) · I. Clark and N. J. Wheeler, *The British origins of nuclear strategy, 1945–1955* (1989) · M. S. Navias, *Nuclear weapons and British strategic planning, 1955–1958* (1991) · W. Scott Lucas, *Divided we stand: Britain, the US and the Suez crisis* (1991) · J. Ramsden, *The age of Balfour and Baldwin, 1902–1940* (1978) · J. Ramsden, *The age of Churchill and Eden, 1940–1957* (1995) · J. Ramsden, *The winds of change: Macmillan to Heath, 1957–1975* (1996) · R. R. James, *Bob Boothby* (1992) · M. Gilbert, *Plough my own furrow: the story of Lord Allen of Hurtwood* (1965) · M. Gilbert, *Winston S. Churchill*, 7: *Road to victory, 1941–1945* (1986) · E. Waugh, *The life of the Right Reverend Ronald Knox* (1959) · private information (2004) [David Dilks] · Burke, *Peerage* · WWW

Archives Bodl. Oxf., corresp. and papers · Bodl. Oxf., diaries and constituency corresp. | Bodl. Oxf., corresp. with Lionel Curtis · Bodl. Oxf., corresp. with Lord Monckton · Bodl. Oxf., letters to Ava, Viscountess Waverley · Bodl. RH, corresp. with Sir R. R. Welensky and few papers relating to Rhodesia · CAC Cam., corresp. with P. G. Buchan-Hepburn · Durham RO, corresp. with Lady Londonderry · Highclere Castle, Hampshire, letters to Lord Porchester · HLRO, corresp. with Lord Beaverbrook · NL Scot., letters to Lord Tweedsmuir · NL Wales, letters to Desmond Donnelly · Nuffield Oxf., corresp. with Lord Cherwell · PRO, CAB 21, 103, 124, 127, 128, 129, 134 · PRO, DO 35, 169, 182 · PRO, FCO 7, 12 · PRO, Foreign Office papers, FO 800/663–690 · PRO, PREM 5, 11 · PRO, T 199 · U. Birm., corresp. with Lord Avon and Lady Avon | FILM BFI NFTVA, *Reputations*, BBC 2, 14 March 1996 · BFI NFTVA, documentary footage · BFI NFTVA, news footage | SOUND BL NSA, current affairs recordings · BL NSA, documentary recordings · BL NSA, news recordings

Likenesses W. Stoneman, photograph, 1947, NPG · A. Newman, photograph, 1954, NPG [see illus.] · V. Weisz (Vicky), cartoons, 1957–63 · J. Gunn, oils, 1960, Carlton Club, London · J. Gunn, oils, 1962, Balliol College, Oxford · D. Levine, ink caricature, 1966, NPG · M. Gerson, photograph, 1967, NPG · A. Conner, bronze bust, 1973, NPG · B. Organ, double portrait, oils, 1980, Oxford University · G. Davies, caricature, plaster head, NPG · H. Powell, pencil drawing, Hertford College, Oxford · photographs, Hult. Arch. · portraits, repro. in R. Dudley Edwards, *Harold Macmillan: a life in pictures* (1983)

Wealth at death £51,114: probate, 1 June 1987, CGPLA Eng. & Wales

Macmillan, Hugh (1833–1903), Free Church of Scotland minister and writer, was born at Aberfeldy, Perthshire, on 17 September 1833, the eldest of the six sons and three daughters of Alexander Macmillan, merchant, and his wife, Margaret Macfarlane. He was educated at Breadalbane Academy, Aberfeldy, and Hill Street Institution, Edinburgh, before entering Edinburgh University in 1847. After graduation he went on to study for the Free Church ministry at New College, Edinburgh. He was licensed by the presbytery of Breadalbane in January 1857, becoming minister of the Free Church at Kirkmichael, Perthshire, in 1859. On 14 June of that year he married Jane, daughter of William Patison of Williamfield, with whom he had five daughters and a son, Hugh Pattison *Macmillan. In 1861 he published *Footnotes from the Page of Nature, or, First Forms of Vegetation*, the first of many popular volumes which dealt with the relationship between religion and science and which drew extensively on his botanical knowledge. He moved to the charge of Free St Peter's Church, Glasgow, in 1864. There he continued to pursue his interest in natural history, an interest informed by extensive foreign travel, and in 1867 he published his best-known work, *Bible Teachings in Nature*. This work was widely translated, and more than 30,000 copies had been printed in the United Kingdom by the time of his death.

In September 1878 Macmillan became minister of the Free West Church, Greenock, where he remained until his retirement from the ministry in 1901. He was honoured at frequent intervals. In 1871 he was awarded the degree of LLD by the University of St Andrews and in the same year he was made a fellow of the Royal Society of Edinburgh. The universities of Edinburgh and Glasgow both awarded him the degree of DD in 1879. He was elected a fellow of the Society of Antiquaries of Scotland in 1883. His own church also recognized him, and he was Thomson lecturer at the Free Church college, Aberdeen, in 1886, Cunningham lecturer at New College, Edinburgh, in 1894, and Gunning lecturer at Edinburgh University in 1897. In that year he was also moderator of the general assembly of the Free Church of Scotland, and in that capacity he attended the diamond jubilee celebrations of Queen Victoria, who was an admirer of his books.

Macmillan's other interests included the highlands and its people, and in this connection he was first chief of the Clan Macmillan Society when it was founded in 1892. As a keen student of art one of his last writings was an appreciation of the work of George Frederick Watts, published posthumously in 1903. Macmillan's prodigious output of writings was testimony to his ceaseless activity and his wide-ranging interests. Their popularity justified the judgement that 'his special mission was that of an exponent and interpreter' (Macmillan, 1907). He died at his home at 2 Murrayfield Road, Edinburgh, on 24 May 1903 and was buried in the Dean cemetery, Edinburgh.

LIONEL ALEXANDER RITCHIE

Sources G. A. Macmillan, preface, in H. Macmillan, *The isles and the Gospel: and other Bible stories* (1907), ix–xviii · J. A. Lamb, ed., *The fasti of the United Free Church of Scotland, 1900–1929* (1956), 160 · *WWW, 1897–1915* · W. Ewing, ed., *Annals of the Free Church of Scotland,* *1843–1900*, 2 vols. (1914) · A. W. Stewart, 'Dr. Hugh MacMillan at home', *Sunday Magazine* (1897), 375–81 · [H. P. Macmillan and others], *In memoriam: Hugh Macmillan* (1903) · *The Scotsman* (25 May 1903) · *Glasgow Herald* (25 May 1903) · *DNB* · H. P. Macmillan, *A man of law's tale* (1952) · m. cert.
Likenesses photograph (in later life), repro. in Macmillan, *The isles and the Gospel*, frontispiece · photograph (in later life), repro. in Macmillan, *Man of law's tale*, facing p. 4
Wealth at death £6238 16s. 8d.: confirmation, 3 July 1903, *CCI*

Macmillan, Hugh Pattison, Baron Macmillan (1873–1952), judge, was born in Glasgow on 20 February 1873, the only son among the six children of the Revd Hugh *Macmillan (1833–1903), a Free Church of Scotland minister, and his wife, Jane, daughter of William Patison, of Edinburgh. Macmillan was educated at the collegiate school, Greenock, at Edinburgh University, where he graduated in 1893 with first-class honours in philosophy, and at Glasgow University, where he obtained his LLB in 1896, becoming Cunninghame scholar. He passed advocate in 1897 after assisting C. J. (later Lord) Guthrie.

Early career While building up his practice at the Scots bar Macmillan acted as reporter for the *Scots Law Times*, as an examiner in law at Glasgow University, and as editor of the *Juridical Review*. In 1901 he married Elizabeth Katherine Grace (*d*. 1967), daughter of William Johnstone Marshall MD, of Greenock; they had no children. Macmillan had no family influence to bring him work, but the care and assiduity with which he conducted his cases soon brought his name to the attention of solicitors. He took silk in 1912 and his practice thereafter continued to grow until he became one of the busiest senior advocates at the Scots bar. He was in great demand in cases which involved municipalities and public bodies and was senior legal assessor to Edinburgh corporation (1920–24) and standing counsel to the convention of royal burghs (1923–30). In 1918 he spent some months as an assistant director of intelligence at the Ministry of Information.

In 1924 the Labour Party, in office for the first time, had no member with sufficient legal qualifications to become lord advocate. Macmillan was neither a member of parliament nor a socialist, and had indeed earlier been a Unionist candidate; but he accepted from Ramsay MacDonald the office of lord advocate. When the Labour government fell Macmillan went to the English bar, establishing himself in chambers in London rather than returning to Scotland, in the reasonable belief that he had promises from both MacDonald and Baldwin, the Conservative leader, that he would in due course be made a lord of appeal in ordinary.

In London, Macmillan enjoyed a varied practice in the House of Lords and the privy council, as well as before parliamentary committees. He was appointed standing counsel for Canada (1928) and for Australia (1929). One of his most distinguished appearances was in 1928 on behalf of the railway companies in the road transport bills in which they obtained power to provide road services in face of increasing competition from bus companies and road hauliers. In 1930 Macmillan was made a lord of appeal in ordinary with the customary life peerage, a post he held

Hugh Pattison Macmillan, Baron Macmillan (1873–1952), by Leonard Campbell Taylor

until 1947. His predecessor, Lord Sumner, warned the new law lord that 'judging is always a stodgy job', but Macmillan purported not to find it so. He delivered some 152 written opinions in the House of Lords and some 75 in the privy council. He nevertheless paid a high price. His problem was accurately diagnosed by Lord Dunedin who in 1935 described Macmillan as being 'very able, but you cannot put your best into law if you have as many irons in the fire as he has' (Heuston, 481). Macmillan's irons were extensive. He was a collector of the famous, and even though he was personally engaging, those who met him found him increasingly tiresome as the years passed. He fancied himself for the lord chancellorship in 1938, and in 1939 he resigned as a lord of appeal to become an unsuccessful minister of information. By 1941 he was back as a lord of appeal.

Judgments Over time a divergence between Macmillan's rhetoric and his performance became more noticeable. Typical of his remarks were announcements that 'the high province of a Supreme Court is to control and develop the law so as to enable it to keep pace with and yet moderate the changing social and economic conditions of the nation' (Macmillan, 220). He admired the fine phrases of Oliver Wendell Holmes about the growth and life of the law; and he speculated about law, ethics, and the judicial process in his writings, a collection of which appeared in 1937 under the title Law and Other Things. His rhetoric was also reflected in early judgments. In a workmen's compensation case in 1931 he declared that precedents in that area should 'be stepping-stones rather than halting

places' (Birch Bros v. Brown, 1931). Macmillan was equally willing to congratulate his colleagues when they overcame precedents of which they disapproved. Indeed, when he wished, Macmillan could manipulate precedent, or torpedo rules with principles, with a felicity of which Mr Justice Cardozo would not have been ashamed. In Penman v. Fife Coal Company Macmillan distinguished out of existence a decision of Lord Herschell's of 1936. A similar skill was exhibited when the house came to consider whether the arbitration clause of a contract could be enforced after a contract was frustrated. The privy council had already decreed that it could not and there were strong dicta in the house by Lord Haldane among others, to the same effect. Although Macmillan conceded that 'in view of their high authority' such dicta were entitled to the most careful consideration, he did 'not think they constitute pronouncements in law by this House such as to be binding on your Lordships' (Heyman v. Darwins Ltd, 1941).

Macmillan was most adept at manipulating 'two competing doctrines' and he was willing 'to consider and accommodate' their respective 'spheres of operation'. He was in the majority in Donoghue v. Stevenson (1932) and it was he who, with Lord Atkin, was largely responsible for the wide ratio that later judges attributed to the decision. His speech has been admired by some, as it again faced the concept of competing doctrines, and had the grand sweep of the Scottish judge accustomed to prefer principle to precedent.

Throughout his career as a law lord Macmillan showed a willingness to treat negligence flexibly and was reluctant to defer automatically to the policy of stare decisis (taking an instrumental rather than a formalistic approach). As the years passed, however, the divergence between rhetoric and reality became more obvious and his impact on the law declined. He was of course sometimes in the majority with lords Atkin and Wright in vital decisions, but he was rarely in the lead. Macmillan was aware of the need to develop law for reasons that ranged from justice to business convenience, but he increasingly lacked the spirit to push his view. His essentially apolitical nature led him to stand increasingly for the status quo. This tendency seemed especially strong after his term as minister of information and was evident to its fullest extent in Liversidge v. Anderson (1941), where he showed himself one of those judges whom Atkin described as 'more executive-minded than the executive'. Macmillan deferred to the views of Atkinson in Halliday's case (1917) and stated his own views in much the same terms. It was not an elegant performance.

Academic lawyers probably overestimate the importance of Liversidge v. Anderson, but in terms of national purpose at large, it is impossible not to note Macmillan's increasingly destructive approach to tax legislation. Despite his views on precedent he often adopted a formalistic approach toward statutory interpretation. In the Duke of Westminster's case (1935), although going by no means as far as lords Tomlin and Russell in promoting tax avoidance, he was 'fully conscious of the anomalous consequences which might conceivably arise in other connections from the course adopted by the respondent'. He refused, however, to concern himself with anything but 'the technical question whether the respondent has brought himself within the language of the income tax rule'.

Moreover, Macmillan, who began to specialize in the increasingly frequent tax appeals, continued to develop this highly artificial approach. In *Inland Revenue Commissioners* v. *Ayrshire Employers Mutual Insurance Association* (1945), when parliament had clearly intended to make the annual surpluses of mutual insurance companies subject to tax, Macmillan found a particularly formalistic argument to show that this had not been the effect of section 31 of the Finance Act of 1933. He was then happily able to announce, 'the legislature has plainly missed fire'. Of this decision, Lord Diplock later said that 'if, as in this case, the Courts can identify the target of Parliamentary legislation their proper function is to see that it is it is hit: not merely to record that it has been missed. Here is judicial legislation at its worst' (Diplock, 10). Yet it was Macmillan who, addressing the Canadian Bar Association on law and order, talked at length about the unsatisfactory state of legislative drafting in England, while his speeches in tax cases could only force parliamentary counsel's office to draft in an increasingly narrow and formalistic way. It was a vicious circle that he did little to ameliorate. If Macmillan began as the bright hope of the House of Lords, he contributed to what Lord Diplock was to call 'the high-water mark of the narrow semantic approach' (ibid.).

Other public appointments Outside his judicial functions, Macmillan is perhaps best known for chairing the Treasury committee on finance and industry (1920–31), which surveyed the nation's financial system in relation to industry. Its report became known by his name, although much of it was written by J. M. Keynes. Macmillan was also chairman of the royal commission on lunacy (1924–6); of the court of inquiry into the coalmining industry dispute (1925); of the subcommittee on the *British Pharmacopoeia* (1926–8); of the Home Office committee on street offences (1927–8); of the shipbuilding industry conferences (1928–30); of the Treasury committee on income tax law codification (1932–6); of the royal commission on Canadian banking and currency (1933); and of the committee on the preservation of works of art in enemy hands (1944–7). He was a member of the political honours committee from 1929 and chairman from 1935. An original trustee of the Pilgrim Trust, he was chairman from 1935 until his death. He was chairman of the court of London University (1929–43) and of the lord chancellor's committee on an institute of advanced legal studies, which was inaugurated in 1948. In addition, he was chairman of the Great Ormond Street Hospital for Sick Children (1928–34); of the King George V memorial fund; of the general committee of the Athenaeum (1935–45); and of the BBC advisory council (1936–40). Other bodies on which he served were the British Museum, the Soane Museum, and the Carnegie Trust for Scottish Universities, the National Trust, King George's Jubilee Trust, and the Society for the Promotion of Nature Reserves. He was president of the Scottish Text Society and was instrumental in founding the Stair Society in

1934. It was largely due to his efforts that the Advocates' Library was taken over as the National Library of Scotland in 1925.

Macmillan received honorary degrees from thirteen universities. In 1937 he was appointed GCVO, and in the following year he was made an honorary burgess of Edinburgh. He had been made a privy councillor and honorary bencher of the Inner Temple during his time as lord advocate. He died at Ewhurst, Surrey, on 5 September 1952. His autobiography, *A Man of Law's Tale*, appeared in 1952, shortly after his death.　　　ROBERT STEVENS

Sources R. Stevens, *Law and politics: the House of Lords as a judicial body, 1800–1976* (1978) · R. F. V. Heuston, *Lives of the lord chancellors, 1885–1940* (1964) · T. Jones, *A diary with letters, 1931–1950* (1954) · K. Diplock, *The courts as legislators* (1965) · *DNB* · H. Macmillan, *Law and other things* (1937)
Archives BL, corresp. and papers relating to British Museum, Add. MSS 54575–54578 · NL Scot., corresp. and papers relating to National Library of Scotland | NL Scot., letters to Lord Haldane · NL Wales, corresp. with Thomas Jones
Likenesses W. Rothenstein, chalk drawing, 1937?, Athenaeum, London · W. Stoneman, photographs, 1937–48, NPG · L. Campbell Taylor, oils, Senate House, London [*see illus.*]
Wealth at death £145,422 8s. 4d.: confirmation, 14 Nov 1952, *CCI*

Macmillan, John (1669–1753), Reformed Presbyterian church minister, the son of John Macmillan, a farmer, was born at Barncauchlaw, Minnigaff, near Newton Stewart, Wigtownshire. South-west Scotland was an area with a close attachment to the covenanter Richard Cameron, and Macmillan grew up amid strong influences towards the old Presbyterian ways, which were increasingly felt to be compromised in the settlement of 1690. While a student in the arts faculty of the University of Edinburgh in 1695–7, he associated with members of the covenanting societies, and he graduated MA on 28 June 1697. It is surmised that he then studied divinity at Edinburgh until 1700, when he became tutor and chaplain to the laird of Broughton. He was also at this period elected an elder of Girthon church, near his home. He was licensed to preach by the Church of Scotland presbytery of Kirkcudbright on 26 November 1700, preached in Balmaghie on 22 December 1700, and was ordained minister of that parish on 18 September of the following year.

Although Macmillan had been ordained in the Church of Scotland the question of covenanting had by no means been settled, and the death of William III reopened the whole matter of the relation between church and state, and of the status of the national covenant and the solemn league and covenant. Macmillan held to a minority view in the presbytery, and by 1703 his relations with his brethren became so acrimonious that he was deposed for disorderly and schismatic practices. Such was the devotion of his parishioners that he continued to preach unhindered until 1715. It was then that his successor William McKie, who had succeeded to the parish in 1710 and had hitherto made do with a barn for a meeting-place, was at last allowed to occupy the pulpit at Balmaghie. Macmillan continued to occupy the manse until 1727.

Since he effectively ceased to be the parish minister of Balmaghie in 1703 Macmillan had been in close touch with the remnant, commonly known as the Cameronians, who refused to grant allegiance to uncovenanted monarch or parliament. On 9 October 1706 he accepted a call to be the minister to the scattered societies, who had not had a minister since the death of James Renwick in 1688, and the defection to the Church of Scotland of William Boyd, Thomas Linning, and Alexander Shields in 1689. In December 1706 Macmillan conducted his first baptisms of children at Crawfordjohn, Lanarkshire. Here, and later when he baptized in Wigtownshire, Kirkcudbrightshire, east Fife, and Perthshire, as well as at other places in Lanarkshire, many of the children were already in their teens, as their parents had waited for a minister whom they could recognize to come. He also conducted marriages, sometimes of several couples at the same time.

The Union of 1707 and the restoration of patronage in the Church of Scotland in 1711 confirmed Macmillan and his friends in their covenanting principles. The covenants were renewed at Auchensaugh in Lanarkshire in July 1712, when between 1000 and 1700 persons gathered to hear Macmillan preach on right covenanting and then to renew their engagements. At the Sunday communion he 'debarred and excommunicated from this holy table of the Lord, Queen and Parliament, and all under them who spread and propagate false and superstitious worship, ay, and while they repent' (Reid, 182). This caused a stir in Scotland as Macmillan consciously identified himself as a successor to former covenanting leaders, such as Donald Cargill.

After leaving the manse at Balmaghie, Macmillan moved to Braehead of Carnwath, Lanarkshire, where from 1736 most of his baptism and marriage services were held. From here he visited and exhorted among the 10,000-strong covenanting community without the help of an ordained minister until in 1743 he was joined by Thomas Nairn, a member of the Associate Synod. A presbytery was then formed which, through Macmillan's influence, became the Reformed Presbyterian church. Although held in high esteem by members of the societies, Macmillan was not immune from criticism if he appeared to compromise with the Church of Scotland. All three of his marriages seem to have been conducted by parish ministers, and he was duly censured. In 1708 he married Jean Gemble, who died childless on 12 June 1711. He married Mary Goldie, *née* Gordon, a widow with children, and the daughter of a covenanting baronet, in 1719; she died in childbirth on 5 May 1723, aged forty-three. Again he married, this time to Grace Russell in 1725. They had several children, the only one surviving his father being John, who became a Reformed Presbyterian church minister.

Macmillan published little. The *True Narrative* was printed in 1704, as were his *Grievances*, which called on the presbytery to restore covenants and the church's spiritual independence. More domestic matters occupied his *Elegy on Mistress Mary Gordon* (1723), and a *Letter to a Dying Friend* (1741). In addition, Macmillan kept a register, first published in 1908, in which he recorded his travels from Balmaghie and later Braehead.

He died at Broomhill, Bothwell, on 1 December 1753, at a time when a division over the doctrine of the atonement was troubling the church. A dissentient group in time formed the Unitarian church in Edinburgh. A memorial to him was placed in the churchyard of Dalserf, Lanarkshire, where he was buried. He was survived by his third wife.

DEREK B. MURRAY

Sources *Fasti Scot.*, 2.392–3 · H. M. B. Reid, *A Cameronian apostle* (1896) · M. Hutchinson, *The Reformed Presbyterian church in Scotland, 1680–1876* (1893) · G. J. Keddie, 'Macmillan, John', *DSCHT* · W. J. Couper, 'The Reformed Presbyterian church in Scotland', *Records of the Scottish Church History Society*, 2 (1925) [whole vol.] · *The register of John Macmillan*, ed. H. Paton (1908)

MacMillan, Sir Kenneth (1929–1992), choreographer, was born on 11 December 1929 at Dunfermline, Fife, the youngest of five children (one of whom died in infancy) of William MacMillan (1891–1946), labourer and cook, and his wife, Edith (1888–1942), daughter of George Shreeve, of Ormesby (near Great Yarmouth) and his wife, Mary Anne (known as Raya).

Early years Kenneth MacMillan's parents met in Norfolk during the First World War, when his father's Scottish regiment was posted at Ormesby. William MacMillan took his growing family back to Scotland but moved to Great Yarmouth in 1935, in search of work. Kenneth went to Northgate infants' school, which was evacuated in 1940 to Upper Broughton in Nottinghamshire; homesick, he insisted on returning to Yarmouth, which was severely bombed during the battle of Britain. He won a scholarship at the age of eleven to Great Yarmouth grammar school, which had been evacuated to Retford, Nottinghamshire, but which allowed its pupils to return home in the holidays in spite of the continued bombing.

It was in Retford that MacMillan discovered ballet, thanks to a local dance teacher, Jean Thomas. He had learned Scottish dancing as a small child in Dunfermline and tap as a boy in Yarmouth, where he performed in end-of-the-pier talent shows and amateur concert parties to entertain the troops. Miss Thomas taught him ballet as well as tap and encouraged him to read about ballet in the local library. 'I was transported into a world which seemed so exotic to me, living at a time when death and destruction was an everyday occurrence' (*Shropshire Star*).

Later, when he became a choreographer, he was determined that the ballets he created should reflect the whole of human experience—death, distress, political oppression, extreme psychological states, as well as the symbolic truths contained in fairy-tale ballets. His boyhood wartime memories inform certain of his works, such as *The Burrow* (1958), *Valley of Shadows* (1983), and *Gloria* (1980), which is dedicated to his father, gassed during the First World War. His mother's death in 1942, when he was twelve, also affected him deeply.

During term time in Retford, MacMillan performed in Jean Thomas's dance concerts as well as taking part in school plays. He kept his dancing activities as secret as he could from his schoolmates, although by the age of fourteen he was already determined to become a ballet dancer. When his grammar school returned to Great Yarmouth in

Sir Kenneth MacMillan (1929–1992), by Yolanda Sonnabend, 1988

1944, he sought out a ballet teacher there, Phyllis Adams, who helped ensure that he was accepted by the Sadler's Wells Ballet School (later the Royal Ballet School) in 1945, when he was fifteen. On his return visits to Yarmouth he would try his hand at choreographing dances for Miss Adams's pupils. He saw his first ballets, danced by Ninette De Valois's Sadler's Wells company, at the New Theatre in London. When the company moved into the Royal Opera House, Covent Garden, in 1946, he appeared, while still a student, in *The Sleeping Beauty*, which reopened the opera house.

Early professional career, 1946–1954 His father died just as MacMillan became a founder member of De Valois's new junior company, first known as the Sadler's Wells Opera Ballet, then Theatre Ballet. It was originally intended as a nursery for young dancers and choreographers, who would then move to the senior company at Covent Garden—as MacMillan did in 1948. He went on its first American tour, dancing the role of Florestan in the last act *pas de trois* in *The Sleeping Beauty* on the company's triumphant opening night in New York in 1949.

Although his career as a dancer was advancing well, MacMillan suffered increasingly from stage fright. De Valois granted him leave of absence early in 1952 and suggested he perform more informally with a small group headed by the young South African choreographer John Cranko. Their performances in Henley-on-Thames helped save the neglected Kenton Theatre, which had been restored by the artist John Piper. During the successful summer season Cranko encouraged MacMillan's interest

in choreography—an ambition deferred in favour of dancing.

Cured of his stage fright, MacMillan rejoined the touring company, the Sadler's Wells Theatre Ballet, in September 1952. Opportunities to choreograph soon arose when the company set up a Sunday workshop under the direction of David Poole. MacMillan's first ballet, *Somnambulism*, was made at short notice in 1953, when a colleague dropped out of the first workshop performance. 'It even surprised me what it was like', MacMillan said in an interview (Gruen). 'I thought when I started doing choreography it was going to be like things that everyone else had done. In point of fact, it came out unlike anything anybody had ever done' (ibid.).

Although dancers of this period, such as Maryon Lane and Pirmin Trecu, confirm that the spiky choreography was new-minted, MacMillan was influenced in his early work by modern ballets of the forties and fifties—in particular, those by Roland Petit and Janine Charrat, danced by visiting French companies, and by Jerome Robbins and Antony Tudor, performed by Ballet Theatre (soon to become American Ballet Theatre). MacMillan also acknowledged the influence of Frederick Ashton, the Royal Ballet's founder-choreographer. 'I certainly learned craftsmanship from him since, when I was a dancer, I was in a lot of his ballets and I saw how a ballet was made' (MacMillan, 9).

MacMillan soon consolidated his initial success by creating *Laiderette* (1954) for the Choreographic Group. Although De Valois found its harpsichord music by Frank Martin unsuitable for inclusion in the touring company's repertory, Marie Rambert snapped up *Laiderette* for her Ballet Rambert, which continued to perform it, to recorded music, until 1967. De Valois promptly commissioned MacMillan's first work for Sadler's Wells Theatre Ballet, *Danses concertantes* (1955), to Igor Stravinsky's music of the same name. Designs by Nicholas Georgiadis, then a young theatre designer at the Slade School of Art, marked the start of a long collaboration between the two men.

Choreography, 1955–1965

His professional debut with *Danses concertantes* showed a talent seething with ideas, bursting to find new ways of using the classical vocabulary … the intoxicating feeling of dance that bubbled wittily and imaginatively, and in such profusion. (Crisp, 'Kenneth MacMillan', 6)

Confident that MacMillan had found his vocation, De Valois agreed that he should give up dancing and become a resident choreographer for the touring company. It presented a programme entirely of his work, including *House of Birds* and *Solitaire*, in June 1956. 'The evening left one in no doubt of MacMillan's arrival among the few creative choreographers', in the opinion of a reviewer (*Ballet Annual*). He was commissioned to create *Noctambules*, his first work for the senior Covent Garden company, in 1956, before taking leave of absence to work with American Ballet Theatre, choreographing *Winter's Eve* and *Journey* for that company's dramatic ballerina, Nora Kaye.

On his return after five months in New York, MacMillan

set about creating *The Burrow* (1958), the first of his signature flesh-and-blood ballets. It was also the first time he used Lynn Seymour, the Canadian dancer who was to become his muse. *The Burrow*, which deals with a group of oppressed people living in terror of 'the knock on the door', has similarities with the story of Anne Frank. It was also a response to the new realism of films and plays of the time.

> Little of what I was seeing then [in ballet] had any contact with a real world of feeling and human behaviour. I wanted to make ballets in which an audience would become caught up with the fate of the characters I showed them. (Crisp, 'The man who makes')

Audiences and critics responded enthusiastically: 'Controversial and stimulating', wrote Clive Barnes, 'this piece [*The Burrow*] seems a landmark destined to do for ballet what *Look Back in Anger* did for the theatre' (*Daily Express*).

Although MacMillan went on to choreograph *The Invitation* (1960), with its graphic depiction of the rape of a young girl (Lynn Seymour), he had also made *Le baiser de la fée* in the same year with Seymour—a response to Stravinsky's score, whose fairy-tale scenario deals with the isolation of the artist from human relationships. However emotionally searing MacMillan's work became in the years that followed, he never totally abandoned the conventions of classical ballet. The two seemingly divergent strands of gritty expressionism and other-worldly fantasy coincided towards the end of his life, when he choreographed *Prince of the Pagodas* (1989), with another elusive fairy-tale scenario, and *The Judas Tree* (1992), which includes a gang rape and a lynching.

MacMillan developed yet a third strand, the plotless ballet, almost as non-representational as its music. After the early *Danses concertantes* he went on to choreograph the pure-dance *Diversions* and *Symphony* in the sixties, as well as two big, ambitious ballets, *The Rite of Spring* and *Song of the Earth*. The Royal Opera House board of governors objected to the use of Mahler's music for a ballet, so MacMillan created *Song of the Earth* for the Stuttgart Ballet in 1965, before it was brought into the Royal Ballet's repertory a year later. The same objections were later raised against his use of Fauré's music for *Requiem* (1976), his memorial to John Cranko, late artistic director of the Stuttgart Ballet (MacMillan created six works in all for the Stuttgart company). *Requiem* was eventually danced by the Royal Ballet in 1983.

In an interview in 1963 MacMillan recognized a prevailing theme in his ballets: 'The more I look at my work, the more it seems that, unwittingly, I choose the lonely, outcast, rejected figure ... it seems to happen unconsciously, as a sort of leitmotif' (MacMillan, 6). His first three-act ballet, however, commissioned by the Royal Ballet for February 1965, was based on the familiar story of *Romeo and Juliet*, to Prokofiev's score. MacMillan already knew Cranko's version for Stuttgart and the Russian production by Leonid Lavrovsky, which had been one of the hits of the Bolshoi's first London season in 1956. But he was determined to bring his own vision of Shakespeare's tragedy to the Royal Opera House stage, with Lynn Seymour and Christopher Gable as the young lovers. 'Their' *Romeo and Juliet* was to be as emotionally immediate as *West Side Story*, while retaining the formal grandeur of a classical ballet. Georgiadis was once again MacMillan's choice of designer.

Seymour and Gable worked closely with the choreographer: their ideas, as well as their physiques and personalities, formed the way the ballet evolved. However, Rudolf Nureyev and Margot Fonteyn were the first-night Romeo and Juliet. Such starry casting in an unproven full-length ballet was a condition for the company's forthcoming American tour, as well as for Paul Czinner's film of the production, made a few months after the première.

Although *Romeo and Juliet* was a huge success with Fonteyn and Nureyev (and the casts that followed), MacMillan felt betrayed by the Royal Ballet management, as did Seymour. Gable, equally disillusioned, gave up dancing for an acting career. MacMillan accepted an offer from the Deutsche Oper in West Berlin to run its ballet company—a decision endorsed by Sir Frederick Ashton, then director of the Royal Ballet. 'I might not have gone if Fred had said I was too valuable to lose', MacMillan told a friend, Gilbert Vernon, 'but he didn't even try to stop me' (private information).

Choreography, 1966–1980 MacMillan left for Berlin in 1966, taking several colleagues with him, including Seymour as his new company's ballerina. It was not a happy experience, though MacMillan created works for the company, including *Concerto* and *Anastasia* (the one-act version) that have been performed by many companies, as well as mounting his own productions of *Swan Lake* and *The Sleeping Beauty*. He found the bureaucracy of a German opera house hard to handle, especially since ballet did not seem a priority. He did not speak German, so he felt cut off from films, theatre, and the outside world: Berlin was a divided city, the western part an allied-controlled enclave. MacMillan became increasingly isolated as his imported entourage moved away to live independent lives.

He had been consulting a psychiatrist before he left for Berlin, suffering from the depression and anxiety attacks that were to dog him all his life. Berlin exacerbated his problems, as did his dependence on alcohol and cigarettes. He had a minor stroke in 1969 from which he soon recovered, shortly after the end of his Berlin appointment. He had already been designated the next artistic director of the Royal Ballet in 1970, after Sir Frederick Ashton's reluctant retirement.

Relations with the Royal Ballet's staff and dancers during the difficult period of transition had been made even more awkward for MacMillan by the opera house management's decision to reorganize its two ballet companies. The touring company was reduced to a small group of soloists: jobs were lost; the re-formed administrative structure of the merged companies was ambiguous, leading to rows and resignations.

MacMillan succeeded, however, in broadening the Royal Ballet's repertory still further by introducing works by other choreographers. Many of his own creations, including a three-act version of *Anastasia*, were not initially well received. As they were revived, they were viewed more favourably. None the less, it would take seventeen years before his *Manon* (1974) was regarded as a modern classic, danced by companies all over the world. Critics of the time were sharply divided over his achievements: his ballets and his artistic policy were attacked by sections of the press in Britain and the United States. During this testing period, he met Deborah Williams, an Australian artist; they married in 1973 following the birth of their daughter, Charlotte.

After seven years as director of the Royal Ballet, MacMillan resigned in 1977 in order to concentrate on choreography. His fourth full-length ballet, *Mayerling* (1978), investigated the tormented psyche of Crown Prince Rudolf and his suicide pact with his young mistress, Mary Vetsera. Scenarios for MacMillan's new one-act ballets were also dark: a disturbed family in *My Brother my Sisters*, a lunatic asylum in *Playground; Valley of Shadows* (based on the novel and film of Giorgio Bassani's *The Garden of the Finzi-Continis*) included scenes in a Nazi concentration camp. *Different Drummer* told the story of George Büchner's *Woyzeck*, another example of man's inhumanity to man.

MacMillan's dance-drama *Isadora* (1981), recreating Isadora Duncan's extravagant life in dance and dialogue, was regarded as an experiment that failed. Although his ballets during this period elicited fine performances, they were not to the taste of an increasingly conservative audience at the Royal Opera House. Televised versions of his work were more successful, including a documentary about *Mayerling* (London Weekend Television, 1978), and another, *A Lot of Happiness* (Granada, 1981), about the process of creating choreography. MacMillan also directed professional theatre productions of August Strindberg's *The Dance of Death* and Tennessee Williams's *Kingdom of Earth*, with mixed results.

MacMillan was knighted in 1983 but felt increasingly that his work, challenging the boundaries of ballet, was ill-appreciated in Britain. He accepted an invitation in 1984 to become artistic associate of American Ballet Theatre, where Mikhail Baryshnikov was then artistic director. MacMillan travelled to the United States to supervise American Ballet Theatre's stagings of his ballets, including *Romeo and Juliet* and a production of *The Sleeping Beauty*, as well as two new works for the company, *Wild Boy* and *Requiem* (to Andrew Lloyd Webber's music). He retained his links with the Royal Ballet, remaining its principal choreographer, while forging new ones with the Australian Ballet and Houston Ballet. During this period of frequent travel, his health deteriorated and he suffered a heart attack in Australia in 1988.

Last years, 1989–1992 Aware that he was living on borrowed time, MacMillan returned to enter a new creative phase with the Royal Ballet. He started work on a long-deferred three-act ballet, *Prince of the Pagodas*, to Benjamin Britten's score. It was to star nineteen-year-old Darcey Bussell in her first major role in 1989. He acquired yet another muse in the former Bolshoi principal dancer, Irek Mukhamedov, who joined the Royal Ballet in 1991. MacMillan

choreographed a gala *pas de deux* for Bussell and Mukhamedov, which became the core of his *Winter Dreams* ballet. His last creation, apart from the dances for the National Theatre's 1992 production of the musical *Carousel*, was *The Judas Tree*, with Mukhamedov as the brutal anti-hero. Controversial to the end, MacMillan invented a tortured, symbolic scenario, built around guilt, betrayal, and murder on a construction site by Canary Wharf, then under development in the East End of London.

By the time of his death MacMillan's reputation as a choreographer had spread worldwide. His ballets, particularly the dramatic, narrative works, have been danced by an increasing number of companies. Roles such as Juliet, Manon, Rudolf, and Mary Vetsera have proved open to interpretation by many dancers from different backgrounds. The Royal Ballet has continued to claim him as its great creative force, along with Frederick Ashton; their ballets have forged its distinctive identity. He was awarded an honorary doctorate by Edinburgh University in 1976 and by the Royal College of Art in 1992.

MacMillan died of a heart attack, backstage, during the first night of the Royal Ballet's revival of *Mayerling* in the Royal Opera House on 29 October 1992. The announcement of his death was made on stage at the end of the ballet—an extraordinarily dramatic, public conclusion to a life in the theatre. He was cremated in London on 6 November 1992; a memorial service was held in Westminster Abbey on 17 February 1993.   JANN PARRY

Sources private information (2004) · E. Thorpe, *Kenneth MacMillan: the man and the ballets* (1985) · L. Seymour and P. Gardner, *Lynn: the autobiography of Lynn Seymour* (1984) · A. Bland, *The Royal Ballet: the first 50 years* (1981) · S. Woodcock, *The Sadler's Wells Royal Ballet* (1991) · A. Kane, 'Kenneth MacMillan: rebel with a cause', *Dancing Times* (Nov 1989), i–viii [dance study suppl.] · C. Crisp, 'Kenneth MacMillan', *About the House*, 8/5 (spring 1990), 4–13 · H. Koegler, 'Kenneth MacMillan: nowhere at home / keine Heimat, nirgends', *Ballet International* (Dec 1989) · D. McMahon, 'MacMillan at sixty', *Dance Theatre Journal* (Feb 1990), 10–12 · M. Hunt, 'Kenneth MacMillan', *Dance Magazine* (Sept 1991) · *Dancing Times* (Dec 1992) · *Financial Times* (30 Oct 1992) · D. Bintley, 'Sir Kenneth MacMillan', *Dance Now* (winter 1992), 42–5 · N. Dromgoole, 'Spotlight on MacMillan', *Dance and Dancers* (March 1983), 20–21 · P. Crookston, 'A childhood: Sir Kenneth MacMillan', *The Times* (6 July 1991) · V. Kewley, 'A life in the day of Sir Kenneth MacMillan', *Sunday Times Magazine* (21 Jan 1990) · C. Crisp, 'The man who makes his emotions dance', *Financial Times* (20 April 1991) · R. Penman, 'Kenneth MacMillan: doing it his way', *Dance Theatre Journal*, 3/1 (1985), 10–12 · R. Billington, 'The Times profile', *The Times* (23 Feb 1984) · R. Christiansen, 'Kenneth MacMillan and the roughing up of ballet', *Dance Theatre Journal* (spring 1997), 10–13 · D. Dougill, 'In the steps of the master', *Sunday Times* (13 Jan 1991) · J. Higgins, 'My brother my sisters', *The Times* (17 May 1978) · J. Gruen and K. MacMillan, interview, 26 July 1972, NYPL for the Performing Arts [tape] · K. MacMillan, interview, *About the House*, 1/2 (1963), 6–9 · *Ballet Annuals*, 1–16 (1947–62) · G. Roberts and K. MacMillan, interview, *Shropshire Star* (5 Nov 1985)

Archives Royal Opera House archives · Theatre Museum | FILM BFI · NYPL for the Performing Arts | SOUND BL NSA, interviews

Likenesses G. Adams, vintage print, 1952, NPG · Y. Sonnabend, oils, 1988, NPG [*see illus.*] · J. Broad, photograph; exhibited in NPG · D. MacMillan, portrait, Royal Opera House, MacMillan Studio · Y. Sonnabend, portrait, NPG · Y. Sonnabend, portrait, Royal Ballet School

Macmillan, Kirkpatrick (*bap.* **1812**, *d.* **1878**), inventor of the pedal bicycle, was born in the parish of Keir near Thornhill, Dumfriesshire, and baptized on 18 September 1812. He was the fifth son (the eldest of whom died aged thirteen) of Robert Macmillan, blacksmith at Courthill smithy in Keir, and his wife, Mary Auld. There were also at least three younger sisters in the family.

Macmillan helped his father at the forge, worked on a neighbouring farm, got a job as a coachman, and at twenty-two became an assistant to the blacksmith of Walter Scott, fifth duke of Buccleuch, at Drumlanrig. Some time afterwards he chanced to see a hobby-horse being ridden along a nearby road, and was struck with the notion of making one for himself. This he did, and when he had learned to ride it he realized what a radical improvement it would be if he could propel it without putting his feet on the ground. At about this time he returned to Courthill to assist his father, and so he was able to use all the resources of the smithy to make the kind of machine that was in his mind. He completed it about the end of 1839, and quickly mastered the art of riding it on the rough country roads, regularly making the 14 mile journey to Dumfries. This first pedal bicycle was propelled by a horizontal reciprocating movement of the rider's feet on the pedals. This movement was transmitted to cranks on the rear wheel by connecting rods; the machine weighed almost exactly half a hundredweight and the physical effort required to ride it must have been very considerable.

In spite of these disadvantages, Macmillan's next exploit, in June 1842, was to ride the 70 miles into Glasgow, a trip which took him two days and resulted in his being fined the sum of 5s. for causing a slight injury to a small girl who ran across his path. He never thought of patenting his invention or trying to make any money out of it, but others who saw it were not slow to realize its potential, and soon copies began to appear and were sold for £6 or £7 each. Gavin Dalzell of Lesmahagow copied his machine in 1846 and passed on the details to so many people that for more than fifty years he was generally regarded as the inventor of the bicycle.

With all these developments Macmillan was quite unconcerned, preferring to enjoy the quiet country life he was used to. Shortly after the death of his father, in 1854 he married Elizabeth Gordon Goldie (*d.* 1865). Of their six children only a son, John, and a daughter survived. After his wife's early death Macmillan's sister Ann became his housekeeper and looked after his two young children. Macmillan died in Courthill on 26 January 1878.

RONALD M. BIRSE, *rev.*

Sources G. Irving, *The devil on wheels* (1986) · N. G. Clayton, 'The first bicycle', *Boneshaker*, 113 (spring 1987) · d. cert.
Wealth at death £234 16s. 7½d.: inventory, 1878, CCI

McMillan, Margaret (1860–1931), socialist propagandist and educationist, was born on 19 July 1860 at Throgg's Neck, Westchester county, New York, the second of the three daughters of James McMillan (*c.*1830–1865), landscape gardener and estate manager, and his wife, Jane (*d.* 1877), daughter of Robert Cameron, factor, of Dochfour,

Margaret McMillan (1860–1931), by Bassano, 1930

Inverness-shire, and his wife, Rachel. Both parents emigrated from Scotland to the United States after their marriage in March 1858. After the death of James McMillan his widow returned to Scotland and her parental home with the two surviving daughters of the marriage (a child named Elizabeth died at the age of three, also in 1865). Margaret McMillan and her sister Rachel *McMillan (1859–1917) grew up and were educated in Inverness.

In biographies published after her death, Margaret McMillan's reputation was established as a 'saviour' and 'champion' of childhood, by her work as an educationist and theorist of progressive nursery education. Her claim to fame during most of her lifetime, however, was as a speaker, propagandist, and journalist for the Independent Labour Party (ILP), which was formed in 1893. (McMillan was an early, though not a founding, member.) As one of the startlingly successful female orators who publicized the work of the late nineteenth-century British socialist parties, she developed a theory of the regenerative and political power of children made healthy, clean, and beautiful by good nutrition and a 'physiological' education that paid equal attention to their physical and intellectual development. By seeing the potential of their own children thus revealed, working-class parents would be moved to embrace socialist principles and vote for the ILP. The practical manifestation of this theory of political agency was the very well-publicized Deptford Camp School (an open-air nursery school) that she founded with Rachel McMillan in 1911. By this time, however, McMillan's focus of interest was child development rather than the role of childhood in the achievement of socialism. Originally her political thesis owed something to the Christian socialism that was later claimed to have formed her, but much more to the continental physiology and reworked faculty psychology (notably the work of Édouard Seguin) that she was so successful in transmitting to popular and professional audiences in late Victorian and Edwardian Britain.

McMillan's main importance now lies in her successful career as a female political propagandist, her original theory of agency and childhood, and the light that both these factors throw on the relationship of the personal and the political in late nineteenth-century British socialism, and on ethical socialism itself. McMillan's reworking of the post-Wordsworthian romantic child into a practical political project is probably her first claim on historical importance. Late in life McMillan attributed all her thinking and educational projects to the influence of her sister Rachel, and Rachel may be placed alongside the other women (notably the duchess of Sutherland in the 1890s, and Nancy Astor in the 1920s) with whom McMillan made intense friendships, and who provided her with intellectual and financial support in her various projects. Of particular interest is the political charisma that McMillan so clearly possessed, and to which there is so much contemporary testimony. The novelty and power of a woman on the political platform, addressing questions of how to live sexually as well as socially, was a feature of the success of all the ILP female orators, though something of McMillan's power must be attributed to the stage training she received in the early 1890s.

After a schooling at Inverness high school and Inverness Academy, McMillan spent time in Frankfurt am Main, Geneva, and Lausanne boarding-schools in preparation for becoming a finishing governess (she was briefly employed as one in Edinburgh, in 1881, between her time in Germany and Switzerland). In later life McMillan frequently attributed her politics to the proto-socialist ideas (notably those of Henry George) that she encountered in these schools. Her time abroad (1878–83) was followed by a period of governessing in the English shires that can be reconstructed only from the fiction she was to produce for the Labour press a few years later, in which a passionate and committed young governess confronts the emptiness and selfishness of bourgeois life, embodied in various ranks of fictionalized female employers. It was from an actual provincial household, the rectory in Ludlow, where she was governess to the daughters of the Revd Edward Clayton, that she dispatched the first of six articles inspired by the London Dock strike of 1889 to the journal the *Christian Socialist*. With the publication of the first of them, she moved to join her sister in London, by now superintendent of a hostel for young working women in Bloomsbury. A period of voluntary work for the settlement movement, membership of the Fabian Society, educational work in the East End, public speaking, investigative journalism, and paid companionship to Lady Meux of the brewing dynasty—who supported McMillan's abortive training as an actress—inscribe a life of heterodox metropolitan leftism between 1889 and 1893. But these years, and involvement with the Labour church, also introduced McMillan to the provincial socialist lecture circuit.

McMillan settled in Bradford in 1893, at a time when other young socialists were relocating themselves in order to make a living from and dedicate a life to the newly formed Independent Labour Party. She taught adults at the Bradford Labour Institute (formed from the local Labour church), continued her travelling propaganda across the north, joined the staff of Robert Blatchford's *Clarion* in 1894, and wrote her first and only novel (*Samson*, 1895) before she was elected to the Bradford school board in November 1894, on the ILP ticket. She served on three boards before she left the city in 1902. Here, in home visiting, school inspection, and contact with parents and children in a textile-producing city that made much use of child labour, lay the roots of McMillan's thinking on childhood and socialism. The need to communicate with working-class parents developed McMillan's techniques of personifying abstract ideas about child development, hygiene, and nutrition; journalism gave her a national audience for a kind of socio-fiction she refined in these years, in which vignettes of child life, labour, and ill health in Bradford served to illuminate broader questions of political principle and action.

The Education Act of 1902 abolished school boards and invested the control and management of elementary schools in county and municipal councils, to which women could not be elected. The move south, to Bromley, in Kent, where Rachel McMillan now lived, was to some extent a repetition of the move made from Ludlow to London a decade before, as McMillan searched for a sphere of action in non-electoral politics. Her output of journalism continued; she took a paid post as lecturer for the Ethical Society, was recruited to the newly formed Workers' Educational Association in 1903, and was elected a member of the Froebel Society executive committee in 1904. She became manager of a group of Deptford elementary schools in 1903. This work, both paid and voluntary, brought her new audiences to whom she could proclaim her thesis of childhood and social renewal. Her journalism became more consistently focused on child development, and her books began to establish her reputation as an educationist rather than as a socialist propagandist.

With her sister, and with financial support from Joseph Fels, the American soap millionaire and disciple of Henry George, McMillan opened a small experimental school clinic at Bow. Here was the germ of the Deptford Clinic (out of which the Camp School grew), started seven years later, in 1910. A campaign for the medical inspection of schoolchildren, which McMillan conducted with much *élan* at ILP and Labour Party conferences and in the Labour press, occupied her in the pre-Deptford years.

The Deptford Camp School was the most famous of McMillan's enterprises, a garden in a slum much visited by journalists and educators, particularly in the years after the First World War. Its principles of management and pedagogy, and McMillan's insistence on economies of scale and a schooling that acknowledged the pattern of working-class life, brought her into conflict with the Nursery School Association (NSA), of which she was elected president in 1923. It was through the NSA that she met Nancy Astor, who was helpful in McMillan's campaigning for a training college, dedicated to her sister's memory. The Rachel McMillan Training College opened in 1930. McMillan spoke on the Conservative platform in Astor's constituency in 1929, an apostasy that can be explained by the status of social mission that the nursery school movement achieved in the 1920s: a claim that moved it beyond party politics for many of its adherents.

McMillan published *Early Childhood* (1900), *Education through the Imagination* (1904; rev. edn, 1923), *The Child and the State* (1911), *The Camp School* (1917), *The Nursery School* (1919), *Life of Rachel McMillan* (1927), and numerous articles and pamphlets. Between 1895 and 1915 she produced on average one article of journalism a week.

McMillan, who was made a Companion of Honour in 1930, died at the Bowden House Nursing Home, Harrow on the Hill, Middlesex, on 29 March 1931 and was interred in the same grave as her sister in Brockley cemetery on 31 March. She was buried by a bishop, with a message of condolence from a queen, and the newspapers made little of her earlier socialism, naming her instead as a great benefactor and saint of childhood.   CAROLYN STEEDMAN

Sources E. Bradburn, *Margaret McMillan: portrait of a pioneer* (1989) · C. Steedman, *Childhood, culture and class in Britain: Margaret McMillan, 1860–1931* (1990) · M. McMillan, *Life of Rachel McMillan* (1927) · A. Mansbridge, *Margaret McMillan, prophet and pioneer* (1932) · M. McMillan, *The child and the state* (1911) · M. McMillan, *The Camp School* (1917) · S. Yeo, 'A new life: the religion of socialism in Britain, 1883–1896', *History Workshop Journal*, 4 (1977), 5–56 · D. Cresswell, *Margaret McMillan: a memoir* (1948) · G. Lowndes, *Margaret McMillan: the children's champion* (1960) · E. Bradburn, *Margaret McMillan: framework and expansion of nursery education* (1976) · *The Times* (30 March 1931) · *Daily Herald* (30 March 1931)
Archives BLPES, British Association for Early Childhood Education collection, Nursery School Association MSS, corresp. with the Independent Labour Party · University of Greenwich | BL, corresp. with Albert Mansbridge, Add. MSS 65196, 65257A · BL, papers relating to Albert Mansbridge's book about Margaret McMillan, Add. MSS 65331, 65345 · BLPES, Francis Johnson collection · U. Lpool L., Sydney Jones Library, corresp. with John Glasier and Katherine Bruce Glasier · U. Reading, Aston MSS · W. Yorks. AS, Miriam Lord collection
Likenesses Russell & Sons, photograph, *c*.1893, repro. in *Labour Prophet* (Sept 1893) · photograph, *c*.1895, repro. in Cresswell, *Margaret McMillan* · Bassano, photograph, 1930, NPG [*see illus.*] · J. Mansbridge, oils, *c*.1931 (after photograph, 1930), Rachel McMillan nursery school, Deptford; repro. in Steedman, *Childhood, culture and class*
Wealth at death £4068 5*s*. 10*d*.: probate, 6 June 1931, *CGPLA Eng. & Wales*

McMillan, Rachel (1859–1917), health visitor and educationist, was born on 25 March 1859 at Throggs Neck, Westchester county, New York, the first of the three daughters of James McMillan (*c*.1830–1865), landscape gardener and estate manager, and his wife, Jane (*d*. 1877), daughter of Robert Cameron, factor, of Dochfour, Inverness-shire, and

his wife, Rachel. Both parents emigrated from Scotland to the United States after their marriage in March 1858. After the death of James McMillan his widow returned to Scotland and her parental home with the two surviving daughters of the marriage (a child named Elizabeth died at the age of three, also in 1865). Rachel and her sister Margaret *McMillan (1860–1931) grew up and were educated in Inverness.

Rachel's claim to fame rests entirely on her sister's assertions and myth making about her. Margaret McMillan professed that the genesis of the famous health centre and Camp School that they ran together in Deptford after 1910 lay with Rachel, and she named the teaching training establishment that she inaugurated in 1930 the Rachel McMillan Training College in acknowledgement of her sister's purported innovations in the field of physiological education. There is absolutely no documentary evidence that Rachel ever did more than support Margaret McMillan in her various endeavours and work with her in Deptford. Rather, Rachel McMillan's interest for modern times must be the way in which she emerged from a traditional and sheltered background of helpful Victorian girlhood to pursue a career in the new forms of social and health-care work that emerged at the end of the nineteenth century. Margaret's valedictory *Life of Rachel McMillan* (1927) contains a classic and much referred to 'conversion to socialism'—not her own, but that of her sister, which is here described as taking place after Rachel's reading of W. T. Stead's *Maiden Tribute of Modern Babylon* (1885). This account has been widely used to inscribe the course of late-nineteenth-century 'ethical socialism'.

At the age of fifteen, Rachel McMillan left Inverness Academy for Coventry, where she spent three years teaching at the Ladies' College there, a school run by two distant female relatives. On the death of her mother and grandfather in 1877 she returned home to nurse her widowed grandmother, a task she undertook for eleven years. There was contact with socialist circles in Edinburgh during these years, through distant cousins. The pages of Margaret McMillan's *Life* that describe Rachel's Edinburgh progress through Socialist League reading groups, earnest study of *Das Kapital*, and William Morris's newspaper *The Commonweal* have been much used by historians of the Independent Labour Party and other socialist groups of the period.

The grandmother, Rachel Cameron, died in July 1888, and Rachel set out on the path of paid employment for the first time in her life. She became junior superintendent of a hostel for working girls in Bloomsbury, London. Though she accompanied her sister in Margaret's early days in Bradford, 'the cradle of socialism', she made the decision to return to London and to train at the Sanitary Institute for the qualification of inspector of nuisances. She gained her certificate in 1895. This qualification opened up a wide range of work for her in the fields of childcare and health visiting. Both McMillan sisters eventually established careers that derived from a new professionalization of childcare.

Rachel McMillan spent some months of 1895 working as

secretary to the Women's Industrial Council in Liverpool, a paid post that drew on her training in health and factory legislation and in environmental health. In 1896 she took up a permanent post in Kent, as a travelling teacher of hygiene. Kent county council did not operate a health visiting scheme, and such a post, which McMillan held until 1913, most likely involved teaching domestic hygiene in rural areas, under the aegis of the Kent technical education committee.

Rachel McMillan lodged in Bromley, and here her sister joined her when she left Bradford in 1902. Margaret's contact with the heterogeneous world of London socialism brought the metropolis to Bromley. In his biography of Margaret McMillan of 1932 Albert Mansbridge remembers meeting Prince Kropotkin, the Lansburys, Margaret Llewelyn Davies, and the countess of Warwick at tea parties in the McMillans' rooms at 51 Tweedy Road, Bromley.

The Deptford Clinic, and the school that developed out of it, brought Rachel McMillan from Kent to Deptford in 1913. She worked full time at the open-air Camp School until her death, much worn-out by managing the Deptford enterprise and nursing her sister through a severe illness. She died at her home, 353 Evelyn Street, Deptford, on 25 March 1917 and was buried in Brockley cemetery on 28 March 1917. Ten years later, in a homage prepared for in many speeches and articles, her sister reinvented her as a pioneer of nursery education and teacher training in the *Life of Rachel McMillan*. The biography also contains one of the most moving and elegiac 'childhoods' in English literature, in which the frail girl-child prefigures the thousands of Bradford and Deptford children who will be 'rescued' by the McMillan sisters in the course of their career. However, the historical record shows Rachel McMillan to have been a hard-working, professionally qualified childcare worker rather than a post-romantic saviour of childhood.   CAROLYN STEEDMAN

Sources C. Steedman, *Childhood, culture and class in Britain: Margaret McMillan, 1860–1931* (1990) • E. Bradburn, *Margaret McMillan: portrait of a pioneer* (1989) • M. McMillan, *Life of Rachel McMillan* (1927) • A. Mansbridge, *Margaret McMillan, prophet and pioneer* (1932) • S. Yeo, 'A new life: the religion of socialism in Britain, 1883–1896', *History Workshop Journal*, 4 (1977), 5–56 • D. Cresswell, *Margaret McMillan: a memoir* (1948) • G. Lowndes, *Margaret McMillan: the children's champion* (1960) • E. Bradburn, *Margaret McMillan: framework and expansion of nursery education* (1976) • d. cert.

Archives BM, Mansbridge MSS, Add. MSS • London School of Economics, Francis Johnson collection • U. Lpool L., Sydney Jones Library, Glasier MSS • U. Reading, Astor MSS • University of Greenwich, Margaret McMillan collection • W. Yorks. AS, Bradford, Miriam Lord collection

Likenesses photograph, *c.*1917, repro. in McMillan, *Life of Rachel McMillan*, cover and frontispiece

Wealth at death £1587 12*s*. 6*d*.: administration, 26 June 1917, CGPLA Eng. & Wales

McMillan, Roderick Macaulay [Roddy] (1923–1979),

actor and playwright, was born on 23 March 1923 in the Anderston district of Glasgow, the second of the two children of Duncan McMillan (1880–1964), a foreman docker, and Rachel Macaulay (1879–1935). Roddy McMillan was born into a Gaelic-speaking family—his father came from Ardnamurchan in Argyll and his mother from the Isle of Harris—and the highland inheritance informed much of his work as an actor and playwright. Religion proved to be unimportant for him despite his strictly Presbyterian upbringing. He was educated at Finnieston public school, Glasgow, leaving at the age of fourteen. The only early sign of performance talent was in playing drums with the Boys' Brigade.

Between 1938 and 1945 McMillan worked briefly as a delivery van boy for a biscuit factory but was soon apprenticed to a glass beveller and lens grinder. He subsequently attended night school as part of his training in the Rolls Royce aero-engineering factory. By 1941 McMillan was taking an interest in amateur acting and, encouraged by the actor Duncan Macrae who had taught him at Finnieston, he joined Glasgow Unity Theatre. He married Jean Alexander Bell (1923–1996) in December 1943; their first daughter, Sine, was born in 1944 and their second, Norma, in 1947.

Unity turned professional in 1946. McMillan decided to stay with them to follow a theatrical career, making his London début in *The Gorbals Story* in February 1948. When Unity broke up, James Bridie was instrumental in McMillan's joining the Glasgow Citizens' Theatre Company in 1950.

McMillan soon established himself as a character actor of considerable stature, with a distinct gift for comedy. His style, described by David Hutchison as 'contemporary urban naturalism' (Hutchison, 5), was clearly the legacy of Unity's repertoire of Russian classics and social realism. McMillan was a regular member of the Citizens' until 1956, acting in a wide range of plays from Shakespeare to new Scottish writers, from J. Bridie and J. B. Priestley to Christmas pantomimes.

However, it was as a playwright that McMillan saw his future. His first play *All in Good Faith*, initially rejected by the Citizens', was eventually produced by them in 1954. The reviews were harshly critical, claiming that it presented an unrealistic picture of contemporary life. McMillan was disillusioned and it was nineteen years before he wrote his second play. Nevertheless the play illustrates his particular gift in utilizing the Scots dialect to communicate with an audience.

With the gradual decline of repertory theatre McMillan moved successfully into television, where he worked regularly from 1959. He was best known in the title role in *The View from Daniel Pike* (1971), as Para Handy in *The Vital Spark* series (1974), and as Choc Minty in *Hazell* (1978). He also enjoyed credits as a supporting actor in films such as *Morning Departure* (1950), *The Battle of the Sexes* (1960), and *Ring of Bright Water* (1969).

It was not until the early 1970s, however, that McMillan really emerged as a leading figure on the Scottish stage when, in an attempt to revive interest in new Scottish drama, Bill Bryden formed a company of leading Scottish actors at Edinburgh's Lyceum Theatre. McMillan played Jake in Bryden's *Willie Rough* (1971) and then, encouraged by Bryden, he wrote *The Bevellers*. The Lyceum's production (1973) was instantly successful with McMillan playing Bob

Darnley. This play became a significant influence on a generation of new Scottish playwrights.

Throughout his life McMillan was keenly interested in Scottish ballads and folk music. He composed and published many songs, including 'Campbeltown Loch'. Theatre was not only his profession but also his private passion. He was on the board of the Duncan Macrae Memorial Trust and between 1953 and 1968 he was an active committee member of Scottish Actors Equity. His only recreation, apart from playwriting, was fly-fishing.

McMillan was a small, stockily built man with sandy coloured hair and a strong and charismatic personality. On his recovery from a period of alcoholism he devoted a considerable time to helping others with similar problems. A man of generous spirit in public and in private, with a pawky sense of humour, he was highly regarded by his colleagues. In 1972 he won a television personality award and in 1979 he became an OBE.

McMillan died suddenly, of a heart attack, at Glasgow Royal Infirmary on 9 July 1979. He was cremated on 12 July at Linn crematorium in Glasgow. In 1982 a new variety of rose, the 'Roddy McMillan', commissioned as a memorial by his friends and colleagues, was introduced at the Chelsea Flower Show. P. S. BARLOW

Sources private information (2004) · BFI · U. Glas. L., special collections department, Scottish Theatre Archive · D. Hutchison, 'Roddy Macmillan and the Scottish theatre', *Cencrastus*, 2 (spring 1980), 5–8 · F. Mackay, 'Arts outlook', *The Scotsman* (28 May 1982) · R. Stevenson and G. Wallace, eds., *Scottish theatre since the seventies* (1996) · *Television Today* (July 1979) · *Glasgow Herald* (July 1979) · *Daily Telegraph* (July 1979) · *International Film Collector* (Sept 1979) · *Photoplay* (Sept 1979) · *The Times* (Nov 1979) · CCI (1980)
Archives U. Glas., photographs, programmes, press cuttings
Likenesses photographs, U. Glas. L., Scottish Theatre Archive
Wealth at death £54,507.73: confirmation, 22 Jan 1980, CCI

McMillan, William (1887–1977), sculptor, was born at Aberdeen on 31 August 1887, the son of William McMillan, master engraver and printer of 37 Powis Place, Aberdeen, and his wife, Jane Knight. He was trained professionally as a sculptor first at the city's art school, Gray's School of Art, and then went on to complete his studies at the Royal College of Art, London (1908–12). In 1916 he married Dorothy (d. 1964), daughter of Maurice Charles Williams, an architect, of Carlisle. There were no children. His early career in London was interrupted almost immediately by the First World War, in which he saw active service in France as an officer with the 5th Oxfordshire and Buckinghamshire light infantry.

Even before the war was over McMillan had begun to establish himself professionally, exhibiting for the first time at the Royal Academy summer exhibition in 1917, and continuing to do so thereafter, with only one exception, every year until 1971. Commissions to design the 'Great War' medal and the victory medal confirmed a reputation which by 1925 had grown sufficiently rapidly for him to be elected an associate of the Royal Academy at the precocious age of thirty-eight; he became a Royal Academician in 1933. In 1929 he was appointed master of the sculpture school in the Royal Academy Schools, a position he held until 1940.

McMillan had the reputation of being a good teacher, relaxed and with a gift for quietly explaining a point. He did not expect or demand followers, nor did he attack those with whom he disagreed. He had in short a sense of the world; this was of considerable importance in a time of revolutionary change in British sculpture, when the impact of European avant-garde ideas began to be felt in Britain through the work of Henry Moore, Barbara Hepworth, and others.

From 1940 until 1966, when he finally gave up the Chelsea studio in Glebe Place which he had used for most of his life, McMillan became involved in a whole series of important public sculptures—among them *King George VI* (1955) in Carlton Gardens, *Sir Walter Raleigh* (1959) in Whitehall, *Alcock and Brown* (1966) at London airport, and the bronze group of *Nereid and Triton with Dolphins* (1948) for the Beatty memorial fountain in Trafalgar Square.

As a sculptor McMillan is notable for working on an exceptionally wide range of subjects—from war memorials to medals, from statues of royalty and generals to works for garden and architectural decoration. All are distinguished by his feeling for the particular material used, and by a strong sense of design and outline. In retrospect, however, it will probably be the imaginative and decorative pieces in native British stones and woods dating from the 1920s and early 1930s that will be seen as his most original and significant contribution to twentieth-century British sculpture. Such attitudes to materials are now so widely accepted that it is hard to imagine the impact in their day of works like *Statuette* (1927), carved in green slate, or the *Birth of Venus*, in Portland stone (1931; Tate Collection), in the Royal Academy. As with all his best sculpture, they have a classical purity of line and a poetic quality that places them among the more distinctive sculptural achievements of the time. McMillan was by nature a conservative, however, and this, combined with his technical skills, drew him increasingly towards public sculpture. The subtle pressure and demands inherent in such work led to a much blander style that is rather more anonymous in character and somewhat dull.

McMillan was an elusive and very private person, fond of a daily routine that took him to the Chelsea Arts Club for lunch and a game of billiards. He was a tall and extremely handsome man, the quizzical expression the chief outward sign of a very dry Scottish sense of humour that led him in younger days to be involved in organizing the Chelsea Arts Ball. He was elected an associate member of the Royal Society of British Sculptors in 1928 and a full member in 1932. He was appointed CVO in 1956. He was also made a freeman of Aberdeen, and the university there conferred upon him an honorary doctorate of law.

McMillan died on 25 September 1977 in hospital at Richmond-on-Thames shortly after his ninetieth birthday, a few days after an assault and robbery in the street had left him badly injured.

NICHOLAS USHERWOOD, *rev.*

Sources *The Times* (28 Sept 1977) · personal knowledge (1986) · private information (1986) [W. Scott] · *CGPLA Eng. & Wales* (1978) · G. Popp and H. Valentine, *Royal Academy of Arts directory of membership: from the foundation in 1768 to 1995, including honorary members* (1996)
Likenesses H. Todd, photograph, 1936, Hult. Arch.
Wealth at death £99,015: probate, 9 Jan 1978, *CGPLA Eng. & Wales*

Macmillan, William Miller (1885–1974), historian, was born in Aberdeen on 1 October 1885, the youngest child in the family of three sons and four daughters of the Revd John Macmillan, Scottish Free Church minister and schoolmaster, who had served as a missionary in India, and his wife, Elizabeth Caid, *née* Lindsay. In 1891 the family emigrated to Cape Colony, and his father lectured at Victoria College, Stellenbosch (later Stellenbosch University) and was in charge of a college hostel. Macmillan was educated at Stellenbosch Boys' High School. In 1903 he went to Merton College, Oxford, as one of the first Rhodes scholars, and in 1906 he gained a second-class degree in modern history. He studied further at Aberdeen, Glasgow, and Berlin before returning to South Africa, where he was appointed lecturer in history and economics at Rhodes University College, Grahamstown, Cape Province, in 1911. Here he embarked on research into poverty and the land question, publishing *The South African Agrarian Problem* (1919).

In 1917 Macmillan took the chair of history at the Johannesburg School of Mines (later the University of the Witwatersrand) where he worked on the radical Scottish missionary Dr John Philip. His analyses of the historic relations of black and white people in the Cape, *The Cape Colour Question* (1927) and *Bantu, Boer and Briton* (1929), illuminated for him 'this African and World Race Problem, ever increasingly urgent in our day'. In *Complex South Africa* (1930) he emphasized the existence of a 'common society', history underpinning his political opposition to the segregation policies of successive South African governments. Membership of the Johannesburg Joint Council of Europeans and Natives, an interracial forum of discussion and protest, led him to advocate co-operation with the progressive black élite, incorporation rather than segregation. Macmillan's personal example inspired a generation of liberal historians: Margaret Hodgson (Ballinger), Cornelius de Kiewiet, J. S. Marais, and Lucy Sutherland. In 1932 his speeches and articles incurred governmental censure of the university. Dissuaded from resigning, Macmillan took extended leave rather than restrain his public utterances. After travelling in Africa he settled in Britain, resigning his chair in 1933.

Without salaried employment, Macmillan turned journalist. Helped by research grants and an association with All Souls College, Oxford, he wrote pioneering studies of social change in Africa which were published as *Africa Emergent* (1938, 1949) and used by Lord Hailey in preparing his *African Survey* (1938). He became a prominent critic of indirect rule and colonial self-sufficiency; in the London Group on African Affairs he opposed the transfer of Bechuanaland, Basutoland, and Swaziland to South Africa. His graphic denunciation of neglect in the West Indies, *Warning from the West Indies* (1936), appeared months before serious West Indian riots, lending force to his advocacy of reconstruction by colonial development. His arguments for revitalizing the colonies were realized in more active policies promoting colonial change. From 1936 he joined the parliamentary labour advisory committee, opposing land bills in Kenya and Southern Rhodesia. From African experience he identified 'the real colonial problem' as 'natural poverty' and 'conquering nature in tropical conditions'. Membership of the advisory committee on education in the colonies (1940–43) confirmed his preoccupation with 'the "emergent" African who must be the architect of the future'; but, as British Council representative in west Africa (1943–5), he became disillusioned with 'the nearly highbrow'.

Macmillan was adopted as Labour candidate for Inverness in 1940, but did not stand at the election of 1945, being out of the country. He was appointed director of colonial studies at the University of St Andrews (1947–54), continuing regular broadcasts as an African observer. As acting professor of history at the University College of the West Indies (1954) he began *The Road to Self-Rule* (1959). While encouraging Westernized intelligentsias, he did not come to terms with their nationalisms, whether he was lecturing in South Africa (1949), advising on local government in Tanganyika (1950), observing the Seretse Khama affair in Bechuanaland (1951), or surveying the possibilities for a Central African Federation (1952). He visited southern Africa regularly until 1973. Honorary degrees were conferred on him by Oxford (1957), Natal (1962), and Edinburgh (1974).

In 1913 Macmillan married Jean, daughter of John Sutherland, headmaster. They had no children. Following their divorce in 1933, he married Mona, daughter of Sir Hugh Justin Tweedie RN. They had two sons and two daughters. Macmillan died on 23 October 1974 at his home, Yew Tree Cottage, Long Wittenham, Berkshire.

DEBORAH LAVIN, *rev.*

Sources W. M. Macmillan, *My South African years* (1975) · M. Macmillan, *Champion of Africa: W. M. Macmillan, the second phase* (privately printed, 1985) · H. Macmillan and S. Marks, eds., *Africa and empire: W. M. Macmillan, historian and social critic* (1989) · L. S. Sutherland, 'William Miller Macmillan: an appreciation', *African affairs*, ed. K. Kirkwood, 3 vols. (1961–9) · *CGPLA Eng. & Wales* (1975)
Archives Bodl. RH, papers, incl. corresp., drafts of speeches, and diaries | Bodl. RH, corresp. with Sir R. R. Welensky
Wealth at death £17,600: probate, 16 Jan 1975, *CGPLA Eng. & Wales*

McMordie [*née* Gray], **Julia** (1860–1942), politician and philanthropist, was born on 30 March 1860 at Cliff Terrace, Hartlepool, co. Durham, the fifth daughter of Sir William *Gray (1823–1898), shipbuilder and shipowner, and his wife, Dorothy (d. 1906), daughter of Captain John Hall RN. A Presbyterian, she was educated at Chislehurst, Kent, but moved to Belfast following her marriage to Robert James McMordie (1849–1914) on 21 May 1886. He was a solicitor in Belfast and also served as Unionist MP for East Belfast and as lord mayor of Belfast from 1910 until his death in 1914. On 23 January 1914, two months before his death, the McMordies were awarded the freedom of the city of Belfast in recognition of their public service. Their children, John Andrew and Elsie Gray, were born on 8 July 1887 and 30 November 1888 respectively.

After her husband's death McMordie's interest in philanthropy and politics continued. She was involved with an array of local organizations in Belfast, including the Samaritan Hospital, the Ulster Hospital for Women and Children, the Girls' Help Society, the Presbyterian Women's and Girls' Union, the Young Women's Christian Association, and the Cripples' Institute. During the First World War she was president of the St John's Women's Voluntary Aid Detachment for Belfast. She was also an active member of the Ulster Women's Unionist Council, serving as an executive committee member and a vice-chairman from 1911 to 1919 and as vice-president from 1919 to 1942.

On 2 September 1918 McMordie became the first female councillor on Belfast corporation, and she served as an alderman from 1920 to 1930. She summed up her interest in municipal affairs in her 1926 electoral manifesto: 'I have tried to do all I could for the best interests of the Ratepayers … I am very much interested in the Health and well being of the Citizens, more especially of the children, … I love the work' (PRO NIre., D.1327/16/1/5).

In 1921 McMordie was one of two women elected to the first parliament of Northern Ireland, standing as a Unionist candidate in South Belfast. Although McMordie had not supported the suffrage movement, much of her parliamentary debate focused on issues relating to women and children. In her maiden speech of 5 April 1922, for instance, she called for an increase in the number of women police officers. She was also anxious to improve educational provisions in Northern Ireland—stressing the importance of employing specially trained teachers for disabled children and of having female school inspectors. Although a staunch unionist and a capable orator, she did not stand for re-election in 1925.

In 1935 McMordie left Belfast, taking up residence in East Cliff, Budleigh Salterton, Devon, in order to be near her family. Various accolades were bestowed on McMordie throughout her life. In 1919 she was appointed CBE and in 1928 she was appointed high sheriff of Belfast, the first woman in Ireland to hold this position. She was a lady of grace of the order of St John of Jerusalem, and was one of the first three women in Ireland to be appointed to the magistracy. In 1936 she was given the honorary degree of LLD from the Queen's University of Belfast.

McMordie died at her daughter's home in King's Cliffe, Oundle, Northamptonshire, on 12 April 1942. She was described as possessing 'gentle dignity, strong courage, and an ever ready will to help' (Belfast Telegraph, 12 May 1921). Perhaps a fitting maxim for her career, which had been dedicated to alleviating 'suffering, and to better the conditions of her fellow beings, the poor, the sick and the children' (Belfast Telegraph, 23 Jan 1928), was one which she used when describing her life: 'I think I can say I have not spared myself' (Belfast News-Letter, 30 April 1930).

DIANE URQUHART

Sources Belfast Telegraph (14 April 1942) · Belfast News-Letter (14 April 1942) · Northern Whig and Belfast Post (15 April 1942) · Thom's Irish who's who (1923) · Who's Who in Northern Ireland (1923) · Who's Who in Northern Ireland (1937) · notebook, PRO NIre., T 1013/2B [listing marriages, births, and deaths of members of Carnmoney Presbyterian Church, co. Antrim] · WWW · electoral manifestos of unionist candidates, 15 Jan 1926, PRO NIre., D 1327/16/1/5 [Pottinger ward, Belfast] · Northern Ireland House of Commons debates, 1921–5 · N. Kinghan, United we stood: the story of the Ulster Women's Unionist Council, 1911–74 (1975) · Belfast Telegraph (12 May 1921) · Belfast Telegraph (23 Jan 1928) · Belfast Telegraph (23 Feb 1928) · Belfast Telegraph (31 Jan 1933) · Belfast Telegraph (1 June 1935) · Belfast News-Letter (30 April 1930) · Northern Whig and Belfast Post (25 April 1935) · Belfast and Northern Ireland Directory (1925) · Belfast and Northern Ireland Directory (1927) · b. cert. · d. cert.

Wealth at death £5537 7s. 3d.: probate, 13 Oct 1942, CGPLA Eng. & Wales

MacMorran, John (d. 1596), merchant and magistrate, may have begun his career as 'domestik and familiar servitor' to Regent Morton (Donaldson, Register of the Privy Seal, 8.684), receiving lands in Renfrewshire in 1576 and a pension of £50 for life the following year. When the regent fell from power MacMorran helped to bring his master's gold and silver to Edinburgh, where it was to be hidden for safety, and after Morton's execution he seems to have had dealings with 'the King's traitors, forfeited and now furth of the realm', presumably some of Morton's friends (Reg. PCS, 504). A John MacMorran features in the privy seal register in October 1582 as 'messenger'; perhaps this was the same man. It is likewise uncertain whether the John MacMorran whose small business in Edinburgh was assessed for tax at £8 in 1581 and £5 in 1583 was Morton's former servant or the latter's son.

It is known, however, that by 1595 John MacMorran was the richest merchant in Edinburgh. He was a bailie, living in a large and luxuriously furnished house in Riddle's Close in the Lawnmarket with his wife, Katherine Hucheson (who outlived him), and their children. He had fine walnut furniture and French chairs, lavish napery and bedding, two silver mazers, a silver saltfat, and a dozen silver spoons. His wardrobe of elegant black clothes included cloaks, doublets, and breeches of taffeta, satin, and plain and figured velvet. Was he wearing his taffeta hat with one of the smart suits when he set out for Edinburgh high school on 15 September 1596? He would have been better advised to put on his steel bonnet covered with black stemming, but he was not expecting any real trouble.

Two days earlier some of the pupils had taken possession of the school, barring the doors against the master, Hercules Rollock. They had a grievance, for the town council had refused to grant them a holiday. Thirty-six hours later, on 15 September, the provost and town council told Bailie MacMorran to take the town officers and resolve the situation. MacMorran arrived at the school, and ordered the pupils to surrender. When they refused, he and the officers picked up a wooden beam and began to ram the back door. Leaning from a window, William Sinclair, one of the pupils, threatened to shoot, but the bailie and his officers ran at the door again. Sinclair fired and MacMorran fell dying to the ground. Horrified, the boys rushed from the building. Sinclair and six others were arrested and held prisoner for more than two months. They had influential parents, however, and were all eventually released. Sinclair, a cousin of the fifth earl of Caithness, later became Sir William Sinclair of Mey.

MacMorran's testament reveals that his shares in the ships *Anna*, *Grace of God*, *Pelican*, *Merting*, *Gud Fortoun*, *Elspeth*, *Flour Delyce*, *Thomas*, and another unnamed vessel were worth more than £4000 Scots. He had £3000 lying at Dieppe and many more thousands in cash in Edinburgh, and with the valuation of his ventures at Bordeaux and elsewhere his estate was worth £21,544 10s. 7d. Scots. He was owed debts amounting to £16,312 13s. 2d., while he himself owed nothing. An English memorandum of 1580 had alleged that a Scottish merchant was considered to be rich if he was worth £1000 sterling, and it has been calculated that MacMorran and his brother Ninian were two of only seven merchants in that category between the years 1570 and 1603. It is ironic that for all his spectacular wealth he died at the hands of a schoolboy in a quarrel about a holiday.   ROSALIND K. MARSHALL

Sources J. G. Fyfe, ed., *Scottish diaries and memoirs, 1550–1746* (1928), 58–9 [Birrel's diary] · J. MacMorran, testament, 10 March 1596 and 23 July 1596, NA Scot., Edinburgh register of testaments, CC8/8/29 · J. R. N. MacPhail, ed., *Papers from the collection of Sir William Fraser*, Scottish History Society, 3rd ser., 5 (1924), 226–9 · G. Donaldson, *James V to James VII* (1965), 251–2 · M. Lynch, *Edinburgh and the Reformation* (1981), 52, 179 · M. H. B. Sanderson, 'The Edinburgh merchants in society, 1570–1603: the evidence of their testaments', *The Renaissance and Reformation in Scotland: essays in honour of Gordon Donaldson*, ed. I. B. Cowan and D. Shaw (1983), 183–99 · *Memoirs of his own life by Sir James Melville of Halhill*, ed. T. Thomson, Bannatyne Club, 18 (1827), 267 · G. Donaldson and others, eds., *Registrum secreti sigilli regum Scotorum / The register of the privy seal of Scotland*, 6 (1963), nos. 684, 864; 8 (1982), no. 958 · *Reg. PCS*, 1st ser., 3.504 · D. Calderwood, *The history of the Kirk of Scotland*, ed. T. Thomson and D. Laing, 8 vols., Wodrow Society, 7 (1842–9), vol. 5, p. 382 · W. Cowan, 'The site of the Black Friars' monastery from the Reformation to the present day', *Book of the Old Edinburgh Club*, 5 (1912), 73–4
Wealth at death £37,861 Scots: NA Scot., Edinburgh register of testaments, 10 March 1596, CC 8/8/29

MacMoyer [Weyer], **Florence** (d. **1713**), informer and schoolmaster, was born in co. Armagh, into a family which since at least the mid-fourteenth century had been hereditary keepers of the Book of Armagh and had as a consequence enjoyed a large landholding under the archbishop. In 1609 this amounted to eight townlands in the barony of Fews, co. Armagh, as well as a house in Armagh town, but in the late 1610s the MacMoyers disappear from the archbishop's rentals, apparently losing their tenancy to an English settler, although as late as 1633 the house in Armagh was still in the possession of one Art MacMoyer. According to an inscription in the Book of Armagh (p. 104*v*), Florence MacMoyer acquired the custody of the book on or before 29 June 1662. He practised as a schoolmaster, no doubt also farming in a small way. According to his subsequent testimony, his brother was recruited into the French army by an Irish officer and he himself was also strongly encouraged to join.

Almost nothing would be known of Florence MacMoyer had he not come forward as a witness at the trial of Oliver Plunket. How he became involved and what were his motives are not entirely clear. His cousin Friar John MacMoyer had been among those Armagh clergy who had been in dispute with Plunket during the 1670s. John was declared apostate in 1678 and by that time had already been seeking Plunket's prosecution for at least two years. While the viceroy in Dublin dismissed John MacMoyer's accusations against Plunket, in the fevered atmosphere of the Popish Plot the authorities in London lent a willing ear. No mention can be found of Florence MacMoyer during the abortive Irish trial of 1680 or the preparations of the winter of 1680–81, but less than a month before Plunket was due to stand trial in London, Florence MacMoyer appeared there, and on 3 May 1681 he was the first witness at the trial. The evidence he gave relied in large part on the elaboration and exaggeration reinterpretation of commonplaces. Crucially, his evidence was entirely hearsay and should have been ruled legally inadmissible in that court.

Soon after Plunket's execution MacMoyer, using the surname Weyer, published a defence entitled *The honesty and true zeal of the kings witnesses justified and vindicated against those unchristian-like equivocal protestations of Dr. Oliver Plunkett, asserting in his last speech his own innocency, being as great damnation to his soul, as any of his former trayterous and hellish practices against his king and countrey, as breathing them upon the point of death, without any time of repenting the enormity of them with true contrition* (1681). In the pamphlet he asserted that his surname was '*Weyer*, and not *MacMoyer*' although he referred to his cousin John as 'Mr Moyre'. He seems to have envisaged a career as an informer: on 23 August he gave information against Lord Blayney, before returning to Ireland the following month. He was paid off in October but on 15 November was informing against Lieutenant Hawkins, the nonconformist son of a London alderman.

However, together with his cousin John, MacMoyer was himself arrested late in 1681. The matter arose out of a letter John MacMoyer had sent Bishop Cusack of Meath before Plunket was arrested, telling Cusack that he was accused of treason and should flee the country. John MacMoyer had clearly been trying to get rid of enemies in the Irish church but had now, together with Florence, 'fallen into the hole which they themselves made', as Cusack put it (Ó Fiaich, 82). A letter of Archbishop John Brenan of 30 June 1683 relates:

> Friar MacMoyer and another Moyer, a relative of his, both accusers of the happy Primate, continue still in prison, where they suffer great privations and are almost dead from hunger, finding none who will give them food, so abhorred are they by all.   (ibid., 83)

How long he spent in prison is not known.

It was in connection with the Plunket trial that the Book of Armagh passed out of the hands of its last keeper, reputedly pawned for £5 in order to cover the cost of MacMoyer's travel to London. Written about 807, the Book of Armagh was a compilation consisting of a Latin New Testament, a collection of patrician documents, and a life of

St Martin. It has been thought that MacMoyer's co-operation in the Plunket trial might have been part of a vain attempt to secure return of the family patrimony that had originally accompanied it.

After the trial MacMoyer apparently attempted to return to his former life. Estate accounts of 1703 show him to have been in possession of a small farmhouse in the townland of Ballintemple. He died on 12 February 1713 and was buried in Ballymoyer churchyard. His tombstone was variously abused and was removed to Ballymoyer House by the Synnott family about 1880 but was subsequently lost during the demolition of the place.

MIHAIL DAFYDD EVANS

Sources T. Ó Fiaich, 'The fall and return of John MacMoyer (and his connection with the trial of Blessed Oliver Plunket)', *Seanchas Ardmhacha*, 3 (1958–9), 50–86 · A. Curtayne, *The trial of Oliver Plunkett* (1953) · J. Gwynn, *Liber Ardmachanus: the Book of Armagh* (1913) · tombstone rubbing, TCD, MS T.2.33

McMullen, John Franklin (1820–1897), banker, was born on 19 May 1820 in Ireland, one of at least three children. His father probably died about 1859. At sixteen McMullen joined the National Bank of Ireland, a newly formed British-owned joint stock bank with a head office in London, as a clerk at its Cork branch. He served as teller and accountant at various branches before being appointed assistant inspector of branches in 1842. Promotion to management of the Waterford branch in 1851 was followed by appointment as an 'inspector of the bank' in January 1853 and manager at Cork in October the same year. He resigned on 19 August 1856, having accepted an appointment with the Union Bank of Australia, a leading Anglo-Australian bank which, like the National, was controlled by a London board. McMullen married Beatrice Carnegie at Tipperary, Ireland in 1884 and their nine children were born in Ireland and Australia.

McMullen arrived in Sydney on the *Simla* on 10 January 1857 and took up his appointment ten days later. Undoubtedly he was appointed to introduce to the Union Bank the skills he had learned in Irish branch banking. As inspector (northern division) of the Union Bank of Australia he was responsible for all branches in New South Wales, Queensland, and New Zealand, and worked jointly with the inspector (southern division), each being separately responsible to the London board. The problems that this system generated were obviated by his appointment in 1859 as inspector and general manager solely responsible for the Australian and New Zealand operations of the bank. At the beginning of his career with the Union Bank he was 'feared and even hated, though his ruthless efficiency was respected' (Butlin, 151). Scathingly critical of the staff when he assumed office, McMullen instituted a clean-up, dismissing and downgrading managers for incompetence and lack of drive. He was to suffer from this same failing towards the end of his twenty-eight years as chief executive.

During McMullen's administration the Union Bank grew substantially, but he was slow to open new branches,

resulting in a loss of market share. Important initiatives were the establishment of the Melbourne Clearing House in 1867 and the introduction of a staff pension and guarantee fund. McMullen also unwittingly set the scene for the banking disasters of the 1890s when in 1863 he urged the board to approve the taking of London deposits. The Union Bank was prudent in handling these deposits, but other banks copied the idea with dire results. McMullen was aware of the difficulties the boom years of the 1880s would bring to the Australian economy and this, together with age and illness, made him more conservative and cautious in expanding the Union's business. However, his successors inherited a business well able to withstand the shock of the 1890s. His strict control over the bank's colonial policy and his failure to delegate caused alarm to the board, particularly when he resisted calls for reorganization of the colonial administration. He grew suspicious of the skills of his own managerial appointees and fell out with a number of his executives. Summoned to London for discussions with the directors (his fourth trip) he tendered his resignation on the grounds of ill health before he could be taken to task. He retired on 24 May 1887. In 1889 he was nevertheless offered, and accepted, a seat on the bank's London board; but he resigned in 1891, again because of ill health.

McMullen was a tall, solid man, with a receding hairline coiffeured in the Regency manner, and he gave the appearance of the authority which was to be expected of an Irish squire. A member of the influential Melbourne Club from 1868 and domineering chairman of the Associated Banks, Victoria, from 1882 until his retirement, his influence on the Australian banking world nevertheless faded fast and his death went unnoticed in Australian newspapers and banking journals. After retirement McMullen lived in England and Ireland, probably as a widower, with no fixed address, and visited Australia. He died at Brewster's Hotel, Lower Baggot Street, Dublin, on 23 June 1897, aged seventy-seven.

T. J. HART

Sources Australia and New Zealand Banking Group Ltd, Melbourne, archive · probate, Public Records Office, Victoria, Australia · *The Argus* [Melbourne] (30 June 1897) · The Royal Bank of Scotland PLC - Archive, London · S. J. Butlin, *Australia and New Zealand Bank: the Bank of Australasia and the Union Bank of Australia Limited, 1828–1951* (1961) · private information (2004)

Likenesses photograph, 1856, Australia and New Zealand Banking Group Ltd, Melbourne, archive

Wealth at death £37,894 0s. 4d.: probate, 30 Nov 1897, CGPLA Ire. · £21,996: probate, 1897, Australia · £8987 19s. 7d.: Irish probate sealed in London, 22 Dec 1897, CGPLA Eng. & Wales

McMullen, Mary [*called* the Female Pedestrian] (*b.* 1763/4?), pedestrian, may have been born in Ireland about 1764. Very little is known about her background or life, except that in the 1820s she achieved, in various places in England, a number of impressive long-distance walking performances under conditions that were, at best, indifferent and sometimes actively hostile. Her most common event was 92 miles in twenty-four hours but she also performed other distances, the shortest known being 20 miles.

Under the name Mrs McMullen or the Female Pedestrian, she journeyed from town to town, arranging and taking part in long-distance performances during which money was collected. To make ends meet she competed regularly, often in front of sizeable crowds, the largest being 6000. In one ten-week period, towards the end of 1826, when she was probably aged sixty-two, there are records of five of her performances—three for 90 or 92 miles, one for 40, and another for 20 miles—and once she completed two performances, each of 92 miles, within four days. It is virtually certain, however, that many of her performances went unrecorded. Despite the many unplanned interruptions, and breaks to eat, drink, and rest, she comfortably completed 20 miles inside four hours, 40 miles inside nine, and 92 miles within twenty-four hours. She was a tall woman who walked in a long dark skirt, white cotton 'waist', coloured scarf, white muslin cap, and black stockings, but without shoes. A half-mile course was usually measured along a public road, which she repeatedly covered throughout the day. Her income was always believed to be meagre, and it was a common experience for her to be impeded by crowds of boys and young men, who had bet against her, and who attempted to stop her completing within the set time. Despite the many impediments she faced, McMullen was said to remain cheerful, and those who saw her frequently commented on her lack of fatigue and the apparent ease with which this 'old woman' performed. Between 1822 and 1827 her son, Bernard, made his living in a similar way and occasionally they travelled together.

Despite these feats, Mary McMullen's efforts did not mark the development of women athletes competing professionally in endurance events, but rather the reverse. Attitudes in the Victorian age to women performing publicly for money, particularly in endurance events, made it increasingly unlikely that this sort of activity would continue to be encouraged, or even tolerated. Another century and a half would have to elapse before women athletes would be able to build on the tradition of Mary McMullen.   PETER F. RADFORD

Sources *London Packet and Chronicle, and Lloyd's Evening Post* (5–7 Nov 1827) · *Annals of Sporting*, 10 (Nov 1826), 305–6 · *Annals of Sporting*, 11 (Jan 1827), 45, 49a–b · P. Egan, *Life in London* (1827)

MacMunn, Charles Alexander (1852–1911), physician and spectroscopist, was born at Seafield House, Easkey, co. Sligo, Ireland, the son of James MacMunn, medical practitioner. MacMunn was educated at Dromore School and entered Trinity College, Dublin, in November 1867. He graduated BA in 1871, MB in 1872, and proceeded MD in 1875 and MA in 1884. After taking his primary medical degree in 1872 he went as an assistant to his cousin James MacMunn (LRCSI, 1822), in practice at 14 Waterloo Road, Wolverhampton. When James died aged sixty-two in November 1873 Charles took over the practice. On 20 January 1874 he married James's daughter, Laetitia, an artist; of their three sons, one, Lionel Alexander, entered medicine and practised as a physician in Birmingham and another, Norman *MacMunn, became a teacher and educationist.

After Laetitia's death, possibly about 1908, Charles married Beatrice, the sister of the channel-swimmer Matthew Webb (1848–1883).

Busy as MacMunn was, he set up in the loft over his stables a laboratory partly equipped by grants from the Birmingham philosophical and royal societies and published *The Spectroscope in Medicine* in 1880. Using a small direct vision spectroscope to replace the eyepiece of a microscope, he examined the absorption bands in spectra transmitted through living tissues, and when he found that the four absorption bands were sharpened by restricting the air supply (by pressing on the coverslip), he realized that the 'natural pigments' producing them played a vital role in cellular respiration. His accounts of 'histohaematins' (in tissues) and 'myohaematin' (in muscle) in the *Philosophical Transactions of the Royal Society* (1886) and *Journal of Physiology* (1887) provided crucial information in deciding the century-old dispute as to whether combustion of foodstuffs occurred in the lungs or the tissues. But MacMunn's work was criticized by Felix Hoppe-Seyler of Freiburg, who abruptly closed the correspondence on the identity of muscle pigments in *Zeitschrift für physiologische Chemie* (1890), which he edited, when his assistant was not able to reproduce MacMunn's findings. The discovery lay fallow until David Keilin, using very similar techniques, showed in 1925 that myohaematin and histohaematin were in fact the cytochromes, which are an integral part of the respiratory chain within mitochondria, the location of internal cellular respiration.

Hoppe-Seyler's autocratic behaviour, which led to neglect of MacMunn's discovery, may have arisen out of pique. When Hoppe-Seyler discovered the absorption spectrum of (reduced) haemoglobin he missed the altered spectrum of oxyhaemoglobin. Two years later George Gabriel Stokes, because of his interest in the nature of colours, correctly surmised the role of haemoglobin in oxygen transport when he showed that the change in colour from venous blue to arterial red blood was due to change in the absorption spectrum; a mathematician had stolen the thunder of a prime physiological chemist.

So that he might not be disturbed while he was preoccupied with his spectroscopic studies MacMunn installed an observation pipe in the wall of his laboratory, and instructed his housekeeper to send callers away. But after the peremptory dismissal of his work his seclusion ended and he began to play an active part in the life of Wolverhampton, taking an especial interest in the volunteer movement before and after distinguished service in south Africa from 1899 to 1902, where Lord Roberts appointed him staff officer to accompany the royal hospitals commission; he was mentioned in dispatches and received the Victoria medal with three clasps. He was the first honorary pathologist to Wolverhampton Royal Hospital.

MacMunn enjoyed conviviality, and excessive alcohol intake may have exacerbated the malaria he contracted during the Second South African War. His health deteriorated and he retired from practice in 1909. He died on 18 February 1911 at 5 Lonsdale Road, Wolverhampton, and after a military funeral service at St Peter's Church he was buried, on 22 February, at Penn Fields, Wolverhampton. He was survived by his second wife. His posthumous *Spectral Analysis Applied to Biology and Medicine* (1914) referred but briefly to the neglected 'respiratory pigments'.

C. S. BREATHNACH

Sources D. Keilin, *The history of cell respiration and cytochrome*, ed. J. Keilin (1970), 86–115 · *BMJ* (4 March 1911), 531 · F. E. Boulton, *Bulletin of the Royal College of Pathologists* (Jan 1986), 8–10 · private information (2004) · G. G. Stokes, letters, CUL, Add. MS 7656 M 187–189 · C. S. Breathnach, 'Old masters', *Irish Journal of Medical Science*, 146 (1977), 185–9 · *The Lancet* (25 Feb 1911), 551–2 · m. cert. · d. cert.
Likenesses B. Clark, photograph, repro. in *BMJ*, 531 · G. Phoenix, portrait, New Cross Hospital, Wolverhampton, department of histopathology
Wealth at death £2862 14s.: probate, 2 May 1911, *CGPLA Eng. & Wales*

MacMunn, Norman (1877–1925), schoolmaster and educationist, was born on 20 July 1877 at Waterloo Road, Wolverhampton, the third son of Charles Alexander *MacMunn (1852–1911), a surgeon and later honorary pathologist at Wolverhampton Royal Hospital, and his first wife, Laetitia (*née* MacMunn). His education from 1882 at a dame-school in Wolverhampton and from 1889 to 1895 at Wolverhampton grammar school he described as 'mental agony', as he worked not on prescribed lines but read voraciously out of school hours. He entered Keble College, Oxford, in 1895 with plans for the church as a career, but he developed an interest in the stage, transferred to Marcon's Hall, Oxford, in 1897, and graduated in 1899 with a third-class degree in English literature. He worked at first in journalism and travelled to Australia and New Zealand, where he spent six years on the *Auckland Star* as literary and drama critic and sub-editor, then returned to England as a reviewer for *The Athenaeum*. He decided to take up educational work, moved to Paris, and taught at the Berlitz School and in a large *lycée*; he was subsequently appointed in 1913 as a teacher of French at King Edward VI Grammar School, Stratford upon Avon.

There MacMunn developed and publicized his 'differential partnership method' of teaching, introducing activity and creativity into the classroom, a system which corresponded with contemporary innovations such as the 'direct method' of language teaching. *A Path to Freedom in the School*, which he published in 1914, was dedicated to the boys of the school for their zeal and sympathy in developing the new freedom, and acknowledged the inspiration of Montessori, Homer Lane, and Edmond Holmes. It expounded a theory of child emancipation, outlined practical solutions, and looked forward to the 'commonwealth school'.

Rejected on health grounds for war service, MacMunn moved in 1914 to West Downs, Winchester, a well-known preparatory school, under its innovating and influential headmaster, Lionel Helbert. There the regime was marked by intense concern for individuals and supportive, familiar relationships with boys. MacMunn was given the freedom to develop his radical new methods, including the establishment of clubs for science, literature, and painting.

In September 1918 MacMunn took a lease on Tiptree Hall, near Kelvedon, Essex, to found a school for war orphans. He worked ceaselessly with his own hands at repairing and furnishing the premises but was hampered by lack of funds. The school opened in January 1919 with twenty boys and girls, but after a year the girls had gone and MacMunn was left with a few of the poorest boys. On 11 November 1919 he married Ethel May Scanlan (*b.* 1881/2), who had joined the staff of the school in the previous March; she was the daughter of William Robert Scanlan, civil engineer. By July 1920 MacMunn had to find homes for his nine orphans and reluctantly took on fee-paying pupils, leading to conflict with parents who rejected the more extreme aspects of his regime, such as a refusal to include compulsory games or to prepare boys for public school. Tiptree was a 'self-governing community' with children free to construct the greater part of their own timetables, and MacMunn described his role as 'chief adviser'. Visitors from many parts of the world included Helen Parkhurst, who developed her own innovatory teaching methods in Dalton, Massachusetts.

From 1914 MacMunn had been active as a contributor to conferences and journals promoting new methods in education, designing, developing, and exhibiting teaching apparatus. Typical was the 'card cyclopaedia', a card catalogue of words and information made collaboratively with his pupils by cutting and pasting extracts from books. In 1921 he published *The Child's Path to Freedom*, a version of his 1914 volume entirely rewritten in the light of six further years of experience. It was a highly successful and influential work, and was posthumously republished in 1926 with a foreword by Percy Nunn. MacMunn drew on Freud and on his own teaching experience. He saw himself as an early pioneer relieved to find acceptance in the climate of Montessorism and the new ideals from 1914 onwards. 'Differentialism' was his own attempt to foster individuality; he worried about the effects of the class lesson on children, and when contemporaries encouraged him to take his theories seriously he was driven to more radical steps. 'To have arrived in practice at the ideal of a school free from rewards and punishment—from compulsion of any sort; ... to have eliminated the class and based all on individual taste and choice—this is to imply a new and not yet easily-digested educational creed' (N. MacMunn, 'The wisdom of educational experiment', *Hibbert Journal*, 1920, 740). He shared with others during and after the First World War the view that traditional school discipline had resulted in German autocracy. In children alone lay the hope of a reformed world. He exhibited the messianic enthusiasm of the first progressives; like others, he acquired the reputation of a crank as he developed his ideas, but his book was widely read, and his ideas widely disseminated among new generations of teachers by John Adams and Percy Nunn.

In January 1924 MacMunn moved his school to Rapallo, Italy, with four boys from Tiptree, and in December the school moved again to San Remo, where it was known as the Home School. The number of boys went up to over twelve, but again he lost many potential pupils because of his unwillingness to compromise with parents. On 8 October 1925 he died at San Remo from bronchopneumonia, and a memorial fund was established by friends and sympathizers who subscribed to bring his card cyclopaedia over from Italy and to give away hundreds of copies of his book to teacher training colleges.

PETER CUNNINGHAM

Sources N. MacMunn, *The child's path to freedom* (1921); later edn (1926), ix–xx [incl. biographical note by M. MacMunn] · R. J. W. Selleck, *English primary education and the progressives, 1914–1939* (1972) · H. Middleton, 'Class teaching through partnership', *The new era in education*, ed. E. Young (1920), 72–9 · J. Adams, *Modern developments in educational practice*, 2nd edn (1928) · J. Ransom, *Schools of tomorrow in England* (1919), 116–24 · B. St G. Drennan, *The Keble College centenary register, 1870–1970* (1970) · [H. R. Thomas and J. Ryan], eds., *Wolverhampton grammar school register, 1515–1920* [1927] · *WWW*, 1897–1915 [Charles Alexander MacMunn] · Venn, *Alum. Cant.* [Vivian Charles MacMunn] · b. cert. · m. cert.
Likenesses photograph, repro. in MacMunn, *The child's path to freedom* (1926), frontispiece
Wealth at death subscription raised on death to return his teaching materials to UK and donate them to training colleges: MacMunn, *Child's path*

Mac Murchada, Diarmait [Dermot MacMurrough; *called* Diarmait na nGall] (*c*.1110–1171), king of Leinster, was the son of Donnchad Mac Murchada, king of Uí Chennselaig and of Leinster, who was slain in battle in Dublin in 1115, and of Órlaith, who was the daughter of Gille Michil Mac Bráenáin of Uí Máel Rubae and Uchdelb, daughter of Cernachán Ua Gairbith, king of Uí Felmeda. During a long career Mac Murchada sought to extend his authority throughout Leinster and beyond, in the process becoming a notable patron of the reformed religious orders as well as extending his influence in more traditional and brutal ways. To posterity he is best known for his appeal in 1166 to Henry II of England for help in the recovery of his kingdom, from which he had been exiled by his enemies; the act has earned him the dubious distinction of being regarded as the instigator of English involvement in Ireland.

Early years Mac Murchada was born about 1110, on the evidence of an entry in the king-list in the *Book of Leinster*. That source attributes to him a forty-six year reign as king of Uí Chennselaig and Leinster, implying that he came to power in 1125–6, following the death of his brother Énna, who died as king of Leinster in 1126; however, the less partisan, though later, *Book of Ballymote* king-list assigns him a forty-year reign, and this corresponds better with the annalistic evidence, where Diarmait first occurs as king of Leinster in 1132. It is not certain whether he should be identified with 'the son of Mac Murchada' who, following the death of Énna, was deposed by Toirdelbach Mór Ua Conchobair (*d*. 1156), king of Connacht and claimant to the high-kingship, who temporarily intruded his own son, Conchobar, as king of Leinster. But Mac Murchada would appear to have had a dynastic rival for the kingship of Uí Chennselaig in Máelsechlainn mac Diarmata meic Murchada, who was slain in 1133 by north Leinster dynasts led by Augaire Ua Tuathail; the latter was himself killed fighting alongside Diarmait in the following year.

The provincial kingship of Leinster A distinction may be drawn between Mac Murchada's patrimonial kingdom of Uí Chennselaig in south Leinster, which was centred on Ferns, Wexford, and with which his lineage was associated from the early historic period, and the provincial or over-kingship of Leinster which his great-grandfather, *Diarmait mac Máel na mBó, succeeded in taking by force in 1052. The over-kingship was much less securely held, particularly in the north Leinster region, and in Osraige on the Munster–Leinster border, and was reliant on the exercise of military force, or the latent threat of it. Mac Murchada's first recorded exploit, which may be equated with his *crech ríg*, or 'royal prey' (that is, his first military expedition whereby he inaugurated his kingship), was his attack in 1132 on the important north Leinster church of Kildare and its abbess, Mór. She had been installed there in 1127 by Ua Conchobair, king of Uí Failgi, at the expense of a daughter of Cerball Mac Fáeláin, king of Uí Fáeláin. Another of Cerball's daughters, Sadb, married Mac Murchada, possibly about 1132. The attack on Kildare may therefore be deemed both to have launched Mac Murchada's bid for the provincial kingship, and also to have avenged the insult to his sister-in-law and the Meic Fáeláin, whose support in north Leinster would have been critical to him in establishing his position as king of Leinster.

The expansion of Mac Murchada's sphere of influence is shown by his fighting a battle in 1134 in alliance with the Hiberno-Norse of Dublin against Conchobar Ua Briain, king of Thomond, the Osraige, and the Hiberno-Norse of Waterford. In 1137 he mustered a fleet of 200 ships drawn from Dublin and Wexford and, this time in alliance with Conchobar Ua Briain, besieged Waterford and carried off the hostages of Donnchad Mac Carthaig, king of Desmond, of Déisi, and of Waterford. Conchobar then submitted to Mac Murchada, in the hope that the latter might secure for him the kingship of Desmond. In 1141 seventeen north Leinster dynasts were killed or blinded by Mac Murchada, an event unprecedented not only for the numbers involved, but also for the fact that it was not the consequence of a military campaign, but appears to have been a deliberate rounding up of political opponents. In 1149 he plundered the church site of Duleek, Meath, signalling his interest in expanding into the east Mide area, into which Tigernán Ua Ruairc, king of Bréifne, was also moving. In 1151 he fought alongside Toirdelbach Ua Conchobair at the battle of Móin Mór, Tipperary, at which Toirdelbach Ua Briain, king of Thomond, suffered a crushing defeat.

In 1152 Mac Murchada abducted Tigernán Ua Ruairc's wife, Derbforgaill, from Mide. She was the daughter of Murchad Ua Máelsechlainn, king of Mide, and according to the seventeenth-century translation of the annals of Clonmacnoise, her brother Máelsechlainn had induced her to solicit Mac Murchada's intervention. The Connacht-oriented annals of Tigernach place the abduction in the context of a joint raid with Toirdelbach Ua Conchobair of Connacht, against Tigernán Ua Ruairc, during which Ua Ruairc suffered a defeat and was temporarily deposed. The annals of the four masters record the participation of Muirchertach Mac Lochlainn, king of Cenél nEógain and claimant to the high-kingship, and state that on the same occasion Mide was divided between Murchad Ua Máelsechlainn and his son, Máelsechlainn, who was granted the eastern portion. It is not impossible that Máelsechlainn had offered the kingship of east Mide to Mac Murchada, along with his sister Derbforgaill, as a means of preventing Ua Ruairc's further encroachment upon that area.

Probably shortly after Derbforgaill's return to Mide in 1153, Mac Murchada married Mór, daughter of Muirchertach Ua Tuathail, king of Uí Muiredaig. He may also be presumed to have supported the promotion of her half-brother, Lorcán Ua Tuathail, to the abbacy of Glendalough, even though the latter's hagiographical life reports that he had been mistreated as a boy while held hostage by Mac Murchada. In 1156 Mac Murchada acknowledged the high-kingship of Muirchertach Mac Lochlainn, who confirmed him in the kingship of Leinster and in 1162 he was present at the Synod of Clane, presided over by Gilla Meic Liac, archbishop of Armagh, where the primacy of Armagh was affirmed, and where Lorcán Ua Tuathail most probably was elected to succeed the dying Gréine as archbishop of Dublin. In the same year the annals of Ulster claim that Mac Murchada obtained 'great power over the Dubliners such as was not obtained for a long time' (Hennessy and MacCarthy, 2.142–3). He had been assisted by Muirchertach Mac Lochlainn, who led a large army to besiege Dublin in 1162. It must have been with Mac Murchada's consent that the Dublin fleet campaigned for six months in 1165 on the Welsh coast in the service of Henry II.

Expulsion and return In 1166 the assassination of his ally, the high-king Muirchertach Mac Lochlainn, occasioned a concerted attack on Mac Murchada by his enemies. Ruaidrí Ua Conchobair, king of Connacht, launched a bid for the high-kingship and succeeded in removing the city of Dublin from Diarmait's control, prompting a revolt by the men of Leinster against the latter's authority. Ua Conchobair led an army into Uí Chennselaig, in advance of which Mac Murchada himself burnt Ferns; a second army, led by Tigernán Ua Ruairc, demolished Diarmait's stone house at Ferns and burnt its *longphort*. Acting as high-king, Ua Conchobair then divided Uí Chennselaig between Diarmait's brother, Murchad (who gave seventeen hostages to Ruaidrí) and Donnchad Mac Gillapátraic, king of Osraige. The Book of Leinster gives 1 August as the date of Mac Murchada's expulsion overseas; he sailed for Bristol and from there travelled on to Aquitaine to secure a personal interview with Henry II, king of England, to seek military aid to help him to recover his kingdom. The request was not unreasonable, considering Henry had hired the Dublin fleet in 1165. Having duly received permission to recruit troops within Henry's dominions, Mac Murchada returned to Bristol, where he was maintained by Robert fitz Harding at the king's expense; it may have been fitz Harding who introduced him to Richard fitz Gilbert de *Clare, earl of Pembroke and lord of Striguil, known as

Strongbow, whom he sought to recruit. By way of inducement, either then, or later in 1170, Mac Murchada offered Strongbow marriage to his daughter, Aífe, and succession to the kingdom of Leinster after his death. Mac Murchada then moved on to south Wales, where he was entertained by Rhys ap Gruffudd, ruler of Deheubarth, and David fitz Gerald, bishop of St David's. There he recruited Robert fitz Stephen and Maurice Fitzgerald (d. 1176), to whom he offered, according to Gerald of Wales, the town of Wexford and two adjoining cantreds.

In autumn 1167 Mac Murchada returned to Leinster with Cambro-Norman mercenaries and re-established himself without difficulty at Ferns, where he was welcomed by the clergy. Ruaidrí Ua Conchobair responded by marching to Uí Chennselaig and exacting both hostages and 100 ounces of gold, the latter as compensation for the abduction of Ua Ruairc's wife in 1152. In the following year Mac Murchada's son, Énna, was blinded by Donnchad Mac Gillapátraic of Osraige, a deed which underlines the threat which Diarmait's recovery of Uí Chennselaig posed to Donnchad. Then in May 1169 Robert fitz Stephen and Hervey de Montmorency landed at Bannow, where Mac Murchada's forces joined them. Together they moved towards Wexford, whose citizens proffered hostages and submitted to Mac Murchada's authority. They then proceeded to campaign in Osraige. Ruaidrí Ua Conchobair responded by again hosting to Uí Chennselaig and exacting additional hostages. About May 1170 Raymond le Gros Fitzgerald, a member of Strongbow's *família*, arrived, following which the men of Waterford suffered a defeat. On 23 August Strongbow himself landed, the city of Waterford was captured on 25 August, and his marriage to Aífe was almost immediately celebrated there. The combined forces of Strongbow and Mac Murchada then marched to Dublin where the city was taken, according to the so-called *Song of Dermot and the Earl*, on 21 September.

Challenge for the high-kingship and death Now in a strong enough position to challenge Ruaidrí Ua Conchobair for the high-kingship, Mac Murchada extended his military activities into Mide, where he plundered the church sites of Clonard, Kells, Dulane, and Slane. Ua Conchobair retaliated by executing the hostages whom he held from Mac Murchada; these included the latter's son, Conchobar, his grandson, the son of Domnall Cáemánach, and the son of his foster brother, Murchad Ua Cáellaide, and their deaths show clearly how serious was the challenge which Mac Murchada now posed to Ua Conchobair's high-kingship. However, Mac Murchada died at Ferns about 1 May 1171. By then he had secured hostages from Mide and Airgialla, and had concluded an alliance with Domnall Mór Ua Briain, king of Thomond, to whom he gave his daughter Órlaith in marriage. She was the child of Sadb, who was also the mother of Donnchad, slain by the Osraige at an unknown date. The mother of his son Conchobar, slain in 1170, and of his daughter Aífe, was Mór. The identity of the mother or mothers of his sons Domnall Cáemánach and Énna, and of his daughter Derbforgaill, who married Domnall Mac Gillamocholmóc, king of Uí Dunchada, is unknown. It is probable that only his relationship with

Mór was recognized as a canonically valid marriage by churchmen.

Ecclesiastical patronage Diarmait Mac Murchada was a notable patron of the church reform movement, skilfully combining support for reform with his own political ambitions. His foundation of a Cistercian abbey at Baltinglass, Wicklow, in 1148 (the confirmation of Henry II's son John as lord of Ireland in 1185 refers to Mac Murchada's charter), elicited a letter of confraternity from Bernard of Clairvaux, possibly at the prompting of Archbishop Malachy of Armagh. Baltinglass Abbey served to neutralize a strategic pass connecting north and south Leinster. With the co-operation of Dungal Ua Cáellaide, bishop of Leighlin (who almost certainly owed his episcopal office to Mac Murchada's patronage), he endowed a Benedictine, subsequently Cistercian, abbey at Killenny, for which an original charter, issued by him about 1162–5, is extant, the earliest of an Irish king. Killenny was strategically located near the pass of Gowran, an important route between Osraige and south Leinster.

With the support of Joseph Ua hAéda, bishop of Ferns (who was almost certainly his nominee for the diocese), Mac Murchada introduced an Augustinian community of Arrouaisian filiation at the seventh-century church site of Ferns, which he endowed with the tithes and first fruits of his demesne throughout Uí Chennselaig and to which he granted his *capellania* (chapel), probably located in his residence at Ferns (which no later than 1166 was built of stone). Although Mac Murchada granted free abbatial election to the community, he reserved to himself and his heirs a right of assent. In the city of Dublin he endowed Holy Trinity Cathedral, the priory of All Hallows (in collaboration with Aéd Ua Cáellaide, bishop of Clogher and head of the Arrouaisian filiation in Ireland), and the Arrouaisian nunnery of St Mary de Hogges, together with its two dependencies at Aghade, Carlow, and Kilculliheen, Waterford. He may also have been responsible for the finely carved Romanesque doorway at Killeshin, Carlow, which shares stylistic features with Baltinglass.

Impact and reputation The assertion by Gerald of Wales that Diarmait Mac Murchada 'brought to prominence men of humble rank' (Giraldus Cambrensis, 40–41) may be substantiated by the rise in the fortunes of his maternal kindred, the Uí Bráenáin, and his foster-kindred, the Uí Cáellaide. He also appears to have settled north Leinster dynasts Ua Briain on assarted land in Dubthír, and Ua Lorcáin in Fothairt in Chairn within Uí Chennselaig. The Leinster ecclesiastic, Aéd Mac Crimthainn, who secured the abbacy of Terryglass in Tipperary in the wake of the battle of Móin Mór in 1151, and whose involvement in the compilation of the Book of Leinster reveals his skills as a propagandist, belonged to the Uí Chremthannáin, who were promoted at the expense of their collaterals, the Uí Mórda of Loígsi. Mac Murchada's personal household included a chancellor (also styled *notarius* and who probably had custody of his seal), a chaplain, a seneschal, and an interpreter. The latter provided information about him to the author of the so-called *Song*

of Dermot and the Earl, who provides a much more positive portrayal, presenting him as 'the noble king, who was of so much worth' (Orpen, 13), than does Gerald of Wales in his *Expugnatio Hibernica*, where Mac Murchada is portrayed as an oppressive ruler given to outbursts of savagery. The sobriquet Diarmait na nGall, 'Diarmait of the Foreigners', although subsequently interpreted as originating from Mac Murchada's recruitment of overseas mercenaries, and used by nationalists as a term of obloquy for his treachery in involving the English in Ireland, more likely derived from his dominance over the Hiberno-Norse of Dublin and Wexford. While contemporary death notices in the Book of Leinster ('Diarmait … died after the victory of extreme unction and penance'; *Book of Leinster*, 1.184) and the annals of Inisfallen record his death neutrally, subsequent accounts are noticeably, and increasingly, hostile, reflecting the historiographical evolution of ever more negative assessments of his career.

M. T. FLANAGAN

Sources W. Stokes, ed., 'The annals of Tigernach [8 pts]', *Revue Celtique*, 16 (1895), 374–419; 17 (1896), 6–33, 119–263, 337–420; 18 (1897), 9–59, 150–97, 267–303, 374–91; pubd sep. (1993) · *AFM* · D. Murphy, ed., *The annals of Clonmacnoise*, trans. C. Mageoghagan (1896); facs. edn (1993), 192–3, 196, 199–200, 202, 205–8 · *Ann. Ulster* · W. M. Hennessy and B. MacCarthy, eds., *Annals of Ulster, otherwise, annals of Senat*, 4 vols. (1887–1901) · W. M. Hennessy, ed. and trans., *The annals of Loch Cé: a chronicle of Irish affairs from AD 1014 to AD 1590*, 2 vols., Rolls Series, 54 (1871) · W. M. Hennessy, ed. and trans., *Chronicum Scotorum: a chronicle of Irish affairs*, Rolls Series, 46 (1866), 332–5 · *Sancti Bernardi opera*, ed. J. Leclercq and others, 8 (Rome, 1977), 513–14 · C. M. Butler and J. H. Bernard, eds., 'The charters of the Cistercian abbey of Duiske in the county of Kilkenny', *Proceedings of the Royal Irish Academy*, 35C (1918–20), 1–188, esp. 5–7 · R. Butler, ed., *Registrum prioratus omnium sanctorum* (1845), 50–51 · Dugdale, *Monasticon*, new edn, 6/2.1141–2 · K. W. Nicholls, 'The charter of John, lord of Ireland, in favour of the Cistercian abbey of Baltinglass', *Peritia*, 4 (1985), 187–206, esp. 191 · C. McNeill, ed., *Calendar of Archbishop Alen's register, c.1172–1534* (1950), 293 · G. H. Orpen, ed. and trans., *The song of Dermot and the earl* (1892) · Giraldus Cambrensis, *Expugnatio Hibernica / The conquest of Ireland*, ed. and trans. A. B. Scott and F. X. Martin (1978) · M. C. Dobbs, ed. and trans., 'The Ban-shenchus [pt 2]', *Revue Celtique*, 48 (1931), 163–234, esp. 191, 198, 231 · R. I. Best and others, eds., *The Book of Leinster, formerly Lebar na Núachongbála*, 6 vols. (1954–83), vol. 1, pp. xvii, 184, 186 · R. Atkinson, ed., *The book of Ballymote: a collection of pieces (prose and verse) in the Irish language*, facs. edn (1887), 55, col. d, ll. 18–26 · M. A. O'Brien, ed., *Corpus genealogiarum Hiberniae* (Dublin, 1962), 13 · D. Ó Corráin, 'The education of Diarmait Mac Murchada', *Ériu*, 28 (1977), 71–81 · B. Ó Cuiv, 'Diarmaid na nGall', *Éigse*, 16 (1975–6), 136–44 · S. Mac Airt, ed. and trans., *The annals of Inisfallen* (1951)

Mac Murchadha, Art Caomhánach [Art Kavanagh MacMurrough; *called* Art Mór Mac Murchadha] (*d.* **1416/17**), chieftain and self-styled king of Leinster, was a descendant of Diarmait Mac Murchada (*d.* 1171) and the son of the Art Caomhánach Mac Murchadha who had died in captivity after his arrest by Lionel of Antwerp, the lieutenant of Ireland, in 1361. He was also known as Art Mór Mac Murchadha. Since 1282 several of his predecessors, including his grandfather and two uncles, had been slain by the English. This violence was in response to a recovery of the military initiative by the Gaelic lords of south-east Ireland, who represented a serious threat to the colony. The revival of the Mic Mhurchadha is reflected in the renewed use of the title *rí Laighean* ('king of Leinster'), which they had virtu-ally abandoned in the thirteenth century.

Mac Murchadha came to prominence in the late 1370s after a tussle for supremacy with a kinsman, Art, son of Diarmaid. The heart of his power lay in the uplands and woods of north Wexford and Carlow surrounding Uí Cheinnsealaigh, the dynastic territory which the Mic Mhurchadha had retained after the Anglo-Norman settle-ment of Leinster. From there he raided widely, menacing south Wexford, together with the Barrow valley and the passes around Carlow, Leighlin, and Gowran, which were crucial for communications between Dublin and the south. He extracted protection money, later known as 'black rent', from places as far apart as Castledermot in Kildare and New Ross in south Wexford. He was also able to make alliances and raise troops in Osraige and Munster. Between 1377 and the arrival of Richard II in 1394, the Dublin authorities were constantly engaged in fighting and negotiating with him. One of his aims was to be accepted by the crown as 'captain of his nation', a status that brought with it an exchequer annuity of 80 marks, which had periodically been paid to his predecessors. His marriage, about 1390, to Elizabeth Calf (or Le Veel), heir of the barons of Norragh in Kildare, was a further source of contention, since the statutes of Kilkenny (1366) had pro-hibited unlicensed marriages between the English and the Irish.

When Richard II landed at Waterford in October 1394, he immediately organized a campaign against Mac Murchadha. His cattle were seized and his lands burned, leading him to submit. The king allowed him to go free while terms were decided. In January 1395 a settlement was reached, by which he, his vassal-lords, and their fight-ing men would leave Leinster and go in the king's army against Irish elsewhere in the island. They were to be com-pensated with lands conquered as a result of this cam-paign. Since Mac Murchadha was to retain Norragh, it can-not have been intended to remove him from Leinster com-pletely. The scheme proved unworkable, not least because most other Gaelic lords soon submitted, and there was lit-tle fighting. After the king left Ireland in May 1395, he maintained diplomatic contacts with the Leinster lords; but the familiar pattern of raid and riposte resumed. When Richard returned to Ireland in May 1399, his chief military target was again Mac Murchadha, who this time managed to frustrate the royal forces until the landing of Bolingbroke in England forced Richard's hasty departure in July. Before the end of 1399 the Irish council reported that Mac Murchadha remained recalcitrant, having sworn that he 'would never be at peace' unless his fee and his wife's lands were restored to him (Graves, 261). Although he recovered both in 1400, the last years of his life saw the usual mixture of war and negotiation. In 1414 he and his sons, Donnchadh and Gearalt, were in bitter conflict with the English of Wexford; in 1415 he sent the abbot of Duiske as his proctor to acknowledge his fealty to Henry V.

Mac Murchadha died in 1416 or early 1417, 'in his own fortress [possibly Ferns, Wexford] ..., after the triumph of unction and penitence' (*Annals of Loch Cé*, 2.147) and was succeeded by Donnchadh. He differed from his predeces-sors in his durability and in the attention he commanded in England. On the one hand he embodied the Gaelic trad-ition. This is the image presented in Jean Creton's chron-icle, both in its famous illustration of his meeting with the earl of Gloucester, and in the claim that he called himself 'excellent king and lord of great Ireland' (*Archaeologia*, 20, 1824, 296). He employed native poets and historians, and bombast pervades a bardic eulogy written in his honour:

His dread lance in graceful hand,
battle fury seizes Art Mac Murchadha;
he can not be spoken to
till he has changed the direction of the foes' lances.
(McKenna, 100)

He used the title 'king of Leinster', and may even have employed the *Dei gratia* formula. On the other hand, he was an astute politician who performed a careful balancing-act, muting his regal pretensions in order to move profitably in the wider world.   ROBIN FRAME

Sources E. Curtis, ed., *Richard II in Ireland, 1394–1395, and submis-sions of the Irish chiefs* (1927) · E. Curtis, 'Unpublished letters from Richard II in Ireland, 1394–5', *Proceedings of the Royal Irish Academy*, 37C (1924–7), 276–303 · D. Johnston, 'Richard II and the submission of Gaelic Ireland', *Irish Historical Studies*, 22 (1980–81), 1–20 · R. Frame, 'Two kings in Leinster: the crown and the MicMhurchadha in the fourteenth century', *Colony and frontier in medieval Ireland: essays presented to J. F. Lydon*, ed. T. B. Barry and others (1995), 155–75 · A. J. Otway-Ruthven, *A history of medieval Ire-land* (1968) · E. Tresham, ed., *Rotulorum patentium et clausorum cancellariae Hiberniae calendarium*, Irish Record Commission (1828) · J. Graves, ed., *A roll of the proceedings of the King's Council in Ireland… AD 1392–93*, Rolls Series, 69 (1877) · W. M. Hennessy, ed. and trans., *The annals of Loch Cé: a chronicle of Irish affairs from AD 1014 to AD 1590*, 2 vols., Rolls Series, 54 (1871) · W. M. Hennessy and B. MacCarthy, eds., *Annals of Ulster, otherwise, annals of Senat*, 4 vols. (1887–1901), vol. 3 · A. M. Freeman, ed. and trans., *Annála Connacht / The annals of Connacht* (1944); repr. (1970) · AFM, 2nd edn · L. McKenna, 'To Art MacMurchadha Caomhánach', *Irish Monthly*, 56 (1928) · [J. Creton], 'Translation of a French metrical history of the deposition of King Richard the Second … with a copy of the original', ed. and trans. J. Webb, *Archaeologia*, 20 (1824), 1–423 · *Oeuvres de Froissart*, ed. K. de Le Hanhove (1871), xv · A. P. Smyth, *Celtic Leinster* (1982) · N. Saul, *Richard II* (1997)
Likenesses portrait (with the earl of Gloucester in 1399), repro. in J. T. Gilbert, ed., *Facsimiles of national manuscripts of Ireland*, 3 (1879), pl. xxxiii

McMurdo, Sir William Montagu Scott

McMurdo, Sir William Montagu Scott (1819–1894), army officer, born on 30 May 1819, was son of Lieutenant-Colonel Archibald McMurdo of Lotus, Loch Arthur, Kirk-cudbrightshire. After attending the Royal Military Col-lege, Sandhurst, he was commissioned ensign in the 8th foot on 1 July 1837, and obtained a lieutenancy in the 22nd foot on 5 January 1841. The regiment went to India in that year, and was stationed at Karachi. It formed part of the force with which Sir Charles James *Napier took the field against the amirs of Sind in December 1842, and McMurdo was placed in charge of the quartermaster-general's department. At the battle of Miani on 17 February 1843 he killed three men, fighting hand to hand, and three more in the battle of Hyderabad on 24 March, where he was himself severely wounded. Two days before, he had been sent with 250 Poona horse to reinforce Major Stack's column on its march to join Napier, and he saved the baggage of the column from capture. He was mentioned in dispatches.

McMurdo became captain in the 28th foot on 8 July 1843, and was transferred to the 78th highlanders on 20 October; but he remained at the head of the quartermaster-general's department in Sind until December 1847, performing the duties 'with great ability and vast labour' (Napier, *Life*, 4.394). He took part in the operations against the hillmen on the right bank of the Indus in 1844–5, where he again distinguished himself by his intrepidity. Napier spoke of him as 'an ornament to Scotland' (ibid., 81), and on 4 September 1844 he married Napier's daughter, Susan Sarah. He received a brevet majority on 18 February 1848. When Napier returned to India as commander-in-chief in 1849, McMurdo went with him as aide-de-camp. He acted as assistant adjutant-general from November 1849 until November 1851, and took part in the operations against the Afridis, including the forcing of the Kohat Pass. In 1850 he published a pamphlet, *Sir Charles Napier's Indian Baggage Corps*, in reply to Colonel Burlton's comments on Napier's letter to Sir John Hobhouse.

McMurdo became lieutenant-colonel in the army on 21 October 1853, and was assistant adjutant-general at Dublin from May 1854 to January 1855. On 2 February he was appointed director-general of the new Land Transport Corps, and was sent to the Crimea, with the local rank of colonel, to reorganize the transport service. This he did with energy, achieving improvement despite difficulties, including dependence on the notoriously inefficient commissariat for forage; McMurdo wrote of Commissary-General James Filder, 'I never … met so disagreeable a coxcomb and so utterly impracticable an official as this little viper' (Sweetman, 55–6). According to John Sweetman, the Land Transport Corps had little impact in the Crimea. On one of his demands the secretary to the Treasury, Sir Charles Trevelyan, had written, 'Col. McMurdo must limit his expenditure'. McMurdo replied: 'When Sir Charles Trevelyan limits the war, I will limit my expenditure' (Hamley, 208). McMurdo also took over the working of the railway. He was made aide-de-camp to the queen and brevet colonel on 11 December 1855, and CB on 2 January 1857. He received the Légion d'honneur (fourth class) and Mejidiye (fourth class).

After the war the Land Transport Corps was converted into the military train, and McMurdo was made colonel-commandant of it on 1 April 1857. In 1859 the volunteer movement began, and from 1860 to January 1865 McMurdo was inspector-general of volunteers, to the great advantage of the force. It was 'a post to which he seems to have had a peculiar call' (*Naval and Military Gazette*, 28 Jan 1865). In 1865, following the suggestion of Charles Manby (secretary of the Institution of Civil Engineers), McMurdo established the engineer and railway volunteer staff corps: the regular army did not have a railway section until 1882. Like other leading volunteers he supported the early-closing movement, to facilitate volunteer activities. He was popular with the volunteers, and when

his house, Rosebank, Fulham (which he had purchased in 1861), burnt down in 1864, the volunteers rebuilt it, as a gift to him. On his retirement as inspector-general he received a testimonial from volunteer officers. He became colonel of the Inns of Court Volunteers on 23 January, and of the engineer and railway volunteer staff corps on 9 February 1865. In 1869 he published *Rifle Volunteers for Field Service: their Arms, Equipment, and Administration*, a pamphlet of advice to the commanding officers of corps. While most regular officers maintained the volunteers were fit only for garrison duties, McMurdo considered they could be used in the field against an invading army, though only after further continuous training.

McMurdo commanded a brigade in the Dublin district from October 1866 to February 1870, and the Rawalpindi district in Bengal from May 1870 to March 1873. He was promoted major-general on 6 March 1868, lieutenant-general on 10 February 1876, and general on 20 May 1878. He was given the colonelcy of the 69th foot in July 1876, and was transferred to the 15th foot in August 1877 and to the 22nd (Cheshire regiment) in June 1888. On 24 May 1881 he was made KCB, and on 1 July was placed on the retired list, being subsequently made GCB (June 1893). He died at Cimiez, Nice, on 2 March 1894. His wife survived him, with several children.   E. M. LLOYD, *rev.* ROGER T. STEARN

Sources *The Times* (3 March 1894) · *Broad Arrow* (10 March 1894) · W. F. P. Napier, *The life and opinions of General Sir Charles James Napier*, 4 vols. (1857) · W. F. P. Napier, *The conquest of Scinde: with some introductory passages in the life of Major-General Sir Charles James Napier*, 2 vols. (1845) · A. W. Kinglake, *The invasion of the Crimea*, [new edn], 9 vols. (1877–88) · E. Hamley, *The war in the Crimea* (1890) · A. D. Lambert, *The Crimean War: British grand strategy, 1853–56* (1990) · J. Sweetman, *War and administration: the significance of the Crimean War for the British army* (1984) · E. M. Spiers, *The late Victorian army, 1868–1902* (1992) · T. A. Heathcote, *The military in British India: the development of British land forces in south Asia, 1600–1947* (1995) · I. F. W. Beckett, *Riflemen form* (1982) · H. Cunningham, *The volunteer force: a social and political history, 1859–1908* (1975) · Boase, *Mod. Eng. biog.* · *CGPLA Eng. & Wales* (1894)

Wealth at death £7260 12s. 3d.: probate, 13 May 1894, *CGPLA Eng. & Wales*

Macmurray, John (1891–1976), moral philosopher, was born on 16 February 1891 in Maxwellton, near Dumfries, Kirkcudbrightshire, the son of James Macmurray (1854–1933), an excise agent in the civil service, and his wife, Mary Anna Grierson (1867–1973). Following a family move to the north-east of Scotland, Macmurray was educated at Aberdeen grammar school and Robert Gordon College—also in Aberdeen—before proceeding to Glasgow University (1909–13) to read classics. In 1913 he secured a Snell exhibition to study at Balliol College, Oxford, but his philosophical studies were interrupted by the outbreak of the First World War.

After the outbreak of war Macmurray joined the medical corps in October 1914. Two years later, however, concluding that he was part of the British war machine, he enlisted as an officer in the Cameron Highlanders. In 1918 he was wounded in the defence of Arras and awarded the MC. He returned to Oxford as the John Locke scholar and completed his degree course in 1919. He had married, in 1916, Elizabeth Hyde Campbell (1891–1982), an artist from

Banchory. As a result of an ectopic pregnancy their marriage was childless.

Macmurray held teaching posts in philosophy at Manchester University (1919–21), Witwatersrand, Johannesburg (1921–2), and Balliol College, Oxford (1923–8) before his appointment in 1928 to the Grote chair of the philosophy of mind and logic at London University. He remained there until 1944, when he returned to Scotland to the chair of moral philosophy at Edinburgh University, the post from which he retired in 1958.

Throughout the 1930s Macmurray established a reputation as a popular, if controversial, BBC radio broadcaster on cultural, political, and ethical topics. He was regarded as an inspirational teacher, particularly in Edinburgh, where philosophy remained a compulsory subject for all arts students. Although his thought was deeply religious he remained outside institutional Christianity, until in 1958 he and his wife took up residence in the Quaker community at Jordans, Buckinghamshire. They were subsequently received into membership of the Society of Friends, whose pacifism and lack of doctrinal definition attracted Macmurray. They lived and worked in the community at Jordans for ten years before returning to Edinburgh. Macmurray died at his Edinburgh home, 8 Mansionhouse Road, on 21 June 1976 and was survived by his wife. He was cremated at Mortonhall crematorium, Edinburgh, on 25 June, and his remains were interred at the Quaker burial-ground in Jordans.

Several publications arose out of Macmurray's 1930s radio broadcasts, including *Freedom in the Modern World* (1932); but his most significant philosophical work were his Gifford lectures, delivered in Glasgow in 1953–4. The two published volumes comprise *The Self as Agent* (1957) and *Persons in Relation* (1961). He was awarded an LLD degree by Glasgow University in 1954.

Macmurray's sympathy for Marxism, particularly in his writings for the Christian left in the 1930s, derives from the view that material and organic processes must be used for the sake of personal freedom. A just socio-economic order and a classless society are necessary conditions of genuine human community. None the less, Macmurray's early affinity with Marxism did not extend to its radical criticism of religion. While hostile to other-worldly forms of Christianity he insisted that religion can enhance personal life. It exercises a vital social function in uniting persons across national and racial boundaries. It enables people to overcome fear of death and of one another. Fear, not hatred, is the antithesis of love. In this respect, ritual and fellowship are primary in religion; belief and doctrine are secondary. Macmurray was here strongly influenced by Hebraic thought forms over against Roman and Greek traditions. For the Old Testament, religion is not a compartment of life. It shapes all of personal, social, and national life. The significance of Jesus resides in his transforming Judaism from a national to a universal religion. His central vision is of the kingdom of God on earth. This regard for Hebrew religion led Macmurray into sharp public criticism of the antisemitism integral to national socialism in the 1930s.

In his Gifford lectures Macmurray's philosophical vision is presented with greater precision. The egocentric and disembodied self of Cartesian thought is roundly attacked. Macmurray substitutes the 'I do' for the 'I think'. The self is more adequately described in terms of agency than thought. The agent is rooted in a material and social world in which identity is determined relationally. In his analysis of the mother–child relation, Macmurray argues that the child's identity is shaped by the intentions of its mother. Skills are acquired through linguistic communication rather than mere instinct. All experience is thus shared experience, and all existence irreducibly social. The child's well-being is dependent both on the mother's continual love and on her willingness to enable her child to become a free agent. A family is maintained by bonds of mutual affection and friendship between all possible pairs of its members. In this respect it is a model for every society. The task of politics is to apply this model under the conditions of economic and social life.

Macmurray's influence continues to grow, as is evident in the recent reissue of his major publications. His philosophical work can now be seen as one of several twentieth-century protests against the distorting effects of Cartesianism. Although his work was largely ignored by the professional guild of philosophers, the relational and holistic description of the self he presents has attracted the attention of social scientists and theologians. A John Macmurray Society was formed in Canada in 1971 and later superseded by the International John Macmurray Association. In the UK, the John Macmurray Fellowship was formed in 1993. His influence upon a generation of students has been significant, if harder to quantify. Macmurray's relational vision of human society now resonates with late twentieth-century communitarian trends in political thought, while the acknowledged influence on Prime Minister Tony Blair's early political development has brought renewed public attention.

DAVID FERGUSSON

Sources *WWW*, 1971–80 · J. Costello, 'The life and thought of John Macmurray', *John Macmurray: critical perspectives*, ed. D. Fergusson and N. Dower (2002) · private information (2004) [J. Costello] · J. E. Costello, *John Macmurray: a biography* (2002)
Archives Regis College, Toronto, collection · U. Edin. L., special collections division, papers | U. Leeds, Brotherton L., letters to Esther Simpson | SOUND BBC archives, London, recordings of (a few) radio broadcasts
Likenesses R. Lyon, portrait, 1957, U. Edin. · photographs, Regis College, Toronto, Macmurray collection
Wealth at death £21,891.95: confirmation, 26 Oct 1976, *CCI*

McMurrich, James Playfair (1859–1939), anatomist in Canada, was born at Toronto, Canada, on 16 October 1859, the son of John McMurrich (1804–1883) and his wife, Janet Dixon. His father was from Paisley, Renfrewshire, and was a member of the legislative council of Canada. Educated at Upper Canada College in Toronto and at the University of Toronto, James McMurrich graduated BA in 1879 and MA in 1881. At the age of twenty-three he became professor of biology at the Ontario Agricultural College (1882–1884), and then went to Johns Hopkins University as instructor in osteology and mammalian anatomy (1884–

1886); at the same time he studied for his PhD degree, which he obtained in 1885.

McMurrich's early academic career was noted for numerous changes and a rapid rise. He held in succession the professorships of biology at Haverford College, Pennsylvania (1886–9), of animal morphology at Clark University, Worcester, Massachusetts (1889–92), of biology at the University of Cincinnati (1892–4), and of anatomy at the University of Michigan (1894–1907). Having refused the chair of anatomy at Yale University he was appointed to Toronto as professor of anatomy in 1907, and he held this chair until his retirement in 1930, when he was made professor emeritus. In 1922 he founded and became the first dean of the school of graduate studies. In 1882 McMurrich had married Katie Moodie (d. 1932), daughter of J. J. Vickers, of Toronto; they had a son and a daughter.

McMurrich was the author of *A Text-Book of Invertebrate Morphology* (1894; 2nd edn, 1896), *The Development of the Human Body* (1902; 7th edn, 1923), and of more than a hundred papers on morphology and embryology. He was a leading authority on the phylogeny of the muscles of the limbs and sea-anemones. He was keenly interested in the history of science, and his *Leonardo da Vinci, the Anatomist (1452–1519)* (1930) is an estimate of Da Vinci's position as an anatomist and physiologist. At the time of his death McMurrich had also assembled considerable material for a projected history of anatomy. He translated Johannes Sobotta's *Atlas and Text Book of Human Anatomy* (1906–7), edited Henry Morris's *Human Anatomy* (4th edn, 1907), and wrote the sections on the muscular and vascular systems in George Arthur Piersol's *Human Anatomy* (1907).

McMurrich was elected FRS (Canada) in 1909 and was posthumously awarded the Flavelle medal in 1939. He was president of the Society of Naturalists (1907), the American Association of Anatomists (1908), the Royal Society of Canada (1922), and the American Association for the Advancement of Science (1922), and he was chairman of the biological board of Canada (1926–34). He was also a member of the North American commission on fisheries investigations (1921–39). He received the honorary degree of LLD from the universities of Michigan (1912), Cincinnati (1923), and Toronto (1931). McMurrich died from coronary thrombosis at his home, 20 Foxbar Road, Toronto, on 9 February 1939.

W. J. BISHOP, rev. MAX SATCHELL

Sources W. R. Bell, 'James Playfair McMurrich (1859–1939): biologist, anatomist, historian', *Medical Press*, 242 (1959), 323 • *The Lancet* (25 Feb 1939), 481 • *WWW* • *DCB*, vol. 11 • *Canadian Medical Association Journal*, 60 (1939), 409 • *The Times* (18 Feb 1939) • A. G. Huntsman, *Proceedings and Transactions of the Royal Society of Canada*, 3rd ser., 33 (1939), section 2, pp. 159–61 [minutes]
Likenesses K. Forbes, oils, University of Toronto, division of anatomy

Macmurrogh, Art. *See* Mac Murchadha, Art Caomhánach (d. 1416/17).

MacMurrough, Dermot. *See* Mac Murchada, Diarmait (c.1110–1171).

MacNab, Sir Allan Napier, baronet (1798–1862), politician and entrepreneur in Canada, was born on 19 February 1798 at Newark, Upper Canada (later Niagara-on-the-Lake, Ontario), the third and first surviving of the seven children of Lieutenant Allan MacNab, a half-pay officer formerly of the Queen's rangers and clerk in the government offices, and his wife, Anne Napier. He grew up in York (later Toronto), the capital of Upper Canada (later Ontario), in a world that was intensely competitive, military, and tory. He was proud of his Scottish ancestry and his family's military traditions, and was determined to escape the penury to which his family had been periodically prone and to make his mark in the world. He was educated somewhat above his origins at the private school of A. W. Carson and later at the nursery of Upper Canada's tory elite, the Home District grammar school. When the Anglo-American War of 1812–14 broke out, he threw himself into it, emerging with the reputation of the boy hero of the war.

On 6 May 1821 MacNab married Elizabeth Brooke (1801/2–1826); they had three children. Baulked in his desire for a career in the British army, in 1826 he gained admission to the bar of Upper Canada and set up his law office in Hamilton, a village of about 200 inhabitants some 45 miles from York on Lake Ontario. As Hamilton entered a period of notable expansion, MacNab's practice thrived exceedingly. Following the death of his first wife, on 29 September 1831 he married Mary Stuart (c.1812–1846), with whom he had three children. On 6 February 1835 he became a bencher of the Law Society of Upper Canada and on 21 January 1838 the first queen's counsel in the province. He had also launched into a wide variety of entrepreneurial activities, notably land speculation and transport promotion, and by 1834 he had begun construction of the mansion, Dundurn, on Burlington Heights, which was to be his home and which remains one of his chief monuments.

In 1830 MacNab was elected a member of the provincial house of assembly for the county of Wentworth, which encompassed Hamilton. At first a moderate tory, he moved significantly to the right during the governorship of Sir Francis Bond Head (1836–8), although he remained deeply interested in economic growth. He was one of Head's most prominent defenders in the crisis of 1836, fully endorsing the view that responsible government would separate Upper Canada from the mother country. That conclusion seemed to MacNab as to other tories to be validated by the rebellion of 1837–8. During the suppression of that uprising MacNab commanded with vigour, ability, and humanity, and his special relationship with the Upper Canadian militia was essential to the government's success. For his efforts he was knighted (March 1838) and hailed as the man who had saved Upper Canada for the British empire.

Imperial policy and Canadian politics now turned in directions MacNab could not approve. He opposed the British government's adoption of responsible government for the Canadas and the terms on which the two provinces were united in 1841. He led the ultra-tory section of the

Conservative Party against the regimes of Lord Sydenham (1841) and Sir Charles Bagot (1842-3) but supported Sir Charles Metcalfe during the crisis of 1843-4. In 1844-7 he was speaker of the house of assembly, a position he had held in Upper Canada from 1837 to 1840, and he helped establish the speaker as an impartial arbiter of debate rather than a party leader. This phase of his career ended dramatically with the controversy over the Rebellion Losses Bill (1849), during which the parliament buildings in Montreal were destroyed by fire. MacNab asserted his ascendancy over the Conservative Party as a whole with highly emotional speeches which kindled public excitement.

By contrast, in the early 1850s MacNab urged his followers to forgive and forget the past. His attempts to chart a new course for the divided and disconsolate Conservatives were initially unpopular. They were also compromised by his increasing preoccupation with railways. In 1845-6 he had revived the Great Western Railway, which was to run between Detroit and Buffalo via Hamilton as a link between rail systems in the American east and the mid-west. In the 1850s he came to symbolize Canada's railway age. As chairman of the assembly's standing committee on railways and telegraph lines, he was reputed to exercise enormous influence. His remark that all his politics were railroads (28 June 1851) was thought to epitomize public life. He was president, director, or parliamentary agent of six railway companies in the 1850s, though in June 1854 he was ousted from the Great Western.

In September 1854 MacNab and the French Canadian A. N. Morin formed the coalition that, as the Conservative Party, was to govern Canada for most of the remainder of the century. It comprised Upper Canadian Conservatives, moderate Reformers, and French-Canadian *bleus*, which was broadly the combination for which MacNab had been working since the early 1840s. During the session of 1856 his performance as leader and premier, which had never been strong, suffered desperately from illness. John A. Macdonald organized the coup that ejected him from office (22 May). Incensed at this treachery, his body swathed in bandages to relieve his gout, MacNab had himself carried into the house, where he defiantly defended himself.

This striking scene ended MacNab's political career. In July 1856 he was granted a baronetcy; the investiture was on 5 February 1858. Increasingly wracked by rheumatism and gout, MacNab died on 8 August 1862 at Dundurn, Hamilton, where he was buried on 11 August. His alleged death-bed conversion to Roman Catholicism after a lifetime's stalwart membership of the Church of England created a final controversy.

In his prime MacNab was a fine man, of above average height, with brown hair, lively eyes, and a large chest. He had great presence. Those he could not charm he bullied. It has been customary to say that his abilities were unequal to the position which force of personality gained for him, and in this there is some truth. Yet he was not without constructive achievement in military, commercial, and political fields. His flair for the dramatic caught the imagination of his contemporaries, and for more than three decades he was a strong and often unpredictable force in the life of his locality and province.

DONALD R. BEER

Sources D. R. Beer, *Sir Allan Napier MacNab* (1984) · T. M. Bailey, ed., *Dictionary of Hamilton biography* (1981) · C. Read and R. J. Stagg, eds., *The rebellion of 1837 in Upper Canada* (1985) · J. K. Johnson, *Becoming prominent: regional leadership in Upper Canada, 1791-1841* (1989) · S. F. Wise, 'Upper Canada and the conservative tradition', *Profiles of a province: studies in the history of Ontario*, ed. E. G. Firth (1967), 20-33 · C. M. Johnston, *The head of the lake* (1958) · G. M. Craig, *Upper Canada: the formative years, 1784-1841* (1963) · J. M. S. Careless, ed., *The pre-confederation premiers: Ontario government leaders, 1841-1867* (1980) · *The Arthur papers*, ed. C. R. Sanderson, 2 (1957) · P. A. Baskerville, 'The boardroom and beyond: aspects of the upper Canadian railroad community', PhD diss., Queen's University, Kingston, Ontario, 1973 · D. McCalla, 'Peter Buchanan, London agent for the Great Western Railway of Canada', *Canadian business history: selected studies, 1497-1971*, ed. D. S. Macmillan (1972), 197-216 · M. Macrae, *MacNab of Dundurn* (1971)

Archives Metropolitan Toronto Reference Library · NA Canada, provincial secretary's correspondence · NA Canada, Upper Canada sundries · University of Toronto, Thomas Fisher Rare Book Library | NA Canada, J. M. Whyte MSS · NA Canada, Buchanan MSS · Queen's University, Kingston, Ontario, J. S. Cartwright MSS

Likenesses oils, *c*.1838, Dundurn Castle, Hamilton · oils, *c*.1853, NA Canada; commissioned by the town of Hamilton · Milne, photograph, *c*.1860, NA Canada · W. Notman, black and white photograph (late in life), NA Canada · J. Partridge, oils (as speaker, 1844-7), NA Canada · group portrait, daguerreotype (in late life; with his family), priv. coll. · lithograph? (after photograph), repro. in *ILN* (12 Jan 1856) · portraits, Metropolitan Toronto Reference Library, John Ross Robertson Collection · portraits, priv. coll.

Wealth at death fighting off bankruptcy; probate sought for $5000 in Canada: Surrogate court records, Public Archives of Ontario, Toronto, R22-6-2 Wentworth county

Macnab, Henry Grey (1760-1823), educationist and mining entrepreneur, was born Henry Macnab on 4 June 1760 at Ulgham, Northumberland, fifth son of James Macnab, gardener, and his wife, Mary Atkinson. By 1771 his father was agent or steward to Sir Henry Grey, second baronet (1722-1808), of Howick, when Henry's eldest sister, Mary, married, at Alnwick, George Johnson (d. 1800), mining engineer and colliery viewer of Walker colliery, Byker, near Newcastle, who was then 'ranked as the greatest viewer in both Tyne and Wear' (Dunn, 1.34-5). Henry's younger sister, Catherine, though under age, also married a viewer, George Allen (b. 1759) of Wallsend, in 1782, when Henry helped deceive Allen about her real age and origins.

Macnab's earliest years are obscure but he acted as a private tutor of elocution and rhetoric at the University of Glasgow for nine years between about 1782 and 1790. He published with the university's printer three books on education and elocution in 1785 and 1786, one dedicated to 'the principal and professors' and another to Edmund Burke. At some time between 1786 and 1791 he added Grey to his name, presumably in honour of his father's employer. In 1791 he accompanied his brother-in-law, George Allen, and another northern geological enthusiast, the painter George Gray, on an expedition to Poland to prospect for coal and other minerals on Prince Adam Czartoryski's estates at Krzeszowice, near Cracow, apparently on instructions from Prince Jozef Poniatowski. Recently advised by Erasmus Darwin on the origin and occurrence of coal, Allen and Gray delivered an enthusiastic report on 16 July, witnessed by Macnab, by which time Allen had already started sinking a pit. But this work can hardly have been acted upon before the Polish revolution was suppressed by Catherine II of Russia in 1792.

Macnab, on his return to Britain, studied medicine at the University of Edinburgh from 1791 to 1793, while his brother-in-law Johnson was busy prospecting for coal in north Skye. After graduating MD at St Andrews on 26 March 1793, Macnab moved to London and spent two years working in London hospitals. He became active in politics and wrote a series of tracts between 1793 and 1801 on the importance of the coal trade, and the effects of its crippling taxation, that he addressed to Pitt and other MPs. His circle of acquaintances now included Joseph Banks, to whom he provided geological data, and he was elected an honorary member of the Newcastle Literary and Philosophical Society in 1794. On 22 July 1795 he married, in London, Caroline Elizabeth Standen (*bap.* 1770) from Wigan, who must have brought him new prosperity, as he spent heavily trying to improve large estates in Shropshire by establishing collieries and quarries at Billingsley and Highley, near Bridgnorth, which he supervised for Johnson. He issued, about 1798, his printed terms for undertaking mineral prospecting. The Shropshire venture, which involved building a new blast furnace at Billingsley, however, proved a financial disaster following Johnson's death there in 1800, and by mid-1801 Macnab was so deep in debt that he was forced to flee to France during the peace of Amiens, to escape his creditors.

When hostilities renewed between Britain and France, Macnab became a prisoner of war, but negotiated to live in Montpellier, where he practised medicine for the next eleven years. He had been liberated by November 1815, when he was in London making his will, but soon returned to France, after becoming physician to the duke of Kent and Strathearn. A keen supporter of the socialist Robert Owen, the duke asked Macnab to visit New Lanark in September 1819 to report on Owen's establishment. Macnab's early doubts on Owen's activities immediately evaporated and he published an enthusiastic report on this visit, and on Owen's educational work at New Lanark in 1819 which was translated into French in 1821. He also published *Observations on the Political, Moral and Religious State of the Civilised World* in 1820. He died in Paris on 3 February 1823 and was buried at Père Lachaise cemetery. His wife almost certainly predeceased him as only his daughter, Elizabeth Caroline, is mentioned in his will of 1815.

H. S. TORRENS

Sources H. S. Torrens, '300 years of oil', *The British Association lectures* (1993), 4–8 · G. Nair and D. Poyner, 'The coming of coal', *Midland History*, 18 (1993), 87–103 · G. Nair, *Highley: the development of a community, 1550–1880* (1988) · E. Mackenzie, *A descriptive and historical account of the town and county of Newcastle upon Tyne*, 2 (1827), 577–8 · P. J. Anderson, ed., *Officers and graduates of University and King's College, Aberdeen, MVD–MDCCCLX*, New Spalding Club, 11 (1893) · M. Dunn, 'History of the viewers', c.1811, Northumbd RO · *GM*, 1st ser., 93/1 (1823), 378–9 · Banks correspondence, BL, Add. MS 33979, 228–229 · Banks correspondence, Sutro Library, San Francisco, USA, COAL 1:13, MIN. 1:12 · *Laws of the Literary and Philosophical Society of Newcastle* (1794), 17 · F.-X. de Feller, *Biographie universelle, ou, Dictionnaire historique des hommes qui se sont fait un nom par leur génie*, ed. C. Weiss and Abbé Busson, new edn, 9 vols. in 8 (Paris, 1847–50), vol. 5, p. 392 · PRO, PROB, 10/4706 · *DNB* · *IGI*

Archives BL, Banks archives, letters · Christ Church Oxf., MSS, MS Estates 84/143–170 · Sutro Library, San Franscisco, Banks archives, letters

Wealth at death left all to daughter (or, if dead, to sisters): will, PRO, PROB 10/4706

Macnab, Iain, of Barachastlain (1890–1967), painter and wood-engraver, was born on 21 October 1890 in Iloilo, Panay, in the Spanish Philippines, the second of four children of John Macnab (1847–1927), of the Hongkong and Shanghai Bank, and his wife, Jessie Mabel Shannan. He went to Kilmalcom in Scotland in 1894, being educated at Edinburgh's Merchiston Castle School, where he exhibited a gift for caricature. He wanted to be a sculptor on leaving school in 1911 but his father forced him into chartered accountancy. Before his finals in 1914 he joined the Highland light infantry and fought at Mons; commissioned into the Argyll and Sutherland Highlanders, he was blown up at Loos in 1916 and was invalided out of the army. Much of the next two years was passed in hospital, with a brief six weeks at the Glasgow School of Art in 1917. His wounds had left him too weak to sculpt and on moving to London in 1918 he studied painting at the Heatherley School of Fine Art. After a spell in Paris in 1919 he returned to Heatherley's as joint principal with Henry Massey.

In 1925 Macnab married the dancer Helen Mary Tench (Helen Wingrave), moved to 33 Warwick Square, Pimlico, London, and there founded the Grosvenor School of Modern Art; among the progressive teachers were the avantgarde linocutters Claude Flight and Cyril Power. Macnab's early printmaking was etching, a dozen by 1927; he then began to engrave in wood and thereafter devoted himself to it, exhibiting widely throughout the 1930s. The school closed for good in 1940; Macnab had two spells in the RAF, being invalided out on each occasion. From 1946 to 1953 he was director of art studies at Heatherley's, now at the Grosvenor site. From there he continued to run the successful Artist Publishing Company. The financial training that he had escaped from was never wasted; of the various art organizations and societies he could be scathing but was in constant demand for his organizational and economic skills, which were the equal of his inspired teaching. All this was achieved with a tremendous sense of humour and kindness, despite the constant pain and repeated hospitalizations caused by the war injuries. A stroke in 1961 ended his engraving, though he continued to paint; he had illustrated six books, exhibiting his cartoonist's eye, and created over seventy independent engravings. He died at St Thomas's Hospital, London on 24 December 1967, and was survived by his wife.

Macnab was elected an associate of the Royal Society of Painter-Printmakers in 1923, a member of the Society of Wood-Engravers in 1932, and of the Royal Institute of Painters in Oils in 1932 (of which he was president 1959–67), and of the Royal Society of Painter-Etchers and

Engravers in 1935. He returned to engraving after the war, unlike so many others, and continued as long as he was physically capable. He was not a visionary thinker but his influence was such that a recognizable Grosvenor-school type of artist came into being; modernist in method and in material, Macnab remained a representational artist, with his interest more in the treatment of a subject than the subject itself, relishing the limitations of wood-engraving. His style, which all his students adopted before adapting it to their own sensibilities, is painterly; yet it has a sculptural feeling for form and structure, and marries modernism with traditional, especially Mediterranean, landscapes and genre scenes. The design is always drawn, blacklines and whitelines engendering one another. Tonal contrasts are achieved in patterned texture and a very deliberate and controlled use of tinting in low relief. In some of the larger works the formality of the composition is startlingly enhanced by the bold placing in the foreground of objects lesser artists would avoid: a glass and soda-siphon, a bowl of fruit and flapping curtain. In the post-war engravings this device, using balcony railings or a vase of flowers, is even more pronounced, first dominating the foreground and then the picture. His *Student's Book of Wood Engraving* (Pitman, 1938), one of two textbooks he wrote, remains influential and a concise statement of what wood-engraving has to offer the artist.

HAL BISHOP

Sources A. Garrett, *Wood engravings and drawings of Iain Macnab of Barachastlain* (1973) [incl. foreword by Brigadier John Francis Macnab of Barravorich] · C. Fitzgerald, 'Iain Macnab of Barachastlain', 'Heatherley's', *Handbook of modern British painting, 1900–1980*, ed. A. Windsor (1992) · A. Windsor, 'The Grosvenor School of Modern Art', *Handbook of modern British painting, 1900–1980*, ed. A. Windsor (1992) · A. Horne, *The dictionary of 20th century British book illustrators* (1994) · K. M. Guichard, *British etchers, 1850–1940*, 2nd edn (1981) · private information (2004) [Barbara Berryman] · 'extracts from a conversation between Peter Barker-Mill [student of Macnab c.1932–1933] and Alan Johnson, 28 May 1989', *Peter Barker Mill* (1989) [exhibition catalogue, Arnolfini Gallery, Bristol] · A. Garrett, *A history of British wood engraving* (1978) · J. Selborne, *British wood-engraved book illustration, 1900–1940* (1998) · D. Buckman, *Dictionary of artists in Britain since 1945* (1998) · J. Hamilton, *Wood engraving and the woodcut in Britain, c.1890–1990* (1994) · B. Peppin and L. Micklethwaite, *Dictionary of British book illustrators: the twentieth century* (1983) · T. Balston, 'English wood engraving, 1900–1950', *Image*, 5 (1950) [re-issued as T. Balston, *English wood engraving, 1900–1950* (1951)] · A. Garrett, ed., *British wood engraving of the 20th century: a personal view* (1980) · R. Garton, *British printmakers, 1855–1955* (1992) · I. Macnab, various articles, *The Artist* (1932–61) · I. Macnab, various articles, *The Studio*, 103–62 (1932–61) · Graves, *RA exhibitors* · *The Times* (27 Dec 1967) · *Society of Wood Engravers Newsletter*, 6 (Jan 1968)

Likenesses I. Macnab, self-portrait, etching, 1944 (*Nude*), repro. in Guichard, *British etchers*, pl. 44 · photograph, repro. in G. B. Harrison, rev., *Selected poems of Robert Browning* (1938)

McNab, William Ramsay (1844–1889), botanist, was born on 9 November 1844 at Edinburgh, the only son of James McNab (1810–1878), horticulturist and principal gardener from 1849 of the Royal Botanic Garden, Edinburgh. He was educated at Edinburgh Academy and studied medicine and botany at the University of Edinburgh, graduating MD in 1866. Thereafter he went to Berlin, where he

studied botany under Alexander Braun and Karl Koch, and pathological anatomy and histology under Rudolf Carl Virchow. Returning to Britain he was assistant physician in the Crichton Royal Institution, Dumfries (1867–70), but abandoned medicine for botany to become professor of natural history at the Royal Agricultural College, Cirencester.

A thorough, precise laboratory demonstrator and a fluent, simple, entertaining lecturer, McNab is credited by the anonymous author of his obituary in *Nature* with introducing to British students, through his lectures at Cirencester in 1871, the incisive experimental methods of Julius Sachs (1832–1897). As no detailed information has been traced about McNab's lecture courses at Cirencester or elsewhere, this particular claim to distinction is difficult to verify; there were others who pioneered the teaching of experimental botany around the same time, such as Thomas Henry Huxley at the Royal School of Mines, and Sydney Vines at Cambridge. Nevertheless, if McNab was indeed teaching Sachs's methods as early as 1871, then that would have preceded both Huxley and Vines.

In March 1872 McNab moved to Dublin as professor of botany in the Royal College of Science, established in 1867 and later incorporated into the National University of Ireland. He had a great appetite for work, voluntarily trebling his work in the Royal College. He contributed various short articles to the *Encyclopaedia Britannica* (9th edn), including 'Vegetable histology', and published two classbooks, *Outlines of Morphology and Physiology* and *Outlines of Classification of Plants* (1878), and numerous brief notes and research papers, especially on plant morphology and physiology.

McNab was married and had children but little is known of the details of his family. His wife signed herself with the initials J. L. (McNab). He was an abrasive, ambitious man, but did not always succeed; for example, he was prevented from obtaining the chair of botany in the University of Glasgow. From 1 April 1878 both the Royal (later National) Botanic Gardens, at Glasnevin, Dublin, and the Royal College of Science were administered by the Department of Science and Art, so McNab sought exclusive facilities at Glasnevin for his teaching and research. The gardens' director, David Moore (1808–1879), was obliged to concede, but feared McNab's ambition (ultimately thwarted) to become director. On 25 March 1880 McNab was appointed scientific superintendent of the Royal Botanic Gardens, without any rights to intervene in administrative or horticultural matters. He was charged to carry out research, report annually on the scientific work of the gardens, and produce a new guidebook (issued in 1885). His subsequent relationship with the curator, David Moore's son Frederick William Moore (1857–1949), was frequently seriously strained.

McNab died of heart disease on 3 December 1889 in Dublin. His wife was left in straitened circumstances, and to support herself and her young children she was obliged to take paying lodgers into her home and to sell her husband's library, scientific instruments, and herbarium. Most of McNab's herbarium, rich in important specimens collected by his grandfather, William McNab (1780–1848) at the Royal Botanic Gardens, Kew, before 1810, and by his father during a visit to North America (1834), is held at the National Botanic Gardens, Glasnevin.

E. CHARLES NELSON

Sources E. C. Nelson and E. M. McCracken, *The brightest jewel: a history of the National Botanic Gardens, Glasnevin, Dublin* (1987) · E. C. Nelson, 'William Ramsay McNab's herbarium in the National Botanic Gardens, Glasnevin', *Glasna*, new ser., 1 (1990), 1–7 · 'Botanical necrology for 1889 … William Ramsay McNab', *Annals of Botany*, 3 (1889–90), 477–9 · *Nature*, 41 (1889–90), 159–60 · *Journal of Botany, British and Foreign*, 28 (1890), 51–2 · S. M. Walters, *The shaping of Cambridge botany* (1981) · misc. MSS, National Botanic Gardens
Archives National Botanic Gardens, Glasnevin, Dublin, Ireland, MSS
Likenesses photograph, *c.*1880, repro. in Nelson, 'William Ramsay McNab's herbarium'

McNabb, Joseph [*name in religion* Vincent McNabb] (1868–1943), theologian and social critic, was born on 8 July 1868 at Portaferry, co. Down, Ireland, the tenth of the eleven children of James McNabb (1823–1911), a master mariner, and his wife, Ann Shields (1830–1901). Both parents came from a seafaring and rural Ulster Catholic background, and family life was devout. McNabb was educated at St Malachy's College, Belfast, apart from one year at St Cuthbert's Grammar School, Newcastle upon Tyne, to where his family had moved in 1882. In November 1885 he joined the English novitiate of the order of Preachers (Dominicans) at Woodchester, Gloucestershire, and received the name in religion of Vincent.

In 1891 McNabb was ordained a priest and continued his studies at the University of Louvain, in Belgium, leaving in July 1894 with the degree of lector in sacred theology. The prevalence of smallholder farms in Belgium made a lasting impression on him. On his return to England he was assigned to teaching Dominican students philosophy and sacred theology at Woodchester (1894–7) and then at Hawkesyard in Staffordshire (1897–1900). He returned to Woodchester as prior, followed by two years (1906–08) of parish work in London, at St Dominic's Priory, Haverstock Hill. He was then sent to Holy Cross Priory, Leicester, as prior until 1914, followed by six years as prior at Hawkesyard. From 1920 until his death he was based at St Dominic's.

McNabb was one of the most widely known Dominicans of the English province. Apart from his work within the order he was well known to Londoners for lively appearances at Speakers' Corner in Hyde Park on behalf of the Catholic Evidence Guild. He presented a memorable figure, always wearing his habit in public, whenever possible walking everywhere in large, heavy duty boots so as to avoid mechanized transport. Many of the most popular of his twenty-five books, such as *The Craft of Prayer* (1935) were collections of talks he had given or articles earlier published in a wide variety of journals. His interest in church unity (see *From a Friar's Cell*, 1923) raised objections from the Holy Office in Rome. He left many unpublished notebooks and papers, lodged in the Dominican Archives. McNabb was also a spiritual director and retreat giver of distinction, and he gave lectures on Aquinas under the

auspices of the University of London extension lectures scheme.

Although he believed that clergy should not meddle in party politics, as a theologian McNabb was convinced of his obligation to contribute to ethical and moral discussion outside the church as well as within. McNabb's fundamental concerns were the family and the poor. Since he considered that the economic and social system of the time, which he termed industrialism, ran counter to what was necessary to support a virtuous life, he believed it necessary to engage in public controversy. From 1912 he was a contributor to Hilaire Belloc's weekly journal, *The Eye-Witness*, and its successors the *New Witness* and *GK's Weekly*. Articles included denunciations of eugenics, arguments in support of striking coalminers, and for a living wage sufficient to keep a family in reasonable comfort. His method of approaching moral and ethical questions was in the tradition of Thomism, a referring of particular situations back to first principles, to what in his terms was primary, and to his chief authorities, the Bible, Aquinas, and the papal social encyclicals, especially Leo XIII's *Rerum novarum* of 1891. In 1917 he met Eric Gill and Hilary Pepler, and under his influence they became Dominican tertiaries, in 1921 forming the craftworker Guild of St Joseph and St Dominic at Ditchling, Sussex. The connection was an important one for all of them, though McNabb later mourned that Ditchling, concentrating on craftwork at the expense of farming, was not sufficiently primary.

From the 1920s McNabb's name became associated with distributism, a social philosophy expounded most notably by Belloc and G. K. Chesterton. Distributists believed that effective liberty could only be realized by the widespread distribution of productive property, and that the family rather than the individual was the basic unit of society. They were against the extension of the role of the state that is inherent in socialism, and also against monopoly capitalism.

McNabb was regarded as a prophetic figure within distributism, in part because his rejection of industrialism was more radical than Belloc or Chesterton's, involving work on the land as constitutive. To his original belief in the primacy of agriculture over commerce and manufacture for all human beings he introduced another element: since the 'leakage' of lapsed Catholics was greater in urban than rural situations, the only hope for the growth of Catholicism in England was for Catholic families to settle on the land: 'Till your soil or kill your soul' (McNabb MSS, Land, 194). *The Church and the Land* (1926) and *Nazareth, or, Social Chaos* (1933) set out his analysis of the need for a return to the land, to self-sufficiency farming, and rejection of machinery. This became McNabb's prevailing preoccupation, and although the majority of his writing and work was more conventionally religious in focus, it is for his insistence on a return to the land that he is best-known. As unemployment increased during the 1930s McNabb inspired the founding of the Catholic land associations, which sought to establish unemployed young Catholic men on small farms.

An ascetic who never compromised in argument or

principle McNabb aroused strong feelings in those who met him. While many who came into contact with him, including Belloc, revered him as little short of a saint, others regarded him as eccentric and fanatical. Some of his brethren found him overly argumentative and dramatic, but he was popular with parishioners, his Dominican biographer noting that he 'always seemed more patient with sin than error' (Valentine, 81). McNabb died from cancer of the throat on 17 June 1943 at St Dominic's Priory, Southampton Road, Haverstock Hill, London. He was buried four days later at Kensal Green cemetery.

ANGELA CUNNINGHAM

Sources F. Valentine, *Father Vincent McNabb, O.P.* (1955) • *Chesterton Review*, 22/1–2 (1996) [Father Vincent McNabb, ed. I. Boyd] • A. Cunningham, 'Prophecy and the poor: Fr Vincent McNabb and distributism', *New Blackfriars* (Feb 1983), 52–64 • Dominican Archives, Blackfriars, Edinburgh, McNabb MSS • E. A. Siderman, *With Father Vincent McNabb at Marble Arch* (1947) • V. McNabb, *Eleven, thank God* (1940) • *The Tablet* (26 June 1943) • F. MacCarthy, *Eric Gill* (1989) **Archives** Blackfriars, George Square, Edinburgh, Dominican Archives
Likenesses J. Gunn, oils, St Dominic's Priory, London

McNachtane, John, of Dundarave (*d.* 1773), customs official and founder of the Beggar's Benison, was the second son of John McNachtane of Dundarave, Argyll (*d.* in or after 1711) and Isobel, daughter of Sir John Campbell of Glenorchy. On his elder brother's death in 1702 he became heir to Dundarave and the chiefship of the McNachtanes. He was a student at Glasgow University in 1706, but did not graduate. He married Isobel Campbell, daughter of a merchant, in 1711 after they had been disciplined for fornication by Inveraray kirk session. Debts had forced his father to dispose of the family lands and, though nominal chief of his clan, McNachtane was forced to seek menial employment. He joined the customs service, being appointed a tidewaiter in Anstruther, Fife, in 1718. By 1720 he had evidently deserted his wife, for she was still in Inveraray when in that year she was disciplined for adultery. McNachtane is alleged to have remarried twice, but the evidence is dubious. He was promoted to collector in the customs service in 1728, and in 1761 was transferred to Edinburgh as one of two inspectors-general of outports.

Though spending his career as a minor official of the Hanoverian regime, McNachtane remained conscious of his ancient blood and resentful of the loss of clan lands (partly brought about by his predecessors' support for the Stuarts). His frustrations reveal themselves in the foundation in Anstruther of the Order of the Beggar's Benison and Merryland (1732–1836). In its early days the club combined, in extremely obscene ritual, myth, and symbolism, subversive themes—libertine sex, Jacobitism, and support for smuggling—with drunken joviality. His impertinent invitation, shortly after the battle of Culloden, to the duke of Cumberland to join the club was, fortunately for McNachtane, never delivered. He was 'sovereign' of the club from about 1745 until his death. Short-lived branches were founded in Edinburgh, Glasgow, and in 1773 at St Petersburg, and many eminent men were recruited as honorary members, including George, prince of Wales

(1783). Having retired from the customs service in 1765 McNachtane died at Springfield, near Edinburgh, on 5 April 1773.

DAVID STEVENSON

Sources *Records of the most ancient and puissant Order of the Beggar's Benison and Merryland, Anstruther*, 2 pts (1892); repr. (1982) • A. I. Macnaughten, *In search of two kinsmen* (1979) • A. I. Macnaughten, *The chiefs of the clan Macnachten and their descendants* (1951) • *Scots Magazine*, 35 (1773), 223 • *Edinburgh Evening Courant* (14 April 1773) • A. G. Cross, 'The Order of the Beggar's Benison in Russia: an unknown episode in Scots-Russian relations in the eighteenth century', *Scottish Slavonic Review*, 3 (autumn 1984), 45–63 • customs establishment books, NA Scot., CE3/1–11 • Leven and Melville muniments, NA Scot., GD 26/11/84 • D. Stevenson, *The Beggar's Benison. Sex clubs of enlightenment Scotland and their rituals* (2001)
Archives NA Scot., CE 3/1–11 • NA Scot., GD 26/11/84

McNaghten, Daniel. *See* McNaughtan, Daniel (1802/3–1865).

Macnaghten, Edward, Baron Macnaghten (1830–1913), judge, the second son of Sir Edmund Francis Workman Macnaghten, second baronet, of Dundarave, co. Antrim, and his wife, Mary Anne, only child of Edward Gwatkin, was born at his father's house in Bloomsbury on 3 February 1830. One of his paternal uncles, Sir William Hay Macnaghten, was murdered at Kabul in December 1841, while another, Edmund Alexander Macnaghten, like his father, was MP for Antrim.

Macnaghten's early years were spent at Roe Park, Limavady, and he attended Dr Cowan's school, The Grange, Sunderland, where many gentrified boys from the north of England and Ireland were then educated. He went to Trinity College, Dublin, in 1847, before proceeding as a scholar to Trinity College, Cambridge, in 1850. He won the Davis university scholarship in 1851, and in 1852 was bracketed senior classic. He was also a senior optime (1852) and won the second chancellor's medal in the same year. He was a serious rower and won the Colquhoun sculls at Cambridge in 1851, the Diamond sculls at Henley in 1852, and twice rowed in the university eight (1851 and 1852). He became a fellow of Trinity in 1853 and an honorary fellow in 1902.

In 1857 Macnaghten was called to the bar at Lincoln's Inn, and for twenty-three years was an equity junior. For a time, in and after 1858, he was secretary to the chancery funds commission. In 1858 he married Frances Arabella (*d.* 1903), the only child of Sir Samuel *Martin, a baron of the exchequer; they had five sons and six daughters.

At the general election of April 1880 Macnaghten was returned for county Antrim as a Conservative MP, and in the same month became queen's counsel. He attached himself first to the rolls court and then to the court of Mr Justice (Sir Joseph William) Chitty; he became a bencher of Lincoln's Inn in 1883 and was treasurer in 1907. In 1883 the earl of Selborne offered him a judgeship, which he refused, to avoid losing his seat to the Liberals. He expected to be appointed as one of the two law officers in Lord Salisbury's first administration, but both appointments went to common lawyers. Macnaghten refused the offer of the home secretaryship made to him personally by Lord Halsbury when Salisbury's second administration was formed in 1886, because he did not want to abandon his career at the bar. He also refused Halsbury's offer of a Chancery judgeship in the following November. However, in January 1887, he was appointed a lord of appeal in ordinary, on the retirement of Lord Blackburn. No practising barrister who had been queen's counsel for less than seven years had ever before been promoted to the House of Lords.

Macnaghten had been elected for North Antrim after the redistribution of seats of 1885, and had spoken in the House of Commons only on Irish topics. He made long speeches on the Land Law (Ireland) Bill on 12 May 1881 and on the Home Rule Bill on 31 May 1886. From the day he entered the House of Lords he took an active part in debate. He generally, but by no means always, spoke on Irish questions and on legal bills. Repeatedly he took charge of bills, and on 6 August 1896 carried against the government an amendment on the Land Law Bill (Ireland) of Gerald Balfour. He was no respecter of persons and did not see why he should bridle his tongue; he once bluntly told Lord Herschell that the latter did not understand the bill he was talking about. In 1903 he was prominent in the committee stage of the Irish Land Bill and carried several amendments, but from that year on he never spoke in debate, although he never ceased to be interested in public affairs, and especially those concerning Ulster. In spite of his high judicial office, and though he was a justice of the peace for county Antrim, where he had a country residence, he signed the Ulster covenant (28 September 1912).

Macnaghten's professional life from 1887 until his death may be traced in twenty-six volumes of the appeal cases and in many volumes of the Indian law reports. In addition to his judicial duties, he was arbitrator in the Portsea Island Building Society inquiry in 1893; chairman of the arbitral tribunal in the boundary dispute between Chile and the Argentine republic in 1899; and, from 1895 until his death, chairman of the Council of Legal Education, and so founder of the system of professional training for the bar.

As a judge, Macnaghten listened with patience and decided without hesitation. It was remarkable how often bench and bar cited a sentence or two of Macnaghten as an authoritative statement of the law. This was largely due to his habit of broadly summarizing the law as the starting point for discussion and judgment, and of using simple yet exact terms. *Van Grutten* v. *Foxwell* (1897) was often quoted to illustrate his characteristic blend of learning, style, and humour, and ability to produce a literary essay from a dry and technical discussion. He could not help being humorous. When he was deeply moved, however, he could use the language of curt sarcasm and of righteous wrath as in *Gluckstein* v. *Barnes* (1900) and his dissenting opinion in *Free Church of Scotland* v. *Overtoun* (1904).

Macnaghten was created GCMG in 1903 and GCB in 1911, the year he succeeded his brother, Francis, as fourth baronet. Lord Macnaghten died at his home, 198 Queen's Gate, London on 17 February 1913. He was succeeded as fifth baronet by his son, Edward Charles Macnaghten (*d.* 1914), who was a leader at the Chancery bar. Sir Edward's two sons, the sixth and seventh baronets, were both killed at the Somme, in July and September 1916 respectively. Lord Macnaghten's second son then succeeded as eighth baronet.   J. A. HAMILTON, *rev.* HUGH MOONEY

Sources W. R. Kennedy, *Law Magazine*, 5th ser., 38 (1912–13), 455 • J. Foster, *Men-at-the-bar: a biographical hand-list of the members of the various inns of court*, 2nd edn (1885), 298 • *The Times* (18 Feb 1913) • *Solicitors' Journal*, 57 (1912–13), 298–9 • *Law Times* (22 Feb 1913), 403, 422 • *Law Journal* (22 Feb 1913), 99, 112–13 • *CGPLA Eng. & Wales* (1913)

Likenesses H. de Glazebrook, oils, 1913, Lincoln's Inn, London; replica, Gov. Art Coll. • C. L. Hartwell, marble bust, Lincoln's Inn, London • Spy [L. Ward], chromolithograph caricature, NPG; repro. in *VF*, 27 (31 Oct 1895), pl. 660

Wealth at death £11,693 9s. 11d.: probate, 15 May 1913, *CGPLA Eng. & Wales*

MacNaghten, John (1723/4–1761), murderer, was son of a gentleman merchant from Benvarden, near Ballymoney, co. Antrim. His father died when he was about six, leaving him an estate worth £500 a year. He was educated at Trinity College, Dublin, but does not appear to have graduated. At college his handsome figure and insinuating address attracted the notice of Clotworthy Skeffington, fourth Viscount Massereene, who introduced him to fashionable society. His passion for gambling soon involved him in debt, but he retrieved his fortune by marrying a Miss Eyre, daughter of Henry Eyre of Rowter, Derbyshire, and sister of the second wife of Massereene's son, also Clotworthy Skeffington, fifth viscount and first earl of Massereene. At the time of his marriage friends made MacNaghten take an oath that he would play no more, but to no avail. About 1750 an attempt to arrest him for debt so alarmed his wife, who was expecting their child, that she went into premature labour and died soon afterwards. In consequence he tried unsuccessfully to commit suicide. Reduced to distress, he obtained through Massereene the collectorship of Coleraine, co. Londonderry, worth about £200 a year. He gambled away more than £800 of the king's money, and in consequence lost his position, and his estate was sequestered.

MacNaghten was then invited to the home of a childhood friend, Andrew Knox of Prehen, co. Londonderry, MP for Donegal, whereupon he at once began to court Knox's fifteen-year-old daughter, Mary Anne, who, though not an heiress, was entitled to a fortune of £5000. She accepted his proposal of marriage against her father's wishes. MacNaghten, however, told her that Knox had secretly consented to their marriage, then persuaded her to read over the marriage service with him in the presence of a witness, and finally claimed her as his wife by law on account of the supposed contract between them. He followed her to Sligo, but was there challenged by a friend of the Knox family, and being wounded was obliged to take refuge in his uncle's house at Londonderry. Meanwhile, the prerogative court of Armagh revoked the pretended contract, and awarded £500 damages to Knox.

MacNaghten, to avoid a suit for these damages, withdrew to England. In August 1761 he returned to Ireland, visited Enniskillen, and, learning that Mary Anne Knox with her mother and aunt were drinking the waters at Swanlinbar, a nearby village, hired a lodging there, disguised as a common sailor. He failed in his attempts to gain an interview with Miss Knox, who was placed under the protection of Lord Mountflorence at Florence Court, co. Fermanagh. MacNaghten then planned an attack on Knox and his family on their way to Dublin for the parliamentary session. On 10 November he, with accomplices, attacked Knox's coach and, meeting with a determined resistance, fatally shot Miss Knox, probably in mistake for her father. MacNaghten, who was himself badly wounded, rode off, but, with a reward of £500 offered, he was captured and lodged in Lifford gaol. He was roughly treated while in custody and went on hunger strike.

At his trial on 8 December MacNaghten declared he had no intention of killing anybody, but had lost control of his actions on being wounded. He strove to save the life of an accomplice, David Dunlap, who was tried with him, alleging that the man was his own tenant and had acted under his influence. Following a fourteen-hour trial he was sentenced to be hanged at Strabane on 15 December 1761. The sentence aroused some public sympathy for MacNaghten, who was thought only to have pursued his wife. As a result there was a general refusal to take part in the work, and the gallows was built by an uncle and some friends of Miss Knox. MacNaghten behaved with the utmost coolness at his execution. He jumped from the gibbet breaking the rope, but he was eventually successfully hanged, aged thirty-eight, and buried with Dunlap in the same grave behind the church of Strabane, co. Tyrone. MacNaghten's celebrated case marked the advent of a new level of violence in abduction cases in Ireland, as witnessed in the Whiteboy agrarian unrest of the 1770s in Munster and Leinster.

GORDON GOODWIN, *rev.* THOMAS P. POWER

Sources J. L. Rayner and G. T. Crook, eds., *The complete Newgate calendar*, 3 (privately printed, London, 1926), 324–30 · *GM*, 1st ser., 31 (1761), 603 · 'A particular account of John MacNaughten, esq., of Benvardon', *Scots Magazine*, 23 (1761), 698–703 · J. E. Walsh, *Sketches of Ireland sixty years ago* (1847), 40–45 · J. Kelly, 'The abduction of women of fortune in eighteenth-century Ireland', *Eighteenth-Century Ireland*, 9 (1994), 7–43

Macnaghten, Sir William Hay, baronet (1793–1841), administrator in India, was born at Fort William, Calcutta, on 24 August 1793, the second son of the sixteen children of Sir Francis Workman Macnaghten (1763–1843) of Dundarave, Antrim, and his wife, Letitia, eldest daughter of Sir William Dunkin, of Clogher, judge of the supreme court of Calcutta. Francis Macnaghten was knighted on becoming a judge of the supreme court of Madras in 1809, in which year he assumed the additional surname and arms of Workman. He was transferred to the supreme court of Calcutta in 1815, retiring eventually in 1825. In 1832, on the death of his elder brother, Edmund Alexander Macnaghten, he succeeded to the chiefship of the clan

Sir William Hay Macnaghten, baronet (1793–1841), by James Atkinson, 1841

Macnaghten and the patrimonial estate of Beardiville; in 1836 he was created a baronet.

William was sent 'home' to be schooled at Charterhouse, and in 1809 returned to India as a cavalry cadet in the Madras army. His first posting with the governor's bodyguard was a leisurely job, and Macnaghten filled his hours learning Persian and Hindi, followed by Tamil, Telugu, Kanarese, and Marathi. In June 1811 he was posted as a cornet to the 4th cavalry at Hyderabad where, under the tutelage of Henry Russell, the resident at the nizam's court, his eyes were opened to the arts of Indian diplomacy. In 1813 he was transferred to the escort of the Mysore resident.

In October 1814 Macnaghten headed north for a place in the Bengal civil service. At the college of Fort William his diligence and cleverness easily marked him out as one of its most distinguished students, and by May 1816 he had conquered Sanskrit and Arabic and won every linguistic prize and medal on the college's books. A sharp-featured, bespectacled young man of expanding girth, he was a courteous companion but somewhat abstracted by the weight of his learning and, as Emily Eden's characterization of him suggests, lesser mortals viewed his attainments with some ambivalence: 'clever and pleasant, speaks Persian rather more fluently than English; Arabic better than Persian; but, for familiar conversation, rather prefers Sanscrit' (Eden, 3–4).

After leaving the college Macnaghten was employed first as an assistant to the registrar of the *sadr diwani adalat* the highest court of appeal in Bengal, and then, from

November 1818, as joint magistrate of Malda, and from February 1820 as acting magistrate of Shahabad. In late 1822 he was appointed registrar of the *sadr diwani adalat*, a good job which enabled him, on 2 August of the following year, to wed Frances (*d.* 1878), daughter of John Livingstone Martyn and widow of Lieutenant-Colonel James McClintock of the Bombay army. Onlookers thought it an odd match: Mrs Macnaghten, described by a recent commentator as a 'cross between Rosamond Vincy and Lady Catherine de Bourgh' (Yapp, 248), was older than her husband, and as pushy and ostentatious as he was reserved and studious. Apparently, however, Macnaghten was devoted to her, and she lived only for his success.

As court registrar, Macnaghten published the first three of six volumes of *Reports of the Cases Determined in the Court of the Nizamat Adawlut* (1827–52), and two genuinely monumental works, *Principles and Precedents of Mohummudan Law* (1825) and *Principles and Precedents of Hindu Law* (2 vols., 1828–9). These latter volumes were a significant addition to the East India Company's tradition of moulding India's vast body of customary and textual law to fit the English notion of precedent, and were used as handbooks by generations of British-Indian judges. Macnaghten's fondness for grand designs, though ultimately fatal, ideally suited him for this bold abridgement and synthesis of Indian experience.

In January 1831 Macnaghten's career soared when the governor-general Lord William Bentinck selected him to be his secretary on a tour to the upper provinces, an engagement which, in 1833, culminated in Macnaghten's appointment as chief secretary of the secret and political department. In October 1837, after four years immersed in the murky and speculative politics of the Great Game, Macnaghten again left Calcutta for the upper provinces, this time in the company of Lord Auckland. The new governor-general's entourage made slow progress up country and, in addition to editing the Arabic text of *A Thousand and One Nights* (4 vols., 1839–42), Macnaghten had time to refine a plan to meet the looming crisis on the north-western frontier. Believing that Ranjit Singh, erstwhile ally and aged ruler of the Punjab, could not live for much longer, Macnaghten argued that the British ought to befriend Afghanistan to counterbalance the Sikhs and to use the country as a buffer against Russia, a menace which then stalked the dreams and waking hours alike of nearly every Briton in India. Macnaghten's plan did away with the old pretence of westward penetration through commerce, and proposed instead an invasion of Afghanistan to oust Dost Muhammad Khan, who was believed to be hostile to the British, and install in his place Shah Shuja, a former amir currently living on British goodwill at Ludhiana.

Auckland was not immediately convinced, but nevertheless he authorized Macnaghten to agree terms with Ranjit Singh about a Sikh invasion of Afghanistan officered by Britons. By July 1838 Macnaghten had concluded treaties with both Ranjit Singh and Shah Shuja and had badgered Auckland into authorizing the invasion.

Once committed, the governor-general did not then complain as Macnaghten edged the Sikhs aside and assembled a large British force for the expedition. Indeed, as proof of his confidence in his political secretary's vision, Auckland made Macnaghten envoy and minister to Kabul, a decision deplored by many frontier specialists who saw him as a desk man, a quintessential civil servant unschooled in the machiavellian politics of Afghanistan.

The march to Afghanistan gave some indication of the troubles ahead. Angered by the ruler of Kalat's inability to secure supplies for the troops, Macnaghten ordered the annexation of three of his provinces to Afghanistan, a policy which eventually necessitated the stationing of British forces there to prop up a new ruler. Against his own rhetoric of minimal intervention, Macnaghten had landed the government of India with a military liability from which it proved impossible to escape.

Initially, however, all was celebration. Kabul was taken on 23 July 1839, and two weeks later Shah Shuja was restored to the throne—although, as Lord Melbourne caustically observed, the terms of his treaty with the envoy made Macnaghten the real king of Afghanistan. Macnaghten quickly saw that British soldiers and money would be needed to prop up Shah Shuja for some time to come, but he had problems with both. The army officers resented being in Afghanistan, jousting with tribesmen in medal-scarce skirmishes; while, on the money side, even though the war's total cost of £8 million was dwarfed by other engagements, it brought no compensating revenue for the British from land taxes or commerce. Moreover, even though Macnaghten himself stuck to the pretence that the British were merely advisers to Shah Shuja, he failed to rein in his subordinate political agents, who behaved like virtual governors in the districts.

As the untenability of the British position emerged, London called for a decisive policy: either annex Afghanistan and hold it by strength, or quit. Neither Auckland nor Macnaghten wanted to take such a decision. Macnaghten, still persisting in the fiction of Shah Shuja's popularity, maintained a ludicrous optimism that the Afghans would soon learn to see the British as friends. As late as August 1841, he chided Henry Rawlinson, his political agent at Kandahar, for seeing Afghanistan as a lost cause: the sort of 'chin-up' talk which had earlier led his disgruntled deputy, Sir Alexander Burnes, to bemoan the 'downright imbecility' of British policy (Yapp, 334).

In the summer of 1841 Macnaghten reluctantly agreed to a policy of retrenchment and intervention, designed to clean up Shah Shuja's government so that it could begin to pay its own way. The feudal cavalry of the chiefs was pruned, and Kabul's bureaucrats were subjected to new surveillance—a dangerous assault on the privileges of two influential classes. Whatever his misgivings, Macnaghten's spirits rocketed on 29 September 1841 when he learned that he had been nominated governor of Bombay. He had been created a baronet in January 1840, but a governorship was the ultimate reward for his exile to Afghanistan. The boon came too late: on 2 November 1841, rebels attacked Burnes's residence in Kabul, killing him and two fellow officers. Rebellion in Kabul was infinitely more dangerous than rural uprisings, and neither Macnaghten nor the military were ready for it. The garrison was unfortified and its commander, General Keith Elphinstone, bedridden. His staff officers were bickering and contentious, looking only to the day they could leave Afghanistan; unable to rally them to fight, Macnaghten was forced to seek a political solution. On 11 December he negotiated the terms of a complete British withdrawal with the rebel leaders, but, when the promised supplies were not forthcoming, he gambled on entering an alternative agreement with Muhammad Akbar Khan, Dost Muhammad's son, who was rumoured to be at loggerheads with the rebels. Macnaghten signed a deal with him on 22 December, but this merely allowed Akbar Khan to enhance his status among his rivals by proving to them that Macnaghten was not to be trusted. The following day, he summoned Macnaghten to an exposed plain outside Kabul. Almost certainly aware that his fate was now sealed, Macnaghten attended the interview accompanied only by captains Trevor, Mackenzie, and Lawrence. On arrival they were seized and carried into the city to their deaths. Akbar Khan himself shot Macnaghten with a pistol given to him by the envoy the day before, whereupon angry city residents hacked his body to pieces and paraded his head and limbs in triumph. Days later, the entire garrison met a similar fate: retreating to Jalalabad, some 4000 soldiers and numerous camp followers were wiped out by freezing weather and snipers.

Back in Calcutta and London, Auckland and Macnaghten were universally condemned for the folly of their Afghan adventure, but in spite of such posthumous unpopularity Macnaghten's formidable widow succeeded in having his remains retrieved from Kabul for interment in the new burial-ground, Circular Road, Calcutta, on 22 April 1843. The couple were childless and the baronetcy became extinct on his death. In 1853 Mrs Macnaghten found a third husband in the second marquess of Headfort. She died in 1878, by which time Macnaghten was beginning to be remembered not just for the fiasco of Kabul but also for his impact on the legal traditions of British India.   KATHERINE PRIOR

Sources M. E. Yapp, *Strategies of British India: Britain, Iran and Afghanistan, 1798–1850* (1980) · BL, Rawlinson MSS · ecclesiastical records, BL OIOC · Burke, *Peerage* (1939) · E. Eden, *Up the country*, ed. E. Thompson, [new edn] (1937) · *DNB* · *The Bengal obituary, or, A record to perpetuate the memory of departed worth*, Holmes & Co. (1848) · V. Eyre, *The military operations at Cabul, which ended in the retreat and destruction of the British army, January 1842* (1843) · J. W. Kaye, *History of the war in Afghanistan*, 2 vols. (1851) · R. L. Arrowsmith, ed., *Charterhouse register, 1769–1872* (1974)
Archives BL OIOC, letter-book, MS Eur. F 335 | BL, letters to Sir Henry Rawlinson, Add. MS 47662 · BL OIOC, letters to W. Pitt Amherst, MS Eur. F 140 · NAM, Sir Abraham Roberts MSS · RS Friends, Lond., Rawlinson MSS · U. Nott. L., letters to Lord William Bentinck
Likenesses J. Atkinson, watercolour drawing, 1841, NPG [*see illus.*] · L. Dickinson, lithograph, NPG; repro. in Eyre, *Portraits of the Cabul Prisoners*

McNair, Arnold Duncan, first Baron McNair (1885–1975), jurist and judge, was born on 4 March 1885 at 52 Lucerne Road, Highbury Fields, London, the eldest child in the family of four sons and one daughter of John McNair (1856–1925) and his wife, Jeannie Ballantyne (1858–1953), teacher, of Paisley. His father, a member of Lloyd's, settled in Sutton, Surrey, had moved to London from Paisley, where his family were weavers of Paisley shawls. Arnold McNair was educated at Aldenham School, then a small school of two hundred boys. He left school at the age of seventeen in order to join his sick uncle, a solicitor with an office in Leadenhall Street in the City of London. Here he completed his articles, passed his examinations, and qualified as a solicitor. After four years, his uncle's health improved, so McNair felt able to try to realize his ambition of going up to Cambridge to read law. Seeking advice about colleges he was told of a very able teacher, W. W. Buckland at Gonville and Caius, but there was some risk as Buckland was said to be in poor health. McNair decided to risk it and won a classical scholarship to Caius which was very necessary for the McNairs were not well off. In the event, Buckland, who later became regius professor of Roman law, lasted into his eighties and took McNair on many vigorous country walks. His supervisions were excellent and McNair learned a great deal from his acute mind and his obvious delight in tackling legal problems.

When he went up to Caius in 1906 McNair was somewhat older than most of his contemporaries but enjoyed his time as an undergraduate. He achieved a double first, being senior in both parts of the law tripos, despite also being president of the union in 1909. He then returned to London where he expected to spend the rest of his life as a solicitor. On 28 March 1912 he married Marjorie (1887–1971), a social worker, daughter of Sir Clement Meacher *Bailhache, an eminent KC; they settled in Highgate and had a son and three daughters. In November 1912 Buckland went to London to offer McNair a lectureship and fellowship at Caius, which he gladly accepted. It was not common in those days for a lecturer in law to become a fellow of his college. Eventually he became also senior tutor of his college, at that time a powerful office. During the First World War he served under the coal controller, was gazetted CBE in 1918, and became secretary to the Sankey commission on the coal industry in 1919.

McNair was called to the bar of Gray's Inn in 1917. After a short spell as reader in the University of London in 1926–7 he returned to Cambridge. He considered his work as a don the most important of his many roles, and he greatly influenced and inspired generations of pupils, his interest in them continuing long after they had gone down. Easily approachable, he received everyone with the same grave and gentle courtesy. A small man, neatly built, he had a ready smile when sharing some gently amusing aspect of whatever he was discussing. He had a light voice, lacking edge, yet clear, because even in conversation his speech was measured. He was a charming and persuasive speaker and a superb lecturer. He would delineate a problem, and after a pause, as though for further reflection, lean over the lectern, eyes wide with discovery, finger raised, to indicate the correct solution in a phrase. Though sceptical about the importance of university boards and committees he served on many and had great influence on them.

His primary interest was the common law and for many years McNair lectured on contract. His classical background showed in his delight in using Latin legal maxims. But he early developed a special interest in international law, though he always urged that international lawyers should first make themselves good private-law lawyers. His constant endeavour was to distinguish and develop what he liked to call 'hard law' as opposed to speculation.

McNair's many writings covered a wide field of international law, English law, and Roman law. In addition to important articles they included: *Legal Effects of War* (1920; 4th edn, 1966), mainly a study of English law; the pioneer work *The Law of the Air*, being his Tagore lectures of 1931 (1932; 3rd edn, 1964); *Roman Law and Common Law* (with W. W. Buckland, 1936); the three volumes of *International Law Opinions* (1956), a collection, with commentary, of opinions of law officers of the crown culled from papers in the Public Record Office; *The Law of Treaties* (1938 and, as a major new treatise, 1961). He also edited the important fourth edition (1926–8) of *International Law* by L. F. L. Oppenheim. In the 1920s he co-operated with Hersch Lauterpacht in founding the *Annual Digest of International Law Cases*, later the *International Law Reports*, which in 1995 celebrated its hundredth volume.

In 1935 McNair succeeded to the Whewell chair in international law at Cambridge, but only two years later left to be vice-chancellor of Liverpool University. He served on many government committees and presided over two royal commissions. He returned to Cambridge in 1945 to be professor of comparative law. The fellows of Caius tried to persuade him to be master, in succession to John Cameron; the only time it is said when the fellows were unanimous in their choice. But he preferred to accept election in 1946 as a judge of the International Court of Justice in The Hague, in succession to Sir Cecil Hurst, and was its president from 1952 to 1955.

McNair was a very good judge, a task to which his scrupulous scholarship and shrewd, cautious, practical sense were ideally suited. He seldom delivered an individual opinion, nearly always preferring to share a broad consensus. His clarity, good sense, and independence were shown by the fact that he twice reached a decision against the United Kingdom. After his retirement from the Hague court he became the first president of the European Court of Human Rights at Strasbourg from 1959 to 1965. He was also president of an Argentine-Chilean court of arbitration to determine a disputed Andes boundary; his award (HMSO, 24 November 1966), delivered when he was eighty-one, showed his shrewdness and effectively disposed of the matter.

McNair's literary interests were Shakespeare and Samuel Johnson. He published *Dr. Johnson and the Law* in 1948 and for a long period was president of the Johnson Society. He became a fellow of the British Academy in 1939, was knighted in 1943, and created Baron McNair of Gleniffer in 1955. He took silk in 1945. He had honorary doctorates from Oxford, Birmingham, Brussels, Glasgow, Liverpool, Reading, and Salonika. In 1959 he was awarded the Manley Hudson gold medal of the American Society of International Law. He was made a bencher of Gray's Inn in 1936 and was its treasurer in 1947. He was president of the Institut de Droit International in 1949–50 and later *président d'honneur*.

McNair died at his home, Lavender Cottage, 25 Storeys Way, Cambridge, on 22 May 1975 and was cremated in Cambridge a week later. He was succeeded in the barony by his son, (Clement) John McNair (*b.* 1915).

R. Y. JENNINGS

Sources *The Times* (24 May 1975) · G. Fitzmaurice, *British Yearbook of International Law*, 47 (1977), xi–xix · personal knowledge (2004) · private information (2004) · CGPLA Eng. & Wales (1975) · Lord McNair and [A. D. McNair], *Selected papers and bibliography*, ed. C. Parry (1974) · R. Y. Jennings, *The discipline of international law: Lord McNair memorial lecture* (1976)
Likenesses P. Dodd, oils, 1959, Gray's Inn, London · W. Bird, photograph, 1964, NPG · P. Dodd, portrait, Gon. & Caius Cam. · P. Dodd, portrait, Peace Palace, The Hague · oils, U. Lpool
Wealth at death £21,150: probate, 11 July 1975, CGPLA Eng. & Wales

McNair, (John) Frederick Adolphus (1828–1910), colonial official and penal reformer, was born at Bath on 23 October 1828, the eldest son of Major Robert McNair, a staff officer. He was educated at King's College, London, and at the School of Mines. In 1844 he was commissioned into the Royal (Madras) Artillery, being promoted captain in 1858, and in 1870 major (retired). He was married twice, first in Madras on 6 November 1849 to Sarah Des Granges (1830–1903), daughter of the Revd J. Paine, with whom he had seven children. A year after her death he married on 25 October 1904, Madalena, *née* Vallance, widow of Surgeon-Major G. Williamson. The marriage in 1869 of McNair's eldest daughter, Elizabeth, to a partner in Singapore's leading firm, Guthries, provided him with an influential link at the height of his own career.

In 1853 McNair was posted to the East India Company's Straits Settlements, to command Madras native infantry detachments first in Malacca and subsequently in Labuan. In 1856, soon after becoming adjutant at the Straits artillery's Singapore headquarters, he was appointed aide-de-camp and private secretary to the governor, E. A. Blundell, and in December 1857 became executive engineer in charge of public works, controlling a labour force of 3000 convicts transported from India and Ceylon. From 1865 to 1867 McNair was back in England as deputy governor in charge of works at Woking prison; but when the Straits Settlements became a crown colony in April 1867 he returned to Singapore as colonial engineer and controller of convicts, with a seat on the legislative council. In 1869 he was appointed to the executive council and became surveyor-general in 1873. On occasion he acted as colonial secretary, and ended his official career in 1884, having been acting lieutenant-governor of Penang since 1881.

McNair gained an international reputation as a prison reformer, his gaol in Singapore drawing official visitors from Java, Siam, and Japan, and becoming a popular tourist attraction. Heavily dependent on convict labour, but compelled through lack of resources to entrust the management of convicts to two European officers—the superintendent and his assistant engineer—the Straits authorities developed an enlightened system to train skilled labour and make convicts largely responsible for supervising themselves. Regulations added by McNair in 1858-9 completed the scheme, which remained in force until convicts were finally removed from the Straits in 1873. The emphasis of the regime was on useful work rather than punishment: on training, responsibility, and eventual rehabilitation into the community as useful citizens. In 1865 the inspector general of gaols, Bengal, pronounced McNair and his two predecessors—also Madras army officers—'entitled to rank in the first class of prison officers and reformers'. An able engineer, noted for his efficiency and discipline, McNair used convict labour to build the Singapore Cathedral, Government House, a modern gaol, and military defences which were specially commended by the governor-general. He started a printing press and even organized convict squads to kill tigers. Fluent in Malay and Hindustani, McNair had great personal influence over convicts, and was called on by former convicts to settle disputes.

McNair was energetic, with a keen, enquiring mind. He was a qualified geologist and a pioneering photographer, and travelled extensively in the interior of the Straits peninsula, sending specimens of woods and metals to India and shells to the British Museum. A dashing, dark-haired, attractive man, kind and hospitable, especially to newcomers, McNair was generally popular. Ambitious and dynamic, he was the confidant of successive governors. He had travelled out on the same ship as Sir Harry Ord, the first colonial governor, and became his most trusted adviser. Ord appointed him to a three-man commission to report on the Malay states in 1871. An enthusiastic advocate of extending British influence, McNair played a significant role in governor Sir Andrew Clarke's decision to install British residents in Perak and Selangor in 1874, and went to Selangor as special commissioner to inquire into piracy. During the 1875-6 disturbances which followed the murder of the first British resident he was appointed chief commissioner in Perak. While recuperating from jungle fever in England, McNair wrote *Perak and the Malays: Sarong and Kris* (1878), a substantial book, drawing heavily on his own experience and illustrated with engravings from his own photographs. He was made CMG in May 1878. McNair visited Siam several times: he accompanied Ord to view the eclipse of the sun in 1868 as King Mongkut's guest, represented the Straits at King Chulalongkorn's coronation in 1873, and acted as secretary to Sir William Robinson's mission to Siam in 1878. McNair was awarded the order of the White Elephant by the king of Siam.

McNair, who was always known by his second forename, retired and returned permanently to Britain in 1884, where he devoted much of his time to writing on Asian topics. His second important book was *Prisoners their Own Warders* (1899), which was a detailed account of the liberal convict system. He died on 17 May 1910 at Belgrave House, Preston Park, Brighton, and was buried in Brighton cemetery.

C. M. Turnbull

Sources W. Makepeace, G. E. Brooke, and R. St J. Braddell, *One hundred years of Singapore*, 2 vols. (1921); repr. (1991) · S. Cunyngham-Brown, *The traders: a story of Britain's south-east Asian commercial adventure* (1971) · J. F. A. McNair and W. D. Bayliss, *Prisoners their own warders* (1899) · F. McNair, *Perak and the Malays* (1878); repr. (1972) · *The Times* (20 May 1910) · DNB · C. N. Parkinson, *British intervention in Malaya, 1867–1877* (1960) · C. D. Cowan, *Nineteenth-century Malaya: the origins of British political control* (1961) · C. B. Buckley, *An anecdotal history of old times in Singapore*, 2 vols. (1902); repr. in 1 vol. (1965); new edn (1984) · Straits Settlements Annual Reports, PRO, CO273 · G. Dana, *Letters of 'Extinguisher' and chronicles of St George* (1870) · m. cert.

Likenesses oils; fomerly in possession of Arthur Wyndham, 1912

Wealth at death £1440 0s. 9d.: probate, 18 June 1910, CGPLA Eng. & Wales

McNair, William Watts (1849–1889), surveyor and explorer, was born on 13 September 1849. He joined the Indian survey department on 1 September 1867. His first twelve years of service were passed with the Rajputana and Mysore topographical parties, and under majors Strahan and Thullier he learned surveying thoroughly. In the autumn of 1879 he was selected to accompany the Khyber column of the Afghan field force, and was present during the fighting before Kabul and the defence of Sherpur in 1879–80. While in Afghanistan he made valuable maps, exploring the Laghman valley and the route to Kafiristan, and he was the first officer to traverse by the same valley the route from Kabul to Jalalabad. South of Kabul he penetrated to the Logar and Wardak valleys. After the war he was engaged in the Kohat survey under Major Thomas Holdich, tracing the frontier line from Kohat to Bannu, and, across the border, surveying part of the valley of the Tochi and mapping some of the Khost district. He was soon transferred to one of the Baluchistan parties, and spent the rest of his life surveying that district; his main work was to carry a series of triangles from the Indus at Dera Ghazi Khan, near the thirtieth parallel, to Quetta.

In 1883, hearing that an Indian explorer known as the Said was about to visit Kafiristan, the mountainous area north of Kabul which was strictly closed to Europeans, McNair volunteered to accompany him disguised as a hakim, or Indian doctor. He obtained a year's leave, and the party crossed the frontier on 13 April. His plane table converted to a prescription book and this and similar ruses for a while prevented his true purpose from being discovered. They passed through the Dir country, and came by the Kotal Pass, at an elevation of 10,450 feet, to Ashreth, and thence to Chitral. He had intended to go northwards, by the Hindu Kush valleys, but after reaching the Dorah Pass and making observations in the Chitral district, he was compelled to return, after his true identity was disclosed. On his return he was officially reprimanded by the viceroy for crossing the frontier into Afghanistan without permission. He published an account of his expedition in the *Proceedings of the Royal Geographical Society* in 1884, and was awarded the Murchison grant.

McNair continued his survey work, but in 1889 was attacked by typhoid fever at Quetta. He managed to reach Mussooree, where he died on 13 August 1889. His journey to Kafiristan was widely praised by contemporaries, pleased that the Russians had been beaten to this remote area and that reports of the area by pandits, particularly the Havildar, had been confirmed.

W. A. J. ARCHBOLD, rev. ELIZABETH BAIGENT

Sources J. E. Howard, *Memoir of W. W. McNair* (1889) · *Proceedings* [Royal Geographical Society], new ser., 11 (1889), 612, 684–6 · C. E. D. Black, *A memoir on the Indian surveys, 1875–1890* (1891) · E. W. C. Sanders, *The military engineer in India*, 2 vols. (1933–5)

Macnally, Leonard (1752–1820), playwright and political informer, was born in Dublin, the only son of William Macnally, merchant of Dublin. According to biographies published in his lifetime, and probably on the basis of information provided by himself, Macnally was related to 'many of the principal Roman Catholic families in Ireland, to the family of Nethscale in Scotland, and Howard in England' (Gilliland). His grandfather is said to have 'made a very considerable personal property' in the development of Georgian Dublin but to have lost it when 'discovered' as a Roman Catholic. His father died in 1756, and as a consequence 'he owes more to nature than to art, and may strictly be said to be a self-educated man ... having received but trifling assistance from private tuition' (ibid.). He had a conversational knowledge of French, acquired through living for a time in Bordeaux. As a child he sustained an injury to the right knee which resulted in lifelong lameness, and when he was about eighteen received a gun wound which necessitated amputation of the thumb on his left hand.

In 1771 Macnally opened a grocery shop in St Mary's Lane, off Capel Street in Dublin, but he entered as a student at both the King's Inns, Dublin, and the Middle Temple, London, in 1774, and was called to the Irish bar in 1776. Finding life as a barrister in Ireland too costly, he returned to London where he was called to the bar on 30 May 1783. He married some time during this period (his wife died on 27 March 1786). He was in London during the Gordon riots in June 1780 and is said to have rescued Dr Thurloe, brother of the lord chancellor and suspected of pro-Catholic sympathies, from the rioters. The law in England, however, proved as unprofitable and unattractive as that in Ireland, and he turned to editing the *Public Ledger*, and to literary work, particularly for the theatre. An early work, *Sentimental Excursions to Windsor and other Places* (1781), ran to two editions. He brought out an opera in Dublin called *The Ruling Passion*, which he followed with a string of Covent Garden productions: *Retaliation* (1782), *Prelude* (1783), *The Coalition* (1783), *Robin Hood, or, Sherwood Forest* (1784), *Fashionable Levities* (1785), *April Fool, or, The Follies of a Night* (1786), and *Richard Coeur de Lion* (1786). All except *Prelude*, *The Coalition*, and *April Fool* were published, and several ran to multiple editions in both London and Dublin. He also published other stage works: *The Apotheosis of Punch* (1779), *Tristram Shandy* (1783), and *Critic upon Critic* (1792). On 16 January 1787 Macnally married Frances (1766–1795), daughter of William I'Anson (or Janson) of

London and Richmond, Yorkshire. Macnally wrote the song 'Sweet lass of Richmond Hill' for her. A daughter was born on 19 January 1788, and they also had a son who died in 1869. After his marriage Macnally returned only once to dramatic production, with *The Cottage Festival* (1796) in Dublin.

On his return to Ireland as a barrister Macnally specialized in defence briefs. These ranged—in 1792, for example—from acting as counsel for Napper Tandy in his action against Lord Westmorland to defending a Dublin gang accused of murder. If he found the law unprofitable it was not through lack of knowledge or skill. His legal publications included: *An Address to the Whig Club* (1790), *Rules of Evidence on Places of the Crown* (1802), and *The Justice of the Peace for Ireland* (1808), all published in Dublin. The last work, which went to two editions, was a multi-volume production that netted Macnally £2500. However, his legal ability was compromised by his political views, and after many years at the bar he was struggling to be appointed as metropolitan stipendiary.

Through the 1790s Macnally's heavy involvement with the United Irishmen occupied much of his time. His first foray into Irish politics had been in London in 1782, with the publication of *The Claims of Ireland, and the Resolutions of the Volunteers Vindicated*, which sought to cast the latter group in a whig light. He became a member of the Dublin Society of United Irishmen at or near its foundation. He was on the committee appointed to prepare a plan for reform, and assisted in the formation of branches of the United Irishmen in provincial towns, acting as secretary at an inaugural meeting at Clonmel in 1792, for example. Among other activities he published verses in the United Irish organ, the *Northern Star*, and fought a duel with Sir Jonah Barrington to vindicate their honour. In the purge of 1794 in which a fifth of the Dublin Society's membership was expelled, Macnally's name was raised, but he was defended by William Drennan: Macnally had 'not been treacherous and I don't think levity a good ground of objection' (*Analecta Hibernica*, 17.127–8). Together with Archibald Rowan and Drennan, he was involved in the publication of a collection of United Irish material which appeared in 1794.

If during his lifetime Macnally was known in the above terms he has since, however, become infamous as the most senior government informer among the United Irishmen. From about 1794, while entertaining the revolutionaries at his home in Dublin at public expense, he betrayed them to the government in a series of regular reports. While no comprehensive study of either his reports or his life has yet been completed, there is evidence that his reports, signed 'J. W.', failed to contain material sufficiently detailed to endanger his colleagues, although early in 1797 he pointed to Lord Edward Fitzgerald as one of the most active and determined of the conspirators. On other occasions reports even took an openly oppositional stance, for example, criticizing the conduct of trials at which defenders were capitally convicted, or after 1798 defending the rebels in Wexford as having treated protestants in their custody 'with great respect'

(Bartlett, 238). That some of his statements could be construed as misinformation—as when in September 1795 he told the authorities that 'Tone keeps quite retired. Study is his object and he is preparing a work for the press', when Wolfe Tone was actually in France making arrangements for the rebellion—seems likely.

However, in addition to providing regular reports, Macnally is known to have handed details of the defence to crown lawyers during the state trials in 1798 and 1803. In 1798 he defended Patrick Finney in conjunction with John Philpot Curran, who was moved to tears by his defence. On 19 September 1803 he also defended Robert Emmet, whom he had sold for £200, and visited him in gaol on the morning of his execution, comforting him with the pious reflection that he would soon meet his mother in heaven. Although the motives for his treachery will never be clear, financial considerations are likely to have been high among Macnally's motivations. He was paid irregularly until 1800, but after that date he received the substantial annual pension of £300 from the secret service fund. It was his son's attempt, after his death, to seek the continuation of this payment that finally resulted in Macnally's treachery being brought to light.

After his second wife's death in 1795 Macnally married Louisa Edgeworth, daughter of the Revd Robert Edgeworth, in May 1799. John O'Keeffe, who knew him well, described Macnally as having 'a handsome, expressive countenance, and fine sparkling dark eyes' (*Recollections of John O'Keeffe*, 1826, 1.45). Macnally died on 13 February 1820 at his home, 22 Harcourt Street, Dublin, and was buried at Donnybrook graveyard. Although he had lived as a protestant, and was openly hostile in his reports about the Roman Catholic clergy, he sent from his deathbed for a Roman Catholic priest and received absolution.

J. M. RIGG, rev. MIHAIL DAFYDD EVANS

Sources T. Gilliland, *The dramatic mirror, containing the history of the stage from the earliest period, to the present time*, 2 vols. (1808) · *The thespian dictionary, or, Dramatic biography of the present age*, 2nd edn (1805) · R. B. MacDowell, *Ireland in the age of imperialism and revolution, 1760–1801* (1979) · J. Killen, *The decade of the United Irishmen, contemporary accounts, 1791–1801* (1997) · J. Smyth, 'Dublin's political underground in the 1790s', *Parliament, politics and people*, ed. G. O'Brien (Dublin, 1989) · T. Bartlett, *The rise and fall of the Irish nation* (Dublin, 1992) · B. Henry, *The Dublin hanged* (1994) · D. Keogh, *The French disease: the Catholic church and radicalism in Ireland, 1790–1800* (Dublin, 1993) · M. Elliott, *Wolfe Tone: prophet of Irish independence* (1989) · E. W. McFarland, *Ireland and Scotland in the age of revolution* (1994) · E. Keane, P. Beryl Phair, and T. U. Sadleir, eds., *King's Inns admission papers, 1607–1867*, IMC (1982) · *N&Q*, 226 (1981), 306–8 · IGI · A. J. Webb, *A compendium of Irish biography* (1878)
Likenesses P. Maguire, stipple (after Irish School, 1775–99), NG Ire.; repro. in *Cyclopaedian Magazine* (1808) · engraving, repro. in Keogh, *The French disease*

MacNalty, Sir Arthur Salusbury (1880–1969), public health administrator, was born on 20 October 1880 at Glenridding, Westmorland, the son of Francis Charles MacNalty, physician, and his wife, Hester Emma Frances, daughter of the Revd Arthur D. Gardner, fellow of Jesus College, Oxford. He spent his early boyhood in the Lake District. He was educated privately in the south while his father was in general medical practice in Winchester. He

was first at Hartley College, Southampton, and later in St Catherine's Society, Oxford, before entering Corpus Christi College, Oxford. He was therefore rather late in taking a degree in natural science (physiology), in which he obtained a second class in 1904; he became MB at the age of twenty-seven, and DM four years later in 1911. In 1913 he married Dorothea (d. 1968), the daughter of the Revd C. H. Simpkinson de Wesselow. They had two daughters.

MacNalty became MRCP in 1925 and was elected a fellow in 1930, having taken the diploma in public health in 1927. His was a slightly unorthodox career in preventive medicine, as he chose to work in the central health department, unlike most of the leading figures in public health, who rose through the services of local authorities in the manner of Sir Arthur Newsholme and Sir George Newman. MacNalty began his career as a clinical physician following a special interest in chest diseases, which led him to the Brompton Hospital, London. Chest diseases at that time meant mainly pulmonary tuberculosis and the central health department—then the Local Government Board—was engaged in the establishment of county and county borough services for the tuberculous. MacNalty was recruited in 1913 to the small team of specialists required to promote a 'sanatorium' and 'dispensary' service throughout the country. Most of his subsequent career was centred upon this service and he did not move around the special sections as most of the more generally trained medical staff were expected to do.

For many years afterwards both medical practitioners and the lay public were seldom aware of the dominant position of tuberculosis control in local authority health responsibilities from 1910 to 1948. MacNalty played a large part in the central guidance of the development of those services. A succession of departmental reports written by MacNalty, culminating in the 1932 report on tuberculosis, testify to his special interest in the epidemiology and treatment of tuberculous infections. He had, however, contributed substantially to the Ministry of Health's work on other infections—especially virus infections of the central nervous system. He was a close friend of Sydney A. Monckton Copeman, the last member of the departmental staff to become a fellow of the Royal Society, and they worked together on virus diseases. It has been said of MacNalty that he was a medical reporter before all else.

MacNalty was a member of the staff transferred to the new Ministry of Health in 1919, and in 1932 he became one of the department's senior medical officers. With the chief medical officer, Sir George Newman, often away, it was thought necessary to have a substitute, and MacNalty was chosen as the unofficial deputy, possibly on account of his compliant characteristics. This in effect made him Newman's heir apparent, and he eventually succeeded him in 1935. At that time MacNalty was not well known among the public health medical staff in the country, but his standing in his own field of medicine was high.

MacNalty was chief medical officer from 1935 for a little over five years. During this period there were preparations for civilian services in time of war, and the Ministry of Health became involved in the hospital building programmes of local authorities and in the development of specialist services. In December 1936 MacNalty was asked to prepare proposals for the provision of specialist and other diagnostic services. He reported that local authority services 'were a more appropriate basis for a comprehensive scheme than the National Health Insurance Scheme', a conclusion supported by his medical colleagues in the department (Webster, 21). The Public Health Laboratory Service was developed from a wartime emergency service, on the basis of a survey initiated by MacNalty. Others were involved in these changes and MacNalty has been given little of the credit for them. In a departmental reorganization in 1940 he retired early, at the age of sixty, to make way for the more dynamic leadership of Wilson Jameson.

In 1941 MacNalty was commissioned by the Nuffield College Reconstruction Survey to contribute to its investigations into the reform of local government. His *Reform of the Public Health Services* was published in 1943. In the pamphlet MacNalty discusses general public health, the central health authorities, and the reconstruction of health and medical services on a comprehensive regional plan. Of particular interest is his claim that in 1939 he had written a memorandum on research in preventive and social medicine for the faculty of medical studies at Oxford University, in which he advocated the establishment of a professorship of preventive and social medicine. The first chair and institute of social medicine was established at Oxford in 1943, when the post was taken up by John Ryle (1889–1950).

MacNalty then turned to the work for which he will be mainly remembered, as editor-in-chief of the official medical history of the war, which he completed shortly before his death in 1969. He gave this work the same devoted attention he had always applied to his writing, and at the same time he indulged his real passion for history, especially medical history. His knowledge of both history and literature was exceptional and his writing extensive.

At the end of his long life (MacNalty died at his home in Bocketts Down Road, Epsom, Surrey, on 17 April 1969), perhaps none remained who had known his whole range of activity and therefore could make a fair assessment. He was an unassertive and reserved man, few of whose staff knew him well, despite his occasional social gestures. Yet he was well liked by those few who came to know him in his later life. He was unfortunate in being thrust into the most responsible medical administrative post in the country at a time when it was exposed to unprecedented strains. One felt he stepped aside with relief; nevertheless, there are few who are prepared to cede leadership gracefully in that way and turn to another career as he did. MacNalty was an honorary fellow of many societies, including the Royal Society of Edinburgh, and was also a freeman of the City of London. He was knighted in 1936.

GEORGE E. GODBER, *rev.* MICHAEL BEVAN

Sources *The Times* (18 Sept 1969) • *The Times* (21 Sept 1969) • personal knowledge (2004) • private information (2004) • C. Webster, *The health services since the war*, 1 (1988) • WWW
Archives Wellcome L. | CAC Cam., A. V. Hill correspondence

Wealth at death £46,457: probate, 25 Nov 1969, *CGPLA Eng. & Wales*

MacNamara, Daniel (1720–1800), lawyer and Roman Catholic activist, was born into the Roman Catholic MacNamara family of Ardcloney, near Killaloe, co. Clare, Ireland; his mother was Mary O'Callaghan. No information has been uncovered about his education. Although in later life he was generally known as Counsellor MacNamara (indicating that he was a barrister), his name is not to be found in any of the registers of the inns of court in London or in the admissions to the King's Inns in Dublin. The probability, then, is that he was an attorney or a solicitor.

Although Catholic lawyers, whether barristers, attorneys, or solicitors, were, prior to the act of 1792, prevented from practising in the courts, they could follow what was known as a chamber practice, in conveyancing, giving legal opinions, lobbying, and as legal advisers. In addition to a highly successful career as a conveyancer, MacNamara was the London agent for several public men in Ireland, including the Irish chief justice, Lord Clonmel, and these retained him at a fixed fee for the purpose of keeping them informed of the political events of the day. MacNamara ensured that he was always in touch with current affairs by keeping open house and table at his villa in Streatham, Surrey, where we are told the élite of London society met and the prince of Wales and men of the highest rank in both houses of parliament were happy to patronize MacNamara's hospitable board.

MacNamara took a deep interest in advancing the cause of his co-religionists, both English and Irish, but it has to be said he was well paid for his services, receiving on one occasion, as a reward from the Irish Catholic Committee, the then colossal sum of £15,500. From the late 1760s onwards he was retained by the Catholic Committee in Dublin to lobby on their behalf with the British government in connection with the various relief measures for Irish Catholics passed between 1774 and 1793. He was also involved, with Edmund Burke, in behind-the-scenes lobbying for the English Relief Act of 1778, under which religious toleration was granted to English Catholics and the penal measures in regard to Catholic ownership of property were repealed.

Although MacNamara was noted for his conviviality, Charles O'Conor, one of the principal Catholic activists in Ireland at that time, found him, as a correspondent, 'a cold one and too laconic for information' (*Letters*, 217). MacNamara died at his home in Streatham on 20 January 1800 and was buried in Streatham churchyard. He was survived by his wife, Catherine. A high earner in his time, he was also a big spender, and by the time of his death his fortune may have been attenuated, for he requested in his will to be buried privately and with as little expense as possible.

PATRICK FAGAN

Sources N. C. MacNamara, *The story of an Irish Sept* [*Macnamara*] (1896), 298–300 • V. B. L. Cloncurry, *Personal recollections of the life and times: with extracts from the correspondence of Valentine, Lord Cloncurry* (1849), 40 • *Letters of Charles O'Conor of Belanagare*, ed. R. E. Ward, J. F.

Wrynne, and C. C. Ward (1988) · C. C. Trench, *Grace's card: Irish Catholic landlords, 1690–1800* (1997) · P. Fagan, *Catholics in a protestant country* (1998), 117 · R. D. Edwards, ed., 'The minute book of the Catholic Committee, 1773–1792', *Archivium Hibernicum*, 9 (1942), 1–172 · will, PRO, PROB 11/1337, sig. 128 · memorial tablet, Streatham church, Streatham, London · NL Ire., MS G.O. 143, fol. 26

Wealth at death probably not substantial; requested cheap, private burial; all to wife except one year's wages to servants: will, PRO, PROB 11/1337, sig. 128

Macnamara, James (1768–1826), naval officer, was descended from an ancient family in Ireland. He entered the navy in 1782 on board the *Gibraltar* (80 guns), bearing the broad pennant of Sir Richard Bickerton. In her he went to the East Indies, where he was taken by Sir Edward Hughes into the *Superb*, his flagship, in which he was present at the action off Cuddalore on 20 June 1783. He afterwards served in the *Europa* flagship at Jamaica, and was promoted lieutenant on 1 December 1788. In 1790 he was in the *Excellent* with Captain Gell, and afterwards in the *Victory*, Lord Hood's flagship. He was again with Hood in the *Victory* in 1793, and on 22 October was promoted commander by him. He was shortly afterwards appointed acting captain of the *Bombay Castle* (74 guns); from her he exchanged into the frigate *Southampton* (32 guns), which he commanded in 1795–6, mostly under Nelson, in the Gulf of Genoa. His post rank was confirmed to date from 6 October 1795. In the battle of Cape St Vincent on 14 February 1797 the *Southampton* was the repeating frigate of the centre of the line. A few months later she returned to England and was paid off. Macnamara was then appointed to the *Cerberus* (32 guns) on the coast of Ireland, later on in the Bay of Biscay, and afterwards in the West Indies; everywhere Macnamara maintained his reputation as a brave and successful officer. After the peace of Amiens the *Cerberus* was for some time employed on the coast of San Domingo, and was paid off in February 1803.

On 6 April 1803 Macnamara fought a duel at Chalk Farm, London, with a Colonel Montgomery. The quarrel arose out of an accidental encounter between the two men's dogs in Hyde Park the same morning. Both men were wounded, Montgomery mortally. The coroner's inquest brought in a verdict of manslaughter; Macnamara was arrested, and tried at the Old Bailey on 22 April. His defence was that the provocation and insult came from Montgomery. He called naval officers, including Hood and Nelson, as witnesses to his being 'the reverse of a quarrelsome man'. The jury returned a verdict of 'not guilty'.

On the renewal of the war Macnamara was appointed to the *Dictator* (64 guns), which he commanded in the North Sea for two years. He afterwards commanded the *Edgar* (74 guns), in the Baltic, and in the Great Belt with Sir Richard Goodwin Keats in 1808. In 1809 he was appointed to the *Berwick* (74 guns), again for service in the North Sea, and on the north coast of France. On 24 March 1811 he chased and, with a small squadron of cruising frigates, drove on shore and destroyed the French frigate *Amazone*, near Cape Barfleur. He was promoted rear-admiral on 4 June 1814, but had no further service. He married, on 26 January 1818, Henrietta, daughter of Henry King of Askham Hall, Westmorland, and widow of Colonel the Hon. George Carleton

(brother of Lord Dorchester), killed at Bergen-op-Zoom in 1814. Macnamara died on 15 January 1826 at Clifton, Bristol. J. K. LAUGHTON, *rev.* ANDREW LAMBERT

Sources D. Syrett and R. L. DiNardo, *The commissioned sea officers of the Royal Navy, 1660–1815*, rev. edn, Occasional Publications of the Navy RS, 1 (1994) · C. Oman, *Nelson* (1947) · J. Marshall, *Royal naval biography*, 1/2 (1823), 685–91 · *GM*, 1st ser., 96/1 (1826), 178–9 · *The dispatches and letters of Vice-Admiral Lord Viscount Nelson*, ed. N. H. Nicolas, 7 vols. (1844–6)

McNamara, Thomas (1808–1892), Roman Catholic priest and college head, was born near Slane, co. Meath. After education at Navan seminary, Meath, he entered St Patrick's College, Maynooth, co. Kildare, in 1825. There he was ordained in 1833. In 1834 he and some associates established Castleknock College, in co. Dublin; after affiliating the college in 1839 with the Congregation of the Mission, an order founded by St Vincent de Paul, they began to give missions throughout Ireland, the first being at Athy, co. Kildare, in 1842.

McNamara took a great interest in deaf mute people, made a special study of ways of educating them, and wrote pamphlets on the subject. He helped to found the Catholic Institution for Deaf and Dumb Mutes at Cabra, near Dublin, in 1846. He was appointed superior of Castleknock College and visitor of the Irish Province of the Congregation of the Mission in 1864, and in 1868 was made rector of the Irish College in Paris, a post which he kept for over twenty years, resigning in 1889. He was the author of various works for the training of Roman Catholic clergy. These include: *Programmes of Sermons and Instructions* (1881), *Sacred Rhetoric, or, The Art of Rhetoric as Applied to the Preaching of the Word of God* (1882), *Enchiridion clericorum: being a Rule of Life for Ecclesiastics* (1882), *Allocutions, or, Short Addresses on Liturgical Observations and Ritual Functions* (1884), and *Pax vobis: being a Popular Exposition of the Seven Sacraments* (1886). McNamara died at St Joseph's, Blackrock, co. Dublin, on 8 March 1892, and was buried on 11 March at Castleknock cemetery. P. L. NOLAN, *rev.* DAVID HUDDLESTON

Sources *Freeman's Journal* [Dublin] (10 March 1892), 5 · *Castleknock College Chronicle* (June 1892), 5–6 · *Irish Daily Independent* (10 March 1892) · M. Purcell, *The story of the Vincentians* (1973)

Macnamara, Thomas James (1861–1931), educationist and politician, was born on 23 August 1861 at the barracks, Montreal, Canada, the son of Thomas Macnamara (*d.* 1899), soldier, and his wife, Elizabeth Harvey.

Following his father's posting to Exeter in 1869 Macnamara was enrolled first at the city's Mint School, then at the St Thomas School. At the age of thirteen he was indentured there as a pupil teacher; he won a queen's scholarship to Borough Road College, which he attended throughout 1880 and 1881. After teaching at the Friends' school, Lancaster, and Spring Grove School, Huddersfield, he became headmaster of the Avon Vale board school, Bristol, in 1884, retaining the post for eight years. Here he secured a reputation as an innovative teacher, was elected to the executive of the National Union of Teachers (NUT) (having made his mark, with James Yoxall, as one of the so-called Indefatigables) and began to contribute to the daily and monthly press. In 1886 he married Rachel Burr

Thomas James Macnamara (1861–1931), by Walter Stoneman, 1920

(*d.* 1955), elder daughter of Angus Cameron, formerly of Aberdeen. Their daughter, Elsie, was born in 1887; their sons, Neil, Brian, and Terence in 1891, 1894, and 1905. In March 1892 he gave up teaching and moved to London on his appointment as editor of the union's weekly journal, *The Schoolmaster*.

In the 1890s, as payment by results was discarded, the provision of an adequate national education system was becoming urgent. Macnamara deployed *The Schoolmaster* to advance NUT causes including better school attendance, teacher superannuation, improved conditions for rural teachers (especially women), and to call for the end of the practice by which children in northern England were permitted to spend half the school day in factories. In November 1894 he was elected as a Progressive to the London school board; here he added the provision of school meals and the abolition of casual child employment to his causes. He succeeded to the presidency of the NUT in April 1896 just as the education minister, Sir John Gorst, was attempting to begin the replacement of the local units of education administration (school boards, set up under the 1870 Education Act and the much older voluntary religious agencies) by county authorities. Macnamara risked a split between voluntary and urban board teacher members by expressing some approval of the bill, only to see it abandoned by the government in June.

In December 1900, when he entered the House of Commons as Liberal MP for North Camberwell (having unsuccessfully contested Deptford in 1895), Macnamara was confident that, through the efforts made by the NUT leadership in highlighting the neglect of rural schools, the membership was now ready to accept county authorities. With his NUT MP colleagues, James Yoxall (Liberal) and Ernest Gray (Unionist), he joined an advisory education group which encouraged A. J. Balfour, soon to be prime minister, to press ahead with comprehensive educational reform. The school boards were duly abolished, county authorities established throughout England and Wales, and voluntary schools permitted to draw on the rates. Macnamara, aware of strong vestigial support among the NUT membership for *ad hoc* administrative units, strove to preserve the London school board, but Balfour was resolute in completing his work; conceding at last that the London county council might effectively add education to its other tasks, Macnamara, still a member, attended the last meeting of the board on 28 April 1904.

Public concern about the rejection of Second South African War volunteers on health grounds provided Macnamara with opportunities to refine the education system. In 1903 the government introduced the so-called model course to improve the physical condition of schoolchildren. Macnamara was instrumental in the appointment of an interdepartmental committee, which introduced more rational physical exercise on a permanent basis. As a witness at the interdepartmental committee on physical deterioration (1904) he advocated local authority action to promote child health and nutrition. The Liberal leadership, however, considered that its priority was the phasing out of voluntary schools and, returned to power, introduced a bill to secure this aim. Macnamara, regarding Balfour's act as more practical, had refused office, but as the bill foundered on House of Lords opposition he was active in the rescue of clauses providing for medical inspections and school meals. Appointed parliamentary secretary to the Local Government Board in February 1907, he resigned from the NUT executive and as editor of *The Schoolmaster*.

What now seemed to be a promising government career was diverted when Asquith succeeded Campbell-Bannerman in April 1908. Macnamara was appointed parliamentary and financial secretary to the Admiralty, a post he was to hold, in peace and war, for twelve years. Though the new prime minister chose to dismiss his achievements, Churchill (first lord 1911–15) left the management of House of Commons business increasingly in his hands, and Balfour (1915–16) commended his tact and judgement in dealing with parliamentary questions on wartime naval expenditure. Later his main functions were to defend the government's record on naval losses, to explain its shipbuilding initiatives and to deal with the increasingly acrimonious issues of labour and pay.

As the war ended Macnamara, now a Coalition Liberal and a close associate of Lloyd George, urgently advocated the adoption of radical policies of social renewal, but the prime minister was preoccupied with the peace settlement and the Irish question. At last, following his valiant effort on behalf of an inadequate coalition candidate in the Spen Valley by-election of December 1919, Macnamara was appointed to the cabinet as minister of labour in March 1920. He was at once confronted with rising unemployment. Until the fall of the coalition in October 1922 he administered what had been set up as a contributory system under the Unemployment Insurance Acts while giving sympathetic consideration to former servicemen; from June 1921, by permitting uncovenanted benefit to be paid, he in effect introduced the principle of automatic entitlement to government assistance for the unemployed.

Macnamara lost his Camberwell seat at the general election of October 1924, and despite efforts to secure re-election at Walsall in 1925 and in 1929 he did not return to parliament. He nevertheless played a significant part in Lloyd George's drive to develop new plans for agricultural and industrial renewal ahead of the 1929 election, drawing on them for his own last published work, *If only we would: some reflections on our social shortcomings with some suggestions for their removal* (1926).

Tall, energetic, cheerful, and one of the most effective platform speakers of his day, Macnamara, in Lloyd George's opinion, 'had a notable career and left his mark on the lives of millions through his unemployment measures' (Taylor, 163). He received the honorary degrees of LLD (St Andrews) in 1898 and MA (Oxford) in 1907, and was sworn of the privy council in 1911. He died on 3 December 1931 at 43 Wimpole Street, London, and his remains were cremated at Golders Green crematorium on 8 December. Rachel Macnamara, one of the first women JPs, survived until 1955.   ROBIN BETTS

Sources R. Betts, *Dr Macnamara, 1861–1931* (1999) · 'In the days of my youth: chapters of autobiography LXXIV: T. J. Macnamara LLD', *Mainly About People* (11 Nov 1899) · 'Thanks to Dr Macnamara', *The Schoolmaster* (6 April 1907) · 'Well-known teachers at work:VI: Mr T. J. Macnamara', *Practical Teacher* (Feb 1892), 424–8 · PRO, parliamentary education committee, 2/5/1901, ED 24/15 65a · *Hansard 5L* (1921) [138.994–1000] · bap. cert. · will, 1927 · C. Hazelhurst and C. Woodland, *Guide to the papers of British cabinet ministers* (1974) · R. S. Churchill, ed., *Winston S. Churchill*, companion vol. 2/3 (1969) · *South London Observer and Camberwell and Peckham Times* (9 Dec 1931) · *My darling pussy: the letters of Lloyd George and Frances Stevenson, 1913–1941*, ed. A. J. P. Taylor (1975) · *CGPLA Eng. & Wales* (1932) · *Daily Telegraph* (9 Dec 1931) · *Schoolmaster and Woman Teacher's Chronicle* (10 Dec 1931) · *Education* (11 Dec 1931)

Archives Bodl. Oxf., corresp. with Viscount Addison · HLRO, corresp. with Andrew Bonar Law · HLRO, letters to David Lloyd George

Likenesses B. Stone, photograph, 1901, NPG · W. Stoneman, photograph, 1920, NPG [*see illus.*] · F. C. Gould, cartoon, repro. in *London* (21 May 1896) · F. C. Gould, cartoon, repro. in *Picture Politics* (Aug 1908) · Matt, portrait, repro. in *Daily Sketch* (28 July 1921) · Spy [L. Ward], caricature, watercolour study, NPG; repro. in *VF* (9 Oct 1907)

Wealth at death £1262 8s. 6d.: probate, 23 Jan 1932, *CGPLA Eng. & Wales*

McNaught, William (1813–1881), mechanical engineer, was born on 27 May 1813 at Sneddon, Paisley, Renfrewshire, the son of John McNaught, steam engineer, and his wife, Mary Lindsay. His parents moved in 1820 to Glasgow, where he received a good education. As he wished to follow in his father's footsteps he was apprenticed at fourteen to Robert Napier at the Vulcan works, Washington

Street, Glasgow. In the evenings he attended science classes at Anderson's University. He showed such competence that when he had completed his apprenticeship at nineteen, he was offered the position of being in charge of the Fort-Gloster mills on the Hooghly River in India. He set off there immediately and remained for four years, but in 1836 returned to Scotland because the climate was affecting his health.

In 1830 McNaught's father had added a revolving cylinder to the steam engine indicator (which traces a diagram of the steam pressure in the cylinder of a steam engine) for carrying the paper on which the trace was drawn. This was a great improvement over James Watt's original device and was awarded the silver medal of the Society of Arts for Scotland because it was much simpler and easier to use. McNaught joined his father in 1838 to manufacture these machines at Robertson Street in Glasgow and helped to introduce them to the various engineers and factories in that area. While advising textile manufacturers on the use of the indicator, McNaught became aware of the need for smoother running, more powerful, and more economical engines. The prevailing type was the single cylinder low-pressure beam engine based on the designs of James Watt, originating about 1784. Arthur Woolf had added a second cylinder alongside the original one to compound them but this layout was unsatisfactory because there was only a short steam pipe connecting the two cylinders with the result that there was considerable overlap of pressures and little improvement in fuel consumption. McNaught took out a patent in 1845 (no. 11001) for an elegant solution which involved few changes to the original engine, though new boilers supplying steam at higher pressures were necessary. He placed a smaller high-pressure cylinder midway between the fulcrum of the beam and the connecting rod on an ordinary beam engine, retaining the original cylinder as the low-pressure one. This layout reduced the pressures on the bearing surfaces and, through the more equal steam pressures in the two cylinders, gave a smoother running engine, especially when compared with William Fairbairn's high-pressure expansive engine. McNaught's primary aims were to increase the power of engines and lessen the strains on the parts. More economical performance was also anticipated. This exceeded his expectations, for some engines gave a saving of fuel of up to 40 per cent (because the long steam pipe connecting the two cylinders acted as a receiver). His layout quickly became very popular, so that in 1849 he left Glasgow and moved to Manchester because orders in Lancashire were so numerous.

McNaught took out at least five further patents, including ones for a steam generator, improved slide valves, and a design of a diagonal engine. That in 1859 for a different arrangement of his compounding cylinders was not as successful as his first which was claimed to have been one of the greatest improvements to the steam engine since it left the hands of James Watt. McNaught was one of the original promoters in 1859 of the Boiler Insurance and Steam Power Co. Ltd. He was a member of the board of directors and was chairman from 1865 until shortly before his death. He died at his home, 16 Clarendon Road, Chorlton upon Medlock, Manchester, on 8 January 1881 after a long illness and was buried in Glasgow. He left a widow, Margaret, whom he had married in Glasgow in 1848, and a grown-up family. Two of his sons carried on their father's business.   RICHARD L. HILLS

Sources *The Engineer*, 51 (1881) · *Engineering* (21 Jan 1881) · A. Rigg, *Practical treatise on the steam engine* (1888) · R. L. Hills, *Power from steam: a history of the stationary steam engine* (1989) · G. B. Williamson, 'Steam engine building in Rochdale', *Transactions of Rochdale Literary and Scientific Society*, 22 (1944–6) · R. S. Burn, *The steam engine: its history and mechanism* (1854) · C. Day, *Indicator diagrams and engine and boiler testing* (1895) · CGPLA Eng. & Wales (1881) · census returns, 1851

Wealth at death under £4000: probate, 27 May 1881, *CGPLA Eng. & Wales*

McNaughtan [McNaghten], **Daniel** (1802/3–1865), criminal lunatic, born in Scotland (probably in Glasgow), was a wood-turner and political radical in Glasgow prior to the events of 20 January 1843 which earned him a place in the legal history of the plea of insanity, as the eponymist of the McNaughtan (or McNaghten) rules. On that day he shot Edward Drummond, private secretary to Sir Robert Peel, mistaking him for the prime minister. Five days later Drummond died of complications from his pistol wound. The assassin was charged with murder in the first degree and tried on 3 and 4 March at the central criminal court in London, the Old Bailey.

McNaughtan's defence rested upon the state of his mind at the time he committed the act, not upon the denial of the act itself. His counsel, Alexander Cockburn, proclaimed McNaughtan 'the victim of a fierce and fearful delusion' that caused him to believe the tories were his enemies. The prosecution argued that McNaughtan was merely insane on the subject of politics and, unless proven to be generally incapable of knowing 'right from wrong', was legally responsible for his crime. The defence responded by introducing the testimony of nine medical experts. When the prosecution chose not to counter this evidence the trial ended, and the jury found McNaughtan 'not guilty by reason of insanity'.

The public—including Queen Victoria, whose assailant in 1840, Edward Oxford, had been found insane—were alarmed by McNaughtan's acquittal. They feared that madmen could now kill with impunity. Debate in the House of Lords established a precedent that continued to exert a powerful influence in Anglo-American law throughout the twentieth century: the 'right from wrong' rules were the sole test of criminal responsibility until 1957, when they were largely replaced by the Scottish concept of 'diminished responsibility'. In the United States the McNaughtan rules remained in effect in twenty-four states at the end of the twentieth century.

Most scholarly interest in McNaughtan has limited itself to legal and psychiatric difficulties in applying the rules. Until recently McNaughtan was universally regarded as a criminal lunatic. New evidence has emerged, however, suggesting McNaughtan was a political activist who was financed to assassinate the prime minister. Banking

Daniel McNaughtan (1802/3–1865), by unknown engraver, pubd 1843

records from the Glasgow and Ship Bank indicate that McNaughtan accumulated most of the £750 found on him at the time of the shooting during the two years prior to the assassination, which he spent travelling round Great Britain and France. There is strong evidence that McNaughtan was intensely involved in radical politics. In 1835, when Abram Duncan came to work as a wood-turner in McNaughtan's shop, Duncan was already a well-known Chartist leader. In the next five years, however, Duncan became the chief spokesman for the trade unions in Glasgow and the west of Scotland. In addition, McNaughtan's reading ticket from the mechanics' institution in Glasgow indicates the former actor and medical student was familiar with the symptoms of insanity, and that he may have been feigning insanity.

On 13 March 1843 Daniel McNaughtan was sent to Bethlem Hospital, St George-in-the-Fields, London, to 'await the Crown's Pleasure'—the equivalent of a life sentence. McNaughtan spent the next twenty-one years confined in a stone cell measuring 8½ by 10½ feet. When Broadmoor opened in 1864 McNaughtan was transferred to the new state criminal lunatic asylum at Crowthorne in Berkshire. By the age of fifty his health had deteriorated and he complained of 'palpitations of the heart'. On 3 May 1865 he 'gradually sank and died at 1:10 a.m.'. A forgotten man, Daniel McNaughtan was buried on the grounds of the asylum. *The Times*, which had devoted much attention to his crime, took no notice of his passing.

RICHARD MORAN

Sources R. Moran, *Knowing right from wrong: the insanity defense of Daniel McNaughtan* (1981) · A. Walk and D. J. West, *Daniel McNaughtan: his trial and the aftermath* (1977) · *The letters of Queen Victoria*, ed. A. C. Benson and Lord Esher [R. B. Brett], 3 vols., 1st ser. (1907), vol. 1 · N. Gash, *Sir Robert Peel: the life of Sir Robert Peel after 1830* (1972) · d. cert.

Archives Bank of Scotland, Edinburgh, archives department, deposit receipt, 5/2/1837–11/7/1844 · Bethlem Royal Hospital, Beckenham, Kent, archives, casebook · Bethlem Royal Hospital, Beckenham, Kent, archives, file · Broadmoor Hospital, Berkshire, archives, casebook · Broadmoor Hospital, Berkshire, archives, file · Faculty of Procurators, Glasgow, annotated roll of Faculty of Procurators in Glasgow, 1668–1874 · PRO, central criminal court, Crim. 1/4/27015 | Bank of Scotland, Edinburgh, archives department, Glasgow Ship, interest receipts, 1/4/1840–29/5/1843, book 2 · Bank of Scotland, Edinburgh, archives department, Trongate branch, 5/2/1837–17/7/1844 · BL, BM 40434/310 · BL, BM 40435/301 · BL, BM 40524/179 · BL, BM 40525/226 · BL, BM 40525/229 · BL, Peel MSS, Add. MS BM 40523/221 · BL, Peel MSS, Add. MS BM 40524/18 · BL, Peel MSS, Add. MS BM 40524/47 · Bodl. Oxf., Graham MSS · HSBC Group Archives, London, London Joint Stock Bank private ledger · PRO, Metropolitan Police, MEPOL 3/17/XL06891 · PRO, central criminal court, Crim. 1/4/x206754 · PRO, Metropolitan Police, MEPOL 3/46/XL06754 · Royal Arch., Queen Victoria's letters, RA 13/61, 62, 66, 14/8, RB 6/32

Likenesses wood-engraving, pubd 1843, NPG [*see illus.*]

Macnaughtan, Sarah Broom (1864–1916), nurse and author, was born at Downhill Gardens in Partick, Lanarkshire, Scotland, on 26 October 1864. She was the fourth daughter of Peter Macnaughtan JP, at the time of her birth secretary of the British India Steam Navigation Company, and his wife, Julia Blackman. Educated at home, she also studied music and painting. She was active in the women's suffrage movement, though never a militant. Travelling, caring for the unfortunate and wounded, and writing characterized her energetic life. A small, delicate-looking woman, only slightly over 5 feet tall, but indefatigable and with substantial private means, she travelled widely in Europe, North and South America, India, Egypt, South Africa, and the Near and Far East from her early adulthood.

Though not a trained nurse, Sarah Macnaughtan tended victims of Balkan wartime atrocities in the 1890s and worked among London's East End poor before serving during the Second South African War as a Red Cross volunteer. She was visiting Canada in 1914 when the First World War began and immediately returned home, where she studied district nursing in Walworth for a month, and on 20 September 1914 sailed for Belgium as head orderly in Mabel Annie St Clair Stobart's hospital unit. After serving courageously during the siege of Antwerp, she left the city on 8 October as it was falling, and on 12 October joined Dr Hector Munro's volunteer ambulance unit at Ostend. The unit moved to Furnes on 22 October; there, early in 1915, with three Belgian sisters, she opened a railway station soup kitchen to provide the otherwise neglected soldiers *en route* for French hospitals with soup, coffee, bread, and dry socks. Shelled out of Furnes at the end of March, she established a second kitchen at Adinkerke station, near La Panne. In summer 1915, refusing pay (she paid her own expenses throughout the war) and although personally disillusioned with war, she delivered thirty-five lectures at munition centres throughout Britain to encourage support of the war effort. In October 1915 she rejoined the Red Cross to serve in Russia but once there found herself frustrated by official delays; her attempt in February 1916 to serve in Persia was aborted by what proved fatal illness. In 1915 she had been awarded the Belgian order of Leopold, and in June 1916 was promoted from honorary associate to lady of grace of the order of the hospital of St John of Jerusalem in England.

Sarah Macnaughtan's literary achievements included a sustained career as writer of popular fiction published both in Britain and the United States, starting in 1894 with the story 'Tom Cophetua' in *Temple Bar*. Her writing is eminently readable, polished, and mildly witty, even if not characteristically profound or innovative. Besides stories in periodicals and one collection, she published thirteen novels, beginning with *Selah Harrison* in 1898, the tale of a reformed Scottish prodigal who dies as a missionary after doing good works in London's East End, and ending with the character studies presented mainly through dialogue of *Some Elderly People and their Young Friends* (1915). Her most skilful novel is the social comedy *The Fortune of Christina M'Nab* (1901), a genial satire of English ways told as the story of a Scottish heiress who ascends the social ladder. Written after a beloved elder brother whom she had gone to Argentina to nurse died of his injuries, *A Lame Dog's Diary* (1905) is a successful *Cranford*-type tale of village life, told through the eyes of a disabled brother who is blessed with a devoted sister. Also drawn from her life transmuted to fiction is the sombre *They who Question*, originally published anonymously in 1914, reissued under signature in 1916, and reflecting the views of an ultimately deeply religious Anglican. Working out her doubts through the characters, she wrestled in this novel with the problem of evil existent despite a loving God. Macnaughtan also published non-fiction, most notably *A Woman's Diary of the War* (1915), recounting principally her work in Belgium and representing but a portion of the closely written diaries she kept for twenty-five years. A more extensive version, *My War Experiences in Two Continents*, including her Russian and Persian ordeals, was posthumously published by her niece, Mrs Lionel Salmon, in 1919, with a pleasant-faced photograph of Macnaughtan (perhaps in her late twenties) as frontispiece. The same portrait appears in the posthumous *My Canadian Memories* (1920), edited by Beatrice Home, reflections on Canadian history and contemporary conditions from her pre-war visit.

Sarah Macnaughtan died at her long-time home, 1 Norfolk Street, Park Lane West, London, on 24 July 1916 of sprue complicated by pernicious anaemia, and was buried in her family's plot at Chart Sutton, Kent.

HARRIET BLODGETT

Sources S. B. Macnaughtan, *A woman's diary of the war* (1915) · S. Macnaughtan, *My war experiences in two continents*, ed. Mrs L. Salmon (1919) · *The Times* (25 July 1916) · *The Times* (29 July 1916), 11 · 'Miss S. Macnaughtan', *The Bookman*, 50 (1916), 162–4 · WWW · J. Sutherland, *The Longman companion to Victorian fiction* (1988) ·

J. Grimes and D. Daims, *Novels in English by women, 1891–1920: a preliminary checklist* (1981) • *The Times* (15 July 1916) • b. cert. • d. cert.
Likenesses E. O. Hoppé, photograph, *c.*1880–1889, repro. in *The Bookman* • E. O. Hoppé, photograph, repro. in Macnaughtan, *My war experiences in two continents*, ed. Salmon
Wealth at death £12,112 7s. 11d.: probate, 27 Sept 1916, *CGPLA Eng. & Wales*

McNaughton, Andrew George Latta (1887–1966), army officer, scientist, and public servant, was born at Moosomin, Saskatchewan, Canada, on 25 February 1887, the elder son of Robert Duncan McNaughton of Moosomin, a prosperous storekeeper of Scottish highland descent, and his wife, Christina Mary Ann, daughter of William Armour, also of Scottish descent. McNaughton grew up in the free pioneer life of the prairies, and was educated at Moosomin public school, Bishop's College School, Lennoxville, Quebec, and McGill University, Montreal (*c.*1907–12), where he read electrical engineering (BSc, 1910), carried out research on high-voltage electricity (MSc, 1912), and remained as lecturer.

He had qualified for a British army commission, but served in the Canadian militia, and was placed on active service in August 1914. He served in France and Belgium as battery commander and heavy artillery brigade commander, and he made his mark as corps counter-battery officer (1917–18). In this novel role he developed successful techniques of flash spotting, sound-ranging, aerial reconnaissance, intelligence recording, and artillery tactics, which much affected military thinking and procedures in these fields. According to one British officer he was 'probably the best and most scientific gunner in any army in the world' (Dear and Foot, 705). He was wounded twice and mentioned in dispatches twice, receiving the DSO in 1917, the CMG in 1919, and an honorary LLD, McGill University (1920) in recognition of 'his remarkable ability as an officer of artillery'. McNaughton had married in 1914 Mabel Clara Stuart, daughter of Godfrey Weir, of Montreal; they had one daughter and three sons, the eldest of whom adopted the surname Leslie. One son, an RCAF officer, was killed in action over Germany in 1942.

McNaughton continued in the Canadian army after the war as director of military training with the rank of acting brigadier-general. In 1921 he attended the Staff College senior division at Camberley where his report called him: 'An officer of exceptional attainments, with immense powers of concentration, and great strength of character'. In 1923 he was appointed deputy chief of the Canadian general staff. In 1927–8 he attended the Imperial Defence College, London. McNaughton was promoted major-general in 1929, and was chief of the Canadian general staff from 1929 to 1935. In 1935, with the deteriorating international situation, he wrote a memorandum warning of Canadian defence deficiencies including lack of anti-aircraft weapons, obsolescence of coastal defences, and inadequate munitions-manufacturing capability. A scientific soldier, he believed in using modern science to keep casualties low. He was adviser to the Canadian delegations to the Imperial Conference (London, 1930) and the armaments limitation conference (Geneva, 1932).

Andrew George Latta McNaughton (1887–1966), by Yousuf Karsh

In this period McNaughton was important not only in the maintenance of some military force in Canada in the face of public lack of interest and parsimony, but in the invention of the cathode ray direction finder, a direct ancestor of radar, in the development of communications and mapping in the Canadian north, in the development of Canada's international and Commonwealth position, in the inception of finite proposals and an unratified treaty for the St Lawrence seaway, in transatlantic air and postal service, and in a Trans-Canada Airway. In the depression he advocated unemployment relief camps and projects. The widespread unemployment and the concentration of the single unemployed in work camps led to problems of public order with which he grappled.

Before the Conservative prime minister R. B. (later Viscount) Bennett was defeated in the 1935 elections, he prevailed upon McNaughton to become president of the National Research Council of Canada (1935–44) which co-ordinated and promoted scientific and industrial research. His character, experience, and talents overcame the suspicions and animosity of the new Liberal government and made it possible for the council to play its part later in the Canadian war effort.

McNaughton was promoted lieutenant-general in 1940, and from December 1939 to December 1943 he commanded, with his usual integrity and drive, the Canadian troops in the United Kingdom as general officer commanding successively of 1st Canadian division, 7th British corps (1940), 1st Canadian corps (1940–2), and the First Canadian Army (1942–3), and prepared them for battle.

Canadian troops served in a succession of European operations and campaigns.

Meanwhile the conflicts arose which led to McNaughton's removal from the command of the First Canadian Army. They raised in personal terms an issue of principle. McNaughton believed that Canada could field and furnish a whole army of volunteer Canadians, under Canadian control but taking its place in the wider scheme. He agreed that parts of it could sometimes be detached, but wanted it to go into battle as a whole Canadian army under his command. The British considered Canadian formations part of their own forces, under Canadian command when purely Canadian, but subject to higher British control in battle, and to the policies which were determined by the British government.

J. L. Ralston, Canadian minister of defence, Lieutenant-General Ken Stuart, the Canadian chief of general staff, and Major-General Harry Crerar, among others, thought that Canadians should fight detached, if necessary, rather than remain unused in the United Kingdom. Thus first a division and an army tank brigade, then an armoured division and a corps headquarters went to Italy, and the rest of the First Canadian Army became in its tactical use a headquarters and Canadian troops at British disposal, dependent on non-Canadians for its supplies. This could work only if its Canadian commanders had the confidence of the British generals under whom they served. In 1943 General Sir Alan Brooke, chief of the Imperial General Staff, and General Sir Bernard Paget, under whose command the First Canadian Army then came, both stated that McNaughton was not suited to command an army in the field. McNaughton, blaming machinations by Ralston and Stuart, resigned in December 1943, amid controversy and mistrust.

McNaughton returned to Canada and in 1944 retired from the army with the rank of full general. He refused to join the political opposition and accepted the invitation of Mackenzie King to become Canada's first Canadian governor-general. Within three weeks and before his appointment was announced, a conscription crisis arose. There were not enough trained infantrymen ready to volunteer for overseas service. Ralston resigned on the conscription issue. King had already appealed to McNaughton to take his place and carry on, without conscription, to save the country from the disunity which had rent it in 1917 on the same issue. In this spirit, to meet a national emergency and for unity as well as from conviction and personal requital, McNaughton accepted and was sworn in on 2 November 1944. Within twenty days the effort to meet the crisis without conscription had failed; King introduced conscription. The government survived. The crisis passed. McNaughton ran for parliament in 1945 at Grey North in February and in Qu'Appelle, his native riding, in the general election of June. In both he was defeated. On 21 August 1945 his resignation was accepted.

McNaughton served as chairman of the Canadian section of the Canada–United States permanent joint board on defence (1945–59); president of the Atomic Energy Control Board of Canada (1946–8); Canadian representative to the United Nations Atomic Energy Commission (1946–50); permanent delegate of Canada to the United Nations (1948–9); and chairman, Canadian section of the International Joint Commission (1950–62). In this last work he opposed the Columbia River treaty providing Canadian water power for American purposes. In and out of office he opposed it and proffered his own plan. He then joined and led a fight to deny Canadian water resources to the United States on a continental basis.

In the midst of this fight McNaughton died at Montebello on 11 July 1966 and was buried in Beechwood cemetery, Ottawa.

Professor F. H. Underhill, an acid and fearless critic, called McNaughton 'the greatest Canadian citizen of his day'. He was a leader who attracted devotion and admiration. He had the gift of convincing whoever he was talking to that they and their opinions mattered to him. But it was by his own devotion to his principles, and by his exceptional talents, that he made his reputation. He fought fiercely and fairly, and to the end. He lost his major battles because his primary ideals of Canadian nationalism were in the wider practical situation secondary, moving only Canadians. Confident, and believing the rightness of his views, he continued bitter against those who thwarted them—Brooke, Ralston, Stuart, and Montgomery—and had ingenuous ignorance of political factors in Mackenzie King's Canada, and an inability to dissemble—failings which were also virtues. He was strikingly photogenic. He was an Anglican, and his recreations included shooting and fishing.

McNaughton was appointed PC (Canada) in 1944, CB in 1935, and CH in 1946, and he received honorary degrees and foreign honours.

PETER WRIGHT, *rev.* ROGER T. STEARN

Sources J. Swettenham, *McNaughton*, 3 vols. (1968–9) · J. Eayrs, *In defence of Canada*, 2 vols. (1964–5) · J. W. Pickersgill and D. F. Forster, *The Mackenzie King record*, 4 vols. (1960–70) · C. P. Stacey, *Six years of war* (1955) · C. P. Stacey, *Arms, men and governments* (1970) · personal knowledge (1981) · *WWW* · F. W. Perry, *The Commonwealth armies: manpower and organisation in two world wars* (1988) · J. B. Brebner, *Canada: a modern history* (1960) · I. C. B. Dear and M. R. D. Foot, eds., *The Oxford companion to the Second World War* (1995)

Archives FILM BFI NFTVA, news footage · IWM FVA, home footage · IWM FVA, news footage | SOUND IWM SA, oral history interview

Likenesses Y. Karsh, photograph, priv. coll. [*see illus.*]

Macnee, Sir Daniel (1806–1882), portrait painter, was born at Fintry, Stirlingshire, the son of Robert Macnee, a farmer, and his wife, Anne Gardner (1785/6–1856). Following the death of his father, he moved to Glasgow with his mother. While in his teens he worked for James Lumsden & Son, the Glasgow publishers, and became a pupil of John Knox (1778–1845), the renowned teacher and portrait, landscape, and panorama painter. His friends and fellow artists included William Leighton Leitch and Horatio McCulloch, with whom he went to work at Cumnock in Ayrshire; Macnee and McCulloch later moved to Edinburgh and were employed by William Home Lizars, the engraver. Macnee continued his art training at the Trustees' Academy.

Macnee's earliest documented works include *Cottage, Near Woodside* (a drawing) and *Portrait of a Lady*, exhibited by the Glasgow Institution for the Encouragement of the Fine Arts in 1821 and 1822. He contributed regularly to the major exhibiting societies, including the Scottish Academy in Edinburgh and the Royal Academy in London, and, in Glasgow, the Dilettanti Society and the West of Scotland Academy of the Fine Arts. His exhibits were primarily subject pictures and portraits.

Macnee became one of Scotland's leading portrait painters, influenced by Sir Henry Raeburn and ranked alongside Sir John Watson Gordon and John Graham Gilbert. His patrons ranged from Glasgow's wealthy merchants to the aristocracy and many pioneering industrialists including James Beaumont Neilson, inventor of the 'hot blast' system which revolutionized the iron industry. In the 1840s Macnee commenced work on *The Hot Blast* (*c.*1843, University of Strathclyde), a group portrait with Neilson and fellow patentees of the system meeting with their legal advisers at the time of the celebrated patent trial of *Neilson v. William Baird & Co.* in Edinburgh in 1843. In 1844 Glasgow town council invited Macnee to paint Queen Victoria's portrait, which, on completion, was put on public display and seen by over 60,000 people in four days. Other subjects include Douglas Jerrold (1853, National Portrait Gallery, London), the journalist and playwright; the Revd Dr Wardlaw (1851, Glasgow Art Gallery and Museum), considered his masterpiece, which received a gold medal at the Paris Universal Exhibition in 1855; and *A Lady in Grey* (1859, National Gallery of Scotland, Edinburgh), a portrait of one of his daughters.

In 1861 Macnee joined the newly founded Glasgow Institute of the Fine Arts. He was chairman of its executive committee and its council and was elected president in 1878. In 1876 he succeeded Sir George Harvey as president of the Royal Scottish Academy, was knighted, and was awarded an honorary degree by the University of Glasgow. He was not connected solely with art organizations: in 1842 he was appointed a trustee of Anderson's University, the precursor of Strathclyde University in Glasgow. Macnee was renowned for his stories and anecdotes: it was claimed in *Memoirs and Portraits of One Hundred Glasgow Men* that 'Thackeray heard him, and pronounced him the prince of *raconteurs*' (Mitchell, Guthrie Smith, and others, 217). In his youth he was described by William Leighton Leitch as a 'slight, elegant young fellow' (ibid., 213–14) and, at his death, as 'one of the best known, and best liked, and most highly gifted Scotchmen of his time' (ibid., 217), by Dr Macgregor, who preached at his funeral.

Macnee was married twice: his first wife, Margaret McGee (or MacGee; *b.* 1809/10), died in 1847; and on 17 November 1859 he married his second cousin Mary Buchanan Macnee, daughter of Peter Macnee of Glengilp. He had several children and was survived by his second wife, two sons (one of whom was also named Daniel), and

three daughters. He died at his home, 6 Learmonth Terrace, Edinburgh, on 17 January 1882 and was buried in the Dean cemetery in that city on 21 January.

GEORGE FAIRFULL SMITH

Sources [J. O. Mitchell, J. Guthrie Smith, and others], 'Sir Daniel Macnee', *Memoirs and portraits of one hundred Glasgow men who have died during the last thirty years*, ed. J. MacLehose, 2 (1886), 213–17 · *The Bailie* (29 Jan 1873), 1–2 · *Glasgow Herald* (19 Jan 1882) · *The Scotsman* (18–23 Jan 1882) · J. L. Caw, *Scottish painting past and present, 1620–1908* (1908) · W. D. McKay, *The Scottish school of painting* (1906) · C. B. de Laperriere, ed., *The Royal Scottish Academy exhibitors, 1826–1990*, 4 vols. (1991), vol. 3 · R. Billcliffe, ed., *The Royal Glasgow Institute of the Fine Arts, 1861–1989: a dictionary of exhibitors at the annual exhibitions*, 4 vols. (1990–92), vol. 3 · R. Brydall, *Art in Scotland, its origin and progress* (1889) · D. Irwin and F. Irwin, *Scottish painters at home and abroad, 1700–1900* (1975) · *The Bailie* (1872–82) · J. Hedderwick, *Backward glances, or, Some personal recollections* (1891) · *DNB* · *CCI* (1882) · *IGI* · *Glasgow Herald* (31 Dec 1847) · *Glasgow Herald* (7 July 1856) · *Glasgow Herald* (18 July 1859)

Archives Royal Scot. Acad., letters | Mitchell L., Glas., Royal Glasgow Institute of the Fine Arts' Archive · Edinburgh

Likenesses D. Brown, photograph, 1855–6, Glasgow School of Art · J. Archer, oils, exh. 1877, Royal Scot. Acad. · W. Graham, photograph (after photograph by T. Annan, *c.*1860–1869), Mitchell L., Glas. · J. Macbeth, oils, Scot. NPG · Maull & Polyblank, carte-de-visite, NPG · caricature, repro. in 'Men you know — no. 15', *The Bailie* (29 Jan 1873) · engraving, repro. in Mitchell, Guthrie Smith, and others, 'Sir Daniel Macnee' · photograph, Mitchell L., Glas., Glasgow City Archives, photographic album of members of the West of Scotland Angling Club · wood-engraving, NPG; repro. in *ILN* (6 May 1876) · woodcut (after photograph by J. Fergus), NPG; repro. in *The Graphic*

Wealth at death £37,192 12s. 0d.: confirmation, 8 March 1882, *CCI*

McNee, Sir John William (1887–1984), physician and pathologist, was born at Murieston, Mount Vernon, Lanarkshire, on 17 December 1887, the son of John McNee, insurance agency inspector, and his wife, Agnes Caven. When the family moved to Newcastle upon Tyne he was educated at the Royal Grammar School there; he later went to Glasgow University and graduated MB, ChB, with honours, in 1909. After appointments held in pathology, with Robert Muir, and in medicine, he worked on a two-year research scholarship with the distinguished pathologist, Professor L. Aschoff, at Freiburg in Germany. He made important observations on haemolytic jaundice in geese, which formed the basis of modern views on the functions of the liver and on reticulo-endothelial cells in the formation of bile—work for which he obtained an MD with gold medal in 1914.

During the First World War McNee served in the Royal Army Medical Corps, attaining the rank of major. He was assistant adviser in pathology to the First Army in France and wrote several articles on gas poisoning, gas gangrene, and trench fever. He was awarded a DSO in 1918 for his war services and was mentioned in dispatches. On the strength of his war work he became a member of the new teaching medical unit at University College Hospital, London, and was later appointed deputy director of that unit and physician to the hospital. While there he conducted some major research, which resulted in the third edition of the textbook (with Sir Humphry Rolleston), *Diseases of the Liver, Gall-Bladder, and Bile-Ducts* (1929). McNee's work on cholesterin metabolism gained him the DSc in 1920. In 1924 he obtained a Rockefeller medical fellowship to Johns Hopkins University at Baltimore, where he investigated bile acids. He was remembered for his work in the USA mainly by the publication of 'The clinical syndrome of thrombosis and the coronary artery', a disorder which had not previously been described in the United Kingdom. This was published in the *Quarterly Journal of Medicine of Britain* (1925), which McNee edited from 1929 to 1948. While in London McNee gave several prestigious lectures, particularly the Lettsomian lecture in 1931 and the Croonian lectures in 1932. He became FRCP (Lond., 1925; Edin., 1943) and FRSE (1940).

In 1936 McNee took up the regius professorship of the practice of medicine at Glasgow University. The new Gardiner Institute of Medicine was purpose built, adjacent to the wards of the Western Infirmary, and provided a combined facility for clinical work, ward teaching, and research. McNee swung himself into the work of developing the department, but there was no question that his ambitions were delayed by the onset of the war in 1939. Since 1935 he had been a consultant physician to the Royal Navy and throughout the Second World War he served with the rank of surgeon rear-admiral to the Royal Navy in Scotland and the western approaches. He organized the medical personnel and equipment of the rescue ships which accompanied the convoys during the war, and he played an important part in instituting a convoy medical code, designed particularly for merchant ships that did not carry a medical officer. During the war McNee still lectured to students, but in the uniform of a rear-admiral—a figure of elegance and panache. After the war he encouraged a group of young colleagues in their researches, and he also helped to establish a Medical Research Council unit on clinical chemotherapy at the Western Infirmary. McNee was involved in several major publications. He not only wrote about his work on the liver and spleen, but he also produced a textbook of medical treatment (1939, with many subsequent editions) with Derrick Dunlop and Stanley Davidson. In 1952 he delivered the Harveian lecture on infective hepatitis. Many honours came his way. He was physician to the king in Scotland (1937–52) and the queen (1952–4), and he was knighted in 1951. He was president of the Royal Medico-Chirurgical Society of Glasgow and of the Gastro-Enterological Society of Great Britain in 1950–51, and of the Association of Physicians of Great Britain and Ireland in 1951–2 when it met in Glasgow. He was also president of the British Medical Association in Glasgow in 1954–5. He had honorary degrees from the National University of Ireland and the universities of Glasgow and Toronto.

In 1923 McNee married Geraldine Zarita Lee (*d.* 1975), daughter of Cecil Henry Arthur Le Bas, stockbroker's clerk, of Charterhouse, London, who was herself at that time a research worker at University College Hospital medical school. They had no children. After McNee's retirement in 1953 they moved to Winchester, Hampshire, where they had a lovely garden containing many rare plants. They were devoted to the countryside and country sports; McNee's favourite sports were fishing and shooting. In his long and happy retirement he was able to express his love of the woods, rivers, and hills through his activities with the Council for the Protection of Rural England, of which he became chairman of the Winchester district branch. He retained his memory and intellectual acuity to the end, despite a degree of Parkinsonism.

McNee was the archetypal modern professor of medicine. He had a remarkably strong base in experimental pathology and as a young man worked with two great pathologists of his generation. He also possessed the charm of the traditional physician. After his wife's death in 1975 McNee experienced an increasing sense of loneliness, but he kept a sharp eye on his old department in Glasgow and wished to be kept up to date on research and progress. He died on 26 January 1984 at his home, Barton Edge, Worthy Road, Winchester and was buried in Winchester. ABRAHAM GOLDBERG, *rev.*

Sources *BMJ* (11 Feb 1984), 494 · personal knowledge (1990)
Archives RCP Lond., corresp. and papers
Likenesses portrait, 1952–3, U. Glas., Archives and Business Records Centre
Wealth at death £783,085: probate, 29 Feb 1984, *CGPLA Eng. & Wales*

MacNeice, (Frederick) Louis (1907–1963), writer, was born at 1 Brookhill Avenue, Belfast, on 12 September 1907, the youngest of three children of John Frederick MacNeice (1866–1942), then rector of Holy Trinity, Belfast, and his wife, Elizabeth Margaret (1866–1914), daughter of Martin Clesham, of co. Galway.

Early years and education Originally a Galway man, Louis MacNeice's father was from 1908 to 1931 rector of Carrickfergus; in those early years his mother was often ill, his father preoccupied and remote: 'My mother was comfort and my father was somewhat alarm' (MacNeice, *Strings are False*, 37). His only brother, William, was what was then termed a mongol, that is, a sufferer from Down's syndrome, and MacNeice was much dependent for company on his sister, Caroline Elizabeth, who was later to marry Sir John Nicholson, third baronet. The death of their mother in 1914 was a severe blow, which threw a sombre shadow over MacNeice's adult recollections of childhood, imparting to much of his poetry a poignant sense of the impermanence of men and things. The children were looked after by a cook and a governess until 1917, when their father brought home a new wife, Georgina Beatrice, second daughter of Thomas Greer, of Sea Park, co. Antrim, and Carrickfergus; she brought 'much comfort and benevolence' (ibid., 61) into their lives. MacNeice's father became bishop of Cashel and Waterford in 1931, bishop of Down and Connor and Dromore in 1935, and died in 1942. In later life MacNeice came to appreciate him, as well as the family background of Galway, Dublin, and Connemara. This acted as a counterpoise to that element of stern Ulster reticence which he did not always find it easy to accept in his own character.

When MacNeice was ten he was sent to Sherborne preparatory school—then a happy place, and he was happy in

Stephen Spender, and published his first book of poems, *Blind Fireworks*. On the security of a lectureship in classics at the University of Birmingham, on 21 June 1930 he married Giovanna Marie Thérèse Babette (Mary) Ezra (1908–1991), daughter of David Ezra and stepdaughter of John Beazley.

Lecturer at Birmingham and emerging poet Industrial Birmingham and its university were a rude shock after the youthful snobberies and 'preciousness' of the Oxford aesthetes; MacNeice had to revise his ideas of how and what to teach, and he confronted the problems inevitable to a man who honestly wants to fulfil his obligations, whether to his employers or to his wife, yet who at a deep level regards his creative writing as more important than anything else. According to his posthumous autobiography, *The Strings are False* (1965), he and his wife at first withdrew from these problems into a 'hothouse' of their private world, in which he wrote a novel, *Roundabout Way* (1932), under the pseudonym Louis Malone. The book he soon came to see as a fake, and it was not a success. But he was unable to shut off the outside world, and at Christmas 1933 he wrote *Eclogue for Christmas* with 'a kind of cold-blooded passion' (MacNeice, *Strings are False*, 146) which surprised him. His son Daniel was born in 1934, and about this time MacNeice also began to take more interest in the life of Birmingham and the university, where there was then a remarkably able group of people; he became a lasting friend of the head of his department, Professor E. R. Dodds, his lifelong mentor who became professor of Greek at Oxford; of Ernest Stahl, a lecturer in German and later Taylor professor at Oxford; and of John Waterhouse, a lecturer in English. And among the students he came to know R. D. Smith, with whom he was later to be associated at the BBC, and Walter Allen. MacNeice was also becoming known as a poet through his contributions to *New Verse* and other periodicals and his second volume of *Poems* (1935), and he was at work, with Dodds's encouragement, on his translation of Aeschylus's *Agamemnon* (1936), which Dodds's successor as professor of Greek at Oxford, Sir Hugh Lloyd-Jones, considered 'the most successful version of any Greek tragedy that anyone in this country has yet produced' (E. R. Dodds, *Missing Persons*, 1977, 116).

Looking grimly at the outside world in 1933 MacNeice had wanted to 'smash the aquarium' (MacNeice, *Strings are False*, 146); instead, in 1935 his own golden bowl was broken when his wife abruptly left him, and their eighteen-month-old son, for an American graduate student. He had to turn his mind to domestic problems, and reconcile himself to the fact of rejection. His autobiography dissimulated the grief and concentrated on the gain of freedom: 'I suddenly realized I was under no more obligations to be respectable' (ibid., 152). But freedom and loneliness made him restless, and at Easter 1936 he and Anthony Blunt visited Spain. His Birmingham years may have made him more conscious of social and political injustice, but he does seem to have seen only the pictures of Spain and not the whole picture, with its intimations of

(Frederick) Louis MacNeice (1907–1963), by Howard Coster, 1942

it. In autumn 1921 he went with an entrance scholarship to Marlborough College, where he enjoyed rugby and running on the downs, and specialized in the classics. John Betjeman, Bernard Spencer, John Hilton, Graham Shepard, and Anthony Blunt were among his contemporaries; all but the first remained lifelong friends. MacNeice matured rapidly and precociously in an aesthetic and intellectual ambience, wrote a great deal of verse, and developed a persona which took pride in an opposition to science as well as religion, a contempt for politics, and a scepticism of all values except the aesthetic.

In 1926 MacNeice won a postmastership to Merton College, but Oxford was at first disappointing: he found much of the work arid, and his Marlborough friends were in other colleges. But he continued to write—chiefly poems and stories of satire and fantasy—and in time became friendly with other poets, notably W. H. Auden, Stephen Spender, and Clere Parsons. He took a first in classical honour moderations in 1928, and eagerly devoured the philosophy prescribed for Greats, ranging beyond it in quest of a system to replace a world founded on the religion he had lost with one founded on reason. But his obsession with the logic of poetry ran counter to any other logic, and his quest did not find a solution either then or later, although it was to be a continuing drive which underlay all his poetry. His Oxford studies did, however, give him a firm intellectual foundation, and in spite of emotional strains, his last year there—1930—was a year of successes. He got a first in *literae humaniores*, edited *Oxford Poetry* with turmoil to come. On his return he felt he could not endure the reminders of his broken marriage, and in summer 1936 accepted a post as lecturer in Greek at Bedford College, London. He then went to Iceland with W. H. Auden, a journey about which they subsequently wrote *Letters from Iceland* (1937).

Move to London and *Autumn Journal* MacNeice discharged his university duties in London punctiliously, although living the literary life and moving gradually away from 'the old gang who were just literary' towards 'the new gang who were all Left' (MacNeice, *Strings are False*, 165). The Group Theatre produced his *Agamemnon* in 1936, which was well received, and, less successfully, his *Out of the Picture* in 1937. His life at this period was 'a whirl of narcotic engagements' (ibid., 165)—parties, private views, and political meetings, and arguments. But although he was left-wing in his sympathies he was never himself formally committed to the revolutionary left, and he found the Communist Party unacceptable; nor can the whirl have been too narcotic, for in the single year 1938 he published another book of poems, *The Earth Compels*; two prose works written to commission, *I Crossed the Minch*, and *Zoo*; and a critical book, *Modern Poetry*, which exhibited a close study of metrics and a keen eye and ear, drew on a wide range in the classics and English, and showed a great balance of judgement. And in August he began a long poem which it took him the rest of the year to finish. *Autumn Journal* (1939), regarded by many as his masterpiece, is *The Prelude* of the 1930s, but it is a dramatic rather than a philosophical poem, sometimes recording emotions as they occur, sometimes recollecting them, but seldom in tranquillity. History is a river on which Wordsworth in his *Prelude* looks back to the rapids of the French Revolution, whereas MacNeice can hear the premonitory thunder of the falls ahead. Memory is a structuring principle of both poems, but in *Autumn Journal* it is a post-Freudian, Proustian memory that flies back and forward like a weaver's shuttle, leaving past and present, public life and private life interwoven on the loom.

The Second World War and the BBC MacNeice paid a second visit to Spain early in 1939 and found it much changed; Barcelona was on the eve of collapse and Franco's cause triumphing. This, and the outbreak of war with Germany, brought his dilemmas to a head: he had also been in the United States that spring, and now, loitering in Ireland, he decided to take leave of absence from Bedford College, and go back to America to see whether he could make a life with the American writer Eleanor Clark whom he had met in New York. His visit was a success, and he enjoyed lecturing at Cornell, but by July 1940 it had become clear to him that if he stayed there he would be 'missing history' ('Traveller's return', *Selected Prose of Louis MacNeice*, ed. A. Heuser, 1990, 83). In the event he was forced to stay on, owing to peritonitis, and he did not get back to England until December. He was rejected for active service because of bad eyesight and in May 1941 joined the BBC features department, which had a covert propaganda brief from the government. There, under Laurence Gilliam, MacNeice applied his mind to the principles and techniques of his new medium and to exploiting it to creative ends. His mastery was apparent in such programmes as the series *The Stones Cry out*, *Alexander Nevsky*, and *Christopher Columbus*. He adapted his old love of the stage to radio drama, and produced at least two memorable contributions: *He had a Date* (1944), an elegy for his friend Graham Shepard who had been killed on convoy duty; and *The Dark Tower* (1946), a synthesis of two favourite themes, the morality quest and the parable.

During the war years MacNeice also produced three more books of poetry, *The Last Ditch* (1940), *Plant and Phantom* (1941), and *Springboard* (1944), and another critical work, *The Poetry of W. B. Yeats* (1941). On 1 July 1942 he made a fresh start in family life by marrying Antoinette Millicent Hedley (Hedli) Anderson (1907–1990), the actress and singer; his son Daniel rejoined him from Ireland, and in 1943 his daughter Corinna was born.

The features department provided MacNeice with security and employment which he found useful, satisfying, and compatible with his vocation as poet. It was natural to continue in this work after the war, more especially as Gilliam had recruited other stimulating colleagues, many of them also poets—W. R. Rodgers, Rayner Heppenstall, Terence Tiller, and, on occasion, Dylan Thomas. Rodgers and Thomas in particular became his close friends, as did Francis (Jack) Dillon, the producer. MacNeice was proud of his skill in this medium and took pleasure in the company and technique of the teams with which he worked. The BBC of those years, and Gilliam particularly, knew how to get loyalty and dedicated work out of the intractable race of poets, and drove them with relaxed reins. MacNeice was given leave to visit Ireland in 1945—an Antaean and necessary return to his origins; his curiosity about the wider world was also given scope and he had many assignments abroad—to Rome, to India and Pakistan (in 1947 and again in 1955), to the United States (1953), to the Gold Coast (1956), and to South Africa (1959).

In 1949, to mark the Goethe bicentenary, the BBC produced MacNeice's version of *Faust*—a major undertaking on which he worked in collaboration with his old friend Ernest Stahl. He had published another collection of poems, *Holes in the Sky* (1948), and the following year *Collected Poems, 1925–1948*. From January to September 1950 he was on leave from the BBC as director of the British Institute in Athens, and he stayed on until the following March as assistant representative of the British Council, which had merged with the British Institute. Again, he led the double life: conscientious in discharging his duties, while writing—in spite of the rueful 'This middle stretch / Of life is bad for poets' ('Day of Renewal', ll. 1–2, *Ten Burnt Offerings*, 65)—the poems published in 1952 as *Ten Burnt Offerings*. Back in London, he was beginning to be strongly conscious of time slipping away, and in elegiac mood he began *Autumn Sequel* (1954), a complement to and reprise of *Autumn Journal*; he was in the midst of writing this when Dylan Thomas died, in November 1953, and grief for that death strongly marked the mood of the poem. He published no more until *Visitations* in 1957—the year in which he received an honorary doctorate from the Queen's University, Belfast. In 1958 he was appointed CBE.

Last years and reputation But some desperate discontent was working in MacNeice, and a desire for renewal. In 1960 he and his second wife separated. He set up house with the actress Mary Wimbush, and in 1961 gave up full-time employment in the BBC to be freer for his own work. He felt himself to be in a fresh creative phase of which *Solstices* (1961) was the first harvest; he delivered the Clark lectures in 1963 (published as *Varieties of Parable* in 1965), and he went to Yorkshire that summer to make a programme, *Persons from Porlock*, which involved recording underground. He insisted on going down with engineers to see that the sound effects were right and caught a severe chill. By the time his sister discovered how ill he was and made him go into hospital it was too late; he died of viral pneumonia at St Leonard's Hospital, Shoreditch, London, on 3 September 1963. After a funeral in London on 7 September, his ashes were interred in Carrodore Churchyard, Ireland.

Before his death MacNeice had been assembling the poems for *The Burning Perch* (1963). Of this he wrote, 'I was taken aback by the high proportion of sombre pieces, ranging from bleak observations to thumbnail nightmares … All I can say is that I did not set out to write this kind of poem: they happened' (*Poetry Book Society Bulletin*, September 1963, 1). It was a central tenet of his critical theory that the poet cannot be completely sure of what he has to say until he has said it, and that he works towards his meaning by a 'dialectic of purification' (MacNeice, *Modern Poetry*, 21). And in a sense what gives MacNeice's poetry its excitement is the tension between his mastery of words and technique, and the uncertainty for which he was trying to find a resolution. It was fortunate for him as a poet that he did not find it, for perplexity over the irreconcilables in life was the yeast that fermented his best work. Any comprehensive theoretical solution would have been sterilizing.

Even so, MacNeice's escape from the frigidities of his classical education had been narrow, as he realized in *Modern Poetry*: 'Marriage at least made me recognize the existence of other people in their own right and not as vicars of my godhead' (MacNeice, *Modern Poetry*, 74). And it was in Birmingham that he learned to respect the ordinary man, and came to form his own conception of what a poet should be: 'able-bodied, fond of talking, a reader of the newspapers, capable of pity and laughter, informed in economics, appreciative of women, involved in personal relationships, actively interested in politics, susceptible to physical impressions' (ibid., 198). But this description omits the qualities which made MacNeice special as a poet: the capacious mind with full memory; the dazzling skill with metaphor and image and symbol; the control of verbal technique—the sharp contemporary tang of his scholar-poet's idiom, ranging from lyric to acute observation, even slapstick; the basic seriousness, the search for a

belief which could explain without destroying the delight of 'The drunkenness of things being various' ('Snow', l. 8, *Collected Poems*, 30). The absence of a firm and forming conviction meant that he was open to experience but often passive in his acceptance of it, however creatively he might give back the experience in poetry. He was himself aware of this: 'But the things that happen to one often seem better than the things one chooses. Even in writing poetry … the few poems or passages which I find wear well have something of accident about them' (MacNeice, *Strings are False*, 220). And in the same passage of his autobiography he expressed the feeling that what makes life worth living is the surrender to the feelings and sensation which the given moment may present.

As poet and critic, and as man—humanist and stoic—MacNeice was all of a piece. Once he had found himself and his deepest themes he developed as a tree develops, the years adding rings and ruggedness to the trunk and density of branch and foliage, but the basic shape not changing. As the tree, rooted where it stands, must accept and surrender to the winds and seasons, so MacNeice stoically and passively accepted whatever life brought him next.   D. M. DAVIN, rev. JON STALLWORTHY

Sources L. MacNeice, *The strings are false*, ed. E. R. Dodds (1965) · L. MacNeice, *Modern poetry: a personal essay* (1938) · J. Stallworthy, *Louis MacNeice* (1995) · m. cert., 1930 · m. cert., 1942 · d. cert.

Archives Bodl. Oxf., corresp. and papers · Bodl. Oxf., papers · Col. U., literary MSS and MSS · King's AC Cam., MSS · State University of New York, MSS and corresp. | Bodl. Oxf., letters to E. R. Dodds · Bodl. Oxf., letters to parents from Sherborne and Marlborough · King's AC Cam., letters to Anthony Blunt | SOUND BL NSA

Likenesses H. Coster, photograph, 1942, NPG [*see illus.*] · N. Sharp, portrait, NPG · F. Topolski, portrait, NPG · death-mask, Bodl. Oxf. · photographs, Bodl. Oxf.

McNeil, Hector (1907–1955), politician, was born at the Temperance Hotel, Garelochhead, Dunbartonshire, on 10 March 1907, the second of seven children of Donald McNeill, journeyman shipwright, and his wife, Margaret McPherson Russell. His father's family originated in the island of Barra and his mother's in Islay. When the family moved to Glasgow, McNeil attended Woodside School and entered Glasgow University with the intention of studying for the ministry. After graduating he decided to make a career in journalism and politics. He held various staff posts on the *Scottish Daily Express*, becoming assistant to the editor in 1938. On 29 April 1939 he married Sheila, daughter of Dr James Craig of Glasgow; they had one son.

McNeil was elected as a Labour councillor on Glasgow town council in 1933 and served until 1936, and again from 1937 to 1938. At the 1935 general election he was narrowly defeated, standing as Labour parliamentary candidate for Glasgow, Kelvingrove. In February 1936 he nearly doubled the previous Labour vote, but was defeated at a by-election contest against Malcolm MacDonald in Ross and Cromarty. He was finally elected MP in July 1941, when he was returned unopposed for Greenock, a constituency he represented until his death.

Hector McNeil (1907–1955), by Bassano, 1946

In 1942–5 McNeil was parliamentary private secretary to Philip Noel-Baker, parliamentary secretary to the Ministry of War Transport. After the election of 1945 Attlee appointed him parliamentary under-secretary of state at the Foreign Office under Ernest Bevin. From October 1946 to February 1950 he was minister of state for foreign affairs. He became the recognized spokesman of the government at the annual general assemblies of the United Nations, and came to be even better known in the United States than he was at home. Indeed he was extremely sensitive to American concerns during his time at the Foreign Office, and was a strong critic of the Soviet Union. He took part in the Paris peace conference of 1946, visited and reported on the political situation in Greece, and was involved in the negotiations leading up to the Brussels treaty in 1948. He led the British delegation to the Economic and Social Council of the United Nations in New York in 1946 and 1947, and took a particular interest in the formation of the International Refugee Organization. He had a close and effective working relationship with Bevin, who seriously considered McNeil as his successor at the Foreign Office, a recommendation rejected by Attlee.

From February 1950 to October 1951 McNeil was secretary of state for Scotland, with a seat in the cabinet. He attempted to enhance the status of his post by refusing to confine himself to speaking solely on Scottish issues, a breach of convention which irritated some of his colleagues. He used his international connections to attract new industries (including IBM) to Clydeside, and he even pressed, without success, for the United Nations Organization to make Edinburgh its temporary base while its permanent home was being built in New York. However, he was criticized in Scotland for devoting more time to his American friends than to Scottish interests. He was resolutely opposed to devolution and endeavoured to prevent an increasingly resurgent Scottish nationalist movement gaining publicity. It was ironic, therefore, that his time at the Scottish Office coincided with the high-profile theft by nationalists of the Stone of Destiny from Westminster Abbey. McNeil took a deep personal interest in the recovery of the stone and the tracking down of the culprits.

After Labour left office in October 1951 McNeil increasingly dedicated himself to his business interests, becoming managing director of the British company producing the *Encyclopaedia Britannica*. His roots in the labour movement were relatively shallow. While he was not unsympathetic to Dalton's hostility to German rearmament in 1952, he was a staunch defender of NATO and was vehemently opposed to the 'third force' and pacifist arguments of the Labour left. He embodied the classless and technocratic ethos of the party's right wing in the immediate post-war years and was a close friend of Hugh Gaitskell. McNeil died of a haemorrhage while on business in New York on 11 October 1955.   MARTIN FRANCIS

Sources *DNB* · *The Times* (12 Oct 1955) · G. Pottinger, *The secretaries of state for Scotland, 1926–1976* (1979) · *The political diary of Hugh Dalton, 1918–1940, 1945–1960*, ed. B. Pimlott (1986) · A. Bullock, *The life and times of Ernest Bevin*, 3 (1983)
Archives NA Scot., private office papers | HLRO, corresp. with Lord Beaverbrook · PRO, official papers, Foreign Office/Scottish Office | FILM BFI NFTVA, documentary footage · BFI NFTVA, news footage
Likenesses Bassano, photograph, 1946, NPG [*see illus.*] · photographs, 1947–50, Hult. Arch.
Wealth at death £1,929 17*s.* 10*d.*: confirmation, 12 Jan 1956, *CCI*

McNeile, (Herman) Cyril [*pseud.* Sapper] (1888–1937), writer, was born at Higher Bore Street, Bodmin, Cornwall, on 28 September 1888, the son of Captain Malcolm McNeile RN, later governor of the royal naval prison, Lewes, and his wife, Christiana Mary, *née* Sloggett. He was educated at Cheltenham College and at the Royal Military Academy, Woolwich, before joining the Royal Engineers in 1907. In 1914 he was gazetted captain and served throughout the First World War, winning the Military Cross. On 31 October 1914 he married Violet Baird (*b.* 1890/91), daughter of Lieutenant-Colonel Arthur Sholto Douglas of the Cameron Highlanders. They had two sons.

As Sapper, McNeile published a number of popular books during the war, including *The Lieutenant and Others* (1915), *Sergeant Michael Cassidy, R.E.* (1915), *Men, Women, and Guns* (1916), and *No Man's Land* (1917). He took his pseudonym from his army experience, the term 'sapper' being the nickname of the Royal Engineers, whose duties entailed mining and tunnelling under enemy lines. McNeile retired from the army in 1919 with the rank of lieutenant-colonel and a year later published *Bulldog Drummond*, an enjoyably implausible thriller, recounting the adventures of one Captain Hugh 'Bulldog' Drummond, 'a demobilised officer who found peace dull'. Drummond, and the gang of loyal clubmen (and the occasional obligatory servant) who followed him, appeared in some seventeen adventures, the first ten of which were written by McNeile. A stage version of *Bulldog Drummond*, starring Sir Gerald Du Maurier, was a hit at Wyndham's Theatre, London, in 1921–2 and was equally successful in New York. The first of many Bulldog Drummond films was made in 1922; the hero has been variously portrayed by Jack Buchanan, Ralph Richardson, John Howard, and Ronald Colman. McNeile wrote a number of other books, all thrillers, notably *Jim Maitland* (1932) and those featuring the private detective Ronald Standish.

As McNeile's scanty *Times* obituary made clear, his own life was relatively quiet: as in the novels of fellow best-selling writers such as P. G. Wodehouse or Agatha Christie, it is the hero who lives the exciting life. But if Wodehouse's aristocratic young men are, as Richard Usborne has remarked, reminiscent of the more intelligent and charming schoolboy of fifteen, then Sapper's heroes, occupying in fictional terms the same sort of London club-land, are at best the heartier type of public-school 'blood', and all too often the more vicious of school bullies. While Christie's characters exhibit the inevitable xenophobia and antisemitism of the period, McNeile's go far beyond the 'polite' norms. His super-villain Carl Petersen and his sidekick-cum-lover, Irma, the slinky epitome of a twenties 'vamp', have no stated nationality, but they are definitely foreign, and as such 'inevitably' evil. Other enemies include the Bolshevik, the 'dago', and especially the Jew. Thirty years on Ian Fleming noted that his hero, James Bond, was Sapper from the waist up and Mickey Spillane below. He referred, presumably, to Drummond's hyped-up patriotism, his lack of intellectual pretension and party-political partiality, and perhaps even his tastes in liquor (Drummond prefers beer, but is not averse to a Martini), but there is a relish in brutality, verging on sadism, that provides a further link between the two.

McNeile died at his home, King's and Princes' Farm, West Chiltington, near Pulborough, Sussex, on 14 August 1937 of illness traceable to his war service. He was survived by his wife. At the time of his death he was working on a stage play, *Bulldog Drummond Again* with his friend Gerard Fairlie, thought to be the model for the eponymous hero. Fairlie went on to write seven more Drummond adventures.   JONATHON GREEN

Sources R. Usborne, *Clubland heroes* (1974) · C. Steinbrenner and O. Penzer, eds., *Encyclopedia of mystery and detection* (1976) · *The Times* (16 Aug 1937) · *DNB* · b. cert. · m. cert. · d. cert. · *CGPLA Eng. & Wales* (1937)
Archives BL, corresp. with Society of Authors, Add. MS 63288
Likenesses H. Coster, photographs, NPG · portrait, repro. in *The Times*
Wealth at death £26,166 19s. 9d.: probate, 28 Oct 1937, *CGPLA Eng. & Wales*

McNeile, Ethel Rhoda (1875–1922), missionary and head-mistress, was born in London on 18 October 1875, the daughter of Hector McNeile (d. 1922), vicar of Bredbury, Cheshire, and his wife, Mary Rosa Lush. Both of her parents were from staunchly evangelical families. Hugh Boyd McNeile, dean of Ripon, was her grandfather, and the novelist (Herman) Cyril McNeile was her cousin. She had three brothers and two sisters. Her father, a brother (Robert Fergus), and sisters (Annie Hilda and Jessie Margaret) all became missionaries of the Church Missionary Society (CMS) and served in Egypt, Palestine, and India.

Ethel McNeile was educated at Queen's School, Chester, from where she was sent to Westfield College, London. Her temperament was rebellious, and she was at this time rebelling against Christianity and women's subordination. She was transferred within a year to the Victoria University of Manchester, where she remained for two years studying mathematics. This opened the way for her to go to Girton College, Cambridge, where she obtained a third class in part one of the classical tripos in 1900. As Cambridge degrees were not yet open to women she subsequently took her MA degree from Trinity College, Dublin. She took up teaching as a profession, first as a classical mistress at Sale high school and afterwards at the City of London Girls' School.

While at Cambridge, Ethel McNeile was deeply troubled by philosophical and theological questions. She was drawn towards theosophy and lectured on behalf of the Theosophical Society, and was secretary of the Manchester ward of the society from 1900 to 1904. In 1904 she set out to India to find her 'master'. While teaching at St Bede's, a Roman Catholic college at Simla, she met Annie Besant, who admitted her into the inner circle of theosophists. But long and frank discussions with a CMS missionary, William Edward Sladen Holland, who had studied philosophy at Oxford, and, most important, her experience of a mystical vision of Christ, induced her to abandon theosophy and return to Christianity. To prepare for missionary educational work she spent some months in England training as a teacher at Cherwell Hall, Oxford. After returning to India she worked for a time with the Zenana Bible and Medical Mission (ZBMM) in Lahore, and joined the staff of the Lady Dufferin Christian Girls' School there. She was accepted by the CMS on 15 January 1907 and was appointed principal of the CMS Normal School at Sigra, Benares. Proficient in Hindi and Urdu, she studied Sanskrit and worked to overcome the shortage of women teachers which seriously hindered women's education in India. A breakdown in her health following a cholera epidemic forced her to return to England in 1911; during the journey home her religious development was influenced by the experience of high mass in St Mark's, Venice, which she attended at the suggestion of Edmund Linwood Strong of the Oxford Mission to Calcutta.

In 1912 Ethel McNeile became principal of the CMS School, Agra, a new girls' school which was to be a sister school to St John's School for Boys. She favoured this idea of linking a girls' school to a boys' school, and taught scripture and English in the boys' school partly to persuade the boys to send girls from their families to school. She organized 'purdah' parties to persuade women to send their daughters. Noting the growing desire among Western-educated Indian men to have their women educated so that they could become their intellectual companions, she proposed that the CMS and ZBMM should found central teaching establishments on the lines of English public schools. Christian missions had long seen women's education as the way to India's regeneration, but mission schools had so far catered mainly for poor orphans and lower-caste girls, and had not cared for the quality of the education imparted. They existed almost solely as evangelistic agencies, whereas she wanted missions to seize the opportunity to establish, in every large city, well-equipped and well-staffed schools for girls from high-caste and élite families who would exercise influence over Indian society in the future. The curriculum was to adapt Western knowledge to Eastern conditions, with more emphasis on domestic education and less on examinations. By linking Indian schools to schools in England she hoped that the former could keep abreast of new methods of teaching and curricular developments.

Ethel McNeile wanted to start a community of CMS women workers with Indians and English women living on equal terms. She felt that Indian women should be trained for leadership, and believed that the work of converting Indians to Christianity should be undertaken by Indians only, rather than by Indians as paid agents of foreigners. This did not meet with the approval of the CMS, and in 1914 she left to enter the Oxford sisterhood at Barisal, Bengal, as Sister Rhoda. She learned Bengali and worked among the untouchables in Barisal and Dacca. The damage to her health from overwork and the damp climate led her to move to the Convent of the Wantage Sisters in Poona in 1918, and from there to the mission in Yerandavana for rest and change.

Sister Rhoda returned to England in March 1919 to join the community of St Mary the Virgin at Wantage, lecturing at St Michael's College, Wantage, to students preparing for foreign missionary work. At the request of the bishop of Oxford, Charles Gore, she wrote *From Theosophy to Christian Faith* (1919). A well-read woman with a questioning mind and a restless spirit, she seems to have found peace during her last years at Wantage, where there is a memorial to her in the chapel. On 19 May 1922 she set out for India on the P. & O. ship *Egypt* to rejoin the mission staff at Poona. On the evening of 20 May 1922, in thick fog off Ushant, the *Egypt* was cut into by the *Seine* and sank within twenty minutes. Sister Rhoda refused to board a lifeboat as there was not room for all. Kneeling on the deck in prayer, comforting other passengers, she went down with the ship.   APARNA BASU

Sources E. R. McNeile, *From theosophy to Christian faith*, 2nd edn (1942) · K. T. Butler and H. I. McMorran, eds., *Girton College register, 1869–1946* (1948) · Sister Rhoda, CSMV (1922) · *Annual Report* [Zenana Bible and Medical Mission] · *The Zenana, or, Women's Work in India* · *Church Missionary Review*

Likenesses photograph, after 1914, repro. in McNeile, *From theosophy to Christian faith*

McNeile, Hugh Boyd

McNeile, Hugh Boyd (1795–1879), dean of Ripon, was born at Ballycastle, co. Antrim, on 15 July 1795, the fourth son of Alexander McNeile JP, deputy lieutenant, and high sheriff of Antrim in 1832, and his wife, Mary, only daughter of John McNeale of Culresheskin, co. Antrim. He was matriculated at Trinity College, Dublin, in 1810, and took his BA in 1815, MA in 1821, and BD and DD in 1847. Subsequently he kept terms at King's Inns, Dublin, and Lincoln's Inn, London, with a view to following a legal and parliamentary career. However, following an evangelical conversion, he was in 1820 ordained to the curacy of Stranorlar, co. Donegal, by William *Magee, then bishop of Raphoe and later archbishop of Dublin, whose daughter Anne (1801/2–1881) he married on 2 May 1822. They were to have nine sons.

In 1822 McNeile was presented by Henry Drummond MP

to the rectory of Albury in Surrey. Proximity to London combined with great ability as a preacher and speaker to enable him quickly to gain a prominent position in Anglican evangelicalism. He was a firm Calvinist and a staunch defender of the established Church of England. He and Drummond became leading supporters of Edward Irving, and shared his convictions regarding the premillennial second advent of Christ. Between 1826 and 1830 McNeile was the moderator at the series of Albury conferences, hosted by Drummond, which was a seminal influence on the development and diffusion of such views. Premillennialism was closely associated in McNeile's mind with a strong interest in missions to the Jews and an intense anti-Catholicism. The latter no doubt also owed something to his Ulster background and his father-in-law's robust protestantism. In 1829 he forcefully denounced Catholic emancipation, which he feared would lead to divine judgment on the nation.

During the early 1830s, as Drummond and the Irvingites set a trajectory which was shortly to take them outside the established churches, McNeile parted company with them, and in 1834 he moved from Albury to become perpetual curate of St Jude's, Liverpool. During the following years he led successful opposition to the Liverpool corporation's attempt to set up a non-sectarian system of education, and was a leading clerical supporter and advocate of the Protestant Association. He was one of the most compelling orators of his generation, having a commanding presence crowned by prematurely white hair, a facility for fluent and logical argument, and a precise and powerful style of utterance. He had a large following, and his capacity to imbue popular prejudice against Roman Catholicism with the dignity of a spiritual crusade gave him enormous and explosive influence on Merseyside. In 1848 his admirers built for him the new church of St Paul's, Princes Park.

McNeile was a leading figure in the opposition to the Maynooth grant in 1845 and to the creation of the Roman Catholic hierarchy in 1850. He also strenuously opposed Tractarianism and liberal theological trends. He published numerous sermons, lectures, and theological treatises. Although he was a man of great abilities, deep faith, and genuine spirituality, the perceived extremism and contentiousness of his views meant that his obvious ambition was frustrated for many years. He became a canon of Chester in 1845, and a residentiary canon in 1860, but it was not until 1868 that Disraeli, in a futile and controversial attempt to strengthen his electoral position by gestures to the protestant gallery, appointed him dean of Ripon. Although now well over seventy, McNeile still had some of his old fire, and he proved to be an energetic dean who completed the restoration of Ripon Minster and whose preaching drew overflowing congregations.

In 1875 failing health led McNeile to resign his deanery, and to retire to Stranorlar House, Bournemouth, where he died on 28 January 1879. His funeral was held in Bournemouth on 1 February. His passing gave rise to a *Times* leader on the decline of the evangelical party in the

Church of England, which was overstated but revealing testimony to the central role McNeile had played in its development over the span of half a century.

JOHN WOLFFE

Sources J. A. Wardle, 'The life and times of the Rev. Dr. Hugh McNeile, DD, 1795–1875', MA diss., University of Manchester, 1981 · J. Wolffe, *The protestant crusade in Great Britain, 1829–1860* (1991) · C. Bullock, *Hugh McNeile and Reformation truth* (1882) · J. Murphy, *The religious problem in English education: the crucial experiment* (1959) · *Random recollections of Exeter Hall in 1834–1837, by one of the protestant party* (1838) · *The Times* (29 Jan 1879) · *The Times* (30 Jan 1879) · G. Butler, *The end of the perfect man* (1879) · Burke, *Gen. GB*
Likenesses R. Smith, engraving, *c*.1835 (after T. C. Thompson), priv. coll. · H. Cousins, mezzotint, pubd 1838 (after T. C. Thompson), BM · G. G. Adams, marble statue, St George's Hall, Liverpool · T. Lupton, mezzotint (after S. Hawksett), BM · D. J. Pound, stipple and line engraving (after photograph by J. T. Foard), NPG · bust, priv. coll.
Wealth at death under £25,000—effects in England: probate, 1 May 1879, *CGPLA Ire.*

McNeill, Duncan, Baron Colonsay and Oronsay (1793–1874), lawyer and politician, was born on 20 August 1793, either on the island of Colonsay or on neighbouring Oronsay, Argyll. He was the second, but eldest surviving, son of John McNeill (1767–1846), owner of the islands, agriculturist, and breeder of highland cattle, and his wife, Hester (*d.* 1843), eldest daughter of Duncan McNeill of Dunmore, Argyll. In his prime McNeill was described as being 6 feet tall and very handsome, and in later life he was said to have a fine, grand face. He never married. His brother was Sir John *McNeill, diplomat, long-serving chairman of the Scottish Poor Law Board of Supervision and inquirer into highland destitution in the late 1840s and into inefficiencies in the Crimea in 1855. McNeill was educated at the University of St Andrews from 1805 to 1809 and took honours in mathematics, graduating MD. He spent three sessions at Edinburgh University, studying metaphysics, psychology, and law, was also during this time a member and president of the Speculative Society, and in 1816 he became a member of the Scottish bar.

McNeill initially took up criminal practice and this resulted in his appointment as an advocate-depute in 1820 and as sheriff of Perthshire in 1824. By the early 1830s, however, he had entered on a period of professional uncertainty. He was rescued from this in November 1834, when he became solicitor-general for Scotland in Sir Robert Peel's first administration. The experience of office was to be short-lived as Peel resigned in April 1835, but McNeill again held this post when Peel returned to office, from September 1841 until October 1842. He was then promoted to be lord advocate in succession to Sir William Rae. In this capacity his biggest legislative achievement was the passing of the Scottish Poor Law Amendment Act in 1845.

His position also now made it necessary for McNeill to have a seat in parliament. Conservative seats were hard to come by in Scotland, but he eventually won Argyll in September 1843. He therefore arrived in the Commons in the immediate aftermath of the Disruption of the Scottish church. He remained loyal to Peel in the split in the Conservative Party caused by the repeal of the corn law, and

Duncan McNeill, Baron Colonsay and Oronsay (1793–1874), by John Phillip, 1866

he left office with him as a free-trade Conservative in July 1846.

McNeill enjoyed a prominent legal practice when out of office; for example, he defended the Glasgow cotton-spinners against a conspiracy to murder charge in 1838. In May 1851 he became an ordinary judge of the court of session, taking the title of Lord Colonsay and Oronsay. Although he owed his appointment to his political opponents, there was self-interest in the generosity shown by Lord John Russell's government. McNeill had been a thorn in the flesh of his successor as lord advocate, Andrew Rutherford, especially over Rutherford's attempts to reform the Scottish marriage law. In 1852, when Lord Justice-General Boyle retired, McNeill was appointed to succeed him in that office and as lord president of the court of session. He held this position until 1867, earning positive contemporary opinions, and was then raised to the peerage as an appeals judge, taking the title Baron Colonsay and Oronsay. He was thus the first Scottish lawyer to be made a law lord. Doubts were expressed at the time about his chances of success in this position and he seems to have been only partly able to confound them. This may have been due to age—he was seventy-three when appointed—but it is more likely that it was due to his innate cautiousness in judgment. Seldom did he go sufficiently beyond the details of a case to lay down a principle which could later be used as a precedent. His political and judicial careers revealed a strong unwillingness to do what was not absolutely necessary. Reaching this position was probably, nevertheless, the high point in his career, in that he did establish a precedent for the appointment of Scottish law lords.

McNeill died at Pau in the French Pyrenees on 31 January 1874. For the last few years of his life he had gone south in the winter to escape the effects of lung disease. His small, private funeral in Edinburgh was said to have reflected a lonely private life; he was buried on 11 February 1874 at Warriston cemetery, Edinburgh.   GORDON F. MILLAR

Sources *Journal of Jurisprudence*, 18 (1874), 157–65 • *Law Times* (7 Feb 1874), 259–60 • *Solicitors' Journal*, 18 (1873–4), 266 • *The Scotsman* (2 Feb 1874) • *The Times* (3 Feb 1874) • *Glasgow Herald* (12 Feb 1874) • G. W. T. Omond, 'Duncan McNeill', *The lord advocates of Scotland, second series, 1834–1880* (1914), 126–46 • *Parliamentary Pocket Companion* (1851) • J. Foster, *Members of parliament, Scotland … 1357–1882*, 2nd edn (privately printed, London, 1882), 237 • *DNB*
Archives BL, corresp. with Sir Robert Peel, Add. MSS 40408–40599 • NA Scot., letters to Lord Dalhousie • U. St Andr., corresp. with James David Forbes
Likenesses T. Duncan, oils, c.1844, Scot. NPG • J. Steell, marble bust, 1856; related plaster bust, Scot. NPG • J. Phillip, oils, 1866, Faculty of Advocates, Parliament Hall, Edinburgh [*see illus.*] • L. Ward, watercolour, 1873, NPG; repro. in *VF* • Rodger of St Andrews, photographs • engraving (after T. Duncan) • portrait, repro. in B. W. Crombie, *Modern Athenians: a series of original portraits of memorable citizens of Edinburgh, 1837–1847* (1882)

MacNeill, Eoin [John] (1867–1945), Irish nationalist and Celtic scholar, was born at Glenarm, co. Antrim, on 15 May 1867, the fourth son and sixth of nine children of Archibald MacNeill (1822–1889), baker, sailor, and merchant, and his wife, Rosetta Macauley (1847/8–1918). James *McNeill was his younger brother. MacNeill was deeply influenced by the distinctive atmosphere of the Glens of Antrim, a Catholic enclave where some Irish was still spoken, while the existence in nearby protestant majority areas of a Presbyterian liberal tradition which distrusted Orangeism as a tool of landlordism encouraged him in persistently underestimating the strength of Ulster Unionism. MacNeill was educated at St Malachy's College, Belfast, where he was further politicized by witnessing sectarian riots.

MacNeill passed first in all Ireland in the senior grade intermediate examination. In 1887, while studying for a degree at the examination-only Royal University of Ireland, he obtained a junior clerkship in the Dublin law courts. At this time he began to learn Irish and was introduced to Celtic scholarship by the historian of early Ireland, Edmund Hogan.

In 1893, with several students of Irish inspired by Douglas Hyde, he founded the Gaelic League and became its first honorary secretary. MacNeill took on much of the organizational work of its early years and edited its successive organs: the *Gaelic Journal*, *Fainne an Lae*, and *An Claideamh Soluis* ('The sword of light'). His Gaelic League

Eoin MacNeill (1867–1945), by unknown photographer, c.1910

work, carried out in time spared from his official duties, involved considerable physical and financial sacrifice. At this time he first befriended P. H. Pearse, whom he recruited to the league executive. On 19 April 1898 MacNeill married Agnes (1872–1953), daughter of James Moore, solicitor, of Ballymena; they had four sons and four daughters. Shortly after his marriage MacNeill suffered a nervous breakdown due to overwork; it left him with an abiding lassitude which may have influenced his passivity in later crises.

From 1904 MacNeill embarked on studies which revolutionized Celtic scholarship. A series of articles (collected in 1921 as *Celtic Ireland*) revised the framework of early Irish history, showing that standard accounts of early Ireland were based on later fabrications by dynastic historians, and that little concrete evidence existed for any period before the fifth century AD. MacNeill showed that scholars who knew Irish language sources only through Victorian translations filtered through the translators' unconscious assumptions misunderstood Gaelic Ireland, implying, for example, that it had no concept of the state as distinct from the ruler. This theory was used by scholars of unionist sympathies to argue that Gaelic society was hopelessly primitive and its destruction necessary to introduce a higher civilization based on law. MacNeill's hostility to the unionist political assumptions of such scholars as the great historian of Norman Ireland, G. H. Orpen, helped him to discover their scholarly errors; it also embroiled him in religious and political polemics whose rancour and overstatements disguise the depth of his scholarship. Reacting against unionist emphasis on law and state administration, and influenced as a devout Catholic by the church's belief that certain spheres of life should be reserved for its influence, he developed a conservative political philosophy, emphasizing the limits on state action.

MacNeill's Catholicism did not prevent him from criticizing church authorities who overstepped their proper sphere; in 1908–9 he led a successful Gaelic League campaign to make Irish essential for matriculation in the new National University of Ireland, despite the opposition of most Catholic bishops, and published *Irish in the National University* (1909). MacNeill became first professor of early and medieval Irish history in the new University College, Dublin, in 1909.

In November 1913, as the home rule crisis developed, MacNeill advocated the formation of nationalist Irish Volunteers in imitation of the (unionist) Ulster Volunteer Force (UVF). He thought that the government could not repress such a movement while leaving the UVF untouched, but combined this with a confused belief that the UVF might be converted to nationalism if it were enlightened about British over-taxation of Ireland. MacNeill's call, taken up by the secret Irish Republican Brotherhood (IRB), aroused popular enthusiasm; the Irish National Volunteers were formed in 1913 with MacNeill as president and most leadership posts held by IRB members. MacNeill, though not a member of the IRB, had separatist sympathies; he thought the Irish Parliamentary Party subservient to the Liberals, and believed that Asquith planned to abandon home rule. MacNeill's correspondence with John Redmond about control of the volunteers combined assurances of loyalty to Redmond with insinuations that by joining the volunteers the Irish people had given MacNeill a mandate which would be betrayed by surrendering control to Redmond.

Redmond temporarily asserted control by threatening to establish a rival organization, but after the outbreak of the First World War, in which Redmond supported the British war effort, the volunteers split. A large majority supported Redmond, but rapidly became inactive; a separatist influenced minority, strong in Dublin, followed MacNeill. From late 1914 to April 1916 MacNeill edited their weekly newspaper, the *Irish Volunteer*.

Two parties developed in the volunteer leadership. MacNeill headed a group advocating a defensive strategy aimed at resisting any attempt to impose conscription or abandon home rule. The other group, secretly preparing a rising during the war, was directed by an IRB committee, led by Thomas Clarke and Sean MacDiarmada, with Pearse as figurehead. MacNeill knew of the rival group, but not the extent of their preparations; he shrank from direct confrontation, fearing the consequences of another split.

In April 1916 the Pearse group, by forging an alleged official document, persuaded MacNeill that a government crackdown was imminent. MacNeill authorized defensive manoeuvres, unaware these were cover for the landing of arms and a full-scale rising on Easter Sunday. When MacNeill discovered this he was horrified, but acquiesced as the plan was too far advanced to be stopped. Later, on hearing that the German ship bearing arms for the rising had been sunk, he published an order cancelling the manoeuvres. The Pearse group ostensibly accepted this, but brought out the Dublin units on Monday. MacNeill's actions still arouse controversy. Sympathizers with the rising leaders claim that he prevented greater success; others argue that he averted unnecessary slaughter. MacNeill took no part in the subsequent week-long Easter rising. He was arrested, tried by court martial, and sentenced to penal servitude for life. He remained in Lewes gaol until amnestied in June 1917. MacNeill then joined the reconstituted Sinn Féin party, and was elected to its executive.

MacNeill became MP for Londonderry City and the National University of Ireland (NUI) in 1918, thereby becoming a member of the revolutionary parliament (Dáil Éireann). In May 1921 he was re-elected for the NUI in the southern House of Commons (and second Dáil), and also returned for Londonderry in the northern House of Commons, where he did not take up his seat. In January 1919 he was appointed minister for finance in the first Dáil, being demoted to industries in April 1919 when Michael Collins assumed control of finance. MacNeill was arrested in a post-Bloody Sunday crackdown by the British government in November 1920, and remained in Mountjoy prison until June 1921, where he spent his time studying early Irish law.

MacNeill supported the Anglo-Irish treaty, and chaired the Dáil debates leading to its ratification, having been elected as speaker in August 1921. In the Irish general election of 1922 he was elected as TD for County Clare. During the civil war of 1922–3 between supporters and opponents of the treaty he defended harsh security measures, including reprisal executions, as upholding the will of the people. MacNeill's son Brian died fighting for the republicans.

From 1922 to 1925 MacNeill was the free state's first minister for education. His tenure was marked by an accommodation with church authority and the imposition of Irish as a compulsory school subject despite protests from many (mostly protestant) parents and teachers. He was diverted from ministerial duties by his nomination in 1924 to the commission determining the boundary between the Irish Free State and Northern Ireland. In the commission's proceedings MacNeill defended the free state claim to most nationalist majority areas, but eventually acquiesced in the decision by the other two members that only small areas should be transferred. When the draft report was leaked to the press MacNeill withdrew his consent and resigned as commissioner and minister under pressure from his government colleagues; after hurried Anglo-Irish negotiations the report was suppressed and the boundary left unchanged. MacNeill's passivity and political maladroitness contributed substantially to the débâcle (he had failed to inform his colleagues of the trend and likely outcome of the commission's proceedings, regarding them as quasi-judicial and therefore confidential), but his emergence as principal scapegoat obscured the extent to which the outcome was predetermined by political circumstances.

MacNeill's political career ended when he unsuccessfully contested the National University constituency in the general election of June 1927. He returned to academic life, working on place names, early Irish law, and Patrician studies (his interest in St Patrick was inspired by the tradition associating the saint with the Glens of Antrim). Some of his Patrician essays were posthumously collected as *St. Patrick* (1964), while a lecture series based on his legal studies appeared in 1932 as *Early Irish Laws and Institutions*. From 1928 he chaired the Irish Manuscripts Commission; from 1936 he was president of the Irish Historical Society, from 1937 to 1940 president of the Royal Society of Antiquaries of Ireland, and from 1940 to 1943 president of the Royal Irish Academy. He retired from his chair in 1941 and died on 15 October 1945 of abdominal cancer at his home, 63 Upper Leeson Street, Dublin. He was buried on 17 October at Kilbarrack cemetery, co. Dublin, after mass at university church, St Stephen's Green.

MacNeill's political career was a sad mixture of incompetence and self-delusion, alternately as figurehead and scapegoat. His death was followed by reaction against many of his scholarly theories, but many of his views were revived by later scholars who emphasize that even his speculations rested on a deep knowledge of the sources. Through his achievements as a language revivalist and one of the greatest Celtic scholars, MacNeill made an enduring contribution to Irish life.   PATRICK MAUME

Sources E. MacNeill, editorials, *Irish Volunteer* (1914–16) • M. Tierney, *Eoin MacNeill: scholar and man of action, 1867–1945*, ed. F. X. Martin (1980) • F. X. Martin and F. J. Byrne, eds., *Eoin MacNeill: the scholar revolutionary* (Shannon, 1973) • E. MacNeill, *Shall Ireland be divided?* (Dublin, 1915) • M. Tierney, Memoir, introduction, in E. MacNeill, *St. Patrick* (Dublin, 1964) • P. Maume, 'Anti-Machiavel: three Ulster nationalists', *Irish Political Studies* (1999) • F. X. Martin, ed., 'Eoin MacNeill on the 1916 rising', *Irish Historical Studies*, 12 (1961), 226–71 • J. A. Gaughan, ed., *The memoirs of Senator Joseph Connolly: a maker of modern Ireland* (Dublin, 1996) • E. MacNeill, *Phases of Irish history* (1919) • E. B. Titley, *Church, state, and the control of schooling in Ireland, 1900–44* (1983) • R. Dudley Edwards, *Patrick Pearse: the triumph of failure* (1977) • E. MacNeill, ed., *An Ulsterman for Ireland … by John Mitchel* (Dublin, 1900) • d. cert.
Archives NL Ire., papers • University College, Dublin, corresp. and papers | NL Ire., letters to Douglas Hyde
Likenesses photograph, c.1910, Hult. Arch. [*see illus.*] • photograph, 1916, repro. in Tierney, *Eoin MacNeill*, frontispiece • photograph, after 1918, repro. in Martin and Byrne, eds., *Eoin MacNeill* • S. O'Sullivan, portrait, University College, Belfast
Wealth at death £1749 6s. 11d.: probate granted to widow, 7 Jan 1946, testamentary calendar 1946 (16), NA Ire.; *CGPLA Éire*

Macneill, Hector (1746–1818), poet, the son of John Macneill (d. c.1777), formerly of the Horse Guards and a retired captain of the 42nd regiment, was born at Rosebank, near Roslin, Edinburghshire, on 22 October 1746. He spent his early youth near Loch Lomond, Stirlingshire, where his father, who had been unfortunate with money, tenanted a farm. His elementary education was at Stirling grammar school, under Dr David Doig, who encouraged his early attempts at writing, and to whom he dedicated his *Will and Jean*.

Aged thirteen or fourteen, Macneill went to Bristol to a relative, a West Indies trader, who interested himself in him as his namesake, and sent him as a prospective sailor on the *Ruby*, bound for St Kitts. Finding that he disliked the sea, Macneill stayed a year with his relative's son in St Kitts, and afterwards served three unhappy years with a

merchant in Guadeloupe. He left for Antigua in 1763 and worked for a short time for his cousin, for little remuneration. He was subsequently assistant to the provost marshal of Grenada at St George's Town for three years. News of the death of his mother and sister caused him to return to Scotland about 1776. Eighteen months later his father died, and he invested the small inheritance he received in an annuity of £80.

By this time Macneill had three dependants to support: two sons, and their mother, whom he did not marry. Needing to earn more money, in 1780 he became assistant secretary, first on Admiral Geary's flagship the *Victory*, with which he served two cruises, then on the flagship of Sir Richard Bickerton in Indian waters, for a further three years. In an interval of peace he visited the caves of Cannara, Ambola, and Elephanta, and described them in *Archaeologia*, 8 (1787). His prospects in India being 'blasted by an unexpected change of administration at home' (author's note to *The Scottish Muse*, 1808, 1.117), he returned to Scotland and hoped to live by writing.

Settling for a time in a farmhouse near Stirling, Macneill found literature unremunerative, and about 1786 he went to Jamaica with influential letters of introduction. An appointment as assistant to the collector of customs came to nothing, and he was forced to stay with a friend. At this time he rediscovered two other friends from his childhood who helped him financially, and he secured jobs for his two sons before he returned to Scotland. During this period, Macneill published a defensive pamphlet, *Observations on the Treatment of the Negroes in Jamaica* (1788), which he later attempted to suppress, claiming that it had represented the views of a friend, not his own.

Macneill had begun writing *The Harp: a Legendary Tale* before going to Jamaica, and completed the poem on the return journey, publishing it in 1789. He stayed for some time with Graham of Gartmore, who is mentioned in the preface, and to whose sister he became engaged. A disagreement put an end to this, and he moved around Argyll, Glasgow, Edinburgh, and St Ninians. He lived for some time with the family of Major Spark, at Viewforth House, Stirling. It was here that he wrote *Scotland's Skaith, or, The History of Will and Jean*, a ballad against drink, published in 1795. This gained him a wide reputation. It went through fourteen editions in twelve months, and its sequel the following year, *The Waes o' War*, was almost as popular. *The Links o' Forth* was published the same year. During this time, he was also a contributor to the *Scots Magazine*.

Around 1799 a six-year illness induced Macneill to return to Jamaica, where his friend John Graham gave him an annuity of £100, and he returned to Scotland a few months later. He settled in Edinburgh, and became a well-known figure on the literary scene. He was respected most for his earlier poetry, including songs such as 'Come under my plaidie', although he continued to write for years to come. He published *The Memoirs of Charles Macpherson, Esq.*, an autobiographical novel, in 1800. *The Poetical Works of Hector Macneill* appeared in 1801, and was republished twice in his lifetime, and again in 1856. *The Pastoral or Lyric Muse of Scotland*, afterwards called *The Scottish Muse*, appeared in 1808. Two anonymous poems, *Town Fashions, or, Modern Manners Delineated* (1810) and *Bygane Times and Late-Come Changes* (1812), demonstrate an impatience with change in his latter years. A second novel, *The Scottish Adventurers*, was also published in 1812. Macneill died on 15 March 1818, in Edinburgh.

T. W. BAYNE, *rev.* SARAH COUPER

Sources *Blackwood*, 4 (1818), 273–7 [abridgment of Macneill's MS autobiography] · C. Rogers, *The modern Scottish minstrel, or, The songs of Scotland of the past half-century*, 1 (1855), 73–81 · Chambers, *Scots.* (1870) · Anderson, *Scot. nat.*, vol. 3 · T. Royle, *The mainstream companion to Scottish literature* (1993), 211 · [J. Robertson], *Lives of Scottish poets*, 3 (1822), 150–66 · *Edinburgh Magazine and Literary Miscellany*, 81 (1818), 396 · private information (2004)

Archives NL Scot., letters to Robert Anderson · NL Scot., letters to Archibald Constable

Likenesses J. Henning, porcelain medallion, 1802, Scot. NPG · plaster medallion, 1802 (after J. Henning), Scot. NPG; version, in possession of W. G. Patterson, 1889 · P. Thomson, line engraving (after William), BM; repro. in H. Macneill, *Works* (1801)

McNeill, James (1869–1938), administrator in India and governor-general of the Irish Free State, was born at Glenarm, co. Antrim, on 27 or 29 March 1869, the youngest son of Archibald McNeill, of Carnegies in the glens, who had been trained as a shipbuilder, owned a bakery which served the coastal area between Cushendun and Cushendall, and also farmed in a small way. His mother was Rosetta Macauley, who on her mother's side traced an ancestry back to the O'Neills, earls of Tyrone, chieftains of Catholic Ulster before the plantations. In the once remote Glens of co. Antrim, justly celebrated for their wild beauty, the Roman Catholics survived as a majority and constituted a little nationalist enclave in the unionist dominion of north-east Ulster. Like the Catholic populations in other parts of the north the people of the glens possessed a strong sentiment of local patriotism, and James McNeill always sustained strong nationalist and united Ireland opinions alongside a pride in his Ulster descent and an appreciation of the Ulster character, without distinction of creed.

McNeill passed his early childhood in the glens, and there acquired a lifelong love of nature and of outdoor life. After attending the local national school he was sent south to his uncle the Revd Charles Macauley, a professor at St Patrick's College, Maynooth, under whose care he remained while he was being educated at Belvedere College, the Jesuit day school in Dublin. He met with so many successes there, particularly in classics and history, that he was advised to direct himself towards the Indian Civil Service. He prepared for the entrance examination at Blackrock College, near Dublin, and afterwards at Emmanuel College, Cambridge, and in 1890 he went out to the Bombay presidency.

McNeill's first important work there was the preparation of the general administration report for 1895–6, the year of the beginning of the bubonic plague epidemic, and by the time of his retirement, during the winter of 1914–15, he was commissioner of the central division of the presidency and an additional member of the central

legislative council of India. His lively sense of Indian grandeur and destinies had won him the trust of the Indian leaders with whom his work brought him in contact. Yet he had not disguised his view that the evolution of India towards political freedom would be a long process owing to the racial and religious complications involved.

In every respect, including that of amusement—he became a fine shot and horseman during these years and an expert at pig-sticking—the life of India suited McNeill; and if he left the service at forty-five, the earliest retiring age, it was not to seek leisure but to place his abilities at the disposal of his native country, then at a crisis of her history.

On his return to Ireland McNeill made his home near Dublin with his brothers Charles and John (Eoin *MacNeill), the latter a prominent figure in the Irish National Volunteers, a leader of Sinn Féin, and, as a scholar, closely associated with the Gaelic revival. Although he was not a participant in the Easter rising of 1916, Eoin MacNeill was compromised in its antecedents and was afterwards arrested, narrowly escaping execution. James McNeill, who had hitherto been chiefly interested in the political and economic aspects of the Gaelic revival, now threw in his lot with the Sinn Féin movement, which triumphed throughout nationalist Ireland at the elections of December 1918. In 1922 McNeill helped to draft the constitution of the Irish Free State, following the Anglo-Irish treaty of December 1921. In 1922 he was also appointed chairman of the Dublin county council, and acted on several occasions as arbiter between employers and workmen.

In 1923 McNeill married Josephine, daughter of James Aherne, of Fermoy, co. Cork; there were no children from the marriage. That year he was sent to London as high commissioner of the Irish Free State, a position for which his long official experience in high administrative posts made him ideally suited. The negative results of the Irish Boundary Commission (1924–5), on which his brother presented the case for Irish unity, were a great disappointment to him, but he remained faithful to the 'Dominion' settlement of 1921, and in December 1927 he accepted the governor-generalship of the Irish Free State.

McNeill took office at a time when the role of governors-general within the evolving British Commonwealth was being clarified. At the same time the Irish Free State government was preoccupied with political and cultural separation from Britain. His office was therefore potentially a difficult one to fulfil and it was made clear to him from the outset that he was neither a representative nor an agent of the British government, but had been appointed by the king solely on the advice of the Irish government. Unlike T. M. Healy, his predecessor in the office, McNeill was a man of gentle speech who had made no personal enemies, and his appointment met with general approval, especially in literary and artistic circles, where his wife had been well known, both in Dublin and in London.

During his time in office McNeill had been scrupulous in acting only on the advice of his executive council, but the accession to power in March 1932 of de Valera's Fianna Fáil, or republican party, made his position untenable. De

Valera felt no personal animosity towards McNeill, but he was determined to abolish the office of governor-general, which he believed represented to Irishmen 'a symbol of our defeat and a badge of our slavery' (Sexton, 122). Matters soon came to a head when in June McNeill was deliberately excluded from the official state reception which marked the Eucharistic Congress in Dublin of 1932. For all the gentleness of his manner there was Ulster iron in McNeill's character and he was particularly angry that a religious occasion should have been thus used to make a political point. He challenged the conduct of the executive council towards his office in a correspondence which he printed, against the council's express wishes, in the *Irish Times* on 12 July 1932. With this act his days as governor-general were effectively numbered.

Personally McNeill would have been glad to resign but, as a matter of principle, he wished to force the executive council to get rid of him by means of the constitutional machinery at its disposal. It was ultimately in accordance with advice tendered by de Valera to George V that McNeill relinquished the office of governor-general in October 1932. He was replaced by 'an inveterate republican who promptly retired into an unprecedented seclusion' (Sexton, 179).

McNeill lived long enough to see the establishment of a new constitution in which the governor-general was replaced by a president and Éire (in English 'Ireland') defined as a republic in 'external association' with the British Commonwealth; but he would have preferred an approach to unity with Ulster to any such constitutional change. He enjoyed six years of retirement on a small estate near Dublin, and died in London on 12 December 1938. He was survived by his wife.

JOSEPH HONE, rev. MARK POTTLE

Sources *The Times* (13 Dec 1938) · *Irish Times* (13 Dec 1938) · J. Ryan, 'Biographical notice', *Studies* (Dec 1945) · D. Gwynn, *The Irish Free State, 1922–1927* (1928) · B. Sexton, *Ireland and the crown, 1922–1936: the governor-generalship of the Irish Free State* (1989) · Venn, *Alum. Cant.*

Archives Plunkett Foundation, Long Hanborough, Oxfordshire, corresp. with Sir Horace Plunkett · TCD, corresp. with Thomas Bodkin

Likenesses S. Purser, oils, priv. coll. · L. Raemakers, crayon drawing, priv. coll.

McNeill, Sir James McFadyen (1892–1964), shipbuilder, was born on 19 August 1892, at 6 Cameron Street, Clydebank, the youngest of three sons of Archibald McNeill (*d.* 1901/2), shipyard foreman, and his wife, Isabella McKinnon, daughter of a farmer on the island of Arran, who died a few days after James was born. The boy was sent to an aunt in Arran, where he spent his early childhood. His father died when he was nine.

McNeill's education began at Clydebank high school, from which a scholarship took him to Allan Glen's school in Glasgow, noted for its technical bias. In 1908 he started an apprenticeship at the shipyard of John Brown & Co. Ltd, Clydebank. Winning a Lloyd's scholarship in naval architecture in 1912, he undertook a sandwich course at the University of Glasgow, combining academic work with practical training in the shipyard, and graduated BSc

Sir James McFadyen McNeill (1892–1964), by Walter Stoneman

in 1915 with special prizes in mathematics, naval architecture, and engineering. Having joined the Royal Naval Volunteer Reserve in 1911, McNeill transferred to the Officers' Training Corps at university, and on graduating was commissioned as a second lieutenant in the Royal Field Artillery Lowland brigade, proceeding to France in 1916. Promoted captain in 1917, he served with the 21st divisional artillery and was awarded the MC at Amiens (1918); then promoted major, he was mentioned in dispatches.

In 1919, McNeill returned to John Brown at Clydebank. He was assistant naval architect from 1922 until 1928, when he became principal naval architect and technical manager. On 8 July 1924 McNeill married Jean Ross (*b.* 1896/7), daughter of Alexander McLaughlan, a Glasgow glass merchant. They had one son.

During the inter-war years McNeill was responsible for the design of a wide variety of ships for different owners and trades, but the work which brought him his greatest acclaim was in the sphere of large passenger liners. As an apprentice he had seen the construction of the *Aquitania* and, in the period after the First World War, he shared in the planning of liners for Canadian Pacific Steamships, New Zealand Shipping Co., Union Castle Line, and other leading companies. He is best remembered for his collaboration with the Cunard Company in the production for their north Atlantic service of the *Queen Mary* and the *Queen Elizabeth*, which went into service in 1936 and 1940 respectively. The considerable advance in size and speed of the *Queen Mary* presented problems in design and construction, which were successfully resolved under

McNeill's assiduous and skilful guidance. Not least of these was the launching of such a large ship in the restricted waters of the River Clyde, and its accomplishment in 1934 was the subject of a classic paper delivered by McNeill to the Institution of Naval Architects in 1935. The respect in which McNeill was held by owners and subcontractors alike was matched by his relations with senior Admiralty officials. They valued greatly his opinions and co-operation, especially during the Second World War, when the Clydebank yard made a singular contribution to naval building.

In 1948 McNeill assumed the office of managing director and in 1953, when the Clydebank works became a separate company in the John Brown Group, he was appointed managing director and deputy chairman. The completion of the Royal Yacht *Britannia* in 1954 brought him his appointment as KCVO. He had already been created CBE in 1950. He retired from executive duties in 1959, and relinquished the deputy chairmanship in 1962.

In addition to his Clydebank posts, McNeill held at various times directorships in the Firth of Clyde Dry Dock Company Ltd, the Rivet, Bolt and Nut Company, the North West Rivet, Bolt and Nut Company Ltd, and the British Linen Bank. His attainments were recognized by his university in 1939 when it conferred on him the honorary degree of LLD. He also greatly prized the fellowship of the Royal Society (1948). In 1950 the Royal Society of Arts named him Royal Designer for Industry. His native town made him a burgess of the burgh of Clydebank. McNeill's concern for the technical institutions of his profession led him to serve as a vice-president of the Institution of Naval Architects, and as president of the Institution of Engineers and Shipbuilders in Scotland (1947–9). In 1956–7 he was chairman of the standing committee of the Association of West European Shipbuilders. In addition he was president of the Shipbuilding Conference (1956–8). He was a member of the general and technical committees of Lloyd's Register of Shipping, and of the court of assistants of the Worshipful Company of Shipwrights.

McNeill had an integrity of purpose and the determination and drive to attain his objectives, coupled with a modesty of manner, which disguised his underlying ability. A staunch member of the Church of Scotland (for a time he was preses of Wellington church in Glasgow), he did not flaunt his beliefs but lived according to them. His busy life did not permit much time for recreation, which for him took the form of an occasional game of golf. McNeill died in Canniesburn Auxiliary Hospital, Bearsden, Glasgow, on 24 July 1964; his wife survived him.

J. BROWN, *rev.*

Sources A. McCance, *Memoirs FRS*, 11 (1965), 127–34 · *The Times* (25 July 1964) · *CGPLA Eng. & Wales* (1964) · b. cert. · m. cert. · d. cert. **Likenesses** W. Bird, photograph, 1963, NPG · W. Stoneman, photograph, RS [*see illus.*] **Wealth at death** £15,614 10s.: confirmation, 18 Sept 1964, *CCI*

McNeill, Sir John (1795–1883), diplomatist and surgeon, born on the island of Colonsay, Argyll, Scotland, was the third of the six sons of John McNeill (1767–1846) of Colonsay and his wife, Hester McNeill (*d.* 1843) of Dunmore, and

Sir John McNeill (1795–1883), by David Octavius Hill and Robert Adamson, 1845

the brother of Duncan *McNeill, Baron Colonsay and Oronsay. He studied medicine at Edinburgh University, where he graduated MD in 1814, at the age of nineteen. On 6 September 1816 he was appointed assistant surgeon on the East India Company's Bombay establishment; he became surgeon on 1 May 1824 and retired from the medical service on 4 June 1836. He was attached to the field force under Colonel East in Cutch and Okamundel in 1818–19 and was afterwards deputy medical storekeeper at the presidency. From 1824 to 1835 he was attached to the East India Company's legation in Persia, at first in medical charge, and latterly as political assistant to the envoy, in which post he displayed great ability. On 30 June 1835 he was appointed secretary of the special embassy sent to Tehran under Henry Ellis to congratulate Mohammed Shah on his accession to the Persian throne. McNeill received permission to wear the Persian decoration of the Sun and Lion of the first class, and on his return home in the spring of 1836 published anonymously a startling anti-Russian pamphlet, *Progress and Present Position of Russia in the East*. He collaborated with J. B. Fraser and David Urquhart in this bout of Russo-phobia.

Palmerston recognized McNeill's ability and sent him to Persia as envoy and minister-plenipotentiary in May 1836 to replace Ellis. However, McNeill's instructions were less energetic than he wished, for he wanted to pursue an active policy of internal political and military reform. Lacking strong support from London and Calcutta, his position was weak when the shah began the siege of Herat in November 1837. Moreover, negotiations over a commercial treaty had almost brought a breakdown in relations with Persia. McNeill unsuccessfully attempted a reconciliation between Herat and Persia, and in June 1838 broke off relations with the shah, his policy of making Persia the agent of British influence a failure. McNeill, having been knighted in 1839, returned to Persia with a new mission in 1841; diplomatic relations were restored in October and a treaty of commerce signed, and he returned home in August 1842.

In 1845 McNeill was appointed chairman of the Board of Supervision entrusted with the working of the new Scottish Poor Law Act of 1845, a post he occupied for thirty-three years. During the potato famine—nearly as disastrous in the western highlands as in Ireland—he conducted a special inquiry into the condition of the western highlands and islands, during which he personally inspected twenty-seven of the most distressed parishes. At the outbreak of war with Russia in 1854, McNeill published revised editions in French and English of his pamphlet *Progress and Present Position of Russia in the East*, with supplementary chapters dealing with the progress of events since 1836, and insisting on the importance to Britain and to Christendom of the autonomy of Turkey and Persia. At the beginning of 1855, when the Crimean disasters had roused public indignation, McNeill and Colonel Alexander Murray Tulloch, an officer of great administrative experience at the War Office, were sent to the Crimea with instructions to report on the whole arrangements and management of the commissariat department and the method of keeping accounts, and to the causes of the delays in unloading and distributing clothing and other stores sent to Balaklava. The commissioners started at once for the seat of war. They took no shorthand writer with them, as the remuneration sanctioned by the Treasury was insufficient to secure a qualified person (A. M. Tulloch, *Crimean Commission*, 1880, 72). The McNeill–Tulloch inquiry was the most effective of the various inquisitions into the Crimean débâcle. It sharply criticized Lord Raglan's personal staff in the Crimea and Commissary-General Filder, and it led to many recriminations as officers sought to clear their names when the report was published in 1856 ('Accounts and papers', *Parl. papers*, 1856, 20). A board of general officers was convened to clear the army, but despite its protestations the McNeill–Tulloch report led to professional reform of the commissariat by the royal warrant of October 1858. Very unusually, the Commons, irritated by executive obfuscation, passed a resolution in 1857 calling for special honours and McNeill soon became a privy councillor and Tulloch a KCB. Oxford University made McNeill a DCL and Edinburgh University chose him as chairman of its amalgamated societies; his inaugural address on competitive examinations was published in 1861.

McNeill married, first, in 1814, Innes, fourth daughter of George Robinson of Clermiston, Midlothian—she died in 1816; second, in 1823, Eliza, third daughter of John Wilson—she died in 1868; third, in 1871, Lady Emma Augusta Campbell, daughter of John, seventh duke of Argyll—she

survived him. He had children, though it is unclear how many and with which wife. He retired as chairman of the Board of Supervision in 1868. He was a fellow of the Royal Society of Edinburgh and an active (founder) member of the Royal Asiatic Society for over sixty years. Despite some recognition, neither his diplomatic nor his military work quite fitted his abilities and he found himself always in an awkward, adversarial relationship to the English establishment. He died at Cannes on 17 May 1883.

H. M. CHICHESTER, rev. H. C. G. MATTHEW

Sources *Dod's Peerage* (1882) · *FO List* · M. E. Yapp, *Strategies of British India: Britain, Iran and Afghanistan, 1798–1850* (1980) · J. B. Kelly, *Britain and the Persian Gulf, 1795–1880* (1968) · J. Sweetman, *War and administration: the significance of the Crimean War for the British army* (1984) · Boase, *Mod. Eng. biog.* · J. W. Kaye, *History of the war in Afghanistan*, 2 vols. (1851) · Anderson, *Scot. nat.*

Archives BL OIOC, corresp. and papers relating to Persia, MS Eur. D 1165 · NA Scot., corresp. and papers · NA Scot., corresp. and papers relating to Crimea · NL Scot., corresp. and papers | BL, corresp. with Lord Aberdeen, Add. MSS 43711–43712, 43238–43239 · BL, corresp. with James Brant, Add. MSS 42512 · BL, corresp. with Florence Nightingale, Add. MS 45768 · Leics. RO, letters to John Paget · NL Scot., letters to Blackwoods · NL Scot., letters to John Paget · NRA, priv. coll., corresp. with James Fraser · U. Durham L., letters to Viscount Ponsonby · U. Southampton L., corresp. with Lord Palmerston

Likenesses D. O. Hill and R. Adamson, photograph, 1845, NPG [*see illus.*] · J. Steell, marble bust, Scot. NPG · G. F. Watts, oils, Inveraray castle, Stratchlyde region · oils, Scot. NPG

Wealth at death £58,322 6s.: confirmation, 15 Aug 1883, *CCI* · £58,000: *DNB*

Macneill, Sir John Benjamin (1792/3–1880), civil engineer, was the son of Captain Torquil Parkes Macneill of Mount Pleasant (now Mount Oliver convent), near Dundalk in co. Louth, Ireland. As a young man he served in the Louth militia, being listed as a lieutenant from 29 April 1811 until the militia was disbanded in 1815.

Macneill first worked as an engineer on roads and bridges around Dundalk under the grand jury system, mainly under the direction of John Foster of Collon, the last speaker of the Irish House of Commons. He then worked in the west of Ireland for Alexander Nimmo before obtaining employment about 1826 with the civil engineer, Thomas Telford, then engaged in road and bridge making in Scotland and England. Macneill became one of Telford's principal assistants or 'deputies' and was entrusted with the improvement of turnpike roads in the north of England, with his headquarters at Daventry, Northamptonshire. Telford appointed him superintendent of the southern division of the Holyhead Road from London to Shrewsbury. He carried out important experiments for Sir Henry Parnell relating to traction on roads, using a dynamometer, and was initially opposed to the introduction of railways. He arrived at the conclusion that the iron-shod feet of horses were more destructive to roads than any other form of contemporary transport. He devised an instrument to be drawn along roads, to indicate their state of repair by monitoring the deflections produced by irregularities in the road surface, tracing them on paper as a continuous curved line. He also devised tables for computing earthwork quantities in canal cuttings and these were published in 1833.

Under Telford (who left him £400 in his will), Macneill acquired great technical and parliamentary experience in engineering matters. After Telford's death in 1834 Macneill built up a considerable practice as a consulting engineer, with offices in London, in Glasgow (where for a short time he was in partnership with James Thompson), and later in Dublin. He constructed the Wishaw and Coltness Railway and other small lines in Scotland, and conducted a series of important experiments in canal-boat traction, suggested by the swift boats carrying sixty passengers and drawn by two horses at the rate of 8 m.p.h., placed by Walter Hunter on the Forth and Clyde Canal. The experiments were published in 1836 in a paper to the Institution of Civil Engineers, for which he received a Telford medal. In 1837 Macneill publicized his system of 'sectio-planography', whereby the heights of all embankments, depths of all cuttings, width of land required, and the necessary gradients were shown at one view. The system was adopted for the preparation of railway plans by the standing orders of the House of Commons. A new system of nomenclature introduced by him, in which slopes (clivities) were distinguished as 'acclivities' and 'declivities', was adopted. When the Irish railway commission began work in 1836 Macneill was entrusted with the surveys of the north of Ireland. He at that time lived with his wife and young family at Mount Pleasant, where he established lime works using a modified Scottish process; this enabled him to improve much unproductive land in the neighbourhood, from which for some years he obtained a large return.

A recommendation of the 1838 House of Commons select committee on education in Ireland that there should be a central polytechnic institute in Dublin moved the board of Trinity College in 1841 to found a school of civil engineering. Macneill was appointed as the first holder of the chair of civil engineering, a post which he held nominally until 1852, when he was succeeded by his assistant, Samuel Downing. He was engineer to many Irish railway schemes, notably the line from Dublin to Drogheda, at the opening of which in 1844 he received a knighthood, the Dublin and Belfast Junction Railway, and the Great Southern and Western Railway from Dublin to Cork. He was the first to introduce wrought-iron lattice girder bridges into the UK, the 140 foot span rail bridge over the Royal Canal near Dublin being erected in 1843, followed in 1855 by the large viaduct over the River Boyne at Drogheda with a central span of 267 feet.

Macneill was tall and strikingly handsome. Although self-taught in technical and scientific subjects, he had a strong interest in matters of science. He was elected a fellow of the Royal Society on 5 April 1838 and regularly attended the meetings of this and other bodies. He became an associate of the Institution of Civil Engineers in 1827 and was transferred to member in 1831. He served on the council from 1837 to 1843. The University of Dublin in 1843 conferred on him an honorary LLD degree, and in 1862 the MA degree. Macneill lacked business acumen and

also contracted for large numbers of shares in uneconomic railway companies. As a result he suffered financially following the railway shares crash of 1866.

Macneill was married, and had two sons and two daughters. His sons, Torquil and Telford, both of whom followed the profession of engineering, predeceased their father. His younger daughter, Grace, became the second wife of Major the Hon. Augustus Jocelyn, second son of the second earl of Roden; she died in 1852. During his later years Macneill went blind, and withdrew from professional pursuits. He moved to London to be near his sons and lived for some time at Surbiton in Surrey and later at 186 Cromwell Road, South Kensington, where he died on 2 March 1880. He was buried in an unmarked grave in Brompton churchyard.   H. M. CHICHESTER, rev. R. C. COX

Sources *The Times* (5 March 1880), 7 • *The Times* (8 March 1880), 8 • *The Engineer* (19 March 1880), 215 • *PICE*, 73 (1882–3), 361–7 • *Dundalk Democrat* (6 March 1880) • *Irish Times* (6 March 1880) • *Dod's Peerage* (1853) • *Engineering* (12 March 1880), 203 • Boase, *Mod. Eng. biog.* • d. cert.
Archives Institution of Engineers of Ireland, letters [copies]
Likenesses oils, Masonic Hall, Dundalk, co. Louth

McNeill, Sir John Carstairs (1831–1904), army officer, was born at Colonsay House, Colonsay, Argyll, on 29 March 1831, the eldest of four sons of Captain Alexander McNeill (1791–1850) of the islands of Colonsay and Oronsay in the Hebrides and his wife, Anne Elizabeth, daughter of John Carstairs of Stratford Green, Essex, and Warboys, Huntingdonshire. Duncan McNeill, Lord Colonsay, the Scottish judge, and Sir John McNeill, the diplomat, were his uncles.

After attending the University of St Andrews, and Addiscombe College from 1849 to 1850, McNeill entered the Bengal army on 9 December 1850 as ensign in the 12th native infantry. He was promoted lieutenant on 30 August 1855 and received the brevet of major for services during the mutiny, in which he won distinction as aide-de-camp to Sir Edward Lugard during the siege and capture of Lucknow. He became captain on 31 August 1860 and major on 8 October 1861, transferring in the latter year to the 107th foot. In New Zealand, as aide-de-camp to General Sir Duncan Cameron, he served through much of the war of 1863–6. He won the Victoria Cross for an act of gallantry near Ohaupo on 30 March 1864, when he was threatened, while carrying dispatches, by a Maori force, and managed to effect the escape of both himself and a private, whose horse had thrown him. McNeill also received the brevet of lieutenant-colonel.

From 1869 to 1872 McNeill was military secretary to Sir John Young, Lord Lisgar, governor-general of Canada, and was on the staff of the Red River expedition under Sir Garnet Wolseley in 1870. He became colonel on 25 April 1872 and was eventually nominated CMG on 2 December 1876 for his Canadian services. He was again with Wolseley as chief of staff in the Second Anglo-Asante War (1873–4), displaying daring, determination, and organizational capacity. However, he was so severely wounded in the wrist at Esaman on 14 October 1873 that he was invalided home, and he declined a staff appointment at Aldershot in 1875

Sir John Carstairs McNeill (1831–1904), by Elliott & Fry

on grounds of recurring fevers. He was made CB on 31 March 1874, by which time he had also been appointed aide-de-camp to the commander-in-chief, George, duke of Cambridge. Then, in November 1874, he became equerry to Queen Victoria, beginning a long association with the royal household, where his love of sport made him a favourite. He also became something of an apologist for Wolseley, who was not so favoured in royal circles. By the queen's command, he accompanied Prince Leopold to Canada and, on his return, was appointed KCMG on 17 August 1880. In 1882 he was promoted major-general and served in the Egyptian campaign as 'bear leader' (Sir Henry Ponsonby to his wife, 23 July 1882, Ponsonby MSS, Add. A 36, 21) to the duke of Connaught, for which he was nominated KCB on 24 November 1882. He later accompanied Connaught on the latter's world tour in 1890.

While McNeill had inherited family estates in the Hebrides—he was made JP and deputy lieutenant for Argyll in 1874—he was not a wealthy man and was reluctant to yield the security of royal employment, declining the Scottish command in 1885 on the grounds of its expense. In 1878 and 1881 he secured the queen's agreement to re-employment at the conclusion of any active service. The queen and Wolseley both pressed his appointment to a brigade command for the 1885 Suakin expedition. However, recriminations were to follow McNeill's action at Tofrek on 22 March. He had led out 3300 fighting men to escort a convoy from Suakin to Tamai. A halt was made at Tofrek but, while a zariba was being formed, the Mahdists attacked in force. After severe fighting, they were driven off with heavy losses but McNeill had suffered 296 casualties and lost over 500 camels. He was accused of being surprised, while his superior, Lieutenant-General Sir Gerald Graham, was criticized for not giving him sufficient mounted troops. Wolseley largely exonerated McNeill when sent to report on the affair, while the queen demanded an inquiry to clear his name. Nevertheless, McNeill never again commanded in the field, and retired in 1890.

Described by Sir Henry Ponsonby as a 'rough noisy soldier and Scottish laird' (Sir Henry Ponsonby to his wife, 4 Nov 1881, Ponsonby MSS, Add. A 36, 20), McNeill was also characterized by Gambier-Parry (119) at Suakin in 1885 as of 'middle stature, somewhat stout, and with a round, red, good humoured face'. According to Gambier-Parry, McNeill 'had a quick, sharp way of asking questions, and a somewhat "stand-off" manner with strangers though when you knew him there was no pleasanter or kinderhearted friend. He possessed also an attractive manner and a cool, quiet way of taking things, which made him to a certain extent popular. He looked as though he had the constitution of a giant and as if he could stand or go through anything' (Gambier-Parry, 119).

In 1898 McNeill was appointed king of arms to the Order of the Bath and, on the accession of Edward VII, was made GCVO on 2 February 1901. He died, unmarried, on 25 May 1904 at St James's Palace, London, and was buried at Oronsay Priory, Argyll.   IAN F. W. BECKETT

Sources Royal Arch., Ponsonby MSS, Add. A 36 · B. Robson, *Fuzzy-wuzzy: the campaigns in the eastern Sudan, 1884–85* (1993) · *In relief of Gordon: Lord Wolseley's campaign journal of the Khartoum relief expedition, 1884–1885*, ed. A. Preston (1967) · N. Frankland, *Witness of a century* (1993) · T. Ryan and B. Parham, *The colonial New Zealand wars* (1986) · J. H. Lehmann, *The model major-general: a biography of Field-Marshal Lord Wolseley* (Boston, 1964) · E. Gambier-Parry, *Suakin, 1885* (1885), 119 · C. N. Robinson, *Celebrities of the army*, 18 pts (1900) · *DNB* · *CCI* (1904)

Archives PRO, Wolseley MSS, Asante journal, Sudan journal, WO 147/3, 147/8 · Royal Arch., army letters, E 30, E 62 · Royal Arch., corresp. on Egyptian campaign, 1882, Z. 176 · Royal Arch., Egypt series, O 24, O 26 | Hove Central Library, Sussex, corresp. with Lady Wolseley, W/P 14 · Royal Arch., Ponsonby MSS, Add. A 36, W 9

Likenesses Elliott & Fry, photograph, NPG [*see illus.*] · wood-engraving (after photograph by W. Notman), NPG; repro. in *ILN* (6 Dec 1873)

Wealth at death £19,147 0s. 5d.: confirmation, 29 July 1904, *CCI*

MacNeill, John Gordon Swift (1849–1926), politician and jurist, was born in Dublin on 11 March 1849, the only son of the evangelical clergyman the Revd John Gordon Swift MacNeill, curate of St James's Church, Dublin, and his wife, Susan Colpoys, daughter of the Revd Henry Tweedy. He was a collateral descendant of the author Jonathan Swift. He entered Trinity College, Dublin, in 1866, and migrated after a year to Christ Church, Oxford, where he read classics, then law and modern history. He graduated BA in 1872 and proceeded MA in 1875. In 1873 he became a student of the Inner Temple and in 1876 was called to the Irish bar. His growing reputation as a legal and constitutional authority led to his election in 1882 as professor of constitutional and criminal law at the King's Inns, Dublin,

John Gordon
Swift MacNeill
(1849–1926), by
James Russell &
Sons, 1887

a post he held until 1888. He took silk in 1893 but, despite his substantial legal reputation, never practised law extensively.

While still a student, MacNeill was active in historical, debating, and political societies: he became in the early 1870s a member of the Home Government Association in Dublin and acted as auditor of the Irish Law Students' Debating Society. He was a member of the council of the Home Government Association and was associated with the initial attempt of Charles Stewart Parnell to win a parliamentary seat in the county Dublin by-election of 1874. During the 1880s he established himself as an effective advocate of home rule, publishing propagandistic works such as *The Irish Parliament: What it Was, and What it Did* (1885), a volume warmly commended by W. E. Gladstone. However, he did not seek a parliamentary seat until standing successfully as the nationalist candidate at the Donegal South by-election on 2 February 1887. He represented this constituency continuously until 1918, when he retired from parliament in the face of the Sinn Féin onslaught. He was among the majority who left committee room 15 with Justin McCarthy on 6 December 1890, thereby parting company with Parnell. He was then an active member of the anti-Parnellite faction until the Irish party was reunited under John Redmond's chairmanship at the beginning of 1900.

Recognized as an expert in parliamentary forms, MacNeill was never an outstanding debater in the House of Commons, although his erudition commanded respect. He mastered the rules and revered the traditions of the House of Commons and, during his early years as an MP, used his knowledge of procedure to abet nationalist obstruction of business. A sincere home-ruler, MacNeill aligned himself on most questions with the radical or left-wing section of British Liberals. In addition to self-government and other Irish issues, he worked for a number of reforms and took an interest in a range of general questions. He argued against the cession of Heligoland to Germany and actively opposed the practice of government ministers serving as directors of public companies:

in March 1892 he successfully moved that the votes of three members of the Conservative government who were directors of the Mombasa Railway be disallowed in a House of Commons division where a conflict of interest was involved. He also showed sympathy for the Boers during the war in southern Africa, and fought for many years to abolish the flogging of boys in the Royal Navy, a practice finally ended in 1906. His part in the abolition campaign was acknowledged by the then Liberal prime minister, Sir Henry Campbell-Bannerman. Finally, MacNeill took pride in his role in the act passed in 1917 to remove British titles from the monarchs of hostile countries. His eccentric though enthusiastic speaking style and championship of unpopular causes gave him a notoriety wickedly captured in several of Harry Furniss's cartoons in *Punch*. Despite his various causes, he had the respect of colleagues, including political opponents, and in 1908 became a member of the committee of privileges of the House of Commons. In 1909 he became professor of constitutional law and of the law of public and private wrongs in the newly constituted National University of Ireland. To this he added the office of clerk of convocation in 1910 and then in 1912 that of dean of the faculty of law.

MacNeill was one of the comparatively few protestants to support home rule throughout his adult life. He was a throwback to the ideals of the nationalist leaders Isaac Butt and Parnell, in that he saw home rule as a means of reconciling communities in Ireland. His background, learning, and ideas made him the true heir of Butt's nationalism, and his support for Irish self-government sprang from a love of his homeland rather than anti-English sentiment. He was among those comfortable with dual loyalties—to both Ireland and Great Britain. Not surprisingly, his cosmopolitan look did not enable him to adapt easily to the more militant and often aggressively Catholic triumphalism of Sinn Féin, and his ambition to be the first speaker of an Irish House of Commons fell victim to the Sinn Féin revolution. He accepted the Irish Free State without enthusiasm, and took little significant part in public life during his final years.

MacNeill died on 24 August 1926 in a Dublin nursing home and was buried at Mount Jerome cemetery, Dublin, three days later. His many writings included two volumes of reminiscences, *What I have Seen and Heard* (1925) and *Studies in the Constitution of the Irish Free State* (1925), the latter of which became an important manual for politicians of the new nation. MacNeill was fond of music, a collector of antiquities, and a devoted walker, preferably to places of archaeological interest. As a lover of dogs, he took an interest in animal welfare and was an opponent of vivisection. He never married and was survived by his sister.

S. L. GWYNN, *rev.* ALAN O'DAY

Sources *The Times* (25 Aug 1926) · *The Times* (27 Aug 1926) · *Irish Times* (25 Aug 1926) · H. Boylan, *A dictionary of Irish biography*, 2nd edn (1988) · *WWBMP* · *Dod's Parliamentary Companion* · J. Loughlin, 'The Irish protestant Home Rule Association and nationalist politics, 1886–1893', *Irish Historical Studies*, 24 (1984–5), 341–60 · F. S. L. Lyons, *The Irish parliamentary party, 1890–1910* (1951) · C. C. O'Brien, *Parnell and his party, 1880–1890* (1957) · F. S. L. Lyons, *John Dillon* (1968) · F. S. L. Lyons, *The fall of Parnell, 1890–1891* (1961) · F. Callanan,

The Parnell split (1992) · J. G. S. MacNeill, *What I have seen and heard* (1925)

Archives Bodl. Oxf., Asquith MSS · NL Ire., Dillon MSS · TCD, corresp. with John Dillon

Likenesses J. Russell & Sons, photograph, 1887, NPG [*see illus.*] · B. Stone, photographs, 1892–1901, NPG · H. Furniss, cartoons, repro. in *Punch* · Spy [L. Ward], chromolithograph, NPG; repro. in *VF* (13 March 1902) · photograph, repro. in *Irish Times* · photograph, repro. in MacNeill, *What I have seen and heard*

Wealth at death £2930 3s. 7d.: probate, 5 Feb 1927, CGPLA *Éire* · £383 1s. 2d.—in England: administration, 18 Jan 1927, CGPLA Eng. & Wales

McNeill, (Florence) Marian (1885–1973), folklorist, was born on 26 March 1885 at Holm, Orkney, the third of four children of Daniel McNeill (1839–1918), a minister of the Free Church of Scotland, and his wife, Jessie Janet Dewar. She received her formal education in Orkney where among her schoolfriends she numbered the future poet and critic Edwin Muir. Marian McNeill graduated MA from Glasgow University in 1912. Before her graduation she travelled in Europe, working as an *assistante anglaise* at the Lycée des Jeunes Filles, Marseilles (1910–11), and then at the Kottbus Höhere Mädchenschule in Germany.

On her return to Scotland in 1912, Marian McNeill was appointed organizer of the Scottish Federation of Women's Suffrage Societies, and in the following year became secretary of the Association for Moral and Social Hygiene, which had been founded in 1870 by Josephine Butler. After the First World War she returned abroad, working as a private teacher of English in Athens (1919–20), during which time she regularly attended social gatherings and poetry readings at the home of the famous Greek poet Angelos Sikelianos. She went back to Scotland to become a freelance journalist and writer. Her first book *Iona: a History of the Island* was published in 1920 and enjoyed considerable popularity, reaching a seventh edition in 1991.

During the 1920s and 1930s Marian McNeill came into regular contact with many leading figures of the Scottish literary renaissance. In 1932 she founded the Clan McNeill Association of Scotland. She also involved herself closely with the politics of Scottish self-government, becoming vice-president of the Scottish National Party. Journalistic contributions to a host of publications including *The Scotsman*, the *Glasgow Herald*, and *Scottish Field* provided her with a regular income. In 1929 she joined the staff of the Scottish National Dictionary Association, as a researcher based in Aberdeen. In that year also her reputation as an authority on Scottish culinary matters became established with the publication of her *The Scots Kitchen: its Traditions and Lore with Old-Time Recipes*. It was the first of several works on Scottish food, which included *The Book of Breakfasts* (1932), *Recommended Recipes* (1948), and *The Scots Cellar: its Traditions and Lore* (1956). *The Scots Kitchen* is an important work, 'full of good scholarship, good wit in its application, and is an excellent and comprehensive survey of the theory and practice of cookery in a country that has always been a responsive friend to France' (*TLS*, 27 June 1929).

A thinly disguised autobiographical novel, *The Road Home*, appeared in 1932; it was to be Marian McNeill's only

venture into fiction. In 1957 however she produced the first volume of her *magnum opus*, *The Silver Bough: a Four Volume Study of the National and Local Festivals of Scotland*. The first volume covered Scottish folklore and folk beliefs, and the second and third volumes provided a calendar of Scottish national festivals. The first volume in particular became a standard work, although there were initial critical misgivings in academic circles. In 1962, for example, the reviewer for the *Times Literary Supplement* observed of volume 3 that:

> although sound enough where it describes what is generally known and traditional, [it] inspires less confidence when the alleged origins are given, and the sources from which Miss McNeill derives her information on this score are not made altogether clear, nor does her bibliography assist her. (*TLS*, 5 Oct 1962)

McNeill was quick to defend her position in a lengthy reply, claiming the work was based on 'living lore acquired, or more correctly imbibed in my childhood in my native Orkneys'. The final volume of *The Silver Bough* (1968) covered the local festivals of Scotland; reviewers once more attacked McNeill's methods and historical accuracy. But Marian McNeill was held in high regard by the Scottish literary establishment, and in the late summer of 1968 the Arts Council for Scotland gave a party for her and the poet Helen B. Cruickshank, both authors being 'in their ninth decade'. In 1962 she had been appointed MBE in the new year honours list. Undeterred by her critics Marian McNeill continued to write about Scottish food, publishing in 1971 a pamphlet entitled *Highland Cookery* in which she continued to extol the virtues of the Scottish larder. Marian McNeill died at her Edinburgh home, 31 St Albans Road, on 22 February 1973 at the age of eighty-seven.   JAMES A. PRATT

Sources H. B. Cruickshank, *Octobiography* (1976) · *The letters of Hugh MacDiarmid*, ed. A. Bold (1984) · W. Ewing, ed., *Annals of the Free Church of Scotland, 1843–1900*, 1 (1914) · J. A. Lamb, ed., *The fasti of the United Free Church of Scotland, 1900–1929* (1956) · H. Henderson, *Alias MacAlias: writings on songs, folk and literature* (1992) · [A. M. Mackenzie], 'The Scots kitchen', *TLS* (27 June 1929), 512 [review] · 'The road home', *TLS* (5 May 1932) · [A. Ross], 'Winter festivities', *TLS* (14 Sept 1962), 692 [review] · F. M. McNeill, 'The silver bough', *TLS* (5 Oct 1962), 777 [letter to the editor] · K. M. Briggs, 'The silver bough', *Folklore*, 73 (1962), 68–9 · 'Festschrift', *TLS* (8 Jan 1971), 42 [review] · *Scottish biographies* (1938) · *WWW* · G. Wright, *MacDiarmid: an illustrated biography* (1977) · *CCI* (1973)

Archives NL Scot., diaries, corresp., and papers | Orkney Archives, Kirkwall, letters to Ernest W. Marwick

Likenesses H. S. Harrison, photograph, 1931, repro. in Wright, *MacDiarmid*, 53 · G. Wright, photograph, 1968, repro. in Wright, *MacDiarmid*, 141

Wealth at death £20,062.98: confirmation, 13 June 1973, *CCI*

McNeill, Ronald John, Baron Cushendun (1861–1934), politician, was born at Torquay, Devon, on 30 April 1861, the only surviving son of Edmund McNeill (1821–1915), a landowner, of Craigdunn, Craigs, near Cushendun, co. Antrim, Ireland, who held land agencies, and his wife, Mary (d. 1909), eldest daughter of Alexander Miller, of Ballycastle, co. Antrim. The McNeills, who had settled in Antrim in 1676, were of Scottish origin; they could trace their descent from Torquil MacNeill, chief of the clan

Neill (*b. c.*1380). Ronald McNeill was educated at Harrow School (1875–80) and at Christ Church, Oxford (1880–84), where he was awarded a second class in modern history. On 9 October 1884 he married Elizabeth Maud (*d.* 1925), fifth daughter of William Bolitho, of Polwithen, Penzance, Cornwall. They had three daughters. He married, second, on 29 December 1930, Catherine Sydney Louisa (*d.* 1939), daughter of Sir Mortimer Reginald Margesson. They had no children.

In 1888 McNeill was called to the bar by Lincoln's Inn, but he abandoned the law for journalism and politics. In 1899 he was appointed assistant editor, and in 1900 editor, of the *St James's Gazette*, a post which he held until 1904. From 1906 to 1911 he was assistant editor of the eleventh edition of the *Encyclopaedia Britannica*, to which he also contributed a range of articles, covering such diverse subjects as recent Australian legislation, the history of the Fenians, and tennis.

McNeill was a determined supporter of tariff reform (a 'whole hogger') and unsuccessfully fought four elections, in West Aberdeenshire (1906), South Aberdeen City (February 1907 and January 1910), and Kirkcudbrightshire (December 1910), before he was elected, unopposed, at a by-election in July 1911, as the Conservative member for the East or St Augustine's division, later known as the Canterbury division, of Kent, which he held until 1927.

As a committed Ulster Unionist, who had published in 1907 *Home Rule: its History and Danger*, McNeill came to prominence as one of the most active of the so-called Conservative 'die-hard' group, which had been formed in 1910 in the disputes over the Conservative response to the reform of the House of Lords. In supporting 'true Tory' policies, as George Wyndham put it in 1911 (Green, 271), the 'die-hards' continued to oppose any thought of home rule for Ireland. The leader of this opposition was Sir Edward Carson, who later described McNeill as 'one of the best and most loyal friends of Ulster which he so deeply loved' (*The Times*, 12). McNeill's passion for this cause, and also his hot-blooded nature, were shown in a celebrated incident during a vote on an amendment to the third Home Rule Bill in November 1912 when, enraged into a 'furious temper' (*Real Old Tory Politics*, 52) by Winston Churchill, who triumphantly waved his handkerchief at the opposition, he threw a copy of the standing orders at Churchill, striking him on the head. During the First World War, McNeill was a chief organizer of the Unionist war committee, which was a focus for Conservative back-bench discontent with the wartime coalition. He opposed the Anglo-Irish treaty of December 1921, which established the Irish Free State, and in the following year he published *Ulster's Stand for Union*, which demonstrated to contemporaries 'the deep and passionate conviction of these dour, determined protestants' (*The Times*, 17). The central argument of this 'classic unionist text' (Bew, 110) was that Ulstermen resorted to militant opposition to home rule only after August 1911, when the House of Lords veto was removed by the passing of the Parliament Act, itself an unconstitutional action, McNeill argued, of the Liberal government.

McNeill supported the moves among Conservatives which led, in October 1922, to the decision to end the coalition with Lloyd George. The new Conservative prime minister, Bonar Law, appointed him parliamentary under-secretary for foreign affairs. This appointment, because McNeill was known largely only as an advocate of often extreme views, caused 'general surprise' even among members of his own party (*The Times*, 17). But he proved himself in this position and was retained there by Baldwin, in his first and second ministries (1923 and 1924). McNeill was sworn of the privy council in 1924, and in November 1925 he became financial secretary to the Treasury. In October 1927 he succeeded Lord Cecil of Chelwood as chancellor of the duchy of Lancaster, which office, together with a seat in the cabinet, he held until 1929. His strong protestant beliefs led him to oppose the introduction of the revised prayer book in 1927. In November 1927 he was raised to the peerage as Baron Cushendun, taking his title from the village in Antrim where he held his property.

For a short time Cushendun held Lord Cecil's office as chief British representative to the League of Nations. In an incident which brought him some degree of fame, during a debate on a Russian proposal for the immediate abolition of all armed forces, in a sitting of the preparatory disarmament commission in March 1928, Cushendun 'submitted the Soviet scheme … to a long and devastating criticism' (*The Times*, 17), which brought cheers from other delegates and much praise in the press. From August to December 1928, when Sir Austen Chamberlain, the foreign secretary, was ill, Cushendun was acting secretary of state for foreign affairs. One of his functions during this time was to sign in Paris on 27 August the Kellogg pact under which war was outlawed.

Cushendun, 6 foot 6 inches tall, and well-built, was an imposing figure. He was also a fine orator. Robert Sanders noted during debates in 1925 that he gave 'about the best speech of the session' (*Real Old Tory Politics*, 223). He died at his home, Glenmona, Cushendun, on 12 October 1934 and was buried at Cushendun on 16 October.

ST JOHN ERVINE, rev. MARC BRODIE

Sources *The Times* (13 Oct 1934) · *Belfast Telegraph* (12 Oct 1934) · *Belfast News-Letter* (13 Oct 1934) · GEC, *Peerage* · J. Turner, *British politics and the Great War: coalition and conflict, 1915–1918* (1992) · R. Blake, *The unknown prime minister: the life and times of Andrew Bonar Law* (1955) · N. Mansergh, *The unresolved question: the Anglo-Irish settlement and its undoing, 1912–1972* (1991) · K. Feiling, *The life of Neville Chamberlain* (1946) · *Real old tory politics: the political diaries of Robert Sanders, Lord Bayford, 1910–35*, ed. J. Ramsden (1984) · E. H. H. Green, *The crisis of conservatism: the politics, economics and ideology of the Conservative Party, 1880–1914* (1995) · A. Jackson, *The Ulster party: Irish unionists in the House of Commons, 1884–1911* (1989) · P. Bew, *Ideology and the Irish question* (1994) · *CGPLA Eng. & Wales* (1935)
Archives PRO NIre. | HLRO, Law MSS · PRO, FO 800/227–8 · U. Birm., Chamberlain MSS | FILM BFI NFTVA, news footage
Likenesses photograph, repro. in *The Times*, 17
Wealth at death £102,682 4s. in England: probate, 11 March 1935, *CGPLA Eng. & Wales* · £10,067 8s.: probate, 30 Jan 1935, *CGPLA NIre.*

MacNeill, Seumas [Seamas, James] (1917–1996), bagpiper and authority on piping, was born James McNeill on 12

Seumas MacNeill (1917–1996), by unknown photographer

September 1917 at 32 Dowanhill Street, Partick, Glasgow, the second of the three children of James McNeill (1883–1953), whose family came from the island of Gigha, and his wife, Christina, *née* Lumsden (1888–1956), a cook, who was from Fife. His father served with the Royal Scots during the First World War, returning to find his job taken by another and his prospects bleak. He had a number of occupations during the depression years, and was considered to be a man of high intelligence employed below his intellectual capacity. Known as James to his family and Jimmy to his hillwalking friends, he chose to use the Gaelic form of his name, Seumas MacNeill, in the piping world. He spent his entire life in Glasgow. He was educated at Hyndland School and at the University of Glasgow, where he took an honours degree in mathematics and natural philosophy (physics), and was awarded the MacKay Smith prize for the most distinguished student in his final honours year. He then attended Jordanhill Teacher Training College for a year, and spent a short time teaching at Glasgow Technical College, before being offered an appointment to the natural philosophy department at Glasgow University. He later became a senior lecturer. He was never tempted to move elsewhere in furtherance of his academic career, and, although a brilliant lecturer and teacher, he made little attempt to pursue research in physics, publishing only one paper. On 8 September 1948 he married Janet Boyd (*b.* 1925), a clerical worker; they had a son, Rory. They lived near the university at 4 Lilybank Gardens, Hillhead, Glasgow, until 1957, when they moved to 22 Mosshead Road, Bearsden.

MacNeill's heart was in piping, and he devoted his

energy almost exclusively to the promotion and development of piping. As Brian Wilson put it in *The Guardian* after MacNeill's death, 'He was at the heart of a series of bold initiatives each of which has survived and flourished down to the present day'. His innovations in the piping world had an influence which would be felt for generations to come. With Thomas Pearston he established the College of Piping in 1944 in a basement in Pitt Street, Glasgow; the college later moved to premises in Otago Street, Glasgow. MacNeill himself was one of its tutors, not content to be a mere figure-head as joint principal (sole principal from 1978). The college had many distinguished pupils, some of whom returned as tutors. It became a centre for the running of the Piobaireachd Society and soon became known as 'The Centre of the Piping World'—a designation awarded by MacNeill himself. MacNeill also founded the monthly magazine the *Piping Times*, which he edited for forty-eight years. It was described as 'always lively due to Seumas's forthright style and liking for a good argument' (Wilson). He was always outspoken in his views, but as a noted piper himself—he won the gold medal for piobaireachd at Oban in 1962—he had a sound basis for his critical opinions. With subscribers all over the world, the historical material accumulated made the magazine an essential work of reference.

MacNeill's published works were not numerous, but proved to be of lasting worth. With Thomas Pearston he published three 'tutors' for the College of Piping; of the first, the *Green Tutor* (1953), more than 245,000 copies were sold in his lifetime, and it was translated into French, German, and Norwegian. It was by far the best seller of any book on piping. In 1990 he added a *Tutor for Piobaireachd*, which was well received. His booklet on piobaireachd, issued in 1968 by the BBC to accompany a series of radio talks and reprinted in 1976, became a classic, as did an article co-authored with John Lenihan, 'An acoustical study of the highland bagpipe' (1954). Both works proved a stepping-stone for later research, and were regarded as authoritative. In 1987 MacNeill and Frank Richardson published *Piobaireachd and its Interpretation*.

As a lecturer MacNeill was supreme. His witty turn of phrase and his enthusiasm held his audiences, some of whom maintained that he was the best lecturer they had ever heard, on any subject. His seminal evening classes on piobaireachd in the 1960s opened many minds to the great classical music of the pipe, and his weekly *Chanter* programmes on the radio will long be remembered. It was said that when he died it would take at least seven good men to replace him in the piping world. Most of his work for piping was not for monetary reward, and he was not a wealthy man. Money meant little to him, other than as a means of furthering the cause of piping.

MacNeill was a tallish, lean, neat man, who wore light-rimmed glasses. His light brown hair receded in his later years. Though not a military man, he bore himself well, and gave an impression of smartness and attention to detail. He often wore a kilt and tweed jacket, a reflection of his passionate loyalty to his country. An award which gave him great pleasure in the 1980s was the loving cup, presented by the city of Glasgow to any citizen deemed to have brought honour to the town. As a young man he made frequent visits to the hills with a group of walking and camping friends. In the late 1940s he was secretary of the Scottish Youth Hostels Association, and he retained his interest in the outdoor life and in the mountains of Scotland. He was a staunch member of the Church of Scotland, actively supporting the work of his local church.

MacNeill was abstemious by nature and his main indulgence was his habit of witticism, often at others' expense. Although he inspired fierce loyalty among his friends, he was a man with many enemies, possibly more than anyone else in the piping world. He was fond of quoting F. D. Roosevelt, 'I hope you will judge me by my enemies', and took gleeful pleasure in stirring controversy. A man of biting wit, he seemed unable to resist the temptation to exercise it, and his rapier thrusts, though brilliantly amusing, were often not appreciated by the victim. He needed as a foil a man such as his friend John MacFadyen to relish his sallies and return them in good measure: exchanges of needle-sharp wit between the two were enjoyed by spectators as if watching a fencing match. Lesser men might, however, be struck hard in their vanity, and some bore a lifelong grudge. Pipers used to say that if you had not been savaged by Seumas, you were a nobody in the piping world. Yet he was not an unkind man: he was capable of great patience and gentle charm, and his courtesy to foreigners was unfailing. What some saw as attacks were often merely exercises of wit, not malice, and subsequent umbrage was frequently the result of misinterpretation of his motives.

As MacNeill grew older he became more bitter, and his attacks became more savage. Dry wit turned acid, and in his last year, clouded by painful illness, he was disappointed in his great aim to have the College of Piping expanded and established as part of a piping centre in a converted building in Cowcaddens, for which a huge amount of money had been raised, much of it by his own efforts. Dispute about his status in the new centre, and other points of disagreement with his fellow fund-raisers, led him to withdraw himself and his college from the project. A disappointed man, whom many considered to have been treated shabbily, he died at his home on 4 April 1996. He had been suffering from cancer of the colon, and as a sick man of nearly eighty years he had not been able to fling himself into the fray as he would have wished. He was survived by his wife. At his own request, he was buried at Riddrie Park cemetery, Glasgow, on 10 April, beside his uncle, Blind Archie McNeill, his piping teacher and beloved mentor.   BRIDGET MACKENZIE

Sources Archives of the College of Piping, 16–24 Otago Street, Glasgow · B. Wilson, *The Guardian* (6 April 1996) · D. MacNeill, *The Herald* (6 April 1996) · *The Scotsman* (13 April 1996) · editorial, *Piper and Drummer* [USA] (Feb 1995) · private information (2004) [family] · J. M. A. Lenihan and S. MacNeill, 'An acoustical study of the highland bagpipe', *Acustica*, 4 (1954) · *Piping Times*, 1/49 (1948–96) [monthly pubn] · b. cert. · d. cert.
Archives College of Piping, 16–24 Otago Street, Glasgow, archives | SOUND College of Piping, Otago Street, Glasgow, tapes of pipers · Radio Scotland, Queen Margaret Drive, Glasgow, BBC Sound Archives, tapes of *Chanter* and other BBC radio programmes
Likenesses photograph, repro. in *Piping Times*, 48/8 (May 1996), cover · photograph, repro. in *The Guardian* · photograph, repro. in *The Herald* · photograph, repro. in *The Scotsman* · photographs, College of Piping, Glasgow [*see illus.*]
Wealth at death £185,876.91: resworn, 3 June 1996, NA Scot., SC/CO 935/124 & 922/1 · £6,452: additional inventory, 24 July 1996, NA Scot., SC/CO 935/124 & 922/1

Mac Néill, Uilliam. *See* Neilson, William (1774–1821).

MacNeven, William James (1763–1841), physician and Irish nationalist, was born on 21 March 1763 at Ballynahowne, near Aughrim in co. Galway, the eldest of the four children of James MacNeven, owner of a small estate, and Rosa Dolphin. His parents were Gaelic-speaking Catholics; according to family tradition, their ancestors had owned large tracts of land in the north of Ireland before being dispossessed and forcibly resettled in Connaught during the Cromwellian era. He was educated at local schools until the age of twelve, when he was sent to Prague to live with his uncle, Baron William O'Kelly MacNeven, the chief physician of the empress Maria Theresa. He attended the medical college at Prague, and graduated from the University of Vienna in 1783. During his years in Europe he became fluent in German and French and developed a strong interest in experimental philosophy.

MacNeven returned to Ireland in 1784 and established his medical practice in Dublin. A 'neat little man of 5 feet 4 inches' (Fitzpatrick, 357), he rapidly acquired a reputation as an energetic individual of 'great genius' (Durey, 126). He entered politics in 1791, when he joined the Catholic Committee, challenged the conciliatory strategy of its leadership, and pressed for Catholic emancipation. In the Catholic convention of 1792 he emerged as a leader of the campaign to extend the 40s. freehold franchise to Catholics. During the early 1790s he became involved in the Society of United Irishmen, and he was elected to its executive in 1797. On the moderate wing of the movement, MacNeven argued that an Irish insurrection should not take place without French assistance; the presence of French troops, he believed, would reduce revolutionary violence and safeguard private property. In June 1797 he travelled to Hamburg, under the alias Williams, and delivered a detailed memorial to the French minister on the state of United Irish forces in Ireland and the best means of effecting an invasion. Proceeding to Paris, he supported the efforts of the United Irish plenipotentiary Edward Lewins to persuade the Directory and General Hoche to organize an expedition to Ireland. MacNeven also attempted, without success, to secure French guarantees that Ireland would not be treated as a conquered country.

Back in Dublin, MacNeven was arrested on 12 March 1798, along with other leaders of the United Irishmen, and was thus in Kilmainham gaol when the rising broke out two months later. In July MacNeven and his fellow prisoners Thomas Addis Emmet and Arthur O'Connor struck a deal with the government; they promised to reveal detailed information about the revolutionary organization in return for their banishment for life to a neutral

William James MacNeven (1763–1841), by T. W. Huffam, pubd 1843 (after James Dowling Herbert)

country. Accordingly, MacNeven described and defended the tenets and tactics of the United Irishmen before the secret committee of the Irish Houses of Lords and Commons on 7 and 8 August, and later published his own version of the examination. He intended to settle in Germany, but was prevented from doing so by the government, which wanted the prisoners safely out of the way in the United States. When Rufus King, the American ambassador to Britain, objected to this plan, the government decided to detain the leading prisoners until the war with France was over. In March 1799 MacNeven and nineteen other prisoners were transferred to Fort George in Scotland, where they remained until the treaty of Amiens in 1802. During his imprisonment MacNeven wrote *An Argument for Independence* (1799), which attacked William Pitt's plans for legislative union between Britain and Ireland.

Upon his release from Fort George in 1802 MacNeven went on a walking tour of Switzerland, which formed the basis for *A Ramble through Swisserland in … 1802* (1803). He spent the winter of 1802–3 in Paris, where he attempted to revive interest in a French expedition to Ireland. When the war between Britain and France resumed in 1803, he joined the French army as a captain in the Irish legion, and drew up a revolutionary proclamation to be distributed among the Irish in the event of an invasion. By the following year, however, he had become increasingly suspicious of France's war aims, and was particularly alarmed by the growing influence of the rival O'Connorite faction within

the Irish legion. Fearing that Napoleon would turn Ireland into a French puppet state, he resigned his commission, left France for the United States, and arrived in New York in July 1805.

In the United States MacNeven resumed his medical practice, received an honorary MD from Columbia College in 1806, and was appointed professor of midwifery in the New York College of Physicians and Surgeons in 1808. After the college was reorganized in 1810, he became professor of chemistry, to which he added materia medica between 1816 and 1820. In 1826 he moved to the newly established Duane Street medical school, where he lectured on materia medica until 1830. Until his retirement in 1839 he continued to practise medicine, and he was appointed hospital inspector during the cholera epidemic of 1832. He was known as the 'father of American chemistry', and his most important scientific publication was his *Exposition of the Atomic Theory of Chymistry* (1819). He also edited William Thomas Brande's *Manual of Chemistry* (1821), which became the standard textbook for students, and was co-editor of the *New York Medical and Philosophical Journal and Review* between 1808 and 1811. On 15 June 1810 he married Jane Margaret Tom, widow of John Tom, merchant of New York, and daughter of Samuel Riker of New Town, Long Island; they had five children.

Along with his compatriots Thomas Addis Emmet and William Sampson, MacNeven was a central figure in New York's Irish-American community. In the words of his friend Thomas O'Connor, MacNeven was 'a member of nearly every society formed in this city, having for its object the honour and interest of his countrymen' (Madden, 3.233). In 1805 MacNeven joined the Friendly Sons of St Patrick and the Hibernian Provident Society. In 1816 he co-founded both the New York Association for the Relief of Emigrant Irishmen and the Shamrock Friendly Society, and petitioned congress to settle Irish immigrants in the Illinois territory. Serving as president of the New York Friends of Ireland in 1828–9, he supported Daniel O'Connell's campaign for Catholic emancipation; in 1831 he reconstituted the Friends of Ireland into an organization for repeal of the Act of Union. Throughout his American career MacNeven encouraged the writing of patriotic Irish literature; his most significant contribution was *Pieces of Irish History* (1807), which attempted to vindicate the United Irishmen in the eyes of the American public.

MacNeven was an active participant in American politics. In New York he belonged to De Witt Clinton's republicans, contributed to the defeat of Rufus King during the assembly elections of 1807, and urged the Irish to fight against the British enemy during the Anglo-American War of 1812–14. His pamphlet *Of the Nature and Functions of Army Staff* (1812) attempted to apply Napoleonic military methods to the organization of the American army. In federal politics MacNeven supported the Democratic Party until 1834, when he opposed President Andrew Jackson's decision to remove the deposits from the United States Bank; Jackson's policy, MacNeven wrote, was 'contrary to the spirit of our constitution, to the principles of genuine liberty, and of republican principles' (Madden, 3.235). This was an unpopular position. MacNeven's daughter recalled that 'a storm of party rage was directed against him' (ibid., 3.207); he was accused of corruption and inconsistency, and his house was attacked by a Jacksonian crowd which included many recent Irish immigrants.

After his retirement in 1839 MacNeven lived with his stepdaughter and his son-in-law, Thomas Addis Emmet, the fifth child of his old friend Thomas Addis Emmet, just outside New York. In November 1840 he was badly hurt when his gig collided with a wagon, and he never fully recovered from the shock. After a long and painful illness he died at his son-in-law's house on 12 July 1841. His funeral service took place at St Patrick's Cathedral, New York, and he was buried at Bowery Bay, Long Island, in the burial-ground of the Riker family.   DAVID A. WILSON

Sources R. R. Madden, *The United Irishmen: their lives and times*, 2nd edn, 3rd ser. (1860), 197–256 · D. Ó Raghallaigh, 'William James MacNeven', *Studies: An Irish Quarterly Review*, 30 (1941), 247–59 · W. J. Fitzpatrick, *Secret service under Pitt* (1892) · M. Durey, *Transatlantic radicals and the early American republic* (1997) · M. Elliott, *Partners in revolution: the United Irishmen and France* (1982) · D. A. Wilson, *United Irishmen, United States: immigrant radicals in the early republic* (1998) · *Memoirs and correspondence of Viscount Castlereagh, second marquess of Londonderry*, ed. C. Vane, marquess of Londonderry, 12 vols. (1848–53), vol. 1, pp. 295–301 · B. Stacey, 'William James MacNeven', *Bulletin of the New York Academy of Medicine*, 41 (Oct 1965), 1037–51 · *DNB* · E. J. Hafner, 'MacNeven, William James', *ANB* · *New York Tribune* (14 July 1841)
Archives Hist. Soc. Penn., Edward Carey Gardiner collection · L. Cong., David Bailie Warden papers · NA Ire., rebellion papers
Likenesses Herbert, engraving, *c*.1797, repro. in Madden, *The United Irishmen, their lives and times* · portrait, 1830–39, repro. in *Catholic encyclopedia* (1910), vol. 9, p. 506 · J. D. Herbert, mezzotint, pubd 1843, NG Ire. · T. W. Huffam, engraving, pubd 1843 (after J. D. Herbert), NG Ire. [see illus.] · group portrait, coloured lithograph (*The United Irish Patriots of 1798*), NPG
Wealth at death left modest inheritance: Madden, *United Irishmen*

MacNicol, Donald (1735–1802), Church of Scotland minister and author, was born in Glenorchy, the son of Nicol MacNicol, tacksman of Socach, and of Mary Stewart of the Invernahyle family. He graduated from St Andrews University in 1756 with an MA and was licensed by the presbytery of Lorn on 3 December 1760. He was ordained on 5 October 1763 in the parish of Saddell and Skipness, Argyll, and was presented by John, duke of Argyll, with the living of Lismore on 3 September 1765.

MacNicol was raised in a family with a long-standing attachment to the Scots Gaelic culture and the oral traditions of the highlands. As a Gaelic speaker who was noted for his learning and excellence as a Gaelic poet, MacNicol developed an early interest in collecting Gaelic poetry and heroic ballads. He also wrote many of the songs of Donnchadh Ban Macan-t-Saoir (Duncan Ban) from the poet's dictation. In the late 1750s and early 1760s James Macpherson, translator and author of *The Poems of Ossian* (1773), had begun collecting Ossianic tales and poems. Macpherson soon realized that MacNicol's collection represented one of the most important compilations of Ossianic and modern poetry that he was likely to secure.

Though the earliest date in his Ossianic collection is 1755 and could not have been the chief source for Macpherson's *Fingal* (1762) and *Temora* (1763), the Celtic scholar Derick Thomson finds MacNicol's collection 'as might be inferred from his background and training … one of the best which we have' (Thomson, *Gaelic Sources*, 8).

MacNicol married Lilias (Lily; *d*. 1831), daughter of Alexander Campbell, in Auchlian, Glenorchy, on 28 November 1771; the couple had sixteen children. Lily was known as a great beauty and though 'MacNicol was considered handsome, he had a badly pocked face, and it took hard and long wooing to win [her]' (Henderson, 344). While MacNicol ministered to his parish a controversy had sprung up in London concerning the authenticity of *The Poems of Ossian* and certain influential readers accused Macpherson of fraud. Samuel Johnson, the well-respected literary critic, found Macpherson's claims for original Ossianic texts unconvincing, and after a trip to the highlands in 1773 in part to examine its culture and social conditions, wrote *A Journey to the Western Islands of Scotland* (1775). Johnson stated briefly his view that the poems of Ossian 'never existed in any other form than that we have seen'. Macpherson's angry response and efforts at having the passage deleted failed when Johnson rebuffed, in his famous letter (20 January 1775), the Scot's supposed threats.

MacNicol, who had followed the Ossian controversy and reacted quickly to Johnson's comments in the *Journey*, was very protective of the honour of Scotland. In a long letter to the Revd John Walker on 22 March 1775 MacNicol complained that Johnson's 'brain [was] deeply intoxicated with national prejudice' (Edinburgh University Library, MS La.III.352; Fleeman, xxxiv–xxxvii). These attacks on Macpherson's work were, he believed, a direct assault on the significance of Gaelic language and culture. William Strahan printed for Thomas Cadell in October 1779 MacNicol's *Remarks on Dr. Samuel Johnson's journey to the Hebrides; in which are contained, observations on the antiquities, language, genius, and manners of the highlanders of Scotland*. MacNicol, who had sent the manuscript to London in the care of several friends, began sarcastically: 'Unfortunately, Dr. Johnson's "Journey" has lain dead in the library, for some time past. This consideration is so discouraging that the writer of the *Remarks* expects little literary reputation and less profit, from his labours' (advertisement). Proceeding in what is a rather tedious detailing of corrections and contradictions of Johnson's *Journey*, MacNicol soon changed his tone and attacked Johnson's character. He decided unequivocally in Macpherson's favour: 'Imposture is the last thing of which a gentleman can be supposed guilty, it is the last thing with which he ought to be charged. To bring forward such an accusation, therefore, without proof to establish it, is a ruffian mode of impeachment' (p. 365).

Scholars studying MacNicol's *Remarks* have searched for examples of unclerical prose asking, for instance, 'is this the "humble and pleasant" paterfamilias of Lismore speaking, or the notorious lecher of London, James Macpherson? Or is it some third person?' (Metzdorf, 53).

Others have decided unequivocally—'no doubt that [Macpherson] intruded some abusive indecencies into the original version' (Fleeman, xxxiv). Without more conclusive evidence the most equitable position is that Macpherson may have interpolated certain passages in MacNicol's book, but the evidence has never fully supported this charge. Certainly someone did touch up MacNicol's manuscript with amendments and additions which James Boswell, among others, found insupportable as an attack on Johnson. While Boswell was deciding on how best to respond, MacNicol had already cancelled two offending passages of nearly six pages in length for subsequent printings of the first edition. Ironically, the uncorrected, uncancelled text would reappear in later editions.

MacNicol continued as a 'humble and pleasant [minister], fulfilling all duties pertaining to his office, being compared to the "minister Paul" for the zeal and frequency of his preaching' (Henderson, 345). His book remained well known, appearing in six editions, the last published in 1887. Johnson, however, reacted by observing that 'the fellow must be a blockhead to bring out an attack that cost five shillings … if they had wit, they should have kept pelting me with pamphlets' (*Laird of Auchinleck*, 223). Later Johnson ghost-wrote in his role as unofficial patron of the Scottish minister, William Shaw, *A Reply to Mr. Clark*, which was appended to the second 'corrected' edition of Shaw's *An Enquiry into the Authenticity of the Poems Ascribed to Ossian* (1782). Beyond answering MacNicol's antagonism, the *Reply* continued the exposé and indictment of Macpherson and other 'forgers' of Highland poetry. MacNicol, who died in Lismore on 28 March 1802, never regretted his part in presenting Ossian and early Gaelic culture to the world.   PAUL J. deGATEGNO

Sources DNB · Fasti Scot. · R. F. Metzdorf, 'M'Nicol, Macpherson, and Johnson', *Eighteenth-century studies in honor of Donald F. Hyde*, ed. W. Bond (1970), 45–61 · G. Henderson, 'Lamh-Sgriobhainnean Mhic-Neacail', *Transactions of the Gaelic Society of Inverness*, 27 (1908–11), 340–409 · J. F. Campbell, *Leabhar na Feinne* (*The Songs of the Fiana*) (1872) · D. S. Thomson, *The Gaelic sources of Macpherson's 'Ossian'* (1952) · D. S. Thomson, ed., *The companion to Gaelic Scotland* (1983) · J. Leyden, *Journal of a tour in the highlands and western islands of Scotland in 1800* (1800) · J. D. Fleeman, introduction, in S. Johnson, *A journey to the western islands of Scotland*, ed. J. D. Fleeman (1985) · Boswell, *Life* · P. J. deGategno, *James Macpherson* (1989) · *Papers of British churchmen, 1780–1940*, HMC (1987) · *Boswell, laird of Auchinleck, 1778–1782*, ed. J. W. Reed and F. A. Pottle (1977), vol. 11 of *The Yale editions of the private papers of James Boswell*, trade edn (1950–89) · R. B. Sher, 'Percy, Shaw, and the Ferguson "cheat": national prejudice in the Ossian wars', *Ossian revisited*, ed. H. Gaskill (1991), 207–45 · F. Stafford, 'Dr Johnson and the ruffian: new evidence in the dispute between Samuel Johnson and James Macpherson', *N&Q*, 234 (1989), 70–77 · T. Costey, 'Johnson's last word on Ossian: ghostwriting for William Shaw', *Aberdeen and the Enlightenment*, ed. J. J. Carter and J. H. Pittock (1987), 375–431
Archives NA Scot., kirk session records · U. Glas. L., special collections department, papers, mainly Gaelic sermons

MacNicol [*married name* Frew], **Elizabeth** [Bessie] (1869–1904), painter, was born on 15 July 1869 at 352 St Vincent Street, Glasgow, the fourth child and elder twin daughter of Peter MacNicol (1839–1903), schoolmaster and later head of Anderston burgh school, and his wife, Mary Ann

Matthews (1839–1903), who were married at Canton, Cardiff, on 28 June 1864. MacNicol's twin brothers died in infancy and two sisters, including her twin, Mary, in early childhood. Despite these tragedies her family background was congenial and supportive and she shared musical talent with her two surviving sisters. She had a lively personality and many friends both male and female. Her health caused concern and in summer she suffered from hayfever. MacNicol studied from 1887 to 1893 at Glasgow School of Art, where women students were welcomed by the charismatic headmaster Francis Newbery, who treated them in the same way as male students. He encouraged MacNicol to continue her studies in Paris at l'Académie Colarossi (1893–4).

MacNicol first drew public attention when she exhibited *A French Girl* (priv. coll.) at the Glasgow Institute in 1895. In 1896 she visited Kirkcudbright and painted Edward Atkinson Hornel, one of the group of painters known as the Glasgow Boys, in his studio (Broughton House, Kirkcudbright). She was influenced by his style of painting and use of colour. MacNicol's Kirkcudbright paintings of young girls under trees with dappled sunlight filtering through foliage also owe much to James Guthrie and David Gauld. Her masterly use of paint textures and attractive colour as in *Under the Apple Tree* (1899; Glasgow Museums and Art Galleries) places her work alongside that of the younger Glasgow Boys. As well as exhibiting in Glasgow and Edinburgh, MacNicol sent paintings to exhibitions in London, Liverpool, and Manchester; to Munich, Ghent, and Vienna on the continent; and to Pittsburgh and St Louis in the United States.

In 1898 MacNicol exhibited *Autumn* (Aberdeen Art Gallery) at the International Society in London, a fancy portrait of a young girl against chestnut leaves. In October 1898 she attended a performance of *Trelawny of the Wells* by Arthur Wing Pinero, and charmed by the Victorian costumes painted *A Girl of the 'Sixties* (Glasgow Museums and Art Galleries). This, the finest of her fancy portraits, was the first of many costume pieces in oils and watercolour. It was shown at her only solo exhibition at Stephen Gooden Art Rooms, Glasgow, in January 1899 and at the International Society in 1901.

On 19 April 1899 MacNicol married Alexander Frew (1861–1908) at her family home, 4 Oakfield Terrace, Glasgow. Frew was a man of many talents and interests, at one time giving up medicine to become a full-time painter specializing in marine subjects. After his marriage he resumed his medical career as a consultant gynaecologist at 12 St James Terrace, Hillhead, Glasgow. A large studio designed for the previous owner allowed MacNicol to paint larger works influenced in colour and composition by J. A. M. Whistler. *Vanity* (priv. coll.), a splendid painting of the back of a nude woman holding a mirror, was exhibited in 1902 at the Glasgow Society of Artists, a new society formed by Frew in criticism of the Royal Glasgow Institute and in imitation of the International Society. *Motherhood* (priv. coll.), a painting of her sister and baby son, and *Baby Crawford* (City Art Centre, Edinburgh) were among later important works, their subject becoming all the more poignant when Bessie MacNicol died in childbirth at home on 4 June 1904, aged thirty-four. The cause of death was given as 'puerperal eclampsia before labour' and her first child was never born. The certificate was signed by Alexander Frew. She was buried on 8 June at Sighthill cemetery, Glasgow. An obituarist commented, 'So brilliant was her work and of such promise that it is felt that her premature death has robbed Scotland of one who should have left a name worthy to rank with the best of her artist sons' (*Glasgow Herald*, 7 June 1904).   Ailsa Tanner

Sources nine letters from Bessie MacNicol to Edward Atkinson Hornel, December 1896 – December 1897, National Trust for Scotland, Broughton House, High Street, Kirkcudbright · letter from Bessie MacNicol to Hugh Hopkins, with a sketch of *A French girl*, priv. coll. · P. Bate, 'In memoriam: Bessie MacNicol, painter', *Scottish Art and Letters*, 3/3 (1904) · G. Eyre-Todd, 'A remarkable career: the late Alexander Frew', *Evening Times* [Glasgow] (16 Jan 1908) · *Glasgow Herald* (7 June 1904) · J. L. Caw, *Scottish painting past and present, 1620–1908* (1908) · J. Burkhauser, ed., *The Glasgow girls: women in art and design, 1880–1920* (1990) · B. Smith, *The life and work of Edward Atkinson Hornel* (1997) · D. Gaze, ed., *Dictionary of women artists*, 2 (1997) · A. Tanner, *Bessie MacNicol: new woman* (1998) [incl. bibliography] · b. cert.

Archives Broughton House, Kirkcudbright, letters to Edward Atkinson Hornel

Likenesses B. MacNicol, drawing, 1893, Ewan Mundy Fine Art, Glasgow · B. MacNicol, oils, *c*.1894, Glasgow Museums and Art Galleries · photographs, priv. coll.

Wealth at death £731 17s. 2d.: confirmation, 23 Jan 1905, *CCI*

MacNish, Robert (1802–1837), physician and writer, one of three sons and four daughters of John William MacNish, surgeon, and his wife, Christian Johnstone Kerr, was born at Henderson's Court, Jamaica Street, Glasgow, on 15 February 1802. Educated first in Glasgow, he was sent when aged seven or eight to the school of the Revd Alexander Easton of Hamilton. MacNish later recalled that, except in drawing, he was considered extremely stupid and was flogged regularly by his teachers. He soon became quite ungovernable. After leaving school he followed his father and grandfather into the medical profession. In 1820 he obtained the degree CM from Glasgow University.

MacNish made what appears to have been a strange choice for his first post in medicine, leaving the bustle of Glasgow for the remoteness of Caithness, where he joined Dr John Henderson in his practice based at Clyth. MacNish found life difficult on two fronts: his relations with Henderson were strained, and the heavy workload of a country practice affected his health. He returned to Glasgow after eighteen months. He had, however, published poetry in the *Inverness Journal*, much of it influenced by the solitude and remoteness of Caithness.

Soon after returning to Glasgow, MacNish left for Paris, where during a stay of a year he attended the lectures of the comparative anatomist Georges Cuvier and the 'inventor' of phrenology, Franz Joseph Gall. On returning to Glasgow, he resumed his medical studies and began to develop his literary career, publishing articles in the *Literary Melange*, *The Emmet*, and Constable's *Edinburgh Review*. In 1825 he became a member of the Faculty of Physicians and Surgeons of Glasgow. MacNish's story 'The Metempsychosis' appeared in *Blackwood's Edinburgh Magazine* in

Robert MacNish (1802–1837), by Daniel Maclise, pubd 1835

May 1826. Influenced by Adelbert von Chamisso's *Peter Schlemihl* (1813), and possibly by James Hogg's *Confessions of a Justified Sinner* (1824), it tells the story of a pact made between the inconsequential Wolstang and the irritable and violent Stadt who agree during a drinking session to exchange bodies. Wolstang then discovers that he can only recover his own bodily form by agreeing to sell his soul. Eventually Wolstang is reunited with his body and in the process has become a firm believer in metempsychosis or the transmigration of the soul.

MacNish published *The Anatomy of Drunkenness* the year after 'The Metempsychosis'. Although he deplored the effects of drunkenness MacNish was keen to acknowledge that 'the pleasures of getting drunk are certainly ecstatic. While the illusion lasts, happiness is complete' (p. 34). The book also dealt with the physiology and pathology of drunkenness, with its effects on sleep, and with delirium tremens. MacNish noted that those suffering the latter were inclined to 'a belief that every person is confederated to ruin him' and often became 'irritated beyond measure by the slightest contradiction' (ibid., 59). He was, however, uncertain about the effects drink had on the personality. On the one hand he believed that in modern society where all is disguise, 'Intoxication tears off the veil, and sets each in his true light' (ibid., 48). The 'drunkard pours out the secrets of his soul. His qualities, good or bad come forth without reserve; and now, if at any time, the human heart may be seen into' (ibid., 35). On the other hand MacNish found himself agreeing with Joseph Addison that drink can produce the opposite effect: 'wine throws a man out of himself, and infuses qualities into the mind which she is a stranger to in her sober moments' (ibid., 49).

During 1829 MacNish, who was of average height and powerfully built, became ill with fever and was confined indoors for five months. He complained to his friend David Moir, another writer and physician, that he found the light intolerable; two months later he was well enough to be able to leave the house only at twilight. Moir noticed how illness had brought about a considerable alteration in his friend:

> His appearance was very much changed, and in the course of a few months, years seemed to have been passing over his head, and leaving their usual effects. The juvenility of his appearance had passed away,—his hearing was considerably impaired; his hair having fallen out was replaced by a wig, and, to aid his sight, he wore spectacles. (MacNish, *The Modern Pythagorean*, 1.146–7)

Not only had he altered physically. Moir noticed that 'The whole nervous system seemed to own an irritability, very different from its accustomed placidity' (ibid., 1.150). MacNish had complained to Moir about his letters not being acknowledged and wrote of 'a conspiracy against me, by all my correspondents not to write to me' (ibid., 1.151). By the beginning of 1830 MacNish had suffered another attack of fever.

It is probable that MacNish wrote the *Philosophy of Sleep* (1830) during his period of illness. Moir claimed that MacNish had struggled to complete the book, identifying the cause as a defect 'in the structure of my mind … my mind just runs one way, and I cannot for the soul of me turn it out of that channel in which it pleases to glide' (MacNish, *The Modern Pythagorean*, 1.168). *Philosophy of Sleep* was strongly influenced by phrenology. In it MacNish describes sleep as being the intermediate state between 'wakefulness and death'. Complete (or healthy) sleep was 'temporary metaphysical death', while imperfect (or diseased) sleep was 'short, feverish and unrefreshing … disturbed by frightful or melancholy dreams' (MacNish, *Philosophy of Sleep*, 1–2). MacNish typically chose to focus on those intermediate states that existed between complete sleep and complete wakefulness: somnambulism, trance, nightmare, reverie, and abstraction.

In May 1833 MacNish visited Edinburgh to study phrenology, during which time he met George Combe. He spent 1834–5 in Paris and other parts of the continent before returning home. On two occasions MacNish offered himself up for character analysis, once by a person named Bennet, and on another occasion, for phrenological analysis, by Robert Cox, nephew of George Combe and secretary of the Edinburgh Phrenological Society. MacNish responded to their findings and these provide some indication of his self-image. He agreed that he found 'self-government no easy task' and confessed to having trouble keeping his temper in an argument, and to a hatred of being contradicted. The disputes of others, though, held a particular fascination for him. 'I am', he wrote, 'immoderately fond of seeing fights, of sparring, and of perusing accounts of battles in the prize-ring' (MacNish,

The Modern Pythagorean, 1.287). It was an aspect of his character to which he returned: 'I like to see drunken squabbles, fights etc., *on* stage, and I am sorry to say, *off* it also. Tragedies I am also fond of' (ibid., 1.299). Brought up in a strict tory household, he had a tendency to side with the opposition 'whatever that may be'. He also liked to make comparisons: of sounds to colours, words to shapes, and shapes to words. While professing to admire beautiful women, marriage held no temptation, as it would require him to be 'obliged to keep very regular hours … I could not tolerate the restraints of married life' (ibid., 1.264). Much of MacNish's writing is concerned with self-division and ambiguity. In this he was part of the nineteenth century's preoccupation with duality, which found perhaps its most famous expression in the work of another Scot, R. L. Stevenson, in *The Strange Case of Dr Jekyll and Mr Hyde* (1886). MacNish's interest in the topic may well have arisen from an awareness of the different elements which made up his own personality.

Early in 1837 MacNish was taken ill with chest pains and fever and fell into a coma. He died in Glasgow on 16 January 1837 and was buried at St Andrew's Episcopal Church.

MICHAEL BEVAN

Sources R. MacNish, *The modern Pythagorean … with the author's life, by his friend D. M. Moir*, 2 vols. (1838) · K. Miller, *Doubles* (1985) · parish register (births), 15 Feb 1802, Glasgow · R. MacNish, *The philosophy of sleep* (1845)
Archives NL Scot., corresp. with George Combe · NL Scot., letters to D. M. Moir
Likenesses T. Dobbie, line engraving (after marble bust by J. Ritchie), BM; repro. in MacNish, *The modern Pythagorean* · D. Maclise, lithograph, BM; repro. in *Fraser's Magazine* (1835) [see illus.]

Mac Nisse mac Faíbrig (d. 507/8). *See under* Ulster, saints of (*act. c.*400–*c.*650).

Macnutt, Derrick Somerset [pseud. Ximenes] (1902–1971), crossword compiler and schoolmaster, was born on 29 March 1902 at Coomrith, Carlisle Road, Eastbourne, Sussex, the elder child and only son of Frederic Brodie Macnutt (1873–1949), curate-in-charge of Christ Church, Wimbledon, and his first wife, Hettie Sina (d. 1945), daughter of the Revd Charles Bullock of Worcester and his second wife, Hester, *née* Savory. His education began at Shrewsbury House preparatory school in Surbiton. In 1915 he gained a scholarship to Marlborough College and in 1920 passed on a classical scholarship to Jesus College, Cambridge, where he won three prizes and graduated with a double first in classics. In 1925 he took up a post teaching classics at St Edmund's School, Canterbury, and in 1928 was appointed senior classics master and housemaster at Christ's Hospital, Horsham. On 30 July 1936 he married the nineteen-year-old Mary Long, daughter of Guy Stephenson Long, rector of Aldington, Kent, the marriage taking place in her father's church. There were three children.

Macnutt had always enjoyed crosswords, especially those set by E. P. Mathers (Torquemada) in *The Observer*. When Mathers died in 1939 Macnutt composed a puzzle in his style by way of a tribute and sent it to the paper. It was published, and he and two others, F. R. Burrow, a Wimbledon tennis referee, and B. G. Whitfield, a master at Eton College, were asked to take over and provide puzzles in a rota. In 1942 Macnutt assumed full charge for all the puzzles and adopted the pseudonym Ximenes, taking it from Francisco Jiménez de Cisneros (1436–1517), the Spanish prelate who was appointed grand inquisitor of Castile following the death of Tomás de Torquemada (1420–1498), the first grand inquisitor. The name was appropriate for one who sought to rack the brains of his victims, and the X was a bonus as a symbol of his means of torture. In all he composed 1200 Ximenes puzzles, the last published posthumously on 30 January 1972. He also compiled some of the Everyman puzzles in *The Observer* as well as more challenging ones for *The Listener* under the name of Tesremos, his middle name reversed.

As a classics teacher, Macnutt had a formidable record. Many of his pupils won Oxbridge scholarships, and he himself was the author of a highly successful Latin course and grammar, written with H. L. O. Flecker and published in 1939. Macnutt's teaching methods in some respects matched those of his cruciverbal eponym. He imposed strict mental discipline on his pupils and coupled it with corporal chastisement in the more recalcitrant cases. The study itself was lined with dictionaries kippered by the 5 ounces a week of the flake that Macnutt had smoked since his undergraduate days. With his plus fours, pebble glasses, booming voice, and extrovert personality, Macnutt remained a force to be reckoned with until his retirement from teaching in 1963.

Macnutt's crossword compilation continued, however, and he was already a cult figure among his loyal solvers. In his final years, about 500 devotees were sending in solutions to his monthly competitions, complete with their own clues. In return they would receive his privately circulated notes. There was a Ximenes tie for the men, a scarf for the women, and a book-plate for merit. At regular intervals there were dinners, the last, in 1968, marking the 1000th Ximenes crossword. The puzzles were always cryptic, in the manner lovingly described by Macnutt in his classic study, *Ximenes on the Art of the Crossword* (1966).

Macnutt died, survived by his wife, of a myocardial infarction on 29 June 1971 at his home, Buckmans, Five Oaks, Billingshurst, Sussex, and was buried at St Peter's Church, Slinfold, Sussex. His mantle as *Observer* compiler passed to Jonathan Crowther (Azed), as he had wished.

ADRIAN ROOM

Sources A. Ellis, 'The clue to Ximenes', *The Observer* (4 July 1971) · [C. M. E. Seaman], 'In memoriam Derrick Macnutt', *The Blue* [magazine of Christ's Hospital], 98/3 (Sept 1971), 248–51 · N. Longmate, *The shaping season* (1998) · *The Times* (2 July 1971) · M. Arnot, *A history of the crossword puzzle* (1982) · A. Robins, *The ABC of crosswords* (1975) · b. cert. · m. cert. · d. cert. · private information (2004)

Likenesses J. Bown, photograph, repro. in D. Manley, *Chambers crossword manual* (1986) · photograph, repro. in Ellis, 'The clue to Ximenes'

Wealth at death £29,924: probate, 27 Oct 1971, *CGPLA Eng. & Wales*

Maconchy, Dame Elizabeth Violet (1907–1994), composer, was born on 19 March 1907 at Silverleys, St Catharine's Estate, Hoddesdon, Hertfordshire, one of three daughters of Gerald Edward Campbell Maconchy (*d.* 1921/2), solicitor, and his wife, Violet Mary, *née* Poe (*c.*1880–*c.*1945). Her parents were both Irish, but lived in Buckinghamshire while Maconchy was a child, returning to her grandparents' residence, Santry Court, near Dublin, for long holidays. About the end of the First World War her father was diagnosed with tuberculosis, and the family moved to Howth, Dublin. Her parents had scant interest in music, but her father played the piano a little, and Maconchy began to compose piano pieces when she was six. She was given piano and music theory lessons while in Dublin, but there was almost no opportunity for her to hear classical music. After her father's death her mother took the family to London, enabling Maconchy to begin her formal musical education at the Royal College of Music (1923–9). She studied the piano with Arthur Alexander, and composition, first with Charles Wood and from 1925 with Ralph Vaughan Williams, who remained a mentor and friend until his death in 1958. Throughout her student years she was strongly encouraged to pursue a career as a composer by her teachers, by the college director, and by a circle of peers who included several lifelong friends, the composers Grace Williams, Dorothy Gow, and Ina Boyle. During this period she became acquainted with Bartók's music, an important influence on the development of her own compositional style.

In 1929 Maconchy won an Octavia travelling scholarship which took her to Paris, Vienna, and Prague, where she had lessons with K. B. Jirák; she first came to public attention when her piano concerto (composed 1928, revised 1929–30) was performed in Prague in March 1930 by Ervín Schulhoff, with Jirák conducting. On 23 August 1930 she married William Richard LeFanu (1904–1995), librarian at the Royal College of Surgeons. Just a week later her suite *The Land* (1929) was performed to great acclaim at a Promenade Concert in London, conducted by Sir Henry Wood. This triumph launched Maconchy into the professional world. In November 1930 three of her songs were published by Oxford University Press, and in 1933 HMV issued her first commercial recording. She was hailed by critics as a leading composer of the younger generation, and her works received performances in public concerts, including the Macnaghten–Lemare concerts, in BBC broadcasts, and at festivals of the International Society for Contemporary Music. Her chamber works in particular—the prize-winning quintet for oboe and strings (1932), the first three string quartets (1932–3, 1936, 1938), and the *Prelude, Interlude and Fugue* for two violins (1934)—were noted for their originality, intensity, rhythmic drive, and taut construction. Her personal life changed course in 1932 when she contracted tuberculosis and was forced to move from London to the Kent countryside. She never lived in London again, but continued to compose steadily. By 1939 her works had been played in eastern Europe, Paris, Germany, the USA, and Australia, as well as in the UK.

In October 1939 Maconchy gave birth to her first child,

Anna, and during the Second World War the family were evacuated to Ludlow in Shropshire. The wartime musical climate inclined away from avant-garde styles, and there were few opportunities for performances in England, though her ballet *Puck Fair* (1939–40) was staged in Dublin in 1941. After the war the family returned south; since their Kent house had been bombed, they moved first to Wickham Bishops in Essex, and in 1954 to a cottage, Shottesbrook, in Boreham, near Chelmsford, which remained Maconchy's home until her death. She gave birth to her second daughter, the composer Nicola LeFanu, in 1947.

In the years immediately following the war Maconchy re-established herself in the musical world as a composer of individuality, resource, and expressivity. She won the Edwin Evans prize for her string quartet no. 5 (1948) and took the London county council prize for coronation year with the overture *Proud Thames* (1952–3). In February–March 1955 the BBC broadcast, as a tribute to her achievements, a special series of concerts featuring the six quartets written to date. Over the following three decades she received numerous commissions from performers, festivals, and organizations, leading her to compose a wide range of works in many genres.

Maconchy's career was underpinned by her extraordinary string quartets, numbering thirteen in all and spanning five decades (1933–83). In contrast to the controlled, contrapuntal austerity of the early works, from the 1960s her style opened out, becoming freer and more expansive. This is evident in the later string quartets, and also in the expressive lyricism of her vocal works, such as the three John Donne settings written for the tenor Peter Pears (1959, 1965), *Ariadne* for soprano and orchestra (1970–71, to words by Cecil Day Lewis), the choral setting *The Leaden Echo and the Golden Echo* (1978, to words by Gerard Manley Hopkins), and the hauntingly beautiful *My Dark Heart* for soprano and six players (1981, to words from Petrarch's sonnets, trans. J. M. Synge).

The 'dramatic counterpoint' inherent in Maconchy's chamber writing laid a foundation for her dramatic stage works. Chamber opera had become a viable genre in postwar Britain following Benjamin Britten's international successes, and, like many British composers, Maconchy turned to this medium, composing a trilogy of one-act operas: *The Sofa* (1956–7, rev. 1966, libretto by Ursula Vaughan Williams), *The Three Strangers* (1957–8, rev. 1977, libretto by Maconchy after Thomas Hardy), and *The Departure* (1960–61, rev. 1977, libretto by Anne Ridler). Her lifelong interest in encouraging children and amateur performers led her to compose choral and orchestral works, such as *An Essex Overture* (1966), written for the Essex Youth Orchestra, and four other stage works, including *The Birds*, 'an extravaganza in one act' (1968, libretto by Maconchy after Aristophanes), and the children's opera *The King of the Golden River* (1975, libretto by Maconchy after John Ruskin). Maconchy also published a number of educational pieces with Faber Music.

Unlike many composers of her time, Maconchy did not supplement her career by teaching composition. Outside composing, she focused on supporting colleagues and encouraging younger composers, and she was highly respected and valued for her important contributions to the profession. She became the first female chairman of the Composers' Guild of Great Britain in 1959 and was for many years associated with the Society for the Promotion of New Music, of which she succeeded to the presidency following Benjamin Britten's death in 1976. She was appointed CBE in 1977 and DBE in 1987. Because she suffered from illness in her final decade, Maconchy's works of the late 1980s proved to be her last: *Butterflies* for voice and harp (1986) and *On St Stephenses Day* for women's chorus (1989). She died in the St Clements Nursing Home, 170 St Clements Hill, Norwich, on 11 November 1994.

JENNIFER DOCTOR

Sources A. Macnaghten, 'Elizabeth Maconchy', *MT*, 96 (1955), 298–302 · 'Elizabeth Maconchy', 1985 [Arts Council videotape directed M. Williams] · N. LeFanu, 'Elizabeth Maconchy', *RCM Magazine*, 83 (1987), 113–14 · N. LeFanu, 'Elizabeth Maconchy', *Reclaiming the muse*, ed. S. Fuller and N. LeFanu, *Contemporary Music Review*, 11 (1994), 201–4 · J. Doctor, '"Working for her own salvation": Vaughan Williams as teacher of Elizabeth Maconchy, Grace Williams and Ina Boyle', *Vaughan Williams in perspective*, ed. L. Foreman (1998), 181–201 · J. Doctor, 'Intersecting circles: the early careers of Elizabeth Maconchy, Elisabeth Lutyens and Grace Williams', *Women and Music Journal*, 2 (1998), 90–109 · [J. Doctor], 'Elizabeth Maconchy (1907–1994)', *A dictionary-catalog of modern British composers*, ed. A. Poulton (Westport, CT, 2000) [detailed works list] · S. Fuller, 'Elizabeth Maconchy', *The Pandora guide to women composers* (1994), 198–202 · H. Cole and J. Doctor, 'Maconchy, Elizabeth', *New Grove*, 2nd edn · *The Times* (12 Nov 1994), 20 · R. R. Bennett, *The Independent* (12 Nov 1994), 42 · *Daily Telegraph* (12 Nov 1994), 19 · H. Cole, *The Guardian* (14 Nov 1994), 12 · *The Gramophone* (Feb 1995), 11 · J. Fowler, *IAWM Journal* (June 1995), 11 · F. Howes, 'The younger generation of composers, iii: Elizabeth Maconchy', *Monthly Musical Record*, 68 (July–Aug 1938), 165–8 · H. Cole, 'Elizabeth Maconchy (born 1907)', *The 80th birthday of Elizabeth Maconchy* (1987) [publisher's leaflet] · J. Skiba, 'Senior British composers, 13: Elizabeth Maconchy', *Composer*, 63 (spring 1978) · F. Maddocks, 'The composer breaks her silence', *The Guardian* (26 July 1983) · C. Heslop, 'Contemporary composers: Elizabeth Maconchy', *Music Teacher*, 66 (April 1987), 23–5 · R. Maycock, 'Inheriting the land', *The Listener* (12 March 1987), 30 · R. Matthew-Walker, 'The early string quartets of Elizabeth Maconchy', *Musical Opinion*, 112 (Nov 1989), 370–74 · 'News and views', *Gramophone*, 67 (Nov 1989), 824 [interview with Maconchy] · C. Roma, 'Choral music of 20th century composers: Elisabeth Lutyens, Elizabeth Maconchy and Thea Musgrave', DMA diss., University of Cincinnati, 1989 · J. Doctor, 'Maconchy's string quartet no. 7 and the BBC', *Musical Objects*, 1 (1995), 5–8 · E. Maconchy, 'Vaughan Williams as teacher', *The Composer*, 2 (March 1959), 18–19 · E. Maconchy, 'Ten days in the USSR', *Performing Right*, 34 (May 1961), 238–9 · E. Maconchy, 'A composer speaks', *Composer*, 42 (1971–2), 25–9 · 'Women in the arts', BBC Radio 3, 24 July 1973 [interview with Maconchy] · b. cert. · d. cert. · private information (2004) [daughter]

Archives BL, MSS · Britten–Pears Library, The Red House, Aldeburgh, Suffolk, MSS · St Hilda's College, Oxford | BBC WAC, contributor files | SOUND BL NSA, personal tape collection

Likenesses K. Church, portrait, 1934, priv. coll. · J. Mendoza, portrait, 1970–79, priv. coll. · photographs, NPG · photographs, Chester Music · photographs, priv. coll.

Maconochie, Alexander [*later* Alexander Maconochie-Welwood], **Lord Meadowbank** (1777–1861), lawyer and politician, was born on 2 March 1777; he was the eldest son of Allan *Maconochie (*bap.* 1748, *d.* 1816), judge and author, and his wife, Elizabeth, third daughter of Robert

Welwood of Garvock and Pitliver in Fife. Maconochie married Anne, the eldest daughter of Robert *Blair of Avontoun, judge, on 29 April 1805. They had five sons and five daughters; the eldest, Allan Alexander, became regius professor of law at Glasgow University and later inherited the family estates.

Maconochie was admitted as an advocate in 1799, probably after having studied law in Edinburgh. He was a member of the Speculative Society at the university and provoked an uproar in 1799 with his opposition to debates on modern political subjects which he feared would turn the society into a Jacobin club. In 1807 he was appointed an advocate-depute. He became sheriff-depute of East Lothian in 1810. A tory of the pre-Reform kind, he was appointed solicitor-general for Scotland in Lord Liverpool's administration in February 1813, and in July 1816 he succeeded Archibald Colquhoun as lord advocate. Maconochie was appointed at a difficult time in Scotland. In the severe economic recession following the conclusion of the Napoleonic wars the lowlands especially were in some degree of political ferment, fuelled by the unemployment and hardship experienced by the urban working class. The government, including Maconochie, was led to believe that a rebellious conspiracy centred on the Glasgow weavers was in preparation in the west of Scotland. Instrumental in this were the reports passed on by the government's 'spy', Alexander Richmond.

As lord advocate Maconochie needed a seat in the House of Commons and he was returned for the borough of Yarmouth on the Isle of Wight at a by-election in February 1817. He spoke for the first time in the House of Commons that same month in support of the first reading of the Habeas Corpus Suspension Bill. He created a great sensation by reading the supposed secret oath, which he stated had been administered to many in Glasgow in connection with the weavers' alleged conspiracy. This was held to have made a great impression on the house and to have contributed to the passing of the first and second readings of the measure that same night. Henry Cockburn states that doubts expressed about the accuracy of his information provoked Maconochie to pledge speedy convictions in proof of it, and that the pledge injuriously affected his methods of prosecuting the subsequent trials for sedition of the various radicals arrested in 1817. Returning to Edinburgh Maconochie conducted the proceedings against (for example) Alexander McLaren, a weaver, and Thomas Baird, a grocer, for sedition. Convictions were obtained, but only by the acceptance of some very wild talk as proof. During the debate on the third reading of the further Habeas Corpus Suspension Bill in June 1817, Maconochie replied to the attacks which had been made on him in the Commons during his absence over these trials. He denied, for instance, any mismanagement of indictments or failure to work with the courts in the proper manner.

The conduct of the proceedings against Andrew McKinley for administering unlawful oaths brought Maconochie further difficulties. This trial had presented the whig side at the Scottish bar—figures such as Murray, Moncreiff, Jeffrey, and Cockburn acting in concert—with a rich opportunity to attack the tory administration of justice in Scotland. Maconochie repeatedly refused the defence access to witnesses and was eventually forced to abandon the trial when the crown's main witness, James Campbell, swore he had been induced by crown officials, not including Maconochie, to give 'appropriate' evidence. Lord Archibald Hamilton's motion in the Commons for the production of the papers in this case (in the context of his charge that crown officials had been guilty of an attempt to procure perjury) was, however, defeated in February 1818.

In March 1818 Maconochie resigned his Yarmouth seat and was returned for the Anstruther district of burghs in Fife, for which he continued to sit until he was made a judge. In the remainder of his time as lord advocate, he was confronted with the pressure for burgh and, by implication, electoral reform, which had as its immediate cause examples of gross financial mismanagement and other corrupt practices, such as the sale of council offices. Maconochie opposed any introduction of a popular element in the election of burgh magistrats, but he did try, unsuccessfully, to pass schemes of burgh reform involving, for example, the creation of a reserve exchequer power to control burgh expenditure.

Maconochie's time as lord advocate cannot be counted a success. In the long term his handling of the trials of 1817 and his inability to deal effectively with a problem like the breakdown in burgh administration merely stored up tension which manifested itself later, for instance in the localized disturbances of the 'radical war' of 1820 in central Scotland. It may therefore have been a relief to the government when Maconochie was appointed an ordinary lord of session and of judiciary in succession to David Douglas, Lord Reston. He took his seat on the bench as Lord Meadowbank on 1 July 1819.

As a judge Maconochie suffered by comparison with his father. The elder Lord Meadowbank had been possessed of philosophical acumen and varied interests. His son was, rather, a man of quick action, painstaking and conscientious, but at the same time petulant and therefore thought to be lacking in weight. According to an apocryphal story from the Parliament House he once asked a counsel who was pleading before him to explain the distinction between the words 'also' and 'likewise', which he had used in his argument. 'Your lordship's father', was the reply, 'was Lord Meadowbank; your lordship is Lord Meadowbank *also* but not *likewise*.' Maconochie resigned his seat on the judicial bench in November 1843. It was rumoured that he was disappointed at not having been chosen earlier in the year to succeed David Boyle as lord justice-clerk; Sir Robert Peel had chosen John Hope.

Maconochie played his part in Edinburgh and Scottish tory society. A noted high point was the toast he proposed to Sir Walter Scott at the first dinner of the Edinburgh Theatrical Fund in February 1827. In the course of his speech Maconochie, with prior consent, revealed Scott's authorship of the Waverley novels. Scott 'pleaded guilty' for the first time in public.

After his resignation Maconochie continued to take an

active part in public affairs connected with Edinburgh and the county. He was a member of the board of manufactures and a vice-president of the Royal Institution. He gave a lot of his time to the improvement of his Meadowbank estate, where as lord advocate he had earlier entertained such luminaries as Archduke Nicholas, afterwards emperor of Russia, and Archduke Maximilian of Austria. On the death of his cousin, Robert Scott Welwood, in June 1854, he inherited the entailed estates of Garvock and Pitliver, and took the additional surname of Welwood. Maconochie died on 30 November 1861 at his home, Meadowbank House, Kirknewton, Midlothian, and was probably buried on the estate.   GORDON F. MILLAR

Sources *Glasgow Herald* (3 Dec 1861) · *The Times* (4 Dec 1861) · G. W. T. Omond, *The lord advocates of Scotland from the close of the fifteenth century to the passing of the Reform Bill*, 2 (1883), 230–55 · *Annual Register* (1862), 467–8 · *Memorials of his time, by Henry Cockburn*, new edn, ed. H. A. Cockburn (1909), 313–20 · Burke, *Gen. GB* (1898), 1567–8 · J. Kay, *A series of original portraits and caricature etchings … with biographical sketches and illustrative anecdotes*, ed. [H. Paton and others], new edn [3rd edn], 2 (1877), 432–3 · *Journal of Henry Cockburn: being a continuation of the 'Memorials of his time', 1831–1854*, 2 (1874), 57 · J. Foster, *Members of parliament, Scotland … 1357–1882*, 2nd edn (privately printed, London, 1882), 237 · J. G. Lockhart, *Memoirs of the life of Sir Walter Scott*, 7 (1838), 21–4 · *The Scotsman* (2 Dec 1861) · Anderson, *Scot. nat.*, 60 · G. Brunton and D. Haig, *An historical account of the senators of the college of justice, from its institution in MDXXXII* (1836), 550 · F. J. Grant, ed., *The Faculty of Advocates in Scotland, 1532–1943*, Scottish RS, 145 (1944), 141 · *DNB*
Archives BL, corresp. with Sir Robert Peel, Add. MSS 40345–40607 · New College, Edinburgh, letters to Thomas Chalmers · NL Scot., corresp. with Sir Thomas Cochrane · NL Scot., corresp. with Lord Melville
Likenesses H. Raeburn, portrait, 1816 · F. Chantrey, bust, AM Oxf. · R. Dighton, coloured etching, NPG · J. Kay, etching, NPG · J. Kay?, two etchings, repro. in Kay, *Series of original portraits and caricature etchings* · M. A. Shee, oils, Scot. NPG

Maconochie [*formerly* M'Konochie], **Sir Alexander** (1787–1860), geographer and penal reformer, was born on 11 February 1787 in Edinburgh, the only child of the second marriage of Alexander M'Konochie (the later spelling was adopted in 1832), a lawyer and commissioner for the board of customs for Scotland, who died in 1795, and his wife, Ann Margaret, who died in 1821. The young Maconochie was placed under the guardianship of Allan Maconochie of Meadowbank, Lord Meadowbank (*bap.* 1748, *d.* 1816), his uncle and later judge of the supreme court of Scotland. Until he was fifteen he had private tuition which concentrated on classics and law, but in August 1803 he was able, apparently against the wishes of his family, to break away to sea by entering the Royal Navy.

During the Napoleonic Wars Maconochie served in the West Indies under Admiral Sir Alexander Cochrane, twice being wounded in action. Promoted lieutenant in the brig *Grasshopper*, he was driven ashore on The Helder in December 1811. He was imprisoned at Verdun for over two years, until 1814. Rejoining the fleet, he saw active service off the North American coast and was promoted to commander in 1815, but was soon paid off. He was placed on the reserve list and returned to Edinburgh; he was retired with the rank of captain in 1855.

In 1816 Maconochie published his first pamphlet, *Considerations on the propriety of establishing a colony on one of the Sandwich Islands*, a work advocating a commercial settlement of the kind which Raffles established three years later at Singapore. In 1818 he published his longest work, a study of the Pacific, which he had never visited: *A summary view of the statistics and existing commerce of the principal shores of the Pacific Ocean*. His geographical writings seem to have been inspired by his interest in promoting commerce and colonization.

In 1822 Maconochie married Mary Hutton Browne (1795–1869), from Bamburgh, Northumberland. They had seven children who, according to Lady Franklin, were brought up with 'a certain outrageous liberality of principle'. As farming in North Queensferry, Fife, proved unprofitable, Maconochie moved to London in 1828. There his renewed acquaintance with Sir John Barrow and Sir John Franklin led to his appointment as secretary to the Royal Geographical Society at its inaugural meeting on 16 July 1830. On 16 November 1833 he became professor of geography at University College, London, the first post of its kind in Great Britain. His inaugural lectures were well attended but thereafter he failed to attract many students. He resigned both positions in 1836 to accompany Sir John Franklin to Van Diemen's Land as his private secretary. (Before embarking he was honoured as knight of the Royal Guelphic Order.) This change of career was apparently prompted by his enthusiasm for further colonial enterprise. On the voyage to Australia, he gave a series of lectures to his fellow passengers entitled 'The natural history of man'. Before he left England, the Society for the Improvement of Prison Discipline had asked him to report on the treatment of convicts in Van Diemen's Land. His report, published in London as a parliamentary paper (*Parl. papers*, 1837–8, 40) was so critical of official policy that Franklin dismissed him. In 1840 he was appointed superintendent of the penal colony on Norfolk Island, where he attempted to put into practice his ideas about reformatory discipline. In 1844, after mixed reports of the outcome of this experiment, he was dismissed by the colonial secretary, Lord Stanley. He returned to England in 1844 but his efforts to persuade the government to establish another penal colony, dismissed by James Stephen as 'so much ill-timed and superficial preaching', were not successful. He published several works on prison discipline, the best known being *Crime and Punishment* (1846), and took an active part in campaigns for penal reform. With the assistance of Matthew Davenport Hill he was appointed governor of the new prison in Birmingham in 1849, but was dismissed within two years. A royal commission of inquiry implicated him in its criticisms of the management of the prison, and a caricature of Maconochie appeared as Captain O'Connor in Charles Reade's novel *It's Never too Late to Mend*, published in 1856. Maconochie had long suffered from liver disease and died of acute peritonitis on 25 October 1860 in Morden, Surrey, where he was buried.

Maconochie took an active part in the establishment of geography in Britain, but it was as a penal reformer that he was most influential. He was the originator of the 'mark' system of prison discipline, which was based on the conviction that the state has a duty to reform criminals, and that positive encouragement was more effective than mere punishment. His belief that prisoners should have an opportunity to earn their release by good behaviour, their progress being measured by 'marks', was criticized by traditionalists as insufficiently punitive. However, his reputation as a pioneer of progressive methods was reaffirmed by subsequent generations of penal reformers. His philosophy was embodied in the declaration of principles at the National Prison Association meeting in Cincinnati in 1877.

M. F. G. SELBY, rev. FELIX DRIVER

Sources J. V. Barry, *Alexander Maconochie of Norfolk Island* (1958) • R. G. Ward, 'Captain Alexander Maconochie', *GJ*, 126 (1960), 458–68 • M. D. Hill, *Our exemplars* (1861), 213–41 • K. Maconochie, 'Alexander Maconochie, sociologist and penal reformer', *Howard Journal*, 9 (1956), 235–41 • R. Hill and F. D. Hill, *The recorder of Birmingham* (1878) • L. Radzinowicz and R. Hood, *A history of English criminal law and its administration from 1750*, 5: *The emergence of penal policy in Victorian and Edwardian England* (1986), vol. 5 • d. cert. • headstone, Morden parish churchyard • J. Clay, *Maconochie's experiment* (2001) **Archives** NHM, reports on Norfolk Island | Mitchell L., NSW, Bourke MSS, report on convicts in Van Dieman's Land, and letters to Sir Richard Bourke • NL Scot., corresp. with George Combe • RGS, letters to Royal Geographical Society • U. Newcastle, letters to Walter Trevelyan • UCL, papers relating to appointment to chair **Likenesses** E. V. Rippingille, portrait, *c.*1836, priv. coll. • C. Essex, bust, *c.*1849; now destroyed • engraving (after C. Essex), repro. in Barry, *Alexander Maconochie*

Maconochie, Allan, of Meadowbank, Lord Meadowbank

(*bap.* **1748**, *d.* **1816**), jurist and judge, was baptized in Edinburgh on 23 January 1748, the only son of Alexander Maconochie of Meadowbank, Edinburghshire (1711–1764?), and his wife, Isabella (*b.* 1725), daughter of the Revd Walter Allan, minister of Colinton. Educated privately by Dr Alexander Adam, later rector of Edinburgh high school, he attended the University of Edinburgh in the 1760s, taking the classes of such luminaries of the Enlightenment as Adam Fergusson, professor of moral philosophy, and Hugh Blair, professor of rhetoric and *belles-lettres*. He also studied Roman law with the professor of civil law, Robert Dick, from 1766 to 1769. He was then apprenticed to Thomas Tod, a well-known writer to the signet.

In 1764, with a group of students that included William Creech, John Bruce, and Henry Mackenzie, Maconochie founded the Speculative Society, soon, for a century or so, to be prominent as 'an institution which has trained more young men to public speaking, talent, and liberal thought than all the other private institutions in Scotland' (*Memorials … by Henry Cockburn*, 73–4). After leaving university he resided at Paris for a short time, before admission as an advocate on 11 December 1770. He entered Lincoln's Inn in London on 16 April 1771 but was not called to the English bar. He subsequently returned to France, where he remained until 1773. On 11 November 1774 he married Elizabeth, third daughter of Robert Welwood of Garvock and Pitliver, Fife. Four sons were born to the marriage: Alexander *Maconochie (1777–1861), later also a judge of

the court of session as Lord Meadowbank; Robert, mintmaster at Madras (1779–1858); James Allan, advocate, sheriff of Orkney and Shetland (1789–1845); and Thomas Tod (*d.* 1847). In 1774 Maconochie was elected to the general assembly of the Church of Scotland as lay representative of the burgh of Dunfermline.

Maconochie was admitted regius professor of public law and the law of nature and nations in the University of Edinburgh on 16 July 1779. He advertised classes each year until he resigned the chair in 1796. In these 'he trace[d] the rise of political institutions from the natural characters and situation of the human species', classifying governments 'according to those general causes to which he attribute[d] the principal varieties in the forms, genius, and revolutions of governments', ultimately endeavouring

> to construct the science of the spirit of laws on a connected view of what might be called the natural history of man as a political agent; and he … conclude[d] his course with treating of the general principles of municipal law, political oeconomy, and the law of nations. (Arnott, 398)

This project, typical of the Scottish Enlightenment, led to his *Essay on the Origin and Progress of the European Legislatures*, published in the *Transactions of the Royal Society of Edinburgh* (1784), of which Maconochie was a fellow and served as vice-president. As a member of the Royal Society of Edinburgh, he sometimes chaired the physical class, and, according to Lord Cockburn, he seemed 'to be equally at home in divinity, agriculture, and geology, in examining mountains, demonstrating his errors to a farmer, and refuting the dogmas of the clergyman' (*Memorials … by Henry Cockburn*, 142–3). In line with this width of knowledge, he published *Directions for Making of Compost Dunghills from Peat* (1802; new edns, 1815, 1842).

Maconochie maintained an active and successful career at the bar. On 18 December 1779 he was elected treasurer of the Faculty of Advocates; part of his task was to sort out the mess left by the somewhat doubtful involvement in the collapse of the Ayr Bank of the previous treasurer, James Balfour of Pilrig (also his predecessor in the chair). In 1788 he became sheriff-depute of Renfrewshire. With his fellow law professor David Hume he was one of the advocates who took the lead in the ejection of Henry Erskine from the office of dean of the Faculty of Advocates in January 1796. He succeeded Alexander Abercromby as an ordinary lord of session, and took his seat on the bench as Lord Meadowbank on 11 March 1796. In the same year he resigned his professorship. Maconochie was appointed a lord of justiciary in place of David Smyth of Methven on 4 September 1804. He was considered by Henry Brougham, who did not compliment others easily, as

> one of the best lawyers—one of the most acute men—a man of large general capacity and of great experience—and, with hardly any exception, certainly with very few exceptions, the most diligent and attentive judge one can remember in the practice of the Scotch law. (*Inglis v. Mansfield*, 1835)

Maconochie took a keen interest in the proposals to reform the court of session in the years after 1800, writing *Considerations on the Introduction of Jury Trial in Civil Causes into Scotland* (1814; 2nd edn, 1815), and was appointed one of the three lords commissioner of the newly appointed jury court on 9 May 1815. His health, however, had already begun to fail, and he took little part in the proceedings of the new court, which was opened for the first time on 22 January 1816. He died at Coates House, near Edinburgh, on 14 June 1816, aged sixty-eight, and was buried in the private burial-ground on the Meadowbank estate, in the parish of Kirknewton, where there is a monument to his memory.

JOHN W. CAIRNS

Sources H. Arnott, *History of Edinburgh*, 2nd edn (1788) • *Memorials of his time, by Henry Cockburn* (1856) • bap. reg. Scot., OPR index, ext 2802210 • U. Edin. L., special collections division, university archives • *Edinburgh Evening Courant* (1779–96) • G. Brunton and D. Haig, *An historical account of the senators of the college of justice, from its institution in MDXXXII* (1832) • N. Campbell and R. M. S. Smellie, *The Royal Society of Edinburgh, 1783–1983* (1983) • NA Scot., SC 70/1/15

Archives Falkirk Museums History Research Centre, Falkirk, Falkirk Archives, letters to William Forbes • NL Scot., letters to Lord Melville

Likenesses J. Brown, pencil drawing, *c.*1780, Scottish Museum of Antiquities, Edinburgh • J. Tassie, paste medallion, 1791, Scot. NPG • J. Kay, caricature, line etching, 1799, NPG • J. Kay, etchings, 1799, Scot. NPG; repro. in J. Kay, *A series of original portraits and caricature etchings … with bibliographical sketches and illustrative anecdotes*, ed. [H. Patton and others], new edn [3rd edn], 2 (1877), nos. 177, 300, 312 • G. Mackenzie, plaster bust, *c.*1820, Royal Society of Edinburgh • H. Raeburn, oils, Scot. NPG

Wealth at death see NA Scot., SC 70/1/15

Macphail, Agnes Campbell (1890–1954), schoolteacher and politician in Canada, was born on 24 March 1890 in a log farmhouse in Proton township in south-western Ontario, Canada, the first of three girls of Dougald MacPhail (1864–1929), a farmer and auctioneer, and his wife, Henrietta Campbell (*d.* 1937), daughter of John Campbell and Jean Black. Her grandparents on both sides had emigrated from Scotland in the middle of the nineteenth century to farm in Ontario.

Growing up on a small farm, the young Agnes Macphail was known as a bright but wilful child who learned readily in the local one-room school. When her parents decided that they could not afford to pay for her to attend high school in the county seat at Owen Sound, she engaged in a successful campaign to reverse their decision. After completing the programme in two rather than four years, she went on to attend teachers' college in Stratford, where she graduated in 1910.

For the next decade Agnes Macphail taught in rural schools in Ontario and Alberta. An innovative teacher with an extroverted personality, she fell in love with a medical student from Queen's University in Kingston, but hopes for marriage were dashed on his return from overseas duty with the Canadian army during the First World War. Increasingly she devoted herself to promoting the United Farmers of Ontario, a new agrarian organization intent on improving rural conditions. She wrote a column for its newspaper, the *Farmer's Sun*, and also acquired skills in public speaking while she organized local clubs for the movement. Runaway inflation during the war and discontent stemming from the imposition of conscription by the federal government in 1917 propelled the United Farmers

into the political arena where, together with other provincial farm organizations, they were known as Progressives.

By 1918 Canadian women had been enfranchised federally. Agnes Macphail decided to seek nomination in the 1921 national election, as one of only three women to stand for the Canadian House of Commons. She alone of the three was successful. She ran on the Farmer–Labour ticket, expressing their grievances with government policy. She remained the sole woman member of the House of Commons until 1935.

Agnes Macphail enjoyed a unique position which allowed her to further women's causes and reform issues more broadly. Even though organized farmers proved ephemeral in federal politics—severely weakened in the election of 1926 and virtually gone in that of 1930—Macphail was influenced by the social democratic thought of the Independent Labour MP from Winnipeg, James Shaver Woodsworth. In parliament she supported progressive legislation such as liberalization of divorce and gender neutral naturalization laws. She assumed the cause of striking coal miners in Cape Breton during the 1920s and also played a role in the negotiations leading to the Old Age Assistance Act of 1927, the first significant social welfare legislation introduced by the Canadian federal government.

As an outspoken advocate of equity feminism Agnes Macphail drew considerable attention from the press. She was an impressive platform speaker who appealed directly to audiences; she employed self-deprecating humour and had a deep voice that broadcast well over the wireless. When she appeared together with Nancy Astor in Montreal in 1922, Canadian newspapers considered that her performance outshone that of her British counterpart. From the writings of Mary Wollstonecraft and John Stuart Mill, Macphail developed an argument for women's equality with men that assailed the dominant presuppositions of her age. 'I am a feminist', she told a rally in Toronto in 1927, 'and I want for women the thing men are not willing to give them—absolute equality. We will not get it this year, but will get it next' (*Farmers' Sun* [Toronto], 20 Jan 1927). Macphail's advocacy of women's rights formed part of a larger programme aimed at making governments more responsive to a greater part of the electorate. While she acknowledged that childbearing punctuated women's lives, she did not believe maternal responsibilities alone were sufficient to make women happy. Like men, women needed gainful employment to find greater satisfaction in life.

Although Agnes Macphail did not subscribe to the view that women possessed a singular ethic apart from men, she became a forceful peace advocate during the 1920s. Active in the Canadian section of the Women's International League for Peace and Freedom, she represented the country at meetings in Washington, Dublin, and Prague. At home Macphail decried the racial attitudes inherited from Britain that had prevented identifiable minorities from being fully integrated into Canadian life, publicly condemning the shootings of Chinese civilians by British and French troops during disruptions in Shanghai in 1927. Some public officials, believing that she was either disloyal or a Bolshevik, refused to allow the member of parliament to use their podiums, but the federal government appointed her as a delegate to the League of Nations in 1929. The first woman to serve the country in a diplomatic capacity, Macphail objected to being relegated to the league's committee on women and secured a place on the disarmament committee, where she served admirably.

As organized farmers ceased to be a direct political force and gradually emerged as the country's most influential lobby, Agnes Macphail helped to launch the Co-operative Commonwealth Federation (CCF). Inspired by the example of Britain's Labour Party, the CCF brought together intellectuals, farmers, and labour in the pursuit of socialism and social democracy. After steering the United Farmers of Ontario into the new movement, Macphail headed the CCF's provincial wing from 1932 to 1934. While the agrarian ideology of the small producer led her to promote co-operatives and she served on the board directing the Ontario United Farmers' Co-operative Company, she regarded capitalism as a system in which elephants danced among chickens while proclaiming 'each for itself'. The CCF itself represented a span on the left ideological spectrum from communist labour advocates to agrarian critics of the old-line parties. When Macphail proved unable to dampen disruptive internal conflicts, the federal leader James Woodsworth disbanded the Ontario CCF in 1934 and Macphail returned to running as a Farmer–Labour candidate.

Failure in political leadership strengthened Agnes Macphail's longstanding resolve to end the barbarism of Canada's penitentiary system. Understanding that countries such as the United Kingdom had initiated programmes to lessen recidivism, she used her position in parliament to attract media attention to the failures of the country's prisons. In a courageous and well-orchestrated campaign in which she was pitted against the forces of government and bureaucracy, she succeeded in 1936 in getting the Liberal government to appoint a royal commission that provided a blueprint for the reform of penitentiaries.

Macphail supplemented her meagre parliamentary stipend through public speaking in Canada and the United States, employing the same New York agent who handled Winston Churchill's North American appearances. While she was protective of her private life, she became personally attached to Robert Gardiner, a federal MP who also headed the United Farmers of Alberta. After wrestling with commitment to her career versus a desire to have children, Macphail broke off her relationship some time after 1935.

Defeated in the 1940 wartime election, when voters overwhelmingly supported the Liberal government, Macphail attempted unsuccessfully to contest a seat in Saskatchewan. After a young cousin shot her father in 1942, Macphail managed to secure the release of the fourteen-year-old from her custody and moved to Toronto, where she raised her. While writing a column on agrarian affairs for a Toronto newspaper in order to earn income, Macphail gained the East York seat in the legislature for the CCF. Defeated in 1945, she was elected again in 1948. In an attempt to capitalize on gains made by Canadian women in the workforce during the Second World War, Macphail spearheaded efforts by her political party to secure genuine pay equity for women and men, rather than the more limited equal pay for work of equal value that Ontario's Progressive Conservative government put into effect in 1952. Following defeat in the 1951 provincial election, Agnes Macphail retired from politics.

While one Canadian magazine equated Macphail's role in Canada with that of the Fabian socialist Beatrice Webb in Britain, the comparison cannot be taken too far. Macphail was a politician rather than an intellectual. Her views, however prescient in their advocacy of women and in preaching the need for governments more responsive to the electorate, fluctuated with changing fortunes during the four decades of her active political life. Unwilling to surrender even to frequent bouts of ill health, Macphail persevered in public life to the point that by 1952 55 per cent of Canadians surveyed in a Gallup poll knew her name. Her example served to inspire many women, notably Thérèse Casgrain, Grace McInnis, and Charlotte Whitton. Ever optimistic of Canada's promise, a trip to Scotland in 1952 confirmed in her mind the wisdom of her grandparents' decision to emigrate. Agnes Macphail died of a heart attack in Wellesley Hospital, Toronto, on 13 February 1954. She was buried at McNeill cemetery near Priceville, Ontario. A bust of Agnes Macphail was installed in Canada's parliament in 1955.

TERRY CROWLEY

Sources T. Crowley, *Agnes Macphail and the politics of equality* (1990) [incl. complete bibliography] · D. Pennington, *Agnes Macphail: reformer* (1989) · M. Stewart and D. French, *Ask no quarter: a biography of Agnes Macphail* (1959) · J. Sangster, *Dreams of equality: women on the Canadian left, 1920–1950* (1989) · *Globe and Mail* [Toronto] (15 Feb 1954)
Archives NA Canada, MSS | NA Canada, CCF MSS and records · Public Archives of Ontario, Toronto, Stewart-French MSS · Saskatchewan Archives Board, Saskatoon, Violet McNaughton MSS · University of Guelph, Ontario, Leonard Harman–UCO collection · University of Toronto, Thomas Fisher Rare Book Library, Woodsworth collection | FILM National Film Board of Canada, Toronto and Ottawa | SOUND NA Canada, National Sound Archives, radio broadcasts from the 1930s and 1940s
Likenesses F. W. de Weldon, bust, erected in 1955, Houses of Parliament, Ottawa; [commissioned by the Women's International League for Peace and Freedom] · Y. Karsh, photograph, University of Guelph, Guelph, Ontario, Leonard Harman–UCO collection
Wealth at death probably very small: Crowley, *Agnes Macphail*

Macphail, Sir (John) Andrew (1864–1938), pathologist and writer, was born at Orwell, Prince Edward Island, on 24 November 1864, the third son of William Macphail, a farmer, and his wife, Catherine Moore, daughter of Finlay Smith. Both were of highland Scottish descent. Macphail was educated locally, accepting a scholarship to the Prince of Wales College, Charlottetown, in 1880, and at the age of nineteen was acting as headmaster of Fanning School,

Prince Edward Island. At McGill University he received a BA degree in 1888, and graduated in medicine in 1891, afterwards travelling to England and studying for a time at the London Hospital. In 1893 he married Georgina Burland (*d.* 1902), a Montreal heiress, with whom he had a son and a daughter.

Macphail's success as a practising specialist and lecturer in pathology in Montreal at the Western Hospital and at the Protestant Hospital for the Insane (1895–1906) led to his appointment in 1907 to the chair of the history of medicine at McGill University, which he held for thirty years. His academic duties and improvement in material circumstances allowed him to devote more time to writing, and in 1907 he undertook the editorship of the *University Magazine*, a quarterly journal of politics and literature sponsored by Dalhousie, McGill, and Toronto universities, which was widely considered at the time to be the leading intellectual review of Canada.

Macphail's reputation as a writer was established by three books published between 1905 and 1910. His *Essay on Puritanism* (1905) was a series of biographical studies of literary and religious figures, and several editions were published in Britain, Canada, and the United States. He followed this success with *Essay on Politics* (1909), in favour of the imperial connection between Canada and England, and *Essays on Fallacy* (1910), a critique of modern theology, education, and the women's suffrage movements. His views, expressed freely in these essays, were often controversial, for while he was a firm Conservative and imperialist, he was a keen free-trader, and his Presbyterianism did not prevent him from being a steady supporter of the Roman Catholic French Canadians. A novel, *The Vine of Sibmah* (1906), was not so well received as the essays, and one other attempt at fiction, *The Land*, a play in one act, failed and was never produced.

In 1911 Macphail combined his literary and medical interests with the founding of the *Canadian Medical Association Journal*. As its first editor he demanded as much from his scientific contributors as he had from his earlier literary ones. As he put it, 'a man who is intelligent enough to be a surgeon, is also intelligent enough to write down what he wants to say in simple, accurate terms' (Macphail, 72). The new publication went on to become Canada's leading medical journal.

The First World War called Macphail to medical service in France with the sixth Canadian field ambulance, and later at the Canadian overseas army's headquarters, where he attained the rank of major. Deeply affected by the horror of the war, he edited an anthology of tragic verse, *The Book of Sorrow* (1916), and published the life and collected poems of his friend John McCrae, the Canadian soldier-poet, under the title *In a Flanders Field* (1918). In 1917 he delivered the Cavendish lecture at Cambridge. For his war services he was knighted in 1918 and appointed OBE in 1919.

After the war, in 1919, an accident impaired his eyesight, forcing him to give up medical practice; he received the honorary degree of LLD from McGill in 1921. He continued to write freely for Canadian and British reviews and to produce books. An English translation (1921) of Louis Hemon's *Marie Chapdelaine* was followed by a controversial and critical volume on the Canadian forces' medical services, which condemned the minister of militia, Sir Sam Hughes (1925). An internationally acclaimed collection of biographies, *Three Persons*, was published in 1929, and in 1930 Macphail was awarded the Lorne Pierce medal of the Royal Society of Canada for outstanding contributions to literature. He also left for posthumous publication a semi-autobiographical volume, *The Master's Wife* (1939), which tells the story of the Macphail family in Canada and was considered by some contemporaries to be the best story ever written of pioneer life in Canada. Macphail died at Montreal on 23 September 1938.

KATHERINE MULLIN

Sources H. J. Morgan, ed., *The Canadian men and women of the time*, 2nd edn (1912) · *The Times* (24 Sept 1938) · W. Toye, ed., *The Oxford companion to Canadian literature* (1983) · *BMJ* (1 Oct 1938), 723 · *The Lancet* (1 Oct 1938), 807 · S. E. D. Shortt, 'Essayist, editor, and physician: the career of Sir Andrew Macphail, 1864–1938', *Canadian Literature*, 96 (1983), 49–58 · J. A. Macphail, 'Style in medical writing', *Canadian Medical Association Journal*, 1 (1911) · *Who's who in Canada* · *DNB*
Archives HLRO, corresp. with Lord Beaverbrook
Likenesses A. Jongers, oils, 1924, repro. in *BMJ*

MacPhail, Duncan (*b. c.*1914). *See under* Knoydart, Seven Men of (*act.* 1948).

Macphail, James (1754–1805), gardener and writer on agriculture, was born in Aberdeenshire, the son of a highland peasant. In his seventeenth year he became a farm labourer, and his wages were 23*s*. 4*d*. for the half-year. After suffering many hardships working in Scotland he moved to England, and in 1785 he became gardener to Lord Hawkesbury (later second earl of Liverpool), at Addiscombe Place, near Croydon, Surrey, where he remained until his death. He invented a new method of cultivating cucumbers, and was very successful at growing pineapples and melons.

In 1794 Macphail published *A treatise on the culture of the cucumber ... to which are added hints and observations on the improvement of agriculture*. With the exception of some remarks on highland farming, based on Macphail's early experiences, *Hints and Observations* consists of paragraphs reprinted verbatim, and without acknowledgement, from Adam Smith's *Wealth of Nations*, the works of Arthur Young, and agricultural reports. They were reprinted separately in 1795. Later works included *Remarks on the present times ... being an introduction to hints and observations ...* (1795), in which Macphail defended himself against the accusation that he held democratic principles, and *The gardener's remembrancer, exhibiting the various natures of earth and degrees of climate best adapted for the growth of trees and ... fruits* (1803), which was reprinted in 1807, with a second edition in 1819.

Macphail died in 1805, probably at Croydon, Surrey.

W. A. S. HEWINS, *rev.* ANNE PIMLOTT BAKER

Sources Desmond, *Botanists* · J. Donaldson, *Agricultural biography* (1854) · J. Macphail, *Remarks on the present times … being an introduction to hints and observations* (1795)
Archives Meterological Office, Bracknell, Berkshire, National Meteorological Archive, meteorological journal relating to Higham Hill

MacPhail, James Robert Nicolson (1858–1933), antiquary, born on 29 June 1858, was the eldest son of James Calder MacPhail, Gaelic-speaking Free Church minister of Pilrig, Edinburgh, and his wife, Anne Badenach, *née* Nicolson. His father co-authored with Robert Rainy, principal of the New College, Edinburgh, the statement for the Free Church and its committee for the highlands presented to the Crofters' Commission of 1883 and printed as item LXXXVII of Appendix A of their report in 1884. MacPhail was educated at the Edinburgh Academy (1868–75), where he was dux, and at Edinburgh University, where he revived the Dialectic Society. After taking his degree he trained for the law in the office of Tods, Murray, and Jamieson, writers to the signet, where experience in preparing the Lauderdale peerage case encouraged his antiquarian interests. He entered the Faculty of Advocates in 1886, became KC in 1910, and was appointed sheriff of Stirling, Dumbarton, and Clackmannan in 1917. He jointly wrote with J. P. Wood *The Law of Arbitration in Scotland* (1900), but his chief intellectual interests were always Scottish history, genealogy, and heraldry; he was considered a high authority on peerage law.

One of MacPhail's early interests was the trial of James Stewart of Acharn for the alleged murder of Colin Campbell of Glenure in 1752, which he detailed in a paper to the Gaelic Society of Inverness read on 30 April 1890; he read another paper on the trial to the same society on 22 February 1900. In the last of the four volumes he edited for the Scottish History Society under the title *Highland Papers*, published by the society in 1914, 1916, 1920, and 1934, he printed marginalia written in a copy of the Trist preserved at Barcaldine Castle. He fully exposed the trial of James of the Glens as a disgraceful miscarriage of justice and the execution of James as judicial murder.

The four volumes of *Highland Papers* (originally collected as manuscripts by Donald Gregory, who died in 1836) put an immense amount of important source material relating to the MacDonalds, the Campbells of Argyll, the MacLeods of Lewis and Harris, the MacLeans of Duart, the Chisholms, the MacRaes, and other highland clans and families at the disposal of highland historians, all edited and annotated with a robust common sense that was never taken in by official propaganda. Sheriff MacPhail was a patriotic Scot; he worked with his father on promoting the movement which led to the appointment of the Crofters' Commission in 1883, and was a prime mover in the agitation for the better housing of the Scottish records and an increase in the staff looking after them. He was chairman of the Scottish Record Society (1931–3), a member of the council of the Scottish History Society from 1892, and chairman from 1922 to 1926. He was a trustee of Sir William Fraser (*d.* 1898), the Scottish genealogist and family historian, and after his appointment as trustee in

1899 spent several years putting these papers in order in his spare time.

In 1900 MacPhail married Nora Helen, younger daughter of General Sir Hugh *Gough and his wife, Annie Margaret; they had two sons and a daughter. MacPhail was known as a tory, but he supported home rule, admired Parnell, and was a founder of the Scottish National Party. He died in Edinburgh on 15 October 1933.

J. L. CAMPBELL

Sources *The Scotsman* (19 Oct 1933) · W. K. Dickson, introduction, *Highland papers*, ed. J. R. N. Macphail, 4, vii–xviii, Scottish History Society, 3rd ser., 22 (1934) · J. R. N. MacPhail, 'An interesting copy of a report on the trial of James Stewart of Acharn', *Transactions of the Gaelic Society of Inverness*, 16 (1889–90), 276–84 · J. R. N. MacPhail, 'Further notes on the trial of James Stewart of Acharn', *Transactions of the Gaelic Society of Inverness*, 24 (1899–1900), 140–56 · *Transactions of the Gaelic Society of Inverness*, 34 · WW · WWW · CCI (1934)
Archives Warks. CRO, genealogical corresp. and papers relating to the Habsburg descent
Likenesses photograph, repro. in MacPhail, ed., *Highland papers*
Wealth at death £4176 17s. 11d.: confirmation, 24 Feb 1934, CCI

Macphee, Alexander (*b. c.*1893). *See under* Knoydart, Seven Men of (*act.* 1948).

Macphee, Donald (*fl.* 1948). *See under* Knoydart, Seven Men of (*act.* 1948).

Macpherson, Annie Parlane (1825–1904), promoter of child emigration, was born on 2 June 1825 in Campsie, by Milton, Stirlingshire, and baptized there on 26 June 1825, the eldest of the seven children of James Macpherson (*d.* 1851), a shoemaker, teacher, and member of the Society of Friends, and his wife, Helen Edwards. She was educated in Glasgow and trained in Froebel's educational methods at the Home and Colonial Training College, London. When her father was appointed superintendent of the Ockham Industrial Schools, Surrey, she acted as his secretary. At the age of nineteen she experienced a religious conversion, possibly connected to the tragic death of her fiancé. Influenced by the revivalist Reginald Radcliffe, she was inspired to undertake evangelical work among the coprolite diggers in Eversden, Cambridgeshire, where she lived from 1858. In 1865 she moved to London. Here she met Clara Lowe and Lady Rowley, who introduced her to mission work in the East End among the young female matchbox makers, whose plight she highlighted in *The Little Matchbox-Makers* (1866). Following an invitation from the Society of Friends to give lectures at the Bedford Institute, she included boys in her rescue mission. She opened a series of 'Revival Homes', named after the evangelical newspaper whose readers supported them, and in 1868 the Home of Industry, at 60 Commercial Street, was acquired to offer work, food and shelter, and basic education and religious instruction.

By 1869 Annie Macpherson had become convinced that emigration was the answer to chronic unemployment, and the Home of Industry assisted 500 people to emigrate to Canada. On a visit to the United States in 1866 she had met charity workers who assisted destitute New York children to move out west, and she adopted a similar plan to send children to homes in rural Canada, a project she outlined in *The Christian*. Sufficient funds were raised for 100 boys to leave for Canada in May 1870. They were accompanied by Annie Macpherson and by Ellen Bilborough, who remained in charge of the Canadian home established at Marchmont, Belleville, Ontario. In 1871 further homes were opened in Ontario at Galt and Knowlton.

Annie Macpherson's homes acted as distributing homes for several other charities, including those of Dr Thomas Barnardo, who had worked with the children at the Home of Industry in its earliest years, and William Quarrier, whom she encouraged to open children's homes in Scotland. When the emigration of poor-law children was approved in 1871 she was also invited by boards of guardians to place pauper children. By 1893, 5730 boys and girls had emigrated through her homes.

Pauper emigration was suspended in 1875 following a critical report by Andrew Doyle to the Local Government Board. It revealed shortcomings in the training and supervision of the children placed by Annie Macpherson and Maria *Rye, another important figure involved in the emigration of children. Their organizations operated in parallel, but their approach was very different and they never co-operated. Maria Rye had the ear of establishment figures and appealed for funds through *The Times*; Annie Macpherson believed in the power of prayer and received donations in response to letters and reports published in *The Christian*. Of the two, Annie Macpherson was the less controversial figure, and her operation was larger, more efficient, and more sympathetic to the children in her care. Although she was less well known in her day, Annie Macpherson's contribution to the history of juvenile emigration was arguably more influential.

An important element of Annie Macpherson's evangelical mission was the training of young Christian workers who helped at the Home of Industry and preached in the East End on Sundays. She established the Bridge of Hope refuge for women, was involved in many other missions, and for more than twenty-five years held a weekly sewing meeting for poor widows. Her sisters were closely involved in her work; Rachel Merry and her family were associated with the Canadian homes, and Louisa Birt ran the Liverpool Sheltering Home. The Macpherson homes were ultimately absorbed into Dr Barnardo's.

Annie Macpherson was a good-looking, warm-hearted woman with a magnetic personality and the power to inspire others. She also 'had her sting and used it, not always wisely, and sometimes too well' (Lowe, 235). She retired in 1902 to Hove, Sussex, where she died at her home, 9 Sackville Road, on 27 November 1904 from bronchitis. A service was held at the Home of Industry, 29 Bethnal Green Road, and she was buried on 3 December 1904 in the City of London cemetery, Ilford, Essex.

JUDY COLLINGWOOD

Sources L. M. Birt, *The children's home-finder: the story of Annie Macpherson and Louisa Birt* (1913) · C. M. S. Lowe, *God's answers: a record of Miss Annie Macpherson's work* (1882) · H. Stretton, 'Women's work for children', *Women's mission: a series of congress papers on the philanthropic work of women by eminent writers*, ed. Baroness Burdett-Coutts (1893) · A. Macpherson, 'Work among poor widows in east London', *Women's mission: a series of congress papers on the philanthropic work of women by eminent writers*, ed. Baroness Burdett-Coutts (1893) · J. Johnson, *Noble women of our time* (1899) · J. Parr, *Labouring children* (1980) · G. Wagner, *Children of the empire* (1982) · *The Christian* (5 May 1870) · *The Revival* (4 March 1869) · *The Revival* (3 June 1869) · IGI · d. cert. · bap. reg. Scot. · *CGPLA Eng. & Wales* (1905)
Archives U. Lpool L., Macpherson Homes, London, registers relating to emigration
Likenesses photograph, repro. in *The Christian* (1 Dec 1904) · photograph, repro. in Birt, *The children's home-finder*
Wealth at death £68 9s. 3d.: probate, 25 Feb 1905, *CGPLA Eng. & Wales*

MacPherson, Colin (1917–1990), Roman Catholic bishop of Argyll and the Isles, was born on 5 August 1917 at Lochboisdale in South Uist, Scotland, the eldest of the three sons and six children of Malcolm MacPherson, a schoolmaster, and his wife, Mary MacMillan. He was educated at the local primary school at Daliburgh, at St Mary's College, Blairs, Aberdeen, and at the Propaganda College, Rome, where he graduated BPhil in 1936 and BTh in 1938. He was ordained on 23 March 1940 and would have gone on to further study had the outbreak of war not necessitated his return to the United Kingdom. He served as the chaplain to the Carmelite convent in Oban and received his first parish appointment, to Knoydart in the west highlands of Scotland, in 1943.

It was there that MacPherson first came to public attention in 1948, when he acted as the spokesman and secretary to the group known as the 'seven men of Knoydart', who carried out protests into the perceived injustices surrounding the allocation of land and other matters on the estate owned by Lord Brocket. In the legal proceedings in the Court of Session which were occasioned by these protests, the agent for the landowner accused Father MacPherson of having 'consistently worked against Lord Brocket' (NA Scot., CS275/1952/4). MacPherson's time in Knoydart was difficult: the population of the area was falling, it was remote, and in 1948 his parochial house burnt down. In 1951 he became the parish priest of St Michael's, Eriskay, and in 1956 he made the short journey to St Mary's, Benbecula, where he remained for a decade. Thus, for much of his early career he was based among the crofting, Roman Catholic, and Gaelic community from which he had come. His position as a native Gaelic speaker and his commitment to his parishioners, in a practical as well as a spiritual manner, were notable. He was a member of the county council of Inverness, was an advocate of agricultural diversity among crofters, and made an especial effort to encourage the rearing of poultry. He also campaigned to improve the housing, educational, and communication facilities of the people of the western isles. His deep commitment to these causes was undoubted and they gave a necessary outlet to his tremendous energies and wide interests beyond the role of a parish priest.

A new phase of MacPherson's career began when he moved to St Mary's, Fort William, in 1966 and was subsequently nominated as bishop of Argyll and the Isles in December 1968. He was the first native Gaelic speaker since the Reformation to be bishop of this diocese, which contained about 12,000 Catholics. His episcopal ordination took place in February 1969 and his predecessor, Bishop McGill, remarked, 'with this rich Island background the Bishop has also an incomparable knowledge of the language, literature and traditions of Gaeldom' (*Oban Times*, 13 Feb 1969). The Scottish highlands are widely perceived to be a bastion of a brand of presbyterianism which takes a much more detached, even hostile, attitude to Gaelic secular culture; McGill's statement is worthy of being read as more than the standard eulogy expected on such occasions.

MacPherson continued to pursue a wide range of interests during his time at St Columba's Cathedral, Oban, by serving, for example, on the religious advisory committees of the BBC and the Independent Television Authority. His knowledge of French and German facilitated his participation in the European episcopal conference. Developments in the diocese during his period as bishop included the opening of new churches on the islands of Mull and Arran, and further plans for a church in the Presbyterian stronghold of Stornoway, on the isle of Lewis. Ironically, the church at Knoydart had to be closed during his time as bishop; one of his obituarists remarked that had the schemes for an expanded crofting community, which he had placed before the board of agriculture for Scotland in 1947 and 1948, been adopted, Inverie 'might have been a much more thriving community' (*The Independent*, 30 March 1990).

MacPherson acted as the Roman Catholic observer at the general assembly of the Church of Scotland in 1974, and in the same year was honoured with the degree of LLD by St Francis Xavier University, Antigonish, Nova Scotia. He died in the County Hospital, Oban, on 24 March 1990 as he was contemplating the fiftieth anniversary of his ordination. At his funeral in St Columba's Cathedral, Oban, on 29 March 1990 his predecessor, Bishop McGill (who had presided at his episcopal ordination twenty-two years earlier), read an address on behalf of Cardinal Gordon Gray. He was buried in Pennygair cemetery, Oban. Bishop MacPherson was the most notable leader of Scottish highland and Gaelic-speaking Catholicism in the twentieth century and the diocese endured difficult times in the period after his death. EWEN A. CAMERON

Sources *The Independent* (30 March 1990) · *Oban Times* (5 Dec 1968) · *Oban Times* (13 Feb 1969) · *Oban Times* (29 March 1990) · *Oban Times* (5 April 1990) · *Scottish Catholic Observer* (6 Dec 1968) · *Scottish Catholic Observer* (7 Feb 1969) · court of session papers, NA Scot., CS 275/1952/4 · C. Johnson, *Scottish Catholic secular clergy, 1878–1989* (1991) · b. cert. · d. cert.
Archives Scottish Catholic Archives, Edinburgh, diocesan archive

Macpherson, David (1746–1816), historian, son of a tailor and clothier, was born at Edinburgh on 26 October 1746. He was probably educated at Edinburgh high school and Edinburgh University, and was afterwards trained as a land surveyor. In this capacity he worked in both Britain and North America, earning enough money to settle, about 1790, with his wife and family, in London and attempt to obtain a livelihood from writing. Losing money

through unfortunate loans he was occasionally in straitened circumstances afterwards, but worked manfully, receiving encouragement from writers like Joseph Ritson and George Chalmers of the *Caledonia*. For some time Macpherson was a deputy keeper of the public records in London, and assisted in preparing for publication the first and part of the second volume of the *Rotuli Scotiae* (2 vols., 1814–19).

Macpherson first demonstrated his talent as a historian in the first edition of Andrew of Wyntoun's manuscript history in the British Library, *De Orygynale Chronykil of Scotland* (2 vols., 1795). An exact piece of scholarship, it contained an elaborate glossary and extensive notes, and was later re-edited, in an enlarged edition, by David Laing for the Historians of Scotland series. In 1796 Macpherson published his *Geographical Illustrations of Scottish History*, but his most celebrated work was his *Annals of Commerce, Fisheries and Navigation* (4 vols., 1805). Although volumes 2 and 3 were largely based on Adam Anderson's *History of Commerce* (1764), volume 4 was an authoritative continuation of Anderson's history to the union with Ireland. The work was well received and Macpherson came to be regarded as a leading authority on the history of Britain's overseas trade. According to George Ellis, 'there are few books of reference whose utility has been more generally acknowledged' (*Edinburgh Review*, 7, 1805, 237). Macpherson's final work was a *History of European Commerce with India* (1812), in which he opposed Adam Smith's view that the East India Company's monopoly was detrimental to the development of trade between India and Europe.

Macpherson died in St Pancras, London, on 1 August 1816. M. J. MERCER

Sources Andrew of Wyntoun, *The orygynale cronykil of Scotland*, [rev. edn], ed. D. Laing, 3 vols. (1872–9), xxxvii–xlix · Anderson, *Scot. nat.* · R. H. I. Palgrave, ed., *Dictionary of political economy*, 3 vols. (1894–9) · Irving, *Scots.* · Allibone, *Dict.* · *GM*, 1st ser., 86/2 (1816), 189

Macpherson, Duncan (1812–1867), military surgeon, was born on 25 September 1812, and trained in medicine at Edinburgh, where he graduated MD in 1835. He was appointed surgeon to the army in Madras in 1836. Between 1840 and 1842 he served with the 37th grenadier regiment in China, and he was severely wounded at Chuenpe (Chuanbi). He told of his experiences in his *Two Years in China* (1842). On his return to India he served chiefly with the irregular horse in the Hyderabad contingent, and on the outbreak of the war with Russia in 1855 he was appointed head of the medical staff of the Turkish contingent on the recommendation of his former commander, Lord Gough. During his time on the Bosphorus he prepared his *Antiquities of Kertch and Researches in the Cimmerian Bosphorus* (1857); this contains a sketch of the history and archaeology as well as of the physical and ethnological features of the country.

Macpherson returned to India and was promoted to the post of inspector-general of the medical service of Madras on 8 January 1858. This infraction of the hitherto sacred rule of seniority, together with the feverish activity of the new inspector in the performance of his duties and his large schemes of reorganization, rendered him not a little 'repugnant to the older official class'. It was, however, generally admitted that he made progress in several important departments of military sanitation. In 1862 he published his *Reports on mountain and marine sanitary; medical and statistical observations on civil stations and military cantonments*.

Macpherson died at Mercara, Coorg, being then honorary physician and honorary surgeon to her majesty, on 8 June 1867. At the time of his death he had been about to be gazetted president of the Madras sanitary commission.

THOMAS SECCOMBE, rev. JAMES MILLS

Sources D. G. Crawford, ed., *Roll of the Indian Medical Service, 1615–1930* (1930) · *The Lancet* (13 July 1867), 56 · *Indian Army List* · *GM*, 4th ser., 4 (1867), 397 · Allibone, *Dict.*

Macpherson, Ewen, of Cluny (1706–1764), Jacobite army officer and clan chieftain, was born on 11 February 1706, probably at Nuid, Badenoch, Inverness-shire, the eldest son of Lachlan Macpherson (1674–1746), originally of Nuid and afterwards of Cluny, and Jean, daughter of Sir Ewen Cameron of Lochiel. In 1591 Macpherson's clan had made a bond of manrent with Gordon, earl of Huntly, and claimed the chieftancy of clan Chattan against the Mackintoshes; in 1672 Donald Macpherson of Cluny applied to the Lyon office as 'the only true representer of the ancient and honourable family of Clan Chattan'. However, the Mackintoshes successfully appealed to the lord Lyon and Donald Macpherson was recognized only as a cadet of Mackintosh of that ilk. At a meeting of clan Chattan held at Moy, Inverness-shire, in 1724, Lachlan Macpherson renounced all claim to the chieftaincy in exchange for the lands of Gallovy, Kinloch, Muckoull, Inverviddan, and Ardverikie around Loch Laggan. In 1744 the Macphersons, attempting to increase their influence and loosen their ties with the Mackintoshes, agreed bonds of friendship and alliance with Cameron of Lochiel and Fraser of Lovat. On 2 March 1742 Ewen Macpherson, then younger of Cluny, married Jean (*d.* in or after 1764), the eldest daughter of Simon Fraser, twelfth Lord Lovat.

In August 1745 Macpherson accepted command of a company in Lord Loudoun's government regiment, despite the fact that the Macphersons had supported the Jacobites in 1715. While still acting as an informant to the lord president, Duncan Forbes of Culloden, Macpherson was kidnapped by his cousin Lochiel on the night of 28 August and brought to Perth. He was kept a prisoner until 7 September when he accepted a commission as a colonel in the Jacobite army. Subsequently Macpherson arrived with forces at Edinburgh and on 29 October 1745 had an audience with Charles Edward Stuart, Jacobite prince of Wales, at Holyrood. Meanwhile, he left 400 men at Alloa to ensure the safe escort of military supplies to Dalkeith and he and Menzies of Shian are reported to have arrived at Dalkeith on 2 November with about 1000 men.

On 18 December Macpherson took part in the attack on the duke of Cumberland's cavalry at Clifton, near Penrith. An observer commented: 'This brave action was chiefly owing to the courage of the Mcphersons, commanded by Clued Mcpherson, their chief, who behaved most gallantly on this occasion' (Blaikie, 186). Macpherson also commanded his men on the left wing of the front line under Lord John Drummond at the battle of Falkirk on 17 January 1746. After Falkirk, Macpherson and Lord George Murray were engaged in capturing government posts in Perthshire and Macpherson was sent to guard the lines of communication around Ruthven. It was here, at Dalmagarry, that he learned from fugitives of the outcome of the battle of Culloden. In June Cluny House, Aberdeenshire, was plundered and burnt by a force under captains George and Hugh Mackay of Reay. Macpherson, the ever ambivalent Jacobite, now became a fugitive from the Hanoverian forces. During this time it was reported that he came off better in a skirmish with government troops in Badenoch. Indeed, in November 1746 it was reported that 'The McDonalds and McPhersons and their followers are still numerous and mostly thieves' and 'a parcel of rebellious rogues' (Terry, 336–7). In depositions made at Westminster in 1746 witnesses described Macpherson as always attired in 'highland dress' and acting 'as an officer at the head of his clan' (Allardyce, 360). Despite their differences in the wake of the battle of Falkirk, Macpherson provided shelter for Prince Charles at his refuge, the 'cage' on Ben Adler overlooking Loch Ericht, in September 1746.

Several months earlier Macpherson had become chief of Cluny following his father's death in July 1746, though for the next nine years he remained an outlaw at Badenoch secure in the 'cage' on Ben Adler. The earl of Albemarle, commander-in-chief of the army in Scotland, ranked Cluny as one of the chiefs of 'some consideration' but failed in his attempts to capture him (Terry, 289), even though government troops were camped near Cluny House for some two years. In February 1747 the lord justice clerk wrote to the duke of Newcastle that Cluny 'seems to be at present the person among the Rebels of most consequence to be laid hold of' and 'still lurking in the Highlands' (Cheyne-Macpherson, 289, 433) despite a reward of £1000 for his capture. Cluny's importance is easy to see; Prince Charles Edward Stuart left him with a large fund of money to be distributed to officers and Jacobite clans to keep them in hope of a further rising. However, these funds, originally as high as £30,000, were the cause of variance among Cluny, the Camerons, and MacDonalds, who did not agree with the way in which they were distributed. In 1748 Cluny's wife gave birth to a son, Duncan, in a kiln for drying corn; the couple also had a daughter, Margaret (*b.* 1743), who married Colonel Duncan Macpherson of Bleaton.

In September 1754 Charles Edward Stuart asked Cluny to come to Paris, and to bring with him whatever funds he still possessed; Cluny escaped to France in 1755. He wrote to Field Marshal Keith from Calais on 4 May 1756 and declared 'tho' my lieving is but small and low, my life is at least much more comfortable than for ten years past' (*Ninth Report*, HMC, 220). However, Prince Charles was far less impressed by Cluny's lack of funds, having expected him to bring to him the remainder of the Loch Arkaig treasure. Cluny further worsened his position by repeatedly denying any knowledge of Stuart jewellery and gold plate which the prince claimed to have left with him for safe keeping before his flight to France. Relations took a final and irrevocable turn when Cluny twice lectured the prince on his need to improve his credibility among his remaining Jacobite sympathizers, not least by his abandonment of alcohol. Charles for his part was enraged by the presumptuousness of such comments—a 'very surprising message delivered in a still more surprising manner' (McLynn, 436)—from an incompetent and dishonest subordinate. Henceforth the prince broke off all relations except for his repeated and unsuccessful hounding of Cluny to disclose the whereabouts of his treasure.

Cluny died on 31 January 1764 at Dunkirk and was buried in the town's Garden of the Carmelites. For Sir John Murray of Broughton he had been 'a man of low stature, very square, of extreme good sense ... determined and resolute with uncommon calmness' (Cheyne-Macpherson, 53). In October 1757 the Cluny estates were among those 'intended to be annexed' (Millar, 347, 350–51). However, by 1763 the estate was being administered by Cluny's brother John Macpherson (1709–1770) of the 78th foot, who was petitioning the courts as tutor for the restoration of the lands to his nephew Duncan (Michie, 338). Duncan was restored in 1784 after the lands had first been offered to the poet James Macpherson. Duncan became lieutenant-colonel of the 3rd foot guards and married (12 June 1798) Catherine, daughter of Sir Evan Cameron of Fassiefiern. He died on 1 August 1817.

The couple's eldest son, **Ewen Macpherson of Cluny** (1804–1884), army officer and landowner, was born on 24 April 1804. He was a captain in the 42nd highlanders and later lieutenant-colonel of the Inverness Highland rifle volunteers until 1882. Created a companion of the Bath by Queen Victoria—who recorded her visit to him at Cluny in her diary in 1847—'Old Cluny' held several prominent public offices, including governor of the Caledonian Bank, director of the Highland Railway, deputy lieutenant of Inverness, and chieftain of the Gaelic Society. He was noted for his attachment to all things highland, and was able to speak Gaelic fluently. He and his wife, Sarah, daughter of Henry Davidson of Tulloch, whom he married on 20 December 1832, had four sons and three daughters. He died at Cluny Castle on 11 January 1884.

DAVIE HORSBURGH

Sources DNB • W. Cheyne-Macpherson, ed., *The chiefs of clan Macpherson* (1947) • C. Sandford Terry, ed., *The Albemarle papers being the correspondence of William Anne, second earl of Albemarle* (1902) • F. McLynn, *Charles Edward Stuart* (1988) • A. H. Millar, ed., *A selection of Scottish forfeited estates papers*, Scottish History Society, 57 (1909) • W. MacLeod, ed., *A list of persons concerned in the rebellion* (1890) • M. Mackintosh, *The clan Mackintosh and the clan Chattan* (1948); rev. edn by L. Mackintosh (1982) • W. B. Blaikie, ed., *Origins of the 'Forty-Five and the papers relating to that rising*, Scottish History Society, 2nd ser., vol. 2 (1916) • J. Stuart, ed., *The miscellany of the Spalding Club*, 2–4, Spalding Club, 6, 16, 20 (1842–9) • *Calendar of the Stuart papers belonging to his majesty the king, preserved at Windsor Castle*, 7 vols., HMC, 56 (1902–23) • J. Allardyce, ed., *Historical papers relating to the Jacobite period, 1699–1750*, 2 vols., New Spalding Club, 14, 16 (1895–6) • *The manuscripts of his grace the duke of Portland*, 10 vols., HMC, 29 (1891–1931), vols. 5–10 • J. G. Michie, ed., *The records of Invercauld* (1901) • V. Gaffney, *The lordship of Strathavon and Tomintoul* (1960) • *Ninth report*, 3 vols., HMC, 8 (1883–4)

Archives West Highland Museum, Fort William, papers relating to uprising of 1745

Wealth at death at time of death was forfeited by crown; granted 6000 livres in 1756 by French crown: HMC, *Ninth report*, 220

Macpherson, Ewen, of Cluny (1804–1884). *See under* Macpherson, Ewen, of Cluny (1706–1764).

Macpherson [*née* Bate], **Gerardine** [Geddie] (1830/31–1878), biographer and book illustrator, was born probably in London, the elder child of Henry Bate, a Leicester artist, and his wife, Louisa, *née* Murphy, the sister of Anna Brownell *Jameson (1794–1860), a well-known writer on art and literature. After Bate went bankrupt in 1839, the childless Mrs Jameson undertook to pay for and superintend his daughter's education. In December 1840 she wrote apprehensively to her friend Ottilie von Goethe that her niece was 'growing a great tall, wild girl, and requires good discipline' (*Letters of Anna Jameson*, 130), but by February 1842 Gerardine (known as Geddie) seems to have been living with her.

In 1846–7 aunt and niece visited France and Italy, mainly to finish Gerardine Bate's education; they travelled with the newly married Robert and Elizabeth Barrett Browning. The romantic atmosphere must have affected the impressionable Gerardine: in Rome she met and fell in love with Robert *Macpherson (1814–1872), a flamboyant Scottish artist who had recently been converted to Roman Catholicism. Stoutly protestant and probably distressed at the prospect of losing her adopted daughter, Jameson strongly disapproved of the attachment. The marriage was delayed by the 1848 revolution in Rome, which further depleted Macpherson's already precarious finances (in 1851, he turned to photography to earn his living); Gerardine Bate appears to have returned to her parents, who did not oppose the match, and in April 1849 Jameson wrote grumpily: 'Gerardine does not go on to my satisfaction' (*Letters of Anna Jameson*, 165). The couple were married on 4 September 1849 in Ealing; in the following year, Mrs Macpherson converted to Catholicism.

Jameson was eventually reconciled to her niece's marriage: in 1855 and 1857, she visited the Macphersons in Rome, attending mass at St Peter's on one occasion to please Gerardine. In 1846–7 Gerardine had designed the engravings for Jameson's *Sacred and Legendary Art* (1848); Jameson now engaged her to provide etchings for the second edition of her *Legends of the Madonna* (1857). Such employment was no doubt welcome: never more than comfortably off, the Macphersons had a growing family and Robert was almost continually in poor health. Gerardine Macpherson was a working wife and mother: she illustrated her husband's *Vatican Sculptures* (1863) and assisted him with his photographic business. Robert Macpherson also dealt in antiquities: responsible for the discovery of Michelangelo's *The Entombment of Christ* in 1846, he hoarded it as a financial security, describing it as

'Gerardine's fortune' and eventually selling it to the National Gallery in 1868 for £2000.

After 1865 Robert Macpherson's health and business both declined, and he died in November 1872, leaving his wife and four surviving children in financial distress. Gerardine Macpherson supported her family by giving lessons in English, acting as an amanuensis, and serving as a newspaper correspondent in Rome during the hot season when the regular correspondents departed. More significantly, she prepared her *Memoirs of the Life of Anna Jameson* (1878), which necessitated a three-month visit to England; the first biography of her aunt, it was published after her death with an introductory preface by a family friend, the novelist Margaret Oliphant. It remained the most important account of Jameson's life and work until it was superseded by Clara Thomas's 1967 biography. Worn out by her many employments, suffering from rheumatism and heart disease, Gerardine Macpherson died in Rome on 24 May 1878; she was buried next to her husband in the cemetery of San Lorenzo.

When first embarking on her niece's education in 1842, Jameson had declared that she would try to 'give her the means of independence [so that] she will not be obliged to marry for money, like so many women of her condition' (*Letters of Anna Jameson*, 135): ironically, as for her aunt, neither education nor marriage ensured financial security (whatever their other benefits) for Gerardine Macpherson. Her plight is indicative of the financial perils of the mid-Victorian middle-class woman; her achievements were the essentially complementary and concealed ones characteristic of the home-educated and amateur woman artist and writer of the 1850s and 1860s.

ROSEMARY MITCHELL

Sources M. O. W. Oliphant, 'Postscript', in G. Macpherson, *Memoirs of the life of Anna Jameson*, ed. M. O. W. Oliphant (1878), xiii–xvii · C. Thomas, *Love and work enough: the life of Anna Jameson* (1967) · M. Munsterberg, 'A biographical sketch of Robert Macpherson', *Art Bulletin*, 68 (1986), 142–53 · *Letters of Anna Jameson to Ottilie von Goethe*, ed. G. H. Needler (1939) · *Anna Jameson: letters and friendships*, ed. B. S. Erskine (1915) · M. Bailey, 'The rediscovery of Michelangelo's *Entombment*: the rescuing of a masterpiece', *Apollo*, 140 (Oct 1994), 30–33

Macpherson, Sir Herbert Taylor (1827–1886), army officer, son of Lieutenant-Colonel Duncan Macpherson, at one time of the 78th highlanders or Ross-shire Buffs, was born at Ardersier, Inverness-shire, on 27 February 1827, and in 1845 was appointed an ensign in his father's former regiment, in which he became lieutenant on 13 July 1848. He served as adjutant of the regiment in the Persian expedition in 1857 and with the force under Sir Henry Havelock at the relief of the residency at Lucknow on 25 September 1857, and in the subsequent defence, for which he was awarded the Victoria Cross. He became captain in the regiment on 5 October 1857, and served under Outram at the defence of the Alambagh, and as brigade major during the final capture of Lucknow, in which he was severely wounded. He was promoted brevet major and granted a year's additional service. He transferred to the 82nd regiment, but after the East India Company's forces passed to

the crown Macpherson was one of the first officers who obtained permission to transfer their services from the British to the Indian army, and became commandant 3rd Gurkha regiment in 1862. In 1859 Macpherson married Maria Elizabeth Henrietta, daughter of Lieutenant-General James Eckford, Indian army; she survived her husband.

Macpherson was appointed major Bengal staff corps in 1865, brevet lieutenant-colonel in 1867, lieutenant-colonel staff corps in 1871, and brevet colonel in 1872. He served in the Hazara (Black Mountain) campaign of 1868, the Lushai expedition in 1871–2 (medal and clasp), and in the Jowaki campaign of 1877, when he was at the forcing of the Bori Pass. In 1878–9 he commanded the 1st brigade of the 1st division of the Khyber column in the Second Anglo-Afghan War. He was made KCB in 1879. In 1880 he was appointed to a brigade in Bengal, with the local rank of major-general.

In 1882 Macpherson became a major-general, and commanded the division of Indian troops sent to Egypt, and was at the battle of Tell al-Kebir. His rapid march with the Indian troops to Zaqaziq, where on the night of the battle of Tell al-Kebir he received a telegram from the commission of pashas at Cairo submitting the army and the country to the khedive, ended Arabi Pasha's rebellion. For some years the telegram was ignored and the credit claimed for the cavalry division of the British army. He received the thanks of parliament and the KCSI.

In August 1886, while commanding the Allahabad division, Macpherson was appointed commander-in-chief at Madras, and, after the failure of the first expedition to Burma to pacify the country, was ordered temporarily to transfer his headquarters there and to remain until the conclusion of operations in the cold season. Macpherson arrived at Rangoon on 9 September and assumed command of the expeditionary force, by then amounting to 30,000 men. He at once proceeded up the Irrawaddy, taking with him a flotilla of river boats carrying the reinforcements he had brought with him from India. He reached Yenangyaung on 14 September, and, after brief delays there and at Prome, arrived at Mandalay on 17 September. The inundations which occurred there soon afterwards caused much sickness among Europeans and the Burmese. Macpherson himself fell ill, having, it was believed, contracted the fever at Mandalay. He abandoned his intention of proceeding to Bhamo, and returned on 12 October to Thayetmyo, and from there proceeded to Prome, where his illness became so severe as to require his removal to Rangoon. He died on board the steamer *Irrawaddy* immediately after leaving Prome for Rangoon on 20 October 1886.

H. M. CHICHESTER, rev. JAMES FALKNER

Sources *Army List* · *Hart's Army List* · *LondG* · T. E. Toomey, *Heroes of the Victoria Cross* (1895) · *Broad Arrow* (23 Oct 1886) · Boase, *Mod. Eng. biog.*

Archives NAM, papers relating to battle of Tell al-Kebir, 6607/20 **Likenesses** black and white photograph, NPG · black and white photograph, repro. in Toomey, *Heroes of the Victoria cross* · chromolithograph (after photograph by P. Vucino & Co.), NPG; repro. in *Pictorial World* (4 Nov 1882) · wood-engraving (after photograph), NPG; repro. in *ILN* (30 Oct 1886)

Wealth at death £750—effects in England: probate, 28 March 1887, *CGPLA Eng. & Wales*

Macpherson, (James) Ian, first Baron Strathcarron (1880–1937), politician, was born at Strone, Kingussie, Inverness-shire, on 14 May 1880, the second of the three sons of James Macpherson JP (1848–1922), farmer of Newtonmore, Inverness-shire, and his wife, Anne (d. 1924), daughter of James Stewart of Strone. Educated locally and at George Watson's College, Edinburgh, he graduated MA and LLB at Edinburgh University, where he was senior president of the Students' Representative Council and president of the Liberal Association. Called to the bar by the Middle Temple in 1906, he combined legal practice with journalism and politics, and after having unsuccessfully contested Wigtownshire and East Renfrewshire at the two general elections of 1910, he was returned at a by-election in 1911 as Liberal member for Ross and Cromarty. He held the seat until his retirement at the end of 1935, for the last four years as a Liberal National. On 24 September 1915 he married Jill (d. 1956), only daughter of George Wood Rhodes, first baronet. They had one son and two daughters.

From 1914 to 1916 Macpherson was parliamentary secretary to the under-secretary of state for war, from 1916 to 1918 under-secretary of state for war, and from 1918 to 1919 vice-president of the army council (deputy secretary of state for war). He was sworn of the privy council in 1918. When the coalition government was reconstituted in January 1919, Macpherson, the youngest minister in the cabinet, was appointed as chief secretary for Ireland. He was an ardent home-ruler, although as a Presbyterian he had sympathies for the north, and refused to co-operate with James MacMahon, the under-secretary, who was a Catholic. He took a tough line on the revolutionary unrest: Sinn Féin was declared a proscribed organization in May 1919, and the Dáil Éireann was declared illegal. Although he believed that repressive measures were insufficient to deal with the situation he was not convinced of the wisdom of the compromise agreed to by the coalition cabinet effectively to partition Ireland through the introduction of separate southern and Ulster 'home rule' parliaments. Macpherson introduced the Government of Ireland Bill early in 1920, 'in a speech which in its lack of conviction may be thought to foreshadow the disillusion with Lloyd George's Irish policy that led to his resignation shortly after' (Mansergh, 116). Macpherson's health had suffered in the job, and the strain of the position was apparent when he told parliament that 'all I can do is stand up and read a carefully prepared answer, prepared by someone else, as best I can' (cited McDowell, 595). Frank Owen suggests his resignation was as much because his 'nerve had gone' as 'he lived in continual terror of assassination' (Owen, 564). Macpherson went to the Ministry of Pensions where he was perhaps more successful, and suited, and there he introduced the Pensions Act of 1922, the keystone of pensions policy until the outbreak of the Second World War. He lost office with the fall of the coalition government in 1922.

Macpherson had continually promoted Scottish interests, and was a keen student of Gaelic. His popularity with his constituents had been increased by his command of the language, for which he had won prizes at university, and his interest in issues of land and afforestation. Lord Alness commented that it was Macpherson who induced him to insert the Gaelic clause in the Education Act of 1918. Macpherson continued with legal work, becoming a KC in 1919, a bencher of his inn in 1930, and recorder of Southend in 1931. He also played a leading role in a number of organizations promoting inter-empire trade.

Combining highland courtesy with the urbanity of a man of the world, Macpherson was popular alike with political friends and with opponents. He was an impressive speaker, and with his command of picturesque imagery and poetic phrase was especially welcome on highland platforms. He received the honorary degree of LLD from Edinburgh University and was a freeman of the royal burgh of Dingwall. Created a baronet in 1933, Macpherson was raised to the peerage as Baron Strathcarron of Banchor, Inverness-shire, in 1936. He died of heart failure at the Coq D'Or restaurant, Stratton Street, London, on 14 August 1937 and was cremated at Golders Green on 18 August.   G. A. WATERS, *rev.* MARC BRODIE

Sources *The Times* (16 Aug 1937) · *The Times* (19 Aug 1937) · Burke, *Peerage* (1999) · N. Mansergh, *The unresolved question: the Anglo-Irish settlement and its undoing, 1912–72* (1991) · F. Owen, *Tempestuous journey: Lloyd George, his life and times* (1954) · R. B. McDowell, 'Administration and the public services, 1870–1921', *A new history of Ireland*, ed. T. W. Moody and others, 6: *Ireland under the Union, 1870–1921* (1996), 571–605 · K. O. Morgan, *Consensus and disunity: the Lloyd George coalition government, 1918–1922* (1979) · WWBMP · b. cert. · *CGPLA Eng. & Wales* (1938)

Archives Bodl. Oxf., corresp. and papers relating to Ireland | HLRO, corresp. with David Lloyd George · HLRO, corresp. with Andrew Bonar Law

Likenesses W. Stoneman, photograph, 1920, NPG · T. Cottrell, cigarette card, NPG

Wealth at death £4431 4s. 10d.: resworn administration, 17 March 1938, *CGPLA Eng. & Wales*

Macpherson, Ian (1905–1944), novelist, was born in Leslie Place, Forres, Moray, on 5 October 1905, the middle of three children, and the only son, of Ewen Macpherson (b. 1863), sheep dealer, and his wife, Mary, whose maiden name was also Macpherson (b. 1870). The family moved to a hill farm at Glensaugh, in Kincardineshire, and Macpherson was educated at Mackie Academy, Stonehaven, where he was dux in 1924. He went to Aberdeen University and in 1928 graduated with first-class honours in English, being awarded the Seafield gold medal. Professor A. A. Jack described him as 'the most distinguished student in the English classes during his four years' study in Aberdeen' (private information), and appointed him to a two-year post as his assistant.

During this period Macpherson wrote his first novel, *Shepherds' Calendar*, which is largely autobiographical, set on a Kincardineshire farm that is recognizably Glensaugh, during and just after the First World War, charting the adolescent development of John Grant. It was published in 1931, the year before Lewis Grassic Gibbon's *Sunset Song*, to which it has been compared; but the distinctive strength of Macpherson's novel lies in the acute psychological perception with which he delineates the triangle of forces within the Grant family, father and mother and son, and the very convincing picture of the day-to-day work of the farm.

In 1930 Macpherson was expected to go off to Cambridge to do postgraduate work to further his academic career, but instead he chose to take a remarkable change of direction. On 10 May of that year he married Elizabeth Cameron (1905–1989), the daughter of the Revd John Cameron and the novelist Margaret Isabel Cameron, *née* Noble, and together they bought a van and spent the summer hawking fruit around Speyside. When winter came they found an abandoned and isolated cottage between Laggan and Dalwhinnie, where they spent the next six years, leading a hand-to-mouth but happy existence, during which period Macpherson did most of his writing. He also pioneered radio discussions with his friend and fellow author John R. Allan.

Macpherson's second novel, *Land of our Fathers*, was published in 1933, and is set virtually on his doorstep in Badenoch and Strathspey. It is a historically significant novel in that it is one of the first to deal with a theme, the highland clearances, which was to become important for other modern Scottish novelists such as Neil Gunn. The novel is centred on James Graeme, a borderer, and his struggle to establish his sheep-farming empire against local antagonism. Like Gunn, Macpherson is anxious to see the clearances as not simply a matter of good and bad. While Graeme rides roughshod over much that is valuable in the old culture, he does produce efficiency and a kind of prosperity. *Pride in the Valley* (1936) is in a sense a sequel to *Land of our Fathers*, in that it is set in the central highlands in the latter half of the nineteenth century, when sheep farming is itself coming under threat from afforestation and deer-stalking. It is a more bitter novel, with a strong sense of the betrayal of the people by the old chief, Cluny Macpherson, in the face of the new commercialism.

Wild Harbour marks a new departure for Macpherson as a novelist, in that instead of being about the past it was about the future. Published in 1936, it is set in 1944, and Macpherson predicts the outbreak of the Second World War, questioning the possibility of isolation and detachment in the face of the horror. His two central characters go off to live in a cave in the highlands, but their sense of natural well-being is undermined by their feeling of betrayal of their kind. As the war intrudes upon them more and more, with armed deserters and marauders scouring the country, they decide they must return. The tragedy is that the dark destiny of modern man belongs to us all, whether we like it or not.

In 1936 Macpherson ended his own isolation when he took a job with a government agency, the Scottish Country Industries Development Trust, which involved his touring the south-west of Scotland, providing support for rural craftsmen. In 1938 he became tenant of the hill farm of Tombain, near Dunphail in Moray. He continued to produce regular journalism but there were no more novels. On 15 July 1944 Macpherson was killed in a motorcycle accident near his home. He was survived by his wife and two young daughters, and was buried in Newtonmore on 17 July 1944.

DOUGLAS F. YOUNG

Sources private information (2004) · D. F. Young, *Highland search: the life and novels of Ian Macpherson* (2002) · E. Macpherson and C. Graham, 'Ian Macpherson', *Leopard Magazine* (May 1979), 19–22 · J. R. Allan, *Northeast lowlands of Scotland* (1952), 180–82 · *Aberdeen University Review*, 31 (1944–6), 127–8 · J. Manson, 'Mearns to Strathspey', *Cencrastus*, 54 (spring–summer 1996), 23–6 · b. cert. · d. cert. **Wealth at death** £1861 1s. 8d.: confirmation, 10 Jan 1945, CCI

MacPherson, James (*c.*1675–1700), thief and reputed musician, is said to have been an illegitimate son of the family of Invershie, Inverness-shire. He was described as 'the son of a gentleman … [and] a gipsy mother', who became 'the leader of one of the gangs of cattle-lifters which roamed over the Province of Moray' (Dick, 476).

At his trial in Banff in November 1700 MacPherson was among those accused as 'Egyptians, soroners, and vagabonds', who 'had a particular language which wes not Irish [Gaelic]' ('Process', 178, 186). They were found guilty of being 'oppressors of his Majesties frie lieges in ane bangstrie [violent] manner, and going up and doune the country armed', being 'thieves, and recepters of thieves' (ibid.). Among other charges MacPherson was accused of having undertaken to cure a man of a boil, and then stolen two mares from the man, which he claimed were payment. MacPherson was taken to Banff's Mercat Cross where he was 'hanged by the neck to the death by the hand of the common executioner' on 16 November 1700 (ibid., 190). The 'Captain' of the group, Peter Broune, who 'played on the wiol', also found guilty, was hanged on 2 April 1701 (ibid., 184).

Broune's role as leader of the criminals, and as fiddler, gradually became attached to MacPherson. In 1769 James Herd published the ballad 'MacPherson's Rant' (similar to the pre-1700 ballad 'Capt. Johnson's Farewell' in the Pepys Collection), which mentioned no music. Robert Burns's new version of the ballad to the tune 'McPherson's Rant' (in print before 1750, and quite likely written to fit the words of the broadside ballad) appeared in James Johnson's *Scots Musical Museum* (1788), as 'Farewell, ye dungeons, dark and strong', with the chorus

> Sae rantingly, sae wantonly,
> Sae dauntingly gaed he,
> He play'd a spring, and danc'd it round
> Below the gallows tree.

Although Burns admitted 'McPherson's Farewell' was his own work, 'excepting the chorus, and one stanza' (Alburger, 71, 217), the words of the chorus may be the first printed indication of a musical MacPherson.

By the end of the nineteenth century writers (including Imlach and Phillips, whose novel *James MacPherson: the Highland Freebooter*, was published in 1894), had turned MacPherson into a handsome, powerful, charismatic man, 'the Rob Roy of the North'. This kept alive the myth that MacPherson had taken up his fiddle on the eve of his execution at Banff, composed and played 'McPherson's Lament', then offered the fiddle to anyone brave enough to take it. When no one did, he broke it over his knee. The broken fiddle and his claymore and targe were said to have been preserved by relatives, and the MacPherson myth was ensured.

MacPherson's worth at his death is unknown, although the trial verdict stated 'their heall moveable goods and gear [were] to be escheat, and inbrought to the Fiscall for his majesties interest' ('Process', 191). The Clan MacPherson Museum, Kingussie, Highland, displays a broken violin described as MacPherson's, while 'his' claymore and targe, 'beyond all doubt genuine; ... the sword, ... a most formidable weapon, requiring both hands to wield it', was in Duff House, Banff, in 1869 (Imlach, 36).

MARY ANNE ALBURGER

Sources M. A. Alburger, *Scottish fiddlers and their music* (1983); repr. (1996) · J. C. Dick, *The songs of Robert Burns*, 2 vols. (1903), 292–3, 475–7 · W. E. Henley and T. F. Henderson, eds., *The poetry of Robert Burns*, 4 (1896–7) · [D. Herd], ed., *Ancient and modern Scottish songs*, new edn, 2 (1869) · J. Imlach, *The history of Banff* (1868) · A. Murdoch, *The fiddle in Scotland* (1888) · J. G. Phillips, *James MacPherson: the highland freebooter* (1894) · 'Process against the Egyptians, at Banff, 1700', *The miscellany of the Spalding Club*, ed. J. Stuart, 3, Spalding Club, 16 (1846), 175–95 · *DNB*

Macpherson, James (1736–1796), writer, was born in the small settlement of Ruthven, near Kingussie, in Badenoch, on 27 October 1736. His father, Andrew, was a small farmer at Invertromie, and his mother, Ellen, was also a Macpherson, both parents distantly related to the chief of the clan Macpherson.

Early years and education The area in which James was born and brought up was still strongly Gaelic. He attended the local parochial school, and possibly a grammar school in Inverness, before enrolling at King's College, Aberdeen, in the 1752–3 session. He seems to have moved to Marischal College in Aberdeen by 1755, probably because lower fees were charged there, and he is thought to have attended classes at the University of Edinburgh as a divinity student in 1755–6. He ran the charity school in Ruthven briefly about 1756 (a fairly standard interlude for divinity students at that time), but seems to have abandoned his divinity career, and switched to acting as a family tutor. He was employed in this way by Graham of Balgowan by 1758, working also as a corrector of the press for Balfour the publisher in Edinburgh.

Macpherson's home area had close involvements with the Jacobite risings of 1715 and 1745. He would have been familiar with the sight of the Ruthven barracks, built in 1718 as part of the mechanism to control the Jacobite highlanders. The Jacobite army set fire to the barracks in February 1746, and it was at Ruthven that the army was disbanded in 1746, after the defeat at Culloden. Some of Macpherson's relatives were actively involved in the 1745 rising. There can be little doubt that such events, and the continuing prejudices against highlanders and their culture, impinged on the young Macpherson as he lived through his teens in the early 1750s. The evidence suggests that he was not strongly literate in Gaelic, but used to living in a Gaelic community, and hearing stories and poems recited, and that these experiences influenced his early writing in various ways.

James Macpherson (1736–1796), by George Romney, 1779–80

Macpherson's university experience brought other literary influences into play. At Aberdeen he developed his study of the classics, and one of his teachers at Marischal College was Thomas Blackwell, who had published his *Enquiry into the Life and Writings of Homer* in 1735. Josef Bysveen, in his *Epic Tradition and Innovation in James Macpherson's Fingal* (1982) argues that Macpherson was strongly influenced in his Ossianic 'epics' by Blackwell's theory of epic. He may also have been influenced by William Lauder's forlorn attempt in 1750 to fabricate originals for Milton's *Paradise Lost*.

Macpherson's interest in composing verse seems to surface during his Aberdeen years, in the form of humorous and satirical pieces about student life there. There are references to this activity in the article on Macpherson in the *Edinburgh Encyclopaedia*, edited by Sir David Brewster in 1830. (Brewster was married to a daughter of Macpherson.) A more serious involvement with verse-making was to appear in the mid-1750s. Bailey Saunders (1894) refers to some early poems in manuscript including 'Death' (an imitation of Robert Blair's 'Grave') and 'The Hunter', influenced by James Thomson's *Seasons*. 'The Hunter' was evidently a predecessor of Macpherson's *The Highlander* which was published in Edinburgh in 1758. About this time Macpherson was also contributing poems to the *Scots Magazine*. One of the earliest, 'On the Death of Marshal Keith', appeared in 1758, with other contributions in 1759. In 1755 he had published an 'imitation' of an ode by Horace in the *Scots Magazine* (see Stafford, 43 ff.).

Early literary contacts and Fragments The build-up to Macpherson's early literary career is attested by these fleeting references to his Aberdeen days, and the influence of the

Badenoch environment, but the most crucial influences surface in his Edinburgh contacts. These can be explored in a little more detail, as there is a considerable bank of evidence available. An influential group of writers, philosophers, and lawmen was building up in Edinburgh at mid-century, and Macpherson's appointment as tutor by Graham of Balgowan seems to have given him an initial entry to this circle. The contacts he developed there were deeply influential, especially from 1759 to 1763, as he built up the bank of writings that were to attract international interest.

Macpherson made the acquaintance of Adam Ferguson, probably on a visit to Ferguson's father's manse in Logierait, accompanying his pupil, the young Graham. Much later, in a letter written in March 1798 (see the *Report to the Highland Society*, appx, 62 ff.), Ferguson recalled hearing, about 1740, a local tailor reciting a heroic ballad in his father's house, and he quotes two lines in badly spelt Gaelic. He then goes on to recall how he had told his college friend John Home about these ballads. It was Ferguson who provided Macpherson with an introduction to John Home, and they had several meetings in the autumn of 1759, at Moffat in the borders. Home urged Macpherson to show him translations of some of the ballads, and Macpherson is said reluctantly to have complied, producing a poem on the death of Oscar (ibid., appx, 69) and other pieces. This encounter led to further contacts in Edinburgh, particularly with Hugh Blair, and the publication in 1760 of Macpherson's *Fragments of Ancient Poetry Collected in the Highlands of Scotland*. This publication stirred up considerable interest, both in Edinburgh and in England, and led to a group of Edinburgh lawyers and literati establishing funds to enable Macpherson to explore this literary area more deeply. He made two trips, the first in August and September 1760 and the second between late October 1760 and early January 1761, visiting Perthshire, Argyllshire, Inverness-shire, and the islands of Skye, North and South Uist, Benbecula, and Mull. He collected manuscripts and oral versions of songs and ballads on these trips.

Macpherson's contacts seem skilfully to have been drawn from both highland and lowland sources. Some of these were friends and relatives in his home area, such as his cousin the Gaelic poet Lachlan Macpherson of Strathmashie. His contact with Adam Ferguson may have led to his correspondence with the Revd James McLagan whose home district was next to Logierait. McLagan was in the process of making a formidable collection of Gaelic poetry, including many ballads, and he supplied Macpherson with a few versions of Ossianic ballads in 1760–61. McLagan was one of a group of St Andrews University graduates who became deeply involved in such collecting, and Macpherson probably got advice from some of these in his tours in Perthshire and Argyllshire. He had been influenced earlier by another St Andrews graduate, Jerome Stone. Stone, from Fife, began teaching in the grammar school at Dunkeld in 1750, and in January 1756 he published an English version of a Gaelic heroic ballad in

the *Scots Magazine*. There can be little doubt that this influenced Macpherson, both as to his interest in collecting ballads and in his style of 'translation'. And a major influence in Macpherson's Ossianic productions was Hugh Blair. Macpherson lived in lodgings in a house below Blair's in Blackfriar's Wynd in Edinburgh, and the two collaborated closely in the production of the books from 1760 to 1763. The exact degree to which Blair either accepted or contributed to the shape and pattern of these is hard to determine, but his influence was very strong.

Ossianic poems It is difficult to resist the idea that by the time Macpherson met Home in 1759 he had already been wondering whether to adapt the Gaelic ballads and present the result to a non-Gaelic public. The speed with which his 'translations' for Home emerged suggests foresight and preparation. His unsuccessful publication *The Highlander* was a foretaste of *Fingal*. He must have considered developing further Jerome Stone's initiative of 1756. And in the 'Preface' to the *Fragments* he hints at the existence of a Gaelic epic: 'In particular there is reason to hope that one work of considerable length, and which deserves to be styled an heroic poem, might be recovered and translated, if encouragement were given to such an undertaking.' He then goes on to give a brief summary of this 'work of considerable length'. And in a footnote to fragment 14 he says 'This is the opening of the epic poem mentioned in the preface.'

The *Fragments* had an enthusiastic reception, and at first there seemed to be a fairly general acceptance of the poems' authenticity. The 'Preface' had stated that 'The translation is extremely literal. Even the arrangement of the words in the original has been imitated.' Some scepticism gradually began to surface, but it was not sufficiently strong to deter progress in the next phase. Macpherson's two extended tours of the highlands produced a significant body of verse, both in manuscript form and in oral transmission. And he drew on the Gaelic expertise of friends and new acquaintances: ministers, landlords, poets, and the custodians of oral tradition.

At the end of the second tour Macpherson spent some time at the home of a friend, the Revd Andrew Gallie, in Brae-Badenoch. Gallie recalls details of this visit in letters he wrote in 1799 and 1801 (*Report to the Highland Society*, 30 ff.). Also in the company was the poet Lachlan Macpherson of Strathmashie, and it emerges, unintentionally on Gallie's part, that Lachlan was making a Gaelic translation of a passage which appears in *Fingal*, book 4. Such translations, or variants of them, were later to be presented as the originals from which James Macpherson's works were translated.

The detailed construction of *Fingal* later continued in Edinburgh. As Blair recalled in 1797 (*Report to the Highland Society*, 59) he and Macpherson met frequently at dinner when Macpherson 'used … to read or repeat to me parts of what he had that day translated'. There can be little doubt that Blair contributed to the discussions, with some of his input appearing in the notes, and possibly in the text also.

From a detailed examination of Macpherson's Ossianic

publications it is clear that he used a range of Gaelic ballads in a variety of ways. Some sixteen or seventeen ballads can be identified, with several used in the *Fragments* and in the translations which were included along with the epic *Fingal*. *Temora* in 1763 has the smallest input from authentic ballads, while *Fingal* has the largest. The ballads are used in a range of different ways: sometimes to provide a basic plot, or an adapted plot, sometimes having a sequence of lines or stanzas loosely translated, with interjections, and often taking names or specific incidents from ballads and using these, or more normally variants of these.

A brief example may be used to illustrate a so-called close translation. This occurs in the opening paragraphs of *Fingal*, book 1. The opening stanza of the Gaelic ballad 'Duan a' Ghairbh' translates 'Arise Hound of Tara [that is, Cuchullin], I see countless ships filling the stormy seas, the ships of the foreigners.' This stanza is used, almost in its entirety, in the opening paragraphs of *Fingal*. The translations, or close adaptations, are italicized here:

> Cuchullin sat by *Tura*'s wall; by the tree of the rustling leaf. … His spear leaned against the mossy rock. His shield lay by him on the grass (…) the scout of the ocean came, Moran the son of Fithil. *Rise*, said the youth, *Cuchullin, rise; I see the ships* of Swaran. Cuchullin, *many* are the foe: *many the heroes of the dark-rolling sea.*

The most detailed account of the sources Macpherson used, and the variety of ways in which he used them, is to be found in Thomson, *The Gaelic Sources of Macpherson's 'Ossian'* (1952).

While using themes, plots, and names from Gaelic ballads, Macpherson also used themes and references from classical and other sources, and added a great quantity of nature description and Romantic episodes. In this he was probably influenced by Thomas Blackwell's theory of epic, and also by what he saw as a need for establishing a heroic past for the highlands and their culture. In doing this he may well have drawn on some acquaintance with Gaelic poetry's deep involvement with nature and landscape, but he carried this involvement to extremes, continually invoking the glories of nature and the terror of its storms, and meshing these with the heroism and suffering of his heroes and their enemies.

Success and controversy *Fingal*'s publication attracted much public attention, with a mixture of acclaim and scepticism. The public interest was great enough to persuade Macpherson to produce another epic, *Temora*, in 1763. This used a Gaelic ballad on the death of Oscar quite extensively in book 1, but after that made hardly any use of Gaelic originals. The overall plot is vague, and the style of writing is less vivid than in *Fingal*. In the introduction and notes to *Temora* he attempts to construct a fictional history of the Caledonians and Scots, arguing that Scotland was the original *Scotia*, and that the Irish Ossianic ballads were borrowed from Scotland. His serious distortion of the evidence aroused Irish resentment. The rather negative reception *Temora* received brought to a close Macpherson's highly active involvement in such writing.

Gradually, in the British Isles, the original acclaim became slanted towards controversy. Thomas Gray's initial enthusiasm was tempered by doubt, while Dr Johnson's reaction was completely sceptical, and also ill-informed, as when he claimed that there were no Gaelic manuscripts aged over 100 years. Johnson's attack aroused the vituperative response of the Revd Donald MacNicol, a prolific collector of Gaelic verse. The controversy continued in press and magazines for many years, and was to become the focus on Macpherson's early writings for long after his death. Too many of the commentators who had Gaelic expertise were unwilling to condemn Macpherson, though they must have realized the falsity of many of his claims.

The controversy had some positive effects in the Gaelic world, promoting a surge of collecting in the remaining years of the eighteenth century and in the nineteenth. McLagan and MacNicol were prominent in this field, as were Ewen MacDiarmid, John Smith, and many others, most of them clergymen. A less creditable result of the Ossianic enthusiasm was the fabrication of Gaelic ballads in the later decades of the eighteenth century.

European reputation In Europe, by contrast, the reaction seems to have been much more positive. The question of authenticity, and the Scottish/English and Scottish/Irish rivalries, did not greatly concern European readers. They seemed more interested in the published works, whatever their origins were. The wildness of the landscape, the strangeness of the characters, and the Romantic interludes, made a strong appeal. The notion of reviving memories of dark ages and prehistoric peoples had its own Romantic appeal, and was to lead to the revival and creation of national epics elsewhere, as with the Finnish *Kalevala*.

The reaction in Germany was the most enthusiastic in the early years after Macpherson's publications, contributing significantly to the *Sturm und Drang* movement. Herder was one of the chief early enthusiasts, and it was at his suggestion that Goethe made some translations of the Scottish poems, and was strongly influenced in *The Sorrows of Young Werther*. Macpherson's strong influence on the European Romantic movement was to continue for decades, fuelled by many translations into European languages, such as Cesarotti's into Italian in 1763, and a French translation in 1774. Napoleon later became an Ossianic enthusiast, and the fascination with the poems spread to other artistic spheres, as in Brahms's and Mendelssohn's music and Alexander Runciman's etchings. Fresh translations continued to appear in the later twentieth century, including a Japanese one in 1971 which rapidly moved to a second edition, and a Russian one in 1983 with a reputed run of 35,000. Oscar and Malvina were often given as names to French children, and Oscar surfaces also in the Swedish royal family of earlier times.

In Britain a two-volume edition of the *Works of Ossian* was published in 1765. This included many minor textual changes and rewriting of notes, and also Blair's 'Critical dissertation'. This was the edition which had a major influence in Europe. A further two-volume edition of the *Poems of Ossian* appeared in 1773, again with a good deal of revision. Among later editions were Malcolm Laing's *The Poems of Ossian* in 1805, and what is probably the most meticulous edition, based on the early publications: Otto L. Jiriczek's *James Macphersons 'Ossian': Faksimile—Neudruck der Erstausgabe von 1762/63 mit Begleitband, die Varianten*, published in Heidelberg in 1940. The *Fragments* appeared in an edition by the Augustan Reprint Society in 1966, with an 'Introduction' by John J. Dunn, and in an edition by Clarsach Publications (Dundee) in 1979. The most recent edition of the entire works is *The Poems of Ossian and Related Works*, published by Edinburgh University Press in 1996. This is edited by Howard Gaskill, and owes much to Jiriczek's edition, but is based textually on the 1765 volumes.

Final years After 1763 Macpherson's involvement with his early works became rather peripheral, apart from the alterations to the 1765 and 1773 editions. Early in 1764 he was appointed secretary to George Johnstone, governor of the Western Provinces. He spent about two years in America and toured the West Indies, returning in 1766 but retaining his salary, which was converted to a pension for life on condition that he devoted himself to political writing in the form of journalism and pamphlets—becoming a kind of spin doctor in modern terminology. He was indebted at various times to the patronage of Lord Bute. In 1771 he published *An Introduction to the History of Great Britain and Ireland*, a work which had a strong Celtic emphasis. In 1773 he published a translation of the *Iliad*, in 1775 the *Papers Containing the Secret History of Great Britain* (a work of some historical importance), and also in 1775 *The History of Great Britain from the Restoration to the Accession of the House of Hanover*.

About 1777 Macpherson became involved with John Macpherson, son of the minister of Sleat in Skye whom he had visited in the early 1760s. John had worked for the nabob of Arcot in India, and he became governor-general in India. He made James Macpherson his agent in London. Then in 1780 James became MP for one of the Cornish boroughs, and held this seat for the rest of his life. He had a secret government pension of £500, and was involved in newspaper presentation of government policy.

By this time Macpherson had acquired fairly substantial wealth, and he used part of it to buy land to the north of Kingussie, and to build an imposing mansion there. He gave it the stylish name of Belleville, and it still adorns the landscape there. Macpherson had retained warm feelings for the place of his birth, and his fellow Gaels there, and was noted for his friendship and hospitality during his annual holidays at Belleville.

Macpherson never married, but his liking for the 'daughters of John Bull', and his own attractiveness, produced several liaisons and three sons and two daughters. He is said to have treated his offspring generously. His eldest son, James, was to succeed to the estate at Belleville, and later it passed to his daughter Juliet, who married David Brewster in 1810, their descendants taking the additional surname of Macpherson.

James Macpherson died at Belleville on 17 February 1796, just short of his sixtieth birthday, and after a lengthy journey to London was buried in the Poets' Corner at the abbey of Westminster.

Investigation of Macpherson's Ossianic work seems to have intensified after his death. He had left £1000 to promote the publication of the originals, so-called. This was in effect the sum collected by a group of highlanders in India, and sent to the Highland Society of London. This was forwarded to Macpherson in 1784, and he replied saying that he would employ his first leisure time on arranging and printing the originals of the *Poems of Ossian*. Various friends became involved in this project, and an elaborate edition was published in 1807, with a Gaelic text manufactured to correspond with the English 'originals', and a superfluous Latin translation and many notes and essays.

In 1805 a much more credible work was published, the *Report to the Highland Society of Scotland*. This consists of a large trawl of letters and reminiscences, many of them produced in response to the society's requests to individuals. These included people who had worked with Macpherson, people from whom he had collected poems, and a good range of independent collectors and knowledgeable Gaels. The report contains much valuable information which has been used by later writers on the controversy.

Over 200 years after Macpherson's death it can at least be said that a more detailed understanding exists of the complexities accompanying his publications of 1760–63 and their wide-ranging influences on literature and culture.

DERICK S. THOMSON

Sources T. Blackwell, *Enquiry into the life and writings of Homer* (1735) • J. Bysveen, *Epic tradition and innovation in James Macpherson's Fingal* (1982) • H. Gaskill, *Ossian revisited* (1991) • H. Gaskill, *The poems of Ossian and related works* (1996) • A. Gillies, *Herder und Ossian* (1933) • O. L. Jiriczek, *James Macpherson's 'Ossian'* (1940) • M. G. H. Pittock, 'James Macpherson and Jacobite code', *Report to the Highland Society* (1805) • B. Saunders, *The life and letters of James Macpherson* (1894) • J. S. Smart, *James Macpherson, an episode in literature* (1905) • F. J. Stafford, *The sublime savage: a study of James Macpherson and the poems of Ossian* (1988) • *From Gaelic to Romantic: Ossianic translations*, ed. F. Stafford and H. Gaskill (1998) • D. S. Thomson, *The Gaelic sources of Macpherson's 'Ossian'* (1952) • D. S. Thomson, 'Bogus Gaelic literature c.1750–c.1820', *Transactions of the Gaelic Society of Glasgow*, 5 (1958) • D. S. Thomson, '"Ossian" Macpherson and the Gaelic world of the eighteenth century', *Aberdeen University Review*, 40 (1963–4), 7–20 • D. S. Thomson, foreword, in J. Macpherson, *Fragments of ancient poetry* (1979) • D. S. Thomson, 'Macpherson's Ossian: ballads to epics', *The Heroic Process*, ed. B. Almqvist and others (1987) • D. S. Thomson, *An introduction to Gaelic poetry*, 2nd edn (1990) • D. S. Thomson, 'James Macpherson: the Gaelic dimension', *From Gaelic to Romantic: Ossianic translations*, ed. F. Stafford and H. Gaskill (1998)

Archives NL Scot., letters • NRA, priv. coll., corresp. • NRA, priv. coll., estate and papers | BL, letters to Warren Hastings, Add. MSS 29142–29164 • BL, corresp. with earl of Liverpool, Add. MSS 38202–38222, 38306–38309 • NA Scot., letters to Allan Macpherson • NRA, priv. coll., letters to W. Duncan, keeper of archives of nabob of Carnatic • NRA, priv. coll., letters relating to East India Co., etc.

Likenesses J. Reynolds, oils, exh. RA 1772, Petworth House, Sussex • J. K. Sherwin, line engraving, pubd 1775 (after J. Reynolds), BM, NPG • G. Romney, oils, 1779–80, NPG [*see illus.*] • oils (after J. Reynolds), Scot. NPG • photogravure (after G. Romney), BM

Macpherson, John (1713–1765), Church of Scotland minister and antiquary, was born on 1 December 1713 at Suardal (Swordale) in Strath on the Isle of Skye, one of three children of Martin Macpherson (1672–1713), minister of Strath, and his wife, Mary, daughter of Lachlan Mackinnon, first laird of Corriechatachan on Skye. Macpherson graduated from King's College, Aberdeen, in 1728 with an MA degree and was licensed by the presbytery of Uist on 12 May 1734. He was ordained on 28 September 1734 in the parish of Barra in the Outer Hebrides, where he began writing verse and published his first work, 'Latin Ode to the Memory of Norman Macleod, Minister of Duirinish', in the *Scots Magazine* (1739). Boswell calls it 'a very pretty ode' (*Boswell's Journal*, 236–7).

On 25 February 1740 Macpherson married Janet Macleod (d. 1748), daughter of Donald Macleod of Bernera (1693–1783), known as the Old Trojan, a fiery Jacobite who fathered twenty-nine children; they had one daughter, Isabella (Isabel; 1742–*c*.1780), and two sons, Martin (1743–1812), later minister of Sleat, and John *Macpherson (*c*.1745–1821), future governor-general of Bengal. Having realized his hope of returning to Skye, Macpherson was transferred to Sleat and the residence at Ostaig on 14 January 1742. He had returned to an island where the principal families, the Macleods and Macdonalds—including a subordinate clan, the Mackinnons—held opposing sympathies, either Jacobite or Hanoverian, but kept their tenants in line with the government. During the critical period of the Jacobite rising of 1745, Macpherson held his living as minister of Sleat and his manse at Ostaig from the principal heritor, Macdonald of Sleat.

An able diplomat, Macpherson avoided political confrontations, focusing instead on the church, literature, and history. In 1747 he published in the *Scots Magazine* a paraphrased Latin version of the *Song of Moses*, with the title *Cantici Mosaici paraphrasis*. Samuel Johnson told Boswell and his Scottish hosts that the work 'did him [Macpherson] honour; that he had a great deal of Latin, and good Latin' (Johnson, 233). Later, with his first cousin the Revd Martin Macpherson of Golspie (1723–1773), he answered the religious treatise of Theophilus Insulanus, the pseudonym of William Macleod, in a *Letter to the Author of the Treatise on the Second Sight* (1759).

On 20 November 1761 Macpherson received a DD degree from King's College, Aberdeen. Persisting in his scholarly work, he agreed to 'enlarge and revise' a work by his friend the Revd Kenneth Macaulay, which appeared in 1764 as *The history of St. Kilda, containing a description of this remarkable island … the manners and customs … the religious and pagan antiquities*. 'But his contribution, although extensive,' J. D. Fleeman allows, 'was not so interesting or so valuable as that made by the Rev. Macaulay' (Johnson, 165). Samuel Johnson was 'fond' of the book, allowing it 'a very pretty piece of topography' (*Boswell's Journal*, 86).

Macpherson's most important work, the posthumous *Critical dissertations on the origin, antiquities, language, government, manners, and religion of the ancient Caledonians, their posterity the Picts, and the British and Irish Scots* (1768), was a response to the Ossian phenomenon prompted by James Macpherson's *Fragments of Ancient Poetry* and his translations of the epics *Fingal* (1762) and *Temora* (1763). An unabashed defender of Ossian and a recognized Celtic authority on antiquities, John had met James Macpherson (no relation) in September 1760 during the latter's search for Ossianic poems in the highlands. Having provided the poet with various documents on Celtic history as well as leads to various Ossian manuscripts, John recited passages of *Fingal* and the fragments often heard in his neighbourhood (Saunders, 123; Stafford, 117, 120). In turn James Macpherson later used material from the minister's *Critical Dissertations*, to which he may have contributed part of the preface, in his dissertations on the epics, as well as his *Introduction to the History of Great Britain and Ireland* (1771), where he again acknowledged John's influence as an advocate of the Caledonian origins of the Scottish nation and as a critic of modern conjectural historians, such as William Robertson, whom John accused of 'looking with too much contempt on the origin of society' (*Critical Dissertations*, 18).

Macpherson, in failing health, had in early 1765 sent a manuscript of the *Critical Dissertations* to London publishers, but with no success. He died at Ostaig on 5 April while revising it. His son John sold the manuscript to William Strahan in January 1767. Whether James Macpherson helped John revise the text before publication remains unclear, but John did compliment his father in the preface to the *Critical Dissertations*: 'being master of Celtic in all its branches, he took pleasure in tracing other languages to that general source of all the ancient and modern tongues of Europe' (*Fasti Scot.*, 7.175). Although the moderate literati of Edinburgh found much to praise in the work, especially its focus on Scotland's national image, Johnson dismissed it, saying, 'you might read half an hour and ask yourself what you had been reading' (Johnson, 165). But the minister had the final word, as his encouragement of Celtic studies and Ossian liberated the literary canon and increased respect for antiquarian studies.

PAUL J. DEGATEGNO

Sources J. N. M. Maclean, 'The early political careers of James "Fingal" Macpherson and Sir John Macpherson', PhD diss., U. Edin., 1967 · *Fasti Scot.*, new edn, vol. 7 · *Boswell for the defence, 1769–1774*, ed. W. K. Wimsatt and F. A. Pottle (1959), vol. 7 of *The Yale editions of the private papers of James Boswell*, trade edn (1950–89) · *Boswell's journal of a tour to the Hebrides with Samuel Johnson*, ed. F. A. Pottle and C. H. Bennett (1936) · H. Gaskill, ed., *Ossian revisited* (1991) · S. Johnson, *A journey to the western islands of Scotland*, ed. J. D. Fleeman (1985) [incl. introduction by J. D. Fleeman] · A. G. Macpherson, 'An old highland genealogy and the evolution of a Scottish clan', *Scottish Studies*, 10 (1966), 1–43 · F. J. Stafford, *The sublime savage: a study of James Macpherson and the poems of Ossian* (1988) · P. deGategno, *James Macpherson* (1989) · H. Weinbrot, *Britannia's issue: the rise of British literature fron Dryden to Ossian* (1993) · B. Saunders, *The life and letters of James Macpherson* (1894) · R. B. Sher, *Church and university in the Scottish Enlightenment: the moderate literati of Edinburgh* (1985) · C. Kidd, *Subverting Scotland's past: Scottish whig historians and the creation of an Anglo-British identity, 1689–c.1830* (1993) · W. Ferguson, *The identity of the Scottish nation* (1998)

Macpherson, Sir John, first baronet (*c*.1745–1821), governor-general of Bengal, may have been born at the

Sir John Macpherson, first baronet (*c*.1745–1821), by Sir Joshua Reynolds, 1778–81?

manse of Sleat in Kilmore, Isle of Skye (A. Mackenzie, *History of the Macleods*, 1889, citing the now missing register of the parish of Sleat in the Isle of Skye). His father, John Macpherson (1713–1765), was a well-educated and cultured Church of Scotland minister; his mother was Janet (*d*. 1748), daughter of Donald Macleod of Bernera and granddaughter of the earl of Seaforth, chief of the powerful Mackenzie clan. Macpherson's father, son of the Revd Martin Macpherson of Strath, had been ordained in 1734, becoming minister of Barra, Outer Hebrides (1734–42), and then taking residence at Ostaig as minister of Sleat (1742–65). His best-known work was the *Critical Dissertations on the Origins … of the Ancient Caledonians* (1768), in which he upheld the significance of the Ossian poems.

In 1760 John, the youngest of three children, began his training for the ministry at King's College, Aberdeen, graduating with an MA in 1764. He then entered the University of Edinburgh (recorded as receiving a degree in November 1768), where he boarded at the home of his tutor, the moral philosopher Adam Ferguson. His father's unexpected death on 5 April 1765 changed his plans, and on 6 March 1767 he accepted the post of purser aboard the East Indiaman *Lord Mansfield*, bound for Madras and commanded by his maternal uncle Captain Alexander Macleod. Macpherson landed on 30 September 1767 and soon introduced himself to Muhammad Ali Khan, nawab of the Carnatic, 'a polite man, of very agreeable address … and the worst man in the world to transact business with' (Warren Hastings to Laurence Sulivan, BL, Add. MS 29126, quoted in Feiling, 406). The nawab, who had been encouraged by the East India Company to pay for various wars

with the French and other Indian princes, borrowed heavily from the company. The interest on the loans was immense and his creditors preyed upon him. Macpherson saw an opportunity of assisting the now desperate nawab, while ensuring his own financial independence. The nawab soon decided upon sending Macpherson back to England as his agent (1768–70) with instructions to seek relief from the home government. After further adventures, including participating in the amphibious assault of Haidar Ali's Fort at Mangalore, he landed at Portsmouth on 14 November 1768. Armed with letters of introduction to the duke of Grafton, the prime minister, from the earl of Warwick (whose sons he had once tutored), Macpherson convinced Grafton and his Treasury secretary, Thomas Bradshaw, of the East India Company's 'oppressive' behaviour toward the Indian prince. The ministry quickly sent out their own representative to Madras 'to decide all questions of peace and war with the native powers' (Feiling, 71; *Letters of Warren Hastings to his Wife*, 212).

On his return to Madras on 23 February 1771 Macpherson had an appointment as a company writer and became friendly with Warren Hastings, who was a second in the council. Macpherson worked diligently to win 'the trust of the Crown's senior servants, the Company's senior servants, and most important of all, [to regain the support of] the Nawab of Arcot' (Maclean, 'Early political careers', 243). Unfortunately, Macpherson saw his hopes for political and financial success slipping away when Hastings left to become governor of Bengal in 1772. Macpherson's duties as mayor of Madras (December 1772–July 1773) and writer did not satisfy him, and he too requested a posting to Bengal. However, he continued to censure the company's actions in Madras. Writing to Hastings in July 1775, for example, he again stressed the predicament of the nawab:

> it is my sincere opinion that if your Board does not speedily supersede the Power of this Government [of Madras] … one of two Events must follow: the ruin of the poor Nabob, or a Convulsion in this ruined Government that the Company may never have strength to recover.   (29 July 1775, BL, Add. MS 29137)

Working in concert with his kinsman, the talented and strategically positioned James Macpherson, then a writer for the North government, John Macpherson was appointed as paymaster to the company army on 3 July 1773. Macpherson increased his financial security through various legal arrangements. Yet his position in the company remained uncertain, and James Macpherson urged his return to England. Events, however, overtook John when he ran foul of the new governor of Madras, George Pigot. Before he could extricate himself and explain his frequent association with the nawab, Pigot accused him of working against company interests and dismissed him from the service on 23 January 1776. His sudden fall seemed all the more harsh since a few months earlier Lauchlin Macleane, a political adventurer *par excellence*, had struck up a close alliance with the nawab. In addition Macleane convinced Hastings to name him as his personal agent to the directors of the company in London.

Until Macleane's unexpected death at sea in 1778, Macpherson had no choice but to work informally and indirectly in support of the nawab's claims, and especially for his own reinstatement. Despite writing of his intention to purchase an estate near Edinburgh, where 'I, or some Macpherson, should have a landed establishment in the warmest part of Caledonia … a resting place' (to James Macpherson, 26 June 1776 BL OIOC, Sir John Macpherson MSS, 122), he decided instead to return to England after receiving assurance from the nawab and Hastings, who both recognized his energy, though each remained suspicious of the other's true intentions.

Macpherson arrived in London in July 1777, and joined James Macpherson in a press campaign in the ministry paper *The Public Advertiser*, to support the nawab and Hastings. Both wrote letters under pseudonyms, and James, whose talents as a pamphleteer were well known, published *A Letter from Mohammed Ali Chan, Nabob of Arcot to the Court of Directors* (1777). Lord North received John Macpherson as confidential agent to the nawab on 15 April 1778. Also on good terms with a former company director in London, Laurence Sulivan, and with North's man of business John Robinson, the Macphersons agreed John would go into parliament to defend him. With the help of his friend Henry Herbert, John secured the unopposed return to the Wiltshire borough of Cricklade in April 1779 and was re-elected in September 1780. Legal action was brought against Macpherson and other electors of Cricklade alleging bribery; the petition was heard in February 1782 when Macpherson's return was declared void and a new election declared. However, with the assistance of Sulivan and the North government, he had already accepted an offer to return to India in January 1781 as a member of the Bengal supreme council and as Warren Hastings's right-hand man.

Macpherson, though often painted as the villain in this scenario, generally remained on Hastings's side throughout the latter's final years as governor-general. As the North ministry sank and the opposition in the Commons supported Edmund Burke and the select committee's investigation into charges of corruption in the company's Indian affairs, Hastings eventually resigned in February 1785. As no new governor-general was immediately appointed, Macpherson succeeded to the chair. In post he initiated sweeping economies, reducing company expenditures, but did little to reverse the historically high rate of corruption, intrigue, and self-serving manipulation within the service. After a short nineteen months of struggle and controversy, he lost his position to Earl Cornwallis on 18 September 1786. However, to soften the blow the government arranged his creation as a baronet on 10 June 1786, assuming later the ascription 'of Calcutta and Lauriston', the latter an estate near Edinburgh. After returning to England in August 1787, his friends suggested he was interested in returning to India as governor-general or as a member of the Bengal supreme council, though this threat had only one intention—securing a company pension. The directors granted him a lump sum of about £15,000, and in 1809 a further £1000 annually.

Able, amiable, highly intelligent, a polymath who reportedly spoke five languages, with striking features, 'regular, pleasing, and expressive', Macpherson was at least 6 feet 3 inches tall (one contemporary report calls him the Gentle Giant at 6 feet 6 inches tall). From 1788 to 1802 he was seen at court with the prince of Wales, with whom he conversed and corresponded. His wealth, easy manner, and intellect assisted him in his travels throughout Europe. In Italy in 1789 he met Leopold, grand duke of Tuscany, later the Habsburg emperor, travelling with him to Venice, Milan, Florence, Pisa, and later to the imperial capital, Vienna. Macpherson maintained a correspondence with many foreign diplomats in Europe during the decade of revolution, suggesting that he was conducting espionage on behalf of his country. In September 1796 he returned to parliament as MP for Horsham, Sussex, which he continued to represent until June 1802. While in England he lived in his lavish London residence, Grove House, 11 Brompton Grove, where he died unmarried on 12 January 1821, secure in his friend John Robinson's regard: 'your merit will be admitted … [it] deserves acknowledgement and reward' (letter to Macpherson, 23 May 1800, BL OIOC, Sir John Macpherson MSS, 38). He was buried at St Anne's Church, Soho.

PAUL J. DEGATEGNO

Sources DNB · *Warren Hastings' letters to Sir John Macpherson*, ed. H. Dodwell (1927) · G. McElroy, 'Ossianic imagination and the history of India: James and John Macpherson as propagandists and intriguers', *Aberdeen and the Enlightenment*, ed. J. Carter and J. Pittock (1987), 363–74 · J. N. M. Maclean, 'The early political careers of James "Fingal" Macpherson and Sir John Macpherson', PhD diss., U. Edin., 1967 · *Fasti Scot.*, new edn, vol. 7 · *The historical and the posthumous memoirs of Sir Nathaniel William Wraxall, 1772–1784*, ed. H. B. Wheatley, 5 vols. (1884) · *The correspondence of Edmund Burke*, 4, ed. J. A. Woods (1963) · P. deGategno, *James Macpherson* (1989) · K. Feiling, *Warren Hastings* (1967) · H. Gaskill, ed., *Ossian revisited* (1991) · *The letters of Warren Hastings to his wife*, ed. S. C. Grier [H. C. Gregg] (1905) · J. Holzman, *The nabobs in England: a study of the returned Anglo-Indian, 1760–1785* (1926) · J. N. M. Maclean, *Reward is secondary: the life of a political adventurer and an inquiry into the mystery of "Junius"* (1963) · A. G. Macpherson, 'An old highland genealogy and the evolution of a Scottish clan', *Scottish Studies*, 10 (1966), 1–43 · P. J. Marshall, *The impeachment of Warren Hastings* (1965) · J. A. Cannon, 'Macpherson, John', HoP, Commons, 1754–90, 3.96–7 · L. S. Sutherland, *The East India Company in eighteenth century politics* (1952)

Archives BL, letters and papers relating to India, Add. MS 69079 · BL OIOC, corresp. and papers relating to India · Bodl. Oxf., papers · NA Scot. · National Archives of India, New Delhi, official papers · NL Scot. · NRA, priv. coll., corresp. and papers · PRO, London | BL, letters to D. Andersson, Add. MS 45417 · BL, corresp. with C. F. Grenville and T. Grenville, Add. MSS 41856–41857, 42071 · BL, letters to Warren Hastings, Add. MSS 29133–29169, 29193 · BL, corresp. with Lord Macartney, Add. MSS 22454–22456 · BL, letters to Lord North, Add. MS 61865 · Bodl. Oxf., corresp. with Lord Macartney · L. Cong., West Florida Commissions · NRA, priv. coll., letters to Sir J. Sinclair · NRA, priv. coll., letters to Lord Shelburne · PRO, letters to William Pitt, PRO 30/8 · Staffs. RO, letters to Lord Dartmouth

Likenesses J. Reynolds, oils, 1778–1781?, Scot. NPG [*see illus.*] · S. W. Reynolds, mezzotint, pubd 1796, BM · R. Earlom, group portrait, mezzotint, pubd 1802 (*The death of the royal tyger*; after J. Zoffany, c.1795), BL OIOC

Wealth at death £247,000 in England and £320,000 in India in October 1796: McElroy, 'Ossianic imagination', 363–74; *Letters to*

the creditors of the House of Boyd, Benfield and Company (1800), Sir John Macpherson papers, BL OIOC, Handlist 178, 185

Macpherson, John (1817–1890), military surgeon and medical writer, was born on 20 May 1817 in Aberdeen, the son of Hugh Macpherson, professor of Greek at the University of Aberdeen, and his wife, Christina MacLeod. He was the brother of the political agent Samuel Charters *Macpherson and the legal writer, William *Macpherson. Macpherson studied medicine at the University of Aberdeen and attended St George's Hospital and Kinnerton Street School in London, and it is presumed that he studied for a short time in Vienna. He became a member of the Royal College of Surgeons in the autumn of 1839, and in December of that year was appointed assistant surgeon in the East India Company's service in Bengal. During his twenty-five years of active working life in India (1839–64) he advanced from assistant surgeon to the 3rd brigade horse artillery in 1840; to second assistant at the Presidency General Hospital with medical charge of the Calcutta native militia in 1845; and to first assistant at the Presidency General Hospital in 1849. He was awarded an honorary MD by the University of Aberdeen in 1845. In accordance with the prevailing East India Company promotion procedure based on length of service, he duly became surgeon in 1853, taking medical charge of the 12th regiment native infantry. In 1856 he became a presidency surgeon, attaining in 1859 the rank of surgeon major in the aftermath of the Indian mutiny. In addition to other official duties such as superintendent-general of vaccine inoculation, he held a number of prestigious and influential positions including that of fellow of the University of Calcutta and president of its faculty of medicine board, as well as the lucrative position of medical officer to St Paul's, one of Calcutta's exclusive public schools.

Although his fame back home in Britain may have been partly a case of mistaken identity (as another medical officer of the same surname, an H. M. Macpherson, excelled in various senior medical positions about the same time), John Macpherson was nevertheless known in Bengal for his historical and clinical research into insanity, dysentery, and the use of quinine and antiperiodics. He went on furlough in 1864 and, on retirement in 1866, pursued a successful career as a medical writer.

Macpherson's seminal *Annals of Cholera* (1872) drew the attention of medical practitioners to the fluctuating appearance patterns of cholera epidemics, the aetiological link with polluted drinking water, and criticized as unfounded the public's and the medical profession's belief that effective drugs for cholera existed. On the basis of thorough historical research and previous clinical studies while assigned to various regiments in India, he stressed that cholera was endemic in India well before the first pandemic of 1817. His earlier *Cholera in its Home* (1866) was at the time referred to by *The Lancet* as 'the best book on the subject'. Macpherson, who lived for a time in Calcutta's well-known Chouringhee Road, was one of those medical practitioners serving in the Indian Medical Service (IMS) who received positive recognition by his peers in Europe, as is indicated by an Irish reviewer of his first

book on cholera who characterized it as evincing an 'acquaintance with the literature on the subject which does no little credit to one who has been so long exposed to the atmosphere of Chouringhee' (*Dublin Medical Journal*, 1866). His various other publications, *The Baths and Wells of Europe* (1869), *Quinine and Antiperiodics* (1856), and *On Bengal Dysentery* (1850), as well as the official *Report on Insanity* (1863), are characterized by what a reviewer in *The Lancet* of *The Baths and Wells of Europe* described as his 'concise and flowing style'. They also highlight his skill in advancing medical knowledge through historical research as well as by up-to-date methods of statistical analysis and clinical experiments. For example, in his report on insanity he challenged the idea that Europeans in tropical climates were prone to suffer from nervous debilitation, considering it as 'too highly coloured' and drawn 'only from the accounts of travellers' (*Calcutta Review*, 26, 1856, 602). Analysing statistical data on the subject he further concluded that, contrary to common belief, insanity was not more prevalent in what were seen to be civilized countries, but simply assumed a different form and was taken more notice of than in countries such as India. In his works *Quinine and Antiperiodics* (1856) and *On Bengal Dysentery* (1850) he scrutinized the effective dosages of quinine and other febrifuges, suggesting that emetics followed by a few doses of febrifuge might suffice to alleviate febrile symptoms, and that on those occasions when sulphate of quinine was scarce, the application of cheaper amorphous solutions of quinine or, in the case of Indians, of 'country substitutes' was an appropriate and effective alternative. In a country where Europeans as well as Indians frequently suffered from various forms of what was then referred to as 'fever', Macpherson's findings were bound to have considerable impact, as his suggestions helped to economize on expenditure for pharmaceuticals, and provided practicable guidelines for those Europeans who worked in remote areas of the empire and relied on self-medication.

Macpherson also researched the value of British and European mineral springs and of popular health spas for various medical conditions, concluding that lay persons and those he termed 'quacks' tended to exaggerate the importance of wells and waters, while medical practitioners underestimated their value. Despite the challenge to British mainstream medical thinking posed by most of Macpherson's writings, his ideas and suggestions were generally well received by medical professionals and by the general public in Britain and other European countries and, in some instances, in British India. Although the authorities in India sanctioned Macpherson's suggestion of a preliminary investigation into the potential medical values of the subcontinent's mineral springs in 1853, they subsequently refused, to his great disappointment, to let him pursue this any further. His father's professional interest in the classics and his frequent meetings with some of Europe's foremost physicians and scientists (such as W. Griesinger, M. von Pettenköfer, and C. A. Wunderlich) may have contributed to Macpherson's wide range of interests and his enquiring approach. His colleagues appreciated that he was 'full of antiquarian lore', widely read, as well as 'warm' yet appropriately 'reserved' (*Lancet*, 727). He married Charlotte Melusina, daughter of John Molesworth Staples, rector of Lissan and Upper Tyrone; Sir John Molesworth *Macpherson was their son. Towards his later years Macpherson suffered from painful intestinal trouble which he might have acquired during his twenty-five years of residence in India. He died on 17 March 1890 at his home, 35 Curzon Street, Mayfair, London, and was survived by his wife.   WALTRAUD ERNST

Sources East-India Register and Directory (1840–60) · *Indian Army and Civil Service List* (1861–7) · *Thacker's Post Office directory: for Bengal ...* (1863–5) · D. G. Crawford, ed., *Roll of the Indian Medical Service, 1615–1930* (1930) · *BMJ* (29 March 1890) · *The Lancet* (29 March 1890) · bap. reg. Scot. · *CGPLA Eng. & Wales* (1890)
Wealth at death £15,021/4/1 in UK: probate, 6 May 1890, *CGPLA Eng. & Wales*

MacPherson, John (*c*.1835–1922), crofter, was born at Glendale, Isle of Skye, the son of Alexander MacPherson and his wife, Flora MacLeod. On 9 March 1865 he married Margaret Maclean; following her death in 1876, on 19 June 1877 he married Mary Macdonald, *née* Mackinnon (*d.* 1906).

MacPherson came to public prominence in the 1880s during the period of land agitation which came to be known as the 'crofters' wars'. These events were centred on the Isle of Skye in the period from 1882 to 1883 and the controversy surrounded estate owners seeking to limit crofters' access to grazing land. A dispute of this type began at Glendale, in the west of the island, in January 1882. The trustees for the late Sir John Macleod, the owner of the Glendale estate, obtained an interdict preventing crofters encroaching on grazing ground at Waterstein. This land had been leased to Nicol Martin, owner of a neighbouring estate, but the lease was due to expire in 1882, and both the Glendale crofters and Sir John MacLeod's factor coveted the land for their own use. Co-ordinated protest, in which MacPherson took a leading part, began in February, and by March this had escalated to threats of a rent strike and land raids. The dispute simmered for the rest of the year and included clashes between estate employees and crofters, including MacPherson, in September and November. In January 1883 a party of sheriff officers and police, attempting to serve notices for breach of interdict, was confronted by a large crowd as they attempted to approach Glendale. A meeting of church ministers, who sought to defuse the situation, and crofters took place in the Free Church at Glendale. The result was the dispatch of the gunboat *Jackal* to Glendale and the arrest of MacPherson and three other ringleaders. They were tried in the Court of Session in Edinburgh in March 1883, found guilty of breach of interdict, and sentenced to two months' imprisonment.

The 'Glendale Martyr', as MacPherson was celebrated, received rousing receptions in Edinburgh and Portree on his release. He arrived home to Glendale just as the royal commission on the grievances of crofters and cottars in the highlands, chaired by Lord Napier, was taking evidence into the crofting issue in that area. On 19 May 1883

he gave evidence in Gaelic about the recent history of the township and the specific grievances of the crofters.

MacPherson's powerful personality was ideal for leadership of the crofters' movement and his habit of opening meetings with charismatic prayers in Gaelic was noted. He became a paid agent of the Highland Land Law Reform Association and spent the summer of 1884 touring the highlands for that organization. In the aftermath of the passage of the Crofters' Holdings (Scotland) Act in 1886, agitation continued in areas of Skye, Tiree, and Lewis and a military expedition was sent to Skye in an attempt to restore order. In November 1886 MacPherson, along with the Revd Malcolm MacCallum, Church of Scotland minister in Waternish, was arrested for inciting others to commit a breach of the peace. On this occasion he was released as there was insufficient evidence for a trial. He was one of the few national leaders of the crofters' movement to emerge for the crofting community. Others such as John Murdoch, Alexander Mackenzie, or the crofter MPs came from urban or journalistic backgrounds. MacPherson's exploits were the subject of Gaelic poetry: 'Duanag don truir ghaidheal a th'ann am priosan dhun Eideann' ('A Poem to the Three Highlanders who are in the Edinburgh Prison') by Alasdair MacIlleathain (Alexander MacLean), and 'Oran Beinn Li' ('Song on Ben Lee') by Mairi Nic-a'-Phearsain (Mary MacPherson). Both poems praise MacPherson's commitment and the effect the experience of imprisonment had on his outlook.

After the effective end of the crofters' wars in 1888, MacPherson faded from the public eye but he remained a powerful figure in the local community of Glendale. He gave evidence to the royal commission on the highlands and islands, chaired by David Brand, in 1893. He was involved in the opposition of a few highland congregations to the union of the United Presbyterian and Free churches in 1900. The estate of Glendale was purchased by the congested districts board in 1904 and the crofters, including MacPherson, were able to purchase their own holdings. MacPherson died of heart disease in Glendale on 16 May 1922 and was buried in the same month in the churchyard of the Old Church there.

EWEN A. CAMERON

Sources I. M. M. MacPhail, *The crofters' war* (1989) · J. Hunter, *The making of the crofting community* (1976), chap. 8 · D. E. Meek, *Tuath is tighearna / Tenants and landlords*, Scottish Gaelic Texts Society, 18 (1995) · G. W. Macpherson, *John MacPherson: the 'Skye martyr'* (1982) · 'Royal commission of inquiry into the condition of crofters and cottars in ... Scotland', *Parl. papers* (1884), vol. 32, C. 3980; vol. 33, C. 3980-I; vol. 34, C. 3980-II; vol. 35, C. 3980-III; vol. 36, C. 3980-IV · 'Royal commission on highlands and islands', *Parl. papers* (1895), 38.1, C. 7668; 38.95, C. 7668-I; vol. 39/1, C. 7668-II; vol. 39/2, C. 7681 · register of births, marriages, and deaths, Portree, Isle of Skye · d. cert.
Likenesses drawing, line, repro. in *ILN*
Wealth at death £96 7*s.* 9*d.*: confirmation, 21 Nov 1922, *CCI*

Macpherson, Sir John Molesworth (1853–1914), administrator and legislative draftsman in India, was born in Calcutta on 8 August 1853. He was the elder son of John *Macpherson MD (1817–1890), of the East India Company's medical service, and nephew of Samuel Charters *Macpherson (1806–1860), of the Madras army, and of William *Macpherson (1812–1893), of the Calcutta bar. His mother was Charlotte Melusina, fifth daughter of John Molesworth Staples, rector of Lissan and Upper Moville, Tyrone. Educated at Westminster School from September 1866 to August 1871, Macpherson was admitted to the Inner Temple in October 1873, called to the bar on 28 June 1876, and enrolled as an advocate of the Calcutta high court that year. His career at the bar was brief; in 1877 he was appointed deputy secretary to the government of India in the legislative department. Acting secretary on several occasions, he was secretary from 1896 until his retirement in 1911. He was created a CSI in June 1897 and was knighted on 12 December 1911. After retirement he was employed by Lord Crewe, secretary of state for India, on a measure to amend and consolidate the conflicting and piecemeal legislation of parliament on India, and was working on this at the time of his death. The measure was finally shaped by Sir Courtenay Ilbert, and became the Government of India Act (1915).

Macpherson married in 1880 Edith Christina (d. 1913), daughter of General Charles Waterloo Hutchinson CB, Royal Engineers, inspector-general of military works in India; they had three sons and one daughter.

Macpherson's career was of a type more common at Whitehall than in India, all in a single office. A legal draftsman's position is necessarily one of self-effacement, and it is difficult to estimate his share in Indian legislation. Its most notable monuments, such as the Transfer of Property Act (1882) and the civil procedure codes (1882 and 1908), were considered in detail by specially appointed committees of the highest legal talent available; and such work as Macpherson may have done on them can hardly have been more than routine. Indeed, he lacked the experience of litigation necessary for more than routine work. However, as he was never the responsible head of the legislative department, he cannot fairly be charged with its conspicuous failures, which were due to a policy of excessive simplification.

Macpherson's reputation was that of a thorough and painstaking official with an intimate knowledge of the details of his office. To this knowledge and experience the rules of procedure for the enlarged Morley–Minto councils (1910) owed much of their success. He was also a valued critic and adviser on the technique of provincial legislation, when it came before the government of India in the ordinary course for approval before enactment. It is, however, with the legislative activities of the foreign department that his name will be longest associated; for the official *Lists of British Enactments in Force in Native States in India* (6 vols., 1888–95) was originally compiled under his guidance, and, though subsequently re-edited, was still familiarly known as 'Macpherson'. He also published *The Law of Mortgage in British India* (1885).

Macpherson was a man of deep piety and a staunch adherent of the Presbyterian church, and he initiated the Simla religious convention. He was happy in his home life

and in a gift for making and retaining a wide circle of friends. He died suddenly at Reigate railway station, Surrey, on 5 January 1914.

S. V. FITZ-GERALD, rev. ROGER T. STEARN

Sources *The Times* (6 Jan 1914) · *Old Westminsters*, vol. 2 · private information (1927) · J. Foster, *Men-at-the-bar: a biographical hand-list of the members of the various inns of court*, 2nd edn (1885) · *Annual Register* (1914) · *WWW*, 1897–1915 · Kelly, *Handbk* (1914) · W. Menski, *Indian legal systems past and present* (1997) · d. cert.

Wealth at death £19,490 4s. 4d.: resworn probate, 6 March 1914, CGPLA Eng. & Wales

Macpherson, Sir John Stuart (1898–1971), governor-general of Nigeria, was born on 25 August 1898 at 23 Duke Street, Edinburgh, the elder son of James Peterkin Macpherson JP of Edinburgh, hotel manager, and his wife, Annabelle Yuill Anderson. He was educated in Edinburgh at George Watson's College and at Edinburgh University (MA, 1921). In 1917 he was commissioned into the Argyll and Sutherland Highlanders. A wound resulted in his having to wear a steel corset for the rest of his life (an extra discomfort in the tropics) and also in total deafness in one ear. Few ever became aware of these constraints.

Passing the eastern cadetships competitive examination, Macpherson was posted in 1921 to the Federated Malay States. He quickly made his mark as a district administrator, and in 1928 he married Joan, elder daughter of Dr W. E. Fry. They had one son, Ian Francis Cluny, who also later joined the colonial service. In 1933 Macpherson's evident potential for a distinguished career in the colonial service was acknowledged by secondment to the Colonial Office. Hardly had he returned to Malaya in 1935 than he was again on the upward ladder: in 1937 in the conventional testing ground of an African secretariat, Lagos, followed in 1939 by promotion to the challenging post of chief secretary of troubled Palestine. The relationship between the youthful Macpherson and his high commissioner, Sir Harold MacMichael, was an instance of affectionate respect between two colonial servants as well as an inspiration to the Palestine service. Years later he was to repeat the closeness of a working relationship with his chief under Alan Lennox-Boyd at the Colonial Office. In 1943 Macpherson's career moved westwards, first as head of the wartime British colonies supply mission in Washington, DC, and then in the dual capacity of comptroller for development and welfare in the West Indies and joint British chairman of the Anglo-American Caribbean commission.

Macpherson's appointment to the governorship of Nigeria in 1948 looked like the triumph of his career. He was, along with Charles Arden-Clarke and Edward Twining, one of the 'young guard' of governors carefully picked by the Colonial Office to replace an older generation such as Arthur Richards (first Baron Milverton) and Sir Philip Mitchell who, in the eyes of such architects of decolonization as Andrew Cohen and his master, the colonial secretary Arthur Creech Jones, were too rooted in pre-war attitudes to adapt with enthusiasm to the new spirit of social engineering and transfer of power. The appointment was all the more surprising within the colonial service where, contrary to common precedent, Macpherson had never been tried out as 'officer administering the government'; but those who had known him in Lagos a decade earlier at once recognized that they were getting the outstanding man of the service. Macpherson's first task was to restore confidence in that service while equally repairing the soured relations between Government House and the nationalist leadership generated by his predecessor. Above all, he had to speed up the protracted constitutional timetable then in place. In this he succeeded, thanks to what the leading American historian of the period called his gift for being 'tactful and conciliatory' (Coleman, 309). He inaugurated nationwide consultation, down to the grass-roots level. An incipient federation was the outcome, accompanied by Macpherson's personal initiative for the accelerated Africanization of the public service.

On retiring from Nigeria in 1955—constitutional changes meant that in 1954 he reassumed the title of governor-general, dormant since 1919—Macpherson was chairman of the 1956 United Nations visiting mission to the trust territories of the Pacific. By his unexpected appointment as permanent under-secretary of state for the colonies in 1956, he became one of the few colonial service officers to assume the top post in the Colonial Office. It was clearly a short-term appointment, arguably calculated to reassure members of the renamed overseas civil service that, at a time when morale might falter as career opportunities shrank with the imminence of independence, at least one of them and not a 'Whitehall warrior' was at the helm.

Retiring in 1959 after a year's extension, Macpherson continued to be active in public life, as chairman of Cable and Wireless Ltd (1962–7), deputy and then chairman of the Basildon New Town Development Corporation (1960–76), vice-president of the Royal Commonwealth and the Royal African societies, and, from 1962, vice-chairman of the advisory committee on distinction awards for consultants. Admired for his ability, diligence, and determination by those who knew him and looked on with affection by all who met him, the ready reference to Jock was a happy recognition of his easy combination of public popularity, private modesty, and personal courtesy.

Macpherson was appointed CMG in 1941, KCMG in 1945, and GCMG in 1951. He was made a knight of the order of St John of Jerusalem in 1952. In 1957 he received the honorary degree of LLD from Edinburgh University. He died on 5 November 1971 at his home, 141 Marsham Court, Marsham Street, Westminster. Lady Macpherson survived her husband. A. H. M. KIRK-GREENE

Sources *The Times* (9 Nov 1971) · interview (recording and transcript), 27 March 1968, Bodl. RH · J. S. Coleman, *Nigeria: background to nationalism* (1958) · D. Goldsworthy, ed., *The conservative government and the end of empire, 1951–1957*, 3 vols. (1994) · private information (1993) · A. H. M. Kirk-Greene, *A biographical dictionary of the British colonial governor* (1980) · H. Foot, *A start in freedom* (1964) · d. cert. · b. cert. · *DNB*

Archives Bodl. RH, Colonial Records Project, MSS · CAC Cam., corresp. with P. G. Buchan-Hepburn | FILM BFI NFTVA, documentary footage
Likenesses W. Stoneman, photograph, 1957, NPG
Wealth at death £52,254: probate, 11 Jan 1972, *CGPLA Eng. & Wales*

McPherson, Joseph Williams (1866–1946), colonial official and anthropologist, was born at Brislington, near Bristol, on 29 August 1866, the youngest of six sons of Dougal McPherson (1824–1883), superintendent of Brislington House Asylum, and his wife, Eliza Williams (1823–1900). Both parents were strict covenanting Christians from the Scottish highlands, where his father had been an estate manager. Joseph was educated at Clifton College, Bristol, and in 1883 entered the Royal College of Science in Dublin, where he converted to Catholicism. In 1887 he won a scholarship to Christ Church, Oxford, to study natural sciences. Nicknamed the Wild One, he accumulated large debts at Oxford—beagling with aristocratic friends was a favourite pastime—and needed to be bailed out by his brothers. After graduating in 1890 with a first in chemistry, he became secretary to the fourth Baron Camoys and then taught science at various public schools in the Bristol area, and was also a senior extension lecturer for Oxford University.

In 1900 McPherson's mother died. They had been close, and he reacted by joining the department of public instruction in the Egyptian government (which had been administered by Britain since the occupation of 1882). His first post on arriving in Cairo in October 1901 was science and mathematics master at the Khedivieh School, the Egyptian equivalent of Eton College. The placement was prestigious, but education ranked low in governmental concerns. Status, however, counted for little with McPherson and he embraced his teaching responsibilities with enthusiasm. Arabic was soon mastered, so allowing direct contact with Egyptians of all backgrounds. Pupils and servants invited him into their homes and to family events. Religious creeds and rituals particularly fascinated him and he attended many weddings, Armenian, Maronite, Coptic, and Greek, as well as Muslim.

Such behaviour placed McPherson apart from the insular British set, but this did not trouble him in the least. In 1904 he transferred to the Ras el Tin School in Alexandria and then to the agricultural college at Giza (on the outskirts of Cairo) in 1907. His scientific expertise won him additional assignments, notably a commission to study the total eclipse of the sun in southern Sudan in 1905. During regular travels around the Middle East and Mediterranean, his imposing physical appearance was often an asset. Though only of medium height, he was rigidly upright and muscular with a large jaw and bushy moustache. A willingness to resolve disputes with his fists was one manifestation of a marked reckless streak. Anthropological curiosity, for instance, was not always the main motive for his visits to Cairo's seedier clubs and brothels, but he was familiar enough with their dangers to carry a pair of knuckledusters or a gun. Speculation on the Alexandria bourse was another activity pursued with gusto:

towards the end of his life he papered a room in his house with worthless share certificates. His personality also demanded periods of solitude, which the Egyptian desert and travel gave him. Linking the gregarious and reflective sides of his character was the spirit of enquiry, underpinned by the Romantic ideal of experience. Teaching jobs and the accompanying long holidays suited him and he shied away from a more focused career.

At first McPherson showed little interest in Egyptian politics. Over two decades of Lord Cromer's firm rule had stabilized the economy and pacified the people. However, the Dinshwai incident of June 1906 (when Egyptian villagers were brutally punished for an affray) broke this calm and Egyptian nationalist pressures sharply mounted. Abroad at the time, McPherson was struck by the tension on his return to Egypt. When Eldon Gorst initiated a policy of liberalization in 1907, McPherson condemned the shift as weakness: 'Egypt for Egyptians—and ruin for all' (Carman and McPherson, 79). Brought up to believe that British imperialism was a force for good, he was unable to understand the nationalist aspirations of the people around him, no matter how deep his sympathy for them in other respects. His view of the 'bigwigs' at the British residency (never especially positive) deteriorated and he declined their invitations to social events. Besides teaching, he worked on a pioneering bilingual science dictionary, published in 1912 as *English–Arabic Vocabulary of Scientific Terms*.

When war broke out in 1914 McPherson was determined to serve his country, despite being close to fifty. The Khedivial Sporting Club in Cairo (renamed the Gezira Sporting Club in December after the deposition of Abbas Hilmi II) formed an all-British reserve unit and McPherson signed up. Known disparagingly as the 'pharaoh's foot', it failed to provide him with the action he desired. He therefore enrolled as a Red Cross officer in July 1915 and went to Gallipoli on board a hospital ship, but was wounded after a week and returned to Egypt. In 1916 he was commissioned in the Camel Transport Corps. The unit, which also comprised Egyptian volunteers, supplied troops in the Sinai desert and carried back the wounded. Captain McPherson's knowledge of local sensitivities was put to good effect in recruitment and requisitioning. Among the British officers, he had a reputation for indulging the natives (for example on Muslim feast days), but he was not averse to using the lash for insubordination or striking the head of a trouble-maker with his gun. In 1917 the campaign moved northwards into Palestine. The 'crusade' (as he called it) to capture the Holy Land thrilled him in a mystical way, particularly because he believed that his mother's spirit resided there. He was greatly disappointed when a bullet wound to his leg forced his retirement from active service in April.

In the following month McPherson was put in charge of Egyptian political prisoners at Giza and promoted to major ('Bimbashi' to the locals). In January 1918 he was appointed acting head of Cairo's secret police, which operated under the overall authority of Thomas Russell Pasha. Although Egypt was entering a period of violent nationalist upheaval (the so-called revolution of 1919), it was nevertheless organized crime that preoccupied McPherson. Breaking up anti-British demonstrations came as something of a relief to him. His method for dispersing a mob was to press a gun to the head of its leader—whom he would personally seize—and then instruct the crowd to move away. This street-level policing reinforced his conviction that Egypt could—and should—be held by force. The vacillating policy of the British residency under Allenby frustrated him. Swift, violent retribution was fundamental to McPherson's mindset.

In 1920 the threat of assassination prompted McPherson to move away from Cairo and, from November, he became passport control and intelligence officer at the Suez canal town of Kantara. The job was undemanding, and he began to recover from the scarring experiences of policing the Cairo underworld. In December 1921 he returned to Cairo for a deskbound position in the War Office's department of public security, but a year later accepted Russell's offer of undercover work directed at drug traffickers. The post was freelance so that Russell would not be implicated if anything went wrong. Disguise was McPherson's forte: his repertory included an 'Armenian Jew of means' and a 'low-class Greek'. Before he retired in 1924, he compiled an index of drug dealers that proved invaluable after the first stringent anti-narcotics laws were passed in 1925.

McPherson used the freedom of retirement to study religious rituals, his lifelong passion. He popularized the results with articles on such topics as the evil eye and Egyptian folk medicine for *John O' London's Weekly*, *Wide World*, and other magazines. He lived in a villa near Giza and cultivated neighbouring fields. Urged by his friend the anthropologist Edward Evans-Pritchard, he wrote *The Moulids of Egypt* (1941), for which he became a noted authority. Many of the 126 religious festivals described have since faded away, making the book of lasting interest. Lawrence Durrell's *Alexandria Quartet* (1957–60) relied heavily on it for descriptions of whirling dances, chants, freak shows, and processions. The ageing McPherson was a well-known figure in Cairo, ambling around on a white mule, and revered by the Egyptian poor as a holy man and seer. This was all the more remarkable because of his earlier public career (his name was often in the newspapers) as head of the secret police.

Bouts of ill health affected McPherson during the Second World War. He was cared for by his servant of thirty years, whose wife and children provided him with a surrogate family. In July 1942 mistaken reports reached Cairo that the line at El Alamein had broken and panic swept the city. Taking his lead from the British embassy, McPherson burnt his papers. He never married and died at home on 22 January 1946. He was buried in Cairo. His posthumous reputation was enhanced by the publication of *Bimbashi McPherson: a Life in Egypt* (1983), a collection of letters to his brothers in England. The book provides a unique worm's-eye view of Cairo's low life. The title of the paperback edition, *The Man who Loved Egypt* (1985), is a fitting memorial.

MICHAEL T. THORNHILL

Sources B. Carman and J. McPherson, eds., *Bimbashi McPherson: a life in Egypt* (1983) • T. W. Russell, *Egyptian service, 1902–1946* (1949) • S. Raafat, 'Gezira Sporting Club milestones', *Egyptian Mail* (10–17 Feb 1996) • S. Robinson, 'Joseph Williams McPherson', gaudy oration, 1996, Christ Church Oxf. • b. cert.
Archives priv. coll., letters | SOUND BL NSA
Likenesses photographs, repro. in Carman and McPherson, eds., *Bimbashi McPherson*
Wealth at death £3635 17s. 6d.: probate, 5 July 1946, CGPLA Eng. & Wales

Macpherson, Lachlan [Lachlann Mac a' Phearsain; *called* Fear Shrath-Mhathaisidh] (*b. c.*1723, *d.* in or before 1780), Gaelic poet and musician, was the only son of John Macpherson (*d.* 1784?), tacksman, and his wife, Jean, daughter of Lachlan Mackintosh of Macintosh. He was the tacksman of Strathmashie, which is located near the village of Laggan in Badenoch, Inverness-shire. He took the field with his father in the Jacobite rising of 1745 and accompanied the clan chief, Ewen Macpherson of Cluny, as far as Derby. He married Mary, daughter of Archibald Butter of Pitlochry, and they had two sons and two daughters.

Lachlan Macpherson's kinsman James Macpherson published *Fragments of Ancient Poetry Collected in the Highlands of Scotland* in June 1760. James then set off in the autumn of the same year on the journey through the highlands that led to the publication of *Fingal* (1761) and *Temora* (1763), purportedly based upon the work of Fingal's son Ossian. In 1805 a report was produced by a committee of the Highland Society of Scotland appointed to inquire into the nature and authenticity of James's poetry. The report includes a letter from Lachlan (appendix, pp. 8–9) saying that he accompanied James during parts of his journey and assisted him in collecting most of the poetry from oral tradition and old manuscripts. Although he travelled with James only on the mainland, Lachlan's reputation as a Gaelic poet, together with his agreeable and polished manners, ensured that they were made welcome in the remoter parts of the highlands. He provided moral support and subsequently helped to prepare material for publication by deciphering ancient scripts, piecing fragments together, and transcribing them in roman characters.

Lachlan Macpherson's involvement with James Macpherson's later poems has been much discussed. Derick Thomson in his essay of 1998 refers to a letter dated 12 March 1799 from Andrew Gallie, minister in the parish of Laggan from 1758 to 1774, to Charles Macintosh, an Edinburgh solicitor. In this letter, printed in the committee's report (pp. 30–37), Gallie describes how he saw James and 'a friend who was at the time with Mr Macpherson and me' working at translations of the retrieved poetry: 'With much labour I have recovered some scattered parts of the translation made at my fire-side, I should rather say of the original translated there, and I communicate to you a few stanzas, taken from the manuscript'. There follow sixteen lines of Gaelic verse. Thomson comments that although these scan decently enough, they are not at all in the style of the ballads. He considers that they correspond closely to a passage in *Fingal* and have strong resemblances to a

passage in the Gaelic version of the poem. The committee asked Gallie who James's friend was and printed his reply of 4 March 1801 (pp. 39–43). Gallie said that the friend was 'alas! no more. His name was Lachlane Macpherson of Strathmashy. He died in the 1767.' It has also been said that after Lachlan's death a paper was found in his handwriting containing a Gaelic version of a poem in the seventh book of *Temora*.

Macpherson did not regard himself as a poet by profession, but rather as a typical tacksman who wrote for his own amusement and that of his friends. He is said to have sat in the porch of his house entertaining everyone with his violin and witty rhymes in the manner of village bards. In later times, on clipping days, his quips and songs were recalled amid general merriment. Over a dozen of his songs survive, many having appeared in Gaelic and in translation in *The Poetry of Badenoch* by Thomas Sinton (1906). One praises the fellowship of whisky; another recounts how Lachlan and his retainers went to the great wood of Loch Laggan to fetch timber for a house. The raft that they built to float the cabers home glided off, carrying one of the men with it. Lachlan sings of the ensuing noise and merriment. The landlord of the stage-house at Dunkeld offended him in some way. Revenge is taken in song by sending an army of mice to ruin the landlord by eating him out of house and home. In 'The White Wedding' he celebrates the marriage of an elderly couple at which all the guests were grey-haired. The old folk rejoice in a gently satirical epithalamium. Others songs are on the theme of hunting and satirize the jingling greed for riches. Perhaps the most serious song laments the death of his clan chieftain, Macpherson of Cluny.

Patrick Macgregor quotes a memorandum written by a Bishop Alexander Macdonell 'shortly before his death'. The author of this memorandum was probably Alexander Macdonald (1755–1837), a Gaelic scholar who was a priest in Perthshire and at a Gaelic chapel in Edinburgh. Macdonald says that all those best acquainted with both James and Lachlan believed that James was not as capable of doing justice to translation from the Gaelic as Lachlan, 'but that gentleman did not live to see the work finished or revised, which is supposed to be the cause of so many mistakes' (Macgregor, 39–40). *Fingal* and *Temora* were published together by James in 1765 as *The Works of Ossian*. Andrew Gallie says that Lachlan Macpherson died in 1767, and John Mackenzie, in *Sar-obair nam bard Gaelach* (1841), that he died 'in the latter end of the 18th century' (pp. 260–63). This is what may have led later writers to say that he lived into the last decade of the century. Derick Thomson in *Gaelic Poetry in the Eighteenth Century* (1993) and in *Companion to Gaelic Scotland* (1994) suggests a date of *c.*1795. However, letters from Macpherson's father and elder son, Alexander, from 1783 and 1780 respectively, which deal with family matters but make no mention of Lachlan, suggest that he had died some time before then (Macpherson of Cluny MSS, NL Scot.).   RICHARD D. JACKSON

Sources R. Douglas and others, *The baronage of Scotland* (1798), 362–3 • A. Macpherson, *Glimpses of church and social life in the highlands in olden times* (1893), 273–4 and 498–500 • Macpherson of

Cluny MSS, NA Scot., GD 80/903/2, 3 and 4 · *Report of the committee of the Highland Society of Scotland appointed to inquire into the nature and authenticity of the poems of Ossian* (1805), 30–32, 43; appx, 8–9 · T. B. Saunders, *The life and letters of James Macpherson* (1894), 117–20, 136–9 · F. J. Stafford, *The sublime savage: a study of James Macpherson and the poems of Ossian* (1988), 116–17, 120, 123–4, 128, 129, 131 · T. McLauchlan and W. F. Skene, eds., *The dean of Lismore's book: a selection of ancient Gaelic poetry* (1862), l–lvii · P. Macgregor, *The genuine remains of Ossian literally translated* (1841), 3, 6, 39–40 · D. S. Thomson, 'James Macpherson: the Gaelic dimension', *From Gaelic to Romantic: Ossianic translations*, ed. F. Stafford and H. Gaskill (Amsterdam and Atlanta, GA, 1998), 20–21 · *Sean dain agus orain Ghaidhealach* (*A collection of ancient and modern Gaelic poems and songs*) (1786), 79–82 · J. Mackenzie, ed., *Sar-obair nam bard Gaelach, or, The beauties of Gaelic poetry* (1841), 260–63 · H. Gaskill and F. Stafford, eds., *The poems of Ossian and related works: James Macpherson* (1996) · D. S. Thomson, *The Gaelic sources of Macpherson's Ossian* (1952), 86–7 · A. M. Sinclair, *The Gaelic bards from 1715 to 1765* (1892), 222–4 · N. Macneill, *The literature of the highlanders*, 2nd edn (1929), 287–92 [with additional chaper by J. Macmaster Campbell] · J. Cameron Lees, *A history of the county of Inverness (mainland)* (1897), 325 · T. Sinton, *The poetry of Badenoch* (1906), viii, xxxvii, 93, 123, 129, 142, 148, 160, 168, 177, 179, 235, 236, 259 · A. G. Macpherson, *A day's march to ruin* (1996) · *A list of persons concerned in the rebellion*, Scottish History Society, 8 (1890), 118 **Archives** NA Scot.

Macpherson, Malcolm (1833–1898), player and teacher of the highland bagpipe, was born on 5 December 1833 at Snizort, Isle of Skye, the son of Angus Macpherson (*c*.1800–*c*.1866), a professional piper, and his wife, Effy MacLeod of Uig in Skye. He was known as Calum Pìobaire ('Malcolm the piper'). Little is known of Malcolm Macpherson's formal schooling, except that he attended Laggan parish school; but in piping he had famous teachers, including his father, Angus MacKay, Archibald Munro, and Alexander Cameron (the elder). He married Ann McDiarmid (*d*. 1903), a midwife from Kildalton, Islay, and they had several sons, three of whom—John (1863–1933), Norman (1869–1947), and Angus (1877–1976)—became champion pipers in their own right.

Following a quarrel with his stepmother, Malcolm Macpherson left home about 1857 for Greenock, where he worked as a labourer, a ship's carpenter, and as piper on the revenue cutter *Prince Albert*. Greenock was the main port of Glasgow, and full of highland people: indeed it was said that one could walk down the high street on a Saturday forenoon and not hear a word of English. There Macpherson studied piobaireachd, the classical music of the highland pipe, with Donald Cameron's brother Sandy (1821–1871), himself an outstanding player (prize pipe, Inverness, 1846; gold medal, Inverness, 1862), and proprietor of the Museum Hotel at 9 William Street in the town centre, a frequent resort of pipers, and only a few minutes' walk from Macpherson's home at 15 Hamilton Street. Sandy Cameron was also pipe-major of the Greenock rifle volunteers and Macpherson played with him in what may have been one of the world's earliest pipe bands.

Malcolm Macpherson went on to become one of the outstanding champion pipers of the second half of the nineteenth century, and won the prize pipe at the Northern Meeting in 1866, and gold medals at Inverness (1871) and Oban (1876). For nearly a generation he plundered the competition circuit at the new-style highland games which were springing up throughout Scotland, winning prizes at Birnam, Portree, Blair Atholl, Aberfeldy, Kingussie, Grantown, and Dunkeld. At the Edinburgh Exhibition of 1886 he gained two gold medals, one of which carried with it the championship of the world for piobaireachd.

About 1866 Macpherson succeeded his father as piper to Macpherson of Cluny (he composed 'The Lament for Cluny Macpherson' on the latter's death in 1886) and his cottage at Catlodge on Speyside, near Kingussie, became a focus for master-class instruction for pipers from all over Scotland. Some of his pupils went on to achieve the highest honours, including John MacDonald of Inverness, Robert Meldrum, Angus MacRae, and William MacLean of Kilcreggan. Macpherson was a superb technician and excelled at heavy bottom-handed tunes such as 'Glengarry's March' and 'My King has Landed in Moidart'. His repertory was very extensive: indeed when asked by a pupil how many piobaireachds he knew, he replied 'Well, once I could play a terrible skelp of tunes, but I believe I could yet manage six twenties'. Malcolm Macpherson is the earliest master teacher of whose methods we have a detailed account. He laid great stress on the traditional oral approach, using canntaireachd, a system in which sung vocables represent the various finger movements on the chanter. His leading pupil, John MacDonald of Inverness, wrote:

> Each morning he used to play Jigs on the chanter while breakfast was being got ready … I can see him now, with his old jacket and his leather sporran, sitting on a stool while the porridge was being brought to the boil. After breakfast he would take his barrow to the peat moss, cut a turf, and build up the fire with wet peat for the day. He would then sit down beside me, take away all books and pipe music, then sing in his own canntaireachd the ground and different variations of the particular piobaireachd he wished me to learn. (MacDonald)

Malcolm Macpherson was the pivotal figure in the Macpherson piping dynasty which, along with the Cameron, McLennan, Bruce, MacKenzie, and MacKay families, was central to the transmission of piobaireachd during the nineteenth century. His grandfather Peter Macpherson is said to have moved from Badenoch to Idrigill in Skye, where he married a sister of the Bruce pipers. His father, Angus, is thought to have studied with Iain Dubh MacCrimmon, John and Peter Bruce, and John MacKay of Raasay. Malcolm himself became the leading piobaireachd player and teacher of his generation. By the beginning of the twentieth century, so important had the family become that folk tales circulated similar to those about the MacCrimmons, concerning dealings with the fairies and access to supernatural powers. The following generation saw John, known familiarly as Jockan (gold medals at Oban, 1889, and Inverness, 1920), and Angus Macpherson (gold medal, Inverness, 1923), rise to eminence: the latter became piper to Andrew Carnegie, and also a prominent composer, judge, and writer. Angus's son Malcolm Ross Macpherson (1906–1966) was also an outstanding performer (gold medal, Inverness, 1927; clasp, Inverness,

1930, 1937) and the main informant for Dr Roderick Ross's *Binneas is Boreraig*, the most important piobaireachd collection published during the second half of the twentieth century.

Malcolm Macpherson died at Catlodge on 9 July 1898 after falling into Loch Coultree attempting to retrieve a lost oar during a fishing expedition. He was buried in the kirkyard at Laggan Bridge on 13 July 1898, with John Macdonald playing 'The Lament for the Children' at the graveside. A memorial at Catlodge was unveiled in August 1960.   WILLIAM DONALDSON

Sources W. Donaldson, *The highland pipe and Scottish society, 1750–1950* (2000) · A. Fairrie, *The Northern Meeting, 1788–1988* (1988) · J. MacDonald, 'The piping reminiscences of John MacDonald M.B.E.', *Oban Times* (4 April 1942) · A. Macpherson, *A highlander looks back* (1953) · R. Ross, *Binneas is Boreraig* (1959–67) · B. Mackenzie, *Piping traditions of the north of Scotland* (1998) · W. MacLean, 'Notices of pipers', *Piping Times*, 42 (1990), 20 · 'Death of well-known champion piper', *Oban Times* (23 July 1898) · J. Campbell, 'Notices of bagpipe makers', *Piping Times*, 51 (1999), 26–9 · J. Campbell, '100 years of piping', *Piper Press* (July 1999), 5–17 · b. cert. · d. cert.
Likenesses photographs, repro. in Campbell, '100 years of piping'

MacPherson, Mary [known as Màiri Mhór nan Òran, Màiri Nighean Ian Bhain] (1821–1898), poet, was born on 10 March 1821 at Skeabost, Skye, the second youngest child of John Macdonald, crofter, known as Ian Bàn Mac Aonghais Oig, and his wife, Flora MacInnes, daughter of Neil MacInnes of Uig, Snizort. Educated at home in domestic skills, she left Skye for Inverness to marry Isaac MacPherson, a shoemaker, on 11 November 1847. He died in 1871 leaving four surviving children. Mary MacPherson was imprisoned on a charge of theft in 1872, and later that year she moved to Glasgow. There she trained as a nurse at the Royal Infirmary gaining a nursing certificate and a diploma in obstetrics. She practised in Greenock and Glasgow until her return to Skye in 1882.

MacPherson found her poetic voice while serving sentence, expressing in Gaelic verse her protestations of innocence and profound sense of outrage. A frequent member of Highland Society céilidhs in Glasgow, she met leading advocates of highland land reform, including John Murdoch, editor of *The Highlander* newspaper, and became well known for her poetry. Her support for Charles Fraser Mackintosh, candidate in the Inverness burghs election of 1874, was declared through her early songs. She later accompanied him during his campaign for election to parliament. A prominent figure during the land league agitation of the 1880s, she recited her Gaelic verses at principal gatherings. Song was a primary vehicle of the dissemination of information to Gaelic speakers without literacy in the language of the printed press. Her poetry, and that of other bards of the land agitation, also provides an essential body of Gaelic evidence relating to the highland land movement. Angus Macbain, the Celtic scholar, believed that her songs contributed to the success of crofter candidates in the 1885–6 elections, and described her as the bard of the movement. Her personal sense of injustice and empathy with the sufferings of her people gave a unique force to her poetry. In 1891 a volume

entitled *Gaelic Songs and Poems, by Mrs Mary Macpherson (Mairi Nighean Ian Bhain)* was published. These were transcribed from her recitation, for although she could read her own poems she could not write them.

A gregarious woman of great physical stature, MacPherson numbered among her friends the scholar Professor John Blackie. He always wore the plaid she made for him, which was placed upon his coffin. Her design was patented as the 'Blackie tartan', which she sold as rugs or wraps. She was the official bard of the Clan Macdonald Society.

After a short illness Mary MacPherson died on 7 November 1898 while visiting Portree, Skye. She was buried on 10 November in Chapel Yard burial-ground, Inverness, where Charles Fraser Mackintosh MP erected a monument. A plaque to her memory was unveiled in 1966 at Skeabost, and a film was made of her life by Comataidh Telebhisein Gaidhlig in 1994.   CHRISTINE LODGE

Sources *Inverness Courier* (11 Nov 1898) [based on that given in *The Scotsman*] · 'Life of the poetess', *Songs and poems by Mrs Mary Macpherson*, ed. A. Macbain (1891) [foreword] · D. E. Meek, 'Gaelic poets of the land agitation', *Transactions of the Gaelic Society of Inverness*, 49 (1974–6), 309–76 · D. E. Meek, *Màiri Mhór nan Òran* (Glasgow, 1977) · D. E. Meek, 'The role of song in the highland land agitation', *Scottish Gaelic Studies*, 16 (1990), 1–53 · A. Nicolson, *History of Skye* (1930) · D. Cooper, *Skye* (1989) · *Scottish Highlander* (30 Oct 1890) [article on forthcoming pubn of *Songs and poems*] · D. S. Thomson, ed., *The companion to Gaelic Scotland* (1983)
Likenesses photographs, Highland Council, Inverness, Highland Photographic Archive, Whyte Collection; repro. in Macbain, ed., *Songs and poems*

Macpherson, Paul (1756–1846), college head, was born into a Roman Catholic family at Scalan, Glenlivet, on 4 March 1756. In June 1767 he was admitted a student in the Scalan seminary, which had been founded by Bishop James Gordon in 1717. Macpherson then spent seven years (1770–77) at the Scots College in Rome, and completed his theological studies at the Scots College at Valladolid in Spain (1777–9). Having been ordained priest by the bishop of Segovia, he joined the Catholic church's Scottish mission, and was stationed successively at Shenval, Banffshire (1779–80), at Aberdeen (1780–83), and at Stobhall, Perthshire. In 1791 he moved to Edinburgh on being appointed procurator of the mission. He was sent to Rome in 1793, where for many years he dealt with the Holy See on matters relating to the Scottish mission.

Following the French occupation of Rome in 1798, Macpherson left the city in possession of valuable Stuart family records and travelled through France and England. He returned two years later, and was the first secular Scottish rector of the Scots College. He was also an agent for the Scottish, and for some years the English, vicars apostolic, and was employed in the same way by a group of Irish bishops. In 1811 he visited Scotland and during this visit became involved in an attempt to rescue Pope Pius VII, then a French prisoner at Savona; he was dispatched on an English frigate from London with ample powers and funds to effect the escape of the pontiff. Spies for the French disclosed the design to the Paris government, and the attempt failed.

Macpherson reopened the Scots College in Rome in 1812 where he remained as rector until 1827. He then resigned from the rectorship and returned to Scotland in May 1827, where he erected a chapel in Glenlivet. In 1834 he made his final journey to Rome where he resumed the office of rector. He died at the Scots College on 24 November 1846.

THOMPSON COOPER, *rev.* MARY CATHERINE MORAN

Sources D. McRoberts, *Abbé Paul Macpherson, 1756–1846* (1946) · C. Johnson, *Developments in the Roman Catholic church in Scotland, 1789–1829* (1983) · *DSCHT* · *Catholic Magazine*, 1 (1831–2), 280 · *GM*, 2nd ser., 27 (1847), 318

Archives Scots College, Rome, corresp. · Scottish Catholic Archives, Edinburgh, notes and papers incl. autobiographical

Macpherson, Robert (1814–1872), photographer and painter, was born in Forfarshire, Scotland, probably on 27 February 1814, and spent most of his professional life in Rome. Little is known of his family background, though it is likely that he was a grandnephew of James *Macpherson (1736–1796), author of the fraudulent Ossianic publication, *Fragments of Ancient Poetry* (1760). The generally accepted view of his early life is that he studied medicine at Edinburgh University (1831–5) and later—possibly about 1838—attended classes at the Royal Scottish Academy of Art. Towards the end of the 1830s he left Scotland for India with the intention of practising as a surgeon; for health reasons, however, he settled in Rome, abandoning his career in medicine to become a painter.

Only moderately successful as an artist, Macpherson found it necessary to undertake freelance work as a journalist, producing articles for *The Times*, the *Daily News*, and *The Athenaeum*. He also practised as a dealer in antiquities and was responsible for the discovery of Michelangelo's *Entombment of Christ*, which he retained as a hedge against financial difficulties, eventually selling it in 1868 to the National Gallery in London for £2000. Gregarious and outgoing, he became a central figure in the community of expatriate artists and intellectuals who congregated in Rome in mid-century, with the sculptor James Gibson and the German painter Peter von Cornelius among his personal friends. In appearance he was the quintessential Scotsman abroad, with flaming red hair, large flowing beard, and full highland costume. In 1847 he became a Roman Catholic, and in the following year fell in love with Gerardine (Geddie) Bate (1830/31–1878) [see Macpherson, Gerardine], the niece and protégée of the renowned art historian Anna Jameson, with whom she had travelled to Rome in the company of Robert and Elizabeth Barrett Browning. Despite her aunt's disapproval, the couple were married on 4 September 1849 in Ealing, Middlesex, Geddie Macpherson converting to Catholicism the following year.

In 1851 Macpherson began experimenting in photography, which he found to be a more lucrative profession than painting. He quickly established himself as one of the leading interpreters of Roman topography, producing nearly 300 views of the city's architectural treasures, as well as numerous reproductions of paintings and sculptures from the papal collections in the Vatican. He used both the albumen and collodion processes, often combining the two, with glass negatives measuring 30.5 centimetres by 40.5, and exposure times varying from two minutes to several days. He also experimented with photolithography, which he tried, without success, to use commercially. Although his work was produced chiefly for sale to the burgeoning tourist trade, it was also regularly included in major exhibitions in London, Edinburgh, and Glasgow. In 1858 he contributed 120 prints to the exhibition of the Architectural Photographic Association. His earlier experience as a painter proved invaluable in the choice of effective viewpoints, and his interpretations of classical architecture were unsurpassed in their aesthetic power and sophistication.

Unlike many of his major rivals, such as the Alinari brothers, Macpherson's commercial activities never grew beyond the scale of a small family business, with many of the practical tasks such as printing and mounting often performed by his wife and mother-in-law. His book *Vatican Sculptures* (1863) was also illustrated with woodcuts by his wife. From about 1865 his career began to falter, and the last years of his life were marked by a steady decline in both his reputation and his health. He died in Rome on 17 November 1872, leaving his wife and their four surviving children, William, Francis, Ada, and Joseph, in a state of acute financial distress. He was buried in the churchyard of San Lorenzo, Rome.

RAY MCKENZIE

Sources M. Munsterberg, 'A biographical sketch of Robert Macpherson', *Art Bulletin*, 68 (1986), 142–53 · G. Macpherson, *Memoirs of the life of Anna Jameson*, ed. M. O. W. Oliphant (1878) · *British Journal of Photography* (6 Dec 1872), 577 · R. McKenzie, 'Scottish photographers in nineteenth-century Italy: Robert Mcpherson and his contemporaries', *History of Photography*, 20 (1996), 33–40 · *Elizabeth Barrett Browning: letters to her sister, 1846–1859*, ed. L. Huxley (1929) · J. E. Freeman, *Gatherings from an artist's portfolio* (1883) · *Letters of Anna Jameson to Ottilie von Goethe*, ed. G. H. Needler (1939) · M. Bailey, 'The rediscovery of Michelangelo's *Entombment*: the rescuing of a masterpiece', *Apollo*, 140 (Oct 1994), 30–33 · d. cert. · *Photographic Notes* (20 Dec 1862), 617 · *Murray's handbook* (1896), xv [Rome] · A. Crawford, 'Robert Macpherson, 1814–72: the foremost photographer of Rome', *Papers of the British School at Rome*, 67 (1999), 353–403

Archives Canadian Centre for Architecture, Montreal, Canada, photographs collection

Macpherson, Samuel Charters (1806–1860), army and political officer in India, born in Old Aberdeen on 7 January 1806, elder brother of John *Macpherson (1817–1890) and of William *Macpherson (1812–1893), was the second son of Hugh Macpherson, professor of Greek at University and King's College, Aberdeen, and his first wife, Anne Maria Charters. He was educated in Edinburgh and at Trinity College, Cambridge, and read for the Scottish bar. In 1827 he sailed for Madras as a cadet; he became lieutenant in 1831 and captain by brevet in 1841.

Macpherson was first engaged on the trigonometrical survey of India, but in 1835 was summoned to rejoin his regiment, which was engaged in operations against the raja of Goomsur in Orissa. In 1837 he was sent by the collector of Ganjam on a mission of survey and inquiry into the unexplored parts of Goomsur. There he made a close study of the Gonds, an aboriginal people then almost unknown. He drew up for the governor-general, Lord

Elphinstone, a report on the Gonds, and the measures to be adopted for the suppression among that people of the meriah, or human sacrifice. A variety of attempts were then made by East India Company officials and soldiers to effect this suppression. However, none met with much success until, in the spring of 1842, Macpherson was himself appointed principal assistant to the collector and political agent in the region. Using his local knowledge, and taking care to conciliate chiefs, priests, and rajas as much as to punish those who carried on the nefarious trade of supplying victims to the Gonds, Macpherson proved highly effective. He also constructed roads, encouraged fairs, and bestowed the meriah girls in marriage on the most influential people in the tribes, making these alliances a passport to the favour of government.

In the districts adjoining Goomsur, however, Macpherson was less successful. There he faced a local uprising, official intrigue and corruption, and disapproval from the provincial government in Madras. In November 1845 his authority was superseded by that of a military commander, and Macpherson and his assistants were ordered to withdraw from the region. Colonel Campbell, his replacement as governor-general's agent for the suppression of meriah sacrifice and female infanticide, also laid charges against him which led to an inquiry lasting a year and a half. The charges, however, were proved to be without foundation and Lord Dalhousie, who was now governor-general, declared that nothing could compensate Macpherson for the infamous treatment he had received.

In August 1853 Macpherson returned to India from sick-leave in Europe and continued his career in the political service. He was appointed in succession political agent at Benares and at Bhopal, but in July 1854, being then brevet major, he was transferred to the more important post of Gwalior, the capital of Sindhia, the most powerful princely ruler in central India. The previous political agent, Sir Robert North Hamilton, was a supporter of Macpherson who himself established close relations with Sindhia's minister Dinkar Rao, a statesman of the first order. Together, Macpherson and Dinkar abolished transit duties, laid out large sums on the roads and public works, drew up a code of law and civil procedure, and put the state's finances in order. Macpherson's support of Dinkar was later repaid with interest. When the Indian mutiny broke out in 1857, it was Dinkar, influenced by Macpherson, who kept the Gwalior contingent and Sindhia's own army from joining the rebels in Delhi.

Macpherson lived to see the uprising suppressed; but the strain upon his health had been too great. He died on 15 April 1860, while on his way to Calcutta. After his death he was gazetted a companion of the Bath.

GORDON GOODWIN, rev. DAVID WASHBROOK

Sources *Memorials of service in India, from the correspondence of the late Major S. C. Macpherson*, ed. W. Macpherson (1865) · Venn, *Alum. Cant.*

Archives BL, Napier MSS

Likenesses stipple, pubd 1865 (after photograph), NPG · portrait, repro. in Macpherson, ed., *Memorials of service in India*, frontispiece

MacPherson, Stewart Myles (1908–1995), radio broadcaster, was born on 29 October 1908 in Winnipeg, Manitoba, Canada, the eldest of three children of Daniel MacPherson, general manager, and his wife, Agnes, née Cuthbert MacPherson, who on marriage became Agnes MacPherson MacPherson. He grew up in Winnipeg, enthusiastic about sport and little else. When his father died, he left high school in his first year and sought work to support his mother. He failed in a number of jobs and at the age of twenty-eight decided to try his luck in England. He travelled across the Atlantic for twenty-three days in a cattle boat and arrived with $11 in his pocket. His first job was as a shoe salesman in Oxford Street, London. But thanks to some Canadian ice hockey playing friends, he was appointed assistant to the press secretary at Wembley stadium. His job was to write the weekly ice hockey programme. When the new season began, he was auditioned by the BBC, and in November 1937 he began a broadcasting career that would make him one of the best-known radio personalities in Britain, a respected war correspondent, and, as the chairman of two well-known radio panel games, a familiar figure on the variety stage.

Although he was new to broadcasting, MacPherson's freshness, his ability to speak clearly and quickly, and his transatlantic accent made him popular with listeners and the BBC. The war threatened to bring his new career to a premature end. The BBC's outside broadcast department was closed and MacPherson went back to Canada. But one man at the BBC—S. J. de Lotbiniere—remembered him when the BBC war reporting unit was formed. MacPherson returned in 1941 and joined a team that would eventually include such distinguished war correspondents as Richard Dimbleby, Wynford Vaughan-Thomas, and Frank Gillard. MacPherson began work in the London blitz and then was attached to the Royal Air Force, flying on bombing missions over Germany. When the invasion of Europe began, he was attached to the US Twelfth Army air group and was one of the reporters on D-day, 6 June 1944. His best-known report came on 17 September 1944. He had flown in a scout plane to meet the First Airborne Army on its flight to Holland and Arnhem: 'The sky was black with transport aircraft, flying in perfect formation. They were completely surrounded by Typhoons, Spitfires, Mustangs, Thunderbolts and Lightning fighters. It was an aerial layer cake' (BBC *War Report*, 17 Sept 1944). *War Report*, broadcast nightly on BBC radio from D-day until VE-day, was personal and informal; an account of what one man had seen and heard. Even though he had no training as a journalist, MacPherson had the eyes, ears, and quick mind, as well as the voice, to shine as a front-line reporter.

After the war MacPherson went back to being a sports commentator. But he secured a wide brief: boxing, golf, speedway, cycling, and the 1948 Olympic games in London. Although he loved his job, he became disenchanted with the BBC's pay structure. As the principal boxing commentator, he was paid 25 guineas per fight. As the presenter of Saturday's *Sports Report* he was paid 15 guineas. When he was invited to chair the panel game *Twenty Questions*, he was eventually paid 50 guineas per programme,

Stewart Myles MacPherson (1908–1995), by Bassano

but only after he had protested and a BBC official agreed to increase his fee, having discovered that Wilfred Pickles was being paid 200 guineas for his role in *Have a Go* (BBC archives).

Twenty Questions flourished under MacPherson's chairmanship, and became one of the longest-running programmes in BBC history. At the same time, MacPherson also chaired a comedy quiz, *Ignorance is Bliss*. The two programmes were quite different: *Twenty Questions* was brisk, entertaining, and unpredictable, *Ignorance is Bliss* was scripted, repetitive, and at times silly. Both series were broadcast 'by arrangement with Maurice Winnick', who became MacPherson's agent. Winnick took both shows on a tour of Britain's variety theatres, with MacPherson in the chair. As a highly paid freelance broadcaster, with a weekly newspaper column, MacPherson became widely known: his square-jawed features, his rimless glasses, and his hair brushed straight back from a high forehead were featured regularly in the national press, and in 1949 Stewie, as he was called, was voted Voice of Britain in the National Radio Awards.

Despite these successes, MacPherson was unsettled in London. His wife, Emily Comfort, whom he had married in 1937, and their two children had gone back to Canada, and when his wartime colleague Ed Murrow offered him a job as a news and sports commentator at the CBS radio station in Minneapolis, MacPherson eventually accepted late in 1949. 'It was', he said later, 'the most agonising decision of my life. I owed a lot to the people of Britain. But as a husband and a father, I felt I had a far greater responsibility to

my family' (Robertson). To signify how much he had meant to Britain, George VI and Queen Elizabeth invited MacPherson to record his final *Twenty Questions* programme at Buckingham Palace.

Minneapolis was not the success MacPherson had expected: CBS sold the radio station in 1960, and MacPherson thought about going back to England. But when an offer came to return to Winnipeg, he accepted a job, first as general manager of Winnipeg Enterprises, a sports organization, and then, when the new television station opened in the city, he was back on the air. One of the first things he did was to revive his old *Twenty Questions* programme. He also introduced television editorials, called *Stew's Views*, and did the occasional sports programme. He retired in 1974 and died in Winnipeg on 16 April 1995. He was survived by his son and daughter, his wife having predeceased him. He was buried on 19 April 1995 in Winnipeg.   PAUL FOX

Sources *The Times* (27 April 1995) · *The Independent* (29 April 1995) · *WWW*, 1991–5 · BBC WAC · BBC *War reports*, BBC Archives · J. Robertson, *Highlights with Stewart Macpherson* (1980) · S. Macpherson, *The mike and I* (1948) · private information (2004) [H. Hacking, J. Robertson] · personal knowledge (2004)
Archives SOUND BL NSA, performance recordings
Likenesses three photographs, 1947–9, Hult. Arch. · Bassano, photograph, NPG [*see illus.*] · A. Wysard, watercolour drawing, NPG · photograph, repro. in *The Times* · photograph, repro. in *The Independent*

Macpherson, William (1812–1893), legal writer, was born in Aberdeen on 19 July 1812, the son of Hugh Macpherson, professor of Greek at King's College, Aberdeen. He was the brother of John *Macpherson (1817–1890), inspector-general of hospitals in India, and of Samuel Charters *Macpherson, political agent in India. He was educated at Charterhouse School and at King's College, Aberdeen (1826–7), before matriculating in Michaelmas 1830 at Trinity College, Cambridge, where he graduated BA in 1834 and MA in 1838. Admitted to the Inner Temple in 1831, he was called to the bar in 1837. In 1841 he published *A Practical Treatise on the Law Relating to Infants*, a well-researched work which attracted notice.

In 1846 Macpherson went to India to practise at the Indian bar, and in 1848 was given by Sir Laurence Peel, chief justice of Bengal, the post of master of equity in the supreme court in Calcutta. On 9 January 1851 he married Diana Macleod Johnston (d. 1880), the only daughter of Dr Johnston of the Madras medical service. Macpherson's *Procedure of the Civil Courts of India* (Calcutta, 1850) immediately became a recognized authority and reached a fifth edition in 1871. He also published *Outlines of the Law of Contracts as Administered in the Courts of British India* (1860). He spent nearly two years (1854–5) in England on leave, and finally left India in March 1859.

In October 1860 Macpherson was appointed editor of the *Quarterly Review* by the publisher, John Murray. He held that post until October 1867, contributing three articles to the review between 1861 and 1864. Also during this period, in 1865, he published *Memorials* of his brother, Samuel Charters Macpherson. In December 1861 Macpherson had become secretary of the Indian law commission, which was appointed to prepare a body of substantive law for India, and he withdrew from literary work in 1867 in order to concentrate on that work. The Indian Succession Act of 1865 illustrates the work of the commission. Owing to the Indian government's desire to exercise more direct control over the undertaking, however, the commission was dissolved in December 1870.

Macpherson then returned to the bar, and practised chiefly before the privy council. His useful *Practice of the Privy Council Judicial Committee*, first published in 1860, reached a second edition in 1873. In 1874 he began reporting the Indian appeals before the privy council for the Council of Law Reporting. In June 1874 he became legal adviser to the India Office, and in September 1879 resigned to become secretary in the judicial department. His nephew John Molesworth *Macpherson became deputy secretary to the government of India in the legislative department in 1877. Macpherson retired from the India Office on 20 February 1882. He died at his home, 3 Kensington Gardens Square, London, on 20 April 1893, and was survived by at least one child.

GORDON GOODWIN, *rev.* CATHERINE PEASE-WATKIN

Sources *The Times* (24 April 1893) · *BL cat.* · private information (1893) · Venn, *Alum. Cant.* · *CGPLA Eng. & Wales* (1893)
Archives Bodl. Oxf., letters to M. P. Edgeworth · Herts. ALS, letters to Lord Lytton
Wealth at death £2639 4s. 8d.: administration with will, 14 June 1893, *CGPLA Eng. & Wales*

PICTURE CREDITS